Chemistry

SEVENTH EDITION

STEVEN S. ZUMDAHL
University of Illinois

SUSAN A. ZUMDAHL
University of Illinois

Succeed in College!

BY WALTER PAUK
Cornell University

JOHN P. FIORE
University of Illinois

HOUGHTON MIFFLIN COMPANY
Boston   New York

CHEMISTRY, SEVENTH EDITION
by Steven S. Zumdahl and Susan A. Zumdahl
Copyright © 2007 by Houghton Mifflin Company. All rights reserved.

Executive Editor: Richard Stratton
Developmental Editor: Rebecca Berardy Schwartz
Senior Project Editor: Cathy Labresh Brooks
Editorial Assistant: Susan Miscio
Senior Art & Design Coordinator: Jill Haber
Composition Buyer: Chuck Dutton
Manufacturing Coordinator: Renee Ostrowski
Senior Marketing Manager: Katherine Greig
Marketing Assistant: Naveen Hariprasad

Cover Image: Masaaki Kazama/Photonica
Photo credits: Page A39.

HOW TO STUDY IN COLLEGE, EIGHTH EDITION
by Walter Pauk and Ross J. Q. Owens
Copyright © 2006 by Houghton Mifflin Company. All rights reserved.

Publisher: Patricia A. Coryell
Senior Sponsoring Editor: Mary Finch
Development Editor: Shani B. Fisher
Editorial Assistants: Andrew Sylvester and Sean McGann
Senior Manufacturing Coordinator: Florence Cadran
Marketing Manager: Elinor Gregory

Custom Publishing Editor: Dan Luciano
Custom Publishing Production Manager: Tina Kozik
Project Coordinator: Jennifer Feltri

This book contains select works from existing Houghton Mifflin Company resources and was produced by Houghton Mifflin Custom Publishing for collegiate use. As such, those adopting and/or contributing to this work are responsible for editorial content, accuracy, continuity and completeness.

ISBN-13: 978-0-618-77083-0
ISBN-10: 0-618-77083-6
N-06320

1 2 3 4 5 6 7 8 9 – AB – 08 07 06

Houghton Mifflin
Custom Publishing

222 Berkeley Street • Boston, MA 02116

Address all correspondence and order information to the above address.

Contents

To the Professor

With this edition of *Chemistry,* students and instructors alike will experience a truly integrated learning program. The textbook's strong emphasis on conceptual learning and problem solving is extended through the numerous online media assignments and activities. It was our mission to create a media program that embodies the spirit of the textbook so that, when instructors and students look online for either study aids or online homework, that each resource supports the goals of the textbook—a strong emphasis on models, real-world applications, and visual learning.

We have gone over every page in the sixth edition thoroughly, fine-tuning in some cases and rewriting in others. In doing so, we have incorporated numerous constructive suggestions from instructors who used the previous edition. Based on this feedback new content has been added, such as the treatment of real gases in Chapter 5, which has been expanded to include a discussion of specific gases, and also coverage of photoelectric effect has been added to Chapter 7. In addition, the *Sample Exercises* in Chapter 2 have been revised to cover the naming of compounds given the formula and the opposite process of writing the formula from the name. To help students review key concepts, the For Review section of each chapter has been reorganized to provide an easy-to-read bulleted summary; this section includes new review questions. The art program has been enhanced to include electrostatic potential maps to show a more accurate distribution of charge in molecules.

In the media program instructors will find a variety of resources to assign additional practice, study, and quiz material. *ChemWork* interactive assignments, end-of-chapter online homework, *HM Testing,* and classroom response system applications allow you to assess students in multiple ways. The Online Study Center promotes self-study with animations, video demonstrations, and practice exercises.

Important Features of *Chemistry*

- *Chemistry* contains numerous discussions, illustrations, and exercises aimed at *overcoming common misconceptions.* It has become increasingly clear from our own teaching experience that students often struggle with chemistry because they misunderstand many of the fundamental concepts. In this text, we have gone to great lengths to provide illustrations and explanations aimed at giving students more accurate pictures of the fundamental ideas of chemistry. In particular, we have attempted to represent the microscopic world of chemistry so that students have a picture in their minds of "what the atoms and molecules are

doing." The art program along with animations emphasize this goal. Also, we have placed a larger emphasis on the qualitative understanding of concepts before quantitative problems are considered. Because using an algorithm to correctly solve a problem often masks misunderstanding—students assume they understand the material because they got the right "answer"—it is important to probe their understanding in other ways. In this vein the text includes a number of Active Learning Questions (previously called In-Class Discussion Questions) at the end of each chapter that are intended for group discussion. It is our experience that students often learn the most when they teach each other. Students are forced to recognize their own lack of conceptual understanding when they try and fail to explain a concept to a colleague.

- With a strong *problem-solving orientation,* this text talks to the student about how to approach and solve chemical problems. We have made a strong pitch to students for using a thoughtful and logical approach rather than simply memorizing procedures. In particular, an innovative method is given for dealing with acid–base equilibria, the material the typical student finds most difficult and frustrating. The key to this approach involves first deciding what species are present in solution, then thinking about the chemical properties of these species. This method provides a general framework for approaching all types of solution equilibria.

- The text contains almost *300 sample exercises,* with many more examples given in the discussions leading to sample exercises or used to illustrate general strategies. When a specific strategy is presented, it is summarized, and the sample exercise that follows it reinforces the step-by-step attack on the problem. In general, in approaching problem solving we emphasize understanding rather than an algorithm-based approach.

- We have presented a thorough *treatment of reactions* that occur in solution, including acid–base reactions. This material appears in Chapter 4, directly after the chapter on chemical stoichiometry, to emphasize the connection between solution reactions and chemical reactions in general. The early presentation of this material provides an opportunity to cover some interesting descriptive chemistry and also supports the lab, which typically involves a great deal of aqueous chemistry. Chapter 4 also includes oxidation–reduction reactions, because a large number of interesting and important chemical reactions involve redox processes. However, coverage of oxidation–reduction is optional at this point and depends on the needs of a specific course.

- *Descriptive chemistry* and chemical principles are thoroughly integrated in this text. Chemical models may appear sterile and confusing without the observations that stimulated their invention. On the other hand, facts without organizing principles may seem overwhelming. A combination of observations and models can make chemistry both interesting and understandable. In addition, in those chapters that deal with the chemistry of the elements systematically, we have made a continuous effort to show how properties and models correlate. Descriptive chemistry is presented in a variety of ways—as applications of the principles in separate sections, in Sample Exercises and exercise sets, in photographs, and in Chemical Impact features.

- Throughout the book a strong *emphasis on models* prevails. Coverage includes how they are constructed, how they are tested, and what we learn when they inevitably fail. Models are developed naturally, with pertinent observations always presented first to show why a particular model was invented.

- Everyday-life *applications* of chemistry that should be of interest to students taking general chemistry appear throughout the text. For example, the Chemical Impact "Pearly Whites" illustrates the procedures for keeping teeth white, and "Thin is In" discusses the new technology being used to produce plasma flat-panel displays. Many industrial applications have also been incorporated into the text.

- A double-helix icon in the *Instructor's Annotated Edition* highlights organic and biological examples of applications that are integrated throughout the text, in end-of-chapter problems, in exercises, or in-text discussions or examples. This feature allows instructors to quickly locate material that will be of particular interest to students in pre-medicine, biology, or other health-related fields.

- Judging from the favorable comments of instructors and students who have used the sixth edition, the text seemed to work very well in a variety of courses. We were especially pleased that *readability* was cited as a key strength when students were asked to assess the text. Thus, although the text has been fine-tuned in many areas, we have endeavored to build on the basic descriptions, strategies, analogies, and explanations that were successful in the previous editions.

New to the Seventh Edition

The seventh edition of *Chemistry* incorporates many significant improvements and is accompanied by new and enhanced media products and support services.

- Electrostatic potential maps have been added to Chapter 8 to show a more accurate distribution of charge in molecules. These maps are based on *ab initio* molecular modeling calculations and provide a convenient method for better student understanding of bond and molecular polarity.

- Additional topics have been added to the text, which include a treatment of real gases in Chapter 5 and coverage of photoelectric effect to Chapter 7. In addition, the Sample Exercises in Chapter 2 have been revised to cover the naming of compounds given the formula and the opposite process of writing the formula from the name.

- The end-of-chapter exercises and problems have been revised, providing approximately 20% new problems, including some that feature molecular art. End-of-chapter problems include: *Active Learning Questions* to test students' conceptual grasp of the material; *Questions* to help review important facts; *Exercises* that are paired and organized by topic; *Additional Exercises,* which are not keyed by topic; *Challenge Problems,* which require students to combine skills and problems; and *Marathon Problems,* which are the most comprehensive and challenging type of problem. New to the seventh edition are *Integrative Problems* that require students to understand multiple concepts across chapters.

- The *For Review* section, at the beginning of the end-of-chapter exercises, has been reorganized to help students more easily identify key concepts and test themselves on these concepts with review questions.

- A large number of new Chemical Impacts have been included in the seventh edition to continue the emphasis on up-to-date application of chemistry in the real world. These essays feature intriguing topics such as "Faux Snow," and "Closest Packing of M&M's®."

- To support the use of active learning in chemical education, we have created new PowerPoint presentations—*Active Learning PowerPoints with Lecture Outlines.* These PowerPoint presentations feature in-class discussion questions called *Reacts,* chemical demonstrations, animations, and figures from the text. This material is designed to help instructors present chemistry using an interactive teaching style, which we believe is most effective in promoting student learning. An *Active Learning Guide* includes the discussion questions and supporting information in a workbook format. The questions are repeated in the workbook (with space to record answers) so that students can focus on participation in class sessions. This guide can then be used effectively for independent student review outside of class.

- The Online Study Center has been enhanced to include a variety of tools to support visual learning and to give students extra practice. A *For Review* section summarizes the key topics of each chapter and helps students visualize the concepts with animations and video demonstrations. *Visualization* quiz questions allow students to test their knowledge of the concepts presented through the animations and video demonstrations. *ACE* practice tests allow students to practice problems on their own, and get immediate feedback. Additional resources include a molecule library, interactive periodic table, and flashcards to help students study key terms.

A very important feature accompanying the seventh edition is the online homework in the Eduspace® online learning tool. In addition to new algorithmic end-of-chapter questions, Eduspace also includes *ChemWork*™ interactive on-line homework. *ChemWork* is structured to help students learn chemistry in a conceptual way and is a series of text-based assignments. The system is modeled on a one-to-one teacher- student problem session. When a student cannot answer a given question, instead of giving him/her the correct answer, a system of interactive hints is available to help them think through each problem. Often the hints are in the form of a question on which the student receives feedback. Links to text material are also available for reference to key concepts at points of learning. The philosophy behind the homework is to help students understand the material so that they can arrive at the correct answer by their own efforts, supported by the kind of help an instructor would provide in a one-to-one tutoring session.

Another important feature of this homework system is that each student, even in a very large course, receives a unique set of tasks for each homework assignment, which is accomplished using random number–generation and similar versions of algorithmic problems. Each student's work is assessed by the system, and the score for each task in the assignment is recorded in the electronic gradebook for immediate access by both student and instructor. The system also encourages increased student responsibility by setting firm deadlines for assignments. From the instructor's perspective, Eduspace encourages student study without the burden of tracking student efforts through grading. Our experience with a similar system at the University of Illinois convinces us that this interactive homework represents an important breakthrough in helping students learn chemistry.

Flexibility of Topic Order

The order of topics in the text was chosen because it is preferred by the majority of instructors. However, we consciously constructed the book so that many other orders are possible. During our tenure at the University of Illinois, for a two-chapter sequence, we used the chapters in this order: 1–6, 13–15, 7–9, 18, 21, 12, 10, 11, 16, 17, and parts of 22. Sections of Chapters 19, 20, and parts of 22 are used throughout the two semesters as appropriate. This order, chosen because of the way the laboratory is organized, is not necessarily recommended, but it illustrates the flexibility of order built into the text.

Some specific points about topic order:

- About half of chemistry courses present kinetics before equilibria; the other half present equilibria first. This text is written to accommodate either order.
- The introductory aspects of thermodynamics are presented relatively early (in Chapter 6) because of the importance of energy in various chemical processes and models, but the more subtle thermodynamic concepts are left until later (Chapter 16). These two chapters may be used together if desired.
- To make the book more flexible, the derivation of the ideal gas law from the kinetic molecular theory and quantitative analysis using spectroscopy are presented in the appendixes. Although mainstream general chemistry courses typically do not cover this material, some courses may find it appropriate. By using the optional material in the appendixes and by assigning the more difficult end-of-chapter exercises (from the additional exercises section), an instructor will find the level of the text appropriate for many majors courses or for other courses requiring a more extensive coverage of these topics.
- Because some courses cover bonding using only a Lewis structure approach, orbitals are not presented in the introductory chapter on bonding (Chapter 8). In Chapter 9 both hybridization and the molecular orbital model are covered, but either or both of these topics may be omitted if desired.
- Chapter 4 can be tailored to fit the specific course involved. Used in its entirety where it stands in the book, it provides interesting examples of descriptive chemistry and supports the laboratory program. Material in this chapter can also be skipped entirely or covered at some later point, whenever appropriate. For example, the sections on oxidation and reduction can be taught with electrochemistry. Although many instructors prefer early introduction of this concept, these sections can be omitted without complication since the next few chapters do not depend on this material.

Supplements

An extensive teaching and learning package has been designed to make this book more useful to both instructors and students.

Technology: For Instructors

Chemistry is accompanied by a complete suite of teaching and learning tools, including the customizable media resources below. Whether online or via CD, these integrated resources are designed to save you time and help make class preparation, presentation, assessment, and course management more efficient and effective.

- **Media Integration Guide for Instructors** is your portal to the digital assets for this text. It includes the CDs described below as well as a user name and password to the Online Teaching Center, giving you instant access to text-related materials.

  HM ClassPrep™ CD includes everything an instructor needs to develop lectures: *Active Learning PowerPoints with Lecture Outlines;* virtually all text figures, tables, and photos in PowerPoint slides and as JPEGs; the *Instructor's Resource Guide* in Word; Word files of the printed *Test Bank;* and Word files of the *Complete Solutions Manual.*

HM Testing™ (powered by *Diploma®*) is Houghton Mifflin's new version of *HM Testing*. It significantly improves on functionality and ease of use by offering instructors all the tools they will need to create, author, deliver, and customize multiple types of tests—including authoring and editing algorithmic questions. New content includes 150 new *Conceptual Questions,* skill-level coding, and preprogrammed, algorithmic questions. HM Testing combines a flexible test-editing program with a comprehensive gradebook function for easy administration and tracking. It enables instructors to administer tests via print, network server, or the web. The HM Testing database contains a wealth of questions and can produce multiple-choice, true/false, fill-in-the-blank, and essay tests. Questions can be customized based on the chapter being covered, the question format, level of difficulty, and specific topics. Available on the HM ClassPrep CD.

HM ClassPresent™ 2006: General Chemistry features new animations and video demonstrations. HM ClassPresent provides a library of high-quality, scaleable lab demonstrations and animations covering core chemistry concepts arranged by chapter and topic. The resources within it can be browsed by thumbnail and description or searched by chapter, title, or keyword. Instructors can export the animations and videos into a variety of presentation formats or use for presentation directly from the CD. Full transcripts accompany all audio commentary to reinforce visual presentations and to cater to different learning styles.

Online Teaching Center includes classroom presentation and preparation materials. Animations; videos; virtually all figures, tables, and photos from the text are available in JPEG and PowerPoint format; the *Transition Guide* from the sixth to seventh edition; *Active Learning PowerPoints with Lecture Outlines;* and classroom response system content are all available online.

Eduspace (powered by Blackboard™), Houghton Mifflin's complete course-management solution, features algorithmic, end-of-chapter questions along with **ChemWork** interactive online homework. Both types of homework problems include links to relevant pages from the text. These integrated resources allow students to reference core concepts at the point of learning. *ChemWork* assignments help students learn the process of thinking like a chemist: as students work through unique, text-based assignments, a system of interactive hints is available to help them think through each problem. Eduspace includes all of Blackboard's powerful features for teaching and learning, and comes preloaded with course materials including videos and animations, and a link to SMARTHINKING™ live online tutoring. Customized functions allow instructors to tailor these materials to their specific needs, select, create and post homework assignments and tests, communicate with students in a variety of different ways, track student progress, and manage their portfolio of course work in the gradebook. To help instructors best utilize the media that accompanies the textbook, lesson plans have been created based on the sections of the book. Each section correlates the relevant *ChemWork* assignments, Visualization (animations and videos), and online end-of-chapter questions. **Please note: instructors who want their students to use Eduspace must request a *Getting Started Guide for Students* which will be bundled free with new copies of the text. Instructors who adopt Eduspace will receive a separate *Getting Started Guide for Instructors* for the program with a passkey to set up their course.**

- **Classroom Response System (CRS)** compatible content on the Online Teaching Center, HM ClassPrep CD, and in Eduspace allows professors to perform "on-the-spot" assessments, deliver quick quizzes, gauge students' understanding of a particular question or concept, and take their class roster easily. Students get immediate feedback on how well they know the content and where they need to improve. Two sets of questions are available in PowerPoint slides: one based on *Test Bank* content and the other with unique, conceptual questions. Both question types are correlated to sections in the textbook. The conceptual questions are also correlated to relevant media and art from the book.

- **TeamUP Integration Services**
  http://teamup.college.hmco.com
  Houghton Mifflin aims to provide customers with quality textbooks, technology, and superior training and implementation services. TeamUP, our integration program, offers flexible, personalized training and consultative services by phone, online, or on campus. Experienced faculty advisors and media specialists will assist you and your department in using our products most effectively.

- **Course-Management Software** is available through *WebCT* and *Blackboard.* These two distributed learning systems allow instructors to create a virtual classroom without any knowledge of HTML. Features include: assessment tools, a gradebook, online file exchange between instructors and students, online syllabi, and course descriptions. The customized *Chemistry* cartridges feature *Test Bank* questions, lecture materials, and study aids related to the text.

Print Supplements: For Instructors

- *Complete Solutions Guide,* by Thomas J. Hummel, Susan Arena Zumdahl, and Steven S. Zumdahl, presents detailed solutions for all of the end-of-chapter exercises in the text for the convenience of faculty and staff involved in instruction and for instructors who wish their students to have solutions for all exercises. Departmental approval is required for the sale of the *Complete Solutions Guide* to students.

- *Instructor's Resource Guide,* by Donald J. DeCoste, includes suggestions for alternative orders of topics, suggested responses to the *Active Learning Questions,* amplification of strategies used in various chapters, lesson plans of media resources correlated to section, answers to *Reacts*, and a section on notes for teaching assistants.

- *Lecture Demonstration Guide,* by Fred Jurgens of the University of Wisconsin—Madison, lists the sources for over 750 classroom demonstrations that can be used in general chemistry courses. Icons in the margins of the *Instructor's Annotated Edition* of the text key the demonstrations to their corresponding text discussions.

- *Instructor's Resource Guide for Experimental Chemistry,* Seventh Edition, by James F. Hall, contains tips including hints on running experiments, approximate times for each experiment, and answers to all prelab and postlab questions posed in the laboratory guide.

- *Bibliobase (www.bibliobase.com)* allows instructors to create a completely customized lab manual by mixing and matching from 88 general chemistry labs—including all the labs from *Experimental Chemistry*—and 56 labs for the course in general, organic, and biochemistry. At the Online Teaching Center, instructors search through the database of labs, make their selections, organize the sequence of the manual, and submit their order via the Internet. Customized, printed, and bound lab manuals are delivered to the bookstore within weeks.

- *Test Item File,* by Steven S. Zumdahl, Susan Arena Zumdahl, and Gretchen Adams (available to adopters), offers a printed version of more than 2000 exam questions, 10 percent of which are new to this edition, referenced to the appropriate text section. Questions are in multiple-choice, open-ended, and true-false formats.

- *Transparencies,* in a full-color set of 255, are available to adopters of the seventh edition of the text.

Technology: For Students

Chemistry is supported by an array of learning tools designed to help students succeed in their chemistry course. It includes the following media resources:

A passkey to the Online Study Center is bound into the front of the textbook. From the Online Study Center, students have access to practice, visualization, and self-study aids. *Visualization* animations and video demonstrations help students see key concepts, and each *Visualization* is accompanied by quiz questions for students' review. A *For Review* section helps students review key topics at a glance and includes video demonstrations and animations for additional reinforcement. *Flashcards* and *ACE* practice tests help students study key concepts and problem-solve. A molecule library, glossary, and interactive periodic table are also available for support. A *Student CD,* with many of these Online Study Center resources, is available upon request for students who do not have Internet access.

Eduspace (powered by *Blackboard*), Houghton Mifflin's complete course-management solution, features algorithmic end-of-chapter questions along with *ChemWork* interactive online homework. Through Eduspace, students can also access the Online Study Center and SMARTHINKING live, online tutoring. Instructors who adopt Eduspace will receive a separate user guide for the program with a passkey to set up their course. Students using Eduspace will also receive a separate user guide and passkey.

SMARTHINKING live, online tutoring is also available free with new books upon instructor request. Students may also purchase stand-alone access to it. SMARTHINKING provides personalized, text-specific tutoring and is available during peak study hours when students need it most. Limits apply; terms and hours of SMARTHINKING service are subject to change.

Print Supplements: For Students

- *Study Guide,* by Paul B. Kelter of the University of Illinois—Urbana. Written to be a self-study aid for students, this guide includes alternate strategies for solving problems, supplemental explanations for the most difficult material, and self-tests. There are approximately 500 worked examples and 1200 practice problems (with answers), designed to give students mastery and confidence.

- *Student Solutions Manual,* by Thomas J. Hummel, Susan Arena Zumdahl, and Steven S. Zumdahl, all of the University of Illinois, Urbana, provides detailed solutions for half of the end-of-chapter exercises (designated by the blue question numbers) using the strategies emphasized in the text. To ensure the accuracy of the solutions, this supplement and the *Complete Solutions Guide* were checked independently by several instructors.

- *Active Learning Guide,* by Donald J. DeCoste. This printed workbook can be used in lecture or recitation in conjunction with the instructor PowerPoint slides. It provides a complete set of *React* questions with space for student answers. Students can use the workbook as a self-study aid outside of class.

- *Solving Equilibrium Problems with Applications to Qualitative Analysis,* by Steven S. Zumdahl. Successfully used by thousands of students, this book offers thorough, step-by-step procedures for solving problems related to equilibria taking place both in the gas phase and in solution. Containing hundreds of sample exercises, test exercises with complete solutions, and end-of-chapter exercises with answers, the text utilizes the same problem-solving methods found in *Chemistry* and is an excellent source of additional drill-type problems. The last chapter presents an exploratory qualitative analysis experiment with explanations based on the principles of aqueous equilibria.

- *Experimental Chemistry,* Seventh Edition, by James F. Hall of the University of Massachusetts—Lowell, provides an extensively revised laboratory program compatible with the text. The 48 experiments present a wide variety of chemistry, and many experiments offer choices of procedures. Safety is strongly emphasized throughout the program.

Acknowledgments: This book represents the efforts of many talented and dedicated people. We particularly want to thank Richard Stratton, Executive Editor, for his vision and oversight of this project. Richard's knowledge, judgment, and enthusiasm have contributed immeasurably to the success of this text. He is not only an outstanding editor but also one of the nicest people in the business.

We also want to thank Cathy Brooks, Senior Project Editor, who did a miraculous job of coordinating the production of an incredibly complex project with grace and good humor. We also especially appreciate the excellent work of Rebecca Berardy Schwartz, Developmental Editor, who managed the revision process in a very supportive and organized manner.

We are especially grateful to Tom Hummel, who managed the revision of the end-of-chapter problems and the solutions manuals. Tom's extensive experience teaching general chemistry and his high standards of accuracy and clarity have resulted in great improvements in the quality of the problems and the solutions in this edition. In addition, we very much appreciate the contributions of Don DeCoste, who has helped us comprehend more clearly the difficulties students have with conceptual understanding and who contributed the Challenge Problems.

We also extend our thanks to Jason Overby, who rendered the electrostatic potential maps and who contributed the Integrative Problems. Our thanks and love also go to Leslie, Steve, Whitney, Scott, Tyler, Sunshine, and Tony for their continuing support.

Thanks to the others at Houghton Mifflin who supplied valuable assistance on this revision: Jill Haber, Senior Art/Design Coordinator; Sharon Donahue, Photo Researcher; Katherine Greig, Senior Marketing Manager; Naveen Hariprasad, Marketing Assistant; and Susan Miscio, Editorial Assistant.

Special thanks go to the following people who helped shape this edition by offering suggestions for its improvement:

Dawood Afzal, Truman State (media reviewer); Carol Anderson, University of Connecticut—Avery Point (media reviewer); Jeffrey R. Appling, Clemson University (media reviewer); Dave Blackburn, University of Minnesota; Robert S. Boikess, Rutgers University; Ken Carter, Truman State (media reviewer); Bette Davidowitz, University of Cape Town; Natalie Foster, Lehigh University; Tracy A. Halmi, Penn State Erie, The Behrend College; Carl A. Hoeger, UC—San Diego; Ahmad Kabbani, Lebanese American University; Arthur Mar, University of Alberta; Jim McCormick, Truman State (media reviewer); Richard Orwell, Blue Ridge Community College (media reviewer); Jason S. Overby, College of Charleston; Robert D. Pike, The College of William and Mary; Daniel Raftery, Purdue University; Jimmy Rogers, University of Texas—Arlington (media reviewer); Raymond Scott, Mary Washington College; Alan Stolzenberg, West Virginia University; Rashmi Venkateswaran, University of Ottawa. *AP reviewers:* Annis Hapkiewicz, Okemos High School; Tina Ohn-Sabatello, Maine Township HS East. *Interactive Course Guide Reviewers:* Lynne C. Cary, Ph.D., Bethel College; Craig C. Martens, University of California—Irvine; Jeffrey P. Osborne, Manchester College; Donald W. Shive, Muhlenberg College; Craig Sockwell, Northwest Shoals Community College; Richard Pennington, College of St. Mary. *Accuracy reviewers:* Linda Bush (textbook reviewer), Jon Booze (media reviewer)

Reviewers of the sixth edition:

Ramesh D. Arasasingham, University of California—Irvine; Stanley A. Bajue, Medgar Evans College, CUNY; V.G. Berner, New Mexico Junior College; Dave Blackburn, University of Minnesota; Steven R. Boone, Central Missouri State University; Gary S. Buckley, Cameron University; Lara L. Chappell, SUNY College at Oswego; David Cramb, University of Calgary; Philip W. Crawford, Southeast Missouri State University; Philip Davis, University of Tennessee; Michael P. Garoutte, Missouri Southern State College; Daniel Graham, Loyola University; David R. Hawkes, Lambuth University; Dale Hawley, Kansas State University; Thomas B. Higgins, Harold Washington College; John C. Hogan, Louisiana State University; Donald P. Land, University of California—Davis; Michael P. Masingale, LeMoyne College; Julie T. Millard, Colby College; Robert H. Paine, Rochester Institute of Technology; Brenda Ross, Cottey College; Jay S. Shore, South Dakota State University; Richard T. Toomey, Northwest Missouri State University; Robert Zoellner, Humboldt State University.

To the Student

*T*he major purpose of this book, of course, is to help you learn chemistry. However, this main thrust is closely linked to two other goals: to show how important and how interesting the subject is, and to show how to think like a chemist. To solve complicated problems the chemist uses logic, trial and error, intuition, and, above all, patience. A chemist is used to being wrong. The important thing is to learn from a mistake, recheck assumptions, and try again. A chemist thrives on puzzles that seem to defy solutions.

Many of you using this text do not plan to be practicing chemists. However, the nonchemist can benefit from the chemist's attitude. Problem solving is important in all professions and in all walks of life. The techniques you will learn from this book will serve you well in any career you choose. Thus, we believe that the study of chemistry has much to offer the nonmajor, including an understanding of many fascinating and important phenomena and a chance to hone problem-solving skills.

This book attempts to present chemistry in a manner that is sensible to the novice. Chemistry is not the result of an inspired vision. It is the product of countless observations and many attempts, using logic and trial and error, to account for these observations. In this book the concepts are developed in a natural way: The observations come first and then models are constructed to explain the observed behavior.

Models are a major focus in this book. The uses and limitations of models are emphasized, and science is treated as a human activity, subject to all the normal human foibles. Mistakes are discussed as well as successes.

A central theme of this book is a thoughtful, systematic approach to problem solving. Learning encompasses much more than simply memorizing facts. Truly educated people use their factual knowledge as a starting point—a base for creative approaches to solving problems.

Read through the material in the text carefully. For most concepts, illustrations or photos will help you visualize what is going on. To further help you visualize concepts by using animations and videos, we have included *Visualization* exercises on the Online Study Center or on an optional free CD. Icons in the text margin signal that there is companion material available on the CD.

Often a given type of problem is "walked through" in the text before the corresponding Sample Exercises appear. Strategies for solving problems are given throughout the text.

Thoroughly examine the Sample Exercises and the problem-solving strategies. The strategies summarize the approach taken in the text; the Sample Exercises follow the strategies step-by-step. Schematics in Chapter 15 also illustrate the logical pathways to solving aqueous equilibrium problems.

Throughout the text, we have used margin notes to highlight key points, to comment on an application of the text material, or to reference material in other parts of the book. Chemical Impact, the boxed feature that appears frequently throughout the text, discusses especially interesting applications of chemistry to the everyday world.

Each chapter has a summary and key terms list for review, and the glossary gives a quick reference for definitions.

Learning chemistry requires working the end-of-chapter exercises assigned by your professor. Answers to exercises denoted by blue question numbers are in the back of the book, and complete solutions to those exercises are in the *Partial Solutions Guide*. To help you assess your level of proficiency, the Online Study Center (college.hmco.com/PIC/zumdahl7e) offers quizzes and electronic homework assignments that feature instant feedback.

The *Study Guide* contains extra practice problems and many worked examples. The supplement, *Solving Equilibrium Problems with Applications to Qualitative Analysis*, reinforces in great detail the text's step-by-step approach to solving equilibrium problems and contains many worked examples and self-quiz questions.

It is very important to use the exercises and electronic homework assignments to your best advantage. Your main goal should not be to simply get the correct answer but to *understand the process* for getting the answer. Memorizing the solutions for specific problems is not a very good way to prepare for an exam. There are too many pigeonholes required to cover every possible problem type. Look within the problem for the solution. Use the concepts you have learned along with a systematic, logical approach to find the solution. Learn to trust yourself to think it out. You will make mistakes, but the important thing is to learn from these errors. The only way to gain confidence is to do lots of practice problems and use these to diagnose your weaknesses.

Be patient and thoughtful and work hard to understand rather than simply memorize. We wish you an interesting and satisfying year.

Features of **Chemistry** Seventh Edition

Conceptual Understanding and Problem Solving

8.13 Molecular Structure: The VSEPR Model

The structures of molecules play a very important role in determining their chemical properties. As we will see later, this is particularly important for biological molecules; a slight change in the structure of a large biomolecule can completely destroy its usefulness to a cell or may even change the cell from a normal one to a cancerous one.

Many accurate methods now exist for determining **molecular structure,** the three-dimensional arrangement of the atoms in a molecule. These methods must be used if precise information about structure is required. However, it is often useful to be able to predict the approximate molecular structure of a molecule. In this section we consider a simple model that allows us to do this. This model, called the **valence shell electron-pair repulsion (VSEPR) model,** is useful in predicting the geometries of molecules formed from nonmetals. The main postulate of this model is that *the structure around a given atom is determined principally by minimizing electron-pair repulsions.* The idea here is that the bonding and nonbonding pairs around a given atom will be positioned as far apart as possible. To see how this model works, we will first consider the molecule $BeCl_2$, which has the Lewis structure

$$:\ddot{Cl}—Be—\ddot{Cl}:$$

> The authors' emphasis on **modeling** (or chemical theories) throughout the text addresses the problem of rote memorization by helping students better understand and appreciate the process of scientific thinking.

> By stressing the limitations and uses of **scientific models**, the authors show students how chemists think and work.

ight Bonding: General Concepts

Fundamental Properties of Models

- Models are human inventions, always based on an incomplete understanding of how nature works. *A model does not equal reality.*

- Models are often wrong. This property derives from the first property. Models are based on speculation and are always oversimplifications.

- Models tend to become more complicated as they age. As flaws are discovered in our models, we "patch" them and thus add more detail.

- It is very important to understand the assumptions inherent in a particular model before you use it to interpret observations or to make predictions. Simple models usually involve very restrictive assumptions and can be expected to yield only qualitative information. Asking for a sophisticated explanation from a simple model is like expecting to get an accurate mass for a diamond using a bathroom scale.

  For a model to be used effectively, we must understand its strengths and weaknesses and ask only appropriate questions. An illustration of this point is the simple aufbau principle used to account for the electron configurations of the elements. Although this model correctly predicts the configuration for most atoms, chromium and copper, for example, do not agree with the predictions. Detailed studies show that the configurations of chromium and copper result from complex electron interactions that are not taken into account in the simple model. However, this does not mean that we should discard the simple model that is so useful for most atoms. Instead, we must apply it with caution and not expect it to be correct in every case.

- When a model is wrong, we often learn much more than when it is right. If a model makes a wrong prediction, it usually means we do not understand some fundamental characteristics of nature. We often learn by making mistakes. (Try to remember this when you get back your next chemistry test.)

8.8 Covalent Bond Energies and Chemical Reactions

In this section we will consider the energies associated with various types of bonds and see how the bonding concept is useful in dealing with the energies of chemical reactions. One important consideration is to establish the sensitivity of a particular type of bond its molecular environment. For example, consider the stepwise decomposition of thane:

Process	Energy Required (kJ/mol)
$CH_4(g) \rightarrow CH_3(g) + H(g)$	435
$CH_3(g) \rightarrow CH_2(g) + H(g)$	453
$CH_2(g) \rightarrow CH(g) + H(g)$	425
$CH(g) \rightarrow C(g) + H(g)$	339
	Total = 1652
	Average = $\dfrac{1652}{4}$ = 413

Sample Exercise 5.5 Avogadro's Law

Avogadro's law also can be written as

$$\frac{V_1}{n_1} = \frac{V_2}{n_2}$$

Suppose we have a 12.2-L sample containing 0.50 mol oxygen gas (O_2) at a pressure of 1 atm and a temperature of 25°C. If all this O_2 were converted to ozone (O_3) at the same temperature and pressure, what would be the volume of the ozone?

Solution

The balanced equation for the reaction is

$$3O_2(g) \longrightarrow 2O_3(g)$$

To calculate the moles of O_3 produced, we must use the appropriate mole ratio:

$$0.50 \text{ mol } O_2 \times \frac{2 \text{ mol } O_3}{3 \text{ mol } O_2} = 0.33 \text{ mol } O_3$$

Avogadro's law states that $V = an$, which can be rearranged to give

$$\frac{V}{n} = a$$

Since a is a constant, an alternative representation is

$$\frac{V_1}{n_1} = a = \frac{V_2}{n_2}$$

where V_1 is the volume of n_1 moles of O_2 gas and V_2 is the volume of n_2 moles of O_3 ga In this case we have

$$n_1 = 0.50 \text{ mol} \qquad n_2 = 0.33 \text{ mol}$$
$$V_1 = 12.2 \text{ L} \qquad V_2 = ?$$

Solving for V_2 gives

$$V_2 = \left(\frac{n_2}{n_1}\right) V_1 = \left(\frac{0.33 \text{ mol}}{0.50 \text{ mol}}\right) 12.2 \text{ L} = 8.1 \text{ L}$$

Reality Check: Note that the volume decreases, as it should, since fewer moles of ga molecules will be present after O_2 is converted to O_3.

See Exercises 5.35 and 5.3

FIGURE 5.10
These balloons each hold 1.0 L of gas at 25°C and 1 atm. Each balloon contains 0.041 mol of gas, or 2.5×10^{22} molecules.

> **Sample Exercises** model a step-by-step approach to solving problems. Cross-references to similar end-of-chapter exercises are provided at the end of each Sample Exercise. **Reality Checks** appear after the solutions in selected exercises, helping students evaluate their answers to ensure that they are reasonable.

Connections

Each chapter begins with an engaging introduction that demonstrates how chemistry is related to everyday life.

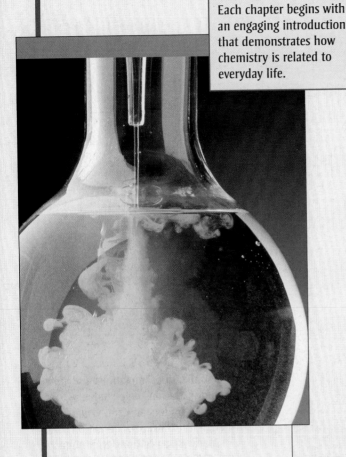

Much of the chemistry that affects each of us occurs among substances dissolved in water. For example, virtually all the chemistry that makes life possible occurs in an aqueous environment. Also, various medical tests involve aqueous reactions, depending heavily on analyses of blood and other body fluids. In addition to the common tests for sugar, cholesterol, and iron, analyses for specific chemical markers allow detection of many diseases before obvious symptoms occur.

Aqueous chemistry is also important in our environment. In recent years, contamination of the groundwater by substances such as chloroform and nitrates has been widely publicized. Water is essential for life, and the maintenance of an ample supply of clean water is crucial to all civilization.

To understand the chemistry that occurs in such diverse places as the human body, the atmosphere, the groundwater, the oceans, the local water treatment plant, your hair as you shampoo it, and so on, we must understand how substances dissolved in water react with each other.

However, before we can understand solution reactions, we need to discuss the nature of solutions in which water is the dissolving medium, or *solvent*. These solutions are called **aqueous solutions**. In this chapter we will study the nature of materials after they are dissolved in water and various types of reactions that occur among these substances. You will see that the procedures developed in Chapter 3 to deal with chemical reactions work very well for reactions that take place in aqueous solutions. To understand the types of reactions that occur in aqueous solutions, we must first explore the types of species present. This requires an understanding of the nature of water.

4.1 Water, the Common Solvent

Water is one of the most important substances on earth. It is essential for sustaining the reactions that keep us alive, but it also affects our lives in many indirect ways. Water helps moderate the earth's temperature; it cools automobile engines, nuclear power plants, and many industrial processes; it provides a means of transportation on the earth's surface and a medium for the growth of a myriad of creatures we use as food; and much more.

One of the most valuable properties of water is its ability to dissolve many different substances. For example, salt "disappears" when you sprinkle it into the water used to cook vegetables, as does sugar when you add it to your iced tea. In each case the "disappearing" substance is obviously still present—you can taste it. What happens when a solid dissolves? To understand this process, we need to consider the nature of water. Liquid water consists of a collection of H_2O molecules. An individual H_2O molecule is "bent" or V-shaped, with an H—O—H angle of approximately 105 degrees:

$$H \overset{105°}{\underset{O}{\frown}} H$$

The O—H bonds in the water molecule are covalent bonds formed by electron sharing between the oxygen and hydrogen atoms. However, the electrons of the bond are not shared equally between these atoms. For reasons we will discuss in later chapters, oxygen has a greater attraction for electrons than does hydrogen. If the electrons were shared equally between the two atoms, both would be electrically neutral because, on average, the number of electrons around each would equal the number of protons in that nucleus.

127

Chemical Impact boxes describe current applications of chemistry. These special-interest boxes cover such topics as preserving works of art, molecules as a means of communication, and the heat of chili peppers.

CHEMICAL IMPACT

The Chemistry of Air Bags

Most experts agree that air bags represent a very important advance in automobile safety. These bags, which are stored in the auto's steering wheel or dash, are designed to inflate rapidly (within about 40 ms) in the event of a crash, cushioning the front-seat occupants against impact. The bags then deflate immediately to allow vision and movement after the crash. Air bags are activated when a severe deceleration (an impact) causes a steel ball to compress a spring and electrically ignite a detonator cap, which, in turn, causes sodium azide (NaN_3) to decompose explosively, forming sodium and nitrogen gas:

$$2NaN_3(s) \longrightarrow 2Na(s) + 3N_2(g)$$

This system works very well and requires a relatively small amount of sodium azide (100 g yields 56 L $N_2(g)$ at 25°C and 1.0 atm).

When a vehicle containing air bags reaches the end of its useful life, the sodium azide present in the activators must be given proper disposal. Sodium azide, besides being explosive, has a toxicity roughly equal to that of sodium cyanide. It also forms hydrazoic acid (HN_3), a toxic, explosive liquid, when treated with acid.

The air bag represents an application of chemistry that has already saved thousands of lives.

Inflated air bags.

Visualization

FIGURE 4.17
Photos and accompanying molecular-level representations illustrating the reaction of KCl(aq) with AgNO₃(aq) to form AgCl(s). Note that it is not possible to have a photo of the mixed solution before the reaction occurs, because it is an imaginary step that we use to help visualize the reaction. Actually, the reaction occurs immediately when the two solutions are mixed.

346 Ch

Since the equation for lattice energy contains the product Q_1Q_2, the lattice energy for a solid with 2+ and 2− ions should be four times that for a solid with 1+ and 1− ions. That is,

$$\frac{(+2)(-2)}{(+1)(-1)} = 4$$

For MgO and NaF, the observed ratio of lattice energies (see Fig. 8.11) is

$$\frac{-3916 \text{ kJ}}{-923 \text{ kJ}} = 4.24$$

more negative than that for combining gaseous Na⁺ and F⁻ ions to form NaF(s). Thus the energy released in forming a solid containing Mg²⁺ and O²⁻ ions rather than Mg⁺ and O⁻ ions more than compensates for the energies required for the processes that produce the Mg²⁺ and O²⁻ ions.

If there is so much lattice energy to be gained in going from singly charged to doubly charged ions in the case of magnesium oxide, why then does solid sodium fluoride contain Na⁺ and F⁻ ions rather than Na²⁺ and F²⁻ ions? We can answer this question by recognizing that both Na⁺ and F⁻ ions have the neon electron configuration. Removal of an electron from Na⁺ requires an extremely large quantity of energy (4560 kJ/mol) because a 2p electron must be removed. Conversely, the addition of an electron to F⁻ would require use of the relatively high-energy 3s orbital, which is also an unfavorable process. Thus we can say that for sodium fluoride the extra energy required to form the doubly charged ions is greater than the gain in lattice energy that would result.

This discussion of the energies involved in the formation of solid ionic compounds illustrates that a variety of factors operate to determine the composition and structure of these compounds. The most important of these factors involve the balancing of the energies required to form highly charged ions and the energy released when highly charged ions combine to form the solid.

8.6 Partial Ionic Character of Covalent Bonds

Recall that when atoms with different electronegativities react to form molecules, the electrons are not shared equally. The possible result is a polar covalent bond or, in the case of a large electronegativity difference, a complete transfer of one or more electrons to form ions. The cases are summarized in Fig. 8.12.

How well can we tell the difference between an ionic bond and a polar covalent bond? The only honest answer to this question is that there are probably no totally ionic bonds between *discrete pairs of atoms*. The evidence for this statement comes from calculations of the percent ionic character for the bonds of various binary compounds in the gas phase. These calculations are based on comparisons of the measured dipole moments for molecules of the type X—Y with the calculated dipole moments for the completely ionic case, X⁺Y⁻. The percent ionic character of a bond can be defined as

$$\text{Percent ionic character of a bond} = \left(\frac{\text{measured dipole moment of X—Y}}{\text{calculated dipole moment of X}^+\text{Y}^-}\right) \times 100\%$$

Application of this definition to various compounds (in the gas phase) gives the results shown in Fig. 8.13, where percent ionic character is plotted versus the difference in the electronegativity values of X and Y. Note from this plot that ionic character increases with electronegativity difference, as expected. However, none of the bonds reaches 100% ionic character, even though compounds with the maximum possible electronegativity differences are considered. Thus, according to this definition, no individual bonds are completely ionic. This conclusion is in contrast to the usual classification of many of these compounds (as ionic solids). All the compounds shown in Fig. 8.13 with more than 50% ionic character are normally considered to be ionic solids. Recall, however, the results in Fig. 8.13 are for the gas p[hase and]

(a)

(b)

(c)

FIGURE 8.12
The three possible types of bonds: (a) a covalent bond formed between identical F atoms; (b) the polar covalent bond of HF, with both ionic and covalent components; and (c) an ionic bond with no electron sharing.

not necessarily be assumed[d]... vored by the multiple ion[s]...

Another complication[s]... contain polyatomic ions. F[or]... contains Na⁺ and SO₄²[⁻]... by covalent bonds. Thus,[]... ambiguous.

Chemistry Animation - Microsoft Internet Explorer

Practice

Active Learning Questions

These questions are designed to be used by groups of students in class. The questions allow students to explore their understanding of concepts through discussion and peer teaching. The real value of these questions is the learning that occurs while students talk to each other about chemical concepts.

1. Consider the following apparatus: a test tube covered with a non-permeable elastic membrane inside a container that is closed with a cork. A syringe goes through the cork.

- Syringe
- Cork
- Membrane

a. As you push down on the syringe, how does the membrane covering the test tube change?

b. You stop pushing the syringe but continue to hold it down. In a few seconds, what happens to the membrane?

2. Figure 5.2 shows a picture of a barometer. Which of the following statements is the best explanation of how this barometer works?

a. Air pressure outside the tube causes the mercury to move in the tube until the air pressure inside and outside the tube is equal.

b. Air pressure inside the tube causes the mercury to move in the tube until the air pressure inside and outside the tube is equal.

c. Air pressure outside the tube counterbalances the weight of the mercury in the tube.

d. Capillary action of the mercury causes the mercury to go up the tube.

e. The vacuum that is formed at the top of the tube holds up the mercury.

Justify your choice, and for the choices you did not pick, explain what is wrong with them. Pictures help!

3. The barometer below shows the level of mercury at a given atmospheric pressure. Fill all the other barometers with mercury for that same atmospheric pressure. Explain your answer.

Hg(l)

---

4. As you increase the temperature of a [gas in a sealed, rigid con]tainer, what happens to the density [of the gas? Would the density] be the same if you did the same [experiment in a container with] a piston at constant pressure? (See [Fig. 5.?])

5. A diagram in a chemistry book [shows a magnified view of a] flask of air as follows:

What do you suppose is between [the] molecules?
a. air
b. dust
c. pollutants
d. oxygen
e. nothing

6. If you put a drinking straw in wa[ter, place your finger over the] opening, and lift the straw out [of the water, some water stays in] the straw. Explain.

7. A chemistry student relates the [following story: I noticed my] tires were a bit low and went to [the gas station, where I filled] the tires. I thought about the kin[etic molecular theory (KMT) and] noticed the tires because the volum[e had increased. After I filled it] was increasing both the press[ure and the volume...] "Hmmm," I thought, "that goes a[gainst what I learned in chem]istry, where I was told pressure [and volume were inversely pro]portional." What is the fault in [the reasoning of the chemistry student] in this situation? Explain *why* we [know that pressure and volume] be inversely related (draw pictu[res and use the KMT].

8. Chemicals *X* and *Y* (both gases) react to form the gas *XY*, but [it] takes a bit of time for the reaction to occur. Both *X* and *Y* [are] placed in a container with a piston (free to move), and you n[otice] the volume. As the reaction occurs, what happens to the volu[me] of the container? (See Fig. 5.18.)

9. Which statement best explains why a hot-air balloon rises wh[en] the air in the balloon is heated?

a. According to Charles's law, the temperature of a gas [is] directly related to its volume. Thus the volume of the ballo[on] increases, making the density smaller. This lifts the ballo[on.]

b. Hot air rises inside the balloon, and this lifts the balloon.

c. The temperature of a gas is directly related to its pressu[re.] The pressure therefore increases, and this lifts the ballo[on.]

d. Some of the gas escapes from the bottom of the balloon, th[us] decreasing the mass of gas in the balloon. This decreases [the] density of the gas in the balloon, which lifts the balloon.

e. Temperature is related to the root mean square velocity of [the] gas molecules. Thus the molecules are moving faster, hitti[ng] the balloon more, and thus lifting the balloon.

Key Terms

Section 5.1
barometer
manometer
mm Hg
torr
standard atmosphere
pascal

Section 5.2
Boyle's law
ideal gas
Charles's law
absolute zero
Avogadro's law

Section 5.3
universal gas constant
ideal gas law

Section 5.4
molar volume
standard temperature and pressure (STP)

Section 5.5
Dalton's law of partial pressures
partial pressure
mole fraction

Section 5.6
kinetic molecular theory (KMT)
root mean square velocity
joule

Section 5.7
diffusion
effusion
Graham's law of effusion

Section 5.8
real gas
van der Waals equation

Section 5.10
atmosphere
air pollution
photochemical smog
acid rain

For Review

State of a gas
- The state of a gas can be described completely by specifying its pressure (P), volume (V), temperature (T) and the amount (moles) of gas present (n)
- Pressure
  - Common units
    - 1 torr = 1 mm Hg
    - 1 atm = 760 torr
  - SI unit: pascal
    - 1 atm = 101,325 Pa

Gas laws
- Discovered by observing the properties of gases
- Boyle's law: $PV = k$
- Charles's law: $V = bT$
- Avogadro's law: $V = an$
- Ideal gas law: $PV = nRT$
- Dalton's law of partial pressures: $P_{total} = P_1 + P_2 + \ldots$ the partial pressure of component n in a mixture of [gases]

Kinetic molecular theory (KMT)
- Model that accounts for ideal gas behavior
- Postulates of the KMT:
  - Volume of gas particles is zero
  - No particle interactions
  - Particles are in constant motion, colliding with [the walls of the container to produce] pressure
  - The average kinetic energy of the gas particle[s is directly related to the] temperature of the gas in kelvins

Gas properties
- The particles in any gas sample have a range of ve[locities]
- The root mean square (rms) velocity for a gas repr[esents the average] of the particle velocities

$$u_{rms} = \sqrt{\frac{3RT}{M}}$$

- Diffusion: the mixing of two or more gases
- Effusion: the process in which a gas passes through a small hole into an empty chamber

Real gas behavior
- Real gases behave ideally only at high temperatures and low pressures
- Understanding how the ideal gas equation must be modified to account for real gas behavior helps us understand how gases behave on a molecular level
- Van der Waals found that to describe real gas behavior we must consider particle interactions and particle volumes

REVIEW QUESTIONS
1. Explain how a barometer and a manometer work to measure the pressure of the atmosphere or the pressure of a gas in a container.

---

226 Chapter Five Gases

25°C. The air has a mole fraction of nitrogen of 0.790, the rest being oxygen.

a. Explain why the balloon would float when heated. Make sure to discuss which factors change and which remain constant, and why this matters. Be complete.

b. Above what temperature would you heat the balloon so that it would float?

123. You have a helium balloon at 1.00 atm and 25°C. You want to make a hot-air balloon with the same volume and same lift as the helium balloon. Assume air is 79.0% nitrogen, 21.0% oxygen by volume. The "lift" of a balloon is given by the difference between the mass of air displaced by the balloon and the mass of gas inside the balloon.

a. Will the temperature in the hot-air balloon have to be higher or lower than 25°C? Explain.

b. Calculate the temperature of the air required for the hot-air balloon to provide the same lift as the helium balloon at 1.00 atm and 25°C. Assume atmospheric conditions are 1.00 atm and 25°C.

4. We state that the ideal gas law tends to hold best at low pressures and high temperatures. Show how the van der Waals equation simplifies to the ideal gas law under these conditions.

5. Atmospheric scientists often use mixing ratios to express the concentrations of trace compounds in air. Mixing ratios are often expressed as ppmv (parts per million volume):

$$ppmv \text{ of } X = \frac{\text{vol. of } X \text{ at STP}}{\text{total vol. of air at STP}} \times 10^6$$

On a recent autumn day, the concentration of carbon monoxide in the air in downtown Denver, Colorado, reached 3.0×10^2 ppmv. The atmospheric pressure at that time was 628 torr, and the temperature was 0°C.

a. What was the partial pressure of CO?

b. What was the concentration of CO in molecules per cubic centimeter?

6. Nitrogen gas (N_2) reacts with hydrogen gas (H_2) to form ammonia gas (NH_3). You have nitrogen and hydrogen gases in a 15.0-L container fitted with a movable piston (the piston allows the container volume to change so as to keep the pressure constant inside the container). Initially the partial pressure of each reactant gas is 1.00 atm. Assume the temperature is constant and that the reaction goes to completion.

a. Calculate the partial pressure of ammonia in the container after the reaction has reached completion.

b. Calculate the volume of the container after the reaction has reached completion.

Integrative Problems

[The]se problems require the integration of multiple concepts to find the [sol]utions.

7. In the presence of nitric acid, UO^{2+} undergoes a redox process. It is converted to UO_2^{2+} and nitric oxide (NO) gas is produced according to the following unbalanced equation:

$$NO_3^-(aq) + UO^{2+}(aq) \longrightarrow NO(g) + UO_2^{2+}(aq)$$

---

[12]. If 2.55×10^2 mL of NO(g) is isolated at 29°C and 1.5 atm, what amount (moles) of UO^{2+} was used in the reaction?

128. Silane, SiH_4, is the silicon analogue of methane, CH_4. It is prepared industrially according to the following equations:

$$Si(s) + 3HCl(g) \longrightarrow HSiCl_3(l) + H_2(g)$$
$$4HSiCl_3(l) \longrightarrow SiH_4(g) + 3SiCl_4(l)$$

a. If 156 mL of $HSiCl_3$ ($d = 1.34$ g/mL) is isolated when 15.0 L of HCl at 10.0 atm and 35°C is used, what is the percent yield of $HSiCl_3$?

b. When 156 mL of $HSiCl_3$ is heated, what volume of SiH_4 at 10.0 atm and 35°C will be obtained if the percent yield of the reaction is 93.1%?

129. Solid thorium(IV) fluoride has a boiling point of 1680°C. What is the density of a sample of gaseous thorium(IV) fluoride at its boiling point under a pressure of 2.5 atm in a 1.7-L container? Which gas will effuse faster at 1680°C, thorium(IV) fluoride or uranium(III) fluoride? How much faster?

130. Natural gas is a mixture of hydrocarbons, primarily methane (CH_4) and ethane (C_2H_6). A typical mixture might have $\chi_{methane} = 0.915$ and $\chi_{ethane} = 0.085$. What are the partial pressures of the two gases in a 15.00-L container of natural gas at 20.°C and 1.44 atm? Assuming complete combustion of both gases in the natural gas sample, what is the total mass of water formed?

Marathon Problem*

This problem is designed to incorporate several concepts and techniques into one situation. Marathon Problems can be used in class by groups of students to help facilitate problem-solving skills.

131. Use the following information to identify element A and compound B, then answer questions a and b.

An empty glass container has a mass of 658.572 g. It has a mass of 659.452 g after it has been filled with nitrogen gas at a pressure of 790. torr and a temperature of 15°C. When the container is evacuated and refilled with a certain element (A) at a pressure of 745 torr and a temperature of 26°C, it has a mass of 660.59 g.

Compound B, a gaseous organic compound that consists of 85.6% carbon and 14.4% hydrogen by mass, is placed in a stainless steel vessel (10.68 L) with excess oxygen gas. The vessel is placed in a constant-temperature bath at 22°C. The pressure in the vessel is 11.98 atm. In the bottom of the vessel is a container that is packed with Ascarite and a desiccant. Ascarite is asbestos impregnated with sodium hydroxide; it quantitatively absorbs carbon dioxide:

$$2NaOH(s) + CO_2(g) \longrightarrow Na_2CO_3(s) + H_2O(l)$$

*Used with permission from the *Journal of Chemical Education*, Vol. 68, No. 11, 1991, pp. 919–922; copyright © 1991, Division of Chemical Education, Inc.

Online Problem Solving and Practice

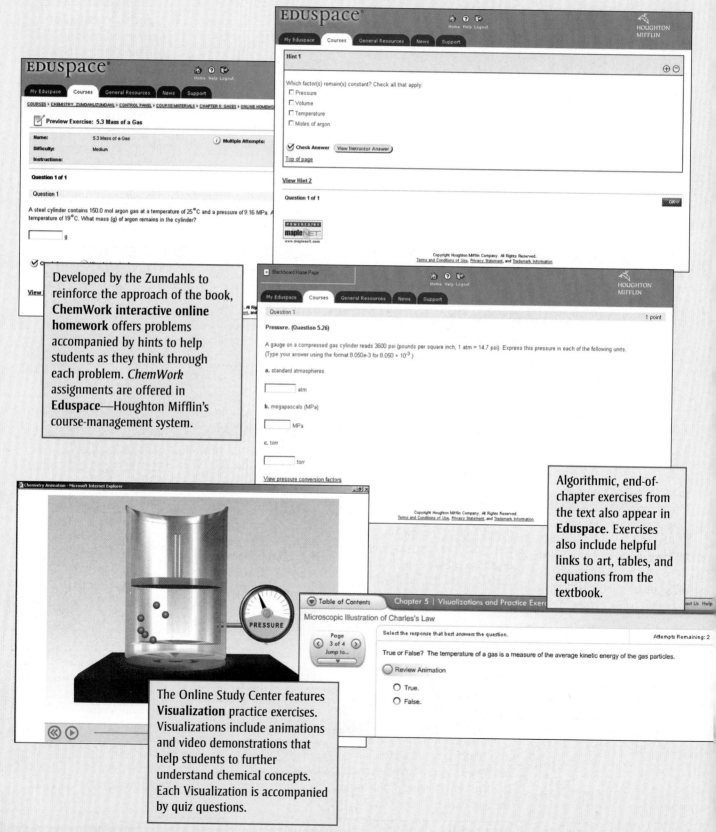

Developed by the Zumdahls to reinforce the approach of the book, **ChemWork interactive online homework** offers problems accompanied by hints to help students as they think through each problem. *ChemWork* assignments are offered in **Eduspace**—Houghton Mifflin's course-management system.

Algorithmic, end-of-chapter exercises from the text also appear in **Eduspace**. Exercises also include helpful links to art, tables, and equations from the textbook.

The Online Study Center features **Visualization** practice exercises. Visualizations include animations and video demonstrations that help students to further understand chemical concepts. Each Visualization is accompanied by quiz questions.

Media Resources for Instructors

HM ClassPrep with **HM Testing (powered by Diploma) CD** is a cross-platform CD that contains extensive text-specific resources for instructors to incorporate into their lecture presentations. These customizable assets include PowerPoint slides, Word files of the printed *Test Bank* and *Solutions Manual*, figures from the text, the *Instructor's Resource Guide* and more. HM Testing (powered by Diploma) is Houghton Mifflin's new flexible test-editing program, which features algorithmically generated questions, conceptual questions, and factual questions coded by level of difficulty to allow you to more easily choose appropriate test items. Select from 2400 test items designed to measure the concepts and principles covered in the seventh edition.

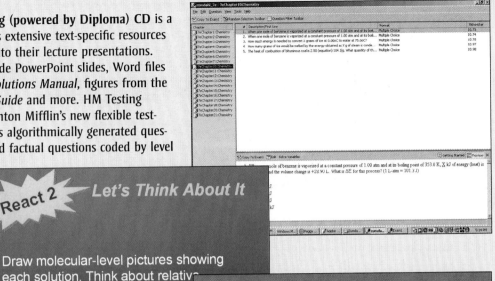

HM ClassPresent includes animations and video demonstrations that can be used to illustrate concepts and ideas that will help students further understand and visualize chemical concepts. Animations and videos can be projected directly from the CD, exported to your computer, and also come embedded in PowerPoint files.

Online Teaching Center for *Chemistry* offers access to lecture preparation materials; PowerPoint presentation resources; JPEGs of virtually all text illustrations, tables, and photos; video demonstrations and animations; molecule library with CHIME; as well as service and support. Also included on the Online Teaching Center, you will find classroom response-system slides. These slides allow you to get on-the-spot feedback on how well your students are grasping key concepts.

Eduspace, featuring online homework, is Houghton Mifflin's course-management system. Eduspace allows for online delivery of course materials, chat and discussion tools, and includes two types of algorithmic online homework: *ChemWork* and end-of-chapter exercises. *ChemWork* helps students learn the process of problem solving with interactive hints that help students think through each problem.

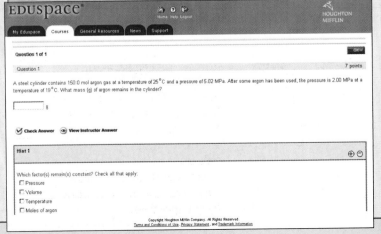

Technological Resources for Students

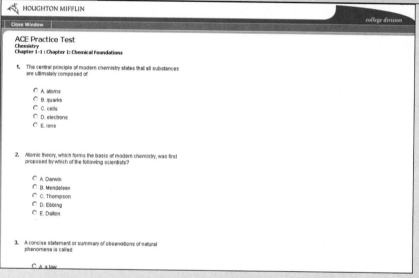

The **Online Study Center** supports the goals of the seventh edition with visualization, practice, and study aids. The *Visualizations* use animations and video demonstrations to help students see the chemistry concepts, and each *Visualization* is accompanied by a set of quiz questions so that students can test their knowledge of the concept.

The Online Study Center also includes an interactive review for each chapter, flashcards of key terms, and *ACE* practice tests, which help students prepare for quizzes and exams. Many of the resources on the Online Study Center are also available on the optional free, student CD-ROM.

Students get access to live, online help through **SMARTHINKING™**. E-structors are available when students need it the most and help students problem-solve rather than supply answers. Available free with new books on instructor's request. Also available via Eduspace.

1 Chemical Foundations

Contents

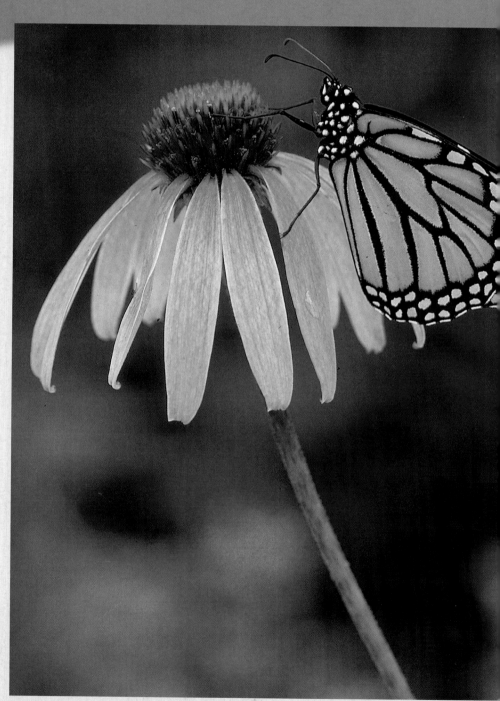

Male Monarch butterflies use the pheromones produced by a gland on their wings to make themselves attractive to females.

W hen you start your car, do you think about chemistry? Probably not, but you should. The power to start your car is furnished by a lead storage battery. How does this battery work, and what does it contain? When a battery goes dead, what does that mean? If you use a friend's car to "jump start" your car, did you know that your battery could explode? How can you avoid such an unpleasant possibility? What is in the gasoline that you put in your tank, and how does it furnish the energy to drive to school? What is the vapor that comes out of the exhaust pipe, and why does it cause air pollution? Your car's air conditioner might have a substance in it that is leading to the destruction of the ozone layer in the upper atmosphere. What are we doing about that? And why is the ozone layer important anyway?

All these questions can be answered by understanding some chemistry. In fact, we'll consider the answers to all these questions in this text.

Chemistry is around you all the time. You are able to read and understand this sentence because chemical reactions are occurring in your brain. The food you ate for breakfast or lunch is now furnishing energy through chemical reactions. Trees and grass grow because of chemical changes.

Chemistry also crops up in some unexpected places. When archaeologist Luis Alvarez was studying in college, he probably didn't realize that the chemical elements iridium and niobium would make him very famous when they helped him solve the problem of the disappearing dinosaurs. For decades scientists had wrestled with the mystery of why the dinosaurs, after ruling the earth for millions of years, suddenly became extinct 65 million years ago. In studying core samples of rocks dating back to that period, Alvarez and his coworkers recognized unusual levels of iridium and niobium in these samples—levels much more characteristic of extraterrestrial bodies than of the earth. Based on these observations, Alvarez hypothesized that a large meteor hit the earth 65 million years ago, changing atmospheric conditions so much that the dinosaurs' food couldn't grow, and they died—almost instantly in the geologic timeframe.

Chemistry is also important to historians. Did you realize that lead poisoning probably was a significant contributing factor to the decline of the Roman Empire? The Romans had high exposure to lead from lead-glazed pottery, lead water pipes, and a sweetening syrup called *sapa* that was prepared by boiling down grape juice in lead-lined vessels. It turns out that one reason for sapa's sweetness was lead acetate ("sugar of lead") that formed as the juice was cooked down. Lead poisoning with its symptoms of lethargy and mental malfunctions certainly could have contributed to the demise of the Roman society.

Chemistry is also apparently very important in determining a person's behavior. Various studies have shown that many personality disorders can be linked directly to imbalances of trace elements in the body. For example, studies on the inmates at Stateville Prison in Illinois have linked low cobalt levels with violent behavior. Lithium salts have been shown to be very effective in controlling the effects of manic depressive disease, and you've probably at some time in your life felt a special "chemistry" for another person. Studies suggest there is literally chemistry going on between two people who are attracted to each other. "Falling in love" apparently causes changes in the chemistry of the brain; chemicals are produced that give that "high" associated with a new relationship. Unfortunately, these chemical effects seem to wear off over time, even if the relationship persists and grows.

The importance of chemistry in the interactions of people should not really surprise us, since we know that insects communicate by emitting and receiving chemical signals via molecules called *pheromones*. For example, ants have a very complicated set of ch signals to signify food sources, danger, and so forth. Also, various female sex attractants have been isolated and used to lure males into traps to control insect populations. It would not be surprising if humans also emitted chemical signals that we were not aware of on a conscious level. Thus chemistry is pretty interesting and pretty important. The main goal of this text is to help you understand the concepts of chemistry so that you can better appreciate the world around you and can be more effective in whatever career you choose.

1.1 Chemistry: An Overview

Since the time of the ancient Greeks, people have wondered about the answer to the question: What is matter made of? For a long time humans have believed that matter is composed of atoms, and in the previous three centuries we have collected much indirect evidence to support this belief. Very recently, something exciting has happened—for the first time we can "see" individual atoms. Of course, we cannot see atoms with the naked eye but must use a special microscope called a scanning tunneling microscope (STM). Although we will not consider the details of its operation here, the STM uses an electron current from a tiny needle to probe the surface of a substance. The STM pictures of several substances are shown in Fig. 1.1. Notice how the atoms are connected to one another by "bridges," which, as we will see, represent the electrons that interconnect atoms.

In addition to "seeing" the atoms in solids such as salt, we have learned how to isolate and view a single atom. For example, the tiny white dot in the center of Fig. 1.2 is a single mercury atom that is held in a special trap.

So, at this point, we are fairly sure that matter consists of individual atoms. The nature of these atoms is quite complex, and the components of atoms don't behave much like the objects we see in the world of our experience. We call this world the *macroscopic world*—the world of cars, tables, baseballs, rocks, oceans, and so forth. One of the main jobs of a scientist is to delve into the macroscopic world and discover its "parts." For example, when you view a beach from a distance, it looks like a continuous solid substance. As you get closer, you see that the beach is really made up of individual grains of sand.

(a)   (b)

FIGURE 1.1
(a) The surface of a single grain of table salt. (b) An oxygen atom (indicated by arrow) on a gallium arsenide surface. (c) Scanning tunneling microscope image showing rows of ring-shaped clusters of benzene molecules on a rhodium surface. Each "doughnut"-shaped image represents a benzene molecule.

(c)

As we examine these grains of sand, we find they are composed of silicon and oxygen atoms connected to each other to form intricate shapes (see Fig. 1.3). One of the main challenges of chemistry is to understand the connection between the macroscopic world that we experience and the *microscopic world* of atoms and molecules. To truly understand chemistry you must learn to think on the atomic level. We will spend much time in this text helping you learn to do that.

One of the amazing things about our universe is that the tremendous variety of substances we find there results from only about 100 different kinds of atoms. You can think of these approximately 100 atoms as the letters in an alphabet out of which all the "words" in the universe are made. It is the way the atoms are organized in a given substance that determines the properties of that substance. For example, water, one of the most common and important substances on earth, is composed of two types of atoms: hydrogen and oxygen. There are two hydrogen atoms and one oxygen atom bound together to form the water molecule:

oxygen atom

hydrogen atom

water molecule

When an electric current passes through it, water is decomposed to hydrogen and oxygen. These *chemical elements* themselves exist naturally as diatomic (two-atom) molecules:

oxygen molecule   written O_2

hydrogen molecule   written H_2

We can represent the decomposition of water to its component elements, hydrogen and oxygen, as follows:

two water molecules written $2H_2O$

electric current

one oxygen molecule written O_2

two hydrogen molecules written $2H_2$

Notice that it takes two molecules of water to furnish the right number of oxygen and hydrogen atoms to allow for the formation of the two-atom molecules. This reaction explains

FIGURE 1.2
A charged mercury atom shows up as a tiny white dot (indicated by the arrow).

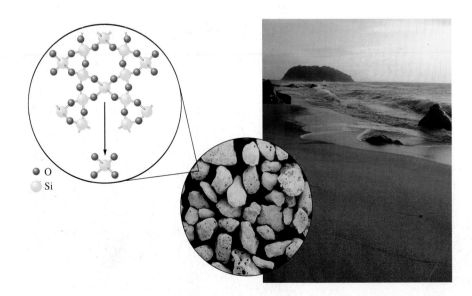

O
Si

FIGURE 1.3
Sand on a beach looks uniform from a distance, but up close the irregular sand grains are visible, and each grain is composed of tiny atoms.

CHEMICAL IMPACT

The Chemistry of Art

The importance of chemistry can show up in some unusual places. For example, a knowledge of chemistry is crucial to authenticating, preserving, and restoring art objects. The J. Paul Getty Museum in Los Angeles has a state-of-the-art chemical laboratory that costs many millions of dollars and employs many scientists. The National Gallery of Art (NGA) in Washington, D.C., also operates a highly sophisticated laboratory that employs 10 people: five chemists, a botanist, an art historian, a technician with a chemistry degree, and two fellows (interns).

One of the chemists at NGA is Barbara Berrie, who specializes in identifying paint pigments. One of her duties is to analyze a painting to see whether the paint pigments are appropriate for the time the picture was supposedly painted and consistent with the pigments known to be used by the artist given credit for the painting. This analysis is one way in which paintings can be authenticated. One of Berrie's recent projects was to analyze the 1617 oil painting *St. Cecilia and an Angel.* Her results showed the painting was the work of two artists of the time, Orazio Gentileschi and Giovanni Lanfranco. Originally the work was thought to be by Gentileschi alone.

Berrie is also working to define the range of colors used by water colorist Winslow Homer (the NGA has 30 Homer paintings in its collection) and to show how his color palette changed over his career. In addition, she is exploring how acidity affects the decomposition of a particular deep green transparent pigment (called copper resinate) used by Italian Renaissance artists so that paintings using this pigment can be better preserved.

Berrie says, "The chemistry I do is not hot-dog chemistry, just good old-fashioned general chemistry."

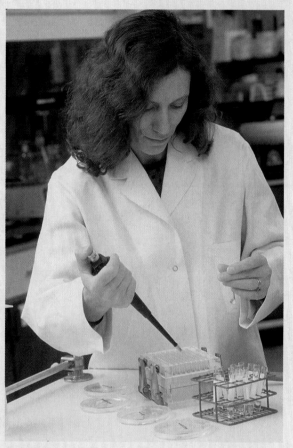

Dr. Barbara Berrie of the National Gallery of Art is shown analyzing the glue used in the wooden supports for a 14th century altar piece.

why the battery in your car can explode if you jump start it improperly. When you hook up the jumper cables, current flows through the dead battery, which contains water (and other things), and causes hydrogen and oxygen to form by decomposition of some of the water. A spark can cause this accumulated hydrogen and oxygen to explode, forming water again.

This example illustrates two of the fundamental concepts of chemistry: (1) matter is composed of various types of atoms, and (2) one substance changes to another by reorganizing the way the atoms are attached to each other.

These are core ideas of chemistry, and we will have much more to say about them.

Science: A Process for Understanding Nature and Its Changes

How do you tackle the problems that confront you in real life? Think about your trip to school. If you live in a city, traffic is undoubtedly a problem you confront daily. How do you decide the best way to drive to school? If you are new in town, you first get a map and look at the possible ways to make the trip. Then you might collect information from people who know the area about the advantages and disadvantages of various routes. Based on this information, you probably try to predict the best route. However, you can find the best route only by trying several of them and comparing the results. After a few experiments with the various possibilities, you probably will be able to select the best way. What you are doing in solving this everyday problem is applying the same process that scientists use to study nature. The first thing you did was collect relevant data. Then you made a prediction, and then you tested it by trying it out. This process contains the fundamental elements of science.

1. Making observations (collecting data)
2. Making a prediction (formulating a hypothesis)
3. Doing experiments to test the prediction (testing the hypothesis)

Scientists call this process the *scientific method*. We will discuss it in more detail in the next section. One of life's most important activities is solving problems—not "plug and chug" exercises, but real problems—problems that have new facets to them, that involve things you may have never confronted before. The more creative you are at solving these problems, the more effective you will be in your career and your personal life. Part of the reason for learning chemistry, therefore, is to become a better problem solver. Chemists are usually excellent problem solvers, because to master chemistry, you have to master the scientific approach. Chemical problems are frequently very complicated—there is usually no neat and tidy solution. Often it is difficult to know where to begin.

1.2 The Scientific Method

Science is a framework for gaining and organizing knowledge. Science is not simply a set of facts but also a plan of action—a *procedure* for processing and understanding certain types of information. Scientific thinking is useful in all aspects of life, but in this text we will use it to understand how the chemical world operates. As we have said in our previous discussion, the process that lies at the center of scientific inquiry is called the **scientific method.** There are actually many scientific methods, depending on the nature of the specific problem under study and on the particular investigator involved. However, it is useful to consider the following general framework for a generic scientific method (see Fig. 1.4):

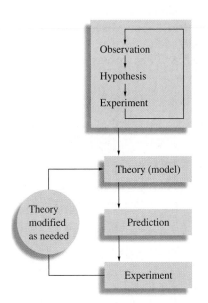

FIGURE 1.4
The fundamental steps of the scientific method.

Steps in the Scientific Method

➡ 1 *Making observations.* Observations may be *qualitative* (the sky is blue; water is a liquid) or *quantitative* (water boils at 100°C; a certain chemistry book weighs 2 kilograms). A qualitative observation does not involve a number. A quantitative observation (called a measurement) involves both a number and a unit.

➡ 2 *Formulating hypotheses.* A hypothesis is a *possible* explanation for an observation.

➡ 3 *Performing experiments.* An experiment is carried out to test a hypothesis. This involves gathering new information that enables a scientist to decide whether

the hypothesis is valid—that is, whether it is supported by the new information learned from the experiment. Experiments always produce new observations, and this brings the process back to the beginning again.

To understand a given phenomenon, these steps are repeated many times, gradually accumulating the knowledge necessary to provide a possible explanation of the phenomenon.

Scientific Models

Once a set of hypotheses that agrees with the various observations is obtained, the hypotheses are assembled into a theory. A **theory,** which is often called a **model,** is a set of tested hypotheses that gives an overall explanation of some natural phenomenon.

It is very important to distinguish between observations and theories. An observation is something that is witnessed and can be recorded. A theory is an *interpretation*—a possible explanation of *why* nature behaves in a particular way. Theories inevitably change as more information becomes available. For example, the motions of the sun and stars have remained virtually the same over the thousands of years during which humans have been observing them, but our explanations—our theories—for these motions have changed greatly since ancient times. (See the Chemical Impact on Observations, Theories, and the Planets on the Web site.)

The point is that scientists do not stop asking questions just because a given theory seems to account satisfactorily for some aspect of natural behavior. They continue doing experiments to refine or replace the existing theories. This is generally done by using the currently accepted theory to make a prediction and then performing an experiment (making a new observation) to see whether the results bear out this prediction.

Always remember that theories (models) are human inventions. They represent attempts to explain observed natural behavior in terms of human experiences. A theory is actually an educated guess. We must continue to do experiments and to refine our theories (making them consistent with new knowledge) if we hope to approach a more nearly complete understanding of nature.

As scientists observe nature, they often see that the same observation applies to many different systems. For example, studies of innumerable chemical changes have shown that the total observed mass of the materials involved is the same before and after the change. Such generally observed behavior is formulated into a statement called a **natural law.** For example, the observation that the total mass of materials is not affected by a chemical change in those materials is called the **law of conservation of mass.**

Note the difference between a natural law and a theory. A natural law is a summary of observed (measurable) behavior, whereas a theory is an explanation of behavior. *A law summarizes what happens; a theory (model) is an attempt to explain why it happens.*

In this section we have described the scientific method as it might ideally be applied (see Fig. 1.5). However, it is important to remember that science does not always progress smoothly and efficiently. For one thing, hypotheses and observations are not totally independent of each other, as we have assumed in the description of the idealized scientific

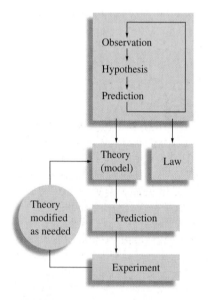

FIGURE 1.5
The various parts of the scientific method.

Robert Boyle (1627–1691) was born in Ireland. He became especially interested in experiments involving air and developed an air pump with which he produced evacuated cylinders. He used these cylinders to show that a feather and a lump of lead fall at the same rate in the absence of air resistance and that sound cannot be produced in a vacuum. His most famous experiments involved careful measurements of the volume of a gas as a function of pressure. In his book *The Skeptical Chymist,* Boyle urged that the ancient view of elements as mystical substances should be abandoned and that an element should instead be defined as anything that cannot be broken down into simpler substances. This conception was an important step in the development of modern chemistry.

CHEMICAL IMPACT

A Note-able Achievement

Post-it Notes, a product of the 3M Corporation, revolutionized casual written communications and personal reminders. Introduced in the United States in 1980, these sticky-but-not-too-sticky notes have now found countless uses in offices, cars, and homes throughout the world.

The invention of sticky notes occurred over a period of about 10 years and involved a great deal of serendipity. The adhesive for Post-it Notes was discovered by Dr. Spencer F. Silver of 3M in 1968. Silver found that when an acrylate polymer material was made in a particular way, it formed cross-linked microspheres. When suspended in a solvent and sprayed on a sheet of paper, this substance formed a "sparse monolayer" of adhesive after the solvent evaporated. Scanning electron microscope images of the adhesive show that it has an irregular surface, a little like the surface of a gravel road. In contrast, the adhesive on cellophane tape looks smooth and uniform, like a superhighway. The bumpy surface of Silver's adhesive caused it to be sticky but not so sticky to produce permanent adhesion, because the number of contact points between the binding surfaces was limited.

When he invented this adhesive, Silver had no specific ideas for its use, so he spread the word of his discovery to his fellow employees at 3M to see if anyone had an application for it. In addition, over the next several years development was carried out to improve the adhesive's properties. It was not until 1974 that the idea for Post-it Notes popped up. One Sunday Art Fry, a chemical engineer for 3M, was singing in his church choir when he became annoyed that the bookmark in his hymnal kept falling out. He thought to himself that it would be nice if the bookmark were sticky enough to stay in place but not so sticky that it couldn't be moved. Luckily, he remembered Silver's glue—and the Post-it Note was born.

For the next three years Fry worked to overcome the manufacturing obstacles associated with the product. By 1977 enough Post-it Notes were being produced to supply 3M's corporate headquarters, where the employees quickly became addicted to their many uses. Post-it Notes are now available in 62 colors and 25 shapes.

In the years since their introduction, 3M has heard some remarkable stories connected to the use of these notes. For example, a Post-it Note was applied to the nose of a corporate jet, where it was intended to be read by the plane's Las Vegas ground crew. Someone forgot to remove it, however. The note was still on the nose of the plane when it landed in Minneapolis, having survived a take-off and landing and speeds of 500 miles per hour at temperatures as low as −56°F. Stories on the 3M Web site also describe how a Post-it Note on the front door of a home survived the 140 mile per hour winds of Hurricane Hugo and how a foreign official accepted Post-it Notes in lieu of cash when a small bribe was needed to cut through bureaucratic hassles.

Post-it Notes have definitely changed the way we communicate and remember things.

method. The coupling of observations and hypotheses occurs because once we begin to proceed down a given theoretical path, our hypotheses are unavoidably couched in the language of that theory. In other words, we tend to see what we expect to see and often fail to notice things that we do not expect. Thus the theory we are testing helps us because it focuses our questions. However, at the very same time, this focusing process may limit our ability to see other possible explanations.

It is also important to keep in mind that scientists are human. They have prejudices; they misinterpret data; they become emotionally attached to their theories and thus lose objectivity; and they play politics. Science is affected by profit motives, budgets, fads, wars, and religious beliefs. Galileo, for example, was forced to recant his astronomical observations in the face of strong religious resistance. Lavoisier, the father of modern chemistry, was beheaded because of his political affiliations. Great progress in the chemistry of nitrogen fertilizers resulted from the desire to produce explosives to fight wars. The progress of science is often affected more by the frailties of humans and their institutions than by the limitations of scientific measuring devices. The scientific methods are only as effective as the humans using them. They do not automatically lead to progress.

CHEMICAL IMPACT

Critical Units!

How important are conversions from one unit to another? If you ask the National Aeronautics and Space Administration (NASA), very important! In 1999 NASA lost a $125 million Mars Climate Orbiter because of a failure to convert from English to metric units.

The problem arose because two teams working on the Mars mission were using different sets of units. NASA's scientists at the Jet Propulsion Laboratory in Pasadena, California, assumed that the thrust data for the rockets on the Orbiter they received from Lockheed Martin Astronautics in Denver, which built the spacecraft, were in metric units. In reality, the units were English. As a result the Orbiter dipped 100 kilometers lower into the Mars atmosphere than planned and the friction from the atmosphere caused the craft to burn up.

NASA's mistake refueled the controversy over whether Congress should require the United States to switch to the metric system. About 95% of the world now uses the metric system, and the United States is slowly switching from English to metric. For example, the automobile industry has adopted metric fasteners and we buy our soda in two-liter bottles.

Units can be very important. In fact, they can mean the difference between life and death on some occasions. In 1983, for example, a Canadian jetliner almost ran out of fuel when someone pumped 22,300 pounds of fuel into the aircraft instead of 22,300 kilograms. Remember to watch your units!

Artist's conception of the lost Mars Climate Orbiter.

Soda is commonly sold in 2-liter bottles—an example of the use of SI units in everyday life.

1.3 Units of Measurement

Making observations is fundamental to all science. A quantitative observation, or *measurement,* always consists of two parts: a *number* and a scale (called a *unit*). Both parts must be present for the measurement to be meaningful.

In this textbook we will use measurements of mass, length, time, temperature, electric current, and the amount of a substance, among others. Scientists recognized long ago that standard systems of units had to be adopted if measurements were to be useful. If every scientist had a different set of units, complete chaos would result. Unfortunately, different standards were adopted in different parts of the world. The two major systems are the *English system* used in the United States and the *metric system* used by most of the rest of the industrialized world. This duality causes a good deal of trouble; for example, parts as simple as bolts are not interchangeable between machines built using the two systems. As a result, the United States has begun to adopt the metric system.

Most scientists in all countries have for many years used the metric system. In 1960, an international agreement set up a system of units called the *International System (le Système International* in French), or the **SI system.** This system is based on the metric system and units derived from the metric system. The fundamental SI units are listed in Table 1.1. We will discuss how to manipulate these units later in this chapter.

Because the fundamental units are not always convenient (expressing the mass of a pin in kilograms is awkward), prefixes are used to change the size of the unit. These are listed in Table 1.2. Some common objects and their measurements in SI units are listed in Table 1.3.

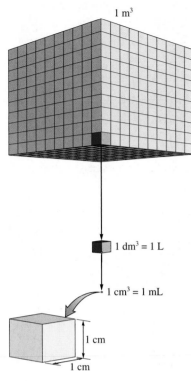

1 m³

1 dm³ = 1 L

1 cm³ = 1 mL

1 cm

1 cm

FIGURE 1.6
The largest cube has sides 1 m in length and a volume of 1 m³. The middle-sized cube has sides 1 dm in length and a volume of 1 dm³, or 1 L. The smallest cube has sides 1 cm in length and a volume of 1 cm³, or 1 mL.

TABLE 1.1 The Fundamental SI Units

Physical Quantity	Name of Unit	Abbreviation
Mass	kilogram	kg
Length	meter	m
Time	second	s
Temperature	kelvin	K
Electric current	ampere	A
Amount of substance	mole	mol
Luminous intensity	candela	cd

One physical quantity that is very important in chemistry is *volume,* which is not a fundamental SI unit but is derived from length. A cube that measures 1 meter (m) on each edge is represented in Fig. 1.6. This cube has a volume of $(1 \text{ m})^3 = 1 \text{ m}^3$. Recognizing that there are 10 decimeters (dm) in a meter, the volume of this cube is $(1 \text{ m})^3 = (10 \text{ dm})^3 = 1000 \text{ dm}^3$. A cubic decimeter, that is $(1 \text{ dm})^3$, is commonly called a *liter (L),* which is a unit of volume slightly larger than a quart. As shown in Fig. 1.6, 1000 liters are contained in a cube with a volume of 1 cubic meter. Similarly, since 1 decimeter equals 10 centimeters (cm), the liter can be divided into 1000 cubes each with a volume of 1 cubic centimeter:

$$1 \text{ liter} = (1 \text{ dm})^3 = (10 \text{ cm})^3 = 1000 \text{ cm}^3$$

Also, since $1 \text{ cm}^3 = 1$ milliliter (mL),

$$1 \text{ liter} = 1000 \text{ cm}^3 = 1000 \text{ mL}$$

Thus 1 liter contains 1000 cubic centimeters, or 1000 milliliters.

Chemical laboratory work frequently requires measurement of the volumes of liquids. Several devices for the accurate determination of liquid volume are shown in Fig. 1.7.

An important point concerning measurements is the relationship between mass and weight. Although these terms are sometimes used interchangeably, they are *not* the same.

TABLE 1.2 The Prefixes Used in the SI System (Those most commonly encountered are shown in blue.)

Prefix	Symbol	Meaning	Exponential Notation*
exa	E	1,000,000,000,000,000,000	10^{18}
peta	P	1,000,000,000,000,000	10^{15}
tera	T	1,000,000,000,000	10^{12}
giga	G	1,000,000,000	10^{9}
mega	M	1,000,000	10^{6}
kilo	k	1,000	10^{3}
hecto	h	100	10^{2}
deka	da	10	10^{1}
—	—	1	10^{0}
deci	d	0.1	10^{-1}
centi	c	0.01	10^{-2}
milli	m	0.001	10^{-3}
micro	μ	0.000001	10^{-6}
nano	n	0.000000001	10^{-9}
pico	p	0.000000000001	10^{-12}
femto	f	0.000000000000001	10^{-15}
atto	a	0.000000000000000001	10^{-18}

*See Appendix 1.1 if you need a review of exponential notation.

TABLE 1.3 Some Examples of Commonly Used Units

Length	A dime is 1 mm thick. A quarter is 2.5 cm in diameter. The average height of an adult man is 1.8 m.
Mass	A nickel has a mass of about 5 g. A 120-lb person has a mass of about 55 kg.
Volume	A 12-oz can of soda has a volume of about 360 mL.

Calibration
mark indicates
25-mL volume

Calibration
mark indicates
250-mL volume

Valve
(stopcock)
controls the
liquid flow

100-mL
graduated cylinder 25-mL pipet 50-mL buret 250-mL
volumetric flask

FIGURE 1.8
An electronic analytical balance.

FIGURE 1.7
Common types of laboratory equipment used to measure liquid volume.

Mass is a measure of the resistance of an object to a change in its state of motion. Mass is measured by the force necessary to give an object a certain acceleration. On earth we use the force that gravity exerts on an object to measure its mass. We call this force the object's **weight.** Since weight is the response of mass to gravity, it varies with the strength of the gravitational field. Therefore, your body mass is the same on the earth or on the moon, but your weight would be much less on the moon than on earth because of the moon's smaller gravitational field.

Because weighing something on a chemical balance (see Fig. 1.8) involves comparing the mass of that object to a standard mass, the terms *weight* and *mass* are sometimes used interchangeably, although this is incorrect.

1.4 Uncertainty in Measurement

The number associated with a measurement is obtained using some measuring device. For example, consider the measurement of the volume of a liquid using a buret (shown in Fig. 1.9 with the scale greatly magnified). Notice that the meniscus of the liquid occurs at about 20.15 milliliters. This means that about 20.15 mL of liquid has been delivered from the buret (if the initial position of the liquid meniscus was 0.00 mL). Note that we must estimate the last number of the volume reading by interpolating between the 0.1-mL marks. Since the last number is estimated, its value may be different if another person makes the same measurement. If five different people read the same volume, the results might be as follows:

FIGURE 1.9
Measurement of volume using a buret. The volume is read at the bottom of the liquid curve (called the meniscus).

Person	Results of Measurement
1	20.15 mL
2	20.14 mL
3	20.16 mL
4	20.17 mL
5	20.16 mL

These results show that the first three numbers (20.1) remain the same regardless of who makes the measurement; these are called *certain* digits. However, the digit to the right of the 1 must be estimated and therefore varies; it is called an *uncertain* digit. We customarily report a measurement by recording all the certain digits plus the *first* uncertain digit. In our example it would not make any sense to try to record the volume of thousandths of a milliliter because the value for hundredths of a milliliter must be estimated when using the buret.

It is very important to realize that a *measurement always has some degree of uncertainty.* The uncertainty of a measurement depends on the precision of the measuring device. For example, using a bathroom scale, you might estimate the mass of a grapefruit to be approximately 1.5 pounds. Weighing the same grapefruit on a highly precise balance might produce a result of 1.476 pounds. In the first case, the uncertainty occurs in the tenths of a pound place; in the second case, the uncertainty occurs in the thousandths of a pound place. Suppose we weigh two similar grapefruits on the two devices and obtain the following results:

A measurement always has some degree of uncertainty.

	Bathroom Scale	Balance
Grapefruit 1	1.5 lb	1.476 lb
Grapefruit 2	1.5 lb	1.518 lb

Do the two grapefruits have the same mass? The answer depends on which set of results you consider. Thus a conclusion based on a series of measurements depends on the certainty of those measurements. For this reason, it is important to indicate the uncertainty in any measurement. This is done by always recording the certain digits and the first uncertain digit (the estimated number). These numbers are called the **significant figures** of a measurement.

Uncertainty in measurement is discussed in more detail in Appendix 1.5.

The convention of significant figures automatically indicates something about the uncertainty in a measurement. The uncertainty in the last number (the estimated number) is usually assumed to be ± 1 unless otherwise indicated. For example, the measurement 1.86 kilograms can be taken to mean 1.86 ± 0.01 kilograms.

Uncertainty in Measurement

In analyzing a sample of polluted water, a chemist measured out a 25.00-mL water sample with a pipet (see Fig. 1.7). At another point in the analysis, the chemist used a graduated cylinder (see Fig. 1.7) to measure 25 mL of a solution. What is the difference between the measurements 25.00 mL and 25 mL?

Solution

Even though the two volume measurements appear to be equal, they really convey different information. The quantity 25 mL means that the volume is between 24 mL and 26 mL, whereas the quantity 25.00 mL means that the volume is between 24.99 mL and 25.01 mL. The pipet measures volume with much greater precision than does the graduated cylinder.

See Question 1.8.

When making a measurement, it is important to record the results to the appropriate number of significant figures. For example, if a certain buret can be read to ± 0.01 mL, you should record a reading of twenty-five milliliters as 25.00 mL, not 25 mL. This way at some later time when you are using your results to do calculations, the uncertainty in the measurement will be known to you.

Precision and Accuracy

Two terms often used to describe the reliability of measurements are *precision* and *accuracy*. Although these words are frequently used interchangeably in everyday life, they have different meanings in the scientific context. **Accuracy** refers to the agreement of a particular value with the true value. **Precision** refers to the degree of agreement among several measurements of the same quantity. Precision reflects the *reproducibility* of a given type of measurement. The difference between these terms is illustrated by the results of three different dart throws shown in Fig. 1.10.

Two different types of errors are illustrated in Fig. 1.10. A **random error** (also called an *indeterminate error*) means that a measurement has an equal probability of being high or low. This type of error occurs in estimating the value of the last digit of a measurement. The second type of error is called **systematic error** (or *determinate error*). This type of error occurs in the same direction each time; it is either always high or always low. Figure 1.10(a) indicates large random errors (poor technique). Figure 1.10(b) indicates small random errors but a large systematic error, and Figure 1.10(c) indicates small random errors and no systematic error.

In quantitative work, precision is often used as an indication of accuracy; we assume that the *average* of a series of precise measurements (which should "average out" the random errors because of their equal probability of being high or low) is accurate, or close to the "true" value. However, this assumption is valid only if systematic errors are absent. Suppose we weigh a piece of brass five times on a very precise balance and obtain the following results:

Weighing	Result
1	2.486 g
2	2.487 g
3	2.485 g
4	2.484 g
5	2.488 g

(a)

(b)

(c)

FIGURE 1.10
The results of several dart throws show the difference between precise and accurate. (a) Neither accurate nor precise (large random errors). (b) Precise but not accurate (small random errors, large systematic error). (c) Bull's-eye! Both precise and accurate (small random errors, no systematic error).

Normally, we would assume that the true mass of the piece of brass is very close to 2.486 grams, which is the average of the five results:

$$\frac{2.486 \text{ g} + 2.487 \text{ g} + 2.485 \text{ g} + 2.484 \text{ g} + 2.488 \text{ g}}{5} = 2.486 \text{ g}$$

However, if the balance has a defect causing it to give a result that is consistently 1.000 gram too high (a systematic error of +1.000 gram), then the measured value of 2.486 grams would be seriously in error. The point here is that high precision among several measurements is an indication of accuracy *only* if systematic errors are absent.

| Sample Exercise 1.2 | **Precision and Accuracy** |

To check the accuracy of a graduated cylinder, a student filled the cylinder to the 25-mL mark using water delivered from a buret (see Fig. 1.7) and then read the volume delivered. Following are the results of five trials:

Trial	Volume Shown by Graduated Cylinder	Volume Shown by the Buret
1	25 mL	26.54 mL
2	25 mL	26.51 mL
3	25 mL	26.60 mL
4	25 mL	26.49 mL
5	25 mL	26.57 mL
Average	25 mL	26.54 mL

Is the graduated cylinder accurate?

Solution

Precision is an indication of accuracy only if there are no systematic errors.

The results of the trials show very good precision (for a graduated cylinder). The student has good technique. However, note that the average value measured using the buret is significantly different from 25 mL. Thus this graduated cylinder is not very accurate. It produces a systematic error (in this case, the indicated result is low for each measurement).

See Question 1.11.

1.5 Significant Figures and Calculations

Calculating the final result for an experiment usually involves adding, subtracting, multiplying, or dividing the results of various types of measurements. Since it is very important that the uncertainty in the final result is known correctly, we have developed rules for counting the significant figures in each number and for determining the correct number of significant figures in the final result.

Rules for Counting Significant Figures

1. *Nonzero integers.* Nonzero integers always count as significant figures.

2. *Zeros.* There are three classes of zeros:

   Leading zeros are never significant figures.

   a. *Leading zeros* are zeros that *precede* all the nonzero digits. These do not count as significant figures. In the number 0.0025, the three zeros simply indicate the position of the decimal point. This number has only two significant figures.

   Captive zeros are always significant figures.

   b. *Captive zeros* are zeros *between* nonzero digits. These always count as significant figures. The number 1.008 has four significant figures.

   Trailing zeros are sometimes significant figures.

   c. *Trailing zeros* are zeros at the *right end* of the number. They are significant only if the number contains a decimal point. The number 100 has only one significant figure, whereas the number 1.00×10^2 has three significant figures. The number one hundred written as 100. also has three significant figures.

   Exact numbers never limit the number of significant figures in a calculation.

3. *Exact numbers.* Many times calculations involve numbers that were not obtained using measuring devices but were determined by counting: 10 experiments, 3 apples, 8 molecules. Such numbers are called *exact numbers*. They can be assumed to have an infinite number of significant figures. Other examples of exact numbers are the 2 in $2\pi r$ (the circumference of a circle) and the 4 and the 3 in $\frac{4}{3}\pi r^3$ (the volume of a sphere). Exact numbers also can arise from definitions. For example, one inch is defined as *exactly* 2.54 centimeters. Thus, in the statement 1 in = 2.54 cm, neither the 2.54 nor the 1 limits the number of significant figures when used in a calculation.

Exponential notation is reviewed in Appendix 1.1.

Note that the number 1.00×10^2 above is written in **exponential notation.** This type of notation has at least two advantages: the number of significant figures can be easily indicated, and fewer zeros are needed to write a very large or very small number. For example, the number 0.000060 is much more conveniently represented as 6.0×10^{25}. (The number has two significant figures.)

| Sample Exercise 1.3 | Significant Figures |

Give the number of significant figures for each of the following results.

a. A student's extraction procedure on tea yields 0.0105 g of caffeine.
b. A chemist records a mass of 0.050080 g in an analysis.
c. In an experiment a span of time is determined to be 8.050×10^{-3} s.

Solution

a. The number contains three significant figures. The zeros to the left of the 1 are leading zeros and are not significant, but the remaining zero (a captive zero) is significant.
b. The number contains five significant figures. The leading zeros (to the left of the 5) are not significant. The captive zeros between the 5 and the 8 are significant, and the trailing zero to the right of the 8 is significant because the number contains a decimal point.
c. This number has four significant figures. Both zeros are significant.

See Exercises 1.25 through 1.28.

To this point we have learned to count the significant figures in a given number. Next, we must consider how uncertainty accumulates as calculations are carried out. The detailed analysis of the accumulation of uncertainties depends on the type of calculation involved and can be complex. However, in this textbook we will employ the following simple rules that have been developed for determining the appropriate number of significant figures in the result of a calculation.

Rules for Significant Figures in Mathematical Operations*

1. *For multiplication or division,* the number of significant figures in the result is the same as the number in the least precise measurement used in the calculation. For example, consider the calculation

$$4.56 \times 1.4 = 6.38 \xrightarrow{\text{Corrected}} 6.4$$

Limiting term has two significant figures   Two significant figures

The product should have only two significant figures, since 1.4 has two significant figures.

2. *For addition or subtraction,* the result has the same number of decimal places as the least precise measurement used in the calculation. For example, consider the sum

$$\begin{array}{r} 12.11 \\ 18.0 \quad \leftarrow \text{Limiting term has one decimal place} \\ \underline{1.013} \\ 31.123 \end{array} \xrightarrow{\text{Corrected}} 31.1$$

One decimal place

The correct result is 31.1, since 18.0 has only one decimal place.

*Although these simple rules work well for most cases, they can give misleading results in certain cases. For more information, see L. M. Schwartz, "Propagation of Significant Figures," *J. Chem. Ed.* **62** (1985): 693; and H. Bradford Thompson, "Is 8°C equal to 50°F?" *J. Chem. Ed.* **68** (1991): 400.

Note that for multiplication and division, significant figures are counted. For addition and subtraction, the decimal places are counted.

In most calculations you will need to round numbers to obtain the correct number of significant figures. The following rules should be applied when rounding.

> ### Rules for Rounding
>
> 1. In a series of calculations, carry the extra digits through to the final result, *then* round.
>
> 2. If the digit to be removed
>   a. is less than 5, the preceding digit stays the same. For example, 1.33 rounds to 1.3.
>   b. is equal to or greater than 5, the preceding digit is increased by 1. For example, 1.36 rounds to 1.4.

Rule 2 is consistent with the operation of electronic calculators.

Although rounding is generally straightforward, one point requires special emphasis. As an illustration, suppose that the number 4.348 needs to be rounded to two significant figures. In doing this, we look *only* at the *first number* to the right of the 3:

$$4.348$$
$$\uparrow$$

Look at this number to
round to two significant figures.

Do not round sequentially. The number 6.8347 rounded to three significant figures is 6.83, not 6.84.

The number is rounded to 4.3 because 4 is less than 5. It is incorrect to round sequentially. For example, do *not* round the 4 to 5 to give 4.35 and then round the 3 to 4 to give 4.4.

When rounding, *use only the first number to the right of the last significant figure.*

It is important to note that Rule 1 above usually will not be followed in the Sample Exercises in this text because we want to show the correct number of significant figures in *each step* of a problem. This same practice is followed for the detailed solutions given in the *Solutions Guide*. However, as stated in Rule 1, the best procedure is to carry extra digits throughout a series of calculations and round to the correct number of significant figures only at the end. This is the practice you should follow. The fact that your rounding procedures are different from those used in this text must be taken into account when you check your answer with the one given at the end of the book or in the *Solutions Guide*. Your answer (based on rounding only at the end of a calculation) may differ in the last place from that given here as the "correct" answer because we have rounded after each step. To help you understand the difference between these rounding procedures, we will consider them further in Sample Exercise 1.4.

Sample Exercise 1.4 | ## Significant Figures in Mathematical Operations

Carry out the following mathematical operations, and give each result with the correct number of significant figures.

a. $1.05 \times 10^{-3} \div 6.135$

b. $21 - 13.8$

c. As part of a lab assignment to determine the value of the gas constant (R), a student measured the pressure (P), volume (V), and temperature (T) for a sample of gas, where

$$R = \frac{PV}{T}$$

The following values were obtained: $P = 2.560$, $T = 275.15$, and $V = 8.8$. (Gases will be discussed in detail in Chapter 5; we will not be concerned at this time about the units for these quantities.) Calculate R to the correct number of significant figures.

This number must be rounded to two significant figures.

Solution

a. The result is 1.71×10^{-4}, which has three significant figures because the term with the least precision (1.05×10^{-3}) has three significant figures.

b. The result is 7 with no decimal point because the number with the least number of decimal places (21) has none.

c.
$$R = \frac{PV}{T} = \frac{(2.560)(8.8)}{275.15}$$

The correct procedure for obtaining the final result can be represented as follows:

$$\frac{(2.560)(8.8)}{275.15} = \frac{22.528}{275.15} = 0.0818753$$
$$= 0.082 = 8.2 \times 10^{-2} = R$$

The final result must be rounded to two significant figures because 8.8 (the least precise measurement) has two significant figures. To show the effects of rounding at intermediate steps, we will carry out the calculation as follows:

Rounded to two significant figures
↓

$$\frac{(2.560)(8.8)}{275.15} = \frac{22.528}{275.15} = \frac{23}{275.15}$$

Now we proceed with the next calculation:

$$\frac{23}{275.15} = 0.0835908$$

Rounded to two significant figures, this result is

$$0.084 = 8.4 \times 10^{-2}$$

Note that intermediate rounding gives a significantly different result than was obtained by rounding only at the end. Again, we must reemphasize that in *your* calculations you should round *only at the end.* However, because rounding is carried out at intermediate steps in this text (to always show the correct number of significant figures), the final answer given in the text may differ slightly from the one you obtain (rounding only at the end).

See Exercises 1.31 through 1.34.

There is a useful lesson to be learned from part c of Sample Exercise 1.4. The student measured the pressure and temperature to greater precision than the volume. A more precise value of R (one with more significant figures) could have been obtained if a more precise measurement of V had been made. As it is, the efforts expended to measure P and T very precisely were wasted. Remember that a series of measurements to obtain some final result should all be done to about the same precision.

TABLE 1.4 English–Metric Equivalents	
Length	1 m = 1.094 yd
	2.54 cm = 1 in
Mass	1 kg = 2.205 lb
	453.6 g = 1 lb
Volume	1 L = 1.06 qt
	1 ft³ = 28.32 L

1.6 Dimensional Analysis

It is often necessary to convert a given result from one system of units to another. The best way to do this is by a method called the **unit factor method,** or more commonly **dimensional analysis.** To illustrate the use of this method, we will consider several unit conversions. Some equivalents in the English and metric systems are listed in Table 1.4. A more complete list of conversion factors given to more significant figures appears in Appendix 6.

Consider a pin measuring 2.85 centimeters in length. What is its length in inches? To accomplish this conversion, we must use the equivalence statement

$$2.54 \text{ cm} = 1 \text{ in}$$

If we divide both sides of this equation by 2.54 centimeters, we get

$$1 = \frac{1 \text{ in}}{2.54 \text{ cm}}$$

This expression is called a *unit factor*. Since 1 inch and 2.54 centimeters are exactly equivalent, multiplying any expression by this unit factor will not change its *value*.

The pin has a length of 2.85 centimeters. Multiplying this length by the appropriate unit factor gives

$$2.85 \text{ cm} \times \frac{1 \text{ in}}{2.54 \text{ cm}} = \frac{2.85}{2.54} \text{ in} = 1.12 \text{ in}$$

Note that the centimeter units cancel to give inches for the result. This is exactly what we wanted to accomplish. Note also that the result has three significant figures, as required by the number 2.85. Recall that the 1 and 2.54 in the conversion factor are exact numbers by definition.

| *Sample Exercise 1.5* | **Unit Conversions I** |

A pencil is 7.00 in long. What is its length in centimeters?

Solution

In this case we want to convert from inches to centimeters. Therefore, we must use the reciprocal of the unit factor used above to do the opposite conversion:

$$7.00 \text{ in} \times \frac{2.54 \text{ cm}}{1 \text{ in}} = (7.00)(2.54) \text{ cm} = 17.8 \text{ cm}$$

Here the inch units cancel, leaving centimeters, as requested.

See Exercises 1.37 and 1.38.

Note that two unit factors can be derived from each equivalence statement. For example, from the equivalence statement 2.54 cm = 1 in, the two unit factors are

$$\frac{2.54 \text{ cm}}{1 \text{ in}} \quad \text{and} \quad \frac{1 \text{ in}}{2.54 \text{ cm}}$$

Consider the direction of the required change to select the correct unit factor.

How do you choose which one to use in a given situation? Simply look at the *direction* of the required change. To change from inches to centimeters, the inches must cancel. Thus the factor 2.54 cm/1 in is used. To change from centimeters to inches, centimeters must cancel, and the factor 1 in/2.54 cm is appropriate.

Converting from One Unit to Another

- To convert from one unit to another, use the equivalence statement that relates the two units.

- Derive the appropriate unit factor by looking at the direction of the required change (to cancel the unwanted units).

- Multiply the quantity to be converted by the unit factor to give the quantity with the desired units.

| Sample Exercise 1.6 | Unit Conversions II |

You want to order a bicycle with a 25.5-in frame, but the sizes in the catalog are given only in centimeters. What size should you order?

Solution

You need to go from inches to centimeters, so 2.54 cm = 1 in is appropriate:

$$25.5 \text{ in} \times \frac{2.54 \text{ cm}}{1 \text{ in}} = 64.8 \text{ cm}$$

See Exercises 1.37 and 1.38.

To ensure that the conversion procedure is clear, a multistep problem is considered in Sample Exercise 1.7.

| Sample Exercise 1.7 | Unit Conversions III |

A student has entered a 10.0-km run. How long is the run in miles?

Solution

This conversion can be accomplished in several different ways. Since we have the equivalence statement 1 m = 1.094 yd, we will proceed by a path that uses this fact. Before we start any calculations, let us consider our strategy. We have kilometers, which we want to change to miles. We can do this by the following route:

$$\text{kilometers} \longrightarrow \text{meters} \longrightarrow \text{yards} \longrightarrow \text{miles}$$

To proceed in this way, we need the following equivalence statements:

$$1 \text{ km} = 1000 \text{ m}$$
$$1 \text{ m} = 1.094 \text{ yd}$$
$$1760 \text{ yd} = 1 \text{ mi}$$

To make sure the process is clear, we will proceed step by step:

Kilometers to Meters:

$$10.0 \text{ km} \times \frac{1000 \text{ m}}{1 \text{ km}} = 1.00 \times 10^4 \text{ m}$$

Meters to Yards:

$$1.00 \times 10^4 \text{ m} \times \frac{1.094 \text{ yd}}{1 \text{ m}} = 1.094 \times 10^4 \text{ yd}$$

Note that we should have only three significant figures in the result. Since this is an intermediate result, however, we will carry the extra digit. Remember, round off only the final result.

Yards to Miles:

$$1.094 \times 10^4 \text{ yd} \times \frac{1 \text{ mi}}{1760 \text{ yd}} = 6.216 \text{ mi}$$

Normally we round to the correct number of significant figures after each step. However, you should round only at the end.

Note in this case that 1 mi equals exactly 1760 yd *by designation*. Thus 1760 is an exact number.

Since the distance was originally given as 10.0 km, the result can have only three significant figures and should be rounded to 6.22 mi. Thus

$$10.0 \text{ km} = 6.22 \text{ mi}$$

Alternatively, we can combine the steps:

$$10.0 \text{ km} \times \frac{1000 \text{ m}}{1 \text{ km}} \times \frac{1.094 \text{ yd}}{1 \text{ m}} \times \frac{1 \text{ mi}}{1760 \text{ yd}} = 6.22 \text{ mi}$$

See Exercises 1.37 and 1.38.

In using dimensional analysis, your verification that everything has been done correctly is that you end up with the correct units. *In doing chemistry problems, you should always include the units for the quantities used.* Always check to see that the units cancel to give the correct units for the final result. This provides a very valuable check, especially for complicated problems.

Study the procedures for unit conversions in the following Sample Exercises.

| **Sample Exercise 1.8** | **Unit Conversion IV** |

The speed limit on many highways in the United States is 55 mi/h. What number would be posted in kilometers per hour?

Solution

Result obtained by rounding only at the end of the calculation

$$\frac{55 \text{ mi}}{\text{h}} \times \frac{1760 \text{ yd}}{1 \text{ mi}} \times \frac{1 \text{ m}}{1.094 \text{ yd}} \times \frac{1 \text{ km}}{1000 \text{ m}} = 88 \text{ km/h}$$

Note that all units cancel except the desired kilometers per hour.

See Exercises 1.43 through 1.45.

| **Sample Exercise 1.9** | **Unit Conversions V** |

A Japanese car is advertised as having a gas mileage of 15 km/L. Convert this rating to miles per gallon.

Solution

Result obtained by rounding only at the end of the calculation

$$\frac{15 \text{ km}}{\text{L}} \times \frac{1000 \text{ m}}{1 \text{ km}} \times \frac{1.094 \text{ yd}}{1 \text{ m}} \times \frac{1 \text{ mi}}{1760 \text{ yd}} \times \frac{1 \text{ L}}{1.06 \text{ qt}} \times \frac{4 \text{ qt}}{1 \text{ gal}} = 35 \text{ mi/gal}$$

See Exercise 1.46.

1.7 Temperature

Three systems for measuring temperature are widely used: the Celsius scale, the Kelvin scale, and the Fahrenheit scale. The first two temperature systems are used in the physical sciences, and the third is used in many of the engineering sciences. Our purpose here is to define the three temperature scales and show how conversions from one scale to another can be performed. Although these conversions can be carried out routinely on most calculators, we will consider the process in some detail here to illustrate methods of problem solving.

The three temperature scales are defined and compared in Fig. 1.11. Note that the size of the temperature unit (the *degree*) is the same for the Kelvin and Celsius scales.

FIGURE 1.11
The three major temperature scales.

The fundamental difference between these two temperature scales is in their zero points. Conversion between these two scales simply requires an adjustment for the different zero points.

$$T_K = T_C + 273.15$$

$$\text{Temperature (Kelvin)} = \text{temperature (Celsius)} + 273.15$$

or

$$T_C = T_K - 273.15$$

$$\text{Temperature (Celsius)} = \text{temperature (Kelvin)} - 273.15$$

For example, to convert 300.00 K to the Celsius scale, we do the following calculation:

$$300.00 - 273.15 = 26.85°C$$

Note that in expressing temperature in Celsius units, the designation °C is used. The degree symbol is not used when writing temperature in terms of the Kelvin scale. The unit of temperature on this scale is called a *kelvin* and is symbolized by the letter K.

Converting between the Fahrenheit and Celsius scales is somewhat more complicated because both the degree sizes and the zero points are different. Thus we need to consider two adjustments: one for degree size and one for the zero point. First, we must account for the difference in degree size. This can be done by reconsidering Fig. 1.11. Notice that since 212°F = 100°C and 32°F = 0°C,

$$212 - 32 = 180 \text{ Fahrenheit degrees} = 100 - 0 = 100 \text{ Celsius degrees}$$

Thus 180° on the Fahrenheit scale is equivalent to 100° on the Celsius scale, and the unit factor is

$$\frac{180°F}{100°C} \quad \text{or} \quad \frac{9°F}{5°C}$$

or the reciprocal, depending on the direction in which we need to go.

Next, we must consider the different zero points. Since 32°F = 0°C, we obtain the corresponding Celsius temperature by first subtracting 32 from the Fahrenheit temperature to account for the different zero points. Then the unit factor is applied to adjust for the difference in the degree size. This process is summarized by the equation

$$(T_F - 32°F)\frac{5°C}{9°F} = T_C \tag{1.1}$$

where T_F and T_C represent a given temperature on the Fahrenheit and Celsius scales, respectively. In the opposite conversion, we first correct for degree size and then correct for the different zero point. This process can be summarized in the following general equation:

$$T_F = T_C \times \frac{9°F}{5°C} + 32°F \tag{1.2}$$

Equations (1.1) and (1.2) are really the same equation in different forms. See if you can obtain Equation (1.2) by starting with Equation (1.1) and rearranging.

Understand the process of converting from one temperature scale to another; do not simply memorize the equations.

At this point it is worthwhile to weigh the two alternatives for learning to do temperature conversions: You can simply memorize the equations, or you can take the time to learn the differences between the temperature scales and to understand the processes involved in converting from one scale to another. The latter approach may take a little more effort, but the understanding you gain will stick with you much longer than the memorized formulas. This choice also will apply to many of the other chemical concepts. Try to think things through!

| Sample Exercise 1.10 | **Temperature Conversions I** |

Normal body temperature is 98.6°F. Convert this temperature to the Celsius and Kelvin scales.

Solution

A physician taking the temperature of a patient.

Rather than simply using the formulas to solve this problem, we will proceed by thinking it through. The situation is diagrammed in Fig. 1.12. First, we want to convert 98.6°F to the Celsius scale. The number of Fahrenheit degrees between 32.0°F and 98.6°F is 66.6°F. We must convert this difference to Celsius degrees:

$$66.6°F \times \frac{5°C}{9°F} = 37.0°C$$

FIGURE 1.12
Normal body temperature on the Fahrenheit, Celsius, and Kelvin scales.

CHEMICAL IMPACT

Faux Snow

Skiing is challenging and fun, but it is also big business. Both skiers and ski operators want the season to last as long as possible. The major factor in maximizing the length of the ski season and in salvaging dry periods during the winter is the ability to "make snow." Machine-made snow is now a required part of maintaining ideal conditions at major ski areas such as Aspen, Breckenridge, and Taos.

Snow is relatively easy to make if the air is cold enough. To manufacture snow, water is cooled to just above 0°C and then pumped at high pressure through a "gun" that produces a fine mist of water droplets that freeze before dropping to the ground. As might be expected, atmospheric conditions are critical when making snow. With an air temperature of −8°C (18°F) or less, untreated water can be used in the snow guns. However, the ideal type of snow for skiing is "powder"—fluffy snow made up of small, individual crystals. To achieve powdery snow requires sufficient nucleation

sites—that is, sites where crystal growth is initiated. This condition can be achieved by "doping" the water with ions such as calcium or magnesium or with fine particles of clay. Also, when the air temperature is between 0°C and −8°C, materials such as silver iodide, detergents, and organic materials may be added to the water to seed the snow.

A discovery at the University of Wisconsin in the 1970s led to the additive most commonly used for snow making. The Wisconsin scientists found that a bacterium (*Pseudomanas syringae*) commonly found in nature makes a protein that acts as a very effective nucleation site for ice formation. In fact, this discovery helped to explain why ice forms at 0°C on the blossoms of fruit trees instead of the water supercooling below 0°C, as pure water does when the temperature is lowered slowly below the freezing point. To help protect fruit blossoms from freeze damage, this bacterium has been genetically modified to remove the ice nucleation protein. As a result, fruit blossoms can survive

---

Thus 98.6°F corresponds to 37.0°C.

Now we can convert to the Kelvin scale:

$$T_K = T_C + 273.15 = 37.0 + 273.15 = 310.2 \text{ K}$$

Note that the final answer has only one decimal place (37.0 is limiting).

See Exercises 1.49, 1.51, and 1.52.

| Sample Exercise 1.11 | **Temperature Conversions II** |

One interesting feature of the Celsius and Fahrenheit scales is that −40°C and −40°F represent the same temperature, as shown in Fig. 1.11. Verify that this is true.

Solution

The difference between 32°F and −40°F is 72°F. The difference between 0°C and −40°C is 40°C. The ratio of these is

$$\frac{72°F}{40°C} = \frac{8 \times 9°F}{8 \times 5°C} = \frac{9°F}{5°C}$$

as required. Thus −40°C is equivalent to −40°F.

See Challenge Problem 1.86.

Since, as shown in Sample Exercise 1.11, −40° on both the Fahrenheit and Celsius scales represents the same temperature, this point can be used as a reference point (like 0°C and 32°F) for a relationship between the two scales:

$$\frac{\text{Number of Fahrenheit degrees}}{\text{Number of Celsius degrees}} = \frac{T_F - (-40)}{T_C - (-40)} = \frac{9°F}{5°C}$$

intact even if the temperature briefly falls below 0°C. (See the Chemical Impact on Organisms and Ice Formation on page 516.) For snow-making purposes, this protein forms the basis for Snowmax (prepared and sold by York Snow of Victor, New York), which is the most popular additive for snow making.

Obviously, snow cannot be made in the summer, so what is a skiing fanatic to do during the warm months? The answer is "dryslope" skiing. Although materials for dryslopes can be manufactured in a variety of ways, polymers are most commonly used for this application. One company that makes a multilayer polymer for artificial ski slopes is Briton Engineering Developments (Yorkshire, England), the producer of Snowflex. Snowflex consists of a slippery polymer fiber placed on top of a shock-absorbing base and lubricated by misting water through holes in its surface. Of course, this virtual skiing is not much like the real thing but it does provide some relief for summer ski withdrawal.

As artificial and synthetic snow amply demonstrate, chemistry makes life more fun.

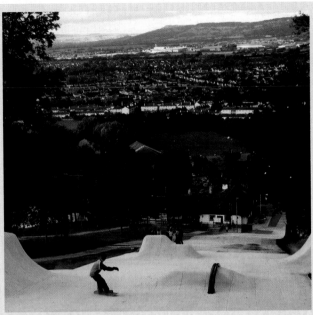

A freestyle ski area at Sheffield Ski Village, in England, uses Snowflex "virtual snow" for year-round fun.

or

$$\frac{T_F + 40}{T_C + 40} = \frac{9°F}{5°C} \qquad (1.3)$$

where T_F and T_C represent the same temperature (but not the same number). This equation can be used to convert Fahrenheit temperatures to Celsius, and vice versa, and may be easier to remember than Equations (1.1) and (1.2).

| Sample Exercise 1.12 | **Temperature Conversions III** |

Liquid nitrogen, which is often used as a coolant for low-temperature experiments, has a boiling point of 77 K. What is this temperature on the Fahrenheit scale?

Solution

We will first convert 77 K to the Celsius scale:

$$T_C = T_K - 273.15 = 77 - 273.15 = -196°C$$

To convert to the Fahrenheit scale, we will use Equation (1.3):

$$\frac{T_F + 40}{T_C + 40} = \frac{9°F}{5°C}$$

$$\frac{T_F + 40}{-196°C + 40} = \frac{T_F + 40}{-156°C} = \frac{9°F}{5°C}$$

$$T_F + 40 = \frac{9°F}{5°C}(-156°C) = -281°F$$

$$T_F = -281°F - 40 = -321°F$$

Liquid nitrogen is so cold that water condenses out of the surrounding air, forming a cloud as the nitrogen is poured.

See Exercises 1.49, 1.51, and 1.52.

1.8 Density

A property of matter that is often used by chemists as an "identification tag" for a substance is **density,** the mass of substance per unit volume of the substance:

$$\text{Density} = \frac{\text{mass}}{\text{volume}}$$

The density of a liquid can be determined easily by weighing an accurately known volume of liquid. This procedure is illustrated in Sample Exercise 1.13.

Sample Exercise 1.13   **Determining Density**

A chemist, trying to identify the main component of a compact disc cleaning fluid, finds that 25.00 cm³ of the substance has a mass of 19.625 g at 20°C. The following are the names and densities of the compounds that might be the main component:

Compound	Density in g/cm³ at 20°C
Chloroform	1.492
Diethyl ether	0.714
Ethanol	0.789
Isopropyl alcohol	0.785
Toluene	0.867

Which of these compounds is the most likely to be the main component of the compact disc cleaner?

Solution

To identify the unknown substance, we must determine its density. This can be done by using the definition of density:

$$\text{Density} = \frac{\text{mass}}{\text{volume}} = \frac{19.625\ \text{g}}{25.00\ \text{cm}^3} = 0.7850\ \text{g/cm}^3$$

This density corresponds exactly to that of isopropyl alcohol, which is therefore the most likely main component of the cleaner. However, note that the density of ethanol is also very close. To be sure that the compound is isopropyl alcohol, we should run several more density experiments. (In the modern laboratory, many other types of tests could be done to distinguish between these two liquids.)

See Exercises 1.55 and 1.56.

There are two ways of indicating units that occur in the denominator. For example, we can write g/cm³ or g cm⁻³. Although we will use the former system here, the other system is widely used.

Besides being a tool for the identification of substances, density has many other uses. For example, the liquid in your car's lead storage battery (a solution of sulfuric acid) changes density because the sulfuric acid is consumed as the battery discharges. In a fully charged battery, the density of the solution is about 1.30 g/cm³. If the density falls below 1.20 g/cm³, the battery will have to be recharged. Density measurement is also used to determine the amount of antifreeze, and thus the level of protection against freezing, in the cooling system of a car.

The densities of various common substances are given in Table 1.5.

TABLE 1.5   Densities of Various Common Substances* at 20°C

Substance	Physical State	Density (g/cm³)
Oxygen	Gas	0.00133
Hydrogen	Gas	0.000084
Ethanol	Liquid	0.789
Benzene	Liquid	0.880
Water	Liquid	0.9982
Magnesium	Solid	1.74
Salt (sodium chloride)	Solid	2.16
Aluminum	Solid	2.70
Iron	Solid	7.87
Copper	Solid	8.96
Silver	Solid	10.5
Lead	Solid	11.34
Mercury	Liquid	13.6
Gold	Solid	19.32

*At 1 atmosphere pressure

1.9 Classification of Matter

Before we can hope to understand the changes we see going on around us—the growth of plants, the rusting of steel, the aging of people, rain becoming more acidic—we must find out how matter is organized. **Matter,** best defined as anything occupying space and having mass, is the material of the universe. Matter is complex and has many levels of organization. In this section we introduce basic ideas about the structure of matter and its behavior.

We will start by considering the definitions of the fundamental properties of matter. Matter exists in three **states:** solid, liquid, and gas. A *solid* is rigid; it has a fixed volume and shape. A *liquid* has a definite volume but no specific shape; it assumes the shape of its container. A *gas* has no fixed volume or shape; it takes on the shape and volume of its container. In contrast to liquids and solids, which are only slightly compressible, gases are highly compressible; it is relatively easy to decrease the volume of a gas. Molecular-level pictures of the three states of water are given in Fig. 1.13. The different properties of ice, liquid water, and steam are determined by the different arrangements of the molecules in these substances. Table 1.5 gives the states of some common substances at 20°C and 1 atmosphere of pressure.

Visualizations:
Structure of a Gas
Structure of a Liquid
Structure of a Solid

Most of the matter around us consists of **mixtures** of pure substances. Wood, gasoline, wine, soil, and air are all mixtures. The main characteristic of a mixture is that it has *variable composition.* For example, wood is a mixture of many substances, the proportions of which vary depending on the type of wood and where it grows. Mixtures can be classified as **homogeneous** (having visibly indistinguishable parts) or **heterogeneous** (having visibly distinguishable parts).

Visualization: Comparison of a Compound and a Mixture

A homogeneous mixture is called a **solution.** Air is a solution consisting of a mixture of gases. Wine is a complex liquid solution. Brass is a solid solution of copper and zinc. Sand in water and iced tea with ice cubes are examples of heterogeneous mixtures. Heterogeneous mixtures usually can be separated into two or more homogeneous mixtures or pure substances (for example, the ice cubes can be separated from the tea).

Visualization: Comparison of a Solution and a Mixture

Mixtures can be separated into pure substances by physical methods. A **pure substance** is one with constant composition. Water is a good illustration of these ideas. As we will discuss in detail later, pure water is composed solely of H_2O molecules,

Visualization: Homogeneous Mixtures: Air and Brass)

FIGURE 1.13
The three states of water (where red spheres represent oxygen atoms and blue spheres represent hydrogen atoms). (a) Solid: the water molecules are locked into rigid positions and are close together. (b) Liquid: the water molecules are still close together but can move around to some extent. (c) Gas: the water molecules are far apart and move randomly.

Solid (Ice)   Liquid (Water)   Gas (Steam)
(a)   (b)   (c)

The term *volatile* refers to the ease with which a substance can be changed to its vapor.

but the water found in nature (groundwater or the water in a lake or ocean) is really a mixture. Seawater, for example, contains large amounts of dissolved minerals. Boiling seawater produces steam, which can be condensed to pure water, leaving the minerals behind as solids. The dissolved minerals in seawater also can be separated out by freezing the mixture, since pure water freezes out. The processes of boiling and freezing are **physical changes:** When water freezes or boils, it changes its state but remains water; it is still composed of H_2O molecules. A physical change is a change in the form of a substance, not in its chemical composition. A physical change can be used to separate a mixture into pure compounds, but it will not break compounds into elements.

One of the most important methods for separating the components of a mixture is **distillation,** a process that depends on differences in the volatility (how readily substances become gases) of the components. In simple distillation, a mixture is heated in a device such as that shown in Fig. 1.14. The most volatile component vaporizes at the lowest temperature, and the vapor passes through a cooled tube (a condenser), where it condenses back into its liquid state.

The simple, one-stage distillation apparatus shown in Fig. 1.14 works very well when only one component of the mixture is volatile. For example, a mixture of water and sand is easily separated by boiling off the water. Water containing dissolved minerals behaves in much the same way. As the water is boiled off, the minerals remain behind as nonvolatile solids. Simple distillation of seawater using the sun as the heat source is an excellent way to desalinate (remove the minerals from) seawater.

However, when a mixture contains several volatile components, the one-step distillation does not give a pure substance in the receiving flask, and more elaborate methods are required.

Another method of separation is simple **filtration,** which is used when a mixture consists of a solid and a liquid. The mixture is poured onto a mesh, such as filter paper, which passes the liquid and leaves the solid behind.

FIGURE 1.14
Simple laboratory distillation apparatus. Cool water circulates through the outer portion of the condenser, causing vapors from the distilling flask to condense into a liquid. The nonvolatile component of the mixture remains in the distilling flask.

A third method of separation is called **chromatography.** Chromatography is the general name applied to a series of methods that employ a system with two *phases* (states) of matter: a mobile phase and a stationary phase. The *stationary phase* is a solid, and the *mobile phase* is either a liquid or a gas. The separation process occurs because the components of the mixture have different affinities for the two phases and thus move through the system at different rates. A component with a high affinity for the mobile phase moves relatively quickly through the chromatographic system, whereas one with a high affinity for the solid phase moves more slowly.

One simple type of chromatography, **paper chromatography,** employs a strip of porous paper, such as filter paper, for the stationary phase. A drop of the mixture to be separated is placed on the paper, which is then dipped into a liquid (the mobile phase) that travels up the paper as though it were a wick (see Fig. 1.15). This method of separating a mixture is often used by biochemists, who study the chemistry of living systems.

It should be noted that when a mixture is separated, the absolute purity of the separated components is an ideal. Because water, for example, inevitably comes into contact with other materials when it is synthesized or separated from a mixture, it is never absolutely pure. With great care, however, substances can be obtained in very nearly pure form.

Pure substances contain compounds (combinations of elements) or free elements. A **compound** is a substance with *constant composition* that can be broken down into elements by chemical processes. An example of a chemical process is the electrolysis of water, in which an electric current is passed through water to break it down into the free elements hydrogen and oxygen. This process produces a chemical change because the water molecules have been broken down. The water is gone, and in its place we have the free elements hydrogen and oxygen. A **chemical change** is one in which a given substance becomes a new substance or substances with different properties and different

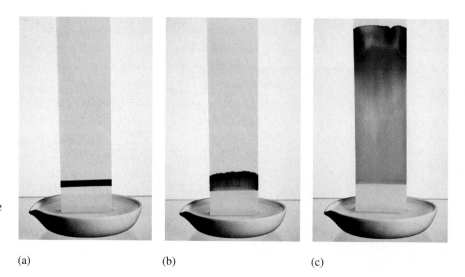

FIGURE 1.15
Paper chromatography of ink. (a) A line of the mixture to be separated is placed at one end of a sheet of porous paper. (b) The paper acts as a wick to draw up the liquid. (c) The component with the weakest attraction for the paper travels faster than the components that cling to the paper.

(a)   (b)   (c)

The element mercury (top left) combines with the element iodine (top right) to form the compound mercuric iodide (bottom). This is an example of a chemical change.

composition. **Elements** are substances that cannot be decomposed into simpler substances by chemical or physical means.

We have seen that the matter around us has various levels of organization. The most fundamental substances we have discussed so far are elements. As we will see in later chapters, elements also have structure: They are composed of atoms, which in turn are composed of nuclei and electrons. Even the nucleus has structure: It is composed of protons and neutrons. And even these can be broken down further, into elementary particles called *quarks*. However, we need not concern ourselves with such details at this point. Figure 1.16 summarizes our discussion of the organization of matter.

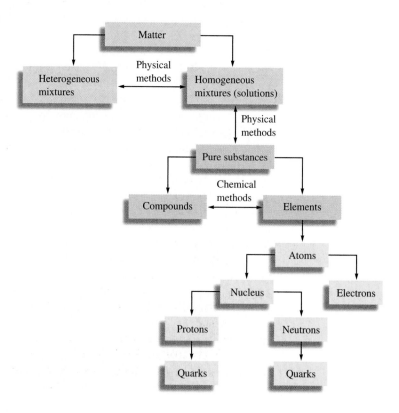

FIGURE 1.16
The organization of matter.

Key Terms

Section 1.2
scientific method
measurement
hypothesis
theory
model
natural law
law of conservation of mass

Section 1.3
SI system
mass
weight

Section 1.4
uncertainty
significant figures
accuracy
precision
random error
systematic error

Section 1.5
exponential notation

Section 1.6
unit factor method
dimensional analysis

Section 1.8
density

Section 1.9
matter
states (of matter)
homogeneous mixture
heterogeneous mixture
solution
pure substance
physical change
distillation
filtration
chromatography
paper chromatography
compound
chemical change
element

For Review

Scientific method
- Make observations
- Formulate hypotheses
- Perform experiments

Models (theories) are explanation of why nature behaves in a particular way.
- They are subject to modification over time and sometimes fail.

Quantitative observations are called measurements.
- Consist of a number and a unit
- Involve some uncertainty
- Uncertainty is indicated by using significant figures
  - Rules to determine significant figures
  - Calculations using significant figures
- Preferred system is SI

Temperature conversions
- $T_K = T_C + 273$
- $T_C = (T_F - 32°F)\left(\dfrac{5°C}{9°F}\right)$
- $T_F = T_C\left(\dfrac{5°F}{9°C}\right) + 32°F$

Density
- $\text{Density} = \dfrac{\text{mass}}{\text{volume}}$

Matter can exist in three states:
- Solid
- Liquid
- Gas

Mixtures can be separated by methods involving only physical changes:
- Distillation
- Filtration
- Chromatography

Compounds can be decomposed to elements only through chemical changes.

REVIEW QUESTIONS

1. Define and explain the differences between the following terms.
   a. law and theory
   b. theory and experiment
   c. qualitative and quantitative
   d. hypothesis and theory
2. Is the scientific method suitable for solving problems only in the sciences? Explain.
3. Which of the following statements (hypotheses) could be tested by quantitative measurement?
   a. Ty Cobb was a better hitter than Pete Rose.
   b. Ivory soap is $99\frac{44}{100}\%$ pure.
   c. Rolaids consumes 47 times its weight in excess stomach acid.

4. For each of the following pieces of glassware, provide a sample measurement and discuss the number of significant figures and uncertainty.

a. b. c.

5. A student performed an analysis of a sample for its calcium content and got the following results:

14.92%   14.91%   14.88%   14.91%

The actual amount of calcium in the sample is 15.70%. What conclusions can you draw about the accuracy and precision of these results?

6. Compare and contrast the multiplication/division significant figure rule to the significant figure rule applied for addition/subtraction mathematical operations.

7. Explain how density can be used as a conversion factor to convert the volume of an object to the mass of the object, and vice versa.

8. On which temperature scale (°F, °C, or K) does 1 degree represent the smallest change in temperature?

9. Distinguish between physical changes and chemical changes.

10. Why is the separation of mixtures into pure or relatively pure substances so important when performing a chemical analysis?

Active Learning Questions

These questions are designed to be used by groups of students in class. The questions allow students to explore their understanding of concepts through discussion and peer teaching. The real value of these questions is the learning that occurs while students talk to each other about chemical concepts.

1. **a.** There are 365 days per year, 24 hours per day, 12 months per year, and 60 minutes per hour. Use these data to determine how many minutes are in a month.
   b. Now use the following data to calculate the number of minutes in a month: 24 hours per day, 60 minutes per hour, 7 days per week, and 4 weeks per month.
   c. Why are these answers different? Which (if any) is more correct? Why?

2. You go to a convenience store to buy candy and find the owner to be rather odd. He allows you to buy pieces in multiples of four, and to buy four, you need $0.23. He only allows you to do this by using 3 pennies and 2 dimes. You have a bunch of pennies and dimes, and instead of counting them, you decide to weigh them.

You have 636.3 g of pennies, and each penny weighs 3.03 g. Each dime weighs 2.29 g. Each piece of candy weighs 10.23 g.
   a. How many pennies do you have?
   b. How many dimes do you need to buy as much candy as possible?
   c. How much should all these dimes weigh?
   d. How many pieces of candy could you buy? (number of dimes from part b)
   e. How much would this candy weigh?
   f. How many pieces of candy could you buy with twice as many dimes?

3. When a marble is dropped into a beaker of water, it sinks to the bottom. Which of the following is the best explanation?
   a. The surface area of the marble is not large enough to be held up by the surface tension of the water.
   b. The mass of the marble is greater than that of the water.
   c. The marble weighs more than an equivalent volume of the water.
   d. The force from dropping the marble breaks the surface tension of the water.
   e. The marble has greater mass and volume than the water.

Justify your choice, and for choices you did not pick, explain what is wrong about them.

4. You have two beakers, one filled to the 100-mL mark with sugar (the sugar has a mass of 180.0 g) and the other filled to the 100-mL mark with water (the water has a mass of 100.0 g). You pour all the sugar and all the water together in a bigger beaker and stir until the sugar is completely dissolved.

   a. Which of the following is true about the mass of the solution? Explain.

     i. It is much greater than 280.0 g.

     ii. It is somewhat greater than 280.0 g.

     iii. It is exactly 280.0 g.

     iv. It is somewhat less than 280.0 g.

     v. It is much less than 280.0 g.

   b. Which of the following is true about the volume of the solution? Explain.

     i. It is much greater than 200.0 mL.

     ii. It is somewhat greater than 200.0 mL.

     iii. It is exactly 200.0 mL.

     iv. It is somewhat less than 200.0 mL.

     v. It is much less than 200.0 mL.

5. You may have noticed that when water boils, you can see bubbles that rise to the surface of the water.

   a. What is inside these bubbles?

     i. air

     ii. hydrogen and oxygen gas

     iii. oxygen gas

     iv. water vapor

     v. carbon dioxide gas

   b. Is the boiling of water a chemical or physical change? Explain.

6. If you place a glass rod over a burning candle, the glass appears to turn black. What is happening to each of the following (physical change, chemical change, both, or neither) as the candle burns? Explain each answer.

   a. the wax   **b.** the wick   **c.** the glass rod

7. Which characteristics of a solid, a liquid, and a gas are exhibited by each of the following substances? How would you classify each substance?

   a. a bowl of pudding   **b.** a bucketful of sand

8. You have water in each graduated cylinder shown:

You then add both samples to a beaker. How would you write the number describing the total volume? What limits the precision of this number?

9. Paracelsus, a sixteenth-century alchemist and healer, adopted as his slogan: "The patients are your textbook, the sickbed is your study." Is this view consistent with using the scientific method?

10. What is wrong with the following statement?

"The results of the experiment do not agree with the theory. Something must be wrong with the experiment."

11. Why is it incorrect to say that the results of a measurement were accurate but not precise?

12. What data would you need to estimate the money you would spend on gasoline to drive your car from New York to Chicago? Provide estimates of values and a sample calculation.

13. Sketch two pieces of glassware: one that can measure volume to the thousandths place and one that can measure volume only to the ones place.

14. You have a 1.0-cm³ sample of lead and a 1.0-cm³ sample of glass. You drop each in separate beakers of water. How do the volumes of water displaced by each sample compare? Explain.

15. Sketch a magnified view (showing atoms/molecules) of each of the following and explain:

   a. a heterogeneous mixture of two different compounds

   b. a homogeneous mixture of an element and a compound

16. You are driving 65 mi/h and take your eyes off the road for "just a second." What distance (in feet) do you travel in this time?

A blue question or exercise number indicates that the answer to that question or exercise appears at the back of this book and a solution appears in the *Solutions Guide*.

Questions

17. The difference between a *law* and a *theory* is the difference between *what* and *why*. Explain.

18. Explain the fundamental steps of the scientific method.

19. A measurement is a quantitative observation involving both a number and a unit. What is a qualitative observation? What are the SI units for mass, length, and volume? What is the assumed uncertainty in a number (unless stated otherwise)? The uncertainty of a measurement depends on the precision of the measuring device. Explain.

20. To determine the volume of a cube, a student measured one of the dimensions of the cube several times. If the true dimension of the cube is 10.62 cm, give an example of four sets of measurements that would illustrate the following.

   a. imprecise and inaccurate data

   b. precise but inaccurate data

   c. precise and accurate data

   Give a possible explanation as to why data can be imprecise or inaccurate. What is wrong with saying a set of measurements is imprecise but accurate?

21. What are significant figures? Show how to indicate the number one thousand to 1 significant figure, 2 significant figures, 3 significant figures, and 4 significant figures. Why is the answer, to

the correct number of significant figures, not 1.0 for the following calculation?

$$\frac{1.5 - 1.0}{0.50} =$$

22. What is the volume per unit mass equal to? What unit conversion would the volume per unit mass be useful for?

23. When the temperature in degrees Fahrenheit (T_F) is plotted versus the temperature in degrees Celsius (T_C), a straight line plot results. A straight line plot also results when T_C is plotted versus T_K (the temperature in degrees Kelvin). Reference Appendix A1.3 and determine the slope and y-intercept of each of these two plots.

24. Give four examples illustrating each of the following terms.
    a. homogeneous mixture   d. element
    b. heterogeneous mixture   e. physical change
    c. compound   f. chemical change

Exercises

In this section similar exercises are paired.

Significant Figures and Unit Conversions

25. Which of the following are exact numbers?
    a. There are *100* cm in 1 m.
    b. One meter equals *1.094* yard.
    c. We can use the equation

    $$°F = \tfrac{9}{5}°C + 32$$

    to convert from Celsius to Fahrenheit temperature. Are the numbers $\tfrac{9}{5}$ and *32* exact or inexact?
    d. $\pi = 3.1415927$.

26. Indicate the number of significant figures in each of the following:
    a. This book contains more than 1000 pages.
    b. A mile is about 5300 ft.
    c. A liter is equivalent to 1.059 qt.
    d. The population of the United States is approaching 3.0×10^2 million.
    e. A kilogram is 1000 g.
    f. The Boeing 747 cruises at around 600 mi/h.

27. How many significant figures are there in each of the following values?
    a. 6.07×10^{-15} e. 463.8052
    b. 0.003840   f. 300
    c. 17.00   g. 301
    d. 8×10^8 h. 300.

28. How many significant figures are in each of the following?
    a. 100   e. 0.0048
    b. 1.0×10^2 f. 0.00480
    c. 1.00×10^3 g. 4.80×10^{-3}
    d. 100.   h. 4.800×10^{-3}

29. Round off each of the following numbers to the indicated number of significant digits and write the answer in standard scientific notation.
    a. 0.00034159 to three digits
    b. 103.351×10^2 to four digits
    c. 17.9915 to five digits
    d. 3.365×10^5 to three digits

30. Use exponential notation to express the number 480 to
    a. one significant figure
    b. two significant figures
    c. three significant figures
    d. four significant figures

31. Evaluate each of the following and write the answer to the appropriate number of significant figures.
    a. $212.2 + 26.7 + 402.09$
    b. $1.0028 + 0.221 + 0.10337$
    c. $52.331 + 26.01 - 0.9981$
    d. $2.01 \times 10^2 + 3.014 \times 10^3$
    e. $7.255 - 6.8350$

32. Perform the following mathematical operations, and express each result to the correct number of significant figures.
    a. $\dfrac{0.102 \times 0.0821 \times 273}{1.01}$
    b. $0.14 \times 6.022 \times 10^{23}$
    c. $4.0 \times 10^4 \times 5.021 \times 10^{-3} \times 7.34993 \times 10^2$
    d. $\dfrac{2.00 \times 10^6}{3.00 \times 10^{-7}}$

33. Perform the following mathematical operations and express the result to the correct number of significant figures.
    a. $\dfrac{2.526}{3.1} + \dfrac{0.470}{0.623} + \dfrac{80.705}{0.4326}$
    b. $(6.404 \times 2.91)/(18.7 - 17.1)$
    c. $6.071 \times 10^{-5} - 8.2 \times 10^{-6} - 0.521 \times 10^{-4}$
    d. $(3.8 \times 10^{-12} + 4.0 \times 10^{-13})/(4 \times 10^{12} + 6.3 \times 10^{13})$
    e. $\dfrac{9.5 + 4.1 + 2.8 + 3.175}{4}$

    (Assume that this operation is taking the average of four numbers. Thus 4 in the denominator is exact.)
    f. $\dfrac{8.925 - 8.905}{8.925} \times 100$

    (This type of calculation is done many times in calculating a percentage error. Assume that this example is such a calculation; thus 100 can be considered to be an exact number.)

34. Perform the following mathematical operations, and express the result to the correct number of significant figures.
    a. $6.022 \times 10^{23} \times 1.05 \times 10^2$
    b. $\dfrac{6.6262 \times 10^{-34} \times 2.998 \times 10^8}{2.54 \times 10^{-9}}$
    c. $1.285 \times 10^{-2} + 1.24 \times 10^{-3} + 1.879 \times 10^{-1}$
    d. $1.285 \times 10^{-2} - 1.24 \times 10^{-3}$
    e. $\dfrac{(1.00866 - 1.00728)}{6.02205 \times 10^{23}}$
    f. $\dfrac{9.875 \times 10^2 - 9.795 \times 10^2}{9.875 \times 10^2} \times 100 \,(100 \text{ is exact})$
    g. $\dfrac{9.42 \times 10^2 + 8.234 \times 10^2 + 1.625 \times 10^3}{3} \,(3 \text{ is exact})$

35. Perform each of the following conversions.
    a. 8.43 cm to millimeters
    b. 2.41×10^2 cm to meters
    c. 294.5 nm to centimeters
    d. 1.445×10^4 m to kilometers

e. 235.3 m to millimeters

f. 903.3 nm to micrometers

36. a. How many kilograms are in one teragram?

b. How many nanometers are in 6.50×10^2 terameters?

c. How many kilograms are in 25 femtograms?

d. How many liters are in 8.0 cubic decimeters?

e. How many microliters are in one milliliter?

f. How many picograms are in one microgram?

37. Perform the following unit conversions.

a. Congratulations! You and your spouse are the proud parents of a new baby, born while you are studying in a country that uses the metric system. The nurse has informed you that the baby weighs 3.91 kg and measures 51.4 cm. Convert your baby's weight to pounds and ounces and her length to inches (rounded to the nearest quarter inch).

b. The circumference of the earth is 25,000 mi at the equator. What is the circumference in kilometers? in meters?

c. A rectangular solid measures 1.0 m by 5.6 cm by 2.1 dm. Express its volume in cubic meters, liters, cubic inches, and cubic feet.

38. Perform the following unit conversions.

a. 908 oz to kilograms

b. 12.8 L to gallons

c. 125 mL to quarts

d. 2.89 gal to milliliters

e. 4.48 lb to grams

f. 550 mL to quarts

39. Use the following exact conversion factors to perform the stated calculations:

$$5\tfrac{1}{2} \text{ yards} = 1 \text{ rod}$$
$$40 \text{ rods} = 1 \text{ furlong}$$
$$8 \text{ furlongs} = 1 \text{ mile}$$

a. The Kentucky Derby race is 1.25 miles. How long is the race in rods, furlongs, meters, and kilometers?

b. A marathon race is 26 miles, 385 yards. What is this distance in rods, furlongs, meters, and kilometers?

40. Although the preferred SI unit of area is the square meter, land is often measured in the metric system in hectares (ha). One hectare is equal to 10,000 m². In the English system, land is often measured in acres (1 acre = 160 rod²). Use the exact conversions and those given in Exercise 39 to calculate the following.

a. 1 ha = ———— km².

b. The area of a 5.5-acre plot of land in hectares, square meters, and square kilometers.

c. A lot with dimensions 120 ft by 75 ft is to be sold for $6500. What is the price per acre? What is the price per hectare?

41. Precious metals and gems are measured in troy weights in the English system:

$$24 \text{ grains} = 1 \text{ pennyweight (exact)}$$
$$20 \text{ pennyweight} = 1 \text{ troy ounce (exact)}$$
$$12 \text{ troy ounces} = 1 \text{ troy pound (exact)}$$
$$1 \text{ grain} = 0.0648 \text{ gram}$$
$$1 \text{ carat} = 0.200 \text{ gram}$$

a. The most common English unit of mass is the pound avoirdupois. What is one troy pound in kilograms and in pounds?

b. What is the mass of a troy ounce of gold in grams and in carats?

c. The density of gold is 19.3 g/cm³. What is the volume of a troy pound of gold?

42. Apothecaries (druggists) use the following set of measures in the English system:

$$20 \text{ grains ap} = 1 \text{ scruple (exact)}$$
$$3 \text{ scruples} = 1 \text{ dram ap (exact)}$$
$$8 \text{ dram ap} = 1 \text{ oz ap (exact)}$$
$$1 \text{ dram ap} = 3.888 \text{ g}$$

a. Is an apothecary grain the same as a troy grain? (See Exercise 41.)

b. 1 oz ap = ———— oz troy.

c. An aspirin tablet contains 5.00×10^2 mg of active ingredient. What mass in grains ap of active ingredient does it contain? What mass in scruples?

d. What is the mass of 1 scruple in grams?

43. Science fiction often uses nautical analogies to describe space travel. If the starship *U.S.S. Enterprise* is traveling at warp factor 1.71, what is its speed in knots and in miles per hour? (Warp 1.71 = 5.00 times the speed of light; speed of light = 3.00×10^8 m/s; 1 knot = 2000 yd/h, exactly.)

44. The world record for the hundred meter dash is 9.77 s. What is the corresponding average speed in units of m/s, km/h, ft/s, and mi/h? At this speed, how long would it take to run 1.00×10^2 yards?

45. Would a car traveling at a constant speed of 65 km/h violate a 40. mi/h speed limit?

46. You pass a road sign saying "New York 112 km." If you drive at a constant speed of 65 mi/h, how long should it take you to reach New York? If your car gets 28 miles to the gallon, how many liters of gasoline are necessary to travel 112 km?

47. If you put 8.21 gallons of gas in your car and it cost you a total of $17.25, what is the cost of gas per liter in Canadian dollars? Assume 0.82 dollar U.S. = 1.00 dollar Canadian.

48. A children's pain relief elixir contains 80. mg acetaminophen per 0.50 teaspoon. The dosage recommended for a child who weighs between 24 and 35 lb is 1.5 teaspoons. What is the range of acetaminophen dosages, expressed in mg acetaminophen/kg body weight, for children who weigh between 24 and 35 lb?

Temperature

49. Convert the following Fahrenheit temperatures to the Celsius and Kelvin scales.

a. $-459°F$, an extremely low temperature

b. $-40.°F$, the answer to a trivia question

c. $68°F$, room temperature

d. $7 \times 10^7 \ °F$, temperature required to initiate fusion reactions in the sun

50. A thermometer gives a reading of $96.1°F \pm 0.2°F$. What is the temperature in °C? What is the uncertainty?

51. Convert the following Celsius temperatures to Kelvin and to Fahrenheit degrees.

a. the temperature of someone with a fever, 39.2°C

b. a cold wintery day, $-25°C$

c. the lowest possible temperature, $-273°C$

d. the melting-point temperature of sodium chloride, 801°C

52. Convert the following Kelvin temperatures to Celsius and Fahrenheit degrees.
  a. the temperature that registers the same value on both the Fahrenheit and Celsius scales, 233 K
  b. the boiling point of helium, 4 K
  c. the temperature at which many chemical quantities are determined, 298 K
  d. the melting point of tungsten, 3680 K

Density

53. A material will float on the surface of a liquid if the material has a density less than that of the liquid. Given that the density of water is approximately 1.0 g/mL, will a block of material having a volume of 1.2×10^4 in^3 and weighing 350 lb float or sink when placed in a reservoir of water?

54. For a material to float on the surface of water, the material must have a density less than that of water (1.0 g/mL) and must not react with the water or dissolve in it. A spherical ball has a radius of 0.50 cm and weighs 2.0 g. Will this ball float or sink when placed in water? (*Note:* Volume of a sphere = $\frac{4}{3}\pi r^3$.)

55. A star is estimated to have a mass of 2×10^{36} kg. Assuming it to be a sphere of average radius 7.0×10^5 km, calculate the average density of the star in units of grams per cubic centimeter.

56. A rectangular block has dimensions 2.9 cm $\times$ 3.5 cm $\times$ 10.0 cm. The mass of the block is 615.0 g. What are the volume and density of the block?

57. Diamonds are measured in carats, and 1 carat = 0.200 g. The density of diamond is 3.51 g/cm^3. What is the volume of a 5.0-carat diamond?

58. The volume of a diamond is found to be 2.8 mL. What is the mass of the diamond in carats? (See Exercise 57.)

59. A sample containing 33.42 g of metal pellets is poured into a graduated cylinder initially containing 12.7 mL of water, causing the water level in the cylinder to rise to 21.6 mL. Calculate the density of the metal.

60. The density of pure silver is 10.5 g/cm^3 at 20°C. If 5.25 g of pure silver pellets is added to a graduated cylinder containing 11.2 mL of water, to what volume level will the water in the cylinder rise?

61. In each of the following pairs, which has the greater mass? (See Table 1.5.)
  a. 1.0 kg of feathers or 1.0 kg of lead
  b. 1.0 mL of mercury or 1.0 mL of water
  c. 19.3 mL of water or 1.00 mL of gold
  d. 75 mL of copper or 1.0 L of benzene

62. Mercury poisoning is a debilitating disease that is often fatal. In the human body, mercury reacts with essential enzymes leading to irreversible inactivity of these enzymes. If the amount of mercury in a polluted lake is 0.4 μg Hg/mL, what is the total mass in kilograms of mercury in the lake? (The lake has a surface area of 100 mi^2 and an average depth of 20 ft.)

63. In each of the following pairs, which has the greater volume?
  a. 1.0 kg of feathers or 1.0 kg of lead
  b. 100 g of gold or 100 g of water
  c. 1.0 L of copper or 1.0 L of mercury

64. Using Table 1.5, calculate the volume of 25.0 g of each of the following substances at 1 atm.
  a. hydrogen gas
  b. water
  c. iron

Chapter 5 discusses the properties of gases. One property unique to gases is that they contain mostly empty space. Explain using the results of your calculations.

65. The density of osmium (the densest metal) is 22.57 g/cm^3. If a 1.00-kg rectangular block of osmium has two dimensions of 4.00 cm $\times$ 4.00 cm, calculate the third dimension of the block.

66. A copper wire (density = 8.96 g/cm^3) has a diameter of 0.25 mm. If a sample of this copper wire has a mass of 22 g, how long is the wire?

Classification and Separation of Matter

67. Match each description below with the following microscopic pictures. More than one picture may fit each description. A picture may be used more than once or not used at all.

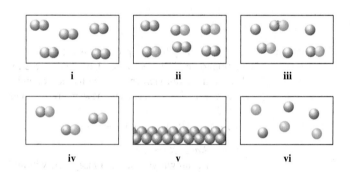

  a. a gaseous compound
  b. a mixture of two gaseous elements
  c. a solid element
  d. a mixture of a gaseous element and a gaseous compound

68. Define the following terms: solid, liquid, gas, pure substance, element, compound, homogeneous mixture, heterogeneous mixture, solution, chemical change, physical change.

69. What is the difference between homogeneous and heterogeneous matter? Classify each of the following as homogeneous or heterogeneous.
  a. a door
  b. the air you breathe
  c. a cup of coffee (black)
  d. the water you drink
  e. salsa
  f. your lab partner

70. Classify each of the following as a mixture or a pure substance.
  a. water   **f.** uranium
  b. blood   **g.** wine
  c. the oceans   **h.** leather
  d. iron   **i.** table salt (NaCl)
  e. brass

Of the pure substances, which are elements and which are compounds?

71. Classify following as physical or chemical changes.
    a. Moth balls gradually vaporize in a closet.
    b. Hydrofluoric acid attacks glass, and is used to etch calibration marks on glass laboratory utensils.
    c. A French chef making a sauce with brandy is able to burn off the alcohol from the brandy, leaving just the brandy flavoring.
    d. Chemistry majors sometimes get holes in the cotton jeans they wear to lab because of acid spills.

72. The properties of a mixture are typically averages of the properties of its components. The properties of a compound may differ dramatically from the properties of the elements that combine to produce the compound. For each process described below, state whether the material being discussed is most likely a mixture or a compound, and state whether the process is a chemical change or a physical change.
    a. An orange liquid is distilled, resulting in the collection of a yellow liquid and a red solid.
    b. A colorless, crystalline solid is decomposed, yielding a pale yellow-green gas and a soft, shiny metal.
    c. A cup of tea becomes sweeter as sugar is added to it.

Additional Exercises

73. For a pharmacist dispensing pills or capsules, it is often easier to weigh the medication to be dispensed rather than to count the individual pills. If a single antibiotic capsule weighs 0.65 g, and a pharmacist weighs out 15.6 g of capsules, how many capsules have been dispensed?

74. In Shakespeare's *Richard III,* the First Murderer says:

    "Take that, and that! [*Stabs Clarence*]
    If that is not enough, I'll drown you in a malmsey butt within!"

    Given that 1 butt = 126 gal, in how many liters of malmsey (a foul brew similar to mead) was the unfortunate Clarence about to be drowned?

75. The contents of one 40. lb bag of topsoil will cover 10. square feet of ground to a depth of 1.0 inch. What number of bags are needed to cover a plot that measures 200. by 300. m to a depth of 4.0 cm?

76. In the opening scenes of the movie *Raiders of the Lost Ark,* Indiana Jones tries to remove a gold idol from a booby-trapped pedestal. He replaces the idol with a bag of sand of approximately equal volume. (Density of gold = 19.32 g/cm^3; density of sand ≈ 2 g/cm^3.)
    a. Did he have a reasonable chance of not activating the mass-sensitive booby trap?
    b. In a later scene he and an unscrupulous guide play catch with the idol. Assume that the volume of the idol is about 1.0 L. If it were solid gold, what mass would the idol have? Is playing catch with it plausible?

77. A column of liquid is found to expand linearly on heating 5.25 cm for a 10.0°F rise in temperature. If the initial temperature of the liquid is 98.6°F, what will the final temperature be in °C if the liquid has expanded by 18.5 cm?

78. A 25.00-g sample of a solid is placed in a graduated cylinder and then the cylinder is filled to the 50.0 mL mark with benzene. The mass of benzene and solid together is 58.80 g. Assuming that the solid is insoluble in benzene and that the density of benzene is 0.880 g/cm^3, calculate the density of the solid.

79. For each of the following, decide which block is more dense: the orange block, the blue block, or it cannot be determined. Explain your answers.

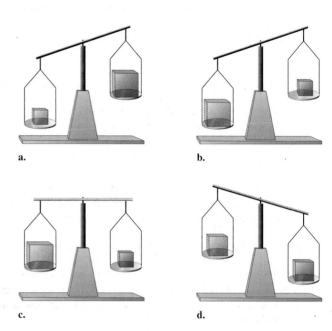

a.   b.

c.   d.

80. According to the *Official Rules of Baseball,* a baseball must have a circumference not more than 9.25 in or less than 9.00 in and a mass not more than 5.25 oz or less than 5.00 oz. What range of densities can a baseball be expected to have? Express this range as a single number with an accompanying uncertainty limit.

81. The density of an irregularly shaped object was determined as follows. The mass of the object was found to be 28.90 g ± 0.03 g. A graduated cylinder was partially filled with water. The reading of the level of the water was 6.4 cm^3 ± 0.1 cm^3. The object was dropped in the cylinder, and the level of the water rose to 9.8 cm^3 ± 0.1 cm^3. What is the density of the object with appropriate error limits? (See Appendix 1.5.)

Challenge Problems

82. Draw a picture showing the markings (graduations) on glassware that would allow you to make each of the following volume measurements of water and explain your answers (the numbers given are as precise as possible).
    a. 128.7 mL   **b.** 18 mL   **c.** 23.45 mL

    If you made the measurements of three samples of water and then poured all of the water together in one container, what total volume of water should you report? Support your answer.

83. Many times errors are expressed in terms of percentage. The percent error is the absolute value of the difference of the true value and the experimental value, divided by the true value, and multiplied by 100.

$$\text{Percent error} = \frac{|\text{true value} - \text{experimental value}|}{\text{true value}} \times 100$$

Calculate the percent error for the following measurements.

a. The density of an aluminum block determined in an experiment was 2.64 g/cm^3. (True value 2.70 g/cm^3.)

b. The experimental determination of iron in iron ore was 16.48%. (True value 16.12%.)

c. A balance measured the mass of a 1.000-g standard as 0.9981 g.

84. A person weighed 15 pennies on a balance and recorded the following masses:

3.112 g	3.109 g	3.059 g
2.467 g	3.079 g	2.518 g
3.129 g	2.545 g	3.050 g
3.053 g	3.054 g	3.072 g
3.081 g	3.131 g	3.064 g

Curious about the results, he looked at the dates on each penny. Two of the light pennies were minted in 1983 and one in 1982. The dates on the 12 heavier pennies ranged from 1970 to 1982. Two of the 12 heavier pennies were minted in 1982.

a. Do you think the Bureau of the Mint changed the way it made pennies? Explain.

b. The person calculated the average mass of the 12 heavy pennies. He expressed this average as 3.0828 g $\pm$ 0.0482 g. What is wrong with the numbers in this result, and how should the value be expressed?

85. On October 21, 1982, the Bureau of the Mint changed the composition of pennies (see Exercise 84). Instead of an alloy of 95% Cu and 5% Zn by mass, a core of 99.2% Zn and 0.8% Cu with a thin shell of copper was adopted. The overall composition of the new penny was 97.6% Zn and 2.4% Cu by mass. Does this account for the difference in mass among the pennies in Exercise 84? Assume the volume of the individual metals that make up each penny can be added together to give the overall volume of the penny, and assume each penny is the same size. (Density of Cu = 8.96 g/cm^3; density of Zn = 7.14 g/cm^3.)

86. Ethylene glycol is the main component in automobile antifreeze. To monitor the temperature of an auto cooling system, you intend to use a meter that reads from 0 to 100. You devise a new temperature scale based on the approximate melting and boiling points of a typical antifreeze solution (-45°C and 115°C). You wish these points to correspond to 0°A and 100°A, respectively.

a. Derive an expression for converting between °A and °C.

b. Derive an expression for converting between °F and °A.

c. At what temperature would your thermometer and a Celsius thermometer give the same numerical reading?

d. Your thermometer reads 86°A. What is the temperature in °C and in °F?

e. What is a temperature of 45°C in °A?

87. Sterling silver is a solid solution of silver and copper. If a piece of a sterling silver necklace has a mass of 105.0 g and a volume of 10.12 mL, calculate the mass percent of copper in the piece of necklace. Assume that the volume of silver present plus the volume of copper present equals the total volume. Refer to Table 1.5.

$$\text{Mass percent of copper} = \frac{\text{mass of copper}}{\text{total mass}} \times 100$$

88. Use molecular-level (microscopic) drawings for each of the following.

a. Show the differences between a gaseous mixture that is a homogeneous mixture of two different compounds, and a gaseous mixture that is a homogeneous mixture of a compound and an element.

b. Show the differences among a gaseous element, a liquid element, and a solid element.

89. Confronted with the box shown in the diagram, you wish to discover something about its internal workings. You have no tools and cannot open the box. You pull on rope B, and it moves rather freely. When you pull on rope A, rope C appears to be pulled slightly into the box. When you pull on rope C, rope A almost disappears into the box.*

a. Based on these observations, construct a model for the interior mechanism of the box.

b. What further experiments could you do to refine your model?

90. An experiment was performed in which an empty 100-mL graduated cylinder was weighed. It was weighed once again after it had been filled to the 10.0-mL mark with dry sand. A 10-mL pipet was used to transfer 10.00 mL of methanol to the cylinder. The sand–methanol mixture was stirred until bubbles no longer emerged from the mixture and the sand looked uniformly wet. The cylinder was then weighed again. Use the data obtained from this experiment (and displayed at the end of this problem) to find the density of the dry sand, the density of methanol, and the density of sand particles. Does the bubbling that occurs when the methanol is added to the dry sand indicate that the sand and methanol are reacting?

Mass of cylinder plus wet sand	45.2613 g
Mass of cylinder plus dry sand	37.3488 g
Mass of empty cylinder	22.8317 g
Volume of dry sand	10.0 mL
Volume of sand + methanol	17.6 mL
Volume of methanol	10.00 mL

---

*From Yoder, Suydam, and Snavely, *Chemistry* (New York: Harcourt Brace Jovanovich, 1975), pp. 9–11.

Integrative Problems

These problems require the integration of multiple concepts to find the solutions.

91. The U.S. trade deficit at the beginning of 2005 was $475,000,000. If the wealthiest 1.00 percent of the U.S. population (297,000,000) contributed an equal amount of money to bring the trade deficit to $0, how many dollars would each person contribute? If one of these people were to pay their share in nickels only, how many nickels are needed? Another person living abroad at the time decides to pay in pounds sterling (£). How many pounds sterling does this person contribute (assume a conversion rate of 1 £ = $ 1.869)?

92. The density of osmium is reported by one source to be 22610 kg/m^3. What is this density in g/cm^3? What is the mass of a block of osmium measuring 10.0 cm × 8.0 cm × 9.0 cm?

93. At the Amundsen-Scott South Pole base station in Antarctica, when the temperature is −100.0°F, researchers who live there can join the "300 Club" by stepping into a sauna heated to 200.0°F then quickly running outside and around the pole that marks the South Pole. What are these temperatures in °C? What are these temperatures in K? If you measured the temperatures only in °C and K, can you become a member of the "300 Club" (that is, is there a 300.-degree difference between the temperature extremes when measured in °C and K?)

Marathon Problem*

This problem is designed to incorporate several concepts and techniques into one situation. Marathon Problems can be used in class by groups of students to help facilitate problem-solving skills.

94. A cylindrical bar of gold that is 1.5 in high and 0.25 in in diameter has a mass of 23.1984 g, as determined on an analytical balance. An empty graduated cylinder is weighed on a triple-beam balance and has a mass of 73.47 g. After pouring a small amount of a liquid into the graduated cylinder, the mass is 79.16 g. When the gold cylinder is placed in the graduated cylinder (the liquid covers the top of the gold cylinder), the volume indicated on the graduated cylinder is 8.5 mL. Assume that the temperature of the gold bar and the liquid are 86°F. If the density of the liquid decreases by 1.0% for each 10.°C rise in temperature (over the range 0 to 50°C), determine

   a. the density of the gold at 86°F.
   b. the density of the liquid at 40.°F.

   Note: Parts a and b can be answered independently.

 Get help understanding core concepts and visualizing molecular-level interactions, and practice problem solving, by visiting the Online Study Center at **college.hmco.com/ PIC/zumdahl7e.**

*Used with permission from the *Journal of Chemical Education,* Vol. 68, No. 11, 1991, pp. 919–922; copyright © 1991, Division of Chemical Education, Inc.

2 Atoms, Molecules, and Ions

Contents

A worker in Thailand piles up salt crystals.

Where does one start in learning chemistry? Clearly we must consider some essential vocabulary and something about the origins of the science before we can proceed very far. Thus, while Chapter 1 provided background on the fundamental ideas and procedures of science in general, Chapter 2 covers the specific chemical background necessary for understanding the material in the next few chapters. The coverage of these topics is necessarily brief at this point. We will develop these ideas more fully as it becomes appropriate to do so. A major goal of this chapter is to present the systems for naming chemical compounds to provide you with the vocabulary necessary to understand this book and to pursue your laboratory studies.

Because chemistry is concerned first and foremost with chemical changes, we will proceed as quickly as possible to a study of chemical reactions (Chapters 3 and 4). However, before we can discuss reactions, we must consider some fundamental ideas about atoms and how they combine.

2.1 The Early History of Chemistry

Chemistry has been important since ancient times. The processing of natural ores to produce metals for ornaments and weapons and the use of embalming fluids are just two applications of chemical phenomena that were utilized prior to 1000 B.C.

The Greeks were the first to try to explain why chemical changes occur. By about 400 B.C. they had proposed that all matter was composed of four fundamental substances: fire, earth, water, and air. The Greeks also considered the question of whether matter is continuous, and thus infinitely divisible into smaller pieces, or composed of small, indivisible particles. Supporters of the latter position were Demokritos* of Abdera (*c.* 460–*c.* 370 B.C.) and Leucippos, who used the term *atomos* (which later became *atoms*) to describe these ultimate particles. However, because the Greeks had no experiments to test their ideas, no definitive conclusion could be reached about the divisibility of matter.

The next 2000 years of chemical history were dominated by a pseudoscience called *alchemy.* Some alchemists were mystics and fakes who were obsessed with the idea of turning cheap metals into gold. However, many alchemists were serious scientists, and this period saw important advances: The alchemists discovered several elements and learned to prepare the mineral acids.

The foundations of modern chemistry were laid in the sixteenth century with the development of systematic metallurgy (extraction of metals from ores) by a German, Georg Bauer (1494–1555), and the medicinal application of minerals by a Swiss alchemist/physician known as Paracelsus (full name: Philippus Theophrastus Bombastus von Hohenheim [1493–1541]).

The first "chemist" to perform truly quantitative experiments was Robert Boyle (1627–1691), who carefully measured the relationship between the pressure and volume of air. When Boyle published his book *The Skeptical Chymist* in 1661, the quantitative sciences of physics and chemistry were born. In addition to his results on the quantitative behavior of gases, Boyle's other major contribution to chemistry consisted of his ideas about the chemical elements. Boyle held no preconceived notion about the number of elements. In his view, a substance was an element unless it could be broken down into two or more simpler substances. As Boyle's experimental definition of an element became generally accepted, the list of known elements began to grow, and the Greek system of

---

*Democritus is an alternate spelling.

CHEMICAL IMPACT

There's Gold in Them There Plants!

Gold has always held a strong allure. For example, the alchemists were obsessed with finding a way to transform cheap metals into gold. Also, when gold was discovered in California in 1849, a frantic rush occurred to that area and other areas in the west. Although gold is still valuable, most of the high-grade gold ores have been exhausted. This leaves the low-grade ores—ores with low concentrations of gold that are expensive to process relative to the amount of gold finally obtained.

Now two scientists have come across a novel way to concentrate the gold from low-grade ores. Christopher Anderson and Robert Brooks of Massey University in Palmerston North, New Zealand, have found plants that accumulate gold atoms as they grow in soil containing gold ore [*Nature* 395 (1998): 553]. The plants brassica (of the mustard family) and chicory seem especially effective as botanical "gold miners." When these plants are dried and burned (after having grown in gold-rich soil), the resulting ash contains approximately 150 ppm (parts per million) of gold. (1 ppm gold represents 1 g of gold in 10^6 g of sample.)

The New Zealand scientists were able to double the amount of gold taken from the soil by the plants by treating the soil with ammonium thiocyanate (NH_4SCN). The thiocyanate, which reacts with the gold, making it more available to the plants, subsequently breaks down in the soil and therefore poses no environmental hazard.

Thus plants seem to hold great promise as gold miners. They are efficient and reliable and will never go on strike.

This plant from the mustard family is a newly discovered source of gold.

four elements finally died. Although Boyle was an excellent scientist, he was not always right. For example, he clung to the alchemists' views that metals were not true elements and that a way would eventually be found to change one metal into another.

The phenomenon of combustion evoked intense interest in the seventeenth and eighteenth centuries. The German chemist Georg Stahl (1660–1734) suggested that a substance he called "phlogiston" flowed out of the burning material. Stahl postulated that a substance burning in a closed container eventually stopped burning because the air in the container became saturated with phlogiston. Oxygen gas, discovered by Joseph Priestley (1733–1804),* an English clergyman and scientist (Fig. 2.1), was found to support vigorous combustion and was thus supposed to be low in phlogiston. In fact, oxygen was originally called "dephlogisticated air."

FIGURE 2.1
The Priestley Medal is the highest honor given by the American Chemical Society. It is named for Joseph Priestley, who was born in England on March 13, 1733. He performed many important scientific experiments, among them the discovery that a gas later identified as carbon dioxide could be dissolved in water to produce *seltzer*. Also, as a result of meeting Benjamin Franklin in London in 1766, Priestley became interested in electricity and was the first to observe that graphite was an electrical conductor. However, his greatest discovery occurred in 1774 when he isolated oxygen by heating mercuric oxide.

Because of his nonconformist political views, Priestley was forced to leave England. He died in the United States in 1804.

---

*Oxygen gas was actually first observed by the Swedish chemist Karl W. Scheele (1742–1786), but because his results were published after Priestley's, the latter is commonly credited with the discovery of oxygen.

2.2 Fundamental Chemical Laws

By the late eighteenth century, combustion had been studied extensively; the gases carbon dioxide, nitrogen, hydrogen, and oxygen had been discovered; and the list of elements continued to grow. However, it was Antoine Lavoisier (1743–1794), a French chemist (Fig. 2.2), who finally explained the true nature of combustion, thus clearing the way for the tremendous progress that was made near the end of the eighteenth century. Lavoisier, like Boyle, regarded measurement as the essential operation of chemistry. His experiments, in which he carefully weighed the reactants and products of various reactions, suggested that *mass is neither created nor destroyed.* Lavoisier's verification of this **law of conservation of mass** was the basis for the developments in chemistry in the nineteenth century.

Lavoisier's quantitative experiments showed that combustion involved oxygen (which Lavoisier named), not phlogiston. He also discovered that life was supported by a process that also involved oxygen and was similar in many ways to combustion. In 1789 Lavoisier published the first modern chemistry textbook, *Elementary Treatise on Chemistry,* in which he presented a unified picture of the chemical knowledge assembled up to that time. Unfortunately, in the same year the text was published, the French Revolution broke out. Lavoisier, who had been associated with collecting taxes for the government, was executed on the guillotine as an enemy of the people in 1794.

After 1800, chemistry was dominated by scientists who, following Lavoisier's lead, performed careful weighing experiments to study the course of chemical reactions and to determine the composition of various chemical compounds. One of these chemists, a Frenchman, Joseph Proust (1754–1826), showed that *a given compound always contains exactly the same proportion of elements by mass.* For example, Proust found that the substance copper carbonate is always 5.3 parts copper to 4 parts oxygen to 1 part carbon (by mass). The principle of the constant composition of compounds, originally called "Proust's law," is now known as the **law of definite proportion.**

Proust's discovery stimulated John Dalton (1766–1844), an English schoolteacher (Fig. 2.3), to think about atoms as the particles that might compose elements. Dalton reasoned that if elements were composed of tiny individual particles, a given compound should always contain the same combination of these atoms. This concept explained why the same relative masses of elements were always found in a given compound.

Oxygen is from the French *oxygène,* meaning "generator of acid," because it was initially considered to be an integral part of all acids.

FIGURE 2.2
Antoine Lavoisier was born in Paris on August 26, 1743. Although Lavoisier's father wanted his son to follow him into the legal profession, young Lavoisier was fascinated by science. From the beginning of his scientific career, Lavoisier recognized the importance of accurate measurements. His careful weighings showed that mass is conserved in chemical reactions and that combustion involves reaction with oxygen. Also, he wrote the first modern chemistry textbook. It is not surprising that Lavoisier is often called the father of modern chemistry.

To help support his scientific work, Lavoisier invested in a private tax-collecting firm and married the daughter of one of the company executives. His connection to the tax collectors proved fatal, for radical French revolutionaries demanded his execution, which occurred on the guillotine on May 8, 1794.

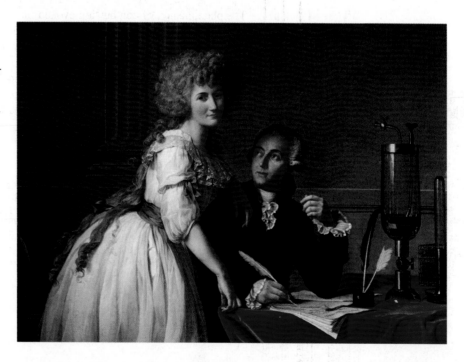

But Dalton discovered another principle that convinced him even more of the existence of atoms. He noted, for example, that carbon and oxygen form two different compounds that contain different relative amounts of carbon and oxygen, as shown by the following data:

	Mass of Oxygen That Combines with 1 g of Carbon
Compound I	1.33 g
Compound II	2.66 g

Dalton noted that compound II contains twice as much oxygen per gram of carbon as compound I, a fact that could easily be explained in terms of atoms. Compound I might be CO, and compound II might be CO_2.* This principle, which was found to apply to compounds of other elements as well, became known as the **law of multiple proportions:** *When two elements form a series of compounds, the ratios of the masses of the second element that combine with 1 gram of the first element can always be reduced to small whole numbers.*

To make sure the significance of this observation is clear, in Sample Exercise 2.1 we will consider data for a series of compounds consisting of nitrogen and oxygen.

Sample Exercise 2.1 | **Illustrating the Law of Multiple Proportions**

The following data were collected for several compounds of nitrogen and oxygen:

	Mass of Nitrogen That Combines with 1 g of Oxygen
Compound A	1.750 g
Compound B	0.8750 g
Compound C	0.4375 g

Show how these data illustrate the law of multiple proportions.

Solution

For the law of multiple proportions to hold, the ratios of the masses of nitrogen combining with 1 gram of oxygen in each pair of compounds should be small whole numbers. We therefore compute the ratios as follows:

$$\frac{A}{B} = \frac{1.750}{0.875} = \frac{2}{1}$$

$$\frac{B}{C} = \frac{0.875}{0.4375} = \frac{2}{1}$$

$$\frac{A}{C} = \frac{1.750}{0.4375} = \frac{4}{1}$$

These results support the law of multiple proportions.

See Exercises 2.27 and 2.28.

---

*Subscripts are used to show the numbers of atoms present. The number 1 is understood (not written). The symbols for the elements and the writing of chemical formulas will be illustrated further in Sections 2.6 and 2.7.

FIGURE 2.3
John Dalton (1766–1844), an Englishman, began teaching at a Quaker school when he was 12. His fascination with science included an intense interest in meteorology, which led to an interest in the gases of the air and their ultimate components, atoms. Dalton is best known for his atomic theory, in which he postulated that the fundamental differences among atoms are their masses. He was the first to prepare a table of relative atomic weights.

Dalton was a humble man with several apparent handicaps: He was not articulate and he was color-blind, a terrible problem for a chemist. Despite these disadvantages, he helped to revolutionize the science of chemistry.

These statements are a modern paraphrase of Dalton's ideas.

The significance of the data in Sample Exercise 2.1 is that compound A contains twice as much nitrogen (N) per gram of oxygen (O) as does compound B and that compound B contains twice as much nitrogen per gram of oxygen as does compound C.

These data can be explained readily if the substances are composed of molecules made up of nitrogen atoms and oxygen atoms. For example, one set of possibilities for compounds A, B, and C is

A: $\dfrac{N}{O} = \dfrac{2}{1}$ B: $\dfrac{N}{O} = \dfrac{1}{1}$ C: $\dfrac{N}{O} = \dfrac{1}{2}$

Now we can see that compound A contains two atoms of N for every atom of O, whereas compound B contains one atom of N per atom of O. That is, compound A contains twice as much nitrogen per given amount of oxygen as does compound B. Similarly, since compound B contains one N per O and compound C contains one N per *two* O's, the nitrogen content of compound C per given amount of oxygen is half that of compound B.

Another set of compounds that fits the data in Sample Exercise 2.1 is

A: $\dfrac{N}{O} = \dfrac{1}{1}$ B: $\dfrac{N}{O} = \dfrac{1}{2}$ C: $\dfrac{N}{O} = \dfrac{1}{4}$

Verify for yourself that these compounds satisfy the requirements.

Still another set that works is

A: $\dfrac{N}{O} = \dfrac{4}{2}$ B: $\dfrac{N}{O} = \dfrac{2}{2}$ C: $\dfrac{N}{O} = \dfrac{2}{4}$

See if you can come up with still another set of compounds that satisfies the data in Sample Exercise 2.1. How many more possibilities are there?

In fact, an infinite number of other possibilities exists. Dalton could not deduce absolute formulas from the available data on relative masses. However, the data on the composition of compounds in terms of the relative masses of the elements supported his hypothesis that each element consisted of a certain type of atom and that compounds were formed from specific combinations of atoms.

2.3 Dalton's Atomic Theory

In 1808 Dalton published *A New System of Chemical Philosophy*, in which he presented his theory of atoms:

1. Each element is made up of tiny particles called atoms.

2. The atoms of a given element are identical; the atoms of different elements are different in some fundamental way or ways.

3. Chemical compounds are formed when atoms of different elements combine with each other. A given compound always has the same relative numbers and types of atoms.

4. Chemical reactions involve reorganization of the atoms—changes in the way they are bound together. The atoms themselves are not changed in a chemical reaction.

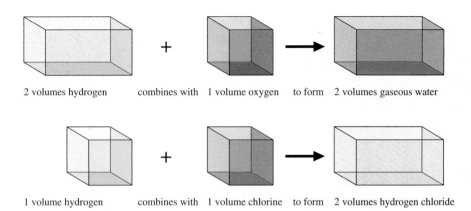

2 volumes hydrogen   combines with   1 volume oxygen   to form   2 volumes gaseous water

1 volume hydrogen   combines with   1 volume chlorine   to form   2 volumes hydrogen chloride

FIGURE 2.4
A representation of some of Gay-Lussac's experimental results on combining gas volumes.

Joseph Louis Gay-Lussac, a French physicist and chemist, was remarkably versatile. Although he is now known primarily for his studies on the combining of volumes of gases, Gay-Lussac was instrumental in the studies of many of the other properties of gases. Some of Gay-Lussac's motivation to learn about gases arose from his passion for ballooning. In fact, he made ascents to heights of over 4 miles to collect air samples, setting altitude records that stood for about 50 years. Gay-Lussac also was the codiscoverer of boron and the developer of a process for manufacturing sulfuric acid. As chief assayer of the French mint, Gay-Lussac developed many techniques for chemical analysis and invented many types of glassware now used routinely in labs. Gay-Lussac spent his last 20 years as a lawmaker in the French government.

It is instructive to consider Dalton's reasoning on the relative masses of the atoms of the various elements. In Dalton's time water was known to be composed of the elements hydrogen and oxygen, with 8 grams of oxygen present for every 1 gram of hydrogen. If the formula for water were OH, an oxygen atom would have to have 8 times the mass of a hydrogen atom. However, if the formula for water were H_2O (two atoms of hydrogen for every oxygen atom), this would mean that each atom of oxygen is 16 times as massive as *each* atom of hydrogen (since the ratio of the mass of one oxygen to that of *two* hydrogens is 8 to 1). Because the formula for water was not then known, Dalton could not specify the relative masses of oxygen and hydrogen unambiguously. To solve the problem, Dalton made a fundamental assumption: He decided that nature would be as simple as possible. This assumption led him to conclude that the formula for water should be OH. He thus assigned hydrogen a mass of 1 and oxygen a mass of 8.

Using similar reasoning for other compounds, Dalton prepared the first table of **atomic masses** (sometimes called **atomic weights** by chemists, since mass is often determined by comparison to a standard mass—a process called *weighing*). Many of the masses were later proved to be wrong because of Dalton's incorrect assumptions about the formulas of certain compounds, but the construction of a table of masses was an important step forward.

Although not recognized as such for many years, the keys to determining absolute formulas for compounds were provided in the experimental work of the French chemist Joseph Gay-Lussac (1778–1850) and by the hypothesis of an Italian chemist named Amadeo Avogadro (1776–1856). In 1809 Gay-Lussac performed experiments in which he measured (under the same conditions of temperature and pressure) the volumes of gases that reacted with each other. For example, Gay-Lussac found that 2 volumes of hydrogen react with 1 volume of oxygen to form 2 volumes of gaseous water and that 1 volume of hydrogen reacts with 1 volume of chlorine to form 2 volumes of hydrogen chloride. These results are represented schematically in Fig. 2.4.

In 1811 Avogadro interpreted these results by proposing that *at the same temperature and pressure, equal volumes of different gases contain the same number of particles.* This assumption (called **Avogadro's hypothesis**) makes sense if the distances between the particles in a gas are very great compared with the sizes of the particles. Under these conditions, the volume of a gas is determined by the number of molecules present, not by the size of the individual particles.

If Avogadro's hypothesis is correct, Gay-Lussac's result,

2 volumes of hydrogen react with 1 volume of oxygen $\longrightarrow$ 2 volumes of water vapor

can be expressed as follows:

2 molecules* of hydrogen react with 1 molecule of oxygen $\longrightarrow$ 2 molecules of water

*A *molecule* is a collection of atoms (see Section 2.6).

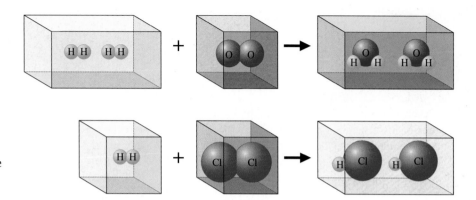

FIGURE 2.5
A representation of combining gases at the molecular level. The spheres represent atoms in the molecules.

These observations can best be explained by assuming that gaseous hydrogen, oxygen, and chlorine are all composed of diatomic (two-atom) molecules: H_2, O_2, and Cl_2, respectively. Gay-Lussac's results can then be represented as shown in Fig. 2.5. (Note that this reasoning suggests that the formula for water is H_2O, not OH as Dalton believed.)

Unfortunately, Avogadro's interpretations were not accepted by most chemists, and a half-century of confusion followed, in which many different assumptions were made about formulas and atomic masses.

During the nineteenth century, painstaking measurements were made of the masses of various elements that combined to form compounds. From these experiments a list of relative atomic masses could be determined. One of the chemists involved in contributing to this list was a Swede named Jöns Jakob Berzelius (1779–1848), who discovered the elements cerium, selenium, silicon, and thorium and developed the modern symbols for the elements used in writing the formulas of compounds.

The Italian chemist Stanislao Cannizzaro (1826–1910) cleared up the confusion in 1860 by doing a series of molar mass determinations that convinced the scientific community that the correct atomic mass of carbon is 12. For more information, see *From Caveman to Chemist* by Hugh Salzberg (American Chemical Society, 1991), p. 223.

2.4   Early Experiments to Characterize the Atom

On the basis of the work of Dalton, Gay-Lussac, Avogadro, and others, chemistry was beginning to make sense. The concept of atoms was clearly a good idea. Inevitably, scientists began to wonder about the nature of the atom. What is an atom made of, and how do the atoms of the various elements differ?

The Electron

The first important experiments that led to an understanding of the composition of the atom were done by the English physicist J. J. Thomson (Fig. 2.6), who studied electrical discharges in partially evacuated tubes called **cathode-ray tubes** (Fig. 2.7) during the period from 1898 to 1903. Thomson found that when high voltage was applied to the tube, a "ray" he called a *cathode ray* (because it emanated from the negative electrode, or cathode) was produced. Because this ray was produced at the negative electrode and was repelled by the negative pole of an applied electric field (see Fig. 2.8), Thomson postulated that the ray was a stream of negatively charged particles, now called **electrons.** From experiments in which he measured the deflection of the beam of electrons in a magnetic field, Thomson determined the *charge-to-mass ratio* of an electron:

$$\frac{e}{m} = -1.76 \times 10^8 \, \text{C/g}$$

where e represents the charge on the electron in coulombs (C) and m represents the electron mass in grams.

FIGURE 2.6
J. J. Thomson (1856–1940) was an English physicist at Cambridge University. He received the Nobel Prize in physics in 1906.

CHEMICAL IMPACT

Berzelius, Selenium, and Silicon

Jöns Jakob Berzelius was probably the best experimental chemist of his generation and, given the crudeness of his laboratory equipment, maybe the best of all time. Unlike Lavoisier, who could afford to buy the best laboratory equipment available, Berzelius worked with minimal equipment in very plain surroundings. One of Berzelius's students described the Swedish chemist's workplace: "The laboratory consisted of two ordinary rooms with the very simplest arrangements; there were neither furnaces nor hoods, neither water system nor gas. Against the walls stood some closets with the chemicals, in the middle the mercury trough and the

blast lamp table. Beside this was the sink consisting of a stone water holder with a stopcock and a pot standing under it. [Next door in the kitchen] stood a small heating furnace."

In these simple facilities Berzelius performed more than 2000 experiments over a 10-year period to determine accurate atomic masses for the 50 elements then known. His success can be seen from the data in the table at left. These remarkably accurate values attest to his experimental skills and patience.

Besides his table of atomic masses, Berzelius made many other major contributions to chemistry. The most important of these was the invention of a simple set of symbols for the elements along with a system for writing the formulas of compounds to replace the awkward symbolic representations of the alchemists. Although some chemists, including Dalton, objected to the new system, it was gradually adopted and forms the basis of the system we use today.

In addition to these accomplishments, Berzelius discovered the elements cerium, thorium, selenium, and silicon. Of these elements, selenium and silicon are particularly important in today's world. Berzelius discovered selenium in 1817 in connection with his studies of sulfuric acid. For years selenium's toxicity has been known, but only recently have we become aware that it may have a positive effect on human

Comparison of Several of Berzelius's Atomic Masses with the Modern Values

Element	Atomic Mass	
	Berzelius's Value	Current Value
Chlorine	35.41	35.45
Copper	63.00	63.55
Hydrogen	1.00	1.01
Lead	207.12	207.2
Nitrogen	14.05	14.01
Oxygen	16.00	16.00
Potassium	39.19	39.10
Silver	108.12	107.87
Sulfur	32.18	32.07

Visualization: Cathode-Ray Tube

One of Thomson's primary goals in his cathode-ray tube experiments was to gain an understanding of the structure of the atom. He reasoned that since electrons could be produced from electrodes made of various types of metals, *all* atoms must contain electrons. Since atoms were known to be electrically neutral, Thomson further assumed that atoms also must contain some positive charge. Thomson postulated that an atom consisted of a

FIGURE 2.7

A cathode-ray tube. The fast-moving electrons excite the gas in the tube, causing a glow between the electrodes. The green color in the photo is due to the response of the screen (coated with zinc sulfide) to the electron beam.

The Alchemists' Symbols for Some Common Elements and Compounds	
Substance	**Alchemists' Symbol**
Silver	☽
Lead	♄
Tin	♃
Platinum	☽⊙
Sulfuric acid	+⊕
Alcohol	∀
Sea salt	⊙

health. Studies have shown that trace amounts of selenium in the diet may protect people from heart disease and cancer. One study based on data from 27 countries showed an inverse relationship between the cancer death rate and the selenium content of soil in a particular region (low cancer death rate in areas with high selenium content). Another research paper reported an inverse relationship between the selenium content of the blood and the incidence of breast cancer in women. A study reported in 1998 used the toenail clippings of 33,737 men to show that selenium seems to protect against prostate cancer. Selenium is also found in the heart muscle and may play an important role in proper heart function. Because of these and other studies, selenium's reputation has improved, and many scientists are now studying its function in the human body.

Silicon is the second most abundant element in the earth's crust, exceeded only by oxygen. As we will see in Chapter 10, compounds involving silicon bonded to oxygen make up most of the earth's sand, rock, and soil. Berzelius prepared silicon in its pure form in 1824 by heating silicon tetrafluoride (SiF_4) with potassium metal. Today, silicon forms the basis for the modern microelectronics industry centered near San Francisco in a place that has come to be known as "Silicon Valley." The technology of the silicon chip (see figure) with its printed circuits has transformed computers from room-sized monsters with thousands of unreliable vacuum tubes to desktop and note-book-sized units with trouble-free "solid-state" circuitry.

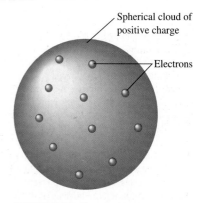
A silicon chip.

See E. J. Holmyard, *Alchemy* (New York: Penguin Books, 1968).

diffuse cloud of positive charge with the negative electrons embedded randomly in it. This model, shown in Fig. 2.9, is often called the *plum pudding model* because the electrons are like raisins dispersed in a pudding (the positive charge cloud), as in plum pudding, a favorite English dessert.

In 1909 Robert Millikan (1868–1953), working at the University of Chicago, performed very clever experiments involving charged oil drops. These experiments allowed

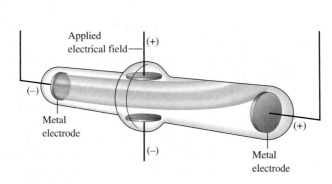

FIGURE 2.8
Deflection of cathode rays by an applied electric field.

FIGURE 2.9
The plum pudding model of the atom.

Visualization: Millikan's Oil Drop Experiment

A technician using a scanner to monitor the uptake of radioactive iodine in a patient's thyroid.

FIGURE 2.10
A schematic representation of the apparatus Millikan used to determine the charge on the electron. The fall of charged oil droplets due to gravity can be halted by adjusting the voltage across the two plates. This voltage and the mass of the oil drop can then be used to calculate the charge on the oil drop. Millikan's experiments showed that the charge on an oil drop is always a whole-number multiple of the electron charge.

FIGURE 2.11
Ernest Rutherford (1871–1937) was born on a farm in New Zealand. In 1895 he placed second in a scholarship competition to attend Cambridge University but was awarded the scholarship when the winner decided to stay home and get married. As a scientist in England, Rutherford did much of the early work on characterizing radioactivity. He named the α and β particles and the γ ray and coined the term *half-life* to describe an important attribute of radioactive elements. His experiments on the behavior of α particles striking thin metal foils led him to postulate the nuclear atom. He also invented the name *proton* for the nucleus of the hydrogen atom. He received the Nobel Prize in chemistry in 1908.

him to determine the magnitude of the electron charge (see Fig. 2.10). With this value and the charge-to-mass ratio determined by Thomson, Millikan was able to calculate the mass of the electron as 9.11×10^{-31} kilogram.

Radioactivity

In the late nineteenth century scientists discovered that certain elements produce high-energy radiation. For example, in 1896 the French scientist Henri Becquerel found accidentally that a piece of a mineral containing uranium could produce its image on a photographic plate in the absence of light. He attributed this phenomenon to a spontaneous emission of radiation by the uranium, which he called **radioactivity.** Studies in the early twentieth century demonstrated three types of radioactive emission: gamma (γ) rays, beta (β) particles, and alpha (α) particles. A γ ray is high-energy "light"; a β particle is a high-speed electron; and an α particle has a 2+ charge, that is, a charge twice that of the electron and with the opposite sign. The mass of an α particle is 7300 times that of the electron. More modes of radioactivity are now known, and we will discuss them in Chapter 18. Here we will consider only α particles because they were used in some crucial early experiments.

The Nuclear Atom

In 1911 Ernest Rutherford (Fig. 2.11), who performed many of the pioneering experiments to explore radioactivity, carried out an experiment to test Thomson's plum pudding model. The experiment involved directing α particles at a thin sheet of metal foil, as illustrated in Fig. 2.12. Rutherford reasoned that if Thomson's model were accurate, the massive α particles should crash through the thin foil like cannonballs through gauze, as shown in Fig. 2.13(a). He expected the α particles to travel through the foil with, at the most, very minor deflections in their paths. The results of the experiment were very different from those Rutherford anticipated. Although most of the α particles passed straight through, many of the particles were deflected at large angles, as shown in Fig. 2.13(b), and some were reflected, never hitting the detector. This outcome was a great surprise to Rutherford. (He wrote that this result was comparable with shooting a howitzer at a piece of paper and having the shell reflected back.)

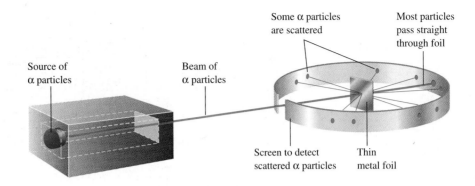

FIGURE 2.12
Rutherford's experiment on α-particle bombardment of metal foil.

Rutherford knew from these results that the plum pudding model for the atom could not be correct. The large deflections of the α particles could be caused only by a center of concentrated positive charge that contains most of the atom's mass, as illustrated in Fig. 2.13(b). Most of the α particles pass directly through the foil because the atom is mostly open space. The deflected α particles are those that had a "close encounter" with the massive positive center of the atom, and the few reflected α particles are those that made a "direct hit" on the much more massive positive center.

In Rutherford's mind these results could be explained only in terms of a **nuclear atom**—an atom with a dense center of positive charge (the **nucleus**) with electrons moving around the nucleus at a distance that is large relative to the nuclear radius.

2.5   The Modern View of Atomic Structure: An Introduction

In the years since Thomson and Rutherford, a great deal has been learned about atomic structure. Because much of this material will be covered in detail in later chapters, only an introduction will be given here. The simplest view of the atom is that it consists of a tiny nucleus (with a diameter of about 10^{-13} cm) and electrons that move about the nucleus at an average distance of about 10^{-8} cm from it (see Fig. 2.14).

The forces that bind the positively charged protons in the nucleus will be discussed in Chapter 18.

As we will see later, the chemistry of an atom mainly results from its electrons. For this reason, chemists can be satisfied with a relatively crude nuclear model. The nucleus is assumed to contain **protons,** which have a positive charge equal in magnitude to the electron's negative charge, and **neutrons,** which have virtually the same mass as a proton but no charge. The masses and charges of the electron, proton, and neutron are shown in Table 2.1.

Visualization: Gold Foil Experiment

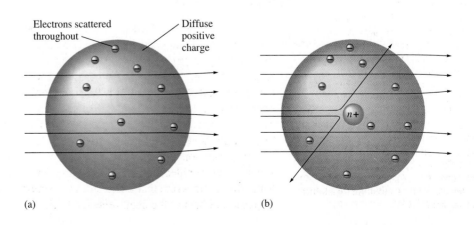

FIGURE 2.13
(a) The expected results of the metal foil experiment if Thomson's model were correct. (b) Actual results.

(a)   (b)

Nucleus

~10^{-13}cm

~10^{-8}cm

FIGURE 2.14
A nuclear atom viewed in cross section. Note that this drawing is not to scale.

The chemistry of an atom arises from its electrons.

If the atomic nucleus were the size of this ball bearing, a typical atom would be the size of this stadium.

Mass number
Atomic number → $_{Z}^{A}X$ ← Element symbol

TABLE 2.1 The Mass and Charge of the Electron, Proton, and Neutron		
Particle	**Mass**	**Charge***
Electron	9.11×10^{-31} kg	$1-$
Proton	1.67×10^{-27} kg	$1+$
Neutron	1.67×10^{-27} kg	None

*The magnitude of the charge of the electron and the proton is 1.60×10^{-19} C.

Two striking things about the nucleus are its small size compared with the overall size of the atom and its extremely high density. The tiny nucleus accounts for almost all the atom's mass. Its great density is dramatically demonstrated by the fact that a piece of nuclear material about the size of a pea would have a mass of 250 million tons!

An important question to consider at this point is, *"If all atoms are composed of these same components, why do different atoms have different chemical properties?"* The answer to this question lies in the number and the arrangement of the electrons. The electrons constitute most of the atomic volume and thus are the parts that "intermingle" when atoms combine to form molecules. Therefore, the number of electrons possessed by a given atom greatly affects its ability to interact with other atoms. As a result, the atoms of different elements, which have different numbers of protons and electrons, show different chemical behavior.

A sodium atom has 11 protons in its nucleus. Since atoms have no net charge, the number of electrons must equal the number of protons. Therefore, a sodium atom has 11 electrons moving around its nucleus. It is *always* true that a sodium atom has 11 protons and 11 electrons. However, each sodium atom also has neutrons in its nucleus, and different types of sodium atoms exist that have different numbers of neutrons. For example, consider the sodium atoms represented in Fig. 2.15. These two atoms are **isotopes,** or *atoms with the same number of protons but different numbers of neutrons.* Note that the symbol for one particular type of sodium atom is written

Mass number
$_{11}^{23}$Na ← Element symbol
Atomic number

where the **atomic number** Z (number of protons) is written as a subscript, and the **mass number** A (the total number of protons and neutrons) is written as a superscript. (The particular atom represented here is called "sodium twenty-three." It has 11 electrons, 11 protons, and 12 neutrons.) Because the chemistry of an atom is due to its electrons, isotopes show almost identical chemical properties. In nature most elements contain mixtures of isotopes.

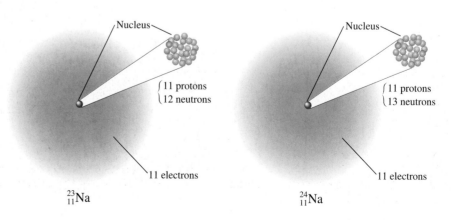

FIGURE 2.15
Two isotopes of sodium. Both have 11 protons and 11 electrons, but they differ in the number of neutrons in their nuclei.

Nucleus
11 protons
12 neutrons
11 electrons
$_{11}^{23}$Na

Nucleus
11 protons
13 neutrons
11 electrons
$_{11}^{24}$Na

CHEMICAL IMPACT

Reading the History of Bogs

Scientists often "read" the history of the earth and its inhabitants using very different "books" than traditional historians. For example, the disappearance of the dinosaurs 65 million years ago in an "instant" of geological time was a great mystery until unusually high iridium and osmium levels were discovered at a position in the earth's crust corresponding to that time. These high levels of iridium and osmium suggested that an extraterrestrial object had struck the earth 65 million years ago with catastrophic results for the dinosaurs. Since then, the huge buried crater caused by the object has been discovered on the Yucatan Peninsula, and virtually everyone is now convinced that this is the correct explanation for the disappearing dinosaurs.

History is also being "read" by scientists studying ice cores from glaciers in Iceland. Now Swiss scientists have found that ancient peat bogs can furnish a reliable historical record. Geochemist William Shotyk of the University of Bern has found a 15,000-year window on history by analyzing the lead content of core samples from a Swiss mountainside peat bog [*Science* 281 (1998): 1635]. Various parts of the core samples were dated by ^{14}C dating techniques (see Chapter 18, Section 18.4, for more information) and analyzed for their scandium and lead contents. Also, the $^{206}Pb/^{207}Pb$ ratio was measured for each sample. These data are represented in the accompanying figure. Notice that the $^{206}Pb/^{207}Pb$ ratio remains very close to 1.20 (see the red band in the figure) from 14,000 years to 3200 years. The value of 1.20 is the same as the average $^{206}Pb/^{207}Pb$ ratio in the earth's soil.

The core also reveals that the total lead and scandium levels increased simultaneously at the 6000-year mark but that the $^{206}Pb/^{207}Pb$ ratio remained close to 1.20. This coincides with the beginning of agriculture in Europe, which caused more soil dust to enter the atmosphere.

Significantly, about 3000 years ago the $^{206}Pb/^{207}Pb$ ratio decreased markedly. This also corresponds in the core sample to an increase in total lead content out of proportion to the increase in scandium. This indicates the lead no longer resulted from soil dust but from other activities of humans—lead mining had begun. Since the 3000-year mark, the $^{206}Pb/^{207}Pb$ ratio has remained well below 1.20, indicating that human use of lead ores has become the dominant source

of airborne lead. This is confirmed by the sharp decline in the ratio beginning 200 years ago that corresponds to the importation into England of Australian lead ores having low $^{206}Pb/^{207}Pb$ ratios.

So far only lead has been used to read the history in the bog. However, Shotyk's group is also measuring the changes in the levels of copper, zinc, cadmium, arsenic, mercury, and antimony. More interesting stories are sure to follow.

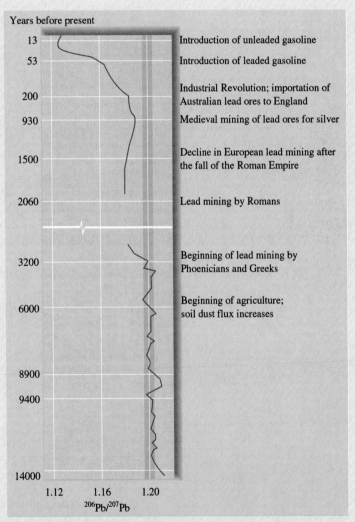

Geochemist William Shotyk's analysis of the lead content of ice core samples reveals a 15,000-year history of lead levels. (Note: Dates are based on calibrated radiocarbon dating. Because the core was retrieved in two segments, a break in data occurs between 2060 and 3200 years before present.)

Sample Exercise 2.2	**Writing the Symbols for Atoms**

Write the symbol for the atom that has an atomic number of 9 and a mass number of 19. How many electrons and how many neutrons does this atom have?

Solution

The atomic number 9 means the atom has 9 protons. This element is called *fluorine,* symbolized by F. The atom is represented as

$$^{19}_{9}\text{F}$$

and is called "fluorine nineteen." Since the atom has 9 protons, it also must have 9 electrons to achieve electrical neutrality. The mass number gives the total number of protons and neutrons, which means that this atom has 10 neutrons.

See Exercises 2.43 through 2.46.

2.6 Molecules and Ions

From a chemist's viewpoint, the most interesting characteristic of an atom is its ability to combine with other atoms to form compounds. It was John Dalton who first recognized that chemical compounds are collections of atoms, but he could not determine the structure of atoms or their means for binding to each other. During the twentieth century we learned that atoms have electrons and that these electrons participate in bonding one atom to another. We will discuss bonding thoroughly in Chapters 8 and 9; here we will introduce some simple bonding ideas that will be useful in the next few chapters.

The forces that hold atoms together in compounds are called **chemical bonds.** One way that atoms can form bonds is by *sharing electrons.* These bonds are called **covalent bonds,** and the resulting collection of atoms is called a **molecule.** Molecules can be represented in several different ways. The simplest method is the **chemical formula,** in which the symbols for the elements are used to indicate the types of atoms present and subscripts are used to indicate the relative numbers of atoms. For example, the formula for carbon dioxide is CO_2, meaning that each molecule contains 1 atom of carbon and 2 atoms of oxygen.

Examples of molecules that contain covalent bonds are hydrogen (H_2), water (H_2O), oxygen (O_2), ammonia (NH_3), and methane (CH_4). More information about a molecule is given by its **structural formula,** in which the individual bonds are shown (indicated by lines). Structural formulas may or may not indicate the actual shape of the molecule. For example, water might be represented as

H—O—H   or

The structure on the right shows the actual shape of the water molecule. Scientists know from experimental evidence that the molecule looks like this. (We will study the shapes of molecules further in Chapter 8.) The structural formula for ammonia is shown in the margin at left.

Note that atoms connected to the central atom by dashed lines are behind the plane of the paper, and atoms connected to the central atom by wedges are in front of the plane of the paper.

In a compound composed of molecules, the individual molecules move around as independent units. For example, a molecule of methane gas can be represented in several ways. The structural formula for methane (CH_4) is shown in Fig. 2.16. The **space-filling**

Visualization: Covalent Bonding

Ammonia

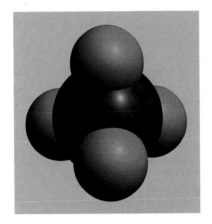

FIGURE 2.16
The structural formula for methane.

H
|
C
H H H
Methane

FIGURE 2.17
Space-filling model of methane. This type of model shows both the relative sizes of the atoms in the molecule and their spatial relationships.

FIGURE 2.18
Ball-and-stick model of methane.

model of methane, which shows the relative sizes of the atoms as well as their relative orientation in the molecule, is given in Fig. 2.17. **Ball-and-stick models** are also used to represent molecules. The ball-and-stick structure of methane is shown in Fig. 2.18.

A second type of chemical bond results from attractions among ions. An **ion** is an atom or group of atoms that has a net positive or negative charge. The best-known ionic compound is common table salt, or sodium chloride, which forms when neutral chlorine and sodium react.

To see how the ions are formed, consider what happens when an electron is transferred from a sodium atom to a chlorine atom (the neutrons in the nuclei will be ignored):

Neutral sodium
atom (Na)

Sodium ion
(Na$^+$)

$11+$ ——— Minus 1 electron ———→ $11+$

10 electrons

11 electrons

Na$^+$ is usually called the *sodium ion* rather than the sodium cation. Also Cl$^-$ is called the *chloride ion* rather than the chloride anion. In general, when a specific ion is referred to, the word *ion* rather than cation or anion is used.

With one electron stripped off, the sodium, with its 11 protons and only 10 electrons, now has a net 1+ charge—it has become a *positive ion*. A positive ion is called a **cation.** The sodium ion is written as Na$^+$, and the process can be represented in shorthand form as

$$Na \longrightarrow Na^+ + e^-$$

If an electron is added to chlorine,

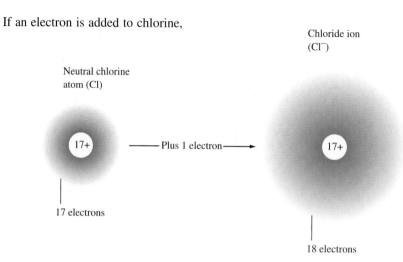

Neutral chlorine
atom (Cl)

— Plus 1 electron ⟶

Chloride ion
(Cl⁻)

17 electrons

18 electrons

the 18 electrons produce a net 1− charge; the chlorine has become an *ion with a negative charge*—an **anion.** The chloride ion is written as Cl⁻, and the process is represented as

$$Cl + e^- \longrightarrow Cl^-$$

Because anions and cations have opposite charges, they attract each other. This *force of attraction between oppositely charged ions* is called **ionic bonding.** As illustrated in Fig. 2.19, sodium metal and chlorine gas (a green gas composed of Cl_2 molecules) react

FIGURE 2.19
Sodium metal (which is so soft it can be cut with a knife and which consists of individual sodium atoms) reacts with chlorine gas (which contains Cl_2 molecules) to form solid sodium chloride (which contains Na^+ and Cl^- ions packed together).

FIGURE 2.20
Ball-and-stick models of the ammonium ion (NH_4^+) and the nitrate ion (NO_3^-).

to form solid sodium chloride, which contains many Na^+ and Cl^- ions packed together and forms the beautiful colorless cubic crystals shown in Fig. 2.19.

A solid consisting of oppositely charged ions is called an **ionic solid,** or a **salt.** Ionic solids can consist of simple ions, as in sodium chloride, or of **polyatomic** (many atom) **ions,** as in ammonium nitrate (NH_4NO_3), which contains ammonium ions (NH_4^+) and nitrate ions (NO_3^-). The ball-and-stick models of these ions are shown in Fig. 2.20.

2.7 An Introduction to the Periodic Table

In a room where chemistry is taught or practiced, a chart called the **periodic table** is almost certain to be found hanging on the wall. This chart shows all the known elements and gives a good deal of information about each. As our study of chemistry progresses, the usefulness of the periodic table will become more obvious. This section will simply introduce it to you.

Visualization: Comparison of a Molecular Compound and an Ionic Compound

A simplified version of the periodic table is shown in Fig. 2.21. The letters in the boxes are the symbols for the elements; these abbreviations are based on the current element names or the original names (see Table 2.2). The number shown above each symbol is the *atomic number* (number of protons) for that element. For example, carbon (C) has atomic number 6, and lead (Pb) has atomic number 82. Most of the elements are **metals.** Metals have characteristic physical properties such as efficient conduction of heat and electricity, malleability (they can be hammered into thin sheets), ductility (they can be pulled into wires), and (often) a lustrous appearance. Chemically, metals tend to *lose* electrons to form positive ions. For example, copper is a typical metal. It is lustrous (although it tarnishes readily); it is an excellent conductor of electricity (it is widely used in electrical wires); and it is readily formed into various shapes, such as pipes for water systems. Copper is also found in many salts, such as the beautiful blue copper sulfate, in which copper is present as Cu^{2+} ions. Copper is a member of the transition metals—the metals shown in the center of the periodic table.

Metals tend to form positive ions; non-metals tend to form negative ions.

The relatively few **nonmetals** appear in the upper-right corner of the table (to the right of the heavy line in Fig. 2.21), except hydrogen, a nonmetal that resides in the upper-left corner. The nonmetals lack the physical properties that characterize the metals. Chemically, they tend to *gain* electrons in reactions with metals to form negative ions. Nonmetals often bond to each other by forming covalent bonds. For example, chlorine is a typical nonmetal. Under normal conditions it exists as Cl_2 molecules; it reacts with metals to form salts containing Cl^- ions (NaCl, for example); and it forms covalent bonds with nonmetals (for example, hydrogen chloride gas, HCl).

Elements in the same vertical column in the periodic table form a *group* (or *family*) and generally have similar properties.

The periodic table is arranged so that elements in the same vertical columns (called **groups** or **families**) have *similar chemical properties.* For example, all of the **alkali metals,** members of Group 1A—lithium (Li), sodium (Na), potassium (K), rubidium (Rb), cesium (Cs), and francium (Fr)—are very active elements that readily form ions with a $1+$ charge when they react with nonmetals. The members of Group 2A—beryllium (Be), magnesium (Mg), calcium (Ca), strontium (Sr), barium (Ba), and radium (Ra)—are called the **alkaline earth metals.** They all form ions with a $2+$ charge when they react with nonmetals. The **halogens,** the members of Group 7A—fluorine (F), chlorine (Cl), bromine (Br), iodine (I), and astatine (At)—all form diatomic molecules. Fluorine, chlorine, bromine, and iodine all react with metals to form salts containing ions with a $1-$ charge (F^-, Cl^-, Br^-, and I^-). The members of Group 8A—helium (He), neon (Ne), argon (Ar), krypton (Kr), xenon (Xe), and radon (Rn)—are known as the **noble gases.** They all exist under normal conditions as monatomic (single-atom) gases and have little chemical reactivity.

Samples of chlorine gas, liquid bromine, and solid iodine.

FIGURE 2.21
The periodic table.

TABLE 2.2 The Symbols for the Elements That Are Based on the Original Names		
Current Name	**Original Name**	**Symbol**
Antimony	Stibium	Sb
Copper	Cuprum	Cu
Iron	Ferrum	Fe
Lead	Plumbum	Pb
Mercury	Hydrargyrum	Hg
Potassium	Kalium	K
Silver	Argentum	Ag
Sodium	Natrium	Na
Tin	Stannum	Sn
Tungsten	Wolfram	W

CHEMICAL IMPACT

Hassium Fits Right in

Hassium, element 108, does not exist in nature but must be made in a particle accelerator. It was first created in 1984 and can be made by shooting magnesium-26 ($^{26}_{12}Mg$) atoms at curium-248 ($^{248}_{96}Cm$) atoms. The collisions between these atoms produce some hassium-265 ($^{265}_{108}Hs$) atoms. The position of hassium in the periodic table (see Fig. 2.21) in the vertical column containing iron, ruthenium, and osmium suggests that hassium should have chemical properties similar to these metals. However, it is not easy to test this prediction—only a few atoms of hassium can be made at a given time and they last for only about 9 seconds. Imagine having to get your next lab experiment done in 9 seconds!

Amazingly, a team of chemists from the Lawrence Berkeley National Laboratory in California, the Paul Scherrer Institute and the University of Bern in Switzerland, and the Institute of Nuclear Chemistry in Germany have done experiments to characterize the chemical behavior of hassium. For example, they have observed that hassium atoms react with oxygen to form a hassium oxide compound of the type expected from its position on the periodic table. The team has also measured other properties of hassium, including the energy released as it undergoes nuclear decay to another atom.

This work would have surely pleased Dmitri Mendeleev (see Fig. 7.23), who originally developed the periodic table and showed its power to predict chemical properties.

Note from Fig. 2.21 that alternate sets of symbols are used to denote the groups. The symbols 1A through 8A are the traditional designations, whereas the numbers 1 to 18 have been suggested recently. In this text the 1A to 8A designations will be used.

The horizontal rows of elements in the periodic table are called **periods.** Horizontal row 1 is called the *first period* (it contains H and He); row 2 is called the *second period* (elements Li through Ne); and so on.

We will learn much more about the periodic table as we continue with our study of chemistry. Meanwhile, when an element is introduced in this text, you should always note its position on the periodic table.

Another format of the periodic table will be discussed in Section 7.11.

2.8 Naming Simple Compounds

When chemistry was an infant science, there was no system for naming compounds. Names such as sugar of lead, blue vitrol, quicklime, Epsom salts, milk of magnesia, gypsum, and laughing gas were coined by early chemists. Such names are called *common names.* As chemistry grew, it became clear that using common names for compounds would lead to unacceptable chaos. Nearly 5 million chemical compounds are currently known. Memorizing common names for these compounds would be an impossible task.

The solution, of course, is to adopt a *system* for naming compounds in which the name tells something about the composition of the compound. After learning the system, a chemist given a formula should be able to name the compound or, given a name, should be able to construct the compound's formula. In this section we will specify the most important rules for naming compounds other than organic compounds (those based on chains of carbon atoms).

We will begin with the systems for naming inorganic **binary compounds**—compounds composed of two elements—which we classify into various types for easier recognition. We will consider both ionic and covalent compounds.

TABLE 2.3   Common Monatomic Cations and Anions

Cation	Name	Anion	Name
H^+	Hydrogen	H^-	Hydride
Li^+	Lithium	F^-	Fluoride
Na^+	Sodium	Cl^-	Chloride
K^+	Potassium	Br^-	Bromide
Cs^+	Cesium	I^-	Iodide
Be^{2+}	Beryllium	O^{2-}	Oxide
Mg^{2+}	Magnesium	S^{2-}	Sulfide
Ca^{2+}	Calcium	N^{3-}	Nitride
Ba^{2+}	Barium	P^{3-}	Phosphide
Al^{3+}	Aluminum		
Ag^+	Silver		

Binary Ionic Compounds (Type I)

Binary ionic compounds contain a positive ion (cation) always written first in the formula and a negative ion (anion). In naming these compounds, the following rules apply:

1. The cation is always named first and the anion second.

A monatomic cation has the same name as its parent element.

2. A monatomic (meaning "one-atom") cation takes its name from the name of the element. For example, Na^+ is called sodium in the names of compounds containing this ion.

3. A monatomic anion is named by taking the root of the element name and adding *-ide*. Thus the Cl^- ion is called chloride.

Some common monatomic cations and anions and their names are given in Table 2.3.

The rules for naming binary ionic compounds are illustrated by the following examples:

In formulas of ionic compounds, simple ions are represented by the element symbol: Cl means Cl^-, Na means Na^+, and so on.

Compound	Ions Present	Name
NaCl	Na^+, Cl^-	Sodium chloride
KI	K^+, I^-	Potassium iodide
CaS	Ca^{2+}, S^{2-}	Calcium sulfide
Li_3N	Li^+, N^{3-}	Lithium nitride
CsBr	Cs^+, Br^-	Cesium bromide
MgO	Mg^{2+}, O^{2-}	Magnesium oxide

Sample Exercise 2.3	**Naming Type I Binary Compounds**

Name each binary compound.

a. CsF   **b.** $AlCl_3$ **c.** LiH

Solution

a. CsF is cesium fluoride.
b. $AlCl_3$ is aluminum chloride.
c. LiH is lithium hydride.

Notice that, in each case, the cation is named first, and then the anion is named.

See Exercise 2.55.

Visualization: Formation of
Ionic Compounds

Formulas from Names

So far we have started with the chemical formula of a compound and decided on its systematic name. The reverse process is also important. For example, given the name calcium hydroxide, we can write the formula as $Ca(OH)_2$ because we know that calcium forms only Ca^{2+} ions and that, since hydroxide is OH^-, two of these anions will be required to give a neutral compound.

Binary Ionic Compounds (Type II)

In the binary ionic compounds considered earlier (Type I), the metal present forms only a single type of cation. That is, sodium forms only Na^+, calcium forms only Ca^{2+}, and so on. However, as we will see in more detail later in the text, there are many metals that form more than one type of positive ion and thus form more than one type of ionic compound with a given anion. For example, the compound $FeCl_2$ contains Fe^{2+} ions, and the compound $FeCl_3$ contains Fe^{3+} ions. In a case such as this, the *charge on the metal ion must be specified*. The systematic names for these two iron compounds are iron(II) chloride and iron(III) chloride, respectively, where the *Roman numeral indicates the charge of the cation.*

Another system for naming these ionic compounds that is seen in the older literature was used for metals that form only two ions. *The ion with the higher charge has a name ending in -ic, and the one with the lower charge has a name ending in -ous.* In this system, for example, Fe^{3+} is called the ferric ion, and Fe^{2+} is called the ferrous ion. The names for $FeCl_3$ and $FeCl_2$ are then ferric chloride and ferrous chloride, respectively. In this text we will use the system that employs Roman numerals. Table 2.4 lists the systematic names for many common type II cations.

TABLE 2.4   Common Type II Cations

Ion	Systematic Name
Fe^{3+}	Iron(III)
Fe^{2+}	Iron(II)
Cu^{2+}	Copper(II)
Cu^+	Copper(I)
Co^{3+}	Cobalt(III)
Co^{2+}	Cobalt(II)
Sn^{4+}	Tin(IV)
Sn^{2+}	Tin(II)
Pb^{4+}	Lead(IV)
Pb^{2+}	Lead(II)
Hg^{2+}	Mercury(II)
Hg_2^{2+}*	Mercury(I)
Ag^+	Silver†
Zn^{2+}	Zinc†
Cd^{2+}	Cadmium†

*Note that mercury(I) ions always occur bound together to form Hg_2^{2+} ions.
†Although these are transition metals, they form only one type of ion, and a Roman numeral is not used.

Sample Exercise 2.4

Formulas from Names for Type I Binary Compounds

Given the following systematic names, write the formula for each compound:

a. potassium iodide
b. calcium oxide
c. gallium bromide

Solution

Name	Formula	Comments
a. potassium iodide	KI	Contains K^+ and I^-.
b. calcium oxide	CaO	Contains Ca^{2+} and O^{2-}.
c. gallium bromide	$GaBr_3$	Contains Ga^{3+} and Br^-. Must have $3Br^-$ to balance charge of Ga^{3+}.

See Exercise 2.55.

Sample Exercise 2.5

Naming Type II Binary Compounds

1. Give the systematic name for each of the following compounds:

   a. CuCl   **b.** HgO   **c.** Fe_2O_3

2. Given the following systematic names, write the formula for each compound:

   a. Manganese(IV) oxide
   b. Lead(II) chloride

Type II binary ionic compounds contain a metal that can form more than one type of cation.

A compound must be electrically neutral.

Solution

All of these compounds include a metal that can form more than one type of cation. Thus we must first determine the charge on each cation. This can be done by recognizing that a compound must be electrically neutral; that is, the positive and negative charges must exactly balance.

1.

Formula	Name	Comments
a. $CuCl$	Copper(I) chloride	Because the anion is Cl^-, the cation must be Cu^+ (for charge balance), which requires a Roman numeral I.
b. HgO	Mercury(II) oxide	Because the anion is O^{2-}, the cation must be Hg^{2+} [mercury(II)].
c. Fe_2O_3	Iron(III) oxide	The three O^{2-} ions carry a total charge of 6−, so two Fe^{3+} ions [iron(III)] are needed to give a 6+ charge.

2.

Name	Formula	Comments
a. Manganese(IV) oxide	MnO_2	Two O^{2-} ions (total charge 4−) are required by the Mn^{4+} ion [manganese(IV)].
b. Lead(II) chloride	$PbCl_2$	Two Cl^- ions are required by the Pb^{2+} ion [lead(II)] for charge balance.

See Exercise 2.56.

A compound containing a transition metal usually requires a Roman numeral in its name.

Note that the use of a Roman numeral in a systematic name is required only in cases where more than one ionic compound forms between a given pair of elements. This case most commonly occurs for compounds containing transition metals, which often form more than one cation. *Elements that form only one cation do not need to be identified by a Roman numeral.* Common metals that do not require Roman numerals are the Group 1A elements, which form only 1+ ions; the Group 2A elements, which form only 2+ ions; and aluminum, which forms only Al^{3+}. The element silver deserves special mention at this point. In virtually all its compounds silver is found as the Ag^+ ion. Therefore, although silver is a transition metal (and can potentially form ions other than Ag^+), silver compounds are usually named without a Roman numeral. Thus $AgCl$ is typically called silver chloride rather than silver(I) chloride, although the latter name is technically correct. Also, a Roman numeral is not used for zinc compounds, since zinc forms only the Zn^{2+} ion.

As shown in Sample Exercise 2.5, when a metal ion is present that forms more than one type of cation, the charge on the metal ion must be determined by balancing the positive and negative charges of the compound. To do this you must be able to recognize the common cations and anions and know their charges (see Tables 2.3 and 2.5).

Crystals of copper(II) sulfate.

| Sample Exercise 2.6 | ## Naming Binary Compounds |

1. Give the systematic name for each of the following compounds:

    a. $CoBr_2$ **b.** $CaCl_2$ **c.** Al_2O_3

2. Given the following systematic names, write the formula for each compound:

    a. Chromium(III) chloride
    b. Gallium iodide

Solution

1.

Formula	Name	Comments
a. $CoBr_2$	Cobalt(II) bromide	Cobalt is a transition metal; the compound name must have a Roman numeral. The two Br^- ions must be balanced by a Co^{2+} ion.
b. $CaCl_2$	Calcium chloride	Calcium, an alkaline earth metal, forms only the Ca^{2+} ion. A Roman numeral is not necessary.
c. Al_2O_3	Aluminum oxide	Aluminum forms only the Al^{3+} ion. A Roman numeral is not necessary.

2.

Name	Formula	Comments
a. Chromium(III) chloride	$CrCl_3$	Chromium(III) indicates that Cr^{3+} is present, so 3 Cl^- ions are needed for charge balance.
b. Gallium iodide	GaI_3	Gallium always forms 3+ ions, so 3 I^- ions are required for charge balance.

See Exercises 2.57 and 2.58.

Various chromium compounds dissolved in water. From left to right: $CrCl_2$, $K_2Cr_2O_7$, $Cr(NO_3)_3$, $CrCl_3$, K_2CrO_4.

The following flowchart is useful when you are naming binary ionic compounds:

The common Type I and Type II ions are summarized in Fig. 2.22. Also shown in Fig. 2.22 are the common monatomic ions.

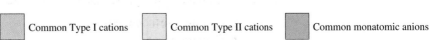

FIGURE 2.22
The common cations and anions.

TABLE 2.5   Common Polyatomic Ions

Ion	Name	Ion	Name
Hg_2^{2+}	Mercury(I)	NCS^-	Thiocyanate
NH_4^+	Ammonium	CO_3^{2-}	Carbonate
NO_2^-	Nitrite	HCO_3^-	Hydrogen carbonate
NO_3^-	Nitrate		(bicarbonate is a widely
SO_3^{2-}	Sulfite		used common name)
SO_4^{2-}	Sulfate	ClO^-	Hypochlorite
HSO_4^-	Hydrogen sulfate	ClO_2^-	Chlorite
	(bisulfate is a widely	ClO_3^-	Chlorate
	used common name)	ClO_4^-	Perchlorate
OH^-	Hydroxide	$C_2H_3O_2^-$	Acetate
CN^-	Cyanide	MnO_4^-	Permanganate
PO_4^{3-}	Phosphate	$Cr_2O_7^{2-}$	Dichromate
HPO_4^{2-}	Hydrogen phosphate	CrO_4^{2-}	Chromate
$H_2PO_4^-$	Dihydrogen phosphate	O_2^{2-}	Peroxide
		$C_2O_4^{2-}$	Oxalate

Ionic Compounds with Polyatomic Ions

We have not yet considered ionic compounds that contain polyatomic ions. For example, the compound ammonium nitrate, NH_4NO_3, contains the polyatomic ions NH_4^+ and NO_3^-. Polyatomic ions are assigned special names that *must be memorized* to name the compounds containing them. The most important polyatomic ions and their names are listed in Table 2.5.

Polyatomic ion formulas must be memorized.

Note in Table 2.5 that several series of anions contain an atom of a given element and different numbers of oxygen atoms. These anions are called **oxyanions.** When there are two members in such a series, the name of the one with the smaller number of oxygen atoms ends in *-ite* and the name of the one with the larger number ends in *-ate*—for example, sulfite (SO_3^{2-}) and sulfate (SO_4^{2-}). When more than two oxyanions make up a series, *hypo-* (less than) and *per-* (more than) are used as prefixes to name the members of the series with the fewest and the most oxygen atoms, respectively. The best example involves the oxyanions containing chlorine, as shown in Table 2.5.

Sample Exercise 2.7   ## Naming Compounds Containing Polyatomic Ions

1. Give the systematic name for each of the following compounds:

   a. Na_2SO_4
   b. KH_2PO_4
   c. $Fe(NO_3)_3$
   d. $Mn(OH)_2$
   e. Na_2SO_3
   f. Na_2CO_3

2. Given the following systematic names, write the formula for each compound:

   a. Sodium hydrogen carbonate
   b. Cesium perchlorate

    c. Sodium hypochlorite
    d. Sodium selenate
    e. Potassium bromate

Solution

1.

Formula	Name	Comments
a. Na_2SO_4	Sodium sulfate	
b. KH_2PO_4	Potassium dihydrogen phosphate	
c. $Fe(NO_3)_3$	Iron(III) nitrate	Transition metal—name must contain a Roman numeral. The Fe^{3+} ion balances three NO_3^- ions.
d. $Mn(OH)_2$	Manganese(II) hydroxide	Transition metal—name must contain a Roman numeral. The Mn^{2+} ion balances three OH^- ions.
e. Na_2SO_3	Sodium sulfite	
f. Na_2CO_3	Sodium carbonate	

2.

Name	Formula	Comments
a. Sodium hydrogen carbonate	$NaHCO_3$	Often called sodium bicarbonate.
b. Cesium perchlorate	$CsClO_4$	
c. Sodium hypochlorite	$NaOCl$	
d. Sodium selenate	Na_2SeO_4	Atoms in the same group, like sulfur and selenium, often form similar ions that are named similarly. Thus SeO_4^{2-} is selenate, like SO_4^{2-} (sulfate).
e. Potassium bromate	$KBrO_3$	As above, BrO_3^- is bromate, like ClO_3^- (chlorate).

See Exercises 2.59 and 2.60.

Binary Covalent Compounds (Type III)

In *binary covalent compounds*, the element names follow the same rules as for binary ionic compounds.

Binary covalent compounds are formed between *two nonmetals*. Although these compounds do not contain ions, they are named very similarly to binary ionic compounds.

In the naming of binary covalent compounds, the following rules apply:

1. The first element in the formula is named first, using the full element name.

2. The second element is named as if it were an anion.

3. Prefixes are used to denote the numbers of atoms present. These prefixes are given in Table 2.6.

4. The prefix *mono-* is never used for naming the first element. For example, CO is called carbon monoxide, *not* monocarbon monoxide.

TABLE 2.6 Prefixes Used to Indicate Number in Chemical Names

Prefix	Number Indicated
mono-	1
di-	2
tri-	3
tetra-	4
penta-	5
hexa-	6
hepta-	7
octa-	8
nona-	9
deca-	10

To see how these rules apply, we will now consider the names of the several covalent compounds formed by nitrogen and oxygen:

Compound	Systematic Name	Common Name
N_2O	Dinitrogen monoxide	Nitrous oxide
NO	Nitrogen monoxide	Nitric oxide
NO_2	Nitrogen dioxide	
N_2O_3	Dinitrogen trioxide	
N_2O_4	Dinitrogen tetroxide	
N_2O_5	Dinitrogen pentoxide	

Notice from the preceding examples that to avoid awkward pronunciations, we often drop the final *o* or *a* of the prefix when the element begins with a vowel. For example, N_2O_4 is called dinitrogen tetroxide, *not* dinitrogen tetraoxide, and CO is called carbon monoxide, *not* carbon monooxide.

Some compounds are always referred to by their common names. The two best examples are water and ammonia. The systematic names for H_2O and NH_3 are never used.

Sample Exercise 2.8

Naming Type III Binary Compounds

1. Name each of the following compounds:

    a. PCl_5
    b. PCl_3
    c. SO_2

2. From the following systematic names, write the formula for each compound:

    a. Sulfur hexafluoride
    b. Sulfur trioxide
    c. Carbon dioxide

Solution

1.

Formula	Name
a. PCl_5	Phosphorus pentachloride
b. PCl_3	Phosphorus trichloride
c. SO_2	Sulfur dioxide

2.

Name	Formula
a. Sulfur hexafluoride	SF_6
b. Sulfur trioxide	SO_3
c. Carbon dioxide	CO_2

See Exercises 2.61 and 2.62.

The rules for naming binary compounds are summarized in Fig. 2.23. Prefixes to indicate the number of atoms are used only in Type III binary compounds (those containing two nonmetals). An overall strategy for naming compounds is given in Fig. 2.24.

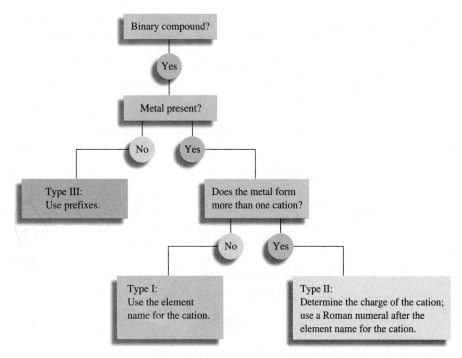

FIGURE 2.23
A flowchart for naming binary compounds.

| Sample Exercise 2.9 | **Naming Various Types of Compounds** |

1. Give the systematic name for each of the following compounds:

   a. P_4O_{10}
   b. Nb_2O_5
   c. Li_2O_2
   d. $Ti(NO_3)_4$

2. Given the following systematic names, write the formula for each compound:

   a. Vanadium(V) fluoride
   b. Dioxygen difluoride
   c. Rubidium peroxide
   d. Gallium oxide

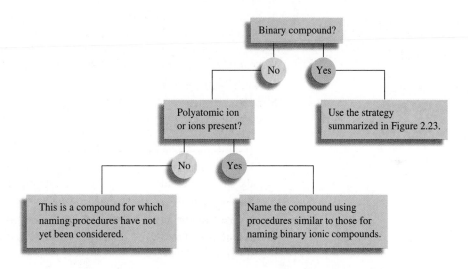

FIGURE 2.24
Overall strategy for naming chemical compounds.

Solution

1.

Compound	Name	Comment
a. P_4O_{10}	Tetraphosphorus decaoxide	Binary covalent compound (Type III), so prefixes are used. The *a* in *deca-* is sometimes dropped.
b. Nb_2O_5	Niobium(V) oxide	Type II binary compound containing Nb^{5+} and O^{2-} ions. Niobium is a transition metal and requires a Roman numeral.
c. Li_2O_2	Lithium peroxide	Type I binary compound containing the Li^+ and O_2^{2-} (peroxide) ions.
d. $Ti(NO_3)_4$	Titanium(IV) nitrate	Not a binary compound. Contains the Ti^{4+} and NO_3^- ions. Titanium is a transition metal and requires a Roman numeral.

2.

Name	Chemical Formula	Comment
a. Vanadium(V) fluoride	VF_5	The compound contains V^{5+} ions and requires five F^- ions for charge balance.
b. Dioxygen difluoride	O_2F_2	The prefix *di-* indicates two of each atom.
c. Rubidium peroxide	Rb_2O_2	Because rubidium is in Group 1A, it forms only 1+ ions. Thus two Rb^+ ions are needed to balance the 2− charge on the peroxide ion (O_2^{2-}).
d. Gallium oxide	Ga_2O_3	Because gallium is in Group 3A, like aluminum, it forms only 3+ ions. Two Ga^{3+} ions are required to balance the charge on three O^{2-} ions.

See Exercises 2.63, 2.65, and 2.66.

Acids

Acids can be recognized by the hydrogen that appears first in the formula.

When dissolved in water, certain molecules produce a solution containing free H^+ ions (protons). These substances, **acids,** will be discussed in detail in Chapters 4, 14, and 15. Here we will simply present the rules for naming acids.

An acid can be viewed as a molecule with one or more H^+ ions attached to an anion. The rules for naming acids depend on whether the anion contains oxygen. If the *anion does not contain oxygen,* the acid is named with the prefix *hydro-* and the suffix *-ic.* For example, when gaseous HCl is dissolved in water, it forms hydrochloric acid. Similarly, HCN and H_2S dissolved in water are called hydrocyanic and hydrosulfuric acids, respectively.

When the *anion contains oxygen,* the acidic name is formed from the root name of the anion with a suffix of *-ic* or *-ous,* depending on the name of the anion.

1. If the anion name ends in *-ate,* the suffix *-ic* is added to the root name. For example, H_2SO_4 contains the sulfate anion (SO_4^{2-}) and is called sulfuric acid; H_3PO_4 contains the phosphate anion (PO_4^{3-}) and is called phosphoric acid; and $HC_2H_3O_2$ contains the acetate ion ($C_2H_3O_2^-$) and is called acetic acid.

2. If the anion has an *-ite* ending, the *-ite* is replaced by *-ous.* For example, H_2SO_3, which contains sulfite (SO_3^{2-}), is named sulfurous acid; and HNO_2, which contains nitrite (NO_2^-), is named nitrous acid.

TABLE 2.7 Names of Acids* That Do Not Contain Oxygen

Acid	Name
HF	Hydrofluoric acid
HCl	Hydrochloric acid
HBr	Hydrobromic acid
HI	Hydroiodic acid
HCN	Hydrocyanic acid
H_2S	Hydrosulfuric acid

*Note that these acids are aqueous solutions containing these substances.

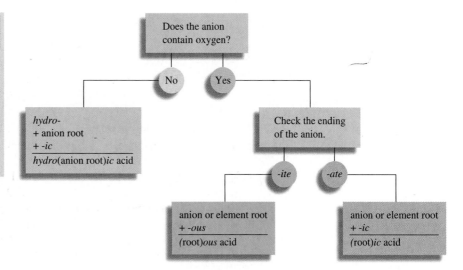

FIGURE 2.25
A flowchart for naming acids. An acid is best considered as one or more H^+ ions attached to an anion.

TABLE 2.8 Names of Some Oxygen-Containing Acids

Acid	Name
HNO_3	Nitric acid
HNO_2	Nitrous acid
H_2SO_4	Sulfuric acid
H_2SO_3	Sulfurous acid
H_3PO_4	Phosphoric acid
$HC_2H_3O_2$	Acetic Acid

The application of these rules can be seen in the names of the acids of the oxyanions of chlorine:

Acid	Anion	Name
$HClO_4$	Perchlor*ate*	Perchlor*ic* acid
$HClO_3$	Chlor*ate*	Chlor*ic* acid
$HClO_2$	Chlor*ite*	Chlor*ous* acid
$HClO$	Hypochlor*ite*	Hypochlor*ous* acid

The names of the most important acids are given in Tables 2.7 and 2.8. An overall strategy for naming acids is shown in Fig. 2.25.

Key Terms

Section 2.2
law of conservation of mass
law of definite proportion
law of multiple proportions

Section 2.3
atomic masses
atomic weights
Avogadro's hypothesis

Section 2.4
cathode-ray tube
electron
radioactivity
nuclear atom
nucleus

Section 2.5
proton
neutron
isotopes
atomic number
mass number

For Review

Fundamental laws
- Conservation of mass
- Definite proportion
- Multiple proportions

Dalton's atomic theory
- All elements are composed of atoms.
- All atoms of a given element are identical.
- Chemical compounds are formed when atoms combine.
- Atoms are not changed in chemical reactions but the way they are bound together changes.

Early atomic experiments and models
- Thomson model
- Millikan experiment
- Rutherford experiment
- Nuclear model

Atomic structure
- Small dense nucleus contains protons and neutrons.
  - Protons—positive charge
  - Neutrons—no charge
- Electrons reside outside the nucleus in the relatively large remaining atomic volume.
  - Electrons—negative charge, small mass (1/1840 of proton)
- Isotopes have the same atomic number but different mass numbers.

Atoms combine to form molecules by sharing electrons to form covalent bonds.
- Molecules are described by chemical formulas.
- Chemical formulas show number and type of atoms.
  - Structural formula
  - Ball-and-stick model
  - Space-filling model

Formation of ions
- Cation—formed by loss of an electron, positive charge
- Anion—formed by gain of an electron, negative charge
- Ionic bonds—formed by interaction of cations and anions

The periodic table organizes elements in order of increasing atomic number.
- Elements with similar properties are in columns, or groups.
- Metals are in the majority and tend to form cations.
- Nonmetals tend to form anions.

Compounds are named using a system of rules depending on the type of compound.
- Binary compounds
  - Type I—contain a metal that always forms the same cation
  - Type II—contain a metal that can form more than one cation
  - Type III—contain two nonmetals
- Compounds containing a polyatomic ion

REVIEW QUESTIONS

1. Use Dalton's atomic theory to account for each of the following.
   a. the law of conservation of mass
   b. the law of definite proportion
   c. the law of multiple proportions
2. What evidence led to the conclusion that cathode rays had a negative charge?
3. What discoveries were made by J. J. Thomson, Henri Becquerel, and Lord Rutherford? How did Dalton's model of the atom have to be modified to account for these discoveries?
4. Consider Ernest Rutherford's alpha-particle bombardment experiment illustrated in Figure 2.12. How did the results of this experiment lead Rutherford away from the plum pudding model of the atom to propose the nuclear model of the atom?
5. Do the proton and the neutron have exactly the same mass? How do the masses of the proton and neutron compare to the mass of the electron? Which particles make the greatest contribution to the mass of an atom? Which particles make the greatest contribution to the chemical properties of an atom?
6. What is the distinction between atomic number and mass number? Between mass number and atomic mass?
7. Distinguish between the terms *family* and *period* in connection with the periodic table. For which of these terms is the term *group* also used?
8. The compounds $AlCl_3$, $CrCl_3$, and ICl_3 have similar formulas, yet each follows a different set of rules to name it. Name these compounds, and then compare and contrast the nomenclature rules used in each case.

9. When metals react with nonmetals, an ionic compound generally results. What is the predicted general formula for the compound formed between an alkali metal and sulfur? Between an alkaline earth metal and nitrogen? Between aluminum and a halogen?
10. How would you name $HBrO_4$, KIO_3, $NaBrO_2$, and HIO? Refer to Table 2.5 and the acid nomenclature discussion in the text.

Active Learning Questions

These questions are designed to be used by groups of students in class. The questions allow students to explore their understanding of concepts through discussion and peer teaching. The real value of these questions is the learning that occurs while students talk to each other about chemical concepts.

1. Which of the following is true about an individual atom? Explain.
   a. An individual atom should be considered to be a solid.
   b. An individual atom should be considered to be a liquid.
   c. An individual atom should be considered to be a gas.
   d. The state of the atom depends on which element it is.
   e. An individual atom cannot be considered to be a solid, liquid, or gas.
   Justify your choice, and for choices you did not pick, explain what is wrong with them.

2. How would you go about finding the number of "chalk molecules" it takes to write your name on the board? Provide an explanation of all you would need to do and a sample calculation.

3. These questions concern the work of J. J. Thomson.
   a. From Thomson's work, which particles do you think he would feel are most important for the formation of compounds (chemical changes) and why?
   b. Of the remaining two subatomic particles, which do you place second in importance for forming compounds and why?
   c. Propose three models that explain Thomson's findings and evaluate them. To be complete you should include Thomson's findings.

4. Heat is applied to an ice cube in a closed container until only steam is present. Draw a representation of this process, assuming you can see it at an extremely high level of magnification. What happens to the size of the molecules? What happens to the total mass of the sample?

5. You have a chemical in a sealed glass container filled with air. The setup is sitting on a balance as shown below. The chemical is ignited by means of a magnifying glass focusing sunlight on the reactant. After the chemical has completely burned, which of the following is true? Explain your answer.

a. The balance will read less than 250.0 g.
b. The balance will read 250.0 g.
c. The balance will read greater than 250.0 g.
d. Cannot be determined without knowing the identity of the chemical.

6. You take three compounds consisting of two elements and decompose them. To determine the relative masses of X, Y, and Z, you collect and weigh the elements, obtaining the following data:

Elements in Compound	Masses of Elements
X and Y	X = 0.4 g, Y = 4.2 g
Y and Z	Y = 1.4 g, Z = 1.0 g
X and Y	X = 2.0 g, Y = 7.0 g

a. What are the assumptions in solving this problem?
b. What are the relative masses of X, Y, and Z?
c. What are the chemical formulas of the three compounds?
d. If you decompose 21 g of compound XY, how much of each element is present?

7. The vitamin niacin (nicotinic acid, $C_6H_5NO_2$) can be isolated from a variety of natural sources such as liver, yeast, milk, and whole grain. It also can be synthesized from commercially available materials. Which source of nicotinic acid, from a nutritional view, is best for use in a multivitamin tablet? Why?

8. One of the best indications of a useful theory is that it raises more questions for further experimentation than it originally answered. Does this apply to Dalton's atomic theory? Give examples.

9. Dalton assumed that all atoms of the same element were identical in all their properties. Explain why this assumption is not valid.

10. Evaluate each of the following as an acceptable name for water:
   a. dihydrogen oxide   c. hydrogen hydroxide
   b. hydroxide hydride   d. oxygen dihydride

11. Why do we call $Ba(NO_3)_2$ barium nitrate, but we call $Fe(NO_3)_2$ iron(II) nitrate?

12. Why is calcium dichloride not the correct systematic name for $CaCl_2$?

13. The common name for NH_3 is ammonia. What would be the systematic name for NH_3? Support your answer.

A blue question or exercise number indicates that the answer to that question or exercise appears at the back of this book and a solution appears in the *Solutions Guide*.

Questions

14. What refinements had to be made in Dalton's atomic theory to account for Gay-Lussac's results on the combining volumes of gases?

15. When hydrogen is burned in oxygen to form water, the composition of water formed does not depend on the amount of oxygen reacted. Interpret this in terms of the law of definite proportion.

16. The two most reactive families of elements are the halogens and the alkali metals. How do they differ in their reactivities?

17. Explain the law of conservation of mass, the law of definite proportion, and the law of multiple proportions.

18. Section 2.3 describes the postulates of Dalton's atomic theory. With some modifications, these postulates hold up very well regarding how we view elements, compounds, and chemical reactions today. Answer the following questions concerning Dalton's atomic theory and the modifications made today.
    a. The atom can be broken down into smaller parts. What are the smaller parts?
    b. How are atoms of hydrogen identical to each other and how can they be different from each other?
    c. How are atoms of hydrogen different from atoms of helium? How can H atoms be similar to He atoms?
    d. How is water different from hydrogen peroxide (H_2O_2) even though both compounds are composed of only hydrogen and oxygen?
    e. What happens in a chemical reaction and why is mass conserved in a chemical reaction?

19. The contributions of J. J. Thomson and Ernest Rutherford led the way to today's understanding of the structure of the atom. What were their contributions?

20. What is the modern view of the structure of the atom?

21. The number of protons in an atom determines the identity of the atom. What does the number and arrangement of the electrons in an atom determine? What does the number of neutrons in an atom determine?

22. Distinguish between the following terms.
    a. molecule versus ion
    b. covalent bonding versus ionic bonding
    c. molecule versus compound
    d. anion versus cation

23. Which of the following statements are true? For the false statements, correct them.
    a. Most of the known elements are metals.
    b. Element 118 should be a nonmetal.
    c. Hydrogen has mostly metallic properties.
    d. A family of elements is also known as a period of elements.
    e. When an alkaline earth metal, A, reacts with a halogen, X, the formula of the covalent compound formed should be A_2X.

24. Each of the following compounds has three possible names listed for it. For each compound, what is the correct name and why aren't the other names used?
    a. N_2O: nitrogen oxide, nitrogen(I) oxide, dinitrogen monoxide
    b. Cu_2O: copper oxide, copper(I) oxide, dicopper monoxide
    c. Li_2O: lithium oxide, lithium(I) oxide, dilithium monoxide

Exercises

In this section similar exercises are paired.

Development of the Atomic Theory

25. When mixtures of gaseous H_2 and gaseous Cl_2 react, a product forms that has the same properties regardless of the relative amounts of H_2 and Cl_2 used.

    a. How is this result interpreted in terms of the law of definite proportion?
    b. When a volume of H_2 reacts with an equal volume of Cl_2 at the same temperature and pressure, what volume of product having the formula HCl is formed?

26. A reaction of 1 liter of chlorine gas (Cl_2) with 3 liters of fluorine gas (F_2) yields 2 liters of a gaseous product. All gas volumes are at the same temperature and pressure. What is the formula of the gaseous product?

27. Hydrazine, ammonia, and hydrogen azide all contain only nitrogen and hydrogen. The mass of hydrogen that combines with 1.00 g of nitrogen for each compound is 1.44×10^{-1} g, 2.16×10^{-1} g, and 2.40×10^{-2} g, respectively. Show how these data illustrate the law of multiple proportions.

28. Consider 100.0-g samples of two different compounds consisting only of carbon and oxygen. One compound contains 27.2 g of carbon and the other has 42.9 g of carbon. How can these data support the law of multiple proportions if 42.9 is not a multiple of 27.2? Show that these data support the law of multiple proportions.

29. Early tables of atomic weights (masses) were generated by measuring the mass of a substance that reacts with 1.00 g of oxygen. Given the following data and taking the atomic mass of hydrogen as 1.00, generate a table of relative atomic masses for oxygen, sodium, and magnesium.

Element	Mass That Combines with 1.00 g Oxygen	Assumed Formula
Hydrogen	0.126 g	HO
Sodium	2.875 g	NaO
Magnesium	1.500 g	MgO

How do your values compare with those in the periodic table? How do you account for any differences?

30. Indium oxide contains 4.784 g of indium for every 1.000 g of oxygen. In 1869, when Mendeleev first presented his version of the periodic table, he proposed the formula In_2O_3 for indium oxide. Before that time it was thought that the formula was InO. What values for the atomic mass of indium are obtained using these two formulas? Assume that oxygen has an atomic mass of 16.00.

The Nature of the Atom

31. From the information in this chapter on the mass of the proton, the mass of the electron, and the sizes of the nucleus and the atom, calculate the densities of a hydrogen nucleus and a hydrogen atom.

32. If you wanted to make an accurate scale model of the hydrogen atom and decided that the nucleus would have a diameter of 1 mm, what would be the diameter of the entire model?

33. In an experiment it was found that the total charge on an oil drop was 5.93×10^{-18} C. How many negative charges does the drop contain?

34. A chemist in a galaxy far, far away performed the Millikan oil drop experiment and got the following results for the charges on

various drops. Use these data to calculate the charge of the electron in zirkombs.

2.56×10^{-12} zirkombs 7.68×10^{-12} zirkombs
3.84×10^{-12} zirkombs 6.40×10^{-13} zirkombs

35. What are the symbols of the following metals: sodium, radium, iron, gold, manganese, lead.

36. What are the symbols of the following nonmetals: fluorine, chlorine, bromine, sulfur, oxygen, phosphorus?

37. Give the names of the metals that correspond to the following symbols: Sn, Pt, Hg, Mg, K, Ag.

38. Give the names of the nonmetals that correspond to the following symbols: As, I, Xe, He, C, Si.

39. a. Classify the following elements as metals or nonmetals:

Mg	Si	Rn
Ti	Ge	Eu
Au	B	Am
Bi	At	Br

b. The distinction between metals and nonmetals is really not a clear one. Some elements, called *metalloids,* are intermediate in their properties. Which of these elements would you reclassify as metalloids? What other elements in the periodic table would you expect to be metalloids?

40. a. List the noble gas elements. Which of the noble gases has only radioactive isotopes? (This situation is indicated on most periodic tables by parentheses around the mass of the element. See inside front cover.)

b. Which lanthanide element and which transition element have only radioactive isotopes?

41. In the periodic table, how many elements are found in
  a. Group 2A?   **c.** the nickel group?
  b. the oxygen family?   **d.** Group 8A?

42. In the periodic table, how many elements are found
  a. in the halogen group?
  b. in the alkali family?
  c. in the lanthanide series?
  d. classified as transition metals?

43. How many protons and neutrons are in the nucleus of each of the following atoms? In a neutral atom of each element, how many electrons are present?
  a. ^{79}Br **d.** ^{133}Cs
  b. ^{81}Br **e.** ^{3}H
  c. ^{239}Pu **f.** ^{56}Fe

44. What number of protons and neutrons are contained in the nucleus of each of the following atoms? Assuming each atom is uncharged, what number of electrons are present?
  a. $^{235}_{92}U$ **d.** $^{208}_{82}Pb$
  b. $^{13}_{6}C$ **e.** $^{86}_{37}Rb$
  c. $^{57}_{26}Fe$ **f.** $^{41}_{20}Ca$

45. Write the atomic symbol ($^{A}_{Z}X$) for each of the following isotopes.
  a. $Z = 8$, number of neutrons $= 9$
  b. the isotope of chlorine in which $A = 37$

  c. $Z = 27$, $A = 60$
  d. number of protons $= 26$, number of neutrons $= 31$
  e. the isotope of I with a mass number of 131
  f. $Z = 3$, number of neutrons $= 4$

46. Write the atomic symbol ($^{A}_{Z}X$) for each of the isotopes described below.
  a. number of protons $= 27$, number of neutrons $= 31$
  b. the isotope of boron with mass number 10
  c. $Z = 12$, $A = 23$
  d. atomic number 53, number of neutrons $= 79$
  e. $Z = 9$, number of neutrons $= 10$
  f. number of protons $= 29$, mass number 65

47. What is the symbol for an ion with 63 protons, 60 electrons, and 88 neutrons? If an ion contains 50 protons, 68 neutrons, and 48 electrons, what is its symbol?

48. What is the symbol of an ion with 16 protons, 18 neutrons, and 18 electrons? What is the symbol for an ion that has 16 protons, 16 neutrons, and 18 electrons?

49. Complete the following table:

Symbol	Number of Protons in Nucleus	Number of Neutrons in Nucleus	Number of Electrons	Net Charge
$^{238}_{92}U$				
	20	20		2+
	23	28	20	
$^{89}_{39}Y$				
	35	44	36	
	15	16		3−

50.

Symbol	Number of Protons in Nucleus	Number of Neutrons in Nucleus	Number of Electrons	Net Charge
$^{53}_{26}Fe^{2+}$				
	26	33		3+
	85	125	86	
	13	14	10	
		76	54	2−

51. For each of the following sets of elements, label each as either noble gases, halogens, alkali metals, alkaline earth metals, or transition metals.
  a. Ti, Fe, Ag   **d.** Ne, Kr, Xe
  b. Mg, Sr, Ba   **e.** F, Br, I
  c. Li, K, Rb

52. Consider the elements of Group 4A (the "carbon family"): C, Si, Ge, Sn, and Pb. What is the trend in metallic character as one goes down this group? What is the trend in metallic character going from left to right across a period in the periodic table?

53. Would you expect each of the following atoms to gain or lose electrons when forming ions? What ion is the most likely in each case?
    a. Ra   c. P   e. Br
    b. In   d. Te   f. Rb

54. For each of the following atomic numbers, use the periodic table to write the formula (including the charge) for the simple *ion* that the element is most likely to form in ionic compounds.
    a. 13   c. 56   e. 87
    b. 34   d. 7   f. 35

Nomenclature

55. Name the compounds in parts a–d and write the formulas for the compounds in parts e–h.
    a. NaBr   e. strontium fluoride
    b. Rb_2O f. aluminum selenide
    c. CaS   g. potassium nitride
    d. AlI_3 h. magnesium phosphide

56. Name the compounds in parts a–d and write the formulas for the compounds in parts e–h.
    a. Hg_2O e. tin(II) nitride
    b. $FeBr_3$ f. cobalt(III) iodide
    c. CoS   g. mercury(II) oxide
    d. $TiCl_4$ h. chromium(VI) sulfide

57. Name each of the following compounds:
    a. CsF   c. Ag_2S e. TiO_2
    b. Li_3N d. MnO_2 f. Sr_3P_2

58. Write the formula for each of the following compounds:
    a. zinc chloride   d. aluminum sulfide
    b. tin(IV) fluoride   e. mercury(I) selenide
    c. calcium nitride   f. silver iodide

59. Name each of the following compounds:
    a. $BaSO_3$ c. $KMnO_4$
    b. $NaNO_2$ d. $K_2Cr_2O_7$

60. Write the formula for each of the following compounds:
    a. chromium(III) hydroxide   c. lead(IV) carbonate
    b. magnesium cyanide   d. ammonium acetate

61. Name each of the following compounds:
    a.

    ● O
    ● N

    b.
    ● I
    ● Cl

    c. SO_2
    d. P_2S_5

62. Write the formula for each of the following compounds:
    a. diboron trioxide   c. dinitrogen monoxide
    b. arsenic pentafluoride   d. sulfur hexachloride

63. Name each of the following compounds:
    a. CuI   c. CoI_2
    b. CuI_2 d. Na_2CO_3

e. $NaHCO_3$ h. NaOCl
f. S_4N_4 i. $BaCrO_4$
g. SF_6 j. NH_4NO_3

64. Name each of the following compounds:
    a. $HC_2H_3O_2$ g. H_2SO_4
    b. NH_4NO_2 h. Sr_3N_2
    c. Co_2S_3 i. $Al_2(SO_3)_3$
    d. ICl   j. SnO_2
    e. $Pb_3(PO_4)_2$ k. Na_2CrO_4
    f. KIO_3 l. HClO

65. Write the formula for each of the following compounds:
    a. sulfur difluoride
    b. sulfur hexafluoride
    c. sodium dihydrogen phosphate
    d. lithium nitride
    e. chromium(III) carbonate
    f. tin(II) fluoride
    g. ammonium acetate
    h. ammonium hydrogen sulfate
    i. cobalt(III) nitrate
    j. mercury(I) chloride
    k. potassium chlorate
    l. sodium hydride

66. Write the formula for each of the following compounds:
    a. chromium(VI) oxide
    b. disulfur dichloride
    c. nickel(II) fluoride
    d. potassium hydrogen phosphate
    e. aluminum nitride
    f. ammonia
    g. manganese(IV) sulfide
    h. sodium dichromate
    i. ammonium sulfite
    j. carbon tetraiodide

67. Write the formula for each of the following compounds:
    a. sodium oxide   h. copper(I) chloride
    b. sodium peroxide   i. gallium arsenide
    c. potassium cyanide   j. cadmium selenide
    d. copper(II) nitrate   k. zinc sulfide
    e. selenium tetrabromide   l. nitrous acid
    f. iodous acid   m. diphosphorus pentoxide
    g. lead(IV) sulfide

68. Write the formula for each of the following compounds:
    a. ammonium hydrogen phosphate
    b. mercury(I) sulfide
    c. silicon dioxide
    d. sodium sulfite
    e. aluminum hydrogen sulfate
    f. nitrogen trichloride
    g. hydrobromic acid
    h. bromous acid
    i. perbromic acid
    j. potassium hydrogen sulfide
    k. calcium iodide
    l. cesium perchlorate

69. Name the following acids illustrated below.

a.   **b.**   **c.**

⚪ H	⚫ C
⚫ N	⚪ S
⚫ O	⚫ P
⚫ Cl	

d.   **e.**

70. Each of the following compounds is incorrectly named. What is wrong with each name, and what is the correct name for each compound?
 a. $FeCl_3$, iron chloride
 b. NO_2, nitrogen(IV) oxide
 c. CaO, calcium(II) monoxide
 d. Al_2S_3, dialuminum trisulfide
 e. $Mg(C_2H_3O_2)_2$, manganese diacetate
 f. $FePO_4$, iron(II) phosphide
 g. P_2S_5, phosphorous sulfide
 h. Na_2O_2, sodium oxide
 i. HNO_3, nitrate acid
 j. H_2S, sulfuric acid

Additional Exercises

71. Chlorine has two natural isotopes: $^{37}_{17}Cl$ and $^{35}_{17}Cl$. Hydrogen reacts with chlorine to form the compound HCl. Would a given amount of hydrogen react with different masses of the two chlorine isotopes? Does this conflict with the law of definite proportion? Why or why not?

72. Which of the following statements is(are) *true?* For the false statements, correct them.
 a. All particles in the nucleus of an atom are charged.
 b. The atom is best described as a uniform sphere of matter in which electrons are embedded.
 c. The mass of the nucleus is only a very small fraction of the mass of the entire atom.
 d. The volume of the nucleus is only a very small fraction of the total volume of the atom.
 e. The number of neutrons in a neutral atom must equal the number of electrons.

73. The isotope of an unknown element, X, has a mass number of 79. The most stable ion of the isotope has 36 electrons and forms a binary compound with sodium having a formula of Na_2X. Which of the following statements is(are) *true?* For the false statements, correct them.
 a. The binary compound formed between X and fluorine will be a covalent compound.
 b. The isotope of X contains 38 protons.
 c. The isotope of X contains 41 neutrons.
 d. The identity of X is strontium, Sr.

74. For each of the following ions, indicate the total number of protons and electrons in the ion. For the positive ions in the list, predict the formula of the simplest compound formed between each positive ion and the oxide ion. For the negative ions in the list, predict the formula of the simplest compound formed between each negative ion and the aluminum ion.
 a. Fe^{2+} **e.** S^{2-}
 b. Fe^{3+} **f.** P^{3-}
 c. Ba^{2+} **g.** Br^-
 d. Cs^+ **h.** N^{3-}

75. The formulas and common names for several substances are given below. Give the systematic names for these substances.
 a. sugar of lead $Pb(C_2H_3O_2)_2$
 b. blue vitrol $CuSO_4$
 c. quicklime   CaO
 d. Epsom salts $MgSO_4$
 e. milk of magnesia $Mg(OH)_2$
 f. gypsum $CaSO_4$
 g. laughing gas N_2O

76. Identify each of the following elements:
 a. a member of the same family as oxygen whose most stable ion contains 54 electrons
 b. a member of the alkali metal family whose most stable ion contains 36 electrons
 c. a noble gas with 18 protons in the nucleus
 d. a halogen with 85 protons and 85 electrons

77. An element's most stable ion forms an ionic compound with bromine, having the formula XBr_2. If the ion of element X has a mass number of 230 and has 86 electrons, what is the identity of the element, and how many neutrons does it have?

78. A certain element has only two naturally occurring isotopes: one with 18 neutrons and the other with 20 neutrons. The element forms 1− charged ions when in ionic compounds. Predict the identity of the element. What number of electrons does the 1− charged ion have?

79. The designations 1A through 8A used for certain families of the periodic table are helpful for predicting the charges on ions in binary ionic compounds. In these compounds, the metals generally take on a positive charge equal to the family number, while the nonmetals take on a negative charge equal to the family number minus eight. Thus the compound between sodium and chlorine contains Na^+ ions and Cl^- ions and has the formula NaCl. Predict the formula and the name of the binary compound formed from the following pairs of elements.
 a. Ca and N   **e.** Ba and I
 b. K and O   **f.** Al and Se
 c. Rb and F   **g.** Cs and P
 d. Mg and S   **h.** In and Br

80. By analogy with phosphorous compounds, name the following: Na_3AsO_4, H_3AsO_4, $Mg_3(SbO_4)_2$.

81. A sample of H_2SO_4 contains 2.02 g of hydrogen, 32.07 g of sulfur, and 64.00 g of oxygen. How many grams of sulfur and grams of oxygen are present in a second sample of H_2SO_4 containing 7.27 g of hydrogen?

82. In a reaction, 34.0 g of chromium(III) oxide reacts with 12.1 g of aluminum to produce chromium and aluminum oxide. If 23.3 g of chromium is produced, what mass of aluminum oxide is produced?

Challenge Problems

83. The elements in one of the groups in the periodic table are often called the coinage metals. Identify the elements in this group based on your own experience.

84. Reaction of 2.0 L of hydrogen gas with 1.0 L of oxygen gas yields 2.0 L of water vapor. All gases are at the same temperature and pressure. Show how these data support the idea that oxygen gas is a diatomic molecule. Must we consider hydrogen to be a diatomic molecule to explain these results?

85. A combustion reaction involves the reaction of a substance with oxygen gas. The complete combustion of any hydrocarbon (binary compound of carbon and hydrogen) produces carbon dioxide and water as the only products. Octane is a hydrocarbon that is found in gasoline. Complete combustion of octane produces 8 liters of carbon dioxide for every 9 liters of water vapor (both measured at the same temperature and pressure). What is the ratio of carbon atoms to hydrogen atoms in a molecule of octane?

86. A chemistry instructor makes the following claim: "Consider that if the nucleus were the size of a grape, the electrons would be about 1 *mile* away on average." Is this claim reasonably accurate? Provide mathematical support.

87. Two elements, R and Q, combine to form two binary compounds. In the first compound, 14.0 g of R combines with 3.00 g of Q. In the second compound, 7.00 g of R combines with 4.50 g of Q. Show that these data are in accord with the law of multiple proportions. If the formula of the second compound is RQ, what is the formula of the first compound?

88. The early alchemists used to do an experiment in which water was boiled for several days in a sealed glass container. Eventually, some solid residue would appear in the bottom of the flask, which was interpreted to mean that some of the water in the flask had been converted into "earth." When Lavoisier repeated this experiment, he found that the water weighed the same before and after heating and the mass of the flask plus the solid residue equaled the original mass of the flask. Were the alchemists correct? Explain what really happened. (This experiment is described in the article by A. F. Scott in *Scientific American,* January 1984.)

89. Each of the following statements is true, but Dalton might have had trouble explaining some of them with his atomic theory. Give explanations for the following statements.

  a. The space-filling models for ethyl alcohol and dimethyl ether are shown below.

        ● C
        ● O
        ○ H

    These two compounds have the same composition by mass (52% carbon, 13% hydrogen, and 35% oxygen), yet the two have different melting points, boiling points, and solubilities in water.

  b. Burning wood leaves an ash that is only a small fraction of the mass of the original wood.

  c. Atoms can be broken down into smaller particles.

  d. One sample of lithium hydride is 87.4% lithium by mass, while another sample of lithium hydride is 74.9% lithium by mass. However, the two samples have the same properties.

90. You have two distinct gaseous compounds made from element X and element Y. The mass percents are as follows:

Compound I: 30.43% X, 69.57% Y
Compound II: 63.64% X, 36.36% Y

In their natural standard states, element X and element Y exist as gases. (Monatomic? Diatomic? Triatomic? That is for you to determine.) When you react "gas X" with "gas Y" to make the products, you get the following data (all at standard pressure and temperature):

1 volume "gas X" + 2 volumes "gas Y" $\longrightarrow$
$$2 \text{ volumes compound I}$$
2 volumes "gas X" + 1 volume "gas Y" $\longrightarrow$
$$2 \text{ volumes compound II}$$

Assume the simplest possible formulas for reactants and products in the chemical equations above. Then, determine the relative atomic masses of element X and element Y.

Integrative Problems

These problems require the integration of multiple concepts to find the solutions.

91. What is the systematic name of Ta_2O_5? If the charge on the metal remained constant and then sulfur was substituted for oxygen, how would the formula change? What is the difference in the total number of protons between Ta_2O_5 and its sulfur analog?

92. A binary ionic compound is known to contain a cation with 51 protons and 48 electrons. The anion contains one-third the number of protons as the cation. The number of electrons in the anion is equal to the number of protons plus 1. What is the formula of this compound? What is the name of this compound?

93. Using the information in Table 2.1, answer the following questions. In an ion with an unknown charge, the total mass of all the electrons was determined to be 2.55×10^{-26} g, while the total mass of its protons was 5.34×10^{-23} g. What is the identity and charge of this ion? What is the symbol and mass number of a neutral atom whose total mass of its electrons is 3.92×10^{-26} g, while its neutrons have a mass of 9.35×10^{-23} g?

Marathon Problem

This problem is designed to incorporate several concepts and techniques into one situation. Marathon Problems can be used in class by groups of students to help facilitate problem-solving skills.

94. You have gone back in time and are working with Dalton on a table of relative masses. Following are his data.

0.602 g gas A reacts with 0.295 g gas B
0.172 g gas B reacts with 0.401 g gas C
0.320 g gas A reacts with 0.374 g gas C

  a. Assuming simplest formulas (AB, BC, and AC), construct a table of relative masses for Dalton.

b. Knowing some history of chemistry, you tell Dalton that if he determines the volumes of the gases reacted at constant temperature and pressure, he need not assume simplest formulas. You collect the following data:

6 volumes gas A + 1 volume gas B → 4 volumes product
1 volume gas B + 4 volumes gas C → 4 volumes product
3 volumes gas A + 2 volumes gas C → 6 volumes product

Write the simplest balanced equations, and find the actual relative masses of the elements. Explain your reasoning.

 Get help understanding core concepts and visualizing molecular-level interactions, and practice problem solving, by visiting the Online Study Center at **college.hmco.com/ PIC/zumdahl7e.**

3 Stoichiometry

Contents

The violent chemical reaction of bromine and phosphorus.

Chemical reactions have a profound effect on our lives. There are many examples: Food is converted to energy in the human body; nitrogen and hydrogen are combined to form ammonia, which is used as a fertilizer; fuels and plastics are produced from petroleum; the starch in plants is synthesized from carbon dioxide and water using energy from sunlight; human insulin is produced in laboratories by bacteria; cancer is induced in humans by substances from our environment; and so on, in a seemingly endless list. The central activity of chemistry is to understand chemical changes such as these, and the study of reactions occupies a central place in this book. We will examine why reactions occur, how fast they occur, and the specific pathways they follow.

In this chapter we will consider the quantities of materials consumed and produced in chemical reactions. This area of study is called **chemical stoichiometry** (pronounced stoy·kē·om′·etry). To understand chemical stoichiometry, you must first understand the concept of relative atomic masses.

3.1 Counting by Weighing

Suppose you work in a candy store that sells gourmet jelly beans by the bean. People come in and ask for 50 beans, 100 beans, 1000 beans, and so on, and you have to count them out—a tedious process at best. As a good problem solver, you try to come up with a better system. It occurs to you that it might be far more efficient to buy a scale and count the jelly beans by weighing them. How can you count jelly beans by weighing them? What information about the individual beans do you need to know?

Assume that all of the jelly beans are identical and that each has a mass of 5 g. If a customer asks for 1000 jelly beans, what mass of jelly beans would be required? Each bean has a mass of 5 g, so you would need 1000 beans × 5 g/bean, or 5000 g (5 kg). It takes just a few seconds to weigh out 5 kg of jelly beans. It would take much longer to count out 1000 of them.

In reality, jelly beans are not identical. For example, let's assume that you weigh 10 beans individually and get the following results:

Bean	Mass
1	5.1 g
2	5.2 g
3	5.0 g
4	4.8 g
5	4.9 g
6	5.0 g
7	5.0 g
8	5.1 g
9	4.9 g
10	5.0 g

Jelly beans can be counted by weighing.

Can we count these nonidentical beans by weighing? Yes. The key piece of information we need is the *average mass* of the jelly beans. Let's compute the average mass for our 10-bean sample.

$$\text{Average mass} = \frac{\text{total mass of beans}}{\text{number of beans}}$$

$$= \frac{5.1 \text{ g} + 5.2 \text{ g} + 5.0 \text{ g} + 4.8 \text{ g} + 4.9 \text{ g} + 5.0 \text{ g} + 5.0 \text{ g} + 5.1 \text{ g} + 4.9 \text{ g} + 5.0 \text{ g}}{10}$$

$$= \frac{50.0}{10} = 5.0 \text{ g}$$

The average mass of a jelly bean is 5.0 g. Thus, to count out 1000 beans, we need to weigh out 5000 g of beans. This sample of beans, in which the beans have an average mass of 5.0 g, can be treated exactly like a sample where all of the beans ae identical. Objects do not need to have identical masses to be counted by weighing. We simply need to know the average mass of the objects. For purposes of counting, the objects *behave as though they were all identical,* as though they each actually had the average mass.

We count atoms in exactly the same way. Because atoms are so small, we deal with samples of matter that contain huge numbers of atoms. Even if we could see the atoms it would not be possible to count them directly. Thus we determine the number of atoms in a given sample by finding its mass. However, just as with jelly beans, to relate the mass to a number of atoms, we must know the average mass of the atoms.

3.2 Atomic Masses

As we saw in Chapter 2, the first quantitative information about atomic masses came from the work of Dalton, Gay-Lussac, Lavoisier, Avogadro, and Berzelius. By observing the proportions in which elements combine to form various compounds, nineteenth-century chemists calculated relative atomic masses. The modern system of atomic masses, instituted in 1961, is based on ^{12}C ("carbon twelve") as the standard. In this system, ^{12}C *is assigned a mass of exactly 12 atomic mass units* (amu), and the masses of all other atoms are given relative to this standard.

The most accurate method currently available for comparing the masses of atoms involves the use of the **mass spectrometer.** In this instrument, diagramed in Fig. 3.1, atoms or molecules are passed into a beam of high-speed electrons, which knock electrons off the atoms or molecules being analyzed and change them into positive ions. An applied

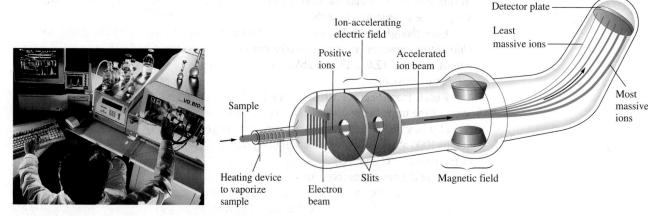

FIGURE 3.1
(left) A scientist injecting a sample into a mass spectrometer. (above) Schematic diagram of a mass spectrometer.

electric field then accelerates these ions into a magnetic field. Because an accelerating ion produces its own magnetic field, an interaction with the applied magnetic field occurs, which tends to change the path of the ion. The amount of path deflection for each ion depends on its mass—the most massive ions are deflected the smallest amount—which causes the ions to separate, as shown in Fig. 3.1. A comparison of the positions where the ions hit the detector plate gives very accurate values of their relative masses. For example, when ^{12}C and ^{13}C are analyzed in a mass spectrometer, the ratio of their masses is found to be

$$\frac{\text{Mass } ^{13}\text{C}}{\text{Mass } ^{12}\text{C}} = 1.0836129$$

Since the atomic mass unit is defined such that the mass of ^{12}C is *exactly* 12 atomic mass units, then on this same scale,

$$\text{Mass of } ^{13}\text{C} = (1.0836129)(12 \text{ amu}) = 13.003355 \text{ amu}$$

↑
Exact number
by definition

The masses of other atoms can be determined in a similar fashion.

The mass for each element is given in the table inside the front cover of this text. This value, even though it is actually a mass, is (for historical reasons) sometimes called the *atomic weight* for each element.

Look at the value of the atomic mass of carbon given in this table. You might expect to see 12, since we said the system of atomic masses is based on ^{12}C. However, the number given for carbon is not 12 but 12.01. Why? The reason for this apparent discrepancy is that the carbon found on earth (natural carbon) is a mixture of the isotopes ^{12}C, ^{13}C, and ^{14}C. All three isotopes have six protons, but they have six, seven, and eight neutrons, respectively. Because natural carbon is a mixture of isotopes, the atomic mass we use for carbon is an *average value* reflecting the average of the isotopes composing it.

The average atomic mass for carbon is computed as follows: It is known that natural carbon is composed of 98.89% ^{12}C atoms and 1.11% ^{13}C atoms. The amount of ^{14}C is negligibly small at this level of precision. Using the masses of ^{12}C (exactly 12 amu) and ^{13}C (13.003355 amu), we can calculate the average atomic mass for natural carbon as follows:

98.89% of 12 amu + 1.11% of 13.0034 amu =
$$(0.9889)(12 \text{ amu}) + (0.0111)(13.0034 \text{ amu}) = 12.01 \text{ amu}$$

In this text we will call the average mass for an element the **average atomic mass** or, simply, the *atomic mass* for that element.

Even though natural carbon does not contain a single atom with mass 12.01, for stoichiometric purposes, we can consider carbon to be composed of only one type of atom with a mass of 12.01. This enables us to count atoms of natural carbon by weighing a sample of carbon.

Recall from Section 3.1 that counting by weighing works if you know the *average* mass of the units being counted. Counting by weighing works just the same for atoms as for jelly beans. For natural carbon with an average mass of 12.01 atomic mass units, to obtain 1000 atoms would require weighing out 12,010 atomic mass units of natural carbon (a mixture of ^{12}C and ^{13}C).

As in the case of carbon, the mass for each element listed in the table inside the front cover of the text is an average value based on the isotopic composition of the naturally occurring element. For instance, the mass listed for hydrogen (1.008) is the average mass for natural hydrogen, which is a mixture of ^{1}H and ^{2}H (deuterium). *No* atom of hydrogen actually has the mass 1.008.

Most elements occur in nature as mixtures of isotopes; thus atomic masses are usually average values.

It is much easier to weigh out 600 hex nuts than count them one by one.

CHEMICAL IMPACT

Buckyballs Teach Some History

About 250 million years ago, 90% of life on earth was destroyed in some sort of cataclysmic event. This event, which ended the Permian period and began the Triassic (the P-T boundary), is the most devastating mass extinction in the earth's history—far surpassing the catastrophe 65 million years ago that wiped out the dinosaurs (the K-T boundary). In 1979 geologist Walter Alvarez and his Nobel Prize–winning physicist father Luis Alvarez suggested that unusually high concentrations of iridium in rocks laid down at the K-T boundary meant that an asteroid had hit the earth, causing tremendous devastation. In the last 20 years much evidence has accumulated to support this hypothesis, including identification of the location of the probable crater caused by the impact in the ocean near Mexico.

Were the P-T boundary extinctions also caused by an extraterrestrial object or by some event on earth, such as a massive volcano explosion? Recent discoveries by geochemists Luann Becker of the University of Washington and

Robert J. Poreda of the University of Rochester seem to strongly support the impact theory. Examining sediment from China and Japan, the team found fullerenes encapsulating argon and helium gas atoms whose isotopic composition indicates that they are extraterrestrial in origin. For example, the ratio of ^3_2He to ^4_2He found in the fullerenes is 100 times greater than the ratio for helium found in the earth's atmosphere. Likewise, the isotopic composition of the fullerene-trapped argon atoms is quite different from that found on earth.

Fullerenes include spherical C_{60} carbon molecules ("buckyballs") whose cavities can trap other atoms such as helium and argon. (See the accompanying figure.) The scientists postulate that the fullerenes originated in stars or collapsing gas clouds where the noble gas atoms were trapped as the fullerenes formed. These fullerenes were then somehow incorporated into the object that eventually hit the earth. Based on the isotopic compositions, the geochemists estimate that the impacting body must have

In addition to being useful for determining accurate mass values for individual atoms, the mass spectrometer is used to determine the isotopic composition of a natural element. For example, when a sample of natural neon is injected into a mass spectrometer, the mass spectrum shown in Fig. 3.2 is obtained. The areas of the "peaks" or the heights of the bars indicate the relative abundances of $^{20}_{10}\text{Ne}$, $^{21}_{10}\text{Ne}$, and $^{22}_{10}\text{Ne}$ atoms.

(a)

(b)

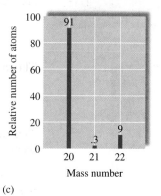

(c)

FIGURE 3.2
(a) Neon gas glowing in a discharge tube. The relative intensities of the signals recorded when natural neon is injected into a mass spectrometer, represented in terms of (b) "peaks" and (c) a bar graph. The relative areas of the peaks are 0.9092 (^{20}Ne), 0.00257 (^{21}Ne), and 0.0882 (^{22}Ne); natural neon is therefore 90.92% ^{20}Ne, 0.257% ^{21}Ne, and 8.82% ^{22}Ne.

been 10 kilometers in diameter, which is comparable in size to the asteroid that is assumed to have killed the dinosaurs.

One factor that had previously cast doubt on an asteroid collision as the cause of the P-T catastrophe was the lack of iridium found in sediments from this period. However, Becker and other scientists argue that this absence probably means the impacting object may have been a comet rather than an asteroid. It is also possible that such a blow could have intensified the volcanism already under way on earth at that time, delivering a "one-two punch" that almost obliterated life on earth, according to Becker.

It is ironic that "buckyballs," which made big news when they were recently synthesized for the first time in the laboratory, actually have been around for millions of years and have some very interesting history to teach us.

Isotope ratios of the noble gas atoms inside celestial buckyballs indicate that these ancient carbon cages formed in a stellar environment, not on earth.

Figure from *Chemical and Engineering News,* Feb. 26, 2001, p. 9. Reprinted by permission of Joseph Wilmhoff.

Sample Exercise 3.1

The Average Mass of an Element

Copper nugget.

FIGURE 3.3
Mass spectrum of natural copper.

When a sample of natural copper is vaporized and injected into a mass spectrometer, the results shown in Fig. 3.3 are obtained. Use these data to compute the average mass of natural copper. (The mass values for ^{63}Cu and ^{65}Cu are 62.93 amu and 64.93 amu, respectively.)

Solution

As shown by the graph, of every 100 atoms of natural copper, 69.09 are ^{63}Cu and 30.91 are ^{65}Cu. Thus the mass of 100 atoms of natural copper is

$$(69.09 \text{ atoms})\left(62.93 \frac{\text{amu}}{\text{atom}}\right) + (30.91 \text{ atoms})\left(64.93 \frac{\text{amu}}{\text{atom}}\right) = 6355 \text{ amu}$$

The *average mass* of a copper atom is

$$\frac{6355 \text{ amu}}{100 \text{ atoms}} = 63.55 \text{ amu/atom}$$

This mass value is used in doing calculations involving the reactions of copper and is the value given in the table inside the front cover of this book.

Reality Check: When you finish a calculation, you should always check whether your answer makes sense. In this case our answer of 63.55 amu is between the masses of the atoms that make up natural copper. This makes sense. The answer could not be smaller than 62.93 amu or larger than 64.93 amu.

See Exercises 3.27 and 3.28.

3.3 The Mole

Because samples of matter typically contain so many atoms, a unit of measure called the *mole* has been established for use in counting atoms. For our purposes, it is most convenient to define the **mole** (abbreviated mol) as *the number equal to the number of carbon atoms in exactly 12 grams of pure ^{12}C.* Techniques such as mass spectrometry, which count atoms very precisely, have been used to determine this number as 6.02214×10^{23} (6.022×10^{23} will be sufficient for our purposes). This number is called **Avogadro's number** to honor his contributions to chemistry. *One mole of something consists of 6.022×10^{23} units of that substance.* Just as a dozen eggs is 12 eggs, a mole of eggs is 6.022×10^{23} eggs.

The magnitude of the number 6.022×10^{23} is very difficult to imagine. To give you some idea, 1 mole of seconds represents a span of time 4 million times as long as the earth has already existed, and 1 mole of marbles is enough to cover the entire earth to a depth of 50 miles! However, since atoms are so tiny, a mole of atoms or molecules is a perfectly manageable quantity to use in a reaction (see Fig. 3.4).

How do we use the mole in chemical calculations? Recall that Avogadro's number is defined as the number of atoms in exactly 12 grams of ^{12}C. This means that 12 grams of ^{12}C contains 6.022×10^{23} atoms. It also means that a 12.01-gram sample of natural carbon contains 6.022×10^{23} atoms (a mixture of ^{12}C, ^{13}C, and ^{14}C atoms, with an average atomic mass of 12.01). Since the ratio of the masses of the samples (12 g/12.01 g) is the same as the ratio of the masses of the individual components (12 amu/12.01 amu), the two samples contain the *same number* of atoms (6.022×10^{23}).

To be sure this point is clear, think of oranges with an average mass of 0.5 pound each and grapefruit with an average mass of 1.0 pound each. Any two sacks for which the sack of grapefruit weighs twice as much as the sack of oranges will contain the same number of pieces of fruit. The same idea extends to atoms. Compare natural carbon (average mass of 12.01) and natural helium (average mass of 4.003). A sample of 12.01 grams of natural carbon contains the same number of atoms as 4.003 grams of natural helium. Both samples contain 1 mole of atoms (6.022×10^{23}). Table 3.1 gives more examples that illustrate this basic idea.

Thus the mole is defined such that a sample of a natural element with a mass equal to the element's atomic mass expressed in grams contains 1 mole of atoms. This definition

The SI definition of the mole is the amount of a substance that contains as many entities as there are in exactly 12 g of carbon-12.

Avogadro's number is 6.022×10^{23}. One mole of anything is 6.022×10^{23} units of that substance.

The mass of 1 mole of an element is equal to its atomic mass in grams.

FIGURE 3.4
Proceeding clockwise from the top, samples containing one mole each of copper, aluminum, iron, sulfur, iodine, and (in the center) mercury.

TABLE 3.1   Comparison of 1 Mole Samples of Various Elements

Element	Number of Atoms Present	Mass of Sample (g)
Aluminum	6.022×10^{23}	26.98
Copper	6.022×10^{23}	63.55
Iron	6.022×10^{23}	55.85
Sulfur	6.022×10^{23}	32.07
Iodine	6.022×10^{23}	126.9
Mercury	6.022×10^{23}	200.6

also fixes the relationship between the atomic mass unit and the gram. Since 6.022×10^{23} atoms of carbon (each with a mass of 12 amu) have a mass of 12 g, then

$$(6.022 \times 10^{23} \text{ atoms})\left(\frac{12 \text{ amu}}{\text{atom}}\right) = 12 \text{ g}$$

and

$$6.022 \times 10^{23} \text{ amu} = 1 \text{ g}$$

Exact
number

This relationship can be used to derive the unit factor needed to convert between atomic mass units and grams.

Sample Exercise 3.2

Determining the Mass of a Sample of Atoms

Americium is an element that does not occur naturally. It can be made in very small amounts in a device known as a *particle accelerator.* Compute the mass in grams of a sample of americium containing six atoms.

Solution

From the table inside the front cover of the text, we note that one americium atom has a mass of 243 amu. Thus the mass of six atoms is

$$6 \text{ atoms} \times 243 \frac{\text{amu}}{\text{atom}} = 1.46 \times 10^3 \text{ amu}$$

Using the relationship

$$6.022 \times 10^{23} \text{ amu} = 1 \text{ g}$$

we write the conversion factor for converting atomic mass units to grams:

$$\frac{1 \text{ g}}{6.022 \times 10^{23} \text{ amu}}$$

The mass of six americium atoms in grams is

$$1.46 \times 10^3 \text{ amu} \times \frac{1 \text{ g}}{6.022 \times 10^{23} \text{ amu}} = 2.42 \times 10^{-21} \text{ g}$$

Reality Check: Since this sample contains only six atoms, the mass should be very small as the amount 2.42×10^{-21} g indicates.

See Exercise 3.33.

CHEMICAL IMPACT

Elemental Analysis Catches Elephant Poachers

In an effort to combat the poaching of elephants by controlling illegal exports of ivory, scientists are now using the isotopic composition of ivory trinkets and elephant tusks to identify the region of Africa where the elephant lived. Using a mass spectrometer, scientists analyze the ivory for the relative amounts of ^{12}C, ^{13}C, ^{14}N, ^{15}N, ^{86}Sr, and ^{87}Sr to determine the diet of the elephant and thus its place of origin. For example, because grasses use a different photosynthetic pathway to produce glucose than do trees, grasses have a slightly different $^{13}C/^{12}C$ ratio from that of trees. They have different ratios because each time a carbon atom is added in going from simpler to more complex compounds, the more massive ^{13}C is disfavored relative to ^{12}C because it reacts more slowly. Because trees use more steps to build up glucose, they end up with a smaller $^{13}C/^{12}C$ ratio in their leaves relative to grasses, and this difference is then reflected in the tissues of elephants. Thus

scientists can tell whether a particular tusk came from a savanna-dwelling elephant (grass-eating) or from a tree-browsing elephant.

Similarly, because the ratios of $^{15}N/^{14}N$ and $^{87}Sr/^{86}Sr$ in elephant tusks also vary depending on the region of Africa the elephant inhabits, they can be used to trace the elephant's origin. In fact, using these techniques, scientists have reported being able to discriminate between elephants living only about 100 miles apart.

There is now international concern about the dwindling elephant populations in Africa—their numbers have decreased significantly in recent years. This concern has led to bans in the export of ivory from many countries in Africa. However, a few nations still allow ivory to be exported. Thus, to enforce the trade restrictions, the origin of a given piece of ivory must be established. It is hoped that the "isotope signature" of the ivory can be used for this purpose.

To do chemical calculations, you must understand what the mole means and how to determine the number of moles in a given mass of a substance. These procedures are illustrated in Sample Exercises 3.3 and 3.4.

| Sample Exercise 3.3 | **Determining Moles of Atoms** |

Aluminum (Al) is a metal with a high strength-to-mass ratio and a high resistance to corrosion; thus it is often used for structural purposes. Compute both the number of moles of atoms and the number of atoms in a 10.0-g sample of aluminum.

(left) Pure aluminum. (right) Aluminum alloys are used for many high-quality bicycle components, such as this chain wheel.

Solution

The mass of 1 mole (6.022×10^{23} atoms) of aluminum is 26.98 g. The sample we are considering has a mass of 10.0 g. Since the mass is less than 26.98 g, this sample contains less than 1 mole of aluminum atoms. We can calculate the number of moles of aluminum atoms in 10.0 g as follows:

$$10.0 \text{ g Al} \times \frac{1 \text{ mol Al}}{26.98 \text{ g Al}} = 0.371 \text{ mol Al atoms}$$

The number of atoms in 10.0 g (0.371 mol) of aluminum is

$$0.371 \text{ mol Al} \times \frac{6.022 \times 10^{23} \text{ atoms}}{1 \text{ mol Al}} = 2.23 \times 10^{23} \text{ atoms}$$

Reality Check: One mole of Al has a mass of 26.98 g and contains 6.022×10^{23} atoms. Our sample is 10.0 g, which is roughly 1/3 of 26.98. Thus the calculated amount should be on the order of 1/3 of 6×10^{23}, which it is.

See Exercise 3.34.

| Sample Exercise 3.4 | ## Calculating Numbers of Atoms |

A silicon chip used in an integrated circuit of a microcomputer has a mass of 5.68 mg. How many silicon (Si) atoms are present in the chip?

Solution

The strategy for doing this problem is to convert from milligrams of silicon to grams of silicon, then to moles of silicon, and finally to atoms of silicon:

Always check to see if your answer is sensible.

Paying careful attention to units and making sure the answer is reasonable can help you detect an inverted conversion factor or a number that was incorrectly entered in your calculator.

$$5.68 \text{ mg Si} \times \frac{1 \text{ g Si}}{1000 \text{ mg Si}} = 5.68 \times 10^{-3} \text{ g Si}$$

$$5.68 \times 10^{-3} \text{ g Si} \times \frac{1 \text{ mol Si}}{28.09 \text{ g Si}} = 2.02 \times 10^{-4} \text{ mol Si}$$

$$2.02 \times 10^{-4} \text{ mol Si} \times \frac{6.022 \times 10^{23} \text{ atoms}}{1 \text{ mol Si}} = 1.22 \times 10^{20} \text{ atoms}$$

Reality Check: Note that 5.68 mg of silicon is clearly much less than 1 mol of silicon (which has a mass of 28.09 g), so the final answer of 1.22×10^{20} atoms (compared with 6.022×10^{23} atoms) is in the right direction.

See Exercise 3.35.

| Sample Exercise 3.5 | ## Calculating the Number of Moles and Mass |

Cobalt (Co) is a metal that is added to steel to improve its resistance to corrosion. Calculate both the number of moles in a sample of cobalt containing 5.00×10^{20} atoms and the mass of the sample.

Solution

Note that the sample of 5.00×10^{20} atoms of cobalt is less than 1 mole (6.022×10^{23} atoms) of cobalt. What fraction of a mole it represents can be determined as follows:

$$5.00 \times 10^{20} \text{ atoms Co} \times \frac{1 \text{ mol Co}}{6.022 \times 10^{23} \text{ atoms Co}} = 8.30 \times 10^{-4} \text{ mol Co}$$

Since the mass of 1 mole of cobalt atoms is 58.93 g, the mass of 5.00×10^{20} atoms can be determined as follows:

$$8.30 \times 10^{-4} \text{ mol Co} \times \frac{58.93 \text{ g Co}}{1 \text{ mol Co}} = 4.89 \times 10^{-2} \text{ g Co}$$

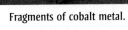

Fragments of cobalt metal.

Reality Check: In this case the sample contains 5×10^{20} atoms, which is approximately 1/1000 of a mole. Thus the sample should have a mass of about $(1/1000)(58.93) \cong 0.06$. Our answer of ~0.05 makes sense.

See Exercise 3.36.

3.4 Molar Mass

A chemical compound is, ultimately, a collection of atoms. For example, methane (the major component of natural gas) consists of molecules that each contain one carbon and four hydrogen atoms (CH_4). How can we calculate the mass of 1 mole of methane; that is, what is the mass of 6.022×10^{23} CH_4 molecules? Since each CH_4 molecule contains one carbon atom and four hydrogen atoms, 1 mole of CH_4 molecules contains 1 mole of carbon atoms and 4 moles of hydrogen atoms. The mass of 1 mole of methane can be found by summing the masses of carbon and hydrogen present:

Mass of 1 mol C	=	12.01 g
Mass of 4 mol H	=	4 × 1.008 g
Mass of 1 mol CH_4	=	16.04 g

In this case, the term 12.01 limits the number of significant figures.

Because 16.04 g represents the mass of 1 mole of methane molecules, it makes sense to call it the *molar mass* for methane. Thus the **molar mass** of a substance is *the mass in grams of one mole of the compound*. Traditionally, the term *molecular weight* has been used for this quantity. However, we will use molar mass exclusively in this text. The molar mass of a known substance is obtained by summing the masses of the component atoms as we did for methane.

A substance's molar mass is the mass in grams of 1 mole of the substance.

Sample Exercise 3.6   Calculating Molar Mass I

Juglone, a dye known for centuries, is produced from the husks of black walnuts. It is also a natural herbicide (weed killer) that kills off competitive plants around the black walnut tree but does not affect grass and other noncompetitive plants. The formula for juglone is $C_{10}H_6O_3$.

a. Calculate the molar mass of juglone.
b. A sample of 1.56×10^{-2} g of pure juglone was extracted from black walnut husks. How many moles of juglone does this sample represent?

Solution

a. The molar mass is obtained by summing the masses of the component atoms. In 1 mole of juglone there are 10 moles of carbon atoms, 6 moles of hydrogen atoms, and 3 moles of oxygen atoms:

10 C:	10 × 12.01 g =	120.1 g
6 H:	6 × 1.008 g =	6.048 g
3 O:	3 × 16.00 g =	48.00 g
Mass of 1 mol $C_{10}H_6O_3$ =		174.1 g

The mass of 1 mole of juglone is 174.1 g, which is the molar mass.

b. The mass of 1 mole of this compound is 174.1 g; thus 1.56×10^{-2} g is much less than a mole. The exact fraction of a mole can be determined as follows:

$$1.56 \times 10^{-2} \text{ g juglone} \times \frac{1 \text{ mol juglone}}{174.1 \text{ g juglone}} = 8.96 \times 10^{-5} \text{ mol juglone}$$

Juglone

See Exercises 3.39 through 3.42.

Sample Exercise 3.7   Calculating Molar Mass II

Calcium carbonate ($CaCO_3$), also called *calcite,* is the principal mineral found in limestone, marble, chalk, pearls, and the shells of marine animals such as clams.

CHEMICAL IMPACT

Measuring the Masses of Large Molecules, or Making Elephants Fly

When a chemist produces a new molecule, one crucial property for making a positive identification is the molecule's mass. There are many ways to determine the molar mass of a compound, but one of the fastest and most accurate methods involves mass spectrometry. This method requires that the substance be put into the gas phase and ionized. The deflection that the resulting ion exhibits as it is accelerated through a magnetic field can be used to obtain a very precise value of its mass. One drawback of this method is that it is difficult to use with large molecules because they are difficult to vaporize. That is, substances that contain large molecules typically have very high boiling points, and these molecules are often damaged when they are vaporized at such high temperatures. A case in point involves proteins, an extremely important class of large biologic molecules that are quite fragile at high temperatures. Typical methods used to obtain the masses of protein molecules are slow and tedious.

Mass spectrometry has not been used previously to obtain protein masses because proteins decompose at the temperatures necessary to vaporize them. However, a new technique called *matrix-assisted laser desorption* has been developed that allows mass spectrometric determination of protein molar masses. In this technique, the large "target" molecule is embedded in a matrix of smaller molecules. The matrix is then placed in a mass spectrometer and blasted with a laser beam, which causes its disintegration. Disintegration of the matrix frees the large target molecule, which is then swept into the mass spectrometer. One researcher involved in this project likened this method to an elephant on top of a tall building: "The elephant must fly if the building is suddenly turned into fine grains of sand."

This technique allows scientists to determine the mass of huge molecules. So far researchers have measured proteins with masses up to 350,000 daltons (1 dalton is the mass of a hydrogen atom). This method, which makes mass spectrometry a routine tool for the determination of protein masses, probably will be extended to even larger molecules such as DNA and could be a revolutionary development in the characterization of biomolecules.

Calcite crystals.

a. Calculate the molar mass of calcium carbonate.
b. A certain sample of calcium carbonate contains 4.86 moles. What is the mass in grams of this sample? What is the mass of the CO_3^{2-} ions present?

Solution

a. Calcium carbonate is an ionic compound composed of Ca^{2+} and CO_3^{2-} ions. In 1 mole of calcium carbonate there are 1 mole of Ca^{2+} ions and 1 mole of CO_3^{2-} ions. The molar mass is calculated by summing the masses of the components:

$$1\ Ca^{2+}: \quad 1 \times 40.08\ g = \quad 40.08\ g$$
$$1\ CO_3^{2-}:$$
$$1\ C: \qquad 1 \times 12.01\ g = \quad 12.01\ g$$
$$3\ O: \qquad 3 \times 16.00\ g = \quad \underline{48.00\ g}$$
$$\text{Mass of 1 mol } CaCO_3 = 100.09\ g$$

Thus the mass of 1 mole of $CaCO_3$ (1 mol Ca^{2+} plus 1 mol CO_3^{2-}) is 100.09 g. This is the molar mass.

b. The mass of 1 mole of $CaCO_3$ is 100.09 g. The sample contains nearly 5 moles, or close to 500 g. The exact amount is determined as follows:

$$4.86\ \text{mol } CaCO_3 \times \frac{100.09\ g\ CaCO_3}{1\ \text{mol } CaCO_3} = 486\ g\ CaCO_3$$

To find the mass of carbonate ions (CO_3^{2-}) present in this sample, we must realize that 4.86 moles of $CaCO_3$ contains 4.86 moles of Ca^{2+} ions and 4.86 moles of CO_3^{2-} ions. The mass of 1 mole of CO_3^{2-} ions is

$$
\begin{array}{ll}
\text{1 C:} & 1 \times 12.01 = 12.01 \text{ g} \\
\text{3 O:} & 3 \times 16.00 = \underline{48.00} \text{ g} \\
\multicolumn{2}{r}{\text{Mass of 1 mol } CO_3^{2-} = 60.01 \text{ g}}
\end{array}
$$

Thus the mass of 4.86 moles of CO_3^{2-} ions is

$$4.86 \ \cancel{\text{mol } CO_3^{2-}} \times \frac{60.01 \text{ g } CO_3^{2-}}{1 \ \cancel{\text{mol } CO_3^{2-}}} = 292 \text{ g } CO_3^{2-}$$

See Exercises 3.43 through 3.46.

Sample Exercise 3.8

Molar Mass and Numbers of Molecules

Isopentyl acetate ($C_7H_{14}O_2$) is the compound responsible for the scent of bananas. A molecular model of isopentyl acetate is shown in the margin below. Interestingly, bees release about 1 μg (1×10^{-6} g) of this compound when they sting. The resulting scent attracts other bees to join the attack. How many molecules of isopentyl acetate are released in a typical bee sting? How many atoms of carbon are present?

Solution

Since we are given a mass of isopentyl acetate and want to find the number of molecules, we must first compute the molar mass:

$$7 \ \cancel{\text{mol}} \text{ C} \times 12.01 \frac{\text{g}}{\cancel{\text{mol}}} = 84.07 \text{ g C}$$

$$14 \ \cancel{\text{mol}} \text{ H} \times 1.008 \frac{\text{g}}{\cancel{\text{mol}}} = 14.11 \text{ g H}$$

$$2 \ \cancel{\text{mol}} \text{ O} \times 16.00 \frac{\text{g}}{\cancel{\text{mol}}} = \frac{32.00 \text{ g O}}{130.18 \text{ g}}$$

This means that 1 mole of isopentyl acetate (6.022×10^{23} molecules) has a mass of 130.18 g.

To find the number of molecules released in a sting, we must first determine the number of moles of isopentyl acetate in 1×10^{-6} g:

$$1 \times 10^{-6} \ \cancel{\text{g } C_7H_{14}O_2} \times \frac{1 \text{ mol } C_7H_{14}O_2}{130.18 \ \cancel{\text{g } C_7H_{14}O_2}} = 8 \times 10^{-9} \text{ mol } C_7H_{14}O_2$$

Since 1 mole is 6.022×10^{23} units, we can determine the number of molecules:

$$8 \times 10^{-9} \ \cancel{\text{mol } C_7H_{14}O_2} \times \frac{6.022 \times 10^{23} \text{ molecules}}{1 \ \cancel{\text{mol } C_7H_{14}O_2}} = 5 \times 10^{15} \text{ molecules}$$

To determine the number of carbon atoms present, we must multiply the number of molecules by 7, since each molecule of isopentyl acetate contains seven carbon atoms:

$$5 \times 10^{15} \ \cancel{\text{molecules}} \times \frac{7 \text{ carbon atoms}}{\cancel{\text{molecule}}} = 4 \times 10^{16} \text{ carbon atoms}$$

Note: In keeping with our practice of always showing the correct number of significant figures, we have rounded after each step. However, if extra digits are carried throughout this problem, the final answer rounds to 3×10^{16}.

See Exercises 3.47 through 3.52.

Isopentyl acetate is released when a bee stings.

 Carbon

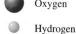 Oxygen

Hydrogen

Isopentyl acetate

To show the correct number of significant figures in each calculation, we round after each step. In your calculations, always carry extra significant figures through to the end; then round.

3.5 Percent Composition of Compounds

There are two common ways of describing the composition of a compound: in terms of the numbers of its constituent atoms and in terms of the percentages (by mass) of its elements. We can obtain the mass percents of the elements from the formula of the compound by comparing the mass of each element present in 1 mole of the compound to the total mass of 1 mole of the compound.

For example, for ethanol, which has the formula C_2H_5OH, the mass of each element present and the molar mass are obtained as follows:

$$\text{Mass of C} = 2 \text{ mol} \times 12.01 \frac{\text{g}}{\text{mol}} = 24.02 \text{ g}$$

$$\text{Mass of H} = 6 \text{ mol} \times 1.008 \frac{\text{g}}{\text{mol}} = 6.048 \text{ g}$$

$$\text{Mass of O} = 1 \text{ mol} \times 16.00 \frac{\text{g}}{\text{mol}} = \underline{16.00 \text{ g}}$$

$$\text{Mass of 1 mol } C_2H_5OH = 46.07 \text{ g}$$

The **mass percent** (often called the *weight percent*) of carbon in ethanol can be computed by comparing the mass of carbon in 1 mole of ethanol to the total mass of 1 mole of ethanol and multiplying the result by 100:

$$\text{Mass percent of C} = \frac{\text{mass of C in 1 mol } C_2H_5OH}{\text{mass of 1 mol } C_2H_5OH} \times 100\%$$

$$= \frac{24.02 \text{ g}}{46.07 \text{ g}} \times 100\% = 52.14\%$$

The mass percents of hydrogen and oxygen in ethanol are obtained in a similar manner:

$$\text{Mass percent of H} = \frac{\text{mass of H in 1 mol } C_2H_5OH}{\text{mass of 1 mol } C_2H_5OH} \times 100\%$$

$$= \frac{6.048 \text{ g}}{46.07 \text{ g}} \times 100\% = 13.13\%$$

$$\text{Mass percent of O} = \frac{\text{mass of O in 1 mol } C_2H_5OH}{\text{mass of 1 mol } C_2H_5OH} \times 100\%$$

$$= \frac{16.00 \text{ g}}{46.07 \text{ g}} \times 100\% = 34.73\%$$

Reality Check: Notice that the percentages add up to 100.00%; this provides a check that the calculations are correct.

Sample Exercise 3.9 | Calculating Mass Percent I

Carvone is a substance that occurs in two forms having different arrangements of the atoms but the same molecular formula ($C_{10}H_{14}O$) and mass. One type of carvone gives caraway seeds their characteristic smell, and the other type is responsible for the smell of spearmint oil. Compute the mass percent of each element in carvone.

Solution

The masses of the elements in 1 mole of carvone are

$$\text{Mass of C in 1 mol} = 10 \text{ mol} \times 12.01 \frac{\text{g}}{\text{mol}} = 120.1 \text{ g}$$

Carvone

$$\text{Mass of H in 1 mol} = 14 \ \cancel{mol} \times 1.008 \frac{g}{\cancel{mol}} = 14.11 \ g$$

$$\text{Mass of O in 1 mol} = 1 \ \cancel{mol} \times 16.00 \frac{g}{\cancel{mol}} = \underline{16.00 \ g}$$

$$\text{Mass of 1 mol } C_{10}H_{14}O = 150.2 \ g$$

Next we find the fraction of the total mass contributed by each element and convert it to a percentage:

$$\text{Mass percent of C} = \frac{120.1 \ g \ C}{150.2 \ g \ C_{10}H_{14}O} \times 100\% = 79.96\%$$

$$\text{Mass percent of H} = \frac{14.11 \ g \ H}{150.2 \ g \ C_{10}H_{14}O} \times 100\% = 9.394\%$$

$$\text{Mass percent of O} = \frac{16.00 \ g \ O}{150.2 \ g \ C_{10}H_{14}O} \times 100\% = 10.65\%$$

Reality Check: Sum the individual mass percent values—they should total to 100% within round-off errors. In this case, the percentages add up to 100.00%.

See Exercises 3.59 and 3.60.

   Calculating Mass Percent II

Although Fleming is commonly given credit for the discovery of penicillin, there is good evidence that penicillium mold extracts were used in the nineteenth century by Lord Joseph Lister to cure infections.

Penicillin, the first of a now large number of antibiotics (antibacterial agents), was discovered accidentally by the Scottish bacteriologist Alexander Fleming in 1928, but he was never able to isolate it as a pure compound. This and similar antibiotics have saved millions of lives that might have been lost to infections. Penicillin F has the formula $C_{14}H_{20}N_2SO_4$. Compute the mass percent of each element.

Solution

The molar mass of penicillin F is computed as follows:

$$C: \quad 14 \ \cancel{mol} \times 12.01 \frac{g}{\cancel{mol}} = 168.1 \ g$$

$$H: \quad 20 \ \cancel{mol} \times 1.008 \frac{g}{\cancel{mol}} = 120.16 \ g$$

$$N: \quad 2 \ \cancel{mol} \times 14.01 \frac{g}{\cancel{mol}} = 28.02 \ g$$

$$S: \quad 1 \ \cancel{mol} \times 32.07 \frac{g}{\cancel{mol}} = 32.07 \ g$$

$$O: \quad 4 \ \cancel{mol} \times 16.00 \frac{g}{\cancel{mol}} = \underline{64.00 \ g}$$

$$\text{Mass of 1 mol } C_{14}H_{20}N_2SO_4 = 312.4 \ g$$

$$\text{Mass percent of C} = \frac{168.1 \ g \ C}{312.4 \ g \ C_{14}H_{20}N_2SO_4} \times 100\% = 53.81\%$$

$$\text{Mass percent of H} = \frac{20.16 \ g \ H}{312.4 \ g \ C_{14}H_{20}N_2SO_4} \times 100\% = 6.453\%$$

$$\text{Mass percent of N} = \frac{28.02 \ g \ N}{312.4 \ g \ C_{14}H_{20}N_2SO_4} \times 100\% = 8.969\%$$

$$\text{Mass percent of S} = \frac{32.07 \ g \ S}{312.4 \ g \ C_{14}H_{20}N_2SO_4} \times 100\% = 10.27\%$$

Penicillin is isolated from a mold that can be grown in large quantities in fermentation tanks.

$$\text{Mass percent of O} = \frac{64.00 \text{ g O}}{312.4 \text{ g C}_{14}\text{H}_{20}\text{N}_2\text{SO}_4} \times 100\% = 20.49\%$$

Reality Check: The percentages add up to 99.99%.

See Exercises 3.61 and 3.62.

3.6 Determining the Formula of a Compound

When a new compound is prepared, one of the first items of interest is the formula of the compound. This is most often determined by taking a weighed sample of the compound and either decomposing it into its component elements or reacting it with oxygen to produce substances such as CO_2, H_2O, and N_2, which are then collected and weighed. A device for doing this type of analysis is shown in Fig. 3.5. The results of such analyses provide the mass of each type of element in the compound, which can be used to determine the mass percent of each element.

We will see how information of this type can be used to compute the formula of a compound. Suppose a substance has been prepared that is composed of carbon, hydrogen, and nitrogen. When 0.1156 gram of this compound is reacted with oxygen, 0.1638 gram of carbon dioxide (CO_2) and 0.1676 gram of water (H_2O) are collected. Assuming that all the carbon in the compound is converted to CO_2, we can determine the mass of carbon originally present in the 0.1156-gram sample. To do this, we must use the fraction (by mass) of carbon in CO_2. The molar mass of CO_2 is

$$\text{C:} \quad 1 \text{ mol} \times 12.01 \frac{\text{g}}{\text{mol}} = 12.01 \text{ g}$$

$$\text{O:} \quad 2 \text{ mol} \times 16.00 \frac{\text{g}}{\text{mol}} = \underline{32.00 \text{ g}}$$

$$\text{Molar mass of CO}_2 = 44.01 \text{ g/mol}$$

CO_2

The fraction of carbon present by mass is

$$\frac{\text{Mass of C}}{\text{Total mass of CO}_2} = \frac{12.01 \text{ g C}}{44.01 \text{ g CO}_2}$$

This factor can now be used to determine the mass of carbon in 0.1638 gram of CO_2:

$$0.1638 \text{ g CO}_2 \times \frac{12.01 \text{ g C}}{44.01 \text{ g CO}_2} = 0.04470 \text{ g C}$$

H_2O

Remember that this carbon originally came from the 0.1156-gram sample of unknown compound. Thus the mass percent of carbon in this compound is

$$\frac{0.04470 \text{ g C}}{0.1156 \text{ g compound}} \times 100\% = 38.67\% \text{ C}$$

FIGURE 3.5
A schematic diagram of the combustion device used to analyze substances for carbon and hydrogen. The sample is burned in the presence of excess oxygen, which converts all its carbon to carbon dioxide and all its hydrogen to water. These products are collected by absorption using appropriate materials, and their amounts are determined by measuring the increase in masses of the absorbents.

The same procedure can be used to find the mass percent of hydrogen in the unknown compound. We assume that all the hydrogen present in the original 0.1156 gram of compound was converted to H_2O. The molar mass of H_2O is 18.02 grams, and the fraction of hydrogen by mass in H_2O is

$$\frac{\text{Mass of H}}{\text{Mass of H}_2\text{O}} = \frac{2.016 \text{ g H}}{18.02 \text{ g H}_2\text{O}}$$

Therefore, the mass of hydrogen in 0.1676 gram of H_2O is

$$0.1676 \text{ g H}_2\text{O} \times \frac{2.016 \text{ g H}}{18.02 \text{ g H}_2\text{O}} = 0.01875 \text{ g H}$$

The mass percent of hydrogen in the compound is

$$\frac{0.01875 \text{ g H}}{0.1156 \text{ g compound}} \times 100\% = 16.22\% \text{ H}$$

The unknown compound contains only carbon, hydrogen, and nitrogen. So far we have determined that it is 38.67% carbon and 16.22% hydrogen. The remainder must be nitrogen:

$$100.00\% - (\underset{\underset{\%\ \text{C}}{\uparrow}}{38.67\%} + \underset{\underset{\%\ \text{H}}{\uparrow}}{16.22\%}) = 45.11\% \text{ N}$$

We have determined that the compound contains 38.67% carbon, 16.22% hydrogen, and 45.11% nitrogen. Next we use these data to obtain the formula.

Since the formula of a compound indicates the *numbers* of atoms in the compound, we must convert the masses of the elements to numbers of atoms. The easiest way to do this is to work with 100.00 grams of the compound. In the present case, 38.67% carbon by mass means 38.67 grams of carbon per 100.00 grams of compound; 16.22% hydrogen means 16.22 grams of hydrogen per 100.00 grams of compound; and so on. To determine the formula, we must calculate the number of carbon atoms in 38.67 grams of carbon, the number of hydrogen atoms in 16.22 grams of hydrogen, and the number of nitrogen atoms in 45.11 grams of nitrogen. We can do this as follows:

$$38.67 \text{ g C} \times \frac{1 \text{ mol C}}{12.01 \text{ g C}} = 3.220 \text{ mol C}$$

$$16.22 \text{ g H} \times \frac{1 \text{ mol H}}{1.008 \text{ g H}} = 16.09 \text{ mol H}$$

$$45.11 \text{ g N} \times \frac{1 \text{ mol N}}{14.01 \text{ g N}} = 3.219 \text{ mol N}$$

Thus 100.00 grams of this compound contains 3.220 moles of carbon atoms, 16.09 moles of hydrogen atoms, and 3.219 moles of nitrogen atoms.

We can find the smallest *whole-number ratio* of atoms in this compound by dividing each of the mole values above by the smallest of the three:

$$\text{C:} \quad \frac{3.220}{3.220} = 1.000 = 1$$

$$\text{H:} \quad \frac{16.09}{3.220} = 4.997 = 5$$

$$\text{N:} \quad \frac{3.219}{3.220} = 1.000 = 1$$

Thus the formula might well be CH_5N. However, it also could be $C_2H_{10}N_2$ or $C_3H_{15}N_3$, and so on—that is, some multiple of the smallest whole-number ratio. Each of these alternatives also has the correct relative numbers of atoms. That is, any molecule that can

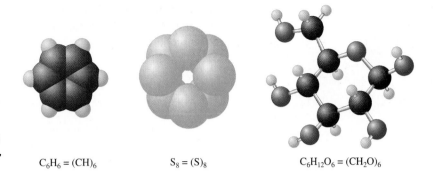

FIGURE 3.6
Examples of substances whose empirical and molecular formulas differ. Notice that molecular formula = (empirical formula)$_n$, where n is an integer.

$C_6H_6 = (CH)_6$ $S_8 = (S)_8$ $C_6H_{12}O_6 = (CH_2O)_6$

Molecular formula = (empirical formula)$_n$, where n is an integer.

be represented as $(CH_5N)_n$, where n is an integer, has the **empirical formula** CH_5N. To be able to specify the exact formula of the molecule involved, the **molecular formula,** we must know the molar mass.

Suppose we know that this compound with empirical formula CH_5N has a molar mass of 31.06 g/mol. How do we determine which of the possible choices represents the molecular formula? Since the molecular formula is always a whole number multiple of the empirical formula, we must first find the empirical formula mass for CH_5N:

$$1 \text{ C:}\quad 1 \times 12.01 \text{ g} = 12.01 \text{ g}$$
$$5 \text{ H:}\quad 5 \times 1.008 \text{ g} = 5.040 \text{ g}$$
$$1 \text{ N:}\quad 1 \times 14.01 \text{ g} = \underline{14.01 \text{ g}}$$
$$\text{Formula mass of } CH_5N = 31.06 \text{ g/mol}$$

This is the same as the known molar mass of the compound. Thus in this case the empirical formula and the molecular formula are the same; this substance consists of molecules with the formula CH_5N. It is quite common for the empirical and molecular formulas to be different; some examples where this is the case are shown in Fig. 3.6.

| Sample Exercise 3.11 | **Determining Empirical and Molecular Formulas I** |

Determine the empirical and molecular formulas for a compound that gives the following percentages upon analysis (in mass percents):

$$71.65\% \text{ Cl} \qquad 24.27\% \text{ C} \qquad 4.07\% \text{ H}$$

The molar mass is known to be 98.96 g/mol.

Solution

First, we convert the mass percents to masses in grams. In 100.00 g of this compound there are 71.65 g of chlorine, 24.27 g of carbon, and 4.07 g of hydrogen. We use these masses to compute the moles of atoms present:

$$71.65 \text{ g Cl} \times \frac{1 \text{ mol Cl}}{35.45 \text{ g Cl}} = 2.021 \text{ mol Cl}$$

$$24.27 \text{ g C} \times \frac{1 \text{ mol C}}{12.01 \text{ g C}} = 2.021 \text{ mol C}$$

$$4.07 \text{ g H} \times \frac{1 \text{ mol H}}{1.008 \text{ g H}} = 4.04 \text{ mol H}$$

Dividing each mole value by 2.021 (the smallest number of moles present), we obtain the empirical formula $ClCH_2$.

FIGURE 3.7
The two forms of dichloroethane.

To determine the molecular formula, we must compare the empirical formula mass with the molar mass. The empirical formula mass is 49.48 g/mol (confirm this). The molar mass is known to be 98.96 g/mol.

$$\frac{\text{Molar mass}}{\text{Empirical formula mass}} = \frac{98.96 \text{ g/mol}}{49.48 \text{ g/mol}} = 2$$
$$\text{Molecular formula} = (\text{ClCH}_2)_2 = \text{Cl}_2\text{C}_2\text{H}_4$$

This substance is composed of molecules with the formula $\text{Cl}_2\text{C}_2\text{H}_4$.

Notice that the method we employ here allows us to determine the molecular formula of a compound but not its structural formula. The compound $\text{Cl}_2\text{C}_2\text{H}_4$ is called *dichloroethane*. There are two forms of this compound, shown in Fig. 3.7. The form on the right was formerly used as an additive in leaded gasoline.

See Exercises 3.57 and 3.58.

Sample Exercise 3.12 | **Determining Empirical and Molecular Formulas II**

A white powder is analyzed and found to contain 43.64% phosphorus and 56.36% oxygen by mass. The compound has a molar mass of 283.88 g/mol. What are the compound's empirical and molecular formulas?

Solution

In 100.00 g of this compound there are 43.64 g of phosphorus and 56.36 g of oxygen. In terms of moles, in 100.00 g of the compound we have

$$43.64 \text{ g P} \times \frac{1 \text{ mol P}}{30.97 \text{ g P}} = 1.409 \text{ mol P}$$

$$56.36 \text{ g O} \times \frac{1 \text{ mol O}}{16.00 \text{ g O}} = 3.523 \text{ mol O}$$

Dividing both mole values by the smaller one gives

$$\frac{1.409}{1.409} = 1 \text{ P} \quad \text{and} \quad \frac{3.523}{1.409} = 2.5 \text{ O}$$

FIGURE 3.8
The structure of P_4O_{10}. Note that some of the oxygen atoms act as "bridges" between the phosphorus atoms. This compound has a great affinity for water and is often used as a desiccant, or drying agent.

This yields the formula $\text{PO}_{2.5}$. Since compounds must contain whole numbers of atoms, the empirical formula should contain only whole numbers. To obtain the simplest set of whole numbers, we multiply both numbers by 2 to give the empirical formula P_2O_5.

To obtain the molecular formula, we must compare the empirical formula mass to the molar mass. The empirical formula mass for P_2O_5 is 141.94.

$$\frac{\text{Molar mass}}{\text{Empirical formula mass}} = \frac{283.88}{141.94} = 2$$

The molecular formula is $(\text{P}_2\text{O}_5)_2$, or P_4O_{10}.
The structural formula of this interesting compound is given in Fig. 3.8.

See Exercise 3.59.

In Sample Exercises 3.11 and 3.12 we found the molecular formula by comparing the empirical formula mass with the molar mass. There is an alternate way to obtain the molecular formula. For example, in Sample Exercise 3.11 we know the molar mass of the compound is 98.96 g/mol. This means that 1 mole of the compound weighs 98.96 grams.

Since we also know the mass percentages of each element, we can compute the mass of each element present in 1 mole of compound:

Chlorine:
$$\frac{71.65 \text{ g Cl}}{100.0 \text{ g compound}} \times \frac{98.96 \text{ g}}{\text{mol}} = \frac{70.90 \text{ g Cl}}{\text{mol compound}}$$

Carbon:
$$\frac{24.27 \text{ g C}}{100.0 \text{ g compound}} \times \frac{98.96 \text{ g}}{\text{mol}} = \frac{24.02 \text{ g C}}{\text{mol compound}}$$

Hydrogen:
$$\frac{4.07 \text{ g H}}{100.0 \text{ g compound}} \times \frac{98.96 \text{ g}}{\text{mol}} = \frac{4.03 \text{ g H}}{\text{mol compound}}$$

Now we can compute moles of atoms present per mole of compound:

Chlorine:
$$\frac{70.90 \text{ g Cl}}{\text{mol compound}} \times \frac{1 \text{ mol Cl}}{35.45 \text{ g Cl}} = \frac{2.000 \text{ mol Cl}}{\text{mol compound}}$$

Carbon:
$$\frac{24.02 \text{ g C}}{\text{mol compound}} \times \frac{1 \text{ mol C}}{12.01 \text{ g C}} = \frac{2.000 \text{ mol C}}{\text{mol compound}}$$

Hydrogen:
$$\frac{4.03 \text{ g H}}{\text{mol compound}} \times \frac{1 \text{ mol H}}{1.008 \text{ g H}} = \frac{4.00 \text{ mol H}}{\text{mol compound}}$$

Thus 1 mole of the compound contains 2 mol Cl atoms, 2 mol C atoms, and 4 mol H atoms, and the molecular formula is $Cl_2C_2H_4$, as obtained in Sample Exercise 3.11.

Sample Exercise 3.13

Determining a Molecular Formula

Caffeine, a stimulant found in coffee, tea, and chocolate, contains 49.48% carbon, 5.15% hydrogen, 28.87% nitrogen, and 16.49% oxygen by mass and has a molar mass of 194.2 g/mol. Determine the molecular formula of caffeine.

Solution

We will first determine the mass of each element in 1 mole (194.2 g) of caffeine:

$$\frac{49.48 \text{ g C}}{100.0 \text{ g caffeine}} \times \frac{194.2 \text{ g}}{\text{mol}} = \frac{96.09 \text{ g C}}{\text{mol caffeine}}$$

$$\frac{5.15 \text{ g H}}{100.0 \text{ g caffeine}} \times \frac{194.2 \text{ g}}{\text{mol}} = \frac{10.0 \text{ g H}}{\text{mol caffeine}}$$

$$\frac{28.87 \text{ g N}}{100.0 \text{ g caffeine}} \times \frac{194.2 \text{ g}}{\text{mol}} = \frac{56.07 \text{ g N}}{\text{mol caffeine}}$$

$$\frac{16.49 \text{ g O}}{100.0 \text{ g caffeine}} \times \frac{194.2 \text{ g}}{\text{mol}} = \frac{32.02 \text{ g O}}{\text{mol caffeine}}$$

Computer-generated molecule of caffeine.

Now we will convert to moles:

Carbon:
$$\frac{96.09 \text{ g C}}{\text{mol caffeine}} \times \frac{1 \text{ mol C}}{12.01 \text{ g C}} = \frac{8.001 \text{ mol C}}{\text{mol caffeine}}$$

Hydrogen:
$$\frac{10.0 \text{ g H}}{\text{mol caffeine}} \times \frac{1 \text{ mol H}}{1.008 \text{ g H}} = \frac{9.92 \text{ mol H}}{\text{mol caffeine}}$$

Nitrogen:
$$\frac{56.07 \text{ g N}}{\text{mol caffeine}} \times \frac{1 \text{ mol N}}{14.01 \text{ g N}} = \frac{4.002 \text{ mol N}}{\text{mol caffeine}}$$

Oxygen:
$$\frac{32.02 \text{ g O}}{\text{mol caffeine}} \times \frac{1 \text{ mol O}}{16.00 \text{ g O}} = \frac{2.001 \text{ mol O}}{\text{mol caffeine}}$$

Rounding the numbers to integers gives the molecular formula for caffeine: $C_8H_{10}N_4O_2$.

See Exercise 3.76.

The methods for obtaining empirical and molecular formulas are summarized as follows:

Empirical Formula Determination

- Since mass percentage gives the number of grams of a particular element per 100 grams of compound, base the calculation on 100 grams of compound. Each percent will then represent the mass in grams of that element.

- Determine the number of moles of each element present in 100 grams of compound using the atomic masses of the elements present.

- Divide each value of the number of moles by the smallest of the values. If each resulting number is a whole number (after appropriate rounding), these numbers represent the subscripts of the elements in the empirical formula.

- If the numbers obtained in the previous step are not whole numbers, multiply each number by an integer so that the results are all whole numbers.

Numbers very close to whole numbers, such as 9.92 and 1.08, should be rounded to whole numbers. Numbers such as 2.25, 4.33, and 2.72 should not be rounded to whole numbers.

Molecular Formula Determination

Method One

- Obtain the empirical formula.

- Compute the mass corresponding to the empirical formula.

- Calculate the ratio

$$\frac{\text{Molar mass}}{\text{Empirical formula mass}}$$

- The integer from the previous step represents the number of empirical formula units in one molecule. When the empirical formula subscripts are multiplied by this integer, the molecular formula results. This procedure is summarized by the equation:

$$\text{Molecular formula} = (\text{empirical formula}) \times \frac{\text{molar mass}}{\text{empirical formula mass}}$$

Method Two

- Using the mass percentages and the molar mass, determine the mass of each element present in one mole of compound.

- Determine the number of moles of each element present in one mole of compound.

- The integers from the previous step represent the subscripts in the molecular formula.

Note that method two assumes that the molar mass of the compound is known accurately.

3.7 Chemical Equations

Chemical Reactions

A chemical change involves a reorganization of the atoms in one or more substances. For example, when the methane (CH_4) in natural gas combines with oxygen (O_2) in the air and burns, carbon dioxide (CO_2) and water (H_2O) are formed. This process is represented by a **chemical equation** with the **reactants** (here methane and oxygen) on the left side of an arrow and the **products** (carbon dioxide and water) on the right side:

$$CH_4 + O_2 \longrightarrow CO_2 + H_2O$$

Reactants   Products

Notice that the atoms have been reorganized. *Bonds have been broken, and new ones have been formed.* It is important to recognize that *in a chemical reaction, atoms are neither created nor destroyed. All atoms present in the reactants must be accounted for among the products.* In other words, there must be the same number of each type of atom on the product side and on the reactant side of the arrow. Making sure that this rule is obeyed is called **balancing a chemical equation** for a reaction.

The equation (shown above) for the reaction between CH_4 and O_2 is not balanced. We can see this from the following representation of the reaction:

Notice that the number of oxygen atoms (in O_2) on the left of the arrow is two, while on the right there are three O atoms (in CO_2 and H_2O). Also, there are four hydrogen atoms (in CH_4) on the left and only two (in H_2O) on the right. Remember that a chemical reaction is simply a rearrangement of the atoms (a change in the way they are organized). Atoms are not created or destroyed in a chemical reaction. Thus the reactants and products must occur in numbers that give the same number of each type of atom among both the reactants and products. Simple trial and error will allow us to figure this out for the reaction of methane with oxygen. The needed numbers of molecules are

Notice that now we have the same number of each type of atom represented among the reactants and the products.

We can represent the preceding situation in a shorthand manner by the following chemical equation:

$$CH_4 + 2O_2 \longrightarrow CO_2 + 2H_2O$$

We can check that the equation is balanced by comparing the number of each type of atom on both sides:

$$CH_4 + 2O_2 \longrightarrow CO_2 + 2H_2O$$

1 C 4 H   1 C   4 H

4 O   2 O   2 O

To summarize, we have

Reactants	Products
1 C	1 C
4 H	4 H
4 O	4 O

Methane reacts with oxygen to produce the flame in a Bunsen burner.

TABLE 3.2   Information Conveyed by the Balanced Equation for the Combustion of Methane

Reactants		Products
$CH_4(g) + 2O_2(g)$	$\longrightarrow$	$CO_2(g) + 2H_2O(g)$
1 molecule + 2 molecules	$\longrightarrow$	1 molecule + 2 molecules
1 mole + 2 moles	$\longrightarrow$	1 mole + 2 moles
6.022×10^{23} molecules + 2 $(6.022 \times 10^{23}$ molecules)	$\longrightarrow$	6.022×10^{23} molecules + 2 $(6.022 \times 10^{23}$ molecules)
16 g + 2 (32 g)		44 g + 2 (18 g)
80 g reactants	$\longrightarrow$	80 g products

The Meaning of a Chemical Equation

Visualization: Oxygen, Hydrogen, Soap Bubbles, and Balloons

The chemical equation for a reaction gives two important types of information: the nature of the reactants and products and the relative numbers of each.

The reactants and products in a specific reaction must be identified by experiment. Besides specifying the compounds involved in the reaction, the equation often gives the *physical states* of the reactants and products:

State	Symbol
Solid	(*s*)
Liquid	(*l*)
Gas	(*g*)
Dissolved in water (in aqueous solution)	(*aq*)

Hydrochloric acid reacts with solid sodium hydrogen carbonate to produce gaseous carbon dioxide.

For example, when hydrochloric acid in aqueous solution is added to solid sodium hydrogen carbonate, the products carbon dioxide gas, liquid water, and sodium chloride (which dissolves in the water) are formed:

$$HCl(aq) + NaHCO_3(s) \longrightarrow CO_2(g) + H_2O(l) + NaCl(aq)$$

The relative numbers of reactants and products in a reaction are indicated by the *coefficients* in the balanced equation. (The coefficients can be determined because we know that the same number of each type of atom must occur on both sides of the equation.) For example, the balanced equation

$$CH_4(g) + 2O_2(g) \longrightarrow CO_2(g) + 2H_2O(g)$$

can be interpreted in several equivalent ways, as shown in Table 3.2. Note that the total mass is 80 grams for both reactants and products. We expect the mass to remain constant, since chemical reactions involve only a rearrangement of atoms. Atoms, and therefore mass, are conserved in a chemical reaction.

From this discussion you can see that a balanced chemical equation gives you a great deal of information.

3.8 Balancing Chemical Equations

Visualization: Conservation of Mass and Balancing Equations

An unbalanced chemical equation is of limited use. Whenever you see an equation, you should ask yourself whether it is balanced. The principle that lies at the heart of the balancing process is that atoms are conserved in a chemical reaction. The same number of each type of atom must be found among the reactants and products. It is also important to recognize that the identities of the reactants and products of a reaction are determined by experimental observation. For example, when liquid ethanol is burned in the presence of sufficient oxygen gas, the products are always carbon dioxide and water. When the equation for this reaction is balanced, the *identities* of the reactants and products must not be changed. *The formulas of the compounds must never be changed in balancing a chemical equation.* That is, the subscripts in a formula cannot be changed, nor can atoms be added or subtracted from a formula.

Most chemical equations can be balanced by inspection, that is, by trial and error. It is always best to start with the most complicated molecules (those containing the greatest number of atoms). For example, consider the reaction of ethanol with oxygen, given by the unbalanced equation

$$C_2H_5OH(l) + O_2(g) \longrightarrow CO_2(g) + H_2O(g)$$

which can be represented by the following molecular models:

Notice that the carbon and hydrogen atoms are not balanced. There are two carbon atoms on the left and one on the right, and there are six hydrogens on the left and two on the right. We need to find the correct numbers of reactants and products so that we have the same number of all types of atoms among the reactants and products. We will balance the equation "by inspection" (a systematic trial-and-error procedure).

The most complicated molecule here is C_2H_5OH. We will begin by balancing the products that contain the atoms in C_2H_5OH. Since C_2H_5OH contains two carbon atoms, we place the coefficient 2 before the CO_2 to balance the carbon atoms:

$$C_2H_5OH(l) + O_2(g) \rightarrow 2CO_2(g) + H_2O(g)$$
2 C atoms   2 C atoms

Since C_2H_5OH contains six hydrogen atoms, the hydrogen atoms can be balanced by placing a 3 before the H_2O:

$$C_2H_5OH(l) + O_2(g) \rightarrow 2CO_2(g) + 3H_2O(g)$$
(5 + 1) H   (3 × 2) H

Last, we balance the oxygen atoms. Note that the right side of the preceding equation contains seven oxygen atoms, whereas the left side has only three. We can correct this by putting a 3 before the O_2 to produce the balanced equation:

$$C_2H_5OH(l) + 3O_2(g) \rightarrow 2CO_2(g) + 3H_2O(g)$$
1 O   6 O   (2 × 2) O   3 O
      7 O   7 O

Now we check:

$$C_2H_5OH(l) + 3O_2(g) \rightarrow 2CO_2(g) + 3H_2O(g)$$
2 C atoms   2 C atoms
6 H atoms   6 H atoms
7 O atoms   7 O atoms

The equation is balanced.

The balanced equation can be represented as follows:

In balancing equations, start with the most complicated molecule.

You can see that all the elements balance.

Writing and Balancing the Equation for a Chemical Reaction

➡ 1 **Determine what reaction is occurring. What are the reactants, the products, and the physical states involved?**

➡ 2 **Write the *unbalanced* equation that summarizes the reaction described in step 1.**

➡ 3 **Balance the equation by inspection, starting with the most complicated molecule(s). Determine what coefficients are necessary so that the same number of each type of atom appears on both reactant and product sides. Do not change the identities (formulas) of any of the reactants or products.**

| *Sample Exercise 3.14* | **Balancing a Chemical Equation I** |

Chromium compounds exhibit a variety of bright colors. When solid ammonium dichromate, $(NH_4)_2Cr_2O_7$, a vivid orange compound, is ignited, a spectacular reaction occurs, as shown in the two photographs on the next page. Although the reaction is actually somewhat more complex, let's assume here that the products are solid chromium(III) oxide, nitrogen gas (consisting of N_2 molecules), and water vapor. Balance the equation for this reaction.

Chromate and dichromate compounds are carcinogens (cancer-inducing agents) and should be handled very carefully.

Solution

➡ 1 From the description given, the reactant is solid ammonium dichromate, $(NH_4)_2Cr_2O_7(s)$, and the products are nitrogen gas, $N_2(g)$, water vapor, $H_2O(g)$, and solid chromium(III) oxide, $Cr_2O_3(s)$. The formula for chromium(III) oxide can be determined by recognizing that the Roman numeral III means that Cr^{3+} ions are present. For a neutral compound, the formula must then be Cr_2O_3, since each oxide ion is O^{2-}.

➡ 2 The unbalanced equation is

$$(NH_4)_2Cr_2O_7(s) \rightarrow Cr_2O_3(s) + N_2(g) + H_2O(g)$$

➡ 3 Note that nitrogen and chromium are balanced (two nitrogen atoms and two chromium atoms on each side), but hydrogen and oxygen are not. A coefficient of 4 for H_2O balances the hydrogen atoms:

$$\underset{(4 \times 2)\,H}{(NH_4)_2Cr_2O_7(s)} \rightarrow Cr_2O_3(s) + N_2(g) + \underset{(4 \times 2)\,H}{4H_2O(g)}$$

Note that in balancing the hydrogen we also have balanced the oxygen, since there are seven oxygen atoms in the reactants and in the products.

Reality Check:

$$2\,N,\ 8\,H,\ 2\,Cr,\ 7\,O \rightarrow 2\,N,\ 8\,H,\ 2\,Cr,\ 7\,O$$

Reactant atoms | Product atoms

The equation is balanced.

See Exercises 3.81 and 3.82.

Decomposition of ammonium dichromate.

| Sample Exercise 3.15 | **Balancing a Chemical Equation II** |

The Ostwald process is described in Section 20.2.

At 1000°C, ammonia gas, NH₃(g), reacts with oxygen gas to form gaseous nitric oxide, NO(g), and water vapor. This reaction is the first step in the commercial production of nitric acid by the Ostwald process. Balance the equation for this reaction.

Solution

The unbalanced equation for the reaction is

$$NH_3(g) + O_2(g) \rightarrow NO(g) + H_2O(g)$$

Because all the molecules in this equation are of about equal complexity, where we start in balancing it is rather arbitrary. Let's begin by balancing the hydrogen. A coefficient of 2 for NH₃ and a coefficient of 3 for H₂O give six atoms of hydrogen on both sides:

$$2NH_3(g) + O_2(g) \rightarrow NO(g) + 3H_2O(g)$$

The nitrogen can be balanced with a coefficient of 2 for NO:

$$2NH_3(g) + O_2(g) \rightarrow 2NO(g) + 3H_2O(g)$$

Finally, note that there are two atoms of oxygen on the left and five on the right. The oxygen can be balanced with a coefficient of $\frac{5}{2}$ for O₂:

$$2NH_3(g) + \frac{5}{2}O_2(g) \rightarrow 2NO(g) + 3H_2O(g)$$

However, the usual custom is to have whole-number coefficients. We simply multiply the entire equation by 2.

$$4NH_3(g) + 5O_2(g) \rightarrow 4NO(g) + 6H_2O(g)$$

Reality Check: There are 4 N, 12 H, and 10 O on both sides, so the equation is balanced.

We can represent this balanced equation visually as

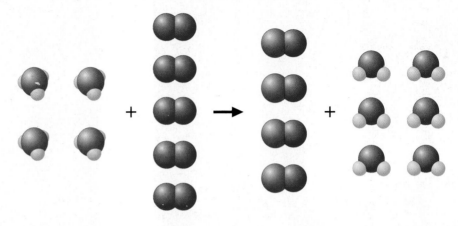

See Exercises 3.83 through 3.88.

3.9 Stoichiometric Calculations: Amounts of Reactants and Products

As we have seen in previous sections of this chapter, the coefficients in chemical equations represent *numbers* of molecules, not masses of molecules. However, when a reaction is to be run in a laboratory or chemical plant, the amounts of substances needed cannot be determined by counting molecules directly. Counting is always done by weighing. In this section we will see how chemical equations can be used to determine the *masses* of reacting chemicals.

To develop the principles for dealing with the stoichiometry of reactions, we will consider the reaction of propane with oxygen to produce carbon dioxide and water. We will consider the question: *"What mass of oxygen will react with 96.1 grams of propane?"* In doing stoichiometry, the first thing we must do is *write the balanced chemical equation* for the reaction. In this case the balanced equation is

> Before doing any calculations involving a chemical reaction, be sure the equation for the reaction is balanced.

$$C_3H_8(g) + 5O_2(g) \longrightarrow 3CO_2(g) + 4H_2O(g)$$

which can be visualized as

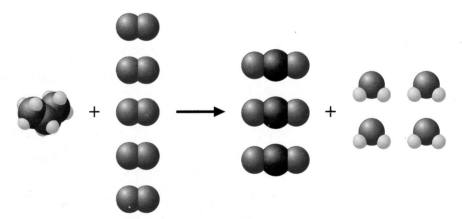

This equation means that 1 mole of C_3H_8 reacts with 5 moles of O_2 to produce 3 moles of CO_2 and 4 moles of H_2O. To use this equation to find the masses of reactants and products, we must be able to convert between masses and moles of substances. Thus we must first ask: *"How many moles of propane are present in 96.1 grams of propane?"* The molar

CHEMICAL IMPACT

High Mountains—Low Octane

The next time that you visit a gas station, take a moment to note the octane rating that accompanies the grade of gasoline that you are purchasing. The gasoline is priced according to its octane rating—a measure of the fuel's antiknock properties. In a conventional internal combustion engine, gasoline vapors and air are drawn into the combustion cylinder on the downward stroke of the piston. This air–fuel mixture is compressed on the upward piston stroke (compression stroke), and a spark from the sparkplug ignites the mix. The rhythmic combustion of the air–fuel mix occurring sequentially in several cylinders furnishes the power to propel the vehicle down the road. Excessive heat and pressure (or poor-quality fuel) within the cylinder may cause the premature combustion of the mixture—commonly known as engine "knock" or "ping." Over time, this engine knock can damage the engine, resulting in inefficient performance and costly repairs.

A consumer typically is faced with three choices of gasoline, with octane ratings of 87 (regular), 89 (midgrade), and 93 (premium). But if you happen to travel or live in the higher elevations of the Rocky Mountain states, you might be surprised to find different octane ratings at the gasoline pumps. The reason for this provides a lesson in stoichiometry. At higher elevations the air is less dense—the volume of oxygen per unit volume of air is smaller. Most engines are designed to achieve a 14:1 oxygen-to-fuel ratio in the cylinder prior to combustion. If less oxygen is available, then less fuel is required to achieve this optimal ratio. In turn, the lower volumes of oxygen and fuel result in a lower pressure in the cylinder. Because high pressure tends to promote knocking, the lower pressure within engine cylinders at higher elevations promotes a more controlled combustion of the air–fuel mixture, and therefore, octane requirements are lower. While consumers in the Rocky Mountain states can purchase three grades of gasoline, the octane ratings of these fuel blends are different from those in the rest of the United States. In Denver, Colorado, regular gasoline is 85 octane, midgrade is 87 octane, and premium is 91 octane—2 points lower than gasoline sold in most of the rest of the country.

mass of propane to three significant figures is 44.1 (that is, $3 \times 12.01 + 8 \times 1.008$). The moles of propane can be calculated as follows:

$$96.1 \ \text{g } C_3H_8 \times \frac{1 \ \text{mol } C_3H_8}{44.1 \ \text{g } C_3H_8} = 2.18 \ \text{mol } C_3H_8$$

Next we must take into account the fact that each mole of propane reacts with 5 moles of oxygen. The best way to do this is to use the balanced equation to construct a **mole ratio.** In this case we want to convert from moles of propane to moles of oxygen. From the balanced equation we see that 5 moles of O_2 is required for each mole of C_3H_8, so the appropriate ratio is

$$\frac{5 \ \text{mol } O_2}{1 \ \text{mol } C_3H_8}$$

Multiplying the number of moles of C_3H_8 by this factor gives the number of moles of O_2 required:

$$2.18 \ \text{mol } C_3H_8 \times \frac{5 \ \text{mol } O_2}{1 \ \text{mol } C_3H_8} = 10.9 \ \text{mol } O_2$$

Notice that the mole ratio is set up so that the moles of C_3H_8 cancel out, and the units that result are moles of O_2.

Since the original question asked for the mass of oxygen needed to react with 96.1 grams of propane, the 10.9 moles of O_2 must be converted to *grams*. Since the molar mass of O_2 is 32.0 g/mol,

$$10.9 \ \text{mol } O_2 \times \frac{32.0 \ \text{g } O_2}{1 \ \text{mol } O_2} = 349 \ \text{g } O_2$$

Therefore, 349 grams of oxygen is required to burn 96.1 grams of propane.

This example can be extended by asking: *"What mass of carbon dioxide is produced when 96.1 grams of propane is combusted with oxygen?"* In this case we must convert between moles of propane and moles of carbon dioxide. This can be accomplished by looking at the balanced equation, which shows that 3 moles of CO_2 is produced for each mole of C_3H_8 reacted. The mole ratio needed to convert from moles of propane to moles of carbon dioxide is

$$\frac{3 \text{ mol } CO_2}{1 \text{ mol } C_3H_8}$$

The conversion is

$$2.18 \text{ mol } C_3H_8 \times \frac{3 \text{ mol } CO_2}{1 \text{ mol } C_3H_8} = 6.54 \text{ mol } CO_2$$

Then, using the molar mass of CO_2 (44.0 g/mol), we calculate the mass of CO_2 produced:

$$6.54 \text{ mol } CO_2 \times \frac{44.0 \text{ g } CO_2}{1 \text{ mol } CO_2} = 288 \text{ g } CO_2$$

We will now summarize the sequence of steps needed to carry out stoichiometric calculations.

$$96.1 \text{ g } C_3H_8 \quad \boxed{\frac{1 \text{ mol } C_3H_8}{44.1 \text{ g } C_3H_8}} \quad 2.18 \text{ mol } C_3H_8 \quad \boxed{\frac{3 \text{ mol } CO_2}{1 \text{ mol } C_3H_8}} \quad 6.54 \text{ mol } CO_2$$

$$\boxed{\frac{44.0 \text{ g } CO_2}{1 \text{ mol } CO_2}} \quad 288 \text{ g } CO_2$$

Calculating Masses of Reactants and Products in Chemical Reactions

➡ 1 **Balance the equation for the reaction.**

➡ 2 **Convert the known mass of the reactant or product to moles of that substance.**

➡ 3 **Use the balanced equation to set up the appropriate mole ratios.**

➡ 4 **Use the appropriate mole ratios to calculate the number of moles of the desired reactant or product.**

➡ 5 **Convert from moles back to grams if required by the problem.**

These steps are summarized by the following diagram:

Sample Exercise 3.16	# Chemical Stoichiometry I

Solid lithium hydroxide is used in space vehicles to remove exhaled carbon dioxide from the living environment by forming solid lithium carbonate and liquid water. What mass of gaseous carbon dioxide can be absorbed by 1.00 kg of lithium hydroxide?

Solution

➥ **1**   Using the description of the reaction, we can write the unbalanced equation:

$$LiOH(s) + CO_2(g) \longrightarrow Li_2CO_3(s) + H_2O(l)$$

The balanced equation is

$$2LiOH(s) + CO_2(g) \longrightarrow Li_2CO_3(s) + H_2O(l)$$

➥ **2**   We convert the given mass of LiOH to moles, using the molar mass of LiOH (6.941 + 16.00 + 1.008 = 23.95 g/mol):

$$1.00 \text{ kg LiOH} \times \frac{1000 \text{ g LiOH}}{1 \text{ kg LiOH}} \times \frac{1 \text{ mol LiOH}}{23.95 \text{ g LiOH}} = 41.8 \text{ mol LiOH}$$

➥ **3**   Since we want to determine the amount of CO_2 that reacts with the given amount of LiOH, the appropriate mole ratio is

$$\frac{1 \text{ mol CO}_2}{2 \text{ mol LiOH}}$$

➥ **4**   We calculate the moles of CO_2 needed to react with the given mass of LiOH using this mole ratio:

$$41.8 \text{ mol LiOH} \times \frac{1 \text{ mol CO}_2}{2 \text{ mol LiOH}} = 20.9 \text{ mol CO}_2$$

➥ **5**   Next we calculate the mass of CO_2, using its molar mass (44.0 g/mol):

$$20.9 \text{ mol CO}_2 \times \frac{44.0 \text{ g CO}_2}{1 \text{ mol CO}_2} = 9.20 \times 10^2 \text{ g CO}_2$$

Thus 920. g of $CO_2(g)$ will be absorbed by 1.00 kg of LiOH(s).

See Exercises 3.89 and 3.90.

Astronaut Sidney M. Gutierrez changes the lithium hydroxide cannisters on space shuttle Columbia. The lithium hydroxide is used to purge carbon dioxide from the air in the shuttle's cabin.

Sample Exercise 3.17	# Chemical Stoichiometry II

Baking soda ($NaHCO_3$) is often used as an antacid. It neutralizes excess hydrochloric acid secreted by the stomach:

$$NaHCO_3(s) + HCl(aq) \longrightarrow NaCl(aq) + H_2O(l) + CO_2(aq)$$

Milk of magnesia, which is an aqueous suspension of magnesium hydroxide, is also used as an antacid:

$$Mg(OH)_2(s) + 2HCl(aq) \longrightarrow 2H_2O(l) + MgCl_2(aq)$$

Which is the more effective antacid per gram, $NaHCO_3$ or $Mg(OH)_2$?

Solution

To answer the question, we must determine the amount of HCl neutralized per gram of $NaHCO_3$ and per gram of $Mg(OH)_2$. Using the molar mass of $NaHCO_3$ (84.01 g/mol), we can determine the moles of $NaHCO_3$ in 1.00 g of $NaHCO_3$:

$$1.00 \text{ g NaHCO}_3 \times \frac{1 \text{ mol NaHCO}_3}{84.01 \text{ g NaHCO}_3} = 1.19 \times 10^{-2} \text{ mol NaHCO}_3$$

Milk of magnesia contains a suspension of $Mg(OH)_2(s)$.

Next we determine the moles of HCl using the mole ratio 1 mol HCl/1 mol $NaHCO_3$:

$$1.19 \times 10^{-2} \text{ mol NaHCO}_3 \times \frac{1 \text{ mol HCl}}{1 \text{ mol NaHCO}_3} = 1.19 \times 10^{-2} \text{ mol HCl}$$

Thus 1.00 g of $NaHCO_3$ will neutralize 1.19×10^{-2} mol HCl.

Using the molar mass of $Mg(OH)_2$ (58.32 g/mol), we determine the moles of $Mg(OH)_2$ in 1.00 g:

$$1.00 \text{ g Mg(OH)}_2 \times \frac{1 \text{ mol Mg(OH)}_2}{58.32 \text{ g Mg(OH)}_2} = 1.71 \times 10^{-2} \text{ mol Mg(OH)}_2$$

To determine the moles of HCl that will react with this amount of $Mg(OH)_2$, we use the mole ratio 2 mol HCl/1 mol $Mg(OH)_2$:

$$1.71 \times 10^{-2} \text{ mol Mg(OH)}_2 \times \frac{2 \text{ mol HCl}}{1 \text{ mol Mg(OH)}_2} = 3.42 \times 10^{-2} \text{ mol HCl}$$

Thus 1.00 g of $Mg(OH)_2$ will neutralize 3.42×10^{-2} mol HCl. It is a better antacid per gram than $NaHCO_3$.

See Exercises 3.91 and 3.92.

3.10 Calculations Involving a Limiting Reactant

The details of the Haber process are discussed in Section 19.2.

Visualization: Limiting Reactant

When chemicals are mixed together to undergo a reaction, they are often mixed in **stoichiometric quantities,** that is, in exactly the correct amounts so that all reactants "run out" (are used up) at the same time. To clarify this concept, let's consider the production of hydrogen for use in the manufacture of ammonia by the **Haber process.** Ammonia, a very important fertilizer itself and a starting material for other fertilizers, is made by combining nitrogen (from the air) with hydrogen according to the equation

$$N_2(g) + 3H_2(g) \longrightarrow 2NH_3(g)$$

Hydrogen can be obtained from the reaction of methane with water vapor:

$$CH_4(g) + H_2O(g) \longrightarrow 3H_2(g) + CO(g)$$

We can illustrate what we mean by stoichiometric quantities by first visualizing the balanced equation as follows:

Since this reaction involves one molecule of methane reacting with one molecule of water, to have stoichiometric amounts of methane and water we must have equal numbers of them, as shown in Fig. 3.9, where several stoichiometric mixtures are shown.

Suppose we want to calculate the mass of water required to react *exactly* with 2.50×10^3 kilograms of methane. That is, how much water will just consume all the 2.50×10^3 kilograms of methane, leaving no methane or water remaining?

To do this calculation, we need to recognize that we need equal numbers of methane and water molecules. Therefore, we first need to find the number of moles of methane molecules in 2.50×10^3 kg (2.50×10^6 g) of methane:

$$2.50 \times 10^6 \text{ g CH}_4 \times \frac{1 \text{ mol CH}_4}{16.04 \text{ g CH}_4} = 1.56 \times 10^5 \text{ mol CH}_4 \text{ molecules}$$

$$\uparrow$$
molar mass of CH_4

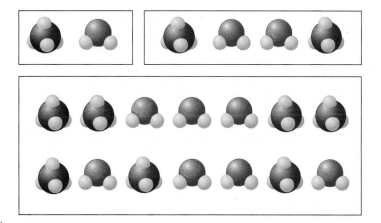

FIGURE 3.9
Three different stoichiometric mixtures of methane and water, which react one-to-one.

This same number of water molecules has a mass determined as follows:

$$1.56 \times 10^5 \text{ mol } H_2O \times \frac{18.02 \text{ g}}{\text{mol } H_2O} = 2.81 \times 10^6 \text{ g } H_2O = 2.81 \times 10^3 \text{ kg } H_2O$$

Thus, if 2.50×10^3 kilograms of methane is mixed with 2.81×10^3 kilograms of water, both reactants will "run out" at the same time. The reactants have been mixed in stoichiometric quantities.

If, on the other hand, 2.50×10^3 kilograms of methane is mixed with 3.00×10^3 kilograms of water, the methane will be consumed before the water runs out. The water will be in *excess*; that is, there will be more water molecules than methane molecules in the reaction mixture. What is the implication of this with respect to the number of product molecules that can form?

To answer this question, consider the situation on a smaller scale. Assume we mix 10 CH_4 molecules and 17 H_2O molecules and let them react. How many H_2 and CO molecules can form?

First picture the mixture of CH_4 and H_2O molecules as shown in Fig. 3.10.

Then imagine that groups consisting of one CH_4 molecule and one H_2O molecule (Fig. 3.10) will react to form three H_2 and one CO molecules (Fig. 3.11).

Notice that products can form only when both CH_4 and H_2O are available to react. Once the 10 CH_4 molecules are used up by reacting with 10 H_2O molecules, the remaining water

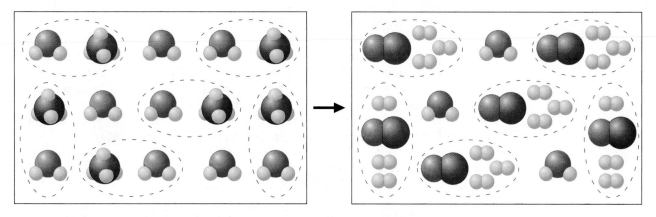

FIGURE 3.10
A mixture of CH_4 and H_2O molecules.

FIGURE 3.11
Methane and water have reacted to form products according to the equation $CH_4 + H_2O \longrightarrow 3H_2 + CO$.

molecules cannot react. They are in excess. Thus the number of products that can form is *limited* by the methane. Once the methane is consumed, no more products can be formed, even though some water still remains. In this situation the amount of methane *limits* the amount of products that can be formed. This brings us to the concept of the **limiting reactant** (or **limiting reagent**), which is the reactant that is consumed first and that therefore limits the amounts of products that can be formed. In any stoichiometry calculation involving a chemical reaction, it is essential to determine which reactant is limiting so as to calculate correctly the amounts of products that will be formed.

To further explore the idea of a limiting reactant, consider the ammonia synthesis reaction:

$$N_2(g) + 3H_2(g) \longrightarrow 2NH_3(g)$$

Assume that 5 N_2 molecules and 9 H_2 molecules are placed in a flask. Is this a stoichiometric mixture of reactants, or will one of them be consumed before the other runs out? From the balanced equation we know that each N_2 molecule requires 3 H_2 molecules for the reaction to occur:

Thus the required H_2/N_2 ratio is $3H_2/1N_2$. In our experiment we have 9 H_2 and 5 N_2, or a ratio of $9H_2/5N_2 = 1.8H_2/1N_2$.

Since the actual ratio (1.8:1) of H_2/N_2 is less than the ratio required by the balanced equation (3:1), there is not enough hydrogen to react with all the nitrogen. That is, the hydrogen will run out first, leaving some unreacted N_2 molecules. We can visualize this as shown in Fig. 3.12.

Figure 3.12 shows that 3 of the N_2 molecules react with the 9 H_2 molecules to produce 6 NH_3 molecules:

$$3N_2 + 9H_2 \longrightarrow 6NH_3$$

This leaves 2 N_2 molecules unreacted—the nitrogen is in excess.

What we have shown here is that in this experiment the hydrogen is the limiting reactant. The amount of H_2 initially present determines the amount of NH_3 that can form. The reaction was not able to use up all the N_2 molecules because the H_2 molecules were all consumed by the first 3 N_2 molecules to react.

Ammonia is dissolved in irrigation water to provide fertilizer for a field of corn.

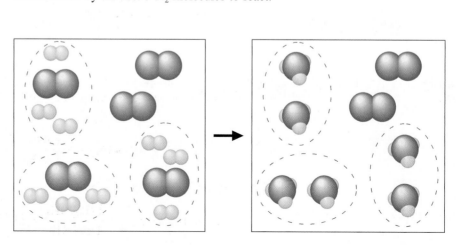

FIGURE 3.12
Hydrogen and nitrogen react to form ammonia according to the equation
$N_2 + 3H_2 \longrightarrow 2NH_3$.

Another way to look at this is to determine how much H_2 would be required by 5 N_2 molecules. Multiplying the balanced equation

$$N_2(g) + 3H_2(g) \longrightarrow 2NH_3(g)$$

by 5 gives

$$5N_2(g) + 15H_2(g) \longrightarrow 10NH_3(g)$$

Thus 5 N_2 molecules would require 15 H_2 molecules and we have only 9. This tells us the same thing we learned earlier—the hydrogen is limiting.

The most important point here is this: *The limiting reactant limits the amount of product that can form.* The reaction that actually occurred was

$$3N_2(g) + 9H_2(g) \longrightarrow 6NH_3(g)$$

not

$$5N_2(g) + 15H_2(g) \longrightarrow 10NH_3(g)$$

Thus 6 NH_3 were formed, not 10 NH_3, because the H_2, not the N_2, was limiting.

In the laboratory or chemical plant we work with much larger quantities than the few molecules of the preceding example. Therefore, we must learn to deal with limiting reactants using moles. The ideas are exactly the same, except that we are using moles of molecules instead of individual molecules. For example, suppose 25.0 kilograms of nitrogen and 5.00 kilograms of hydrogen are mixed and reacted to form ammonia. How do we calculate the mass of ammonia produced when this reaction is run to completion (until one of the reactants is completely consumed)?

As in the preceding example, we must use the balanced equation

$$N_2(g) + 3H_2(g) \longrightarrow 2NH_3(g)$$

to determine whether nitrogen or hydrogen is the limiting reactant and then to determine the amount of ammonia that is formed. We first calculate the moles of reactants present:

$$25.0 \text{ kg } N_2 \times \frac{1000 \text{ g } N_2}{1 \text{ kg } N_2} \times \frac{1 \text{ mol } N_2}{28.0 \text{ g } N_2} = 8.93 \times 10^2 \text{ mol } N_2$$

$$5.00 \text{ kg } H_2 \times \frac{1000 \text{ g } H_2}{1 \text{ kg } H_2} \times \frac{1 \text{ mol } H_2}{2.016 \text{ g } H_2} = 2.48 \times 10^3 \text{ mol } H_2$$

Since 1 mol N_2 reacts with 3 mol H_2, the number of moles of H_2 that will react exactly with 8.93×10^2 mol N_2 is

$$8.93 \times 10^2 \text{ mol } N_2 \times \frac{3 \text{ mol } H_2}{1 \text{ mol } N_2} = 2.68 \times 10^3 \text{ mol } H_2$$

Thus 8.93×10^2 mol N_2 requires 2.68×10^3 mol H_2 to react completely. However, in this case, only 2.48×10^3 mol H_2 is present. This means that the hydrogen will be consumed before the nitrogen. Thus hydrogen is the *limiting reactant* in this particular situation, and we must use the amount of hydrogen to compute the quantity of ammonia formed:

Always determine which reactant is limiting.

$$2.48 \times 10^3 \text{ mol } H_2 \times \frac{2 \text{ mol } NH_3}{3 \text{ mol } H_2} = 1.65 \times 10^3 \text{ mol } NH_3$$

Converting moles to kilograms gives

$$1.65 \times 10^3 \text{ mol } NH_3 \times \frac{17.0 \text{ g } NH_3}{1 \text{ mol } NH_3} = 2.80 \times 10^4 \text{ g } NH_3 = 28.0 \text{ kg } NH_3$$

Note that to determine the limiting reactant, we could have started instead with the given amount of hydrogen and calculated the moles of nitrogen required:

$$2.48 \times 10^3 \; \text{mol H}_2 \times \frac{1 \; \text{mol N}_2}{3 \; \text{mol H}_2} = 8.27 \times 10^2 \; \text{mol N}_2$$

Thus 2.48×10^3 mol H_2 requires 8.27×10^2 mol N_2. Since 8.93×10^2 mol N_2 is actually present, the nitrogen is in excess. The hydrogen will run out first, and thus again we find that hydrogen limits the amount of ammonia formed.

A related but simpler way to determine which reactant is limiting is to compare the mole ratio of the substances required by the balanced equation with the mole ratio of reactants actually present. For example, in this case the mole ratio of H_2 to N_2 required by the balanced equation is

$$\frac{3 \; \text{mol H}_2}{1 \; \text{mol N}_2}$$

That is,

$$\frac{\text{mol H}_2}{\text{mol N}_2} \; (\text{required}) = \frac{3}{1} = 3$$

In this experiment we have 2.48×10^3 mol H_2 and 8.93×10^2 mol N_2. Thus the ratio

$$\frac{\text{mol H}_2}{\text{mol N}_2} \; (\text{actual}) = \frac{2.48 \times 10^3}{8.93 \times 10^2} = 2.78$$

Since 2.78 is less than 3, the actual mole ratio of H_2 to N_2 is too small, and H_2 must be limiting. If the actual H_2 to N_2 mole ratio had been greater than 3, then the H_2 would have been in excess and the N_2 would be limiting.

Sample Exercise 3.18

Stoichiometry: Limiting Reactant

Nitrogen gas can be prepared by passing gaseous ammonia over solid copper(II) oxide at high temperatures. The other products of the reaction are solid copper and water vapor. If a sample containing 18.1 g of NH_3 is reacted with 90.4 g of CuO, which is the limiting reactant? How many grams of N_2 will be formed?

Solution

From the description of the problem, we can obtain the following balanced equation:

$$2NH_3(g) + 3CuO(s) \longrightarrow N_2(g) + 3Cu(s) + 3H_2O(g)$$

Next we must compute the moles of NH_3 (molar mass = 17.03 g/mol) and of CuO (molar mass = 79.55 g/mol):

$$18.1 \; \text{g NH}_3 \times \frac{1 \; \text{mol NH}_3}{17.03 \; \text{g NH}_3} = 1.06 \; \text{mol NH}_3$$

$$90.4 \; \text{g CuO} \times \frac{1 \; \text{mol CuO}}{79.55 \; \text{g CuO}} = 1.14 \; \text{mol CuO}$$

To determine the limiting reactant, we use the mole ratio for CuO and NH_3:

$$1.06 \; \text{mol NH}_3 \times \frac{3 \; \text{mol CuO}}{2 \; \text{mol NH}_3} = 1.59 \; \text{mol CuO}$$

Thus 1.59 mol CuO is required to react with 1.06 mol NH_3. Since only 1.14 mol CuO is actually present, the amount of CuO is limiting; CuO will run out before NH_3 does. We can verify this conclusion by comparing the mole ratio of CuO and NH_3 required by the balanced equation

$$\frac{\text{mol CuO}}{\text{mol NH}_3}(\text{required}) = \frac{3}{2} = 1.5$$

with the mole ratio actually present

$$\frac{\text{mol CuO}}{\text{mol NH}_3}(\text{actual}) = \frac{1.14}{1.06} = 1.08$$

Since the actual ratio is too small (smaller than 1.5), CuO is the limiting reactant.

Because CuO is the limiting reactant, we must use the amount of CuO to calculate the amount of N_2 formed. From the balanced equation, the mole ratio between CuO and N_2 is

$$\frac{1 \text{ mol N}_2}{3 \text{ mol CuO}}$$

$$1.14 \text{ mol CuO} \times \frac{1 \text{ mol N}_2}{3 \text{ mol CuO}} = 0.380 \text{ mol N}_2$$

Using the molar mass of N_2 (28.0 g/mol), we can calculate the mass of N_2 produced:

$$0.380 \text{ mol N}_2 \times \frac{28.0 \text{ g N}_2}{1 \text{ mol N}_2} = 10.6 \text{ g N}_2$$

See Exercises 3.99 through 3.101.

The amount of a product formed when the limiting reactant is completely consumed is called the **theoretical yield** of that product. In Sample Exercise 3.18, 10.6 grams of nitrogen represents the theoretical yield. This is the *maximum amount* of nitrogen that can be produced from the quantities of reactants used. Actually, the amount of product predicted by the theoretical yield is seldom obtained because of side reactions (other reactions that involve one or more of the reactants or products) and other complications. The *actual yield* of product is often given as a percentage of the theoretical yield. This is called the **percent yield:**

Percent yield is important as an indicator of the efficiency of a particular laboratory or industrial reaction.

$$\frac{\text{Actual yield}}{\text{Theoretical yield}} \times 100\% = \text{percent yield}$$

For example, if the reaction considered in Sample Exercise 3.18 actually gave 6.63 grams of nitrogen instead of the predicted 10.6 grams, the percent yield of nitrogen would be

$$\frac{6.63 \text{ g N}_2}{10.6 \text{ g N}_2} \times 100\% = 62.5\%$$

Methanol

| Sample Exercise 3.19 | Calculating Percent Yield |

Methanol (CH_3OH), also called *methyl alcohol,* is the simplest alcohol. It is used as a fuel in race cars and is a potential replacement for gasoline. Methanol can be manufactured by combination of gaseous carbon monoxide and hydrogen. Suppose 68.5 kg CO(g) is reacted with 8.60 kg H_2(g). Calculate the theoretical yield of methanol. If 3.57×10^4 g CH_3OH is actually produced, what is the percent yield of methanol?

Solution

First, we must find out which reactant is limiting. The balanced equation is

$$2H_2(g) + CO(g) \longrightarrow CH_3OH(l)$$

Next we must calculate the moles of reactants:

$$68.5 \text{ kg CO} \times \frac{1000 \text{ g CO}}{1 \text{ kg CO}} \times \frac{1 \text{ mol CO}}{28.02 \text{ g CO}} = 2.44 \times 10^3 \text{ mol CO}$$

$$8.60 \text{ kg H}_2 \times \frac{1000 \text{ g H}_2}{1 \text{ kg H}_2} \times \frac{1 \text{ mol H}_2}{2.016 \text{ g H}_2} = 4.27 \times 10^3 \text{ mol H}_2$$

To determine which reactant is limiting, we compare the mole ratio of H_2 and CO required by the balanced equation

$$\frac{\text{mol H}_2}{\text{mol CO}} \text{ (required)} = \frac{2}{1} = 2$$

with the actual mole ratio

$$\frac{\text{mol H}_2}{\text{mol CO}} \text{ (actual)} = \frac{4.27 \times 10^3}{2.44 \times 10^3} = 1.75$$

Since the actual mole ratio of H_2 to CO is smaller than the required ratio, *H_2 is limiting.* We therefore must use the amount of H_2 and the mole ratio between H_2 and CH_3OH to determine the maximum amount of methanol that can be produced:

$$4.27 \times 10^3 \text{ mol H}_2 \times \frac{1 \text{ mol CH}_3\text{OH}}{2 \text{ mol H}_2} = 2.14 \times 10^3 \text{ mol CH}_3\text{OH}$$

Using the molar mass of CH_3OH (32.04 g/mol), we can calculate the theoretical yield in grams:

$$2.14 \times 10^3 \text{ mol CH}_3\text{OH} \times \frac{32.04 \text{ g CH}_3\text{OH}}{1 \text{ mol CH}_3\text{OH}} = 6.86 \times 10^4 \text{ g CH}_3\text{OH}$$

Thus, from the amount of reactants given, the maximum amount of CH_3OH that can be formed is 6.86×10^4 g. This is the *theoretical yield.*

The percent yield is

$$\frac{\text{Actual yield (grams)}}{\text{Theoretical yield (grams)}} \times 100 = \frac{3.57 \times 10^4 \text{ g CH}_3\text{OH}}{6.86 \times 10^4 \text{ g CH}_3\text{OH}} \times 100\% = 52.0\%$$

See Exercises 3.103 and 3.104.

Methanol is used as a fuel in Indianapolis-type racing cars.

Solving a Stoichiometry Problem Involving Masses of Reactants and Products

➡ 1 **Write and balance the equation for the reaction.**

➡ 2 **Convert the known masses of substances to moles.**

➡ 3 **Determine which reactant is limiting.**

➡ 4 **Using the amount of the limiting reactant and the appropriate mole ratios, compute the number of moles of the desired product.**

➡ 5 **Convert from moles to grams, using the molar mass.**

This process is summarized in the diagram below:

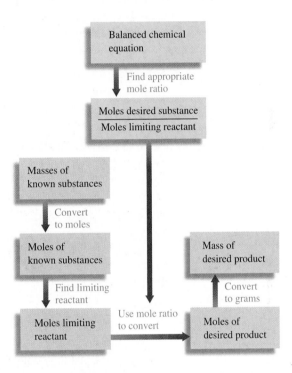

Key Terms

chemical stoichiometry

Section 3.2
mass spectrometer
average atomic mass

Section 3.3
mole
Avogadro's number

Section 3.4
molar mass

Section 3.5
mass percent

Section 3.6
empirical formula
molecular formula

For Review

Stoichiometry
- Deals with the amounts of substances consumed and/or produced in a chemical reaction.
- We count atoms by measuring the mass of the sample.
- To relate mass and the number of atoms, the average atomic mass is required.

Mole
- The amount of carbon atoms in exactly 12 g of pure ^{12}C
- 6.022×10^{23} units of a substance
- The mass of one mole of an element = the atomic mass in grams

Molar mass
- Mass (g) of one mole of a compound or element
- Obtained for a compound by finding the sum of the average masses of its constituent atoms

Percent composition
- The mass percent of each element in a compound
- Mass percent $= \dfrac{\text{mass of element in 1 mole of substance}}{\text{mass of 1 mole of substance}} \times 100\%$

Empirical formula
- The simplest whole-number ratio of the various types of atoms in a compound
- Can be obtained from the mass percent of elements in a compound

Molecular formula
- For molecular substances:
  - The formula of the constituent molecules
  - Always an integer multiple of the empirical formula
- For ionic substances:
  - The same as the empirical formula

Chemical reactions
- Reactants are turned into products.
- Atoms are neither created nor destroyed.
- All of the atoms present in the reactants must also be present in the products.

Characteristics of a chemical equation
- Represents a chemical reaction
- Reactants on the left side of the arrow, products on the right side
- When balanced, gives the relative numbers of reactant and product molecules or ions

Stoichiometry calculations
- Amounts of reactants consumed and products formed can be determined from the balanced chemical equation.
- The limiting reactant is the one consumed first, thus limiting the amount of product that can form.

Yield
- The theoretical yield is the maximum amount that can be produced from a given amount of the limiting reactant.
- The actual yield, the amount of product actually obtained, is always less than the theoretical yield.
- Percent yield $= \dfrac{\text{actual yield (g)}}{\text{theoretical yield (g)}} \times 100\%$

REVIEW QUESTIONS

1. Explain the concept of "counting by weighing" using marbles as your example.
2. Atomic masses are relative masses. What does this mean?
3. The atomic mass of boron (B) is given in the periodic table as 10.81, yet no single atom of boron has a mass of 10.81 amu. Explain.
4. What three conversion factors and in what order would you use them to convert the mass of a compound into atoms of a particular element in that compound—for example, from 1.00 g aspirin ($C_9H_8O_4$) to number of hydrogen atoms in the 1.00-g sample?
5. Figure 3.5 illustrates a schematic diagram of a combustion device used to analyze organic compounds. Given that a certain amount of a compound containing carbon, hydrogen, and oxygen is combusted in this device, explain how the data relating to the mass of CO_2 produced and the mass of H_2O produced can be manipulated to determine the empirical formula.

6. What is the difference between the empirical and molecular formulas of a compound? Can they ever be the same? Explain.

7. Consider the hypothetical reaction between A_2 and AB pictured below.

What is the balanced equation? If 2.50 mol A_2 is reacted with excess AB, what amount (moles) of product will form? If the mass of AB is 30.0 amu and the mass of A_2 is 40.0 amu, what is the mass of the product? If 15.0 g of AB is reacted, what mass of A_2 is required to react with all of the AB, and what mass of product is formed?

8. What is a limiting reactant problem? Explain two different strategies that can be used to solve limiting reactant problems.

9. Consider the following mixture of $SO_2(g)$ and $O_2(g)$.

If $SO_2(g)$ and $O_2(g)$ react to form $SO_3(g)$, draw a representation of the product mixture assuming the reaction goes to completion. What is the limiting reactant in the reaction? If 96.0 g of SO_2 reacts with 32.0 g O_2, what mass of product will form?

10. Why is the actual yield of a reaction often less than the theoretical yield?

Active Learning Questions

These questions are designed to be used by groups of students in class. The questions allow students to explore their understanding of concepts through discussion and peer teaching. The real value of these questions is the learning that occurs while students talk to each other about chemical concepts.

1. The following are actual student responses to the question: Why is it necessary to balance chemical equations?
   a. The chemicals will not react until you have added the correct mole ratios.
   b. The correct products will not be formed unless the right amount of reactants have been added.
   c. A certain number of products cannot be formed without a certain number of reactants.
   d. The balanced equation tells you how much reactant you need and allows you to predict how much product you'll make.
   e. A mole-to-mole ratio must be established for the reaction to occur as written.

   Justify the best choice, and for choices you did not pick, explain what is wrong with them.

2. What information do we get from a formula? From an equation?

3. You are making cookies and are missing a key ingredient—eggs. You have most of the other ingredients needed to make the cookies, except you have only 1.33 cups of butter and no eggs. You note that the recipe calls for 2 cups of butter and 3 eggs (plus the other ingredients) to make 6 dozen cookies. You call a friend and have him bring you some eggs.
   a. What number of eggs do you need?
   b. If you use all the butter (and get enough eggs), what number of cookies will you make?

   Unfortunately, your friend hangs up before you tell him how many eggs you need. When he arrives, he has a surprise for you—to save time, he has broken them all in a bowl for you. You ask him how many he brought, and he replies, "I can't remember." You weigh the eggs and find that they weigh 62.1 g. Assuming that an average egg weighs 34.21 g,
   a. What quantity of butter is needed to react with all the eggs?
   b. What number of cookies can you make?
   c. Which will you have left over, eggs or butter?
   d. What quantity is left over?

4. Nitrogen (N_2) and hydrogen (H_2) react to form ammonia (NH_3).

   Consider the mixture of N_2 (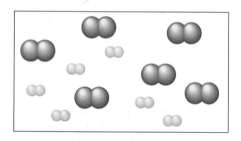) and H_2 ( ) in a

   closed container as illustrated below:

   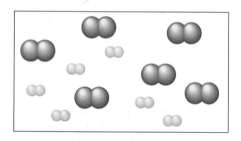

   Assuming the reaction goes to completion, draw a representation of the product mixture. Explain how you arrived at this representation.

5. For the preceding question, which of the following equations best represents the reaction?
   a. $6N_2 + 6H_2 \longrightarrow 4NH_3 + 4N_2$
   b. $N_2 + H_2 \longrightarrow NH_3$
   c. $N + 3H \longrightarrow NH_3$
   d. $N_2 + 3H_2 \longrightarrow 2NH_3$
   e. $2N_2 + 6H_2 \longrightarrow 4NH_3$

   Justify your choice, and for choices you did not pick, explain what is wrong with them.

6. You know that chemical A reacts with chemical B. You react 10.0 g A with 10.0 g B. What information do you need to determine the amount of product that will be produced? Explain.

7. A new grill has a mass of 30.0 kg. You put 3.0 kg of charcoal in the grill. You burn all the charcoal and the grill has a mass of 30.0 kg. What is the mass of the gases given off? Explain.

8. Consider an iron bar on a balance as shown.

   As the iron bar rusts, which of the following is true? Explain your answer.
   a. The balance will read less than 75.0 g.
   b. The balance will read 75.0 g.
   c. The balance will read greater than 75.0 g.
   d. The balance will read greater than 75.0 g, but if the bar is removed, the rust is scraped off, and the bar replaced, the balance will read 75.0 g.

9. You may have noticed that water sometimes drips from the exhaust of a car as it is running. Is this evidence that there is at least a small amount of water originally present in the gasoline? Explain.

Questions 10 and 11 deal with the following situation: You react chemical A with chemical B to make one product. It takes 100 g of A to react completely with 20 g B.

10. What is the mass of the product?
   a. less than 10 g
   b. between 20 and 100 g
   c. between 100 and 120 g
   d. exactly 120 g
   e. more than 120 g

11. What is true about the chemical properties of the product?
   a. The properties are more like chemical A.
   b. The properties are more like chemical B.
   c. The properties are an average of those of chemical A and chemical B.
   d. The properties are not necessarily like either chemical A or chemical B.
   e. The properties are more like chemical A or more like chemical B, but more information is needed.

   Justify your choice, and for choices you did not pick, explain what is wrong with them.

12. Is there a difference between a homogeneous mixture of hydrogen and oxygen in a 2:1 mole ratio and a sample of water vapor? Explain.

13. Chlorine exists mainly as two isotopes, ^{37}Cl and ^{35}Cl. Which is more abundant? How do you know?

14. The average mass of a carbon atom is 12.011. Assuming you could pick up one carbon atom, estimate the chance that you would randomly get one with a mass of 12.011. Support your answer.

15. Can the subscripts in a chemical formula be fractions? Explain. Can the coefficients in a balanced chemical equation be fractions? Explain. Changing the subscripts of chemicals can balance the equations mathematically. Why is this unacceptable?

16. Consider the equation $2A + B \longrightarrow A_2B$. If you mix 1.0 mol of A with 1.0 mol of B, what amount (moles) of A_2B can be produced?

17. According to the law of conservation of mass, mass cannot be gained or destroyed in a chemical reaction. Why can't you simply add the masses of two reactants to determine the total mass of product?

18. Which of the following pairs of compounds have the same *empirical* formula?
  a. acetylene, C_2H_2, and benzene, C_6H_6
  b. ethane, C_2H_6, and butane, C_4H_{10}
  c. nitrogen dioxide, NO_2, and dinitrogen tetroxide, N_2O_4
  d. diphenyl ether, $C_{12}H_{10}O$, and phenol, C_6H_5OH

A blue question or exercise number indicates that the answer to that question or exercise appears at the back of the book and a solution appears in the *Solutions Guide*.

Questions

19. Reference section 3.2 to find the atomic masses of ^{12}C and ^{13}C, the relative abundance of ^{12}C and ^{13}C in natural carbon, and the average mass (in amu) of a carbon atom. If you had a sample of natural carbon containing exactly 10,000 atoms, determine the number of ^{12}C and ^{13}C atoms present. What would be the average mass (in amu) and the total mass (in amu) of the carbon atoms in this 10,000-atom sample? If you had a sample of natural carbon containing 6.0221×10^{23} atoms, determine the number of ^{12}C and ^{13}C atoms present. What would be the average mass (in amu) and the total mass (in amu) of this 6.0221×10^{23} atom sample? Given that $1 \text{ g} = 6.0221 \times 10^{23}$ amu, what is the total mass of 1 mol of natural carbon in units of grams?

20. Avogadro's number, molar mass, and the chemical formula of a compound are three useful conversion factors. What unit conversions can be accomplished using these conversion factors?

21. If you had a mol of U.S. dollar bills and equally distributed the money to all of the people of the world, how rich would every person be? Assume a world population of 6 billion.

22. What is the difference between the molar mass and the empirical formula mass of a compound? When are these masses the same and when are they different? When different, how is the molar mass related to the empirical formula mass?

23. How is the mass percent of elements in a compound different for a 1.0-g sample versus a 100.-g sample versus a 1-mol sample of the compound?

24. A balanced chemical equation contains a large amount of information. What information is given in a balanced equation?

25. Consider the following generic reaction:

$$A_2B_2 + 2C \longrightarrow 2CB \text{ and } 2A$$

What steps and information are necessary to perform the following determinations assuming that 1.00×10^4 molecules of A_2B_2 are reacted with excess C?
  a. mass of CB produced
  b. atoms of A produced
  c. mol of C reacted
  d. percent yield of CB

26. Consider the following generic reaction:

$$Y_2 + 2XY \longrightarrow 2XY_2$$

In a limiting reactant problem, a certain quantity of each reactant is given and you are usually asked to calculate the mass of product formed. If 10.0 g of Y_2 is reacted with 10.0 g of XY, outline two methods you could use the determine which reactant is limiting (runs out first) and thus determines the mass of product formed. A method sometimes used to solve limiting reactant problems is to assume each reactant is limiting and then calculate the mass of product formed from each given quantity of reactant. How does this method work in determining which reactant is limiting?

Exercises

In this section similar exercises are paired.

Atomic Masses and the Mass Spectrometer

27. An element consists of 1.40% of an isotope with mass 203.973 amu, 24.10% of an isotope with mass 205.9745 amu, 22.10% of an isotope with mass 206.9759 amu, and 52.40% of an isotope with mass 207.9766 amu. Calculate the average atomic mass and identify the element.

28. An element "X" has five major isotopes, which are listed below along with their abundances. What is the element?

Isotope	Percent Natural Abundance	Atomic Mass
^{46}X	8.00%	45.95269
^{47}X	7.30%	46.951764
^{48}X	73.80%	47.947947
^{49}X	5.50%	48.947841
^{50}X	5.40%	49.944792

29. The element rhenium (Re) has two naturally occurring isotopes, ^{185}Re and ^{187}Re, with an average atomic mass of 186.207 amu. Rhenium is 62.60% ^{187}Re, and the atomic mass of ^{187}Re is 186.956 amu. Calculate the mass of ^{185}Re.

30. Assume silicon has three major isotopes in nature as shown in the table below. Fill in the missing information.

Isotope	Mass (amu)	Abundance
^{28}Si	27.98	_____
^{29}Si	_____	4.70%
^{32}Si	29.97	3.09%

31. The mass spectrum of bromine (Br_2) consists of three peaks with the following characteristics:

Mass (amu)	Relative Size
157.84	0.2534
159.84	0.5000
161.84	0.2466

How do you interpret these data?

32. Gallium arsenide, GaAs, has gained widespread use in semi-conductor devices that convert light and electrical signals in fiber-optic communications systems. Gallium consists of 60.% ^{69}Ga and 40.% ^{71}Ga. Arsenic has only one naturally occurring isotope, ^{75}As. Gallium arsenide is a polymeric material, but its mass spectrum shows fragments with the formulas GaAs and Ga_2As_2. What would the distribution of peaks look like for these two fragments?

Moles and Molar Masses

33. Calculate the mass of 500. atoms of iron (Fe).

34. What number of Fe atoms and what amount (moles) of Fe atoms are in 500.0 g of iron?

35. Diamond is a natural form of pure carbon. What number of atoms of carbon are in a 1.00-carat diamond (1.00 carat = 0.200 g)?

36. A diamond contains 5.0×10^{21} atoms of carbon. What amount (moles) of carbon and what mass (grams) of carbon are in this diamond?

37. Aluminum metal is produced by passing an electric current through a solution of aluminum oxide (Al_2O_3) dissolved in molten cryolite (Na_3AlF_6). Calculate the molar masses of Al_2O_3 and Na_3AlF_6.

38. The Freons are a class of compounds containing carbon, chlorine, and fluorine. While they have many valuable uses, they have been shown to be responsible for depletion of the ozone in the upper atmosphere. In 1991, two replacement compounds for Freons went into production: HFC-134a (CH_2FCF_3) and HCFC-124 ($CHClFCF_3$). Calculate the molar masses of these two compounds.

39. Calculate the molar mass of the following substances.

a. ○ H ● N

b. ○ H ● N

c. $(NH_4)_2Cr_2O_7$

40. Calculate the molar mass of the following substances.

a. ○ O ● P

b. $Ca_3(PO_4)_2$ **c.** Na_2HPO_4

41. What amount (moles) of compound is present in 1.00 g of each of the compounds in Exercise 39?

42. What amount (moles) of compound is present in 1.00 g of each of the compounds in Exercise 40?

43. What mass of compound is present in 5.00 mol of each of the compounds in Exercise 39?

44. What mass of compound is present in 5.00 mol of each of the compounds in Exercise 40?

45. What mass of nitrogen is present in 5.00 mol of each of the compounds in Exercise 39?

46. What mass of phosphorus is present in 5.00 mol of each of the compounds in Exercise 40?

47. What number of molecules (or formula units) are present in 1.00 g of each of the compounds in Exercise 39?

48. What number of molecules (or formula units) are present in 1.00 g of each of the compounds in Exercise 40?

49. What number of atoms of nitrogen are present in 1.00 g of each of the compounds in Exercise 39?

50. What number of atoms of phosphorus are present in 1.00 g of each of the compounds in Exercise 40?

51. Ascorbic acid, or vitamin C ($C_6H_8O_6$), is an essential vitamin. It cannot be stored by the body and must be present in the diet. What is the molar mass of ascorbic acid? Vitamin C tablets are taken as a dietary supplement. If a typical tablet contains 500.0 mg of vitamin C, what amount (moles) and what number of molecules of vitamin C does it contain?

52. The molecular formula of acetylsalicylic acid (aspirin), one of the most commonly used pain relievers, is $C_9H_8O_4$.
a. Calculate the molar mass of aspirin.
b. A typical aspirin tablet contains 500. mg of $C_9H_8O_4$. What amount (moles) of $C_9H_8O_4$ molecules and what number of molecules of acetylsalicylic acid are in a 500.-mg tablet?

53. What amount (moles) are represented by each of these samples?
a. 150.0 g Fe_2O_3 **c.** 1.5×10^{16} molecules of BF_3
b. 10.0 mg NO_2

54. What amount (moles) is represented by each of these samples?
a. 20.0 mg caffeine, $C_8H_{10}N_4O_2$
b. 2.72×10^{21} molecules of ethanol, C_2H_5OH
c. 1.50 g of dry ice, CO_2

55. What number of atoms of nitrogen are present in 5.00 g of each of the following?
a. glycine, $C_2H_5O_2N$ **c.** calcium nitrate
b. magnesium nitride   **d.** dinitrogen tetroxide

56. Complete the following table.

Mass of Sample	Moles of Sample	Molecules in Sample	Total Atoms in Sample
4.24 g C_6H_6			
	0.224 mol H_2O		
		2.71×10^{22} molecules CO_2	
			3.35×10^{22} total atoms in CH_3OH sample

57. Aspartame is an artificial sweetener that is 160 times sweeter than sucrose (table sugar) when dissolved in water. It is marketed

as Nutra-Sweet. The molecular formula of aspartame is $C_{14}H_{18}N_2O_5$.
a. Calculate the molar mass of aspartame.
b. What amount (moles) of molecules are present in 10.0 g aspartame?
c. Calculate the mass in grams of 1.56 mol aspartame.
d. What number of molecules are in 5.0 mg aspartame?
e. What number of atoms of nitrogen are in 1.2 g aspartame?
f. What is the mass in grams of 1.0×10^9 molecules of aspartame?
g. What is the mass in grams of one molecule of aspartame?

58. Chloral hydrate ($C_2H_3Cl_3O_2$) is a drug formerly used as a sedative and hypnotic. It is the compound used to make "Mickey Finns" in detective stories.
a. Calculate the molar mass of chloral hydrate.
b. What amount (moles) of $C_2H_3Cl_3O_2$ molecules are in 500.0 g chloral hydrate?
c. What is the mass in grams of 2.0×10^{-2} mol chloral hydrate?
d. What number of chlorine atoms are in 5.0 g chloral hydrate?
e. What mass of chloral hydrate would contain 1.0 g Cl?
f. What is the mass of exactly 500 molecules of chloral hydrate?

Percent Composition

59. Calculate the percent composition by mass of the following compounds that are important starting materials for synthetic polymers:
a. $C_3H_4O_2$ (acrylic acid, from which acrylic plastics are made)
b. $C_4H_6O_2$ (methyl acrylate, from which Plexiglas is made)
c. C_3H_3N (acrylonitrile, from which Orlon is made)

60. Anabolic steroids are performance enhancement drugs whose use has been banned from most major sporting activities. One anabolic steroid is fluoxymesterone ($C_{20}H_{29}FO_3$). Calculate the percent composition by mass of fluoxymesterone.

61. Several important compounds contain only nitrogen and oxygen. Place the following compounds in order of increasing mass percent of nitrogen.
a. NO, a gas formed by the reaction of N_2 with O_2 in internal combustion engines
b. NO_2, a brown gas mainly responsible for the brownish color of photochemical smog
c. N_2O_4, a colorless liquid used as fuel in space shuttles
d. N_2O, a colorless gas sometimes used as an anesthetic by dentists (known as laughing gas)

62. Arrange the following substances in order of increasing mass percent of carbon.
a. caffeine, $C_8H_{10}N_4O_2$
b. sucrose, $C_{12}H_{22}O_{11}$
c. ethanol, C_2H_5OH

63. Vitamin B_{12}, cyanocobalamin, is essential for human nutrition. It is concentrated in animal tissue but not in higher plants. Although nutritional requirements for the vitamin are quite low, people who abstain completely from animal products may develop a deficiency anemia. Cyanocobalamin is the form used in vitamin supplements. It contains 4.34% cobalt by mass. Calculate the molar mass of cyanocobalamin, assuming that there is one atom of cobalt in every molecule of cyanocobalamin.

64. Fungal laccase, a blue protein found in wood-rotting fungi, is 0.390% Cu by mass. If a fungal laccase molecule contains 4 copper atoms, what is the molar mass of fungal laccase?

Empirical and Molecular Formulas

65. Express the composition of each of the following compounds as the mass percents of its elements.
a. formaldehyde, CH_2O
b. glucose, $C_6H_{12}O_6$
c. acetic acid, $HC_2H_3O_2$

66. Considering your answer to Exercise 65, which type of formula, empirical or molecular, can be obtained from elemental analysis that gives percent composition?

67. Give the empirical formula for each of the compounds represented below.

a.   b.

c.

⚪	H
⚪	O
⚪	N
⚫	C
⚪	P

d.

68. Determine the molecular formulas to which the following empirical formulas and molar masses pertain.
a. SNH (188.35 g/mol)
b. $NPCl_2$ (347.64 g/mol)
c. CoC_4O_4 (341.94 g/mol)
d. SN (184.32 g/mol)

69. The compound adrenaline contains 56.79% C, 6.56% H, 28.37% O, and 8.28% N by mass. What is the empirical formula for adrenaline?

70. The most common form of nylon (nylon-6) is 63.68% carbon, 12.38% nitrogen, 9.80% hydrogen, and 14.14% oxygen. Calculate the empirical formula for nylon-6.

71. There are two binary compounds of mercury and oxygen. Heating either of them results in the decomposition of the compound, with oxygen gas escaping into the atmosphere while leaving a residue of pure mercury. Heating 0.6498 g of one of the compounds leaves a residue of 0.6018 g. Heating 0.4172 g of the other compound results in a mass loss of 0.016 g. Determine the empirical formula of each compound.

72. A sample of urea contains 1.121 g N, 0.161 g H, 0.480 g C, and 0.640 g O. What is the empirical formula of urea?

73. A compound containing only sulfur and nitrogen is 69.6% S by mass; the molar mass is 184 g/mol. What are the empirical and molecular formulas of the compound?

74. Determine the molecular formula of a compound that contains 26.7% P, 12.1% N, and 61.2% Cl, and has a molar mass of 580 g/mol.

75. Adipic acid is an organic compound composed of 49.31% C, 43.79% O, and the rest hydrogen. If the molar mass of adipic acid is 146.1 g/mol, what are the empirical and molecular formulas for adipic acid?

76. Maleic acid is an organic compound composed of 41.39% C, 3.47% H, and the rest oxygen. If 0.129 mol of maleic acid has a mass of 15.0 g, what are the empirical and molecular formulas of maleic acid?

77. Many homes in rural America are heated by propane gas, a compound that contains only carbon and hydrogen. Complete combustion of a sample of propane produced 2.641 g of carbon dioxide and 1.442 g of water as the only products. Find the empirical formula of propane.

78. A compound contains only C, H, and N. Combustion of 35.0 mg of the compound produces 33.5 mg CO_2 and 41.1 mg H_2O. What is the empirical formula of the compound?

79. Cumene is a compound containing only carbon and hydrogen that is used in the production of acetone and phenol in the chemical industry. Combustion of 47.6 mg cumene produces some CO_2 and 42.8 mg water. The molar mass of cumene is between 115 and 125 g/mol. Determine the empirical and molecular formulas.

80. A compound contains only carbon, hydrogen, and oxygen. Combustion of 10.68 mg of the compound yields 16.01 mg CO_2 and 4.37 mg H_2O. The molar mass of the compound is 176.1 g/mol. What are the empirical and molecular formulas of the compound?

Balancing Chemical Equations

81. Give the balanced equation for each of the following chemical reactions:
   a. Glucose ($C_6H_{12}O_6$) reacts with oxygen gas to produce gaseous carbon dioxide and water vapor.
   b. Solid iron(III) sulfide reacts with gaseous hydrogen chloride to form solid iron(III) chloride and hydrogen sulfide gas.
   c. Carbon disulfide liquid reacts with ammonia gas to produce hydrogen sulfide gas and solid ammonium thiocyanate (NH_4SCN).

82. Give the balanced equation for each of the following.
   a. The combustion of ethanol (C_2H_5OH) forms carbon dioxide and water vapor. A combustion reaction refers to a reaction of a substance with oxygen gas.
   b. Aqueous solutions of lead(II) nitrate and sodium phosphate are mixed, resulting in the precipitate formation of lead(II) phosphate with aqueous sodium nitrate as the other product.

   c. Solid zinc reacts with aqueous HCl to form aqueous zinc chloride and hydrogen gas.
   d. Aqueous strontium hydroxide reacts with aqueous hydrobromic acid to produce water and aqueous strontium bromide.

83. Balance the following equations:
   a. $Ca(OH)_2(aq) + H_3PO_4(aq) \rightarrow H_2O(l) + Ca_3(PO_4)_2(s)$
   b. $Al(OH)_3(s) + HCl(aq) \rightarrow AlCl_3(aq) + H_2O(l)$
   c. $AgNO_3(aq) + H_2SO_4(aq) \rightarrow Ag_2SO_4(s) + HNO_3(aq)$

84. Balance each of the following chemical equations.
   a. $KO_2(s) + H_2O(l) \rightarrow KOH(aq) + O_2(g) + H_2O_2(aq)$
   b. $Fe_2O_3(s) + HNO_3(aq) \rightarrow Fe(NO_3)_3(aq) + H_2O(l)$
   c. $NH_3(g) + O_2(g) \rightarrow NO(g) + H_2O(g)$
   d. $PCl_5(l) + H_2O(l) \rightarrow H_3PO_4(aq) + HCl(g)$
   e. $CaO(s) + C(s) \rightarrow CaC_2(s) + CO_2(g)$
   f. $MoS_2(s) + O_2(g) \rightarrow MoO_3(s) + SO_2(g)$
   g. $FeCO_3(s) + H_2CO_3(aq) \rightarrow Fe(HCO_3)_2(aq)$

85. Balance the following equations representing combustion reactions:
   a.

   b.

   c. $C_{12}H_{22}O_{11}(s) + O_2(g) \rightarrow CO_2(g) + H_2O(g)$
   d. $Fe(s) + O_2(g) \rightarrow Fe_2O_3(s)$
   e. $FeO(s) + O_2(g) \rightarrow Fe_2O_3(s)$

86. Balance the following equations:
   a. $Cr(s) + S_8(s) \rightarrow Cr_2S_3(s)$
   b. $NaHCO_3(s) \xrightarrow{\text{Heat}} Na_2CO_3(s) + CO_2(g) + H_2O(g)$
   c. $KClO_3(s) \xrightarrow{\text{Heat}} KCl(s) + O_2(g)$
   d. $Eu(s) + HF(g) \rightarrow EuF_3(s) + H_2(g)$

87. Silicon is produced for the chemical and electronics industries by the following reactions. Give the balanced equation for each reaction.
   a. $SiO_2(s) + C(s) \xrightarrow[\text{arc furnace}]{\text{Electric}} Si(s) + CO(g)$
   b. Silicon tetrachloride is reacted with very pure magnesium, producing silicon and magnesium chloride.
   c. $Na_2SiF_6(s) + Na(s) \rightarrow Si(s) + NaF(s)$

88. Glass is a mixture of several compounds, but a major constituent of most glass is calcium silicate, $CaSiO_3$. Glass can be etched by treatment with hydrofluoric acid; HF attacks the calcium silicate of the glass, producing gaseous and water-soluble products (which can be removed by washing the glass). For example, the volumetric glassware in chemistry laboratories is often graduated by using this process. Balance the following equation for the reaction of hydrofluoric acid with calcium silicate.

$$CaSiO_3(s) + HF(aq) \rightarrow CaF_2(aq) + SiF_4(g) + H_2O(l)$$

Reaction Stoichiometry

89. Over the years, the thermite reaction has been used for welding railroad rails, in incendiary bombs, and to ignite solid-fuel rocket motors. The reaction is

$$Fe_2O_3(s) + 2Al(s) \longrightarrow 2Fe(l) + Al_2O_3(s)$$

What masses of iron(III) oxide and aluminum must be used to produce 15.0 g iron? What is the maximum mass of aluminum oxide that could be produced?

90. The reaction between potassium chlorate and red phosphorus takes place when you strike a match on a matchbox. If you were to react 52.9 g of potassium chlorate ($KClO_3$) with excess red phosphorus, what mass of tetraphosphorus decaoxide (P_4O_{10}) would be produced?

$$KClO_3(s) + P_4(s) \longrightarrow P_4O_{10}(s) + KCl(s) \quad \text{(unbalanced)}$$

91. The reusable booster rockets of the U.S. space shuttle employ a mixture of aluminum and ammonium perchlorate for fuel. A possible equation for this reaction is

$$3Al(s) + 3NH_4ClO_4(s) \longrightarrow$$
$$Al_2O_3(s) + AlCl_3(s) + 3NO(g) + 6H_2O(g)$$

What mass of NH_4ClO_4 should be used in the fuel mixture for every kilogram of Al?

92. One of relatively few reactions that takes place directly between two solids at room temperature is

$$Ba(OH)_2 \cdot 8H_2O(s) + NH_4SCN(s) \longrightarrow$$
$$Ba(SCN)_2(s) + H_2O(l) + NH_3(g)$$

In this equation, the $\cdot 8H_2O$ in $Ba(OH)_2 \cdot 8H_2O$ indicates the presence of eight water molecules. This compound is called barium hydroxide octahydrate.
   a. Balance the equation.
   b. What mass of ammonium thiocyanate (NH_4SCN) must be used if it is to react completely with 6.5 g barium hydroxide octahydrate?

93. Bacterial digestion is an economical method of sewage treatment. The reaction

$$5CO_2(g) + 55NH_4^+(aq) + 76O_2(g) \xrightarrow{\text{bacteria}}$$
$$\underset{\text{bacterial tissue}}{C_5H_7O_2N(s)} + 54NO_2^-(aq) + 52H_2O(l) + 109H^+(aq)$$

is an intermediate step in the conversion of the nitrogen in organic compounds into nitrate ions. What mass of bacterial tissue is produced in a treatment plant for every 1.0×10^4 kg of wastewater containing 3.0% NH_4^+ ions by mass? Assume that 95% of the ammonium ions are consumed by the bacteria.

94. Phosphorus can be prepared from calcium phosphate by the following reaction:

$$2Ca_3(PO_4)_2(s) + 6SiO_2(s) + 10C(s) \longrightarrow$$
$$6CaSiO_3(s) + P_4(s) + 10CO(g)$$

Phosphorite is a mineral that contains $Ca_3(PO_4)_2$ plus other non-phosphorus-containing compounds. What is the maximum amount of P_4 that can be produced from 1.0 kg of phosphorite if the phorphorite sample is 75% $Ca_3(PO_4)_2$ by mass? Assume an excess of the other reactants.

95. Aspirin ($C_9H_8O_4$) is synthesized by reacting salicylic acid ($C_7H_6O_3$) with acetic anhydride ($C_4H_6O_3$). The balanced equation is

$$C_7H_6O_3 + C_4H_6O_3 \longrightarrow C_9H_8O_4 + HC_2H_3O_2$$

   a. What mass of acetic anhydride is needed to completely consume 1.00×10^2 g salicylic acid?
   b. What is the maximum mass of aspirin (the theoretical yield) that could be produced in this reaction?

96. The space shuttle environmental control system handles excess CO_2 (which the astronauts breathe out; it is 4.0% by mass of exhaled air) by reacting it with lithium hydroxide, LiOH, pellets to form lithium carbonate, Li_2CO_3, and water. If there are 7 astronauts on board the shuttle, and each exhales 20. L of air per minute, how long could clean air be generated if there were 25,000 g of LiOH pellets available for each shuttle mission? Assume the density of air is 0.0010 g/mL.

Limiting Reactants and Percent Yield

97. Consider the reaction between $NO(g)$ and $O_2(g)$ represented below.

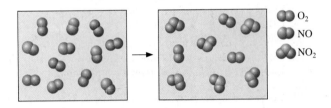

What is the balanced equation for this reaction and what is the limiting reactant?

98. Consider the following reaction:

$$4NH_3(g) + 5O_2(g) \longrightarrow 4NO(g) + 6H_2O(g)$$

If a container were to have 10 molecules of O_2 and 10 molecules of NH_3 initially, how many total molecules (reactants plus products) would be present in the container after this reaction goes to completion?

99. Hydrogen peroxide is used as a cleaning agent in the treatment of cuts and abrasions for several reasons. It is an oxidizing agent that can directly kill many microorganisms; it decomposes upon contact with blood, releasing elemental oxygen gas (which inhibits the growth of anaerobic microorganisms); and it foams upon contact with blood, which provides a cleansing action. In the laboratory, small quantities of hydrogen peroxide can be prepared by the action of an acid on an alkaline earth metal peroxide, such as barium peroxide:

$$BaO_2(s) + 2HCl(aq) \longrightarrow H_2O_2(aq) + BaCl_2(aq)$$

What mass of hydrogen peroxide should result when 1.50 g of barium peroxide is treated with 25.0 mL of hydrochloric acid solution containing 0.0272 g of HCl per mL? What mass of which reagent is left unreacted?

100. Consider the following unbalanced equation:

$$Ca_3(PO_4)_2(s) + H_2SO_4(aq) \longrightarrow CaSO_4(s) + H_3PO_4(aq)$$

What masses of calcium sulfate and phosphoric acid can be produced from the reaction of 1.0 kg calcium phosphate with 1.0 kg concentrated sulfuric acid (98% H_2SO_4 by mass)?

101. Hydrogen cyanide is produced industrially from the reaction of gaseous ammonia, oxygen, and methane:

$$2NH_3(g) + 3O_2(g) + 2CH_4(g) \longrightarrow 2HCN(g) + 6H_2O(g)$$

If 5.00×10^3 kg each of NH_3, O_2, and CH_4 are reacted, what mass of HCN and of H_2O will be produced, assuming 100% yield?

102. Acrylonitrile (C_3H_3N) is the starting material for many synthetic carpets and fabrics. It is produced by the following reaction.

$$2C_3H_6(g) + 2NH_3(g) + 3O_2(g) \longrightarrow 2C_3H_3N(g) + 6H_2O(g)$$

If 15.0 g C_3H_6, 10.0 g O_2, and 5.00 g NH_3 are reacted, what mass of acrylonitrile can be produced, assuming 100% yield?

103. A student prepared aspirin in a laboratory experiment using the reaction in Exercise 95. The student reacted 1.50 g salicylic acid with 2.00 g acetic anhydride. The yield was 1.50 g aspirin. Calculate the theoretical yield and the percent yield for this experiment.

104. DDT, an insecticide harmful to fish, birds, and humans, is produced by the following reaction:

$$2C_6H_5Cl + C_2HOCl_3 \longrightarrow C_{14}H_9Cl_5 + H_2O$$
$$\text{chlorobenzene} \quad \text{chloral} \quad \quad \text{DDT}$$

In a government lab, 1142 g of chlorobenzene is reacted with 485 g of chloral.
a. What mass of DDT is formed?
b. Which reactant is limiting? Which is in excess?
c. What mass of the excess reactant is left over?
d. If the actual yield of DDT is 200.0 g, what is the percent yield?

105. Bornite (Cu_3FeS_3) is a copper ore used in the production of copper. When heated, the following reaction occurs:

$$2Cu_3FeS_3(s) + 7O_2(g) \longrightarrow 6Cu(s) + 2FeO(s) + 6SO_2(g)$$

If 2.50 metric tons of bornite is reacted with excess O_2 and the process has an 86.3% yield of copper, what mass of copper is produced?

106. Consider the following unbalanced reaction:

$$P_4(s) + F_2(g) \longrightarrow PF_3(g)$$

What mass of F_2 is needed to produce 120. g of PF_3 if the reaction has a 78.1% yield? 99.8g F₂ produce PF3

Additional Exercises

107. A given sample of a xenon fluoride compound contains molecules of the type XeF_n, where n is some whole number. Given that 9.03×10^{20} molecules of XeF_n weighs 0.368 g, determine the value for n in the formula.

108. Many cereals are made with high moisture content so that the cereal can be formed into various shapes before it is dried. A cereal product containing 58% H_2O by mass is produced at the rate

of 1000. kg/h. What mass of water must be evaporated per hour if the final product contains only 20.% water?

109. Consider the reaction

$$2H_2(g) + O_2(g) \longrightarrow 2H_2O(g)$$

Identify the limiting reagent in each of the reaction mixtures given below:
a. 50 molecules of H_2 and 25 molecules of O_2
b. 100 molecules of H_2 and 40 molecules of O_2
c. 100 molecules of H_2 and 100 molecules of O_2
d. 0.50 mol H_2 and 0.75 mol O_2
e. 0.80 mol H_2 and 0.75 mol O_2
f. 1.0 g H_2 and 0.25 mol O_2
g. 5.00 g H_2 and 56.00 g O_2

110. Some bismuth tablets, a medication used to treat upset stomachs, contain 262 mg of bismuth subsalicylate, $C_7H_5BiO_4$, per tablet. Assuming two tablets are digested, calculate the mass of bismuth consumed.

111. The empirical formula of styrene is CH; the molar mass of styrene is 104.14 g/mol. What number of H atoms are present in a 2.00-g sample of styrene?

112. Terephthalic acid is an important chemical used in the manufacture of polyesters and plasticizers. It contains only C, H, and O. Combustion of 19.81 mg terephthalic acid produces 41.98 mg CO_2 and 6.45 mg H_2O. If 0.250 mol of terephthalic acid has a mass of 41.5 g, determine the molecular formula for terephthalic acid.

113. A sample of a hydrocarbon (a compound consisting of only carbon and hydrogen) contains 2.59×10^{23} atoms of hydrogen and is 17.3% hydrogen by mass. If the molar mass of the hydrocarbon is between 55 and 65 g/mol, what amount (moles) of compound are present, and what is the mass of the sample?

114. A binary compound between an unknown element E and hydrogen contains 91.27% E and 8.73% H by mass. If the formula of the compound is E_3H_8, calculate the atomic mass of E.

115. A 0.755-g sample of hydrated copper(II) sulfate

$$CuSO_4 \cdot xH_2O$$

was heated carefully until it had changed completely to anhydrous copper(II) sulfate ($CuSO_4$) with a mass of 0.483 g. Determine the value of x. [This number is called the *number of waters of hydration* of copper(II) sulfate. It specifies the number of water molecules per formula unit of $CuSO_4$ in the hydrated crystal.]

116. ABS plastic is a tough, hard plastic used in applications requiring shock resistance. The polymer consists of three monomer units: acrylonitrile (C_3H_3N), butadiene (C_4H_6), and styrene (C_8H_8).
a. A sample of ABS plastic contains 8.80% N by mass. It took 0.605 g of Br_2 to react completely with a 1.20-g sample of ABS plastic. Bromine reacts 1:1 (by moles) with the butadiene molecules in the polymer and nothing else. What is the percent by mass of acrylonitrile and butadiene in this polymer?
b. What are the relative numbers of each of the monomer units in this polymer?

117. A sample of LSD (D-lysergic acid diethylamide, $C_{24}H_{30}N_3O$) is added to some table salt (sodium chloride) to form a mixture. Given that a 1.00-g sample of the mixture undergoes combustion to produce 1.20 g of CO_2, what is the mass percentage of LSD in the mixture?

118. Methane (CH_4) is the main component of marsh gas. Heating methane in the presence of sulfur produces carbon disulfide and hydrogen sulfide as the only products.

    a. Write the balanced chemical equation for the reaction of methane and sulfur.

    b. Calculate the theoretical yield of carbon disulfide when 120. g of methane is reacted with an equal mass of sulfur.

119. A potential fuel for rockets is a combination of B_5H_9 and O_2. The two react according to the following balanced equation:

$$2B_5H_9(l) + 12O_2(g) \longrightarrow 5B_2O_3(s) + 9H_2O(g)$$

If one tank in a rocket holds 126 g of B_5H_9 and another tank holds 192 g of O_2, what mass of water can be produced when the entire contents of each tank react together?

120. Silver sulfadiazine burn-treating cream creates a barrier against bacterial invasion and releases antimicrobial agents directly into the wound. If 25.0 g of Ag_2O is reacted with 50.0 g of $C_{10}H_{10}N_4SO_2$, what mass of silver sulfadiazine, $AgC_{10}H_9N_4SO_2$, can be produced, assuming 100% yield?

$$Ag_2O(s) + 2C_{10}H_{10}N_4SO_2(s) \longrightarrow 2AgC_{10}H_9N_4SO_2(s) + H_2O(l)$$

121. An iron ore sample contains Fe_2O_3 plus other impurities. A 752-g sample of impure iron ore is heated with excess carbon, producing 453 g of pure iron by the following reaction:

$$Fe_2O_3(s) + 3C(s) \longrightarrow 2Fe(s) + 3CO(g)$$

What is the mass percent of Fe_2O_3 in the impure iron ore sample? Assume that Fe_2O_3 is the only source of iron and that the reaction is 100% efficient.

122. Commercial brass, an alloy of Zn and Cu, reacts with hydrochloric acid as follows:

$$Zn(s) + 2HCl(aq) \longrightarrow ZnCl_2(aq) + H_2(g)$$

(Cu does not react with HCl.) When 0.5065 g of a certain brass alloy is reacted with excess HCl, 0.0985 g $ZnCl_2$ is eventually isolated.

    a. What is the composition of the brass by mass?

    b. How could this result be checked without changing the above procedure?

123. Vitamin A has a molar mass of 286.4 g/mol and a general molecular formula of C_xH_yE, where E is an unknown element. If vitamin A is 83.86% C and 10.56% H by mass, what is the molecular formula of vitamin A?

Challenge Problems

124. Natural rubidium has the average mass of 85.4678 and is composed of isotopes ^{85}Rb (mass $= 84.9117$) and ^{87}Rb. The ratio of atoms $^{85}Rb/^{87}Rb$ in natural rubidium is 2.591. Calculate the mass of ^{87}Rb.

125. A compound contains only carbon, hydrogen, nitrogen, and oxygen. Combustion of 0.157 g of the compound produced 0.213 g CO_2 and 0.0310 g H_2O. In another experiment, it is found that 0.103 g of the compound produces 0.0230 g NH_3. What is the empirical formula of the compound? *Hint:* Combustion involves reacting with excess O_2. Assume that all the carbon ends up in CO_2 and all the hydrogen ends up in H_2O. Also assume that all the nitrogen ends up in the NH_3 in the second experiment.

126. Nitric acid is produced commercially by the Ostwald process, represented by the following equations:

$$4NH_3(g) + 5O_2(g) \longrightarrow 4NO(g) + 6H_2O(g)$$
$$2NO(g) + O_2(g) \longrightarrow 2NO_2(g)$$
$$3NO_2(g) + H_2O(l) \longrightarrow 2HNO_3(aq) + NO(g)$$

What mass of NH_3 must be used to produce 1.0×10^6 kg HNO_3 by the Ostwald process? Assume 100% yield in each reaction and assume that the NO produced in the third step is not recycled.

127. Consider a 5.430-g mixture of FeO and Fe_3O_4. You react this mixture with an excess of oxygen to form 5.779 g Fe_2O_3. Calculate the percent by mass of FeO in the original mixture.

128. A 9.780-g gaseous mixture contains ethane (C_2H_6) and propane (C_3H_8). Complete combustion to form carbon dioxide and water requires 1.120 mol of oxygen. Calculate the mass percent of ethane in the original mixture.

129. Zinc and magnesium metal each react with hydrochloric acid to make chloride salts of the respective metals, and hydrogen gas. A 10.00-g mixture of zinc and magnesium produces 0.5171 g of hydrogen gas upon being mixed with an excess of hydrochloric acid. Determine the percent magnesium by mass in the original mixture.

130. A 2.077-g sample of an element, which has an atomic mass between 40 and 55, reacts with oxygen to form 3.708 g of an oxide. Determine the formula of the oxide (and identify the element).

131. Consider a gaseous binary compound with a molar mass of 62.09 g/mol. When 1.39 g of this compound is completely burned in excess oxygen, 1.21 g of water is formed. Determine the formula of the compound. Assume water is the only product that contains hydrogen.

132. A 2.25-g sample of scandium metal is reacted with excess hydrochloric acid to produce 0.1502 g hydrogen gas. What is the formula of the scandium chloride produced in the reaction?

133. In the production of printed circuit boards for the electronics industry, a 0.60-mm layer of copper is laminated onto an insulating plastic board. Next, a circuit pattern made of a chemically resistant polymer is printed on the board. The unwanted copper is removed by chemical etching, and the protective polymer is finally removed by solvents. One etching reaction is

$$Cu(NH_3)_4Cl_2(aq) + 4NH_3(aq) + Cu(s) \longrightarrow 2Cu(NH_3)_4Cl(aq)$$

A plant needs to manufacture 10,000 printed circuit boards, each 8.0×16.0 cm in area. An average of 80.% of the copper is removed from each board (density of copper $= 8.96$ g/cm^3). What masses of $Cu(NH_3)_4Cl_2$ and NH_3 are needed to do this? Assume 100% yield.

134. The aspirin substitute, acetaminophen ($C_8H_9O_2N$), is produced by the following three-step synthesis:

    I. $C_6H_5O_3N(s) + 3H_2(g) + HCl(aq) \longrightarrow$
$$C_6H_8ONCl(s) + 2H_2O(l)$$

II. $C_6H_8ONCl(s) + NaOH(aq) \longrightarrow$
$$C_6H_7ON(s) + H_2O(l) + NaCl(aq)$$

III. $C_6H_7ON(s) + C_4H_6O_3(l) \longrightarrow$
$$C_8H_9O_2N(s) + HC_2H_3O_2(l)$$

The first two reactions have percent yields of 87% and 98% by mass, respectively. The overall reaction yields 3 mol of acetaminophen product for every 4 mol of $C_6H_5O_3N$ reacted.
   a. What is the percent yield by mass for the overall process?
   b. What is the percent yield by mass of step III?

135. An element X forms both a dichloride (XCl_2) and a tetrachloride (XCl_4). Treatment of 10.00 g XCl_2 with excess chlorine forms 12.55 g XCl_4. Calculate the atomic mass of X, and identify X.

136. When $M_2S_3(s)$ is heated in air, it is converted to $MO_2(s)$. A 4.000-g sample of $M_2S_3(s)$ shows a decrease in mass of 0.277 g when it is heated in air. What is the average atomic mass of M?

137. When aluminum metal is heated with an element from Group 6A of the periodic table, an ionic compound forms. When the experiment is performed with an unknown Group 6A element, the product is 18.56% Al by mass. What is the formula of the compound?

138. A sample of a mixture containing only sodium chloride and potassium chloride has a mass of 4.000 g. When this sample is dissolved in water and excess silver nitrate is added, a white solid (silver chloride) forms. After filtration and drying, the solid silver chloride has the mass 8.5904 g. Calculate the mass percent of each mixture component.

139. Ammonia reacts with O_2 to form either $NO(g)$ or $NO_2(g)$ according to these unbalanced equations:

$$NH_3(g) + O_2(g) \longrightarrow NO(g) + H_2O(g)$$
$$NH_3(g) + O_2(g) \longrightarrow NO_2(g) + H_2O(g)$$

In a certain experiment 2.00 mol of $NH_3(g)$ and 10.00 mol of $O_2(g)$ are contained in a closed flask. After the reaction is complete, 6.75 mol of $O_2(g)$ remains. Calculate the number of moles of $NO(g)$ in the product mixture: (*Hint:* You cannot do this problem by adding the balanced equations, because you cannot assume that the two reactions will occur with equal probability.)

140. You take 1.00 g of an aspirin tablet (a compound consisting solely of carbon, hydrogen, and oxygen), burn it in air, and collect 2.20 g CO_2 and 0.400 g H_2O. You know that the molar mass of aspirin is between 170 and 190 g/mol. Reacting 1 mole of salicylic acid with 1 mole of acetic anhydride ($C_4H_6O_3$) gives you 1 mole of aspirin and 1 mole of acetic acid ($C_2H_4O_2$). Use this information to determine the molecular formula of salicylic acid.

Integrative Problems

These problems require the integration of multiple concepts to find the solutions.

141. With the advent of techniques such as scanning tunneling microscopy, it is now possible to "write" with individual atoms by manipulating and arranging atoms on an atomic surface.
   a. If an image is prepared by manipulating iron atoms and their total mass is 1.05×10^{-20} g, what number of iron atoms were used?

b. If the image is prepared on a platinum surface that is exactly 20 platinum atoms high and 14 platinum atoms wide, what is the mass (grams) of the atomic surface?
   c. If the atomic surface were changed to ruthenium atoms and the same surface mass as determined in part b is used, what number of ruthenium atoms is needed to construct the surface?

142. Tetrodotoxin is a toxic chemical found in fugu pufferfish, a popular but rare delicacy in Japan. This compound has a LD_{50} (the amount of substance that is lethal to 50.% of a population sample) of 10. μg per kg of body mass. Tetrodotoxin is 41.38% carbon by mass, 13.16% nitrogen by mass, and 5.37% hydrogen by mass, with the remaining amount consisting of oxygen. What is the empirical formula of tetrodotoxin? If three molecules of tetrodotoxin has a mass of 1.59×10^{-21} g, what is the molecular formula of tetrodotoxin? What number of molecules of tetrodotoxin would be the LD_{50} dosage for a person weighing 165 lb?

143. An ionic compound MX_3 is prepared according to the following unbalanced chemical equation.

$$M + X_2 \longrightarrow MX_3$$

A 0.105-g sample of X_2 contains 8.92×10^{20} molecules. The compound MX_3 consists of 54.47% X by mass. What are the identities of M and X, and what is the correct name for MX_3? Starting with 1.00 g each of M and X_2, what mass of MX_3 can be prepared?

144. The compound As_2I_4 is synthesized by reaction of arsenic metal with arsenic triiodide. If a solid cubic block of arsenic ($d = 5.72$ g/cm^3) that is 3.00 cm on edge is allowed to react with 1.01×10^{24} molecules of arsenic triiodide, how much As_2I_4 can be prepared? If the percent yield of As_2I_4 was 75.6%, what mass of As_2I_4 was actually isolated?

Marathon Problems

These problems are designed to incorporate several concepts and techniques into one situation. Marathon Problems can be used in class by groups of students to help facilitate problem-solving skills.

***145.** From the information below, determine the mass of substance C that will be formed if 45.0 grams of substance A reacts with 23.0 grams of substance B. (Assume that the reaction between A and B goes to completion.)
   a. Substance A is a gray solid that consists of an alkaline earth metal and carbon (37.5% by mass). It reacts with substance B to produce substances C and D. Forty million trillion formula units of A have a mass of 4.26 milligrams.
   b. 47.9 grams of substance B contains 5.36 grams of hydrogen and 42.5 grams of oxygen.
   c. When 10.0 grams of C is burned in excess oxygen, 33.8 grams of carbon dioxide and 6.92 grams of water are produced. A mass spectrum of substance C shows a parent molecular ion with a mass-to-charge ratio of 26.
   d. Substance D is the hydroxide of the metal in substance A.

---

*Used with permission from the *Journal of Chemical Education,* Vol. 68, No. 11, 1991, pp. 919–922; copyright © 1991, Division of Chemical Education, Inc.

146. Consider the following balanced chemical equation:

$$A + 5B \longrightarrow 3C + 4D$$

a. Equal masses of A and B are reacted. Complete each of the following with either "A is the limiting reactant because _____"; "B is the limiting reactant because _____"; or "we cannot determine the limiting reactant because _____".

  i. If the molar mass of A is greater than the molar mass of B, then

  ii. If the molar mass of B is greater than the molar mass of A, then

b. The products of the reaction are carbon dioxide (C) and water (D). Compound A has the same molar mass as carbon dioxide. Compound B is a diatomic molecule. Identify compound B and support your answer.

c. Compound A is a hydrocarbon that is 81.71% carbon by mass. Determine its empirical and molecular formulas.

Get help understanding core concepts and visualizing molecular-level interactions, and practice problem solving, by visiting the Online Study Center at **college.hmco.com/ PIC/zumdahl7e.**

4 Types of Chemical Reactions and Solution Stoichiometry

Contents

Yellow lead(II) iodide is produced when lead(II) nitrate is mixed with potassium iodide.

*M*uch of the chemistry that affects each of us occurs among substances dissolved in water. For example, virtually all the chemistry that makes life possible occurs in an aqueous environment. Also, various medical tests involve aqueous reactions, depending heavily on analyses of blood and other body fluids. In addition to the common tests for sugar, cholesterol, and iron, analyses for specific chemical markers allow detection of many diseases before obvious symptoms occur.

Aqueous chemistry is also important in our environment. In recent years, contamination of the groundwater by substances such as chloroform and nitrates has been widely publicized. Water is essential for life, and the maintenance of an ample supply of clean water is crucial to all civilization.

To understand the chemistry that occurs in such diverse places as the human body, the atmosphere, the groundwater, the oceans, the local water treatment plant, your hair as you shampoo it, and so on, we must understand how substances dissolved in water react with each other.

However, before we can understand solution reactions, we need to discuss the nature of solutions in which water is the dissolving medium, or *solvent*. These solutions are called **aqueous solutions.** In this chapter we will study the nature of materials after they are dissolved in water and various types of reactions that occur among these substances. You will see that the procedures developed in Chapter 3 to deal with chemical reactions work very well for reactions that take place in aqueous solutions. To understand the types of reactions that occur in aqueous solutions, we must first explore the types of species present. This requires an understanding of the nature of water.

4.1 Water, the Common Solvent

Water is one of the most important substances on earth. It is essential for sustaining the reactions that keep us alive, but it also affects our lives in many indirect ways. Water helps moderate the earth's temperature; it cools automobile engines, nuclear power plants, and many industrial processes; it provides a means of transportation on the earth's surface and a medium for the growth of a myriad of creatures we use as food; and much more.

One of the most valuable properties of water is its ability to dissolve many different substances. For example, salt "disappears" when you sprinkle it into the water used to cook vegetables, as does sugar when you add it to your iced tea. In each case the "disappearing" substance is obviously still present—you can taste it. What happens when a solid dissolves? To understand this process, we need to consider the nature of water. Liquid water consists of a collection of H_2O molecules. An individual H_2O molecule is "bent" or V-shaped, with an H—O—H angle of approximately 105 degrees:

$$H \overset{105°}{\underset{O}{\diagup\diagdown}} H$$

The O—H bonds in the water molecule are covalent bonds formed by electron sharing between the oxygen and hydrogen atoms. However, the electrons of the bond are not shared equally between these atoms. For reasons we will discuss in later chapters, oxygen has a greater attraction for electrons than does hydrogen. If the electrons were shared equally between the two atoms, both would be electrically neutral because, on average, the number of electrons around each would equal the number of protons in that nucleus.

FIGURE 4.1
(top) The water molecule is polar. (bottom) A space-filling model of the water molecule.

Visualization: The Dissolution of a Solid in a Liquid

However, because the oxygen atom has a greater attraction for electrons, the shared electrons tend to spend more time close to the oxygen than to either of the hydrogens. Thus the oxygen atom gains a slight excess of negative charge, and the hydrogen atoms become slightly positive. This is shown in Fig. 4.1, where δ (delta) indicates a *partial* charge (*less than one unit of charge*). Because of this unequal charge distribution, water is said to be a **polar molecule.** It is this polarity that gives water its great ability to dissolve compounds.

A schematic of an ionic solid dissolving in water is shown in Fig. 4.2. Note that the "positive ends" of the water molecules are attracted to the negatively charged anions and that the "negative ends" are attracted to the positively charged cations. This process is called **hydration.** The hydration of its ions tends to cause a salt to "fall apart" in the water, or to dissolve. The strong forces present among the positive and negative ions of the solid are replaced by strong water–ion interactions.

It is very important to recognize that when ionic substances (salts) dissolve in water, they break up into the *individual* cations and anions. For instance, when ammonium nitrate (NH_4NO_3) dissolves in water, the resulting solution contains NH_4^+ and NO_3^- ions moving around independently. This process can be represented as

$$NH_4NO_3(s) \xrightarrow{\text{H}_2\text{O}(l)} NH_4^+(aq) + NO_3^-(aq)$$

where (*aq*) designates that the ions are hydrated by unspecified numbers of water molecules.

The **solubility** of ionic substances in water varies greatly. For example, sodium chloride is quite soluble in water, whereas silver chloride (contains Ag^+ and Cl^- ions) is only very slightly soluble. The differences in the solubilities of ionic compounds in water typically depend on the relative attractions of the ions for each other (these forces hold the solid together) and the attractions of the ions for water molecules (which cause the solid to disperse [dissolve] in water). Solubility is a complex topic that we will explore in much more detail in Chapter 11. However, the most important thing to remember at

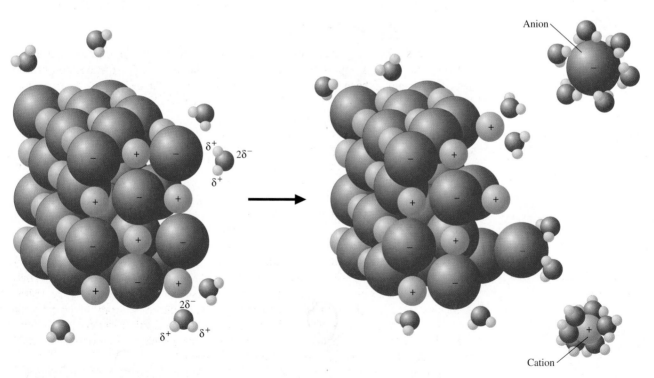

FIGURE 4.2
Polar water molecules interact with the positive and negative ions of a salt, assisting in the dissolving process.

FIGURE 4.3
(a) The ethanol molecule contains a polar O—H bond similar to those in the water molecule. (b) The polar water molecule interacts strongly with the polar O—H bond in ethanol. This is a case of "like dissolving like."

this point is that when an ionic solid does dissolve in water, the ions become hydrated and are dispersed (move around independently).

Water also dissolves many nonionic substances. Ethanol (C_2H_5OH), for example, is very soluble in water. Wine, beer, and mixed drinks are aqueous solutions of ethanol and other substances. Why is ethanol so soluble in water? The answer lies in the structure of the alcohol molecules, which is shown in Fig. 4.3(a). The molecule contains a polar O—H bond like those in water, which makes it very compatible with water. The interaction of water with ethanol is represented in Fig. 4.3(b).

Many substances do not dissolve in water. Pure water will not, for example, dissolve animal fat, because fat molecules are nonpolar and do not interact effectively with polar water molecules. In general, polar and ionic substances are expected to be more soluble in water than nonpolar substances. "Like dissolves like" is a useful rule for predicting solubility. We will explore the basis for this generalization when we discuss the details of solution formation in Chapter 11.

4.2 The Nature of Aqueous Solutions: Strong and Weak Electrolytes

As we discussed in Chapter 2, a solution is a homogeneous mixture. It is the same throughout (the first sip of a cup of coffee is the same as the last), but its composition can be varied by changing the amount of dissolved substances (one can make weak or strong coffee). In this section we will consider what happens when a substance, the **solute**, is dissolved in liquid water, the **solvent.**

One useful property for characterizing a solution is its **electrical conductivity,** its ability to conduct an electric current. This characteristic can be checked conveniently by using an apparatus like the ones shown in Figure 4.4. If the solution in the container conducts electricity, the bulb lights. Pure water is not an electrical conductor. However, some aqueous solutions conduct current very efficiently, and the bulb shines very brightly; these solutions contain **strong electrolytes.** Other solutions conduct only a small current, and the bulb glows dimly; these solutions contain **weak electrolytes.** Some solutions permit no current to flow, and the bulb remains unlit; these solutions contain **nonelectrolytes.**

The basis for the conductivity properties of solutions was first correctly identified by Svante Arrhenius (1859–1927), then a Swedish graduate student in physics, who carried out research on the nature of solutions at the University of Uppsala in the early 1880s. Arrhenius came to believe that the conductivity of solutions arose from the presence of ions, an idea that was at first scorned by the majority of the scientific establishment. However, in the late 1890s when atoms were found to contain charged particles, the ionic theory suddenly made sense and became widely accepted.

As Arrhenius postulated, the extent to which a solution can conduct an electric current depends directly on the number of ions present. Some materials, such as sodium chloride, readily produce ions in aqueous solution and thus are strong electrolytes. Other substances,

Visualization: Electrolytes

An *electrolyte* is a substance that when dissolved in water produces a solution that can conduct electricity.

Visualization: Electrolyte Behavior

FIGURE 4.4
Electrical conductivity of aqueous solutions. The circuit will be completed and will allow current to flow only when there are charge carriers (ions) in the solution. *Note:* Water molecules are present but not shown in these pictures. (a) A hydrochloric acid solution, which is a strong electrolyte, contains ions that readily conduct the current and give a brightly lit bulb. (b) An acetic acid solution, which is a weak electrolyte, contains only a few ions and does not conduct as much current as a strong electrolyte. The bulb is only dimly lit. (c) A sucrose solution, which is a nonelectrolyte, contains no ions and does not conduct a current. The bulb remains unlit.

(a)   (b)   (c)

such as acetic acid, produce relatively few ions when dissolved in water and are weak electrolytes. A third class of materials, such as sugar, form virtually no ions when dissolved in water and are nonelectrolytes.

Strong Electrolytes

Strong electrolytes are substances that are completely ionized when they are dissolved in water, as represented in Fig. 4.4(a). We will consider several classes of strong electrolytes: (1) soluble salts, (2) strong acids, and (3) strong bases.

As shown in Fig. 4.2, a salt consists of an array of cations and anions that separate and become hydrated when the salt dissolves. For example, when NaCl dissolves in water, it produces hydrated Na^+ and Cl^- ions in the solution (see Fig. 4.5). Virtually no NaCl

NaCl(*s*)
dissolves

Na^+ Cl^-

FIGURE 4.5
When solid NaCl dissolves, the Na^+ and Cl^- ions are randomly dispersed in the water.

FIGURE 4.6
HCl(*aq*) is completely ionized.

+ H⁺
● Cl⁻

The Arrhenius definition of an acid is a substance that produces H⁺ ions in solution.

Strong electrolytes dissociate (ionize) completely in aqueous solution.

Perchloric acid, HClO₄(*aq*), is another strong acid.

units are present. Thus NaCl is a strong electrolyte. It is important to recognize that these aqueous solutions contain millions of water molecules that we will not include in our molecular-level drawings.

One of Arrhenius's most important discoveries concerned the nature of acids. Acidity was first associated with the sour taste of citrus fruits. In fact, the word *acid* comes directly from the Latin word *acidus,* meaning "sour." The mineral acids sulfuric acid (H_2SO_4) and nitric acid (HNO_3), so named because they were originally obtained by the treatment of minerals, were discovered around 1300.

Although acids were known for hundreds of years before the time of Arrhenius, no one had recognized their essential nature. In his studies of solutions, Arrhenius found that when the substances HCl, HNO_3, and H_2SO_4 were dissolved in water, they behaved as strong electrolytes. He postulated that this was the result of ionization reactions in water, for example:

$$HCl \xrightarrow{H_2O} H^+(aq) + Cl^-(aq)$$
$$HNO_3 \xrightarrow{H_2O} H^+(aq) + NO_3^-(aq)$$
$$H_2SO_4 \xrightarrow{H_2O} H^+(aq) + HSO_4^-(aq)$$

Thus Arrhenius proposed that an ***acid*** *is a substance that produces H^+ ions (protons) when it is dissolved in water.*

Studies of conductivity show that when HCl, HNO_3, and H_2SO_4 are placed in water, *virtually every molecule ionizes.* These substances are strong electrolytes and are thus called **strong acids.** All three are very important chemicals, and much more will be said about them as we proceed. However, at this point the following facts are important:

Sulfuric acid, nitric acid, and hydrochloric acid are aqueous solutions and should be written in chemical equations as $H_2SO_4(aq)$, $HNO_3(aq)$, and HCl(*aq*), respectively, although they often appear without the (*aq*) symbol.

A strong acid is one that completely dissociates into its ions. Thus, if 100 molecules of HCl are dissolved in water, 100 H^+ ions and 100 Cl^- ions are produced. Virtually no HCl molecules exist in aqueous solutions (see Fig. 4.6).

Sulfuric acid is a special case. The formula H_2SO_4 indicates that this acid can produce two H^+ ions per molecule when dissolved in water. However, only the first H^+ ion is completely dissociated. The second H^+ ion can be pulled off under certain conditions, which we will discuss later. Thus an aqueous solution of H_2SO_4 contains mostly H^+ ions and HSO_4^- ions.

Another important class of strong electrolytes consists of the **strong bases,** soluble ionic compounds containing the hydroxide ion (OH^-). When these compounds are dissolved in water, the cations and OH^- ions separate and move independently. Solutions containing bases have a bitter taste and a slippery feel. The most common basic solutions are those produced when solid sodium hydroxide (NaOH) or potassium hydroxide (KOH) is dissolved in water to produce ions, as follows (see Fig. 4.7):

$$NaOH(s) \xrightarrow{H_2O} Na^+(aq) + OH^-(aq)$$
$$KOH(s) \xrightarrow{H_2O} K^+(aq) + OH^-(aq)$$

● OH⁻
+ Na⁺

FIGURE 4.7
An aqueous solution of sodium hydroxide.

Weak electrolytes dissociate (ionize) only to a small extent in aqueous solution.

Weak Electrolytes

Weak electrolytes are substances that exhibit a small degree of ionization in water. That is, they produce relatively few ions when dissolved in water, as shown in Fig. 4.4(b). The most common weak electrolytes are weak acids and weak bases.

CHEMICAL IMPACT

Arrhenius: A Man with Solutions

Science is a human endeavor, subject to human frailties and governed by personalities, politics, and prejudices. One of the best illustrations of the often bumpy path of the advancement of scientific knowledge is the story of Swedish chemist Svante Arrhenius.

When Arrhenius began studies toward his doctorate at the University of Uppsala around 1880, he chose to investigate the passage of electricity through solutions, a mystery that had baffled scientists for a century. The first experiments had been done in the 1770s by Cavendish, who compared the conductivity of salt solution with that of rain water using his own physiologic reaction to the electric shocks he received! Arrhenius had an array of instruments to measure electric current, but the process of carefully weighing, measuring, and recording data from a multitude of experiments was a tedious one.

After his long series of experiments was performed, Arrhenius quit his laboratory bench and returned to his country

Svante August Arrhenius.

The main acidic component of vinegar is acetic acid ($HC_2H_3O_2$). The formula is written to indicate that acetic acid has two chemically distinct types of hydrogen atoms. Formulas for acids are often written with the acidic hydrogen atom or atoms (any that will produce H^+ ions in solution) listed first. If any nonacidic hydrogens are present, they are written later in the formula. Thus the formula $HC_2H_3O_2$ indicates one acidic and three nonacidic hydrogen atoms. The dissociation reaction for acetic acid in water can be written as follows:

$$HC_2H_3O_2(aq) \overset{H_2O}{\rightleftharpoons} H^+(aq) + C_2H_3O_2^-(aq)$$

Acetic acid is very different from the strong acids because only about 1% of its molecules dissociate in aqueous solutions at typical concentrations. For example, in a solution containing 0.1 mole of $HC_2H_3O_2$ per liter, for every 100 molecules of $HC_2H_3O_2$ originally dissolved in water, approximately 99 molecules of $HC_2H_3O_2$ remain intact (see Fig. 4.8). That is, only one molecule out of every 100 dissociates (to produce one H^+ ion and one $C_2H_3O_2^-$ ion).

Because acetic acid is a weak electrolyte, it is called a **weak acid.** Any acid, such as acetic acid, that *dissociates (ionizes) only to a slight extent in aqueous solutions is called a weak acid.* In Chapter 14 we will explore the subject of weak acids in detail.

The most common weak base is ammonia (NH_3). When ammonia is dissolved in water, it reacts as follows:

$$NH_3(aq) + H_2O(l) \longrightarrow NH_4^+(aq) + OH^-(aq)$$

The solution is *basic* because OH^- ions are produced. Ammonia is called a **weak base** because *the resulting solution is a weak electrolyte;* that is, very few ions are formed. In fact, in a solution containing 0.1 mole of NH_3 per liter, for every 100 molecules of NH_3

⬤ Hydrogen

⬤ Oxygen

⬤ Carbon

FIGURE 4.8
Acetic acid ($HC_2H_3O_2$) exists in water mostly as undissociated molecules. Only a small percentage of the molecules are ionized.

home to try to formulate a model that could account for his data. He wrote, "I got the idea in the night of the 17th of May in the year 1883, and I could not sleep that night until I had worked through the whole problem." His idea was that ions were responsible for conducting electricity through a solution.

Back at Uppsala, Arrhenius took his doctoral dissertation containing the new theory to his advisor, Professor Cleve, an eminent chemist and the discoverer of the elements holmium and thulium. Cleve's uninterested response was what Arrhenius had expected. It was in keeping with Cleve's resistance to new ideas—he had not even accepted Mendeleev's periodic table, introduced 10 years earlier.

It is a long-standing custom that before a doctoral degree is granted, the dissertation must be defended before a panel of professors. Although this procedure is still followed at most universities today, the problems are usually worked out in private with the evaluating professors before the actual defense. However, when Arrhenius did it, the dissertation defense was an open debate, which could be rancorous and humiliating. Knowing that it would be unwise to antagonize his professors, Arrhenius downplayed his convictions about

his new theory as he defended his dissertation. His diplomacy paid off: He was awarded his degree, albeit reluctantly, because the professors still did not believe his model and considered him to be a marginal scientist, at best.

Such a setback could have ended his scientific career, but Arrhenius was a crusader; he was determined to see his theory triumph. He promptly embarked on a political campaign, enlisting the aid of several prominent scientists, to get his theory accepted.

Ultimately, the ionic theory triumphed. Arrhenius's fame spread, and honors were heaped on him, culminating in the Nobel Prize in chemistry in 1903. Not one to rest on his laurels, Arrhenius turned to new fields, including astronomy; he formulated a new theory that the solar system may have come into being through the collision of stars. His exceptional versatility led him to study the use of serums to fight disease, energy resources and conservation, and the origin of life.

Additional insight on Arrhenius and his scientific career can be obtained from his address on receiving the Willard Gibbs Award. See *Journal of the American Chemical Society* 36 (1912): 353.

● Hydrogen

● Oxygen

● Nitrogen

FIGURE 4.9
The reaction of NH_3 in water.

originally dissolved, only one NH_4^+ ion and one OH^- ion are produced; 99 molecules of NH_3 remain unreacted (see Fig. 4.9).

Nonelectrolytes

Nonelectrolytes are substances that dissolve in water but do not produce any ions, as shown in Fig. 4.4(c). An example of a nonelectrolyte is ethanol (see Fig. 4.3 for the structural formula). When ethanol dissolves, entire C_2H_5OH molecules are dispersed in the water. Since the molecules do not break up into ions, the resulting solution does not conduct an electric current. Another common nonelectrolyte is table sugar (sucrose, $C_{12}H_{22}O_{11}$), which is very soluble in water but which produces no ions when it dissolves. The sucrose molecules remain intact.

4.3 The Composition of Solutions

Chemical reactions often take place when two solutions are mixed. To perform stoichiometric calculations in such cases, we must know two things: (1) the *nature of the reaction,* which depends on the exact forms the chemicals take when dissolved, and (2) the *amounts of chemicals* present in the solutions, usually expressed as concentrations.

The concentration of a solution can be described in many different ways, as we will see in Chapter 11. At this point we will consider only the most commonly used expression of concentration, **molarity** (*M*), which is defined as *moles of solute per volume of solution in liters:*

$$M = \text{molarity} = \frac{\text{moles of solute}}{\text{liters of solution}}$$

A solution that is 1.0 molar (written as 1.0 *M*) contains 1.0 mole of solute per liter of solution.

| Sample Exercise 4.1 | Calculation of Molarity I |

Calculate the molarity of a solution prepared by dissolving 11.5 g of solid NaOH in enough water to make 1.50 L of solution.

Solution

To find the molarity of the solution, we first compute the number of moles of solute using the molar mass of NaOH (40.00 g/mol):

$$11.5 \text{ g NaOH} \times \frac{1 \text{ mol NaOH}}{40.00 \text{ g NaOH}} = 0.288 \text{ mol NaOH}$$

Then we divide by the volume of the solution in liters:

$$\text{Molarity} = \frac{\text{mol solute}}{\text{L solution}} = \frac{0.288 \text{ mol NaOH}}{1.50 \text{ L solution}} = 0.192 \; M \text{ NaOH}$$

See Exercises 4.21 and 4.22.

| Sample Exercise 4.2 | Calculation of Molarity II |

Calculate the molarity of a solution prepared by dissolving 1.56 g of gaseous HCl in enough water to make 26.8 mL of solution.

Solution

First we calculate the number of moles of HCl (molar mass = 36.46 g/mol):

$$1.56 \text{ g HCl} \times \frac{1 \text{ mol HCl}}{36.46 \text{ g HCl}} = 4.28 \times 10^{-2} \text{ mol HCl}$$

Next we must change the volume of the solution to liters:

$$26.8 \text{ mL} \times \frac{1 \text{ L}}{1000 \text{ mL}} = 2.68 \times 10^{-2} \text{ L}$$

Finally, we divide the moles of solution by the liters of solution:

$$\text{Molarity} = \frac{4.28 \times 10^{-2} \text{ mol HCl}}{2.68 \times 10^{-2} \text{ L solution}} = 1.60 \; M \text{ HCl}$$

See Exercises 4.21 and 4.22.

It is important to realize that the conventional description of a solution's concentration may not accurately reflect the true composition of the solution. Solution concentration is always given in terms of the form of the solute *before* it dissolves. For example, when a solution is described as being 1.0 *M* NaCl, this means that the solution was prepared by dissolving 1.0 mole of solid NaCl in enough water to make 1.0 liter of solution; it does not mean that the solution contains 1.0 mole of NaCl units. Actually, the solution contains 1.0 mole of Na^+ ions and 1.0 mole of Cl^- ions. This situation is further illustrated in Sample Exercise 4.3.

| Sample Exercise 4.3 | Concentrations of Ions I |

Give the concentration of each type of ion in the following solutions:

a. 0.50 *M* $Co(NO_3)_2$
b. 1 *M* $Fe(ClO_4)_3$

Solution

a. When solid $Co(NO_3)_2$ dissolves, the cobalt(II) cation and the nitrate anions separate:

$$Co(NO_3)_2(s) \xrightarrow{\text{H}_2\text{O}} Co^{2+}(aq) + 2NO_3^-(aq)$$

For each mole of $Co(NO_3)_2$ that is dissolved, the solution contains 1 mol Co^{2+} ions and 2 mol NO_3^- ions. Thus a solution that is 0.50 M $Co(NO_3)_2$ contains 0.50 M Co^{2+} and (2×0.50) M NO_3^- or 1.0 M NO_3^-.

b. When solid $Fe(ClO_4)_3$ dissolves, the iron(III) cation and the perchlorate anions separate:

$$Fe(ClO_4)_3(s) \xrightarrow{\text{H}_2\text{O}} Fe^{3+}(aq) + 3ClO_4^-(aq)$$

Thus a solution that is described as 1 M $Fe(ClO_4)_3$ actually contains 1 M Fe^{3+} ions and 3 M ClO_4^- ions.

See Exercises 14.23 and 14.24.

An aqueous solution of $Co(NO_3)_2$.

$$M = \frac{\text{moles of solute}}{\text{liters of solution}}$$

Often chemists need to determine the number of moles of solute present in a given volume of a solution of known molarity. The procedure for doing this is easily derived from the definition of molarity. If we multiply the molarity of a solution by the volume (in liters) of a particular sample of the solution, we get the moles of solute present in that sample:

$$\text{Liters of solution} \times \text{molarity} = \text{liters of solution} \times \frac{\text{moles of solute}}{\text{liters of solution}} = \text{moles of solute}$$

This procedure is demonstrated in Sample Exercises 4.4 and 4.5.

| Sample Exercise 4.4 | **Concentrations of Ions II** |

Calculate the number of moles of Cl^- ions in 1.75 L of 1.0×10^{-3} M $ZnCl_2$.

Solution

When solid $ZnCl_2$ dissolves, it produces ions as follows:

$$ZnCl_2(s) \xrightarrow{\text{H}_2\text{O}} Zn^{2+}(aq) + 2Cl^-(aq)$$

Thus a 1.0×10^{-3} M $ZnCl_2$ solution contains 1.0×10^{-3} M Zn^{2+} ions and 2.0×10^{-3} M Cl^- ions. To calculate the moles of Cl^- ions in 1.75 L of the 1.0×10^{-3} M $ZnCl_2$ solution, we must multiply the volume times the molarity:

$$1.75 \text{ L solution} \times 2.0 \times 10^{-3} \, M \, Cl^- = 1.75 \text{ L solution} \times \frac{2.0 \times 10^{-3} \text{ mol } Cl^-}{\text{L solution}}$$

$$= 3.5 \times 10^{-3} \text{ mol } Cl^-$$

See Exercise 4.25.

| Sample Exercise 4.5 | **Concentration and Volume** |

Typical blood serum is about 0.14 M NaCl. What volume of blood contains 1.0 mg NaCl?

Solution

We must first determine the number of moles represented by 1.0 mg NaCl (molar mass = 58.45 g/mol):

$$1.0 \text{ mg NaCl} \times \frac{1 \text{ g NaCl}}{1000 \text{ mg NaCl}} \times \frac{1 \text{ mol NaCl}}{58.45 \text{ g NaCl}} = 1.7 \times 10^{-5} \text{ mol NaCl}$$

Next, we must determine what volume of 0.14 M NaCl solution contains 1.7×10^{-5} mol NaCl. There is some volume, call it V, that when multiplied by the molarity of this solution will yield 1.7×10^{-5} mol NaCl. That is:

$$V \times \frac{0.14 \text{ mol NaCl}}{\text{L solution}} = 1.7 \times 10^{-5} \text{ mol NaCl}$$

We want to solve for the volume:

$$V = \frac{1.7 \times 10^{-5} \text{ mol NaCl}}{\dfrac{0.14 \text{ mol NaCl}}{\text{L solution}}} = 1.2 \times 10^{-4} \text{ L solution}$$

Thus 0.12 mL of blood contains 1.7×10^{-5} mol NaCl or 1.0 mg NaCl.

See Exercises 4.27 and 4.28.

A **standard solution** is a *solution whose concentration is accurately known.* Standard solutions, often used in chemical analysis, can be prepared as shown in Fig. 4.10 and in Sample Exercise 4.6.

| Sample Exercise 4.6 | # Solutions of Known Concentration |

To analyze the alcohol content of a certain wine, a chemist needs 1.00 L of an aqueous 0.200 M $K_2Cr_2O_7$ (potassium dichromate) solution. How much solid $K_2Cr_2O_7$ must be weighed out to make this solution?

Solution

We must first determine the moles of $K_2Cr_2O_7$ required:

$$1.00 \text{ L solution} \times \frac{0.200 \text{ mol } K_2Cr_2O_7}{\text{L solution}} = 0.200 \text{ mol } K_2Cr_2O_7$$

FIGURE 4.10

Steps involved in the preparation of a standard aqueous solution. (a) Put a weighed amount of a substance (the solute) into the volumetric flask, and add a small quantity of water. (b) Dissolve the solid in the water by gently swirling the flask (*with the stopper in place*). (c) Add more water (with gentle swirling) until the level of the solution just reaches the mark etched on the neck of the flask. Then mix the solution thoroughly by inverting the flask several times.

This amount can be converted to grams using the molar mass of $K_2Cr_2O_7$ (294.18 g/mol).

$$0.200 \text{ mol } K_2Cr_2O_7 \times \frac{294.20 \text{ g } K_2Cr_2O_7}{\text{mol } K_2Cr_2O_7} = 58.8 \text{ g } K_2Cr_2O_7$$

Thus, to make 1.00 L of 0.200 M $K_2Cr_2O_7$, the chemist must weigh out 58.8 g $K_2Cr_2O_7$, transfer it to a 1.00-L volumetric flask, and add distilled water to the mark on the flask.

See Exercises 4.29a and c and 4.30c and e.

Dilution

Visualization: Dilution

Dilution with water does not alter the numbers of moles of solute present.

To save time and space in the laboratory, routinely used solutions are often purchased or prepared in concentrated form (called *stock solutions*). Water is then added to achieve the molarity desired for a particular solution. This process is called **dilution.** For example, the common acids are purchased as concentrated solutions and diluted as needed. A typical dilution calculation involves determining how much water must be added to an amount of stock solution to achieve a solution of the desired concentration. The key to doing these calculations is to remember that

Moles of solute after dilution = moles of solute before dilution

because only water (no solute) is added to accomplish the dilution.

For example, suppose we need to prepare 500. mL of 1.00 M acetic acid ($HC_2H_3O_2$) from a 17.4 M stock solution of acetic acid. What volume of the stock solution is required? The first step is to determine the number of moles of acetic acid in the final solution by multiplying the volume by the molarity (remembering that the volume must be changed to liters):

$$500. \text{ mL solution} \times \frac{1 \text{ L solution}}{1000 \text{ mL solution}} \times \frac{1.00 \text{ mol } HC_2H_3O_2}{\text{L solution}} = 0.500 \text{ mol } HC_2H_3O_2$$

Thus we need to use a volume of 17.4 M acetic acid that contains 0.500 mol $HC_2H_3O_2$. That is,

$$V \times \frac{17.4 \text{ mol } HC_2H_3O_2}{\text{L solution}} = 0.500 \text{ mol } HC_2H_3O_2$$

Solving for V gives

$$V = \frac{0.500 \text{ mol } HC_2H_3O_2}{\dfrac{17.4 \text{ mol } HC_2H_3O_2}{\text{L solution}}} = 0.0287 \text{ L or } 28.7 \text{ mL solution}$$

Thus, to make 500 mL of a 1.00 M acetic acid solution, we can take 28.7 mL of 17.4 M acetic acid and dilute it to a total volume of 500 mL with distilled water.

A dilution procedure typically involves two types of glassware: a pipet and a volumetric flask. A *pipet* is a device for accurately measuring and transferring a given volume of solution. There are two common types of pipets: *volumetric* (or *transfer*) *pipets* and *measuring pipets,* as shown in Fig. 4.11. Volumetric pipets come in specific sizes, such as 5 mL, 10 mL, 25 mL, and so on. Measuring pipets are used to measure volumes for which a volumetric pipet is not available. For example, we would use a measuring pipet as shown in Fig. 4.12 on page 139 to deliver 28.7 mL of 17.4 M acetic acid into a 500-mL volumetric flask and then add water to the mark to perform the dilution described above.

Calibration mark

(a)   (b)

FIGURE 4.11
(a) A measuring pipet is graduated and can be used to measure various volumes of liquid accurately. (b) A volumetric (transfer) pipet is designed to measure one volume accurately. When filled to the mark, it delivers the volume indicated on the pipet.

CHEMICAL IMPACT

Tiny Laboratories

One of the major impacts of modern technology is to make things smaller. The best example is the computer. Calculations that 30 years ago required a machine the size of a large room now can be carried out on a hand-held calculator. This tendency toward miniaturization is also having a major impact on the science of chemical analysis. Using the techniques of computer chip makers, researchers are now constructing minuscule laboratories on the surface of a tiny chip made of silicon, glass, or plastic (see photo). Instead of electrons, 10^{-6} to 10^{-9} L of liquids moves between reaction chambers on the chip through tiny capillaries. The chips typically contain no moving parts. Instead of conventional pumps, the chip-based laboratories use voltage differences to move liquids that contain ions from one reaction chamber to another.

Microchip laboratories have many advantages. They require only tiny amounts of sample. This is especially advantageous for expensive, difficult-to-prepare materials or in cases such as criminal investigations, where only small amounts of evidence may exist. The chip laboratories also minimize contamination because they represent a "closed system" once the material has been introduced to the chip. In addition, the chips can be made to be disposable to prevent cross-contamination of different samples.

The chip laboratories present some difficulties not found in macroscopic laboratories. The main problem concerns the large surface area of the capillaries and reaction chambers relative to the sample volume. Molecules or biological cells in the sample solution encounter so much "wall" that they may undergo unwanted reactions with the wall materials. Glass seems to present the least of these problems, and the walls of silicon chip laboratories can be protected by formation of relatively inert silicon dioxide. Because plastic is inexpensive, it seems a good choice for disposable chips, but plastic also is the most reactive with the samples and the least durable of the available materials.

Caliper Technologies Corporation, of Palo Alto, California, is working toward creating a miniature chemistry laboratory about the size of a toaster that can be used with "plug-in" chip-based laboratories. Various chips would be furnished with the unit that would be appropriate for different types of analyses. The entire unit would be connected to a computer to collect and analyze the data. There is even the possibility that these "laboratories" could be used in the home to perform analyses such as blood sugar and blood cholesterol and to check for the presence of bacteria such as *E. coli* and many others. This would revolutionize the health care industry.

Plastic chips such as this one made by Caliper Technologies are being used to perform laboratory procedures traditionally done with test tubes.

Adapted from "The Incredible Shrinking Laboratory," by Corinna Wu, as appeared in *Science News,* Vol. 154, August 15, 1998, p. 104.

Sample Exercise 4.7   ## Concentration and Volume

What volume of 16 *M* sulfuric acid must be used to prepare 1.5 L of a 0.10 *M* H_2SO_4 solution?

Solution

We must first determine the moles of H_2SO_4 in 1.5 L of 0.10 *M* H_2SO_4:

$$1.5 \text{ L solution} \times \frac{0.10 \text{ mol } H_2SO_4}{\text{L solution}} = 0.15 \text{ mol } H_2SO_4$$

FIGURE 4.12
(a) A measuring pipet is used to transfer 28.7 mL of 17.4 M acetic acid solution to a volumetric flask. (b) Water is added to the flask to the calibration mark. (c) The resulting solution is 1.00 M acetic acid.

Next we must find the volume of 16 M H_2SO_4 that contains 0.15 mol H_2SO_4:

$$V \times \frac{16 \text{ mol } H_2SO_4}{\text{L solution}} = 0.15 \text{ mol } H_2SO_4$$

Solving for V gives

$$V = \frac{0.15 \text{ mol } H_2SO_4}{\dfrac{16 \text{ mol } H_2SO_4}{1 \text{ L solution}}} = 9.4 \times 10^{-3} \text{ L or } 9.4 \text{ mL solution}$$

In diluting an acid, "Do what you oughta, always add acid to water."

Thus, to make 1.5 L of 0.10 M H_2SO_4 using 16 M H_2SO_4, we must take 9.4 mL of the concentrated acid and dilute it with water to 1.5 L. The correct way to do this is to add the 9.4 mL of acid to about 1 L of distilled water and then dilute to 1.5 L by adding more water.

See Exercises 4.29b and d and 4.30a, b, and d.

As noted earlier, the central idea in performing the calculations associated with dilutions is to recognize that the moles of solute are not changed by the dilution. Another way to express this condition is by the following equation:

$$M_1 V_1 = M_2 V_2$$

where M_1 and V_1 represent the molarity and volume of the original solution (before dilution) and M_2 and V_2 represent the molarity and volume of the diluted solution. This equation makes sense because

$$M_1 \times V_1 = \text{mol solute before dilution}$$
$$= \text{mol solute after dilution} = M_2 \times V_2$$

Repeat Sample Exercise 4.7 using the equation $M_1V_1 = M_2V_2$. Note that in doing so

$$M_1 = 16\,M \qquad M_2 = 0.10\,M \qquad V_2 = 1.5\,\text{L}$$

and V_1 is the unknown quantity sought. The equation $M_1V_1 = M_2V_2$ always holds for a dilution. This equation will be easy for you to remember if you understand where it comes from.

4.4 Types of Chemical Reactions

Although we have considered many reactions so far in this text, we have examined only a tiny fraction of the millions of possible chemical reactions. To make sense of all these reactions, we need some system for grouping reactions into classes. Although there are many different ways to do this, we will use the system most commonly used by practicing chemists:

Types of Solution Reactions

- **Precipitation reactions**
- **Acid–base reactions**
- **Oxidation–reduction reactions**

Virtually all reactions can be put into one of these classes. We will define and illustrate each type in the following sections.

4.5 Precipitation Reactions

When two solutions are mixed, an insoluble substance sometimes forms; that is, a solid forms and separates from the solution. Such a reaction is called a **precipitation reaction,** and the solid that forms is called a **precipitate.** For example, a precipitation reaction occurs when an aqueous solution of potassium chromate, $K_2CrO_4(aq)$, which is yellow, is added to a colorless aqueous solution containing barium nitrate, $Ba(NO_3)_2(aq)$. As shown in Fig. 4.13, when these solutions are mixed, a yellow solid forms. What is the equation that describes this chemical change? To write the equation, we must know the identities of the reactants and products. The reactants have already been described: $K_2CrO_4(aq)$ and $Ba(NO_3)_2(aq)$. Is there some way we can predict the identities of the products? In particular, what is the yellow solid?

   The best way to predict the identity of this solid is to think carefully about what products are possible. To do this, we need to know what species are present in the solution after the two reactant solutions are mixed. First, let's think about the nature of each reactant solution. The designation $Ba(NO_3)_2(aq)$ means that barium nitrate (a white solid) has been dissolved in water. Notice that barium nitrate contains the Ba^{2+} and NO_3^- ions. *Remember: In virtually every case, when a solid containing ions dissolves in water, the ions separate* and move around independently. That is, $Ba(NO_3)_2(aq)$ does not contain $Ba(NO_3)_2$ units; it contains separated Ba^{2+} and NO_3^- ions. See Fig. 4.14(a).

   Similarly, since solid potassium chromate contains the K^+ and CrO_4^{2-} ions, an aqueous solution of potassium chromate (which is prepared by dissolving solid K_2CrO_4 in water) contains these separated ions, as shown in Fig. 4.14(b).

   We can represent the mixing of $K_2CrO_4(aq)$ and $Ba(NO_3)_2(aq)$ in two ways. First, we can write

$$K_2CrO_4(aq) + Ba(NO_3)_2(aq) \longrightarrow \text{products}$$

FIGURE 4.13
When yellow aqueous potassium chromate is added to a colorless barium nitrate solution, yellow barium chromate precipitates.

A *precipitation reaction* also can be called a *double displacement reaction.*

Visualization: Precipitation Reactions

The quantitative aspects of precipitation reactions are covered in Chapter 15.

When ionic compounds dissolve in water, the *resulting solution contains the separated ions.*

FIGURE 4.14
Reactant solutions: (a) $Ba(NO_3)_2(aq)$ and (b) $K_2CrO_4(aq)$.

(a)   (b)

However, a much more accurate representation is

$$\underbrace{2K^+(aq) + CrO_4^{2-}(aq)}_{\substack{\text{The ions in} \\ K_2CrO_4(aq)}} + \underbrace{Ba^{2+}(aq) + 2NO_3^-(aq)}_{\substack{\text{The ions in} \\ Ba(NO_3)_2(aq)}} \longrightarrow \text{products}$$

Thus the mixed solution contains the ions:

$$K^+ \qquad CrO_4^{2-} \qquad Ba^{2+} \qquad NO_3^-$$

as illustrated in Fig. 4.15(a).

How can some or all of these ions combine to form a yellow solid? This is not an easy question to answer. In fact, predicting the products of a chemical reaction is one of the hardest things a beginning chemistry student is asked to do. Even an experienced chemist, when confronted with a new reaction, is often not sure what will happen. The chemist tries to think of the various possibilities, considers the likelihood of each

(a)   (b)   (c)

FIGURE 4.15
The reaction of $K_2CrO_4(aq)$ and $Ba(NO_3)_2(aq)$. (a) The molecular-level "picture" of the mixed solution before any reaction has occurred. (b) The molecular-level "picture" of the solution after the reaction has occurred to form $BaCrO_4(s)$. *Note:* $BaCrO_4(s)$ is not molecular. It actually contains Ba^{2+} and CrO_4^{2-} ions packed together in a lattice. (c) A photo of the solution after the reaction has occurred, showing the solid $BaCrO_4$ on the bottom.

possibility, and then makes a prediction (an educated guess). Only after identifying each product *experimentally* is the chemist sure what reaction has taken place. However, an educated guess is very useful because it provides a place to start. It tells us what kinds of products we are most likely to find. We already know some things that will help us predict the products of the above reaction.

1. When ions form a solid compound, the compound must have a zero net charge. Thus the products of this reaction must contain *both anions and cations*. For example, K^+ and Ba^{2+} could not combine to form the solid, nor could CrO_4^{2-} and NO_3^-.

2. Most ionic materials contain only two types of ions: one type of cation and one type of anion (for example, NaCl, KOH, Na_2SO_4, K_2CrO_4, $Co(NO_3)_2$, NH_4Cl, Na_2CO_3).

The possible combinations of a given cation and a given anion from the list of ions K^+, CrO_4^{2-}, Ba^{2+}, and NO_3^- are

$$K_2CrO_4 \qquad KNO_3 \qquad BaCrO_4 \qquad Ba(NO_3)_2$$

Which of these possibilities is most likely to represent the yellow solid? We know it's not K_2CrO_4 or $Ba(NO_3)_2$. They are the reactants. They were present (dissolved) in the separate solutions that were mixed. The only real possibilities for the solid that formed are

$$KNO_3 \quad \text{and} \quad BaCrO_4$$

To decide which of these most likely represents the yellow solid, we need more facts. An experienced chemist knows that the K^+ ion and the NO_3^- ion are both colorless. Thus, if the solid is KNO_3, it should be white, not yellow. On the other hand, the CrO_4^{2-} ion is yellow (note in Fig. 4.14 that $K_2CrO_4(aq)$ is yellow). Thus the yellow solid is almost certainly $BaCrO_4$. Further tests show that this is the case.

So far we have determined that one product of the reaction between $K_2CrO_4(aq)$ and $Ba(NO_3)_2(aq)$ is $BaCrO_4(s)$, but what happened to the K^+ and NO_3^- ions? The answer is that these ions are left dissolved in the solution; KNO_3 does not form a solid when the K^+ and NO_3^- ions are present in this much water. In other words, if we took solid KNO_3 and put it in the same quantity of water as is present in the mixed solution, it would dissolve. Thus, when we mix $K_2CrO_4(aq)$ and $Ba(NO_3)_2(aq)$, $BaCrO_4(s)$ forms, but KNO_3 is left behind in solution (we write it as $KNO_3(aq)$). Thus the overall equation for this precipitation reaction using the formulas of the reactants and products is

$$K_2CrO_4(aq) + Ba(NO_3)_2(aq) \longrightarrow BaCrO_4(s) + 2KNO_3(aq)$$

As long as water is present, the KNO_3 remains dissolved as separated ions. (See Fig. 4.15 to help visualize what is happening in this reaction. Note the solid $BaCrO_4$ on the bottom of the container, while the K^+ and NO_3^- ions remain dispersed in the solution.) If we removed the solid $BaCrO_4$ and then evaporated the water, white solid KNO_3 would be obtained; the K^+ and NO_3^- ions would assemble themselves into solid KNO_3 when the water is removed.

Now let's consider another example. When an aqueous solution of silver nitrate is added to an aqueous solution of potassium chloride, a white precipitate forms, as shown in Fig. 4.16. We can represent what we know so far as

$$AgNO_3(aq) + KCl(aq) \longrightarrow \text{unknown white solid}$$

Remembering that when ionic substances dissolve in water, the ions separate, we can write

$$\underbrace{Ag^+, NO_3^-}_{\substack{\text{In silver} \\ \text{nitrate} \\ \text{solution}}} + \underbrace{K^+, Cl^-}_{\substack{\text{In potassium} \\ \text{chloride} \\ \text{solution}}} \longrightarrow \underbrace{Ag^+, NO_3^-, K^+, Cl^-}_{\substack{\text{Combined solution,} \\ \text{before reaction}}} \longrightarrow \text{white solid}$$

FIGURE 4.16
Precipitation of silver chloride by mixing solutions of silver nitrate and potassium chloride. The K^+ and NO_3^- ions remain in solution.

Since we know the white solid must contain both positive and negative ions, the possible compounds that can be assembled from this collection of ions are

$$AgNO_3 \qquad KCl \qquad AgCl \qquad KNO_3$$

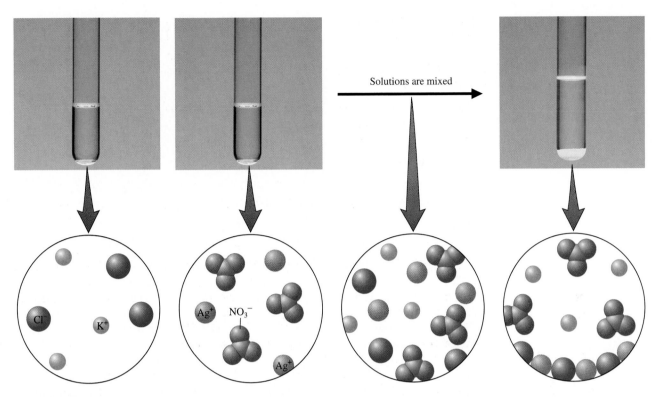

FIGURE 4.17
Photos and accompanying molecular-level representations illustrating the reaction of KCl(*aq*) with AgNO₃(*aq*) to form AgCl(*s*). Note that it is not possible to have a photo of the mixed solution before the reaction occurs, because it is an imaginary step that we use to help visualize the reaction. Actually, the reaction occurs immediately when the two solutions are mixed.

Visualization: Reactions of Silver I

Since $AgNO_3$ and KCl are the substances dissolved in the two reactant solutions, we know that they do not represent the white solid product. Therefore, the only real possibilities are

$$AgCl \quad and \quad KNO_3$$

From the first example considered, we know that KNO_3 is quite soluble in water. Thus solid KNO_3 will not form when the reactant solids are mixed. The product must be $AgCl(s)$ (which can be proved by experiment to be true). The overall equation for the reaction now can be written

$$AgNO_3(aq) + KCl(aq) \longrightarrow AgCl(s) + KNO_3(aq)$$

Figure 4.17 shows the result of mixing aqueous solutions of $AgNO_3$ and KCl, including a microscopic visualization of the reaction.

Notice that in these two examples we had to apply both concepts (solids must have a zero net charge) and facts (KNO_3 is very soluble in water, CrO_4^{2-} is yellow, and so on). Doing chemistry requires both understanding ideas and remembering key information. Predicting the identity of the solid product in a precipitation reaction requires knowledge of the solubilities of common ionic substances. As an aid in predicting the products of precipitation reactions, some simple solubility rules are given in Table 4.1. You should memorize these rules.

The phrase *slightly soluble* used in the solubility rules in Table 4.1 means that the tiny amount of solid that dissolves is not noticeable. The solid appears to be insoluble to the naked eye. Thus the terms *insoluble* and *slightly soluble* are often used interchangeably.

Note that the information in Table 4.1 allows us to predict that AgCl is the white solid formed when solutions of $AgNO_3$ and KCl are mixed. Rules 1 and 2 indicate that KNO_3 is soluble, and Rule 3 states that AgCl is insoluble.

TABLE 4.1   Simple Rules for the Solubility of Salts in Water

1. Most nitrate (NO_3^-) salts are soluble.

2. Most salts containing the alkali metal ions (Li^+, Na^+, K^+, Cs^+, Rb^+) and the ammonium ion (NH_4^+) are soluble.

3. Most chloride, bromide, and iodide salts are soluble. Notable exceptions are salts containing the ions Ag^+, Pb^{2+}, and Hg_2^{2+}.

4. Most sulfate salts are soluble. Notable exceptions are $BaSO_4$, $PbSO_4$, Hg_2SO_4, and $CaSO_4$.

5. Most hydroxide salts are only slightly soluble. The important soluble hydroxides are NaOH and KOH. The compounds $Ba(OH)_2$, $Sr(OH)_2$, and $Ca(OH)_2$ are marginally soluble.

6. Most sulfide (S^{2-}), carbonate (CO_3^{2-}), chromate (CrO_4^{2-}), and phosphate (PO_4^{3-}) salts are only slightly soluble.

Visualization: Solubility Rules

When solutions containing ionic substances are mixed, it will be helpful in determining the products if you think in terms of *ion interchange.* For example, in the preceding discussion we considered the results of mixing $AgNO_3(aq)$ and $KCl(aq)$. In determining the products, we took the cation from one reactant and combined it with the anion of the other reactant:

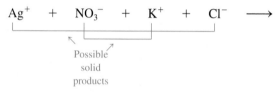

$$Ag^+ \quad + \quad NO_3^- \quad + \quad K^+ \quad + \quad Cl^- \quad \longrightarrow$$

Possible
solid
products

The solubility rules in Table 4.1 allow us to predict whether either product forms as a solid.

To begin, focus on the ions in solution before any reaction occurs.

The key to dealing with the chemistry of an aqueous solution is first to *focus on the actual components of the solution before any reaction occurs* and then to figure out how these components will react with each other. Sample Exercise 4.8 illustrates this process for three different reactions.

Sample Exercise 4.8   ## Predicting Reaction Products

Using the solubility rules in Table 4.1, predict what will happen when the following pairs of solutions are mixed.

a. $KNO_3(aq)$ and $BaCl_2(aq)$
b. $Na_2SO_4(aq)$ and $Pb(NO_3)_2(aq)$
c. $KOH(aq)$ and $Fe(NO_3)_3(aq)$

Solution

a. The formula $KNO_3(aq)$ represents an aqueous solution obtained by dissolving solid KNO_3 in water to form a solution containing the hydrated ions $K^+(aq)$ and $NO_3^-(aq)$. Likewise, $BaCl_2(aq)$ represents a solution formed by dissolving solid $BaCl_2$ in water to produce $Ba^{2+}(aq)$ and $Cl^-(aq)$. When these two solutions are mixed, the resulting solution contains the ions K^+, NO_3^-, Ba^{2+}, and Cl^-. All ions are hydrated, but the (aq) is omitted for simplicity. To look for possible solid products, combine the cation from one reactant with the anion from the other:

$$K^+ \quad + \quad NO_3^- \quad + \quad Ba^{2+} \quad + \quad Cl^- \quad \longrightarrow$$

Possible
solid products

Lead sulfate is a white solid.

Note from Table 4.1 that the rules predict that both KCl and $Ba(NO_3)_2$ are soluble in water. Thus no precipitate forms when $KNO_3(aq)$ and $BaCl_2(aq)$ are mixed. All the ions remain dissolved in solution. No chemical reaction occurs.

b. Using the same procedures as in part a, we find that the ions present in the combined solution before any reaction occurs are Na^+, SO_4^{2-}, Pb^{2+}, and NO_3^-. The possible salts that could form precipitates are

$$Na^+ \quad + \quad SO_4^{2-} \quad + \quad Pb^{2+} \quad + \quad NO_3^- \quad \longrightarrow$$

The compound $NaNO_3$ is soluble, but $PbSO_4$ is insoluble (see Rule 4 in Table 4.1). When these solutions are mixed, $PbSO_4$ will precipitate from the solution. The balanced equation is

$$Na_2SO_4(aq) + Pb(NO_3)_2(aq) \longrightarrow PbSO_4(s) + 2NaNO_3(aq)$$

c. The combined solution (before any reaction occurs) contains the ions K^+, OH^-, Fe^{3+}, and NO_3^-. The salts that might precipitate are KNO_3 and $Fe(OH)_3$. The solubility rules in Table 4.1 indicate that both K^+ and NO_3^- salts are soluble. However, $Fe(OH)_3$ is only slightly soluble (Rule 5) and hence will precipitate. The balanced equation is

$$3KOH(aq) + Fe(NO_3)_3(aq) \longrightarrow Fe(OH)_3(s) + 3KNO_3(aq)$$

See Exercises 4.37 and 4.38.

Solid $Fe(OH)_3$ forms when aqueous KOH and $Fe(NO_3)_3$ are mixed.

4.6 Describing Reactions in Solution

In this section we will consider the types of equations used to represent reactions in solution. For example, when we mix aqueous potassium chromate with aqueous barium nitrate, a reaction occurs to form a precipitate ($BaCrO_4$) and dissolved potassium nitrate. So far we have written the overall or **formula equation** for this reaction:

$$K_2CrO_4(aq) + Ba(NO_3)_2(aq) \longrightarrow BaCrO_4(s) + 2KNO_3(aq)$$

Although the formula equation shows the reactants and products of the reaction, it does not give a correct picture of what actually occurs in solution. As we have seen, aqueous solutions of potassium chromate, barium nitrate, and potassium nitrate contain individual ions, not collections of ions, as implied by the formula equation. Thus the **complete ionic equation**

A strong electrolyte is a substance that completely breaks apart into ions when dissolved in water.

$$2K^+(aq) + CrO_4^{2-}(aq) + Ba^{2+}(aq) + 2NO_3^-(aq) \longrightarrow$$
$$BaCrO_4(s) + 2K^+(aq) + 2NO_3^-(aq)$$

better represents the actual forms of the reactants and products in solution. *In a complete ionic equation, all substances that are strong electrolytes are represented as ions.*

The complete ionic equation reveals that only some of the ions participate in the reaction. The K^+ and NO_3^- ions are present in solution both before and after the reaction. The ions that do not participate directly in the reaction are called **spectator ions.** The ions that participate in this reaction are the Ba^{2+} and CrO_4^{2-} ions, which combine to form solid $BaCrO_4$:

Net ionic equations include only those components that undergo changes in the reaction.

$$Ba^{2+}(aq) + CrO_4^{2-}(aq) \longrightarrow BaCrO_4(s)$$

This equation, called the **net ionic equation,** includes only those solution components directly involved in the reaction. Chemists usually write the net ionic equation for a reaction in solution because it gives the actual forms of the reactants and products and includes only the species that undergo a change.

> ### Three Types of Equations Are Used to Describe Reactions in Solution
>
> - The **formula equation** gives the overall reaction stoichiometry but not necessarily the actual forms of the reactants and products in solution.
>
> - The **complete ionic equation** represents as ions all reactants and products that are strong electrolytes.
>
> - The **net ionic equation** includes only those solution components undergoing a change. Spectator ions are not included.

Sample Exercise 4.9   **Writing Equations for Reactions**

For each of the following reactions, write the formula equation, the complete ionic equation, and the net ionic equation.

a. Aqueous potassium chloride is added to aqueous silver nitrate to form a silver chloride precipitate plus aqueous potassium nitrate.

b. Aqueous potassium hydroxide is mixed with aqueous iron(III) nitrate to form a precipitate of iron(III) hydroxide and aqueous potassium nitrate.

Solution

a. Formula Equation

$$KCl(aq) + AgNO_3(aq) \longrightarrow AgCl(s) + KNO_3(aq)$$

Complete Ionic Equation
(*Remember:* Any ionic compound dissolved in water will be present as the separated ions.)

$$K^+(aq) + Cl^-(aq) + Ag^+(aq) + NO_3^-(aq) \longrightarrow AgCl(s) + K^+(aq) + NO_3^-(aq)$$

Spectator ion   Spectator ion   Solid, not written as separate ions   Spectator ion   Spectator ion

Canceling the spectator ions

$$\cancel{K^+}(aq) + Cl^-(aq) + Ag^+(aq) + \cancel{NO_3^-}(aq) \longrightarrow AgCl(s) + \cancel{K^+}(aq) + \cancel{NO_3^-}(aq)$$

gives the following net ionic equation.

Net Ionic Equation

$$Cl^-(aq) + Ag^+(aq) \longrightarrow AgCl(s)$$

b. Formula Equation

$$3KOH(aq) + Fe(NO_3)_3(aq) \longrightarrow Fe(OH)_3(s) + 3KNO_3(aq)$$

Complete Ionic Equation

$$3K^+(aq) + 3OH^-(aq) + Fe^{3+}(aq) + 3NO_3^-(aq) \longrightarrow$$
$$Fe(OH)_3(s) + 3K^+(aq) + 3NO_3^-(aq)$$

Net Ionic Equation

$$3OH^-(aq) + Fe^{3+}(aq) \longrightarrow Fe(OH)_3(s)$$

See Exercises 4.39 through 4.44.

4.7 Stoichiometry of Precipitation Reactions

In Chapter 3 we covered the principles of chemical stoichiometry: the procedures for calculating quantities of reactants and products involved in a chemical reaction. Recall that in performing these calculations we first convert all quantities to moles and then use the coefficients of the balanced equation to assemble the appropriate mole ratios. In cases where reactants are mixed we must determine which reactant is limiting, since the reactant that is consumed first will limit the amounts of products formed. *These same principles apply to reactions that take place in solutions.* However, two points about solution reactions need special emphasis. The first is that it is sometimes difficult to tell immediately what reaction will occur when two solutions are mixed. Usually we must do some thinking about the various possibilities and then decide what probably will happen. The first step in this process *always* should be to write down the species that are actually present in the solution, as we did in Section 4.5. The second special point about solution reactions is that to obtain the moles of reactants we must use the volume of the solution and its molarity. This procedure was covered in Section 4.3.

We will introduce stoichiometric calculations for reactions in solution in Sample Exercise 4.10.

Sample Exercise 4.10

Determining the Mass of Product Formed

Calculate the mass of solid NaCl that must be added to 1.50 L of a 0.100 M AgNO$_3$ solution to precipitate all the Ag$^+$ ions in the form of AgCl.

Solution

When added to the AgNO$_3$ solution (which contains Ag$^+$ and NO$_3^-$ ions), the solid NaCl dissolves to yield Na$^+$ and Cl$^-$ ions. Thus the mixed solution contains the ions

$$Ag^+ \qquad NO_3^- \qquad Na^+ \qquad Cl^-$$

Note from Table 4.1 that NaNO$_3$ is soluble and AgCl is insoluble. Therefore, solid AgCl forms according to the following net ionic equation:

$$Ag^+(aq) + Cl^-(aq) \longrightarrow AgCl(s)$$

In this case we must add enough Cl$^-$ ions to react with all the Ag$^+$ ions present. Thus we must calculate the moles of Ag$^+$ ions present in 1.50 L of a 0.100 M AgNO$_3$ solution (remember that a 0.100 M AgNO$_3$ solution contains 0.100 M Ag$^+$ ions and 0.100 M NO$_3^-$ ions):

$$1.50 \cancel{L} \times \frac{0.100 \text{ mol Ag}^+}{\cancel{L}} = 0.150 \text{ mol Ag}^+$$

Because Ag$^+$ and Cl$^-$ react in a 1:1 ratio, 0.150 mol Cl$^-$ ions and thus 0.150 mol NaCl are required. We calculate the mass of NaCl required as follows:

$$0.150 \cancel{\text{ mol NaCl}} \times \frac{58.45 \text{ g NaCl}}{\cancel{\text{mol NaCl}}} = 8.77 \text{ g NaCl}$$

See Exercise 4.47.

Notice from Sample Exercise 4.10 that the procedures for doing stoichiometric calculations for solution reactions are very similar to those for other types of reactions. It is useful to think in terms of the following steps for reactions in solution.

Solving Stoichiometry Problems for Reactions in Solution

➡ 1 **Identify the species present in the combined solution, and determine what reaction occurs.**

➡ 2 **Write the balanced net ionic equation for the reaction.**

➡ 3 **Calculate the moles of reactants.**

➡ 4 **Determine which reactant is limiting.**

➡ 5 **Calculate the moles of product or products, as required.**

➡ 6 **Convert to grams or other units, as required.**

| Sample Exercise 4.11 | # Determining the Mass of Product Formed |

When aqueous solutions of Na_2SO_4 and $Pb(NO_3)_2$ are mixed, $PbSO_4$ precipitates. Calculate the mass of $PbSO_4$ formed when 1.25 L of 0.0500 M $Pb(NO_3)_2$ and 2.00 L of 0.0250 M Na_2SO_4 are mixed.

Solution

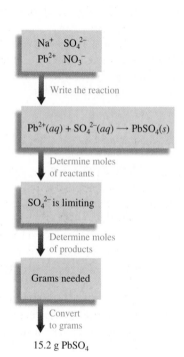

➡ **1** *Identify the species present in the combined solution, and determine what reaction occurs.* When the aqueous solutions of Na_2SO_4 (containing Na^+ and SO_4^{2-} ions) and $Pb(NO_3)_2$ (containing Pb^{2+} and NO_3^- ions) are mixed, the resulting solution contains the ions Na^+, SO_4^{2-}, Pb^{2+}, and NO_3^-. Since $NaNO_3$ is soluble and $PbSO_4$ is insoluble (see Rule 4 in Table 4.1), solid $PbSO_4$ will form.

➡ **2** *Write the balanced net ionic equation for the reaction.* The net ionic equation is

$$Pb^{2+}(aq) + SO_4^{2-}(aq) \longrightarrow PbSO_4(s)$$

➡ **3** *Calculate the moles of reactants.* Since 0.0500 M $Pb(NO_3)_2$ contains 0.0500 M Pb^{2+} ions, we can calculate the moles of Pb^{2+} ions in 1.25 L of this solution as follows:

$$1.25 \, \cancel{L} \times \frac{0.0500 \text{ mol } Pb^{2+}}{\cancel{L}} = 0.0625 \text{ mol } Pb^{2+}$$

The 0.0250 M Na_2SO_4 solution contains 0.0250 M SO_4^{2-} ions, and the number of moles of SO_4^{2-} ions in 2.00 L of this solution is

$$2.00 \, \cancel{L} \times \frac{0.0250 \text{ mol } SO_4^{2-}}{\cancel{L}} = 0.0500 \text{ mol } SO_4^{2-}$$

➡ **4** *Determine which reactant is limiting.* Because Pb^{2+} and SO_4^{2-} react in a 1:1 ratio, the amount of SO_4^{2-} will be limiting (0.0500 mol SO_4^{2-} is less than 0.0625 mol Pb^{2+}).

➡ **5** *Calculate the moles of product.* Since the Pb^{2+} ions are present in excess, only 0.0500 mol of solid $PbSO_4$ will be formed.

➡ **6** *Convert to grams of product.* The mass of $PbSO_4$ formed can be calculated using the molar mass of $PbSO_4$ (303.3 g/mol):

$$0.0500 \, \cancel{\text{mol } PbSO_4} \times \frac{303.3 \text{ g } PbSO_4}{1 \, \cancel{\text{mol } PbSO_4}} = 15.2 \text{ g } PbSO_4$$

See Exercises 4.49 and 4.50.

4.8 Acid–Base Reactions

Visualization: Proton Transfer

The Brønsted–Lowry concept of acids and bases will be discussed in detail in Chapter 14.

Earlier in this chapter we considered Arrhenius's concept of acids and bases: An acid is a substance that produces H^+ ions when dissolved in water, and a base is a substance that produces OH^- ions. Although these ideas are fundamentally correct, it is convenient to have a more general definition of a base, which includes substances that do not contain OH^- ions. Such a definition was provided by Johannes N. Brønsted (1879–1947) and Thomas M. Lowry (1874–1936), who defined acids and bases as follows:

> An **acid** is a proton donor.

> A **base** is a proton acceptor.

How do we know when to expect an acid–base reaction? One of the most difficult tasks for someone inexperienced in chemistry is to predict what reaction might occur when two solutions are mixed. With precipitation reactions, we found that the best way to deal with this problem is to focus on the species actually present in the mixed solution. This idea also applies to acid–base reactions. For example, when an aqueous solution of hydrogen chloride (HCl) is mixed with an aqueous solution of sodium hydroxide (NaOH), the combined solution contains the ions H^+, Cl^-, Na^+, and OH^-. The separated ions are present because HCl is a strong acid and NaOH is a strong base. How can we predict what reaction occurs, if any? First, will NaCl precipitate? From Table 4.1 we can see that NaCl is soluble in water and thus will not precipitate. Therefore, the Na^+ and Cl^- ions are spectator ions. On the other hand, because water is a nonelectrolyte, large quantities of H^+ and OH^- ions cannot coexist in solution. They react to form H_2O molecules:

$$H^+(aq) + OH^-(aq) \longrightarrow H_2O(l)$$

This is the net ionic equation for the reaction that occurs when aqueous solutions of HCl and NaOH are mixed.

Next, consider mixing an aqueous solution of acetic acid ($HC_2H_3O_2$) with an aqueous solution of potassium hydroxide (KOH). In our earlier discussion of conductivity we said that an aqueous solution of acetic acid is a weak electrolyte. This tells us that acetic acid does not dissociate into ions to any great extent. In fact, in 0.1 M $HC_2H_3O_2$ approximately 99% of the $HC_2H_3O_2$ molecules remain undissociated. However, when solid KOH is dissolved in water, it dissociates completely to produce K^+ and OH^- ions. Therefore, in the solution formed by mixing aqueous solutions of $HC_2H_3O_2$ and KOH, *before any reaction occurs*, the principal species are $HC_2H_3O_2$, K^+, and OH^-. What reaction will occur? A possible precipitation reaction could occur between K^+ and OH^-. However, we know that KOH is soluble, so precipitation does not occur. Another possibility is a reaction involving the hydroxide ion (a proton acceptor) and some proton donor. Is there a source of protons in the solution? The answer is yes—the $HC_2H_3O_2$ molecules. The OH^- ion has such a strong affinity for protons that it can strip them from the $HC_2H_3O_2$ molecules. The net ionic equation for this reaction is

$$OH^-(aq) + HC_2H_3O_2(aq) \longrightarrow H_2O(l) + C_2H_3O_2^-(aq)$$

This reaction illustrates a very important general principle: *The hydroxide ion is such a strong base that for purposes of stoichiometric calculations it can be assumed to react completely with any weak acid that we will encounter.* Of course, OH^- ions also react completely with the H^+ ions in solutions of strong acids.

We will now deal with the stoichiometry of acid–base reactions in aqueous solutions. The procedure is fundamentally the same as that used previously for precipitation reactions.

Performing Calculations for Acid–Base Reactions

Species present

↓ Write the reaction

Balanced net ionic equation

↓ Determine moles of reactants

Identify limiting reactant

↓ Determine moles of products

Check units of products

➡ **1** **List the species present in the combined solution** *before any reaction occurs,* **and decide what reaction will occur.**

➡ **2** **Write the balanced net ionic equation for this reaction.**

➡ **3** **Calculate the moles of reactants. For reactions in solution, use the volumes of the original solutions and their molarities.**

➡ **4** **Determine the limiting reactant where appropriate.**

➡ **5** **Calculate the moles of the required reactant or product.**

➡ **6** **Convert to grams or volume (of solution), as required.**

An acid–base reaction is often called a **neutralization reaction.** When just enough base is added to react exactly with the acid in a solution, we say the acid has been *neutralized.*

Sample Exercise 4.12 | **Neutralization Reactions I**

What volume of a 0.100 *M* HCl solution is needed to neutralize 25.0 mL of 0.350 *M* NaOH?

Solution

➡ **1** *List the species present in the combined solution before any reaction occurs, and decide what reaction will occur.* The species present in the mixed solutions before any reaction occurs are

$$\underbrace{\text{H}^+ \quad \text{Cl}^-}_{\text{From HCl}(aq)} \qquad \underbrace{\text{Na}^+ \quad \text{OH}^-}_{\text{From NaOH}(aq)}$$

What reaction will occur? The two possibilities are

$$\text{Na}^+(aq) + \text{Cl}^-(aq) \longrightarrow \text{NaCl}(s)$$
$$\text{H}^+(aq) + \text{OH}^-(aq) \longrightarrow \text{H}_2\text{O}(l)$$

Since we know that NaCl is soluble, the first reaction does not take place (Na$^+$ and Cl$^-$ are spectator ions). However, as we have seen before, the reaction of the H$^+$ and OH$^-$ ions to form H$_2$O does occur.

➡ **2** *Write the balanced net ionic equation.* The balanced net ionic equation for this reaction is

$$\text{H}^+(aq) + \text{OH}^-(aq) \longrightarrow \text{H}_2\text{O}(l)$$

➡ **3** *Calculate the moles of reactants.* The number of moles of OH$^-$ ions in the 25.0-mL sample of 0.350 *M* NaOH is

$$25.0 \text{ mL NaOH} \times \frac{1 \text{ L}}{1000 \text{ mL}} \times \frac{0.350 \text{ mol OH}^-}{\text{L NaOH}} = 8.75 \times 10^{-3} \text{ mol OH}^-$$

➡ **4** *Determine the limiting reactant.* This problem requires the addition of just enough H$^+$ ions to react exactly with the OH$^-$ ions present. Thus we need not be concerned with determining a limiting reactant.

➡ **5** *Calculate the moles of reactant needed.* Since H$^+$ and OH$^-$ ions react in a 1:1 ratio, 8.75×10^{-3} mol H$^+$ ions is required to neutralize the OH$^-$ ions present.

➡ **6** *Convert to volume required.* The volume *V* of 0.100 *M* HCl required to furnish 8.75×10^{-3} mol H$^+$ ions can be calculated as follows:

$$V \times \frac{0.100 \text{ mol H}^+}{\text{L}} = 8.75 \times 10^{-3} \text{ mol H}^+$$

Solving for *V* gives

$$V = \frac{8.75 \times 10^{-3} \text{ mol H}^+}{\dfrac{0.100 \text{ mol H}^+}{\text{L}}} = 8.75 \times 10^{-2} \text{ L}$$

H$^+$ Cl$^-$
Na$^+$ OH$^-$

Write the reaction

H$^+$(aq) + OH$^-$(aq) $\longrightarrow$ H$_2$O(l)

Moles OH$^-$ $\longrightarrow$ 8.75 × 10^{-3}

No limiting reactant

Moles H$^+$ $\longrightarrow$ 8.75 × 10^{-3}

Volume needed

Convert to volume

87.5 mL of 0.100 *M* HCl needed

Thus 8.75×10^{-2} L (87.5 mL) of 0.100 M HCl is required to neutralize 25.0 mL of 0.350 M NaOH.

See Exercises 4.59 and 4.60.

| **Sample Exercise 4.13** | ## Neutralization Reactions II |

In a certain experiment, 28.0 mL of 0.250 M HNO$_3$ and 53.0 mL of 0.320 M KOH are mixed. Calculate the amount of water formed in the resulting reaction. What is the concentration of H$^+$ or OH$^-$ ions in excess after the reaction goes to completion?

Solution

The species available for reaction are

$$\underbrace{H^+ \quad NO_3^-}_{\substack{\text{From HNO}_3 \\ \text{solution}}} \qquad \underbrace{K^+ \quad OH^-}_{\substack{\text{From KOH} \\ \text{solution}}}$$

Since KNO$_3$ is soluble, K$^+$ and NO$_3^-$ are spectator ions, so the net ionic equation is

$$H^+(aq) + OH^-(aq) \longrightarrow H_2O(l)$$

We next compute the amounts of H$^+$ and OH$^-$ ions present:

$$28.0 \text{ mL HNO}_3 \times \frac{1 \text{ L}}{1000 \text{ mL}} \times \frac{0.250 \text{ mol H}^+}{\text{L HNO}_3} = 7.00 \times 10^{-3} \text{ mol H}^+$$

$$53.0 \text{ mL KOH} \times \frac{1 \text{ L}}{1000 \text{ mL}} \times \frac{0.320 \text{ mol OH}^-}{\text{L KOH}} = 1.70 \times 10^{-2} \text{ mol OH}^-$$

Since H$^+$ and OH$^-$ react in a 1:1 ratio, the limiting reactant is H$^+$. This means that 7.00×10^{-3} mol H$^+$ ions will react with 7.00×10^{-3} mol OH$^-$ ions to form 7.00×10^{-3} mol H$_2$O.

The amount of OH$^-$ ions in excess is obtained from the following difference:

$$\text{Original amount} - \text{amount consumed} = \text{amount in excess}$$

$$1.70 \times 10^{-2} \text{ mol OH}^- - 7.00 \times 10^{-3} \text{ mol OH}^- = 1.00 \times 10^{-2} \text{ mol OH}^-$$

The volume of the combined solution is the sum of the individual volumes:

$$\text{Original volume of HNO}_3 + \text{original volume of KOH} = \text{total volume}$$

$$28.0 \text{ mL} + 53.0 \text{ mL} = 81.0 \text{ mL} = 8.10 \times 10^{-2} \text{ L}$$

Thus the molarity of OH$^-$ ions in excess is

$$\frac{\text{mol OH}^-}{\text{L solution}} = \frac{1.00 \times 10^{-2} \text{ mol OH}^-}{8.10 \times 10^{-2} \text{ L}} = 0.123 \text{ M OH}^-$$

See Exercises 4.61 and 4.62.

Acid–Base Titrations

Volumetric analysis is a technique for determining the amount of a certain substance by doing a titration. A **titration** involves delivery (from a buret) of a measured volume of a solution of known concentration (the *titrant*) into a solution containing the substance being analyzed (the *analyte*). The titrant contains a substance that reacts in a known manner with the analyte. The point in the titration where enough titrant has been added to react exactly with the analyte is called the **equivalence point** or the **stoichiometric point.** This point is often marked by an **indicator,** a substance added at the beginning of the titration that changes color at (or very near) the equivalence point. The point where the indicator

Visualization: Neutralization of a Strong Acid by a Strong Base

Ideally, the endpoint and stoichiometric point should coincide.

actually changes color is called the **endpoint** of the titration. The goal is to choose an indicator such that the endpoint (where the indicator changes color) occurs exactly at the equivalence point (where just enough titrant has been added to react with all the analyte).

The following three requirements must be met for a titration to be successful:

1. The exact reaction between titrant and analyte must be known (and rapid).

2. The stoichiometric (equivalence) point must be marked accurately.

3. The volume of titrant required to reach the stoichiometric point must be known accurately.

When the analyte is a base or an acid, the required titrant is a strong acid or strong base, respectively. This procedure is called an *acid–base titration.* An indicator very commonly used for acid–base titrations is phenolphthalein, which is colorless in an acidic solution and pink in a basic solution. Thus, when an acid is titrated with a base, the phenolphthalein remains colorless until after the acid is consumed and the first drop of excess base is added. In this case, the endpoint (the solution changes from colorless to pink) occurs approximately one drop of base beyond the stoichiometric point. This type of titration is illustrated in the three photos in Fig. 4.18.

We will deal with the acid–base titrations only briefly here but will return to the topic of titrations and indicators in more detail in Chapter 15. The titration of an acid with a standard solution containing hydroxide ions is described in Sample Exercise 4.15. In Sample Exercise 4.14 we show how to determine accurately the concentration of a sodium hydroxide solution. This procedure is called *standardizing the solution.*

FIGURE 4.18
The titration of an acid with a base. (a) The titrant (the base) is in the buret, and the flask contains the acid solution along with a small amount of indicator. (b) As base is added drop by drop to the acid solution in the flask during the titration, the indicator changes color, but the color disappears on mixing. (c) The stoichiometric (equivalence) point is marked by a permanent indicator color change. The volume of base added is the difference between the final and initial buret readings.

Sample Exercise 4.14

Neutralization Titration

K$^+$ HC$_8$H$_4$O$_4$$^-$

A student carries out an experiment to standardize (determine the exact concentration of) a sodium hydroxide solution. To do this, the student weighs out a 1.3009-g sample of potassium hydrogen phthalate (KHC$_8$H$_4$O$_4$, often abbreviated KHP). KHP (molar mass 204.22 g/mol) has one acidic hydrogen. The student dissolves the KHP in distilled water, adds phenolphthalein as an indicator, and titrates the resulting solution with the sodium hydroxide solution to the phenolphthalein endpoint. The difference between the final and initial buret readings indicates that 41.20 mL of the sodium hydroxide solution is required to react exactly with the 1.3009 g KHP. Calculate the concentration of the sodium hydroxide solution.

Solution

Aqueous sodium hydroxide contains the Na$^+$ and OH$^-$ ions, and KHC$_8$H$_4$O$_4$ dissolves in water to give the K$^+$ and HC$_8$H$_4$O$_4$$^-$ ions. As the titration proceeds, the mixed solution contains the following ions: K$^+$, HC$_8$H$_4$O$_4$$^-$, Na$^+$, and OH$^-$. The OH$^-$ will remove an H$^+$ from the HC$_8$H$_4$O$_4$$^-$ to give the following net ionic reaction:

$$HC_8H_4O_4{}^-(aq) + OH^-(aq) \longrightarrow H_2O(l) + C_8H_4O_4{}^{2-}(aq)$$

Since the reaction exhibits 1:1 stoichiometry, we know that 41.20 mL of the sodium hydroxide solution must contain exactly the same number of moles of OH$^-$ as there are moles of HC$_8$H$_4$O$_4$$^-$ in 1.3009 g KHC$_8$H$_4$O$_4$.

We calculate the moles of KHC$_8$H$_4$O$_4$ in the usual way:

$$1.3009 \text{ g } \cancel{KHC_8H_4O_4} \times \frac{1 \text{ mol KHC}_8\text{H}_4\text{O}_4}{204.22 \text{ g } \cancel{KHC_8H_4O_4}} = 6.3701 \times 10^{-3} \text{ mol KHC}_8\text{H}_4\text{O}_4$$

This means that 6.3701×10^{-3} mol OH$^-$ must be added to react with the 6.3701×10^{-3} mol HC$_8$H$_4$O$_4$$^-$. Thus 41.20 mL ($4.120 \times 10^{-2}$ L) of the sodium hydroxide solution must contain 6.3701×10^{-3} mol OH$^-$ (and Na$^+$), and the concentration of the sodium hydroxide solution is

$$\text{Molarity of NaOH} = \frac{\text{mol NaOH}}{\text{L solution}} = \frac{6.3701 \times 10^{-3} \text{ mol NaOH}}{4.120 \times 10^{-2} \text{ L}}$$

$$= 0.1546 \text{ } M$$

This standard sodium hydroxide solution can now be used in other experiments (see Sample Exercise 4.15).

See Exercises 4.63 and 4.66.

Sample Exercise 4.15

Neutralization Analysis

An environmental chemist analyzed the effluent (the released waste material) from an industrial process known to produce the compounds carbon tetrachloride (CCl$_4$) and benzoic acid (HC$_7$H$_5$O$_2$), a weak acid that has one acidic hydrogen atom per molecule. A sample of this effluent weighing 0.3518 g was shaken with water, and the resulting aqueous solution required 10.59 mL of 0.1546 M NaOH for neutralization. Calculate the mass percent of HC$_7$H$_5$O$_2$ in the original sample.

Solution

In this case, the sample was a mixture containing CCl$_4$ and HC$_7$H$_5$O$_2$, and it was titrated with OH$^-$ ions. Clearly, CCl$_4$ is not an acid (it contains no hydrogen atoms), so we can assume it does not react with OH$^-$ ions. However, HC$_7$H$_5$O$_2$ is an acid that donates one H$^+$ ion per molecule to react with an OH$^-$ ion as follows:

$$HC_7H_5O_2(aq) + OH^-(aq) \longrightarrow H_2O(l) + C_7H_5O_2{}^-(aq)$$

Although $HC_7H_5O_2$ is a weak acid, the OH^- ion is such a strong base that we can assume that each OH^- ion added will react with a $HC_7H_5O_2$ molecule until all the benzoic acid is consumed.

We must first determine the number of moles of OH^- ions required to react with all the $HC_7H_5O_2$:

$$10.59 \text{ mL NaOH} \times \frac{1 \text{ L}}{1000 \text{ mL}} \times \frac{0.1546 \text{ mol OH}^-}{\text{L NaOH}} = 1.637 \times 10^{-3} \text{ mol OH}^-$$

This number is also the number of moles of $HC_7H_5O_2$ present. The number of grams of the acid is calculated using its molar mass (122.12 g/mol):

$$1.637 \times 10^{-3} \text{ mol HC}_7\text{H}_5\text{O}_2 \times \frac{122.12 \text{ g HC}_7\text{H}_5\text{O}_2}{1 \text{ mol HC}_7\text{H}_5\text{O}_2} = 0.1999 \text{ g HC}_7\text{H}_5\text{O}_2$$

The mass percent of $HC_7H_5O_2$ in the original sample is

$$\frac{0.1999 \text{ g}}{0.3518 \text{ g}} \times 100 = 56.82\%$$

See Exercise 4.65.

The first step in the analysis of a complex solution is to write down the components and focus on the chemistry of each one. When a strong electrolyte is present, write it as separated ions.

In doing problems involving titrations, you must first decide what reaction is occurring. Sometimes this seems difficult because the titration solution contains several components. *The key to success is to first write down all the components in the solution and focus on the chemistry of each one.* We have been emphasizing this approach in dealing with the reactions between ions in solution. Make it a habit to write down the components of solutions before trying to decide what reaction(s) might take place as you attempt the end-of-chapter problems involving titrations.

4.9 Oxidation–Reduction Reactions

We have seen that many important substances are ionic. Sodium chloride, for example, can be formed by the reaction of elemental sodium and chlorine:

$$2Na(s) + Cl_2(g) \longrightarrow 2NaCl(s)$$

In this reaction, solid sodium, which contains neutral sodium atoms, reacts with chlorine gas, which contains diatomic Cl_2 molecules, to form the ionic solid NaCl, which contains Na^+ and Cl^- ions. This process is represented in Fig. 4.19. *Reactions like this one, in which one or more electrons are transferred, are called* **oxidation–reduction reactions** *or* **redox reactions.**

Many important chemical reactions involve oxidation and reduction. Photosynthesis, which stores energy from the sun in plants by converting carbon dioxide and water to sugar, is a very important oxidation–reduction reaction. In fact, most reactions used for energy production are redox reactions. In humans, the oxidation of sugars, fats, and proteins provides the energy necessary for life. Combustion reactions, which provide most of the energy to power our civilization, also involve oxidation and reduction. An example is the reaction of methane with oxygen:

$$CH_4(g) + 2O_2(g) \longrightarrow CO_2(g) + 2H_2O(g) + \text{energy}$$

Even though none of the reactants or products in this reaction is ionic, the reaction is still assumed to involve a transfer of electrons from carbon to oxygen. To explain this, we must introduce the concept of oxidation states.

Visualization: Zinc and Iodine

Visualization: Barking Dogs: Reaction of Phosphorus

Visualization: Dry Ice and Magnesium

Visualization: Sugar and Potassium Chlorate

FIGURE 4.19
The reaction of solid sodium and gaseous chlorine to form solid sodium chloride.

2Na(s)
Sodium

+

Cl₂(g)
Chlorine

2NaCl(s)
Sodium chloride

Oxidation States

The concept of **oxidation states** (also called *oxidation numbers*) provides a way to keep track of electrons in oxidation–reduction reactions, particularly redox reactions involving covalent substances. Recall that electrons are shared by atoms in covalent bonds. The oxidation states of atoms in covalent compounds are obtained by arbitrarily assigning the electrons (which are actually shared) to particular atoms. We do this as follows: For a covalent bond between two identical atoms, the electrons are split equally between the two. In cases where two different atoms are involved (and the electrons are thus shared unequally), the shared electrons are assigned completely to the atom that has the stronger attraction for electrons. For example, recall from the discussion of the water molecule in Section 4.1 that oxygen has a greater attraction for electrons than does hydrogen. Therefore, in assigning the oxidation state of oxygen and hydrogen in H_2O, we assume that the oxygen atom actually possesses all the electrons. Recall that a hydrogen atom has one electron. Thus, in water, oxygen has formally "taken" the electrons from two hydrogen atoms. This gives the oxygen an *excess* of two electrons (its oxidation state is -2) and leaves each hydrogen with no electrons (the oxidation state of each hydrogen is thus $+1$).

We define the *oxidation states* (or *oxidation numbers*) of the atoms in a covalent compound as the imaginary charges the atoms would have if the shared electrons were divided equally between identical atoms bonded to each other or, for different atoms, were all assigned to the atom in each bond that has the greater attraction for electrons. Of course,

CHEMICAL IMPACT

Iron Zeroes in on Pollution

Treating groundwater contaminated with pollutants is typically very complicated and very expensive. However, chemists have discovered a low-tech, economical method for treating the contaminated groundwater near a former semiconductor manufacturing plant in Sunnyvale, California. They have replaced the elaborate decontamination machinery used at the site for more than a decade with 220 tons of iron filings buried in a giant trough. Because there are no pumps to maintain and no electricity to purchase, this simple system will save approximately $300,000 per year. The property, which was thought to be unusable for the 30-year lifetime of the old clean-up process because of the need for constant monitoring and access, can now be used immediately.

A schematic of the iron treatment method is shown in the accompanying figure. At Sunnyvale, the iron barrier is 40 feet long, 4 feet wide, and 20 feet deep. In the 4 days it takes for contaminated water to seep through the wall of iron,

the chlorinated organic contaminants are degraded into products that are then themselves decomposed to simpler substances. According to engineers on the site, the polluted water that seeps through the wall meets Environmental Protection Agency (EPA) standards when it emerges on the other side.

How does iron metal clean up contaminated groundwater? It's a result of the ability of iron metal (oxidation state = 0) to act as a reducing agent toward the chlorine-containing organic pollutant molecules. The reaction can be represented as follows:

$$Fe(s) + RCl(aq) + H^+(aq) \longrightarrow$$
$$Fe^{2+}(aq) + RH(aq) + Cl^-(aq)$$

where RCl represents a chlorinated organic molecule. The reaction appears to involve a direct reaction between the metal and an RCl molecule adsorbed on the metal surface.

for ionic compounds containing monatomic ions, the oxidation states of the ions are equal to the ion charges.

These considerations lead to a series of rules for assigning oxidation states that are summarized in Table 4.2. Application of these simple rules allows the assignment of oxidation states in most compounds. To apply these rules recognize that *the sum of the oxidation states must be zero for an electrically neutral compound*. For an ion, the sum of the oxidation states must equal the charge of the ion. The principles are illustrated by Sample Exercise 4.16.

Oxidation of copper metal by nitric acid. The copper atoms lose two electrons to form Cu^{2+} ions, which give a deep green color that becomes turquoise when diluted with water.

TABLE 4.2 Rules for Assigning Oxidation States

The Oxidation State of . . .	Summary	Examples
• An atom in an element is zero	Element: 0	$Na(s)$, $O_2(g)$, $O_3(g)$, $Hg(l)$
• A monatomic ion is the same as its charge	Monatomic ion: charge of ion	Na^+, Cl^-
• Fluorine is −1 in its compounds	Fluorine: −1	HF, PF_3
• Oxygen is usually −2 in its compounds Exception: peroxides (containing O_2^{2-}) in which oxygen is −1	Oxygen: −2	H_2O, CO_2
• Hydrogen is +1 in its covalent compounds	Hydrogen: +1	H_2O, HCl, NH_3

In addition to decomposing chlorinated organic contaminants, iron appears to be useful against other pollutants as well. Iron can degrade dye wastes from textile mills and can reduce soluble Cr(VI) compounds to insoluble Cr(III) products, which are much less harmful. Iron's reducing abilities also appear useful in removing radioactive technetium, a common pollutant at nuclear processing facilities. Iron also appears to be effective for removing nitrates from the soil.

Other metals, such as zinc, tin, and palladium, have shown promise for use in groundwater clean-up, too. These metals generally react more quickly than iron but are more expensive and pose their own environmental hazards.

Inexpensive and environmentally benign, iron seems to be the metal of choice for most groundwater clean-up. It's cheap, it's effective, it's almost a miracle!

Reproduced with permission from *Chemical & Engineering News,* July 3, 1995, 73(27), p. 20. Copyright © 1995 American Chemical Society.

It is worthwhile to note at this point that the convention is to write actual charges on ions as $n+$ or $n-$, the number being written *before* the plus or minus sign. On the other hand, oxidation states (not actual charges) are written $+n$ or $-n$, the number being written *after* the plus or minus sign.

Sample Exercise 4.16

Assigning Oxidation States

Assign oxidation states to all atoms in the following.

a. CO_2
b. SF_6
c. NO_3^-

Solution

a. Since we have a specific rule for the oxidation state of oxygen, we will assign its value first. The oxidation state of oxygen is -2. The oxidation state of the carbon atom can be determined by recognizing that since CO_2 has no charge, the sum of the oxidation states for oxygen and carbon must be zero. Since each oxygen is -2 and there are two oxygen atoms, the carbon atom must be assigned an oxidation state of $+4$:

$$CO_2$$

$+4 \qquad -2$ for each oxygen

We can check the assigned oxidation states by noting that when the number of atoms is taken into account, the sum is zero as required:

$$1(+4) + 2(-2) = 0$$

No. of C atoms   No. of O atoms

b. Since we have no rule for sulfur, we first assign the oxidation state of each fluorine as −1. The sulfur must then be assigned an oxidation state of +6 to balance the total of −6 from the fluorine atoms:

$$SF_6$$

+6   −1 for each fluorine

Reality Check: +6 + 6(−1) = 0

c. Oxygen has an oxidation state of −2. Because the sum of the oxidation states of the three oxygens is −6 and the net charge on the NO_3^- ion is 1−, the nitrogen must have an oxidation state of +5:

$$NO_3^-$$

+5   −2 for each oxygen

Reality Check: +5 + 3(−2) = −1

Note that in this case the sum must be −1 (the overall charge on the ion).

See Exercises 4.67 through 4.70.

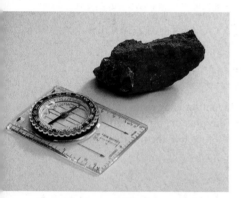

Magnetite is a magnetic ore containing Fe_3O_4. Note that the compass needle points toward the ore.

We need to make one more point about oxidation states, and this can be illustrated by the compound Fe_3O_4, which is the main component in magnetite, an iron ore that accounts for the reddish color of many types of rocks and soils. To determine the oxidation states in Fe_3O_4, we first assign each oxygen atom its usual oxidation state of −2. The three iron atoms must yield a total of +8 to balance the total of −8 from the four oxygens. This means that each iron atom has an oxidation state of $+\frac{8}{3}$. A noninteger value for the oxidation state may seem strange because charge is expressed in whole numbers. However, although they are rare, noninteger oxidation states do occur because of the rather arbitrary way that electrons are divided up by the rules in Table 4.2. For Fe_3O_4, for example, the rules assume that all the iron atoms are equal, when in fact this compound can best be viewed as containing four O^{2-} ions, two Fe^{3+} ions, and one Fe^{2+} ion per formula unit. (Note that the "average" charge on iron works out to be $\frac{8}{3}+$, which is equal to the oxidation state we determined above.) Noninteger oxidation states should not intimidate you. They are used in the same way as integer oxidation states—for keeping track of electrons.

The Characteristics of Oxidation–Reduction Reactions

Oxidation–reduction reactions are characterized by a transfer of electrons. In some cases, the transfer occurs in a literal sense to form ions, such as in the reaction

$$2Na(s) + Cl_2(g) \longrightarrow 2NaCl(s)$$

However, sometimes the transfer is less obvious. For example, consider the combustion of methane (the oxidation state for each atom is given):

$$CH_4(g) + 2O_2(g) \longrightarrow CO_2(g) + 2H_2O(g)$$

Oxidation
state   −4   +1   0   +4   −2   +1   −2
              (each H)   (each O)(each H)

Note that the oxidation state for oxygen in O_2 is 0 because it is in elemental form. In this reaction there are no ionic compounds, but we can still describe the process in terms of a transfer of electrons. Note that carbon undergoes a change in oxidation state from −4 in CH_4 to +4 in CO_2. Such a change can be accounted for by a loss of eight electrons (the symbol e^- stands for an electron);

$$CH_4 \longrightarrow CO_2 + 8e^-$$

−4   +4

CHEMICAL IMPACT

Pearly Whites

People have long been concerned about the "whiteness" of their teeth. In the Middle Ages the local barber-surgeon would whiten teeth using nitric acid—a procedure fraught with dangers, including the fact that nitric acid dissolves tooth enamel, which in turn leads to massive tooth decay. Today many safer procedures are available for keeping teeth sparkling white.

The outer layer of teeth, the enamel, consists of the mineral hydroxyapatite, which contains calcium phosphate. Underneath the enamel is dentin, an off-white mixture of calcium phosphate and collagen that protects the nerves and blood vessels at the center of the tooth.

The discoloration of teeth is usually due to colored molecules in our diet from sources such as blueberries, red wine, and coffee. The tar from cigarettes also stains teeth. Aging is another factor. As we get older, chemical changes occur that cause the dentin to become more yellow.

The stains produced when colored molecules are adsorbed to the surfaces of teeth can be removed by brushing. Toothpastes contain abrasives such as tiny particles of silica,

aluminum oxide, calcium carbonate, or calcium phosphate to help scrub off adsorbed stains.

Stains due to molecules lying below the surface are usually attacked with an oxidizing agent, hydrogen peroxide (H_2O_2). As H_2O_2 breaks down into water and oxygen, intermediates are produced that react with and decompose the molecules that produce teeth discoloration.

Off-the-shelf teeth whiteners typically contain carbamide peroxide (a 1:1 mixture of urea and hydrogen peroxide), glycerin, stannate and pyrophosphate salts (preservatives), and flavoring agents. These whiteners come in a form that can be brushed directly onto the teeth or are embedded in a plastic strip that can be stuck to the teeth. Because these products have a low strength for safety reasons, it may take several weeks of applying them for full whitening to occur.

Whitening treatments by dentists often involve the application of substances containing more than 30% hydrogen peroxide. These substances must be used with the appropriate protection of the tissues surrounding the teeth. Keeping your teeth white is another example of chemistry in action.

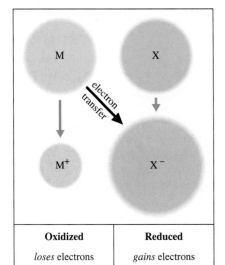

Oxidized	Reduced
loses electrons	*gains* electrons
oxidation state *increases*	oxidation state *decreases*
reducing agent	*oxidizing* agent

FIGURE 4.20
A summary of an oxidation–reduction process, in which M is oxidized and X is reduced.

On the other hand, each oxygen changes from an oxidation state of 0 in O_2 to -2 in H_2O and CO_2, signifying a gain of two electrons per atom. Since four oxygen atoms are involved, this is a gain of eight electrons:

$$2O_2 + 8e^- \longrightarrow CO_2 + 2H_2O$$
$$\quad\;\; 0 \qquad\qquad\qquad 4(-2) = -8$$

No change occurs in the oxidation state of hydrogen, and it is not formally involved in the electron-transfer process.

With this background, we can now define some important terms. **Oxidation** is an *increase* in oxidation state (a loss of electrons). **Reduction** is a *decrease* in oxidation state (a gain of electrons). Thus in the reaction

$$2Na(s) + Cl_2(g) \longrightarrow 2NaCl(s)$$
$$\quad\; 0 \qquad\; 0 \qquad\qquad +1 \;\; -1$$

sodium is oxidized and chlorine is reduced. In addition, Cl_2 is called the **oxidizing agent (electron acceptor),** and Na is called the **reducing agent (electron donor).** These terms are summarized in Fig. 4.20.

Concerning the reaction

$$CH_4(g) + 2O_2(g) \longrightarrow CO_2(g) + 2H_2O(g)$$
$$-4 \;\; +1 \qquad\quad 0 \qquad\qquad +4 \;\; -2 \qquad\; +1 \;\; -2$$

CHEMICAL IMPACT

Aging: Does It Involve Oxidation?

Although aging is supposed to bring wisdom, almost no one wants to get old. Along with wisdom, aging brings wrinkles, loss of physical strength, and greater susceptibility to disease.

Why do we age? No one knows for certain, but many scientists think that oxidation plays a major role. The oxygen molecule and other oxidizing agents in the body apparently can extract single electrons from the large molecules that make up cell membranes, thus making them very reactive. Subsequently, these activated molecules can link up, changing the properties of the cell membrane. At some point, enough of these reactions have occurred that the body's immune system comes to view the changed cell as an "enemy" and destroys it. This is particularly detrimental to the organism when the cells involved are irreplaceable. Nerve

cells, for example, fall into this category. They rarely regenerate in an adult.

The body has defenses against oxidation, such as vitamin E, a well-known antioxidant. Studies have shown that red blood cells age much faster than normal when they are deficient in vitamin E. Based on studies such as these, some have suggested large doses of vitamin E as a preventive measure against aging, but there is no solid evidence that this practice has any impact on aging.

Another protective antioxidant found in our bodies is superoxide dismutase (SOD), which protects us from the superoxide ion O_2^-, a powerful oxidizing agent that is particularly damaging to vital enzymes. The importance of SOD in opposing the aging process is indicated from the results of a study by Dr. Richard Cutler at the Gerontology Research

---

Oxidation is an increase in oxidation state. *Reduction* is a decrease in oxidation state.

A helpful mnemonic device is OIL RIG (**O**xidation **I**nvolves **L**oss; **R**eduction **I**nvolves **G**ain). Another common mnemonic is LEO says GER. (**L**oss of **E**lectrons, **O**xidation; **G**ain of **E**lectrons, **R**eduction).

An oxidizing agent is reduced and a reducing agent is oxidized in a redox reaction.

we can say the following:

Carbon is oxidized because there has been an increase in its oxidation state (carbon has formally lost electrons).

Oxygen is reduced because there has been a decrease in its oxidation state (oxygen has formally gained electrons).

CH_4 is the reducing agent.

O_2 is the oxidizing agent.

Note that when the oxidizing or reducing agent is named, the *whole compound* is specified, not just the element that undergoes the change in oxidation state.

| Sample Exercise 4.17 | **Oxidation–Reduction Reactions I** |

When powdered aluminum metal is mixed with pulverized iodine crystals and a drop of water is added to help the reaction get started, the resulting reaction produces a great deal of energy. The mixture bursts into flames, and a purple smoke of I_2 vapor is produced from the excess iodine. The equation for the reaction is

$$2Al(s) + 3I_2(s) \longrightarrow 2AlI_3(s)$$

For this reaction, identify the atoms that are oxidized and reduced, and specify the oxidizing and reducing agents.

Solution

The first step is to assign oxidation states:

$$2Al(s) + 3I_2(s) \longrightarrow 2AlI_3(s)$$

Finely ground aluminum and iodine are mixed and react vigorously to form aluminum iodide after a drop of water is added. The purple cloud is excess iodine vaporized by the heat of the reaction.

Center of the National Institutes of Health in Baltimore that showed a strong correlation between the life spans of a dozen mammalian species and their levels of SOD. Human SOD is now being produced by the techniques of biotechnology in amounts that will enable scientists to carefully study its effects on aging and on various diseases such as rheumatoid arthritis and muscular dystrophy. Although SOD is available in health food stores in forms to be taken orally, this practice is useless because the SOD is digested (broken down into simpler substances) before it can reach the bloodstream.

Research does indicate that consuming certain foods may retard the aging process. For example, a recent study of 8000 male Harvard graduates found that chocolate and candy eaters live almost a year longer than those who abstain. Although the researchers from Harvard School of Public Health are not certain of the mechanism for this effect, they suggest that the antioxidants present in chocolate may provide the health benefits. For example, chocolate contains phenols,

antioxidants that are also present in wine, another substance that seems to promote good health if used in moderation.

Oxidation is only one possible cause for aging. Research continues on many fronts to try to discover why we get "older" as time passes.

Can eating chocolate slow down the aging process?

Since each aluminum atom changes its oxidation state from 0 to +3 (an increase in oxidation state), aluminum is *oxidized.* On the other hand, the oxidation state of each iodine atom decreases from 0 to −1, and iodine is *reduced.* Since Al furnishes electrons for the reduction of iodine, it is the *reducing agent;* I_2 is the *oxidizing agent.*

See Exercises 4.71 and 4.72.

Sample Exercise 4.18 | ## Oxidation–Reduction Reactions II

Metallurgy, the process of producing a metal from its ore, always involves oxidation–reduction reactions. In the metallurgy of galena (PbS), the principal lead-containing ore, the first step is the conversion of lead sulfide to its oxide (a process called *roasting*):

$$2PbS(s) + 3O_2(g) \longrightarrow 2PbO(s) + 2SO_2(g)$$

The oxide is then treated with carbon monoxide to produce the free metal:

$$PbO(s) + CO(g) \longrightarrow Pb(s) + CO_2(g)$$

For each reaction, identify the atoms that are oxidized and reduced, and specify the oxidizing and reducing agents.

Solution

For the first reaction, we can assign the following oxidation states:

$$2PbS(s) + 3O_2(g) \longrightarrow 2PbO(s) + 2SO_2(g)$$
$$\text{+2} \quad \text{−2} \qquad 0 \qquad \text{+2} \quad \text{−2} \qquad \text{+4} \quad \text{−2 (each O)}$$

The oxidation state for the sulfur atom increases from −2 to +4. Thus sulfur is oxidized. The oxidation state for each oxygen atom decreases from 0 to −2. Oxygen is reduced. The oxidizing agent (that accepts the electrons) is O_2, and the reducing agent (that donates electrons) is PbS.

For the second reaction we have

$$PbO(s) + CO(g) \longrightarrow Pb(s) + CO_2(g)$$

$$\begin{matrix} +2 & -2 & +2 & -2 & & 0 & & +4 & -2 \text{ (each O)} \end{matrix}$$

Lead is reduced (its oxidation state decreases from +2 to 0), and carbon is oxidized (its oxidation state increases from +2 to +4). PbO is the oxidizing agent, and CO is the reducing agent.

See Exercises 4.71 and 4.72.

4.10 Balancing Oxidation–Reduction Equations

Oxidation–reduction reactions in aqueous solutions are often complicated, which means that it can be difficult to balance their equations by simple inspection. In this section we will discuss a special technique for balancing the equations of redox reactions that occur in aqueous solutions. It is called the *half-reaction method*.

The Half-Reaction Method for Balancing Oxidation–Reduction Reactions in Aqueous Solutions

For oxidation–reduction reactions that occur in aqueous solution, it is useful to separate the reaction into two **half-reactions:** one involving oxidation and the other involving reduction. For example, consider the unbalanced equation for the oxidation–reduction reaction between cerium(IV) ion and tin(II) ion:

$$Ce^{4+}(aq) + Sn^{2+}(aq) \longrightarrow Ce^{3+}(aq) + Sn^{4+}(aq)$$

This reaction can be separated into a half-reaction involving the substance being *reduced,*

$$Ce^{4+}(aq) \longrightarrow Ce^{3+}(aq)$$

and one involving the substance being *oxidized,*

$$Sn^{2+}(aq) \longrightarrow Sn^{4+}(aq)$$

The general procedure is to balance the equations for the half-reactions separately and then to add them to obtain the overall balanced equation. The half-reaction method for balancing oxidation–reduction equations differs slightly depending on whether the reaction takes place in acidic or basic solution.

The Half-Reaction Method for Balancing Equations for Oxidation–Reduction Reactions Occurring in Acidic Solution

➡ **1 Write separate equations for the oxidation and reduction half-reactions.**

➡ **2 For each half-reaction,**
   a. Balance all the elements except hydrogen and oxygen.
   b. Balance oxygen using H_2O.

c. Balance hydrogen using H^+.
d. Balance the charge using electrons.

➡ **3 If necessary, multiply one or both balanced half-reactions by an integer to equalize the number of electrons transferred in the two half-reactions.**

➡ **4 Add the half-reactions, and cancel identical species.**

➡ **5 Check that the elements and charges are balanced.**

These steps are summarized by the following flowchart:

We will illustrate this method by balancing the equation for the reaction between permanganate and iron(II) ions in acidic solution:

$$MnO_4^-(aq) + Fe^{2+}(aq) \xrightarrow{\text{Acid}} Fe^{3+}(aq) + Mn^{2+}(aq)$$

This reaction can be used to analyze iron ore for its iron content.

➡ **1** *Identify and write equations for the half-reactions.* The oxidation states for the half-reaction involving the permanganate ion show that manganese is reduced:

$$MnO_4^- \longrightarrow Mn^{2+}$$
$$\overset{+7}{} \quad \overset{-2\,\text{(each O)}}{} \quad \overset{+2}{}$$

This is the *reduction half-reaction.* The other half-reaction involves the oxidation of iron(II) to iron(III) ion and is the *oxidation half-reaction:*

$$Fe^{2+} \longrightarrow Fe^{3+}$$
$$\overset{+2}{} \qquad \overset{+3}{}$$

➡ **2** *Balance each half-reaction.* For the reduction reaction, we have

$$MnO_4^-(aq) \longrightarrow Mn^{2+}(aq)$$

a. The manganese is balanced.
b. We balance oxygen by adding $4H_2O$ to the right side of the equation:

$$MnO_4^-(aq) \longrightarrow Mn^{2+}(aq) + 4H_2O(l)$$

c. Next, we balance hydrogen by adding $8H^+$ to the left side:

$$8H^+(aq) + MnO_4^-(aq) \longrightarrow Mn^{2+}(aq) + 4H_2O(l)$$

d. All the elements have been balanced, but we need to balance the charge using electrons. At this point we have the following overall charges for reactants and products in the reduction half-reaction:

$$\underbrace{8H^+(aq) + MnO_4^-(aq)}_{\underbrace{8+ \quad + \quad 1-}_{7+}} \longrightarrow \underbrace{Mn^{2+}(aq) + 4H_2O(l)}_{\underbrace{2+ \quad + \quad 0}_{2+}}$$

We can equalize the charges by adding five electrons to the left side:

$$\underbrace{5e^- + 8H^+(aq) + MnO_4^-(aq)}_{2+} \longrightarrow \underbrace{Mn^{2+}(aq) + 4H_2O(l)}_{2+}$$

Both the *elements* and the *charges* are now balanced, so this represents the balanced reduction half-reaction. The fact that five electrons appear on the reactant side of the equation makes sense, since five electrons are required to reduce MnO_4^- (Mn has an oxidation state of $+7$) to Mn^{2+} (Mn has an oxidation state of $+2$).

For the oxidation reaction

$$Fe^{2+}(aq) \longrightarrow Fe^{3+}(aq)$$

the elements are balanced, and we must simply balance the charge:

$$\underbrace{Fe^{2+}(aq)}_{2+} \longrightarrow \underbrace{Fe^{3+}(aq)}_{3+}$$

One electron is needed on the right side to give a net $2+$ charge on both sides:

$$\underbrace{Fe^{2+}(aq)}_{2+} \longrightarrow \underbrace{Fe^{3+}(aq) + e^-}_{2+}$$

The number of electrons gained in the reduction half-reaction must equal the number of electrons lost in the oxidation half-reaction.

➡ **3** *Equalize the electron transfer in the two half-reactions.* Since the reduction half-reaction involves a transfer of five electrons and the oxidation half-reaction involves a transfer of only one electron, the oxidation half-reaction must be multiplied by 5:

$$5Fe^{2+}(aq) \longrightarrow 5Fe^{3+}(aq) + 5e^-$$

➡ **4** *Add the half-reactions.* The half-reactions are added to give

$$5e^- + 5Fe^{2+}(aq) + MnO_4^-(aq) + 8H^+(aq) \longrightarrow$$
$$5Fe^{3+}(aq) + Mn^{2+}(aq) + 4H_2O(l) + 5e^-$$

Note that the electrons cancel (as they must) to give the final balanced equation:

$$5Fe^{2+}(aq) + MnO_4^-(aq) + 8H^+(aq) \longrightarrow 5Fe^{3+}(aq) + Mn^{2+}(aq) + 4H_2O(l)$$

➡ **5** *Check that elements and charges are balanced.*

Elements balance: 5Fe, 1Mn, 4O, 8H $\longrightarrow$ 5Fe, 1Mn, 4O, 8H

Charges balance: $5(2+) + (1-) + 8(1+) = 17+ \longrightarrow$
$$5(3+) + (2+) + 0 = 17+$$

The equation is balanced.

Sample Exercise 4.19	## Balancing Oxidation–Reduction Reactions (Acidic)

Potassium dichromate ($K_2Cr_2O_7$) is a bright orange compound that can be reduced to a blue-violet solution of Cr^{3+} ions. Under certain conditions, $K_2Cr_2O_7$ reacts with ethyl alcohol (C_2H_5OH) as follows:

$$H^+(aq) + Cr_2O_7{}^{2-}(aq) + C_2H_5OH(l) \longrightarrow Cr^{3+}(aq) + CO_2(g) + H_2O(l)$$

Balance this equation using the half-reaction method.

Solution

➡ **1** The reduction half-reaction is

$$Cr_2O_7{}^{2-}(aq) \longrightarrow Cr^{3+}(aq)$$

Chromium is reduced from an oxidation state of $+6$ in $Cr_2O_7{}^{2-}$ to one of $+3$ in Cr^{3+}. The oxidation half-reaction is

$$C_2H_5OH(l) \longrightarrow CO_2(g)$$

Carbon is oxidized from an oxidation state of -2 in C_2H_5OH to $+4$ in CO_2.

➡ **2** Balancing all elements except hydrogen and oxygen in the first half-reaction, we have

$$Cr_2O_7{}^{2-}(aq) \longrightarrow 2Cr^{3+}(aq)$$

Balancing oxygen using H_2O, we have

$$Cr_2O_7{}^{2-}(aq) \longrightarrow 2Cr^{3+}(aq) + 7H_2O(l)$$

Balancing hydrogen using H^+, we have

$$14H^+(aq) + Cr_2O_7{}^{2-}(aq) \longrightarrow 2Cr^{3+}(aq) + 7H_2O(l)$$

Balancing the charge using electrons, we have

$$6e^- + 14H^+(aq) + Cr_2O_7{}^{2-}(aq) \longrightarrow 2Cr^{3+}(aq) + 7H_2O(l)$$

When potassium dichromate reacts with ethanol, a blue-violet solution containing Cr^{3+} is formed.

Next, we turn to the oxidation half-reaction

$$C_2H_5OH(l) \longrightarrow CO_2(g)$$

Balancing carbon, we have

$$C_2H_5OH(l) \longrightarrow 2CO_2(g)$$

Balancing oxygen using H_2O, we have

$$C_2H_5OH(l) + 3H_2O(l) \longrightarrow 2CO_2(g)$$

Balancing hydrogen using H^+, we have

$$C_2H_5OH(l) + 3H_2O(l) \longrightarrow 2CO_2(g) + 12H^+(aq)$$

We then balance the charge by adding $12e^-$ to the right side:

$$C_2H_5OH(l) + 3H_2O(l) \longrightarrow 2CO_2(g) + 12H^+(aq) + 12e^-$$

3 In the reduction half-reaction there are 6 electrons on the left-hand side, and there are 12 electrons on the right-hand side of the oxidation half-reaction. Thus we multiply the reduction half-reaction by 2 to give

$$12e^- + 28H^+(aq) + 2Cr_2O_7^{2-}(aq) \longrightarrow 4Cr^{3+}(aq) + 14H_2O(l)$$

4 Adding the half-reactions and canceling identical species, we have

Reduction Half-Reaction: $12e^- + 28H^+(aq) + 2Cr_2O_7^{2-}(aq) \longrightarrow 4Cr^{3+}(aq) + 14H_2O(l)$

Oxidation Half-Reaction: $C_2H_5OH(l) + 3H_2O(l) \longrightarrow 2CO_2(g) + 12H^+(aq) + 12e^-$

Complete Reaction: $16H^+(aq) + 2Cr_2O_7^{2-}(aq) + C_2H_5OH(l) \longrightarrow 4Cr^{3+} + 11H_2O(l) + 2CO_2(g)$

5 Check that elements and charges are balanced.

Elements balance: $22H, 4Cr, 15O, 2C \longrightarrow 22H, 4Cr, 15O, 2C$

Charges balance: $+16 + 2(-2) + 0 = +12 \longrightarrow 4(+3) + 0 + 0 = +12$

See Exercises 4.73 and 4.74.

Oxidation–reduction reactions can occur in basic solutions (the reactions involve OH^- ions) as well as in acidic solution (the reactions involve H^+ ions). The half-reaction method for balancing equations is slightly different for the two cases.

The Half-Reaction Method for Balancing Equations for Oxidation–Reduction Reactions Occurring in Basic Solution

1 Use the half-reaction method as specified for acidic solutions to obtain the final balanced equation *as if H^+ ions were present.*

2 To both sides of the equation obtained above, add a number of OH^- ions that is equal to the number of H^+ ions. (We want to eliminate H^+ by forming H_2O.)

3 Form H_2O on the side containing both H^+ and OH^- ions, and eliminate the number of H_2O molecules that appear on both sides of the equation.

4 Check that elements and charges are balanced.

This method is summarized by the following flowchart:

We will illustrate how this method is applied in Sample Exercise 4.20.

Sample Exercise 4.20

Balancing Oxidation–Reduction Reactions (Basic)

Silver is sometimes found in nature as large nuggets; more often it is found mixed with other metals and their ores. An aqueous solution containing cyanide ion is often used to extract the silver using the following reaction that occurs in basic solution:

$$Ag(s) + CN^-(aq) + O_2(g) \xrightarrow{\text{Basic}} Ag(CN)_2^-(aq)$$

Balance this equation using the half-reaction method.

Solution

➥ **1** Balance the equation as if H^+ ions were present. Balance the oxidation half-reaction:

$$CN^-(aq) + Ag(s) \longrightarrow Ag(CN)_2^-(aq)$$

Balance carbon and nitrogen:

$$2CN^-(aq) + Ag(s) \longrightarrow Ag(CN)_2^-(aq)$$

Balance the charge:

$$2CN^-(aq) + Ag(s) \longrightarrow Ag(CN)_2^-(aq) + e^-$$

Balance the reduction half-reaction:

$$O_2(g) \longrightarrow$$

Balance oxygen:

$$O_2(g) \longrightarrow 2H_2O(l)$$

Balance hydrogen:

$$O_2(g) + 4H^+(aq) \longrightarrow 2H_2O(l)$$

Balance the charge:

$$4e^- + O_2(g) + 4H^+(aq) \longrightarrow 2H_2O(l)$$

Multiply the balanced oxidation half-reaction by 4:

$$8CN^-(aq) + 4Ag(s) \longrightarrow 4Ag(CN)_2^-(aq) + 4e^-$$

Add the half-reactions, and cancel identical species:

Oxidation Half-Reaction: $8CN^-(aq) + 4Ag(s) \longrightarrow 4Ag(CN)_2^-(aq) + 4e^-$

Reduction Half-Reaction: $4e^- + O_2(g) + 4H^+(aq) \longrightarrow 2H_2O(l)$

Complete Reaction: $8CN^-(aq) + 4Ag(s) + O_2(g) + 4H^+(aq) \longrightarrow 4Ag(CN)_2^-(aq) + 2H_2O(l)$

➥ **2** Add OH^- ions to both sides of the balanced equation to eliminate the H^+ ions. We need to add $4OH^-$ to each side:

$$8CN^-(aq) + 4Ag(s) + O_2(g) + \underbrace{4H^+(aq) + 4OH^-(aq)}_{4H_2O(l)} \longrightarrow$$
$$4Ag(CN)_2^-(aq) + 2H_2O(l) + 4OH^-(aq)$$

➥ **3** Eliminate as many H_2O molecules as possible:

$$8CN^-(aq) + 4Ag(s) + O_2(g) + 2H_2O(l) \longrightarrow 4Ag(CN)_2^-(aq) + 4OH^-(aq)$$

➥ **4** Check that elements and charges are balanced.

Elements balance: $8C, 8N, 4Ag, 4O, 4H \longrightarrow 8C, 8N, 4Ag, 4O, 4H$

Charges balance: $8(1-) + 0 + 0 + 0 = 8- \longrightarrow 4(1-) + 4(1-) = 8-$

See Exercises 4.75 and 4.76.

Key Terms

aqueous solution

Section 4.1
polar molecule
hydration
solubility

Section 4.2
solute
solvent
electrical conductivity
strong electrolyte
weak electrolyte
nonelectrolyte
acid
strong acid
strong base
weak acid
weak base

For Review

Chemical reactions in solution are very important in everyday life.

Water is a polar solvent that dissolves many ionic and polar substances.

Electrolytes
- Strong electolyte: 100% dissociated to produce separate ions; strongly conducts an electric current
- Weak electrolyte: Only a small percentage of dissolved molecules produce ions; weakly conducts an electric current
- Nonelectrolyte: Dissolved substance produces no ions; does not conduct an electric current

Acids and bases
- Arrhenius model
  - Acid: produces H^+
  - Base: produces OH^-

- Brønsted–Lowry model
  - Acid: proton donor
  - Base: proton acceptor
- Strong acid: completely dissociates into separated H^+ and anions
- Weak acid: dissociates to a slight extent

Molarity
- One way to describe solution composition

$$\text{Molarity } (M) = \frac{\text{moles of solute}}{\text{volume of solution (L)}}$$

- Moles solute = volume of solution (L) × molarity
- Standard solution: molarity is accurately known

Dilution
- Solvent is added to reduce the molarity
- Moles of solute after dilution = moles of solute before dilution

$$M_1V_1 = M_2V_2$$

Types of equations that describe solution reactions
- Formula equation: all reactants and products are written as complete formulas
- Complete ionic equation: all reactants and products that are strong electrolytes are written as separated ions
- Net ionic equation: only those compounds that undergo a change are written; spectator ions are not included

Solubility rules
- Based on experiment observation
- Help predict the outcomes of precipitation reactions

Important types of solution reactions
- Acid–base reactions: involve a transfer of H^+ ions
- Precipitation reactions: formation of a solid occurs
- Oxidation–reduction reactions: involve electron transfer

Titrations
- Measures the volume of a standard solution (titrant) needed to react with a substance in solution
- Stoichiometric (equivalence) point: the point at which the required amount of titrant has been added to exactly react with the substance being analyzed
- Endpoint: the point at which a chemical indicator changes color

Oxidation–reduction reactions
- Oxidation states are assigned using a set of rules to keep track of electron flow
- Oxidation: increase in oxidation state (a loss of electrons)
- Reduction: decrease in oxidation state (a gain of electrons)
- Oxidizing agent: gains electrons (is reduced)
- Reducing agent: loses electrons (is oxidized)
- Equations for oxidation–reduction reactions are usually balanced by the half-reaction method

REVIEW QUESTIONS

1. The (*aq*) designation listed after a solute indicates the process of hydration. Using KBr(*aq*) and C_2H_5OH(*aq*) as your examples, explain the process of hydration for soluble ionic compounds and for soluble covalent compounds.

2. Characterize strong electrolytes versus weak electrolytes versus nonelectrolytes. Give examples of each. How do you experimentally determine whether a soluble substance is a strong electrolyte, weak electrolyte, or nonelectrolyte?

3. Distinguish between the terms *slightly soluble* and *weak electrolyte*.
4. Molarity is a conversion factor relating moles of solute in solution to the volume of the solution. How does one use molarity as a conversion factor to convert from moles of solute to volume of solution, and from volume of solution to moles of solute present?
5. What is a dilution? What stays constant in a dilution? Explain why the equation $M_1V_1 = M_2V_2$ works for dilution problems.
6. When the following beakers are mixed, draw a molecular-level representation of the product mixture (see Fig. 4.17).

7. Differentiate between the formula equation, the complete ionic equation, and the net ionic equation. For each reaction in Question 6, write all three balanced equations.
8. What is an acid–base reaction? Strong bases are soluble ionic compounds that contain the hydroxide ion. List the strong bases. When a strong base reacts with an acid, what is always produced? Explain the terms *titration, stoichiometric point, neutralization,* and *standardization*.
9. Define the terms *oxidation, reduction, oxidizing agent,* and *reducing agent*. Given a chemical reaction, how can you tell if it is a redox reaction?
10. What is a half-reaction? Why must the number of electrons lost in the oxidation equal the number of electrons gained in a reduction? Summarize briefly the steps in the half-reaction method for balancing redox reactions. What two items must be balanced in a redox reaction (or any reaction)?

Active Learning Questions

These questions are designed to be used by groups of students in class. The questions allow students to explore their understanding of concepts through discussion and peer teaching. The real value of these questions is the learning that occurs while students talk to each other about chemical concepts.

1. Assume you have a highly magnified view of a solution of HCl that allows you to "see" the HCl. Draw this magnified view. If you dropped in a piece of magnesium, the magnesium would disappear and hydrogen gas would be released. Represent this change using symbols for the elements, and write out the balanced equation.
2. You have a solution of table salt in water. What happens to the salt concentration (increases, decreases, or stays the same) as the solution boils? Draw pictures to explain your answer.

3. You have a sugar solution (solution A) with concentration x. You pour one-fourth of this solution into a beaker, and add an equivalent volume of water (solution B).
   a. What is the ratio of sugar in solutions A and B?
   b. Compare the volumes of solutions A and B.
   c. What is the ratio of the concentrations of sugar in solutions A and B?
4. You add an aqueous solution of lead nitrate to an aqueous solution of potassium iodide. Draw highly magnified views of each solution individually, and the mixed solution including any product that forms. Write the balanced equation for the reaction.
5. Order the following molecules from lowest to highest oxidation state of the nitrogen atom: HNO_3, NH_4Cl, N_2O, NO_2, $NaNO_2$.
6. Why is it that when something gains electrons, it is said to be *reduced?* What is being reduced?

7. Consider separate aqueous solutions of HCl and H_2SO_4 with the same molar concentrations. You wish to neutralize an aqueous solution of NaOH. For which acid solution would you need to add more volume (in milliliters) to neutralize the base?
   a. the HCl solution
   b. the H_2SO_4 solution
   c. You need to know the acid concentrations to answer this question.
   d. You need to know the volume and concentration of the NaOH solution to answer this question.
   e. c and d
   Explain.

8. Draw molecular-level pictures to differentiate between concentrated and dilute solutions.

A blue question or exercise number indicates that the answer to that question or exercise appears at the back of this book and a solution appears in the *Solutions Guide*.

Questions

9. Differentiate between what happens when the following are dissolved in water.
   a. polar solute versus nonpolar solute
   b. KF versus $C_6H_{12}O_6$
   c. RbCl versus AgCl
   d. HNO_3 versus CO

10. A student wants to prepare 1.00 L of a 1.00 M solution of NaOH (molar mass = 40.00 g/mol). If solid NaOH is available, how would the student prepare this solution? If 2.00 M NaOH is available, how would the student prepare the solution? To help insure three significant figures in the NaOH molarity, to how many significant figures should the volumes and mass be determined?

11. List the formulas of three soluble bromide salts and three insoluble bromide salts. Do the same exercise for sulfate salts, hydroxide salts, and phosphate salts (list three soluble salts and three insoluble salts). List the formulas for six insoluble Pb^{2+} salts and one soluble Pb^{2+} salt.

12. When 1.0 mol of solid lead nitrate is added to 2.0 mol of aqueous potassium iodide, a yellow precipitate forms. After the precipitate settles to the bottom, does the solution above the precipitate conduct electricity? Explain. Write the complete ionic equation to help you answer this question.

13. What is an acid and what is a base? An acid–base reaction is sometimes called a proton-transfer reaction. Explain.

14. A student had 1.00 L of a 1.00 M acid solution. Much to the surprise of the student, it took 2.00 L of 1.00 M NaOH solution to react completely with the acid. Explain why it took twice as much NaOH to react with all of the acid.

   In a different experiment, a student had 10.0 mL of 0.020 M HCl. Again, much to the surprise of the student, it took only 5.00 mL of 0.020 M strong base to react completely with the HCl. Explain why it took only half as much strong base to react with all of the HCl.

15. Differentiate between the following terms.
   a. species reduced versus the reducing agent
   b. species oxidized versus the oxidizing agent
   c. oxidation state versus actual charge

16. When balancing reactions in Chapter 3, we did not mention that reactions must be charge balanced as well as mass balanced. What do *charge balanced* and *mass balanced* mean? How are redox reactions charge balanced?

Exercises

In this section similar exercises are paired.

Aqueous Solutions: Strong and Weak Electrolytes

17. Show how each of the following strong electrolytes "breaks up" into its component ions upon dissolving in water by drawing molecular-level pictures.
   a. NaBr   **f.** $FeSO_4$
   b. $MgCl_2$ **g.** $KMnO_4$
   c. $Al(NO_3)_3$ **h.** $HClO_4$
   d. $(NH_4)_2SO_4$ **i.** $NH_4C_2H_3O_2$ (ammonium acetate)
   e. NaOH

18. Match each name below with the following microscopic pictures of that compound in aqueous solution.

   i   ii   iii   iv

   a. barium nitrate   **c.** potassium carbonate
   b. sodium chloride   **d.** magnesium sulfate
   Which picture best represents $HNO_3(aq)$? Why aren't any of the pictures a good representation of $HC_2H_3O_2(aq)$?

19. Calcium chloride is a strong electrolyte and is used to "salt" streets in the winter to melt ice and snow. Write a reaction to show how this substance breaks apart when it dissolves in water.

20. Commercial cold packs and hot packs are available for treating athletic injuries. Both types contain a pouch of water and a dry chemical. When the pack is struck, the pouch of water breaks, dissolving the chemical, and the solution becomes either hot or cold. Many hot packs use magnesium sulfate, and many cold packs use ammonium nitrate. Write reactions to show how these strong electrolytes break apart when they dissolve in water.

Solution Concentration: Molarity

21. Calculate the molarity of each of these solutions.
   a. A 5.623-g sample of $NaHCO_3$ is dissolved in enough water to make 250.0 mL of solution.
   b. A 184.6-mg sample of $K_2Cr_2O_7$ is dissolved in enough water to make 500.0 mL of solution.
   c. A 0.1025-g sample of copper metal is dissolved in 35 mL of concentrated HNO_3 to form Cu^{2+} ions and then water is added to make a total volume of 200.0 mL. (Calculate the molarity of Cu^{2+}.)

22. A solution of ethanol (C_2H_5OH) in water is prepared by dissolving 75.0 mL of ethanol (density = 0.79 g/cm^3) in enough water to make 250.0 mL of solution. What is the molarity of the ethanol in this solution?

23. Calculate the concentration of all ions present in each of the following solutions of strong electrolytes.
    a. 0.100 mol of $Ca(NO_3)_2$ in 100.0 mL of solution
    b. 2.5 mol of Na_2SO_4 in 1.25 L of solution
    c. 5.00 g of NH_4Cl in 500.0 mL of solution
    d. 1.00 g K_3PO_4 in 250.0 mL of solution

24. Calculate the concentration of all ions present in each of the following solutions of strong electrolytes.
    a. 0.0200 mol of sodium phosphate in 10.0 mL of solution
    b. 0.300 mol of barium nitrate in 600.0 mL of solution
    c. 1.00 g of potassium chloride in 0.500 L of solution
    d. 132 g of ammonium sulfate in 1.50 L of solution

25. Which of the following solutions of strong electrolytes contains the largest number of moles of chloride ions: 100.0 mL of 0.30 M $AlCl_3$, 50.0 mL of 0.60 M $MgCl_2$, or 200.0 mL of 0.40 M $NaCl$?

26. Which of the following solutions of strong electrolytes contains the largest number of ions: 100.0 mL of 0.100 M $NaOH$, 50.0 mL of 0.200 M $BaCl_2$, or 75.0 mL of 0.150 M Na_3PO_4?

27. What mass of $NaOH$ is contained in 250.0 mL of a 0.400 M sodium hydroxide solution?

28. If 10. g of $AgNO_3$ is available, what volume of 0.25 M $AgNO_3$ solution can be prepared?

29. Describe how you would prepare 2.00 L of each of the following solutions.
    a. 0.250 M $NaOH$ from solid $NaOH$
    b. 0.250 M $NaOH$ from 1.00 M $NaOH$ stock solution
    c. 0.100 M K_2CrO_4 from solid K_2CrO_4
    d. 0.100 M K_2CrO_4 from 1.75 M K_2CrO_4 stock solution

30. How would you prepare 1.00 L of a 0.50 M solution of each of the following?
    a. H_2SO_4 from "concentrated" (18 M) sulfuric acid
    b. HCl from "concentrated" (12 M) reagent
    c. $NiCl_2$ from the salt $NiCl_2 \cdot 6H_2O$
    d. HNO_3 from "concentrated" (16 M) reagent
    e. Sodium carbonate from the pure solid

31. A solution is prepared by dissolving 10.8 g ammonium sulfate in enough water to make 100.0 mL of stock solution. A 10.00-mL sample of this stock solution is added to 50.00 mL of water. Calculate the concentration of ammonium ions and sulfate ions in the final solution.

32. Calculate the sodium ion concentration when 70.0 mL of 3.0 M sodium carbonate is added to 30.0 mL of 1.0 M sodium bicarbonate.

33. A standard solution is prepared for the analysis of fluoxymesterone ($C_{20}H_{29}FO_3$), an anabolic steroid. A stock solution is first prepared by dissolving 10.0 mg of fluoxymesterone in enough water to give a total volume of 500.0 mL. A 100.0-μL aliquot (portion) of this solution is diluted to a final volume of 100.0 mL. Calculate the concentration of the final solution in terms of molarity.

34. A stock solution containing Mn^{2+} ions was prepared by dissolving 1.584 g pure manganese metal in nitric acid and diluting to a final volume of 1.000 L. The following solutions were then prepared by dilution:

    For solution A, 50.00 mL of stock solution was diluted to 1000.0 mL.

    For solution B, 10.00 mL of solution A was diluted to 250.0 mL.
    For solution C, 10.00 mL of solution B was diluted to 500.0 mL.

    Calculate the concentrations of the stock solution and solutions A, B, and C.

Precipitation Reactions

35. On the basis of the general solubility rules given in Table 4.1, predict which of the following substances are likely to be soluble in water.
    a. aluminum nitrate
    b. magnesium chloride
    c. rubidium sulfate
    d. nickel(II) hydroxide
    e. lead(II) sulfide
    f. magnesium hydroxide
    g. iron(III) phosphate

36. On the basis of the general solubility rules given in Table 4.1, predict which of the following substances are likely to be soluble in water.
    a. zinc chloride
    b. lead(II) nitrate
    c. lead(II) sulfate
    d. sodium iodide
    e. cobalt(III) sulfide
    f. chromium(III) hydroxide
    g. magnesium carbonate
    h. ammonium carbonate

37. When the following solutions are mixed together, what precipitate (if any) will form?
    a. $FeSO_4(aq) + KCl(aq)$
    b. $Al(NO_3)_3(aq) + Ba(OH)_2(aq)$
    c. $CaCl_2(aq) + Na_2SO_4(aq)$
    d. $K_2S(aq) + Ni(NO_3)_2(aq)$

38. When the following solutions are mixed together, what precipitate (if any) will form?
    a. $Hg_2(NO_3)_2(aq) + CuSO_4(aq)$
    b. $Ni(NO_3)_2(aq) + CaCl_2(aq)$
    c. $K_2CO_3(aq) + MgI_2(aq)$
    d. $Na_2CrO_4(aq) + AlBr_3(aq)$

39. For the reactions in Exercise 37, write the balanced formula equation, complete ionic equation, and net ionic equation. If no precipitate forms, write "No reaction."

40. For the reactions in Exercise 38, write the balanced formula equation, complete ionic equation, and net ionic equation. If no precipitate forms, write "No reaction."

41. Write the balanced formula and net ionic equation for the reaction that occurs when the contents of the two beakers are added together. What colors represent the spectator ions in each reaction?

a.

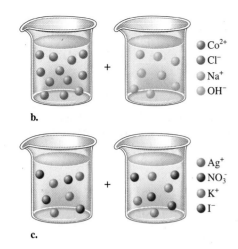

b.

c.

42. Give an example how each of the following insoluble ionic compounds could be produced using a precipitation reaction. Write the balanced formula equation for each reaction.
a. $Fe(OH)_3(s)$ **c.** $PbSO_4(s)$
b. $Hg_2Cl_2(s)$ **d.** $BaCrO_4(s)$

43. Write net ionic equations for the reaction, if any, that occurs when aqueous solutions of the following are mixed.
a. ammonium sulfate and barium nitrate
b. lead(II) nitrate and sodium chloride
c. sodium phosphate and potassium nitrate
d. sodium bromide and rubidium chloride
e. copper(II) chloride and sodium hydroxide

44. Write net ionic equations for the reaction, if any, that occurs when aqueous solutions of the following are mixed.
a. chromium(III) chloride and sodium hydroxide
b. silver nitrate and ammonium carbonate
c. copper(II) sulfate and mercury(I) nitrate
d. strontium nitrate and potassium iodide

45. Separate samples of a solution of an unknown soluble ionic compound are treated with KCl, Na_2SO_4, and NaOH. A precipitate forms only when Na_2SO_4 is added. Which cations could be present in the unknown soluble ionic compound?

46. A sample may contain any or all of the following ions: Hg_2^{2+}, Ba^{2+}, and Mn^{2+}.
a. No precipitate formed when an aqueous solution of NaCl was added to the sample solution.
b. No precipitate formed when an aqueous solution of Na_2SO_4 was added to the sample solution.
c. A precipitate formed when the sample solution was made basic with NaOH.
Which ion or ions are present in the sample solution?

47. What mass of Na_2CrO_4 is required to precipitate all of the silver ions from 75.0 mL of a 0.100 M solution of $AgNO_3$?

48. What volume of 0.100 M Na_3PO_4 is required to precipitate all the lead(II) ions from 150.0 mL of 0.250 M $Pb(NO_3)_2$?

49. What mass of solid aluminum hydroxide can be produced when 50.0 mL of 0.200 M $Al(NO_3)_3$ is added to 200.0 mL of 0.100 M KOH?

50. What mass of barium sulfate can be produced when 100.0 mL of a 0.100 M solution of barium chloride is mixed with 100.0 mL of a 0.100 M solution of iron(III) sulfate?

51. How many grams of silver chloride can be prepared by the reaction of 100.0 mL of 0.20 M silver nitrate with 100.0 mL of 0.15 M calcium chloride? Calculate the concentrations of each ion remaining in solution after precipitation is complete.

52. The drawings below represent aqueous solutions. Solution A is 2.00 L of a 2.00 M aqueous solution of copper(II) nitrate. Solution B is 2.00 L of a 3.00 M aqueous solution of potassium hydroxide.

A   B

a. Draw a picture of the solution made by mixing solutions A and B together after the precipitation reaction takes place. Make sure this picture shows the correct relative volume compared to solutions A and B, and the correct relative number of ions, along with the correct relative amount of solid formed.
b. Determine the concentrations (in M) of all ions left in solution (from part a) and the mass of solid formed.

53. A 1.42-g sample of a pure compound, with formula M_2SO_4, was dissolved in water and treated with an excess of aqueous calcium chloride, resulting in the precipitation of all the sulfate ions as calcium sulfate. The precipitate was collected, dried, and found to weigh 1.36 g. Determine the atomic mass of M, and identify M.

54. You are given a 1.50-g mixture of sodium nitrate and sodium chloride. You dissolve this mixture into 100 mL of water and then add an excess of 0.500 M silver nitrate solution. You produce a white solid, which you then collect, dry, and measure. The white solid has a mass of 0.641 g.
a. If you had an extremely magnified view of the solution (to the atomic-molecular level), list the species you would see (include charges, if any).
b. Write the balanced net ionic equation for the reaction that produces the solid. Include phases and charges.
c. Calculate the percent sodium chloride in the original unknown mixture.

Acid–Base Reactions

55. Write the balanced formula, complete ionic, and net ionic equations for each of the following acid–base reactions.
a. $HClO_4(aq) + Mg(OH)_2(s) \rightarrow$
b. $HCN(aq) + NaOH(aq) \rightarrow$
c. $HCl(aq) + NaOH(aq) \rightarrow$

56. Write the balanced formula, complete ionic, and net ionic equations for each of the following acid–base reactions.
a. $HNO_3(aq) + Al(OH)_3(s) \rightarrow$
b. $HC_2H_3O_2(aq) + KOH(aq) \rightarrow$
c. $Ca(OH)_2(aq) + HCl(aq) \rightarrow$

57. Write the balanced formula, complete ionic, and net ionic equations for the reactions that occur when the following are mixed.
a. potassium hydroxide (aqueous) and nitric acid
b. barium hydroxide (aqueous) and hydrochloric acid
c. perchloric acid [$HClO_4(aq)$] and solid iron(III) hydroxide

58. Write the balanced formula, complete ionic, and net ionic equations for the reactions that occur when the following are mixed.

a. solid silver hydroxide and hydrobromic acid
b. aqueous strontium hydroxide and hydroiodic acid
c. solid chromium(III) hydroxide and nitric acid

59. What volume of each of the following acids will react completely with 50.00 mL of 0.200 M NaOH?

a. 0.100 M HCl
b. 0.150 M HNO_3
c. 0.200 M $HC_2H_3O_2$ (1 acidic hydrogen)

60. What volume of each of the following bases will react completely with 25.00 mL of 0.200 M HCl?

a. 0.100 M NaOH
b. 0.0500 M $Ba(OH)_2$
c. 0.250 M KOH

61. Hydrochloric acid (75.0 mL of 0.250 M) is added to 225.0 mL of 0.0550 M $Ba(OH)_2$ solution. What is the concentration of the excess H^+ or OH^- ions left in this solution?

62. A student mixes four reagents together, thinking that the solutions will neutralize each other. The solutions mixed together are 50.0 mL of 0.100 M hydrochloric acid, 100.0 mL of 0.200 M of nitric acid, 500.0 mL of 0.0100 M calcium hydroxide, and 200.0 mL of 0.100 M rubidium hydroxide. Is the resulting solution neutral? If not, calculate the concentration of excess H^+ or OH^- ions left in solution.

63. A 25.00-mL sample of hydrochloric acid solution requires 24.16 mL of 0.106 M sodium hydroxide for complete neutralization. What is the concentration of the original hydrochloric acid solution?

64. What volume of 0.0200 M calcium hydroxide is required to neutralize 35.00 mL of 0.0500 M nitric acid?

65. A student titrates an unknown amount of potassium hydrogen phthalate ($KHC_8H_4O_4$, often abbreviated as KHP) with 20.46 mL of a 0.1000 M NaOH solution. KHP (molar mass = 204.22 g/mol) has one acidic hydrogen. What mass of KHP was titrated (reacted completely) by the sodium hydroxide solution?

66. The concentration of a certain sodium hydroxide solution was determined by using the solution to titrate a sample of potassium hydrogen phthalate (abbreviated as KHP). KHP is an acid with one acidic hydrogen and a molar mass of 204.22 g/mol. In the titration, 34.67 mL of the sodium hydroxide solution was required to react with 0.1082 g KHP. Calculate the molarity of the sodium hydroxide.

Oxidation–Reduction Reactions

67. Assign oxidation states for all atoms in each of the following compounds.

a. $KMnO_4$
b. NiO_2
c. $Na_4Fe(OH)_6$
d. $(NH_4)_2HPO_4$
e. P_4O_6
f. Fe_3O_4
g. $XeOF_4$
h. SF_4
i. CO
j. $C_6H_{12}O_6$

68. Assign oxidation states for all atoms in each of the following compounds.

a. UO_2^{2+}
b. As_2O_3
c. $NaBiO_3$
d. As_4
e. $HAsO_2$
f. $Mg_2P_2O_7$
g. $Na_2S_2O_3$
h. Hg_2Cl_2
i. $Ca(NO_3)_2$

69. Assign the oxidation state for nitrogen in each of the following.

a. Li_3N
b. NH_3
c. N_2H_4
d. NO
e. N_2O
f. NO_2
g. NO_2^-
h. NO_3^-
i. N_2

70. Assign oxidation numbers to all the atoms in each of the following.

a. $SrCr_2O_7$
b. $CuCl_2$
c. O_2
d. H_2O_2
e. $MgCO_3$
f. Ag
g. $PbSO_3$
h. PbO_2
i. $Na_2C_2O_4$
j. CO_2
k. $(NH_4)_2Ce(SO_4)_3$
l. Cr_2O_3

71. Specify which of the following are oxidation–reduction reactions, and identify the oxidizing agent, the reducing agent, the substance being oxidized, and the substance being reduced.

a. $Cu(s) + 2Ag^+(aq) \rightarrow 2Ag(s) + Cu^{2+}(aq)$
b. $HCl(g) + NH_3(g) \rightarrow NH_4Cl(s)$
c. $SiCl_4(l) + 2H_2O(l) \rightarrow 4HCl(aq) + SiO_2(s)$
d. $SiCl_4(l) + 2Mg(s) \rightarrow 2MgCl_2(s) + Si(s)$
e. $Al(OH)_4^-(aq) \rightarrow AlO_2^-(aq) + 2H_2O(l)$

72. Specify which of the following equations represent oxidation–reduction reactions, and indicate the oxidizing agent, the reducing agent, the species being oxidized, and the species being reduced.

a. $CH_4(g) + H_2O(g) \rightarrow CO(g) + 3H_2(g)$
b. $2AgNO_3(aq) + Cu(s) \rightarrow Cu(NO_3)_2(aq) + 2Ag(s)$
c. $Zn(s) + 2HCl(aq) \rightarrow ZnCl_2(aq) + H_2(g)$
d. $2H^+(aq) + 2CrO_4^{2-}(aq) \rightarrow Cr_2O_7^{2-}(aq) + H_2O(l)$

73. Balance the following oxidation–reduction reactions that occur in acidic solution.

a. $Zn(s) + HCl(aq) \rightarrow Zn^{2+}(aq) + H_2(g) + Cl^-(aq)$
b. $I^-(aq) + ClO^-(aq) \rightarrow I_3^-(aq) + Cl^-(aq)$
c. $As_2O_3(s) + NO_3^-(aq) \rightarrow H_3AsO_4(aq) + NO(g)$
d. $Br^-(aq) + MnO_4^-(aq) \rightarrow Br_2(l) + Mn^{2+}(aq)$
e. $CH_3OH(aq) + Cr_2O_7^{2-}(aq) \rightarrow CH_2O(aq) + Cr^{3+}(aq)$

74. Balance the following oxidation–reduction reactions that occur in acidic solution using the half-reaction method.

a. $Cu(s) + NO_3^-(aq) \rightarrow Cu^{2+}(aq) + NO(g)$
b. $Cr_2O_7^{2-}(aq) + Cl^-(aq) \rightarrow Cr^{3+}(aq) + Cl_2(g)$
c. $Pb(s) + PbO_2(s) + H_2SO_4(aq) \rightarrow PbSO_4(s)$
d. $Mn^{2+}(aq) + NaBiO_3(s) \rightarrow Bi^{3+}(aq) + MnO_4^-(aq)$
e. $H_3AsO_4(aq) + Zn(s) \rightarrow AsH_3(g) + Zn^{2+}(aq)$

75. Balance the following oxidation–reduction reactions that occur in basic solution.

a. $Al(s) + MnO_4^-(aq) \rightarrow MnO_2(s) + Al(OH)_4^-(aq)$
b. $Cl_2(g) \rightarrow Cl^-(aq) + OCl^-(aq)$
c. $NO_2^-(aq) + Al(s) \rightarrow NH_3(g) + AlO_2^-(aq)$

76. Balance the following oxidation–reduction reactions that occur in basic solution.
    a. $Cr(s) + CrO_4^{2-}(aq) \rightarrow Cr(OH)_3(s)$
    b. $MnO_4^-(aq) + S^{2-}(aq) \rightarrow MnS(s) + S(s)$
    c. $CN^-(aq) + MnO_4^-(aq) \rightarrow CNO^-(aq) + MnO_2(s)$

77. Chlorine gas was first prepared in 1774 by C. W. Scheele by oxidizing sodium chloride with manganese(IV) oxide. The reaction is

    $$NaCl(aq) + H_2SO_4(aq) + MnO_2(s) \longrightarrow$$
    $$Na_2SO_4(aq) + MnCl_2(aq) + H_2O(l) + Cl_2(g)$$

    Balance this equation.

78. Gold metal will not dissolve in either concentrated nitric acid or concentrated hydrochloric acid. It will dissolve, however, in aqua regia, a mixture of the two concentrated acids. The products of the reaction are the $AuCl_4^-$ ion and gaseous NO. Write a balanced equation for the dissolution of gold in aqua regia.

Additional Exercises

79. Which of the following statements is (are) true? For the false statements, correct them.
    a. A concentrated solution in water will always contain a strong or weak electrolyte.
    b. A strong electrolyte will break up into ions when dissolved in water.
    c. An acid is a strong electrolyte.
    d. All ionic compounds are strong electrolytes in water.

80. A 230.-mL sample of a 0.275 M $CaCl_2$ solution is left on a hot plate overnight; the following morning, the solution is 1.10 M. What volume of water evaporated from the 0.275 M $CaCl_2$ solution?

81. Using the general solubility rules given in Table 4.1, name three reagents that would form precipitates with each of the following ions in aqueous solution. Write the net ionic equation for each of your suggestions.
    a. chloride ion   d. sulfate ion
    b. calcium ion   e. mercury(I) ion, Hg_2^{2+}
    c. iron(III) ion   f. silver ion

82. Consider a 1.50-g mixture of magnesium nitrate and magnesium chloride. After dissolving this mixture in water, 0.500 M silver nitrate is added dropwise until precipitate formation is complete. The mass of the white precipitate formed is 0.641 g.
    a. Calculate the mass percent of magnesium chloride in the mixture.
    b. Determine the minimum volume of silver nitrate that must have been added to ensure complete formation of the precipitate.

83. A 1.00-g sample of an alkaline earth metal chloride is treated with excess silver nitrate. All of the chloride is recovered as 1.38 g of silver chloride. Identify the metal.

84. A mixture contains only NaCl and $Al_2(SO_4)_3$. A 1.45-g sample of the mixture is dissolved in water and an excess of NaOH is added, producing a precipitate of $Al(OH)_3$. The precipitate is filtered, dried, and weighed. The mass of the precipitate is 0.107 g. What is the mass percent of $Al_2(SO_4)_3$ in the sample?

85. Saccharin ($C_7H_5NO_3S$) is sometimes dispensed in tablet form. Ten tablets with a total mass of 0.5894 g were dissolved in water. They were oxidized to convert all the sulfur to sulfate ion, which was precipitated by adding an excess of barium chloride solution. The mass of $BaSO_4$ obtained was 0.5032 g. What is the average mass of saccharin per tablet? What is the average mass percent of saccharin in the tablets?

86. A mixture contains only NaCl and $Fe(NO_3)_3$. A 0.456-g sample of the mixture is dissolved in water, and an excess of NaOH is added, producing a precipitate of $Fe(OH)_3$. The precipitate is filtered, dried, and weighed. Its mass is 0.107 g. Calculate the following.
    a. the mass of iron in the sample
    b. the mass of $Fe(NO_3)_3$ in the sample
    c. the mass percent of $Fe(NO_3)_3$ in the sample

87. A student added 50.0 mL of an NaOH solution to 100.0 mL of 0.400 M HCl. The solution was then treated with an excess of aqueous chromium(III) nitrate, resulting in formation of 2.06 g of precipitate. Determine the concentration of the NaOH solution.

88. What acid and what strong base would react in aqueous solution to produce the following salts in the formula equation? Write the balanced formula equation for each reaction.
    a. potassium perchlorate
    b. cesium nitrate
    c. calcium iodide

89. A 10.00-mL sample of vinegar, an aqueous solution of acetic acid ($HC_2H_3O_2$), is titrated with 0.5062 M NaOH, and 16.58 mL is required to reach the equivalence point.
    a. What is the molarity of the acetic acid?
    b. If the density of the vinegar is 1.006 g/cm³, what is the mass percent of acetic acid in the vinegar?

90. When hydrochloric acid reacts with magnesium metal, hydrogen gas and aqueous magnesium chloride are produced. What volume of 5.0 M HCl is required to react completely with 3.00 g of magnesium?

91. A 2.20-g sample of an unknown acid (empirical formula = $C_3H_4O_3$) is dissolved in 1.0 L of water. A titration required 25.0 mL of 0.500 M NaOH to react completely with all the acid present. Assuming the unknown acid has one acidic proton per molecule, what is the molecular formula of the unknown acid?

92. Carminic acid, a naturally occurring red pigment extracted from the cochineal insect, contains only carbon, hydrogen, and oxygen. It was commonly used as a dye in the first half of the nineteenth century. It is 53.66% C and 4.09% H by mass. A titration required 18.02 mL of 0.0406 M NaOH to neutralize 0.3602 g carminic acid. Assuming that there is only one acidic hydrogen per molecule, what is the molecular formula of carminic acid?

93. A 30.0-mL sample of an unknown strong base is neutralized after the addition of 12.0 mL of a 0.150 M HNO_3 solution. If the unknown base concentration is 0.0300 M, give some possible identities for the unknown base.

94. Many oxidation–reduction reactions can be balanced by inspection. Try to balance the following reactions by inspection. In each reaction, identify the substance reduced and the substance oxidized.
    a. $Al(s) + HCl(aq) \rightarrow AlCl_3(aq) + H_2(g)$
    b. $CH_4(g) + S(s) \rightarrow CS_2(l) + H_2S(g)$
    c. $C_3H_8(g) + O_2(g) \rightarrow CO_2(g) + H_2O(l)$
    d. $Cu(s) + Ag^+(aq) \rightarrow Ag(s) + Cu^{2+}(aq)$

95. One of the classical methods for the determination of the manganese content in steel is to convert all the manganese to the deeply colored permanganate ion and then to measure the absorption of light. The steel is dissolved in nitric acid, producing the manganese(II) ion and nitrogen dioxide gas. This solution is then reacted with an acidic solution containing periodate ion; the products are the permanganate and iodate ions. Write balanced chemical equations for both these steps.

Challenge Problems

96. The units of parts per million (ppm) and parts per billion (ppb) are commonly used by environmental chemists. In general, 1 ppm means 1 part of solute for every 10^6 parts of solution. Mathematically, by mass:

$$\text{ppm} = \frac{\mu\text{g solute}}{\text{g solution}} = \frac{\text{mg solute}}{\text{kg solution}}$$

In the case of very dilute aqueous solutions, a concentration of 1.0 ppm is equal to 1.0 μg of solute per 1.0 mL, which equals 1.0 g solution. Parts per billion is defined in a similar fashion. Calculate the molarity of each of the following aqueous solutions.
   a. 5.0 ppb Hg in H_2O
   b. 1.0 ppb $CHCl_3$ in H_2O
   c. 10.0 ppm As in H_2O
   d. 0.10 ppm DDT ($C_{14}H_9Cl_5$) in H_2O

97. In most of its ionic compounds, cobalt is either Co(II) or Co(III). One such compound, containing chloride ion and waters of hydration, was analyzed, and the following results were obtained. A 0.256-g sample of the compound was dissolved in water, and excess silver nitrate was added. The silver chloride was filtered, dried, and weighed, and it had a mass of 0.308 g. A second sample of 0.416 g of the compound was dissolved in water, and an excess of sodium hydroxide was added. The hydroxide salt was filtered and heated in a flame, forming cobalt(III) oxide. The mass of cobalt(III) oxide formed was 0.145 g.
   a. What is the percent composition, by mass, of the compound?
   b. Assuming the compound contains one cobalt atom per formula unit, what is the molecular formula?
   c. Write balanced equations for the three reactions described.

98. Polychlorinated biphenyls (PCBs) have been used extensively as dielectric materials in electrical transformers. Because PCBs have been shown to be potentially harmful, analysis for their presence in the environment has become very important. PCBs are manufactured according to the following generic reaction:

$$C_{12}H_{10} + nCl_2 \rightarrow C_{12}H_{10-n}Cl_n + nHCl$$

This reaction results in a mixture of PCB products. The mixture is analyzed by decomposing the PCBs and then precipitating the resulting Cl^- as AgCl.
   a. Develop a general equation that relates the average value of n to the mass of a given mixture of PCBs and the mass of AgCl produced.
   b. A 0.1947-g sample of a commercial PCB yielded 0.4791 g of AgCl. What is the average value of n for this sample?

99. You have two 500.0 mL aqueous solutions. Solution A is a solution of silver nitrate, and solution B is a solution of potassium chromate. The masses of the solutes in each of the solutions are the same. When the solutions are added together, a blood-red precipitate forms. After the reaction has gone to completion, you dry the solid and find that it has a mass of 331.8 g.
   a. Calculate the concentration of the potassium ions in the original potassium chromate solution.
   b. Calculate the concentration of the chromate ions in the final solution.

100. A sample is a mixture of KCl and KBr. When 0.1024 g of the sample is dissolved in water and reacted with excess silver nitrate, 0.1889 g solid is obtained. What is the composition by mass percent of the original mixture?

101. You are given a solid that is a mixture of Na_2SO_4 and K_2SO_4. A 0.205-g sample of the mixture is dissolved in water. An excess of an aqueous solution of $BaCl_2$ is added. The $BaSO_4$ that is formed is filtered, dried, and weighed. Its mass is 0.298 g. What mass of SO_4^{2-} ion is in the sample? What is the mass percent of SO_4^{2-} ion in the sample? What are the percent compositions by mass of Na_2SO_4 and K_2SO_4 in the sample?

102. Zinc and magnesium metal each react with hydrochloric acid according to the following equations:

$$Zn(s) + 2HCl(aq) \longrightarrow ZnCl_2(aq) + H_2(g)$$
$$Mg(s) + 2HCl(aq) \longrightarrow MgCl_2(aq) + H_2(g)$$

A 10.00-g mixture of zinc and magnesium is reacted with the stoichiometric amount of hydrochloric acid. The reaction mixture is then reacted with 156 mL of 3.00 M silver nitrate to produce the maximum possible amount of silver chloride.
   a. Determine the percent magnesium by mass in the original mixture.
   b. If 78.0 mL of HCl was added, what was the concentration of the HCl?

103. You made 100.0 mL of a lead(II) nitrate solution for lab but forgot to cap it. The next lab session you noticed that there was only 80.0 mL left (the rest had evaporated). In addition, you forgot the initial concentration of the solution. You decide to take 2.00 mL of the solution and add an excess of a concentrated sodium chloride solution. You obtain a solid with a mass of 3.407 g. What was the concentration of the original lead(II) nitrate solution?

104. Consider reacting copper(II) sulfate with iron. Two possible reactions can occur, as represented by the following equations.

copper(II) sulfate(aq) + iron(s) $\longrightarrow$
$\quad$ copper(s) + iron(II) sulfate(aq)
copper(II) sulfate(aq) + iron(s) $\longrightarrow$
$\quad$ copper(s) + iron(III) sulfate(aq)

You place 87.7 mL of a 0.500 M solution of copper(II) sulfate in a beaker. You then add 2.00 g of iron filings to the copper(II) sulfate solution. After one of the above reactions occurs, you isolate 2.27 g of copper. Which equation above describes the reaction that occurred? Support your answer.

105. Consider an experiment in which two burets, Y and Z, are simultaneously draining into a beaker that initially contained 275.0 mL of 0.300 M HCl. Buret Y contains 0.150 M NaOH and buret Z contains 0.250 M KOH. The stoichiometric point in the titration is reached 60.65 minutes after Y and Z were started simultaneously. The total volume in the beaker at the stoichiometric point is 655 mL. Calculate the flow rates of burets Y and Z. Assume the flow rates remain constant during the experiment.

106. Complete and balance each acid–base reaction.
  a. $H_3PO_4(aq) + NaOH(aq) \rightarrow$
    Contains three acidic hydrogens
  b. $H_2SO_4(aq) + Al(OH)_3(s) \rightarrow$
    Contains two acidic hydrogens
  c. $H_2Se(aq) + Ba(OH)_2(aq) \rightarrow$
    Contains two acidic hydrogens
  d. $H_2C_2O_4(aq) + NaOH(aq) \rightarrow$
    Contains two acidic hydrogens

107. What volume of 0.0521 M $Ba(OH)_2$ is required to neutralize exactly 14.20 mL of 0.141 M H_3PO_4? Phosphoric acid contains three acidic hydrogens.

108. A 10.00-mL sample of sulfuric acid from an automobile battery requires 35.08 mL of 2.12 M sodium hydroxide solution for complete neutralization. What is the molarity of the sulfuric acid? Sulfuric acid contains two acidic hydrogens.

109. Some of the substances commonly used in stomach antacids are MgO, $Mg(OH)_2$, and $Al(OH)_3$.
  a. Write a balanced equation for the neutralization of hydrochloric acid by each of these substances.
  b. Which of these substances will neutralize the greatest amount of 0.10 M HCl per gram?

110. A 6.50-g sample of a diprotic acid requires 137.5 mL of a 0.750 M NaOH solution for complete reaction. Determine the molar mass of the acid.

111. Citric acid, which can be obtained from lemon juice, has the molecular formula $C_6H_8O_7$. A 0.250-g sample of citric acid dissolved in 25.0 mL of water requires 37.2 mL of 0.105 M NaOH for complete neutralization. What number of acidic hydrogens per molecule does citric acid have?

112. Balance the following equations by the half-reaction method.
  a. $Fe(s) + HCl(aq) \rightarrow HFeCl_4(aq) + H_2(g)$
  b. $IO_3^-(aq) + I^-(aq) \xrightarrow{\text{Acid}} I_3^-(aq)$
  c. $Cr(NCS)_6^{4-}(aq) + Ce^{4+}(aq) \xrightarrow{\text{Acid}}$
    $Cr^{3+}(aq) + Ce^{3+}(aq) + NO_3^-(aq) + CO_2(g) + SO_4^{2-}(aq)$
  d. $CrI_3(s) + Cl_2(g) \xrightarrow{\text{Base}} CrO_4^{2-}(aq) + IO_4^-(aq) + Cl^-(aq)$
  e. $Fe(CN)_6^{4-}(aq) + Ce^{4+}(aq) \xrightarrow{\text{Base}}$
    $Ce(OH)_3(s) + Fe(OH)_3(s) + CO_3^{2-}(aq) + NO_3^-(aq)$
  f. $Fe(OH)_2(s) + H_2O_2(aq) \xrightarrow{\text{Base}} Fe(OH)_3(s)$

113. It took 25.06 ±0.05 mL of a sodium hydroxide solution to titrate a 0.4016-g sample of KHP (see Exercise 65). Calculate the concentration and uncertainty in the concentration of the sodium hydroxide solution. (See Appendix 1.5.) Neglect any uncertainty in the mass.

Integrative Problems

These problems require the integration of multiple concepts to find the solutions.

114. Tris(pentafluorophenyl)borane, commonly known by its acronym BARF, is frequently used to initiate polymerization of ethylene or propylene in the presence of a catalytic transition metal compound. It is composed solely of C, F, and B; it is 42.23% C by mass and 55.66% F by mass.
  a. What is the empirical formula of BARF?
  b. A 2.251-g sample of BARF dissolved in 347.0 mL of solution produces a 0.01267 M solution. What is the molecular formula of BARF?

115. In a 1-L beaker, 203 mL of 0.307 M ammonium chromate was mixed with 137 mL of 0.269 M chromium(III) nitrite to produce ammonium nitrite and chromium(III) chromate. Write the balanced chemical reaction occurring here. If the percent yield of the reaction was 88.0%, how much chromium(III) chromate was isolated?

116. The vanadium in a sample of ore is converted to VO^{2+}. The VO^{2+} ion is subsequently titrated with MnO_4^- in acidic solution to form $V(OH)_4^+$ and manganese(II) ion. To titrate the solution, 26.45 mL of 0.02250 M MnO_4^- was required. If the mass percent of vanadium in the ore was 58.1%, what was the mass of the ore sample? Which of the four transition metal ions in this titration has the highest oxidation state?

117. The unknown acid H_2X can be neutralized completely by OH^- according to the following (unbalanced) equation:

$$H_2X(aq) + OH^- \longrightarrow X^{2-} + H_2O$$

The ion formed as a product, X^{2-}, was shown to have 36 total electrons. What is element X? Propose a name for H_2X? To completely neutralize a sample of H_2X, 35.6 mL of 0.175 M OH^- solution was required. What was the mass of the H_2X sample used?

Marathon Problems

These problems are designed to incorporate several concepts and techniques into one situation. Marathon Problems can be used in class by groups of students to help facilitate problem-solving skills.

118. Three students were asked to find the identity of the metal in a particular sulfate salt. They dissolved a 0.1472-g sample of the salt in water and treated it with excess barium chloride, resulting in the precipitation of barium sulfate. After the precipitate had been filtered and dried, it weighed 0.2327 g.

Each student analyzed the data independently and came to different conclusions. Pat decided that the metal was titanium. Chris thought it was sodium. Randy reported that it was gallium. What formula did each student assign to the sulfate salt?

Look for information on the sulfates of gallium, sodium, and titanium in this text and reference books such as the *CRC Handbook of Chemistry and Physics*. What further tests would you suggest to determine which student is most likely correct?

119. You have two 500.0-mL aqueous solutions. Solution A is a solution of a metal nitrate that is 8.246% nitrogen by mass. The ionic compound in solution B consists of potassium, chromium, and oxygen; chromium has an oxidation state of +6 and there are 2 potassiums and 1 chromium in the formula. The masses of the solutes in each of the solutions are the same. When the solutions are added together, a blood-red precipitate forms. After the reaction has gone to completion, you dry the solid and find that it has a mass of 331.8 g.
  a. Identify the ionic compounds in solution A and solution B.
  b. Identify the blood-red precipitate.
  c. Calculate the concentration (molarity) of all ions in the original solutions.
  d. Calculate the concentration (molarity) of all ions in the final solution.

 Get help understanding core concepts and visualizing molecular-level interactions, and practice problem solving, by visiting the Online Study Center at **college.hmco.com/ PIC/zumdahl7e.**

5 Gases

Contents

The steaming fumaroles located in Bjarnarflag, Iceland release a variety of gases.

Matter exists in three distinct physical states: gas, liquid, and solid. Although relatively few substances exist in the gaseous state under typical conditions, gases are very important. For example, we live immersed in a gaseous solution. The earth's atmosphere is a mixture of gases that consists mainly of elemental nitrogen (N_2) and oxygen (O_2). The atmosphere both supports life and acts as a waste receptacle for the exhaust gases that accompany many industrial processes. The chemical reactions of these waste gases in the atmosphere lead to various types of pollution, including smog and acid rain. The gases in the atmosphere also shield us from harmful radiation from the sun and keep the earth warm by reflecting heat radiation back toward the earth. In fact, there is now great concern that an increase in atmospheric carbon dioxide, a product of the combustion of fossil fuels, is causing a dangerous warming of the earth.

In this chapter we will look carefully at the properties of gases. First we will see how measurements of gas properties lead to various types of laws—statements that show how the properties are related to each other. Then we will construct a model to explain why gases behave as they do. This model will show how the behavior of the individual particles of a gas leads to the observed properties of the gas itself (a collection of many, many particles).

The study of gases provides an excellent example of the scientific method in action. It illustrates how observations lead to natural laws, which in turn can be accounted for by models.

5.1 Pressure

A gas uniformly fills any container, is easily compressed, and mixes completely with any other gas. One of the most obvious properties of a gas is that it exerts pressure on its surroundings. For example, when you blow up a balloon, the air inside pushes against the elastic sides of the balloon and keeps it firm.

As mentioned earlier, the gases most familiar to us form the earth's atmosphere. The pressure exerted by this gaseous mixture that we call air can be dramatically demonstrated by the experiment shown in Fig. 5.1. A small volume of water is placed in a metal can,

As a gas, water occupies 1200 times as much space as it does as a liquid at 25°C and atmospheric pressure.

Visualization: Collapsing Can

FIGURE 5.1
The pressure exerted by the gases in the atmosphere can be demonstrated by boiling water in a large metal can (a) and then turning off the heat and sealing the can. As the can cools, the water vapor condenses, lowering the gas pressure inside the can. This causes the can to crumple (b).

179

FIGURE 5.2
A torricellian barometer. The tube, completely filled with mercury, is inverted in a dish of mercury. Mercury flows out of the tube until the pressure of the column of mercury (shown by the black arrow) "standing on the surface" of the mercury in the dish is equal to the pressure of the air (shown by the purple arrows) on the rest of the surface of the mercury in the dish.

Soon after Torricelli died, a German physicist named Otto von Guericke invented an air pump. In a famous demonstration for the King of Prussia in 1663, Guericke placed two hemispheres together, pumped the air out of the resulting sphere through a valve, and showed that teams of horses could not pull the hemispheres apart. Then, after secretly opening the air valve, Guericke easily separated the hemispheres by hand. The King of Prussia was so impressed that he awarded Guericke a lifetime pension!

and the water is boiled, which fills the can with steam. The can is then sealed and allowed to cool. Why does the can collapse as it cools? It is the atmospheric pressure that crumples the can. When the can is cooled after being sealed so that no air can flow in, the water vapor (steam) condenses to a very small volume of liquid water. As a gas, the water filled the can, but when it is condensed to a liquid, the liquid does not come close to filling the can. The H_2O molecules formerly present as a gas are now collected in a very small volume of liquid, and there are very few molecules of gas left to exert pressure outward and counteract the air pressure. As a result, the pressure exerted by the gas molecules in the atmosphere smashes the can.

A device to measure atmospheric pressure, the **barometer,** was invented in 1643 by an Italian scientist named Evangelista Torricelli (1608–1647), who had been a student of Galileo. Torricelli's barometer is constructed by filling a glass tube with liquid mercury and inverting it in a dish of mercury, as shown in Fig. 5.2. Notice that a large quantity of mercury stays in the tube. In fact, at sea level the height of this column of mercury averages 760 mm. Why does this mercury stay in the tube, seemingly in defiance of gravity? Figure 5.2 illustrates how the pressure exerted by the atmospheric gases on the surface of mercury in the dish keeps the mercury in the tube.

Atmospheric pressure results from the mass of the air being pulled toward the center of the earth by gravity—in other words, it results from the weight of the air. Changing weather conditions cause the atmospheric pressure to vary, so the height of the column of Hg supported by the atmosphere at sea level varies; it is not always 760 mm. The meteorologist who says a "low" is approaching means that the atmospheric pressure is going to decrease. This condition often occurs in conjunction with a storm.

Atmospheric pressure also varies with altitude. For example, when Torricelli's experiment is done in Breckenridge, Colorado (elevation 9600 feet), the atmosphere supports a column of mercury only about 520 mm high because the air is "thinner." That is, there is less air pushing down on the earth's surface at Breckenridge than at sea level.

Units of Pressure

Because instruments used for measuring pressure, such as the **manometer** (Fig. 5.3), often contain mercury, the most commonly used units for pressure are based on the height

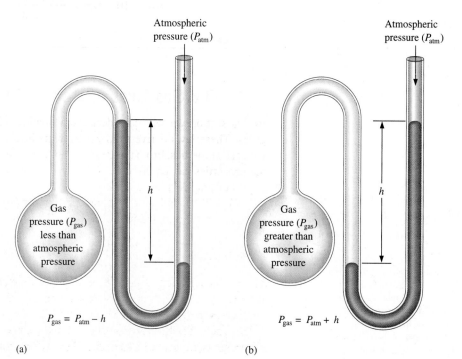

FIGURE 5.3
A simple manometer, a device for measuring the pressure of a gas in a container. The pressure of the gas is given by h (the difference in mercury levels) in units of torr (equivalent to mm Hg). (a) Gas pressure = atmospheric pressure − h. (b) Gas pressure = atmospheric pressure + h.

of the mercury column (in millimeters) that the gas pressure can support. The unit **mm Hg** (millimeter of mercury) is often called the **torr** in honor of Torricelli. The terms *torr* and *mm Hg* are used interchangeably by chemists. A related unit for pressure is the **standard atmosphere** (abbreviated atm):

$$1 \text{ standard atmosphere} = 1 \text{ atm} = 760 \text{ mm Hg} = 760 \text{ torr}$$

However, since pressure is defined as force per unit area,

$$\text{Pressure} = \frac{\text{force}}{\text{area}}$$

the fundamental units of pressure involve units of force divided by units of area. In the SI system, the unit of force is the newton (N) and the unit of area is meters squared (m^2). (For a review of the SI system, see Chapter 1.) Thus the unit of pressure in the SI system is newtons per meter squared (N/m^2) and is called the **pascal** (Pa). In terms of pascals, the standard atmosphere is

$$1 \text{ standard atmosphere} = 101{,}325 \text{ Pa}$$

Thus 1 atmosphere is about 10^5 pascals. Since the pascal is so small, and since it is not commonly used in the United States, we will use it sparingly in this book. However, converting from torrs or atmospheres to pascals is straightforward, as shown in Sample Exercise 5.1.

Checking tire pressure.

| *Sample Exercise 5.1* | **Pressure Conversions** |

The pressure of a gas is measured as 49 torr. Represent this pressure in both atmospheres and pascals.

1 atm = 760 mm Hg
= 760 torr
= 101,325 Pa
= 29.92 in Hg
= 14.7 lb/in²

Solution

$$49 \text{ torr} \times \frac{1 \text{ atm}}{760 \text{ torr}} = 6.4 \times 10^{-2} \text{ atm}$$

$$6.4 \times 10^{-2} \text{ atm} \times \frac{101{,}325 \text{ Pa}}{1 \text{ atm}} = 6.5 \times 10^3 \text{ Pa}$$

See Exercises 5.27 and 5.28.

5.2 The Gas Laws of Boyle, Charles, and Avogadro

In this section we will consider several mathematical laws that relate the properties of gases. These laws derive from experiments involving careful measurements of the relevant gas properties. From these experimental results, the mathematical relationships among the properties can be discovered. These relationships are often represented pictorially by means of graphs (plots).

We will take a historical approach to these laws to give you some perspective on the scientific method in action.

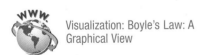

Visualization: Boyle's Law: A Graphical View

Boyle's Law

The first quantitative experiments on gases were performed by an Irish chemist, Robert Boyle (1627–1691). Using a J-shaped tube closed at one end (Fig. 5.4), which he reportedly set up in the multistory entryway of his house, Boyle studied the relationship between the pressure of the trapped gas and its volume. Representative values from Boyle's experiments are given in Table 5.1. These data show that the product of the pressure and

FIGURE 5.4
A J-tube similar to the one used by Boyle.

Boyle's law: $V \propto 1/P$ at constant temperature.

Graphing is reviewed in Appendix 1.3.

TABLE 5.1   Actual Data from Boyle's Experiment

Volume (in³)	Pressure (in Hg)	Pressure × Volume (in Hg × in³)
117.5	12.0	14.1×10^2
87.2	16.0	14.0×10^2
70.7	20.0	14.1×10^2
58.8	24.0	14.1×10^2
44.2	32.0	14.1×10^2
35.3	40.0	14.1×10^2
29.1	48.0	14.0×10^2

volume for the trapped air sample is constant within the accuracies of Boyle's measurements (note the third column in Table 5.1). This behavior can be represented by the equation

$$PV = k$$

which is called **Boyle's law** and where k is a constant for a given sample of air at a specific temperature.

It is convenient to represent the data in Table 5.1 by using two different plots. The first type of plot, P versus V, forms a curve called a *hyperbola* shown in Fig. 5.5(a). Looking at this plot, note that as the volume drops by about half (from 58.8 to 29.1), the pressure doubles (from 24.0 to 48.0). In other words, there is an *inverse relationship* between pressure and volume. The second type of plot can be obtained by rearranging Boyle's law to give

$$V = \frac{k}{P} = k\frac{1}{P}$$

which is the equation for a straight line of the type

$$y = mx + b$$

where m represents the slope and b the intercept of the straight line. In this case, $y = V$, $x = 1/P$, $m = k$, and $b = 0$. Thus a plot of V versus $1/P$ using Boyle's data gives a straight line with an intercept of zero, as shown in Fig. 5.5(b).

In the three centuries since Boyle carried out his studies, the sophistication of measuring techniques has increased tremendously. The results of highly accurate measurements show that Boyle's law holds precisely only at very low pressures. Measurements at higher pressures reveal that PV is not constant but varies as the pressure is varied. Results for several gases at pressures below 1 atm are shown in Fig. 5.6. Note the very small changes that occur in the product PV as the pressure is changed at these low pressures. Such changes become

FIGURE 5.5
Plotting Boyle's data from Table 5.1. (a) A plot of P versus V shows that the volume doubles as the pressure is halved. (b) A plot of V versus $1/P$ gives a straight line. The slope of this line equals the value of the constant k.

(a)

(b)

FIGURE 5.6
A plot of PV versus P for several gases at pressures below 1 atm. An ideal gas is expected to have a constant value of PV, as shown by the dotted line. Carbon dioxide shows the largest change in PV, and this change is actually quite small: PV changes from about 22.39 L · atm at 0.25 atm to 22.26 L · atm at 1.00 atm. Thus Boyle's law is a good approximation at these relatively low pressures.

more significant at much higher pressures, where the complex nature of the dependence of PV on pressure becomes more obvious. We will discuss these deviations and the reasons for them in detail in Section 5.8. *A gas that strictly obeys Boyle's law is called an* **ideal gas.** We will describe the characteristics of an ideal gas more completely in Section 5.3.

One common use of Boyle's law is to predict the new volume of a gas when the pressure is changed (at constant temperature), or vice versa. Because deviations from Boyle's law are so slight at pressures close to 1 atm, in our calculations we will assume that gases obey Boyle's law (unless stated otherwise).

| Sample Exercise 5.2 | **Boyle's Law I** |

Sulfur dioxide (SO_2), a gas that plays a central role in the formation of acid rain, is found in the exhaust of automobiles and power plants. Consider a 1.53-L sample of gaseous SO_2 at a pressure of 5.6×10^3 Pa. If the pressure is changed to 1.5×10^4 Pa at a constant temperature, what will be the new volume of the gas?

Solution

We can solve this problem using Boyle's law,

$$PV = k$$

which also can be written as

$$P_1V_1 = k = P_2V_2 \quad \text{or} \quad P_1V_1 = P_2V_2$$

where the subscripts 1 and 2 represent two states (conditions) of the gas (both at the same temperature). In this case,

$$P_1 = 5.6 \times 10^3 \text{ Pa} \qquad P_2 = 1.5 \times 10^4 \text{ Pa}$$
$$V_1 = 1.53 \text{ L} \qquad\qquad V_2 = ?$$

We can solve the preceding equation for V_2:

$$V_2 = \frac{P_1V_1}{P_2} = \frac{5.6 \times 10^3 \text{ Pa} \times 1.53 \text{ L}}{1.5 \times 10^4 \text{ Pa}} = 0.57 \text{ L}$$

The new volume will be 0.57 L.

See Exercise 5.33.

5.6 × 10³ Pa   1.5 × 10⁴ Pa

$V = 1.53$ L $V = ?$
As pressure increases, the volume of SO_2 decreases.

Boyle's law also can be written as
$$P_1V_1 = P_2V_2$$

Always check that your answer makes physical (common!) sense.

The fact that the volume decreases in Sample Exercise 5.2 makes sense because the pressure was increased. *To help eliminate errors, make it a habit to check whether an answer to a problem makes physical sense.*

We mentioned before that Boyle's law is only approximately true for real gases. To determine the significance of the deviations, studies of the effect of changing pressure on the volume of a gas are often done, as shown in Sample Exercise 5.3.

| Sample Exercise 5.3 | **Boyle's Law II** |

In a study to see how closely gaseous ammonia obeys Boyle's law, several volume measurements were made at various pressures, using 1.0 mol NH_3 gas at a temperature of 0°C. Using the results listed on the following page, calculate the Boyle's law constant for NH_3 at the various pressures.

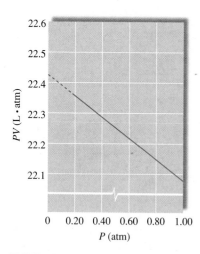

FIGURE 5.7
A plot of PV versus P for 1 mol of ammonia. The dashed line shows the extrapolation of the data to zero pressure to give the "ideal" value of PV of 22.41 L · atm.

Experiment	Pressure (atm)	Volume (L)
1	0.1300	172.1
2	0.2500	89.28
3	0.3000	74.35
4	0.5000	44.49
5	0.7500	29.55
6	1.000	22.08

Solution

To determine how closely NH_3 gas follows Boyle's law under these conditions, we calculate the value of k (in L · atm) for each set of values:

Experiment	1	2	3	4	5	6
$k = PV$	22.37	22.32	22.31	22.25	22.16	22.08

Although the deviations from true Boyle's law behavior are quite small at these low pressures, note that the value of k changes regularly in one direction as the pressure is increased. Thus, to calculate the "ideal" value of k for NH_3, we can plot PV versus P, as shown in Fig. 5.7, and extrapolate (extend the line beyond the experimental points) back to zero pressure, where, for reasons we will discuss later, a gas behaves most ideally. The value of k obtained by this extrapolation is 22.41 L · atm. Notice that this is the same value obtained from similar plots for the gases CO_2, O_2, and Ne at 0°C, as shown in Fig. 5.6.

See Exercise 5.97.

Charles's Law

In the century following Boyle's findings, scientists continued to study the properties of gases. One of these scientists was a French physicist, Jacques Charles (1746–1823), who was the first person to fill a balloon with hydrogen gas and who made the first solo balloon flight. Charles found in 1787 that the volume of a gas at constant pressure increases *linearly* with the temperature of the gas. That is, a plot of the volume of a gas (at constant pressure) versus its temperature (°C) gives a straight line. This behavior is shown for samples of several gases in Fig. 5.8. The slopes of the lines in this graph are different

Visualization: Liquid Nitrogen and Balloons

FIGURE 5.8
Plots of V versus T (°C) for several gases. The solid lines represent experimental measurements on gases. The dashed lines represent extrapolation of the data into regions where these gases would become liquids or solids. Note that the samples of the various gases contain different numbers of moles.

A snowmaking machine, in which water is blown through nozzles by compressed air. The mixture is cooled by expansion to form ice crystals of snow.

FIGURE 5.9
Plots of V versus T as in Fig. 5.8, except here the Kelvin scale is used for temperature.

Visualization: Charles's Law: A Graphical View

Charles's law: $V \propto T$ (expressed in K) of constant pressure.

because the samples contain different numbers of moles of gas. A very interesting feature of these plots is that the volumes of all the gases extrapolate to zero at the same temperature, $-273.2°C$. On the Kelvin temperature scale this point is defined as 0 K, which leads to the following relationship between the Kelvin and Celsius scales:

$$K = °C + 273$$

When the volumes of the gases shown in Fig. 5.8 are plotted versus temperature on the Kelvin scale, the plots in Fig. 5.9 result. In this case, the volume of each gas is *directly proportional to temperature* and extrapolates to zero when the temperature is 0 K. This behavior is represented by the equation known as **Charles's law,**

$$V = bT$$

where T is in kelvins and b is a proportionality constant.

Before we illustrate the uses of Charles's law, let us consider the importance of 0 K. At temperatures below this point, the extrapolated volumes would become negative. The fact that a gas cannot have a negative volume suggests that 0 K has a special significance. In fact, 0 K is called **absolute zero,** and there is much evidence to suggest that this temperature cannot be attained. Temperatures of approximately 0.000001 K have been produced in laboratories, but 0 K has never been reached.

| Sample Exercise 5.4 | **Charles's Law** |

A sample of gas at 15°C and 1 atm has a volume of 2.58 L. What volume will this gas occupy at 38°C and 1 atm?

Solution

Charles's law, which describes the dependence of the volume of a gas on temperature at constant pressure, can be used to solve this problem. Charles's law in the form $V = bT$ can be rearranged to

$$\frac{V}{T} = b$$

Charles's law also can be written as
$$\frac{V_1}{T_1} = \frac{V_2}{T_2}$$

An equivalent statement is

$$\frac{V_1}{T_1} = b = \frac{V_2}{T_2}$$

where the subscripts 1 and 2 represent two states for a given sample of gas at constant pressure. In this case, we are given the following (note that the temperature values *must* be changed to the Kelvin scale):

$$T_1 = 15°C + 273 = 288 \text{ K} \qquad T_2 = 38°C + 273 = 311 \text{ K}$$
$$V_1 = 2.58 \text{ L} \qquad V_2 = ?$$

Solving for V_2 gives

$$V_2 = \left(\frac{T_2}{T_1}\right)V_1 = \left(\frac{311 \text{ K}}{288 \text{ K}}\right)2.58 \text{ L} = 2.79 \text{ L}$$

Reality Check: The new volume is greater than the initial volume, which makes physical sense because the gas will expand as it is heated.

See Exercise 5.35.

Avogadro's Law

In Chapter 2 we noted that in 1811 the Italian chemist Avogadro postulated that equal volumes of gases at the same temperature and pressure contain the same number of "particles." This observation is called **Avogadro's law,** which is illustrated by Fig. 5.10. Stated mathematically, Avogadro's law is

$$V = an$$

where V is the volume of the gas, n is the number of moles of gas particles, and a is a proportionality constant. This equation states that *for a gas at constant temperature and pressure, the volume is directly proportional to the number of moles of gas.* This relationship is obeyed closely by gases at low pressures.

| Sample Exercise 5.5 | Avogadro's Law |

Avogadro's law also can be written as

$$\frac{V_1}{n_1} = \frac{V_2}{n_2}$$

Suppose we have a 12.2-L sample containing 0.50 mol oxygen gas (O_2) at a pressure of 1 atm and a temperature of 25°C. If all this O_2 were converted to ozone (O_3) at the same temperature and pressure, what would be the volume of the ozone?

Solution

The balanced equation for the reaction is

$$3O_2(g) \longrightarrow 2O_3(g)$$

To calculate the moles of O_3 produced, we must use the appropriate mole ratio:

$$0.50 \ \text{mol} \ O_2 \times \frac{2 \ \text{mol} \ O_3}{3 \ \text{mol} \ O_2} = 0.33 \ \text{mol} \ O_3$$

Avogadro's law states that $V = an$, which can be rearranged to give

$$\frac{V}{n} = a$$

Since a is a constant, an alternative representation is

$$\frac{V_1}{n_1} = a = \frac{V_2}{n_2}$$

where V_1 is the volume of n_1 moles of O_2 gas and V_2 is the volume of n_2 moles of O_3 gas. In this case we have

$$n_1 = 0.50 \ \text{mol} \qquad n_2 = 0.33 \ \text{mol}$$
$$V_1 = 12.2 \ \text{L} \qquad V_2 = ?$$

Solving for V_2 gives

$$V_2 = \left(\frac{n_2}{n_1}\right)V_1 = \left(\frac{0.33 \ \text{mol}}{0.50 \ \text{mol}}\right)12.2 \ \text{L} = 8.1 \ \text{L}$$

Reality Check: Note that the volume decreases, as it should, since fewer moles of gas molecules will be present after O_2 is converted to O_3.

See Exercises 5.35 and 5.36.

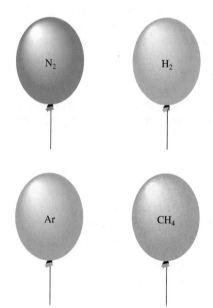

FIGURE 5.10
These balloons each hold 1.0 L of gas at 25°C and 1 atm. Each balloon contains 0.041 mol of gas, or 2.5×10^{22} molecules.

5.3 The Ideal Gas Law

We have considered three laws that describe the behavior of gases as revealed by experimental observations:

Boyle's law:	$V = \dfrac{k}{P}$	(at constant T and n)
Charles's law:	$V = bT$	(at constant P and n)
Avogadro's law:	$V = an$	(at constant T and P)

These relationships, which show how the volume of a gas depends on pressure, temperature, and number of moles of gas present, can be combined as follows:

$$V = R\left(\frac{Tn}{P}\right)$$

$$R = 0.08206 \frac{L \cdot atm}{K \cdot mol}$$

where R is the combined proportionality constant called the **universal gas constant.** When the pressure is expressed in atmospheres and the volume in liters, R has the value 0.08206 L · atm/K · mol. The preceding equation can be rearranged to the more familiar form of the **ideal gas law:**

$$PV = nRT$$

Visualization: The Ideal Gas Law, $PV = nRT$

The ideal gas law is an *equation of state* for a gas, where the state of the gas is its condition at a given time. A particular *state* of a gas is described by its pressure, volume, temperature, and number of moles. Knowledge of any three of these properties is enough to completely define the state of a gas, since the fourth property can then be determined from the equation for the ideal gas law.

The ideal gas law applies best at pressures smaller than 1 atm.

It is important to recognize that the ideal gas law is an empirical equation—it is based on experimental measurements of the properties of gases. A gas that obeys this equation is said to behave *ideally*. The ideal gas equation is best regarded as a limiting law—it expresses behavior that real gases *approach* at low pressures and high temperatures. Therefore, an ideal gas is a hypothetical substance. However, most gases obey the ideal gas equation closely enough at pressures below 1 atm that only minimal errors result from assuming ideal behavior. Unless you are given information to the contrary, you should assume ideal gas behavior when solving problems involving gases in this text.

The ideal gas law can be used to solve a variety of problems. Sample Exercise 5.6 demonstrates one type, where you are asked to find one property characterizing the state of a gas, given the other three.

| *Sample Exercise 5.6* | **Ideal Gas Law I** |

A sample of hydrogen gas (H_2) has a volume of 8.56 L at a temperature of 0°C and a pressure of 1.5 atm. Calculate the moles of H_2 molecules present in this gas sample.

Solution

Solving the ideal gas law for n gives

$$n = \frac{PV}{RT}$$

In this case $P = 1.5$ atm, $V = 8.56$ L, $T = 0°C + 273 = 273$ K, and $R = 0.08206$ L · atm/K · mol. Thus

$$n = \frac{(1.5 \text{ atm})(8.56 \text{ L})}{\left(0.08206 \dfrac{L \cdot atm}{K \cdot mol}\right)(273 \text{ K})} = 0.57 \text{ mol}$$

See Exercises 5.37 through 5.42.

The reaction of zinc with hydrochloric acid to produce bubbles of hydrogen gas.

The ideal gas law is also used to calculate the changes that will occur when the conditions of the gas are changed.

| Sample Exercise 5.7 | **Ideal Gas Law II** |

Suppose we have a sample of ammonia gas with a volume of 7.0 mL at a pressure of 1.68 atm. The gas is compressed to a volume of 2.7 mL at a constant temperature. Use the ideal gas law to calculate the final pressure.

Solution

The basic assumption we make when using the ideal gas law to describe a change in state for a gas is that the equation applies equally well to both the initial and the final states. In dealing with a change in state, we always *place the variables that change on one side of the equals sign and the constants on the other.* In this case the pressure and volume change, and the temperature and the number of moles remain constant (as does R, by definition). Thus we write the ideal gas law as

$$PV = nRT$$

$\nearrow$ Change $\nwarrow$ Remain constant

Since n and T remain the same in this case, we can write $P_1V_1 = nRT$ and $P_2V_2 = nRT$. Combining these gives

$$P_1V_1 = nRT = P_2V_2 \quad \text{or} \quad P_1V_1 = P_2V_2$$

We are given $P_1 = 1.68$ atm, $V_1 = 7.0$ mL, and $V_2 = 2.7$ mL. Solving for P_2 thus gives

$$P_2 = \left(\frac{V_1}{V_2}\right)P_1 = \left(\frac{7.0 \text{ mL}}{2.7 \text{ mL}}\right)1.68 \text{ atm} = 4.4 \text{ atm}$$

Reality Check: Does this answer make sense? The volume decreased (at constant temperature), so the pressure should increase, as the result of the calculation indicates. Note that the calculated final pressure is 4.4 atm. Most gases do not behave ideally above 1 atm. Therefore, we might find that if we *measured* the pressure of this gas sample, the observed pressure would differ slightly from 4.4 atm.

See Exercises 5.43 and 5.44.

As pressure increases, the volume decreases.

| Sample Exercise 5.8 | **Ideal Gas Law III** |

A sample of methane gas that has a volume of 3.8 L at 5°C is heated to 86°C at constant pressure. Calculate its new volume.

Solution

To solve this problem, we take the ideal gas law and segregate the changing variables and the constants by placing them on opposite sides of the equation. In this case, volume and temperature change, and the number of moles and pressure (and, of course, R) remain constant. Thus $PV = nRT$ becomes

$$\frac{V}{T} = \frac{nR}{P}$$

which leads to

$$\frac{V_1}{T_1} = \frac{nR}{P} \quad \text{and} \quad \frac{V_2}{T_2} = \frac{nR}{P}$$

Combining these gives

$$\frac{V_1}{T_1} = \frac{nR}{P} = \frac{V_2}{T_2} \quad \text{or} \quad \frac{V_1}{T_1} = \frac{V_2}{T_2}$$

We are given

$$T_1 = 5°C + 273 = 278 \text{ K} \qquad T_2 = 86°C + 273 = 359 \text{ K}$$
$$V_1 = 3.8 \text{ L} \qquad\qquad\qquad V_2 = ?$$

Thus

$$V_2 = \frac{T_2 V_1}{T_1} = \frac{(359 \text{ K})(3.8 \text{ L})}{278 \text{ K}} = 4.9 \text{ L}$$

Reality Check: Is the answer sensible? In this case the temperature increased (at constant pressure), so the volume should increase. Thus the answer makes sense.

See Exercises 5.45 and 5.46.

The problem in Sample Exercise 5.8 could be described as a "Charles's law problem," whereas the problem in Sample Exercise 5.7 might be called a "Boyle's law problem." In both cases, however, we started with the ideal gas law. The real advantage of using the ideal gas law is that it applies to virtually any problem dealing with gases and is easy to remember.

Sample Exercise 5.9	**Ideal Gas Law IV**

A sample of diborane gas (B_2H_6), a substance that bursts into flame when exposed to air, has a pressure of 345 torr at a temperature of −15°C and a volume of 3.48 L. If conditions are changed so that the temperature is 36°C and the pressure is 468 torr, what will be the volume of the sample?

Solution

Visualization: Changes in Gas Volume, Pressure, and Concentration

Since, for this sample, pressure, temperature, and volume all change while the number of moles remains constant, we use the ideal gas law in the form

$$\frac{PV}{T} = nR$$

which leads to

$$\frac{P_1 V_1}{T_1} = nR = \frac{P_2 V_2}{T_2} \quad \text{or} \quad \frac{P_1 V_1}{T_1} = \frac{P_2 V_2}{T_2}$$

Then

$$V_2 = \frac{T_2 P_1 V_1}{T_1 P_2}$$

We have

$$P_1 = 345 \text{ torr} \qquad\qquad P_2 = 468 \text{ torr}$$
$$T_1 = -15°C + 273 = 258 \text{ K} \qquad T_2 = 36°C + 273 = 309 \text{ K}$$
$$V_1 = 3.48 \text{ L} \qquad\qquad\quad V_2 = ?$$

Thus

$$V_2 = \frac{(309 \text{ K})(345 \text{ torr})(3.48 \text{ L})}{(258 \text{ K})(468 \text{ torr})} = 3.07 \text{ L}$$

See Exercises 5.47 and 5.48.

Always convert the temperature to the Kelvin scale when applying the ideal gas law.

Since the equation used in Sample Exercise 5.9 involves a *ratio* of pressures, it was unnecessary to convert pressures to units of atmospheres. The units of torrs cancel. (You will obtain the same answer by inserting $P_1 = \frac{345}{760}$ and $P_2 = \frac{468}{760}$ into the equation.) However, temperature *must always* be converted to the Kelvin scale; since this conversion involves *addition* of 273, the conversion factor does not cancel. Be careful.

One of the many other types of problems dealing with gases that can be solved using the ideal gas law is illustrated in Sample Exercise 5.10.

| **Ideal Gas Law V**

A sample containing 0.35 mol argon gas at a temperature of 13°C and a pressure of 568 torr is heated to 56°C and a pressure of 897 torr. Calculate the change in volume that occurs.

Solution

We use the ideal gas law to find the volume for each set of conditions:

State 1	State 2
$n_1 = 0.35$ mol	$n_2 = 0.35$ mol
$P_1 = 568 \text{ torr} \times \dfrac{1 \text{ atm}}{760 \text{ torr}} = 0.747$ atm	$P_2 = 897 \text{ torr} \times \dfrac{1 \text{ atm}}{760 \text{ torr}} = 1.18$ atm
$T_1 = 13°C + 273 = 286$ K	$T_2 = 56°C + 273 = 329$ K

Solving the ideal gas law for volume gives

$$V_1 = \frac{n_1 R T_1}{P_1} = \frac{(0.35 \text{ mol})(0.08206 \text{ L} \cdot \text{atm/K} \cdot \text{mol})(286 \text{ K})}{(0.747 \text{ atm})} = 11 \text{ L}$$

and

$$V_2 = \frac{n_2 R T_2}{P_2} = \frac{(0.35 \text{ mol})(0.08206 \text{ L} \cdot \text{atm/K} \cdot \text{mol})(329 \text{ K})}{(1.18 \text{ atm})} = 8.0 \text{ L}$$

Thus, in going from state 1 to state 2, the volume changes from 11 L to 8.0 L. The change in volume, ΔV (Δ is the Greek capital letter delta), is then

$$\Delta V = V_2 - V_1 = 8.0 \text{ L} - 11 \text{ L} = -3 \text{ L}$$

The *change* in volume is negative because the volume decreases. Note that for this problem (unlike Sample Exercise 5.9) the pressures must be converted from torrs to atmospheres, as required by the atmosphere part of the units for R, since each volume was found separately and the conversion factor does not cancel.

See Exercise 5.49.

Argon glowing in a discharge tube.

When 273.15 K is used in this calculation, the molar volume obtained in Sample Exercise 5.3 is the same value as 22.41 L.

5.4 Gas Stoichiometry

Suppose we have 1 mole of an ideal gas at 0°C (273.2 K) and 1 atm. From the ideal gas law, the volume of the gas is given by

$$V = \frac{nRT}{P} = \frac{(1.000 \text{ mol})(0.08206 \text{ L} \cdot \text{atm/K} \cdot \text{mol})(273.2 \text{ K})}{1.000 \text{ atm}} = 22.42 \text{ L}$$

TABLE 5.2   Molar Volumes for Various Gases at 0°C and 1 atm

Gas	Molar Volume (L)
Oxygen (O_2)	22.397
Nitrogen (N_2)	22.402
Hydrogen (H_2)	22.433
Helium (He)	22.434
Argon (Ar)	22.397
Carbon dioxide (CO_2)	22.260
Ammonia (NH_3)	22.079

FIGURE 5.11
22.4 L of a gas would just fit into this box.

This volume of 22.42 liters is the **molar volume** of an ideal gas (at 0°C and 1 atm). The measured molar volumes of several gases are listed in Table 5.2. Note that the molar volumes of some of the gases are very close to the ideal value, while others deviate significantly. Later in this chapter we will discuss some of the reasons for the deviations.

The conditions 0°C and 1 atm, called **standard temperature and pressure** (abbreviated **STP**), are common reference conditions for the properties of gases. For example, the molar volume of an ideal gas is 22.42 liters at STP (see Fig. 5.11).

STP: 0°C and 1 atm

Sample Exercise 5.11   Gas Stoichiometry I

A sample of nitrogen gas has a volume of 1.75 L at STP. How many moles of N_2 are present?

Solution

We could solve this problem by using the ideal gas equation, but we can take a shortcut by using the molar volume of an ideal gas at STP. Since 1 mole of an ideal gas at STP has a volume of 22.42 L, 1.75 L of N_2 at STP will contain less than 1 mole. We can find how many moles using the ratio of 1.75 L to 22.42 L:

$$1.75 \text{ L } N_2 \times \frac{1 \text{ mol } N_2}{22.42 \text{ L } N_2} = 7.81 \times 10^{-2} \text{ mol } N_2$$

See Exercises 5.51 and 5.52.

Many chemical reactions involve gases. By assuming ideal behavior for these gases, we can carry out stoichiometric calculations if the pressure, volume, and temperature of the gases are known.

Sample Exercise 5.12   Gas Stoichiometry II

Quicklime (CaO) is produced by the thermal decomposition of calcium carbonate ($CaCO_3$). Calculate the volume of CO_2 at STP produced from the decomposition of 152 g $CaCO_3$ by the reaction

$$CaCO_3(s) \longrightarrow CaO(s) + CO_2(g)$$

Solution

We employ the same strategy we used in the stoichiometry problems earlier in this book. That is, we compute the number of moles of $CaCO_3$ consumed and the number of moles of CO_2 produced. The moles of CO_2 can then be converted to volume using the molar volume of an ideal gas.

Using the molar mass of $CaCO_3$ (100.09 g/mol), we can calculate the number of moles of $CaCO_3$:

$$152 \text{ g } CaCO_3 \times \frac{1 \text{ mol } CaCO_3}{100.09 \text{ g } CaCO_3} = 1.52 \text{ mol } CaCO_3$$

Since each mole of $CaCO_3$ produces a mole of CO_2, 1.52 mol CO_2 will be formed. We can compute the volume of CO_2 at STP by using the molar volume:

$$1.52 \text{ mol } CO_2 \times \frac{22.42 \text{ L } CO_2}{1 \text{ mol } CO_2} = 34.1 \text{ L } CO_2$$

Thus the decomposition of 152 g $CaCO_3$ produces 34.1 L CO_2 at STP.

See Exercises 5.53 through 5.56.

Remember that the molar volume of an ideal gas is 22.42 L when measured at STP.

Note that in Sample Exercise 5.12 the final step involved calculation of the volume of gas from the number of moles. Since the conditions were specified as STP, we were able to use the molar volume of a gas at STP. If the conditions of a problem are different from STP, the ideal gas law must be used to compute the volume.

Gas Stoichiometry III

A sample of methane gas having a volume of 2.80 L at 25°C and 1.65 atm was mixed with a sample of oxygen gas having a volume of 35.0 L at 31°C and 1.25 atm. The mixture was then ignited to form carbon dioxide and water. Calculate the volume of CO_2 formed at a pressure of 2.50 atm and a temperature of 125°C.

Solution

From the description of the reaction, the unbalanced equation is

$$CH_4(g) + O_2(g) \longrightarrow CO_2(g) + H_2O(g)$$

which can be balanced to give

$$CH_4(g) + 2O_2(g) \longrightarrow CO_2(g) + 2H_2O(g)$$

Next, we must find the limiting reactant, which requires calculating the numbers of moles of each reactant. We convert the given volumes of methane and oxygen to moles using the ideal gas law as follows:

$$n_{CH_4} = \frac{PV}{RT} = \frac{(1.65 \text{ atm})(2.80 \text{ L})}{(0.08206 \text{ L} \cdot \text{ atm}/K \cdot \text{ mol})(298 \text{ K})} = 0.189 \text{ mol}$$

$$n_{O_2} = \frac{PV}{RT} = \frac{(1.25 \text{ atm})(35.0 \text{ L})}{(0.08206 \text{ L} \cdot \text{ atm}/K \cdot \text{ mol})(304 \text{ K})} = 1.75 \text{ mol}$$

In the balanced equation for the combustion reaction, 1 mol CH_4 requires 2 mol O_2. Thus the moles of O_2 required by 0.189 mol CH_4 can be calculated as follows:

$$0.189 \text{ mol } CH_4 \times \frac{2 \text{ mol } O_2}{1 \text{ mol } CH_4} = 0.378 \text{ mol } O_2$$

Since 1.75 mol O_2 is available, O_2 is in excess. The limiting reactant is CH_4. The number of moles of CH_4 available must be used to calculate the number of moles of CO_2 produced:

$$0.189 \ \text{mol CH}_4 \times \frac{1 \ \text{mol CO}_2}{1 \ \text{mol CH}_4} = 0.189 \ \text{mol CO}_2$$

Since the conditions stated are not STP, we must use the ideal gas law to calculate the volume:

$$V = \frac{nRT}{P}$$

In this case $n = 0.189$ mol, $T = 125°C + 273 = 398$ K, $P = 2.50$ atm, and $R = 0.08206$ L $\cdot$ atm/K $\cdot$ mol. Thus

$$V = \frac{(0.189 \ \text{mol})(0.08206 \ \text{L} \cdot \text{atm/K} \cdot \text{mol})(398 \ \text{K})}{2.50 \ \text{atm}} = 2.47 \ \text{L}$$

This represents the volume of CO_2 produced under these conditions.

See Exercises 5.57 and 5.58.

Molar Mass of a Gas

One very important use of the ideal gas law is in the calculation of the molar mass (molecular weight) of a gas from its measured density. To see the relationship between gas density and molar mass, consider that the number of moles of gas n can be expressed as

$$n = \frac{\text{grams of gas}}{\text{molar mass}} = \frac{\text{mass}}{\text{molar mass}} = \frac{m}{\text{molar mass}}$$

Substitution into the ideal gas equation gives

$$P = \frac{nRT}{V} = \frac{(m/\text{molar mass})RT}{V} = \frac{m(RT)}{V(\text{molar mass})}$$

$\text{Density} = \dfrac{\text{mass}}{\text{volume}}$

However, m/V is the gas density d in units of grams per liter. Thus

$$P = \frac{dRT}{\text{molar mass}}$$

or

$$\text{Molar mass} = \frac{dRT}{P} \qquad (5.1)$$

Thus, if the density of a gas at a given temperature and pressure is known, its molar mass can be calculated.

| Sample Exercise 5.14 | ## Gas Density/Molar Mass |

The density of a gas was measured at 1.50 atm and 27°C and found to be 1.95 g/L. Calculate the molar mass of the gas.

Solution

Using Equation (5.1), we calculate the molar mass as follows:

$$\text{Molar mass} = \frac{dRT}{P} = \frac{\left(1.95 \ \dfrac{\text{g}}{\text{L}}\right)\left(0.08206 \ \dfrac{\text{L} \cdot \text{atm}}{\text{K} \cdot \text{mol}}\right)(300. \ \text{K})}{1.50 \ \text{atm}} = 32.0 \ \text{g/mol}$$

Reality Check: These are the units expected for molar mass.

See Exercises 5.61 through 5.64.

You could memorize the equation involving gas density and molar mass, but it is better simply to remember the total gas equation, the definition of density, and the relationship between number of moles and molar mass. You can then derive the appropriate equation when you need it. This approach ensures that you understand the concepts and means one less equation to memorize.

5.5 Dalton's Law of Partial Pressures

Among the experiments that led John Dalton to propose the atomic theory were his studies of mixtures of gases. In 1803 Dalton summarized his observations as follows: *For a mixture of gases in a container, the total pressure exerted is the sum of the pressures that each gas would exert if it were alone.* This statement, known as **Dalton's law of partial pressures,** can be expressed as follows:

$$P_{TOTAL} = P_1 + P_2 + P_3 + \cdots$$

where the subscripts refer to the individual gases (gas 1, gas 2, and so on). The symbols P_1, P_2, P_3, and so on represent each **partial pressure,** the pressure that a particular gas would exert if it were alone in the container.

Assuming that each gas behaves ideally, the partial pressure of each gas can be calculated from the ideal gas law:

$$P_1 = \frac{n_1 RT}{V}, \qquad P_2 = \frac{n_2 RT}{V}, \qquad P_3 = \frac{n_3 RT}{V}, \qquad \cdots$$

The total pressure of the mixture P_{TOTAL} can be represented as

$$P_{TOTAL} = P_1 + P_2 + P_3 + \cdots = \frac{n_1 RT}{V} + \frac{n_2 RT}{V} + \frac{n_3 RT}{V} + \cdots$$

$$= (n_1 + n_2 + n_3 + \cdots)\left(\frac{RT}{V}\right)$$

$$= n_{TOTAL}\left(\frac{RT}{V}\right)$$

where n_{TOTAL} is the sum of the numbers of moles of the various gases. Thus, for a mixture of ideal gases, it is the *total number of moles of particles* that is important, not the identity or composition of the involved gas particles. This idea is illustrated in Fig. 5.12.

FIGURE 5.12
The partial pressure of each gas in a mixture of gases in a container depends on the number of moles of that gas. The total pressure is the sum of the partial pressures and depends on the total moles of gas particles present, no matter what they are.

This important observation indicates some fundamental characteristics of an ideal gas. The fact that the pressure exerted by an ideal gas is not affected by the identity (composition) of the gas particles reveals two things about ideal gases: (1) the volume of the individual gas particle must not be important, and (2) the forces among the particles must not be important. If these factors were important, the pressure exerted by the gas would depend on the nature of the individual particles. These observations will strongly influence the model that we will eventually construct to explain ideal gas behavior.

Sample Exercise 5.15

Dalton's Law I

Mixtures of helium and oxygen can be used in scuba diving tanks to help prevent "the bends." For a particular dive, 46 L He at 25°C and 1.0 atm and 12 L O_2 at 25°C and 1.0 atm were pumped into a tank with a volume of 5.0 L. Calculate the partial pressure of each gas and the total pressure in the tank at 25°C.

Solution

The first step is to calculate the number of moles of each gas using the ideal gas law in the form:

$$n = \frac{PV}{RT}$$

$$n_{He} = \frac{(1.0 \text{ atm})(46 \text{ L})}{(0.08206 \text{ L} \cdot \text{atm/K} \cdot \text{mol})(298 \text{ K})} = 1.9 \text{ mol}$$

$$n_{O_2} = \frac{(1.0 \text{ atm})(12 \text{ L})}{(0.08206 \text{ L} \cdot \text{atm/K} \cdot \text{mol})(298 \text{ K})} = 0.49 \text{ mol}$$

The tank containing the mixture has a volume of 5.0 L, and the temperature is 25°C. We can use these data and the ideal gas law to calculate the partial pressure of each gas:

$$P = \frac{nRT}{V}$$

$$P_{He} = \frac{(1.9 \text{ mol})(0.08206 \text{ L} \cdot \text{atm/K} \cdot \text{mol})(298 \text{ K})}{5.0 \text{ L}} = 9.3 \text{ atm}$$

$$P_{O_2} = \frac{(0.49 \text{ mol})(0.08206 \text{ L} \cdot \text{atm/K} \cdot \text{mol})(298 \text{ K})}{5.0 \text{ L}} = 2.4 \text{ atm}$$

The total pressure is the sum of the partial pressures:

$$P_{TOTAL} = P_{He} + P_{O_2} = 9.3 \text{ atm} + 2.4 \text{ atm} = 11.7 \text{ atm}$$

See Exercises 5.65 and 5.66.

At this point we need to define the **mole fraction:** *the ratio of the number of moles of a given component in a mixture to the total number of moles in the mixture.* The Greek lowercase letter chi (*X*) is used to symbolize the mole fraction. For example, for a given component in a mixture, the mole fraction X_1 is

$$X_1 = \frac{n_1}{n_{TOTAL}} = \frac{n_1}{n_1 + n_2 + n_3 + \cdots}$$

CHEMICAL IMPACT

Separating Gases

Assume you work for an oil company that owns a huge natural gas reservoir containing a mixture of methane and nitrogen gases. In fact, the gas mixture contains so much nitrogen that it is unusable as a fuel. Your job is to separate the nitrogen (N_2) from the methane (CH_4). How might you accomplish this task? You clearly need some sort of "molecular filter" that will stop the slightly larger methane molecules (size $\approx$ 430 pm) and allow the nitrogen molecules (size $\approx$ 410 pm) to pass through. To accomplish the separation of molecules so similar in size will require a very precise "filter."

The good news is that such a filter exists. Recent work by Steven Kuznick and Valerie Bell at Engelhard Corporation in New Jersey and Michael Tsapatsis at the University of Massachusetts has produced a "molecular sieve" in which the pore (passage) sizes can be adjusted precisely enough to separate N_2 molecules from CH_4 molecules. The material involved is a special hydrated titanosilicate (contains H_2O, Ti, Si, O, and Sr) compound patented by Engelhard known as ETS-4 (Engelhard TitanoSilicate-4). When sodium ions are substituted for the strontium ions in ETS-4 and the new material is carefully dehydrated, a uniform and controllable pore-size reduction occurs (see figure). The researchers have shown that the material can be used to separate N_2 ($\approx$ 410 pm) from O_2 ($\approx$ 390 pm). They have also shown that it is possible to reduce the nitrogen content of natural gas from 18% to less than 5% with a 90% recovery of methane.

Molecular sieve framework of titanium (blue), silicon (green), and oxygen (red) atoms contracts on heating—at room temperature (left), d = 4.27 Å; at 250°C (right), d = 3.94 Å.

From the ideal gas equation we know that the number of moles of a gas is directly proportional to the pressure of the gas, since

$$n = P\left(\frac{V}{RT}\right)$$

That is, for each component in the mixture,

$$n_1 = P_1\left(\frac{V}{RT}\right), \qquad n_2 = P_2\left(\frac{V}{RT}\right), \qquad \cdots$$

Therefore, we can represent the mole fraction in terms of pressures:

$$\chi_1 = \frac{n_1}{n_{\text{TOTAL}}} = \frac{\overbrace{P_1(V/RT)}^{n_1}}{\underbrace{P_1(V/RT)}_{n_1} + \underbrace{P_2(V/RT)}_{n_2} + \underbrace{P_3(V/RT)}_{n_3} + \cdots}$$

$$= \frac{(V/RT)P_1}{(V/RT)(P_1 + P_2 + P_3 + \cdots)}$$

$$= \frac{P_1}{P_1 + P_2 + P_3 + \cdots} = \frac{P_1}{P_{\text{TOTAL}}}$$

In fact, the mole fraction of each component in a mixture of ideal gases is directly related to its partial pressure:

$$\chi_2 = \frac{n_2}{n_{\text{TOTAL}}} = \frac{P_2}{P_{\text{TOTAL}}}$$

CHEMICAL IMPACT

The Chemistry of Air Bags

Most experts agree that air bags represent a very important advance in automobile safety. These bags, which are stored in the auto's steering wheel or dash, are designed to inflate rapidly (within about 40 ms) in the event of a crash, cushioning the front-seat occupants against impact. The bags then deflate immediately to allow vision and movement after the crash. Air bags are activated when a severe deceleration (an impact) causes a steel ball to compress a spring and electrically ignite a detonator cap, which, in turn, causes sodium azide (NaN_3) to decompose explosively, forming sodium and nitrogen gas:

$$2NaN_3(s) \longrightarrow 2Na(s) + 3N_2(g)$$

This system works very well and requires a relatively small amount of sodium azide (100 g yields 56 L $N_2(g)$ at 25°C and 1.0 atm).

When a vehicle containing air bags reaches the end of its useful life, the sodium azide present in the activators must be given proper disposal. Sodium azide, besides being explosive, has a toxicity roughly equal to that of sodium cyanide. It also forms hydrazoic acid (HN_3), a toxic and explosive liquid, when treated with acid.

The air bag represents an application of chemistry that has already saved thousands of lives.

Inflated air bags.

Sample Exercise 5.16	## Dalton's Law II

The partial pressure of oxygen was observed to be 156 torr in air with a total atmospheric pressure of 743 torr. Calculate the mole fraction of O_2 present.

Solution

The mole fraction of O_2 can be calculated from the equation

$$\chi_{O_2} = \frac{P_{O_2}}{P_{TOTAL}} = \frac{156 \text{ torr}}{743 \text{ torr}} = 0.210$$

Note that the mole fraction has no units.

See Exercise 5.69.

The expression for the mole fraction,

$$\chi_1 = \frac{P_1}{P_{TOTAL}}$$

can be rearranged to give

$$P_1 = \chi_1 \times P_{TOTAL}$$

That is, *the partial pressure of a particular component of a gaseous mixture is the mole fraction of that component times the total pressure.*

FIGURE 5.13
The production of oxygen by thermal decomposition of $KClO_3$. The MnO_2 is mixed with the $KClO_3$ to make the reaction faster.

| Sample Exercise 5.17 | Dalton's Law III |

The mole fraction of nitrogen in the air is 0.7808. Calculate the partial pressure of N_2 in air when the atmospheric pressure is 760. torr.

Solution

The partial pressure of N_2 can be calculated as follows:

$$P_{N_2} = \chi_{N_2} \times P_{TOTAL} = 0.7808 \times 760. \text{ torr} = 593 \text{ torr}$$

See Exercise 5.70.

Collecting a Gas over Water

Vapor pressure will be discussed in detail in Chapter 10. A table of water vapor pressure values is given in Section 10.8.

A mixture of gases results whenever a gas is collected by displacement of water. For example, Fig. 5.13 shows the collection of oxygen gas produced by the decomposition of solid potassium chlorate. In this situation, the gas in the bottle is a mixture of water vapor and the oxygen being collected. Water vapor is present because molecules of water escape from the surface of the liquid and collect in the space above the liquid. Molecules of water also return to the liquid. When the rate of escape equals the rate of return, the number of water molecules in the vapor state remains constant, and thus the pressure of water vapor remains constant. This pressure, which depends on temperature, is called the *vapor pressure of water.*

| Sample Exercise 5.18 | **Gas Collection over Water** |

A sample of solid potassium chlorate ($KClO_3$) was heated in a test tube (see Fig. 5.13) and decomposed by the following reaction:

$$2KClO_3(s) \longrightarrow 2KCl(s) + 3O_2(g)$$

The oxygen produced was collected by displacement of water at 22°C at a total pressure of 754 torr. The volume of the gas collected was 0.650 L, and the vapor pressure of water at 22°C is 21 torr. Calculate the partial pressure of O_2 in the gas collected and the mass of $KClO_3$ in the sample that was decomposed.

Solution

First we find the partial pressure of O_2 from Dalton's law of partial pressures:

$$P_{TOTAL} = P_{O_2} + P_{H_2O} = P_{O_2} + 21 \text{ torr} = 754 \text{ torr}$$

Thus

$$P_{O_2} = 754 \text{ torr} - 21 \text{ torr} = 733 \text{ torr}$$

Now we use the ideal gas law to find the number of moles of O_2:

$$n_{O_2} = \frac{P_{O_2}V}{RT}$$

In this case,

$$P_{O_2} = 733 \text{ torr} = \frac{733 \text{ torr}}{760 \text{ torr/atm}} = 0.964 \text{ atm}$$

$$V = 0.650 \text{ L}$$

$$T = 22°C + 273 = 295 \text{ K}$$

$$R = 0.08206 \text{ L} \cdot \text{atm/K} \cdot \text{mol}$$

Thus

$$n_{O_2} = \frac{(0.964 \text{ atm})(0.650 \text{ L})}{(0.08206 \text{ L} \cdot \text{atm/K} \cdot \text{mol})(295 \text{ K})} = 2.59 \times 10^{-2} \text{ mol}$$

Next we will calculate the moles of $KClO_3$ needed to produce this quantity of O_2. From the balanced equation for the decomposition of $KClO_3$, we have a mole ratio of 2 mol $KClO_3$/3 mol O_2. The moles of $KClO_3$ can be calculated as follows:

$$2.59 \times 10^{-2} \text{ mol } O_2 \times \frac{2 \text{ mol } KClO_3}{3 \text{ mol } O_2} = 1.73 \times 10^{-2} \text{ mol } KClO_3$$

Using the molar mass of $KClO_3$ (122.6 g/mol), we calculate the grams of $KClO_3$:

$$1.73 \times 10^{-2} \text{ mol } KClO_3 \times \frac{122.6 \text{ g } KClO_3}{1 \text{ mol } KClO_3} = 2.12 \text{ g } KClO_3$$

Thus the original sample contained 2.12 g $KClO_3$.

See Exercises 5.71 through 5.73.

5.6 The Kinetic Molecular Theory of Gases

We have so far considered the behavior of gases from an experimental point of view. Based on observations from different types of experiments, we know that at pressures of less than 1 atm most gases closely approach the behavior described by the ideal gas law. Now we want to construct a model to explain this behavior.

Before we do this, let's briefly review the scientific method. Recall that a law is a way of generalizing behavior that has been observed in many experiments. Laws are very useful, since they allow us to predict the behavior of similar systems. For example, if a chemist prepares a new gaseous compound, a measurement of the gas density at known pressure and temperature can provide a reliable value for the compound's molar mass.

However, although laws summarize observed behavior, they do not tell us *why* nature behaves in the observed fashion. This is the central question for scientists. To try to answer this question, we construct theories (build models). The models in chemistry consist of speculations about what the individual atoms or molecules (microscopic particles) might be doing to cause the observed behavior of the macroscopic systems (collections of very large numbers of atoms and molecules).

A model is considered successful if it explains the observed behavior in question and predicts correctly the results of future experiments. It is important to understand that a model can never be proved absolutely true. In fact, *any model is an approximation* by its

(a)   (b)

FIGURE 5.14
(a) One mole of $N_2(l)$ has a volume of approximately 35 mL and a density of 0.81 g/mL. (b) One mole of $N_2(g)$ has a volume of 22.4 L (STP) and a density of 1.2×10^{-3} g/mL. Thus the ratio of the volumes of gaseous N_2 and liquid N_2 is 22.4/0.035 = 640 and the spacing of the molecules is 9 times farther apart in $N_2(g)$.

Visualization: Visualizing Molecular Motion: Single Molecule

Visualization: Visualizing Molecular Motion: Many Molecules

Visualization: Boyle's Law: A Molecular-Level View

very nature and is bound to fail at some point. Models range from the simple to the extraordinarily complex. We use simple models to predict approximate behavior and more complicated models to account very precisely for observed quantitative behavior. In this text we will stress simple models that provide an approximate picture of what might be happening and that fit the most important experimental results.

An example of this type of model is the **kinetic molecular theory (KMT),** a simple model that attempts to explain the properties of an ideal gas. This model is based on speculations about the behavior of the individual gas particles (atoms or molecules). The postulates of the kinetic molecular theory as they relate to the particles of an ideal gas can be stated as follows:

1. The particles are so small compared with the distances between them that *the volume of the individual particles can be assumed to be negligible* (zero). See Fig. 5.14.

2. *The particles are in constant motion. The collisions of the particles with the walls of the container are the cause of the pressure exerted by the gas.*

3. *The particles are assumed to exert no forces on each other;* they are assumed neither to attract nor to repel each other.

4. *The average kinetic energy of a collection of gas particles is assumed to be directly proportional to the Kelvin temperature of the gas.*

Of course, the molecules in a real gas have finite volumes and do exert forces on each other. Thus *real gases* do not conform to these assumptions. However, we will see that these postulates do indeed explain *ideal gas* behavior.

The true test of a model is how well its predictions fit the experimental observations. The postulates of the kinetic molecular model picture an ideal gas as consisting of particles having no volume and no attractions for each other, and the model assumes that the gas produces pressure on its container by collisions with the walls.

Let's consider how this model accounts for the properties of gases as summarized by the ideal gas law: $PV = nRT$.

Pressure and Volume (Boyle's Law)

We have seen that for a given sample of gas at a given temperature (n and T are constant) that if the volume of a gas is decreased, the pressure increases:

$$P = (nRT)\frac{1}{V}$$

↑
Constant

FIGURE 5.15
The effects of decreasing the volume of a sample of gas at constant temperature.

This makes sense based on the kinetic molecular theory, since a decrease in volume means that the gas particles will hit the wall more often, thus increasing pressure, as illustrated in Fig. 5.15.

Pressure and Temperature

From the ideal gas law we can predict that for a given sample of an ideal gas at a constant volume, the pressure will be directly proportional to the temperature:

$$P = \left(\frac{nR}{V}\right)T$$

$\uparrow$
Constant

The KMT accounts for this behavior because when the temperature of a gas increases, the speeds of its particles increase, the particles hitting the wall with greater force and greater frequency. Since the volume remains the same, this would result in increased gas pressure, as illustrated in Fig. 5.16.

Volume and Temperature (Charles's Law)

The ideal gas law indicates that for a given sample of gas at a constant pressure, the volume of the gas is directly proportional to the temperature in kelvins:

$$V = \left(\frac{nR}{P}\right)T$$

$\uparrow$
Constant

Visualization: Charles's Law: A Molecular-Level View

This can be visualized from the KMT, as shown in Fig. 5.17. When the gas is heated to a higher temperature, the speeds of its molecules increase and thus they hit the walls more often and with more force. The only way to keep the pressure constant in this situation is to increase the volume of the container. This compensates for the increased particle speeds.

FIGURE 5.16
The effects of increasing the temperature of a sample of gas at constant volume.

FIGURE 5.17
The effects of increasing the temperature of a sample of gas at constant pressure.

Volume and Number of Moles (Avogadro's Law)

The ideal gas law predicts that the volume of a gas at a constant temperature and pressure depends directly on the number of gas particles present:

$$V = \left(\frac{RT}{P}\right)n$$

$\uparrow$
Constant

This makes sense in terms of the KMT, because an increase in the number of gas particles at the same temperature would cause the pressure to increase if the volume were held constant (see Fig. 5.18). The only way to return the pressure to its original value is to increase the volume.

It is important to recognize that the volume of a gas (at constant P and T) depends only on the *number* of gas particles present. The individual volumes of the particles are not a factor because the particle volumes are so small compared with the distances between the particles (for a gas behaving ideally).

Mixture of Gases (Dalton's Law)

The observation that the total pressure exerted by a mixture of gases is the sum of the pressures of the individual gases is expected because the KMT assumes that all gas particles are independent of each other and that the volumes of the individual particles are unimportant. Thus the identities of the gas particles do not matter.

Deriving the Ideal Gas Law

We have shown qualitatively that the assumptions of the KMT successfully account for the observed behavior of an ideal gas. We can go further. By applying the principles of physics to the assumptions of the KMT, we can in effect derive the ideal gas law.

FIGURE 5.18
The effects of increasing the number of moles of gas particles at constant temperature and pressure.

As shown in detail in Appendix 2, we can apply the definitions of velocity, momentum, force, and pressure to the collection of particles in an ideal gas and *derive* the following expression for pressure:

$$P = \frac{2}{3}\left[\frac{nN_A(\frac{1}{2}m\overline{u^2})}{V}\right]$$

where P is the pressure of the gas, n is the number of moles of gas, N_A is Avogadro's number, m is the mass of each particle, $\overline{u^2}$ is the average of the square of the velocities of the particles, and V is the volume of the container.

The quantity $\frac{1}{2}m\overline{u^2}$ represents the average kinetic energy of a gas particle. If the average kinetic energy of an individual particle is multiplied by N_A, the number of particles in a mole, we get the average kinetic energy for a mole of gas particles:

$$(KE)_{avg} = N_A(\tfrac{1}{2}m\overline{u^2})$$

Kinetic energy (KE) given by the equation $KE = \frac{1}{2}m\overline{u^2}$ is the energy due to the motion of a particle. We will discuss this further in Section 6.1.

Using this definition, we can rewrite the expression for pressure as

$$P = \frac{2}{3}\left[\frac{n(KE)_{avg}}{V}\right] \quad \text{or} \quad \frac{PV}{n} = \frac{2}{3}(KE)_{avg}$$

Visualization: Liquid Nitrogen and Balloons

The fourth postulate of the kinetic molecular theory is that the average kinetic energy of the particles in the gas sample is directly proportional to the temperature in Kelvins. Thus, since $(KE)_{avg} \propto T$, we can write

$$\frac{PV}{n} = \frac{2}{3}(KE)_{avg} \propto T \quad \text{or} \quad \frac{PV}{n} \propto T$$

Note that this expression has been *derived* from the assumptions of the kinetic molecular theory. How does it compare to the ideal gas law—the equation obtained from experiment? Compare the ideal gas law,

$$\frac{PV}{n} = RT \quad \text{From experiment}$$

with the result from the kinetic molecular theory,

$$\frac{PV}{n} \propto T \quad \text{From theory}$$

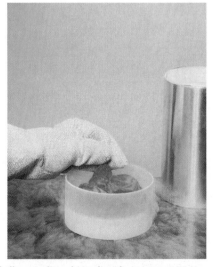

(a) A balloon filled with air at room temperature. (b) The balloon is dipped into liquid nitrogen at 77 K. (c) The balloon collapses as the molecules inside slow down due to the decreased temperature. Slower molecules produce a lower pressure.

These expressions have exactly the same form if R, the universal gas constant, is considered the proportionality constant in the second case.

The agreement between the ideal gas law and the predictions of the kinetic molecular theory gives us confidence in the validity of the model. The characteristics we have assumed for ideal gas particles must agree, at least under certain conditions, with their actual behavior.

The Meaning of Temperature

We have seen from the kinetic molecular theory that the Kelvin temperature indicates the average kinetic energy of the gas particles. The exact relationship between temperature and average kinetic energy can be obtained by combining the equations:

$$\frac{PV}{n} = RT = \frac{2}{3}(KE)_{avg}$$

which yields the expression

$$(KE)_{avg} = \frac{3}{2}RT$$

This is a very important relationship. It summarizes the meaning of the Kelvin temperature of a gas: The Kelvin temperature is an index of the random motions of the particles of a gas, with higher temperature meaning greater motion. (As we will see in Chapter 10, temperature is an index of the random motions in solids and liquids as well as in gases.)

Root Mean Square Velocity

In the equation from the kinetic molecular theory, the average velocity of the gas particles is a special kind of average. The symbol $\overline{u^2}$ means the average of the *squares* of the particle velocities. The square root of $\overline{u^2}$ is called the **root mean square velocity** and is symbolized by u_{rms}:

$$u_{rms} = \sqrt{\overline{u^2}}$$

We can obtain an expression for u_{rms} from the equations

$$(KE)_{avg} = N_A(\tfrac{1}{2}m\overline{u^2}) \quad \text{and} \quad (KE)_{avg} = \frac{3}{2}RT$$

Combination of these equations gives

$$N_A(\tfrac{1}{2}m\overline{u^2}) = \frac{3}{2}RT \quad \text{or} \quad \overline{u^2} = \frac{3RT}{N_A m}$$

Taking the square root of both sides of the last equation produces

$$\sqrt{\overline{u^2}} = u_{rms} = \sqrt{\frac{3RT}{N_A m}}$$

In this expression m represents the mass in kilograms of a single gas particle. When N_A, the number of particles in a mole, is multiplied by m, the product is the mass of a *mole* of gas particles in *kilograms*. We will call this quantity M. Substituting M for $N_A m$ in the equation for u_{rms}, we obtain

$$u_{rms} = \sqrt{\frac{3RT}{M}}$$

Before we can use this equation, we need to consider the units for R. So far we have used 0.08206 L · atm/K · mol as the value of R. But to obtain the desired units (meters

$$R = 0.08206 \frac{L \cdot atm}{K \cdot mol}$$

$$R = 8.3145 \frac{J}{K \cdot mol}$$

per second) for u_{rms}, R must be expressed in different units. As we will see in more detail in Chapter 6, the energy unit most often used in the SI system is the joule (J). A **joule** is defined as a kilogram meter squared per second squared (kg $\cdot$ m^2/s^2). When R is converted to include the unit of joules, it has the value 8.3145 J/K $\cdot$ mol. When R in these units is used in the expression $\sqrt{3RT/M}$, u_{rms} is obtained in the units of meters per second as desired.

| Sample Exercise 5.19 | **Root Mean Square Velocity** |

Calculate the root mean square velocity for the atoms in a sample of helium gas at 25°C.

Solution

The formula for root mean square velocity is

$$u_{rms} = \sqrt{\frac{3RT}{M}}$$

Visualization: Kinetic-Molecular Theory/Heat Transfer

In this case $T = 25°C + 273 = 298$ K, $R = 8.3145$ J/K $\cdot$ mol, and M is the mass of a mole of helium in kilograms:

$$M = 4.00 \frac{g}{mol} \times \frac{1 \text{ kg}}{1000 \text{ g}} = 4.00 \times 10^{-3} \text{ kg/mol}$$

Thus

$$u_{rms} = \sqrt{\frac{3\left(8.3145 \frac{J}{K \cdot mol}\right)(298 \text{ K})}{4.00 \times 10^{-3} \frac{kg}{mol}}} = \sqrt{1.86 \times 10^6 \frac{J}{kg}}$$

Since the units of J are kg $\cdot$ m^2/s^2, this expression becomes

$$\sqrt{1.86 \times 10^6 \frac{kg \cdot m^2}{kg \cdot s^2}} = 1.36 \times 10^3 \text{ m/s}$$

Note that the resulting units (m/s) are appropriate for velocity.

See Exercises 5.79 and 5.80.

FIGURE 5.19
Path of one particle in a gas. Any given particle will continuously change its course as a result of collisions with other particles, as well as with the walls of the container.

So far we have said nothing about the range of velocities actually found in a gas sample. In a real gas there are large numbers of collisions between particles. For example, as we will see in the next section, when an odorous gas such as ammonia is released in a room, it takes some time for the odor to permeate the air. This delay results from collisions between the NH_3 molecules and the O_2 and N_2 molecules in the air, which greatly slow the mixing process.

If the path of a particular gas particle could be monitored, it would look very erratic, something like that shown in Fig. 5.19. The average distance a particle travels between collisions in a particular gas sample is called the *mean free path*. It is typically a very small distance (1×10^{-7} m for O_2 at STP). One effect of the many collisions among gas particles is to produce a large range of velocities as the particles collide and exchange kinetic energy. Although u_{rms} for oxygen gas at STP is approximately 500 meters per second, the majority of O_2 molecules do not have this velocity. The actual distribution of molecular velocities for oxygen gas at STP is shown in Fig. 5.20. This figure shows the relative number of gas molecules having each particular velocity.

We are also interested in the effect of *temperature* on the velocity distribution in a gas. Figure 5.21 shows the velocity distribution for nitrogen gas at three temperatures. Note that as the temperature is increased, the curve peak moves toward higher values and the range

Relative number of O₂ molecules with given velocity

0   4×10^2 8×10^2
Molecular velocity (m/s)

FIGURE 5.20
A plot of the relative number of O_2 molecules that have a given velocity at STP.

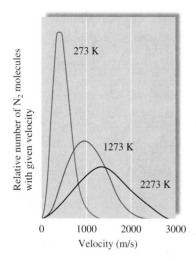

FIGURE 5.21
A plot of the relative number of N_2 molecules that have a given velocity at three temperatures. Note that as the temperature increases, both the average velocity and the spread of velocities increase.

Visualization: Effusion of a Gas

In Graham's law the units for molar mass can be g/mol or kg/mol, since the units cancel in the ratio $\sqrt{M_2}/\sqrt{M_1}$.

of velocities becomes much larger. The peak of the curve reflects the most probable velocity (the velocity found most often as we sample the movement of the various particles in the gas). Because the kinetic energy increases with temperature, it makes sense that the peak of the curve should move to higher values as the temperature of the gas is increased.

5.7 Effusion and Diffusion

We have seen that the postulates of the kinetic molecular theory, when combined with the appropriate physical principles, produce an equation that successfully fits the experimentally observed behavior of gases as they approach ideal behavior. Two phenomena involving gases provide further tests of this model.

Diffusion is the term used to describe the mixing of gases. When a small amount of pungent-smelling ammonia is released at the front of a classroom, it takes some time before everyone in the room can smell it, because time is required for the ammonia to mix with the air. The rate of diffusion is the rate of the mixing of gases. **Effusion** is the term used to describe the passage of a gas through a tiny orifice into an evacuated chamber, as shown in Fig. 5.22. The rate of effusion measures the speed at which the gas is transferred into the chamber.

Effusion

Thomas Graham (1805–1869), a Scottish chemist, found experimentally that the rate of effusion of a gas is inversely proportional to the square root of the mass of its particles. Stated in another way, the relative rates of effusion of two gases at the same temperature and pressure are given by the inverse ratio of the square roots of the masses of the gas particles:

$$\frac{\text{Rate of effusion for gas 1}}{\text{Rate of effusion for gas 2}} = \frac{\sqrt{M_2}}{\sqrt{M_1}}$$

where M_1 and M_2 represent the molar masses of the gases. This equation is called **Graham's law of effusion.**

| Sample Exercise 5.20 | **Effusion Rates** |

Calculate the ratio of the effusion rates of hydrogen gas (H_2) and uranium hexafluoride (UF_6), a gas used in the enrichment process to produce fuel for nuclear reactors (see Fig. 5.23).

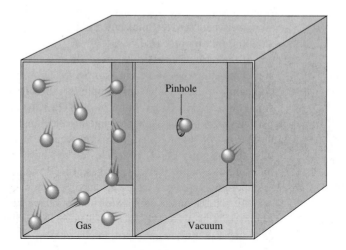

FIGURE 5.22
The effusion of a gas into an evacuated chamber. The rate of effusion (the rate at which the gas is transferred across the barrier through the pin hole) is inversely proportional to the square root of the mass of the gas molecules.

FIGURE 5.23
Relative molecular speed distribution of H_2 and UF_6.

Solution

First we need to compute the molar masses: Molar mass of H_2 = 2.016 g/mol, and molar mass of UF_6 = 352.02 g/mol. Using Graham's law,

$$\frac{\text{Rate of effusion for } H_2}{\text{Rate of effusion for } UF_6} = \frac{\sqrt{M_{UF_6}}}{\sqrt{M_{H_2}}} = \sqrt{\frac{352.02}{2.016}} = 13.2$$

The effusion rate of the very light H_2 molecules is about 13 times that of the massive UF_6 molecules.

See Exercises 5.85 through 5.88.

Does the kinetic molecular model for gases correctly predict the relative effusion rates of gases summarized by Graham's law? To answer this question, we must recognize that the effusion rate for a gas depends directly on the average velocity of its particles. The faster the gas particles are moving, the more likely they are to pass through the effusion orifice. This reasoning leads to the following *prediction* for two gases at the same pressure and temperature (T):

$$\frac{\text{Effusion rate for gas 1}}{\text{Effusion rate for gas 2}} = \frac{u_{rms} \text{ for gas 1}}{u_{rms} \text{ for gas 2}} = \frac{\sqrt{\dfrac{3RT}{M_1}}}{\sqrt{\dfrac{3RT}{M_2}}} = \frac{\sqrt{M_2}}{\sqrt{M_1}}$$

This equation is identical to Graham's law. Thus the kinetic molecular model does fit the experimental results for the effusion of gases.

Diffusion

Visualization: Diffusion of Gases

Diffusion is frequently illustrated by the lecture demonstration represented in Fig. 5.24, in which two cotton plugs soaked in ammonia and hydrochloric acid are simultaneously placed at the ends of a long tube. A white ring of ammonium chloride (NH_4Cl) forms where the NH_3 and HCl molecules meet several minutes later:

$$NH_3(g) + HCl(g) \longrightarrow NH_4Cl(s)$$
White solid

Visualization: Gaseous Ammonia and Hydrochloric Acid

FIGURE 5.24
(above right) When HCl(g) and NH_3(g) meet in the tube, a white ring of $NH_4Cl(s)$ forms. (above left) A demonstration of the relative diffusion rates of NH_3 and HCl molecules through air. Two cotton plugs, one dipped in HCl(aq) and one dipped in NH_3(aq), are simultaneously inserted into the ends of the tube. Gaseous NH_3 and HCl vaporizing from the cotton plugs diffuse toward each other and, where they meet, react to form $NH_4Cl(s)$.

As a first approximation we might expect that the distances traveled by the two gases are related to the relative velocities of the gas molecules:

$$\frac{\text{Distance traveled by NH}_3}{\text{Distance traveled by HCl}} = \frac{u_{\text{rms}} \text{ for NH}_3}{u_{\text{rms}} \text{ for HCl}} = \sqrt{\frac{M_{\text{HCl}}}{M_{\text{NH}_3}}} = \sqrt{\frac{36.5}{17}} = 1.5$$

However, careful experiments produce an observed ratio of less than 1.5, indicating that a quantitative analysis of diffusion requires a more complex analysis.

The diffusion of the gases through the tube is surprisingly slow in light of the fact that the velocities of HCl and NH_3 molecules at 25°C are about 450 and 660 meters per second, respectively. Why does it take several minutes for the NH_3 and HCl molecules to meet? The answer is that the tube contains air and thus the NH_3 and HCl molecules undergo many collisions with O_2 and N_2 molecules as they travel through the tube. Because so many collisions occur when gases mix, diffusion is quite complicated to describe theoretically.

5.8 Real Gases

An ideal gas is a hypothetical concept. No gas *exactly* follows the ideal gas law, although many gases come very close at low pressures and/or high temperatures. Thus ideal gas behavior can best be thought of as the behavior *approached by real gases* under certain conditions.

We have seen that a very simple model, the kinetic molecular theory, by making some rather drastic assumptions (no interparticle interactions and zero volume for the gas particles), successfully explains ideal behavior. However, it is important that we examine real gas behavior to see how it differs from that predicted by the ideal gas law and to determine what modifications are needed in the kinetic molecular theory to explain the observed behavior. Since a model is an approximation and will inevitably fail, we must be ready to learn from such failures. In fact, we often learn more about nature from the failures of our models than from their successes.

We will examine the experimentally observed behavior of real gases by measuring the pressure, volume, temperature, and number of moles for a gas and noting how the quantity PV/nRT depends on pressure. Plots of PV/nRT versus P are shown for several gases in Fig. 5.25. For an ideal gas, PV/nRT equals 1 under all conditions, but notice that for real gases, PV/nRT approaches 1 only at very low pressures (typically below 1 atm). To illustrate the effect of temperature, PV/nRT is plotted versus P for nitrogen gas at several temperatures in Fig. 5.26. Note that the behavior of the gas appears to become more nearly ideal as the temperature is increased. The most important conclusion to be drawn from these figures is that a real gas typically exhibits behavior that is closest to ideal behavior at *low pressures* and *high temperatures.*

One of the most important procedures in science is correcting our models as we collect more data. We will understand more clearly how gases actually behave if we can figure out how to correct the simple model that explains the ideal gas law so that the new model fits the behavior we actually observe for gases. So the question is: How can we modify the assumptions of the kinetic molecular theory to fit the behavior of real gases? The first person to do important work in this area was Johannes van der Waals (1837–1923), a physics professor at the University of Amsterdam who in 1910 received a Nobel Prize for his work. To follow his analysis, we start with the ideal gas law,

$$P = \frac{nRT}{V}$$

Remember that this equation describes the behavior of a hypothetical gas consisting of volumeless entities that do not interact with each other. In contrast, a real gas consists of atoms or molecules that have finite volumes. Therefore, the volume available to a given particle in a real gas is less than the volume of the container because the gas particles themselves take up some of the space. To account for this discrepancy, van der Waals

FIGURE 5.25
Plots of PV/nRT versus P for several gases (200 K). Note the significant deviations from ideal behavior ($PV/nRT = 1$). The behavior is close to ideal only at low pressures (less than 1 atm).

FIGURE 5.26
Plots of PV/nRT versus P for nitrogen gas at three temperatures. Note that although nonideal behavior is evident in each case, the deviations are smaller at the higher temperatures.

represented the actual volume as the volume of the container V minus a correction factor for the volume of the molecules nb, where n is the number of moles of gas and b is an empirical constant (one determined by fitting the equation to the experimental results). Thus the volume *actually available* to a given gas molecule is given by the difference $V - nb$.

This modification of the ideal gas equation leads to the equation

$$P' = \frac{nRT}{V - nb}$$

The volume of the gas particles has now been taken into account.

The next step is to allow for the attractions that occur among the particles in a real gas. The effect of these attractions is to make the observed pressure P_{obs} smaller than it would be if the gas particles did not interact:

$$P_{obs} = (P' - \text{correction factor}) = \left(\frac{nRT}{V - nb} - \text{correction factor} \right)$$

This effect can be understood using the following model. When gas particles come close together, attractive forces occur, which cause the particles to hit the wall very slightly less often than they would in the absence of these interactions (see Fig. 5.27).

The size of the correction factor depends on the concentration of gas molecules defined in terms of moles of gas particles per liter (n/V). The higher the concentration, the more likely a pair of gas particles will be close enough to attract each other. For large numbers of particles, the number of interacting *pairs* of particles depends on the square of the number of particles and thus on the square of the concentration, or $(n/V)^2$. This can be justified as follows: In a gas sample containing N particles, there are $N - 1$ partners available for each particle, as shown in Fig. 5.28. Since the $1 \cdots 2$ pair is the same as the $2 \cdots 1$ pair, this analysis counts each pair twice. Thus, for N particles, there are $N(N - 1)/2$ pairs. If N is a very large number, $N - 1$ approximately equals N, giving $N^2/2$ possible pairs. Thus the pressure, corrected for the attractions of the particles, has the form

$$P_{obs} = P' - a \left(\frac{n}{V} \right)^2$$

where a is a proportionality constant (which includes the factor of $\frac{1}{2}$ from $N^2/2$). The value of a for a given real gas can be determined from observing the actual behavior of that gas. Inserting the corrections for both the volume of the particles and the attractions of the particles gives the equation

$$P_{obs} = \frac{nRT}{V - \underline{nb}} - a\underline{\left(\frac{n}{V} \right)^2}$$

Observed	Volume	Volume	Pressure
pressure	of the	correction	correction
	container		

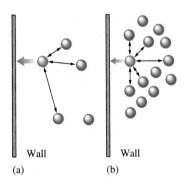

FIGURE 5.27
(a) Gas at low concentration—relatively few interactions between particles. The indicated gas particle exerts a pressure on the wall close to that predicted for an ideal gas. (b) Gas at high concentration—many more interactions between particles. The indicated gas particle exerts a much lower pressure on the wall than would be expected in the absence of interactions.

P′ is corrected for the finite volume of the particles. The attractive forces have not yet been taken into account.

The attractive forces among molecules will be discussed in Chapter 10.

We have now corrected for both the finite volume and the attractive forces of the particles.

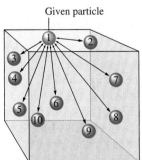

Given particle

Gas sample with ten particles

FIGURE 5.28
Illustration of pairwise interactions among gas particles. In a sample with 10 particles, each particle has 9 possible partners, to give $10(9)/2 = 45$ distinct pairs. The factor of $\frac{1}{2}$ arises because when particle ① is the particle of interest we count the ① $\cdots$ ② pair, and when particle ② is the particle of interest we count the ② $\cdots$ ① pair. However, ① $\cdots$ ② and ② $\cdots$ ① are the same pair that we have counted twice. Therefore, we must divide by 2 to get the actual number of pairs.

(a)   (b)

FIGURE 5.29
The volume taken up by the gas particles themselves is less important at (a) large container volume (low pressure) than at (b) small container volume (high pressure).

This equation can be rearranged to give the **van der Waals equation:**

$$\left[P_{obs} + a\left(\frac{n}{V}\right)^2 \right] \times \underbrace{(V - nb)}_{} = nRT$$

$$\underbrace{\text{Corrected pressure}}_{P_{ideal}} \qquad \underbrace{\text{Corrected volume}}_{V_{ideal}}$$

P_{obs} is usually called just P.

The values of the weighting factors a and b are determined for a given gas by fitting experimental behavior. That is, a and b are varied until the best fit of the observed pressure is obtained under all conditions. The values of a and b for various gases are given in Table 5.3.

Experimental studies indicate that the changes van der Waals made in the basic assumptions of the kinetic molecular theory correct the major flaws in the model. First, consider the effects of volume. For a gas at low pressure (large volume), the volume of the container is very large compared with the volumes of the gas particles. That is, in this case the volume available to the gas is essentially equal to the volume of the container, and the gas behaves ideally. On the other hand, for a gas at high pressure (small container volume), the volume of the particles becomes significant so that the volume available to the gas is significantly less than the container volume. These cases are illustrated in Fig. 5.29. Note from Table 5.3 that the volume correction constant b generally increases with the size of the gas molecule, which gives further support to these arguments.

The fact that a real gas tends to behave more ideally at high temperatures also can be explained in terms of the van der Waals model. At high temperatures the particles are moving so rapidly that the effects of interparticle interactions are not very important.

The corrections to the kinetic molecular theory that van der Waals found necessary to explain real gas behavior make physical sense, which makes us confident that we understand the fundamentals of gas behavior at the particle level. This is significant because so much important chemistry takes place in the gas phase. In fact, the mixture of gases called the atmosphere is vital to our existence. In Section 5.10 we consider some of the important reactions that occur in the atmosphere.

TABLE 5.3   Values of the van der Waals Constants for Some Common Gases

Gas	$a\left(\dfrac{\text{atm} \cdot \text{L}^2}{\text{mol}^2}\right)$	$b\left(\dfrac{\text{L}}{\text{mol}}\right)$
He	0.0341	0.0237
Ne	0.211	0.0171
Ar	1.35	0.0322
Kr	2.32	0.0398
Xe	4.19	0.0511
H_2	0.244	0.0266
N_2	1.39	0.0391
O_2	1.36	0.0318
Cl_2	6.49	0.0562
CO_2	3.59	0.0427
CH_4	2.25	0.0428
NH_3	4.17	0.0371
H_2O	5.46	0.0305

5.9 Characteristics of Several Real Gases

We can understand gas behavior more completely if we examine the characteristics of several common gases. Note from Figure 5.25 that the gases H_2, N_2, CH_4, and CO_2 show different behavior when the compressibility $\left(\frac{PV}{nRT}\right)$ is plotted versus P. For example, notice that the plot for $H_2(g)$ never drops below the ideal value (1.0) in contrast to all the other gases. What is special about H_2 compared to these other gases? Recall from Section 5.8 that the reason that the compressibility of a real gas falls below 1.0 is that the actual (observed) pressure is lower than the pressure expected for an ideal gas due to the intermolecular attractions that occur in real gases. This must mean that H_2 molecules have very low attractive forces for each other. This idea is borne out by looking at the van der Waals *a* value for H_2 in Table 5.3. Note that H_2 has the lowest value among the gases H_2, N_2, CH_4, and CO_2. Remember that the value of *a* reflects how much of a correction must be made to adjust the observed pressure up to the expected ideal pressure:

$$P_{ideal} = P_{observed} + a\left(\frac{n}{V}\right)^2$$

A low value for *a* reflects weak intermolecular forces among the gas molecules.

Also notice that although the compressibility for N_2 dips below 1.0, it does not show as much deviation as that for CH_4, which in turn does not show as much deviation as the compressibility for CO_2. Based on this behavior we can surmise that the importance of intermolecular interactions increases in this order:

$$H_2 < N_2 < CH_4 < CO_2$$

This order is reflected by the relative *a* values for these gases in Table 5.3. In Section 10.1, we will see how these variations in intermolecular interactions can be explained. The main point to be made here is that real gas behavior can tell us about the relative importance of intermolecular attractions among gas molecules.

5.10 Chemistry in the Atmosphere

The most important gases to us are those in the **atmosphere** that surrounds the earth's surface. The principal components are N_2 and O_2, but many other important gases, such as H_2O and CO_2, are also present. The average composition of the earth's atmosphere near sea level, with the water vapor removed, is shown in Table 5.4. Because of gravitational effects, the composition of the earth's atmosphere is not constant; heavier molecules tend to be near the earth's surface, and light molecules tend to migrate to higher altitudes, with some eventually escaping into space. The atmosphere is a highly complex and dynamic system, but for convenience we divide it into several layers based on the way the temperature changes with altitude. (The lowest layer, called the *troposphere,* is shown in Fig. 5.30.) Note that in contrast to the complex temperature profile of the atmosphere, the pressure decreases in a regular way with increasing altitude.

The chemistry occurring in the higher levels of the atmosphere is mostly determined by the effects of high-energy radiation and particles from the sun and other sources in space. In fact, the upper atmosphere serves as an important shield to prevent this high-energy radiation from reaching the earth, where it would damage the relatively fragile molecules sustaining life. In particular, the ozone in the upper atmosphere helps prevent high-energy ultraviolet radiation from penetrating to the earth. Intensive research is in progress to determine the natural factors that control the ozone concentration and how it is affected by chemicals released into the atmosphere.

The chemistry occurring in the troposphere, the layer of atmosphere closest to the earth's surface, is strongly influenced by human activities. Millions of tons of gases and particulates are released into the troposphere by our highly industrial civilization. Actually, it is amazing that the atmosphere can absorb so much material with relatively small permanent changes (so far).

Significant changes, however, are occurring. Severe **air pollution** is found around many large cities, and it is probable that long-range changes in our planet's weather are taking place. We will discuss some of the long-range effects of pollution in Chapter 6. In this section we will deal with short-term, localized effects of pollution.

The two main sources of pollution are transportation and the production of electricity. The combustion of petroleum in vehicles produces CO, CO_2, NO, and NO_2, along with unburned molecules from petroleum. When this mixture is trapped close to the ground in stagnant air, reactions occur producing chemicals that are potentially irritating and harmful to living systems.

TABLE 5.4 Atmospheric Composition Near Sea Level (Dry Air)*

Component	Mole Fraction
N_2	0.78084
O_2	0.20948
Ar	0.00934
CO_2	0.000345
Ne	0.00001818
He	0.00000524
CH_4	0.00000168
Kr	0.00000114
H_2	0.0000005
NO	0.0000005
Xe	0.000000087

*The atmosphere contains various amounts of water vapor depending on conditions.

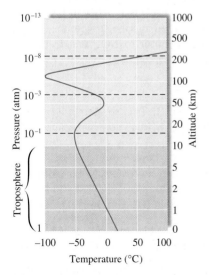

FIGURE 5.30
The variation of temperature (blue) and pressure (dashed lines) with altitude. Note that the pressure steadily decreases with altitude, but the temperature increases and decreases.

CHEMICAL IMPACT

Acid Rain: A Growing Problem

Rainwater, even in pristine wilderness areas, is slightly acidic because some of the carbon dioxide present in the atmosphere dissolves in the raindrops to produce H^+ ions by the following reaction:

$$H_2O(l) + CO_2(g) \longrightarrow H^+(aq) + HCO_3^-(aq)$$

This process produces only very small concentrations of H^+ ions in the rainwater. However, gases such as NO_2 and SO_2, which are by-products of energy use, can produce significantly higher H^+ concentrations. Nitrogen dioxide reacts with water to give a mixture of nitrous acid and nitric acid:

$$2NO_2(g) + H_2O(l) \longrightarrow HNO_2(aq) + HNO_3(aq)$$

Sulfur dioxide is oxidized to sulfur trioxide, which then reacts with water to form sulfuric acid:

$$2SO_2(g) + O_2(g) \longrightarrow 2SO_3(g)$$
$$SO_3(g) + H_2O(l) \longrightarrow H_2SO_4(aq)$$

The damage caused by the acid formed in polluted air is a growing worldwide problem. Lakes are dying in Norway, the forests are under stress in Germany, and buildings and statues are deteriorating all over the world.

The Field Museum in Chicago contains more white Georgia marble than any other structure in the world. But nearly 70 years of exposure to the elements has taken such a toll on it that the building has recently undergone a multimillion-dollar renovation to replace the damaged marble with freshly quarried material.

What is the chemistry of the deterioration of marble by sulfuric acid? Marble is produced by geologic processes at high temperatures and pressures from limestone, a sedimentary rock formed by slow deposition of calcium carbonate from the shells of marine organisms. Limestone and marble are chemically identical ($CaCO_3$) but differ in physical properties; limestone is composed of smaller particles of calcium carbonate and is thus more porous and more workable. Although both limestone and marble are used for buildings, marble can be polished to a higher sheen and is often preferred for decorative purposes.

Both marble and limestone react with sulfuric acid to form calcium sulfate. The process can be represented most

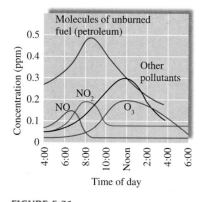

FIGURE 5.31

Concentration (in molecules per million molecules of "air") for some smog components versus time of day.

(From "Photochemistry of Air Pollution," by P. A. Leighton, in *Physical Chemistry: A Series of Monographs,* edited by Eric Hutchinson and P. Van Rysselberghe, copyright 1961 and renewed 1989, Elsevier Science (USA), reproduced by permission of the publisher.)

The OH radical has no charge [it has one fewer electron than the hydroxide ion (OH^-)].

The complex chemistry of polluted air appears to center around the nitrogen oxides (NO_x). At the high temperatures found in the gasoline and diesel engines of cars and trucks, N_2 and O_2 react to form a small quantity of NO that is emitted into the air with the exhaust gases (see Fig. 5.31). This NO is immediately oxidized in air to NO_2, which, in turn, absorbs energy from sunlight and breaks up into nitric oxide and free oxygen atoms:

$$NO_2(g) \xrightarrow{\text{Radiant energy}} NO(g) + O(g)$$

Oxygen atoms are very reactive and can combine with O_2 to form *ozone:*

$$O(g) + O_2(g) \longrightarrow O_3(g)$$

Ozone is also very reactive and can react directly with other pollutants, or the ozone can absorb light and break up to form an energetically excited O_2 molecule (O_2^*) and an energetically excited oxygen atom (O^*). The latter species readily reacts with a water molecule to form two hydroxyl radicals (OH):

$$O^* + H_2O \longrightarrow 2OH$$

The hydroxyl radical is a very reactive oxidizing agent. For example, OH can react with NO_2 to form nitric acid:

$$OH + NO_2 \longrightarrow HNO_3$$

The OH radical also can react with the unburned hydrocarbons in the polluted air to produce chemicals that cause the eyes to water and burn and are harmful to the respiratory system.

simply as

$$CaCO_3(s) + H_2SO_4(aq) \longrightarrow$$
$$Ca^{2+}(aq) + SO_4^{2-}(aq) + H_2O(l) + CO_2(g)$$

In this equation the calcium sulfate is represented by separate hydrated ions because calcium sulfate is quite water soluble and dissolves in rainwater. Thus, in areas bathed by rainwater, the marble slowly dissolves away.

In areas of the building protected from the rain, the calcium sulfate can form the mineral gypsum ($CaSO_4 \cdot 2H_2O$). The $\cdot 2H_2O$ in the formula of gypsum indicates the presence of two water molecules (called *waters of hydration*) for each $CaSO_4$ formula unit in the solid. The smooth surface of the marble is thus replaced by a thin layer of gypsum, a more porous material that binds soot and dust.

What can be done to protect limestone and marble structures from this kind of damage? Of course, one approach is to lower sulfur dioxide emissions from power plants (see Fig. 5.33). In addition, scientists are experimenting with coatings to protect marble from the acidic atmosphere. However, a coating can do more harm than good unless it "breathes." If moisture trapped beneath the coating freezes, the expanding ice can fracture the marble. Needless to say, it is difficult to find a coating that will allow water, but not acid, to pass—but the search continues.

The damaging effects of acid rain can be seen by comparing these photos of a decorative statue on the Field Museum in Chicago. The first photo was taken about 1920, the second in 1990.

The end product of this whole process is often referred to as **photochemical smog,** so called because light is required to initiate some of the reactions. The production of photochemical smog can be understood more clearly by examining as a group the reactions discussed above:

$$NO_2(g) \longrightarrow NO(g) + O(g)$$
$$O(g) + O_2(g) \longrightarrow O_3(g)$$
$$NO(g) + \tfrac{1}{2}O_2(g) \longrightarrow NO_2(g)$$

Net reaction:
$$\tfrac{3}{2}O_2(g) \longrightarrow O_3(g)$$

Although represented here as O_2, the actual oxidant for NO is OH or an organic peroxide such as CH_3COO, formed by oxidation of organic pollutants.

Note that the NO_2 molecules assist in the formation of ozone without being themselves used up. The ozone formed then leads to the formation of OH and other pollutants.

We can observe this process by analyzing polluted air at various times during a day (see Fig. 5.31). As people drive to work between 6 and 8 a.m., the amounts of NO, NO_2, and unburned molecules from petroleum increase. Later, as the decomposition of NO_2 occurs, the concentration of ozone and other pollutants builds up. Current efforts to combat the formation of photochemical smog are focused on cutting down the amounts of molecules from unburned fuel in automobile exhaust and designing engines that produce less nitric oxide.

The other major source of pollution results from burning coal to produce electricity. Much of the coal found in the Midwest contains significant quantities of sulfur, which, when burned, produces sulfur dioxide:

$$S \text{ (in coal)} + O_2(g) \longrightarrow SO_2(g)$$

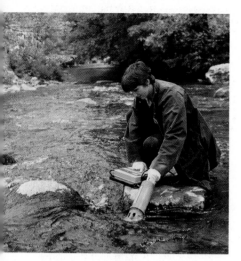

FIGURE 5.32
An environmental officer in Wales tests the pH of water.

A further oxidation reaction occurs when sulfur dioxide is changed to sulfur trioxide in the air:*

$$2SO_2(g) + O_2(g) \longrightarrow 2SO_3(g)$$

The production of sulfur trioxide is significant because it can combine with droplets of water in the air to form sulfuric acid:

$$SO_3(g) + H_2O(l) \longrightarrow H_2SO_4(aq)$$

Sulfuric acid is very corrosive to both living things and building materials. Another result of this type of pollution is **acid rain.** In many parts of the northeastern United States and southeastern Canada, acid rain has caused some freshwater lakes to become too acidic to support any life (Fig. 5.32).

The problem of sulfur dioxide pollution is made more complicated by the energy crisis. As petroleum supplies dwindle and the price increases, our dependence on coal will probably grow. As supplies of low-sulfur coal are used up, high-sulfur coal will be utilized. One way to use high-sulfur coal without further harming the air quality is to remove the sulfur dioxide from the exhaust gas by means of a system called a *scrubber* before it is emitted from the power plant stack. A common method of scrubbing is to blow powdered limestone ($CaCO_3$) into the combustion chamber, where it is decomposed to lime and carbon dioxide:

$$CaCO_3(s) \longrightarrow CaO(s) + CO_2(g)$$

The lime then combines with the sulfur dioxide to form calcium sulfite:

$$CaO(s) + SO_2(g) \longrightarrow CaSO_3(s)$$

To remove the calcium sulfite and any remaining unreacted sulfur dioxide, an aqueous suspension of lime is injected into the exhaust gases to produce a *slurry* (a thick suspension), as shown in Fig. 5.33.

Unfortunately, there are many problems associated with scrubbing. The systems are complicated and expensive and consume a great deal of energy. The large quantities of calcium sulfite produced in the process present a disposal problem. With a typical scrubber, approximately 1 ton of calcium sulfite per year is produced per person served by the power plant. Since no use has yet been found for this calcium sulfite, it is usually buried in a landfill. As a result of these difficulties, air pollution by sulfur dioxide continues to be a major problem, one that is expensive in terms of damage to the environment and human health as well as in monetary terms.

FIGURE 5.33
A schematic diagram of the process for scrubbing sulfur dioxide from stack gases in power plants.

*This reaction is very slow unless solid particles are present. See Chapter 12 for a discussion.

Key Terms

For Review

State of a gas

- The state of a gas can be described completely by specifying its pressure (P), volume (V), temperature (T) and the amount (moles) of gas present (n)
- Pressure
  - Common units

    $1 \text{ torr} = 1 \text{ mm Hg}$

    $1 \text{ atm} = 760 \text{ torr}$

  - SI unit: pascal

    $1 \text{ atm} = 101{,}325 \text{ Pa}$

Gas laws

- Discovered by observing the properties of gases
- Boyle's law: $PV = k$
- Charles's law: $V = bT$
- Avogadro's law: $V = an$
- Ideal gas law: $PV = nRT$
- Dalton's law of partial pressures: $P_{total} = P_1 + P_2 + P_3 + \cdots$, where P_n represents the partial pressure of component n in a mixture of gases

Kinetic molecular theory (KMT)

- Model that accounts for ideal gas behavior
- Postulates of the KMT:
  - Volume of gas particles is zero
  - No particle interactions
  - Particles are in constant motion, colliding with the container walls to produce pressure
  - The average kinetic energy of the gas particles is directly proportional to the temperature of the gas in kelvins

Gas properties

- The particles in any gas sample have a range of velocities
- The root mean square (rms) velocity for a gas represents the average of the squares of the particle velocities

$$u_{rms} = \sqrt{\frac{3RT}{M}}$$

- Diffusion: the mixing of two or more gases
- Effusion: the process in which a gas passes through a small hole into an empty chamber

Real gas behavior

- Real gases behave ideally only at high temperatures and low pressures
- Understanding how the ideal gas equation must be modified to account for real gas behavior helps us understand how gases behave on a molecular level
- Van der Waals found that to describe real gas behavior we must consider particle interactions and particle volumes

REVIEW QUESTIONS

1. Explain how a barometer and a manometer work to measure the pressure of the atmosphere or the pressure of a gas in a container.

2. What are Boyle's law, Charles's law, and Avogadro's law? What plots do you make to show a linear relationship for each law?

3. Show how Boyle's law, Charles's law, and Avogadro's law are special cases of the ideal gas law. Using the ideal gas law, determine the relationship between P and n (at constant V and T) and between P and T (at constant V and n).

4. Rationalize the following observations.
   a. Aerosol cans will explode if heated.
   b. You can drink through a soda straw.
   c. A thin-walled can will collapse when the air inside is removed by a vacuum pump.
   d. Manufacturers produce different types of tennis balls for high and low elevations.

5. Consider the following balanced equation in which gas X forms gas X_2:

$$2X(g) \rightarrow X_2(g)$$

Equal moles of X are placed in two separate containers. One container is rigid so the volume cannot change; the other container is flexible so the volume changes to keep the internal pressure equal to the external pressure. The above reaction is run in each container. What happens to the pressure and density of the gas inside each container as reactants are converted to products?

6. Use the postulates of the kinetic molecular theory (KMT) to explain why Boyle's law, Charles's law, Avogadro's law, and Dalton's law of partial pressures hold true for ideal gases. Use the KMT to explain the P versus n (at constant V and T) relationship and the P versus T (at constant V and n) relationship.

7. Consider the following velocity distribution curves A and B.

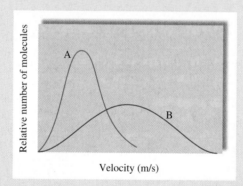

a. If the plots represent the velocity distribution of 1.0 L of He(g) at STP versus 1.0 L of $Cl_2(g)$ at STP, which plot corresponds to each gas? Explain your reasoning.

b. If the plots represent the velocity distribution of 1.0 L of $O_2(g)$ at temperatures of 273 K versus 1273 K, which plot corresponds to each temperature? Explain your reasoning. Under which temperature condition would the $O_2(g)$ sample behave most ideally? Explain.

8. Briefly describe two methods one might use to find the molar mass of a newly synthesized gas for which a molecular formula was not known.

9. In the van der Waals equation, why is a term added to the observed pressure and why is a term subtracted from the container volume to correct for nonideal gas behavior?

10. Why do real gases not always behave ideally? Under what conditions does a real gas behave most ideally? Why?

Active Learning Questions

These questions are designed to be used by groups of students in class. The questions allow students to explore their understanding of concepts through discussion and peer teaching. The real value of these questions is the learning that occurs while students talk to each other about chemical concepts.

1. Consider the following apparatus: a test tube covered with a non-permeable elastic membrane inside a container that is closed with a cork. A syringe goes through the cork.

   — Syringe

   — Cork

   — Membrane

   a. As you push down on the syringe, how does the membrane covering the test tube change?
   b. You stop pushing the syringe but continue to hold it down. In a few seconds, what happens to the membrane?

2. Figure 5.2 shows a picture of a barometer. Which of the following statements is the best explanation of how this barometer works?
   a. Air pressure outside the tube causes the mercury to move in the tube until the air pressure inside and outside the tube is equal.
   b. Air pressure inside the tube causes the mercury to move in the tube until the air pressure inside and outside the tube is equal.
   c. Air pressure outside the tube counterbalances the weight of the mercury in the tube.
   d. Capillary action of the mercury causes the mercury to go up the tube.
   e. The vacuum that is formed at the top of the tube holds up the mercury.

   Justify your choice, and for the choices you did not pick, explain what is wrong with them. Pictures help!

3. The barometer below shows the level of mercury at a given atmospheric pressure. Fill all the other barometers with mercury for that same atmospheric pressure. Explain your answer.

   Hg(*l*)

4. As you increase the temperature of a gas in a sealed, rigid container, what happens to the density of the gas? Would the results be the same if you did the same experiment in a container with a piston at constant pressure? (See Figure 5.17.)

5. A diagram in a chemistry book shows a magnified view of a flask of air as follows:

   What do you suppose is between the dots (the dots represent air molecules)?
   a. air
   b. dust
   c. pollutants
   d. oxygen
   e. nothing

6. If you put a drinking straw in water, place your finger over the opening, and lift the straw out of the water, some water stays in the straw. Explain.

7. A chemistry student relates the following story: I noticed my tires were a bit low and went to the gas station. As I was filling the tires, I thought about the kinetic molecular theory (KMT). I noticed the tires because the volume was low, and I realized that I was increasing both the pressure and volume of the tires. "Hmmm," I thought, "that goes against what I learned in chemistry, where I was told pressure and volume are inversely proportional." What is the fault in the logic of the chemistry student in this situation? Explain *why* we think pressure and volume to be inversely related (draw pictures and use the KMT).

8. Chemicals *X* and *Y* (both gases) react to form the gas *XY*, but it takes a bit of time for the reaction to occur. Both *X* and *Y* are placed in a container with a piston (free to move), and you note the volume. As the reaction occurs, what happens to the volume of the container? (See Fig. 5.18.)

9. Which statement best explains why a hot-air balloon rises when the air in the balloon is heated?
   a. According to Charles's law, the temperature of a gas is directly related to its volume. Thus the volume of the balloon increases, making the density smaller. This lifts the balloon.
   b. Hot air rises inside the balloon, and this lifts the balloon.
   c. The temperature of a gas is directly related to its pressure. The pressure therefore increases, and this lifts the balloon.
   d. Some of the gas escapes from the bottom of the balloon, thus decreasing the mass of gas in the balloon. This decreases the density of the gas in the balloon, which lifts the balloon.
   e. Temperature is related to the root mean square velocity of the gas molecules. Thus the molecules are moving faster, hitting the balloon more, and thus lifting the balloon.

   Justify your choice, and for the choices you did not pick, explain what is wrong with them.

10. Draw a highly magnified view of a sealed, rigid container filled with a gas. Then draw what it would look like if you cooled the gas significantly but kept the temperature above the boiling point of the substance in the container. Also draw what it would look like if you heated the gas significantly. Finally, draw what each situation would look like if you evacuated enough of the gas to decrease the pressure by a factor of 2.

11. If you release a helium balloon, it soars upward and eventually pops. Explain this behavior.

12. If you have any two gases in different containers that are the same size at the same pressure and same temperature, what is true about the moles of each gas? Why is this true?

13. Explain the following seeming contradiction: You have two gases, A and B, in two separate containers of equal volume and at equal pressure and temperature. Therefore, you must have the same number of moles of each gas. Because the two temperatures are equal, the average kinetic energies of the two samples are equal. Therefore, since the energy given such a system will be converted to translational motion (that is, move the molecules), the root mean square velocities of the two are equal, and thus the particles in each sample move, on average, with the same relative speed. Since A and B are different gases, they each must have a different molar mass. If A has higher molar mass than B, the particles of A must be hitting the sides of the container with more force. Thus the pressure in the container of gas A must be higher than that in the container with gas B. However, one of our initial assumptions was that the pressures were equal.

14. You have a balloon covering the mouth of a flask filled with air at 1 atm. You apply heat to the bottom of the flask until the volume of the balloon is equal to that of the flask.
    a. Which has more air in it, the balloon or the flask? Or do both have the same amount? Explain.
    b. In which is the pressure greater, the balloon or the flask? Or is the pressure the same? Explain.

15. How does Dalton's law of partial pressures help us with our model of ideal gases? That is, what postulates of the kinetic molecular theory does it support?

Questions

16. At room temperature, water is a liquid with a molar volume of 18 mL. At 105°C and 1 atm pressure, water is a gas and has a molar volume of over 30 L. Explain the large difference in molar volumes.

17. If a barometer were built using water ($d = 1.0$ g/cm^3) instead of mercury ($d = 13.6$ g/cm^3), would the column of water be higher than, lower than, or the same as the column of mercury at 1.00 atm? If the level is different, by what factor? Explain.

18. A bag of potato chips is packed and sealed in Los Angeles, California, and then shipped to Lake Tahoe, Nevada, during ski season. It is noticed that the volume of the bag of potato chips has increased upon its arrival in Lake Tahoe. What external conditions would most likely cause the volume increase?

19. Boyle's law can be represented graphically in several ways. Which of the following plots does *not* correctly represent Boyle's law (assuming constant T and n)? Explain.

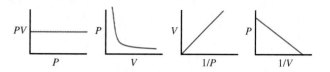

20. As weather balloons rise from the earth's surface, the pressure of the atmosphere becomes less, tending to cause the volume of the balloons to expand. However, the temperature is much lower in the upper atmosphere than at sea level. Would this temperature effect tend to make such a balloon expand or contract? Weather balloons do, in fact, expand as they rise. What does this tell you?

21. Which noble gas has the smallest density at STP? Explain.

22. Consider two different containers, each filled with 2 moles of Ne(g). One of the containers is rigid and has constant volume. The other container is flexible (like a balloon) and is capable of changing its volume to keep the external pressure and internal pressure equal to each other. If you raise the temperature in both containers, what happens to the pressure and density of the gas inside each container? Assume a constant external pressure.

23. Do all the molecules in a 1-mol sample of CH$_4$(g) have the same kinetic energy at 273 K? Do all molecules in a 1-mol sample of N$_2$(g) have the same velocity at 546 K? Explain.

24. Consider the following samples of gases at the same temperature.

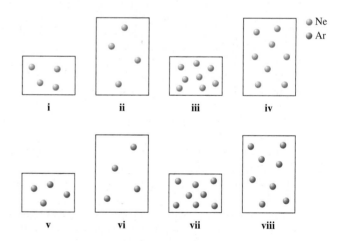

Arrange each of these samples in order from lowest to highest:
    a. pressure
    b. average kinetic energy
    c. density
    d. root mean square velocity
Note: Some samples of gases may have equal values for these attributes. Assume the larger containers have a volume twice the volume of the smaller containers and assume the mass of an argon atom is twice the mass of a neon atom.

25. As NH$_3$(g) is decomposed into nitrogen gas and hydrogen gas at constant pressure and temperature, the volume of the product gases collected is twice the volume of NH$_3$ reacted. Explain. As NH$_3$(g)

is decomposed into nitrogen gas and hydrogen gas at constant volume and temperature, the total pressure increases by some factor. Why the increase in pressure and by what factor does the total pressure increase when reactants are completely converted into products? How do the partial pressures of the product gases compare to each other and to the initial pressure of NH_3?

26. Which of the following statements is (are) true? For the false statements, correct them.

a. At constant temperature, the lighter the gas molecules, the faster the average velocity of the gas molecules.

b. At constant temperature, the heavier the gas molecules, the larger the average kinetic energy of the gas molecules.

c. A real gas behaves most ideally when the container volume is relatively large and the gas molecules are moving relatively quickly.

d. As temperature increases, the effect of interparticle interactions on gas behavior is increased.

e. At constant V and T, as gas molecules are added into a container, the number of collisions per unit area increases resulting in a higher pressure.

f. The kinetic molecular theory predicts that pressure is inversely proportional to temperature at constant volume and mol of gas.

Exercises

In this section similar exercises are paired.

Pressure

27. Freon-12 (CF_2Cl_2) is commonly used as the refrigerant in central home air conditioners. The system is initially charged to a pressure of 4.8 atm. Express this pressure in each of the following units (1 atm = 14.7 psi).
a. mm Hg   **b.** torr   **c.** Pa   **d.** psi

28. A gauge on a compressed gas cylinder reads 2200 psi (pounds per square inch; 1 atm = 14.7 psi). Express this pressure in each of the following units.
a. standard atmospheres
b. megapascals (MPa)
c. torr

29. A sealed-tube manometer (as shown below) can be used to measure pressures below atmospheric pressure. The tube above the mercury is evacuated. When there is a vacuum in the flask, the mercury levels in both arms of the U-tube are equal. If a gaseous sample is introduced into the flask, the mercury levels are different. The difference h is a measure of the pressure of the gas inside the flask. If h is equal to 6.5 cm, calculate the pressure in the flask in torr, pascals, and atmospheres.

30. If the sealed-tube manometer in Exercise 29 had a height difference of 20.0 inches between the mercury levels, what is the pressure in the flask in torr and atmospheres?

31. A diagram for an open-tube manometer is shown below.

Atmosphere

If the flask is open to the atmosphere, the mercury levels are equal. For each of the following situations where a gas is contained in the flask, calculate the pressure in the flask in torr, atmospheres, and pascals.

Atmosphere (760. torr)   Flask   118 mm   **a.**

Atmosphere (760. torr)   Flask   215 mm   **b.**

c. Calculate the pressures in the flask in parts a and b (in torr) if the atmospheric pressure is 635 torr.

32. a. If the open-tube manometer in Exercise 31 contains a nonvolatile silicone oil (density = 1.30 g/cm³) instead of mercury (density = 13.6 g/cm³), what are the pressures in the flask as shown in parts a and b in torr, atmospheres, and pascals?

b. What advantage would there be in using a less dense fluid than mercury in a manometer used to measure relatively small differences in pressure?

Gas Laws

33. A particular balloon is designed by its manufacturer to be inflated to a volume of no more than 2.5 L. If the balloon is filled with 2.0 L of helium at sea level, is released, and rises to an altitude at which the atmospheric pressure is only 500. mm Hg, will the balloon burst? (Assume temperature is constant.)

34. A balloon is filled to a volume of 7.00×10^2 mL at a temperature of 20.0°C. The balloon is then cooled at constant pressure to a temperature of 1.00×10^2 K. What is the final volume of the balloon?

35. An 11.2-L sample of gas is determined to contain 0.50 mol of N_2. At the same temperature and pressure, how many moles of gas would there be in a 20.-L sample?

36. Consider the following chemical equation.

$$2NO_2(g) \longrightarrow N_2O_4(g)$$

If 25.0 mL of NO_2 gas is completely converted to N_2O_4 gas under the same conditions, what volume will the N_2O_4 occupy?

37. Complete the following table for an ideal gas.

	P(atm)	V(L)	n(mol)	T
a.	5.00		2.00	155°C
b.	0.300	2.00		155 K
c.	4.47	25.0	2.01	
d.		2.25	10.5	75°C

38. Complete the following table for an ideal gas.

	P	V	n	T
a.	7.74×10^3 Pa	12.2 mL		25°C
b.		43.0 mL	0.421 mol	223 K
c.	455 torr		4.4×10^{-2} mol	331°C
d.	745 mm Hg	11.2 L	0.401 mol	

39. Suppose two 200.0-L tanks are to be filled separately with the gases helium and hydrogen. What mass of each gas is needed to produce a pressure of 135 atm in its respective tank at 24°C?

40. A flask that can withstand an internal pressure of 2500 torr, but no more, is filled with a gas at 21.0°C and 758 torr and heated. At what temperature will it burst?

41. A 2.50-L container is filled with 175 g argon.
   a. If the pressure is 10.0 atm, what is the temperature?
   b. If the temperature is 225 K, what is the pressure?

42. A person accidentally swallows a drop of liquid oxygen, $O_2(l)$, which has a density of 1.149 g/mL. Assuming the drop has a volume of 0.050 mL, what volume of gas will be produced in the person's stomach at body temperature (37°C) and a pressure of 1.0 atm?

43. A gas sample containing 1.50 mol at 25°C exerts a pressure of 400. torr. Some gas is *added* to the same container and the temperature is increased to 50.°C. If the pressure increases to 800. torr, how many moles of gas were added to the container? Assume a constant-volume container.

44. A bicycle tire is filled with air to a pressure of 100. psi at a temperature of 19°C. Riding the bike on asphalt on a hot day increases the temperature of the tire to 58°C. The volume of the tire increases by 4.0%. What is the new pressure in the bicycle tire?

45. Consider two separate gas containers at the following conditions:

Container A	**Container B**
Contents: $SO_2(g)$	Contents: unknown gas
Pressure = P_A	Pressure = P_B
Moles of gas = 1.0 mol	Moles of gas = 2.0 mol
Volume = 1.0 L	Volume = 2.0 L
Temperature = 7°C	Temperature = 287°C

How is the pressure in container B related to the pressure in container A?

46. A container is filled with an ideal gas to a pressure of 40.0 atm at 0°C.
   a. What will be the pressure in the container if it is heated to 45°C?
   b. At what temperature would the pressure be 1.50×10^2 atm?
   c. At what temperature would the pressure be 25.0 atm?

47. An ideal gas is contained in a cylinder with a volume of 5.0×10^2 mL at a temperature of 30.°C and a pressure of 710. torr. The gas is then compressed to a volume of 25 mL, and the temperature is raised to 820.°C. What is the new pressure of the gas?

48. A compressed gas cylinder contains 1.00×10^3 g of argon gas. The pressure inside the cylinder is 2050. psi (pounds per square inch) at a temperature of 18°C. How much gas remains in the cylinder if the pressure is decreased to 650. psi at a temperature of 26°C?

49. A sealed balloon is filled with 1.00 L of helium at 23°C and 1.00 atm. The balloon rises to a point in the atmosphere where the pressure is 220. torr and the temperature is −31°C. What is the change in volume of the balloon as it ascends from 1.00 atm to a pressure of 220. torr?

50. A hot-air balloon is filled with air to a volume of 4.00×10^3 m³ at 745 torr and 21°C. The air in the balloon is then heated to 62°C, causing the balloon to expand to a volume of 4.20×10^3 m³. What is the ratio of the number of moles of air in the heated balloon to the original number of moles of air in the balloon? (*Hint:* Openings in the balloon allow air to flow in and out. Thus the pressure in the balloon is always the same as that of the atmosphere.)

Gas Density, Molar Mass, and Reaction Stoichiometry

51. Consider the following reaction:

$$4Al(s) + 3O_2(g) \rightarrow 2Al_2O_3(s)$$

It takes 2.00 L of pure oxygen gas at STP to react completely with a certain sample of aluminum. What is the mass of aluminum reacted?

52. A student adds 4.00 g of dry ice (solid CO_2) to an empty balloon. What will be the volume of the balloon at STP after all the dry ice sublimes (converts to gaseous CO_2)?

53. Air bags are activated when a severe impact causes a steel ball to compress a spring and electrically ignite a detonator cap. This causes sodium azide (NaN_3) to decompose explosively according to the following reaction:

$$2NaN_3(s) \longrightarrow 2Na(s) + 3N_2(g)$$

What mass of $NaN_3(s)$ must be reacted to inflate an air bag to 70.0 L at STP?

54. Concentrated hydrogen peroxide solutions are explosively decomposed by traces of transition metal ions (such as Mn or Fe):

$$2H_2O_2(aq) \rightarrow 2H_2O(l) + O_2(g)$$

What volume of pure $O_2(g)$, collected at 27°C and 746 torr, would be generated by decomposition of 125 g of a 50.0% by mass hydrogen peroxide solution? Ignore any water vapor that may be present.

55. In 1897 the Swedish explorer Andreé tried to reach the North Pole in a balloon. The balloon was filled with hydrogen gas. The hydrogen gas was prepared from iron splints and diluted sulfuric acid. The reaction is

$$Fe(s) + H_2SO_4(aq) \longrightarrow FeSO_4(aq) + H_2(g)$$

The volume of the balloon was 4800 m³ and the loss of hydrogen gas during filling was estimated at 20.%. What mass of iron splints and 98% (by mass) H_2SO_4 were needed to ensure the complete filling of the balloon? Assume a temperature of 0°C, a pressure of 1.0 atm during filling, and 100% yield.

56. Sulfur trioxide, SO_3, is produced in enormous quantities each year for use in the synthesis of sulfuric acid.

$$S(s) + O_2(g) \rightarrow SO_2(g)$$
$$2SO_2(g) + O_2(g) \rightarrow 2SO_3(g)$$

What volume of $O_2(g)$ at 350.°C and a pressure of 5.25 atm is needed to completely convert 5.00 g of sulfur to sulfur trioxide?

57. Consider the reaction between 50.0 mL of liquid methyl alcohol, CH_3OH (density = 0.850 g/mL), and 22.8 L of O_2 at 27°C and a pressure of 2.00 atm. The products of the reaction are $CO_2(g)$ and $H_2O(g)$. Calculate the number of moles of H_2O formed if the reaction goes to completion.

58. Urea (H_2NCONH_2) is used extensively as a nitrogen source in fertilizers. It is produced commercially from the reaction of ammonia and carbon dioxide:

$$2NH_3(g) + CO_2(g) \xrightarrow[\text{Pressure}]{\text{Heat}} H_2NCONH_2(s) + H_2O(g)$$

Ammonia gas at 223°C and 90. atm flows into a reactor at a rate of 500. L/min. Carbon dioxide at 223°C and 45 atm flows into the reactor at a rate of 600. L/min. What mass of urea is produced per minute by this reaction assuming 100% yield?

59. Hydrogen cyanide is prepared commercially by the reaction of methane, $CH_4(g)$, ammonia, $NH_3(g)$, and oxygen, $O_2(g)$, at high temperature. The other product is gaseous water.
  a. Write a chemical equation for the reaction.
  b. What volume of $HCN(g)$ can be obtained from 20.0 L $CH_4(g)$, 20.0 L $NH_3(g)$, and 20.0 L $O_2(g)$? The volumes of all gases are measured at the same temperature and pressure.

60. Methanol, CH_3OH, can be produced by the following reaction:

$$CO(g) + 2H_2(g) \longrightarrow CH_3OH(g)$$

Hydrogen at STP flows into a reactor at a rate of 16.0 L/min. Carbon monoxide at STP flows into the reactor at a rate of 25.0 L/min. If 5.30 g of methanol is produced per minute, what is the percent yield of the reaction?

61. An unknown diatomic gas has a density of 3.164 g/L at STP. What is the identity of the gas?

62. A compound has the empirical formula CHCl. A 256-mL flask, at 373 K and 750. torr, contains 0.800 g of the gaseous compound. Give the molecular formula.

63. Uranium hexafluoride is a solid at room temperature, but it boils at 56°C. Determine the density of uranium hexafluoride at 60.°C and 745 torr.

64. Given that a sample of air is made up of nitrogen, oxygen, and argon in the mole fractions 78% N_2, 21% O_2, and 1.0% Ar, what is the density of air at standard temperature and pressure?

Partial Pressure

65. A piece of solid carbon dioxide, with a mass of 7.8 g, is placed in a 4.0-L otherwise empty container at 27°C. What is the pressure in the container after all the carbon dioxide vaporizes? If 7.8 g solid carbon dioxide were placed in the same container but it already contained air at 740 torr, what would be the partial pressure of carbon dioxide and the total pressure in the container after the carbon dioxide vaporizes?

66. A mixture of 1.00 g H_2 and 1.00 g He is placed in a 1.00-L container at 27°C. Calculate the partial pressure of each gas and the total pressure.

67. Consider the flasks in the following diagram. What are the final partial pressures of H_2 and N_2 after the stopcock between the two flasks is opened? (Assume the final volume is 3.00 L.) What is the total pressure (in torr)?

2.00 L H_2
475 torr

1.00 L N_2
0.200 atm

68. Consider the flask apparatus in Exercise 67, which now contains 2.00 L of H_2 at a pressure of 360. torr and 1.00 L of N_2 at an unknown pressure. If the total pressure in the flasks is 320. torr after the stopcock is opened, determine the initial pressure of N_2 in the 1.00-L flask.

69. The partial pressure of $CH_4(g)$ is 0.175 atm and that of $O_2(g)$ is 0.250 atm in a mixture of the two gases.
a. What is the mole fraction of each gas in the mixture?
b. If the mixture occupies a volume of 10.5 L at 65°C, calculate the total number of moles of gas in the mixture.
c. Calculate the number of grams of each gas in the mixture.

70. A 1.00-L gas sample at 100.°C and 600. torr contains 50.0% helium and 50.0% xenon by mass. What are the partial pressures of the individual gases?

71. Small quantities of hydrogen gas can be prepared in the laboratory by the addition of aqueous hydrochloric acid to metallic zinc.

$$Zn(s) + 2HCl(aq) \rightarrow ZnCl_2(aq) + H_2(g)$$

Typically, the hydrogen gas is bubbled through water for collection and becomes saturated with water vapor. Suppose 240. mL of hydrogen gas is collected at 30.°C and has a total pressure of 1.032 atm by this process. What is the partial pressure of hydrogen gas in the sample? How many grams of zinc must have reacted to produce this quantity of hydrogen? (The vapor pressure of water is 32 torr at 30.°C.)

72. Helium is collected over water at 25°C and 1.00 atm total pressure. What total volume of gas must be collected to obtain 0.586 g of helium? (At 25°C the vapor pressure of water is 23.8 torr.)

73. At elevated temperatures, sodium chlorate decomposes to produce sodium chloride and oxygen gas. A 0.8765-g sample of impure sodium chlorate was heated until the production of oxygen gas ceased. The oxygen gas collected over water occupied 57.2 mL at a temperature of 22°C and a pressure of 734 torr. Calculate the mass percent of $NaClO_3$ in the original sample. (At 22°C the vapor pressure of water is 19.8 torr.)

74. Xenon and fluorine will react to form binary compounds when a mixture of these two gases is heated to 400°C in a nickel reaction vessel. A 100.0-mL nickel container is filled with xenon and fluorine, giving partial pressures of 1.24 atm and 10.10 atm, respectively, at a temperature of 25°C. The reaction vessel is heated to 400°C to cause a reaction to occur and then cooled to a temperature at which F_2 is a gas and the xenon fluoride compound produced is a nonvolatile solid. The remaining F_2 gas is transferred to another 100.0-mL nickel container, where the pressure of F_2 at 25°C is 7.62 atm. Assuming all of the xenon has reacted, what is the formula of the product?

75. Hydrogen azide, HN_3, decomposes on heating by the following *unbalanced* reaction:

$$HN_3(g) \longrightarrow N_2(g) + H_2(g)$$

If 3.0 atm of pure $HN_3(g)$ is decomposed initially, what is the final total pressure in the reaction container? What are the partial pressures of nitrogen and hydrogen gas? Assume the volume and temperature of the reaction container are constant.

76. Some very effective rocket fuels are composed of lightweight liquids. The fuel composed of dimethylhydrazine [$(CH_3)_2N_2H_2$] mixed with dinitrogen tetroxide was used to power the Lunar Lander in its missions to the moon. The two components react according to the following equation:

$$(CH_3)_2N_2H_2(l) + 2N_2O_4(l) \longrightarrow 3N_2(g) + 4H_2O(g) + 2CO_2(g)$$

If 150 g of dimethylhydrazine reacts with excess dinitrogen tetroxide and the product gases are collected at 27°C in an evacuated 250-L tank, what is the partial pressure of nitrogen gas produced and what is the total pressure in the tank assuming the reaction has 100% yield?

Kinetic Molecular Theory and Real Gases

77. Calculate the average kinetic energies of CH_4 and N_2 molecules at 273 K and 546 K.

78. A 100.-L flask contains a mixture of methane, CH_4, and argon at 25°C. The mass of argon present is 228 g and the mole fraction of methane in the mixture is 0.650. Calculate the total kinetic energy of the gaseous mixture.

79. Calculate the root mean square velocities of CH_4 and N_2 molecules at 273 K and 546 K.

80. Consider separate 1.0-L samples of $He(g)$ and $UF_6(g)$, both at 1.00 atm and containing the same number of moles. What ratio of temperatures for the two samples would produce the same root mean square velocity?

81. Consider a 1.0-L container of neon gas at STP. Will the average kinetic energy, average velocity, and frequency of collisions of gas molecules with the walls of the container increase, decrease, or remain the same under each of the following conditions?
a. The temperature is increased to 100°C.
b. The temperature is decreased to −50°C.
c. The volume is decreased to 0.5 L.
d. The number of moles of neon is doubled.

82. Consider two gases, A and B, each in a 1.0-L container with both gases at the same temperature and pressure. The mass of gas A in the container is 0.34 g and the mass of gas B in the container is 0.48 g.

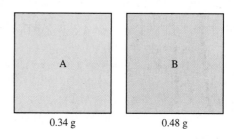

0.34 g   0.48 g

a. Which gas sample has the most molecules present? Explain.

b. Which gas sample has the largest average kinetic energy? Explain.

c. Which gas sample has the fastest average velocity? Explain.

d. How can the pressure in the two containers be equal to each other since the larger gas B molecules collide with the container walls more forcefully?

83. Consider three identical flasks filled with different gases.

Flask A: CO at 760 torr and 0°C

Flask B: N_2 at 250 torr and 0°C

Flask C: H_2 at 100 torr and 0°C

a. In which flask will the molecules have the greatest average kinetic energy?

b. In which flask will the molecules have the greatest average velocity?

84. Consider separate 1.0-L gaseous samples of H_2, Xe, Cl_2, and O_2 all at STP.

a. Rank the gases in order of increasing average kinetic energy.

b. Rank the gases in order of increasing average velocity.

c. How can separate 1.0-L samples of O_2 and H_2 each have the same average velocity?

85. Freon-12 is used as a refrigerant in central home air conditioners. The rate of effusion of Freon-12 to Freon-11 (molar mass = 137.4 g/mol) is 1.07:1. The formula of Freon-12 is one of the following: CF_4, CF_3Cl, CF_2Cl_2, $CFCl_3$, or CCl_4. Which formula is correct for Freon-12?

86. The rate of effusion of a particular gas was measured and found to be 24.0 mL/min. Under the same conditions, the rate of effusion of pure methane (CH_4) gas is 47.8 mL/min. What is the molar mass of the unknown gas?

87. One way of separating oxygen isotopes is by gaseous diffusion of carbon monoxide. The gaseous diffusion process behaves like an effusion process. Calculate the relative rates of effusion of $^{12}C^{16}O$, $^{12}C^{17}O$, and $^{12}C^{18}O$. Name some advantages and disadvantages of separating oxygen isotopes by gaseous diffusion of carbon dioxide instead of carbon monoxide.

88. It took 4.5 minutes for 1.0 L helium to effuse through a porous barrier. How long will it take for 1.0 L Cl_2 gas to effuse under identical conditions?

89. Calculate the pressure exerted by 0.5000 mol N_2 in a 1.0000-L container at 25.0°C

a. using the ideal gas law.

b. using the van der Waals equation.

c. Compare the results.

90. Calculate the pressure exerted by 0.5000 mol N_2 in a 10.000-L container at 25.0°C

a. using the ideal gas law.

b. using the van der Waals equation.

c. Compare the results.

d. Compare the results with those in Exercise 89.

Atmosphere Chemistry

91. Use the data in Table 5.4 to calculate the partial pressure of He in dry air assuming that the total pressure is 1.0 atm. Assuming a temperature of 25°C, calculate the number of He atoms per cubic centimeter.

92. A 1.0-L sample of air is collected at 25°C at sea level (1.00 atm). Estimate the volume this sample of air would have at an altitude of 15 km (see Fig. 5.30).

93. Write reactions to show how nitric and sulfuric acids are produced in the atmosphere.

94. Write reactions to show how the nitric and sulfuric acids in acid rain react with marble and limestone. (Both marble and limestone are primarily calcium carbonate.)

Additional Exercises

95. Draw a qualitative graph to show how the first property varies with the second in each of the following (assume 1 mol of an ideal gas and T in kelvins).

a. PV versus V with constant T

b. P versus T with constant V

c. T versus V with constant P

d. P versus V with constant T

e. P versus $1/V$ with constant T

f. PV/T versus P

96. At STP, 1.0 L Br_2 reacts completely with 3.0 L F_2, producing 2.0 L of a product. What is the formula of the product? (All substances are gases.)

97. A form of Boyle's law is $PV = k$ (at constant T and n). Table 5.1 contains actual data from pressure–volume experiments conducted by Robert Boyle. The value of k in most experiments is 14.1×10^2 in Hg · in³. Express k in units of atm · L. In Sample Exercise 5.3, k was determined for NH_3 at various pressures and volumes. Give some reasons why the k values differ so dramatically between Sample Exercise 5.3 and Table 5.1.

98. An ideal gas at 7°C is in a spherical flexible container having a radius of 1.00 cm. The gas is heated at constant pressure to 88°C. Determine the radius of the spherical container after the gas is heated. (Volume of a sphere = $4/3\pi r^3$.)

99. A 2.747-g sample of manganese metal is reacted with excess HCl gas to produce 3.22 L of $H_2(g)$ at 373 K and 0.951 atm and a manganese chloride compound ($MnCl_x$). What is the formula of the manganese chloride compound produced in the reaction?

100. Equal moles of hydrogen gas and oxygen gas are mixed in a flexible reaction vessel and then sparked to initiate the formation of gaseous water. Assuming that the reaction goes to completion, what is the ratio of the final volume of the gas mixture to the initial volume of the gas mixture if both volumes are measured at the same temperature and pressure?

101. A 15.0-L tank is filled with H_2 to a pressure of 2.00×10^2 atm. How many balloons (each 2.00 L) can be inflated to a pressure of 1.00 atm from the tank? Assume that there is no temperature change and that the tank cannot be emptied below 1.00 atm pressure.

102. A spherical glass container of unknown volume contains helium gas at 25°C and 1.960 atm. When a portion of the helium is withdrawn and adjusted to 1.00 atm at 25°C, it is found to have a volume of 1.75 cm^3. The gas remaining in the first container shows a pressure of 1.710 atm. Calculate the volume of the spherical container.

103. A 2.00-L sample of $O_2(g)$ was collected over water at a total pressure of 785 torr and 25°C. When the $O_2(g)$ was dried (water vapor removed), the gas had a volume of 1.94 L at 25°C and 785 torr. Calculate the vapor pressure of water at 25°C.

104. A 20.0-L stainless steel container was charged with 2.00 atm of hydrogen gas and 3.00 atm of oxygen gas. A spark ignited the mixture, producing water. What is the pressure in the tank at 25°C? at 125°C?

105. Metallic molybdenum can be produced from the mineral molybdenite, MoS_2. The mineral is first oxidized in air to molybdenum trioxide and sulfur dioxide. Molybdenum trioxide is then reduced to metallic molybdenum using hydrogen gas. The balanced equations are

$$MoS_2(s) + \tfrac{7}{2}O_2(g) \rightarrow MoO_3(s) + 2SO_2(g)$$
$$MoO_3(s) + 3H_2(g) \rightarrow Mo(s) + 3H_2O(l)$$

Calculate the volumes of air and hydrogen gas at 17°C and 1.00 atm that are necessary to produce 1.00×10^3 kg of pure molybdenum from MoS_2. Assume air contains 21% oxygen by volume and assume 100% yield for each reaction.

106. Nitric acid is produced commercially by the Ostwald process. In the first step ammonia is oxidized to nitric oxide:

$$4NH_3(g) + 5O_2(g) \rightarrow 4NO(g) + 6H_2O(g)$$

Assume this reaction is carried out in the apparatus diagramed below.

2.00 L NH$_3$	1.00 L O$_2$
0.500 atm	1.50 atm

The stopcock between the two reaction containers is opened, and the reaction proceeds using proper catalysts. Calculate the partial pressure of NO after the reaction is complete. Assume 100% yield for the reaction, assume the final container volume is 3.00 L, and assume the temperature is constant.

107. In the "Méthode Champenoise," grape juice is fermented in a wine bottle to produce sparkling wine. The reaction is

$$C_6H_{12}O_6(aq) \longrightarrow 2C_2H_5OH(aq) + 2CO_2(g)$$

Fermentation of 750. mL grape juice (density = 1.0 g/cm^3) is allowed to take place in a bottle with a total volume of 825 mL until 12% by volume is ethanol (C_2H_5OH). Assuming that the CO_2 is insoluble in H_2O (actually, a wrong assumption), what

would be the pressure of CO_2 inside the wine bottle at 25°C? (The density of ethanol is 0.79 g/cm^3.)

108. One of the chemical controversies of the nineteenth century concerned the element beryllium (Be). Berzelius originally claimed that beryllium was a trivalent element (forming Be^{3+} ions) and that it gave an oxide with the formula Be_2O_3. This resulted in a calculated atomic mass of 13.5 for beryllium. In formulating his periodic table, Mendeleev proposed that beryllium was divalent (forming Be^{2+} ions) and that it gave an oxide with the formula BeO. This assumption gives an atomic mass of 9.0. In 1894, A. Combes (*Comptes Rendus* 1894, p. 1221) reacted beryllium with the anion $C_5H_7O_2^-$ and measured the density of the gaseous product. Combes's data for two different experiments are as follows:

	I	II
Mass	0.2022 g	0.2224 g
Volume	22.6 cm^3	26.0 cm^3
Temperature	13°C	17°C
Pressure	765.2 mm Hg	764.6 mm

If beryllium is a divalent metal, the molecular formula of the product will be $Be(C_5H_7O_2)_2$; if it is trivalent, the formula will be $Be(C_5H_7O_2)_3$. Show how Combes's data help to confirm that beryllium is a divalent metal.

109. The nitrogen content of organic compounds can be determined by the Dumas method. The compound in question is first reacted by passage over hot $CuO(s)$:

$$\text{Compound} \xrightarrow[\text{CuO}(s)]{\text{Hot}} N_2(g) + CO_2(g) + H_2O(g)$$

The product gas is then passed through a concentrated solution of KOH to remove the CO_2. After passage through the KOH solution, the gas contains N_2 and is saturated with water vapor. In a given experiment a 0.253-g sample of a compound produced 31.8 mL N_2 saturated with water vapor at 25°C and 726 torr. What is the mass percent of nitrogen in the compound? (The vapor pressure of water at 25°C is 23.8 torr.)

110. A compound containing only C, H, and N yields the following data.
  i. Complete combustion of 35.0 mg of the compound produced 33.5 mg of CO_2 and 41.1 mg of H_2O.
  ii. A 65.2-mg sample of the compound was analyzed for nitrogen by the Dumas method (see Exercise 109), giving 35.6 mL of N_2 at 740. torr and 25°C.
  iii. The effusion rate of the compound as a gas was measured and found to be 24.6 mL/min. The effusion rate of argon gas, under identical conditions, is 26.4 mL/min.
What is the molecular formula of the compound?

111. An organic compound contains C, H, N, and O. Combustion of 0.1023 g of the compound in excess oxygen yielded 0.2766 g of CO_2 and 0.0991 g of H_2O. A sample of 0.4831 g of the compound was analyzed for nitrogen by the Dumas method (see Exercise 109). At STP, 27.6 mL of dry N_2 was obtained. In a third experiment, the density of the compound as a gas was found to be 4.02 g/L at 127°C and 256 torr. What are the empirical and molecular formulas of the compound?

112. Consider the following diagram:

Container A (with porous walls) is filled with air at STP. It is then inserted into a large enclosed container (B), which is then flushed with $H_2(g)$. What will happen to the pressure inside container A? Explain your answer.

113. Without looking at tables of values, which of the following gases would you expect to have the largest value of the van der Waals constant b: H_2, N_2, CH_4, C_2H_6, or C_3H_8? From the values in Table 5.3 for the van der Waals constant a for the gases H_2, CO_2, N_2, and CH_4, predict which of these gas molecules show the strongest intermolecular attractions.

Challenge Problems

114. An important process for the production of acrylonitrile (C_3H_3N) is given by the following reaction:

$$2C_3H_6(g) + 2NH_3(g) + 3O_2(g) \longrightarrow 2C_3H_3N(g) + 6H_2O(g)$$

A 150.-L reactor is charged to the following partial pressures at 25°C:

$$P_{C_3H_6} = 0.500 \text{ MPa}$$
$$P_{NH_3} = 0.800 \text{ MPa}$$
$$P_{O_2} = 1.500 \text{ MPa}$$

What mass of acrylonitrile can be produced from this mixture (Mpa = 10^6 Pa)?

115. A chemist weighed out 5.14 g of a mixture containing unknown amounts of BaO(s) and CaO(s) and placed the sample in a 1.50-L flask containing $CO_2(g)$ at 30.0°C and 750. torr. After the reaction to form $BaCO_3(s)$ and $CaCO_3(s)$ was completed, the pressure of $CO_2(g)$ remaining was 230. torr. Calculate the mass percentages of CaO(s) and BaO(s) in the mixture.

116. A mixture of chromium and zinc weighing 0.362 g was reacted with an excess of hydrochloric acid. After all the metals in the mixture reacted, 225 mL of dry hydrogen gas was collected at 27°C and 750. torr. Determine the mass percent Zn in the metal sample. [Zinc reacts with hydrochloric acid to produce zinc chloride and hydrogen gas; chromium reacts with hydrochloric acid to produce chromium(III) chloride and hydrogen gas.]

117. Consider a sample of a hydrocarbon (a compound consisting of only carbon and hydrogen) at 0.959 atm and 298 K. Upon combusting the entire sample in oxygen, you collect a mixture of gaseous carbon dioxide and water vapor at 1.51 atm and 375 K. This mixture has a density of 1.391 g/L and occupies a volume four times as large as that of the pure hydrocarbon. Determine the molecular formula of the hydrocarbon.

118. You have an equimolar mixture of the gases SO_2 and O_2, along with some He, in a container fitted with a piston. The density of this mixture at STP is 1.924 g/L. Assume ideal behavior and constant temperature and pressure.
  a. What is the mole fraction of He in the original mixture?
  b. The SO_2 and O_2 react to completion to form SO_3. What is the density of the gas mixture after the reaction is complete?

119. Methane (CH_4) gas flows into a combustion chamber at a rate of 200. L/min at 1.50 atm and ambient temperature. Air is added to the chamber at 1.00 atm and the same temperature, and the gases are ignited.
  a. To ensure complete combustion of CH_4 to $CO_2(g)$ and $H_2O(g)$, three times as much oxygen as is necessary is reacted. Assuming air is 21 mole percent O_2 and 79 mole percent N_2, calculate the flow rate of air necessary to deliver the required amount of oxygen.
  b. Under the conditions in part a, combustion of methane was not complete as a mixture of $CO_2(g)$ and $CO(g)$ was produced. It was determined that 95.0% of the carbon in the exhaust gas was present in CO_2. The remainder was present as carbon in CO. Calculate the composition of the exhaust gas in terms of mole fraction of CO, CO_2, O_2, N_2, and H_2O. Assume CH_4 is completely reacted and N_2 is unreacted.

120. A steel cylinder contains 5.00 mol of graphite (pure carbon) and 5.00 mol of O_2. The mixture is ignited and all the graphite reacts. Combustion produces a mixture of CO gas and CO_2 gas. After the cylinder has cooled to its original temperature, it is found that the pressure of the cylinder has increased by 17.0%. Calculate the mole fractions of CO, CO_2, and O_2 in the final gaseous mixture.

121. The total mass that can be lifted by a balloon is given by the difference between the mass of air displaced by the balloon and the mass of the gas inside the balloon. Consider a hot-air balloon that approximates a sphere 5.00 m in diameter and contains air heated to 65°C. The surrounding air temperature is 21°C. The pressure in the balloon is equal to the atmospheric pressure, which is 745 torr.
  a. What total mass can the balloon lift? Assume that the average molar mass of air is 29.0 g/mol. (*Hint:* Heated air is less dense than cool air.)
  b. If the balloon is filled with enough helium at 21°C and 745 torr to achieve the same volume as in part a, what total mass can the balloon lift?
  c. What mass could the hot-air balloon in part a lift if it were on the ground in Denver, Colorado, where a typical atmospheric pressure is 630. torr?

122. You have a sealed, flexible balloon filled with argon gas. The atmospheric pressure is 1.00 atm and the temperature is

25°C. The air has a mole fraction of nitrogen of 0.790, the rest being oxygen.

a. Explain why the balloon would float when heated. Make sure to discuss which factors change and which remain constant, and why this matters. Be complete.

b. Above what temperature would you heat the balloon so that it would float?

123. You have a helium balloon at 1.00 atm and 25°C. You want to make a hot-air balloon with the same volume and same lift as the helium balloon. Assume air is 79.0% nitrogen, 21.0% oxygen by volume. The "lift" of a balloon is given by the difference between the mass of air displaced by the balloon and the mass of gas inside the balloon.

a. Will the temperature in the hot-air balloon have to be higher or lower than 25°C? Explain.

b. Calculate the temperature of the air required for the hot-air balloon to provide the same lift as the helium balloon at 1.00 atm and 25°C. Assume atmospheric conditions are 1.00 atm and 25°C.

124. We state that the ideal gas law tends to hold best at low pressures and high temperatures. Show how the van der Waals equation simplifies to the ideal gas law under these conditions.

125. Atmospheric scientists often use mixing ratios to express the concentrations of trace compounds in air. Mixing ratios are often expressed as ppmv (parts per million volume):

$$\text{ppmv of } X = \frac{\text{vol. of } X \text{ at STP}}{\text{total vol. of air at STP}} \times 10^6$$

On a recent autumn day, the concentration of carbon monoxide in the air in downtown Denver, Colorado, reached 3.0×10^2 ppmv. The atmospheric pressure at that time was 628 torr, and the temperature was 0°C.

a. What was the partial pressure of CO?

b. What was the concentration of CO in molecules per cubic centimeter?

126. Nitrogen gas (N_2) reacts with hydrogen gas (H_2) to form ammonia gas (NH_3). You have nitrogen and hydrogen gases in a 15.0-L container fitted with a movable piston (the piston allows the container volume to change so as to keep the pressure constant inside the container). Initially the partial pressure of each reactant gas is 1.00 atm. Assume the temperature is constant and that the reaction goes to completion.

a. Calculate the partial pressure of ammonia in the container after the reaction has reached completion.

b. Calculate the volume of the container after the reaction has reached completion.

Integrative Problems

These problems require the integration of multiple concepts to find the solutions.

127. In the presence of nitric acid, UO^{2+} undergoes a redox process. It is converted to UO_2^{2+} and nitric oxide (NO) gas is produced according to the following unbalanced equation:

$$NO_3^-(aq) + UO^{2+}(aq) \longrightarrow NO(g) + UO_2^{2+}(aq)$$

If 2.55×10^2 mL of NO(g) is isolated at 29°C and 1.5 atm, what amount (moles) of UO^{2+} was used in the reaction?

128. Silane, SiH_4, is the silicon analogue of methane, CH_4. It is prepared industrially according to the following equations:

$$Si(s) + 3HCl(g) \longrightarrow HSiCl_3(l) + H_2(g)$$
$$4HSiCl_3(l) \longrightarrow SiH_4(g) + 3SiCl_4(l)$$

a. If 156 mL of $HSiCl_3$ ($d = 1.34$ g/mL) is isolated when 15.0 L of HCl at 10.0 atm and 35°C is used, what is the percent yield of $HSiCl_3$?

b. When 156 mL of $HSiCl_3$ is heated, what volume of SiH_4 at 10.0 atm and 35°C will be obtained if the percent yield of the reaction is 93.1%?

129. Solid thorium(IV) fluoride has a boiling point of 1680°C. What is the density of a sample of gaseous thorium(IV) fluoride at its boiling point under a pressure of 2.5 atm in a 1.7-L container? Which gas will effuse faster at 1680°C, thorium(IV) fluoride or uranium(III) fluoride? How much faster?

130. Natural gas is a mixture of hydrocarbons, primarily methane (CH_4) and ethane (C_2H_6). A typical mixture might have $\chi_{methane} = 0.915$ and $\chi_{ethane} = 0.085$. What are the partial pressures of the two gases in a 15.00-L container of natural gas at 20.°C and 1.44 atm? Assuming complete combustion of both gases in the natural gas sample, what is the total mass of water formed?

Marathon Problem*

This problem is designed to incorporate several concepts and techniques into one situation. Marathon Problems can be used in class by groups of students to help facilitate problem-solving skills.

131. Use the following information to identify element A and compound B, then answer questions a and b.

An empty glass container has a mass of 658.572 g. It has a mass of 659.452 g after it has been filled with nitrogen gas at a pressure of 790. torr and a temperature of 15°C. When the container is evacuated and refilled with a certain element (A) at a pressure of 745 torr and a temperature of 26°C, it has a mass of 660.59 g.

Compound B, a gaseous organic compound that consists of 85.6% carbon and 14.4% hydrogen by mass, is placed in a stainless steel vessel (10.68 L) with excess oxygen gas. The vessel is placed in a constant-temperature bath at 22°C. The pressure in the vessel is 11.98 atm. In the bottom of the vessel is a container that is packed with Ascarite and a desiccant. Ascarite is asbestos impregnated with sodium hydroxide; it quantitatively absorbs carbon dioxide:

$$2NaOH(s) + CO_2(g) \longrightarrow Na_2CO_3(s) + H_2O(l)$$

---

*Used with permission from the *Journal of Chemical Education,* Vol. 68, No. 11, 1991, pp. 919–922; copyright © 1991, Division of Chemical Education, Inc.

The desiccant is anhydrous magnesium perchlorate, which quantitatively absorbs the water produced by the combustion reaction as well as the water produced by the above reaction. Neither the Ascarite nor the desiccant reacts with compound B or oxygen. The total mass of the container with the Ascarite and desiccant is 765.3 g.

The combustion reaction of compound B is initiated by a spark. The pressure immediately rises, then begins to decrease, and finally reaches a steady value of 6.02 atm. The stainless steel vessel is carefully opened, and the mass of the container inside the vessel is found to be 846.7 g.

A and B react quantitatively in a 1:1 mole ratio to form one mole of the single product, gas C.

a. How many grams of C will be produced if 10.0 L of A and 8.60 L of B (each at STP) are reacted by opening a stopcock connecting the two samples?

b. What will be the total pressure in the system?

 Get help understanding core concepts and visualizing molecular-level interactions, and practice problem solving, by visiting the Online Study Center at **college.hmco.com/PIC/zumdahl7e.**

6 Thermochemistry

Contents

Hot lava flowing into the ocean in Hawaii Volcanoes National Park creates clouds of steam.

E nergy is the essence of our very existence as individuals and as a society. The food that we eat furnishes the energy to live, work, and play, just as the coal and oil consumed by manufacturing and transportation systems power our modern industrialized civilization.

In the past, huge quantities of carbon-based fossil fuels have been available for the taking. This abundance of fuels has led to a world society with a voracious appetite for energy, consuming millions of barrels of petroleum every day. We are now dangerously dependent on the dwindling supplies of oil, and this dependence is an important source of tension among nations in today's world. In an incredibly short time we have moved from a period of ample and cheap supplies of petroleum to one of high prices and uncertain supplies. If our present standard of living is to be maintained, we must find alternatives to petroleum. To do this, we need to know the relationship between chemistry and energy, which we explore in this chapter.

There are additional problems with fossil fuels. The waste products from burning fossil fuels significantly affect our environment. For example, when a carbon-based fuel is burned, the carbon reacts with oxygen to form carbon dioxide, which is released into the atmosphere. Although much of this carbon dioxide is consumed in various natural processes such as photosynthesis and the formation of carbonate materials, the amount of carbon dioxide in the atmosphere is steadily increasing. This increase is significant because atmospheric carbon dioxide absorbs heat radiated from the earth's surface and radiates it back toward the earth. Since this is an important mechanism for controlling the earth's temperature, many scientists fear that an increase in the concentration of carbon dioxide will warm the earth, causing significant changes in climate. In addition, impurities in the fossil fuels react with components of the air to produce air pollution. We discussed some aspects of this problem in Chapter 5.

Just as energy is important to our society on a macroscopic scale, it is critically important to each living organism on a microscopic scale. The living cell is a miniature chemical factory powered by energy from chemical reactions. The process of cellular respiration extracts the energy stored in sugars and other nutrients to drive the various tasks of the cell. Although the extraction process is more complex and more subtle, the energy obtained from "fuel" molecules by the cell is the same as would be obtained from burning the fuel to power an internal combustion engine.

Whether it is an engine or a cell that is converting energy from one form to another, the processes are all governed by the same principles, which we will begin to explore in this chapter. Additional aspects of energy transformation will be covered in Chapter 16.

6.1 The Nature of Energy

Although the concept of energy is quite familiar, energy itself is rather difficult to define precisely. We will define **energy** as the *capacity to do work or to produce heat*. In this chapter we will concentrate specifically on the heat transfer that accompanies chemical processes.

One of the most important characteristics of energy is that it is conserved. The **law of conservation of energy** states that *energy can be converted from one form to another but can be neither created nor destroyed*. That is, the energy of the universe is constant. Energy can be classified as either potential or kinetic energy. **Potential energy** is energy due to position or composition. For example, water behind a dam has potential energy that can be converted to work when the water flows down through turbines, thereby creating

One interesting definition of energy is that which is needed to oppose natural attractions (for example, gravity and electrostatic attractions).

The total energy content of the universe is constant.

(a) Initial

(b) Final

FIGURE 6.1
(a) In the initial positions, ball A has a higher potential energy than ball B. (b) After A has rolled down the hill, the potential energy lost by A has been converted to random motions of the components of the hill (frictional heating) and to the increase in the potential energy of B.

Heat involves a transfer of energy.

This infrared photo of a house shows where energy leaks occur. The more red the color, the more energy (heat) is leaving the house.

Visualization: Coffee Creamer Flammability

electricity. Attractive and repulsive forces also lead to potential energy. The energy released when gasoline is burned results from differences in attractive forces between the nuclei and electrons in the reactants and products. The **kinetic energy** of an object is energy due to the motion of the object and depends on the mass of the object m and its velocity v: $KE = \frac{1}{2}mv^2$.

Energy can be converted from one form to another. For example, consider the two balls in Fig. 6.1(a). Ball A, because of its higher position initially, has more potential energy than ball B. When A is released, it moves down the hill and strikes B. Eventually, the arrangement shown in Fig. 6.1(b) is achieved. What has happened in going from the initial to the final arrangement? The potential energy of A has decreased, but since energy is conserved, all the energy lost by A must be accounted for. How is this energy distributed?

Initially, the potential energy of A is changed to kinetic energy as the ball rolls down the hill. Part of this kinetic energy is then transferred to B, causing it to be raised to a higher final position. Thus the potential energy of B has been increased. However, since the final position of B is lower than the original position of A, some of the energy is still unaccounted for. Both balls in their final positions are at rest, so the missing energy cannot be due to their motions. What has happened to the remaining energy?

The answer lies in the interaction between the hill's surface and the ball. As ball A rolls down the hill, some of its kinetic energy is transferred to the surface of the hill as heat. This transfer of energy is called *frictional heating*. The temperature of the hill increases very slightly as the ball rolls down.

Before we proceed further, it is important to recognize that heat and temperature are decidedly different. As we saw in Chapter 5, *temperature* is a property that reflects the random motions of the particles in a particular substance. **Heat,** on the other hand, involves the *transfer* of energy between two objects due to a temperature difference. Heat is not a substance contained by an object, although we often talk of heat as if this were true.

Note that in going from the initial to the final arrangements in Fig. 6.1, ball B gains potential energy because work was done by ball A on B. **Work** is defined as force acting over a distance. Work is required to raise B from its original position to its final one. Part of the original energy stored as potential energy in A has been transferred through work to B, thereby increasing B's potential energy. Thus there are two ways to transfer energy: through work and through heat.

In rolling to the bottom of the hill shown in Fig. 6.1, ball A will always lose the same amount of potential energy. However, the way that this energy transfer is divided between work and heat depends on the specific conditions—the **pathway.** For example, the surface of the hill might be so rough that the energy of A is expended completely through frictional heating; A is moving so slowly when it hits B that it cannot move B to the next level. In this case, no work is done. Regardless of the condition of the hill's surface, the *total energy* transferred will be constant. However, the amounts of heat and work will differ. Energy change is independent of the pathway; however, work and heat are both dependent on the pathway.

This brings us to a very important concept: the **state function** or **state property.** A state function refers to a property of the system that depends only on its *present state.* A state function (property) does not depend in any way on the system's past (or future). In other words, the value of a state function does not depend on how the system arrived at the present state; it depends only on the characteristics of the present state. This leads to a very important characteristic of a state function: A change in this function (property) in going from one state to another state is independent of the particular pathway taken between the two states.

A nonscientific analogy that illustrates the difference between a state function and a nonstate function is elevation on the earth's surface and distance between two points. In traveling from Chicago (elevation 674 ft) to Denver (elevation 5280 ft), the change in elevation is always $5280 - 674 = 4606$ ft regardless of the route taken between the two cities. The distance traveled, however, depends on how you make the trip. Thus elevation is a function that does not depend on the route (pathway) but distance is pathway dependent. Elevation is a state function and distance is not.

Energy is a state function; work and heat are not.

Of the functions considered in our present example, energy is a state function, but work and heat are not state functions.

Chemical Energy

The ideas we have just illustrated using mechanical examples also apply to chemical systems. The combustion of methane, for example, is used to heat many homes in the United States:

$$CH_4(g) + 2O_2(g) \longrightarrow CO_2(g) + 2H_2O(g) + \text{energy (heat)}$$

To discuss this reaction, we divide the universe into two parts: the system and the surroundings. The **system** is the part of the universe on which we wish to focus attention; the **surroundings** include everything else in the universe. In this case we define the system as the reactants and products of the reaction. The surroundings consist of the reaction container (a furnace, for example), the room, and anything else other than the reactants and products.

When a reaction results in the evolution of heat, it is said to be **exothermic** (*exo-* is a prefix meaning "out of"); that is, energy flows *out of the system.* For example, in the combustion of methane, energy flows out of the system as heat. Reactions that absorb energy from the surroundings are said to be **endothermic.** When the heat flow is *into a system,* the process is endothermic. For example, the formation of nitric oxide from nitrogen and oxygen is endothermic:

$$N_2(g) + O_2(g) + \text{energy (heat)} \longrightarrow 2NO(g)$$

Where does the energy, released as heat, come from in an exothermic reaction? The answer lies in the difference in potential energies between the products and the reactants. Which has lower potential energy, the reactants or the products? We know that total energy is conserved and that energy flows from the system into the surroundings in an exothermic reaction. This means that *the energy gained by the surroundings must be equal to the energy lost by the system.* In the combustion of methane, the energy content of the system decreases, which means that 1 mole of CO_2 and 2 moles of H_2O molecules (the products) possess less potential energy than do 1 mole of CH_4 and 2 moles of O_2 molecules (the reactants). The heat flow into the surroundings results from a lowering of the potential energy of the reaction system. This always holds true. *In any exothermic reaction, some of the potential energy stored in the chemical bonds is being converted to thermal energy (random kinetic energy) via heat.*

The energy diagram for the combustion of methane is shown in Fig. 6.2, where $\Delta(PE)$ represents the *change* in potential energy stored in the bonds of the products as compared with the bonds of the reactants. In other words, this quantity represents the difference between

Visualization: Sugar and Potassium Chlorate

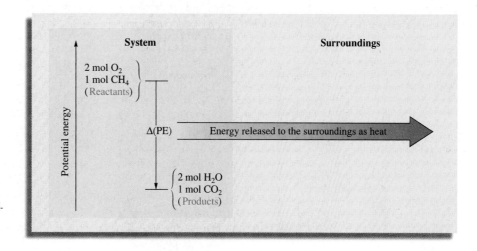

FIGURE 6.2
The combustion of methane releases the quantity of energy $\Delta(PE)$ to the surroundings via heat flow. This is an exothermic process.

FIGURE 6.3
The energy diagram for the reaction of nitrogen and oxygen to form nitric oxide. This is an endothermic process: Heat [equal in magnitude to $\Delta(PE)$] flows into the system from the surroundings.

the energy required to break the bonds in the reactants and the energy released when the bonds in the products are formed. In an exothermic process, the bonds in the products are stronger (on average) than those of the reactants. That is, more energy is released by forming the new bonds in the products than is consumed to break the bonds in the reactants. The net result is that the quantity of energy $\Delta(PE)$ is transferred to the surroundings through heat.

For an endothermic reaction, the situation is reversed, as shown in Fig. 6.3. Energy that flows into the system as heat is used to increase the potential energy of the system. In this case the products have higher potential energy (weaker bonds on average) than the reactants.

The study of energy and its interconversions is called **thermodynamics.** The law of conservation of energy is often called the **first law of thermodynamics** and is stated as follows: *The energy of the universe is constant.*

The **internal energy** E of a system can be defined most precisely as the sum of the kinetic and potential energies of all the "particles" in the system. The internal energy of a system can be changed by a flow of work, heat, or both. That is,

$$\Delta E = q + w$$

where ΔE represents the change in the system's internal energy, q represents heat, and w represents work.

Thermodynamic quantities always consist of two parts: a *number*, giving the magnitude of the change, and a *sign*, indicating the direction of the flow. *The sign reflects the system's point of view.* For example, if a quantity of energy flows *into* the system via heat (an endothermic process), q is equal to $+x$, where the *positive* sign indicates that the *system's energy is increasing.* On the other hand, when energy flows *out of* the system via heat (an exothermic process), q is equal to $-x$, where the *negative* sign indicates that the *system's energy is decreasing.*

In this text the same conventions also apply to the flow of work. If the system does work on the surroundings (energy flows out of the system), w is negative. If the surroundings do work on the system (energy flows into the system), w is positive. We define work from the system's point of view to be consistent for all thermodynamic quantities. That is, in this convention the signs of both q and w reflect what happens to the system; thus we use $\Delta E = q + w$.

In this text we *always* take the system's point of view. This convention is not followed in every area of science. For example, engineers are in the business of designing machines to do work, that is, to make the system (the machine) transfer energy to its surroundings through work. Consequently, engineers define work from the surroundings' point of view. In their convention, work that flows out of the system is treated as positive because the energy of the surroundings has increased. The first law of thermodynamics is then written $\Delta E = q - w'$, where w' signifies work from the surroundings' point of view.

The convention in this text is to take the system's point of view; $q = -x$ denotes an exothermic process, and $q = +x$ denotes an endothermic one.

| Sample Exercise 6.1 | **Internal Energy** |

Calculate ΔE for a system undergoing an endothermic process in which 15.6 kJ of heat flows and where 1.4 kJ of work is done on the system.

The joule (J) is the fundamental SI unit for energy:

$$J = \frac{kg \cdot m^2}{s^2}$$

One kilojoule (kJ) $= 10^3$ J.

Solution

We use the equation

$$\Delta E = q + w$$

where $q = +15.6$ kJ, since the process is endothermic, and $w = +1.4$ kJ, since work is done on the system. Thus

$$\Delta E = 15.6 \text{ kJ} + 1.4 \text{ kJ} = 17.0 \text{ kJ}$$

The system has gained 17.0 kJ of energy.

See Exercises 6.21 and 6.22.

Visualization: Work versus Energy Flow

A common type of work associated with chemical processes is work done by a gas (through *expansion*) or work done to a gas (through *compression*). For example, in an automobile engine, the heat from the combustion of the gasoline expands the gases in the cylinder to push back the piston, and this motion is then translated into the motion of the car.

Suppose we have a gas confined to a cylindrical container with a movable piston as shown in Fig. 6.4, where F is the force acting on a piston of area A. Since pressure is defined as force per unit area, the pressure of the gas is

$$P = \frac{F}{A}$$

Work is defined as force applied over a distance, so if the piston moves a distance Δh, as shown in Fig. 6.4, then the work done is

$$\text{Work} = \text{force} \times \text{distance} = F \times \Delta h$$

Since $P = F/A$ or $F = P \times A$, then

$$\text{Work} = F \times \Delta h = P \times A \times \Delta h$$

Since the volume of a cylinder equals the area of the piston times the height of the cylinder (Fig. 6.4), the change in volume ΔV resulting from the piston moving a distance Δh is

$$\Delta V = \text{final volume} - \text{initial volume} = A \times \Delta h$$

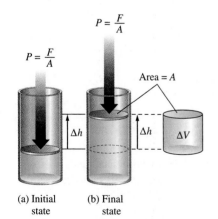

FIGURE 6.4
(a) The piston, moving a distance Δh against a pressure P, does work on the surroundings. (b) Since the volume of a cylinder is the area of the base times its height, the change in volume of the gas is given by $\Delta h \times A = \Delta V$.

Substituting $\Delta V = A \times \Delta h$ into the expression for work gives

$$\text{Work} = P \times A \times \Delta h = P\Delta V$$

This gives us the *magnitude* (size) of the work required to expand a gas ΔV against a pressure P.

What about the sign of the work? The gas (the system) is expanding, moving the piston against the pressure. Thus the system is doing work on the surroundings, so from the system's point of view the sign of the work should be negative.

For an *expanding* gas, ΔV is a positive quantity because the volume is increasing. Thus ΔV and w must have opposite signs, which leads to the equation

w and *P*Δ*V* have opposite signs because when the gas expands (ΔV is positive), work flows into the surroundings (*w* is negative).

$$w = -P\Delta V$$

Note that for a gas expanding against an external pressure P, w is a negative quantity as required, since work flows out of the system. When a gas is *compressed,* ΔV is a negative quantity (the volume decreases), which makes w a positive quantity (work flows into the system).

| Sample Exercise 6.2 | *PV* Work |

Calculate the work associated with the expansion of a gas from 46 L to 64 L at a constant external pressure of 15 atm.

Solution

For a gas at constant pressure,

$$w = -P\Delta V$$

For an ideal gas, work can occur only when its volume changes. Thus, if a gas is heated at constant volume, the pressure increases but no work occurs.

In this case $P = 15$ atm and $\Delta V = 64 - 46 = 18$ L. Hence

$$w = -15 \text{ atm} \times 18 \text{ L} = -270 \text{ L} \cdot \text{atm}$$

Note that since the gas expands, it does work on its surroundings.

Reality Check: Energy flows out of the gas, so w is a negative quantity.

See Exercises 6.25 through 6.27.

In dealing with "*PV* work," keep in mind that the P in $P\Delta V$ always refers to the external pressure—the pressure that causes a compression or that resists an expansion.

| Sample Exercise 6.3 | Internal Energy, Heat, and Work |

A balloon is being inflated to its full extent by heating the air inside it. In the final stages of this process, the volume of the balloon changes from 4.00×10^6 L to 4.50×10^6 L by the addition of 1.3×10^8 J of energy as heat. Assuming that the balloon expands against a constant pressure of 1.0 atm, calculate ΔE for the process. (To convert between $L \cdot$ atm and J, use $1 \text{ L} \cdot \text{atm} = 101.3$ J.)

Solution

To calculate ΔE, we use the equation

$$\Delta E = q + w$$

Since the problem states that 1.3×10^8 J of energy is *added* as heat,

$$q = +1.3 \times 10^8 \text{ J}$$

A propane burner is used to heat the air in a hot-air balloon.

The work done can be calculated from the expression

$$w = -P\Delta V$$

In this case $P = 1.0$ atm and

$$\Delta V = V_{\text{final}} - V_{\text{initial}}$$
$$= 4.50 \times 10^6 \text{ L} - 4.00 \times 10^6 \text{ L} = 0.50 \times 10^6 \text{ L} = 5.0 \times 10^5 \text{ L}$$

Thus

$$w = -1.0 \text{ atm} \times 5.0 \times 10^5 \text{ L} = -5.0 \times 10^5 \text{ L} \cdot \text{atm}$$

Note that the negative sign for w makes sense, since the gas is expanding and thus doing work on the surroundings.

To calculate ΔE, we must sum q and w. However, since q is given in units of J and w is given in units of L · atm, we must change the work to units of joules:

$$w = -5.0 \times 10^5 \text{ L} \cdot \text{atm} \times \frac{101.3 \text{ J}}{\text{L} \cdot \text{atm}} = -5.1 \times 10^7 \text{ J}$$

Then

$$\Delta E = q + w = (+1.3 \times 10^8 \text{ J}) + (-5.1 \times 10^7 \text{ J}) = 8 \times 10^7 \text{ J}$$

Reality Check: Since more energy is added through heating than the gas expends doing work, there is a net increase in the internal energy of the gas in the balloon. Hence ΔE is positive.

See Exercises 6.28 through 6.30.

6.2 Enthalpy and Calorimetry

Enthalpy

So far we have discussed the internal energy of a system. A less familiar property of a system is its **enthalpy,** H, which is defined as

$$H = E + PV$$

where E is the internal energy of the system, P is the pressure of the system, and V is the volume of the system.

Since internal energy, pressure, and volume are all state functions, *enthalpy is also a state function.* But what exactly is enthalpy? To help answer this question, consider a process carried out at constant pressure and where the only work allowed is pressure–volume work ($w = -P\Delta V$). Under these conditions, the expression

> Enthalpy is a state function. A change in enthalpy does not depend on the pathway between two states.

$$\Delta E = q_P + w$$

becomes

$$\Delta E = q_P - P\Delta V$$

> Recall from the previous section that w and $P\Delta V$ have opposite signs:
>
> $$w = -P\Delta V$$

or

$$q_P = \Delta E + P\Delta V$$

where q_P is the heat at constant pressure.

We will now relate q_P to a change in enthalpy. The definition of enthalpy is $H = E + PV$. Therefore, we can say

$$\text{Change in } H = (\text{change in } E) + (\text{change in } PV)$$

or

$$\Delta H = \Delta E + \Delta(PV)$$

Since P is constant, the change in PV is due only to a change in volume. Thus

$$\Delta(PV) = P\Delta V$$

and

$$\Delta H = \Delta E + P\Delta V$$

This expression is identical to the one we obtained for q_P:

$$q_P = \Delta E + P\Delta V$$

Thus, for a process carried out at constant pressure and where the only work allowed is that from a volume change, we have

$$\Delta H = q_P$$

$\Delta H = q$ *only* at constant pressure.

At constant pressure (where only PV work is allowed), the change in enthalpy ΔH of the system is equal to the energy flow as heat. This means that for a reaction studied at constant pressure, the flow of heat is a measure of the change in enthalpy for the system. For this reason, the terms *heat of reaction* and *change in enthalpy* are used interchangeably for reactions studied at constant pressure.

The change in enthalpy of a system has no easily interpreted meaning except at constant pressure, where $\Delta H =$ heat.

For a chemical reaction, the enthalpy change is given by the equation

$$\Delta H = H_{products} - H_{reactants}$$

At constant pressure, exothermic means ΔH is negative; endothermic means ΔH is positive.

In a case in which the products of a reaction have a greater enthalpy than the reactants, ΔH will be positive. Thus heat will be absorbed by the system, and the reaction is endothermic. On the other hand, if the enthalpy of the products is less than that of the reactants, ΔH will be negative. In this case the overall decrease in enthalpy is achieved by the generation of heat, and the reaction is exothermic.

| Sample Exercise 6.4 | **Enthalpy** |

When 1 mole of methane (CH_4) is burned at constant pressure, 890 kJ of energy is released as heat. Calculate ΔH for a process in which a 5.8-g sample of methane is burned at constant pressure.

Solution

At constant pressure, 890 kJ of energy per mole of CH_4 is produced as heat:

$$q_P = \Delta H = -890 \text{ kJ/mol } CH_4$$

Note that the minus sign indicates an exothermic process. In this case, a 5.8-g sample of CH_4 (molar mass = 16.0 g/mol) is burned. Since this amount is smaller than 1 mole, less than 890 kJ will be released as heat. The actual value can be calculated as follows:

$$5.8 \text{ g } CH_4 \times \frac{1 \text{ mol } CH_4}{16.0 \text{ g } CH_4} = 0.36 \text{ mol } CH_4$$

and

$$0.36 \text{ mol } CH_4 \times \frac{-890 \text{ kJ}}{\text{mol } CH_4} = -320 \text{ kJ}$$

Thus, when a 5.8-g sample of CH_4 is burned at constant pressure,

$$\Delta H = \text{heat flow} = -320 \text{ kJ}$$

See Exercises 6.35 through 6.38.

TABLE 6.1 The Specific Heat Capacities of Some Common Substances	
Substance	Specific Heat Capacity (J/°C · g)
$H_2O(l)$	4.18
$H_2O(s)$	2.03
Al(s)	0.89
Fe(s)	0.45
Hg(l)	0.14
C(s)	0.71

Specific heat capacity: the energy required to raise the temperature of one gram of a substance by one degree Celsius.

Molar heat capacity: the energy required to raise the temperature of one mole of a substance by one degree Celsius.

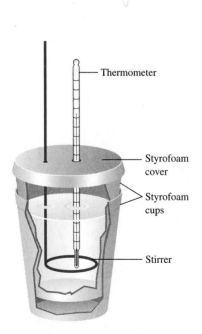

FIGURE 6.5
A coffee-cup calorimeter made of two Styrofoam cups.

Calorimetry

The device used experimentally to determine the heat associated with a chemical reaction is called a **calorimeter. Calorimetry,** the science of measuring heat, is based on observing the temperature change when a body absorbs or discharges energy as heat. Substances respond differently to being heated. One substance might require a great deal of heat energy to raise its temperature by one degree, whereas another will exhibit the same temperature change after absorbing relatively little heat. The **heat capacity** C of a substance, which is a measure of this property, is defined as

$$C = \frac{\text{heat absorbed}}{\text{increase in temperature}}$$

When an element or a compound is heated, the energy required will depend on the amount of the substance present (for example, it takes twice as much energy to raise the temperature of two grams of water by one degree than it takes to raise the temperature of one gram of water by one degree). Thus, in defining the heat capacity of a substance, the amount of substance must be specified. If the heat capacity is given *per gram* of substance, it is called the **specific heat capacity,** and its units are J/°C · g or J/K · g. If the heat capacity is given *per mole* of the substance, it is called the **molar heat capacity,** and it has the units J/°C · mol or J/K · mol. The specific heat capacities of some common substances are given in Table 6.1. Note from this table that the heat capacities of metals are very different from that of water. It takes much less energy to change the temperature of a gram of a metal by 1°C than for a gram of water.

Although the calorimeters used for highly accurate work are precision instruments, a very simple calorimeter can be used to examine the fundamentals of calorimetry. All we need are two nested Styrofoam cups with a cover through which a stirrer and thermometer can be inserted, as shown in Fig. 6.5. This device is called a "coffee-cup calorimeter." The outer cup is used to provide extra insulation. The inner cup holds the solution in which the reaction occurs.

The measurement of heat using a simple calorimeter such as that shown in Fig. 6.5 is an example of **constant-pressure calorimetry,** since the pressure (atmospheric pressure) remains constant during the process. Constant-pressure calorimetry is used in determining the changes in enthalpy (heats of reactions) for reactions occurring in solution. Recall that under these conditions, the change in enthalpy equals the heat.

For example, suppose we mix 50.0 mL of 1.0 M HCl at 25.0°C with 50.0 mL of 1.0 M NaOH also at 25°C in a calorimeter. After the reactants are mixed by stirring, the temperature is observed to increase to 31.9°C. As we saw in Section 4.8, the net ionic equation for this reaction is

$$H^+(aq) + OH^-(aq) \longrightarrow H_2O(l)$$

When these reactants (each originally at the same temperature) are mixed, the temperature of the mixed solution is observed to increase. Therefore, the chemical reaction must be releasing energy as heat. This released energy increases the random motions of the solution components, which in turn increases the temperature. The quantity of energy released can be determined from the temperature increase, the mass of solution, and the specific heat capacity of the solution. For an approximate result, we will assume that the calorimeter does not absorb or leak any heat and that the solution can be treated as if it were pure water with a density of 1.0 g/mL.

We also need to know the heat required to raise the temperature of a given amount of water by 1°C. Table 6.1 lists the specific heat capacity of water as 4.18 J/°C · g. This means that 4.18 J of energy is required to raise the temperature of 1 gram of water by 1°C.

CHEMICAL IMPACT

Nature Has Hot Plants

The voodoo lily is a beautiful, seductive—and foul-smelling—plant. The exotic-looking lily features an elaborate reproductive mechanism—a purple spike that can reach nearly 3 feet in length and is cloaked by a hoodlike leaf. But approach to the plant reveals bad news—it smells terrible!

Despite its antisocial odor, this putrid plant has fascinated biologists for many years because of its ability to generate heat. At the peak of its metabolic activity, the plant's blossom can be as much as 15°C above its ambient temperature. To generate this much heat, the metabolic rate of the plant must be close to that of a flying hummingbird!

What's the purpose of this intense heat production? For a plant faced with limited food supplies in the very competitive tropical climate where it grows, heat production seems like a great waste of energy. The answer to this mystery is that the voodoo lily is pollinated mainly by carrion-loving insects. Thus the lily prepares a malodorous mixture of chemicals characteristic of rotting meat, which it then "cooks" off into the surrounding air to attract flesh-feeding beetles and flies. Then, once the insects enter the pollination chamber, the high temperatures there (as high as 110°F) cause the insects to remain very active to better carry out their pollination duties.

The voodoo lily is only one of many such thermogenic (heat-producing) plants. Another interesting example is the eastern skunk cabbage, which produces enough heat to bloom inside of a snow bank by creating its own ice caves. These plants are of special interest to biologists because they provide opportunities to study metabolic reactions that are quite subtle in "normal" plants. For example, recent studies have shown that salicylic acid, the active form of aspirin, is probably very important in producing the metabolic bursts in thermogenic plants.

Besides studying the dramatic heat effects in thermogenic plants, biologists are also interested in calorimetric

---

If two reactants at the same temperature are mixed and the resulting solution gets warmer, this means the reaction taking place is exothermic. An endothermic reaction cools the solution.

From these assumptions and definitions, we can calculate the heat (change in enthalpy) for the neutralization reaction:

Energy released by the reaction

= energy absorbed by the solution

= specific heat capacity × mass of solution × increase in temperature

$= s \times m \times \Delta T$

In this case the increase in temperature $(\Delta T) = 31.9°C - 25.0°C = 6.9°C$, and the mass of solution $(m) = 100.0 \text{ mL} \times 1.0 \text{ g/mL} = 1.0 \times 10^2$ g. Thus

$$\text{Energy released} = s \times m \times \Delta T$$

$$= \left(4.18 \frac{\text{J}}{°C \cdot g}\right)(1.0 \times 10^2 \text{ g})(6.9°C)$$

$$= 2.9 \times 10^3 \text{ J}$$

How much energy would have been released if twice these amounts of solutions had been mixed? The answer is that twice as much energy would have been produced. The heat of a reaction is an *extensive property;* it depends directly on the amount of substance, in this case on the amounts of reactants. In contrast, an *intensive property* is not related to the amount of a substance. For example, temperature is an intensive property.

Enthalpies of reaction are often expressed in terms of moles of reacting substances. The number of moles of H^+ ions consumed in the preceding experiment is

$$50.0 \text{ mL} \times \frac{1 \text{ L}}{1000 \text{ mL}} \times \frac{1.0 \text{ mol}}{\text{L}} H^+ = 5.0 \times 10^{-2} \text{ mol } H^+$$

Thus 2.9×10^3 J heat was released when 5.0×10^{-2} mol H^+ ions reacted, or

$$\frac{2.9 \times 10^3 \text{ J}}{5.0 \times 10^{-2} \text{ mol } H^+} = 5.8 \times 10^4 \text{ J/mol}$$

studies of regular plants. For example, very precise calorimeters have been designed that can be used to study the heat produced, and thus the metabolic activities, of clumps of cells no larger than a bread crumb. Several scientists have suggested that a single calorimetric measurement taking just a few minutes on a tiny plant might be useful in predicting the growth rate of the mature plant throughout its lifetime. If true, this would provide a very efficient method for selecting the plants most likely to thrive as adults.

Because the study of the heat production by plants is an excellent way to learn about plant metabolism, this continues to be a "hot" area of research.

The voodoo lily attracts pollinating insects with its foul odor.

Notice that in this example we mentally keep track of the direction of the energy flow and assign the correct sign at the end of the calculation.

of heat released per 1.0 mol H^+ ions neutralized. Thus the *magnitude* of the enthalpy change per mole for the reaction

$$H^+(aq) + OH^-(aq) \longrightarrow H_2O(l)$$

is 58 kJ/mol. Since heat is *evolved*, $\Delta H = -58$ kJ/mol.

Sample Exercise 6.5   ## Constant-Pressure Calorimetry

When 1.00 L of 1.00 M $Ba(NO_3)_2$ solution at 25.0°C is mixed with 1.00 L of 1.00 M Na_2SO_4 solution at 25°C in a calorimeter, the white solid $BaSO_4$ forms and the temperature of the mixture increases to 28.1°C. Assuming that the calorimeter absorbs only a negligible quantity of heat, that the specific heat capacity of the solution is 4.18 J/°C · g, and that the density of the final solution is 1.0 g/mL, calculate the enthalpy change per mole of $BaSO_4$ formed.

Solution

The ions present before any reaction occurs are Ba^{2+}, NO_3^-, Na^+, and SO_4^{2-}. The Na^+ and NO_3^- ions are spectator ions, since $NaNO_3$ is very soluble in water and will not precipitate under these conditions. The net ionic equation for the reaction is therefore

$$Ba^{2+}(aq) + SO_4^{2-}(aq) \longrightarrow BaSO_4(s)$$

Since the temperature increases, formation of the solid $BaSO_4$ must be exothermic; ΔH will be negative.

Heat evolved by reaction

= heat absorbed by solution

= specific heat capacity × mass of solution × increase in temperature

Since 1.00 L of each solution is used, the total solution volume is 2.00 L, and

$$\text{Mass of solution} = 2.00 \cancel{L} \times \frac{1000 \cancel{mL}}{1 \cancel{L}} \times \frac{1.0 \text{ g}}{\cancel{mL}} = 2.0 \times 10^3 \text{ g}$$

$$\text{Temperature increase} = 28.1°C - 25.0°C = 3.1°C$$

$$\text{Heat evolved} = (4.18 \text{ J}/°\cancel{C} \cdot \cancel{g})(2.0 \times 10^3 \cancel{g})(3.1°\cancel{C}) = 2.6 \times 10^4 \text{ J}$$

Thus

$$q = q_P = \Delta H = -2.6 \times 10^4 \text{ J}$$

Since 1.0 L of 1.0 M $Ba(NO_3)_2$ contains 1 mol Ba^{2+} ions and 1.0 L of 1.0 M Na_2SO_4 contains 1.0 mol SO_4^{2-} ions, 1.0 mol solid $BaSO_4$ is formed in this experiment. Thus the enthalpy change per mole of $BaSO_4$ formed is

$$\Delta H = -2.6 \times 10^4 \text{ J/mol} = -26 \text{ kJ/mol}$$

See Exercises 6.51 through 6.54.

Calorimetry experiments also can be performed at **constant volume.** For example, when a photographic flashbulb flashes, the bulb becomes very hot, because the reaction of the zirconium or magnesium wire with the oxygen inside the bulb is exothermic. The reaction occurs inside the flashbulb, which is rigid and does not change volume. Under these conditions, no work is done (because the volume must change for pressure–volume work to be performed). To study the energy changes in reactions under conditions of constant volume, a "bomb calorimeter" (Fig. 6.6) is used. Weighed reactants are placed inside a rigid steel container (the "bomb") and ignited. The energy change is determined by measuring the increase in the temperature of the water and other calorimeter parts. For a constant-volume process, the change in volume ΔV is equal to zero, so work (which is $-P\Delta V$) is also equal to zero. Therefore,

$$\Delta E = q + w = q = q_V \qquad \text{(constant volume)}$$

FIGURE 6.6
A bomb calorimeter. The reaction is carried out inside a rigid steel "bomb" (photo of actual disassembled "bomb" shown on right), and the heat evolved is absorbed by the surrounding water and other calorimeter parts. The quantity of energy produced by the reaction can be calculated from the temperature increase.

CHEMICAL IMPACT

Firewalking: Magic or Science?

For millennia people have been amazed at the ability of Eastern mystics to walk across beds of glowing coals without any apparent discomfort. Even in the United States, thousands of people have performed feats of firewalking as part of motivational seminars. How is this possible? Do firewalkers have supernatural powers?

Actually, there are good scientific explanations, based on the concepts covered in this chapter, of why firewalking is possible. The first important factor concerns the heat capacity of feet. Because human tissue is mainly composed of water, it has a relatively large specific heat capacity. This means that a large amount of energy must be transferred from the coals to significantly change the temperature of the feet. During the brief contact between feet and coals, there is relatively little time for energy flow so the feet do not reach a high enough temperature to cause damage.

Second, although the surface of the coals has a very high temperature, the red hot layer is very thin. Therefore, the quantity of energy available to heat the feet is smaller than might be expected. This factor points to the difference between temperature and heat. Temperature reflects the *intensity* of the random kinetic energy in a given sample of matter. The amount of energy available for heat flow, on the other hand, depends on the quantity of matter at a given temperature—10 grams of matter at a given temperature contains 10 times as much thermal

A group of firewalkers in Japan.

energy as 1 gram of the same matter. This is why the tiny spark from a sparkler does not hurt when it hits your hand. The spark has a very high temperature but has so little mass that no significant energy transfer occurs to your hand. This same argument applies to the very thin hot layer on the coals.

Thus, although firewalking is an impressive feat, there are several sound scientific reasons why it is possible (with the proper training and a properly prepared bed of coals).

Suppose we wish to measure the energy of combustion of octane (C_8H_{18}), a component of gasoline. A 0.5269-g sample of octane is placed in a bomb calorimeter known to have a heat capacity of 11.3 kJ/°C. This means that 11.3 kJ of energy is required to raise the temperature of the water and other parts of the calorimeter by 1°C. The octane is ignited in the presence of excess oxygen, and the temperature increase of the calorimeter is 2.25°C. The amount of energy released is calculated as follows:

Energy released by the reaction

$$= \text{temperature increase} \times \text{energy required to change the temperature by 1°C}$$

$$= \Delta T \times \text{heat capacity of calorimeter}$$

$$= 2.25°C \times 11.3 \text{ kJ/°C} = 25.4 \text{ kJ}$$

This means that 25.4 kJ of energy was released by the combustion of 0.5269 g octane.

The number of moles of octane is

$$0.5269 \; \text{g octane} \times \frac{1 \; \text{mol octane}}{114.2 \; \text{g octane}} = 4.614 \times 10^{-3} \; \text{mol octane}$$

Since 25.4 kJ of energy was released for 4.614×10^{-3} mol octane, the energy released per mole is

$$\frac{25.4 \; \text{kJ}}{4.614 \times 10^{-3} \; \text{mol}} = 5.50 \times 10^3 \; \text{kJ/mol}$$

Since the reaction is exothermic, ΔE is negative:

$$\Delta E_{\text{combustion}} = -5.50 \times 10^3 \; \text{kJ/mol}$$

Note that since no work is done in this case, ΔE is equal to the heat.

$$\Delta E = q + w = q \qquad \text{since } w = 0$$

Thus $q = -5.50 \times 10^3$ kJ/mol.

Sample Exercise 6.6

Constant-Volume Calorimetry

Hydrogen's potential as a fuel is discussed in Section 6.6.

It has been suggested that hydrogen gas obtained by the decomposition of water might be a substitute for natural gas (principally methane). To compare the energies of combustion of these fuels, the following experiment was carried out using a bomb calorimeter with a heat capacity of 11.3 kJ/°C. When a 1.50-g sample of methane gas was burned with excess oxygen in the calorimeter, the temperature increased by 7.3°C. When a 1.15-g sample of hydrogen gas was burned with excess oxygen, the temperature increase was 14.3°C. Calculate the energy of combustion (per gram) for hydrogen and methane.

Solution

We calculate the energy of combustion for methane using the heat capacity of the calorimeter (11.3 kJ/°C) and the observed temperature increase of 7.3°C:

$$\text{Energy } \textit{released} \text{ in the combustion of 1.5 g CH}_4 = (11.3 \; \text{kJ/°C})(7.3\text{°C})$$

$$= 83 \; \text{kJ}$$

The direction of energy flow is indicated by words in this example. Using signs to designate the direction of energy flow:

$$\Delta E_{\text{combustion}} = -55 \; \text{kJ/g}$$

for methane and

$$\Delta E_{\text{combustion}} = -141 \; \text{kJ/g}$$

for hydrogen.

$$\text{Energy } \textit{released} \text{ in the combustion of 1 g CH}_4 = \frac{83 \; \text{kJ}}{1.5 \; \text{g}} = 55 \; \text{kJ/g}$$

Similarly, for hydrogen

$$\text{Energy } \textit{released} \text{ in the combustion of 1.15 g H}_2 = (11.3 \; \text{kJ/°C})(14.3\text{°C})$$

$$= 162 \; \text{kJ}$$

$$\text{Energy } \textit{released} \text{ in the combustion of 1 g H}_2 = \frac{162 \; \text{kJ}}{1.15 \; \text{g}} = 141 \; \text{kJ/g}$$

The energy released in the combustion of 1 g hydrogen is approximately 2.5 times that for 1 g methane, indicating that hydrogen gas is a potentially useful fuel.

See Exercises 6.55 and 6.56.

6.3 Hess's Law

Since enthalpy is a state function, the change in enthalpy in going from some initial state to some final state is independent of the pathway. This means that *in going from a particular set of reactants to a particular set of products, the change in enthalpy is the same whether the reaction takes place in one step or in a series of steps.* This principle is known as **Hess's law** and can be illustrated by examining the oxidation of nitrogen to produce nitrogen dioxide. The overall reaction can be written in one step, where the enthalpy change is represented by ΔH_1.

ΔH is not dependent on the reaction pathway.

$$N_2(g) + 2O_2(g) \longrightarrow 2NO_2(g) \qquad \Delta H_1 = 68 \; \text{kJ}$$

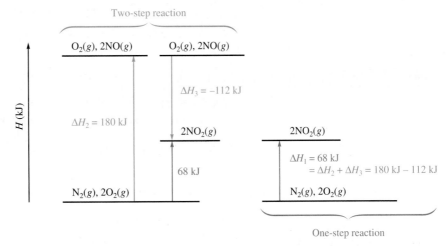

FIGURE 6.7
The principle of Hess's law. The same change in enthalpy occurs when nitrogen and oxygen react to form nitrogen dioxide, regardless of whether the reaction occurs in one (red) or two (blue) steps.

Visualization: Hess's Law

This reaction also can be carried out in two distinct steps, with enthalpy changes designated by ΔH_2 and ΔH_3:

$$N_2(g) + O_2(g) \longrightarrow 2NO(g) \qquad\qquad \Delta H_2 = 180 \text{ kJ}$$
$$2NO(g) + O_2(g) \longrightarrow 2NO_2(g) \qquad\qquad \Delta H_3 = -112 \text{ kJ}$$

Net reaction: $N_2(g) + 2O_2(g) \longrightarrow 2NO_2(g) \qquad \Delta H_2 + \Delta H_3 = 68 \text{ kJ}$

Note that the sum of the two steps gives the net, or overall, reaction and that

$$\Delta H_1 = \Delta H_2 + \Delta H_3 = 68 \text{ kJ}$$

The principle of Hess's law is shown schematically in Fig. 6.7.

Characteristics of Enthalpy Changes

Reversing the direction of a reaction changes the sign of ΔH.

To use Hess's law to compute enthalpy changes for reactions, it is important to understand two characteristics of ΔH for a reaction:

1. If a reaction is reversed, the sign of ΔH is also reversed.

2. The magnitude of ΔH is directly proportional to the quantities of reactants and products in a reaction. If the coefficients in a balanced reaction are multiplied by an integer, the value of ΔH is multiplied by the same integer.

Both these rules follow in a straightforward way from the properties of enthalpy changes. The first rule can be explained by recalling that the *sign* of ΔH indicates the *direction* of the heat flow at constant pressure. If the direction of the reaction is reversed, the direction of the heat flow also will be reversed. To see this, consider the preparation of xenon tetrafluoride, which was the first binary compound made from a noble gas:

$$Xe(g) + 2F_2(g) \longrightarrow XeF_4(s) \qquad \Delta H = -251 \text{ kJ}$$

Crystals of xenon tetrafluoride, the first reported binary compound containing a noble gas element.

This reaction is exothermic, and 251 kJ of energy flows into the surroundings as heat. On the other hand, if the colorless XeF_4 crystals are decomposed into the elements, according to the equation

$$XeF_4(s) \longrightarrow Xe(g) + 2F_2(g)$$

the opposite energy flow occurs because 251 kJ of energy must be added to the system to produce this endothermic reaction. Thus, for this reaction, $\Delta H = +251$ kJ.

The second rule comes from the fact that ΔH is an extensive property, depending on the amount of substances reacting. For example, since 251 kJ of energy is evolved for the reaction

$$Xe(g) + 2F_2(g) \longrightarrow XeF_4(s)$$

then for a preparation involving twice the quantities of reactants and products, or

$$2Xe(g) + 4F_2(g) \longrightarrow 2XeF_4(s)$$

twice as much heat would be evolved:

$$\Delta H = 2(-251 \text{ kJ}) = -502 \text{ kJ}$$

Sample Exercise 6.7

Hess's Law I

Two forms of carbon are *graphite,* the soft, black, slippery material used in "lead" pencils and as a lubricant for locks, and *diamond,* the brilliant, hard gemstone. Using the enthalpies of combustion for graphite (-394 kJ/mol) and diamond (-396 kJ/mol), calculate ΔH for the conversion of graphite to diamond:

$$C_{graphite}(s) \longrightarrow C_{diamond}(s)$$

Solution

The combustion reactions are

$$C_{graphite}(s) + O_2(g) \longrightarrow CO_2(g) \qquad \Delta H = -394 \text{ kJ}$$
$$C_{diamond}(s) + O_2(g) \longrightarrow CO_2(g) \qquad \Delta H = -396 \text{ kJ}$$

Note that if we reverse the second reaction (which means we must change the sign of ΔH) and sum the two reactions, we obtain the desired reaction:

$$
\begin{array}{ll}
C_{graphite}(s) + O_2(g) \longrightarrow CO_2(g) & \Delta H = -394 \text{ kJ} \\
\underline{CO_2(g) \longrightarrow C_{diamond}(s) + O_2(g)} & \underline{\Delta H = -(-396 \text{ kJ})} \\
C_{graphite}(s) \longrightarrow C_{diamond}(s) & \Delta H = 2 \text{ kJ}
\end{array}
$$

Thus 2 kJ of energy is required to change 1 mol graphite to diamond. This process is endothermic.

See Exercises 6.57 and 6.58.

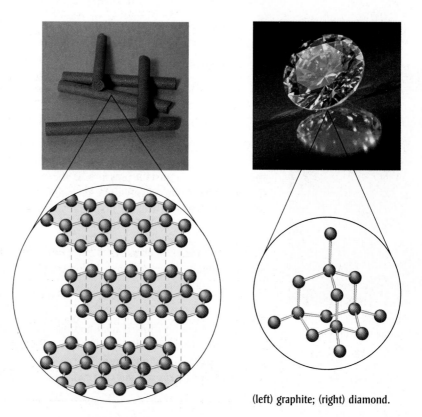

(left) graphite; (right) diamond.

| Sample Exercise 6.8 | **Hess's Law II** |

Diborane (B_2H_6) is a highly reactive boron hydride that was once considered as a possible rocket fuel for the U.S. space program. Calculate ΔH for the synthesis of diborane from its elements, according to the equation

$$2B(s) + 3H_2(g) \longrightarrow B_2H_6(g)$$

using the following data:

Reaction	ΔH
(a) $2B(s) + \frac{3}{2}O_2(g) \longrightarrow B_2O_3(s)$	-1273 kJ
(b) $B_2H_6(g) + 3O_2(g) \longrightarrow B_2O_3(s) + 3H_2O(g)$	-2035 kJ
(c) $H_2(g) + \frac{1}{2}O_2(g) \longrightarrow H_2O(l)$	-286 kJ
(d) $H_2O(l) \longrightarrow H_2O(g)$	44 kJ

Solution

To obtain ΔH for the required reaction, we must somehow combine equations (a), (b), (c), and (d) to produce that reaction and add the corresponding ΔH values. This can best be done by focusing on the reactants and products of the required reaction. The reactants are $B(s)$ and $H_2(g)$, and the product is $B_2H_6(g)$. How can we obtain the correct equation? Reaction (a) has $B(s)$ as a reactant, as needed in the required equation. Thus reaction (a) will be used as it is. Reaction (b) has $B_2H_6(g)$ as a reactant, but this substance is needed as a product. Thus reaction (b) must be reversed, and the sign of ΔH must be changed accordingly. Up to this point we have

| (a) | $2B(s) + \frac{3}{2}O_2(g) \longrightarrow B_2O_3(s)$ | $\Delta H = -1273$ kJ |
| $-$(b) | $B_2O_3(s) + 3H_2O(g) \longrightarrow B_2H_6(g) + 3O_2(g)$ | $\Delta H = -(-2035$ kJ$)$ |

Sum: $B_2O_3(s) + 2B(s) + \frac{3}{2}O_2(g) + 3H_2O(g) \longrightarrow B_2O_3(s) + B_2H_6(g) + 3O_2(g)$ $\Delta H = 762$ kJ

Deleting the species that occur on both sides gives

$$2B(s) + 3H_2O(g) \longrightarrow B_2H_6(g) + \tfrac{3}{2}O_2(g) \qquad \Delta H = 762 \text{ kJ}$$

We are closer to the required reaction, but we still need to remove $H_2O(g)$ and $O_2(g)$ and introduce $H_2(g)$ as a reactant. We can do this using reactions (c) and (d). If we multiply reaction (c) and its ΔH value by 3 and add the result to the preceding equation, we have

| | $2B(s) + 3H_2O(g) \longrightarrow B_2H_6(g) + \frac{3}{2}O_2(g)$ | $\Delta H = 762$ kJ |
| $3 \times$ (c) | $3[H_2(g) + \frac{1}{2}O_2(g) \longrightarrow H_2O(l)]$ | $\Delta H = 3(-286$ kJ$)$ |

Sum: $2B(s) + 3H_2(g) + \frac{3}{2}O_2(g) + 3H_2O(g) \longrightarrow B_2H_6(g) + \frac{3}{2}O_2(g) + 3H_2O(l)$ $\Delta H = -96$ kJ

We can cancel the $\frac{3}{2}O_2(g)$ on both sides, but we cannot cancel the H_2O because it is gaseous on one side and liquid on the other. This can be solved by adding reaction (d), multiplied by 3:

| | $2B(s) + 3H_2(g) + 3H_2O(g) \longrightarrow B_2H_6(g) + 3H_2O(l)$ | $\Delta H = -96$ kJ |
| $3 \times$ (d) | $3[H_2O(l) \longrightarrow H_2O(g)]$ | $\Delta H = 3(44$ kJ$)$ |

$2B(s) + 3H_2(g) + 3H_2O(g) + 3H_2O(l) \longrightarrow B_2H_6(g) + 3H_2O(l) + 3H_2O(g)$ $\Delta H = +36$ kJ

This gives the reaction required by the problem:

$$2B(s) + 3H_2(g) \longrightarrow B_2H_6(g) \qquad \Delta H = +36 \text{ kJ}$$

Thus ΔH for the synthesis of 1 mol diborane from the elements is $+36$ kJ.

See Exercises 6.59 through 6.64.

Hints for Using Hess's Law

Calculations involving Hess's law typically require that several reactions be manipulated and combined to finally give the reaction of interest. In doing this procedure you should

- Work *backward* from the required reaction, using the reactants and products to decide how to manipulate the other given reactions at your disposal

- Reverse any reactions as needed to give the required reactants and products

- Multiply reactions to give the correct numbers of reactants and products

This process involves some trial and error, but it can be very systematic if you always allow the final reaction to guide you.

6.4 Standard Enthalpies of Formation

For a reaction studied under conditions of constant pressure, we can obtain the enthalpy change using a calorimeter. However, this process can be very difficult. In fact, in some cases it is impossible, since certain reactions do not lend themselves to such study. An example is the conversion of solid carbon from its graphite form to its diamond form:

$$C_{graphite}(s) \longrightarrow C_{diamond}(s)$$

The value of ΔH for this process cannot be obtained by direct measurement in a calorimeter because the process is much too slow under normal conditions. However, as we saw in Sample Exercise 6.7, ΔH for this process can be calculated from heats of combustion. This is only one example of how useful it is to be able to *calculate* ΔH values for chemical reactions. We will next show how to do this using standard enthalpies of formation.

The **standard enthalpy of formation** (ΔH_f°) of a compound is defined as the *change in enthalpy that accompanies the formation of one mole of a compound from its elements with all substances in their standard states.*

A *degree symbol* on a thermodynamic function, for example, ΔH°, indicates that the corresponding process has been carried out under standard conditions. The **standard state** for a substance is a precisely defined reference state. Because thermodynamic functions often depend on the concentrations (or pressures) of the substances involved, we must use a common reference state to properly compare the thermodynamic properties of two substances. This is especially important because, for most thermodynamic properties, we can measure only *changes* in the property. For example, we have no method for determining absolute values of enthalpy. We can measure enthalpy changes (ΔH values) only by performing heat-flow experiments.

Recently, the International Union of Pure and Applied Chemists (IUPAC) has adopted 1 bar (100,000 Pa) as the standard pressure instead of 1 atm (101,305 Pa). Both standards are now in wide use.

Standard state is *not* the same as the standard temperature and pressure (STP) for a gas (discussed in Section 5.4).

Conventional Definitions of Standard States

For a Compound

- The standard state of a gaseous substance is a pressure of exactly 1 atmosphere.

- For a pure substance in a condensed state (liquid or solid), the standard state is the pure liquid or solid.

- For a substance present in a solution, the standard state is a concentration of exactly 1 *M*.

For an Element

- The standard state of an element is the form in which the element exists under conditions of 1 atmosphere and 25°C. (The standard state for oxygen is $O_2(g)$ at a pressure of 1 atmosphere; the standard state for sodium is $Na(s)$; the standard state for mercury is $Hg(l)$; and so on.)

Brown nitrogen dioxide gas.

TABLE 6.2 Standard Enthalpies of Formation for Several Compounds at 25°C

Compound	ΔH_f° (kJ/mol)
$NH_3(g)$	−46
$NO_2(g)$	34
$H_2O(l)$	−286
$Al_2O_3(s)$	−1676
$Fe_2O_3(s)$	−826
$CO_2(g)$	−394
$CH_3OH(l)$	−239
$C_8H_{18}(l)$	−269

Several important characteristics of the definition of the enthalpy of formation will become clearer if we again consider the formation of nitrogen dioxide from the elements in their standard states:

$$\tfrac{1}{2}N_2(g) + O_2(g) \longrightarrow NO_2(g) \qquad \Delta H_f^\circ = 34 \text{ kJ/mol}$$

Note that the reaction is written so that both elements are in their standard states, and 1 mole of product is formed. Enthalpies of formation are *always* given per mole of product with the product in its standard state.

The formation reaction for methanol is written as

$$C(s) + 2H_2(g) + \tfrac{1}{2}O_2(g) \longrightarrow CH_3OH(l) \qquad \Delta H_f^\circ = -239 \text{ kJ/mol}$$

The standard state of carbon is graphite, the standard states for oxygen and hydrogen are the diatomic gases, and the standard state for methanol is the liquid.

The ΔH_f° values for some common substances are shown in Table 6.2. More values are found in Appendix 4. The importance of the tabulated ΔH_f° values is that enthalpies for many reactions can be calculated using these numbers. To see how this is done, we will calculate the standard enthalpy change for the combustion of methane:

$$CH_4(g) + 2O_2(g) \longrightarrow CO_2(g) + 2H_2O(l)$$

Enthalpy is a state function, so we can invoke Hess's law and choose *any* convenient pathway from reactants to products and then sum the enthalpy changes along the chosen pathway. A convenient pathway, shown in Fig. 6.8, involves taking the reactants apart to the respective elements in their standard states in reactions (a) and (b) and then forming the products from these elements in reactions (c) and (d). This general pathway will work for any reaction, since atoms are conserved in a chemical reaction.

Note from Fig. 6.8 that reaction (a), where methane is taken apart into its elements,

$$CH_4(g) \longrightarrow C(s) + 2H_2(g)$$

is just the reverse of the formation reaction for methane:

$$C(s) + 2H_2(g) \longrightarrow CH_4(g) \qquad \Delta H_f^\circ = -75 \text{ kJ/mol}$$

Since reversing a reaction means changing the sign of ΔH but keeping the magnitude the same, ΔH for reaction (a) is $-\Delta H_f^\circ$, or 75 kJ. Thus $\Delta H^\circ_{(a)} = 75$ kJ.

Next we consider reaction (b). Here oxygen is already an element in its standard state, so no change is needed. Thus $\Delta H^\circ_{(b)} = 0$.

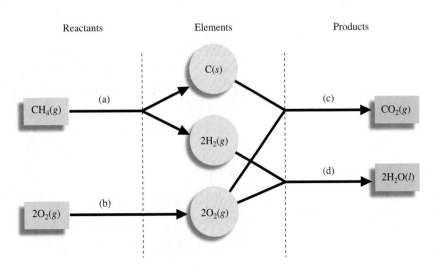

FIGURE 6.8
In this pathway for the combustion of methane, the reactants are first taken apart in reactions (a) and (b) to form the constituent elements in their standard states, which are then used to assemble the products in reactions (c) and (d).

The next steps, reactions (c) and (d), use the elements formed in reactions (a) and (b) to form the products. Note that reaction (c) is simply the formation reaction for carbon dioxide:

$$C(s) + O_2(g) \longrightarrow CO_2(g) \qquad \Delta H_f^\circ = -394 \text{ kJ/mol}$$

and

$$\Delta H^\circ_{(c)} = \Delta H_f^\circ \text{ for } CO_2(g) = -394 \text{ kJ}$$

Reaction (d) is the formation reaction for water:

$$H_2(g) + \tfrac{1}{2}O_2(g) \longrightarrow H_2O(l) \qquad \Delta H_f^\circ = -286 \text{ kJ/mol}$$

However, since 2 moles of water are required in the balanced equation, we must form 2 moles of water from the elements:

$$2H_2(g) + O_2(g) \longrightarrow 2H_2O(l)$$

Thus

$$\Delta H^\circ_{(d)} = 2 \times \Delta H_f^\circ \text{ for } H_2O(l) = 2(-286 \text{ kJ}) = -572 \text{ kJ}$$

We have now completed the pathway from the reactants to the products. The change in enthalpy for the reaction is the sum of the ΔH values (including their signs) for the steps:

$$\Delta H^\circ_{\text{reaction}}$$
$$= \Delta H^\circ_{(a)} + \Delta H^\circ_{(b)} + \Delta H^\circ_{(c)} + \Delta H^\circ_{(d)}$$
$$= [-\Delta H_f^\circ \text{ for } CH_4(g)] + 0 + [\Delta H_f^\circ \text{ for } CO_2(g)] + [2 \times \Delta H_f^\circ \text{ for } H_2O(l)]$$
$$= -(-75 \text{ kJ}) + 0 + (-394 \text{ kJ}) + (-572 \text{ kJ})$$
$$= -891 \text{ kJ}$$

This process is diagramed in Fig. 6.9. Notice that the reactants are taken apart and converted to elements [not necessary for $O_2(g)$] that are then used to form products. You can see that this is a very exothermic reaction because very little energy is required to convert the reactants to the respective elements but a great deal of energy is released when these elements form the products. This is why this reaction is so useful for producing heat to warm homes and offices.

Let's examine carefully the pathway we used in this example. First, the reactants were broken down into the elements in their standard states. This process involved reversing

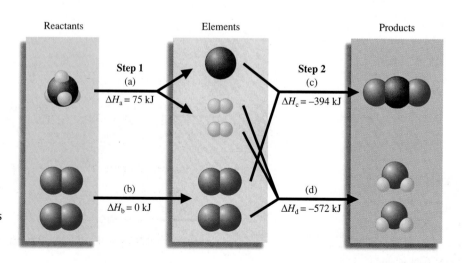

FIGURE 6.9
A schematic diagram of the energy changes for the reaction $CH_4(g) + 2O_2(g) \rightarrow CO_2(g) + 2H_2O(l)$.

Reactants   Elements   Products

Step 1
(a)
$\Delta H_a = 75$ kJ

Step 2
(c)
$\Delta H_c = -394$ kJ

(b)
$\Delta H_b = 0$ kJ

(d)
$\Delta H_d = -572$ kJ

Subtraction means to reverse the sign and add.

the formation reactions and thus switching the signs of the enthalpies of formation. The products were then constructed from these elements. This involved formation reactions and thus enthalpies of formation. We can summarize this entire process as follows: *The enthalpy change for a given reaction can be calculated by subtracting the enthalpies of formation of the reactants from the enthalpies of formation of the products.* Remember to multiply the enthalpies of formation by integers as required by the balanced equation. This statement can be represented symbolically as follows:

$$\Delta H^{\circ}_{\text{reaction}} = \Sigma n_{\text{p}}\Delta H^{\circ}_{\text{f}}(\text{products}) - \Sigma n_{\text{r}}\Delta H^{\circ}_{\text{f}}(\text{reactants}) \qquad (6.1)$$

where the symbol Σ (sigma) means "to take the sum of the terms," and n_{p} and n_{r} represent the moles of each product or reactant, respectively.

Elements in their standard states are not included in enthalpy calculations using $\Delta H^{\circ}_{\text{f}}$ values.

Elements are not included in the calculation because elements require no change in form. We have in effect *defined* the enthalpy of formation of an element in its standard state as zero, since we have chosen this as our reference point for calculating enthalpy changes in reactions.

Keep in Mind the Following Key Concepts When Doing Enthalpy Calculations:

- When a reaction is reversed, the magnitude of ΔH remains the same, but its sign changes.

- When the balanced equation for a reaction is multiplied by an integer, the value of ΔH for that reaction must be multiplied by the same integer.

- The change in enthalpy for a given reaction can be calculated from the enthalpies of formation of the reactants and products:

$$\Delta H^{\circ}_{\text{reaction}} = \Sigma n_{\text{p}}\Delta H^{\circ}_{\text{f}}(\text{products}) - \Sigma n_{\text{r}}\Delta H^{\circ}_{\text{f}}(\text{reactants})$$

- Elements in their standard states are not included in the $\Delta H_{\text{reaction}}$ calculations. That is, $\Delta H^{\circ}_{\text{f}}$ for an element in its standard state is zero.

| Sample Exercise 6.9 | **Enthalpies from Standard Enthalpies of Formation I** |

Using the standard enthalpies of formation listed in Table 6.2, calculate the standard enthalpy change for the overall reaction that occurs when ammonia is burned in air to form nitrogen dioxide and water. This is the first step in the manufacture of nitric acid.

$$4NH_3(g) + 7O_2(g) \longrightarrow 4NO_2(g) + 6H_2O(l)$$

Solution

We will use the pathway in which the reactants are broken down into elements in their standard states, which are then used to form the products (see Fig. 6.10).

➡ **1** *Decomposition of $NH_3(g)$ into elements* (reaction (a) in Fig. 6.10). The first step is to decompose 4 moles of NH_3 into N_2 and H_2:

$$4NH_3(g) \longrightarrow 2N_2(g) + 6H_2(g)$$

The preceding reaction is 4 times the *reverse* of the formation reaction for NH_3:

$$\tfrac{1}{2}N_2(g) + \tfrac{3}{2}H_2(g) \longrightarrow NH_3(g) \qquad \Delta H^{\circ}_{\text{f}} = -46 \text{ kJ/mol}$$

Thus

$$\Delta H^{\circ}_{(a)} = 4 \text{ mol}[-(-46 \text{ kJ/mol})] = 184 \text{ kJ}$$

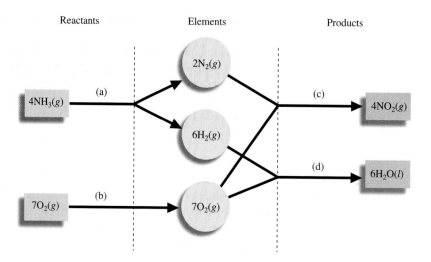

Reactants   Elements   Products

FIGURE 6.10
A pathway for the combustion of ammonia.

➥ **2**   *Elemental oxygen* (reaction (b) in Fig. 6.10). Since $O_2(g)$ is an element in its standard state, $\Delta H^\circ_{(b)} = 0$.

We now have the elements $N_2(g)$, $H_2(g)$, and $O_2(g)$, which can be combined to form the products of the overall reaction.

➥ **3**   *Synthesis of $NO_2(g)$ from elements* (reaction (c) in Fig. 6.10). The overall reaction equation has 4 moles of NO_2. Thus the required reaction is 4 times the formation reaction for NO_2:

$$4 \times [\tfrac{1}{2}N_2(g) + O_2(g) \longrightarrow NO_2(g)]$$

and

$$\Delta H^\circ_{(c)} = 4 \times \Delta H^\circ_f \text{ for } NO_2(g)$$

From Table 6.2, ΔH°_f for $NO_2(g) = 34$ kJ/mol and

$$\Delta H^\circ_{(c)} = 4 \text{ mol} \times 34 \text{ kJ/mol} = 136 \text{ kJ}$$

➥ **4**   *Synthesis of $H_2O(l)$ from elements* (reaction (d) in Fig. 6.10). Since the overall equation for the reaction has 6 moles of $H_2O(l)$, the required reaction is 6 times the formation reaction for $H_2O(l)$:

$$6 \times [H_2(g) + \tfrac{1}{2}O_2(g) \longrightarrow H_2O(l)]$$

and

$$\Delta H^\circ_{(d)} = 6 \times \Delta H^\circ_f \text{ for } H_2O(l)$$

From Table 6.2, ΔH°_f for $H_2O(l) = -286$ kJ/mol and

$$\Delta H^\circ_{(d)} = 6 \text{ mol} (-286 \text{ kJ/mol}) = -1716 \text{ kJ}$$

To summarize, we have done the following:

$$4NH_3(g) \xrightarrow{\Delta H^\circ_{(a)}} \left\{ \begin{array}{l} 2N_2(g) + 6H_2(g) \\ 7O_2(g) \end{array} \right.$$

$$7O_2(g) \xrightarrow{\Delta H^\circ_{(b)}}$$

$$\left. \begin{array}{l} \xrightarrow{\Delta H^\circ_{(c)}} 4NO_2(g) \\ \xrightarrow{\Delta H^\circ_{(d)}} 6H_2O(l) \end{array} \right.$$

Elements in their
standard states

We add the $\Delta H°$ values for the steps to get $\Delta H°$ for the overall reaction:

$$\Delta H°_{\text{reaction}} = \Delta H°_{(a)} + \Delta H°_{(b)} + \Delta H°_{(c)} + \Delta H°_{(d)}$$
$$= \left[4 \times -\Delta H°_{\text{f}} \text{ for } NH_3(g) \right] + 0 + \left[4 \times \Delta H°_{\text{f}} \text{ for } NO_2(g) \right]$$
$$+ \left[6 \times \Delta H°_{\text{f}} \text{ for } H_2O(l) \right]$$
$$= \left[4 \times \Delta H°_{\text{f}} \text{ for } NO_2(g) \right] + \left[6 \times \Delta H°_{\text{f}} \text{ for } H_2O(l) \right]$$
$$- \left[4 \times \Delta H°_{\text{f}} \text{ for } NH_3(g) \right]$$
$$= \Sigma n_{\text{p}} \Delta H°_{\text{f}}(\text{products}) - \Sigma n_{\text{r}} \Delta H°_{\text{f}}(\text{reactants})$$

Remember that elemental reactants and products do not need to be included, since $\Delta H°_{\text{f}}$ for an element in its standard state is zero. Note that we have again obtained Equation (6.1). The final solution is

$$\Delta H°_{\text{reaction}} = \left[4 \times (34 \text{ kJ}) \right] + \left[6 \times (-286 \text{ kJ}) \right] - \left[4 \times (-46 \text{ kJ}) \right]$$
$$= -1396 \text{ kJ}$$

See Exercises 6.67 and 6.68.

Now that we have shown the basis for Equation (6.1), we will make direct use of it to calculate ΔH for reactions in succeeding exercises.

Sample Exercise 6.10

Enthalpies from Standard Enthalpies of Formation II

Visualization: Thermite Reaction

Using enthalpies of formation, calculate the standard change in enthalpy for the thermite reaction:

$$2Al(s) + Fe_2O_3(s) \longrightarrow Al_2O_3(s) + 2Fe(s)$$

This reaction occurs when a mixture of powdered aluminum and iron(III) oxide is ignited with a magnesium fuse.

Solution

We use Equation (6.1):

$$\Delta H° = \Sigma n_{\text{p}} \Delta H°_{\text{f}}(\text{products}) - \Sigma n_{\text{r}} \Delta H°_{\text{f}}(\text{reactants})$$

where

$$\Delta H°_{\text{f}} \text{ for } Fe_2O_3(s) = -826 \text{ kJ/mol}$$
$$\Delta H°_{\text{f}} \text{ for } Al_2O_3(s) = -1676 \text{ kJ/mol}$$
$$\Delta H°_{\text{f}} \text{ for } Al(s) = \Delta H°_{\text{f}} \text{ for } Fe(s) = 0$$

Thus

$$\Delta H°_{\text{reaction}} = \Delta H°_{\text{f}} \text{ for } Al_2O_3(s) - \Delta H°_{\text{f}} \text{ for } Fe_2O_3(s)$$
$$= -1676 \text{ kJ} - (-826 \text{ kJ}) = -850. \text{ kJ}$$

This reaction is so highly exothermic that the iron produced is initially molten. This process is often used as a lecture demonstration and also has been used in welding massive steel objects such as ships' propellers.

The thermite reaction is one of the most energetic chemical reactions known.

See Exercises 6.71 and 6.72.

Enthalpies from Standard Enthalpies of Formation III

Methanol (CH_3OH) is often used as a fuel in high-performance engines in race cars. Using the data in Table 6.2, compare the standard enthalpy of combustion per gram of methanol with that per gram of gasoline. Gasoline is actually a mixture of compounds, but assume for this problem that gasoline is pure liquid octane (C_8H_{18}).

Solution

The combustion reaction for methanol is

$$2CH_3OH(l) + 3O_2(g) \longrightarrow 2CO_2(g) + 4H_2O(l)$$

Using the standard enthalpies of formation from Table 6.2 and Equation (6.1), we have

$$\Delta H°_{reaction} = 2 \times \Delta H°_f \text{ for } CO_2(g) + 4 \times \Delta H°_f \text{ for } H_2O(l) -$$
$$2 \times \Delta H°_f \text{ for } CH_3OH(l)$$
$$= 2 \times (-394 \text{ kJ}) + 4 \times (-286 \text{ kJ}) - 2 \times (-239 \text{ kJ})$$
$$= -1454 \text{ kJ}$$

Thus 1454 kJ of heat is evolved when 2 moles of methanol burn. The molar mass of methanol is 32.0 g/mol. This means that 1454 kJ of energy is produced when 64.0 g methanol burns. The enthalpy of combustion per gram of methanol is

$$\frac{-1454 \text{ kJ}}{64.0 \text{ g}} = -22.7 \text{ kJ/g}$$

The combustion reaction for octane is

$$2C_8H_{18}(l) + 25O_2(g) \longrightarrow 16CO_2(g) + 18H_2O(l)$$

Using the standard enthalpies of information from Table 6.2 and Equation (6.1), we have

$$\Delta H°_{reaction} = 16 \times \Delta H°_f \text{ for } CO_2(g) + 18 \times \Delta H°_f \text{ for } H_2O(l) -$$
$$2 \times \Delta H°_f \text{ for } C_8H_{18}(l)$$
$$= 16 \times (-394 \text{ kJ}) + 18 \times (-286 \text{ kJ}) - 2 \times (-269 \text{ kJ})$$
$$= -1.09 \times 10^4 \text{ kJ}$$

This is the amount of heat evolved when 2 moles of octane burn. Since the molar mass of octane is 114.2 g/mol, the enthalpy of combustion per gram of octane is

$$\frac{-1.09 \times 10^4 \text{ kJ}}{2(114.2 \text{ g})} = -47.8 \text{ kJ/g}$$

The enthalpy of combustion per gram of octane is approximately twice that per gram of methanol. On this basis, gasoline appears to be superior to methanol for use in a racing car, where weight considerations are usually very important. Why, then, is methanol used in racing cars? The answer is that methanol burns much more smoothly than gasoline in high-performance engines, and this advantage more than compensates for its weight disadvantage.

See Exercise 6.77.

6.5 Present Sources of Energy

Woody plants, coal, petroleum, and natural gas hold a vast amount of energy that originally came from the sun. By the process of photosynthesis, plants store energy that can be claimed by burning the plants themselves or the decay products that have been converted

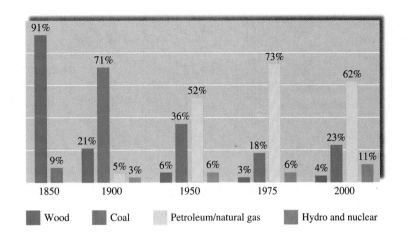

FIGURE 6.11
Energy sources used in the United States.

■ Wood   ■ Coal   ▨ Petroleum/natural gas   ■ Hydro and nuclear

This oil rig in Norway is the largest in the world.

TABLE 6.3   Names and Formulas for Some Common Hydrocarbons

Formula	Name
CH_4	Methane
C_2H_6	Ethane
C_3H_8	Propane
C_4H_{10}	Butane
C_5H_{12}	Pentane
C_6H_{14}	Hexane
C_7H_{16}	Heptane
C_8H_{18}	Octane

over millions of years to **fossil fuels.** Although the United States currently depends heavily on petroleum for energy, this dependency is a relatively recent phenomenon, as shown in Fig. 6.11. In this section we discuss some sources of energy and their effects on the environment.

Petroleum and Natural Gas

Although how they were produced is not completely understood, petroleum and natural gas were most likely formed from the remains of marine organisms that lived approximately 500 million years ago. **Petroleum** is a thick, dark liquid composed mostly of compounds called *hydrocarbons* that contain carbon and hydrogen. (Carbon is unique among elements in the extent to which it can bond to itself to form chains of various lengths.) Table 6.3 gives the formulas and names for several common hydrocarbons. **Natural gas,** usually associated with petroleum deposits, consists mostly of methane, but it also contains significant amounts of ethane, propane, and butane.

The composition of petroleum varies somewhat, but it consists mostly of hydrocarbons having chains that contain from 5 to more than 25 carbons. To be used efficiently, the petroleum must be separated into fractions by boiling. The lighter molecules (having the lowest boiling points) can be boiled off, leaving the heavier ones behind. The commercial uses of various petroleum fractions are shown in Table 6.4.

The petroleum era began when the demand for lamp oil during the Industrial Revolution outstripped the traditional sources: animal fats and whale oil. In response to this increased demand, Edwin Drake drilled the first oil well in 1859 at Titusville, Pennsylvania. The petroleum from this well was refined to produce *kerosene* (fraction C_{10}–C_{18}), which served as an excellent lamp oil. *Gasoline* (fraction C_5–C_{10}) had limited use and was often discarded. However, this situation soon changed. The development of the electric light decreased the need for kerosene, and the advent of the "horseless carriage" with its gasoline-powered engine signaled the birth of the gasoline age.

As gasoline became more important, new ways were sought to increase the yield of gasoline obtained from each barrel of petroleum. William Burton invented a process at Standard Oil of Indiana called *pyrolytic (high-temperature) cracking*. In this process, the heavier molecules of the kerosene fraction are heated to about 700°C, causing them to break (crack) into the smaller molecules of hydrocarbons in the gasoline fraction. As cars became larger, more efficient internal combustion engines were designed. Because of the uneven burning of the gasoline then available, these engines "knocked," producing unwanted noise and even engine damage. Intensive research to find additives that would promote smoother burning produced tetraethyl lead, $(C_2H_5)_4Pb$, a very effective "antiknock" agent.

TABLE 6.4   Uses of the Various Petroleum Fractions

Petroleum Fraction in Terms of Numbers of Carbon Atoms	Major Uses
$C_5–C_{10}$	Gasoline
$C_{10}–C_{18}$	Kerosene
	Jet fuel
$C_{15}–C_{25}$	Diesel fuel
	Heating oil
	Lubricating oil
$>C_{25}$	Asphalt

Coal has variable composition depending on both its age and location.

The electromagnetic spectrum, including visible and infrared radiation, is discussed in Chapter 7.

The addition of tetraethyl lead to gasoline became a common practice, and by 1960, gasoline contained as much as 3 grams of lead per gallon. As we have discovered so often in recent years, technological advances can produce environmental problems. To prevent air pollution from automobile exhaust, catalytic converters have been added to car exhaust systems. The effectiveness of these converters, however, is destroyed by lead. The use of leaded gasoline also greatly increased the amount of lead in the environment, where it can be ingested by animals and humans. For these reasons, the use of lead in gasoline has been phased out, requiring extensive (and expensive) modifications of engines and of the gasoline refining process.

Coal

Coal was formed from the remains of plants that were buried and subjected to high pressure and heat over long periods of time. Plant materials have a high content of cellulose, a complex molecule whose empirical formula is CH_2O but whose molar mass is around 500,000 g/mol. After the plants and trees that flourished on the earth at various times and places died and were buried, chemical changes gradually lowered the oxygen and hydrogen content of the cellulose molecules. Coal "matures" through four stages: lignite, subbituminous, bituminous, and anthracite. Each stage has a higher carbon-to-oxygen and carbon-to-hydrogen ratio; that is, the relative carbon content gradually increases. Typical elemental compositions of the various coals are given in Table 6.5. The energy available from the combustion of a given mass of coal increases as the carbon content increases. Therefore, anthracite is the most valuable coal, and lignite the least valuable.

Coal is an important and plentiful fuel in the United States, currently furnishing approximately 23% of our energy. As the supply of petroleum dwindles, the share of the energy supply from coal is expected to increase. However, coal is expensive and dangerous to mine underground, and the strip mining of fertile farmland in the Midwest or of scenic land in the West causes obvious problems. In addition, the burning of coal, especially high-sulfur coal, yields air pollutants such as sulfur dioxide, which, in turn, can lead to acid rain, as we learned in Chapter 5. However, even if coal were pure carbon, the carbon dioxide produced when it was burned would still have significant effects on the earth's climate.

Effects of Carbon Dioxide on Climate

The earth receives a tremendous quantity of radiant energy from the sun, about 30% of which is reflected back into space by the earth's atmosphere. The remaining energy passes through the atmosphere to the earth's surface. Some of this energy is absorbed by plants for photosynthesis and some by the oceans to evaporate water, but most of it is absorbed by soil, rocks, and water, increasing the temperature of the earth's surface. This energy is in turn radiated from the heated surface mainly as *infrared radiation,* often called *heat radiation.*

TABLE 6.5   Elemental Composition of Various Types of Coal

| Type of Coal | Mass Percent of Each Element | | | | |
	C	H	O	N	S
Lignite	71	4	23	1	1
Subbituminous	77	5	16	1	1
Bituminous	80	6	8	1	5
Anthracite	92	3	3	1	1

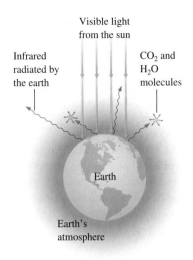

FIGURE 6.12
The earth's atmosphere is transparent to visible light from the sun. This visible light strikes the earth, and part of it is changed to infrared radiation. The infrared radiation from the earth's surface is strongly absorbed by CO_2, H_2O, and other molecules present in smaller amounts (for example, CH_4 and N_2O) in the atmosphere. In effect, the atmosphere traps some of the energy, acting like the glass in a greenhouse and keeping the earth warmer than it would otherwise be.

The average temperature of the earth's surface is 298 K. It would be 255 K without the "greenhouse gases."

The atmosphere, like window glass, is transparent to visible light but does not allow all the infrared radiation to pass back into space. Molecules in the atmosphere, principally H_2O and CO_2, strongly absorb infrared radiation and radiate it back toward the earth, as shown in Fig. 6.12, so a net amount of thermal energy is retained by the earth's atmosphere, causing the earth to be much warmer than it would be without its atmosphere. In a way, the atmosphere acts like the glass of a greenhouse, which is transparent to visible light but absorbs infrared radiation, thus raising the temperature inside the building. This **greenhouse effect** is seen even more spectacularly on Venus, where the dense atmosphere is thought to be responsible for the high surface temperature of that planet.

Thus the temperature of the earth's surface is controlled to a significant extent by the carbon dioxide and water content of the atmosphere. The effect of atmospheric moisture (humidity) is apparent in the Midwest. In summer, when the humidity is high, the heat of the sun is retained well into the night, giving very high nighttime temperatures. On the other hand, in winter, the coldest temperatures always occur on clear nights, when the low humidity allows efficient radiation of energy back into space.

The atmosphere's water content is controlled by the water cycle (evaporation and precipitation), and the average remains constant over the years. However, as fossil fuels have been used more extensively, the carbon dioxide concentration has increased by about 16% from 1880 to 1980. Comparisons of satellite data have now produced evidence that the greenhouse effect has significantly warmed the earth's atmosphere. The data compare the same areas in both 1979 and 1997. The analysis shows that more infrared radiation was blocked by CO_2, methane, and other greenhouse gases. This *could* increase the earth's average temperature by as much as 3°C, causing dramatic changes in climate and greatly affecting the growth of food crops.

How well can we predict long-term effects? Because weather has been studied for a period of time that is minuscule compared with the age of the earth, the factors that control the earth's climate in the long range are not clearly understood. For example, we do not understand what causes the earth's periodic ice ages. So it is difficult to estimate the impact of the increasing carbon dioxide levels.

In fact, the variation in the earth's average temperature over the past century is somewhat confusing. In the northern latitudes during the past century, the average temperature rose by 0.8°C over a period of 60 years, then cooled by 0.5°C during the next 25 years, and finally warmed by 0.2°C in the succeeding 15 years. Such fluctuations do not match the steady increase in carbon dioxide. However, in southern latitudes and near the equator during the past century, the average temperature showed a steady rise totaling 0.4°C.

Sheep grazing on a ranch in Australia.

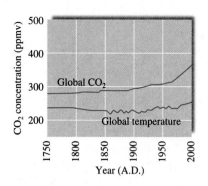

FIGURE 6.13
The atmospheric CO_2 concentration and the average global temperature over the last 250 years. Note the significant increase in CO_2 concentration in the last 50 years.

(Source: National Assessment Synthesis Team, *Climate Change Impacts on the United States: The Potential Consequences of Climate, Variability and Change, Overview,* Report for the U.S. Global Change Research Program, Cambridge University Press, Cambridge, UK, p. 13, 2000.)

This figure is in reasonable agreement with the predicted effect of the increasing carbon dioxide concentration over that period. Another significant fact is that the past 10 years constitute the warmest decade on record.

Although the exact relationship between the carbon dioxide concentration in the atmosphere and the earth's temperature is not known at present, one thing is clear: The increase in the atmospheric concentration of carbon dioxide is quite dramatic (see Fig. 6.13). We must consider the implications of this increase as we consider our future energy needs.

Methane is another greenhouse gas that is 21 times more potent than carbon dioxide. This fact is particularly significant for countries with lots of animals, because methane is produced by methanogenic archae that live in the animals' rumen. For example, sheep and cattle produce about 14% of Australia's total greenhouse emissions. To reduce this level, Australia has initiated a program to vaccinate sheep and cattle to lower the number of archae present in their digestive systems. It is hoped that this effort will reduce by 20% the amount of methane emitted by these animals.

6.6 New Energy Sources

As we search for the energy sources of the future, we need to consider economic, climatic, and supply factors. There are several potential energy sources: the sun (solar), nuclear processes (fission and fusion), biomass (plants), and synthetic fuels. Direct use of the sun's radiant energy to heat our homes and run our factories and transportation systems seems a sensible long-term goal. But what do we do now? Conservation of fossil fuels is one obvious step, but substitutes for fossil fuels also must be found. We will discuss some alternative sources of energy here. Nuclear power will be considered in Chapter 21.

Coal Conversion

One alternative energy source involves using a traditional fuel—coal—in new ways. Since transportation costs for solid coal are high, more energy-efficient fuels are being developed from coal. One possibility is to produce a gaseous fuel. Substances like coal that contain large molecules have high boiling points and tend to be solids or thick liquids. To convert coal from a solid to a gas therefore requires reducing the size of the molecules; the coal structure must be broken down in a process called *coal gasification.* This is done by treating the coal with oxygen and steam at high temperatures to break many of the carbon–carbon bonds. These bonds are replaced by carbon–hydrogen and carbon–oxygen bonds as the coal fragments react with the water and oxygen. The process is represented in Fig. 6.14. The desired product is a mixture of carbon monoxide and hydrogen called *synthetic gas,* or **syngas,** and methane (CH_4) gas. Since all the components of this product can react with oxygen to release heat in a combustion reaction, this gas is a useful fuel.

One of the most important considerations in designing an industrial process is efficient use of energy. In coal gasification, some of the reactions are exothermic:

$$C(s) + 2H_2(g) \longrightarrow CH_4(g) \qquad \Delta H° = -75 \text{ kJ}$$
$$C(s) + \tfrac{1}{2}O_2(g) \longrightarrow CO(g) \qquad \Delta H° = -111 \text{ kJ}$$
$$C(s) + O_2(g) \longrightarrow CO_2(g) \qquad \Delta H° = -394 \text{ kJ}$$

Other gasification reactions are endothermic, for example:

$$C(s) + H_2O(g) \longrightarrow H_2(g) + CO(g) \qquad \Delta H° = 131 \text{ kJ}$$

An industrial process must be energy efficient.

If such conditions as the rate of feed of coal, air, and steam are carefully controlled, the correct temperature can be maintained in the process without using any external energy source. That is, an energy balance is maintained.

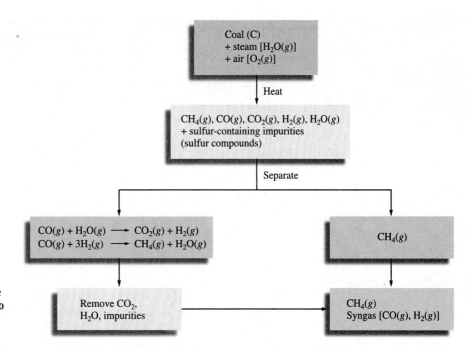

FIGURE 6.14
Coal gasification. Reaction of coal with a mixture of steam and air breaks down the large hydrocarbon molecules in the coal to smaller gaseous molecules, which can be used as fuels.

Presently only a few plants in the United States use syngas produced on site to produce electricity. These plants are being used to evaluate the economic feasibility of producing electrical power by coal gasification.

Although syngas can be used directly as a fuel, it is also important as a raw material to produce other fuels. For example, syngas can be converted directly to methanol:

$$CO(g) + 2H_2(g) \longrightarrow CH_3OH(l)$$

Methanol is used in the production of synthetic fibers and plastics and also can be used as a fuel. In addition, it can be converted directly to gasoline. Approximately half of South Africa's gasoline supply comes from methanol produced from syngas.

In addition to coal gasification, the formation of *coal slurries* is another new use of coal. A slurry is a suspension of fine particles in a liquid, and coal must be pulverized and mixed with water to form a slurry. The slurry can be handled, stored, and burned in ways similar to those used for *residual oil,* a heavy fuel oil from petroleum accounting for almost 15% of U.S. petroleum imports. One hope is that coal slurries might replace solid coal and residual oil as fuels for electricity-generating power plants. However, the water needed for slurries might place an unacceptable burden on water resources, especially in the western states.

Hydrogen as a Fuel

If you have ever seen a lecture demonstration where hydrogen–oxygen mixtures were ignited, you have witnessed a demonstration of hydrogen's potential as a fuel. The combustion reaction is

$$H_2(g) + \tfrac{1}{2}O_2(g) \longrightarrow H_2O(l) \qquad \Delta H° = -286 \text{ kJ}$$

As we saw in Sample Exercise 6.6, the heat of combustion of $H_2(g)$ per gram is approximately 2.5 times that of natural gas. In addition, hydrogen has a real advantage over fossil fuels in that the only product of hydrogen combustion is water; fossil fuels also produce carbon dioxide. However, even though it appears that hydrogen is a very logical choice as a major fuel for the future, there are three main problems: the cost of production, storage, and transport.

The main engines in the space shuttle Endeavour use hydrogen and oxygen as fuel.

CHEMICAL IMPACT

Farming the Wind

In the Midwest the wind blows across fields of corn, soybeans, wheat, and wind turbines—wind turbines? It turns out that the wind that seems to blow almost continuously across the plains is now becoming the latest cash crop. One of these new-breed wind farmers is Daniel Juhl, who recently erected 17 wind turbines on six acres of land near Woodstock, Minnesota. These turbines can generate as much as 10 megawatts (MW) of electricity, which Juhl sells to the local electrical utility.

There is plenty of untapped wind-power in the United States. Wind mappers rate regions on a scale of 1 to 6 (with 6 being the best) to indicate the quality of the wind resource. Wind farms are now being developed in areas rated from 4 to 6. The farmers who own the land welcome the increased income derived from the wind blowing across their land. Economists estimate that each acre devoted to wind turbines

can pay royalties to the farmers of as much as $8000 per year, or many times the revenue from growing corn on that same land. Daniel Juhl claims that farmers who construct the turbines themselves can realize as much as $20,000 per year per turbine. Globally, wind generation of electricity has nearly quadrupled in the last five years and is expected to increase by about 60% per year in the United States. The economic feasibility of wind-generated electricity has greatly improved in the last 30 years as the wind turbines have become more efficient. Today's turbines can produce electricity that costs about the same as that from other sources. The most impressive thing about wind power is the magnitude of the supply. According to the American Wind Energy Association in Washington, D.C., the wind-power potential in the United States is comparable or larger than the energy resources under the sands of Saudi Arabia.

First let's look at the production problem. Although hydrogen is very abundant on earth, virtually none of it exists as the free gas. Currently, the main source of hydrogen gas is from the treatment of natural gas with steam:

$$CH_4(g) + H_2O(g) \longrightarrow 3H_2(g) + CO(g)$$

We can calculate ΔH for this reaction using Equation (6.1):

$$\Delta H^\circ = \Sigma n_p \Delta H_f^\circ(\text{products}) - \Sigma n_r \Delta H_f^\circ(\text{reactants})$$
$$= \Delta H_f^\circ \text{ for } CO(g) - \Delta H_f^\circ \text{ for } CH_4(g) - \Delta H_f^\circ \text{ for } H_2O(g)$$
$$= -111 \text{ kJ} - (-75 \text{ kJ}) - (-242 \text{ kJ}) = 206 \text{ kJ}$$

Note that this reaction is highly endothermic; treating methane with steam is not an efficient way to obtain hydrogen for fuel. It would be much more economical to burn the methane directly.

A virtually inexhaustible supply of hydrogen exists in the waters of the world's oceans. However, the reaction

$$H_2O(l) \longrightarrow H_2(g) + \tfrac{1}{2}O_2(g)$$

requires 286 kJ of energy per mole of liquid water, and under current circumstances, large-scale production of hydrogen from water is not economically feasible. However, several methods for such production are currently being studied: electrolysis of water, thermal decomposition of water, thermochemical decomposition of water, and biological decomposition of water.

Electrolysis of water involves passing an electric current through it, as shown in Fig. 1.16 in Chapter 1. The present cost of electricity makes the hydrogen produced by electrolysis too expensive to be competitive as a fuel. However, if in the future we develop more efficient sources of electricity, this situation could change.

Recent research at the University of Minnesota by Lanny Schmidt and his coworkers suggests that corn could be a feasible source of hydrogen. In this process the starch from the corn is fermented to produce alcohol, which is then decomposed in a special

Electrolysis will be discussed in Chapter 17.

The biggest hurdle that must be overcome before wind power can become a significant electricity producer in the United States is construction of the transmission infrastructure—the power lines needed to move the electricity from the rural areas to the cities where most of the power is used. For example, the hundreds of turbines planned in southwest Minnesota in a development called Buffalo Ridge could supply enough electricity to power 1 million homes if transmission problems can be solved.

Another possible scenario for wind farms is to use the electrical power generated to decompose water to produce hydrogen gas that could be carried to cities by pipelines and used as a fuel. One real benefit of hydrogen is that it produces water as its only combustion product. Thus, it is essentially pollution-free.

Within a few years wind power could be a major source of electricity. There could be a fresh wind blowing across the energy landscape of the United States in the near future.

This State Line Wind Project along the Oregon-Washington border uses approximately 399 wind turbines to create enough electricity to power some 70,000 households.

reactor at 140°C with a rhodium and cerium oxide catalyst to give hydrogen. These scientists indicate that enough hydrogen gas can be obtained from a few ounces of ethanol to generate electricity to run six 60-watt bulbs for an hour.

Thermal decomposition is another method for producing hydrogen from water. This involves heating the water to several thousand degrees, where it spontaneously decomposes into hydrogen and oxygen. However, attaining temperatures in this range would be very expensive even if a practical heat source and a suitable reaction container were available.

In the thermochemical decomposition of water, chemical reactions, as well as heat, are used to "split" water into its components. One such system involves the following reactions (the temperature required for each is given in parentheses):

$$2HI \longrightarrow I_2 + H_2 \qquad (425°C)$$
$$2H_2O + SO_2 + I_2 \longrightarrow H_2SO_4 + 2HI \qquad (90°C)$$
$$\underline{H_2SO_4 \longrightarrow SO_2 + H_2O + \tfrac{1}{2}O_2 \qquad (825°C)}$$

Net reaction: $H_2O \longrightarrow H_2 + \tfrac{1}{2}O_2$

Note that the HI is not consumed in the net reaction. Note also that the maximum temperature required is 825°C, a temperature that is feasible if a nuclear reactor is used as a heat source. A current research goal is to find a system for which the required temperatures are low enough that sunlight can be used as the energy source.

But what about the organisms that decompose water without the aid of electricity or high temperatures? In the process of photosynthesis, green plants absorb carbon dioxide and water and use them along with energy from the sun to produce the substances needed for growth. Scientists have studied photosynthesis for years, hoping to get answers to humanity's food and energy shortages. At present, much of this research involves attempts to modify the photosynthetic process so that plants will release hydrogen gas from water instead of using the hydrogen to produce complex compounds. Small-scale experiments have shown that under certain conditions plants do produce hydrogen gas, but the yields are far from being commercially useful. At this point the economical production of hydrogen gas remains unrealized.

The storage and transportation of hydrogen also present problems. First, on metal surfaces the H_2 molecule decomposes to atoms. Since the atoms are so small, they can migrate into the metal, causing structural changes that make it brittle. This might lead to a pipeline failure if hydrogen were pumped under high pressure.

An additional problem is the relatively small amount of energy that is available *per unit volume* of hydrogen gas. Although the energy available per gram of hydrogen is significantly greater than that per gram of methane, the energy available per given volume of hydrogen is about one-third that available from the same volume of methane. This is demonstrated in Sample Exercise 6.12.

Although the use of hydrogen as a fuel solves some of the problems associated with fossil fuels, it does present some potential environmental problems of its own. Studies by John M. Eiler and his colleagues at California Institute of Technology indicate that, if hydrogen becomes a major source of energy, accidental leakage of the gas into the atmosphere could pose a threat. The Cal Tech scientists calculate that leakage could raise the concentration of H_2 in the atmosphere from its natural level of 0.5 part per million to more than 2 parts per million. As some of the H_2 eventually finds its way into the upper atmosphere, it would react with O_2 to form water, which would increase the number of ice crystals. This could lead to the destruction of some of the protective ozone because many of the chemical reactions that destroy ozone occur on the surfaces of ice crystals. However, as is the usual case with environmental issues, the situation is complicated. The scenario suggested by Eiler's team may not happen because the leaked H_2 could be consumed by soil microbes that use hydrogen as a nutrient. In fact, Eiler's studies show that 90% of the H_2 emitted into the atmosphere today from sources such as motor vehicles and forest fires is eventually absorbed by soil organisms.

The evaluation of hydrogen as a fuel illustrates how complex and interconnected the economic and environmental issues are.

Sample Exercise 6.12

Enthalpies of Combustion

Compare the energy available from the combustion of a given volume of methane and the same volume of hydrogen at the same temperature and pressure.

Solution

In Sample Exercise 6.6 we calculated the heat released for the combustion of methane and hydrogen: 55 kJ/g CH_4 and 141 kJ/g H_2. We also know from our study of gases that 1 mol $H_2(g)$ has the same volume as 1 mol $CH_4(g)$ at the same temperature and pressure (assuming ideal behavior). Thus, for molar volumes of both gases under the same conditions of temperature and pressure,

$$\frac{\text{Enthalpy of combustion of 1 molar volume of } H_2(g)}{\text{Enthalpy of combustion of 1 molar volume of } CH_4(g)}$$

$$= \frac{\text{enthalpy of combustion per mole of } H_2}{\text{enthalpy of combustion per mole of } CH_4}$$

$$= \frac{(-141 \text{ kJ/g})(2.02 \text{ g } H_2/\text{mol } H_2)}{(-55 \text{ kJ/g})(16.04 \text{ g } CH_4/\text{mol } CH_4)}$$

$$= \frac{-285}{-882} \approx \frac{1}{3}$$

Thus about three times the volume of hydrogen gas is needed to furnish the same energy as a given volume of methane.

See Exercise 6.78.

Could hydrogen be considered as a potential fuel for automobiles? This is an intriguing question. The internal combustion engines in automobiles can be easily adapted to burn hydrogen. In fact, BMW is now experimenting with a fleet of cars powered by hydrogen-burning internal combustion engines. However, the primary difficulty is the storage of enough hydrogen to give an automobile a reasonable range. This is illustrated by Sample Exercise 6.13.

Sample Exercise 6.13 **Comparing Enthalpies of Combustion**

Assuming that the combustion of hydrogen gas provides three times as much energy per gram as gasoline, calculate the volume of liquid H_2 (density = 0.0710 g/mL) required to furnish the energy contained in 80.0 L (about 20 gal) of gasoline (density = 0.740 g/mL). Calculate also the volume that this hydrogen would occupy as a gas at 1.00 atm and 25°C.

Solution

The mass of 80.0 L gasoline is

$$80.0 \, \text{L} \times \frac{1000 \, \text{mL}}{1 \, \text{L}} \times \frac{0.740 \, \text{g}}{\text{mL}} = 59,200 \, \text{g}$$

Since H_2 furnishes three times as much energy per gram as gasoline, only a third as much liquid hydrogen is needed to furnish the same energy:

$$\text{Mass of } H_2(l) \text{ needed} = \frac{59,200 \, \text{g}}{3} = 19,700 \, \text{g}$$

Since density = mass/volume, then volume = mass/density, and the volume of $H_2(l)$ needed is

$$V = \frac{19,700 \, \text{g}}{0.0710 \, \text{g/mL}}$$
$$= 2.77 \times 10^5 \, \text{mL} = 277 \, \text{L}$$

Thus 277 L of liquid H_2 is needed to furnish the same energy of combustion as 80.0 L of gasoline.

To calculate the volume that this hydrogen would occupy as a gas at 1.00 atm and 25°C, we use the ideal gas law:

$$PV = nRT$$

In this case

$P = 1.00$ atm, $T = 273 + 25°C = 298$ K, and $R = 0.08206$ L · atm/K · mol.

Also,

$$n = 19,700 \, \text{g } H_2 \times \frac{1 \, \text{mol } H_2}{2.02 \, \text{g } H_2} = 9.75 \times 10^3 \, \text{mol } H_2$$

Thus

$$V = \frac{nRT}{P} = \frac{(9.75 \times 10^3 \, \text{mol})(0.08206 \, \text{L · atm/K · mol})(298 \, \text{K})}{1.00 \, \text{atm}}$$
$$= 2.38 \times 10^5 \, \text{L} = 238,000 \, \text{L}$$

At 1 atm and 25°C, the hydrogen gas needed to replace 20 gal of gasoline occupies a volume of 238,000 L.

See Exercises 6.79 and 6.80.

CHEMICAL IMPACT

Veggie Gasoline?

Gasoline usage is as high as ever, and world petroleum supplies will eventually dwindle. One possible alternative to petroleum as a source of fuels and lubricants is vegetable oil—the same vegetable oil we now use to cook french fries. Researchers believe that the oils from soybeans, corn, canola, and sunflowers all have the potential to be used in cars as well as on salads.

The use of vegetable oil for fuel is not a new idea. Rudolf Diesel reportedly used peanut oil to run one of his engines at the Paris Exposition in 1900. In addition, ethyl alcohol has been used widely as a fuel in South America and as a fuel additive in the United States.

This promotion bus both advertises biodiesel and demonstrates its usefulness

You can see from Sample Exercise 6.13 that an automobile would need a huge tank to hold enough hydrogen gas (at 1 atm) to have a typical mileage range. Clearly, hydrogen must be stored as a liquid or in some other way. Is this feasible? Because of its very low boiling point (20 K), storage of liquid hydrogen requires a superinsulated container that can withstand high pressures. Storage in this manner would be both expensive and hazardous because of the potential for explosion. Thus storage of hydrogen in the individual automobile as a liquid does not seem practical.

A much better alternative seems to be the use of metals that absorb hydrogen to form solid metal hydrides:

$$H_2(g) + M(s) \longrightarrow MH_2(s)$$

Metal hydrides are discussed in Chapter 18.

To use this method of storage, hydrogen gas would be pumped into a tank containing the solid metal in powdered form, where it would be absorbed to form the hydride, whose volume would be little more than that of the metal alone. This hydrogen would then be available for combustion in the engine by release of $H_2(g)$ from the hydride as needed:

$$MH_2(s) \longrightarrow M(s) + H_2(g)$$

Several types of solids that absorb hydrogen to form hydrides are being studied for use in hydrogen-powered vehicles. The most likely use of hydrogen in automobiles will be to power fuel cells (see Section 17.5). Ford, Honda, and Toyota are all experimenting with cars powered by hydrogen fuel cells.

Other Energy Alternatives

Many other energy sources are being considered for future use. The western states, especially Colorado, contain huge deposits of *oil shale,* which consists of a complex carbon-based material called *kerogen* contained in porous rock formations. These deposits have the potential of being a larger energy source than the vast petroleum deposits of the Middle East. The main problem with oil shale is that the trapped fuel is not fluid and cannot

Biodiesel, a fuel made by esterifying the fatty acids found in vegetable oil, has some real advantages over regular diesel fuel. Biodiesel produces fewer pollutants such as particulates, carbon monoxide, and complex organic molecules, and since vegetable oils have no sulfur, there is no noxious sulfur dioxide in the exhaust gases. Also, biodiesel can run in existing engines with little modification. In addition, biodiesel is much more biodegradable than petroleum-based fuels, so spills cause less environmental damage.

Of course, biodiesel also has some serious drawbacks. The main one is that it costs about three times as much as regular diesel fuel. Biodiesel also produces more nitrogen oxides in the exhaust than conventional diesel fuel and is less stable in storage. Biodiesel also can leave more gummy deposits in engines and must be "winterized" by removing components that tend to solidify at low temperatures.

The best solution may be to use biodiesel as an additive to regular diesel fuel. One such fuel is known as B20 because it is 20% biodiesel and 80% conventional diesel fuel. B20 is especially attractive because of the higher lubricating ability of vegetable oils, thus reducing diesel engine wear.

Vegetable oils are also being looked at as replacements for motor oils and hydraulic fluids. Tests of a sunflower seed–based engine lubricant manufactured by Renewable Lubricants of Hartville, Ohio, have shown satisfactory lubricating ability while lowering particle emissions. In addition, Lou Honary and his colleagues at the University of Northern Iowa have developed BioSOY, a vegetable oil–based hydraulic fluid for use in heavy machinery.

Veggie oil fuels and lubricants seem to have a growing market as petroleum supplies wane and as environmental laws become more stringent. In Germany's Black Forest region, for example, environmental protection laws require that farm equipment use only vegetable oil fuels and lubricants. In the near future there may be veggie oil in your garage as well as in your kitchen.

Adapted from "Fill 'Er Up . . . with Veggie Oil," by Corinna Wu, as appeared in *Science News*, Vol. 154, December 5, 1998, p. 364.

be pumped. To recover the fuel, the rock must be heated to a temperature of 250°C or higher to decompose the kerogen to smaller molecules that produce gaseous and liquid products. This process is expensive and yields large quantities of waste rock, which have a negative environmental impact.

Ethanol (C_2H_5OH) is another fuel with the potential to supplement, if not replace, gasoline. The most common method of producing ethanol is fermentation, a process in which sugar is changed to alcohol by the action of yeast. The sugar can come from virtually any source, including fruits and grains, although fuel-grade ethanol would probably come mostly from corn. Car engines can burn pure alcohol or *gasohol,* an alcohol–gasoline mixture (10% ethanol in gasoline), with little modification. Gasohol is now widely available in the United States. The use of pure alcohol as a motor fuel is not feasible in most of the United States because it does not vaporize easily when temperatures are low. However, pure ethanol could be a very practical fuel in warm climates. For example, in Brazil, large quantities of ethanol fuel are being produced for cars.

Methanol (CH_3OH), an alcohol similar to ethanol, which has been used successfully for many years in race cars, is now being evaluated as a motor fuel in California. A major gasoline retailer has agreed to install pumps at 25 locations to dispense a fuel that is 85% methanol and 15% gasoline for use in specially prepared automobiles. The California Energy Commission feels that methanol has great potential for providing a secure, long-term energy supply that would alleviate air quality problems. Arizona and Colorado are also considering methanol as a major source of portable energy.

Another potential source of liquid fuels is oil squeezed from seeds (*seed oil*). For example, some farmers in North Dakota, South Africa, and Australia are now using sunflower oil to replace diesel fuel. Oil seeds, found in a wide variety of plants, can be processed to produce an oil composed mainly of carbon and hydrogen, which of course reacts with oxygen to produce carbon dioxide, water, and heat. It is hoped that oil-seed plants can be developed that will thrive under soil and climatic conditions unsuitable for corn and wheat. The main advantage of seed oil as a fuel is that it is renewable. Ideally, fuel would be grown just like food crops.

The sugars in corn are fermented and used to produce ethanol, an additive for gasoline.

Key Terms

For Review

Energy
- The capacity to do work or produce heat
- Is conserved (first law of thermodynamics)
- Can be converted from one form to another
- Is a state function
- Potential energy: stored energy
- Kinetic energy: energy due to motion
- The internal energy for a system is the sum of its potential and kinetic energies
- The internal energy of a system can be changed by work and heat:

$$\Delta E = q + w$$

Work
- Force applied over a distance
- For an expanding/contracting gas
- Not a state function

$$w = -P\Delta V$$

Heat
- Energy flow due to a temperature difference
- Exothermic: energy as heat flows out of a system
- Endothermic: energy as heat flows into a system
- Not a state function
- Measured for chemical reactions by calorimetry

Enthalpy
- $H = E + PV$
- Is a state function
- Hess's law: the change in enthalpy in going from a given set of reactants to a given set of products is the same whether the process takes place in one step or a series of steps
- Standard enthalpies of formation (ΔH_f°) can be used to calculate ΔH for a chemical reaction

$$\Delta H_{reaction}^\circ = \sum n_p \Delta H_f^\circ (\text{products}) - \sum n_r \Delta H^\circ (\text{reactants})$$

Energy use
- Energy sources from fossil fuels are associated with difficult supply and environmental impact issues
- The greenhouse effect results from release into the atmosphere of gases, including carbon dioxide, that strongly absorb infrared radiation, thus warming the earth
- Alternative fuels are being sought to replace fossil fuels:
  - Hydrogen
  - Syngas from coal
  - Biofuels from plants such as corn and certain seed-producing plants

REVIEW QUESTIONS

1. Define the following terms: potential energy, kinetic energy, path-dependent function, state function, system, surroundings.

2. Consider the following potential energy diagrams for two different reactions.

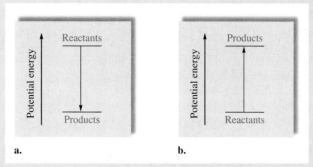

a.   b.

Which plot represents an exothermic reaction? In plot a, do the reactants on average have stronger or weaker bonds than the products? In plot b, reactants must gain potential energy to convert to products. How does this occur?

3. What is the first law of thermodynamics? How can a system change its internal energy, E? What are the sign conventions for thermodynamic quantities used in this text?

4. When a gas expands, what is the sign of w? Why? When a gas contracts, what is the sign of w? Why? What are the signs of q and w for the process of boiling water?

5. What is the heat gained/released at constant pressure equal to (q_P = ?)? What is the heat gained/released at constant volume equal to (q_V = ?)? Explain why ΔH is obtained directly from a coffee-cup calorimeter, whereas ΔE is obtained directly from a bomb calorimeter.

6. High-quality audio amplifiers generate large amounts of heat. To dissipate the heat and prevent damage to the electronic components, heat-radiating metal fins are used. Would it be better to make these fins out of iron or aluminum? Why? (See Table 6.1 for specific heat capacities.)

7. Explain how calorimetry works to calculate ΔH or ΔE for a reaction. Does the temperature of the calorimeter increase or decrease for an endothermic reaction? For an exothermic reaction? Explain.

8. What is Hess's law? When a reaction is reversed, what happens to the sign and magnitude of ΔH for that reversed reaction? When the coefficients in a balanced reaction are multiplied by a factor n, what happens to the sign and magnitude of ΔH for that multiplied reaction?

9. Define the standard enthalpy of formation. What are standard states for elements and for compounds? Using Hess's law, illustrate why the formula $\Delta H^{\circ}_{\text{reaction}} = \Sigma n_p \Delta H^{\circ}_f$ (products) $- \Sigma n_r \Delta H^{\circ}_f$ (reactants) works to calculate ΔH° for a reaction.

10. What are some of the problems associated with the world's dependence on fossil fuels? What are some alternative fuels for petroleum products?

Active Learning Questions

These questions are designed to be used by groups of students in class. The questions allow students to explore their understanding of concepts through discussion and peer teaching. The real value of these questions is the learning that occurs while students talk to each other about chemical concepts.

1. Objects placed together eventually reach the same temperature. When you go into a room and touch a piece of metal in that room, it feels colder than a piece of plastic. Explain.

2. What is meant by the term *lower in energy?* Which is lower in energy, a mixture of hydrogen and oxygen gases or liquid water? How do you know? Which of the two is more stable? How do you know?

3. A fire is started in a fireplace by striking a match and lighting crumpled paper under some logs. Explain all the energy transfers in this scenario using the terms *exothermic, endothermic, system, surroundings, potential energy,* and *kinetic energy* in the discussion.

4. Liquid water turns to ice. Is this process endothermic or exothermic? Explain what is occurring using the terms *system, surroundings, heat, potential energy,* and *kinetic energy* in the discussion.

5. Consider the following statements: "Heat is a form of energy, and energy is conserved. The heat lost by a system must be equal to the amount of heat gained by the surroundings. Therefore, heat is conserved." Indicate everything you think is correct in these statements. Indicate everything you think is incorrect. Correct the incorrect statements and explain.

6. Consider 5.5 L of a gas at a pressure of 3.0 atm in a cylinder with a movable piston. The external pressure is changed so that the volume changes to 10.5 L.
   a. Calculate the work done, and indicate the correct sign.
   b. Use the preceding data but consider the process to occur in two steps. At the end of the first step, the volume is 7.0 L. The second step results in a final volume of 10.5 L. Calculate the work done, and indicate the correct sign.
   c. Calculate the work done if after the first step the volume is 8.0 L and the second step leads to a volume of 10.5 L. Does the work differ from that in part b? Explain.

7. In Question 6 the work calculated for the different conditions in the various parts of the question was different even though the system had the same initial and final conditions. Based on this information, is work a state function?
   a. Explain how you know that work is not a state function.
   b. Why does the work increase with an increase in the number of steps?
   c. Which two-step process resulted in more work, when the first step had the bigger change in volume or when the second step had the bigger change in volume? Explain.

8. Photosynthetic plants use the following reaction to produce glucose, cellulose, and so forth:

$$6CO_2(g) + 6H_2O(l) \xrightarrow{\text{Sunlight}} C_6H_{12}O_6(s) + 6O_2(g)$$

How might extensive destruction of forests exacerbate the greenhouse effect?

A blue question or exercise number indicates that the answer to that question or exercise appears at the back of this book and a solution appears in the *Solutions Guide.*

Questions

9. Consider an airplane trip from Chicago, Illinois to Denver, Colorado. List some path-dependent functions and some state functions for the plane trip

10. How is average bond strength related to relative potential energies of the reactants and the products?

11. Assuming gasoline is pure $C_8H_{18}(l)$, predict the signs of q and w for the process of combusting gasoline into $CO_2(g)$ and $H_2O(g)$.

12. What is the difference between ΔH and ΔE?

13. The enthalpy of combustion of $CH_4(g)$ when $H_2O(l)$ is formed is $^-891$ kJ/mol and the enthalpy of combustion of $CH_4(g)$ when $H_2O(g)$ is formed is $^-803$ kJ/mol. Use these data and Hess's law to determine the enthalpy of vaporization for water.

14. Standard enthalpies of formation are relative values. What are ΔH_f° values relative to?

15. What is incomplete combustion of fossil fuels? Why can this be a problem?

16. Explain the advantages and disadvantages of hydrogen as an alternative fuel.

Exercises

In this section similar exercises are paired.

Potential and Kinetic Energy

17. Calculate the kinetic energy of a baseball (mass = 5.25 oz) with a velocity of 1.0×10^2 mi/h.

18. Calculate the kinetic energy of a 1.0×10^{-5}-g object with a velocity of 2.0×10^5 cm/s.

19. Which has the greater kinetic energy, an object with a mass of 2.0 kg and a velocity of 1.0 m/s or an object with a mass of 1.0 kg and a velocity of 2.0 m/s?

20. Consider the accompanying diagram. Ball A is allowed to fall and strike ball B. Assume that all of ball A's energy is transferred to ball B, at point I, and that there is no loss of energy to other sources. What is the kinetic energy and the potential energy of ball B at point II? The potential energy is given by PE = mgz, where m is the mass in kilograms, g is the gravitational constant (9.81 m/s^2), and z is the distance in meters.

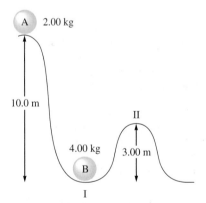

Heat and Work

21. Calculate ΔE for each of the following.
   a. $q = -47$ kJ, $w = +88$ kJ
   b. $q = +82$ kJ, $w = -47$ kJ
   c. $q = +47$ kJ, $w = 0$
   d. In which of these cases do the surroundings do work on the system?

22. A system undergoes a process consisting of the following two steps:

   Step 1: The system absorbs 72 J of heat while 35 J of work is done on it.

Step 2: The system absorbs 35 J of heat while performing 72 J of work.

Calculate ΔE for the overall process.

23. If the internal energy of a thermodynamic system is increased by 300. J while 75 J of expansion work is done, how much heat was transferred and in which direction, to or from the system?

24. Calculate the internal energy change for each of the following.
    a. One hundred (100.) joules of work are required to compress a gas. At the same time, the gas releases 23 J of heat.
    b. A piston is compressed from a volume of 8.30 L to 2.80 L against a constant pressure of 1.90 atm. In the process, there is a heat gain by the system of 350. J.
    c. A piston expands against 1.00 atm of pressure from 11.2 L to 29.1 L. In the process, 1037 J of heat is absorbed.

25. A sample of an ideal gas at 15.0 atm and 10.0 L is allowed to expand against a constant external pressure of 2.00 atm at a constant temperature. Calculate the work in units of kJ for the gas expansion. (*Hint:* Boyle's law applies.)

26. A piston performs work of 210. L atm on the surroundings, while the cylinder in which it is placed expands from 10. L to 25 L. At the same time, 45 J of heat is transferred from the surroundings to the system. Against what pressure was the piston working?

27. Consider a mixture of air and gasoline vapor in a cylinder with a piston. The original volume is 40. cm^3. If the combustion of this mixture releases 950. J of energy, to what volume will the gases expand against a constant pressure of 650. torr if all the energy of combustion is converted into work to push back the piston?

28. As a system increases in volume, it absorbs 52.5 J of energy in the form of heat from the surroundings. The piston is working against a pressure of 0.500 atm. The final volume of the system is 58.0 L. What was the initial volume of the system if the internal energy of the system decreased by 102.5 J?

29. A balloon filled with 39.1 mol helium has a volume of 876 L at 0.0°C and 1.00 atm pressure. The temperature of the balloon is increased to 38.0°C as it expands to a volume of 998 L, the pressure remaining constant. Calculate q, w, and ΔE for the helium in the balloon. (The molar heat capacity for helium gas is 20.8 J/°C · mol.)

30. One mole of $H_2O(g)$ at 1.00 atm and 100.°C occupies a volume of 30.6 L. When one mole of $H_2O(g)$ is condensed to one mole of $H_2O(l)$ at 1.00 atm and 100.°C, 40.66 kJ of heat is released. If the density of $H_2O(l)$ at this temperature and pressure is 0.996 g/cm^3, calculate ΔE for the condensation of one mole of water at 1.00 atm and 100.°C.

Properties of Enthalpy

31. One of the components of polluted air is NO. It is formed in the high-temperature environment of internal combustion engines by the following reaction:

$$N_2(g) + O_2(g) \longrightarrow 2NO(g) \qquad \Delta H = 180 \text{ kJ}$$

Why are high temperatures needed to convert N_2 and O_2 to NO?

32. The reaction

$$SO_3(g) + H_2O(l) \longrightarrow H_2SO_4(aq)$$

is the last step in the commercial production of sulfuric acid. The enthalpy change for this reaction is −227 kJ. In designing a sulfuric acid plant, is it necessary to provide for heating or cooling of the reaction mixture? Explain.

33. Are the following processes exothermic or endothermic?
    a. When solid KBr is dissolved in water, the solution gets colder.
    b. Natural gas (CH_4) is burned in a furnace.
    c. When concentrated H_2SO_4 is added to water, the solution gets very hot.
    d. Water is boiled in a teakettle.

34. Are the following processes exothermic or endothermic?
    a. the combustion of gasoline in a car engine
    b. water condensing on a cold pipe
    c. $CO_2(s) \longrightarrow CO_2(g)$
    d. $F_2(g) \longrightarrow 2F(g)$

35. The overall reaction in a commercial heat pack can be represented as

$$4Fe(s) + 3O_2(g) \longrightarrow 2Fe_2O_3(s) \qquad \Delta H = -1652 \text{ kJ}$$

    a. How much heat is released when 4.00 mol iron is reacted with excess O_2?
    b. How much heat is released when 1.00 mol Fe_2O_3 is produced?
    c. How much heat is released when 1.00 g iron is reacted with excess O_2?
    d. How much heat is released when 10.0 g Fe and 2.00 g O_2 are reacted?

36. Consider the following reaction:

$$2H_2(g) + O_2(g) \longrightarrow 2H_2O(l) \qquad \Delta H = -572 \text{ kJ}$$

    a. How much heat is evolved for the production of 1.00 mol of $H_2O(l)$?
    b. How much heat is evolved when 4.03 g of hydrogen is reacted with excess oxygen?
    c. How much heat is evolved when 186 g of oxygen is reacted wih excess hydrogen?
    d. The total volume of hydrogen gas needed to fill the *Hindenburg* was 2.0 × 10^8 L at 1.0 atm and 25°C. How much heat was evolved when the *Hindenburg* exploded, assuming all of the hydrogen reacted?

37. Consider the combustion of propane:

$$C_3H_8(g) + 5O_2(g) \longrightarrow 3CO_2(g) + 4H_2O(l) \quad \Delta H = -2221 \text{ kJ}$$

Assume that all the heat in Sample Exercise 6.3 comes from the combustion of propane. What mass of propane must be burned to furnish this amount of energy assuming the heat transfer process is 60.% efficient?

38. Consider the following reaction:

$$CH_4(g) + 2O_2(g) \longrightarrow CO_2(g) + 2H_2O(l) \qquad \Delta H = -891 \text{ kJ}$$

Calculate the enthalpy change for each of the following cases:
    a. 1.00 g methane is burned in excess oxygen.
    b. 1.00 × 10^3 L methane gas at 740. torr and 25°C is burned in excess oxygen.

39. For the process $H_2O(l) \longrightarrow H_2O(g)$ at 298 K and 1.0 atm, ΔH is more positive than ΔE by 2.5 kJ/mol. What does the 2.5 kJ/mol quantity represent?

40. For the following reactions at constant pressure, predict if $\Delta H > \Delta E$, $\Delta H < \Delta E$, or $\Delta H = \Delta E$.
    a. $2HF(g) \longrightarrow H_2(g) + F_2(g)$
    b. $N_2(g) + 3H_2(g) \longrightarrow 2NH_3(g)$
    c. $4NH_3(g) + 5O_2(g) \longrightarrow 4NO(g) + 6H_2O(g)$

Calorimetry and Heat Capacity

41. Consider the substances in Table 6.1. Which substance requires the largest amount of energy to raise the temperature of 25.0 g of the substance from 15.0°C to 37.0°C? Calculate the energy. Which substance in Table 6.1 has the largest temperature change when 550. g of the substance absorbs 10.7 kJ of energy? Calculate the temperature change.

42. The specific heat capacity of silver is 0.24 J/°C · g.
    a. Calculate the energy required to raise the temperature of 150.0 g Ag from 273 K to 298 K.
    b. Calculate the energy required to raise the temperature of 1.0 mol Ag by 1.0°C (called the *molar heat capacity* of silver).
    c. It takes 1.25 kJ of energy to heat a sample of pure silver from 12.0°C to 15.2°C. Calculate the mass of the sample of silver.

43. A 5.00-g sample of one of the substances listed in Table 6.1 was heated from 25.2°C to 55.1°C, requiring 133 J to do so. What substance was it?

44. It takes 585 J of energy to raise the temperature of 125.6 g mercury from 20.0°C to 53.5°C. Calculate the specific heat capacity and the molar heat capacity of mercury.

45. A 30.0-g sample of water at 280. K is mixed with 50.0 g of water at 330. K. Calculate the final temperature of the mixture assuming no heat loss to the surroundings.

46. A biology experiment requires the preparation of a water bath at 37.0°C (body temperature). The temperature of the cold tap water is 22.0°C, and the temperature of the hot tap water is 55.0°C. If a student starts with 90.0 g of cold water, what mass of hot water must be added to reach 37.0°C?

47. A 5.00-g sample of aluminum pellets (specific heat capacity = 0.89 J/°C · g) and a 10.00-g sample of iron pellets (specific heat capacity = 0.45 J/°C · g) are heated to 100.0°C. The mixture of hot iron and aluminum is then dropped into 97.3 g of water at 22.0°C. Calculate the final temperature of the metal and water mixture, assuming no heat loss to the surroundings.

48. Hydrogen gives off 120. J/g of energy when burned in oxygen, and methane gives off 50. J/g under the same circumstances. If a mixture of 5.0 g of hydrogen and 10. g of methane is burned, and the heat released is transferred to 50.0 g of water at 25.0°C, what final temperature will be reached by the water?

49. A 150.0-g sample of a metal at 75.0°C is added to 150.0 g of H_2O at 15.0°C. The temperature of the water rises to 18.3°C. Calculate the specific heat capacity of the metal, assuming that all the heat lost by the metal is gained by the water.

50. A 110.-g sample of copper (specific heat capacity = 0.20 J/°C · g) is heated to 82.4°C and then placed in a container of water at 22.3°C. The final temperature of the water and copper is 24.9°C. What is the mass of the water in the container, assuming that all the heat lost by the copper is gained by the water?

51. In a coffee-cup calorimeter, 50.0 mL of 0.100 M $AgNO_3$ and 50.0 mL of 0.100 M HCl are mixed to yield the following reaction:

$$Ag^+(aq) + Cl^-(aq) \longrightarrow AgCl(s)$$

The two solutions were initially at 22.60°C, and the final temperature is 23.40°C. Calculate the heat that accompanies this reaction in kJ/mol of AgCl formed. Assume that the combined solution has a mass of 100.0 g and a specific heat capacity of 4.18 J/°C · g.

52. In a coffee-cup calorimeter, 1.60 g of NH_4NO_3 is mixed with 75.0 g of water at an initial temperature of 25.00°C. After dissolution of the salt, the final temperature of the calorimeter contents is 23.34°C. Assuming the solution has a heat capacity of 4.18 J/°C · g and assuming no heat loss to the calorimeter, calculate the enthalpy change for the dissolution of NH_4NO_3 in units of kJ/mol.

53. Consider the dissolution of $CaCl_2$:

$$CaCl_2(s) \longrightarrow Ca^{2+}(aq) + 2Cl^-(aq) \qquad \Delta H = -81.5 \text{ kJ}$$

An 11.0-g sample of $CaCl_2$ is dissolved in 125 g of water, with both substances at 25.0°C. Calculate the final temperature of the solution assuming no heat lost to the surroundings and assuming the solution has a specific heat capacity of 4.18 J/°C · g.

54. Consider the reaction

$$2HCl(aq) + Ba(OH)_2(aq) \longrightarrow BaCl_2(aq) + 2H_2O(l) \\ \Delta H = -118 \text{ kJ}$$

Calculate the heat when 100.0 mL of 0.500 M HCl is mixed with 300.0 mL of 0.100 M $Ba(OH)_2$. Assuming that the temperature of both solutions was initially 25.0°C and that the final mixture has a mass of 400.0 g and a specific heat capacity of 4.18 J/°C · g, calculate the final temperature of the mixture.

55. The heat capacity of a bomb calorimeter was determined by burning 6.79 g of methane (energy of combustion = −802 kJ/mol CH_4) in the bomb. The temperature changed by 10.8°C.
    a. What is the heat capacity of the bomb?
    b. A 12.6-g sample of acetylene, C_2H_2, produced a temperature increase of 16.9°C in the same calorimeter. What is the energy of combustion of acetylene (in kJ/mol)?

56. A 0.1964-g sample of quinone ($C_6H_4O_2$) is burned in a bomb calorimeter that has a heat capacity of 1.56 kJ/°C. The temperature of the calorimeter increases by 3.2°C. Calculate the energy of combustion of quinone per gram and per mole.

Hess's Law

57. The enthalpy of combustion of solid carbon to form carbon dioxide is −393.7 kJ/mol carbon, and the enthalpy of combustion of carbon monoxide to form carbon dioxide is −283.3 kJ/mol CO. Use these data to calculate ΔH for the reaction

$$2C(s) + O_2(g) \longrightarrow 2CO(g)$$

58. Combustion reactions involve reacting a substance with oxygen. When compounds containing carbon and hydrogen are combusted, carbon dioxide and water are the products. Using the enthalpies of combustion for C_4H_4 (-2341 kJ/mol), C_4H_8 (-2755 kJ/mol), and H_2 (-286 kJ/mol), calculate ΔH for the reaction

$$C_4H_4(g) + 2H_2(g) \longrightarrow C_4H_8(g)$$

59. Given the following data

$$NH_3(g) \longrightarrow \tfrac{1}{2}N_2(g) + \tfrac{3}{2}H_2(g) \qquad \Delta H = 46 \text{ kJ}$$
$$2H_2(g) + O_2(g) \longrightarrow 2H_2O(g) \qquad \Delta H = -484 \text{ kJ}$$

calculate ΔH for the reaction

$$2N_2(g) + 6H_2O(g) \longrightarrow 3O_2(g) + 4NH_3(g)$$

On the basis of the enthalpy change, is this a useful reaction for the synthesis of ammonia?

60. Given the following data

$$2ClF(g) + O_2(g) \longrightarrow Cl_2O(g) + F_2O(g) \qquad \Delta H = 167.4 \text{ kJ}$$
$$2ClF_3(g) + 2O_2(g) \longrightarrow Cl_2O(g) + 3F_2O(g) \qquad \Delta H = 341.4 \text{ kJ}$$
$$2F_2(g) + O_2(g) \longrightarrow 2F_2O(g) \qquad \Delta H = -43.4 \text{ kJ}$$

calculate ΔH for the reaction

$$ClF(g) + F_2(g) \longrightarrow ClF_3(g)$$

61. Given the following data

$$2O_3(g) \longrightarrow 3O_2(g) \qquad \Delta H = -427 \text{ kJ}$$
$$O_2(g) \longrightarrow 2O(g) \qquad \Delta H = +495 \text{ kJ}$$
$$NO(g) + O_3(g) \longrightarrow NO_2(g) + O_2(g) \qquad \Delta H = -199 \text{ kJ}$$

calculate ΔH for the reaction

$$NO(g) + O(g) \longrightarrow NO_2(g)$$

62. The bombardier beetle uses an explosive discharge as a defensive measure. The chemical reaction involved is the oxidation of hydroquinone by hydrogen peroxide to produce quinone and water:

$$C_6H_4(OH)_2(aq) + H_2O_2(aq) \longrightarrow C_6H_4O_2(aq) + 2H_2O(l)$$

Calculate ΔH for this reaction from the following data:

$$C_6H_4(OH)_2(aq) \longrightarrow C_6H_4O_2(aq) + H_2(g)$$
$$\Delta H = +177.4 \text{ kJ}$$
$$H_2(g) + O_2(g) \longrightarrow H_2O_2(aq) \qquad \Delta H = -191.2 \text{ kJ}$$
$$H_2(g) + \tfrac{1}{2}O_2(g) \longrightarrow H_2O(g) \qquad \Delta H = -241.8 \text{ kJ}$$
$$H_2O(g) \longrightarrow H_2O(l) \qquad \Delta H = -43.8 \text{ kJ}$$

63. Given the following data

$$Ca(s) + 2C(graphite) \longrightarrow CaC_2(s) \qquad \Delta H = -62.8 \text{ kJ}$$
$$Ca(s) + \tfrac{1}{2}O_2(g) \longrightarrow CaO(s) \qquad \Delta H = -635.5 \text{ kJ}$$
$$CaO(s) + H_2O(l) \longrightarrow Ca(OH)_2(aq) \qquad \Delta H = -653.1 \text{ kJ}$$
$$C_2H_2(g) + \tfrac{5}{2}O_2(g) \longrightarrow 2CO_2(g) + H_2O(l) \qquad \Delta H = -1300. \text{ kJ}$$
$$C(graphite) + O_2(g) \longrightarrow CO_2(g) \qquad \Delta H = -393.5 \text{ kJ}$$

calculate ΔH for the reaction

$$CaC_2(s) + 2H_2O(l) \longrightarrow Ca(OH)_2(aq) + C_2H_2(g)$$

64. Given the following data

$$P_4(s) + 6Cl_2(g) \longrightarrow 4PCl_3(g) \qquad \Delta H = -1225.6 \text{ kJ}$$
$$P_4(s) + 5O_2(g) \longrightarrow P_4O_{10}(s) \qquad \Delta H = -2967.3 \text{ kJ}$$
$$PCl_3(g) + Cl_2(g) \longrightarrow PCl_5(g) \qquad \Delta H = -84.2 \text{ kJ}$$
$$PCl_3(g) + \tfrac{1}{2}O_2(g) \longrightarrow Cl_3PO(g) \qquad \Delta H = -285.7 \text{ kJ}$$

calculate ΔH for the reaction

$$P_4O_{10}(s) + 6PCl_5(g) \longrightarrow 10Cl_3PO(g)$$

Standard Enthalpies of Formation

65. Give the definition of the standard enthalpy of formation for a substance. Write separate reactions for the formation of NaCl, H_2O, $C_6H_{12}O_6$, and $PbSO_4$ that have $\Delta H°$ values equal to $\Delta H_f°$ for each compound.

66. Write reactions for which the enthalpy change will be
   a. $\Delta H_f°$ for solid aluminum oxide.
   b. The standard enthalpy of combustion of liquid ethanol, $C_2H_5OH(l)$.
   c. The standard enthalpy of neutralization of sodium hydroxide solution by hydrochloric acid.
   d. $\Delta H_f°$ for gaseous vinyl chloride, $C_2H_3Cl(g)$.
   e. The enthalpy of combustion of liquid benzene, $C_6H_6(l)$.
   f. The enthalpy of solution of solid ammonium bromide.

67. Use the values of $\Delta H_f°$ in Appendix 4 to calculate $\Delta H°$ for the following reactions.
   a.

$$\bullet N \quad \bullet H \quad \bullet O \quad \bullet C$$

   b. $Ca_3(PO_4)_2(s) + 3H_2SO_4(l) \longrightarrow 3CaSO_4(s) + 2H_3PO_4(l)$
   c. $NH_3(g) + HCl(g) \longrightarrow NH_4Cl(s)$

68. Use the values of $\Delta H_f°$ in Appendix 4 to calculate $\Delta H°$ for the following reactions. (See Exercise 67.)
   a.

   b. $SiCl_4(l) + 2H_2O(l) \longrightarrow SiO_2(s) + 4HCl(aq)$
   c. $MgO(s) + H_2O(l) \longrightarrow Mg(OH)_2(s)$

69. The Ostwald process for the commercial production of nitric acid from ammonia and oxygen involves the following steps:

$$4NH_3(g) + 5O_2(g) \longrightarrow 4NO(g) + 6H_2O(g)$$
$$2NO(g) + O_2(g) \longrightarrow 2NO_2(g)$$
$$3NO_2(g) + H_2O(l) \longrightarrow 2HNO_3(aq) + NO(g)$$

   a. Use the values of $\Delta H_f°$ in Appendix 4 to calculate the value of $\Delta H°$ for each of the preceding reactions.
   b. Write the overall equation for the production of nitric acid by the Ostwald process by combining the preceding equations. (Water is also a product.) Is the overall reaction exothermic or endothermic?

70. Calculate $\Delta H°$ for each of the following reactions using the data in Appendix 4:

$$4Na(s) + O_2(g) \longrightarrow 2Na_2O(s)$$

$$2Na(s) + 2H_2O(l) \longrightarrow 2NaOH(aq) + H_2(g)$$

$$2Na(s) + CO_2(g) \longrightarrow Na_2O(s) + CO(g)$$

Explain why a water or carbon dioxide fire extinguisher might not be effective in putting out a sodium fire.

71. The reusable booster rockets of the space shuttle use a mixture of aluminum and ammonium perchlorate as fuel. A possible reaction is

$$3Al(s) + 3NH_4ClO_4(s)$$
$$\longrightarrow Al_2O_3(s) + AlCl_3(s) + 3NO(g) + 6H_2O(g)$$

Calculate $\Delta H°$ for this reaction.

72. The space shuttle orbiter utilizes the oxidation of methylhydrazine by dinitrogen tetroxide for propulsion:

$$4N_2H_3CH_3(l) + 5N_2O_4(l) \longrightarrow 12H_2O(g) + 9N_2(g) + 4CO_2(g)$$

Calculate $\Delta H°$ for this reaction.

73. Consider the reaction

$$2ClF_3(g) + 2NH_3(g) \longrightarrow N_2(g) + 6HF(g) + Cl_2(g)$$
$$\Delta H° = -1196 \text{ kJ}$$

Calculate $\Delta H_f°$ for $ClF_3(g)$.

74. The standard enthalpy of combustion of ethene gas, $C_2H_4(g)$, is -1411.1 kJ/mol at 298 K. Given the following enthalpies of formation, calculate $\Delta H_f°$ for $C_2H_4(g)$.

$$CO_2(g) \quad -393.5 \text{ kJ/mol}$$
$$H_2O(l) \quad -285.8 \text{ kJ/mol}$$

Energy Consumption and Sources

75. Ethanol (C_2H_5OH) has been proposed as an alternative fuel. Calculate the standard of enthalpy of combustion per gram of liquid ethanol.

76. Methanol (CH_3OH) has also been proposed as an alternative fuel. Calculate the standard enthalpy of combustion per gram of liquid methanol and compare this answer to that for ethanol in Exercise 75.

77. Some automobiles and buses have been equipped to burn propane (C_3H_8). Compare the amounts of energy that can be obtained per gram of $C_3H_8(g)$ and per gram of gasoline, assuming that gasoline is pure octane, $C_8H_{18}(l)$. (See Sample Exercise 6.11.) Look up the boiling point of propane. What disadvantages are there to using propane instead of gasoline as a fuel?

78. Acetylene (C_2H_2) and butane (C_4H_{10}) are gaseous fuels with enthalpies of combustion of -49.9 kJ/g and -49.5 kJ/g, respectively. Compare the energy available from the combustion of a given volume of acetylene to the combustion energy from the same volume of butane at the same temperature and pressure.

79. Assume that 4.19×10^6 kJ of energy is needed to heat a home. If this energy is derived from the combustion of methane (CH_4), what volume of methane, measured at STP, must be burned? ($\Delta H°_{\text{combustion}}$ for $CH_4 = -891$ kJ/mol)

80. The complete combustion of acetylene, $C_2H_2(g)$, produces 1300. kJ of energy per mole of acetylene consumed. How many grams of acetylene must be burned to produce enough heat to raise the temperature of 1.00 gal of water by 10.0°C if the process is 80.0% efficient? Assume the density of water is 1.00 g/cm³.

Additional Exercises

81. Three gas-phase reactions were run in a constant-pressure piston apparatus as illustrated below. For each reaction, give the balanced reaction and predict the sign of w (the work done) for the reaction.

a.

b.

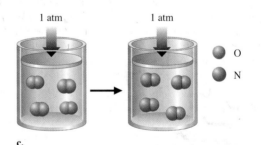

c.

If just the balanced reactions were given, how could you predict the sign of w for a reaction?

82. Consider the following changes:

a. $N_2(g) \longrightarrow N_2(l)$
b. $CO(g) + H_2O(g) \longrightarrow H_2(g) + CO_2(g)$
c. $Ca_3P_2(s) + 6H_2O(l) \longrightarrow 3Ca(OH)_2(s) + 2PH_3(g)$
d. $2CH_3OH(l) + 3O_2(g) \longrightarrow 2CO_2(g) + 4H_2O(l)$
e. $I_2(s) \longrightarrow I_2(g)$

At constant temperature and pressure, in which of these changes is work done by the system on the surroundings? By the surroundings on the system? In which of them is no work done?

83. Consider the following cyclic process carried out in two steps on a gas:

Step 1: 45 J of heat is added to the gas, and 10. J of expansion work is performed.

Step 2: 60. J of heat is removed from the gas as the gas is compressed back to the initial state.

Calculate the work for the gas compression in Step 2.

84. Calculate $\Delta H°$ for the reaction

$$2K(s) + 2H_2O(l) \longrightarrow 2KOH(aq) + H_2(g)$$

A 5.00-g chunk of potassium is dropped into 1.00 kg water at 24.0°C. What is the final temperature of the water after the preceding reaction occurs? Assume that all the heat is used to raise the temperature of the water. (Never run this reaction. It is very dangerous; it bursts into flame!)

85. The enthalpy of neutralization for the reaction of a strong acid with a strong base is -56 kJ/mol of water produced. How much energy will be released when 200.0 mL of 0.400 M HCl is mixed with 150.0 mL of 0.500 M NaOH?

86. When 1.00 L of 2.00 M Na_2SO_4 solution at 30.0°C is added to 2.00 L of 0.750 M $Ba(NO_3)_2$ solution at 30.0°C in a calorimeter, a white solid ($BaSO_4$) forms. The temperature of the mixture increases to 42.0°C. Assuming that the specific heat capacity of the solution is 6.37 J/°C · g and that the density of the final solution is 2.00 g/mL, calculate the enthalpy change per mole of $BaSO_4$ formed.

87. If a student performs an endothermic reaction in a calorimeter, how does the calculated value of ΔH differ from the actual value if the heat exchanged with the calorimeter is not taken into account?

88. In a bomb calorimeter, the reaction vessel is surrounded by water that must be added for each experiment. Since the amount of water is not constant from experiment to experiment, the mass of water must be measured in each case. The heat capacity of the calorimeter is broken down into two parts: the water and the calorimeter components. If a calorimeter contains 1.00 kg water and has a total heat capacity of 10.84 kJ/°C, what is the heat capacity of the calorimeter components?

89. The bomb calorimeter in Exercise 88 is filled with 987 g of water. The initial temperature of the calorimeter contents is 23.32°C. A 1.056-g sample of benzoic acid ($\Delta E_{comb} = -26.42$ kJ/g) is combusted in the calorimeter. What is the final temperature of the calorimeter contents?

90. Given the following data

$$Fe_2O_3(s) + 3CO(g) \longrightarrow 2Fe(s) + 3CO_2(g) \qquad \Delta H° = -23 \text{ kJ}$$
$$3Fe_2O_3(s) + CO(g) \longrightarrow 2Fe_3O_4(s) + CO_2(g) \qquad \Delta H° = -39 \text{ kJ}$$
$$Fe_3O_4(s) + CO(g) \longrightarrow 3FeO(s) + CO_2(g) \qquad \Delta H° = +18 \text{ kJ}$$

calculate $\Delta H°$ for the reaction

$$FeO(s) + CO(g) \longrightarrow Fe(s) + CO_2(g)$$

91. At 298 K, the standard enthalpies of formation for $C_2H_2(g)$ and $C_6H_6(l)$ are 227 kJ/mol and 49 kJ/mol, respectively.
a. Calculate $\Delta H°$ for

$$C_6H_6(l) \longrightarrow 3C_2H_2(g)$$

b. Both acetylene (C_2H_2) and benzene (C_6H_6) can be used as fuels. Which compound would liberate more energy per gram when combusted in air?

92. Using the following data, calculate the standard heat of formation of $ICl(g)$ in kJ/mol:

$$Cl_2(g) \longrightarrow 2Cl(g) \qquad \Delta H° = 242.3 \text{ kJ}$$
$$I_2(g) \longrightarrow 2I(g) \qquad \Delta H° = 151.0 \text{ kJ}$$
$$ICl(g) \longrightarrow I(g) + Cl(g) \qquad \Delta H° = 211.3 \text{ kJ}$$
$$I_2(s) \longrightarrow I_2(g) \qquad \Delta H° = 62.8 \text{ kJ}$$

93. Calculate $\Delta H°$ for each of the following reactions, which occur in the atmosphere.
a. $C_2H_4(g) + O_3(g) \longrightarrow CH_3CHO(g) + O_2(g)$
b. $O_3(g) + NO(g) \longrightarrow NO_2(g) + O_2(g)$
c. $SO_3(g) + H_2O(l) \longrightarrow H_2SO_4(aq)$
d. $2NO(g) + O_2(g) \longrightarrow 2NO_2(g)$

Challenge Problems

94. Consider 2.00 mol of an ideal gas that is taken from state A ($P_A = 2.00$ atm, $V_A = 10.0$ L) to state B ($P_B = 1.00$ atm, $V_B = 30.0$ L) by two different pathways:

These pathways are summarized on the following graph of P versus V:

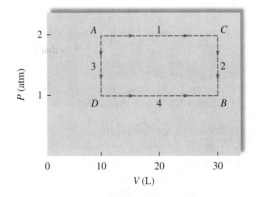

Calculate the work (in units of J) associated with the two pathways. Is work a state function? Explain.

95. Combustion of table sugar produces $CO_2(g)$ and $H_2O(l)$. When 1.46 g of table sugar is combusted in a constant-volume (bomb) calorimeter, 24.00 kJ of heat is liberated.
a. Assuming that table sugar is pure sucrose, $C_{12}H_{22}O_{11}(s)$, write the balanced equation for the combustion reaction.

b. Calculate ΔE in kJ/mol $C_{12}H_{22}O_{11}$ for the combustion reaction of sucrose.

c. Calculate ΔH in kJ/mol $C_{12}H_{22}O_{11}$ for the combustion reaction of sucrose at 25°C.

96. The sun supplies energy at a rate of about 1.0 kilowatt per square meter of surface area (1 watt = 1 J/s). The plants in an agricultural field produce the equivalent of 20. kg of sucrose ($C_{12}H_{22}O_{11}$) per hour per hectare (1 ha = 10,000 m^2). Assuming that sucrose is produced by the reaction

$$12CO_2(g) + 11H_2O(l) \longrightarrow C_{12}H_{22}O_{11}(s) + 12O_2(g)$$
$$\Delta H = 5640 \text{ kJ}$$

calculate the percentage of sunlight used to produce the sucrose—that is, determine the efficiency of photosynthesis.

97. The best solar panels currently available are about 13% efficient in converting sunlight to electricity. A typical home will use about 40. kWh of electricity per day (1 kWh = 1 kilowatt hour; 1 kW = 1000 J/s). Assuming 8.0 hours of useful sunlight per day, calculate the minimum solar panel surface area necessary to provide all of a typical home's electricity. (See Exercise 96 for the energy rate supplied by the sun.)

98. On Easter Sunday, April 3, 1983, nitric acid spilled from a tank car near downtown Denver, Colorado. The spill was neutralized with sodium carbonate:

$$2HNO_3(aq) + Na_2CO_3(s) \longrightarrow 2NaNO_3(aq) + H_2O(l) + CO_2(g)$$

a. Calculate $\Delta H°$ for this reaction. Approximately 2.0×10^4 gal nitric acid was spilled. Assume that the acid was an aqueous solution containing 70.0% HNO_3 by mass with a density of 1.42 g/cm^3. How much sodium carbonate was required for complete neutralization of the spill, and how much heat was evolved? ($\Delta H_f°$ for $NaNO_3(aq) = -467$ kJ/mol)

b. According to *The Denver Post* for April 4, 1983, authorities feared that dangerous air pollution might occur during the neutralization. Considering the magnitude of $\Delta H°$, what was their major concern?

99. A piece of chocolate cake contains about 400 Calories. A nutritional Calorie is equal to 1000 calories (thermochemical calories), which is equal to 4.184 kJ. How many 8-in-high steps must a 180-lb man climb to expend the 400 Cal from the piece of cake? See Exercise 20 for the formula for potential energy.

100. The standard enthalpy of formation of $H_2O(l)$ at 298 K is -285.8 kJ/mol. Calculate the change in internal energy for the following process at 298 K and 1 atm:

$$H_2O(l) \longrightarrow H_2(g) + \tfrac{1}{2}O_2(g) \qquad \Delta E° = \text{?}$$

(*Hint:* Using the ideal gas equation, derive an expression for work in terms of *n*, *R*, and *T*.)

101. You have a 1.00-mol sample of water at $-30.$°C and you heat it until you have gaseous water at 140.°C. Calculate *q* for the entire process. Use the following data.

$$\text{Specific heat capacity of ice} = 2.03 \text{ J/°C} \cdot \text{g}$$
$$\text{Specific heat capacity of water} = 4.18 \text{ J/°C} \cdot \text{g}$$
$$\text{Specific heat capacity of steam} = 2.02 \text{ J/°C} \cdot \text{g}$$

$$H_2O(s) \longrightarrow H_2O(l) \qquad \Delta H_{fusion} = 6.02 \text{ kJ/mol (at 0°C)}$$
$$H_2O(l) \longrightarrow H_2O(g) \qquad \Delta H_{vaporization} = 40.7 \text{ kJ/mol (at 100.°C)}$$

102. A 500.0-g sample of an element at 195°C is dropped into an ice–water mixture; 109.5 g of ice melts and an ice–water mixture remains. Calculate the specific heat of the element. See Exercise 101 for pertinent information.

Integrative Problems

These problems require the integration of multiple concepts to find the solutions.

103. The preparation of $NO_2(g)$ from $N_2(g)$ and $O_2(g)$ is an endothermic reaction:

$$N_2(g) + O_2(g) \longrightarrow NO_2(g) \text{ (unbalanced)}$$

The enthalpy change of reaction for the balanced equation (with lowest whole-number coefficients) is $\Delta H = 67.7$ kJ. If 2.50×10^2 mL of $N_2(g)$ at 100.°C and 3.50 atm and 4.50×10^2 mL of $O_2(g)$ at 100.°C and 3.50 atm are mixed, what amount of heat is necessary to synthesize $NO_2(g)$?

104. Nitromethane, CH_3NO_2, can be used as a fuel. When the liquid is burned, the (unbalanced) reaction is mainly

$$CH_3NO_2(l) + O_2(g) \longrightarrow CO_2(g) + N_2(g) + H_2O(g)$$

a. The standard enthalpy change of reaction ($\Delta H°_{rxn}$) for the balanced reaction (with lowest whole-number coefficients) is -1288.5 kJ. Calculate the $\Delta H_f°$ for nitromethane.

b. A 15.0-L flask containing a sample of nitromethane is filled with O_2 and the flask is heated to 100.°C. At this temperature, and after the reaction is complete, the total pressure of all the gases inside the flask is 950. torr. If the mole fraction of nitrogen ($X_{nitrogen}$) is 0.134 after the reaction is complete, what mass of nitrogen was produced?

105. A cubic piece of uranium metal (specific heat capacity = 0.117 J/°C · g) at 200.0°C is dropped into 1.00 L of deuterium oxide ("heavy water," specific heat capacity = 4.211 J/°C · g) at 25.5°C. The final temperature of the uranium and deuterium oxide mixture is 28.5°C. Given the densities of uranium (19.05 g/cm^3) and deuterium oxide (1.11 g/mL), what is the edge length of the cube of uranium?

Marathon Problems*

These problems are designed to incorporate several concepts and techniques into one situation. Marathon Problems can be used in class by groups of students to help facilitate problem-solving skills.

106. A sample consisting of 22.7 g of a nongaseous, unstable compound X is placed inside a metal cylinder with a radius of 8.00 cm, and a piston is carefully placed on the surface of the compound so that, for all practical purposes, the distance between the bottom of the cylinder and the piston is zero. (A hole in the piston allows trapped air to escape as the piston is placed on the compound; then this hole is plugged so that nothing in-

---

*Used with permission from the *Journal of Chemical Education*, Vol. 68, No. 11, 1991, pp. 919–922; copyright © 1991, Division of Chemical Education, Inc.

side the cylinder can escape.) The piston-and-cylinder apparatus is carefully placed in 10.00 kg of water at 25.00°C. The barometric pressure is 778 torr.

When the compound spontaneously decomposes, the piston moves up, the temperature of the water reaches a maximum of 29.52°C, and then it gradually decreases as the water loses heat to the surrounding air. The distance between the piston and the bottom of the cylinder, at the maximum temperature, is 59.8 cm. Chemical analysis shows that the cylinder contains 0.300 mol carbon dioxide, 0.250 mol liquid water, 0.025 mol oxygen gas, and an undetermined amount of a gaseous element A.

It is known that the enthalpy change for the decomposition of X, according to the reaction described above, is −1893 kJ/mol X. The standard enthalpies of formation for gaseous carbon dioxide and liquid water are −393.5 kJ/mol and −286 kJ/mol, respectively. The heat capacity for water is 4.184 J/°C · g. The conversion factor between L · atm and J can be determined from the two values for the gas constant R, namely, 0.08206 L · atm/mol · K and 8.3145 J/mol · K. The vapor pressure of water at 29.5°C is 31 torr. Assume that the heat capacity of the piston-and-cylinder apparatus is negligible and that the piston has negligible mass.

Given the preceding information, determine

a. The formula for X.

b. The pressure–volume work (in kJ) for the decomposition of the 22.7-g sample of X.

c. The *molar* change in internal energy for the decomposition of X and the approximate standard enthalpy of formation for X.

107. A gaseous hydrocarbon reacts completely with oxygen gas to form carbon dioxide and water vapor. Given the following data, determine ΔH_f° for the hydrocarbon:

$$\Delta H_{rxn}^\circ = -2044.5 \text{ kJ/mol hydrocarbon}$$

$$\Delta H_f^\circ (CO_2) = -393.5 \text{ kJ/mol}$$

$$\Delta H_f^\circ (H_2O) = -242 \text{ kJ/mol}$$

Density of CO_2 and H_2O product mixture at 1.00 atm, 200.°C = 0.751g/L

The density of the hydrocarbon is less than the density of Kr at the same conditions.

 Get help understanding core concepts and visualizing molecular-level interactions, and practice problem solving, by visiting the Online Study Center at **College.hmco.com/ PIC/Zumdahl7e.**

7 Atomic Structure and Periodicity

Contents

Light refracted through a prism.

In the past 200 years, a great deal of experimental evidence has accumulated to support the atomic model. This theory has proved to be both extremely useful and physically reasonable. When atoms were first suggested by the Greek philosophers Democritus and Leucippus about 400 B.C., the concept was based mostly on intuition. In fact, for the following 20 centuries, no convincing experimental evidence was available to support the existence of atoms. The first real scientific data were gathered by Lavoisier and others from quantitative measurements of chemical reactions. The results of these stoichiometric experiments led John Dalton to propose the first systematic atomic theory. Dalton's theory, although crude, has stood the test of time extremely well.

Once we came to "believe in" atoms, it was logical to ask: What is the nature of an atom? Does an atom have parts, and if so, what are they? In Chapter 2 we considered some of the experiments most important for shedding light on the nature of the atom. Now we will see how the atomic theory has evolved to its present state.

One of the most striking things about the chemistry of the elements is the periodic repetition of properties. There are several groups of elements that show great similarities in chemical behavior. As we saw in Chapter 2, these similarities led to the development of the periodic table of the elements. In this chapter we will see that the modern theory of atomic structure accounts for periodicity in terms of the electron arrangements in atoms.

However, before we examine atomic structure, we must consider the revolution that took place in physics in the first 30 years of the twentieth century. During that time, experiments were carried out, the results of which could not be explained by the theories of classical physics developed by Isaac Newton and many others who followed him. A radical new theory called *quantum mechanics* was developed to account for the behavior of light and atoms. This "new physics" provides many surprises for humans who are used to the macroscopic world, but it seems to account flawlessly (within the bounds of necessary approximations) for the behavior of matter.

As the first step in our exploration of this revolution in science we will consider the properties of light, more properly called *electromagnetic radiation*.

7.1 Electromagnetic Radiation

One of the ways that energy travels through space is by **electromagnetic radiation.** The light from the sun, the energy used to cook food in a microwave oven, the X rays used by dentists, and the radiant heat from a fireplace are all examples of electromagnetic radiation. Although these forms of radiant energy seem quite different, they all exhibit the same type of wavelike behavior and travel at the speed of light in a vacuum.

Waves have three primary characteristics: wavelength, frequency, and speed. **Wavelength** (symbolized by the lowercase Greek letter lambda, λ) is the *distance between two consecutive peaks or troughs in a wave,* as shown in Fig. 7.1. The **frequency** (symbolized by the lowercase Greek letter nu, ν) is defined as the *number of waves (cycles) per second that pass a given point in space*. Since all types of electromagnetic radiation travel at the speed of light, short-wavelength radiation must have a high frequency. You can see this in Fig. 7.1, where three waves are shown traveling between two points at constant speed. Note that the wave with the shortest wavelength (λ_3) has the highest frequency and the wave with the longest wavelength (λ_1) has the lowest frequency. This implies an inverse relationship between wavelength and frequency, that is, $\lambda \propto 1/\nu$, or

$$\lambda\nu = c$$

Wavelength λ and frequency ν are inversely related.

c = speed of light
  = 2.9979×10^8 m/s

Visualization: Electromagnetic Wave

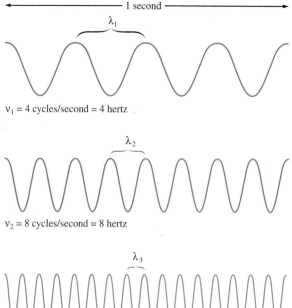

1 second

λ_1

$\nu_1 = 4$ cycles/second = 4 hertz

λ_2

$\nu_2 = 8$ cycles/second = 8 hertz

λ_3

$\nu_3 = 16$ cycles/second = 16 hertz

FIGURE 7.1
The nature of waves. Note that the radiation with the shortest wavelength has the highest frequency.

Although the waves associated with light are not obvious to the naked eye, ocean waves provide a familiar source of recreation.

where λ is the wavelength in meters, ν is the frequency in cycles per second, and c is the speed of light (2.9979×10^8 m/s). In the SI system, cycles is understood, and the unit per second becomes 1/s, or s^{-1}, which is called the *hertz* (abbreviated Hz).

Electromagnetic radiation is classified as shown in Fig. 7.2. Radiation provides an important means of energy transfer. For example, the energy from the sun reaches the earth mainly in the form of visible and ultraviolet radiation, whereas the glowing coals of a fireplace transmit heat energy by infrared radiation. In a microwave oven the water molecules in food absorb microwave radiation, which increases their motions. This energy is then transferred to other types of molecules via collisions, causing an increase in the food's temperature. As we proceed in the study of chemistry, we will consider many of the classes of electromagnetic radiation and the ways in which they affect matter.

FIGURE 7.2
Classification of electromagnetic radiation.
Spectrum adapted by permission from C. W. Keenan, D. C. Kleinfelter, and J. H. Wood, *General College Chemistry*, 6th ed. (New York: Harper & Row, 1980).

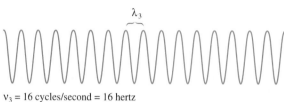

Wavelength in meters

| 10^{-12} | 10^{-10} | 10^{-8} | 4×10^{-7} | 7×10^{-7} | 10^{-4} | 10^{-2} | 1 | 10^2 | 10^4 |

Gamma rays | X rays | Ultraviolet | Visible | Infrared | Microwaves | Radio waves

FM   Shortwave   AM

4×10^{-7} 5×10^{-7} 6×10^{-7} 7×10^{-7}

CHEMICAL IMPACT

Flies That Dye

Mediterranean and Mexican fruit flies are formidable pests that have the potential to seriously damage several important fruit crops. Because of this, there have been several widely publicized sprayings of residential areas in southern California with the pesticide malathion to try to control fruit flies. Now there may be a better way to kill fruit flies—with a blend of two common dyes (red dye no. 28 and yellow dye no. 8) long used to color drugs and cosmetics. One of the most interesting things about this new pesticide is that it is activated by light. After an insect eats the blend of dyes, the molecules absorb light (through the insect's transparent body), which causes them to generate oxidizing agents that attack the proteins and cell membranes in the bug's body. Death occurs within 12 hours.

The sunlight that turns on the dye's toxicity after the fly ingests it also degrades the dye in the environment, making it relatively safe. It appears likely that in the near future the fruit fly will "dye" with little harm to the environment.

| *Sample Exercise 7.1* | **Frequency of Electromagnetic Radiation** |

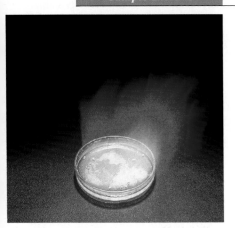

When a strontium salt is dissolved in methanol (with a little water) and ignited, it gives a brilliant red flame. The red color is produced by emission of light when electrons, excited by the energy of the burning methanol, fall back to their ground states.

The brilliant red colors seen in fireworks are due to the emission of light with wavelengths around 650 nm when strontium salts such as $Sr(NO_3)_2$ and $SrCO_3$ are heated. (This can be easily demonstrated in the lab by dissolving one of these salts in methanol that contains a little water and igniting the mixture in an evaporating dish.) Calculate the frequency of red light of wavelength 6.50×10^2 nm.

Solution

We can convert wavelength to frequency using the equation

$$\lambda \nu = c \quad \text{or} \quad \nu = \frac{c}{\lambda}$$

where $c = 2.9979 \times 10^8$ m/s. In this case $\lambda = 6.50 \times 10^2$ nm. Changing the wavelength to meters, we have

$$6.50 \times 10^2 \text{ nm} \times \frac{1 \text{ m}}{10^9 \text{ nm}} = 6.50 \times 10^{-7} \text{ m}$$

and

$$\nu = \frac{c}{\lambda} = \frac{2.9979 \times 10^8 \text{ m/s}}{6.50 \times 10^{-7} \text{ m}} = 4.61 \times 10^{14} \text{ s}^{-1} = 4.61 \times 10^{14} \text{ Hz}$$

See Exercises 7.31 and 7.32.

7.2 The Nature of Matter

It is probably fair to say that at the end of the nineteenth century, physicists were feeling rather smug. Theories could explain phenomena as diverse as the motions of the planets and the dispersion of visible light by a prism. Rumor has it that students were being discouraged from pursuing physics as a career because it was felt that all the major problems had been solved, or at least described in terms of the current physical theories.

At the end of the nineteenth century, the idea prevailed that matter and energy were distinct. Matter was thought to consist of particles, whereas energy in the form of light (electromagnetic radiation) was described as a wave. Particles were things that had mass and whose position in space could be specified. Waves were described as massless and delocalized; that is, their position in space could not be specified. It also was assumed that there was no intermingling of matter and light. Everything known before 1900 seemed to fit neatly into this view.

Visualization: Electrified Pickle

When alternating current at 110 volts is applied to a dill pickle, a glowing discharge occurs. The current flowing between the electrodes (forks), which is supported by the Na^+ and Cl^- ions present, apparently causes some sodium atoms to form in an excited state. When these atoms relax to the ground state, they emit visible light at 589 nm, producing the yellow glow reminiscent of sodium vapor lamps.

At the beginning of the twentieth century, however, certain experimental results suggested that this picture was incorrect. The first important advance came in 1900 from the German physicist Max Planck (1858–1947). Studying the radiation profiles emitted by solid bodies heated to incandescence, Planck found that the results could not be explained in terms of the physics of his day, which held that matter could absorb or emit any quantity of energy. Planck could account for these observations only by postulating that energy can be gained or lost only in *whole-number multiples* of the quantity $h\nu$, where h is a constant called **Planck's constant,** determined by experiment to have the value 6.626×10^{-34} J · s. That is, the change in energy for a system ΔE can be represented by the equation

$$\Delta E = nh\nu$$

where n is an integer (1, 2, 3, . . .), h is Planck's constant, and ν is the frequency of the electromagnetic radiation absorbed or emitted.

Planck's result was a real surprise. It had always been assumed that the energy of matter was continuous, which meant that the transfer of any quantity of energy was possible. Now it seemed clear that energy is in fact **quantized** and can occur only in discrete units of size $h\nu$. Each of these small "packets" of energy is called a *quantum*. A system can transfer energy only in whole quanta. Thus energy seems to have particulate properties.

Energy can be gained or lost only in integer multiples of $h\nu$.

Planck's constant $= 6.626 \times 10^{-34}$ J · s.

Sample Exercise 7.2

The Energy of a Photon

The blue color in fireworks is often achieved by heating copper(I) chloride (CuCl) to about 1200°C. Then the compound emits blue light having a wavelength of 450 nm. What is the increment of energy (the quantum) that is emitted at 4.50×10^2 nm by CuCl?

Solution

The quantum of energy can be calculated from the equation

$$\Delta E = h\nu$$

The frequency ν for this case can be calculated as follows:

$$\nu = \frac{c}{\lambda} = \frac{2.9979 \times 10^8 \text{ m/s}}{4.50 \times 10^{-7} \text{ m}} = 6.66 \times 10^{14} \text{ s}^{-1}$$

So

$$\Delta E = h\nu = (6.626 \times 10^{-34} \text{ J} \cdot \text{s})(6.66 \times 10^{14} \text{ s}^{-1}) = 4.41 \times 10^{-19} \text{ J}$$

A sample of CuCl emitting light at 450 nm can lose energy only in increments of 4.41×10^{-19} J, the size of the quantum in this case.

See Exercises 7.33 and 7.34.

The next important development in the knowledge of atomic structure came when Albert Einstein (see Fig. 7.3) proposed that electromagnetic radiation is itself quantized. Einstein suggested that electromagnetic radiation can be viewed as a stream of "particles" called **photons.** The energy of each photon is given by the expression

$$E_{\text{photon}} = h\nu = \frac{hc}{\lambda}$$

Visualization: Photoelectric Effect

where h is Planck's constant, ν is the frequency of the radiation, and λ is the wavelength of the radiation.

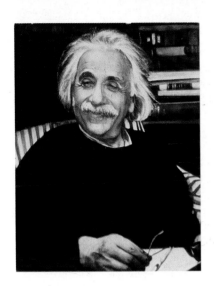

FIGURE 7.3
Albert Einstein (1879–1955) was born in Germany. Nothing in his early development suggested genius; even at the age of 9 he did not speak clearly, and his parents feared that he might be handicapped. When asked what profession Einstein should follow, his school principal replied, "It doesn't matter; he'll never make a success of anything." When he was 10, Einstein entered the Luitpold Gymnasium (high school), which was typical of German schools of that time in being harshly disciplinarian. There he developed a deep suspicion of authority and a skepticism that encouraged him to question and doubt—valuable qualities in a scientist. In 1905, while a patent clerk in Switzerland, Einstein published a paper explaining the photoelectric effect via the quantum theory. For this revolutionary thinking he received a Nobel Prize in 1921. Highly regarded by this time, he worked in Germany until 1933, when Hitler's persecution of the Jews forced him to come to the United States. He worked at the Institute for Advanced Studies in Princeton, New Jersey, until his death in 1955.

Einstein was undoubtedly the greatest physicist of our age. Even if someone else had derived the theory of relativity, his other work would have ensured his ranking as the second greatest physicist of his time. Our concepts of space and time were radically changed by ideas he first proposed when he was 26 years old. From then until the end of his life, he attempted unsuccessfully to find a single unifying theory that would explain all physical events.

The Photoelectric Effect

Einstein arrived at this conclusion through his analysis of the **photoelectric effect** (for which he later was awarded the Nobel Prize). The photoelectric effect refers to the phenomenon in which electrons are emitted from the surface of a metal when light strikes it. The following observations characterize the photoelectric effect.

1. Studies in which the frequency of the light is varied show that no electrons are emitted by a given metal below a specific threshold frequency ν_0.

2. For light with frequency lower than the threshold frequency, no electrons are emitted regardless of the intensity of the light.

3. For light with frequency greater than the threshold frequency, the number of electrons emitted increases with the intensity of the light.

4. For light with frequency greater than the threshold frequency, the kinetic energy, of the emitted electrons increases linearly with the frequency of the light.

These observations can be explained by assuming that electromagnetic radiation is quantized (consists of photons), and that the threshold frequency represents the minimum energy required to remove the electron from the metal's surface.

$$\text{Minimum energy required to remove an electron} = E_0 = h\nu_0$$

Because a photon with energy less than E_0 ($\nu < \nu_0$) cannot remove an electron, light with a frequency less than the threshold frequency produces no electrons. On the other hand, for light where $\nu > \nu_0$, the energy in excess of that required to remove the electron is given to the electron as kinetic energy (KE):

$$\text{KE}_{\text{electron}} = \tfrac{1}{2}mv^2 = h\nu - h\nu_0$$

Mass of electron   Velocity of electron   Energy of incident photon   Energy required to remove electron from metal's surface

Because in this picture the intensity of light is a measure of the number of photons present in a given part of the beam, a greater intensity means that more photons are available to release electrons (as long as $\nu > \nu_0$ for the radiation).

In a related development, Einstein derived the famous equation

$$E = mc^2$$

in his *special theory of relativity* published in 1905. The main significance of this equation is that *energy has mass*. This is more apparent if we rearrange the equation in the following form:

$$m = \frac{E}{c^2}$$

$\uparrow$ Mass $E \leftarrow$ Energy $c^2 \nwarrow$ Speed of light

CHEMICAL IMPACT

Chemistry That Doesn't Leave You in the Dark

In the animal world, the ability to see at night provides predators with a distinct advantage over their prey. The same advantage can be gained by military forces and law enforcement agencies around the world through the use of recent advances in night vision technology.

All types of night vision equipment are electro-optical devices that amplify existing light. A lens collects light and focuses it on an image intensifier. The image intensifier is based on the photoelectric effect—materials that give off electrons when light is shined on them. Night vision intensifiers use semiconductor-based materials to produce large numbers of electrons for a given input of photons. The emitted electrons are then directed onto a screen covered with compounds that phosphoresce (glow when struck by electrons). While television tubes use various phosphors to produce color pictures, night vision devices use phosphors that appear green, because the human eye can distinguish more shades of green than any other color. The viewing screen shows an image that otherwise would be invisible to the naked eye during nighttime viewing.

Current night vision devices use gallium arsenide (GaAs)–based intensifiers that can amplify input light as much as 50,000 times. These devices are so sensitive they can use starlight to produce an image. It is also now possible to use light (infrared) that cannot be sensed with the human eye to create an image.

This technology, while developed originally for military and law enforcement applications, is now becoming available to the consumer. For example, Cadillac included night vision as an option on its cars for the year 2000. As night-imaging technology improves and costs become less prohibitive, a whole new world is opening up for the technophile—after the sun goes down.

A night vision photo of the midair refueling of a U.S. Air Force plane.

Using this form of the equation, we can calculate the mass associated with a given quantity of energy. For example, we can calculate the *apparent* mass of a photon. For electromagnetic radiation of wavelength λ, the energy of each photon is given by the expression

$$E_{\text{photon}} = \frac{hc}{\lambda}$$

Then the apparent mass of a photon of light with wavelength λ is given by

$$m = \frac{E}{c^2} = \frac{hc/\lambda}{c^2} = \frac{h}{\lambda c}$$

Does a photon really have mass? The answer *appears to be* yes. In 1922 American physicist Arthur Compton (1892–1962) performed experiments involving collisions of X rays and electrons that showed that photons do exhibit the apparent mass calculated from the preceding equation. However, it is clear that photons do not have mass in the classical sense. A photon has mass only in a relativistic sense—it has no rest mass.

Note that the apparent mass of a photon depends on its wavelength. The mass of a photon at rest is thought to be zero, although we never observe it at rest.

Light as a wave phenomenon

Light as a stream of photons

FIGURE 7.4
Electromagnetic radiation exhibits wave properties and particulate properties. The energy of each photon of the radiation is related to the wavelength and frequency by the equation $E_{\text{photon}} = h\nu = hc/\lambda$.

We can summarize the important conclusions from the work of Planck and Einstein as follows:

Energy is quantized. It can occur only in discrete units called quanta.

Electromagnetic radiation, which was previously thought to exhibit only wave properties, seems to show certain characteristics of particulate matter as well. This phenomenon is sometimes referred to as the **dual nature of light** and is illustrated in Fig. 7.4.

Thus light, which previously was thought to be purely wavelike, was found to have certain characteristics of particulate matter. But is the opposite also true? That is, does matter that is normally assumed to be particulate exhibit wave properties? This question was raised in 1923 by a young French physicist named Louis de Broglie (1892–1987). To see how de Broglie supplied the answer to this question, recall that the relationship between mass and wavelength for electromagnetic radiation is $m = h/\lambda c$. For a particle with velocity v, the corresponding expression is

Do not confuse ν (frequency) with v (velocity).

$$m = \frac{h}{\lambda v}$$

Rearranging to solve for λ, we have

$$\lambda = \frac{h}{mv}$$

This equation, called *de Broglie's equation,* allows us to calculate the wavelength for a particle, as shown in Sample Exercise 7.3.

| Sample Exercise 7.3 | **Calculations of Wavelength** |

Compare the wavelength for an electron (mass $= 9.11 \times 10^{-31}$ kg) traveling at a speed of 1.0×10^7 m/s with that for a ball (mass $= 0.10$ kg) traveling at 35 m/s.

Solution

We use the equation $\lambda = h/mv$, where

$$h = 6.626 \times 10^{-34} \text{ J} \cdot \text{s} \quad \text{or} \quad 6.626 \times 10^{-34} \text{ kg} \cdot \text{m}^2/\text{s}$$

since

$$1 \text{ J} = 1 \text{ kg} \cdot \text{m}^2/\text{s}^2$$

For the electron,

$$\lambda_e = \frac{6.626 \times 10^{-34} \frac{\text{kg} \cdot \text{m} \cdot \text{m}}{\text{s}}}{(9.11 \times 10^{-31} \text{ kg})(1.0 \times 10^7 \text{ m/s})} = 7.27 \times 10^{-11} \text{ m}$$

For the ball,

$$\lambda_b = \frac{6.626 \times 10^{-34} \frac{\text{kg} \cdot \text{m} \cdot \text{m}}{\text{s}}}{(0.10 \text{ kg})(35 \text{ m/s})} = 1.9 \times 10^{-34} \text{ m}$$

See Exercises 7.41 through 7.44.

Notice from Sample Exercise 7.3 that the wavelength associated with the ball is incredibly short. On the other hand, the wavelength of the electron, although still quite small, happens to be on the same order as the spacing between the atoms in a typical crystal. This is important because, as we will see presently, it provides a means for testing de Broglie's equation.

CHEMICAL IMPACT

Thin Is In

Since the beginning of television about 75 years ago, TV sets have been built around cathode ray tubes (CRTs) in which a "gun" fires electrons at a screen containing phosphors (compounds that emit colored light when excited by some energy source). Although CRT televisions produce excellent pictures, big-screen TVs are very thick and very heavy. Several new technologies are now being used that reduce the bulk of color monitors. One such approach involves a plasma flat-panel display. As the name suggests, the major advantage of these screens is that they are very thin and relatively light.

All color monitors work by manipulating millions of pixels, each of which contains red, blue, and green color-producing phosphors. By combining these three fundamental colors with various weightings, all colors of the rainbow can be generated, thereby producing color images on the monitor. The various types of monitors differ in the energy source used to excite the phosphors. Whereas a CRT monitor uses an electron gun as the energy source, a plasma monitor uses an applied voltage to produce gas-phase ions and electrons, which, when they recombine, emit ultraviolet light. This light, in turn, excites the phosphors.

Plasma monitors have pixel compartments that contain xenon and neon gas. Each pixel consists of three subpixels: one containing a red phosphor, one with a green phosphor, and one with a blue phosphor. Two perpendicular sets of electrodes define a matrix around the subpixels:

Electrodes

Electrodes

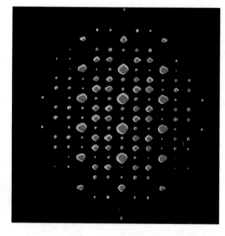

Diffraction results when light is scattered from a regular array of points or lines. You may have noticed the diffraction of light from the ridges and grooves of a compact disc. The colors result because the various wavelengths of visible light are not all scattered in the same way. The colors are "separated," giving the same effect as light passing through a prism. Just as a regular arrangement of ridges and grooves produces diffraction, so does a regular array of atoms or ions in a crystal, as shown in the photographs below. For example, when X rays are directed onto a crystal of sodium chloride, with its regular array of Na^+ and Cl^- ions, the scattered radiation produces a **diffraction pattern** of bright spots and dark areas on a photographic plate, as shown in Fig. 7.5(a). This occurs because the scattered light can interfere constructively (the peaks and troughs of the beams are in phase) to produce a bright spot [Fig. 7.5(b)] or destructively (the peaks and troughs are out of phase) to produce a dark area [Fig. 7.5(c)].

A diffraction pattern can only be explained in terms of waves. Thus this phenomenon provides a test for the postulate that particles such as electrons have wavelengths. As we saw in Sample Exercise 7.3, an electron with a velocity of 10^7 m/s (easily achieved by acceleration of the electron in an electric field) has a wavelength of about 10^{-10} m, which is roughly the distance between the ions in a crystal such as sodium chloride. This is important because diffraction occurs most efficiently when the spacing between the scattering points is about the same as the wavelength of the wave being diffracted. Thus, if electrons really do have an associated wavelength, a crystal should diffract electrons. An experiment to test this idea was carried out in 1927 by C. J. Davisson and

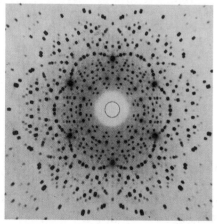

(top) The pattern produced by electron diffraction of a titanium/nickel alloy. (bottom) Pattern produced by X-ray diffraction of a beryl crystal.

One set of the electrodes is above the pixels, and the perpendicular set is below the pixels. When the computer managing the image places a voltage difference across a given subpixel, electrons are removed from the xenon and neon atoms present to form a plasma (cations and electrons). When the cations recombine with the electrons, photons of light are emitted that are absorbed by the phosphor compound, which then emits red, green, or blue light. By controlling the size of the voltage on a given subpixel, a given pixel can produce a variety of colors. When all of the pixels are excited appropriately, a color image is produced.

The plasma display makes it possible to have a large, yet relatively thin screen. Since each pixel is energized individually, this display looks bright and clear from almost any angle. The main disadvantage of this technology is its relatively high cost. However, as advances are being made, the price is falling significantly. CRT monitors may soon be of interest only to antique collectors.

A plasma display from Sony.

L. H. Germer at Bell Laboratories. When they directed a beam of electrons at a nickel crystal, they observed a diffraction pattern similar to that seen from the diffraction of X rays. This result verified de Broglie's relationship, at least for electrons. Larger chunks of matter, such as balls, have such small wavelengths (see Sample Exercise 7.3) that they are impossible to verify experimentally. However, we believe that all matter obeys de Broglie's equation.

Now we have come full circle. Electromagnetic radiation, which at the turn of the twentieth century was thought to be a pure waveform, was found to possess particulate properties. Conversely, electrons, which were thought to be particles, were found to have a wavelength associated with them. The significance of these results is that matter and energy are not distinct.

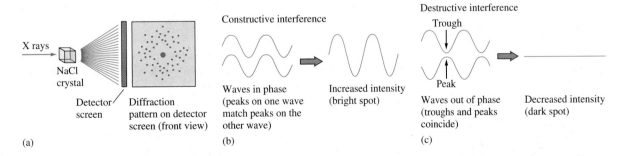

FIGURE 7.5
(a) Diffraction occurs when electromagnetic radiation is scattered from a regular array of objects, such as the ions in a crystal of sodium chloride. The large spot in the center is from the main incident beam of X rays. (b) Bright spots in the diffraction pattern result from *constructive interference* of waves. The waves are in phase; that is, their peaks match. (c) Dark areas result from *destructive interference* of waves. The waves are out of phase; the peaks of one wave coincide with the troughs of another wave.

Energy is really a form of matter, and all matter shows the same types of properties. That is, *all matter exhibits both particulate and wave properties.* Large pieces of matter, such as baseballs, exhibit predominantly particulate properties. The associated wavelength is so small that it is not observed. Very small "bits of matter," such as photons, while showing some particulate properties, exhibit predominantly wave properties. Pieces of matter with intermediate mass, such as electrons, show clearly both the particulate and wave properties of matter.

7.3 The Atomic Spectrum of Hydrogen

As we saw in Chapter 2, key information about the atom came from several experiments carried out in the early twentieth century, in particular Thomson's discovery of the electron and Rutherford's discovery of the nucleus. Another important experiment was the study of the emission of light by excited hydrogen atoms. When a sample of hydrogen gas receives a high-energy spark, the H_2 molecules absorb energy, and some of the H—H bonds are broken. The resulting hydrogen atoms are *excited;* that is, they contain excess energy, which they release by emitting light of various wavelengths to produce what is called the *emission spectrum* of the hydrogen atom.

To understand the significance of the hydrogen emission spectrum, we must first describe the **continuous spectrum** that results when white light is passed through a prism, as shown in Fig. 7.6(a). This spectrum, like the rainbow produced when sunlight is

A beautiful rainbow.

Visualization: Refraction of White Light

Visualization: The Line Spectrum of Hydrogen

Visualization: Flame Tests

FIGURE 7.6
(a) A continuous spectrum containing all wavelengths of visible light (indicated by the initial letters of the colors of the rainbow). (b) The hydrogen line spectrum contains only a few discrete wavelengths.

Spectrum adapted by permission from C. W. Keenan, D. C. Kleinfelter, and J. H. Wood, *General College Chemistry,* 6th ed. (New York: Harper & Row, 1980).

(a)

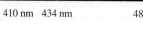

410 nm 434 nm   486 nm   656 nm

(b)

FIGURE 7.7
A change between two discrete energy levels emits a photon of light.

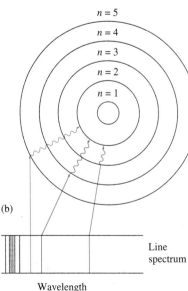

dispersed by raindrops, contains *all* the wavelengths of visible light. In contrast, when the hydrogen emission spectrum in the visible region is passed through a prism, as shown in Fig. 7.6(b), we see only a few lines, each of which corresponds to a discrete wavelength. The hydrogen emission spectrum is called a **line spectrum.**

What is the significance of the line spectrum of hydrogen? It indicates that *only certain energies are allowed for the electron in the hydrogen atom.* In other words, the energy of the electron in the hydrogen atom is *quantized.* This observation ties in perfectly with the postulates of Max Planck discussed in Section 7.2. Changes in energy between discrete energy levels in hydrogen will produce only certain wavelengths of emitted light, as shown in Fig. 7.7. For example, a given change in energy from a high to a lower level would give a wavelength of light that can be calculated from Planck's equation:

$$\Delta E = h\nu = \frac{hc}{\lambda}$$

Change in energy — Frequency of light emitted — Wavelength of light emitted

The discrete line spectrum of hydrogen shows that only certain energies are possible; that is, the electron energy levels are quantized. In contrast, if any energy level were allowed, the emission spectrum would be continuous.

7.4 The Bohr Model

In 1913, a Danish physicist named Niels Bohr (1885–1962), aware of the experimental results we have just discussed, developed a **quantum model** for the hydrogen atom. Bohr proposed that the *electron in a hydrogen atom moves around the nucleus only in certain allowed circular orbits.* He calculated the radii for these allowed orbits by using the theories of classical physics and by making some new assumptions.

From classical physics Bohr knew that a particle in motion tends to move in a straight line and can be made to travel in a circle only by application of a force toward the center of the circle. Thus Bohr reasoned that the tendency of the revolving electron to fly off the atom must be just balanced by its attraction for the positively charged nucleus. But classical physics also decreed that a charged particle under acceleration should radiate energy. Since an electron revolving around the nucleus constantly changes its direction, it is constantly accelerating. Therefore, the electron should emit light and lose energy—and thus be drawn into the nucleus. This, of course, does not correlate with the existence of stable atoms.

Clearly, an atomic model based solely on the theories of classical physics was untenable. Bohr also knew that the correct model had to account for the experimental spectrum of hydrogen, which showed that only certain electron energies were allowed. The experimental data were absolutely clear on this point. Bohr found that his model would fit the experimental results if he assumed that the angular momentum of the electron (angular momentum equals the product of mass, velocity, and orbital radius) could occur only in certain increments. It was not clear why this should be true, but with this assumption, Bohr's model gave hydrogen atom energy levels consistent with the hydrogen emission spectrum. The model is represented pictorially in Fig. 7.8.

FIGURE 7.8
Electronic transitions in the Bohr model for the hydrogen atom. (a) An energy-level diagram for electronic transitions. (b) An orbit-transition diagram, which accounts for the experimental spectrum. (Note that the orbits shown are schematic. They are not drawn to scale.) (c) The resulting line spectrum on a photographic plate. Note that the lines in the visible region of the spectrum correspond to transitions from higher levels to the $n = 2$ level.

The J in Equation (7.1) stands for joules.

Niels Hendrik David Bohr (1885–1962) as a boy lived in the shadow of his younger brother Harald, who played on the 1908 Danish Olympic Soccer Team and later became a distinguished mathematician. In school, Bohr received his poorest marks in composition and struggled with writing during his entire life. In fact, he wrote so poorly that he was forced to dictate his Ph.D. thesis to his mother. Nevertheless, Bohr was a brilliant physicist. After receiving his Ph.D. in Denmark, he constructed a quantum model for the hydrogen atom by the time he was 27. Even though his model later proved to be incorrect, Bohr remained a central figure in the drive to understand the atom. He was awarded the Nobel Prize in physics in 1922.

Although we will not show the derivation here, the most important equation to come from Bohr's model is the expression for the *energy levels available to the electron in the hydrogen atom:*

$$E = -2.178 \times 10^{-18} \text{ J} \left(\frac{Z^2}{n^2} \right) \tag{7.1}$$

in which n is an integer (the larger the value of n, the larger is the orbit radius) and Z is the nuclear charge. Using Equation (7.1), Bohr was able to calculate hydrogen atom energy levels that exactly matched the values obtained by experiment.

The negative sign in Equation (7.1) simply means that the energy of the electron bound to the nucleus is lower than it would be if the electron were at an infinite distance ($n = \infty$) from the nucleus, where there is no interaction and the energy is zero:

$$E = -2.178 \times 10^{-18} \text{ J} \left(\frac{Z^2}{\infty} \right) = 0$$

The energy of the electron in any orbit is negative relative to this reference state.

Equation (7.1) can be used to calculate the change in energy of an electron when the electron changes orbits. For example, suppose an electron in level $n = 6$ of an excited hydrogen atom falls back to level $n = 1$ as the hydrogen atom returns to its lowest possible energy state, its **ground state.** We use Equation (7.1) with $Z = 1$, since the hydrogen nucleus contains a single proton. The energies corresponding to the two states are as follows:

For $n = 6$: $E_6 = -2.178 \times 10^{-18} \text{ J} \left(\frac{1^2}{6^2} \right) = -6.050 \times 10^{-20} \text{ J}$

For $n = 1$: $E_1 = -2.178 \times 10^{-18} \text{ J} \left(\frac{1^2}{1^2} \right) = -2.178 \times 10^{-18} \text{ J}$

Note that for $n = 1$ the electron has a more negative energy than it does for $n = 6$, which means that the electron is more tightly bound in the smallest allowed orbit.

The change in energy ΔE when the electron falls from $n = 6$ to $n = 1$ is

$$\begin{aligned} \Delta E &= \text{energy of final state} - \text{energy of initial state} \\ &= E_1 - E_6 = (-2.178 \times 10^{-18} \text{ J}) - (-6.050 \times 10^{-20} \text{ J}) \\ &= -2.117 \times 10^{-18} \text{ J} \end{aligned}$$

The negative sign for the *change* in energy indicates that the atom has *lost* energy and is now in a more stable state. The energy is carried away from the atom by the production (emission) of a photon.

The wavelength of the emitted photon can be calculated from the equation

$$\Delta E = h \left(\frac{c}{\lambda} \right) \quad \text{or} \quad \lambda = \frac{hc}{\Delta E}$$

where ΔE represents the change in energy of the atom, which equals the energy of the emitted photon. We have

$$\lambda = \frac{hc}{\Delta E} = \frac{(6.626 \times 10^{-34} \text{ J} \cdot \text{s})(2.9979 \times 10^{8} \text{ m/s})}{2.117 \times 10^{-18} \text{ J}} = 9.383 \times 10^{-8} \text{ m}$$

Note that for this calculation the absolute value of ΔE is used (we have not included the negative sign). In this case we indicate the direction of energy flow by saying that a photon of wavelength 9.383×10^{-8} m has been *emitted* from the hydrogen atom. Simply plugging the negative value of ΔE into the equation would produce a negative value for λ, which is physically meaningless.

Sample Exercise 7.4 ## Energy Quantization in Hydrogen

Calculate the energy required to excite the hydrogen electron from level $n = 1$ to level $n = 2$. Also calculate the wavelength of light that must be absorbed by a hydrogen atom in its ground state to reach this excited state.*

Solution

Using Equation (7.1) with $Z = 1$, we have

$$E_1 = -2.178 \times 10^{-18} \text{ J}\left(\frac{1^2}{1^2}\right) = -2.178 \times 10^{-18} \text{ J}$$

$$E_2 = -2.178 \times 10^{-18} \text{ J}\left(\frac{1^2}{2^2}\right) = -5.445 \times 10^{-19} \text{ J}$$

$$\Delta E = E_2 - E_1 = (-5.445 \times 10^{-19} \text{ J}) - (-2.178 \times 10^{-18} \text{ J}) = 1.633 \times 10^{-18} \text{ J}$$

The positive value for ΔE indicates that the system has gained energy. The wavelength of light that must be *absorbed* to produce this change is

Note from Fig. 7.2 that the light required to produce the transition from the $n = 1$ to $n = 2$ level in hydrogen lies in the ultraviolet region.

$$\lambda = \frac{hc}{\Delta E} = \frac{(6.626 \times 10^{-34} \text{ J} \cdot \text{s})(2.9979 \times 10^8 \text{ m/s})}{1.633 \times 10^{-18} \text{ J}}$$
$$= 1.216 \times 10^{-7} \text{ m}$$

See Exercises 7.45 and 7.46.

At this time we must emphasize two important points about the Bohr model:

1. The model correctly fits the quantized energy levels of the hydrogen atom and postulates only certain allowed circular orbits for the electron.

2. As the electron becomes more tightly bound, its energy becomes more negative relative to the zero-energy reference state (corresponding to the electron being at infinite distance from the nucleus). As the electron is brought closer to the nucleus, energy is released from the system.

Using Equation (7.1), we can derive a general equation for the electron moving from one level (n_{initial}) to another level (n_{final}):

$$\Delta E = \text{energy of level } n_{\text{final}} - \text{energy of level } n_{\text{initial}}$$
$$= E_{\text{final}} - E_{\text{initial}}$$
$$= (-2.178 \times 10^{-18} \text{ J})\left(\frac{1^2}{n_{\text{final}}^2}\right) - (-2.178 \times 10^{-18} \text{ J})\left(\frac{1^2}{n_{\text{initial}}^2}\right)$$
$$= -2.178 \times 10^{-18} \text{ J}\left(\frac{1}{n_{\text{final}}^2} - \frac{1}{n_{\text{initial}}^2}\right) \tag{7.2}$$

Equation (7.2) can be used to calculate the energy change between *any* two energy levels in a hydrogen atom, as shown in Sample Exercise 7.5.

---

*After this exercise we will no longer show cancellation marks. However, the same process for canceling units applies throughout this text.

CHEMICAL IMPACT

Fireworks

The art of using mixtures of chemicals to produce explosives is an ancient one. Black powder—a mixture of potassium nitrate, charcoal, and sulfur—was being used in China well before 1000 A.D. and has been used subsequently through the centuries in military explosives, in construction blasting, and for fireworks. The DuPont Company, now a major chemical manufacturer, started out as a manufacturer of black powder. In fact, the founder, Eleuthère duPont, learned the manufacturing technique from none other than Lavoisier.

Before the nineteenth century, fireworks were confined mainly to rockets and loud bangs. Orange and yellow colors came from the presence of charcoal and iron filings. However, with the great advances in chemistry in the nineteenth century, new compounds found their way into fireworks. Salts of copper, strontium, and barium added brilliant colors. Magnesium and aluminum metals gave a dazzling white light. Fireworks, in fact, have changed very little since then.

How do fireworks produce their brilliant colors and loud bangs? Actually, only a handful of different chemicals are responsible for most of the spectacular effects. To produce the noise and flashes, an oxidizer (an oxidizing agent) and a fuel (a reducing agent) are used. A common mixture involves potassium perchlorate ($KClO_4$) as the oxidizer and aluminum and sulfur as the fuel. The perchlorate oxidizes the fuel in a very exothermic reaction, which produces a brilliant flash, due to the aluminum, and a loud report from the rapidly expanding gases produced. For a color effect, an element with a colored emission spectrum is included. Recall that the electrons in atoms can be raised to higher-energy orbitals when the atoms absorb energy. The excited atoms can then release this excess energy by emitting light of specific wavelengths, often in the visible region. In fireworks, the energy to excite the electrons comes from the reaction between the oxidizer and fuel.

Yellow colors in fireworks are due to the 589-nm emission of sodium ions. Red colors come from strontium salts emitting at 606 nm and from 636 to 688 nm. This red color is familiar from highway safety flares. Barium salts give a green color in fireworks, due to a series of emission lines

Quick-burning fuse

Twine

Delay fuses (slow-burning)

Heavy cardboard barriers

Side fuse (fast fuse)

Colored-paper fuse end

Cross fuse (fast fuse)

Paper wrapper

Red star composition

Blue star composition

"Flash and sound" mixture ($KClO_4$/S/Al)

Black powder propellant

Steel mortar buried in ground

A typical aerial shell used in fireworks displays. Time-delayed fuses cause a shell to explode in stages. In this case a red starburst occurs first, followed by a blue starburst, and finally a flash and loud report. (Reprinted with permission from *Chemical & Engineering News*, June 29, 1981, p. 24. Copyright © 1981, American Chemical Society.)

between 505 and 535 nm. A really good blue color, however, is hard to obtain. Copper salts give a blue color, emitting in the 420- to 460-nm region. But difficulties occur because the oxidizing agent, potassium chlorate ($KClO_3$), reacts with copper salts to form copper chlorate, a highly explosive compound that is dangerous to store. (The use of $KClO_3$ in fireworks has been largely abandoned because of its explosive hazards.) Paris green, a copper salt containing arsenic, was once used extensively but is now considered to be too toxic.

In recent years the colors produced by fireworks have become more intense because of the formation of metal chlorides during the burning process. These gaseous metal chloride molecules produce colors much more brilliant than do the metal atoms by themselves. For example, strontium chloride produces a much brighter red than do strontium atoms.

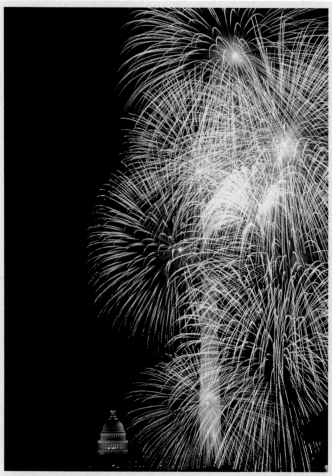

Fireworks in Washington, D.C.

Thus, chlorine-donating compounds are now included in many fireworks shells.

A typical aerial shell is shown in the diagram. The shell is launched from a mortar (a steel cylinder) using black powder as the propellant. Time-delayed fuses are used to fire the shell in stages. A list of chemicals commonly used in fireworks is given in the table.

Although you might think that the chemistry of fireworks is simple, the achievement of the vivid white flashes and the brilliant colors requires complex combinations of chemicals. For example, because the white flashes produce high flame temperatures, the colors tend to wash out. Thus oxidizers such as $KClO_4$ are commonly used with fuels that produce relatively low flame temperatures. An added difficulty, however, is that perchlorates are very sensitive to accidental ignition and are therefore quite hazardous. Another problem arises from the use of sodium salts. Because sodium produces an extremely bright yellow emission, sodium salts cannot be used when other colors are desired. Carbon-based fuels also give a yellow flame that masks other colors, and this limits the use of organic compounds as fuels. You can see that the manufacture of fireworks that produce the desired effects and are also safe to handle requires careful selection of chemicals. And, of course, there is still the dream of a deep blue flame.

Chemicals Commonly Used in the Manufacture of Fireworks

Oxidizers	Fuels	Special Effects
Potassium nitrate	Aluminum	Red flame: strontium nitrate, strontium carbonate
Potassium chlorate	Magnesium	Green flame: barium nitrate, barium chlorate
Potassium perchlorate	Titanium	Blue flame: copper carbonate, copper sulfate, copper oxide
Ammonium perchlorate	Charcoal	Yellow flame: sodium oxalate, cryolite (Na_3AlF_6)
Barium nitrate	Sulfur	White flame: magnesium, aluminum
Barium chlorate	Antimony sulfide	Gold sparks: iron filings, charcoal
Strontium nitrate	Dextrin	White sparks: aluminum, magnesium, aluminum–magnesium alloy, titanium
	Red gum	Whistle effect: potassium benzoate or sodium salicylate
	Polyvinyl chloride	White smoke: mixture of potassium nitrate and sulfur
		Colored smoke: mixture of potassium chlorate, sulfur, and organic dye

Sample Exercise 7.5	**Electron Energies**

Calculate the energy required to remove the electron from a hydrogen atom in its ground state.

Solution

Removing the electron from a hydrogen atom in its ground state corresponds to taking the electron from $n_{\text{initial}} = 1$ to $n_{\text{final}} = \infty$. Thus

$$\Delta E = -2.178 \times 10^{-18} \text{ J}\left(\frac{1}{n_{\text{final}}^2} - \frac{1}{n_{\text{initial}}^2}\right)$$

$$= -2.178 \times 10^{-18} \text{ J}\left(\frac{1}{\infty} - \frac{1}{1^2}\right)$$

$$= -2.178 \times 10^{-18} \text{ J}(0 - 1) = 2.178 \times 10^{-18} \text{ J}$$

The energy required to remove the electron from a hydrogen atom in its ground state is 2.178×10^{-18} J.

See Exercises 7.51 and 7.52.

Visualization: Flame Tests

Although Bohr's model fits the energy levels for hydrogen, it is a fundamentally incorrect model for the hydrogen atom.

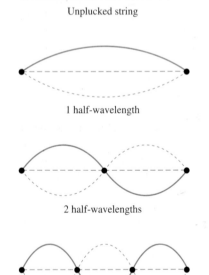

Unplucked string

1 half-wavelength

2 half-wavelengths

3 half-wavelengths

FIGURE 7.9
The standing waves caused by the vibration of a guitar string fastened at both ends. Each dot represents a node (a point of zero displacement).

At first Bohr's model appeared to be very promising. The energy levels calculated by Bohr closely agreed with the values obtained from the hydrogen emission spectrum. However, when Bohr's model was applied to atoms other than hydrogen, it did not work at all. Although some attempts were made to adapt the model using elliptical orbits, it was concluded that Bohr's model is fundamentally incorrect. The model is, however, very important historically, because it showed that the observed quantization of energy in atoms could be explained by making rather simple assumptions. Bohr's model paved the way for later theories. It is important to realize, however, that the current theory of atomic structure is in no way derived from the Bohr model. Electrons do *not* move around the nucleus in circular orbits, as we shall see later in this chapter.

7.5 The Quantum Mechanical Model of the Atom

By the mid-1920s it had become apparent that the Bohr model could not be made to work. A totally new approach was needed. Three physicists were at the forefront of this effort: Werner Heisenberg (1901–1976), Louis de Broglie (1892–1987), and Erwin Schrödinger (1887–1961). The approach they developed became known as *wave mechanics* or, more commonly, *quantum mechanics.* As we have already seen, de Broglie originated the idea that the electron, previously considered to be a particle, also shows wave properties. Pursuing this line of reasoning, Schrödinger, an Austrian physicist, decided to attack the problem of atomic structure by giving emphasis to the wave properties of the electron. To Schrödinger and de Broglie, the electron bound to the nucleus seemed similar to a **standing wave,** and they began research on a wave mechanical description of the atom.

The most familiar example of standing waves occurs in association with musical instruments such as guitars or violins, where a string attached at both ends vibrates to produce a musical tone. The waves are described as "standing" because they are stationary;

Wave-generating apparatus.

(a)

(b)

(c)

FIGURE 7.10

The hydrogen electron visualized as a standing wave around the nucleus. The circumference of a particular circular orbit would have to correspond to a whole number of wavelengths, as shown in (a) and (b), or else destructive interference occurs, as shown in (c). This is consistent with the fact that only certain electron energies are allowed; the atom is quantized. (Although this idea encouraged scientists to use a wave theory, it does not mean that the electron really travels in circular orbits.)

the waves do not travel along the length of the string. The motions of the string can be explained as a combination of simple waves of the type shown in Fig. 7.9. The dots in this figure indicate the nodes, or points of zero lateral (sideways) displacement, for a given wave. Note that there are limitations on the allowed wavelengths of the standing wave. Each end of the string is fixed, so there is always a node at each end. This means that there must be a whole number of *half* wavelengths in any of the allowed motions of the string (see Fig. 7.9). Standing waves can be illustrated using the wave generator shown in the photo below.

A similar situation results when the electron in the hydrogen atom is imagined to be a standing wave. As shown in Fig. 7.10, only certain circular orbits have a circumference into which a whole number of wavelengths of the standing electron wave will "fit." All other orbits would produce destructive interference of the standing electron wave and are not allowed. This seemed like a possible explanation for the observed quantization of the hydrogen atom, so Schrödinger worked out a model for the hydrogen atom in which the electron was assumed to behave as a standing wave.

It is important to recognize that Schrödinger could not be sure that this idea would work. The test had to be whether or not the model would correctly fit the experimental data on hydrogen and other atoms. The physical principles for describing standing waves were well known in 1925 when Schrödinger decided to treat the electron in this way. His mathematical treatment is too complicated to be detailed here. However, the form of Schrödinger's equation is

$$\hat{H}\psi = E\psi$$

where ψ, called the **wave function,** is a function of the coordinates (x, y, and z) of the electron's position in three-dimensional space and $\hat{H}$ represents a set of mathematical instructions called an *operator.* In this case, the operator contains mathematical terms that produce the total energy of the atom when they are applied to the wave function. E represents the total energy of the atom (the sum of the potential energy due to the attraction between the proton and electron and the kinetic energy of the moving electron). When this equation is analyzed, many solutions are found. Each solution consists of a wave function ψ that is characterized by a particular value of E. A specific wave function is often called an **orbital.**

To illustrate the most important ideas of the **quantum (wave) mechanical model** of the atom, we will first concentrate on the wave function corresponding to the lowest energy for the hydrogen atom. This wave function is called the 1*s* orbital. The first point of interest is to explore the meaning of the word *orbital.* As we will see, this is not a trivial matter. One thing is clear: An orbital is *not* a Bohr orbit. The electron in the hydrogen 1*s* orbital is not moving around the nucleus in a circular orbit. How, then, is the electron moving? The answer is quite surprising: *We do not know.* The wave function gives us no information about the detailed pathway of the electron. This is somewhat disturbing. When we solve problems involving the motions of particles in the macroscopic world, we are able to predict their pathways. For example, when two billiard balls with known velocities collide, we can predict their motions after the collision. However, we cannot predict the electron's motion from the 1*s* orbital function. Does this mean that the theory is wrong? Not necessarily: We have already learned that an electron does not behave much like a billiard ball, so we must examine the situation closely before we discard the theory.

To help us understand the nature of an orbital, we need to consider a principle discovered by Werner Heisenberg, one of the primary developers of quantum mechanics. Heisenberg's mathematical analysis led him to a surprising conclusion: *There is a fundamental limitation to just how precisely we can know both the position and momentum of a particle at a given time.* This is a statement of the **Heisenberg uncertainty principle.** Stated mathematically, the uncertainty principle is

$$\Delta x \cdot \Delta(mv) \geq \frac{h}{4\pi}$$

where Δx is the uncertainty in a particle's position, $\Delta(mv)$ is the uncertainty in a particle's momentum, and h is Planck's constant. Thus the minimum uncertainty in the product $\Delta \cdot \Delta(mv)$ is $h/4\pi$. What this equation really says is that the more accurately we know a particle's position, the less accurately we can know its momentum, and vice versa. This limitation is so small for large particles such as baseballs or billiard balls that it is unnoticed. However, for a small particle such as the electron, the limitation becomes quite important. Applied to the electron, the uncertainty principle implies that we cannot know the exact motion of the electron as it moves around the nucleus. It is therefore not appropriate to assume that the electron is moving around the nucleus in a well-defined orbit, as in the Bohr model.

The Physical Meaning of a Wave Function

Given the limitations indicated by the uncertainty principle, what then is the physical meaning of a wave function for an electron? That is, what is an atomic orbital? Although the wave function itself has no easily visualized meaning, the square of the function does have a definite physical significance. *The square of the function indicates the probability of finding an electron near a particular point in space.* For example, suppose we have two positions in space, one defined by the coordinates x_1, y_1, and z_1 and the other by the coordinates x_2, y_2, and z_2. The relative probability of finding the electron at positions 1 and 2 is given by substituting the values of x, y, and z for the two positions into the wave function, squaring the function value, and computing the following ratio:

$$\frac{[\psi(x_1, y_1, z_1)]^2}{[\psi(x_2, y_2, z_2)]^2} = \frac{N_1}{N_2}$$

The quotient N_1/N_2 is the ratio of the probabilities of finding the electron at positions 1 and 2. For example, if the value of the ratio N_1/N_2 is 100, the electron is 100 times more likely to be found at position 1 than at position 2. The model gives no information concerning when the electron will be at either position or how it moves between the positions. This vagueness is consistent with the concept of the Heisenberg uncertainty principle.

The square of the wave function is most conveniently represented as a **probability distribution,** in which the intensity of color is used to indicate the probability value near a given point in space. The probability distribution for the hydrogen $1s$ wave function (orbital) is shown in Fig. 7.11(a). The best way to think about this diagram is as a three-dimensional time exposure with the electron as a tiny moving light. The more times the electron visits a particular point, the darker the negative becomes. Thus the darkness of a point indicates the probability of finding an electron at that position. This diagram is also known as an *electron density map; electron density* and *electron probability* mean the same thing. When a chemist uses the term *atomic orbital,* he or she is probably picturing an electron density map of this type.

Another way of representing the electron probability distribution for the $1s$ wave function is to calculate the probability at points along a line drawn outward in any direction from the nucleus. The result is shown in Fig. 7.11(b). Note that the probability of finding the electron at a particular position is greatest close to the nucleus and drops off rapidly as the distance from the nucleus increases. We are also interested in knowing the *total* probability of finding the electron in the hydrogen atom at a particular *distance* from the nucleus. Imagine that the space around the hydrogen nucleus is made up of a series of thin spherical shells (rather like layers in an onion), as shown in Fig. 7.12(a). When the total probability of finding the electron in each spherical shell is plotted versus the distance from the nucleus, the plot in Fig. 7.12(b) is obtained. This graph is called the **radial probability distribution.**

The maximum in the curve occurs because of two opposing effects. The probability of finding an electron at a particular position is greatest near the nucleus, but the volume

Probability is the likelihood, or odds, that something will occur.

(a)

Probability (R^2)

Distance from nucleus (r)

(b)

FIGURE 7.11
(a) The probability distribution for the hydrogen $1s$ orbital in three-dimensional space. (b) The probability of finding the electron at points along a line drawn from the nucleus outward in any direction for the hydrogen $1s$ orbital.

(a)   (b)

1 Å $= 10^{-10}$ m; the angstrom is most often used as the unit for atomic radius because of its convenient size. Another convenient unit is the picometer:

1 pm $= 10^{-12}$ m

Visualization: 1s Orbital

of the spherical shell increases with distance from the nucleus. Therefore, as we move away from the nucleus, the probability of finding the electron at a given position decreases, but we are summing more positions. Thus the total probability increases to a certain radius and then decreases as the electron probability at each position becomes very small. For the hydrogen 1s orbital, the maximum radial probability (the distance at which the electron is most likely to be found) occurs at a distance of 5.29×10^{-2} nm or 0.529 Å from the nucleus. Interestingly, this is exactly the radius of the innermost orbit in the Bohr model. Note that in Bohr's model the electron is assumed to have a circular path and so is *always* found at this distance. In the quantum mechanical model, the specific electron motions are unknown, and this is the *most probable* distance at which the electron is found.

One more characteristic of the hydrogen 1s orbital that we must consider is its size. As we can see from Fig. 7.11, the size of this orbital cannot be defined precisely, since the probability never becomes zero (although it drops to an extremely small value at large values of r). So, in fact, the hydrogen 1s orbital has no distinct size. However, it is useful to have a definition of relative orbital size. *The definition most often used by chemists to describe the size of the hydrogen 1s orbital is the radius of the sphere that encloses 90% of the total electron probability.* That is, 90% of the time the electron is inside this sphere.

So far we have described only the lowest-energy wave function in the hydrogen atom, the 1s orbital. Hydrogen has many other orbitals, which we will describe in the next section. However, before we proceed, we should summarize what we have said about the meaning of an atomic orbital. An orbital is difficult to define precisely at an introductory level. Technically, an orbital is a wave function. However, it is usually most helpful to picture an orbital as a three-dimensional electron density map. That is, an electron "in" a particular atomic orbital is assumed to exhibit the electron probability indicated by the orbital map.

7.6 Quantum Numbers

When we solve the Schrödinger equation for the hydrogen atom, we find many wave functions (orbitals) that satisfy it. Each of these orbitals is characterized by a series of numbers called **quantum numbers,** which describe various properties of the orbital:

The **principal quantum number** (n) has integral values: 1, 2, 3, ... The principal quantum number is related to the size and energy of the orbital. As n increases, the orbital becomes larger and the electron spends more time farther from the nucleus. An increase in n also means higher energy, because the electron is less tightly bound to the nucleus, and the energy is less negative.

The **angular momentum quantum number** (ℓ) has integral values from 0 to $n - 1$ for each value of n. This quantum number is related to the shape of atomic orbitals. The value of ℓ for a particular orbital is commonly assigned a letter: $\ell = 0$ is called s;

TABLE 7.1   The Angular Momentum Quantum Numbers and Corresponding Letters Used to Designate Atomic Orbitals

Value of ℓ	0	1	2	3	4
Letter Used	s	p	d	f	g

Number of Orbitals per Subshell

$s = 1$
$p = 3$
$d = 5$
$f = 7$
$g = 9$

TABLE 7.2   Quantum Numbers for the First Four Levels of Orbitals in the Hydrogen Atom

n	ℓ	Orbital Designation	m_ℓ	Number of Orbitals
1	0	1s	0	1
2	0	2s	0	1
	1	2p	$-1, 0, +1$	3
3	0	3s	0	1
	1	3p	$-1, 0, 1$	3
	2	3d	$-2, -1, 0, 1, 2$	5
4	0	4s	0	1
	1	4p	$-1, 0, 1$	3
	2	4d	$-2, -1, 0, 1, 2$	5
	3	4f	$-3, -2, -1, 0, 1, 2, 3$	7

$\ell = 1$ is called p; $\ell = 2$ is called d; $\ell = 3$ is called f. This system arises from early spectral studies and is summarized in Table 7.1.

The **magnetic quantum number** (m_ℓ) has integral values between ℓ and $-\ell$, including zero. The value of m_ℓ is related to the orientation of the orbital in space relative to the other orbitals in the atom.

The first four levels of orbitals in the hydrogen atom are listed with their quantum numbers in Table 7.2. Note that each set of orbitals with a given value of ℓ (sometimes called a **subshell**) is designated by giving the value of n and the letter for ℓ. Thus an orbital where $n = 2$ and $\ell = 1$ is symbolized as 2p. There are three 2p orbitals, which have different orientations in space. We will describe these orbitals in the next section.

$n = 1, 2, 3, ..$
$\ell = 0, 1, ... (n - 1)$
$m_\ell = -\ell, ... 0, ... +\ell$

Sample Exercise 7.6	**Electron Subshells**

For principal quantum level $n = 5$, determine the number of allowed subshells (different values of ℓ), and give the designation of each.

Solution

For $n = 5$, the allowed values of ℓ run from 0 to 4 ($n - 1 = 5 - 1$). Thus the subshells and their designations are

$\ell = 0$	$\ell = 1$	$\ell = 2$	$\ell = 3$	$\ell = 4$
5s	5p	5d	5f	5g

See Exercises 7.57 through 7.59.

7.7 Orbital Shapes and Energies

We have seen that the meaning of an orbital is represented most clearly by a probability distribution. Each orbital in the hydrogen atom has a unique probability distribution. We also saw that another means of representing an orbital is by the surface that surrounds 90% of the total electron probability. These two types of representations for the hydrogen 1*s*, 2*s*, and 3*s* orbitals are shown in Fig. 7.13. Note the characteristic spherical shape of each of the *s* orbitals. Note also that the 2*s* and 3*s* orbitals contain areas of high probability separated by areas of zero probability. These latter areas are called **nodal surfaces,** or simply **nodes.** The number of nodes increases as *n* increases. For *s* orbitals, the number of nodes is given by $n - 1$. For our purposes, however, we will think of *s* orbitals only in terms of their overall spherical shape, which becomes larger as the value of *n* increases.

The two types of representations for the 2*p* orbitals (there are no 1*p* orbitals) are shown in Fig. 7.14. Note that the *p* orbitals are not spherical like *s* orbitals but have two *lobes* separated by a node at the nucleus. The *p* orbitals are labeled according to the axis of the *xyz* coordinate system along which the lobes lie. For example, the 2*p* orbital with lobes centered along the *x* axis is called the $2p_x$ orbital.

At this point it is useful to remember that mathematical functions have signs. For example, a simple sine wave (see Fig. 7.1) oscillates from positive to negative and repeats this pattern. Atomic orbital functions also have signs. The functions for *s* orbitals are positive everywhere in three-dimensional space. That is, when the *s* orbital function is evaluated at any point in space, it results in a positive number. In contrast, the *p* orbital functions have different signs in different regions of space. For example, the p_z orbirtal has a positive sign in all the regions of space in which *z* is positive and has a negative sign when *z* is negative. This behavior is indicated in Fig. 7.14(b) by the positive and negative signs inside their boundary surfaces. It is important to understand that these are mathematical signs, not charges. Just as a sine wave has alternating positive and negative phases, so too *p* orbitals have positive and negative phases. The phases of the p_x, p_y, and p_z orbitals are indicated in Fig. 7.14(b).

As you might expect from our discussion of the *s* orbitals, the 3*p* orbitals have a more complex probability distribution than that of the 2*p* orbitals (see Fig. 7.15), but they can still be represented by the same boundary surface shapes. The surfaces just grow larger as the value of *n* increases.

There are no *d* orbitals that correspond to principal quantum levels $n = 1$ and $n = 2$. The *d* orbitals ($\ell = 2$) first occur in level $n = 3$. The five 3*d* orbitals have the shapes shown in Fig. 7.16. The *d* orbitals have two different fundamental shapes. Four of the orbitals (d_{xz}, d_{yz}, d_{xy}, and $d_{x^2-y^2}$) have four lobes centered in the plane indicated in the orbital label. Note that d_{xy} and $d_{x^2-y^2}$ are both centered in the *xy* plane; however, the lobes of $d_{x^2-y^2}$ lie *along* the *x* and *y* axes, while the lobes of d_{xy} lie *between* the axes. The fifth orbital, d_{z^2}, has a unique shape with two lobes along the *z* axis and a belt centered in the *xy* plane. The *d* orbitals for levels $n > 3$ look like the 3*d* orbitals but have larger lobes.

The *f* orbitals first occur in level $n = 4$, and as might be expected, they have shapes even more complex than those of the *d* orbitals. Figure 7.17 shows representations of the 4*f* orbitals ($\ell = 3$) along with their designations. These orbitals are not involved in the bonding in any of the compounds we will consider in this text. Their shapes and labels are simply included for completeness.

So far we have talked about the shapes of the hydrogen atomic orbitals but not about their energies. For the hydrogen atom, the energy of a particular orbital is determined by its value of *n*. Thus *all* orbitals with the same value of *n* have the *same energy*—they are said to be **degenerate.** This is shown in Fig. 7.18, where the energies for the orbitals in the first three quantum levels for hydrogen are shown.

n value
↓
$2p_x$ ← orientation in space
↑
ℓ value

Node

Nodes

1*s*

2*s*

(a)

3*s*

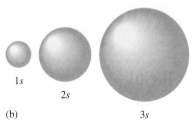

1*s*

2*s*

(b)

3*s*

FIGURE 7.13
Two representations of the hydrogen 1*s*, 2*s*, and 3*s* orbitals. (a) The electron probability distribution. (b) The surface that contains 90% of the total electron probability (the size of the orbital, by definition).

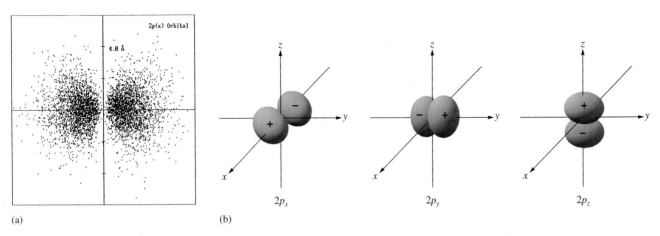

(a)

(b)

FIGURE 7.14
Representation of the 2p orbitals. (a) The electron probability distribution for a 2p orbital. (Generated from a program by Robert Allendoerfer on Project SERAPHIM disk PC 2402; reprinted with permission.) (b) The boundary surface representations of all three 2p orbitals. Note that the signs inside the surface indicate the phases (signs) of the orbital in that region of space.

Hydrogen's single electron can occupy any of its atomic orbitals. However, in the lowest energy state, the *ground state,* the electron resides in the 1s orbital. If energy is put into the atom, the electron can be transferred to a higher-energy orbital, producing an *excited state.*

A Summary of the Hydrogen Atom

- In the quantum (wave) mechanical model, the electron is viewed as a standing wave. This representation leads to a series of wave functions (orbitals) that describe the possible energies and spatial distributions available to the electron.

- In agreement with the Heisenberg uncertainty principle, the model cannot specify the detailed electron motions. Instead, the square of the wave function represents the probability distribution of the electron in that orbital. This allows us to picture orbitals in terms of probability distributions, or electron density maps.

- The size of an orbital is arbitrarily defined as the surface that contains 90% of the total electron probability.

- The hydrogen atom has many types of orbitals. In the ground state, the single electron resides in the 1s orbital. The electron can be excited to higher-energy orbitals if energy is put into the atom.

FIGURE 7.15
A cross section of the electron probability distribution for a 3p orbital.

7.8 Electron Spin and the Pauli Principle

The concept of **electron spin** was developed by Samuel Goudsmit and George Uhlenbeck while they were graduate students at the University of Leyden in the Netherlands. They found that a fourth quantum number (in addition to n, ℓ, and m_ℓ) was necessary to account for the details of the emission spectra of atoms. The spectral data indicate that the electron has a magnetic moment with two possible orientations when the atom is placed in an external magnetic field. Since they knew from classical physics that a spinning charge produces a magnetic moment, it seemed reasonable to assume that the electron could have two spin states, thus producing the two oppositely directed magnetic moments

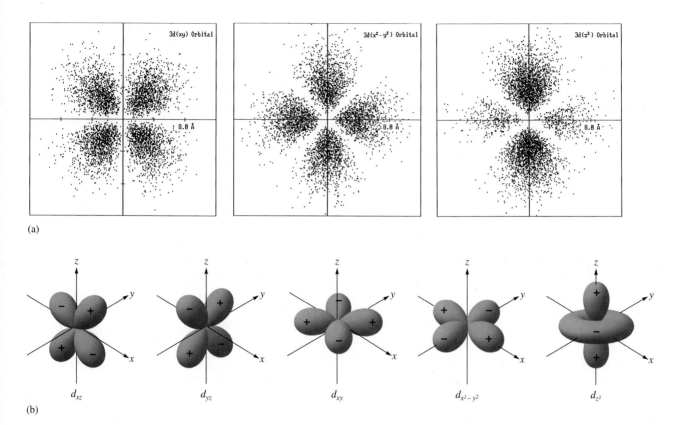

(a)

(b)

FIGURE 7.16
Representation of the 3*d* orbitals. (a) Electron density plots of selected 3*d* orbitals. (Generated from a program by Robert Allendoerfer on Project SERAPHIM disk PC 2402; reprinted with permission.) (b) The boundary surfaces of all five 3*d* orbitals, with the signs (phases) indicated.

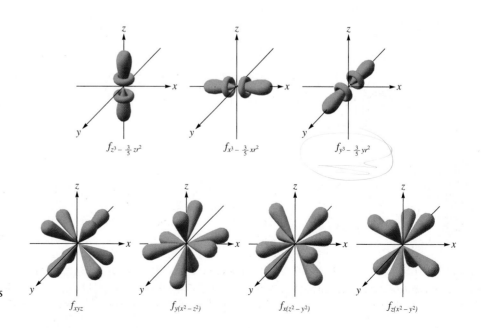

FIGURE 7.17
Representation of the 4*f* orbitals in terms of their boundary surfaces.

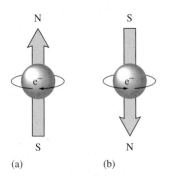

FIGURE 7.18
Orbital energy levels for the hydrogen atom.

$$m_s = +\tfrac{1}{2} \text{ or } -\tfrac{1}{2}$$

Each orbital can hold a maximum of two electrons.

FIGURE 7.19
A picture of the spinning electron. Spinning in one direction, the electron produces the magnetic field oriented as shown in (a). Spinning in the opposite direction, it gives a magnetic field of the opposite orientation, as shown in (b).

(see Fig. 7.19). The new quantum number adopted to describe this phenomenon, called the **electron spin quantum number** (m_s), can have only one of two values, $+\tfrac{1}{2}$ and $-\tfrac{1}{2}$. We can interpret this to mean that the electron can spin in one of two opposite directions, although other interpretations also have been suggested.

For our purposes, the main significance of electron spin is connected with the postulate of Austrian physicist Wolfgang Pauli (1900–1958): *In a given atom no two electrons can have the same set of four quantum numbers* (*n, ℓ, m_ℓ, and m_s*). This is called the **Pauli exclusion principle.** Since electrons in the same orbital have the same values of *n*, *ℓ*, and *m_ℓ*, this postulate says that they must have different values of *m_s*. Then, since only two values of *m_s* are allowed, *an orbital can hold only two electrons, and they must have opposite spins.* This principle will have important consequences as we use the atomic model to account for the electron arrangements of the atoms in the periodic table.

7.9 Polyelectronic Atoms

The quantum mechanical model gives a description of the hydrogen atom that agrees very well with experimental data. However, the model would not be very useful if it did not account for the properties of all the other atoms as well.

To see how the model applies to **polyelectronic atoms,** that is, atoms with more than one electron, let's consider helium, which has two protons in its nucleus and two electrons:

$$2+ \begin{array}{l} e^- \\ e^- \end{array}$$

Three energy contributions must be considered in the description of the helium atom: (1) the kinetic energy of the electrons as they move around the nucleus, (2) the potential energy of attraction between the nucleus and the electrons, and (3) the potential energy of repulsion between the two electrons.

Although the helium atom can be readily described in terms of the quantum mechanical model, the Schrödinger equation that results cannot be solved exactly. The difficulty arises in dealing with the repulsions between the electrons. Since the electron pathways are unknown, the electron repulsions cannot be calculated exactly. This is called the *electron correlation problem.*

The electron correlation problem occurs with all polyelectronic atoms. To treat these systems using the quantum mechanical model, we must make approximations. Most commonly, the approximation used is to treat each electron as if it were moving in a *field of charge that is the net result of the nuclear attraction and the average repulsions of all the other electrons.*

For example, consider the sodium atom, which has 11 electrons:

Now let's single out the outermost electron and consider the forces this electron feels. The electron clearly is attracted to the highly charged nucleus. However, the electron also feels the repulsions caused by the other 10 electrons. The net effect is that the electron is not

FIGURE 7.20
A comparison of the radial probability distributions of the 2s and 2p orbitals.

(a)

(b)

FIGURE 7.21
(a) The radial probability distribution for an electron in a 3s orbital. Although a 3s electron is mostly found far from the nucleus, there is a small but significant probability (shown by the arrows) of its being found close to the nucleus. The 3s electron penetrates the shield of inner electrons. (b) The radial probability distribution for the 3s, 3p, and 3d orbitals. The arrows indicate that the s orbital (red arrow) allows greater electron penetration than the p orbital (yellow arrow) does; the d orbital allows minimal electron penetration.

bound nearly as tightly to the nucleus as it would be if the other electrons were not present. We say that the electron is *screened* or *shielded* from the nuclear charge by the repulsions of the other electrons.

This picture of polyelectronic atoms leads to *hydrogenlike orbitals* for these atoms. They have the same general shapes as the orbitals for hydrogen, but their sizes and energies are different. The differences occur because of the interplay between nuclear attraction and the electron repulsions.

One especially important difference between polyelectronic atoms and the hydrogen atom is that for hydrogen all the orbitals in a given principal quantum level have the same energy (they are said to be *degenerate*). This is not the case for polyelectronic atoms, where we find that for a given principal quantum level the orbitals vary in energy as follows:

$$E_{ns} < E_{np} < E_{nd} < E_{nf}$$

In other words, when electrons are placed in a particular quantum level, they "prefer" the orbitals in the order s, p, d, and then f. Why does this happen? Although the concept of orbital energies is a complicated matter, we can qualitatively understand why the 2s orbital has a lower energy than the 2p orbital in a polyelectronic atom by looking at the probability profiles of these orbitals (see Fig. 7.20). Notice that the 2p orbital has its maximum probability closer to the nucleus than for the 2s. This might lead us to predict that the 2p would be preferable (lower energy) to the 2s orbital. However, notice the small hump of electron density that occurs in the 2s profile very near the nucleus. This means that although an electron in the 2s orbital spends most of its time a little farther from the nucleus than does an electron in the 2p orbital, it spends a small but very significant amount of time very near the nucleus. We say that the 2s electron *penetrates* to the nucleus more than one in the 2p orbital. This *penetration effect* causes an electron in a 2s orbital to be attracted to the nucleus more strongly than an electron in a 2p orbital. That is, the 2s orbital is lower in energy than the 2p orbitals in a polyelectronic atom.

The same thing happens in the other principal quantum levels as well. Figure 7.21 shows the radial probability profiles for the 3s, 3p, and 3d orbitals. Note again the hump in the 3s profile very near the nucleus. The innermost hump for the 3p is farther out, which causes the energy of the 3s orbital to be lower than that of the 3p. Notice that the 3d orbital has its maximum probability closer to the nucleus than either the 3s or 3p does, but its absence of probability near the nucleus causes it to be highest in energy of the three orbitals. The relative energies of the orbitals for n = 3 are

$$E_{3s} < E_{3p} < E_{3d}$$

In general, the more effectively an orbital allows its electron to penetrate the shielding electrons to be close to the nuclear charge, the lower is the energy of that orbital.

A summary diagram of the orders of the orbital energies for polyelectronic atoms is represented in Fig. 7.22. We will use these orbitals in Section 7.11 to show how the electrons are arranged in polyelectronic atoms.

7.10 The History of the Periodic Table

The modern periodic table contains a tremendous amount of useful information. In this section we will discuss the origin of this valuable tool; later we will see how the quantum mechanical model for the atom explains the periodicity of chemical properties. Certainly the greatest triumph of the quantum mechanical model is its ability to account for the arrangement of the elements in the periodic table.

The periodic table was originally constructed to represent the patterns observed in the chemical properties of the elements. As chemistry progressed during the eighteenth and nineteenth centuries, it became evident that the earth is composed of a great many

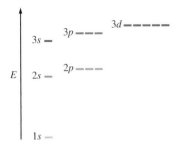

FIGURE 7.22

The orders of the energies of the orbitals in the first three levels of polyelectronic atoms.

elements with very different properties. Things are much more complicated than the simple model of earth, air, fire, and water suggested by the ancients. At first, the array of elements and properties was bewildering. Gradually, however, patterns were noticed.

The first chemist to recognize patterns was Johann Dobereiner (1780–1849), who found several groups of three elements that have similar properties, for example, chlorine, bromine, and iodine. However, as Dobereiner attempted to expand this model of *triads* (as he called them) to the rest of the known elements, it became clear that it was severely limited.

The next notable attempt was made by the English chemist John Newlands, who in 1864 suggested that elements should be arranged in *octaves,* based on the idea that certain properties seemed to repeat for every eighth element in a way similar to the musical scale, which repeats for every eighth tone. Even though this model managed to group several elements with similar properties, it was not generally successful.

The present form of the periodic table was conceived independently by two chemists: the German Julius Lothar Meyer (1830–1895) and Dmitri Ivanovich Mendeleev (1834–1907), a Russian (Fig. 7.23). Usually Mendeleev is given most of the credit, because it was he who emphasized how useful the table could be in predicting the existence and properties of still unknown elements. For example, in 1872 when Mendeleev first published his table (see Fig. 7.24), the elements gallium, scandium, and germanium were unknown. Mendeleev correctly predicted the existence and properties of these elements from gaps in his periodic table. The data for germanium (which Mendeleev called "*ekasilicon*") are shown in Table 7.3. Note the excellent agreement between the actual values and Mendeleev's predictions, which were based on the properties of other members in the group of elements similar to germanium.

Using his table, Mendeleev also was able to correct several values for atomic masses. For example, the original atomic mass of 76 for indium was based on the assumption that indium oxide had the formula InO. This atomic mass placed indium, which has metallic properties, among the nonmetals. Mendeleev assumed the atomic mass was probably incorrect and proposed that the formula of indium oxide was really In_2O_3. Based on this correct formula, indium has an atomic mass of approximately 113, placing the element among the metals. Mendeleev also corrected the atomic masses of beryllium and uranium.

Because of its obvious usefulness, Mendeleev's periodic table was almost universally adopted, and it remains one of the most valuable tools at the chemist's disposal. For example, it is still used to predict the properties of elements recently discovered, as shown in Table 7.4.

A current version of the periodic table is shown inside the front cover of this book. The only fundamental difference between this table and that of Mendeleev is that it lists the elements in order by atomic number rather than by atomic mass. The reason for this will become clear later in this chapter as we explore the electron arrangements of the atom. Another recent format of the table is discussed in the following section.

FIGURE 7.23

Dmitri Ivanovich Mendeleev (1834–1907), born in Siberia as the youngest of 17 children, taught chemistry at the University of St. Petersburg. In 1860 Mendeleev heard the Italian chemist Cannizzaro lecture on a reliable method for determining the correct atomic masses of the elements. This important development paved the way for Mendeleev's own brilliant contribution to chemistry—the periodic table. In 1861 Mendeleev returned to St. Petersburg, where he wrote a book on organic chemistry. Later Mendeleev also wrote a book on inorganic chemistry, and he was struck by the fact that the systematic approach characterizing organic chemistry was lacking in inorganic chemistry. In attempting to systematize inorganic chemistry, he eventually arranged the elements in the form of the periodic table.

Mendeleev was a versatile genius who was interested in many fields of science. He worked on many problems associated with Russia's natural resources, such as coal, salt, and various metals. Being particularly interested in the petroleum industry, he visited the United States in 1876 to study the Pennsylvania oil fields. His interests also included meteorology and hot-air balloons. In 1887 he made an ascent in a balloon to study a total eclipse of the sun.

TABELLE II

REIHEN	GRUPPE I. — R²O	GRUPPE II. — RO	GRUPPE III. — R²O³	GRUPPE IV. RH⁴ RO²	GRUPPE V. RH³ R²O⁵	GRUPPE VI. RH² RO³	GRUPPE VII. RH R²O⁷	GRUPPE VIII. — RO⁴
1	H = 1							
2	Li = 7	Be = 9,4	B = 11	C = 12	N = 14	O = 16	F = 19	
3	Na = 23	Mg = 24	Al = 27,3	Si = 28	P = 31	S = 32	Cl = 35,5	
4	K = 39	Ca = 40	— = 44	Ti = 48	V = 51	Cr = 52	Mn = 55	Fe = 56, Co = 59, Ni = 59, Cu = 63.
5	(Cu = 63)	Zn = 65	— = 68	— = 72	As = 75	Se = 78	Br = 80	
6	Rb = 85	Sr = 87	?Yt = 88	Zr = 90	Nb = 94	Mo = 96	— = 100	Ru = 104, Rh = 104, Pd = 106, Ag = 108.
7	(Ag = 108)	Cd = 112	In = 113	Sn = 118	Sb = 122	Te = 125	J = 127	
8	Cs = 133	Ba = 137	?Di = 138	?Ce = 140	—	—	—	
9	(—)		—	—	—	—	—	
10	—	—	?Er = 178	?La = 180	Ta = 182	W = 184	—	Os = 195, Ir = 197, Pt = 198, Au = 199.
11	(Au = 199)	Hg = 200	Tl = 204	Pb = 207	Bi = 208	—	—	
12	—	—	—	Th = 231	—	U = 240	—	

FIGURE 7.24
Mendeleev's early periodic table, published in 1872. Note the spaces left for missing elements with atomic masses 44, 68, 72, and 100.
(From *Annalen der Chemie und Pharmacie*, VIII, Supplementary Volume for 1872, page 511.)

TABLE 7.3   Comparison of the Properties of Germanium as Predicted by Mendeleev and as Actually Observed

Properties of Germanium	Predicted in 1871	Observed in 1886
Atomic weight	72	72.3
Density	5.5 g/cm³	5.47 g/cm³
Specific heat	0.31 J/(°C · g)	0.32 J/(°C · g)
Melting point	Very high	960°C
Oxide formula	RO_2	GeO_2
Oxide density	4.7 g/cm³	4.70 g/cm³
Chloride formula	RCl_4	$GeCl_4$
bp of chloride	100°C	86°C

TABLE 7.4   Predicted Properties of Elements 113 and 114

Property	Element 113	Element 114
Chemically like	Thallium	Lead
Atomic mass	297	298
Density	16 g/mL	14 g/mL
Melting point	430°C	70°C
Boiling point	1100°C	150°C

CHEMICAL IMPACT

The Growing Periodic Table

The periodic table of the elements has undergone significant changes since Mendeleev published his first version in 1869. In particular, in the past 60 years we have added 20 new elements beyond uranium. These so-called transuranium elements all have been synthesized using particle accelerators.

Edwin M. McMillan and Phillip H. Abelson succeeded in synthesizing the first transuranium element, neptunium (element 93), at the University of California, Berkeley, in 1940. In 1941, Glenn T. Seaborg synthesized and identified element 94 (plutonium), and over the next several years, researchers under his direction at UC Berkeley discovered nine other transuranium elements. In 1945 Seaborg suggested that the elements heavier than element 89 (actinium) were misplaced as transition metals and should be relocated on the periodic table in a series below the transition metals

Dr. Glenn Seaborg.

(the actinide series). Seaborg was awarded a Nobel Prize in chemistry in 1951 for his contributions.

7.11 The Aufbau Principle and the Periodic Table

We can use the quantum mechanical model of the atom to show how the electron arrangements in the hydrogenlike atomic orbitals of the various atoms account for the organization of the periodic table. Our main assumption here is that all atoms have the same type of orbitals as have been described for the hydrogen atom. *As protons are added one by one to the nucleus to build up the elements, electrons are similarly added to these hydrogenlike orbitals.* This is called the **aufbau principle.**

Hydrogen has one electron, which occupies the $1s$ orbital in its ground state. The configuration for hydrogen is written as $1s^1$, which can be represented by the following *orbital diagram:*

Aufbau is German for "building up."

H ($Z = 1$)
He ($Z = 2$)
Li ($Z = 3$)
Be ($Z = 4$)
B ($Z = 5$)
etc.
($Z =$ atomic number)

H: $1s^1$ $1s$ [↑] $2s$ [ ] $2p$ [ ][ ][ ]

The arrow represents an electron spinning in a particular direction.

The next element, *helium,* has two electrons. Since two electrons with opposite spins can occupy an orbital, according to the Pauli exclusion principle, the electrons for helium are in the $1s$ orbital with opposite spins, producing a $1s^2$ configuration:

He: $1s^2$ $1s$ [↑↓] $2s$ [ ] $2p$ [ ][ ][ ]

Lithium has three electrons, two of which can go into the $1s$ orbital before the orbital is filled. Since the $1s$ orbital is the only orbital for $n = 1$, the third electron will occupy the lowest-energy orbital with $n = 2$, or the $2s$ orbital, giving a $1s^2 2s^1$ configuration:

Li: $1s^2 2s^1$ $1s$ [↑↓] $2s$ [↑] $2p$ [ ][ ][ ]

In recent years, three major research facilities have taken the lead in synthesizing new elements. Along with UC Berkeley, Nuclear Research in Dubna, Russia, and GSI in Darmstadt, Germany, were responsible for synthesizing elements 104–112 by the end of 1996.

As it turned out, naming the new elements has caused more controversy than anything else connected with their discovery. Traditionally, the discoverer of an element is allowed to name it. However, because there is some dispute among the researchers at Berkeley, Darmstadt, and Dubna about who really discovered the various elements, competing names were submitted. After years of controversy, the International Union of Pure and Applied Chemistry (IUPAC) finally settled on the names listed in the accompanying table.

The name for element 106 in honor of Glenn Seaborg caused special controversy because an element had never before been named for a living person (Dr. Seaborg died in 1999). However, because of Seaborg's commanding stature

in the scientific community, the name seaborgium was adopted.

Names for the elements beyond 111 have not been decided, and these elements are represented on many periodic tables with three letters that symbolize their atomic numbers. More traditional names will no doubt be assigned in due time (hopefully with a minimum of controversy).

Atomic Number	Name	Symbol
104	Rutherfordium	Rf
105	Dubium	Db
106	Seaborgium	Sg
107	Bohrium	Bh
108	Hassium	Hs
109	Meitnerium	Mt
110	Darmstadtium	Ds
111	Roentgenium	Rg

The next element, *beryllium,* has four electrons, which occupy the 1s and 2s orbitals:

$$\text{Be:} \quad 1s^2 2s^2$$

Boron has five electrons, four of which occupy the 1s and 2s orbitals. The fifth electron goes into the second type of orbital with $n = 2$, the 2p orbitals:

$$\text{B:} \quad 1s^2 2s^2 2p^1$$

Since all the 2p orbitals have the same energy (are degenerate), it does not matter which 2p orbital the electron occupies.

Carbon is the next element and has six electrons. Two electrons occupy the 1s orbital, two occupy the 2s orbital, and two occupy 2p orbitals. Since there are three 2p orbitals with the same energy, the mutually repulsive electrons will occupy *separate* 2p orbitals. This behavior is summarized by **Hund's rule** (named for the German physicist F. H. Hund), which states that *the lowest energy configuration for an atom is the one having the maximum number of unpaired electrons allowed by the Pauli principle in a particular set of degenerate orbitals.* By convention, the unpaired electrons are represented as having parallel spins (with spin "up").

The configuration for carbon could be written $1s^2 2s^2 2p^1 2p^1$ to indicate that the electrons occupy separate 2p orbitals. However, the configuration is usually given as $1s^2 2s^2 2p^2$, and it is understood that the electrons are in different 2p orbitals. The orbital diagram for carbon is

For an atom with unfilled subshells, the lowest energy is achieved by electrons occupying separate orbitals with parallel spins, as far as allowed by the Pauli exclusion principle.

$$\text{C:} \quad 1s^2 2s^2 2p^2$$

Note that the unpaired electrons in the 2p orbitals are shown with parallel spins.

The configuration for *nitrogen,* which has seven electrons, is $1s^2 2s^2 2p^3$. The three electrons in the $2p$ orbitals occupy separate orbitals with parallel spins:

$$\text{N:} \quad 1s^2 2s^2 2p^3 \qquad \begin{array}{ccc} 1s & 2s & 2p \\ \boxed{\uparrow\downarrow} & \boxed{\uparrow\downarrow} & \boxed{\uparrow\,\uparrow\,\uparrow} \end{array}$$

The configuration for *oxygen,* which has eight electrons, is $1s^2 2s^2 2p^4$. One of the $2p$ orbitals is now occupied by a pair of electrons with opposite spins, as required by the Pauli exclusion principle:

$$\text{O:} \quad 1s^2 2s^2 2p^4 \qquad \begin{array}{ccc} 1s & 2s & 2p \\ \boxed{\uparrow\downarrow} & \boxed{\uparrow\downarrow} & \boxed{\uparrow\downarrow\,\uparrow\,\uparrow} \end{array}$$

The orbital diagrams and electron configurations for *fluorine* (nine electrons) and *neon* (ten electrons) are as follows:

$$\begin{array}{lll} & & \quad 1s \quad\quad 2s \quad\quad\quad 2p \\ \text{F:} & 1s^2 2s^2 2p^5 & \boxed{\uparrow\downarrow} \quad \boxed{\uparrow\downarrow} \quad \boxed{\uparrow\downarrow\,\uparrow\downarrow\,\uparrow} \\ \text{Ne:} & 1s^2 2s^2 2p^6 & \boxed{\uparrow\downarrow} \quad \boxed{\uparrow\downarrow} \quad \boxed{\uparrow\downarrow\,\uparrow\downarrow\,\uparrow\downarrow} \end{array}$$

With neon, the orbitals with $n = 1$ and $n = 2$ are now completely filled.

For *sodium,* the first ten electrons occupy the $1s$, $2s$, and $2p$ orbitals, and the eleventh electron must occupy the first orbital with $n = 3$, the $3s$ orbital. The electron configuration for sodium is $1s^2 2s^2 2p^6 3s^1$. To avoid writing the inner-level electrons, this configuration is often abbreviated as $[\text{Ne}]3s^1$, where $[\text{Ne}]$ represents the electron configuration of neon, $1s^2 2s^2 2p^6$.

The next element, *magnesium,* has the configuration $1s^2 2s^2 2p^6 3s^2$, or $[\text{Ne}]3s^2$. Then the next six elements, *aluminum* through *argon,* have configurations obtained by filling the $3p$ orbitals one electron at a time. Figure 7.25 summarizes the electron configurations of the first 18 elements by giving the number of electrons in the type of orbital occupied last.

At this point it is useful to introduce the concept of **valence electrons,** *the electrons in the outermost principal quantum level of an atom.* The valence electrons of the nitrogen atom, for example, are the $2s$ and $2p$ electrons. For the sodium atom, the valence electron is the electron in the $3s$ orbital, and so on. Valence electrons are the most important electrons to chemists because they are involved in bonding, as we will see in the next two chapters. The inner electrons are known as **core electrons.**

Note in Fig. 7.25 that a very important pattern is developing: *The elements in the same group (vertical column of the periodic table) have the same valence electron configuration.* Remember that Mendeleev originally placed the elements in groups based on similarities in chemical properties. Now we understand the reason behind these

---

[Ne] is shorthand for $1s^2 2s^2 2p^6$.

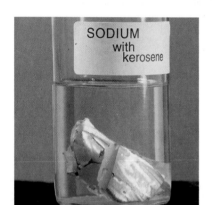

Sodium metal is so reactive that it is stored under kerosene to protect it from the oxygen in the air.

A vial containing potassium metal. The sealed vial contains an inert gas to protect the potassium from reacting with oxygen.

FIGURE 7.25
The electron configurations in the type of orbital occupied last for the first 18 elements.

H $1s^1$								He $1s^2$
Li $2s^1$	Be $2s^2$		B $2p^1$	C $2p^2$	N $2p^3$	O $2p^4$	F $2p^5$	Ne $2p^6$
Na $3s^1$	Mg $3s^2$		Al $3p^1$	Si $3p^2$	P $3p^3$	S $3p^4$	Cl $3p^5$	Ar $3p^6$

groupings. Elements with the same valence electron configuration show similar chemical behavior.

The element after argon is *potassium*. Since the 3*p* orbitals are fully occupied in argon, we might expect the next electron to go into a 3*d* orbital (recall that for $n = 3$ the orbitals are 3*s*, 3*p*, and 3*d*). However, the chemistry of potassium is clearly very similar to that of lithium and sodium, indicating that the last electron in potassium occupies the 4*s* orbital instead of one of the 3*d* orbitals, a conclusion confirmed by many types of experiments. The electron configuration of potassium is

$$\text{K:} \quad 1s^2 2s^2 2p^6 3s^2 3p^6 4s^1 \quad \text{or} \quad [\text{Ar}]4s^1$$

The next element is *calcium:*

$$\text{Ca:} \quad [\text{Ar}]4s^2$$

The next element, *scandium,* begins a series of 10 elements (scandium through zinc) called the **transition metals,** whose configurations are obtained by adding electrons to the five 3*d* orbitals. The configuration of scandium is

$$\text{Sc:} \quad [\text{Ar}]4s^2 3d^1$$

That of *titanium* is

$$\text{Ti:} \quad [\text{Ar}]4s^2 3d^2$$

And that of *vanadium* is

$$\text{V:} \quad [\text{Ar}]4s^2 3d^3$$

Chromium is the next element. The expected configuration is $[\text{Ar}]4s^2 3d^4$. However, the observed configuration is

$$\text{Cr:} \quad [\text{Ar}]4s^1 3d^5$$

The explanation for this configuration of chromium is beyond the scope of this book. In fact, chemists are still disagreeing over the exact cause of this anomaly. Note, however, that the observed configuration has both the 4*s* and 3*d* orbitals half-filled. This is a good way to remember the correct configuration.

The next four elements, *manganese* through *nickel,* have the expected configurations:

$$\text{Mn:} \quad [\text{Ar}]4s^2 3d^5 \qquad \text{Co:} \quad [\text{Ar}]4s^2 3d^7$$
$$\text{Fe:} \quad [\text{Ar}]4s^2 3d^6 \qquad \text{Ni:} \quad [\text{Ar}]4s^2 3d^8$$

The configuration for *copper* is expected to be $[\text{Ar}]4s^2 3d^9$. However, the observed configuration is

$$\text{Cu:} \quad [\text{Ar}]4s^1 3d^{10}$$

In this case, a half-filled 4*s* orbital and a filled set of 3*d* orbitals characterize the actual configuration.

Zinc has the expected configuration:

$$\text{Zn:} \quad [\text{Ar}]4s^2 3d^{10}$$

The configurations of the transition metals are shown in Fig. 7.26. After that, the next six elements, *gallium* through *krypton,* have configurations that correspond to filling the 4*p* orbitals (see Fig. 7.26).

The entire periodic table is represented in Fig. 7.27 in terms of which orbitals are being filled. The valence electron configurations are given in Fig. 7.28. From these two figures, note the following additional points:

1. The $(n + 1)s$ orbitals always fill before the *nd* orbitals. For example, the 5*s* orbitals fill in rubidium and strontium before the 4*d* orbitals fill in the second row of transition

Calcium metal.

Chromium is often used to plate bumpers and hood ornaments, such as this statue of Mercury found on a 1929 Buick.

The $(n + 1)s$ orbital fills before the *nd* orbitals.

FIGURE 7.26
Electron configurations for potassium through krypton. The transition metals (scandium through zinc) have the general configuration $[Ar]4s^23d^n$, except for chromium and copper.

metals (yttrium through cadmium). This early filling of the s orbitals can be explained by the penetration effect. For example, the $4s$ orbital allows for so much more penetration to the vicinity of the nucleus that it becomes lower in energy than the $3d$ orbital. Thus the $4s$ fills before the $3d$. The same things can be said about the $5s$ and $4d$, the $6s$ and $5d$, and the $7s$ and $6d$ orbitals.

2. After lanthanum, which has the configuration $[Xe]6s^25d^1$, a group of 14 elements called the **lanthanide series,** or the **lanthanides,** occurs. This series of elements corresponds to the filling of the seven $4f$ orbitals. Note that sometimes an electron occupies a $5d$ orbital instead of a $4f$ orbital. This occurs because the energies of the $4f$ and $5d$ orbitals are very similar.

3. After actinium, which has the configuration $[Rn]7s^26d^1$, a group of 14 elements called the **actinide series,** or the **actinides,** occurs. This series corresponds to the filling of the seven $5f$ orbitals. Note that sometimes one or two electrons occupy the $6d$ orbitals instead of the $5f$ orbitals, because these orbitals have very similar energies.

Lanthanides are elements in which the $4f$ orbitals are being filled.

Actinides are elements in which the $5f$ orbitals are being filled.

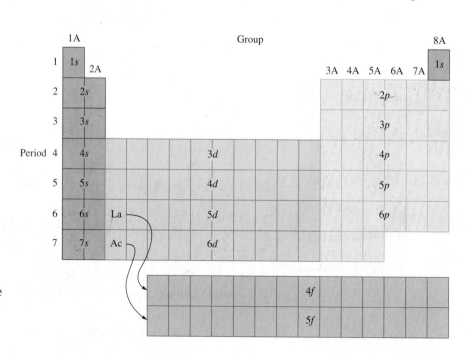

FIGURE 7.27
The orbitals being filled for elements in various parts of the periodic table. Note that in going along a horizontal row (a period), the $(n + 1)s$ orbital fills before the nd orbital. The group labels indicate the number of valence electrons (ns plus np electrons) for the elements in each group.

The group label tells the total number of valence electrons for that group.

4. The group labels for Groups 1A, 2A, 3A, 4A, 5A, 6A, 7A, and 8A indicate the *total number* of valence electrons for the atoms in these groups. For example, all the elements in Group 5A have the configuration ns^2np^3. (The *d* electrons fill one period late and are usually not counted as valence electrons.) The meaning of the group labels for the transition metals is not as clear as for the Group A elements, and these will not be used in this text.

5. The groups labeled 1A, 2A, 3A, 4A, 5A, 6A, 7A, and 8A are often called the **main-group,** or **representative, elements.** Every member of these groups has the same valence electron configuration.

The International Union of Pure and Applied Chemistry (IUPAC), a body of scientists organized to standardize scientific conventions, has recommended a new form for the periodic table, which the American Chemical Society has adopted (see the blue numbers in Fig. 7.28). In this new version the group number indicates the number of *s*, *p*, and *d* electrons added since the last noble gas. We will not use the new format in this book, but you

FIGURE 7.28
The periodic table with atomic symbols, atomic numbers, and partial electron configurations.

should be aware that the familiar periodic table may be soon replaced by this or a similar format.

The results considered in this section are very important. We have seen that the quantum mechanical model can be used to explain the arrangement of the elements in the periodic table. This model allows us to understand that the similar chemistry exhibited by the members of a given group arises from the fact that they all have the same valence electron configuration. Only the principal quantum number of the valence orbitals changes in going down a particular group.

It is important to be able to give the electron configuration for each of the main-group elements. This is most easily done by using the periodic table. If you understand how the table is organized, it is not necessary to memorize the order in which the orbitals fill. Review Figs. 7.27 and 7.28 to make sure that you understand the correspondence between the orbitals and the periods and groups.

When an electron configuration is given in this text, the orbitals are listed in the order in which they fill.

Cr: $[Ar]4s^13d^5$
Cu: $[Ar]4s^13d^{10}$

Predicting the configurations of the transition metals ($3d$, $4d$, and $5d$ elements), the lanthanides ($4f$ elements), and the actinides ($5f$ elements) is somewhat more difficult because there are many exceptions of the type encountered in the first-row transition metals (the $3d$ elements). You should memorize the configurations of chromium and copper, the two exceptions in the first-row transition metals, since these elements are often encountered.

| Sample Exercise 7.7 | **Electron Configurations** |

Give the electron configurations for sulfur (S), cadmium (Cd), hafnium (Hf), and radium (Ra) using the periodic table inside the front cover of this book.

Solution

Sulfur is element 16 and resides in Period 3, where the $3p$ orbitals are being filled (see Fig. 7.29). Since sulfur is the fourth among the "$3p$ elements," it must have four $3p$ electrons. Its configuration is

$$S: 1s^22s^22p^63s^23p^4 \quad \text{or} \quad [Ne]3s^23p^4$$

Cadmium is element 48 and is located in Period 5 at the end of the $4d$ transition metals, as shown in Fig. 7.29. It is the tenth element in the series and thus has 10 electrons in the $4d$ orbitals, in addition to the 2 electrons in the $5s$ orbital. The configuration is

$$Cd: 1s^22s^22p^63s^23p^64s^23d^{10}4p^65s^24d^{10} \quad \text{or} \quad [Kr]5s^24d^{10}$$

Hafnium is element 72 and is found in Period 6, as shown in Fig. 7.29. Note that it occurs just after the lanthanide series. Thus the $4f$ orbitals are already filled. Hafnium is

FIGURE 7.29
The positions of the elements considered in Sample Exercise 7.7.

the second member of the $5d$ transition series and has two $5d$ electrons. The configuration is

$$\text{Hf:} \quad 1s^2 2s^2 2p^6 3s^2 3p^6 4s^2 3d^{10} 4p^6 5s^2 4d^{10} 5p^6 6s^2 4f^{14} 5d^2 \quad \text{or} \quad [\text{Xe}] 6s^2 4f^{14} 5d^2$$

Radium is element 88 and is in Period 7 (and Group 2A), as shown in Fig. 7.29. Thus radium has two electrons in the $7s$ orbital, and the configuration is

$$\text{Ra:} \quad 1s^2 2s^2 2p^6 3s^2 3p^6 4s^2 3d^{10} 4p^6 5s^2 4d^{10} 5p^6 6s^2 4f^{14} 5d^{10} 6p^6 7s^2 \quad \text{or} \quad [\text{Rn}] 7s^2$$

See Exercises 7.69 through 7.72.

7.12 Periodic Trends in Atomic Properties

We have developed a fairly complete picture of polyelectronic atoms. Although the model is rather crude because the nuclear attractions and electron repulsions are simply lumped together, it is very successful in accounting for the periodic table of elements. We will next use the model to account for the observed trends in several important atomic properties: ionization energy, electron affinity, and atomic size.

Ionization Energy

Ionization energy is the energy required to remove an electron from a gaseous atom or ion:

$$X(g) \longrightarrow X^+(g) + e^-$$

where the atom or ion is assumed to be in its ground state.

To introduce some of the characteristics of ionization energy, we will consider the energy required to remove several electrons in succession from aluminum in the gaseous state. The ionization energies are

$$
\begin{aligned}
\text{Al}(g) &\longrightarrow \text{Al}^+(g) + e^- & I_1 &= 580 \text{ kJ/mol} \\
\text{Al}^+(g) &\longrightarrow \text{Al}^{2+}(g) + e^- & I_2 &= 1815 \text{ kJ/mol} \\
\text{Al}^{2+}(g) &\longrightarrow \text{Al}^{3+}(g) + e^- & I_3 &= 2740 \text{ kJ/mol} \\
\text{Al}^{3+}(g) &\longrightarrow \text{Al}^{4+}(g) + e^- & I_4 &= 11,600 \text{ kJ/mol}
\end{aligned}
$$

Several important points can be illustrated from these results. In a stepwise ionization process, it is always the highest-energy electron (the one bound least tightly) that is removed first. The **first ionization energy** I_1 is the energy required to remove the highest-energy electron of an atom. The first electron removed from the aluminum atom comes from the $3p$ orbital (Al has the electron configuration $[\text{Ne}]3s^2 3p^1$). The second electron comes from the $3s$ orbital (since Al$^+$ has the configuration $[\text{Ne}]3s^2$). Note that the value of I_1 is considerably smaller than the value of I_2, the **second ionization energy.**

This makes sense for several reasons. The primary factor is simply charge. Note that the first electron is removed from a neutral atom (Al), whereas the second electron is removed from a 1+ ion (Al$^+$). The increase in positive charge binds the electrons more firmly, and the ionization energy increases. The same trend shows up in the third (I_3) and fourth (I_4) ionization energies, where the electron is removed from the Al^{2+} and Al^{3+} ions, respectively.

The increase in successive ionization energies for an atom also can be interpreted using our simple model for polyelectronic atoms. The increase in ionization energy from I_1 to I_2 makes sense because the first electron is removed from a $3p$ orbital that is higher in energy than the $3s$ orbital from which the second electron is removed. The largest jump in ionization energy by far occurs in going from the third ionization energy (I_3) to the fourth (I_4). This is so because I_4 corresponds to removing a core electron (Al^{3+} has the configuration $1s^2 2s^2 2p^6$), and core electrons are bound much more tightly than valence electrons.

Ionization energy results in the formation of a **positive** ion.

Setting the aluminum cap on the Washington Monument in 1884. At that time, aluminum was regarded as a precious metal.

TABLE 7.5 Successive Ionization Energies in Kilojoules per Mole for the Elements in Period 3

Element	I_1	I_2	I_3	I_4	I_5	I_6	I_7
Na	495	4560		Core electrons*			
Mg	735	1445	7730				
Al	580	1815	2740	11,600			
Si	780	1575	3220	4350	16,100		
P	1060	1890	2905	4950	6270	21,200	
S	1005	2260	3375	4565	6950	8490	27,000
Cl	1255	2295	3850	5160	6560	9360	11,000
Ar	1527	2665	3945	5770	7230	8780	12,000

*Note the large jump in ionization energy in going from removal of valence electrons to removal of core electrons.

General decrease ↑

General increase →

TABLE 7.6 First Ionization Energies for the Alkali Metals and Noble Gases

Atom	I_1(kJ/mol)
Group 1A	
Li	520
Na	495
K	419
Rb	409
Cs	382
Group 8A	
He	2377
Ne	2088
Ar	1527
Kr	1356
Xe	1176
Rn	1042

Table 7.5 gives the values of ionization energies for all the Period 3 elements. Note the large jump in energy in each case in going from removal of valence electrons to removal of core electrons.

The values of the first ionization energies for the elements in the first six periods of the periodic table are graphed in Fig. 7.30. Note that in general as we go *across a period from left to right, the first ionization energy increases.* This is consistent with the idea that electrons added in the same principal quantum level do not completely shield the increasing nuclear charge caused by the added protons. Thus electrons in the same principal quantum level are generally more strongly bound as we move to the right on the periodic table, and there is a general increase in ionization energy values as electrons are added to a given principal quantum level.

On the other hand, *first ionization energy decreases in going down a group.* This can be seen most clearly by focusing on the Group 1A elements (the alkali metals) and the Group 8A elements (the noble gases), as shown in Table 7.6. The main reason for the decrease in ionization energy in going down a group is that the electrons being removed are, on average, farther from the nucleus. As *n* increases, the size of the orbital increases, and the electron is easier to remove.

First ionization energy increases across a period and decreases down a group.

FIGURE 7.30
The values of first ionization energy for the elements in the first six periods. In general, ionization energy decreases in going down a group. For example, note the decrease in values for Group 1A and Group 8A. In general, ionization energy increases in going left to right across a period. For example, note the sharp increase going across Period 2 from lithium through neon.

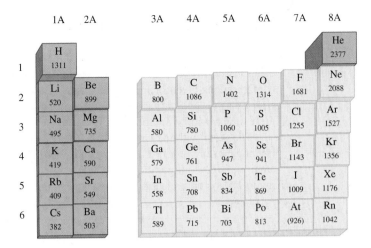

FIGURE 7.31
Trends in ionization energies (kJ/mol) for the representative elements.

In Fig. 7.30 we see that there are some discontinuities in ionization energy in going across a period. For example, for Period 2, discontinuities occur in going from beryllium to boron and from nitrogen to oxygen. These exceptions to the normal trend can be explained in terms of electron repulsions. The decrease in ionization energy in going from beryllium to boron reflects the fact that the electrons in the filled $2s$ orbital provide some shielding for electrons in the $2p$ orbital from the nuclear charge. The decrease in ionization energy in going from nitrogen to oxygen reflects the extra electron repulsions in the doubly occupied oxygen $2p$ orbital.

The ionization energies for the representative elements are summarized in Fig. 7.31.

| Sample Exercise 7.8 | **Trends in Ionization Energies** |

The first ionization energy for phosphorus is 1060 kJ/mol, and that for sulfur is 1005 kJ/mol. Why?

Solution

Phosphorus and sulfur are neighboring elements in Period 3 of the periodic table and have the following valence electron configurations: Phosphorus is $3s^2 3p^3$, and sulfur is $3s^2 3p^4$.

Ordinarily, the first ionization energy increases as we go across a period, so we might expect sulfur to have a greater ionization energy than phosphorus. However, in this case the fourth p electron in sulfur must be placed in an already occupied orbital. The electron–electron repulsions that result cause this electron to be more easily removed than might be expected.

See Exercises 7.93 and 7.94.

| Sample Exercise 7.9 | **Ionization Energies** |

Consider atoms with the following electron configurations:

$$1s^2 2s^2 2p^6$$
$$1s^2 2s^2 2p^6 3s^1$$
$$1s^2 2s^2 2p^6 3s^2$$

Which atom has the largest first ionization energy, and which one has the smallest second ionization energy? Explain your choices.

Solution

The atom with the largest value of I_1 is the one with the configuration $1s^2 2s^2 2p^6$ (this is the neon atom), because this element is found at the right end of Period 2. Since the $2p$ electrons do not shield each other very effectively, I_1 will be relatively large. The other configurations given include $3s$ electrons. These electrons are effectively shielded by the core electrons and are farther from the nucleus than the $2p$ electrons in neon. Thus I_1 for these atoms will be smaller than for neon.

The atom with the smallest value of I_2 is the one with the configuration $1s^2 2s^2 2p^6 3s^2$ (the magnesium atom). For magnesium, both I_1 and I_2 involve valence electrons. For the atom with the configuration $1s^2 2s^2 2p^6 3s^1$ (sodium), the second electron lost (corresponding to I_2) is a core electron (from a $2p$ orbital).

See Exercises 7.121 and 7.123.

Electron Affinity

Electron affinity is associated with the production of a **negative** ion.

Electron affinity *is the energy change associated with the addition of an electron to a gaseous atom:*

$$X(g) + e^- \longrightarrow X^-(g)$$

The sign convention for electron affinity values follows the convention for energy changes used in Chapter 6.

Because two different conventions have been used, there is a good deal of confusion in the chemical literature about the signs for electron affinity values. Electron affinity has been defined in many textbooks as the energy *released* when an electron is added to a gaseous atom. This convention requires that a positive sign be attached to an exothermic addition of an electron to an atom, which opposes normal thermodynamic conventions. Therefore, in this book we define electron affinity as a *change* in energy, which means that if the addition of the electron is exothermic, the corresponding value for electron affinity will carry a negative sign.

Figure 7.32 shows the electron affinity values for the atoms among the first 20 elements that form stable, isolated negative ions—that is, the atoms that undergo the addition of an electron as shown above. As expected, all these elements have negative (exothermic) electron affinities. Note that the *more negative* the energy, the greater the quantity of energy released. Although electron affinities generally become more negative from left to right across a period, there are several exceptions to this rule in each period. The dependence of electron affinity on atomic number can be explained by considering the changes in electron repulsions as a function of electron configurations. For example, the fact that the nitrogen atom does not form a stable, isolated $N^-(g)$ ion, whereas carbon forms $C^-(g)$, reflects the difference in the electron configurations of these atoms. An electron added to nitrogen ($1s^2 2s^2 2p^3$) to form the $N^-(g)$ ion ($1s^2 2s^2 2p^4$) would have to occupy a $2p$ orbital that already contains one electron. The extra repulsion between the electrons in this doubly occupied orbital causes $N^-(g)$ to be unstable. When an electron is added to carbon ($1s^2 2s^2 2p^2$) to form the $C^-(g)$ ion ($1s^2 2s^2 2p^3$), no such extra repulsions occur.

In contrast to the nitrogen atom, the oxygen atom can add one electron to form the stable $O^-(g)$ ion. Presumably oxygen's greater nuclear charge compared with that of nitrogen

FIGURE 7.32
The electron affinity values for atoms among the first 20 elements that form stable, isolated X^- ions. The lines shown connect adjacent elements. The absence of a line indicates missing elements (He, Be, N, Ne, Mg, and Ar) whose atoms do not add an electron exothermically and thus do not form stable, isolated X^- ions.

TABLE 7.7 Electron Affinities of the Halogens

Atom	Electron Affinity (kJ/mol)
F	−327.8
Cl	−348.7
Br	−324.5
I	−295.2

is sufficient to overcome the repulsion associated with putting a second electron into an already occupied $2p$ orbital. However, it should be noted that a second electron *cannot* be added to an oxygen atom $[O^-(g) + e^- \not\rightarrow O^{2-}(g)]$ to form an isolated oxide ion. This outcome seems strange in view of the many stable oxide compounds (MgO, Fe_2O_3, and so on) that are known. As we will discuss in detail in Chapter 8, the O^{2-} ion is stabilized in ionic compounds by the large attractions that occur among the positive ions and the oxide ions.

When we go down a group, electron affinity should become more positive (less energy released), since the electron is added at increasing distances from the nucleus. Although this is generally the case, the changes in electron affinity in going down most groups are relatively small, and numerous exceptions occur. This behavior is demonstrated by the electron affinities of the Group 7A elements (the halogens) shown in Table 7.7. Note that the range of values is quite small compared with the changes that typically occur across a period. Also note that although chlorine, bromine, and iodine show the expected trend, the energy released when an electron is added to fluorine is smaller than might be expected. This smaller energy release has been attributed to the small size of the $2p$ orbitals. Because the electrons must be very close together in these orbitals, there are unusually large electron–electron repulsions. In the other halogens with their larger orbitals, the repulsions are not as severe.

Atomic Radius

FIGURE 7.33
The radius of an atom (*r*) is defined as half the distance between the nuclei in a molecule consisting of identical atoms.

Just as the size of an orbital cannot be specified exactly, neither can the size of an atom. We must make some arbitrary choices to obtain values for **atomic radii.** These values can be obtained by measuring the distances between atoms in chemical compounds. For example, in the bromine molecule, the distance between the two nuclei is known to be 228 pm. The bromine atomic radius is assumed to be half this distance, or 114 pm, as shown in Fig. 7.33. These radii are often called *covalent atomic radii* because of the way they are determined (from the distances between atoms in covalent bonds).

For nonmetallic atoms that do not form diatomic molecules, the atomic radii are estimated from their various covalent compounds. The radii for metal atoms (called *metallic radii*) are obtained from half the distance between metal atoms in solid metal crystals.

The values of the atomic radii for the representative elements are shown in Fig. 7.34. Note that these values are significantly smaller than might be expected from the 90% electron density volumes of isolated atoms, because when atoms form bonds, their electron "clouds" interpenetrate. However, these values form a self-consistent data set that can be used to discuss the trends in atomic radii.

Note from Fig. 7.34 that the atomic radii decrease in going from left to right across a period. This decrease can be explained in terms of the increasing effective nuclear charge (decreasing shielding) in going from left to right. This means that the valence electrons are drawn closer to the nucleus, decreasing the size of the atom.

Atomic radius increases down a group, because of the increases in the orbital sizes in successive principal quantum levels.

Visualization: Determining the Atomic Radius of a Nonmetal (Chlorine)

Visualization: Determining the Atomic Radius of a Nonmetal (Carbon)

Sample Exercise 7.10

Trends in Radii

Predict the trend in radius for the following ions: Be^{2+}, Mg^{2+}, Ca^{2+}, and Sr^{2+}.

Solution

All these ions are formed by removing two electrons from an atom of a Group 2A element. In going from beryllium to strontium, we are going down the group, so the sizes increase:

$$Be^{2+} < Mg^{2+} < Ca^{2+} < Sr^{2+}$$

Smallest radius   Largest radius

See Exercises 7.85, 7.86, and 7.89.

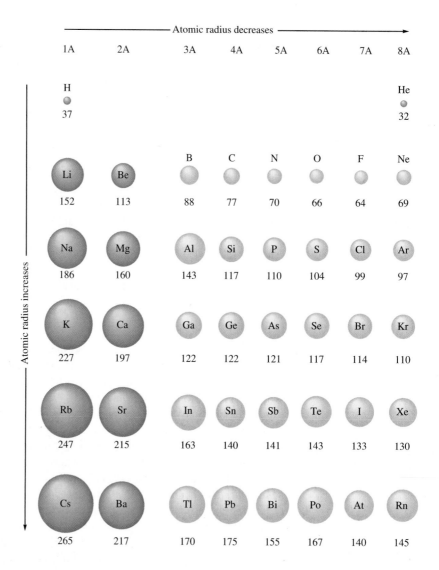

FIGURE 7.34
Atomic radii (in picometers) for selected atoms. Note that atomic radius decreases going across a period and increases going down a group. The values for the noble gases are estimated, because data from bonded atoms are lacking.

7.13 The Properties of a Group: The Alkali Metals

We have seen that the periodic table originated as a way to portray the systematic properties of the elements. Mendeleev was primarily responsible for first showing its usefulness in correlating and predicting the elemental properties. In this section we will summarize much of the information available from the table. We also will illustrate the usefulness of the table by discussing the properties of a representative group, the alkali metals.

Information Contained in the Periodic Table

1. The essence of the periodic table is that the groups of representative elements exhibit similar chemical properties that change in a regular way. The quantum mechanical model of the atom has allowed us to understand the basis for the similarity of properties in a group—that each group member has the same valence electron configuration. *It is the number and type of valence electrons that primarily determine an atom's chemistry.*

2. One of the most valuable types of information available from the periodic table is the electron configuration of any representative element. If you understand the organization

FIGURE 7.35
Special names for groups in the periodic table.

of the table, you will not need to memorize electron configurations for these elements. Although the predicted electron configurations for transition metals are sometimes incorrect, this is not a serious problem. You should, however, memorize the configurations of two exceptions, chromium and copper, since these $3d$ transition elements are found in many important compounds.

3. As we mentioned in Chapter 2, certain groups in the periodic table have special names. These are summarized in Fig. 7.35. Groups are often referred to by these names, so you should learn them.

Metals and nonmetals were first discussed in Chapter 2.

4. The most basic division of the elements in the periodic table is into metals and nonmetals. The most important chemical property of a metal atom is the tendency to give up one or more electrons to form a positive ion; metals tend to have low ionization energies. The metallic elements are found on the left side of the table, as shown in Fig. 7.35. The most chemically reactive metals are found on the lower left-hand portion of the table, where the ionization energies are smallest. The most distinctive chemical property of a nonmetal atom is the ability to gain one or more electrons to form an anion when reacting with a metal. Thus nonmetals are elements

with large ionization energies and the most negative electron affinities. The nonmetals are found on the right side of the table, with the most reactive ones in the upper right-hand corner, except for the noble gas elements, which are quite unreactive. The division into metals and nonmetals shown in Fig. 7.35 is only approximate. Many elements along the division line exhibit both metallic and nonmetallic properties under certain circumstances. These elements are often called **metalloids,** or sometimes **semimetals.**

The Alkali Metals

The metals of Group 1A, the alkali metals, illustrate very well the relationships among the properties of the elements in a group. Lithium, sodium, potassium, rubidium, cesium, and francium are the most chemically reactive of the metals. We will not discuss francium here because it occurs in nature in only very small quantities. Although hydrogen is found in Group 1A of the periodic table, it behaves as a nonmetal, in contrast to the other members of that group. The fundamental reason for hydrogen's nonmetallic character is its very small size (see Fig. 7.34). The electron in the small $1s$ orbital is bound tightly to the nucleus.

Hydrogen will be discussed further in Chapter 19.

Some important properties of the first five alkali metals are shown in Table 7.8. The data in Table 7.8 show that in going down the group, the first ionization energy decreases and the atomic radius increases. This agrees with the general trends discussed in Section 7.12.

The overall increase in density in going down Group 1A is typical of all groups. This occurs because atomic mass generally increases more rapidly than atomic size. Thus there is more mass per unit volume for each succeeding element.

Other groups will be discussed in Chapters 19 and 20.

The smooth decrease in melting point and boiling point in going down Group 1A is not typical; in most other groups more complicated behavior occurs. Note that the melting point of cesium is only 29°C. Cesium can be melted readily using only the heat from your hand. This is very unusual—metals typically have rather high melting points. For example, tungsten melts at 3410°C. The only other metals with low melting points are mercury (mp −38°C) and gallium (mp 30°C).

Oxidation–reduction reactions were discussed in Chapter 4.

The chemical property most characteristic of a metal is the ability to lose its valence electrons. The Group 1A elements are very reactive. They have low ionization energies and react with nonmetals to form ionic solids. A typical example involves the reaction of sodium with chlorine to form sodium chloride:

$$2Na(s) + Cl_2(g) \longrightarrow 2NaCl(s)$$

where sodium chloride contains Na^+ and Cl^- ions. This is an oxidation–reduction reaction in which chlorine oxidizes sodium. In the reactions between metals and nonmetals,

TABLE 7.8 Properties of Five Alkali Metals

Element	Valence Electron Configuration	Density at 25°C (g/cm³)	mp (°C)	bp (°C)	First Ionization Energy (kJ/mol)	Atomic (covalent) Radius (pm)	Ionic (M⁺) Radius (pm)
Li	$2s^1$	0.53	180	1330	520	152	60
Na	$3s^1$	0.97	98	892	495	186	95
K	$4s^1$	0.86	64	760	419	227	133
Rb	$5s^1$	1.53	39	668	409	247	148
Cs	$6s^1$	1.87	29	690	382	265	169

CHEMICAL IMPACT

Potassium—Too Much of a Good Thing Can Kill You

Potassium is widely recognized as an essential element. In fact, our daily requirement for potassium is more than twice that for sodium. Because most foods contain potassium, serious deficiency of this element in humans is rare. However, potassium deficiency can be caused by kidney malfunction or by the use of certain diuretics. Potassium deficiency leads to muscle weakness, irregular heartbeat, and depression.

Potassium is found in the fluids of the body as the K^+ ion, and its presence is essential to the operation of our nervous system. The passage of impulses along the nerves requires the flow of K^+ (and Na^+) through channels in the membranes of the nerve cells. Failure of this ion flow prevents nerve transmissions and results in death. For example, the black mamba snake kills its victims by injecting a venom that blocks the potassium channels in the nerve cells.

Although a steady intake of potassium is essential to preserve life, ironically, too much potassium can be lethal. In fact, the deadly ingredient in the drug mixture used for executing criminals is potassium chloride. Injection of a large amount of a potassium chloride solution produces an excess of K^+ ion in

The black mamba snake's venom kills by blocking the potassium channels in the nerve cells of victims.

the fluids surrounding the cells and prevents the essential flow of K^+ out the cells to allow nerve impulses to occur. This causes the heart to stop beating. Unlike other forms of execution, death by lethal injection of potassium chloride does not harm the organs of the body. Thus condemned criminals who are executed in this manner could potentially donate their organs for transplants. However, this idea is very controversial.

---

it is typical for the nonmetal to behave as the oxidizing agent and the metal to behave as the reducing agent, as shown by the following reactions:

$$2Na(s) + S(s) \longrightarrow Na_2S(s)$$
$$\text{Contains } Na^+ \text{ and } S^{2-} \text{ ions}$$

$$6Li(s) + N_2(g) \longrightarrow 2Li_3N(s)$$
$$\text{Contains } Li^+ \text{ and } N^{3-} \text{ ions}$$

$$2Na(s) + O_2(g) \longrightarrow Na_2O_2(s)$$
$$\text{Contains } Na^+ \text{ and } O_2{}^{2-} \text{ ions}$$

For reactions of the types just shown, the relative reducing powers of the alkali metals can be predicted from the first ionization energies listed in Table 7.8. Since it is much easier to remove an electron from a cesium atom than from a lithium atom, cesium should be the better reducing agent. The expected trend in reducing ability is

$$Cs > Rb > K > Na > Li$$

This order is observed experimentally for direct reactions between the solid alkali metals and nonmetals. However, this is not the order for reducing ability found when the alkali

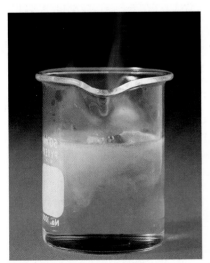

Potassium reacts violently with water.

TABLE 7.9 Hydration Energies for Li$^+$, Na$^+$, and K$^+$ Ions

Ion	Hydration Energy (kJ/mol)
Li$^+$	-510
Na$^+$	-402
K$^+$	-314

metals react in aqueous solution. For example, the reduction of water by an alkali metal is very vigorous and exothermic:

$$2M(s) + 2H_2O(l) \longrightarrow H_2(g) + 2M^+(aq) + 2OH^-(aq) + \text{energy}$$

The order of reducing abilities observed for this reaction for the first three group members is

$$\text{Li} > \text{K} > \text{Na}$$

In the gas phase potassium loses an electron more easily than sodium, and sodium more easily than lithium. Thus it is surprising that lithium is the best reducing agent toward water.

This reversal occurs because the formation of the M$^+$ ions in aqueous solution is strongly influenced by the hydration of these ions by the polar water molecules. The *hydration energy* of an ion represents the change in energy that occurs when water molecules attach to the M$^+$ ion. The hydration energies for the Li$^+$, Na$^+$, and K$^+$ ions (shown in Table 7.9) indicate that the process is exothermic in each case. However, nearly twice as much energy is released by the hydration of the Li$^+$ ion as for the K$^+$ ion. This difference is caused by size effects; the Li$^+$ ion is much smaller than the K$^+$ ion, and thus its *charge density* (charge per unit volume) is also much greater. This means that the polar water molecules are more strongly attracted to the small Li$^+$ ion. Because the Li$^+$ ion is so strongly hydrated, its formation from the lithium atom occurs more readily than the formation of the K$^+$ ion from the potassium atom. Although a potassium atom in the gas phase loses its valence electron more readily than a lithium atom in the gas phase, the opposite is true in aqueous solution. This anomaly is an example of the importance of the polarity of the water molecule in aqueous reactions.

There is one more surprise involving the highly exothermic reactions of the alkali metals with water. Experiments show that in water lithium is the best reducing agent, so we might expect that lithium should react the most violently with water. However, this is not true. Sodium and potassium react much more vigorously. Why is this so? The answer lies in the relatively high melting point of lithium. When sodium and potassium react with water, the heat evolved causes them to melt, giving a larger area of contact with water. Lithium, on the other hand, does not melt under these conditions and reacts more slowly. This illustrates the important principle (which we will discuss in detail in Chapter 12) that the energy change for a reaction and the rate at which it occurs are not necessarily related.

In this section we have seen that the trends in atomic properties summarized by the periodic table can be a great help in understanding the chemical behavior of the elements. This fact will be emphasized over and over as we proceed in our study of chemistry.

Key Terms

Section 7.1
electromagnetic radiation
wavelength
frequency

Section 7.2
Planck's constant
quantization
photon
photoelectric effect
$E = mc^2$
dual nature of light
diffraction
diffraction pattern

Section 7.3
continuous spectrum
line spectrum

For Review

Electromagnetic radiation
- Characterized by its wavelength (λ), frequency (ν), and speed ($c = 2.9979 \times 10^8$ m/s)

$$\lambda \nu = c$$

- Can be viewed as a stream of "particles" called photons, each with energy $h\nu$, where h is Planck's constant (6.626×10^{-34} J $\cdot$ s)

Photoelectric effect
- When light strikes a metal surface, electrons are emitted
- Analysis of the kinetic energy and numbers of the emitted electrons led Einstein to suggest that electromagnetic radiation can be viewed as a stream of photons

Hydrogen spectrum
- The emission spectrum of hydrogen shows discrete wavelengths
- Indicates that hydrogen has discrete energy levels

Bohr model of the hydrogen atom

- Using the data from the hydrogen spectrum and assuming angular momentum to be quantized, Bohr devised a model in which the electron traveled in circular orbits
- Although an important pioneering effort, this model proved to be entirely incorrect

Wave (quantum) mechanical model

- An electron is described as a standing wave
- The square of the wave function (often called an orbital) gives a probability distribution for the electron position
- The exact position of the electron is never known, which is consistent with the Heisenberg uncertainty principle: it is impossible to know accurately both the position and the momentum of a particle simultaneously
- Probability maps are used to define orbital shapes
- Orbitals are characterized by the quantum numbers n, ℓ, and m_ℓ

Electron spin

- Described by the spin quantum number m_s which can have values of $\pm\frac{1}{2}$
- Pauli exclusion principle: no two electrons in a given atom can have the same set of quantum numbers n, ℓ, m_ℓ, and m_s
- Only two electrons with opposite spins can occupy a given orbital

Periodic table

- By populating the orbitals from the wave mechanical model (the aufbau principle), the form of the periodic table can be explained
- According to the wave mechanical model, atoms in a given group have the same valence (outer) electron configuration
- The trends in properties such as ionization energies and atomic radii can be explained in terms of the concepts of nuclear attraction, electron repulsions, shielding, and penetration

REVIEW QUESTIONS

1. Four types of electromagnetic radiation (EMR) are ultraviolet, microwaves, gamma rays, and visible. All of these types of EMR can be characterized by wavelength, frequency, photon energy, and speed of travel. Define these terms and rank the four types of electromagnetic radiation in order of increasing wavelength, frequency, photon energy, and speed.

2. Characterize the Bohr model of the atom. In the Bohr model, what do we mean when we say something is quantized? How does the Bohr model of the hydrogen atom explain the hydrogen emission spectrum? Why is the Bohr model fundamentally incorrect?

3. What experimental evidence supports the quantum theory of light? Explain the wave-particle duality of all matter. For what size particles must one consider both the wave and the particle properties?

4. List the most important ideas of the quantum mechanical model of the atom. Include in your discussion the terms or names *wave function, orbital, Heisenberg uncertainty principle, de Broglie, Schrödinger,* and *probability distribution.*

5. What are quantum numbers? What information do we get from the quantum numbers n, ℓ, and m_ℓ? We define a spin quantum number (m_s), but do we know that an electron literally spins?

6. How do $2p$ orbitals differ from each other? How do $2p$ and $3p$ orbitals differ from each other? What is a nodal surface in an atomic orbital? What is wrong with $1p$, $1d$, $2d$, $1f$, $2f$, and $3f$ orbitals? Explain what we mean when we say that a $4s$ electron is more penetrating than a $3d$ electron.

7. Four blocks of elements in a periodic table refer to various atomic orbitals being filled. What are the four blocks and the corresponding orbitals? How do you get the energy ordering of the atomic orbitals from the periodic table? What is the aufbau principle? Hund's rule? The Pauli exclusion principle? There are two common exceptions to the ground-state electron configuration for elements 1–36 as predicted by the periodic table. What are they?

8. What is the difference between core electrons and valence electrons? Why do we emphasize the valence electrons in an atom when discussing atomic properties? What is the relationship between valence electrons and elements in the same group of the periodic table?

9. Using the element phosphorus as an example, write the equation for a process in which the energy change will correspond to the ionization energy and to the electron affinity.

   Explain why the first ionization energy tends to increase as one proceeds from left to right across a period. Why is the first ionization energy of aluminum lower than that of magnesium, and the first ionization energy of sulfur lower than that of phosphorus?

   Why do the successive ionization energies of an atom always increase? Note the successive ionization energies for silicon given in Table 7.5. Would you expect to see any large jumps between successive ionization energies of silicon as you removed all the electrons, one by one, beyond those shown in the table?

10. The radius trend and the ionization energy trend are exact opposites. Does this make sense? Define electron affinity. Electron affinity values are both exothermic (negative) and endothermic (positive). However, ionization energy values are always endothermic (positive). Explain.

Active Learning Questions

These questions are designed to be used by groups of students in class. The questions allow students to explore their understanding of concepts through discussion and peer teaching. The real value of these questions is the learning that occurs while students talk to each other about chemical concepts.

1. What does it mean for something to have wavelike properties? Particulate properties? Electromagnetic radiation can be discussed in terms of both particles and waves. Explain the experimental verification for each of these views.

2. Defend and criticize Bohr's model. Why was it reasonable that such a model was proposed, and what evidence was there that it "works"? Why do we no longer "believe" in it?

3. The first four ionization energies for the elements X and Y are shown below. The units are not kJ/mol.

	X	Y
First	170	200
Second	350	400
Third	1800	3500
Fourth	2500	5000

   Identify the elements X and Y. There may be more than one correct answer, so explain completely.

4. Compare the first ionization energy of helium to its second ionization energy, remembering that both electrons come from the $1s$ orbital. Explain the difference without using actual numbers from the text.

5. Which has the larger second ionization energy, lithium or beryllium? Why?

6. Explain why a graph of ionization energy versus atomic number (across a row) is not linear. Where are the exceptions? Why are there exceptions?

7. Without referring to your text, predict the trend of second ionization energies for the elements sodium through argon. Compare your answer with Table 7.5. Explain any differences.

8. Account for the fact that the line that separates the metals from the nonmetals on the periodic table is diagonal downward to the right instead of horizontal or vertical.

9. Explain *electron* from a quantum mechanical perspective, including a discussion of atomic radii, probabilities, and orbitals.

10. Choose the best response for the following. The ionization energy for the chlorine atom is equal in magnitude to the electron affinity for
   a. the Cl atom.
   b. the Cl^- ion.
   c. the Cl^+ ion.
   d. the F atom.
   e. none of these.

Explain each choice. Justify your choice, and for the choices you did not select, explain what is incorrect about them.

11. Consider the following statement: "The ionization energy for the potassium atom is negative, because when K loses an electron to become K^+, it achieves a noble gas electron configuration." Indicate everything that is correct in this statement. Indicate everything that is incorrect. Correct the incorrect information and explain.

12. In going across a row of the periodic table, electrons are added and ionization energy generally increases. In going down a column of the periodic table, electrons are also being added but ionization energy decreases. Explain.

13. How does probability fit into the description of the atom?

14. What is meant by an *orbital?*

A blue question or exercise number indicates that the answer to that question or exercise appears at the back of the book and a solution appears in the *Solutions Guide.*

Questions

15. What type of relationship (direct or inverse) exists between wavelength, frequency, and photon energy? What does a photon energy unit of a Joule equal?

16. Explain the photoelectric effect.

17. How does the wavelength of a fast-pitched baseball compare to the wavelength of an electron traveling at 1/10 the speed of light? What is the significance of this comparison? See Sample Exercise 7.3.

18. The Bohr model only works for one electron species. Why do we discuss it in this text (what's good about it)?

19. Describe the significance of the radial probability distribution shown in Fig. 7.12(b).

20. The periodic table consists of four blocks of elements which correspond to *s*, *p*, *d*, and *f* orbitals being filled. After *f* orbitals come *g* and *h* orbitals. In theory, if a *g* block and an *h* block of elements existed, how long would the rows of *g* and *h* elements be in this theoretical periodic table?

21. Many times the claim is made that subshells half-filled with electrons are particularly stable. Can you suggest a possible physical basis for this claim?

22. Diagonal relationships in the periodic table exist as well as the vertical relationships. For example, Be and Al are similar in some of their properties, as are B and Si. Rationalize why these diagonal relationships hold for properties such as size, ionization energy, and electron affinity.

23. Elements with very large ionization energies also tend to have highly exothermic electron affinities. Explain. Which group of elements would you expect to be an exception to this statement?

24. The changes in electron affinity as one goes down a group in the periodic table are not nearly as large as the variations in ionization energies. Why?

25. Why is it much harder to explain the line spectra of polyelectronic atoms and ions than it is to explain the line spectra of hydrogen and hydrogenlike ions?

26. Scientists use emission spectra to confirm the presence of an element in materials of unknown composition. Why is this possible?

27. Does the minimization of electron–electron repulsions correlate with Hund's rule?

28. In the hydrogen atom, what is the physical significance of the state for which $n = \infty$ and $E = 0$?

29. The work function is the energy required to remove an electron from an atom on the surface of a metal. How does this definition differ from that for ionization energy?

30. Many more anhydrous lithium salts are hygroscopic (readily absorb water) than are those of the other alkali metals. Explain.

Exercises

In this section similar exercises are paired.

Light and Matter

31. Photosynthesis uses 660-nm light to convert CO_2 and H_2O into glucose and O_2. Calculate the frequency of this light.

32. An FM radio station broadcasts at 99.5 MHz. Calculate the wavelength of the corresponding radio waves.

33. Microwave radiation has a wavelength on the order of 1.0 cm. Calculate the frequency and the energy of a single photon of this radiation. Calculate the energy of an Avogadro's number of photons (called an *einstein*) of this radiation.

34. A photon of ultraviolet (UV) light possesses enough energy to mutate a strand of human DNA. What is the energy of a single UV photon and a mole of UV photons having a wavelength of 25 nm?

35. Consider the following waves representing electromagnetic radiation:

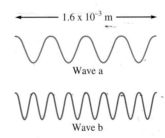

Wave a

Wave b

Which wave has the longer wavelength? Calculate the wavelength. Which wave has the higher frequency and larger photon energy? Calculate these values. Which wave has the faster velocity? What type of electromagnetic radiation are illustrated?

36. One type of electromagnetic radiation has a frequency of 107.1 MHz, another type has a wavelength of 2.12×10^{-10} m, and another type of electromagnetic radiation has photons with energy equal to 3.97×10^{-19} J/photon. Identify each type of electromagnetic radiation and place them in order of increasing photon energy and increasing frequency.

37. Carbon absorbs energy at a wavelength of 150. nm. The total amount of energy emitted by a carbon sample is 1.98×10^5 J. Calculate the number of carbon atoms present in the sample, assuming that each atom emits one photon.

38. A carbon–oxygen double bond in a certain organic molecule absorbs radiation that has a frequency of 6.0×10^{13} s^{-1}.
a. What is the wavelength of this radiation?
b. To what region of the spectrum does this radiation belong?
c. What is the energy of this radiation per photon? Per mole of photons?
d. A carbon–oxygen bond in a different molecule absorbs radiation with frequency equal to 5.4×10^{13} s^{-1}. Is this radiation more or less energetic?

39. The work function of an element is the energy required to remove an electron from the surface of the solid element. The work function for lithium is 279.7 kJ/mol (that is, it takes 279.7 kJ of energy to remove one mole of electrons from one mole of Li atoms on the surface of Li metal). What is the maximum wavelength of light that can remove an electron from an atom on the surface of lithium metal?

40. It takes 208.4 kJ of energy to remove 1 mole of electrons from an atom on the surface of rubidium metal. How much energy does it take to remove a single electron from an atom on the surface of solid rubidium? What is the maximum wavelength of light capable of doing this?

41. Calculate the de Broglie wavelength for each of the following.
a. an electron with a velocity 10.% of the speed of light
b. a tennis ball (55 g) served at 35 m/s ($\sim$80 mi/h)

42. Neutron diffraction is used in determining the structures of molecules.
a. Calculate the de Broglie wavelength of a neutron moving at 1.00% of the speed of light.
b. Calculate the velocity of a neutron with a wavelength of 75 pm (1 pm = 10^{-12} m).

43. A particle has a velocity that is 90.% of the speed of light. If the wavelength of the particle is 1.5×10^{-15} m, calculate the mass of the particle.

44. Calculate the velocities of electrons with de Broglie wavelengths of 1.0×10^2 nm and 1.0 nm, respectively.

Hydrogen Atom: The Bohr Model

45. Calculate the wavelength of light emitted when each of the following transitions occur in the hydrogen atom. What type of electromagnetic radiation is emitted in each transition?
a. $n = 3 \rightarrow n = 2$
b. $n = 4 \rightarrow n = 2$
c. $n = 2 \rightarrow n = 1$

46. Calculate the wavelength of light emitted when each of the following transitions occur in the hydrogen atom. What type of electromagnetic radiation is emitted in each transition?
a. $n = 4 \rightarrow n = 3$
b. $n = 5 \rightarrow n = 4$
c. $n = 5 \rightarrow n = 3$

47. Using vertical lines, indicate the transitions from Exercise 45 on an energy-level diagram for the hydrogen atom (see Fig. 7.8).

48. Using vertical lines, indicate the transitions from Exercise 46 on an energy-level diagram for the hydrogen atom (see Fig. 7.8).

49. Does a photon of visible light ($\lambda \approx 400$ to 700 nm) have sufficient energy to excite an electron in a hydrogen atom from the $n = 1$ to the $n = 5$ energy state? from the $n = 2$ to the $n = 6$ energy state?

50. An electron is excited from the $n = 1$ ground state to the $n = 3$ state in a hydrogen atom. Which of the following statements are true? Correct the false statements to make them true.
a. It takes more energy to ionize (completely remove) the electron from $n = 3$ than from the ground state.
b. The electron is farther from the nucleus on average in the $n = 3$ state than in the $n = 1$ state.
c. The wavelength of light emitted if the electron drops from $n = 3$ to $n = 2$ will be shorter than the wavelength of light emitted if the electron falls from $n = 3$ to $n = 1$.
d. The wavelength of light emitted when the electron returns to the ground state from $n = 3$ will be the same as the wavelength of light absorbed to go from $n = 1$ to $n = 3$.
e. For $n = 3$, the electron is in the first excited state.

51. Calculate the maximum wavelength of light capable of removing an electron for a hydrogen atom from the energy state characterized by $n = 1$: by $n = 2$.

52. Consider an electron for a hydrogen atom in an excited state. The maximum wavelength of electromagnetic radiation that can completely remove (ionize) the electron from the H atom is 1460 nm. What is the initial excited state for the electron ($n = $?)?

53. An excited hydrogen atom with an electron in the $n = 5$ state emits light having a frequency of 6.90×10^{14} s^{-1}. Determine the principal quantum level for the final state in this electronic transition.

54. An excited hydrogen atom emits light with a wavelength of 397.2 nm to reach the energy level for which $n = 2$. In which principal quantum level did the electron begin?

Quantum Mechanics, Quantum Numbers, and Orbitals

55. Using the Heisenberg uncertainty principle, calculate Δx for each of the following.
a. an electron with $\Delta v = 0.100$ m/s
b. a baseball (mass = 145 g) with $\Delta v = 0.100$ m/s
c. How does the answer in part a compare with the size of a hydrogen atom?
d. How does the answer in part b correspond to the size of a baseball?

56. The Heisenberg uncertainty principle can be expressed in the form

$$\Delta E \cdot \Delta t \geq \frac{h}{4\pi}$$

where E represents energy and t represents time. Show that the units for this form are the same as the units for the form used in this chapter:

$$\Delta x \cdot \Delta(mv) \geq \frac{h}{4\pi}$$

57. What are the possible values for the quantum numbers n, ℓ, and m_ℓ?

58. Which of the following orbital designations are incorrect: 1s, 1p, 7d, 9s, 3f, 4f, 2d?

59. Which of the following sets of quantum numbers are not allowed in the hydrogen atom? For the sets of quantum numbers that are incorrect, state what is wrong in each set.
   a. $n = 3, \ell = 2, m_\ell = 2$
   b. $n = 4, \ell = 3, m_\ell = 4$
   c. $n = 0, \ell = 0, m_\ell = 0$
   d. $n = 2, \ell = -1, m_\ell = 1$

60. Which of the following sets of quantum numbers are not allowed? For each incorrect set, state why it is incorrect.
   a. $n = 3, \ell = 3, m_\ell = 0, m_s = -\frac{1}{2}$
   b. $n = 4, \ell = 3, m_\ell = 2, m_s = -\frac{1}{2}$
   c. $n = 4, \ell = 1, m_\ell = 1, m_s = +\frac{1}{2}$
   d. $n = 2, \ell = 1, m_\ell = -1, m_s = -1$
   e. $n = 5, \ell = -4, m_\ell = 2, m_s = +\frac{1}{2}$
   f. $n = 3, \ell = 1, m_\ell = 2, m_s = -\frac{1}{2}$

61. What is the physical significance of the value of ψ^2 at a particular point in an atomic orbital?

62. In defining the sizes of orbitals, why must we use an arbitrary value, such as 90% of the probability of finding an electron in that region?

Polyelectronic Atoms

63. How many orbitals in an atom can have the designation 5p, $3d_{z^2}$, 4d, n = 5, n = 4?

64. How many electrons in an atom can have the designation 1p, $6d_{x^2-y^2}$, 4f, $7p_y$, 2s, n = 3?

65. Give the maximum number of electrons in an atom that can have these quantum numbers:
   a. $n = 4$
   b. $n = 5, m_\ell = +1$
   c. $n = 5, m_s = +\frac{1}{2}$
   d. $n = 3, \ell = 2$
   e. $n = 2, \ell = 1$

66. Give the maximum number of electrons in an atom that can have these quantum numbers:
   a. $n = 0, \ell = 0, m_\ell = 0$
   b. $n = 2, \ell = 1, m_\ell = -1, m_s = -\frac{1}{2}$
   c. $n = 3, m_s = +\frac{1}{2}$
   d. $n = 2, \ell = 2$
   e. $n = 1, \ell = 0, m_\ell = 0$

67. Draw atomic orbital diagrams representing the ground-state electron configuration for each of the following elements.
   a. Na
   b. Co
   c. Kr
   How many unpaired electrons are present in each element?

68. For elements 1–36, there are two exceptions to the filling order as predicted from the periodic table. Draw the atomic orbital diagrams for the two exceptions and indicate how many unpaired electrons are present.

69. The elements Si, Ga, As, Ge, Al, Cd, S, and Se are all used in the manufacture of various semiconductor devices. Write the expected electron configuration for these atoms.

70. The elements Cu, O, La, Y, Ba, Tl, and Bi are all found in high-temperature ceramic superconductors. Write the expected electron configuration for these atoms.

71. Write the expected electron configurations for each of the following atoms: Sc, Fe, P, Cs, Eu, Pt, Xe, Br.

72. Write the expected electron configurations for each of the following atoms: Cl, Sb, Sr, W, Pb, Cf.

73. Write the expected ground-state electron configuration for the following.
   a. the element with one unpaired 5p electron that forms a covalent with compound fluorine
   b. the (as yet undiscovered) alkaline earth metal after radium
   c. the noble gas with electrons occupying 4f orbitals
   d. the first-row transition metal with the most unpaired electrons

74. Using only the periodic table inside the front cover of the text, write the expected ground-state electron configurations for
   a. the third element in Group 5A.
   b. element number 116.
   c. an element with three unpaired 5d electrons.
   d. the halogen with electrons in the 6p atomic orbitals.

75. In the ground state of mercury, Hg,
   a. how many electrons occupy atomic orbitals with n = 3?
   b. how many electrons occupy d atomic orbitals?
   c. how many electrons occupy p_z atomic orbitals?
   d. how many electrons have spin "up" ($m_s = +\frac{1}{2}$)?

76. In the ground state of element 115, Uup,
   a. how many electrons have n = 5 as one of their quantum numbers?
   b. how many electrons have $\ell = 3$ as one of their quantum numbers?
   c. how many electrons have $m_\ell = 1$ as one of their quantum numbers?
   d. how many electrons have $m_s = -\frac{1}{2}$ as one of their quantum numbers?

77. Give a possible set of values of the four quantum numbers for all the electrons in a boron atom and a nitrogen atom if each is in the ground state.

78. Give a possible set of values of the four quantum numbers for the 4s and 3d electrons in titanium.

79. A certain oxygen atom has the electron configuration $1s^2 2s^2 2p_x^2 2p_y^2$. How many unpaired electrons are present? Is this an excited state of oxygen? In going from this state to the ground state would energy be released or absorbed?

80. Which of the following electron configurations correspond to an excited state? Identify the atoms and write the ground-state electron configuration where appropriate.
   a. $1s^2 2s^2 3p^1$
   b. $1s^2 2s^2 2p^6$
   c. $1s^2 2s^2 2p^4 3s^1$
   d. $[Ar]4s^2 3d^5 4p^1$
   How many unpaired electrons are present in each of these species?

81. Which of elements 1–36 have two unpaired electrons in the ground state?

82. Which of elements 1–36 have one unpaired electron in the ground state?

83. One bit of evidence that the quantum mechanical model is "correct" lies in the magnetic properties of matter. Atoms with unpaired electrons are attracted by magnetic fields and thus are said to exhibit *paramagnetism*. The degree to which this effect is observed is directly related to the number of unpaired electrons present in the atom. Consider the ground-state electron configurations for Li, N, Ni, Te, Ba, and Hg. Which of these atoms would be expected to be paramagnetic, and how many unpaired electrons are present in each paramagnetic atom?

84. How many unpaired electrons are present in each of the following in the ground state: O, O^+, O^-, Os, Zr, S, F, Ar?

The Periodic Table and Periodic Properties

85. Arrange the following groups of atoms in order of increasing size.
a. Te, S, Se
b. K, Br, Ni
c. Ba, Si, F

86. Arrange the following groups of atoms in order of increasing size.
a. Rb, Na, Be
b. Sr, Se, Ne
c. Fe, P, O

87. Arrange the atoms in Exercise 85 in order of increasing first ionization energy.

88. Arrange the atoms in Exercise 86 in order of increasing first ionization energy.

89. In each of the following sets, which atom or ion has the smallest radius?
a. H, He
b. Cl, In, Se
c. element 120, element 119, element 117
d. Nb, Zn, Si
e. Na^-, Na, Na^+

90. In each of the following sets, which atom or ion has the smallest ionization energy?
a. Ca, Sr, Ba
b. K, Mn, Ga
c. N, O, F
d. S^{2-}, S, S^{2+}
e. Cs, Ge, Ar

91. Element 106 has been named seaborgium, Sg, in honor of Glenn Seaborg, discoverer of the first transuranium element.
a. Write the expected electron configuration for element 106.
b. What other element would be most like element 106 in its properties?
c. Write the formula for a possible oxide and a possible oxyanion of element 106.

92. Predict some of the properties of element 117 (the symbol is Uus, following conventions proposed by the International Union of Pure and Applied Chemistry, or IUPAC).

a. What will be its electron configuration?
b. What element will it most resemble chemically?
c. What will be the formula of the neutral binary compounds it forms with sodium, magnesium, carbon, and oxygen?
d. What oxyanions would you expect Uus to form?

93. The first ionization energies of As and Se are 0.947 and 0.941 MJ/mol, respectively. Rationalize these values in terms of electron configurations.

94. Rank the elements Be, B, C, N, and O in order of increasing first ionization energy. Explain your reasoning.

95. For each of the following pairs of elements

$$(C \text{ and } N) \qquad (Ar \text{ and } Br)$$

pick the atom with
a. more favorable (exothermic) electron affinity.
b. higher ionization energy.
c. larger size.

96. For each of the following pairs of elements

$$(Mg \text{ and } K) \qquad (F \text{ and } Cl)$$

pick the atom with
a. more favorable (exothermic) electron affinity.
b. higher ionization energy.
c. larger size.

97. The electron affinities of the elements from aluminum to chlorine are −44, −120, −74, −200.4, and −384.7 kJ/mol, respectively. Rationalize the trend in these values.

98. The electron affinity for sulfur is more exothermic than that for oxygen. How do you account for this?

99. Order each of the following sets from the least exothermic electron affinity to the most exothermic electron affinity.
a. F, Cl, Br, I   **b.** N, O, F

100. Which has the more negative electron affinity, the oxygen atom or the O^- ion? Explain your answer.

101. Write equations corresponding to the following.
a. The fourth ionization energy of Se
b. The electron affinity of S^-
c. The electron affinity of Fe^{3+}
d. The ionization energy of Mg

102. Using data from the text, determine the following values (justify your answer):
a. the electron affinity of Mg^{2+}
b. the ionization energy of Cl^-
c. the electron affinity of Cl^+
d. the ionization energy of Mg^- (Electron affinity of Mg = 230 kJ/mol)

Alkali Metals

103. An ionic compound of potassium and oxygen has the empirical formula KO. Would you expect this compound to be potassium(II) oxide or potassium peroxide? Explain.

104. Give the name and formula of each of the binary compounds formed from the following elements.
a. Li and N
b. Na and Br
c. K and S

105. Cesium was discovered in natural mineral waters in 1860 by R. W. Bunsen and G. R. Kirchhoff using the spectroscope they invented in 1859. The name came from the Latin *caesius* ("sky blue") because of the prominent blue line observed for this element at 455.5 nm. Calculate the frequency and energy of a photon of this light.

106. The bright yellow light emitted by a sodium vapor lamp consists of two emission lines at 589.0 and 589.6 nm. What are the frequency and the energy of a photon of light at each of these wavelengths? What are the energies in kJ/mol?

107. Does the information on alkali metals in Table 7.8 of the text confirm the general periodic trends in ionization energy and atomic radius? Explain.

108. Predict the atomic number of the next alkali metal after francium and give its ground-state electron configuration.

109. Complete and balance the equations for the following reactions.
 a. $Li(s) + N_2(g) \rightarrow$
 b. $Rb(s) + S(s) \rightarrow$

110. Complete and balance the equations for the following reactions.
 a. $Cs(s) + H_2O(l) \rightarrow$
 b. $Na(s) + Cl_2(g) \rightarrow$

Additional Exercises

111. Photogray lenses incorporate small amounts of silver chloride in the glass of the lens. When light hits the AgCl particles, the following reaction occurs:

$$AgCl \xrightarrow{h\nu} Ag + Cl$$

The silver metal that is formed causes the lenses to darken. The enthalpy change for this reaction is 3.10×10^2 kJ/mol. Assuming all this energy must be supplied by light, what is the maximum wavelength of light that can cause this reaction?

112. A certain microwave oven delivers 750. watts (joule/s) of power to a coffee cup containing 50.0 g of water at 25.0°C. If the wavelength of microwaves in the oven is 9.75 cm, how long does it take, and how many photons must be absorbed, to make the water boil? The specific heat capacity of water is 4.18 J/°C · g and assume only the water absorbs the energy of the microwaves.

113. Mars is roughly 60 million km from earth. How long does it take for a radio signal originating from earth to reach Mars?

114. Consider the following approximate visible light spectrum:

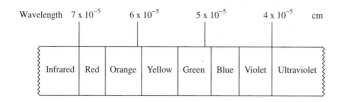

Barium emits light in the visible region of the spectrum. If each photon of light emitted from barium has an energy of 3.59×10^{-19} J, what color of visible light is emitted?

115. One of the visible lines in the hydrogen emission spectrum corresponds to the $n = 6$ to $n = 2$ electronic transition. What color light is this transition? See Exercise 114.

116. Using Fig. 7.28, list the elements (ignore the lanthanides and actinides) that have ground-state electron configurations that differ from those we would expect from their positions in the periodic table.

117. Are the following statements true for the hydrogen atom only, true for all atoms, or not true for any atoms?
 a. The principal quantum number completely determines the energy of a given electron.
 b. The angular momentum quantum number, ℓ, determines the shapes of the atomic orbitals.
 c. The magnetic quantum number, m_ℓ, determines the direction that the atomic orbitals point in space.

118. Although no currently known elements contain electrons in *g* orbitals in the ground state, it is possible that these elements will be found or that electrons in excited states of known elements could be in *g* orbitals. For *g* orbitals, the value of ℓ is 4. What is the lowest value of *n* for which *g* orbitals could exist? What are the possible values of m_ℓ? How many electrons could a set of *g* orbitals hold?

119. Consider the representations of the *p* and *d* atomic orbitals in Figs. 7.14 and 7.16. What do the $+$ and $-$ signs indicate?

120. Total radial probability distributions for the helium, neon, and argon atoms are shown in the following graph. How can one interpret the shapes of these curves in terms of electron configurations, quantum numbers, and nuclear charges?

121. The following graph plots the first, second, and third ionization energies for Mg, Al, and Si.

Without referencing the text, which plot corresponds to which element? In one of the plots, there is a huge jump in energy between I_2 and I_3, unlike in the other two plots. Explain this phenomenon.

122. An ion having a 4+ charge and a mass of 49.9 amu has 2 electrons with principal quantum number $n = 1$, 8 electrons with $n = 2$, and 10 electrons with $n = 3$. Supply as many of the properties for the ion as possible from the information given. *Hint:* In forming ions for this species, the $4s$ electrons are lost before the $3d$ electrons.
   a. the atomic number
   b. total number of s electrons
   c. total number of p electrons
   d. total number of d electrons
   e. the number of neutrons in the nucleus
   f. the ground-state electron configuration of the neutral atom

123. The successive ionization energies for an unknown element are
   $I_1 = 896$ kJ/mol
   $I_2 = 1752$ kJ/mol
   $I_3 = 14{,}807$ kJ/mol
   $I_4 = 17{,}948$ kJ/mol
   To which family in the periodic table does the unknown element most likely belong?

124. An unknown element is a nonmetal and has a valence electron configuration of ns^2np^4.
   a. How many valence electrons does this element have?
   b. What are some possible identities for this element?
   c. What is the formula of the compound this element would form with potassium?
   d. Would this element have a larger or smaller radius than barium?
   e. Would this element have a greater or smaller ionization energy than fluorine?

125. Using data from this chapter, calculate the change in energy expected for each of the following processes.
   a. $Na(g) + Cl(g) \rightarrow Na^+(g) + Cl^-(g)$
   b. $Mg(g) + F(g) \rightarrow Mg^+(g) + F^-(g)$
   c. $Mg^+(g) + F(g) \rightarrow Mg^{2+}(g) + F^-(g)$
   d. $Mg(g) + 2F(g) \rightarrow Mg^{2+}(g) + 2F^-(g)$

Challenge Problems

126. One of the emission spectral lines for Be^{3+} has a wavelength of 253.4 nm for an electronic transition that begins in the state with $n = 5$. What is the principal quantum number of the lower-energy state corresponding to this emission? (*Hint:* The Bohr model can be applied to one-electron ions. Don't forget the Z factor: Z = nuclear charge = atomic number.)

127. The figure below represents part of the emission spectrum for a one-electron ion in the gas phase. All the lines result from electronic transitions from excited states to the $n = 3$ state. (See Exercise 126.)

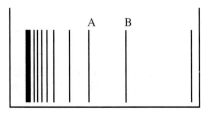

Wavelength →

a. What electronic transitions correspond to lines A and B?
b. If the wavelength of line B is 142.5 nm, calculate the wavelength of line A.

128. When the excited electron in a hydrogen atom falls from $n = 5$ to $n = 2$, a photon of blue light is emitted. if an excited electron in He^+ falls from $n = 4$, to which energy level must it fall so that a similar blue light (as with the hydrogen) is emitted? Prove it. (See Exercise 126.)

129. The wave function for the $2p_z$ orbital in the hydrogen atom is

$$\psi_{2p_z} = \frac{1}{4\sqrt{2\pi}} \left(\frac{Z}{a_0}\right)^{3/2} \sigma e^{-\sigma/2} \cos\theta$$

where a_0 is the value for the radius of the first Bohr orbit in meters (5.29×10^{-11}), σ is $Z(r/a_0)$, r is the value for the distance from the nucleus in meters, and θ is an angle. Calculate the value of $\psi_{2p_z}{}^2$ at $r = a_0$ for $\theta = 0$ (z axis) and for $\theta = 90°$ (xy plane).

130. Answer the following questions assuming that m_s could have three values rather than two and that the rules for n, ℓ, and m_ℓ are the normal ones.
   a. How many electrons would an orbital be able to hold?
   b. How many elements would the first and second periods in the periodic table contain?
   c. How many elements would be contained in the first transition metal series?
   d. How many electrons would the set of $4f$ orbitals be able to hold?

131. Assume that we are in another universe with different physical laws. Electrons in this universe are described by four quantum numbers with meanings similar to those we use. We will call these quantum numbers p, q, r, and s. The rules for these quantum numbers are as follows:

$p = 1, 2, 3, 4, 5, \dots$.
q takes on positive odd integer and $q \leq p$.
r takes on all even integer values from $-q$ to $+q$. (Zero is considered an even number.)
$s = +\frac{1}{2}$ or $-\frac{1}{2}$

   a. Sketch what the first four periods of the periodic table will look like in this universe.
   b. What are the atomic numbers of the first four elements you would expect to be least reactive?
   c. Give an example, using elements in the first four rows, of ionic compounds with the formulas XY, XY_2, X_2Y, XY_3, and X_2Y_3.
   d. How many electrons can have $p = 4$, $q = 3$?
   e. How many electrons can have $p = 3$, $q = 0$, $r = 0$?
   f. How many electrons can have $p = 6$?

132. Without looking at data in the text, sketch a qualitative graph of the third ionization energy versus atomic number for the elements Na through Ar, and explain your graph.

133. The following numbers are the ratios of second ionization energy to first ionization energy:

Na: 9.2
Mg: 2.0
Al: 3.1
Si: 2.0

P: 1.8
S: 2.3
Cl: 1.8
Ar: 1.8

Explain these relative numbers.

134. We expect the atomic radius to increase going down a group in the periodic table. Can you suggest why the atomic radius of hafnium breaks this rule? (See data below.)

Atomic Radii, in pm			
Sc	157	Ti	147.7
Y	169.3	Zr	159.3
La	191.5	Hf	147.6

135. Consider the following ionization energies for aluminum:

$$Al(g) \longrightarrow Al^+(g) + e^- \qquad I_1 = 580 \text{ kJ/mol}$$
$$Al^+(g) \longrightarrow Al^{2+}(g) + e^- \qquad I_2 = 1815 \text{ kJ/mol}$$
$$Al^{2+}(g) \longrightarrow Al^{3+}(g) + e^- \qquad I_3 = 2740 \text{ kJ/mol}$$
$$Al^{3+}(g) \longrightarrow Al^{4+}(g) + e^- \qquad I_4 = 11,600 \text{ kJ/mol}$$

a. Account for the trend in the values of the ionization energies.
b. Explain the large increase between I_3 and I_4.
c. Which one of the four ions has the greatest electron affinity? Explain.
d. List the four aluminum ions given in order of increasing size, and explain your ordering. (*Hint:* Remember that most of the size of an atom or ion is due to its electrons.)

136. While Mendeleev predicted the existence of several undiscovered elements, he did not predict the existence of the noble gases, the lanthanides, or the actinides. Propose reasons why Mendeleev was not able to predict the existence of the noble gases.

137. An atom of a particular element is traveling at 1.00% of the speed of light. The de Broglie wavelength is found to be 3.31×10^{-3} pm. Which element is this? Prove it.

Integrative Problems

These problems require the integration of multiple concepts to find the solutions.

138. As the weapons officer aboard the *Starship Chemistry,* it is your duty to configure a photon torpedo to remove an electron from the outer hull of an enemy vessel. You know that the work function (the binding energy of the electron) of the hull of the enemy ship is 7.52×10^{-19} J.

a. What wavelength does your photon torpedo need to be to eject an electron?
b. You find an extra photon torpedo with a wavelength of 259 nm and fire it at the enemy vessel. Does this photon torpedo do any damage to the ship (does it eject an electron)?
c. If the hull of the enemy vessel is made of the element with an electron configuration of $[Ar]4s^13d^{10}$, what metal is this?

139. Francium, Fr, is a radioactive element found in some uranium minerals and is formed as a result of the decay of actinium.
a. What are the electron configurations of francium and its predicted most common ion?
b. It has been estimated that at any one time, there is only one (1.0) ounce of francium on earth. Assuming this is true, what number of francium atoms exist on earth?
c. The longest-lived isotope of francium is ^{223}Fr. What is the total mass in grams of the neutrons in one atom of this isotope?

140. Answer the following questions based on the given electron configurations and identify the elements.
a. Arrange these atoms in order of increasing size: $[Kr]5s^24d^{10}5p^6$; $[Kr]5s^24d^{10}5p^1$; $[Kr]5s^24d^{10}5p^3$.
b. Arrange these atoms in order of decreasing first ionization energy: $[Ne]3s^23p^5$; $[Ar]4s^23d^{10}4p^3$; $[Ar]4s^23d^{10}4p^5$.

Marathon Problem*

This problem is designed to incorporate several concepts and techniques into one situation. Marathon Problems can be used in class by groups of students to help facilitate problem-solving skills.

141. From the information below, identify element X.
a. The wavelength of the radio waves sent by an FM station broadcasting at 97.1 MHz is 30.0 million (3.00×10^7) times greater than the wavelength corresponding to the energy difference between a particular excited state of the hydrogen atom and the ground state.
b. Let *V* represent the principal quantum number for the valence shell of element X. If an electron in the hydrogen atom falls from shell *V* to the inner shell corresponding to the excited state mentioned above in part a, the wavelength of light emitted is the same as the wavelength of an electron moving at a speed of 570. m/s.
c. The number of unpaired electrons for element X in the ground state is the same as the maximum number of electrons in an atom that can have the quantum number designations $n = 2$, $m_\ell = -1$, and $m_s = -\frac{1}{2}$.
d. Let *A* equal the charge of the stable ion that would form when the undiscovered element 120 forms ionic compounds. This value of *A* also represents the angular momentum quantum number for the subshell containing the unpaired electron(s) for element X.

 Get help understanding core concepts and visualizing molecular-level interactions, and practice problem solving, by visiting the Online Study Center at **college.hmco.com/ PIC/zumdahl7e.**

*Used with permission from the *Journal of Chemical Education,* Vol. 68, No. 11, 1991, pp. 919–922; copyright © 1991, Division of Chemical Education, Inc.

8 Bonding: General Concepts

Contents

Carbon forms very stable spherical C$_{60}$ molecules.

As we examine the world around us, we find it to be composed almost entirely of compounds and mixtures of compounds: Rocks, coal, soil, petroleum, trees, and human bodies are all complex mixtures of chemical compounds in which different kinds of atoms are bound together. Substances composed of unbound atoms do exist in nature, but they are very rare. Examples are the argon in the atmosphere and the helium mixed with natural gas reserves.

The manner in which atoms are bound together has a profound effect on chemical and physical properties. For example, graphite is a soft, slippery material used as a lubricant in locks, and diamond is one of the hardest materials known, valuable both as a gemstone and in industrial cutting tools. Why do these materials, both composed solely of carbon atoms, have such different properties? The answer, as we will see, lies in the bonding in these substances.

Silicon and carbon are next to each other in Group 4A of the periodic table. From our knowledge of periodic trends, we might expect SiO_2 and CO_2 to be very similar. But SiO_2 is the empirical formula of silica, which is found in sand and quartz, and carbon dioxide is a gas, a product of respiration. Why are they so different? We will be able to answer this question after we have developed models for bonding.

Molecular bonding and structure play the central role in determining the course of all chemical reactions, many of which are vital to our survival. Later in this book we will demonstrate their importance by showing how enzymes facilitate complex chemical reactions, how genetic characteristics are transferred, and how hemoglobin in the blood carries oxygen throughout the body. All of these fundamental biological reactions hinge on the geometric structures of molecules, sometimes depending on very subtle differences in molecular shape to channel the chemical reaction one way rather than another.

Many of the world's current problems require fundamentally chemical answers: disease and pollution control, the search for new energy sources, the development of new fertilizers to increase crop yields, the improvement of the protein content in various staple grains, and many more. To understand the behavior of natural materials, we must understand the nature of chemical bonding and the factors that control the structures of

Quartz grows in beautiful, regular crystals.

compounds. In this chapter we will present various classes of compounds that illustrate the different types of bonds and then develop models to describe the structure and bonding that characterize materials found in nature. Later these models will be useful in understanding chemical reactions.

8.1 Types of Chemical Bonds

What is a chemical bond? There is no simple and yet complete answer to this question. In Chapter 2 we defined bonds as forces that hold groups of atoms together and make them function as a unit.

There are many types of experiments we can perform to determine the fundamental nature of materials. For example, we can study physical properties such as melting point, hardness, and electrical and thermal conductivity. We can also study solubility characteristics and the properties of the resulting solutions. To determine the charge distribution in a molecule, we can study its behavior in an electric field. We can obtain information about the strength of a bonding interaction by measuring the **bond energy,** which is the energy required to break the bond.

There are several ways in which atoms can interact with one another to form aggregates. We will consider several specific examples to illustrate the various types of chemical bonds.

Earlier, we saw that when solid sodium chloride is dissolved in water, the resulting solution conducts electricity, a fact that helps to convince us that sodium chloride is composed of Na^+ and Cl^- ions. Therefore, when sodium and chlorine react to form sodium chloride, electrons are transferred from the sodium atoms to the chlorine atoms to form Na^+ and Cl^- ions, which then aggregate to form solid sodium chloride. Why does this happen? The best simple answer is that *the system can achieve the lowest possible energy by behaving in this way.* The attraction of a chlorine atom for the extra electron and the very strong mutual attractions of the oppositely charged ions provide the driving forces for the process. The resulting solid sodium chloride is a very sturdy material; it has a melting point of approximately 800°C. The bonding forces that produce this great thermal stability result from the electrostatic attractions of the closely packed, oppositely charged ions. This is an example of **ionic bonding.** Ionic substances are formed when an atom that loses electrons relatively easily reacts with an atom that has a high affinity for electrons. That is, an **ionic compound** results when a metal reacts with a nonmetal.

The energy of interaction between a pair of ions can be calculated using **Coulomb's law** in the form

$$E = (2.31 \times 10^{-19} \text{ J} \cdot \text{nm})\left(\frac{Q_1 Q_2}{r}\right)$$

where E has units of joules, r is the distance between the ion centers in nanometers, and Q_1 and Q_2 are the numerical ion charges.

For example, in solid sodium chloride the distance between the centers of the Na^+ and Cl^- ions is 2.76 Å (0.276 nm), and the ionic energy per pair of ions is

$$E = (2.31 \times 10^{-19} \text{ J} \cdot \text{nm})\left[\frac{(+1)(-1)}{0.276 \text{ nm}}\right] = -8.37 \times 10^{-19} \text{ J}$$

where the negative sign indicates an attractive force. That is, the *ion pair has lower energy than the separated ions.*

Coulomb's law also can be used to calculate the repulsive energy when two like-charged ions are brought together. In this case the calculated value of the energy will have a positive sign.

We have seen that a bonding force develops when two different types of atoms react to form oppositely charged ions. But how does a bonding force develop between two

0.276 nm

Na^+ Cl^-

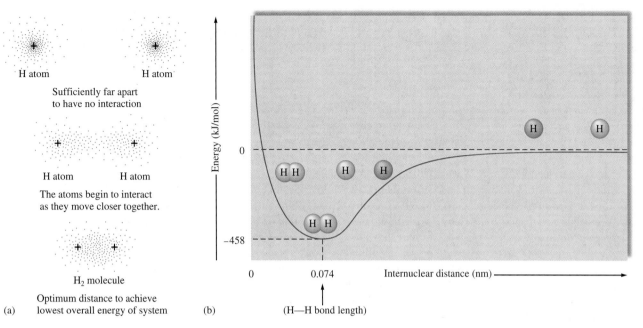

FIGURE 8.1
(a) The interaction of two hydrogen atoms. (b) Energy profile as a function of the distance between the nuclei of the hydrogen atoms. As the atoms approach each other (right side of graph), the energy decreases until the distance reaches 0.074 nm (0.74 Å) and then begins to increase again due to repulsions.

identical atoms? Let's explore this situation from a very simple point of view by considering the energy terms that result when two hydrogen atoms are brought close together, as shown in Fig. 8.1(a). When hydrogen atoms are brought close together, there are two unfavorable potential energy terms, proton–proton repulsion and electron–electron repulsion, and one favorable term, proton–electron attraction. Under what conditions will the H_2 molecule be favored over the separated hydrogen atoms? That is, what conditions will favor bond formation? The answer lies in the strong tendency in nature for any system to achieve the lowest possible energy. A bond will form (that is, the two hydrogen atoms will exist as a molecular unit) if the system can lower its total energy in the process.

In this case, then, the hydrogen atoms will position themselves so that the system will achieve the lowest possible energy; the system will act to minimize the sum of the positive (repulsive) energy terms and the negative (attractive) energy term. The distance where the energy is minimal is called the **bond length.** The total energy of this system as a function of distance between the hydrogen nuclei is shown in Fig. 8.1(b). Note several important features of this diagram:

> The energy terms involved are the net potential energy that results from the attractions and repulsions among the charged particles and the kinetic energy due to the motions of the electrons.

> The zero point of energy is defined with the atoms at infinite separation.

> At very short distances the energy rises steeply because of the importance of the repulsive forces when the atoms are very close together.

> The bond length is the distance at which the system has minimum energy.

In the H_2 molecule, the electrons reside primarily in the space between the two nuclei, where they are attracted simultaneously by both protons. This positioning is precisely what leads to the stability of the H_2 molecule compared with two separated hydrogen

A bond will form if the energy of the aggregate is lower than that of the separated atoms.

Potential energy was discussed in Chapter 6.

CHEMICAL IMPACT

No Lead Pencils

Did you ever wonder why the part of a pencil that makes the mark is called the "lead"? Pencils have no lead in them now—and they never have. Apparently the association between writing and the element lead arose during the Roman Empire, when lead rods were used as writing utensils because they leave a gray mark on paper. Many centuries later, in 1564, a deposit of a black substance found to be very useful for writing was discovered in Borrowdale, England. This substance, originally called "black lead," was shown in 1879 by Swedish chemist Carl Scheele to be a form of carbon and was subsequently named graphite (after the Greek *graphein,* meaning "to write").

Originally, chunks of graphite from Borrowdale, called marking stones, were used as writing instruments. Later,

sticks of graphite were used. Because graphite is brittle, the sticks needed reinforcement. At first they were wrapped in string, which was unwound as the core wore down. Eventually, graphite rods were tied between two wooden slats or inserted into hollowed-out wooden sticks to form the first crude pencils.

Although Borrowdale graphite was pure enough to use directly, most graphite must be mixed with other materials to be useful for writing instruments. In 1795, the French chemist Nicolas-Jaques Conté invented a process in which graphite is mixed with clay and water to produce pencil "lead," a recipe that is still used today. In modern pencil manufacture, graphite and clay are mixed and crushed into a fine powder to which water is added. After the gray sludge

atoms. The potential energy of each electron is lowered because of the increased attractive forces in this area. When we say that a bond is formed between the hydrogen atoms, we mean that the H_2 molecule is more stable than two separated hydrogen atoms by a certain quantity of energy (the bond energy).

We can also think of a bond in terms of forces. The simultaneous attraction of each electron by the protons generates a force that pulls the protons toward each other and that just balances the proton–proton and electron–electron repulsive forces at the distance corresponding to the bond length.

The type of bonding we encounter in the hydrogen molecule and in many other molecules in which *electrons are shared by nuclei* is called **covalent bonding.**

Ionic and covalent bonds are the extreme bond types.

So far we have considered two extreme types of bonding. In ionic bonding the participating atoms are so different that one or more electrons are transferred to form oppositely charged ions, which then attract each other. In covalent bonding two identical atoms share electrons equally. The bonding results from the mutual attraction of the two nuclei for the shared electrons. Between these extremes are intermediate cases in which the atoms are not so different that electrons are completely transferred but are different enough that unequal sharing results, forming what is called a **polar covalent bond.** An example of this type of bond occurs in the hydrogen fluoride (HF) molecule. When a sample of hydrogen fluoride gas is placed in an electric field, the molecules tend to orient themselves as shown in Fig. 8.2, with the fluoride end closest to the positive pole and the hydrogen end closest to the negative pole. This result implies that the HF molecule has the following charge distribution:

$$\underset{\delta+ \quad \delta-}{\text{H—F}}$$

where δ (lowercase delta) is used to indicate a fractional charge. This same effect was noted in Chapter 4, where many of water's unusual properties were attributed to the polar O—H bonds in the H_2O molecule.

Visualization: Polar Molecules

The most logical explanation for the development of the partial positive and negative charges on the atoms (bond polarity) in such molecules as HF and H_2O is that the is blended for several days, it is dried, ground up again, and mixed with more water to give a gray paste. The paste is extruded through a metal tube to form thin rods, which are then cut into pencil-length pieces called "leads." These leads are heated in an oven to 1000°C until they are smooth and hard. The ratio of clay to graphite is adjusted to vary the hardness of the lead——the more clay in the mix, the harder the lead and the lighter the line it makes.

Pencils are made from a slat of wood with several grooves cut in it to hold the leads. A similar grooved slat is then placed on top and glued to form a "sandwich" from which individual pencils are cut, sanded smooth, and painted. Although many types of wood have been used over the years to make pencils, the current favorite is incense cedar from the Sierra Nevada Mountains of California.

Modern pencils are simple but amazing instruments. The average pencil can write approximately 45,000 words, which is equivalent to a line 35 miles long. The graphite in a pencil is easily transferred to paper because graphite contains layers of carbon atoms bound together in a "chicken-wire" structure. Although the bonding *within* each layer is very strong, the bonding *between* layers is weak, giving graphite its slippery, soft nature. In this way, graphite is much different from diamond, the other common elemental form of carbon. In diamond the carbon atoms are bound tightly in all three dimensions, making it extremely hard—the hardest natural substance.

Pencils are very useful——especially for doing chemistry problems——because we can erase our mistakes. Most pencils used in the United States have erasers (first attached to pencils in 1858), although most European pencils do not. Laid end-to end, the number of pencils made in the United States each year would circle the earth about 15 times. Pencils illustrate how useful a simple substance like graphite can be.

electrons in the bonds are not shared equally. For example, we can account for the polarity of the HF molecule by assuming that the fluorine atom has a stronger attraction for the shared electrons than the hydrogen atom. Likewise, in the H_2O molecule the oxygen atom appears to attract the shared electrons more strongly than the hydrogen atoms do. Because bond polarity has important chemical implications, we find it useful to quantify the ability of an atom to attract shared electrons. In the next section we show how this is done.

8.2 Electronegativity

The different affinities of atoms for the electrons in a bond are described by a property called **electronegativity:** *the ability of an atom in a molecule to attract shared electrons to itself.*

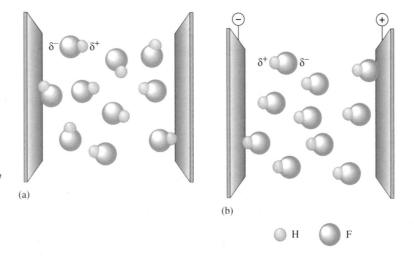

FIGURE 8.2
The effect of an electric field on hydrogen fluoride molecules. (a) When no electric field is present, the molecules are randomly oriented. (b) When the field is turned on, the molecules tend to line up with their negative ends toward the positive pole and their positive ends toward the negative pole.

Increasing electronegativity ⟶

FIGURE 8.3
The Pauling electronegativity values. Electronegativity generally increases across a period and decreases down a group.

The most widely accepted method for determining values of electronegativity is that of Linus Pauling (1901–1995), an American scientist who won the Nobel Prizes for both chemistry and peace. To understand Pauling's model, consider a hypothetical molecule HX. The relative electronegativities of the H and X atoms are determined by comparing the measured H—X bond energy with the "expected" H—X bond energy, which is an average of the H—H and X—X bond energies:

$$\text{Expected H—X bond energy} = \frac{\text{H—H bond energy} + \text{X—X bond energy}}{2}$$

The difference (Δ) between the actual (measured) and expected bond energies is

$$\Delta = (\text{H—X})_{\text{act}} - (\text{H—X})_{\text{exp}}$$

If H and X have identical electronegativities, $(\text{H—X})_{\text{act}}$ and $(\text{H—X})_{\text{exp}}$ are the same, and Δ is 0. On the other hand, if X has a greater electronegativity than H, the shared electron(s) will tend to be closer to the X atom. The molecule will be polar, with the following charge distribution:

$$\text{H—X}$$
$$\delta+ \quad \delta-$$

Note that this bond can be viewed as having an ionic as well as a covalent component. The attraction between the partially (and oppositely) charged H and X atoms will lead to a greater bond strength. Thus $(\text{H—X})_{\text{act}}$ will be larger than $(\text{H—X})_{\text{exp}}$. The greater is the difference in the electronegativities of the atoms, the greater is the ionic component of the bond and the greater is the value of Δ. Thus the relative electronegativities of H and X can be assigned from the Δ values.

Electronegativity values have been determined by this process for virtually all the elements; the results are given in Fig. 8.3. Note that electronegativity generally increases going from left to right across a period and decreases going down a group for the representative elements. The range of electronegativity values is from 4.0 for fluorine to 0.7 for cesium.

The relationship between electronegativity and bond type is shown in Table 8.1. For identical atoms (an electronegativity difference of zero), the electrons in the bond are shared equally, and no polarity develops. When two atoms with very different electronegativities

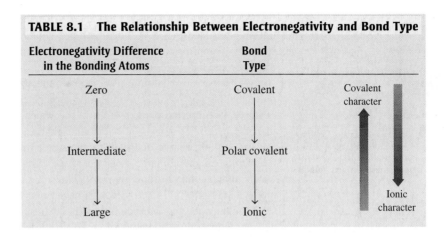

TABLE 8.1 The Relationship Between Electronegativity and Bond Type

Electronegativity Difference in the Bonding Atoms	Bond Type	
Zero	Covalent	Covalent character
Intermediate	Polar covalent	
Large	Ionic	Ionic character

interact, electron transfer can occur to form the ions that make up an ionic substance. Intermediate cases give polar covalent bonds with unequal electron sharing.

Sample Exercise 8.1

Relative Bond Polarities

Order the following bonds according to polarity: H—H, O—H, Cl—H, S—H, and F—H.

Solution

The polarity of the bond increases as the difference in electronegativity increases. From the electronegativity values in Fig. 8.3, the following variation in bond polarity is expected (the electronegativity value appears in parentheses below each element):

$$H—H < S—H < Cl—H < O—H < F—H$$
$$(2.1)(2.1) \quad (2.5)(2.1) \quad (3.0)(2.1) \quad (3.5)(2.1) \quad (4.0)(2.1)$$

Electronegativity difference   0   0.4   0.9   1.4   1.9

Covalent bond ———————→ Polar covalent bond
Polarity increases

See Exercises 8.31 and 8.32.

8.3 Bond Polarity and Dipole Moments

We have seen that when hydrogen fluoride is placed in an electric field, the molecules have a preferential orientation (see Fig. 8.2). This follows from the charge distribution in the HF molecule, which has a positive end and a negative end. A molecule such as HF that has a center of positive charge and a center of negative charge is said to be **dipolar,** or to have a **dipole moment.** The dipolar character of a molecule is often represented by an arrow pointing to the negative charge center with the tail of the arrow indicating the positive center of charge:

δ^+ δ^-

FIGURE 8.4
An electrostatic potential map of HF. Red indicates the most electron-rich area (the fluorine atom) and blue indicates the most electron-poor region (the hydrogen atom).

Another way to represent the charge distribution in HF is by an electrostatic potential diagram (see Fig. 8.4). For this representation the colors of visible light are used to show the variation in charge distribution. Red indicates the most electron-rich region of the molecule and blue indicates the most electron-poor region.

Of course, any diatomic (two-atom) molecule that has a polar bond also will show a molecular dipole moment. Polyatomic molecules also can exhibit dipolar behavior. For example, because the oxygen atom in the water molecule has a greater electronegativity than the hydrogen atoms, the molecular charge distribution is that shown in Fig. 8.5(a). Because of this charge distribution, the water molecule behaves in an electric field as if it had two centers of charge—one positive and one negative—as shown in Fig. 8.5(b). The water molecule has a dipole moment. The same type of behavior is observed for the NH_3 molecule (Fig. 8.6). Some molecules have polar bonds but do not have a dipole moment. This occurs when the individual bond polarities are arranged in such a way that they cancel each other out. An example is the CO_2 molecule, which is a linear molecule that has the charge distribution shown in Fig. 8.7. In this case the opposing bond polarities cancel out, and the carbon dioxide molecule does not have a dipole moment. There is no preferential way for this molecule to line up in an electric field. (Try to find a preferred orientation to make sure you understand this concept.)

There are many cases besides that of carbon dioxide where the bond polarities oppose and exactly cancel each other. Some common types of molecules with polar bonds but no dipole moment are shown in Table 8.2.

FIGURE 8.5
(a) The charge distribution in the water molecule. (b) The water molecule in an electric field. (c) The electrostatic potential diagram of the water molecule.

(a)   (b)   (c)

FIGURE 8.6
(a) The structure and charge distribution of the ammonia molecule. The polarity of the N—H bonds occurs because nitrogen has a greater electronegativity than hydrogen. (b) The dipole moment of the ammonia molecule oriented in an electric field. (c) The electrostatic potential diagram for ammonia.

(a)   (b)   (c)

FIGURE 8.7
(a) The carbon dioxide molecule. (b) The opposed bond polarities cancel out, and the carbon dioxide molecule has no dipole moment. (c) The electrostatic potential diagram for carbon dioxide.

(a)   (b)   (c)

TABLE 8.2   Types of Molecules with Polar Bonds but No Resulting Dipole Moment

Type		Cancellation of Polar Bonds	Example	Ball-and-Stick Model
Linear molecules with two identical bonds	B—A—B CO_2	←—+ +—→		
Planar molecules with three identical bonds 120 degrees apart	B, A, B B, 120°		SO_3	
Tetrahedral molecules with four identical bonds 109.5 degrees apart	B, A, B, B		CCl_4	

| *Sample Exercise 8.2* | **Bond Polarity and Dipole Moment** |

For each of the following molecules, show the direction of the bond polarities and indicate which ones have a dipole moment: HCl, Cl_2, SO_3 (a planar molecule with the oxygen atoms spaced evenly around the central sulfur atom), CH_4 [tetrahedral (see Table 8.2) with the carbon atom at the center], and H_2S (V-shaped with the sulfur atom at the point).

Solution

The HCl molecule: In Fig. 8.3, we see that the electronegativity of chlorine (3.0) is greater than that of hydrogen (2.1). Thus the chlorine will be partially negative, and the hydrogen will be partially positive. The HCl molecule has a dipole moment:

The Cl₂ molecule: The two chlorine atoms share the electrons equally. No bond polarity occurs, and the Cl_2 molecule has no dipole moment.

The SO₃ molecule: The electronegativity of oxygen (3.5) is greater than that of sulfur (2.5). This means that each oxygen will have a partial negative charge, and the sulfur will have a partial positive charge:

The presence of polar bonds does not always yield a polar molecule.

The bond polarities arranged symmetrically as shown cancel, and the molecule has no dipole moment. This molecule is the second type shown in Table 8.2.

The CH₄ molecule: Carbon has a slightly higher electronegativity (2.5) than does hydrogen (2.1). This leads to small partial positive charges on the hydrogen atoms and a small partial negative charge on the carbon:

This case is similar to the third type in Table 8.2, and the bond polarities cancel. The molecule has no dipole moment.

The H₂S molecule: Since the electronegativity of sulfur (2.5) is slightly greater than that of hydrogen (2.1), the sulfur will have a partial negative charge, and the hydrogen atoms will have a partial positive charge, which can be represented as

This case is analogous to the water molecule, and the polar bonds result in a dipole moment oriented as shown:

See Exercise 8.114.

8.4 Ions: Electron Configurations and Sizes

The description of the electron arrangements in atoms that emerged from the quantum mechanical model has helped a great deal in our understanding of what constitutes a stable compound. In virtually every case the atoms in a stable compound have a noble gas arrangement of electrons. Nonmetallic elements achieve a noble gas electron configuration either by sharing electrons with other nonmetals to form covalent bonds or by taking electrons from metals to form ions. In the second case, the nonmetals form anions, and the metals form cations. The generalizations that apply to electron configurations in stable compounds are as follows:

Atoms in stable compounds usually have a noble gas electron configuration.

• When *two nonmetals* react to form a covalent bond, they share electrons in a way that completes the valence electron configurations of both atoms. That is, both nonmetals attain noble gas electron configurations.

- When *a nonmetal and a representative-group metal* react to form a binary ionic compound, the ions form so that the valence electron configuration of the nonmetal achieves the electron configuration of the next noble gas atom and the valence orbitals of the metal are emptied. In this way both ions achieve noble gas electron configurations.

These generalizations apply to the vast majority of compounds and are important to remember. We will deal with covalent bonds more thoroughly later, but now we will consider what implications these rules hold for ionic compounds.

Predicting Formulas of Ionic Compounds

In the solid state of an ionic compound the ions are relatively close together, and many ions are simultaneously interacting:

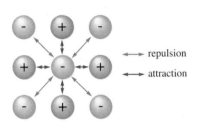

repulsion

attraction

In the gas phase of an ionic substance the ions would be relatively far apart and would not contain large groups of ions:

At the beginning of this discussion it should be emphasized that when chemists use the term *ionic compound,* they are usually referring to the solid state of that compound. In the solid state the ions are close together. That is, solid ionic compounds contain a large collection of positive and negative ions packed together in a way that minimizes the $\ominus\cdot\cdot\ominus$ and $\oplus\cdot\cdot\oplus$ repulsions and maximizes the $\oplus\cdot\cdot\ominus$ attractions. This situation stands in contrast to the gas phase of an ionic substance, where the ions are quite far apart on average. In the gas phase, a pair of ions may get close enough to interact, but large collections of ions do not exist. Thus, when we speak in this text of the stability of an ionic compound, we are referring to the solid state, where the large attractive forces present among oppositely charged ions tend to stabilize (favor the formation of) the ions. For example, as we mentioned in the preceding chapter, the O^{2-} ion is not stable as an isolated, gas-phase species but, of course, is very stable in many solid ionic compounds. That is, $MgO(s)$, which contains Mg^{2+} and O^{2-} ions, is very stable, but the isolated, gas-phase ion pair $Mg^{2+}\cdot\cdot O^{2-}$ is not energetically favorable in comparison with the separate neutral gaseous atoms. Thus you should keep in mind that in this section, and in most other cases where we are describing the nature of ionic compounds, the discussion usually refers to the solid state, where many ions are simultaneously interacting.

To illustrate the principles of electron configurations in stable, solid ionic compounds, we will consider the formation of an ionic compound from calcium and oxygen. We can predict what compound will form by considering the valence electron configurations of the two atoms:

$$Ca: \quad [Ar]4s^2$$
$$O: \quad [He]2s^22p^4$$

From Fig. 8.3 we see that the electronegativity of oxygen (3.5) is much greater than that of calcium (1.0). Because of this large difference, electrons will be transferred from calcium to oxygen to form oxygen anions and calcium cations in the compound. How many electrons are transferred? We can base our prediction on the observation that noble gas configurations are generally the most stable. Note that oxygen needs two electrons to fill its $2s$ and $2p$ valence orbitals and to achieve the configuration of neon ($1s^22s^22p^6$). And by losing two electrons, calcium can achieve the configuration of argon. Two electrons are therefore transferred:

$$Ca + O \longrightarrow Ca^{2+} + O^{2-}$$
$$\underbrace{\qquad}_{2e^-}$$

Visualization: Formation of Ionic Compounds

To predict the formula of the ionic compound, we simply recognize that chemical compounds are always electrically neutral—they have the same quantities of positive and negative charges. In this case we have equal numbers of Ca^{2+} and O^{2-} ions, and the empirical formula of the compound is CaO.

The same principles can be applied to many other cases. For example, consider the compound formed between aluminum and oxygen. Because aluminum has the configuration $[Ne]3s^23p^1$, it loses three electrons to form the Al^{3+} ion and thus achieves the neon

A bauxite mine. Bauxite contains Al_2O_3, the main source of aluminum.

configuration. Therefore, the Al^{3+} and O^{2-} ions form in this case. Since the compound must be electrically neutral, there must be three O^{2-} ions for every two Al^{3+} ions, and the compound has the empirical formula Al_2O_3.

Table 8.3 shows common elements that form ions with noble gas electron configurations in ionic compounds. In losing electrons to form cations, metals in Group 1A lose one electron, those in Group 2A lose two electrons, and those in Group 3A lose three electrons. In gaining electrons to form anions, nonmetals in Group 7A (the halogens) gain one electron, and those in Group 6A gain two electrons. Hydrogen typically behaves as a nonmetal and can gain one electron to form the hydride ion (H^-), which has the electron configuration of helium.

There are some important exceptions to the rules discussed here. For example, tin forms both Sn^{2+} and Sn^{4+} ions, and lead forms both Pb^{2+} and Pb^{4+} ions. Also, bismuth forms Bi^{3+} and Bi^{5+} ions, and thallium forms Tl^+ and Tl^{3+} ions. There are no simple explanations for the behavior of these ions. For now, just note them as exceptions to the very useful rule that ions generally adopt noble gas electron configurations in ionic compounds. Our discussion here refers to representative metals. The transition metals exhibit more complicated behavior, forming a variety of ions that will be considered in Chapter 21.

Sizes of Ions

Ion size plays an important role in determining the structure and stability of ionic solids, the properties of ions in aqueous solution, and the biologic effects of ions. As with atoms, it is impossible to define precisely the sizes of ions. Most often, ionic radii are determined

TABLE 8.3   Common Ions with Noble Gas Configurations in Ionic Compounds

Group 1A	Group 2A	Group 3A	Group 6A	Group 7A	Electron Configuration
H^-, Li^+	Be^{2+}				[He]
Na^+	Mg^{2+}	Al^{3+}	O^{2-}	F^-	[Ne]
K^+	Ca^{2+}		S^{2-}	Cl^-	[Ar]
Rb^+	Sr^{2+}		Se^{2-}	Br^-	[Kr]
Cs^+	Ba^{2+}		Te^{2-}	I^-	[Xe]

from the measured distances between ion centers in ionic compounds. This method, of course, involves an assumption about how the distance should be divided up between the two ions. Thus you will note considerable disagreement among ionic sizes given in various sources. Here we are mainly interested in trends and will be less concerned with absolute ion sizes.

Various factors influence ionic size. We will first consider the relative sizes of an ion and its parent atom. Since a positive ion is formed by removing one or more electrons from a neutral atom, the resulting cation is smaller than its parent atom. The opposite is true for negative ions; the addition of electrons to a neutral atom produces an anion significantly larger than its parent atom.

It is also important to know how the sizes of ions vary depending on the positions of the parent elements in the periodic table. Figure 8.8 shows the sizes of the most important ions (each with a noble gas configuration) and their position in the periodic table. Note that ion size increases down a group. The changes that occur horizontally are complicated because of the change from predominantly metals on the left-hand side of the periodic table to nonmetals on the right-hand side. A given period thus contains both elements that give up electrons to form cations and ones that accept electrons to form anions.

One trend worth noting involves the relative sizes of a set of **isoelectronic ions**—*ions containing the same number of electrons.* Consider the ions O^{2-}, F^-, Na^+, Mg^{2+}, and Al^{3+}. Each of these ions has the neon electron configuration. How do the sizes of these ions vary? In general, there are two important facts to consider in predicting the relative sizes of ions: the number of electrons and the number of protons. Since these ions are isoelectronic, the number of electrons is 10 in each case. Electron repulsions therefore should be about the same in all cases. However, the number of protons increases from 8 to 13 as we go from the O^{2-} ion to the Al^{3+} ion. Thus, in going from O^{2-} to Al^{3+}, the 10 electrons experience a greater attraction as the positive charge on the nucleus increases. This causes the ions to become smaller. You can confirm this by looking at Fig. 8.8. In general, for a series of isoelectronic ions, the size decreases as the nuclear charge Z increases.

Visualization: Ionic Radii

For isoelectronic ions, size decreases as Z increases.

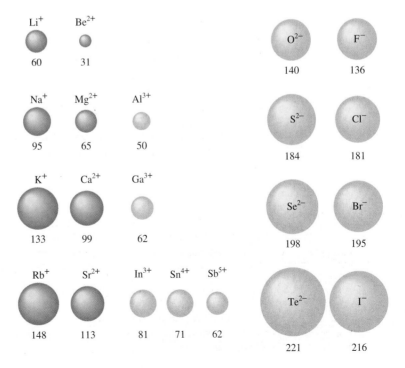

FIGURE 8.8
Sizes of ions related to positions of the elements on the periodic table. Note that size generally increases down a group. Also note that in a series of isoelectronic ions, size decreases with increasing atomic number. The ionic radii are given in units of picometers.

| Sample Exercise 8.3 | ### Relative Ion Size I |

Arrange the ions Se^{2-}, Br^-, Rb^+, and Sr^{2+} in order of decreasing size.

Solution

This is an isoelectronic series of ions with the krypton electron configuration. Since these ions all have the same number of electrons, their sizes will depend on the nuclear charge. The Z values are 34 for Se^{2-}, 35 for Br^-, 37 for Rb^+, and 38 for Sr^{2+}. Since the nuclear charge is greatest for Sr^{2+}, it is the smallest of these ions. The Se^{2-} ion is largest:

$$Se^{2-} > Br^- > Rb^+ > Sr^{2+}$$
$$\uparrow \qquad\qquad\qquad \uparrow$$
$$\text{Largest} \qquad\qquad \text{Smallest}$$

See Exercises 8.37 and 8.38.

| Sample Exercise 8.4 | ### Relative Ion Size II |

Choose the largest ion in each of the following groups.

a. Li^+, Na^+, K^+, Rb^+, Cs^+
b. Ba^{2+}, Cs^+, I^-, Te^{2-}

Solution

a. The ions are all from Group 1A elements. Since size increases down a group (the ion with the greatest number of electrons is largest), Cs^+ is the largest ion.
b. This is an isoelectronic series of ions, all of which have the xenon electron configuration. The ion with the smallest nuclear charge is largest:

$$Te^{2-} > \quad I^- \quad > \quad Cs^+ \quad > \quad Ba^{2+}$$
$$Z = 52 \quad Z = 53 \quad Z = 55 \quad Z = 56$$

See Exercises 8.39 and 8.40.

8.5 Energy Effects in Binary Ionic Compounds

In this section we will introduce the factors that influence the stability and the structures of solid binary ionic compounds. We know that metals and nonmetals react by transferring electrons to form cations and anions that are mutually attractive. The resulting ionic solid forms because the aggregated oppositely charged ions have a lower energy than the original elements. Just how strongly the ions attract each other in the solid state is indicated by the **lattice energy**—*the change in energy that takes place when separated gaseous ions are packed together to form an ionic solid:*

$$M^+(g) + X^-(g) \longrightarrow MX(s)$$

The structures of ionic solids will be discussed in detail in Chapter 10.

The lattice energy is often defined as the energy *released* when an ionic solid forms from its ions. However, in this book the sign of an energy term is always determined from the system's point of view: negative if the process is exothermic, positive if endothermic. Thus, using this convention, the lattice energy has a negative sign.

We can illustrate the energy changes involved in the formation of an ionic solid by considering the formation of solid lithium fluoride from its elements:

$$Li(s) + \tfrac{1}{2}F_2(g) \longrightarrow LiF(s)$$

To see the energy terms associated with this process, we take advantage of the fact that energy is a state function and break this reaction into steps, the sum of which gives the overall reaction.

Lithium fluoride.

➡ **1**   Sublimation of solid lithium. Sublimation involves taking a substance from the solid state to the gaseous state:

$$Li(s) \longrightarrow Li(g)$$

The enthalpy of sublimation for Li(s) is 161 kJ/mol.

➡ **2**   Ionization of lithium atoms to form Li$^+$ ions in the gas phase:

$$Li(g) \longrightarrow Li^+(g) + e^-$$

This process corresponds to the first ionization energy for lithium, which is 520 kJ/mol.

➡ **3**   Dissociation of fluorine molecules. We need to form a mole of fluorine atoms by breaking the F—F bonds in a half mole of F$_2$ molecules:

$$\tfrac{1}{2}F_2(g) \longrightarrow F(g)$$

The energy required to break this bond is 154 kJ/mol. In this case we are breaking the bonds in a half mole of fluorine, so the energy required for this step is (154 kJ)/2, or 77 kJ.

➡ **4**   Formation of F$^-$ ions from fluorine atoms in the gas phase:

$$F(g) + e^- \longrightarrow F^-(g)$$

The energy change for this process corresponds to the electron affinity of fluorine, which is −328 kJ/mol.

➡ **5**   Formation of solid lithium fluoride from the gaseous Li$^+$ and F$^-$ ions:

$$Li^+(g) + F^-(g) \longrightarrow LiF(s)$$

This corresponds to the lattice energy for LiF, which is −1047 kJ/mol.

Since the sum of these five processes yields the desired overall reaction, the sum of the individual energy changes gives the overall energy change:

Process	Energy Change (kJ)
$Li(s) \rightarrow Li(g)$	161
$Li(g) \rightarrow Li^+(g) + e^-$	520
$\tfrac{1}{2}F_2(g) \rightarrow F(g)$	77
$F(g) + e^- \rightarrow F^-(g)$	−328
$Li^+(g) + F^-(g) \rightarrow LiF(s)$	−1047
Overall: $Li(s) + \tfrac{1}{2}F_2(g) \rightarrow LiF(s)$	−617 kJ (per mole of LiF)

In doing this calculation, we have ignored the small difference between ΔH_{sub} and ΔE_{sub}.

This process is summarized by the energy diagram in Fig. 8.9. Note that the formation of solid lithium fluoride from its elements is highly exothermic, mainly because of the very large negative lattice energy. A great deal of energy is released when the ions combine to form the solid. In fact, note that the energy released when an electron is added to a fluorine atom to form the F$^-$ ion (328 kJ/mol) is not enough to remove an electron from lithium (520 kJ/mol). That is, when a metallic lithium atom reacts with a nonmetallic fluorine atom to form *separated* ions,

$$Li(g) + F(g) \longrightarrow Li^+(g) + F^-(g)$$

the process is endothermic and thus unfavorable. Clearly, then, the main impetus for the formation of an ionic compound rather than a covalent compound results from the strong mutual attractions among the Li$^+$ and F$^-$ ions in the solid. The lattice energy is the dominant energy term.

Visualization: Born–Haber Cycle for NaCl(s)

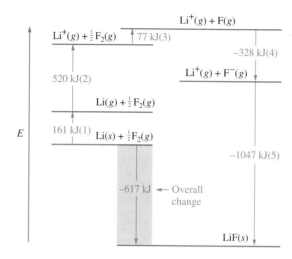

FIGURE 8.9
The energy changes involved in the formation of solid lithium fluoride from its elements. The numbers in parentheses refer to the reaction steps discussed in the text.

(a)

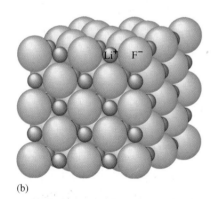

(b)

FIGURE 8.10
The structure of lithium fluoride. (a) Represented by ball-and-stick model. Note that each Li^+ ion is surrounded by six F^- ions, and each F^- ion is surrounded by six Li^+ ions. (b) Represented with the ions shown as spheres. The structure is determined by packing the spherical ions in a way that both maximizes the ionic attractions and minimizes the ionic repulsions.

The structure of solid lithium fluoride is represented in Fig. 8.10. Note the alternating arrangement of the Li^+ and F^- ions. Also note that each Li^+ is surrounded by six F^- ions, and each F^- ion is surrounded by six Li^+ ions. This structure can be rationalized by assuming that the ions behave as hard spheres that pack together in a way that both maximizes the attractions among the oppositely charged ions and minimizes the repulsions among the identically charged ions.

All the binary ionic compounds formed by an alkali metal and a halogen have the structure shown in Fig. 8.10, except for the cesium salts. The arrangement of ions shown in Fig. 8.10 is often called the *sodium chloride structure,* after the most common substance that possesses it.

Lattice Energy Calculations

In discussing the energetics of the formation of solid lithium fluoride, we emphasized the importance of lattice energy in contributing to the stability of the ionic solid. Lattice energy can be represented by a modified form of Coulomb's law:

$$\text{Lattice energy} = k\left(\frac{Q_1 Q_2}{r}\right)$$

where k is a proportionality constant that depends on the structure of the solid and the electron configurations of the ions, Q_1 and Q_2 are the charges on the ions, and r is the shortest distance between the centers of the cations and anions. Note that the lattice energy has a negative sign when Q_1 and Q_2 have opposite signs. This result is expected, since bringing cations and anions together is an exothermic process. Also note that the process becomes more exothermic as the ionic charges increase and as the distances between the ions in the solid decrease.

The importance of the charges in ionic solids can be illustrated by comparing the energies involved in the formation of NaF(s) and MgO(s). These solids contain the isoelectronic ions Na^+, F^-, Mg^{2+}, and O^{2-}. The energy diagram for the formation of the two solids is given in Fig. 8.11. Note several important features:

The energy released when the gaseous Mg^{2+} and O^{2-} ions combine to form solid MgO is much greater (more than four times greater) than that released when the gaseous Na^+ and F^- ions combine to form solid NaF.

The energy required to remove two electrons from the magnesium atom (735 kJ/mol for the first and 1445 kJ/mol for the second, yielding a total of 2180 kJ/mol) is much greater than the energy required to remove one electron from a sodium atom (495 kJ/mol).

FIGURE 8.11
Comparison of the energy changes involved in the formation of solid sodium fluoride and solid magnesium oxide. Note the large lattice energy for magnesium oxide (where doubly charged ions are combining) compared with that for sodium fluoride (where singly charged ions are combining).

Energy (737 kJ/mol) is required to add two electrons to the oxygen atom in the gas phase. Addition of the first electron is exothermic (-141 kJ/mol), but addition of the second electron is quite endothermic (878 kJ/mol). This latter energy must be obtained indirectly, since the $O^{2-}(g)$ ion is not stable.

In view of the facts that twice as much energy is required to remove the second electron from magnesium as to remove the first and that addition of an electron to the gaseous O^- ion is quite endothermic, it seems puzzling that magnesium oxide contains Mg^{2+} and O^{2-} ions rather than Mg^+ and O^- ions. The answer lies in the lattice energy. Note that the lattice energy for combining gaseous Mg^{2+} and O^{2-} ions to form $MgO(s)$ is 3000 kJ/mol

Since the equation for lattice energy contains the product Q_1Q_2, the lattice energy for a solid with 2+ and 2− ions should be four times that for a solid with 1+ and 1− ions. That is,

$$\frac{(+2)(-2)}{(+1)(-1)} = 4$$

For MgO and NaF, the observed ratio of lattice energies (see Fig. 8.11) is

$$\frac{-3916 \text{ kJ}}{-923 \text{ kJ}} = 4.24$$

more negative than that for combining gaseous Na^+ and F^- ions to form NaF(s). Thus the energy released in forming a solid containing Mg^{2+} and O^{2-} ions rather than Mg^+ and O^- ions more than compensates for the energies required for the processes that produce the Mg^{2+} and O^{2-} ions.

If there is so much lattice energy to be gained in going from singly charged to doubly charged ions in the case of magnesium oxide, why then does solid sodium fluoride contain Na^+ and F^- ions rather than Na^{2+} and F^{2-} ions? We can answer this question by recognizing that both Na^+ and F^- ions have the neon electron configuration. Removal of an electron from Na^+ requires an extremely large quantity of energy (4560 kJ/mol) because a $2p$ electron must be removed. Conversely, the addition of an electron to F^- would require use of the relatively high-energy $3s$ orbital, which is also an unfavorable process. Thus we can say that for sodium fluoride the extra energy required to form the doubly charged ions is greater than the gain in lattice energy that would result.

This discussion of the energies involved in the formation of solid ionic compounds illustrates that a variety of factors operate to determine the composition and structure of these compounds. The most important of these factors involve the balancing of the energies required to form highly charged ions and the energy released when highly charged ions combine to form the solid.

8.6 Partial Ionic Character of Covalent Bonds

Recall that when atoms with different electronegativities react to form molecules, the electrons are not shared equally. The possible result is a polar covalent bond or, in the case of a large electronegativity difference, a complete transfer of one or more electrons to form ions. The cases are summarized in Fig. 8.12.

How well can we tell the difference between an ionic bond and a polar covalent bond? The only honest answer to this question is that there are probably no totally ionic bonds between *discrete pairs of atoms*. The evidence for this statement comes from calculations of the percent ionic character for the bonds of various binary compounds in the gas phase. These calculations are based on comparisons of the measured dipole moments for molecules of the type X—Y with the calculated dipole moments for the completely ionic case, X^+Y^-. The percent ionic character of a bond can be defined as

$$\text{Percent ionic character of a bond} = \left(\frac{\text{measured dipole moment of X—Y}}{\text{calculated dipole moment of } X^+Y^-} \right) \times 100\%$$

Application of this definition to various compounds (in the gas phase) gives the results shown in Fig. 8.13, where percent ionic character is plotted versus the difference in the electronegativity values of X and Y. Note from this plot that ionic character increases with electronegativity difference, as expected. However, none of the bonds reaches 100% ionic character, even though compounds with the maximum possible electronegativity differences are considered. Thus, according to this definition, no individual bonds are completely ionic. This conclusion is in contrast to the usual classification of many of these compounds (as ionic solids). All the compounds shown in Fig. 8.13 with more than 50% ionic character are normally considered to be ionic solids. Recall, however, that the results in Fig. 8.13 are for the gas phase, where individual XY molecules exist. These results cannot necessarily be assumed to apply to the solid state, where the existence of ions is favored by the multiple ion interactions.

Another complication in identifying ionic compounds is that many substances contain polyatomic ions. For example, NH_4Cl contains NH_4^+ and Cl^- ions, and Na_2SO_4 contains Na^+ and SO_4^{2-} ions. The ammonium and sulfate ions are held together by covalent bonds. Thus, calling NH_4Cl and Na_2SO_4 ionic compounds is somewhat ambiguous.

(a)

(b)

(c)

FIGURE 8.12

The three possible types of bonds: (a) a covalent bond formed between identical F atoms; (b) the polar covalent bond of HF, with both ionic and covalent components; and (c) an ionic bond with no electron sharing.

FIGURE 8.13
The relationship between the ionic character of a covalent bond and the electronegativity difference of the bonded atoms. Note that the compounds with ionic character greater than 50% are normally considered to be ionic compounds.

We will avoid these problems by adopting an operational definition of ionic compounds: *Any compound that conducts an electric current when melted will be classified as ionic.*

8.7 The Covalent Chemical Bond: A Model

Before we develop specific models for covalent chemical bonding, it will be helpful to summarize some of the concepts introduced in this chapter.

What is a chemical bond? Chemical bonds can be viewed as forces that cause a group of atoms to behave as a unit.

Why do chemical bonds occur? There is no principle of nature that states that bonds are favored or disfavored. Bonds are neither inherently "good" nor inherently "bad" as far as nature is concerned; *bonds result from the tendency of a system to seek its lowest possible energy.* From a simplistic point of view, bonds occur when collections of atoms are more stable (lower in energy) than the separate atoms. For example, approximately 1652 kJ of energy is required to break a mole of methane (CH_4) molecules into separate C and H atoms. Or, taking the opposite view, 1652 kJ of energy is released when 1 mole of methane is formed from 1 mole of gaseous C atoms and 4 moles of gaseous H atoms. Thus we can say that 1 mole of CH_4 molecules in the gas phase is 1652 kJ lower in energy than 1 mole of carbon atoms plus 4 moles of hydrogen atoms. Methane is therefore a stable molecule relative to its separated atoms.

We find it useful to interpret molecular stability in terms of a model called a *chemical bond.* To understand why this model was invented, let's continue with methane, which consists of four hydrogen atoms arranged at the corners of a tetrahedron around a carbon atom:

A tetrahedron has four equal triangular faces.

Given this structure, it is natural to envision four individual C—H interactions (we call them *bonds*). The energy of stabilization of CH_4 is divided equally among the four bonds to give an average C—H bond energy per mole of C—H bonds:

$$\frac{1652 \text{ kJ/mol}}{4} = 413 \text{ kJ/mol}$$

Next, consider methyl chloride, which consists of CH_3Cl molecules having the structure

Experiments have shown that approximately 1578 kJ of energy is required to break down 1 mole of gaseous CH_3Cl molecules into gaseous carbon, chlorine, and hydrogen atoms. The reverse process can be represented as

$$C(g) + Cl(g) + 3H(g) \longrightarrow CH_3Cl(g) + 1578 \text{ kJ/mol}$$

A mole of gaseous methyl chloride is lower in energy by 1578 kJ than its separate gaseous atoms. Thus a mole of methyl chloride is held together by 1578 kJ of energy. Again, it is very useful to divide this energy into individual bonds. Methyl chloride can be visualized as containing one C—Cl bond and three C—H bonds. If we assume arbitrarily that a C—H interaction represents the same quantity of energy in any situation (that is, that the strength of a C—H bond is independent of its molecular environment), we can do the following bookkeeping:

$$1 \text{ mol C—Cl bonds plus 3 mol C—H bonds} = 1578 \text{ kJ}$$
$$\text{C—Cl bond energy} + 3(\text{average C—H bond energy}) = 1578 \text{ kJ}$$
$$\text{C—Cl bond energy} + 3(413 \text{ kJ/mol}) = 1578 \text{ kJ}$$
$$\text{C—Cl bond energy} = 1578 - 1239 = 339 \text{ kJ/mol}$$

These assumptions allow us to associate given quantities of energy with C—H and C—Cl bonds.

It is important to note that the bond concept is a human invention. Bonds provide a method for dividing up the energy evolved when a stable molecule is formed from its component atoms. Thus in this context a bond represents a quantity of energy obtained from the overall molecular energy of stabilization in a rather arbitrary way. This is not to say that the concept of individual bonds is a bad idea. In fact, the modern concept of the chemical bond, conceived by the American chemists G. N. Lewis and Linus Pauling, is one of the most useful ideas chemists have ever developed.

Models: An Overview

The framework of chemistry, like that of any science, consists of *models*—attempts to explain how nature operates on the microscopic level based on experiences in the macroscopic world. To understand chemistry, one must understand its models and how they are used. We will use the concept of bonding to reemphasize the important characteristics of models, including their origin, structure, and uses.

Models originate from our observations of the properties of nature. For example, the concept of bonds arose from the observations that most chemical processes involve collections of atoms and that chemical reactions involve rearrangements of the ways the atoms are grouped. Therefore, to understand reactions, we must understand the forces that bind atoms together.

In natural processes there is a tendency toward lower energy. Collections of atoms therefore occur because the aggregated state has lower energy than the separated atoms. Why? As we saw earlier in this chapter, the best explanations for the energy change involve

Bonding is a model proposed to explain molecular stability.

atoms sharing electrons or atoms transferring electrons to become ions. In the case of electron sharing, we find it convenient to assume that individual bonds occur between pairs of atoms. Let's explore the validity of this assumption and see how it is useful.

In a diatomic molecule such as H_2, it is natural to assume that a bond exists between the atoms, holding them together. It is also useful to assume that individual bonds are present in polyatomic molecules such as CH_4. Therefore, instead of thinking of CH_4 as a unit with a stabilization energy of 1652 kJ per mole, we choose to think of CH_4 as containing four C—H bonds, each worth 413 kJ of energy per mole of bonds. Without this concept of individual bonds in molecules, chemistry would be hopelessly complicated. There are millions of different chemical compounds, and if each of these compounds had to be considered as an entirely new entity, the task of understanding chemical behavior would be overwhelming.

The bonding model provides a framework to systematize chemical behavior by enabling us to think of molecules as collections of common fundamental components. For example, a typical biomolecule, such as a protein, contains hundreds of atoms and might seem discouragingly complex. However, if we think of a protein as constructed of individual bonds, C—C, C—H, C—N, C—O, N—H, and so on, it helps tremendously in predicting and understanding the protein's behavior. The essential idea is that we expect a given bond to behave about the same in any molecular environment. Used in this way, the model of the chemical bond has helped chemists to systematize the reactions of the millions of existing compounds.

In addition to being useful, the bonding model is physically sensible. It makes sense that atoms can form stable groups by sharing electrons; shared electrons give a lower energy state because they are simultaneously attracted by two nuclei.

Also, as we will see in the next section, bond energy data support the existence of discrete bonds that are relatively independent of the molecular environment. It is very important to remember, however, that the chemical bond is only a model. Although our concept of discrete bonds in molecules agrees with many of our observations, some molecular properties require that we think of a molecule as a whole, with the electrons free to move through the entire molecule. This is called *delocalization* of the electrons, a concept that will be discussed more completely in the next chapter.

The concept of individual bonds makes it much easier to deal with complex molecules such as DNA. A small segment of a DNA molecule is shown here.

Fundamental Properties of Models

- Models are human inventions, always based on an incomplete understanding of how nature works. *A model does not equal reality.*

- Models are often wrong. This property derives from the first property. Models are based on speculation and are always oversimplifications.

- Models tend to become more complicated as they age. As flaws are discovered in our models, we "patch" them and thus add more detail.

- It is very important to understand the assumptions inherent in a particular model before you use it to interpret observations or to make predictions. Simple models usually involve very restrictive assumptions and can be expected to yield only qualitative information. Asking for a sophisticated explanation from a simple model is like expecting to get an accurate mass for a diamond using a bathroom scale.

  For a model to be used effectively, we must understand its strengths and weaknesses and ask only appropriate questions. An illustration of this point is the simple aufbau principle used to account for the electron configurations of the elements. Although this model correctly predicts the configuration for most atoms, chromium and copper, for example, do not agree with the predictions. Detailed studies show that the configurations of chromium and copper result from complex electron interactions that are not taken into account in the simple model. However, this does not mean that we should discard the simple model that is so useful for most atoms. Instead, we must apply it with caution and not expect it to be correct in every case.

- When a model is wrong, we often learn much more than when it is right. If a model makes a wrong prediction, it usually means we do not understand some fundamental characteristics of nature. We often learn by making mistakes. (Try to remember this when you get back your next chemistry test.)

8.8 Covalent Bond Energies and Chemical Reactions

In this section we will consider the energies associated with various types of bonds and see how the bonding concept is useful in dealing with the energies of chemical reactions. One important consideration is to establish the sensitivity of a particular type of bond to its molecular environment. For example, consider the stepwise decomposition of methane:

Process	Energy Required (kJ/mol)
$CH_4(g) \rightarrow CH_3(g) + H(g)$	435
$CH_3(g) \rightarrow CH_2(g) + H(g)$	453
$CH_2(g) \rightarrow CH(g) + H(g)$	425
$CH(g) \rightarrow C(g) + H(g)$	339

$$\text{Total} = 1652$$

$$\text{Average} = \frac{1652}{4} = 413$$

Although a C—H bond is broken in each case, the energy required varies in a nonsystematic way. This example shows that the C—H bond is somewhat sensitive to its environment. We use the *average* of these individual bond dissociation energies even though this quantity only approximates the energy associated with a C—H bond in a particular molecule. The degree of sensitivity of a bond to its environment also can be seen

TABLE 8.4 Average Bond Energies (kJ/mol)

Single Bonds								Multiple Bonds	
H—H	432	N—H	391	I—I	149			C=C	614
H—F	565	N—N	160	I—Cl	208			C≡C	839
H—Cl	427	N—F	272	I—Br	175			O=O	495
H—Br	363	N—Cl	200					C=O*	745
H—I	295	N—Br	243			S—H	347	C≡O	1072
		N—O	201			S—F	327	N=O	607
C—H	413	O—H	467			S—Cl	253	N=N	418
C—C	347	O—O	146			S—Br	218	N≡N	941
C—N	305	O—F	190			S—S	266	C≡N	891
C—O	358	O—Cl	203					C=N	615
C—F	485	O—I	234			Si—Si	340		
C—Cl	339					Si—H	393		
C—Br	276	F—F	154			Si—C	360		
C—I	240	F—Cl	253			Si—O	452		
C—S	259	F—Br	237						
		Cl—Cl	239						
		Cl—Br	218						
		Br—Br	193						

*C=O(CO$_2$) = 799

from experimental measurements of the energy required to break the C—H bond in the following molecules:

Molecule	Measured C—H Bond Energy (kJ/mol)
HCBr$_3$	380
HCCl$_3$	380
HCF$_3$	430
C$_2$H$_6$	410

These data show that the C—H bond strength varies significantly with its environment, but the concept of an average C—H bond strength remains useful to chemists. The average values of bond energies for various types of bonds are listed in Table 8.4.

So far we have discussed bonds in which one pair of electrons is shared. This type of bond is called a **single bond.** As we will see in more detail later, atoms sometimes share two pairs of electrons, forming a **double bond,** or share three pairs of electrons, forming a **triple bond.** The bond energies for these *multiple bonds* are also given in Table 8.4.

A relationship also exists between the number of shared electron pairs and the bond length. As the number of shared electrons increases, the bond length shortens. This relationship is shown for selected bonds in Table 8.5.

Bond Energy and Enthalpy

Bond energy values can be used to calculate approximate energies for reactions. To illustrate how this is done, we will calculate the change in energy that accompanies the following reaction:

$$H_2(g) + F_2(g) \longrightarrow 2HF(g)$$

This reaction involves breaking one H—H and one F—F bond and forming two H—F bonds. For bonds to be broken, energy must be *added* to the system—an endothermic

TABLE 8.5 Bond Lengths for Selected Bonds

Bond	Bond Type	Bond Length (pm)	Bond Energy (kJ/mol)
C—C	Single	154	347
C=C	Double	134	614
C≡C	Triple	120	839
C—O	Single	143	358
C=O	Double	123	745
C—N	Single	143	305
C=N	Double	138	615
C≡N	Triple	116	891

process. Consequently, the energy terms associated with bond breaking have *positive* signs. The formation of a bond *releases* energy, an exothermic process, so the energy terms associated with bond making carry a *negative* sign. We can write the enthalpy change for a reaction as follows:

ΔH = sum of the energies required to break old bonds (positive signs) plus the sum of the energies released in the formation of new bonds (negative signs)

This leads to the expression

$$\Delta H = \underbrace{\Sigma D \text{ (bonds broken)}}_{\text{Energy required}} - \underbrace{\Sigma D \text{ (bonds formed)}}_{\text{Energy released}}$$

where Σ represents the sum of terms, and D represents the bond energy per mole of bonds. (D *always* has a positive sign.)

In the case of the formation of HF,

$$\Delta H = D_{H-H} + D_{F-F} - 2D_{H-F}$$

$$= 1 \text{ mol} \times \frac{432 \text{ kJ}}{\text{mol}} + 1 \text{ mol} \times \frac{154 \text{ kJ}}{\text{mol}} - 2 \text{ mol} \times \frac{565 \text{ kJ}}{\text{mol}}$$

$$= -544 \text{ kJ}$$

Thus, when 1 mol $H_2(g)$ and 1 mol $F_2(g)$ react to form 2 mol HF(g), 544 kJ of energy should be released.

This result can be compared with the calculation of ΔH for this reaction from the standard enthalpy of formation for HF (-271 kJ/mol):

$$\Delta H° = 2 \text{ mol} \times (-271 \text{ kJ/mol}) = -542 \text{ kJ}$$

Thus the use of bond energies to calculate ΔH works quite well in this case.

Sample Exercise 8.5 | ## ΔH from Bond Energies

Using the bond energies listed in Table 8.4, calculate ΔH for the reaction of methane with chlorine and fluorine to give Freon-12 (CF_2Cl_2).

$$CH_4(g) + 2Cl_2(g) + 2F_2(g) \longrightarrow CF_2Cl_2(g) + 2HF(g) + 2HCl(g)$$

Solution

The idea here is to break the bonds in the gaseous reactants to give individual atoms and then assemble these atoms into the gaseous products by forming new bonds:

$$\text{Reactants} \xrightarrow[\text{required}]{\text{Energy}} \text{atoms} \xrightarrow[\text{released}]{\text{Energy}} \text{products}$$

We then combine the energy changes to calculate ΔH:

ΔH = energy required to break bonds − energy released when bonds form

where the minus sign gives the correct sign to the energy terms for the exothermic processes.

Reactant Bonds Broken:

CH_4: 4 mol C—H $4 \text{ mol} \times \dfrac{413 \text{ kJ}}{\text{mol}} = 1652 \text{ kJ}$

$2Cl_2$: 2 mol Cl—Cl $2 \text{ mol} \times \dfrac{239 \text{ kJ}}{\text{mol}} = 478 \text{ kJ}$

$2F_2$: 2 mol F—F $2 \text{ mol} \times \dfrac{154 \text{ kJ}}{\text{mol}} = 308 \text{ kJ}$

Total energy required = 2438 kJ

Product Bonds Formed:

CF_2Cl_2: 2 mol C—F $2 \text{ mol} \times \dfrac{485 \text{ kJ}}{\text{mol}} = 970 \text{ kJ}$

and

2 mol C—Cl $2 \text{ mol} \times \dfrac{339 \text{ kJ}}{\text{mol}} = 3678 \text{ kJ}$

HF: 2 mol H—F $2 \text{ mol} \times \dfrac{565 \text{ kJ}}{\text{mol}} = 1130 \text{ kJ}$

HCl: 2 mol H—Cl $2 \text{ mol} \times \dfrac{427 \text{ kJ}}{\text{mol}} = 3854 \text{ kJ}$

Total energy released = 3632 kJ

We now can calculate ΔH:

ΔH = energy required to break bonds − energy released when bonds form

= 2438 kJ − 3632 kJ

= −1194 kJ

Since the sign of the value for the enthalpy change is negative, this means that 1194 kJ of energy is released per mole of CF_2Cl_2 formed.

See Exercises 8.53 through 8.60.

8.9 The Localized Electron Bonding Model

So far we have discussed the general characteristics of the chemical bonding model and have seen that properties such as bond strength and polarity can be assigned to individual bonds. In this section we introduce a specific model used to describe covalent bonds. We need a simple model that can be applied easily even to very complicated molecules and that can be used routinely by chemists to interpret and organize the wide variety of chemical phenomena. The model that serves this purpose is the **localized electron (LE) model,** which assumes that *a molecule is composed of atoms that are bound together by sharing pairs of electrons using the atomic orbitals of the bound atoms.* Electron pairs in the molecule are assumed to be localized on a particular atom or in the space between two atoms. Those pairs of electrons localized on an atom are called **lone pairs,** and those found in the space between the atoms are called **bonding pairs.**

As we will apply it, the LE model has three parts:

1. Description of the valence electron arrangement in the molecule using Lewis structures (will be discussed in the next section).

2. Prediction of the geometry of the molecule using the valence shell electron-pair repulsion (VSEPR) model (will be discussed in Section 8.13).

3. Description of the type of atomic orbitals used by the atoms to share electrons or hold lone pairs (will be discussed in Chapter 9).

8.10 Lewis Structures

The **Lewis structure** of a molecule shows how the valence electrons are arranged among the atoms in the molecule. These representations are named after G. N. Lewis (Fig. 8.14). The rules for writing Lewis structures are based on observations of thousands of molecules. From experiment, chemists have learned that the *most important requirement for the formation of a stable compound is that the atoms achieve noble gas electron configurations.*

We have already seen that when metals and nonmetals react to form binary ionic compounds, electrons are transferred and the resulting ions typically have noble gas electron configurations. An example is the formation of KBr, where the K^+ ion has the [Ar] electron configuration and the Br^- ion has the [Kr] electron configuration. In writing Lewis structures, the rule is that *only the valence electrons are included.* Using dots to represent electrons, the Lewis structure for KBr is

No dots are shown on the K^+ ion because it has no valence electrons. The Br^- ion is shown with eight electrons because it has a filled valence shell.

Next we will consider Lewis structures for molecules with covalent bonds, involving elements in the first and second periods. The principle of achieving a noble gas electron configuration applies to these elements as follows:

- Hydrogen forms stable molecules where it shares two electrons. That is, it follows a **duet rule.** For example, when two hydrogen atoms, each with one electron, combine to form the H_2 molecule, we have

By sharing electrons, each hydrogen in H_2, in effect, has two electrons; that is, each hydrogen has a filled valence shell.

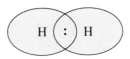

- Helium does not form bonds because its valence orbital is already filled; it is a noble gas. Helium has the electron configuration $1s^2$ and can be represented by the Lewis structure

He :

Lewis structures show only valence electrons.

FIGURE 8.14
G. N. Lewis (1875–1946).

- The second-row nonmetals carbon through fluorine form stable molecules when they are surrounded by enough electrons to fill the valence orbitals, that is, the $2s$ and the three $2p$ orbitals. Since eight electrons are required to fill these orbitals, these elements typically obey the **octet rule;** they are surrounded by eight electrons. An example is the F_2 molecule, which has the following Lewis structure:

F atom with seven valence electrons F_2 molecule   F atom with seven valence electrons

Note that each fluorine atom in F_2 is, in effect, surrounded by eight electrons, two of which are shared with the other atom. This is a *bonding pair* of electrons, as discussed earlier. Each fluorine atom also has three pairs of electrons not involved in bonding. These are the *lone pairs.*

- Neon does not form bonds because it already has an octet of valence electrons (it is a noble gas). The Lewis structure is

$$: \overset{..}{\underset{..}{Ne}} :$$

Note that only the valence electrons of the neon atom ($2s^2 2p^6$) are represented by the Lewis structure. The $1s^2$ electrons are core electrons and are not shown.

From the preceding discussion we can formulate the following rules for writing the Lewis structures of molecules containing atoms from the first two periods.

Steps for Writing Lewis Structures

➡ 1 **Sum the valence electrons from all the atoms. Do not worry about keeping track of which electrons come from which atoms. It is the *total* number of electrons that is important.**

➡ 2 **Use a pair of electrons to form a bond between each pair of bound atoms.**

➡ 3 **Arrange the remaining electrons to satisfy the duet rule for hydrogen and the octet rule for the second-row elements.**

To see how these steps are applied, we will draw the Lewis structures of a few molecules. We will first consider the water molecule and follow the previous steps.

➡ 1 We sum the *valence* electrons for H_2O as shown:

$$1 + 1 + 6 = 8 \text{ valence electrons}$$
$$\nearrow \quad \nearrow \quad \nearrow$$
$$H \quad H \quad O$$

➡ 2 Using a pair of electrons per bond, we draw in the two O—H single bonds:

$$H—O—H$$

Note that *a line instead of a pair of dots is used to indicate each pair* of *bonding electrons.* This is the standard notation.

➡ 3 We distribute the remaining electrons to achieve a noble gas electron configuration for each atom. Since four electrons have been used in forming the two bonds, four electrons (8 − 4) remain to be distributed. Hydrogen is satisfied with two electrons (duet rule), but oxygen needs eight electrons to have a noble gas configuration. Thus the remaining

Carbon, nitrogen, oxygen, and fluorine always obey the octet rule in stable molecules.

four electrons are added to oxygen as two lone pairs. Dots are used to represent the lone pairs:

H—O—H represents H:O:H

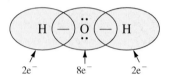

This is the correct Lewis structure for the water molecule. Each hydrogen has two electrons and the oxygen has eight, as shown below:

$$H \left(-\right) \ddot{\underset{..}{O}} \left(-\right) H$$

2e⁻   8e⁻   2e⁻

As a second example, let's write the Lewis structure for carbon dioxide. Summing the valence electrons gives

$$4 + 6 + 6 = 16$$
$$\nearrow \quad \nearrow \quad \nearrow$$
$$C \quad O \quad O$$

After forming a bond between the carbon and each oxygen,

$$O—C—O$$

the remaining electrons are distributed to achieve noble gas configurations on each atom. In this case we have 12 electrons (16 − 4) remaining after the bonds are drawn. The distribution of these electrons is determined by a trial-and-error process. We have 6 pairs of electrons to distribute. Suppose we try 3 pairs on each oxygen to give

$$:\ddot{\underset{..}{O}}—C—\ddot{\underset{..}{O}}:$$

Is this correct? To answer this question, we need to check two things:

1. The total number of electrons. There are 16 valence electrons in this structure, which is the correct number.

2. The octet rule for each atom. Each oxygen has 8 electrons, but the carbon has only 4. This cannot be the correct Lewis structure.

O=C=O represents

O::C::O

How can we arrange the 16 available electrons to achieve an octet for each atom? Suppose there are 2 shared pairs between the carbon and each oxygen:

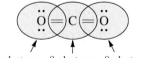

8 electrons   8 electrons   8 electrons

Now each atom is surrounded by 8 electrons, and the total number of electrons is 16, as required. This is the correct Lewis structure for carbon dioxide, which has two double bonds and four lone pairs.

Finally, let's consider the Lewis structure of the CN⁻ (cyanide) ion. Summing the valence electrons, we have

$$CN^-$$
$$\diagup \diagup \diagup$$
$$4 + 5 + 1 = 10$$

Note that the negative charge means an extra electron is present. After drawing a single bond (C—N), we distribute the remaining electrons to achieve a noble gas configuration for each atom. Eight electrons remain to be distributed. We can try various possibilities, for example:

$$\ddot{C}—\ddot{N}$$

This structure is incorrect because C and N have only six electrons each instead of eight. The correct arrangement is

$$[\,:C\!\equiv\!N:\,]^-$$

(Satisfy yourself that both carbon and nitrogen have eight electrons.)

| Sample Exercise 8.6 | **Writing Lewis Structures** |

Give the Lewis structure for each of the following.

a. HF	**d.** CH_4
b. N_2	**e.** CF_4
c. NH_3	**f.** NO^+

Solution

In each case we apply the three steps for writing Lewis structures. Recall that lines are used to indicate shared electron pairs and that dots are used to indicate nonbonding pairs (lone pairs). We have the following tabulated results:

	Total Valence Electrons	Draw Single Bonds	Calculate Number of Electrons Remaining	Use Remaining Electrons to Achieve Noble Gas Configurations	Check Number of Electrons
a. HF	$1 + 7 = 8$	H—F	6	H—$\ddot{\underset{..}{F}}$:	H, 2 F, 8
b. N_2	$5 + 5 = 10$	N—N	8	:N≡N:	N, 8
c. NH_3	$5 + 3(1) = 8$	H—N—H | H	2	H—$\ddot{N}$—H | H	H, 2 N, 8
d. CH_4	$4 + 4(1) = 8$	H | H—C—H | H	0	H | H—C—H | H	H, 2 C, 8
e. CF_4	$4 + 4(7) = 32$	F | F—C—F | F	24	:$\ddot{F}$: | :$\ddot{F}$—C—$\ddot{F}$: | :$\ddot{F}$:	F, 8 C, 8
f. NO^+	$5 + 6 - 1 = 10$	N—O	8	$[:N\!\equiv\!O:]^+$	N, 8 O, 8

See Exercises 8.67 and 8.68.

CHEMICAL IMPACT

Nitrogen Under Pressure

The element nitrogen exists at normal temperatures and pressures as a gas containing N_2, a molecule with a very strong triple bond. In the gas phase the diatomic molecules move around independently with almost no tendency to associate with each other. Under intense pressure, however, nitrogen changes to a dramatically different form. This conclusion was reached at the Carnegie Institution in Washington, D.C., by Mikhail Erements and his colleagues, who subjected nitrogen to a pressure of 2.4 million atmospheres in a special diamond anvil press. Under this tremendous pressure the bonds of the N_2 molecules break and a substance containing an aggregate of nitrogen atoms forms. In other words, under great pressure elemental nitrogen changes from a substance containing diatomic molecules to one containing many nitrogen atoms bonded to each other. Interestingly, this substance remains intact even after the pressure is released—as long as the temperature remains at 100 K. This new form of nitrogen has a very high potential energy relative to N_2. Thus this substance would be an extraordinarily powerful propellant or explosive if enough of it could be made. This new form of nitrogen is also a semiconductor for electricity; normal nitrogen gas is an insulator.

The newly discovered form of nitrogen is significant for several reasons. For one thing, it may help us understand the nature of the interiors of the giant gas planets such as Jupiter. Also, their success in changing nitrogen to an atomic solid encourages high-pressure scientists who are trying to

A diamond anvil cell used to study materials at very high pressures.

accomplish the same goal with hydrogen. It is surprising that nitrogen, which has diatomic molecules containing bonds more than twice as strong as those in hydrogen, will form an atomic solid at these pressures but hydrogen does not. Hydrogen remains a molecular solid at far greater pressures than nitrogen can endure.

When writing Lewis structures, do not worry about which electrons come from which atoms in a molecule. The best way to look at a molecule is to regard it as a new entity that uses all the available valence electrons of the atoms to achieve the lowest possible energy.* The valence electrons belong to the molecule, rather than to the individual atoms. Simply distribute all valence electrons so that the various rules are satisfied, without regard for the origin of each particular electron.

8.11 Exceptions to the Octet Rule

The localized electron model is a simple but very successful model, and the rules we have used for Lewis structures apply to most molecules. However, with such a simple model, some exceptions are inevitable. Boron, for example, tends to form compounds in which the boron atom has fewer than eight electrons around it—it does not have a complete octet. Boron trifluoride (BF_3), a gas at normal temperatures and pressures, reacts very

---

*In a sense this approach corrects for the fact that the localized electron model overemphasizes that a molecule is simply a sum of its parts—that is, that the atoms retain their individual identities in the molecule.

energetically with molecules such as water and ammonia that have available electron pairs (lone pairs). The violent reactivity of BF_3 with electron-rich molecules arises because the boron atom is electron-deficient. Boron trifluoride has 24 valence electrons. The Lewis structure often drawn for BF_3 is

Note that in this structure boron has only 6 electrons around it. The octet rule for boron can be satisfied by drawing a structure with a double bond, such as

Recent studies indicate that double bonding may be important in BF_3. However, the boron atom in BF_3 certainly behaves as if it is electron-deficient, as indicated by the re-activity of BF_3 toward electron-rich molecules, for example, toward NH_3 to form H_3NBF_3:

In this stable compound, boron has an octet of electrons.

It is characteristic of boron to form molecules in which the boron atom is electron-deficient. On the other hand, carbon, nitrogen, oxygen, and fluorine can be counted on to obey the octet rule.

Some atoms exceed the octet rule. This behavior is observed only for those elements in Period 3 of the periodic table and beyond. To see how this arises, we will consider the Lewis structure for sulfur hexafluoride (SF_6), a well-known and very stable molecule. The sum of the valence electrons is

$$6 + 6(7) = 48 \text{ electrons}$$

Indicating the single bonds gives the structure on the left below:

We have used 12 electrons to form the S—F bonds, which leaves 36 electrons. Since fluor-ine always follows the octet rule, we complete the six fluorine octets to give the structure on the right above. This structure uses all 48 valence electrons for SF_6, but sulfur has 12 electrons around it; that is, sulfur *exceeds* the octet rule. How can this happen?

To answer this question, we need to consider the different types of valence orbitals characteristic of second- and third-period elements. The second-row elements have $2s$ and $2p$ valence orbitals, and the third-row elements have $3s$, $3p$, and $3d$ orbitals. The $3s$ and $3p$ orbitals fill with electrons in going from sodium to argon, but the $3d$ orbitals remain empty. For example, the valence orbital diagram for a sulfur atom is

Third-row elements can exceed the octet rule.

The localized electron model assumes that the empty $3d$ orbitals can be used to accommodate extra electrons. Thus the sulfur atom in SF_6 can have 12 electrons around it by using the $3s$ and $3p$ orbitals to hold 8 electrons, with the extra 4 electrons placed in the formerly empty $3d$ orbitals.

Lewis Structures: Comments About the Octet Rule

- The second-row elements C, N, O, and F should always be assumed to obey the octet rule.

- The second-row elements B and Be often have fewer than eight electrons around them in their compounds. These electron-deficient compounds are very reactive.

- The second-row elements never exceed the octet rule, since their valence orbitals ($2s$ and $2p$) can accommodate only eight electrons.

- Third-row and heavier elements often satisfy the octet rule but can exceed the octet rule by using their empty valence d orbitals.

- When writing the Lewis structure for a molecule, satisfy the octet rule for the atoms first. If electrons remain after the octet rule has been satisfied, then place them on the elements having available d orbitals (elements in Period 3 or beyond).

Whether the atoms that exceed the octet rule actually place the extra electrons in their d orbitals is a matter of controversy among theoretical chemists. We will not consider this issue in this text.

| Sample Exercise 8.7 | **Lewis Structures for Molecules That Violate the Octet Rule I** |

Write the Lewis structure for PCl_5.

Solution

We can follow the same stepwise procedure we used above for sulfur hexafluoride.

➡ **1** Sum the valence electrons.

$$5 + 5(7) = 40 \text{ electrons}$$
$$\underset{P}{\uparrow} \quad \underset{Cl}{\uparrow}$$

➡ **2** Indicate single bonds between bound atoms.

➡ **3** Distribute the remaining electrons. In this case, 30 electrons ($40 - 10$) remain. These are used to satisfy the octet rule for each chlorine atom. The final Lewis structure is

Note that phosphorus, which is a third-row element, has exceeded the octet rule by two electrons.

See Exercises 8.71 and 8.72.

In the PCl_5 and SF_6 molecules, the central atoms (P and S, respectively) must have the extra electrons. However, in molecules having more than one atom that can exceed the octet rule, it is not always clear which atom should have the extra electrons. Consider the Lewis structure for the triiodide ion (I_3^-), which has

$$3(7) + 1 = 22 \text{ valence electrons}$$

↑   ↑
1   1 − charge

Indicating the single bonds gives I—I—I. At this point, 18 electrons (22 − 4) remain. Trial and error will convince you that one of the iodine atoms must exceed the octet rule, but *which* one?

The rule we will follow is that *when it is necessary to exceed the octet rule for one of several third-row (or higher) elements, assume that the extra electrons should be placed on the central atom.*

Thus for I_3^- the Lewis structure is

$$\left[\, :\ddot{\underset{..}{I}}-\ddot{\underset{..}{I}}-\ddot{\underset{..}{I}}: \,\right]^-$$

where the central iodine exceeds the octet rule. This structure agrees with known properties of I_3^-.

Lewis Structures for Molecules That Violate the Octet Rule II

Write the Lewis structure for each molecule or ion.

a. ClF_3 **b.** XeO_3 **c.** $RnCl_2$ **d.** $BeCl_2$ **e.** ICl_4^-

Solution

a. The chlorine atom (third row) accepts the extra electrons.

b. All atoms obey the octet rule.

c. Radon, a noble gas in Period 6, accepts the extra electrons.

d. Beryllium is electron-deficient.

$$:\ddot{\underset{..}{Cl}}-Be-\ddot{\underset{..}{Cl}}:$$

e. Iodine exceeds the octet rule.

See Exercises 8.71 and 8.72.

8.12 Resonance

Sometimes more than one valid Lewis structure (one that obeys the rules we have outlined) is possible for a given molecule. Consider the Lewis structure for the nitrate ion (NO_3^-), which has 24 valence electrons. To achieve an octet of electrons around each atom, a structure like this is required:

If this structure accurately represents the bonding in NO_3^-, there should be two types of N---O bonds observed in the molecule: one shorter bond (the double bond) and two identical longer ones (the two single bonds). However, experiments clearly show that NO_3^- exhibits only *one* type of N---O bond with a length and strength *between* those expected for a single bond and a double bond. Thus, although the structure we have shown above is a valid Lewis structure, it does *not* correctly represent the bonding in NO_3^-. This is a serious problem, and it means that the model must be modified.

Look again at the proposed Lewis structure for NO_3^-. There is no reason for choosing a particular oxygen atom to have the double bond. There are really three valid Lewis structures:

Is any of these structures a correct description of the bonding in NO_3^-? No, because NO_3^- does not have one double and two single bonds—it has three equivalent bonds. We can solve this problem by making the following assumption: The correct description of NO_3^- is *not given by any one* of the three Lewis structures but is given only by the *superposition of all three.*

The nitrate ion does not exist as any of the three extreme structures but exists as an average of all three. **Resonance** *is invoked when more than one valid Lewis structure can be written for a particular molecule.* The resulting electron structure of the molecule is given by the average of these **resonance structures.** This situation is usually represented by double-headed arrows as follows:

Note that in all these resonance structures the arrangement of the nuclei is the same. Only the placement of the electrons differs. The arrows do not mean that the molecule "flips" from one resonance to another. They simply show that the *actual structure is an average of the three resonance structures.*

The concept of resonance is necessary because the localized electron model postulates that electrons are localized between a given pair of atoms. However, nature does not really operate this way. Electrons are really delocalized—they can move around the entire molecule. The valence electrons in the NO_3^- molecule distribute themselves to provide equivalent N---O bonds. Resonance is necessary to compensate for the defective assumption of the localized electron model. However, this model is so useful that we retain the concept of localized electrons and add resonance to allow the model to treat species such as NO_3^-.

Resonance Structures

Describe the electron arrangement in the nitrite anion (NO_2^-) using the localized electron model.

Solution

We will follow the usual procedure for obtaining the Lewis structure for the NO_2^- ion. In NO_2^- there are $5 + 2(6) + 1 = 18$ valence electrons. Indicating the single bonds gives the structure

$$O\!-\!N\!-\!O$$

The remaining 14 electrons ($18 - 4$) can be distributed to produce these structures:

$$\left[\overset{\cdot\cdot}{\underset{:O \qquad O:}{N}} \right]^- \longleftrightarrow \left[\overset{\cdot\cdot}{\underset{:O \qquad O:}{N}} \right]^-$$

This is a resonance situation. Two equivalent Lewis structures can be drawn. *The electronic structure of the molecule is correctly represented not by either resonance structure but by the average of the two.* There are two equivalent N--O bonds, each one intermediate between a single and a double bond.

See Exercises 8.73 through 8.78.

Odd-Electron Molecules

Relatively few molecules formed from nonmetals contain odd numbers of electrons. One common example is nitric oxide (NO), which is formed when nitrogen and oxygen gases react at the high temperatures in automobile engines. Nitric oxide is emitted into the air, where it immediately reacts with oxygen to form gaseous nitrogen dioxide (NO_2), another odd-electron molecule.

Since the localized electron model is based on pairs of electrons, it does not handle odd-electron cases in a natural way. To treat odd-electron molecules, a more sophisticated model is needed.

Formal Charge

Equivalent Lewis structures contain the same numbers of single and multiple bonds. For example, the resonance structures for O_3

$$\overset{\cdot\cdot}{\underset{:O \qquad \cdot O\cdot}{O}} \quad \text{and} \quad \overset{\cdot\cdot}{\underset{\cdot O\cdot \qquad O:}{O}}$$

are equivalent Lewis structures. These are equally important in describing the bonding in O_3. Nonequivalent Lewis structures contain different numbers of single and multiple bonds.

Molecules or polyatomic ions containing atoms that can exceed the octet rule often have many nonequivalent Lewis structures, all of which obey the rules for writing Lewis structures. For example, as we will see in detail below, the sulfate ion has a Lewis structure with all single bonds and several Lewis structures that contain double bonds. How do we decide which of the many possible Lewis structures best describes the actual bonding in sulfate? One method is to estimate the charge on each atom in the various possible Lewis structures and use these charges to select the most appropriate structure(s). We will see below how this is done, but first we must decide on a method to assign atomic charges in molecules.

In Chapter 4 we discussed one system for obtaining charges, called *oxidation states.* However, in assigning oxidation states, we always count *both* the shared electrons as belonging to the more electronegative atom in a bond. This practice leads to highly exaggerated estimates of charge. In other words, although oxidation states are useful for bookkeeping electrons in redox reactions, they are not realistic estimates of the actual charges on individual atoms in a molecule, so they are not suitable for judging the appropriateness of Lewis structures. Another definition of the charge on an atom in a molecule, the formal charge, can, however, be used to evaluate Lewis structures. As we will see below, the **formal charge** of an atom in a molecule is *the difference between the number of valence electrons on the free atom and the number of valence electrons assigned to the atom in the molecule.*

Therefore, to determine the formal charge of a given atom in a molecule, we need to know two things:

1. The number of valence electrons on the free neutral atom (which has zero net charge because the number of electrons equals the number of protons)

2. The number of valence electrons "belonging" to the atom in a molecule

We then compare these numbers. If in the molecule the atom has the same number of valence electrons as it does in the free state, the positive and negative charges just balance, and it has a formal charge of zero. If the atom has one more valence electron in a molecule than it has as a free atom, it has a formal charge of -1, and so on. Thus the formal charge on an atom in a molecule is defined as

Formal charge = (number of valence electrons on free atom)
$\qquad$ − (number of valence electrons assigned to the atom in the molecule)

To compute the formal charge of an atom in a molecule, we assign the valence electrons in the molecule to the various atoms, making the following assumptions:

1. Lone pair electrons belong entirely to the atom in question.

2. Shared electrons are *divided equally* between the two sharing atoms.

Thus the number of valence electrons assigned to a given atom is calculated as follows:

(Valence electrons)$_{\text{assigned}}$ = (number of lone pair electrons)
$\qquad$ $+ \frac{1}{2}$ (number of shared electrons)

We will illustrate the procedure for calculating formal charges by considering two of the possible Lewis structures for the sulfate ion, which has 32 valence electrons. For the Lewis structure

each oxygen atom has 6 lone pair electrons and shares 2 electrons with the sulfur atom. Thus, using the preceding assumptions, each oxygen is assigned 7 valence electrons.

Valence electrons assigned to each oxygen = $6 \; plus \; \frac{1}{2}(2) = 7$

Lone pair electrons $\qquad$ Shared electrons

Formal charge on oxygen = $6 \; minus \; 7 = -1$

Valence electrons on a free O atom $\qquad$ Valence electrons assigned to each O in SO_4^{2-}

The formal charge on each oxygen is -1.

For the sulfur atom there are no lone pair electrons, and eight electrons are shared with the oxygen atoms. Thus, for sulfur,

$$\text{Valence electrons assigned to sulfur} = 0 \; plus \; \tfrac{1}{2}(8) = 4$$

↑   ↑
Lone   Shared
pair   electrons
electrons

$$\text{Formal charge on sulfur} = 6 \; minus \; 4 = 2$$

↑   ↑
Valence electrons
on a free S atom
Valence
electrons
assigned to S
in SO_4^{2-}

A second possible Lewis structure is

$$\left[\begin{array}{c} \overset{\cdot\cdot}{\underset{\cdot\cdot}{O}} \\ \| \\ :\overset{\cdot\cdot}{\underset{\cdot\cdot}{O}}\!-\!S\!-\!\overset{\cdot\cdot}{\underset{\cdot\cdot}{O}}: \\ \| \\ \underset{\cdot\cdot}{\overset{\cdot\cdot}{O}} \end{array}\right]^{2-}$$

In this case the formal charges are as follows:

For oxygen atoms with single bonds:

$$\text{Valence electrons assigned} = 6 + \tfrac{1}{2}(2) = 7$$
$$\text{Formal charge} = 6 - 7 = -1$$

For oxygen atoms with double bonds:

$$\text{Valence electrons assigned} = 4 + \tfrac{1}{2}(4) = 6$$

↑
Each double
bond has 4
electrons

$$\text{Formal charge} = 6 - 6 = 0$$

For the sulfur atom:

$$\text{Valence electrons assigned} = 0 + \tfrac{1}{2}(12) = 6$$
$$\text{Formal charge} = 6 - 6 = 0$$

We will use two fundamental assumptions about formal charges to evaluate Lewis structures:

1. Atoms in molecules try to achieve formal charges as close to zero as possible.

2. Any negative formal charges are expected to reside on the most electronegative atoms.

We can use these principles to evaluate the two Lewis structures for sulfate given previously. Notice that in the structure with only single bonds, each oxygen has a formal charge of -1, while the sulfur has a formal charge of $+2$. In contrast, in the structure with two double bonds and two single bonds, the sulfur and two oxygen atoms have a formal charge of 0, while two oxygens have a formal charge of -1. Based on the assumptions given above, the structure with two double bonds is preferred—it has lower formal charges and the -1 formal charges are on electronegative oxygen atoms. Thus, for the sulfate ion, we might expect resonance structures such as

to more closely describe the bonding than the Lewis structure with only single bonds.

Rules Governing Formal Charge

- To calculate the formal charge on an atom:

  1. Take the sum of the lone pair electrons and one-half the shared electrons. This is the number of valence electrons assigned to the atom in the molecule.

  2. Subtract the number of assigned electrons from the number of valence electrons on the free, neutral atom to obtain the formal charge.

- The sum of the formal charges of all atoms in a given molecule or ion must equal the overall charge on that species.

- If nonequivalent Lewis structures exist for a species, those with formal charges closest to zero and with any negative formal charges on the most electronegative atoms are considered to best describe the bonding in the molecule or ion.

Sample Exercise 8.10

Formal Charges

Give possible Lewis structures for XeO_3, an explosive compound of xenon. Which Lewis structure or structures are most appropriate according to the formal charges?

Solution

For XeO_3 (26 valence electrons) we can draw the following possible Lewis structures (formal charges are indicated in parentheses):

Based on the ideas of formal charge, we would predict that the Lewis structures with the lower values of formal charge would be most appropriate for describing the bonding in XeO_3.

See Exercises 8.81 through 8.86.

As a final note, there are a couple of cautions about formal charge to keep in mind. First, although formal charges are closer to actual atomic charges in molecules than are oxidation states, formal charges still provide only *estimates* of charge—they should not be taken as actual atomic charges. Second, the evaluation of Lewis structures using formal charge ideas can lead to erroneous predictions. Tests based on experiments must be used to make the final decisions on the correct description of the bonding in a molecule or polyatomic ion.

8.13 Molecular Structure: The VSEPR Model

The structures of molecules play a very important role in determining their chemical properties. As we will see later, this is particularly important for biological molecules; a slight change in the structure of a large biomolecule can completely destroy its usefulness to a cell or may even change the cell from a normal one to a cancerous one.

Many accurate methods now exist for determining **molecular structure,** the three-dimensional arrangement of the atoms in a molecule. These methods must be used if precise information about structure is required. However, it is often useful to be able to predict the approximate molecular structure of a molecule. In this section we consider a simple model that allows us to do this. This model, called the **valence shell electron-pair repulsion (VSEPR) model,** is useful in predicting the geometries of molecules formed from nonmetals. The main postulate of this model is that *the structure around a given atom is determined principally by minimizing electron-pair repulsions.* The idea here is that the bonding and nonbonding pairs around a given atom will be positioned as far apart as possible. To see how this model works, we will first consider the molecule $BeCl_2$, which has the Lewis structure

$$: \overset{..}{Cl} - Be - \overset{..}{Cl} :$$

Note that there are two pairs of electrons around the beryllium atom. What arrangement of these electron pairs allows them to be as far apart as possible to minimize the repulsions? Clearly, the best arrangement places the pairs on opposite sides of the beryllium atom at 180 degrees from each other:

This is the maximum possible separation for two electron pairs. Once we have determined the optimal arrangement of the electron pairs around the central atom, we can specify the molecular structure of $BeCl_2$, that is, the positions of the atoms. Since each electron pair on beryllium is shared with a chlorine atom, the molecule has a **linear structure** with a 180-degree bond angle:

Next, let's consider BF_3, which has the Lewis structure

Here the boron atom is surrounded by three pairs of electrons. What arrangement will minimize the repulsions? The electron pairs are farthest apart at angles of 120 degrees:

Visualization:VSEPR

$BeCl_2$ has only four electrons around Be and is expected to be very reactive with electron-pair donors.

Visualization: VSEPR: Two Electron Pairs

Visualization: VSEPR: Three Electron Pairs

Since each of the electron pairs is shared with a fluorine atom, the molecular structure will be

This is a planar (flat) and triangular molecule, which is commonly described as a **trigonal planar structure.**

Next, let's consider the methane molecule, which has the Lewis structure

There are four pairs of electrons around the central carbon atom. What arrangement of these electron pairs best minimizes the repulsions? First, let's try a square planar arrangement:

The carbon atom and the electron pairs are centered in the plane of the paper, and the angles between the pairs are all 90 degrees.

Is there another arrangement with angles greater than 90 degrees that would put the electron pairs even farther away from each other? The answer is yes. The **tetrahedral structure** has angles of 109.5 degrees:

It can be shown that this is the maximum possible separation of four pairs around a given atom. This means that *whenever four pairs of electrons are present around an atom, they should always be arranged tetrahedrally.*

Now that we have the electron-pair arrangement that gives the least repulsion, we can determine the positions of the atoms and thus the molecular structure of CH_4. In methane, each of the four electron pairs is shared between the carbon atom and a hydrogen atom. Thus the hydrogen atoms are placed as in Fig. 8.15, and the molecule has a tetrahedral structure with the carbon atom at the center.

Recall that the main idea of the VSEPR model is to find the arrangement of electron pairs around the central atom that minimizes the repulsions. Then we can determine the molecular structure from knowing how the electron pairs are shared with the peripheral atoms. Use the following steps to predict the structure of a molecule using the VSEPR model.

FIGURE 8.15
The molecular structure of methane. The tetrahedral arrangement of electron pairs produces a tetrahedral arrangement of hydrogen atoms.

Steps to Apply the VSEPR Model

➥ 1 **Draw the Lewis structure for the molecule.**

➥ 2 **Count the electron pairs and arrange them in the way that minimizes repulsion (that is, put the pairs as far apart as possible).**

➥ 3 **Determine the positions of the atoms from the *way the electron pairs are shared.***

➥ 4 **Determine the name of the molecular structure from the *positions of the atoms.***

We will predict the structure of ammonia (NH_3) using this stepwise approach.

➥ 1   Draw the Lewis structure:

$$H—\overset{\cdot\cdot}{N}—H$$
$$\underset{H}{|}$$

➥ 2   Count the pairs of electrons and arrange them to minimize repulsions. The NH_3 molecule has four pairs of electrons: three bonding pairs and one nonbonding pair. From the discussion of the methane molecule, we know that the best arrangement of four electron pairs is a tetrahedral array, as shown in Fig. 8.16(a).

➥ 3   Determine the positions of the atoms. The three H atoms share electron pairs, as shown in Fig. 8.16(b).

➥ 4   Name the molecular structure. It is very important to recognize that the *name* of the molecular structure is always based on the *positions of the atoms.* The placement of the electron pairs determines the structure, but the name is based on the positions of the atoms. Thus it is incorrect to say that the NH_3 molecule is tetrahedral. It has a tetrahedral arrangement of electron pairs but not a tetrahedral arrangement of atoms. The molecular structure of ammonia is a **trigonal pyramid** (one side is different from the other three) rather than a tetrahedron, as shown in Fig. 8.16(c).

When four uniform balloons are tied together, they naturally form a tetrahedral shape.

| *Sample Exercise 8.11* | **Prediction of Molecular Structure I** |

Describe the molecular structure of the water molecule.

Solution

The Lewis structure for water is

$$H—\overset{\cdot\cdot}{\underset{\cdot\cdot}{O}}—H$$

There are four pairs of electrons: two bonding pairs and two nonbonding pairs. To minimize repulsions, these are best arranged in a tetrahedral array, as shown in Fig. 8.17(a).

FIGURE 8.16
(a) The tetrahedral arrangement of electron pairs around the nitrogen atom in the ammonia molecule. (b) Three of the electron pairs around nitrogen are shared with hydrogen atoms as shown and one is a lone pair. Although the arrangement of *electron pairs* is tetrahedral, as in the methane molecule, the hydrogen atoms in the ammonia molecule occupy only three corners of the tetrahedron. A lone pair occupies the fourth corner. (c) Note that molecular geometry is trigonal pyramidal, not tetrahedral.

(a)   (b)   (c)

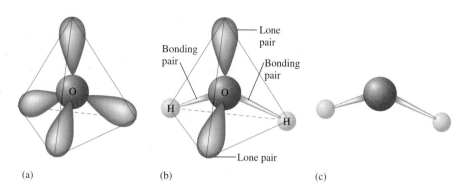

FIGURE 8.17
(a) The tetrahedral arrangement of the four electron pairs around oxygen in the water molecule. (b) Two of the electron pairs are shared between oxygen and the hydrogen atoms and two are lone pairs. (c) The V-shaped molecular structure of the water molecule.

(a)   (b)   (c)

Although H_2O has a tetrahedral arrangement of electron pairs, it is not a tetrahedral molecule. The atoms in the H_2O molecule form a V shape, as shown in Fig. 8.17(b) and (c).

See Exercises 8.91 and 8.92.

From Sample Exercise 8.11 we see that the H_2O molecule is V-shaped, or bent, because of the presence of the lone pairs. If no lone pairs were present, the molecule would be linear, the polar bonds would cancel, and the molecule would have no dipole moment. This would make water very different from the polar substance so familiar to us.

From the previous discussion we would predict that the H—X—H bond angle (where X is the central atom) in CH_4, NH_3, and H_2O should be the tetrahedral angle of 109.5 degrees. Experimental studies, however, show that the actual bond angles are those given in Fig. 8.18. What significance do these results have for the VSEPR model? One possible point of view is that we should be pleased to have the observed angles so close to the tetrahedral angle. The opposite view is that the deviations are significant enough to require modification of the simple model so that it can more accurately handle similar cases. We will take the latter view.

Let us examine the following data:

	CH_4	NH_3	H_2O
Number of Lone Pairs	0	1	2
Bond Angle	109.5°	107°	104.5°

One interpretation of the trend observed here is that lone pairs require more space than bonding pairs; in other words, as the number of lone pairs increases, the bonding pairs are increasingly squeezed together.

FIGURE 8.18
The bond angles in the CH_4, NH_3, and H_2O molecules. Note that the bond angle between bonding pairs decreases as the number of lone pairs increases. Note that all of the angles in CH_4 are 109.5 degrees and all of the angles in NH_3 are 107 degrees.

Methane   Ammonia   Water

(a)

(b)

FIGURE 8.19

(a) In a bonding pair of electrons, the electrons are shared by two nuclei. (b) In a lone pair, both electrons must be close to a single nucleus and tend to take up more of the space around that atom.

This interpretation seems to make physical sense if we think in the following terms. A bonding pair is shared between two nuclei, and the electrons can be close to either nucleus. They are relatively confined between the two nuclei. A lone pair is localized on only one nucleus, and both electrons will be close only to that nucleus, as shown schematically in Fig. 8.19. These pictures help us understand why a lone pair may require more space near an atom than a bonding pair.

As a result of these observations, we make the following addition to the original postulate of the VSEPR model: *Lone pairs require more room than bonding pairs and tend to compress the angles between the bonding pairs.*

So far we have considered cases with two, three, and four electron pairs around the central atom. These are summarized in Table 8.6.

Table 8.7 summarizes the structures possible for molecules in which there are four electron pairs around the central atom with various numbers of atoms bonded to it. Note that molecules with four pairs of electrons around the central atom can be tetrahedral (AB_4), trigonal pyramidal (AB_3), and V-shaped (AB_2).

For five pairs of electrons, there are several possible choices. The one that produces minimum repulsion is a **trigonal bipyramid.** Note from Table 8.6 that this arrangement

TABLE 8.6   Arrangements of Electron Pairs Around an Atom Yielding Minimum Repulsion

Number of Electron Pairs	Arrangement of Electron Pairs		Example
2	Linear		
3	Trigonal planar		
4	Tetrahedral		
5	Trigonal bipyramidal		
6	Octahedral		

TABLE 8.7 Structures of Molecules That Have Four Electron Pairs Around the Central Atom

Electron-Pair Arrangement	Molecular Structure
	Tetrahedral
	Trigonal pyramid
	V-shaped (bent)

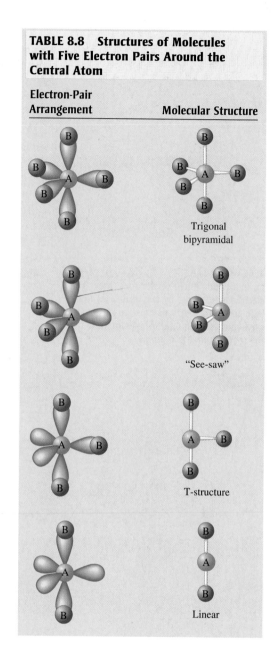

TABLE 8.8 Structures of Molecules with Five Electron Pairs Around the Central Atom

Electron-Pair Arrangement	Molecular Structure
	Trigonal bipyramidal
	"See-saw"
	T-structure
	Linear

has two different angles, 90 degrees and 120 degrees. As the name suggests, the structure formed by this arrangement of pairs consists of two trigonal-based pyramids that share a common base. Table 8.8 summarizes the structures possible for molecules in which there are five electron pairs around the central atom with various numbers of atoms bonded to it. Note that molecules with five pairs of electrons around the central atom can be trigonal bipyramidal (AB_5), see-saw (AB_4), T-shaped (AB_3), and linear (AB_2).

Six pairs of electrons can best be arranged around a given atom with 90-degree angles to form an **octahedral structure,** as shown in Table 8.6.

To use the VSEPR model to determine the geometric structures of molecules, you should memorize the relationships between the number of electron pairs and their best arrangement.

| Sample Exercise 8.12 | Prediction of Molecular Structure II |

When phosphorus reacts with excess chlorine gas, the compound phosphorus pentachloride (PCl_5) is formed. In the gaseous and liquid states, this substance consists of PCl_5 molecules, but in the solid state it consists of a $1:1$ mixture of PCl_4^+ and PCl_6^- ions. Predict the geometric structures of PCl_5, PCl_4^+, and PCl_6^-.

Solution

The Lewis structure for PCl_5 is shown. Five pairs of electrons around the phosphorus atom require a trigonal bipyramidal arrangement (see Table 8.6). When the chlorine atoms are included, a trigonal bipyramidal molecule results:

The Lewis structure for the PCl_4^+ ion ($5 + 4(7) - 1 = 32$ valence electrons) is shown below. There are four pairs of electrons surrounding the phosphorus atom in the PCl_4^+ ion, which requires a tetrahedral arrangement of the pairs. Since each pair is shared with a chlorine atom, a tetrahedral PCl_4^+ cation results.

The Lewis structure for PCl_6^- ($5 + 6(7) + 1 = 48$ valence electrons) is shown below. Since phosphorus is surrounded by six pairs of electrons, an octahedral arrangement is required to minimize repulsions, as shown below in the center. Since each electron pair is shared with a chlorine atom, an octahedral PCl_6^- anion is predicted.

See Exercises 8.89, 8.90, 8.93, and 8.94.

| Sample Exercise 8.13 | Prediction of Molecular Structure III |

Because the noble gases have filled s and p valence orbitals, they were not expected to be chemically reactive. In fact, for many years these elements were called *inert gases* because of this supposed inability to form any compounds. However, in the early 1960s several compounds of krypton, xenon, and radon were synthesized. For example, a team at the

Argonne National Laboratory produced the stable colorless compound xenon tetrafluoride (XeF_4). Predict its structure and whether it has a dipole moment.

Solution

The Lewis structure for XeF_4 is

The xenon atom in this molecule is surrounded by six pairs of electrons, which means an octahedral arrangement.

The structure predicted for this molecule will depend on how the lone pairs and bonding pairs are arranged. Consider the two possibilities shown in Fig. 8.20. The bonding pairs are indicated by the presence of the fluorine atoms. Since the structure predicted differs in the two cases, we must decide which of these arrangements is preferable. The key is to look at the lone pairs. In the structure in part (a), the lone pair–lone pair angle is 90 degrees; in the structure in part (b), the lone pairs are separated by 180 degrees. Since lone pairs require more room than bonding pairs, a structure with two lone pairs at 90 degrees is unfavorable. Thus the arrangement in Fig. 8.20(b) is preferred, and the molecular structure is predicted to be square planar. Note that this molecule is *not* described as being octahedral. There is an *octahedral arrangement of electron pairs,* but the *atoms* form a **square planar structure.**

Although each Xe—F bond is polar (fluorine has a greater electronegativity than xenon), the square planar arrangement of these bonds causes the polarities to cancel.

Thus XeF_4 has no dipole moment, as shown in the margin.

See Exercises 8.95 through 8.98.

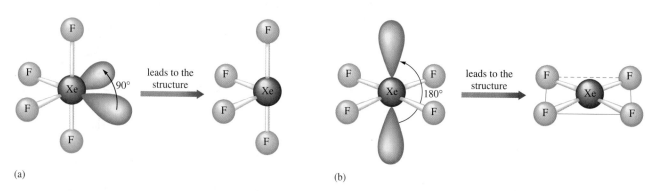

FIGURE 8.20
Possible electron-pair arrangements for XeF_4. Since arrangement (a) has lone pairs at 90 degrees from each other, it is less favorable than arrangement (b), where the lone pairs are at 180 degrees.

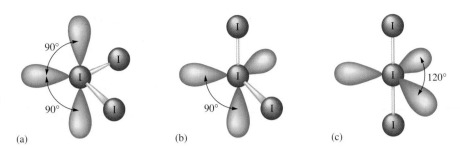

FIGURE 8.21
Three possible arrangements of the electron pairs in the I$_3^-$ ion. Arrangement (c) is preferred because there are no 90-degree lone pair–lone pair interactions.

We can further illustrate the use of the VSEPR model for molecules or ions with lone pairs by considering the triiodide ion (I$_3^-$).

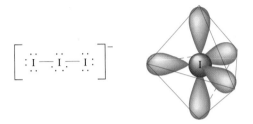

The central iodine atom has five pairs around it, which requires a trigonal bipyramidal arrangement. Several possible arrangements of lone pairs are shown in Fig. 8.21. Note that structures (a) and (b) have lone pairs at 90 degrees, whereas in (c) all lone pairs are at 120 degrees. Thus structure (c) is preferred. The resulting molecular structure for I$_3^-$ is linear:

$$[I\!-\!I\!-\!I]^-$$

The VSEPR Model and Multiple Bonds

So far in our treatment of the VSEPR model we have not considered any molecules with multiple bonds. To see how these molecules are handled by this model, let's consider the NO$_3^-$ ion, which requires three resonance structures to describe its electronic structure:

The NO$_3^-$ ion is known to be planar with 120-degree bond angles:

This planar structure is the one expected for three pairs of electrons around a central atom, which means that *a double bond should be counted as one effective pair* in using the VSEPR model. This makes sense because the two pairs of electrons involved in the double bond are *not* independent pairs. Both the electron pairs must be in the space between the nuclei of the two atoms to form the double bond. In other words, the double bond acts as one center of electron density to repel the other pairs of electrons. The same holds true for triple bonds. This leads us to another general rule: *For the VSEPR model, multiple bonds count as one effective electron pair.*

The molecular structure of nitrate also shows us one more important point: *When a molecule exhibits resonance, any one of the resonance structures can be used to predict the molecular structure using the VSEPR model.* These rules are illustrated in Sample Exercise 8.14.

Sample Exercise 8.14 | ## Structures of Molecules with Multiple Bonds

Predict the molecular structure of the sulfur dioxide molecule. Is this molecule expected to have a dipole moment?

Solution

First, we must determine the Lewis structure for the SO_2 molecule, which has 18 valence electrons. The expected resonance structures are

To determine the molecular structure, we must count the electron pairs around the sulfur atom. In each resonance structure the sulfur has one lone pair, one pair in a single bond, and one double bond. Counting the double bond as one pair yields three effective pairs around the sulfur. According to Table 8.6, a trigonal planar arrangement is required, which yields a V-shaped molecule:

Thus the structure of the SO_2 molecule is expected to be V-shaped, with a 120-degree bond angle. The molecule has a dipole moment directed as shown:

Since the molecule is V-shaped, the polar bonds do not cancel.

See Exercises 8.99 and 8.100.

It should be noted at this point that lone pairs that are oriented at least 120 degrees from other pairs do not produce significant distortions of bond angles. For example, the angle in the SO_2 molecule is actually quite close to 120 degrees. We will follow the

FIGURE 8.22
The molecular structure of methanol.
(a) The arrangement of electron pairs and atoms around the carbon atom. (b) The arrangement of bonding and lone pairs around the oxygen atom. (c) The molecular structure.

general principle that *a 120-degree angle provides lone pairs with enough space so that distortions do not occur. Angles less than 120 degrees are distorted when lone pairs are present.*

Molecules Containing No Single Central Atom

So far we have considered molecules consisting of one central atom surrounded by other atoms. The VSEPR model can be readily extended to more complicated molecules, such as methanol (CH_3OH). This molecule is represented by the following Lewis structure:

$$
\begin{array}{c}
H \\
| \\
H - C - \ddot{O} - H \\
| \\
H
\end{array}
$$

The molecular structure can be predicted from the arrangement of pairs around the carbon and oxygen atoms. Note that there are four pairs of electrons around the carbon, which requires a tetrahedral arrangement, as shown in Fig. 8.22(a). The oxygen also has four pairs, which requires a tetrahedral arrangement. However, in this case the tetrahedron will be slightly distorted by the space requirements of the lone pairs [Fig. 8.22(b)]. The overall geometric arrangement for the molecule is shown in Fig. 8.22(c).

> ### Summary of the VSEPR Model
>
> The rules for using the VSEPR model to predict molecular structure follow:
>
> - Determine the Lewis structure(s) for the molecule.
> - For molecules with resonance structures, use any of the structures to predict the molecular structure.
> - Sum the electron pairs around the central atom.
> - In counting pairs, count each multiple bond as a single effective pair.
> - The arrangement of the pairs is determined by minimizing electron-pair repulsions. These arrangements are shown in Table 8.6.
> - Lone pairs require more space than bonding pairs do. Choose an arrangement that gives the lone pairs as much room as possible. Recognize that the lone pairs may produce a slight distortion of the structure at angles less than 120 degrees.

The VSEPR Model—How Well Does It Work?

The VSEPR model is very simple. There are only a few rules to remember, yet the model correctly predicts the molecular structures of most molecules formed from nonmetallic elements. Molecules of any size can be treated by applying the VSEPR model to each appropriate atom (those bonded to at least two other atoms) in the molecule. Thus we can use this model to predict the structures of molecules with hundreds of atoms. It does,

CHEMICAL IMPACT

Chemical Structure and Communication: Semiochemicals

In this chapter we have stressed the importance of being able to predict the three-dimensional structure of a molecule. Molecular structure is important because of its effect on chemical reactivity. This is especially true in biological systems, where reactions must be efficient and highly specific. Among the hundreds of types of molecules in the fluids of a typical biological system, the appropriate reactants must find and react only with each other—-they must be very discriminating. This specificity depends largely on structure. The molecules are constructed so that only the appropriate partners can approach each other in a way that allows reaction.

Another area where molecular structure is central is in the use of molecules as a means of communication. Examples of a chemical communication occur in humans in the conduction of nerve impulses across synapses, the control of the manufacture and storage of key chemicals in cells, and the senses of smell and taste. Plants and animals also use chemical communication. For example, ants lay down a chemical trail so that other ants can find a particular food supply. Ants also warn their fellow workers of approaching danger by emitting certain chemicals.

The queen bee secretes a chemical that prevents the worker bees from raising a competitive sovereign.

Molecules convey messages by fitting into appropriate receptor sites in a very specific way, which is determined by their structure. When a molecule occupies a receptor site, chemical processes are stimulated that produce the appropriate response. Sometimes receptors can be fooled, as in the use of artificial sweeteners—-molecules fit the sites on the taste buds that stimulate a "sweet" response in the brain, but they are not metabolized in the same way as natural sugars. Similar deception is useful in insect control. If an area is sprayed

however, fail in a few instances. For example, phosphine (PH_3), which has a Lewis structure analogous to that of ammonia,

$$H-\overset{..}{\underset{|}{P}}-H \qquad H-\overset{..}{\underset{|}{N}}-H$$
$$\quad\;\; H \qquad\qquad\quad\;\; H$$

would be predicted to have a molecular structure similar to that for NH_3, with bond angles of approximately 107 degrees. However, the bond angles of phosphine are actually 94 degrees. There are ways of explaining this structure, but more rules have to be added to the model.

This again illustrates the point that simple models are bound to have exceptions. In introductory chemistry we want to use simple models that fit the majority of cases; we are willing to accept a few failures rather than complicate the model. The amazing thing about the VSEPR model is that such a simple model predicts correctly the structures of so many molecules.

with synthetic female sex attractant molecules, the males of that species become so confused that mating does not occur.

A *semiochemical* is a molecule that delivers a message between members of the same or different species of plant or animal. There are three groups of these chemical messengers: allomones, kairomones, and pheromones. Each is of great ecological importance.

An *allomone* is defined as a chemical that somehow gives adaptive advantage to the producer. For example, leaves of the black walnut tree contain a herbicide, juglone, that appears after the leaves fall to the ground. Juglone is not toxic to grass or certain grains, but it is effective against plants such as apple trees that would compete for the available water and food supplies.

Antibiotics are also allomones, since the microorganisms produce them to inhibit other species from growing near them.

Many plants produce bad-tasting chemicals to protect themselves from plant-eating insects and animals. The familiar compound nicotine deters animals from eating the tobacco plant. The millipede sends an unmistakable "back off" message by squirting a predator with benzaldehyde and hydrogen cyanide.

Defense is not the only use of allomones, however. Flowers use scent as a way to attract pollinating insects. Honeybees, for instance, are guided to alfalfa and flowers by a series of sweet-scented compounds.

Kairomones are chemical messengers that bring advantageous news to the receiver, and the floral scents are kairomones from the honeybees' viewpoint. Many predators are guided by kairomones emitted by their food. For example, apple skins exude a chemical that attracts the codling moth larva. In some cases kairomones help the underdog.

Certain marine mollusks can pick up the "scent" of their predators, the sea stars, and make their escape.

Pheromones are chemicals that affect receptors of the same species as the donor. That is, they are specific within a species. *Releaser pheromones* cause an immediate reaction in the receptor, and *primer pheromones* cause long-term effects. Examples of releaser pheromones are sex attractants of insects, generated in some species by the males and in others by the females. Sex pheromones also have been found in plants and mammals.

Alarm pheromones are highly volatile compounds (ones easily changed to a gas) released to warn of danger. Honeybees produce isoamyl acetate ($C_7H_{14}O_2$) in their sting glands. Because of its high volatility, this compound does not linger after the state of alert is over. Social behavior in insects is characterized by the use of *trail pheromones,* which are used to indicate a food source. Social insects such as bees, ants, wasps, and termites use these substances. Since trail pheromones are less volatile compounds, the indicators persist for some time.

Primer pheromones, which cause long-term behavioral changes, are harder to isolate and identify. One example, however, is the "queen substance" produced by queen honeybees. All the eggs in a colony are laid by one queen bee. If she is removed from the hive or dies, the worker bees are activated by the absence of the queen substance and begin to feed royal jelly to bee larvae so as to raise a new queen. The queen substance also prevents the development of the workers' ovaries so that only the queen herself can produce eggs.

Many studies of insect pheromones are now under way in the hope that they will provide a method of controlling insects that is more efficient and safer than the current chemical pesticides.

NH₃

PH₃

Key Terms

For Review

Chemical bonds
- Hold groups of atoms together
- Occur when a group of atoms can lower its total energy by aggregating
- Types of chemical bonds
  - Ionic: electrons are transferred to form ions
  - Covalent: equal sharing of electrons
  - Polar covalent: unequal electron sharing
- Percent ionic character of a bond X—Y

$$\frac{\text{Measured dipole moment of X—Y}}{\text{Calculated dipole moment for X}^+\text{Y}^-} \times 100\%$$

- Electronegativity: the relative ability of an atom to attract shared electrons
  - The polarity of a bond depends on the electronegativity difference of the bonded atoms
- The spacial arrangement of polar bonds in a molecule determines whether the molecule has a dipole moment

Ionic bonding
- An ion has a different size than its parent atom
  - An anion is larger than its parent ion
  - A cation is smaller than its parent atom
- Lattice energy: the change in energy when ions are packed together to form an ionic solid

Bond energy
- The energy necessary to break a covalent bond
- Increases as the number of shared pairs increases
- Can be used to estimate the enthalpy change for a chemical reaction

Lewis structures
- Show how the valence electron pairs are arranged among the atoms in a molecule or polyatomic ion
- Stable molecules usually contain atoms that have their valence orbitals filled
  - Leads to a duet rule for hydrogen
  - Leads to an octet rule for second-row elements
  - The atoms of elements in the third row and beyond can exceed the octet rule
- Several equivalent Lewis structures can be drawn for some molecules, a concept called resonance
- When several nonequivalent Lewis structures can be drawn for a molecule, formal charge is often used to choose the most appropriate structure(s)

VSEPR model
- Based on the idea that electron pairs will be arranged around a central atom in a way that minimizes the electron repulsions
- Can be used to predict the geometric structure of most molecules

REVIEW QUESTIONS

1. Distinguish between the terms *electronegativity* versus *electron affinity, covalent bond* versus *ionic bond,* and *pure covalent bond* versus *polar covalent bond.*

Characterize the types of bonds in terms of electronegativity difference. Energetically, why do ionic and covalent bonds form?

2. When an element forms an anion, what happens to the radius? When an element forms a cation, what happens to the radius? Why? Define the term *isoelectronic*. When comparing sizes of ions, which ion has the largest radius and which ion has the smallest radius in an isoelectronic series? Why?

3. Define the term *lattice energy*. Why, energetically, do ionic compounds form? Figure 8.11 illustrates the energy changes involved in the formation of $MgO(s)$ and $NaF(s)$. Why is the lattice energy of $MgO(s)$ so different from that of $NaF(s)$? The magnesium oxide is composed of Mg^{2+} and O^{2-} ions. Energetically, why does $Mg^{2+}O^{2-}$ form and not Mg^+O^-? Why doesn't $Mg^{3+}O^{3-}$ form?

4. Explain how bond energies can be used to estimate ΔH for a reaction. Why is this an estimate of ΔH? How do the product bond strengths compare to the reactant bond strengths for an exothermic reaction? For an endothermic reaction? What is the relationship between the number of bonds between two atoms and bond strength? Bond length?

5. Give a rationale for the octet rule and the duet rule for H in terms of orbitals. Give the steps for drawing a Lewis structure for a molecule or ion. In general, molecules and ions always follow the octet rule unless it is impossible. The three types of exceptions are molecules/ions with too few electrons, molecules/ions with an odd number of electrons, and molecules/ions with too many electrons. Which atoms sometimes have fewer than 8 electrons around them? Give an example. Which atoms sometimes have more than 8 electrons around them? Give some examples. Why are odd-electron species generally very reactive and uncommon? Give an example of an odd-electron molecule.

6. Explain the terms *resonance* and *delocalized electrons*. When a substance exhibits resonance, we say that none of the individual Lewis structures accurately portrays the bonding in the substance. Why do we draw resonance structures?

7. Define formal charge and explain how to calculate it. What is the purpose of the formal charge? Organic compounds are composed mostly of carbon and hydrogen, but also may have oxygen, nitrogen, and/or halogens in the formula. Formal charge arguments work very well for organic compounds when drawing the best Lewis structure. How do C, H, N, O, and Cl satisfy the octet rule in organic compounds so as to have a formula charge of zero?

8. Explain the main postulate of the VSEPR model. List the five base geometries (along with bond angles) that most molecules or ions adopt to minimize electron-pair repulsions. Why are bond angles sometimes slightly less than predicted in actual molecules as compared to what is predicted by the VSEPR model?

9. Give two requirements that should be satisfied for a molecule to be polar. Explain why CF_4 and XeF_4 are nonpolar compounds (have no dipole moments) while SF_4 is polar (has a dipole moment). Is CO_2 polar? What about COS? Explain.

10. Consider the following compounds: CO_2, SO_2, KrF_2, SO_3, NF_3, IF_3, CF_4, SF_4, XeF_4, PF_5, IF_5, and SCl_6. These 12 compounds are all examples of different molecular structures. Draw the Lewis structures for each and predict the molecular structure. Predict the bond angles and the polarity of each. (A polar molecule has a dipole moment, while a nonpolar molecule does not.) See Exercises 89 and 90 for the molecular structures based on the trigonal bipyramid and the octahedral geometries.

Active Learning Questions

These questions are designed to be used by groups of students in class. The questions allow students to explore their understanding of concepts through discussion and peer teaching. The real value of these questions is the learning that occurs while students talk to each other about chemical concepts.

1. Explain the electronegativity trends across a row and down a column of the periodic table. Compare these trends with those of ionization energies and atomic radii. How are they related?

2. The ionic compound AB is formed. The charges on the ions may be $+1$, -1; $+2$, -2; $+3$, -3; or even larger. What are the factors that determine the charge for an ion in an ionic compound?

3. Using only the periodic table, predict the most stable ion for Na, Mg, Al, S, Cl, K, Ca, and Ga. Arrange these from largest to smallest radius, and explain why the radius varies as it does. Compare your predictions with Fig. 8.8.

4. The bond energy for a C—H bond is about 413 kJ/mol in CH_4 but 380 kJ/mol in $CHBr_3$. Although these values are relatively close in magnitude, they are different. Explain why they are different. Does the fact that the bond energy is lower in $CHBr_3$ make any sense? Why?

5. Consider the following statement: "Because oxygen wants to have a negative two charge, the second electron affinity is more negative than the first." Indicate everything that is correct in this statement. Indicate everything that is incorrect. Correct the incorrect statements and explain.

6. Which has the greater bond lengths: NO_2^- or NO_3^-? Explain.

7. The following ions are best described with resonance structures. Draw the resonance structures, and using formal charge arguments, predict the best Lewis structure for each ion.
   a. NCO^-
   b. CNO^-

8. Would you expect the electronegativity of titanium to be the same in the species Ti, Ti^{2+}, Ti^{3+}, and Ti^{4+}? Explain.

9. The second electron affinity values for both oxygen and sulfur are unfavorable (endothermic). Explain.

10. What is meant by a chemical bond? Why do atoms form bonds with each other? Why do some elements exist as molecules in nature instead of as free atoms?

11. Why are some bonds ionic and some covalent?

12. Does a Lewis structure tell which electrons come from which atoms? Explain.

A blue question or exercise number indicates that the answer to that question or exercise appears at the back of this book and a solution appears in the *Solutions Guide*.

Questions

13. Some plant fertilizer compounds are $(NH_4)_2SO_4$, $Ca_3(PO_4)_2$, K_2O, P_2O_5, and KCl. Which of these compounds contain both ionic and covalent bonds?

14. Some of the important properties of ionic compounds are as follows:
    i. low electrical conductivity as solids and high conductivity in solution or when molten

    ii. relatively high melting and boiling points
    iii. brittleness
    iv. solubility in polar solvents
    How does the concept of ionic bonding discussed in this chapter account for these properties?

15. What is the electronegativity trend? Where does hydrogen fit into the electronegativity trend for the other elements in the periodic table?

16. Give one example of a compound having a linear molecular structure that has an overall dipole moment (is polar) and one example that does not have an overall dipole moment (is nonpolar). Do the same for molecules that have trigonal planar and tetrahedral molecular structures.

17. When comparing the size of different ions, the general radii trend discussed in Chapter 7 is generally not very useful. What do you concentrate on when comparing sizes of ions to each other or when comparing the size of an ion to its neutral atom?

18. In general, the higher the charge on the ions in an ionic compound, the more favorable the lattice energy. Why do some stable ionic compounds have $+1$ charged ions even though $+4$, $+5$, $+6$, charged ions would have a more favorable lattice energy?

19. Combustion reactions of fossil fuels provide most of the energy needs of the world. Why are combustion reactions of fossil fuels so exothermic?

20. Which of the following statements is(are) true? Correct the false statements.
    a. It is impossible to satisfy the octet rule for all atoms in XeF_2.
    b. Because SF_4 exists, then OF_4 should also exist because oxygen is in the same family as sulfur.
    c. The bond in NO^+ should be stronger than the bond in NO^-.
    d. As predicted from the two Lewis structures for ozone, one oxygen-oxygen bond is stronger than the other oxygen-oxygen bond.

21. Three resonance structures can be drawn for CO_2. Which resonance structure is best from a formal charge standpoint?

22. Which of the following statements is(are) true? Correct the false statements.
    a. The molecules SeS_3, SeS_2, PCl_5, $TeCl_4$, ICl_3, and $XeCl_2$ all exhibit at least one bond angle which is approximately $120°$.
    b. The bond angle in SO_2 should be similar to the bond angle in CS_2 or SCl_2.
    c. Of the compounds CF_4, KrF_4, and SeF_4, only SeF_4 exhibits an overall dipole moment (is polar).
    d. Central atoms in a molecule adopt a geometry of the bonded atoms and lone pairs about the central atom in order to maximize electron repulsions.

Exercises

In this section similar exercises are paired.

Chemical Bonds and Electronegativity

23. Without using Fig. 8.3, predict the order of increasing electronegativity in each of the following groups of elements.
    a. C, N, O   c. Si, Ge, Sn
    b. S, Se, Cl   d. Tl, S, Ge

24. Without using Fig. 8.3, predict the order of increasing electronegativity in each of the following groups of elements.
   a. Na, K, Rb   **c.** F, Cl, Br
   b. B, O, Ga   **d.** S, O, F

25. Without using Fig. 8.3, predict which bond in each of the following groups will be the most polar.
   a. C—F, Si—F, Ge—F
   b. P—Cl or S—Cl
   c. S—F, S—Cl, S—Br
   d. Ti—Cl, Si—Cl, Ge—Cl

26. Without using Fig. 8.3, predict which bond in each of the following groups will be the most polar.
   a. C—H, Si—H, Sn—H
   b. Al—Br, Ga—Br, In—Br, Tl—Br
   c. C—O or Si—O
   d. O—F or O—Cl

27. Repeat Exercises 23 and 25, this time using the values for the electronegativities of the elements given in Fig. 8.3. Are there differences in your answers?

28. Repeat Exercises 24 and 26, this time using the values for the electronegativities of the elements given in Fig. 8.3. Are there differences in your answers?

29. Which of the following incorrectly shows the bond polarity? Show the correct bond polarity for those that are incorrect.
   a. $^{\delta+}$H—F$^{\delta-}$ **d.** $^{\delta+}$Br—Br$^{\delta-}$
   b. $^{\delta+}$Cl—I$^{\delta-}$ **e.** $^{\delta+}$O—P$^{\delta-}$
   c. $^{\delta+}$Si—S$^{\delta-}$

30. Indicate the bond polarity (show the partial positive and partial negative ends) in the following bonds.
   a. C—O   **d.** Br—Te
   b. P—H   **e.** Se—S
   c. H—Cl

31. Hydrogen has an electronegativity value between boron and carbon and identical to phosphorus. With this in mind, rank the following bonds in order of decreasing polarity: P—H, O—H, N—H, F—H, C—H.

32. Rank the following bonds in order of increasing ionic character: N—O, Ca—O, C—F, Br—Br, K—F.

Ions and Ionic Compounds

33. Write electron configurations for the most stable ion formed by each of the elements Fr, Be, P, Cl, and Se (when in stable ionic compounds).

34. Write electron configurations for
   a. the cations Mg^{2+}, K^+, and Al^{3+}.
   b. the anions N^{3-}, O^{2-}, F^-, and Te^{2-}.

35. Which of the following ions have noble gas electron configurations?
   a. Fe^{2+}, Fe^{3+}, Sc^{3+}, Co^{3+}
   b. Tl^+, Te^{2-}, Cr^{3+}
   c. Pu^{4+}, Ce^{4+}, Ti^{4+}
   d. Ba^{2+}, Pt^{2+}, Mn^{2+}

36. What noble gas has the same election configuration as each of the ions in the following compounds?
   a. cesium sulfide
   b. strontium fluoride

c. calcium nitride
d. aluminum bromide

37. Give three ions that are isoelectronic with xenon. Place these ions in order of increasing size.

38. Consider the ions Sc^{3+}, Cl^-, K^+, Ca^{2+}, and S^{2-}. Match these ions to the following pictures that represent the relative sizes of the ions.

39. For each of the following groups, place the atoms and/or ions in order of decreasing size.
   a. Cu, Cu^+, Cu^{2+}
   b. Ni^{2+}, Pd^{2+}, Pt^{2+}
   c. O, O^-, O^{2-}
   d. La^{3+}, Eu^{3+}, Gd^{3+}, Yb^{3+}
   e. Te^{2-}, I^-, Cs^+, Ba^{2+}, La^{3+}

40. For each of the following groups, place the atoms and/or ions in order of decreasing size.
   a. V, V^{2+}, V^{3+}, V^{5+}
   b. Na^+, K^+, Rb^+, Cs^+
   c. Te^{2-}, I^-, Cs^+, Ba^{2+}
   d. P, P^-, P^{2-}, P^{3-}
   e. O^{2-}, S^{2-}, Se^{2-}, Te^{2-}

41. Predict the empirical formulas of the ionic compounds formed from the following pairs of elements. Name each compound.
   a. Al and S   **c.** Mg and Cl
   b. K and N   **d.** Cs and Br

42. Predict the empirical formulas of the ionic compounds formed from the following pairs of elements. Name each compound.
   a. Ga and I   **c.** Sr and F
   b. Na and O   **d.** Ca and P

43. Which compound in each of the following pairs of ionic substances has the most exothermic lattice energy? Justify your answers.
   a. NaCl, KCl
   b. LiF, LiCl
   c. $Mg(OH)_2$, MgO
   d. $Fe(OH)_2$, $Fe(OH)_3$
   e. NaCl, Na_2O
   f. MgO, BaS

44. Which compound in each of the following pairs of ionic substances has the most exothermic lattice energy? Justify your answers.
   a. LiF, CsF
   b. NaBr, NaI
   c. $BaCl_2$, BaO
   d. Na_2SO_4, $CaSO_4$
   e. KF, K_2O
   f. Li_2O, Na_2S

45. Use the following data to estimate ΔH_f° for potassium chloride.

$$K(s) + \tfrac{1}{2}Cl_2(g) \longrightarrow KCl(s)$$

Lattice energy	−690. kJ/mol
Ionization energy for K	419 kJ/mol
Electron affinity of Cl	−349 kJ/mol
Bond energy of Cl_2	239 kJ/mol
Enthalpy of sublimation for K	64 kJ/mol

46. Use the following data to estimate ΔH_f° for magnesium fluoride.

$$Mg(s) + F_2(g) \longrightarrow MgF_2(s)$$

Lattice energy	−3916 kJ/mol
First ionization energy of Mg	735 kJ/mol
Second ionization energy of Mg	1445 kJ/mol
Electron affinity of F	−328 kJ/mol
Bond energy of F_2	154 kJ/mol
Enthalpy of sublimation of Mg	150. kJ/mol

47. Consider the following energy changes:

	ΔH (kJ/mol)
$Mg(g) \rightarrow Mg^+(g) + e^-$	735
$Mg^+(g) \rightarrow Mg^{2+}(g) + e^-$	1445
$O(g) + e^- \rightarrow O^-(g)$	−141
$O^-(g) + e^- \rightarrow O^{2-}(g)$	878

Magnesium oxide exists as $Mg^{2+}O^{2-}$ and not as Mg^+O^-. Explain.

48. Compare the electron affinity of fluorine to the ionization energy of sodium. Is the process of an electron being "pulled" from the sodium atom to the fluorine atom exothermic or endothermic? Why is NaF a stable compound? Is the overall formation of NaF endothermic or exothermic? How can this be?

49. LiI(s) has a heat of formation of −272 kJ/mol and a lattice energy of −753 kJ/mol. The ionization energy of Li(g) is 520. kJ/mol, the bond energy of $I_2(g)$ is 151 kJ/mol, and the electron affinity of I(g) is −295 kJ/mol. Use these data to determine the heat of sublimation of Li(s).

50. Use the following data to estimate ΔH for the reaction $S^-(g) + e^- \rightarrow S^{2-}(g)$. Include an estimate of uncertainty.

	ΔH_f°	Lattice Energy	I.E. of M	ΔH_{sub} of M
Na_2S	−365	−2203	495	109
K_2S	−381	−2052	419	90
Rb_2S	−361	−1949	409	82
Cs_2S	−360	−1850	382	78

$$S(s) \longrightarrow S(g) \qquad \Delta H = 277 \text{ kJ/mol}$$
$$S(g) + e^- \longrightarrow S^-(g) \qquad \Delta H = -200 \text{ kJ/mol}$$

Assume that all values are known to ±1 kJ/mol.

51. Rationalize the following lattice energy values:

Compound	Lattice Energy (kJ/mol)
CaSe	−2862
Na_2Se	−2130
CaTe	−2721
Na_2Te	−2095

52. The lattice energies of $FeCl_3$, $FeCl_2$, and Fe_2O_3 are (in no particular order) −2631, −5359, and −14,774 kJ/mol. Match the appropriate formula to each lattice energy. Explain.

Bond Energies

53. Use bond energy values (Table 8.4) to estimate ΔH for each of the following reactions in the gas phase.
   a. $H_2 + Cl_2 \rightarrow 2HCl$
   b. $N \equiv N + 3H_2 \rightarrow 2NH_3$

54. Use bond energy values (Table 8.4) to estimate ΔH for each of the following reactions.

a.

$$H-C \equiv N(g) + 2H_2(g) \longrightarrow H-\overset{\overset{\displaystyle H}{|}}{\underset{\underset{\displaystyle H}{|}}{C}}-N(g)$$
(with H H on the N)

b.

$$\underset{H}{\overset{H}{>}}N-N\underset{H}{\overset{H}{<}} (l) + 2F_2(g) \longrightarrow N \equiv N(g) + 4HF(g)$$

55. Use bond energies (Table 8.4) to predict ΔH for the isomerization of methyl isocyanide to acetonitrile:

$$CH_3N \equiv C(g) \longrightarrow CH_3C \equiv N(g)$$

56. Acetic acid is responsible for the sour taste of vinegar. It can be manufactured using the following reaction:

$$CH_3OH(g) + C \equiv O(g) \longrightarrow CH_3\overset{\overset{\displaystyle O}{\|}}{C}-OH(l)$$

Use tabulated values of bond energies (Table 8.4) to estimate ΔH for this reaction.

57. Use bond energies to predict ΔH for the combustion of ethanol:

$$C_2H_5OH(l) + 3O_2(g) \rightarrow 2CO_2(g) + 3H_2O(g)$$

58. Use bond energies to estimate ΔH for the combustion for one mole of acetylene:

$$C_2H_2(g) + \tfrac{5}{2}O_2(g) \longrightarrow 2CO_2(g) + H_2O(g)$$

59. Use bond energies to estimate ΔH for the following reaction:

$$H_2O_2(aq) + CH_3OH(aq) \longrightarrow H_2CO(aq) + 2H_2O(l)$$

60. The space shuttle orbiter utilizes the oxidation of methyl hydrazine by dinitrogen tetroxide for propulsion:

$$5N_2O_4(l) + 4N_2H_3CH_3(l) \longrightarrow 12H_2O(g) + 9N_2(g) + 4CO_2(g)$$

Use bond energies to estimate ΔH for this reaction. The structures for the reactants are:

$+$

61. Consider the following reaction:

$\Delta H = -549\,\text{kJ}$

Estimate the carbon–fluorine bond energy given that the C—C bond energy is 347 kJ/mol, the C=C bond energy is 614 kJ/mol, and the F—F bond energy is 154 kJ/mol.

62. Consider the following reaction:

$$A_2 + B_2 \longrightarrow 2AB \qquad \Delta H = -285\,\text{kJ}$$

The bond energy for A_2 is one-half the amount of the AB bond energy. The bond energy of $B_2 = 432$ kJ/mol. What is the bond energy of A_2?

63. Compare your answers from parts a and b of Exercise 53 with ΔH values calculated for each reaction using standard enthalpies of formation in Appendix 4. Do enthalpy changes calculated from bond energies give a reasonable estimate of the actual values?

64. Compare your answer from Exercise 56 to the ΔH value calculated from standard enthalpies of formation in Appendix 4. Explain any discrepancies.

65. The standard enthalpies of formation for $S(g)$, $F(g)$, $SF_4(g)$, and $SF_6(g)$ are $+278.8$, $+79.0$, -775, and -1209 kJ/mol, respectively.
    a. Use these data to estimate the energy of an S—F bond.
    b. Compare your calculated values to the value given in Table 8.4. What conclusions can you draw?
    c. Why are the $\Delta H_{\text{f}}^{\circ}$ values for $S(g)$ and $F(g)$ not equal to zero, since sulfur and fluorine are elements?

66. Use the following standard enthalpies of formation to estimate the N—H bond energy in ammonia: $N(g)$, 472.7 kJ/mol; $H(g)$, 216.0 kJ/mol; $NH_3(g)$, -46.1 kJ/mol. Compare your value to the one in Table 8.4.

Lewis Structures and Resonance

67. Write Lewis structures that obey the octet rule for each of the following.
    a. HCN   d. NH_4^+ g. CO_2
    b. PH_3 e. H_2CO h. O_2
    c. $CHCl_3$ f. SeF_2 i. HBr
    Except for HCN and H_2CO, the first atom listed is the central atom. For HCN and H_2CO, carbon is the central atom.

68. Write Lewis structures that obey the octet rule for each of the following molecules and ions. (In each case the first atom listed is the central atom.)
    a. $POCl_3$, SO_4^{2-}, XeO_4, PO_4^{3-}, ClO_4^-
    b. NF_3, SO_3^{2-}, PO_3^{3-}, ClO_3^-

c. ClO_2^-, SCl_2, PCl_2^-
d. Considering your answers to parts a, b, and c, what conclusions can you draw concerning the structures of species containing the same number of atoms and the same number of valence electrons?

69. One type of exception to the octet rule are compounds with central atoms having fewer than eight electrons around them. BeH_2 and BH_3 are examples of this type of exception. Draw the Lewis structures for BeH_2 and BH_3.

70. Lewis structures can be used to understand why some molecules react in certain ways. Write the Lewis structures for the reactants and products in the reactions described below.
    a. Nitrogen dioxide dimerizes to produce dinitrogen tetroxide.
    b. Boron trihydride accepts a pair of electrons from ammonia, forming BH_3NH_3.
    Give a possible explanation for why these two reactions occur.

71. The most common type of exception to the octet rule are compounds or ions with central atoms having more than eight electrons around them. PF_5, SF_4, ClF_3 and Br_3^- are examples of this type of exception. Draw the Lewis structure for these compounds or ions. Which elements, when they have to, can have more than eight electrons around them? How is this rationalized?

72. SF_6, ClF_5, and XeF_4 are three compounds whose central atoms do not follow the octet rule. Draw Lewis structures for these compounds.

73. Write Lewis structures for the following. Show all resonance structures where applicable.
    a. NO_2^-, NO_3^-, N_2O_4 (N_2O_4 exists as O_2N—NO_2.)
    b. OCN^-, SCN^-, N_3^- (Carbon is the central atom in OCN^- and SCN^-.)

74. Some of the important pollutants in the atmosphere are ozone (O_3), sulfur dioxide, and sulfur trioxide. Write Lewis structures for these three molecules. Show all resonance structures where applicable.

75. Benzene (C_6H_6) consists of a six-membered ring of carbon atoms with one hydrogen bonded to each carbon. Write Lewis structures for benzene, including resonance structures.

76. Borazine ($B_3N_3H_6$) has often been called "inorganic" benzene. Write Lewis structures for borazine. Borazine contains a six-membered ring of alternating boron and nitrogen atoms with one hydrogen bonded to each boron and nitrogen.

77. An important observation supporting the concept of resonance in the localized electron model was that there are only three different structures of dichlorobenzene ($C_6H_4Cl_2$). How does this fact support the concept of resonance (see Exercise 75)?

78. Consider the following bond lengths:

    C—O 143 pm   C=O 123 pm   C≡O 109 pm

    In the CO_3^{2-} ion, all three C—O bonds have identical bond lengths of 136 pm. Why?

79. Place the species below in order of shortest to longest nitrogen–nitrogen bond.

    $$N_2 \qquad N_2F_4 \qquad N_2F_2$$

    (N_2F_4 exists as F_2N—NF_2, and N_2F_2 exists as FN—NF.)

80. Order the following species with respect to carbon–oxygen bond length (longest to shortest).

$$CO, \quad CO_2, \quad CO_3^{2-}, \quad CH_3OH$$

What is the order from the weakest to the strongest carbon–oxygen bond? (CH_3OH exists as $H_3C—OH$.)

Formal Charge

81. Write Lewis structures that obey the octet rule for the following species. Assign the formal charge for each central atom.

a. $POCl_3$ **e.** SO_2Cl_2
b. SO_4^{2-} **f.** XeO_4
c. ClO_4^- **g.** ClO_3^-
d. PO_4^{3-} **h.** NO_4^{3-}

82 Write Lewis structures for the species in Exercise 81 that involve minimum formal charges.

83. Write the Lewis structure for O_2F_2 (O_2F_2 exists as F—O—O—F). Assign oxidation states and formal charges to the atoms in O_2F_2. This compound is a vigorous and potent oxidizing and fluorinating agent. Are oxidation states or formal charges more useful in accounting for these properties of O_2F_2?

84. Oxidation of the cyanide ion produces the stable cyanate ion, OCN^-. The fulminate ion, CNO^-, on the other hand, is very unstable. Fulminate salts explode when struck; $Hg(CNO)_2$ is used in blasting caps. Write the Lewis structures and assign formal charges for the cyanate and fulminate ions. Why is the fulminate ion so unstable? (C is the central atom in OCN^- and N is the central atom in CNO^-.)

85. When molten sulfur reacts with chlorine gas, a vile-smelling orange liquid forms that has an empirical formula of SCl. The structure of this compound has a formal charge of zero on all elements in the compound. Draw the Lewis structure for the vile-smelling orange liquid.

86. Nitrous oxide (N_2O) has three possible Lewis structures:

$$:N{=}N{=}O: \longleftrightarrow :N{\equiv}N{-}\ddot{O}: \longleftrightarrow :\ddot{N}{-}N{\equiv}O:$$

Given the following bond lengths,

N—N	167 pm	N=O	115 pm
N=N	120 pm	N—O	147 pm
N≡N	110 pm		

rationalize the observations that the N—N bond length in N_2O is 112 pm and that the N—O bond length is 119 pm. Assign formal charges to the resonance structures for N_2O. Can you eliminate any of the resonance structures on the basis of formal charges? Is this consistent with observation?

Molecular Structure and Polarity

87. Predict the molecular structure and bond angles for each molecule or ion in Exercises 67 and 73.

88. Predict the molecular structure and bond angles for each molecule or ion in Exercises 68 and 74.

89. There are several molecular structures based on the trigonal bipyramid geometry (see Table 8.6). Three such structures are

Linear   T-shaped   See-saw

Which of the compounds in Exercises 71 and 72 have these molecular structures?

90. Two variations of the octahedral geometry (see Table 8.6) are illustrated below.

Square planar   Square pyramid

Which of the compounds in Exercises 71 and 72 have these molecular structures?

91. Predict the molecular structure (including bond angles) for each of the following.

a. SeO_3
b. SeO_2

92. Predict the molecular structure (including bond angles) for each of the following.

a. PCl_3
b. SCl_2
c. SiF_4

93. Predict the molecular structure (including bond angles) for each of the following. (See Exercises 89 and 90.)

a. $XeCl_2$
b. ICl_3
c. TeF_4
d. PCl_5

94. Predict the molecular structure (including bond angles) for each of the following. (See Exercises 89 and 90.)

a. ICl_5
b. $XeCl_4$
c. $SeCl_6$

95. Which of the molecules in Exercise 91 have dipole moments (are polar)?

96. Which of the molecules in Exercise 92 have dipole moments (are polar)?

97. Which of the molecules in Exercise 93 have dipole moments (are polar)?

98. Which of the molecules in Exercise 94 have dipole moments (are polar)?

99. Write Lewis structures and predict the molecular structures of the following. (See Exercises 89 and 90.)

a. OCl_2, KrF_2, BeH_2, SO_2
b. SO_3, NF_3, IF_3
c. CF_4, SeF_4, KrF_4
d. IF_5, AsF_5

Which of these compounds are polar?

100. Write Lewis structures and predict whether each of the following is polar or nonpolar.
   a. HOCN (exists as HO—CN)
   b. COS
   c. XeF_2
   d. CF_2Cl_2
   e. SeF_6
   f. H_2CO (C is the central atom.)

101. Consider the following Lewis structure where E is an unknown element:

$$\left[\ddot{:O}-E-\ddot{O}: \atop :\ddot{O}: \right]^{-}$$

What are some possible identities for element E? Predict the molecular structure (including bond angles) for this ion.

102. Consider the following Lewis structure where E is an unknown element:

$$\left[:\ddot{F}-E \begin{matrix} \ddot{O}: \\ \ddot{F}: \end{matrix} \right]^{2-}$$

What are some possible identities for element E? Predict the molecular structure (including bond angles) for this ion. (See Exercises 89 and 90.)

103. The molecules BF_3, CF_4, CO_2, PF_5, and SF_6 are all nonpolar, even though they all contain polar bonds. Why?

104. Two different compounds have the formula XeF_2Cl_2. Write Lewis structures for these two compounds, and describe how measurement of dipole moments might be used to distinguish between them.

Additional Exercises

105. Arrange the following in order of increasing radius and increasing ionization energy.
   a. N^+, N, N^-
   b. Se, Se^-, Cl, Cl^+
   c. Br^-, Rb^+, Sr^{2+}

106. For each of the following, write an equation that corresponds to the energy given.
   a. lattice energy of NaCl
   b. lattice energy of NH_4Br
   c. lattice energy of MgS
   d. O=O double bond energy beginning with $O_2(g)$ as a reactant

107. Use bond energies (Table 8.4), values of electron affinities (Table 7.7), and the ionization energy of hydrogen (1312 kJ/mol) to estimate ΔH for each of the following reactions.
   a. $HF(g) \rightarrow H^+(g) + F^-(g)$
   b. $HCl(g) \rightarrow H^+(g) + Cl^-(g)$
   c. $HI(g) \rightarrow H^+(g) + I^-(g)$
   d. $H_2O(g) \rightarrow H^+(g) + OH^-(g)$
   (Electron affinity of $OH(g) = -180.$ kJ/mol.)

108. Write Lewis structures for CO_3^{2-}, HCO_3^-, and H_2CO_3. When acid is added to an aqueous solution containing carbonate or bicarbonate ions, carbon dioxide gas is formed. We generally say that carbonic acid (H_2CO_3) is unstable. Use bond energies to estimate ΔH for the reaction (in the gas phase)

$$H_2CO_3 \longrightarrow CO_2 + H_2O$$

Specify a possible cause for the instability of carbonic acid.

109. Which member of the following pairs would you expect to be more energetically stable? Justify each choice.
   a. NaBr or $NaBr_2$
   b. ClO_4 or ClO_4^-
   c. SO_4 or XeO_4
   d. OF_4 or SeF_4

110. What do each of the following sets of compounds/ions have in common with each other?
   a. SO_3, NO_3^-, CO_3^{2-}
   b. O_3, SO_2, NO_2^-

111. What do each of the following sets of compounds/ions have in common with each other? See your Lewis structures for Exercises 91 through 94.
   a. $XeCl_4$, $XeCl_2$
   b. ICl_5, TeF_4, ICl_3, PCl_3, SCl_2, SeO_2

112. Although both Br_3^- and I_3^- ions are known, the F_3^- ion has not been observed. Explain.

113. Refer back to Exercises 81 and 82. Would you make the same prediction for the molecular structure for each case using the Lewis structure obtained in Exercise 81 as compared with the one obtained in Exercise 82?

114. Which of the following molecules have dipole moments? For the molecules that are polar, indicate the polarity of each bond and the direction of the net dipole moment of the molecule.
   a. CH_2Cl_2, $CHCl_3$, CCl_4
   b. CO_2, N_2O
   c. PH_3, NH_3

115. The structure of TeF_5^- is

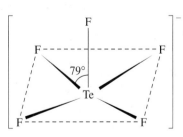

Draw a complete Lewis structure for TeF_5^-, and explain the distortion from the ideal square pyramidal structure. (See Exercise 90.)

Challenge Problems

116. An alternative definition of electronegativity is

$$\text{Electronegativity} = \text{constant (I.E.} - \text{E.A.)}$$

where I.E. is the ionization energy and E.A. is the electron affinity using the sign conventions of this book. Use data in

Chapter 7 to calculate the (I.E. − E.A.) term for F, Cl, Br, and I. Do these values show the same trend as the electronegativity values given in this chapter? The first ionization energies of the halogens are 1678, 1255, 1138, and 1007 kJ/mol, respectively. (*Hint:* Choose a constant so that the electronegativity of fluorine equals 4.0. Using this constant, calculate relative electronegativities for the other halogens and compare to values given in the text.)

117. Calculate the standard heat of formation of the compound $ICl(g)$ at 25°C, and show your work. (*Hint:* Use Table 8.4 and Appendix 4.)

118. Given the following information:

Heat of sublimation of $Li(s)$ = 166 kJ/mol
Bond energy of HCl = 427 kJ/mol
Ionization energy of $Li(g)$ = 520. kJ/mol
Electron affinity of $Cl(g)$ = −349 kJ/mol
Lattice energy of $LiCl(s)$ = −829 kJ/mol
Bond energy of H_2 = 432 kJ/mol

Calculate the net change in energy for the following reaction:

$$2Li(s) + 2HCl(g) \longrightarrow 2LiCl(s) + H_2(g)$$

119. Use data in this chapter (and Chapter 7) to discuss why MgO is an ionic compound but CO is not an ionic compound.

120. Think of forming an ionic compound as three steps (this is a simplification, as with all models): (1) removing an electron from the metal; (2) adding an electron to the nonmetal; and (3) allowing the metal cation and nonmetal anion to come together.
    a. What is the sign of the energy change for each of these three processes?
    b. In general, what is the sign of the sum of the first two processes? Use examples to support your answer.
    c. What must be the sign of the sum of the three processes?
    d. Given your answer to part c, why do ionic bonds occur?
    e. Given your above explanations, why is NaCl stable but not Na_2Cl? $NaCl_2$? What about MgO compared to MgO_2? Mg_2O?

121. The compound NF_3 is quite stable, but NCl_3 is very unstable (NCl_3 was first synthesized in 1811 by P. L. Dulong, who lost three fingers and an eye studying its properties). The compounds NBr_3 and NI_3 are unknown, although the explosive compound $NI_3 \cdot NH_3$ is known. Account for the instability of these halides of nitrogen.

122. Three processes that have been used for the industrial manufacture of acrylonitrile (CH_2CHCN), an important chemical used in the manufacture of plastics, synthetic rubber, and fibers, are shown below. Use bond energy values (Table 8.4) to estimate ΔH for each of the reactions.

a.

b. $4CH_2{=}CHCH_3 + 6NO \xrightarrow[Ag]{700°C}$
$$4CH_2{=}CHCN + 6H_2O + N_2$$
The nitrogen–oxygen bond energy in nitric oxide (NO) is 630. kJ/mol.

c. $2CH_2{=}CHCH_3 + 2NH_3 + 3O_2 \xrightarrow[425-510°C]{Catalyst}$
$$2CH_2{=}CHCN + 6H_2O$$

d. Is the elevated temperature noted in parts b and c needed to provide energy to endothermic reactions?

123. The compound hexaazaisowurtzitane is the highest-energy explosive known (*C & E News,* Jan. 17, 1994, p. 26). The compound, also known as CL-20, was first synthesized in 1987. The method of synthesis and detailed performance data are still classified because of CL-20's potential military application in rocket boosters and in warheads of "smart" weapons. The structure of CL-20 is

CL-20

In such shorthand structures, each point where lines meet represents a carbon atom. In addition, the hydrogens attached to the carbon atoms are omitted; each of the six carbon atoms has one hydrogen atom attached. Finally, assume that the two O atoms in the NO_2 groups are attached to N with one single bond and one double bond.

Three possible reactions for the explosive decomposition of CL-20 are
    i. $C_6H_6N_{12}O_{12}(s) \rightarrow 6CO(g) + 6N_2(g) + 3H_2O(g) + \frac{3}{2}O_2(g)$
    ii. $C_6H_6N_{12}O_{12}(s) \rightarrow 3CO(g) + 3CO_2(g) + 6N_2(g) + 3H_2O(g)$
    iii. $C_6H_6N_{12}O_{12}(s) \rightarrow 6CO_2(g) + 6N_2(g) + 3H_2(g)$
    a. Use bond energies to estimate ΔH for these three reactions.
    b. Which of the above reactions releases the largest amount of energy per kilogram of CL-20?

124. Many times extra stability is characteristic of a molecule or ion in which resonance is possible. How could this be used to explain the acidities of the following compounds? (The acidic hydrogen is marked by an asterisk.) Part c shows resonance in the C_6H_5 ring.

125. Peroxyacetyl nitrate, or PAN, is present in photochemical smog. Draw Lewis structures (including resonance forms) for PAN. The skeletal arrangement is

126. Draw a Lewis structure for the *N,N*-dimethylformamide molecule. The skeletal structure is

$$\underset{\displaystyle\text{CH}_3}{\text{H}-\text{C}-\text{N}-\text{CH}_3}$$

(with O double-bonded above C)

Various types of evidence lead to the conclusion that there is some double bond character to the C—N bond. Draw one or more resonance structures that support this observation.

127. Predict the molecular structure for each of the following. (See Exercises 89 and 90.)
   a. BrFI$_2$
   b. XeO$_2$F$_2$
   c. TeF$_2$Cl$_3{}^-$
   For each formula there are at least two different structures that can be drawn using the same central atom. Draw all possible structures for each formula.

128. The study of carbon-containing compounds and their properties is called *organic chemistry*. Besides carbon atoms, organic compounds also can contain hydrogen, oxygen, and nitrogen atoms (as well as other types of atoms). A common trait of simple organic compounds is to have Lewis structures where all atoms have a formal charge of zero. Consider the following incomplete Lewis structure for an organic compound called *histidine* (an amino acid, which is the building block of all proteins found in our bodies):

Draw a complete Lewis structure for histidine in which all atoms have a formal charge of zero. What should be the approximate bond angles about the carbon atom labeled 1 and the nitrogen atom labeled 2?

129. Using bond energies, estimate ΔH for the following reaction:

$$\text{CH}_3\text{CH}_2\text{OH}(aq) + \text{HOCCH}_3(aq) \longrightarrow \text{CH}_3\text{CH}_2\text{OCCH}_3(aq) + \text{H}_2\text{O}(l)$$

(each acetyl group shown with O double-bonded to C)

130. Consider the following computer-generated model of caffeine.

H
O
N
C

Draw a Lewis structure for caffeine in which all atoms have a formal charge of zero.

Integrative Problems

These problems require the integration of multiple concepts to find the solutions.

131. A compound, XF$_5$, is 42.81% fluorine by mass. Identify the element X. What is the molecular structure of XF$_5$?

132. A polyatomic ion is composed of C, N, and an unknown element X. The skeletal Lewis structure of this polyatomic ion is [X—C—N]$^-$. The ion X^{2-} has an electron configuration of [Ar]$4s^2 3d^{10} 4p^6$. What is element X? Knowing the identity of X, complete the Lewis structure of the polyatomic ion, including all important resonance structures.

133. Identify the following elements based on their electron configurations and rank them in order of increasing electronegativity: [Ar]$4s^1 3d^5$; [Ne]$3s^2 3p^3$; [Ar]$4s^2 3d^{10} 4p^3$; [Ne]$3s^2 3p^5$.

Marathon Problem

This problem is designed to incorporate several concepts and techniques into one situation. Marathon Problems can be used in class by groups of students to help facilitate problem-solving skills.

134. Identify the five compounds of H, N, and O described below. For each compound, write a Lewis structure that is consistent with the information given.
   a. All the compounds are electrolytes, although not all of them are strong electrolytes. Compounds C and D are ionic and compound B is covalent.
   b. Nitrogen occurs in its highest possible oxidation state in compounds A and C; nitrogen occurs in its lowest possible oxidation state in compounds C, D, and E. The formal charge on both nitrogens in compound C is +1; the formal charge on the only nitrogen in compound B is 0.
   c. Compounds A and E exist in solution. Both solutions give off gases. Commercially available concentrated solutions of compound A are normally 16 *M*. The commercial, concentrated solution of compound E is 15 *M*.
   d. Commercial solutions of compound E are labeled with a misnomer that implies that a binary, gaseous compound of nitrogen and hydrogen has reacted with water to produce ammonium ions and hydroxide ions. Actually, this reaction occurs to only a slight extent.
   e. Compound D is 43.7% N and 50.0% O by mass. If compound D were a gas at STP, it would have a density of 2.86 g/L.
   f. A formula unit of compound C has one more oxygen than a formula unit of compound D. Compounds C and A have one ion in common when compound A is acting as a strong electrolyte.
   g. Solutions of compound C are weakly acidic; solutions of compound A are strongly acidic; solutions of compounds B and E are basic. The titration of 0.726 g of compound B requires 21.98 mL of 1.000 *M* HCl for complete neutralization.

WWW Get help understanding core concepts and visualizing molecular-level interactions, and practice problem solving, by visiting the Online Study Center at **college.hmco.com/PIC/zumdahl 7e.**

9 Covalent Bonding: Orbitals

Contents

A close-up of soap bubbles reveals their geometric shapes.

In Chapter 8 we discussed the fundamental concepts of bonding and introduced the most widely used simple model for covalent bonding: the localized electron model. We saw the usefulness of a bonding model as a means for systematizing chemistry by allowing us to look at molecules in terms of individual bonds. We also saw that molecular structure can be predicted by minimizing electron-pair repulsions. In this chapter we will examine bonding models in more detail, particularly focusing on the role of orbitals.

9.1 Hybridization and the Localized Electron Model

As we saw in Chapter 8, the localized electron model views a molecule as a collection of atoms bound together by sharing electrons between their atomic orbitals. The arrangement of valence electrons is represented by the Lewis structure (or structures, where resonance occurs), and the molecular geometry can be predicted from the VSEPR model. In this section we will describe the atomic orbitals used to share electrons and hence to form the bonds.

sp³ Hybridization

Visualization: Hybridization: sp³

The valence orbitals are the orbitals associated with the highest principal quantum level that contains electrons on a given atom.

Let us reconsider the bonding in methane, which has the Lewis structure and molecular geometry shown in Fig. 9.1. In general, we assume that bonding involves only the valence orbitals. This means that the hydrogen atoms in methane use $1s$ orbitals. The valence orbitals of a carbon atom are the $2s$ and $2p$ orbitals shown in Fig. 9.2. In thinking about how carbon can use these orbitals to bond to the hydrogen atoms, we can see two related problems:

1. Using the $2p$ and $2s$ atomic orbitals will lead to two different types of C—H bonds: (a) those from the overlap of a $2p$ orbital of carbon and a $1s$ orbital of hydrogen (there will be three of these) and (b) those from the overlap of a $2s$ orbital of carbon and a $1s$ orbital of hydrogen (there will be one of these). This is a problem because methane is known to have four identical C—H bonds.

2. Since the carbon $2p$ orbitals are mutually perpendicular, we might expect the three C—H bonds formed with these orbitals to be oriented at 90-degree angles:

$$\begin{array}{c} \text{H} \\ 90° \quad \text{C} \; \text{H} \quad 90° \\ \text{H} \quad 90° \end{array}$$

However, the methane molecule is known by experiment to be tetrahedral with bond angles of 109.5 degrees.

Hybridization is a modification of the localized electron model to account for the observation that atoms often seem to use special atomic orbitals in forming molecules.

sp^3 hybridization gives a tetrahedral set of orbitals.

This analysis leads to one of two conclusions: Either the simple localized electron model is wrong or carbon adopts a set of atomic orbitals other than its "native" $2s$ and $2p$ orbitals to bond to the hydrogen atoms in forming the methane molecule. The second conclusion seems more reasonable. The $2s$ and $2p$ orbitals present on an *isolated* carbon atom may not be the best set of orbitals for bonding; a new set of atomic

FIGURE 9.1
(a) The Lewis structure of the methane molecule. (b) The tetrahedral molecular geometry of the methane molecule.

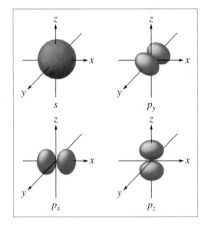

FIGURE 9.2
The valence orbitals on a free carbon atom: $2s$, $2p_x$, $2p_y$, and $2p_z$.

orbitals might better serve the carbon atom in forming molecules. To account for the known structure of methane, it makes sense to assume that the carbon atom has four equivalent atomic orbitals, arranged tetrahedrally. In fact, such a set of orbitals can be obtained quite readily by combining the carbon $2s$ and $2p$ orbitals, as shown schematically in Fig. 9.3. This mixing of the native atomic orbitals to form special orbitals for bonding is called **hybridization.** The four new orbitals are called sp^3 orbitals because they are formed from one $2s$ and three $2p$ orbitals (s^1p^3). We say that the carbon atom undergoes sp^3 **hybridization** or is sp^3 **hybridized.** The four sp^3 orbitals are identical in shape, each one having a large lobe and a small lobe (see Fig. 9.4). The four orbitals are oriented in space so that the large lobes form a tetrahedral arrangement, as shown in Fig. 9.3.

The hybridization of the carbon $2s$ and $2p$ orbitals also can be represented by an orbital energy-level diagram, as shown in Fig. 9.5. Note that electrons have been omitted because we do not need to be concerned with the electron arrangements on the individual atoms—it is the total number of electrons and the arrangement of these electrons in the *molecule* that are important. We are assuming that carbon's atomic orbitals are rearranged to accommodate the best electron arrangement for the molecule as a whole. The new sp^3 atomic orbitals on carbon are used to share electron pairs with the $1s$ orbitals from the four hydrogen atoms, as shown in Fig. 9.6 on page 393.

At this point let's summarize the bonding in the methane molecule. The experimentally known structure of this molecule can be explained if we assume that the carbon atom adopts a special set of atomic orbitals. These new orbitals are obtained by combining the $2s$ and the three $2p$ orbitals of the carbon atom to produce four identically shaped orbitals that are oriented toward the corners of a tetrahedron and are used to bond to the hydrogen atoms. Thus the four sp^3 orbitals on carbon in methane are postulated to account for its known structure.

Remember this principle: *Whenever a set of equivalent tetrahedral atomic orbitals is required by an atom, this model assumes that the atom adopts a set of sp^3 orbitals; the atom becomes sp^3 hybridized.*

It is really not surprising that an atom in a molecule might adopt a different set of atomic orbitals (called **hybrid orbitals**) from those it has in the free state. It does not seem unreasonable that to achieve minimum energy, an atom uses one set of atomic orbitals in the free state and a different set in a molecule. This is consistent with the idea that a molecule is more than simply a sum of its parts. What the atoms in a molecule were

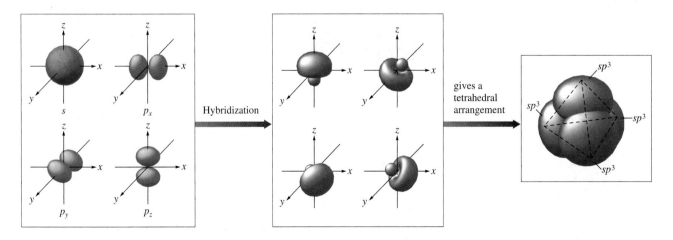

FIGURE 9.3
The "native" $2s$ and three $2p$ atomic orbitals characteristic of a free carbon atom are combined to form a new set of four sp^3 orbitals. The small lobes of the orbitals are usually omitted from diagrams for clarity.

FIGURE 9.4
Cross section of an sp^3 orbital. This shows a "slice" of the electron density of the sp^3 orbitals illustrated in the center diagram of Fig. 9.3.
(Generated from a program by Robert Allendoerfer on Project SERAPHIM disk PC2402; printed with permission.)

FIGURE 9.5
An energy-level diagram showing the formation of four sp^3 orbitals.

like before the molecule was formed is not as important as how the electrons are best arranged in the molecule. Therefore, this model assumes that the individual atoms respond as needed to achieve the minimum energy for the molecule.

Sample Exercise 9.1

The Localized Electron Model I

Describe the bonding in the ammonia molecule using the localized electron model.

Solution

A complete description of the bonding involves three steps:

1. Writing the Lewis structure
2. Determining the arrangement of electron pairs using the VSEPR model
3. Determining the hybrid atomic orbitals needed to describe the bonding in the molecule

The Lewis structure for NH_3 is

$$H—\overset{\cdot\cdot}{\underset{|}{N}}—H$$
$$H$$

The four electron pairs around the nitrogen atom require a tetrahedral arrangement to minimize repulsions. We have seen that a tetrahedral set of sp^3 hybrid orbitals is obtained by combining the $2s$ and three $2p$ orbitals. In the NH_3 molecule three of the sp^3 orbitals are used to form bonds to the three hydrogen atoms, and the fourth sp^3 orbital holds the lone pair, as shown in Fig. 9.7.

See Exercise 9.15.

FIGURE 9.6
The tetrahedral set of four sp^3 orbitals of the carbon atom are used to share electron pairs with the four $1s$ orbitals of the hydrogen atoms to form the four equivalent C—H bonds. This accounts for the known tetrahedral structure of the CH_4 molecule.

FIGURE 9.7
The nitrogen atom in ammonia is sp^3 hybridized.

sp^2 Hybridization

Ethylene (C_2H_4) is an important starting material in the manufacture of plastics. The C_2H_4 molecule has 12 valence electrons and the following Lewis structure:

We saw in Chapter 8 that a double bond acts as one effective pair, so in the ethylene molecule each carbon is surrounded by three effective pairs. This requires a trigonal planar arrangement with bond angles of 120 degrees. What orbitals do the carbon atoms in this molecule employ? The molecular geometry requires a set of orbitals in one plane at angles

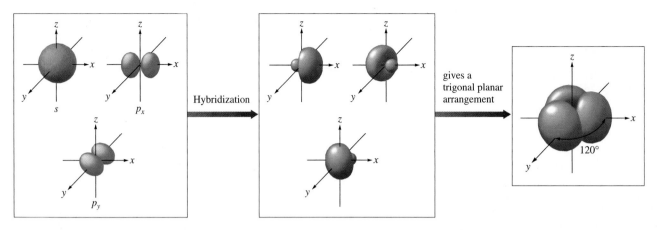

FIGURE 9.8
The hybridization of the *s*, p_x, and p_y atomic orbitals results in the formation of three sp^2 orbitals centered in the *xy* plane. The large lobes of the orbitals lie in the plane at angles of 120 degrees and point toward the corners of a triangle.

A double bond acts as one effective electron pair.

of 120 degrees. Since the 2*s* and 2*p* valence orbitals of carbon do not have the required arrangement, we need a set of hybrid orbitals.

The sp^3 orbitals we have just considered will not work because they are at angles of 109.5 degrees rather than the required 120 degrees. In ethylene the carbon atom must hybridize in a different manner. A set of three orbitals arranged at 120-degree angles in the same plane can be obtained by combining one *s* orbital and two *p* orbitals, as shown in Fig. 9.8. The orbital energy-level diagram for this arrangement is shown in Fig. 9.9. Since one 2*s* and two 2*p* orbitals are used to form these hybrid orbitals, this is called **sp^2 hybridization.** Note from Fig. 9.8 that the plane of the sp^2 hybridized orbitals is determined by which *p* orbitals are used. Since in this case we have arbitrarily decided to use the p_x and p_y orbitals, the hybrid orbitals are centered in the *xy* plane.

sp^2 hybridization gives a trigonal planar arrangement of atomic orbitals.

In forming the sp^2 orbitals, one 2*p* orbital on carbon has not been used. This remaining *p* orbital (p_z) is oriented perpendicular to the plane of the sp^2 orbitals, as shown in Fig. 9.10.

Note in Fig. 9.10 and the figures that follow that the orbital lobes are artificially narrowed to more clearly show their relative orientations.

Now we will see how these orbitals can be used to account for the bonds in ethylene. The three sp^2 orbitals on each carbon can be used to share electrons, as shown in Fig. 9.11. In each of these bonds, the electron pair is shared in an area centered on a line running between the atoms. This type of covalent bond is called a **sigma (σ) bond.** In the ethylene molecule, the σ bonds are formed using sp^2 orbitals on each carbon atom and the 1*s* orbital on each hydrogen atom.

How can we explain the double bond between the carbon atoms? In the σ bond the electron pair occupies the space between the carbon atoms. The second bond must therefore result from sharing an electron pair in the space *above and below* the σ bond. This type of bond can be formed using the 2*p* orbital perpendicular to the sp^2 hybrid orbitals on each carbon atom (refer to Fig. 9.10). These parallel *p* orbitals can share an electron pair, which occupies the space above and below a line joining the atoms, to form a **pi (π) bond,** as shown in Fig. 9.12.

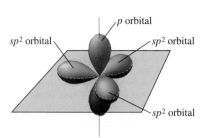

FIGURE 9.10
When an *s* and two *p* orbitals are mixed to form a set of three *sp²* orbitals, one *p* orbital remains unchanged and is perpendicular to the plane of the hybrid orbitals. Note that in this figure and those that follow, the orbitals are drawn with narrowed lobes to show their orientations more clearly.

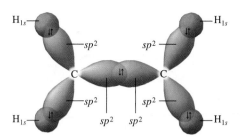

FIGURE 9.11
The *σ* bonds in ethylene. Note that for each bond the shared electron pair occupies the region directly between the atoms.

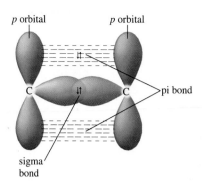

FIGURE 9.12
A carbon–carbon double bond consists of a *σ* bond and a *π* bond. In the *σ* bond the shared electrons occupy the space directly between the atoms. The *π* bond is formed from the unhybridized *p* orbitals on the two carbon atoms. In a *π* bond the shared electron pair occupies the space above and below a line joining the atoms.

Visualization: Hybridization: *sp²*

Visualization: Formation of C=C Double Bond in Ethylene

Note that *σ* bonds are formed from orbitals whose lobes point toward each other, but *π* bonds result from parallel orbitals. A *double bond always consists of one σ bond,* where the electron pair is located directly between the atoms, *and one π bond,* where the shared pair occupies the space above and below the *σ* bond.

We can now completely specify the orbitals that this model assumes are used to form the bonds in the ethylene molecule. As shown in Fig. 9.13, the carbon atoms use *sp²* hybrid orbitals to form the *σ* bonds to the hydrogen atoms and to each other, and they use *p* to form the *π* bond with each other. Note that we have accounted fully for the Lewis structure of ethylene with its carbon–carbon double bond and carbon–hydrogen single bonds.

This example illustrates an important general principle of this model: *Whenever an atom is surrounded by three effective pairs, a set of sp² hybrid orbitals is required.*

sp Hybridization

Another type of hybridization occurs in carbon dioxide, which has the following Lewis structure:

$$\ddot{O}=C=\ddot{O}$$

In the CO_2 molecule the carbon atom has two effective pairs that will be arranged at an angle of 180 degrees. We therefore need a pair of atomic orbitals oriented in opposite directions. This requires a new type of hybridization, since neither *sp³* nor *sp²* hybrid

Visualization: Hybridization: *sp*

FIGURE 9.13
(a) The orbitals used to form the bonds in ethylene. (b) The Lewis structure for ethylene.

(a)   (b)

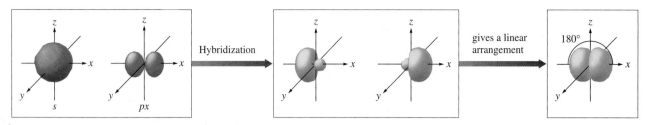

FIGURE 9.14
When one *s* orbital and one *p* orbital are hybridized, a set of two *sp* orbitals oriented at 180 degrees results.

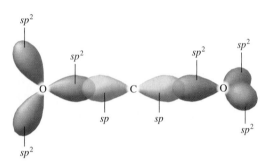

FIGURE 9.15
The hybrid orbitals in the CO_2 molecule.

FIGURE 9.16
The orbital energy-level diagram for the formation of *sp* hybrid orbitals on carbon.

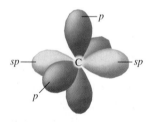

FIGURE 9.17
The orbitals of an *sp* hybridized carbon atom.

More rigorous theoretical models of CO_2 indicate that each of the oxygen atoms uses two *p* orbitals simultaneously to form the pi bonds to the carbon atom, thus leading to unusually strong C=O bonds.

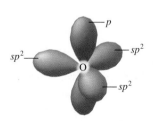

FIGURE 9.18
The orbital arrangement for an *sp²* hybridized oxygen atom.

orbitals will fit this case. To obtain two hybrid orbitals arranged at 180 degrees requires *sp* **hybridization,** involving one *s* orbital and one *p* orbital, as shown in Fig. 9.14.

In terms of this model, *two effective pairs around an atom will always require sp hybridization of that atom.* The *sp* orbitals of carbon in carbon dioxide can be seen in Fig. 9.15, and the corresponding orbital energy-level diagram for their formation is given in Fig. 9.16. These *sp* hybrid orbitals are used to form the σ bonds between the carbon and the oxygen atoms. Note that two 2*p* orbitals remain unchanged on the *sp* hybridized carbon. These are used to form the π bonds with the oxygen atoms.

In the CO_2 molecule each oxygen atom* has three effective pairs around it, requiring a trigonal planar arrangement of the pairs. Since a trigonal set of hybrid orbitals requires sp^2 hybridization, each oxygen atom is sp^2 hybridized. One *p* orbital on each oxygen is unchanged and is used for the π bond with the carbon atom.

Now we are ready to use our model to describe the bonding in carbon dioxide. The *sp* orbitals on carbon form σ bonds with the sp^2 orbitals on the two oxygen atoms (Fig. 9.15). The remaining sp^2 orbitals on the oxygen atoms hold lone pairs. The π bonds between the carbon atom and each oxygen atom are formed by the overlap of parallel 2*p* orbitals. The *sp* hybridized carbon atom has two unhybridized *p* orbitals, pictured in Fig. 9.17. Each of these *p* orbitals is used to form a π bond with an oxygen atom (see Fig. 9.18). The total bonding picture for the CO_2 molecule is shown in Fig. 9.19. Note that this picture of the bonding neatly explains the arrangement of electrons predicted by the Lewis structure.

Another molecule whose bonding can be described by *sp* hybridization is acetylene (C_2H_2), which has the systematic name ethyne. The Lewis structure for acetylene is

$$H-C \equiv C-H$$

---

*We will assume that minimizing electron repulsions also is important for the peripheral atoms in a molecule and apply the VSEPR model to these atoms as well.

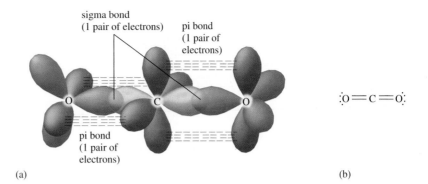

FIGURE 9.19
(a) The orbitals used to form the bonds in carbon dioxide. Note that the carbon–oxygen double bonds each consist of one σ bond and one π bond. (b) The Lewis structure for carbon dioxide.

Because the triple bond counts as one effective repulsive unit, each carbon has two effective pairs, which requires a linear arrangement. Thus each carbon atom requires sp hybridization, leaving two unchanged p orbitals (see Fig. 9.16). One of the oppositely oriented (see Fig. 9.14) sp orbitals is used to form a bond to the hydrogen atom; the other sp orbital overlaps with the similar sp orbital on the other carbon to form the sigma bond. The two pi bonds are formed from the overlap of the two p orbitals on each carbon. This accounts for the triple bond (one sigma and two pi bonds) in acetylene.

| Sample Exercise 9.2 | The Localized Electron Model II |

Describe the bonding in the N_2 molecule.

Solution

The Lewis structure for the nitrogen molecule is

$$: N \equiv N :$$

where each nitrogen atom is surrounded by two effective pairs. (Remember that a multiple bond counts as one effective pair.) This gives a linear arrangement (180 degrees) requiring a pair of oppositely directed orbitals. This situation requires sp hybridization. Each nitrogen atom in the nitrogen molecule has two sp hybrid orbitals and two unchanged p orbitals, as shown in Fig. 9.20(a). The sp orbitals are used to form the σ bond between the nitrogen atoms and to hold lone pairs, as shown in Fig. 9.20(b). The p orbitals are used to form the two π bonds [see Fig. 9.20(c)]; each pair of overlapping parallel p orbitals holds one electron pair. Such bonding accounts for the electron arrangement given by the Lewis structure. The triple bond consists of a σ bond (overlap of two sp orbitals) and two π bonds (each one from an overlap of two p orbitals). In addition, a lone pair occupies an sp orbital on each nitrogen atom.

See Exercises 9.17 and 9.18.

dsp^3 Hybridization

To illustrate the treatment of a molecule in which the central atom exceeds the octet rule, consider the bonding in the phosphorus pentachloride molecule (PCl_5). The Lewis structure

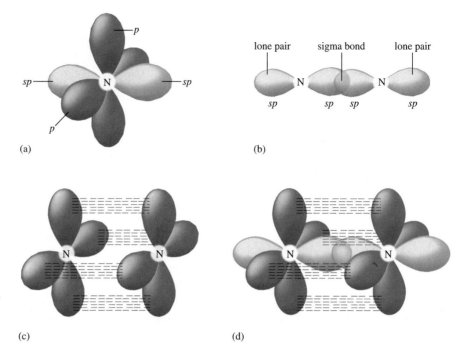

FIGURE 9.20
(a) An *sp* hybridized nitrogen atom. There are two *sp* hybrid orbitals and two unhybridized *p* orbitals. (b) The σ bond in the N₂ molecule. (c) The two π bonds in N₂ are formed when electron pairs are shared between two sets of parallel *p* orbitals. (d) The total bonding picture for N₂.

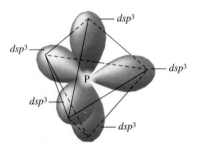

FIGURE 9.21
A set of *dsp³* hybrid orbitals on a phosphorus atom. Note that the set of five *dsp³* orbitals has a trigonal bipyramidal arrangement. (Each *dsp³* orbital also has a small lobe that is not shown in this diagram.)

shows that the phosphorus atom is surrounded by five electron pairs. Since five pairs require a trigonal bipyramidal arrangement, we need a trigonal bipyramidal set of atomic orbitals on phosphorus. Such a set of orbitals is formed by ***dsp³* hybridization** of one *d* orbital, one *s* orbital, and three *p* orbitals, as shown in Fig. 9.21.

The *dsp³* hybridized phosphorus atom in the PCl₅ molecule uses its five *dsp³* orbitals to share electrons with the five chlorine atoms. *Note that a set of five effective pairs around a given atom always requires a trigonal bipyramidal arrangement, which in turn requires* *dsp³* *hybridization of that atom.*

The Lewis structure for PCl₅ shows that each chlorine atom is surrounded by four electron pairs. This requires a tetrahedral arrangement, which in turn requires a set of four *sp³* orbitals on each chlorine atom.

Now we can describe the bonding in the PCl₅ molecule. The five P—Cl σ bonds are formed by sharing electrons between a *dsp³* orbital* on the phosphorus atom and an *sp³* orbital on each chlorine.[†] The other *sp³* orbitals on each chlorine hold lone pairs. This is shown in Fig. 9.22.

| *Sample Exercise 9.3* | **The Localized Electron Model III** |

Describe the bonding in the triiodide ion (I₃⁻).

Solution

The Lewis structure for I₃⁻

$$\left[:\ddot{\text{I}}—\ddot{\text{I}}—\ddot{\text{I}}: \right]^{-}$$

---

*There is considerable controversy about whether the *d* orbitals are as heavily involved in the bonding in these molecules as this model predicts. However, this matter is beyond the scope of this text.
[†]Although we have no way of proving conclusively that each chlorine is *sp³* hybridized, we assume that minimizing electron-pair repulsions is as important for peripheral atoms as for the central atom. Thus we will apply the VSEPR model and hybridization to both central and peripheral atoms.

(a)

FIGURE 9.22
(a) The structure of the PCl$_5$ molecule.
(b) The orbitals used to form the bonds in PCl$_5$. The phosphorus uses a set of five dsp^3 orbitals to share electron pairs with sp^3 orbitals on the five chlorine atoms. The other sp^3 orbitals on each chlorine atom hold lone pairs.

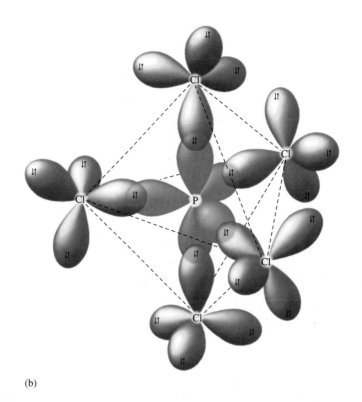

(b)

shows that the central iodine atom has five pairs of electrons (see Section 8.11). A set of five pairs requires a trigonal bipyramidal arrangement, which in turn requires a set of dsp^3 orbitals. The outer iodine atoms have four pairs of electrons, which calls for a tetrahedral arrangement and sp^3 hybridization.

Thus the central iodine is dsp^3 hybridized. Three of these hybrid orbitals hold lone pairs, and two of them overlap with sp^3 orbitals of the other two iodine atoms to form σ bonds.

See Exercise 9.23.

d^2sp^3 hybridization gives six orbitals arranged octahedrally.

d^2sp^3 Hybridization

Some molecules have six pairs of electrons around a central atom; an example is sulfur hexafluoride (SF$_6$), which has the Lewis structure

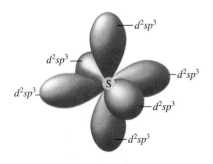

FIGURE 9.23
An octahedral set of d^2sp^3 orbitals on a sulfur atom. The small lobe of each hybrid orbital has been omitted for clarity.

This requires an octahedral arrangement of pairs and in turn an octahedral set of six hybrid orbitals, or **d^2sp^3 hybridization,** in which two d orbitals, one s orbital, and three p orbitals are combined (see Fig. 9.23). Note that *six electron pairs around an atom are always arranged octahedrally and require d^2sp^3 hybridization of the atom.* Each of the d^2sp^3 orbitals on the sulfur atom is used to bond to a fluorine atom. Since there are four pairs on each fluorine atom, the fluorine atoms are assumed to be sp^3 hybridized.

| Sample Exercise 9.4 | **The Localized Electron Model IV** |

How is the xenon atom in XeF_4 hybridized?

Solution

As seen in Sample Exercise 8.13, XeF_4 has six pairs of electrons around xenon that are arranged octahedrally to minimize repulsions. An octahedral set of six atomic orbitals is required to hold these electrons, and the xenon atom is d^2sp^3 hybridized.

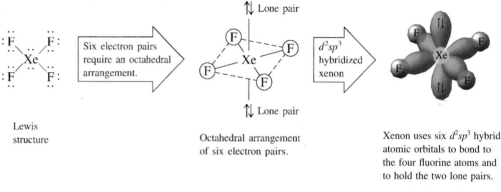

Lewis structure

Six electron pairs require an octahedral arrangement.

Octahedral arrangement of six electron pairs.

d^2sp^3 hybridized xenon

Xenon uses six d^2sp^3 hybrid atomic orbitals to bond to the four fluorine atoms and to hold the two lone pairs.

See Exercise 9.24.

The Localized Electron Model: A Summary

The description of a molecule using the localized electron model involves three distinct steps.

Localized Electron Model

➡ 1 **Draw the Lewis structure(s).**

➡ 2 **Determine the arrangement of electron pairs using the VSEPR model.**

➡ 3 **Specify the hybrid orbitals needed to accommodate the electron pairs.**

It is important to do the steps in this order. For a model to be successful, it must follow nature's priorities. In the case of bonding, it seems clear that the tendency for a molecule to minimize its energy is more important than the maintenance of the characteristics of atoms as they exist in the free state. The atoms adjust to meet the "needs" of the molecule. When considering the bonding in a particular molecule, therefore, we always start with the molecule rather than the component atoms. In the molecule the electrons will be arranged to give each atom a noble gas configuration, where possible, and to minimize electron-pair repulsions. We then assume that the atoms adjust their orbitals by hybridization to allow the molecule to adopt the structure that gives the minimum energy.

In applying the localized electron model, we must remember not to overemphasize the characteristics of the separate atoms. It is not where the valence electrons originate that is important; it is where they are needed in the molecule to achieve stability. In the same vein, it is not the orbitals in the isolated atom that matter, but which orbitals the molecule requires for minimum energy.

The requirements for the various types of hybridization are summarized in Fig. 9.24 on the following page.

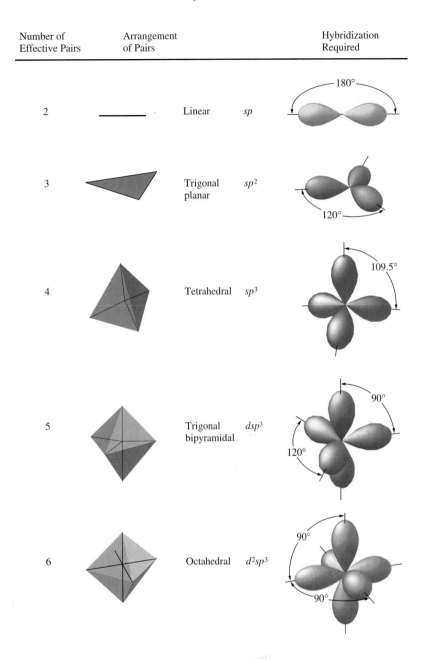

Number of Effective Pairs	Arrangement of Pairs		Hybridization Required
2	——	Linear	sp
3		Trigonal planar	sp^2
4		Tetrahedral	sp^3
5		Trigonal bipyramidal	dsp^3
6		Octahedral	d^2sp^3

FIGURE 9.24
The relationship of the number of effective pairs, their spatial arrangement, and the hybrid orbital set required.

| Sample Exercise 9.5 | ## The Localized Electron Model V |

For each of the following molecules or ions, predict the hybridization of each atom, and describe the molecular structure.

a. CO   **b.** BF_4^- **c.** XeF_2

Solution

a. The CO molecule has 10 valence electrons, and its Lewis structure is

$$: C \equiv O :$$

Each atom has two effective pairs, which means that both are sp hybridized. The triple bond consists of a σ bond produced by overlap of an sp orbital from each atom and two π bonds produced by overlap of $2p$ orbitals from each atom. The lone pairs are in sp orbitals. Since the CO molecule has only two atoms, it must be linear.

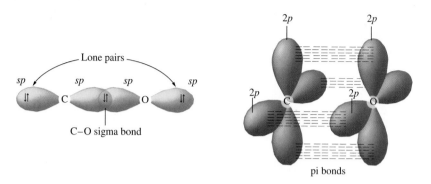

b. The BF_4^- ion has 32 valence electrons. The Lewis structure shows four pairs of electrons around the boron atom, which means a tetrahedral arrangement:

This requires sp^3 hybridization of the boron atom. Each fluorine atom also has four electron pairs and can be assumed to be sp^3 hybridized (only one sp^3 orbital is shown for each fluorine atom). The BF_4^- ion's molecular structure is tetrahedral.

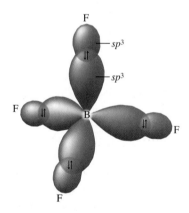

c. The XeF_2 molecule has 22 valence electrons. The Lewis structure shows five electron pairs on the xenon atom, which requires a trigonal bipyramidal arrangement:

Note that the lone pairs are placed in the plane where they are 120 degrees apart. To accommodate five pairs at the vertices of a trigonal bipyramid requires that the xenon atom adopt a set of five dsp^3 orbitals. Each fluorine atom has four electron pairs and can be assumed to be sp^3 hybridized. The XeF_2 molecule has a linear arrangement of atoms.

See Exercises 9.27 and 9.28.

9.2 The Molecular Orbital Model

Molecular orbital theory parallels the atomic theory discussed in Chapter 7.

We have seen that the localized electron model is of great value in interpreting the structure and bonding of molecules. However, there are some problems with this model. For example, it incorrectly assumes that electrons are localized, and so the concept of resonance must be added. Also, the model does not deal effectively with molecules containing unpaired electrons. And finally, the model gives no direct information about bond energies.

Another model often used to describe bonding is the **molecular orbital model.** To introduce the assumptions, methods, and results of this model, we will consider the simplest of all molecules, H_2, which consists of two protons and two electrons. A very stable molecule, H_2 is lower in energy than the separated hydrogen atoms by 432 kJ/mol.

Since the hydrogen molecule consists of protons and electrons, the same components found in separated hydrogen atoms, it seems reasonable to use a theory similar to the atomic theory discussed in Chapter 7, which assumes that the electrons in an atom exist in orbitals of a given energy. Can we apply this same type of model to the hydrogen molecule? Yes. In fact, describing the H_2 molecule in terms of quantum mechanics is quite straightforward.

However, even though it is formulated rather easily, this problem cannot be solved exactly. The difficulty is the same as that in dealing with polyelectronic atoms—the electron correlation problem. Since we do not know the details of the electron movements, we cannot deal with the electron–electron interactions in a specific way. We need to make approximations that allow a solution of the problem but do not destroy the model's physical integrity. The success of these approximations can only be measured by comparing predictions based on theory with experimental observations. In this case we will see that the simplified model works very well.

Just as atomic orbitals are solutions to the quantum mechanical treatment of atoms, **molecular orbitals (MOs)** are solutions to the molecular problem. Molecular orbitals

FIGURE 9.26
(a) The MO energy-level diagram for the H_2 molecule. (b) The shapes of the MOs are obtained by squaring the wave functions for MO_1 and MO_2. The positions of the nuclei are indicated by •.

have many of the same characteristics as atomic orbitals. Two of the most important are that they can hold two electrons with opposite spins and that the square of the molecular orbital wave function indicates electron probability.

We will now describe the bonding in the hydrogen molecule using this model. The first step is to obtain the hydrogen molecule's orbitals, a process that is greatly simplified if we assume that the molecular orbitals can be constructed from the hydrogen 1s atomic orbitals.

When the quantum mechanical equations for the hydrogen molecule are solved, two molecular orbitals result, which can be represented as

$$MO_1 = 1s_A + 1s_B$$
$$MO_2 = 1s_A - 1s_B$$

where $1s_A$ and $1s_B$ represent the 1s orbitals from the two separated hydrogen atoms. This process is shown schematically in Fig. 9.25.

The orbital properties of most interest are size, shape (described by the electron probability distribution), and energy. These properties for the hydrogen molecular orbitals are represented in Fig. 9.26. From Fig. 9.26 we can note several important points:

1. The electron probability of both molecular orbitals is centered along the line passing through the two nuclei. For MO_1 the greatest electron probability is *between* the nuclei, and for MO_2 it is on *either side* of the nuclei. This type of electron distribution is described as *sigma* (σ), as in the localized electron model. Accordingly, we refer to MO_1 and MO_2 as **sigma (σ) molecular orbitals.**

2. In the molecule only the molecular orbitals are available for occupation by electrons. The 1s atomic orbitals of the hydrogen atoms no longer exist, because the H_2 molecule—a new entity—has its own set of new orbitals.

3. MO_1 is lower in energy than the 1s orbitals of free hydrogen atoms, while MO_2 is higher in energy than the 1s orbitals. This fact has very important implications for the stability of the H_2 molecule, since if the two electrons (one from each hydrogen atom) occupy the lower-energy MO_1, they will have lower energy than they do in the two separate hydrogen atoms. This situation favors molecule formation, because nature tends to seek the lowest energy state. That is, the driving force for molecule formation is that the molecular orbital available to the two electrons has lower energy than the atomic orbitals these electrons occupy in the separated atoms. This situation is favorable to bonding, or *probonding.*

    On the other hand, if the two electrons were forced to occupy the higher-energy MO_2, they would be definitely *antibonding.* In this case, these electrons would have lower energy in the separated atoms than in the molecule, and the separated state would be favored. Of course, since the lower-energy MO_1 *is* available, the two electrons occupy that MO and the molecule is stable.

    We have seen that the molecular orbitals of the hydrogen molecule fall into two classes: bonding and antibonding. A **bonding molecular orbital** is *lower in energy than the atomic orbitals of which it is composed.* Electrons in this type of orbital will favor the molecule; that is, they will favor bonding. An **antibonding molecular orbital** is *higher in energy than the atomic orbitals of which it is composed.* Electrons in this type of orbital will favor the separated atoms (they are antibonding). Figure 9.27 illustrates these ideas.

4. Figure 9.26 shows that for the bonding molecular orbital in the H_2 molecule the electrons have the greatest probability of being between the nuclei. This is exactly what we would expect, since the electrons can lower their energies by being simultaneously attracted by both nuclei. On the other hand, the electron distribution for the

Bonding will result if the molecule has lower energy than the separated atoms.

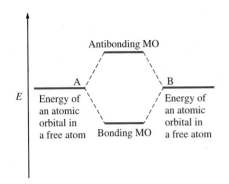

FIGURE 9.27
Bonding and antibonding molecular orbitals (MOs).

FIGURE 9.28
A molecular orbital energy-level diagram for the H_2 molecule.

Although the model predicts that H_2^- should be stable, this ion has never been observed, again emphasizing the perils of simple models.

FIGURE 9.29
The molecular orbital energy-level diagram for the H_2^- ion.

antibonding molecular orbital is such that the electrons are mainly outside the space between the nuclei. This type of distribution is not expected to provide any bonding force. In fact, it causes the electrons to be higher in energy than in the separated atoms. Thus the molecular orbital model produces electron distributions and energies that agree with our basic ideas of bonding. This fact reassures us that the model is physically reasonable.

5. The labels on molecular orbitals indicate their symmetry (shape), the parent atomic orbitals, and whether they are bonding or antibonding. Antibonding character is indicated by an asterisk. For the H_2 molecule, both MOs have σ symmetry, and both are constructed from hydrogen $1s$ atomic orbitals. The molecular orbitals for H_2 are therefore labeled as follows:

$$MO_1 = \sigma_{1s}$$
$$MO_2 = \sigma_{1s}{}^*$$

6. Molecular electron configurations can be written in much the same way as atomic (electron) configurations. Since the H_2 molecule has two electrons in the σ_{1s} molecular orbital, the electron configuration is $\sigma_{1s}{}^2$.

7. Each molecular orbital can hold two electrons, but the spins must be opposite.

8. Orbitals are conserved. The number of molecular orbitals will always be the same as the number of atomic orbitals used to construct them.

Many of the above points are summarized in Fig. 9.28.

Now suppose we could form the H_2^- ion from a hydride ion (H^-) and a hydrogen atom. Would this species be stable? Since the H^- ion has the configuration $1s^2$ and the H atom has a $1s^1$ configuration, we will use $1s$ atomic orbitals to construct the MO diagram for the H_2^- ion, as shown in Fig. 9.29. The electron configuration for H_2^- is $(\sigma_{1s})^2(\sigma_{1s}{}^*)^1$.

The key idea is that the H_2^- ion will be stable if it has a lower energy than its separated parts. From Fig. 9.29 we see that in going from the separated H^- ion and H atom to the H_2^- ion, the model predicts that two electrons are lowered in energy and one electron is raised in energy. In other words, two electrons are bonding and one electron is antibonding. Since more electrons favor bonding, H_2^- is predicted to be a stable entity—a bond has formed. But how would we expect the bond strengths in the molecules of H_2 and H_2^- to compare?

In the formation of the H_2 molecule, two electrons are lowered in energy and no electrons are raised in energy compared with the parent atoms. When H_2^- is formed, two electrons are lowered in energy and one is raised, producing *a net lowering of the energy of only one electron*. Thus the model predicts that H_2 is *twice as stable* as H_2^- with respect to their separated components. In other words, the bond in the H_2 molecule is predicted to be about twice as strong as the bond in the H_2^- ion.

Bond Order

To indicate bond strength, we use the concept of bond order. **Bond order** is *the difference between the number of bonding electrons and the number of antibonding electrons divided by 2.*

$$\text{Bond order} = \frac{\text{number of bonding electrons} - \text{number of antibonding electrons}}{2}$$

We divide by 2 because, from the localized electron model, we are used to thinking of bonds in terms of *pairs* of electrons.

FIGURE 9.30
The molecular orbital energy-level diagram for the He$_2$ molecule.

Since the H$_2$ molecule has two bonding electrons and no antibonding electrons, the bond order is

$$\text{Bond order} = \frac{2 - 0}{2} = 1$$

The H$_2{}^-$ ion has two bonding electrons and one antibonding electron; the bond order is

$$\text{Bond order} = \frac{2 - 1}{2} = \frac{1}{2}$$

Bond order is an indication of bond strength because it reflects the difference between the number of bonding electrons and the number of antibonding electrons. *Larger bond order means greater bond strength.*

We will now apply the molecular orbital model to the helium molecule (He$_2$). Does this model predict that this molecule will be stable? Since the He atom has a $1s^2$ configuration, $1s$ orbitals are used to construct the molecular orbitals, and the molecule will have four electrons. From the diagram shown in Fig. 9.30 it is apparent that two electrons are raised in energy and two are lowered in energy. Thus the bond order is zero:

$$\frac{2 - 2}{2} = 0$$

This implies that the He$_2$ molecule is *not* stable with respect to the two free He atoms, which agrees with the observation that helium gas consists of individual He atoms.

9.3 Bonding in Homonuclear Diatomic Molecules

In this section we consider *homonuclear diatomic molecules* (those composed of two identical atoms) of elements in Period 2 of the periodic table. Since the lithium atom has a $1s^2 2s^1$ electron configuration, it would seem that we should use the Li $1s$ and $2s$ orbitals to form the molecular orbitals of the Li$_2$ molecule. However, the $1s$ orbitals on the lithium atoms are much smaller than the $2s$ orbitals and therefore do not overlap in space to any appreciable extent (see Fig. 9.31). Thus the two electrons in each $1s$ orbital can be assumed to be localized and not to participate in the bonding. *To participate in molecular orbitals, atomic orbitals must overlap in space.* This means that only the valence orbitals of the atoms contribute significantly to the molecular orbitals of a particular molecule.

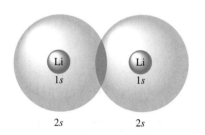

FIGURE 9.31
The relative sizes of the lithium $1s$ and $2s$ atomic orbitals.

FIGURE 9.32
The molecular orbital energy-level diagram for the Li$_2$ molecule.

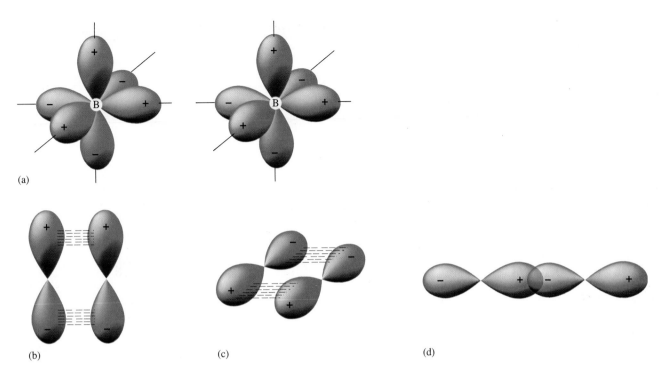

FIGURE 9.33
(a) The three mutually perpendicular 2p orbitals on two adjacent boron atoms. The signs indicate the orbital phases. Two pairs of parallel p orbitals can overlap, as shown in (b) and (c), and the third pair can overlap head-on, as shown in (d).

The molecular orbital diagram of the Li_2 molecule and the shapes of its bonding and antibonding MOs are shown in Fig. 9.32. The electron configuration for Li_2 (valence electrons only) is σ_{2s}^2, and the bond order is

$$\frac{2 - 0}{2} = 1$$

The Li_2 is a stable molecule (has lower energy than two separated lithium atoms). However, this does not mean that Li_2 is the most stable form of elemental lithium. In fact, at normal temperature and pressure, lithium exists as a solid containing many lithium atoms bound to each other.

For the beryllium molecule (Be_2) the bonding and antibonding orbitals both contain two electrons. In this case the bond order is $(2 - 2)/2 = 0$, and since Be_2 is not more stable than two separated Be atoms, no molecule forms. However, beryllium metal contains many beryllium atoms bonded to each other and is stable for reasons we will discuss in Chapter 10.

Since the boron atom has a $1s^2 2s^2 2p^1$ configuration, we describe the B_2 molecule by considering how p atomic orbitals combine to form molecular orbitals. Recall that p orbitals have two lobes and that they occur in sets of three mutually perpendicular orbitals [see Fig. 9.33(a)]. When two B atoms approach each other, two pairs of p orbitals can overlap in a parallel fashion [Fig. 9.33(b) and (c)] and one pair can overlap head-on [Fig. 9.33(d)].

First, let's consider the molecular orbitals from the head-on overlap, as shown in Fig. 9.34(a). Note that the electrons in the bonding MO are, as expected, concentrated between the nuclei, and the electrons in the antibonding MO are concentrated outside the area between the two nuclei. Also, both these MOs are σ molecular orbitals. The

Beryllium metal.

Visualization: Pi Bonding and Antibonding Orbitals

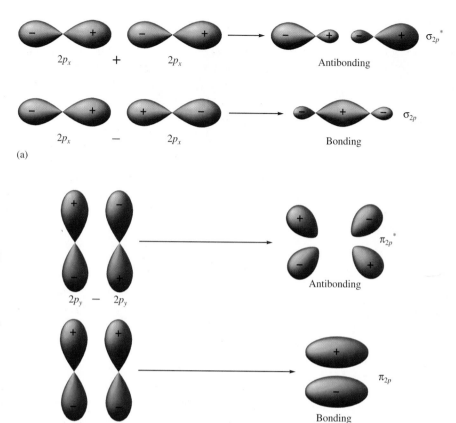

FIGURE 9.34
(a) The two *p* orbitals on the boron atoms that overlap head-on combine to form σ bonding and antibonding orbitals. The bonding orbital is formed by reversing the sign of the right orbital so the positive phases of both orbitals match between the nuclei to produce constructive interference. This leads to enhanced electron probability between the nuclei. The antibonding orbital is formed by the direct combination of the orbitals, which gives destructive interference of the positive phase of one orbital with the negative phase of the second orbital. This produces a node between the nuclei, which gives decreased electron probability. (b) When the parallel *p* orbitals are combined with the positive and negative phases matched, constructive interference occurs, giving a bonding π orbital. When the orbitals have opposite phases (the signs of one orbital are reversed), destructive interference occurs, resulting in an antibonding π orbital.

p orbitals that overlap in a parallel fashion also produce bonding and antibonding orbitals [Fig. 9.34(b)]. Since the electron probability lies above and below the line between the nuclei, both the orbitals are **pi (π) molecular orbitals.** They are designated as π_{2p} for the bonding MO and $\pi_{2p}*$ for the antibonding MO.

Let's try to make an educated guess about the relative energies of the σ and π molecular orbitals formed from the 2*p* atomic orbitals. Would we expect the electrons to prefer the σ bonding orbital (where the electron probability is concentrated in the area between the nuclei) or the π bonding orbital? The σ orbital would seem to have the lower energy, since the electrons are closest to the two nuclei. This agrees with the observation that σ interactions are stronger than π interactions.

Figure 9.35 gives the molecular orbital energy-level diagram *expected* when the two sets of 2*p* orbitals on the boron atoms combine to form molecular orbitals. Note that there are two π bonding orbitals at the same energy (degenerate orbitals) formed from the two pairs of parallel *p* orbitals, and there are two degenerate π antibonding orbitals. The energy of the π_{2p} orbitals is expected to be higher than that of the σ_{2p} orbital because σ interactions are generally stronger than π interactions.

To construct the total molecular orbital diagram for the B_2 molecule, we make the assumption that the 2*s* and 2*p* orbitals combine separately (in other words, there is no 2*s*–2*p* mixing). The resulting diagram is shown in Fig. 9.36. Note that B_2 has six *valence* electrons. (Remember the 1*s* orbitals and electrons are assumed not to participate in the bonding.) This diagram predicts the bond order:

$$\frac{4-2}{2} = 1$$

Therefore, B_2 should be a stable molecule.

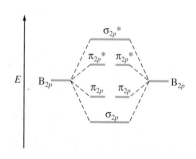

FIGURE 9.35
The *expected* molecular orbital energy-level diagram resulting from the combination of the 2*p* orbitals on two boron atoms.

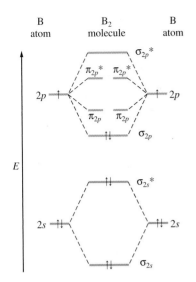

FIGURE 9.36
The *expected* molecular orbital energy-level diagram for the B_2 molecule.

FIGURE 9.37
Diagram of the kind of apparatus used to measure the paramagnetism of a sample. A paramagnetic sample will appear heavier when the electromagnet is turned on because the sample is attracted into the inducing magnetic field.

Paramagnetism

At this point we need to discuss an additional molecular property—magnetism. Most materials have no magnetism until they are placed in a magnetic field. However, in the presence of such a field, magnetism of two types can be induced. **Paramagnetism** causes the substance to be attracted into the inducing magnetic field. **Diamagnetism** causes the substance to be repelled from the inducing magnetic field. Figure 9.37 illustrates how paramagnetism is measured. The sample is weighed with the electromagnet turned off and then weighed again with the electromagnet turned on. An increase in weight when the field is turned on indicates the sample is paramagnetic. Studies have shown that *paramagnetism is associated with unpaired electrons and diamagnetism is associated with paired electrons.* Any substance that has both paired and unpaired electrons will exhibit a net paramagnetism, since the effect of paramagnetism is much stronger than that of diamagnetism.

The molecular orbital energy-level diagram represented in Fig. 9.36 predicts that the B_2 molecule will be diamagnetic, since the MOs contain only paired electrons. However, experiments show that B_2 is actually paramagnetic with two unpaired electrons. Why does the model yield the wrong prediction? This is yet another illustration of how models are developed and used. In general, we try to use the simplest possible model that accounts for all the important observations. In this case, although the simplest model successfully describes the diatomic molecules up to B_2, it certainly is suspect if it cannot describe the B_2 molecule correctly. This means we must either discard the model or find a way to modify it.

Let's consider one assumption that we made. In our treatment of B_2, we have assumed that the s and p orbitals combine separately to form molecular orbitals. Calculations show that when the s and p orbitals are allowed to mix in the same molecular orbital, a different energy-level diagram results for B_2 (see Fig. 9.38). Note that even though the s and p contributions to the MOs are no longer separate, we retain the simple orbital designations. The energies of π_{2p} and σ_{2p} orbitals are reversed by p–s mixing, and the σ_{2s} and the σ_{2s}^* orbitals are no longer equally spaced relative to the energy of the free $2s$ orbital.

When the six valence electrons for the B_2 molecule are placed in the modified energy-level diagram, each of the last two electrons goes into one of the degenerate π_{2p} orbitals. This produces a paramagnetic molecule in agreement with experimental results. Thus, when the model is extended to allow p–s mixing in molecular orbitals, it predicts the correct magnetism. Note that the bond order is $(4 - 2)/2 = 1$, as before.

The remaining diatomic molecules of the elements in Period 2 can be described using similar ideas. For example, the C_2 and N_2 molecules use the same set of orbitals as for B_2 (see Fig. 9.38). Because the importance of $2s$–$2p$ mixing decreases across the period, the σ_{2p} and π_{2p} orbitals revert to the order expected in the absence of $2s$–$2p$ mixing for the molecules O_2 and F_2, as shown in Fig. 9.39.

Several significant points arise from the orbital diagrams, bond strengths, and bond lengths summarized in Fig. 9.39 for the Period 2 diatomics:

1. There are definite correlations between bond order, bond energy, and bond length. As the bond order predicted by the molecular orbital model increases, the bond energy increases and the bond length decreases. This is a clear indication that the bond order predicted by the model accurately reflects bond strength, and it strongly supports the reasonableness of the MO model.

2. Comparison of the bond energies of the B_2 and F_2 molecules indicates that bond order cannot automatically be associated with a particular bond energy. Although both molecules have a bond order of 1, the bond in B_2 appears to be about twice as strong as the bond in F_2. As we will see in our later discussion of the halogens, F_2 has an unusually weak single bond due to larger than usual electron–electron repulsions (there are 14 valence electrons on the small F_2 molecule).

3. Note the very large bond energy associated with the N_2 molecule, which the molecular orbital model predicts will have a bond order of 3, a triple bond. The very strong bond in N_2 is the principal reason that many nitrogen-containing compounds are used as high explosives. The reactions involving these explosives give the very stable N_2 molecule as a product, thus releasing large quantities of energy.

Visualization: Magnetic Properties of Liquid Nitrogen and Oxygen

4. The O_2 molecule is known to be paramagnetic. This can be very convincingly demonstrated by pouring liquid oxygen between the poles of a strong magnet, as shown in Fig. 9.40. The oxygen remains there until it evaporates. Significantly, the molecular orbital model correctly predicts oxygen's paramagnetism, while the localized electron model predicts a diamagnetic molecule.

Sample Exercise 9.6   The Molecular Orbital Model I

For the species O_2, O_2^+, and O_2^-, give the electron configuration and the bond order for each. Which has the strongest bond?

Solution

The O_2 molecule has 12 valence electrons $(6 + 6)$; O_2^+ has 11 valence electrons $(6 + 6 - 1)$; and O_2^- has 13 valence electrons $(6 + 6 + 1)$. We will assume that the ions

FIGURE 9.38
The *correct* molecular orbital energy-level diagram for the B_2 molecule. When p–s mixing is allowed, the energies of the σ_{2p} and π_{2p} orbitals are reversed. The two electrons from the B $2p$ orbitals now occupy separate, degenerate π_{2p} molecular orbitals and thus have parallel spins. Therefore, this diagram explains the observed paramagnetism of B_2.

Visualization: Molecular Orbital Diagram (N_2)

FIGURE 9.39
The molecular orbital energy-level diagrams, bond orders, bond energies, and bond lengths for the diatomic molecules B_2 through F_2. Note that for O_2 and F_2 the σ_{2p} orbital is lower in energy than the π_{2p} orbitals.

	B_2	C_2	N_2	O_2	F_2
Magnetism	Para-magnetic	Dia-magnetic	Dia-magnetic	Para-magnetic	Dia-magnetic
Bond order	1	2	3	2	1
Observed bond dissociation energy (kJ/mol)	290	620	942	495	154
Observed bond length (pm)	159	131	110	121	143

can be treated using the same molecular orbital diagram as for the neutral diatomic molecule:

The electron configuration for each species can then be taken from the diagram:

$$O_2: \quad (\sigma_{2s})^2(\sigma_{2s}*)^2(\sigma_{2p})^2(\pi_{2p})^4(\pi_{2p}*)^2$$
$$O_2{}^+: \quad (\sigma_{2s})^2(\sigma_{2s}*)^2(\sigma_{2p})^2(\pi_{2p})^4(\pi_{2p}*)^1$$
$$O_2{}^-: \quad (\sigma_{2s})^2(\sigma_{2s}*)^2(\sigma_{2p})^2(\pi_{2p})^4(\pi_{2p}*)^3$$

The bond orders are:

$$\text{For } O_2: \quad \frac{8-4}{2} = 2$$

$$\text{For } O_2{}^+: \quad \frac{8-3}{2} = 2.5$$

$$\text{For } O_2{}^-: \quad \frac{8-5}{2} = 1.5$$

Thus $O_2{}^+$ is expected to have the strongest bond of the three species.

See Exercises 9.39 and 9.40.

Sample Exercise 9.7   **The Molecular Orbital Model II**

Use the molecular orbital model to predict the bond order and magnetism of each of the following molecules.

a. Ne_2
b. P_2

Solution

a. The valence orbitals for Ne are $2s$ and $2p$. Thus we can use the molecular orbitals we have already constructed for the diatomic molecules of the Period 2 elements. The Ne_2 molecule has 16 valence electrons (8 from each atom). Placing these electrons in the appropriate molecular orbitals produces the following diagram:

The bond order is $(8 - 8)/2 = 0$, and Ne_2 does not exist.

b. The P_2 molecule contains phosphorus atoms from the third row of the periodic table. We will assume that the diatomic molecules of the Period 3 elements can be

Visualization: Magnetic Properties of Liquid Nitrogen and Oxygen

treated in a way very similar to that which we have used so far. Thus we will draw the MO diagram for P_2 analogous to that for N_2. The only change will be that the molecular orbitals will be formed from $3s$ and $3p$ atomic orbitals. The P_2 model has 10 valence electrons (5 from each phosphorus atom). The resulting molecular orbital diagram is

$$
E \quad
\begin{array}{ll}
\sigma_{3p}{}^{*} & \text{——} \\[4pt]
\pi_{3p}{}^{*} & \text{— —} \\[4pt]
\sigma_{3p} & \uparrow\downarrow \\[4pt]
\pi_{3p} & \uparrow\downarrow \;\; \uparrow\downarrow \\[4pt]
\sigma_{3s}{}^{*} & \uparrow\downarrow \\[4pt]
\sigma_{3s} & \uparrow\downarrow
\end{array}
$$

The molecule has a bond order of 3 and is expected to be diamagnetic.

See Exercises 9.37 through 9.42.

9.4 Bonding in Heteronuclear Diatomic Molecules

In this section we will deal with selected examples of **heteronuclear** (different atoms) **diatomic molecules.** A special case involves molecules containing atoms adjacent to each other in the periodic table. Since the atoms involved in such a molecule are so similar, we can use the molecular orbital diagram for homonuclear molecules. For example, we can predict the bond order and magnetism of nitric oxide (NO) by placing its 11 valence electrons (5 from nitrogen and 6 from oxygen) in the molecular orbital energy-level diagram shown in Fig. 9.41. The molecule should be paramagnetic and has a bond order of

$$
\frac{8-3}{2} = 2.5
$$

Experimentally, nitric oxide is indeed found to be paramagnetic. Notice that this odd-electron molecule is described very naturally by the MO model. In contrast, the localized electron model, in the simple form used in this text, cannot be used readily to treat such molecules.

FIGURE 9.41
The molecular orbital energy-level diagram for the NO molecule. We assume that orbital order is the same as that for N_2. The bond order is 2.5.

| Sample Exercise 9.8 | **The Molecular Orbital Model III** |

Use the molecular orbital model to predict the magnetism and bond order of the NO^{+} and CN^{-} ions.

Solution

The NO^{+} ion has 10 valence electrons $(5 + 6 - 1)$. The CN^{-} ion also has 10 valence electrons $(4 + 5 + 1)$. Both ions are therefore diamagnetic and have a bond order derived from the equation

$$
\frac{8-2}{2} = 3
$$

The molecular orbital diagram for these two ions is the same (see Fig. 9.42).

See Exercises 9.43 and 9.44.

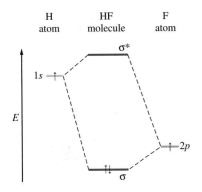

FIGURE 9.42
The molecular orbital energy-level diagram for both the NO⁺ and CN⁻ ions.

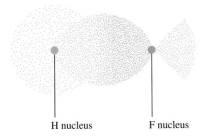

FIGURE 9.43
A partial molecular orbital energy-level diagram for the HF molecule.

When the two atoms of a diatomic molecule are very different, the energy-level diagram for homonuclear molecules can no longer be used. A new diagram must be devised for each molecule. We will illustrate this case by considering the hydrogen fluoride (HF) molecule. The electron configurations of the hydrogen and fluorine atoms are $1s^1$ and $1s^2 2s^2 2p^5$, respectively. To keep things as simple as possible, we will assume that fluorine uses only one of its $2p$ orbitals to bond to hydrogen. Thus the molecular orbitals for HF will be composed of fluorine $2p$ and hydrogen $1s$ orbitals. Figure 9.43 gives the partial molecular orbital energy-level diagram for HF, focusing only on the orbitals involved in the bonding. We are assuming that fluorine's other valence electrons remain localized on the fluorine. The $2p$ orbital of fluorine is shown at a lower energy than the $1s$ orbital of hydrogen on the diagram because fluorine binds its valence electrons more tightly. Thus the $2p$ electron on a free fluorine atom is at lower energy than the $1s$ electron on a free hydrogen atom. The diagram predicts that the HF molecule should be stable because both electrons are lowered in energy relative to their energy in the free hydrogen and fluorine atoms, which is the driving force for bond formation.

Because the fluorine $2p$ orbital is lower in energy than the hydrogen $1s$ orbital, the electrons prefer to be closer to the fluorine atom. That is, the σ molecular orbital containing the bonding electron pair shows greater electron probability close to the fluorine (see Fig. 9.44). The electron pair is not shared equally. This causes the fluorine atom to have a slight excess of negative charge and leaves the hydrogen atom partially positive. This is *exactly* the bond polarity observed for HF. Thus the molecular orbital model accounts in a straightforward way for the different electronegativities of hydrogen and fluorine and the resulting unequal charge distribution.

9.5 Combining the Localized Electron and Molecular Orbital Models

One of the main difficulties with the localized electron model is its assumption that electrons are localized. This problem is most apparent with molecules for which several valid Lewis structures can be drawn. It is clear that none of these structures taken alone adequately describes the electronic structure of the molecule. The concept of resonance was invented to solve this problem. However, even with resonance included, the localized electron model does not describe molecules and ions such as O_3 and NO_3^- in a very satisfying way.

It would seem that the ideal bonding model would be one with the simplicity of the localized electron model but with the delocalization characteristic of the molecular orbital model. We can achieve this by combining the two models to describe molecules that require resonance. Note that for species such as O_3 and NO_3^- the double bond changes position in the resonance structures (see Fig. 9.45). Since a double bond involves one σ and one π bond, there is a σ bond between all bound atoms in each resonance structure. It is really the π bond that has different locations in the various resonance structures.

Therefore we conclude that the σ bonds in a molecule can be described as being localized with no apparent problems. It is the π bonding that must be treated as being

FIGURE 9.44
The electron probability distribution in the bonding molecular orbital of the HF molecule. Note the greater electron density close to the fluorine atom.

FIGURE 9.45
The resonance structures for O_3 and NO_3^-. Note that it is the double bond that occupies various positions in the resonance structures.

CHEMICAL IMPACT

What's Hot?

One of the best things about New Mexico is the food. Authentic New Mexican cuisine employs liberal amounts of green and red chilies—often called chili peppers. Chilies apparently originated in parts of South America and were spread north by birds. When Columbus came to North America, which he originally thought was India, he observed the natives using chilies for spicing foods. When he took chilies back to Europe, Columbus mistakenly called them peppers and the name stuck.

The spicy payload of chilies is delivered mainly by the chemical capsaicin, which has the following structure:

Capsaicin was isolated as a pure substance by L. T. Thresh in 1846. Since then substituted capsaicins have also been found in chilies. The spicy power of chilies derives mostly from capsaicin and dihydrocapsaicin.

The man best known for explaining the "heat" of chilies is Wilbur Scoville, who defined the Scoville unit for measuring chili power. He arbitrarily established the hotness of pure capsaicin as 16 million. On this scale a typical green or red chili has a rating of about 2500 Scoville units. You may have had an encounter with habanero chilies that left you looking for a firehose to put out the blaze in your mouth—habaneros have a Scoville rating of about 500,000! Capsaicin has found many uses outside of cooking. It is used in pepper sprays and repellant sprays for many garden pests, although birds are unaffected by capsaicin. Capsaicin also stimulates the body's circulation and causes pain receptors to release endorphins, similar to the effect produced by intense exercise. Instead of jogging you may want to sit on the couch eating chilies. Either way you are going to sweat.

In molecules that require resonance, it is the π bonding that is most clearly delocalized.

delocalized. Thus, for molecules that require resonance, we will use the localized electron model to describe the σ bonding and the molecular orbital model to describe the π bonding. This allows us to keep the bonding model as simple as possible and yet give a more physically accurate description of such molecules.

We will illustrate the general method by considering the bonding in benzene, an important industrial chemical that must be handled carefully because it is a known carcinogen. The benzene molecule (C_6H_6) consists of a planar hexagon of carbon atoms with one hydrogen atom bound to each carbon atom, as shown in Fig. 9.46(a). In the molecule all six C—C bonds are known to be equivalent. To explain this fact, the localized electron model must invoke resonance [see Fig. 9.46(b)].

A better description of the bonding in benzene results when we use a combination of the models, as described above. In this description it is assumed that the σ bonds of carbon involve sp^2 orbitals, as shown in Fig. 9.47. These σ bonds are all centered in the plane of the molecule.

FIGURE 9.46

(a) The benzene molecule consists of a ring of six carbon atoms with one hydrogen atom bound to each carbon; all atoms are in the same plane. All the C—C bonds are known to be equivalent. (b) Two of the resonance structures for the benzene molecule. The localized electron model must invoke resonance to account for the six equal C—C bonds.

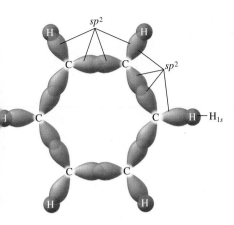

FIGURE 9.47
The σ bonding system in the benzene molecule.

Since each carbon atom is sp^2 hybridized, a p orbital perpendicular to the plane of the ring remains on each carbon atom. These six p orbitals can be used to form π molecular orbitals, as shown in Fig. 9.48(a). The electrons in the resulting π molecular orbitals are delocalized above and below the plane of the ring, as shown in Fig. 9.48(b). This gives six equivalent C—C bonds, as required by the known structure of the benzene molecule. The benzene structure is often written as

to indicate the **delocalized π bonding** in the molecule.

Very similar treatments can be applied to other planar molecules for which resonance is required by the localized electron model. For example, the NO_3^- ion can be described using the π molecular orbital system shown in Fig. 9.49. In this molecule each atom is assumed to be sp^2 hybridized, which leaves one p orbital on each atom perpendicular to the plane of the ion. These p orbitals can combine to form the π molecular orbital system.

FIGURE 9.48
(a) The π molecular orbital system in benzene is formed by combining the six p orbitals from the six sp^2 hybridized carbon atoms. (b) The electrons in the resulting π molecular orbitals are delocalized over the entire ring of carbon atoms, giving six equivalent bonds. A composite of these orbitals is represented here.

(a)

(b)

Visualization: Pi Bonding in the Nitrate Ion

FIGURE 9.49
(a) The p orbitals used to form the π bonding system in the NO_3^- ion. (b) A representation of the delocalization of the electrons in the π molecular orbital system of the NO_3^- ion.

(a)

(b)

Key Terms

For Review

Two widely used bonding models
- Localized electron model
- Molecular orbital model

Localized electron model
- Molecule is pictured as a group of atoms sharing electron pairs between atomic orbitals
- Hybrid orbitals, which are combinations of the "native" atomic orbitals, are often required to account for the molecular structure
  - Four electron pairs (tetrahedral arrangement) require sp^3 orbitals
  - Three electron pairs (trigonal planar arrangement) require sp^2 orbitals
  - Two electron pairs (linear arrangement) requires sp orbitals

Two types of bonds
- Sigma: electrons are shared in the area centered on a line joining the atoms
- Pi: a shared electron pair occupies the space above and below the line joining the atoms

Molecular orbital model
- A molecule is assumed to be a new entity consisting of positively charged nuclei and electrons
- The electrons in the molecule are contained in molecular orbitals, which in the simplest form of the model are constructed from the atomic orbitals of the constituent atoms
- The model correctly predicts relative bond strength, magnetism, and bond polarity
- It correctly portrays electrons as being delocalized in polyatomic molecules
- The main disadvantage of the model is that it is difficult to apply qualitatively to polyatomic molecules

Molecular orbitals are classified in two ways: energy and shape
- Energy
  - A bonding MO is lower in energy than the atomic orbitals from which it is constructed. Electrons in this type of MO are lower in energy in the molecule than in the separated atoms and thus favor molecule formation.
  - An antibonding MO is higher in energy than the atomic orbitals from which it is constructed. Electrons in this type of MO are higher in energy in the molecule than in the separated atoms and thus do not favor molecule formation.
- Shape (symmetry)
  - Sigma (σ) MOs have their electron probability centered on a line passing through the nuclei
  - Pi (π) MOs have their electron probability concentrated above and below the line connecting the nuclei

Bond order is an index of bond strength

$$\text{Bond order} = \frac{\text{number of bonding electrons} - \text{number of antibonding electrons}}{2}$$

Molecules that require the concept of resonance in the localized electron model can be more accurately described by combining the localized electron and molecular orbital models
- The σ bonds are localized
- The π bonds are delocalized

REVIEW QUESTIONS

1. Why do we hybridize atomic orbitals to explain the bonding in covalent compounds? What type of bonds form from hybrid orbitals, sigma or pi? Explain.

2. What hybridization is required for central atoms that have a tetrahedral arrangement of electron pairs? A trigonal planar arrangement of electron pairs? A linear arrangement of electron pairs? How many unhybridized p atomic orbitals are present when a central atom exhibits tetrahedral geometry? Trigonal planar geometry? Linear geometry? What are the unhybridized p atomic orbitals used for?

3. Describe the bonding in H_2S, CH_4, H_2CO, and HCN using the localized electron model.

4. What hybridization is required for central atoms exhibiting trigonal bipyramidal geometry? Octahedral geometry? Describe the bonding of PF_5, SF_4, SF_6, and IF_5 using the localized electron model.

5. Electrons in σ bonding molecular orbitals are most likely to be found in the region between the two bonded atoms. Why does this arrangement favor bonding? In a σ antibonding orbital, where are the electrons most likely to be found in relation to the nuclei in a bond?

6. Show how $2s$ orbitals combine to form σ bonding and σ antibonding molecular orbitals. Show how $2p$ orbitals overlap to form σ bonding, π bonding, π antibonding, and σ antibonding molecular orbitals.

7. What are the relationships among bond order, bond energy, and bond length? Which of these can be measured? Distinguish between the terms *paramagnetic* and *diamagnetic*. What type of experiment can be done to determine if a material is paramagnetic?

8. How does molecular orbital theory explain the following observations?
   a. H_2 is stable, while He_2 is unstable.
   b. B_2 and O_2 are paramagnetic, while C_2, N_2, and F_2 are diamagnetic.
   c. N_2 has a very large bond energy associated with it.
   d. NO^+ is more stable than NO^-.

9. Consider the heteronuclear diatomic molecule HF. Explain in detail how molecular orbital theory is applied to describe the bonding in HF.

10. What is delocalized π bonding and what does it explain? Explain the delocalized π bonding system in C_6H_6 (benzene) and O_3 (ozone).

Active Learning Questions

These questions are designed to be used by groups of students in class. The questions allow students to explore their understanding of concepts through discussion and peer teaching. The real value of these questions is the learning that occurs while students talk to each other about chemical concepts.

1. What are molecular orbitals? How do they compare with atomic orbitals? Can you tell by the shape of the bonding and antibonding orbitals which is lower in energy? Explain.

2. Explain the difference between the σ and π MOs for homonuclear diatomic molecules. How are bonding and antibonding orbitals different? Why are there two π MOs and one σ MO? Why are the π MOs degenerate?

3. Compare Figs. 9.36 and 9.38. Why are they different? Because B_2 is known to be paramagnetic, the π_{2p} and σ_{2p} molecular orbitals must be switched from the first prediction. What is the rationale for this? Why might one expect the σ_{2p} to be lower in energy than the π_{2p}? Why can't we use diatomic oxygen to help us decide whether the σ_{2p} or π_{2p} is lower in energy?

4. Which of the following would you expect to be more favorable energetically? Explain.
   a. An H_2 molecule in which enough energy is added to excite one electron from the bonding to the antibonding MO
   b. Two separate H atoms

5. Draw the Lewis structure for HCN. Indicate the hybrid orbitals, and draw a picture showing all the bonds between the atoms, labeling each bond as σ or π.

6. Which is the more correct statement: "The methane molecule (CH_4) is a tetrahedral molecule because it is sp^3 hybridized" or "The methane molecule (CH_4) is sp^3 hybridized because it is a tetrahedral molecule"? What, if anything, is the difference between these two statements?

A blue question or exercise number indicates that the answer to that question or exercise appears at the back of this book and a solution appears in the *Solutions Guide*.

Questions

7. In the hybrid orbital model, compare and contrast σ bonds versus π bonds. What orbitals form the σ bonds and what orbitals form the π bonds? Assume the z-axis is the internuclear axis.

8. In the molecular orbital model, compare and contrast σ versus π bonds. What orbitals form the σ bonds and what orbitals form the π bonds? Assume the z-axis is the internuclear axis.

9. Why are *d* orbitals sometimes used to form hybrid orbitals? Which period of elements does not use *d* orbitals for hybridization? If necessary, which *d* orbitals (3d, 4d, 5d, or 6d) would sulfur use to form hybrid orbitals requiring *d* atomic orbitals? Answer the same question for arsenic and for iodine.

10. The atoms in a single bond can rotate about the internuclear axis without breaking the bond. The atoms in a double and triple bond cannot rotate about the internuclear axis unless the bond is broken. Why?

11. Compare and contrast bonding versus antibonding molecular orbitals.

12. What modification to the molecular orbital model was made from the experimental evidence that B_2 is paramagnetic?

13. Why does the molecular orbital model do a better job in explaining the bonding in NO^- and NO than the hybrid orbital model?

14. The three NO bonds in NO_3^- are all equivalent in length and strength. How is this explained even though any valid Lewis structure for NO_3^- has one double bond and two single bonds to nitrogen?

Exercises

In this section similar exercises are paired.

The Localized Electron Model and Hybrid Orbitals

15. Use the localized electron model to describe the bonding in H_2O.

16. Use the localized electron model to describe the bonding in CCl_4.

17. Use the localized electron model to describe the bonding in H_2CO (carbon is the central atom).

18. Use the localized electron model to describe the bonding in C_2H_2 (exists as HCCH).

19. The space-filling models of ethane and ethanol are shown below.

Ethane   Ethanol
(C_2H_6)   (C_2H_5OH)

C
H
O

Use the localized electron model to describe the bonding in ethane and ethanol.

20. The space-filling models of hydrogen cyanide and phosgene are shown below.

Hydrogen cyanide   Phosgene
(HCN)   ($COCl_2$)

C
H
O
N
Cl

Use the localized electron model to describe the bonding in hydrogen cyanide and phosgene.

21. Give the expected hybridization of the central atom for the molecules or ions in Exercises 67 and 73 from Chapter 8.

22. Give the expected hybridization of the central atom for the molecules or ions in Exercises 68 and 74 from Chapter 8.

23. Give the expected hybridization of the central atom for the molecules or ions in Exercise 71 from Chapter 8.

24. Give the expected hybridization of the central atom for the molecules in Exercise 72 from Chapter 8.

25. Give the expected hybridization of the central atom for the molecules in Exercises 91 and 92 from Chapter 8.

26. Give the expected hybridization of the central atom for the molecules in Exercises 93 and 94 from Chapter 8.

27. For each of the following molecules, write the Lewis structure(s), predict the molecular structure (including bond angles), give the expected hybrid orbitals on the central atom, and predict the overall polarity.

a. CF_4 e. BeH_2 i. KrF_4
b. NF_3 f. TeF_4 j. SeF_6
c. OF_2 g. AsF_5 k. IF_5
d. BF_3 h. KrF_2 l. IF_3

28. For each of the following molecules or ions that contain sulfur, write the Lewis structure(s), predict the molecular structure (including bond angles), and give the expected hybrid orbitals for sulfur.

a. SO_2
b. SO_3
c. $S_2O_3^{2-}$ $\left[\begin{array}{c} O \\ | \\ S-S-O \\ | \\ O \end{array} \right]^{2-}$
d. $S_2O_8^{2-}$ $\left[\begin{array}{c} O \quad\quad O \\ | \quad\quad\quad | \\ O-S-O-O-S-O \\ | \quad\quad\quad | \\ O \quad\quad O \end{array} \right]^{2-}$
e. SO_3^{2-}
f. SO_4^{2-}
g. SF_2
h. SF_4
i. SF_6
j. F_3S-SF
k. SF_5^+

29. Why must all six atoms in C_2H_4 be in the same plane?

30. The allene molecule has the following Lewis structure:

Are all four hydrogen atoms in the same plane? If not, what is their spatial relationship? Explain.

31. Biacetyl and acetoin are added to margarine to make it taste more like butter.

Biacetyl   Acetoin

Complete the Lewis structures, predict values for all C—C—O bond angles, and give the hybridization of the carbon atoms in these two compounds. Are the four carbons and two oxygens in biacetyl in the same plane? How many σ bonds and how many π bonds are there in biacetyl and acetoin?

32. Many important compounds in the chemical industry are derivatives of ethylene (C_2H_4). Two of them are acrylonitrile and methyl methacrylate.

Acrylonitrile   Methyl methacrylate

Complete the Lewis structures, showing all lone pairs. Give approximate values for bond angles *a* through *f*. Give the hybridization of all carbon atoms. In acrylonitrile, how many of the atoms in the molecule lie in the same plane? How many σ bonds and how many π bonds are there in methyl methacrylate and acrylonitrile?

33. One of the first drugs to be approved for use in treatment of acquired immune deficiency syndrome (AIDS) was azidothymidine (AZT). Complete the Lewis structure for AZT.

a. How many carbon atoms are sp^3 hybridized?
b. How many carbon atoms are sp^2 hybridized?
c. Which atom is sp hybridized?
d. How many σ bonds are in the molecule?
e. How many π bonds are in the molecule?
f. What is the N—N—N bond angle in the azide ($—N_3$) group?
g. What is the H—O—C bond angle in the side group attached to the five-membered ring?
h. What is the hybridization of the oxygen atom in the $—CH_2OH$ group?

34. Hot and spicy foods contain molecules that stimulate pain-detecting nerve endings. Two such molecules are piperine and capsaicin:

Piperine

Capsaicin

Piperine is the active compound in white and black pepper, and capsaicin is the active compound in chili peppers. The ring structures in piperine and capsaicin are shorthand notation. Each point where lines meet represents a carbon atom.

a. Complete the Lewis structure for piperine and capsaicin showing all lone pairs of electrons.
b. How many carbon atoms are sp, sp^2, and sp^3 hybridized in each molecule?
c. Which hybrid orbitals are used by the nitrogen atoms in each molecule?
d. Give approximate values for the bond angles marked *a* through *l* in the above structures.

The Molecular Orbital Model

35. Which of the following are predicted by the molecular orbital model to be stable diatomic species?
a. H_2^+, H_2, H_2^-, H_2^{2-}
b. He_2^{2+}, He_2^+, He_2

36. Which of the following are predicted by the molecular orbital model to be stable diatomic species?
a. N_2^{2-}, O_2^{2-}, F_2^{2-} **b.** Be_2, B_2, Ne_2

37. Using the molecular orbital model, write electron configurations for the following diatomic species and calculate the bond orders. Which ones are paramagnetic?
a. Li_2 **b.** C_2 **c.** S_2

38. Consider the following electron configuration:

$$(\sigma_{3s})^2(\sigma_{3s}^*)^2(\sigma_{3p})^2(\pi_{3p})^4(\pi_{3p}^*)^4$$

Give four species that, in theory, would have this electron configuration

39. Using molecular orbital theory, explain why the removal of one electron in O_2 strengthens bonding, while the removal of one electron in N_2 weakens bonding.

40. Using the molecular orbital model to describe the bonding in F_2^+, F_2, and F_2^-, predict the bond orders and the relative bond lengths for these three species. How many unpaired electrons are present in each species?

41. Which charge(s) for the N_2 molecule would give a bond order of 2.5?

42. A Lewis structure obeying the octet rule can be drawn for O_2 as follows:

$$:\ddot{O}=\ddot{O}:$$

Use the molecular orbital energy-level diagram for O_2 to show that the above Lewis structure corresponds to an excited state.

43. Using the molecular orbital model, write electron configurations for the following diatomic species and calculate the bond orders. Which ones are paramagnetic? Place the species in order of increasing bond length and bond energy.
    a. CO   b. CO^+ c. CO^{2+}

44. Using the molecular orbital model, write electron configurations for the following diatomic species and calculate the bond orders. Which ones are paramagnetic? Place the species in order of increasing bond length and bond energy.
    a. NO^+ b. NO   c. NO^-

45. In which of the following diatomic molecules would the bond strength be expected to weaken as an electron is removed to form the positive charged ion?
    a. H_2 c. C_2^{2-}
    b. B_2 d. OF

46. In terms of the molecular orbital model, which species in each of the following two pairs will most likely be the one to gain an electron? Explain.

    CN or NO
    O_2^{2+} or N_2^{2+}

47. Show how two $2p$ atomic orbitals can combine to form a σ or a π molecular orbital.

48. Show how a hydrogen $1s$ atomic orbital and a fluorine $2p$ atomic orbital overlap to form bonding and antibonding molecular orbitals in the hydrogen fluoride molecule. Are these molecular orbitals σ or π molecular orbitals?

49. Use Figs. 9.43 and 9.44 to answer the following questions.
    a. Would the bonding molecular orbital in HF place greater electron density near the H or the F atom? Why?
    b. Would the bonding molecular orbital have greater fluorine $2p$ character, greater hydrogen $1s$ character, or an equal contribution from both? Why?

c. Answer the previous two questions for the antibonding molecular orbital in HF.

50. The diatomic molecule OH exists in the gas phase. The bond length and bond energy have been measured to be 97.06 pm and 424.7 kJ/mol, respectively. Assume that the OH molecule is analogous to the HF molecule discussed in the chapter and that molecular orbitals result from the overlap of a lower-energy p_z orbital from oxygen with the higher-energy $1s$ orbital of hydrogen (the O—H bond lies along the z-axis).
    a. Which of the two molecular orbitals will have the greater hydrogen $1s$ character?
    b. Can the $2p_x$ orbital of oxygen form molecular orbitals with the $1s$ orbital of hydrogen? Explain.
    c. Knowing that only the $2p$ orbitals of oxygen will interact significantly with the $1s$ orbital of hydrogen, complete the molecular orbital energy-level diagram for OH. Place the correct number of electrons in the energy levels.
    d. Estimate the bond order for OH.
    e. Predict whether the bond order of OH^+ will be greater than, less than, or the same as that of OH. Explain.

51. Describe the bonding in the O_3 molecule and the NO_2^- ion using the localized electron model. How would the molecular orbital model describe the π bonding in these two species?

52. Describe the bonding in the CO_3^{2-} ion using the localized electron model. How would the molecular orbital model describe the π bonding in this species?

Additional Exercises

53. Draw the Lewis structures, predict the molecular structures, and describe the bonding (in terms of the hybrid orbitals for the central atom) for the following.
    a. XeO_3 d. $XeOF_2$
    b. XeO_4 e. XeO_3F_2
    c. $XeOF_4$

54. $FClO_2$ and F_3ClO can both gain a fluoride ion to form stable anions. F_3ClO and F_3ClO_2 will both lose a fluoride ion to form stable cations. Draw the Lewis structures and describe the hybrid orbitals used by chlorine in these ions.

55. Vitamin B_6 is an organic compound whose deficiency in the human body can cause apathy, irritability, and an increased susceptibility to infections. Below is an incomplete Lewis structure for vitamin B_6. Complete the Lewis structure and answer the following questions. *Hint:* Vitamin B_6 can be classified as an organic compound (a compound based on carbon atoms). The majority of Lewis structures for simple organic compounds have all atoms with a formal charge of zero. Therefore, add lone pairs and multiple bonds to the structure below to give each atom a formal charge of zero.

a. How many σ bonds and π bonds exist in vitamin B₆?

b. Give approximate values for the bond angles marked *a* through *g* in the structure.

c. How many carbon atoms are *sp²* hybridized?

d. How many carbon, oxygen, and nitrogen atoms are *sp³* hybridized?

e. Does vitamin B₆ exhibit delocalized π bonding? Explain.

56. Aspartame is an artificial sweetener marketed under the name Nutra-Sweet. A partial Lewis structure for aspartame is shown below.

Note that the six-sided ring is shorthand notation for a benzene ring (—C₆H₅). Benzene is discussed in Section 9.5. Complete the Lewis structure for aspartame. How many C and N atoms exhibit *sp²* hybridization? How many C and O atoms exhibit *sp³* hybridization? How many σ and π bonds are in aspartame? Aspartame is an organic compound and the Lewis structure follows the guidelines outlined in Exercise 55.

57. Using bond energies from Table 8.4, estimate the barrier to rotation about a carbon–carbon double bond. To do this, consider what must happen to go from

to

in terms of making and breaking chemical bonds; that is, what must happen in terms of the π bond?

58. The three most stable oxides of carbon are carbon monoxide (CO), carbon dioxide (CO₂), and carbon suboxide (C₃O₂). The space-filling models for these three compounds are

For each oxide, draw the Lewis structure, predict the molecular structure, and describe the bonding (in terms of the hybrid orbitals for the carbon atoms).

59. Complete the Lewis structures of the following molecules. Predict the molecular structure, polarity, bond angles, and hybrid orbitals used by the atoms marked by asterisks for each molecule.

a. BH₃

$$H—\overset{\displaystyle |}{\underset{\displaystyle H}{B^*}}—H$$

b. N₂F₂

F—N*—N*—F

c. C₄H₆

$$H—\overset{H}{\underset{H}{C^*}}—\overset{H}{\underset{H}{C^*}}—C^*—C^*—H$$

d. ICl₃

$$Cl—\overset{\displaystyle |}{\underset{\displaystyle Cl}{I^*}}—Cl$$

60. Complete the following resonance structures for POCl₃.

$$\underset{(A)}{Cl—\overset{O}{\underset{\displaystyle Cl}{P}}—Cl} \longleftrightarrow \underset{(B)}{Cl—\overset{O}{\underset{\displaystyle Cl}{\overset{\|}{P}}}—Cl}$$

a. Would you predict the same molecular structure from each resonance structure?

b. What is the hybridization of P in each structure?

c. What orbitals can the P atom use to form the π bond in structure B?

d. Which resonance structure would be favored on the basis of formal charges?

61. The N₂O molecule is linear and polar.

a. On the basis of this experimental evidence, which arrangement, NNO or NON, is correct? Explain your answer.

b. On the basis of your answer to part a, write the Lewis structure of N₂O (including resonance forms). Give the formal charge on each atom and the hybridization of the central atom.

c. How would the multiple bonding in :N≡N—O̤: be described in terms of orbitals?

62. Describe the bonding in NO⁺, NO⁻, and NO using both the localized electron and molecular orbital models. Account for any discrepancies between the two models.

63. Describe the bonding in the first excited state of N₂ (the one closest in energy to the ground state) using the molecular orbital model. What differences do you expect in the properties of the molecule in the ground state as compared to the first excited state? (An excited state of a molecule corresponds to an electron arrangement other than that giving the lowest possible energy.)

64. Acetylene (C₂H₂) can be produced from the reaction of calcium carbide (CaC₂) with water. Use both the localized electron and molecular orbital models to describe the bonding in the acetylide anion (C₂²⁻).

65. Using an MO energy-level diagram, would you expect F₂ to have a lower or higher first ionization energy than atomic fluorine? Why?

66. Show how a d_{xz} atomic orbital and a p_z atomic orbital combine to form a bonding molecular orbital. Assume the *x*-axis is the internuclear axis. Is a σ or a π molecular orbital formed? Explain.

67. What type of molecular orbital would result from the in phase combination of two d_{xz} atomic orbitals shown below? Assume the x-axis is the internuclear axis.

68. Consider three molecules: A, B, and C. Molecule A has a hybridization of sp^3. Molecule B has two more effective pairs (electron pairs around the central atom) than molecule A. Molecule C consists of two σ bonds and two π bonds. Give the molecular structure, hybridization, bond angles, and an example for each molecule.

Challenge Problems

69. Consider your Lewis structure for the computer-generated model of caffeine shown in Exercise 130 of Chapter 8. How many C and N atoms are sp^2 hybridized in your Lewis structure for caffeine? How many C and N atoms are sp^3 hybridized? sp hybridized? How many σ and π bonds are in your Lewis structure?

70. The space-filling model for benzoic acid is shown below.

Benzoic acid
($C_6H_5CO_2H$)

Describe the bonding in benzoic acid using the localized electron model combined with the molecular orbital model.

71. Two structures can be drawn by cyanuric acid:

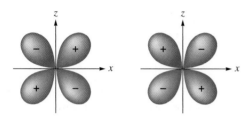

a. Are these two structures the same molecule? Explain.
b. Give the hybridization of the carbon and nitrogen atoms in each structure.
c. Use bond energies (Table 8.4) to predict which form is more stable; that is, which contains the strongest bonds.

72. Cholesterol ($C_{27}H_{46}O$) has the following structure:

In such shorthand structures, each point where lines meet represents a carbon atom and most H atoms are not shown. Draw the complete structure showing all carbon and hydrogen atoms. (There will be four bonds to each carbon atom.) Indicate which carbon atoms use sp^2 or sp^3 hybrid orbitals. Are all carbon atoms in the same plane, as implied by the structure?

73. Cyanamide (H_2NCN), an important industrial chemical, is produced by the following steps:

$$CaC_2 + N_2 \longrightarrow CaNCN + C$$

$$CaNCN \xrightarrow{Acid} \underset{\text{Cyanamide}}{H_2NCN}$$

Calcium cyanamide (CaNCN) is used as a direct-application fertilizer, weed killer, and cotton defoliant. It is also used to make cyanamide, dicyandiamide, and melamine plastics:

$$H_2NCN \xrightarrow{Acid} NCNC(NH_2)_2$$
$$\text{Dicyandiamide}$$

$$NCNC(NH_2)_2 \xrightarrow[NH_3]{Heat}$$

Melamine
(π bonds
not shown)

a. Write Lewis structures for NCN^{2-}, H_2NCN, dicyandiamide, and melamine, including resonance structures where appropriate.
b. Give the hybridization of the C and N atoms in each species.
c. How many σ bonds and how many π bonds are in each species?
d. Is the ring in melamine planar?
e. There are three different C—N bond distances in dicyandiamide, $NCNC(NH_2)_2$, and the molecule is nonlinear. Of all the resonance structures you drew for this molecule, predict which should be the most important.

74. In Exercise 75 in Chapter 8, the Lewis structures for benzene (C_6H_6) were drawn. Using one of the Lewis structures, estimate ΔH_f° for $C_6H_6(g)$ using bond energies and given that the standard enthalpy of formation of $C(g)$ is 717 kJ/mol. The experimental ΔH_f° value of $C_6H_6(g)$ is 83 kJ/mol. Explain the discrepancy between the experimental value and the calculated ΔH_f° value for $C_6H_6(g)$.

75. A flask containing gaseous N_2 is irradiated with 25-nm light.
   a. Using the following information, indicate what species can form in the flask during irradiation.

$$N_2(g) \longrightarrow 2N(g) \qquad \Delta H = 941 \text{ kJ/mol}$$
$$N_2(g) \longrightarrow N_2^+(g) + e^- \qquad \Delta H = 1501 \text{ kJ/mol}$$
$$N(g) \longrightarrow N^+(g) + e^- \qquad \Delta H = 1402 \text{ kJ/mol}$$

   b. What range of wavelengths will produce atomic nitrogen in the flask but will not produce any ions?
   c. Explain why the first ionization energy of N_2 (1501 kJ/mol) is greater than the first ionization energy of atomic nitrogen (1402 kJ/mol).

76. As compared with CO and O_2, CS and S_2 are very unstable molecules. Give an explanation based on the relative abilities of the sulfur and oxygen atoms to form π bonds.

77. Values of measured bond energies may vary greatly depending on the molecule studied. Consider the following reactions:

$$NCl_3(g) \longrightarrow NCl_2(g) + Cl(g) \qquad \Delta H = 375 \text{ kJ/mol}$$
$$ONCl(g) \longrightarrow NO(g) + Cl(g) \qquad \Delta H = 158 \text{ kJ/mol}$$

Rationalize the difference in the values of ΔH for these reactions, even though each reaction appears to involve only the breaking of one N—Cl bond. (*Hint:* Consider the bond order of the NO bond in ONCl and in NO.)

78. Use the MO model to explain the bonding in BeH_2. When constructing the MO energy-level diagram, assume that the Be's $1s$ electrons are not involved in bond formation.

79. Carbon monoxide (CO) forms bonds to a variety of metals and metal ions. Its ability to bond to iron in hemoglobin is the reason that CO is so toxic. The bond carbon monoxide forms to metals is through the carbon atom:

$$M—C≡O$$

   a. On the basis of electronegativities, would you expect the carbon atom or the oxygen atom to form bonds to metals?
   b. Assign formal charges to the atoms in CO. Which atom would you expect to bond to a metal on this basis?
   c. In the MO model, bonding MOs place more electron density near the more electronegative atom. (See the HF molecule, Figs. 9.43 and 9.44.) Antibonding MOs place more electron density near the less electronegative atom in the diatomic molecule. Use the MO model to predict which atom of carbon monoxide should form bonds to metals.

80. Arrange the following from lowest to highest ionization energy: O, O_2, O_2^-, O_2^+. Explain your answer.

81. Use the MO model to determine which of the following has the smallest ionization energy: N_2, O_2, N_2^{2-}, N_2^-, O_2^+. Explain your answer.

82. Given that the ionization energy of F_2^- is 290 kJ, do the following:
   a. Calculate the bond energy of F_2^-. You will need to look up the bond energy of F_2 and ionization energy of F^-.
   b. Explain the difference in bond energy between F_2^- and F_2 using MO theory.

Integrative Problems

These problems require the integration of multiple concepts to find the solutions.

83. As the head engineer of your starship in charge of the warp drive, you notice that the supply of dilithium is critically low. While searching for a replacement fuel, you discover some diboron, B_2.
   a. What is the bond order in Li_2 and B_2?
   b. How many electrons must be removed from B_2 to make it isoelectronic with Li_2 so that it might be used in the warp drive?
   c. The reaction to make B_2 isoelectronic with Li_2 is generalized (where n = number of electrons determined in part b) as follows:

$$B_2 \rightarrow B_2^{n+} + ne^- \qquad \Delta H = 6455 \text{ kJ/mol}$$

How much energy is needed to ionize 1.5 kg of B_2 to the desired isoelectronic species?

84. An unusual category of acids known as superacids, which are defined as any acid stronger than 100% sulfuric acid, can be prepared by seemingly simple reactions similar to the one below. In this example, the reaction of anhydrous HF with SbF_5 produces the superacid $[H_2F]^+[SbF_6]^-$:

$$2HF(l) + SbF_5(l) \rightarrow [H_2F]^+[SbF_6]^-(l)$$

   a. What are the molecular structures of all species in this reaction? What are the hybridizations of the central atoms in each species?
   b. What mass of $[H_2F]^+[SbF_6]^-$ can be prepared when 2.93 mL of anhydrous HF (density = 0.975 g/mL) and 10.0 mL of SbF_5 (density = 3.10 g/mL) are allowed to react?

85. Determine the molecular structure and hybridization of the central atom X in the polyatomic ion XY_3^+ given the following information: A neutral atom of X contains 36 electrons, and the element Y makes an anion with a 1– charge, which has the electron configuration $1s^2 2s^2 2p^6$.

 Get help understanding core concepts and visualizing molecular-level interactions, and practice problem solving by visiting the Online Study Center at **college.hmco.com/ PIC/zumdahl7e.**

10 Liquids and Solids

Contents

Karst formation in Phang Nga Bay, Thailand at sunset. The Karst is limestone that has eroded into these formations rising out of the sea.

You have only to think about water to appreciate how different the three states of matter are. Flying, swimming, and ice skating are all done in contact with water in its various forms. Clearly, the arrangements of the water molecules must be significantly different in its gas, liquid, and solid forms.

In Chapter 5 we saw that a gas can be pictured as a substance whose component particles are far apart, are in rapid random motion, and exert relatively small forces on each other. The kinetic molecular model was constructed to account for the ideal behavior that most gases approach at high temperatures and low pressures.

Solids are obviously very different from gases. A gas has low density and high compressibility and completely fills its container. Solids have much greater densities, are compressible only to a very slight extent, and are rigid—a solid maintains its shape irrespective of its container. These properties indicate that the components of a solid are close together and exert large attractive forces on each other.

The properties of liquids lie somewhere between those of solids and gases but not midway between, as can be seen from some of the properties of the three states of water. For example, compare the enthalpy change for the melting of ice at 0°C (the heat of fusion) with that for vaporizing liquid water at 100°C (the heat of vaporization):

$$H_2O(s) \longrightarrow H_2O(l) \qquad \Delta H°_{fus} = 6.02 \text{ kJ/mol}$$
$$H_2O(l) \longrightarrow H_2O(g) \qquad \Delta H°_{vap} = 40.7 \text{ kJ/mol}$$

These values show a much greater change in structure in going from the liquid to the gaseous state than in going from the solid to the liquid state. This suggests that there are extensive attractive forces among the molecules in liquid water, similar to but not as strong as those in the solid state.

The relative similarity of the liquid and solid states also can be seen in the densities of the three states of water. As shown in Table 10.1, the densities for liquid and solid water are quite close.* Compressibilities also can be used to explore the relationship among water's states. At 25°C, the density of liquid water changes from 0.99707 g/cm^3 at a pressure of 1 atm to 1.046 g/cm^3 at 1065 atm. Given the large change in pressure, this is a very small variation in the density. Ice also shows little variation in density with increased pressure. On the other hand, at 400°C, the density of gaseous water changes from 3.26×10^{-4} g/cm^3 at 1 atm pressure to 0.157 g/cm^3 at 242 atm—a huge variation.

The conclusion is clear. The liquid and solid states show many similarities and are strikingly different from the gaseous state, as shown schematically in Fig. 10.1. We must bear this in mind as we develop models for the structures of solids and liquids.

We will proceed in our study of liquids and solids by first considering the properties and structures of liquids and solids. Then we will consider the changes in state that occur between solid and liquid, liquid and gas, and solid and gas.

Visualization: Intermolecular Forces: London Dispersion Forces

---

*Although the densities of solid and liquid water are quite similar, as is typical for most substances, water is quite unusual in that the density of its solid state is slightly less than that of its liquid state. For most substances, the density of the solid state is slightly greater than that of the liquid state.

TABLE 10.1 Densities of the Three States of Water

State	Density (g/cm³)
Solid (0°C, 1 atm)	0.9168
Liquid (25°C, 1 atm)	0.9971
Gas (400°C, 1 atm)	3.26×10^{-4}

Gas　　　　Liquid　　　　Solid

FIGURE 10.1
Schematic representations of the three states of matter.

10.1 Intermolecular Forces

In Chapters 8 and 9 we saw that atoms can form stable units called *molecules* by sharing electrons. This is called *intramolecular* (within the molecule) *bonding*. In this chapter we consider the properties of the **condensed states** of matter (liquids and solids) and the forces that cause the aggregation of the components of a substance to form a liquid or a solid. These forces may involve covalent or ionic bonding, or they may involve weaker interactions usually called **intermolecular forces** (because they occur between, rather than within, molecules).

It is important to recognize that when a substance such as water changes from solid to liquid to gas, *the molecules remain intact*. The changes in states are due to changes in the forces *among* the molecules rather than in those *within* the molecules. In ice, as we will see later in this chapter, the molecules are virtually locked in place, although they can vibrate about their positions. If energy is added, the motions of the molecules increase, and they eventually achieve the greater movement and disorder characteristic of liquid water. The ice has melted. As more energy is added, the gaseous state is eventually reached, with the individual molecules far apart and interacting relatively little. However, the gas still consists of water molecules. It would take much energy to overcome the covalent bonds and decompose the water molecules into their component atoms. This can be seen by comparing the energy needed to vaporize 1 mole of liquid water (40.7 kJ) with that needed to break the O—H bonds in 1 mole of water molecules (934 kJ).

Dipole–Dipole Forces

As we saw in Section 8.3, molecules with polar bonds often behave in an electric field as if they had a center of positive charge and a center of negative charge. That is, they exhibit a dipole moment. Molecules with dipole moments can attract each other electrostatically by lining up so that the positive and negative ends are close to each other, as shown in Fig. 10.2(a). This is called a **dipole–dipole attraction.** In a condensed state such as a liquid, where many molecules are in close proximity, the dipoles find the best compromise between attraction and repulsion. That is, the molecules orient themselves to maximize the ⊕---⊖ interactions and to minimize ⊕---⊕ and ⊖---⊖ interactions, as represented in Fig. 10.2(b).

Dipole–dipole forces are typically only about 1% as strong as covalent or ionic bonds, and they rapidly become weaker as the distance between the dipoles increases. At low pressures in the gas phase, where the molecules are far apart, these forces are relatively unimportant.

Particularly strong dipole–dipole forces, however, are seen among molecules in which hydrogen is bound to a highly electronegative atom, such as nitrogen, oxygen, or fluorine. Two factors account for the strengths of these interactions: the great polarity of the bond and the close approach of the dipoles, allowed by the very small size of the hydrogen atom. Because dipole–dipole attractions of this type are so unusually strong, they are given a special name—**hydrogen bonding.** Figure 10.3 shows hydrogen bonding among water

---

Intermolecular forces were introduced in Chapter 5 to explain nonideal gas behavior.

Remember that temperature is a measure of the random motions of the particles in a substance.

Dipole–dipole forces are forces that act between polar molecules.

Visualization: Intermolecular Forces: Dipole–Dipole Forces

Visualization: Intermolecular Forces: Hydrogen Bonding Forces

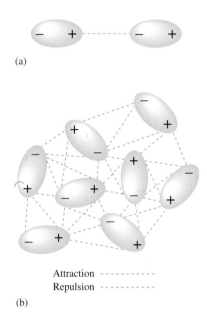

(a)

(b)

FIGURE 10.2
(a) The electrostatic interaction of two polar molecules. (b) The interaction of many dipoles in a condensed state.

Attraction ----------
Repulsion ----------

(a)   (b)

FIGURE 10.3
(a) The polar water molecule. (b) Hydrogen bonding among water molecules. Note that the small size of the hydrogen atom allows for close interactions.

molecules, which occurs between the partially positive H atoms and the lone pairs on adjacent water molecules.

Hydrogen bonding has a very important effect on physical properties. For example, the boiling points for the covalent hydrides of the elements in Groups 4A, 5A, 6A, and 7A are given in Fig. 10.4. Note that the nonpolar tetrahedral hydrides of Group 4A show a steady increase in boiling point with molar mass (that is, in going down the group), whereas, for the other groups, the lightest member has an unexpectedly high boiling point. Why? The answer lies in the especially large hydrogen bonding interactions that exist among the smallest molecules with the most polar X—H bonds. These unusually strong hydrogen bonding forces are due primarily to two factors. One factor is the relatively large electronegativity values of the lightest elements in each group, which leads to especially polar X—H bonds. The second factor is the small size of the first element of each group, which allows for the close approach of the dipoles, further strengthening the intermolecular forces. Because the interactions among the molecules containing the lightest elements in Groups 5A and 6A are so strong, an unusually large quantity of energy must be supplied

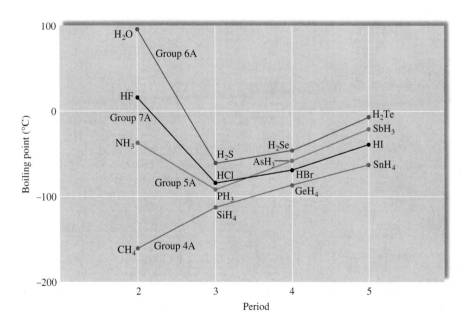

FIGURE 10.4
The boiling points of the covalent hydrides of the elements in Groups 4A, 5A, 6A, and 7A.

Boiling point will be defined precisely in Section 10.8.

to overcome these interactions and separate the molecules to produce the gaseous state. These molecules will remain together in the liquid state even at high temperatures—hence the very high boiling points.

Hydrogen bonding is also important in organic molecules (molecules with a carbon chain backbone). For example, the alcohols methanol (CH_3OH) and ethanol (CH_3CH_2OH) have much higher boiling points than would be expected from their molar masses because of the polar O—H bonds in these molecules, which produce hydrogen bonding.

London Dispersion Forces

Even molecules without dipole moments must exert forces on each other. We know this because all substances—even the noble gases—exist in the liquid and solid states under certain conditions. The forces that exist among noble gas atoms and nonpolar molecules are called **London dispersion forces.** To understand the origin of these forces, let's consider a pair of noble gas atoms. Although we usually assume that the electrons of an atom are uniformly distributed about the nucleus, this is apparently not true at every instant. As the electrons move about the nucleus, a momentary nonsymmetrical electron distribution can develop that produces a temporary dipolar arrangement of charge. The formation of this temporary dipole can, in turn, affect the electron distribution of a neighboring atom. That is, this *instantaneous dipole* that occurs accidentally in a given atom can then *induce* a similar dipole in a neighboring atom, as represented in Fig. 10.5(a). This phenomenon leads to an interatomic attraction that is relatively weak and short-lived but that can be very significant especially for large atoms (see below). For these interactions to become strong enough to produce a solid, the motions of the atoms must be greatly slowed down. This explains, for instance, why the noble gas elements have such low freezing points (see Table 10.2).

Note from Table 10.2 that the freezing point rises going down the group. The principal cause for this trend is that as the atomic number increases, the number of electrons increases, and there is an increased chance of the occurrence of momentary dipole interactions. We describe this phenomenon using the term *polarizability,* which indicates the

TABLE 10.2 The Freezing Points of the Group 8A Elements

Element	Freezing Point (°C)
Helium*	−269.7
Neon	−248.6
Argon	−189.4
Krypton	−157.3
Xenon	−111.9

*Helium is the only element that will not freeze by lowering its temperature at 1 atm. Pressure must be applied to freeze helium.

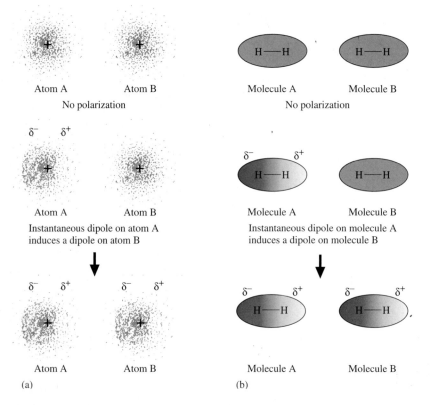

FIGURE 10.5
(a) An instantaneous polarization can occur on atom A, creating an instantaneous dipole. This dipole creates an induced dipole on neighboring atom B. (b) Nonpolar molecules such as H_2 also can develop instantaneous and induced dipoles.

Atom A   Atom B
No polarization

Molecule A   Molecule B
No polarization

δ^- δ^+

Atom A   Atom B
Instantaneous dipole on atom A induces a dipole on atom B

δ^- δ^+

Molecule A   Molecule B
Instantaneous dipole on molecule A induces a dipole on molecule B

δ^- δ^+ δ^- δ^+

Atom A   Atom B

(a)

δ^- δ^+ δ^- δ^+

Molecule A   Molecule B

(b)

ease with which the electron "cloud" of an atom can be distorted to give a dipolar charge distribution. Thus we say that large atoms with many electrons exhibit a higher polarizability than small atoms. This means that the importance of London dispersion forces increases greatly as the size of the atom increases.

These same ideas also apply to nonpolar molecules such as H_2, CH_4, CCl_4, and CO_2 [see Fig. 10.5(b)]. Since none of these molecules has a permanent dipole moment, their principal means of attracting each other is through London dispersion forces.

10.2 The Liquid State

Liquids and liquid solutions are vital to our lives. Of course, water is the most important liquid. Besides being essential to life, water provides a medium for food preparation, for transportation, for cooling in many types of machines and industrial processes, for recreation, for cleaning, and for a myriad of other uses.

Liquids exhibit many characteristics that help us understand their nature. We have already mentioned their low compressibility, lack of rigidity, and high density compared with gases. Many of the properties of liquids give us direct information about the forces that exist among the particles. For example, when a liquid is poured onto a solid surface, it tends to bead as droplets, a phenomenon that depends on the intermolecular forces. Although molecules in the interior of the liquid are completely surrounded by other molecules, those at the liquid surface are subject to attractions only from the side and from below (Fig. 10.6). The effect of this uneven pull on the surface molecules tends to draw them into the body of the liquid and causes a droplet of liquid to assume the shape that has the minimum surface area—a sphere.

To increase a liquid's surface area, molecules must move from the interior of the liquid to the surface. This requires energy, since some intermolecular forces must be overcome. The resistance of a liquid to an increase in its surface area is called the **surface tension** of the liquid. As we would expect, liquids with relatively large intermolecular forces, such as those with polar molecules, tend to have relatively high surface tensions.

Polar liquids typically exhibit **capillary action,** the spontaneous rising of a liquid in a narrow tube. Two different types of forces are responsible for this property: *cohesive forces,* the intermolecular forces among the molecules of the liquid, and *adhesive forces,* the forces between the liquid molecules and their container. We have already seen how cohesive forces operate among polar molecules. Adhesive forces occur when a container is made of a substance that has polar bonds. For example, a glass surface contains many oxygen atoms with partial negative charges that are attractive to the positive end of a polar molecule such as water. This ability of water to "wet" glass makes it creep up the walls of the tube where the water surface touches the glass. This, however, tends to increase the surface area of the water, which is opposed by the cohesive forces that try to minimize the surface. Thus, because water has both strong cohesive (intermolecular) forces and strong adhesive forces to glass, it "pulls itself" up a glass capillary tube (a tube with a small diameter) to a height where the weight of the column of water just balances the water's tendency to be attracted to the glass surface. The concave shape of the meniscus (see Fig. 10.7) shows that water's adhesive forces toward the glass are stronger than its cohesive forces. A nonpolar liquid such as mercury (see Fig. 10.7) shows a convex meniscus. This behavior is characteristic of a liquid in which the cohesive forces are stronger than the adhesive forces toward glass.

Another property of liquids strongly dependent on intermolecular forces is **viscosity,** a measure of a liquid's resistance to flow. As might be expected, liquids with large intermolecular forces tend to be highly viscous. For example, glycerol, whose structure is

$$H-\overset{\displaystyle H}{\underset{\displaystyle H}{\overset{|}{\underset{|}{C}}}}-O-H$$
$$H-\overset{|}{\underset{|}{C}}-O-H$$
$$H-\overset{|}{\underset{|}{C}}-O-H$$

The dispersion forces in molecules with large atoms are quite significant and are often actually more important than dipole–dipole forces.

For a given volume, a sphere has a smaller surface area than any other shape.

Surface tension: The resistance of a liquid to an increase in its surface area.

The composition of glass is discussed in Section 10.5.

Viscosity: A measure of a liquid's resistance to flow.

FIGURE 10.6
A molecule in the interior of a liquid is attracted by the molecules surrounding it, whereas a molecule at the surface of a liquid is attracted only by molecules below it and on each side.

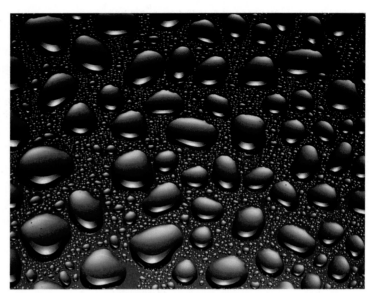

Beads of water on a waxed car finish. The nonpolar component of the wax causes the water to form approximately spherical droplets.

FIGURE 10.7
Nonpolar liquid mercury forms a convex meniscus in a glass tube, whereas polar water forms a concave meniscus.

Glycerol

has an unusually high viscosity due mainly to its high capacity to form hydrogen bonds using its O—H groups (see margin).

Molecular complexity also leads to higher viscosity because very large molecules can become entangled with each other. For example, gasoline, a nonviscous liquid, contains hydrocarbon molecules of the type CH_3—$(CH_2)_n$—CH_3, where n varies from about 3 to 8. However, grease, which is very viscous, contains much larger hydrocarbon molecules in which n varies from 20 to 25.

Structural Model for Liquids

In many respects, the development of a structural model for liquids presents greater challenges than the development of such a model for the other two states of matter. In the gaseous state the particles are so far apart and are moving so rapidly that intermolecular forces are negligible under most circumstances. This means that we can use a relatively simple model for gases. In the solid state, although the intermolecular forces are large, the molecular motions are minimal, and fairly simple models are again possible. The liquid state, however, has both strong intermolecular forces *and* significant molecular motions. Such a situation precludes the use of really simple models for liquids. Recent advances in *spectroscopy,* the study of the manner in which substances interact with electromagnetic radiation, make it possible to follow the very rapid changes that occur in liquids. As a result, our models of liquids are becoming more accurate. As a starting point, a typical liquid might best be viewed as containing a large number of regions where the arrangements of the components are similar to those found in the solid, but with more disorder, and a smaller number of regions where holes are present. The situation is highly dynamic, with rapid fluctuations occurring in both types of regions.

10.3 An Introduction to Structures and Types of Solids

There are many ways to classify solids, but the broadest categories are **crystalline solids,** those with a highly regular arrangement of their components, and **amorphous solids,** those with considerable disorder in their structures.

FIGURE 10.8
Two crystalline solids: pyrite (left), amethyst (right).

The regular arrangement of the components of a crystalline solid at the microscopic level produces the beautiful, characteristic shapes of crystals, such as those shown in Fig. 10.8. The positions of the components in a crystalline solid are usually represented by a **lattice,** a three-dimensional system of points designating the positions of the components (atoms, ions, or molecules) that make up the substance. The *smallest repeating unit* of the lattice is called the **unit cell.** Thus a particular lattice can be generated by repeating the unit cell in all three dimensions to form the extended structure. Three common unit cells and their lattices are shown in Fig. 10.9. Note from Fig. 10.9 that the extended structure in each case can be viewed as a series of repeating unit cells that share common faces in the interior of the solid.

Although we will concentrate on crystalline solids in this book, there are many important noncrystalline (amorphous) materials. An example is common glass, which is best pictured as a solution in which the components are "frozen in place" before they can achieve an ordered arrangement. Although glass is a solid (it has a rigid shape), a great deal of disorder exists in its structure.

X-Ray Analysis of Solids

The structures of crystalline solids are most commonly determined by **X-ray diffraction.** Diffraction occurs when beams of light are scattered from a regular array of points in which the spacings between the components are comparable with the wavelength of the light. Diffraction is due to constructive interference when the waves of parallel beams are in phase and to destructive interference when the waves are out of phase.

When X rays of a single wavelength are directed at a crystal, a diffraction pattern is obtained, as we saw in Fig. 7.5. The light and dark areas on the photographic plate occur because the waves scattered from various atoms may reinforce or cancel each other (see Fig. 10.10). The key to whether the waves reinforce or cancel is the difference in distance traveled by the waves after they strike the atoms. The waves are in phase before they are reflected, so if the difference in distance traveled is an *integral number of wavelengths,* the waves will still be in phase.

Since the distance traveled depends on the distance between the atoms, the diffraction pattern can be used to determine the interatomic spacings. The exact relationship can be worked out using the diagram in Fig. 10.11, which shows two in-phase waves being reflected by atoms in two different layers in a crystal. The extra distance traveled by the lower wave is the sum of the distances xy and yz, and the waves will be in phase after reflection if

$$xy + yz = n\lambda \qquad (10.1)$$

Unit cell   Lattice   Space-filling unit cell   Example

FIGURE 10.9
Three cubic unit cells and the corresponding lattices. Note that only parts of spheres on the corners and faces of the unit cells reside inside the unit cell, as shown by the "cutoff" versions.

where n is an integer and λ is the wavelength of the X rays. Using trigonometry (see Fig. 10.11), we can show that

$$xy + yz = 2d \sin \theta \qquad (10.2)$$

where d is the distance between the atoms and θ is the angle of incidence and reflection. Combining Equation (10.1) and Equation (10.2) gives

$$n\lambda = 2d \sin \theta \qquad (10.3)$$

Equation (10.3) is called the *Bragg equation* after William Henry Bragg (1862–1942) and his son William Lawrence Bragg (1890–1972), who shared the Nobel Prize in physics in 1915 for their pioneering work in X-ray crystallography.

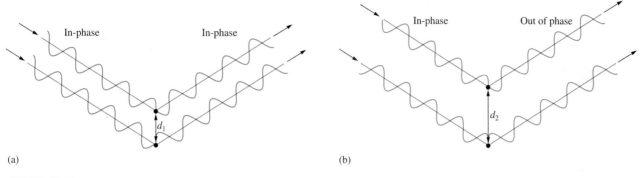

FIGURE 10.10
X rays scattered from two different atoms may reinforce (constructive interference) or cancel (destructive interference) one another. (a) Both the incident rays and the reflected rays are also in phase. In this case, d_1 is such that the difference in the distances traveled by the two rays is a whole number of wavelengths. (b) The incident rays are in phase but the reflected rays are exactly out of phase. In this case d_2 is such that the difference in distances traveled by the two rays is an odd number of half wavelengths.

A diffractometer is a computer-controlled instrument used for carrying out the X-ray analysis of crystals. It rotates the crystal with respect to the X-ray beam and collects the data produced by the scattering of the X rays from the various planes of atoms in the crystal. The results are then analyzed by computer.

The techniques for crystal structure analysis have reached a level of sophistication that allows the determination of very complex structures, such as those important in biological systems. For example, the structures of several enzymes have been determined, thus enabling biochemists to understand how they perform their functions. We will explore this topic further in Chapter 12. Using X-ray diffraction, we can gather data on bond lengths and angles and in so doing can test the predictions of our models of molecular geometry.

Sample Exercise 10.1   ## Using the Bragg Equation

X rays of wavelength 1.54 Å were used to analyze an aluminum crystal. A reflection was produced at $\theta = 19.3$ degrees. Assuming $n = 1$, calculate the distance d between the planes of atoms producing this reflection.

Solution

To determine the distance between the planes, we use Equation (10.3) with $n = 1$, $\lambda = 1.54$ Å, and $\theta = 19.3$ degrees. Since $2d \sin \theta = n\lambda$,

$$d = \frac{n\lambda}{2 \sin \theta} = \frac{(1)(1.54 \text{ Å})}{(2)(0.3305)} = 2.33 \text{ Å} = 233 \text{ pm}$$

See Exercises 10.41 through 10.44.

Graduate student Maria Zhuravlera operating an X-ray diffractometer at Michigan State University.

FIGURE 10.11
Reflection of X rays of wavelength λ from a pair of atoms in two different layers of a crystal. The lower wave travels an extra distance equal to the sum of *xy* and *yz*. If this distance is an integral number of wavelengths ($n = 1, 2, 3, \ldots$), the waves will reinforce each other when they exit the crystal.

CHEMICAL IMPACT

Smart Fluids

Matter seems to be getting smarter these days. Increasingly, we have discovered materials that can remember their initial shape after being deformed or can sense and respond to their environment. In particular, valuable new materials have been formulated whose properties can be changed instantly by applying a magnetic or electric field.

One example of such a substance is a fluid whose flow characteristics (rheology) can be changed from free flowing to almost solid in about 0.01 second by the application of an electromagnetic field. This "magnetorheological" (MR) fluid was developed by Lord Corporation. Working in collaboration with Delphi Corporation, the company is applying the fluid in suspension control of General Motors automobiles such as Cadillacs and Corvettes. The so-called Magneride system has sensors that monitor the road surface and provide information about what suspension damping is needed. In response, a message is instantly sent to an electromagnetic coil in the shock absorbers, which adjusts the viscosity of the MR fluid to provide continuously variable damping. The result: an amazingly smooth ride and unerring road-holding ability.

The MR fluid is composed of a synthetic oil in which particles of an iron-containing compound are suspended. When

Magnetic field off
Magnetic particles flow randomly

Magnetic field on
Applied field (H) creates structure that increases viscosity

the magnetic field is turned off, these particles flow freely in all directions (see the figure above). When the field is turned on, the particles aggregate into chains that line up perpendicular to the flow of the fluid, thereby increasing its viscosity in proportion to the strength of the applied field.

Many other applications of MR fluids besides auto suspensions are under development. For example, this technology is being used in a prosthesis (see below) for above-the-knee amputees, which gives them a more natural gait and improves stair climbing. One very large-scale application is in Japan's National Museum of Emerging Science and Innovation, where an MR fluid is being used in dampers to protect the building against earthquake damage. Large MR-fluid dampers are also being used for stabilizing bridges such as the Dong Ting Lake Bridge in China's Hunan province to steady it in high winds.

This High Intelligence Prosthesis for the knee uses an MR fluid damper to provide motion that closely duplicates the natural movement of the knee joint.

Types of Crystalline Solids

There are many different types of crystalline solids. For example, although both sugar and salt dissolve readily in water, the properties of the resulting solutions are quite different. The salt solution readily conducts an electric current, whereas the sugar solution does not. This behavior arises from the nature of the components in these two solids. Common salt (NaCl) is an ionic solid; it contains Na^+ and Cl^- ions. When solid sodium chloride dissolves in the polar water, sodium and chloride ions are distributed throughout the resulting solution and are free to conduct electric current. Table sugar (sucrose), on the other hand, is composed of neutral molecules that are dispersed throughout the water when the solid dissolves. No ions are present, and the resulting solution does not conduct electricity. These examples illustrate two important types of solids: **ionic solids,** represented by sodium chloride, and **molecular solids,** represented by sucrose. Ionic solids have ions at the points of the lattice that describes the structure of the solid. A molecular solid, on the other hand, has discrete covalently bonded molecules at each of its lattice points. Ice is a molecular solid that has an H_2O molecule at each point (see Fig. 10.12).

Buckminsterfullerene, C_{60}, is a particular member of the fullerene family.

A third type of solid is represented by elements such as carbon (which exists in the forms graphite, diamond, and the fullerenes), boron, silicon, and all metals. These substances all have atoms at the lattice points that describe the structure of the solid. Therefore, we call solids of this type **atomic solids.** Examples of these three types of solids are shown in Fig. 10.12.

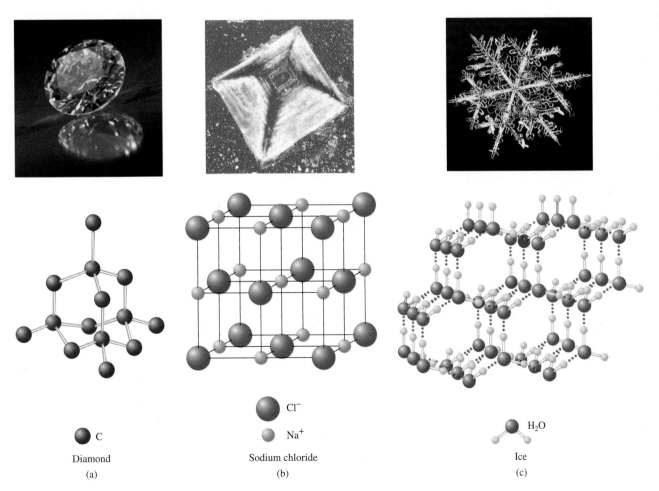

Cl$^-$

Na$^+$

H$_2$O

C

Diamond

Sodium chloride

Ice

(a)

(b)

(c)

FIGURE 10.12

Examples of three types of crystalline solids. Only part of the structure is shown in each case. (a) An atomic solid. (b) An ionic solid. (c) A molecular solid. The dotted lines show the hydrogen bonding interactions among the polar water molecules.

TABLE 10.3   Classification of Solids

| | Atomic Solids | | | | |
	Metallic	*Network*	*Group 8A*	*Molecular Solids*	*Ionic Solids*
Components That Occupy the Lattice Points:	Metal atoms	Nonmetal atoms	Group 8A atoms	Discrete molecules	Ions
Bonding:	Delocalized covalent	Directional covalent (leading to giant molecules)	London dispersion forces	Dipole–dipole and/or London dispersion forces	Ionic

To summarize, we find it convenient to classify solids according to what type of component occupies the lattice points. This leads to the classifications *atomic solids* (atoms at the lattice points), *molecular solids* (discrete, relatively small molecules at the lattice points), and *ionic solids* (ions at the lattice points). In addition, atomic solids are placed into the following subgroups based on the bonding that exists among the atoms in the solid: *metallic solids, network solids,* and *Group 8A solids.* In metallic solids, a special type of delocalized nondirectional covalent bonding occurs. In network solids, the atoms bond to each other with strong directional covalent bonds that lead to giant molecules, or networks, of atoms. In the Group 8A solids, the noble gas elements are attracted to each other with London dispersion forces. The classification of solids is summarized in Table 10.3.

The internal forces in a solid determine the properties of the solid.

The markedly different bonding present in the various atomic solids leads to dramatically different properties for the resulting solids. For example, although argon, copper, and diamond all are atomic solids, they have strikingly different properties. Argon (a Group 8A solid) has a very low melting point ($-189°C$), whereas diamond (a network solid) and copper (a metallic solid) melt at high temperatures (about 3500 and 1083°C, respectively). Copper is an excellent conductor of electricity, whereas argon and diamond are both insulators. Copper can be easily changed in shape; it is both malleable (can be formed into thin sheets) and ductile (can be pulled into a wire). Diamond, on the other hand, is the hardest natural substance known. We will explore the structure and bonding of atomic solids in the next two sections.

10.4 Structure and Bonding in Metals

Metals are characterized by high thermal and electrical conductivity, malleability, and ductility. As we will see, these properties can be traced to the nondirectional covalent bonding found in metallic crystals.

The closest packing model for metallic crystals assumes that metal atoms are uniform, hard spheres.

A metallic crystal can be pictured as containing spherical atoms packed together and bonded to each other equally in all directions. We can model such a structure by packing uniform, hard spheres in a manner that most efficiently uses the available space. Such an arrangement is called **closest packing.** The spheres are packed in layers, as shown in Fig. 10.13, in which each sphere is surrounded by six others. In the second layer the spheres do not lie directly over those in the first layer. Instead, each one occupies an indentation (or dimple) formed by three spheres in the first layer. In the third layer the spheres can occupy the dimples of the second layer in two possible ways: They can occupy positions so that each sphere in the third layer lies directly over a sphere in the first layer (the *aba* arrangement; Fig. 10.13a), or they can occupy positions so that no sphere in the third layer lies over one in the first layer (the *abc* arrangement; Fig. 10.13b).

Visualization: Electron Sea Model

The *aba* arrangement has the *hexagonal* unit cell shown in Fig. 10.14, and the resulting structure is called the **hexagonal closest packed (hcp) structure.** The *abc* arrangement has a *face-centered cubic* unit cell, as shown in Fig. 10.15, and the resulting structure is

(a) *abab* — Closest packing

Top view   Top view   Side view

FIGURE 10.13
The closest packing arrangement of uniform spheres. In each layer a given sphere is surrounded by six others, creating six dimples, only three of which can be occupied in the next layer. (a) *aba* packing: The second layer is like the first, but it is displaced so that each sphere in the second layer occupies a dimple in the first layer. The spheres in the third layer occupy dimples in the second layer so that the spheres in the third layer lie directly over those in the first layer (*aba*). (b) *abc* packing: The spheres in the third layer occupy dimples in the second layer so that no spheres in the third layer lie above any in the first layer (*abc*). The fourth layer is like the first.

(b) *abca* — Closest packing

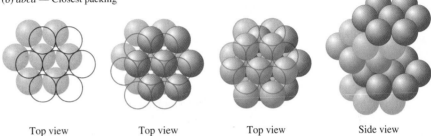

Top view   Top view   Top view   Side view

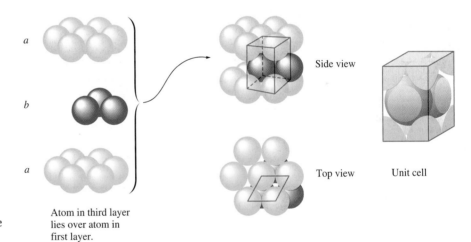

Side view

Top view

Unit cell

FIGURE 10.14
When spheres are closest packed so that the spheres in the third layer are directly over those in the first layer *(aba)*, the unit cell is the hexagonal prism illustrated here in red.

a

b

a

Atom in third layer lies over atom in first layer.

a

c

b

a

An atom in every fourth layer lies over an atom in the first layer.

Unit cell

FIGURE 10.15
When spheres are packed in the *abc* arrangement, the unit cell is face-centered cubic. To make the cubic arrangement easier to see, the vertical axis has been tilted as shown.

CHEMICAL IMPACT

Seething Surfaces

When we picture a solid, we think of the particles as being packed closely together with relatively little motion. The particles are thought to vibrate randomly about their positions but stay in nearly the same place. Recent research, however, indicates surface particles are a great deal more mobile than was previously thought. Independent teams of scientists from the University of Leiden in the Netherlands and Sandia National Laboratory in New Mexico have found a surprising amount of atom-swapping occurring on the surface of a copper crystal.

The Dutch scientist Raoul van Gastel and his colleagues used a scanning tunneling microscope (STM) to study the surface of a copper crystal containing indium atom impurities. They noted that a given patch of surface would stay the same for several scans and then, suddenly, the indium atoms would appear at different places. Surprisingly, the indium atoms seemed to make "long jumps," moving as many as five atom positions between scans. The most likely explanation for these movements is a "hole" created by a copper atom escaping the surface. This hole moves around as other atoms shift to fill it in succession (see accompanying figure). The best analogy to the movement of the hole is the toy slide puzzle with 15 numbered pieces and one missing

piece in a 4 × 4 array. The object of the game is to slide a piece into the hole and then repeat the process until the numbers appear in order.

The hole on the copper surface moves very fast—up to 100 million times per second—shuffling copper atoms and allowing the indium atoms to change positions. Van Gastel believes that all of the observed motion results from just a few fast-moving holes. In fact, he suggests that just one in 6 billion copper atoms is missing at a given time, analogous to one person in the entire earth's population. Its absence causes a given atom on the surface to move every 30 or 40 seconds. Brian Swartzentruber of Sandia National Laboratories came to similar conclusions using an STM to track the movement of palladium atoms on a copper surface.

These results have important implications. For example, metal surfaces are often used to speed up particular reactions. The motions on the metal surface could significantly influence the way that reactants interact with the surface. Also, a lot of effort is now being expended to construct tiny "machines" (called nanoscale devices) by assembling individual atoms on a solid surface. These devices could be literally torn apart by excess surface motions.

A section of a surface containing copper atoms (red) and an indium atom (yellow). A hole due to a missing copper atom is shown on the left. The blue line on the right shows the movement of this hole. As an atom moves to fill the hole, the hole moves as well. In the process, the indium atom jumps to a new position.

A toy slide puzzle.

Reprinted with permission from *Physical Review Letters,* Feb. 19, 2001, Volume 86, Issue 5, "Nothing Moves A Surface: Vacancy Mediated Surface Diffusion" by Dr. Raoul van Gastel et al, pp. 1562–1565. Copyright © 2001 by the American Physical Society.

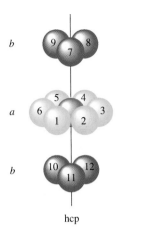

FIGURE 10.16
The indicated sphere has 12 nearest neighbors.

called the **cubic closest packed (ccp) structure.** Note that in the hcp structure the spheres in every other layer occupy the same vertical position (*ababab* · · ·), whereas in the ccp structure the spheres in every fourth layer occupy the same vertical position (*abcabca* · · ·). A characteristic of both structures is that each sphere has 12 equivalent nearest neighbors: 6 in the same layer, 3 in the layer above, and 3 in the layer below (that form the dimples). This is illustrated for the hcp structure in Fig. 10.16.

Knowing the *net* number of spheres (atoms) in a particular unit cell is important for many applications involving solids. To illustrate how to find the net number of spheres in a unit cell, we will consider a face-centered cubic unit cell (Fig. 10.17). Note that this unit cell is defined by the *centers* of the spheres on the cube's corners. Thus 8 cubes share a given sphere, so $\frac{1}{8}$ of this sphere lies inside each unit cell. Since a cube has 8 corners, there are $8 \times \frac{1}{8}$ pieces, or enough to put together 1 whole sphere. The spheres at the center of each face are shared by 2 unit cells, so $\frac{1}{2}$ of each lies inside a particular unit cell. Since the cube has 6 faces, we have $6 \times \frac{1}{2}$ pieces, or enough to construct 3 whole spheres. Thus the net number of spheres in a face-centered cubic unit cell is

$$\left(8 \times \frac{1}{8}\right) + \left(6 \times \frac{1}{2}\right) = 4$$

Sample Exercise 10.2   ## Calculating the Density of a Closest Packed Solid

Silver crystallizes in a cubic closest packed structure. The radius of a silver atom is 144 pm. Calculate the density of solid silver.

Solution

Density is mass per unit volume. Thus we need to know how many silver atoms occupy a given volume in the crystal. The structure is cubic closest packed, which means the unit cell is face-centered cubic, as shown in the accompanying figure.

We must find the volume of this unit cell for silver and the net number of atoms it contains. Note that in this structure the atoms touch along the diagonals for each

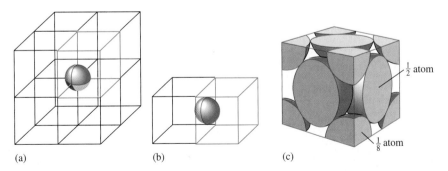

(a)   (b)   (c)

FIGURE 10.17
The net number of spheres in a face-centered cubic unit cell. (a) Note that the sphere on a corner of the colored cell is shared with 7 other unit cells (a total of 8). Thus $\frac{1}{8}$ of such a sphere lies within a given unit cell. Since there are 8 corners in a cube, there are 8 of these $\frac{1}{8}$ pieces, or 1 net sphere. (b) The sphere on the center of each face is shared by 2 unit cells, and thus each unit cell has $\frac{1}{2}$ of each of these types of spheres. There are 6 of these $\frac{1}{2}$ spheres to give 3 net spheres. (c) Thus the face-centered cubic unit cell contains 4 net spheres (all of the pieces can be assembled to give 4 spheres).

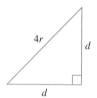

face and not along the edges of the cube. Thus the length of the diagonal is $r + 2r + r$, or $4r$. We use this fact to find the length of the edge of the cube by the Pythagorean theorem:

$$d^2 + d^2 = (4r)^2$$
$$2d^2 = 16r^2$$
$$d^2 = 8r^2$$
$$d = \sqrt{8r^2} = r\sqrt{8}$$

Since $r = 144$ pm for a silver atom,

$$d = (144 \text{ pm})(\sqrt{8}) = 407 \text{ pm}$$

The volume of the unit cell is d^3, which is $(407 \text{ pm})^3$, or $6.74 \times 10^7 \text{ pm}^3$. We convert this to cubic centimeters as follows:

$$6.74 \times 10^7 \text{ pm}^3 \times \left(\frac{1.00 \times 10^{-10} \text{ cm}}{\text{pm}}\right)^3 = 6.74 \times 10^{-23} \text{ cm}^3$$

Since we know that the net number of atoms in the face-centered cubic unit cell is 4, we have 4 silver atoms contained in a volume of $6.74 \times 10^{-23} \text{ cm}^3$. The density is therefore

$$\text{Density} = \frac{\text{mass}}{\text{volume}} = \frac{(4 \text{ atoms})(107.9 \text{ g/mol})(1 \text{ mol}/6.022 \times 10^{23} \text{ atoms})}{6.74 \times 10^{-23} \text{ cm}^3}$$
$$= 10.6 \text{ g/cm}^3$$

See Exercises 10.45 through 10.48.

Crystalline silver contains cubic closest packed silver atoms.

Examples of metals that form cubic closest packed solids are aluminum, iron, copper, cobalt, and nickel. Magnesium and zinc are hexagonal closest packed. Calcium and certain other metals can crystallize in either of these structures. Some metals, however, assume structures that are not closest packed. For example, the alkali metals have structures characterized by a *body-centered cubic (bcc) unit cell* (see Fig. 10.9), where the spheres touch along the body diagonal of the cube. In this structure, each sphere has 8 nearest neighbors (count the number of atoms around the atom at the center of the unit cell), as compared with 12 in the closest packed structures. Why a particular metal adopts the structure it does is not well understood.

Bonding Models for Metals

Malleable: Can be pounded into thin sheets.

Ductile: Can be drawn to form a wire.

Any successful bonding model for metals must account for the typical physical properties of metals: malleability, ductility, and the efficient and uniform conduction of heat and electricity in all directions. Although the shapes of most pure metals can be changed relatively easily, most metals are durable and have high melting points. These facts indicate that the bonding in most metals is both *strong* and *nondirectional*. That is, although it is difficult to separate metal atoms, it is relatively easy to move them, provided the atoms stay in contact with each other.

The simplest picture that explains these observations is the *electron sea model*, which envisions a regular array of metal cations in a "sea" of valence electrons (see Fig. 10.18). The mobile electrons can conduct heat and electricity, and the metal ions can be easily moved around as the metal is hammered into a sheet or pulled into a wire.

CHEMICAL IMPACT

Closest Packing of M & Ms

Although we usually think of scientists as dealing with esoteric and often toxic materials, sometimes they surprise us. For example, scientists at several prestigious universities have lately shown a lot of interest in M & M candies.

To appreciate the scientists' interest in M & Ms, we must consider the importance of packing atoms, molecules, or microcrystals in understanding the structures of solids. The most efficient use of space is the closest packing of uniform spheres, where 74% of the space is occupied by the spheres and 26% of space is left unoccupied. Although the structures of most pure metals can be explained in terms of closest packing, most other substances—such as many alloys and ceramics—consist of random arrays of microscopic particles. For this reason, it is of interest to study how such objects pack in a random way.

When uniform spheres, such as marbles, are poured into a large container, the resulting random packing of the spheres results in only 64% of the space being occupied by the spheres. Thus it was very surprising when Princeton University chemist Salvatore Torquato and his colleagues at Cornell and North Carolina Central Universities discovered that, when the ellipsoidal-shaped M & Ms are poured into a large container, the candies occupy 73.5% of the available space. In other words, the randomly packed M & Ms occupy space with almost the same efficiency as closest packed spheres do.

Why do randomly packed ellipsoids occupy space so much more efficiently than randomly packed spheres? The

scientists speculate that because the ellipsoids can tip and rotate in ways that spheres cannot, they can pack more closely to their neighbors.

According to Torquato, these results are important because they will help us better understand the properties of disordered materials ranging from powders to glassy solids. He also says that M & Ms make ideal test objects because they are inexpensive and uniform and "you can eat the experiment afterward."

A related model that gives a more detailed view of the electron energies and motions is the **band model,** or **molecular orbital (MO) model,** for metals. In this model, the electrons are assumed to travel around the metal crystal in molecular orbitals formed from the valence atomic orbitals of the metal atoms (Fig. 10.19).

Recall that in the MO model for the gaseous Li_2 molecule (Section 9.3), two widely spaced molecular orbital energy levels (bonding and antibonding) result when two identical atomic orbitals interact. However, when many metal atoms interact,

FIGURE 10.18
The electron sea model for metals postulates a regular array of cations in a "sea" of valence electrons. (a) Representation of an alkali metal (Group 1A) with one valence electron. (b) Representation of an alkaline earth metal (Group 2A) with two valence electrons.

(a)

(b)

Number of interacting atomic orbitals

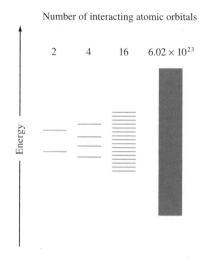

FIGURE 10.19
The molecular orbital energy levels produced when various numbers of atomic orbitals interact. Note that for two atomic orbitals two rather widely spaced energy levels result. (Recall the description of H_2 in Section 9.2.) As more atomic orbitals are available to form molecular orbitals, the resulting energy levels are more closely spaced, finally producing a band of very closely spaced orbitals.

as in a metal crystal, the large number of resulting molecular orbitals become more closely spaced and finally form a virtual continuum of levels, called *bands,* as shown in Fig. 10.19.

As an illustration, picture a magnesium metal crystal, which has an hcp structure. Since each magnesium atom has one $3s$ and three $3p$ valence atomic orbitals, a crystal with n magnesium atoms has available $n(3s)$ and $3n(3p)$ orbitals to form the molecular orbitals, as illustrated in Fig. 10.20. Note that the core electrons are localized, as shown by their presence in the energy "well" around each magnesium atom. However, the valence electrons occupy closely spaced molecular orbitals, which are only partially filled.

The existence of empty molecular orbitals close in energy to filled molecular orbitals explains the thermal and electrical conductivity of metal crystals. Metals conduct electricity and heat very efficiently because of the availability of highly mobile electrons. For example, when an electric potential is placed across a strip of metal, for current to flow, electrons must be free to move. In the band model for metals, the electrons in partially filled bonds are mobile. These conduction electrons are free to travel throughout the metal crystal as dictated by the potential imposed on the metal. The molecular orbitals occupied by these conducting electrons are called *conduction bands.* These mobile electrons also account for the efficiency of the conduction of heat through metals. When one end of a metal rod is heated, the mobile electrons can rapidly transmit the thermal energy to the other end.

Metal Alloys

Because of the nature of the structure and bonding of metals, other elements can be introduced into a metallic crystal relatively easily to produce substances called alloys. An **alloy** is best defined as *a substance that contains a mixture of elements and has metallic properties.* Alloys can be conveniently classified into two types.

FIGURE 10.20
(left) A representation of the energy levels (bands) in a magnesium crystal. The electrons in the $1s$, $2s$, and $2p$ orbitals are close to the nuclei and thus are localized on each magnesium atom as shown. However, the $3s$ and $3p$ valence orbitals overlap and mix to form molecular orbitals. Electrons in these energy levels can travel throughout the crystal. (right) Crystals of magnesium grown from a vapor.

CHEMICAL IMPACT

What Sank the Titanic?

On April 12, 1912, the steamship *Titanic* struck an iceberg in the North Atlantic approximately 100 miles south of the Grand Banks of Newfoundland and within 3 hours was resting on the bottom of the ocean. Of her more than 2300 passengers and crew, over 1500 lost their lives. While the tragic story of the *Titanic* has never faded from the minds and imaginations of the generations that followed, the 1985 discovery of the wreck by a joint Franco-American expedition at a depth of 12,612 feet rekindled the world's interest in the "greatest oceangoing vessel" ever built. The discovery also would reveal important scientific clues as to why and how the *Titanic* sank so quickly in the frigid waters of the North Atlantic.

The *Titanic* was designed to be virtually "unsinkable," and even in the worst-case scenario, a head-on collision with another ocean liner, the ship was engineered to take from one to three days to sink. Thus its quick trip to the bottom has puzzled scientists for years. In 1991, Steve Blasco, an ocean-floor geologist for the Canadian Department of Natural Resources, led a scientific expedition to the wreck. On one of 17 dives to the site, Blasco's team recovered a piece of steel that appeared to be a part of the *Titanic*'s hull. Unlike modern steel, which would have shown evidence of bending in a collision, the steel recovered from the *Titanic* appeared to have shattered on impact with the iceberg. This suggested that the metal might not have been as ductile (*ductility* is the ability to stretch without breaking) as it should have been. In 1994, tests were conducted on small pieces of metal, called *coupons*, cut from the recovered piece of hull. These samples shattered without bending. Further analysis showed that the steel used to construct the hull of the *Titanic* was high in sulfur content, and it is known that sulfur occlusions tend to make steel more brittle. This evidence suggests that the quality of the steel used to make the hull of the *Titanic* may very well have been an important factor that led to the rapid sinking of the ship.

But—not so fast. The *Titanic* continues to provoke controversy. A team of naval engineers and scientists recently have concluded that it was not brittle steel but faulty rivets that doomed the *Titanic*. During expeditions in 1996 and 1998 conducted by RMS Titanic, Inc., more samples of *Titanic*'s steel and rivets were obtained for further study. Analysis of these samples by a team headed by Tim Foecke of the National Institute of Standards and Technology (NIST) shows that the rivets contain three times the expected amount of silicate slag. Foecke and his colleagues argue that the high slag content resulted in weak rivets that snapped in large numbers when the collision occurred, mortally wounding the ship.

What sank the *Titanic?* It hit an iceberg. The details remain to be figured out.

Bow of the Titanic under $2\frac{1}{2}$ miles of water.

Brass

(a)

copper

zinc

Steel

(b)

iron

• carbon

FIGURE 10.21
Two types of alloys.

Visualization: Homogeneous
Mixtures: Air and Brass

(a)   Diamond

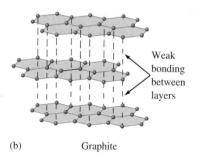

Weak
bonding
between
layers

(b)   Graphite

FIGURE 10.22
The structures of diamond and graphite. In
each case only a small part of the entire
structure is shown.

TABLE 10.4   The Composition of the Two Brands of Steel Tubing Commonly Used to Make Lightweight Racing Bicycles

Brand of Tubing	% C	% Si	% Mn	% Mo	% Cr
Reynolds	0.25	0.25	1.3	0.20	—
Columbus	0.25	0.30	0.65	0.20	1.0

In a **substitutional alloy** some of the host metal atoms are *replaced* by other metal atoms of similar size. For example, in brass, approximately one-third of the atoms in the host copper metal have been replaced by zinc atoms, as shown in Fig. 10.21(a). Sterling silver (93% silver and 7% copper), pewter (85% tin, 7% copper, 6% bismuth, and 2% antimony), and plumber's solder (95% tin and 5% antimony) are other examples of substitutional alloys.

An **interstitial alloy** is formed when some of the interstices (holes) in the closest packed metal structure are occupied by small atoms, as shown in Fig. 10.21(b). Steel, the best-known interstitial alloy, contains carbon atoms in the holes of an iron crystal. The presence of the interstitial atoms changes the properties of the host metal. Pure iron is relatively soft, ductile, and malleable due to the absence of directional bonding. The spherical metal atoms can be rather easily moved with respect to each other. However, when carbon, which forms strong directional bonds, is introduced into an iron crystal, the presence of the directional carbon–iron bonds makes the resulting alloy harder, stronger, and less ductile than pure iron. The amount of carbon directly affects the properties of steel. *Mild steels,* containing less than 0.2% carbon, are ductile and malleable and are used for nails, cables, and chains. *Medium steels,* containing 0.2 to 0.6% carbon, are harder than mild steels and are used in rails and structural steel beams. *High-carbon steels,* containing 0.6 to 1.5% carbon, are tough and hard and are used for springs, tools, and cutlery.

Many types of steel also contain elements in addition to iron and carbon. Such steels are often called *alloy steels,* and they can be viewed as being mixed interstitial (carbon) and substitutional (other metals) alloys. Bicycle frames, for example, are constructed from a wide variety of alloy steels. The compositions of the two brands of steel tubing most commonly used in expensive racing bicycles are given in Table 10.4.

10.5 Carbon and Silicon: Network Atomic Solids

Many atomic solids contain strong directional covalent bonds to form a solid that might best be viewed as a "giant molecule." We call these substances **network solids.** In contrast to metals, these materials are typically brittle and do not efficiently conduct heat or electricity. To illustrate network solids, in this section we will discuss two very important elements, carbon and silicon, and some of their compounds.

The two most common forms of carbon, diamond and graphite, are typical network solids. In diamond, the hardest naturally occurring substance, each carbon atom is surrounded by a tetrahedral arrangement of other carbon atoms to form a huge molecule [see Fig. 10.22(a)]. This structure is stabilized by covalent bonds, which, in terms of the localized electron model, are formed by the overlap of sp^3 hybridized carbon atomic orbitals.

It is also useful to consider the bonding among the carbon atoms in diamond in terms of the molecular orbital model. Energy-level diagrams for diamond and a typical metal are given in Fig. 10.23. Recall that the conductivity of metals can be explained by

FIGURE 10.23
Partial representation of the molecular orbital energies in (a) diamond and (b) a typical metal.

Graphite and diamond, two forms of carbon.

postulating that electrons are excited from filled levels into the very near empty levels, or conduction bands. However, note that in the energy-level diagram for diamond there is *a large gap between the filled and the empty levels.* This means that electrons cannot be transferred easily to the empty conduction bands. As a result, diamond is not expected to be a good electrical conductor. In fact, this prediction of the model agrees exactly with the observed behavior of diamond, which is known to be an electrical insulator—it does not conduct an electric current.

Graphite is very different from diamond. While diamond is hard, basically colorless, and an insulator, graphite is slippery, black, and a conductor. These differences, of course, arise from the differences in bonding in the two types of solids. In contrast to the tetrahedral arrangement of carbon atoms in diamond, the structure of graphite is based on layers of carbon atoms arranged in fused six-membered rings, as shown in Fig. 10.22(b). Each carbon atom in a particular layer of graphite is surrounded by the three other carbon atoms in a trigonal planar arrangement with 120-degree bond angles. The localized electron model predicts sp^2 hybridization in this case. The three sp^2 orbitals on each carbon are used to form σ bonds with three other carbon atoms. One $2p$ orbital remains unhybridized on each carbon and is perpendicular to the plane of carbon atoms, as shown in Fig. 10.24.

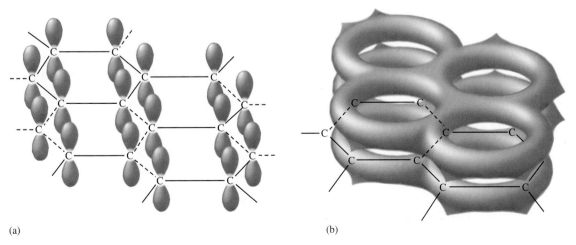

(a)

(b)

FIGURE 10.24
The *p* orbitals (a) perpendicular to the plane of the carbon ring system in graphite can combine to form (b) an extensive π-bonding network.

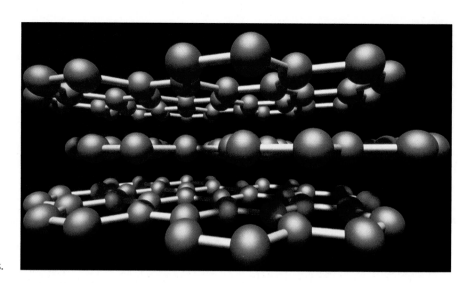

FIGURE 10.25
Graphite consists of layers of carbon atoms.

Computer-generated model of silica.

These orbitals combine to form a group of closely spaced π molecular orbitals that are important in two ways. First, they contribute significantly to the stability of the graphite layers because of the π bond formation. Second, the π molecular orbitals with their delocalized electrons account for the electrical conductivity of graphite. These closely spaced orbitals are exactly analogous to the conduction bands found in metal crystals.

Graphite is often used as a lubricant in locks (where oil is undesirable because it collects dirt). The slipperiness that is characteristic of graphite can be explained by noting that graphite has very strong bonding *within* the layers of carbon atoms but little bonding *between* the layers (the valence electrons are all used to form σ and π bonds among carbons within the layers). This arrangement allows the layers to slide past one another quite readily. Graphite's layered structure is shown in Fig. 10.25. This is in contrast to diamond, which has uniform bonding in all directions in the crystal.

Because of their extreme hardness, diamonds are used extensively in industrial cutting implements. Thus it is desirable to convert cheaper graphite to diamond. As we might expect from the higher density of diamond (3.5 g/cm^3) compared with that of graphite (2.2 g/cm^3), this transformation can be accomplished by applying very high pressures to graphite. The application of 150,000 atm of pressure at 2800°C converts graphite virtually completely to diamond. The high temperature is required to break the strong bonds in graphite so the rearrangement can occur.

Silicon is an important constituent of the compounds that make up the earth's crust. In fact, silicon is to geology as carbon is to biology. Just as carbon compounds are the basis for most biologically significant systems, silicon compounds are fundamental to most of the rocks, sands, and soils found in the earth's crust. However, although carbon and silicon are next to each other in Group 4A of the periodic table, the carbon-based compounds of biology and the silicon-based compounds of geology have markedly different structures. Carbon compounds typically contain long strings of carbon–carbon bonds, whereas the most stable silicon compounds involve chains with silicon–oxygen bonds.

The fundamental silicon–oxygen compound is **silica**, which has the empirical formula SiO_2. Knowing the properties of the similar compound carbon dioxide, one might expect silica to be a gas that contains discrete SiO_2 molecules. In fact, nothing could be further from the truth—quartz and some types of sand are typical of the materials composed of silica. What accounts for this difference? The answer lies in the bonding.

The bonding in the CO_2 molecule was described in Section 9.1.

Recall that the Lewis structure of CO_2 is

$$\ddot{O}\!=\!C\!=\!\ddot{O}$$

and that each $C\!=\!O$ bond can be viewed as a combination of a σ bond involving a carbon sp hybrid orbital and a π bond involving a carbon $2p$ orbital. On the contrary, silicon cannot use its valence $3p$ orbitals to form strong π bonds with oxygen, mainly because of the larger size of the silicon atom and its orbitals, which results in less effective overlap with the smaller oxygen orbitals. Therefore, instead of forming π bonds, the silicon atom satisfies the octet rule by forming single bonds with four oxygen atoms, as shown in the representation of the structure of quartz in Fig. 10.26. Note that each silicon atom is at the center of a tetrahedral arrangement of oxygen atoms, which are shared with other silicon atoms. Although the empirical formula for quartz is SiO_2, the structure is based on a *network* of SiO_4 tetrahedra with shared oxygen atoms rather than discrete SiO_2 molecules. It is obvious that the differing abilities of carbon and silicon to form π bonds with oxygen have profound effects on the structures and properties of CO_2 and SiO_2.

Compounds closely related to silica and found in most rocks, soils, and clays are the **silicates.** Like silica, the silicates are based on interconnected SiO_4 tetrahedra. However, in contrast to silica, where the O/Si ratio is 2:1, silicates have O/Si ratios greater than 2:1 and contain silicon–oxygen *anions*. This means that to form the neutral solid silicates, cations are needed to balance the excess negative charge. In other words, silicates are salts containing metal cations and polyatomic silicon–oxygen anions. Examples of important silicate anions are shown in Fig. 10.27.

When silica is heated above its melting point (about 1600°C) and cooled rapidly, an amorphous solid called a **glass** results (see Fig. 10.28). Note that a glass contains

FIGURE 10.26
(top) The structure of quartz (empirical formula SiO_2). Quartz contains chains of SiO_4 tetrahedra (bottom) that share oxygen atoms.

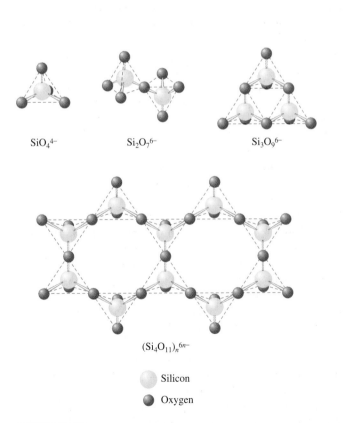

SiO_4^{4-} $Si_2O_7^{6-}$ $Si_3O_9^{6-}$

$(Si_4O_{11})_n^{6n-}$

○ Silicon
● Oxygen

FIGURE 10.27
Examples of silicate anions, all of which are based on SiO_4^{4-} tetrahedra.

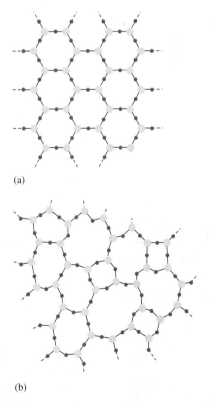

(a)

(b)

FIGURE 10.28
Two-dimensional representations of (a) a quartz crystal and (b) a quartz glass.

TABLE 10.5   Compositions of Some Common Types of Glass

Type of Glass	Percentages of Various Components						
	SiO_2	CaO	Na_2O	B_2O_3	Al_2O_3	K_2O	MgO
Window (soda-lime glass)	72	11	13	—	0.3	3.8	—
Cookware (aluminosilicate glass)	55	15	—	—	20	—	10
Heat-resistant (borosilicate glass)	76	3	5	13	2	0.5	—
Optical	69	12	6	0.3	—	12	—

A glass pitcher being manufactured.

a good deal of disorder, in contrast to the crystalline nature of quartz. Glass more closely resembles a very viscous solution than it does a crystalline solid. Common glass results when substances such as Na_2CO_3 are added to the silica melt, which is then cooled. The properties of glass can be varied greatly by varying the additives. For example, addition of B_2O_3 produces a glass (called *borosilicate glass*) that expands and contracts little under large temperature changes. Thus it is useful for labware and cooking utensils. The most common brand name for this glass is Pyrex. The addition of K_2O produces an especially hard glass that can be ground to the precise shapes needed for eyeglass and contact lenses. The compositions of several types of glass are shown in Table 10.5.

Ceramics

Ceramics are typically made from clays (which contain silicates) and hardened by firing at high temperatures. Ceramics are nonmetallic materials that are strong, brittle, and resistant to heat and attack by chemicals.

Like glass, ceramics are based on silicates, but with that the resemblance ends. Glass can be melted and remelted as often as desired, but once a ceramic has been hardened, it is resistant to extremely high temperatures. This behavior results from the very different structures of glasses and ceramics. A glass is a *homogeneous,* noncrystalline "frozen solution," and a ceramic is *heterogeneous.* A ceramic contains two phases: minute crystals of silicates that are suspended in a glassy cement.

To understand how ceramics harden, it is necessary to know something about the structure of clays. Clays are formed by the weathering action of water and carbon dioxide on the mineral feldspar, which is a mixture of silicates with empirical formulas such as $K_2O \cdot Al_2O_3 \cdot 6SiO_2$ and $Na_2O \cdot Al_2O_3 \cdot 6SiO_2$. Feldspar is really an *aluminosilicate* in which aluminum as well as silicon atoms are part of the oxygen-bridged polyanion. The weathering of feldspar produces kaolinite, consisting of tiny thin platelets with the empirical formula $Al_2Si_2O_5(OH)_4$. When dry, the platelets cling together; when water is present, they can slide over one another, giving clay its plasticity. As clay dries, the platelets begin to interlock again. When the remaining water is driven off during firing, the silicates and cations form a glass that binds the tiny crystals of kaolinite.

Ceramics have a very long history. Rocks, which are natural ceramic materials, served as the earliest tools. Later, clay vessels dried in the sun or baked in fires served as containers for food and water. These early vessels were no doubt crude and quite porous. With the discovery of glazing, which probably occurred about 3000 B.C. in Egypt, pottery became more serviceable as well as more beautiful. Prized porcelain is essentially the same material as crude earthenware, but specially selected clays and glazings are used for porcelain and the clay object is fired at a very high temperature.

An artist paints a ceramic vase before glazing.

CHEMICAL IMPACT

Golfing with Glass

You probably can guess what material traditionally was used to construct the "woods" used in golf. Modern technology has changed things. Like the bats used in college baseball, most "woods" are now made of metal. While bats are made of aluminum, golf club heads are often made of stainless steel or titanium.

Metals and their alloys usually form crystals that contain highly ordered arrangements of atoms. However, a company called Liquidmetal Golf of Laguna Niguel, California, has begun producing golf clubs containing glass—metallic glass. The company has found that when molten mixtures of titanium, zirconium, nickel, beryllium, and copper are cooled, they solidify, forming a glass. Unlike crystalline materials that contain a regular array of atoms, glasses are amorphous—the atoms are randomly scattered throughout the solid.

These golf clubs with metallic glass inserts have some unusual characteristics. Golfers who have tried the clubs say they combine hardness with a "soft feel." Studies show that the glass transfers more of the energy of the golf swing to the ball with less impact to the golfer's hands than with regular metal woods.

One of the fortunate properties of this five-component metallic glass (invented in 1992 by William L. Johnson and Atakan Peker at the California Institute of Technology) is that it can be cooled relatively slowly to form the glass. This allows manufacture of relatively large glass objects such as inserts for golf club heads. Most mixtures of metals that form glasses must be cooled very rapidly to obtain the glass, which results in tiny particles of glass leading to powders.

Golf clubs with a titanium shell and metallic glass inserts.

David S. Lee, head of manufacturing at Liquidmetal Golf, says that golf clubs were an obvious first application for this five-component glass because golfers are used to paying high prices for clubs that employ new technology. Liquidmetal Golf is now looking for other applications of this new glass. How about glass bicycle frames?

Although ceramics have been known since antiquity, they are not obsolete materials. On the contrary, ceramics constitute one of the most important classes of "high-tech" materials. Because of their stability at high temperatures and resistance to corrosion, ceramics seem an obvious choice for constructing jet and automobile engines in which the greatest fuel efficiencies are possible at very high temperatures. But ceramics are brittle—they break rather than bend—which limits their usefulness. However, more flexible ceramics can be obtained by adding small amounts of organic polymers. Taking their cue from natural "organoceramics" such as teeth and shells of sea creatures that contain small amounts of organic polymers, materials scientists have found that incorporating tiny amounts of long organic molecules into ceramics as they form produces materials that are much less subject to fracture. These materials should be useful for lighter, more durable engine parts, as well as for flexible superconducting wire and microelectronic devices. In addition, these organoceramics hold great promise for prosthetic devices such as artificial bones.

Semiconductors

n-type semiconductor

(a)

p-type semiconductor

(b)

FIGURE 10.29
(a) A silicon crystal doped with arsenic, which has one more valence electron than silicon. (b) A silicon crystal doped with boron, which has one less electron than silicon.

Electrons must be in singly occupied molecular orbitals to conduct a current.

Elemental silicon has the same structure as diamond, as might be expected from its position in the periodic table (in Group 4A directly under carbon). Recall that in diamond there is a large energy gap between the filled and empty molecular orbitals (see Fig. 10.23). This gap prevents excitation of electrons to the empty molecular orbitals (conduction bands) and makes diamond an insulator. In silicon the situation is similar, but the energy gap is smaller. A few electrons can cross the gap at 25°C, making silicon a **semiconducting element,** or **semiconductor.** In addition, at higher temperatures, where more energy is available to excite electrons into the conduction bands, the conductivity of silicon increases. This is typical behavior for a semiconducting element and is in contrast to that of metals, whose conductivity decreases with increasing temperature.

The small conductivity of silicon can be enhanced at normal temperatures if the silicon crystal is *doped* with certain other elements. For example, when a small fraction of silicon atoms is replaced by arsenic atoms, each having *one more* valence electron than silicon, extra electrons become available for conduction, as shown in Fig. 10.29(a). This produces an **n-type semiconductor,** a substance whose conductivity is increased by doping it with atoms having more valence electrons than the atoms in the host crystal. These extra electrons lie close in energy to the conduction bands and can be easily excited into these levels, where they can conduct an electric current [see Fig. 10.30(a)].

We also can enhance the conductivity of silicon by doping the crystal with an element such as boron, which has only three valence electrons, *one less* than silicon. Because boron has one less electron than is required to form the bonds with the surrounding silicon atoms, an electron vacancy, or *hole,* is created, as shown in Fig. 10.29(b). As an electron fills this hole, it leaves a new hole, and this process can be repeated. Thus the hole advances through the crystal in a direction opposite to movement of the electrons jumping to fill the hole. Another way of thinking about this phenomenon is that in pure silicon each atom has four valence electrons and the low-energy molecular orbitals are exactly filled. Replacing silicon atoms with boron atoms leaves vacancies in these molecular orbitals, as shown in Fig. 10.30(b). This means that there is only one electron in some of the molecular orbitals, and these unpaired electrons can function as conducting electrons. Thus the substance becomes a better conductor. When semiconductors are doped with atoms having fewer valence electrons than the atoms of the host crystal, they are called **p-type semiconductors,** so named because the positive holes can be viewed as the charge carriers.

Most important applications of semiconductors involve connection of a p-type and an n-type to form a **p–n junction.** Figure 10.31(a) shows a typical junction; the red dots

FIGURE 10.30
Energy-level diagrams for (a) an n-type semiconductor and (b) a p-type semiconductor.

(a)

(b)

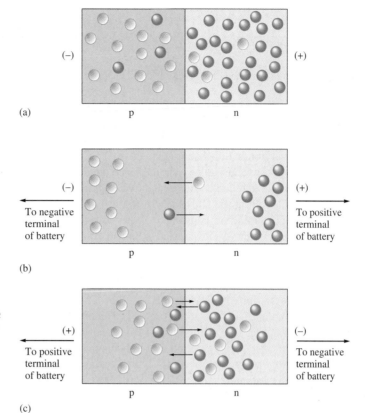

(a)

(b)

(c)

FIGURE 10.31

The p–n junction involves the contact of a p-type and an n-type semiconductor. (a) The charge carriers of the p-type region are holes (⬤). In the n-type region the charge carriers are electrons (⬤). (b) No current flows (reverse bias). (c) Current readily flows (forward bias). Note that each electron that crosses the boundary leaves a hole behind. Thus the electrons and the holes move in opposite directions.

Printed circuits are discussed in the Chemical Impact feature on page 452.

represent excess electrons in the n-type semiconductor, and the white circles represent holes (electron vacancies) in the p-type semiconductor. At the junction, a small number of electrons migrate from the n-type region into the p-type region, where there are vacancies in the low-energy molecular orbitals. The effect of these migrations is to place a negative charge on the p-type region (since it now has a surplus of electrons) and a positive charge on the n-type region (since it has lost electrons, leaving holes in its low-energy molecular orbitals). This charge buildup, called the *contact potential,* or *junction potential,* prevents further migration of electrons.

Now suppose an external electric potential is applied by connecting the negative terminal of a battery to the p-type region and the positive terminal to the n-type region. The situation represented in Fig. 10.31(b) results. Electrons are drawn toward the positive terminal, and the resulting holes move toward the negative terminal—exactly opposite to the natural flow of electrons at the p–n junction. The junction resists the imposed current flow in this direction and is said to be under *reverse bias.* No current flows through the system.

On the other hand, if the battery is connected so that the negative terminal is connected to the n-type region and the positive terminal is connected to the p-type region [Fig. 10.31(c)], the movement of electrons (and holes) is in the favored direction. The junction has low resistance, and a current flows easily. The junction is said to be under *forward bias.*

A p–n junction makes an excellent *rectifier,* a device that produces a pulsating direct current (flows in one direction) from alternating current (flows in both directions alternately). When placed in a circuit where the potential is constantly reversing, a p–n junction transmits current only under forward bias, thus converting the alternating current to direct current. Radios, computers, and other electronic devices formerly

CHEMICAL IMPACT

Transistors and Printed Circuits

Transistors have had an immense impact on the technology of electronic devices for which signal amplification is needed, such as communications equipment and computers. Before the invention of the transistor at Bell Laboratories in 1947, amplification was provided exclusively by vacuum tubes, which were both bulky and unreliable. The first electronic digital computer, ENIAC, built at the University of Pennsylvania, had 19,000 vacuum tubes and consumed 150,000 watts of electricity. Because of the discovery and development of the transistor and the printed circuit, a handheld calculator run by a small battery now has the same computing power as ENIAC.

A *junction transistor* is made by joining n-type and p-type semiconductors so as to form an n–p–n or a p–n–p junction. The former type is shown in Fig. 10.32. In this diagram the input signal (to be amplified) occurs in circuit 1, which has a small resistance and a forward-biased n–p junction (junction 1). As the voltage of the input signal to this circuit varies, the current in the circuit varies, which means there is a change in the number of electrons crossing the n–p junction. Circuit 2 has a relatively large resistance and is under reverse bias. The key to operation of the transistor is that current only flows in circuit 2 when electrons crossing junction 1 also cross junction 2 and travel to the positive terminal. Since the current in circuit 1 determines the number of electrons crossing junction 1, the number of electrons available to cross junction 2 is also directly proportional to the current in circuit 1. The current in circuit 2 therefore varies depending on the current in circuit 1.

The voltage V, current I, and resistance R in a circuit are related by the equation

$$V = IR$$

Since circuit 2 has a large resistance, a given current in circuit 2 produces a larger voltage than the same current in circuit 1, which has a small resistance. Thus a signal or variable voltage in circuit 1, such as might be produced by a human voice on a telephone, is reproduced in circuit 2, but with much greater voltage changes. That is, the input signal has been *amplified* by the junction transistor. This device, which has replaced the large vacuum tube, is a tiny component of a printed circuit on a silicon chip.

Silicon chips are really "planar" transistors constructed from thin layers of n-type and p-type regions connected by conductors. A chip less than 1 cm wide can contain hundreds of printed circuits and be used in computers, radios, and televisions.

A printed circuit has many n–p–n junction transistors. Fig. 10.33 illustrates the formation of one transistor area. The chip begins as a thin wafer of silicon that has been doped with an n-type impurity. A protective layer of silicon dioxide is then produced on the wafer by exposing it in a furnace to an oxidizing atmosphere. The next step is to produce a p-type semiconductor. To do this, the surface of the oxide is covered by a polymeric photoresist, as shown in Fig. 10.33(a). A template that only allows light to shine through in selected areas is then placed on top [Fig. 10.33(b)], and light is shown on the chip. The photoresist

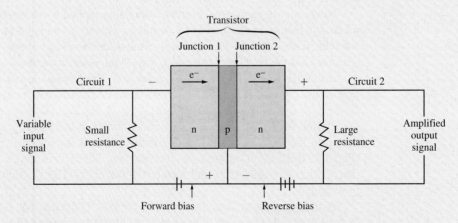

FIGURE 10.32
A schematic of two circuits connected by a transistor. The signal in circuit 1 is amplified in circuit 2.

that has been exposed to light undergoes a chemical change that causes its solubility to be different from the unexposed photoresist. The exposed photoresist is dissolved using selective solvents [Fig. 10.33(c)], and the exposed area is treated with an etching solution to dissolve the oxide coating [Fig. 10.33(d)]. When the remaining photoresist is dissolved, the silicon wafer has its oxide coating intact except at the one spot (of diameter x), as shown in Fig. 10.33(d).

Exposing the wafer to a p-type impurity such as boron at about 1000°C causes a p-type semiconductor area to be formed in the exposed spot as the boron atoms diffuse into the silicon crystal [Fig. 10.33(e)]. Next, to form a small n-type area in the center of the p-type region, the wafer is again placed in the oxidizing furnace to be recoated over its entire surface with oxide. Then a new photoresist covering is applied, which is illuminated through a template with a transparent area indicated by y [Fig. 10.33(f)]. The photoresist and oxide are then removed from the illuminated area, and the wafer is exposed to an n-type impurity to form a small n-type region as shown in Fig. 10.33(g). Next, conductors are layered onto the chip giving the finished transistor [Fig. 10.33(h)], which has two circuits connected through an n–p–n junction (see Fig. 10.32). This transistor then becomes a part of a large circuit layered onto the chip and interconnected by conductors.

The method given here for producing a printed circuit does not represent the latest technology in this field. The manufacture of printed circuits is a highly competitive business, and changes in methodology occur almost daily.

FIGURE 10.33
The steps for forming a transistor in a crystal of initially pure silicon.

used bulky, unreliable vacuum tubes as rectifiers. The p–n junction has revolutionized electronics; modern solid-state components contain p–n junctions in printed circuits.

10.6 Molecular Solids

So far we have considered solids in which atoms occupy the lattice positions. In some of these substances (network solids), the solid can be considered to be one giant molecule. In addition, there are many types of solids that contain discrete molecular units at each lattice position. A common example is ice, where the lattice positions are occupied by water molecules [see Fig. 10.12(c)]. Other examples are dry ice (solid carbon dioxide), some forms of sulfur that contain S_8 molecules [Fig. 10.34(a)], and certain forms of phosphorus that contain P_4 molecules [Fig. 10.34(b)]. These substances are characterized by strong covalent bonding *within* the molecules but relatively weak forces *between* the molecules. For example, it takes only 6 kJ of energy to melt 1 mole of solid water (ice) because only intermolecular (H_2O—H_2O) interactions must be overcome. However, 470 kJ of energy is required to break 1 mole of covalent O—H bonds. The differences between the covalent bonds within the molecules and the forces between the molecules are apparent from the comparison of the interatomic and intermolecular distances in solids shown in Table 10.6.

The forces that exist among the molecules in a molecular solid depend on the nature of the molecules. Many molecules such as CO_2, I_2, P_4, and S_8 have no dipole moment, and the intermolecular forces are London dispersion forces. Because these forces are often relatively small, we might expect all these substances to be gaseous at 25°C, as is the case for carbon dioxide. However, as the size of the molecules increases, the London forces become quite large, causing many of these substances to be solids at 25°C.

When molecules do have dipole moments, their intermolecular forces are significantly greater, especially when hydrogen bonding is possible. Water molecules are particularly well suited to interact with each other because each molecule has two polar O—H bonds and two lone pairs on the oxygen atom. This can lead to the association

Visualization: Molecular Solids

A "steaming" piece of dry ice.

FIGURE 10.34
(a) Sulfur crystals (yellow) contain S_8 molecules. (b) White phosphorus (containing P_4 molecules) is so reactive with the oxygen in air that it must be stored under water.   (a)   (b)

CHEMICAL IMPACT

Explosive Sniffer

These days security is at the top of everyone's list of important concerns, especially for those people who are responsible for the safety of our transportation systems. In particular, airports need speedy and sensitive detectors for explosives. Plastic explosives are especially tricky to detect because they do not respond to metal detectors, and they can be shaped into innocent-looking objects to avoid X-ray detection. However, a team of scientists at Oak Ridge National Laboratory led by Thomas Thundat has just published a description of an inexpensive device that is extremely sensitive to two N-containing compounds found in plastic explosives. The key part of this detection device is a tiny (180-micrometer), V-shaped cantilever made of silicon. The cantilever is shown in the accompanying photo next to a human hair for size comparison.

The upper surface of the cantilever was first coated with a layer of gold and then a one-molecule-thick layer of an acid that binds to each of the two N-containing molecules to be detected: pentaerythritol tetranitrate (PETN) and hexahydro-1,3,5-triazine (RDX). When a stream of air containing tiny amounts of PETN or RDX passes over the cantilever, these molecules bind to the cantilever, causing it to bend "like a diving board." This bending is not due to the added mass of the attached PETN and RDX. Rather, the deformation occurs because the area of the cantilever surface where binding takes place stretches relative to the unbound areas. A laser pointed at the cantilever detects the bending motion when PETN or RDX (or both) is present. The device's sensitivity is quite remarkable: 14 parts per trillion of PETN and 30 parts per trillion of RDX.

All in all, this device appears very promising for detecting plastic explosives in luggage. The cantilevers are inexpensive to construct (approximately $1), and the entire device is about the size of a shoe box. Also, the Oak Ridge team can fabricate thousands of cantilevers in one device. By putting different coatings on the cantilever arms, it should be possible to detect many other types of chemicals and possible biological agents.

This detector looks like a very promising addition to our arsenal of security devices.

When explosive compounds bind to these V-shaped cantilevers, the microscopic structures, which are about the width of a hair, bend and produce a signal.

TABLE 10.6 Comparison of Atomic Separations Within Molecules (Covalent Bonds) and Between Molecules (Intermolecular Interactions)

Solid	Distance Between Atoms in Molecule*	Closest Distance Between Molecules in the Solid
P_4	220 pm	380 pm
S_8	206 pm	370 pm
Cl_2	199 pm	360 pm

*The shorter distances within the molecules indicate stronger bonding.

of four hydrogen atoms with each oxygen: two by covalent bonds and two by dipole forces:

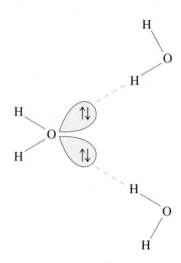

Note the two relatively short covalent oxygen–hydrogen bonds and the two longer oxygen–hydrogen dipole interactions that can be seen in the ice structure in Fig. 10.12(c).

10.7 Ionic Solids

Ionic solids are stable, high-melting substances held together by the strong electrostatic forces that exist between oppositely charged ions. The principles governing the structures of ionic solids were introduced in Section 8.5. In this section we will review and extend these principles.

The structures of most binary ionic solids, such as sodium chloride, can be explained by the closest packing of spheres. Typically, the larger ions, usually the anions, are packed in one of the closest packing arrangements (hcp or ccp), and the smaller cations fit into holes among the closest packed anions. The packing is done in a way that maximizes the electrostatic attractions among oppositely charged ions and minimizes the repulsions among ions with like charges.

There are three types of holes in closest packed structures:

1. Trigonal holes are formed by three spheres in the same layer [Fig. 10.35(a)].

2. Tetrahedral holes are formed when a sphere sits in the dimple of three spheres in an adjacent layer [Fig. 10.35(b)].

3. Octahedral holes are formed between two sets of three spheres in adjoining layers of the closest packed structures [Fig. 10.35(c)].

For spheres of a given diameter, the holes increase in size in the order

$$\text{trigonal} < \text{tetrahedral} < \text{octahedral}$$

In fact, trigonal holes are so small that they are never occupied in binary ionic compounds. Whether the tetrahedral or octahedral holes in a given binary ionic solid are occupied depends mainly on the *relative* sizes of the anion and cation. For example, in zinc sulfide the S^{2-} ions (ionic radius = 180 pm) are arranged in a cubic closest packed structure with the smaller Zn^{2+} ions (ionic radius = 70 pm) in the tetrahedral holes. The locations of the tetrahedral holes in the face-centered cubic unit cell of the ccp structure are shown in Fig. 10.36(a). Note from this figure that there are eight tetrahedral holes in the unit cell. Also recall from the discussion in Section 10.4 that there are four net spheres in the

(a)

(b)

(c)

FIGURE 10.35
The holes that exist among closest packed uniform spheres. (a) The trigonal hole formed by three spheres in a given plane. (b) The tetrahedral hole formed when a sphere occupies a dimple formed by three spheres in an adjacent layer. (c) The octahedral hole formed by six spheres in two adjacent layers.

Trigonal hole

Tetrahedral hole

Octahedral hole

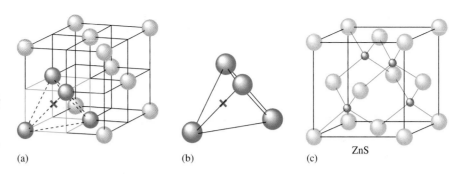

FIGURE 10.36
(a) The location (X) of a tetrahedral hole in the face-centered cubic unit cell. (b) One of the tetrahedral holes. (c) The unit cell for ZnS where the S^{2-} ions (yellow) are closest packed with the Zn^{2+} ions (red) in alternating tetrahedral holes.

(a)   (b)   (c) ZnS

face-centered cubic unit cell. Thus there are *twice as many tetrahedral holes as packed anions* in the closest packed structure. Zinc sulfide must have the same number of S^{2-} ions and Zn^{2+} ions to achieve electrical neutrality. Thus in the zinc sulfide structure only *half* the tetrahedral holes contain Zn^{2+} ions, as shown in Fig. 10.36(c).

The structure of sodium chloride can be described in terms of a cubic closest packed array of Cl^- ions with Na^+ ions in all the octahedral holes. The locations of the octahedral holes in the face-centered cubic unit cell are shown in Fig. 10.37(a). The easiest octahedral hole to find in this structure is the one at the center of the cube. Note that this hole is surrounded by six spheres, as is required to form an octahedron. The remaining octahedral holes are shared with other unit cells and are more difficult to visualize. However, it can be shown that the number of octahedral holes in the ccp structure is the *same* as the number of packed anions. Figure 10.37(b) shows the structure for sodium chloride that results from Na^+ ions filling all the octahedral holes in a ccp array of Cl^- ions.

> Closest packed structures contain twice as many tetrahedral holes as packed spheres. Closest packed structures contain the same number of octahedral holes as packed spheres.

A great variety of ionic solids exists. Our purpose in this section is not to give an exhaustive treatment of ionic solids, but to emphasize the fundamental principles governing their structures. As we have seen, the most useful model for explaining the structures of these solids regards the ions as hard spheres that are packed to maximize attractions and minimize repulsions.

| *Sample Exercise 10.3* | Determining the Number of Ions in a Unit Cell |

Determine the net number of Na^+ and Cl^- ions in the sodium chloride unit cell.

Solution

Visualization: Structure of an Ionic Solid (NaCl).

Note from Fig. 10.37(b) that the Cl^- ions are cubic closest packed and thus form a face-centered cubic unit cell. There is a Cl^- ion on each corner and one at the center of each face of the cube. Thus the net number of Cl^- ions present in a unit cell is

$$8(\tfrac{1}{8}) + 6(\tfrac{1}{2}) = 4$$

FIGURE 10.37
(a) The locations (gray X) of the octahedral holes in the face-centered cubic unit cell. (b) Representation of the unit cell for solid NaCl. The Cl^- ions (green spheres) have a ccp arrangement with Na^+ ions (gray spheres) in all the octahedral holes. Note that this representation shows the idealized closest packed structure of NaCl. In the actual structure, the Cl^- ions do not quite touch.

(a)   (b)

The Na^+ ions occupy the octahedral holes located in the center of the cube and midway along each edge. The Na^+ ion in the center of the cube is contained entirely in the unit cell, whereas those on the edges are shared by four unit cells (four cubes share a common edge). Since the number of edges in a cube is 12, the net number of Na^+ ions present is

$$1(1) + 12(\tfrac{1}{4}) = 4$$

We have shown that the net number of ions in a unit cell is 4 Na^+ ions and 4 Cl^- ions, which agrees with the 1:1 stoichiometry of sodium chloride.

See Exercises 10.61 through 10.68.

In this chapter we have considered various types of solids. Table 10.7 summarizes these types of solids and some of their properties.

TABLE 10.7   Types and Properties of Solids

Type of Solid:	Atomic			Molecular	Ionic
	Network	**Metallic**	**Group 8A**		
Structural Unit:	Atom	Atom	Atom	Molecule	Ion
Type of Bonding:	Directional covalent bonds	Nondirectional covalent bonds involving electrons that are delocalized throughout the crystal	London dispersion forces	Polar molecules: dipole–dipole interactions Nonpolar molecules: London dispersion forces	Ionic
Typical Properties:	Hard	Wide range of hardness		Soft	Hard
	High melting point	Wide range of melting points	Very low melting point	Low melting point	High melting point
	Insulator	Conductor		Insulator	Insulator
Examples:	Diamond	Silver Iron Brass	Argon(s)	Ice (solid H_2O) Dry ice (solid CO_2)	Sodium chloride Calcium fluoride

| Sample Exercise 10.4 | Types of Solids |

Using Table 10.7, classify each of the following substances according to the type of solid it forms.

a. Gold
b. Carbon dioxide
c. Lithium fluoride
d. Krypton

Solution

a. Solid gold is an atomic solid with metallic properties.
b. Solid carbon dioxide contains nonpolar carbon dioxide molecules and is a molecular solid.
c. Solid lithium fluoride contains Li^+ and F^- ions and is a binary ionic solid.
d. Solid krypton contains krypton atoms that can interact only through London dispersion forces. It is an atomic solid but has properties characteristic of a molecular solid with nonpolar molecules.

See Exercises 10.71 and 10.72.

10.8 Vapor Pressure and Changes of State

Now that we have considered the general properties of the three states of matter, we can explore the processes by which matter changes state. One very familiar example of a change in state occurs when a liquid evaporates from an open container. This is clear evidence that the molecules of a liquid can escape the liquid's surface and form a gas, a process called **vaporization,** or **evaporation.** Vaporization is endothermic because energy is required to overcome the relatively strong intermolecular forces in the liquid. The energy required to vaporize 1 mole of a liquid at a pressure of 1 atm is called the **heat of vaporization,** or the **enthalpy of vaporization,** and is usually symbolized as ΔH_{vap}.

Vapor is the usual term for the gas phase of a substance that exists as a solid or liquid at 25°C and 1 atm.

ΔH_{vap} for water at 100°C is 40.7 kJ/mol.

The endothermic nature of vaporization has great practical significance; in fact, one of the most important roles that water plays in our world is to act as a coolant. Because of the strong hydrogen bonding among its molecules in the liquid state, water has an unusually large heat of vaporization (40.7 kJ/mol). A significant portion of the sun's energy that reaches earth is spent evaporating water from the oceans, lakes, and rivers rather than warming the earth. The vaporization of water is also crucial to the body's temperature-control system through evaporation of perspiration.

Vapor Pressure

When a liquid is placed in a closed container, the amount of liquid at first decreases but eventually becomes constant. The decrease occurs because there is an initial net transfer of molecules from the liquid to the vapor phase (Fig. 10.38). This evaporation process occurs at a constant rate at a given temperature (see Fig. 10.39). However, the reverse process is different. Initially, as the number of vapor molecules increases, so does the rate of return of these molecules to the liquid. The process by which vapor molecules re-form a liquid is called **condensation.** Eventually, enough vapor molecules are present above the liquid so that the rate of condensation equals the rate of evaporation (see Fig. 10.39). *At this point no further net change occurs in the amount of liquid or vapor because the two opposite processes exactly balance each other;* the system is at **equilibrium.** Note that this system is highly *dynamic* on the molecular level—molecules are constantly escaping from and entering the liquid at a high rate. However, there is no *net* change because the two opposite processes just *balance* each other.

(a)   (b)

FIGURE 10.38
Behavior of a liquid in a closed container. (a) Initially, net evaporation occurs as molecules are transferred from the liquid to the vapor phase, so the amount of liquid decreases. (b) As the number of vapor molecules increases, the rate of return to the liquid (condensation) increases, until finally the rate of condensation equals the rate of evaporation. The system is at equilibrium, and no further changes occur in the amounts of vapor or liquid.

FIGURE 10.39
The rates of condensation and evaporation over time for a liquid sealed in a closed container. The rate of evaporation remains constant and the rate of condensation increases as the number of molecules in the vapor phase increases, until the two rates become equal. At this point, the equilibrium vapor pressure is attained.

The pressure of the vapor present at equilibrium is called the **equilibrium vapor pressure,** or more commonly, the **vapor pressure** of the liquid. A simple barometer can measure the vapor pressure of a liquid, as shown in Fig. 10.40(a). The liquid is injected at the bottom of the tube of mercury and floats to the surface because the mercury is so dense. A portion of the liquid evaporates at the top of the column, producing a vapor whose pressure pushes some mercury out of the tube. When the system reaches equilibrium, the vapor pressure can be determined from the change in the height of the mercury column since

A system at equilibrium is dynamic on the molecular level but shows no macroscopic changes.

$$P_{\text{atmosphere}} = P_{\text{vapor}} + P_{\text{Hg column}}$$

Thus
$$P_{\text{vapor}} = P_{\text{atmosphere}} - P_{\text{Hg column}}$$

The vapor pressures of liquids vary widely [see Fig. 10.40(b)]. Liquids with high vapor pressures are said to be *volatile*—they evaporate rapidly from an open dish. The vapor pressure of a liquid is principally determined by the size of the *intermolecular forces* in the liquid. Liquids in which the intermolecular forces are large have relatively low vapor

FIGURE 10.40
(a) The vapor pressure of a liquid can be measured easily using a simple barometer of the type shown here. (b) The three liquids, water, ethanol (C_2H_5OH), and diethyl ether [$(C_2H_5)_2O$], have quite different vapor pressures. Ether is by far the most volatile of the three. Note that in each case a little liquid remains (floating on the mercury).

FIGURE 10.41
The number of molecules in a liquid with a given energy versus kinetic energy at two temperatures. Part (a) shows a lower temperature than that in part (b). Note that the proportion of molecules with enough energy to escape the liquid to the vapor phase (indicated by shaded areas) increases dramatically with temperature. This causes vapor pressure to increase markedly with temperature.

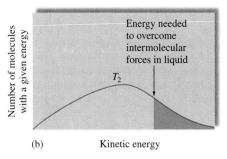

(a)   Kinetic energy   (b)   Kinetic energy

pressures because the molecules need high energies to escape to the vapor phase. For example, although water has a much lower molar mass than diethyl ether, the strong hydrogen-bonding forces that exist among water molecules in the liquid cause water's vapor pressure to be much lower than that of diethyl ether [see Fig. 10.40(b)]. In general, substances with large molar masses have relatively low vapor pressures, mainly because of the large dispersion forces. The more electrons a substance has, the more polarizable it is, and the greater the dispersion forces are.

Measurements of the vapor pressure for a given liquid at several temperatures show that *vapor pressure increases significantly with temperature.* Figure 10.41 illustrates the distribution of molecular kinetic energy present in a liquid at two different temperatures. To overcome the intermolecular forces in a liquid, a molecule must have sufficient kinetic energy. As the temperature of the liquid is increased, the fraction of molecules having the minimum energy needed to overcome these forces and escape to the vapor phase increases markedly. Thus the vapor pressure of a liquid increases dramatically with temperature. Values for water at several temperatures are given in Table 10.8.

The quantitative nature of the temperature dependence of vapor pressure can be represented graphically. Plots of vapor pressure versus temperature for water, ethanol, and diethyl ether are shown in Fig. 10.42(a). Note the nonlinear increase in vapor pressure for all the liquids as the temperature is increased. We find that a straight line can be obtained by plotting $\ln(P_{vap})$ versus $1/T$, where T is the Kelvin temperature, as shown in Fig. 10.42(b). We can represent this behavior by the equation

$$\ln(P_{vap}) = -\frac{\Delta H_{vap}}{R}\left(\frac{1}{T}\right) + C \tag{10.4}$$

where ΔH_{vap} is the enthalpy of vaporization, R is the universal gas constant, and C is a constant characteristic of a given liquid. The symbol *ln* means that the natural logarithm of the vapor pressure is taken.

Equation (10.4) is the equation for a straight line of the form $y = mx + b$, where

$$y = \ln(P_{vap})$$

$$x = \frac{1}{T}$$

$$m = \text{slope} = -\frac{\Delta H_{vap}}{R}$$

$$b = \text{intercept} = C$$

TABLE 10.8   The Vapor Pressure of Water as a Function of Temperature

T (°C)	P (torr)
0.0	4.579
10.0	9.209
20.0	17.535
25.0	23.756
30.0	31.824
40.0	55.324
60.0	149.4
70.0	233.7
90.0	525.8

Natural logarithms are reviewed in Appendix 1.2.

Sample Exercise 10.5   **Determining Enthalpies of Vaporization**

Using the plots in Fig. 10.42(b), determine whether water or diethyl ether has the larger enthalpy of vaporization.

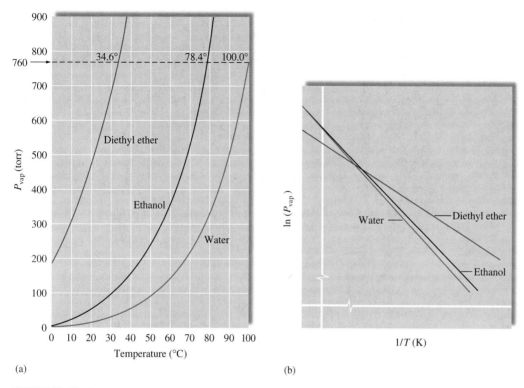

FIGURE 10.42
(a) The vapor pressure of water, ethanol, and diethyl ether as a function of temperature. (b) Plots of ln(P_{vap}) versus 1/T (Kelvin temperature) for water, ethanol, and diethyl ether.

Solution

When ln(P_{vap}) is plotted versus 1/T, the slope of the resulting straight line is

$$-\frac{\Delta H_{vap}}{R}$$

Note from Fig. 10.42(b) that the slopes of the lines for water and diethyl ether are both negative, as expected, and that the line for ether has the smaller slope. Thus ether has the smaller value of ΔH_{vap}. This makes sense because the hydrogen bonding in water causes it to have a relatively large enthalpy of vaporization.

See Exercise 10.79.

Equation (10.4) is important for several reasons. For example, we can determine the heat of vaporization for a liquid by measuring P_{vap} at several temperatures and then evaluating the slope of a plot of ln(P_{vap}) versus 1/T. On the other hand, if we know the values of ΔH_{vap} and P_{vap} at one temperature, we can use Equation (10.4) to calculate P_{vap} at another temperature. This can be done by recognizing that the constant C does not depend on temperature. Thus at two temperatures T_1 and T_2 we can solve Equation (10.4) for C and then write the equality

$$\ln(P_{vap,T_1}) + \frac{\Delta H_{vap}}{RT_1} = C = \ln(P_{vap,T_2}) + \frac{\Delta H_{vap}}{RT_2}$$

This can be rearranged to

$$\ln(P_{vap,T_1}) - \ln(P_{vap,T_2}) = \frac{\Delta H_{vap}}{R}\left(\frac{1}{T_2} - \frac{1}{T_1}\right)$$

Equation (10.5) is called the *Clausius–Clapeyron equation.*

or

$$\ln\left(\frac{P_{vap,T_1}}{P_{vap,T_2}}\right) = \frac{\Delta H_{vap}}{R}\left(\frac{1}{T_2} - \frac{1}{T_1}\right) \qquad (10.5)$$

| Sample Exercise 10.6 | ## Calculating Vapor Pressure |

The vapor pressure of water at 25°C is 23.8 torr, and the heat of vaporization of water at 25°C is 43.9 kJ/mol. Calculate the vapor pressure of water at 50.°C.

Solution

We will use Equation (10.5):

In solving this problem, we ignore the fact that ΔH_{vap} is slightly temperature dependent.

$$\ln\left(\frac{P_{vap,T_1}}{P_{vap,T_2}}\right) = \frac{\Delta H_{vap}}{R}\left(\frac{1}{T_2} - \frac{1}{T_1}\right)$$

For water we have

$$P_{vap,T_1} = 23.8 \text{ torr}$$
$$T_1 = 25 + 273 = 298 \text{ K}$$
$$T_2 = 50. + 273 = 323 \text{ K}$$
$$\Delta H_{vap} = 43.9 \text{ KJ/mol} = 43,900 \text{ J/mol}$$
$$R = 8.3145 \text{ J/K mol}$$

Thus

$$\ln\left(\frac{23.8 \text{ torr}}{P_{vap,T_2}\,(\text{torr})}\right) = \frac{43,900 \text{ J/mol}}{8.3145 \text{ J/K mol}}\left(\frac{1}{323 \text{ K}} - \frac{1}{298 \text{ K}}\right)$$

$$\ln\left(\frac{23.8}{P_{vap,T_2}}\right) = -1.37$$

Phase changes of carbon dioxide are discussed in Section 10.9.

Taking the antilog (see Appendix 1.2) of both sides gives

$$\frac{23.8}{P_{vap,T_2}} = 0.254$$

$$P_{vap,T_2} = 93.7 \text{ torr}$$

See Exercises 10.81 through 10.84.

Like liquids, solids have vapor pressures. Figure 10.43 shows iodine vapor in equilibrium with solid iodine in a closed flask. Under normal conditions iodine **sublimes;** that is, it goes directly from the solid to the gaseous state without passing through the liquid state. **Sublimation** also occurs with dry ice (solid carbon dioxide).

Sublimation: A process in which a substance goes directly from the solid to the gaseous state.

Changes of State

What happens when a solid is heated? Typically, it will melt to form a liquid. If the heating continues, the liquid will at some point boil and form the vapor phase. This process can be represented by a **heating curve:** a plot of temperature versus time for a process where energy is added at a constant rate.

The heating curve for water is given in Fig. 10.44. As energy flows into the ice, the random vibrations of the water molecules increase as the temperature rises. Eventually, the molecules become so energetic that they break loose from their lattice positions, and the change from solid to liquid occurs. This is indicated by a plateau at 0°C on the

Visualization: Changes of State

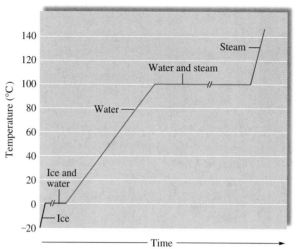

FIGURE 10.44
The heating curve (not drawn to scale) for a given quantity of water where energy is added at a constant rate. The plateau at the boiling point is longer than the plateau at the melting point because it takes almost seven times more energy (and thus seven times the heating time) to vaporize liquid water than to melt ice. The slopes of the other lines are different because the different states of water have different molar heat capacities (the energy required to raise the temperature of 1 mole of a substance by 1°C).

Ionic solids such as NaCl and NaF have very high melting points and enthalpies of fusion because of the strong ionic forces in these solids. At the other extreme is $O_2(s)$, a molecular solid containing nonpolar molecules with weak intermolecular forces. (See Table 10.9.)

The melting and boiling points will be defined more precisely later in this section.

heating curve. At this temperature, called the *melting point,* all the added energy is used to disrupt the ice structure by breaking the hydrogen bonds, thus increasing the potential energy of the water molecules. The enthalpy change that occurs at the melting point when a solid melts is called the **heat of fusion,** or more accurately, the **enthalpy of fusion,** ΔH_{fus}. The melting points and enthalpies of fusion for several representative solids are listed in Table 10.9.

The temperature remains constant until the solid has completely changed to liquid; then it begins to increase again. At 100°C the liquid water reaches its *boiling point,* and the temperature then remains constant as the added energy is used to vaporize the liquid. When the liquid is completely changed to vapor, the temperature again begins to rise. Note that changes of state are physical changes; although intermolecular forces have been overcome, no chemical bonds have been broken. If the water vapor were heated to much higher temperatures, the water molecules would break down into the individual atoms. This would

TABLE 10.9   Melting Points and Enthalpies of Fusion for Several Representative Solids

Compound	Melting Point (°C)	Enthalpy of Fusion (kJ/mol)
O_2	−218	0.45
HCl	−114	1.99
HI	−51	2.87
CCl_4	−23	2.51
$CHCl_3$	−64	9.20
H_2O	0	6.02
NaF	992	29.3
NaCl	801	30.2

FIGURE 10.45
The vapor pressures of solid and liquid water as a function of temperature. The data for liquid water below 0°C are obtained from supercooled water. The data for solid water above 0°C are estimated by extrapolation of vapor pressure from below 0°C.

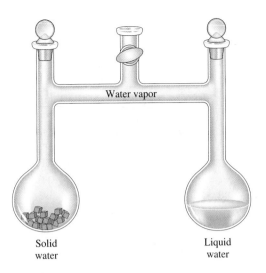

FIGURE 10.46
An apparatus that allows solid and liquid water to interact only through the vapor state.

be a chemical change, since covalent bonds are broken. We no longer have water after this occurs.

The melting and boiling points for a substance are determined by the vapor pressures of the solid and liquid states. Figure 10.45 shows the vapor pressures of solid and liquid water as functions of temperature near 0°C Note that below 0°C the vapor pressure of ice is less than the vapor pressure of liquid water. Also note that the vapor pressure of ice has a larger temperature dependence than that of the liquid. That is, the vapor pressure of ice increases more rapidly for a given rise in temperature than does the vapor pressure of water. Thus, as the temperature of the solid is increased, a point is eventually reached where the *liquid and solid have identical vapor pressures*. This is the melting point.

These concepts can be demonstrated experimentally using the apparatus illustrated in Fig. 10.46, where ice occupies one compartment and liquid water the other. Consider the following cases.

Case 1
A temperature at which the vapor pressure of the solid is greater than that of the liquid. At this temperature the solid requires a higher pressure than the liquid does to be in equilibrium with the vapor. Thus, as vapor is released from the solid to try to achieve equilibrium, the liquid will absorb vapor in an attempt to reduce the vapor pressure to its equilibrium value. The net effect is a conversion from solid to liquid through the vapor phase. In fact, no solid can exist under these conditions. The amount of solid will steadily decrease and the volume of liquid will increase. Finally, there will be only liquid in the right compartment, which will come to equilibrium with the water vapor, and no further changes will occur in the system. This temperature must be above the melting point of ice, since only the liquid state can exist.

Case 2
A temperature at which the vapor pressure of the solid is less than that of the liquid. This is the opposite of the situation in case 1. In this case, the liquid requires a higher pressure than the solid does to be in equilibrium with the vapor, so the liquid will gradually disappear, and the amount of ice will increase. Finally, only the solid will remain, which will achieve equilibrium with the vapor. This temperature must be *below the melting point* of ice, since only the solid state can exist.

Constant pressure
of 1 atmosphere

— Movable
   piston

— Liquid water

FIGURE 10.47
Water in a closed system with a pressure of 1 atm exerted on the piston. No bubbles can form within the liquid as long as the vapor pressure is less than 1 atm.

Case 3

A temperature at which the vapor pressures of the solid and liquid are identical. In this case, the solid and liquid states have the same vapor pressure, so they can coexist in the apparatus at equilibrium simultaneously with the vapor. This temperature represents the *freezing point* where both the solid and liquid states can exist.

We can now describe the melting point of a substance more precisely. The **normal melting point** is defined as *the temperature at which the solid and liquid states have the same vapor pressure under conditions where the total pressure is 1 atmosphere.*

Boiling occurs when the vapor pressure of a liquid becomes equal to the pressure of its environment. The **normal boiling point** of a liquid is *the temperature at which the vapor pressure of the liquid is exactly 1 atmosphere.* This concept is illustrated in Fig. 10.47. At temperatures where the vapor pressure of the liquid is less than 1 atmosphere, no bubbles of vapor can form because the pressure on the surface of the liquid is greater than the pressure in any spaces in the liquid where the bubbles are trying to form. Only when the liquid reaches a temperature at which the pressure of vapor in the spaces in the liquid is 1 atmosphere can bubbles form and boiling occur.

However, changes of state do not always occur exactly at the boiling point or melting point. For example, water can be readily **supercooled;** that is, it can be cooled below 0°C at 1 atm pressure and remain in the liquid state. Supercooling occurs because, as it is cooled, the water may not achieve the degree of organization necessary to form ice at 0°C, and thus it continues to exist as the liquid. At some point the correct ordering occurs and ice rapidly forms, releasing energy in the exothermic process and bringing the temperature back up to the melting point, where the remainder of the water freezes (see Fig. 10.48).

A liquid also can be **superheated,** or raised to temperatures above its boiling point, especially if it is heated rapidly. Superheating can occur because bubble formation in the interior of the liquid requires that many high-energy molecules gather in the same vicinity, and this may not happen at the boiling point, especially if the liquid is heated rapidly. If the liquid becomes superheated, the vapor pressure in the liquid is greater than the atmospheric pressure. Once a bubble does form, since its internal pressure is greater than that of the atmosphere, it can burst before rising to the surface, blowing the surrounding liquid out of the container. This is called *bumping* and has ruined many experiments. It can be avoided by adding boiling chips to the flask containing the liquid. Boiling chips are bits of porous ceramic material containing trapped air that escapes on heating, forming tiny bubbles that act as "starters" for vapor bubble formation. This allows a smooth onset of boiling as the boiling point is reached.

Boiling chip releasing air bubbles acts as a nucleating agent for the bubbles that form when water boils.

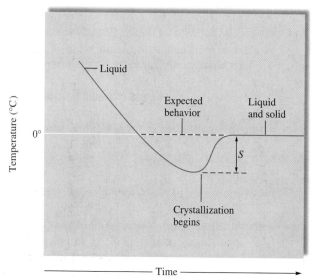

FIGURE 10.48
The supercooling of water. The extent of supercooling is given by *S*.

10.9 Phase Diagrams

A **phase diagram** is a convenient way of representing the phases of a substance as a function of temperature and pressure. For example, the phase diagram for water (Fig. 10.49) shows which state exists at a given temperature and pressure. It is important to recognize that a phase diagram describes conditions and events in a *closed* system of the type represented in Fig. 10.47, where no material can escape into the surroundings and no air is present. Notice that the diagram is not drawn to scale (neither axis is linear). This is done to emphasize certain features of the diagram that will be discussed below.

To show how to interpret the phase diagram for water, we will consider heating experiments at several pressures, shown by the dashed lines in Fig. 10.50.

Experiment 1

Pressure is 1 atm. This experiment begins with the cylinder shown in Fig. 10.47 completely filled with ice at a temperature of $-20°C$ and the piston exerting a pressure of 1 atm directly on the ice (there is no air space). Since at temperatures below $0°C$ the vapor pressure of ice is less than 1 atm—which is the constant external pressure on the piston—no vapor is present in the cylinder. As the cylinder is heated, ice is the only component until the temperature reaches $0°C$, where the ice changes to liquid water as energy is added. This is the normal melting point of water. Note that under these conditions no vapor exists in the system. The vapor pressures of the solid and liquid are equal, but this vapor pressure is less than 1 atm, so no water vapor can exist. This is true on the solid/liquid line everywhere except at the triple point (see Experiment 3 below). When the solid has completely changed to liquid, the temperature again rises. At this point, the cylinder contains only liquid water. *No vapor is present* because the vapor pressure of liquid water under these conditions is less than 1 atm, the constant external pressure on the piston. Heating continues until the temperature of the liquid water reaches $100°C$. At this point, the vapor pressure of liquid water is 1 atm, and boiling occurs, with the liquid changing to vapor. This is the normal boiling point of water. After the liquid has been completely converted to steam, the temperature again rises as the heating continues. The cylinder now contains only water vapor.

Experiment 2

Pressure is 2.0 torr. Again, we start with ice as the only component in the cylinder at $-20°C$. The pressure exerted by the piston in this case is only 2.0 torr. As heating proceeds, the temperature rises to $-10°C$, where the ice changes directly to vapor, a process known as *sublimation*. Sublimation occurs when the vapor pressure of ice is equal to the

FIGURE 10.49
The phase diagram for water. T_m represents the normal melting point; T_3 and P_3 denote the triple point; T_b represents the normal boiling point; T_c represents the critical temperature; P_c represents the critical pressure. The negative slope of the solid/liquid line reflects the fact that the density of ice is less than that of liquid water. (Note that this line extends indefinitely, as indicated by the arrow.)

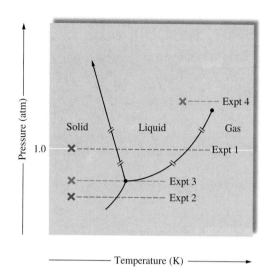

FIGURE 10.50
Diagrams of various heating experiments on samples of water in a closed system.

external pressure, which in this case is only 2.0 torr. No liquid water appears under these conditions because the vapor pressure of liquid water is always greater than 2.0 torr, and thus it cannot exist at this pressure. If liquid water were placed in a cylinder under such a low pressure, it would vaporize immediately at temperatures above −10°C or freeze at temperatures below −10°C.

Experiment 3

Pressure is 4.58 torr. Again, we start with ice as the only component in the cylinder at −20°C. In this case the pressure exerted on the ice by the piston is 4.58 torr. As the cylinder is heated, no new phase appears until the temperature reaches 0.01°C (273.16 K). At this point, called the **triple point,** solid and liquid water have identical vapor pressures of 4.58 torr. Thus *at 0.01°C (273.16 K) and 4.58 torr all three states of water are present.* In fact, *only* under these conditions can all three states of water coexist in a closed system.

Experiment 4

Pressure is 225 atm. In this experiment we start with liquid water in the cylinder at 300°C; the pressure exerted by the piston on the water is 225 atm. Liquid water can be present at this temperature because of the high external pressure. As the temperature increases, something happens that we did not see in the first three experiments: The liquid gradually changes into a vapor but goes through an intermediate "fluid" region, which is neither true liquid nor vapor. This is quite unlike the behavior at lower temperatures and pressures, say at 100°C. and 1 atm, where the temperature remains constant while a definite phase change from liquid to vapor occurs. This unusual behavior occurs because the conditions are beyond the critical point for water. The **critical temperature** can be defined as the temperature above which the vapor cannot be liquefied no matter what pressure is applied. The **critical pressure** is the pressure required to produce liquefaction *at the* critical temperature. Together, the critical temperature and the critical pressure define the **critical point.** For water the critical point is 374°C and 218 atm. Note that the liquid/vapor line on the phase diagram for water ends at the critical point. Beyond this point the transition from one state to another involves the intermediate "fluid" region just described.

Applications of the Phase Diagram for Water

There are several additional interesting features of the phase diagram for water. Note that the solid/liquid boundary line has a negative slope. This means that the melting point of ice *decreases* as the external pressure *increases*. This behavior, which is opposite to that

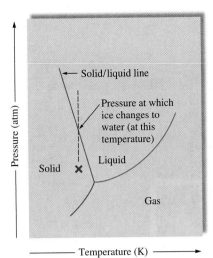

FIGURE 10.51
The phase diagram for water. At point X on the phase diagram, water is a solid. However, as the external pressure is increased while the temperature remains constant (indicated by the vertical dotted line), the solid/liquid line is crossed and the ice melts.

Visualization: Boiling Water with Ice Water

Water boils at 89°C in Leadville, Colorado.

The effect of pressure on ice allows this skater to glide smoothly.

observed for most substances, occurs because the density of ice is *less* than that of liquid water at the melting point. The maximum density of water occurs at 4°C; when liquid water freezes, its volume increases.

We can account for the effect of pressure on the melting point of water using the following reasoning. At the melting point, liquid and solid water coexist—they are in dynamic equilibrium, since the rate at which ice is melting is just balanced by the rate at which the water is freezing. What happens if we apply pressure to this system? When subjected to increased pressure, matter reduces its volume. This behavior is most dramatic for gases but also occurs for condensed states. Since a given mass of ice at 0°C has a larger volume than the same mass of liquid water, the system can reduce its volume in response to the increased pressure by changing to liquid. Thus at 0°C and an external pressure greater than 1 atm, water is liquid. In other words, the freezing point of water is less than 0°C when the pressure is greater than 1 atm.

Figure 10.51 illustrates the effect of pressure on ice. At the point X on the phase diagram, ice is subjected to increased pressure at constant temperature. Note that as the pressure is increased, the solid/liquid line is crossed, indicating that the ice melts. This phenomenon may be important in ice skating. The narrow blade of the skate exerts a large pressure, since the skater's weight is supported by the small area of the blade. Also, the frictional heating due to the moving skate contributes to the melting of the ice.* After the blade passes, the liquid refreezes as normal pressure and temperature return. Without this lubrication effect due to the thawing ice, ice skating would not be the smooth, graceful activity that many people enjoy.

Ice's lower density has other implications. When water freezes in a pipe or an engine block, it will expand and break the container. This is why water pipes are insulated in cold climates and antifreeze is used in water-cooled engines. The lower density of ice also means that ice formed on rivers and lakes will float, providing a layer of insulation that helps prevent bodies of water from freezing solid in the winter. Aquatic life can therefore continue to live through periods of freezing temperatures.

A liquid boils at the temperature where the vapor pressure of the liquid equals the external pressure. Thus the boiling point of a substance, like the melting point, depends on the external pressure. This is why water boils at different temperatures at different elevations (see Table 10.10), and any cooking carried out in boiling water will be affected by this variation. For example, it takes longer to hard-boil an egg in Leadville, Colorado (elevation: 10,150 ft), than in San Diego, California (sea level), since water boils at a lower temperature in Leadville.

As we mentioned earlier, the phase diagram for water describes a closed system. Therefore, we must be very cautious in using the phase diagram to explain the behavior of water in a natural setting, such as on the earth's surface. For example, in dry climates (low humidity), snow and ice seem to sublime—a minimum amount of slush is produced. Wet clothes put on an outside line at temperatures below 0°C freeze and then dry while frozen. However, the phase diagram (Fig. 10.47) shows that ice should *not* be able to sublime at normal atmospheric pressures. What is happening in these cases? Ice in the natural environment is not in a closed system. The pressure is provided by the atmosphere rather than by a solid piston. This means that the vapor produced over the ice can escape from the immediate region as soon as it is formed. The vapor does not come to equilibrium with the solid, and the ice slowly disappears. Sublimation, which seems forbidden by the phase diagram, does in fact occur under these conditions, although it is not the sublimation under equilibrium conditions described by the phase diagram.

---

*The physics of ice skating is quite complex, and there is disagreement about whether the pressure or the frictional heating of the ice skate is most important. See "Letter to the Editor," by R. Silberman, *J. Chem. Ed.* **65** (1988): 186.

CHEMICAL IMPACT

Making Diamonds at Low Pressures: Fooling Mother Nature

In 1955 Robert H. Wentorf, Jr., accomplished something that borders on alchemy—he turned peanut butter into diamonds. He and his coworkers at the General Electric Research and Development Center also changed roofing pitch, wood, coal, and many other carbon-containing materials into diamonds, using a process involving temperatures of $\approx 2000°C$ and pressures of $\approx 10^5$ atm. Although the first diamonds made by this process looked like black sand because of the impurities present, the process has now been developed to a point such that beautiful, clear, gem-quality diamonds can be produced. General Electric now has the capacity to produce 150 million carats (30,000 kg) of diamonds annually (virtually all of which is "diamond grit" used for industrial purposes such as abrasive coatings on cutting tools). The production of large, gem-quality diamonds by this process is still too expensive to compete with the natural sources of these stones. However, this may change as methods are developed for making diamonds at low pressures.

The high temperatures and pressures used in the GE process for making diamonds make sense if one looks at the accompanying phase diagram for carbon. Note that graphite—not diamond—is the most stable form of carbon

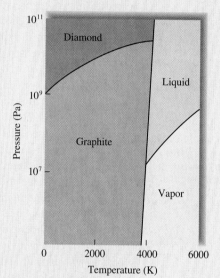

The phase diagram for carbon.

under ordinary conditions of temperature and pressure. However, diamond becomes more stable than graphite at very high pressures (as one would expect from the greater

A carbon dioxide fire extinguisher.

TABLE 10.10   Boiling Point of Water at Various Locations

Location	Feet Above Sea Level	P_{atm} (torr)	Boiling Point (°C)
Top of Mt. Everest, Tibet	29,028	240	70
Top of Mt. McKinley, Alaska	20,320	340	79
Top of Mt. Whitney, Calif.	14,494	430	85
Leadville, Colo.	10,150	510	89
Top of Mt. Washington, N.H.	6,293	590	93
Boulder, Colo.	5,430	610	94
Madison, Wis.	900	730	99
New York City, N.Y.	10	760	100
Death Valley, Calif.	−282	770	100.3

The Phase Diagram for Carbon Dioxide

The phase diagram for carbon dioxide (Fig. 10.52) differs from that for water. The solid/liquid line has a positive slope, since solid carbon dioxide is more dense than liquid carbon dioxide. The triple point for carbon dioxide occurs at 5.1 atm and −56.6°C, and the critical point occurs at 72.8 atm and 31°C. At a pressure of 1 atm, solid carbon dioxide sublimes density of diamond). The high temperature used in the GE process is necessary to disrupt the bonds in graphite so that diamond (the most stable form of carbon at the high pressures used in the process) can form. Once the diamond is produced, the elemental carbon is "trapped" in this form at normal conditions (25°C, 1 atm) because the reaction back to the graphite form is so slow. That is, even though graphite is more stable than diamond at 25°C and 1 atm, diamond can exist almost indefinitely because the conversion to graphite is a very *slow* reaction. As a result, diamonds formed at the high pressures found deep in the earth's crust can be brought to the earth's surface by natural geologic processes and continue to exist for millions of years.*

We have seen that diamond formed in the laboratory at high pressures is "trapped" in this form, but this process is very expensive. Can diamond be formed at low pressures? The phase diagram for carbon says no. However, researchers have found that under the right conditions diamonds can be

"grown" at low pressures. The process used is called *chemical vapor deposition* (*CVD*). CVD uses an energy source to release carbon atoms from a compound such as methane into a steady flow of hydrogen gas (some of which is dissociated to produce hydrogen atoms). The carbon atoms then deposit as a diamond film on a surface maintained at a temperature between 600 and 900°C. Why does diamond form on this surface rather than the favored graphite? Nobody is sure, but it has been suggested that at these relatively high temperatures the diamond structure grows faster than the graphite structure and so diamond is favored under these conditions. It also has been suggested that the hydrogen atoms present react much faster with graphite fragments than with diamond fragments, effectively removing any graphite from the growing film. Once it forms, of course, diamond is trapped. The major advantage of CVD is that there is no need for the extraordinarily high pressures used in the traditional process for synthesizing diamonds.

The first products with diamond films are already on the market. Audiophiles can buy tweeters that have diaphragms coated with a thin diamond film that limits sound distortion. Watches with diamond-coated crystals are planned, as are diamond-coated windows in infrared scanning devices used in analytical instruments and missile guidance systems. These applications represent only the beginning for diamond-coated products.

*In Morocco, a 50-km-long slab called Beni Bousera contains chunks of graphite that were probably once diamonds formed in the deposit when it was buried 150 km underground. As this slab slowly rose to the surface over millions of years, the very slow reaction changing diamond to graphite had time to occur. On the other hand, in the diamond-rich kimberlite deposits in South Africa, which rise to the surface much faster, the diamonds have not had sufficient time to revert to graphite.

at −78°C, a property that leads to its common name, *dry ice*. No liquid phase occurs under normal atmospheric conditions, making dry ice a convenient refrigerant.

Carbon dioxide is often used in fire extinguishers, where it exists as a liquid at 25°C under high pressures. Liquid carbon dioxide released from the extinguisher into the environment at 1 atm immediately changes to a vapor. Being heavier than air, this vapor smothers the fire by keeping oxygen away from the flame. The liquid/vapor transition is highly endothermic, so cooling also results, which helps to put out the fire.

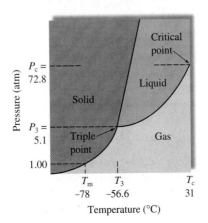

FIGURE 10.52
The phase diagram for carbon dioxide. The liquid state does not exist at a pressure of 1 atm. The solid/liquid line has a positive slope, since the density of solid carbon dioxide is greater than that of liquid carbon dioxide.

Key Terms

For Review

Condensed states of matter: liquids and solids
- Held together by forces among the component molecules, atoms, or ions
- Liquids exhibit properties such as surface tension, capillary action, and viscosity that depend on the forces among the components

Dipole–dipole forces
- Attractions among molecules with dipole moments
- Hydrogen bonding is a particularly strong form of dipole–dipole attraction
  - Occurs in molecules containing hydrogen bonded to a highly electronegative element such as nitrogen, oxygen, or fluorine
  - Produces unusually high boiling points

London dispersion forces
- Caused by instantaneous dipoles that form in atoms or nonpolar molecules

Crystalline solids
- Have a regular arrangement of components often represented as a lattice; the smallest repeating unit of the lattice is called the unit cell
- Classified by the types of components:
  - Atomic solids (atoms)
  - Ionic solids (ions)
  - Molecular solids (molecules)
- Arrangement of the components can be determined by X-ray analysis

Metals
- Structure is modeled by assuming atoms to be uniform spheres
  - Closest packing
    - Hexagonal
    - Cubic
- Metallic bonding can be described in terms of two models
  - Electron sea model: valence electrons circulate freely among the metal cations
  - Band model: electrons are assumed to occupy molecular orbitals
    - Conduction bands: closely spaced molecular orbitals with empty electron spaces
- Alloys: mixtures with metallic properties
  - Substitutional
  - Interstitial

Network solids
- Contain giant networks of atoms covalently bound together
- Examples are diamond and graphite
- Silicates are network solids containing Si—O—Si bridges that form the basis for many rocks, clays, and ceramics

Semiconductors
- Very pure silicon is "doped" with other elements
  - n-type: doping atoms typically contain five valence electrons (one more than silicon)
  - p-type: doping elements typically contain three valence electrons
- Modern electronics are based on devices with p–n junctions

Molecular solids
- Components are discrete molecules
- Intermolecular forces are typically weak, leading to relatively low boiling and melting points

Ionic solids

- Components are ions
- Interionic forces are relatively strong, leading to solids with high melting and boiling points
- Many structures consist of closest packing of the larger ions with the smaller ions in tetrahedral or octahedral holes

Phase changes

- The change from liquid to gas (vapor) is called vaporization or evaporation
- Condensation is the reverse of vaporization
- Equilibrium vapor pressure: the pressure that occurs over a liquid or solid in a closed system when the rate of evaporation equals the rate of condensation
    - Liquids whose components have high intermolecular forces have relatively low vapor pressures
    - Normal boiling point: the temperature at which the vapor pressure of a liquid equals one atmosphere
    - Normal melting point: the temperature at which a solid and its liquid have the same vapor pressure (at 1 atm external pressure)
- Phase diagram
    - Shows what state exists at a given temperature and pressure in a closed system
    - Triple point: temperature at which all three phases exist simultaneously
    - Critical point: defined by the critical temperature and pressure
        - Critical temperature: the temperature above which the vapor cannot be liquefied no matter the applied pressure
        - Critical pressure: the pressure required to produce liquefaction at the critical temperature

REVIEW QUESTIONS

1. What are intermolecular forces? How do they differ from intramolecular forces? What are dipole–dipole forces? How do typical dipole–dipole forces differ from hydrogen-bonding interactions? In what ways are they similar? What are London dispersion forces? How do typical London dispersion forces differ from dipole–dipole forces? In what ways are they similar? Describe the relationship between molecular size and strength of London dispersion forces. Place the major types of intermolecular forces in order of increasing strength. Is there some overlap? That is, can the strongest London dispersion forces be greater than some dipole–dipole forces? Give an example of such an instance.

2. Define the following terms and describe how each depends on the strength of the intermolecular forces.
    a. surface tension
    b. viscosity
    c. melting point
    d. boiling point
    e. vapor pressure

3. Compare and contrast solids versus liquids versus gases.

4. Distinguish between the items in the following pairs.
    a. crystalline solid; amorphous solid
    b. ionic solid; molecular solid
    c. molecular solid; network solid
    d. metallic solid; network solid

5. What is a lattice? What is a unit cell? Describe a simple cubic unit cell. How many net atoms are contained in a simple cubic unit cell? How is the radius of the atom

related to the cube edge length for a simple cubic unit cell? Answer the same questions for the body-centered cubic unit cell and for the face-centered unit cell.

6. What is closest packing? What is the difference between hexagonal closest packing and cubic closest packing? What is the unit cell for each closest packing?

7. Use the band model to describe differences among insulators, conductors, and semiconductors. Also use the band model to explain why each of the following increases the conductivity of a semiconductor.
   a. increasing the temperature
   b. irradiating with light
   c. adding an impurity
   How do conductors and semiconductors differ as to the effect of temperature on electrical conductivity? How can an n-type semiconductor be produced from pure germanium? How can a p-type semiconductor be produced from pure germanium?

8. Describe, in general, the structures of ionic solids. Compare and contrast the structure of sodium chloride and zinc sulfide. How many tetrahedral holes and octahedral holes are there per closest packed anion? In zinc sulfide, why are only one-half of the tetrahedral holes filled with cations?

9. Define each of the following.
   a. evaporation
   b. condensation
   c. sublimation
   d. boiling
   e. melting
   f. enthalpy of vaporization
   g. enthalpy of fusion
   h. heating curve
   Why is the enthalpy of vaporization for water much greater than its enthalpy of fusion? What does this say about the changes in intermolecular forces in going from solid to liquid to vapor? What do we mean when we say that a liquid is *volatile?* Do volatile liquids have large or small vapor pressures at room temperature? What strengths of intermolecular forces occur in highly volatile liquids?

10. Compare and contrast the phase diagrams of water versus carbon dioxide. Why doesn't CO_2 have a normal melting point and a normal boiling point, whereas water does? The slopes of the solid–liquid lines in the phase diagrams of H_2O and CO_2 are different. What do the slopes of the solid–liquid lines indicate in terms of the relative densities of the solid and liquid states for each substance? How do the melting points of H_2O and CO_2 depend on pressure? How do the boiling points of H_2O and CO_2 depend on pressure? Rationalize why the critical temperature for H_2O is greater than that for CO_2.

Active Learning Questions

These questions are designed to be used by groups of students in class. The questions allow students to explore their understanding of concepts through discussion and peer teaching. The real value of these questions is the learning that occurs while students talk to each other about chemical concepts.

1. It is possible to balance a paper clip on the surface of water in a beaker. If you add a bit of soap to the water, however, the paper clip sinks. Explain how the paper clip can float and why it sinks when soap is added.

2. Consider a sealed container half-filled with water. Which statement best describes what occurs in the container?
   a. Water evaporates until the air is saturated with water vapor; at this point, no more water evaporates.
   b. Water evaporates until the air is overly saturated (supersaturated) with water, and most of this water recondenses; this cycle continues until a certain amount of water vapor is present, and then the cycle ceases.
   c. Water does not evaporate because the container is sealed.
   d. Water evaporates, and then water evaporates and recondenses simultaneously and continuously.

e. Water evaporates until it is eventually all in vapor form.

Explain each choice. Justify your choice, and for choices you did not pick, explain what is wrong with them.

3. Explain the following: You add 100 mL of water to a 500-mL round-bottom flask and heat the water until it is boiling. You remove the heat and stopper the flask, and the boiling stops. You then run cool water over the neck of the flask, and the boiling begins again. It seems as though you are boiling water by cooling it.

4. Is it possible for the dispersion forces in a particular substance to be stronger than the hydrogen bonding forces in another substance? Explain your answer.

5. Does the nature of intermolecular forces change when a substance goes from a solid to a liquid, or from a liquid to a gas? What causes a substance to undergo a phase change?

6. Why do liquids have a vapor pressure? Do all liquids have vapor pressures? Explain. Do solids exhibit vapor pressure? Explain. How does vapor pressure change with changing temperature? Explain.

7. Water in an open beaker evaporates over time. As the water is evaporating, is the vapor pressure increasing, decreasing, or staying the same? Why?

8. What is the vapor pressure of water at 100°C? How do you know?

9. Refer to Fig. 10.44. Why doesn't temperature increase continuously over time? That is, why does the temperature stay constant for periods of time?

10. Which are stronger, intermolecular or intramolecular forces for a given molecule? What observation(s) have you made that support this? Explain.

11. Why does water evaporate?

A blue question or exercise number indicates that the answer to that question or exercise appears at the back of this book and a solution appears in the *Solutions Guide*.

Questions

12. The nonpolar hydrocarbon $C_{25}H_{52}$ is a solid at room temperature. Its boiling point is greater than 400°C. Which has the stronger intermolecular forces, $C_{25}H_{52}$ or H_2O? Explain your answer.

13. Atoms are assumed to touch in closest packed structures, yet every closest packed unit cell contains a significant amount of empty space. Why?

14. Define *critical temperature* and *critical pressure*. In terms of the kinetic molecular theory, why is it impossible for a substance to exist as a liquid above its critical temperature?

15. Use the kinetic molecular theory to explain why a liquid gets cooler as it evaporates from an insulated container.

16. Will a crystalline solid or an amorphous solid give a simpler X-ray diffraction pattern? Why?

17. What is an alloy? Explain the differences in structure between substitutional and interstitial alloys. Give an example of each type.

18. Describe what is meant by a dynamic equilibrium in terms of the vapor pressure of a liquid.

19. How does each of the following affect the rate of evaporation of a liquid in an open dish?
  a. intermolecular forces
  b. temperature
  c. surface area

20. When a person has a severe fever, one therapy used to reduce the fever is an "alcohol rub." Explain how the evaporation of alcohol from a person's skin removes heat energy from the body.

21. When wet laundry is hung on a clothesline on a cold winter day, it will freeze but eventually dry. Explain.

22. Why is a burn from steam typically much more severe than a burn from boiling water?

23. You have three covalent compounds with three very different boiling points. All of the compounds have similar molar mass and relative shape. Explain how these three compounds could have very different boiling points.

24. Compare and contrast the structures of the following solids.
  a. diamond versus graphite
  b. silica versus silicates versus glass

25. Compare and contrast the structures of the following solids.
  a. $CO_2(s)$ versus $H_2O(s)$
  b. $NaCl(s)$ versus $CsCl(s)$; See Exercise 61 for the structures.

26. Silicon carbide (SiC) is an extremely hard substance that acts as an electrical insulator. Propose a structure for SiC.

27. A plot of $\ln P_{vap}$ versus $1/T$ (K) is linear with a negative slope. Why is this the case?

28. Iodine, like most substances, exhibits only three phases; solid, liquid, and vapor. The triple point of iodine is at 90 torr and 115°C. Which of the following statements concerning liquid I_2 must be true? Explain your answer.
  a. $I_2(l)$ is more dense than $I_2(g)$.
  b. $I_2(l)$ cannot exist above 115°C.
  c. $I_2(l)$ cannot exist at 1 atmosphere pressure.
  d. $I_2(l)$ cannot have a vapor pressure greater than 90 torr.
  e. $I_2(l)$ cannot exist at a pressure of 10 torr.

Exercises

In this section similar exercises are paired.

Intermolecular Forces and Physical Properties

29. Identify the most important types of interparticle forces present in the solids of each of the following substances.
  a. Ar   **e.** CH_4
  b. HCl   **f.** CO
  c. HF   **g.** $NaNO_3$
  d. $CaCl_2$

30. Identify the most important types of interparticle forces present in the solids of each of the following substances.
  a. NH_4Cl
  b. Teflon, $CF_3(CF_2CF_2)_nCF_3$
  c. Polyethylene, $CH_3(CH_2CH_2)_nCH_3$
  d. $CHCl_3$
  e. NH_3
  f. NO
  g. BF_3

31. Predict which substance in each of the following pairs would have the greater intermolecular forces.
  a. CO_2 or OCS
  b. SeO_2 or SO_2
  c. $CH_3CH_2CH_2NH_2$ or $H_2NCH_2CH_2NH_2$
  d. CH_3CH_3 or H_2CO
  e. CH_3OH or H_2CO

32. Consider the compounds Cl_2, HCl, F_2, NaF, and HF. Which compound has a boiling point closest to that of argon? Explain.

33. Rationalize the difference in boiling points for each of the following pairs of substances:
  a. *n*-pentane $CH_3CH_2CH_2CH_2CH_3$ 36.2°C

  neopentane $H_3C-\overset{\overset{\displaystyle CH_3}{|}}{\underset{\underset{\displaystyle CH_3}{|}}{C}}-CH_3$ 9.5°C

  b. HF   20°C
     HCl   −85°C
  c. HCl   −85°C
     LiCl   1360°C
  d. *n*-pentane $CH_3CH_2CH_2CH_2CH_3$ 36.2°C
     n-hexane $CH_3CH_2CH_2CH_2CH_2CH_3$ 69°C

34. Consider the following compounds and formulas. (*Note:* The formulas are written in such a way as to give you an idea of the structure.)

  ethanol: CH_3CH_2OH
  dimethyl ether: CH_3OCH_3
  propane: $CH_3CH_2CH_3$

  The boiling points of these compounds are (in no particular order) −42.1°C, −23°C, and 78.5°C. Match the boiling points to the correct compounds.

35. In each of the following groups of substances, pick the one that has the given property. Justify your answer.
  a. highest boiling point: HBr, Kr, or Cl_2
  b. highest freezing point: H_2O, NaCl, or HF
  c. lowest vapor pressure at 25°C: Cl_2, Br_2, or I_2
  d. lowest freezing point: N_2, CO, or CO_2
  e. lowest boiling point: CH_4, CH_3CH_3, or $CH_3CH_2CH_3$
  f. highest boiling point: HF, HCl, or HBr
  g. lowest vapor pressure at 25°C: $CH_3CH_2CH_3$, $CH_3\overset{\overset{\displaystyle O}{||}}{C}CH_3$, or $CH_3CH_2CH_2OH$

36. In each of the following groups of substances, pick the one that has the given property. Justify each answer.
  a. highest boiling point: CCl_4, CF_4, CBr_4
  b. lowest freezing point: LiF, F_2, HCl
  c. smallest vapor pressure at 25°C: CH_3OCH_3, CH_3CH_2OH, $CH_3CH_2CH_3$
  d. greatest viscosity: H_2S, HF, H_2O_2

  e. greatest heat of vaporization: H_2CO, CH_3CH_3, CH_4
  f. smallest enthalpy of fusion: I_2, CsBr, CaO

Properties of Liquids

37. The shape of the meniscus of water in a glass tube is different from that of mercury in a glass tube. Why?

H_2O in glass   Hg in glass

38. Explain why water forms into beads on a waxed car finish.

39. Hydrogen peroxide (H_2O_2) is a syrupy liquid with a relatively low vapor pressure and a normal boiling point of 152.2°C. Rationalize the differences of these physical properties from those of water.

40. Carbon diselenide (CSe_2) is a liquid at room temperature. The normal boiling point is 125°C, and the melting point is −45.5°C. Carbon disulfide (CS_2) is also a liquid at room temperature with normal boiling and melting points of 46.5°C and −111.6°C, respectively. How do the strengths of the intermolecular forces vary from CO_2 to CS_2 to CSe_2? Explain.

Structures and Properties of Solids

41. X rays from a copper X-ray tube ($\lambda = 154$ pm) were diffracted at an angle of 14.22 degrees by a crystal of silicon. Assuming first-order diffraction ($n = 1$ in the Bragg equation), what is the interplanar spacing in silicon?

42. The second-order diffraction ($n = 2$) for a gold crystal is at an angle of 22.20° for X rays of 154 pm. What is the spacing between these crystal planes?

43. A topaz crystal has an interplanar spacing (*d*) of 1.36 Å (1 Å = 1×10^{-10} m). Calculate the wavelength of the X ray that should be used if $\theta = 15.0°$ (assume $n = 1$).

44. X rays of wavelength 2.63 Å were used to analyze a crystal. The angle of first-order diffraction ($n = 1$ in the Bragg equation) was 15.55 degrees. What is the spacing between crystal planes, and what would be the angle for second-order diffraction ($n = 2$)?

45. Calcium has a cubic closest packed structure as a solid. Assuming that calcium has an atomic radius of 197 pm, calculate the density of solid calcium.

46. Nickel has a face-centered cubic unit cell. The density of nickel is 6.84 g/cm³. Calculate a value for the atomic radius of nickel.

47. A certain form of lead has a cubic closest packed structure with an edge length of 492 pm. Calculate the value of the atomic radius and the density of lead.

48. You are given a small bar of an unknown metal X. You find the density of the metal to be 10.5 g/cm³. An X-ray diffraction experiment measures the edge of the face-centered cubic unit cell as 4.09 Å (1 Å = 10⁻¹⁰ m). Identify X.

49. Titanium metal has a body-centered cubic unit cell. The density of titanium is 4.50 g/cm³. Calculate the edge length of the unit cell and a value for the atomic radius of titanium. (*Hint:* In a body-centered arrangement of spheres, the spheres touch across the body diagonal.)

50. Barium has a body-centered cubic structure. If the atomic radius of barium is 222 pm, calculate the density of solid barium.

51. The radius of gold is 144 pm, and the density is 19.32 g/cm³. Does elemental gold have a face-centered cubic structure or a body-centered cubic structure?

52. The radius of tungsten is 137 pm and the density is 19.3 g/cm³. Does elemental tungsten have a face-centered cubic structure or a body-centered cubic structure?

53. What fraction of the total volume of a cubic closest packed structure is occupied by atoms? (*Hint:* $V_{sphere} = \frac{4}{3}\pi r^3$.) What fraction of the total volume of a simple cubic structure is occupied by atoms? Compare the answers.

54. Iron has a density of 7.86 g/cm³ and crystallizes in a body-centered cubic lattice. Show that only 68% of a body-centered lattice is actually occupied by atoms, and determine the atomic radius of iron.

55. Explain how doping silicon with either phosphorus or gallium increases the electrical conductivity over that of pure silicon.

56. Explain how a p–n junction makes an excellent rectifier.

57. Selenium is a semiconductor used in photocopying machines. What type of semiconductor would be formed if a small amount of indium impurity is added to pure selenium?

58. The Group 3A/Group 5A semiconductors are composed of equal amounts of atoms from Group 3A and Group 5A—for example, InP and GaAs. These types of semiconductors are used in light-emitting diodes and solid-state lasers. What would you add to make a p-type semiconductor from pure GaAs? How would you dope pure GaAs to make an n-type semiconductor?

59. The band gap in aluminum phosphide (AlP) is 2.5 electron-volts (1eV = 1.6 × 10⁻¹⁹ J). What wavelength of light is emitted by an AlP diode?

60. An aluminum antimonide solid-state laser emits light with a wavelength of 730. nm. Calculate the band gap in joules.

61. The structures of some common crystalline substances are shown below. Show that the net composition of each unit cell corresponds to the correct formula of each substance.

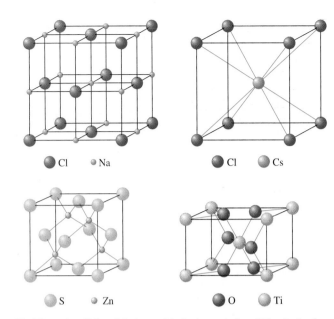

Cl Na   Cl Cs

S Zn   O Ti

62. The unit cell for nickel arsenide is shown below. What is the formula of this compound?

Ni
As

63. Cobalt fluoride crystallizes in a closest packed array of fluoride ions with the cobalt ions filling one-half of the octahedral holes. What is the formula of this compound?

64. The compounds Na₂O, CdS, and ZrI₄ all can be described as cubic closest packed anions with the cations in tetrahedral holes. What fraction of the tetrahedral holes is occupied for each case?

65. What is the formula for the compound that crystallizes with a cubic closest packed array of sulfur ions, and that contains zinc ions in $\frac{1}{8}$ of the tetrahedral holes and aluminum ions in $\frac{1}{2}$ of the octahedral holes?

66. Assume the two-dimensional structure of an ionic compound, M_xA_y, is

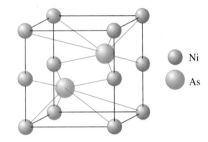

What is the empirical formula of this ionic compound?

67. A certain metal fluoride crystallizes in such a way that the fluoride ions occupy simple cubic lattice sites, while the metal ions occupy the body centers of *half* the cubes. What is the formula of the metal fluoride?

68. The structure of manganese fluoride can be described as a simple cubic array of manganese ions with fluoride ions at the center of each edge of the cubic unit cell. What is the charge of the manganese ions in this compound?

69. The unit cell of MgO is shown below.

Does MgO have a structure like that of NaCl or ZnS? If the density of MgO is 3.58 g/cm^3, estimate the radius (in centimeters) of the O^{2-} anions and the Mg^{2+} cations.

70. The CsCl structure is a simple cubic array of chloride ions with a cesium ion at the center of each cubic array (see Exercise 61). Given that the density of cesium chloride is 3.97 g/cm^3, and assuming that the chloride and cesium ions touch along the body diagonal of the cubic unit cell, calculate the distance between the centers of adjacent Cs$^+$ and Cl$^-$ ions in the solid. Compare this value with the expected distance based on the sizes of the ions. The ionic radius of Cs$^+$ is 169 pm, and the ionic radius of Cl$^-$ is 181 pm.

71. What type of solid will each of the following substances form?
    a. CO$_2$ e. Ru   i. NaOH
    b. SiO$_2$ f. I$_2$ j. U
    c. Si   g. KBr   k. CaCO$_3$
    d. CH$_4$ h. H$_2$O   l. PH$_3$

72. What type of solid will each of the following substances form?
    a. diamond   e. KCl   i. Ar
    b. PH$_3$ f. quartz   j. Cu
    c. H$_2$ g. NH$_4$NO$_3$ k. C$_6$H$_{12}$O$_6$
    d. Mg   h. SF$_2$

73. The memory metal, nitinol, is an alloy of nickel and titanium. It is called a *memory metal* because after being deformed, a piece of nitinol wire will return to its original shape. The structure of nitinol consists of a simple cubic array of Ni atoms and an inner penetrating simple cubic array of Ti atoms. In the extended lattice, a Ti atom is found at the center of a cube of Ni atoms; the reverse is also true.
    a. Describe the unit cell for nitinol.
    b. What is the empirical formula of nitinol?
    c. What are the coordination numbers (number of nearest neighbors) of Ni and Ti in nitinol?

74. The unit cell for a pure xenon fluoride compound is shown below. What is the formula of the compound?

Xenon

Fluorine

75. Perovskite is a mineral containing calcium, titanium, and oxygen. Two different representations of the unit cell are shown below. Show that both these representations give the same formula and the same number of oxygen atoms around each titanium atom.

Titanium

Calcium

Oxygen

76. A mineral crystallizes in a cubic closest packed array of oxygen ions with aluminum ions in some of the octahedral holes and magnesium ions in some of the tetrahedral holes. Deduce the formula of this mineral and predict the fraction of octahedral holes and tetrahedral holes that are filled by the various cations.

77. Materials containing the elements Y, Ba, Cu, and O that are superconductors (electrical resistance equals zero) at temperatures

Barium   Oxygen   Copper   Yttrium

(a) Ideal perovskite structure

(b) Actual structure of superconductor

above that of liquid nitrogen were recently discovered. The structures of these materials are based on the perovskite structure. Were they to have the ideal perovskite structure, the superconductor would have the structure shown in part (a) of the figure above.

a. What is the formula of this ideal perovskite material?

b. How is this structure related to the perovskite structure shown in Exercise 75?

These materials, however, do not act as superconductors unless they are deficient in oxygen. The structure of the actual superconducting phase appears to be that shown in part (b) of the figure.

c. What is the formula of this material?

78. The structures of another class of ceramic, high-temperature superconductors are shown in the figure below.

a. Determine the formula of each of these four superconductors.

b. One of the structural features that appears to be essential for high-temperature superconductivity is the presence of planar sheets of copper and oxygen atoms. As the number of sheets in each unit cell increases, the temperature for the onset of superconductivity increases. Order the four structures from lowest to the highest superconducting temperature.

c. Assign oxidation states to Cu in each structure assuming Tl exists as Tl^{3+}. The oxidation states of Ca, Ba, and O are assumed to be +2, +2, and −2, respectively.

d. It also appears that copper must display a mixture of oxidation states for a material to exhibit superconductivity. Explain how this occurs in these materials as well as in the superconductor in Exercise 77.

- Ti
- O
- Ca
- Ba
- Cu

(a) (b)

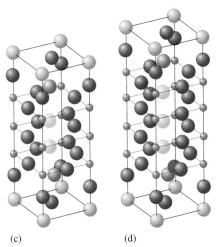

(c) (d)

Phase Changes and Phase Diagrams

79. Plot the following data and determine ΔH_{vap} for magnesium and lithium. In which metal is the bonding stronger?

Vapor Pressure (mm Hg)	Temperature (°C)	
	Li	Mg
1.	750.	620.
10.	890.	740.
100.	1080.	900.
400.	1240.	1040.
760.	1310.	1110.

80. From the following data for liquid nitric acid, determine its heat of vaporization and normal boiling point.

Temperature (°C)	Vapor Pressure (mm Hg)
0.	14.4
10.	26.6
20.	47.9
30.	81.3
40.	133
50.	208
80.	670.

81. In Breckenridge, Colorado, the typical atmospheric pressure is 520. torr. What is the boiling point of water ($\Delta H_{vap} = 40.7$ kJ/mol) in Breckenridge?

82. What pressure would have to be applied to steam at 350.°C to condense the steam to liquid water ($\Delta H_{vap} = 40.7$ kJ/mol)?

83. Carbon tetrachloride, CCl_4, has a vapor pressure of 213 torr at 40.°C and 836 torr at 80.°C. What is the normal boiling point of CCl_4?

84. The normal boiling point for acetone is 56.5°C. At an elevation of 5300 ft the atmospheric pressure is 630. torr. What would be the boiling point of acetone ($\Delta H_{vap} = 32.0$ kJ/mol) at this elevation? What would be the vapor pressure of acetone at 25.0°C at this elevation?

85. A substance, X, has the following properties:

		Specific Heat Capacities	
ΔH_{vap}	20. kJ/mol	C(s)	3.0 J/g · °C
ΔH_{fus}	5.0 kJ/mol	C(l)	2.5 J/g · °C
bp	75°C	C(g)	1.0 J/g · °C
mp	−15°C		

Sketch a heating curve for substance X starting at −50.°C.

86. Given the data in Exercise 85 on substance X, calculate the energy that must be removed to convert 250. g of substance X from a gas at 100.°C to a solid at −50.°C. Assume X has a molar mass of 75.0 g/mol.

87. How much energy does it take to convert 0.500 kg ice at $-20.°C$ to steam at $250.°C$? Specific heat capacities: ice, 2.03 J/g · °C; liquid, 4.2 J/g · °C; steam, 2.0 J/g · °C, $\Delta H_{vap} = 40.7$ kJ/mol, $\Delta H_{fus} = 6.02$ kJ/mol.

88. Consider a 75.0-g sample of $H_2O(g)$ at 125°C. What phase or phases are present when 215 kJ of energy is removed from this sample? (See Exercise 87.)

89. An ice cube tray contains enough water at 22.0°C to make 18 ice cubes that each have a mass of 30.0 g. The tray is placed in a freezer that uses CF_2Cl_2 as a refrigerant. The heat of vaporization of CF_2Cl_2 is 158 J/g. What mass of CF_2Cl_2 must be vaporized in the refrigeration cycle to convert all the water at 22.0°C to ice at $-5.0°C$? The heat capacities for $H_2O(s)$ and $H_2O(l)$ are 2.03 J/g · °C and 4.18 J/g · °C, respectively, and the enthalpy of fusion for ice is 6.02 kJ/mol.

90. A 0.250-g chunk of sodium metal is cautiously dropped into a mixture of 50.0 g of water and 50.0 g of ice, both at 0°C. The reaction is

$$2Na(s) + 2H_2O(l) \longrightarrow 2NaOH(aq) + H_2(g) \quad \Delta H = -368 \text{ kJ}$$

Will the ice melt? Assuming the final mixture has a specific heat capacity of 4.18 J/g · °C, calculate the final temperature. The enthalpy of fusion for ice is 6.02 kJ/mol.

91. Consider the phase diagram given below. What phases are present at points A through H? Identify the triple point, normal boiling point, normal freezing point, and critical point. Which phase is denser, solid or liquid?

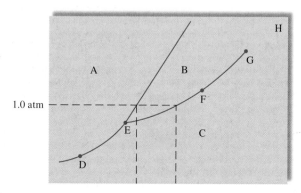

92. Sulfur exhibits two solid phases, rhombic and monoclinic. Use the accompanying phase diagram for sulfur to answer the following questions. (The phase diagram is not to scale.)

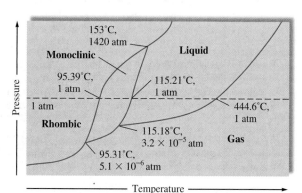

a. How many triple points are in the phase diagram?
b. What phases are in equilibrium at each of the triple points?
c. What is the stable phase at 1 atm and 100.°C?
d. What are the normal melting point and the normal boiling point of sulfur?
e. Which is the densest phase?
f. At a pressure of 1.0×10^{-5} atm, can rhombic sulfur sublime?
g. What phase changes occur when the pressure on a sample of sulfur at 100.°C is increased from 1.0×10^{-8} atm to 1500 atm?

93. Use the accompanying phase diagram for carbon to answer the following questions.
a. How many triple points are in the phase diagram?
b. What phases can coexist at each triple point?
c. What happens if graphite is subjected to very high pressures at room temperature?
d. If we assume that the density increases with an increase in pressure, which is more dense, graphite or diamond?

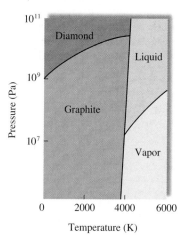

94. Like most substances, bromine exists in one of the three typical phases. Br_2 has a normal melting point of $-7.2°C$ and a normal boiling point of 59°C. The triple point for Br_2 is $-7.3°C$ and 40 torr, and the critical point is 320°C and 100 atm. Using this information, sketch a phase diagram for bromine indicating the points described above. Based on your phase diagram, order the three phases from least dense to most dense. What is the stable phase of Br_2 at room temperature and 1 atm? Under what temperature conditions can liquid bromine never exist? What phase changes occur as the temperature of a sample of bromine at 0.10 atm is increased from $-50°C$ to 200°C?

95. The melting point of a fictional substance X is 225°C at 10.0 atm. If the density of the solid phase of X is 2.67 g/cm^3 and the density of the liquid phase is 2.78 g/cm^3 at 10.0 atm, predict whether the normal melting point of X will be less than, equal to, or greater than 225°C. Explain.

96. Consider the following data for xenon:

Triple point:	$-121°C$, 280 torr
Normal melting point:	$-112°C$
Normal boiling point:	$-107°C$

Which is more dense, Xe(s), or Xe(l)? How do the melting point and boiling point of xenon depend on pressure?

Additional Exercises

97. Rationalize why chalk (calcium carbonate) has a higher melting point than motor oil (large compounds made from carbon and hydrogen), which has a higher melting point than water, which engages in relatively strong hydrogen-bonding interactions.

98. Rationalize the differences in physical properties in terms of intermolecular forces for the following organic compounds. Compare the first three substances with each other, compare the last three with each other, and then compare all six. Can you account for any anomalies?

	bp (°C)	mp (°C)	ΔH_{vap} (kJ/mol)
Benzene, C_6H_6	80	6	33.9
Naphthalene, $C_{10}H_8$	218	80	51.5
Carbon tetrachloride	76	−23	31.8
Acetone, CH_3COCH_3	56	−95	31.8
Acetic acid, CH_3CO_2H	118	17	39.7
Benzoic acid, $C_6H_5CO_2H$	249	122	68.2

99. Consider the following vapor pressure versus temperature plot for three different substances A, B, and C.

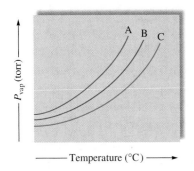

If the three substances are CH_4, SiH_4, and NH_3, match each curve to the correct substance.

100. Consider the following enthalpy changes:

$$F^- + HF \longrightarrow FHF^- \quad \Delta H = -155 \text{ kJ/mol}$$
$$(CH_3)_2C{=}O + HF \longrightarrow (CH_3)_2C{=}O \text{---} HF$$
$$\Delta H = -46 \text{ kJ/mol}$$
$$H_2O(g) + HOH(g) \longrightarrow H_2O \text{---} HOH \text{ (in ice)}$$
$$\Delta H = -21 \text{ kJ/mol}$$

How do the strengths of hydrogen bonds vary with the electronegativity of the element to which hydrogen is bonded? Where in the preceding series would you expect hydrogen bonds of the following type to fall?

$$\text{—N---HO—} \quad \text{and} \quad \text{—N---H—N}$$

101. How could you tell experimentally if TiO_2 is an ionic solid or a network solid?

102. Boron nitride (BN) exists in two forms. The first is a slippery solid formed from the reaction of BCl_3 with NH_3, followed by heating in an ammonia atmosphere at 750°C. Subjecting the first form of BN to a pressure of 85,000 atm at 1800°C produces a second form that is the second hardest substance known. Both forms of BN remain solids to 3000°C. Suggest structures for the two forms of BN.

103. Consider the following data concerning four different substances.

Compound	Conducts Electricity as a Solid	Other Properties
B_2H_6	no	gas at 25°C
SiO_2	no	high mp
CsI	no	aqueous solution conducts electricity
W	yes	high mp

Label the four substances as either ionic, network, metallic, or molecular solids.

104. A 20.0-g sample of ice at −10.0°C is mixed with 100.0 g of water at 80.0°C. Calculate the final temperature of the mixture assuming no heat loss to the surroundings. The heat capacities of $H_2O(s)$ and $H_2O(l)$ are 2.03 and 4.18 J/g · °C, respectively, and the enthalpy of fusion for ice is 6.02 kJ/mol.

105. In regions with dry climates, evaporative coolers are used to cool air. A typical electric air conditioner is rated at 1.00×10^4 Btu/h (1 Btu, or British thermal unit = amount of energy to raise the temperature of 1 lb of water by 1°F). How much water must be evaporated each hour to dissipate as much heat as a typical electric air conditioner?

106. The critical point of NH_3 is 132°C and 111 atm, and the critical point of N_2 is −147°C and 34 atm. Which of these substances cannot be liquefied at room temperature no matter how much pressure is applied? Explain.

Challenge Problems

107. When 1 mol of benzene is vaporized at a constant pressure of 1.00 atm and its boiling point of 353.0 K, 30.79 kJ of energy (heat) is absorbed and the volume change is +28.90 L. What are ΔE and ΔH for this process?

108. You and a friend each synthesize a compound with the formula $XeCl_2F_2$. Your compound is a liquid and your friend's compound is a gas (at the same conditions of temperature and pressure). Explain how the two compounds with the same formulas can exist in different phases at the same conditions of pressure and temperature.

109. Using the heats of fusion and vaporization for water given in Exercise 87, calculate the change in enthalpy for the sublimation of water:

$$H_2O(s) \longrightarrow H_2O(g)$$

Using the ΔH value given in Exercise 100 and the number of hydrogen bonds formed with each water molecule, estimate what portion of the intermolecular forces in ice can be accounted for by hydrogen bonding.

110. Oil of wintergreen, or methyl salicylate, has the following structure:

$mp = -8°C$

Methyl-4-hydroxybenzoate is another molecule with exactly the same molecular formula; it has the following structure:

$mp = 127°C$

Account for the large difference in the melting points of the two substances.

111. Consider the following melting point data:

Compound:	NaCl	MgCl$_2$	AlCl$_3$	SiCl$_4$	PCl$_3$	SCl$_2$	Cl$_2$
mp (°C):	801	708	190	−70	−91	−78	−101
Compound:	NaF	MgF$_2$	AlF$_3$	SiF$_4$	PF$_5$	SF$_6$	F$_2$
mp (°C):	997	1396	1040	−90	−94	−56	−220

Account for the trends in melting points in terms of interparticle forces.

112. MnO has either the NaCl type structure or the CsCl type structure (see Exercise 70). The edge length of the MnO unit cell is 4.47×10^{-8} cm and the density of MnO is 5.28 g/cm^3.
   a. Does MnO crystallize in the NaCl or the CsCl type structure?
   b. Assuming that the ionic radius of oxygen is 140. pm, estimate the ionic radius of manganese.

113. Some ionic compounds contain a mixture of different charged cations. For example, some titanium oxides contain a mixture of Ti^{2+} and Ti^{3+} ions. Consider a certain oxide of titanium that is 28.31% oxygen by mass and contains a mixture of Ti^{2+} and Ti^{3+} ions. Determine the formula of the compound and the relative numbers of Ti^{2+} and Ti^{3+} ions.

114. Spinel is a mineral that contains 37.9% aluminum, 17.1% magnesium, and 45.0% oxygen, by mass, and has a density of 3.57 g/cm^3. The edge of the cubic unit cell measures 809 pm. How many of each type of ion are present in the unit cell?

115. Mn crystallizes in the same type of cubic unit cell as Cu. Assuming that the radius of Mn is 5.6% larger than the radius of Cu and the density of copper is 8.96 g/cm^3, calculate the density of Mn.

116. You are asked to help set up a historical display in the park by stacking some cannonballs next to a Revolutionary War cannon. You are told to stack them by starting with a triangle in which each side is composed of four touching cannonballs. You are to continue stacking them until you have a single ball on the top centered over the middle of the triangular base.
   a. How many cannonballs do you need?
   b. What type of closest packing is displayed by the cannonballs?
   c. The four corners of the pyramid of cannonballs form the corners of what type of regular geometric solid?

117. Some water is placed in a sealed glass container connected to a vacuum pump (a device used to pump gases from a container), and the pump is turned on. The water appears to boil and then freezes. Explain these changes using the phase diagram for water. What would happen to the ice if the vacuum pump was left on indefinitely?

118. The molar enthalpy of vaporization of water at 373 K and 1.00 atm is 40.7 kJ/mol. What fraction of this energy is used to change the internal energy of the water, and what fraction is used to do work against the atmosphere? (*Hint:* Assume that water vapor is an ideal gas.)

119. For a simple cubic array, solve for the volume of an interior sphere (cubic hole) in terms of the radius of a sphere in the array.

120. Consider two different compounds, each with the formula C$_2$H$_6$O. One of these compounds is a liquid at room conditions and the other is a gas. Write Lewis structures consistent with this observation and explain your answer. *Hint:* the oxygen atom in both structures satisfies the octet rule with two bonds and two lone pairs.

Integrative Problems

These problems require the integration of multiple concepts to find the solutions.

121. A 0.132-mol sample of an unknown semiconducting material with the formula XY has a mass of 19.0 g. The element X has an electron configuration of [Kr]$5s^2 4d^{10}$. What is this semiconducting material? A small amount of the Y atoms in the semiconductor is replaced with an equivalent amount of atoms with and electron configuration of [Ar]$4s^2 3d^{10} 4p^5$. Does this correspond to n-type or p-type doping?

122. A metal burns in air at 600°C under high pressure to form an oxide with formula MO$_2$. This compound is 23.72% oxygen by mass. The distance between touching atoms in a cubic closest packed crystal of this metal is 269.0 pm. What is this metal? What is its density?

123. One method of preparing elemental mercury involves roasting cinnabar (HgS) in quicklime (CaO) at 600.°C followed by condensation of the mercury vapor. Given the heat of vaporization of mercury (296 J/g) and the vapor pressure of mercury at 25.0°C (2.56×10^{-3} torr), what is the vapor pressure of the condensed mercury at 300.°C? How many atoms of mercury are present in the mercury vapor at 300.°C if the reaction is conducted in a closed 15.0-L container?

Marathon Problem

This problem is designed to incorporate several concepts and techniques into one situation. Marathon Problems can be used in class by groups of students to help facilitate problem-solving skills.

124. General Zod has sold Lex Luthor what Zod claims to be a new copper-colored form of kryptonite, the only substance that can harm Superman. Lex, not believing in honor among thieves, decided to carry out some tests on the supposed kryptonite. From previous tests, Lex knew that kryptonite is a metal having a specific heat capacity of 0.082 J/g · °C, and a density of 9.2 g/cm^3.

Lex Luthor's first experiment was an attempt to find the specific heat capacity of kryptonite. He dropped a 10 g ± 3 g sample of the metal into a boiling water bath at a temperature of 100.0°C ± 0.2°C. He waited until the metal had reached the bath temperature and then quickly transferred it to 100 g ± 3 g of water that was contained in a calorimeter at an initial temperature of 25.0°C ± 0.2°C. The final temperature of the metal and water was 25.2°C. Based on these results, is it possible to distinguish between copper and kryptonite? Explain.

When Lex found that his results from the first experiment were inconclusive, he decided to determine the density of the sample. He managed to steal a better balance and determined the mass of another portion of the purported kryptonite to be 4 g ± 1 g. He dropped this sample into water contained in a 25-mL graduated cylinder and found that it displaced a volume of 0.42 mL ± 0.02 mL. Is the metal copper or kryptonite? Explain.

Lex was finally forced to determine the crystal structure of the metal General Zod had given him. He found that the cubic unit cell contained 4 atoms and had an edge length of 600. pm. Explain how this information enabled Lex to identify the metal as copper or kryptonite.

Will Lex be going after Superman with the kryptonite or seeking revenge on General Zod? What improvements could he have made in his experimental techniques to avoid performing the crystal structure determination?

Get help understanding core concepts and visualizing molecular-level interactions, and practice problem solving, by visiting the Online Study Center at **college.hmco.com/ PIC/zumdahl7e.**

11 Properties of Solutions

Contents

Opals are formed from colloidal suspensions of silica when the liquid evaporates.

M ost of the substances we encounter in daily life are mixtures: Wood, milk, gasoline, champagne, seawater, shampoo, steel, and air are common examples. When the components of a mixture are uniformly intermingled—that is, when a mixture is homogeneous—it is called a *solution*. Solutions can be gases, liquids, or solids, as shown in Table 11.1. However, we will be concerned in this chapter with the properties of liquid solutions, particularly those containing water. As we saw in Chapter 4, many essential chemical reactions occur in aqueous solutions because water is capable of dissolving so many substances.

11.1 Solution Composition

Because a mixture, unlike a chemical compound, has a variable composition, the relative amounts of substances in a solution must be specified. The qualitative terms *dilute* (relatively little solute present) and *concentrated* (relatively large amount of solute) are often used to describe solution content, but we need to define solution composition more precisely to perform calculations. For example, in dealing with the stoichiometry of solution reactions in Chapter 4, we found it useful to describe solution composition in terms of **molarity,** or the number of moles of solute per liter of solution (symbolized by M).

Other ways of describing solution composition are also useful. **Mass percent** (sometimes called *weight percent*) is the percent by mass of the solute in the solution:

$$\text{Mass percent} = \left(\frac{\text{mass of solute}}{\text{mass of solution}} \right) \times 100\%$$

Another way of describing solution composition is the **mole fraction** (symbolized by the Greek lowercase letter chi, χ), the ratio of the number of moles of a given component to the total number of moles of solution. For a two-component solution, where n_A and n_B represent the number of moles of the two components,

$$\text{Mole fraction of component A} = \chi_A = \frac{n_A}{n_A + n_B}$$

A solute is the substance being dissolved. The solvent is the dissolving medium.

$$\text{Molarity} = \frac{\text{moles of solute}}{\text{liters of solution}}$$

When liquids are mixed, the liquid present in the largest amount is called the *solvent*.

TABLE 11.1 Various Types of Solutions

Example	State of Solution	State of Solute	State of Solvent
Air, natural gas	Gas	Gas	Gas
Vodka in water, antifreeze	Liquid	Liquid	Liquid
Brass	Solid	Solid	Solid
Carbonated water (soda)	Liquid	Gas	Liquid
Seawater, sugar solution	Liquid	Solid	Liquid
Hydrogen in platinum	Solid	Gas	Solid

In very dilute aqueous solutions, the magnitude of the molality and the molarity are almost the same.

Still another way of describing solution composition is **molality** (symbolized by m), the number of moles of solute per *kilogram of solvent:*

$$\text{Molality} = \frac{\text{moles of solute}}{\text{kilogram of solvent}}$$

| Sample Exercise 11.1 | **Various Methods for Describing Solution Composition** |

A solution is prepared by mixing 1.00 g ethanol (C_2H_5OH) with 100.0 g water to give a final volume of 101 mL. Calculate the molarity, mass percent, mole fraction, and molality of ethanol in this solution.

Solution

Since molarity depends on the volume of the solution, it changes slightly with temperature. Molality is independent of temperature because it depends only on mass.

Molarity: The moles of ethanol can be obtained from its molar mass (46.07 g/mol):

$$1.00 \text{ g } C_2H_5OH \times \frac{1 \text{ mol } C_2H_5OH}{46.07 \text{ g } C_2H_5OH} = 2.17 \times 10^{-2} \text{ mol } C_2H_5OH$$

$$\text{Volume} = 101 \text{ mL} \times \frac{1 \text{ L}}{1000 \text{ mL}} = 0.101 \text{ L}$$

$$\text{Molarity of } C_2H_5OH = \frac{\text{moles of } C_2H_5OH}{\text{liters of solution}} = \frac{2.17 \times 10^{-2} \text{ mol}}{0.101 \text{ L}}$$

$$= 0.215 \text{ } M$$

Mass percent:

$$\text{Mass percent } C_2H_5OH = \left(\frac{\text{mass of } C_2H_5OH}{\text{mass of solution}} \right) \times 100\%$$

$$= \left(\frac{1.00 \text{ g } C_2H_5OH}{100.0 \text{ g } H_2O + 1.00 \text{ g } C_2H_5OH} \right) \times 100\%$$

$$= 0.990\% \text{ } C_2H_5OH$$

Mole fraction:

$$\text{Mole fraction of } C_2H_5OH = \frac{n_{C_2H_5OH}}{n_{C_2H_5OH} + n_{H_2O}}$$

$$n_{H_2O} = 100.0 \text{ g } H_2O \times \frac{1 \text{ mol } H_2O}{18.0 \text{ g } H_2O} = 5.56 \text{ mol}$$

$$\chi_{C_2H_5OH} = \frac{2.17 \times 10^{-2} \text{ mol}}{2.17 \times 10^{-2} \text{ mol} + 5.56 \text{ mol}}$$

$$= \frac{2.17 \times 10^{-2}}{5.58} = 0.00389$$

Molality:

$$\text{Molality of } C_2H_5OH = \frac{\text{moles of } C_2H_5OH}{\text{kilogram of } H_2O} = \frac{2.17 \times 10^{-2} \text{ mol}}{100.0 \text{ g} \times \dfrac{1 \text{ kg}}{1000 \text{ g}}}$$

$$= \frac{2.17 \times 10^{-2} \text{ mol}}{0.1000 \text{ kg}}$$

$$= 0.217 \text{ } m$$

See Exercises 11.25 through 11.27.

TABLE 11.2   The Molar Mass, Equivalent Mass, and Relationship of Molarity and Normality for Several Acids and Bases

Acid or Base	Molar Mass	Equivalent Mass	Relationship of Molarity and Normality
HCl	36.5	36.5	$1\,M = 1\,N$
H_2SO_4	98	$\dfrac{98}{2} = 49$	$1\,M = 2\,N$
NaOH	40	40	$1\,M = 1\,N$
$Ca(OH)_2$	74	$\dfrac{74}{2} = 37$	$1\,M = 2\,N$

The definition of an equivalent depends on the reaction taking place in the solution.

The quantity we call *equivalent mass* here traditionally has been called *equivalent weight.*

Oxidation–reduction half-reactions were discussed in Section 4.10.

Another concentration measure sometimes encountered is **normality** (symbolized by N). Normality is defined as the number of *equivalents* per liter of solution, where the definition of an equivalent depends on the reaction taking place in the solution. *For an acid–base reaction,* the equivalent is the mass of acid or base that can furnish or accept exactly 1 mole of protons (H^+ ions). In Table 11.2 note, for example, that the equivalent mass of sulfuric acid is the molar mass divided by 2, since each mole of H_2SO_4 can furnish 2 moles of protons. The equivalent mass of calcium hydroxide is also half the molar mass, since each mole of $Ca(OH)_2$ contains 2 moles of OH^- ions that can react with 2 moles of protons. The equivalent is defined so that 1 equivalent of acid will react with exactly 1 equivalent of base.

For oxidation–reduction reactions, the equivalent is defined as the quantity of oxidizing or reducing agent that can accept or furnish 1 mole of electrons. Thus 1 equivalent of reducing agent will react with exactly 1 equivalent of oxidizing agent. The equivalent mass of an oxidizing or reducing agent can be calculated from the number of electrons in its half-reaction. For example, MnO_4^- reacting in acidic solution absorbs five electrons to produce Mn^{2+}:

$$MnO_4^- + 5e^- + 8H^+ \longrightarrow Mn^{2+} + 4H_2O$$

Since the MnO_4^- ion present in 1 mole of $KMnO_4$ consumes 5 moles of electrons, the equivalent mass is the molar mass divided by 5:

$$\text{Equivalent mass of } KMnO_4 = \frac{\text{molar mass}}{5} = \frac{158\text{ g}}{5} = 31.6\text{ g}$$

Calculating Various Methods of Solution Composition from the Molarity

Sample Exercise 11.2

The electrolyte in automobile lead storage batteries is a 3.75 M sulfuric acid solution that has a density of 1.230 g/mL. Calculate the mass percent, molality, and normality of the sulfuric acid.

Solution

The density of the solution in grams per liter is

$$1.230\,\frac{g}{mL} \times \frac{1000\text{ mL}}{1\text{ L}} = 1.230 \times 10^3\text{ g/L}$$

Thus 1 liter of this solution contains 1230. g of the mixture of sulfuric acid and water. Since the solution is 3.75 M, we know that 3.75 mol H_2SO_4 is present per liter of solution. The number of grams of H_2SO_4 present is

$$3.75\text{ mol} \times \frac{98.1\text{ g }H_2SO_4}{1\text{ mol}} = 368\text{ g }H_2SO_4$$

A modern 12-volt lead storage battery of the type used in automobiles.

CHEMICAL IMPACT

Electronic Ink

The printed page has been a primary means of communication for over 3000 years, and researchers at the Massachusetts Institute of Technology (MIT) believe they have discovered why. It seems that the brain responds positively to fixed images on a sheet of paper, particularly those areas of the brain that store and process "spatial maps." In comparison, information displayed on computer screens or TV screens seems to lack some of the visual signals that stimulate the learning centers of the brain to retain knowledge. While modern technology provides us with many other media by which we can communicate, the appeal of written words on a piece of paper remains. Surprisingly, the technology of printing has changed very little since the invention of the printing press—that is, until now.

In the past several years Joseph M. Jacobson and his students at MIT have developed a prototype of a self-printing page. The key to this self-printing "paper" is microencapsulation technology—the same technology that is used in "carbonless" carbon paper and "scratch-and-sniff" cologne and perfume advertisements in magazines. Jacobson's system involves the use of millions of transparent fluid-filled capsules containing microscopic particles. These particles are colored and positively charged on one side and white and negatively charged on the other. When an electric field is selectively applied to the capsules, the white side of the microparticles can be oriented upward or the colored side can be caused to flip up. Appropriate application of an electric field can orient the particles in such a way as to produce words, and once the words have been created, virtually no more energy is needed to keep the particles in place. An image can be maintained on a page with consumption of only 50 millionths of an amp of power! The entire display is about 200 μm thick (2.5 times that of paper)

The amount of water present in 1 liter of solution is obtained from the difference

$$1230. \text{ g solution} - 368 \text{ g H}_2\text{SO}_4 = 862 \text{ g H}_2\text{O}$$

Since we now know the masses of the solute and solvent, we can calculate the mass percent.

$$\text{Mass percent H}_2\text{SO}_4 = \frac{\text{mass of H}_2\text{SO}_4}{\text{mass of solution}} \times 100\% = \frac{368 \text{ g}}{1230. \text{ g}} \times 100\%$$
$$= 29.9\% \text{ H}_2\text{SO}_4$$

From the moles of solute and the mass of solvent we can calculate the molality.

$$\text{Molality of H}_2\text{SO}_4 = \frac{\text{moles H}_2\text{SO}_4}{\text{kilogram of H}_2\text{O}}$$
$$= \frac{3.75 \text{ mol H}_2\text{SO}_4}{862 \text{ g H}_2\text{O} \times \dfrac{1 \text{ kg H}_2\text{O}}{1000 \text{ g H}_2\text{O}}} = 4.35 \text{ } m$$

Since each sulfuric acid molecule can furnish two protons, 1 mol H_2SO_4 represents 2 equivalents. Thus a solution with 3.75 mol H_2SO_4 per liter contains $2 \times 3.75 = 7.50$ equivalents per liter, and the normality is 7.50 N.

See Exercise 11.31.

11.2 The Energies of Solution Formation

Dissolving solutes in liquids is very common. We dissolve salt in the water used to cook vegetables, sugar in iced tea, stains in cleaning fluid, gaseous carbon dioxide in water to make soda water, ethanol in gasoline to make gasohol, and so on.

and is so flexible and durable that it can be curled around a pencil and can operate at temperatures from −4 to 158°F. Presently, print resolution is not as good as a modern laser printer, but reduction of the microencapsulated particles from 50 to 40 μm should produce print that rivals the quality of the laser printer.

The first commercial applications of this technology are expected to appear in retail stores across the country in the form of electronic signs that can be updated instantly from a central location. The present technology is a long way from being able to create electronic books, but this is the eventual goal of Jacobson's research team. It seems very likely that this electronic ink technology will contribute greatly to the evolution of the printed page over the next century.

Signs like this one created by E Ink are the first to use electronic ink, which can be updated from a computer inside the store or from a remote location.

DDT

Polar solvents dissolve polar solutes; nonpolar solvents dissolve nonpolar solutes.

Solubility is important in other ways. For example, because the pesticide DDT is fat-soluble, it is retained and concentrated in animal tissues, where it causes detrimental effects. This is why DDT, even though it is effective for killing mosquitos, has been banned in the United States. Also, the solubility of various vitamins is important in determining correct dosages. The insolubility of barium sulfate means it can be used safely to improve X rays of the gastrointestinal tract, even though Ba^{2+} ions are quite toxic.

What factors affect solubility? The cardinal rule of solubility is *like dissolves like*. We find that we must use a polar solvent to dissolve a polar or ionic solute and a nonpolar solvent to dissolve a nonpolar solute. Now we will try to understand why this behavior occurs. To simplify the discussion, we will assume that the formation of a liquid solution takes place in three distinct steps.

➡ 1 **Separating the solute into its individual components (expanding the solute).**

➡ 2 **Overcoming intermolecular forces in the solvent to make room for the solute (expanding the solvent).**

➡ 3 **Allowing the solute and solvent to interact to form the solution.**

These steps are illustrated in Fig. 11.1. Steps 1 and 2 require energy, since forces must be overcome to expand the solute and solvent. Step 3 usually releases energy. In other words, steps 1 and 2 are endothermic, and step 3 is often exothermic. The enthalpy change associated with the formation of the solution, called the **enthalpy (heat) of solution** (ΔH_{soln}), is the sum of the ΔH values for the steps:

$$\Delta H_{soln} = \Delta H_1 + \Delta H_2 + \Delta H_3$$

The enthalpy of solution is the sum of the energies used in expanding both solvent and solute and the energy of solvent–solute interaction.

where ΔH_{soln} may have a positive sign (energy absorbed) or a negative sign (energy released), as shown in Fig. 11.2.

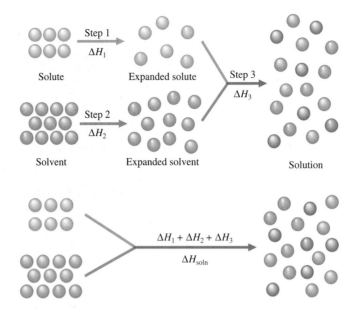

FIGURE 11.1
The formation of a liquid solution can be divided into three steps: (1) expanding the solute, (2) expanding the solvent, and (3) combining the expanded solute and solvent to form the solution.

ΔH_1 is expected to be small for nonpolar solutes but can be large for large molecules.

To illustrate the importance of the various energy terms in the equation for ΔH_{soln}, we will consider two specific cases. First, we know that oil is not soluble in water. When oil tankers leak, the petroleum forms an oil slick that floats on the water and is eventually carried onto the beaches. We can explain the immiscibility of oil and water by considering the energy terms involved. Oil is a mixture of nonpolar molecules that interact through London dispersion forces, which depend on molecule size. We expect ΔH_1 to be small for a typical nonpolar solute, but it will be relatively large for the large oil molecules. The term ΔH_3 will be small, since interactions between the nonpolar solute molecules and the polar water molecules will be negligible. However, ΔH_2 will be large and positive because it takes considerable energy to overcome the hydrogen bonding forces among the water molecules to expand the solvent. Thus ΔH_{soln} will be large and positive because of the ΔH_1 and ΔH_2 terms. Since a large amount of energy would have to be expended to form an oil–water solution, this process does not occur to any appreciable extent. These same arguments hold true for any nonpolar solute and polar solvent—the combination of a nonpolar solute and a highly polar solvent is not expected to produce a solution.

FIGURE 11.2
The heat of solution (a) ΔH_{soln} has a negative sign (the process is exothermic) if step 3 releases more energy than that required by steps 1 and 2. (b) ΔH_{soln} has a positive sign (the process is endothermic) if steps 1 and 2 require more energy than is released in step 3. (If the energy changes for steps 1 and 2 equal that for step 3, then ΔH_{soln} is zero.)

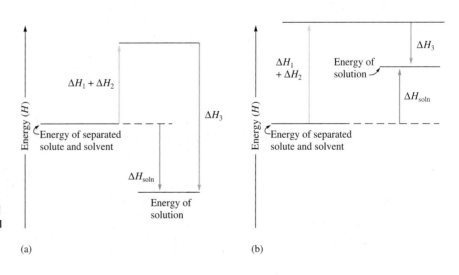

As a second case, let's consider the solubility of an ionic solute, such as sodium chloride, in water. Here the term ΔH_1 is large and positive because the strong ionic forces in the crystal must be overcome, and ΔH_2 is large and positive because hydrogen bonds must be broken in the water. Finally, ΔH_3 is large and negative because of the strong interactions between the ions and the water molecules. In fact, the exothermic and endothermic terms essentially cancel, as shown from the known values:

$$NaCl(s) \longrightarrow Na^+(g) + Cl^-(g) \qquad \Delta H_1 = 786 \text{ kJ/mol}$$
$$H_2O(l) + Na^+(g) + Cl^-(g) \longrightarrow Na^+(aq) + Cl^-(aq) \qquad \Delta H_{hyd} = \Delta H_2 + \Delta H_3$$
$$= -783 \text{ kJ/mol}$$

Here the **enthalpy (heat) of hydration** (ΔH_{hyd}) combines the terms ΔH_2 (for expanding the solvent) and ΔH_3 (for solvent–solute interactions). The heat of hydration represents the enthalpy change associated with the dispersal of a gaseous solute in water. Thus the heat of solution for dissolving sodium chloride is the sum of ΔH_1 and ΔH_{hyd}:

$$\Delta H_{soln} = 786 \text{ kJ/mol} - 783 \text{ kJ/mol} = 3 \text{ kJ/mol}$$

The factors that act as driving forces for a process are discussed more fully in Chapter 16.

Note that ΔH_{soln} is small but positive; the dissolving process requires a small amount of energy. Then why is NaCl so soluble in water? The answer lies in nature's tendency toward higher probability of the mixed state. That is, processes naturally run in the direction that leads to the most probable state. For example, imagine equal numbers of orange and yellow spheres separated by a partition, as shown in Fig. 11.3(a). If we remove the partition and shake the container, the spheres will mix [Fig. 11.3(b)], and no amount of shaking will cause them to return to the state of separated orange and yellow. Why? The mixed state is simply much more likely to occur (more probable) than the original separate state because there are many more ways of placing the spheres to give a mixed state than a separated state. This is a general principle. *One factor that favors a process is an increase in probability.*

But energy considerations are also important. *Processes that require large amounts of energy tend not to occur.* Since dissolving 1 mole of solid NaCl requires only a small amount of energy, the solution forms, presumably because of the large increase in the probability of the state when the solute and solvent are mixed.

The various possible cases for solution formation are summarized in Table 11.3. Note that in two cases, polar–polar and nonpolar–nonpolar, the heat of solution is expected to be small. In these cases, the solution forms because of the increase in the probability of the mixed state. In the other cases (polar–nonpolar and nonpolar–polar), the heat of solution is expected to be large and positive, and the large quantity of energy required acts to prevent the solution from forming. Although this discussion has greatly oversimplified the complex driving forces for solubility, these ideas are a useful starting point for understanding the observation that *like dissolves like.*

Gasoline floating on water. Since gasoline is nonpolar, it is immiscible with water, because water contains polar molecules.

FIGURE 11.3
(a) Orange and yellow spheres separated by a partition in a closed container. (b) The spheres after the partition is removed and the container has been shaken for some time.

(a)

(b)

TABLE 11.3 The Energy Terms for Various Types of Solutes and Solvents

	ΔH_1	ΔH_2	ΔH_3	ΔH_{soln}	Outcome
Polar solute, polar solvent	Large	Large	Large, negative	Small	Solution forms
Nonpolar solute, polar solvent	Small	Large	Small	Large, positive	No solution forms
Nonpolar solute, nonpolar solvent	Small	Small	Small	Small	Solution forms
Polar solute, nonpolar solvent	Large	Small	Small	Large, positive	No solution forms

Hexane

Liquid methanol

Grease

Sample Exercise 11.3

Differentiating Solvent Properties

Decide whether liquid hexane (C_6H_{14}) or liquid methanol (CH_3OH) is the more appropriate solvent for the substances grease ($C_{20}H_{42}$) and potassium iodide (KI).

Solution

Hexane is a nonpolar solvent because it contains C—H bonds. Thus hexane will work best for the nonpolar solute grease. Methanol has an O—H group that makes it significantly polar. Thus it will serve as the better solvent for the ionic solid KI.

See Exercises 11.37 through 11.39.

www. Visualization: Ammonia Fountain

www. Visualization: Micelle Formation: The Cleansing Action of Soap

11.3 Factors Affecting Solubility

Structure Effects

In the last section we saw that solubility is favored if the solute and solvent have similar polarities. Since it is the molecular structure that determines polarity, there should be a definite connection between structure and solubility. Vitamins provide an excellent example of the relationship among molecular structure, polarity, and solubility.

Recently, there has been considerable publicity about the pros and cons of consuming large quantities of vitamins. For example, large doses of vitamin C have been advocated to combat various illnesses, including the common cold. Vitamin E has been extolled as a youth-preserving elixir and a protector against the carcinogenic (cancer-causing) effects of certain chemicals. However, there are possible detrimental effects from taking large amounts of some vitamins, depending on their solubilities.

Vitamins can be divided into two classes: *fat-soluble* (vitamins A, D, E, and K) and *water-soluble* (vitamins B and C). The reason for the differing solubility characteristics can be seen by comparing the structures of vitamins A and C (Fig. 11.4). Vitamin A, composed mostly of carbon and hydrogen atoms that have similar electronegativities, is virtually nonpolar. This causes it to be soluble in nonpolar materials such as body fat, which is also largely composed of carbon and hydrogen, but not soluble in polar solvents such as water. On the other hand, vitamin C has many polar O—H and C—O bonds, making the molecule polar and thus water-soluble. We often describe nonpolar materials such as vitamin A as *hydrophobic* (water-fearing) and polar substances such as vitamin C as *hydrophilic* (water-loving).

Because of their solubility characteristics, the fat-soluble vitamins can build up in the fatty tissues of the body. This has both positive and negative effects. Since these vitamins

Vitamin A

Vitamin C

FIGURE 11.4
The molecular structures of (a) vitamin A (nonpolar, fat-soluble) and (b) vitamin C (polar, water-soluble). The circles in the structural formulas indicate polar bonds. Note that vitamin C contains far more polar bonds than vitamin A.

can be stored, the body can tolerate for a time a diet deficient in vitamins A, D, E, or K. Conversely, if excessive amounts of these vitamins are consumed, their buildup can lead to the illness *hypervitaminosis.*

In contrast, the water-soluble vitamins are excreted by the body and must be consumed regularly. This fact was first recognized when the British navy discovered that scurvy, a disease often suffered by sailors, could be prevented if the sailors regularly ate fresh limes (which are a good source of vitamin C) when aboard ship (hence the name "limey" for the British sailor).

Pressure Effects

While pressure has little effect on the solubilities of solids or liquids, it does significantly increase the solubility of a gas. Carbonated beverages, for example, are always bottled at high pressures of carbon dioxide to ensure a high concentration of carbon dioxide in the liquid. The fizzing that occurs when you open a can of soda results from the escape of gaseous carbon dioxide because under these conditions the pressure of CO_2 above the solution is now much lower than that used in the bottling process.

The increase in gas solubility with pressure can be understood from Fig. 11.5. Figure 11.5(a) shows a gas in equilibrium with a solution; that is, the gas molecules are entering and leaving the solution at the same rate. If the pressure is suddenly increased [Fig. 11.5(b)], the number of gas molecules per unit volume increases, and the gas enters the solution at a higher rate than it leaves. As the concentration of dissolved gas increases, the rate of the escape of the gas also increases until a new equilibrium is reached [Fig. 11.5(c)], where the solution contains more dissolved gas than before.

Carbonation in a bottle of soda.

CHEMICAL IMPACT

Ionic Liquids?

So far in this text, you have seen that ionic substances are stable solids with high melting points. For example, sodium chloride has a melting point near 800°C. One of the "hottest" areas of current chemical research is ionic liquids—substances composed of ions that are liquids at normal temperatures and pressures. This unusual behavior results from the differences in the sizes of the anions and cations in the ionic liquids. Dozens of small anions, such as BF_4^- (tetrafluoroborate) or PF_6^- (hexafluorophosphate), can be paired with thousands of large cations, such as 1-hexyl-3-methylimidazolium or 1-butyl-3-methylimidazolium (parts a and b respectively, in the accompanying figure). These substances remain liquids because the bulky, asymmetrical cations do not pack together efficiently with the smaller,

symmetrical anions. In contrast, in sodium chloride the ions can pack very efficiently to form a compact, orderly arrangement, leading to maximum cation–anion attractions and thus a high melting point.

The excitement being generated by these ionic liquids arises from many factors. For one thing, almost an infinite variety of ionic liquids are possible due to the large variety of bulky cations and small anions available. According to Kenneth R. Seddon, Director of QUILL (Queen's University Ionic Liquid Laboratory) in Northern Ireland, a *trillion* ionic liquids are possible. Another great advantage of these liquids is their long liquid range, typically from −100°C to 200°C.

In addition, the cations in the liquids can be designed to perform specific functions. For example, chemist James

The relationship between gas pressure and the concentration of dissolved gas is given by **Henry's law:**

$$C = kP$$

where C represents the concentration of the dissolved gas, k is a constant characteristic of a particular solution, and P represents the partial pressure of the gaseous solute above the solution. In words, Henry's law states that *the amount of a gas dissolved in a solution is directly proportional to the pressure of the gas above the solution.*

Henry's law is obeyed most accurately for dilute solutions of gases that do not dissociate in or react with the solvent. For example, Henry's law is obeyed by oxygen gas in water, but it does *not* correctly represent the behavior of gaseous hydrogen chloride in water because of the dissociation reaction

William Henry (1774–1836), a close friend of John Dalton, formulated his law in 1801.

Henry's law holds only when there is no chemical reaction between the solute and solvent.

$$HCl(g) \xrightarrow{\text{H}_2\text{O}} H^+(aq) + Cl^-(aq)$$

FIGURE 11.5
(a) A gaseous solute in equilibrium with a solution. (b) The piston is pushed in, which increases the pressure of the gas and the number of gas molecules per unit volume. This causes an increase in the rate at which the gas enters the solution, so the concentration of dissolved gas increases. (c) The greater gas concentration in the solution causes an increase in the rate of escape. A new equilibrium is reached.

(a)

(b)

(c)

Solution

H. Davis, of the University of South Alabama in Mobile, has designed various cations that will attract potentially harmful ions such as mercury, cadmium, uranium, and americium (the latter two are commonly found in nuclear waste materials) and leach them out of contaminated solutions. Davis has also developed cations that will remove H_2S (which produces SO_2 when the gas is burned) and CO_2 (which does not burn) from natural gas. Potentially, these ionic solutions might also be used to remove CO_2 from the exhaust gases of fossil-fuel–burning power plants to lessen the "greenhouse effect."

(a)　　　　　　　　　　　　　　　　(b)

The biggest obstacle to the widespread use of ionic liquids is their cost. Normal organic solvents used in industry typically cost a few cents per liter, but ionic liquids can cost hundreds of times that amount. However, the environmentally friendly nature of ionic liquids (they produce no vapors because the ions are not volatile) and the flexibility of these substances as reaction media make them very attractive. As a consequence, efforts are under way to make their use economically feasible.

The term *ionic liquid* may have seemed like an oxymoron in the past, but these substances have a very promising future.

Sample Exercise 11.4　　**Calculations Using Henry's Law**

A certain soft drink is bottled so that a bottle at 25°C contains CO_2 gas at a pressure of 5.0 atm over the liquid. Assuming that the partial pressure of CO_2 in the atmosphere is 4.0×10^{-4} atm, calculate the equilibrium concentrations of CO_2 in the soda both before and after the bottle is opened. The Henry's law constant for CO_2 in aqueous solution is 3.1×10^{-2} mol/L · atm at 25°C.

Solution

We can write Henry's law for CO_2 as

$$C_{CO_2} = k_{CO_2}P_{CO_2}$$

where $k_{CO_2} = 3.1 \times 10^{-2}$ mol/L · atm. In the *unopened* bottle, $P_{CO_2} = 5.0$ atm and

$$C_{CO_2} = k_{CO_2}P_{CO_2} = (3.1 \times 10^{-2} \text{ mol/L} \cdot \text{atm})(5.0 \text{ atm}) = 0.16 \text{ mol/L}$$

In the *opened* bottle, the CO_2 in the soda eventually reaches equilibrium with the atmospheric CO_2, so $P_{CO_2} = 4.0 \times 10^{-4}$ atm and

$$C_{CO_2} = k_{CO_2}P_{CO_2} = \left(3.1 \times 10^{-2} \frac{\text{mol}}{\text{L} \cdot \text{atm}}\right)(4.0 \times 10^{-4} \text{ atm}) = 1.2 \times 10^{-5} \text{ mol/L}$$

Note the large change in concentration of CO_2. This is why soda goes "flat" after being open for a while.

See Exercises 11.43 and 11.44.

Temperature Effects (for Aqueous Solutions)

ΔH°_{soln} refers to the formation of a 1.0 *M* ideal solution and is not necessarily relevant to the process of dissolving a solid in a saturated solution. Thus ΔH°_{soln} is of limited use in predicting the variation of solubility with temperature.

Everyday experiences of dissolving substances such as sugar may lead you to think that solubility always increases with temperature. This is not the case. The dissolving of a solid occurs *more rapidly* at higher temperatures, but the amount of solid that can be dissolved may increase or decrease with increasing temperature. The effect of temperature on the solubility in water of several solids is shown in Fig. 11.6. Note that although the solubility of most solids in water increases with temperature, the solubilities of some substances (such as sodium sulfate and cerium sulfate) decrease with increasing temperature.

Predicting the temperature dependence of solubility is very difficult. For example, although there is some correlation between the sign of ΔH°_{soln} and the variation of solubility with temperature, important exceptions exist.* The only sure way to determine the temperature dependence of a solid's solubility is by experiment.

The behavior of gases dissolving in water appears less complex. The solubility of a gas in water typically decreases with increasing temperature,† as is shown for several cases in Fig. 11.7. This temperature effect has important environmental implications because of the widespread use of water from lakes and rivers for industrial cooling. After being used, the water is returned to its natural source at a higher than ambient temperature (**thermal pollution** has occurred). Because it is warmer, this water contains less than the normal concentration of oxygen and is also less dense; it tends to "float" on the colder water below, thus blocking normal oxygen absorption. This effect can be especially important in deep lakes. The warm upper layer can seriously decrease the amount of oxygen available to aquatic life in the deeper layers of the lake.

The decreasing solubility of gases with increasing temperature is also responsible for the formation of *boiler scale*. As we will see in more detail in Chapter 14, the bicarbonate ion is formed when carbon dioxide is dissolved in water containing the carbonate ion:

$$CO_3^{2-}(aq) + CO_2(aq) + H_2O(l) \longrightarrow 2HCO_3^-(aq)$$

When the water also contains Ca^{2+} ions, this reaction is especially important—calcium bicarbonate is soluble in water, but calcium carbonate is insoluble. When the water is heated, the carbon dioxide is driven off. For the system to replace the lost carbon dioxide, the reverse reaction must occur:

$$2HCO_3^-(aq) \longrightarrow H_2O(l) + CO_2(aq) + CO_3^{2-}(aq)$$

This reaction, however, also increases the concentration of carbonate ions, causing solid calcium carbonate to form. This solid is the boiler scale that coats the walls of containers such as industrial boilers and tea kettles. Boiler scale reduces the efficiency of heat transfer and can lead to blockage of pipes (see Fig. 11.8).

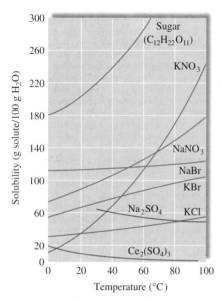

FIGURE 11.6
The solubilities of several solids as a function of temperature. Note that while most substances become more soluble in water with increasing temperature, sodium sulfate and cerium sulfate become less soluble.

FIGURE 11.7
The solubilities of several gases in water as a function of temperature at a constant pressure of 1 atm of gas above the solution.

FIGURE 11.8
A pipe with accumulated mineral deposits. The cross section clearly indicates the reduction in pipe capacity.

---

*For more information see R. S. Treptow, "Le Châtelier's Principle Applied to the Temperature Dependence of Solubility," *J. Chem. Ed.* **61** (1984): 499.
†The opposite behavior is observed for most nonaqueous solvents.

CHEMICAL IMPACT

The Lake Nyos Tragedy

On August 21, 1986, a cloud of gas suddenly boiled from Lake Nyos in Cameroon, killing nearly 2000 people. Although at first it was speculated that the gas was hydrogen sulfide, it now seems clear it was carbon dioxide. What would cause Lake Nyos to emit this huge, suffocating cloud of CO_2? Although the answer may never be known for certain, many scientists believe that the lake suddenly "turned over," bringing to the surface water that contained huge quantities of dissolved carbon dioxide. Lake Nyos is a deep lake that is thermally stratified: Layers of warm, less dense water near the surface float on the colder, denser water layers near the lake's bottom. Under normal conditions the lake stays this way; there is little mixing among the different layers. Scientists believe that over hundreds or thousands of years, carbon dioxide gas had seeped into the cold water at the lake's bottom and dissolved in great amounts because of the large pressure of CO_2 present (in accordance with Henry's law). For some reason on August 21, 1986, the lake apparently suffered an overturn, possibly due to wind or to unusual cooling of the lake's surface by monsoon clouds. This caused water that was greatly supersaturated with CO_2 to reach the surface and release tremendous quantities of gaseous CO_2 that suffocated thousands of humans and animals before they knew what hit them—a tragic, monumental illustration of Henry's law.

Lake Nyos in Cameroon.

Since 1986 the scientists studying Lake Nyos and nearby Lake Monoun have observed a rapid recharging of the CO_2 levels in the deep waters of these lakes, causing concern that another deadly gas release could occur at any time. Apparently the only way to prevent such a disaster is to pump away the CO_2-charged deep water in the two lakes. Scientists at a conference to study this problem in 1994 recommended such a solution, but it has not yet been funded by Cameroon.

11.4 The Vapor Pressures of Solutions

Liquid solutions have physical properties significantly different from those of the pure solvent, a fact that has great practical importance. For example, we add antifreeze to the water in a car's cooling system to prevent freezing in winter and boiling in summer. We also melt ice on sidewalks and streets by spreading salt. These preventive measures work because of the solute's effect on the solvent's properties.

To explore how a nonvolatile solute affects a solvent, we will consider the experiment represented in Fig. 11.9, in which a sealed container encloses a beaker containing an aqueous sulfuric acid solution and a beaker containing pure water. Gradually, the volume of the sulfuric acid solution increases and the volume of the pure water decreases. Why? We can explain this observation if the vapor pressure of the pure solvent is greater than that of the solution. Under these conditions, the pressure of vapor necessary to achieve equilibrium with the pure solvent is greater than that required to reach equilibrium with the aqueous acid solution. Thus, as the pure solvent emits vapor to attempt to reach equilibrium, the aqueous sulfuric acid solution absorbs vapor to try to lower the vapor pressure toward its equilibrium value. This process results in a net transfer of water from the pure water through the vapor phase to the sulfuric acid solution. The system can reach an equilibrium vapor pressure only when all the water is transferred to the solution. This

A nonvolatile solute has no tendency to escape from solution into the vapor phase.

FIGURE 11.9
An aqueous solution and pure water in a closed environment. (a) Initial stage. (b) After a period of time, the water is transferred to the solution.

(a) Water   Aqueous solution

(b) Aqueous solution

experiment is just one of many observations indicating that the presence of a *nonvolatile solute lowers the vapor pressure of a solvent.*

We can account for this behavior in terms of the simple model shown in Fig. 11.10. The dissolved nonvolatile solute decreases the number of solvent molecules per unit volume and it should proportionately lower the escaping tendency of the solvent molecules. For example, in a solution consisting of half nonvolatile solute molecules and half solvent molecules, we might expect the observed vapor pressure to be half that of the pure solvent, since only half as many molecules can escape. In fact, this is what is observed.

Detailed studies of the vapor pressures of solutions containing nonvolatile solutes were carried out by François M. Raoult (1830–1901). His results are described by the equation known as **Raoult's law:**

$$P_{soln} = \chi_{solvent} P^0_{solvent}$$

where P_{soln} is the observed vapor pressure of the solution, $\chi_{solvent}$ is the mole fraction of solvent, and $P^0_{solvent}$ is the vapor pressure of the pure solvent. Note that for a solution of half solute and half solvent molecules, $\chi_{solvent}$ is 0.5, so the vapor pressure of the solution is half that of the pure solvent. On the other hand, for a solution in which three-fourths of the solution molecules are solvent, $\chi_{solvent} = \frac{3}{4} = 0.75$, and $P_{soln} = 0.75 P^0_{solvent}$. The idea is that the nonvolatile solute simply dilutes the solvent.

Visualization: Vapor Pressure Lowering: Liquid/Vapor Equilibrium
Visualization: Vapor Pressure Lowering: Addition of a Solute
Visualization: Vapor Pressure Lowering: Solution/Vapor Equilibrium

FIGURE 11.10
The presence of a nonvolatile solute inhibits the escape of solvent molecules from the liquid and so lowers the vapor pressure of the solvent.

Pure solvent   Solution with a nonvolatile solute

Raoult's law states that the vapor pressure of a solution is directly proportional to the mole fraction of solvent present.

Raoult's law is a linear equation of the form $y = mx + b$, where $y = P_{soln}$, $x = \chi_{solvent}$, $m = P^0_{solvent}$, and $b = 0$. Thus a plot of P_{soln} versus $\chi_{solvent}$ gives a straight line with a slope equal to $P^0_{solvent}$, as shown in Fig. 11.11.

Sample Exercise 11.5

Calculating the Vapor Pressure of a Solution

Calculate the expected vapor pressure at 25°C for a solution prepared by dissolving 158.0 g of common table sugar (sucrose, molar mass = 342.3 g/mol) in 643.5 cm³ of water. At 25°C, the density of water is 0.9971 g/cm³ and the vapor pressure is 23.76 torr.

Solution

We will use Raoult's law in the form

$$P_{soln} = \chi_{H_2O} P^0_{H_2O}$$

To calculate the mole fraction of water in the solution, we must first determine the number of moles of sucrose:

$$\text{Moles of sucrose} = 158.0 \text{ g sucrose} \times \frac{1 \text{ mol sucrose}}{342.3 \text{ g sucrose}}$$

$$= 0.4616 \text{ mol sucrose}$$

To determine the moles of water present, we first convert volume to mass using the density:

$$643.5 \text{ cm}^3 \text{ H}_2\text{O} \times \frac{0.9971 \text{ g H}_2\text{O}}{\text{cm}^3 \text{ H}_2\text{O}} = 641.6 \text{ g H}_2\text{O}$$

The number of moles of water is therefore

$$641.6 \text{ g H}_2\text{O} \times \frac{1 \text{ mol H}_2\text{O}}{18.01 \text{ g H}_2\text{O}} = 35.63 \text{ mol H}_2\text{O}$$

The mole fraction of water in the solution is

$$\chi_{H_2O} = \frac{\text{mol H}_2\text{O}}{\text{mol H}_2\text{O} + \text{mol sucrose}} = \frac{35.63 \text{ mol}}{35.63 \text{ mol} + 0.4616 \text{ mol}}$$

$$= \frac{35.63 \text{ mol}}{36.09 \text{ mol}} = 0.9873$$

Then
$$P_{soln} = \chi_{H_2O} P^0_{H_2O} = (0.9873)(23.76 \text{ torr}) = 23.46 \text{ torr}$$

Thus the vapor pressure of water has been lowered from 23.76 torr in the pure state to 23.46 torr in the solution. The vapor pressure has been lowered by 0.30 torr.

See Exercises 11.45 and 11.46.

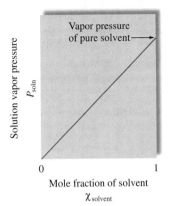

FIGURE 11.11
For a solution that obeys Raoult's law, a plot of P_{soln} versus $\chi_{solvent}$ gives a straight line.

The phenomenon of the lowering of the vapor pressure gives us a convenient way to "count" molecules and thus provides a means for experimentally determining molar masses. Suppose a certain mass of a compound is dissolved in a solvent and the vapor pressure of the resulting solution is measured. Using Raoult's law, we can determine the number of moles of solute present. Since the mass of this number of moles is known, we can calculate the molar mass.

The lowering of vapor pressure depends on the number of solute particles present in the solution.

We also can use vapor pressure measurements to characterize solutions. For example, 1 mole of sodium chloride dissolved in water lowers the vapor pressure approximately twice as much as expected because the solid has two ions per formula unit, which separate when it dissolves. Thus vapor pressure measurements can give valuable information about the nature of the solute after it dissolves.

CHEMICAL IMPACT

Spray Power

Products in aerosol cans are widely used in our society. We use hairsprays, mouth sprays, shaving cream, whipped cream, spray paint, spray cleaners, and many others. As in the case of most consumer products, chemistry plays an important role in making aerosol products work.

An aerosol is a mixture of small particles (solids or liquids) dispersed in some sort of medium (a gas or a liquid). An inspection of the ingredients in an aerosol can reveals a long list of chemical substances, all of which fall into one of three categories: (1) an active ingredient, (2) an inactive ingredient, or (3) a propellant. The active ingredients perform the functions for which the product was purchased (for example, the resins in hairspray). It is very important that the contents of an aerosol can be chemically compatible. If an undesired chemical reaction were to occur inside the can, it is likely that the product would be unable to perform its function. The inactive ingredients serve to keep the product properly mixed and prevent chemical reactions within the can prior to application. The propellant delivers the product out of the can.

Most aerosol products contain liquefied hydrocarbon propellants* such as propane (C_3H_8) and butane (C_4H_{10}). While these molecules are extremely flammable, they are excellent propellants, and they also help to disperse and mix the components of the aerosol can as they are delivered. These propellants have critical temperatures above room temperature,

Insecticide is sprayed from an aerosol can.

*For foods delivered by aerosol cans, propane and butane are obviously not appropriate propellants. For substances such as whipped cream, the propellant N_2O is often used.

| Sample Exercise 11.6 | Calculating the Vapor Pressure of a Solution Containing Ionic Solute |

Predict the vapor pressure of a solution prepared by mixing 35.0 g solid Na_2SO_4 (molar mass = 142 g/mol) with 175 g water at 25°C. The vapor pressure of pure water at 25°C is 23.76 torr.

Solution

First, we need to know the mole fraction of H_2O.

$$n_{H_2O} = 175 \text{ g } H_2O \times \frac{1 \text{ mol } H_2O}{18.0 \text{ g } H_2O} = 9.72 \text{ mol } H_2O$$

$$n_{Na_2SO_4} = 35.0 \text{ g } Na_2SO_4 \times \frac{1 \text{ mol } Na_2SO_4}{142 \text{ g } Na_2SO_4} = 0.246 \text{ mol } Na_2SO_4$$

It is essential to recognize that when 1 mole of solid Na_2SO_4 dissolves, it produces 2 mol Na^+ ions and 1 mol SO_4^{2-} ions. Thus the number of solute particles present in this solution is three times the number of moles of solute dissolved:

$$n_{solute} = 3(0.246) = 0.738 \text{ mol}$$

$$\chi_{H_2O} = \frac{n_{H_2O}}{n_{solute} + n_{H_2O}} = \frac{9.72 \text{ mol}}{0.738 \text{ mol} + 9.72 \text{ mol}} = \frac{9.72}{10.458} = 0.929$$

which means that the intermolecular forces among their molecules are strong enough to form a liquid when pressure is applied. In the highly pressurized aerosol can, the liquid phase of the propellant is in equilibrium with the gaseous phase of the propellant in the head space of the can. The ability of the propellant to maintain this equilibrium is the key to how the aerosol can works. All aerosol cans are constructed in a similar way (see accompanying diagram). At the top of the can is a valve (acts to open and seal the can) and an actuator (to open the valve). Pushing the actuator opens the valve, and the propellant gas escapes through a long tube (the dip tube) that extends from the bottom of the can. With the valve open, the propellant, at a greater pressure than the atmosphere, escapes through the dip tube, carrying the active ingredient(s) with it. The rapidly expanding gas propels the contents from the can and in some instances (for example, shaving cream, carpet shampoo) produces a foam. After each use, the remaining propellant in the can reestablishes equilibrium between the liquid and gaseous phases, keeping the pressure constant within the can as long as sufficient propellant remains. The trick is to have the active and inactive ingredients and the propellant run out at the same time. Given the nature of the most common propellants, you can understand the warning about not putting the "empty" cans in a fire.

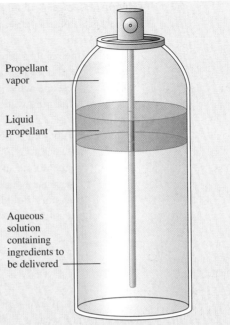

An aerosol can for delivery of an active ingredient dissolved in an aqueous solution.

Now we can use Raoult's law to predict the vapor pressure:

$$P_{soln} = \chi_{H_2O} P^0_{H_2O} = (0.929)(23.76 \text{ torr}) = 22.1 \text{ torr}$$

See Exercise 11.48.

Nonideal Solutions

So far we have assumed that the solute is nonvolatile and so does not contribute to the vapor pressure over the solution. However, for liquid–liquid solutions where both components are volatile, a modified form of Raoult's law applies:

$$P_{TOTAL} = P_A + P_B = \chi_A P^0_A + \chi_B P^0_B$$

where P_{TOTAL} represents the total vapor pressure of a solution containing A and B, χ_A and χ_B are the mole fractions of A and B, P^0_A and P^0_B are the vapor pressures of pure A and pure B, and P_A and P_B are the partial pressures resulting from molecules of A and of B in the vapor above the solution (see Fig. 11.12).

FIGURE 11.12
When a solution contains two volatile components, both contribute to the total vapor pressure. Note that in this case the solution contains equal numbers of the components and ◐ but the vapor contains more ◐ than ◐. This means that component ◐ is more volatile (has a higher vapor pressure as a pure liquid) than component ◐.

A liquid–liquid solution that obeys Raoult's law is called an **ideal solution.** Raoult's law is to solutions what the ideal gas law is to gases. As with gases, ideal behavior for solutions is never perfectly achieved but is sometimes closely approached. Nearly ideal behavior is often observed when the solute–solute, solvent–solvent, and solute–solvent interactions are very similar. That is, in solutions where the solute and solvent are very much alike, the solute simply acts to dilute the solvent. However, if the solvent has a special affinity for the solute, such as if hydrogen bonding occurs, the tendency of the solvent molecules to escape will be lowered more than expected. The observed vapor pressure will be *lower* than the value predicted by Raoult's law; there will be a *negative deviation from Raoult's law.*

When a solute and solvent release large quantities of energy in the formation of a solution, that is, when ΔH_{soln} is large and negative, we can assume that strong interactions exist between the solute and solvent. In this case we expect a negative deviation from Raoult's law, because both components will have a lower escaping tendency in the solution than in the pure liquids. This behavior is illustrated by an acetone–water solution, where the molecules can hydrogen-bond effectively:

Strong solute–solvent interaction gives a vapor pressure lower than that predicted by Raoult's law.

$$CH_3 \\ \diagdown \\ C=O\text{---}H\text{---}O \\ \diagup \diagup \\ CH_3 \delta- \delta+ H$$

In contrast, if two liquids mix endothermically, it indicates that the solute–solvent interactions are weaker than the interactions among the molecules in the pure liquids. More energy is required to expand the liquids than is released when the liquids are mixed. In this case the molecules in the solution have a higher tendency to escape than expected, and *positive* deviations from Raoult's law are observed (see Fig. 11.13). An example of this case is provided by a solution of ethanol and hexane, whose Lewis structures are as follows:

Ethanol   Hexane

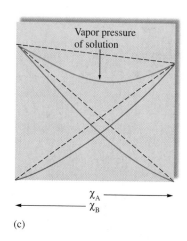

(a)   (b)   (c)

FIGURE 11.13

Vapor pressure for a solution of two volatile liquids. (a) The behavior predicted for an ideal liquid–liquid solution by Raoult's law. (b) A solution for which P_{TOTAL} is larger than the value calculated from Raoult's law. This solution shows a positive deviation from Raoult's law. (c) A solution for which P_{TOTAL} is smaller than the value calculated from Raoult's law. This solution shows a negative deviation from Raoult's law.

TABLE 11.4   Summary of the Behavior of Various Types of Solutions

Interactive Forces Between Solute (A) and Solvent (B) Particles	ΔH_{soln}	ΔT for Solution Formation	Deviation from Raoult's Law	Example
$A \leftrightarrow A, B \leftrightarrow B \equiv A \leftrightarrow B$	Zero	Zero	None (ideal solution)	Benzene–toluene
$A \leftrightarrow A, B \leftrightarrow B < A \leftrightarrow B$	Negative (exothermic)	Positive	Negative	Acetone–water
$A \leftrightarrow A, B \leftrightarrow B > A \leftrightarrow B$	Positive (endothermic)	Negative	Positive	Ethanol–hexane

Benzene   Toluene

The polar ethanol and the nonpolar hexane molecules are not able to interact effectively. Thus the enthalpy of solution is positive, as is the deviation from Raoult's law.

Finally, for a solution of very similar liquids, such as benzene and toluene (shown in margin), the enthalpy of solution is very close to zero, and thus the solution closely obeys Raoult's law (ideal behavior).

A summary of the behavior of various types of solutions is given in Table 11.4.

Calculating the Vapor Pressure of a Solution Containing Two Liquids

Sample Exercise 11.7

Acetone

Chloroform

A solution is prepared by mixing 5.81 g acetone (C_3H_6O, molar mass = 58.1 g/mol) and 11.9 g chloroform ($HCCl_3$, molar mass = 119.4 g/mol). At 35°C, this solution has a total vapor pressure of 260. torr. Is this an ideal solution? The vapor pressures of pure acetone and pure chloroform at 35°C are 345 and 293 torr, respectively.

Solution

To decide whether this solution behaves ideally, we first calculate the expected vapor pressure using Raoult's law:

$$P_{TOTAL} = \chi_A P_A^0 + \chi_C P_C^0$$

where A stands for acetone and C stands for chloroform. The calculated value can then be compared with the observed vapor pressure.

First, we must calculate the number of moles of acetone and chloroform:

$$5.81 \text{ g acetone} \times \frac{1 \text{ mol acetone}}{58.1 \text{ g acetone}} = 0.100 \text{ mol acetone}$$

$$11.9 \text{ g chloroform} \times \frac{1 \text{ mol chloroform}}{119 \text{ g chloroform}} = 0.100 \text{ mol chloroform}$$

Since the solution contains equal numbers of moles of acetone and chloroform, that is,

$$\chi_A = 0.500 \quad \text{and} \quad \chi_C = 0.500$$

the expected vapor pressure is

$$P_{TOTAL} = (0.500)(345 \text{ torr}) + (0.500)(293 \text{ torr}) = 319 \text{ torr}$$

In this case the usually nonpolar C—H bond is strongly polarized by the three attached, highly electronegative chlorine atoms, thus producing hydrogen bonding.

Comparing this value with the observed pressure of 260. torr shows that the solution does not behave ideally. The observed value is lower than that expected. This negative deviation from Raoult's law can be explained in terms of the hydrogen bonding interaction

$$
\begin{array}{c}
CH_3 \\
 \diagdown \\
 C{=}O\text{---}H{-}C{-}Cl \\
 \diagup | \\
CH_3 \delta- \delta+ Cl
\end{array}
$$

Acetone   Chloroform

which lowers the tendency of these molecules to escape from the solution.

See Exercises 11.55 and 11.56.

11.5 Boiling-Point Elevation and Freezing-Point Depression

In the preceding section we saw how a solute affects the vapor pressure of a liquid solvent. Because changes of state depend on vapor pressure, the presence of a solute also affects the freezing point and boiling point of a solvent. Freezing-point depression, boiling-point elevation, and osmotic pressure (discussed in Section 11.6) are called **colligative properties.** As we will see, they are grouped together because they depend only on the number, and not on the identity, of the solute particles in an ideal solution. Because of their direct relationship to the number of solute particles, the colligative properties are very useful for characterizing the nature of a solute after it is dissolved in a solvent and for determining molar masses of substances.

Normal boiling point was defined in Section 10.8.

Visualization: Boiling-Point Elevation: Liquid/Vapor Equilibrium
Visualization: Boiling-Point Elevation: Addition of a Solute
Visualization: Boiling-Point Elevation: Solution/Vapor Equilibrium

Boiling-Point Elevation

The normal boiling point of a liquid occurs at the temperature where the vapor pressure is equal to 1 atmosphere. We have seen that a nonvolatile solute lowers the vapor pressure of the solvent. Therefore, such a solution must be heated to a higher temperature than the boiling point of the pure solvent to reach a vapor pressure of 1 atmosphere. This means that *a nonvolatile solute elevates the boiling point of the solvent.* Figure 11.14 shows the phase diagram for an aqueous solution containing a nonvolatile solute. Note that the liquid/vapor line is shifted to higher temperatures than those for pure water.

FIGURE 11.14
Phase diagrams for pure water (red lines) and for an aqueous solution containing a nonvolatile solute (blue lines). Note that the boiling point of the solution is higher than that of pure water. Conversely, the freezing point of the solution is lower than that of pure water. The effect of a nonvolatile solute is to extend the liquid range of a solvent.

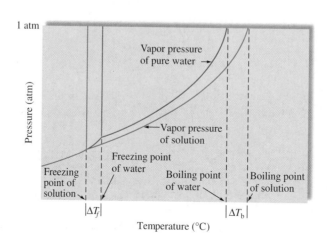

TABLE 11.5 Molal Boiling-Point Elevation Constants (K_b) and Freezing-Point Depression Constants (K_f) for Several Solvents

Solvent	Boiling Point (°C)	K_b (°C · kg/mol)	Freezing Point (°C)	K_f (°C · kg/mol)
Water (H_2O)	100.0	0.51	0	1.86
Carbon tetrachloride (CCl_4)	76.5	5.03	−22.99	30.
Chloroform ($CHCl_3$)	61.2	3.63	−63.5	4.70
Benzene (C_6H_6)	80.1	2.53	5.5	5.12
Carbon disulfide (CS_2)	46.2	2.34	−111.5	3.83
Ethyl ether ($C_4H_{10}O$)	34.5	2.02	−116.2	1.79
Camphor ($C_{10}H_{16}O$)	208.0	5.95	179.8	40.

As you might expect, the magnitude of the boiling-point elevation depends on the concentration of the solute. The change in boiling point can be represented by the equation

$$\Delta T = K_b m_{solute}$$

where ΔT is the boiling-point elevation, or the difference between the boiling point of the solution and that of the pure solvent, K_b is a constant that is characteristic of the solvent and is called the **molal boiling-point elevation constant,** and m_{solute} is the *molality* of the solute in the solution.

Values of K_b for some common solvents are given in Table 11.5. The molar mass of a solute can be determined from the observed boiling-point elevation, as shown in Sample Exercise 11.8.

Sample Exercise 11.8

Calculating the Molar Mass by Boiling-Point Elevation

A solution was prepared by dissolving 18.00 g glucose in 150.0 g water. The resulting solution was found to have a boiling point of 100.34°C. Calculate the molar mass of glucose. Glucose is a molecular solid that is present as individual molecules in solution.

Solution

We make use of the equation

$$\Delta T = K_b m_{solute}$$

where
$$\Delta T = 100.34°C - 100.00°C = 0.34°C$$

From Table 11.5, for water $K_b = 0.51$. The molality of this solution then can be calculated by rearranging the boiling-point elevation equation to give

$$m_{solute} = \frac{\Delta T}{K_b} = \frac{0.34°C}{0.51°C \cdot kg/mol} = 0.67 \text{ mol/kg}$$

The solution was prepared using 0.1500 kg water. Using the definition of molality, we can find the number of moles of glucose in the solution.

$$m_{solute} = 0.67 \text{ mol/kg} = \frac{\text{mol solute}}{\text{kg solvent}} = \frac{n_{glucose}}{0.1500 \text{ kg}}$$

$$n_{glucose} = (0.67 \text{ mol/kg})(0.1500 \text{ kg}) = 0.10 \text{ mol}$$

Thus 0.10 mol glucose has a mass of 18.00 g, and 1.0 mol glucose has a mass of 180 g (10×18.00 g). The molar mass of glucose is 180 g/mol.

See Exercise 11.58.

Sugar dissolved in water to make candy causes the boiling point to be elevated above 100°C.

Melting point and *freezing point* both refer to the temperature where the solid and liquid coexist.

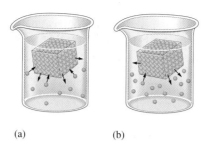

FIGURE 11.15
(a) Ice in equilibrium with liquid water.
(b) Ice in equilibrium with liquid water containing a dissolved solute (shown in pink).

(a)   (b)

Freezing-Point Depression

Visualization: Freezing-Point Depression: Solid/Liquid Equilibrium
Visualization: Freezing-Point Depression: Addition of a Solute
Visualization: Freezing-Point Depression: Solid/Solution Equilibrium

When a solute is dissolved in a solvent, the freezing point of the solution is lower than that of the pure solvent. Why? Recall that the vapor pressures of ice and liquid water are the same at 0°C. Suppose a solute is dissolved in water. The resulting solution will not freeze at 0°C because *the water in the solution has a lower vapor pressure than that of pure ice.* No ice will form under these conditions. However, the vapor pressure of ice decreases more rapidly than that of liquid water as the temperature decreases. Therefore, as the solution is cooled, the vapor pressure of the ice and that of the liquid water in the solution will eventually become equal. The temperature at which this occurs is the new freezing point of the solution and is below 0°C. The freezing point has been *depressed.*

We can account for this behavior in terms of the simple model shown in Fig. 11.15. The presence of the solute lowers the rate at which molecules in the liquid return to the solid state. Thus, for an aqueous solution, only the liquid state is found at 0°C. As the solution is cooled, the rate at which water molecules leave the solid ice decreases until this rate and the rate of formation of ice become equal and equilibrium is reached. This is the freezing point of the water in the solution.

Because a solute lowers the freezing point of water, compounds such as sodium chloride and calcium chloride are often spread on streets and sidewalks to prevent ice from forming in freezing weather. Of course, if the outside temperature is lower than the freezing point of the resulting salt solution, ice forms anyway. So this procedure is not effective at extremely cold temperatures.

The solid/liquid line for an aqueous solution is shown on the phase diagram for water in Fig. 11.14. Since the presence of a solute elevates the boiling point and depresses the freezing point of the solvent, adding a solute has the effect of extending the liquid range.

The equation for freezing-point depression is analogous to that for boiling-point elevation:

$$\Delta T = K_f m_{solute}$$

where ΔT is the freezing-point depression, or the difference between the freezing point of the pure solvent and that of the solution, and K_f is a constant that is characteristic of a particular solvent and is called the **molal freezing-point depression constant.** Values of K_f for common solvents are listed in Table 11.5.

Like the boiling-point elevation, the observed freezing-point depression can be used to determine molar masses and to characterize solutions.

Spreading salt on a highway.

| *Sample Exercise 11.9* | **Freezing-Point Depression** |

Ethylene glycol

What mass of ethylene glycol ($C_2H_6O_2$, molar mass = 62.1 g/mol), the main component of antifreeze, must be added to 10.0 L of water to produce a solution for use in a car's radiator that freezes at $-10.0°F$ ($-23.3°C$)? Assume the density of water is exactly 1 g/mL.

The addition of antifreeze lowers the freezing point of water in a car's radiator.

Solution

The freezing point must be lowered from 0°C to −23.3°C. To determine the molality of ethylene glycol needed to accomplish this, we can use the equation

$$\Delta T = K_f m_{solute}$$

where $\Delta T = 23.3°C$ and $K_f = 1.86$ (from Table 11.5). Solving for the molality gives

$$m_{solute} = \frac{\Delta T}{K_f} = \frac{23.3°C}{1.86°C \cdot kg/mol} = 12.5 \ mol/kg$$

This means that 12.5 mol ethylene glycol must be added per kilogram of water. We have 10.0 L, or 10.0 kg, of water. Therefore, the total number of moles of ethylene glycol needed is

$$\frac{12.5 \ mol}{kg} \times 10.0 \ kg = 1.25 \times 10^2 \ mol$$

The mass of ethylene glycol needed is

$$1.25 \times 10^2 \ mol \times \frac{62.1 \ g}{mol} = 7.76 \times 10^3 \ g \ (or \ 7.76 \ kg)$$

See Exercises 11.61 and 11.62.

Sample Exercise 11.10

Determining Molar Mass by Freezing-Point Depression

A chemist is trying to identify a human hormone that controls metabolism by determining its molar mass. A sample weighing 0.546 g was dissolved in 15.0 g benzene, and the freezing-point depression was determined to be 0.240°C. Calculate the molar mass of the hormone.

Solution

From Table 11.5, K_f for benzene is 5.12°C · kg/mol, so the molality of the hormone is

$$m_{hormone} = \frac{\Delta T}{K_f} = \frac{0.240°C}{5.12°C \cdot kg/mol} = 4.69 \times 10^{-2} \ mol/kg$$

The moles of hormone can be obtained from the definition of molality:

$$4.69 \times 10^{-2} \ mol/kg = m_{solute} = \frac{mol \ hormone}{0.0150 \ kg \ benzene}$$

or

$$mol \ hormone = \left(4.69 \times 10^{-2} \frac{mol}{kg}\right)(0.0150 \ kg) = 7.04 \times 10^{-4} \ mol$$

Since 0.546 g hormone was dissolved, 7.04×10^{-4} mol hormone has a mass of 0.546 g, and

$$\frac{0.546 \ g}{7.04 \times 10^{-4} \ mol} = \frac{x \ g}{1.00 \ mol}$$

$$x = 776 \ g/mol$$

Thus the molar mass of the hormone is 776 g/mol.

See Exercises 11.63 and 11.64.

11.6 Osmotic Pressure

Osmotic pressure, another of the colligative properties, can be understood from Fig. 11.16. A solution and pure solvent are separated by a **semipermeable membrane,** which allows *solvent but not solute* molecules to pass through. As time passes, the volume of the solution increases and that of the solvent decreases. This flow of solvent into the solution through the semipermeable membrane is called **osmosis.** Eventually the liquid levels stop changing, indicating that the system has reached equilibrium. Because the liquid levels are different at this point, there is a greater hydrostatic pressure on the solution than on the pure solvent. This excess pressure is called the **osmotic pressure.**

We can take another view of this phenomenon, as illustrated in Fig. 11.17. Osmosis can be prevented by applying a pressure to the solution. *The minimum pressure that stops the osmosis is equal to the osmotic pressure of the solution.* A simple model to explain osmotic pressure can be constructed as shown in Fig. 11.18. The membrane allows only solvent molecules to pass through. However, the initial rates of solvent transfer to and from the solution are not the same. The solute particles interfere with the passage of solvent, so the rate of transfer is slower from the solution to the solvent than in the reverse direction. Thus there is a net transfer of solvent molecules into the solution, which causes the solution volume to increase. As the solution level rises in the tube, the resulting pressure exerts an extra "push" on the solvent molecules in the solution, forcing them back through the membrane. Eventually, enough pressure develops so that the solvent transfer becomes equal in both directions. At this point, equilibrium is achieved and the levels stop changing.

Osmotic pressure can be used to characterize solutions and determine molar masses, as can the other colligative properties, but osmotic pressure is particularly useful because a small concentration of solute produces a relatively large osmotic pressure.

Experiments show that the dependence of the osmotic pressure on solution concentration is represented by the equation

$$\Pi = MRT$$

where Π is the osmotic pressure in atmospheres, M is the molarity of the solution, R is the gas law constant, and T is the Kelvin temperature.

A molar mass determination using osmotic pressure is illustrated in Sample Exercise 11.11.

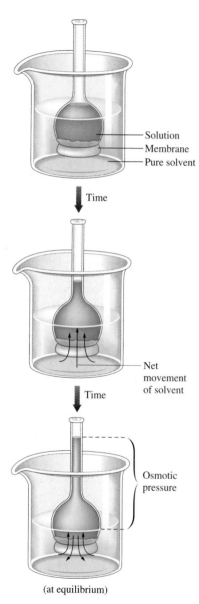

Time

Time

FIGURE 11.16
A tube with a bulb on the end that is covered by a semipermeable membrane. The solution is inside the tube and is bathed in the pure solvent. There is a net transfer of solvent molecules into the solution until the hydrostatic pressure equalizes the solvent flow in both directions.

Solution
Membrane
Pure solvent

Net movement of solvent

Osmotic pressure

(at equilibrium)

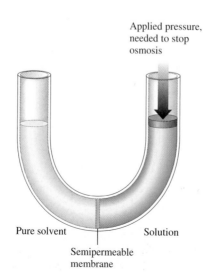

Applied pressure, needed to stop osmosis

Pure solvent   Solution

Semipermeable membrane

FIGURE 11.17
The normal flow of solvent into the solution (osmosis) can be prevented by applying an external pressure to the solution. The minimum pressure required to stop the osmosis is equal to the osmotic pressure of the solution.

FIGURE 11.18
(a) A pure solvent and its solution (containing a nonvolatile solute) are separated by a semipermeable membrane through which solvent molecules (blue) can pass but solute molecules (green) cannot. The rate of solvent transfer is greater from solvent to solution than from solution to solvent. (b) The system at equilibrium, where the rate of solvent transfer is the same in both directions.

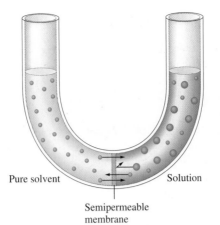

Pure solvent   Solution

Semipermeable
membrane

(a)

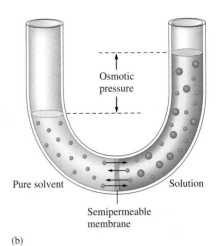

Osmotic
pressure

Pure solvent   Solution

Semipermeable
membrane

(b)

| Sample Exercise 11.11 | **Determining Molar Mass from Osmotic Pressure** |

To determine the molar mass of a certain protein, 1.00×10^{-3} g of it was dissolved in enough water to make 1.00 mL of solution. The osmotic pressure of this solution was found to be 1.12 torr at 25.0°C. Calculate the molar mass of the protein.

Solution

We use the equation

$$\Pi = MRT$$

In this case we have

$$\Pi = 1.12 \text{ torr} \times \frac{1 \text{ atm}}{760 \text{ torr}} = 1.47 \times 10^{-3} \text{ atm}$$

$$R = 0.08206 \text{ L} \cdot \text{atm/K} \cdot \text{mol}$$

$$T = 25.0 + 273 = 298 \text{ K}$$

Note that the osmotic pressure must be converted to atmospheres because of the units of R.

Solving for M gives

$$M = \frac{1.47 \times 10^{-3} \text{ atm}}{(0.08206 \text{ L} \cdot \text{atm/K} \cdot \text{mol})(298 \text{ K})} = 6.01 \times 10^{-5} \text{ mol/L}$$

Since 1.00×10^{-3} g protein was dissolved in 1 mL solution, the mass of protein per liter of solution is 1.00 g. The solution's concentration is 6.01×10^{-5} mol/L. This concentration is produced from 1.00×10^{-3} g protein per milliliter, or 1.00 g/L. Thus 6.01×10^{-5} mol protein has a mass of 1.00 g and

$$\frac{1.00 \text{ g}}{6.01 \times 10^{-5} \text{ mol}} = \frac{x \text{ g}}{1.00 \text{ mol}}$$

$$x = 1.66 \times 10^{4} \text{ g}$$

Measurements of osmotic pressure generally give much more accurate molar mass values than those from freezing-point or boiling-point changes.

The molar mass of the protein is 1.66×10^{4} g/mol. This molar mass may seem very large, but it is relatively small for a protein.

See Exercise 11.66.

In osmosis, a semipermeable membrane prevents transfer of *all* solute particles. A similar phenomenon, called **dialysis,** occurs at the walls of most plant and animal cells.

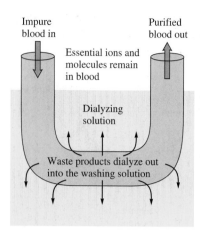

FIGURE 11.19
Representation of the functioning of an artificial kidney.

Patient undergoing dialysis.

However, in this case the membrane allows transfer of both solvent molecules and *small* solute molecules and ions. One of the most important applications of dialysis is the use of artificial kidney machines to purify the blood. The blood is passed through a cellophane tube, which acts as the semipermeable membrane. The tube is immersed in a dialyzing solution (see Fig. 11.19). This "washing" solution contains the same concentrations of ions and small molecules as blood but has none of the waste products normally removed by the kidneys. The resulting dialysis (movement of waste molecules into the washing solution) cleanses the blood.

Solutions that have identical osmotic pressures are said to be **isotonic solutions.** Fluids administered intravenously must be isotonic with body fluids. For example, if red blood cells are bathed in a hypertonic solution, which is a solution having an osmotic pressure higher than that of the cell fluids, the cells will shrivel because of a net transfer of water out of the cells. This phenomenon is called *crenation.* The opposite phenomenon, called *hemolysis,* occurs when cells are bathed in a hypotonic solution, a solution with an osmotic pressure lower than that of the cell fluids. In this case, the cells rupture because of the flow of water into the cells.

We can use the phenomenon of crenation to our advantage. Food can be preserved by treating its surface with a solute that gives a solution that is hypertonic to bacteria cells. Bacteria on the food then tend to shrivel and die. This is why salt can be used to protect meat and sugar can be used to protect fruit.

The brine used in pickling causes the cucumbers to shrivel.

| Sample Exercise 11.12 | **Isotonic Solutions** |

What concentration of sodium chloride in water is needed to produce an aqueous solution isotonic with blood ($\Pi = 7.70$ atm at 25°C)?

Solution

We can calculate the molarity of the solute from the equation

$$\Pi = MRT \quad \text{or} \quad M = \frac{\Pi}{RT}$$

$$M = \frac{7.70 \text{ atm}}{(0.08206 \text{ L} \cdot \text{atm/K} \cdot \text{mol})(298 \text{ K})} = 0.315 \text{ mol/L}$$

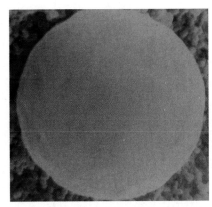

Red blood cells in three stages of osmosis. (a) The normal shape of a red blood cell. (b) This cell has shrunk because water moved out of it by osmosis. (c) This cell is swollen with water that has moved into it by osmosis.

This represents the total molarity of solute particles. But NaCl gives two ions per formula unit. Therefore, the concentration of NaCl needed is $\frac{0.315\ M}{2} = 0.1575\ M = 0.158\ M$. That is,

$$NaCl \longrightarrow Na^+ + Cl^-$$

0.1575 M   0.1575 M   0.1575 M

0.315 M

See Exercise 11.68.

Reverse Osmosis

If a solution in contact with pure solvent across a semipermeable membrane is subjected to an external pressure larger than its osmotic pressure, **reverse osmosis** occurs. The pressure will cause a net flow of solvent from the solution to the solvent, as shown in Fig. 11.20. In reverse osmosis, the semipermeable membrane acts as a "molecular filter" to remove solute particles. This fact is applicable to the **desalination** (removal of dissolved salts) of seawater, which is highly hypertonic to body fluids and thus is not drinkable.

As the population of the Sun Belt areas of the United States increases, more demand will be placed on the limited supplies of fresh water there. One obvious source of fresh water is from the desalination of seawater. Various schemes have been suggested, including solar evaporation, reverse osmosis, and even a plan for towing icebergs from Antarctica. The problem, of course, is that all the available processes are expensive. However, as water shortages increase, desalination is becoming necessary. For example, the first full-time public desalination plant in the United States started operations on Catalina Island, just off the coast of California (see Fig. 11.21). This plant, which can produce 132,000 gallons of drinkable water from the Pacific Ocean every day, operates by reverse osmosis. Powerful pumps, developing over 800 lb/in² of pressure, are employed to force seawater through synthetic semipermeable membranes.

Catalina Island's plant may be just the beginning. The city of Santa Barbara opened a $40 million desalination plant in 1992 that can produce 8 million gallons of drinking water per day, and other plants are in the planning stages.

A small-scale, manually operated reverse osmosis desalinator has been developed by the U.S. Navy to provide fresh water on life rafts. Potable water can be supplied by this desalinator at the rate of 1.25 gallons of water per hour—enough to keep 25 people alive. This compact desalinator, which weighs only 10 pounds, can now replace the bulky cases of fresh water formerly stored in Navy life rafts.

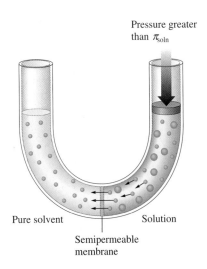

Pressure greater than π_{soln}

Pure solvent

Solution

Semipermeable membrane

FIGURE 11.20
Reverse osmosis. A pressure greater than the osmotic pressure of the solution is applied, which causes a net flow of solvent molecules (blue) from the solution to the pure solvent. The solute molecules (green) remain behind.

(b)

FIGURE 11.21
(a) Residents of Catalina Island off the coast of southern California are benefiting from a new desalination plant that can supply 132,000 gallons a day, or one-third of the island's daily needs. (b) Machinery in the desalination plant for Catalina Island.

11.7 Colligative Properties of Electrolyte Solutions

As we have seen previously, the colligative properties of solutions depend on the total concentration of solute particles. For example, a 0.10 *m* glucose solution shows a freezing point depression of 0.186°C:

$$\Delta T = K_f m = (1.86°C \cdot kg/mol)(0.100 \ mol/kg) = 0.186°C$$

On the other hand, a 0.10 *m* sodium chloride solution should show a freezing-point depression of 0.37°C, since the solution is 0.10 *m* Na⁺ ions and 0.10 *m* Cl⁻ ions. Therefore, the solution contains a total of 0.20 *m* solute particles, and $\Delta T = (1.86°C \cdot kg/mol)$ (0.20 mol/kg) = 0.37°C.

The relationship between the moles of solute dissolved and the moles of particles in solution is usually expressed using the **van't Hoff factor,** *i:*

$$i = \frac{\text{moles of particles in solution}}{\text{moles of solute dissolved}}$$

Dutch chemist J. H. van't Hoff (1852–1911) received the first Nobel Prize in chemistry in 1901.

FIGURE 11.22
In an aqueous solution a few ions aggregate, forming ion pairs that behave as a unit.

The *expected* value for *i* can be calculated for a salt by noting the number of ions per formula unit. For example, for NaCl, *i* is 2; for K_2SO_4, *i* is 3; and for $Fe_3(PO_4)_2$, *i* is 5. These calculated values assume that when a salt dissolves, it completely dissociates into its component ions, which then move around independently. This assumption is not always true. For example, the freezing-point depression observed for 0.10 *m* NaCl is 1.87 times that for 0.10 *m* glucose rather than twice as great. That is, for a 0.10 *m* NaCl solution the observed value for *i* is 1.87 rather than 2. Why? The best explanation is that **ion pairing** occurs in solution (see Fig. 11.22). At a given instant a small percentage of the sodium and chloride ions are paired and thus count as a single particle. In general, ion pairing is most important in concentrated solutions. As the solution becomes more dilute,

TABLE 11.6   Expected and Observed Values of the van't Hoff Factor for 0.05 *m* Solutions of Several Electrolytes

Electrolyte	*i* (expected)	*i* (observed)
NaCl	2.0	1.9
$MgCl_2$	3.0	2.7
$MgSO_4$	2.0	1.3
$FeCl_3$	4.0	3.4
HCl	2.0	1.9
Glucose*	1.0	1.0

*A nonelectrolyte shown for comparison.

the ions are farther apart and less ion pairing occurs. For example, in a 0.0010 *m* NaCl solution, the observed value of *i* is 1.97, which is very close to the expected value.

Ion pairing occurs to some extent in all electrolyte solutions. Table 11.6 shows expected and observed values of *i* for a given concentration of various electrolytes. Note that the deviation of *i* from the expected value tends to be greatest where the ions have multiple charges. This is expected because ion pairing ought to be most important for highly charged ions.

The colligative properties of electrolyte solutions are described by including the van't Hoff factor in the appropriate equation. For example, for changes in freezing and boiling points, the modified equation is

$$\Delta T = imK$$

where *K* represents the freezing-point depression or boiling-point elevation constant for the solvent.

For the osmotic pressure of electrolyte solutions, the equation is

$$\Pi = iMRT$$

Sample Exercise 11.13 | **Osmotic Pressure**

The observed osmotic pressure for a 0.10 *M* solution of $Fe(NH_4)_2(SO_4)_2$ at 25°C is 10.8 atm. Compare the expected and experimental values for *i*.

Solution

The ionic solid $Fe(NH_4)_2(SO_4)_2$ dissociates in water to produce 5 ions:

$$Fe(NH_4)_2(SO_4)_2 \xrightarrow{H_2O} Fe^{2+} + 2NH_4^+ + 2SO_4^{2-}$$

Thus the expected value for *i* is 5. We can obtain the experimental value for *i* by using the equation for osmotic pressure:

$$\Pi = iMRT \quad \text{or} \quad i = \frac{\Pi}{MRT}$$

where $\Pi = 10.8$ atm, $M = 0.10$ mol/L, $R = 0.08206$ L · atm/K · mol, and $T = 25 + 273 = 298$ K. Substituting these values into the equation gives

$$i = \frac{\Pi}{MRT} = \frac{10.8 \text{ atm}}{(0.10 \text{ mol/L})(0.08206 \text{ L · atm/K · mol})(298 \text{ K})} = 4.4$$

The experimental value for *i* is less than the expected value, presumably because of ion pairing.

See Exercises 11.73 and 11.74.

CHEMICAL IMPACT

The Drink of Champions—Water

In 1965, the University of Florida football team, the Gators, participated in a research program to test a sports drink formula containing a mixture of carbohydrates and electrolytes. The drink was used to help prevent dehydration caused by extreme workouts in the hot Florida climate. The Gators' success that season was in part attributed to their use of the sports drink formula. In 1967, a modified form of this formula was marketed with the name Gatorade. Today, Gatorade leads sales in sports drinks, but many other brands have entered a market where annual sales exceed $700 million!

During moderate- to high-intensity exercise, glycogen (a fuel reserve that helps maintain normal body processes) can be depleted within 60 to 90 minutes. Blood sugar levels drop as the glycogen reserves are used up, and lactic acid (a by-product of glucose metabolism) builds up in muscle tissue causing fatigue and muscle cramps. Muscles also generate a large amount of heat that must be dissipated. Water, which has a large specific heat capacity, is used to take heat away from these muscles. Sweating and evaporative cooling help the body maintain a constant temperature, but at a huge cost. During a high-intensity workout in hot weather, anywhere from 1 to 3 quarts of water can be lost from sweating per hour. Sweating away more than 2% of your body weight—a quart for every 100 pounds—can put a large stress on the heart, increasing body temperature and decreasing performance. Excessive sweating also results in the loss of sodium and potassium ions—two very important electrolytes that are present in the fluids inside and outside cells.

All the major sports drinks contain three main ingredients—carbohydrates in the form of simple sugars such as

FIGURE 11.24

A representation of two colloidal particles. In each the center particle is surrounded by a layer of positive ions, with negative ions in the outer layer. Thus, although the particles are electrically neutral, they still repel each other because of their outer negative layer of ions.

11.8 Colloids

Mud can be suspended in water by vigorous stirring. When the stirring stops, most of the particles rapidly settle out, but even after several days some of the smallest particles remain suspended. Although undetected in normal lighting, their presence can be demonstrated by shining a beam of intense light through the suspension. The beam is visible from the side because the light is scattered by the suspended particles (Fig. 11.23). In a true solution, on the other hand, the beam is invisible from the side because the individual ions and molecules dispersed in the solution are too small to scatter visible light.

The scattering of light by particles is called the **Tyndall effect** and is often used to distinguish between a suspension and a true solution.

A suspension of tiny particles in some medium is called a **colloidal dispersion,** or a **colloid.** The suspended particles are single large molecules or aggregates of molecules or ions ranging in size from 1 to 1000 nm. Colloids are classified according to the states of the dispersed phase and the dispersing medium. Table 11.7 summarizes various types of colloids.

What stabilizes a colloid? Why do the particles remain suspended rather than forming larger aggregates and precipitating out? The answer is complicated, but the main factor seems to be *electrostatic repulsion*. A colloid, like all other macroscopic substances, is electrically neutral. However, when a colloid is placed in an electric field, the dispersed particles all migrate to the same electrode and thus must all have the same charge. How is this possible? The center of a colloidal particle (a tiny ionic crystal, a group of molecules, or a single large molecule) attracts from the medium a layer of ions, all of the same charge. This group of ions, in turn, attracts another layer of oppositely charged ions, as shown in Fig. 11.24. Because the colloidal particles all have an outer layer of ions with the same charge, they repel each other and do not easily aggregate to form particles that are large enough to precipitate.

sucrose, glucose, and fructose; electrolytes, including sodium and potassium ions; and water. Because these are the three major substances lost through sweating, good scientific reasoning suggests that drinking sports drinks should improve performance. But just how effectively do sports drinks deliver on their promises?

Recent studies have confirmed that athletes who eat a balanced diet and drink plenty of water are just as well off as those who consume sports drinks. A sports drink may have only one advantage over drinking water—it tastes better than water to most athletes. And if a drink tastes better, it will encourage more consumption, thus keeping cells hydrated.

Since most of the leading sports drinks contain the same ingredients in similar concentrations, taste may be the single most important factor in choosing your drink. If you are not interested in any particular sports drink, drink plenty of water. The key to quality performance is to keep your cells hydrated.

For healthy athletes, drinking water during exercise may be as effective as drinking sports drinks.

Adapted with permission from "Sports Drinks: Don't Sweat the Small Stuff," by Tim Graham, *ChemMatters*, February 1999, p. 11.

TABLE 11.7   Types of Colloids

Examples	Dispersing Medium	Dispersed Substance	Colloid Type
Fog, aerosol sprays	Gas	Liquid	Aerosol
Smoke, airborne bacteria	Gas	Solid	Aerosol
Whipped cream, soap suds	Liquid	Gas	Foam
Milk, mayonnaise	Liquid	Liquid	Emulsion
Paint, clays, gelatin	Liquid	Solid	Sol
Marshmallow, polystyrene foam	Solid	Gas	Solid foam
Butter, cheese	Solid	Liquid	Solid emulsion
Ruby glass	Solid	Solid	Solid sol

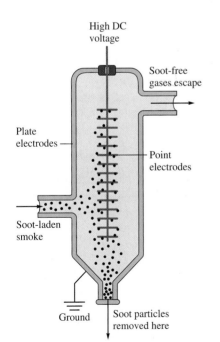

FIGURE 11.25

The Cottrell precipitator installed in a smokestack. The charged plates attract the colloidal particles because of their ion layers and thus remove them from the smoke.

The destruction of a colloid, called **coagulation,** usually can be accomplished either by heating or by adding an electrolyte. Heating increases the velocities of the colloidal particles, causing them to collide with enough energy that the ion barriers are penetrated and the particles can aggregate. Because this process is repeated many times, the particle grows to a point where it settles out. Adding an electrolyte neutralizes the adsorbed ion layers. This is why clay suspended in rivers is deposited where the river reaches the ocean, forming the deltas characteristic of large rivers like the Mississippi. The high salt content of the seawater causes the colloidal clay particles to coagulate.

The removal of soot from smoke is another example of the coagulation of a colloid. When smoke is passed through an electrostatic precipitator (Fig. 11.25), the suspended solids are removed. The use of precipitators has produced an immense improvement in the air quality of heavily industrialized cities.

CHEMICAL IMPACT

Organisms and Ice Formation

The ice-cold waters of the polar oceans are teeming with fish that seem immune to freezing. One might think that these fish have some kind of antifreeze in their blood. However, studies show that they are protected from freezing in a very different way from the way antifreeze protects our cars. As we have seen in this chapter, solutes such as sugar, salt, and ethylene glycol lower the temperature at which the solid and liquid phases of water can coexist. However, the fish could not tolerate high concentrations of solutes in their blood because of the osmotic pressure effects. Instead, they are protected by proteins in their blood. These proteins allow the water in the bloodstream to be supercooled—exist below 0°C—without forming ice. They apparently coat the surface of each tiny ice crystal, as soon as it begins to form, preventing it from growing to a size that would cause biologic damage.

Although it might at first seem surprising, this research on polar fish has attracted the attention of ice cream manufacturers. Premium quality ice cream is smooth; it does not have large ice crystals in it. The makers of ice cream would like to incorporate these polar fish proteins, or molecules that behave similarly, into ice cream to prevent the growth of ice crystals during storage.

Fruit and vegetable growers have a similar interest: They also want to prevent ice formation that damages their crops during an unusual cold wave. However, this is a very different kind of problem than keeping polar fish from freezing. Many types of fruits and vegetables are colonized by

An Antarctic fish, *Chaerophalus aceratus.*

bacteria that manufacture a protein that *encourages* freezing by acting as a nucleating agent to start an ice crystal. Chemists have identified the offending protein in the bacteria and the gene that is responsible for making it. They have learned to modify the genetic material of these bacteria in a way that removes their ability to make the protein that encourages ice crystal formation. If testing shows that these modified bacteria have no harmful effects on the crop or the environment, the original bacteria strain will be replaced with the new form so that ice crystals will not form so readily when a cold snap occurs.

Key Terms

Section 11.1
molarity
mass percent
mole fraction
molality
normality

Section 11.2
enthalpy (heat) of solution
enthalpy (heat) of hydration

Section 11.3
Henry's law
thermal pollution

Section 11.4
Raoult's law
ideal solution

For Review

Solution composition
- Molarity (M): moles solute per liter of solution
- Mass percent: ratio of mass of solute to mass of solution times 100%
- Mole fraction (X): ratio of moles of a given component to total moles of all components
- Molality (m): moles solute per mass of solvent (in kg)
- Normality (N): number of equivalents per liter of solution

Enthalpy of solution (ΔH_{soln})
- The enthalpy change accompanying solution formation
- Can be partitioned into
  - The energy required to overcome the solute–solute interactions
  - The energy required to "make holes" in the solvent
  - The energy associated with solute–solvent interactions

Factors That affect solubility
- Polarity of solute and solvent
  - "Like dissolves like" is a useful generalization
- Pressure increases the solubility of gases in a solvent
  - Henry's law: $C = kP$
- Temperature effects
  - Increased temperature decreases the solubility of a gas in water
  - Most solids are more soluble at higher temperatures but important exceptions exist

Vapor pressure of solutions
- A solution containing a nonvolatile solute has a lower vapor pressure than a solution of the pure solvent
- Raoult's law defines an ideal solution

$$P_{vapor}^{soln} = \chi_{solvent} P_{vapor}^{solvent}$$

  - Solutions in which the solute–solvent attractions differ from the solute–solute and solvent–solvent attractions violate Raoult's law

Colligative properties
- Depend on the number of solute particles present
- Boiling-point elevation: $\Delta T = K_b m_{solute}$
- Freezing-point lowering: $\Delta T = K_f m_{solute}$
- Osmotic pressure: $\Pi = MRT$
  - Osmosis occurs when a solution and pure solvent are separated by a semipermeable membrane that allows solvent molecules to pass but not solute particles
  - Reverse osmosis occurs when the applied pressure is greater than the osmotic pressure of the solution
- Because colligative properties depend on the number of particles, solutes that break into several ions when they dissolve have an effect proportional to the number of ions produced
  - The van't Hoff factor i represents the number of ions produced by each formula unit of solute

Colloids
- A suspension of tiny particles stabilized by electrostatic repulsion among the ion layers surrounding the individual particles
- Can be coagulated (destroyed) by heating or adding an electrolyte

REVIEW QUESTIONS

1. The four most common ways to describe solution composition are mass percent, mole fraction, molarity, and molality. Define each of these solution composition terms. Why is molarity temperature-dependent, whereas the other three solution composition terms are temperature-independent?
2. Using KF as an example, write equations that refer to ΔH_{soln} and ΔH_{hyd}. Lattice energy was defined in Chapter 8 as ΔH for the reaction $K^+(g) + F^-(g) \longrightarrow KF(s)$. Show how you would utilize Hess's law to calculate ΔH_{soln} from ΔH_{hyd} and ΔH_{LE} for KF, where ΔH_{LE} = lattice energy ΔH_{soln} for KF, as for other soluble ionic compounds, is a relatively small number. How can this be since ΔH_{hyd} and ΔH_{LE} are relatively large negative numbers?
3. What does the axiom "like dissolves like" mean? There are four types of solute/solvent combinations: polar solutes in polar solvents, nonpolar solutes in polar solvents, and so on. For each type of solution, discuss the magnitude of ΔH_{soln}.
4. Structure, pressure, and temperature all have an effect on solubility.
   Discuss each of their effects. What is Henry's law? Why does Henry's law not work for $HCl(g)$? What do the terms *hydrophobic* and *hydrophilic* mean?

5. Define the terms in Raoult's law. Figure 11.9 illustrates the net transfer of water molecules from pure water to an aqueous solution of a nonvolatile solute. Explain why eventually all of the water from the beaker of pure water will transfer to the aqueous solution. If the experiment illustrated in Fig. 11.9 was performed using a volatile solute, what would happen? How do you calculate the total vapor pressure when both the solute and solvent are volatile?

6. In terms of Raoult's law, distinguish between an ideal liquid–liquid solution and a nonideal liquid–liquid solution. If a solution is ideal, what is true about ΔH_{soln}, ΔT for the solution formation, and the interactive forces within the pure solute and pure solvent as compared to the interactive forces within the solution. Give an example of an ideal solution. Answer the previous two questions for solutions that exhibit either negative or positive deviations from Raoult's law.

7. Vapor-pressure lowering is a colligative property, as are freezing-point depression and boiling-point elevation. What is a colligative property? Why is the freezing point depressed for a solution as compared to the pure solvent? Why is the boiling point elevated for a solution as compared to the pure solvent? Explain how to calculate ΔT for a freezing-point depression problem or a boiling-point elevation problem. Of the solvents listed in Table 11.5, which would have the largest freezing-point depression for a 0.50 molal solution? Which would have the smallest boiling-point elevation for a 0.50 molal solution?

   A common application of freezing-point depression and boiling-point elevation experiments is to provide a means to calculate the molar mass of a nonvolatile solute. What data are needed to calculate the molar mass of a nonvolatile solute? Explain how you would manipulate these data to calculate the molar mass of the nonvolatile solute.

8. What is osmotic pressure? How is osmotic pressure calculated? Molarity units are used in the osmotic pressure equation. When does the molarity of a solution approximately equal the molality of the solution? Before refrigeration was common, many foods were preserved by salting them heavily, and many fruits were preserved by mixing them with a large amount of sugar (fruit preserves). How do salt and sugar act as preservatives? Two applications of osmotic pressure are dialysis and desalination. Explain these two processes.

9. Distinguish between a strong electrolyte, a weak electrolyte, and a nonelectrolyte. How can colligative properties be used to distinguish between them? What is the van't Hoff factor? Why is the observed freezing-point depression for electrolyte solutions sometimes less than the calculated value? Is the discrepancy greater for concentrated or dilute solutions?

10. What is a colloidal dispersion? Give some examples of colloids. The Tyndall effect is often used to distinguish between a colloidal suspension and a true solution. Explain. The destruction of a colloid is done through a process called coagulation. What is coagulation?

Active Learning Questions

These questions are designed to be used by groups of students in class. The questions allow students to explore their understanding of concepts through discussion and peer teaching. The real value of these questions is the learning that occurs while students talk to each other about chemical concepts.

1. Consider Fig. 11.9. According to the caption and picture, water seems to go from one beaker to another.

   a. Explain why this occurs.

   b. The explanation in the text uses terms such as *vapor pressure* and *equilibrium*. Explain what these have to do with the phenomenon. For example, what is coming to equilibrium?

   c. Does all the water end up in the second beaker?

   d. Is water evaporating from the beaker containing the solution? If so, is the rate of evaporation increasing, decreasing, or staying constant?

   Draw pictures to illustrate your explanations.

2. Once again, consider Fig. 11.9. Suppose instead of having a nonvolatile solute in the solvent in one beaker, the two beakers contain different volatile liquids. That is, suppose one beaker contains liquid A (P_{vap} = 50 torr) and the other beaker contains liquid B (P_{vap} = 100 torr). Explain what happens as time passes. How is this similar to the first case (shown in the figure)? How is it different?

3. Assume that you place a freshwater plant into a saltwater solution and examine it under a microscope. What happens to the plant cells? What if you placed a saltwater plant in pure water? Explain. Draw pictures to illustrate your explanations.

4. How does ΔH_{soln} relate to deviations from Raoult's law? Explain.

5. You have read that adding a solute to a solvent can both increase the boiling point and decrease the freezing point. A friend of yours explains it to you like this: "The solute and solvent can be like salt in water. The salt gets in the way of freezing in that it blocks the water molecules from joining together. The salt acts like a strong bond holding the water molecules together so that it is harder to boil." What do you say to your friend?

6. You drop an ice cube (made from pure water) into a saltwater solution at 0°C. Explain what happens and why.

7. Using the phase diagram for water and Raoult's law, explain why salt is spread on the roads in winter (even when it is below freezing).

8. You and your friend are each drinking cola from separate 2-L bottles. Both colas are equally carbonated. You are able to drink 1 L of cola, but your friend can drink only about half a liter. You each close the bottles and place them in the refrigerator. The next day when you each go to get the colas, whose will be more carbonated and why?

A blue question or exercise number indicates that the answer to that question or exercise appears at the back of this book and a solution appears in the *Solutions Guide*.

Solution Review

If you have trouble with these exercises, review Sections 4.1 to 4.3 in Chapter 4.

9. Rubbing alcohol contains 585 g of isopropanol (C_3H_7OH) per liter (aqueous solution). Calculate the molarity.

10. What volume of a 0.580 M solution of $CaCl_2$ contains 1.28 g of solute?

11. Calculate the sodium ion concentration when 70.0 mL of 3.0 M sodium carbonate is added to 30.0 mL of 1.0 M sodium bicarbonate.

12. Write equations showing the ions present after the following strong electrolytes are dissolved in water.
a. HNO_3 **d.** $SrBr_2$ **g.** NH_4NO_3
b. Na_2SO_4 **e.** $KClO_4$ **h.** $CuSO_4$
c. $Al(NO_3)_3$ **f.** NH_4Br **i.** $NaOH$

Questions

13. Rationalize the temperature dependence of the solubility of a gas in water in terms of the kinetic molecular theory.

14. The weak electrolyte $NH_3(g)$ does not obey Henry's law. Why? $O_2(g)$ obeys Henry's law in water but not in blood (an aqueous solution). Why?

15. The two beakers in the sealed container illustrated below contain pure water and an aqueous solution of a volatile solute.

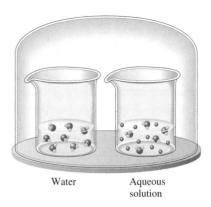

Water   Aqueous
                  solution

If the solute is less volatile than water, explain what will happen to the volumes in the two containers as time passes.

16. The following plot shows the vapor pressure of various solutions of components A and B at some temperature.

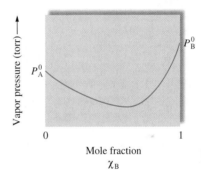

Which of the following statements is false concerning solutions of A and B?
a. The solutions exhibit negative deviations from Raoult's law.
b. ΔH_{mix} for the solutions should be exothermic.
c. The intermolecular forces are stronger in solution than in either pure A or pure B.
d. Pure liquid B is more volatile than pure liquid A.
e. The solution with χ_B = 0.6 will have a lower boiling point than either pure A or pure B.

17. When pure methanol is mixed with water, the resulting solution feels warm. Would you expect this solution to be ideal? Explain.

18. Detergent molecules can stabilize the emulsion of oil in water as well as remove dirt from soiled clothes. A typical detergent is sodium dodecylsulfate, or SDS, and it has a formula of $CH_3(CH_2)_{10}CH_2SO_4^-Na^+$. In aqueous solution, SDS suspends oil or dirt by forming small aggregates of detergent anions called *micelles*. Propose a structure for micelles.

19. For an acid or a base, when is the normality of a solution equal to the molarity of the solution and when are the two concentration units different?

20. In order for sodium chloride to dissolve in water, a small amount of energy must be added during solution formation. This is not energetically favorable. Why is NaCl so soluble in water?

21. Which of the following statements is(are) true? Correct the false statements.
    a. The vapor pressure of a solution is directly related to the mole fraction of solute.
    b. When a solute is added to water, the water in solution has a lower vapor pressure than that of pure ice at 0°C.
    c. Colligative properties depend only on the identity of the solute and not on the number of solute particles present.
    d. When sugar is added to water, the boiling point of the solution increases above 100°C because sugar has a higher boiling point than water.

22. Is the following statement true of false? Explain your answer. When determining the molar mass of a solute using boiling point of freezing point data, camphor would be the best solvent choice of all of the solvents listed in Table 11.5.

23. Explain the terms isotonic solution, crenation, and hemolysis.

24. What is ion pairing?

Exercises

In this section similar exercises are paired.

Concentration of Solutions

25. A solution of phosphoric acid was made by dissolving 10.0 g of H_3PO_4 in 100.0 mL of water. The resulting volume was 104 mL. Calculate the density, mole fraction, molarity, and molality of the solution. Assume water has a density of 1.00 g/cm³.

26. An aqueous antifreeze solution is 40.0% ethylene glycol ($C_2H_6O_2$) by mass. The density of the solution is 1.05 g/cm³. Calculate the molality, molarity, and mole fraction of the ethylene glycol.

27. Common commercial acids and bases are aqueous solutions with the following properties:

	Density (g/cm³)	Mass Percent of Solute
Hydrochloric acid	1.19	38
Nitric acid	1.42	70.
Sulfuric acid	1.84	95
Acetic acid	1.05	99
Ammonia	0.90	28

Calculate the molarity, molality, and mole fraction of each of the preceding reagents.

28. In lab you need to prepare at least 100 mL of each of the following solutions. Explain how you would proceed using the given information.
    a. 2.0 m KCl in water (density of $H_2O = 1.00$ g/cm³)
    b. 15% NaOH by mass in water ($d = 1.00$ g/cm³)
    c. 25% NaOH by mass in CH_3OH ($d = 0.79$ g/cm³)
    d. 0.10 mole fraction of $C_6H_{12}O_6$ in water ($d = 1.00$ g/cm³)

29. A solution is prepared by mixing 25 mL pentane (C_5H_{12}, $d = 0.63$ g/cm³) with 45 mL hexane (C_6H_{14}, $d = 0.66$ g/cm³). Assuming that the volumes add on mixing, calculate the mass percent, mole fraction, molality, and molarity of the pentane.

30. A bottle of wine contains 12.5% ethanol by volume. The density of ethanol (C_2H_5OH) is 0.789 g/cm³. Calculate the concentration of ethanol in wine in terms of mass percent and molality.

31. A 1.37 M solution of citric acid ($H_3C_6H_5O_7$) in water has a density of 1.10 g/cm³. Calculate the mass percent, molality, mole fraction, and normality of the citric acid. Citric acid has three acidic protons.

32. Calculate the molarity and mole fraction of acetone in a 1.00 m solution of acetone (CH_3COCH_3) in ethanol (C_2H_5OH). (Density of acetone = 0.788 g/cm³; density of ethanol = 0.789 g/cm³.) Assume that the volumes of acetone and ethanol add.

Energetics of Solutions and Solubility

33. The lattice energy* of NaI is −686 kJ/mol, and the enthalpy of hydration is −694 kJ/mol. Calculate the enthalpy of solution per mole of solid NaI. Describe the process to which this enthalpy change applies.

34. a. Use the following data to calculate the enthalpy of hydration for calcium chloride and calcium iodide.

	Lattice Energy	ΔH_{soln}
$CaCl_2(s)$	−2247 kJ/mol	−46 kJ/mol
$CaI_2(s)$	−2059 kJ/mol	−104 kJ/mol

    b. Based on your answers to part a, which ion, Cl^- or I^-, is more strongly attracted to water?

35. Although $Al(OH)_3$ is insoluble in water, NaOH is very soluble. Explain in terms of lattice energies.

36. The high melting points of ionic solids indicate that a lot of energy must be supplied to separate the ions from one another. How is it possible that the ions can separate from one another when soluble ionic compounds are dissolved in water, often with essentially no temperature change?

37. Which solvent, water or carbon tetrachloride, would you choose to dissolve each of the following?
    a. KrF_2 e. MgF_2
    b. SF_2 f. CH_2O
    c. SO_2 g. $CH_2{=}CH_2$
    d. CO_2

38. Which solvent, water or hexane (C_6H_{14}), would you choose to dissolve each of the following?
    a. NaCl   c. octane (C_8H_{18})
    b. HF   d. $(NH_4)_2SO_4$

39. What factors cause one solute to be more strongly attracted to water than another? For each of the following pairs, predict which substance would be more soluble in water.
    a. CH_3CH_2OH or $CH_3CH_2CH_3$
    b. $CHCl_3$ or CCl_4
    c. CH_3CH_2OH or $CH_3(CH_2)_{14}CH_2OH$

*Lattice energy was defined in Chapter 8 as the energy change for the process $M^+(g) + X^-(g) \rightarrow MX(s)$.

40. Which ion in each of the following pairs would you expect to be more strongly hydrated? Why?
  a. Na^+ or Mg^{2+} **d.** F^- or Br^-
  b. Mg^{2+} or Be^{2+} **e.** Cl^- or ClO_4^-
  c. Fe^{2+} or Fe^{3+} **f.** ClO_4^- or SO_4^{2-}

41. Rationalize the trend in water solubility for the following simple alcohols:

Alcohol	Solubility (g/100 g H_2O at 20°C)
Methanol, CH_3OH	Soluble in all proportions
Ethanol, CH_3CH_2OH	Soluble in all proportions
Propanol, $CH_3CH_2CH_2OH$	Soluble in all proportions
Butanol, $CH_3(CH_2)_2CH_2OH$	8.14
Pentanol, $CH_3(CH_2)_3CH_2OH$	2.64
Hexanol, $CH_3(CH_2)_4CH_2OH$	0.59
Heptanol, $CH_3(CH_2)_5CH_2OH$	0.09

42. The solubility of benzoic acid ($HC_7H_5O_2$),

is 0.34 g/100 mL in water at 25°C and is 10.0 g/100 mL in benzene (C_6H_6) at 25°C. Rationalize this solubility behavior. (*Hint:* Benzoic acid forms a dimer in benzene.) Would benzoic acid be more or less soluble in a 0.1 M NaOH solution than it is in water? Explain.

43. The solubility of nitrogen in water is 8.21×10^{-4} mol/L at 0°C when the N_2 pressure above water is 0.790 atm. Calculate the Henry's law constant for N_2 in units of mol/L · atm for Henry's law in the form $C = kP$, where C is the gas concentration in mol/L. Calculate the solubility of N_2 in water when the partial pressure of nitrogen above water is 1.10 atm at 0°C.

44. In Exercise 107 in Chapter 5, the pressure of CO_2 in a bottle of sparkling wine was calculated assuming that the CO_2 was insoluble in water. This was a bad assumption. Redo this problem by assuming that CO_2 obeys Henry's law. Use the data given in that problem to calculate the partial pressure of CO_2 in the gas phase and the solubility of CO_2 in the wine at 25°C. The Henry's law constant for CO_2 is 3.1×10^{-2} mol/L · atm at 25°C with Henry's law in the form $C = kP$, where C is the concentration of the gas in mol/L.

Vapor Pressures of Solutions

45. Glycerin, $C_3H_8O_3$, is a nonvolatile liquid. What is the vapor pressure of a solution made by adding 164 g of glycerin to 338 mL of H_2O at 39.8°C? The vapor pressure of pure water at 39.8°C is 54.74 torr and its density is 0.992 g/cm³.

46. The vapor pressure of a solution containing 53.6 g glycerin ($C_3H_8O_3$) in 133.7 g ethanol (C_2H_5OH) is 113 torr at 40°C. Calculate the vapor pressure of pure ethanol at 40°C assuming that glycerin is a nonvolatile, nonelectrolyte solute in ethanol.

47. At a certain temperature, the vapor pressure of pure benzene (C_6H_6) is 0.930 atm. A solution was prepared by dissolving 10.0 g of a nondissociating, nonvolatile solute in 78.11 g of benzene at that temperature. The vapor pressure of the solution was found to be 0.900 atm. Assuming the solution behaves ideally, determine the molar mass of the solute.

48. A solution of sodium chloride in water has a vapor pressure of 19.6 torr at 25°C. What is the mole fraction of NaCl solute particles in this solution? What would be the vapor pressure of this solution at 45°C? The vapor pressure of pure water is 23.8 torr at 25°C and 71.9 torr at 45°C and assume sodium chloride exists as Na^+ and Cl^- ions in solution.

49. Pentane (C_5H_{12}) and hexane (C_6H_{14}) form an ideal solution. At 25°C the vapor pressures of pentane and hexane are 511 and 150. torr, respectively. A solution is prepared by mixing 25 mL pentane (density, 0.63 g/mL) with 45 mL hexane (density, 0.66 g/mL).
  a. What is the vapor pressure of the resulting solution?
  b. What is the composition by mole fraction of pentane in the vapor that is in equilibrium with this solution?

50. A solution is prepared by mixing 0.0300 mol CH_2Cl_2 and 0.0500 mol CH_2Br_2 at 25°C. Assuming the solution is ideal, calculate the composition of the vapor (in terms of mole fractions) at 25°C. At 25°C, the vapor pressures of pure CH_2Cl_2 and pure CH_2Br_2 are 133 and 11.4 torr, respectively.

51. What is the composition of a methanol (CH_3OH)–propanol ($CH_3CH_2CH_2OH$) solution that has a vapor pressure of 174 torr at 40°C? At 40°C, the vapor pressures of pure methanol and pure propanol are 303 and 44.6 torr, respectively. Assume the solution is ideal.

52. Benzene and toluene form an ideal solution. Consider a solution of benzene and toluene prepared at 25°C. Assuming the mole fractions of benzene and toluene in the vapor phase are equal, calculate the composition of the solution. At 25°C the vapor pressures of benzene and toluene are 95 and 28 torr, respectively.

53. Which of the following will have the lowest total vapor pressure at 25°C?
  a. pure water (vapor pressure = 23.8 torr at 25°C)
  b. a solution of glucose in water with $X_{C_6H_{12}O_6} = 0.01$
  c. a solution of sodium chloride in water with $X_{NaCl} = 0.01$
  d. a solution of methanol in water with $X_{CH_3OH} = 0.2$ (Consider the vapor pressure of both methanol [143 torr at 25°C] and water.)

54. Which of the choices in Exercise 53 has the highest vapor pressure?

55. A solution is made by mixing 50.0 g acetone (CH_3COCH_3) and 50.0 g methanol (CH_3OH). What is the vapor pressure of this solution at 25°C? What is the composition of the vapor expressed as a mole fraction? Assume ideal solution and gas behavior. (At 25°C the vapor pressures of pure acetone and pure methanol are 271 and 143 torr, respectively.) The actual vapor pressure of this solution is 161 torr. Explain any discrepancies.

56. The vapor pressures of several solutions of water–propanol ($CH_3CH_2CH_2OH$) were determined at various compositions, with the following data collected at 45°C:

X_{H_2O}	Vapor pressure (torr)
0	74.0
0.15	77.3
0.37	80.2
0.54	81.6
0.69	80.6
0.83	78.2
1.00	71.9

a. Are solutions of water and propanol ideal? Explain.
b. Predict the sign of ΔH_{soln} for water–propanol solutions.
c. Are the interactive forces between propanol and water molecules weaker than, stronger than, or equal to the interactive forces between the pure substances? Explain.
d. Which of the solutions in the data would have the lowest normal boiling point?

Colligative Properties

57. A solution is prepared by dissolving 27.0 g of urea, $(NH_2)_2CO$, in 150.0 g of water. Calculate the boiling point of the solution. Urea is a nonelectrolyte.

58. A 2.00-g sample of a large biomolecule was dissolved in 15.0 g of carbon tetrachloride. The boiling point of this solution was determined to be 77.85°C. Calculate the molar mass of the biomolecule. For carbon tetrachloride, the boiling-point constant is 5.03°C · kg/mol, and the boiling point of pure carbon tetrachloride is 76.50°C.

59. What mass of glycerin ($C_3H_8O_3$), a nonelectrolyte, must be dissolved in 200.0 g water to give a solution with a freezing point of −1.50°C?

60. The freezing point of t-butanol is 25.50°C and K_f is 9.1°C · kg/mol. Usually t-butanol absorbs water on exposure to air. If the freezing point of a 10.0-g sample of t-butanol is 24.59°C, how many grams of water are present in the sample?

61. Calculate the freezing point and boiling point of an antifreeze solution that is 50.0% by mass of ethylene glycol ($HOCH_2CH_2OH$) in water. Ethylene glycol is a nonelectrolyte.

62. What volume of ethylene glycol ($C_2H_6O_2$), a nonelectrolyte, must be added to 15.0 L of water to produce an antifreeze solution with a freezing point of −25.0°C? What is the boiling point of this solution? (The density of ethylene glycol is 1.11 g/cm³, and the density of water is 1.00 g/cm³.)

63. Thyroxine, an important hormone that controls the rate of metabolism in the body, can be isolated from the thyroid gland. When 0.455 g of thyroxine is dissolved in 10.0 g of benzene, the freezing point of the solution is depressed by 0.300°C. What is the molar mass of thyroxine? See Table 11.5.

64. Anthraquinone contains only carbon, hydrogen, and oxygen and has an empirical formula of C_7H_4O. The freezing point of camphor is lowered by 22.3°C when 1.32 g anthraquinone is dissolved in 11.4 g camphor. Determine the molecular formula of anthraquinone.

65. a. Calculate the freezing-point depression and osmotic pressure at 25°C of an aqueous solution containing 1.0 g/L of a protein (molar mass = 9.0×10^4 g/mol) if the density of the solution is 1.0 g/cm³.
b. Considering your answer to part a, which colligative property, freezing-point depression or osmotic pressure, would be better used to determine the molar masses of large molecules? Explain.

66. An aqueous solution of 10.00 g of catalase, an enzyme found in the liver, has a volume of 1.00 L at 27°C. The solution's osmotic pressure at 27°C is found to be 0.74 torr. Calculate the molar mass of catalase.

67. If the human eye has an osmotic pressure of 8.00 atm at 25°C, what concentration of solute particles in water will provide an isotonic eyedrop solution (a solution with equal osmotic pressure)?

68. How would you prepare 1.0 L of an aqueous solution of sodium chloride having an osmotic pressure of 15 atm at 22°C? Assume sodium chloride exists as Na^+ and Cl^- ions in solution.

Properties of Electrolyte Solutions

69. Consider the following solutions:
0.010 m Na_3PO_4 in water
0.020 m $CaBr_2$ in water
0.020 m KCl in water
0.020 m HF in water (HF is a weak acid.)
a. Assuming complete dissociation of the soluble salts, which solution(s) would have the same boiling point as 0.040 m $C_6H_{12}O_6$ in water? $C_6H_{12}O_6$ is a nonelectrolyte.
b. Which solution would have the highest vapor pressure at 28°C?
c. Which solution would have the largest freezing-point depression?

70. From the following:

pure water
solution of $C_{12}H_{22}O_{11}$ (m = 0.01) in water
solution of NaCl (m = 0.01) in water
solution of $CaCl_2$ (m = 0.01) in water

choose the one with the

a. highest freezing point.
b. lowest freezing point.
c. highest boiling point.
d. lowest boiling point.
e. highest osmotic pressure.

71. Calculate the freezing point and the boiling point of each of the following aqueous solutions. (Assume complete dissociation.)
a. 0.050 m $MgCl_2$
b. 0.050 m $FeCl_3$

72. A water desalination plant is set up near a salt marsh containing water that is 0.10 M NaCl. Calculate the minimum pressure that must be applied at 20.°C to purify the water by reverse osmosis. Assume NaCl is completely dissociated.

73. Use the following data for three aqueous solutions of $CaCl_2$ to calculate the apparent value of the van't Hoff factor.

Molality	Freezing-Point Depression (°C)
0.0225	0.110
0.0910	0.440
0.278	1.330

74. Calculate the freezing point and the boiling point of each of the following solutions using the observed van't Hoff factors in Table 11.6.
   a. 0.050 *m* $MgCl_2$ **b.** 0.050 *m* $FeCl_3$

75. In the winter of 1994, record low temperatures were registered throughout the United States. For example, in Champaign, Illinois, a record low of $-29°F$ was registered. At this temperature can salting icy roads with $CaCl_2$ be effective in melting the ice?
   a. Assume *i* = 3.00 for $CaCl_2$.
   b. Assume the average value of *i* from Exercise 73.
   (The solubility of $CaCl_2$ in cold water is 74.5 g per 100.0 g of water.)

76. A 0.500-g sample of a compound is dissolved in enough water to form 100.0 mL of solution. This solution has an osmotic pressure of 2.50 atm at 25°C. If each molecule of the solute dissociates into two particles (in this solvent), what is the molar mass of this solute?

Additional Exercises

77. In a coffee-cup calorimeter, 1.60 g of NH_4NO_3 was mixed with 75.0 g of water at an initial temperature of 25.00°C. After dissolution of the salt, the final temperature of the calorimeter contents was 23.34°C.
   a. Assuming the solution has a heat capacity of 4.18 J/g · °C, and assuming no heat loss to the calorimeter, calculate the enthalpy of solution (ΔH_{soln}) for the dissolution of NH_4NO_3 in units of kJ/mol.
   b. If the enthalpy of hydration for NH_4NO_3 is $-630.$ kJ/mol, calculate the lattice energy of NH_4NO_3.

78. In flushing and cleaning columns used in liquid chromatography to remove adsorbed contaminants, a series of solvents is used. Hexane (C_6H_{14}), chloroform ($CHCl_3$), methanol (CH_3OH), and water are passed through the column in that order. Rationalize the order in terms of intermolecular forces and the mutual solubility (miscibility) of the solvents.

79. Explain the following on the basis of the behavior of atoms and/or ions.
   a. Cooking with water is faster in a pressure cooker than in an open pan.
   b. Salt is used on icy roads.
   c. Melted sea ice from the Artic Ocean produces fresh water.
   d. $CO_2(s)$ (dry ice) does not have a normal boiling point under normal atmospheric conditions, even though CO_2 is a liquid in fire extinguishers.
   e. Adding a solute to a solvent extends the liquid phase over a larger temperature range.

80. The term "proof" is defined as twice the percent by volume of pure ethanol in solution. Thus, a solution that is 95% (by volume) ethanol is 190 proof. What is the molarity of ethanol in a 92 proof ethanol/water solution? Assume the density of ethanol, C_2H_5OH, is 0.79 g/cm³ and the density of water is 1.0 g/cm³.

81. At 25°C, the vapor in equilibrium with a solution containing carbon disulfide and acetonitrile has a total pressure of 263 torr and is 85.5 mole percent carbon disulfide. What is the mole fraction of carbon disulfide in the solution? At 25°C, the vapor pressure of carbon disulfide is 375 torr. Assume the solution and vapor exhibit ideal behavior.

82. If the fluid inside a tree is about 0.1 *M* more concentrated in solute than the groundwater that bathes the roots, how high will a column of fluid rise in the tree at 25°C? Assume that the density of the fluid is 1.0 g/cm³. (The density of mercury is 13.6 g/cm³.)

83. An unknown compound contains only carbon, hydrogen, and oxygen. Combustion analysis of the compound gives mass percents of 31.57% C and 5.30% H. The molar mass is determined by measuring the freezing-point depression of an aqueous solution. A freezing point of $-5.20°C$ is recorded for a solution made by dissolving 10.56 g of the compound in 25.0 g water. Determine the empirical formula, molar mass, and molecular formula of the compound. Assume that the compound is a nonelectrolyte.

84. Consider the following:

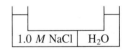

   What would happen to the level of liquid in the two arms if the semipermeable membrane separating the two liquids were permeable to
   a. H_2O only?   **b.** H_2O, Na^+, and Cl^-?

85. Consider an aqueous solution containing sodium chloride that has a density of 1.01 g/mL. Assume the solution behaves ideally. The freezing point of this solution at 1.0 atm is $-1.28°C$. Calculate the percent composition of this solution (by mass).

86. What stabilizes a colloidal suspension? Explain why adding heat or adding an electrolyte can cause the suspended particles to settle out.

87. The freezing point of an aqueous solution is $-2.79°C$.
   a. Determine the boiling point of this solution.
   b. Determine the vapor pressure (in mm Hg) of this solution at 25°C (the vapor pressure of pure water at 25°C is 23.76 mm Hg).
   c. Explain any assumptions you make in solving parts a and b.

Challenge Problems

88. The vapor pressure of pure benzene is 750.0 torr and the vapor pressure of toluene is 300.0 torr at a certain temperature. You make a solution by pouring "some" benzene with "some" toluene. You then place this solution in a closed container and wait for the vapor to come into equilibrium with the solution. Next, you condense the vapor. You put this liquid (the condensed vapor) in a closed container and wait for the vapor to come into equilibrium with the solution. You then condense this vapor and find the mole fraction of benzene in this vapor to be 0.714. Determine the mole fraction of benzene in the original solution assuming the solution behaves ideally.

89. Liquid A has vapor pressure *x*, and liquid B has vapor pressure *y*. What is the mole fraction of the liquid mixture if the vapor above the solution is 30.% A by moles? 50.% A? 80.% A? (Calculate in terms of *x* and *y*.)
   Liquid A has vapor pressure *x*, liquid B has vapor pressure *y*. What is the mole fraction of the vapor above the solution if the liquid mixture is 30.% A by moles? 50.% A? 80.% A? (Calculate in terms of *x* and *y*.)

90. Erythrocytes are red blood cells containing hemoglobin. In a saline solution they shrivel when the salt concentration is high and swell when the salt concentration is low. In a 25°C aqueous solution of NaCl, whose freezing point is −0.406°C, erythrocytes neither swell nor shrink. If we want to calculate the osmotic pressure of the solution inside the erythrocytes under these conditions, what do we need to assume? Why? Estimate how good (or poor) of an assumption this is. Make this assumption and calculate the osmotic pressure of the solution inside the erythrocytes.

91. You make 20.0 g of a sucrose ($C_{12}H_{22}O_{11}$) and NaCl mixture and dissolve it in 1.00 kg of water. The freezing point of this solution is found to be −0.426°C. Assuming ideal behavior, calculate the mass percent composition of the original mixture, and the mole fraction of sucrose in the original mixture.

92. An aqueous solution is 1.00% NaCl by mass and has a density of 1.071 g/cm³ at 25°C. The observed osmotic pressure of this solution is 7.83 atm at 25°C.

   a. What fraction of the moles of NaCl in this solution exist as ion pairs?

   b. Calculate the freezing point that would be observed for this solution.

93. The vapor in equilibrium with a pentane–hexane solution at 25°C has a mole fraction of pentane equal to 0.15 at 25°C. What is the mole fraction of pentane in the solution? (See Exercise 49 for the vapor pressures of the pure liquids.)

94. A forensic chemist is given a white solid that is suspected of being pure cocaine ($C_{17}H_{21}NO_4$, molar mass = 303.35 g/mol). She dissolves 1.22 ± 0.01 g of the solid in 15.60 ± 0.01 g benzene. The freezing point is lowered by 1.32 ± 0.04°C.

   a. What is the molar mass of the substance? Assuming that the percent uncertainty in the calculated molar mass is the same as the percent uncertainty in the temperature change, calculate the uncertainty in the molar mass.

   b. Could the chemist unequivocally state that the substance is cocaine? For example, is the uncertainty small enough to distinguish cocaine from codeine ($C_{18}H_{21}NO_3$, molar mass = 299.36 g/mol)?

   c. Assuming that the absolute uncertainties in the measurements of temperature and mass remain unchanged, how could the chemist improve the precision of her results?

95. A 1.60-g sample of a mixture of naphthalene ($C_{10}H_8$) and anthracene ($C_{14}H_{10}$) is dissolved in 20.0 g benzene (C_6H_6). The freezing point of the solution is 2.81°C. What is the composition as mass percent of the sample mixture? The freezing point of benzene is 5.51°C, and K_f is 5.12°C · kg/mol.

96. A solid mixture contains $MgCl_2$ and NaCl. When 0.5000 g of this solid is dissolved in enough water to form 1.000 L of solution, the osmotic pressure at 25.0°C is observed to be 0.3950 atm. What is the mass percent of $MgCl_2$ in the solid? (Assume ideal behavior for the solution.)

97. Formic acid (HCO_2H) is a monoprotic acid that ionizes only partially in aqueous solutions. A 0.10 *M* formic acid solution is 4.2% ionized. Assuming that the molarity and molality of the solution

are the same, calculate the freezing point and the boiling point of 0.10 *M* formic acid.

98. Specifications for lactated Ringer's solution, which is used for intravenous (IV) injections, are as follows to reach 100. mL of solution:

   285–315 mg Na^+
   14.1–17.3 mg K^+
   4.9–6.0 mg Ca^{2+}
   368–408 mg Cl^-
   231–261 mg lactate, $C_3H_5O_3{}^-$

   a. Specify the amounts of NaCl, KCl, $CaCl_2 \cdot 2H_2O$, and $NaC_3H_5O_3$ needed to prepare 100. mL of lactated Ringer's solution.

   b. What is the range of the osmotic pressure of the solution at 37°C, given the above specifications?

99. In some regions of the southwest United States, the water is very hard. For example, in Las Cruces, New Mexico, the tap water contains about 560 μg of dissolved solids per milliliter. Reverse osmosis units are marketed in this area to soften water. A typical unit exerts a pressure of 8.0 atm and can produce 45 L of water per day.

   a. Assuming all of the dissolved solids are $MgCO_3$ and assuming a temperature of 27°C, what total volume of water must be processed to produce 45 L of pure water?

   b. Would the same system work for purifying seawater? (Assume seawater is 0.60 *M* NaCl.)

Integrative Problems

These problems require the integration of multiple concepts to find the solutions.

100. Creatinine, $C_4H_7N_3O$, is a by-product of muscle metabolism, and creatinine levels in the body are known to be a fairly reliable indicator of kidney function. The normal level of creatinine in the blood for adults is approximately 1.0 mg per deciliter (dL) of blood. If the density of blood is 1.025 g/mL, calculate the molality of a normal creatinine level in a 10.0-mL blood sample. What is the osmotic pressure of this solution at 25.0°C?

101. An aqueous solution containing 0.250 mol of Q, a strong electrolyte, in 5.00×10^2 g of water freezes at −2.79°C. What is the van't Hoff factor for Q? The molal freezing-point depression constant for water is 1.86°C · kg/mol. What is the formula of Q if it is 38.68% chlorine by mass and there are twice as many anions as cations in one formula unit of Q?

102. Patients undergoing an upper gastrointestinal tract laboratory test are typically given an X-ray contrast agent that aids with the radiologic imaging of the anatomy. One such contrast agent is sodium diatrizoate, a nonvolatile water-soluble compound. A 0.378 *m* solution is prepared by dissolving 38.4 g of sodium diatrizoate (NaDTZ) in 1.60×10^2 mL of water at 31.2°C (the density of water at 31.2°C is 0.995 g/mL). What is the molar mass of sodium diatrizoate? What is the vapor pressure of this solution if the vapor pressure of pure water at 31.2°C is 34.1 torr?

Marathon Problem*

This problem is designed to incorporate several concepts and techniques into one situation. Marathon Problems can be used in class by groups of students to help facilitate problem-solving skills.

103. Using the following information, identify the strong electrolyte whose general formula is

$$M_x(A)_y \cdot zH_2O$$

Ignore the effect of interionic attractions in the solution.

a. A^{n-} is a common oxyanion. When 30.0 mg of the anhydrous sodium salt containing this oxyanion (Na_nA, where $n = 1, 2,$ or 3) is reduced, 15.26 mL of 0.02313 M reducing agent is required to react completely with the Na_nA present. Assume a 1:1 mole ratio in the reaction.

b. The cation is derived from a silvery white metal that is relatively expensive. The metal itself crystallizes in a body-centered cubic unit cell and has an atomic radius of 198.4 pm. The solid, pure metal has a density of 5.243 g/cm³. The oxidation number of M in the strong electrolyte in question is +3.

c. When 33.45 mg of the compound is present (dissolved) in 10.0 mL of aqueous solution at 25°C, the solution has an osmotic pressure of 558 torr.

Get help understanding core concepts and visualizing molecular-level interactions, and practice problem solving, by visiting the Online Study Center at **college.hmco.com/ PIC/zumdahl7e.**

*This Marathon Problem was developed by James H. Burness, Penn State University, York Campus. Reprinted with permission from the *Journal of Chemical Education,* Vol. 68, No. 11, 1991, pp. 919–922; copyright © 1991, Division of Chemical Education, Inc.

12 Chemical Kinetics

Contents

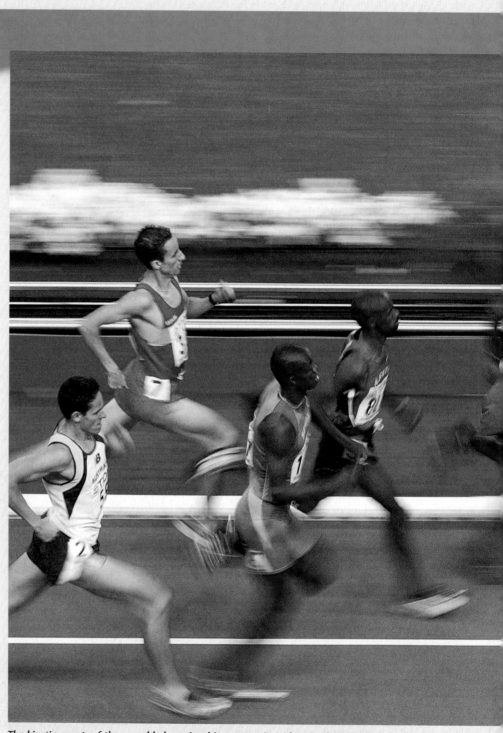

The kinetic energy of these world championship runners is evident in the 800-meter race at Saint-Denis, France.

The applications of chemistry focus largely on chemical reactions, and the commercial use of a reaction requires knowledge of several of its characteristics, including its stoichiometry, energetics, and rate. A reaction is defined by its reactants and products, whose identity must be learned by experiment. Once the reactants and products are known, the equation for the reaction can be written and balanced, and stoichiometric calculations can be carried out. Another very important characteristic of a reaction is its spontaneity. Spontaneity refers to the *inherent tendency* for the process to occur; however, it implies nothing about speed. *Spontaneous does not mean fast.* There are many spontaneous reactions that are so slow that no apparent reaction occurs over a period of weeks or years at normal temperatures. For example, there is a strong inherent tendency for gaseous hydrogen and oxygen to combine, that is,

$$2H_2(g) + O_2(g) \longrightarrow 2H_2O(l)$$

but in fact the two gases can coexist indefinitely at 25°C. Similarly, the gaseous reactions

$$H_2(g) + Cl_2(g) \longrightarrow 2HCl(g)$$
$$N_2(g) + 3H_2(g) \longrightarrow 2NH_3(g)$$

are both highly likely to occur from a thermodynamic standpoint, but we observe no reactions under normal conditions. In addition, the process of changing diamond to graphite is spontaneous but is so slow that it is not detectable.

To be useful, reactions must occur at a reasonable rate. To produce the 20 million tons of ammonia needed each year for fertilizer, we cannot simply mix nitrogen and hydrogen gases at 25°C and wait for them to react. It is not enough to understand the stoichiometry and thermodynamics of a reaction; we also must understand the factors that govern the rate of the reaction. The area of chemistry that concerns reaction rates is called **chemical kinetics.**

One of the main goals of chemical kinetics is to understand the steps by which a reaction takes place. This series of steps is called the *reaction mechanism.* Understanding the mechanism allows us to find ways to facilitate the reaction. For example, the Haber process for the production of ammonia requires high temperatures to achieve commercially feasible reaction rates. However, even higher temperatures (and more cost) would be required without the use of iron oxide, which speeds up the reaction.

In this chapter we will consider the main ideas of chemical kinetics. We will explore rate laws, reaction mechanisms, and simple models for chemical reactions.

Visualization: Coffee Creamer Flammability

12.1 Reaction Rates

The kinetics of air pollution is discussed in Section 12.8.

To introduce the concept of the rate of a reaction, we will consider the decomposition of nitrogen dioxide, a gas that causes air pollution. Nitrogen dioxide decomposes to nitric oxide and oxygen as follows:

$$2NO_2(g) \longrightarrow 2NO(g) + O_2(g)$$

Suppose in a particular experiment we start with a flask of nitrogen dioxide at 300°C and measure the concentrations of nitrogen dioxide, nitric oxide, and oxygen as the nitrogen dioxide decomposes. The results of this experiment are summarized in Table 12.1, and the data are plotted in Fig. 12.1.

The energy required for athletic exertion, the breaching of an Orca whale, and the combustion of fuel in a race car all result from chemical reactions.

Note from these results that the concentration of the reactant (NO_2) decreases with time and the concentrations of the products (NO and O_2) increase with time (see Fig. 12.2). Chemical kinetics deals with the speed at which these changes occur. The speed, or *rate*, of a process is defined as the change in a given quantity over a specific period of time. For chemical reactions, the quantity that changes is the amount or concentration of a reactant or product. So the **reaction rate** of a chemical reaction is defined as the *change in concentration of a reactant or product per unit time:*

$$\text{Rate} = \frac{\text{concentration of A at time } t_2 - \text{concentration of A at time } t_1}{t_2 - t_1}$$

[A] means concentration of A in mol/L.

$$= \frac{\Delta[A]}{\Delta t}$$

TABLE 12.1   Concentrations of Reactant and Products as a Function of Time for the Reaction $2NO_2(g) \rightarrow 2NO(g) + O_2(g)$ (at 300°C)

Time (±1 s)	Concentration (mol/L)		
	NO_2	NO	O_2
0	0.0100	0	0
50	0.0079	0.0021	0.0011
100	0.0065	0.0035	0.0018
150	0.0055	0.0045	0.0023
200	0.0048	0.0052	0.0026
250	0.0043	0.0057	0.0029
300	0.0038	0.0062	0.0031
350	0.0034	0.0066	0.0033
400	0.0031	0.0069	0.0035

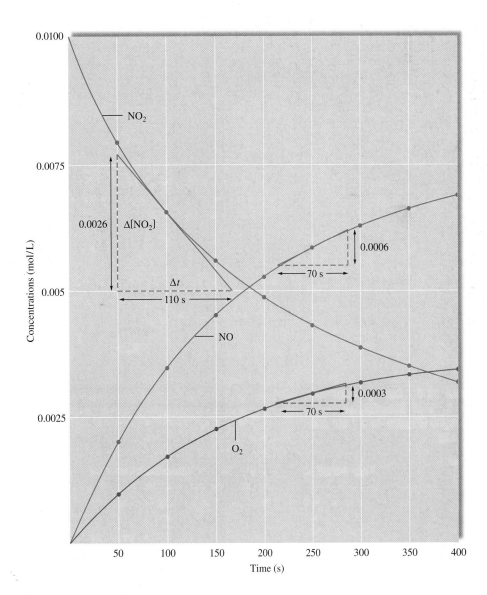

FIGURE 12.1
Starting with a flask of nitrogen dioxide at 300°C, the concentrations of nitrogen dioxide, nitric oxide, and oxygen are plotted versus time.

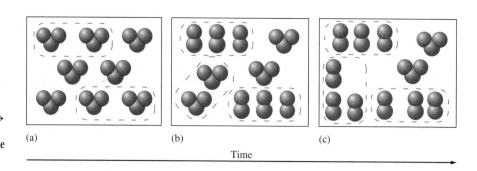

FIGURE 12.2
Representation of the reaction $2NO_2(g) \rightarrow 2NO(g) + O_2(g)$. (a) The reaction at the very beginning ($t = 0$). (b) and (c) As time passes, NO_2 is converted to NO and O_2.

(a)   (b)   (c)

Time

where A is the reactant or product being considered, and the square brackets indicate concentration in mol/L. As usual, the symbol Δ indicates a *change* in a given quantity. Note that a change can be positive (increase) or negative (decrease), thus leading to a positive or negative reaction rate by this definition. However, for convenience, we will always define the rate as a positive quantity, as we will see.

Now let us calculate the average rate at which the concentration of NO_2 changes over the first 50 seconds of the reaction using the data given in Table 12.1.

$$\frac{\text{Change in } [NO_2]}{\text{Time elapsed}} = \frac{\Delta[NO_2]}{\Delta t}$$

$$= \frac{[NO_2]_{t=50} - [NO_2]_{t=0}}{50.\,s - 0\,s}$$

$$= \frac{0.0079\ \text{mol/L} - 0.0100\ \text{mol/L}}{50.\,s}$$

$$= -4.2 \times 10^{-5}\ \text{mol/L} \cdot s$$

Note that since the concentration of NO_2 decreases with time, $\Delta[NO_2]$ is a negative quantity. Because it is customary to work with *positive* reaction rates, we define the rate of this particular reaction as

$$\text{Rate} = -\frac{\Delta[NO_2]}{\Delta t}$$

Appendix 1.3 reviews slopes of straight lines.

Since the concentrations of reactants always decrease with time, any rate expression involving a reactant will include a negative sign. The average rate of this reaction from 0 to 50 seconds is then

$$\text{Rate} = -\frac{\Delta[NO_2]}{\Delta t}$$

$$= -(-4.2 \times 10^{-5}\ \text{mol/L} \cdot s)$$

$$= 4.2 \times 10^{-5}\ \text{mol/L} \cdot s$$

TABLE 12.2 Average Rate (in mol/L · s) of Decomposition of Nitrogen Dioxide as a Function of Time*

$\dfrac{\Delta[NO_2]}{\Delta t}$	Time Period (s)
4.2×10^{-5}	$0 \rightarrow 50$
2.8×10^{-5}	$50 \rightarrow 100$
2.0×10^{-5}	$100 \rightarrow 150$
1.4×10^{-5}	$150 \rightarrow 200$
1.0×10^{-5}	$200 \rightarrow 250$

*Note that the *rate* decreases with time.

The average rates for this reaction during several other time intervals are given in Table 12.2. *Note that the rate is not constant but decreases with time.* The rates given in Table 12.2 are *average rates* over 50-second time intervals. The value of the rate at a particular time (the **instantaneous rate**) can be obtained by computing the slope of a line tangent to the curve at that point. Figure 12.1 shows a tangent drawn at $t = 100$ seconds. The *slope* of this line gives the rate at $t = 100$ seconds as follows:

$$\text{Slope of the tangent line} = \frac{\text{change in } y}{\text{change in } x}$$

$$= \frac{\Delta[NO_2]}{\Delta t}$$

Los Angeles on a clear day, and on a day when air pollution is significant.

But

$$\text{Rate} = -\frac{\Delta[NO_2]}{\Delta t}$$

Therefore,

$$\text{Rate} = -(\text{slope of the tangent line})$$
$$= -\left(\frac{-0.0026 \text{ mol/L}}{110 \text{ s}}\right)$$
$$= 2.4 \times 10^{-5} \text{ mol/L} \cdot \text{s}$$

So far we have discussed the rate of this reaction only in terms of the reactant. The rate also can be defined in terms of the products. However, in doing so we must take into account the coefficients in the balanced equation for the reaction, because the stoichiometry determines the relative rates of consumption of reactants and generation of products. For example, in the reaction we are considering,

$$2NO_2(g) \longrightarrow 2NO(g) + O_2(g)$$

both the reactant NO_2 and the product NO have a coefficient of 2, so NO is produced at the same rate as NO_2 is consumed. We can verify this from Fig. 12.1. Note that the curve for NO is the same shape as the curve for NO_2, except that it is inverted, or flipped over. This means that, at any point in time, the slope of the tangent to the curve for NO will be the negative of the slope to the curve for NO_2. (Verify this at the point $t = 100$ seconds on both curves.) In the balanced equation, the product O_2 has a coefficient of 1, which means it is produced half as fast as NO, since NO has a coefficient of 2. That is, the rate of NO production is twice the rate of O_2 production.

We also can verify this fact from Fig. 12.1. For example, at $t = 250$ seconds,

$$\text{Slope of the tangent to the NO curve} = \frac{6.0 \times 10^{-4} \text{ mol/L}}{70. \text{ s}}$$
$$= 8.6 \times 10^{-6} \text{ mol/L} \cdot \text{s}$$
$$\text{Slope of the tangent to the O}_2 \text{ curve} = \frac{3.0 \times 10^{-4} \text{ mol/L}}{70. \text{ s}}$$
$$= 4.3 \times 10^{-6} \text{ mol/L} \cdot \text{s}$$

The slope at $t = 250$ seconds on the NO curve is twice the slope of that point on the O_2 curve, showing that the rate of production of NO is twice that of O_2.

The rate information can be summarized as follows:

Rate of consumption of NO_2	=	rate of production of NO	=	2(rate of production of O_2)

$$-\frac{\Delta[NO_2]}{\Delta t} = \frac{\Delta[NO]}{\Delta t} = 2\left(\frac{\Delta[O_2]}{\Delta t}\right)$$

We have seen that the rate of a reaction is not constant, but that it changes with time. This is so because the concentrations change with time (Fig. 12.1).

Because the reaction rate changes with time, and because the rate is different (by factors that depend on the coefficients in the balanced equation) depending on which reactant or product is being studied, we must be very specific when we describe a rate for a chemical reaction.

12.2 Rate Laws: An Introduction

Chemical reactions are *reversible*. In our discussion of the decomposition of nitrogen dioxide, we have so far considered only the *forward reaction*, as shown here:

$$2NO_2(g) \longrightarrow 2NO(g) + O_2(g)$$

However, the *reverse reaction* also can occur. As NO and O_2 accumulate, they can react to re-form NO_2:

$$O_2(g) + 2NO(g) \longrightarrow 2NO_2(g)$$

When gaseous NO_2 is placed in an otherwise empty container, initially the dominant reaction is

$$2NO_2(g) \longrightarrow 2NO(g) + O_2(g)$$

When forward and reverse reaction rates are equal, there will be no changes in the concentrations of reactants or products. This is called *chemical equilibrium* and is discussed fully in Chapter 13.

and the change in the concentration of NO_2 ($\Delta[NO_2]$) depends only on the forward reaction. However, after a period of time, enough products accumulate so that the reverse reaction becomes important. Now $\Delta[NO_2]$ depends on the *difference in the rates of the forward and reverse reactions*. This complication can be avoided if we study the rate of a reaction under conditions where the reverse reaction makes only a negligible contribution. Typically, this means that we must study a reaction at a point soon after the reactants are mixed, before the products have had time to build up to significant levels.

If we choose conditions where the reverse reaction can be neglected, the *reaction rate will depend only on the concentrations of the reactants*. For the decomposition of nitrogen dioxide, we can write

$$\text{Rate} = k[NO_2]^n \qquad (12.1)$$

Such an expression, which shows how the rate depends on the concentrations of reactants, is called a **rate law**. The proportionality constant k, called the **rate constant,** and n, called the **order** of the reactant, must both be determined by experiment. The order of a reactant can be an integer (including zero) or a fraction. For the relatively simple reactions we will consider in this book, the orders will often be positive integers.

Note two important points about Equation (12.1):

1. The concentrations of the products do not appear in the rate law because the reaction rate is being studied under conditions where the reverse reaction does not contribute to the overall rate.

2. The value of the exponent n must be determined by experiment; it cannot be written from the balanced equation.

Before we go further we must define exactly what we mean by the term *rate* in Equation (12.1). In Section 12.1 we saw that reaction rate means a change in concentration per unit time. However, which reactant or product concentration do we choose in defining the rate? For example, for the decomposition of NO_2 to produce O_2 and NO considered in Section 12.1, we could define the rate in terms of any of these three species. However, since O_2 is produced only half as fast as NO, we must be careful to specify which species we are talking about in a given case. For instance, we might choose to define the reaction rate in terms of the consumption of NO_2:

$$\text{Rate} = -\frac{\Delta[NO_2]}{\Delta t} = k[NO_2]^n$$

On the other hand, we could define the rate in terms of the production of O_2:

$$\text{Rate}' = \frac{\Delta[O_2]}{\Delta t} = k'[NO_2]^n$$

Note that because $2NO_2$ molecules are consumed for every O_2 molecule produced,

$$\text{Rate} = 2 \times \text{rate}'$$

or

$$k[NO_2]^n = 2k'[NO_2]^n$$

and

$$k = 2 \times k'$$

Thus the value of the rate constant depends on how the rate is defined.

In this text we will always be careful to define exactly what is meant by the rate for a given reaction so that there will be no confusion about which specific rate constant is being used.

Types of Rate Laws

Notice that the rate law we have used to this point expresses rate as a function of concentration. For example, for the decomposition of NO_2 we have defined

$$\text{Rate} = -\frac{\Delta[NO_2]}{\Delta t} = k[NO_2]^n$$

which tells us (once we have determined the value of n) exactly how the rate depends on the concentration of the reactant, NO_2. A rate law that expresses how the *rate depends on concentration* is technically called the **differential rate law,** but it is often simply called the **rate law.** Thus when we use the term *the rate law* in this text, we mean the expression that gives the rate as a function of concentration.

The name *differential rate law* comes from a mathematical term. We will regard it simply as a label. The terms *differential rate law* and *rate law* will be used interchangeably in this text.

A second kind of rate law, the **integrated rate law,** also will be important in our study of kinetics. The integrated rate law expresses how the *concentrations depend on time.* Although we will not consider the details here, a given differential rate law is always related to a certain type of integrated rate law, and vice versa. That is, if we determine the differential rate law for a given reaction, we automatically know the form of the integrated rate law for the reaction. This means that once we determine experimentally either type of rate law for a reaction, we also know the other one.

Which rate law we choose to determine by experiment often depends on what types of data are easiest to collect. If we can conveniently measure how the rate changes as the concentrations are changed, we can readily determine the differential (rate/concentration) rate law. On the other hand, if it is more convenient to measure the concentration as a function of time, we can determine the form of the integrated (concentration/time) rate law. We will discuss how rate laws are actually determined in the next several sections.

Why are we interested in determining the rate law for a reaction? How does it help us? It helps us because we can work backward from the rate law to infer the steps by which the reaction occurs. Most chemical reactions do not take place in a single step but result from a series of sequential steps. To understand a chemical reaction, we must learn what these steps are. For example, a chemist who is designing an insecticide may study the reactions involved in the process of insect growth to see what type of molecule might interrupt this series of reactions. Or an industrial chemist may be trying to make a given reaction occur faster. To accomplish this, he or she must know which step is slowest, because it is that step that must be speeded up. Thus a chemist is usually not interested in a rate law for its own sake but because of what it reveals about the steps by which a reaction occurs. We will develop a process for finding the reaction steps in this chapter.

Rate Laws: A Summary

- There are two types of rate laws.

  1. The *differential rate law* (often called simply the *rate law*) shows how the rate of a reaction depends on concentrations.

  2. The *integrated rate law* shows how the concentrations of species in the reaction depend on time.

- Because we typically consider reactions only under conditions where the reverse reaction is unimportant, our rate laws will involve only concentrations of reactants.

- Because the differential and integrated rate laws for a given reaction are related in a well-defined way, the experimental determination of *either* of the rate laws is sufficient.

- Experimental convenience usually dictates which type of rate law is determined experimentally.

- Knowing the rate law for a reaction is important mainly because we can usually infer the individual steps involved in the reaction from the specific form of the rate law.

12.3 Determining the Form of the Rate Law

The first step in understanding how a given chemical reaction occurs is to determine the *form* of the rate law. That is, we need to determine experimentally the power to which each reactant concentration must be raised in the rate law. In this section we will explore ways to obtain the differential rate law for a reaction. First, we will consider the decomposition of dinitrogen pentoxide in carbon tetrachloride solution:

$$2N_2O_5(soln) \longrightarrow 4NO_2(soln) + O_2(g)$$

Data for this reaction at 45°C are listed in Table 12.3 and plotted in Fig. 12.3. In this reaction the oxygen gas escapes from the solution and thus does not react with the nitrogen dioxide, so we do not have to be concerned about the effects of the reverse reaction at any time over the life of the reaction. That is, the reverse reaction is negligible at all times over the course of this reaction.

Evaluation of the reaction rates at concentrations of N_2O_5 of 0.90 M and 0.45 M, by taking the slopes of the tangents to the curve at these points (see Fig. 12.3), yields the following data:

TABLE 12.3 Concentration/ Time Data for the Reaction $2N_2O_5(soln) \rightarrow 4NO_2(soln) + O_2(g)$ (at 45°C)

$[N_2O_5]$ (mol/L)	Time (s)
1.00	0
0.88	200
0.78	400
0.69	600
0.61	800
0.54	1000
0.48	1200
0.43	1400
0.38	1600
0.34	1800
0.30	2000

$[N_2O_5]$	Rate (mol/L · s)
0.90 M	5.4×10^{-4}
0.45 M	2.7×10^{-4}

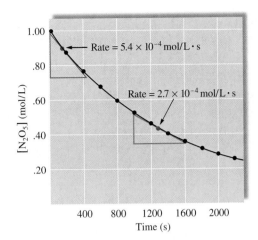

FIGURE 12.3
A plot of the concentration of N_2O_5 as a function of time for the reaction $2N_2O_5(soln) \rightarrow 4NO_2(soln) + O_2(g)$ (at 45°C). Note that the reaction rate at $[N_2O_5] = 0.90\ M$ is twice that at $[N_2O_5] = 0.45\ M$.

Visualization: Decomposition of N_2O_5

First order: rate $= k[A]$. Doubling the concentration of A doubles the reaction rate.

Note that when $[N_2O_5]$ is halved, the rate is also halved. This means that the rate of this reaction depends on the concentration of N_2O_5 to the *first power*. In other words, the (differential) rate law for this reaction is

$$\text{Rate} = -\frac{\Delta[N_2O_5]}{\Delta t} = k[N_2O_5]^1 = k[N_2O_5]$$

Thus the reaction is *first order* in N_2O_5. Note that for this reaction the order is *not* the same as the coefficient of N_2O_5 in the balanced equation for the reaction. This reemphasizes the fact that the order of a particular reactant must be obtained by *observing* how the reaction rate depends on the concentration of that reactant.

We have seen that by determining the instantaneous rate at two different reactant concentrations, the rate law for the decomposition of N_2O_5 is shown to have the form

$$\text{Rate} = -\frac{\Delta[A]}{\Delta t} = k[A]$$

where A represents N_2O_5.

Method of Initial Rates

The value of the initial rate is determined for each experiment at the same value of t as close to $t = 0$ as possible.

One common method for experimentally determining the form of the rate law for a reaction is the **method of initial rates**. The **initial rate** of a reaction is the instantaneous rate determined just after the reaction begins (just after $t = 0$). The idea is to determine the instantaneous rate before the initial concentrations of reactants have changed significantly. Several experiments are carried out using different initial concentrations, and the initial rate is determined for each run. The results are then compared to see how the initial rate depends on the initial concentrations. This allows the form of the rate law to be determined. We will illustrate the method of initial rates using the following equation:

Visualization: Reaction Rate and Concentration

$$NH_4^+(aq) + NO_2^-(aq) \longrightarrow N_2(g) + 2H_2O(l)$$

Table 12.4 gives initial rates obtained from three experiments involving different initial concentrations of reactants. The general form of the rate law for this reaction is

$$\text{Rate} = -\frac{\Delta[NH_4^+]}{\Delta t} = k[NH_4^+]^n[NO_2^-]^m$$

We can determine the values of n and m by observing how the initial rate depends on the initial concentrations of NH_4^+ and NO_2^-. In Experiments 1 and 2, where the initial

TABLE 12.4   Initial Rates from Three Experiments for the Reaction $NH_4^+(aq) + NO_2^-(aq) \rightarrow N_2(g) + 2H_2O(l)$

Experiment	Initial Concentration of NH_4^+	Initial Concentration of NH_2^-	Initial Rate (mol/L · s)
1	0.100 M	0.0050 M	1.35×10^{-7}
2	0.100 M	0.010 M	2.70×10^{-7}
3	0.200 M	0.010 M	5.40×10^{-7}

concentration of NH_4^+ remains the same but the initial concentration of NO_2^- doubles, the observed initial rate also doubles. Since

$$\text{Rate} = k[NH_4^+]^n[NO_2^-]^m$$

we have for Experiment 1

$$\text{Rate} = 1.35 \times 10^{-7} \text{ mol/L} \cdot \text{s} = k(0.100 \text{ mol/L})^n(0.0050 \text{ mol/L})^m$$

and for Experiment 2

$$\text{Rate} = 2.70 \times 10^{-7} \text{ mol/L} \cdot \text{s} = k(0.100 \text{ mol/L})^n(0.010 \text{ mol/L})^m$$

The ratio of these rates is

$$\frac{\text{Rate 2}}{\text{Rate 1}} = \underbrace{\frac{2.70 \times 10^{-7} \text{ mol/L} \cdot \text{s}}{1.35 \times 10^{-7} \text{ mol/L} \cdot \text{s}}}_{2.00} = \frac{k(\cancel{0.100 \text{ mol/L}})^n(0.010 \text{ mol/L})^m}{k(\cancel{0.100 \text{ mol/L}})^n(0.0050 \text{ mol/L})^m}$$

$$= \frac{(0.010 \text{ mol/L})^m}{(0.0050 \text{ mol/L})^m} = (2.0)^m$$

Rates 1, 2, and 3 were determined at the same value of t (very close to $t = 0$).

Thus

$$\frac{\text{Rate 2}}{\text{Rate 1}} = 2.00 = (2.0)^m$$

which means the value of m is 1. The rate law for this reaction is first order in the reactant NO_2^-.

A similar analysis of the results for Experiments 2 and 3 yields the ratio

$$\frac{\text{Rate 3}}{\text{Rate 2}} = \frac{5.40 \times 10^{-7} \text{ mol/L} \cdot \text{s}}{2.70 \times 10^{-7} \text{ mol/L} \cdot \text{s}} = \frac{(0.200 \text{ mol/L})^n}{(0.100 \text{ mol/L})^n}$$

$$= 2.00 = \left(\frac{0.200}{0.100}\right)^n = (2.00)^n$$

The value of n is also 1.

We have shown that the values of n and m are both 1 and the rate law is

$$\text{Rate} = k[NH_4^+][NO_2^-]$$

This rate law is first order in both NO_2^- and NH_4^+. Note that it is merely a coincidence that n and m have the same values as the coefficients of NH_4^+ and NO_2^- in the balanced equation for the reaction.

Overall reaction order is the sum of the orders for the various reactants.

The **overall reaction order** is the sum of n and m. For this reaction, $n + m = 2$. The reaction is second order overall.

The value of the rate constant k can now be calculated using the results of *any* of the three experiments shown in Table 12.4. From the data for Experiment 1, we know that

$$\text{Rate} = k[NH_4^+][NO_2^-]$$
$$1.35 \times 10^{-7}\,\text{mol/L} \cdot \text{s} = k(0.100\,\text{mol/L})(0.0050\,\text{mol/L})$$

Then

$$k = \frac{1.35 \times 10^{-7}\,\text{mol/L} \cdot \text{s}}{(0.100\,\text{mol/L})(0.0050\,\text{mol/L})} = 2.7 \times 10^{-4}\,\text{L/mol} \cdot \text{s}$$

| Sample Exercise 12.1 | Determining a Rate Law |

The reaction between bromate ions and bromide ions in acidic aqueous solution is given by the equation

$$BrO_3^-(aq) + 5Br^-(aq) + 6H^+(aq) \longrightarrow 3Br_2(l) + 3H_2O(l)$$

Table 12.5 gives the results from four experiments. Using these data, determine the orders for all three reactants, the overall reaction order, and the value of the rate constant.

Solution

The general form of the rate law for this reaction is

$$\text{Rate} = k[BrO_3^-]^n[Br^-]^m[H^+]^p$$

We can determine the values of n, m, and p by comparing the rates from the various experiments. To determine the value of n, we use the results from Experiments 1 and 2, in which only $[BrO_3^-]$ changes:

$$\frac{\text{Rate 2}}{\text{Rate 1}} = \frac{1.6 \times 10^{-3}\,\text{mol/L} \cdot \text{s}}{8.0 \times 10^{-4}\,\text{mol/L} \cdot \text{s}} = \frac{k(0.20\,\text{mol/L})^n(0.10\,\text{mol/L})^m(0.10\,\text{mol/L})^p}{k(0.10\,\text{mol/L})^n(0.10\,\text{mol/L})^m(0.10\,\text{mol/L})^p}$$

$$2.0 = \left(\frac{0.20\,\text{mol/L}}{0.10\,\text{mol/L}}\right)^n = (2.0)^n$$

Thus n is equal to 1.

To determine the value of m, we use the results from Experiments 2 and 3, in which only $[Br^-]$ changes:

$$\frac{\text{Rate 3}}{\text{Rate 2}} = \frac{3.2 \times 10^{-3}\,\text{mol/L} \cdot \text{s}}{1.6 \times 10^{-3}\,\text{mol/L} \cdot \text{s}} = \frac{k(0.20\,\text{mol/L})^n(0.20\,\text{mol/L})^m(0.10\,\text{mol/L})^p}{k(0.20\,\text{mol/L})^n(0.10\,\text{mol/L})^m(0.10\,\text{mol/L})^p}$$

$$2.0 = \left(\frac{0.20\,\text{mol/L}}{0.10\,\text{mol/L}}\right)^m = (2.0)^m$$

Thus m is equal to 1.

TABLE 12.5 The Results from Four Experiments to Study the Reaction
$BrO_3^-(aq) + 5Br^-(aq) + 6H^+(aq) \rightarrow 3Br_2(l) + 3H_2O(l)$

Experiment	Initial Concentration of BrO_3^- (mol/L)	Initial Concentration of Br^- (mol/L)	Initial Concentration of H^+ (mol/L)	Measured Initial Rate (mol/L · s)
1	0.10	0.10	0.10	8.0×10^{-4}
2	0.20	0.10	0.10	1.6×10^{-3}
3	0.20	0.20	0.10	3.2×10^{-3}
4	0.10	0.10	0.20	3.2×10^{-3}

To determine the value of p, we use the results from Experiments 1 and 4, in which $[BrO_3^-]$ and $[Br^-]$ are constant but $[H^+]$ differs:

$$\frac{\text{Rate 4}}{\text{Rate 1}} = \frac{3.2 \times 10^{-3} \text{ mol/L} \cdot \text{s}}{8.0 \times 10^{-4} \text{ mol/L} \cdot \text{s}} = \frac{k(0.10 \text{ mol/L})^n(0.10 \text{ mol/L})^m(0.20 \text{ mol/L})^p}{k(0.10 \text{ mol/L})^n(0.10 \text{ mol/L})^m(0.10 \text{ mol/L})^p}$$

$$4.0 = \left(\frac{0.20 \text{ mol/L}}{0.10 \text{ mol/L}}\right)^p$$

$$4.0 = (2.0)^p = (2.0)^2$$

Thus p is equal to 2.

The rate of this reaction is first order in BrO_3^- and Br^- and second order in H^+. The overall reaction order is $n + m + p = 4$.

The rate law can now be written

$$\text{Rate} = k[BrO_3^-][Br^-][H^+]^2$$

The value of the rate constant k can be calculated from the results of any of the four experiments. For Experiment 1, the initial rate is 8.0×10^{-4} mol/L $\cdot$ s and $[BrO_3^-] = 0.100\,M$, $[Br^-] = 0.10\,M$, and $[H^+] = 0.10\,M$. Using these values in the rate law gives

$$8.0 \times 10^{-4} \text{ mol/L} \cdot \text{s} = k(0.10 \text{ mol/L})(0.10 \text{ mol/L})(0.10 \text{ mol/L})^2$$

$$8.0 \times 10^{-4} \text{ mol/L} \cdot \text{s} = k(1.0 \times 10^{-4} \text{ mol}^4/\text{L}^4)$$

$$k = \frac{8.0 \times 10^{-4} \text{ mol/L} \cdot \text{s}}{1.0 \times 10^{-4} \text{ mol}^4/\text{L}^4} = 8.0 \text{ L}^3/\text{mol}^3 \cdot \text{s}$$

Reality Check: Verify that the same value of k can be obtained from the results of the other experiments.

See Exercises 12.25 through 12.28.

12.4 The Integrated Rate Law

The rate laws we have considered so far express the rate as a function of the reactant concentrations. It is also useful to be able to express the reactant concentrations as a function of time, given the (differential) rate law for the reaction. In this section we show how this is done.

We will proceed by first looking at reactions involving a single reactant:

$$aA \longrightarrow \text{products}$$

all of which have a rate law of the form

$$\text{Rate} = -\frac{\Delta[A]}{\Delta t} = k[A]^n$$

We will develop the integrated rate laws individually for the cases $n = 1$ (first order), $n = 2$ (second order), and $n = 0$ (zero order).

First-Order Rate Laws

For the reaction

$$2N_2O_5(soln) \longrightarrow 4NO_2(soln) + O_2(g)$$

we have found that the rate law is

$$\text{Rate} = -\frac{\Delta[N_2O_5]}{\Delta t} = k[N_2O_5]$$

Since the rate of this reaction depends on the concentration of N_2O_5 to the first power, it is a **first-order reaction.** This means that if the concentration of N_2O_5 in a flask were suddenly doubled, the rate of production of NO_2 and O_2 also would double. This rate law can be put into a different form using a calculus operation known as integration, which yields the expression

$$\ln[N_2O_5] = -kt + \ln[N_2O_5]_0$$

Appendix 1.2 contains a review of logarithms.

where ln indicates the natural logarithm, t is the time, $[N_2O_5]$ is the concentration of N_2O_5 at time t, and $[N_2O_5]_0$ is the initial concentration of N_2O_5 (at $t = 0$, the start of the experiment). Note that such an equation, called the *integrated rate law,* expresses the *concentration of the reactant as a function of time.*

For a chemical reaction of the form

$$aA \longrightarrow \text{products}$$

where the kinetics are first order in [A], the rate law is

$$\text{Rate} = -\frac{\Delta[A]}{\Delta t} = k[A]$$

and the **integrated first-order rate law** is

$$\ln[A] = -kt + \ln[A]_0 \tag{12.2}$$

There are several important things to note about Equation (12.2):

An integrated rate law relates concentration to reaction time.

1. The equation shows how the concentration of A depends on time. If the initial concentration of A and the rate constant k are known, the concentration of A at any time can be calculated.

2. Equation (12.2) is of the form $y = mx + b$, where a plot of y versus x is a straight line with slope m and intercept b. In Equation (12.2),

$$y = \ln[A] \qquad x = t \qquad m = -k \qquad b = \ln[A]_0$$

For a first-order reaction, a plot of ln[A] versus t is always a straight line.

Thus, for a first-order reaction, plotting the natural logarithm of concentration versus time always gives a straight line. This fact is often used to test whether a reaction is first order. For the reaction

$$aA \longrightarrow \text{products}$$

the *reaction is first order in A if a plot of ln[A] versus t is a straight line.* Conversely, if this plot is not a straight line, the reaction is not first order in A.

3. This integrated rate law for a first-order reaction also can be expressed in terms of a *ratio* of [A] and $[A]_0$ as follows:

$$\ln\left(\frac{[A]_0}{[A]}\right) = kt$$

| Sample Exercise 12.2 | **First-Order Rate Laws I** |

The decomposition of N_2O_5 in the gas phase was studied at constant temperature.

$$2N_2O_5(g) \longrightarrow 4NO_2(g) + O_2(g)$$

$\ln[N_2O_5]$	Time (s)
-2.303	0
-2.649	50
-2.996	100
-3.689	200
-4.382	300
-5.075	400

FIGURE 12.4
A plot of $\ln[N_2O_5]$ versus time.

The following results were collected:

$[N_2O_5]$ (mol/L)	Time (s)
0.1000	0
0.0707	50
0.0500	100
0.0250	200
0.0125	300
0.00625	400

Using these data, verify that the rate law is first order in $[N_2O_5]$, and calculate the value of the rate constant, where the rate $= -\Delta[N_2O_5]/\Delta t$.

Solution

We can verify that the rate law is first order in $[N_2O_5]$ by constructing a plot of $\ln[N_2O_5]$ versus time. The values of $\ln[N_2O_5]$ at various times are given in the table above and the plot of $\ln[N_2O_5]$ versus time is shown in Fig. 12.4. The fact that the plot is a straight line confirms that the reaction is first order in N_2O_5, since it follows the equation $\ln[N_2O_5] = -kt + \ln[N_2O_5]_0$.

Since the reaction is first order, the slope of the line equals $-k$, where

$$\text{Slope} = \frac{\text{change in } y}{\text{change in } x} = \frac{\Delta y}{\Delta x} = \frac{\Delta(\ln[N_2O_5])}{\Delta t}$$

Since the first and last points are exactly on the line, we will use these points to calculate the slope:

$$\text{Slope} = \frac{-5.075 - (-2.303)}{400.\,\text{s} - 0\,\text{s}} = \frac{-2.772}{400.\,\text{s}} = -6.93 \times 10^{-3}\,\text{s}^{-1}$$

$$k = -(\text{slope}) = 6.93 \times 10^{-3}\,\text{s}^{-1}$$

See Exercise 12.31.

Sample Exercise 12.3   ## First-Order Rate Laws II

Using the data given in Sample Exercise 12.2, calculate $[N_2O_5]$ at 150 s after the start of the reaction.

Solution

We know from Sample Exercise 12.2 that $[N_2O_5] = 0.0500$ mol/L at 100 s and $[N_2O_5] = 0.0250$ mol/L at 200 s. Since 150 s is halfway between 100 and 200 s, it is tempting to assume that we can simply use an arithmetic average to obtain $[N_2O_5]$ at that time. This is incorrect because it is $\ln[N_2O_5]$, not $[N_2O_5]$, that is directly proportional to t. To calculate $[N_2O_5]$ after 150 s, we use Equation (12.2):

$$\ln[N_2O_5] = -kt + \ln[N_2O_5]_0$$

where $t = 150.$ s, $k = 6.93 \times 10^{-3}\,s^{-1}$ (as determined in Sample Exercise 12.2), and $[N_2O_5]_0 = 0.1000$ mol/L.

$$\ln([N_2O_5])_{t=150} = -(6.93 \times 10^{-3}\,s^{-1})(150.\,s) + \ln(0.100)$$
$$= -1.040 - 2.303 = -3.343$$
$$[N_2O_5]_{t=150} = \text{antilog}(-3.343) = 0.0353 \text{ mol/L}$$

The antilog operation means to exponentiate (see Appendix 1.2).

Note that this value of $[N_2O_5]$ is *not* halfway between 0.0500 and 0.0250 mol/L.

See Exercise 12.31.

Half-Life of a First-Order Reaction

WWW
Visualization: Half-Life of Reactions

The time required for a reactant to reach half its original concentration is called the **half-life of a reactant** and is designated by the symbol $t_{1/2}$. For example, we can calculate the half-life of the decomposition reaction discussed in Sample Exercise 12.2. The data plotted in Fig. 12.5 show that the half-life for this reaction is 100 seconds. We can see this by considering the following numbers:

$[N_2O_5]$(mol/L)	t (s)		
0.100	0	$\Delta t = 100$ s;	$\dfrac{[N_2O_5]_{t=100}}{[N_2O_5]_{t=0}} = \dfrac{0.050}{0.100} = \dfrac{1}{2}$
0.0500	100	$\Delta t = 100$ s;	$\dfrac{[N_2O_5]_{t=200}}{[N_2O_5]_{t=100}} = \dfrac{0.025}{0.050} = \dfrac{1}{2}$
0.0250	200	$\Delta t = 100$ s;	$\dfrac{[N_2O_5]_{t=300}}{[N_2O_5]_{t=200}} = \dfrac{0.0125}{0.0250} = \dfrac{1}{2}$
0.0125	300		

FIGURE 12.5
A plot of $[N_2O_5]$ versus time for the decomposition reaction of N_2O_5.

Note that it *always* takes 100 seconds for $[N_2O_5]$ to be halved in this reaction.

A general formula for the half-life of a first-order reaction can be derived from the integrated rate law for the general reaction

$$aA \longrightarrow products$$

If the reaction is first order in $[A]$,

$$\ln\left(\frac{[A]_0}{[A]}\right) = kt$$

By definition, when $t = t_{1/2}$,

$$[A] = \frac{[A]_0}{2}$$

Then, for $t = t_{1/2}$, the integrated rate law becomes

$$\ln\left(\frac{[A]_0}{[A]_0/2}\right) = kt_{1/2}$$

or

$$\ln(2) = kt_{1/2}.$$

Substituting the value of $\ln(2)$ and solving for $t_{1/2}$ gives

$$t_{1/2} = \frac{0.693}{k} \tag{12.3}$$

For a first-order reaction, $t_{1/2}$ is independent of the initial concentration.

This is the *general equation for the half-life of a first-order reaction*. Equation (12.3) can be used to calculate $t_{1/2}$ if k is known or k if $t_{1/2}$ is known. Note that for a first-order reaction, *the half-life does not depend on concentration*.

| Sample Exercise 12.4 | **Half-Life for First-Order Reaction** |

A certain first-order reaction has a half-life of 20.0 minutes.

a. Calculate the rate constant for this reaction.
b. How much time is required for this reaction to be 75% complete?

Solution

a. Solving Equation (12.3) for k gives

$$k = \frac{0.693}{t_{1/2}} = \frac{0.693}{20.0 \text{ min}} = 3.47 \times 10^{-2} \text{ min}^{-1}$$

b. We use the integrated rate law in the form

$$\ln\left(\frac{[A]_0}{[A]}\right) = kt$$

If the reaction is 75% complete, 75% of the reactant has been consumed, leaving 25% in the original form:

$$\frac{[A]}{[A]_0} \times 100\% = 25\%$$

This means that

$$\frac{[A]}{[A]_0} = 0.25 \quad \text{or} \quad \frac{[A]_0}{[A]} = \frac{1}{0.25} = 4.0$$

Then

$$\ln\left(\frac{[A]_0}{[A]}\right) = \ln(4.0) = kt = \left(\frac{3.47 \times 10^{-2}}{\text{min}}\right)t$$

and
$$t = \frac{\ln(4.0)}{3.47 \times 10^{-2} \, / \, \text{min}} = 40. \text{ min}$$

Thus it takes 40. minutes for this particular reaction to reach 75% completion.

Let's consider another way of solving this problem using the definition of half-life. After one half-life the reaction has gone 50% to completion. If the initial concentration were 1.0 mol/L, after one half-life the concentration would be 0.50 mol/L. One more half-life would produce a concentration of 0.25 mol/L. Comparing 0.25 mol/L with the original 1.0 mol/L shows that 25% of the reactant is left after two half-lives. This is a general result. (What percentage of reactant remains after three half-lives?) Two half-lives for this reaction is 2(20.0 min), or 40.0 min, which agrees with the preceding answer.

See Exercises 12.32 and 12.42 through 12.44.

Second-Order Rate Laws

For a general reaction involving a single reactant, that is,

$$aA \longrightarrow \text{products}$$

that is second order in A, the rate law is

Second order: rate $= k[A]^2$. Doubling the concentration of A quadruples the reaction rate; tripling the concentration of A increases the rate by nine times.

$$\text{Rate} = -\frac{\Delta[A]}{\Delta t} = k[A]^2 \tag{12.4}$$

The **integrated second-order rate law** has the form

$$\frac{1}{[A]} = kt + \frac{1}{[A]_0} \tag{12.5}$$

Note the following characteristics of Equation (12.5):

For second-order reactions, a plot of $1/[A]$ versus t will be linear.

1. A plot of $1/[A]$ versus t will produce a straight line with a slope equal to k.

2. Equation (12.5) shows how [A] depends on time and can be used to calculate [A] at any time t, provided k and $[A]_0$ are known.

When one half-life of the second-order reaction has elapsed ($t = t_{1/2}$), by definition,

$$[A] = \frac{[A]_0}{2}$$

Equation (12.5) then becomes

$$\frac{1}{\dfrac{[A]_0}{2}} = kt_{1/2} + \frac{1}{[A]_0}$$

$$\frac{2}{[A]_0} - \frac{1}{[A]_0} = kt_{1/2}$$

$$\frac{1}{[A]_0} = kt_{1/2}$$

Solving for $t_{1/2}$ gives *the expression for the half-life of a second-order reaction:*

$$t_{1/2} = \frac{1}{k[A]_0} \tag{12.6}$$

| | Sample Exercise 12.5 | Determining Rate Laws |

Butadiene reacts to form its dimer according to the equation

$$2C_4H_6(g) \longrightarrow C_8H_{12}(g)$$

The following data were collected for this reaction at a given temperature:

$[C_4H_6]$ (mol/L)	Time (± 1 s)
0.01000	0
0.00625	1000
0.00476	1800
0.00370	2800
0.00313	3600
0.00270	4400
0.00241	5200
0.00208	6200

a. Is this reaction first order or second order?
b. What is the value of the rate constant for the reaction?
c. What is the half-life for the reaction under the conditions of this experiment?

Solution

a. To decide whether the rate law for this reaction is first order or second order, we must see whether the plot of $\ln[C_4H_6]$ versus time is a straight line (first order) or the plot of $1/[C_4H_6]$ versus time is a straight line (second order). The data necessary to make these plots are as follows:

t (s)	$\dfrac{1}{[C_4H_6]}$	$\ln[C_4H_4]$
0	100	−4.605
1000	160	−5.075
1800	210	−5.348
2800	270	−5.599
3600	320	−5.767
4400	370	−5.915
5200	415	−6.028
6200	481	−6.175

The resulting plots are shown in Fig. 12.6. Since the $\ln[C_4H_6]$ versus t plot [Fig. 12.6(a)] is not a straight line, the reaction is *not* first order. The reaction is, however, second order, as shown by the linearity of the $1/[C_4H_6]$ versus t plot [Fig. 12.6(b)]. Thus we can now write the rate law for this second-order reaction:

$$\text{Rate} = -\frac{\Delta[C_4H_6]}{\Delta t} = k[C_4H_6]^2$$

b. For a second-order reaction, a plot of $1/[C_4H_6]$ versus t produces a straight line of slope k. In terms of the standard equation for a straight line, $y = mx + b$, we have $y = 1/[C_4H_6]$ and $x = t$. Thus the slope of the line can be expressed as follows:

$$\text{Slope} = \frac{\Delta y}{\Delta x} = \frac{\Delta\left(\dfrac{1}{[C_4H_6]}\right)}{\Delta t}$$

Butadiene (C_4H_6)

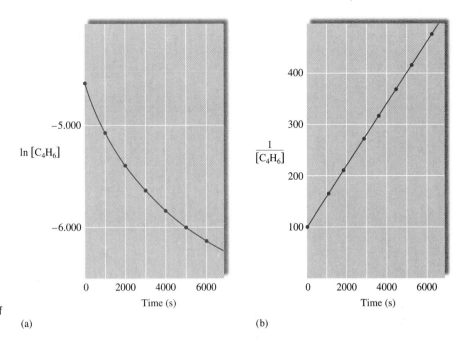

FIGURE 12.6
(a) A plot of $\ln[C_4H_6]$ versus t. (b) A plot of $1/[C_4H_6]$ versus t.

(a)   (b)

Using the points at $t = 0$ and $t = 6200$, we can find the rate constant for the reaction:

$$k = \text{slope} = \frac{(481 - 100)\,\text{L/mol}}{(6200. - 0)\,\text{s}} = \frac{381}{6200.}\,\text{L/mol} \cdot \text{s} = 6.14 \times 10^{-2}\,\text{L/mol} \cdot \text{s}$$

c. The expression for the half-life of a second-order reaction is

$$t_{1/2} = \frac{1}{k[A]_0}$$

In this case $k = 6.14 \times 10^{-2}$ L/mol · s (from part b) and $[A]_0 = [C_4H_6]_0 = 0.01000\ M$ (the concentration at $t = 0$). Thus

$$t_{1/2} = \frac{1}{(6.14 \times 10^{-2}\,\text{L/mol} \cdot \text{s})(1.000 \times 10^{-2}\,\text{mol/L})} = 1.63 \times 10^3\,\text{s}$$

The initial concentration of C_4H_6 is halved in 1630 s.

See Exercises 12.33, 12.34, 12.45, and 12.46.

For a second-order reaction, $t_{1/2}$ is dependent on $[A]_0$. For a first-order reaction, $t_{1/2}$ is independent of $[A]_0$.

It is important to recognize the difference between the half-life for a first-order reaction and the half-life for a second-order reaction. For a second-order reaction, $t_{1/2}$ depends on both k and $[A]_0$; for a first-order reaction, $t_{1/2}$ depends only on k. For a first-order reaction, a constant time is required to reduce the concentration of the reactant by half, and then by half again, and so on, as the reaction proceeds. From Sample Exercise 12.5 we can see that this is *not* true for a second-order reaction. For that second-order reaction, we found that the first half-life (the time required to go from $[C_4H_6] = 0.010\ M$ to $[C_4H_6] = 0.0050\ M$) is 1630 seconds. We can estimate the second half-life from the concentration data as a function of time. Note that to reach $0.0024\ M\ C_4H_6$ (approximately $0.0050/2$) requires 5200 seconds of reaction time. Thus to get from $0.0050\ M\ C_4H_6$ to $0.0024\ M\ C_4H_6$ takes 3570 seconds ($5200 - 1630$). The second half-life is much longer than the first. This pattern is characteristic of second-order reactions. In fact, *for a second-order reaction, each successive half-life is double the preceding one* (provided the effects

For each successive half-life, $[A]_0$ is halved. Since $t_{1/2} = 1/k[A]_0$, $t_{1/2}$ doubles.

of the reverse reaction can be ignored, as we are assuming here). Prove this to yourself by examining the equation $t_{1/2} = 1/(k[A]_0)$.

Zero-Order Rate Laws

Most reactions involving a single reactant show either first-order or second-order kinetics. However, sometimes such a reaction can be a **zero-order reaction.** The rate law for a zero-order reaction is

$$\text{Rate} = k[A]^0 = k(1) = k$$

A zero-order reaction has a constant rate.

For a zero-order reaction, the rate is constant. It does not change with concentration as it does for first-order or second-order reactions.

The **integrated rate law for a zero-order reaction** is

$$[A] = -kt + [A]_0 \tag{12.7}$$

In this case a plot of $[A]$ versus t gives a straight line of slope $-k$, as shown in Fig. 12.7.

The expression for the half-life of a zero-order reaction can be obtained from the integrated rate law. By definition, $[A] = [A]_0/2$ when $t = t_{1/2}$, so

$$\frac{[A]_0}{2} = -kt_{1/2} + [A]_0$$

or

$$kt_{1/2} = \frac{[A]_0}{2k}$$

Solving for $t_{1/2}$ gives

$$t_{1/2} = \frac{[A]_0}{2k} \tag{12.8}$$

Zero-order reactions are most often encountered when a substance such as a metal surface or an enzyme is required for the reaction to occur. For example, the decomposition reaction

$$2N_2O(g) \longrightarrow 2N_2(g) + O_2(g)$$

occurs on a hot platinum surface. When the platinum surface is completely covered with N_2O molecules, an increase in the concentration of N_2O has no effect on the rate, since only those N_2O molecules on the surface can react. Under these conditions, *the rate is a constant* because it is controlled by what happens on the platinum surface rather than by the total concentration of N_2O, as illustrated in Fig. 12.8. This reaction also can occur at high temperatures with no platinum surface present, but under these conditions, it is not zero order.

Integrated Rate Laws for Reactions with More Than One Reactant

So far we have considered the integrated rate laws for simple reactions with only one reactant. Special techniques are required to deal with more complicated reactions. Let's consider the reaction

$$BrO_3^-(aq) + 5Br^-(aq) + 6H^+(aq) \longrightarrow 3Br_2(l) + 3H_2O(l)$$

From experimental evidence we know that the rate law is

$$\text{Rate} = -\frac{\Delta[BrO_3^-]}{\Delta t} = k[BrO_3^-][Br^-][H^+]^2$$

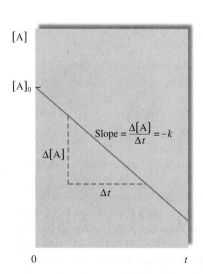

$$\text{Slope} = \frac{\Delta[A]}{\Delta t} = -k$$

FIGURE 12.7
A plot of $[A]$ versus t for a zero-order reaction.

FIGURE 12.8
The decomposition reaction $2N_2O(g) \rightarrow 2N_2(g) + O_2(g)$ takes place on a platinum surface. Although $[N_2O]$ is twice as great in (b) as in (a), the rate of decomposition of N_2O is the same in both cases because the platinum surface can accommodate only a certain number of molecules. As a result, this reaction is zero order.

$\bullet\bullet\bullet$ N_2O

(a)   (b)

Suppose we run this reaction under conditions where $[BrO_3^-]_0 = 1.0 \times 10^{-3} \, M$, $[Br^-]_0 = 1.0 \, M$, and $[H^+]_0 = 1.0 \, M$. As the reaction proceeds, $[BrO_3^-]$ decreases significantly, but because the Br^- ion and H^+ ion concentrations are so large initially, relatively little of these two reactants is consumed. Thus $[Br^-]$ and $[H^+]$ remain *approximately constant.* In other words, under the conditions where the Br^- ion and H^+ ion concentrations are much larger than the BrO_3^- ion concentration, we can assume that throughout the reaction

$$[Br^-] = [Br^-]_0 \quad \text{and} \quad [H^+] = [H^+]_0$$

This means that the rate law can be written

$$\text{Rate} = k[Br^-]_0[H^+]_0^2[BrO_3^-] = k'[BrO_3^-]$$

where, since $[Br^-]_0$ and $[H^+]_0$ are constant,

$$k' = k[Br^-]_0[H^+]_0^2$$

The rate law

$$\text{Rate} = k'[BrO_3^-]$$

is first order. However, since this law was obtained by simplifying a more complicated one, it is called a **pseudo-first-order rate law.** Under the conditions of this experiment, a plot of $\ln[BrO_3^-]$ versus t will give a straight line where the slope is equal to $-k'$. Since $[Br^-]_0$ and $[H^+]_0$ are known, the value of k can be calculated from the equation

$$k' = k[Br^-]_0[H^+]_0^2$$

which can be rearranged to give

$$k = \frac{k'}{[Br^-]_0[H^+]_0^2}$$

Note that the kinetics of complicated reactions can be studied by observing the behavior of one reactant at a time. If the concentration of one reactant is much smaller than the concentrations of the others, then the amounts of those reactants present in large concentrations will not change significantly and can be regarded as constant. The change in concentration with time of the reactant present in a relatively small amount can then be used to determine the order of the reaction in that component. This technique allows us to determine rate laws for complex reactions.

12.5 Rate Laws: A Summary

In the last several sections we have developed the following important points:

1. To simplify the rate laws for reactions, we have always assumed that the rate is being studied under conditions where only the forward reaction is important. This produces rate laws that contain only reactant concentrations.

2. There are two types of rate laws.
   a. The *differential rate law* (often called the *rate law*) shows how the rate depends on the concentrations. The forms of the rate laws for zero-order, first-order, and second-order kinetics of reactions with single reactants are shown in Table 12.6.
   b. The *integrated rate law* shows how concentration depends on time. The integrated rate laws corresponding to zero-order, first-order, and second- order kinetics of one-reactant reactions are given in Table 12.6.

3. Whether we determine the differential rate law or the integrated rate law depends on the type of data that can be collected conveniently and accurately. Once we have experimentally determined either type of rate law, we can write the other for a given reaction.

4. The most common method for experimentally determining the differential rate law is the method of initial rates. In this method several experiments are run at different initial concentrations and the instantaneous rates are determined for each at the same value of t (as close to $t = 0$ as possible). The point is to evaluate the rate before the concentrations change significantly from the initial values. From a comparison of the initial rates and the initial concentrations the dependence of the rate on the concentrations of various reactants can be obtained—that is, the order in each reactant can be determined.

5. To experimentally determine the integrated rate law for a reaction, concentrations are measured at various values of t as the reaction proceeds. Then the job is to see which integrated rate law correctly fits the data. Typically this is done visually by ascertaining which type of plot gives a straight line. A summary for one-reactant reactions is given in Table 12.6. Once the correct straight-line plot is found, the correct integrated rate law can be chosen and the value of k obtained from the slope. Also, the (differential) rate law for the reaction can then be written.

Visualization: Rate Laws

TABLE 12.6 Summary of the Kinetics for Reactions of the Type aA → Products That Are Zero, First, or Second Order in [A]

	Order		
	Zero	*First*	*Second*
Rate Law:	$\text{Rate} = k$	$\text{Rate} = k[A]$	$\text{Rate} = k[A]^2$
Integrated Rate Law:	$[A] = -kt + [A]_0$	$\ln[A] = -kt + \ln[A]_0$	$\dfrac{1}{[A]} = kt + \dfrac{1}{[A]_0}$
Plot Needed to Give a Straight Line: Relationship of Rate Constant to the Slope of Straight Line:	$[A]$ versus t Slope $= -k$	$\ln[A]$ versus t Slope $= -k$	$\dfrac{1}{[A]}$ versus t Slope $= k$
Half-Life:	$t_{1/2} = \dfrac{[A]_0}{2k}$	$t_{1/2} = \dfrac{0.693}{k}$	$t_{1/2} = \dfrac{1}{k[A]_0}$

6. The integrated rate law for a reaction that involves several reactants can be treated by choosing conditions such that the concentration of only one reactant varies in a given experiment. This is done by having the concentration of one reactant remain small compared with the concentrations of all the others, causing a rate law such as

$$\text{Rate} = k[A]^n[B]^m[C]^p$$

to reduce to

$$\text{Rate} = k'[A]^n$$

where $k' = k[B]_0^m[C]_0^p$ and $[B]_0 \gg [A]_0$ and $[C]_0 \gg [A]_0$. The value of n is obtained by determining whether a plot of $[A]$ versus t is linear ($n = 0$), a plot of $\ln[A]$ versus t is linear ($n = 1$), or a plot of $1/[A]$ versus t is linear ($n = 2$). The value of k' is determined from the slope of the appropriate plot. The values of m, p, and k can be found by determining the value of k' at several different concentrations of B and C.

12.6 Reaction Mechanisms

Visualization: Oscillating Reaction

Most chemical reactions occur by a *series of steps* called the **reaction mechanism.** To understand a reaction, we must know its mechanism, and one of the main purposes for studying kinetics is to learn as much as possible about the steps involved in a reaction. In this section we explore some of the fundamental characteristics of reaction mechanisms.

Consider the reaction between nitrogen dioxide and carbon monoxide:

$$NO_2(g) + CO(g) \longrightarrow NO(g) + CO_2(g)$$

The rate law for this reaction is known from experiment to be

$$\text{Rate} = k[NO_2]^2$$

A balanced equation does not tell us *how* the reactants become products.

As we will see below, this reaction is more complicated than it appears from the balanced equation. This is quite typical; the balanced equation for a reaction tells us the reactants, the products, and the stoichiometry but gives no direct information about the reaction mechanism.

For the reaction between nitrogen dioxide and carbon monoxide, the mechanism is thought to involve the following steps:

$$NO_2(g) + NO_2(g) \xrightarrow{k_1} NO_3(g) + NO(g)$$
$$NO_3(g) + CO(g) \xrightarrow{k_2} NO_2(g) + CO_2(g)$$

An intermediate is formed in one step and used up in a subsequent step and so is never seen as a product.

where k_1 and k_2 are the rate constants of the individual reactions. In this mechanism, gaseous NO_3 is an **intermediate,** a species that is neither a reactant nor a product but that is formed and consumed during the reaction sequence. This reaction is illustrated in Fig. 12.9.

Step 1

Step 2

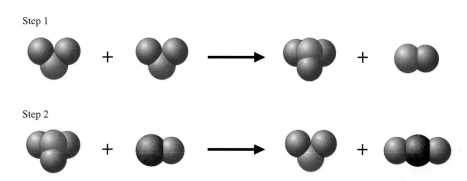

FIGURE 12.9
A molecular representation of the elementary steps in the reaction of NO_2 and CO.

TABLE 12.7 Examples of Elementary Steps

Elementary Step	Molecularity	Rate Law
A → products	*Uni*molecular	Rate = $k[A]$
A + A → products	*Bi*molecular	Rate = $k[A]^2$
(2A → products)		
A + B → products	*Bi*molecular	Rate = $k[A][B]$
A + A + B → products	*Ter*molecular	Rate = $k[A]^2[B]$
(2A + B → products)		
A + B + C → products	*Ter*molecular	Rate = $k[A][B][C]$

Each of these two reactions is called an **elementary step,** *a reaction whose rate law can be written from its molecularity.* **Molecularity** is defined as the number of species that must collide to produce the reaction indicated by that step. A reaction involving one molecule is called a **unimolecular step.** Reactions involving the collision of two and three species are termed **bimolecular** and **termolecular,** respectively. Termolecular steps are quite rare, because the probability of three molecules colliding simultaneously is very small. Examples of these three types of elementary steps and the corresponding rate laws are shown in Table 12.7. Note from Table 12.7 that the rate law for an elementary step follows *directly* from the molecularity of that step. For example, for a bimolecular step the rate law is always second order, either of the form $k[A]^2$ for a step with a single reactant or of the form $k[A][B]$ for a step involving two reactants.

The prefix *uni-* means one, *bi-* means two, and *ter-* means three.

A unimolecular elementary step is always first order, a bimolecular step is always second order, and so on.

We can now define a reaction mechanism more precisely. It is a *series of elementary steps that must satisfy two requirements:*

1. The sum of the elementary steps must give the overall balanced equation for the reaction.

2. The mechanism must agree with the experimentally determined rate law.

To see how these requirements are applied, we will consider the mechanism given above for the reaction of nitrogen dioxide and carbon monoxide. First, note that the sum of the two steps gives the overall balanced equation:

$$NO_2(g) + NO_2(g) \longrightarrow NO_3(g) + NO(g)$$
$$NO_3(g) + CO(g) \longrightarrow NO_2(g) + CO_2(g)$$
$$\overline{NO_2(g) + NO_2(g) + NO_3(g) + CO(g) \longrightarrow NO_3(g) + NO(g) + NO_2(g) + CO_2(g)}$$

Overall reaction: $NO_2(g) + CO(g) \longrightarrow NO(g) + CO_2(g)$

The first requirement for a correct mechanism is met. To see whether the mechanism meets the second requirement, we need to introduce a new idea: the **rate-determining step.** Multistep reactions often have one step that is much slower than all the others. Reactants can become products only as fast as they can get through this slowest step. That is, the overall reaction can be no faster than the slowest, or rate-determining, step in the sequence. An analogy for this situation is the pouring of water rapidly into a container through a funnel. The water collects in the container at a rate that is essentially determined by the size of the funnel opening and not by the rate of pouring.

A reaction is only as fast as its slowest step.

Which is the rate-determining step in the reaction of nitrogen dioxide and carbon monoxide? Let's *assume* that the first step is rate-determining and the second step is relatively fast:

$$NO_2(g) + NO_2(g) \longrightarrow NO_3(g) + ONO(g) \quad \text{Slow (rate-determining)}$$
$$NO_3(g) + CO(g) \longrightarrow NO_2(g) + CO_2(g) \quad \text{Fast}$$

What we have really assumed here is that the formation of NO_3 occurs much more slowly than its reaction with CO. The rate of CO_2 production is then controlled by the rate of formation of NO_3 in the first step. Since this is an elementary step, we can write the rate law from the molecularity. The bimolecular first step has the rate law

$$\text{Rate of formation of } NO_3 = \frac{\Delta[NO_3]}{\Delta t} = k_1[NO_2]^2$$

Since the overall reaction rate can be no faster than the slowest step,

$$\text{Overall rate} = k_1[NO_2]^2$$

Note that this rate law agrees with the experimentally determined rate law given earlier. The mechanism we assumed above satisfies the two requirements stated earlier and *may* be the correct mechanism for the reaction.

How does a chemist deduce the mechanism for a given reaction? The rate law is always determined first. Then, using chemical intuition and following the two rules given on the previous page, the chemist constructs possible mechanisms and tries, with further experiments, to eliminate those that are least likely. *A mechanism can never be proved absolutely.* We can only say that a mechanism that satisfies the two requirements is *possibly* correct. Deducing mechanisms for chemical reactions can be difficult and requires skill and experience. We will only touch on this process in this text.

Sample Exercise 12.6	## Reaction Mechanisms

The balanced equation for the reaction of the gases nitrogen dioxide and fluorine is

$$2NO_2(g) + F_2(g) \longrightarrow 2NO_2F(g)$$

The experimentally determined rate law is

$$\text{Rate} = k[NO_2][F_2]$$

A suggested mechanism for this reaction is

$$NO_2 + F_2 \xrightarrow{k_1} NO_2F + F \qquad \text{Slow}$$
$$F + NO_2 \xrightarrow{k_2} NO_2F \qquad \text{Fast}$$

Is this an acceptable mechanism? That is, does it satisfy the two requirements?

Solution

The first requirement for an acceptable mechanism is that the sum of the steps should give the balanced equation:

$$NO_2 + F_2 \longrightarrow NO_2F + F$$
$$\underline{F + NO_2 \longrightarrow NO_2F}$$
$$2NO_2 + F_2 + \cancel{F} \longrightarrow 2NO_2F + \cancel{F}$$

Overall reaction: $\qquad 2NO_2 + F_2 \longrightarrow 2NO_2F$

The first requirement is met.

The second requirement is that the mechanism must agree with the experimentally determined rate law. Since the proposed mechanism states that the first step is rate-determining, the overall reaction rate must be that of the first step. The first step is bimolecular, so the rate law is

$$\text{Rate} = k_1[NO_2][F_2]$$

This has the same form as the experimentally determined rate law. The proposed mechanism is acceptable because it satisfies both requirements. (Note that we have not proved that it is *the correct* mechanism.)

See Exercises 12.51 and 12.52.

Although the mechanism given in Sample Exercise 12.6 has the correct stoichiometry and fits the observed rate law, other mechanisms may also satisfy these requirements. For example, the mechanism might be

$$NO_2 + F_2 \longrightarrow NOF_2 + O \qquad \text{Slow}$$
$$NO_2 + O \longrightarrow NO_3 \qquad \text{Fast}$$
$$NOF_2 + NO_2 \longrightarrow NO_2F + NOF \qquad \text{Fast}$$
$$NO_3 + NOF \longrightarrow NO_2F + NO_2 \qquad \text{Fast}$$

To decide on the most probable mechanism for the reaction, the chemist doing the study would have to perform additional experiments.

12.7 A Model for Chemical Kinetics

How do chemical reactions occur? We already have given some indications. For example, we have seen that the rates of chemical reactions depend on the concentrations of the reacting species. The initial rate for the reaction

$$aA + bB \longrightarrow \text{products}$$

can be described by the rate law

$$\text{Rate} = k[A]^n[B]^m$$

where the order of each reactant depends on the detailed reaction mechanism. This explains why reaction rates depend on concentration. But what about some of the other factors affecting reaction rates? For example, how does temperature affect the speed of a reaction?

We can answer this question qualitatively from our experience. We have refrigerators because food spoilage is retarded at low temperatures. The combustion of wood occurs at a measurable rate only at high temperatures. An egg cooks in boiling water much faster at sea level than in Leadville, Colorado (elevation 10,000 ft), where the boiling point of water is approximately 90°C. These observations and others lead us to conclude that *chemical reactions speed up when the temperature is increased.* Experiments have shown that virtually all rate constants show an exponential increase with absolute temperature, as represented in Fig. 12.10.

In this section we discuss a model used to account for the observed characteristics of reaction rates. This model, called the **collision model,** is built around the central idea that *molecules must collide to react.* We have already seen how this assumption explains the concentration dependence of reaction rates. Now we need to consider whether this model can account for the observed temperature dependence of reaction rates.

The kinetic molecular theory of gases predicts that an increase in temperature raises molecular velocities and so increases the frequency of collisions between molecules. This idea agrees with the observation that reaction rates are greater at higher temperatures. Thus there is qualitative agreement between the collision model and experimental observations. However, it is found that the rate of reaction is much smaller than the calculated collision frequency in a collection of gas particles. This must mean that *only a small fraction of the collisions produces a reaction.* Why?

k

T (K)

FIGURE 12.10
A plot showing the exponential dependence of the rate constant on absolute temperature. The exact temperature dependence of k is different for each reaction. This plot represents the behavior of a rate constant that doubles for every increase in temperature of 10 K.

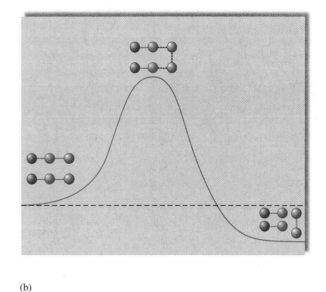

(a)   (b)

FIGURE 12.11
(a) The change in potential energy as a function of reaction progress for the reaction $2BrNO \rightarrow 2NO + Br_2$. The activation energy E_a represents the energy needed to disrupt the BrNO molecules so that they can form products. The quantity ΔE represents the net change in energy in going from reactant to products. (b) A molecular representation of the reaction.

This question was first addressed in the 1880s by Svante Arrhenius. He proposed the existence of a *threshold energy,* called the **activation energy,** that must be overcome to produce a chemical reaction. Such a proposal makes sense, as we can see by considering the decomposition of BrNO in the gas phase:

$$2BrNO(g) \longrightarrow 2NO(g) + Br_2(g)$$

In this reaction two Br—N bonds must be broken and one Br—Br bond must be formed. Breaking a Br—N bond requires considerable energy (243 kJ/mol), which must come from somewhere. The collision model postulates that the energy comes from the kinetic energies possessed by the reacting molecules before the collision. This kinetic energy is changed into potential energy as the molecules are distorted during a collision to break bonds and rearrange the atoms into the product molecules.

We can envision the reaction progress as shown in Fig. 12.11. The arrangement of atoms found at the top of the potential energy "hill," or barrier, is called the **activated complex,** or **transition state.** The conversion of BrNO to NO and Br_2 is exothermic, as indicated by the fact that the products have lower potential energy than the reactant. However, ΔE has no effect on the rate of the reaction. Rather, the rate depends on the size of the activation energy E_a.

The main point here is that a certain minimum energy is required for two BrNO molecules to "get over the hill" so that products can form. This energy is furnished by the energy of the collision. A collision between two BrNO molecules with small kinetic energies will not have enough energy to get over the barrier. At a given temperature only a certain fraction of the collisions possesses enough energy to be effective (to result in product formation).

We can be more precise by recalling from Chapter 5 that a distribution of velocities exists in a sample of gas molecules. Therefore, a distribution of collision energies also exists, as shown in Fig. 12.12 for two different temperatures. Figure 12.12 also shows the activation energy for the reaction in question. Only collisions with energy greater than

Visualization: Transition States and Activation Energy

The higher the activation energy, the slower the reaction at a given temperature.

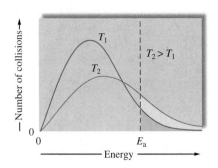

FIGURE 12.12
Plot showing the number of collisions with a particular energy at T_1 and T_2, where $T_2 > T_1$.

the activation energy are able to react (get over the barrier). At the lower temperature, T_1, the fraction of effective collisions is quite small. However, as the temperature is increased to T_2, the fraction of collisions with the required activation energy increases dramatically. When the temperature is doubled, the fraction of effective collisions much more than doubles. In fact, the fraction of effective collisions increases *exponentially* with temperature. This is encouraging for our theory; remember that rates of reactions are observed to increase exponentially with temperature. Arrhenius postulated that the number of collisions having an energy greater than or equal to the activation energy is given by the expression:

Number of collisions with the activation energy = (total number of collisions)$e^{-E_a/RT}$

where E_a is the activation energy, R is the universal gas constant, and T is the Kelvin temperature. The factor $e^{-E_a/RT}$ represents the fraction of collisions with energy E_a or greater at temperature T.

We have seen that not all molecular collisions are effective in producing chemical reactions because a minimum energy is required for the reaction to occur. There is, however, another complication. Experiments show that the *observed reaction rate is considerably smaller than the rate of collisions with enough energy to surmount the barrier.* This means that many collisions, even though they have the required energy, still do not produce a reaction. Why not?

The answer lies in the **molecular orientations** during collisions. We can illustrate this using the reaction between two BrNO molecules, as shown in Fig. 12.13. Some collision orientations can lead to reaction, and others cannot. Therefore, we must include a correction factor to allow for collisions with nonproductive molecular orientations.

To summarize, two requirements must be satisfied for reactants to collide successfully (to rearrange to form products):

1. The collision must involve enough energy to produce the reaction; that is, the collision energy must equal or exceed the activation energy.

2. The relative orientation of the reactants must allow formation of any new bonds necessary to produce products.

Taking these factors into account, we can represent the rate constant as

$$k = zpe^{-E_a/RT}$$

Visualization: The Gas Phase Reaction of NO and Cl_2

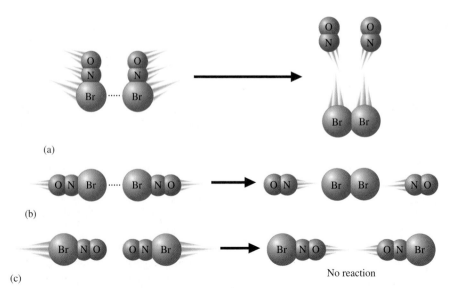

(a)

(b)

(c)

No reaction

FIGURE 12.13
Several possible orientations for a collision between two BrNO molecules. Orientations (a) and (b) can lead to a reaction, but orientation (c) cannot.

A snowy tree cricket. The frequency of a cricket's chirps depends on the temperature of the cricket.

where z is the collision frequency, p is called the **steric factor** (always less than 1) and reflects the fraction of collisions with effective orientations, and $e^{-E_a/RT}$ represents the fraction of collisions with sufficient energy to produce a reaction. This expression is most often written in form

$$k = Ae^{-E_a/RT} \qquad (12.9)$$

which is called the **Arrhenius equation.** In this equation, A replaces zp and is called the **frequency factor** for the reaction.

Taking the natural logarithm of each side of the Arrhenius equation gives

$$\ln(k) = -\frac{E_a}{R}\left(\frac{1}{T}\right) + \ln(A) \qquad (12.10)$$

Equation (12.10) is a linear equation of the type $y = mx + b$, where $y = \ln(k)$, $m = -E_a/R = $ slope, $x = 1/T$, and $b = \ln(A) = $ intercept. Thus, for a reaction where the rate constant obeys the Arrhenius equation, a plot of $\ln(k)$ versus $1/T$ gives a straight line. The slope and intercept can be used to determine, respectively, the values of E_a and A characteristic of that reaction. The fact that most rate constants obey the Arrhenius equation to a good approximation indicates that the collision model for chemical reactions is physically reasonable.

| Sample Exercise 12.7 | **Determining Activation Energy I** |

The reaction

$$2N_2O_5(g) \longrightarrow 4NO_2(g) + O_2(g)$$

was studied at several temperatures, and the following values of k were obtained:

k (s^{-1})	T (°C)
2.0×10^{-5}	20
7.3×10^{-5}	30
2.7×10^{-4}	40
9.1×10^{-4}	50
2.9×10^{-3}	60

Calculate the value of E_a for this reaction.

Solution

To obtain the value of E_a, we need to construct a plot of $\ln(k)$ versus $1/T$. First, we must calculate values of $\ln(k)$ and $1/T$, as shown below:

T (°C)	T (K)	$1/T$ (K)	k (s^{-1})	$\ln(k)$
20	293	3.41×10^{-3}	2.0×10^{-5}	-10.82
30	303	3.30×10^{-3}	7.3×10^{-5}	-9.53
40	313	3.19×10^{-3}	2.7×10^{-4}	-8.22
50	323	3.10×10^{-3}	9.1×10^{-4}	-7.00
60	333	3.00×10^{-3}	2.9×10^{-3}	-5.84

FIGURE 12.14
Plot of ln(k) versus 1/T for the reaction $2N_2O_5(g) \rightarrow 4NO_2(g) + O_2(g)$. The value of the activation energy for this reaction can be obtained from the slope of the line, which equals $-E_a/R$.

The plot of ln(k) versus $1/T$ is shown in Fig. 12.14, where the slope

$$\frac{\Delta\ln(k)}{\Delta\left(\frac{1}{T}\right)}$$

is found to be -1.2×10^4 K. The value of E_a can be determined by solving the following equation:

$$\text{Slope} = -\frac{E_a}{R}$$

$$E_a = -R(\text{slope}) = -(8.3145 \text{ J/K} \cdot \text{mol})(-1.2 \times 10^4 \text{ K})$$
$$= 1.0 \times 10^5 \text{ J/mol}$$

Thus the value of the activation energy for this reaction is 1.0×10^5 J/mol.

See Exercises 12.57 and 12.58.

The most common procedure for finding E_a for a reaction involves measuring the rate constant k at several temperatures and then plotting ln(k) versus $1/T$, as shown in Sample Exercise 12.7. However, E_a also can be calculated from the values of k at only two temperatures by using a formula that can be derived as follows from Equation (12.10).
At temperature T_1, where the rate constant is k_1,

$$\ln(k_1) = -\frac{E_a}{RT_1} + \ln(A)$$

At temperature T_2, where the rate constant is k_2,

$$\ln(k_2) = -\frac{E_a}{RT_2} + \ln(A)$$

Subtracting the first equation from the second gives

$$\ln(k_2) - \ln(k_1) = \left[-\frac{E_a}{RT_2} + \ln(A) \right] - \left[-\frac{E_a}{RT_1} + \ln(A) \right]$$

$$= -\frac{E_a}{RT_2} + \frac{E_a}{RT_1}$$

And

$$\ln\left(\frac{k_2}{k_1}\right) = \frac{E_a}{R}\left(\frac{1}{T_1} - \frac{1}{T_2}\right) \qquad (12.11)$$

Therefore, the values of k_1 and k_2 measured at temperatures T_1 and T_2 can be used to calculate E_a, as shown in Sample Exercise 12.8.

Sample Exercise 12.8	## Determining Activation Energy II

The gas-phase reaction between methane and diatomic sulfur is given by the equation

$$CH_4(g) + 2S_2(g) \longrightarrow CS_2(g) + 2H_2S(g)$$

At 550°C the rate constant for this reaction is 1.1 L/mol · s, and at 625°C the rate constant is 6.4 L/mol · s. Using these values, calculate E_a for this reaction.

Solution

The relevant data are shown in the following table:

k (L/mol · s)	T (°C)	T (K)
$1.1 = k_1$	550	$823 = T_1$
$6.4 = k_2$	625	$898 = T_2$

Substituting these values into Equation (12.11) gives

$$\ln\left(\frac{6.4}{1.1}\right) = \frac{E_a}{8.3145 \text{ J/K} \cdot \text{mol}}\left(\frac{1}{823 \text{ K}} - \frac{1}{898 \text{ K}}\right)$$

Solving for E_a gives

$$E_a = \frac{(8.3145 \text{ J/K} \cdot \text{mol})\ln\left(\dfrac{6.4}{1.1}\right)}{\left(\dfrac{1}{823 \text{ K}} - \dfrac{1}{898 \text{ K}}\right)}$$

$$= 1.4 \times 10^5 \text{ J/mol}$$

See Exercises 12.59 through 12.62.

12.8 Catalysis

We have seen that the rate of a reaction increases dramatically with temperature. If a particular reaction does not occur fast enough at normal temperatures, we can speed it up by raising the temperature. However, sometimes this is not feasible. For example, living cells can survive only in a rather narrow temperature range, and the human body is designed to operate at an almost constant temperature of 98.6°F. But many of the complicated biochemical reactions keeping us alive would be much too slow at this temperature without intervention. We exist only because the body contains many substances called **enzymes,** which increase the rates of these reactions. In fact, almost every biologically important reaction is assisted by a specific enzyme.

FIGURE 12.15
Energy plots for a catalyzed and an uncatalyzed pathway for a given reaction.

Visualization: Heterogeneous Catalysis

These cookies contain partially hydrogenated vegetable oil.

FIGURE 12.16
Effect of a catalyst on the number of reaction-producing collisions. Because a catalyst provides a reaction pathway with a lower activation energy, a much greater fraction of the collisions is effective for the catalyzed pathway (b) than for the uncatalyzed pathway (a) (at a given temperature). This allows reactants to become products at a much higher rate, even though there is no temperature increase.

Although it is possible to use higher temperatures to speed up commercially important reactions, such as the Haber process for synthesizing ammonia, this is very expensive. In a chemical plant an increase in temperature means significantly increased costs for energy. The use of an appropriate catalyst allows a reaction to proceed rapidly at a relatively low temperature and can therefore hold down production costs.

A **catalyst** is *a substance that speeds up a reaction without being consumed itself.* Just as virtually all vital biologic reactions are assisted by enzymes (biologic catalysts), almost all industrial processes also involve the use of catalysts. For example, the production of sulfuric acid uses vanadium(V) oxide, and the Haber process uses a mixture of iron and iron oxide.

How does a catalyst work? Remember that for each reaction a certain energy barrier must be surmounted. How can we make a reaction occur faster without raising the temperature to increase the molecular energies? The solution is to provide a new pathway for the reaction, one with a *lower activation energy.* This is what a catalyst does, as is shown in Fig. 12.15. Because the catalyst allows the reaction to occur with a lower activation energy, a much larger fraction of collisions is effective at a given temperature, and the reaction rate is increased. This effect is illustrated in Fig. 12.16. Note from this diagram that although a catalyst lowers the activation energy E_a for a reaction, it does not affect the energy difference ΔE between products and reactants.

Catalysts are classified as homogeneous or heterogeneous. A **homogeneous catalyst** is one that is *present in the same phase as the reacting molecules.* A **heterogeneous catalyst** exists *in a different phase,* usually as a solid.

Heterogeneous Catalysis

Heterogeneous catalysis most often involves gaseous reactants being adsorbed on the surface of a solid catalyst. **Adsorption** refers to the collection of one substance on the surface of another substance; *absorption* refers to the penetration of one substance into another. Water is *absorbed* by a sponge.

An important example of heterogeneous catalysis occurs in the hydrogenation of unsaturated hydrocarbons, compounds composed mainly of carbon and hydrogen with some carbon–carbon double bonds. Hydrogenation is an important industrial process used to change unsaturated fats, occurring as oils, to saturated fats (solid shortenings such as Crisco) in which the C=C bonds have been converted to C—C bonds through addition of hydrogen.

A simple example of hydrogenation involves ethylene:

$$
\underset{\text{Ethylene}}{\overset{\displaystyle \mathrm{H}\mathrm{H}}{\underset{\displaystyle \mathrm{H}\mathrm{H}}{\mathrm{C}{=}\mathrm{C}}}}(g) + \mathrm{H}_2(g) \longrightarrow \underset{\text{Ethane}}{\mathrm{H}{-}\underset{\mathrm{H}}{\overset{\mathrm{H}}{\mathrm{C}}}{-}\underset{\mathrm{H}}{\overset{\mathrm{H}}{\mathrm{C}}}{-}\mathrm{H}}(g)
$$

This reaction is quite slow at normal temperatures, mainly because the strong bond in the hydrogen molecule results in a large activation energy for the reaction. However, the

(a)

(b)

(a) Metal surface

(b)

(c)

(d)

Carbon

Hydrogen

FIGURE 12.17
Heterogeneous catalysis of the hydrogenation of ethylene. (a) The reactants above the metal surface. (b) Hydrogen is adsorbed onto the metal surface, forming metal–hydrogen bonds and breaking the H—H bonds. The π bond in ethylene is broken and metal–carbon bonds are formed during adsorption. (c) The adsorbed molecules and atoms migrate toward each other on the metal surface, forming new C—H bonds. (d) The C atoms in ethane (C_2H_6) have completely saturated bonding capacities and so cannot bind strongly to the metal surfaces. The C_2H_6 molecule thus escapes.

reaction rate can be greatly increased by using a solid catalyst of platinum, palladium, or nickel. The hydrogen and ethylene adsorb on the catalyst surface, where the reaction occurs. The main function of the catalyst apparently is to allow formation of metal–hydrogen interactions that weaken the H—H bonds and facilitate the reaction. The mechanism is illustrated in Fig. 12.17.

Typically, heterogeneous catalysis involves four steps:

1. Adsorption and activation of the reactants

2. Migration of the adsorbed reactants on the surface

3. Reaction of the adsorbed substances

4. Escape, or *desorption,* of the products

Heterogeneous catalysis also occurs in the oxidation of gaseous sulfur dioxide to gaseous sulfur trioxide. This process is especially interesting because it illustrates both positive and negative consequences of chemical catalysis.

The negative side is the formation of damaging air pollutants. Recall that sulfur dioxide, a toxic gas with a choking odor, is formed whenever sulfur-containing fuels are burned. However, it is sulfur trioxide that causes most of the environmental damage, mainly through the production of acid rain. When sulfur trioxide combines with a droplet of water, sulfuric acid is formed:

$$H_2O(l) + SO_3(g) \longrightarrow H_2SO_4(aq)$$

This sulfuric acid can cause considerable damage to vegetation, buildings and statues, and fish populations.

Sulfur dioxide is *not* rapidly oxidized to sulfur trioxide in clean, dry air. Why, then, is there a problem? The answer is catalysis. Dust particles and water droplets catalyze the reaction between SO_2 and O_2 in the air.

On the positive side, the heterogeneous catalysis of the oxidation of SO_2 is used to advantage in the manufacture of sulfuric acid, where the reaction of O_2 and SO_2 to form SO_3 is catalyzed by a solid mixture of platinum and vanadium(V) oxide.

Heterogeneous catalysis is also utilized in the catalytic converters in automobile exhaust systems. The exhaust gases, containing compounds such as nitric oxide, carbon monoxide, and unburned hydrocarbons, are passed through a converter containing beads of solid catalyst (see Fig. 12.18). The catalyst promotes the conversion of carbon monoxide to carbon dioxide, hydrocarbons to carbon dioxide and water, and nitric oxide to nitrogen gas to lessen the environmental impact of the exhaust gases. However, this beneficial catalysis can, unfortunately, be accompanied by the unwanted catalysis of the oxidation of SO_2 to SO_3, which reacts with the moisture present to form sulfuric acid.

Because of the complex nature of the reactions that take place in the converter, a mixture of catalysts is used. The most effective catalytic materials are transition metal oxides and noble metals such as palladium and platinum.

Homogeneous Catalysis

A homogeneous catalyst exists in the same phase as the reacting molecules. There are many examples in both the gas and liquid phases. One such example is the unusual catalytic behavior of nitric oxide toward ozone. In the troposphere, that part of the atmosphere closest to earth, nitric oxide catalyzes ozone production. However, in the upper atmosphere it catalyzes the decomposition of ozone. Both these effects are unfortunate environmentally.

In the lower atmosphere, NO is produced in any high-temperature combustion process where N_2 is present. The reaction

$$N_2(g) + O_2(g) \longrightarrow 2NO(g)$$

CHEMICAL IMPACT

Automobiles: Air Purifiers?

Outlandish as it may seem, a new scheme has been proposed to turn automobiles into air purifiers, devouring the pollutants ozone and carbon monoxide. Engelhard Corporation, an Iselin, New Jersey, company that specializes in the manufacture of catalytic converters for automotive exhaust systems, has developed a catalyst that decomposes ozone to oxygen and converts carbon monoxide to carbon dioxide. Engelhard proposes to paint the catalyst on auto-mobile radiators and air-conditioner compressors where fans draw large volumes of air for cooling purposes. The catalyst works well at the warm temperatures present on the surfaces of these devices. The idea is to let cars destroy pollutants using nothing but the catalyst and waste radiator heat.

It's an intriguing idea. The residents of Los Angeles drive nearly 300 million miles every day. At that rate, they could process a lot of air.

Visualization: Homogeneous Catalysis

is very slow at normal temperatures because of the very strong N≡N and O=O bonds. However, at elevated temperatures, such as those found in the internal combustion engines of automobiles, significant quantities of NO form. Some of this NO is converted back to N_2 in the catalytic converter, but significant amounts escape into the atmosphere to react with oxygen:

$$2NO(g) + O_2(g) \longrightarrow 2NO_2(g)$$

In the atmosphere, NO_2 can absorb light and decompose as follows:

$$NO_2(g) \xrightarrow{\text{Light}} NO(g) + O(g)$$

The oxygen atom is very reactive and can combine with oxygen molecules to form ozone:

$$O_2(g) + O(g) \longrightarrow O_3(g)$$

Ozone is a powerful oxidizing agent that can react with other air pollutants to form substances irritating to the eyes and lungs, and is itself very toxic.

In this series of reactions, nitric oxide is acting as a true catalyst because it assists the production of ozone without being consumed itself. This can be seen by summing the reactions:

Although O_2 is represented here as the oxidizing agent for NO, the actual oxidizing agent is probably some type of peroxide compound produced by reaction of oxygen with pollutants. The direct reaction of NO and O_2 is very slow.

$$
\begin{aligned}
NO(g) + \tfrac{1}{2}O_2(g) &\longrightarrow NO_2(g) \\
NO_2(g) &\xrightarrow{\text{Light}} NO(g) + O(g) \\
O_2(g) + O(g) &\longrightarrow O_3(g) \\
\hline
\tfrac{3}{2}O_2(g) &\longrightarrow O_3(g)
\end{aligned}
$$

FIGURE 12.18
The exhaust gases from an automobile engine are passed through a catalytic converter to minimize environmental damage.

In the upper atmosphere, the presence of nitric oxide has the opposite effect—the depletion of ozone. The series of reactions involved is

$$NO(g) + O_3(g) \longrightarrow NO_2(g) + O_2(g)$$
$$\underline{O(g) + NO_2(g) \longrightarrow NO(g) + O_2(g)}$$
$$O(g) + O_3(g) \longrightarrow 2O_2(g)$$

Nitric oxide is again catalytic, but here its effect is to change O_3 to O_2. This is a potential problem because O_3, which absorbs ultraviolet light, is necessary to protect us from the harmful effects of this high-energy radiation. That is, we want O_3 in the upper atmosphere to block ultraviolet radiation from the sun but not in the lower atmosphere, where we would have to breathe it and its oxidation products.

The ozone layer is also threatened by *Freons,* a group of stable, noncorrosive compounds, until recently, used as refrigerants and as propellants in aerosol cans. The most commonly used substance of this type was Freon-12 (CCl_2F_2). The chemical inertness of Freons makes them valuable but also creates a problem, since they remain in the environment a long time. Eventually, they migrate into the upper atmosphere to be decomposed by high-energy light. Among the decomposition products are chlorine atoms:

Freon-12

$$CCl_2F_2(g) \xrightarrow{\text{Light}} CClF_2(g) + Cl(g)$$

These chlorine atoms can catalyze the decomposition of ozone:

$$Cl(g) + O_3(g) \longrightarrow ClO(g) + O_2(g)$$
$$\underline{O(g) + ClO(g) \longrightarrow Cl(g) + O_2(g)}$$
$$O(g) + O_3(g) \longrightarrow 2O_2(g)$$

Ozone

The problem of Freons has been brought into strong focus by the discovery of a mysterious "hole" in the ozone layer in the stratosphere over Antarctica. Studies performed there to find the reason for the hole have found unusually high levels of chlorine monoxide (ClO). This strongly implicates the Freons in the atmosphere as being responsible for the ozone destruction.

Because they pose environmental problems, Freons have been banned by international agreement. Substitute compounds are now being used.

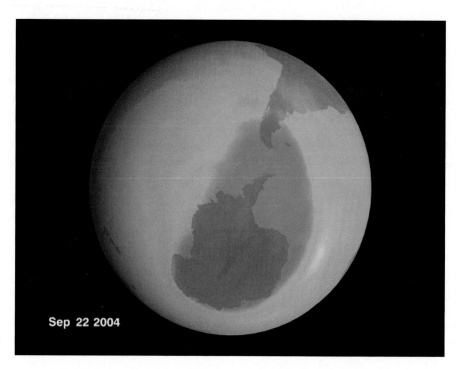

This graphic shows data from the Total Ozone Mapping Spectrometer (TOMS) Earth Probe.

Sep 22 2004

CHEMICAL IMPACT

Enzymes: Nature's Catalysts

The most impressive examples of homogeneous catalysis occur in nature, where the complex reactions necessary for plant and animal life are made possible by enzymes. Enzymes are large molecules specifically tailored to facilitate a given type of reaction. Usually enzymes are proteins, an important class of biomolecules constructed from α-amino acids that have the general structure

where R represents any one of 20 different substituents. These amino acid molecules can be "hooked together" to form a *polymer* (a word meaning "many parts") called a *protein*. The general structure of a protein can be represented as follows:

Since specific proteins are needed by the human body, the proteins in food must be broken into their constituent amino acids, which are then used to construct new proteins in the body's cells. The reaction in which a protein is broken down one amino acid at a time is shown in Fig. 12.19. Note that in this reaction a water molecule reacts with a protein molecule to produce an amino acid and a new protein containing one less amino acid. Without the enzymes found in human cells, this reaction would be much too slow to be useful. One of these enzymes is *carboxypeptidase-A,* a zinc-containing protein (Fig. 12.20).

Carboxypeptidase-A captures the protein to be acted on (called the *substrate*) in a special groove and positions the substrate so that the end is in the active site, where the catalysis occurs (Fig. 12.21). Note that the Zn^{2+} ion bonds to the oxygen of the C=O (carbonyl) group. This polarizes the electron density in the carbonyl group, allowing the neigh-

FIGURE 12.19
The removal of the end amino acid from a protein by reaction with a molecule of water. The products are an amino acid and a new, smaller protein.

boring C—N bond to be broken much more easily. When the reaction is completed, the remaining portion of the substrate protein and the newly formed amino acid are released by the enzyme.

The process just described for carboxypeptidase-A is characteristic of the behavior of other enzymes. Enzyme catalysis can be represented by the series of reactions shown below:

$$E + S \longrightarrow E \cdot S$$
$$E \cdot S \longrightarrow E + P$$

where E represents the enzyme, S represents the substrate, E · S represents the enzyme–substrate complex, and P represents the products. The enzyme and substrate form a complex, where the reaction occurs. The enzyme then releases the product and is ready to repeat the process. The most amazing thing about enzymes is their efficiency. Because an enzyme plays its catalytic role over and over and very rapidly, only a tiny amount of enzyme is required. This makes the isolation of enzymes for study quite difficult.

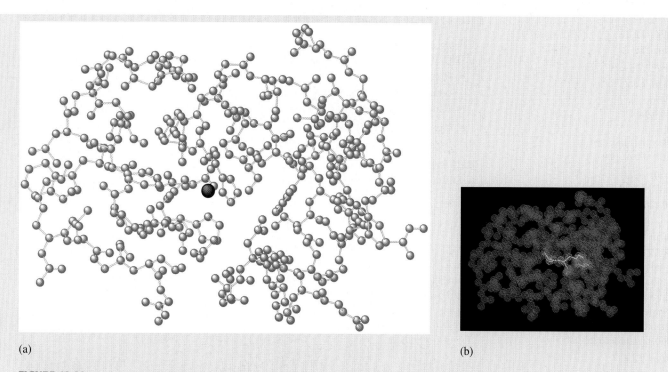

(a)   (b)

FIGURE 12.20
(a) The structure of the enzyme carboxypeptidase-A, which contains 307 amino acids. The zinc ion is shown above as a black sphere in the center. (b) Carboxypeptidase-A with a substrate (pink) in place.

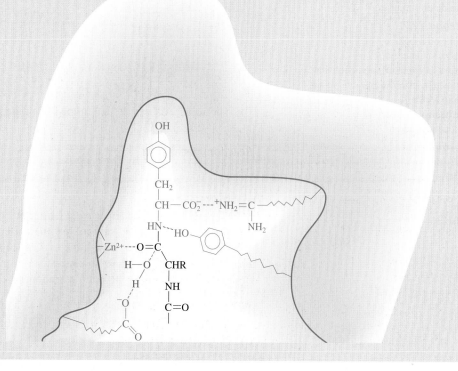

FIGURE 12.21
Protein–substrate interaction. The substrate is shown in black and red, with the red representing the terminal amino acid. Blue indicates side chains from the enzyme that help bind the substrate.

Key Terms

chemical kinetics

Section 12.1
reaction rate
instantaneous rate

Section 12.2
rate law
rate constant
order
(differential) rate law
integrated rate law

Section 12.3
method of initial rates
initial rate
overall reaction order

Section 12.4
first-order reaction
integrated first-order rate law
half-life of a reactant
integrated second-order rate law
zero-order reaction
integrated zero-order rate law
pseudo-first-order rate law

Section 12.6
reaction mechanism
intermediate
elementary step
molecularity
unimolecular step
bimolecular step
termolecular step
rate-determining step

Section 12.7
collision model
activation energy
activated complex (transition state)
molecular orientations
steric factor
Arrhenius equation
frequency factor

Section 12.8
enzyme
catalyst
homogeneous catalyst
heterogeneous catalyst
adsorption

For Review

Chemical kinetics

- The study of the factors that control the rate (speed) of a chemical reaction
  - Rate is defined in terms of the change in concentration of a given reaction component per unit time
  - Kinetic measurements are often made under conditions where the reverse reaction is insignificant
- The kinetic and thermodynamic properties of a reaction are not fundamentally related

Rate laws

- Differential rate law: describes the rate as a function of concentration

$$\text{Rate} = -\frac{\Delta[A]}{\Delta t} = k[A]^n$$

  - k is the rate constant
  - n is the order; not related to the coefficients in the balanced equation
- Integrated rate law: describes the concentration as a function of time
  - For a reaction of the type

$$aA \longrightarrow \text{products}$$

  for which

$$\text{Rate} = k[A]^n$$

$n = 0$:	$[A] = -kt + [A]_0$
	$t_{1/2} = \dfrac{[A]_0}{2k}$
$n = 1$:	$\ln[A] = -kt + \ln[A]_0$
	$t_{1/2} = \dfrac{0.693}{k}$
$n = 2$:	$\dfrac{1}{[A]} = kt + \dfrac{1}{[A]_0}$
	$t_{1/2} = \dfrac{1}{k[A]_0}$

  - The value of k can be determined from the plot of the appropriate function of [A] versus t

Reaction mechanism

- Series of elementary steps by which an overall reaction occurs
  - Elementary step: rate law for the step can be written from the molecularity of the reaction
- Two requirements for an acceptable mechanism:
  - The elementary steps sum to give the correct overall balanced equation
  - The mechanism agrees with the experimentally determined rate law
- Simple reactions can have an elementary step that is slower than all of the other steps; which is called the rate-determining step.

Kinetic models

- The simplest model to account for reaction kinetics is the collision model
  - Molecules must collide to react
  - The collision kinetic energy furnishes the potential energy needed to enable the reactants to rearrange to form products

- A certain threshold energy called the activation energy (E_a) is necessary for a reaction to occur
- The relative orientations of the colliding reactants are also a determining factor in the reaction rate
- This model leads to the Arrhenius equation:

$$k = Ae^{-E_a/RT}$$

- A depends on the collision frequency and relative orientation of the molecules
- The value of E_a can be found by obtaining the values of k at several temperatures

Catalyst

- Speeds up a reaction without being consumed
- Works by providing a lower-energy pathway for the reaction
- Enzymes are biological catalysts
- Catalysts can be classified as homogeneous or heterogeneous
  - Homogeneous: exist in the same phase as the reactants
  - Heterogeneous: exist in a different phase than the reactants

REVIEW QUESTIONS

1. Define *reaction rate.* Distinguish between the initial rate, average rate, and instantaneous rate of a chemical reaction. Which of these rates is usually fastest? The initial rate is the rate used by convention. Give a possible explanation as to why.

2. Distinguish between the differential rate law and the integrated rate law. Which of these is often called just the "rate law"? What is k in a rate law, and what are orders in a rate law? Explain.

3. One experimental procedure that can be used to determine the rate law of a reaction is the method of initial rates. What data are gathered in the method of initial rates, and how are these data manipulated to determine k and the orders of the species in the rate law? Are the units for k, the rate constant, the same for all rate laws? Explain. If a reaction is first order in A, what happens to the rate if [A] is tripled? If the initial rate for a reaction increases by a factor of 16 when [A] is quadrupled, what is the order of n? If a reaction is third order in A and [A] is doubled, what happens to the initial rate? If a reaction is zero order, what effect does [A] have on the initial rate of a reaction?

4. The initial rate for a reaction is equal to the slope of the tangent line at $t \approx 0$ in a plot of [A] versus time. From calculus, initial rate $= \dfrac{-d[A]}{dt}$. Therefore, the differential rate law for a reaction is Rate $= \dfrac{-d[A]}{dt} = k[A]^n$. Assuming you have some calculus in your background, derive the zero-, first-, and second-order integrated rate laws using the differential rate law.

5. Consider the zero-, first-, and second-order integrated rate laws. If you have concentration versus time data for some species in a reaction, what plots would you make to "prove" a reaction is either zero, first, or second order? How would the rate constant, k, be determined from such a plot? What does the y-intercept equal in each plot? When a rate law contains the concentration of two or more species, how can plots be used to determine k and the orders of the species in the rate law?

6. Derive expressions for the half-life of zero-, first-, and second-order reactions using the integrated rate law for each order. How does each half-life depend on

concentration? If the half-life for a reaction is 20. seconds, what would be the second half-life assuming the reaction is either zero, first, or second order?

7. Define each of the following.
   a. elementary step
   b. molecularity
   c. reaction mechanism
   d. intermediate
   e. rate-determining step

   What two requirements must be met to call a mechanism plausible? Why say a "plausible" mechanism instead of the "correct" mechanism? Is it true that most reactions occur by a one-step mechanism? Explain.

8. What is the premise underlying the collision model? How is the rate affected by each of the following?
   a. activation energy
   b. temperature
   c. frequency of collisions
   d. orientation of collisions

   Sketch a potential energy versus reaction progress plot for an endothermic reaction and for an exothermic reaction. Show ΔE and E_a in both plots. When concentrations and temperatures are equal, would you expect the rate of the forward reaction to be equal to, greater than, or less than the rate of the reverse reaction if the reaction is exothermic? Endothermic?

9. Give the Arrhenius equation. Take the natural log of both sides and place this equation in the form of a straight-line equation ($y = mx + b$). What data would you need and how would you graph those data to get a linear relationship using the Arrhenius equation? What does the slope of the straight line equal? What does the y-intercept equal? What are the units of R in the Arrhenius equation? Explain how if you know the rate constant value at two different temperatures, you can determine the activation energy for the reaction.

10. Why does a catalyst increase the rate of a reaction? What is the difference between a homogeneous catalyst and a heterogeneous catalyst? Would a given reaction necessarily have the same rate law for both a catalyzed and an uncatalyzed pathway? Explain.

Active Learning Questions*

These questions are designed to be used by groups of students in class. The questions allow students to explore their understanding of concepts through discussion and peer teaching. The real value of these questions is the learning that occurs while students talk to each other about chemical concepts.

1. Define *stability* from both a kinetic and thermodynamic perspective. Give examples to show the differences in these concepts.

2. Describe at least two experiments you could perform to determine a rate law.

3. Make a graph of [A] versus time for zero-, first-, and second-order reactions. From these graphs, compare successive half-lives.

4. How does temperature affect k, the rate constant? Explain.

5. Consider the following statements: "In general, the rate of a chemical reaction increases a bit at first because it takes a while for the reaction to get 'warmed up.' After that, however, the rate of the reaction decreases because its rate is dependent on the concentrations of the reactants, and these are decreasing." Indicate everything that is correct in these statements, and indicate everything that is incorrect. Correct the incorrect statements and explain.

6. For the reaction A + B → C, explain at least two ways in which the rate law could be zero order in chemical A.

7. A friend of yours states, "A balanced equation tells us how chemicals interact. Therefore, we can determine the rate law directly from the balanced equation." What do you tell your friend?

8. Provide a conceptual rationale for the differences in the half-lives of zero-, first-, and second-order reactions.

---

*In the Questions and the Exercises, the term *rate law* always refers to the differential rate law.

A blue question or exercise number indicates that the answer to that question or exercise appears at the back of this book and a solution appears in the *Solutions Guide*.

Questions

9. Define what is meant by unimolecular and bimolecular steps. Why are termolecular steps infrequently seen in chemical reactions?

10. Hydrogen reacts explosively with oxygen. However, a mixture of H_2 and O_2 can exist indefinitely at room temperature. Explain why H_2 and O_2 do not react under these conditions.

11. For the reaction

$$2H_2(g) + 2NO(g) \longrightarrow N_2(g) + 2H_2O(g)$$

the observed rate law is

$$Rate = k[NO]^2[H_2]$$

Which of the changes listed below would affect the value of the rate constant k?
a. increasing the partial pressure of hydrogen gas
b. changing the temperature
c. using an appropriate catalyst

12. The rate law for a reaction can be determined only from experiment and not from the balanced equation. Two experimental procedures were outlined in Chapter 12. What are these two procedures? Explain how each method is used to determine rate laws.

13. Table 12.2 illustrates how the average rate of a reaction decreases with time. Why does the average rate decrease with time? How does the instantaneous rate of a reaction depend on time? Why are initial rates used by convention?

14. The type of rate law for a reaction, either the differential rate law or the integrated rate, is usually determined by which data is easiest to collect. Explain.

15. The initial rate of a reaction doubles as the concentration of one of the reactants is quadrupled. What is the order of this reactant? If a reactant has a -1 order, what happens to the initial rate when the concentration of that reactant increases by a factor of two?

16. Reactions that require a metal catalyst are often zero order after a certain amount of reactant(s) are present. Explain.

17. The central idea of the collision model is that molecules must collide in order to react. Give two reasons why not all collisions of reactant molecules result in product formation.

18. Would the slope of a ln k versus $1/T$ (K) plot for a catalyzed reaction be more of less negative than the slope of the ln k versus $1/T$ (K) plot for the uncatalyzed reaction? Explain.

Exercises

In this section similar exercises are paired.

Reaction Rates

19. Consider the reaction

$$4PH_3(g) \longrightarrow P_4(g) + 6H_2(g)$$

If, in a certain experiment, over a specific time period, 0.0048 mol PH_3 is consumed in a 2.0-L container each second of reaction, what are the rates of production of P_4 and H_2 in this experiment?

20. In the Haber process for the production of ammonia,

$$N_2(g) + 3H_2(g) \longrightarrow 2NH_3(g)$$

what is the relationship between the rate of production of ammonia and the rate of consumption of hydrogen?

21. At 40°C, $H_2O_2(aq)$ will decompose according to the following reaction:

$$2H_2O_2(aq) \longrightarrow 2H_2O(l) + O_2(g)$$

The following data were collected for the concentration of H_2O_2 at various times.

Time (s)	[H₂O₂] (mol/L)
0	1.000
2.16×10^4	0.500
4.32×10^4	0.250

a. Calculate the average rate of decomposition of H_2O_2 between 0 and 2.16×10^4 s. Use this rate to calculate the average rate of production of $O_2(g)$ over the same time period.
b. What are these rates for the time period 2.16×10^4 s to 4.32×10^4 s?

22. Consider the general reaction

$$1aA + 2bB \longrightarrow 3cC$$

and the following average rate data over some time period Δt:

$$-\frac{\Delta A}{\Delta t} = 0.0080 \text{ mol/L} \cdot \text{s}$$

$$-\frac{\Delta B}{\Delta t} = 0.0120 \text{ mol/L} \cdot \text{s}$$

$$\frac{\Delta C}{\Delta t} = 0.0160 \text{ mol/L} \cdot \text{s}$$

Determine a set of possible coefficients to balance this general reaction.

23. What are the units for each of the following if the concentrations are expressed in moles per liter and the time in seconds?
a. rate of a chemical reaction
b. rate constant for a zero-order rate law
c. rate constant for a first-order rate law
d. rate constant for a second-order rate law
e. rate constant for a third-order rate law

24. The rate law for the reaction

$$Cl_2(g) + CHCl_3(g) \longrightarrow HCl(g) + CCl_4(g)$$

is $$Rate = k[Cl_2]^{1/2}[CHCl_3]$$

What are the units for k, assuming time in seconds and concentration in mol/L?

Rate Laws from Experimental Data: Initial Rates Method

25. The reaction

$$2NO(g) + Cl_2(g) \longrightarrow 2NOCl(g)$$

was studied at $-10°C$. The following results were obtained where

$$\text{Rate} = -\frac{\Delta[Cl_2]}{\Delta t}$$

$[NO]_0$ (mol/L)	$[Cl_2]_0$ (mol/L)	Initial Rate (mol/L $\cdot$ min)
0.10	0.10	0.18
0.10	0.20	0.36
0.20	0.20	1.45

a. What is the rate law?
b. What is the value of the rate constant?

26. The reaction

$$2I^-(aq) + S_2O_8^{2-}(aq) \longrightarrow I_2(aq) + 2SO_4^{2-}(aq)$$

was studied at $25°C$. The following results were obtained where

$$\text{Rate} = -\frac{\Delta[S_2O_8^{2-}]}{\Delta t}$$

$[I^-]_0$ (mol/L)	$[S_2O_8^{2-}]_0$ (mol/L)	Initial Rate (mol/L $\cdot$ s)
0.080	0.040	12.5×10^{-6}
0.040	0.040	6.25×10^{-6}
0.080	0.020	6.25×10^{-6}
0.032	0.040	5.00×10^{-6}
0.060	0.030	7.00×10^{-6}

a. Determine the rate law.
b. Calculate a value for the rate constant for each experiment and an average value for the rate constant.

27. The decomposition of nitrosyl chloride was studied:

$$2NOCl(g) \rightleftharpoons 2NO(g) + Cl_2(g)$$

The following data were obtained where

$$\text{Rate} = -\frac{\Delta[NOCl]}{\Delta t}$$

$[NOCl]_0$ (molecules/cm^3)	Initial Rate (molecules/cm^3 $\cdot$ s)
3.0×10^{16}	5.98×10^4
2.0×10^{16}	2.66×10^4
1.0×10^{16}	6.64×10^3
4.0×10^{16}	1.06×10^5

a. What is the rate law?
b. Calculate the rate constant.

c. Calculate the rate constant when concentrations are given in moles per liter.

28. The following data were obtained for the gas-phase decomposition of dinitrogen pentoxide,

$$2N_2O_5(g) \longrightarrow 4NO_2(g) + O_2(g)$$

$[N_2O_5]_0$ (mol/L)	Initial Rate (mol/L $\cdot$ s)
0.0750	8.90×10^{-4}
0.190	2.26×10^{-3}
0.275	3.26×10^{-3}
0.410	4.85×10^{-3}

Defining the rate as $-\Delta[N_2O_5]/\Delta t$, write the rate law and calculate the value of the rate constant.

29. The rate of the reaction between hemoglobin (Hb) and carbon monoxide (CO) was studied at $20°C$. The following data were collected with all concentration units in μmol/L. (A hemoglobin concentration of 2.21 μmol/L is equal to 2.21×10^{-6} mol/L.)

$[Hb]_0$ (μmol/L)	$[CO]_0$ (μmol/L)	Initial Rate (μmol/L $\cdot$ s)
2.21	1.00	0.619
4.42	1.00	1.24
4.42	3.00	3.71

a. Determine the orders of this reaction with respect to Hb and CO.
b. Determine the rate law.
c. Calculate the value of the rate constant.
d. What would be the initial rate for an experiment with $[Hb]_0 = 3.36$ μmol/L and $[CO]_0 = 2.40$ μmol/L?

30. The following data were obtained for the reaction

$$2ClO_2(aq) + 2OH^-(aq) \longrightarrow ClO_3^-(aq) + ClO_2^-(aq) + H_2O(l)$$

where

$$\text{Rate} = -\frac{\Delta[ClO_2]}{\Delta t}$$

$[ClO_2]_0$ (mol/L)	$[OH^-]_0$ (mol/L)	Initial Rate (mol/L $\cdot$ s)
0.0500	0.100	5.75×10^{-2}
0.100	0.100	2.30×10^{-1}
0.100	0.0500	1.15×10^{-1}
.175	.0844	?

a. Determine the rate law and the value of the rate constant.
b. What would be the initial rate for an experiment with $[ClO_2]_0 = 0.175$ mol/L and $[OH^-]_0 = 0.0844$ mol/L?

Integrated Rate Laws

31. The decomposition of hydrogen peroxide was studied, and the following data were obtained at a particular temperature:

Time (s)	[H$_2$O$_2$] (mol/L)
0	1.00
120 ± 1	0.91
300 ± 1	0.78
600 ± 1	0.59
1200 ± 1	0.37
1800 ± 1	0.22
2400 ± 1	0.13
3000 ± 1	0.082
3600 ± 1	0.050

Assuming that

$$\text{Rate} = -\frac{\Delta[H_2O_2]}{\Delta t}$$

determine the rate law, the integrated rate law, and the value of the rate constant. Calculate [H$_2$O$_2$] at 4000. s after the start of the reaction.

32. A certain reaction has the following general form:

$$aA \longrightarrow bB$$

At a particular temperature and [A]$_0$ = 2.00 × 10^{-2} M, concentration versus time data were collected for this reaction, and a plot of ln[A] versus time resulted in a straight line with a slope value of −2.97 × 10^{-2} min^{-1}.
a. Determine the rate law, the integrated rate law, and the value of the rate constant for this reaction.
b. Calculate the half-life for this reaction.
c. How much time is required for the concentration of A to decrease to 2.50 × 10^{-3} M?

33. The rate of the reaction

$$NO_2(g) + CO(g) \longrightarrow NO(g) + CO_2(g)$$

depends only on the concentration of nitrogen dioxide below 225°C. At a temperature below 225°C, the following data were collected:

Time (s)	[NO$_2$] (mol/L)
0	0.500
1.20 × 10^3	0.444
3.00 × 10^3	0.381
4.50 × 10^3	0.340
9.00 × 10^3	0.250
1.80 × 10^4	0.174

Determine the rate law, the integrated law, and the value of the rate constant. Calculate [NO$_2$] at 2.70 × 10^4 s after the start of the reaction.

34. A certain reaction has the following general form:

$$aA \longrightarrow bB$$

At a particular temperature and [A]$_0$ = 2.80 × 10^{-3} M, concentration versus time data were collected for this reaction, and a plot of 1/[A] versus time resulted in a straight line with a slope value of +3.60 × 10^{-2} L/mol · s.
a. Determine the rate law, the integrated rate law, and the value of the rate constant for this reaction.
b. Calculate the half-life for this reaction.
c. How much time is required for the concentration of A to decrease to 7.00 × 10^{-4} M?

35. The decomposition of ethanol (C$_2$H$_5$OH) on an alumina (Al$_2$O$_3$) surface

$$C_2H_5OH(g) \longrightarrow C_2H_4(g) + H_2O(g)$$

was studied at 600 K. Concentration versus time data were collected for this reaction, and a plot of [A] versus time resulted in a straight line with a slope of −4.00 × 10^{-5} mol/L · s.
a. Determine the rate law, the integrated rate law, and the value of the rate constant for this reaction.
b. If the initial concentration of C$_2$H$_5$OH was 1.25 × 10^{-2} M, calculate the half-life for this reaction.
c. How much time is required for all the 1.25 × 10^{-2} M C$_2$H$_5$OH to decompose?

36. At 500 K in the presence of a copper surface, ethanol decomposes according to the equation

$$C_2H_5OH(g) \longrightarrow CH_3CHO(g) + H_2(g)$$

The pressure of C$_2$H$_5$OH was measured as a function of time and the following data were obtained:

Time (s)	$P_{C_2H_5OH}$ (torr)
0	250.
100.	237
200.	224
300.	211
400.	198
500.	185

Since the pressure of a gas is directly proportional to the concentration of gas, we can express the rate law for a gaseous reaction in terms of partial pressures. Using the above data, deduce the rate law, the integrated rate law, and the value of the rate constant, all in terms of pressure units in atm and time in seconds. Predict the pressure of C$_2$H$_5$OH after 900. s from the start of the reaction. (*Hint:* To determine the order of the reaction with respect to C$_2$H$_5$OH, compare how the pressure of C$_2$H$_5$OH decreases with each time listing.)

37. The dimerization of butadiene

$$2C_4H_6(g) \longrightarrow C_8H_{12}(g)$$

was studied at 500. K, and the following data were obtained:

Time (s)	$[C_4H_6]$ (mol/L)
195	1.6×10^{-2}
604	1.5×10^{-2}
1246	1.3×10^{-2}
2180	1.1×10^{-2}
6210	0.68×10^{-2}

Assuming that

$$\text{Rate} = -\frac{\Delta[C_4H_6]}{\Delta t}$$

determine the form of the rate law, the integrated rate law, and the rate constant for this reaction. (These are actual experimental data, so they may not give a perfectly straight line.)

38. The rate of the reaction

$$O(g) + NO_2(g) \longrightarrow NO(g) + O_2(g)$$

was studied at a certain temperature.
a. In the first set of experiments, NO_2 was in large excess, at a concentration of 1.0×10^{13} molecules/cm³ with the following data collected:

Time (s)	[O] (atoms/cm³)
0	5.0×10^9
1.0×10^{-2}	1.9×10^9
2.0×10^{-2}	6.8×10^8
3.0×10^{-2}	2.5×10^8

What is the order of the reaction with respect to oxygen atoms?
b. The reaction is known to be first order with respect to NO_2. Determine the overall rate law and the value of the rate constant.

39. Experimental data for the reaction

$$A \longrightarrow 2B + C$$

have been plotted in the following three different ways (with concentration units in mol/L):

What is the order of the reaction with respect to A and what is the initial concentration of A?

40. Consider the data plotted in Exercise 39 when answering the following questions.
a. What is the concentration of A after 9 s?
b. What are the first three half-lives for this experiment?

41. The reaction

$$A \longrightarrow B + C$$

is known to be zero order in A and to have a rate constant of 5.0×10^{-2} mol/L · s at 25°C. An experiment was run at 25°C where $[A]_0 = 1.0 \times 10^{-3}$ M.
a. Write the integrated rate law for this reaction.
b. Calculate the half-life for the reaction.
c. Calculate the concentration of B after 5.0×10^{-3} s has elapsed.

42. The radioactive isotope ^{32}P decays by first-order kinetics and has a half-life of 14.3 days. How long does it take for 95.0% of a sample of ^{32}P to decay?

43. A first-order reaction is 75.0% complete in 320. s.
a. What are the first and second half-lives for this reaction?
b. How long does it take for 90.0% completion?

44. The rate law for the decomposition of phosphine (PH_3) is

$$\text{Rate} = -\frac{\Delta[PH_3]}{\Delta t} = k[PH_3]$$

It takes 120. s for 1.00 M PH_3 to decrease to 0.250 M. How much time is required for 2.00 M PH_3 to decrease to a concentration of 0.350 M? $.250 = -K (120_{sec}) + log 1.00$

$151.55 G.$

45. Consider the following initial rate data for the decomposition of compound AB to give A and B:

$[AB]_0$ (mol/L)	Initial Rate (mol/L · s)
0.200	3.20×10^{-3}
0.400	1.28×10^{-2}
0.600	2.88×10^{-2}

Determine the half-life for the decomposition reaction initially having 1.00 M AB present.

46. The rate law for the reaction

$$2NOBr(g) \longrightarrow 2NO(g) + Br_2(g)$$

at some temperature is

$$\text{Rate} = -\frac{\Delta[\text{NOBr}]}{\Delta t} = k[\text{NOBr}]^2$$

a. If the half-life for this reaction is 2.00 s when $[\text{NOBr}]_0 = 0.900\ M$, calculate the value of k for this reaction.
b. How much time is required for the concentration of NOBr to decrease to 0.100 M?

47. For the reaction A $\rightarrow$ products, successive half-lives are observed to be 10.0, 20.0, and 40.0 min for an experiment in which $[\text{A}]_0 = 0.10\ M$. Calculate the concentration of A at the following times.
   a. 80.0 min
   b. 30.0 min

48. Consider the hypothetical reaction

$$\text{A} + \text{B} + 2\text{C} \longrightarrow 2\text{D} + 3\text{E}$$

where the rate law is

$$\text{Rate} = -\frac{\Delta[\text{A}]}{\Delta t} = k[\text{A}][\text{B}]^2$$

An experiment is carried out where $[\text{A}]_0 = 1.0 \times 10^{-2}\ M$, $[\text{B}]_0 = 3.0\ M$, and $[\text{C}]_0 = 2.0\ M$. The reaction is started, and after 8.0 seconds, the concentration of A is $3.8 \times 10^{-3}\ M$.
   a. Calculate k for this reaction.
   b. Calculate the half-life for this experiment.
   c. Calculate the concentration of A after 13.0 seconds.
   d. Calculate the concentration of C after 13.0 seconds.

Reaction Mechanisms

49. Write the rate laws for the following elementary reactions.
   a. $\text{CH}_3\text{NC}(g) \rightarrow \text{CH}_3\text{CN}(g)$
   b. $\text{O}_3(g) + \text{NO}(g) \rightarrow \text{O}_2(g) + \text{NO}_2(g)$
   c. $\text{O}_3(g) \rightarrow \text{O}_2(g) + \text{O}(g)$
   c. $\text{O}_3(g) + \text{O}(g) \rightarrow 2\text{O}_2(g)$

50. The mechanisms shown below have been proposed to explain the kinetics of the reaction considered in Question 11. Which of the following are acceptable mechanisms? Explain.

Mechanism I:

$$2\text{H}_2(g) + 2\text{NO}(g) \longrightarrow \text{N}_2(g) + 2\text{H}_2\text{O}(g)$$

Mechanism II:

$$\text{H}_2(g) + \text{NO}(g) \longrightarrow \text{H}_2\text{O}(g) + \text{N}(g) \qquad \text{Slow}$$
$$\text{N}(g) + \text{NO}(g) \longrightarrow \text{N}_2(g) + \text{O}(g) \qquad \text{Fast}$$
$$\text{H}_2(g) + \text{O}(g) \longrightarrow \text{H}_2\text{O}(g) \qquad \text{Fast}$$

Mechanism III:

$$\text{H}_2(g) + 2\text{NO}(g) \longrightarrow \text{N}_2\text{O}(g) + \text{H}_2\text{O}(g) \qquad \text{Slow}$$
$$\text{N}_2\text{O}(g) + \text{H}_2(g) \longrightarrow \text{N}_2(g) + \text{H}_2\text{O}(g) \qquad \text{Fast}$$

51. A proposed mechanism for a reaction is

$$\text{C}_4\text{H}_9\text{Br} \longrightarrow \text{C}_4\text{H}_9^+ + \text{Br}^- \qquad \text{Slow}$$
$$\text{C}_4\text{H}_9^+ + \text{H}_2\text{O} \longrightarrow \text{C}_4\text{H}_9\text{OH}_2^+ \qquad \text{Fast}$$
$$\text{C}_4\text{H}_9\text{OH}_2^+ + \text{H}_2\text{O} \longrightarrow \text{C}_4\text{H}_9\text{OH} + \text{H}_3\text{O}^+ \qquad \text{Fast}$$

Write the rate law expected for this mechanism. What is the overall balanced equation for the reaction? What are the intermediates in the proposed mechanism?

52. The mechanism for the reaction of nitrogen dioxide with carbon monoxide to form nitric oxide and carbon dioxide is thought to be

$$\text{NO}_2 + \text{NO}_2 \longrightarrow \text{NO}_3 + \text{NO} \qquad \text{Slow}$$
$$\text{NO}_3 + \text{CO} \longrightarrow \text{NO}_2 + \text{CO}_2 \qquad \text{Fast}$$

Write the rate law expected for this mechanism. What is the overall balanced equation for the reaction?

Temperature Dependence of Rate Constants and the Collision Model

53. For the following reaction profile, indicate
   a. the positions of reactants and products.
   b. the activation energy.
   c. ΔE for the reaction.

E

—— Reaction coordinate ——→

54. Draw a rough sketch of the energy profile for each of the following cases:
   a. $\Delta E = +10$ kJ/mol, $E_a = 25$ kJ/mol
   b. $\Delta E = -10$ kJ/mol, $E_a = 50$ kJ/mol
   c. $\Delta E = -50$ kJ/mol, $E_a = 50$ kJ/mol

55. The activation energy for the reaction

$$\text{NO}_2(g) + \text{CO}(g) \longrightarrow \text{NO}(g) + \text{CO}_2(g)$$

is 125 kJ/mol, and ΔE for the reaction is -216 kJ/mol. What is the activation energy for the reverse reaction $[\text{NO}(g) + \text{CO}_2(g) \longrightarrow \text{NO}_2(g) + \text{CO}(g)]$?

56. For a certain process, the activation energy is greater for the forward reaction than for the reverse reaction. Does this reaction have a positive or negative value for ΔE?

57. The rate constant for the gas-phase decomposition of N_2O_5,

$$\text{N}_2\text{O}_5 \longrightarrow 2\text{NO}_2 + \tfrac{1}{2}\text{O}_2$$

has the following temperature dependence:

T (K)	k (s^{-1})
338	4.9×10^{-3}
318	5.0×10^{-4}
298	3.5×10^{-5}

Make the appropriate graph using these data, and determine the activation energy for this reaction.

58. The reaction

$$(CH_3)_3CBr + OH^- \longrightarrow (CH_3)_3COH + Br^-$$

in a certain solvent is first order with respect to $(CH_3)_3CBr$ and zero order with respect to OH^-. In several experiments, the rate constant k was determined at different temperatures. A plot of $\ln(k)$ versus $1/T$ was constructed resulting in a straight line with a slope value of -1.10×10^4 K and y-intercept of 33.5. Assume k has units of s^{-1}.

a. Determine the activation energy for this reaction.
b. Determine the value of the frequency factor A.
c. Calculate the value of k at 25°C.

59. The activation energy for the decomposition of $HI(g)$ to $H_2(g)$ and $I_2(g)$ is 186 kJ/mol. The rate constant at 555 K is 3.52×10^{-7} L/mol · s. What is the rate constant at 645 K?

60. A first-order reaction has rate constants of $4.6 \times 10^{-2}\,s^{-1}$ and $8.1 \times 10^{-2}\,s^{-1}$ at 0°C and 20.°C, respectively. What is the value of the activation energy?

61. A certain reaction has an activation energy of 54.0 kJ/mol. As the temperature is increased from 22°C to a higher temperature, the rate constant increases by a factor of 7.00. Calculate the higher temperature.

62. Chemists commonly use a rule of thumb that an increase of 10 K in temperature doubles the rate of a reaction. What must the activation energy be for this statement to be true for a temperature increase from 25 to 35°C?

63. Which of the following reactions would you expect to proceed at a faster rate at room temperature? Why? (*Hint:* Think about which reaction would have the lower activation energy.)

$$2Ce^{4+}(aq) + Hg_2^{2+}(aq) \longrightarrow 2Ce^{3+}(aq) + 2Hg^{2+}(aq)$$
$$H_3O^+(aq) + OH^-(aq) \longrightarrow 2H_2O(l)$$

64. One reason suggested for the instability of long chains of silicon atoms is that the decomposition involves the transition state shown below:

The activation energy for such a process is 210 kJ/mol, which is less than either the Si—Si or the Si—H bond energy. Why would a similar mechanism not be expected to play a very important role in the decomposition of long chains of carbon atoms as seen in organic compounds?

Catalysts

65. One mechanism for the destruction of ozone in the upper atmosphere is

$O_3(g) + NO(g) \longrightarrow NO_2(g) + O_2(g)$	Slow
$NO_2(g) + O(g) \longrightarrow NO(g) + O_2(g)$	Fast

Overall reaction $O_3(g) + O(g) \longrightarrow 2O_2(g)$

a. Which species is a catalyst?
b. Which species is an intermediate?
c. E_a for the uncatalyzed reaction

$$O_3(g) + O(g) \longrightarrow 2O_2$$

is 14.0 kJ. E_a for the same reaction when catalyzed is 11.9 kJ. What is the ratio of the rate constant for the catalyzed reaction to that for the uncatalyzed reaction at 25°C? Assume that the frequency factor A is the same for each reaction.

66. One of the concerns about the use of Freons is that they will migrate to the upper atmosphere, where chlorine atoms can be generated by the following reaction:

$$CCl_2F_2 \xrightarrow{\ h\nu\ } CF_2Cl + Cl$$
Freon-12

Chlorine atoms can act as a catalyst for the destruction of ozone. The activation energy for the reaction

$$Cl + O_3 \longrightarrow ClO + O_2$$

is 2.1 kJ/mol. Which is the more effective catalyst for the destruction of ozone, Cl or NO? (See Exercise 65.)

67. Assuming that the mechanism for the hydrogenation of C_2H_4 given in Section 12.8 is correct, would you predict that the product of the reaction of C_2H_4 with D_2 would be CH_2D—CH_2D or CHD_2—CH_3? How could the reaction of C_2H_4 with D_2 be used to confirm the mechanism for the hydrogenation of C_2H_4 given in Section 12.8?

68. The decomposition of NH_3 to N_2 and H_2 was studied on two surfaces:

Surface	E_a (kJ/mol)
W	163
Os	197

Without a catalyst, the activation energy is 335 kJ/mol.

a. Which surface is the better heterogeneous catalyst for the decomposition of NH_3? Why?
b. How many times faster is the reaction at 298 K on the W surface compared with the reaction with no catalyst present? Assume that the frequency factor A is the same for each reaction.
c. The decomposition reaction on the two surfaces obeys a rate law of the form

$$\text{Rate} = k\frac{[NH_3]}{[H_2]}$$

How can you explain the inverse dependence of the rate on the H_2 concentration?

69. A famous chemical demonstration is the "magic genie" procedure, in which hydrogen peroxide decomposes to water and oxygen gas with the aid of a catalyst. The activation energy of this (uncatalyzed) reaction is 70.0 kJ/mol. When the catalyst is added, the activation energy (at 20.°C) is 42.0 kJ/mol. Theoretically, to what temperature (°C) would one have to heat the hydrogen peroxide solution so that the rate of the uncatalyzed reaction is equal to the rate of the catalyzed reaction at 20.°C? Assume the frequency factor A is constant and assume the initial concentrations are the same.

70. The activation energy for a reaction is changed from 184 kJ/mol to 59.0 kJ/mol at 600. K by the introduction of a catalyst. If the uncatalyzed reaction takes about 2400 years to occur, about how long will the catalyzed reaction take? Assume the frequency factor A is constant and assume the initial concentrations are the same.

Additional Exercises

71. The reaction

$$2NO(g) + O_2(g) \longrightarrow 2NO_2(g)$$

was studied, and the following data were obtained where

$$\text{Rate} = -\frac{\Delta[O_2]}{\Delta t}$$

$[NO]_0$ (molecules/cm³)	$[O_2]_0$ (molecules/cm³)	Initial Rate (molecules/cm³ · s)
1.00×10^{18}	1.00×10^{18}	2.00×10^{16}
3.00×10^{18}	1.00×10^{18}	1.80×10^{17}
2.50×10^{18}	2.50×10^{18}	3.13×10^{17}

What would be the initial rate for an experiment where $[NO]_0 = 6.21 \times 10^{18}$ molecules/cm³ and $[O_2]_0 = 7.36 \times 10^{18}$ molecules/cm³?

72. Sulfuryl chloride (SO_2Cl_2) decomposes to sulfur dioxide (SO_2) and chlorine (Cl_2) by reaction in the gas phase. The following pressure data were obtained when a sample containing 5.00×10^{-2} mol sulfuryl chloride was heated to 600. K in a 5.00×10^{-1}-L container.

Time (hours):	0.00	1.00	2.00	4.00	8.00	16.00
$P_{SO_2Cl_2}$ (atm):	4.93	4.26	3.52	2.53	1.30	0.34

Defining the rate as $-\dfrac{\Delta[SO_2Cl_2]}{\Delta t}$,

a. determine the value of the rate constant for the decomposition of sulfuryl chloride at 600. K.
b. what is the half-life of the reaction?
c. what fraction of the sulfuryl chloride remains after 20.0 h?

73. For the reaction

$$2N_2O_5(g) \longrightarrow 4NO_2(g) + O_2(g)$$

the following data were collected, where

$$\text{Rate} = -\frac{\Delta[N_2O_5]}{\Delta t}$$

Time (s)	T = 338 K $[N_2O_5]$	T = 318 K $[N_2O_5]$
0	1.00×10^{-1} M	1.00×10^{-1} M
100.	6.14×10^{-2} M	9.54×10^{-2} M
300.	2.33×10^{-2} M	8.63×10^{-2} M
600.	5.41×10^{-3} M	7.43×10^{-2} M
900.	1.26×10^{-3} M	6.39×10^{-2} M

Calculate E_a for this reaction.

74. Experimental values for the temperature dependence of the rate constant for the gas-phase reaction

$$NO + O_3 \longrightarrow NO_2 + O_2$$

are as follows:

T (K)	k (L/mol · s)
195	1.08×10^9
230.	2.95×10^9
260.	5.42×10^9
298	12.0×10^9
369	35.5×10^9

Make the appropriate graph using these data, and determine the activation energy for this reaction.

75. For enzyme-catalyzed reactions that follow the mechanism

$$E + S \rightleftharpoons E \cdot S$$
$$E \cdot S \rightleftharpoons E + P$$

a graph of the rate as a function of [S], the concentration of the substrate, has the following appearance:

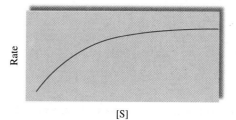

Note that at higher substrate concentrations the rate no longer changes with [S]. Suggest a reason for this.

76. The activation energy of a certain uncatalyzed biochemical reaction is 50.0 kJ/mol. In the presence of a catalyst at 37°C, the rate constant for the reaction increases by a factor of 2.50×10^3 as compared with the uncatalyzed reaction. Assuming the frequency factor A is the same for both the catalyzed and uncatalyzed reactions, calculate the activation energy for the catalyzed reaction.

77. Consider the reaction

$$3A + B + C \rightarrow D + E$$

where the rate law is defined as

$$-\frac{\Delta[A]}{\Delta t} = k[A]^2[B][C]$$

An experiment is carried out where $[B]_0 = [C]_0 = 1.00\ M$ and $[A]_0 = 1.00 \times 10^{-4}\ M$.

a. If after 3.00 min, $[A] = 3.26 \times 10^{-5}\ M$, calculate the value of k.

b. Calculate the half-life for this experiment.

c. Calculate the concentration of B and the concentration of A after 10.0 min.

Challenge Problems

78. Consider a reaction of the type aA $\rightarrow$ products, in which the rate law is found to be rate = $k[A]^3$ (termolecular reactions are improbable but possible). If the first half-life of the reaction is found to be 40. s, what is the time for the second half-life? *Hint:* Using your calculus knowledge, derive the integrated rate law from the differential rate law for a termolecular reaction:

$$\text{Rate} = \frac{-d[A]}{dt} = k[A]^3$$

79. A study was made of the effect of the hydroxide concentration on the rate of the reaction

$$I^-(aq) + OCl^-(aq) \longrightarrow IO^-(aq) + Cl^-(aq)$$

The following data were obtained:

$[I^-]_0$ (mol/L)	$[OCl^-]_0$ (mol/L)	$[OH^-]_0$ (mol/L)	Initial Rate (mol/L · s)
0.0013	0.012	0.10	9.4×10^{-3}
0.0026	0.012	0.10	18.7×10^{-3}
0.0013	0.0060	0.10	4.7×10^{-3}
0.0013	0.018	0.10	14.0×10^{-3}
0.0013	0.012	0.050	18.7×10^{-3}
0.0013	0.012	0.20	4.7×10^{-3}
0.0013	0.018	0.20	7.0×10^{-3}

Determine the rate law and the value of the rate constant for this reaction.

80. Two isomers (A and B) of a given compound dimerize as follows:

$$2A \xrightarrow{k_1} A_2$$
$$2B \xrightarrow{k_2} B_2$$

Both processes are known to be second order in reactant, and k_1 is known to be 0.250 L/mol · s at 25°C. In a particular experiment A and B were placed in separate containers at 25°C, where $[A]_0 = 1.00 \times 10^{-2}\ M$ and $[B]_0 = 2.50 \times 10^{-2}\ M$. It was found that after each reaction had progressed for 3.00 min, $[A] = 3.00[B]$. In this case the rate laws are defined as

$$\text{Rate} = -\frac{\Delta[A]}{\Delta t} = k_1[A]^2$$

$$\text{Rate} = -\frac{\Delta[B]}{\Delta t} = k_2[B]^2$$

a. Calculate the concentration of A_2 after 3.00 min.

b. Calculate the value of k_2.

c. Calculate the half-life for the experiment involving A.

81. The reaction

$$NO(g) + O_3(g) \longrightarrow NO_2(g) + O_2(g)$$

was studied by performing two experiments. In the first experiment the rate of disappearance of NO was followed in the presence of a large excess of O_3. The results were as follows ($[O_3]$ remains effectively constant at 1.0×10^{14} molecules/cm³):

Time (ms)	[NO] (molecules/cm³)
0	6.0×10^8
100 ± 1	5.0×10^8
500 ± 1	2.4×10^8
700 ± 1	1.7×10^8
1000 ± 1	9.9×10^7

In the second experiment [NO] was held constant at 2.0×10^{14} molecules/cm³. The data for the disappearance of O_3 are as follows:

Time (ms)	$[O_3]$ (molecules/cm³)
0	1.0×10^{10}
50 ± 1	8.4×10^9
100 ± 1	7.0×10^9
200 ± 1	4.9×10^9
300 ± 1	3.4×10^9

a. What is the order with respect to each reactant?

b. What is the overall rate law?

c. What is the value of the rate constant from each set of experiments?

$$\text{Rate} = k'[NO]^x \qquad \text{Rate} = k''[O_3]^y$$

d. What is the value of the rate constant for the overall rate law?

$$\text{Rate} = k[NO]^x[O_3]^y$$

82. Most reactions occur by a series of steps. The energy profile for a certain reaction that proceeds by a two-step mechanism is

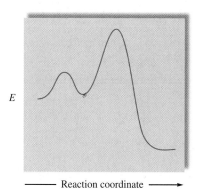

E

———— Reaction coordinate ————→

On the energy profile, indicate

a. The positions of reactants and products.

b. The activation energy for the overall reaction.

c. ΔE for the reaction.

d. Which point on the plot represents the energy of the intermediate in the two-step reaction?

e. Which step in the mechanism for this reaction is rate determining, the first or the second step? Explain.

83. Experiments during a recent summer on a number of fireflies (small beetles, *Lampyridaes photinus*) showed that the average interval between flashes of individual insects was 16.3 s at 21.0°C and 13.0 s at 27.8°C.

a. What is the apparent activation energy of the reaction that controls the flashing?

b. What would be the average interval between flashes of an individual firefly at 30.0°C?

c. Compare the observed intervals and the one you calculated in part b to the rule of thumb that the Celsius temperature is 54 minus twice the interval between flashes.

84. The decomposition of $NO_2(g)$ occurs by the following bimolecular elementary reaction:

$$2NO_2(g) \longrightarrow 2NO(g) + O_2(g)$$

The rate constant at 273 K is 2.3×10^{-12} L/mol · s, and the activation energy is 111 kJ/mol. How long will it take for the concentration of $NO_2(g)$ to decrease from an initial partial pressure of 2.5 atm to 1.5 atm at 500. K? Assume ideal gas behavior.

85. The following data were collected in two studies of the reaction

$$2A + B \longrightarrow C + D$$

Time (s)	Experiment 1 [A] (mol/L) × 10⁻²	Experiment 2 [A] (mol/L) × 10⁻²
0	10.0	10.0
20.	6.67	5.00
40.	5.00	3.33
60.	4.00	2.50
80.	3.33	2.00
100.	2.86	1.67
120.	2.50	1.43

In experiment 1, $[B]_0 = 5.0\ M$.

In experiment 2, $[B]_0 = 10.0\ M$.

$$\text{Rate} = \frac{-\Delta[A]}{\Delta t}$$

a. Why is [B] much greater than [A]?

b. Give the rate law and value for k for this reaction.

86. The following data were collected in two studies of the reaction

$$2H_2(g) + 2NO(g) \longrightarrow N_2(g) + 2H_2O(g)$$

Time (s)	Experiment 1 [H₂] (mol/L)	Experiment 2 [H₂] (mol/L)
0.	1.0×10^{-2}	1.0×10^{-2}
10.	8.4×10^{-3}	5.0×10^{-3}
20.	7.1×10^{-3}	2.5×10^{-3}
30.	?	1.3×10^{-3}
40.	5.0×10^{-3}	6.3×10^{-4}

In experiment 1, $[NO]_0 = 10.0\ M$.

In experiment 2, $[NO]_0 = 20.0\ M$.

$$\text{Rate} = \frac{-\Delta[H_2]}{\Delta t}$$

a. Use the concentration versus time data to determine the rate law for the reaction.

b. Solve for the rate constant (k) for the reaction. Include units.

c. Calculate the concentration of H_2 in experiment 1 at $t = 30.$ s.

87. Consider the hypothetical reaction

$$A + B + 2C \longrightarrow 2D + 3E$$

In a study of this reaction three experiments were run at the same temperature. The rate is defined as $-\Delta[B]/\Delta t$.

Experiment 1:

$$[A]_0 = 2.0\ M \quad [B]_0 = 1.0 \times 10^{-3}\ M \quad [C]_0 = 1.0\ M$$

[B] (mol/L)	Time (s)
2.7×10^{-4}	1.0×10^5
1.6×10^{-4}	2.0×10^5
1.1×10^{-4}	3.0×10^5
8.5×10^{-5}	4.0×10^5
6.9×10^{-5}	5.0×10^5
5.8×10^{-5}	6.0×10^5

Experiment 2:

$$[A]_0 = 1.0 \times 10^{-2}\ M \quad [B]_0 = 3.0\ M \quad [C]_0 = 1.0\ M$$

[A] (mol/L)	Time (s)
8.9×10^{-3}	1.0
7.1×10^{-3}	3.0
5.5×10^{-3}	5.0
3.8×10^{-3}	8.0
2.9×10^{-3}	10.0
2.0×10^{-3}	13.0

Experiment 3:

$$[A]_0 = 10.0\ M \quad [B]_0 = 5.0\ M \quad [C]_0 = 5.0 \times 10^{-1}\ M$$

[C] (mol/L)	Time (s)
0.43	1.0×10^{-2}
0.36	2.0×10^{-2}
0.29	3.0×10^{-2}
0.22	4.0×10^{-2}
0.15	5.0×10^{-2}
0.08	6.0×10^{-2}

Write the rate law for this reaction, and calculate the rate constant.

88. Hydrogen peroxide and the iodide ion react in acidic solution as follows:

$$H_2O_2(aq) + 3I^-(aq) + 2H^+(aq) \longrightarrow I_3^-(aq) + 2H_2O(l)$$

The kinetics of this reaction were studied by following the decay of the concentration of H_2O_2 and constructing plots of $\ln[H_2O_2]$ versus time. All the plots were linear and all solutions had $[H_2O_2]_0 = 8.0 \times 10^{-4}$ mol/L. The slopes of these straight lines depended on the initial concentrations of I^- and H^+. The results follow:

$[I^-]_0$ (mol/L)	$[H^+]_0$ (mol/L)	Slope (min^{-1})
0.1000	0.0400	-0.120
0.3000	0.0400	-0.360
0.4000	0.0400	-0.480
0.0750	0.0200	-0.0760
0.0750	0.0800	-0.118
0.0750	0.1600	-0.174

The rate law for this reaction has the form

$$\text{Rate} = \frac{-\Delta[H_2O_2]}{\Delta t} = (k_1 + k_2[H^+])[I^-]^m[H_2O_2]^n$$

a. Specify the order of this reaction with respect to $[H_2O_2]$ and $[I^-]$.
b. Calculate the values of the rate constants, k_1 and k_2.

c. What reason could there be for the two-term dependence of the rate on $[H^+]$?

Integrative Problems

These problems require the integration of multiple concepts to find the solutions.

89. Sulfuryl chloride undergoes first-order decomposition at 320.°C with a half-life of 8.75 h.

$$SO_2Cl_2(g) \longrightarrow SO_2(g) + Cl_2(g)$$

What is the value of the rate constant, k, in s^{-1}? If the initial pressure of SO_2Cl_2 is 791 torr and the decomposition occurs in a 1.25-L container, how many molecules of SO_2Cl_2 remain after 12.5 h?

90. Upon dissolving InCl(s) in HCl, In$^+$(aq) undergoes a disproportionation reaction according to the following unbalanced equation:

$$In^+(aq) \longrightarrow In(s) + In^{3+}(aq)$$

This disproportionation follows first-order kinetics with a half-life of 667 s. What is the concentration of In$^+$(aq) after 1.25 h if the initial solution of In$^+$(aq) was prepared by dissolving 2.38 g of InCl(s) in 5.00×10^2 mL of dilute HCl? What mass of In(s) is formed after 1.25 h?

91. The decomposition of iodoethane in the gas phase proceeds according to the following equation:

$$C_2H_5I(g) \longrightarrow C_2H_4(g) + HI(g)$$

At 660. K, $k = 7.2 \times 10^{-4}$ s^{-1}; at 720. K, $k = 1.7 \times 10^{-2}$ s^{-1}. What is the rate constant for this first-order decomposition at 325°C? If the initial pressure of iodoethane is 894 torr at 245°C, what is the pressure of iodoethane after three half-lives?

Marathon Problem

This problem is designed to incorporate several concepts and techniques into one situation. Marathon Problems can be used in class by groups of students to help facilitate problem-solving skills.

92. Consider the following reaction:

$$CH_3X + Y \longrightarrow CH_3Y + X$$

At 25°C, the following two experiments were run, yielding the following data:

Experiment 1: $[Y]_0 = 3.0\ M$

[CH$_3$X] (mol/L)	Time (h)
7.08×10^{-3}	1.0
4.52×10^{-3}	1.5
2.23×10^{-3}	2.3
4.76×10^{-4}	4.0
8.44×10^{-5}	5.7
2.75×10^{-5}	7.0

Experiment 2: $[Y]_0 = 4.5\ M$

[CH$_3$X] (mol/L)	Time (h)
4.50×10^{-3}	0
1.70×10^{-3}	1.0
4.19×10^{-4}	2.5
1.11×10^{-4}	4.0
2.81×10^{-5}	5.5

Experiments also were run at 85°C. The value of the rate constant at 85°C was found to be 7.88×10^8 (with the time in units of hours), where $[CH_3X]_0 = 1.0 \times 10^{-2}\ M$ and $[Y]_0 = 3.0\ M$.

a. Determine the rate law and the value of k for this reaction at 25°C.

b. Determine the half-life at 85°C.

c. Determine E_a for the reaction.

d. Given that the C—X bond energy is known to be about 325 kJ/mol, suggest a mechanism that explains the results in parts a and c.

 Get help understanding core concepts and visualizing molecular-level interactions, and practice problem solving, by visiting the Online Study Center at **college.hmco.com/ PIC/zumdahl7e.**

13 Chemical Equilibrium

Contents

*I*n doing stoichiometry calculations we assumed that reactions proceed to completion, that is, until one of the reactants runs out. Many reactions do proceed essentially to completion. For such reactions it can be assumed that the reactants are quantitatively converted to products and that the amount of limiting reactant that remains is negligible. On the other hand, there are many chemical reactions that stop far short of completion. An example is the dimerization of nitrogen dioxide:

$$NO_2(g) + NO_2(g) \longrightarrow N_2O_4(g)$$

The reactant, NO_2, is a dark brown gas, and the product, N_2O_4, is a colorless gas. When NO_2 is placed in an evacuated, sealed glass vessel at 25°C, the initial dark brown color decreases in intensity as it is converted to colorless N_2O_4. However, even over a long period of time, the contents of the reaction vessel do not become colorless. Instead, the intensity of the brown color eventually becomes constant, which means that the concentration of NO_2 is no longer changing. This is illustrated on the molecular level in Fig. 13.1. This observation is a clear indication that the reaction has stopped short of completion. In fact, the system has reached **chemical equilibrium,** *the state where the concentrations of all reactants and products remain constant with time.*

Any chemical reactions carried out in a closed vessel will reach equilibrium. For some reactions the equilibrium position so favors the products that the reaction appears to have gone to completion. We say that the equilibrium position for such reactions lies *far to the right* (in the direction of the products). For example, when gaseous hydrogen and oxygen are mixed in stoichiometric quantities and react to form water vapor, the reaction proceeds essentially to completion. The amounts of the reactants that remain when the system reaches equilibrium are so tiny as to be negligible. By contrast, some reactions occur only to a slight extent. For example, when solid CaO is placed in a closed vessel at 25°C, the decomposition to solid Ca and gaseous O_2 is virtually undetectable. In cases like this, the equilibrium position is said to lie *far to the left* (in the direction of the reactants).

In this chapter we will discuss how and why a chemical system comes to equilibrium and the characteristics of equilibrium. In particular, we will discuss how to calculate the concentrations of the reactants and products present for a given system at equilibrium.

13.1 The Equilibrium Condition

Since no changes occur in the concentrations of reactants or products in a reaction system at equilibrium, it may appear that everything has stopped. However, this is not the case. On the molecular level, there is frantic activity. Equilibrium is not static but is a highly *dynamic* situation. The concept of chemical equilibrium is analogous to the flow of cars across a bridge connecting two island cities. Suppose the traffic flow on the bridge

Equilibrium is a dynamic situation.

The effect of temperature on the endothermic, aqueous equilibrium:

$$Co(H_2O)_6{}^{2+} + 4Cl^- \rightleftharpoons CoCl_4{}^{2-} + 6H_2O$$
$$\text{Pink} \qquad\qquad\qquad \text{Blue}$$

The violet solution in the center is at 25°C and contains significant quantities of both pink $Co(H_2O)_6{}^{2+}$ and blue $CoCl_4{}^{2-}$. When the solution is cooled, it turns pink because the equilibrium is shifted to the left. Heating the solution favors the blue $CoCl_4{}^{2-}$ ions.

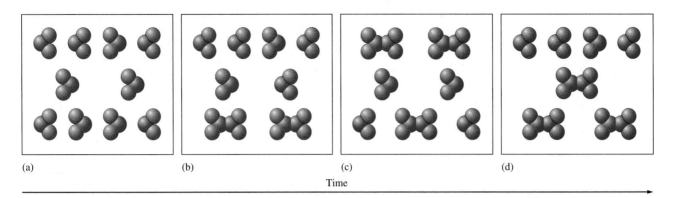

(a)   (b)   (c)   (d)

Time

FIGURE 13.1
A molecular representation of the reaction $2NO_2(g) \rightarrow N_2O_4(g)$ over time in a closed vessel. Note that the numbers of NO_2 and N_2O_4 in the container become constant (c and d) after sufficient time has passed.

is the same in both directions. It is obvious that there is motion, since one can see the cars traveling back and forth across the bridge, but the number of cars in each city is not changing because equal numbers of cars are entering and leaving. The result is no *net* change in the car population.

To see how this concept applies to chemical reactions, consider the reaction between steam and carbon monoxide in a closed vessel at a high temperature where the reaction takes place rapidly:

$$H_2O(g) + CO(g) \rightleftharpoons H_2(g) + CO_2(g)$$

Assume that the same number of moles of gaseous CO and gaseous H_2O are placed in a closed vessel and allowed to react. The plots of the concentrations of reactants and products versus time are shown in Fig. 13.2. Note that since CO and H_2O were originally present in equal molar quantities, and since they react in a 1:1 ratio, the concentrations of the two gases are always equal. Also, since H_2 and CO_2 are formed in equal amounts, they are always present in the same concentrations.

Figure 13.2 is a profile of the progress of the reaction. When CO and H_2O are mixed, they immediately begin to react to form H_2 and CO_2. This leads to a decrease in the concentrations of the reactants, but the concentrations of the products, which were initially at zero, are increasing. Beyond a certain time, indicated by the dashed line in Fig. 13.2, the concentrations of reactants and products no longer change—equilibrium has been reached. Unless the system is somehow disturbed, no further changes in concentrations will occur. Note that although the equilibrium position lies far to the right, the concentrations of reactants never go to zero; the reactants will always be present in small but constant concentrations. This is shown on the microscopic level in Fig. 13.3.

What would happen to the gaseous equilibrium mixture of reactants and products represented in Fig. 13.3, parts (c) and (d), if we injected some $H_2O(g)$ into the box? To answer this question, we need to be sure we understand the equilibrium condition: The

FIGURE 13.2
The changes in concentrations with time for the reaction $H_2O(g) + CO(g) \rightleftharpoons H_2(g) + CO_2(g)$ when equimolar quantities of $H_2O(g)$ and $CO(g)$ are mixed.

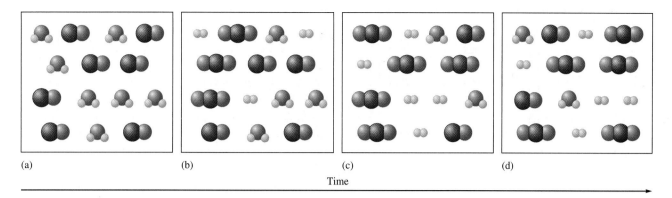

(a)   (b)   (c)   (d)

Time

FIGURE 13.3
(a) H_2O and CO are mixed in equal numbers and begin to react (b) to form CO_2 and H_2. After time has passed, equilibrium is reached (c) and the numbers of reactant and product molecules then remain constant over time (d).

concentrations of reactants and products remain constant at equilibrium because the forward and reverse reaction rates are equal. If we inject some H_2O molecules, what will happen to the forward reaction: $H_2O + CO \rightarrow H_2 + CO_2$? It will speed up because more H_2O molecules means more collisions between H_2O and CO molecules. This in turn will form more products and will cause the reverse reaction $H_2O + CO \leftarrow H_2 + CO_2$ to speed up. Thus the system will change until the forward and reverse reaction rates again become equal. Will this new equilibrium position contain more or fewer product molecules than are shown in Fig. 13.3(c) and (d)? Think about this carefully. If you are not sure of the answer now, keep reading. We will consider this type of situation in more detail later in this chapter.

Why does equilibrium occur? We saw in Chapter 12 that molecules react by colliding with one another, and the more collisions, the faster the reaction. This is why reaction rates depend on concentrations. In this case the concentrations of H_2O and CO are lowered by the forward reaction:

$$H_2O + CO \longrightarrow H_2 + CO_2$$

As the concentrations of the reactants decrease, the forward reaction slows down (Fig. 13.4). As in the bridge traffic analogy, there is also a reverse direction:

$$H_2O + CO \longleftarrow H_2 + CO_2$$

Initially in this experiment no H_2 and CO_2 were present, and this reverse reaction could not occur. However, as the forward reaction proceeds, the concentrations of H_2 and CO_2 build up, and the rate of the reverse reaction increases (Fig. 13.4) as the forward reaction slows down. Eventually, the concentrations reach levels where the rate of the forward reaction equals the rate of the reverse reaction. The system has reached equilibrium.

A double arrow ($\rightleftharpoons$) is used to show that a reaction can occur in either direction.

FIGURE 13.4
The changes with time in the rates of forward and reverse reactions for $H_2O(g) + CO(g) \rightleftharpoons H_2(g) + CO_2(g)$ when equimolar quantities of $H_2O(g)$ and $CO(g)$ are mixed. The rates do not change in the same way with time because the forward reaction has a much larger rate constant than the reverse reaction.

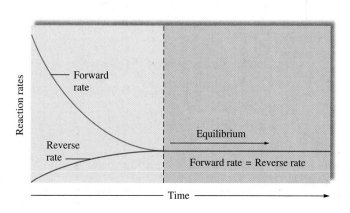

Reaction rates

Forward rate

Reverse rate

Equilibrium

Forward rate = Reverse rate

Time

The relationship between equilibrium and thermodynamics is explored in Section 16.8.

The equilibrium position of a reaction—left, right, or somewhere in between—is determined by many factors: the initial concentrations, the relative energies of the reactants and products, and the relative degree of "organization" of the reactants and products. Energy and organization come into play because nature tries to achieve minimum energy and maximum disorder, as we will show in detail in Chapter 16. For now, we will simply view the equilibrium phenomenon in terms of the rates of opposing reactions.

The Characteristics of Chemical Equilibrium

To explore the important characteristics of chemical equilibrium, we will consider the synthesis of ammonia from elemental nitrogen and hydrogen:

$$N_2(g) + 3H_2(g) \rightleftharpoons 2NH_3(g)$$

The United States produces about 20 million tons of ammonia annually.

This process is of great commercial value because ammonia is an important fertilizer for the growth of corn and other crops. Ironically, this beneficial process was discovered in Germany just before World War I in a search for ways to produce nitrogen-based explosives. In the course of this work, German chemist Fritz Haber (1868–1934) pioneered the large-scale production of ammonia.

When gaseous nitrogen, hydrogen, and ammonia are mixed in a closed vessel at 25°C, no apparent change in the concentrations occurs over time, regardless of the original amounts of the gases. Why? There are two possible reasons why the concentrations of the reactants and products of a given chemical reaction remain unchanged when mixed.

Molecules with strong bonds produce large activation energies and tend to react slowly at 25°C.

1. The system is at chemical equilibrium.

2. The forward and reverse reactions are so slow that the system moves toward equilibrium at a rate that cannot be detected.

The second reason applies to the nitrogen, hydrogen, and ammonia mixture at 25°C. As we saw in Chapters 8 and 9, the N_2 molecule has a very strong triple bond (941 kJ/mol) and thus is very unreactive. Also, the H_2 molecule has an unusually strong single bond (432 kJ/mol). Therefore, mixtures of N_2, H_2, and NH_3 at 25°C can exist with no apparent change over long periods of time, unless a catalyst is introduced to speed up the forward and reverse reactions. Under appropriate conditions, the system does reach equilibrium, as shown in Fig. 13.5. Note that because of the reaction stoichiometry, H_2 disappears three times as fast as N_2 does and NH_3 forms twice as fast as N_2 disappears.

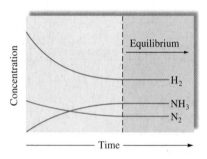

FIGURE 13.5
A concentration profile for the reaction $N_2(g) + 3H_2(g) \rightleftharpoons 2NH_3(g)$ when only $N_2(g)$ and $H_2(g)$ are mixed initially.

13.2 The Equilibrium Constant

Science is fundamentally empirical—it is based on experiment. The development of the equilibrium concept is typical. From their observations of many chemical reactions, two Norwegian chemists, Cato Maximilian Guldberg (1836–1902) and Peter Waage (1833–1900), proposed in 1864 the **law of mass action** as a general description of the equilibrium condition. Guldberg and Waage postulated that for a reaction of the type

The law of mass action is based on experimental observation.

$$jA + kB \rightleftharpoons lC + mD$$

where A, B, C, and D represent chemical species and j, k, l, and m are their coefficients in the balanced equation, the law of mass action is represented by the following **equilibrium expression:**

$$K = \frac{[C]^l[D]^m}{[A]^j[B]^k}$$

The square brackets indicate the concentrations of the chemical species *at equilibrium*, and K is a constant called the **equilibrium constant.**

| Sample Exercise 13.1 | Writing Equilibrium Expressions |

Write the equilibrium expression for the following reaction:

$$4NH_3(g) + 7O_2(g) \rightleftharpoons 4NO_2(g) + 6H_2O(g)$$

Solution

Applying the law of mass action gives

The square brackets indicate concentration in units of mol/L.

Coefficient of NO_2

Coefficient of H_2O

$$K = \frac{[NO_2]^4[H_2O]^6}{[NH_3]^4[O_2]^7}$$

Coefficient of O_2

Coefficient of NH_3

See Exercise 13.17.

The value of the equilibrium constant at a given temperature can be calculated if we know the equilibrium concentrations of the reaction components, as illustrated in Sample Exercise 13.2.

It is very important to note at this point that the equilibrium constants are customarily given without units. The reason for this is beyond the scope of this text, but it involves corrections for the nonideal behavior of the substances taking part in the reaction. When these corrections are made, the units cancel out and the corrected K has no units. Thus we will not use units for K in this text.

| Sample Exercise 13.2 | Calculating the Values of K |

The following equilibrium concentrations were observed for the Haber process at 127°C:

$$[NH_3] = 3.1 \times 10^{-2} \text{ mol/L}$$
$$[N_2] = 8.5 \times 10^{-1} \text{ mol/L}$$
$$[H_2] = 3.1 \times 10^{-3} \text{ mol/L}$$

a. Calculate the value of K at 127°C for this reaction.

b. Calculate the value of the equilibrium constant at 127°C for the reaction

$$2NH_3(g) \rightleftharpoons N_2(g) + 3H_2(g)$$

c. Calculate the value of the equilibrium constant at 127°C for the reaction given by the equation

$$\tfrac{1}{2}N_2(g) + \tfrac{3}{2}H_2(g) \rightleftharpoons NH_3(g)$$

Solution

a. The balanced equation for the Haber process is

$$N_2(g) + 3H_2(g) \rightleftharpoons 2NH_3(g)$$

Thus

$$K = \frac{[NH_3]^2}{[N_2][H_2]^3} = \frac{(3.1 \times 10^{-2})^2}{(8.5 \times 10^{-1})(3.1 \times 10^{-3})^3}$$
$$= 3.8 \times 10^4$$

Note that K is written without units.

b. This reaction is written in the reverse order from the equation given in part a. This leads to the equilibrium expression

$$K' = \frac{[N_2][H_2]^3}{[NH_3]^2}$$

which is the reciprocal of the expression used in part a. Therefore,

$$K' = \frac{[N_2][H_2]^3}{[NH_3]^2} = \frac{1}{K} = \frac{1}{3.8 \times 10^4} = 2.6 \times 10^{-5}$$

c. We use the law of mass action:

$$K'' = \frac{[NH_3]}{[N_2]^{1/2}[H_2]^{3/2}}$$

If we compare this expression to that obtained in part a, we see that since

$$\frac{[NH_3]}{[N_2]^{1/2}[H_2]^{3/2}} = \left(\frac{[NH_3]^2}{[N_2][H_2]^3}\right)^{1/2}$$

$$K'' = K^{1/2}$$

Thus

$$K'' = K^{1/2} = (3.8 \times 10^4)^{1/2} = 1.9 \times 10^2$$

See Exercises 13.19 and 13.21 through 13.24.

We can draw some important conclusions from the results of Sample Exercise 13.2. For a reaction of the form

$$jA + kB \rightleftharpoons lC + mD$$

the equilibrium expression is

$$K = \frac{[C]^l[D]^m}{[A]^j[B]^k}$$

If this reaction is reversed, then the new equilibrium expression is

$$K' = \frac{[A]^j[B]^k}{[C]^l[D]^m} = \frac{1}{K}$$

If the original reaction is multiplied by some factor n to give

$$njA + nkB \rightleftharpoons nlC + nmD$$

the equilibrium expression becomes

$$K'' = \frac{[C]^{nl}[D]^{nm}}{[A]^{nj}[B]^{nk}} = K^n$$

We Can Summarize These Conclusions About the Equilibrium Expression as Follows:

- The equilibrium expression for a reaction is the reciprocal of that for the reaction written in reverse.

- When the balanced equation for a reaction is multiplied by a factor n, the equilibrium expression for the new reaction is the original expression raised to the nth power. Thus $K_{new} = (K_{original})^n$.

- K values are customarily written without units.

The law of mass action applies to solution and gaseous equilibria.

A cross section showing how anhydrous ammonia is injected into the soil to act as a fertilizer.

For a reaction at a given temperature, there are many equilibrium positions but only one value for K.

The law of mass action is widely applicable. It correctly describes the equilibrium behavior of an amazing variety of chemical systems in solution and in the gas phase. Although, as we will see later, corrections must be applied in certain cases, such as for concentrated aqueous solutions and for gases at high pressures, the law of mass action provides a remarkably accurate description of all types of chemical equilibria.

Consider again the ammonia synthesis reaction. The equilibrium constant K always has the same value at a given temperature. At 500°C the value of K is 6.0×10^{-2}. Whenever N_2, H_2, and NH_3 are mixed together at this temperature, the system will always come to an equilibrium position such that

$$\frac{[NH_3]^2}{[N_2][H_2]^3} = 6.0 \times 10^{-2}$$

This expression has the same value at 500°C, *regardless of the amounts of the gases that are mixed together initially.*

Although the special ratio of products to reactants defined by the equilibrium expression is constant for a given reaction system at a given temperature, the *equilibrium concentrations will not always be the same.* Table 13.1 gives three sets of data for the synthesis of ammonia, showing that even though the individual sets of equilibrium concentrations are quite different for the different situations, the *equilibrium constant, which depends on the ratio of the concentrations, remains the same* (within experimental error). Note that subscript zeros indicate initial concentrations.

Each *set of equilibrium concentrations* is called an **equilibrium position.** It is essential to distinguish between the equilibrium constant and the equilibrium positions for a given reaction system. There is only *one* equilibrium constant for a particular system at a particular temperature, but there are an *infinite* number of equilibrium positions. The specific equilibrium position adopted by a system depends on the initial concentrations, but the equilibrium constant does not.

Sample Exercise 13.3 Equilibrium Positions

The following results were collected for two experiments involving the reaction at 600°C between gaseous sulfur dioxide and oxygen to form gaseous sulfur trioxide:

Experiment 1		Experiment 2	
Initial	*Equilibrium*	*Initial*	*Equilibrium*
$[SO_2]_0 = 2.00\ M$	$[SO_2] = 1.50\ M$	$[SO_2]_0 = 0.500\ M$	$[SO_2] = 0.590\ M$
$[O_2]_0 = 1.50\ M$	$[O_2] = 1.25\ M$	$[O_2]_0 = 0$	$[O_2] = 0.0450\ M$
$[SO_3]_0 = 3.00\ M$	$[SO_3] = 3.50\ M$	$[SO_3]_0 = 0.350\ M$	$[SO_3] = 0.260\ M$

Show that the equilibrium constant is the same in both cases.

Solution

The balanced equation for the reaction is

$$2SO_2(g) + O_2(g) \rightleftharpoons 2SO_3(g)$$

From the law of mass action,

$$K = \frac{[SO_3]^2}{[SO_2]^2[O_2]}$$

TABLE 13.1 Results of Three Experiments for the Reaction $N_2(g) + 3H_2(g) \rightleftharpoons 2NH_3(g)$

Experiment	Initial Concentrations	Equilibrium Concentrations	$K = \dfrac{[NH_3]^2}{[N_2][H_2]^3}$
I	$[N_2]_0 = 1.000\ M$ $[H_2]_0 = 1.000\ M$ $[NH_3]_0 = 0$	$[N_2] = 0.921\ M$ $[H_2] = 0.763\ M$ $[NH_3] = 0.157\ M$	$K = 6.02 \times 10^{-2}$
II	$[N_2]_0 = 0$ $[H_2]_0 = 0$ $[NH_3]_0 = 1.000\ M$	$[N_2] = 0.399\ M$ $[H_2] = 1.197\ M$ $[NH_3] = 0.203\ M$	$K = 6.02 \times 10^{-2}$
III	$[N_2]_0 = 2.00\ M$ $[H_2]_0 = 1.00\ M$ $[NH_3]_0 = 3.00\ M$	$[N_2] = 2.59\ M$ $[H_2] = 2.77\ M$ $[NH_3] = 1.82\ M$	$K = 6.02 \times 10^{-2}$

For Experiment 1,

$$K_1 = \frac{(3.50)^2}{(1.50)^2(1.25)} = 4.36$$

For Experiment 2,

$$K_2 = \frac{(0.260)^2}{(0.590)^2(0.0450)} = 4.32$$

The value of K is constant, within experimental error.

See Exercise 13.24.

13.3 Equilibrium Expressions Involving Pressures

So far we have been describing equilibria involving gases in terms of concentrations. Equilibria involving gases also can be described in terms of pressures. The relationship between the pressure and the concentration of a gas can be seen from the ideal gas equation:

The ideal gas equation was discussed in Section 5.3.

$$PV = nRT \quad \text{or} \quad P = \left(\frac{n}{V}\right)RT = CRT$$

where C equals n/V, or the number of moles n of gas per unit volume V. Thus C represents the *molar concentration of the gas.*

For the ammonia synthesis reaction, the equilibrium expression can be written in terms of concentrations, that is,

$$K = \frac{[NH_3]^2}{[N_2][H_2]^3} = \frac{C_{NH_3}^{\ 2}}{(C_{N_2})(C_{H_2}^{\ 3})} = K_c$$

or in terms of the *equilibrium partial pressures of the gases,* that is,

$$K_p = \frac{P_{NH_3}^{\ 2}}{(P_{N_2})(P_{H_2}^{\ 3})}$$

K involves concentrations; K_p involves pressures. In some books, the symbol K_c is used instead of K.

Both the symbols K and K_c are used commonly for an equilibrium constant in terms of concentrations. We will always use K in this book. The symbol K_p represents an equilibrium constant in terms of partial pressures.

| *Sample Exercise 13.4* | **Calculating Values of K_p** |

The reaction for the formation of nitrosyl chloride

$$2NO(g) + Cl_2(g) \rightleftharpoons 2NOCl(g)$$

was studied at 25°C. The pressures at equilibrium were found to be

$$P_{NOCl} = 1.2 \text{ atm}$$
$$P_{NO} = 5.0 \times 10^{-2} \text{ atm}$$
$$P_{Cl_2} = 3.0 \times 10^{-1} \text{ atm}$$

Calculate the value of K_p for this reaction at 25°C.

Solution

For this reaction,

$$K_p = \frac{P_{NOCl}^2}{(P_{NO_2})^2(P_{Cl_2})} = \frac{(1.2)^2}{(5.0 \times 10^{-2})^2(3.0 \times 10^{-1})}$$
$$= 1.9 \times 10^3$$

See Exercises 13.25 and 13.26.

The relationship between K and K_p for a particular reaction follows from the fact that for an ideal gas, $C = P/RT$. For example, for the ammonia synthesis reaction,

$$P = CRT \quad \text{or} \quad C = \frac{P}{RT}$$

$$K = \frac{[NH_3]^2}{[N_2][H_2]^3} = \frac{C_{NH_3}^2}{(C_{N_2})(C_{H_2}^3)}$$

$$= \frac{\left(\dfrac{P_{NH_3}}{RT}\right)^2}{\left(\dfrac{P_{N_2}}{RT}\right)\left(\dfrac{P_{H_2}}{RT}\right)^3} = \frac{P_{NH_3}^2}{(P_{N_2})(P_{H_2}^3)} \times \frac{\left(\dfrac{1}{RT}\right)^2}{\left(\dfrac{1}{RT}\right)^4}$$

$$= \frac{P_{NH_3}^2}{(P_{N_2})(P_{H_2}^3)} (RT)^2$$

$$= K_p(RT)^2$$

However, for the synthesis of hydrogen fluoride from its elements,

$$H_2(g) + F_2(g) \rightleftharpoons 2HF(g)$$

the relationship between K and K_p is given by

$$K = \frac{[HF]^2}{[H_2][F_2]} = \frac{C_{HF}^2}{(C_{H_2})(C_{F_2})}$$

$$= \frac{\left(\dfrac{P_{HF}}{RT}\right)^2}{\left(\dfrac{P_{H_2}}{RT}\right)\left(\dfrac{P_{F_2}}{RT}\right)} = \frac{P_{HF}^2}{(P_{H_2})(P_{F_2})}$$

$$= K_p$$

Thus, for this reaction, K is equal to K_p. This equality occurs because the sum of the coefficients on either side of the balanced equation is identical, so the terms in RT cancel out. In the equilibrium expression for the ammonia synthesis reaction, the sum of the powers in the numerator is different from that in the denominator, and K does not equal K_p.

For the general reaction

$$jA + kB \rightleftharpoons lC + mD$$

the relationship between K and K_p is

$$K_p = K(RT)^{\Delta n}$$

where Δn is the sum of the coefficients of the *gaseous* products minus the sum of the co-efficients of the *gaseous* reactants. This equation is quite easy to derive from the definitions of K and K_p and the relationship between pressure and concentration. For the preceding general reaction,

$$K_p = \frac{(P_C{}^l)(P_D{}^m)}{(P_A{}^j)(P_B{}^k)} = \frac{(C_C \times RT)^l(C_D \times RT)^m}{(C_A \times RT)^j(C_B \times RT)^k}$$

$$= \frac{(C_C{}^l)(C_D{}^m)}{(C_A{}^j)(C_B{}^k)} \times \frac{(RT)^{l+m}}{(RT)^{j+k}} = K(RT)^{(l+m)-(j+k)}$$

$$= K(RT)^{\Delta n}$$

Δn always involves products minus reactants.

where $\Delta n = (l + m) - (j + k)$, the difference in the sums of the coefficients for the gaseous products and reactants.

Sample Exercise 13.5

Calculating K from K_p

Using the value of K_p obtained in Sample Exercise 13.4, calculate the value of K at 25°C for the reaction

$$2NO(g) + Cl_2(g) \rightleftharpoons 2NOCl(g)$$

Solution

From the value of K_p, we can calculate K using

$$K_p = K(RT)^{\Delta n}$$

where $T = 25 + 273 = 298$ K and

$$\Delta n = 2 - (2 + 1) = -1$$

Sum of product coefficients   Sum of reactant coefficients

$$\Delta n$$
$$\downarrow$$

Thus

$$K_p = K(RT)^{-1} = \frac{K}{RT}$$

and

$$K = K_p(RT)$$
$$= (1.9 \times 10^3)(0.08206)(298)$$
$$= 4.6 \times 10^4$$

See Exercises 13.27 and 13.28.

13.4 Heterogeneous Equilibria

So far we have discussed equilibria only for systems in the gas phase, where all reactants and products are gases. These are **homogeneous equilibria.** However, many equilibria involve more than one phase and are called **heterogeneous equilibria.** For example, the thermal decomposition of calcium carbonate in the commercial preparation of lime occurs by a reaction involving both solid and gas phases:

$$CaCO_3(s) \rightleftharpoons CaO(s) + CO_2(g)$$
$$\uparrow$$
$$\text{Lime}$$

Straightforward application of the law of mass action leads to the equilibrium expression

$$K' = \frac{[CO_2][CaO]}{[CaCO_3]}$$

However, experimental results show that the *position of a heterogeneous equilibrium does not depend on the amounts of pure solids or liquids present* (see Fig. 13.6). The fundamental reason for this behavior is that the concentrations of pure solids and liquids cannot change. Thus the equilibrium expression for the decomposition of solid calcium carbonate might be represented as

$$K' = \frac{[CO_2]C_1}{C_2}$$

where C_1 and C_2 are constants representing the concentrations of the solids CaO and $CaCO_3$, respectively. This expression can be rearranged to give

$$\frac{C_2 K'}{C_1} = K = [CO_2]$$

We can generalize from this result as follows: If pure solids or pure liquids are involved in a chemical reaction, their concentrations *are not included in the equilibrium expression* for the reaction. This simplification occurs *only* with pure solids or liquids, not with solutions or gases, since in these last two cases the concentrations can vary.

For example, in the decomposition of liquid water to gaseous hydrogen and oxygen,

$$2H_2O(l) \rightleftharpoons 2H_2(g) + O_2(g)$$

where

$$K = [H_2]^2[O_2] \quad \text{and} \quad K_p = (P_{H_2}{}^2)(P_{O_2})$$

water is not included in either equilibrium expression because it is a pure liquid. However, if the reaction were carried out under conditions where the water is a gas rather than a liquid, that is,

$$2H_2O(g) \rightleftharpoons 2H_2(g) + O_2(g)$$

Lime is among the top five chemicals manufactured in the United States in terms of the amount produced.

The concentrations of pure liquids and solids are constant.

The Seven Sisters chalk cliffs in East Sussex, England. The chalk is made up of compressed calcium carbonate skeletons of microscopic algae from the late Cretaceous Period.

FIGURE 13.6
The position of the equilibrium $CaCO_3(s) \rightleftharpoons CaO(s) + CO_2(g)$ does not depend on the amounts of $CaCO_3(s)$ and $CaO(s)$ present.

CO₂

CaCO₃

CaO

(a)

(b)

then

$$K = \frac{[H_2]^2[O_2]}{[H_2O]^2} \quad \text{and} \quad K_p = \frac{(P_{H_2}^{\,2})(P_{O_2})}{P_{H_2O}^{\,2}}$$

because the concentration or pressure of water vapor can change.

Sample Exercise 13.6 | **Equilibrium Expressions for Heterogeneous Equilibria**

Write the expressions for K and K_p for the following processes:

a. Solid phosphorus pentachloride decomposes to liquid phosphorus trichloride and chlorine gas.

b. Deep blue solid copper(II) sulfate pentahydrate is heated to drive off water vapor to form white solid copper(II) sulfate.

Solution

a. The reaction is

$$PCl_5(s) \rightleftharpoons PCl_3(l) + Cl_2(g)$$

The equilibrium expressions are

$$K = [Cl_2] \quad \text{and} \quad K_p = P_{Cl_2}$$

In this case neither the pure solid PCl_5 nor the pure liquid PCl_3 is included in the equilibrium expressions.

b. The reaction is

$$CuSO_4 \cdot 5H_2O(s) \rightleftharpoons CuSO_4(s) + 5H_2O(g)$$

The equilibrium expressions are

$$K = [H_2O]^5 \quad \text{and} \quad K_p = (P_{H_2O})^5$$

The solids are not included.

See Exercise 13.29.

Hydrated copper(II) sulfate on the left. Water applied to anhydrous copper(II) sulfate, on the right, forms the hydrated compound.

13.5 Applications of the Equilibrium Constant

Knowing the equilibrium constant for a reaction allows us to predict several important features of the reaction: the tendency of the reaction to occur (but not the speed of the reaction), whether a given set of concentrations represents an equilibrium condition, and the equilibrium position that will be achieved from a given set of initial concentrations.

To introduce some of these ideas, we will first consider the reaction

where ○ and ● represent two different types of atoms. Assume that this reaction has an equilibrium constant equal to 16.

In a given experiment, the two types of molecules are mixed together in the following amounts:

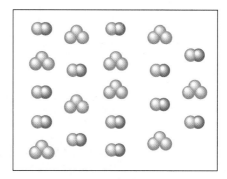

After the system reacts and comes to equilibrium, what will the system look like? We know that at equilibrium the ratio

$$\frac{(N_{\text{○○}})(N_{\text{△}})}{(N_{\text{△}})(N_{\text{○○}})} = 16$$

must be satisfied, where each N represents the number of molecules of each type. We originally have 9 △ molecules and 12 ○○ molecules. As a place to start, let's just assume that 5 △ molecules disappear for the system to reach equilibrium. Since equal numbers of the △ and ○○ molecules react, this means that 5 ○○ molecules also will disappear. This also means that 5 ○○ molecules and 5 △ molecules will be formed. We can summarize as follows:

Initial Conditions	New Conditions
9 △ molecules	9 − 5 = 4 △ molecules
12 ○○ molecules	12 − 5 = 7 ○○ molecules
0 △ molecules	0 + 5 = 5 △ molecules
0 ○○ molecules	0 + 5 = 5 ○○ molecules

Do the new conditions represent equilibrium for this reaction system? We can find out by taking the ratio of the numbers of molecules:

$$\frac{(N_{\text{○○}})(N_{\text{△}})}{(N_{\text{△}})(N_{\text{○○}})} = \frac{(5)(5)}{(4)(7)} = 0.9$$

Thus this is not an equilibrium position because the ratio is not 16, as required for equilibrium. In which direction must the system move to achieve equilibrium? Since the observed ratio is smaller than 16, we must increase the numerator and decrease the denominator: The system needs to move to the right (toward more products) to achieve equilibrium. That is, more than 5 of the original reactant molecules must disappear to reach equilibrium for this system. How can we find the correct number? Since we do not know the number of molecules that need to disappear to reach equilibrium, let's call this number x. Now we can set up a table similar to the one we used earlier:

Initial Conditions		Equilibrium Conditions
9 ⬡ molecules	x ⬡ disappear	$9 - x$ ⬡ molecules
12 ⬭ molecules	x ⬭ disappear	$12 - x$ ⬭ molecules
0 ⬡ molecules	x ⬡ form	x ⬡ molecules
0 ⬭ molecules	x ⬭ form	x ⬭ molecules

For the system to be at equilibrium, we know that the following ratio must be satisfied:

$$\frac{(N_{\text{⬭}})(N_{\text{⬡}})}{(N_{\text{⬡}})(N_{\text{⬭}})} = 16 = \frac{(x)(x)}{(9 - x)(12 - x)}$$

The easiest way to solve for x here is by trial and error. From our previous discussion we know that x is greater than 5. Also, we know that it must be less than 9 because we have only 9 ⬡ molecules to start. We can't use all of them or we will have a zero in the denominator, which causes the ratio to be infinitely large. By trial and error, we find that $x = 8$ because

$$\frac{(x)(x)}{(9 - x)(12 - x)} = \frac{(8)(8)}{(9 - 8)(12 - 8)} = \frac{64}{4} = 16$$

The equilibrium mixture can be pictured as follows:

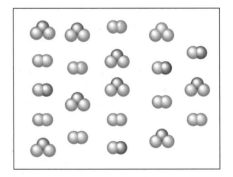

Note that it contains 8 ⬭ molecules, 8 ⬡ molecules, 1 ⬡ molecule, and 4 ⬭ molecules as required.

This pictorial example should help you understand the fundamental ideas of equilibrium. Now we will proceed to a more systematic quantitative treatment of chemical equilibrium.

The Extent of a Reaction

The inherent tendency for a reaction to occur is indicated by the magnitude of the equilibrium constant. A value of K much larger than 1 means that at equilibrium the reaction

(b)

FIGURE 13.7
(a) A physical analogy illustrating the difference between thermodynamic and kinetic stabilities. The boulder is thermodynamically more stable (lower potential energy) in position *B* than in position *A* but cannot get over the hump *H*. (b) The reactants H_2 and O_2 have a strong tendency to form H_2O. That is, H_2O has lower energy than H_2 and O_2. However, the large activation energy E_a prevents the reaction at 25°C. In other words, the magnitude of *K* for the reaction depends on ΔE, but the reaction rate depends on E_a.

system will consist of mostly products—the equilibrium lies to the right. Another way of saying this is that reactions with very large equilibrium constants go essentially to completion. On the other hand, a very small value of *K* means that the system at equilibrium will consist of mostly reactants—the equilibrium position is far to the left. The given reaction does not occur to any significant extent.

It is important to understand that *the size of K and the time required to reach equilibrium are not directly related.* The time required to achieve equilibrium depends on the reaction rate, which is determined by the size of the activation energy. The size of *K* is determined by thermodynamic factors such as the difference in energy between products and reactants. This difference is represented in Fig. 13.7 and will be discussed in detail in Chapter 16.

Reaction Quotient

When the reactants and products of a given chemical reaction are mixed, it is useful to know whether the mixture is at equilibrium or, if not, the direction in which the system must shift to reach equilibrium. If the concentration of one of the reactants or products is zero, the system will shift in the direction that produces the missing component. However, if all the initial concentrations are nonzero, it is more difficult to determine the direction of the move toward equilibrium. To determine the shift in such cases, we use the **reaction quotient, Q.** The reaction quotient is obtained by applying the law of mass action using *initial concentrations* instead of equilibrium concentrations. For example, for the synthesis of ammonia

$$N_2(g) + 3H_2(g) \rightleftharpoons 2NH_3(g)$$

the expression for the reaction quotient is

$$Q = \frac{[NH_3]_0^2}{[N_2]_0[H_2]_0^3}$$

where the subscript zeros indicate initial concentrations.

To determine in which direction a system will shift to reach equilibrium, we compare the values of *Q* and *K*. There are three possible cases:

1. *Q is equal to K.* The system is at equilibrium; no shift will occur.

2. *Q is greater than K.* In this case, the ratio of initial concentrations of products to initial concentrations of reactants is too large. To reach equilibrium, a net change of products to reactants must occur. The system *shifts to the left,* consuming products and forming reactants, until equilibrium is achieved.

3. *Q is less than K.* In this case, the ratio of initial concentrations of products to initial concentrations of reactants is too small. The *system must shift to the right,* consuming reactants and forming products, to attain equilibrium.

Sample Exercise 13.7   **Using the Reaction Quotient**

For the synthesis of ammonia at 500°C, the equilibrium constant is 6.0×10^{-2}. Predict the direction in which the system will shift to reach equilibrium in each of the following cases:

a. $[NH_3]_0 = 1.0 \times 10^{-3}\,M$; $[N_2]_0 = 1.0 \times 10^{-5}\,M$; $[H_2]_0 = 2.0 \times 10^{-3}\,M$
b. $[NH_3]_0 = 2.00 \times 10^{-4}\,M$; $[N_2]_0 = 1.50 \times 10^{-5}\,M$; $[H_2]_0 = 3.54 \times 10^{-1}\,M$
c. $[NH_3]_0 = 1.0 \times 10^{-4}\,M$; $[N_2]_0 = 5.0\,M$; $[H_2]_0 = 1.0 \times 10^{-2}\,M$

Solution

a. First we calculate the value of Q:

$$Q = \frac{[NH_3]_0^2}{[N_2]_0[H_2]_0^3} = \frac{(1.0 \times 10^{-3})^2}{(1.0 \times 10^{-5})(2.0 \times 10^{-3})^3}$$
$$= 1.3 \times 10^7$$

Since $K = 6.0 \times 10^{-2}$, Q is much greater than K. To attain equilibrium, the concentrations of the products must be decreased and the concentrations of the reactants increased. The system will shift to the left:

$$N_2 + 3H_2 \longleftarrow 2NH_3$$

b. We calculate the value of Q:

$$Q = \frac{[NH_3]_0^2}{[N_2]_0[H_2]_0^3} = \frac{(2.00 \times 10^{-4})^2}{(1.50 \times 10^{-5})(3.54 \times 10^{-1})^3}$$
$$= 6.01 \times 10^{-2}$$

In this case $Q = K$, so the system is at equilibrium. No shift will occur.

c. The value of Q is

$$Q = \frac{[NH_3]_0^2}{[N_2]_0[H_2]_0^3} = \frac{(1.0 \times 10^{-4})^2}{(5.0)(1.0 \times 10^{-2})^3}$$
$$= 2.0 \times 10^{-3}$$

Here Q is less than K, so the system will shift to the right to attain equilibrium by increasing the concentration of the product and decreasing the reactant concentrations:

$$N_2 + 3H_2 \longrightarrow 2NH_3$$

See Exercises 13.33 through 13.36.

Calculating Equilibrium Pressures and Concentrations

A typical equilibrium problem involves finding the equilibrium concentrations (or pressures) of reactants and products, given the value of the equilibrium constant and the initial concentrations (or pressures). However, since such problems sometimes become complicated mathematically, we will develop useful strategies for solving them by considering cases for which we know one or more of the equilibrium concentrations (or pressures).

Sample Exercise 13.8   **Calculating Equilibrium Pressures I**

Dinitrogen tetroxide in its liquid state was used as one of the fuels on the lunar lander for the NASA Apollo missions. In the gas phase it decomposes to gaseous nitrogen dioxide:

$$N_2O_4(g) \rightleftharpoons 2NO_2(g)$$

Consider an experiment in which gaseous N_2O_4 was placed in a flask and allowed to reach equilibrium at a temperature where $K_p = 0.133$. At equilibrium, the pressure of N_2O_4 was found to be 2.71 atm. Calculate the equilibrium pressure of $NO_2(g)$.

Apollo II lunar landing module at Tranquility Base, 1969.

Solution

We know that the equilibrium pressures of the gases NO_2 and N_2O_4 must satisfy the relationship

$$K_p = \frac{P_{NO_2}{}^2}{P_{N_2O_4}} = 0.133$$

Since we know $P_{N_2O_4}$, we can simply solve for P_{NO_2}:

$$P_{NO_2}{}^2 = K_p(P_{N_2O_4}) = (0.133)(2.71) = 0.360$$

Therefore,

$$P_{NO_2} = \sqrt{0.360} = 0.600$$

See Exercises 13.37 and 13.38.

| Sample Exercise 13.9 | **Calculating Equilibrium Pressures II** |

At a certain temperature a 1.00-L flask initially contained 0.298 mol $PCl_3(g)$ and 8.70×10^{-3} mol $PCl_5(g)$. After the system had reached equilibrium, 2.00×10^{-3} mol $Cl_2(g)$ was found in the flask. Gaseous PCl_5 decomposes according to the reaction

$$PCl_5(g) \rightleftharpoons PCl_3(g) + Cl_2(g)$$

Calculate the equilibrium concentrations of all species and the value of K.

Solution

The equilibrium expression for this reaction is

$$K = \frac{[Cl_2][PCl_3]}{[PCl_5]}$$

To find the value of K, we must calculate the equilibrium concentrations of all species and then substitute these quantities into the equilibrium expression. The best method for finding the equilibrium concentrations is to begin with the initial concentrations, which we will define as the concentrations before any shift toward equilibrium has occurred. We will then modify these initial concentrations appropriately to find the equilibrium concentrations.

The initial concentrations are

$$[Cl_2]_0 = 0$$

$$[PCl_3]_0 = \frac{0.298 \text{ mol}}{1.00 \text{ L}} = 0.298 \, M$$

$$[PCl_5]_0 = \frac{8.70 \times 10^{-3} \text{ mol}}{1.00 \text{ L}} = 8.70 \times 10^{-3} \, M$$

Next we find the change required to reach equilibrium. Since no Cl_2 was initially present but $2.00 \times 10^{-3} \, M$ Cl_2 is present at equilibrium, 2.00×10^{-3} mol PCl_5 must have decomposed to form 2.00×10^{-3} mol Cl_2 and 2.00×10^{-3} mol PCl_3. In other words, to reach equilibrium, the reaction shifted to the right:

$$PCl_5(g) \longrightarrow PCl_3(g) + Cl_2(g)$$
$$2.00 \times 10^{-3} \text{ mol} \longrightarrow 2.00 \times 10^{-3} \text{ mol} + 2.00 \times 10^{-3} \text{ mol}$$

↑
Net amount of PCl_5
decomposed

↖ ↗
Net amounts of
products formed

Now we apply this change to the initial concentrations to obtain the equilibrium concentrations:

$$[Cl_2] = 0 + \frac{2.00 \times 10^{-3} \text{ mol}}{1.00 \text{ L}} = 2.00 \times 10^{-3} \, M$$
$$\big([Cl_2]_0$$

$$[PCl_3] = 0.298 \, M + \frac{2.00 \times 10^{-3} \text{ mol}}{1.00 \text{ L}} = 0.300 \, M$$
$$\big([PCl_3]_0$$

$$[PCl_5] = 8.70 \times 10^{-3} \, M - \frac{2.00 \times 10^{-3} \text{ mol}}{1.00 \text{ L}} = 6.70 \times 10^{-3} \, M$$
$$\big([PCl_5]_0$$

These equilibrium concentrations can now be used to find K:

$$K = \frac{[Cl_2][PCl_3]}{[PCl_5]} = \frac{(2.00 \times 10^{-3})(0.300)}{6.70 \times 10^{-3}}$$
$$= 8.96 \times 10^{-2}$$

See Exercises 13.39 through 13.42.

Sometimes we are not given any of the equilibrium concentrations (or pressures), only the initial values. Then we must use the stoichiometry of the reaction to express concentrations (or pressures) at equilibrium in terms of the initial values. This is illustrated in Sample Exercise 13.10.

| Sample Exercise 13.10 | **Calculating Equilibrium Concentrations I** |

Carbon monoxide reacts with steam to produce carbon dioxide and hydrogen. At 700 K the equilibrium constant is 5.10. Calculate the equilibrium concentrations of all species if 1.000 mol of each component is mixed in a 1.000-L flask.

Solution

The balanced equation for the reaction is

$$CO(g) + H_2O(g) \rightleftharpoons CO_2(g) + H_2(g)$$

and

$$K = \frac{[CO_2][H_2]}{[CO][H_2O]} = 5.10$$

Next we calculate the initial concentrations:

$$[CO]_0 = [H_2O]_0 = [CO_2]_0 = [H_2]_0 = \frac{1.000 \text{ mol}}{1.000 \text{ L}} = 1.000 \, M$$

Is the system at equilibrium, and if not, which way will it shift to reach the equilibrium position? These questions can be answered by calculating Q:

$$Q = \frac{[CO_2]_0[H_2]_0}{[CO]_0[H_2O]_0} = \frac{(1.000 \text{ mol/L})(1.000 \text{ mol/L})}{(1.000 \text{ mol/L})(1.000 \text{ mol/L})} = 1.000$$

Since Q is less than K, the system is not at equilibrium initially but must shift to the right.

What are the equilibrium concentrations? As before, we start with the initial concentrations and modify them to obtain the equilibrium concentrations. We must ask this question: How much will the system shift to the right to attain the equilibrium condition? In Sample Exercise 13.9 the change needed for the system to reach equilibrium was given. However, in this case we do not have this information.

Since the required change in concentrations is unknown at this point, we will define it in terms of x. Let's assume that x mol/L CO must react for the system to reach equilibrium. This means that the initial concentration of CO will decrease by x mol/L:

$$[CO] = [CO]_0 - x$$

$$\underset{\text{Equilibrium}}{\uparrow} \qquad \underset{\text{Initial}}{\uparrow} \quad \underset{\text{Change}}{\uparrow}$$

Since each CO molecule reacts with one H_2O molecule, the concentration of water vapor also must decrease by x mol/L:

$$[H_2O] = [H_2O]_0 - x$$

As the reactant concentrations decrease, the product concentrations increase. Since all the coefficients are 1 in the balanced reaction, 1 mol CO reacting with 1 mol H_2O will produce 1 mol CO_2 and 1 mol H_2. Or in the present case, to reach equilibrium, x mol/L CO will react with x mol/L H_2O to give an additional x mol/L CO_2 and x mol/L H_2:

$$xCO + xH_2O \longrightarrow xCO_2 + xH_2$$

Thus the initial concentrations of CO_2 and H_2 will increase by x mol/L:

$$[CO_2] = [CO_2]_0 + x$$
$$[H_2] = [H_2]_0 + x$$

Now we have all the equilibrium concentrations defined in terms of the initial concentrations and the change x:

Initial Concentration (mol/L)	Change (mol/L)	Equilibrium Concentration (mol/L)
$[CO]_0 = 1.000$	$-x$	$1.000 - x$
$[H_2O]_0 = 1.000$	$-x$	$1.000 - x$
$[CO_2]_0 = 1.000$	$+x$	$1.000 + x$
$[H_2]_0 = 1.000$	$+x$	$1.000 + x$

Note that the sign of x is determined by the direction of the shift. In this example, the system shifts to the right, so the product concentrations increase and the reactant concentrations decrease. Also note that because the coefficients in the balanced equation are all 1, the magnitude of the change is the same for all species.

Now since we know that the equilibrium concentrations must satisfy the equilibrium expression, we can find the value of x by substituting these concentrations into the expression

$$K = 5.10 = \frac{[CO_2][H_2]}{[CO][H_2O]} = \frac{(1.000 + x)(1.000 + x)}{(1.000 - x)(1.000 - x)} = \frac{(1.000 + x)^2}{(1.000 - x)^2}$$

Since the right side of the equation is a perfect square, the solution of the problem can be simplified by taking the square root of both sides:

$$\sqrt{5.10} = 2.26 = \frac{1.000 + x}{1.000 - x}$$

Multiplying and collecting terms gives

$$x = 0.387 \text{ mol/L}$$

Thus the system shifts to the right, consuming 0.387 mol/L CO and 0.387 mol/L H_2O and forming 0.387 mol/L CO_2 and 0.387 mol/L H_2.

Now the equilibrium concentrations can be calculated:

$$[CO] = [H_2O] = 1.000 - x = 1.000 - 0.387 = 0.613 \, M$$
$$[CO_2] = [H_2] = 1.000 + x = 1.000 + 0.387 = 1.387 \, M$$

Reality Check: These values can be checked by substituting them back into the equilibrium expression to make sure they give the correct value for K:

$$K = \frac{[CO_2][H_2]}{[CO][H_2O]} = \frac{(1.387)^2}{(0.613)^2} = 5.12$$

This result is the same as the given value of K (5.10) within round-off error, so the answer must be correct.

See Exercise 13.45.

| Sample Exercise 13.11 | **Calculating Equilibrium Concentrations II** |

Assume that the reaction for the formation of gaseous hydrogen fluoride from hydrogen and fluorine has an equilibrium constant of 1.15×10^2 at a certain temperature. In a particular experiment, 3.000 mol of each component was added to a 1.500-L flask. Calculate the equilibrium concentrations of all species.

Solution

The balanced equation for the reaction is

$$H_2(g) + F_2(g) \rightleftharpoons 2HF(g)$$

The equilibrium expression is

$$K = 1.15 \times 10^2 = \frac{[HF]^2}{[H_2][F_2]}$$

We first calculate the initial concentrations:

$$[HF]_0 = [H_2]_0 = [F_2]_0 = \frac{3.000 \text{ mol}}{1.500 \text{ L}} = 2.000 \, M$$

Then we find the value of Q:

$$Q = \frac{[HF]_0^2}{[H_2]_0[F_2]_0} = \frac{(2.000)^2}{(2.000)(2.000)} = 1.000$$

Since Q is much less than K, the system must shift to the right to reach equilibrium.

What change in the concentrations is necessary? Since this is presently unknown, we will define the change needed in terms of x. Let x equal the number of moles per liter of H_2 consumed to reach equilibrium. The stoichiometry of the reaction shows that x mol/L F_2 also will be consumed and $2x$ mol/L HF will be formed:

$$H_2(g) \;+\; F_2(g) \;\longrightarrow\; 2HF(g)$$
$$x\ \text{mol/L} + x\ \text{mol/L} \longrightarrow 2x\ \text{mol/L}$$

Now the equilibrium concentrations can be expressed in terms of x:

Initial Concentration (mol/L)	Change (mol/L)	Equilibrium Concentration (mol/L)
$[H_2]_0 = 2.000$	$-x$	$[H_2] = 2.000 - x$
$[F_2]_0 = 2.000$	$-x$	$[F_2] = 2.000 - x$
$[HF]_0 = 2.000$	$+2x$	$[HF] = 2.000 + 2x$

These concentrations can be represented in a shorthand table as follows:

We often refer to this form as an **ICE** table (indicated by the first letters of Initial, Change, and Equilibrium).

	$H_2(g)$	$+$	$F_2(g)$	$\rightleftharpoons$	$2HF(g)$
Initial:	2.000		2.000		2.000
Change:	$-x$		$-x$		$+2x$
Equilibrium:	$2.000 - x$		$2.000 - x$		$2.000 + 2x$

To solve for x, we substitute the equilibrium concentrations into the equilibrium expression:

$$K = 1.15 \times 10^2 = \frac{[HF]^2}{[H_2][F_2]} = \frac{(2.000 + 2x)^2}{(2.000 - x)^2}$$

The right side of this equation is a perfect square, so taking the square root of both sides gives

$$\sqrt{1.15 \times 10^2} = \frac{2.000 + 2x}{2.000 - x}$$

which yields $x = 1.528$. The equilibrium concentrations can now be calculated:

$$[H_2] = [F_2] = 2.000\ M - x = 0.472\ M$$
$$[HF] = 2.000\ M + 2x = 5.056\ M$$

Reality Check: Checking these values by substituting them into the equilibrium expression gives

$$\frac{[HF]^2}{[H_2][F_2]} = \frac{(5.056)^2}{(0.472)^2} = 1.15 \times 10^2$$

which agrees with the given value of K.

See Exercise 13.46.

13.6 Solving Equilibrium Problems

We have already considered most of the strategies needed to solve equilibrium problems. The typical procedure for analyzing a chemical equilibrium problem can be summarized as follows:

Procedure for Solving Equilibrium Problems

➡ 1 **Write the balanced equation for the reaction.**

➡ 2 **Write the equilibrium expression using the law of mass action.**

➡ 3 **List the initial concentrations.**

➡ 4 **Calculate Q, and determine the direction of the shift to equilibrium.**

➡ 5 **Define the change needed to reach equilibrium, and define the equilibrium concentrations by applying the change to the initial concentrations.**

➡ 6 **Substitute the equilibrium concentrations into the equilibrium expression, and solve for the unknown.**

➡ 7 **Check your calculated equilibrium concentrations by making sure they give the correct value of K.**

So far we have been careful to choose systems in which we can solve for the unknown by taking the square root of both sides of the equation. However, this type of system is not really very common, and we must now consider a more typical problem. Suppose for a synthesis of hydrogen fluoride from hydrogen and fluorine, 3.000 mol H_2 and 6.000 mol F_2 are mixed in a 3.000-L flask. Assume that the equilibrium constant for the synthesis reaction at this temperature is 1.15×10^2. We calculate the equilibrium concentration of each component as follows:

➡ 1 We begin, as usual, by writing the balanced equation for the reaction:

$$H_2(g) + F_2(g) \rightleftharpoons 2HF(g)$$

➡ 2 The equilibrium expression is

$$K = 1.15 \times 10^2 = \frac{[HF]^2}{[H_2][F_2]}$$

➡ 3 The initial concentrations are

$$[H_2]_0 = \frac{3.000 \text{ mol}}{3.000 \text{ L}} = 1.000 \ M$$

$$[F_2]_0 = \frac{6.000 \text{ mol}}{3.000 \text{ L}} = 2.000 \ M$$

$$[HF]_0 = 0$$

➡ 4 There is no need to calculate Q because no HF is present initially, and we know that the system must shift to the right to reach equilibrium.

➡ 5 If we let x represent the number of moles per liter of H_2 consumed to reach equilibrium, we can represent the equilibrium concentrations as follows:

	$H_2(g)$	+	$F_2(g)$	$\rightleftharpoons$	$2HF(g)$
Initial:	1.000		2.000		0
Change:	$-x$		$-x$		$+2x$
Equilibrium:	$1.000 - x$		$2.000 - x$		$2x$

➡ **6** Substituting the equilibrium concentrations into the equilibrium expression gives

$$K = 1.15 \times 10^2 = \frac{[HF]^2}{[H_2][F_2]} = \frac{(2x)^2}{(1.000 - x)(2.000 - x)}$$

Since the right side of this equation is not a perfect square, we cannot take the square root of both sides, but must use some other procedure.

First, do the indicated multiplication:

$$(1.000 - x)(2.000 - x)(1.15 \times 10^2) = (2x)^2$$

or $\qquad (1.15 \times 10^2)x^2 - 3.000(1.15 \times 10^2)x + 2.000(1.15 \times 10^2) = 4x^2$

and collect terms

$$(1.11 \times 10^2)x^2 - (3.45 \times 10^2)x + 2.30 \times 10^2 = 0$$

This is a quadratic equation of the general form

$$ax^2 + bx + c = 0$$

Use of the quadratic formula is explained in Appendix 1.4.

where the roots can be obtained from the quadratic formula:

$$x = \frac{-b \pm \sqrt{b^2 - 4ac}}{2a}$$

In this example, $a = 1.11 \times 10^2$, $b = -3.45 \times 10^2$, and $c = 2.30 \times 10^2$. Substituting these values into the quadratic formula gives two values for x:

$$x = 2.14 \text{ mol/L} \quad \text{and} \quad x = 0.968 \text{ mol/L}$$

Both these results cannot be valid (since a *given* set of initial concentrations leads to only *one* equilibrium position). How can we choose between them? Since the expression for the equilibrium concentration of H_2 is

$$[H_2] = 1.000 \, M - x$$

the value of x cannot be 2.14 mol/L (because subtracting 2.14 M from 1.000 M gives a negative concentration of H_2, which is physically impossible). Thus the correct value for x is 0.968 mol/L, and the equilibrium concentrations are as follows:

$$[H_2] = 1.000 \, M - 0.968 \, M = 3.2 \times 10^{-2} \, M$$
$$[F_2] = 2.000 \, M - 0.968 \, M = 1.032 \, M$$
$$[HF] = 2(0.968 \, M) = 1.936 \, M$$

Reality Check:

➡ **7** We can check these concentrations by substituting them into the equilibrium expression:

$$\frac{[HF]^2}{[H_2][F_2]} = \frac{(1.936)^2}{(3.2 \times 10^{-2})(1.032)} = 1.13 \times 10^2$$

This value is in close agreement with the given value for K (1.15×10^2), so the calculated equilibrium concentrations are correct.

This procedure is further illustrated for a problem involving pressures in Sample Exercise 13.12.

| Sample Exercise 13.12 | **Calculating Equilibrium Pressures** |

Assume that gaseous hydrogen iodide is synthesized from hydrogen gas and iodine vapor at a temperature where the equilibrium constant is 1.00×10^2. Suppose HI at 5.000×10^{-1} atm, H_2 at 1.000×10^{-2} atm, and I_2 at 5.000×10^{-3} atm are mixed in a 5.000-L flask. Calculate the equilibrium pressures of all species.

Solution

The balanced equation for this process is

$$H_2(g) + I_2(g) \rightleftharpoons 2HI(g)$$

and the equilibrium expression in terms of pressure is

$$K_p = \frac{P_{HI}^2}{(P_{H_2})(P_{I_2})} = 1.00 \times 10^2$$

The given initial pressures are

$$P_{HI}^0 = 5.000 \times 10^{-1} \text{ atm}$$
$$P_{H_2}^0 = 1.000 \times 10^{-2} \text{ atm}$$
$$P_{I_2}^0 = 5.000 \times 10^{-3} \text{ atm}$$

The value of Q for this system is

$$Q = \frac{(P_{HI}^0)^2}{(P_{H_2}^0)(P_{I_2}^0)} = \frac{(5.000 \times 10^{-1} \text{ atm})^2}{(1.000 \times 10^{-2} \text{ atm})(5.000 \times 10^{-3} \text{ atm})} = 5.000 \times 10^3$$

Since Q is greater than K, the system will shift to the left to reach equilibrium.

So far we have used moles or concentrations in stoichiometric calculations. However, it is equally valid to use pressures for a gas-phase system at constant temperature and volume because in this case pressure is directly proportional to the number of moles:

$$P = n\left(\frac{RT}{V}\right) \longleftarrow \text{ Constant if constant } T \text{ and } V$$

Thus we can represent the change needed to achieve equilibrium in terms of pressures.

Let x be the change in pressure (in atm) of H_2 as the system shifts left toward equilibrium. This leads to the following equilibrium pressures:

	$H_2(g)$	$+$	$I_2(g)$	$\rightleftharpoons$	$2HI(g)$
Initial:	1.000×10^{-2}		5.000×10^{-3}		5.000×10^{-1}
Change:	$+x$		$+x$		$-2x$
Equilibrium:	$1.000 \times 10^{-2} + x$		$5.000 \times 10^{-3} + x$		$5.000 \times 10^{-1} - 2x$

Substitution into the equilibrium expression gives

$$K_p = \frac{(P_{HI})^2}{(P_{H_2})(P_{I_2})} = \frac{(5.000 \times 10^{-1} - 2x)^2}{(1.000 \times 10^{-2} + x)(5.000 \times 10^{-3} + x)}$$

Multiplying and collecting terms yield the quadratic equation where $a = 9.60 \times 10^1$, $b = 3.5$, and $c = -2.45 \times 10^{-1}$:

$$(9.60 \times 10^1)x^2 + 3.5x - (2.45 \times 10^{-1}) = 0$$

From the quadratic formula, the correct value for x is $x = 3.55 \times 10^{-2}$ atm. The equilibrium pressures can now be calculated from the expressions involving x:

$$P_{HI} = 5.000 \times 10^{-1} \text{ atm} - 2(3.55 \times 10^{-2}) \text{ atm} = 4.29 \times 10^{-1} \text{ atm}$$
$$P_{H_2} = 1.000 \times 10^{-2} \text{ atm} + 3.55 \times 10^{-2} \text{ atm} = 4.55 \times 10^{-2} \text{ atm}$$
$$P_{I_2} = 5.000 \times 10^{-3} \text{ atm} + 3.55 \times 10^{-2} \text{ atm} = 4.05 \times 10^{-2} \text{ atm}$$

Reality Check:

$$\frac{P_{HI}^2}{P_{H_2} \cdot P_{I_2}} = \frac{(4.29 \times 10^{-1})^2}{(4.55 \times 10^{-2})(4.05 \times 10^{-2})} = 99.9$$

This agrees with the given value of K (1.00×10^2), so the calculated equilibrium concentrations are correct.

See Exercises 13.47 through 13.50.

Treating Systems That Have Small Equilibrium Constants

We have seen that fairly complicated calculations are often necessary to solve equilibrium problems. However, under certain conditions, simplifications are possible that greatly reduce the mathematical difficulties. For example, gaseous NOCl decomposes to form the gases NO and Cl_2. At 35°C the equilibrium constant is 1.6×10^{-5}. In an experiment in which 1.0 mol NOCl is placed in a 2.0-L flask, what are the equilibrium concentrations?

The balanced equation is

$$2NOCl(g) \rightleftharpoons 2NO(g) + Cl_2(g)$$

and

$$K = \frac{[NO]^2[Cl_2]}{[NOCl]^2} = 1.6 \times 10^{-5}$$

The initial concentrations are

$$[NOCl]_0 = \frac{1.0 \text{ mol}}{2.0 \text{ L}} = 0.50 \, M \qquad [NO]_0 = 0 \qquad [Cl_2]_0 = 0$$

Since there are no products initially, the system will move to the right to reach equilibrium. We will define x as the change in concentration of Cl_2 needed to reach equilibrium. The changes in the concentrations of NOCl and NO can then be obtained from the balanced equation:

$$2NOCl(g) \longrightarrow 2NO(g) + Cl_2(g)$$
$$2x \longrightarrow 2x + x$$

The concentrations can be summarized as follows:

	$2NOCl(g)$	$\rightleftharpoons$	$2NO(g)$	$+$	$Cl_2(g)$
Initial:	0.50		0		0
Change:	$-2x$		$+2x$		$+x$
Equilibrium:	$0.50 - 2x$		$2x$		x

The equilibrium concentrations must satisfy the equilibrium expression

$$K = 1.6 \times 10^{-5} = \frac{[NO]^2[Cl_2]}{[NOCl]^2} = \frac{(2x)^2(x)}{(0.50 - 2x)^2}$$

Multiplying and collecting terms will give an equation with terms containing x^3, x^2, and x, which requires complicated methods to solve directly. However, we can avoid this situation by recognizing that since K is so small (1.6×10^{-5}), the system will not proceed far to the right to reach equilibrium. That is, x *represents a relatively small number.* The consequence of this fact is that the term $(0.50 - 2x)$ can be approximated by 0.50. That is, when x is small,

$$0.50 - 2x \approx 0.50$$

Approximations can simplify complicated math, but their validity should be checked carefully.

Making this approximation allows us to simplify the equilibrium expression:

$$1.6 \times 10^{-5} = \frac{(2x)^2(x)}{(0.50 - 2x)^2} \approx \frac{(2x)^2(x)}{(0.50)^2} = \frac{4x^3}{(0.50)^2}$$

Solving for x^3 gives

$$x^3 = \frac{(1.6 \times 10^{-5})(0.50)^2}{4} = 1.0 \times 10^{-6}$$

and $x = 1.0 \times 10^{-2}$.

How valid is this approximation? If $x = 1.0 \times 10^{-2}$, then

$$0.50 - 2x = 0.50 - 2(1.0 \times 10^{-2}) = 0.48$$

The difference between 0.50 and 0.48 is 0.02, or 4% of the initial concentration of NOCl, a relatively small discrepancy that will have little effect on the outcome. That is, since $2x$ is very small compared with 0.50, the value of x obtained in the approximate solution should be very close to the exact value. We use this approximate value of x to calculate the equilibrium concentrations:

$$[NOCl] = 0.50 - 2x \approx 0.50 \, M$$
$$[NO] = 2x = 2(1.0 \times 10^{-2} \, M) = 2.0 \times 10^{-2} \, M$$
$$[Cl_2] = x = 1.0 \times 10^{-2} \, M$$

Reality Check:

$$\frac{[NO]^2[Cl_2]}{[NOCl]^2} = \frac{(2.0 \times 10^{-2})^2(1.0 \times 10^{-2})}{(0.50)^2} = 1.6 \times 10^{-5}$$

Since the given value of K is 1.6×10^{-5}, these calculated concentrations are correct.

This problem was much easier to solve than it appeared at first because the *small value of K and the resulting small shift to the right to reach equilibrium allowed simplification.*

13.7 Le Châtelier's Principle

It is important to understand the factors that control the *position* of a chemical equilibrium. For example, when a chemical is manufactured, the chemists and chemical engineers in charge of production want to choose conditions that favor the desired product as much as possible. That is, they want the equilibrium to lie far to the right. When Fritz Haber was developing the process for the synthesis of ammonia, he did extensive studies on how temperature and pressure affect the equilibrium concentration of ammonia. Some of his results are given in Table 13.2. Note that the equilibrium amount of NH_3 increases

TABLE 13.2 The Percent by Mass of NH_3 at Equilibrium in a Mixture of N_2, H_2, and NH_3 as a Function of Temperature and Total Pressure*

Temperature (°C)	Total Pressure		
	300 atm	*400 atm*	*500 atm*
400	48% NH_3	55% NH_3	61% NH_3
500	26% NH_3	32% NH_3	38% NH_3
600	13% NH_3	17% NH_3	21% NH_3

*Each experiment was begun with a 3:1 mixture of H_2 and N_2.

with an increase in pressure but decreases as the temperature is increased. Thus the amount of NH_3 present at equilibrium is favored by conditions of low temperature and high pressure.

However, this is not the whole story. Carrying out the process at low temperatures is not feasible because then the reaction is too slow. Even though the equilibrium tends to shift to the right as the temperature is lowered, the attainment of equilibrium would be much too slow at low temperatures to be practical. This emphasizes once again that we must study both the thermodynamics and the kinetics of a reaction before we really understand the factors that control it.

We can qualitatively predict the effects of changes in concentration, pressure, and temperature on a system at equilibrium by using **Le Châtelier's principle,** which states that *if a change is imposed on a system at equilibrium, the position of the equilibrium will shift in a direction that tends to reduce that change.* Although this rule sometimes over-simplifies the situation, it works remarkably well.

Visualization: Le Châtelier's Principle

The Effect of a Change in Concentration

To see how we can predict the effect of change in concentration on a system at equilibrium, we will consider the ammonia synthesis reaction. Suppose there is an equilibrium position described by these concentrations:

$$[N_2] = 0.399\ M \qquad [H_2] = 1.197\ M \qquad [NH_3] = 0.202\ M$$

What will happen if 1.000 mol/L N_2 is suddenly injected into the system? We can answer this question by calculating the value of Q. The concentrations before the system adjusts are

$$[N_2]_0 = 0.399\ M + 1.000\ M = 1.399\ M$$

$$\uparrow$$
Added N_2

$$[H_2]_0 = 1.197\ M$$
$$[NH_3]_0 = 0.202\ M$$

Note we are labeling these as "initial concentrations" because the system is no longer at equilibrium. Then

$$Q = \frac{[NH_3]_0^2}{[N_2]_0[H_2]_0^3} = \frac{(0.202)^2}{(1.399)(1.197)^3} = 1.70 \times 10^{-2}$$

Since we are not given the value of K, we must calculate it from the first set of equilibrium concentrations:

$$K = \frac{[NH_3]^2}{[N_2][H_2]^3} = \frac{(0.202)^2}{(0.399)(1.197)^3} = 5.96 \times 10^{-2}$$

As expected, Q is less than K because the concentration of N_2 was increased.

The system will shift to the right to come to the new equilibrium position. Rather than do the calculations, we simply summarize the results:

Equilibrium Position I		Equilibrium Position II
$[N_2] = 0.399\ M$	1.000 mol/L	$[N_2] = 1.348\ M$
$[H_2] = 1.197\ M$	of N_2 added $\longrightarrow$	$[H_2] = 1.044\ M$
$[NH_3] = 0.202\ M$		$[NH_3] = 0.304\ M$

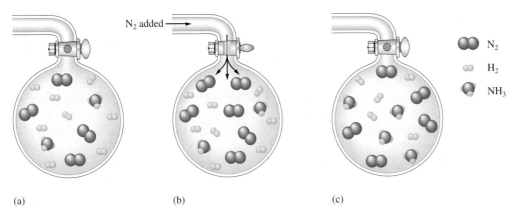

(a)   (b)   (c)

FIGURE 13.8
(a) The initial equilibrium mixture of N_2, H_2, and NH_3. (b) Addition of N_2. (c) The new equilibrium position for the system containing more N_2 (due to addition of N_2), less H_2, and more NH_3 than in (a).

Note from these data that the equilibrium position does in fact shift to the right: The concentration of H_2 decreases, the concentration of NH_3 increases, and of course, since nitrogen is added, the concentration of N_2 shows an increase relative to the amount present in the original equilibrium position. (However, notice that the nitrogen showed a decrease relative to the amount present immediately after addition of the 1.000 mol N_2.)

We can understand this shift by thinking about reaction rates. When we add N_2 molecules to the system, the number of collisions between N_2 and H_2 will increase, thus increasing the rate of the forward reaction and in turn increasing the rate of formation of NH_3 molecules. More NH_3 molecules will in turn lead to a higher rate for the reverse reaction. Eventually, the forward and reverse reaction rates will again become equal, and the system will reach its new equilibrium position.

We can predict this shift qualitatively by using Le Châtelier's principle. Since the change imposed is the addition of nitrogen, Le Châtelier's principle predicts that the system will shift in a direction that consumes nitrogen. This reduces the effect of the addition. Thus Le Châtelier's principle correctly predicts that adding nitrogen will cause the equilibrium to shift to the right (see Fig. 13.8).

If ammonia had been added instead of nitrogen, the system would have shifted to the left to consume ammonia. So another way of stating Le Châtelier's principle is to say that *if a component (reactant or product) is added to a reaction system at equilibrium (at constant T and P or constant T and V), the equilibrium position will shift in the direction that lowers the concentration of that component. If a component is removed, the opposite effect occurs.*

> The system shifts in the direction that compensates for the imposed change.

Sample Exercise 13.13   ## Using Le Châtelier's Principle I

Arsenic can be extracted from its ores by first reacting the ore with oxygen (called *roasting*) to form solid As_4O_6, which is then reduced using carbon:

$$As_4O_6(s) + 6C(s) \rightleftharpoons As_4(g) + 6CO(g)$$

Predict the direction of the shift of the equilibrium position in response to each of the following changes in conditions.

a. Addition of carbon monoxide

b. Addition or removal of carbon or tetraarsenic hexoxide (As_4O_6)

c. Removal of gaseous arsenic (As_4)

Solution

a. Le Châtelier's principle predicts that the shift will be away from the substance whose concentration is increased. The equilibrium position will shift to the left when carbon monoxide is added.

b. Since the amount of a pure solid has no effect on the equilibrium position, changing the amount of carbon or tetraarsenic hexoxide will have no effect.

c. If gaseous arsenic is removed, the equilibrium position will shift to the right to form more products. In industrial processes, the desired product is often continuously removed from the reaction system to increase the yield.

See Exercise 13.57.

The Effect of a Change in Pressure

Basically, there are three ways to change the pressure of a reaction system involving gaseous components:

1. Add or remove a gaseous reactant or product.

2. Add an inert gas (one not involved in the reaction).

3. Change the volume of the container.

We have already considered the addition or removal of a reactant or product. When an inert gas is added, there is no effect on the equilibrium position. *The addition of an inert gas increases the total pressure but has no effect on the concentrations or partial pressures of the reactants or products.* That is, in this case the added molecules do not participate in the reaction in any way and thus cannot affect the equilibrium in any way. Thus the system remains at the original equilibrium position.

When the volume of the container is changed, the concentrations (and thus the partial pressures) of both reactants and products are changed. We could calculate Q and predict the direction of the shift. However, for systems involving gaseous components, there is an easier way: We focus on the volume. The central idea is that *when the volume of the*

Visualization: Equilibrium Decomposition of N_2O_4

(a) Brown $NO_2(g)$ and colorless $N_2O_4(g)$ in equilibrium in a syringe. (b) The volume is suddenly decreased, giving a greater concentration of both N_2O_4 and NO_2 (indicated by the darker brown color). (c) A few seconds after the sudden volume decrease, the color is much lighter brown as the equilibrium shifts the brown $NO_2(g)$ to colorless $N_2O_4(g)$ as predicted by Le Châtelier's principle, since in the equilibrium

$$2NO_2(g) \rightleftharpoons N_2O_4(g)$$

the product side has the smaller number of molecules.

(a)

(b)

(c)

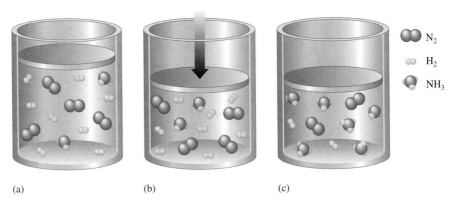

FIGURE 13.9
(a) A mixture of $NH_3(g)$, $N_2(g)$, and $H_2(g)$ at equilibrium. (b) The volume is suddenly decreased. (c) The new equilibrium position for the system containing more NH_3 and less N_2 and H_2. The reaction $N_2(g) + 3H_2(g) \rightleftharpoons 2NH_3(g)$ shifts to the right (toward the side with fewer molecules) when the container volume is decreased.

(a)   (b)   (c)

container holding a gaseous system is reduced, the system responds by reducing its own volume. This is done by decreasing the total number of gaseous molecules in the system.

To see that this is true, we can rearrange the ideal gas law to give

$$V = \left(\frac{RT}{P}\right)n$$

or at constant T and P,

$$V \propto n$$

That is, at constant temperature and pressure, the volume of a gas is directly proportional to the number of moles of gas present.

Suppose we have a mixture of the gases nitrogen, hydrogen, and ammonia at equilibrium (Fig. 13.9). If we suddenly reduce the volume, what will happen to the equilibrium position? The reaction system can reduce its volume by reducing the number of molecules present. This means that the reaction

$$N_2(g) + 3H_2(g) \rightleftharpoons 2NH_3(g)$$

will shift to the right, since in this direction four molecules (one of nitrogen and three of hydrogen) react to produce two molecules (of ammonia), thus *reducing the total number of gaseous molecules present*. The new equilibrium position will be farther to the right than the original one. That is, the equilibrium position will shift toward the side of the reaction involving the smaller number of gaseous molecules in the balanced equation.

The opposite is also true. When the container volume is increased, the system will shift so as to increase its volume. An increase in volume in the ammonia synthesis system will produce a shift to the left to increase the total number of gaseous molecules present.

| Sample Exercise 13.14 | **Using Le Châtelier's Principle II** |

Predict the shift in equilibrium position that will occur for each of the following processes when the volume is reduced.

a. The preparation of liquid phosphorus trichloride by the reaction

$$P_4(s) + 6Cl_2(g) \rightleftharpoons 4PCl_3(l)$$

b. The preparation of gaseous phosphorus pentachloride according to the equation

$$PCl_3(g) + Cl_2(g) \rightleftharpoons PCl_5(g)$$

c. The reaction of phosphorus trichloride with ammonia:

$$PCl_3(g) + 3NH_3(g) \rightleftharpoons P(NH_2)_3(g) + 3HCl(g)$$

Solution

a. Since P_4 and PCl_3 are a pure solid and a pure liquid, respectively, we need to consider only the effect of the change in volume on Cl_2. The volume is decreased, so the position of the equilibrium will shift to the right, since the reactant side contains six gaseous molecules and the product side has none.

b. Decreasing the volume will shift the given reaction to the right, since the product side contains only one gaseous molecule while the reactant side has two.

c. Both sides of the balanced reaction equation have four gaseous molecules. A change in volume will have no effect on the equilibrium position. There is no shift in this case.

See Exercise 13.58.

The Effect of a Change in Temperature

It is important to realize that although the changes we have just discussed may alter the equilibrium *position,* they do not alter the equilibrium *constant.* For example, the addition of a reactant shifts the equilibrium position to the right but has no effect on the value of the equilibrium constant; the new equilibrium concentrations satisfy the original equilibrium constant.

The effect of temperature on equilibrium is different, however, because *the value of K changes with temperature.* We can use Le Châtelier's principle to predict the direction of the change.

The synthesis of ammonia from nitrogen and hydrogen is exothermic. We can represent this by treating energy as a product:

$$N_2(g) + 3H_2(g) \rightleftharpoons 2NH_3(g) + 92 \text{ kJ}$$

If energy is added to this system at equilibrium by heating it, Le Châtelier's principle predicts that the shift will be in the direction that consumes energy, that is, to the left. Note that this shift decreases the concentration of NH_3 and increases the concentrations of N_2

Of course, energy is not a chemical product of this reaction, but thinking of it in this way makes it easy to apply Le Châtelier's principle.

Shifting the $N_2O_4(g) \rightarrow 2NO_2(g)$ equilibrium by changing the temperature. (a) At 100°C the flask is definitely reddish brown due to a large amount of NO_2 present. (b) At 0°C the equilibrium is shifted toward colorless $N_2O_4(g)$.

TABLE 13.3   Observed Value of K for the Ammonia Synthesis Reaction as a Function of Temperature*

Temperature (K)	K
500	90
600	3
700	0.3
800	0.04

*For this exothermic reaction, the value of K decreases as the temperature increases, as predicted by Le Châtelier's principle.

and H_2, thus *decreasing the value of K*. The experimentally observed change in K with temperature for this reaction is indicated in Table 13.3. The value of K decreases with increased temperature, as predicted.

On the other hand, for an endothermic reaction, such as the decomposition of calcium carbonate,

$$556 \text{ kJ} + CaCO_3(s) \rightleftharpoons CaO(s) + CO_2(g)$$

an increase in temperature will cause the equilibrium to shift to the right and the value of K to increase.

In summary, to use Le Châtelier's principle to describe the effect of a temperature change on a system at equilibrium, treat energy as a reactant (in an endothermic process) or as a product (in an exothermic process), and predict the direction of the shift in the same way as when an actual reactant or product is added or removed. Although Le Châtelier's principle cannot predict the size of the change in K, it does correctly predict the direction of the change.

Sample Exercise 13.15	**Using Le Châtelier's Principle III**

For each of the following reactions, predict how the value of K changes as the temperature is increased.

TABLE 13.4   Shifts in the Equilibrium Position for the Reaction 58 kJ + $N_2O_4(g)$ $\rightleftharpoons$ 2NO$_2$(g)

Change	Shift
Addition of $N_2O_4(g)$	Right
Addition of $NO_2(g)$	Left
Removal of $N_2O_4(g)$	Left
Removal of $NO_2(g)$	Right
Addition of He(g)	None
Decrease container volume	Left
Increase container volume	Right
Increase temperature	Right
Decrease temperature	Left

a. $N_2(g) + O_2(g) \rightleftharpoons 2NO(g)$ $\Delta H° = 181 \text{ kJ}$
b. $2SO_2(g) + O_2(g) \rightleftharpoons 2SO_3(g)$ $\Delta H° = -198 \text{ kJ}$

Solution

a. This is an endothermic reaction, as indicated by the positive value for $\Delta H°$. Energy can be viewed as a reactant, and K increases (the equilibrium shifts to the right) as the temperature is increased.

b. This is an exothermic reaction (energy can be regarded as a product). As the temperature is increased, the value of K decreases (the equilibrium shifts to the left).

See Exercises 13.63 and 13.64.

We have seen how Le Châtelier's principle can be used to predict the effect of several types of changes on a system at equilibrium. To summarize these ideas, Table 13.4 shows how various changes affect the equilibrium position of the endothermic reaction

$$N_2O_4(g) \rightleftharpoons 2NO_2(g) \qquad \Delta H° = 58 \text{ kJ}$$

Key Terms

chemical equilibrium

Section 13.2
law of mass action
equilibrium expression
equilibrium constant
equilibrium position

Section 13.4
homogeneous equilibria
heterogeneous equilibria

Section 13.5
reaction quotient, Q

Section 13.7
Le Châtelier's principle

For Review

Chemical equilibrium
- When a reaction takes place in a closed system, it reaches a condition where the concentrations of the reactants and products remain constant over time
- Dynamic state: reactants and products are interconverted continually
  - Forward rate = reverse rate
- The law of mass action: for the reaction

$$jA + kB \rightleftharpoons mC + nD$$

$$K = \frac{[C]^m[D]^n}{[A]^j[B]^k} = \text{equilibrium constant}$$

- A pure liquid or solid is never included in the equilibrium expression
- For a gas-phase reaction the reactants and products can be described in terms of their partial pressures and the equilibrium constant is called K_p:

$$K_p = K(RT)^{\Delta n}$$

where Δn is the sum of the coefficients of the gaseous products minus the sum of the coefficients of the gaseous reactants

Equilibrium position

- A set of reactant and product concentrations that satisfies the equilibrium constant expression
  - There is one value of K for a given system at a given temperature
  - There are an infinite number of equilibrium positions at a given temperature depending on the initial concentrations
- A small value of K means the equilibrium lies to the left; a large value of K means the equilibrium lies to the right
  - The size of K has no relationship to the speed at which equilibrium is achieved
- Q, the reaction quotient, applies the law of mass action to initial concentrations rather than equilibrium concentrations
  - If $Q > K$, the system will shift to the left to achieve equilibrium
  - If $Q < K$, the system will shift to the right to achieve equilibrium
- Finding the concentrations that characterize a given equilibrium position:

  1. Start with the given initial concentrations (pressures)
  2. Define the change needed to reach equilibrium
  3. Apply the change to the initial concentrations (pressures) and solve for the equilibrium concentrations (pressures)

Le Châtelier's principle

- Enables qualitative prediction of the effects of changes in concentration, pressure, and temperature on a system at equilibrium
- If a change in conditions is imposed on a system at equilibrium, the system will shift in a direction that compensates for the imposed change
  - In other words, when a stress is placed on a system at equilibrium, the system shifts in the direction that relieves the stress

REVIEW QUESTIONS

1. Characterize a system at chemical equilibrium with respect to each of the following.
   a. the rates of the forward and reverse reactions
   b. the overall composition of the reaction mixture
   For a general reaction $3A(g) + B(g) \longrightarrow 2C(g)$, if one starts an experiment with only reactants present, show what the plot of concentrations of A, B, and C versus time would look like. Also sketch the plot illustrating the rate of the forward reaction and rate of the reverse reaction versus time.
2. What is the law of mass action? Is it true that the value of K depends on the amounts of reactants and products mixed together initially? Explain. Is it true that reactions with large equilibrium constant values are very fast? Explain. There is only one value of the equilibrium constant for a particular system at a particular temperature, but there is an infinite number of equilibrium positions. Explain.
3. Consider the following reactions at some temperature:

$$2NOCl(g) \rightleftharpoons 2NO(g) + Cl_2(g) \qquad K = 1.6 \times 10^{-5}$$
$$2NO(g) \rightleftharpoons N_2(g) + O_2(g) \qquad K = 1 \times 10^{31}$$

For each reaction, assume some quantities of the reactants were placed in separate containers and allowed to come to equilibrium. Describe the relative amounts of reactants and products that would be present at equilibrium. At equilibrium, which is faster, the forward or reverse reaction in each case?

4. What is the difference between K and K_p? When does $K = K_p$ for a reaction? When does $K \neq K_p$ for a reaction? If the coefficients in a reaction equation are tripled, how is the new value of K related to the initial value of K? If a reaction is reversed, how is the value of K_p for the reversed reaction related to the value of K_p for the initial reaction?

5. What are homogeneous equilibria? Heterogeneous equilibria? What is the difference in writing K expressions for homogeneous versus heterogeneous reactions? Summarize which species are included in the K expression and which species are not included.

6. Distinguish between the terms *equilibrium constant* and *reaction quotient*. When $Q = K$, what does this say about a reaction? When $Q < K$, what does this say about a reaction? When $Q > K$, what does this say about a reaction?

7. Summarize the steps for solving equilibrium problems (see the beginning of Section 13.6). In general, when solving an equilibrium problem, you should always set up an ICE table. What is an ICE table?

8. A common type of reaction we will study is that having a very small K value ($K \ll 1$). Solving for equilibrium concentrations in an equilibrium problem usually requires many mathematical operations to be performed. However, the math involved when solving equilibrium problems for reactions having small K values ($K \ll 1$) is simplified. What assumption is made when solving the equilibrium concentrations for reactions with small K values? Whenever assumptions are made, they must be checked for validity. In general, the "5% rule" is used to check the validity of assuming x (or $2x$, $3x$, and so on) is very small compared to some number. When x (or $2x$, $3x$, and so on) is less than 5% of the number the assumption was made against, then the assumption is said to be valid. If the 5% rule fails, what do you do to solve for the equilibrium concentrations?

9. What is Le Châtelier's principle? Consider the reaction $2NOCl(g) \rightleftharpoons 2NO(g) + Cl_2(g)$. If this reaction is at equilibrium, what happens when the following changes occur?
   a. $NOCl(g)$ is added.
   b. $NO(g)$ is added.
   c. $NOCl(g)$ is removed.
   d. $Cl_2(g)$ is removed.
   e. The container volume is decreased.
   For each of these changes, what happens to the value of K for the reaction as equilibrium is reached again? Give an example of a reaction for which the addition or removal of one of the reactants or products has no effect on the equilibrium position.
   In general, how will the equilibrium position of a gas-phase reaction be affected if the volume of the reaction vessel changes? Are there reactions that will not have their equilibria shifted by a change in volume? Explain. Why does changing the pressure in a rigid container by adding an inert gas not shift the equilibrium position for a gas-phase reaction?

10. The only "stress" (change) that also changes the value of K is a change in temperature. For an exothermic reaction, how does the equilibrium position change as temperature increases, and what happens to the value of K? Answer the same questions for an endothermic reaction. If the value of K increases with a decrease in temperature, is the reaction exothermic or endothermic? Explain.

Active Learning Questions

These questions are designed to be used by groups of students in class. The questions allow students to explore their understanding of concepts through discussion and peer teaching. The real value of these questions is the learning that occurs while students talk to each other about chemical concepts.

1. Consider an equilibrium mixture of four chemicals (A, B, C, and D, all gases) reacting in a closed flask according to the equation:

$$A + B \rightleftharpoons C + D$$

   a. You add more A to the flask. How does the concentration of each chemical compare to its original concentration after equilibrium is reestablished? Justify your answer.
   b. You have the original setup at equilibrium, and add more D to the flask. How does the concentration of each chemical compare to its original concentration after equilibrium is reestablished? Justify your answer.

2. The boxes shown below represent a set of initial conditions for the reaction:

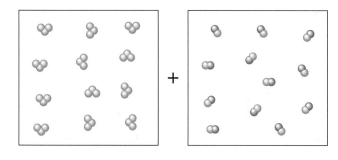

$$K = 25$$

   Draw a quantitative molecular picture that shows what this system looks like after the reactants are mixed in one of the boxes and the system reaches equilibrium. Support your answer with calculations.

3. For the reaction $H_2(g) + I_2(g) \rightleftharpoons 2HI(g)$, consider two possibilities: (a) you mix 0.5 mol of each reactant, allow the system to come to equilibrium, and then add another mole of H_2 and allow the system to reach equilibrium again, or (b) you mix 1.5 mol H_2 and 0.5 mol I_2 and allow the system to reach equilibrium. Will the final equilibrium mixture be different for the two procedures? Explain.

4. Given the reaction $A(g) + B(g) \rightleftharpoons C(g) + D(g)$, consider the following situations:
   i. You have 1.3 M A and 0.8 M B initially.
   ii. You have 1.3 M A, 0.8 M B, and 0.2 M C initially.
   iii. You have 2.0 M A and 0.8 M B initially.

   Order the preceding situations in terms of increasing equilibrium concentration of D. Explain your order. Then give the order in terms of increasing equilibrium concentration of B and explain.

5. Consider the reaction $A(g) + 2B(g) \rightleftharpoons C(g) + D(g)$ in a 1.0-L rigid flask. Answer the following questions for each situation (a–d):
   i. Estimate a range (as small as possible) for the requested substance. For example, [A] could be between 95 M and 100 M.
   ii. Explain how you decided on the limits for the estimated range.
   iii. Indicate what other information would enable you to narrow your estimated range.
   iv. Compare the estimated concentrations for a through d, and explain any differences.

   a. If at equilibrium [A] = 1 M, and then 1 mol C is added, estimate the value for [A] once equilibrium is reestablished.
   b. If at equilibrium [B] = 1 M, and then 1 mol C is added, estimate the value for [B] once equilibrium is reestablished.
   c. If at equilibrium [C] = 1 M, and then 1 mol C is added, estimate the value for [C] once equilibrium is reestablished.
   d. If at equilibrium [D] = 1 M, and then 1 mol C is added, estimate the value for [D] once equilibrium is reestablished.

6. Consider the reaction $A(g) + B(g) \rightleftharpoons C(g) + D(g)$. A friend asks the following: "I know we have been told that if a mixture of A, B, C, and D is at equilibrium and more of A is added, more C and D will form. But how can more C and D form if we do not add more B?" What do you tell your friend?

7. Consider the following statements: "Consider the reaction $A(g) + B(g) \rightleftharpoons C(g)$, for which at equilibrium [A] = 2 M, [B] = 1 M, and [C] = 4 M. To a 1-L container of the system at equilibrium you add 3 moles of B. A possible equilibrium condition is [A] = 1 M, [B] = 3 M, and [C] = 6 M because in both cases $K = 2$." Indicate everything that is correct in these statements and everything that is incorrect. Correct the incorrect statements, and explain.

8. Le Châtelier's principle is stated (Section 13.7) as follows: "If a change is imposed on a system at equilibrium, the position of the equilibrium will shift in a direction that tends to reduce that change." The system $N_2 + 3H_2 \rightleftharpoons 2NH_3$ is used as an example in which the addition of nitrogen gas at equilibrium results in a decrease in H_2 concentration and an increase in NH_3 concentration. In the experiment the volume is assumed to be constant. On the other hand, if N_2 is added to the reaction system in a container with a piston so that the pressure can be held constant, the amount of NH_3 actually could decrease and the concentration of H_2 would increase as equilibrium is reestablished. Explain how this can happen. Also, if you consider this same system at equilibrium, the addition of an inert gas, holding the pressure constant, *does* affect the equilibrium position. Explain why the addition of an inert gas to this system in a rigid container does not affect the equilibrium position.

A blue question or exercise number indicates that the answer to that question or exercise appears at the back of this book and a solution appears in the *Solutions Guide.*

Questions

9. Consider the following reaction:

$$H_2O(g) + CO(g) \rightleftharpoons H_2(g) + CO_2(g)$$

Amounts of H_2O, CO, H_2, and CO_2 are put into a flask so that the composition corresponds to an equilibrium position. If the CO placed in the flask is labeled with radioactive ^{14}C, will ^{14}C be found only in CO molecules for an indefinite period of time? Explain.

10. Consider the same reaction as in Exercise 9. In one experiment 1.0 mol $H_2O(g)$ and 1.0 mol $CO(g)$ are put into a flask and heated to 350°C. In a second experiment 1.0 mol $H_2(g)$ and 1.0 mol $CO_2(g)$ are put into another flask with the same volume as the first. This mixture is also heated to 350°C. After equilibrium is reached, will there be any difference in the composition of the mixtures in the two flasks?

11. Consider the following reaction at some temperature:

$$H_2O(g) + CO(g) \rightleftharpoons H_2(g) + CO_2(g) \qquad K = 2.0$$

Some molecules of H_2O and CO are placed in a 1.0-L container as shown below.

When equilibrium is reached, how many molecules of H_2O, CO, H_2 and CO_2 are present? Do this problem by trial and error—that is, if two molecules of CO react, is this equilibrium; if three molecules of CO react, is this equilibrium; and so on.

12. Consider the following generic reaction:

$$2A_2B(g) \rightleftharpoons 2A_2(g) + B_2(g)$$

Some molecules of A_2B are placed in a 1.0-L container. As time passes, several snapshots of the reaction mixture are taken as illustrated below.

Which illustration is the first to represent an equilibrium mixture? Explain. How many molecules of A_2B reacted initially?

13. Explain the difference between K, K_p, and Q.

14. Consider the following reactions.

$$H_2(g) + I_2(g) \longrightarrow 2HI(g) \quad \text{and} \quad H_2(g) + I_2(s) \longrightarrow 2HI(g)$$

List two property differences between these two reactions that relate to equilibrium.

15. For a typical equilibrium problem, the value of K and the initial reaction conditions are given for a specific reaction, and you are asked to calculate the equilibrium concentrations. Many of these calculations involve solving a quadratic or cubic equation. What can you do to avoid solving a quadratic or cubic equation and still come up with reasonable equilibrium concentrations?

16. Which of the following statements is(are) true? Correct the false statement(s).
   a. When a reactant is added to a system at equilibrium at a given temperature, the reaction will shift right to reestablish equilibrium.
   b. When a product is added to a system at equilibrium at a given temperature, the value of K for the reaction will increase when equilibrium is reestablished.
   c. When temperature is increased for a reaction at equilibrium, the value of K for the reaction will increase.
   d. When the volume of a reaction container is increased for a system at equilibrium at a given temperature, the reaction will shift left to reestablish equilibrium.
   e. Addition of a catalyst (a substance that increases the speed of the reaction) has no effect on the equilibrium position.

Exercises

In this section similar exercises are paired.

The Equilibrium Constant

17. Write the equilibrium expression (K) for each of the following gas-phase reactions.
   a. $N_2(g) + O_2(g) \rightleftharpoons 2NO(g)$
   b. $N_2O_4(g) \rightleftharpoons 2NO_2(g)$
   c. $SiH_4(g) + 2Cl_2(g) \rightleftharpoons SiCl_4(g) + 2H_2(g)$
   d. $2PBr_3(g) + 3Cl_2(g) \rightleftharpoons 2PCl_3(g) + 3Br_2(g)$

18. Write the equilibrium expression (K_p) for each reaction in Exercise 17.

19. At a given temperature, $K = 1.3 \times 10^{-2}$ for the reaction

$$N_2(g) + 3H_2(g) \rightleftharpoons 2NH_3(g)$$

Calculate values of K for the following reactions at this temperature.
   a. $\frac{1}{2}N_2(g) + \frac{3}{2}H_2(g) \rightleftharpoons NH_3(g)$
   b. $2NH_3(g) \rightleftharpoons N_2(g) + 3H_2(g)$
   c. $NH_3(g) \rightleftharpoons \frac{1}{2}N_2(g) + \frac{3}{2}H_2(g)$
   d. $2N_2(g) + 6H_2(g) \rightleftharpoons 4NH_3(g)$

20. For the reaction

$$H_2(g) + Br_2(g) \rightleftharpoons 2HBr(g)$$

$K_p = 3.5 \times 10^4$ at 1495 K. What is the value of K_p for the following reactions at 1495 K?
   a. $HBr(g) \rightleftharpoons \frac{1}{2}H_2(g) + \frac{1}{2}Br_2(g)$
   b. $2HBr(g) \rightleftharpoons H_2(g) + Br_2(g)$
   c. $\frac{1}{2}H_2(g) + \frac{1}{2}Br_2(g) \rightleftharpoons HBr(g)$

21. For the reaction

$$2NO(g) + 2H_2(g) \rightleftharpoons N_2(g) + 2H_2O(g)$$

it is determined that, at equilibrium at a particular temperature, the concentrations are as follows: $[NO(g)] = 8.1 \times 10^{-3} M$, $[H_2(g)] = 4.1 \times 10^{-5} M$, $[N_2(g)] = 5.3 \times 10^{-2} M$, and $[H_2O(g)] = 2.9 \times 10^{-3} M$. Calculate the value of K for the reaction at this temperature.

22. For the reaction

$$N_2(g) + 3Cl_2(g) \rightleftharpoons 2NCl_3(g)$$

an analysis of an equilibrium mixture is performed at a certain temperature. It is found that $[NCl_3(g)] = 1.9 \times 10^{-1} M$, $[N_2(g)] = 1.4 \times 10^{-3} M$, and $[Cl_2(g)] = 4.3 \times 10^{-4} M$. Calculate K for the reaction at this temperature.

23. At a particular temperature, a 3.0-L flask contains 2.4 mol Cl_2, 1.0 mol NOCl, and 4.5×10^{-3} mol NO. Calculate K at this temperature for the following reaction:

$$2NOCl(g) \rightleftharpoons 2NO(g) + Cl_2(g)$$

24. At a particular temperature a 2.00-L flask at equilibrium contains 2.80×10^{-4} mol N_2, 2.50×10^{-5} mol O_2, and 2.00×10^{-2} mol N_2O. Calculate K at this temperature for the reaction

$$2N_2(g) + O_2(g) \rightleftharpoons 2N_2O(g)$$

If $[N_2] = 2.00 \times 10^{-4} M$, $[N_2O] = 0.200 M$, and $[O_2] = 0.00245 M$, does this represent a system at equilibrium?

25. The following equilibrium pressures at a certain temperature were observed for the reaction

$$2NO_2(g) \rightleftharpoons 2NO(g) + O_2(g)$$

$$P_{NO_2} = 0.55 \text{ atm}$$
$$P_{NO} = 6.5 \times 10^{-5} \text{ atm}$$
$$P_{O_2} = 4.5 \times 10^{-5} \text{ atm}$$

Calculate the value for the equilibrium constant K_p at this temperature.

26. The following equilibrium pressures were observed at a certain temperature for the reaction

$$N_2(g) + 3H_2(g) \rightleftharpoons 2NH_3(g)$$

$$P_{NH_3} = 3.1 \times 10^{-2} \text{ atm}$$
$$P_{N_2} = 8.5 \times 10^{-1} \text{ atm}$$
$$P_{H_2} = 3.1 \times 10^{-3} \text{ atm}$$

Calculate the value for the equilibrium constant K_p at this temperature.
If $P_{N_2} = 0.525$ atm, $P_{NH_3} = 0.0167$ atm, and $P_{H_2} = 0.00761$ atm, does this represent a system at equilibrium?

27. At $327°$, the equilibrium concentrations are $[CH_3OH] = 0.15 M$, $[CO] = 0.24 M$, and $[H_2] = 1.1 M$ for the reaction

$$CH_3OH(g) \rightleftharpoons CO(g) + 2H_2(g)$$

Calculate K_p at this temperature.

28. At 1100 K, $K_p = 0.25$ for the reaction

$$2SO_2(g) + O_2(g) \rightleftharpoons 2SO_3(g)$$

What is the value of K at this temperature?

29. Write expressions for K and K_p for the following reactions.
   a. $2NH_3(g) + CO_2(g) \rightleftharpoons N_2CH_4O(s) + H_2O(g)$
   b. $2NBr_3(s) \rightleftharpoons N_2(g) + 3Br_2(g)$
   c. $2KClO_3(s) \rightleftharpoons 2KCl(s) + 3O_2(g)$
   d. $CuO(s) + H_2(g) \rightleftharpoons Cu(l) + H_2O(g)$

30. For which reactions in Exercise 29 is K_p equal to K?

31. Consider the following reaction at a certain temperature:

$$4Fe(s) + 3O_2(g) \rightleftharpoons 2Fe_2O_3(s)$$

An equilibrium mixture contains 1.0 mol Fe, 1.0×10^{-3} mol O_2, and 2.0 mol Fe_2O_3 all in a 2.0-L container. Calculate the value of K for this reaction.

32. In a study of the reaction

$$3Fe(s) + 4H_2O(g) \rightleftharpoons Fe_3O_4(s) + 4H_2(g)$$

at 1200 K it was observed that when the equilibrium partial pressure of water vapor is 15.0 torr, that total pressure at equilibrium is 36.3 torr. Calculate the value of K_p for this reaction at 1200 K. *Hint:* Apply Dalton's law of partial pressures.

Equilibrium Calculations

33. The equilibrium constant, K, is 2.4×10^3 at a certain temperature for the reaction

$$2NO(g) \rightleftharpoons N_2(g) + O_2(g)$$

For which of the following sets of conditions is the system at equilibrium? For those that are not at equilibrium, in which direction will the system shift?
   a. A 1.0-L flask contains 0.024 mol NO, 2.0 mol N_2, and 2.6 mol O_2.
   b. A 2.0-L flask contains 0.032 mol NO, 0.62 mol N_2, and 4.0 mol O_2.
   c. A 3.0-L flask contains 0.060 mol NO, 2.4 mol N_2, and 1.7 mol O_2.

34. The equilibrium constant, K_p, is 2.4×10^3 at a certain temperature for the reaction

$$2NO(g) \rightleftharpoons N_2(g) + O_2(g)$$

For which of the following sets of conditions is the system at equilibrium? For those that are not at equilibrium, in which direction will the system shift?
   a. $P_{NO} = 0.010$ atm, $P_{N_2} = 0.11$ atm, $P_{O_2} = 2.0$ atm
   b. $P_{NO} = 0.0078$ atm, $P_{N_2} = 0.36$ atm, $P_{O_2} = 0.67$ atm
   c. $P_{NO} = 0.0062$ atm, $P_{N_2} = 0.51$ atm, $P_{O_2} = 0.18$ atm

35. At 900°C, $K_p = 1.04$ for the reaction

$$CaCO_3(s) \rightleftharpoons CaO(s) + CO_2(g)$$

At a low temperature, dry ice (solid CO_2), calcium oxide, and calcium carbonate are introduced into a 50.0-L reaction chamber. The temperature is raised to 900°C, resulting in the dry ice converting to gaseous CO_2. For the following mixtures, will the initial amount of calcium oxide increase, decrease, or remain the same as the system moves toward equilibrium at 900°C?

a. 655 g $CaCO_3$, 95.0 g CaO, P_{CO_2} = 2.55 atm
b. 780 g $CaCO_3$, 1.00 g CaO, P_{CO_2} = 1.04 atm
c. 0.14 g $CaCO_3$, 5000 g CaO, P_{CO_2} = 1.04 atm
d. 715 g $CaCO_3$, 813 g CaO, P_{CO_2} = 0.211 atm

36. Ethyl acetate is synthesized in a nonreacting solvent (not water) according to the following reaction:

$$CH_3CO_2H + C_2H_5OH \rightleftharpoons CH_3CO_2C_2H_5 + H_2O \qquad K = 2.2$$
Acetic acid   Ethanol   Ethyl acetate

For the following mixtures (a–d), will the concentration of H_2O increase, decrease, or remain the same as equilibrium is established?

a. $[CH_3CO_2C_2H_5]$ = 0.22 M, $[H_2O]$ = 0.10 M, $[CH_3CO_2H]$ = 0.010 M, $[C_2H_5OH]$ = 0.010 M
b. $[CH_3CO_2C_2H_5]$ = 0.22 M, $[H_2O]$ = 0.0020 M, $[CH_3CO_2H]$ = 0.0020 M, $[C_2H_5OH]$ = 0.10 M
c. $[CH_3CO_2C_2H_5]$ = 0.88 M, $[H_2O]$ = 0.12 M, $[CH_3CO_2H]$ = 0.044 M, $[C_2H_5OH]$ = 6.0 M
d. $[CH_3CO_2C_2H_5]$ = 4.4 M, $[H_2O]$ = 4.4 M, $[CH_3CO_2H]$ = 0.88 M, $[C_2H_5OH]$ = 10.0 M
e. What must the concentration of water be for a mixture with $[CH_3CO_2C_2H_5]$ = 2.0 M, $[CH_3CO_2H]$ = 0.10 M, $[C_2H_5OH]$ = 5.0 M to be at equilibrium?
f. Why is water included in the equilibrium expression for this reaction?

37. For the reaction

$$2H_2O(g) \rightleftharpoons 2H_2(g) + O_2(g)$$

$K = 2.4 \times 10^{-3}$ at a given temperature. At equilibrium it is found that $[H_2O(g)]$ = 1.1×10^{-1} M and $[H_2(g)]$ = 1.9×10^{-2} M. What is the concentration of $O_2(g)$ under these conditions?

38. The reaction

$$2NO(g) + Br_2(g) \rightleftharpoons 2NOBr(g)$$

has K_p = 109 at 25°C. If the equilibrium partial pressure of Br_2 is 0.0159 atm and the equilibrium partial pressure of NOBr is 0.0768 atm, calculate the partial pressure of NO at equilibrium.

39. A 1.00-L flask was filled with 2.00 mol gaseous SO_2 and 2.00 mol gaseous NO_2 and heated. After equilibrium was reached, it was found that 1.30 mol gaseous NO was present. Assume that the reaction

$$SO_2(g) + NO_2(g) \rightleftharpoons SO_3(g) + NO(g)$$

occurs under these conditions. Calculate the value of the equilibrium constant, K, for this reaction.

40. A sample of $S_8(g)$ is placed in an otherwise empty rigid container at 1325 K at an initial pressure of 1.00 atm, where it decomposes to $S_2(g)$ by the reaction

$$S_8(g) \rightleftharpoons 4S_2(g)$$

At equilibrium, the partial pressure of S_8 is 0.25 atm. Calculate K_p for this reaction at 1325 K.

41. At a particular temperature, 12.0 mol of SO_3 is placed into a 3.0-L rigid container, and the SO_3 dissociates by the reaction

$$2SO_3(g) \rightleftharpoons 2SO_2(g) + O_2(g)$$

At equilibrium, 3.0 mol of SO_2 is present. Calculate K for this reaction.

42. At a certain temperature, 4.0 mol NH_3 is introduced into a 2.0-L container, and the NH_3 partially dissociates by the reaction

$$2NH_3(g) \rightleftharpoons N_2(g) + 3H_2(g)$$

At equilibrium, 2.0 mol NH_3 remains. What is the value of K for this reaction?

43. An initial mixture of nitrogen gas and hydrogen gas is reacted in a rigid container at a certain temperature by the reaction

$$3H_2(g) + N_2(g) \rightleftharpoons 2NH_3(g)$$

At equilibrium, the concentrations are $[H_2]$ = 5.0 M, $[N_2]$ = 8.0 M, and $[NH_3]$ = 4.0 M. What were the concentrations of nitrogen gas and hydrogen gas that were reacted initially?

44. Nitrogen gas (N_2) reacts with hydrogen gas (H_2) to form ammonia (NH_3). At 200°C in a closed container, 1.00 atm of nitrogen gas is mixed with 2.00 atm of hydrogen gas. At equilibrium, the total pressure is 2.00 atm. Calculate the partial pressure of hydrogen gas at equilibrium.

45. At a particular temperature, K = 3.75 for the reaction

$$SO_2(g) + NO_2(g) \rightleftharpoons SO_3(g) + NO(g)$$

If all four gases had initial concentrations of 0.800 M, calculate the equilibrium concentrations of the gases.

46. At a particular temperature, K = 1.00×10^2 for the reaction

$$H_2(g) + I_2(g) \rightleftharpoons 2HI(g)$$

In an experiment, 1.00 mol H_2, 1.00 mol I_2, and 1.00 mol HI are introduced into a 1.00-L container. Calculate the concentrations of all species when equilibrium is reached.

47. At 2200°C, K_p = 0.050 for the reaction

$$N_2(g) + O_2(g) \rightleftharpoons 2NO(g)$$

What is the partial pressure of NO in equilibrium with N_2 and O_2 that were placed in a flask at initial pressures of 0.80 and 0.20 atm, respectively?

48. At 25°C, K = 0.090 for the reaction

$$H_2O(g) + Cl_2O(g) \rightleftharpoons 2HOCl(g)$$

Calculate the concentrations of all species at equilibrium for each of the following cases.
a. 1.0 g H_2O and 2.0 g Cl_2O are mixed in a 1.0-L flask.
b. 1.0 mol pure HOCl is placed in a 2.0-L flask.

49. At 1100 K, K_p = 0.25 for the reaction

$$2SO_2(g) + O_2(g) \rightleftharpoons 2SO_3(g)$$

Calculate the equilibrium partial pressures of SO_2, O_2, and SO_3 produced from an initial mixture in which P_{SO_2} = P_{O_2} = 0.50 atm and P_{SO_3} = 0. (*Hint:* If you don't have a graphing calculator, then use the method of successive approximations to solve, as discussed in Appendix 1.4.)

50. At a particular temperature, $K_p = 0.25$ for the reaction

$$N_2O_4(g) \rightleftharpoons 2NO_2(g)$$

a. A flask containing only N_2O_4 at an initial pressure of 4.5 atm is allowed to reach equilibrium. Calculate the equilibrium partial pressures of the gases.

b. A flask containing only NO_2 at an initial pressure of 9.0 atm is allowed to reach equilibrium. Calculate the equilibrium partial pressures of the gases.

c. From your answers to parts a and b, does it matter from which direction an equilibrium position is reached?

51. At 35°C, $K = 1.6 \times 10^{-5}$ for the reaction

$$2NOCl(g) \rightleftharpoons 2NO(g) + Cl_2(g)$$

Calculate the concentrations of all species at equilibrium for each of the following original mixtures.

a. 2.0 mol pure NOCl in a 2.0-L flask

b. 1.0 mol NOCl and 1.0 mol NO in a 1.0-L flask

c. 2.0 mol NOCl and 1.0 mol Cl_2 in a 1.0-L flask

52. At a particular temperature, $K = 4.0 \times 10^{-7}$ for the reaction

$$N_2O_4(g) \rightleftharpoons 2NO_2(g)$$

In an experiment, 1.0 mol N_2O_4 is placed in a 10.0-L vessel. Calculate the concentrations of N_2O_4 and NO_2 when this reaction reaches equilibrium.

53. At a particular temperature, $K = 2.0 \times 10^{-6}$ for the reaction

$$2CO_2(g) \rightleftharpoons 2CO(g) + O_2(g)$$

If 2.0 mol CO_2 is initially placed into a 5.0-L vessel, calculate the equilibrium concentrations of all species.

54. Lexan is a plastic used to make compact discs, eyeglass lenses, and bullet-proof glass. One of the compounds used to make Lexan is phosgene ($COCl_2$), an extremely poisonous gas. Phosgene decomposes by the reaction

$$COCl_2(g) \rightleftharpoons CO(g) + Cl_2(g)$$

for which $K_p = 6.8 \times 10^{-9}$ at 100°C. If pure phosgene at an initial pressure of 1.0 atm decomposes, calculate the equilibrium pressures of all species.

55. At 25°C, $K_p = 2.9 \times 10^{-3}$ for the reaction

$$NH_4OCONH_2(s) \rightleftharpoons 2NH_3(g) + CO_2(g)$$

In an experiment carried out at 25°C, a certain amount of NH_4OCONH_2 is placed in an evacuated rigid container and allowed to come to equilibrium. Calculate the total pressure in the container at equilibrium.

56. A sample of solid ammonium chloride was placed in an evacuated container and then heated so that it decomposed to ammonia gas and hydrogen chloride gas. After heating, the total pressure in the container was found to be 4.4 atm. Calculate K_p at this temperature for the decomposition reaction

$$NH_4Cl(s) \rightleftharpoons NH_3(g) + HCl(g)$$

Le Châtelier's Principle

57. Suppose the reaction system

$$UO_2(s) + 4HF(g) \rightleftharpoons UF_4(g) + 2H_2O(g)$$

has already reached equilibrium. Predict the effect that each of the following changes will have on the equilibrium position. Tell whether the equilibrium will shift to the right, will shift to the left, or will not be affected.

a. Additional $UO_2(s)$ is added to the system.

b. The reaction is performed in a glass reaction vessel; $HF(g)$ attacks and reacts with glass.

c. Water vapor is removed.

58. Predict the shift in the equilibrium position that will occur for each of the following reactions when the volume of the reaction container is increased.

a. $N_2(g) + 3H_2(g) \rightleftharpoons 2NH_3(g)$

b. $PCl_5(g) \rightleftharpoons PCl_3(g) + Cl_2(g)$

c. $H_2(g) + F_2(g) \rightleftharpoons 2HF(g)$

d. $COCl_2(g) \rightleftharpoons CO(g) + Cl_2(g)$

e. $CaCO_3(s) \rightleftharpoons CaO(s) + CO_2(g)$

59. An important reaction in the commercial production of hydrogen is

$$CO(g) + H_2O(g) \rightleftharpoons H_2(g) + CO_2(g) + \text{Heat}$$

How will this system at equilibrium shift in each of the five following cases?

a. Gaseous carbon dioxide is removed.

b. Water vapor is added.

c. The pressure is increased by adding helium gas.

d. The temperature is increased (the reaction is exothermic).

e. The pressure is increased by decreasing the volume of the reaction container.

60. What will happen to the number of moles of SO_3 in equilibrium with SO_2 and O_2 in the reaction

$$2SO_3(g) \rightleftharpoons 2SO_2(g) + O_2(g) \qquad \Delta H° = 197 \text{ kJ}$$

in each of the following cases?

a. Oxygen gas is added.

b. The pressure is increased by decreasing the volume of the reaction container.

c. The pressure is increased by adding argon gas.

d. The temperature is decreased.

e. Gaseous sulfur dioxide is removed.

61. In which direction will the position of the equilibrium

$$2HI(g) \rightleftharpoons H_2(g) + I_2(g)$$

be shifted for each of the following changes?

a. $H_2(g)$ is added.

b. $I_2(g)$ is removed.

c. $HI(g)$ is removed.

d. Some $Ar(g)$ is added.

e. The volume of the container is doubled.

f. The temperature is decreased (the reaction is exothermic).

62. Hydrogen for use in ammonia production is produced by the reaction

$$\text{Energy} + CH_4(g) + H_2O(g) \xrightarrow[750°C]{\text{Ni catalyst}} CO(g) + 3H_2(g)$$

What will happen to a reaction mixture at equilibrium if
a. $H_2O(g)$ is removed?
b. the temperature is increased (the reaction is endothermic)?
c. an inert gas is added? ⟶ *beel. 606)!*
d. $CO(g)$ is removed?
e. the volume of the container is tripled? ⟶ *608*

63. Old-fashioned "smelling salts" consist of ammonium carbonate, $(NH_4)_2CO_3$. The reaction for the decomposition of ammonium carbonate

phuck + $(NH_4)_2CO_3(s) \rightleftharpoons 2NH_3(g) + CO_2(g) + H_2O(g)$

is endothermic. Would the smell of ammonia increase or decrease as the temperature is increased?

64. Ammonia is produced by the Haber process, in which nitrogen and hydrogen are reacted directly using an iron mesh impregnated with oxides as a catalyst. For the reaction   *ΔH+, ∆H⁻*

oheory $N_2(g) + 3H_2(g) \rightleftharpoons 2NH_3(g) + E$ *cre...*

equilibrium constants (K_p values) as a function of temperature are

300°C, 4.34×10^{-3}
500°C, 1.45×10^{-5} *↑Energy*
600°C, 2.25×10^{-6}

Is the reaction exothermic or endothermic? *Kp ↓*

Additional Exercises

65. Calculate a value for the equilibrium constant for the reaction

$$O_2(g) + O(g) \rightleftharpoons O_3(g)$$

given

$$NO_2(g) \xrightarrow{hv} NO(g) + O(g) \qquad K = 6.8 \times 10^{-49}$$
$$O_3(g) + NO(g) \rightleftharpoons NO_2(g) + O_2(g) \qquad K = 5.8 \times 10^{-34}$$

Hint: When reactions are added together, the equilibrium expressions are multiplied.

66. At 25°C, $K_p \approx 1 \times 10^{-31}$ for the reaction

$$N_2(g) + O_2(g) \rightleftharpoons 2NO(g)$$

a. Calculate the concentration of NO, in molecules/cm³, that can exist in equilibrium in air at 25°C. In air, $P_{N_2} = 0.8$ atm and $P_{O_2} = 0.2$ atm.
b. Typical concentrations of NO in relatively pristine environments range from 10^8 to 10^{10} molecules/cm³. Why is there a discrepancy between these values and your answer to part a?

67. The gas arsine, AsH_3, decomposes as follows:

$$2AsH_3(g) \rightleftharpoons 2As(s) + 3H_2(g)$$

In an experiment at a certain temperature, pure $AsH_3(g)$ was placed in an empty, rigid, sealed flask at a pressure of 392.0 torr. After 48 hours the pressure in the flask was observed to be constant at 488.0 torr.
a. Calculate the equilibrium pressure of $H_2(g)$.
b. Calculate K_p for this reaction.

68 At a certain temperature, $K = 9.1 \times 10^{-4}$ for the reaction

$$FeSCN^{2+}(aq) \rightleftharpoons Fe^{3+}(aq) + SCN^-(aq)$$

Calculate the concentrations of Fe^{3+}, SCN^-, and $FeSCN^{2+}$ in a solution that is initially 2.0 M $FeSCN^{2+}$.

69. For the reaction

$$PCl_5(g) \rightleftharpoons PCl_3(g) + Cl_2(g)$$

at 600. K, the equilibrium constant, K_p, is 11.5. Suppose that 2.450 g of PCl_5 is placed in an evacuated 500.-mL bulb, which is then heated to 600. K.
a. What would be the pressure of PCl_5 if it did not dissociate?
b. What is the partial pressure of PCl_5 at equilibrium?
c. What is the total pressure in the bulb at equilibrium?
d. What is the degree of dissociation of PCl_5 at equilibrium?

70. At 25°C, gaseous SO_2Cl_2 decomposes to $SO_2(g)$ and $Cl_2(g)$ to the extent that 12.5% of the original SO_2Cl_2 (by moles) has decomposed to reach equilibrium. The total pressure (at equilibrium) is 0.900 atm. Calculate the value of K_p for this system.

71. For the following reaction at a certain temperature

$$H_2(g) + F_2(g) \rightleftharpoons 2HF(g)$$

it is found that the equilibrium concentrations in a 5.00-L rigid container are $[H_2] = 0.0500$ M, $[F_2] = 0.0100$ M, and $[HF] = 0.400$ M. If 0.200 mol of F_2 is added to this equilibrium mixture, calculate the concentrations of all gases once equilibrium is reestablished.

72. Consider the reaction

$$Fe^{3+}(aq) + SCN^-(aq) \rightleftharpoons FeSCN^{2+}(aq)$$

How will the equilibrium position shift if
a. water is added, doubling the volume?
b. $AgNO_3(aq)$ is added? (AgSCN is insoluble.)
c. $NaOH(aq)$ is added? [$Fe(OH)_3$ is insoluble.]
d. $Fe(NO_3)_3(aq)$ is added?

73. Chromium(VI) forms two different oxyanions, the orange dichromate ion, $Cr_2O_7^{2-}$, and the yellow chromate ion, CrO_4^{2-}. (See the following photos.) The equilibrium reaction between the two ions is

$$Cr_2O_7^{2-}(aq) + H_2O(l) \rightleftharpoons 2CrO_4^{2-}(aq) + 2H^+(aq)$$

Explain why orange dichromate solutions turn yellow when sodium hydroxide is added.

74. The synthesis of ammonia gas from nitrogen gas and hydrogen gas represents a classic case in which a knowledge of kinetics and equilibrium was used to make a desired chemical reaction economically feasible. Explain how each of the following conditions helps to maximize the yield of ammonia.
  a. running the reaction at an elevated temperature
  b. removing the ammonia from the reaction mixture as it forms
  c. using a catalyst
  d. running the reaction at high pressure

75. Suppose $K = 4.5 \times 10^{-3}$ at a certain temperature for the reaction

$$PCl_5(g) \rightleftharpoons PCl_3(g) + Cl_2(g)$$

If it is found that the concentration of PCl_5 is twice the concentration of PCl_3, what must be the concentration of Cl_2 under these conditions?

76. For the reaction below, $K_p = 1.16$ at 800.°C.

$$CaCO_3(s) \rightleftharpoons CaO(s) + CO_2(g)$$

If a 20.0-g sample of $CaCO_3$ is put into a 10.0-L container and heated to 800.°C, what percentage by mass of the $CaCO_3$ will react to reach equilibrium?

77. A 2.4156-g sample of PCl_5 was placed in an empty 2.000-L flask and allowed to decompose to PCl_3 and Cl_2 at 250.0°C:

$$PCl_5(g) \rightleftharpoons PCl_3(g) + Cl_2(g)$$

At equilibrium the total pressure inside the flask was observed to be 358.7 torr. Calculate the partial pressure of each gas at equilibrium and the value of K_p at 250.0°C.

78. Consider the decomposition of the compound $C_5H_6O_3$ as follows:

$$C_5H_6O_3(g) \longrightarrow C_2H_6(g) + 3CO(g)$$

When a 5.63-g sample of pure $C_5H_6O_3(g)$ was sealed into an otherwise empty 2.50-L flask and heated to 200.°C, the pressure in the flask gradually rose to 1.63 atm and remained at that value. Calculate K for this reaction.

Challenge Problems

79. At 35°C, $K = 1.6 \times 10^{-5}$ for the reaction

$$2NOCl(g) \rightleftharpoons 2NO(g) + Cl_2(g)$$

If 2.0 mol NO and 1.0 mol Cl_2 are placed into a 1.0-L flask, calculate the equilibrium concentrations of all species.

80. Nitric oxide and bromine at initial partial pressures of 98.4 and 41.3 torr, respectively, were allowed to react at 300. K. At equilibrium the total pressure was 110.5 torr. The reaction is

$$2NO(g) + Br_2(g) \rightleftharpoons 2NOBr(g)$$

  a. Calculate the value of K_p.
  b. What would be the partial pressures of all species if NO and Br_2, both at an initial partial pressure of 0.30 atm, were allowed to come to equilibrium at this temperature?

81. At 25°C, $K_p = 5.3 \times 10^5$ for the reaction

$$N_2(g) + 3H_2(g) \rightleftharpoons 2NH_3(g)$$

When a certain partial pressure of $NH_3(g)$ is put into an otherwise empty rigid vessel at 25°C, equilibrium is reached when

50.0% of the original ammonia has decomposed. What was the original partial pressure of ammonia before any decomposition occurred?

82. Consider the reaction

$$P_4(g) \longrightarrow 2P_2(g)$$

where $K_p = 1.00 \times 10^{-1}$ at 1325 K. In an experiment where $P_4(g)$ is placed into a container at 1325 K, the equilibrium mixture of $P_4(g)$ and $P_2(g)$ has a total pressure of 1.00 atm. Calculate the equilibrium pressures of $P_4(g)$ and $P_2(g)$. Calculate the fraction (by moles) of $P_4(g)$ that has dissociated to reach equilibrium.

83. The partial pressures of an equilibrium mixture of $N_2O_4(g)$ and $NO_2(g)$ are $P_{N_2O_4} = 0.34$ atm and $P_{NO_2} = 1.20$ atm at a certain temperature. The volume of the container is doubled. Find the partial pressures of the two gases when a new equilibrium is established.

84. At 125°C, $K_p = 0.25$ for the reaction

$$2NaHCO_3(s) \rightleftharpoons Na_2CO_3(s) + CO_2(g) + H_2O(g)$$

A 1.00-L flask containing 10.0 g $NaHCO_3$ is evacuated and heated to 125°C.
  a. Calculate the partial pressures of CO_2 and H_2O after equilibrium is established.
  b. Calculate the masses of $NaHCO_3$ and Na_2CO_3 present at equilibrium.
  c. Calculate the minimum container volume necessary for all of the $NaHCO_3$ to decompose.

85. An 8.00-g sample of SO_3 was placed in an evacuated container, where it decomposed at 600°C according to the following reaction:

$$SO_3(g) \rightleftharpoons SO_2(g) + \tfrac{1}{2}O_2(g)$$

At equilibrium the total pressure and the density of the gaseous mixture were 1.80 atm and 1.60 g/L, respectively. Calculate K_p for this reaction.

86. A sample of iron(II) sulfate was heated in an evacuated container to 920 K, where the following reactions occurred:

$$2FeSO_4(s) \rightleftharpoons Fe_2O_3(s) + SO_3(g) + SO_2(g)$$
$$SO_3(g) \rightleftharpoons SO_2(g) + \tfrac{1}{2}O_2(g)$$

After equilibrium was reached, the total pressure was 0.836 atm and the partial pressure of oxygen was 0.0275 atm. Calculate K_p for each of these reactions.

87. At 5000 K and 1.000 atm, 83.00% of the oxygen molecules in a sample have dissociated to atomic oxygen. At what pressure will 95.0% of the molecules dissociate at this temperature?

88. A sample of $N_2O_4(g)$ is placed in an empty cylinder at 25°C. After equilibrium is reached the total pressure is 1.5 atm and 16% (by moles) of the original $N_2O_4(g)$ has dissociated to $NO_2(g)$.
  a. Calculate the value of K_p for this dissociation reaction at 25°C.
  b. If the volume of the cylinder is increased until the total pressure is 1.0 atm (the temperature of the system remains constant), calculate the equilibrium pressure of $N_2O_4(g)$ and $NO_2(g)$.
  c. What percentage (by moles) of the original $N_2O_4(g)$ is dissociated at the new equilibrium position (total pressure = 1.00 atm)?

89. A sample of gaseous nitrosyl bromide, NOBr, was placed in a rigid flask, where it decomposed at 25°C according to the following reaction:

$$2NOBr(g) \rightleftharpoons 2NO(g) + Br_2(g)$$

At equilibrium the total pressure and the density of the gaseous mixture were found to be 0.0515 atm and 0.1861 g/L, respectively. Calculate the value of K_p for this reaction.

90. The equilibrium constant K_p for the reaction

$$CCl_4(g) \rightleftharpoons C(s) + 2Cl_2(g)$$

at 700°C is 0.76 atm. Determine the initial pressure of carbon tetrachloride that will produce a total equilibrium pressure of 1.20 atm at 700°C.

Integrative Problems

These problems require the integration of multiple concepts to find the solutions.

91. For the reaction

$$NH_3(g) + H_2S(g) \rightleftharpoons NH_4HS(s)$$

$K = 400.$ at 35.0°C. If 2.00 mol each of NH_3, H_2S, and NH_4HS are placed in a 5.00-L vessel, what mass of NH_4HS will be present at equilibrium? What is the pressure of H_2S at equilibrium?

92. Given $K = 3.50$ at 45°C for the reaction

$$A(g) + B(g) \rightleftharpoons C(g)$$

and $K = 7.10$ at 45°C for the reaction

$$2A(g) + D(g) \rightleftharpoons C(g)$$

what is the value of K at the same temperature for the reaction

$$C(g) + D(g) \rightleftharpoons 2B(g)$$

What is the value of K_p at 45°C for the reaction? Starting with 1.50 atm partial pressures of both C and D, what is the mole fraction of B once equilibrium is reached?

93. The hydrocarbon naphthalene was frequently used in mothballs until recently, when it was discovered that human inhalation of naphthalene vapors can lead to hemolytic anemia. Naphthalene is 93.71% carbon by mass and a 0.256-mol sample of naphthalene has a mass of 32.8 g. What is the molecular formula of naphthalene? This compound works as a pesticide in mothballs by sublimation of the solid so that it fumigates enclosed spaces with its vapors according to the equation

$$naphthalene(s) \rightleftharpoons naphthalene(g) \quad K = 4.29 \times 10^{-6} \text{ (at 298 K)}$$

If 3.00 g of solid naphthalene is placed into an enclosed space with a volume of 5.00 L at 25°C, what percentage of the naphthalene will have sublimed once equilibrium has been established?

Marathon Problem*

This problem is designed to incorporate several concepts and techniques into one situation. Marathon Problems can be used in class by groups of students to help facilitate problem-solving skills.

94. Consider the reaction

$$A(g) + B(g) \rightleftharpoons C(g)$$

for which $K = 1.30 \times 10^2$. Assume that 0.406 mol C(g) is placed in the cylinder represented below. The temperature is 300.0 K, and the barometric pressure on the piston (which is assumed to be massless and frictionless) is constant at 1.00 atm. The original volume (before the 0.406 mol C(g) begins to decompose) is 10.00 L. What is the volume in the cylinder at equilibrium?

P = 1.00 atm

Original volume = 10.00 L

T = 300.0 K

0.406 mole of pure C(g) (initially)

Get help understanding core concepts and visualizing molecular-level interactions, and practice problem solving, by visiting the Online Study Center at **college.hmco.com/ PIC/zumdahl7e.**

*Used with permission from the *Journal of Chemical Education,* Vol. 68, No. 11, 1991, pp. 919–922; copyright © 1991, Division of Chemical Education, Inc.

14 Acids and Bases

Contents

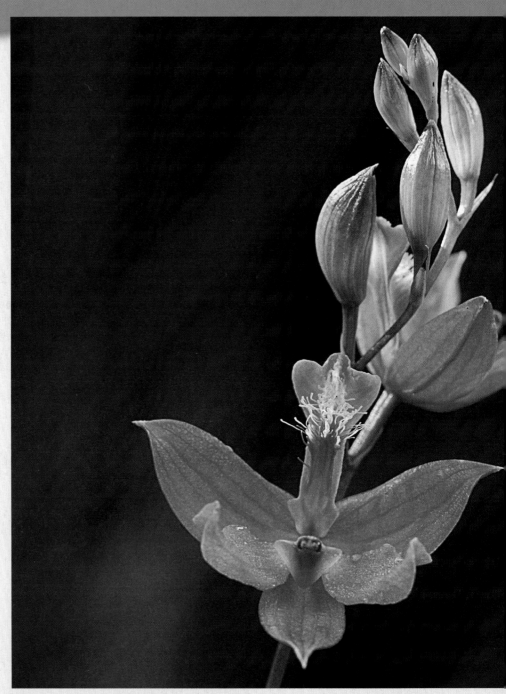

This grass pink orchid thrives in the acidic soil of a bog meadow at Illinois Beach State Park.

In this chapter we reencounter two very important classes of compounds, acids and bases. We will explore their interactions and apply the fundamentals of chemical equilibria discussed in Chapter 13 to systems involving proton-transfer reactions.

Acid–base chemistry is important in a wide variety of everyday applications. There are complex systems in our bodies that carefully control the acidity of our blood, since even small deviations may lead to serious illness and death. The same sensitivity exists in other life forms. If you have ever had tropical fish or goldfish, you know how important it is to monitor and control the acidity of the water in the aquarium.

Acids and bases are also important in industry. For example, the vast quantity of sulfuric acid manufactured in the United States each year is needed to produce fertilizers, polymers, steel, and many other materials.

The influence of acids on living things has assumed special importance in the United States, Canada, and Europe in recent years as a result of the phenomenon of acid rain (see the Chemical Impact in Chapter 5). This problem is complex and has diplomatic and economic overtones that make it all the more difficult to solve.

14.1 The Nature of Acids and Bases

Don't taste chemicals!

Acids and bases were first discussed in Section 4.2.

Acids were first recognized as a class of substances that taste sour. Vinegar tastes sour because it is a dilute solution of acetic acid; citric acid is responsible for the sour taste of a lemon. Bases, sometimes called *alkalis,* are characterized by their bitter taste and slippery feel. Commercial preparations for unclogging drains are highly basic.

The first person to recognize the essential nature of acids and bases was Svante Arrhenius. Based on his experiments with electrolytes, Arrhenius postulated that *acids produce hydrogen ions in aqueous solution, while bases produce hydroxide ions.* At the time, the **Arrhenius concept** of acids and bases was a major step forward in quantifying acid–base chemistry, but this concept is limited because it applies only to aqueous solutions and allows for only one kind of base—the hydroxide ion. A more general definition of acids and bases was suggested by the Danish chemist Johannes Brønsted (1879–1947) and the English chemist Thomas Lowry (1874–1936). In terms of the **Brønsted–Lowry model,** *an acid is a proton (H$^+$) donor, and a base is a proton acceptor.* For example, when gaseous HCl dissolves in water, each HCl molecule donates a proton to a water molecule and so qualifies as a Brønsted–Lowry acid. The molecule that accepts the proton, in this case water, is a Brønsted–Lowry base.

To understand how water can act as a base, we need to remember that the oxygen of the water molecule has two unshared electron pairs, either of which can form a covalent bond with an H$^+$ ion. When gaseous HCl dissolves, the following reaction occurs:

$$H-\overset{\cdot\cdot}{\underset{|}{O}}: + H-\overset{\cdot\cdot}{\underset{\cdot\cdot}{Cl}}: \longrightarrow \left[H-\overset{\cdot\cdot}{\underset{|}{O}}-H\right]^+ + \left[:\overset{\cdot\cdot}{\underset{\cdot\cdot}{Cl}}:\right]^-$$

Note that the proton is transferred from the HCl molecule to the water molecule to form H_3O^+, which is called the **hydronium ion.** This reaction is represented in Fig. 14.1 using molecular models.

Common household substances that contain acids and bases. Vinegar is a dilute solution of acetic acid. Drain cleaners contain strong bases such as sodium hydroxide.

The general reaction that occurs when an acid is dissolved in water can best be represented as

Recall that (*aq*) means the substance is hydrated.

$$\underset{\text{Acid}}{\text{HA}(aq)} + \underset{\text{Base}}{\text{H}_2\text{O}(l)} \;\rightleftharpoons\; \underset{\substack{\text{Conjugate}\\\text{acid}}}{\text{H}_3\text{O}^+(aq)} + \underset{\substack{\text{Conjugate}\\\text{base}}}{\text{A}^-(aq)} \qquad (14.1)$$

This representation emphasizes the significant role of the polar water molecule in pulling the proton from the acid. Note that the **conjugate base** is everything that remains of the acid molecule after a proton is lost. The **conjugate acid** is formed when the proton is transferred to the base. A **conjugate acid–base pair** consists of two substances related to each other by the donating and accepting of a single proton. In Equation (14.1) there are two conjugate acid–base pairs: HA and A$^-$ and H$_2$O and H$_3$O$^+$. This reaction is represented by molecular models in Fig. 14.2.

It is important to note that Equation (14.1) really represents *a competition for the proton between the two bases H₂O and A⁻*. If H$_2$O is a much stronger base than A$^-$, that is, if H$_2$O has a much greater affinity for H$^+$ than does A$^-$, the equilibrium position will be far to the right; most of the acid dissolved will be in the ionized form. Conversely, if A$^-$ is a much stronger base than H$_2$O, the equilibrium position will lie far to the left. In this case most of the acid dissolved will be present at equilibrium as HA.

Visualization: Acid Ionization Equilibrium

The equilibrium expression for the reaction given in Equation (14.1) is

$$K_\text{a} = \frac{[\text{H}_3\text{O}^+][\text{A}^-]}{[\text{HA}]} = \frac{[\text{H}^+][\text{A}^-]}{[\text{HA}]} \qquad (14.2)$$

In this chapter we will always represent an acid as simply dissociating. This does not mean we are using the Arrhenius model for acids. Since water does not affect the equilibrium position, it is simply easier to leave it out of the acid dissociation reaction.

where K_a is called the **acid dissociation constant.** Both H$_3$O$^+$(*aq*) and H$^+$(*aq*) are commonly used to represent the hydrated proton. In this book we will often use simply H$^+$, but you should remember that it is hydrated in aqueous solutions.

In Chapter 13 we saw that the concentration of a pure solid or a pure liquid is always omitted from the equilibrium expression. In a dilute solution we can assume that the

FIGURE 14.1
The reaction of HCl and H₂O.

FIGURE 14.2
The reaction of an acid HA with water to form H_3O^+ and a conjugate base A^-.

concentration of liquid water remains essentially constant when an acid is dissolved. Thus the term $[H_2O]$ is not included in Equation (14.2), and the equilibrium expression for K_a has the same form as that for the simple dissociation into ions:

$$HA(aq) \rightleftharpoons H^+(aq) + A^-(aq)$$

You should not forget, however, that water plays an important role in causing the acid to ionize.

Note that K_a is the equilibrium constant for the reaction in which a proton is removed from HA to form the conjugate base A^-. We use K_a to represent *only* this type of reaction. Knowing this, you can write the K_a expression for any acid, even one that is totally unfamiliar to you. As you do Sample Exercise 14.1, focus on the definition of the reaction corresponding to K_a.

Sample Exercise 14.1	**Acid Dissociation (Ionization) Reactions**

Write the simple dissociation (ionization) reaction (omitting water) for each of the following acids.

a. Hydrochloric acid (HCl)
b. Acetic acid ($HC_2H_3O_2$)
c. The ammonium ion (NH_4^+)
d. The anilinium ion ($C_6H_5NH_3^+$)
e. The hydrated aluminum(III) ion $[Al(H_2O)_6]^{3+}$

Solution

a. $HCl(aq) \rightleftharpoons H^+(aq) + Cl^-(aq)$
b. $HC_2H_3O_2(aq) \rightleftharpoons H^+(aq) + C_2H_3O_2^-(aq)$
c. $NH_4^+(aq) \rightleftharpoons H^+(aq) + NH_3(aq)$
d. $C_6H_5NH_3^+(aq) \rightleftharpoons H^+(aq) + C_6H_5NH_2(aq)$
e. Although this formula looks complicated, writing the reaction is simple if you concentrate on the meaning of K_a. Removing a proton, which can come only from one of the water molecules, leaves one OH^- and five H_2O molecules attached to the Al^{3+} ion. So the reaction is

$$Al(H_2O)_6^{3+}(aq) \rightleftharpoons H^+(aq) + Al(H_2O)_5OH^{2+}(aq)$$

See Exercises 14.27 and 14.28.

The Brønsted–Lowry model is not limited to aqueous solutions; it can be extended to reactions in the gas phase. For example, we discussed the reaction between gaseous hydrogen chloride and ammonia when we studied diffusion (Section 5.7):

$$NH_3(g) + HCl(g) \rightleftharpoons NH_4Cl(s)$$

In this reaction, a proton is donated by the hydrogen chloride to the ammonia, as shown by these Lewis structures:

When HCl(g) and NH$_3$(g) meet in a tube, a white ring of NH$_4$Cl(s) forms.

FIGURE 14.3
The reaction of NH_3 with HCl to form NH_4^+ and Cl^-.

Note that this is not considered an acid–base reaction according to the Arrhenius concept. Figure 14.3 shows a molecular representation of this reaction.

14.2 Acid Strength

The strength of an acid is defined by the equilibrium position of its dissociation (ionization) reaction:

$$HA(aq) + H_2O(l) \rightleftharpoons H_3O^+(aq) + A^-(aq)$$

A **strong acid** is one for which *this equilibrium lies far to the right*. This means that almost all the original HA is dissociated (ionized) at equilibrium [see Fig. 14.4(a)]. There is an important connection between the strength of an acid and that of its conjugate base. *A strong acid yields a weak conjugate base*—one that has a low affinity for a proton. A strong acid also can be described as an acid whose conjugate base is a much weaker base than water (see Fig. 14.5). In this case the water molecules win the competition for the H^+ ions.

> A strong acid has a weak conjugate base.

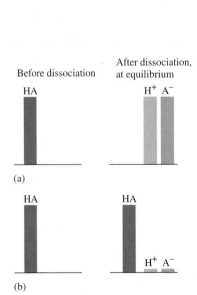

FIGURE 14.4
Graphic representation of the behavior of acids of different strengths in aqueous solution. (a) A strong acid. (b) A weak acid.

FIGURE 14.5
The relationship of acid strength and conjugate base strength for the reaction

$$HA(aq) + H_2O(l) \rightleftharpoons H_3O^+(aq) + A^-(aq)$$

Acid   Conjugate base

TABLE 14.1   Various Ways to Describe Acid Strength

Property	Strong Acid	Weak Acid
K_a value	K_a is large	K_a is small
Position of the dissociation (ionization) equilibrium	Far to the right	Far to the left
Equilibrium concentration of H^+ compared with original concentration of HA	$[H^+] \approx [HA]_0$	$[H^+] \ll [HA]_0$
Strength of conjugate base compared with that of water	A^- much weaker base than H_2O	A^- much stronger base than H_2O

$\ll$ means much less than.
$\gg$ means much greater than.

Perchloric acid can explode if handled improperly.

Conversely, a **weak acid** is one for which *the equilibrium lies far to the left.* Most of the acid originally placed in the solution is still present as HA at equilibrium. That is, a weak acid dissociates only to a very small extent in aqueous solution [see Fig. 14.4(b)]. In contrast to a strong acid, a weak acid has a conjugate base that is a much stronger base than water. In this case a water molecule is not very successful in pulling an H^+ ion from the conjugate base. *The weaker the acid, the stronger its conjugate base.*

The various ways of describing the strength of an acid are summarized in Table 14.1. Strong and weak acids are represented pictorially in Fig. 14.6.

The common strong acids are sulfuric acid [$H_2SO_4(aq)$], hydrochloric acid [$HCl(aq)$], nitric acid [$HNO_3(aq)$], and perchloric acid [$HClO_4(aq)$]. Sulfuric acid is actually a **diprotic acid,** an acid having two acidic protons. The acid H_2SO_4 is a strong acid, virtually 100% dissociated (ionized) in water:

$$H_2SO_4(aq) \longrightarrow H^+(aq) + HSO_4^-(aq)$$

The HSO_4^- ion, however, is a weak acid:

$$HSO_4^-(aq) \rightleftharpoons H^+(aq) + SO_4^{2-}(aq)$$

Most acids are **oxyacids,** in which the acidic proton is attached to an oxygen atom. The strong acids mentioned above, except hydrochloric acid, are typical examples. Many common weak acids, such as phosphoric acid (H_3PO_4), nitrous acid (HNO_2), and

Sulfuric acid
(H_2SO_4)

Nitric acid
(HNO_3)

Perchloric acid
($HClO_4$)

FIGURE 14.6
(a) A strong acid HA is completely ionized in water. (b) A weak acid HB exists mostly as undissociated HB molecules in water. Note that the water molecules are not shown in this figure.

Phosphoric acid
(H_3PO_4)

Nitrous acid
(HNO_2)

Hypochlorous acid
(HOCl)

Acidic H

Acetic acid
(CH_3CO_2H)

Acidic H

Benzoic acid
($C_6H_5CO_2H$)

Appendix 5.1 contains a table of K_a values.

TABLE 14.2   Values of K_a for Some Common Monoprotic Acids

Formula	Name	Value of K_a*
HSO_4^-	Hydrogen sulfate ion	1.2×10^{-2}
$HClO_2$	Chlorous acid	1.2×10^{-2}
$HC_2H_2ClO_2$	Monochloracetic acid	1.35×10^{-3}
HF	Hydrofluoric acid	7.2×10^{-4}
HNO_2	Nitrous acid	4.0×10^{-4}
$HC_2H_3O_2$	Acetic acid	1.8×10^{-5}
$[Al(H_2O)_6]^{3+}$	Hydrated aluminum(III) ion	1.4×10^{-5}
HOCl	Hypochlorous acid	3.5×10^{-8}
HCN	Hydrocyanic acid	6.2×10^{-10}
NH_4^+	Ammonium ion	5.6×10^{-10}
HOC_6H_5	Phenol	1.6×10^{-10}

Increasing acid strength →

*The units of K_a are customarily omitted.

hypochlorous acid (HOCl), are also oxyacids. **Organic acids,** those with a carbon atom backbone, commonly contain the **carboxyl group:**

$$-C\overset{\displaystyle O}{\underset{\displaystyle O-H}{}}$$

Acids of this type are usually weak. Examples are acetic acid (CH_3COOH), often written $HC_2H_3O_2$, and benzoic acid (C_6H_5COOH). Note that the remainder of the hydrogens in these molecules are not acidic—they do not form H^+ in water.

There are some important acids in which the acidic proton is attached to an atom other than oxygen. The most significant of these are the hydrohalic acids HX, where X represents a halogen atom.

Table 14.2 contains a list of common **monoprotic acids** (those having *one* acidic proton) and their K_a values. Note that the strong acids are not listed. When a strong acid molecule such as HCl, for example, is placed in water, the position of the dissociation equilibrium

$$HCl(aq) + H_2O(l) \rightleftharpoons H^+(aq) + Cl^-(aq)$$

lies so far to the right that [HCl] cannot be measured accurately. This prevents an accurate calculation of K_a:

$$K_a = \frac{[H^+][Cl^-]}{[HCl]}$$

Very small and highly uncertain

Sample Exercise 14.2 | Relative Base Strength

Using Table 14.2, arrange the following species according to their strengths as bases: H_2O, F^-, Cl^-, NO_2^-, and CN^-.

Solution

Remember that water is a stronger base than the conjugate base of a strong acid but a weaker base than the conjugate base of a weak acid. This leads to the following order:

$$Cl^- < H_2O < \text{conjugate bases of weak acids}$$

Weakest bases ⟶ Strongest bases

We can order the remaining conjugate bases by recognizing that the strength of an acid is *inversely related* to the strength of its conjugate base. Since from Table 14.2 we have

$$K_a \text{ for HF} > K_a \text{ for HNO}_2 > K_a \text{ for HCN}$$

the base strengths increase as follows:

$$\text{F}^- < \text{NO}_2^- < \text{CN}^-$$

The combined order of increasing base strength is

$$\text{Cl}^- < \text{H}_2\text{O} < \text{F}^- < \text{NO}_2^- < \text{CN}^-$$

See Exercises 14.33 through 14.36.

Water as an Acid and a Base

A substance is said to be **amphoteric** if it can behave either as an acid or as a base. Water is the most common **amphoteric substance.** We can see this clearly in the **autoionization** of water, which involves the transfer of a proton from one water molecule to another to produce a hydroxide ion and a hydronium ion:

$$H_2O + H_2O \rightleftharpoons H_3O^+ + OH^-$$
acid(1)   base(1)   acid(2)   base(2)

In this reaction, also illustrated in Fig. 14.7, one water molecule acts as an acid by furnishing a proton, and the other acts as a base by accepting the proton.

Autoionization can occur in other liquids besides water. For example, in liquid ammonia the autoionization reaction is

The autoionization reaction for water

$$2\text{H}_2\text{O}(l) \rightleftharpoons \text{H}_3\text{O}^+(aq) + \text{OH}^-(aq)$$

leads to the equilibrium expression

$$K_w = [\text{H}_3\text{O}^+][\text{OH}^-] = [\text{H}^+][\text{OH}^-]$$

where K_w, called the **ion-product constant** (or the **dissociation constant** for water), always refers to the autoionization of water.

Experiment shows that at 25°C in pure water,

$$[\text{H}^+] = [\text{OH}^-] = 1.0 \times 10^{-7} M$$

which means that at 25°C

$$K_w = [\text{H}^+][\text{OH}^-] = (1.0 \times 10^{-7})(1.0 \times 10^{-7})$$
$$= 1.0 \times 10^{-14}$$

$K_w = [\text{H}^+][\text{OH}^-]$
$= 1.0 \times 10^{-14}$

FIGURE 14.7
Two water molecules react to form H_3O^+ and OH^-.

It is important to recognize the meaning of K_w. In any aqueous solution at 25°C, *no matter what it contains,* the product of $[H^+]$ and $[OH^-]$ must always equal 1.0×10^{-14}. There are three possible situations:

1. A neutral solution, where $[H^+] = [OH^-]$.

2. An acidic solution, where $[H^+] > [OH^-]$.

3. A basic solution, where $[OH^-] > [H^+]$.

In each case, however, at 25°C,

$$K_w = [H^+][OH^-] = 1.0 \times 10^{-14}$$

Sample Exercise 14.3

Calculating $[H^+]$ and $[OH^-]$

Calculate $[H^+]$ or $[OH^-]$ as required for each of the following solutions at 25°C, and state whether the solution is neutral, acidic, or basic.

a. $1.0 \times 10^{-5}\, M\, OH^-$
b. $1.0 \times 10^{-7}\, M\, OH^-$
c. $10.0\, M\, H^+$

Solution

a. $K_w = [H^+][OH^-] = 1.0 \times 10^{-14}$. Since $[OH^-]$ is $1.0 \times 10^{-5}\, M$, solving for $[H^+]$ gives

$$[H^+] = \frac{1.0 \times 10^{-14}}{[OH^-]} = \frac{1.0 \times 10^{-14}}{1.0 \times 10^{-5}} = 1.0 \times 10^{-9}\, M$$

Since $[OH^-] > [H^+]$, the solution is basic.

Visualization: Self-Ionization of Water

b. As in part a, solving for $[H^+]$ gives

$$[H^+] = \frac{1.0 \times 10^{-14}}{[OH^-]} = \frac{1.0 \times 10^{-14}}{1.0 \times 10^{-7}} = 1.0 \times 10^{-7}\, M$$

Since $[H^+] = [OH^-]$, the solution is neutral.

c. Solving for $[OH^-]$ gives

$$[OH^-] = \frac{1.0 \times 10^{-14}}{[H^+]} = \frac{1.0 \times 10^{-14}}{10.0} = 1.0 \times 10^{-15}\, M$$

Since $[H^+] > [OH^-]$, the solution is acidic.

See Exercises 14.37 and 14.38.

Since K_w is an equilibrium constant, it varies with temperature. The effect of temperature is considered in Sample Exercise 14.4.

Sample Exercise 14.4

Autoionization of Water

At 60°C, the value of K_w is 1×10^{-13}.

a. Using Le Châtelier's principle, predict whether the reaction

$$2H_2O(l) \rightleftharpoons H_3O^+(aq) + OH^-(aq)$$

is exothermic or endothermic.

b. Calculate $[H^+]$ and $[OH^-]$ in a neutral solution at 60°C.

Solution

a. K_w *increases* from 1×10^{-14} at 25°C to 1×10^{-13} at 60°C. Le Châtelier's principle states that if a system at equilibrium is heated, it will adjust to consume energy. Since the value of K_w increases with temperature, we must think of energy as a reactant, and so the process must be endothermic.

b. At 60°C,

$$[H^+][OH^-] = 1 \times 10^{-13}$$

For a neutral solution,

$$[H^+] = [OH^-] = \sqrt{1 \times 10^{-13}} = 3 \times 10^{-7} \, M$$

See Exercise 14.39.

Visualization: The pH Scale

The pH scale is a compact way to represent solution acidity.

Appendix 1.2 has a review of logs.

14.3 The pH Scale

Because $[H^+]$ in an aqueous solution is typically quite small, the **pH scale** provides a convenient way to represent solution acidity. The pH is a log scale based on 10, where

$$pH = -\log[H^+]$$

Thus for a solution where

$$[H^+] = 1.0 \times 10^{-7} \, M$$
$$pH = -(-7.00) = 7.00$$

At this point we need to discuss significant figures for logarithms. The rule is that *the number of decimal places in the log is equal to the number of significant figures in the original number.* Thus

$$[H^+] = 1.0 \times 10^{-9} \, M$$
$$pH = 9.00$$

2 significant figures

2 decimal places

Similar log scales are used for representing other quantities; for example,

$$pOH = -\log[OH^-]$$
$$pK = -\log K$$

Since pH is a log scale based on 10, *the pH changes by 1 for every power of 10 change in [H⁺].* For example, a solution of pH 3 has an H^+ concentration 10 times that of a solution of pH 4 and 100 times that of a solution of pH 5. Also note that because pH is defined as $-\log[H^+]$, *the pH decreases as [H⁺] increases.* The pH scale and the pH values for several common substances are shown in Fig. 14.8.

The pH of a solution is usually measured using a pH meter, an electronic device with a probe that can be inserted into a solution of unknown pH. The probe contains an acidic aqueous solution enclosed by a special glass membrane that allows migration of H^+ ions. If the unknown solution has a different pH from the solution in the probe, an electric potential results, which is registered on the meter (see Fig. 14.9).

Sample Exercise 14.5 | Calculating pH and pOH

The pH meter is discussed more fully in Section 17.4.

Calculate pH and pOH for each of the following solutions at 25°C.

a. $1.0 \times 10^{-3} \, M \, OH^-$
b. $1.0 \, M \, OH^+$

CHEMICAL IMPACT

Arnold Beckman, Man of Science

Arnold Beckman died at age 104 in May 2004. Beckman's leadership of science and business spans virtually the entire twentieth century. He was born in 1900 in Cullom, Illinois, a town of 500 people that had no electricity or telephones. Beckman says, "In Cullom we were forced to improvise. I think it was a good thing."

The son of a blacksmith, Beckman had his interest in science awakened at age nine. At that time, in the attic of his house he discovered *J. Dorman Steele's Fourteen Weeks in Chemistry,* a book containing instructions for doing chemistry experiments. Beckman became so fascinated with chemistry that his father built him a small "chemistry shed" in the back yard for his tenth birthday.

Beckman's interest in chemistry was fostered by his high school teachers, and he eventually attended the University of Illinois, Urbana–Champaign. He graduated with

Arnold Beckman.

a bachelor's degree in chemical engineering in 1922 and stayed one more year to get a master's degree. He then went to Caltech, where he earned a Ph.D. and became a faculty member.

[H⁺] scale figure:

[H⁺]	pH	
10^{-14}	14	← 1 *M* NaOH
10^{-13}	13	
Basic 10^{-12}	12	← Ammonia
		(Household
10^{-11}	11	cleaner)
10^{-10}	10	
10^{-9}	9	
10^{-8}	8	
		← Blood
Neutral 10^{-7}	7	← Pure water
		← Milk
10^{-6}	6	
10^{-5}	5	
10^{-4}	4	
10^{-3}	3	← Vinegar
		← Lemon juice
Acidic 10^{-2}	2	← Stomach acid
10^{-1}	1	
1	0	← 1 *M* HCl

FIGURE 14.8
The pH scale and pH values of some common substances.

Solution

a.
$$[H^+] = \frac{K_w}{[OH^-]} = \frac{1.0 \times 10^{-14}}{1.0 \times 10^{-3}} = 1.0 \times 10^{-11}\ M$$

$$pH = -\log[H^+] = -\log(1.0 \times 10^{-11}) = 11.00$$

$$pOH = -\log[OH^-] = -\log(1.0 \times 10^{-3}) = 3.00$$

b.
$$[OH^-] = \frac{K_w}{[H^+]} = \frac{1.0 \times 10^{-14}}{1.0} = 1.0 \times 10^{-14}\ M$$

$$pH = -\log[H^+] = -\log(1.0) = 0.00$$

$$pOH = -\log[OH^-] = -\log(1.0 \times 10^{-14}) = 14.00$$

See Exercise 14.41.

It is useful to consider the log form of the expression

$$K_w = [H^+][OH^-]$$

FIGURE 14.9
pH meters are used to measure acidity.

Beckman was always known for his inventiveness. As a youth he designed a pressurized fuel system for his Model T Ford to overcome problems with its normal gravity feed fuel system—you had to *back* it up steep hills to keep it from starving for fuel. In 1927 he applied for his first patent: a buzzer to alert drivers that they were speeding.

In 1935 Beckman invented something that would cause a revolution in scientific instrumentation. A college friend who worked in a laboratory in the California citrus industry needed an accurate, convenient way to measure the acidity of orange juice. In response, Beckman invented the pH meter, which he initially called the acidimeter. This compact, sturdy device was an immediate hit. It signaled a new era in scientific instrumentation. In fact, business was so good that Beckman left Caltech to head his own company.

Over the years Beckman invented many other devices, including an improved potentiometer and an instrument for measuring the light absorbed by molecules. At age 65 he retired as president of Beckman Instruments (headquartered in Fullerton, California). After a merger the company be-

came Beckman Coulter; it had sales of more than $2 billion in 2003.

After stepping down as president of Beckman Instruments, Beckman began a new career—donating his wealth for the improvement of science. In 1984 he and Mabel, his wife of 58 years, donated $40 million to his alma mater—the University of Illinois—to fund the Beckman Institute. The Beckmans have also funded many other research institutes, including one at Caltech, and formed a foundation that currently gives $20 million each year to various scientific endeavors.

Arnold Beckman was a man known for his incredible creativity but even more he was recognized as a man of absolute integrity. Mr. Beckman has important words for us: "Whatever you do, be enthusiastic about it."

Note: You can see Arnold Beckman's biography at the Chemical Heritage Foundation Web site (http://www.chemheritage.org).

That is,

$$\log K_w = \log[H^+] + \log[OH^-]$$

or

$$-\log K_w = -\log[H^+] - \log[OH^-]$$

Thus

$$pK_w = pH + pOH \qquad (14.3)$$

Since $K_w = 1.0 \times 10^{-14}$,

$$pK_w = -\log(1.0 \times 10^{-14}) = 14.00$$

Thus, for *any* aqueous solution at 25°C, pH and pOH add up to 14.00:

$$pH + pOH = 14.00 \qquad (14.4)$$

Sample Exercise 14.6

Calculating pH

The pH of a sample of human blood was measured to be 7.41 at 25°C. Calculate pOH, $[H^+]$, and $[OH^-]$ for the sample.

Solution

Since pH + pOH = 14.00,

$$pOH = 14.00 - pH = 14.00 - 7.41 = 6.59$$

To find $[H^+]$ we must go back to the definition of pH:

$$pH = -\log[H^+]$$

Thus

$$7.41 = -\log[H^+] \quad \text{or} \quad \log[H^+] = -7.41$$

We need to know the *antilog* of -7.41. As shown in Appendix 1.2, taking the antilog is the same as exponentiation; that is,

antilog(n) = log$^{-1}(n)$

$$\text{antilog}(n) = 10^n$$

Since pH = $-\log[H^+]$,

$$-\text{pH} = \log[H^+]$$

and $[H^+]$ can be calculated by taking the antilog of $-\text{pH}$:

$$[H^+] = \text{antilog}(-\text{pH})$$

In the present case,

$$[H^+] = \text{antilog}(-\text{pH}) = \text{antilog}(-7.41) = 10^{-7.41} = 3.9 \times 10^{-8}$$

Similarly, $[OH^-] = \text{antilog}(-\text{pOH})$, and

$$[OH^-] = \text{antilog}(-6.59) = 10^{-6.59} = 2.6 \times 10^{-7} \, M$$

See Exercises 14.42 through 14.46.

Now that we have considered all the fundamental definitions relevant to acid–base solutions, we can proceed to a quantitative description of the equilibria present in these solutions. The main reason that acid–base problems sometimes seem difficult is that a typical aqueous solution contains many components, so the problems tend to be complicated. However, you can deal with these problems successfully if you use the following general strategies:

- *Think chemistry.* Focus on the solution components and their reactions. It will almost always be possible to choose one reaction that is the most important.

- *Be systematic.* Acid–base problems require a step-by-step approach.

- *Be flexible.* Although all acid–base problems are similar in many ways, important differences do occur. Treat each problem as a separate entity. Do not try to force a given problem into matching any you have solved before. Look for both the similarities and the differences.

- *Be patient.* The complete solution to a complicated problem cannot be seen immediately in all its detail. Pick the problem apart into its workable steps.

- *Be confident.* Look within the problem for the solution, and let the problem guide you. Assume that you can think it out. Do not rely on memorizing solutions to problems. In fact, memorizing solutions is usually detrimental because you tend to try to force a new problem to be the same as one you have seen before. *Understand and think; don't just memorize.*

14.4 Calculating the pH of Strong Acid Solutions

When we deal with acid–base equilibria, *we must focus on the solution components and their chemistry.* For example, what species are present in a 1.0 M solution of HCl? Since hydrochloric acid is a strong acid, we assume that it is completely dissociated. Thus, although the label on the bottle says 1.0 M HCl, the solution contains virtually no HCl molecules. Typically, container labels indicate the substance(s) used to make up the solution but do not necessarily describe the solution components after dissolution. Thus a 1.0 M HCl solution contains H^+ and Cl^- ions rather than HCl molecules.

The next step in dealing with aqueous solutions is to determine which components are significant and which can be ignored. We need to focus on the **major species,** those solution components present in relatively large amounts. In 1.0 M HCl, for example, the major species are H^+, Cl^-, and H_2O. Since this is a very acidic solution, OH^- is present

Common Strong Acids
HCl(*aq*)
HNO_3(*aq*)
H_2SO_4(*aq*)
$HClO_4$(*aq*)

only in tiny amounts and is classified as a minor species. In attacking acid–base problems, the importance of *writing the major species in the solution* as the first step cannot be overemphasized. *This single step is the key to solving these problems successfully.*

Always write the major species present in the solution.

To illustrate the main ideas involved, let us calculate the pH of 1.0 *M* HCl. We first list the major species: H^+, Cl^-, and H_2O. Since we want to calculate the pH, we will focus on those major species that can furnish H^+. Obviously, we must consider H^+ from the dissociation of HCl. However, H_2O also furnishes H^+ by autoionization, which is often represented by the simple dissociation reaction

$$H_2O(l) \rightleftharpoons H^+(aq) + OH^-(aq)$$

The H^+ from the strong acid drives the equilibrium $H_2O \rightleftharpoons H^+ + OH^-$ to the left.

However, is autoionization an important source of H^+ ions? In pure water at 25°C, $[H^+]$ is 10^{-7} *M*. In 1.0 *M* HCl solution, the water will produce even less than 10^{-27} *M* H^+, since by Le Châtelier's principle the H^+ from the dissociated HCl will drive the position of the water equilibrium to the left. Thus the amount of H^+ contributed by water is negligible compared with the 1.0 *M* H^+ from the dissociation of HCl. Therefore, we can say that $[H^+]$ in the solution is 1.0 *M*. The pH is then

$$pH = -\log[H^+] = -\log(1.0) = 0$$

| Sample Exercise 14.7 | **pH of Strong Acids** |

In pure water, only 10^{-7} *M* H^+ is produced.

a. Calculate the pH of 0.10 *M* HNO_3.
b. Calculate the pH of 1.0×10^{-10} *M* HCl.

Solution

Major Species

H^+

NO_3^-

H_2O

a. Since HNO_3 is a strong acid, the major species in solution are

$$H^+, \quad NO_3^-, \quad \text{and} \quad H_2O$$

The concentration of HNO_3 is virtually zero, since the acid completely dissociates in water. Also, $[OH^-]$ will be very small because the H^+ ions from the acid will drive the equilibrium

$$H_2O(l) \rightleftharpoons H^+(aq) + OH^-(aq)$$

to the left. That is, this is an acidic solution where $[H^+] \gg [OH^-]$, so $[OH^-] \ll 10^{-7}$ *M*. The sources of H^+ are

1. H^+ from HNO_3 (0.10 *M*)
2. H^+ from H_2O

The number of H^+ ions contributed by the autoionization of water will be very small compared with the 0.10 *M* contributed by the HNO_3 and can be neglected. Since the dissolved HNO_3 is the only important source of H^+ ions in this solution,

$$[H^+] = 0.10 \; M \quad \text{and} \quad pH = -\log(0.10) = 1.00$$

b. Normally, in an aqueous solution of HCl the major species are H^+, Cl^-, and H_2O. However, in this case the amount of HCl in solution is so small that it has no effect; the only major species is H_2O. Thus the pH will be that of pure water, or pH = 7.00.

See Exercises 14.47 and 14.48.

14.5 Calculating the pH of Weak Acid Solutions

Since a weak acid dissolved in water can be viewed as a prototype of almost any equilibrium occurring in aqueous solution, we will proceed carefully and systematically. Although some of the procedures we develop here may seem unnecessary, they will become essential as the problems become more complicated. We will develop the necessary strategies by calculating the pH of a 1.00 M solution of HF ($K_a = 7.2 \times 10^{-4}$).

The first step, as always, is to *write the major species in the solution.* From its small K_a value, we know that hydrofluoric acid is a weak acid and will be dissociated only to a slight extent. Thus, when we write the major species, the hydrofluoric acid will be represented in its dominant form, as HF. The major species in solution are HF and H_2O.

The next step (since this is a pH problem) is to decide which of the major species can furnish H^+ ions. Actually, both major species can do so:

$$HF(aq) \rightleftharpoons H^+(aq) + F^-(aq) \qquad K_a = 7.2 \times 10^{-4}$$
$$H_2O(l) \rightleftharpoons H^+(aq) + OH^-(aq) \qquad K_w = 1.0 \times 10^{-14}$$

In aqueous solutions, however, typically one source of H^+ can be singled out as dominant. By comparing K_a for HF with K_w for H_2O, we see that hydrofluoric acid, although weak, is still a much stronger acid than water. Thus we will assume that hydrofluoric acid will be the dominant source of H^+. We will ignore the tiny contribution by water.

Therefore, it is the dissociation of HF that will determine the equilibrium concentration of H^+ and hence the pH:

$$HF(aq) \rightleftharpoons H^+(aq) + F^-(aq)$$

The equilibrium expression is

$$K_a = 7.2 \times 10^{-4} = \frac{[H^+][F^-]}{[HF]}$$

To solve the equilibrium problem, we follow the procedures developed in Chapter 13 for gas-phase equilibria. First, we list the initial concentrations, the *concentrations before the reaction of interest has proceeded to equilibrium.* Before any HF dissociates, the concentrations of the species in the equilibrium are

$$[HF]_0 = 1.00\ M \quad [F^-]_0 = 0 \quad [H^+]_0 = 10^{-7}\ M \approx 0$$

(Note that the zero value for $[H^+]_0$ is an approximation, since we are neglecting the H^+ ions from the autoionization of water.)

The next step is to determine the change required to reach equilibrium. Since some HF will dissociate to come to equilibrium (but this amount is presently unknown), we let x be the change in the concentration of HF that is required to achieve equilibrium. That is, we assume that x mol/L HF will dissociate to produce x mol/L H^+ and x mol/L F^- as the system adjusts to its equilibrium position. Now the equilibrium concentrations can be defined in terms of x:

$$[HF] = [HF]_0 - x = 1.00 - x$$
$$[F^-] = [F^-]_0 + x = 0 + x = x$$
$$[H^+] = [H^+]_0 + x \approx 0 + x = x$$

Substituting these equilibrium concentrations into the equilibrium expression gives

$$K_a = 7.2 \times 10^{-4} = \frac{[H^+][F^-]}{[HF]} = \frac{(x)(x)}{1.00 - x}$$

This expression produces a quadratic equation that can be solved using the quadratic formula, as for the gas-phase systems in Chapter 13. However, since K_a for HF is so small, HF will dissociate only slightly, and x is expected to be small. This will allow us to simplify the calculation. If x is very small compared to 1.00, the term in the denominator can be approximated as follows:

$$1.00 - x \approx 1.00$$

First, *always* write the major species present in the solution.

Major Species

 HF

 H_2O

The equilibrium expression then becomes

$$7.2 \times 10^{-4} = \frac{(x)(x)}{1.00 - x} \approx \frac{(x)(x)}{1.00}$$

which yields

$$x^2 \approx (7.2 \times 10^{-4})(1.00) = 7.2 \times 10^{-4}$$
$$x \approx \sqrt{7.2 \times 10^{-4}} = 2.7 \times 10^{-2}$$

The validity of an approximation should always be checked.

How valid is the approximation that $[HF] = 1.00\ M$? Because this question will arise often in connection with acid–base equilibrium calculations, we will consider it carefully. *The validity of the approximation depends on how much accuracy we demand for the calculated value of [H⁺].* Typically, the K_a values for acids are known to an accuracy of only about $\pm 5\%$. It is reasonable therefore to apply this figure when determining the validity of the approximation

$$[HA]_0 - x \approx [HA]_0$$

We will use the following test. First, we calculate the value of x by making the approximation

$$K_a = \frac{x^2}{[HA]_0 - x} \approx \frac{x^2}{[HA]_0}$$

where

$$x^2 \approx K_a[HA]_0 \quad \text{and} \quad x \approx \sqrt{K_a[HA]_0}$$

We then compare the sizes of x and $[HA]_0$. If the expression

$$\frac{x}{[HA]_0} \times 100\%$$

is less than or equal to 5%, the value of x is small enough that the approximation

$$[HA]_0 - x \approx [HA]_0$$

will be considered valid.

In our example,

$$x = 2.7 \times 10^{-2}\ \text{mol/L}$$
$$[HA]_0 = [HF]_0 = 1.00\ \text{mol/L}$$

and

$$\frac{x}{[HA]_0} \times 100 = \frac{2.7 \times 10^{-2}}{1.00} \times 100\% = 2.7\%$$

The approximation we made is considered valid, and the value of x calculated using that approximation is acceptable. Thus

$$x = [H^+] = 2.7 \times 10^{-2}\ M \quad \text{and} \quad pH = -\log(2.7 \times 10^{-2}) = 1.57$$

This problem illustrates all the important steps for solving a typical equilibrium problem involving a weak acid. These steps are summarized as follows:

Solving Weak Acid Equilibrium Problems

⇨ 1 **List the major species in the solution.**

⇨ 2 **Choose the species that can produce H⁺, and write balanced equations for the reactions producing H⁺.**

⇨ 3 **Using the values of the equilibrium constants for the reactions you have written, decide which equilibrium will dominate in producing H⁺.**

⇨ 4 **Write the equilibrium expression for the dominant equilibrium.**

The K_a values for various weak acids are given in Table 14.2 and in Appendix 5.1.

➡ 5 **List the initial concentrations of the species participating in the dominant equilibrium.**

➡ 6 **Define the change needed to achieve equilibrium; that is, define x.**

➡ 7 **Write the equilibrium concentrations in terms of x.**

➡ 8 **Substitute the equilibrium concentrations into the equilibrium expression.**

➡ 9 **Solve for x the "easy" way, that is, by assuming that $[HA]_0 - x \approx [HA]_0$.**

➡ 10 **Use the 5% rule to verify whether the approximation is valid.**

➡ 11 **Calculate $[H^+]$ and pH.**

We use this systematic approach in Sample Exercise 14.8.

Sample Exercise 14.8

The pH of Weak Acids

The hypochlorite ion (OCl^-) is a strong oxidizing agent often found in household bleaches and disinfectants. It is also the active ingredient that forms when swimming pool water is treated with chlorine. In addition to its oxidizing abilities, the hypochlorite ion has a relatively high affinity for protons (it is a much stronger base than Cl^-, for example) and forms the weakly acidic hypochlorous acid ($HOCl$, $K_a = 3.5 \times 10^{-8}$). Calculate the pH of a 0.100 M aqueous solution of hypochlorous acid.

Major Species

 HOCl

 H₂O

Swimming pool water must be frequently tested for pH and chlorine content.

Solution

➡ 1 We list the major species. Since HOCl is a weak acid and remains mostly undissociated, the major species in a 0.100 M HOCl solution are

$$HOCl \quad \text{and} \quad H_2O$$

➡ 2 Both species can produce H^+:

$$HOCl(aq) \rightleftharpoons H^+(aq) + OCl^-(aq) \qquad K_a = 3.5 \times 10^{-8}$$
$$H_2O(l) \rightleftharpoons H^+(aq) + OH^-(aq) \qquad K_w = 1.0 \times 10^{-14}$$

➡ 3 Since HOCl is a significantly stronger acid than H_2O, it will dominate in the production of H^+.

➡ 4 We therefore use the following equilibrium expression:

$$K_a = 3.5 \times 10^{-8} = \frac{[H^+][OCl^-]}{[HOCl]}$$

➡ 5 The initial concentrations appropriate for this equilibrium are

$$[HOCl]_0 = 0.100 \, M$$
$$[OCl^-]_0 = 0$$
$$[H^+]_0 \approx 0 \qquad \text{(We neglect the contribution from H}_2\text{O.)}$$

➡ 6 Since the system will reach equilibrium by the dissociation of HOCl, let x be the amount of HOCl (in mol/L) that dissociates in reaching equilibrium.

➡ 7 The equilibrium concentrations in terms of x are

$$[HOCl] = [HOCl]_0 - x = 0.100 - x$$
$$[OCl^-] = [OCl^-]_0 + x = 0 + x = x$$
$$[H^+] = [H^+]_0 + x \approx 0 + x = x$$

➡ 8 Substituting these concentrations into the equilibrium expression gives

$$K_a = 3.5 \times 10^{-8} = \frac{(x)(x)}{0.100 - x}$$

➡ **9** Since K_a is so small, we can expect a small value for x. Thus we make the approximation $[HA]_0 - x \approx [HA]_0$,   or $0.100 - x \approx 0.100$, which leads to the expression

$$K_a = 3.5 \times 10^{-8} = \frac{x^2}{0.100 - x} \approx \frac{x^2}{0.100}$$

Solving for x gives

$$x = 5.9 \times 10^{-5}$$

➡ **10** The approximation $0.100 - x \approx 0.100$ must be validated. To do this, we compare x to $[HOCl]_0$:

$$\frac{x}{[HA]_0} \times 100 = \frac{x}{[HOCl]_0} \times 100 = \frac{5.9 \times 10^{-5}}{0.100} \times 100 = 0.059\%$$

Since this value is much less than 5%, the approximation is considered valid.

➡ **11** We calculate $[H^+]$ and pH:

$$[H^+] = x = 5.9 \times 10^{-5}\,M \qquad \text{and} \qquad pH = 4.23$$

See Exercises 14.53 through 14.55.

The pH of a Mixture of Weak Acids

The same systematic approach applies to all solution equilibria.

Sometimes a solution contains two weak acids of very different strengths. This case is considered in Sample Exercise 14.9. Note that the steps are again followed (though not labeled).

Sample Exercise 14.9 | ## The pH of Weak Acid Mixtures

Calculate the pH of a solution that contains $1.00\,M$ HCN ($K_a = 6.2 \times 10^{-10}$) and $5.00\,M$ HNO$_2$ ($K_a = 4.0 \times 10^{-4}$). Also calculate the concentration of cyanide ion (CN^-) in this solution at equilibrium.

Solution

Since HCN and HNO$_2$ are both weak acids and are largely undissociated, the major species in the solution are

Major Species

 HCN

 HNO$_2$

H$_2$O

$$\text{HCN,} \quad \text{HNO}_2, \quad \text{and} \quad \text{H}_2\text{O}$$

All three of these components produce H^+:

$$HCN(aq) \rightleftharpoons H^+(aq) + CN^-(aq) \qquad K_a = 6.2 \times 10^{-10}$$
$$HNO_2(aq) \rightleftharpoons H^+(aq) + NO_2^-(aq) \qquad K_a = 4.0 \times 10^{-4}$$
$$H_2O(l) \rightleftharpoons H^+(aq) + OH^-(aq) \qquad K_w = 1.0 \times 10^{-14}$$

A mixture of three acids might lead to a very complicated problem. However, the situation is greatly simplified by the fact that even though HNO$_2$ is a weak acid, it is much stronger than the other two acids present (as revealed by the K values). Thus HNO$_2$ can be assumed to be the dominant producer of H^+, and we will focus on the equilibrium expression

$$K_a = 4.0 \times 10^{-4} = \frac{[H^+][NO_2^-]}{[HNO_2]}$$

The initial concentrations, the definition of x, and the equilibrium concentrations are as follows:

Initial Concentration (mol/L)		Equilibrium Concentration (mol/L)
$[HNO_2]_0 = 5.00$	$\xrightarrow{\substack{x \text{ mol/L } HNO_2 \\ \text{dissociates}}}$	$[HNO_2] = 5.00 - x$
$[NO_2^-]_0 = 0$		$[NO_2^-] = x$
$[H^+]_0 \approx 0$		$[H^+] = x$

It is convenient to represent these concentrations in the following shorthand form (called an ICE table):

To avoid clutter we do not show the units of concentration in the ICE tables. All terms have units of mol/L.

	$HNO_2(aq)$	$\rightleftharpoons$	$H^-(aq)$	$+$	$NO_2^-(aq)$
Initial:	5.00		0		0
Change:	$-x$		$+x$		$+x$
Equilibrium:	$5.00 - x$		x		x

Substituting the equilibrium concentrations in the equilibrium expression and making the approximation that $5.00 - x = 5.00$ give

$$K_a = 4.0 \times 10^{-4} = \frac{(x)(x)}{5.00 - x} \approx \frac{x^2}{5.00}$$

We solve for x:

$$x = 4.5 \times 10^{-2}$$

Using the 5% rule, we show that the approximation is valid:

$$\frac{x}{[HNO_2]_0} \times 100 = \frac{4.5 \times 10^{-2}}{5.00} \times 100 = 0.90\%$$

Therefore,

$$[H^+] = x = 4.5 \times 10^{-2} M \quad \text{and} \quad pH = 1.35$$

We also want to calculate the equilibrium concentration of cyanide ion in this solution. The CN^- ions in this solution come from the dissociation of HCN:

$$HCN(aq) \rightleftharpoons H^+(aq) + CN^-(aq)$$

Although the position of this equilibrium lies far to the left and does not contribute *significantly* to $[H^+]$, HCN is the *only source* of CN^-. Thus we must consider the extent of the dissociation of HCN to calculate $[CN^-]$. The equilibrium expression for the preceding reaction is

$$K_a = 6.2 \times 10^{-10} = \frac{[H^+][CN^-]}{[HCN]}$$

We know $[H^+]$ for this solution from the results of the first part of the problem. It is important to understand that *there is only one kind of H^+ in this solution.* It does not matter from which acid the H^+ ions originate. The equilibrium $[H^+]$ we need to insert into the HCN equilibrium expression is $4.5 \times 10^{-2} M$, even though the H^+ was contributed almost entirely from the dissociation of HNO_2. What is [HCN] at equilibrium? We know $[HCN]_0 = 1.00 \, M$, and since K_a for HCN is so small, a negligible amount of HCN will dissociate. Thus

$$[HCN] = [HCN]_0 - \text{amount of HCN dissociated} \approx [HCN]_0 = 1.00 \, M$$

Since $[H^+]$ and $[HCN]$ are known, we can find $[CN^-]$ from the equilibrium expression:

$$K_a = 6.2 \times 10^{-10} = \frac{[H^+][CN^-]}{[HCN]} = \frac{(4.5 \times 10^{-2})[CN^-]}{1.00}$$

$$[CN^-] = \frac{(6.2 \times 10^{-10})(1.00)}{4.5 \times 10^{-2}} = 1.4 \times 10^{-8}\,M$$

Note the significance of this result. Since $[CN^-] = 1.4 \times 10^{-8}\,M$ and HCN is the only source of CN^-, this means that only 1.4×10^{-8} mol/L of HCN dissociated. This is a very small amount compared with the initial concentration of HCN, which is exactly what we would expect from its very small K_a value, and $[HCN] = 1.00\,M$ as assumed.

See Exercises 14.61 and 14.62.

Percent Dissociation

Percent dissociation is also known as *percent ionization.*

It is often useful to specify the amount of weak acid that has dissociated in achieving equilibrium in an aqueous solution. The **percent dissociation** is defined as follows:

$$\text{Percent dissociation} = \frac{\text{amount dissociated (mol/L)}}{\text{initial concentration (mol/L)}} \times 100\% \qquad (14.5)$$

For example, we found earlier that in a $1.00\,M$ solution of HF, $[H^+] = 2.7 \times 10^{-2}\,M$. To reach equilibrium, 2.7×10^{-2} mol/L of the original $1.00\,M$ HF dissociates, so

$$\text{Percent dissociation} = \frac{2.7 \times 10^{-2}\,\text{mol/L}}{1.00\,\text{mol/L}} \times 100\% = 2.7\%$$

For a given weak acid, the percent dissociation increases as the acid becomes more dilute. For example, the percent dissociation of acetic acid ($HC_2H_3O_2$, $K_a = 1.8 \times 10^{-5}$) is significantly greater in a $0.10\,M$ solution than in a $1.0\,M$ solution, as demonstrated in Sample Exercise 14.10.

| *Sample Exercise 14.10* | ## Calculating Percent Dissociation |

Calculate the percent dissociation of acetic acid ($K_a = 1.8 \times 10^{-5}$) in each of the following solutions.

a. $1.00\,M\ HC_2H_3O_2$
b. $0.100\,M\ HC_2H_3O_2$

Solution

Major Species

$HC_2H_3O_2$

H_2O

a. Since acetic acid is a weak acid, the major species in this solution are $HC_2H_3O_2$ and H_2O. Both species are weak acids, but acetic acid is a much stronger acid than water. Thus the dominant equilibrium will be

$$HC_2H_3O_2(aq) \rightleftharpoons H^+(aq) + C_2H_3O_2{}^-(aq)$$

and the equilibrium expression is

$$K_a = 1.8 \times 10^{-5} = \frac{[H^+][C_2H_3O_2{}^-]}{[HC_2H_3O_2]}$$

The initial concentrations, definition of x, and equilibrium concentrations are:

	$HC_2H_3O_2(aq)$	$\rightleftharpoons$	$H^+(aq)$	$+$	$C_2H_3O_2{}^-(aq)$
Initial:	1.00		0		0
Change:	$-x$		x		x
Equilibrium:	$1.00 - x$		x		x

An acetic acid solution, which is a weak electrolyte, contains only a few ions and does not conduct as much current as a strong electrolyte. The bulb is only dimly lit.

Inserting the equilibrium concentrations into the equilibrium expression and making the usual approximation that x is small compared with $[HA]_0$ give

$$K_a = 1.8 \times 10^{-5} = \frac{[H^+][C_2H_3O_2^-]}{[HC_2H_3O_2]} = \frac{(x)(x)}{1.00 - x} \approx \frac{x^2}{1.00}$$

Thus

$$x^2 \approx 1.8 \times 10^{-5} \quad \text{and} \quad x \approx 4.2 \times 10^{-3}$$

The approximation $1.00 - x \approx 1.00$ is valid by the 5% rule (check this yourself), so

$$[H^+] = x = 4.2 \times 10^{-3} \, M$$

The percent dissociation is

$$\frac{[H^+]}{[HC_2H_3O_2]_0} \times 100 = \frac{4.2 \times 10^{-3}}{1.00} \times 100\% = 0.42\%$$

b. This is a similar problem, except that in this case $[HC_2H_3O_2] = 0.100 \, M$. Analysis of the problem leads to the expression

$$K_a = 1.8 \times 10^{-5} = \frac{[H^+][C_2H_3O_2^-]}{[HC_2H_3O_2]} = \frac{(x)(x)}{0.100 - x} \approx \frac{x^2}{0.100}$$

Thus

$$x = [H^+] = 1.3 \times 10^{-3} \, M$$

and

$$\text{Percent dissociation} = \frac{1.3 \times 10^{-3}}{0.10} \times 100\% = 1.3\%$$

See Exercises 14.63 and 14.64.

The results in Sample Exercise 14.10 show two important facts. The concentration of H^+ ion at equilibrium is smaller in the 0.10 M acetic acid solution than in the 1.0 M acetic acid solution, as we would expect. However, the percent dissociation is significantly greater in the 0.10 M solution than in the 1.0 M solution. This is a general result. *For solutions of any weak acid HA, $[H^+]$ decreases as $[HA]_0$ decreases, but the percent dissociation increases as $[HA]_0$ decreases.* This phenomenon can be explained as follows.

The more dilute the weak acid solution, the greater is the percent dissociation.

Consider the weak acid HA with the initial concentration $[HA]_0$, where at equilibrium

$$[HA] = [HA]_0 - x \approx [HA]_0$$
$$[H^+] = [A^-] = x$$

Thus

$$K_a = \frac{[H^+][A^-]}{[HA]} \approx \frac{(x)(x)}{[HA]_0}$$

Now suppose enough water is added suddenly to dilute the solution by a factor of 10. The new concentrations before any adjustment occurs are

$$[A^-]_{new} = [H^+]_{new} = \frac{x}{10}$$

$$[HA]_{new} = \frac{[HA]_0}{10}$$

and Q, the reaction quotient, is

$$Q = \frac{\left(\dfrac{x}{10}\right)\left(\dfrac{x}{10}\right)}{\dfrac{[HA]_0}{10}} = \frac{1(x)(x)}{10[HA]_0} = \frac{1}{10}K_a$$

Since Q is less than K_a, the system must adjust to the right to reach the new equilibrium position. Thus the percent dissociation increases when the acid is diluted. This behavior

CHEMICAL IMPACT

Household Chemistry

Common household bleach is an aqueous solution containing approximately 5% sodium hypochlorite, a potent oxidizing agent that can react with and decolorize chemicals that cause stains. Bleaching solutions are manufactured by dissolving chlorine gas in a sodium hydroxide solution to give the reaction

$$Cl_2(g) + 2OH^-(aq) \rightleftharpoons OCl^-(aq) + Cl^-(aq) + H_2O(l)$$

As long as the pH of this solution is maintained above 8, the OCl^- ion is the predominant chlorine-containing species. However, if the solution is made acidic (the $[OH^-]$ lowered), elemental chlorine (Cl_2) is favored, and since Cl_2 is much less soluble in water than is sodium hypochlorite, Cl_2 gas is suddenly evolved from the solution. This is why labels on bottles of bleach carry warnings about mixing the bleach with other cleaning solutions. For example, toilet bowl cleaners usually contain acids such as H_3PO_4 or HSO_4^- and have pH values around 2. Mixing toilet bowl cleaner with bleach can lead to a very dangerous evolution of chlorine gas.

In addition, if bleach is mixed with a cleaning agent containing ammonia, the chlorine and ammonia can react to produce chloramines, such as NH_2Cl, $NHCl_2$, and NCl_3. These compounds produce acrid fumes that can cause respiratory distress.

HOUSEHOLD USE

Toilet bowls. Flush toilet. Pour 1 cup of bleach into bowl. Brush. Let stand 10 minutes before flushing again.

Kitchen sinks. Cover stains with 1 gallon of water before adding 2/3 cup of Safeway Regular Ultra Bleach. Let stand 5 minutes before rinsing.

Bathtubs and showers, floors, vinyl, tile, woodwork and appliances. Clean with a solution of 2/3 cup of bleach per gallon of warm water. Let stand 5 minutes before rinsing.

DANGER: CORROSIVE.
Contains Sodium Hypochlorite
Contains No Phosphates

Causes substantial but temporary eye injury. Avoid contact with eyes or on clothing. Harmful if swallowed. May irritate skin. For prolonged use, wear gloves. **Treatment:** If in eyes rinse with plenty of water for 15 minutes. If swallowed, drink a glassful of water. Call physician or Poison Control Center in either case. If in contact with skin wash skin thoroughly with soap and water. **Add only to water, do not mix with acid or other household chemicals** such as toilet bowl cleaners, ammonia or rust removers. To do so may release hazardous gases. Prolonged contact with metal may cause pitting or discoloration. **Storage and disposal:** Store in a cool dry area, away from direct sunlight and heat to avoid deterioration. Do not reuse empty container; instead, rinse and put in trash collection.

The label on this bleach bottle warns of the hazards of mixing cleaning solutions.

---

is summarized in Fig. 14.10. In Sample Exercise 14.11 we see how the percent dissociation can be used to calculate the K_a value for a weak acid.

Sample Exercise 14.11

Calculating K_a from Percent Dissociation

Lactic acid ($HC_3H_5O_3$) is a waste product that accumulates in muscle tissue during exertion, leading to pain and a feeling of fatigue. In a 0.100 M aqueous solution, lactic acid is 3.7% dissociated. Calculate the value of K_a for this acid.

Solution

From the small value for the percent dissociation, it is clear that $HC_3H_5O_3$ is a weak acid. Thus the major species in the solution are the undissociated acid and water:

$$HC_3H_5O_3 \quad \text{and} \quad H_2O$$

However, even though $HC_3H_5O_3$ is a weak acid, it is a much stronger acid than water and will be the dominant source of H^+ in the solution. The dissociation reaction is

$$HC_3H_5O_3(aq) \rightleftharpoons H^+(aq) + C_3H_5O_3^-(aq)$$

and the equilibrium expression is

$$K_a = \frac{[H^+][C_3H_5O_3^-]}{[HC_3H_5O_3]}$$

More concentrated　　**More dilute**

Acid concentration

Percent dissociation

H^+ concentration

FIGURE 14.10
The effect of dilution on the percent dissociation and $[H^+]$ of a weak acid solution.

Major Species

$HC_3H_5O_3$

H_2O

Strenuous exercise causes a buildup of lactic acid in muscle tissues.

In a basic solution at 25°C, pH > 7.

Visualization: Limewater and Carbon Dioxide

The initial and equilibrium concentrations are as follows:

Initial Concentration (mol/L)		Equilibrium Concentration (mol/L)
$[HC_3H_5O_3]_0 = 0.10$		$[HC_3H_5O_3] = 0.10 - x$
$[C_3H_5O_3^-]_0 = 0$	$\xrightarrow[\substack{HC_3H_5O_3 \\ dissociates}]{x \text{ mol/L}}$	$[C_3H_5O_3^-] = x$
$[H^+]_0 \approx 0$		$[H^+] = x$

The change needed to reach equilibrium can be obtained from the percent dissociation and Equation (14.5). For this acid,

$$\text{Percent dissociation} = 3.7\% = \frac{x}{[HC_3H_5O_3]_0} \times 100\% = \frac{x}{0.10} \times 100\%$$

and

$$x = \frac{3.7}{100}(0.10) = 3.7 \times 10^{-3} \text{ mol/L}$$

Now we can calculate the equilibrium concentrations:

$$[HC_3H_5O_3] = 0.10 - x = 0.10 \, M \qquad \text{(to the correct number of significant figures)}$$
$$[C_3H_5O_3^-] = [H^+] = x = 3.7 \times 10^{-3} \, M$$

These concentrations can now be used to calculate the value of K_a for lactic acid:

$$K_a = \frac{[H^+][C_3H_5O_3^-]}{[HC_3H_5O_3]} = \frac{(3.7 \times 10^{-3})(3.7 \times 10^{-3})}{0.10} = 1.4 \times 10^{-4}$$

See Exercises 14.65 and 14.66.

14.6 Bases

According to the Arrhenius concept, a base is a substance that produces OH^- ions in aqueous solution. According to the Brønsted–Lowry model, a base is a proton acceptor. The bases sodium hydroxide (NaOH) and potassium hydroxide (KOH) fulfill both criteria. They contain OH^- ions in the solid lattice and, behaving as strong electrolytes, dissociate completely when dissolved in aqueous solution:

$$NaOH(s) \longrightarrow Na^+(aq) + OH^-(aq)$$

leaving virtually no undissociated NaOH. Thus a 1.0 *M* NaOH solution really contains 1.0 *M* Na^+ and 1.0 *M* OH^-. Because of their complete dissociation, NaOH and KOH are called **strong bases** in the same sense as we defined strong acids.

All the hydroxides of the Group 1A elements (LiOH, NaOH, KOH, RbOH, and CsOH) are strong bases, but only NaOH and KOH are common laboratory reagents, because the lithium, rubidium, and cesium compounds are expensive. The alkaline earth (Group 2A) hydroxides—$Ca(OH)_2$, $Ba(OH)_2$, and $Sr(OH)_2$—are also strong bases. For these compounds, two moles of hydroxide ion are produced for every mole of metal hydroxide dissolved in aqueous solution.

The alkaline earth hydroxides are not very soluble and are used only when the solubility factor is not important. In fact, the low solubility of these bases can sometimes be an advantage. For example, many antacids are suspensions of metal hydroxides, such as aluminum hydroxide and magnesium hydroxide. The low solubility of these compounds prevents a large hydroxide ion concentration that would harm the tissues of the mouth, esophagus, and stomach. Yet these suspensions furnish plenty of

An antacid containing aluminum and magnesium hydroxides.

Calcium carbonate is also used in scrubbing, as discussed in Section 5.10.

hydroxide ion to react with the stomach acid, since the salts dissolve as this reaction proceeds.

Calcium hydroxide, $Ca(OH)_2$, often called **slaked lime,** is widely used in industry because it is inexpensive and plentiful. For example, slaked lime is used in scrubbing stack gases to remove sulfur dioxide from the exhaust of power plants and factories. In the scrubbing process a suspension of slaked lime is sprayed into the stack gases to react with sulfur dioxide gas according to the following steps:

$$SO_2(g) + H_2O(l) \rightleftharpoons H_2SO_3(aq)$$
$$Ca(OH)_2(aq) + H_2SO_3(aq) \rightleftharpoons CaSO_3(s) + 2H_2O(l)$$

Slaked lime is also widely used in water treatment plants for softening hard water, which involves the removal of ions, such as Ca^{2+} and Mg^{2+}, that hamper the action of detergents. The softening method most often employed in water treatment plants is the **lime–soda process,** in which *lime* (CaO) and *soda ash* (Na_2CO_3) are added to the water. As we will see in more detail later in this chapter, the CO_3^{2-} ion reacts with water to produce the HCO_3^- ion. When the lime is added to the water, it forms slaked lime, that is,

$$CaO(s) + H_2O(l) \longrightarrow Ca(OH)_2(aq)$$

which then reacts with the HCO_3^- ion from the added soda ash and the Ca^{2+} ion in the hard water to produce calcium carbonate:

$$Ca(OH)_2(aq) + \underset{\underset{\text{From hard water}}{\nearrow}}{Ca^{2+}}(aq) + 2HCO_3^-(aq) \longrightarrow 2CaCO_3(s) + 2H_2O(l)$$

Thus, for every mole of $Ca(OH)_2$ consumed, 1 mole of Ca^{2+} is removed from the hard water, thereby softening it. Some hard water naturally contains bicarbonate ions. In this case, no soda ash is needed—simply adding the lime produces the softening.

Calculating the pH of a strong base solution is relatively simple, as illustrated in Sample Exercise 14.12.

Sample Exercise 14.12 | **The pH of Strong Bases**

Calculate the pH of a $5.0 \times 10^{-2}\,M$ NaOH solution.

Major Species

 Na^+

 OH^-

 H_2O

Solution

The major species in this solution are

$$\underbrace{Na^+, \quad OH^-,}_{\text{From NaOH}} \quad \text{and} \quad H_2O$$

Although autoionization of water also produces OH^- ions, the pH will be dominated by the OH^- ions from the dissolved NaOH. Thus, in the solution,

$$[OH^-] = 5.0 \times 10^{-2}\,M$$

and the concentration of H^+ can be calculated from K_w:

$$[H^+] = \frac{K_w}{[OH^-]} = \frac{1.0 \times 10^{-14}}{5.0 \times 10^{-2}} = 2.0 - 10^{-13}\,M$$
$$pH = 12.70$$

Note that this is a basic solution for which

$$[OH^-] > [H^+] \quad \text{and} \quad pH > 7$$

The added OH^- from the salt has shifted the water autoionization equilibrium

$$H_2O(l) \rightleftharpoons H^+(aq) + OH^-(aq)$$

to the left, significantly lowering $[H^+]$ compared with that in pure water.

See Exercises 14.77 through 14.80.

A base does not have to contain hydroxide ion.

Many types of proton acceptors (bases) do not contain the hydroxide ion. However, when dissolved in water, these substances increase the concentration of hydroxide ion because of their reaction with water. For example, ammonia reacts with water as follows:

$$NH_3(aq) + H_2O(l) \rightleftharpoons NH_4^+(aq) + OH^-(aq)$$

The ammonia molecule accepts a proton and thus functions as a base. Water is the acid in this reaction. Note that even though the base ammonia contains no hydroxide ion, it still increases the concentration of hydroxide ion to yield a basic solution.

Bases such as ammonia typically have at least one unshared pair of electrons that is capable of forming a bond with a proton. The reaction of an ammonia molecule with a water molecule can be represented as follows:

$$H-\overset{H}{\underset{H}{N}}: \quad H-\overset{..}{\underset{H}{O}}: \quad \rightleftharpoons \quad H-\overset{H}{\underset{H}{N^+}}-H \; + \; :\overset{..}{\underset{..}{O}}-H^-$$

There are many bases like ammonia that produce hydroxide ion by reaction with water. In most of these bases, the lone pair is located on a nitrogen atom. Some examples are

| Methylamine | Dimethylamine | Trimethylamine | Ethylamine | Pyridine |

Note that the first four bases can be thought of as substituted ammonia molecules with hydrogen atoms replaced by methyl (CH_3) or ethyl (C_2H_5) groups. The pyridine molecule is like benzene

except that a nitrogen atom replaces one of the carbon atoms in the ring. The general reaction between a base B and water is given by

$$\underset{\text{Base}}{B(aq)} + \underset{\text{Acid}}{H_2O(l)} \rightleftharpoons \underset{\substack{\text{Conjugate} \\ \text{acid}}}{BH^+(aq)} + \underset{\substack{\text{Conjugate} \\ \text{base}}}{OH^-(aq)} \qquad (14.6)$$

The equilibrium constant for this general reaction is

Appendix 5.3 contains a table of K_b values.

$$K_b = \frac{[BH^+][OH^-]}{[B]}$$

where K_b *always refers to the reaction of a base with water to form the conjugate acid and the hydroxide ion.*

Bases of the type represented by B in Equation (14.6) compete with OH^-, a very strong base, for the H^+ ion. Thus their K_b values tend to be small (for example, for ammonia, $K_b = 1.8 \times 10^{-5}$), and they are called **weak bases.** The values of K_b for some common weak bases are listed in Table 14.3.

TABLE 14.3   Values of K_b for Some Common Weak Bases

Name	Formula	Conjugate Acid	K_b
Ammonia	NH_3	NH_4^+	1.8×10^{-5}
Methylamine	CH_3NH_2	$CH_3NH_3^+$	4.38×10^{-4}
Ethylamine	$C_2H_5NH_2$	$C_2H_5NH_3^+$	5.6×10^{-4}
Aniline	$C_6H_5NH_2$	$C_6H_5NH_3^+$	3.8×10^{-10}
Pyridine	C_5H_5N	$C_5H_5NH^+$	1.7×10^{-9}

Visualization: Brønsted–Lowry Reaction

Typically, pH calculations for solutions of weak bases are very similar to those for weak acids, as illustrated by Sample Exercises 14.13 and 14.14.

Sample Exercise 14.13

The pH of Weak Bases I

Calculate the pH for a 15.0 M solution of NH_3 ($K_b = 1.8 \times 10^{-5}$).

Solution

Since ammonia is a weak base, as can be seen from its small K_b value, most of the dissolved NH_3 will remain as NH_3. Thus the major species in solution are

$$NH_3 \quad \text{and} \quad H_2O$$

Major Species

 NH_3

 H_2O

Both these substances can produce OH^- according to the reactions

$$NH_3(aq) + H_2O(l) \rightleftharpoons NH_4^+(aq) + OH^-(aq) \qquad K_b = 1.8 \times 10^{-5}$$
$$H_2O(l) \rightleftharpoons H^+(aq) + OH^-(aq) \qquad K_w = 1.0 \times 10^{-14}$$

However, the contribution from water can be neglected, since $K_b \gg K_w$. The equilibrium for NH_3 will dominate, and the equilibrium expression to be used is

$$K_b = 1.8 \times 10^{-5} = \frac{[NH_4^+][OH^-]}{[NH_3]}$$

The appropriate concentrations are

Refer to the steps for solving weak acid equilibrium problems. Use the same systematic approach for weak base equilibrium problems.

Initial Concentration (mol/L)		Equilibrium Concentration (mol/L)
$[NH_3]_0 = 15.0$	x mol/L	$[NH_3] = 15.0 - x$
$[NH_4^+]_0 = 0$	NH_3 reacts with	$[NH_4^+] = x$
$[OH^-]_0 \approx 0$	H_2O to reach equilibrium	$[OH^-] = x$

In terms of an ICE table, these concentrations are:

	$NH_3(aq)$	$+$	$H_2O(l)$	$\rightleftharpoons$	$NH_4^+(aq)$	$+$	$OH^-(aq)$
Initial:	15.0		—		0		0
Change:	$-x$		—		$+x$		$+x$
Equilibrium:	$15.0 - x$		—		x		x

CHEMICAL IMPACT

Amines

We have seen that many bases have nitrogen atoms with one lone pair and can be viewed as substituted ammonia molecules, with the general formula $R_xNH_{(3-x)}$. Compounds of this type are called **amines.** Amines are widely distributed in animals and plants, and complex amines often serve as messengers or regulators. For example, in the human nervous system, there are two amine stimulants, *norepinephrine* and *adrenaline*.

Norepinephrine

Adrenaline

Ephedrine, widely used as a decongestant, was a known drug in China over 2000 years ago. Indians in Mexico and the Southwest have used the hallucinogen *mescaline,* extracted from the peyote cactus, for centuries.

Ephedrine

Mescaline

Substituting the equilibrium concentrations into the equilibrium expression and making the usual approximation gives

$$K_b = 1.8 \times 10^{-5} = \frac{[NH_4^+][OH^-]}{[NH_3]} = \frac{(x)(x)}{15.0 - x} \approx \frac{x^2}{15.0}$$

Thus

$$x \approx 1.6 \times 10^{-2}$$

The 5% rule validates the approximation (check it yourself), so

$$[OH^-] = 1.6 \times 10^{-2} \, M$$

Since we know that K_w must be satisfied for this solution, we can calculate $[H^+]$ as follows:

$$[H^+] = \frac{K_w}{[OH^-]} = \frac{1.0 \times 10^{-14}}{1.6 \times 10^{-2}} = 6.3 \times 10^{-13} \, M$$

Therefore,

$$pH = -\log(6.3 \times 10^{-13}) = 12.20$$

See Exercises 14.83 and 14.84.

Sample Exercise 14.13 illustrates how a typical weak base equilibrium problem should be solved. Note two additional important points:

A table of K_b values for bases is also given in Appendix 5.3.

1. We calculated $[H^+]$ from K_w and then calculated the pH, but another method is available. The pOH could have been calculated from $[OH^-]$ and then used in Equation (14.3):

$$pK_w = 14.00 = pH + pOH$$
$$pH = 14.00 - pOH$$

Many other drugs, such as codeine and quinine, are amines, but they are usually not used in their pure amine forms. Instead, they are treated with an acid to become acid salts. An example of an acid salt is ammonium chloride, obtained by the reaction

$$NH_3 + HCl \longrightarrow NH_4Cl$$

Amines also can be protonated in this way. The resulting acid salt, written as AHCl (where A represents the amine), contains AH^+ and Cl^-. In general, the acid salts are more stable and more soluble in water than the parent amines. For instance, the parent amine of the well-known local anesthetic *novocaine* is insoluble in water, whereas the acid salt is much more soluble.

Peyote cactus growing on a rock.

Novocaine hydrochloride

2. In a 15.0 M NH_3 solution, the equilibrium concentrations of NH_4^+ and OH^- are each 1.6×10^{-2} M. Only a small percentage,

$$\frac{1.6 \times 10^{-2}}{15.0} \times 100\% = 0.11\%$$

of the ammonia reacts with water. Bottles containing 15.0 M NH_3 solution are often labeled 15.0 M NH_4OH, but as you can see from these results, 15.0 M NH_3 is actually a much more accurate description of the solution contents.

| *Sample Exercise 14.14* | **The pH of Weak Bases II** |

Calculate the pH of a 1.0 M solution of methylamine ($K_b = 4.38 \times 10^{-4}$).

Solution

Major Species

 CH_3NH_2

 H_2O

Since methylamine (CH_3NH_2) is a weak base, the major species in solution are

$$CH_3NH_2 \quad \text{and} \quad H_2O$$

Both are bases; however, water can be neglected as a source of OH^-, so the dominant equilibrium is

$$CH_3NH_2(aq) + H_2O(l) \rightleftharpoons CH_3NH_3^+(aq) + OH^-(aq)$$

and

$$K_b = 4.38 \times 10^{-4} = \frac{[CH_3NH_3^+][OH^-]}{[CH_3NH_2]}$$

The ICE table is:

	$CH_3NH_2(aq)$	+	$H_2O(l)$	$\rightleftharpoons$	$CH_3NH_3^+(aq)$	+	$OH^-(aq)$
Initial:	1.0		—		0		0
Change:	$-x$		—		$+x$		$+x$
Equilibrium:	$1.0 - x$		—		x		x

Substituting the equilibrium concentrations in the equilibrium expression and making the usual approximation give

$$K_b = 4.38 \times 10^{-4} = \frac{[CH_3NH_3^+][OH^-]}{[CH_3NH_2]} = \frac{(x)(x)}{1.0 - x} \approx \frac{x^2}{1.0}$$

and

$$x \approx 2.1 \times 10^{-2}$$

The approximation is valid by the 5% rule, so

$$[OH^-] = x = 2.1 \times 10^{-2}\ M$$
$$pOH = 1.68$$
$$pH = 14.00 - 1.68 = 12.32$$

See Exercises 14.85 and 14.86.

14.7 Polyprotic Acids

Some important acids, such as sulfuric acid (H_2SO_4) and phosphoric acid (H_3PO_4), can furnish more than one proton and are called **polyprotic acids.** A polyprotic acid always dissociates in a *stepwise* manner, one proton at a time. For example, the diprotic (two-proton) acid carbonic acid (H_2CO_3), which is so important in maintaining a constant pH in human blood, dissociates in the following steps:

$$H_2CO_3(aq) \rightleftharpoons H^+(aq) + HCO_3^-(aq) \quad K_{a_1} = \frac{[H^+][HCO_3^-]}{[H_2CO_3]} = 4.3 \times 10^{-7}$$

$$HCO_3^-(aq) \rightleftharpoons H^+(aq) + CO_3^{2-}(aq) \quad K_{a_2} = \frac{[H^+][CO_3^{2-}]}{[HCO_3^-]} = 5.6 \times 10^{-11}$$

The successive K_a values for the dissociation equilibria are designated K_{a_1} and K_{a_2}. Note that the conjugate base HCO_3^- of the first dissociation equilibrium becomes the acid in the second step.

Carbonic acid is formed when carbon dioxide gas is dissolved in water. In fact, the first dissociation step for carbonic acid is best represented by the reaction

$$CO_2(aq) + H_2O(l) \rightleftharpoons H^+(aq) + HCO_3^-(aq)$$

since relatively little H_2CO_3 actually exists in solution. However, it is convenient to consider CO_2 in water as H_2CO_3 so that we can treat such solutions using the familiar dissociation reactions for weak acids.

Phosphoric acid is a **triprotic acid** (three protons) that dissociates in the following steps:

$$H_3PO_4(aq) \rightleftharpoons H^+(aq) + H_2PO_4^-(aq) \quad K_{a_1} = \frac{[H^+][H_2PO_4^-]}{[H_3PO_4]} = 7.5 \times 10^{-3}$$

$$H_2PO_4^-(aq) \rightleftharpoons H^+(aq) + HPO_4^{2-}(aq) \quad K_{a_2} = \frac{[H^+][HPO_4^{2-}]}{[H_2PO_4^-]} = 6.2 \times 10^{-8}$$

$$HPO_4^{2-}(aq) \rightleftharpoons H^+(aq) + PO_4^{3-}(aq) \quad K_{a_3} = \frac{[H^+][PO_4^{3-}]}{[HPO_4^{2-}]} = 4.8 \times 10^{-13}$$

TABLE 14.4 Stepwise Dissociation Constants for Several Common Polyprotic Acids

Name	Formula	K_{a_1}	K_{a_2}	K_{a_3}
Phosphoric acid	H_3PO_4	7.5×10^{-3}	6.2×10^{-8}	4.8×10^{-13}
Arsenic acid	H_3AsO_4	5×10^{-3}	8×10^{-8}	6×10^{-10}
Carbonic acid	H_2CO_3	4.3×10^{-7}	5.6×10^{-11}	
Sulfuric acid	H_2SO_4	Large	1.2×10^{-2}	
Sulfurous acid	H_2SO_3	1.5×10^{-2}	1.0×10^{-7}	
Hydrosulfuric acid*	H_2S	1.0×10^{-7}	$\sim 10^{-19}$	
Oxalic acid	$H_2C_2O_4$	6.5×10^{-2}	6.1×10^{-5}	
Ascorbic acid (vitamin C)	$H_2C_6H_6O_6$	7.9×10^{-5}	1.6×10^{-12}	

*The K_{a_2} value for H_2S is very uncertain. Because it is so small, the K_{a_2} value is very difficult to measure accurately.

For a typical weak polyprotic acid,

$$K_{a_1} > K_{a_2} > K_{a_3}$$

A table of K_a values for polyprotic acids is also given in Appendix 5.2.

That is, the acid involved in each step of the dissociation is successively weaker, as shown by the stepwise dissociation constants given in Table 14.4. These values indicate that the loss of a second or third proton occurs less readily than loss of the first proton. This is not surprising; as the negative charge on the acid increases, it becomes more difficult to remove the positively charged proton.

Although we might expect the pH calculations for solutions of polyprotic acids to be complicated, the most common cases are surprisingly straightforward. To illustrate, we will consider a typical case, phosphoric acid, and a unique case, sulfuric acid.

Phosphoric Acid

Phosphoric acid is typical of most polyprotic acids in that the successive K_a values are very different. For example, the ratios of successive K_a values (from Table 14.4) are

$$\frac{K_{a_1}}{K_{a_2}} = \frac{7.5 \times 10^{-3}}{6.2 \times 10^{-8}} = 1.2 \times 10^5$$

$$\frac{K_{a_2}}{K_{a_3}} = \frac{6.2 \times 10^{-8}}{4.8 \times 10^{-13}} = 1.3 \times 10^5$$

Thus the relative acid strengths are

$$H_3PO_4 \gg H_2PO_4^- \gg HPO_4^{2-}$$

For a typical polyprotic acid in water, only the first dissociation step is important in determining the pH.

This means that in a solution prepared by dissolving H_3PO_4 in water, *only the first dissociation step makes an important contribution to $[H^+]$.* This greatly simplifies the pH calculations for phosphoric acid solutions, as is illustrated in Sample Exercise 14.15.

Sample Exercise 14.15 **The pH of a Polyprotic Acid**

Calculate the pH of a 5.0 M H_3PO_4 solution and the equilibrium concentrations of the species H_3PO_4, $H_2PO_4^-$, HPO_4^{2-}, and PO_4^{3-}.

Major Species

 H_3PO_4

 H_2O

Solution

The major species in solution are

$$H_3PO_4 \quad \text{and} \quad H_2O$$

None of the dissociation products of H_3PO_4 is written, since the K_a values are all so small that they will be minor species. The dominant equilibrium is the dissociation of H_3PO_4:

$$H_3PO_4(aq) \rightleftharpoons H^+(aq) + H_2PO_4^-(aq)$$

where

$$K_{a_1} = 7.5 \times 10^{-3} = \frac{[H^+][H_2PO_4^-]}{[H_3PO_4]}$$

The ICE table is:

	$H_3PO_4(aq)$	$\rightleftharpoons$	$H^+(aq)$	$+$	$H_2PO_4^-(aq)$
Initial:	5.0		0		0
Change:	$-x$		$+x$		$+x$
Equilibrium:	$5.0 - x$		x		x

Substituting the equilibrium concentrations into the expression for K_{a_1} and making the usual approximation give

$$K_{a_1} = 7.5 \times 10^{-3} = \frac{[H^+][H_2PO_4^-]}{[H_3PO_4]} = \frac{(x)(x)}{5.0 - x} \approx \frac{x^2}{5.0}$$

Thus

$$x \approx 1.9 \times 10^{-1}$$

Since 1.9×10^{-1} is less than 5% of 5.0, the approximation is acceptable, and

$$[H^+] = x = 0.19 \, M$$
$$pH = 0.72$$

So far we have determined that

$$[H^+] = [H_2PO_4^-] = 0.19 \, M$$

and

$$[H_3PO_4] = 5.0 - x = 4.8 \, M$$

The concentration of HPO_4^{2-} can be obtained by using the expression for K_{a_2}:

$$K_{a_2} = 6.2 \times 10^{-8} = \frac{[H^+][HPO_4^{2-}]}{[H_2PO_4^-]}$$

where

$$[H^+] = [H_2PO_4^-] = 0.19 \, M$$

Thus

$$[HPO_4^{2-}] = K_{a_2} = 6.2 \times 10^{-8} \, M$$

To calculate $[PO_4^{3-}]$, we use the expression for K_{a_3} and the values of $[H^+]$ and $[HPO_4^{2-}]$ calculated previously:

$$K_{a_3} = \frac{[H^+][PO_4^{3-}]}{[HPO_4^{2-}]} = 4.8 \times 10^{-13} = \frac{0.19[PO_4^{3-}]}{(6.2 \times 10^{-8})}$$

$$[PO_4^{3-}] = \frac{(4.8 \times 10^{-13})(6.2 \times 10^{-8})}{0.19} = 1.6 \times 10^{-19} \, M$$

These results show that the second and third dissociation steps do not make an important contribution to $[H^+]$. This is apparent from the fact that $[HPO_4^{2-}]$ is 6.2×10^{-8} M, which means that only 6.2×10^{-8} mol/L $H_2PO_4^-$ has dissociated. The value of $[PO_4^{3-}]$ shows that the dissociation of HPO_4^{2-} is even smaller. We must, however, use the second and third dissociation steps to calculate $[HPO_4^{2-}]$ and $[PO_4^{3-}]$, since these steps are the only sources of these ions.

See Exercises 14.95 and 14.96.

Sulfuric Acid

Sulfuric acid is unique among the common acids in that it is *a strong acid in its first dissociation step and a weak acid in its second step:*

$$H_2SO_4(aq) \longrightarrow H^+(aq) + HSO_4^-(aq) \quad K_{a_1} \text{ is very large}$$
$$HSO_4^-(aq) \rightleftharpoons H^+(aq) + SO_4^{2-}(aq) \quad K_{a_2} = 1.2 \times 10^{-2}$$

Sample Exercise 14.16 illustrates how to calculate the pH for sulfuric acid solutions.

| Sample Exercise 14.16 | **The pH of Sulfuric Acid** |

Calculate the pH of a 1.0 M H_2SO_4 solution.

Solution

The major species in the solution are

$$H^+, HSO_4^-, \quad \text{and} \quad H_2O$$

where the first two ions are produced by the complete first dissociation step of H_2SO_4. The concentration of H^+ in this solution will be at least 1.0 M, since this amount is produced by the first dissociation step of H_2SO_4. We must now answer this question: Does the HSO_4^- ion dissociate enough to produce a significant contribution to the concentration of H^+? This question can be answered by calculating the equilibrium concentrations for the dissociation reactions of HSO_4^-:

$$HSO_4^-(aq) \rightleftharpoons H^+(aq) + SO_4^{2-}(aq)$$

where
$$K_{a_2} = 1.2 \times 10^{-2} = \frac{[H^+][SO_4^{2-}]}{[HSO_4^-]}$$

The ICE table is:

	$HSO_4^-(aq)$	$\rightleftharpoons$	$H^+(aq)$	+	$SO_4^{2-}(aq)$
Initial:	1.0		1.0		0
Change:	$-x$		$+x$		$+x$
Equilibrium:	$1.0 - x$		$1.0 + x$		x

Note that $[H^+]_0$ is not equal to zero, as it usually is for a weak acid, because the first dissociation step has already occurred. Substituting the equilibrium concentrations into the expression for K_{a_2} and making the usual approximation give

$$K_{a_2} = 1.2 \times 10^{-2} = \frac{[H^+][SO_4^{2-}]}{[HSO_4^-]} = \frac{(1.0 + x)(x)}{1.0 - x} \approx \frac{(1.0)(x)}{(1.0)}$$

Thus
$$x \approx 1.2 \times 10^{-2}$$

Since 1.2×10^{-2} is 1.2% of 1.0, the approximation is valid according to the 5% rule. Note that x is not equal to $[H^+]$ in this case. Instead,

$$[H^+] = 1.0\,M + x = 1.0\,M + (1.2 \times 10^{-2})\,M$$
$$= 1.0\,M \quad \text{(to the correct number of significant figures)}$$

Thus the dissociation of HSO_4^- does not make a significant contribution to the concentration of H^+, and

$$[H^+] = 1.0\,M \quad \text{and} \quad pH = 0.00$$

See Exercise 14.97.

Major Species

 H^+

 HSO_4^-

H_2O

A bottle of sulfuric acid.

Only in dilute H_2SO_4 solutions does the second dissociation step contribute significantly to $[H^+]$.

Sample Exercise 14.16 illustrates the most common case for sulfuric acid in which only the first dissociation makes an important contribution to the concentration of H^+. In solutions more dilute than 1.0 M (for example, 0.10 M H_2SO_4), the dissociation of HSO_4^- is important, and solving the problem requires use of the quadratic formula, as shown in Sample Exercise 14.17.

| Sample Exercise 14.17 | **The pH of Sulfuric Acid** |

Calculate the pH of a 1.00×10^{-2} M H_2SO_4 solution.

Solution

The major species in solution are

$$H^+, \quad HSO_4^-, \quad \text{and} \quad H_2O$$

Proceeding as in Sample Exercise 14.16, we consider the dissociation of HSO_4^-, which leads to the following ICE table:

Major Species

H^+

HSO_4^-

H_2O

	$HSO_4^-(aq)$	$\rightleftharpoons$	$H^+(aq)$	$+$	$SO_4^{2-}(aq)$
Initial:	0.0100		0.0100		0
			From dissociation of H_2SO_4		
Change:	$-x$		$+x$		$+x$
Equilibrium:	$0.0100 - x$		$0.0100 + x$		x

Substituting the equilibrium concentrations into the expression for K_{a_2} gives

$$1.2 \times 10^{-2} = K_{a_2} = \frac{[H^+][SO_4^{2-}]}{[HSO_4^-]} = \frac{(0.0100 + x)(x)}{(0.0100 - x)}$$

If we make the usual approximation, then $0.0100 + x \approx 0.0100$ and $0.0100 - x \approx 0.0100$, and we have

$$1.2 \times 10^{-2} = \frac{(0.0100 + x)(x)}{(0.0100 - x)} \approx \frac{(0.0100)x}{(0.0100)}$$

The calculated value of x is

$$x = 1.2 \times 10^{-2} = 0.012$$

This value is larger than 0.010, clearly a ridiculous result. Thus we cannot make the usual approximation and must instead solve the quadratic equation. The expression

$$1.2 \times 10^{-2} = \frac{(0.0100 + x)(x)}{(0.0100 - x)}$$

leads to
$$(1.2 \times 10^{-2})(0.0100 - x) = (0.0100 + x)(x)$$
$$(1.2 \times 10^{-4}) - (1.2 \times 10^{-2})x = (1.0 \times 10^{-2})x + x^2$$
$$x^2 + (2.2 \times 10^{-2})x - (1.2 \times 10^{-4}) = 0$$

This equation can be solved using the quadratic formula

$$x = \frac{-b \pm \sqrt{b^2 - 4ac}}{2a}$$

where $a = 1$, $b = 2.2 \times 10^{-2}$, and $c = -1.2 \times 10^{-4}$. Use of the quadratic formula gives one negative root (which cannot be correct) and one positive root,

$$x = 4.5 \times 10^{-3}$$

Thus $[\text{H}^+] = 0.0100 + x = 0.0100 + 0.0045 = 0.0145$

and $\text{pH} = 1.84$

Note that in this case the second dissociation step produces about half as many H^+ ions as the initial step does.

This problem also can be solved by successive approximations, a method illustrated in Appendix 1.4.

See Exercise 14.98.

Characteristics of Weak Polyprotic Acids

1. Typically, successive K_a values are so much smaller than the first value that only the first dissociation step makes a significant contribution to the equilibrium concentration of H^+. This means that the calculation of the pH for a solution of a typical weak polyprotic acid is identical to that for a solution of a weak monoprotic acid.

2. Sulfuric acid is unique in being a strong acid in its first dissociation step and a weak acid in its second step. For relatively concentrated solutions of sulfuric acid (1.0 M or higher), the large concentration of H^+ from the first dissociation step represses the second step, which can be neglected as a contributor of H^+ ions. For dilute solutions of sulfuric acid, the second step does make a significant contribution, and the quadratic equation must be used to obtain the total H^+ concentration.

14.8 Acid–Base Properties of Salts

Salt is simply another name for *ionic compound*. When a salt dissolves in water, we assume that it breaks up into its ions, which move about independently, at least in dilute solutions. Under certain conditions, these ions can behave as acids or bases. In this section we explore such reactions.

Salts That Produce Neutral Solutions

Recall that the conjugate base of a strong acid has virtually no affinity for protons in water. This is why strong acids completely dissociate in aqueous solution. Thus, when anions such as Cl^- and NO_3^- are placed in water, they do not combine with H^+ and have no effect on the pH. Cations such as K^+ and Na^+ from strong bases have no affinity for H^+, nor can they produce H^+, so they too have no effect on the pH of an aqueous solution. *Salts that consist of the cations of strong bases and the anions of strong acids have no effect on $[\text{H}^+]$ when dissolved in water.* This means that aqueous solutions of salts such as KCl, NaCl, NaNO_3, and KNO_3 are neutral (have a pH of 7).

The salt of a strong acid and a strong base gives a neutral solution.

Salts That Produce Basic Solutions

In an aqueous solution of sodium acetate ($\text{NaC}_2\text{H}_3\text{O}_2$), the major species are

$$\text{Na}^+, \quad \text{C}_2\text{H}_3\text{O}_2^-, \quad \text{and} \quad \text{H}_2\text{O}$$

What are the acid–base properties of each component? The Na^+ ion has neither acid nor base properties. The $\text{C}_2\text{H}_3\text{O}_2^-$ ion is the conjugate base of acetic acid, a weak acid. This means that $\text{C}_2\text{H}_3\text{O}_2^-$ has a significant affinity for a proton and is a base. Finally, water is a weakly amphoteric substance.

Major Species

 Na^+

 $\text{C}_2\text{H}_3\text{O}_2^-$

H_2O

The pH of this solution will be determined by the $C_2H_3O_2^-$ ion. Since $C_2H_3O_2^-$ is a base, it will react with the best proton donor available. In this case, water is the *only* source of protons, and the reaction between the acetate ion and water is

$$C_2H_3O_2^-(aq) + H_2O(l) \rightleftharpoons HC_2H_3O_2(aq) + OH^-(aq) \qquad (14.7)$$

Note that this reaction, which yields a base solution, involves a *base reacting with water to produce hydroxide ion and a conjugate acid*. We have defined K_b as the equilibrium constant for such a reaction. In this case,

$$K_b = \frac{[HC_2H_3O_2][OH^-]}{[C_2H_3O_2^-]}$$

The value of K_a for acetic acid is well known (1.8×10^{-5}). But how can we obtain the K_b value for the acetate ion? The answer lies in the relationships among K_a, K_b, and K_w. Note that when the expression for K_a for acetic acid is multiplied by the expression for K_b for the acetate ion, the result is K_w:

$$K_a \times K_b = \frac{[H^+][\cancel{C_2H_3O_2^-}]}{[\cancel{HC_2H_3O_2}]} \times \frac{[\cancel{HC_2H_3O_2}][OH^-]}{[\cancel{C_2H_3O_2^-}]} = [H^+][OH^-] = K_w$$

This is a very important result. For any weak acid and its conjugate base,

$$K_a \times K_b = K_w$$

Thus, when either K_a or K_b is known, the other can be calculated. For the acetate ion,

$$K_b = \frac{K_w}{K_a \text{ (for } HC_2H_3O_2)} = \frac{1.0 \times 10^{-14}}{1.8 \times 10^{-5}} = 5.6 \times 10^{-10}$$

This is the K_b value for the reaction described by Equation (14.7). Note that it is obtained from the K_a value of the parent weak acid, in this case acetic acid. The sodium acetate solution is an example of an important general case. *For any salt whose cation has neutral properties (such as Na^+ or K^+) and whose anion is the conjugate base of a weak acid, the aqueous solution will be basic. The K_b value for the anion can be obtained from the relationship $K_b = K_w/K_a$.* Equilibrium calculations of this type are illustrated in Sample Exercise 14.18.

A basic solution is formed if the anion of the salt is the conjugate base of a weak acid.

Salts as Weak Bases

Calculate the pH of a 0.30 M NaF solution. The K_a value for HF is 7.2×10^{-4}.

Solution

The major species in solution are

$$Na^+, F^-, \quad \text{and} \quad H_2O$$

Since HF is a weak acid, the F^- ion must have a significant affinity for protons, and the dominant reaction will be

$$F^-(aq) + H_2O(l) \rightleftharpoons HF(aq) + OH^-(aq)$$

which yields the K_b expression

$$K_b = \frac{[HF][OH^-]}{[F^-]}$$

The value of K_b can be calculated from K_w and the K_a value for HF:

$$K_b = \frac{K_w}{K_a \text{ (for HF)}} = \frac{1.0 \times 10^{-14}}{7.2 \times 10^{-4}} = 1.4 \times 10^{-11}$$

Major Species

 Na^+

 F^-

 H_2O

The corresponding ICE table is:

	$F^-(aq)$	$+$	$H_2O(l)$	$\rightleftharpoons$	$HF(aq)$	$+$	$OH^-(aq)$
Initial:	0.30		—		0		≈ 0
Change:	$-x$		—		$+x$		$+x$
Equilibrium:	$0.30 - x$		—		x		x

Thus

$$K_b = 1.4 \times 10^{-11} = \frac{[HF][OH^-]}{[F^-]} = \frac{(x)(x)}{0.30 - x} \approx \frac{x^2}{0.30}$$

and

$$x \approx 2.0 \times 10^{-6}$$

The approximation is valid by the 5% rule, so

$$[OH^-] = x = 2.0 \times 10^{-6}\,M$$
$$pOH = 5.69$$
$$pH = 14.00 - 5.69 = 8.31$$

As expected, the solution is basic.

See Exercise 14.103.

Base Strength in Aqueous Solutions

To emphasize the concept of base strength, let us consider the basic properties of the cyanide ion. One relevant reaction is the dissociation of hydrocyanic acid in water:

$$HCN(aq) + H_2O(l) \rightleftharpoons H_3O^+(aq) + CN^-(aq) \qquad K_a = 6.2 \times 10^{-10}$$

Since HCN is such a weak acid, CN^- appears to be a *strong* base, showing a very high affinity for H^+ *compared to H_2O*, with which it is competing. However, we also need to look at the reaction in which cyanide ion reacts with water:

$$CN^-(aq) + H_2O(l) \rightleftharpoons HCN(aq) + OH^-(aq)$$

where

$$K_b = \frac{K_w}{K_a} = \frac{1.0 \times 10^{-14}}{6.2 \times 10^{-10}} = 1.6 \times 10^{-5}$$

In this reaction CN^- appears to be a weak base; the K_b value is only 1.6×10^{-5}. What accounts for this apparent difference in base strength? The key idea is that in the reaction of CN^- with H_2O, *CN^- is competing with OH^- for H^+, instead of competing with H_2O,* as it does in the HCN dissociation reaction. These equilibria show the following relative base strengths:

$$OH^- > CN^- > H_2O$$

Similar arguments can be made for other "weak" bases, such as ammonia, the acetate ion, the fluoride ion, and so on.

Salts That Produce Acidic Solutions

Some salts produce acidic solutions when dissolved in water. For example, when solid NH_4Cl is dissolved in water, NH_4^+ and Cl^- ions are present, with NH_4^+ behaving as a weak acid:

$$NH_4^+(aq) \rightleftharpoons NH_3(aq) + H^+(aq)$$

The Cl^- ion, having virtually no affinity for H^+ in water, does not affect the pH of the solution.

In general, *salts in which the anion is not a base and the cation is the conjugate acid of a weak base produce acidic solutions.*

Sample Exercise 14.19	Salts as Weak Acids I

Calculate the pH of a 0.10 M NH_4Cl solution. The K_b value for NH_3 is 1.8×10^{-5}.

Solution

The major species in solution are

$$NH_4^+, \quad Cl^-, \quad \text{and} \quad H_2O$$

Major Species

Cl^-

NH_4^+

H_2O

Note that both NH_4^+ and H_2O can produce H^+. The dissociation reaction for the NH_4^+ ion is

$$NH_4^+(aq) \rightleftharpoons NH_3(aq) + H^+(aq)$$

for which
$$K_a = \frac{[NH_3][H^+]}{[NH_4^+]}$$

Note that although the K_b value for NH_3 is given, the reaction corresponding to K_b is not appropriate here, since NH_3 is not a major species in the solution. Instead, the given value of K_b is used to calculate K_a for NH_4^+ from the relationship

$$K_a \times K_b = K_w$$

Thus
$$K_a \text{ (for } NH_4^+) = \frac{K_w}{K_b \text{ (for } NH_3)} = \frac{1.0 \times 10^{-14}}{1.8 \times 10^{-5}} = 5.6 \times 10^{-10}$$

Although NH_4^+ is a very weak acid, as indicated by its K_a value, it is stronger than H_2O and will dominate in the production of H^+. Thus we will focus on the dissociation reaction of NH_4^+ to calculate the pH in this solution.

We solve the weak acid problem in the usual way:

	$NH_4^+(aq)$	$\rightleftharpoons$	$H^+(aq)$	$+$	$NH_3(aq)$
Initial:	0.10		≈ 0		0
Change:	$-x$		$+x$		$+x$
Equilibrium:	$0.10 - x$		x		x

Thus

$$5.6 \times 10^{-10} = K_a = \frac{[H^+][NH_3]}{[NH_4^+]} = \frac{(x)(x)}{0.10 - x} \approx \frac{x^2}{0.10}$$

$$x \approx 7.5 \times 10^{-6}$$

The approximation is valid by the 5% rule, so

$$[H^+] = x = 7.5 \times 10^{-6} \, M \quad \text{and} \quad pH = 5.13$$

See Exercise 14.104.

A second type of salt that produces an acidic solution is one that contains a *highly charged metal ion*. For example, when solid aluminum chloride ($AlCl_3$) is dissolved in water, the resulting solution is significantly acidic. Although the Al^{3+} ion is not itself a Brønsted–Lowry acid, the hydrated ion $Al(H_2O)_6^{3+}$ formed in water is a weak acid:

$$Al(H_2O)_6^{3+}(aq) \rightleftharpoons Al(OH)(H_2O)_5^{2+}(aq) + H^+(aq)$$

The high charge on the metal ion polarizes the O—H bonds in the attached water molecules, making the hydrogens in these water molecules more acidic than those in free water molecules. Typically, the higher the charge on the metal ion, the stronger the acidity of the hydrated ion.

Section 14.9 contains a further discussion of the acidity of hydrated ions.

Sample Exercise 14.20

Salts as Weak Acids II

Calculate the pH of a 0.010 M $AlCl_3$ solution. The K_a value for $Al(H_2O)_6^{3+}$ is 1.4×10^{-5}.

Solution

The major species in solution are

$$Al(H_2O)_6^{3+}, \quad Cl^-, \quad \text{and} \quad H_2O$$

Since the $Al(H_2O)_6^{3+}$ ion is a stronger acid than water, the dominant equilibrium is

$$Al(H_2O)_6^{3+}(aq) \rightleftharpoons Al(OH)(H_2O)_5^{2+}(aq) + H^+(aq)$$

and

$$1.4 \times 10^{-5} = K_a = \frac{[Al(OH)(H_2O)_5^{2+}][H^+]}{[Al(H_2O)_6^{3+}]}$$

This is a typical weak acid problem, which we can solve with the usual procedure:

Major Species

Cl^-

$Al(H_2O)_6^{3+}$

H_2O

	$Al(H_2O)_6^{3+}(aq)$	$\rightleftharpoons$	$Al(OH)(H_2O)_5^{2+}(aq)$	$+$	$H^+(aq)$
Initial:	0.010		0		≈ 0
Change:	$-x$		$+x$		$+x$
Equilibrium:	$0.010 - x$		x		x

Thus

$$1.4 \times 10^{-5} = K_a = \frac{[Al(OH)(H_2O)_5^{2+}][H^+]}{[Al(H_2O)_6^{3+}]} = \frac{(x)(x)}{0.010 - x} \approx \frac{x^2}{0.010}$$

$$x \approx 3.7 \times 10^{-4}$$

Since the approximation is valid by the 5% rule,

$$[H^+] = x = 3.7 \times 10^{-4}\, M \quad \text{and} \quad pH = 3.43$$

See Exercises 14.109 and 14.110.

TABLE 14.5 Qualitative Prediction of pH for Solutions of Salts for Which Both Cation and Anion Have Acidic or Basic Properties

$K_a > K_b$	pH < 7 (acidic)
$K_b > K_a$	pH > 7 (basic)
$K_a = K_b$	pH $= 7$ (neutral)

So far we have considered salts in which only one of the ions has acidic or basic properties. For many salts, such as ammonium acetate ($NH_4C_2H_3O_2$), both ions can affect the pH of the aqueous solution. Because the equilibrium calculations for these cases can be quite complicated, we will consider only the qualitative aspects of such problems. We can predict whether the solution will be basic, acidic, or neutral by comparing the K_a value for the acidic ion with the K_b value for the basic ion. If the K_a value for the acidic ion is larger than the K_b value for the basic ion, the solution will be acidic. If the K_b value is larger than the K_a value, the solution will be basic. Equal K_a and K_b values mean a neutral solution. These facts are summarized in Table 14.5.

| Sample Exercise 14.21 | The Acid–Base Properties of Salts |

Predict whether an aqueous solution of each of the following salts will be acidic, basic, or neutral.

a. $NH_4C_2H_3O_2$ **b.** NH_4CN **c.** $Al_2(SO_4)_3$

Solution

a. The ions in solution are NH_4^+ and $C_2H_3O_2^-$. As we mentioned previously, K_a for NH_4^+ is 5.6×10^{-10} and K_b for $C_2H_3O_2^-$ is 5.6×10^{-10}. Thus K_a for NH_4^+ is equal to K_b for $C_2H_3O_2^-$, and the solution will be neutral (pH = 7).

b. The solution will contain NH_4^+ and CN^- ions. The K_a value for NH_4^+ is 5.6×10^{-10} and

$$K_b(\text{for } CN^-) = \frac{K_w}{K_a(\text{for HCN})} = 1.6 \times 10^{-5}$$

Since K_b for CN^- is much larger than K_a for NH_4^+, CN^- is a much stronger base than NH_4^+ is an acid. This solution will be basic.

c. The solution will contain $Al(H_2O)_6^{3+}$ and SO_4^{2-} ions. The K_a value for $Al(H_2O)_6^{3+}$ is 1.4×10^{-5}, as given in Sample Exercise 14.20. We must calculate K_b for SO_4^{2-}. The HSO_4^- ion is the conjugate acid of SO_4^{2-}, and its K_a value is K_{a_2} for sulfuric acid, or 1.2×10^{-2}. Therefore,

$$K_b(\text{for } SO_4^{2-}) = \frac{K_w}{K_{a_2}(\text{for sulfuric acid})}$$
$$= \frac{1.0 \times 10^{-14}}{1.2 \times 10^{-2}} = 8.3 \times 10^{-13}$$

This solution will be acidic, since K_a for $Al(H_2O)_6^{3+}$ is much greater than K_b for SO_4^{2-}.

See Exercises 14.111 and 14.112.

The acid–base properties of aqueous solutions of various salts are summarized in Table 14.6.

TABLE 14.6 Acid–Base Properties of Various Types of Salts

Type of Salt	Examples	Comment	pH of Solution
Cation is from strong base; anion is from strong acid	KCl, KNO₃, NaCl, NaNO₃	Neither acts as an acid or a base	Neutral
Cation is from strong base; anion is from weak acid	NaC₂H₃O₂, KCN, NaF	Anion acts as a base; cation has no effect on pH	Basic
Cation is conjugate acid of weak base; anion is from strong acid	NH₄Cl, NH₄NO₃	Cation acts as acid; anion has no effect on pH	Acidic
Cation is conjugate acid of weak base; anion is conjugate base of weak acid	NH₄C₂H₃O₂, NH₄CN	Cation acts as an acid; anion acts as a base	Acidic if $K_a > K_b$, basic if $K_b > K_a$, neutral if $K_a = K_b$
Cation is highly charged metal ion; anion is from strong acid	Al(NO₃)₃, FeCl₃	Hydrated cation acts as an acid; anion has no effect on pH	Acidic

14.9 The Effect of Structure on Acid–Base Properties

Further aspects of acid strengths are discussed in Section 20.7.

TABLE 14.7   Bond Strengths and Acid Strengths for Hydrogen Halides

H—X Bond	Bond Strength (kJ/mol)	Acid Strength in Water
H—F	565	Weak
H—Cl	427	Strong
H—Br	363	Strong
H—I	295	Strong

We have seen that when a substance is dissolved in water, it produces an acidic solution if it can donate protons and produces a basic solution if it can accept protons. What structural properties of a molecule cause it to behave as an acid or as a base?

Any molecule containing a hydrogen atom is potentially an acid. However, many such molecules show no acidic properties. For example, molecules containing C—H bonds, such as chloroform ($CHCl_3$) and nitromethane (CH_3NO_2), do not produce acidic aqueous solutions because a C—H bond is both strong and nonpolar and thus there is no tendency to donate protons. On the other hand, although the H—Cl bond in gaseous hydrogen chloride is slightly stronger than a C—H bond, it is much more polar, and this molecule readily dissociates when dissolved in water.

Thus there are two main factors that determine whether a molecule containing an X—H bond will behave as a Brønsted–Lowry acid: the strength of the bond and the polarity of the bond.

To explore these factors let's consider the relative acid strengths of the hydrogen halides. The bond polarities vary as shown

$$H—F > H—Cl > H—Br > H—I$$

Most polar   Least polar

because electronegativity decreases going down the group. Based on the high polarity of the H—F bond, we might expect hydrogen fluoride to be a very strong acid. In fact, among HX molecules, HF is the only weak acid ($K_a = 7.2 \times 10^{-4}$) when dissolved in water. The H—F bond is unusually strong, as shown in Table 14.7, and thus is difficult to break. This contributes significantly to the reluctance of the HF molecules to dissociate in water.

Another important class of acids are the oxyacids, which as we saw in Section 14.2 characteristically contain the grouping H—O—X. Several series of oxyacids are listed with their K_a values in Table 14.8. Note from these data that for a given series the acid strength increases with an increase in the number of oxygen atoms attached to the central atom. For example, in the series containing chlorine and a varying number of oxygen atoms, HOCl is a weak acid, but the acid strength is successively greater as the number of oxygen atoms increases. This happens because the very electronegative oxygen atoms are able to draw electrons away from the chlorine atom and the O—H bond, as shown in Fig. 14.11. The net effect is to both polarize and weaken the O—H bond; this effect becomes more important as the number of attached oxygen atoms increases. This means that a proton is most readily produced by the molecule with the largest number of attached oxygen atoms ($HClO_4$).

This type of behavior is also observed for hydrated metal ions. Earlier in this chapter we saw that highly charged metal ions such as Al^{3+} produce acidic solutions. The acidity of the water molecules attached to the metal ion is increased by the attraction of electrons to the positive metal ion:

$$Al^{3+}—O\begin{matrix} H \\ \\ H \end{matrix}$$

The greater the charge on the metal ion, the more acidic the hydrated ion becomes.

For acids containing the H—O—X grouping, the greater the ability of X to draw electrons toward itself, the greater the acidity of the molecule. Since the electronegativity of X reflects its ability to attract the electrons involved in bonding, we might expect acid strength to depend on the electronegativity of X. In fact, there is an excellent correlation between the electronegativity of X and the acid strength for oxyacids, as shown in Table 14.9.

FIGURE 14.11
The effect of the number of attached oxygens on the O—H bond in a series of chlorine oxyacids. As the number of oxygen atoms attached to the chlorine atom increases, they become more effective at withdrawing electron density from the O—H bond, thereby weakening and polarizing it. This increases the tendency for the molecule to produce a proton, and so its acid strength increases.

TABLE 14.8   Several Series of Oxyacids and Their K_a Values

Oxyacid	Structure	K_a Value
$HClO_4$	H—O—Cl with three O	Large (~10^7)
$HClO_3$	H—O—Cl with two O	~1
$HClO_2$	H—O—Cl—O	1.2×10^{-2}
HClO	H—O—Cl	3.5×10^{-8}
H_2SO_4	H—O—S with O—H and O	Large
H_2SO_3	H—O—S with O—H and O	1.5×10^{-2}
HNO_3	H—O—N with two O	Large
HNO_2	H—O—N—O	4.0×10^{-4}

TABLE 14.9   Comparison of Electronegativity of X and K_a Value for a Series of Oxyacids

Acid	X	Electronegativity of X	K_a for Acid
HOCl	Cl	3.0	4×10^{-8}
HOBr	Br	2.8	2×10^{-9}
HOI	I	2.5	2×10^{-11}
$HOCH_3$	CH_3	2.3 (for carbon in CH_3)	~10^{-15}

14.10 Acid–Base Properties of Oxides

A compound containing the H—O—X group will produce an acidic solution in water if the O—X bond is strong and covalent. If the O—X bond is ionic, the compound will produce a basic solution in water.

We have just seen that molecules containing the grouping H—O—X can behave as acids and that the acid strength depends on the electron-withdrawing ability of X. But substances with this grouping also can behave as bases if the hydroxide ion instead of a proton is produced. What determines which behavior will occur? The answer lies mainly in the nature of the O—X bond. If X has a relatively high electronegativity, the O—X bond will be covalent and strong. When the compound containing the H—O—X grouping is dissolved in water, the O—X bond will remain intact. It will be the polar and relatively weak H—O bond that will tend to break, releasing a proton. On the other hand, if X has a very low electronegativity, the O—X bond will be ionic and subject to being broken in polar water. Examples are the ionic substances NaOH and KOH that dissolve in water to give the metal cation and the hydroxide ion.

We can use these principles to explain the acid–base behavior of oxides when they are dissolved in water. For example, when a covalent oxide such as sulfur trioxide is dissolved in water, an acidic solution results because sulfuric acid is formed:

$$SO_3(g) + H_2O(l) \longrightarrow H_2SO_4(aq)$$

The structure of H_2SO_4 is shown in the margin. In this case, the strong, covalent O—S bonds remain intact and the H—O bonds break to produce protons. Other common covalent oxides that react with water to form acidic solutions are sulfur dioxide, carbon dioxide, and nitrogen dioxide, as shown by the following reactions:

$$SO_2(g) + H_2O(l) \longrightarrow H_2SO_3(aq)$$
$$CO_2(g) + H_2O(l) \longrightarrow H_2CO_3(aq)$$
$$2NO_2(g) + H_2O(l) \longrightarrow HNO_3(aq) + HNO_2(aq)$$

Thus, when a covalent oxide dissolves in water, an acidic solution forms. These oxides are called **acidic oxides.**

On the other hand, when an ionic oxide dissolves in water, a basic solution results, as shown by the following reactions:

$$CaO(s) + H_2O(l) \longrightarrow Ca(OH)_2(aq)$$
$$K_2O(s) + H_2O(l) \longrightarrow 2KOH(aq)$$

These reactions can be explained by recognizing that the oxide ion has a high affinity for protons and reacts with water to produce hydroxide ions:

$$O^{2-}(aq) + H_2O(l) \longrightarrow 2OH^-(aq)$$

Thus the most ionic oxides, such as those of the Group 1A and 2A metals, produce basic solutions when they are dissolved in water. As a result, these oxides are called **basic oxides.**

14.11 The Lewis Acid–Base Model

We have seen that the first successful conceptualization of acid–base behavior was proposed by Arrhenius. This useful but limited model was replaced by the more general Brønsted–Lowry model. An even more general model for acid–base behavior was suggested by G. N. Lewis in the early 1920s. A **Lewis acid** is an *electron-pair acceptor,* and a **Lewis base** is an *electron-pair donor.* Another way of saying this is that a Lewis acid has an empty atomic orbital that it can use to accept (share) an electron pair from a molecule that has a lone pair of electrons (Lewis base). The three models for acids and bases are summarized in Table 14.10.

TABLE 14.10   Three Models for Acids and Bases

Model	Definition of Acid	Definition of Base
Arrhenius	H^+ producer	OH^- producer
Brønsted–Lowry	H^+ donor	H^+ acceptor
Lewis	Electron-pair acceptor	Electron-pair donor

Note that Brønsted–Lowry acid–base reactions (proton donor–proton acceptor reactions) are encompassed by the Lewis model. For example, the reaction between a proton and an ammonia molecule, that is,

$$\text{H}^+ + :\text{N}-\text{H} \longrightarrow \left[\text{H}-\text{N}-\text{H}\right]^+$$

Lewis acid   Lewis base

can be represented as a reaction between an electron-pair acceptor (H^+) and an electron-pair donor (NH_3). The same holds true for a reaction between a proton and a hydroxide ion:

$$\text{H}^+ + [:\ddot{\text{O}}-\text{H}]^- \longrightarrow \text{O}:$$

Lewis acid   Lewis base

The Lewis model encompasses the Brønsted–Lowry model, but the reverse is not true.

The real value of the Lewis model for acids and bases is that it covers many reactions that do not involve Brønsted–Lowry acids. For example, consider the gas-phase reaction between boron trifluoride and ammonia.

$$:\ddot{\text{F}}-\text{B}-\ddot{\text{F}}: + :\text{N}-\text{H} \longrightarrow :\ddot{\text{F}}-\text{B}-\text{N}-\text{H}$$

Lewis acid   Lewis base

Here the electron-deficient BF_3 molecule (there are only six electrons around the boron) completes its octet by reacting with NH_3, which has a lone pair of electrons. (see Fig. 14.12.) In fact, as mentioned in Chapter 8, the electron deficiency of boron trifluoride makes it very reactive toward any electron-pair donor. That is, it is a strong Lewis acid.

The hydration of a metal ion, such as Al^{3+}, also can be viewed as a Lewis acid–base reaction:

$$\text{Al}^{3+} + 6\left(:\ddot{\text{O}}\right) \longrightarrow \left[\text{Al}-\left(\ddot{\text{O}}\right)_6\right]^{3+}$$

Lewis acid   Lewis base

FIGURE 14.12
Reaction of BF_3 with NH_3.

FIGURE 14.13
The $Al(H_2O)_6^{3+}$ ion.

Here the Al^{3+} ion accepts one electron pair from each of six water molecules to form $Al(H_2O)_6^{3+}$ (see Fig. 14.13).

In addition, the reaction between a covalent oxide and water to form a Brønsted–Lowry acid can be defined as a Lewis acid–base reaction. An example is the reaction between sulfur trioxide and water:

Note that as the water molecule attaches to sulfur trioxide, a proton shift occurs to form sulfuric acid.

Sample Exercise 14.22

Lewis Acids and Bases

For each reaction, identify the Lewis acid and base.

a. $Ni^{2+}(aq) + 6NH_3(aq) \longrightarrow Ni(NH_3)_6^{2+}(aq)$
b. $H^+(aq) + H_2O(aq) \rightleftharpoons H_3O^+(aq)$

Solution

a. Each NH_3 molecule donates an electron pair to the Ni^{2+} ion:

The nickel(II) ion is the Lewis acid, and ammonia is the Lewis base.
b. The proton is the Lewis acid and the water molecule is the Lewis base:

See Exercises 14.119 and 14.120.

CHEMICAL IMPACT

Self-Destructing Paper

The New York City Public Library has 88 miles of bookshelves, and on 36 miles of these shelves the books are quietly disintegrating between their covers. In fact, an estimated 40% of the books in the major research collections in the United States will soon be too fragile to handle.

The problem results from the acidic paper widely used in printing books in the past century. Ironically, books from the eighteenth, seventeenth, sixteenth, and even fifteenth century are in much better shape. Gutenberg Bibles contain paper that is in remarkably good condition. In those days, paper was made by hand from linen or rags, but in the nineteenth century, the demand for cheap paper skyrocketed. Paper manufacturers found that paper could be made economically, by machine, using wood pulp. To size the paper (that is, fill in microscopic holes to lower absorption of moisture and prevent seeping or spreading of inks), alum $[Al_2(SO_4)_3]$ was added in large amounts.

A book ravaged by the decomposition of acidic paper.

Because the hydrated aluminum ion $[Al(H_2O)_6^{3+}]$ is an acid $(K_a \approx 10^{-5})$, paper manufactured using alum is quite acidic.

14.12 Strategy for Solving Acid–Base Problems: A Summary

In this chapter we have encountered many different situations involving aqueous solutions of acids and bases, and in the next chapter we will encounter still more. In solving for the equilibrium concentrations in these aqueous solutions, it is tempting to create a pigeonhole for each possible situation and to memorize the procedures necessary to deal with that particular case. This approach is just not practical and usually leads to frustration: Too many pigeonholes are required—there seems to be an infinite number of cases. But you can handle any case successfully by taking a systematic, patient, and thoughtful approach. When analyzing an acid–base equilibrium problem, do *not* ask yourself how a memorized solution can be used to solve the problem. Instead, ask this question: *What are the major species in the solution and what is their chemical behavior?*

The most important part of doing a complicated acid–base equilibrium problem is the analysis you do at the beginning of a problem.

What major species are present?

Does a reaction occur that can be assumed to go to completion?

What equilibrium dominates the solution?

Let the problem guide you. Be patient.

The following steps outline a general strategy for solving problems involving acid–base equilibria.

Over time this acidity causes the paper fibers to disintegrate; the pages of books fall apart when they are used.

One could transfer the contents of the threatened books to microfilm, but that would be a very slow and expensive process. Can the books be chemically treated to neutralize the acid and stop the deterioration? Yes. In fact, you know enough chemistry at this point to design the treatment patented in 1936 by Otto Schierholz. He dipped individual pages in solutions of alkaline earth bicarbonate salts [$Mg(HCO_3)_2$, $Ca(HCO_3)_2$, and so on]. The HCO_3^- ions present in these solutions react with the H^+ in the paper to give CO_2 and H_2O. This treatment works well and is used today to preserve especially important works, but it is slow and labor-intensive.

It would be much more economical if large numbers of books could be treated at one time without disturbing the bindings. However, soaking entire books in an aqueous solution is out of the question. A logical question then is: Are there gaseous bases that could be used to neutralize the acid? Certainly; the organic amines (general formula, RNH_2) are bases, and those with low molar masses are gases under normal conditions. Experiments in which books were treated using ammonia, butylamine ($CH_3CH_2CH_2CH_2NH_2$), and other amines have shown that the method works, but only for a short time. The amines do enter the paper and neutralize the acid, but being volatile, they gradually evaporate, leaving the paper in its original acidic condition.

A much more effective treatment involves diethylzinc [$(CH_3CH_2)_2Zn$], which boils at $117°C$ and 1 atm. Diethylzinc (DEZ) reacts with oxygen or water to produce ZnO as follows:

$$(CH_3CH_2)_2Zn(g) + 7O_2(g) \longrightarrow$$
$$ZnO(s) + 4CO_2(g) + 5H_2O(g)$$
$$(CH_3CH_2)_2Zn(g) + H_2O(g) \longrightarrow ZnO(s) + 2CH_3CH_3(g)$$

The solid zinc oxide produced in these reactions is deposited among the paper fibers, and being a basic oxide, it neutralizes the acid present as shown in the equation

$$ZnO + 2H^+ \longrightarrow Zn^{2+} + H_2O$$

One major problem is that DEZ ignites spontaneously on contact with air. Therefore, this treatment must be carried out in a chamber filled mainly with $N_2(g)$, where the amount of O_2 present can be rigorously controlled. The pressure in the chamber must be maintained well below one atmosphere both to lower the boiling point of DEZ and to remove excess moisture from the book's pages. Several major DEZ fires have slowed its implementation as a book preservative. However, the Library of Congress has designed a new DEZ treatment plant that includes a chamber large enough for approximately 9000 books to be treated at one time.

Solving Acid–Base Problems

➡ 1 List the major species in solution.

➡ 2 Look for reactions that can be assumed to go to completion—for example, a strong acid dissociating or H^+ reacting with OH^-.

➡ 3 For a reaction that can be assumed to go to completion:
a. Determine the concentration of the products.
b. Write down the major species in solution after the reaction.

➡ 4 Look at each major component of the solution and decide if it is an acid or a base.

➡ 5 Pick the equilibrium that will control the pH. Use known values of the dissociation constants for the various species to help decide on the dominant equilibrium.
a. Write the equation for the reaction and the equilibrium expression.
b. Compute the initial concentrations (assuming the dominant equilibrium has not yet occurred, that is, no acid dissociation, and so on).
c. Define x.
d. Compute the equilibrium concentrations in terms of x.
e. Substitute the concentrations into the equilibrium expression, and solve for x.
f. Check the validity of the approximation.
g. Calculate the pH and other concentrations as required.

Although these steps may seem somewhat cumbersome, especially for simpler problems, they will become increasingly helpful as the aqueous solutions become more complicated. If you develop the habit of approaching acid–base problems systematically, the more complex cases will be much easier to manage.

Key Terms

For Review

Models for acids and bases

- Arrhenius model
  - Acids produce H^+ in solution
  - Bases produce OH^- in solution
- Brønsted–Lowry model
  - An acid is a proton donor
  - A base is a proton acceptor
  - In this model an acid molecule reacts with a water molecule, which behaves as a base:

$$HA(aq) + H_2O(l) \rightleftharpoons H_3O^+(aq) + A^-(aq)$$

  Acid   Base   Conjugate   Conjugate
                                 acid   base

  to form a new acid (conjugate acid) and a new base (conjugate base).
- Lewis model
  - A Lewis acid is an electron-pair acceptor
  - A Lewis base is an electron-pair donor

Acid–base equilibrium

- The equilibrium constant for an acid dissociating (ionizing) in water is called K_a
- The K_a expression is

$$K_a = \frac{[H_3O^+][A^-]}{[HA]}$$

which is often simplified as

$$K_a = \frac{[H^+][A^-]}{[HA]}$$

- $[H_2O]$ is never included because it is assumed to be constant

Acid strength

- A strong acid has a very large K_a value
  - The acid completely dissociates (ionizes) in water
  - The dissociation (ionization) equilibrium position lies all the way to the right
  - Strong acids have very weak conjugate bases
  - The common strong acids are nitric acid [$HNO_3(aq)$], hydrochloric acid [$HCl(aq)$], sulfuric acid [$H_2SO(aq)$] and perchloric acid [$HClO_4(aq)$]
- A weak acid has a small K_a value
  - The acid dissociates (ionizes) to only a slight extent
  - The dissociation (ionization) equilibrium position lies far to the left
  - Weak acids have relatively strong conjugate bases
  - Percent dissociation of a weak acid

$$\% \text{ dissociation} = \frac{\text{amount dissociated (mol/L)}}{\text{initial concentration (mol/L)}} \times 100\%$$

  - The smaller the percent dissociation, the weaker the acid
  - Dilution of a weak acid increases its percent dissociation

Autoionization of water

- Water is an amphoteric substance: it behaves as both an acid and a base
- Water reacts with itself in an acid–base reaction

$$H_2O(l) + H_2O(l) \rightleftharpoons H_3O^+(aq) + OH^-(aq)$$

which leads to the equilibrium expression

$$K_w = [H_3O^+][OH^-] \quad \text{or} \quad [H^+][OH^-] = K_w$$

- K_w is the ion-product constant for water
- At 25°C in pure water $[H^+] = [OH^-] = 1.0 \times 10^{-7}$, so $K_w = 1.0 \times 10^{-14}$
- Acidic solution: $[H^+] > [OH^-]$
- Basic solution: $[OH^-] > [H^+]$
- Neutral solution: $[H^+] = [OH^-]$

The pH scale
- $pH = -\log[H^+]$
- Since pH is a log scale, the pH changes by 1 for every 10-fold change in $[H^+]$
- The log scale is also used for $[OH^-]$ and for K_a values

$$pOH = -\log[OH^-]$$
$$pK_a = -\log K_a$$

Bases
- Strong bases are hydroxide salts, such as NaOH and KOH
- Weak bases react with water to produce OH^-

$$B(aq) + H_2O(l) \rightleftharpoons BH^+(aq) + OH^-(aq)$$

- The equilibrium constant for this reaction is called K_b where

$$K_b = \frac{[BH^+][OH^-]}{[B]}$$

- In water a base B is always competing with OH^- for a proton (H^+), so K_b values tend to be very small, thus making B a weak base (compared to OH^-)

Polyprotic acids
- A polyprotic acid has more than one acidic proton
- Polyprotic acids dissociate one proton at a time
  - Each step has a characteristic K_a value
  - Typically for a weak polyprotic acid, $K_{a_1} > K_{a_2} > K_{a_3}$
- Sulfuric acid is unique
  - It is a strong acid in the first dissociation step (K_{a_1} is very large)
  - It is a weak acid in the second step

Acid–base properties of salts
- Can produce acidic, basic, or neutral solutions
- Salts that contain:
  - Cations of strong bases and anions of strong acids produce neutral solutions
  - Cations of strong bases and anions of weak acids produce basic solutions
  - Cations of weak bases and anions of strong acids produce acidic solutions
- Acidic solutions are produced by salts containing a highly charged metal cation—for example, Al^{3+} and Fe^{3+}

Effect of structure on acid–base properties
- Many substances that function as acids or bases contain the H—O—X grouping
  - Molecules in which the O—X bond is strong and covalent tend to behave as acids
    - As X becomes more electronegative, the acid becomes stronger
  - When the O—X bond is ionic, the substance behaves as a base, releasing OH^- ions in water

REVIEW QUESTIONS

1. Define each of the following:
   a. Arrhenius acid
   b. Brønsted–Lowry acid
   c. Lewis acid
   Which of the definitions is most general? Write reactions to justify your answer.

2. Define or illustrate the meaning of the following terms:
   a. K_a reaction
   b. K_a equilibrium constant
   c. K_b reaction
   d. K_b equilibrium constant
   e. conjugate acid–base pair

3. Define or illustrate the meaning of the following terms:
   a. amphoteric
   b. K_w reaction
   c. K_w equilibrium constant
   d. pH
   e. pOH
   f. pK_w
   Give the conditions for a neutral solution at 25°C, in terms of [H^+], pH, and the relationship between [H^+] and [OH^-]. Do the same for an acidic solution and for a basic solution. As a solution becomes more acidic, what happens to pH, pOH, [H^+], and [OH^-]? As a solution becomes more basic, what happens to pH, pOH, [H^+], and [OH^-]?

4. How is acid strength related to the value of K_a? What is the difference between strong acids versus weak acids (see Table 14.1)? As the strength of an acid increases, what happens to the strength of the conjugate base? How is base strength related to the value of K_b? As the strength of a base increases, what happens to the strength of the conjugate acid?

5. Two strategies are followed when solving for the pH of an acid in water. What is the strategy for calculating the pH of a strong acid in water? What major assumptions are made when solving strong acid problems? The best way to recognize strong acids is to memorize them. List the six common strong acids (the two not listed in the text are HBr and HI).

   Most acids, by contrast, are weak acids. When solving for the pH of a weak acid in water, you must have the K_a value. List two places in this text that provide K_a values for weak acids. You can utilize these tables to help you recognize weak acids. What is the strategy for calculating the pH of a weak acid in water? What assumptions are generally made? What is the 5% rule? If the 5% rule fails, how do you calculate the pH of a weak acid in water?

6. Two strategies are also followed when solving for the pH of a base in water. What is the strategy for calculating the pH of a strong base in water? List the strong bases mentioned in the text that should be committed to memory. Why is calculating the pH of $Ca(OH)_2$ solutions a little more difficult than calculating the pH of NaOH solutions?

   Most bases are weak bases. The presence of what element most commonly results in basic properties for an organic compound? What is present on this element in compounds that allows it to accept a proton?

   Table 14.3 and Appendix 5 of the text list K_b values for some weak bases. What strategy is used to solve for the pH of a weak base in water? What assumptions are made when solving for the pH of weak base solutions? If the 5% rule fails, how do you calculate the pH of a weak base in water?

7. Table 14.4 lists the stepwise K_a values for some polyprotic acids. What is the difference between a monoprotic acid, a diprotic acid, and a triprotic acid? Most polyprotic acids are weak acids; the major exception is H_2SO_4. To solve for the pH of a solution of H_2SO_4, you must solve a strong acid problem as well as a weak acid problem. Explain. Write out the reactions that refer to K_{a_1} and K_{a_2} for H_2SO_4.

   For H_3PO_4, $K_{a_1} = 7.5 \times 10^{-3}$, $K_{a_2} = 6.2 \times 10^{-8}$, and $K_{a_3} = 4.8 \times 10^{-13}$. Write out the reactions that refer to the K_{a_1}, K_{a_2}, and K_{a_3} equilibrium constants. What are the three acids in a solution of H_3PO_4? Which acid is strongest? What are the three conjugate bases in a solution of H_3PO_4? Which conjugate base is strongest? Summarize the strategy for calculating the pH of a polyprotic acid in water.

8. For conjugate acid–base pairs, how are K_a and K_b related? Consider the reaction of acetic acid in water

$$CH_3CO_2H(aq) + H_2O(l) \rightleftharpoons CH_3CO_2^-(aq) + H_3O^+(aq)$$

   where $K_a = 1.8 \times 10^{-5}$.
   a. Which two bases are competing for the proton?
   b. Which is the stronger base?
   c. In light of your answer to part b, why do we classify the acetate ion ($CH_3CO_2^-$) as a weak base? Use an appropriate reaction to justify your answer.

   In general, as base strength increases, conjugate acid strength decreases. Explain why the conjugate acid of the weak base NH_3 is a weak acid.

   To summarize, the conjugate base of a weak acid is a weak base and the conjugate acid of a weak base is a weak acid (weak gives you weak). Assuming K_a for a monoprotic strong acid is 1×10^6, calculate K_b for the conjugate base of this strong acid. Why do conjugate bases of strong acids have no basic properties in water? List the conjugate bases of the six common strong acids. To tie it all together, some instructors have students think of Li^+, K^+, Rb^+, Cs^+, Ca^{2+}, Sr^{2+}, and Ba^{2+} as the conjugate acids of the strong bases LiOH, KOH, RbOH, CsOH, $Ca(OH)_2$, $Sr(OH)_2$, and $Ba(OH)_2$. Although not technically correct, the conjugate acid strength of these cations is similar to the conjugate base strength of the strong acids. That is, these cations have no acidic properties in water; similarly, the conjugate bases of strong acids have no basic properties (strong gives you worthless). Fill in the blanks with the correct response. The conjugate base of a weak acid is a _____ base. The conjugate acid of a weak base is a _____ acid. The conjugate base of a strong acid is a _____ base. The conjugate acid of a strong base is a _____ acid. (*Hint:* Weak gives you weak and strong gives you worthless.)

9. What is a salt? List some anions that behave as weak bases in water. List some anions that have no basic properties in water. List some cations that behave as weak acids in water. List some cations that have no acidic properties in water. Using these lists, give some formulas for salts that have only weak base properties in water. What strategy would you use to solve for the pH of these basic salt solutions? Identify some salts that have only weak acid properties in water. What strategy would you use to solve for the pH of these acidic salt solutions? Identify some salts that have no acidic or basic properties in water (produce neutral solutions). When a salt contains both a weak acid ion and a weak base ion, how do you predict whether the solution pH is acidic, basic, or neutral?

10. For oxyacids, how does acid strength depend on
    a. the strength of the bond to the acidic hydrogen atom?
    b. the electronegativity of the element bonded to the oxygen atom that bears the acidic hydrogen?
    c. the number of oxygen atoms?
    How does the strength of a conjugate base depend on these factors?
        What type of solution forms when a nonmetal oxide dissolves in water? Give an example of such an oxide. What type of solution forms when a metal oxide dissolves in water? Give an example of such an oxide.

Active Learning Questions

These questions are designed to be used by groups of students in class. The questions allow students to explore their understanding of concepts through discussion and peer teaching. The real value of these questions is the learning that occurs while students talk to each other about chemical concepts.

1. Consider two beakers of pure water at different temperatures. How do their pH values compare? Which is more acidic? more basic? Explain.

2. Differentiate between the terms *strength* and *concentration* as they apply to acids and bases. When is HCl strong? Weak? Concentrated? Dilute? Answer the same questions for ammonia. Is the conjugate base of a weak acid a strong base?

3. Sketch two graphs: (a) percent dissociation for weak acid HA versus the initial concentration of HA ($[HA]_0$) and (b) H^+ concentration versus $[HA]_0$. Explain both.

4. Consider a solution prepared by mixing a weak acid HA and HCl. What are the major species? Explain what is occurring in solution. How would you calculate the pH? What if you added NaA to this solution? Then added NaOH?

5. Explain why salts can be acidic, basic, or neutral, and show examples. Do this without specific numbers.

6. Consider two separate aqueous solutions: one of a weak acid HA and one of HCl. Assuming you started with 10 molecules of each:
   a. Draw a picture of what each solution looks like at equilibrium.
   b. What are the major species in each beaker?
   c. From your pictures, calculate the K_a values of each acid.
   d. Order the following from the strongest to the weakest base: H_2O, A^-, Cl^-. Explain your order.

7. You are asked to calculate the H^+ concentration in a solution of $NaOH(aq)$. Because sodium hydroxide is a base, can we say there is no H^+, since having H^+ would imply that the solution is acidic?

8. Consider a solution prepared by mixing a weak acid HA, HCl, and NaA. Which of the following statements best describes what happens?

a. The H^+ from the HCl reacts completely with the A^- from the NaA. Then the HA dissociates somewhat.

b. The H^+ from the HCl reacts somewhat with the A^- from the NaA to make HA, while the HA is dissociating. Eventually you have equal amounts of everything.

c. The H^+ from the HCl reacts somewhat with the A^- from the NaA to make HA while the HA is dissociating. Eventually all the reactions have equal rates.

d. The H^+ from the HCl reacts completely with the A^- from the NaA. Then the HA dissociates somewhat until "too much" H^+ and A^- are formed, so the H^+ and A^- react to form HA, and so on. Eventually equilibrium is reached.

Justify your choice, and for choices you did not pick, explain what is wrong with them.

9. Consider a solution formed by mixing 100.0 mL of 0.10 M HA ($K_a = 1.0 \times 10^{-6}$), 100.00 mL of 0.10 M NaA, and 100.0 mL of 0.10 M HCl. In calculating the pH for the final solution, you would make some assumptions about the order in which various reactions occur to simplify the calculations. State these assumptions. Does it matter whether the reactions actually occur in the assumed order? Explain.

10. A certain sodium compound is dissolved in water to liberate Na^+ ions and a certain negative ion. What evidence would you look for to determine whether the anion is behaving as an acid or a base? How could you tell whether the anion is a strong base? Explain how the anion could behave simultaneously as an acid and a base.

11. Acids and bases can be thought of as chemical opposites (acids are proton donors, and bases are proton acceptors). Therefore, one might think that $K_a = 1/K_b$. Why isn't this the case? What is the relationship between K_a and K_b? Prove it with a derivation.

12. Consider two solutions of the salts $NaX(aq)$ and $NaY(aq)$ at equal concentrations. What would you need to know to determine which solution has the higher pH? Explain how you would decide (perhaps even provide a sample calculation).

13. What is meant by *pH*? True or false: A strong acid solution always has a lower pH than a weak acid solution. Explain.

14. Why is the pH of water at 25°C equal to 7.00?

15. Can the pH of a solution be negative? Explain.

A blue question or exercise number indicates that the answer to that question or exercise appears at the back of this book and a solution appears in the *Solutions Guide*.

Questions

16. Why is H_3O^+ the strongest acid and OH^- the strongest base that can exist in significant amounts in aqueous solutions?

17. How many significant figures are there in the numbers: 10.78, 6.78, 0.78? If these were pH values, to how many significant figures can you express the $[H^+]$? Explain any discrepancies between your answers to the two questions.

18. In terms of orbitals and electron arrangements, what must be present for a molecule or an ion to act as a Lewis acid? What must be present for a molecule or an ion to act as a Lewis base?

19. Give three example solutions that fit each of the following descriptions.
  a. A strong electrolyte solution that is very acidic.
  b. A strong electrolyte solution that is slightly acidic.
  c. A strong electrolyte solution that is very basic.
  d. A strong electrolyte solution that is slightly basic.
  e. A strong electrolyte solution that is neutral.

20. Derive an expression for the relationship between pK_a and pK_b for a conjugate acid–base pair. ($pK = -\log K$.)

21. Consider the following statements. Write out an example reaction and K expression that is associated with each statement.
  a. The autoionization of water.
  b. An acid reacts with water to produce the conjugate base of the acid and the hydronium ion.
  c. A base reacts with water to produce the conjugate acid of the base and the hydroxide ion.

22. Which of the following statements is(are) true? Correct the false statements.
  a. When a base is dissolved in water, the lowest possible pH of the solution is 7.0.
  b. When an acid is dissolved in water, the lowest possible pH is 0.
  c. A strong acid solution will have a lower pH than a weak acid solution.
  d. A 0.0010 M $Ba(OH)_2$ solution has a pOH that is twice the pOH value of a 0.0010 M KOH solution.

23. Consider the following mathematical expressions.
  a. $[H^+] = [HA]_o$
  b. $[H^+] = (K_a \times [HA]_o)^{1/2}$
  c. $[OH^-] = 2[B]_o$
  d. $[OH^-] = (K_b \times [B]_o)^{1/2}$

  For each expression, give three solutions where the mathematical expression would give a good approximation for the $[H^+]$ or $[OH^-]$. $[Ha_o]$ and $[B]$ represent initial concentrations of an acid or a base.

24. Consider a 0.10 M H_2CO_3 solution and a 0.10 M H_2SO_4 solution. Without doing any detailed calculations, choose one of the following statements that best describes the $[H^+]$ of each solution and explain your answer.
  a. The $[H^+]$ is less than 0.10 M.
  b. The $[H^+]$ is 0.10 M.

  c. The $[H^+]$ is between 0.10 M and 0.20 M.
  d. The $[H^+]$ is 0.20 M.

25. Of the hydrogen halides, only HF is a weak acid. Give a possible explanation.

26. Explain why the following are done, both of which are related to acid/base chemistry.
  a. Power plants burning coal with high sulfur content use scrubbers to help eliminate sulfur emissions.
  b. A gardener mixes lime (CaO) into the soil of his garden.

Exercises

In this section similar exercises are paired.

Nature of Acids and Bases

27. Write balanced equations that describe the following reactions.
  a. the dissociation of perchloric acid in water
  b. the dissociation of propanoic acid ($CH_3CH_2CO_2H$) in water
  c. the dissociation of ammonium ion in water

28. Write the dissociation reaction and the corresponding K_a equilibrium expression for each of the following acids in water.
  a. HCN
  b. HOC_6H_5
  c. $C_6H_5NH_3^+$

29. For each of the following aqueous reactions, identify the acid, the base, the conjugate base, and the conjugate acid.
  a. $H_2O + H_2CO_3 \rightleftharpoons H_3O^+ + HCO_3^-$
  b. $C_5H_5NH^+ + H_2O \rightleftharpoons C_5H_5N + H_3O^+$
  c. $HCO_3^- + C_5H_5NH^+ \rightleftharpoons H_2CO_3 + C_5H_5N$

30. For each of the following aqueous reactions, identify the acid, the base, the conjugate base, and the conjugate acid.
  a. $Al(H_2O)_6^{3+} + H_2O \rightleftharpoons H_3O^+ + Al(H_2O)_5(OH)^{2+}$
  b. $H_2O + HONH_3^+ \rightleftharpoons HONH_2 + H_3O^+$
  c. $HOCl + C_6H_5NH_2 \rightleftharpoons OCl^- + C_6H_5NH_3^+$

31. Classify each of the following as a strong acid or a weak acid.

  a.   **b.**   **c.**   **d.**

H
O
Cl
S

32. Consider the following illustrations:

H^+
A^-
B^-

Which beaker best illustrates what happens when the following acids are dissolved in water?

a. HNO_2 d. HF
b. HNO_3 e. $HC_2H_3O_2$
c. HCl

33. Use Table 14.2 to order the following from the strongest to the weakest acid.

$$HClO_2, \quad H_2O, \quad NH_4^+, \quad HClO_4$$

34. Use Table 14.2 to order the following from the strongest to the weakest base.

$$ClO_2^-, \quad H_2O, \quad NH_3, \quad ClO_4^-$$

35. You may need Table 14.2 to answer the following questions.
    a. Which is the stronger acid, HCl or H_2O?
    b. Which is the stronger acid, H_2O or HNO_2?
    c. Which is the stronger acid, HCN or HOC_6H_5?

36. You may need Table 14.2 to answer the following questions.
    a. Which is the stronger base, Cl^- or H_2O?
    b. Which is the stronger base, H_2O or NO_2^-?
    c. Which is the stronger base, CN^- or $OC_6H_5^-$?

Autoionization of Water and the pH Scale

37. Calculate the $[OH^-]$ of each of the following solutions at 25°C. Identify each solution as neutral, acidic, or basic.
    a. $[H^+] = 1.0 \times 10^{-7} M$ c. $[H^+] = 12 M$
    b. $[H^+] = 8.3 \times 10^{-16} M$ d. $[H^+] = 5.4 \times 10^{-5} M$

38. Calculate the $[H^+]$ of each of the following solutions at 25°C. Identify each solution as neutral, acidic, or basic.
    a. $[OH^-] = 1.5 M$ c. $[OH^-] = 1.0 \times 10^{-7} M$
    b. $[OH^-] = 3.6 \times 10^{-15} M$ d. $[OH^-] = 7.3 \times 10^{-4} M$

39. Values of K_w as a function of temperature are as follows:

Temperature (°C)	K_w
0	1.14×10^{-15}
25	1.00×10^{-14}
35	2.09×10^{-14}
40.	2.92×10^{-14}
50.	5.47×10^{-14}

    a. Is the autoionization of water exothermic or endothermic?
    b. Calculate $[H^+]$ and $[OH^-]$ in a neutral solution at 50.°C.

40. At 40°C the value of K_w is 2.92×10^{-14}.
    a. Calculate the $[H^+]$ and $[OH^-]$ in pure water at 40°C.
    b. What is the pH of pure water at 40°C?
    c. If the hydroxide ion concentration in a solution is 0.10 M, what is the pH at 40°C?

41. Calculate the pH and pOH of the solutions in Exercises 37 and 38.

42. Calculate $[H^+]$ and $[OH^-]$ for each solution at 25°C. Identify each solution as neutral, acidic, or basic.
    a. pH = 7.40 (the normal pH of blood)
    b. pH = 15.3

c. pH = -1.0
d. pH = 3.20
e. pOH = 5.0
f. pOH = 9.60

43. Fill in the missing information in the following table.

	pH	pOH	$[H^+]$	$[OH^-]$	Acidic, Basic, or Neutral?
Solution a	6.88				
Solution b				$8.4 \times 10^{-14} M$	
Solution c		3.11			
Solution d			$1.0 \times 10^{-7} M$		

44. Fill in the missing information in the following table.

	pH	pOH	$[H^+]$	$[OH^-]$	Acidic, Basic, or Neutral?
Solution a	9.63				
Solution b				$3.9 \times 10^{-6} M$	
Solution c			0.027 M		
Solution d		12.2			

45. The pH of a sample of gastric juice in a person's stomach is 2.1. Calculate the pOH, $[H^+]$, and $[OH^-]$ for this sample. Is gastric juice acidic or basic?

46. The pOH of a sample of baking soda dissolved in water is 5.74 at 25°C. Calculate the pH, $[H^+]$, and $[OH^-]$ for this sample. Is the solution acidic or basic?

Solutions of Acids

47. What are the major species present in 0.250 M solutions of each of the following acids? Calculate the pH of each of these solutions.
    a. $HClO_4$ b. HNO_3

48. Calculate the pH of each of the following solutions of a strong acid in water.
    a. 0.10 M HCl   c. $1.0 \times 10^{-11} M$ HCl
    b. 5.0 M HCl

49. A solution is prepared by adding 50.0 mL of 0.050 M HCl to 150.0 mL of 0.10 M HNO_3. Calculate the concentrations of all species in this solution.

50. A solution is prepared by mixing 90.0 mL of 5.00 M HCl and 30.0 mL of 8.00 M HNO_3. Water is then added until the final volume is 1.00 L. Calculate $[H^+]$, $[OH^-]$, and the pH for this solution.

reactions causing the solution to be acidic or basic. The relevant K_a and K_b values are found in Tables 14.2 and 14.3.

a. KCl   c. CH_3NH_3Cl e. NH_4F Acidic

b. $NH_4C_2H_3O_2$ d. KF basic   f. CH_3NH_3CN basic

Relationships Between Structure and Strengths of Acids and Bases

113. Place the species in each of the following groups in order of increasing acid strength. Explain the order you chose for each group.

a. HIO_3, $HBrO_3$ c. HOCl, HOI

b. HNO_2, HNO_3 d. H_3PO_4, H_3PO_3

114. Place the species in each of the following groups in order of increasing base strength. Give your reasoning in each case.

a. IO_3^-, BrO_3^- b. NO_2^-, NO_3^- c. OCl^-, OI^-

115. Place the species in each of the following groups in order of increasing acid strength.

a. H_2O, H_2S, H_2Se (bond energies: H—O, 467 kJ/mol; H—S, 363 kJ/mol; H—Se, 276 kJ/mol)

b. CH_3CO_2H, FCH_2CO_2H, F_2CHCO_2H, F_3CCO_2H

c. NH_4^+, $HONH_3^+$

d. NH_4^+, PH_4^+ (bond energies: N—H, 391 kJ/mol; P—H, 322 kJ/mol)

Give reasons for the orders you chose.

116. Using your results from Exercise 115, place the species in each of the following groups in order of increasing base strength.

a. OH^-, SH^-, SeH^- b. NH_3, PH_3 c. NH_3, $HONH_2$

117. Will the following oxides give acidic, basic, or neutral solutions when dissolved in water? Write reactions to justify your answers.

a. CaO   b. SO_2 c. Cl_2O

118. Will the following oxides give acidic, basic, or neutral solutions when dissolved in water? Write reactions to justify your answers.

a. Li_2O b. CO_2 c. SrO

Lewis Acids and Bases

119. Identify the Lewis acid and the Lewis base in each of the following reactions.

a. $B(OH)_3(aq) + H_2O(l) \rightleftharpoons B(OH)_4^-(aq) + H^+(aq)$

b. $Ag^+(aq) + 2NH_3(aq) \rightleftharpoons Ag(NH_3)_2^+(aq)$

c. $BF_3(g) + F^-(aq) \rightleftharpoons BF_4^-(aq)$

120. Identify the Lewis acid and the Lewis base in each of the following reactions.

a. $Fe^{3+}(aq) + 6H_2O(l) \rightleftharpoons Fe(H_2O)_6^{3+}(aq)$

b. $H_2O(l) + CN^-(aq) \rightleftharpoons HCN(aq) + OH^-(aq)$

c. $HgI_2(s) + 2I^-(aq) \rightleftharpoons HgI_4^{2-}(aq)$

121. Aluminum hydroxide is an amphoteric substance. It can act as either a Brønsted–Lowry base or a Lewis acid. Write a reaction showing $Al(OH)_3$ acting as a base toward H^+ and as an acid toward OH^-.

122. Zinc hydroxide is an amphoteric substance. Write equations that describe $Zn(OH)_2$ acting as a Brønsted–Lowry base toward H^+ and as a Lewis acid toward OH^-.

123. Would you expect Fe^{3+} or Fe^{2+} to be the stronger Lewis acid? Explain.

124. Use the Lewis acid–base model to explain the following reaction.

$$CO_2(g) + H_2O(l) \longrightarrow H_2CO_3(aq)$$

Additional Exercises

125. A 10.0-mL sample of an HCl solution has a pH of 2.000. What volume of water must be added to change the pH to 4.000?

126. Which of the following represent conjugate acid–base pairs? For those pairs that are not conjugates, write the correct conjugate acid or base for each species in the pair.

a. H_2O, OH^- c. H_3PO_4, $H_2PO_4^-$

b. H_2SO_4, SO_4^{2-} d. $HC_2H_3O_2$, $C_2H_3O_2^-$

127. A solution is made by adding 50.0 mL of 0.200 M acetic acid ($K_a = 1.8 \times 10^{-5}$) to 50.0 mL of 1.00×10^{-3} M HCl.

a. Calculate the pH of the solution.

b. Calculate the acetate ion concentration.

128. You have 100.0 g of saccharin, a sugar substitute, and you want to prepare a pH = 5.75 solution. What volume of solution can be prepared? For saccharin, $HC_7H_4NSO_3$, $pK_a = 11.70$ ($pK_a = -\log K_a$).

129. A solution is tested for pH and conductivity as pictured below:

The solution contains one of the following substances: HCl, NaOH, NH_4Cl, HCN, NH_3, HF, or NaCN. If the solute concentration is about 1.0 M, what is the identity of the solute?

130. A 0.25-g sample of lime (CaO) is dissolved in enough water to make 1500 mL of solution. Calculate the pH of the solution.

131. At 25°C, a saturated solution of benzoic acid ($K_a = 6.4 \times 10^{-5}$) has a pH of 2.80. Calculate the water solubility of benzoic acid in moles per liter.

132. Calculate the pH and $[S^{2-}]$ in a 0.10 M H_2S solution. Assume $K_{a_1} = 1.0 \times 10^{-7}$; $K_{a_2} = 1.0 \times 10^{-19}$.

133. A typical vitamin C tablet (containing pure ascorbic acid, $H_2C_6H_6O_6$) weighs 500. mg. One vitamin C tablet is dissolved in enough water to make 200.0 mL of solution. Calculate the pH of this solution. Ascorbic acid is a diprotic acid.

134. Calculate the pH of an aqueous solution containing 1.0×10^{-2} M HCl, 1.0×10^{-2} M H_2SO_4, and 1.0×10^{-2} M HCN.

135. Acrylic acid (CH_2=$CHCO_2H$) is a precursor for many important plastics. K_a for acrylic acid is 5.6×10^{-5}.
    a. Calculate the pH of a 0.10 M solution of acrylic acid.
    b. Calculate the percent dissociation of a 0.10 M solution of acrylic acid.
    c. Calculate the pH of a 0.050 M solution of sodium acrylate ($NaC_3H_3O_2$).

136. A 0.20 M sodium chlorobenzoate ($NaC_7H_4ClO_2$) solution has a pH of 8.65. Calculate the pH of a 0.20 M chlorobenzoic acid ($HC_7H_4ClO_2$) solution.

137. The equilibrium constant K_a for the reaction

$$Fe(H_2O)_6^{3+}(aq) + H_2O(l) \rightleftharpoons$$
$$Fe(H_2O)_5(OH)^{2+}(aq) + H_3O^+(aq)$$

is 6.0×10^{-3}.
    a. Calculate the pH of a 0.10 M solution of $Fe(H_2O)_6^{3+}$.
    b. Will a 1.0 M solution of iron(II) nitrate have a higher or lower pH than a 1.0 M solution of iron(III) nitrate? Explain.

138. Rank the following 0.10 M solutions in order of increasing pH.
    a. HI, HF, NaF, NaI
    b. NH_4Br, HBr, KBr, NH_3
    c. $C_6H_5NH_3NO_3$, $NaNO_3$, NaOH, HOC_6H_5, KOC_6H_5, $C_6H_5NH_2$, HNO_3

139. Is an aqueous solution of $NaHSO_4$ acidic, basic, or neutral? What reaction occurs with water? Calculate the pH of a 0.10 M solution of $NaHSO_4$.

140. Calculate [CO_3^{2-}] in a 0.010 M solution of CO_2 in water (H_2CO_3). If all the CO_3^{2-} in this solution comes from the reaction

$$HCO_3^-(aq) \rightleftharpoons H^+(aq) + CO_3^{2-}(aq)$$

what percentage of the H^+ ions in the solution is a result of the dissociation of HCO_3^-? When acid is added to a solution of sodium hydrogen carbonate ($NaHCO_3$), vigorous bubbling occurs. How is this reaction related to the existence of carbonic acid (H_2CO_3) molecules in aqueous solution?

141. Hemoglobin (abbreviated Hb) is a protein that is responsible for the transport of oxygen in the blood of mammals. Each hemoglobin molecule contains four iron atoms that are the binding sites for O_2 molecules. The oxygen binding is pH dependent. The relevant equilibrium reaction is

$$HbH_4^{4+}(aq) + 4O_2(g) \rightleftharpoons Hb(O_2)_4(aq) + 4H^+(aq)$$

Use Le Châtelier's principle to answer the following.
    a. What form of hemoglobin, HbH_4^{4+} or $Hb(O_2)_4$, is favored in the lungs? What form is favored in the cells?
    b. When a person hyperventilates, the concentration of CO_2 in the blood is decreased. How does this affect the oxygen-binding equilibrium? How does breathing into a paper bag help to counteract this effect?
    c. When a person has suffered a cardiac arrest, injection of a sodium bicarbonate solution is given. Why is this necessary?

142. Calculate the value for the equilibrium constant for each of the following aqueous reactions.
    a. $NH_3 + H_3O^+ \rightleftharpoons NH_4^+ + H_2O$
    b. $NO_2^- + H_3O^+ \rightleftharpoons HNO_2 + H_2O$
    c. $NH_4^+ + OH^- \rightleftharpoons NH_3 + H_2O$
    d. $HNO_2 + OH^- \rightleftharpoons H_2O + NO_2^-$

143. Students are often surprised to learn that organic acids, such as acetic acid, contain —OH groups. Actually, all oxyacids contain hydroxyl groups. Sulfuric acid, usually written as H_2SO_4, has the structural formula $SO_2(OH)_2$, where S is the central atom. Identify the acids whose structural formulas are shown below. Why do they behave as acids, while NaOH and KOH are bases?
    a. $SO(OH)_2$ b. $ClO_2(OH)$ c. $HPO(OH)_2$

Challenge Problems

144. The pH of 1.0×10^{-8} M hydrochloric acid is not 8.00. The correct pH can be calculated by considering the relationship between the molarities of the three principal ions in the solution (H^+, Cl^-, and OH^-). These molarities can be calculated from algebraic equations that can be derived from the considerations given below.
    a. The solution is electrically neutral.
    b. The hydrochloric acid can be assumed to be 100% ionized.
    c. The product of the molarities of the hydronium ions and the hydroxide ions must equal K_w.
    Calculate the pH of a 1.0×10^{-8} HCl solution.

145. Calculate the pH of a 1.0×10^{-7} M solution of NaOH in water.

146. Calculate [OH^-] in a 3.0×10^{-7} M solution of $Ca(OH)_2$.

147. Consider 50.0 mL of a solution of weak acid HA = $K_a(1.00 \times 10^{-6})$, which has a pH of 4.000. What volume of water must be added to make the pH = 5.000?

148. Making use of the assumptions we ordinarily make in calculating the pH of an aqueous solution of a weak acid, calculate the pH of a 1.0×10^{-6} M solution of hypobromous acid (HBrO, $K_a = 2 \times 10^{-9}$). What is wrong with your answer? Why is it wrong? Without trying to solve the problem, tell what has to be included to solve the problem correctly.

149. Calculate the pH of a 0.200 M solution of C_5H_5NHF. *Hint:* C_5H_5NHF is a salt composed of $C_5H_5NH^+$ and F^- ions. The principal equilibrium in this solution is the best acid reacting with the best base; the reaction for the principal equilibrium is

$$C_5H_5NH^+(aq) + F^-(aq) \rightleftharpoons$$
$$C_5H_5N(aq) + HF(aq) \quad K = 8.2 \times 10^{-3}$$

150. Determine the pH of a 0.50 M solution of NH_4OCl. See Exercise 149.

151. Calculate [OH^-] in a solution obtained by adding 0.0100 mol of solid NaOH to 1.00 L of 15.0 M NH_3.

152. What mass of NaOH(s) must be added to 1.0 L of 0.050 M NH_3 to ensure that the percent ionization of NH_3 is no greater than 0.0010%? Assume no volume change on addition of NaOH.

153. A certain acid, HA, has a vapor density of 5.11 g/L when in the gas phase at a temperature of 25°C and a pressure of 1.00 atm. When 1.50 g of this acid is dissolved in enough water to make 100.0 mL of solution, the pH is found to be 1.80. Calculate K_a for the acid.

154. Calculate the mass of sodium hydroxide that must be added to 1.00 L of 1.00 M $HC_2H_3O_2$ to double the pH of the solution (assume that the NaOH does not change the volume of the solution).

155. Consider the species PO_4^{3-}, HPO_4^{2-}, and $H_2PO_4^-$. Each ion can act as a base in water. Determine the K_b value for each of these species. Which species is the strongest base?

156. Calculate the pH of a 0.10 M solution of sodium phosphate. See Exercise 155.

157. Will 0.10 M solutions of the following salts be acidic, basic, or neutral? See Appendix 5 for K_a values.
  a. ammonium bicarbonate
  b. sodium dihydrogen phosphate
  c. sodium hydrogen phosphate
  d. ammonium dihydrogen phosphate
  e. ammonium formate

158. a. The principal equilibrium in a solution of $NaHCO_3$ is

$$HCO_3^-(aq) + HCO_3^-(aq) \rightleftharpoons H_2CO_3(aq) + CO_3^{2-}(aq)$$

  Calculate the value of the equilibrium constant for this reaction.
  b. At equilibrium, what is the relationship between $[H_2CO_3]$ and $[CO_3^{2-}]$?
  c. Using the equilibrium

$$H_2CO_3(aq) \rightleftharpoons 2H^+(aq) + CO_3^{2-}(aq)$$

  derive an expression for the pH of the solution in terms of K_{a_1} and K_{a_2} using the result from part b.
  d. What is the pH of a solution of $NaHCO_3$?

159. A 0.100-g sample of the weak acid HA (molar mass = 100.0 g/mol) is dissolved in 500.0 g of water. The freezing point of the resulting solution is $-0.0056°C$. Calculate the value of K_a for this acid. Assume molarity equals molarity in this solution.

160. A sample containing 0.0500 mol of $Fe_2(SO_4)_3$ is dissolved in enough water to make 1.00 L of solution. This solution contains hydrated SO_4^{2-} and $Fe(H_2O)_6^{3+}$ ions. The latter behaves as an acid:

$$Fe(H_2O)_6^{3+}(aq) \rightleftharpoons Fe(H_2O)_5OH^{2+}(aq) + H^+(aq)$$

  a. Calculate the expected osmotic pressure of this solution at 25°C if the above dissociation is negligible.
  b. The actual osmotic pressure of the solution is 6.73 atm at 25°C. Calculate K_a for the dissociation reaction of $Fe(H_2O)_6^{3+}$. (To do this calculation, you must assume that none of the ions goes through the semipermeable membrane. Actually, this is not a great assumption for the tiny H^+ ion.)

Integrative Problems

These problems require the integration of multiple concepts to find the solutions.

161. A 2.14-g sample of sodium hypoiodite is dissolved in water to make 1.25 L of solution. The solution pH is 11.32. What is K_b for the hypoiodite ion?

162. Isocyanic acid (HNCO) can be prepared by heating sodium cyanate in the presence of solid oxalic acid according to the equation

$$2NaOCN(s) + H_2C_2O_4(s) \longrightarrow 2HNCO(l) + Na_2C_2O_4(s)$$

Upon isolating pure $HNCO(l)$, an aqueous solution of HNCO can be prepared by dissolving the liquid HNCO in water. What is the pH of a 100.-mL solution of HNCO prepared from the reaction of 10.0 g each of NaOCN and $H_2C_2O_4$, assuming all of the HNCO produced is dissolved in solution? (K_a of HNCO = 1.2×10^{-4}.)

163. Papaverine hydrochloride (abbreviated $papH^+Cl^-$; molar mass = 378.85 g/mol) is a drug that belongs to a group of medicines called vasodilators, which cause blood vessels to expand, thereby increasing blood flow. This drug is the conjugate acid of the weak base papaverine (abbreviated pap; $K_b = 8.33 \times 10^{-9}$ at 35.0°C). Calculate the pH of a 30.0 mg/mL aqueous dose of $papH^+Cl^-$ prepared at 35.0°C. K_w at 35.0°C is 2.1×10^{-14}.

Marathon Problems*

These problems are designed to incorporate several concepts and techniques into one situation. Marathon Problems can be used in class by groups of students to help facilitate problem-solving skills.

164. Captain Kirk, of the Starship *Enterprise*, has been told by his superiors that only a chemist can be trusted with the combination to the safe containing the dilithium crystals that power the ship. The combination is the pH of solution A, described below, followed by the pH of solution C. (Example: If the pH of solution A is 3.47 and that of solution C is 8.15, then the combination to the safe is 3-47-8-15.) The chemist must determine the combination using only the information below (all solutions are at 25°C):

Solution A is 50.0 mL of a 0.100 M solution of the weak monoprotic acid HX.
Solution B is a 0.0500 M solution of the salt NaX. It has a pH of 10.02.
Solution C is made by adding 15.0 mL of 0.250 M KOH to solution A.
What is the combination to the safe?

165. For the following, mix equal volumes of one solution from Group I with one solution from Group II to achieve the indicated pH. Calculate the pH of each solution.

Group I: 0.20 M NH_4Cl, 0.20 M HCl, 0.20 M $C_6H_5NH_3Cl$, 0.20 M $(C_2H_5)_3NHCl$
Group II: 0.20 M KOI, 0.20 M NaCN, 0.20 M KOCl, 0.20 M $NaNO_2$

  a. the solution with the lowest pH
  b. the solution with the highest pH
  c. the solution with the pH closest to 7.00

 Get help understanding core concepts and visualizing molecular-level interactions, and practice problem solving, by visiting the Online Study Center at **college.hmco.com/ PIC/zumdahl7e.**

*Used with permission from the *Journal of Chemical Education,* Vol. 68, No. 11, 1991, pp. 919–922; copyright © 1991, Division of Chemical Education, Inc.

15 Applications of Aqueous Equilibria

Contents

Stalactites are formed when carbonate minerals dissolve in ground water acidified by carbon dioxide and then solidify when the water evaporates.

M uch important chemistry, including almost all the chemistry of the natural world, occurs in aqueous solution. We have already introduced one very significant class of aqueous equilibria, acid–base reactions. In this chapter we consider more applications of acid–base chemistry and introduce two additional types of aqueous equilibria, those involving the solubility of salts and those involving the formation of complex ions.

The interplay of acid–base, solubility, and complex ion equilibria is often important in natural processes, such as the weathering of minerals, the uptake of nutrients by plants, and tooth decay. For example, limestone ($CaCO_3$) will dissolve in water made acidic by dissolved carbon dioxide:

$$CO_2(aq) + H_2O(l) \rightleftharpoons H^+(aq) + HCO_3^-(aq)$$
$$H^+(aq) + CaCO_3(s) \rightleftharpoons Ca^{2+}(aq) + HCO_3^-(aq)$$

This two-step process and its reverse account for the formation of limestone caves and the stalactites and stalagmites found therein. In the forward direction of the process, the acidic water (containing carbon dioxide) dissolves the underground limestone deposits, thereby forming a cavern. The reverse process occurs as the water drips from the ceiling of the cave, and the carbon dioxide is lost to the air. This causes solid calcium carbonate to form, producing stalactites on the ceiling and stalagmites where the drops hit the cave floor.

Before we consider the other types of aqueous equilibria, we will deal with acid–base equilibria in more detail.

Acid–Base Equilibria

15.1 Solutions of Acids or Bases Containing a Common Ion

In Chapter 14 we were concerned with calculating the equilibrium concentrations of species (particularly H^+ ions) in solutions containing an acid or a base. In this section we discuss solutions that contain not only the weak acid HA but also its salt NaA. Although this appears to be a new type of problem, we will see that this case can be handled rather easily using the procedures developed in Chapter 14.

Suppose we have a solution containing the weak acid hydrofluoric acid (HF, $K_a = 7.2 \times 10^{-4}$) and its salt sodium fluoride (NaF). Recall that when a salt dissolves in water, it breaks up completely into its ions—it is a strong electrolyte:

$$NaF(s) \xrightarrow{H_2O(l)} Na^+(aq) + F^-(aq)$$

Since hydrofluoric acid is a weak acid and only slightly dissociated, the major species in the solution are HF, Na^+, F^-, and H_2O. The **common ion** in this solution is F^-, since it is produced by both hydrofluoric acid and sodium fluoride. What effect does the presence of the dissolved sodium fluoride have on the dissociation equilibrium of hydrofluoric acid?

To answer this question, we compare the extent of dissociation of hydrofluoric acid in two different solutions, the first containing 1.0 *M* HF and the second containing 1.0 *M* HF and 1.0 M NaF. By Le Châtelier's principle, we would expect the dissociation equilibrium for HF

$$HF(aq) \rightleftharpoons H^+(aq) + F^-(aq)$$

in the second solution to be *driven to the left by the presence of F⁻ ions from the NaF.* Thus the extent of dissociation of HF will be *less* in the presence of dissolved NaF:

$$HF(aq) \rightleftharpoons H^+(aq) + F^-(aq)$$

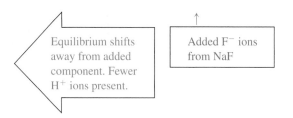

| Equilibrium shifts away from added component. Fewer H⁺ ions present. | Added F⁻ ions from NaF |

The common ion effect is an application of Le Châtelier's principle.

The shift in equilibrium position that occurs because of the addition of an ion already involved in the equilibrium reaction is called the **common ion effect.** This effect makes a solution of NaF and HF less acidic than a solution of HF alone.

The common ion effect is quite general. For example, solid NH_4Cl added to a 1.0 M NH_3 solution produces additional ammonium ions:

$$NH_4Cl(s) \xrightarrow{H_2O} NH_4^+(aq) + Cl^-(aq)$$

and this causes the position of the ammonia–water equilibrium to shift to the left:

$$NH_3(aq) + H_2O(l) \rightleftharpoons NH_4^+(aq) + OH^-(aq)$$

This reduces the equilibrium concentration of OH^- ions.

The common ion effect is also important in solutions of polyprotic acids. The production of protons by the first dissociation step greatly inhibits the succeeding dissociation steps, which, of course, also produce protons, the common ion in this case. We will see later in this chapter that the common ion effect is also important in dealing with the solubility of salts.

Equilibrium Calculations

The procedures for finding the pH of a solution containing a weak acid or base plus a common ion are very similar to the procedures, which we covered in Chapter 14, for solutions containing the acids or bases alone. For example, in the case of a weak acid, the only important difference is that the initial concentration of the anion A^- is not zero in a solution that also contains the salt NaA. Sample Exercise 15.1 illustrates a typical example using the same general approach we developed in Chapter 14.

| *Sample Exercise 15.1* | **Acidic Solutions Containing Common Ions** |

In Section 14.5 we found that the equilibrium concentration of H^+ in a 1.0 M HF solution is $2.7 \times 10^{-2} M$, and the percent dissociation of HF is 2.7%. Calculate $[H^+]$ and the percent dissociation of HF in a solution containing 1.0 M HF ($K_a = 7.2 \times 10^{-4}$) and 1.0 M NaF.

Major Species

F⁻

Na⁺

HF

H₂O

Solution

As the aqueous solutions we consider become more complex, it is more important than ever to be systematic and to *focus on the chemistry* occurring in the solution before thinking about mathematical procedures. The way to do this is *always* to write the major species first and consider the chemical properties of each one.

In a solution containing 1.0 M HF and 1.0 M NaF, the major species are

$$HF, \quad F^-, \quad Na^+, \quad and \quad H_2O$$

We know that Na^+ ions have neither acidic nor basic properties and that water is a very weak acid (or base). Therefore, the important species are HF and F^-, which participate in the acid dissociation equilibrium that controls $[H^+]$ in this solution. That is, the position of the equilibrium

$$HF(aq) \rightleftharpoons H^+(aq) + F^-(aq)$$

will determine $[H^+]$ in the solution. The equilibrium expression is

$$K_a = \frac{[H^+][F^-]}{[HF]} = 7.2 \times 10^{-4}$$

The important concentrations are shown in the following table.

Initial Concentration (mol/L)		Equilibrium Concentration (mol/L)
$[HF]_0 = 1.0$ (from dissolved HF)		$[HF] = 1.0 - x$
$[F^-]_0 = 1.0$ (from dissolved NaF)	$\xrightarrow[\text{dissociates}]{x \text{ mol/L HF}}$	$[F^-] = 1.0 + x$
$[H^+]_0 = 0$ (neglect contribution from H₂O)		$[H^+] = x$

Note that $[F^-]_0 = 1.0 \, M$ because of the dissolved sodium fluoride and that at equilibrium $[F^-] > 1.0 \, M$ because when the acid dissociates it produces F^- as well as H^+. Then

$$K_a = 7.2 \times 10^{-4} = \frac{[H^+][F^-]}{[HF]} = \frac{(x)(1.0 + x)}{1.0 - x} \approx \frac{(x)(1.0)}{1.0}$$

(since x is expected to be small).

Solving for x gives

$$x = \frac{1.0}{1.0}(7.2 \times 10^{-4}) = 7.2 \times 10^{-4}$$

Noting that x is small compared to 1.0, we conclude that this result is acceptable. Thus

$$[H^+] = x = 7.2 \times 10^{-4} \, M \qquad \text{(The pH is 3.14.)}$$

The percent dissociation of HF in this solution is

$$\frac{[H^+]}{[HF]_0} \times 100 = \frac{7.2 \times 10^{-4} \, M}{1.0 \, M} \times 100 = 0.072\%$$

Compare these values for $[H^+]$ and percent dissociation of HF with those for a 1.0 M HF solution, where $[H^+] = 2.7 \times 10^{-2} \, M$ and the percent dissociation is 2.7%. The large difference shows clearly that the presence of the F^- ions from the dissolved NaF greatly inhibits the dissociation of HF. The position of the acid dissociation equilibrium has been shifted to the left by the presence of F^- ions from NaF.

See Exercises 15.25 and 15.26.

15.2 Buffered Solutions

The most important application of acid–base solutions containing a common ion is for buffering. A **buffered solution** is one that *resists a change in its pH* when either hydroxide ions or protons are added. The most important practical example of a buffered solution is our blood, which can absorb the acids and bases produced in biologic reactions without changing its pH. A constant pH for blood is vital because cells can survive only in a very narrow pH range.

A buffered solution may contain a *weak* acid and its salt (for example, HF and NaF) or a *weak* base and its salt (for example, NH_3 and NH_4Cl). By choosing the appropriate components, a solution can be buffered at virtually any pH.

In treating buffered solutions in this chapter, we will start by considering the equilibrium calculations. We will then use these results to show how buffering works. That is, we will answer the question: How does a buffered solution resist changes in pH when an acid or a base is added?

As you do the calculations associated with buffered solutions, keep in mind that these are merely solutions containing weak acids or bases, and the procedures required are the same ones we have already developed. Be sure to use the systematic approach introduced in Chapter 14.

The most important buffering system in the blood involves HCO_3^- and H_2CO_3.

The systematic approach developed in Chapter 14 for weak acids and bases applies to buffered solutions.

The pH of a Buffered Solution I

Notice as you do this problem that it is exactly like examples you have seen in Chapter 14.

A buffered solution contains 0.50 M acetic acid ($HC_2H_3O_2$, $K_a = 1.8 \times 10^{-5}$) and 0.50 M sodium acetate ($NaC_2H_3O_2$). Calculate the pH of this solution.

Solution

The major species in the solution are

$$HC_2H_3O_2, \quad Na^+, \quad C_2H_3O_2^-, \quad \text{and} \quad H_2O$$

↑	↑	↑	↑
Weak acid	Neither acid nor base	Base (conjugate base of $HC_2H_3O_2$)	Very weak acid or base

Examination of the solution components leads to the conclusion that the acetic acid dissociation equilibrium, which involves both $HC_2H_3O_2$ and $C_2H_3O_2^-$, will control the pH of the solution:

$$HC_2H_3O_2(aq) \rightleftharpoons H^+(aq) + C_2H_3O_2^-(aq)$$

$$K_a = 1.8 \times 10^{-5} = \frac{[H^+][C_2H_3O_2^-]}{[HC_2H_3O_2]}$$

The concentrations are as follows:

Initial Concentration (mol/L)		Equilibrium Concentration (mol/L)
$[HC_2H_3O_2]_0 = 0.50$	x mol/L of $HC_2H_3O_2$ dissociates to reach equilibrium	$[HC_2H_3O_2] = 0.50 - x$
$[C_2H_3O_2^-]_0 = 0.50$		$[C_2H_3O_2^-] = 0.50 + x$
$[H^+]_0 \approx 0$		$[H^+] = x$

Major Species

 $HC_2H_3O_2$

 $C_2H_3O_2^-$

Na^+

H_2O

A digital pH meter shows the pH of the buffered solution to be 4.740.

The corresponding ICE table is

	$HC_2H_3O_2(aq)$	$\rightleftharpoons$	$H^+(aq)$	$+$	$C_2H_3O_2^-(aq)$
Initial:	0.50		≈ 0		0.50
Change:	$-x$		$+x$		$+x$
Equilibrium:	$0.50 - x$		x		$0.50 + x$

Then

$$K_a = 1.8 \times 10^{-5} = \frac{[H^+][C_2H_3O_2^-]}{[HC_2H_3O_2]} = \frac{(x)(0.50 + x)}{0.50 - x} \approx \frac{(x)(0.50)}{0.50}$$

and

$$x \approx 1.8 \times 10^{-5}$$

The approximations are valid (by the 5% rule), so

$$[H^+] = x = 1.8 \times 10^{-5}\, M \quad \text{and} \quad \text{pH} = 4.74$$

See Exercises 15.33 and 15.34.

Sample Exercise 15.3	**pH Changes in Buffered Solutions**

Calculate the change in pH that occurs when 0.010 mol solid NaOH is added to 1.0 L of the buffered solution described in Sample Exercise 15.2. Compare this pH change with that which occurs when 0.010 mol solid NaOH is added to 1.0 L of water.

Major Species

$HC_2H_3O_2$

$C_2H_3O_2^-$

Na^+

OH^-

H_2O

Solution

Since the added solid NaOH will completely dissociate, the major species in solution *before any reaction occurs* are $HC_2H_3O_2$, Na^+, $C_2H_3O_2^-$, OH^-, and H_2O. Note that the solution contains a relatively large amount of the very strong base hydroxide ion, which has a great affinity for protons. The best source of protons is the acetic acid, and the reaction that will occur is

$$OH^- + HC_2H_3O_2 \longrightarrow H_2O + C_2H_3O_2^-$$

Although acetic acid is a weak acid, the hydroxide ion is such a strong base that the reaction above will *proceed essentially to completion* (until the OH^- ions are consumed).

The best approach to this problem involves two distinct steps: (1) assume that the reaction goes to completion, and carry out the stoichiometric calculations, and then (2) carry out the equilibrium calculations.

1. *The stoichiometry problem.* The stoichiometry for the reaction is shown below.

Major Species

$HC_2H_3O_2$

$C_2H_3O_2^-$

Na^+

H_2O

	$HC_2H_3O_2$	$+$	OH^-	$\longrightarrow$	$C_2H_3O_2^-$	$+$	H_2O
Before reaction:	1.0 L × 0.50 *M* = 0.50 mol		0.010 mol		1.0 L × 0.50 *M* = 0.50 mol		
After reaction:	0.50 − 0.010 = 0.49 mol		0.010 − 0.010 = 0 mol		0.50 + 0.010 = 0.51 mol		

Note that 0.010 mol $HC_2H_3O_2$ has been converted to 0.010 mol $C_2H_3O_2^-$ by the added OH^-.

(top) Pure water at pH 7.000. (bottom) When 0.01 mol NaOH is added to 1.0 L of pure water, the pH jumps to 12.000.

2. *The equilibrium problem.* After the reaction between OH^- and $HC_2H_3O_2$ is complete, the major species in solution are

$$HC_2H_3O_2, \quad Na^+, \quad C_2H_3O_2^-, \quad \text{and} \quad H_2O$$

The dominant equilibrium involves the dissociation of acetic acid.

This problem is then very similar to that in Sample Exercise 15.2. The only difference is that the addition of 0.010 mol OH^- has consumed some $HC_2H_3O_2$ and produced some $C_2H_3O_2^-$, yielding the following ICE table:

	$HC_2H_3O_2(aq)$	$\rightleftharpoons$	$H^+(aq)$	$+$	$C_2H_3O_2^-(aq)$
Initial:	0.49		0		0.51
Change:	$-x$		$+x$		$+x$
Equilibrium:	$0.49 - x$		x		$0.51 + x$

Note that the initial concentrations are defined after the reaction with OH^- is complete but before the system adjusts to equilibrium. Following the usual procedure gives

$$K_a = 1.8 \times 10^{-5} = \frac{[H^+][C_2H_3O_2^-]}{[HC_2H_3O_2]} = \frac{(x)(0.51 + x)}{0.49 - x} \approx \frac{(x)(0.51)}{0.49}$$

and

$$x \approx 1.7 \times 10^{-5}$$

The approximations are valid (by the 5% rule), so

$$[H^+] = x = 1.7 \times 10^{-5} \quad \text{and} \quad pH = 4.76$$

The change in pH produced by the addition of 0.01 mol OH^- to this buffered solution is then

$$\underset{\substack{\uparrow \\ \text{New solution}}}{4.76} - \underset{\substack{\uparrow \\ \text{Original solution}}}{4.74} = +0.02$$

The pH increased by 0.02 pH units.

Now compare this with what happens when 0.01 mol solid NaOH is added to 1.0 L water to give 0.01 M NaOH. In this case $[OH^-] = 0.01\ M$ and

$$[H^+] = \frac{K_w}{[OH^-]} = \frac{1.0 \times 10^{-14}}{1.0 \times 10^{-2}} = 1.0 \times 10^{-12}$$

$$pH = 12.00$$

Thus the change in pH is

$$\underset{\substack{\uparrow \\ \text{New solution}}}{12.00} - \underset{\substack{\uparrow \\ \text{Pure water}}}{7.00} = +5.00$$

The increase is 5.00 pH units. Note how well the buffered solution resists a change in pH as compared with pure water.

See Exercises 15.35 and 15.36.

Sample Exercises 15.2 and 15.3 represent typical buffer problems that involve all the concepts that you need to know to handle buffered solutions containing weak acids. Pay special attention to the following points:

1. Buffered solutions are simply solutions of weak acids or bases containing a common ion. The pH calculations on buffered solutions require exactly the same procedures introduced in Chapter 14. *This is not a new type of problem.*

2. When a strong acid or base is added to a buffered solution, it is best to deal with the stoichiometry of the resulting reaction first. After the stoichiometric calculations are completed, then consider the equilibrium calculations. This procedure can be presented as follows:

Buffering: How Does It Work?

Visualization: Buffers

Sample Exercises 15.2 and 15.3 demonstrate the ability of a buffered solution to absorb hydroxide ions without a significant change in pH. *But how does a buffer work?* Suppose a buffered solution contains relatively large quantities of a weak acid HA and its conjugate base A^-. When hydroxide ions are added to the solution, since the weak acid represents the best source of protons, the following reaction occurs:

$$OH^- + HA \longrightarrow A^- + H_2O$$

The net result is that OH^- ions are not allowed to accumulate but are replaced by A^- ions.

The stability of the pH under these conditions can be understood by examining the equilibrium expression for the dissociation of HA:

$$K_a = \frac{[H^+][A^-]}{[HA]}$$

or, rearranging,

$$[H^+] = K_a \frac{[HA]}{[A^-]}$$

In a buffered solution the pH is governed by the ratio $[HA]/[A^-]$.

In other words, the *equilibrium concentration of H^+, and thus the pH, is determined by the ratio $[HA]/[A^-]$*. When OH^- ions are added, HA is converted to A^-, and the ratio $[HA]/[A^-]$ decreases. However, *if the amounts of HA and A^- originally present are very large compared with the amount of OH^- added,* the change in the $[HA]/[A^-]$ ratio will be small.

In Sample Exercises 15.2 and 15.3,

$$\frac{[HA]}{[A^-]} = \frac{0.50}{0.50} = 1.0 \quad \text{Initially}$$

$$\frac{[HA]}{[A^-]} = \frac{0.49}{0.51} = 0.96 \quad \text{After adding 0.01 mol/L OH}^-$$

The change in the ratio $[HA]/[A^-]$ is very small. Thus the $[H^+]$ and the pH remain essentially constant.

The essence of buffering, then, is that $[HA]$ and $[A^-]$ are large compared with the amount of OH^- added. Thus, when the OH^- is added, the concentrations of HA and A^- change, but only by small amounts. Under these conditions, the $[HA]/[A^-]$ ratio and thus the $[H^+]$ remain virtually constant.

Visualization: Adding an Acid to a Buffer

Similar reasoning applies when protons are added to a buffered solution of a weak acid and a salt of its conjugate base. Because the A^- ion has a high affinity for H^+, the added H^+ ions react with A^- to form the weak acid:

$$H^+ + A^- \longrightarrow HA$$

and free H^+ ions do not accumulate. In this case there will be a net change of A^- to HA. However, if $[A^-]$ and $[HA]$ are large compared with the $[H^+]$ added, little change in the pH will occur.

The form of the acid dissociation equilibrium expression

$$[H^+] = K_a\frac{[HA]}{[A^-]} \tag{15.1}$$

is often useful for calculating $[H^+]$ in a buffered solution, since $[HA]$ and $[A^-]$ are known. For example, to calculate $[H^+]$ in a buffered solution containing 0.10 M HF ($K_a = 7.2 \times 10^{-4}$) and 0.30 M NaF, we simply substitute into Equation (15.1):

$$[H^+] = (7.2 \times 10^{-4})\frac{0.10}{0.30} = 2.4 \times 10^{-4}\,M$$

Another useful form of Equation (15.1) can be obtained by taking the negative log of both sides:

$$-\log[H^+] = -\log(K_a) - \log\left(\frac{[HA]}{[A^-]}\right)$$

That is,

$$pH = pK_a - \log\left(\frac{[HA]}{[A^-]}\right)$$

or, where inverting the log term reverses the sign:

$$pH = pK_a + \log\left(\frac{[A^-]}{[HA]}\right) = pK_a + \log\left(\frac{[base]}{[acid]}\right) \qquad (15.2)$$

This log form of the expression for K_a is called the **Henderson–Hasselbalch equation** and is useful for calculating the pH of solutions when the ratio $[HA]/[A^-]$ is known.

For a particular buffering system (conjugate acid–base pair), all solutions that have the same ratio $[A^-]/[HA]$ will have the same pH. For example, a buffered solution containing 5.0 M $HC_2H_3O_2$ and 3.0 M $NaC_2H_3O_2$ will have the same pH as one containing 0.050 M $HC_2H_3O_2$ and 0.030 M $NaC_2H_3O_2$. This can be shown as follows:

System	$[A^-]/[HA]$
5.0 M $HC_2H_3O_2$ and 3.0 M $NaC_2H_3O_2$	$\dfrac{3.0\,M}{5.0\,M} = 0.60$
0.050 M $HC_2H_3O_2$ and 0.030 M $NaC_2H_3O_2$	$\dfrac{0.030\,M}{0.050\,M} = 0.60$

Therefore,

$$pH = pK_a + \log\left(\frac{[C_2H_3O_2^-]}{[HC_2H_3O_2]}\right) = 4.74 + \log(0.60) = 4.74 - 0.22 = 4.52$$

Note that in using this equation we have assumed that the equilibrium concentrations of A^- and HA are equal to the initial concentrations. That is, we are assuming the validity of the approximations

$$[A^-] = [A^-]_0 + x \approx [A^-]_0 \quad \text{and} \quad [HA] = [HA]_0 - x \approx [HA]_0$$

where x is the amount of acid that dissociates. Since the initial concentrations of HA and A^- are relatively large in a buffered solution, this assumption is generally acceptable.

| *Sample Exercise 15.4* | **The pH of a Buffered Solution II** |

Calculate the pH of a solution containing 0.75 M lactic acid ($K_a = 1.4 \times 10^{-4}$) and 0.25 M sodium lactate. Lactic acid ($HC_3H_5O_3$) is a common constituent of biologic systems. For example, it is found in milk and is present in human muscle tissue during exertion.

Major Species

$HC_3H_5O_3$

$C_3H_5O_3^-$

Na^+

H_2O

Solution

The major species in solution are

$$HC_3H_5O_3, \quad Na^+, \quad C_3H_5O_3^-, \quad \text{and} \quad H_2O$$

Since Na^+ has no acid–base properties and H_2O is a weak acid or base, the pH will be controlled by the lactic acid dissociation equilibrium:

$$HC_3H_5O_3(aq) \rightleftharpoons H^+(aq) + C_3H_5O_3^-(aq)$$

$$K_a = \frac{[H^+][C_3H_5O_3^-]}{[HC_3H_5O_3]} = 1.4 \times 10^{-4}$$

Since $[HC_3H_5O_3]_0$ and $[C_3H_5O_3^-]_0$ are relatively large,

$$[HC_3H_5O_3] \approx [HC_3H_5O_3]_0 = 0.75 \ M$$

and

$$[C_3H_5O_3^-] \approx [C_3H_5O_3^-]_0 = 0.25 \ M$$

Thus, using the rearranged K_a expression, we have

$$[H^+] = K_a \frac{[HC_3H_5O_3]}{[C_3H_5O_3^-]} = (1.4 \times 10^{-4}) \frac{(0.75 \ M)}{(0.25 \ M)} = 4.2 \times 10^{-4} \ M$$

and

$$pH = -\log(4.2 \times 10^{-4}) = 3.38$$

Alternatively, we could use the Henderson–Hasselbalch equation:

$$pH = pK_a + \log\left(\frac{[C_3H_5O_3^-]}{[HC_3H_5O_3]}\right) = 3.85 + \log\left(\frac{0.25 \ M}{0.75 \ M}\right) = 3.38$$

See Exercises 15.37 and 15.38.

Buffered solutions also can be formed from a weak base and the corresponding conjugate acid. In these solutions, the weak base B reacts with any H^+ added:

$$B + H^+ \longrightarrow BH^+$$

and the conjugate acid BH^+ reacts with any added OH^-:

$$BH^+ + OH^- \longrightarrow B + H_2O$$

The approach needed to perform pH calculations for these systems is virtually identical to that used above. This makes sense because, as is true of all buffered solutions, a weak acid (BH^+) and a weak base (B) are present. A typical case is illustrated in Sample Exercise 15.5.

| Sample Exercise 15.5 | **The pH of a Buffered Solution III** |

A buffered solution contains 0.25 M NH_3 ($K_b = 1.8 \times 10^{-5}$) and 0.40 M NH_4Cl. Calculate the pH of this solution.

Major Species

 Cl^-

 NH_4^+

 NH_3

H_2O

Solution

The major species in solution are

$$NH_3, \quad \underbrace{NH_4^+, \quad Cl^-,}_{\text{From the dissolved } NH_4Cl} \quad \text{and} \quad H_2O$$

Since Cl^- is such a weak base and water is a weak acid or base, the important equilibrium is

$$NH_3(aq) + H_2O(l) \rightleftharpoons NH_4^+(aq) + OH^-(aq)$$

and

$$K_b = 1.8 \times 10^{-5} = \frac{[NH_4^+][OH^-]}{[NH_3]}$$

The appropriate ICE table is:

	$NH_3(aq)$	$+$	$H_2O(l)$	$\rightleftharpoons$	$NH_4^+(aq)$	$+$	$OH^-(aq)$
Initial:	0.25		—		0.40		≈ 0
Change:	$-x$		—		$+x$		$+x$
Equilibrium:	$0.25 - x$		—		$0.40 + x$		x

Then

$$K_b = 1.8 \times 10^{-5} = \frac{[NH_4^+][OH^-]}{[NH_3]} = \frac{(0.40 + x)(x)}{0.25 - x} \approx \frac{(0.40)(x)}{0.25}$$

and
$$x \approx 1.1 \times 10^{-5}$$

The approximations are valid (by the 5% rule), so

$$[OH^-] = x = 1.1 \times 10^{-5}$$
$$pOH = 4.95$$
$$pH = 14.00 - 4.95 = 9.05$$

This case is typical of a buffered solution in that the initial and equilibrium concentrations of buffering materials are essentially the same.

Alternative Solution

There is another way of looking at this problem. Since the solution contains relatively large quantities of *both* NH_4^+ and NH_3, we can use the equilibrium

$$NH_3(aq) + H_2O(l) \rightleftharpoons NH_4^+(aq) + OH^-(aq)$$

to calculate $[OH^-]$ and then calculate $[H^+]$ from K_w as we have just done. Or we can use the dissociation equilibrium for NH_4^+, that is,

$$NH_4^+(aq) \rightleftharpoons NH_3(aq) + H^+(aq)$$

to calculate $[H^+]$ directly. *Either choice will give the same answer,* since the same equilibrium concentrations of NH_3 and NH_4^+ must satisfy both equilibria.

We can obtain the K_a value for NH_4^+ from the given K_b value for NH_3, since $K_a \times K_b = K_w$:

$$K_a = \frac{K_w}{K_b} = \frac{1.0 \times 10^{-14}}{1.8 \times 10^{-5}} = 5.6 \times 10^{-10}$$

Then, using the Henderson–Hasselbalch equation, we have

$$pH = pK_a + \log\left(\frac{[base]}{[acid]}\right)$$
$$= 9.25 + \log\left(\frac{0.25\,M}{0.40\,M}\right) = 9.25 - 0.20 = 9.05$$

See Exercises 15.37 and 15.38.

Adding Strong Acid to a Buffered Solution I

Calculate the pH of the solution that results when 0.10 mol gaseous HCl is added to 1.0 L of the buffered solution from Sample Exercise 15.5.

Solution

Before any reaction occurs, the solution contains the following major species:

$$NH_3, \quad NH_4^+, \quad Cl^-, \quad H^+, \quad \text{and} \quad H_2O$$

What reaction can occur? We know that H^+ will not react with Cl^- to form HCl. In contrast to Cl^-, the NH_3 molecule has a great affinity for protons (this is demonstrated by the fact that NH_4^+ is such a weak acid [$K_a = 5.6 \times 10^{-10}$]). Thus NH_3 will react with H^+ to form NH_4^+:

$$NH_3(aq) + H^+(aq) \longrightarrow NH_4^+(aq)$$

Major Species

 Cl^-

 H^+

 NH_4^+

 NH_3

H_2O

Since this reaction can be assumed to go essentially to completion to form the very weak acid NH_4^+, we will do the stoichiometry calculations before we consider the equilibrium calculations. That is, we will let the reaction run to completion and then consider the equilibrium. The stoichiometry calculations for this process are shown below.

Remember: Think about the chemistry first. Ask yourself if a reaction will occur among the major species.

	NH_3	$+$	H^+	$\longrightarrow$	NH_4^+
Before reaction:	(1.0 L)(0.25 M) = 0.25 mol		0.10 mol ↑ Limiting reactant		(1.0 L)(0.40 M) = 0.40 mol
After reaction:	0.25 − 0.10 = 0.15 mol		0		0.40 + 0.10 = 0.50 mol

Major Species

Cl^-

 NH_4^+

 NH_3

H_2O

After the reaction goes to completion, the solution contains the major species

$$NH_3, \quad NH_4^+, \quad Cl^-, \quad \text{and} \quad H_2O$$

and

$$[NH_3]_0 = \frac{0.15 \text{ mol}}{1.0 \text{ L}} = 0.15 \, M$$

$$[NH_4^+]_0 = \frac{0.50 \text{ mol}}{1.0 \text{ L}} = 0.50 \, M$$

We can use the Henderson–Hasselbalch equation, where

$$[\text{Base}] = [NH_3] \approx [NH_3]_0 = 0.15 \, M$$
$$[\text{Acid}] = [NH_4^+] \approx [NH_4^+]_0 = 0.50 \, M$$

Then

$$\text{pH} = \text{p}K_a + \log\left(\frac{[NH_3]}{[NH_4^+]}\right)$$

$$= 9.25 + \log\left(\frac{0.15 \, M}{0.50 \, M}\right) = 9.25 - 0.52 = 8.73$$

Note that the addition of HCl only slightly decreases the pH, as we would expect in a buffered solution.

See Exercise 15.39.

Summary of the Most Important Characteristics of Buffered Solutions

- Buffered solutions contain relatively large concentrations of a weak acid and the corresponding weak base. They can involve a weak acid HA and the conjugate base A^- or a weak base B and the conjugate acid BH^+.

- When H^+ is added to a buffered solution, it reacts essentially to completion with the weak base present:

$$H^+ + A^- \longrightarrow HA \quad \text{or} \quad H^+ + B \longrightarrow BH^+$$

- When OH^- is added to a buffered solution, it reacts essentially to completion with the weak acid present:

$$OH^- + HA \longrightarrow A^- + H_2O \quad \text{or} \quad OH^- + BH^+ \longrightarrow B + H_2O$$

- The pH in the buffered solution is determined by the ratio of the concentrations of the weak acid and weak base. As long as this ratio remains virtually constant, the pH will remain virtually constant. This will be the case as long as the concentrations of the buffering materials (HA and A⁻ or B and BH⁺) are large compared with the amounts of H⁺ or OH⁻ added.

15.3 Buffering Capacity

A buffer with a large capacity contains large concentrations of the buffering components.

The **buffering capacity** of a buffered solution represents the amount of protons or hydroxide ions the buffer can absorb without a significant change in pH. A buffer with a large capacity contains large concentrations of buffering components and so can absorb a relatively large amount of protons or hydroxide ions and show little pH change. *The pH of a buffered solution is determined by the ratio [A⁻]/[HA]. The capacity of a buffered solution is determined by the magnitudes of [HA] and [A⁻].*

| *Sample Exercise 15.7* | **Adding Strong Acid to a Buffered Solution II** |

Calculate the change in pH that occurs when 0.010 mol gaseous HCl is added to 1.0 L of each of the following solutions:

$$\text{Solution A:} \quad 5.00 \ M \ HC_2H_3O_2 \quad \text{and} \quad 5.00 \ M \ NaC_2H_3O_2$$
$$\text{Solution B:} \quad 0.050 \ M \ HC_2H_3O_2 \quad \text{and} \quad 0.050 \ M \ NaC_2H_3O_2$$

For acetic acid, $K_a = 1.8 \times 10^{-5}$.

Solution

For both solutions the initial pH can be determined from the Henderson–Hasselbalch equation:

$$pH = pK_a + \log\left(\frac{[C_2H_3O_2^-]}{[HC_2H_3O_2]}\right)$$

In each case, $[C_2H_3O_2^-] = [HC_2H_3O_2]$. Therefore, the initial pH for both A and B is

$$pH = pK_a + \log(1) = pK_a = -\log(1.8 \times 10^{-5}) = 4.74$$

After the addition of HCl to each of these solutions, the major species *before any reaction occurs* are

$$HC_2H_3O_2, \quad Na^+, \quad C_2H_3O_2^-, \quad \underbrace{H^+, \quad Cl^-}_{\text{From the added HCl}}, \quad \text{and} \quad H_2O$$

Will any reactions occur among these species? Note that we have a relatively large quantity of H⁺, which will readily react with any effective base. We know that Cl⁻ will not react with H⁺ to form HCl in water. However, $C_2H_3O_2^-$ will react with H⁺ to form the weak acid $HC_2H_3O_2$:

$$H^+(aq) + C_2H_3O_2^-(aq) \longrightarrow HC_2H_3O_2(aq)$$

Because $HC_2H_3O_2$ is a weak acid, we assume that this reaction runs to completion; the 0.010 mol of added H⁺ will convert 0.010 mol $C_2H_3O_2^-$ to 0.010 mol $HC_2H_3O_2$.

For solution A (since the solution volume is 1.0 L, the number of moles equals the molarity), the following calculations apply:

Major Species

 Cl⁻

 $HC_2H_3O_2$

 $C_2H_3O_2^-$

 Na⁺

H⁺

H_2O

	H⁺	+	$C_2H_3O_2^-$	$\longrightarrow$	$HC_2H_3O_2$
Before reaction:	0.010 *M*		5.00 *M*		5.00 *M*
After reaction:	0		4.99 *M*		5.01 *M*

The new pH can be obtained by substituting the new concentrations into the Henderson–Hasselbalch equation:

$$pH = pK_a + \log\left(\frac{[C_2H_3O_2^-]}{[HC_2H_3O_2]}\right)$$

$$= 4.74 + \log\left(\frac{4.99}{5.01}\right) = 4.74 - 0.0017 = 4.74$$

There is virtually no change in pH for solution A when 0.010 mol gaseous HCl is added.

For solution B, the following calculations apply:

	H^+	+	$C_2H_3O_2^-$	$\longrightarrow$	$HC_2H_3O_2$
Before reaction:	0.010 M		0.050 M		0.050 M
After reaction:	0		0.040 M		0.060 M

The new pH is

$$pH = 4.74 + \log\left(\frac{0.040}{0.060}\right)$$

$$= 4.74 - 0.18 = 4.56$$

Although the pH change for solution B is small, a change did occur, which is in contrast to solution A.

These results show that solution A, which contains much larger quantities of buffering components, has a much higher buffering capacity than solution B.

See Exercises 15.39 and 15.40.

We have seen that the pH of a buffered solution depends on the ratio of the concentrations of buffering components. When this ratio is least affected by added protons or hydroxide ions, the solution is the most resistant to a change in pH. To find the ratio that gives optimal buffering, let's suppose we have a buffered solution containing a large concentration of acetate ion and only a small concentration of acetic acid. Addition of protons to form acetic acid will produce a relatively large *percent* change in the concentration of acetic acid and so will produce a relatively large change in the ratio $[C_2H_3O_2^-]/[HC_2H_3O_2]$ (see Table 15.1). Similarly, if hydroxide ions are added to remove some acetic acid, the percent change in the concentration of acetic acid is again large. The same effects are seen if the initial concentration of acetic acid is large and that of acetate ion is small.

TABLE 15.1 Change in $[C_2H_3O_2^-]/[HC_2H_3O_2]$ for Two Solutions When 0.01 mol H^+ Is Added to 1.0 L of Each

Solution	$\left(\dfrac{[C_2H_3O_2^-]}{[HC_2H_3O_2]}\right)_{orig}$	$\left(\dfrac{[C_2H_3O_2^-]}{[HC_2H_3O_2]}\right)_{new}$	Change	Percent Change
A	$\dfrac{1.00\ M}{1.00\ M} = 1.00$	$\dfrac{0.99\ M}{1.01\ M} = 0.98$	$1.00 \rightarrow 0.98$	2.00%
B	$\dfrac{1.00\ M}{0.01\ M} = 100$	$\dfrac{0.99\ M}{0.02\ M} = 49.5$	$100 \rightarrow 49.5$	50.5%

Because large changes in the ratio $[A^-]/[HA]$ will produce large changes in pH, we want to avoid this situation for the most effective buffering. This type of reasoning leads us to the general conclusion that optimal buffering occurs when $[HA]$ is equal to $[A^-]$. It is for this condition that the ratio $[A^-]/[HA]$ is most resistant to change when H^+ or OH^- is added to the buffered solution. This means that when choosing the buffering components for a specific application, we want $[A^-]/[HA]$ to equal 1. It follows that since

$$pH = pK_a + \log\left(\frac{[A^-]}{[HA]}\right) = pK_a + \log(1) = pK_a$$

the *pK_a of the weak acid to be used in the buffer should be as close as possible to the desired pH.* For example, suppose we need a buffered solution with a pH of 4.00. The most effective buffering will occur when $[HA]$ is equal to $[A^-]$. From the Henderson–Hasselbalch equation,

$$pH = pK_a + \log\left(\frac{[A^-]}{[HA]}\right)$$

4.00 is wanted   Ratio = 1 for most effective buffer

That is, $4.00 = pK_a + \log(1) = pK_a + 0$ and $pK_a = 4.00$

Thus the best choice of a weak acid is one that has $pK_a = 4.00$ or $K_a = 1.0 \times 10^{-4}$.

Sample Exercise 15.8 | **Preparing a Buffer**

A chemist needs a solution buffered at pH 4.30 and can choose from the following acids (and their sodium salts):

a. chloroacetic acid ($K_a = 1.35 \times 10^{-3}$)
b. propanoic acid ($K_a = 1.3 \times 10^{-5}$)
c. benzoic acid ($K_a = 6.4 \times 10^{-5}$)
d. hypochlorous acid ($K_a = 3.5 \times 10^{-8}$)

Calculate the ratio $[HA]/[A^-]$ required for each system to yield a pH of 4.30. Which system will work best?

Solution

A pH of 4.30 corresponds to

$$[H^+] = 10^{-4.30} = \text{antilog}(-4.30) = 5.0 \times 10^{-5}\,M$$

Since K_a values rather than pK_a values are given for the various acids, we use Equation (15.1)

$$[H^+] = K_a\frac{[HA]}{[A^-]}$$

rather than the Henderson–Hasselbalch equation. We substitute the required $[H^+]$ and K_a for each acid into Equation (15.1) to calculate the ratio $[HA]/[A^-]$ needed in each case.

Acid	$[H^+] = K_a \dfrac{[HA]}{[A^-]}$	$\dfrac{[HA]}{[A^-]}$
a. Chloroacetic	$5.0 \times 10^{-5} = 1.35 \times 10^{-3}\left(\dfrac{[HA]}{[A^-]}\right)$	3.7×10^{-2}
b. Propanoic	$5.0 \times 10^{-5} = 1.3 \times 10^{-5}\left(\dfrac{[HA]}{[A^-]}\right)$	3.8
c. Benzoic	$5.0 \times 10^{-5} = 6.4 \times 10^{-5}\left(\dfrac{[HA]}{[A^-]}\right)$	0.78
d. Hypochlorous	$5.0 \times 10^{-5} = 3.5 \times 10^{-8}\left(\dfrac{[HA]}{[A^-]}\right)$	1.4×10^{3}

Since $[HA]/[A^-]$ for benzoic acid is closest to 1, the system of benzoic acid and its sodium salt will be the best choice among those given for buffering a solution at pH 4.3. This example demonstrates the principle that the optimal buffering system has a pK_a value close to the desired pH. The pK_a for benzoic acid is 4.19.

See Exercises 15.45 and 15.46.

15.4 Titrations and pH Curves

As we saw in Chapter 4, a titration is commonly used to determine the amount of acid or base in a solution. This process involves a solution of known concentration (the titrant) delivered from a buret into the unknown solution until the substance being analyzed is just consumed. The stoichiometric (equivalence) point is often signaled by the color change of an indicator. In this section we will discuss the pH changes that occur during an acid–base titration. We will use this information later to show how an appropriate indicator can be chosen for a particular titration.

The progress of an acid–base titration is often monitored by plotting the pH of the solution being analyzed as a function of the amount of titrant added. Such a plot is called a **pH curve** or **titration curve**.

Strong Acid–Strong Base Titrations

The net ionic reaction for a strong acid–strong base titration is

$$H^+(aq) + OH^-(aq) \longrightarrow H_2O(l)$$

To compute $[H^+]$ at a given point in the titration, we must determine the amount of H^+ that remains at that point and divide by the total volume of the solution. Before we proceed, we need to consider a new unit, which is especially convenient for titrations. Since titrations usually involve small quantities (burets are typically graduated in milliliters), the mole is inconveniently large. Therefore, we will use the **millimole** (abbreviated **mmol**), which, as the prefix indicates, is a thousandth of a mole:

$$1 \text{ mmol} = \frac{1 \text{ mol}}{1000} = 10^{-3} \text{ mol}$$

A setup used to do the pH titration of an acid or a base.

So far we have defined molarity only in terms of moles per liter. We can now define it in terms of *millimoles per milliliter,* as shown below:

$$\text{Molarity} = \frac{\text{mol solute}}{\text{L solution}} = \frac{\dfrac{\text{mol solute}}{1000}}{\dfrac{\text{L solution}}{1000}} = \frac{\text{mmol solute}}{\text{mL solution}}$$

1 millimole $= 1 \times 10^{-3}$ mol
1 mL $= 1 \times 10^{-3}$ L

$$\frac{\text{mmol}}{\text{mL}} = \frac{\text{mol}}{\text{L}} = M$$

A 1.0 M solution thus contains 1.0 mole of solute per liter of solution or, *equivalently,* 1.0 millimole of solute per milliliter of solution. Just as we obtain the number of moles of solute from the product of the volume in liters and the molarity, we obtain the number of millimoles of solute from the product of the volume in milliliters and the molarity:

$$\text{Number of mmol} = \text{volume (in mL)} \times \text{molarity}$$

CASE STUDY: *Strong Acid–Strong Base Titration*

We will illustrate the calculations involved in a strong acid–strong base titration by considering the titration of 50.0 mL of 0.200 M HNO$_3$ with 0.100 M NaOH. We will calculate the pH of the solution at selected points during the course of the titration, where specific volumes of 0.100 M NaOH have been added.

A. No NaOH has been added.

Since HNO$_3$ is a strong acid (is completely dissociated), the solution contains the major species

$$\text{H}^+, \quad \text{NO}_3^-, \quad \text{and} \quad \text{H}_2\text{O}$$

and the pH is determined by the H$^+$ from the nitric acid. Since 0.200 M HNO$_3$ contains 0.200 M H$^+$,

$$[\text{H}^+] = 0.200 \, M \quad \text{and} \quad \text{pH} = 0.699$$

B. 10.0 mL of 0.100 M NaOH has been added.

In the mixed solution *before any reaction occurs,* the major species are

$$\text{H}^+, \quad \text{NO}_3^-, \quad \text{Na}^+, \quad \text{OH}^-, \quad \text{and} \quad \text{H}_2\text{O}$$

Note that large quantities of both H$^+$ and OH$^-$ are present. The 1.00 mmol (10.0 mL $\times$ 0.100 M) of added OH$^-$ will react with 1.00 mmol H$^+$ to form water:

	H$^+$	+	OH$^-$	$\longrightarrow$	H$_2$O
Before reaction:	50.0 mL $\times$ 0.200 M = 10.0 mmol		10.0 mL $\times$ 0.100 M = 1.00 mmol		
After reaction:	10.0 − 1.00 = 9.0 mmol		1.00 − 1.00 = 0		

After the reaction, the solution contains

$$\text{H}^+, \quad \text{NO}_3^-, \quad \text{Na}^+, \quad \text{and} \quad \text{H}_2\text{O} \text{ (the OH}^- \text{ ions have been consumed)}$$

and the pH will be determined by the H$^+$ remaining:

The final solution volume is the sum of the original volume of HNO$_3$ and the volume of added NaOH.

$$[\text{H}^+] = \frac{\text{mmol H}^+ \text{ left}}{\text{volume of solution (mL)}} = \frac{9.0 \text{ mmol}}{(50.0 + 10.0) \text{ mL}} = 0.15 \, M$$

Original volume of HNO$_3$ solution   Volume of NaOH added

$$\text{pH} = -\log(0.15) = 0.82$$

C. 20.0 mL (total) of 0.100 *M* NaOH has been added.

We consider this point from the perspective that a total of 20.0 mL NaOH has been added to the *original* solution, rather than that 10.0 mL has been added to the solution from point B. It is best to go back to the original solution each time so that a mistake made at an earlier point does not show up in each succeeding calculation. As before, the added OH⁻ will react with H⁺ to form water:

	H^+	$+$	OH^-	$\longrightarrow$	H_2O
Before reaction:	50.0 mL × 0.200 *M* = 10.0 mmol		20.0 mL × 0.100 *M* = 2.00 mmol		
After reaction:	10.0 − 2.00 = 8.00 mmol		2.00 − 2.00 = 0 mmol		

After the reaction

$$[H^+] = \frac{8.00 \text{ mmol}}{(50.0 + 20.0) \text{ mL}} = 0.11 \, M \quad \text{(H}^+ \text{ remaining)}$$

$$pH = 0.942$$

D. 50.0 mL (total) of 0.100 *M* NaOH has been added.

Proceeding exactly as for points B and C, the pH is found to be 1.301.

E. 100.0 mL (total) of 0.100 *M* NaOH has been added.

At this point the amount of NaOH that has been added is

$$100.0 \text{ mL} \times 0.100 \, M = 10.0 \text{ mmol}$$

The original amount of nitric acid was

$$50.0 \text{ mL} \times 0.200 \, M = 10.0 \text{ mmol}$$

Equivalence (stoichiometric) point: The point in the titration where an amount of base has been added to exactly react with all the acid originally present.

Enough OH⁻ has been added to react exactly with the H⁺ from the nitric acid. This is the **stoichiometric point**, or **equivalence point**, of the titration. At this point the major species in solution are

$$Na^+, \quad NO_3^-, \quad \text{and} \quad H_2O$$

Since Na⁺ has no acid or base properties and NO₃⁻ is the anion of the strong acid HNO₃ and is therefore a very weak base, neither NO₃⁻ nor Na⁺ affects the pH, and the solution is neutral (the pH is 7.00).

F. 150.0 mL (total) of 0.100 *M* NaOH has been added.

The stoichiometric calculations for the titration reaction are as follows:

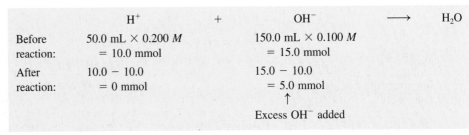

	H^+	$+$	OH^-	$\longrightarrow$	H_2O
Before reaction:	50.0 mL × 0.200 *M* = 10.0 mmol		150.0 mL × 0.100 *M* = 15.0 mmol		
After reaction:	10.0 − 10.0 = 0 mmol		15.0 − 10.0 = 5.0 mmol		

Excess OH⁻ added

Now OH$^-$ is *in excess* and will determine the pH:

$$[OH^-] = \frac{mmol\ OH^-\ in\ excess}{volume\ (mL)} = \frac{5.0\ mmol}{(50.0 + 150.0)\ mL} = \frac{5.0\ mmol}{200.0\ mL} = 0.025\ M$$

Since $[H^+][OH^-] = 1.0 \times 10^{-14}$,

$$[H^+] = \frac{1.0 \times 10^{-14}}{2.5 \times 10^{-2}} = 4.0 \times 10^{-13}\ M \qquad and \qquad pH = 12.40$$

G. 200.0 mL (total) of 0.100 M NaOH has been added.
Proceeding as for point F, the pH is found to be 12.60.

The results of these calculations are summarized by the pH curve shown in Fig. 15.1. Note that the pH changes very gradually until the titration is close to the equivalence point, where a dramatic change occurs. This behavior is due to the fact that early in the titration there is a relatively large amount of H$^+$ in the solution, and the addition of a given amount of OH$^-$ thus produces a small change in pH. However, near the equivalence point [H$^+$] is relatively small, and the addition of a small amount of OH$^-$ produces a large change.

The pH curve in Fig. 15.1, typical of the titration of a strong acid with a strong base, has the following characteristics:

Before the equivalence point, [H$^+$] (and hence the pH) can be calculated by dividing the number of millimoles of H$^+$ remaining by the total volume of the solution in millimeters.

At the equivalence point, the pH is 7.00.

After the equivalence point, [OH$^-$] can be calculated by dividing the number of millimoles of excess OH$^-$ by the total volume of the solution. Then [H$^+$] is obtained from K_w.

The titration of a strong base with a strong acid requires reasoning very similar to that used above, except, of course, that OH$^-$ is in excess before the equivalence point and H$^+$ is in excess after the equivalence point. The pH curve for the titration of 100.0 mL of 0.50 M NaOH with 1.0 M HCl is shown in Fig. 15.2.

FIGURE 15.1
The pH curve for the titration of 50.0 mL of 0.200 M HNO$_3$ with 0.100 M NaOH. Note that the equivalence point occurs at 100.0 mL of NaOH added, the point where exactly enough OH$^-$ has been added to react with all the H$^+$ originally present. The pH of 7 at the equivalence point is characteristic of a strong acid–strong base titration.

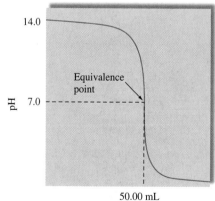

FIGURE 15.2
The pH curve for the titration of 100.0 mL of 0.50 M NaOH with 1.0 M HCl. The equivalence point occurs at 50.00 mL of HCl added, since at this point 5.0 mmol H$^+$ has been added to react with the original 5.0 mmol OH$^-$.

Titrations of Weak Acids with Strong Bases

We have seen that since strong acids and strong bases are completely dissociated, the calculations to obtain the pH curves for titrations involving the two are quite straightforward. However, when the acid being titrated is a weak acid, there is a major difference: To calculate $[H^+]$ after a certain amount of strong base has been added, we must deal with the weak acid dissociation equilibrium. We have dealt with this same situation earlier in this chapter when we treated buffered solutions. Calculation of the pH curve for a titration of a weak acid with a strong base really amounts to a series of buffer problems. In performing these calculations it is very important to remember that even though the acid is weak, it *reacts essentially to completion* with hydroxide ion, a very strong base.

Calculating the pH curve for a weak acid–strong base titration involves a two-step procedure.

Treat the stoichiometry and equilibrium problems separately.

➡ 1 *A stoichiometry problem.* **The reaction of hydroxide ion with the weak acid is assumed to run to completion, and the concentrations of the acid *remaining* and the conjugate base *formed* are determined.**

➡ 2 *An equilibrium problem.* **The position of the weak acid equilibrium is determined, and the pH is calculated.**

It is *essential* to do these steps *separately*. Note that the procedures necessary to do these calculations have all been used before.

CASE STUDY: *Weak Acid–Strong Base Titration*

As an illustration, we will consider the titration of 50.0 mL of 0.10 M acetic acid ($HC_2H_3O_2$, $K_a = 1.8 \times 10^{-5}$) with 0.10 M NaOH. As before, we will calculate the pH at various points representing volumes of added NaOH.

A. No NaOH has been added.

This is a typical weak acid calculation of the type introduced in Chapter 14. The pH is 2.87. (Check this yourself.)

B. 10.0 mL of 0.10 M NaOH has been added.

The major species in the mixed solution *before any reaction takes place* are

$$HC_2H_3O_2, \quad OH^-, \quad Na^+, \quad \text{and} \quad H_2O$$

The strong base OH^- will react with the strongest proton donor, which in this case is $HC_2H_3O_2$.

The Stoichiometry Problem

You are again doing exactly the same type of calculation already considered in Chapter 14.

	OH^-	+	$HC_2H_3O_2$	$\longrightarrow$	$C_2H_3O_2^-$	+	H_2O
Before reaction:	10 mL × 0.10 M = 1.0 mmol		50.0 mL × 0.10 M = 5.0 mmol		0 mmol		
After reaction:	1.0 − 1.0 = 0 mmol ↑ Limiting reactant		5.0 − 1.0 = 4.0 mmol		1.0 mmol ↑ Formed by the reaction		

The Equilibrium Problem

We examine the major components left in the solution *after the reaction takes place* to decide on the dominant equilibrium. The major species are

$$HC_2H_3O_2, \quad C_2H_3O_2^-, \quad Na^+, \quad \text{and} \quad H_2O$$

Since $HC_2H_3O_2$ is a much stronger acid than H_2O, and since $C_2H_3O_2^-$ is the conjugate base of $HC_2H_3O_2$, the pH will be determined by the position of the acetic acid dissociation equilibrium:

$$HC_2H_3O_2(aq) \rightleftharpoons H^+(aq) + C_2H_3O_2^-(aq)$$

where

$$K_a = \frac{[H^+][C_2H_3O_2^-]}{[HC_2H_3O_2]}$$

We follow the usual steps to complete the equilibrium calculations:

	Initial Concentration			Equilibrium Concentration
The initial concentrations are defined after the reaction with OH^- has gone to completion but before any dissociation of $HC_2H_3O_2$ occurs.	$[HC_2H_3O_2]_0 = \dfrac{4.0 \text{ mmol}}{(50.0 + 10.0) \text{ mL}} = \dfrac{4.0}{60.0}$	$\xrightarrow[\text{dissociates}]{x \text{ mmol/mL} \atop HC_2H_3O_2}$		$[HC_2H_3O_2] = \dfrac{4.0}{60.0} - x$
	$[C_2H_3O_2^-]_0 = \dfrac{1.0 \text{ mmol}}{(50.0 + 10.0) \text{ mL}} = \dfrac{1.0}{60.0}$			$[C_2H_3O_2^-] = \dfrac{1.0}{60.0} + x$
	$[H^+]_0 \approx 0$			$[H^+] = x$

The appropriate ICE table is

	$HC_2H_3O_2(aq)$	$\rightleftharpoons$	$H^+(aq)$	+	$C_2H_3O_2^-(aq)$
Initial:	$\dfrac{4.0}{60.0}$		≈ 0		$\dfrac{1.0}{60.0}$
Change:	$-x$		$+x$		$+x$
Equilibrium:	$\dfrac{4.0}{60.0} - x$		x		$\dfrac{1.0}{60.0} + x$

Therefore,

$$1.8 \times 10^{-5} = K_a = \frac{[H^+][C_2H_3O_2^-]}{[HC_2H_3O_2]} = \frac{x\left(\dfrac{1.0}{60.0} + x\right)}{\dfrac{4.0}{60.0} - x} \approx \frac{x\left(\dfrac{1.0}{60.0}\right)}{\dfrac{4.0}{60.0}} = \left(\dfrac{1.0}{4.0}\right)x$$

Note that the approximations made are well within the 5% rule.

$$x = \left(\frac{4.0}{1.0}\right)(1.8 \times 10^{-5}) = 7.2 \times 10^{-5} = [H^+] \quad \text{and} \quad pH = 4.14$$

C. 25.0 mL (total) of 0.10 M NaOH has been added.

The procedure here is very similar to that used at point B and will only be summarized briefly. The stoichiometry problem is summarized as follows:

	OH^-	+	$HC_2H_3O_2$	$\longrightarrow$	$C_2H_3O_2^-$	+	H_2O
Before reaction:	25.0 mL × 0.10 M = 2.5 mmol		50.0 mL × 0.10 M = 5.0 mmol		0 mmol		
After reaction:	2.5 − 2.5 = 0		5.0 − 2.5 = 2.5 mmol		2.5 mmol		

After the reaction, the major species in solution are

$$HC_2H_3O_2, \quad C_2H_3O_2^-, \quad Na^+, \quad \text{and} \quad H_2O$$

The equilibrium that will control the pH is

$$HC_2H_3O_2(aq) \rightleftharpoons H^+(aq) + C_2H_3O_2^-(aq)$$

and the pertinent concentrations are as follows:

Initial Concentration		Equilibrium Concentration
$[HC_2H_3O_2]_0 = \dfrac{2.5 \text{ mmol}}{(50.0 + 25.0) \text{ mL}}$	$\xrightarrow[\text{dissociates}]{x \text{ mmol/mL} \\ HC_2H_3O_2}$	$[HC_2H_3O_2] = \dfrac{2.5}{75.0} - x$
$[C_2H_3O_2^-]_0 = \dfrac{2.5 \text{ mmol}}{(50.0 + 25.0) \text{ mL}}$		$[C_2H_3O_2^-] = \dfrac{2.5}{75.0} + x$
$[H^+]_0 \approx 0$		$[H^+] = x$

The corresponding ICE table is

	$HC_2H_3O_2(aq)$	$\rightleftharpoons$	$H^+(aq)$	$+$	$C_2H_3O_2^-(aq)$
Initial:	$\dfrac{2.5}{75.0}$		≈ 0		$\dfrac{2.5}{75.0}$
Change:	$-x$		$+x$		$+x$
Equilibrium:	$\dfrac{2.5}{75.0} - x$		x		$\dfrac{2.5}{75.0} + x$

Therefore,

$$1.8 \times 10^{-5} = K_a = \frac{[H^+][C_2H_3O_2^-]}{[HC_2H_3O_2]} = \frac{x\left(\dfrac{2.5}{75.0} + x\right)}{\dfrac{2.5}{75.0} - x} \approx \frac{x\left(\dfrac{2.5}{75.0}\right)}{\dfrac{2.5}{75.0}}$$

$$x = 1.8 \times 10^{-5} = [H^+] \quad \text{and} \quad pH = 4.74$$

This is a special point in the titration because it is *halfway to the equivalence point*. The original solution, 50.0 mL of 0.10 M $HC_2H_3O_2$, contained 5.0 mmol $HC_2H_3O_2$. Thus 5.0 mmol OH^- is required to reach the equivalence point. That is, 50 mL NaOH is required, since

$$(50.0 \text{ mL})(0.10 \ M) = 5.0 \text{ mmol}$$

After 25.0 mL NaOH has been added, half the original $HC_2H_3O_2$ has been converted to $C_2H_3O_2^-$. At this point in the titration $[HC_2H_3O_2]_0$ is equal to $[C_2H_3O_2^-]_0$. We can neglect the effect of dissociation; that is,

$$[HC_2H_3O_2] = [HC_2H_3O_2]_0 - x \approx [HC_2H_3O_2]_0$$
$$[C_2H_3O_2^-] = [C_2H_3O_2^-]_0 + x \approx [C_2H_3O_2^-]_0$$

At this point, half the acid has been used up, so

$$[HC_2H_3O_2] = [C_2H_3O_2^-]$$

The expression for K_a at the halfway point is

$$K_a = \frac{[H^+][C_2H_3O_2^-]}{[HC_2H_3O_2]} = \frac{[H^+][C_2H_3O_2^-]_0}{[HC_2H_3O_2]_0} = [H^+]$$

Equal at the halfway point

Then, *at the halfway point* in the titration,

$$[H^+] = K_a \quad \text{and} \quad pH = pK_a$$

D. 40.0 mL (total) of 0.10 M NaOH has been added.

The procedures required here are the same as those used for points B and C. The pH is 5.35. (Check this yourself.)

E. 50.0 mL (total) of 0.10 M NaOH has been added.

This is the equivalence point of the titration; 5.0 mmol OH^- has been added, which will just react with the 5.0 mmol $HC_2H_3O_2$ originally present. At this point the solution contains the major species

$$Na^+, \quad C_2H_3O_2^-, \quad \text{and} \quad H_2O$$

Note that the solution contains $C_2H_3O_2^-$, which is a base. Remember that a base wants to combine with a proton, and the only source of protons in this solution is water. Thus the reaction will be

$$C_2H_3O_2^-(aq) + H_2O(l) \rightleftharpoons HC_2H_3O_2(aq) + OH^-(aq)$$

This is a *weak base* reaction characterized by K_b:

$$K_b = \frac{[HC_2H_3O_2][OH^-]}{[C_2H_3O_2^-]} = \frac{K_w}{K_a} = \frac{1.0 \times 10^{-14}}{1.8 \times 10^{-5}} = 5.6 \times 10^{-10}$$

The relevant concentrations are as follows:

Initial Concentration (before any $C_2H_3O_2^-$ reacts with H_2O)		Equilibrium Concentration
$[C_2H_3O_2^-]_0 = \dfrac{5.0 \text{ mmol}}{(50.0 + 50.0) \text{ mL}}$ $= 0.050 \ M$	$\xrightarrow[\text{with } H_2O]{\begin{array}{c} x \text{ mmol/mL} \\ C_2H_3O_2^- \text{ reacts} \end{array}}$	$[C_2H_3O_2^-] = 0.050 - x$
$[OH^-]_0 \approx 0$		$[OH^-] = x$
$[HC_2H_3O_2]_0 = 0$		$[HC_2H_3O_2] = x$

The corresponding ICE table is

	$C_2H_3O_2^-(aq)$	$+$	$H_2O(l)$	$\rightleftharpoons$	$HC_2H_3O_2(aq)$	$+$	$OH^-(aq)$
Initial:	0.050		—		0		≈ 0
Change:	$-x$		—		$+x$		$+x$
Equilibrium:	$0.050 - x$		—		x		x

Therefore,

$$5.6 \times 10^{-10} = K_b = \frac{[HC_2H_3O_2][OH^-]}{[C_2H_3O_2^-]} = \frac{(x)(x)}{0.050 - x} \approx \frac{x^2}{0.050}$$

$$x \approx 5.3 \times 10^{-6}$$

The approximation is valid (by the 5% rule), so

$$[OH^-] = 5.3 \times 10^{-6} \ M$$

and

$$[H^+][OH^-] = K_w = 1.0 \times 10^{-14}$$

$$[H^+] = 1.9 \times 10^{-9} \ M$$

$$pH = 8.72$$

This is another important result: *The pH at the equivalence point of a titration of a weak acid with a strong base is always greater than 7.* This is so because the anion of the acid, which remains in solution at the equivalence point, is a base. In contrast, for the titration of a strong acid with a strong base, the pH at the equivalence point is 7.0, because the anion remaining in this case is *not* an effective base.

F. 60.0 mL (total) of 0.10 *M* NaOH has been added.

At this point, excess OH^- has been added. The stoichiometric calculations are as follows:

	OH^-	+	$HC_2H_3O_2$	$\longrightarrow$	$C_2H_3O_2^-$	+	H_2O
Before reaction:	60.0 mL × 0.10 *M* = 6.0 mmol		50.0 mL × 0.10 *M* = 5.0 mmol		0 mmol		
After reaction:	6.0 − 5.0 = 1.0 mmol in excess		5.0 − 5.0 = 0		5.0 mmol		

After the reaction is complete, the solution contains the major species

$$Na^+,\quad C_2H_3O_2^-,\quad OH^-,\quad \text{and}\quad H_2O$$

There are two bases in this solution, OH^- and $C_2H_3O_2^-$. However, $C_2H_3O_2^-$ is a weak base compared with OH^-. Therefore, the amount of OH^- produced by reaction of $C_2H_3O_2^-$ with H_2O will be small compared with the excess OH^- already in solution. You can verify this conclusion by looking at point E, where only $5.3 \times 10^{-6}\,M\ OH^-$ was produced by $C_2H_3O_2^-$. The amount in this case will be even smaller, since the excess OH^- will push the K_b equilibrium to the left.

Thus the pH is determined by the excess OH^-:

$$[OH^-] = \frac{\text{mmol of } OH^- \text{ in excess}}{\text{volume (in mL)}} = \frac{1.0\ \text{mmol}}{(50.0 + 60.0)\ \text{mL}}$$
$$= 9.1 \times 10^{-3}\ M$$

and
$$[H^+] = \frac{1.0 \times 10^{-14}}{9.1 \times 10^{-3}} = 1.1 \times 10^{-12}\ M$$

$$pH = 11.96$$

G. 75.0 mL (total) of 0.10 *M* NaOH has been added.

The procedure needed here is very similar to that for point F. The pH is 12.30. (Check this yourself.)

The pH curve for this titration is shown in Fig. 15.3. It is important to note the differences between this curve and that in Fig. 15.1. For example, the shapes of the plots are

FIGURE 15.3
The pH curve for the titration of 50.0 mL of 0.100 *M* $HC_2H_3O_2$ with 0.100 *M* NaOH. Note that the equivalence point occurs at 50.0 mL of NaOH added, where the amount of added OH^- exactly equals the original amount of acid. The pH at the equivalence point is greater than 7.0 because the $C_2H_3O_2^-$ ion present at this point is a base and reacts with water to produce OH^-.

Vol NaOH

The equivalence point is defined by the stoichiometry, not by the pH.

quite different before the equivalence point, although they are very similar after that point. (The shapes of the strong and weak acid curves are the same after the equivalence points because excess OH^- controls the pH in this region in both cases.) Near the beginning of the titration of the weak acid, the pH increases more rapidly than it does in the strong acid case. It levels off near the halfway point and then increases rapidly again. The leveling off near the halfway point is caused by buffering effects. Earlier in this chapter we saw that optimal buffering occurs when [HA] is equal to $[A^-]$. This is exactly the case at the halfway point of the titration. As we can see from the curve, the pH changes least rapidly in this region of the titration.

The other notable difference between the curves for strong and weak acids is the value of the pH at the equivalence point. For the titration of a strong acid, the equivalence point occurs at pH 7. For the titration of a weak acid, the pH at the equivalence point is greater than 7 because of the basicity of the conjugate base of the weak acid.

It is important to understand that the equivalence point in an acid–base titration is *defined by the stoichiometry, not by the pH.* The equivalence point occurs when enough titrant has been added to react exactly with all the acid or base being titrated.

Sample Exercise 15.9 | Titration of a Weak Acid

Hydrogen cyanide gas (HCN), a powerful respiratory inhibitor, is highly toxic. It is a very weak acid ($K_a = 6.2 \times 10^{-10}$) when dissolved in water. If a 50.0-mL sample of 0.100 M HCN is titrated with 0.100 M NaOH, calculate the pH of the solution

a. after 8.00 mL of 0.100 M NaOH has been added.
b. at the halfway point of the titration.
c. at the equivalence point of the titration.

Solution

a. *The stoichiometry problem.* After 8.00 mL of 0.100 M NaOH has been added, the following calculations apply:

	HCN	+	OH^-	$\longrightarrow$	CN^-	+	H_2O
Before reaction:	50.0 mL × 0.100 M = 5.00 mmol		8.00 mL × 0.100 M = 0.800 mmol		0 mmol		
After reaction:	5.00 − 0.800 = 4.20 mmol		0.800 − 0.800 = 0		0.800 mmol		

The equilibrium problem. Since the solution contains the major species

$$HCN, \quad CN^-, \quad Na^+, \quad \text{and} \quad H_2O$$

the position of the acid dissociation equilibrium

$$HCN(aq) \rightleftharpoons H^+(aq) + CN^-(aq)$$

will determine the pH.

Initial Concentration		Equilibrium Concentration
$[HCN]_0 = \dfrac{4.2 \text{ mmol}}{(50.0 + 8.0) \text{ mL}}$		$[HCN] = \dfrac{4.2}{58.0} - x$
$[CN^-]_0 = \dfrac{0.800 \text{ mmol}}{(50.0 + 8.0) \text{ mL}}$	$\xrightarrow[\text{dissociates}]{\substack{x \text{ mmol/mL} \\ \text{HCN}}}$	$[CN^-] = \dfrac{0.80}{58.0} + x$
$[H^+]_0 \approx 0$		$[H^+] = x$

The corresponding ICE table is

	HCN(aq)	$\rightleftharpoons$	H⁺(aq)	+	CN⁻(aq)
Initial:	$\dfrac{4.2}{58.0}$		≈ 0		$\dfrac{0.80}{58.0}$
Change:	$-x$		$+x$		$+x$
Equilibrium:	$\dfrac{4.2}{58.0} - x$		x		$\dfrac{0.80}{58.0} + x$

Substituting the equilibrium concentrations into the expression for K_a gives

The approximations made here are well within the 5% rule.

$$6.2 \times 10^{-10} = K_a = \frac{[\text{H}^+][\text{CN}^-]}{[\text{HCN}]} = \frac{x\left(\dfrac{0.80}{58.0} + x\right)}{\dfrac{4.2}{58.0} - x} \approx \frac{x\left(\dfrac{0.80}{58.0}\right)}{\left(\dfrac{4.2}{58.0}\right)} = x\left(\frac{0.80}{4.2}\right)$$

$$x = 3.3 \times 10^{-9}\,M = [\text{H}^+] \quad \text{and} \quad \text{pH} = 8.49$$

b. *At the halfway point of the titration.* The amount of HCN originally present can be obtained from the original volume and molarity:

$$50.0\ \text{mL} \times 0.100\,M = 5.00\ \text{mmol}$$

Thus the halfway point will occur when 2.50 mmol OH⁻ has been added:

$$\text{Volume of NaOH (in mL)} \times 0.100\,M = 2.50\ \text{mmol OH}^-$$

or

$$\text{Volume of NaOH} = 25.0\ \text{mL}$$

As was pointed out previously, at the halfway point [HCN] is equal to [CN⁻] and pH is equal to $\text{p}K_a$. Thus, after 25.0 mL of 0.100 *M* NaOH has been added,

$$\text{pH} = \text{p}K_a = -\log(6.2 \times 10^{-10}) = 9.21$$

c. *At the equivalence point.* The equivalence point will occur when a total of 5.00 mmol OH⁻ has been added. Since the NaOH solution is 0.100 *M*, the equivalence point occurs when 50.0 mL NaOH has been added. This amount will form 5.00 mmol CN⁻. The major species in solution at the equivalence point are

$$\text{CN}^-, \quad \text{Na}^+, \quad \text{and} \quad \text{H}_2\text{O}$$

Thus the reaction that will control the pH involves the basic cyanide ion extracting a proton from water:

$$\text{CN}^-(aq) + \text{H}_2\text{O}(l) \rightleftharpoons \text{HCN}(aq) + \text{OH}^-(aq)$$

and

$$K_b = \frac{K_w}{K_a} = \frac{1.0 \times 10^{-14}}{6.2 \times 10^{-10}} = 1.6 \times 10^{-5} = \frac{[\text{HCN}][\text{OH}^-]}{[\text{CN}^-]}$$

Initial Concentration		Equilibrium Concentration
$[\text{CN}^-]_0 = \dfrac{5.00\ \text{mmol}}{(50.0 + 50.0)\ \text{mL}}$		$[\text{CN}^-] = (5.00 \times 10^{-2}) - x$
$= 5.00 \times 10^{-2}\,M$	*x* mmol/mL of	
$[\text{HCN}]_0 = 0$	$\xrightarrow[\text{with H}_2\text{O}]{\text{CN}^-\ \text{reacts}}$	$[\text{HCN}] = x$
$[\text{OH}^-]_0 \approx 0$		$[\text{OH}^-] = x$

The corresponding ICE table is

	$CN^-(aq)$	$+$	$H_2O(l)$	$\rightleftharpoons$	$HCN(aq)$	$+$	$OH^-(aq)$
Initial:	0.050		—		0		0
Change:	$-x$		—		$+x$		$+x$
Equilibrium:	$0.050 - x$		—		x		x

Substituting the equilibrium concentrations into the expression for K_b and solving in the usual way gives

$$[OH^-] = x = 8.9 \times 10^{-4}$$

Then, from K_w, we have

$$[H^+] = 1.1 \times 10^{-11} \quad \text{and} \quad \text{pH} = 10.96$$

See Exercises 15.55, 15.57, and 15.58.

The amount of acid present, not its strength, determines the equivalence point.

Two important conclusions can be drawn from a comparison of the titration of 50.0 mL of 0.1 M acetic acid covered earlier in this section and that of 50.0 mL of 0.1 M hydrocyanic acid analyzed in Sample Exercise 15.9. First, the same amount of 0.1 M NaOH is required to reach the equivalence point in both cases. The fact that HCN is a much weaker acid than $HC_2H_3O_2$ has no bearing on the amount of base required. It is the *amount* of acid, not its strength, that determines the equivalence point. Second, the pH value at the equivalence point *is* affected by the acid strength. For the titration of acetic acid, the pH at the equivalence point is 8.72; for the titration of hydrocyanic acid, the pH at the equivalence point is 10.96. This difference occurs because the CN^- ion is a much stronger base than the $C_2H_3O_2^-$ ion. Also, the pH at the halfway point of the titration is much higher for HCN than for $HC_2H_3O_2$, again because of the greater base strength of the CN^- ion (or equivalently, the smaller acid strength of HCN).

The strength of a weak acid has a significant effect on the shape of its pH curve. Figure 15.4 shows pH curves for 50-mL samples of 0.10 M solutions of various acids titrated with 0.10 M NaOH. Note that the equivalence point occurs in each case when the same volume of 0.10 M NaOH has been added but that the shapes of the curves are dramatically different. The weaker the acid, the greater the pH value at the equivalence point. In particular, note that the vertical region that surrounds the equivalence point becomes shorter as the acid being titrated becomes weaker. We will see in the next section that the choice of an indicator is more limited for such a titration.

Besides being used to analyze for the amount of acid or base in a solution, titrations can be used to determine the values of equilibrium constants, as shown in Sample Exercise 15.10.

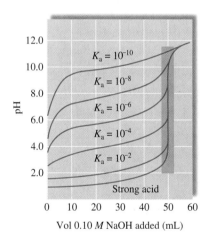

FIGURE 15.4
The pH curves for the titrations of 50.0-mL samples of 0.10 M acids with various K_a values with 0.10 M NaOH.

Calculation of K_a

Sample Exercise 15.10

Calculating K_a

A chemist has synthesized a monoprotic weak acid and wants to determine its K_a value. To do so, the chemist dissolves 2.00 mmol of the solid acid in 100.0 mL water and titrates the resulting solution with 0.0500 M NaOH. After 20.0 mL NaOH has been added, the pH is 6.00. What is the K_a value for the acid?

Solution

The stoichiometry problem. We represent the monoprotic acid as HA. The stoichiometry for the titration reaction is shown below.

	HA	+	OH$^-$	$\longrightarrow$	A$^-$	+	H$_2$O
Before reaction:	2.00 mmol		20.0 mL $\times$ 0.0500 M = 1.00 mmol		0 mmol		
After reaction:	2.00 $-$ 1.00 = 1.00 mmol		1.00 $-$ 1.00 = 0		1.00 mmol		

The equilibrium problem. After the reaction the solution contains the major species

$$HA, \quad A^-, \quad Na^+, \quad \text{and} \quad H_2O$$

The pH will be determined by the equilibrium

$$HA(aq) \rightleftharpoons H^+(aq) + A^-(aq)$$

for which

$$K_a = \frac{[H^+][A^-]}{[HA]}$$

Initial Concentration		**Equilibrium Concentration**
$[HA]_0 = \dfrac{1.00 \text{ mmol}}{(100.0 + 20.0) \text{ mL}}$ $= 8.33 \times 10^{-3} M$	$\xrightarrow[\text{dissociates}]{x \text{ mmol/mL HA}}$	$[HA] = 8.33 \times 10^{-3} - x$
$[A^-] = \dfrac{1.00 \text{ mmol}}{(100.0 + 20.0) \text{ mL}}$ $= 8.33 \times 10^{-3} M$		$[A^-] = 8.33 \times 10^{-3} + x$
$[H^+]_0 \approx 0$		$[H^+] = x$

The corresponding ICE table is

	HA(aq)	$\rightleftharpoons$	H$^+$(aq)	+	A$^-$(aq)
Initial:	8.33×10^{-3}		≈ 0		8.33×10^{-3}
Change:	$-x$		$+x$		$+x$
Equilibrium:	$8.33 \times 10^{-3} - x$		x		$8.33 \times 10^{-3} + x$

Note that x is known here because the pH at this point is known to be 6.00. Thus

$$x = [H^+] = \text{antilog}(-pH) = 1.0 \times 10^{-6} M$$

Substituting the equilibrium concentrations into the expression for K_a allows calculation of the K_a value:

$$
\begin{aligned}
K_a = \frac{[H^+][A^-]}{[HA]} &= \frac{x(8.33 \times 10^{-3} + x)}{(8.33 \times 10^{-3}) - x} \\
&= \frac{(1.0 \times 10^{-6})(8.33 \times 10^{-3} + 1.0 \times 10^{-6})}{(8.33 \times 10^{-3}) - (1.0 \times 10^{-6})} \\
&\approx \frac{(1.0 \times 10^{-6})(8.33 \times 10^{-3})}{8.33 \times 10^{-3}} = 1.0 \times 10^{-6}
\end{aligned}
$$

There is an easier way to think about this problem. The original solution contained 2.00 mmol of HA, and since 20.0 mL of added 0.0500 M NaOH contains 1.0 mmol OH^-, this is the halfway point in the titration (where $[HA]$ is equal to $[A^-]$). Thus

$$[H^+] = K_a = 1.0 \times 10^{-6}$$

See Exercise 15.63.

Titrations of Weak Bases with Strong Acids

Titrations of weak bases with strong acids can be treated using the procedures we introduced previously. As always, you should *think first about the major species in solution* and decide whether a reaction occurs that runs essentially to completion. If such a reaction does occur, let it run to completion and do the stoichiometric calculations. Finally, choose the dominant equilibrium and calculate the pH.

CASE STUDY: *Weak Base–Strong Acid Titration*

The calculations involved for the titration of a weak base with a strong acid will be illustrated by the titration of 100.0 mL of 0.050 M NH_3 with 0.10 M HCl.

Before the addition of any HCl.
1. Major species:

$$NH_3 \quad \text{and} \quad H_2O$$

NH_3 is a base and will seek a source of protons. In this case H_2O is the only available source.

2. No reactions occur that go to completion, since NH_3 cannot readily take a proton from H_2O. This is evidenced by the small K_b value for NH_3.

3. The equilibrium that controls the pH involves the reaction of ammonia with water:

$$NH_3(aq) + H_2O(l) \rightleftharpoons NH_4^+(aq) + OH^-(aq)$$

Use K_b to calculate $[OH^-]$. Although NH_3 is a weak base (compared with OH^-), it produces much more OH^- in this reaction than is produced from the autoionization of H_2O.

Before the equivalence point.
1. Major species (before any reaction occurs):

$$NH_3, \quad \underbrace{H^+, \quad Cl^-}_{\substack{\text{From added} \\ \text{HCl}}}, \quad \text{and} \quad H_2O$$

2. The NH_3 will react with H^+ from the added HCl:

$$NH_3(aq) + H^+(aq) \rightleftharpoons NH_4^+(aq)$$

This reaction proceeds essentially to completion because the NH_3 readily reacts with a free proton. This case is much different from the previous case, where H_2O was the only source of protons. The stoichiometric calculations are then carried out using the known volume of 0.10 M HCl added.

3. After the reaction of NH_3 with H^+ is run to completion, the solution contains the following major species:

$$NH_3, \quad \underset{\substack{\uparrow \\ \text{Formed in} \\ \text{titration reaction}}}{NH_4^+}, \quad Cl^-, \quad \text{and} \quad H_2O$$

Note that the solution contains NH_3 and NH_4^+, and the equilibria involving these species will determine $[H^+]$. You can use either the dissociation reaction of NH_4^+

$$NH_4^+(aq) \rightleftharpoons NH_3(aq) + H^+(aq)$$

or the reaction of NH_3 with H_2O

$$NH_3(aq) + H_2O(l) \rightleftharpoons NH_4^+(aq) + OH^-(aq)$$

At the equivalence point.

1. By definition, the equivalence point occurs when all the original NH_3 is converted to NH_4^+. Thus the major species in solution are

$$NH_4^+, \quad Cl^-, \quad \text{and} \quad H_2O$$

2. No reactions occur that go to completion.

3. The dominant equilibrium (the one that controls the $[H^+]$) will be the dissociation of the weak acid NH_4^+, for which

$$K_a = \frac{K_w}{K_b(\text{for } NH_3)}$$

Beyond the equivalence point.

1. Excess HCl has been added, and the major species are

$$H^+, \quad NH_4^+, \quad Cl^-, \quad \text{and} \quad H_2O$$

2. No reaction occurs that goes to completion.

3. Although NH_4^+ will dissociate, it is such a weak acid that $[H^+]$ will be determined simply by the excess H^+:

$$[H^+] = \frac{\text{mmol } H^+ \text{ in excess}}{\text{mL solution}}$$

The results of these calculations are shown in Table 15.2. The pH curve is shown in Fig. 15.5.

TABLE 15.2 Summary of Results for the Titration of 100.0 mL 0.050 M NH_3 with 0.10 M HCl

Volume of 0.10 M HCl Added (mL)	$[NH_3]_0$	$[NH_4^+]_0$	$[H^+]$	pH
0	0.05 M	0	1.1×10^{-11} M	10.96
10.0	$\dfrac{4.0 \text{ mmol}}{(100 + 10) \text{ mL}}$	$\dfrac{1.0 \text{ mmol}}{(100 + 10) \text{ mL}}$	1.4×10^{-10} M	9.85
25.0*	$\dfrac{2.5 \text{ mmol}}{(100 + 25) \text{ mL}}$	$\dfrac{2.5 \text{ mmol}}{(100 + 25) \text{ mL}}$	5.6×10^{-10} M	9.25
50.0†	0	$\dfrac{5.0 \text{ mmol}}{(100 + 50) \text{ mL}}$	4.3×10^{-6} M	5.36
60.0‡	0	$\dfrac{5.0 \text{ mmol}}{(100 + 60) \text{ mL}}$	$\dfrac{1.0 \text{ mmol}}{160 \text{ mL}}$ $= 6.2 \times 10^{-3}$ M	2.21

*Halfway point
†Equivalence point
‡$[H^+]$ determined by the 1.0 mmol of excess H^+

FIGURE 15.5
The pH curve for the titration of 100.0 mL of 0.050 *M* NH₃ with 0.10 *M* HCl. Note the pH at the equivalence point is less than 7, since the solution contains the weak acid NH_4^+.

15.5 Acid–Base Indicators

There are two common methods for determining the equivalence point of an acid–base titration:

1. Use a pH meter (see Fig. 14.9) to monitor the pH and then plot the titration curve. The center of the vertical region of the pH curve indicates the equivalence point (for example, see Figs. 15.1 through 15.5).

2. Use an **acid–base indicator,** which marks the end point of a titration by changing color. Although the *equivalence point of a titration, defined by the stoichiometry, is not necessarily the same as the end point* (where the indicator changes color), careful selection of the indicator will ensure that the error is negligible.

The most common acid–base indicators are complex molecules that are themselves weak acids (represented by HIn). They exhibit one color when the proton is attached to the molecule and a different color when the proton is absent. For example, **phenolphthalein,** a commonly used indicator, is colorless in its HIn form and pink in its In⁻, or basic, form. The actual structures of the two forms of phenolphthalein are shown in Fig. 15.6.

To see how molecules such as phenolphthalein function as indicators, consider the following equilibrium for some hypothetical indicator HIn, a weak acid with $K_a = 1.0 \times 10^{-8}$.

(Colorless acid form, HIn)

(Pink base form, In⁻)

FIGURE 15.6
The acid and base forms of the indicator phenolphthalein. In the acid form (HIn), the molecule is colorless. When a proton (plus H_2O) is removed to give the base form (In⁻), the color changes to pink.

The indicator phenolphthalein is colorless in acidic solution and pink in basic solution.

$$HIn(aq) \rightleftharpoons H^+(aq) + In^-(aq)$$
$$\underset{\text{Red}}{} \qquad\qquad \underset{\text{Blue}}{}$$

$$K_a = \frac{[H^+][In^-]}{[HIn]}$$

By rearranging, we get

$$\frac{K_a}{[H^+]} = \frac{[In^-]}{[HIn]}$$

Suppose we add a few drops of this indicator to an acidic solution whose pH is 1.0 ($[H^+] = 1.0 \times 10^{-1}$). Then

$$\frac{K_a}{[H^+]} = \frac{1.0 \times 10^{-8}}{1.0 \times 10^{-1}} = 10^{-7} = \frac{1}{10,000,000} = \frac{[In^-]}{[HIn]}$$

The *end point* is defined by the change in color of the indicator. The *equivalence point* is defined by the reaction stoichiometry.

This ratio shows that the predominant form of the indicator is HIn, resulting in a red solution. As OH^- is added to this solution in a titration, $[H^+]$ decreases and the equilibrium shifts to the right, changing HIn to In^-. At some point in a titration, enough of the In^- form will be present in the solution so that a purple tint will be noticeable. That is, a color change from red to reddish purple will occur.

How much In^- must be present for the human eye to detect that the color is different from the original one? For most indicators, about a tenth of the initial form must be converted to the other form before a new color is apparent. We will assume, then, that in the titration of an acid with a base, the color change will occur at a pH where

$$\frac{[In^-]}{[HIn]} = \frac{1}{10}$$

Sample Exercise 15.11	**Indicator Color Change**

Bromthymol blue, an indicator with a K_a value of 1.0×10^{-7}, is yellow in its HIn form and blue in its In^- form. Suppose we put a few drops of this indicator in a strongly acidic solution. If the solution is then titrated with NaOH, at what pH will the indicator color change first be visible?

Methyl orange indicator is yellow in basic solution and red in acidic solution.

(a)   (b)   (c)

FIGURE 15.7
(a) Yellow acid form of bromthymol blue; (b) a greenish tint is seen when the solution contains 1 part blue and 10 parts yellow; (c) blue basic form.

Solution

For bromthymol blue,

$$K_a = 1.0 \times 10^{-7} = \frac{[H^+][In^-]}{[HIn]}$$

We assume that the color change is visible when

$$\frac{[In^-]}{[HIn]} = \frac{1}{10}$$

That is, we assume that we can see the first hint of a greenish tint (yellow plus a little blue) when the solution contains 1 part blue and 10 parts yellow (see Fig. 15.7). Thus

$$K_a = 1.0 \times 10^{-7} = \frac{[H^+](1)}{10}$$

$$[H^+] = 1.0 \times 10^{-6} \quad \text{or} \quad pH = 6.00$$

The color change is first visible at pH 6.00.

See Exercises 15.65 through 15.68.

The Henderson–Hasselbalch equation is very useful in determining the pH at which an indicator changes color. For example, application of Equation (15.2) to the K_a expression for the general indicator HIn yields

$$pH = pK_a + \log\left(\frac{[In^-]}{[HIn]}\right)$$

where K_a is the dissociation constant for the acid form of the indicator (HIn). Since we assume that the color change is visible when

$$\frac{[In^-]}{[HIn]} = \frac{1}{10}$$

we have the following equation for determining the pH at which the color change occurs:

$$pH = pK_a + \log(\tfrac{1}{10}) = pK_a - 1$$

For bromthymol blue ($K_a = 1 \times 10^{-7}$, or $pK_a = 7$), the pH at the color change is

$$pH = 7 - 1 = 6$$

as we calculated in Sample Exercise 15.11.

When a basic solution is titrated, the indicator HIn will initially exist as In$^-$ in solution, but as acid is added, more HIn will be formed. In this case the color change will be visible when there is a mixture of 10 parts In$^-$ and 1 part HIn. That is, a color change from blue to blue-green will occur (see Fig. 15.7) due to the presence of some of the yellow HIn molecules. This color change will be first visible when

$$\frac{[\text{In}^-]}{[\text{HIn}]} = \frac{10}{1}$$

Note that this is the reciprocal of the ratio for the titration of an acid. Substituting this ratio into the Henderson–Hasselbalch equation gives

$$pH = pK_a + \log(\tfrac{10}{1}) = pK_a + 1$$

For bromthymol blue ($pK_a = 7$), we have a color change at

$$pH = 7 + 1 = 8$$

In summary, when bromthymol blue is used for the titration of an acid, the starting form will be HIn (yellow), and the color change occurs at a pH of about 6. When bromthymol blue is used for the titration of a base, the starting form is In$^-$ (blue), and the color change occurs at a pH of about 8. Thus the useful pH range for bromthymol blue is

$$pK_a(\text{bromthymol blue}) \pm 1 = 7 \pm 1$$

or from 6 to 8. This is a general result. For a typical acid–base indicator with dissociation constant K_a, the color transition occurs over a range of pH values given by $pK_a \pm 1$. The useful pH ranges for several common indicators are shown in Fig. 15.8.

When we choose an indicator for a titration, we want the indicator end point (where the color changes) and the titration equivalence point to be as close as possible. Choosing an indicator is easier if there is a large change in pH near the equivalence point of the titration. The dramatic change in pH near the equivalence point in a strong acid–strong base titration (Figs. 15.1 and 15.2) produces a sharp end point; that is, the complete color change (from the acid-to-base or base-to-acid colors) usually occurs over one drop of added titrant.

What indicator should we use for the titration of 100.00 mL of 0.100 M HCl with 0.100 M NaOH? We know that the equivalence point occurs at pH 7.00. In the initially acidic solution, the indicator will be predominantly in the HIn form. As OH$^-$ ions are added, the pH increases rather slowly at first (see Fig. 15.1) and then rises rapidly at the equivalence point. This sharp change causes the indicator dissociation equilibrium

$$\text{HIn} \rightleftharpoons \text{H}^+ + \text{In}^-$$

to shift suddenly to the right, producing enough In$^-$ ions to give a color change. Since we are titrating an acid, the indicator is predominantly in the acid form initially. Therefore, the first observable color change will occur at a pH where

$$\frac{[\text{In}^-]}{[\text{HIn}]} = \frac{1}{10}$$

Thus

$$pH = pK_a + \log(\tfrac{1}{10}) = pK_a - 1$$

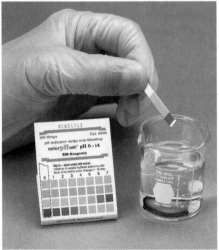

Universal indicator paper can be used to estimate the pH of a solution.

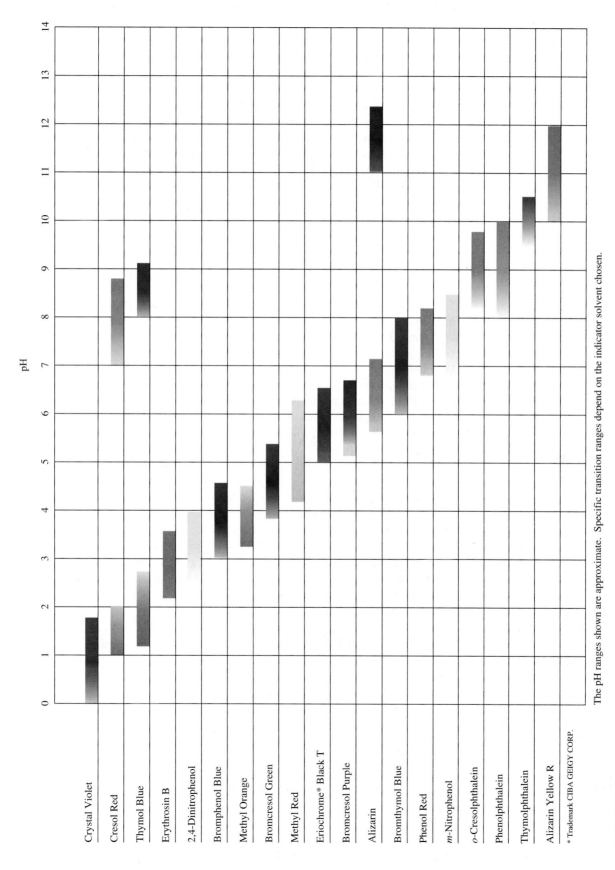

The pH ranges shown are approximate. Specific transition ranges depend on the indicator solvent chosen.

FIGURE 15.8
The useful pH ranges for several common indicators. Note that most indicators have a useful range of about two pH units, as predicted by the expression $pK_a \pm 1$.

* Trademark CIBA GEIGY CORP.

TABLE 15.3 Selected pH Values Near the Equivalence Point in the Titration of 100.0 mL of 0.10 _M_ HCl with 0.10 _M_ NaOH

NaOH Added (mL)	pH
99.99	5.3
100.00	7.0
100.01	8.7

If we want an indicator that changes color at pH 7, we can use this relationship to find the pK_a value for a suitable indicator:

$$pH = 7 = pK_a - 1 \quad \text{or} \quad pK_a = 7 + 1 = 8$$

Thus an indicator with a pK_a value of 8 ($K_a = 1 \times 10^{-8}$) changes color at about pH 7 and is ideal for marking the end point for a strong acid–strong base titration.

How crucial is it for a strong acid–strong base titration that the indicator change color exactly at pH 7? We can answer this question by examining the pH change near the equivalence point of the titration of 100 mL of 0.10 _M_ HCl and 0.10 _M_ NaOH. The data for a few points at or near the equivalence point are shown in Table 15.3. Note that in going from 99.99 to 100.01 mL of added NaOH solution (about half of a drop), the pH changes from 5.3 to 8.7—a very dramatic change. This behavior leads to the following general conclusions about indicators for a strong acid–strong base titration:

Indicator color changes will be sharp, occurring with the addition of a single drop of titrant.

There is a wide choice of suitable indicators. The results will agree within one drop of titrant, using indicators with end points as far apart as pH 5 and pH 9 (see Fig. 15.9).

The titration of weak acids is somewhat different. Figure 15.4 shows that the weaker the acid being titrated, the smaller the vertical area around the equivalence point. This allows much less flexibility in choosing the indicator. We must choose an indicator whose useful pH range has a midpoint as close as possible to the pH at the equivalence point. For example, we saw earlier that in the titration of 0.1 _M_ HC$_2$H$_3$O$_2$ with 0.1 _M_ NaOH the pH at the equivalence point is 8.7 (see Fig. 15.3). A good indicator choice would be phenolphthalein, since its useful pH range is 8 to 10. Thymol blue (changes color, pH 8–9) also would be acceptable, but methyl red would not. The choice of an indicator is illustrated graphically in Fig. 15.10.

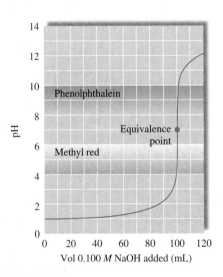

FIGURE 15.9
The pH curve for the titration of 100.0 mL of 0.10 _M_ HCl with 0.10 _M_ NaOH. Note that the end points of phenolphthalein and methyl red occur at virtually the same amounts of added NaOH.

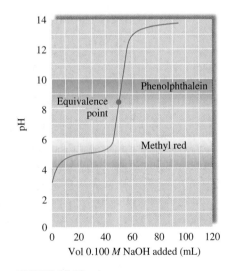

FIGURE 15.10
The pH curve for the titration of 50 mL of 0.1 _M_ HC$_2$H$_3$O$_2$ with 0.1 _M_ NaOH. Phenolphthalein will give an end point very close to the equivalence point of the titration. Methyl red would change color well before the equivalence point (so the end point would be very different from the equivalence point) and would not be a suitable indicator for this titration.

Solubility Equilibria

15.6 Solubility Equilibria and the Solubility Product

Solubility is a very important phenomenon. The fact that substances such as sugar and table salt dissolve in water allows us to flavor foods easily. The fact that calcium sulfate is less soluble in hot water than in cold water causes it to coat tubes in boilers, reducing thermal efficiency. Tooth decay involves solubility: When food lodges between the teeth, acids form that dissolve tooth enamel, which contains a mineral called *hydroxyapatite,* $Ca_5(PO_4)_3OH$. Tooth decay can be reduced by treating teeth with fluoride (see Chemical Impact, p. 720). Fluoride replaces the hydroxide in hydroxyapatite to produce the corresponding fluorapatite, $Ca_5(PO_4)_3F$, and calcium fluoride, CaF_2, both of which are less soluble in acids than the original enamel. Another important consequence of solubility involves the use of a suspension of barium sulfate to improve the clarity of X rays of the gastrointestinal tract. The very low solubility of barium sulfate, which contains the toxic ion Ba^{2+}, makes ingestion of the compound safe.

In this section we consider the equilibria associated with solids dissolving to form aqueous solutions. We will assume that when a typical ionic solid dissolves in water, it dissociates completely into separate hydrated cations and anions. For example, calcium fluoride dissolves in water as follows:

$$CaF_2(s) \xrightarrow{\text{H}_2\text{O}} Ca^{2+}(aq) + 2F^-(aq)$$

When the solid salt is first added to the water, no Ca^{2+} and F^- ions are present. However, as the dissolution proceeds, the concentrations of Ca^{2+} and F^- increase, making it more and more likely that these ions will collide and re-form the solid phase. Thus two competing processes are occurring—the dissolution reaction and its reverse:

$$Ca^{2+}(aq) + 2F^-(aq) \longrightarrow CaF_2(s)$$

Ultimately, dynamic equilibrium is reached:

$$CaF_2(s) \rightleftharpoons Ca^{2+}(aq) + 2F^-(aq)$$

At this point no more solid dissolves (the solution is said to be *saturated*).

We can write an equilibrium expression for this process according to the law of mass action:

$$K_{sp} = [Ca^{2+}][F^-]^2$$

where $[Ca^{2+}]$ and $[F^-]$ are expressed in mol/L. The constant K_{sp} is called the **solubility product constant** or simply the **solubility product** for the equilibrium expression.

Since CaF_2 is a pure solid, it is not included in the equilibrium expression. The fact that the amount of excess solid present does not affect the position of the solubility equilibrium might seem strange at first; more solid means more surface area exposed to the solvent, which would seem to result in greater solubility. This is not the case, however. When the ions in solution re-form the solid, they do so on the surface of the solid. Thus doubling the surface area of the solid not only doubles the rate of dissolving, but also doubles the rate of re-formation of the solid. The amount of excess solid present therefore has no effect on the equilibrium position. Similarly, although either increasing the surface area by grinding up the solid or stirring the solution speeds up the attainment of equilibrium, neither procedure changes the amount of solid dissolved at equilibrium. Neither the amount of excess solid nor the size of the particles present will shift the *position* of the solubility equilibrium.

It is very important to distinguish between the *solubility* of a given solid and its *solubility product*. The solubility product is an *equilibrium constant* and has only *one* value

Adding F^- to drinking water is controversial. See Geoff Rayner-Canham, "Fluoride: Trying to Separate Fact from Fallacy," *Chem 13 News,* Sept. 2001, pp. 16–19.

For simplicity, we will ignore the effects of ion associations in these solutions.

An X ray of the lower gastrointestinal tract using barium sulfate.

Pure liquids and pure solids are never included in an equilibrium expression (Section 13.4).

TABLE 15.4 K_{sp} Values at 25°C for Common Ionic Solids

Ionic Solid	K_{sp} (at 25°C)	Ionic Solid	K_{sp} (at 25°C)	Ionic Solid	K_{sp} (at 25°C)
Fluorides		Hg_2CrO_4*	2×10^{-9}	$Co(OH)_2$	2.5×10^{-16}
BaF_2	2.4×10^{-5}	$BaCrO_4$	8.5×10^{-11}	$Ni(OH)_2$	1.6×10^{-16}
MgF_2	6.4×10^{-9}	Ag_2CrO_4	9.0×10^{-12}	$Zn(OH)_2$	4.5×10^{-17}
PbF_2	4×10^{-8}	$PbCrO_4$	2×10^{-16}	$Cu(OH)_2$	1.6×10^{-19}
SrF_2	7.9×10^{-10}			$Hg(OH)_2$	3×10^{-26}
CaF_2	4.0×10^{-11}	Carbonates		$Sn(OH)_2$	3×10^{-27}
		$NiCO_3$	1.4×10^{-7}	$Cr(OH)_3$	6.7×10^{-31}
Chlorides		$CaCO_3$	8.7×10^{-9}	$Al(OH)_3$	2×10^{-32}
$PbCl_2$	1.6×10^{-5}	$BaCO_3$	1.6×10^{-9}	$Fe(OH)_3$	4×10^{-38}
$AgCl$	1.6×10^{-10}	$SrCO_3$	7×10^{-10}	$Co(OH)_3$	2.5×10^{-43}
Hg_2Cl_2*	1.1×10^{-18}	$CuCO_3$	2.5×10^{-10}		
		$ZnCO_3$	2×10^{-10}	Sulfides	
Bromides		$MnCO_3$	8.8×10^{-11}	MnS	2.3×10^{-13}
$PbBr_2$	4.6×10^{-6}	$FeCO_3$	2.1×10^{-11}	FeS	3.7×10^{-19}
$AgBr$	5.0×10^{-13}	Ag_2CO_3	8.1×10^{-12}	NiS	3×10^{-21}
Hg_2Br_2*	1.3×10^{-22}	$CdCO_3$	5.2×10^{-12}	CoS	5×10^{-22}
		$PbCO_3$	1.5×10^{-15}	ZnS	2.5×10^{-22}
Iodides		$MgCO_3$	6.8×10^{-6}	SnS	1×10^{-26}
PbI_2	1.4×10^{-8}	Hg_2CO_3*	9.0×10^{-15}	CdS	1.0×10^{-28}
AgI	1.5×10^{-16}			PbS	7×10^{-29}
Hg_2I_2*	4.5×10^{-29}	Hydroxides		CuS	8.5×10^{-45}
		$Ba(OH)_2$	5.0×10^{-3}	Ag_2S	1.6×10^{-49}
Sulfates		$Sr(OH)_2$	3.2×10^{-4}	HgS	1.6×10^{-54}
$CaSO_4$	6.1×10^{-5}	$Ca(OH)_2$	1.3×10^{-6}		
Ag_2SO_4	1.2×10^{-5}	$AgOH$	2.0×10^{-8}	Phosphates	
$SrSO_4$	3.2×10^{-7}	$Mg(OH)_2$	8.9×10^{-12}	Ag_3PO_4	1.8×10^{-18}
$PbSO_4$	1.3×10^{-8}	$Mn(OH)_2$	2×10^{-13}	$Sr_3(PO_4)_2$	1×10^{-31}
$BaSO_4$	1.5×10^{-9}	$Cd(OH)_2$	5.9×10^{-15}	$Ca_3(PO_4)_2$	1.3×10^{-32}
		$Pb(OH)_2$	1.2×10^{-15}	$Ba_3(PO_4)_2$	6×10^{-39}
Chromates		$Fe(OH)_2$	1.8×10^{-15}	$Pb_3(PO_4)_2$	1×10^{-54}
$SrCrO_4$	3.6×10^{-5}				

*Contains Hg_2^{2+} ions. $K = [Hg_2^{2+}][X^-]^2$ for Hg_2X_2 salts, for example.

Visualization: Solution
Equilibrium

Visualization: Supersaturated
Sodium Acetate

K_{sp} is an equilibrium constant; solubility is an equilibrium position.

for a given solid at a given temperature. Solubility, on the other hand, is an *equilibrium position*. In pure water at a specific temperature a given salt has a particular solubility. On the other hand, if a common ion is present in the solution, the solubility varies according to the concentration of the common ion. However, in all cases the product of the ion concentrations must satisfy the K_{sp} expression. The K_{sp} values at 25°C for many common ionic solids are listed in Table 15.4. The units are customarily omitted.

Solving solubility equilibria problems requires many of the same procedures we have used to deal with acid–base equilibria, as illustrated in Sample Exercises 15.12 and 15.13.

Sample Exercise 15.12 Calculating K_{sp} from Solubility I

Copper(I) bromide has a measured solubility of 2.0×10^{-4} mol/L at 25°C. Calculate its K_{sp} value.

Solution

In this experiment the solid was placed in contact with water. Thus, before any reaction occurred, the system contained solid CuBr and H_2O. The process that occurs is the dissolving of CuBr to form the separated Cu^+ and Br^- ions:

$$CuBr(s) \rightleftharpoons Cu^+(aq) + Br^-(aq)$$

where $$K_{sp} = [Cu^+][Br^-]$$

Initially, the solution contains no Cu^+ or Br^-, so the initial concentrations are

$$[Cu^+]_0 = [Br^-]_0 = 0$$

The equilibrium concentrations can be obtained from the measured solubility of CuBr, which is 2.0×10^{-4} mol/L. This means that 2.0×10^{-4} mol solid CuBr dissolves per 1.0 L of solution to come to equilibrium with the excess solid. The reaction is

$$CuBr(s) \longrightarrow Cu^+(aq) + Br^-(aq)$$

Thus

2.0×10^{-4} mol/L CuBr(s)

$$\longrightarrow 2.0 \times 10^{-4} \text{ mol/L } Cu^+(aq) + 2.0 \times 10^{-4} \text{ mol/L } Br^-(aq)$$

We can now write the equilibrium concentrations:

$$[Cu^+] = [Cu^+]_0 + \text{change to reach equilibrium}$$
$$= 0 + 2.0 \times 10^{-4} \text{ mol/L}$$

and

$$[Br^-] = [Br^-]_0 + \text{change to reach equilibrium}$$
$$= 0 + 2.0 \times 10^{-4} \text{ mol/L}$$

These equilibrium concentrations allow us to calculate the value of K_{sp} for CuBr:

$$K_{sp} = [Cu^+][Br^-] = (2.0 \times 10^{-4} \text{ mol/L})(2.0 \times 10^{-4} \text{ mol/L})$$
$$= 4.0 \times 10^{-8} \text{ mol}^2/L^2 = 4.0 \times 10^{-8}$$

The units for K_{sp} values are usually omitted.

See Exercise 15.77.

Sample Exercise 15.13

Calculating K_{sp} from Solubility II

Calculate the K_{sp} value for bismuth sulfide (Bi_2S_3), which has a solubility of 1.0×10^{-15} mol/L at 25°C.

Solution

The system initially contains H_2O and solid Bi_2S_3, which dissolves as follows:

$$Bi_2S_3(s) \rightleftharpoons 2Bi^{3+}(aq) + 3S^{2-}(aq)$$

Therefore, $$K_{sp} = [Bi^{3+}]^2[S^{2-}]^3$$

Since no Bi^{3+} and S^{2-} ions were present in solution before the Bi_2S_3 dissolved,

$$[Bi^{3+}]_0 = [S^{2-}]_0 = 0$$

Thus the equilibrium concentrations of these ions will be determined by the amount of salt that dissolves to reach equilibrium, which in this case is 1.0×10^{-15} mol/L. Since each Bi_2S_3 unit contains $2Bi^{3+}$ and $3S^{2-}$ ions:

1.0×10^{-15} mol/L $Bi_2S_3(s)$

$$\longrightarrow 2(1.0 \times 10^{-15} \text{ mol/L}) Bi^{3+}(aq) + 3(1.0 \times 10^{-15} \text{ mol/L}) S^{2-}(aq)$$

The equilibrium concentrations are

$$[Bi^{3+}] = [Bi^{3+}]_0 + \text{change} = 0 + 2.0 \times 10^{-15} \text{ mol/L}$$
$$[S^{2-}] = [S^{2-}]_0 + \text{change} = 0 + 3.0 \times 10^{-15} \text{ mol/L}$$

Then

$$K_{sp} = [Bi^{3+}]^2[S^{2-}]^3 = (2.0 \times 10^{-15})^2(3.0 \times 10^{-15})^3 = 1.1 \times 10^{-73}$$

See Exercises 15.78 through 15.80.

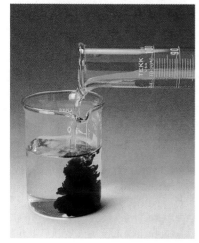

Precipitation of bismuth sulfide.

Sulfide is a very basic anion and really exists in water as HS^-. We will not consider this complication.

Solubilities must be expressed in mol/L in K_{sp} calculations.

CHEMICAL IMPACT

The Chemistry of Teeth

If dental chemistry continues to progress at the present rate, tooth decay may soon be a thing of the past. Cavities are holes that develop in tooth enamel, which is composed of the mineral hydroxyapatite, $Ca_5(PO_4)_3OH$. Recent research has shown that there is constant dissolving and re-forming of the tooth mineral in the saliva at the tooth's surface. Demineralization (dissolving of tooth enamel) is mainly caused by weak acids in the saliva created by bacteria as they metabolize carbohydrates in food. (The solubility of $Ca_5(PO_4)_3OH$ in acidic saliva should come as no surprise to you if you understand how pH affects the solubility of a salt with basic anions.)

In the first stages of tooth decay, parts of the tooth surface become porous and spongy and develop swiss-cheese-like holes that, if untreated, eventually turn into cavities (see photo). However, recent results indicate that if the affected tooth is bathed in a solution containing appropriate amounts of Ca^{2+}, PO_4^{3-}, and F^-, it remineralizes. Because the F^- replaces OH^- in the tooth mineral ($Ca_5(PO_4)_3OH$ is changed to $Ca_5(PO_4)_3F$), the remineralized area is more resistant to future decay, since fluoride is a weaker base than hydroxide ion. In addition, it has been shown that the presence of Sr^{2+} in the remineralizing fluid significantly increases resistance to decay.

If these results hold up under further study, the work of dentists will change dramatically. Dentists will be much

X-ray photo showing decay (dark area) on the molar (right).

more involved in preventing damage to teeth than in repairing damage that has already occurred. One can picture the routine use of a remineralization rinse that will repair problem areas before they become cavities. Dental drills could join leeches as a medical anachronism.

We have seen that the experimentally determined solubility of an ionic solid can be used to calculate its K_{sp} value.* The reverse is also possible: The solubility of an ionic solid can be calculated if its K_{sp} value is known.

Sample Exercise 15.14

Calculating Solubility from K_{sp}

The K_{sp} value for copper(II) iodate, $Cu(IO_3)_2$, is 1.4×10^{-7} at 25°C. Calculate its solubility at 25°C.

Solution

The system initially contains H_2O and solid $Cu(IO_3)_2$, which dissolves according to the following equilibrium:

$$Cu(IO_3)_2(s) \rightleftharpoons Cu^{2+}(aq) + 2IO_3^-(aq)$$

Therefore,
$$K_{sp} = [Cu^{2+}][IO_3^-]^2$$

---

*This calculation assumes that all the dissolved solid is present as separated ions. In some cases, such as $CaSO_4$, large numbers of ion pairs exist in solution, so this method yields an incorrect value for K_{sp}.

To find the solubility of $Cu(IO_3)_2$, we must find the equilibrium concentrations of the Cu^{2+} and IO_3^- ions. We do this in the usual way by specifying the initial concentrations (before any solid has dissolved) and then defining the change required to reach equilibrium. Since in this case we do not know the solubility, we will assume that x mol/L of the solid dissolves to reach equilibrium. The 1:2 stoichiometry of the salt means that

$$x \text{ mol/L } Cu(IO_3)_2(s) \longrightarrow x \text{ mol/L } Cu^{2+}(aq) + 2x \text{ mol/L } IO_3^-(aq)$$

The concentrations are as follows:

Initial Concentration (mol/L) (before any $Cu(IO_3)_2$ dissolves)		Equilibrium Concentration (mol/L)
$[Cu^{2+}]_0 = 0$ $[IO_3^-]_0 = 0$	x mol/L dissolves $\xrightarrow{\text{to reach equilibrium}}$	$[Cu^{2+}] = x$ $[IO_3^-] = 2x$

Substituting the equilibrium concentrations into the expression for K_{sp} gives

$$1.4 \times 10^{-7} = K_{sp} = [Cu^{2+}][IO_3^-]^2 = (x)(2x)^2 = 4x^3$$

Then

$$x = \sqrt[3]{3.5 \times 10^{-8}} = 3.3 \times 10^{-3} \text{ mol/L}$$

Thus the solubility of solid $Cu(IO_3)_2$ is 3.3×10^{-3} mol/L.

See Exercises 15.81 and 15.82.

Relative Solubilities

A salt's K_{sp} value gives us information about its solubility. However, we must be careful in using K_{sp} values to predict the *relative* solubilities of a group of salts. There are two possible cases:

1. The salts being compared produce the same number of ions. For example, consider

$$AgI(s) \qquad K_{sp} = 1.5 \times 10^{-16}$$
$$CuI(s) \qquad K_{sp} = 5.0 \times 10^{-12}$$
$$CaSO_4(s) \qquad K_{sp} = 6.1 \times 10^{-5}$$

Each of these solids dissolves to produce two ions:

$$\text{Salt} \rightleftharpoons \text{cation} + \text{anion}$$
$$K_{sp} = [\text{cation}][\text{anion}]$$

If x is the solubility in mol/L, then at equilibrium

$$[\text{Cation}] = x$$
$$[\text{Anion}] = x$$
$$K_{sp} = [\text{cation}][\text{anion}] = x^2$$
$$x = \sqrt{K_{sp}} = \text{solubility}$$

Therefore, in this case we can compare the solubilities for these solids by comparing the K_{sp} values:

$$CaSO_4(s) \quad > CuI(s) > \quad AgI(s)$$

Most soluble; largest K_{sp} Least soluble; smallest K_{sp}

TABLE 15.5   Calculated Solubilities for CuS, Ag₂S, and Bi₂S₃ at 25°C

Salt	K_{sp}	Calculated Solubility (mol/L)
CuS	8.5×10^{-45}	9.2×10^{-23}
Ag₂S	1.6×10^{-49}	3.4×10^{-17}
Bi₂S₃	1.1×10^{-73}	1.0×10^{-15}

2. The salts being compared produce different numbers of ions. For example, consider

$$CuS(s) \qquad K_{sp} = 8.5 \times 10^{-45}$$
$$Ag_2S(s) \qquad K_{sp} = 1.6 \times 10^{-49}$$
$$Bi_2S_3(s) \qquad K_{sp} = 1.1 \times 10^{-73}$$

Because these salts produce different numbers of ions when they dissolve, the K_{sp} values cannot be compared *directly* to determine relative solubilities. In fact, if we calculate the solubilities (using the procedure in Sample Exercise 15.14), we obtain the results summarized in Table 15.5. The order of solubilities is

$$\underset{\text{Most soluble}}{Bi_2S_3(s)} \; > Ag_2S(s) > \; \underset{\text{Least soluble}}{CuS(s)}$$

which is opposite to the order of the K_{sp} values.

Remember that relative solubilities can be predicted by comparing K_{sp} values *only* for salts that produce the same total number of ions.

Common Ion Effect

So far we have considered ionic solids dissolved in pure water. We will now see what happens when the water contains an ion in common with the dissolving salt. For example, consider the solubility of solid silver chromate (Ag_2CrO_4, $K_{sp} = 9.0 \times 10^{-12}$) in a 0.100 M solution of $AgNO_3$. Before any Ag_2CrO_4 dissolves, the solution contains the major species Ag^+, NO_3^-, and H_2O, with solid Ag_2CrO_4 on the bottom of the container. Since NO_3^- is not found in Ag_2CrO_4, we can ignore it. The relevant initial concentrations (before any Ag_2CrO_4 dissolves) are

$$[Ag^+]_0 = 0.100 \; M \text{ (from the dissolved } AgNO_3)$$
$$[CrO_4^{2-}]_0 = 0$$

The system comes to equilibrium as the solid Ag_2CrO_4 dissolves according to the reaction

$$Ag_2CrO_4(s) \rightleftharpoons 2Ag^+(aq) + CrO_4^{2-}(aq)$$

for which

$$K_{sp} = [Ag^+]^2[CrO_4^{2-}] = 9.0 \times 10^{-12}$$

We assume that x mol/L of Ag_2CrO_4 dissolves to reach equilibrium, which means that

$$x \text{ mol/L } Ag_2CrO_4(s) \longrightarrow 2x \text{ mol/L } Ag^+(aq) + x \text{ mol/L } CrO_4^{2-}$$

Now we can specify the equilibrium concentrations in terms of x:

$$[Ag^+] = [Ag^+]_0 + \text{change} = 0.100 + 2x$$
$$[CrO_4^{2-}] = [CrO_4^{2-}]_0 + \text{change} = 0 + x = x$$

Substituting these concentrations into the expression for K_{sp} gives

$$9.0 \times 10^{-12} = [Ag^+]^2[CrO_4^{2-}] = (0.100 + 2x)^2(x)$$

A potassium chromate solution being added to aqueous silver nitrate, forming silver chromate.

The mathematics required here appear to be complicated, since the multiplication of terms on the right-hand side produces an expression that contains an x^3 term. However, as is usually the case, we can make simplifying assumptions. Since the K_{sp} value for Ag_2CrO_4 is small (the position of the equilibrium lies far to the left), x is expected to be small compared with 0.100 M. Therefore, $0.100 + 2x \approx 0.100$, which allows simplification of the expression:

$$9.0 \times 10^{-12} = (0.100 + 2x)^2(x) \approx (0.100)^2(x)$$

Then
$$x \approx \frac{9.0 \times 10^{-12}}{(0.100)^2} = 9.0 \times 10^{-10} \text{ mol/L}$$

Since x is much less than 0.100 M, the approximation is valid (by the 5% rule). Thus

$$\text{Solubility of } Ag_2CrO_4 \text{ in } 0.100 \ M \ AgNO_3 = x = 9.0 \times 10^{-10} \text{ mol/L}$$

and the equilibrium concentrations are

$$[Ag^+] = 0.100 + 2x = 0.100 + 2(9.0 \times 10^{-10}) = 0.100 \ M$$
$$[CrO_4^{2-}] = x = 9.0 \times 10^{-10} \ M$$

Now we compare the solubilities of Ag_2CrO_4 in pure water and in 0.100 M $AgNO_3$:

$$\text{Solubility of } Ag_2CrO_4 \text{ in pure water} = 1.3 \times 10^{-4} \text{ mol/L}$$
$$\text{Solubility of } Ag_2CrO_4 \text{ in } 0.100 \ M \ AgNO_3 = 9.0 \times 10^{-10} \text{ mol/L}$$

Note that the solubility of Ag_2CrO_4 is much less in the presence of Ag^+ ions from $AgNO_3$. This is another example of the common ion effect. The solubility of a solid is lowered if the solution already contains ions common to the solid.

| *Sample Exercise 15.15* | ## Solubility and Common Ions |

Calculate the solubility of solid CaF_2 ($K_{sp} = 4.0 \times 10^{-11}$) in a 0.025 M NaF solution.

Solution

Before any CaF_2 dissolves, the solution contains the major species Na^+, F^-, and H_2O. The solubility equilibrium for CaF_2 is

$$CaF_2(s) \rightleftharpoons Ca^{2+}(aq) + 2F^-(aq)$$

and
$$K_{sp} = 4.0 \times 10^{-11} = [Ca^{2+}][F^-]^2$$

Initial Concentration (mol/L) (before any CaF₂ dissolves)		Equilibrium Concentration (mol/L)
$[Ca^{2+}]_0 = 0$ $[F^-]_0 = 0.025 \ M$ ↗ From 0.025 M NaF	x mol/L CaF₂ dissolves ⟶ to reach equilibrium	$[Ca^{2+}] = x$ $[F^-] = 0.025 + 2x$ ↗ ↗ From NaF From CaF₂

Substituting the equilibrium concentrations into the expression for K_{sp} gives

$$K_{sp} = 4.0 \times 10^{-11} = [Ca^{2+}][F^-]^2 = (x)(0.025 + 2x)^2$$

Assuming that $2x$ is negligible compared with 0.025 (since K_{sp} is small) gives

$$4.0 \times 10^{-11} \approx (x)(0.025)^2$$
$$x \approx 6.4 \times 10^{-8}$$

The approximation is valid (by the 5% rule), and

$$\text{Solubility} = x = 6.4 \times 10^{-8} \text{ mol/L}$$

Thus 6.4×10^{-8} mol solid CaF_2 dissolves per liter of the 0.025 M NaF solution.

See Exercises 15.89 through 15.92.

pH and Solubility

The pH of a solution can greatly affect a salt's solubility. For example, magnesium hydroxide dissolves according to the equilibrium

$$Mg(OH)_2(s) \rightleftharpoons Mg^{2+}(aq) + 2OH^-(aq)$$

Addition of OH^- ions (an increase in pH) will, by the common ion effect, force the equilibrium to the left, decreasing the solubility of $Mg(OH)_2$. On the other hand, an addition of H^+ ions (a decrease in pH) increases the solubility, because OH^- ions are removed from solution by reacting with the added H^+ ions. In response to the lower concentration of OH^-, the equilibrium position moves to the right. This is why a suspension of solid $Mg(OH)_2$, known as *milk of magnesia,* dissolves as required in the stomach to combat excess acidity.

This idea also applies to salts with other types of anions. For example, the solubility of silver phosphate (Ag_3PO_4) is greater in acid than in pure water because the PO_4^{3-} ion is a strong base that reacts with H^+ to form the HPO_4^{2-} ion. The reaction

$$H^+ + PO_4^{3-} \longrightarrow HPO_4^{2-}$$

occurs in acidic solution, thus lowering the concentration of PO_4^{3-} and shifting the solubility equilibrium

$$Ag_3PO_4(s) \rightleftharpoons 3Ag^+(aq) + PO_4^{3-}(aq)$$

to the right. This, in turn, increases the solubility of silver phosphate.

Silver chloride (AgCl), however, has the same solubility in acid as in pure water. Why? Since the Cl^- ion is a very weak base (that is, HCl is a very strong acid), no HCl molecules are formed. Thus the addition of H^+ to a solution containing Cl^- does not affect $[Cl^-]$ and has no effect on the solubility of a chloride salt.

The general rule is that if the anion X^- is an effective base—that is, if HX is a weak acid—the salt MX will show increased solubility in an acidic solution. Examples of common anions that are effective bases are OH^-, S^{2-}, CO_3^{2-}, $C_2O_4^{2-}$, and CrO_4^{2-}. Salts containing these anions are much more soluble in an acidic solution than in pure water.

As mentioned at the beginning of this chapter, one practical result of the increased solubility of carbonates in acid is the formation of huge limestone caves such as Mammoth Cave in Kentucky and Carlsbad Caverns in New Mexico. Carbon dioxide dissolved in groundwater makes it acidic, increasing the solubility of calcium carbonate and eventually producing huge caverns. As the carbon dioxide escapes to the air, the pH of the dripping water goes up and the calcium carbonate precipitates, forming stalactites and stalagmites.

15.7 Precipitation and Qualitative Analysis

So far we have considered solids dissolving in solutions. Now we will consider the reverse process—the formation of a solid from solution. When solutions are mixed, various reactions can occur. We have already considered acid–base reactions in some detail. In this section we show how to predict whether a precipitate will form when two solutions are mixed. We will use the **ion product,** which is defined just like the expression for K_{sp} for a given solid except that *initial concentrations are used* instead of equilibrium concentrations. For solid CaF_2, the expression for the ion product Q is written

$$Q = [Ca^{2+}]_0[F^-]_0^2$$

If we add a solution containing Ca^{2+} ions to a solution containing F^- ions, a precipitate may or may not form, depending on the concentrations of these ions in the resulting mixed solution. To predict whether precipitation will occur, we consider the relationship between Q and K_{sp}.

Q is used here in a very similar way to the use of the reaction quotient in Chapter 13.

If Q is greater than K_{sp}, precipitation occurs and will continue until the concentrations are reduced to the point that they satisfy K_{sp}.

If Q is less than K_{sp}, no precipitation occurs.

Sample Exercise 15.16 | **Determining Precipitation Conditions**

A solution is prepared by adding 750.0 mL of 4.00×10^{-3} M $Ce(NO_3)_3$ to 300.0 mL of 2.00×10^{-2} M KIO_3. Will $Ce(IO_3)_3$ ($K_{sp} = 1.9 \times 10^{-10}$) precipitate from this solution?

Solution

First, we calculate $[Ce^{3+}]_0$ and $[IO_3^-]_0$ in the mixed solution before any reaction occurs:

$$[Ce^{3+}]_0 = \frac{(750.0 \text{ mL})(4.00 \times 10^{-3} \text{ mmol/mL})}{(750.0 + 300.0) \text{ mL}} = 2.86 \times 10^{-3} \text{ } M$$

$$[IO_3^-]_0 = \frac{(300.0 \text{ mL})(2.00 \times 10^{-2} \text{ mmol/mL})}{(750.0 + 300.0) \text{ mL}} = 5.71 \times 10^{-3} \text{ } M$$

The ion product for $Ce(IO_3)_3$ is

$$Q = [Ce^{3+}]_0[IO_3^-]_0^3 = (2.86 \times 10^{-3})(5.71 \times 10^{-3})^3 = 5.32 \times 10^{-10}$$

Since Q is greater than K_{sp}, $Ce(IO_3)_3$ will precipitate from the mixed solution.

See Exercises 15.97 and 15.98.

For $Ce(IO_3)_3(s)$, $K_{sp} = [Ce^{3+}][IO_3^-]^3$.

Sometimes we want to do more than simply predict whether precipitation will occur; we may want to calculate the equilibrium concentrations in the solution after precipitation occurs. For example, let us calculate the equilibrium concentrations of Pb^{2+} and I^- ions in a solution formed by mixing 100.0 mL of 0.0500 M $Pb(NO_3)_2$ and 200.0 mL of 0.100 M NaI. First, we must determine whether solid PbI_2 ($K_{sp} = 1.4 \times 10^{-8}$) forms when the solutions are mixed. To do so, we need to calculate $[Pb^{2+}]_0$ and $[I^-]_0$ before any reaction occurs:

$$[Pb^{2+}]_0 = \frac{\text{mmol } Pb^{2+}}{\text{mL solution}} = \frac{(100.0 \text{ mL})(0.0500 \text{ mmol/mL})}{300.0 \text{ mL}} = 1.67 \times 10^{-2} \text{ } M$$

$$[I^-]_0 = \frac{\text{mmol } I^-}{\text{mL solution}} = \frac{(200.0 \text{ mL})(0.100 \text{ mmol/mL})}{300.0 \text{ mL}} = 6.67 \times 10^{-2} \text{ } M$$

The ion product for PbI_2 is

$$Q = [Pb^{2+}]_0[I^-]_0^2 = (1.67 \times 10^{-2})(6.67 \times 10^{-2})^2 = 7.43 \times 10^{-5}$$

Since Q is greater than K_{sp}, a precipitate of PbI_2 will form.

Since the K_{sp} for PbI_2 is quite small (1.4×10^{-8}), only very small quantities of Pb^{2+} and I^- can coexist in aqueous solution. In other words, when Pb^{2+} and I^- are mixed, most of these ions will precipitate out as PbI_2. That is, the reaction

$$Pb^{2+}(aq) + 2I^-(aq) \longrightarrow PbI_2(s)$$

> The equilibrium constant for formation of solid PbI_2 is $1/K_{sp}$, or 7×10^7, so this equilibrium lies far to the right.

(which is the reverse of the dissolution reaction) goes essentially to completion.

If, when two solutions are mixed, a reaction occurs that goes virtually to completion, it is essential to do the stoichiometry calculations before considering the equilibrium calculations. Therefore, in this case we let the system go completely in the direction toward which it tends. Then we will let it adjust back to equilibrium. If we let Pb^{2+} and I^- react to completion, we have the following concentrations:

	Pb^{2+}	$+$	$2I^-$	$\longrightarrow$	PbI_2
Before reaction:	(100.0 mL)(0.0500 M) = 5.00 mmol		(200.0 mL)(0.100 M) = 20.0 mmol		The amount of PbI_2 formed does not influence the equilibrium.
After reaction:	0 mmol		20.0 − 2(5.00) = 10.0 mmol		

> In this reaction 10 mmol I^- is in excess.

Next we must allow the system to adjust to equilibrium. At equilibrium $[Pb^{2+}]$ is not actually zero because the reaction does not go quite to completion. The best way to think about this is that once the PbI_2 is formed, a very small amount redissolves to reach equilibrium. Since I^- is in excess, the PbI_2 is dissolving into a solution that contains 10.0 mmol I^- per 300.0 mL of solution, or 3.33×10^{-2} M I^-.

We could state this problem as follows: What is the solubility of solid PbI_2 in a 3.33×10^{-2} M NaI solution? The lead iodide dissolves according to the equation

$$PbI_2(s) \rightleftharpoons Pb^{2+}(aq) + 2I^-(aq)$$

The concentrations are as follows:

Initial Concentration (mol/L)		Equilibrium Concentration (mol/L)
$[Pb^{2+}]_0 = 0$ $[I^-]_0 = 3.33 \times 10^{-2}$	$\xrightarrow[\text{dissolves}]{x \text{ mol/L} \atop PbI_2(s)}$	$[Pb^{2+}] = x$ $[I^-] = 3.33 \times 10^{-2} + 2x$

Substituting into the expression for K_{sp} gives

$$K_{sp} = 1.4 \times 10^{-8} = [Pb^{2+}][I^-]^2 = (x)(3.33 \times 10^{-2} + 2x)^2 \approx (x)(3.33 \times 10^{-2})^2$$

Then
$$[Pb^{2+}] = x = 1.3 \times 10^{-5} \, M$$
$$[I^-] = 3.33 \times 10^{-2} \, M$$

Note that $3.33 \times 10^{-2} \gg 2x$, so the approximation is valid. These Pb^{2+} and I^- concentrations thus represent the equilibrium concentrations present in a solution formed by mixing 100.0 mL of 0.0500 M $Pb(NO_3)_2$ and 200.0 mL of 0.100 M NaI.

Sample Exercise 15.17   Precipitation

A solution is prepared by mixing 150.0 mL of 1.00×10^{-2} M $Mg(NO_3)_2$ and 250.0 mL of 1.00×10^{-1} M NaF. Calculate the concentrations of Mg^{2+} and F^- at equilibrium with solid MgF_2 ($K_{sp} = 6.4 \times 10^{-9}$).

Solution

The first step is to determine whether solid MgF_2 forms. To do this, we need to calculate the concentrations of Mg^{2+} and F^- in the mixed solution and find Q:

$$[Mg^{2+}]_0 = \frac{\text{mmol } Mg^{2+}}{\text{mL solution}} = \frac{(150.0 \text{ mL})(1.00 \times 10^{-2} M)}{400.0 \text{ mL}} = 3.75 \times 10^{-3} M$$

$$[F^-]_0 = \frac{\text{mmol } F^-}{\text{mL solution}} = \frac{(250.0 \text{ mL})(1.00 \times 10^{-1} M)}{400.0 \text{ mL}} = 6.25 \times 10^{-2} M$$

$$Q = [Mg^{2+}]_0[F^-]_0^2 = (3.75 \times 10^{-3})(6.25 \times 10^{-2})^2 = 1.46 \times 10^{-5}$$

Since Q is greater than K_{sp}, solid MgF_2 will form.

The next step is to run the precipitation reaction to completion:

	Mg^{2+}	$+$	$2F^-$	$\longrightarrow$	$MgF_2(s)$
Before reaction:	$(150.0)(1.00 \times 10^{-2})$ $= 1.50$ mmol		$(250.0)(1.00 \times 10^{-1})$ $= 25.0$ mmol		
After reaction:	$1.50 - 1.50 = 0$		$25.0 - 2(1.50)$ $= 22.0$ mmol		

Note that excess F^- remains after the precipitation reaction goes to completion. The concentration is

$$[F^-]_{\text{excess}} = \frac{22.0 \text{ mmol}}{400.0 \text{ mL}} = 5.50 \times 10^{-2} M$$

Although we have assumed that the Mg^{2+} is completely consumed, we know that $[Mg^{2+}]$ will not be zero at equilibrium. We can compute the equilibrium $[Mg^{2+}]$ by letting MgF_2 redissolve to satisfy the expression for K_{sp}. How much MgF_2 will dissolve in a $5.50 \times 10^{-2} M$ NaF solution? We proceed as usual:

$$MgF_2(s) \rightleftharpoons Mg^{2+}(aq) + 2F^-(aq)$$
$$K_{sp} = [Mg^{2+}][F^-]^2 = 6.4 \times 10^{-9}$$

Initial Concentration (mol/L)		Equilibrium Concentration (mol/L)
$[Mg^{2+}]_0 = 0$ $[F^-]_0 = 5.50 \times 10^{-2}$	$\xrightarrow[\text{dissolves}]{\substack{x \text{ mol/L} \\ MgF_2(s)}}$	$[Mg^{2+}] = x$ $[F^-] = 5.50 \times 10^{-2} + 2x$

$$K_{sp} = 6.4 \times 10^{-9} = [Mg^{2+}][F^-]^2$$
$$= (x)(5.50 \times 10^{-2} + 2x)^2 \approx (x)(5.50 \times 10^{-2})^2$$
$$[Mg^{2+}] = x = 2.1 \times 10^{-6} M$$
$$[F^-] = 5.50 \times 10^{-2} M$$

See Exercises 15.99 and 15.100.

Selective Precipitation

The approximations made here fall within the 5% rule.

Mixtures of metal ions in aqueous solution are often separated by **selective precipitation,** that is, by using a reagent whose anion forms a precipitate with only one or a few of the metal ions in the mixture. For example, suppose we have a solution containing both Ba^{2+} and Ag^+ ions. If NaCl is added to the solution, AgCl precipitates as a white solid, but since $BaCl_2$ is soluble, the Ba^{2+} ions remain in solution.

Sample Exercise 15.18 ## Selective Precipitation

A solution contains 1.0×10^{-4} M Cu^+ and 2.0×10^{-3} M Pb^{2+}. If a source of I^- is added gradually to this solution, will PbI_2 ($K_{sp} = 1.4 \times 10^{-8}$) or CuI ($K_{sp} = 5.3 \times 10^{-12}$) precipitate first? Specify the concentration of I^- necessary to begin precipitation of each salt.

Solution

For PbI_2, the K_{sp} expression is

$$1.4 \times 10^{-8} = K_{sp} = [Pb^{2+}][I^-]^2$$

Since $[Pb^{2+}]$ in this solution is known to be 2.0×10^{-3} M, the greatest concentration of I^- that can be present without causing precipitation of PbI_2 can be calculated from the K_{sp} expression:

$$1.4 \times 10^{-8} = [Pb^{2+}][I^-]^2 = (2.0 \times 10^{-3})[I^-]^2$$
$$[I^-] = 2.6 \times 10^{-3} \ M$$

Any I^- in excess of this concentration will cause solid PbI_2 to form.

Similarly, for CuI, the K_{sp} expression is

$$5.3 \times 10^{-12} = K_{sp} = [Cu^+][I^-] = (1.0 \times 10^{-4})[I^-]$$

and

$$[I^-] = 5.3 \times 10^{-8} \ M$$

A concentration of I^- in excess of 5.3×10^{-8} M will cause formation of solid CuI.

As I^- is added to the mixed solution, CuI will precipitate first, since the $[I^-]$ required is less. Therefore, Cu^+ would be separated from Pb^{2+} using this reagent.

See Exercises 15.101 and 15.102.

We can compare K_{sp} values to find relative solubilities because FeS and MnS produce the same number of ions in solution.

Since metal sulfide salts differ dramatically in their solubilities, the sulfide ion is often used to separate metal ions by selective precipitation. For example, consider a solution containing a mixture of 10^{-3} M Fe^{2+} and 10^{-3} M Mn^{2+}. Since FeS ($K_{sp} = 3.7 \times 10^{-19}$) is much less soluble than MnS ($K_{sp} = 2.3 \times 10^{-13}$), careful addition of S^{2-} to the mixture will precipitate Fe^{2+} as FeS, leaving Mn^{2+} in solution.

One real advantage of the sulfide ion as a precipitating reagent is that because it is basic, its concentration can be controlled by regulating the pH of the solution. H_2S is a diprotic acid that dissociates in two steps:

$$H_2S \rightleftharpoons H^+ + HS^- \qquad K_{a_1} = 1.0 \times 10^{-7}$$
$$HS^- \rightleftharpoons H^+ + S^{2-} \qquad K_{a_2} \approx 10^{-19}$$

Note from the small K_{a_2} value that S^{2-} ions have a high affinity for protons. In an acidic solution (large $[H^+]$), $[S^{2-}]$ will be relatively small, since under these conditions the dissociation equilibria will lie far to the left. On the other hand, in basic solutions $[S^{2-}]$ will be relatively large, since the very small value of $[H^+]$ will pull both equilibria to the right, producing S^{2-}.

FIGURE 15.11
The separation of Cu^{2+} and Hg^{2+} from Ni^{2+} and Mn^{2+} using H_2S. At a low pH, $[S^{2-}]$ is relatively low and only the very insoluble HgS and CuS precipitate. When OH^- is added to lower $[H^+]$, the value of $[S^{2-}]$ increases, and MnS and NiS precipitate.

Flame test for potassium.

Flame test for sodium.

This means that the most insoluble sulfide salts, such as CuS ($K_{sp} = 8.5 \times 10^{-45}$) and HgS ($K_{sp} = 1.6 \times 10^{-54}$), can be precipitated from an acidic solution, leaving the more soluble ones, such as MnS ($K_{sp} = 2.3 \times 10^{-13}$) and NiS ($K_{sp} = 3 \times 10^{-21}$), still dissolved. The manganese and nickel sulfides can then be precipitated by making the solution slightly basic. This procedure is diagramed in Fig. 15.11.

Qualitative Analysis

The classic scheme for **qualitative analysis** of a mixture containing all the common cations (listed in Fig. 15.12) involves first separating them into five major groups based on solubilities. (These groups are not directly related to the groups of the periodic table.) Each group is then treated further to separate and identify the individual ions. We will be concerned here only with separation of the major groups.

Group I—Insoluble chlorides

When dilute aqueous HCl is added to a solution containing a mixture of the common cations, only Ag^+, Pb^{2+}, and Hg_2^{2+} will precipitate out as insoluble chlorides. All other chlorides are soluble and remain in solution. The Group I precipitate is removed, leaving the other ions in solution for treatment with sulfide ion.

Group II—Sulfides insoluble in acid solution

After the insoluble chlorides are removed, the solution is still acidic, since HCl was added. If H_2S is added to this solution, only the most insoluble sulfides (those of Hg^{2+}, Cd^{2+}, Bi^{3+}, Cu^{2+}, and Sn^{4+}) will precipitate, since $[S^{2-}]$ is relatively low because of the high concentration of H^+. The more soluble sulfides will remain dissolved under these conditions, and the precipitate of the insoluble salt is removed.

Group III—Sulfides insoluble in basic solution

The solution is made basic at this stage, and more H_2S is added. As we saw earlier, a basic solution produces a higher $[S^{2-}]$, which leads to precipitation of the more soluble sulfides. The cations precipitated as sulfides at this stage are Co^{2+}, Zn^{2+}, Mn^{2+}, Ni^{2+}, and Fe^{2+}. If any Cr^{3+} and Al^{3+} ions are present, they also will precipitate, but as insoluble hydroxides (remember the solution is now basic). The precipitate is separated from the solution containing the rest of the ions.

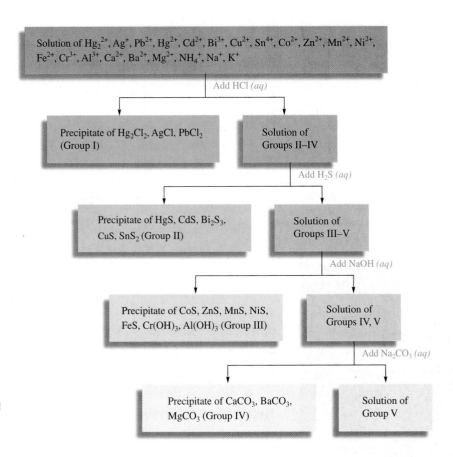

FIGURE 15.12
A schematic diagram of the classic method for separating the common cations by selective precipitation.

Group IV—Insoluble carbonates

At this point, all the cations have been precipitated except those from Groups 1A and 2A of the periodic table. The Group 2A cations form insoluble carbonates and can be precipitated by the addition of CO_3^{2-}. For example, Ba^{2+}, Ca^{2+}, and Mg^{2+} form solid carbonates and can be removed from the solution.

From left to right, cadmium sulfide, chromium(III) hydroxide, aluminum hydroxide, and nickel(II) hydroxide.

Group V—Alkali metal and ammonium ions
The only ions remaining in solution at this point are the Group 1A cations and the NH_4^+ ion, all of which form soluble salts with the common anions. The Group 1A cations are usually identified by the characteristic colors they produce when heated in a flame. These colors are due to the emission spectra of these ions.

The qualitative analysis scheme for cations based on the selective precipitation procedure described above is summarized in Fig. 15.12.

Complex Ion Equilibria

15.8 Equilibria Involving Complex Ions

A **complex ion** is a charged species consisting of a metal ion surrounded by *ligands*. A ligand is simply a Lewis base—a molecule or ion having a lone electron pair that can be donated to an empty orbital on the metal ion to form a covalent bond. Some common ligands are H_2O, NH_3, Cl^-, and CN^-. The number of ligands attached to a metal ion is called the *coordination number*. The most common coordination numbers are 6, for example, in $Co(H_2O)_6^{2+}$ and $Ni(NH_3)_6^{2+}$; 4, for example, in $CoCl_4^{2-}$ and $Cu(NH_3)_4^{2+}$; and 2, for example, in $Ag(NH_3)_2^+$; but others are known.

$CoCl_4^{2-}$

The properties of complex ions will be discussed in more detail in Chapter 21. For now, we will just look at the equilibria involving these species. Metal ions add ligands one at a time in steps characterized by equilibrium constants called **formation constants** or **stability constants.** For example, when solutions containing Ag^+ ions and NH_3 molecules are mixed, the following reactions take place:

$$Ag^+ + NH_3 \rightleftharpoons Ag(NH_3)^+ \qquad K_1 = 2.1 \times 10^3$$
$$Ag(NH_3)^+ + NH_3 \rightleftharpoons Ag(NH_3)_2^+ \qquad K_2 = 8.2 \times 10^3$$

where K_1 and K_2 are the formation constants for the two steps. In a solution containing Ag^+ and NH_3, all the species NH_3, Ag^+, $Ag(NH_3)^+$, and $Ag(NH_3)_2^+$ exist at equilibrium. Calculating the concentrations of all these components can be complicated. However, usually the total concentration of the ligand is much larger than the total concentration of the metal ion, and approximations can greatly simplify the problems.

For example, consider a solution prepared by mixing 100.0 mL of 2.0 M NH_3 with 100.0 mL of 1.0×10^{-3} M $AgNO_3$. *Before any reaction occurs,* the mixed solution contains the major species Ag^+, NO_3^-, NH_3, and H_2O. What reaction or reactions will occur in this solution? From our discussions of acid–base chemistry, we know that one reaction is

$$NH_3(aq) + H_2O(l) \rightleftharpoons NH_4^+(aq) + OH^-(aq)$$

However, we are interested in the reaction between NH_3 and Ag^+ to form complex ions, and since the position of the preceding equilibrium lies far to the left (K_b for NH_3 is 1.8×10^{-5}), we can neglect the amount of NH_3 used up in the reaction with water. Therefore, before any complex ion formation, the concentrations in the mixed solution are

$$[Ag^+]_0 = \frac{(100.0 \text{ mL})(1.0 \times 10^{-3} M)}{(200.0 \text{ mL})} = 5.0 \times 10^{-4} M$$

Total volume

$$[NH_3]_0 = \frac{(100.0 \text{ mL})(2.0 M)}{(200.0 \text{ mL})} = 1.0 M$$

A solution containing the blue $CoCl_4^{2-}$ complex ion.

As mentioned already, the Ag^+ ion reacts with NH_3 in a stepwise fashion to form $AgNH_3^+$ and then $Ag(NH_3)_2^+$:

$$Ag^+ + NH_3 \rightleftharpoons Ag(NH_3)^+ \qquad K_1 = 2.1 \times 10^3$$
$$Ag(NH_3)^+ + NH_3 \rightleftharpoons Ag(NH_3)_2^+ \qquad K_2 = 8.2 \times 10^3$$

Since both K_1 and K_2 are large, and since there is a large excess of NH_3, *both reactions can be assumed to go essentially to completion.* This is equivalent to writing the net reaction in the solution as follows:

$$Ag^+ + 2NH_3 \longrightarrow Ag(NH_3)_2^+$$

The relevant stoichiometric calculations are as follows:

	Ag^+	$+$	$2NH_3$	$\longrightarrow$	$Ag(NH_3)_2^+$
Before reaction:	$5.0 \times 10^{-4}\ M$		$1.0\ M$		0
After reaction:	0		$1.0 - 2(5.0 \times 10^{-4}) \approx 1.0\ M$		$5.0 \times 10^{-4}\ M$

Twice as much NH_3 as Ag^+ is required

Note that in this case we have used molarities when performing the stoichiometry calculations and we have assumed this reaction to be complete, using all the original Ag^+ to form $Ag(NH_3)_2^+$. In reality, a *very small amount* of the $Ag(NH_3)_2^+$ formed will dissociate to produce small amounts of $Ag(NH_3)^+$ and Ag^+. However, since the amount of $Ag(NH_3)_2^+$ dissociating will be so small, we can safely assume that $[Ag(NH_3)_2^+]$ is $5.0 \times 10^{-4}\ M$ at equilibrium. Also, we know that since so little NH_3 has been consumed, $[NH_3]$ is $1.0\ M$ at equilibrium. We can use these concentrations to calculate $[Ag^+]$ and $[Ag(NH_3)^+]$ using the K_1 and K_2 expressions.

To calculate the equilibrium concentration of $Ag(NH_3)^+$, we use

$$K_2 = 8.2 \times 10^3 = \frac{[Ag(NH_3)_2^+]}{[Ag(NH_3)^+][NH_3]}$$

since $[Ag(NH_3)_2^+]$ and $[NH_3]$ are known. Rearranging and solving for $[Ag(NH_3)^+]$ give

$$[Ag(NH_3)^+] = \frac{[Ag(NH_3)_2^+]}{K_2[NH_3]} = \frac{5.0 \times 10^{-4}}{(8.2 \times 10^3)(1.0)} = 6.1 \times 10^{-8}\ M$$

Now the equilibrium concentration of Ag^+ can be calculated using K_1:

$$K_1 = 2.1 \times 10^3 = \frac{[Ag(NH_3)^+]}{[Ag^+][NH_3]} = \frac{6.1 \times 10^{-8}}{[Ag^+](1.0)}$$

$$[Ag^+] = \frac{6.1 \times 10^{-8}}{(2.1 \times 10^3)(1.0)} = 2.9 \times 10^{-11}\ M$$

So far we have assumed that $Ag(NH_3)_2^+$ is the dominant silver-containing species in solution. Is this a valid assumption? The calculated concentrations are

$$[Ag(NH_3)_2^+] = 5.0 \times 10^{-4}\ M$$
$$[Ag(NH_3)^+] = 6.1 \times 10^{-8}\ M$$
$$[Ag^+] = 2.9 \times 10^{-11}\ M$$

These values clearly support the conclusion that

$$[Ag(NH_3)_2^+] \gg [Ag(NH_3)^+] \gg [Ag^+]$$

Essentially all the Ag^+ ions originally present end up in $Ag(NH_3)_2^+$.

Thus the assumption that $Ag(NH_3)_2{}^+$ is the dominant Ag^+-containing species is valid, and the calculated concentrations are correct.

This analysis shows that although complex ion equilibria have many species present and look complicated, the calculations are actually quite straightforward, especially if the ligand is present in large excess.

Complex Ions

Calculate the concentrations of Ag^+, $Ag(S_2O_3)^-$, and $Ag(S_2O_3)_2{}^{3-}$ in a solution prepared by mixing 150.0 mL of 1.00×10^{-3} M $AgNO_3$ with 200.0 mL of 5.00 M $Na_2S_2O_3$. The stepwise formation equilibria are

$$Ag^+ + S_2O_3{}^{2-} \rightleftharpoons Ag(S_2O_3)^- \qquad K_1 = 7.4 \times 10^8$$
$$Ag(S_2O_3)^- + S_2O_3{}^{2-} \rightleftharpoons Ag(S_2O_3)_2{}^{3-} \qquad K_2 = 3.9 \times 10^4$$

Solution

The concentrations of the ligand and metal ion in the mixed solution *before any reaction occurs* are

$$[Ag^+]_0 = \frac{(150.0 \text{ mL})(1.00 \times 10^{-3}\,M)}{(150.0 \text{ mL} + 200.0 \text{ mL})} = 4.29 \times 10^{-4}\,M$$

$$[S_2O_3{}^{2-}]_0 = \frac{(200.0 \text{ mL})(5.00\,M)}{(150.0 \text{ mL} + 200.0 \text{ mL})} = 2.86\,M$$

$Ag(S_2O_3)_2{}^{3-}$

Since $[S_2O_3{}^{2-}]_0 \gg [Ag^+]_0$, and since K_1 and K_2 are large, both formation reactions can be assumed to go to completion, and the net reaction in the solution is as follows:

	Ag^+	+	$2S_2O_3{}^{2-}$	$\longrightarrow$	$Ag(S_2O_3)_2{}^{3-}$
Before reaction:	$4.29 \times 10^{-4}\,M$		$2.86\,M$		0
After reaction:	~ 0		$2.86 - 2(4.29 \times 10^{-4})$ $\approx 2.86\,M$		$4.29 \times 10^{-4}\,M$

Note that Ag^+ is limiting and that the amount of $S_2O_3{}^{2-}$ consumed is negligible. Also note that since all these species are in the same solution, the molarities can be used to do the stoichiometry problem.

Of course, the concentration of Ag^+ is not zero at equilibrium, and there is some $Ag(S_2O_3)^-$ in the solution. To calculate the concentrations of these species, we must use the K_1 and K_2 expressions. We can calculate the concentration of $Ag(S_2O_3)^-$ from K_2:

$$3.9 \times 10^4 = K_2 = \frac{[Ag(S_2O_3)_2{}^{3-}]}{[Ag(S_2O_3)^-][S_2O_3{}^{2-}]} = \frac{4.29 \times 10^{-4}}{[Ag(S_2O_3)^-](2.86)}$$

$$[Ag(S_2O_3)^-] = 3.8 \times 10^{-9}\,M$$

We can calculate $[Ag^+]$ from K_1:

$$7.4 \times 10^8 = K_1 = \frac{[Ag(S_2O_3)^-]}{[Ag^+][S_2O_3{}^{2-}]} = \frac{3.8 \times 10^{-9}}{[Ag^+](2.86)}$$

$$[Ag^+] = 1.8 \times 10^{-18}\,M$$

These results show that $[Ag(S_2O_3)_2{}^{3-}] \gg [Ag(S_2O_3)^-] \gg [Ag^+]$

(top) Aqueous ammonia is added to silver chloride (white). (bottom) Silver chloride, insoluble in water, dissolves to form $Ag(NH_3)_2^+(aq)$ and $Cl^-(aq)$.

Thus the assumption is valid that essentially all the original Ag^+ is converted to $Ag(S_2O_3)_2^{3-}$ at equilibrium.

See Exercises 15.109 and 15.110.

Complex Ions and Solubility

Often ionic solids that are very nearly water-insoluble must be dissolved somehow in aqueous solutions. For example, when the various qualitative analysis groups are precipitated out, the precipitates must be redissolved to separate the ions within each group. Consider a solution of cations that contains Ag^+, Pb^{2+}, and Hg_2^{2+}, among others. When dilute aqueous HCl is added to this solution, the Group I ions will form the insoluble chlorides AgCl, $PbCl_2$, and Hg_2Cl_2. Once this mixed precipitate is separated from the solution, it must be redissolved to identify the cations individually. How can this be done? We know that some solids are more soluble in acidic than in neutral solutions. What about chloride salts? For example, can AgCl be dissolved by using a strong acid? The answer is no, because Cl^- ions have virtually no affinity for H^+ ions in aqueous solution. The position of the dissolution equilibrium

$$AgCl(s) \rightleftharpoons Ag^+(aq) + Cl^-(aq)$$

is not affected by the presence of H^+.

How can we pull the dissolution equilibrium to the right, even though Cl^- is an extremely weak base? The key is to lower the concentration of Ag^+ in solution by forming complex ions. For example, Ag^+ reacts with excess NH_3 to form the stable complex ion $Ag(NH_3)_2^+$. As a result, AgCl is quite soluble in concentrated ammonia solutions. The relevant reactions are

$$AgCl(s) \rightleftharpoons Ag^+ + Cl^- \qquad K_{sp} = 1.6 \times 10^{-10}$$
$$Ag^+ + NH_3 \rightleftharpoons Ag(NH_3)^+ \qquad K_1 = 2.1 \times 10^3$$
$$Ag(NH_3)^+ + NH_3 \rightleftharpoons Ag(NH_3)_2^+ \qquad K_2 = 8.2 \times 10^3$$

The Ag^+ ion produced by dissolving solid AgCl combines with NH_3 to form $Ag(NH_3)_2^+$, which causes more AgCl to dissolve, until the point at which

$$[Ag^+][Cl^-] = K_{sp} = 1.6 \times 10^{-10}$$

Here $[Ag^+]$ refers only to the Ag^+ ion that is present as a separate species in solution. It is *not* the total silver content of the solution, which is

$$[Ag]_{\text{total dissolved}} = [Ag^+] + [Ag(NH_3)^+] + [Ag(NH_3)_2^+]$$

For reasons discussed in the previous section, virtually all the Ag^+ from the dissolved AgCl ends up in the complex ion $Ag(NH_3)_2^+$. Thus we can represent the dissolving of solid AgCl in excess NH_3 by the equation

$$AgCl(s) + 2NH_3(aq) \rightleftharpoons Ag(NH_3)_2^+(aq) + Cl^-(aq)$$

When reactions are added, the equilibrium constant for the overall process is the product of the constants for the individual reactions.

Since this equation is the *sum of the three stepwise reactions* given above, the equilibrium constant for the reaction is the product of the constants for the three reactions. (Demonstrate this to yourself by multiplying together the three expressions for K_{sp}, K_1, and K_2.) The equilibrium expression is

$$K = \frac{[Ag(NH_3)_2^+][Cl^-]}{[NH_3]^2}$$
$$= K_{sp} \times K_1 \times K_2 = (1.6 \times 10^{-10})(2.1 \times 10^3)(8.2 \times 10^3) = 2.8 \times 10^{-3}$$

Using this expression, we will now calculate the solubility of solid AgCl in a 10.0 M NH_3 solution. If we let x be the solubility (in mol/L) of AgCl in the solution, we can then write the following expressions for the equilibrium concentrations of the pertinent species:

$$[Cl^-] = x$$
$$[Ag(NH_3)_2^+] = x$$

x mol/L of AgCl dissolves to produce x mol/L of Cl^- and x mol/L of $Ag(NH_3)_2^+$

$$[NH_3] = 10.0 - 2x$$

Formation of x mol/L of $Ag(NH_3)_2^+$ requires $2x$ mol/L of NH_3, since each complex ion contains two NH_3 ligands

Substituting these concentrations into the equilibrium expression gives

$$K = 2.8 \times 10^{-3} = \frac{[Ag(NH_3)_2^+][Cl^-]}{[NH_3]^2} = \frac{(x)(x)}{(10.0 - 2x)^2} = \frac{x^2}{(10.0 - 2x)^2}$$

No approximations are necessary here. Taking the square root of both sides of the equation gives

$$\sqrt{2.8 \times 10^{-3}} = \frac{x}{10.0 - 2x}$$

$$x = 0.48 \text{ mol/L} = \text{solubility of AgCl}(s) \text{ in } 10.0 \; M \; NH_3$$

Thus the solubility of AgCl in 10.0 M NH_3 is much greater than its solubility in pure water, which is

$$\sqrt{K_{sp}} = 1.3 \times 10^{-5} \text{ mol/L}$$

In this chapter we have considered two strategies for dissolving a water-insoluble ionic solid. If the *anion* of the solid is a good base, the solubility is greatly increased by acidifying the solution. In cases where the anion is not sufficiently basic, the ionic solid often can be dissolved in a solution containing a ligand that forms stable complex ions with its *cation*.

Sometimes solids are so insoluble that combinations of reactions are needed to dissolve them. For example, to dissolve the extremely insoluble HgS ($K_{sp} = 10^{-54}$), it is necessary to use a mixture of concentrated HCl and concentrated HNO_3, called *aqua regia*. The H^+ ions in the aqua regia react with the S^{2-} ions to form H_2S, and Cl^- reacts with Hg^{2+} to form various complex ions, including $HgCl_4^{2-}$. In addition, NO_3^- oxidizes S^{2-} to elemental sulfur. These processes lower the concentrations of Hg^{2+} and S^{2-} and thus promote the solubility of HgS.

Since the solubility of many salts increases with temperature, simple heating is sometimes enough to make a salt sufficiently soluble. For example, earlier in this section we considered the mixed chloride precipitates of the Group I ions—$PbCl_2$, AgCl, and Hg_2Cl_2. The effect of temperature on the solubility of $PbCl_2$ is such that we can precipitate $PbCl_2$ with cold aqueous HCl and then redissolve it by heating the solution to near boiling. The silver and mercury(I) chlorides remain precipitated, since they are not significantly soluble in hot water. However, solid AgCl can be dissolved using aqueous ammonia. The solid Hg_2Cl_2 reacts with NH_3 to form a mixture of elemental mercury and $HgNH_2Cl$:

$$Hg_2Cl_2(s) + 2NH_3(aq) \longrightarrow \underset{\text{White}}{HgNH_2Cl(s)} + \underset{\text{Black}}{Hg(l)} + NH_4^+(aq) + Cl^-(aq)$$

The mixed precipitate appears gray. This is an oxidation–reduction reaction in which one mercury(I) ion in Hg_2Cl_2 is oxidized to Hg^{2+} in $HgNH_2Cl$ and the other mercury(I) ion is reduced to Hg, or elemental mercury.

The treatment of the Group I ions is summarized in Fig. 15.13. Note that the presence of Pb^{2+} is confirmed by adding CrO_4^{2-}, which forms bright yellow lead(II) chromate

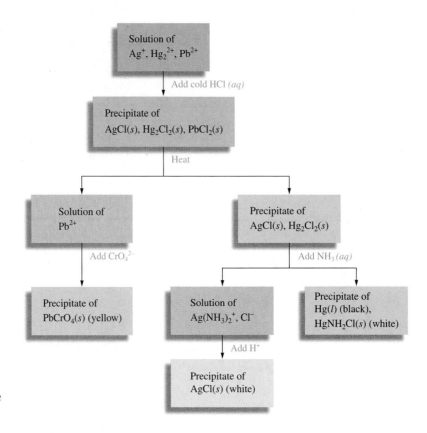

FIGURE 15.13
The separation of the Group I ions in the classic scheme of qualitative analysis.

($PbCrO_4$). Also note that H^+ added to a solution containing $Ag(NH_3)_2^+$ reacts with the NH_3 to form NH_4^+, destroying the $Ag(NH_3)_2^+$ complex. Silver chloride then re-forms:

$$2H^+(aq) + Ag(NH_3)_2^+(aq) + Cl^-(aq) \longrightarrow 2NH_4^+(aq) + AgCl(s)$$

Note that the qualitative analysis of cations by selective precipitation involves all the types of reactions we have discussed and represents an excellent application of the principles of chemical equilibrium.

Key Terms

Section 15.1
common ion
common ion effect

Section 15.2
buffered solution
Henderson–Hasselbalch equation

Section 15.3
buffering capacity

Section 15.4
pH curve (titration curve)
millimole (mmol)
equivalence point (stoichiometric point)

For Review

Buffered solutions
- Contains a weak acid (HA) and its salt (NaA) or a weak base (B) and its salt (BHCl)
- Resists a change in its pH when H^+ or OH^- is added
- For a buffered solution containing HA and A^-
  - The Henderson–Hasselbalch equation is useful:

$$pH = pK_a + \log\left(\frac{[A^-]}{[HA]}\right)$$

  - The capacity of the buffered solution depends on the amounts of HA and A^- present

- The most efficient buffering occurs when the $\dfrac{[A^-]}{[HA]}$ ratio is close to 1
- Buffering works because the amounts of HA (which reacts with added OH^-) and A^- (which reacts with added H^+) are large enough that the $\dfrac{[A^-]}{[HA]}$ ratio does not change significantly when strong acids or bases are added

Acid–base titrations

- The progress of a titration is represented by plotting the pH of the solution versus the volume of added titrant; the resulting graph is called a pH curve or titration curve
- Strong acid–strong base titrations show a sharp change in pH near the equivalence point
- The shape of the pH curve for a strong base–strong acid titration is quite different before the equivalence point from the shape of the pH curve for a strong base–weak acid titration
  - The strong base–weak acid pH curve shows the effects of buffering before the equivalence point
  - For a strong base–weak acid titration, the pH is greater than 7 at the equivalence point because of the basic properties of A^-
- Indicators are sometimes used to mark the equivalence point of an acid–base titration
  - The end point is where the indicator changes color
  - The goal is to have the end point and the equivalence point be as close as possible

Solids dissolving in water

- For a slightly soluble salt, an equilibrium is set up between the excess solid (MX) and the ions in solution

$$MX(s) \rightleftharpoons M^+(aq) + X^-(aq)$$

- The corresponding constant is called K_{sp}:

$$K_{sp} = [M^+][X^-]$$

  - The solubility of $MX(s)$ is decreased by the presence from another source of either M^+ or X^-; this is called the common ion effect
- Predicting whether precipitation will occur when two solutions are mixed involves calculating Q for the initial concentrations
  - If $Q > K_{sp}$, precipitation occurs
  - If $Q \leq K_{sp}$, no precipitation occurs

REVIEW QUESTIONS

1. What is meant by the presence of a common ion? How does the presence of a common ion affect an equilibrium such as

$$HNO_2(aq) \rightleftharpoons H^+(aq) + NO_2^-(aq)$$

   What is an acid–base solution called that contains a common ion?
2. Define a buffer solution. What makes up a buffer solution? How do buffers absorb added H^+ or OH^- with little pH change?

   Is it necessary that the concentrations of the weak acid and the weak base in a buffered solution be equal? Explain. What is the pH of a buffer when the weak acid and conjugate base concentrations are equal?

   A buffer generally contains a weak acid and its weak conjugate base, or a weak base and its weak conjugate acid, in water. You can solve for the pH by setting up the equilibrium problem using the K_a reaction of the weak acid or the

K_b reaction of the conjugate base. Both reactions give the same answer for the pH of the solution. Explain.

A third method that can be used to solve for the pH of a buffer solution is the Henderson–Hasselbalch equation. What is the Henderson–Hasselbalch equation? What assumptions are made when using this equation?

3. One of the most challenging parts of solving acid–base problems is writing out the correct reaction. When a strong acid or a strong base is added to solutions, they are great at what they do and we always react them first. If a strong acid is added to a buffer, what reacts with the H^+ from the strong acid and what are the products? If a strong base is added to a buffer, what reacts with the OH^- from the strong base and what are the products? Problems involving the reaction of a strong acid or strong base are assumed to be stoichiometry problems and not equilibrium problems. What is assumed when a strong acid or strong base reacts to make it a stoichiometry problem?

A good buffer generally contains relatively equal concentrations of weak acid and conjugate base. If you wanted to buffer a solution at pH = 4.00 or pH = 10.00, how would you decide which weak acid–conjugate base or weak base–conjugate acid pair to use? The second characteristic of a good buffer is good buffering capacity. What is the *capacity* of a buffer? How do the following buffers differ in capacity? How do they differ in pH?

0.01 *M* acetic acid/0.01 *M* sodium acetate

0.1 *M* acetic acid/0.1 *M* sodium acetate

1.0 *M* acetic acid/1.0 *M* sodium acetate

4. Draw the general titration curve for a strong acid titrated by a strong base. At the various points in the titration, list the major species present before any reaction takes place and the major species present after any reaction takes place. What reaction takes place in a strong acid–strong base titration? How do you calculate the pH at the various points along the curve? What is the pH at the equivalence point for a strong acid–strong base titration? Why? Answer the same questions for a strong base–strong acid titration. Compare and contrast a strong acid–strong base titration versus a strong base–strong acid titration.

5. Sketch the titration curve for a weak acid titrated by a strong base. When performing calculations concerning weak acid–strong base titrations, the general two-step procedure is to solve a stoichiometry problem first, then to solve an equilibrium problem to determine the pH. What reaction takes place in the stoichiometry part of the problem? What is assumed about this reaction?

At the various points in your titration curve, list the major species present after the strong base (NaOH, for example) reacts to completion with the weak acid, HA. What equilibrium problem would you solve at the various points in your titration curve to calculate the pH? Why is pH > 7.0 at the equivalence point of a weak acid–strong base titration? Does the pH at the halfway point to equivalence have to be less than 7.0? What does the pH at the halfway point equal? Compare and contrast the titration curves for a strong acid–strong base titration and a weak acid–strong base titration.

6. Sketch the titration curve for a weak base titrated by a strong acid. Weak base–strong acid titration problems also follow a two-step procedure. What reaction takes place in the stoichiometry part of the problem? What is assumed about this reaction? At the various points in your titration curve, list the major species present after the strong acid (HNO_3, for example) reacts to completion with the weak base, B. What equilibrium problem would you solve at the various points in your titration curve to calculate the pH? Why is pH < 7.0 at the equivalence point of a weak base–strong acid titration? If pH = 6.0 at the

halfway point to equivalence, what is the K_b value for the weak base titrated? Compare and contrast the titration curves for a strong base–strong acid titration and a weak base–strong acid titration.

7. What is an acid–base indicator? Define the equivalence (stoichiometric) point and the end point of a titration. Why should you choose an indicator so that the two points coincide? Do the pH values of the two points have to be within ± 0.01 pH unit of each other? Explain. Why does an indicator change from its acid color to its base color over a range of pH values? In general, when do color changes start to occur for indicators? Can the indicator thymol blue contain only a single $-CO_2H$ group and no other acidic or basic functional group? Explain.

8. To what reaction does the solubility product constant, K_{sp}, refer? Table 15.4 lists K_{sp} values for several ionic solids. For any of these ionic compounds, you should be able to calculate the solubility. What is the solubility of a salt, and what procedures do you follow to calculate the solubility of a salt? How would you calculate the K_{sp} value for a salt given the solubility?

Under what circumstances can you compare the relative solubilities of two salts directly by comparing the values of their solubility products? When can relative solubilities not be compared based on K_{sp} values? What is a common ion and how does its presence affect the solubility? List some salts whose solubility increases as the pH becomes more acidic. What is true about the anions in these salts? List some salts whose solubility remains unaffected by the solution pH. What is true about the anions in these salts?

9. What is the difference between the ion product, Q, and the solubility product, K_{sp}? What happens when $Q > K_{sp}$? $Q < K_{sp}$? $Q = K_{sp}$? Mixtures of metal ions in aqueous solution can sometimes be separated by selective precipitation. What is selective precipitation? If a solution contained 0.10 M Mg^{2+}, 0.10 M Ca^{2+}, and 0.10 M Ba^{2+}, how could addition of NaF be used to separate the cations out of solution—that is, what would precipitate first, then second, then third? How could addition of K_3PO_4 be used to separate out the cations in a solution that 1.0 M Ag^+, 1.0 M Pb^{2+}, and 1.0 M Sr^{2+}?

10. What is a complex ion? The stepwise formation constants for the complex ion $Cu(NH_3)_4^{2+}$ are $K_1 \approx 1 \times 10^3$, $K_2 \approx 1 \times 10^4$, $K_3 \approx 1 \times 10^3$, and $K_4 \approx 1 \times 10^3$. Write the reactions that refer to each of these formation constants. Given that the values of the formation constants are large, what can you deduce about the equilibrium concentration of $Cu(NH_3)_4^{2+}$ versus the equilibrium concentration of Cu^{2+}? When 5 M ammonia is added to a solution containing $Cu(OH)_2(s)$, the precipitate will eventually dissolve in solution. Why? If 5 M HNO_3 is then added, the $Cu(OH)_2$ precipitate re-forms. Why? In general, what effect does the ability of a cation to form a complex ion have on the solubility of salts containing that cation?

Active Learning Questions

These questions are designed to be used by groups of students in class. The questions allow students to explore their understanding of concepts through discussion and peer teaching. The real value of these questions is the learning that occurs while students talk to each other about chemical concepts.

1. What are the major species in solution after $NaHSO_4$ is dissolved in water? What happens to the pH of the solution as more $NaHSO_4$ is added? Why? Would the results vary if baking soda ($NaHCO_3$) were used instead?

2. A friend asks the following: "Consider a buffered solution made up of the weak acid HA and its salt NaA. If a strong base like NaOH is added, the HA reacts with the OH^- to form A^-. Thus the amount of acid (HA) is decreased, and the amount of base (A^-) is increased. Analogously, adding HCl to the buffered solution forms more of the acid (HA) by reacting with the base (A^-). Thus how can we claim that a buffered solution resists changes in the pH of the solution?" How would you explain buffering to this friend?

3. Mixing together solutions of acetic acid and sodium hydroxide can make a buffered solution. Explain. How does the amount of

each solution added change the effectiveness of the buffer? Would a buffer solution made by mixing HCl and NaOH be effective? Explain.

4. Sketch two pH curves, one for the titration of a weak acid with a strong base and one for a strong acid with a strong base. How are they similar? How are they different? Account for the similarities and the differences.

5. Sketch a pH curve for the titration of a weak acid (HA) with a strong base (NaOH). List the major species and explain how you would go about calculating the pH of the solution at various points, including the halfway point and the equivalence point.

6. Devise as many ways as you can to experimentally determine the K_{sp} value of a solid. Explain why each of these would work.

7. You are browsing through the *Handbook of Hypothetical Chemistry* when you come across a solid that is reported to have a K_{sp} value of zero in water at 25°C. What does this mean?

8. A friend tells you: "The constant K_{sp} of a salt is called the solubility product constant and is calculated from the concentrations of ions in the solution. Thus, if salt A dissolves to a greater extent than salt B, salt A must have a higher K_{sp} than salt B." Do you agree with your friend? Explain.

9. Explain the following phenomenon: You have a test tube with about 20 mL of silver nitrate solution. Upon adding a few drops of sodium chromate solution, you notice a red solid forming in a relatively clear solution. Upon adding a few drops of a sodium chloride solution to the same test tube, you notice a white solid and a pale yellow solution. Use the K_{sp} values in the book to support your explanation, and include the balanced reactions.

10. What happens to the K_{sp} value of a solid as the temperature of the solution changes? Consider both increasing and decreasing temperatures, and explain your answer.

11. Which is more likely to dissolve in an acidic solution, silver sulfide or silver chloride? Why?

12. You have two salts, AgX and AgY, with very similar K_{sp} values. You know that the K_a value for HX is much greater than the K_a value for HY. Which salt is more soluble in an acidic solution? Explain.

A blue question or exercise number indicates that the answer to that question or exercise appears at the back of this book and a solution appears in the *Solutions Guide*.

Questions

13. The common ion effect for weak acids is to significantly decrease the dissociation of the acid in water. The common ion effect for ionic solids (salts) is to significantly decrease the solubility of the ionic compound in water. Explain both of these common ion effects.

14. Consider a buffer solution where [weak acid] > [conjugate base]. How is the pH of the solution related to the pK_a value of the weak acid? If [conjugate base] > [weak acid], how is pH related to pK_a?

15. A best buffer has about equal quantities of weak acid and conjugate base present as well as having a large concentration of each species present. Explain.

16. Consider the following four titrations.
    i. 100.0 mL of 0.10 M HCl titrated by 0.10 M NaOH
    ii. 100.0 mL of 0.10 M NaOH titrated by 0.10 M HCl
    iii. 100.0 mL of 0.10 M CH$_3$NH$_2$ titrated by 0.10 M HCl
    iv. 100.0 mL of 0.10 M HF titrated by 0.10 M NaOH
    Rank the titrations in order of:
    a. increasing volume of titrant added to reach the equivalence point.
    b. increasing pH initially before any titrant has been added.
    c. increasing pH at the halfway point in equivalence.
    d. increasing pH at the equivalence point.
    How would the rankings change if C$_5$H$_5$N replaced CH$_3$NH$_2$ and if HOC$_6$H$_5$ replaced HF?

17. Figure 15.4 shows the pH curves for the titrations of six different acids by NaOH. Make a similar plot for the titration of three different bases by 0.10 M HCl. Assume 50.0 mL of 0.20 M of the bases and assume the three bases are a strong base (KOH), a weak base with $K_b = 1 \times 10^{-5}$, and another weak base with $K_b = 1 \times 10^{-10}$.

18. Acid–base indicators mark the end point of titrations by "magically" turning a different color. Explain the "magic" behind acid–base indicators.

19. The salts in Table 15.4, with the possible exception of the hydroxide salts, have one of the following mathematical relationships between the K_{sp} value and the molar solubility, s.
    i. $K_{sp} = s^2$ iii. $K_{sp} = 27s^4$
    ii. $K_{sp} = 4s^3$ iv. $K_{sp} = 108s^5$
    For each mathematical relationship, give an example of a salt in Table 15.4 that exhibits that relationship.

20. List some ways one can increase the solubility of a salt in water.

Exercises

In this section similar exercises are paired.

Buffers

21. A certain buffer is made by dissolving NaHCO$_3$ and Na$_2$CO$_3$ in some water. Write equations to show how this buffer neutralizes added H$^+$ and OH$^-$.

22. A buffer is prepared by dissolving HONH$_2$ and HONH$_3$NO$_3$ in some water. Write equations to show how this buffer neutralizes added H$^+$ and OH$^-$.

23. Calculate the pH of each of the following solutions.
    a. 0.100 M propanoic acid (HC$_3$H$_5$O$_2$, $K_a = 1.3 \times 10^{-5}$)
    b. 0.100 M sodium propanoate (NaC$_3$H$_5$O$_2$)
    c. pure H$_2$O
    d. a mixture containing 0.100 M HC$_3$H$_5$O$_2$ and 0.100 M NaC$_3$H$_5$O$_2$

24. Calculate the pH of each of the following solutions.
    a. 0.100 M HONH$_2$ ($K_b = 1.1 \times 10^{-8}$)
    b. 0.100 M HONH$_3$Cl
    c. pure H$_2$O
    d. a mixture containing 0.100 M HONH$_2$ and 0.100 M HONH$_3$Cl

25. Compare the percent dissociation of the acid in Exercise 23a with the percent dissociation of the acid in Exercise 23d. Explain the large difference in percent dissociation of the acid.

26. Compare the percent ionization of the base in Exercise 24a with the percent ionization of the base in Exercise 24d. Explain any differences.

27. Calculate the pH after 0.020 mol HCl is added to 1.00 L of each of the four solutions in Exercise 23.

28. Calculate the pH after 0.020 mol HCl is added to 1.00 L of each of the four solutions in Exercise 24.

29. Calculate the pH after 0.020 mol NaOH is added to 1.00 L of each of the four solutions in Exercise 23.

30. Calculate the pH after 0.020 mol NaOH is added to 1.00 L of each of the solutions in Exercise 24.

31. Which of the solutions in Exercise 23 shows the least change in pH upon the addition of acid or base? Explain.

32. Which of the solutions in Exercise 24 is a buffered solution?

33. Calculate the pH of a solution that is 1.00 M HNO_2 and 1.00 M $NaNO_2$.

34. Calculate the pH of a solution that is 0.60 M HF and 1.00 M KF.

35. Calculate the pH after 0.10 mol of NaOH is added to 1.00 L of the solution in Exercise 33, and calculate the pH after 0.20 mol of HCl is added to 1.00 L of the solution in Exercise 33.

36. Calculate the pH after 0.10 mol of NaOH is added to 1.00 L of the solution in Exercise 34, and calculate the pH after 0.20 mol of HCl is added to 1.00 L of the solution in Exercise 34.

37. Calculate the pH of a buffer solution prepared by dissolving 21.46 g of benzoic acid ($HC_7H_5O_2$) and 37.68 g of sodium benzoate in 200.0 mL of solution.

38. A buffered solution is made by adding 50.0 g NH_4Cl to 1.00 L of a 0.75 M solution of NH_3. Calculate the pH of the final solution. (Assume no volume change.)

39. Calculate the pH after 0.010 mol gaseous HCl is added to 250.0 mL of each of the following buffered solutions.
a. 0.050 M NH_3/0.15 M NH_4Cl
b. 0.50 M NH_3/1.50 M NH_4Cl
Do the two original buffered solutions differ in their pH or their capacity? What advantage is there in having a buffer with a greater capacity?

40. An aqueous solution contains dissolved $C_6H_5NH_3Cl$ and $C_6H_5NH_2$. The concentration of $C_6H_5NH_2$ is 0.50 M and pH is 4.20.
a. Calculate the concentration of $C_6H_5NH_3^+$ in this buffer solution.
b. Calculate the pH after 4.0 g of NaOH(s) is added to 1.0 L of this solution. (Neglect any volume change.)

41. Calculate the mass of sodium acetate that must be added to 500.0 mL of 0.200 M acetic acid to form a pH = 5.00 buffer solution.

42. What volumes of 0.50 M HNO_2 and 0.50 M $NaNO_2$ must be mixed to prepare 1.00 L of a solution buffered at pH = 3.55?

43. Consider a solution that contains both C_5H_5N and $C_5H_5NHNO_3$. Calculate the ratio $[C_5H_5N]/[C_5H_5NH^+]$ if the solution has the following pH values.
a. pH = 4.50   **c.** pH = 5.23
b. pH = 5.00   **d.** pH = 5.50

44. a. Carbonate buffers are important in regulating the pH of blood at 7.40. What is the concentration ratio of CO_2 (usually written H_2CO_3) to HCO_3^- in blood at pH = 7.40?

$$H_2CO_3(aq) \rightleftharpoons HCO_3^-(aq) + H^+(aq) \quad K_a = 4.3 \times 10^{-7}$$

b. Phosphate buffers are important in regulating the pH of intracellular fluids at pH values generally between 7.1 and 7.2. What is the concentration ratio of $H_2PO_4^-$ to HPO_4^{2-} in intracellular fluid at pH = 7.15?

$$H_2PO_4^-(aq) \rightleftharpoons HPO_4^{2-}(aq) + H^+(aq) \quad K_a = 6.2 \times 10^{-8}$$

c. Why is a buffer composed of H_3PO_4 and $H_2PO_4^-$ ineffective in buffering the pH of intracellular fluid?

$$H_3PO_4(aq) \rightleftharpoons H_2PO_4^-(aq) + H^+(aq) \quad K_a = 7.5 \times 10^{-3}$$

45. Consider the acids in Table 14.2. Which acid would be the best choice for preparing a pH = 7.00 buffer? Explain how to make 1.0 L of this buffer.

46. Consider the bases in Table 14.3. Which base would be the best choice for preparing a pH = 5.00 buffer? Explain how to make 1.0 L of this buffer.

47. Which of the following mixtures would result in buffered solutions when 1.0 L of each of the two solutions are mixed?
a. 0.1 M KOH and 0.1 M CH_3NH_3Cl
b. 0.1 M KOH and 0.2 M CH_3NH_2
c. 0.2 M KOH and 0.1 M CH_3NH_3Cl
d. 0.1 M KOH and 0.2 M CH_3NH_3Cl

48. Which of the following mixtures would result in a buffered solution when 1.0 L of each of the two solutions are mixed?
a. 0.2 M HNO_3 and 0.4 M $NaNO_3$
b. 0.2 M HNO_3 and 0.4 M HF
c. 0.2 M HNO_3 and 0.4 M NaF
d. 0.2 M HNO_3 and 0.4 M NaOH

49. How many moles of NaOH must be added to 1.0 L of 2.0 M $HC_2H_3O_2$ to produce a solution buffered at each pH?
a. pH = pK_a **b.** pH = 4.00   **c.** pH = 5.00

50. Calculate the number of moles of HCl(g) that must be added to 1.0 L of 1.0 M $NaC_2H_3O_2$ to produce a solution buffered at each pH.
a. pH = pK_a **b.** pH = 4.20   **c.** pH = 5.00

Acid–Base Titrations

51. Consider the titration of a generic weak acid HA with a strong base that gives the following titration curve:

On the curve, indicate the points that correspond to the following:
a. the stoichiometric (equivalence) point
b. the region with maximum buffering
c. pH = pK_a
d. pH depends only on [HA]
e. pH depends only on [A$^-$]
f. pH depends only on the amount of excess strong base added

52. Sketch the titration curve for the titration of a generic weak base B with a strong acid. The titration reaction is

$$B + H^+ \rightleftharpoons BH^+$$

On this curve, indicate the points that correspond to the following:
a. the stoichiometric (equivalence) point
b. the region with maximum buffering
c. pH = pK_a
d. pH depends only on [B]
e. pH depends only on [BH$^+$]
f. pH depends only on the amount of excess strong acid added

53. Consider the titration of 40.0 mL of 0.200 M HClO$_4$ by 0.100 M KOH. Calculate the pH of the resulting solution after the following volumes of KOH have been added.
a. 0.0 mL   d. 80.0 mL
b. 10.0 mL   e. 100.0 mL
c. 40.0 mL

54. Consider the titration of 80.0 mL of 0.100 M Ba(OH)$_2$ by 0.400 M HCl. Calculate the pH of the resulting solution after the following volumes of HCl have been added.
a. 0.0 mL   d. 40.0 mL
b. 20.0 mL   e. 80.0 mL
c. 30.0 mL

55. Consider the titration of 100.0 mL of 0.200 M acetic acid (K_a = 1.8 × 10^{-5}) by 0.100 M KOH. Calculate the pH of the resulting solution after the following volumes of KOH have been added.
a. 0.0 mL   d. 150.0 mL
b. 50.0 mL   e. 200.0 mL
c. 100.0 mL   f. 250.0 mL

56. Consider the titration of 100.0 mL of 0.100 M H$_2$NNH$_2$ (K_b = 3.0 × 10^{-6}) by 0.200 M HNO$_3$. Calculate the pH of the resulting solution after the following volumes of HNO$_3$ have been added.
a. 0.0 mL   d. 40.0 mL
b. 20.0 mL   e. 50.0 mL
c. 25.0 mL   f. 100.0 mL

57. A 25.0-mL sample of 0.100 M lactic acid (HC$_3$H$_5$O$_3$, pK_a = 3.86) is titrated with 0.100 M NaOH solution. Calculate the pH after the addition of 0.0 mL, 4.0 mL, 8.0 mL, 12.5 mL, 20.0 mL, 24.0 mL, 24.5 mL, 24.9 mL, 25.0 mL, 25.1 mL, 26.0 mL, 28.0 mL, and 30.0 mL of the NaOH. Plot the results of your calculations as pH versus milliliters of NaOH added.

58. Repeat the procedure in Exercise 57, but for the titration of 25.0 mL of 0.100 M propanoic acid (HC$_3$H$_5$O$_2$, K_a = 1.3 × 10^{-5}) with 0.100 M NaOH.

59. Repeat the procedure in Exercise 57, but for the titration of 25.0 mL of 0.100 M NH$_3$ (K_b = 1.8 × 10^{-5}) with 0.100 M HCl.

60. Repeat the procedure in Exercise 57, but for the titration of 25.0 mL of 0.100 M pyridine with 0.100 M hydrochloric acid (K_b for pyridine is 1.7 × 10^{-9}). Do not do the points at 24.9 and 25.1 mL.

61. Calculate the pH at the halfway point and at the equivalence point for each of the following titrations.
a. 100.0 mL of 0.10 M HC$_7$H$_5$O$_2$ (K_a = 6.4 × 10^{-5}) titrated by 0.10 M NaOH
b. 100.0 mL of 0.10 M C$_2$H$_5$NH$_2$ (K_b = 5.6 × 10^{-4}) titrated by 0.20 M HNO$_3$
c. 100.0 mL of 0.50 M HCl titrated by 0.25 M NaOH

62. In the titration of 50.0 mL of 1.0 M methylamine, CH$_3$NH$_2$ (K_b = 4.4 × 10^{-4}), with 0.50 M HCl, calculate the pH under the following conditions.
a. after 50.0 mL of 0.50 M HCl has been added
b. at the stoichiometric point

63. You have 75.0 mL of 0.10 M HA. After adding 30.0 mL of 0.10 M NaOH, the pH is 5.50. What is the K_a value of HA?

64. A sample of an ionic compound NaA, where A$^-$ is the anion of a weak acid, was dissolved in enough water to make 100.0 mL of solution and was then titrated with 0.100 M HCl. After 500.0 mL of HCl was added, the pH was measured and found to be 5.00. The experimenter found that 1.00 L of 0.100 M HCl was required to reach the stoichiometric point of the titration.
a. What is the K_b value for A$^-$?
b. Calculate the pH of the solution at the stoichiometric point of the titration.

Indicators

65. Two drops of indicator HIn (K_a = 1.0 × 10^{-9}), where HIn is yellow and In$^-$ is blue, are placed in 100.0 mL of 0.10 M HCl.
a. What color is the solution initially?
b. The solution is titrated with 0.10 M NaOH. At what pH will the color change (yellow to greenish yellow) occur?
c. What color will the solution be after 200.0 mL of NaOH has been added?

66. Methyl red has the following structure:

It undergoes a color change from red to yellow as a solution gets more basic. Calculate an approximate pH range for which methyl red is useful. What is the color change and the pH at the color change when a weak acid is titrated with a strong base using methyl red as an indicator? What is the color change and the pH at the color change when a weak base is titrated with a strong acid using methyl red as an indicator? For which of these two types of titrations is methyl red a possible indicator?

67. Potassium hydrogen phthalate, known as KHP (molar mass = 204.22 g/mol), can be obtained in high purity and is used to determine the concentration of solutions of strong bases by the reaction

$$HP^-(aq) + OH^-(aq) \longrightarrow H_2O(l) + P^{2-}(aq)$$

If a typical titration experiment begins with approximately 0.5 g of KHP and has a final volume of about 100 mL, what is an appropriate indicator to use? The pK_a for HP^- is 5.51.

68. A certain indicator HIn has a pK_a of 3.00 and a color change becomes visible when 7.00% of the indicator has been converted to In^-. At what pH is this color change visible?

69. Which of the indicators in Fig. 15.8 could be used for the titrations in Exercises 53 and 55?

70. Which of the indicators in Fig. 15.8 could be used for the titrations in Exercises 54 and 56?

71. Which of the indicators in Fig. 15.8 could be used for the titrations in Exercises 57 and 59?

72. Which of the indicators in Fig. 15.8 could be used for the titrations in Exercises 58 and 60?

73. Estimate the pH of a solution in which bromcresol green is blue and thymol blue is yellow. (See Fig. 15.8.)

74. A solution has a pH of 7.0. What would be the color of the solution if each of the following indicators were added? (See Fig. 15.8.)
a. thymol blue   **c.** methyl red
b. bromthymol blue   **d.** crystal violet

Solubility Equilibria

75. Write balanced equations for the dissolution reactions and the corresponding solubility product expressions for each of the following solids.
a. $AgC_2H_3O_2$ **b.** $Al(OH)_3$ **c.** $Ca_3(PO_4)_2$

76. Write balanced equations for the dissolution reactions and the corresponding solubility product expressions for each of the following solids.
a. Ag_2CO_3 **b.** $Ce(IO_3)_3$ **c.** BaF_2

77. Use the following data to calculate the K_{sp} value for each solid.
a. The solubility of CaC_2O_4 is 6.1×10^{-3} g/L.
b. The solubility of BiI_3 is 1.32×10^{-5} mol/L.

78. Use the following data to calculate the K_{sp} value for each solid.
a. The solubility of $Pb_3(PO_4)_2$ is 6.2×10^{-12} mol/L.
b. The solubility of Li_2CO_3 is 7.4×10^{-2} mol/L.

79. The concentration of Pb^{2+} in a solution saturated with $PbBr_2(s)$ is 2.14×10^{-2} M. Calculate K_{sp} for $PbBr_2$.

80. The concentration of Ag^+ in a solution saturated with $Ag_2C_2O_4(s)$ is 2.2×10^{-4} M. Calculate K_{sp} for $Ag_2C_2O_4$.

81. Calculate the solubility of each of the following compounds in moles per liter. Ignore any acid–base properties.
a. Ag_3PO_4, $K_{sp} = 1.8 \times 10^{-18}$
b. $CaCO_3$, $K_{sp} = 8.7 \times 10^{-9}$
c. Hg_2Cl_2, $K_{sp} = 1.1 \times 10^{-18}$ (Hg_2^{2+} is the cation in solution.)

82. Calculate the solubility of each of the following compounds in moles per liter. Ignore any acid–base properties.
a. PbI_2, $K_{sp} = 1.4 \times 10^{-8}$
b. $CdCO_3$, $K_{sp} = 5.2 \times 10^{-12}$
c. $Sr_3(PO_4)_2$, $K_{sp} = 1 \times 10^{-31}$

83. The solubility of the ionic compound M_2X_3, having a molar mass of 288 g/mol, is 3.60×10^{-7} g/L. Calculate the K_{sp} of the compound.

84. A solution contains 0.018 mol each of I^-, Br^-, and Cl^-. When the solution is mixed with 200. mL of 0.24 M $AgNO_3$, what mass of $AgCl(s)$ precipitates out, and what is the $[Ag^+]$? Assume no volume change.

$$AgI, K_{sp} = 1.5 \times 10^{-16}$$
$$AgBr, K_{sp} = 5.0 \times 10^{-13}$$
$$AgCl, K_{sp} = 1.6 \times 10^{-10}$$

85. Calculate the molar solubility of $Co(OH)_3$, $K_{sp} = 2.5 \times 10^{-43}$.

86. Calculate the molar solubility of $Cd(OH)_2$, $K_{sp} = 5.9 \times 10^{-11}$.

87. For each of the following pairs of solids, determine which solid has the smallest molar solubility.
a. $CaF_2(s)$, $K_{sp} = 4.0 \times 10^{-11}$, or $BaF_2(s)$, $K_{sp} = 2.4 \times 10^{-5}$
b. $Ca_3(PO_4)_2(s)$, $K_{sp} = 1.3 \times 10^{-32}$, or $FePO_4(s)$, $K_{sp} = 1.0 \times 10^{-22}$

88. For each of the following pairs of solids, determine which solid has the smallest molar solubility.
a. FeC_2O_4, $K_{sp} = 2.1 \times 10^{-7}$, or $Cu(IO_4)_2$, $K_{sp} = 1.4 \times 10^{-7}$
b. Ag_2CO_3, $K_{sp} = 8.1 \times 10^{-12}$, or $Mn(OH)_2$, $K_{sp} = 2 \times 10^{-13}$

89. Calculate the solubility (in moles per liter) of $Fe(OH)_3$ ($K_{sp} = 4 \times 10^{-38}$) in each of the following.
a. water
b. a solution buffered at pH = 5.0
c. a solution buffered at pH = 11.0

90. The K_{sp} for silver sulfate (Ag_2SO_4) is 1.2×10^{-5}. Calculate the solubility of silver sulfate in each of the following.
a. water   **b.** 0.10 M $AgNO_3$ **c.** 0.20 M K_2SO_4

91. Calculate the solubility of solid $Ca_3(PO_4)_2$ ($K_{sp} = 1.3 \times 10^{-32}$) in a 0.20 M Na_3PO_4 solution.

92. The solubility of $Ce(IO_3)_3$ in a 0.20 M KIO_3 solution is 4.4×10^{-8} mol/L. Calculate K_{sp} for $Ce(IO_3)_3$.

93. What mass of ZnS ($K_{sp} = 2.5 \times 10^{-22}$) will dissolve in 300.0 mL of 0.050 M $Zn(NO_3)_2$? Ignore the basic properties of S^{2-}.

94. The concentration of Mg^{2+} in seawater is 0.052 M. At what pH will 99% of the Mg^{2+} be precipitated as the hydroxide salt? [K_{sp} for $Mg(OH)_2 = 8.9 \times 10^{-12}$.]

95. Which of the substances in Exercises 81 and 82 show increased solubility as the pH of the solution becomes more acidic? Write equations for the reactions that occur to increase the solubility.

96. For which salt in each of the following groups will the solubility depend on pH?
a. AgF, AgCl, AgBr   **c.** $Sr(NO_3)_2$, $Sr(NO_2)_2$
b. $Pb(OH)_2$, $PbCl_2$ **d.** $Ni(NO_3)_2$, $Ni(CN)_2$

97. Will a precipitate form when 75.0 mL of 0.020 M $BaCl_2$ and 125 mL of 0.040 M Na_2SO_4 are mixed together?

98. Will a precipitate form when 100.0 mL of 4.0×10^{-4} M $Mg(NO_3)_2$ is added to 100.0 mL of 2.0×10^{-4} M NaOH?

99. Calculate the final concentrations of $K^+(aq)$, $C_2O_4^{2-}(aq)$, $Ba^{2+}(aq)$, and $Br^-(aq)$ in a solution prepared by adding 0.100 L of 0.200 M $K_2C_2O_4$ to 0.150 L of 0.250 M $BaBr_2$. (For BaC_2O_4, $K_{sp} = 2.3 \times 10^{-8}$.)

100. A solution is prepared by mixing 50.0 mL of 0.10 M $Pb(NO_3)_2$ with 50.0 mL of 1.0 M KCl. Calculate the concentrations of Pb^{2+} and Cl^- at equilibrium. K_{sp} for $PbCl_2(s)$ is 1.6×10^{-5}.

101. A solution contains 1.0×10^{-5} M Na_3PO_4. What is the minimum concentration of $AgNO_3$ that would cause precipitation of solid Ag_3PO_4 ($K_{sp} = 1.8 \times 10^{-18}$)?

102. A solution contains 0.25 M $Ni(NO_3)_2$ and 0.25 M $Cu(NO_3)_2$. Can the metal ions be separated by slowly adding Na_2CO_3? Assume that for successful separation 99% of the metal ion must be precipitated before the other metal ion begins to precipitate, and assume no volume change on addition of Na_2CO_3.

Complex Ion Equilibria

103. Write equations for the stepwise formation of each of the following complex ions.
a. $Ni(CN)_4^{2-}$
b. $V(C_2O_4)_3^{3-}$

104. Write equations for the stepwise formation of each of the following complex ions.
a. CoF_6^{3-}
b. $Zn(NH_3)_4^{2+}$

105. Given the following data,

$Mn^{2+}(aq) + C_2O_4^{2-}(aq) \rightleftharpoons MnC_2O_4(aq)$ $K_1 = 7.9 \times 10^3$
$MnC_2O_4(aq) + C_2O_4^{2-}(aq) \rightleftharpoons Mn(C_2O_4)_2^{2-}(aq)$
                                                          $K_2 = 7.9 \times 10^1$

calculate the value for the overall formation constant for $Mn(C_2O_4)_2^{2-}$:

$$K = \frac{[Mn(C_2O_4)_2^{2-}]}{[Mn^{2+}][C_2O_4^{2-}]^2}$$

106. In the presence of CN^-, Fe^{3+} forms the complex ion $Fe(CN)_6^{3-}$. The equilibrium concentrations of Fe^{3+} and $Fe(CN)_6^{3-}$ are 8.5×10^{-40} M and 1.5×10^{-3} M, respectively, in a 0.11 M KCN solution. Calculate the value for the overall formation constant of $Fe(CN)_6^{3-}$.

$Fe^{3+}(aq) + 6CN^-(aq) \rightleftharpoons Fe(CN)_6^{3-}$ $K_{overall} = ?$

107. When aqueous KI is added gradually to mercury(II) nitrate, an orange precipitate forms. Continued addition of KI causes the precipitate to dissolve. Write balanced equations to explain these observations. (*Hint:* Hg^{2+} reacts with I^- to form HgI_4^{2-}.)

108. As sodium chloride solution is added to a solution of silver nitrate, a white precipitate forms. Ammonia is added to the mixture and the precipitate dissolves. When potassium bromide solution is then added, a pale yellow precipitate appears. When a solution of sodium thiosulfate is added, the yellow precipitate dissolves. Finally, potassium iodide is added to the solution and a yellow precipitate forms. Write reactions for all the changes mentioned above. What conclusions can you draw concerning the sizes of the K_{sp} values for AgCl, AgBr, and AgI?

109. The overall formation constant for HgI_4^{2-} is 1.0×10^{30}. That is,

$$1.0 \times 10^{30} = \frac{[HgI_4^{2-}]}{[Hg^{2+}][I^-]^4}$$

What is the concentration of Hg^{2+} in 500.0 mL of a solution that was originally 0.010 M Hg^{2+} and 0.78 M I^-? The reaction is

$$Hg^{2+}(aq) + 4I^-(aq) \rightleftharpoons HgI_4^{2-}(aq)$$

110. A solution is formed by mixing 50.0 mL of 10.0 M NaX with 50.0 mL of 2.0×10^{-3} M $CuNO_3$. Assume that Cu(I) forms complex ions with X^- as follows:

$Cu^+(aq) + X^-(aq) \rightleftharpoons CuX(aq)$ $K_1 = 1.0 \times 10^2$
$CuX(aq) + X^-(aq) \rightleftharpoons CuX_2^-(aq)$ $K_2 = 1.0 \times 10^4$
$CuX_2^-(aq) + X^-(aq) \rightleftharpoons CuX_3^{2-}(aq)$ $K_3 = 1.0 \times 10^3$

with an overall reaction

$Cu^+(aq) + 3X^-(aq) \rightleftharpoons CuX_3^{2-}(aq)$ $K = 1.0 \times 10^9$

Calculate the following concentrations at equilibrium.
a. CuX_3^{2-} **b.** CuX_2^- **c.** Cu^+

111. a. Calculate the molar solubility of AgI in pure water. K_{sp} for AgI is 1.5×10^{-16}.
b. Calculate the molar solubility of AgI in 3.0 M NH_3. The overall formation constant for $Ag(NH_3)_2^+$ is 1.7×10^7.
c. Compare the calculated solubilities from parts a and b. Explain any differences.

112. Solutions of sodium thiosulfate are used to dissolve unexposed AgBr ($K_{sp} = 5.0 \times 10^{-13}$) in the developing process for black-and-white film. What mass of AgBr can dissolve in 1.00 L of 0.500 M $Na_2S_2O_3$? Ag^+ reacts with $S_2O_3^{2-}$ to form a complex ion:

$$Ag^+(aq) + 2S_2O_3^{2-}(aq) \rightleftharpoons Ag(S_2O_3)_2^{3-}(aq)$$
$$K = 2.9 \times 10^{13}$$

113. K_f for the complex ion $Ag(NH_3)_2^+$ is 1.7×10^7. K_{sp} for AgCl is 1.6×10^{-10}. Calculate the molar solubility of AgCl in 1.0 M NH_3.

114. The copper(I) ion forms a chloride salt that has $K_{sp} = 1.2 \times 10^{-6}$. Copper(I) also forms a complex ion with Cl^-:

$$Cu^+(aq) + 2Cl^-(aq) \rightleftharpoons CuCl_2^-(aq)$$ $K = 8.7 \times 10^4$

a. Calculate the solubility of copper(I) chloride in pure water. (Ignore $CuCl_2^-$ formation for part a.)
b. Calculate the solubility of copper(I) chloride in 0.10 M NaCl.

115. A series of chemicals were added to some $AgNO_3(aq)$. NaCl(aq) was added first to the silver nitrate solution with the end result shown below in test tube 1, $NH_3(aq)$ was then added with the end result shown in test tube 2, and $HNO_3(aq)$ was added last with the end result shown in test tube 3.

Explain the results shown in each test tube. Include a balanced equation for the reaction(s) taking place.

116. The solubility of copper(II) hydroxide in water can be increased by adding either the base NH_3 or the acid HNO_3. Explain. Would added NH_3 or HNO_3 have the same effect on the solubility of silver acetate or silver chloride? Explain.

Additional Exercises

117. Derive an equation analogous to the Henderson–Hasselbalch equation but relating pOH and pK_b of a buffered solution composed of a weak base and its conjugate acid, such as NH_3 and NH_4^+.

118. a. Calculate the pH of a buffered solution that is 0.100 M in $C_6H_5CO_2H$ (benzoic acid, $K_a = 6.4 \times 10^{-5}$) and 0.100 M in $C_6H_5CO_2Na$.

  b. Calculate the pH after 20.0% (by moles) of the benzoic acid is converted to benzoate anion by addition of strong acid. Use the dissociation equilibrium

$$C_6H_5CO_2H(aq) \rightleftharpoons C_6H_5CO_2^-(aq) + H^+(aq)$$

  to calculate the pH.

  c. Do the same as in part b, but use the following equilibrium to calculate the pH:

$$C_6H_5CO_2^-(aq) + H_2O(l) \rightleftharpoons C_6H_5CO_2H(aq) + OH^-(aq)$$

  d. Do your answers in parts b and c agree? Explain.

119. Consider a solution containing 0.10 M ethylamine ($C_2H_5NH_2$), 0.20 M $C_2H_5NH_3^+$, and 0.20 M Cl^-.

  a. Calculate the pH of this solution.

  b. Calculate the pH after 0.050 mol of KOH(s) is added to 1.00 L of this solution. (Ignore any volume changes.)

120. You make 1.00 L of a buffered solution (pH = 4.00) by mixing acetic acid and sodium acetate. You have 1.00 M solutions of each component of the buffered solution. What volume of each solution do you mix to make such a buffered solution?

121. You have the following reagents on hand:

Solids (pKa of Acid Form Is Given)	Solutions
Benzoic acid (4.19)	5.0 M HCl
Sodium acetate (4.74)	1.0 M acetic acid (4.74)
Potassium fluoride (3.14)	2.6 M NaOH
Ammonium chloride (9.26)	1.0 M HOCl (7.46)

What combinations of reagents would you use to prepare buffers at the following pH values?
  a. 3.0   **b.** 4.0   **c.** 5.0   **d.** 7.0   **e.** 9.0

122. Tris(hydroxymethyl)aminomethane, commonly called TRIS or Trizma, is often used as a buffer in biochemical studies. Its buffering range is pH 7 to 9, and K_b is 1.19×10^{-6} for the aqueous reaction

$$(HOCH_2)_3CNH_2 + H_2O \rightleftharpoons (HOCH_2)_3CNH_3^+ + OH^-$$
$$\text{TRIS} \qquad\qquad\qquad \text{TRISH}^+$$

  a. What is the optimal pH for TRIS buffers?

  b. Calculate the ratio [TRIS]/[TRISH$^+$] at pH = 7.00 and at pH = 9.00.

  c. A buffer is prepared by diluting 50.0 g TRIS base and 65.0 g TRIS hydrochloride (written as TRISHCl) to a total volume of

2.0 L. What is the pH of this buffer? What is the pH after 0.50 mL of 12 M HCl is added to a 200.0-mL portion of the buffer?

123. Calculate the value of the equilibrium constant for each of the following reactions in aqueous solution.

  a. $HC_2H_3O_2 + OH^- \rightleftharpoons C_2H_3O_2^- + H_2O$
  b. $C_2H_3O_2^- + H^+ \rightleftharpoons HC_2H_3O_2$
  c. $HCl + NaOH \rightleftharpoons NaCl + H_2O$

124. The following plot shows the pH curves for the titrations of various acids by 0.10 M NaOH (all of the acids were 50.0-mL samples of 0.10 M concentration).

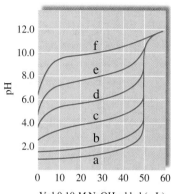

  a. Which pH curve corresponds to the weakest acid?

  b. Which pH curve corresponds to the strongest acid? Which point on the pH curve would you examine to see if this acid is a strong acid or a weak acid (assuming you did not know the initial concentration of the acid)?

  c. Which pH curve corresponds to an acid with $K_a \approx 1 \times 10^{-6}$?

125. Calculate the volume of 1.50×10^{-2} M NaOH that must be added to 500.0 mL of 0.200 M HCl to give a solution that has pH = 2.15.

126. Repeat the procedure in Exercise 57, but for the titration of 25.0 mL of 0.100 M HNO_3 with 0.100 M NaOH.

127. The active ingredient in aspirin is acetylsalicylic acid. A 2.51-g sample of acetylsalicylic acid required 27.36 mL of 0.5106 M NaOH for complete reaction. Addition of 13.68 mL of 0.5106 M HCl to the flask containing the aspirin and the sodium hydroxide produced a mixture with pH = 3.48. Find the molar mass of acetylsalicylic acid and its K_a value. State any assumptions you must make to reach your answer.

128. One method for determining the purity of aspirin (empirical formula, $C_9H_8O_4$) is to hydrolyze it with NaOH solution and then to titrate the remaining NaOH. The reaction of aspirin with NaOH is as follows:

$$C_9H_8O_4(s) + 2OH^-(aq)$$
$$\text{Aspirin} \xrightarrow[\text{10 min}]{\text{Boil}} C_7H_5O_3^-(aq) + C_2H_3O_2^-(aq) + H_2O(l)$$
$$\qquad\qquad\quad \text{Salicylate ion} \qquad \text{Acetate ion}$$

A sample of aspirin with a mass of 1.427 g was boiled in 50.00 mL of 0.500 M NaOH. After the solution was cooled, it took 31.92 mL of 0.289 M HCl to titrate the excess NaOH. Calculate the purity of the aspirin. What indicator should be used for this titration? Why?

129. A certain acetic acid solution has pH = 2.68. Calculate the volume of 0.0975 M KOH required to reach the equivalence point in the titration of 25.0 mL of the acetic acid solution.

130. A 0.210-g sample of an acid (molar mass = 192 g/mol) is titrated with 30.5 mL of 0.108 M NaOH to a phenolphthalein end point. Is the acid monoprotic, diprotic, or triprotic?

131. A student intends to titrate a solution of a weak monoprotic acid with a sodium hydroxide solution but reverses the two solutions and places the weak acid solution in the buret. After 23.75 mL of the weak acid solution has been added to 50.0 mL of the 0.100 M NaOH solution, the pH of the resulting solution is 10.50. Calculate the original concentration of the solution of weak acid.

132. A student titrates an unknown weak acid, HA, to a pale pink phenolphthalein end point with 25.0 mL of 0.100 M NaOH. The student then adds 13.0 mL of 0.100 M HCl. The pH of the resulting solution is 4.7. How is the value of pK_a for the unknown acid related to 4.7?

133. a. Using the K_{sp} value for $Cu(OH)_2$ (1.6×10^{-19}) and the overall formation constant for $Cu(NH_3)_4^{2+}$ (1.0×10^{13}), calculate the value for the equilibrium constant for the following reaction:

$$Cu(OH)_2(s) + 4NH_3(aq) \rightleftharpoons Cu(NH_3)_4^{2+}(aq) + 2OH^-(aq)$$

b. Use the value of the equilibrium constant you calculated in part a to calculate the solubility (in mol/L) of $Cu(OH)_2$ in 5.0 M NH_3. In 5.0 M NH_3 the concentration of OH^- is 0.0095 M.

134. The solubility rules outlined in Chapter 4 say that $Ba(OH)_2$, $Sr(OH)_2$, and $Ca(OH)_2$ are marginally soluble hydroxides. Calculate the pH of a saturated solution of each of these marginally soluble hydroxides.

135. The K_{sp} of hydroxyapatite, $Ca_5(PO_4)_3OH$, is 6.8×10^{-37}. Calculate the solubility of hydroxyapatite in pure water in moles per liter. How is the solubility of hydroxyapatite affected by adding acid? When hydroxyapatite is treated with fluoride, the mineral fluorapatite, $Ca_5(PO_4)_3F$, forms. The K_{sp} of this substance is 1×10^{-60}. Calculate the solubility of fluorapatite in water. How do these calculations provide a rationale for the fluoridation of drinking water?

136. In the chapter discussion of precipitate formation, we ran the precipitation reaction to completion and then let some of the precipitate redissolve to get back to equilibrium. To see why, redo Sample Exercise 15.17, where

Initial Concentration (mol/L)	Equilibrium Concentration (mol/L)
$[Mg^{2+}]_0 = 3.75 \times 10^{-3}$	
$[F^-]_0 = 6.25 \times 10^{-2}$	
	$[Mg^{2+}] = 3.75 \times 10^{-3} - y$
x mol/Mg^{2+}	$[F^-] = 6.25 \times 10^{-2} - 2y$
reacts to form MgF_2	

137. Calculate the concentration of Pb^{2+} in each of the following.
a. a saturated solution of $Pb(OH)_2$, $K_{sp} = 1.2 \times 10^{-15}$
b. a saturated solution of $Pb(OH)_2$ buffered at pH = 13.00

c. Ethylenediaminetetraacetate ($EDTA^{4-}$) is used as a complexing agent in chemical analysis and has the following structure:

$$\begin{array}{c} ^-O_2C-CH_2 \\ ^-O_2C-CH_2 \end{array} N-CH_2-CH_2-N \begin{array}{c} CH_2-CO_2^- \\ CH_2-CO_2^- \end{array}$$

Ethylenediaminetetraacetate

Solutions of $EDTA^{4-}$ are used to treat heavy metal poisoning by removing the heavy metal in the form of a soluble complex ion. The complex ion virtually eliminates the heavy metal ions from reacting with biochemical systems. The reaction of $EDTA^{4-}$ with Pb^{2+} is

$$Pb^{2+}(aq) + EDTA^{4-}(aq) \rightleftharpoons PbEDTA^{2-}(aq)$$
$$K = 1.1 \times 10^{18}$$

Consider a solution with 0.010 mol $Pb(NO_3)_2$ added to 1.0 L of an aqueous solution buffered at pH = 13.00 and containing 0.050 M Na_4EDTA. Does $Pb(OH)_2$ precipitate from this solution?

Challenge Problems

138. Another way to treat data from a pH titration is to graph the absolute value of the change in pH per change in milliliters added versus milliliters added ($\Delta pH/\Delta mL$ versus mL added). Make this graph using your results from Exercise 57. What advantage might this method have over the traditional method for treating titration data?

139. A buffer is made using 45.0 mL of 0.750 M $HC_3H_5O_2$ ($K_a = 1.3 \times 10^{-5}$) and 55.0 mL of 0.700 M $NaC_3H_5O_2$. What volume of 0.10 M NaOH must be added to change the pH of the original buffer solution by 2.5%?

140. A 0.400 M solution of ammonia was titrated with hydrochloric acid to the equivalence point, where the total volume was 1.50 times the original volume. At what pH does the equivalence point occur?

141. What volume of 0.0100 M NaOH must be added to 1.00 L of 0.0500 M HOCl to achieve a pH of 8.00?

142. Consider a solution formed by mixing 50.0 mL of 0.100 M H_2SO_4, 30.0 mL of 0.100 M HOCl, 25.0 mL of 0.200 M NaOH, 25.0 mL of 0.100 M $Ba(OH)_2$, and 10.0 mL of 0.150 M KOH. Calculate the pH of this solution.

143. When a diprotic acid, H_2A, is titrated by NaOH, the protons on the diprotic acid are generally removed one at a time, resulting in a pH curve that has the following generic shape:

Vol NaOH added

a. Notice that the plot has essentially two titration curves. If the first equivalence point occurs at 100.0 mL of NaOH added, what volume of NaOH added corresponds to the second equivalence point?

b. For the following volumes of NaOH added, list the major species present after the OH$^-$ reacts completely.
   i. 0 mL NaOH added
   ii. between 0 and 100.0 mL NaOH added
   iii. 100.0 mL NaOH added
   iv. between 100.0 and 200.0 mL NaOH added
   v. 200.0 mL NaOH added
   vi. after 200.0 mL NaOH added

c. If the pH at 50.0 mL of NaOH added is 4.0 and the pH at 150.0 mL of NaOH added is 8.0, determine the values K_{a_1} and K_{a_2} for the diprotic acid.

144. The titration of Na$_2$CO$_3$ with HCl has the following qualitative profile:

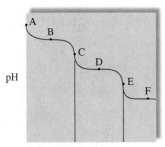

mL HCl

a. Identify the major species in solution as points A–F.

b. Calculate the pH at the halfway points to equivalence, B and D. *Hint:* Refer to Exercise 143.

145. A few drops of each of the indicators shown in the accompanying table were placed in separate portions of a 1.0 M solution of a weak acid, HX. The results are shown in the last column of the table. What is the approximate pH of the solution containing HX? Calculate the approximate value of K_a for HX.

Indicator	Color of HIn	Color of In$^-$	pK$_a$ of HIn	HX
Bromphenol blue	Yellow	Blue	4.0	Blue
Bromcresol purple	Yellow	Purple	6.0	Yellow
Bromcresol green	Yellow	Blue	4.8	Green
Alizarin	Yellow	Red	6.5	Yellow

146. Consider a solution made by mixing 500.0 mL of 4.0 M NH$_3$ and 500.0 mL of 0.40 M AgNO$_3$. Ag$^+$ reacts with NH$_3$ to form AgNH$_3^+$ and Ag(NH$_3$)$_2^+$:

$$Ag^+ + NH_3 \rightleftharpoons AgNH_3^+ \qquad K_1 = 2.1 \times 10^3$$
$$AgNH_3^+ + NH_3 \rightleftharpoons Ag(NH_3)_2^+ \qquad K_2 = 8.2 \times 10^3$$

Determine the concentration of all species in solution.

147. What is the maximum possible concentration of Ni^{2+} ion in water at 25°C that is saturated with 0.10 M H$_2$S and maintained at pH 3.0 with HCl?

148. You add an excess of solid MX in 250 g of water. You measure the freezing point and find it to be −0.028°C. What is the K_{sp} of the solid? Assume the density of the solution is 1.0 g/cm^3.

149. a. Calculate the molar solubility of SrF$_2$ in water, ignoring the basic properties of F$^-$. (For SrF$_2$, $K_{sp} = 7.9 \times 10^{-10}$.)

b. Would the measured molar solubility of SrF$_2$ be greater than or less than the value calculated in part a? Explain.

c. Calculate the molar solubility of SrF$_2$ in a solution buffered at pH = 2.00. (K_a for HF is 7.2×10^{-4}.)

150. A solution saturated with a salt of the type M$_3$X$_2$ has an osmotic pressure of 2.64×10^{-2} atm at 25°C. Calculate the K_{sp} value for the salt, assuming ideal behavior.

Integrative Problems

These problems require the integration of multiple concepts to find the solutions.

151. A buffer solution is prepared by mixing 75.0 mL of 0.275 M fluorobenzoic acid (C$_7$H$_5$O$_2$F) with 55.0 mL of 0.472 M sodium fluorobenzoate. The pK_a of this weak acid is 2.90. What is the pH of the buffer solution?

152. The K_{sp} for Q, a slightly soluble ionic compound composed of M$_2^{2+}$ and X$^-$ ions, is 4.5×10^{-29}. The electron configuration of M$^+$ is [Xe]$6s^14f^{14}5d^{10}$. The X$^-$ anion has 54 electrons. What is the molar solubility of Q in a solution of NaX prepared by dissolving 1.98 g of NaX in 150. mL of water?

153. Calculate the pH of a solution prepared by mixing 250. mL of 0.174 m aqueous HF (density = 1.10 g/mL) with 38.7 g of an aqueous solution that is 1.50% NaOH by mass (density = 1.02 g/mL). (K_a for HF = 7.2×10^{-4}.)

Marathon Problem*

This problem is designed to incorporate several concepts and techniques into one situation. Marathon Problems can be used in class by groups of students to help facilitate problem-solving skills.

154. A 225-mg sample of a diprotic acid is dissolved in enough water to make 250. mL of solution. The pH of this solution is 2.06. A saturated solution of calcium hydroxide ($K_{sp} = 1.3 \times 10^{-6}$) is prepared by adding excess calcium hydroxide to pure water and then removing the undissolved solid by filtration. Enough of the calcium hydroxide solution is added to the solution of the acid to reach the second equivalence point. The pH at the second equivalence point (as determined by a pH meter) is 7.96. The first dissociation constant for the acid (K_{a_1}) is 5.90×10^{-2}. Assume that the volumes of the solutions are additive, all solutions are at 25°C, and that K_{a_1} is at least 1000 times greater than K_{a_2}.

a. Calculate the molar mass of the acid.

b. Calculate the second dissociation constant for the acid (K_{a_2}).

 Get help understanding core concepts and visualizing molecular-level interactions, and practice problem solving, by visiting the Online Study Center at **college.hmco.com/PIC/zumdahl7e.**

*Used with permission from the *Journal of Chemical Education,* Vol. 68, No. 11, 1991, pp. 919–922; copyright © 1991, Division of Chemical Education, Inc.

16 Spontaneity, Entropy, and Free Energy

Contents

Solid carbon dioxide (dry ice), when placed in water, causes violent bubbling as gaseous CO_2 is released. The "fog" is moisture condensed from the cold air.

*T*he *first law of thermodynamics* is a statement of the law of conservation of energy: Energy can be neither created nor destroyed. In other words, *the energy of the universe is constant.* Although the total energy is constant, the various forms of energy can be interchanged in physical and chemical processes. For example, if you drop a book, some of the initial potential energy of the book is changed to kinetic energy, which is then transferred to the atoms in the air and the floor as random motion. The net effect of this process is to change a given quantity of potential energy to exactly the same quantity of thermal energy. Energy has been converted from one form to another, but the same quantity of energy exists before and after the process.

Now let's consider a chemical example. When methane is burned in excess oxygen, the major reaction is

$$CH_4(g) + 2O_2(g) \longrightarrow CO_2(g) + 2H_2O(g) + energy$$

This reaction produces a quantity of energy, which is released as heat. This energy flow results from the lowering of the potential energy stored in the bonds of CH_4 and O_2 as they react to form CO_2 and H_2O. This is illustrated in Fig. 16.1. Potential energy has been converted to thermal energy, but the energy content of the universe has remained constant in accordance with the first law of thermodynamics.

The first law of thermodynamics is used mainly for energy bookkeeping, that is, to answer such questions as

How much energy is involved in the change?

Does energy flow into or out of the system?

What form does the energy finally assume?

The first law of thermodynamics: The energy of the universe is constant.

Although the first law of thermodynamics provides the means for accounting for energy, it gives no hint as to why a particular process occurs in a given direction. This is the main question to be considered in this chapter.

16.1 Spontaneous Processes and Entropy

Spontaneous does not mean fast.

A process is said to be *spontaneous* if it *occurs without outside intervention.* **Spontaneous processes** may be fast or slow. As we will see in this chapter, thermodynamics can tell us the *direction* in which a process will occur but can say nothing about the *speed* of the process. As we saw in Chapter 12, the rate of a reaction depends on many factors, such as activation energy, temperature, concentration, and catalysts, and we were able to explain these effects using a simple collision model. In describing a chemical reaction, the discipline of chemical kinetics focuses on the pathway between reactants and products; thermodynamics considers only the initial and final states and does not require knowledge of the pathway between reactants and products (see Fig. 16.2).

FIGURE 16.1
When methane and oxygen react to form carbon dioxide and water, the products have lower potential energy than the reactants. This change in potential energy results in energy flow (heat) to the surroundings.

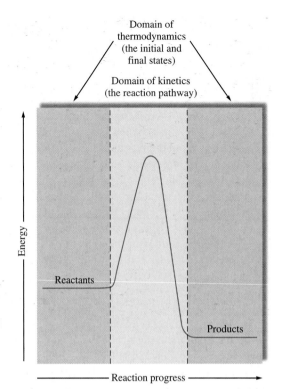

Domain of
thermodynamics
(the initial and
final states)

Domain of kinetics
(the reaction pathway)

Reactants

Products

Energy

Reaction progress

FIGURE 16.2
The rate of a reaction depends on the pathway from reactants to products; this is the domain of kinetics. Thermodynamics tells us whether a reaction is spontaneous based only on the properties of the reactants and products. The predictions of thermodynamics do not require knowledge of the pathway between reactants and products.

In summary, thermodynamics lets us predict whether a process will occur but gives no information about the amount of time required for the process. For example, according to the principles of thermodynamics, a diamond should change spontaneously to graphite. The fact that we do not observe this process does not mean the prediction is wrong; it simply means the process is very slow. Thus we need both thermodynamics and kinetics to describe reactions fully.

To explore the idea of spontaneity, consider the following physical and chemical processes:

A ball rolls down a hill but never spontaneously rolls back up the hill.

If exposed to air and moisture, steel rusts spontaneously. However, the iron oxide in rust does not spontaneously change back to iron metal and oxygen gas.

A gas fills its container uniformly. It never spontaneously collects at one end of the container.

Heat flow always occurs from a hot object to a cooler one. The reverse process never occurs spontaneously.

Wood burns spontaneously in an exothermic reaction to form carbon dioxide and water, but wood is not formed when carbon dioxide and water are heated together.

At temperatures below 0°C, water spontaneously freezes, and at temperatures above 0°C, ice spontaneously melts.

What thermodynamic principle will provide an explanation of why, under a given set of conditions, each of these diverse processes occurs in one direction and never in the reverse? In searching for an answer, we could explain the behavior of a ball on a hill in terms of gravity. But what does gravity have to do with the rusting of a nail or the freezing of water? Early developers of thermodynamics thought that exothermicity might be the key—that a process would be spontaneous if it were exothermic. Although this factor

Plant materials burn to form carbon dioxide and water.

A disordered pile of playing cards.

Probability refers to likelihood.

Visualization: Entropy

does appear to be important, since many spontaneous processes are exothermic, it is not the total answer. For example, the melting of ice, which occurs spontaneously at temperatures greater than 0°C, is an endothermic process.

What common characteristic causes the processes listed above to be spontaneous in one direction only? After many years of observation, scientists have concluded that the characteristic common to all spontaneous processes is an increase in a property called **entropy,** denoted by the symbol S. *The driving force for a spontaneous process is an increase in the entropy of the universe.*

What is entropy? Although there is no simple definition that is completely accurate, *entropy can be viewed as a measure of molecular randomness or disorder.* The natural progression of things is from order to disorder, from lower entropy to higher entropy. To illustrate the natural tendency toward disorder, you only have to think about the condition of your room. Your room naturally tends to get messy (disordered), because an ordered room requires everything to be in its place. There are simply many more ways for things to be out of place than for them to be in their places.

As another example, suppose you have a deck of playing cards ordered in some particular way. You throw these cards into the air and pick them all up at random. Looking at the new sequence of the cards, you would be very surprised to find that it matched the original order. Such an event would be possible, but *very improbable*. There are billions of ways for the deck to be disordered, but only one way to be ordered according to your definition. Thus the chances of picking the cards up out of order are much greater than the chance of picking them up in order. It is natural for disorder to increase.

Entropy is a thermodynamic function that describes the *number of arrangements* (positions and/or energy levels) that are *available to a system* existing in a given state. Entropy is closely associated with probability. The key concept is that the more ways a particular state can be achieved, the greater is the likelihood (probability) of finding that state. In other words, *nature spontaneously proceeds toward the states that have the highest probabilities of existing.* This conclusion is not surprising at all. The difficulty comes in connecting this concept to real-life processes. For example, what does the spontaneous rusting of steel have to do with probability? Understanding the connection between entropy and spontaneity will allow us to answer such questions. We will begin to explore this connection by considering a very simple process, the expansion of an ideal gas into

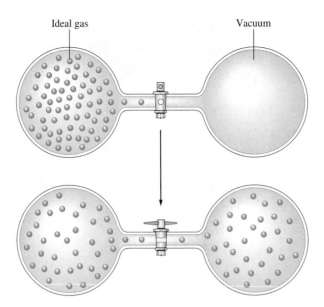

FIGURE 16.3
The expansion of an ideal gas into an evacuated bulb.

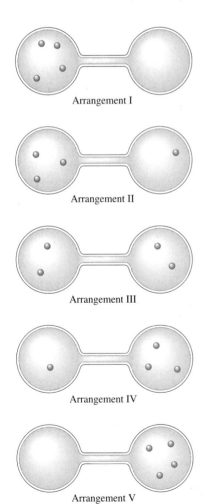

Arrangement I

Arrangement II

Arrangement III

Arrangement IV

Arrangement V

FIGURE 16.4
Possible arrangements (states) of four molecules in a two-bulbed flask.

a vacuum, as represented in Fig. 16.3. Why is this process spontaneous? The driving force is probability. Because there are more ways of having the gas evenly spread throughout the container than there are ways for it to be in any other possible state, the gas spontaneously attains the uniform distribution.

To understand this conclusion, we will greatly simplify the system and consider the possible arrangements of only four gas molecules in the two-bulbed container (Fig. 16.4). How many ways can each arrangement (state) be achieved? Arrangements I and V can be achieved in only one way—all the molecules must be in one end. Arrangements II and V can be achieved in four ways, as shown in Table 16.1. Each configuration that gives a particular arrangement is called a *microstate*. Arrangement I has one microstate, and arrangement II has four microstates. Arrangement III can be achieved in six ways (six microstates), as shown in Table 16.1. *Which arrangement is most likely to occur?* The one that can be achieved in the greatest number of ways. Thus arrangement III is most probable. The relative probabilities of arrangements III, II, and I are 6 : 4 : 1. We have discovered an important principle: The probability of occurrence of a particular arrangement (state) depends on the number of ways (microstates) in which that arrangement can be achieved.

The consequences of this principle are dramatic for large numbers of molecules. One gas molecule in the flask in Fig. 16.4 has one chance in two of being in the left bulb. We say that the probability of finding the molecule in the left bulb is $\frac{1}{2}$. For two molecules in the flask, there is one chance in two of finding each molecule in the left bulb, so there is one chance in four ($\frac{1}{2} \times \frac{1}{2} = \frac{1}{4}$) that *both* molecules will be in the left bulb. As the number of molecules increases, the relative probability of finding all of them in the left bulb decreases, as shown in Table 16.2. For 1 mole of gas, the probability of finding all the molecules in the left bulb is so small that this arrangement would "never" occur.

Thus a gas placed in one end of a container will spontaneously expand to fill the entire vessel evenly because, for a large number of gas molecules, there is a huge number of microstates in which equal numbers of molecules are in both ends. On the other hand, the opposite process,

into or out of the system as heat. To understand this, suppose an exothermic process transfers 50 J of energy as heat to the surroundings, where it becomes thermal energy, that is, kinetic energy associated with the random motions of atoms. Thus this flow of energy into the surroundings increases the random motions of atoms there and thereby increases the entropy of the surroundings. The sign of ΔS_{surr} is positive. When an endothermic process occurs in the system, it produces the opposite effect. Heat flows from the surroundings to the system, and the random motions of the atoms in the surroundings decrease, decreasing the entropy of the surroundings. The vaporization of water is an endothermic process. Thus, for this change of state, ΔS_{surr} is negative.

Remember it is the sign of ΔS_{univ} that tells us whether the vaporization of water is spontaneous. We have seen that ΔS_{sys} is positive and favors the process and that ΔS_{surr} is negative and unfavorable. Thus the components of ΔS_{univ} are in opposition. Which one controls the situation? The answer *depends on the temperature.* We know that at a pressure of 1 atmosphere, water changes spontaneously from liquid to gas at all temperatures above 100°C. Below 100°C, the opposite process (condensation) is spontaneous.

Since ΔS_{sys} and ΔS_{surr} are in opposition for the vaporization of water, the temperature must have an effect on the relative importance of these two terms. To understand why this is so, we must discuss in more detail the factors that control the entropy changes in the surroundings. The central idea is that *the entropy changes in the surroundings are primarily determined by heat flow.* An exothermic process in the system increases the entropy of the surroundings, because the resulting energy flow increases the random motions in the surroundings. This means that exothermicity is an important driving force for spontaneity. In earlier chapters we have seen that a system tends to undergo changes that lower its energy. We now understand the reason for this tendency. When a system at constant temperature moves to a lower energy, the energy it gives up is transferred to the surroundings, leading to an increase in entropy there.

The significance of exothermicity as a driving force *depends on the temperature at which the process occurs.* That is, the magnitude of ΔS_{surr} depends on the temperature at which the heat is transferred. We will not attempt to prove this fact here. Instead, we offer an analogy. Suppose that you have $50 to give away. Giving it to a millionaire would not create much of an impression—a millionaire has money to spare. However, to a poor college student, $50 would represent a significant sum and would be received with considerable joy. The same principle can be applied to energy transfer via the flow of heat. If 50 J of energy is transferred to the surroundings, the impact of that event depends greatly on the temperature. If the temperature of the surroundings is very high, the atoms there are in rapid motion. The 50 J of energy will not make a large percent change in these motions. On the other hand, if 50 J of energy is transferred to the surroundings at a very low temperature, where atomic motion is slow, the energy will cause a large percent change in these motions. *The impact of the transfer of a given quantity of energy as heat to or from the surroundings will be greater at lower temperatures.*

For our purposes, there are two important characteristics of the entropy changes that occur in the surroundings:

1. *The sign of ΔS_{surr} depends on the direction of the heat flow.* At constant temperature, an exothermic process in the system causes heat to flow into the surroundings, increasing the random motions and thus the entropy of the surroundings. For this case, ΔS_{surr} is positive. The opposite is true for an endothermic process in a system at constant temperature. Note that although the driving force described here really results from the change in entropy, it is often described in terms of energy: Nature tends to seek the lowest possible energy.

2. *The magnitude of ΔS_{surr} depends on the temperature.* The transfer of a given quantity of energy as heat produces a much greater percent change in the randomness of the surroundings at a low temperature than it does at a high temperature. Thus ΔS_{surr} depends directly on the quantity of heat transferred and inversely on temperature. In

Boiling water to form steam increases its volume and thus its entropy.

In an endothermic process, heat flows from the surroundings into the system. In an exothermic process, heat flows into the surroundings from the system.

In a process occurring at constant temperature, the tendency for the system to lower its energy results from the positive value of ΔS_{surr}.

other words, the tendency for the system to lower its energy becomes a more important driving force at lower temperatures.

$$
\begin{array}{c}
\text{Driving force} \\
\text{provided by} \\
\text{the energy flow} \\
\text{(heat)}
\end{array}
=
\begin{array}{c}
\text{magnitude of the} \\
\text{entropy change of} \\
\text{the surroundings}
\end{array}
=
\frac{\text{quantity of heat (J)}}{\text{temperature (K)}}
$$

These ideas are summarized as follows:

Exothermic process:
ΔS_{surr} = positive

Exothermic process: $\qquad \Delta S_{surr} = +\dfrac{\text{quantity of heat (J)}}{\text{temperature (K)}}$

Endothermic process:
ΔS_{surr} = negative

Endothermic process: $\qquad \Delta S_{surr} = -\dfrac{\text{quantity of heat (J)}}{\text{temperature (K)}}$

We can express ΔS_{surr} in terms of the change in enthalpy ΔH for a process occurring at constant pressure, since

$$\text{Heat flow (constant } P) = \text{change in enthalpy} = \Delta H$$

When no subscript is present, the quantity (for example, ΔH) refers to the system.

Recall that ΔH consists of two parts: a sign and a number. The *sign* indicates the direction of flow, where a plus sign means into the system (endothermic) and a minus sign means out of the system (exothermic). The *number* indicates the quantity of energy.

Combining all these concepts produces the following definition of ΔS_{surr} for a reaction that takes place under conditions of constant temperature (in kelvins) and pressure:

$$\Delta S_{surr} = -\frac{\Delta H}{T}$$

The minus sign changes the point of view from the system to the surroundings.

The minus sign is necessary because the sign of ΔH is determined with respect to the reaction system, and this equation expresses a property of the surroundings. This means that if the reaction is exothermic, ΔH has a negative sign, but since heat flows into the surroundings, ΔS_{surr} is positive.

Sample Exercise 16.4 ## Determining ΔS_{surr}

In the metallurgy of antimony, the pure metal is recovered via different reactions, depending on the composition of the ore. For example, iron is used to reduce antimony in sulfide ores:

$$Sb_2S_3(s) + 3Fe(s) \longrightarrow 2Sb(s) + 3FeS(s) \qquad \Delta H = -125 \text{ kJ}$$

Carbon is used as the reducing agent for oxide ores:

$$Sb_4O_6(s) + 6C(s) \longrightarrow 4Sb(s) + 6CO(g) \qquad \Delta H = 778 \text{ kJ}$$

Calculate ΔS_{surr} for each of these reactions at 25°C and 1 atm.

Solution

We use

$$\Delta S_{surr} = -\frac{\Delta H}{T}$$

where $\qquad T = 25 + 273 = 298 \text{ K}$

For the sulfide ore reaction,

$$\Delta S_{surr} = -\frac{-125 \text{ kJ}}{298 \text{ K}} = 0.419 \text{ kJ/K} = 419 \text{ J/K}$$

The mineral stibnite contains Sb_2S_3.

TABLE 16.3   Interplay of ΔS_{sys} and ΔS_{surr} in Determining the Sign of ΔS_{univ}

Signs of Entropy Changes			
ΔS_{sys}	ΔS_{surr}	ΔS_{univ}	*Process Spontaneous?*
+	+	+	Yes
−	−	−	No (reaction will occur in opposite direction)
+	−	?	Yes, if ΔS_{sys} has a larger magnitude than ΔS_{surr}
−	+	?	Yes, if ΔS_{surr} has a larger magnitude than ΔS_{sys}

Note that ΔS_{surr} is positive, as it should be, since this reaction is exothermic and heat flow occurs to the surroundings, increasing the randomness of the surroundings.

For the oxide ore reaction,

$$\Delta S_{surr} = -\frac{778 \text{ kJ}}{298} = -2.61 \text{ kJ/K} = -2.61 \times 10^3 \text{ J/K}$$

In this case ΔS_{surr} is negative because heat flow occurs from the surroundings to the system.

See Exercises 16.25 and 16.26.

We have seen that the spontaneity of a process is determined by the entropy change it produces in the universe. We also have seen that ΔS_{univ} has two components, ΔS_{sys} and ΔS_{surr}. If for some process both ΔS_{sys} and ΔS_{surr} are positive, then ΔS_{univ} is positive, and the process is spontaneous. If, on the other hand, both ΔS_{sys} and ΔS_{surr} are negative, the process does not occur in the direction indicated but is spontaneous in the opposite direction. Finally, if ΔS_{sys} and ΔS_{surr} have opposite signs, the spontaneity of the process depends on the sizes of the opposing terms. These cases are summarized in Table 16.3.

We can now understand why spontaneity is often dependent on temperature and thus why water spontaneously freezes below 0°C and melts above 0°C. The term ΔS_{surr} is temperature-dependent. Since

$$\Delta S_{surr} = -\frac{\Delta H}{T}$$

at constant pressure, the value of ΔS_{surr} changes markedly with temperature. The magnitude of ΔS_{surr} will be very small at high temperatures and will increase as the temperature decreases. That is, exothermicity is most important as a driving force at low temperatures.

16.4 Free Energy

The symbol *G* for free energy honors Josiah Willard Gibbs (1839–1903), who was professor of mathematical physics at Yale University from 1871 to 1903. He laid the foundations of many areas of thermodynamics, particularly as they apply to chemistry.

So far we have used ΔS_{univ} to predict the spontaneity of a process. However, another thermodynamic function is also related to spontaneity and is especially useful in dealing with the temperature dependence of spontaneity. This function is called the **free energy,** which is symbolized by *G* and defined by the relationship

$$G = H - TS$$

where *H* is the enthalpy, *T* is the Kelvin temperature, and *S* is the entropy.

Visualization: Spontaneous
Reactions

For a process that occurs at constant temperature, the change in free energy (ΔG) is given by the equation

$$\Delta G = \Delta H - T\Delta S$$

Note that all quantities here refer to the system. From this point on we will follow the usual convention that when no subscript is included, the quantity refers to the system.

To see how this equation relates to spontaneity, we divide both sides of the equation by $-T$ to produce

$$-\frac{\Delta G}{T} = -\frac{\Delta H}{T} + \Delta S$$

Remember that at constant temperature and pressure

$$\Delta S_{surr} = -\frac{\Delta H}{T}$$

So we can write

$$-\frac{\Delta G}{T} = -\frac{\Delta H}{T} + \Delta S = \Delta S_{surr} + \Delta S = \Delta S_{univ}$$

We have shown that

$$\Delta S_{univ} = -\frac{\Delta G}{T} \qquad \text{at constant } T \text{ and } P$$

This result is very important. It means that a process carried out at constant temperature and pressure will be spontaneous only if ΔG is negative. That is, *a process (at constant T and P) is spontaneous in the direction in which the free energy decreases* ($-\Delta G$ means $+\Delta S_{univ}$).

Now we have two functions that can be used to predict spontaneity: the entropy of the universe, which applies to all processes, and free energy, which can be used for processes carried out at constant temperature and pressure. Since so many chemical reactions occur under the latter conditions, free energy is the more useful to chemists.

Let's use the free energy equation to predict the spontaneity of the melting of ice:

$$H_2O(s) \longrightarrow H_2O(l)$$

The superscript degree symbol (°) indicates all substances are in their standard states.

for which $\Delta H° = 6.03 \times 10^3$ J/mol   and $\Delta S° = 22.1$ J/K · mol

Results of the calculations of ΔS_{univ} and $\Delta G°$ at $-10°C$, $0°C$, and $10°C$ are shown in Table 16.4. These data predict that the process is spontaneous at $10°C$; that is, ice melts at this temperature because ΔS_{univ} is positive and $\Delta G°$ is negative. The opposite is true at $-10°C$, where water freezes spontaneously.

To review the definitions of standard states, see page 246.

Why is this so? The answer lies in the fact that ΔS_{sys} ($\Delta S°$) and ΔS_{surr} oppose each other. The term $\Delta S°$ favors the melting of ice because of the increase in positional entropy, and ΔS_{surr} favors the freezing of water because it is an exothermic process. At temperatures below

TABLE 16.4   Results of the Calculation of ΔS_{univ} and $\Delta G°$ for the Process $H_2O(s) \rightarrow H_2O(l)$ at $-10°C$, $0°C$, and $10°C$*

T (°C)	T (K)	$\Delta H°$ (J/mol)	$\Delta S°$ (J/K · mol)	$\Delta S_{surr} = -\dfrac{\Delta H°}{T}$ (J/K · mol)	$\Delta S_{univ} = \Delta S° + \Delta S_{surr}$ (J/K · mol)	$T\Delta S°$ (J/mol)	$\Delta G° = \Delta H° - T\Delta S°$ (J/mol)
-10	263	6.03×10^3	22.1	-22.9	-0.8	5.81×10^3	$+2.2 \times 10^2$
0	273	6.03×10^3	22.1	-22.1	0	6.03×10^3	0
10	283	6.03×10^3	22.1	-21.3	$+0.8$	6.25×10^3	-2.2×10^2

*Note that at $10°C$, $\Delta S°$ (ΔS_{sys}) controls, and the process occurs even though it is endothermic. At $-10°C$, the magnitude of ΔS_{surr} is larger than that of $\Delta S°$, so the process is spontaneous in the opposite (exothermic) direction.

0°C, the change of state occurs in the exothermic direction because ΔS_{surr} is larger in magnitude than ΔS_{sys}. But above 0°C the change occurs in the direction in which ΔS_{sys} is favorable, since in this case ΔS_{sys} is larger in magnitude than ΔS_{surr}. At 0°C the *opposing tendencies just balance,* and the two states coexist; there is no driving force in either direction. An equilibrium exists between the two states of water. Note that ΔS_{univ} is equal to 0 at 0°C.

We can reach the same conclusions by examining $\Delta G°$. At $-10°$, $\Delta G°$ is positive because the $\Delta H°$ term is larger than the $T\Delta S°$ term. The opposite is true at 10°C. At 0°C, $\Delta H°$ is equal to $T\Delta S°$ and $\Delta G°$ is equal to 0. This means that solid H_2O and liquid H_2O have the same free energy at 0°C ($\Delta G° = G_{liquid} - G_{solid}$), and the system is at equilibrium.

We can understand the temperature dependence of spontaneity by examining the behavior of ΔG. For a process occurring at constant temperature and pressure,

$$\Delta G = \Delta H - T\Delta S$$

If ΔH and ΔS favor opposite processes, spontaneity will depend on temperature in such a way that the exothermic direction will be favored at low temperatures. For example, for the process

$$H_2O(s) \longrightarrow H_2O(l)$$

ΔH is positive and ΔS is positive. The natural tendency for this system to lower its energy is in opposition to its natural tendency to increase its positional randomness. At low temperatures, ΔH dominates, and at high temperatures, ΔS dominates. The various possible cases are summarized in Table 16.5.

Sample Exercise 16.5   ## Free Energy and Spontaneity

At what temperatures is the following process spontaneous at 1 atm?

$$Br_2(l) \longrightarrow Br_2(g)$$
$$\Delta H° = 31.0 \text{ kJ/mol} \quad \text{and} \quad \Delta S° = 93.0 \text{ J/K} \cdot \text{mol}$$

What is the normal boiling point of liquid Br_2?

Solution

The vaporization process will be spontaneous at all temperatures where $\Delta G°$ is negative. Note that $\Delta S°$ favors the vaporization process because of the increase in positional entropy, and $\Delta H°$ favors the *opposite* process, which is exothermic. These opposite tendencies will exactly balance at the boiling point of liquid Br_2, since at this temperature liquid and gaseous Br_2 are in equilibrium ($\Delta G° = 0$). We can find this temperature by setting $\Delta G° = 0$ in the equation

$$\Delta G° = \Delta H° - T\Delta S°$$
$$0 = \Delta H° - T\Delta S°$$
$$\Delta H° = T\Delta S°$$

Note that although ΔH and ΔS are somewhat temperature-dependent, it is a good approximation to assume they are constant over a relatively small temperature range.

TABLE 16.5   Various Possible Combinations of ΔH and ΔS for a Process and the Resulting Dependence of Spontaneity on Temperature

Case	Result
ΔS positive, ΔH negative	Spontaneous at all temperatures
ΔS positive, ΔH positive	Spontaneous at high temperatures (where exothermicity is relatively unimportant)
ΔS negative, ΔH negative	Spontaneous at low temperatures (where exothermicity is dominant)
ΔS negative, ΔH positive	Process not spontaneous at *any* temperature (reverse process is spontaneous at *all* temperatures)

Then
$$T = \frac{\Delta H^\circ}{\Delta S^\circ} = \frac{3.10 \times 10^4 \text{ J/mol}}{93.0 \text{ J/K} \cdot \text{mol}} = 333 \text{ K}$$

At temperatures above 333 K, $T\Delta S^\circ$ has a larger magnitude than ΔH°, and ΔG° (or $\Delta H^\circ - T\Delta S^\circ$) is negative. Above 333 K, the vaporization process is spontaneous; the opposite process occurs spontaneously below this temperature. At 333 K, liquid and gaseous Br_2 coexist in equilibrium. These observations can be summarized as follows (the pressure is 1 atm in each case):

1. $T > 333$ K. The term ΔS° controls. The increase in entropy when liquid Br_2 is vaporized is dominant.

2. $T < 333$ K. The process is spontaneous in the direction in which it is exothermic. The term ΔH° controls.

3. $T = 333$ K. The opposing driving forces are just balanced ($\Delta G^\circ = 0$), and the liquid and gaseous phases of bromine coexist. This is the normal boiling point.

See Exercises 16.29 through 16.31.

16.5 Entropy Changes in Chemical Reactions

The second law of thermodynamics tells us that a process will be spontaneous if the entropy of the universe increases when the process occurs. We saw in Section 16.4 that for a process at constant temperature and pressure, we can use the change in free energy of the system to predict the sign of ΔS_{univ} and thus the direction in which it is spontaneous. So far we have applied these ideas only to physical processes, such as changes of state and the formation of solutions. However, the main business of chemistry is studying chemical reactions, and, therefore, we want to apply the second law to reactions.

First, we will consider the entropy changes accompanying chemical reactions that occur under conditions of constant temperature and pressure. As for the other types of processes we have considered, the entropy changes in the *surroundings* are determined by the heat flow that occurs as the reaction takes place. However, the entropy changes in the *system* (the reactants and products of the reaction) are determined by positional probability.

For example, in the ammonia synthesis reaction

$$N_2(g) + 3H_2(g) \longrightarrow 2NH_3(g)$$

four reactant molecules become two product molecules, lowering the number of independent units in the system, which leads to less positional disorder.

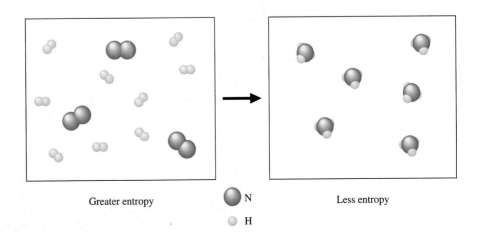

Greater entropy   ● N   Less entropy
                     ● H

Fewer molecules mean fewer possible configurations. To help clarify this idea, consider a special container with a million compartments, each large enough to hold a hydrogen molecule. Thus there are a million ways one H_2 molecule can be placed in this container. But suppose we break the H—H bond and place the two independent H atoms in the same container. A little thought will convince you that there are *many* more than a million ways to place the two separate atoms. The number of arrangements possible for the two independent atoms is much greater than the number for the molecule. Thus for the process

$$H_2 \longrightarrow 2H$$

positional entropy increases.

Does positional entropy increase or decrease when the following reaction takes place?

$$4NH_3(g) + 5O_2(g) \longrightarrow 4NO(g) + 6H_2O(g)$$

In this case 9 gaseous molecules are changed to 10 gaseous molecules, and the positional entropy increases. There are more independent units as products than as reactants. In general, when a reaction involves gaseous molecules, *the change in positional entropy is dominated by the relative numbers of molecules of gaseous reactants and products.* If the number of molecules of the gaseous products is greater than the number of molecules of the gaseous reactants, positional entropy typically increases, and ΔS will be positive for the reaction.

Sample Exercise 16.6

Predicting the Sign of $\Delta S°$

Predict the sign of $\Delta S°$ for each of the following reactions.

a. The thermal decomposition of solid calcium carbonate:

$$CaCO_3(s) \longrightarrow CaO(s) + CO_2(g)$$

b. The oxidation of SO_2 in air:

$$2SO_2(g) + O_2(g) \longrightarrow 2SO_3(g)$$

Solution

a. Since in this reaction a gas is produced from a solid reactant, the positional entropy increases, and $\Delta S°$ is positive.

b. Here three molecules of gaseous reactants become two molecules of gaseous products. Since the number of gas molecules decreases, positional entropy decreases, and $\Delta S°$ is negative.

See Exercises 16.33 and 16.34.

In thermodynamics it is the *change* in a certain function that is usually important. The change in enthalpy determines if a reaction is exothermic or endothermic at constant pressure. The change in free energy determines if a process is spontaneous at constant temperature and pressure. It is fortunate that changes in thermodynamic functions are sufficient for most purposes, since absolute values for many thermodynamic characteristics of a system, such as enthalpy or free energy, cannot be determined.

However, we can assign absolute entropy values. Consider a solid at 0 K, where molecular motion virtually ceases. If the substance is a perfect crystal, its internal arrangement is absolutely regular (see Fig. 16.5(a)). There is only *one way* to achieve this perfect order: Every particle must be in its place. For example, with N coins there is only one

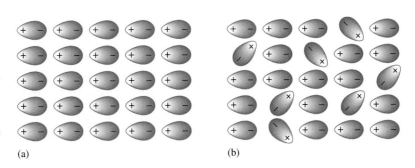

FIGURE 16.5
(a) A perfect crystal of hydrogen chloride at 0 K; the dipolar HCl molecules are represented by ⊕|⊖. The entropy is zero (S = 0) for this perfect crystal at 0 K.
(b) As the temperature rises above 0 K, lattice vibrations allow some dipoles to change their orientations, producing some disorder and an increase in entropy (S > 0).

(a)   (b)

A perfect crystal at 0 K is an unattainable ideal, taken as a standard but never actually observed.

way to achieve the state of all heads. Thus a perfect crystal represents the lowest possible entropy; that is, *the entropy of a perfect crystal at 0 K is zero.* This is a statement of the **third law of thermodynamics.**

As the temperature of a perfect crystal is increased, the random vibrational motions increase, and disorder increases within the crystal [see Fig. 16.5(b)]. Thus the entropy of a substance increases with temperature. Since S is zero for a perfect crystal at 0 K, the entropy value for a substance at a particular temperature can be calculated by knowing the temperature dependence of entropy. (We will not show such calculations here.)

The standard entropy values represent the increase in entropy that occurs when a substance is heated from 0 K to 298 K at 1 atm pressure.

The *standard entropy values* $S°$ of many common substances at 298 K and 1 atm are listed in Appendix 4. From these values you will see that the entropy of a substance does indeed increase in going from solid to liquid to gas. One especially interesting feature of this table is the very low $S°$ value for diamond. The structure of diamond is highly ordered, with each carbon strongly bound to a tetrahedral arrangement of four other carbon atoms (see Section 10.5, Fig. 10.22). This type of structure allows very little disorder and has a very low entropy, even at 298 K. Graphite has a slightly higher entropy because its layered structure allows for a little more disorder.

Because *entropy is a state function of the system* (it is not pathway-dependent), the entropy change for a given chemical reaction can be calculated by taking the difference between the standard entropy values of products and those of the reactants:

$$\Delta S°_{\text{reaction}} = \Sigma n_p S°_{\text{products}} - \Sigma n_r S°_{\text{reactants}}$$

where, as usual, Σ represents the sum of the terms. It is important to note that entropy is an extensive property (it depends on the amount of substance present). This means that the number of moles of a given reactant (n_r) or product (n_p) must be taken into account.

Sample Exercise 16.7   ## Calculating $\Delta S°$

Calculate $\Delta S°$ at 25°C for the reaction

$$2\text{NiS}(s) + 3\text{O}_2(g) \longrightarrow 2\text{SO}_2(g) + 2\text{NiO}(s)$$

given the following standard entropy values:

Substance	$S°$ (J/K · mol)
$\text{SO}_2(g)$	248
$\text{NiO}(s)$	38
$\text{O}_2(g)$	205
$\text{NiS}(s)$	53

Solution

Since

$$\Delta S° = \Sigma n_p S°_{products} - \Sigma n_r S°_{reactants}$$

$$= 2S°_{SO_2(g)} + 2S°_{NiO(s)} - 2S°_{NiS(s)} - 3S°_{O_2(s)}$$

$$= 2\text{ mol}\left(248 \frac{J}{K \cdot mol}\right) + 2\text{ mol}\left(38 \frac{J}{K \cdot mol}\right)$$

$$\quad -2\text{ mol}\left(53 \frac{J}{K \cdot mol}\right) - 3\text{ mol}\left(205 \frac{J}{K \cdot mol}\right)$$

$$= 496 \text{ J/K} + 76 \text{ J/K} - 106 \text{ J/K} - 615 \text{ J/K}$$

$$= -149 \text{ J/K}$$

We would expect $\Delta S°$ to be negative because the number of gaseous molecules decreases in this reaction.

See Exercise 16.37.

Sample Exercise 16.8 **Calculating $\Delta S°$**

Calculate $\Delta S°$ for the reduction of aluminum oxide by hydrogen gas:

$$Al_2O_3(s) + 3H_2(g) \longrightarrow 2Al(s) + 3H_2O(g)$$

Use the following standard entropy values:

Substance	$S°$ (J/K · mol)
$Al_2O_3(s)$	51
$H_2(g)$	131
$Al(s)$	28
$H_2O(g)$	189

Solution

$$\Delta S° = \Sigma n_p S°_{products} - \Sigma n_r S°_{reactants}$$

$$= 2S°_{Al(s)} + 3S°_{H_2O(g)} - 3S°_{H_2(g)} - S°_{Al_2O_3(s)}$$

$$= 2\text{ mol}\left(28 \frac{J}{K \cdot mol}\right) + 3\text{ mol}\left(189 \frac{J}{K \cdot mol}\right)$$

$$\quad -3\text{ mol}\left(131 \frac{J}{K \cdot mol}\right) - 1\text{ mol}\left(51 \frac{J}{K \cdot mol}\right)$$

$$= 56 \text{ J/K} + 567 \text{ J/K} - 393 \text{ J/K} - 51 \text{ J/K}$$

$$= 179 \text{ J/K}$$

See Exercises 16.38 through 16.40.

The reaction considered in Sample Exercise 16.8 involves 3 moles of hydrogen gas on the reactant side and 3 moles of water vapor on the product side. Would you expect ΔS to be large or small for such a case? We have assumed that ΔS depends on the relative numbers of molecules of gaseous reactants and products. Based on this assumption, ΔS should be near zero for this reaction. However, ΔS is large and

Vibrations

Rotation

FIGURE 16.6
The H_2O molecule can vibrate and rotate in several ways, some of which are shown here. This freedom of motion leads to a higher entropy for water than for a substance like hydrogen, a simple diatomic molecule with fewer possible motions.

The value of $\Delta G°$ tells us nothing about the rate of a reaction, only its eventual equilibrium position.

positive. Why is this so? The large value for ΔS results from the difference in the entropy values for hydrogen gas and water vapor. The reason for this difference can be traced to the difference in molecular structure. Because it is a nonlinear, triatomic molecule, H_2O has more rotational and vibrational motions (see Fig. 16.6) than does the diatomic H_2 molecule. Thus the standard entropy value for $H_2O(g)$ is greater than that for $H_2(g)$. Generally, *the more complex the molecule, the higher the standard entropy value.*

16.6 Free Energy and Chemical Reactions

For chemical reactions we are often interested in the **standard free energy change** ($\Delta G°$), *the change in free energy that will occur if the reactants in their standard states are converted to the products in their standard states.* For example, for the ammonia synthesis reaction at 25°C,

$$N_2(g) + 3H_2(g) \rightleftharpoons 2NH_3(g) \qquad \Delta G° = -33.3 \text{ kJ} \qquad (16.1)$$

This $\Delta G°$ value represents the change in free energy when 1 mol nitrogen gas at 1 atm reacts with 3 mol hydrogen gas at 1 atm to produce 2 mol gaseous NH_3 at 1 atm.

It is important to recognize that the standard free energy change for a reaction is not measured directly. For example, we can measure heat flow in a calorimeter to determine $\Delta H°$, but we cannot measure $\Delta G°$ this way. The value of $\Delta G°$ for the ammonia synthesis in Equation (16.1) was *not* obtained by mixing 1 mol N_2 and 3 mol H_2 in a flask and measuring the change in free energy as 2 mol NH_3 formed. For one thing, if we mixed 1 mol N_2 and 3 mol H_2 in a flask, the system would go to equilibrium rather than to completion. Also, we have no instrument that measures free energy. However, while we cannot directly measure $\Delta G°$ for a reaction, we can calculate it from other measured quantities, as we will see later in this section.

Why is it useful to know $\Delta G°$ for a reaction? As we will see in more detail later in this chapter, knowing the $\Delta G°$ values for several reactions allows us to compare the relative tendency of these reactions to occur. The more negative the value of $\Delta G°$, the further a reaction will go to the right to reach equilibrium. We must use standard-state free energies to make this comparison because free energy varies with pressure or concentration. Thus, to get an accurate comparison of reaction tendencies, we must compare all reactions under the same pressure or concentration conditions. We will have more to say about the significance of $\Delta G°$ later.

There are several ways to calculate $\Delta G°$. One common method uses the equation

$$\Delta G° = \Delta H° - T\Delta S°$$

which applies to a reaction carried out at constant temperature. For example, for the reaction

$$C(s) + O_2(g) \longrightarrow CO_2(g)$$

the values of $\Delta H°$ and $\Delta S°$ are known to be -393.5 kJ and 3.05 J/K, respectively, and $\Delta G°$ can be calculated at 298 K as follows:

$$\begin{aligned}
\Delta G° &= \Delta H° - T\Delta S° \\
&= -3.935 \times 10^5 \text{ J} - (298 \text{ K})(3.05 \text{ J/K}) \\
&= -3.944 \times 10^5 \text{ J} \\
&= -394.4 \text{ kJ (per mole of } CO_2)
\end{aligned}$$

| Sample Exercise 16.9 | Calculating $\Delta H°$, $\Delta S°$, and $\Delta G°$ |

Consider the reaction

$$2SO_2(g) + O_2(g) \longrightarrow 2SO_3(g)$$

carried out at 25°C and 1 atm. Calculate $\Delta H°$, $\Delta S°$, and $\Delta G°$ using the following data:

Substance	$\Delta H_f°$ (kJ/mol)	$S°$ (J/K · mol)
$SO_2(g)$	−297	248
$SO_3(g)$	−396	257
$O_2(g)$	0	205

Solution

The value of $\Delta H°$ can be calculated from the enthalpies of formation using the equation we discussed in Section 6.4:

$$\Delta H° = \Sigma n_p \Delta H_{f\ (\text{products})}° - \Sigma n_r \Delta H_{f\ (\text{reactants})}°$$

Then

$$\Delta H° = 2\Delta H_{f\ (SO_3(g))}° - 2\Delta H_{f\ (SO_2(g))}° - \Delta H_{f\ (O_2(g))}°$$
$$= 2\ \text{mol}(-396\ \text{kJ/mol}) - 2\ \text{mol}(-297\ \text{kJ/mol}) - 0$$
$$= -792\ \text{kJ} + 594\ \text{kJ}$$
$$= -198\ \text{kJ}$$

The value of $\Delta S°$ can be calculated using the standard entropy values and the equation discussed in Section 16.5:

$$\Delta S° = \Sigma n_p S_{\text{products}}° - \Sigma n_r S_{\text{reactants}}°$$

Thus

$$\Delta S° = 2S_{SO_3(g)}° - 2S_{SO_2(g)}° - S_{O_2(g)}°$$
$$= 2\ \text{mol}(257\ \text{J/K · mol}) - 2\ \text{mol}(248\ \text{J/K · mol}) - 1\ \text{mol}(205\ \text{J/K · mol})$$
$$= 514\ \text{J/K} - 496\ \text{J/K} - 205\ \text{J/K}$$
$$= -187\ \text{J/K}$$

We would expect $\Delta S°$ to be negative because three molecules of gaseous reactants give two molecules of gaseous products.

The value of $\Delta G°$ can now be calculated from the equation

$$\Delta G° = \Delta H° - T\Delta S°$$
$$= -198\ \text{kJ} - (298\ \text{K})\left(-187\ \frac{\text{J}}{\text{K}}\right)\left(\frac{1\ \text{kJ}}{1000\ \text{J}}\right)$$
$$= -198\ \text{kJ} + 55.7\ \text{kJ} = -142\ \text{kJ}$$

See Exercises 16.45 through 16.47.

A second method for calculating ΔG for a reaction takes advantage of the fact that, like enthalpy, *free energy is a state function.* Therefore, we can use procedures for finding ΔG that are similar to those for finding ΔH using Hess's law.

To illustrate this method for calculating the free energy change, we will obtain $\Delta G°$ for the reaction

$$2CO(g) + O_2(g) \longrightarrow 2CO_2(g) \qquad (16.2)$$

from the following data:

$$2CH_4(g) + 3O_2(g) \longrightarrow 2CO(g) + 4H_2O(g) \qquad \Delta G° = -1088 \text{ kJ} \qquad (16.3)$$
$$CH_4(g) + 2O_2(g) \longrightarrow CO_2(g) + 2H_2O(g) \qquad \Delta G° = -801 \text{ kJ} \qquad (16.4)$$

Note that $CO(g)$ is a reactant in Equation (16.2). This means that Equation (16.3) must be reversed, since $CO(g)$ is a product in that reaction as written. When a reaction is reversed, the sign of $\Delta G°$ is also reversed. In Equation (16.4), $CO_2(g)$ is a product, as it is in Equation (16.2), but only one molecule of CO_2 is formed. Thus Equation (16.4) must be multiplied by 2, which means the $\Delta G°$ value for Equation (16.4) also must be multiplied by 2. Free energy is an extensive property, since it is defined by two extensive properties, H and S.

Reversed Equation (16.3)
$$2CO(g) + 4H_2O(g) \longrightarrow 2CH_4(g) + 3O_2(g) \qquad \Delta G° = -(-1088 \text{ kJ})$$

$2 \times$ Equation (16.4)
$$\underline{2CH_4(g) + 4O_2(g) \longrightarrow 2CO_2(g) + 4H_2O(g) \qquad \Delta G° = 2(-801 \text{ kJ})}$$

$$2CO(g) + O_2(g) \longrightarrow 2CO_2(g) \qquad \Delta G° = -(-1088 \text{ kJ})$$
$$+ 2(-801 \text{ kJ})$$
$$= -514 \text{ kJ}$$

This example shows that the ΔG values for reactions are manipulated in exactly the same way as the ΔH values.

Sample Exercise 16.10   # Calculating $\Delta G°$

Graphite

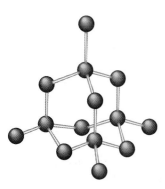

Diamond

Using the following data (at 25°C)

$$C_{diamond}(s) + O_2(g) \longrightarrow CO_2(g) \qquad \Delta G° = -397 \text{ kJ} \qquad (16.5)$$
$$C_{graphite}(s) + O_2(g) \longrightarrow CO_2(g) \qquad \Delta G° = -394 \text{ kJ} \qquad (16.6)$$

calculate $\Delta G°$ for the reaction

$$C_{diamond}(s) \longrightarrow C_{graphite}(s)$$

Solution

We reverse Equation (16.6) to make graphite a product, as required, and then add the new equation to Equation (16.5):

$$C_{diamond}(s) + O_2(g) \longrightarrow CO_2(g) \qquad \Delta G° = -397 \text{ kJ}$$

Reversed Equation (16.6)
$$\underline{CO_2(g) \longrightarrow C_{graphite}(s) + O_2(g) \qquad \Delta G° = -(-394 \text{ kJ})}$$

$$C_{diamond}(s) \longrightarrow C_{graphite}(s) \qquad \Delta G° = -397 \text{ kJ} + 394 \text{ kJ}$$
$$= -3 \text{ kJ}$$

Since $\Delta G°$ is negative for this process, diamond should spontaneously change to graphite at 25°C and 1 atm. However, the reaction is so slow under these conditions that we do not observe the process. This is another example of kinetic rather than thermodynamic control of a reaction. We can say that diamond is kinetically stable with respect to graphite even though it is thermodynamically unstable.

See Exercises 16.51 and 16.52.

In Sample Exercise 16.10 we saw that the process

$$C_{diamond}(s) \longrightarrow C_{graphite}(s)$$

is spontaneous but very slow at 25°C and 1 atm. The reverse process can be made to occur at high temperatures and pressures. Diamond has a more compact structure and thus a higher density than graphite, so exerting very high pressure causes it to become thermodynamically favored. If high temperatures are also used to make the process fast enough to be feasible, diamonds can be made from graphite. The conditions typically used involve temperatures greater than 1000°C and pressures of about 10^5 atm. About half of all industrial diamonds are made this way.

A third method for calculating the free energy change for a reaction uses standard free energies of formation. The **standard free energy of formation** (ΔG_f°) of a substance

> The standard state of an element is its most stable state of 25°C and 1 atm.

is defined as the *change in free energy that accompanies the formation of 1 mole of that substance from its constituent elements with all reactants and products in their standard states.* For the formation of glucose ($C_6H_{12}O_6$), the appropriate reaction is

$$6C(s) + 6H_2(g) + 3O_2(g) \longrightarrow C_6H_{12}O_6(s)$$

The standard free energy associated with this process is called the *free energy of formation of glucose.* Values of the standard free energy of formation are useful in calculating ΔG° for specific chemical reactions using the equation

> Calculating ΔG° is very similar to calculating ΔH°, as shown in Section 6.4.

$$\Delta G^\circ = \Sigma n_p \Delta G_{f \text{ (products)}}^\circ - \Sigma n_r \Delta G_{f \text{ (reactants)}}^\circ$$

Values of ΔG_f° for many common substances are listed in Appendix 4. Note that, analogous to the enthalpy of formation, *the standard free energy of formation of an element in its standard state is zero.* Also note that the number of moles of each reactant (n_r) and product (n_p) must be used when calculating ΔG° for a reaction.

| Sample Exercise 16.11 | Calculating ΔG° |

Methanol is a high-octane fuel used in high-performance racing engines. Calculate ΔG° for the reaction

$$2CH_3OH(g) + 3O_2(g) \longrightarrow 2CO_2(g) + 4H_2O(g)$$

given the following free energies of formation:

Substance	ΔG_f° (kJ/mol)
$CH_3OH(g)$	−163
$O_2(g)$	0
$CO_2(g)$	−394
$H_2O(g)$	−229

Solution

We use the equation

$$\Delta G^\circ = \Sigma n_p \Delta G_{f \text{ (products)}}^\circ - \Sigma n_r \Delta G_{f \text{ (reactants)}}^\circ$$
$$= 2\Delta G_{f\,(CO_2(g))}^\circ + 4\Delta G_{f\,(H_2O(g))}^\circ - 3\Delta G_{f\,(O_2(g))}^\circ - 2\Delta G_{f\,(CH_3OH(g))}^\circ$$
$$= 2 \text{ mol}(-394 \text{ kJ/mol}) + 4 \text{ mol}(-229 \text{ kJ/mol}) - 3(0)$$
$$\qquad -2 \text{ mol}(-163 \text{ kJ/mol})$$
$$= -1378 \text{ kJ}$$

The large magnitude and the negative sign of $\Delta G°$ indicate that this reaction is very favorable thermodynamically.

See Exercises 16.53 through 16.55.

| Sample Exercise 16.12 | **Free Energy and Spontaneity** |

Ethylene

Ethanol

A chemical engineer wants to determine the feasibility of making ethanol (C_2H_5OH) by reacting water with ethylene (C_2H_4) according to the equation

$$C_2H_4(g) + H_2O(l) \longrightarrow C_2H_5OH(l)$$

Is this reaction spontaneous under standard conditions?

Solution

To determine the spontaneity of this reaction under standard conditions, we must determine $\Delta G°$ for the reaction. We can do this using standard free energies of formation at 25° from Appendix 4:

$$\Delta G°_{f\ (C_2H_5OH(l))} = -175 \text{ kJ/mol}$$
$$\Delta G°_{f\ (H_2O(l))} = -237 \text{ kJ/mol}$$
$$\Delta G°_{f\ (C_2H_4(g))} = 68 \text{ kJ/mol}$$

Then

$$\Delta G° = \Delta G°_{f\ (C_2H_5OH(l))} - \Delta G°_{f\ (H_2O(l))} - \Delta G°_{f\ (C_2H_4(g))}$$
$$= -175 \text{ kJ} - (-237 \text{ kJ}) - 68 \text{ kJ}$$
$$= -6 \text{ kJ}$$

Thus the process is spontaneous under standard conditions at 25°C.

See Exercise 16.56.

Although the reaction considered in Sample Exercise 16.12 is spontaneous, other features of the reaction must be studied to see if the process is feasible. For example, the chemical engineer will need to study the kinetics of the reaction to determine whether it is fast enough to be useful and, if it is not, whether a catalyst can be found to enhance the rate. In doing these studies, the engineer must remember that $\Delta G°$ depends on temperature:

$$\Delta G° = \Delta H° - T\Delta S°$$

Thus, if the process must be carried out at high temperatures to be fast enough to be feasible, $\Delta G°$ must be recalculated at that temperature from the $\Delta H°$ and $\Delta S°$ values for the reaction.

16.7 The Dependence of Free Energy on Pressure

In this chapter we have seen that a system at constant temperature and pressure will proceed spontaneously in the direction that lowers its free energy. This is why reactions proceed until they reach equilibrium. As we will see later in this section, *the equilibrium position represents the lowest free energy value available to a particular reaction system.* The free energy of a reaction system changes as the reaction proceeds, because free energy is dependent on the pressure of a gas or on the concentration of species in solution. We will deal only with the pressure dependence of the free energy of an ideal gas. The dependence of free energy on concentration can be developed using similar reasoning.

To understand the pressure dependence of free energy, we need to know how pressure affects the thermodynamic functions that comprise free energy, that is, enthalpy and entropy (recall that $G = H - TS$). For an ideal gas, enthalpy is not pressure-dependent. However, entropy *does* depend on pressure because of its dependence on volume. Consider 1 mole of an ideal gas at a given temperature. At a volume of 10.0 L, the gas has many more positions available for its molecules than if its volume is 1.0 L. The positional entropy is greater in the larger volume. In summary, at a given temperature for 1 mole of ideal gas

$$S_{\text{large volume}} > S_{\text{small volume}}$$

or, since pressure and volume are inversely related,

$$S_{\text{low pressure}} > S_{\text{high pressure}}$$

We have shown qualitatively that the entropy and therefore the free energy of an ideal gas depend on its pressure. Using a more detailed argument, which we will not consider here, it can be shown that

$$G = G° + RT \ln(P)$$

where $G°$ is the free energy of the gas at a pressure of 1 atm, G is the free energy of the gas at a pressure of P atm, R is the universal gas constant, and T is the Kelvin temperature.

To see how the change in free energy for a reaction depends on pressure, we will consider the ammonia synthesis reaction

$$N_2(g) + 3H_2(g) \longrightarrow 2NH_3(g)$$

In general, $\qquad\qquad \Delta G = \Sigma n_p G_{\text{products}} - \Sigma n_r G_{\text{reactants}}$

For this reaction $\qquad \Delta G = 2G_{NH_3} - G_{N_2} - 3G_{H_2}$

See Appendix 1.2 to review logarithms.

where
$$G_{NH_3} = G°_{NH_3} + RT \ln(P_{NH_3})$$
$$G_{N_2} = G°_{N_2} + RT \ln(P_{N_2})$$
$$G_{H_2} = G°_{H_2} + RT \ln(P_{H_2})$$

Substituting these values into the equation gives

$$\Delta G = 2[G°_{NH_3} + RT \ln(P_{NH_3})] - [G°_{N_2} + RT \ln(P_{N_2})] - 3[G°_{H_2} + RT \ln(P_{H_2})]$$
$$= 2G°_{NH_3} - G°_{N_2} - 3G°_{H_2} + 2RT \ln(P_{NH_3}) - RT \ln(P_{N_2}) - 3RT \ln(P_{H_2})$$
$$= \underbrace{(2G°_{NH_3} - G°_{N_2} - 3G°_{H_2})}_{\Delta G° \text{ reaction}} + RT[2 \ln(P_{NH_3}) - \ln(P_{N_2}) - 3 \ln(P_{H_2})]$$

The first term (in parentheses) is $\Delta G°$ for the reaction. Thus we have

$$\Delta G = \Delta G°_{\text{reaction}} + RT[2 \ln(P_{NH_3}) - \ln(P_{N_2}) - 3 \ln(P_{H_2})]$$

and since
$$2 \ln(P_{NH_3}) = \ln(P_{NH_3}{}^2)$$
$$-\ln(P_{N_2}) = \ln\left(\frac{1}{P_{N_2}}\right)$$
$$-3 \ln(P_{H_2}) = \ln\left(\frac{1}{P_{H_2}{}^3}\right)$$

the equation becomes

$$\Delta G = \Delta G° + RT \ln\left(\frac{P_{NH_3}{}^2}{(P_{N_2})(P_{H_2}{}^3)}\right)$$

But the term

$$\frac{P_{NH_3}^2}{(P_{N_2})(P_{H_2}^3)}$$

is the reaction quotient Q discussed in Section 13.5. Therefore, we have

$$\Delta G = \Delta G° + RT \ln(Q)$$

where Q is the reaction quotient (from the law of mass action), T is the temperature (K), R is the gas law constant and is equal to 8.3145 J/K · mol, $\Delta G°$ is the free energy change for the reaction with all reactants and products at a pressure of 1 atm, and ΔG is the free energy change for the reaction for the specified pressures of reactants and products.

| *Sample Exercise 16.13* | ## Calculating $\Delta G°$ |

One method for synthesizing methanol (CH_3OH) involves reacting carbon monoxide and hydrogen gases:

$$CO(g) + 2H_2(g) \longrightarrow CH_3OH(l)$$

Calculate ΔG at 25°C for this reaction where carbon monoxide gas at 5.0 atm and hydrogen gas at 3.0 atm are converted to liquid methanol.

Solution

To calculate ΔG for this process, we use the equation

$$\Delta G = \Delta G° + RT \ln(Q)$$

We must first compute $\Delta G°$ from standard free energies of formation (see Appendix 4). Since

$$\Delta G°_{f\,(CH_3OH(l))} = -166 \text{ kJ}$$
$$\Delta G°_{f\,(H_2(g))} = 0$$
$$\Delta G°_{f\,(CO(g))} = -137 \text{ kJ}$$
$$\Delta G° = -166 \text{ kJ} - (-137 \text{ kJ}) - 0 = -29 \text{ kJ} = -2.9 \times 10^4 \text{ J}$$

Note that this is the value of $\Delta G°$ for the reaction of 1 mol CO with 2 mol H_2 to produce 1 mol CH_3OH. We might call this the value of $\Delta G°$ for one "round" of the reaction or for one mole of the reaction. Thus the $\Delta G°$ value might better be written as -2.9×10^4 J/mol of reaction, or -2.9×10^4 J/mol rxn.

We can now calculate ΔG using

$$\Delta G° = -2.9 \times 10^4 \text{ J/mol rxn}$$
$$R = 8.3145 \text{ J/K} \cdot \text{mol}$$
$$T = 273 + 25 = 298 \text{ K}$$
$$Q = \frac{1}{(P_{CO})(P_{H_2}^2)} = \frac{1}{(5.0)(3.0)^2} = 2.2 \times 10^{-2}$$

Note in this case that ΔG is defined for "one mole of the reaction," that is, for 1 mol CO(g) reacting with 2 mol $H_2(g)$ to form 1 mol $CH_3OH(l)$. Thus ΔG, $\Delta G°$, and $RT \ln(Q)$ all have units of J/mol of reaction. In this case the units of R are actually J/K · mol of reaction, although they are usually not written this way.

Note that the pure liquid methanol is not included in the calculation of Q. Then

$$\Delta G = \Delta G° + RT \ln(Q)$$
$$= (-2.9 \times 10^4 \text{ J/mol rxn}) + (8.3145 \text{ J/K} \cdot \text{mol rxn})(298 \text{ K}) \ln(2.2 \times 10^{-2})$$
$$= (-2.9 \times 10^4 \text{ J/mol rxn}) - (9.4 \times 10^3 \text{ J/mol rxn}) = -3.8 \times 10^4 \text{ J/mol rxn}$$
$$= -38 \text{ kJ/mol rxn}$$

Note that ΔG is significantly more negative than $\Delta G°$, implying that the reaction is more spontaneous at reactant pressures greater than 1 atm. We might expect this result from Le Châtelier's principle.

See Exercises 16.57 and 16.58.

The Meaning of ΔG for a Chemical Reaction

In this section we have learned to calculate ΔG for chemical reactions under various conditions. For example, in Sample Exercise 16.13 the calculations show that the formation of $CH_3OH(l)$ from $CO(g)$ at 5.0 atm reacting with $H_2(g)$ at 3.0 atm is spontaneous. What does this result mean? Does it mean that if we mixed 1.0 mol $CO(g)$ and 2.0 mol $H_2(g)$ together at pressures of 5.0 and 3.0 atm, respectively, that 1.0 mol $CH_3OH(l)$ would form in the reaction flask? The answer is no. This answer may surprise you in view of what has been said in this section. It is true that 1.0 mol $CH_3OH(l)$ has a lower free energy than 1.0 mol $CO(g)$ at 5.0 atm plus 2.0 mol $H_2(g)$ at 3.0 atm. However, when $CO(g)$ and $H_2(g)$ are mixed under these conditions, there is *an even lower free energy available to this system than 1.0 mol pure $CH_3OH(l)$.* For reasons we will discuss shortly, *the system can achieve the lowest possible free energy by going to equilibrium, not by going to completion.* At the equilibrium position, some of the $CO(g)$ and $H_2(g)$ will remain in the reaction flask. So even though 1.0 mol pure $CH_3OH(l)$ is at a lower free energy than 1.0 mol $CO(g)$ and 2.0 mol $H_2(g)$ at 5.0 and 3.0 atm, respectively, the reaction system will stop short of forming 1.0 mol $CH_3OH(l)$. The reaction stops short of completion because the equilibrium mixture of $CH_3OH(l)$, $CO(g)$, and $H_2(g)$ exists at the lowest possible free energy available to the system.

To illustrate this point, we will explore a mechanical example. Consider balls rolling down the two hills shown in Fig. 16.7. Note that in both cases point B has a lower potential energy than point A.

In Fig. 16.7(a) the ball will roll to point B. This diagram is analogous to a phase change. For example, at 25°C ice will spontaneously change completely to liquid water, because the latter has the lowest free energy. In this case liquid water is the only choice. There is no intermediate mixture of ice and water with lower free energy.

The situation is different for a chemical reaction system, as illustrated in Fig. 16.7(b). In Fig. 16.7(b) the ball will not get to point B because there is a lower potential energy at point C. Like the ball, a chemical system will seek the *lowest possible* free energy, which, for reasons we will discuss below, is the equilibrium position.

Therefore, although the value of ΔG for a given reaction system tells us whether the products or reactants are favored under a given set of conditions, it does not mean that the system will proceed to pure products (if ΔG is negative) or remain at pure reactants (if ΔG is positive). Instead, the system will spontaneously go to the equilibrium position,

FIGURE 16.7
Schematic representations of balls rolling down two types of hills.

(a)

(b)

the lowest possible free energy available to it. In the next section we will see that the value of $\Delta G°$ for a particular reaction tells us exactly where this position will be.

16.8 Free Energy and Equilibrium

When the components of a given chemical reaction are mixed, they will proceed, rapidly or slowly depending on the kinetics of the process, to the equilibrium position. In Chapter 13 we defined the equilibrium position as the point at which the forward and reverse reaction rates are equal. In this chapter we look at equilibrium from a thermodynamic point of view, and we find that the **equilibrium point** *occurs at the lowest value of free energy available to the reaction system.* As it turns out, the two definitions give the same equilibrium state, which must be the case for both the kinetic and thermodynamic models to be valid.

To understand the relationship of free energy to equilibrium, let's consider the following simple hypothetical reaction:

$$A(g) \rightleftharpoons B(g)$$

where 1.0 mole of gaseous A is initially placed in a reaction vessel at a pressure of 2.0 atm. The free energies for A and B are diagramed as shown in Fig. 16.8(a). As A reacts to form B, the total free energy of the system changes, yielding the following results:

$$\text{Free energy of A} = G_A = G_A° + RT \ln(P_A)$$
$$\text{Free energy of B} = G_B = G_B° + RT \ln(P_B)$$
$$\text{Total free energy of system} = G = G_A + G_B$$

As A changes to B, G_A will decrease because P_A is decreasing [Fig. 16.8(b)]. In contrast, G_B will increase because P_B is increasing. The reaction will proceed to the right as long as the total free energy of the system decreases (as long as G_B is less than G_A). At some point the pressures of A and B reach the values P_A^e and P_B^e that make G_A equal to G_B. *The system has reached equilibrium* [Fig. 16.8(c)]. Since A at pressure P_A^e and B at pressure P_B^e have the same free energy (G_A equals G_B), ΔG is zero for A at pressure P_A^e changing to B at pressure P_B^e. *The system has reached minimum free energy.* There is no longer any driving force to change A to B or B to A, so the system remains at this position (the pressures of A and B remain constant).

Suppose that for the experiment described above the plot of free energy versus the mole fraction of A reacted is defined as shown in Fig. 16.9(a). In this experiment, minimum free energy is reached when 75% of A has been changed to B. At this point, the pressure of A is 0.25 times the original pressure, or

$$(0.25)(2.0 \text{ atm}) = 0.50 \text{ atm}$$

The pressure of B is

$$(0.75)(2.0 \text{ atm}) = 1.5 \text{ atm}$$

FIGURE 16.8
(a) The initial free energies of A and B. (b) As $A(g)$ changes to $B(g)$, the free energy of A decreases and that of B increases. (c) Eventually, pressures of A and B are achieved such that $G_A = G_B$, the equilibrium position.

FIGURE 16.9
(a) The change in free energy to reach equilibrium, beginning with 1.0 mol $A(g)$ at $P_A = 2.0$ atm. (b) The change in free energy to reach equilibrium, beginning with 1.0 mol $B(g)$ at $P_B = 2.0$ atm. (c) The free energy profile for $A(g) \rightleftharpoons B(g)$ in a system containing 1.0 mol (A plus B) at $P_{TOTAL} = 2.0$ atm. Each point on the curve corresponds to the total free energy of the system for a given combination of A and B.

Since this is the equilibrium position, we can use the equilibrium pressures to calculate a value for K for the reaction in which A is converted to B at this temperature:

$$K = \frac{P_B^e}{P_A^e} = \frac{1.5 \text{ atm}}{0.50 \text{ atm}} = 3.0$$

For the reaction $A(g) \rightleftharpoons B(g)$, the pressure is constant during the reaction, since the same number of gas molecules is always present.

Exactly the same equilibrium point would be achieved if we placed 1.0 mol pure $B(g)$ in the flask at a pressure of 2.0 atm. In this case B would change to A until equilibrium $(G_B = G_A)$ is reached. This is shown in Fig. 16.9(b).

The overall free energy curve for this system is shown in Fig. 16.9(c). Note that any mixture of $A(g)$ and $B(g)$ containing 1.0 mol (A plus B) at a total pressure of 2.0 atm will react until it reaches the minimum in the curve.

In summary, when substances undergo a chemical reaction, the reaction proceeds to the minimum free energy (equilibrium), which corresponds to the point where

$$G_{\text{products}} = G_{\text{reactants}} \quad \text{or} \quad \Delta G = G_{\text{products}} - G_{\text{reactants}} = 0$$

We can now establish a quantitative relationship between free energy and the value of the equilibrium constant. We have seen that

$$\Delta G = \Delta G° + RT \ln(Q)$$

and at equilibrium ΔG equals 0 and Q equals K.

So
$$\Delta G = 0 = \Delta G° + RT \ln(K)$$

or
$$\Delta G° = -RT \ln(K)$$

We must note the following characteristics of this very important equation.

Case 1: $\Delta G° = 0$. When $\Delta G°$ equals zero for a particular reaction, the free energies of the reactants and products are equal when all components are in the standard states (1 atm for gases). The system is at equilibrium when the pressures of all reactants and products are 1 atm, which means that K equals 1.

Case 2: $\Delta G° < 0$. In this case $\Delta G°$ $(G°_{\text{products}} - G°_{\text{reactants}})$ is negative, which means that

$$G°_{\text{products}} < G°_{\text{reactants}}$$

If a flask contains the reactants and products, all at 1 atm, the system will *not* be at equilibrium. Since $G°_{\text{products}}$ is less than $G°_{\text{reactants}}$, the system will adjust to the right to reach equilibrium. In this case K will be *greater than 1,* since the pressures of the products at equilibrium will be greater than 1 atm and the pressures of the reactants at equilibrium will be less than 1 atm.

Case 3: $\Delta G° > 0$. Since $\Delta G°$ $(G°_{\text{products}} - G°_{\text{reactants}})$ is positive,

$$G°_{\text{reactants}} < G°_{\text{products}}$$

If a flask contains the reactants and products, all at 1 atm, the system will *not* be at equilibrium. In this case the system will adjust to the left (toward the reactants, which have a lower free energy) to reach equilibrium. The value of K will be *less than 1,* since at equilibrium the pressures of the reactants will be greater than 1 atm and the pressures of the products will be less than 1 atm.

These results are summarized in Table 16.6. The value of K for a specific reaction can be calculated from the equation

$$\Delta G° = -RT \ln(K)$$

as is shown in Sample Exercises 16.14 and 16.15.

TABLE 16.6   Qualitative Relationship Between the Change in Standard Free Energy and the Equilibrium Constant for a Given Reaction

$\Delta G°$	K
$\Delta G° = 0$	$K = 1$
$\Delta G° < 0$	$K > 1$
$\Delta G° > 0$	$K < 1$

| *Sample Exercise 16.14* | **Free Energy and Equilibrium I** |

Consider the ammonia synthesis reaction

$$N_2(g) + 3H_2(g) \rightleftharpoons 2NH_3(g)$$

where $\Delta G° = -33.3$ kJ per mole of N_2 consumed at 25°C. For each of the following mixtures of reactants and products at 25°C, predict the direction in which the system will shift to reach equilibrium.

a. $P_{NH_3} = 1.00$ atm, $P_{N_2} = 1.47$ atm, $P_{H_2} = 1.00 \times 10^{-2}$ atm
b. $P_{NH_3} = 1.00$ atm, $P_{N_2} = 1.00$ atm, $P_{H_2} = 1.00$ atm

Solution

a. We can predict the direction of reaction to equilibrium by calculating the value of ΔG using the equation

The units of ΔG, $\Delta G°$, and $RT \ln (Q)$ all refer to the balanced reaction with all amounts expressed in moles. We might say that the units are joules per "mole of reaction," although only the "per mole" is indicated for R (as is customary).

$$\Delta G = \Delta G° + RT \ln(Q)$$

where

$$Q = \frac{P_{NH_3}{}^2}{(P_{N_2})(P_{H_2}{}^3)} = \frac{(1.00)^2}{(1.47)(1.00 \times 10^{-2})^3} = 6.80 \times 10^5$$

$$T = 25 + 273 = 298 \text{ K}$$

$$R = 8.3145 \text{ J/K} \cdot \text{mol}$$

and

$$\Delta G° = -33.3 \text{ kJ/mol} = -3.33 \times 10^4 \text{ J/mol}$$

Then

$$\Delta G = (-3.33 \times 10^4 \text{ J/mol}) + (8.3145 \text{ J/K} \cdot \text{mol})(298 \text{ K}) \ln(6.8 \times 10^5)$$
$$= (-3.33 \times 10^4 \text{ J/mol}) + (3.33 \times 10^4 \text{ J/mol}) = 0$$

Since $\Delta G = 0$, the reactants and products have the same free energies at these partial pressures. The system is already at equilibrium, and no shift will occur.

b. The partial pressures given here are all 1.00 atm, which means that the system is in the standard state. That is,

$$\Delta G = \Delta G° + RT \ln(Q) = \Delta G° + RT \ln\frac{(1.00)^2}{(1.00)(1.00)^3}$$
$$= \Delta G° + RT \ln(1.00) = \Delta G° + 0 = \Delta G°$$

For this reaction at 25°C,

$$\Delta G° = -33.3 \text{ kJ/mol}$$

The negative value for $\Delta G°$ means that in their standard states the products have a lower free energy than the reactants. Thus the system will move to the right to reach equilibrium. That is, K is greater than 1.

See Exercise 16.59.

| *Sample Exercise 16.15* | **Free Energy and Equilibrium II** |

The overall reaction for the corrosion (rusting) of iron by oxygen is

$$4Fe(s) + 3O_2(g) \rightleftharpoons 2Fe_2O_3(s)$$

Using the following data, calculate the equilibrium constant for this reaction at 25°C.

Substance	ΔH_f° (kJ/mol)	S° (J/K · mol)
$Fe_2O_3(s)$	−826	90
$Fe(s)$	0	27
$O_2(g)$	0	205

Solution

To calculate K for this reaction, we will use the equation

$$\Delta G^\circ = -RT \ln(K)$$

We must first calculate ΔG° from

$$\Delta G^\circ = \Delta H^\circ - T\Delta S^\circ$$

where

$$\Delta H^\circ = 2\Delta H_{f\,(Fe_2O_3(s))}^\circ - 3\Delta H_{f\,(O_2(g))}^\circ - 4\Delta H_{f\,(Fe(s))}^\circ$$
$$= 2\,mol(-826\,kJ/mol) - 0 - 0$$
$$= -1652\,kJ = -1.652 \times 10^6\,J$$
$$\Delta S^\circ = 2S_{Fe_2O_3}^\circ - 3S_{O_2}^\circ - 4S_{Fe}^\circ$$
$$= 2\,mol(90\,J/K \cdot mol) - 3\,mol(205\,J/K \cdot mol) - 4\,mol(27\,J/K \cdot mol)$$
$$= -543\,J/K$$

and
$$T = 273 + 25 = 298\,K$$

Then
$$\Delta G^\circ = \Delta H^\circ - T\Delta S^\circ = (-1.652 \times 10^6\,J) - (298\,K)(-543\,J/K)$$
$$= -1.490 \times 10^6\,J$$

and
$$\Delta G^\circ = -RT\ln(K) = -1.490 \times 10^6\,J = -(8.3145\,J/K \cdot mol)(298\,K)\ln(K)$$

Thus
$$\ln(K) = \frac{1.490 \times 10^6}{2.48 \times 10^3} = 601$$

and
$$K = e^{601}$$

This is a very large equilibrium constant. The rusting of iron is clearly very favorable from a thermodynamic point of view.

See Exercise 16.62.

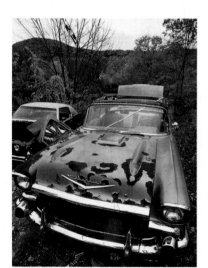

Formation of rust on bare steel is a spontaneous process.

The Temperature Dependence of K

In Chapter 13 we used Le Châtelier's principle to predict qualitatively how the value of K for a given reaction would change with a change in temperature. Now we can specify the quantitative dependence of the equilibrium constant on temperature from the relationship

$$\Delta G^\circ = -RT\ln(K) = \Delta H^\circ - T\Delta S^\circ$$

We can rearrange this equation to give

$$\ln(K) = -\frac{\Delta H^\circ}{RT} + \frac{\Delta S^\circ}{R} = -\frac{\Delta H^\circ}{R}\left(\frac{1}{T}\right) + \frac{\Delta S^\circ}{R}$$

Note that this is a linear equation of the form $y = mx + b$, where $y = \ln(K)$, $m = -\Delta H°/R =$ slope, $x = 1/T$, and $b = \Delta S°/R =$ intercept. This means that if values of K for a given reaction are determined at various temperatures, a plot of $\ln(K)$ versus $1/T$ will be linear, with slope $-\Delta H°/R$ and intercept $\Delta S°/R$. This result assumes that both $\Delta H°$ and $\Delta S°$ are independent of temperature over the temperature range considered. This assumption is a good approximation over a relatively small temperature range.

16.9 Free Energy and Work

One of the main reasons we are interested in physical and chemical processes is that we want to use them to do work for us, and we want this work done as efficiently and economically as possible. We have already seen that at constant temperature and pressure, the sign of the change in free energy tells us whether a given process is spontaneous. This is very useful information because it prevents us from wasting effort on a process that has no inherent tendency to occur. Although a thermodynamically favorable chemical reaction may not occur to any appreciable extent because it is too slow, it makes sense in this case to try to find a catalyst to speed up the reaction. On the other hand, if the reaction is prevented from occurring by its thermodynamic characteristics, we would be wasting our time looking for a catalyst.

In addition to its qualitative usefulness (telling us whether a process is spontaneous), the change in free energy is important quantitatively because it can tell us how much work can be done with a given process. In fact, the *maximum possible useful work obtainable from a process at constant temperature and pressure is equal to the change in free energy:*

$$w_{\text{max}} = \Delta G$$

Note that "*PV* work" is not counted as useful work here.

This relationship explains why this function is called the *free* energy. Under certain conditions, ΔG for a spontaneous process represents the energy that is *free to do useful work.* On the other hand, for a process that is not spontaneous, the value of ΔG tells us the minimum amount of work that must be *expended* to make the process occur.

Knowing the value of ΔG for a process thus gives us valuable information about how close the process is to 100% efficiency. For example, when gasoline is burned in a car's engine, the work produced is about 20% of the maximum work available.

For reasons we will only briefly introduce in this book, the amount of work we actually obtain from a spontaneous process is *always* less than the maximum possible amount.

To explore this idea more fully, let's consider an electric current flowing through the starter motor of a car. The current is generated from a chemical change in a battery, and we can calculate ΔG for the battery reaction and so determine the energy available to do work. Can we use all this energy to do work? No, because a current flowing through a wire causes frictional heating, and the greater the current, the greater the heat. This heat represents wasted energy—it is not useful for running the starter motor. We can minimize this energy waste by running very low currents through the motor circuit. However, zero current flow would be necessary to eliminate frictional heating entirely, and we cannot derive any work from the motor if no current flows. This represents the difficulty in which nature places us. Using a process to do work requires that some of the energy be wasted, and usually the faster we run the process, the more energy we waste.

Achieving the maximum work available from a spontaneous process can occur only via a hypothetical pathway. Any real pathway wastes energy. If we could discharge the battery infinitely slowly by an infinitesimal current flow, we would achieve the maximum useful work. Also, if we could then recharge the battery using an infinitesimally small

FIGURE 16.10
A battery can do work by sending current to a starter motor. The battery can then be recharged by forcing current through it in the opposite direction. If the current flow in both processes is infinitesimally small, $w_1 = w_2$. This is a *reversible process.* But if the current flow is finite, as it would be in any real case, $w_2 > w_1$. This is an *irreversible process* (the *universe is different* after the cyclic process occurs). All real processes are irreversible.

current, exactly the same amount of energy would be used to return the battery to its original state. After we cycle the battery in this way, the universe (the system and surroundings) is exactly the same as it was before the cyclic process. This is a **reversible process** (see Fig. 16.10).

However, if the battery is discharged to run the starter motor and then recharged using a *finite* current flow, as is the case in reality, *more* work will always be required to recharge the battery than the battery produces as it discharges. This means that even though the battery (the system) has returned to its original state, the surroundings have not, because the surroundings had to furnish a net amount of work as the battery was cycled. The *universe is different* after this cyclic process is performed, and this function is called an **irreversible process.** *All real processes are irreversible.*

In general, after any real cyclic process is carried out in a system, the surroundings have less ability to do work and contain more thermal energy. In other words, *in any real cyclic process in the system, work is changed to heat in the surroundings, and the entropy of the universe increases.* This is another way of stating the second law of thermodynamics.

Thus thermodynamics tells us the work potential of a process and then tells us that we can never achieve this potential. In this spirit, thermodynamicist Henry Bent has paraphrased the first two laws of thermodynamics as follows:

First law: You can't win, you can only break even.

Second law: You can't break even.

When energy is used to do work, it becomes less organized and less concentrated and thus less useful.

The ideas we have discussed in this section are applicable to the energy crisis that will probably increase in severity over the next 25 years. The crisis is obviously not one of supply; the first law tells us that the universe contains a constant supply of energy. The problem is the availability of *useful* energy. *As we use energy, we degrade its usefulness.* For example, when gasoline reacts with oxygen in the combustion reaction, the change in potential energy results in heat flow. Thus the energy concentrated in the bonds of the gasoline and oxygen molecules ends up *spread* over the surroundings as thermal energy, where it is much more difficult to harness for useful work. This is a way in which the entropy of the universe increases: Concentrated energy becomes spread out—more disordered and less useful. Thus the crux of the energy problem is that we are rapidly consuming the concentrated energy found in fossil fuels. It took millions of years to concentrate the sun's energy in these fuels, and we will consume these same fuels in a few hundred years. Thus we must use these energy sources as wisely as possible.

Key Terms

For Review

First law of thermodynamics
- States that the energy of the universe is constant
- Provides a way to keep track of energy as it changes form
- Gives no information about why a particular process occurs in a given direction

Second law of thermodynamics
- States that for any spontaneous process there is always an increase in the entropy of the universe
- Entropy(S) is a thermodynamic function that describes the number of arrangements (positions and/or energy levels) available to a system existing in a given state
  - Nature spontaneously proceeds toward states that have the highest probability of occurring
  - Using entropy, thermodynamics can predict the direction in which a process will occur spontaneously

$$\Delta S_{univ} = \Delta S_{sys} + \Delta S_{surr}$$

  - For a spontaneous process, ΔS_{univ} must be positive
  - For a process at constant temperature and pressure:
    - ΔS_{sys} is dominated by "positional" entropy
      For a chemical reaction, ΔS_{sys} is dominated by changes in the number of gaseous molecules
    - ΔS_{surr} is determined by heat:

$$\Delta S_{surr} = -\frac{\Delta H}{T}$$

      ΔS_{surr} is positive for an exothermic process (ΔH is negative)
      Because ΔS_{surr} depends inversely on T, exothermicity becomes a more important driving force at low temperatures
- Thermodynamics cannot predict the rate at which a system will spontaneously change; the principles of kinetics are necessary to do this

Third law of thermodynamics
- States that the entropy of a perfect crystal at 0 K is zero

Free energy (*G*)
- Free energy is a state function:

$$G = H - TS$$

- A process occurring at constant temperature and pressure is spontaneous in the direction in which its free energy decreases ($\Delta G < 0$)
- For a reaction the standard free energy change ($\Delta G°$) is the change in free energy that occurs when reactants in their standard states are converted to products in their standard states
- The standard free energy change for a reaction can be determined from the standard free energies of formation ($\Delta G_f°$) of the reactants and products:

$$\Delta G° = \Sigma n_p \Delta G_f°(\text{products}) - \Sigma n_r \Delta G_f°(\text{reactants})$$

- Free energy depends on temperature and pressure:

$$G = G° + RT \ln P$$

TABLE 16.1 The Microstates That Give a Particular Arrangement (State)

Arrangement	Microstates

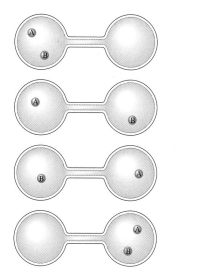

For two molecules in the flask, there are four possible microstates:

Thus there is one chance in four of finding

TABLE 16.2 Probability of Finding All the Molecules in the Left Bulb as a Function of the Total Number of Molecules

Number of Molecules	Relative Probability of Finding All Molecules in the Left Bulb
1	$\dfrac{1}{2}$
2	$\dfrac{1}{2} \times \dfrac{1}{2} = \dfrac{1}{2^2} = \dfrac{1}{4}$
3	$\dfrac{1}{2} \times \dfrac{1}{2} \times \dfrac{1}{2} = \dfrac{1}{2^3} = \dfrac{1}{8}$
5	$\dfrac{1}{2} \times \dfrac{1}{2} \times \dfrac{1}{2} \times \dfrac{1}{2} \times \dfrac{1}{2} = \dfrac{1}{2^5} = \dfrac{1}{32}$
10	$\dfrac{1}{2^{10}} = \dfrac{1}{1024}$
n	$\dfrac{1}{2^n} = \left(\dfrac{1}{2}\right)^n$
6×10^{23} (1 mole)	$\left(\dfrac{1}{2}\right)^{6 \times 10^{23}} \approx 10^{-(2 \times 10^{23})}$

although not impossible, is *highly* improbable, since only one microstate leads to this arrangement. Therefore, this process does not occur spontaneously.

The type of probability we have been considering in this example is called **positional probability** because it depends on the number of configurations in space (positional microstates) that yield a particular state. A gas expands into a vacuum to give a uniform distribution because the expanded state has the highest positional probability, that is, the largest entropy, of the states available to the system.

Positional probability is also illustrated by changes of state. In general, positional entropy increases in going from solid to liquid to gas. A mole of a substance has a much smaller volume in the solid state than it does in the gaseous state. In the solid state, the molecules are close together, with relatively few positions available to them; in the gaseous state, the molecules are far apart, with many more positions available to them. The liquid state is closer to the solid state than it is to the gaseous state in these terms. We can summarize these comparisons as follows:

> Solid, liquid, and gaseous states were compared in Chapter 10.

> Solids are more ordered than liquids or gases and thus have lower entropy.

$$S_{\text{solid}} \quad < \quad S_{\text{liquid}} \quad \lll \quad S_{\text{gas}}$$

> The tendency to mix is due to the increased volume available to the particles of each component of the mixture. For example, when two liquids are mixed, the molecules of each liquid have more available volume and thus more available positions.

Positional entropy is also very important in the formation of solutions. In Chapter 11 we saw that solution formation is favored by the natural tendency for substances to mix. We can now be more precise. The entropy change associated with the mixing of two pure substances is expected to be positive. An increase in entropy is expected because there are many more microstates for the mixed condition than for the separated condition. This effect is due principally to the increased volume available to a given "particle" after mixing occurs. For example, when two liquids are mixed to form a solution, the molecules of each liquid have more available volume and thus more available positions. Therefore, the increase in positional entropy associated with mixing favors the formation of solutions.

| Sample Exercise 16.1 | **Positional Entropy** |

For each of the following pairs, choose the substance with the higher positional entropy (per mole) at a given temperature.

a. Solid CO_2 and gaseous CO_2
b. N_2 gas at 1 atm and N_2 gas at 1.0×10^{-2} atm

Solution

a. Since a mole of gaseous CO_2 has the greater volume by far, the molecules have many more available positions than in a mole of solid CO_2. Thus gaseous CO_2 has the higher positional entropy.

b. A mole of N_2 gas at 1×10^{-2} atm has a volume 100 times that (at a given temperature) of a mole of N_2 gas at 1 atm. Thus N_2 gas at 1×10^{-2} atm has the higher positional entropy.

See Exercise 16.23.

| Sample Exercise 16.2 | **Predicting Entropy Changes** |

Predict the sign of the entropy change for each of the following processes.

a. Solid sugar is added to water to form a solution.
b. Iodine vapor condenses on a cold surface to form crystals.

Solution

a. The sugar molecules become randomly dispersed in the water when the solution forms and thus have access to a larger volume and a larger number of possible positions. The positional disorder is increased, and there will be an increase in entropy. ΔS is positive, since the final state has a larger entropy than the initial state, and $\Delta S = S_{final} - S_{initial}$.
b. Gaseous iodine is forming a solid. This process involves a change from a relatively large volume to a much smaller volume, which results in lower positional disorder. For this process ΔS is negative (the entropy decreases).

See Exercise 16.24.

16.2 Entropy and the Second Law of Thermodynamics

We have seen that processes are spontaneous when they result in an increase in disorder. Nature always moves toward the most probable state available to it. We can state this principle in terms of entropy: *In any spontaneous process there is always an increase in the entropy of the universe.* This is the **second law of thermodynamics.** Contrast this with the first law of thermodynamics, which tells us that the energy of the universe is constant. Energy is conserved in the universe, but entropy is not. In fact, the second law can be paraphrased as follows: *The entropy of the universe is increasing.*

As in Chapter 6, we find it convenient to divide the universe into a system and the surroundings. Thus we can represent the change in the entropy of the universe as

$$\Delta S_{univ} = \Delta S_{sys} + \Delta S_{surr}$$

where ΔS_{sys} and ΔS_{surr} represent the changes in entropy that occur in the system and surroundings, respectively.

To predict whether a given process will be spontaneous, we must know the sign of ΔS_{univ}. If ΔS_{univ} is positive, the entropy of the universe increases, and the process is spontaneous in the direction written. If ΔS_{univ} is negative, the process is spontaneous in the *opposite* direction. If ΔS_{univ} is zero, the process has no tendency to occur, and the system is at equilibrium. To predict whether a process is spontaneous, we must consider the entropy changes that occur both in the system and in the surroundings and then take their sum.

> The total energy of the universe is constant, but the entropy is increasing.

| Sample Exercise 16.3 | **The Second Law** |

In a living cell, large molecules are assembled from simple ones. Is this process consistent with the second law of thermodynamics?

Solution

To reconcile the operation of an order-producing cell with the second law of thermodynamics, we must remember that ΔS_{univ}, not ΔS_{sys}, must be positive for a process to be spontaneous. A process for which ΔS_{sys} is negative can be spontaneous if the associated ΔS_{surr} is both larger and positive. The operation of a cell is such a process.

See Questions 16.7 and 16.8.

CHEMICAL IMPACT

Entropy: An Organizing Force?

In this text we have emphasized the meaning of the second law of thermodynamics—that the entropy of the universe is always increasing. Although the results of all our experiments support this conclusion, this does not mean that order cannot appear spontaneously in a given part of the universe. The best example of this phenomenon involves the assembly of cells in living organisms. Of course, when a process that creates an ordered system is examined in detail, it is found that other parts of the process involve an increase in disorder such that the sum of all the entropy changes is positive. In fact, scientists are now finding that the search for maximum entropy in one part of a system can be a powerful force for organization in another part of the system.

To understand how entropy can be an organizing force, look at the accompanying figure. In a system containing large and small "balls" as shown in the figure, the small balls can "herd" the large balls into clumps in the corners and near the walls. This clears out the maximum space for the small balls so that they can move more freely, thus maximizing the entropy of the system, as demanded by the second law of thermodynamics.

In essence, the ability to maximize entropy by sorting different-sized objects creates a kind of attractive force, called a *depletion*, or *excluded-volume, force*. These "entropic forces" operate for objects in the size range of approximately 10^{-8} to approximately 10^{-6} m. For entropy-induced ordering to occur, the particles must be constantly jostling each other and must be constantly agitated by solvent molecules, thus making gravity unimportant.

There is increasing evidence that entropic ordering is important in many biological systems. For example, this phenomenon seems to be responsible for the clumping of sickle-cell hemoglobin in the presence of much smaller proteins that act as the "smaller balls." Entropic forces also have been linked to the clustering of DNA in cells without nuclei, and Allen Minton of the National Institutes of Health in Bethesda, Maryland, is studying the role of entropic forces in the binding of proteins to cell membranes.

Entropic ordering also appears in nonbiological settings, especially in the ways polymer molecules clump together. For example, polymers added to paint to improve the flow characteristics of the paint actually caused it to coagulate because of depletion forces.

Thus, as you probably have concluded already, entropy is a complex issue. As entropy drives the universe to its ultimate death of maximum chaos, it provides some order along the way.

16.3 The Effect of Temperature on Spontaneity

To explore the interplay of ΔS_{sys} and ΔS_{surr} in determining the sign of ΔS_{univ}, we will first discuss the change of state for one mole of water from liquid to gas,

$$H_2O(l) \longrightarrow H_2O(g)$$

considering the water to be the system and everything else the surroundings.

What happens to the entropy of water in this process? A mole of liquid water (18 grams) has a volume of approximately 18 mL. A mole of gaseous water at 1 atmosphere and 100°C occupies a volume of approximately 31 liters. Clearly, there are many more positions available to the water molecules in a volume of 31 L than in 18 mL, and the vaporization of water is favored by this increase in positional probability. That is, for this process the entropy of the system increases; ΔS_{sys} has a positive sign.

What about the entropy change in the surroundings? Although we will not prove it here, entropy changes in the surroundings are determined primarily by the flow of energy

- This relationship can be used to derive the relationship between $\Delta G°$ for a reaction and the value of its equilibrium constant K:

$$\Delta G° = -RT \ln K$$

- For $\Delta G° = 0$, $K = 1$
- For $\Delta G° < 0$, $K > 1$
- For $\Delta G° > 0$, $K < 1$

- The maximum possible useful work obtainable from a process at constant temperature and pressure is equal to the change in free energy:

$$w_{max} = \Delta G$$

- In any real process, $w < w_{max}$
- When energy is used to do work in a real process, the energy of the universe remains constant but the usefulness of the energy decreases
  - Concentrated energy is spread out in the surroundings as thermal energy

REVIEW QUESTIONS

1. Define the following:
   a. spontaneous process
   b. entropy
   c. positional probability
   d. system
   e. surroundings
   f. universe

2. What is the second law of thermodynamics? For any process, there are four possible sign combinations for ΔS_{sys} and ΔS_{surr}. Which sign combination(s) always give a spontaneous process? Which sign combination(s) always give a nonspontaneous process? Which sign combination(s) may or may not give a spontaneous process?

3. What determines ΔS_{surr} for a process? To calculate ΔS_{surr} at constant pressure and temperature, we use the following equation: $\Delta S_{surr} = -\Delta H/T$. Why does a minus sign appear in the equation, and why is ΔS_{surr} inversely proportional to temperature?

4. The free energy change, ΔG, for a process at constant temperature and pressure is related to ΔS_{univ} and reflects the spontaneity of the process. How is ΔG related to ΔS_{univ}? When is a process spontaneous? Nonspontaneous? At equilibrium? ΔG is a composite term composed of ΔH, T, and ΔS. What is the ΔG equation? Give the four possible sign combinations for ΔH and ΔS. What temperatures are required for each sign combination to yield a spontaneous process? If ΔG is positive, what does it say about the reverse process? How does the $\Delta G = \Delta H - T\Delta S$ equation reduce when at the melting-point temperature of a solid-to-liquid phase change or at the boiling-point temperature of a liquid-to-gas phase change? What is the sign of ΔG for the solid-to-liquid phase change at temperatures above the freezing point? What is the sign of ΔG for the liquid-to-gas phase change at temperatures below the boiling point?

5. What is the third law of thermodynamics? What are standard entropy values, $S°$, and how are these $S°$ values (listed in Appendix 4) used to calculate $\Delta S°$ for a reaction? How would you use Hess's law to calculate $\Delta S°$ for a reaction? What does the superscript ° indicate?

   Predicting the sign of $\Delta S°$ for a reaction is an important skill to master. For a gas-phase reaction, what do you concentrate on to predict the sign of $\Delta S°$? For a phase change, what do you concentrate on to predict the sign of $\Delta S°$?

That is, how are S°_{solid}, S°_{liquid}, and S°_{gas} related to one another? When a solute dissolves in water, what is usually the sign of ΔS° for this process?

6. What is the standard free energy change, ΔG°, for a reaction? What is the standard free energy of formation, ΔG°_f, for a substance? How are ΔG°_f values used to calculate ΔG°_{rxn}? How can you use Hess's law to calculate ΔG°_{rxn}? How can you use ΔH° and ΔS° values to calculate ΔG°_{rxn}? Of the functions ΔH°, ΔS°, and ΔG°, which depends most strongly on temperature? When ΔG° is calculated at temperatures other than 25°C, what assumptions are generally made concerning ΔH° and ΔS°?

7. If you calculate a value for ΔG° for a reaction using the values of ΔG°_f in Appendix 4 and get a negative number, is it correct to say that the reaction is always spontaneous? Why or why not? Free energy changes also depend on concentration. For gases, how is G related to the pressure of the gas? What are standard pressures for gases and standard concentrations for solutes? How do you calculate ΔG for a reaction at nonstandard conditions? The equation to determine ΔG at nonstandard conditions has Q in it: What is Q? A reaction is spontaneous as long as ΔG is negative; that is, reactions always proceed as long as the products have a lower free energy than the reactants. What is so special about equilibrium? Why don't reactions move away from equilibrium?

8. Consider the equation $\Delta G = \Delta G^\circ + RT \ln(Q)$. What is the value of ΔG for a reaction at equilibrium? What does Q equal at equilibrium? At equilibrium, the previous equation reduces to $\Delta G^\circ = -RT \ln(K)$. When $\Delta G^\circ > 0$, what does it indicate about K? When $\Delta G^\circ < 0$, what does it indicate about K? When $\Delta G^\circ = 0$, what does it indicate about K? ΔG predicts spontaneity for a reaction, whereas ΔG° predicts the equilibrium position. Explain what this statement means. Under what conditions can you use ΔG° to determine the spontaneity of a reaction?

9. Even if ΔG is negative, the reaction may not occur. Explain the interplay between the thermodynamics and the kinetics of a reaction. High temperatures are favorable to a reaction kinetically but may be unfavorable to a reaction thermodynamically. Explain.

10. Discuss the relationship between w_{max} and the magnitude and sign of the free energy change for a reaction. Also discuss w_{max} for real processes. What is a reversible process?

Active Learning Questions

These questions are designed to be used by groups of students in class. The questions allow students to explore their understanding of concepts through discussion and peer teaching. The real value of these questions is the learning that occurs while students talk to each other about chemical concepts.

1. For the process $A(l) \longrightarrow A(g)$, which direction is favored by changes in energy probability? Positional probability? Explain your answers. If you wanted to favor the process as written, would you raise or lower the temperature of the system? Explain.

2. For a liquid, which would you expect to be larger, ΔS_{fusion} or $\Delta S_{evaporation}$? Why?

3. Gas A_2 reacts with gas B_2 to form gas AB at a constant temperature. The bond energy of AB is much greater than that of either reactant. What can be said about the sign of ΔH? ΔS_{surr}? ΔS? Explain how potential energy changes for this process. Explain how random kinetic energy changes during the process.

4. What types of experiments can be carried out to determine whether a reaction is spontaneous? Does spontaneity have any relationship to the final equilibrium position of a reaction? Explain.

5. A friend tells you, "Free energy G and pressure P are related by the equation $G = G^\circ + RT \ln(P)$. Also, G is related to the equilibrium constant K in that when $G_{products} = G_{reactants}$, the system is at equilibrium. Therefore, it must be true that a system is at equilibrium when all the pressures are equal." Do you agree with this friend? Explain.

6. You remember that ΔG° is related to $RT \ln(K)$ but cannot remember if it's $RT \ln(K)$ or $-RT \ln(K)$. Realizing what ΔG° and K mean, how can you figure out the correct sign?

A blue question or exercise number indicates that the answer to that question or exercise appears at the back of this book and a solution appears in the *Solutions Guide*.

Questions

7. The synthesis of glucose directly from CO_2 and H_2O and the synthesis of proteins directly from amino acids are both nonspontaneous processes under standard conditions. Yet it is necessary for these to occur for life to exist. In light of the second law of thermodynamics, how can life exist?

8. When the environment is contaminated by a toxic or potentially toxic substance (for example, from a chemical spill or the use of insecticides), the substance tends to disperse. How is this consistent with the second law of thermodynamics? In terms of the second law, which requires the least work: cleaning the environment after it has been contaminated or trying to prevent the contamination before it occurs? Explain.

9. A green plant synthesizes glucose by photosynthesis, as shown in the reaction

$$6CO_2(g) + 6H_2O(l) \longrightarrow C_6H_{12}O_6(s) + 6O_2(g)$$

Animals use glucose as a source of energy:

$$C_6H_{12}O_6(s) + 6O_2(g) \longrightarrow 6CO_2(g) + 6H_2O(l)$$

If we were to assume that both these processes occur to the same extent in a cyclic process, what thermodynamic property must have a nonzero value?

10. Human DNA contains almost twice as much information as is needed to code for all the substances produced in the body. Likewise, the digital data sent from *Voyager II* contained one redundant bit out of every two bits of information. The Hubble space telescope transmits three redundant bits for every bit of information. How is entropy related to the transmission of information? What do you think is accomplished by having so many redundant bits of information in both DNA and the space probes?

11. Entropy has been described as "time's arrow." Interpret this view of entropy.

12. A mixture of hydrogen gas and chlorine gas remains unreacted until it is exposed to ultraviolet light from a burning magnesium strip. Then the following reaction occurs very rapidly:

$$H_2(g) + Cl_2(g) \longrightarrow 2HCl(g)$$

Explain.

13. Table 16.1 shows the possible arrangements of four molecules in a two-bulbed flask. What are the possible arrangements if there is one molecule in this two-bulbed flask or two molecules or three molecules? For each, what arrangement is most likely?

14. ΔS_{surr} is sometime called the energy disorder term. Explain.

15. The third law of thermodynamics states that the entropy of a perfect crystal at 0 K is zero. In Appendix 4, $F^-(aq)$, $OH^-(aq)$, and $S^{2-}(aq)$ all have negative standard entropy values. How can $S°$ values be less than zero?

16. The deciding factor on why HF is a weak acid and not a strong acid like the other hydrogen halides is entropy. What occurs when HF dissociates in water as compared to the other hydrogen halides?

17. List three different ways to calculate the standard free energy change, $\Delta G°$, for a reaction at 25°C? How is $\Delta G°$ estimated at temperatures other than 25°C? What assumptions are made?

18. What information can be determined from ΔG for a reaction? Does one get the same information from $\Delta G°$, the standard free energy change? $\Delta G°$ allows determination of the equilibrium constant K for a reaction. How? How can one estimate the value of K at temperatures other than 25°C for a reaction? How can one estimate the temperature where $K = 1$ for a reaction? Do all reactions have a specific temperature where $K = 1$?

Exercises

In this section similar exercises are paired.

Spontaneity, Entropy, and the Second Law of Thermodynamics: Free Energy

19. Which of the following processes are spontaneous?
    a. Salt dissolves in H_2O.
    b. A clear solution becomes a uniform color after a few drops of dye are added.
    c. Iron rusts.
    d. You clean your bedroom.

20. Which of the following processes are spontaneous?
    a. A house is built.
    b. A satellite is launched into orbit.
    c. A satellite falls back to earth.
    d. The kitchen gets cluttered.

21. Consider the following energy levels, each capable of holding two objects:

$$E = 2 \text{ kJ} \underline{\hspace{1cm}}$$
$$E = 1 \text{ kJ} \underline{\hspace{1cm}}$$
$$E = 0 \quad \underline{XX}$$

Draw all the possible arrangements of the two identical particles (represented by X) in the three energy levels. What total energy is most likely, that is, occurs the greatest number of times? Assume that the particles are indistinguishable from each other.

22. Redo Exercise 21 with two particles A and B, which can be distinguished from each other.

23. Choose the compound with the greatest positional probability in each case.
    a. 1 mol H_2 (at STP) or 1 mol H_2 (at 100°C, 0.5 atm)
    b. 1 mol N_2 (at STP) or 1 mol N_2 (at 100 K, 2.0 atm)
    c. 1 mol $H_2O(s)$ (at 0°C) or 1 mol $H_2O(l)$ (at 20°C)

24. Which of the following involve an increase in the entropy of the system?
    a. melting of a solid
    b. sublimation
    c. freezing
    d. mixing
    e. separation
    f. boiling

25. Predict the sign of ΔS_{surr} for the following processes.
    a. $H_2O(l) \longrightarrow H_2O(g)$
    b. $CO_2(g) \longrightarrow CO_2(s)$

26. Calculate ΔS_{surr} for the following reactions at 25°C and 1 atm.
   a. $C_3H_8(g) + 5O_2(g) \longrightarrow 3CO_2(g) + 4H_2O(l)$ $\Delta H° = -2221$ kJ
   b. $2NO_2(g) \longrightarrow 2NO(g) + O_2(g)$ $\Delta H° = 112$ kJ

27. Given the values of ΔH and ΔS, which of the following changes will be spontaneous at constant T and P?
   a. $\Delta H = +25$ kJ, $\Delta S = +5.0$ J/K, $T = 300.$ K
   b. $\Delta H = +25$ kJ, $\Delta S = +100.$ J/K, $T = 300.$ K
   c. $\Delta H = -10.$ kJ, $\Delta S = +5.0$ J/K, $T = 298$ K
   d. $\Delta H = -10.$ kJ, $\Delta S = -40.$ J/K, $T = 200.$ K

28. At what temperatures will the following processes be spontaneous?
   a. $\Delta H = -18$ kJ and $\Delta S = -60.$ J/K
   b. $\Delta H = +18$ kJ and $\Delta S = +60.$ J/K
   c. $\Delta H = +18$ kJ and $\Delta S = -60.$ J/K
   d. $\Delta H = -18$ kJ and $\Delta S = +60.$ J/K

29. Ethanethiol (C_2H_5SH; also called ethyl mercaptan) is commonly added to natural gas to provide the "rotten egg" smell of a gas leak. The boiling point of ethanethiol is 35°C and its heat of vaporization is 27.5 kJ/mol. What is the entropy of vaporization for this substance?

30. For mercury, the enthalpy of vaporization is 58.51 kJ/mol and the entropy of vaporization is 92.92 J/K · mol. What is the normal boiling point of mercury?

31. For ammonia (NH_3), the enthalpy of fusion is 5.65 kJ/mol and the entropy of fusion is 28.9 J/K · mol.
   a. Will $NH_3(s)$ spontaneously melt at 200. K?
   b. What is the approximate melting point of ammonia?

32. The enthalpy of vaporization of ethanol is 38.7 kJ/mol at its boiling point (78°C). Determine ΔS_{sys}, ΔS_{surr}, and ΔS_{univ} when 1.00 mol of ethanol is vaporized at 78°C and 1.00 atm.

Chemical Reactions: Entropy Changes and Free Energy

33. Predict the sign of $\Delta S°$ for each of the following changes.
   a.

   b. $AgCl(s) \longrightarrow Ag^+(aq) + Cl^-(aq)$
   c. $2H_2(g) + O_2(g) \longrightarrow 2H_2O(l)$
   d. $H_2O(l) \longrightarrow H_2O(g)$

34. Predict the sign of $\Delta S°$ for each of the following changes.
   a. $Na(s) + \frac{1}{2}Cl_2(g) \longrightarrow NaCl(s)$
   b. $N_2(g) + 3H_2(g) \longrightarrow 2NH_3(g)$
   c. $NaCl(s) \longrightarrow Na^+(aq) + Cl^-(aq)$
   d. $NaCl(s) \longrightarrow NaCl(l)$

35. For each of the following pairs of substances, which substance has the greater value of $S°$?
   a. $C_{graphite}(s)$ or $C_{diamond}(s)$
   b. $C_2H_5OH(l)$ or $C_2H_5OH(g)$
   c. $CO_2(s)$ or $CO_2(g)$

36. For each of the following pairs, which substance has the greater value of S?
   a. N_2O (at 0 K) or He (at 10 K)
   b. $N_2O(g)$ (at 1 atm, 25°C) or He(g) (at 1 atm, 25°C)
   c. $H_2O(s)$ (at 0°C) or $H_2O(l)$ (at 0°C)

37. Predict the sign of $\Delta S°$ and then calculate $\Delta S°$ for each of the following reactions.
   a. $2H_2S(g) + SO_2(g) \longrightarrow 3S_{rhombic}(s) + 2H_2O(g)$
   b. $2SO_3(g) \longrightarrow 2SO_2(g) + O_2(g)$
   c. $Fe_2O_3(s) + 3H_2(g) \longrightarrow 2Fe(s) + 3H_2O(g)$

38. Predict the sign of $\Delta S°$ and then calculate $\Delta S°$ for each of the following reactions.
   a. $H_2(g) + \frac{1}{2}O_2(g) \longrightarrow H_2O(l)$
   b. $2CH_3OH(g) + 3O_2(g) \longrightarrow 2CO_2(g) + 4H_2O(g)$
   c. $HCl(g) \longrightarrow H^+(aq) + Cl^-(aq)$

39. For the reaction

$$C_2H_2(g) + 4F_2(g) \longrightarrow 2CF_4(g) + H_2(g)$$

$\Delta S°$ is equal to -358 J/K. Use this value and data from Appendix 4 to calculate the value of $S°$ for $CF_4(g)$.

40. For the reaction

$$2Al(s) + 3Br_2(l) \longrightarrow 2AlBr_3(s)$$

$\Delta S°$ is equal to -144 J/K. Use this value and data from Appendix 4 to calculate the value of $S°$ for solid aluminum bromide.

41. It is quite common for a solid to change from one structure to another at a temperature below its melting point. For example, sulfur undergoes a phase change from the rhombic crystal structure to the monoclinic crystal form at temperatures above 95°C.
   a. Predict the signs of ΔH and ΔS for the process $S_{rhombic} \longrightarrow S_{monoclinic}$.
   b. Which form of sulfur has the more ordered crystalline structure?

42. When most biologic enzymes are heated they lose their catalytic activity. The change

$$\text{original enzyme} \longrightarrow \text{new form}$$

that occurs on heating is endothermic and spontaneous. Is the structure of the original enzyme or its new form more ordered? Explain.

43. Consider the reaction

$$2O(g) \longrightarrow O_2(g)$$

   a. Predict the signs of ΔH and ΔS.
   b. Would the reaction be more spontaneous at high or low temperatures?

44. Hydrogen cyanide is produced industrially by the following exothermic reaction:

$$2NH_3(g) + 3O_2(g) + 2CH_4(g) \xrightarrow[\text{Pt-Rh}]{1000°C} 2HCN(g) + 6H_2O(g)$$

Is the high temperature needed for thermodynamic or kinetic reasons?

45. From data in Appendix 4, calculate $\Delta H°$, $\Delta S°$, and $\Delta G°$ for each of the following reactions at 25°C.

a. $CH_4(g) + 2O_2(g) \longrightarrow CO_2(g) + 2H_2O(g)$
b. $6CO_2(g) + 6H_2O(l) \longrightarrow C_6H_{12}O_6(s) + 6O_2(g)$
Glucose
c. $P_4O_{10}(s) + 6H_2O(l) \longrightarrow 4H_3PO_4(s)$
d. $HCl(g) + NH_3(g) \longrightarrow NH_4Cl(s)$

46. The decomposition of ammonium dichromate $[(NH_4)_2Cr_2O_7]$ is called the "volcano" demonstration for its fiery display. The decomposition reaction involves breaking down ammonium dichromate into nitrogen gas, water vapor, and solid chromium(III) oxide. From the data in Appendix 4 and given $\Delta H_f^\circ = -23$ kJ/mol and $\Delta S^\circ = 114$ J/K · mol for $(NH_4)_2Cr_2O_7$, calculate ΔG° for the "volcano" reaction and calculate ΔG_f° for ammonium dichromate.

47. For the reaction at 298 K,

$$2NO_2(g) \rightleftharpoons N_2O_4(g)$$

the values of ΔH° and ΔS° are -58.03 kJ and -176.6 J/K, respectively. What is the value of ΔG° at 298 K? Assuming that ΔH° and ΔS° do not depend on temperature, at what temperature is $\Delta G^\circ = 0$? Is ΔG° negative above or below this temperature?

48. At 100.°C and 1.00 atm, $\Delta H^\circ = 40.6$ kJ/mol for the vaporization of water. Estimate ΔG° for the vaporization of water at 90.°C and 110.°C. Assume ΔH° and ΔS° at 100.°C and 1.00 atm do not depend on temperature.

49. Using data from Appendix 4, calculate ΔH°, ΔS°, and ΔG° for the following reactions that produce acetic acid:

$$CH_4(g) + CO_2(g) \rightarrow CH_3\overset{\displaystyle O}{\overset{\displaystyle \|}{C}}\!-\!OH(l)$$

$$CH_3OH(g) + CO(g) \rightarrow CH_3\overset{\displaystyle O}{\overset{\displaystyle \|}{C}}\!-\!OH(l)$$

Which reaction would you choose as a commercial method for producing acetic acid (CH_3CO_2H) at standard conditions? What temperature conditions would you choose for the reaction? Assume ΔH° and ΔS° do not depend on temperature.

50. Consider two reactions for the production of ethanol:

$$C_2H_4(g) + H_2O(g) \longrightarrow CH_3CH_2OH(l)$$
$$C_2H_6(g) + H_2O(g) \longrightarrow CH_3CH_2OH(l) + H_2(g)$$

Which would be the more thermodynamically feasible at standard conditions? Why?

51. Given the following data:

$$2H_2(g) + C(s) \longrightarrow CH_4(g) \qquad \Delta G^\circ = -51 \text{ kJ}$$
$$2H_2(g) + O_2(g) \longrightarrow 2H_2O(l) \qquad \Delta G^\circ = -474 \text{ kJ}$$
$$C(s) + O_2(g) \longrightarrow CO_2(g) \qquad \Delta G^\circ = -394 \text{ kJ}$$

Calculate ΔG° for $CH_4(g) + 2O_2(g) \rightarrow CO_2(g) + 2H_2O(l)$.

52. Given the following data:

$$2C_6H_6(l) + 15O_2(g) \longrightarrow 12CO_2(g) + 6H_2O(l)$$
$$\Delta G^\circ = -6399 \text{ kJ}$$
$$C(s) + O_2(g) \longrightarrow CO_2(g) \qquad\qquad \Delta G^\circ = -394 \text{ kJ}$$
$$H_2(g) + \tfrac{1}{2}O_2(g) \longrightarrow H_2O(l) \qquad\quad \Delta G^\circ = -237 \text{ kJ}$$

calculate ΔG° for the reaction

$$6C(s) + 3H_2(g) \longrightarrow C_6H_6(l)$$

53. For the reaction

$$SF_4(g) + F_2(g) \longrightarrow SF_6(g)$$

the value of ΔG° is -374 kJ. Use this value and data from Appendix 4 to calculate the value of ΔG_f° for $SF_4(g)$.

54. The value of ΔG° for the reaction

$$2C_4H_{10}(g) + 13O_2(g) \longrightarrow 8CO_2(g) + 10H_2O(l)$$

is -5490. kJ. Use this value and data from Appendix 4 to calculate the standard free energy of formation for $C_4H_{10}(g)$.

55. Assuming standard conditions, can the following reaction take place at room temperature?

$$3Cl_2(g) + 2CH_4(g) \longrightarrow CH_3Cl(g) + CH_2Cl_2(g) + 3HCl(g)$$
$$\Delta G^\circ (CH_4) = -50.72 \text{ kJ/mol} \qquad \Delta G^\circ (CH_3Cl) = -57.37 \text{ kJ/mol}$$
$$\Delta G^\circ (CH_2Cl_2) = -68.85 \text{ kJ/mol} \quad \Delta G^\circ (HCl) = -95.30 \text{ kJ/mol}$$

56. Consider the reaction

$$2POCl_3(g) \longrightarrow 2PCl_3(g) + O_2(g)$$

a. Calculate ΔG° for this reaction. The ΔG_f° values for $POCl_3(g)$ and $PCl_3(g)$ are -502 kJ/mol and -270. kJ/mol, respectively.
b. Is this reaction spontaneous under standard conditions at 298 K?
c. The value of ΔS° for this reaction is 179 J/K. At what temperatures is this reaction spontaneous at standard conditions? Assume that ΔH° and ΔS° do not depend on temperature.

Free Energy: Pressure Dependence and Equilibrium

57. Using data from Appendix 4, calculate ΔG for the reaction

$$NO(g) + O_3(g) \longrightarrow NO_2(g) + O_2(g)$$

for these conditions:

$$T = 298 \text{ K}$$
$$P_{NO} = 1.00 \times 10^{-6} \text{ atm}, \ P_{O_3} = 2.00 \times 10^{-6} \text{ atm}$$
$$P_{NO_2} = 1.00 \times 10^{-7} \text{ atm}, \ P_{O_2} = 1.00 \times 10^{-3} \text{ atm}$$

58. Using data from Appendix 4, calculate ΔG for the reaction

$$2H_2S(g) + SO_2(g) \rightleftharpoons 3S_{rhombic}(s) + 2H_2O(g)$$

for the following conditions at 25°C:

$$P_{H_2S} = 1.0 \times 10^{-4} \text{ atm}$$
$$P_{SO_2} = 1.0 \times 10^{-2} \text{ atm}$$
$$P_{H_2O} = 3.0 \times 10^{-2} \text{ atm}$$

59. Consider the reaction

$$2NO_2(g) \rightleftharpoons N_2O_4(g)$$

For each of the following mixtures of reactants and products at 25°C, predict the direction in which the reaction will shift to reach equilibrium.
a. $P_{NO_2} = P_{N_2O_4} = 1.0$ atm
b. $P_{NO_2} = 0.21$ atm, $P_{N_2O_4} = 0.50$ atm
c. $P_{NO_2} = 0.29$ atm, $P_{N_2O_4} = 1.6$ atm

60. Consider the following reaction:

$$N_2(g) + 3H_2(g) \rightleftharpoons 2NH_3(g)$$

Calculate ΔG for this reaction under the following conditions (assume an uncertainty of ± 1 in all quantities):
a. $T = 298$ K, $P_{N_2} = P_{H_2} = 200$ atm, $P_{NH_3} = 50$ atm
b. $T = 298$ K, $P_{N_2} = 200$ atm, $P_{H_2} = 600$ atm, $P_{NH_3} = 200$ atm

61. Consider the following reaction at 25.0°C:

$$2NO_2(g) \rightleftharpoons N_2O_4(g)$$

The values of $\Delta H°$ and $\Delta S°$ are -58.03 kJ/mol and -176.6 J/K · mol, respectively. Calculate the value of K at 25.0°C. Assuming $\Delta H°$ and $\Delta S°$ are temperature independent, estimate the value of K at 100.0°C.

62. Consider the reaction

$$H_2(g) + Cl_2(g) \rightleftharpoons 2HCl(g)$$

a. Calculate $\Delta H°$, $\Delta S°$, $\Delta G°$, and K (at 298 K) using data in Appendix 4.
b. If $H_2(g)$, $Cl_2(g)$, and $HCl(g)$ are placed in a flask such that the pressure of each gas is 1 atm, in which direction will the system shift to reach equilibrium at 25°C?

63. Calculate $\Delta G°$ for $H_2O(g) + \frac{1}{2}O_2(g) \rightleftharpoons H_2O_2(g)$ at 600. K, using the following data:

$H_2(g) + O_2(g) \rightleftharpoons H_2O_2(g)$ $K = 2.3 \times 10^6$ at 600. K
$2H_2(g) + O_2(g) \rightleftharpoons 2H_2O(g)$ $K = 1.8 \times 10^{37}$ at 600. K

64. The Ostwald process for the commercial production of nitric acid involves three steps:

$$4NH_3(g) + 5O_2(g) \xrightarrow[825°C]{Pt} 4NO(g) + 6H_2O(g)$$
$$2NO(g) + O_2(g) \longrightarrow 2NO_2(g)$$
$$3NO_2(g) + H_2O(l) \longrightarrow 2HNO_3(l) + NO(g)$$

a. Calculate $\Delta H°$, $\Delta S°$, $\Delta G°$, and K (at 298 K) for each of the three steps in the Ostwald process (see Appendix 4).
b. Calculate the equilibrium constant for the first step at 825°C, assuming $\Delta H°$ and $\Delta S°$ do not depend on temperature.
c. Is there a thermodynamic reason for the high temperature in the first step assuming standard conditions?

65. Consider the following reaction at 800. K:

$$N_2(g) + 3F_2(g) \longrightarrow 2NF_3(g)$$

An equilibrium mixture contains the following partial pressures: $P_{N_2} = 0.021$ atm, $P_{F_2} = 0.063$ atm, $P_{NF_3} = 0.48$ atm. Calculate $\Delta G°$ for the reaction at 800. K.

66. Consider the following reaction at 298 K:

$$2SO_2(g) + O_2(g) \longrightarrow 2SO_3(g)$$

An equilibrium mixture contains $O_2(g)$ and $SO_3(g)$ at partial pressures of 0.50 atm and 2.0 atm, respectively. Using data from Appendix 4, determine the equilibrium partial pressure of SO_2 in the mixture. Will this reaction be most favored at a high or a low temperature, assuming standard conditions?

67. Consider the relationship:

$$\ln(K) = \frac{-\Delta H°}{RT} + \frac{\Delta S°}{R}$$

The equilibrium constant for some hypothetical process was determined as a function of temperature (in Kelvin) with the results plotted below.

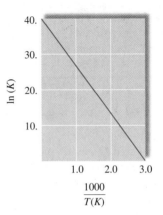

From the plot, determine the values of $\Delta H°$ and $\Delta S°$ for this process. What would be the major difference in the $\ln(K)$ versus $1/T$ plot for an endothermic process as compared to an exothermic process?

68. The equilibrium constant K for the reaction

$$2Cl(g) \rightleftharpoons Cl_2(g)$$

was measured as a function of temperature (Kelvin). A graph of $\ln K$ versus $1/T$ for this reaction gives a straight line with a slope of 1.352×10^4 K and a y-intercept of -14.51. Determine the values of $\Delta H°$ and $\Delta S°$ for this reaction. Reference Exercise 67.

Additional Exercises

69. Using Appendix 4 and the following data, determine $S°$ for $Fe(CO)_5(g)$.

$Fe(s) + 5CO(g) \longrightarrow Fe(CO)_5(g)$ $\Delta S° = ?$
$Fe(CO)_5(l) \longrightarrow Fe(CO)_5(g)$ $\Delta S° = 107$ J/K
$Fe(s) + 5CO(g) \longrightarrow Fe(CO)_5(l)$ $\Delta S° = -677$ J/K

70. Some water is placed in a coffee-cup calorimeter. When 1.0 g of an ionic solid is added, the temperature of the solution increases from 21.5°C to 24.2°C as the solid dissolves. For the dissolving process, what are the signs for ΔS_{sys}, ΔS_{surr}, and ΔS_{univ}?

71. Consider the following system at equilibrium at 25°C:

$$PCl_3(g) + Cl_2(g) \rightleftharpoons PCl_5(g)   \Delta G° = -92.50 \text{ kJ}$$

What will happen to the ratio of partial pressure of PCl_5 to partial pressure of PCl_3 if the temperature is raised? Explain completely.

72. Calculate the entropy change for the vaporization of liquid methane and liquid hexane using the following data.

	Boiling Point (1 atm)	ΔH_{vap}
Methane	112 K	8.20 kJ/mol
Hexane	342 K	28.9 kJ/mol

Compare the molar volume of gaseous methane at 112 K with that of gaseous hexane at 342 K. How do the differences in molar volume affect the values of ΔS_{vap} for these liquids?

73. As $O_2(l)$ is cooled at 1 atm, it freezes at 54.5 K to form solid I. At a lower temperature, solid I rearranges to solid II, which has a different crystal structure. Thermal measurements show that ΔH for the I → II phase transition is −743.1 J/mol, and ΔS for the same transition is −17.0 J/K · mol. At what temperature are solids I and II in equilibrium?

74. Consider the following reaction:

$$H_2O(g) + Cl_2O(g) \rightleftharpoons 2HOCl(g) \qquad K_{298} = 0.090$$

For $Cl_2O(g)$,

$$\Delta G_f^{\circ} = 97.9 \text{ kJ/mol}$$
$$\Delta H_f^{\circ} = 80.3 \text{ kJ/mol}$$
$$S^{\circ} = 266.1 \text{ J/K} \cdot \text{mol}$$

a. Calculate ΔG° for the reaction using the equation $\Delta G^{\circ} = -RT \ln(K)$.

b. Use bond energy values (Table 8.4) to estimate ΔH° for the reaction.

c. Use the results from parts a and b to estimate ΔS° for the reaction.

d. Estimate ΔH_f° and S° for HOCl(g).

e. Estimate the value of K at 500. K.

f. Calculate ΔG at 25°C when $P_{H_2O} = 18$ torr, $P_{Cl_2O} = 2.0$ torr, and $P_{HOCl} = 0.10$ torr.

75. Carbon monoxide is toxic because it bonds much more strongly to the iron in hemoglobin (Hgb) than does O_2. Consider the following reactions and approximate standard free energy changes:

$$Hgb + O_2 \longrightarrow HgbO_2 \qquad \Delta G^{\circ} = -70 \text{ kJ}$$
$$Hgb + CO \longrightarrow HgbCO \qquad \Delta G^{\circ} = -80 \text{ kJ}$$

Using these data, estimate the equilibrium constant value at 25°C for the following reaction:

$$HgbO_2 + CO \rightleftharpoons HgbCO + O_2$$

76. Using the following data, calculate the value of K_{sp} for $Ba(NO_3)_2$, one of the *least* soluble of the common nitrate salts.

Species	ΔG_f°
$Ba^{2+}(aq)$	−561 kJ/mol
$NO_3^-(aq)$	−109 kJ/mol
$Ba(NO_3)_2(s)$	−797 kJ/mol

77. In the text the equation

$$\Delta G = \Delta G^{\circ} + RT \ln(Q)$$

was derived for gaseous reactions where the quantities in Q were expressed in units of pressure. We also can use units of mol/L for the quantities in Q, specifically for aqueous reactions. With this in mind, consider the reaction

$$HF(aq) \rightleftharpoons H^+(aq) + F^-(aq)$$

for which $K_a = 7.2 \times 10^{-4}$ at 25°C. Calculate ΔG for the reaction under the following conditions at 25°C.

a. $[HF] = [H^+] = [F^-] = 1.0 \ M$
b. $[HF] = 0.98 \ M, [H^+] = [F^-] = 2.7 \times 10^{-2} \ M$
c. $[HF] = [H^+] = [F^-] = 1.0 \times 10^{-5} \ M$
d. $[HF] = [F^-] = 0.27 \ M, [H^+] = 7.2 \times 10^{-4} \ M$
e. $[HF] = 0.52 \ M, [F^-] = 0.67 \ M, [H^+] = 1.0 \times 10^{-3} \ M$

Based on the calculated ΔG values, in what direction will the reaction shift to reach equilibrium for each of the five sets of conditions?

78. Many biochemical reactions that occur in cells require relatively high concentrations of potassium ion (K^+). The concentration of K^+ in muscle cells is about 0.15 M. The concentration of K^+ in blood plasma is about 0.0050 M. The high internal concentration in cells is maintained by pumping K^+ from the plasma. How much work must be done to transport 1.0 mol K^+ from the blood to the inside of a muscle cell at 37°C, normal body temperature? When 1.0 mol K^+ is transferred from blood to the cells, do any other ions have to be transported? Why or why not?

79. Cells use the hydrolysis of adenosine triphosphate, abbreviated as ATP, as a source of energy. Symbolically, this reaction can be written as

$$ATP(aq) + H_2O(l) \longrightarrow ADP(aq) + H_2PO_4^-(aq)$$

where ADP represents adenosine diphosphate. For this reaction, $\Delta G^{\circ} = -30.5$ kJ/mol.

a. Calculate K at 25°C.

b. If all the free energy from the metabolism of glucose

$$C_6H_{12}O_6(s) + 6O_2(g) \longrightarrow 6CO_2(g) + 6H_2O(l)$$

goes into forming ATP from ADP, how many ATP molecules can be produced for every molecule of glucose?

c. Much of the ATP formed from metabolic processes is used to provide energy for transport of cellular components. What amount (mol) of ATP must be hydrolyzed to provide the energy for the transport of 1.0 mol of K^+ from the blood to the inside of a muscle cell at 37°C as described in Exercise 78?

80. One reaction that occurs in human metabolism is

$$HO_2CCH_2CH_2CHCO_2H(aq) + NH_3(aq) \rightleftharpoons$$
$$\overset{|}{NH_2}$$
Glutamic acid

$$\overset{O}{\overset{\|}{H_2NCCH_2CH_2CHCO_2H}}(aq) + H_2O(l)$$
$$\overset{|}{NH_2}$$
Glutamine

For this reaction $\Delta G° = 14$ kJ at 25°C.

a. Calculate K for this reaction at 25°C.

b. In a living cell this reaction is coupled with the hydrolysis of ATP. (See Exercise 79.) Calculate $\Delta G°$ and K at 25°C for the following reaction:

Glutamic acid(aq) + ATP(aq) + NH$_3$(aq) $\rightleftharpoons$
Glutamine(aq) + ADP(aq) + H$_2$PO$_4^-$(aq)

81. Consider the reactions

$$Ni^{2+}(aq) + 6NH_3(aq) \longrightarrow Ni(NH_3)_6^{2+}(aq) \quad (1)$$
$$Ni^{2+}(aq) + 3en(aq) \longrightarrow Ni(en)_3^{2+}(aq) \quad (2)$$

where

$$en = H_2N—CH_2—CH_2—NH_2$$

The ΔH values for the two reactions are quite similar, yet $K_{\text{reaction 2}} > K_{\text{reaction 1}}$. Explain.

82. Use the equation in Exercise 67 to determine $\Delta H°$ and $\Delta S°$ for the autoionization of water:

$$H_2O(l) \rightleftharpoons H^+(aq) + OH^-(aq)$$

T(°C)	K_w
0	1.14×10^{-15}
25	1.00×10^{-14}
35	2.09×10^{-14}
40.	2.92×10^{-14}
50.	5.47×10^{-14}

83. Consider the reaction

$$Fe_2O_3(s) + 3H_2(g) \longrightarrow 2Fe(s) + 3H_2O(g)$$

Assuming $\Delta H°$ and $\Delta S°$ do not depend on temperature, calculate the temperature where $K = 1.00$ for this reaction.

Challenge Problems

84. Liquid water at 25°C is introduced into an evacuated, insulated vessel. Identify the signs of the following thermodynamic functions for the process that occurs: ΔH, ΔS, ΔT_{water}, ΔS_{surr}, ΔS_{univ}.

85. Using data from Appendix 4, calculate $\Delta H°$, $\Delta G°$, and K (at 298 K) for the production of ozone from oxygen:

$$3O_2(g) \rightleftharpoons 2O_3(g)$$

At 30 km above the surface of the earth, the temperature is about 230. K and the partial pressure of oxygen is about 1.0×10^{-3} atm. Estimate the partial pressure of ozone in equilibrium with oxygen at 30 km above the earth's surface. Is it reasonable to assume that the equilibrium between oxygen and ozone is maintained under these conditions? Explain.

86. Entropy can be calculated by a relationship proposed by Ludwig Boltzmann:

$$S = k \ln(W)$$

where $k = 1.38 \times 10^{-23}$ J/K and W is the number of ways a particular state can be obtained. (This equation is engraved on Boltzmann's tombstone.) Calculate S for the three arrangements of particles in Table 16.1.

87. a. Using the free energy profile for a simple one-step reaction, show that at equilibrium $K = k_f/k_r$, where k_f and k_r are the rate constants for the forward and reverse reactions. *Hint:* Use the relationship $\Delta G° = -RT \ln(K)$ and represent k_f and k_r using the Arrhenius equation ($k = Ae^{-E_a/RT}$).

b. Why is the following statement false? "A catalyst can increase the rate of a forward reaction but not the rate of the reverse reaction."

88. Consider the reaction

$$H_2(g) + Br_2(g) \rightleftharpoons 2HBr(g)$$

where $\Delta H° = -103.8$ kJ/mol. In a particular experiment, equal moles of H$_2$(g) at 1.00 atm and Br$_2$(g) at 1.00 atm were mixed in a 1.00-L flask at 25°C and allowed to reach equilibrium. Then the molecules of H$_2$ at equilibrium were counted using a very sensitive technique, and 1.10×10^{13} molecules were found. For this reaction, calculate the values of K, $\Delta G°$, and $\Delta S°$.

89. Consider the system

$$A(g) \longrightarrow B(g)$$

at 25°C.

a. Assuming that $G_A° = 8996$ J/mol and $G_B° = 11,718$ J/mol, calculate the value of the equilibrium constant for this reaction.

b. Calculate the equilibrium pressures that result if 1.00 mol A(g) at 1.00 atm and 1.00 mol B(g) at 1.00 atm are mixed at 25°C.

c. Show by calculations that $\Delta G = 0$ at equilibrium.

90. The equilibrium constant for a certain reaction decreases from 8.84 to 3.25×10^{-2} when the temperature increases from 25°C to 75°C. Estimate the temperature where $K = 1.00$ for this reaction. Estimate the value of $\Delta S°$ for this reaction. *Hint:* Manipulate the equation in Exercise 67.

91. If wet silver carbonate is dried in a stream of hot air, the air must have a certain concentration level of carbon dioxide to prevent silver carbonate from decomposing by the reaction

$$Ag_2CO_3(s) \rightleftharpoons Ag_2O(s) + CO_2(g)$$

$\Delta H°$ for this reaction is 79.14 kJ/mol in the temperature range of 25 to 125°C. Given that the partial pressure of carbon dioxide in equilibrium with pure solid silver carbonate is 6.23×10^{-3} torr at 25°C, calculate the partial pressure of CO_2 necessary to prevent decomposition of Ag_2CO_3 at 110.°C. *Hint:* Manipulate the equation in Exercise 67.

92. Carbon tetrachloride (CCl_4) and benzene (C_6H_6) form ideal solutions. Consider an equimolar solution of CCl_4 and C_6H_6 at 25°C. The vapor above the solution is collected and condensed. Using the following data, determine the composition in mole fraction of the condensed vapor.

Substance	ΔG_f°
$C_6H_6(l)$	124.50 kJ/mol
$C_6H_6(g)$	129.66 kJ/mol
$CCl_4(l)$	−65.21 kJ/mol
$CCl_4(g)$	−60.59 kJ/mol

93. Some nonelectrolyte solute (molar mass = 142 g/mol) was dissolved in 150. mL of a solvent (density = 0.879 g/cm³). The elevated boiling point of the solution was 355.4 K. What mass of solute was dissolved in the solvent? For the solvent, the enthalpy of vaporization is 33.90 kJ/mol, the entropy of vaporization is 95.95 J/K · mol, and the boiling-point elevation constant is 2.5 K · kg/mol.

94. You have a 1.00-L sample of hot water (90.0°C) sitting open in a 25.0°C room. Eventually the water cools to 250°C while the temperature of the room remains unchanged. Calculate ΔS_{surr} for this process. Assume the density of water is 1.00 g/cm³ over this temperature range, and the heat capacity of water is constant over this temperature range and equal to 75.4 J/K · mol.

95. Consider a weak acid, HX. If a 0.10 M solution of HX has a pH of 5.83 at 25°C, what is ΔG° for the acid's dissociation reaction at 25°C?

96. Sodium chloride is added to water (at 25°C) until it is saturated. Calculate the Cl^- concentration in such a solution.

Species	ΔG° (kJ/mol)
NaCl(s)	−384
Na⁺(aq)	−262
Cl⁻(aq)	−131

Integrative Problems

These problems require the integration of multiple concepts to find the solutions.

97. For the equilibrium

$$A(g) + 2B(g) \rightleftharpoons C(g)$$

the initial concentrations are [A] = [B] = [C] = 0.100 atm. Once equilibrium has been established, it is found that [C] = 0.040 atm. What is ΔG° for this reaction at 25°C?

98. What is the pH of a 0.125 M solution of the weak base B if $\Delta H^\circ = -28.0$ kJ and $\Delta S^\circ = -175$ J/K for the following equilibrium reaction at 25°C?

$$B(aq) + H_2O(l) \rightleftharpoons BH^+(aq) + OH^-(aq)$$

Marathon Problem

This problem is designed to incorporate several concepts and techniques into one situation. Marathon Problems can be used in class by groups of students to help facilitate problem-solving skills.

99. Impure nickel, refined by smelting sulfide ores in a blast furnace, can be converted into metal from 99.90% to 99.99% purity by the Mond process. The primary reaction involved in the Mond process is

$$Ni(s) + 4CO(g) \rightleftharpoons Ni(CO)_4(g)$$

a. Without referring to Appendix 4, predict the sign of ΔS° for the above reaction. Explain.

b. The spontaneity of the above reaction is temperature dependent. Predict the sign of ΔS_{surr} for this reaction. Explain.

c. For $Ni(CO)_4(g)$, $\Delta H_f^\circ = -607$ kJ/mol and $S^\circ = 417$ J/K · mol at 298 K. Using these values and data in Appendix 4, calculate ΔH° and ΔS° for the above reaction.

d. Calculate the temperature at which $\Delta G^\circ = 0$ ($K = 1$) for the above reaction, assuming that ΔH° and ΔS° do not depend on temperature.

e. The first step of the Mond process involves equilibrating impure nickel with $CO(g)$ and $Ni(CO)_4(g)$ at about 50°C. The purpose of this step is to convert as much nickel as possible into the gas phase. Calculate the equilibrium constant for the above reaction at 50.°C.

f. In the second step of the Mond process, the gaseous $Ni(CO)_4$ is isolated and heated to 227°C. The purpose of this step is to deposit as much nickel as possible as pure solid (the reverse of the above reaction). Calculate the equilibrium constant for the above reaction at 227°C.

g. Why is temperature increased for the second step of the Mond process?

h. The Mond process relies on the volatility of $Ni(CO)_4$ for its success. Only pressures and temperatures at which $Ni(CO)_4$ is a gas are useful. A recently developed variation of the Mond process carries out the first step at higher pressures and a temperature of 152°C. Estimate the maximum pressure of $Ni(CO)_4(g)$ that can be attained before the gas will liquefy at 152°C. The boiling point for $Ni(CO)_4$ is 42°C and the enthalpy of vaporization is 29.0 kJ/mol.
[*Hint:* The phase change reaction and the corresponding equilibrium expression are

$$Ni(CO)_4(l) \rightleftharpoons Ni(CO)_4(g) \qquad K = P_{Ni(CO)_4}$$

$Ni(CO)_4(g)$ will liquefy when the pressure of $Ni(CO)_4$ is greater than the K value.]

Get help understanding core concepts and visualizing molecular-level interactions, and practice problem solving, by visiting the Online Study Center at **college.hmco.com/PIC/zumdahl7e.**

17 Electrochemistry

Contents

A nickel half-electroplated with copper.

*E*lectrochemistry constitutes one of the most important interfaces between chemistry and everyday life. Every time you start your car, turn on your calculator, look at your digital watch, or listen to a radio at the beach, you are depending on electrochemical reactions. Our society sometimes seems to run almost entirely on batteries. Certainly the advent of small, dependable batteries along with silicon-chip technology has made possible the tiny calculators, tape recorders, and clocks that we take for granted.

Electrochemistry is important in other less obvious ways. For example, the corrosion of iron, which has tremendous economic implications, is an electrochemical process. In addition, many important industrial materials such as aluminum, chlorine, and sodium hydroxide are prepared by electrolytic processes. In analytical chemistry, electrochemical techniques employ electrodes that are specific for a given molecule or ion, such as H^+ (pH meters), F^-, Cl^-, and many others. These increasingly important methods are used to analyze for trace pollutants in natural waters or for the tiny quantities of chemicals in human blood that may signal the development of a specific disease.

Electrochemistry is best defined as *the study of the interchange of chemical and electrical energy*. It is primarily concerned with two processes that involve oxidation–reduction reactions: the generation of an electric current from a spontaneous chemical reaction and the opposite process, the use of a current to produce chemical change.

17.1 Galvanic Cells

As we discussed in detail in Section 4.9, an **oxidation–reduction (redox) reaction** involves a transfer of electrons from the **reducing agent** to the **oxidizing agent.** Recall that **oxidation** involves a *loss of electrons* (an increase in oxidation number) and that **reduction** involves a *gain of electrons* (a decrease in oxidation number).

To understand how a redox reaction can be used to generate a current, let's consider the reaction between MnO_4^- and Fe^{2+}:

$$8H^+(aq) + MnO_4^-(aq) + 5Fe^{2+}(aq) \longrightarrow Mn^{2+}(aq) + 5Fe^{3+}(aq) + 4H_2O(l)$$

In this reaction, Fe^{2+} is oxidized and MnO_4^- is reduced; electrons are transferred from Fe^{2+} (the reducing agent) to MnO_4^- (the oxidizing agent).

It is useful to break a redox reaction into **half-reactions,** one involving oxidation and one involving reduction. For the reaction above, the half-reactions are

Balancing half-reactions is discussed in Section 4.10.

$$\text{Reduction:} \quad 8H^+ + MnO_4^- + 5e^- \longrightarrow Mn^{2+} + 4H_2O$$
$$\text{Oxidation:} \quad 5(Fe^{2+} \longrightarrow Fe^{3+} + e^-)$$

The multiplication of the second half-reaction by 5 indicates that this reaction must occur five times for each time the first reaction occurs. The balanced overall reaction is the sum of the half-reactions.

When MnO_4^- and Fe^{2+} are present in the same solution, the electrons are transferred directly when the reactants collide. Under these conditions, no useful work is obtained from the chemical energy involved in the reaction, which instead is released as heat. How can we harness this energy? The key is to separate the oxidizing agent from the reducing agent, thus requiring the electron transfer to occur through a wire. The current produced in the wire by the electron flow can then be directed through a device, such as an electric motor, to provide useful work.

FIGURE 17.1
Schematic of a method to separate the oxidizing and reducing agents of a redox reaction. (The solutions also contain counterions to balance the charge.)

For example, consider the system illustrated in Fig. 17.1. If our reasoning has been correct, electrons should flow through the wire from Fe^{2+} to MnO_4^-. However, when we construct the apparatus as shown, no flow of electrons is apparent. Why? Careful observation shows that when we connect the wires from the two compartments, current flows for an instant and then ceases. The current stops flowing because of charge buildups in the two compartments. If electrons flowed from the right to the left compartment in the apparatus as shown, the left compartment (receiving electrons) would become negatively charged, and the right compartment (losing electrons) would become positively charged. Creating a charge separation of this type requires a large amount of energy. Thus sustained electron flow cannot occur under these conditions.

However, we can solve this problem very simply. The solutions must be connected so that ions can flow to keep the net charge in each compartment zero. This connection might involve a **salt bridge** (a U-tube filled with an electrolyte) or a **porous disk** in a tube connecting the two solutions (see Fig. 17.2). Either of these devices allows ions to flow without extensive mixing of the solutions. When we make the provision for ion flow, the circuit is complete. Electrons flow through the wire from reducing agent to oxidizing agent, and ions flow from one compartment to the other to keep the net charge zero.

A galvanic cell uses a spontaneous redox reaction to produce a current that can be used to do work.

We now have covered all the essential characteristics of a **galvanic cell,** *a device in which chemical energy is changed to electrical energy.* (The opposite process is called *electrolysis* and will be considered in Section 17.7.)

The reaction in an electrochemical cell occurs at the interface between the electrode and the solution where the electron transfer occurs. The electrode compartment in which *oxidation* occurs is called the **anode;** the electrode compartment in which *reduction* occurs is called the **cathode** (see Fig. 17.3).

Oxidation occurs at the anode. Reduction occurs at the cathode.

FIGURE 17.2
Galvanic cells can contain a salt bridge as in (a) or a porous-disk connection as in (b). A salt bridge contains a strong electrolyte held in a Jello-like matrix. A porous disk contains tiny passages that allow hindered flow of ions.

(a)   (b)

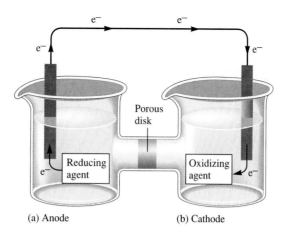

FIGURE 17.3
An electrochemical process involves electron transfer at the interface between the electrode and the solution. (a) The species in the solution acting as the reducing agent supplies electrons to the anode. (b) The species in the solution acting as the oxidizing agent receives electrons from the cathode.

(a) Anode   (b) Cathode

Cell Potential

Visualization: Voltaic Cell:
Cathode Reaction

Visualization: Voltaic Cell:
Anode Reaction

A volt is 1 joule of work per coulomb of charge transferred: 1 V = 1 J/C.

A galvanic cell consists of an oxidizing agent in one compartment that pulls electrons through a wire from a reducing agent in the other compartment. The "pull," or driving force, on the electrons is called the **cell potential** ($\mathscr{E}_{cell}$), or the **electromotive force** (emf) of the cell. The unit of electrical potential is the **volt** (abbreviated V), which is defined as 1 joule of work per coulomb of charge transferred.

How can we measure the cell potential? One possible instrument is a crude **voltmeter,** which works by drawing current through a known resistance. However, when current flows through a wire, the frictional heating that occurs wastes some of the potentially useful energy of the cell. A traditional voltmeter will therefore measure a potential that is less than the maximum cell potential. The key to determining the maximum potential is to do the measurement under conditions of zero current so that no energy is wasted. Traditionally, this has been accomplished by inserting a variable-voltage device (powered from an external source) in *opposition* to the cell potential. The voltage on this instrument (called a **potentiometer**) is adjusted until no current flows in the cell circuit. Under such conditions, the cell potential is equal in magnitude and opposite in sign to the voltage setting of the potentiometer. This value represents the *maximum* cell potential, since no energy is wasted heating the wire. More recently, advances in electronic technology have allowed the design of *digital voltmeters* that draw only a negligible amount of current (see Fig. 17.4). Since these instruments are more convenient to use, they have replaced potentiometers in the modern laboratory.

Digital
voltmeter

FIGURE 17.4
Digital voltmeters draw only a negligible current and are convenient to use.

17.2 Standard Reduction Potentials

The reaction in a galvanic cell is always an oxidation–reduction reaction that can be broken down into two half-reactions. It would be convenient to assign a potential to *each* half-reaction so that when we construct a cell from a given pair of half-reactions we can obtain the cell potential by summing the half-cell potentials. For example, the observed potential for the cell shown in Fig. 17.5(a) is 0.76 V, and the cell reaction* is

$$2H^+(aq) + Zn(s) \longrightarrow Zn^{2+}(aq) + H_2(g)$$

For this cell, the anode compartment contains a zinc metal electrode with Zn^{2+} and SO_4^{2-} ions in aqueous solution. The anode reaction is the oxidation half-reaction:

$$Zn \longrightarrow Zn^{2+} + 2e^-$$

The zinc metal, in producing Zn^{2+} ions that go into solution, is giving up electrons, which flow through the wire. For now, we will assume that all cell components are in their standard states, so in this case the solution in the anode compartment will contain 1 M Zn^{2+}. The cathode reaction of this cell is the reduction half-reaction:

$$2H^+ + 2e^- \longrightarrow H_2$$

The cathode consists of a platinum electrode (used because it is a chemically inert conductor) in contact with 1 M H^+ ions and bathed by hydrogen gas at 1 atm. Such an electrode, called the **standard hydrogen electrode,** is shown in Fig. 17.5(b).

Although we can measure the *total* potential of this cell (0.76 V), there is no way to measure the potentials of the individual electrode processes. Thus, if we want potentials for the half-reactions (half-cells), we must arbitrarily divide the total cell potential. For example, if we assign the reaction

$$2H^+ + 2e^- \longrightarrow H_2$$

The name *galvanic cell* honors Luigi Galvani (1737–1798), an Italian scientist generally credited with the discovery of electricity. These cells are sometimes called *voltaic cells* after Alessandro Volta (1745–1827), another Italian, who first constructed cells of this type around 1800.

An electrochemical cell with a measured potential of 1.10 V.

FIGURE 17.5
(a) A galvanic cell involving the reactions $Zn \rightarrow Zn^{2+} + 2e^-$ (at the anode) and $2H^+ + 2e^- \rightarrow H_2$ (at the cathode) has a potential of 0.76 V. (b) The standard hydrogen electrode where $H_2(g)$ at 1 atm is passed over a platinum electrode in contact with 1 M H^+ ions. This electrode process (assuming ideal behavior) is arbitrarily assigned a value of exactly zero volts.

*In this text we will follow the convention of indicating the physical states of the reactants and products only in the overall redox reaction. For simplicity, half-reactions will *not* include the physical states.

where $[H^+] = 1\ M$ and $P_{H_2} = 1$ atm

a potential of exactly zero volts, then the reaction

$$Zn \longrightarrow Zn^{2+} + 2e^-$$

will have a potential of 0.76 V because

$$\mathscr{E}^\circ_{cell} = \mathscr{E}^\circ_{H^+ \to H_2} + \mathscr{E}^\circ_{Zn \to Zn^{2+}}$$
$$\uparrow \qquad\qquad \uparrow \qquad\qquad \uparrow$$
$$0.76\ V \qquad 0\ V \qquad 0.76\ V$$

where the superscript $^\circ$ indicates that *standard states* are employed. In fact, by setting the standard potential for the half-reaction $2H^+ + 2e^- \to H_2$ equal to zero, we can assign values to all other half-reactions.

For example, the measured potential for the cell shown in Fig. 17.6 is 1.10 V. The cell reaction is

$$Zn(s) + Cu^{2+}(aq) \longrightarrow Zn^{2+}(aq) + Cu(s)$$

which can be divided into the half-reactions

$$\text{Anode:} \qquad Zn \longrightarrow Zn^{2+} + 2e^-$$
$$\text{Cathode:} \qquad Cu^{2+} + 2e^- \longrightarrow Cu$$

Then

$$\mathscr{E}^\circ_{cell} = \mathscr{E}^\circ_{Zn \to Zn^{2+}} + \mathscr{E}^\circ_{Cu^{2+} \to Cu}$$

Visualization: Electrochemical Half-Reactions in a Galvanic Cell

Standard states were discussed in Section 6.4.

Visualization: Zinc/Copper Cells with Lemons

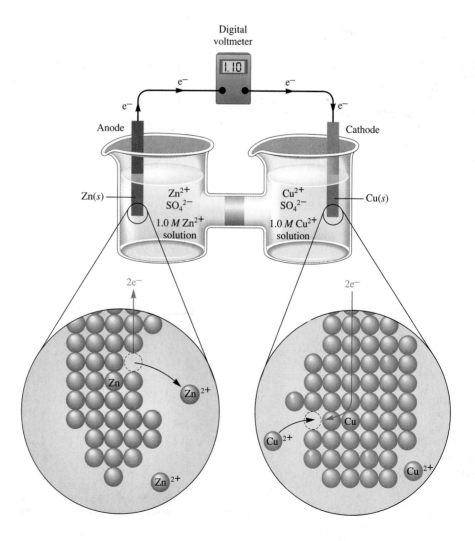

FIGURE 17.6
A galvanic cell involving the half-reactions $Zn \to Zn^{2+} + 2e^-$ (anode) and $Cu^{2+} + 2e^- \to Cu$ (cathode), with $\mathscr{E}^\circ_{cell} = 1.10$ V.

Since $\mathscr{E}^\circ_{Zn \rightarrow Zn^{2+}}$ was earlier assigned a value of 0.76 V, the value of $\mathscr{E}^\circ_{Cu^{2+} \rightarrow Cu}$ must be 0.34 V because

$$1.10 \text{ V} = 0.76 \text{ V} + 0.34 \text{ V}$$

The standard hydrogen potential is the reference potential against which all half-reaction potentials are assigned.

The scientific community has universally accepted the half-reaction potentials based on the assignment of zero volts to the process $2H^+ + 2e^- \rightarrow H_2$ (under standard conditions where ideal behavior is assumed). However, before we can use these values to calculate cell potentials, we need to understand several essential characteristics of half-cell potentials.

The accepted convention is to give the potentials of half-reactions as *reduction* processes. For example:

$$2H^+ + 2e^- \longrightarrow H_2$$
$$Cu^{2+} + 2e^- \longrightarrow Cu$$
$$Zn^{2+} + 2e^- \longrightarrow Zn$$

Visualization: Galvanic (Voltaic) Cells

All half-reactions are given as reduction processes in standard tables.

The $\mathscr{E}^\circ$ values corresponding to reduction half-reactions with all solutes at 1 M and all gases at 1 atm are called **standard reduction potentials.** Standard reduction potentials for the most common half-reactions are given in Table 17.1 and Appendix 5.5.

Combining two half-reactions to obtain a balanced oxidation–reduction reaction often requires two manipulations:

1. One of the reduction half-reactions must be reversed (since redox reactions must involve a substance being oxidized and a substance being reduced). The half-reaction with the largest positive potential will run as written (as a reduction), and the other

TABLE 17.1   Standard Reduction Potentials at 25°C (298 K) for Many Common Half-Reactions

Half-Reaction	$\mathscr{E}^\circ$ (V)	Half-Reaction	$\mathscr{E}^\circ$ (V)
$F_2 + 2e^- \rightarrow 2F^-$	2.87	$O_2 + 2H_2O + 4e^- \rightarrow 4OH^-$	0.40
$Ag^{2+} + e^- \rightarrow Ag^+$	1.99	$Cu^{2+} + 2e^- \rightarrow Cu$	0.34
$Co^{3+} + e^- \rightarrow Co^{2+}$	1.82	$Hg_2Cl_2 + 2e^- \rightarrow 2Hg + 2Cl^-$	0.27
$H_2O_2 + 2H^- + 2e^- \rightarrow 2H_2O$	1.78	$AgCl + e^- \rightarrow Ag + Cl^-$	0.22
$Ce^{4+} + e^- \rightarrow Ce^{3+}$	1.70	$SO_4^{2-} + 4H^+ + 2e^- \rightarrow H_2SO_3 + H_2O$	0.20
$PbO_2 + 4H^+ + SO_4^{2-} + 2e^- \rightarrow PbSO_4 + 2H_2O$	1.69	$Cu^{2+} + e^- \rightarrow Cu^+$	0.16
$MnO_4^- + 4H^+ + 3e^- \rightarrow MnO_2 + 2H_2O$	1.68	$2H^+ + 2e^- \rightarrow H_2$	0.00
$2e^- + 2H^+ + IO_4^- \rightarrow IO_3^- + H_2O$	1.60	$Fe^{3+} + 3e^- \rightarrow Fe$	−0.036
$MnO_4^- + 8H^+ + 5e^- \rightarrow Mn^{2+} + 4H_2O$	1.51	$Pb^{2+} + 2e^- \rightarrow Pb$	−0.13
$Au^{3+} + 3e^- \rightarrow Au$	1.50	$Sn^{2+} + 2e^- \rightarrow Sn$	−0.14
$PbO_2 + 4H^+ + 2e^- \rightarrow Pb^{2+} + 2H_2O$	1.46	$Ni^{2+} + 2e^- \rightarrow Ni$	−0.23
$Cl_2 + 2e^- \rightarrow 2Cl^-$	1.36	$PbSO_4 + 2e^- \rightarrow Pb + SO_4^{2-}$	−0.35
$Cr_2O_7^{2-} + 14H^+ + 6e^- \rightarrow 2Cr^{3+} + 7H_2O$	1.33	$Cd^{2+} + 2e^- \rightarrow Cd$	−0.40
$O_2 + 4H^+ + 4e^- \rightarrow 2H_2O$	1.23	$Fe^{2+} + 2e^- \rightarrow Fe$	−0.44
$MnO_2 + 4H^+ + 2e^- \rightarrow Mn^{2+} + 2H_2O$	1.21	$Cr^{3+} + e^- \rightarrow Cr^{2+}$	−0.50
$IO_3^- + 6H^+ + 5e^- \rightarrow \frac{1}{2}I_2 + 3H_2O$	1.20	$Cr^{3+} + 3e^- \rightarrow Cr$	−0.73
$Br_2 + 2e^- \rightarrow 2Br^-$	1.09	$Zn^{2+} + 2e^- \rightarrow Zn$	−0.76
$VO_2^+ + 2H^+ + e^- \rightarrow VO^{2+} + H_2O$	1.00	$2H_2O + 2e^- \rightarrow H_2 + 2OH^-$	−0.83
$AuCl_4^- + 3e^- \rightarrow Au + 4Cl^-$	0.99	$Mn^{2+} + 2e^- \rightarrow Mn$	−1.18
$NO_3^- + 4H^+ + 3e^- \rightarrow NO + 2H_2O$	0.96	$Al^{3+} + 3e^- \rightarrow Al$	−1.66
$ClO_2 + e^- \rightarrow ClO_2^-$	0.954	$H_2 + 2e^- \rightarrow 2H^-$	−2.23
$2Hg^{2+} + 2e^- \rightarrow Hg_2^{2+}$	0.91	$Mg^{2+} + 2e^- \rightarrow Mg$	−2.37
$Ag^+ + e^- \rightarrow Ag$	0.80	$La^{3+} + 3e^- \rightarrow La$	−2.37
$Hg_2^{2+} + 2e^- \rightarrow 2Hg$	0.80	$Na^+ + e^- \rightarrow Na$	−2.71
$Fe^{3+} + e^- \rightarrow Fe^{2+}$	0.77	$Ca^{2+} + 2e^- \rightarrow Ca$	−2.76
$O_2 + 2H^+ + 2e^- \rightarrow H_2O_2$	0.68	$Ba^{2+} + 2e^- \rightarrow Ba$	−2.90
$MnO_4^- + e^- \rightarrow MnO_4^{2-}$	0.56	$K^+ + e^- \rightarrow K$	−2.92
$I_2 + 2e^- \rightarrow 2I^-$	0.54	$Li^+ + e^- \rightarrow Li$	−3.05
$Cu^+ + e^- \rightarrow Cu$	0.52		

When a half-reaction is reversed, the sign of $\mathscr{E}°$ is reversed.

half-reaction will be forced to run in reverse (will be the oxidation reaction). The net potential of the cell will be the *difference* between the two. Since the reduction process occurs at the cathode and the oxidation process occurs at the anode, we can write

$$\mathscr{E}°_{cell} = \mathscr{E}°\,(\text{cathode}) - \mathscr{E}°\,(\text{anode})$$

Because subtraction means "change the sign and add," in the examples done here we will change the sign of the oxidation (anode) reaction when we reverse it and add it to the reduction (cathode) reaction.

2. Since the number of electrons lost must equal the number gained, the half-reactions must be multiplied by integers as necessary to achieve the balanced equation. However, the *value of $\mathscr{E}°$ is not changed* when a half-reaction is multiplied by an integer. Since a standard reduction potential is an *intensive property* (it does not depend on how many times the reaction occurs), the potential is *not* multiplied by the integer required to balance the cell reaction.

When a half-reaction is multiplied by an integer, $\mathscr{E}°$ remains the same.

Consider a galvanic cell based on the redox reaction

$$Fe^{3+}(aq) + Cu(s) \longrightarrow Cu^{2+}(aq) + Fe^{2+}(aq)$$

The pertinent half-reactions are

$$Fe^{3+} + e^- \longrightarrow Fe^{2+} \qquad \mathscr{E}° = 0.77 \text{ V} \qquad (1)$$
$$Cu^{2+} + 2e^- \longrightarrow Cu \qquad \mathscr{E}° = 0.34 \text{ V} \qquad (2)$$

To balance the cell reaction and calculate the standard cell potential, reaction (2) must be reversed:

$$Cu \longrightarrow Cu^{2+} + 2e^- \qquad -\mathscr{E}° = -0.34 \text{ V}$$

Visualization: Copper Metal in Water
Visualization: Copper Metal in Sulfuric Acid
Visualization: Copper Metal in Hydrochloric Acid
Visualization: Copper Metal in Nitric Acid

Note the change in sign for the $\mathscr{E}°$ value. Now, since each Cu atom produces two electrons but each Fe^{3+} ion accepts only one electron, reaction (1) must be multiplied by 2:

$$2Fe^{3+} + 2e^- \longrightarrow 2Fe^{2+} \qquad \mathscr{E}° = 0.77 \text{ V}$$

Note that $\mathscr{E}°$ is not changed in this case.

Now we can obtain the balanced cell reaction by summing the appropriately modified half-reactions:

$$2Fe^{3+} + 2e^- \longrightarrow 2Fe^{2+} \qquad\qquad \mathscr{E}\,(\text{cathode}) = 0.77 \text{ V}$$
$$Cu \longrightarrow Cu^{2+} + 2e^- \qquad\qquad -\mathscr{E}\,(\text{anode}) = -0.34 \text{ V}$$

Cell reaction: $Cu(s) + 2Fe^{3+}(aq) \longrightarrow Cu^{2+}(aq) + 2Fe^{2+}(aq)$
$$\mathscr{E}°_{cell} = \mathscr{E}°\,(\text{cathode}) - \mathscr{E}°\,(\text{anode})$$
$$= 0.77 \text{ V} - 0.34 \text{ V} = 0.43 \text{ V}$$

Sample Exercise 17.1 ## Galvanic Cells

a. Consider a galvanic cell based on the reaction

$$Al^{3+}(aq) + Mg(s) \longrightarrow Al(s) + Mg^{2+}(aq)$$

The half-reactions are

$$Al^{3+} + 3e^- \longrightarrow Al \qquad \mathscr{E}° = -1.66 \text{ V} \qquad (1)$$
$$Mg^{2+} + 2e^- \longrightarrow Mg \qquad \mathscr{E}° = -2.37 \text{ V} \qquad (2)$$

Give the balanced cell reaction and calculate $\mathscr{E}°$ for the cell.

b. A galvanic cell is based on the reaction

$$MnO_4^-(aq) + H^+(aq) + ClO_3^-(aq) \longrightarrow ClO_4^-(aq) + Mn^{2+}(aq) + H_2O(l)$$

The half-reactions are

$$MnO_4^- + 5e^- + 8H^+ \longrightarrow Mn^{2+} + 4H_2O \qquad \mathscr{E}° = 1.51 \text{ V} \qquad (1)$$

$$ClO_4^- + 2H^+ + 2e^- \longrightarrow ClO_3^- + H_2O \qquad \mathscr{E}° = 1.19 \text{ V} \qquad (2)$$

Give the balanced cell reaction and calculate $\mathscr{E}°$ for the cell.

Solution

a. The half-reaction involving magnesium must be reversed and since this is the oxidation process, it is the anode:

$$Mg \longrightarrow Mg^{2+} + 2e^- \qquad -\mathscr{E}° \text{ (anode)} = -(-2.37 \text{ V}) = 2.37 \text{ V}$$

Also, since the two half-reactions involve different numbers of electrons, they must be multiplied by integers as follows:

$$2(Al^{3+} + 3e^- \longrightarrow Al) \qquad \mathscr{E}° \text{ (cathode)} = -1.66 \text{ V}$$

$$\underline{3(Mg \longrightarrow Mg^{2+} + 2e^-) \qquad -\mathscr{E}° \text{ (anode)} = \quad 2.37 \text{ V}}$$

$$2Al^{3+}(aq) + 3Mg(s) \longrightarrow 2Al(s) + 3Mg^{2+}(aq) \qquad \mathscr{E}°_{cell} = \mathscr{E}° \text{ (cathode)} - \mathscr{E}° \text{ (anode)}$$

$$= -1.66 \text{ V} + 2.37 \text{ V} = 0.71 \text{ V}$$

b. Half-reaction (2) must be reversed (it is the anode), and both half-reactions must be multiplied by integers to make the number of electrons equal:

$$2(MnO_4^- + 5e^- + 8H^+ \longrightarrow Mn^{2+} + 4H_2O) \qquad \mathscr{E}° \text{ (cathode)} = \quad 1.51 \text{ V}$$

$$\underline{5(ClO_3^- + H_2O \longrightarrow ClO_4^- + 2H^+ + 2e^-) \qquad -\mathscr{E}° \text{ (anode)} = -1.19 \text{ V}}$$

$$2MnO_4^-(aq) + 6H^+(aq) + 5ClO_3^-(aq) \longrightarrow \qquad \mathscr{E}°_{cell} = \mathscr{E}° \text{ (cathode)} - \mathscr{E}° \text{ (anode)}$$

$$2Mn^{2+}(aq) + 3H_2O(l) + 5ClO_4^-(aq) \qquad = 1.51 \text{ V} - 1.19 \text{ V} = 0.32 \text{ V}$$

See Exercises 17.27 and 17.28.

Line Notation

We now will introduce a handy line notation used to describe electrochemical cells. In this notation the anode components are listed on the left and the cathode components are listed on the right, separated by double vertical lines (indicating the salt bridge or porous disk). For example, the line notation for the cell described in Sample Exercise 17.1(a) is

$$Mg(s)|Mg^{2+}(aq)||Al^{3+}(aq)|Al(s)$$

In this notation a phase difference (boundary) is indicated by a single vertical line. Thus, in this case, vertical lines occur between the solid Mg metal and the Mg^{2+} in aqueous solution and between solid Al and Al^{3+} in aqueous solution. Also note that the substance constituting the anode is listed at the far left and the substance constituting the cathode is listed at the far right.

For the cell described in Sample Exercise 17.1(b), all the components involved in the oxidation–reduction reaction are ions. Since none of these dissolved ions can serve as an electrode, a nonreacting (inert) conductor must be used. The usual choice is platinum. Thus, for the cell described in Sample Exercise 17.1(b), the line notation is

$$Pt(s)|ClO_3^-(aq), ClO_4^-(aq), H^+(aq)||H^+(aq), MnO_4^-(aq), Mn^{2+}(aq)|Pt(s)$$

Complete Description of a Galvanic Cell

Next we want to consider how to describe a galvanic cell fully, given just its half-reactions. This description will include the cell reaction, the cell potential, and the physical setup of the cell. Let's consider a galvanic cell based on the following half-reactions:

$$Fe^{2+} + 2e^- \longrightarrow Fe \qquad\qquad \mathscr{E}° = -0.44 \text{ V}$$
$$MnO_4^- + 5e^- + 8H^+ \longrightarrow Mn^{2+} + 4H_2O \qquad \mathscr{E}° = 1.51 \text{ V}$$

In a working galvanic cell, one of these reactions must run in reverse. Which one?

We can answer this question by considering the sign of the potential of a working cell: *A cell will always run spontaneously in the direction that produces a positive cell potential.* Thus, in the present case, it is clear that the half-reaction involving iron must be reversed, since this choice leads to a positive cell potential:

$$Fe \longrightarrow Fe^{2+} + 2e^- \qquad -\mathscr{E}° = 0.44 \text{ V} \qquad \text{Anode reaction}$$
$$MnO_4^- + 5e^- + 8H^+ \longrightarrow Mn^{2+} + 4H_2O \qquad \mathscr{E}° = 1.51 \text{ V} \qquad \text{Cathode reaction}$$

where $\qquad \mathscr{E}°_{cell} = \mathscr{E}° \text{ (cathode)} - \mathscr{E}° \text{ (anode)} = 1.51 \text{ V} + 0.44 \text{ V} = 1.95 \text{ V}$

The balanced cell reaction is obtained as follows:

$$5(Fe \longrightarrow Fe^{2+} + 2e^-)$$
$$\underline{2(MnO_4^- + 5e^- + 8H^+ \longrightarrow Mn^{2+} + 4H_2O)}$$
$$2MnO_4^-(aq) + 5Fe(s) + 16H^+(aq) \longrightarrow 5Fe^{2+}(aq) + 2Mn^{2+}(aq) + 8H_2O(l)$$

Now consider the physical setup of the cell, shown schematically in Fig. 17.7. In the left compartment the active components in their standard states are pure metallic iron (Fe) and $1.0 \text{ } M \text{ } Fe^{2+}$. The anion present depends on the iron salt used. In this compartment the anion does not participate in the reaction but simply balances the charge. The half-reaction that takes place at this electrode is

$$Fe \longrightarrow Fe^{2+} + 2e^-$$

which is an oxidation reaction, so this compartment is the anode. The electrode consists of pure iron metal.

In the right compartment the active components in their standard states are $1.0 \text{ } M$ MnO_4^-, $1.0 \text{ } M \text{ } H^+$, and $1.0 \text{ } M \text{ } Mn^{2+}$, with appropriate unreacting ions (often called *counterions*) to balance the charge. The half-reaction in this compartment is

$$MnO_4^- + 5e^- + 8H^+ \longrightarrow Mn^{2+} + 4H_2O$$

which is a reduction reaction, so this compartment is the cathode. Since neither MnO_4^- nor Mn^{2+} ions can serve as the electrode, a nonreacting conductor such as platinum must be employed.

The next step is to determine the direction of electron flow. In the left compartment the half-reaction involves the oxidation of iron:

$$Fe \longrightarrow Fe^{2+} + 2e^-$$

In the right compartment the half-reaction is the reduction of MnO_4^-:

$$MnO_4^- + 5e^- + 8H^+ \longrightarrow Mn^{2+} + 4H_2O$$

Thus the electrons flow from Fe to MnO_4^- in this cell, or from the anode to the cathode, as is always the case. The line notation for this cell is

$$Fe(s)|Fe^{2+}(aq)||MnO_4^-(aq), Mn^{2+}(aq)|Pt(s)$$

A complete description of a galvanic cell usually includes four items:

- The cell potential (always positive for a galvanic cell where $\mathscr{E}°_{cell} = \mathscr{E}° \text{ (cathode)} - \mathscr{E}° \text{ (anode)}$ and the balanced cell reaction.

- The direction of electron flow, obtained by inspecting the half-reactions and using the direction that gives a positive $\mathscr{E}°_{cell}$.

A galvanic cell runs spontaneously in the direction that gives a positive value for $\mathscr{E}_{cell}$.

FIGURE 17.7
The schematic of a galvanic cell based on the half-reactions:

$$Fe \longrightarrow Fe^{2+} + 2e^-$$
$$MnO_4^- + 5e^- + 8H^+ \longrightarrow Mn^{2+} + 4H_2O$$

- Designation of the anode and cathode.

- The nature of each electrode and the ions present in each compartment. A chemically inert conductor is required if none of the substances participating in the half-reaction is a conducting solid.

Sample Exercise 17.2

Description of a Galvanic Cell

Describe completely the galvanic cell based on the following half-reactions under standard conditions:

$$Ag^+ + e^- \longrightarrow Ag \qquad \mathscr{E}° = 0.80 \text{ V} \qquad (1)$$
$$Fe^{3+} + e^- \longrightarrow Fe^{2+} \qquad \mathscr{E}° = 0.77 \text{ V} \qquad (2)$$

Solution

Item 1 Since a positive $\mathscr{E}°_{cell}$ value is required, reaction (2) must run in reverse:

$$Ag^+ + e^- \longrightarrow Ag \qquad \mathscr{E}° \text{ (cathode) } = 0.80 \text{ V}$$
$$Fe^{2+} \longrightarrow Fe^{3+} + e^- \qquad -\mathscr{E}° \text{ (anode) } = -0.77 \text{ V}$$

Cell reaction: $Ag^+(aq) + Fe^{2+}(aq) \longrightarrow Fe^{3+}(aq) + Ag(s)$ $\mathscr{E}°_{cell} = 0.03 \text{ V}$

Item 2 Since Ag^+ receives electrons and Fe^{2+} loses electrons in the cell reaction, the electrons will flow from the compartment containing Fe^{2+} to the compartment containing Ag^+.

Item 3 Oxidation occurs in the compartment containing Fe^{2+} (electrons flow from Fe^{2+} to Ag^+). Hence this compartment functions as the anode. Reduction occurs in the compartment containing Ag^+, so this compartment functions as the cathode.

Item 4 The electrode in the Ag/Ag^+ compartment is silver metal, and an inert conductor, such as platinum, must be used in the Fe^{2+}/Fe^{3+} compartment. Appropriate counterions are assumed to be present. The diagram for this cell is shown in Fig. 17.8. The line notation for this cell is

$$Pt(s)|Fe^{2+}(aq), Fe^{3+}(aq)||Ag^+(aq)|Ag(s)$$

See Exercises 17.29 and 17.30.

FIGURE 17.8
Schematic diagram for the galvanic cell based on the half-reactions

$$Ag^+ + e^- \longrightarrow Ag$$
$$Fe^{2+} \longrightarrow Fe^{3+} + e^-$$

17.3 Cell Potential, Electrical Work, and Free Energy

So far we have considered electrochemical cells in a very practical fashion without much theoretical background. The next step will be to explore the relationship between thermodynamics and electrochemistry.

The work that can be accomplished when electrons are transferred through a wire depends on the "push" (the thermodynamic driving force) behind the electrons. This driving force (the emf) is defined in terms of a *potential difference* (in volts) between two points in the circuit. Recall that a volt represents a joule of work per coulomb of charge transferred:

$$\text{emf} = \text{potential difference (V)} = \frac{\text{work (J)}}{\text{charge (C)}}$$

Thus 1 joule of work is produced or required (depending on the direction) when 1 coulomb of charge is transferred between two points in the circuit that differ by a potential of 1 volt.

In this book, *work is viewed from the point of view of the system*. Thus work flowing out of the system is indicated by a minus sign. When a cell produces a current, the cell

Using a battery-powered drill to insert a screw.

potential is positive, and the current can be used to do work—to run a motor, for instance. Thus the cell potential $\mathscr{E}$ and the work w have opposite signs:

$$\mathscr{E} = \frac{-w}{q} \begin{array}{l} \leftarrow \text{Work} \\ \leftarrow \text{Charge} \end{array}$$

Therefore,
$$-w = q\mathscr{E}$$

From this equation it can be seen that the maximum work in a cell would be obtained at the maximum cell potential:

$$-w_{max} = q\mathscr{E}_{max} \quad \text{or} \quad w_{max} = -q\mathscr{E}_{max}$$

Work is never the maximum possible if any current is flowing.

However, there is a problem. To obtain electrical work, current must flow. When current flows, some energy is inevitably wasted through frictional heating, and the maximum work is not obtained. This reflects the important general principle introduced in Section 16.9: *In any real, spontaneous process some energy is always wasted—the actual work realized is always less than the calculated maximum.* This is a consequence of the fact that the entropy of the universe must increase in any spontaneous process. Recall from Section 16.9 that the only process from which maximum work could be realized is the hypothetical reversible process. For a galvanic cell this would involve an infinitesimally small current flow and thus an infinite amount of time to do the work. Even though we can never achieve the maximum work through the actual discharge of a galvanic cell, we can measure the maximum potential. There is negligible current flow when a cell potential is measured with a potentiometer or an efficient digital voltmeter. No current flow implies no waste of energy, so the potential measured is the maximum.

Although we can never actually realize the maximum work from a cell reaction, the value for it is still useful in evaluating the efficiency of a real process based on the cell reaction. For example, suppose a certain galvanic cell has a maximum potential (at zero current) of 2.50 V. In a particular experiment 1.33 moles of electrons were passed through this cell at an average actual potential of 2.10 V. The actual work done is

$$w = -q\mathscr{E}$$

where $\mathscr{E}$ represents the actual potential difference at which the current flowed (2.10 V or 2.10 J/C) and q is the quantity of charge in coulombs transferred. The charge on 1 mole of electrons is a constant called the **faraday** (abbreviated F), which has the value *96,485 coulombs of charge per mole of electrons.* Thus q equals the number of moles of electrons times the charge per mole of electrons:

$$q = nF = 1.33 \text{ mol e}^- \times 96,485 \text{ C/mol e}^-$$

Then, for the preceding experiment, the actual work is

$$w = -q\mathscr{E} = -(1.33 \text{ mol e}^- \times 96,485 \text{ C/mol e}^-) \times (2.10 \text{ J/C})$$
$$= -2.69 \times 10^5 \text{ J}$$

For the maximum possible work, the calculation is similar, except that the maximum potential is used:

$$w_{max} = -q\mathscr{E}$$
$$= -\left(1.33 \text{ mol e}^- \times 96,485 \frac{\text{C}}{\text{mol e}^-}\right)\left(2.50 \frac{\text{J}}{\text{C}}\right)$$
$$= -3.21 \times 10^5 \text{ J}$$

Thus, in its actual operation, the efficiency of this cell is

$$\frac{w}{w_{max}} \times 100\% = \frac{-2.69 \times 10^5 \text{ J}}{-3.21 \times 10^5 \text{ J}} \times 100\% = 83.8\%$$

Michael Faraday lecturing at the Royal Institution before Prince Albert and others (1855). The faraday was named in honor of Michael Faraday (1791–1867), an Englishman who may have been the greatest experimental scientist of the nineteenth century. Among his many achievements were the invention of the electric motor and generator and the development of the principles of electrolysis.

Next we want to relate the potential of a galvanic cell to free energy. In Section 16.9 we saw that for a process carried out at constant temperature and pressure, the change in free energy equals the maximum useful work obtainable from that process:

$$w_{max} = \Delta G$$

For a galvanic cell,

$$w_{max} = -q\mathscr{E}_{max} = \Delta G$$

Since

$$q = nF$$

we have

$$\Delta G = -q\mathscr{E}_{max} = -nF\mathscr{E}_{max}$$

From now on the subscript on $\mathscr{E}_{max}$ will be deleted, with the understanding that any potential given in this book is the maximum potential. Thus

$$\Delta G = -nF\mathscr{E}$$

For standard conditions,

$$\Delta G° = -nF\mathscr{E}°$$

This equation states that *the maximum cell potential is directly related to the free energy difference between the reactants and the products in the cell.* This relationship is important because it provides an experimental means to obtain ΔG for a reaction. It also confirms that a galvanic cell will run in the direction that gives a positive value for $\mathscr{E}_{cell}$; a positive $\mathscr{E}_{cell}$ value corresponds to a negative ΔG value, which is the condition for spontaneity.

Sample Exercise 17.3

Calculating $\Delta G°$ for a Cell Reaction

Using the data in Table 17.1, calculate $\Delta G°$ for the reaction

$$Cu^{2+}(aq) + Fe(s) \longrightarrow Cu(s) + Fe^{2+}(aq)$$

Is this reaction spontaneous?

Solution

The half-reactions are

$$
\begin{array}{ll}
Cu^{2+} + 2e^- \longrightarrow Cu & \mathscr{E}° \text{ (cathode)} = 0.34 \text{ V} \\
\underline{\phantom{Cu^{2+} +} Fe \longrightarrow Fe^{2+} + 2e^-} & \underline{-\mathscr{E}° \text{ (anode)} = 0.44 \text{ V}} \\
Cu^{2+} + Fe \longrightarrow Fe^{2+} + Cu & \mathscr{E}°_{cell} = 0.78 \text{ V}
\end{array}
$$

We can calculate $\Delta G°$ from the equation

$$\Delta G° = -nF\mathscr{E}°$$

Since two electrons are transferred per atom in the reaction, 2 moles of electrons are required per mole of reactants and products. Thus $n = 2$ mol e^-, $F = 96,485$ C/mol e^-, and $\mathscr{E}° = 0.78$ V $= 0.78$ J/C. Therefore,

$$\Delta G° = -(2 \text{ mol } e^-)\left(96,485 \frac{C}{\text{mol } e^-}\right)\left(0.78 \frac{J}{C}\right)$$

$$= -1.5 \times 10^5 \text{ J}$$

The process is spontaneous, as indicated by both the negative sign of $\Delta G°$ and the positive sign of $\mathscr{E}°_{cell}$.

This reaction is used industrially to deposit copper metal from solutions resulting from the dissolving of copper ores.

See Exercises 17.37 and 17.38.

Sample Exercise 17.4	**Predicting Spontaneity**

Using the data from Table 17.1, predict whether 1 M HNO_3 will dissolve gold metal to form a 1 M Au^{3+} solution.

Solution

The half-reaction for HNO_3 acting as an oxidizing agent is

$$NO_3^- + 4H^+ + 3e^- \longrightarrow NO + 2H_2O \qquad \mathscr{E}° \text{ (cathode)} = 0.96 \text{ V}$$

The reaction for the oxidation of solid gold to Au^{3+} ions is

$$Au \longrightarrow Au^{3+} + 3e^- \qquad -\mathscr{E}° \text{ (anode)} = -1.50 \text{ V}$$

The sum of these half-reactions gives the required reaction:

$$Au(s) + NO_3^-(aq) + 4H^+(aq) \longrightarrow Au^{3+}(aq) + NO(g) + 2H_2O(l)$$

and $\qquad \mathscr{E}°_{cell} = \mathscr{E}° \text{ (cathode)} - \mathscr{E}° \text{ (anode)} = 0.96 \text{ V} - 1.50 \text{ V} = -0.54 \text{ V}$

Since the $\mathscr{E}°$ value is negative, the process will *not* occur under standard conditions. That is, gold will not dissolve in 1 M HNO_3 to give 1 M Au^{3+}. In fact, a mixture (1:3 by volume) of concentrated nitric and hydrochloric acids, called *aqua regia,* is required to dissolve gold.

See Exercises 17.37 and 17.38.

A gold ring does not dissolve in nitric acid.

17.4 Dependence of Cell Potential on Concentration

So far we have described cells under standard conditions. In this section we consider the dependence of the cell potential on concentration. Under standard conditions (all concentrations 1 M), the cell with the reaction

$$Cu(s) + 2Ce^{4+}(aq) \longrightarrow Cu^{2+}(aq) + 2Ce^{3+}(aq)$$

has a potential of 1.36 V. What will the cell potential be if $[Ce^{4+}]$ is greater than 1.0 M? This question can be answered qualitatively in terms of Le Châtelier's principle. An increase in the concentration of Ce^{4+} will favor the forward reaction and thus increase the driving force on the electrons. The cell potential will increase. On the other hand, an increase in the concentration of a product (Cu^{2+} or Ce^{3+}) will oppose the forward reaction, thus decreasing the cell potential.

These ideas are illustrated in Sample Exercise 17.5.

Sample Exercise 17.5	**The Effects of Concentration on** $\mathscr{E}$

For the cell reaction

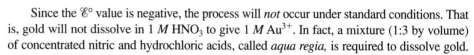

$$2Al(s) + 3Mn^{2+}(aq) \longrightarrow 2Al^{3+}(aq) + 3Mn(s) \qquad \mathscr{E}°_{cell} = 0.48 \text{ V}$$

predict whether $\mathscr{E}_{cell}$ is larger or smaller than $\mathscr{E}°_{cell}$ for the following cases.

a. $[Al^{3+}] = 2.0 \, M, [Mn^{2+}] = 1.0 \, M$
b. $[Al^{3+}] = 1.0 \, M, [Mn^{2+}] = 3.0 \, M$

Solution

a. A product concentration has been raised above 1.0 M. This will oppose the cell reaction and will cause $\mathscr{E}_{cell}$ to be less than $\mathscr{E}°_{cell}$ ($\mathscr{E}_{cell} < 0.48$ V).
b. A reactant concentration has been increased above 1.0 M, and $\mathscr{E}_{cell}$ will be greater than $\mathscr{E}°_{cell}$ ($\mathscr{E}_{cell} > 0.48$ V).

See Exercise 17.51.

A concentration cell with 1.0 M Cu^{2+} on the right and 0.010 M Cu^{2+} on the left.

FIGURE 17.9
A concentration cell that contains a silver electrode and aqueous silver nitrate in both compartments. Because the right compartment contains 1 M Ag$^+$ and the left compartment contains 0.1 M Ag$^+$, there will be a driving force to transfer electrons from left to right. Silver will be deposited on the right electrode, thus lowering the concentration of Ag$^+$ in the right compartment. In the left compartment the silver electrode dissolves (producing Ag$^+$ ions) to raise the concentration of Ag$^+$ in solution.

Concentration Cells

Because cell potentials depend on concentration, we can construct galvanic cells where both compartments contain the same components but at different concentrations. For example, in the cell in Fig. 17.9, both compartments contain aqueous AgNO$_3$, but with different molarities. Let's consider the potential of this cell and the direction of electron flow. The half-reaction relevant to both compartments of this cell is

$$\text{Ag}^+ + \text{e}^- \longrightarrow \text{Ag} \qquad \mathscr{E}° = 0.80 \text{ V}$$

If the cell had 1 M Ag$^+$ in both compartments,

$$\mathscr{E}°_{\text{cell}} = 0.80 \text{ V} - 0.80 \text{ V} = 0 \text{ V}$$

However, in the cell described here, the concentrations of Ag$^+$ in the two compartments are 1 M and 0.1 M. Because the concentrations of Ag$^+$ are unequal, the half-cell potentials will not be identical, and the cell will exhibit a positive voltage. In which direction will the electrons flow in this cell? The best way to think about this question is to recognize that nature will try to equalize the concentrations of Ag$^+$ in the two compartments. This can be done by transferring electrons from the compartment containing 0.1 M Ag$^+$ to the one containing 1 M Ag$^+$ (left to right in Fig. 17.9). This electron transfer will produce more Ag$^+$ in the left compartment and consume Ag$^+$ (to form Ag) in the right compartment.

A cell in which both compartments have the same components but at different concentrations is called a **concentration cell.** The difference in concentration is the only factor that produces a cell potential in this case, and the voltages are typically small.

Sample Exercise 17.6 ## Concentration Cells

Determine the direction of electron flow and designate the anode and cathode for the cell represented in Fig. 17.10.

Solution

The concentrations of Fe^{2+} ion in the two compartments can (eventually) be equalized by transferring electrons from the left compartment to the right. This will cause Fe^{2+} to be formed in the left compartment, and iron metal will be deposited (by reducing Fe^{2+} ions to Fe) on the right electrode. Since electron flow is from left to right, oxidation occurs in the left compartment (the anode) and reduction occurs in the right (the cathode).

See Exercise 17.52.

FIGURE 17.10
A concentration cell containing iron electrodes and different concentrations of Fe^{2+} ion in the two compartments.

The Nernst Equation

The dependence of the cell potential on concentration results directly from the dependence of free energy on concentration. Recall from Chapter 16 that the equation

$$\Delta G = \Delta G° + RT \ln(Q)$$

where Q is the reaction quotient, was used to calculate the effect of concentration on ΔG. Since $\Delta G = -nF\mathscr{E}$ and $\Delta G° = -nF\mathscr{E}°$, the equation becomes

$$-nF\mathscr{E} = -nF\mathscr{E}° + RT \ln(Q)$$

Dividing each side of the equation by $-nF$ gives

$$\mathscr{E} = \mathscr{E}° - \frac{RT}{nF} \ln(Q) \tag{17.1}$$

Nernst was one of the pioneers in the development of electrochemical theory and is generally given credit for first stating the third law of thermodynamics. He won the Nobel Prize in chemistry in 1920.

Equation (17.1), which gives the relationship between the cell potential and the concentrations of the cell components, is commonly called the **Nernst equation,** after the German chemist Walther Hermann Nernst (1864–1941).

The Nernst equation is often given in a form that is valid at 25°C:

$$\mathscr{E} = \mathscr{E}° - \frac{0.0591}{n} \log(Q)$$

Using this relationship, we can calculate the potential of a cell in which some or all of the components are not in their standard states.

For example, $\mathscr{E}°_{cell}$ is 0.48 V for the galvanic cell based on the reaction

$$2Al(s) + 3Mn^{2+}(aq) \longrightarrow 2Al^{3+}(aq) + 3Mn(s)$$

Consider a cell in which

$$[Mn^{2+}] = 0.50\,M \quad \text{and} \quad [Al^{3+}] = 1.50\,M$$

The cell potential at 25°C for these concentrations can be calculated using the Nernst equation:

$$\mathscr{E}_{cell} = \mathscr{E}°_{cell} - \frac{0.0591}{n} \log(Q)$$

We know that

$$\mathscr{E}°_{cell} = 0.48\text{ V}$$

and

$$Q = \frac{[Al^{3+}]^2}{[Mn^{2+}]^3} = \frac{(1.50)^2}{(0.50)^3} = 18$$

Since the half-reactions are

$$\begin{aligned} \text{Oxidation:} \quad & 2Al \longrightarrow 2Al^{3+} + 6e^- \\ \text{Reduction:} \quad & 3Mn^{2+} + 6e^- \longrightarrow 3Mn \end{aligned}$$

we know that

$$n = 6$$

Thus

$$\mathscr{E}_{cell} = 0.48 - \frac{0.0591}{6} \log(18)$$

$$= 0.48 - \frac{0.0591}{6}(1.26) = 0.48 - 0.01 = 0.47\text{ V}$$

Note that the cell voltage decreases slightly because of the nonstandard concentrations. This change is consistent with the predictions of Le Châtelier's principle (see Sample Exercise 17.5). In this case, since the reactant concentration is lower than 1.0 *M* and the product concentration is higher than 1.0 *M*, $\mathscr{E}_{cell}$ is less than $\mathscr{E}°_{cell}$.

The potential calculated from the Nernst equation is the maximum potential before any current flow has occurred. As the cell discharges and current flows from anode to cathode, the concentrations will change, and as a result, $\mathscr{E}_{cell}$ will change. In fact, *the cell will spontaneously discharge until it reaches equilibrium,* at which point

$$Q = K \text{ (the equilibrium constant)} \quad \text{and} \quad \mathscr{E}_{cell} = 0$$

A "dead" battery is one in which the cell reaction has reached equilibrium, and there is no longer any chemical driving force to push electrons through the wire. In other words, *at equilibrium, the components in the two cell compartments have the same free energy, and $\Delta G = 0$ for the cell reaction at the equilibrium concentrations.* The cell no longer has the ability to do work.

Sample Exercise 17.7	**The Nernst Equation**

Describe the cell based on the following half-reactions:

$$VO_2^+ + 2H^+ + e^- \longrightarrow VO^{2+} + H_2O \qquad \mathscr{E}° = 1.00 \text{ V} \qquad (1)$$

$$Zn^{2+} + 2e^- \longrightarrow Zn \qquad \mathscr{E}° = -0.76 \text{ V} \qquad (2)$$

where

$$T = 25°C$$
$$[VO_2^+] = 2.0 \, M$$
$$[H^+] = 0.50 \, M$$
$$[VO^{2+}] = 1.0 \times 10^{-2} \, M$$
$$[Zn^{2+}] = 1.0 \times 10^{-1} \, M$$

Solution

The balanced cell reaction is obtained by reversing reaction (2) and multiplying reaction (1) by 2:

2 × reaction (1)	$2VO_2^+ + 4H^+ + 2e^- \longrightarrow 2VO^{2+} + 2H_2O$	$\mathscr{E}°$ (cathode) = 1.00 V
Reaction (2) reversed	$Zn \longrightarrow Zn^{2+} + 2e^-$	$-\mathscr{E}°$ (anode) = 0.76 V

Cell reaction: $2VO_2^+(aq) + 4H^+(aq) + Zn(s) \longrightarrow 2VO^{2+}(aq) + 2H_2O(l) + Zn^{2+}(aq)$ $\mathscr{E}°_{cell} = 1.76 \text{ V}$

Since the cell contains components at concentrations other than 1 M, we must use the Nernst equation, where $n = 2$ (since two electrons are transferred), to calculate the cell potential. At 25°C we can use the equation

$$\mathscr{E} = \mathscr{E}°_{cell} - \frac{0.0591}{n} \log(Q)$$

$$= 1.76 - \frac{0.0591}{2} \log\left(\frac{[Zn^{2+}][VO^{2+}]^2}{[VO_2^+]^2[H^+]^4}\right)$$

$$= 1.76 - \frac{0.0591}{2} \log\left(\frac{(1.0 \times 10^{-1})(1.0 \times 10^{-2})^2}{(2.0)^2(0.50)^4}\right)$$

$$= 1.76 - \frac{0.0591}{2} \log(4 \times 10^{-5}) = 1.76 + 0.13 = 1.89 \text{ V}$$

The cell diagram is given in Fig. 17.11.

FIGURE 17.11
Schematic diagram of the cell described in Sample Exercise 17.7.

See Exercises 17.55 through 17.58.

Reference solution of
dilute hydrochloric acid

Silver wire coated with
silver chloride

Thin-walled membrane

FIGURE 17.12
A glass electrode contains a reference solution of dilute hydrochloric acid in contact with a thin glass membrane in which a silver wire coated with silver chloride has been embedded. When the electrode is dipped into a solution containing H^+ ions, the electrode potential is determined by the difference in $[H^+]$ between the two solutions.

Ion-Selective Electrodes

Because the cell potential is sensitive to the concentrations of the reactants and products involved in the cell reaction, measured potentials can be used to determine the concentration of an ion. A pH meter (see Fig. 14.9) is a familiar example of an instrument that measures concentration using an observed potential. The pH meter has three main components: a standard electrode of known potential, a special **glass electrode** that changes potential depending on the concentration of H^+ ions in the solution into which it is dipped, and a potentiometer that measures the potential between the electrodes. The potentiometer reading is automatically converted electronically to a direct reading of the pH of the solution being tested.

The glass electrode (see Fig. 17.12) contains a reference solution of dilute hydrochloric acid in contact with a thin glass membrane. The electrical potential of the glass electrode depends on the difference in $[H^+]$ between the reference solution and the solution into which it is dipped. Thus the electrical potential varies with the pH of the solution being tested.

Electrodes that are sensitive to the concentration of a particular ion are called **ion-selective electrodes,** of which the glass electrode for pH measurement is just one example. Glass electrodes can be made sensitive to such ions as Na^+, K^+, or NH_4^+ by changing the composition of the glass. Other ions can be detected if an appropriate crystal replaces the glass membrane. For example, a crystal of lanthanum(III) fluoride (LaF_3) can be used in an electrode to measure $[F^-]$. Solid silver sulfide (Ag_2S) can be used to measure $[Ag^+]$ and $[S^{2-}]$. Some of the ions that can be detected by ion-selective electrodes are listed in Table 17.2.

Calculation of Equilibrium Constants for Redox Reactions

The quantitative relationship between $\mathscr{E}°$ and $\Delta G°$ allows calculation of equilibrium constants for redox reactions. For a cell at equilibrium,

$$\mathscr{E}_{cell} = 0 \quad \text{and} \quad Q = K$$

Applying these conditions to the Nernst equation valid at 25°C,

$$\mathscr{E} = \mathscr{E}° - \frac{0.0591}{n} \log(Q)$$

TABLE 17.2 Some Ions Whose Concentrations Can Be Detected by Ion-Selective Electrodes

Cations	Anions
H^+	Br^-
Cd^{2+}	Cl^-
Ca^{2+}	CN^-
Cu^{2+}	F^-
K^+	NO_3^-
Ag^+	S^{2-}
Na^+	

gives

$$0 = \mathscr{E}° - \frac{0.0591}{n} \log(K)$$

or

$$\log(K) = \frac{n\mathscr{E}°}{0.0591} \quad \text{at } 25°C$$

| Sample Exercise 17.8 | ### Equilibrium Constants from Cell Potentials |

For the oxidation–reduction reaction

$$S_4O_6^{2-}(aq) + Cr^{2+}(aq) \longrightarrow Cr^{3+}(aq) + S_2O_3^{2-}(aq)$$

the appropriate half-reactions are

$$S_4O_6^{2-} + 2e^- \longrightarrow 2S_2O_3^{2-} \qquad \mathscr{E}° = 0.17 \text{ V} \qquad (1)$$
$$Cr^{3+} + e^- \longrightarrow Cr^{2+} \qquad \mathscr{E}° = -0.50 \text{ V} \qquad (2)$$

Balance the redox reaction, and calculate $\mathscr{E}°$ and K (at 25°C).

Solution

To obtain the balanced reaction, we must reverse reaction (2), multiply it by 2, and add it to reaction (1):

Reaction (1)	$S_4O_6^{2-} + 2e^- \longrightarrow 2S_2O_3^{2-}$	$\mathscr{E}°$ (cathode) = 0.17 V
2 × reaction (2) reversed	$2(Cr^{2+} \longrightarrow Cr^{3+} + e^-)$	$-\mathscr{E}°$ (anode) = $-(-0.50)$ V
Cell reaction:	$2Cr^{2+}(aq) + S_4O_6^{2-}(aq) \longrightarrow 2Cr^{3+}(aq) + 2S_2O_3^{2-}(aq)$	$\mathscr{E}° = 0.67$ V

In this reaction, 2 moles of electrons are transferred for every unit of reaction, that is, for every 2 mol Cr^{2+} reacting with 1 mol $S_4O_6^{2-}$ to form 2 mol Cr^{3+} and 2 mol $S_2O_3^{2-}$. Thus $n = 2$. Then

$$\log(K) = \frac{n\mathscr{E}°}{0.0591} = \frac{2(0.67)}{0.0591} = 22.6$$

The value of K is found by taking the antilog of 22.6:

$$K = 10^{22.6} = 4 \times 10^{22}$$

This very large equilibrium constant is not unusual for a redox reaction.

The blue solution contains Cr^{2+} ions, and the green solution contains Cr^{3+} ions.

See Exercises 17.65, 17.66, 17.69, and 17.70.

17.5 Batteries

A **battery** is a galvanic cell or, more commonly, a group of galvanic cells connected in series, where the potentials of the individual cells add to give the total battery potential. Batteries are a source of direct current and have become an essential source of portable power in our society. In this section we examine the most common types of batteries. Some new batteries currently being developed are described at the end of the chapter.

Lead Storage Battery

Since about 1915 when self-starters were first used in automobiles, the **lead storage battery** has been a major factor in making the automobile a practical means of transportation. This type of battery can function for several years under temperature extremes from $-30°F$ to $120°F$ and under incessant punishment from rough roads.

CHEMICAL IMPACT

Printed Batteries

Soon you may reach for a compact disc in your local record store and, as you touch it, the package will start playing one of the songs on the disc. Or you may stop to look at a product because the package begins to glow as you pass it in the store. These effects could happen soon thanks to the invention of a flexible, superthin battery that can actually be printed onto the package. This battery was developed by Power Paper, Ltd., a company founded by Baruch Levanon and several colleagues.

The battery developed by Power Paper consists of five layers of zinc (anode) and manganese dioxide (cathode) and is only 0.5 millimeter thick. The battery can be printed onto paper with a regular printing press and appears to present no environmental hazards.

The new battery has been licensed by International Paper Company, which intends to use it to bring light, sound, and other special effects to packaging to entice potential customers. You might see talking, singing, or glowing packages on the shelves within a year or two.

A CD case with an ultrathin battery that can be "printed" on packages like ink.

H₂SO₄
electrolyte
solution

Anode (lead
grid filled with
spongy lead)

Cathode (lead
grid filled with
spongy PbO₂)

FIGURE 17.13
One of the six cells in a 12-V lead storage battery. The anode consists of a lead grid filled with spongy lead, and the cathode is a lead grid filled with lead dioxide. The cell also contains 38% (by mass) sulfuric acid.

In this battery, lead serves as the anode, and lead coated with lead dioxide serves as the cathode. Both electrodes dip into an electrolyte solution of sulfuric acid. The electrode reactions are

Anode reaction:	$Pb + HSO_4^- \longrightarrow PbSO_4 + H^+ + 2e^-$
Cathode reaction:	$PbO_2 + HSO_4^- + 3H^+ + 2e^- \longrightarrow PbSO_4 + 2H_2O$

Cell reaction: $Pb(s) + PbO_2(s) + 2H^+(aq) + 2HSO_4^-(aq) \longrightarrow 2PbSO_4(s) + 2H_2O(l)$

The typical automobile lead storage battery has six cells connected in series. Each cell contains multiple electrodes in the form of grids (Fig. 17.13) and produces approximately 2 V, to give a total battery potential of about 12 V. Note from the cell reaction that sulfuric acid is consumed as the battery discharges. This lowers the density of the electrolyte solution from its initial value of about 1.28 g/cm³ in the fully charged battery. As a result, the condition of the battery can be monitored by measuring the density of the sulfuric acid solution. The solid lead sulfate formed in the cell reaction during discharge adheres to the grid surfaces of the electrodes. The battery is recharged by forcing current through it in the opposite direction to reverse the cell reaction. A car's battery is continuously charged by an alternator driven by the automobile engine.

An automobile with a dead battery can be "jump-started" by connecting its battery to the battery in a running automobile. This process can be dangerous, however, because the resulting flow of current causes electrolysis of water in the dead battery, producing hydrogen and oxygen gases (see Section 17.7 for details). Disconnecting the jumper cables after the disabled car starts causes an arc that can ignite the gaseous

CHEMICAL IMPACT

Thermophotovoltaics: Electricity from Heat

A photovoltaic cell transforms the energy of sunlight into an electric current. These devices are used to power calculators, electric signs in rural areas, experimental cars, and an increasing number of other devices. But what happens at night or on cloudy days? Usually photovoltaic power sources employ a battery as a reserve energy source when light levels are low.

Now there is an emerging technology, called *thermophotovoltaics* (TPV), that uses a heat source instead of the sun for energy. These devices can operate at night or on an overcast day without a battery. Although TPV devices could use many different sources of heat, the examples currently under development use a propane burner. To produce an electric current, the radiant heat from the burner is used to excite a "radiator," a device that emits infrared (IR) radiation when heated. The emitted IR radiation then falls on a "converter," which is a semiconductor that contains p–n junctions. The IR radiation excites electrons from valence bands to conduction bands in the semiconductor so that the electrons can flow as a current. A schematic of a TPV generator is illustrated in the diagram.

TPV technology has advanced recently because researchers have found that it is possible to use radiators such as silicon carbide, which can operate at relatively low temperatures (approximately 1000°C), with III–V semiconductor converters such as gallium antimonide (GSb) or gallium arsenide (GaAs). While development work continues on many fronts, the first commercial TPV product is being marketed by JX Crystals of Issaquah, Washington. The product—Midnight Sun—is a propane-powered TPV generator that can produce 30 watts of electricity and is intended for use on boats to charge the batteries that power navigation and other essential equipment. Although at $3000 the TPV generator is more expensive than a conventional diesel-powered generator, Midnight Sun is silent and more reliable because it has no moving parts.

Although TPV technology is still in its infancy, it has many possible uses. The utilization of industrial waste heat—generated by glass and steel manufacturing and other industries—could establish a huge market for TPV. For example, two-thirds of the energy used in the manufacture of glass ends up as waste heat. If a significant quantity of this

mixture. If this happens, the battery may explode, ejecting corrosive sulfuric acid. This problem can be avoided by connecting the ground jumper cable to a part of the engine remote from the battery. Any arc produced when this cable is disconnected will then be harmless.

Traditional types of storage batteries require periodic "topping off" because the water in the electrolyte solution is depleted by the electrolysis that accompanies the charging process. Recent types of batteries have electrodes made of an alloy of calcium and lead that inhibits the electrolysis of water. These batteries can be sealed, since they require no addition of water.

It is rather amazing that in the 85 years in which lead storage batteries have been used, no better system has been found. Although a lead storage battery does provide excellent service, it has a useful lifetime of 3 to 5 years in an automobile. While it might seem that the battery could undergo an indefinite number of discharge/charge cycles, physical damage from road shock and chemical side-reactions eventually cause it to fail.

Other Batteries

— Anode
(zinc inner case)

— Cathode
(graphite rod)

— Paste of MnO_2, NH_4Cl, and carbon

FIGURE 17.14
A common dry cell battery.

The calculators, electronic games, digital watches, and portable CD players that are so familiar to us are all powered by small, efficient batteries. The common **dry cell battery** was invented more than 100 years ago by George Leclanché (1839–1882), a French chemist. In its *acid version,* the dry cell battery contains a zinc inner case that acts as the anode and a carbon rod in contact with a moist paste of solid MnO_2, solid NH_4Cl, and carbon that acts as the cathode (Fig. 17.14). The half-reactions are complex but can be

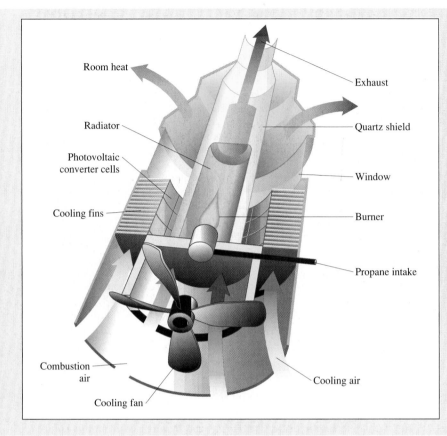

now wasted energy could be used to produce electricity, this would have tremendous fiscal implications.

Another promising application of TPV technology is for cars with hybrid energy sources. For example, an experimental electric car built at Western Washington University uses a 10-kW TPV generator to supplement the batteries that serve as the main power source.

Projections indicate that TPV devices could account for $500 million in sales by 2005, mainly by substituting TPV generators for small diesel-powered generators used on boats and by the military in the field. It appears that this technology has a hot future.

Diagram of a TPV generator.

approximated as follows:

Anode reaction: $$Zn \longrightarrow Zn^{2+} + 2e^-$$

Cathode reaction: $$2NH_4^+ + 2MnO_2 + 2e^- \longrightarrow Mn_2O_3 + 2NH_3 + H_2O$$

This cell produces a potential of about 1.5 V.

In the *alkaline version* of the dry cell battery, the solid NH_4Cl is replaced with KOH or NaOH. In this case the half-reactions can be approximated as follows:

Anode reaction: $$Zn + 2OH^- \longrightarrow ZnO + H_2O + 2e^-$$

Cathode reaction: $$2MnO_2 + H_2O + 2e^- \longrightarrow Mn_2O_3 + 2OH^-$$

The alkaline dry cell lasts longer mainly because the zinc anode corrodes less rapidly under basic conditions than under acidic conditions.

Other types of useful batteries include the *silver cell*, which has a Zn anode and a cathode that employs Ag_2O as the oxidizing agent in a basic environment. *Mercury cells*, often used in calculators, have a Zn anode and a cathode involving HgO as the oxidizing agent in a basic medium (see Fig. 17.15).

An especially important type of battery is the *nickel–cadmium battery,* in which the electrode reactions are

Anode reaction: $$Cd + 2OH^- \longrightarrow Cd(OH)_2 + 2e^-$$

Cathode reaction: $$NiO_2 + 2H_2O + 2e^- \longrightarrow Ni(OH)_2 + 2OH^-$$

Batteries for electronic watches are, by necessity, very tiny.

As in the lead storage battery, the products adhere to the electrodes. Therefore, a nickel–cadmium battery can be recharged an indefinite number of times.

CHEMICAL IMPACT

Fuel Cells for Cars

Your next car may be powered by a fuel cell. Until recently only affordable to NASA, fuel cells are now ready to become practical power plants in cars. Many car companies are testing vehicles that should be commercially available by 2004 or 2005. All of these vehicles are powered by hydrogen–oxygen fuel cells (see Fig. 17.16).

One of the most common types of fuel cells for automobiles uses a proton-exchange membrane (PEM). When H_2 releases electrons at the anode, H^+ ions form and then travel through the membrane to the cathode, where they combine with O_2 and electrons to form water. This cell generates about 0.7 V of power. To achieve the desired power level, several cells are stacked in series. Fuel cells of this type have appeared in several prototype vehicles, such as Nissan's Xterra FCV, Ford's Focus FCV, and DaimlerChrysler's Mercedes Benz NECAR 5 (see photo).

A gathering of several cars powered by fuel cells at Los Angeles Memorial Coliseum.

The main question yet to be answered deals with whether the fuel cells in these cars will be fueled by H_2 stored on board or by H_2 made from gasoline or methanol as it is needed. The latter systems include an onboard reformer that uses catalysts to produce H_2 from other fuels. The on-board storage of hydrogen could take place in a tank at high pressure (approximately 5000 psi) or it could utilize a metal-hydride–based solid. Energy Conversion Devices (ECD) of Troy, Michigan, is developing a storage system based on a magnesium alloy that absorbs H_2 to form a magnesium hydride. The H_2 gas can be released from this solid by heating it to 300°C. According to ECD, the alloy can be fully charged with H_2 in about 5 minutes, achieving a hydrogen density of 103 g/L. This density compares to 71 g/L for liquid hydrogen and 31 g/L for gaseous hydrogen at 5000 psi. ECD claims its storage system furnishes enough H_2 to power a fuel-cell car for 300 miles of driving.

Clearly, fuel-cell–powered cars are on the near horizon.

Fuel Cells

A **fuel cell** is *a galvanic cell for which the reactants are continuously supplied.* To illustrate the principles of fuel cells, let's consider the exothermic redox reaction of methane with oxygen:

$$CH_4(g) + 2O_2(g) \longrightarrow CO_2(g) + 2H_2O(g) + \text{energy}$$

FIGURE 17.15
A mercury battery of the type used in calculators.

Cathode (steel)

Insulation

Anode (zinc container)

Paste of HgO (oxidizing agent) in a basic medium of KOH and $Zn(OH)_2$

FIGURE 17.16
Schematic of the hydrogen–oxygen fuel cell.

Usually the energy from this reaction is released as heat to warm homes and to run machines. However, in a fuel cell designed to use this reaction, the energy is used to produce an electric current: The electrons flow from the reducing agent (CH_4) to the oxidizing agent (O_2) through a conductor.

The U.S. space program has supported extensive research to develop fuel cells. The space shuttle uses a fuel cell based on the reaction of hydrogen and oxygen to form water:

$$2H_2(g) + O_2(g) \longrightarrow 2H_2O(l)$$

A schematic of a fuel cell that employs this reaction is shown in Fig. 17.16. The half-reactions are

Anode reaction: $\quad 2H_2 + 4OH^- \longrightarrow 4H_2O + 4e^-$

Cathode reaction: $\quad 4e^- + O_2 + 2H_2O \longrightarrow 4OH^-$

A cell of this type weighing about 500 pounds has been designed for space vehicles, but this fuel cell is not practical enough for general use as a source of portable power. However, current research on portable electrochemical power is now proceeding at a rapid pace. In fact, cars powered by fuel cells are now being tested on the streets.

Fuel cells are also finding use as permanent power sources. For example, a power plant built in New York City contains stacks of hydrogen–oxygen fuel cells, which can be rapidly put on-line in response to fluctuating power demands. The hydrogen gas is obtained by decomposing the methane in natural gas. A plant of this type also has been constructed in Tokyo.

In addition, new fuel cells are under development that can use fuels such as methane and diesel directly without having to produce hydrogen first.

17.6 Corrosion

Corrosion can be viewed as the process of returning metals to their natural state—the ores from which they were originally obtained. Corrosion involves oxidation of the metal. Since corroded metal often loses its structural integrity and attractiveness, this spontaneous process has great economic impact. Approximately one-fifth of the iron and steel produced annually is used to replace rusted metal.

Metals corrode because they oxidize easily. Table 17.1 shows that, with the exception of gold, those metals commonly used for structural and decorative purposes all have standard reduction potentials less positive than that of oxygen gas. When any of these half-reactions is reversed (to show oxidation of the metal) and combined with the reduction half-reaction for oxygen, the result is a positive $\mathscr{E}°$ value. Thus the oxidation of most metals by oxygen is spontaneous (although we cannot tell from the potential how fast it will occur).

Some metals, such as copper, gold, silver, and platinum, are relatively difficult to oxidize. These are often called *noble metals*.

In view of the large difference in reduction potentials between oxygen and most metals, it is surprising that the problem of corrosion does not completely prevent the use of metals in air. However, most metals develop a thin oxide coating, which tends to protect their internal atoms against further oxidation. The metal that best demonstrates this phenomenon is aluminum. With a reduction potential of -1.7 V, aluminum should be easily oxidized by O_2. According to the apparent thermodynamics of the reaction, an aluminum airplane could dissolve in a rainstorm. The fact that this very active metal can be used as a structural material is due to the formation of a thin, adherent layer of aluminum oxide (Al_2O_3), more properly represented as $Al_2(OH)_6$, which greatly inhibits further corrosion. The potential of the "passive," oxide-coated aluminum is -0.6 V, a value that causes it to behave much like a noble metal.

Iron also can form a protective oxide coating. This coating is not an infallible shield against corrosion, however; when steel is exposed to oxygen in moist air, the oxide that forms tends to scale off and expose new metal surfaces to corrosion.

CHEMICAL IMPACT

Paint That Stops Rust—Completely

Traditionally, paint has provided the most economical method for protecting steel against corrosion. However, as people who live in the Midwest know well, paint cannot prevent a car from rusting indefinitely. Eventually, flaws develop in the paint that allow the ravages of rusting to take place.

This situation may soon change. Chemists at Glidden Research Center in Ohio have developed a paint called Rustmaster Pro that worked so well to prevent rusting in its initial tests that the scientists did not believe their results. Steel coated with the new paint showed no signs of rusting after an astonishing 10,000 hours of exposure in a salt spray chamber at 38°C.

Rustmaster is a water-based polymer formulation that prevents corrosion in two different ways. First, the polymer layer that cures in air forms a barrier impenetrable to both oxygen and water vapor. Second, the chemicals in the coating react with the steel surface to produce an interlayer between the metal and the polymer coating. This interlayer is a complex mineral called *pyroaurite* that contains cations of the form $[M_{1-x}Z_x(OH)_2]^{x+}$, where M is a 2+ ion (Mg^{2+}, Fe^{2+}, Zn^{2+}, Co^{2+}, or Ni^{2+}), Z is a 3+ ion (Al^{3+}, Fe^{3+}, Mn^{3+}, Co^{3+}, or Ni^{3+}), and x is a number between 0 and 1. The anions in pyroaurite are typically CO_3^{2-}, Cl^-, and/or SO_4^{2-}.

This pyroaurite interlayer is the real secret of the paint's effectiveness. Because the corrosion of steel has an electrochemical mechanism, motion of ions must be possible between the cathodic and anodic areas on the surface of the steel for rusting to occur. However, the pyroaurite interlayer grows into the neighboring polymer layer, thus preventing this crucial movement of ions. In effect, this layer prevents corrosion in the same way that removing the salt bridge prevents current from flowing in a galvanic cell.

In addition to having an extraordinary corrosion-fighting ability, Rustmaster yields an unusually small quantity of volatile solvents as it dries. A typical paint can produce from 1 to 5 kg of volatiles per gallon; Rustmaster produces only 0.05 kg. This paint may signal a new era in corrosion prevention.

The corrosion products of noble metals such as copper and silver are complex and affect the use of these metals as decorative materials. Under normal atmospheric conditions, copper forms an external layer of greenish copper carbonate called *patina. Silver tarnish* is silver sulfide (Ag_2S), which in thin layers gives the silver surface a richer appearance. Gold, with a positive standard reduction potential of 1.50 V, significantly larger than that for oxygen (1.23 V), shows no appreciable corrosion in air.

Corrosion of Iron

Since steel is the main structural material for bridges, buildings, and automobiles, controlling its corrosion is extremely important. To do this, we must understand the corrosion mechanism. Instead of being a direct oxidation process as we might expect, the corrosion of iron is an electrochemical reaction, as shown in Fig. 17.17.

FIGURE 17.17
The electrochemical corrosion of iron.

(Anode reaction: $Fe \longrightarrow Fe^{2+} + 2e^-$)   (Cathode reaction: $O_2 + 2H_2O + 4e^- \longrightarrow 4OH^-$)

Steel has a nonuniform surface because the chemical composition is not completely homogeneous. Also, physical strains leave stress points in the metal. These nonuniformities cause areas where the iron is more easily oxidized (*anodic regions*) than it is at others (*cathodic regions*). In the anodic regions each iron atom gives up two electrons to form the Fe^{2+} ion:

$$Fe \longrightarrow Fe^{2+} + 2e^-$$

The electrons that are released flow through the steel, as they do through the wire of a galvanic cell, to a cathodic region, where they react with oxygen:

$$O_2 + 2H_2O + 4e^- \longrightarrow 4OH^-$$

The Fe^{2+} ions formed in the anodic regions travel to the cathodic regions through the moisture on the surface of the steel, just as ions travel through a salt bridge in a galvanic cell. In the cathodic regions Fe^{2+} ions react with oxygen to form rust, which is hydrated iron(III) oxide of variable composition:

$$4Fe^{2+}(aq) + O_2(g) + (4 + 2n)H_2O(l) \longrightarrow 2Fe_2O_3 \cdot nH_2O(s) + 8H^+(aq)$$
$$\text{Rust}$$

Because of the migration of ions and electrons, rust often forms at sites that are remote from those where the iron dissolved to form pits in the steel. The degree of hydration of the iron oxide affects the color of the rust, which may vary from black to yellow to the familiar reddish brown.

The electrochemical nature of the rusting of iron explains the importance of moisture in the corrosion process. Moisture must be present to act as a kind of salt bridge between anodic and cathodic regions. Steel does not rust in dry air, a fact that explains why cars last much longer in the arid Southwest than in the relatively humid Midwest. Salt also accelerates rusting, a fact all too easily recognized by car owners in the colder parts of the United States, where salt is used on roads to melt snow and ice. The severity of rusting is greatly increased because the dissolved salt on the moist steel surface increases the conductivity of the aqueous solution formed there and thus accelerates the electrochemical corrosion process. Chloride ions also form very stable complex ions with Fe^{3+}, and this factor tends to encourage the dissolving of the iron, again accelerating the corrosion.

Prevention of Corrosion

Prevention of corrosion is an important way of conserving our natural resources of energy and metals. The primary means of protection is the application of a coating, most commonly paint or metal plating, to protect the metal from oxygen and moisture. Chromium and tin are often used to plate steel (see Section 17.8) because they oxidize to form a durable, effective oxide coating. Zinc, also used to coat steel in a process called **galvanizing,** forms a mixed oxide–carbonate coating. Since zinc is a more active metal than iron, as the potentials for the oxidation half-reactions show,

$$Fe \longrightarrow Fe^{2+} + 2e^- \qquad -\mathscr{E}° = 0.44 \text{ V}$$
$$Zn \longrightarrow Zn^{2+} + 2e^- \qquad -\mathscr{E}° = 0.76 \text{ V}$$

any oxidation that occurs dissolves zinc rather than iron. Recall that the reaction with the most positive standard potential has the greatest thermodynamic tendency to occur. Thus zinc acts as a "sacrificial" coating on steel.

Alloying is also used to prevent corrosion. *Stainless steel* contains chromium and nickel, both of which form oxide coatings that change steel's reduction potential to one characteristic of the noble metals. In addition, a new technology is now being developed

FIGURE 17.18
Cathodic protection of an underground pipe.

to create surface alloys. That is, instead of forming a metal alloy such as stainless steel, which has the same composition throughout, a cheaper carbon steel is treated by ion bombardment to produce a thin layer of stainless steel or other desirable alloy on the surface. In this process, a "plasma" or "ion gas" of the alloying ions is formed at high temperatures and is then directed onto the surface of the metal.

Cathodic protection is a method most often employed to protect steel in buried fuel tanks and pipelines. An active metal, such as magnesium, is connected by a wire to the pipeline or tank to be protected (Fig. 17.18). Because the magnesium is a better reducing agent than iron, electrons are furnished by the magnesium rather than by the iron, keeping the iron from being oxidized. As oxidation occurs, the magnesium anode dissolves, and so it must be replaced periodically. Ships' hulls are protected in a similar way by attaching bars of titanium metal to the steel hull (Fig. 17.18). In salt water the titanium acts as the anode and is oxidized instead of the steel hull (the cathode).

17.7 Electrolysis

An electrolytic cell uses electrical energy to produce a chemical change that would otherwise not occur spontaneously.

A galvanic cell produces current when an oxidation–reduction reaction proceeds spontaneously. A similar apparatus, an **electrolytic cell,** uses electrical energy to produce chemical change. The process of **electrolysis** involves *forcing a current through a cell to produce a chemical change for which the cell potential is negative;* that is, electrical work causes an otherwise nonspontaneous chemical reaction to occur. Electrolysis has great practical importance; for example, charging a battery, producing aluminum metal, and chrome plating an object are all done electrolytically.

To illustrate the difference between a galvanic cell and an electrolytic cell, consider the cell shown in Fig. 17.19(a) as it runs spontaneously to produce 1.10 V. In this *galvanic* cell the reaction at the anode is

$$Zn \longrightarrow Zn^{2+} + 2e^-$$

whereas at the cathode the reaction is

$$Cu^{2+} + 2e^- \longrightarrow Cu$$

Figure 17.19(b) shows an external power source forcing electrons through the cell in the *opposite* direction to that in (a). This requires an external potential greater than 1.10 V, which must be applied in opposition to the natural cell potential. This device is an *electrolytic cell.* Notice that since electron flow is opposite in the two cases, the anode and cathode are reversed between (a) and (b). Also, ion flow through the salt bridge is opposite in the two cells.

Now we will consider the stoichiometry of electrolytic processes, that is, *how much chemical change occurs with the flow of a given current for a specified time.* Suppose we wish to determine the mass of copper that is plated out when a current of 10.0 amps

FIGURE 17.19

(a) A standard galvanic cell based on the spontaneous reaction

$$Zn + Cu^{2+} \longrightarrow Zn^{2+} + Cu$$

(b) A standard electrolytic cell. A power source forces the opposite reaction

$$Cu + Zn^{2+} \longrightarrow Cu^{2+} + Zn$$

(an **ampere** [amp], abbreviated A, is *1 coulomb of charge per second*) is passed for 30.0 minutes through a solution containing Cu^{2+}. *Plating* means depositing the neutral metal on the electrode by reducing the metal ions in solution. In this case each Cu^{2+} ion requires two electrons to become an atom of copper metal:

$$Cu^{2+}(aq) + 2e^- \longrightarrow Cu(s)$$

This reduction process will occur at the cathode of the electrolytic cell.

To solve this stoichiometry problem, we need the following steps:

current and time	$\xrightarrow{1}$	quantity of charge in coulombs	$\xrightarrow{2}$	moles of electrons	$\xrightarrow{3}$	moles of copper	$\xrightarrow{4}$	grams of copper

➠ **1** **Since an amp is a coulomb of charge per second, we multiply the current by the time in seconds to obtain the total coulombs of charge passed into the Cu^{2+} solution at the cathode:**

$$\text{Coulombs of charge} = \text{amps} \times \text{seconds} = \frac{C}{s} \times s$$

$$= 10.0\frac{C}{s} \times 30.0 \text{ min} \times 60.0 \frac{s}{\text{min}}$$

$$= 1.80 \times 10^4 \text{ C}$$

➠ **2** **Since 1 mole of electrons carries a charge of 1 faraday, or 96,485 coulombs, we can calculate the number of moles of electrons required to carry 1.80×10^4 coulombs of charge:**

$$1.80 \times 10^4 \text{ C} \times \frac{1 \text{ mol e}^-}{96,485 \text{ C}} = 1.87 \times 10^{-1} \text{ mol e}^-$$

This means that 0.187 mole of electrons flowed into the Cu^{2+} solution.

➡ 3 Each Cu^{2+} ion requires two electrons to become a copper atom. Thus each mole of electrons produces $\frac{1}{2}$ mole of copper metal:

$$1.87 \times 10^{-1} \text{ mol e}^- \times \frac{1 \text{ mol Cu}}{2 \text{ mol e}^-} = 9.35 \times 10^{-2} \text{ mol Cu}$$

➡ 4 We now know the moles of copper metal plated onto the cathode, and we can calculate the mass of copper formed:

$$9.35 \times 10^{-2} \text{ mol Cu} \times \frac{63.546 \text{ g}}{\text{mol Cu}} = 5.94 \text{ g Cu}$$

| Sample Exercise 17.9 | **Electroplating** |

Sample Exercise 17.9 describes only the half-cell of interest. There also must be an anode at which oxidation is occurring.

How long must a current of 5.00 A be applied to a solution of Ag^+ to produce 10.5 g silver metal?

Solution

In this case, we must use the steps given earlier in reverse:

| grams of silver | → | moles of silver | → | moles of electrons required | → | coulombs of charge required | → | time required for plating |

$$10.5 \text{ g Ag} \times \frac{1 \text{ mol Ag}}{107.868 \text{ g Ag}} = 9.73 \times 10^{-2} \text{ mol Ag}$$

Each Ag^+ ion requires one electron to become a silver atom:

$$Ag^+ + e^- \longrightarrow Ag$$

Thus 9.73×10^{-2} mol of electrons is required, and we can calculate the quantity of charge carried by these electrons:

$$9.73 \times 10^{-2} \text{ mol e}^- \times \frac{96,485 \text{ C}}{\text{mol e}^-} = 9.39 \times 10^3 \text{ C}$$

The 5.00 A (5.00 C/s) of current must produce 9.39×10^3 C of charge. Thus

$$\left(5.00 \frac{C}{s}\right) \times (\text{time, in s}) = 9.39 \times 10^3 \text{ C}$$

$$\text{Time} = \frac{9.39 \times 10^3}{5.00} \text{ s} = 1.88 \times 10^3 \text{ s} = 31.3 \text{ min}$$

See Exercises 17.77 through 17.80.

Electrolysis of Water

We have seen that hydrogen and oxygen combine spontaneously to form water and that the accompanying decrease in free energy can be used to run a fuel cell to produce electricity. The reverse process, which is of course nonspontaneous, can be forced by electrolysis:

Anode reaction:	$2H_2O \longrightarrow O_2 + 4H^+ + 4e^-$	$-\mathscr{E}° = -1.23$ V
Cathode reaction:	$4H_2O + 4e^- \longrightarrow 2H_2 + 4OH^-$	$\mathscr{E}° = -0.83$ V
Net reaction:	$6H_2O \longrightarrow 2H_2 + O_2 + \underbrace{4(H^+ + OH^-)}_{4H_2O}$	$\mathscr{E}° = -2.06$ V

or

$$2H_2O \longrightarrow 2H_2 + O_2$$

Visualization: Electrolysis of Water

FIGURE 17.20
The electrolysis of water produces hydrogen gas at the cathode (on the right) and oxygen gas at the anode (on the left).

Note that these potentials assume an anode chamber with 1 M H^+ and a cathode chamber with 1 M OH^-. In pure water, where $[H^+] = [OH^-] = 10^{-7}$ M, the potential for the overall process is -1.23 V.

In practice, however, if platinum electrodes connected to a 6-V battery are dipped into pure water, no reaction is observed because pure water contains so few ions that only a negligible current can flow. However, addition of even a small amount of a soluble salt causes an immediate evolution of bubbles of hydrogen and oxygen, as illustrated in Fig. 17.20.

Electrolysis of Mixtures of Ions

Suppose a solution in an electrolytic cell contains the ions Cu^{2+}, Ag^+, and Zn^{2+}. If the voltage is initially very low and is gradually turned up, in which order will the metals be plated out onto the cathode? This question can be answered by looking at the standard reduction potentials of these ions:

$$Ag^+ + e^- \longrightarrow Ag \qquad \mathscr{E}° = 0.80 \text{ V}$$
$$Cu^{2+} + 2e^- \longrightarrow Cu \qquad \mathscr{E}° = 0.34 \text{ V}$$
$$Zn^{2+} + 2e^- \longrightarrow Zn \qquad \mathscr{E}° = -0.76 \text{ V}$$

Remember that the more *positive* the $\mathscr{E}°$ value, the more the reaction has a tendency to proceed in the direction indicated. Of the three reactions listed, the reduction of Ag^+ occurs most easily, and the order of oxidizing ability is

$$Ag^+ > Cu^{2+} > Zn^{2+}$$

This means that silver will plate out first as the potential is increased, followed by copper, and finally zinc.

Sample Exercise 17.10	**Relative Oxidizing Abilities**

An acidic solution contains the ions Ce^{4+}, VO_2^+, and Fe^{3+}. Using the $\mathscr{E}°$ values listed in Table 17.1, give the order of oxidizing ability of these species and predict which one will be reduced at the cathode of an electrolytic cell at the lowest voltage.

Solution

The half-reactions and $\mathscr{E}°$ values are

$$Ce^{4+} + e^- \longrightarrow Ce^{3+} \qquad \mathscr{E}° = 1.70 \text{ V}$$
$$VO_2^+ + 2H^+ + e^- \longrightarrow VO^{2+} + H_2O \qquad \mathscr{E}° = 1.00 \text{ V}$$
$$Fe^{3+} + e^- \longrightarrow Fe^{2+} \qquad \mathscr{E}° = 0.77 \text{ V}$$

The order of oxidizing ability is therefore

$$Ce^{4+} > VO_2^+ > Fe^{3+}$$

The Ce^{4+} ion will be reduced at the lowest voltage in an electrolytic cell.

See Exercise 17.89.

The principle described in this section is very useful, but it must be applied with some caution. For example, in the electrolysis of an aqueous solution of sodium chloride, we should be able to use $\mathscr{E}°$ values to predict the products. Of the major species in the solution

CHEMICAL IMPACT

The Chemistry of Sunken Treasure

When the galleon *Atocha* was destroyed on a reef by a hurricane in 1622, it was bound for Spain carrying approximately 47 tons of copper, gold, and silver from the New World. The bulk of the treasure was silver bars and coins packed in wooden chests. When treasure hunter Mel Fisher salvaged the silver in 1985, corrosion and marine growth had transformed the shiny metal into something that looked like coral. Restoring the silver to its original condition required an understanding of the chemical changes that had occurred in 350 years of being submerged in the ocean. Much of this chemistry we have already considered at various places in this text.

As the wooden chests containing the silver decayed, the oxygen supply was depleted, favoring the growth of certain bacteria that use the sulfate ion rather than oxygen as an oxidizing agent to generate energy. As these bacteria consume sulfate ions, they release hydrogen sulfide gas that reacts with silver to form black silver sulfide:

$$2Ag(s) + H_2S(aq) \longrightarrow Ag_2S(s) + H_2(g)$$

Thus, over the years, the surface of the silver became covered with a tightly adhering layer of corrosion, which fortunately protected the silver underneath and thus prevented total conversion of the silver to silver sulfide.

Silver coins and tankards salvaged from the wreck of the *Atocha*.

(Na^+, Cl^-, and H_2O), only Cl^- and H_2O can be readily oxidized. The half-reactions (written as oxidization processes) are

$$2Cl^- \longrightarrow Cl_2 + 2e^- \qquad -\mathscr{E}° = -1.36 \text{ V}$$
$$2H_2O \longrightarrow O_2 + 4H^+ + 4e^- \qquad -\mathscr{E}° = -1.23 \text{ V}$$

Since water has the more positive potential, we would expect to see O_2 produced at the anode because it is easier (thermodynamically) to oxidize H_2O than Cl^-. Actually, this does not happen. As the voltage is increased in the cell, the Cl^- ion is the first to be oxidized. A much higher potential than expected is required to oxidize water. The voltage required in excess of the expected value (called the *overvoltage*) is much greater for the production of O_2 than for Cl_2, which explains why chlorine is produced first.

The causes of overvoltage are very complex. Basically, the phenomenon is caused by difficulties in transferring electrons from the species in the solution to the atoms on the electrode across the electrode–solution interface. Because of this situation, $\mathscr{E}°$ values must be used cautiously in predicting the actual order of oxidation or reduction of species in an electrolytic cell.

Another change that took place as the wood decomposed was the formation of carbon dioxide. This shifted the equilibrium that is present in the ocean,

$$CO_2(aq) + H_2O(l) \rightleftharpoons HCO_3^-(aq) + H^+(aq)$$

to the right, producing higher concentrations of HCO_3^-. In turn, the HCO_3^- reacted with Ca^{2+} ions present in the seawater to form calcium carbonate:

$$Ca^{2+}(aq) + HCO_3^-(aq) \rightleftharpoons CaCO_3(s) + H^+(aq)$$

Calcium carbonate is the main component of limestone. Thus, over time, the corroded silver coins and bars became encased in limestone.

Both the limestone formation and the corrosion had to be dealt with. Since $CaCO_3$ contains the basic anion CO_3^{2-}, acid dissolves limestone:

$$2H^+(aq) + CaCO_3(s) \longrightarrow Ca^{2+}(aq) + CO_2(g) + H_2O(l)$$

Soaking the mass of coins in a buffered acidic bath for several hours allowed the individual pieces to be separated, and the black Ag_2S on the surfaces was revealed. An abrasive could not be used to remove this corrosion; it would have destroyed the details of the engraving—a very valuable feature of the coins to a historian or a collector—and it would have washed away some of the silver. Instead, the corrosion reaction was reversed through electrolytic reduction. The coins were connected to the cathode of an electrolytic cell in a dilute sodium hydroxide solution as represented in the figure.

As electrons flow, the Ag^+ ions in the silver sulfide are reduced to silver metal:

$$Ag_2S + 2e^- \longrightarrow Ag + S^{2-}$$

As a by-product, bubbles of hydrogen gas from the reduction of water form on the surface of the coins:

$$2H_2O + 2e^- \longrightarrow H_2(g) + 2OH^-$$

The agitation caused by the bubbles loosens the flakes of metal sulfide and helps clean the coins.

These procedures have made it possible to restore the treasure to very nearly its condition when the *Atocha* sailed many years ago.

17.8 Commercial Electrolytic Processes

The chemistry of metals is characterized by their ability to donate electrons to form ions. Because metals are typically such good reducing agents, most are found in nature in *ores,* mixtures of ionic compounds often containing oxide, sulfide, and silicate anions. The noble metals, such as gold, silver, and platinum, are more difficult to oxidize and are often found as pure metals.

Production of Aluminum

Aluminum is one of the most abundant elements on earth, ranking third behind oxygen and silicon. Since aluminum is a very active metal, it is found in nature as its oxide in an ore called *bauxite* (named after Les Baux, France, where it was discovered in 1821). Production of aluminum metal from its ore proved to be more difficult than production of most other metals. In 1782 Lavoisier recognized aluminum to be a metal "whose affinity for oxygen is so strong that it cannot be overcome by any known reducing agent." As a result, pure aluminum metal remained unknown. Finally, in 1854

FIGURE 17.21
Charles Martin Hall (1863–1914) was a student at Oberlin College in Ohio when he first became interested in aluminum. One of his professors commented that anyone who could manufacture aluminum cheaply would make a fortune, and Hall decided to give it a try. The 21-year-old Hall worked in a wooden shed near his house with an iron frying pan as a container, a blacksmith's forge as a heat source, and galvanic cells constructed from fruit jars. Using these crude galvanic cells, Hall found that he could produce aluminum by passing a current through a molten Al_2O_3/Na_3AlF_6 mixture. By a strange coincidence, Paul Heroult, a Frenchman who was born and died in the same years as Hall, made the same discovery at about the same time.

a process was found for producing metallic aluminum using sodium, but aluminum remained a very expensive rarity. In fact, it is said that Napoleon III served his most honored guests with aluminum forks and spoons, while the others had to settle for gold and silver utensils.

The breakthrough came in 1886 when two men, Charles M. Hall in the United States and Paul Heroult in France, almost simultaneously discovered a practical electrolytic process for producing aluminum (see Fig. 17.21). The key factor in the *Hall–Heroult process* is the use of molten cryolite (Na_3AlF_6) as the solvent for the aluminum oxide.

Electrolysis is possible only if ions can move to the electrodes. A common method for producing ion mobility is dissolving the substance to be electrolyzed in water. This is not possible in the case of aluminum because water is more easily reduced than Al^{3+}, as the following standard reduction potentials show:

$$Al^{3+} + 3e^- \longrightarrow Al \qquad \mathscr{E}° = -1.66 \text{ V}$$
$$2H_2O + 2e^- \longrightarrow H_2 + 2OH^- \qquad \mathscr{E}° = -0.83 \text{ V}$$

Thus aluminum metal cannot be plated out of an aqueous solution of Al^{3+}.

Ion mobility also can be produced by melting the salt. But the melting point of solid Al_2O_3 is much too high (2050°C) to allow practical electrolysis of the molten oxide. A mixture of Al_2O_3 and Na_3AlF_6, however, has a melting point of 1000°C, and the resulting molten mixture can be used to obtain aluminum metal electrolytically. Because of this discovery by Hall and Heroult, the price of aluminum plunged (see Table 17.3), and its use became economically feasible.

Bauxite is not pure aluminum oxide (called *alumina*); it also contains the oxides of iron, silicon, and titanium, and various silicate materials. To obtain the pure hydrated alumina ($Al_2O_3 \cdot nH_2O$), the crude bauxite is treated with aqueous sodium hydroxide. Being amphoteric, alumina dissolves in the basic solution:

$$Al_2O_3(s) + 2OH^-(aq) \longrightarrow 2AlO_2^-(aq) + H_2O(l)$$

The other metal oxides, which are basic, remain as solids. The solution containing the aluminate ion (AlO_2^-) is separated from the sludge of the other oxides and is acidified with carbon dioxide gas, causing the hydrated alumina to reprecipitate:

$$2CO_2(g) + 2AlO_2^-(aq) + (n + 1)H_2O(l) \longrightarrow 2HCO_3^-(aq) + Al_2O_3 \cdot nH_2O(s)$$

The purified alumina is then mixed with cryolite and melted, and the aluminum ion is reduced to aluminum metal in an electrolytic cell of the type shown in Fig. 17.22. Because the electrolyte solution contains a large number of aluminum-containing ions, the chemistry is not completely clear. However, the alumina probably reacts with the cryolite anion as follows:

$$Al_2O_3 + 4AlF_6^{3-} \longrightarrow 3Al_2OF_6^{2-} + 6F^-$$

The electrode reactions are thought to be

Cathode reaction: $\qquad AlF_6^{3-} + 3e^- \longrightarrow Al + 6F^-$
Anode reaction: $\quad 2Al_2OF_6^{2-} + 12F^- + C \longrightarrow 4AlF_6^{3-} + CO_2 + 4e^-$

The overall cell reaction can be written as

$$2Al_2O_3 + 3C \longrightarrow 4Al + 3CO_2$$

The aluminum produced in this electrolytic process is 99.5% pure. To be useful as a structural material, aluminum is alloyed with metals such as zinc (used for trailer and aircraft construction) and manganese (used for cooking utensils, storage tanks, and highway signs). The production of aluminum consumes about 5% of all the electricity used in the United States.

TABLE 17.3　The Price of Aluminum over the Past Century

Date	Price of Aluminum ($/lb)*
1855	100,000
1885	100
1890	2
1895	0.50
1970	0.30
1980	0.80
1990	0.74

*Note the precipitous drop in price after the discovery of the Hall–Heroult process.

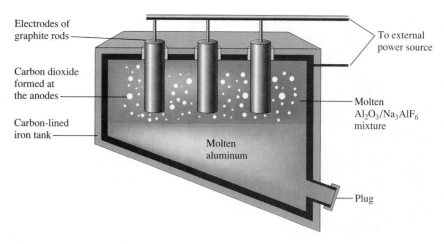

Electrodes of
graphite rods

Carbon dioxide
formed at
the anodes

Carbon-lined
iron tank

To external
power source

Molten
Al_2O_3/Na_3AlF_6
mixture

Molten
aluminum

Plug

FIGURE 17.22

A schematic diagram of an electrolytic cell for producing aluminum by the Hall–Heroult process. Because molten aluminum is more dense than the mixture of molten cryolite and alumina, it settles to the bottom of the cell and is drawn off periodically. The graphite electrodes are gradually eaten away and must be replaced from time to time. The cell operates at a current flow of up to 250,000 A.

Electrorefining of Metals

Purification of metals is another important application of electrolysis. For example, impure copper from the chemical reduction of copper ore is cast into large slabs that serve as the anodes for electrolytic cells. Aqueous copper sulfate is the electrolyte, and thin sheets of ultrapure copper function as the cathodes (see Fig. 17.23).

The main reaction at the anode is

$$Cu \longrightarrow Cu^{2+} + 2e^-$$

Other metals such as iron and zinc are also oxidized from the impure anode:

$$Zn \longrightarrow Zn^{2+} + 2e^-$$
$$Fe \longrightarrow Fe^{2+} + 2e^-$$

FIGURE 17.23

Ultrapure copper sheets that serve as the cathodes are lowered between slabs of impure copper that serve as the anodes into a tank containing an aqueous solution of copper sulfate ($CuSO_4$). It takes about four weeks for the anodes to dissolve and for the pure copper to be deposited on the cathodes.

(a)

(b)

FIGURE 17.24
(a) A silver-plated teapot. Silver plating is often used to beautify and protect cutlery and items of table service.
(b) Schematic of the electroplating of a spoon. The item to be plated is the cathode, and the anode is a silver bar.
Silver is plated out at the cathode: $Ag^+ + e^- \rightarrow Ag$. Note that a salt bridge is not needed here because Ag^+ ions
are involved at both electrodes.

Noble metal impurities in the anode are not oxidized at the voltage used; they fall to the
bottom of the cell to form a sludge, which is processed to remove the valuable silver, gold,
and platinum.

The Cu^{2+} ions from the solution are deposited onto the cathode

$$Cu^{2+} + 2e^- \longrightarrow Cu$$

producing copper that is 99.95% pure.

Metal Plating

Metals that readily corrode can often be protected by the application of a thin coating of
a metal that resists corrosion. Examples are "tin" cans, which are actually steel cans with
a thin coating of tin, and chrome-plated steel bumpers for automobiles.

An object can be plated by making it the cathode in a tank containing ions of the
plating metal. The silver plating of a spoon is shown schematically in Fig. 17.24(b). In
an actual plating process, the solution also contains ligands that form complexes with the
silver ion. By lowering the concentration of Ag^+ in this way, a smooth, even coating of
silver is obtained.

Electrolysis of Sodium Chloride

Addition of a nonvolatile solute lowers the
melting point of the solvent, molten NaCl
in this case.

Sodium metal is mainly produced by the electrolysis of molten sodium chloride. Because
solid NaCl has a rather high melting point (800°C), it is usually mixed with solid $CaCl_2$ to
lower the melting point to about (600°C). The mixture is then electrolyzed in a **Downs cell,**
as illustrated in Fig. 17.25, where the reactions are

Anode reaction: $\qquad\qquad 2Cl^- \longrightarrow Cl_2 + 2e^-$

Cathode reaction: $\qquad Na^+ + e^- \longrightarrow Na$

Cl$_2$ gas

Liquid sodium metal

Molten mixture of NaCl and CaCl$_2$

Cathode

Cathode

Iron screen

Iron screen

Anode

FIGURE 17.25
The Downs cell for the electrolysis of molten sodium chloride. The cell is designed so that the sodium and chlorine produced cannot come into contact with each other to re-form NaCl.

At the temperatures in the Downs cell, the sodium is liquid and is drained off, then cooled, and cast into blocks. Because it is so reactive, sodium must be stored in an inert solvent, such as mineral oil, to prevent its oxidation.

Electrolysis of aqueous sodium chloride (brine) is an important industrial process for the production of chlorine and sodium hydroxide. In fact, this process is the second largest consumer of electricity in the United States, after the production of aluminum. Sodium is not produced in this process under normal circumstances because H$_2$O is more easily reduced than Na$^+$, as the standard reduction potentials show:

$$Na^+ + e^- \longrightarrow Na \qquad \mathscr{E}° = -2.71 \text{ V}$$
$$2H_2O + 2e^- \longrightarrow H_2 + 2OH^- \qquad \mathscr{E}° = -0.83 \text{ V}$$

Hydrogen, not sodium, is produced at the cathode.

For the reasons we discussed in Section 17.7, chlorine gas is produced at the anode. Thus the electrolysis of brine produces hydrogen and chlorine:

Anode reaction: $\qquad 2Cl^- \longrightarrow Cl_2 + 2e^-$

Cathode reaction: $\qquad 2H_2O + 2e^- \longrightarrow H_2 + 2OH^-$

It leaves a solution containing dissolved NaOH and NaCl.

The contamination of the sodium hydroxide by NaCl can be virtually eliminated using a special **mercury cell** for electrolyzing brine (see Fig. 17.26). In this cell, mercury is the conductor at the cathode, and because hydrogen gas has an extremely high overvoltage with a mercury electrode, Na$^+$ is reduced instead of H$_2$O. The resulting sodium metal dissolves in the mercury, forming a liquid alloy, which is then pumped to a chamber where the dissolved sodium reacts with water to produce hydrogen:

$$2Na(s) + 2H_2O(l) \longrightarrow 2Na^+(aq) + 2OH^-(aq) + H_2(g)$$

Relatively pure solid NaOH can be recovered from the aqueous solution, and the regenerated mercury is then pumped back to the electrolysis cell. This process, called the **chlor–alkali process,** was the main method for producing chlorine and sodium hydroxide in the United States for many years. However, because of the environmental problems associated with the mercury cell, it has been largely displaced in the

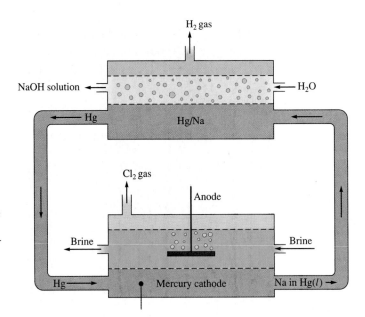

FIGURE 17.26
The mercury cell for production of chlorine and sodium hydroxide. The large overvoltage required to produce hydrogen at a mercury electrode means that Na^+ ions are reduced rather than water. The sodium formed dissolves in the liquid mercury and is pumped to a chamber where it reacts with water.

chlor–alkali industry by other technologies. In the United States, nearly 75% of the chlor–alkali production is now carried out in diaphragm cells. In a diaphragm cell the cathode and anode are separated by a diaphragm that allows passage of H_2O molecules, Na^+ ions, and, to a limited extent, Cl^- ions. The diaphragm does not allow OH^- ions to pass through it. Thus the H_2 and OH^- formed at the cathode are kept separate from the Cl_2 formed at the anode. The major disadvantage of this process is that the aqueous effluent pumped from the cathode compartment contains a mixture of sodium hydroxide and unreacted sodium chloride, which must be separated if pure sodium hydroxide is a desired product.

In the past 30 years, a new process has been developed in the chlor–alkali industry that employs a membrane to separate the anode and cathode compartments in brine electrolysis cells. The membrane is superior to a diaphragm because the membrane is impermeable to anions. Only cations can flow through the membrane. Because neither Cl^- nor OH^- ions can pass through the membrane separating the anode and cathode compartments, NaCl contamination of the NaOH formed at the cathode does not occur. Although membrane technology is now just becoming prominent in the United States, it is the dominant method for chlor–alkali production in Japan.

Key Terms

electrochemistry

Section 17.1
oxidation–reduction (redox) reaction
reducing agent
oxidizing agent
oxidation
reduction
half-reactions
salt bridge
porous disk
galvanic cell
anode
cathode

For Review

Electrochemistry
- The study of the interchange of chemical and electrical energy
- Employs oxidation–reduction reactions
- Galvanic cell: chemical energy is transformed into electrical energy by separating the oxidizing and reducing agents and forcing the electrons to travel through a wire
- Electrolytic cell: electrical energy is used to produce a chemical change

Galvanic cell
- Anode: the electrode where oxidation occurs
- Cathode: the electrode where reduction occurs

- The driving force behind the electron transfer is called the cell potential ($\mathscr{E}_{cell}$)
  - The potential is measured in units of volts (V), defined as a joule of work per coulomb of charge:

$$\mathscr{E}(V) = \frac{-\text{work (J)}}{\text{charge (C)}} = -\frac{w}{q}$$

  - A system of half-reactions, called standard reduction potentials, can be used to calculate the potentials of various cells
    - The half-reaction $2H^+ + 2e^- \longrightarrow H_2$ is arbitrarily assigned a potential of 0 V

Free energy and work
- The maximum work that a cell can perform is

$$-w_{max} = q\mathscr{E}_{max}$$

where $\mathscr{E}_{max}$ represents the cell potential when no current is flowing
- The actual work obtained from a cell is always less than the maximum because energy is lost through frictional heating of the wire when current flows
- For a process carried out at constant temperature and pressure, the change in free energy equals the maximum useful work obtainable from that process:

$$\Delta G = w_{max} = -q\mathscr{E}_{max} = -nF\mathscr{E}$$

where F (faraday) equals 96,485 C and n is the number of moles of electrons transferred in the process

Concentration cell
- A galvanic cell in which both compartments have the same components but at different concentrations
- The electrons flow in the direction that tends to equalize the concentrations

Nernst equation
- Shows how the cell potential depends on the concentrations of the cell components:

$$\mathscr{E} = \mathscr{E}_0 - \frac{0.0591}{n} \log Q \quad \text{at } 25°C$$

- When a galvanic cell is at equilibrium, $\mathscr{E} = 0$ and $Q = K$

Batteries
- A battery consists of a galvanic cell or group of cells connected in series that serve as a source of direct current
- Lead storage battery
  - Anode: lead
  - Cathode: lead coated with PbO_2
  - Electrolyte: $H_2SO_4(aq)$
- Dry cell battery
  - Contains a moist paste instead of a liquid electrolyte
  - Anode: usually Zn
  - Cathode: carbon rod in contact with an oxidizing agent (which varies depending on the application)

Fuel cells
- Galvanic cells in which the reactants are continuously supplied
- The H_2/O_2 fuel cell is based on the reaction between H_2 and O_2 to form water

Corrosion
- Involves the oxidation of metals to form mainly oxides and sulfides

- Some metals, such as aluminum and chromium, form a thin protective oxide coating that prevents further corrosion
- The corrosion of iron to form rust is an electrochemical process
  - The Fe^{2+} ions formed at anodic areas of the surface migrate through the moisture layer to cathodic regions, where they react with oxygen from the air
  - Iron can be protected from corrosion by coating it with paint or with a thin layer of metal such as chromium, tin, or zinc; by alloying; and by cathodic protection

Electrolysis
- Used to place a thin coating of metal onto steel
- Used to produce pure metals such as aluminum and copper

REVIEW QUESTIONS

1. What is electrochemistry? What are redox reactions? Explain the difference between a galvanic and an electrolytic cell.

2. Galvanic cells harness spontaneous oxidation–reduction reactions to produce work by producing a current. They do so by controlling the flow of electrons from the species oxidized to the species reduced. How is a galvanic cell designed? What is in the cathode compartment? The anode compartment? What purpose do electrodes serve? Which way do electrons always flow in the wire connecting the two electrodes in a galvanic cell? Why is it necessary to use a salt bridge or a porous disk in a galvanic cell? Which way do cations flow in the salt bridge? Which way do the anions flow? What is a cell potential and what is a volt?

3. Table 17.1 lists common half-reactions along with the standard reduction potential associated with each half-reaction. These standard reduction potentials are all relative to some standard. What is the standard (zero point)? If $\mathscr{E}°$ is positive for a half-reaction, what does it mean? If $\mathscr{E}°$ is negative for a half-reaction, what does it mean? Which species in Table 17.1 is most easily reduced? Least easily reduced? The reverse of the half-reactions in Table 17.1 are the oxidation half-reactions. How are standard oxidation potentials determined? In Table 17.1, which species is the best reducing agent? The worst reducing agent?

   To determine the standard cell potential for a redox reaction, the standard reduction potential is added to the standard oxidation potential. What must be true about this sum if the cell is to be spontaneous (produce a galvanic cell)? Standard reduction and oxidation potentials are intensive. What does this mean? Summarize how line notation is used to describe galvanic cells.

4. Consider the equation $\Delta G° = -nF\mathscr{E}°$. What are the four terms in this equation? Why does a minus sign appear in the equation? What does the superscript $°$ indicate?

5. The Nernst equation allows determination of the cell potential for a galvanic cell at nonstandard conditions. Write out the Nernst equation. What are nonstandard conditions? What do $\mathscr{E}$, $\mathscr{E}°$, n, and Q stand for in the Nernst equation? What does the Nernst equation reduce to when a redox reaction is at equilibrium? What are the signs of $\Delta G°$ and $\mathscr{E}°$ when $K < 1$? When $K > 1$? When $K = 1$? Explain the following statement: $\mathscr{E}$ determines spontaneity, while $\mathscr{E}°$ determines the equilibrium position. Under what conditions can you use $\mathscr{E}°$ to predict spontaneity?

6. What are concentration cells? What is $\mathscr{E}°$ in a concentration cell? What is the driving force for a concentration cell to produce a voltage? Is the higher or the lower ion concentration solution present at the anode? When the anode ion concentration is decreased and/or the cathode ion concentration is increased, both

give rise to larger cell potentials. Why? Concentration cells are commonly used to calculate the value of equilibrium constants for various reactions. For example, the silver concentration cell illustrated in Fig. 17.9 can be used to determine the K_{sp} value for AgCl(s). To do so, NaCl is added to the anode compartment until no more precipitate forms. The [Cl$^-$] in solution is then determined somehow. What happens to $\mathscr{E}_{cell}$ when NaCl is added to the anode compartment? To calculate the K_{sp} value, [Ag$^+$] must be calculated. Given the value of $\mathscr{E}_{cell}$, how is [Ag$^+$] determined at the anode?

7. Batteries are galvanic cells. What happens to $\mathscr{E}_{cell}$ as a battery discharges? Does a battery represent a system at equilibrium? Explain. What is $\mathscr{E}_{cell}$ when a battery reaches equilibrium? How are batteries and fuel cells alike? How are they different? The U.S. space program utilizes hydrogen–oxygen fuel cells to produce power for its spacecraft. What is a hydrogen–oxygen fuel cell?

8. Not all spontaneous redox reactions produce wonderful results. Corrosion is an example of a spontaneous redox process that has negative effects. What happens in the corrosion of a metal such as iron? What must be present for the corrosion of iron to take place? How can moisture and salt increase the severity of corrosion? Explain how the following protect metals from corrosion:
   a. paint
   b. durable oxide coatings
   c. galvanizing
   d. sacrificial metal
   e. alloying
   f. cathodic protection

9. What characterizes an electrolytic cell? What is an ampere? When the current applied to an electrolytic cell is multiplied by the time in seconds, what quantity is determined? How is this quantity converted to moles of electrons required? How are moles of electrons required converted to moles of metal plated out? What does plating mean? How do you predict the cathode and the anode half-reactions in an electrolytic cell? Why is the electrolysis of molten salts much easier to predict in terms of what occurs at the anode and cathode than the electrolysis of aqueous dissolved salts? What is overvoltage?

10. Electrolysis has many important industrial applications. What are some of these applications? The electrolysis of molten NaCl is the major process by which sodium metal is produced. However, the electrolysis of aqueous NaCl does not produce sodium metal under normal circumstances. Why? What is purification of a metal by electrolysis?

Active Learning Questions

These questions are designed to be used by groups of students in class. The questions allow students to explore their understanding of concepts through discussion and peer teaching. The real value of these questions is the learning that occurs while students talk to each other about chemical concepts.

1. Sketch a galvanic cell, and explain how it works. Look at Figs. 17.1 and 17.2. Explain what is occurring in each container and why the cell in Fig. 17.2 "works" but the one in Fig. 17.1 does not.

2. In making a specific galvanic cell, explain how one decides on the electrodes and the solutions to use in the cell.

3. You want to "plate out" nickel metal from a nickel nitrate solution onto a piece of metal inserted into the solution. Should you use copper or zinc? Explain.

4. A copper penny can be dissolved in nitric acid but not in hydrochloric acid. Using reduction potentials from the book, show why this is so. What are the products of the reaction? Newer pennies contain a mixture of zinc and copper. What happens to the zinc in the penny when the coin is placed in nitric acid? Hydrochloric acid? Support your explanations with data from the book, and include balanced equations for all reactions.

5. Sketch a cell that forms iron metal from iron(II) while changing chromium metal to chromium(III). Calculate the voltage, show

the electron flow, label the anode and cathode, and balance the overall cell equation.

6. Which of the following is the best reducing agent: F_2, H_2, Na, Na^+, F^-? Explain. Order as many of these species as possible from the best to the worst oxidizing agent. Why can't you order all of them? From Table 17.1 choose the species that is the best oxidizing agent. Choose the best reducing agent. Explain.

7. You are told that metal A is a better reducing agent than metal B. What, if anything, can be said about A^+ and B^+? Explain.

8. Explain the following relationships: ΔG and w, cell potential and w, cell potential and ΔG, cell potential and Q. Using these relationships, explain how you could make a cell in which both electrodes are the same metal and both solutions contain the same compound, but at different concentrations. Why does such a cell run spontaneously?

9. Explain why cell potentials are not multiplied by the coefficients in the balanced redox equation. (Use the relationship between ΔG and cell potential to do this.)

10. What is the difference between $\mathscr{E}$ and $\mathscr{E}°$? When is $\mathscr{E}$ equal to zero? When is $\mathscr{E}°$ equal to zero? (Consider "regular" galvanic cells as well as concentration cells.)

11. Consider the following galvanic cell:

What happens to $\mathscr{E}$ as the concentration of Zn^{2+} is increased? As the concentration of Ag^+ is increased? What happens to $\mathscr{E}°$ in these cases?

12. Look up the reduction potential for Fe^{3+} to Fe^{2+}. Look up the reduction potential for Fe^{2+} to Fe. Finally, look up the reduction potential for Fe^{3+} to Fe. You should notice that adding the reduction potentials for the first two does not give the potential for the third. Why not? Show how you can use the first two potentials to calculate the third potential.

A blue question or exercise number indicates that the answer to that question or exercise appears at the back of this book and a solution appears in the *Solutions Guide*.

Review of Oxidation–Reduction Reactions

If you have trouble with these exercises, you should review Sections 4.9 and 4.10.

13. Define *oxidation* and *reduction* in terms of both change in oxidation number and electron loss or gain.

14. Assign oxidation numbers to all the atoms in each of the following.

a. HNO_3 e. $C_6H_{12}O_6$ i. $Na_2C_2O_4$
b. $CuCl_2$ f. Ag   j. CO_2
c. O_2 g. $PbSO_4$ k. $(NH_4)_2Ce(SO_4)_3$
d. H_2O_2 h. PbO_2 l. Cr_2O_3

15. Specify which of the following equations represent oxidation–reduction reactions, and indicate the oxidizing agent, the reducing agent, the species being oxidized, and the species being reduced.

a. $CH_4(g) + H_2O(g) \rightarrow CO(g) + 3H_2(g)$
b. $2AgNO_3(aq) + Cu(s) \rightarrow Cu(NO_3)_2(aq) + 2Ag(s)$
c. $Zn(s) + 2HCl(aq) \rightarrow ZnCl_2(aq) + H_2(g)$
d. $2H^+(aq) + 2CrO_4^{2-}(aq) \rightarrow Cr_2O_7^{2-}(aq) + H_2O(l)$

16. Balance each of the following equations by the half-reaction method for the pH conditions specified.

a. $Cr(s) + NO_3^-(aq) \rightarrow Cr^{3+}(aq) + NO(g)$ (acidic)
b. $Al(s) + MnO_4^-(aq) \rightarrow Al^{3+}(aq) + Mn^{2+}(aq)$ (acidic)
c. $CH_3OH(aq) + Ce^{4+}(aq) \rightarrow CO_2(aq) + Ce^{3+}(aq)$ (acidic)
d. $PO_3^{3-}(aq) + MnO_4^-(aq) \rightarrow$
$$PO_4^{3-}(aq) + MnO_2(s)   \text{(basic)}$$
e. $Mg(s) + OCl^-(aq) \rightarrow Mg(OH)_2(s) + Cl^-(aq)$ (basic)
f. $H_2CO(aq) + Ag(NH_3)_2^+(aq) \rightarrow$
$$HCO_3^-(aq) + Ag(s) + NH_3(aq)   \text{(basic)}$$

Questions

17. When magnesium metal is added to a beaker of $HCl(aq)$, a gas is produced. Knowing that magnesium is oxidized and that hydrogen is reduced, write the balanced equation for the reaction. How many electrons are transferred in the balanced equation? What quantity of useful work can be obtained when Mg is added directly to the beaker of HCl? How can you harness this reaction to do useful work?

18. How can one construct a galvanic cell from two substances, each having a negative standard reduction potential?

19. The free energy change for a reaction, ΔG, is an extensive property. What is an extensive property? Surprisingly, one can calculate ΔG from the cell potential, $\mathscr{E}$, for the reaction. This is surprising because $\mathscr{E}$ is an intensive property. How can the extensive property ΔG be calculated from the intensive property $\mathscr{E}$?

20. What is wrong with the following statement: The best concentration cell will consist of the substance having the most positive standard reduction potential. What drives a concentration cell to produce a large voltage?

21. When jump-starting a car with a dead battery, the ground jumper should be attached to a remote part of the engine block. Why?

22. In theory, most metals should easily corrode in air. Why? A group of metals called the noble metals are relatively difficult to corrode in air. Some noble metals include: gold, platinum, and silver. Reference Table 17.1 to come up with a possible reason why the noble metals are relatively difficult to corrode.

23. Consider the electrolysis of a molten salt of some metal. What information must you know to calculate the mass of metal plated out in the electrolytic cell?

24. Although aluminum is one of the most abundant elements on earth, production of pure Al proved very difficult until the late 1800s. At this time, the Hall–Heroult process made it relatively easy to produce pure Al. Why was pure Al so difficult to produce and what was the key discovery behind the Hall–Heroult process?

Exercises

In this section similar exercises are paired.

Galvanic Cells, Cell Potentials, Standard Reduction Potentials, and Free Energy

25. Sketch the galvanic cells based on the following overall reactions. Show the direction of electron flow and identify the cathode and anode. Give the overall balanced reaction. Assume that all concentrations are 1.0 M and that all partial pressures are 1.0 atm.
  a. $Cr^{3+}(aq) + Cl_2(g) \rightleftharpoons Cr_2O_7^{2-}(aq) + Cl^-(aq)$
  b. $Cu^{2+}(aq) + Mg(s) \rightleftharpoons Mg^{2+}(aq) + Cu(s)$

26. Sketch the galvanic cells based on the following overall reactions. Show the direction of electron flow, the direction of ion migration through the salt bridge, and identify the cathode and anode. Give the overall balanced reaction. Assume that all concentrations are 1.0 M and that all partial pressures are 1.0 atm.
  a. $IO_3^-(aq) + Fe^{2+}(aq) \rightleftharpoons Fe^{3+}(aq) + I_2(aq)$
  b. $Zn(s) + Ag^+(aq) \rightleftharpoons Zn^{2+}(aq) + Ag(s)$

27. Calculate $\mathscr{E}°$ values for the galvanic cells in Exercise 25.

28. Calculate $\mathscr{E}°$ values for the galvanic cells in Exercise 26.

29. Sketch the galvanic cells based on the following half-reactions. Show the direction of electron flow, show the direction of ion migration through the salt bridge, and identify the cathode and anode. Give the overall balanced reaction, and determine $\mathscr{E}°$ for the galvanic cells. Assume that all concentrations are 1.0 M and that all partial pressures are 1.0 atm.
  a. $Cl_2 + 2e^- \rightarrow 2Cl^-$ $\quad \mathscr{E}° = 1.36$ V
  $Br_2 + 2e^- \rightarrow 2Br^-$ $\quad \mathscr{E}° = 1.09$ V
  b. $MnO_4^- + 8H^+ + 5e^- \rightarrow Mn^{2+} + 4H_2O$ $\quad \mathscr{E}° = 1.51$ V
  $IO_4^- + 2H^+ + 2e^- \rightarrow IO_3^- + H_2O$ $\quad \mathscr{E}° = 1.60$ V

30. Sketch the galvanic cells based on the following half-reactions. Show the direction of electron flow, show the direction of ion migration through the salt bridge, and identify the cathode and anode. Give the overall balanced reaction, and determine $\mathscr{E}°$ for the galvanic cells. Assume that all concentrations are 1.0 M and that all partial pressures are 1.0 atm.
  a. $H_2O_2 + 2H^+ + 2e^- \rightarrow 2H_2O$ $\quad \mathscr{E}° = 1.78$ V
  $O_2 + 2H^+ + 2e^- \rightarrow H_2O_2$ $\quad \mathscr{E}° = 0.68$ V
  b. $Mn^{2+} + 2e^- \rightarrow Mn$ $\quad \mathscr{E}° = -1.18$ V
  $Fe^{3+} + 3e^- \rightarrow Fe$ $\quad \mathscr{E}° = -0.036$ V

31. Give the standard line notation for each cell in Exercises 25 and 29.

32. Give the standard line notation for each cell in Exercises 26 and 30.

33. Consider the following galvanic cells:

(a)   (b)

For each galvanic cell, give the balanced cell reaction and determine $\mathscr{E}°$. Standard reduction potentials are found in Table 17.1.

34. Give the balanced cell reaction and determine $\mathscr{E}°$ for the galvanic cells based on the following half-reactions. Standard reduction potentials are found in Table 17.1.
  a. $Cr_2O_7^{2-} + 14H^+ + 6e^- \rightarrow 2Cr^{3+} + 7H_2O$
  $H_2O_2 + 2H^+ + 2e^- \rightarrow 2H_2O$
  b. $2H^+ + 2e^- \rightarrow H_2$
  $Al^{3+} + 3e^- \rightarrow Al$

35. Calculate $\mathscr{E}°$ values for the following cells. Which reactions are spontaneous as written (under standard conditions)? Balance the reactions. Standard reduction potentials are found in Table 17.1.
  a. $MnO_4^-(aq) + I^-(aq) \rightleftharpoons I_2(aq) + Mn^{2+}(aq)$
  b. $MnO_4^-(aq) + F^-(aq) \rightleftharpoons F_2(g) + Mn^{2+}(aq)$

36. Calculate $\mathscr{E}°$ values for the following cells. Which reactions are spontaneous as written (under standard conditions)? Balance the reactions that are not already balanced. Standard reduction potentials are found in Table 17.1.
  a. $H_2(g) \rightleftharpoons H^+(aq) + H^-(aq)$
  b. $Au^{3+}(aq) + Ag(s) \rightleftharpoons Ag^+(aq) + Au(s)$

37. Chlorine dioxide (ClO_2), which is produced by the reaction

$$2NaClO_2(aq) + Cl_2(g) \longrightarrow 2ClO_2(g) + 2NaCl(aq)$$

has been tested as a disinfectant for municipal water treatment. Using data from Table 17.1, calculate $\mathscr{E}°$ and $\Delta G°$ at 25°C for the production of ClO_2.

38. The amount of manganese in steel is determined by changing it to permanganate ion. The steel is first dissolved in nitric acid, producing Mn^{2+} ions. These ions are then oxidized to the deeply colored MnO_4^- ions by periodate ion (IO_4^-) in acid solution.
  a. Complete and balance an equation describing each of the above reactions.
  b. Calculate $\mathscr{E}°$ and $\Delta G°$ at 25°C for each reaction.

39. Calculate the maximum amount of work that can be obtained from the galvanic cells at standard conditions in Exercise 33.

40. Calculate the maximum amount of work that can be obtained from the galvanic cells at standard conditions in Exercise 34.

41. Calculate $\mathscr{E}°$ for the reaction

$$CH_3OH(l) + \tfrac{3}{2}O_2(g) \longrightarrow CO_2(g) + 2H_2O(l)$$

using values of $\Delta G_f°$ in Appendix 4.

42. The equation $\Delta G° = -nF\mathscr{E}°$ also can be applied to half-reactions. Use standard reduction potentials to estimate $\Delta G_f°$ for $Fe^{2+}(aq)$ and $Fe^{3+}(aq)$. ($\Delta G_f°$ for $e^- = 0$.)

43. Using data from Table 17.1, place the following in order of increasing strength as oxidizing agents (all under standard conditions).

$$Cd^{2+}, \quad IO_3^-, \quad K^+, \quad H_2O, \quad AuCl_4^-, \quad I_2$$

44. Using data from Table 17.1, place the following in order of increasing strength as reducing agents (all under standard conditions).

$$Cu^+, \quad F^-, \quad H^-, \quad H_2O, \quad I_2, \quad K$$

45. Answer the following questions using data from Table 17.1 (all under standard conditions).
   a. Is $H^+(aq)$ capable of oxidizing $Cu(s)$ to $Cu^{2+}(aq)$?
   b. Is $Fe^{3+}(aq)$ capable of oxidizing $I^-(aq)$?
   c. Is $H_2(g)$ capable of reducing $Ag^+(aq)$?
   d. Is $Fe^{2+}(aq)$ capable of reducing $Cr^{3+}(aq)$ to $Cr^{2+}(aq)$?

46. Consider only the species (at standard conditions)

$$Na^+, \quad Cl^-, \quad Ag^+, \quad Ag, \quad Zn^{2+}, \quad Zn, \quad Pb$$

in answering the following questions. Give reasons for your answers. (Use data from Table 17.1.)
   a. Which is the strongest oxidizing agent?
   b. Which is the strongest reducing agent?
   c. Which species can be oxidized by $SO_4^{2-}(aq)$ in acid?
   d. Which species can be reduced by $Al(s)$?

47. Use the table of standard reduction potentials (Table 17.1) to pick a reagent that is capable of each of the following oxidations (under standard conditions in acidic solution).
   a. Oxidize Br^- to Br_2 but not oxidize Cl^- to Cl_2
   b. Oxidize Mn to Mn^{2+} but not oxidize Ni to Ni^{2+}

48. Use the table of standard reduction potentials (Table 17.1) to pick a reagent that is capable of each of the following reductions (under standard conditions in acidic solution).
   a. Reduce Cu^{2+} to Cu but not reduce Cu^{2+} to Cu^+.
   b. Reduce Br_2 to Br^- but not reduce I_2 to I^-.

49. Hydrazine is somewhat toxic. Use the half-reactions shown below to explain why household bleach (a highly alkaline solution of sodium hypochlorite) should not be mixed with household ammonia or glass cleansers that contain ammonia.

$$ClO^- + H_2O + 2e^- \longrightarrow 2OH^- + Cl^- \qquad \mathscr{E}° = 0.90 \text{ V}$$
$$N_2H_4 + 2H_2O + 2e^- \longrightarrow 2NH_3 + 2OH^- \qquad \mathscr{E}° = -0.10 \text{ V}$$

50. The compound with the formula TlI_3 is a black solid. Given the following standard reduction potentials,

$$Tl^{3+} + 2e^- \longrightarrow Tl^+ \qquad \mathscr{E}° = 1.25 \text{ V}$$
$$I_3^- + 2e^- \longrightarrow 3I^- \qquad \mathscr{E}° = 0.55 \text{ V}$$

would you formulate this compound as thallium(III) iodide or thallium(I) triiodide?

The Nernst Equation

51. A galvanic cell is based on the following half-reactions at 25°C:

$$Ag^+ + e^- \longrightarrow Ag$$
$$H_2O_2 + 2H^+ + 2e^- \longrightarrow 2H_2O$$

Predict whether $\mathscr{E}_{cell}$ is larger or smaller than $\mathscr{E}°_{cell}$ for the following cases.
   a. $[Ag^+] = 1.0 \, M$, $[H_2O_2] = 2.0 \, M$, $[H^+] = 2.0 \, M$
   b. $[Ag^+] = 2.0 \, M$, $[H_2O_2] = 1.0 \, M$, $[H^+] = 1.0 \times 10^{-7} \, M$

52. Consider the concentration cell in Fig. 17.10. If the Fe^{2+} concentration in the right compartment is changed from $0.1 \, M$ to $1 \times 10^{-7} \, M \, Fe^{2+}$, predict the direction of electron flow, and designate the anode and cathode compartments.

53. Consider the concentration cell shown below. Calculate the cell potential at 25°C when the concentration of Ag^+ in the compartment on the right is the following.
   a. $1.0 \, M$
   b. $2.0 \, M$
   c. $0.10 \, M$
   d. $4.0 \times 10^{-5} \, M$
   e. Calculate the potential when both solutions are $0.10 \, M$ in Ag^+. For each case, also identify the cathode, the anode, and the direction in which electrons flow.

54. Consider a concentration cell similar to the one shown in Exercise 53, except that both electrodes are made of Ni and in the left-hand compartment $[Ni^{2+}] = 1.0 \, M$. Calculate the cell potential at 25°C when the concentration of Ni^{2+} in the compartment on the right has each of the following values.
   a. $1.0 \, M$
   b. $2.0 \, M$
   c. $0.10 \, M$
   d. $4.0 \times 10^{-5} \, M$
   e. Calculate the potential when both solutions are $2.5 \, M$ in Ni^{2+}. For each case, also identify the cathode, anode, and the direction in which electrons flow.

55. The overall reaction in the lead storage battery is

$$Pb(s) + PbO_2(s) + 2H^+(aq) + 2HSO_4^-(aq) \longrightarrow$$
$$2PbSO_4(s) + 2H_2O(l)$$

Calculate $\mathscr{E}$ at 25°C for this battery when $[H_2SO_4] = 4.5 \, M$, that is, $[H^+] = [HSO_4^-] = 4.5 \, M$. At 25°C, $\mathscr{E}° = 2.04$ V for the lead storage battery.

56. Calculate the pH of the cathode compartment for the following reaction given $\mathscr{E}_{cell} = 3.01$ V when $[Cr^{3+}] = 0.15 \, M$, $[Al^{3+}] = 0.30 \, M$, and $[Cr_2O_7^{2-}] = 0.55 \, M$.

$$2Al(s) + Cr_2O_7^{2-}(aq) + 14H^+(aq) \rightarrow$$
$$2Al^{3+}(aq) + 2Cr^{3+}(aq) + 7H_2O(l)$$

57. Consider the cell described below:

$$Zn|Zn^{2+}(1.00 \, M)||Cu^{2+}(1.00 \, M)|Cu$$

Calculate the cell potential after the reaction has operated long enough for the $[Zn^{2+}]$ to have changed by 0.20 mol/L. (Assume $T = 25°C$.)

58. Consider the cell described below:

$$Al|Al^{3+}(1.00 \, M)||Pb^{2+}(1.00 \, M)|Pb$$

Calculate the cell potential after the reaction has operated long enough for the $[Al^{3+}]$ to have changed by 0.60 mol/L. (Assume $T = 25°C$.)

59. An electrochemical cell consists of a standard hydrogen electrode and a copper metal electrode.
    a. What is the potential of the cell at 25°C if the copper electrode is placed in a solution in which $[Cu^{2+}] = 2.5 \times 10^{-4}$ M?
    b. The copper electrode is placed in a solution of unknown $[Cu^{2+}]$. The measured potential at 25°C is 0.195 V. What is $[Cu^{2+}]$? (Assume Cu^{2+} is reduced.)

60. An electrochemical cell consists of a nickel metal electrode immersed in a solution with $[Ni^{2+}] = 1.0$ M separated by a porous disk from an aluminum metal electrode.
    a. What is the potential of this cell at 25°C if the aluminum electrode is placed in a solution in which $[Al^{3+}] = 7.2 \times 10^{-3}$ M?
    b. When the aluminum electrode is placed in a certain solution in which $[Al^{3+}]$ is unknown, the measured cell potential at 25°C is 1.62 V. Calculate $[Al^{3+}]$ in the unknown solution. (Assume Al is oxidized.)

61. An electrochemical cell consists of a standard hydrogen electrode and a copper metal electrode. If the copper electrode is placed in a solution of 0.10 M NaOH that is saturated with $Cu(OH)_2$, what is the cell potential at 25°C? (For $Cu(OH)_2$, $K_{sp} = 1.6 \times 10^{-19}$.)

62. An electrochemical cell consists of a nickel metal electrode immersed in a solution with $[Ni^{2+}] = 1.0$ M separated by a porous disk from an aluminum metal electrode immersed in a solution with $[Al^{3+}] = 1.0$ M. Sodium hydroxide is added to the aluminum compartment, causing $Al(OH)_3(s)$ to precipitate. After precipitation of $Al(OH)_3$ has ceased, the concentration of OH^- is 1.0×10^{-4} M and the measured cell potential is 1.82 V. Calculate the K_{sp} value for $Al(OH)_3$.

$$Al(OH)_3(s) \rightleftharpoons Al^{3+}(aq) + 3OH^-(aq) \quad K_{sp} = ?$$

63. Consider a concentration cell that has both electrodes made of some metal M. Solution A in one compartment of the cell contains 1.0 M M^{2+}. Solution B in the other cell compartment has a volume of 1.00 L. At the beginning of the experiment 0.0100 mol of $M(NO_3)_2$ and 0.0100 mol of Na_2SO_4 are dissolved in solution B (ignore volume changes), where the reaction

$$M^{2+}(aq) + SO_4^{2-}(aq) \rightleftharpoons MSO_4(s)$$

occurs. For this reaction equilibrium is rapidly established, whereupon the cell potential is found to be +0.44 V at 25°C. Assume that the process

$$M^{2+} + 2e^- \longrightarrow M$$

has a standard reduction potential of −0.31 V and that no other redox process occurs in the cell. Calculate the value of K_{sp} for $MSO_4(s)$ at 25°C.

64. You have a concentration cell in which the cathode has a silver electrode with 0.10 M Ag^+. The anode also has a silver electrode with $Ag^+(aq)$, 0.050 M $S_2O_3^{2-}$, and 1.0×10^{-3} M $Ag(S_2O_3)_2^{3-}$. You read the voltage to be 0.76 V.

a. Calculate the concentration of Ag^+ at the cathode.
b. Determine the value of the equilibrium constant for the formation of $Ag(S_2O_3)_2^{3-}$.

$$Ag^+(aq) + 2S_2O_3^{2-}(aq) \rightleftharpoons Ag(S_2O_3)_2^{3-}(aq) \quad K = ?$$

65. Calculate $\Delta G°$ and K at 25°C for the reactions in Exercises 25 and 29.

66. Calculate $\Delta G°$ and K at 25°C for the reactions in Exercises 26 and 30.

67. An excess of finely divided iron is stirred up with a solution that contains Cu^{2+} ion, and the system is allowed to come to equilibrium. The solid materials are then filtered off, and electrodes of solid copper and solid iron are inserted into the remaining solution. What is the value of the ratio $[Fe^{2+}]/[Cu^{2+}]$ at 25°C?

68. Consider the following reaction:

$$Ni^{2+}(aq) + Sn(s) \rightarrow Ni(s) + Sn^{2+}(aq)$$

Determine the minimum ratio of $[Sn^{2+}]/[Ni^{2+}]$ necessary to make this reaction spontaneous as written.

69. Under standard conditions, what reaction occurs, if any, when each of the following operations is performed?
    a. Crystals of I_2 are added to a solution of NaCl.
    b. Cl_2 gas is bubbled into a solution of NaI.
    c. A silver wire is placed in a solution of $CuCl_2$.
    d. An acidic solution of $FeSO_4$ is exposed to air.
    For the reactions that occur, write a balanced equation and calculate $\mathscr{E}°$, $\Delta G°$, and K at 25°C.

70. A disproportionation reaction involves a substance that acts as both an oxidizing and a reducing agent, producing higher and lower oxidation states of the same element in the products. Which of the following disproportionation reactions are spontaneous under standard conditions? Calculate $\Delta G°$ and K at 25°C for those reactions that are spontaneous under standard conditions.
    a. $2Cu^+(aq) \rightarrow Cu^{2+}(aq) + Cu(s)$
    b. $3Fe^{2+}(aq) \rightarrow 2Fe^{3+}(aq) + Fe(s)$
    c. $HClO_2(aq) \rightarrow ClO_3^-(aq) + HClO(aq)$ (unbalanced)
    Use the half-reactions:

$$ClO_3^- + 3H^+ + 2e^- \longrightarrow HClO_2 + H_2O \quad \mathscr{E}° = 1.21 \text{ V}$$
$$HClO_2 + 2H^+ + 2e^- \longrightarrow HClO + H_2O \quad \mathscr{E}° = 1.65 \text{ V}$$

71. Consider the galvanic cell based on the following half-reactions:

$$Au^{3+} + 3e^- \longrightarrow Au \quad \mathscr{E}° = 1.50 \text{ V}$$
$$Tl^+ + e^- \longrightarrow Tl \quad \mathscr{E}° = -0.34 \text{ V}$$

a. Determine the overall cell reaction and calculate $\mathscr{E}°_{cell}$.
b. Calculate $\Delta G°$ and K for the cell reaction at 25°C.
c. Calculate $\mathscr{E}_{cell}$ at 25°C when $[Au^{3+}] = 1.0 \times 10^{-2}$ M and $[Tl^+] = 1.0 \times 10^{-4}$ M.

72. Consider the following galvanic cell at 25°C:

$$Pt|Cr^{2+}(0.30 \text{ } M), Cr^{3+}(2.0 \text{ } M)||Co^{2+}(0.20 \text{ } M)|Co$$

The overall reaction and equilibrium constant value are

$$2Cr^{2+}(aq) + Co^{2+}(aq) \longrightarrow$$
$$2Cr^{3+}(aq) + Co(s) \quad K = 2.79 \times 10^7$$

Calculate the cell potential, $\mathscr{E}$, for this galvanic cell and ΔG for the cell reaction at these conditions.

73. Calculate K_{sp} for iron(II) sulfide given the following data:

$$FeS(s) + 2e^- \rightarrow Fe(s) + S^{2-}(aq) \qquad \mathscr{E}° = -1.01 \text{ V}$$
$$Fe^{2+}(aq) + 2e^- \rightarrow Fe(s) \qquad \mathscr{E}° = -0.44 \text{ V}$$

74. For the following half-reaction, $\mathscr{E}° = -2.07$ V:

$$AlF_6{}^{3-} + 3e^- \longrightarrow Al + 6F^-$$

Using data from Table 17.1, calculate the equilibrium constant at 25°C for the reaction

$$Al^{3+}(aq) + 6F^-(aq) \rightleftharpoons AlF_6{}^{3-}(aq) \quad K = ?$$

75. Calculate the value of the equilibrium constant for the reaction of zinc metal in a solution of silver nitrate at 25°C.

76. The solubility product for $CuI(s)$ is 1.1×10^{-12}. Calculate the value of $\mathscr{E}°$ for the half-reaction

$$CuI + e^- \longrightarrow Cu + I^-$$

Electrolysis

77. How long will it take to plate out each of the following with a current of 100.0 A?
   a. 1.0 kg Al from aqueous Al^{3+}
   b. 1.0 g Ni from aqueous Ni^{2+}
   c. 5.0 mol Ag from aqueous Ag^+

78. The electrolysis of BiO^+ produces pure bismuth. How long would it take to produce 10.0 g of Bi by the electrolysis of a BiO^+ solution using a current of 25.0 A?

79. What mass of each of the following substances can be produced in 1.0 h with a current of 15 A?
   a. Co from aqueous Co^{2+} **c.** I_2 from aqueous KI
   b. Hf from aqueous Hf^{4+} **d.** Cr from molten CrO_3

80. Aluminum is produced commercially by the electrolysis of Al_2O_3 in the presence of a molten salt. If a plant has a continuous capacity of 1.00 million amp, what mass of aluminum can be produced in 2.00 h?

81. An unknown metal M is electrolyzed. It took 74.1 s for a current of 2.00 amp to plate out 0.107 g of the metal from a solution containing $M(NO_3)_3$. Identify the metal.

82. Electrolysis of an alkaline earth metal chloride using a current of 5.00 A for 748 s deposits 0.471 g of metal at the cathode. What is the identity of the alkaline earth metal chloride?

83. What volume of F_2 gas, at 25°C and 1.00 atm, is produced when molten KF is electrolyzed by a current of 10.0 A for 2.00 h? What mass of potassium metal is produced? At which electrode does each reaction occur?

84. What volumes of $H_2(g)$ and $O_2(g)$ at STP are produced from the electrolysis of water by a current of 2.50 A in 15.0 min?

85. One of the few industrial-scale processes that produce organic compounds electrochemically is used by the Monsanto Company to produce 1,4-dicyanobutane. The reduction reaction is

$$2CH_2{=}CHCN + 2H^+ + 2e^- \longrightarrow NC{-}(CH_2)_4{-}CN$$

The $NC{-}(CH_2)_4{-}CN$ is then chemically reduced using hydrogen gas to $H_2N{-}(CH_2)_6{-}NH_2$, which is used in the production of nylon. What current must be used to produce 150. kg of $NC{-}(CH_2)_4{-}CN$ per hour?

86. A single Hall–Heroult cell (as shown in Fig. 17.22) produces about 1 ton of aluminum in 24 hours. What current must be used to accomplish this?

87. It took 2.30 min using a current of 2.00 A to plate out all the silver from 0.250 L of a solution containing Ag^+. What was the original concentration of Ag^+ in the solution?

88. A solution containing Pt^{4+} is electrolyzed with a current of 4.00 A. How long will it take to plate out 99% of the platinum in 0.50 L of a 0.010 M solution of Pt^{4+}?

89. A solution at 25°C contains 1.0 M Cd^{2+}, 1.0 M Ag^+, 1.0 M Au^{3+}, and 1.0 M Ni^{2+} in the cathode compartment of an electrolytic cell. Predict the order in which the metals will plate out as the voltage is gradually increased.

90. Consider the following half-reactions:

$$IrCl_6{}^{3-} + 3e^- \longrightarrow Ir + 6Cl^- \qquad \mathscr{E}° = 0.77 \text{ V}$$
$$PtCl_4{}^{2-} + 2e^- \longrightarrow Pt + 4Cl^- \qquad \mathscr{E}° = 0.73 \text{ V}$$
$$PdCl_4{}^{2-} + 2e^- \longrightarrow Pd + 4Cl^- \qquad \mathscr{E}° = 0.62 \text{ V}$$

A hydrochloric acid solution contains platinum, palladium, and iridium as chloro-complex ions. The solution is a constant 1.0 M in chloride ion and 0.020 M in each complex ion. Is it feasible to separate the three metals from this solution by electrolysis? (Assume that 99% of a metal must be plated out before another metal begins to plate out.)

91. What reactions take place at the cathode and the anode when each of the following is electrolyzed?
   a. molten $NiBr_2$ **b.** molten AlF_3 **c.** molten MnI_2

92. What reactions take place at the cathode and the anode when each of the following is electrolyzed? (Assume standard conditions.)
   a. 1.0 M $NiBr_2$ solution
   b. 1.0 M AlF_3 solution
   c. 1.0 M MnI_2 solution

Additional Exercises

93. The saturated calomel electrode, abbreviated SCE, is often used as a reference electrode in making electrochemical measurements. The SCE is composed of mercury in contact with a saturated solution of calomel (Hg_2Cl_2). The electrolyte solution is saturated KCl. $\mathscr{E}_{SCE}$ is +0.242 V relative to the standard hydrogen electrode. Calculate the potential for each of the following galvanic cells containing a saturated calomel electrode and the given half-cell components at standard conditions. In each case, indicate whether the SCE is the cathode or the anode. Standard reduction potentials are found in Table 17.1.

a. $Cu^{2+} + 2e^- \longrightarrow Cu$
b. $Fe^{3+} + e^- \longrightarrow Fe^{2+}$
c. $AgCl + e^- \longrightarrow Ag + Cl^-$
d. $Al^{3+} + 3e^- \longrightarrow Al$
e. $Ni^{2+} + 2e^- \longrightarrow Ni$

94. Consider the following half-reactions:

$$Pt^{2+} + 2e^- \longrightarrow Pt \qquad \mathscr{E}° = 1.188 \text{ V}$$
$$PtCl_4^{2-} + 2e^- \longrightarrow Pt + 4Cl^- \qquad \mathscr{E}° = 0.755 \text{ V}$$
$$NO_3^- + 4H^+ + 3e^- \longrightarrow NO + 2H_2O \qquad \mathscr{E}° = 0.96 \text{ V}$$

Explain why platinum metal will dissolve in aqua regia (a mixture of hydrochloric and nitric acids) but not in either concentrated nitric or concentrated hydrochloric acid individually.

95. Consider the standard galvanic cell based on the following half-reactions

$$Cu^{2+} + 2e^- \longrightarrow Cu$$
$$Ag^+ + e^- \longrightarrow Ag$$

The electrodes in this cell are $Ag(s)$ and $Cu(s)$. Does the cell potential increase, decrease, or remain the same when the following changes occur to the standard cell?
a. $CuSO_4(s)$ is added to the copper half-cell compartment (assume no volume change).
b. $NH_3(aq)$ is added to the copper half-cell compartment. *Hint:* Cu^{2+} reacts with NH_3 to form $Cu(NH_3)_4^{2+}(aq)$.
c. $NaCl(s)$ is added to the silver half-cell compartment. *Hint:* Ag^+ reacts with Cl^- to form $AgCl(s)$.
d. Water is added to both half-cell compartments until the volume of solution is doubled.
e. The silver electrode is replaced with a platinum electrode.

$$Pt^{2+} + 2e^- \longrightarrow Pt \qquad \mathscr{E}° = 1.19 \text{ V}$$

96. A standard galvanic cell is constructed so that the overall cell reaction is

$$2Al^{3+}(aq) + 3M(s) \longrightarrow 3M^{2+}(aq) + 2Al(s)$$

where M is an unknown metal. If $\Delta G° = -411$ kJ for the overall cell reaction, identify the metal used to construct the standard cell.

97. The black silver sulfide discoloration of silverware can be removed by heating the silver article in a sodium carbonate solution in an aluminum pan. The reaction is

$$3Ag_2S(s) + 2Al(s) \rightleftharpoons 6Ag(s) + 3S^{2-}(aq) + 2Al^{3+}(aq)$$

a. Using data in Appendix 4, calculate $\Delta G°$, K, and $\mathscr{E}°$ for the above reaction at 25°C. (For $Al^{3+}(aq)$, $\Delta G_f° = -480.$ kJ/mol.)
b. Calculate the value of the standard reduction potential for the following half-reaction:

$$2e^- + Ag_2S(s) \longrightarrow 2Ag(s) + S^{2-}(aq)$$

98. In 1973 the wreckage of the Civil War ironclad USS *Monitor* was discovered near Cape Hatteras, North Carolina. (The *Monitor* and the CSS *Virginia* [formerly the USS *Merrimack*] fought the first battle between iron-armored ships.) In 1987 investigations were begun to see if the ship could be salvaged. It was reported in *Time* (June 22, 1987) that scientists were considering adding sacrificial anodes of zinc to the rapidly

corroding metal hull of the *Monitor*. Describe how attaching zinc to the hull would protect the *Monitor* from further corrosion.

99. When aluminum foil is placed in hydrochloric acid, nothing happens for the first 30 seconds or so. This is followed by vigorous bubbling and the eventual disappearance of the foil. Explain these observations.

100. Which of the following statements concerning corrosion is/are true? For the false statements, correct them.
a. Corrosion is an example of an electrolytic process.
b. Corrosion of steel involves the reduction of iron coupled with the oxidation of oxygen.
c. Steel rusts more easily in the dry (arid) Southwest states than in the humid Midwest states.
d. Salting roads in the winter has the added benefit of hindering the corrosion of steel.
e. The key to cathodic protection is to connect via a wire a metal more easily oxidized than iron to the steel surface to be protected.

101. A patent attorney has asked for your advice concerning the merits of a patent application that describes a single aqueous galvanic cell capable of producing a 12-V potential. Comment.

102. The overall reaction and equilibrium constant value for a hydrogen–oxygen fuel cell at 298 K is

$$2H_2(g) + O_2(g) \longrightarrow 2H_2O(l) \qquad K = 1.28 \times 10^{83}$$

a. Calculate $\mathscr{E}°$ and $\Delta G°$ at 298 K for the fuel cell reaction.
b. Predict the signs of $\Delta H°$ and $\Delta S°$ for the fuel cell reaction.
c. As temperature increases, does the maximum amount of work obtained from the fuel cell reaction increase, decrease, or remain the same? Explain.

103. What is the maximum work that can be obtained from a hydrogen–oxygen fuel cell at standard conditions that produces 1.00 kg of water at 25°C? Why do we say that this is the maximum work that can be obtained? What are the advantages and disadvantages in using fuel cells rather than the corresponding combustion reactions to produce electricity?

104. The overall reaction and standard cell potential at 25°C for the rechargeable nickel–cadmium alkaline battery is

$$Cd(s) + NiO_2(s) + 2H_2O(l) \longrightarrow$$
$$Ni(OH)_2(s) + Cd(OH)_2(s) \qquad \mathscr{E}° = 1.10 \text{ V}$$

For every mole of Cd consumed in the cell, what is the maximum useful work that can be obtained at standard conditions?

105. An experimental fuel cell has been designed that uses carbon monoxide as fuel. The overall reaction is

$$2CO(g) + O_2(g) \longrightarrow 2CO_2(g)$$

The two half-cell reactions are

$$CO + O^{2-} \longrightarrow CO_2 + 2e^-$$
$$O_2 + 4e^- \longrightarrow 2O^{2-}$$

The two half-reactions are carried out in separate compartments connected with a solid mixture of CeO_2 and Gd_2O_3. Oxide ions can move through this solid at high temperatures (about 800°C). ΔG for the overall reaction at 800°C under certain concentration conditions is -380 kJ. Calculate the cell potential for this fuel cell at the same temperature and concentration conditions.

106. A fuel cell designed to react grain alcohol with oxygen has the following net reaction:

$$C_2H_5OH(l) + 3O_2(g) \longrightarrow 2CO_2(g) + 3H_2O(l)$$

The maximum work 1 mol of alcohol can yield by this process is 1320 kJ. What is the theoretical maximum voltage this cell can achieve?

107. Gold is produced electrochemically from an aqueous solution of $Au(CN)_2^-$ containing an excess of CN^-. Gold metal and oxygen gas are produced at the electrodes. What amount (moles) of O_2 will be produced during the production of 1.00 mol of gold?

108. In the electrolysis of a sodium chloride solution, what volume of $H_2(g)$ is produced in the same time it takes to produce 257 L of $Cl_2(g)$, with both volumes measured at 50.°C and 2.50 atm?

109. An aqueous solution of an unknown salt of ruthenium is electrolyzed by a current of 2.50 A passing for 50.0 min. If 2.618 g Ru is produced at the cathode, what is the charge on the ruthenium ions in solution?

110. It takes 15 kWh (kilowatt-hours) of electrical energy to produce 1.0 kg of aluminum metal from aluminum oxide by the Hall–Heroult process. Compare this to the amount of energy necessary to melt 1.0 kg of aluminum metal. Why is it economically feasible to recycle aluminum cans? (The enthalpy of fusion for aluminum metal is 10.7 kJ/mol [1 watt = 1 J/s].)

Challenge Problems

111. Combine the equations

$$\Delta G° = -nF\mathscr{E}° \quad \text{and} \quad \Delta G° = \Delta H° - T\Delta S°$$

to derive an expression for $\mathscr{E}°$ as a function of temperature. Describe how one can graphically determine $\Delta H°$ and $\Delta S°$ from measurements of $\mathscr{E}°$ at different temperatures, assuming that $\Delta H°$ and $\Delta S°$ do not depend on temperature. What property would you look for in designing a reference half-cell that would produce a potential relatively stable with respect to temperature?

112. The overall reaction in the lead storage battery is

$$Pb(s) + PbO_2(s) + 2H^+(aq) + 2HSO_4^-(aq) \longrightarrow 2PbSO_4(s) + 2H_2O(l)$$

a. For the cell reaction $\Delta H° = -315.9$ kJ and $\Delta S° = 263.5$ J/K. Calculate $\mathscr{E}°$ at $-20.°C$. Assume $\Delta H°$ and $\Delta S°$ do not depend on temperature.

b. Calculate $\mathscr{E}$ at $-20.°C$ when $[HSO_4^-] = [H^+] = 4.5\ M$.

c. Consider your answer to Exercise 55. Why does it seem that batteries fail more often on cold days than on warm days?

113. Consider the following galvanic cell:

Calculate the K_{sp} value for $Ag_2SO_4(s)$. Note that to obtain silver ions in the right compartment (the cathode compartment), excess solid Ag_2SO_4 was added and some of the salt dissolved.

114. A zinc–copper battery is constructed as follows at 25°C:

$$Zn\,|\,Zn^{2+}(0.10\ M)\,||\,Cu^{2+}(2.50\ M)\,|\,Cu$$

The mass of each electrode is 200. g.

a. Calculate the cell potential when this battery is first connected.

b. Calculate the cell potential after 10.0 A of current has flowed for 10.0 h. (Assume each half-cell contains 1.00 L of solution.)

c. Calculate the mass of each electrode after 10.0 h.

d. How long can this battery deliver a current of 10.0 A before it goes dead?

115. A galvanic cell is based on the following half-reactions:

$$Fe^{2+} + 2e^- \longrightarrow Fe(s) \qquad \mathscr{E}° = -0.440\ V$$
$$2H^+ + 2e^- \longrightarrow H_2(g) \qquad \mathscr{E}° = 0.000\ V$$

where the iron compartment contains an iron electrode and $[Fe^{2+}] = 1.00 \times 10^{-3}\ M$ and the hydrogen compartment contains a platinum electrode, $P_{H_2} = 1.00$ atm, and a weak acid, HA, at an initial concentration of $1.00\ M$. If the observed cell potential is 0.333 V at 25°C, calculate the K_a value for the weak acid HA.

116. Consider a cell based on the following half-reactions:

$$Au^{3+} + 3e^- \longrightarrow Au \qquad \mathscr{E}° = 1.50\ V$$
$$Fe^{3+} + e^- \longrightarrow Fe^{2+} \qquad \mathscr{E}° = 0.77\ V$$

a. Draw this cell under standard conditions, labeling the anode, the cathode, the direction of electron flow, and the concentrations, as appropriate.

b. When enough $NaCl(s)$ is added to the compartment containing gold to make the $[Cl^-] = 0.10\ M$, the cell potential is observed to be 0.31 V. Assume that Au^{3+} is reduced and assume that the reaction in the compartment containing gold is

$$Au^{3+}(aq) + 4Cl^-(aq) \rightleftharpoons AuCl_4^-(aq)$$

Calculate the value of K for this reaction at 25°C.

117. The measurement of pH using a glass electrode obeys the Nernst equation. The typical response of a pH meter at 25.00°C is given by the equation

$$\mathscr{E}_{meas} = \mathscr{E}_{ref} + 0.05916\ \text{pH}$$

where $\mathscr{E}_{ref}$ contains the potential of the reference electrode and all other potentials that arise in the cell that are not related to the hydrogen ion concentration. Assume that $\mathscr{E}_{ref} = 0.250$ V and that $\mathscr{E}_{meas} = 0.480$ V.

a. What is the uncertainty in the values of pH and $[H^+]$ if the uncertainty in the measured potential is ± 1 mV (± 0.001 V)?

b. To what precision must the potential be measured for the uncertainty in pH to be ± 0.02 pH unit?

118. Zirconium is one of the few metals that retains its structural integrity upon exposure to radiation. For this reason, the fuel rods in most nuclear reactors are made of zirconium. Answer the following questions about the redox properties of zirconium based on the half-reaction

$$ZrO_2 \cdot H_2O + H_2O + 4e^- \longrightarrow Zr + 4OH^- \qquad \mathscr{E}° = -2.36\ V$$

a. Is zirconium metal capable of reducing water to form hydrogen gas at standard conditions?

b. Write a balanced equation for the reduction of water by zirconium metal.

c. Calculate $\mathscr{E}°$, $\Delta G°$, and K for the reduction of water by zirconium metal.

d. The reduction of water by zirconium occurred during the accident at Three Mile Island, Pennsylvania, in 1979. The hydrogen produced was successfully vented and no chemical explosion occurred. If 1.00×10^3 kg of Zr reacts, what mass of H_2 is produced? What volume of H_2 at 1.0 atm and 1000.°C is produced?

e. At Chernobyl, USSR, in 1986, hydrogen was produced by the reaction of superheated steam with the graphite reactor core:

$$C(s) + H_2O(g) \longrightarrow CO(g) + H_2(g)$$

A chemical explosion involving the hydrogen gas did occur at Chernobyl. In light of this fact, do you think it was a correct decision to vent the hydrogen and other radioactive gases into the atmosphere at Three Mile Island? Explain.

119. A galvanic cell is based on the following half-reactions:

$$Ag^+ + e^- \longrightarrow Ag(s) \qquad \mathscr{E}° = 0.80 \text{ V}$$
$$Cu^{2+} + 2e^- \longrightarrow Cu(s) \qquad \mathscr{E}° = 0.34 \text{ V}$$

In this cell, the silver compartment contains a silver electrode and excess $AgCl(s)$ ($K_{sp} = 1.6 \times 10^{-10}$), and the copper compartment contains a copper electrode and $[Cu^{2+}] = 2.0 M$.

a. Calculate the potential for this cell at 25°C.

b. Assuming 1.0 L of 2.0 M Cu^{2+} in the copper compartment, calculate the moles of NH_3 that would have to be added to give a cell potential of 0.52 V at 25°C (assume no volume change on addition of NH_3).

$$Cu^{2+}(aq) + 4NH_3(aq) \rightleftharpoons$$
$$Cu(NH_3)_4{}^{2+}(aq) \qquad K = 1.0 \times 10^{13}$$

120. Given the following two standard reduction potentials,

$$M^{3+} + 3e^- \to M \qquad \mathscr{E}° = -0.10 \text{ V}$$
$$M^{2+} + 2e^- \to M \qquad \mathscr{E}° = -0.50 \text{ V}$$

solve for the standard reduction potential of the half-reaction

$$M^{3+} + e^- \to M^{2+}$$

(*Hint:* You must use the extensive property $\Delta G°$ to determine the standard reduction potential.)

121. You make a galvanic cell with a piece of nickel, 1.0 M $Ni^{2+}(aq)$, a piece of silver, and 1.0 M $Ag^+(aq)$. Calculate the concentrations of $Ag^+(aq)$ and $Ni^{2+}(aq)$ once the cell is "dead."

122. A chemist wishes to determine the concentration of $CrO_4{}^{2-}$ electrochemically. A cell is constructed consisting of a saturated calomel electrode (SCE; see Exercise 93) and a silver wire coated with Ag_2CrO_4. The $\mathscr{E}°$ value for the following half-reaction is $+0.446$ V relative to the standard hydrogen electrode:

$$Ag_2CrO_4 + 2e^- \longrightarrow 2Ag + CrO_4{}^{2-}$$

a. Calculate $\mathscr{E}_{cell}$ and ΔG at 25°C for the cell reaction when $[CrO_4{}^{2-}] = 1.00$ mol/L.

b. Write the Nernst equation for the cell. Assume that the SCE concentrations are constant.

c. If the coated silver wire is placed in a solution (at 25°C) in which $[CrO_4{}^{2-}] = 1.00 \times 10^{-5} M$, what is the expected cell potential?

d. The measured cell potential at 25°C is 0.504 V when the coated wire is dipped into a solution of unknown $[CrO_4{}^{2-}]$. What is $[CrO_4{}^{2-}]$ for this solution?

e. Using data from this problem and from Table 17.1, calculate the solubility product (K_{sp}) for Ag_2CrO_4.

123. You have a concentration cell with Cu electrodes and $[Cu^{2+}] = 1.00 M$ (right side) and $1.0 \times 10^{-4} M$ (left side).

a. Calculate the potential for this cell at 25°C.

b. The Cu^{2+} ion reacts with NH_3 to form $Cu(NH_3)_4{}^{2+}$ where the stepwise formation constants are $K_1 = 1.0 \times 10^3$, $K_2 = 1.0 \times 10^4$, $K_3 = 1.0 \times 10^3$, and $K_4 = 1.0 \times 10^3$. Calculate the new cell potential after enough NH_3 is added to the left cell compartment such that at equilibrium $[NH_3] = 2.0 M$.

124. When copper reacts with nitric acid, a mixture of $NO(g)$ and $NO_2(g)$ is evolved. The volume ratio of the two product gases depends on the concentration of the nitric acid according to the equilibrium

$$2H^+(aq) + 2NO_3{}^-(aq) + NO(g) \rightleftharpoons 3NO_2(g) + H_2O(l)$$

Consider the following standard reduction potentials at 25°C:

$$3e^- + 4H^+(aq) + NO_3{}^-(aq) \longrightarrow NO(g) + 2H_2O(l)$$
$$\mathscr{E}° = 0.957 \text{ V}$$

$$e^- + 2H^+(aq) + NO_3{}^-(aq) \longrightarrow NO_2(g) + 2H_2O(l)$$
$$\mathscr{E}° = 0.775 \text{ V}$$

a. Calculate the equilibrium constant for the above reaction.

b. What concentration of nitric acid will produce a NO and NO_2 mixture with only 0.20% NO_2 (by moles) at 25°C and 1.00 atm? Assume that no other gases are present and that the change in acid concentration can be neglected.

Integrative Problems

These problems require the integration of multiple concepts to find the solutions.

125. The following standard reduction potentials have been determined for the aqueous chemistry of indium:

$$In^{3+}(aq) + 2e^- \longrightarrow In^+(aq) \qquad \mathscr{E}° = -0.444 \text{ V}$$
$$In^+(aq) + e^- \longrightarrow In(s) \qquad \mathscr{E}° = -0.126 \text{ V}$$

a. What is the equilibrium constant for the disproportionation reaction, where a species is both oxidized and reduced, shown below?

$$3In^+(aq) \longrightarrow 2In(s) + In^{3+}(aq)$$

b. What is $\Delta G_f°$ for $In^+(aq)$ if $\Delta G_f° = -97.9$ kJ/mol for $In^{3+}(aq)$?

126. An electrochemical cell is set up using the following balanced reaction:

$$M^{a+}(aq) + N(s) \longrightarrow N^{2+}(aq) + M(s)$$

Given the standard reduction potentials are:

$$M^{a+} + ae^- \longrightarrow M \qquad \mathscr{E}° = +0.400 \text{ V}$$
$$N^{2+} + 2e^- \longrightarrow N \qquad \mathscr{E}° = +0.240 \text{ V}$$

The cell contains 0.10 M N^{2+} and produces a voltage of 0.180 V. If the concentration of M^{a+} is such that the value of the reaction quotient Q is 9.32×10^{-3}, calculate $[M^{a+}]$. Calculate w_{max} for this electrochemical cell.

127. Three electrochemical cells were connected in series so that the same quantity of electrical current passes through all three cells. In the first cell, 1.15 g of chromium metal was deposited from a chromium(III) nitrate solution. In the second cell, 3.15 g of osmium was deposited from a solution made of Os^{n+} and nitrate ions. What is the name of the salt? In the third cell, the electrical charge passed through a solution containing X^{2+} ions caused deposition of 2.11 g of metallic X. What is the electron configuration of X?

Marathon Problems

These problems are designed to incorporate several concepts and techniques into one situation. Marathon Problems can be used in class by groups of students to help facilitate problem-solving skills.

128. A galvanic cell is based on the following half-reactions:

$$Cu^{2+}(aq) + 2e^- \longrightarrow Cu(s) \qquad \mathscr{E}° = 0.34 \text{ V}$$
$$V^{2+}(aq) + 2e^- \longrightarrow V(s) \qquad \mathscr{E}° = -1.20 \text{ V}$$

In this cell, the copper compartment contains a copper electrode and $[Cu^{2+}] = 1.00\ M$, and the vanadium compartment contains

a vanadium electrode and V^{2+} at an unknown concentration. The compartment containing the vanadium (1.00 L of solution) was titrated with 0.0800 M H_2EDTA^{2-}, resulting in the reaction

$$H_2EDTA^{2-}(aq) + V^{2+}(aq)$$
$$\rightleftharpoons VEDTA^{2-}(aq) + 2H^+(aq) \qquad K = ?$$

The potential of the cell was monitored to determine the stoichiometric point for the process, which occurred at a volume of 500.0 mL of H_2EDTA^{2-} solution added. At the stoichiometric point, $\mathscr{E}_{cell}$ was observed to be 1.98 V. The solution was buffered at a pH of 10.00.

a. Calculate $\mathscr{E}_{cell}$ before the titration was carried out.
b. Calculate the value of the equilibrium constant, K, for the titration reaction.
c. Calculate $\mathscr{E}_{cell}$ at the halfway point in the titration.

129. The table below lists the cell potentials for the 10 possible galvanic cells assembled from the metals A, B, C, D, and E, and their respective 1.00 M 2+ ions in solution. Using the data in the table, establish a standard reduction potential table similar to Table 17.1 in the text. Assign a reduction potential of 0.00 V to the half-reaction that falls in the middle of the series. You should get two different tables. Explain why, and discuss what you could do to determine which table is correct.

	A(s) in A²⁺(aq)	B(s) in B²⁺(aq)	C(s) in C²⁺(aq)	D(s) in D²⁺(aq)
E(s) in E²⁺(aq)	0.28 V	0.81 V	0.13 V	1.00 V
D(s) in D²⁺(aq)	0.72 V	0.19 V	1.13 V	—
C(s) in C²⁺(aq)	0.41 V	0.94 V	—	—
B(s) in B²⁺(aq)	0.53 V	—	—	—

Get help understanding core concepts and visualizing molecular-level interactions, and practice problem solving, by visiting the Online Study Center at **college.hmco.com/ PIC/zumdahl7e.**

18 The Nucleus: A Chemist's View

Contents

Workers inside a giant chamber at the National Ignition Facility in California. This chamber will be used to induce nuclear fusion by aiming 192 lasers at a pellet of fuel.

*S*ince the chemistry of an atom is determined by the number and arrangement of its electrons, the properties of the nucleus are not of primary importance to chemists. In the simplest view, the nucleus provides the positive charge to bind the electrons in atoms and molecules. However, a quick reading of any daily newspaper will show you that the nucleus and its properties have an important impact on our society. This chapter considers those aspects of the nucleus about which everyone should have some knowledge.

Several aspects of the nucleus are immediately impressive: its very small size, its very large density, and the magnitude of the energy that holds it together. The radius of a typical nucleus appears to be about 10^{-13} cm. This can be compared to the radius of a typical atom, which is on the order of 10^{-8} cm. A visualization will help you appreciate the small size of the nucleus: If the nucleus of the hydrogen atom were the size of a Ping-Pong ball, the electron in the $1s$ orbital would be, on average, 0.5 kilometer (0.3 mile) away. The density of the nucleus is equally impressive—approximately 1.6×10^{14} g/cm^3. A sphere of nuclear material the size of a Ping-Pong ball would have a mass of 2.5 *billion tons!* In addition, the energies involved in nuclear processes are typically millions of times larger than those associated with normal chemical reactions. This fact makes nuclear processes very attractive for feeding the voracious energy appetite of our civilization.

Atomos, the Greek root of the word *atom,* means "indivisible." It was originally believed that the atom was the ultimate indivisible particle of which all matter was composed. However, as we discussed in Chapter 2, Lord Rutherford showed in 1911 that the atom is not homogeneous, but rather has a dense, positively charged center surrounded by electrons. Subsequently, scientists have learned that the nucleus of the atom can be subdivided into particles called **neutrons** and **protons.** In fact, in the past two decades it has become apparent that even the protons and neutrons are composed of smaller particles called *quarks.*

For most purposes, the nucleus can be regarded as a collection of **nucleons** (neutrons and protons), and the internal structures of these particles can be ignored. As we discussed in Chapter 2, the number of protons in a particular nucleus is called the **atomic number** (Z), and the sum of the neutrons and protons is the **mass number** (A). Atoms that have identical atomic numbers but different mass number values are called **isotopes.** However, we usually do not use the singular form *isotope* to refer to a particular member of a group of isotopes. Rather, we use the term *nuclide.* A **nuclide** is a unique atom, represented by the symbol

$$^A_Z X$$

> The atomic number Z is the number of protons in a nucleus; the mass number A is the sum of protons and neutrons in a nucleus.

> The term *isotopes* refers to a group of nuclides with the same atomic number. Each individual atom is properly called a *nuclide,* not an isotope.

where X represents the symbol for a particular element. For example, the following nuclides constitute the isotopes of carbon: carbon-12 ($^{12}_6$C), carbon-13 ($^{13}_6$C), and carbon-14 ($^{14}_6$C).

18.1 Nuclear Stability and Radioactive Decay

Nuclear stability is the central topic of this chapter and forms the basis for all the important applications related to nuclear processes. Nuclear stability can be considered from both a kinetic and a thermodynamic point of view. **Thermodynamic stability,** as we will use the term here, refers to the potential energy of a particular nucleus as compared with the sum of the potential energies of its component protons and neutrons. We will use the term **kinetic stability** to describe the probability that a nucleus will undergo decomposition to form a different nucleus—a process called **radioactive decay.** We will consider radioactivity in this section.

Many nuclei are radioactive; that is, they decompose, forming another nucleus and producing one or more particles. An example is carbon-14, which decays as follows:

$$^{14}_{6}C \longrightarrow \, ^{14}_{7}N + \, ^{0}_{-1}e$$

where $^{0}_{-1}e$ represents an electron, which is called a **beta particle,** or **β particle,** in nuclear terminology. This equation is typical of those representing radioactive decay in that both A and Z must be conserved. That is, the Z values must give the same sum on both sides of the equation ($6 = 7 - 1$), as must the A values ($14 = 14 + 0$).

Of the approximately 2000 known nuclides, only 279 are stable with respect to radioactive decay. Tin has the largest number of stable isotopes—10.

It is instructive to examine how the numbers of neutrons and protons in a nucleus are related to its stability with respect to radioactive decay. Figure 18.1 shows a plot of the positions of the stable nuclei as a function of the number of protons (Z) and the number of neutrons ($A - Z$). The stable nuclides are said to reside in the **zone of stability.**

The following are some important observations concerning radioactive decay:

- All nuclides with 84 or more protons are unstable with respect to radioactive decay.

- Light nuclides are stable when Z equals $A - Z$, that is, when the neutron/proton ratio is 1. However, for heavier elements the neutron/proton ratio required for stability is greater than 1 and increases with Z.

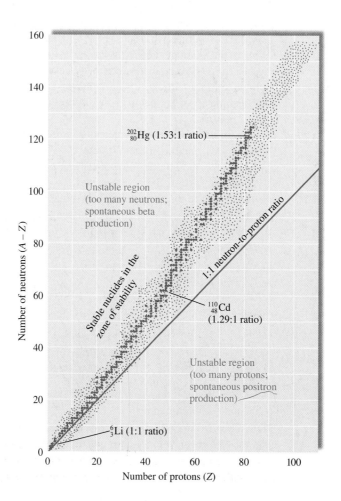

FIGURE 18.1

The zone of stability. The red dots indicate the nuclides that *do not* undergo radioactive decay. Note that as the number of protons in a nuclide increases, the neutron/proton ratio required for stability also increases.

TABLE 18.1 Number of Stable Nuclides Related to Numbers of Protons and Neutrons

Number of Protons	Number of Neutrons	Number of Stable Nuclides	Examples
Even	Even	168	$^{12}_{6}C$, $^{16}_{8}O$
Even	Odd	57	$^{13}_{6}C$, $^{47}_{22}Ti$
Odd	Even	50	$^{19}_{9}F$, $^{23}_{11}Na$
Odd	Odd	4	$^{2}_{1}H$, $^{6}_{3}Li$

Note: Even numbers of protons and neutrons seem to favor stability.

- Certain combinations of protons and neutrons seem to confer special stability. For example, nuclides with even numbers of protons and neutrons are more often stable than those with odd numbers, as shown by the data in Table 18.1.

- There are also certain specific numbers of protons or neutrons that produce especially stable nuclides. These *magic numbers* are 2, 8, 20, 28, 50, 82, and 126. This behavior parallels that for atoms in which certain numbers of electrons (2, 10, 18, 36, 54, and 86) produce special chemical stability (the noble gases).

Types of Radioactive Decay

Radioactive nuclei can undergo decomposition in various ways. These decay processes fall into two categories: those that involve a change in the mass number of the decaying nucleus and those that do not. We will consider the former type of process first.

An **alpha particle,** or **α particle,** is a helium nucleus ($^{4}_{2}He$). **Alpha-particle production** is a very common mode of decay for heavy radioactive nuclides. For example, $^{238}_{92}U$, the predominant (99.3%) isotope of natural uranium, decays by α-particle production:

α-particle production involves a change in *A* for the decaying nucleus; β-particle production has no effect on *A*.

$$^{238}_{92}U \longrightarrow {}^{4}_{2}He + {}^{234}_{90}Th$$

Another α-particle producer is $^{230}_{90}Th$:

$$^{230}_{90}Th \longrightarrow {}^{4}_{2}He + {}^{226}_{88}Ra$$

Visualization: Nuclear Particles

Another decay process in which the mass number of the decaying nucleus changes is **spontaneous fission,** the splitting of a heavy nuclide into two lighter nuclides with similar mass numbers. Although this process occurs at an extremely slow rate for most nuclides, it is important in some cases, such as for $^{254}_{98}Cf$, where spontaneous fission is the predominant mode of decay.

The most common decay process in which the mass number of the decaying nucleus remains constant is **β-particle production.** For example, the thorium-234 nuclide produces a β particle and is converted to protactinium-234:

$$^{234}_{90}Th \longrightarrow {}^{234}_{91}Pa + {}^{0}_{-1}e$$

Iodine-131 is also a β-particle producer:

$$^{131}_{53}I \longrightarrow {}^{0}_{-1}e + {}^{131}_{54}Xe$$

The β particle is assigned the mass number 0, since its mass is tiny compared with that of a proton or neutron. Because the value of Z is -1 for the β particle, the atomic number for the new nuclide is greater by 1 than for the original nuclide. Thus *the net effect of β-particle production is to change a neutron to a proton.* We therefore expect nuclides that lie above the zone of stability (those nuclides whose neutron/proton ratios are too high) to be β-particle producers.

It should be pointed out that although the β particle is an electron, the emitting nucleus does not contain electrons. As we shall see later in this chapter, a given quantity of energy (which is best regarded as a form of matter) can become a particle (another form of matter) under certain circumstances. The unstable nuclide creates an electron as it releases energy in the decay process. The electron thus results from the decay process rather than being present before the decay occurs. Think of this as somewhat like talking: Words are not stored inside us but are formed as we speak. Later in this chapter we will discuss in more detail this very interesting phenomenon where matter in the form of particles and matter in the form of energy can interchange.

A **gamma ray,** or **γ ray,** refers to a high-energy photon. Frequently, γ-ray production accompanies nuclear decays and particle reactions, such as in the α-particle decay of $^{238}_{92}U$:

$$^{238}_{92}U \longrightarrow {}^{4}_{2}He + {}^{234}_{90}Th + 2\,{}^{0}_{0}\gamma$$

where two γ rays of different energies are produced in addition to the α particle. The emission of γ rays is one way a nucleus with excess energy (in an excited nuclear state) can relax to its ground state.

Positron production occurs for nuclides that are below the zone of stability (those nuclides whose neutron/proton ratios are too small). The positron is a particle with the same mass as the electron but opposite charge. An example of a nuclide that decays by positron production is sodium-22:

$$^{22}_{11}Na \longrightarrow {}^{0}_{1}e + {}^{22}_{10}Ne$$

Note that *the net effect is to change a proton to a neutron,* causing the product nuclide to have a higher neutron/proton ratio than the original nuclide.

Besides being oppositely charged, the positron shows an even more fundamental difference from the electron: It is the *antiparticle* of the electron. When a positron collides with an electron, the particulate matter is changed to electromagnetic radiation in the form of high-energy photons:

$$^{0}_{-1}e + {}^{0}_{1}e \longrightarrow 2\,{}^{0}_{0}\gamma$$

This process, which is characteristic of matter–antimatter collisions, is called *annihilation* and is another example of the interchange of the forms of matter.

Electron capture is a process in which one of the inner-orbital electrons is captured by the nucleus, as illustrated by the process

$$^{201}_{80}Hg + \underbrace{^{0}_{-1}e}_{\text{Inner-orbital electron}} \longrightarrow {}^{201}_{79}Au + {}^{0}_{0}\gamma$$

This reaction would have been of great interest to the alchemists, but unfortunately it does not occur at a rate that would make it a practical means for changing mercury to gold. Gamma rays are always produced along with electron capture to release excess energy. The various types of radioactive decay are summarized in Table 18.2.

Sample Exercise 18.1 | ## Nuclear Equations I

Write balanced equations for each of the following processes.

a. $^{11}_{6}C$ produces a positron.

b. $^{241}_{83}Bi$ produces a β particle.

c. $^{237}_{93}Np$ produces an α particle.

TABLE 18.2   Various Types of Radioactive Processes Showing the Changes That Take Place in the Nuclides

Process	Change in A	Change in Z	Change in Neutron/Proton Ratio	Example
β-particle (electron) production	0	+1	Decrease	$^{227}_{89}\text{Ac} \longrightarrow {}^{227}_{90}\text{Th} + {}^{0}_{-1}\text{e}$
Positron production	0	−1	Increase	$^{13}_{7}\text{N} \longrightarrow {}^{13}_{6}\text{C} + {}^{0}_{1}\text{e}$
Electron capture	0	−1	Increase	$^{73}_{33}\text{As} + {}^{0}_{-1}\text{e} \longrightarrow {}^{73}_{32}\text{Ge}$
α-particle production	−4	−2	Increase	$^{210}_{84}\text{Po} \longrightarrow {}^{206}_{82}\text{Pb} + {}^{4}_{2}\text{He}$
γ-ray production	0	0	—	Excited nucleus $\longrightarrow$ ground-state nucleus $+ {}^{0}_{0}\gamma$
Spontaneous fission	—	—	—	$^{254}_{98}\text{Cf} \longrightarrow$ lighter nuclides $+$ neutrons

Solution

a. We must find the product nuclide represented by $^{A}_{Z}\text{X}$ in the following equation:

$$^{11}_{6}\text{C} \longrightarrow {}^{0}_{1}\text{e} + {}^{A}_{Z}\text{X}$$
$$\uparrow$$
$$\text{Positron}$$

We can find the identity of $^{A}_{Z}\text{X}$ by recognizing that the total of the Z and A values must be the same on both sides of the equation. Thus for X, Z must be $6 - 1 = 5$ and A must be $11 - 0 = 11$. Therefore, $^{A}_{Z}\text{X}$ is $^{11}_{5}\text{B}$. (The fact that Z is 5 tells us that the nuclide is boron.) Thus the balanced equation is

$$^{11}_{6}\text{C} \longrightarrow {}^{0}_{1}\text{e} + {}^{11}_{5}\text{B}$$

b. Knowing that a β particle is represented by $^{0}_{-1}\text{e}$ and that Z and A are conserved, we can write

$$^{214}_{83}\text{Bi} \longrightarrow {}^{0}_{-1}\text{e} + {}^{214}_{84}\text{X}$$

so $^{A}_{Z}\text{X}$ must be $^{214}_{84}\text{Po}$.

c. Since an α particle is represented by $^{4}_{2}\text{He}$, the balanced equation must be

$$^{237}_{93}\text{Np} \longrightarrow {}^{4}_{2}\text{He} + {}^{233}_{91}\text{Pa}$$

See Exercises 18.11 and 18.12.

Sample Exercise 18.2	**Nuclear Equations II**

In each of the following nuclear reactions, supply the missing particle.

a. $^{195}_{79}\text{Au} + ? \rightarrow {}^{195}_{78}\text{Pt}$

b. $^{38}_{19}\text{K} \rightarrow {}^{38}_{18}\text{Ar} + ?$

Solution

a. Since A does not change and Z decreases by 1, the missing particle must be an electron:

$$^{195}_{79}\text{Au} + {}^{0}_{-1}\text{e} \longrightarrow {}^{195}_{78}\text{Pt}$$

This is an example of electron capture.

b. To conserve Z and A, the missing particle must be a positron:

$$^{38}_{19}\text{K} \longrightarrow {}^{38}_{18}\text{Ar} + {}^{0}_{1}\text{e}$$

Thus potassium-38 decays by positron production.

See Exercises 18.13 and 18.14.

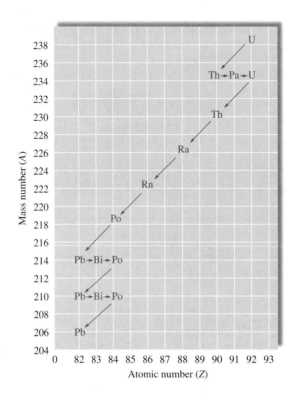

FIGURE 18.2
The decay series from $^{238}_{92}$U to $^{206}_{82}$Pb. Each nuclide in the series except $^{206}_{82}$Pb. is unstable, and the successive transformations (shown by the arrows) continue until $^{206}_{82}$Pb is finally formed. Note that horizontal arrows indicate processes where A is unchanged, while diagonal arrows signify that both A and Z change.

Often a radioactive nucleus cannot reach a stable state through a single decay process. In such a case, a **decay series** occurs until a stable nuclide is formed. A well-known example is the decay series that starts with $^{238}_{92}$U and ends with $^{206}_{82}$Pb, as shown in Fig. 18.2. Similar series exist for $^{235}_{92}$U:

$$^{235}_{92}\text{U} \xrightarrow[\text{decays}]{\text{Series of}} {}^{207}_{82}\text{Pb}$$

and for $^{232}_{90}$Th:

$$^{232}_{90}\text{Th} \xrightarrow[\text{decays}]{\text{Series of}} {}^{208}_{82}\text{Pb}$$

18.2 The Kinetics of Radioactive Decay

In a sample containing radioactive nuclides of a given type, each nuclide has a certain probability of undergoing decay. Suppose that a sample of 1000 atoms of a certain nuclide produces 10 decay events per hour. This means that over the span of an hour, 1 out of every 100 nuclides will decay. Given that this probability of decay is characteristic for this type of nuclide, we could predict that a 2000-atom sample would give 20 decay events per hour. Thus, for radioactive nuclides, the **rate of decay,** which is the negative of the change in the number of nuclides per unit time

$$\left(-\frac{\Delta N}{\Delta t}\right)$$

Rates of reaction are discussed in Chapter 12.

is directly proportional to the number of nuclides N in a given sample:

$$\text{Rate} = -\frac{\Delta N}{\Delta t} \propto N$$

The negative sign is included because the number of nuclides is decreasing. We now insert a proportionality constant k to give

$$\text{Rate} = -\frac{\Delta N}{\Delta t} = kN$$

This is the rate law for a first-order process, as we saw in Chapter 12. As shown in Section 12.4, the integrated first-order rate law is

$$\ln\left(\frac{N}{N_0}\right) = -kt$$

where N_0 represents the original number of nuclides (at $t = 0$) and N represents the number *remaining* at time t.

Half-Life

Visualization: Half-Life of Nuclear Decay

The **half-life** ($t_{1/2}$) of a radioactive sample is defined as the time required for the number of nuclides to reach half the original value ($N_0/2$). We can use this definition in connection with the integrated first-order rate law (as we did in Section 12.4) to produce the following expression for $t_{1/2}$:

$$t_{1/2} = \frac{\ln(2)}{k} = \frac{0.693}{k}$$

Thus, if the half-life of a radioactive nuclide is known, the rate constant can be easily calculated, and vice versa.

Sample Exercise 18.3	**Kinetics of Nuclear Decay I**

Technetium-99m is used to form pictures of internal organs in the body and is often used to assess heart damage. The *m* for this nuclide indicates an excited nuclear state that decays to the ground state by gamma emission. The rate constant for decay of $^{99m}_{43}\text{Tc}$ is known to be 1.16×10^{-1}/h. What is the half-life of this nuclide?

Solution

The half-life can be calculated from the expression

$$t_{1/2} = \frac{0.693}{k} = \frac{0.693}{1.16 \times 10^{-1}/\text{h}}$$
$$= 5.98 \text{ h}$$

Thus it will take 5.98 h for a given sample of technetium-99m to decrease to half the original number of nuclides.

See Exercise 18.21.

The image of a bone scan of a normal chest (posterior view). Radioactive technetium-99m is injected into the patient and is then concentrated in bones, allowing a physician to look for abnormalities such as might be caused by cancer.

The harmful effects of radiation will be discussed in Section 18.7.

As we saw in Section 12.4, the half-life for a first-order process is constant. This is shown for the β-particle decay of strontium-90 in Fig. 18.3; it takes 28.8 years for each halving of the amount of $^{90}_{38}\text{Sr}$. Contamination of the environment with $^{90}_{38}\text{Sr}$ poses serious health hazards because of the similar chemistry of strontium and calcium (both are in Group 2A). Strontium-90 in grass and hay is incorporated into cow's milk along with calcium and is then passed on to humans, where it lodges in the bones. Because of its relatively long half-life, it persists for years in humans, causing radiation damage that may lead to cancer.

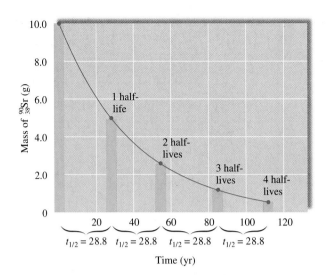

FIGURE 18.3
The decay of a 10.0-g sample of strontium-90 over time. Note that the half-life is a constant 28.8 years.

<table>
<tr><td>Sample Exercise 18.4</td><td></td></tr>
</table>

Kinetics of Nuclear Decay II

The half-life of molybdenum-99 is 67.0 h. How much of a 1.000-mg sample of $^{99}_{42}$Mo is left after 335 h?

Solution

The easiest way to solve this problem is to recognize that 335 h represents five half-lives for $^{99}_{42}$Mo:

$$335 = 5 \times 67.0$$

We can sketch the change that occurs, as is shown in Fig. 18.4. Thus, after 335 h, 0.031 mg $^{99}_{42}$Mo remains.

See Exercise 18.23.

The half-lives of radioactive nuclides vary over a tremendous range. For example, $^{144}_{60}$Nd has a half-life of 5×10^{15} years, while $^{214}_{84}$Po has a half-life of 2×10^{-4} second. To give you some perspective on this, the half-lives of the nuclides in the $^{238}_{92}$U decay series are given in Table 18.3.

FIGURE 18.4
The change in the amount of $^{99}_{42}$Mo with time ($t_{1/2} = 67$ h).

TABLE 18.3 The Half-Lives of Nuclides in the $^{238}_{92}U$ Decay Series

Nuclide	Particle Produced	Half-Life
Uranium-238 ($^{238}_{92}U$)	α	4.51×10^9 years
↓		
Thorium-234 ($^{234}_{90}Th$)	β	24.1 days
↓		
Protactinium-234 ($^{234}_{91}Pa$)	β	6.75 hours
↓		
Uranium-234 ($^{234}_{92}U$)	α	2.48×10^5 years
↓		
Thorium-230 ($^{230}_{90}Th$)	α	8.0×10^4 years
↓		
Radium-226 ($^{226}_{88}Ra$)	α	1.62×10^3 years
↓		
Radon-222 ($^{222}_{86}Rn$)	α	3.82 days
↓		
Polonium-218 ($^{218}_{84}Po$)	α	3.1 minutes
↓		
Lead-214 ($^{214}_{82}Pb$)	β	26.8 minutes
↓		
Bismuth-214 ($^{214}_{83}Bi$)	β	19.7 minutes
↓		
Polonium-214 ($^{214}_{84}Po$)	α	1.6×10^{-4} second
↓		
Lead-210 ($^{210}_{82}Pb$)	β	20.4 years
↓		
Bismuth-210 ($^{210}_{83}Bi$)	β	5.0 days
↓		
Polonium-210 ($^{210}_{84}Po$)	α	138.4 days
↓		
Lead-206 ($^{206}_{82}Pb$)	—	Stable

18.3 Nuclear Transformations

In 1919 Lord Rutherford observed the first **nuclear transformation,** *the change of one element into another.* He found that by bombarding $^{14}_{7}N$ with α particles, the nuclide $^{17}_{8}O$ could be produced:

$$^{14}_{7}N + ^{4}_{2}He \longrightarrow ^{17}_{8}O + ^{1}_{1}H$$

Fourteen years later, Irene Curie and her husband Frederick Joliot observed a similar transformation from aluminum to phosphorus:

$$^{27}_{13}Al + ^{4}_{2}He \longrightarrow ^{30}_{15}P + ^{1}_{0}n$$

where $^{1}_{0}n$ represents a neutron.

Over the years, many other nuclear transformations have been achieved, mostly using **particle accelerators,** which, as the name reveals, are devices used to give particles very high velocities. Because of the electrostatic repulsion between the target nucleus and a positive ion, accelerators are needed when positive ions are used as bombarding particles. The particle, accelerated to a very high velocity, can overcome the repulsion and penetrate the target nucleus, thus effecting the transformation. A schematic diagram of one type of particle accelerator, the **cyclotron,** is shown in Fig. 18.5. The ion is introduced at the center of the cyclotron and is accelerated in an expanding spiral path by use of alternating electric fields in the presence of a magnetic field. The **linear accelerator**

CHEMICAL IMPACT

Stellar Nucleosynthesis

How did all the matter around us originate? The scientific answer to this question is a theory called *stellar nucleosynthesis*—literally, the formation of nuclei in stars.

Many scientists believe that our universe originated as a cloud of neutrons that became unstable and produced an immense explosion, giving this model its name—*the big bang theory*. The model postulates that, following the initial explosion, neutrons decomposed into protons and electrons,

$$_{0}^{1}n \longrightarrow {}_{1}^{1}H + {}_{-1}^{0}e$$

which eventually recombined to form clouds of hydrogen. Over the eons, gravitational forces caused many of these hydrogen clouds to contract and heat up sufficiently to reach temperatures where proton fusion was possible, which released large quantities of energy. When the tendency to expand due to the heat from fusion and the tendency to contract due to the forces of gravity are balanced, a stable young star such as our sun can be formed.

Eventually, when the supply of hydrogen is exhausted, the core of the star will again contract with further heating until temperatures are reached where fusion of helium nuclei can occur, leading to the formation of $_{6}^{12}C$ and $_{8}^{16}O$ nuclei. In turn, when the supply of helium nuclei runs out, further contraction and heating will occur, until fusion of heavier nuclei takes place. This process occurs repeatedly, forming heavier and heavier nuclei until iron nuclei are formed. Because the iron nucleus is the most stable of all, energy is required to fuse iron nuclei. This endothermic fusion process cannot furnish energy to sustain the star, and therefore it cools to a small, dense *white dwarf.*

illustrated in Fig. 18.6 employs changing electric fields to achieve high velocities on a linear pathway.

In addition to positive ions, neutrons are often employed as bombarding particles to effect nuclear transformations. Because neutrons are uncharged and thus not repelled electrostatically by a target nucleus, they are readily absorbed by many nuclei, leading to new nuclides. The most common source of neutrons for this purpose is a fission reactor (see Section 18.6).

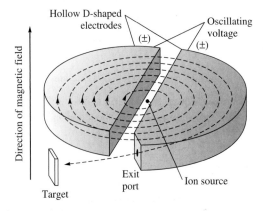

FIGURE 18.5
A schematic diagram of a cyclotron. The ion is introduced in the center and is pulled back and forth between the hollow D-shaped electrodes by constant reversals of the electric field. Magnets above and below these electrodes produce a spiral path that expands as the particle velocity increases. When the particle has sufficient speed, it exits the accelerator and is directed at the target nucleus.

The evolution just described is characteristic of small and medium-sized stars. Much larger stars, however, become unstable at some time during their evolution and undergo a *supernova explosion.* In this explosion, some medium-mass nuclei are fused to form heavy elements. Also, some light nuclei capture neutrons. These neutron-rich nuclei then produce β particles, increasing their atomic number with each event. This eventually leads to heavy nuclei. In fact, almost all nuclei heavier than iron are thought to originate from supernova explosions. The debris of a supernova explosion thus contains a large variety of elements and might eventually form a solar system such as our own.

Although other theories for the origin of matter have been suggested, there is much evidence to support the big bang theory, and it continues to be widely accepted.

Image of a portion of the Cygnus Loop supernova remnant, taken by the Hubble space telescope.

For more information see V. E. Viola, "Formation of the chemical elements and the evolution of our universe," *J. Chem. Ed.* **67** (1990): 723.

A physicist works with a small cyclotron at the University of California at Berkeley.

By using neutron and positive-ion bombardment, scientists have been able to extend the periodic table. Prior to 1940, the heaviest known element was uranium ($Z = 92$), but in 1940, neptunium ($Z = 93$) was produced by neutron bombardment of $^{238}_{92}\text{U}$. The process initially gives $^{239}_{92}\text{U}$, which decays to $^{239}_{93}\text{Np}$ by β-particle production:

$$^{238}_{92}\text{U} + ^{1}_{0}\text{n} \longrightarrow ^{239}_{92}\text{U} \xrightarrow[t_{1/2} = 23 \text{ min}]{} ^{238}_{92}\text{Np} + ^{0}_{-1}\text{p}$$

In the years since 1940, the elements with atomic numbers 93 through 112, called the **transuranium elements,*** have been synthesized. Many of these elements have very short half-lives, as shown in Table 18.4. As a result, only a few atoms of some have ever been formed. This, of course, makes the chemical characterization of these elements extremely difficult.

FIGURE 18.6
Schematic diagram of a linear accelerator, which uses a changing electric field to accelerate a positive ion along a linear path. As the ion leaves the source, the odd-numbered tubes are negatively charged, and the even-numbered tubes are positively charged. The positive ion is thus attracted into tube 1. As the ion leaves tube 1, the tube polarities are reversed. Now tube 1 is positive, repelling the positive ion, and tube 2 is negative, attracting the positive ion. This process continues, eventually producing high particle velocity.

*For more information see G. B. Kauffman, "Beyond uranium," *Chem. Eng. News* (Nov. 19, 1990): 18.

TABLE 18.4 Syntheses of Some of the Transuranium Elements

Element	Neutron Bombardment	Half-Life
Neptunium (Z = 93)	$^{238}_{92}U + ^{1}_{0}n \longrightarrow ^{239}_{93}Np + ^{0}_{-1}e$	2.35 days ($^{239}_{93}Np$)
Plutonium (Z = 94)	$^{239}_{93}Np \longrightarrow ^{239}_{94}Pu + ^{0}_{-1}e$	24,400 years ($^{239}_{94}Pu$)
Americium (Z = 95)	$^{239}_{94}Pu + 2\,^{1}_{0}n \longrightarrow ^{241}_{94}Pu \longrightarrow ^{241}_{95}Am + ^{0}_{-1}e$	458 years ($^{241}_{95}Am$)

Element	Positive-Ion Bombardment	Half-Life
Curium (Z = 96)	$^{239}_{94}Pu + ^{4}_{2}He \longrightarrow ^{242}_{96}Cm + ^{1}_{0}n$	163 days ($^{242}_{96}Cm$)
Californium (Z = 98)	$^{242}_{96}Cm + ^{4}_{2}He \longrightarrow ^{245}_{98}Cf + ^{1}_{0}n$	44 minutes ($^{245}_{98}Cf$)
	or $^{238}_{92}U + ^{12}_{6}C \longrightarrow ^{246}_{98}Cf + 4\,^{1}_{0}n$	
Rutherfordium (Z = 104)	$^{249}_{98}Cf + ^{12}_{6}C \longrightarrow ^{257}_{104}Rf + 4\,^{1}_{0}n$	
Dubnium (Z = 105)	$^{249}_{98}Cf + ^{15}_{7}N \longrightarrow ^{260}_{105}Db + 4\,^{1}_{0}n$	
Seaborgium (Z = 106)	$^{249}_{98}Cf + ^{18}_{8}O \longrightarrow ^{263}_{106}Sg + 4\,^{1}_{0}n$	

18.4 Detection and Uses of Radioactivity

Although various instruments measure radioactivity levels, the most familiar of them is the **Geiger–Müller counter,** or **Geiger counter** (see Fig. 18.7). This instrument takes advantage of the fact that the high-energy particles from radioactive decay processes produce ions when they travel through matter. The probe of the Geiger counter is filled with argon gas, which can be ionized by a rapidly moving particle. This reaction is demonstrated by the equation:

$$Ar(g) \xrightarrow[\text{particle}]{\text{High-energy}} Ar^{+}(g) + e^{-}$$

Normally, a sample of argon gas will not conduct a current when an electrical potential is applied. However, the formation of ions and electrons produced by the passage of the high-energy particle allows a momentary current to flow. Electronic devices detect this current flow, and the number of these events can be counted. Thus the decay rate of the radioactive sample can be determined.

Another instrument often used to detect levels of radioactivity is a **scintillation counter,** which takes advantage of the fact that certain substances, such as zinc sulfide,

Geiger counters are often called *survey meters* in the industry.

Visualization: Geiger Counter

FIGURE 18.7
A schematic representation of a Geiger–Müller counter. The high-energy radioactive particle enters the window and ionizes argon atoms along its path. The resulting ions and electrons produce a momentary current pulse, which is amplified and counted.

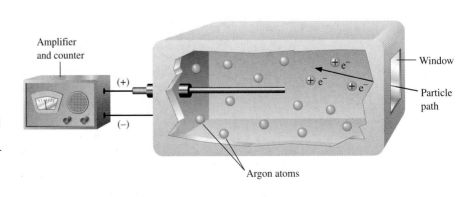

give off light when they are struck by high-energy radiation. A photocell senses the flashes of light that occur as the radiation strikes and thus measures the number of decay events per unit of time.

Dating by Radioactivity

Archeologists, geologists, and others involved in reconstructing the ancient history of the earth rely heavily on radioactivity to provide accurate dates for artifacts and rocks. A method that has been very important for dating ancient articles made from wood or cloth is **radiocarbon dating,** or **carbon-14 dating,** a technique originated in the 1940s by Willard Libby, an American chemist who received a Nobel Prize for his efforts in this field.

Radiocarbon dating is based on the radioactivity of the nuclide $^{14}_{6}C$, which decays via β-particle production:

$$^{14}_{6}C \longrightarrow \, ^{0}_{-1}e + \, ^{14}_{7}N$$

Carbon-14 is continuously produced in the atmosphere when high-energy neutrons from space collide with nitrogen-14:

$$^{14}_{7}N + \, ^{1}_{0}n \longrightarrow \, ^{14}_{6}C + \, ^{1}_{1}H$$

Brigham Young researcher Scott Woodward taking a bone sample for carbon-14 dating at an archeological site in Egypt.

Radioactive nuclides are often called *radionuclides*. Carbon dating is based on the radionuclide $^{14}_{6}C$.

The $^{14}_{6}C/^{12}_{6}C$ ratio is the basis for carbon-14 dating.

Thus carbon-14 is continuously produced by this process, and it continuously decomposes through β-particle production. Over the years, the rates for these two processes have become equal, and like a participant in a chemical reaction at equilibrium, the amount of $^{14}_{6}C$ that is present in the atmosphere remains approximately constant.

Carbon-14 can be used to date wood and cloth artifacts because the $^{14}_{6}C$, along with the other carbon isotopes in the atmosphere, reacts with oxygen to form carbon dioxide. A living plant consumes carbon dioxide in the photosynthesis process and incorporates the carbon, including $^{14}_{6}C$, into its molecules. As long as the plant lives, the $^{14}_{6}C/^{12}_{6}C$ ratio in its molecules remains the same as in the atmosphere because of the continuous uptake of carbon. However, as soon as a tree is cut to make a wooden bowl or a flax plant is harvested to make linen, the $^{14}_{6}C/^{12}_{6}C$ ratio begins to decrease because of the radioactive decay of $^{14}_{6}C$ (the $^{12}_{6}C$ nuclide is stable). Since the half-life of $^{14}_{6}C$ is 5730 years, a wooden bowl found in an archeological dig showing a $^{14}_{6}C/^{12}_{6}C$ ratio that is half that found in currently living trees is approximately 5730 years old. This reasoning assumes that the current $^{14}_{6}C/^{12}_{6}C$ ratio is the same as that found in ancient times.

Dendrochronologists, scientists who date trees from annual growth rings, have used data collected from long-lived species of trees, such as bristlecone pines and sequoias, to show that the $^{14}_{6}C$ content of the atmosphere has changed significantly over the ages. These data have been used to derive correction factors that allow very accurate dates to be determined from the observed $^{14}_{6}C/^{12}_{6}C$ ratio in an artifact, especially for artifacts 10,000 years old or younger. Recent measurements of uranium/thorium ratios in ancient coral indicate that dates in the 20,000- to 30,000-year range may have errors as large as 3000 years. As a result, efforts are now being made to recalibrate the $^{14}_{6}C$ dates over this period.

A dendrochronologist cutting a section from a dead tree in South Africa.

Sample Exercise 18.5

^{14}C Dating

The remnants of an ancient fire in a cave in Africa showed a $^{14}_{6}C$ decay rate of 3.1 counts per minute per gram of carbon. Assuming that the decay rate of $^{14}_{6}C$ in freshly cut wood (corrected for changes in the $^{14}_{6}C$ content of the atmosphere) is 13.6 counts per minute per gram of carbon, calculate the age of the remnants. The half-life of $^{14}_{6}C$ is 5730 years.

Solution

The key to solving this problem is to realize that the decay rates given are directly proportional to the number of $^{14}_{6}C$ nuclides present. Radioactive decay follows first-order kinetics:

$$\text{Rate} = kN$$

Thus

$$\frac{3.1 \text{ counts/min} \cdot \text{g}}{13.6 \text{ counts/min} \cdot \text{g}} = \frac{\text{rate at time } t}{\text{rate at time } 0} = \frac{kN}{kN_0}$$

Number of nuclides
↙ present at time t

↖ Number of nuclides
present at time 0

$$= \frac{N}{N_0} = 0.23$$

We can now use the integrated first-order rate law:

$$\ln\left(\frac{N}{N_0}\right) = -kt$$

where

$$k = \frac{0.693}{t_{1/2}} = \frac{0.693}{5730 \text{ years}}$$

to solve for t, the time elapsed since the campfire:

$$\ln\left(\frac{N}{N_0}\right) = \ln(0.23) = -\left(\frac{0.693}{5730 \text{ years}}\right)t$$

Solving this equation gives $t = 12,000$ years; the campfire in the cave occurred about 12,000 years ago.

See Exercises 18.31 and 18.32.

One drawback of radiocarbon dating is that a fairly large piece of the object (from a half to several grams) must be burned to form carbon dioxide, which is then analyzed for radioactivity. Another method for counting $^{14}_{6}C$ nuclides avoids destruction of a significant portion of a valuable artifact. This technique, requiring only about 10^{-3} g, uses a mass spectrometer (see Chapter 3), in which the carbon atoms are ionized and accelerated through a magnetic field that deflects their path. Because of their different masses, the various ions are deflected by different amounts and can be counted separately. This allows a very accurate determination of the $^{14}_{6}C/^{12}_{6}C$ ratio in the sample.

In their attempts to establish the geologic history of the earth, geologists have made extensive use of radioactivity. For example, since $^{238}_{92}U$ decays to the stable $^{206}_{82}Pb$ nuclide, the ratio of $^{206}_{82}Pb$ to $^{238}_{92}U$ in a rock can, under favorable circumstances, be used to estimate the age of the rock. The radioactive nuclide $^{176}_{71}Lu$, which decays to $^{176}_{72}Hf$, has a half-life of 37 billion years (only 186 nuclides out of 10 trillion decay each year!). Thus this nuclide can be used to date very old rocks. With this technique, scientists have estimated that the earth's crust formed 4.3 billion years ago.

| Sample Exercise 18.6 | **Dating by Radioactivity** |

Because the half-life of $^{238}_{92}U$ is very long compared with those of the other members of the decay series (see Table 18.3) to reach $^{206}_{82}Pb$, the number of nuclides present in intermediate stages of decay is negligible. That is, once a $^{238}_{92}U$ nuclide starts to decay, it reaches $^{206}_{82}Pb$ relatively fast.

A rock containing $^{238}_{92}U$ and $^{206}_{82}Pb$ was examined to determine its approximate age. Analysis showed the ratio of $^{206}_{82}Pb$ atoms to $^{238}_{92}U$ atoms to be 0.115. Assuming that no lead was originally present, that all the $^{206}_{82}Pb$ formed over the years has remained in the rock, and that the number of nuclides in intermediate stages of decay between $^{238}_{92}U$ and $^{206}_{82}Pb$ is negligible, calculate the age of the rock. The half-life of $^{238}_{92}U$ is 4.5×10^9 years.

Solution

This problem can be solved using the integrated first-order rate law:

$$\ln\left(\frac{N}{N_0}\right) = -kt = -\left(\frac{0.693}{4.5 \times 10^9 \text{ years}}\right)t$$

where N/N_0 represents the ratio of $^{238}_{92}U$ atoms now found in the rock to the number present when the rock was formed. We are assuming that each $^{206}_{82}Pb$ nuclide present must have come from decay of a $^{238}_{92}U$ atom:

$$^{238}_{92}U \longrightarrow {}^{206}_{82}Pb$$

Thus

| Number of $^{238}_{92}U$ atoms originally present | = | number of $^{206}_{82}Pb$ atoms now present | + | number of $^{238}_{92}U$ atoms now present |

$$\frac{\text{Atoms of } ^{206}_{82}Pb \text{ now present}}{\text{Atoms of } ^{238}_{92}U \text{ now present}} = 0.115 = \frac{0.115}{1.000} = \frac{115}{1000}$$

Think carefully about what this means. For every 1115 $^{238}_{92}U$ atoms originally present in the rock, 115 have been changed to $^{206}_{82}Pb$ and 1000 remain as $^{238}_{92}U$. Thus

$$\frac{N}{N_0} = \frac{^{238}_{92}U}{^{206}_{82}Pb + {}^{238}_{92}U} = \frac{1000}{1115} = 0.8969$$

$$\ln\left(\frac{N}{N_0}\right) = \ln(0.8969) = -\left(\frac{0.693}{4.5 \times 10^9 \text{ years}}\right)t$$

$$t = 7.1 \times 10^8 \text{ years}$$

This is the approximate age of the rock. It was formed sometime in the Cambrian period.

See Exercises 18.33 and 18.34.

Medical Applications of Radioactivity

Although the rapid advances of the medical sciences in recent decades are due to many causes, one of the most important has been the discovery and use of **radiotracers,** radioactive nuclides that can be introduced into organisms in food or drugs and whose pathways can be *traced* by monitoring their radioactivity. For example, the incorporation of nuclides such as $^{14}_6C$ and $^{32}_{15}P$ into nutrients has produced important information about metabolic pathways.

Iodine-131 has proved very useful in the diagnosis and treatment of illnesses of the thyroid gland. Patients drink a solution containing small amounts of $Na^{131}I$, and the uptake of the iodine by the thyroid gland is monitored with a scanner (see Fig. 18.8).

A pellet containing radioactive ^{131}I.

FIGURE 18.8
After consumption of $Na^{131}I$, the patient's thyroid is scanned for radioactivity levels to determine the efficiency of iodine absorption. (left) A normal thyroid. (right) An enlarged thyroid.

TABLE 18.5   Some Radioactive Nuclides, with Half-Lives and Medical Applications as Radiotracers

Nuclide	Half-Life	Area of the Body Studied
^{131}I	8.1 days	Thyroid
^{59}Fe	45.1 days	Red blood cells
^{99}Mo	67 hours	Metabolism
^{32}P	14.3 days	Eyes, liver, tumors
^{51}Cr	27.8 days	Red blood cells
^{87}Sr	2.8 hours	Bones
^{99m}Tc	6.0 hours	Heart, bones, liver, and lungs
^{133}Xe	5.3 days	Lungs
^{24}Na	14.8 hours	Circulatory system

Thallium-201 can be used to assess the damage to the heart muscle in a person who has suffered a heart attack, because thallium is concentrated in healthy muscle tissue. Technetium-99m is also taken up by normal heart tissue and is used for damage assessment in a similar way.

Radiotracers provide sensitive and noninvasive methods for learning about biologic systems, for detection of disease, for monitoring the action and effectiveness of drugs, and for early detection of pregnancy, and their usefulness should continue to grow. Some useful radiotracers are listed in Table 18.5.

18.5 Thermodynamic Stability of the Nucleus

We can determine the thermodynamic stability of a nucleus by calculating the change in potential energy that would occur if that nucleus were formed from its constituent protons and neutrons. For example, let's consider the hypothetical process of forming a $^{16}_{8}O$ nucleus from eight neutrons and eight protons:

$$8 \, ^{1}_{0}n + 8 \, ^{1}_{1}H \longrightarrow \, ^{16}_{8}O$$

The energy change associated with this process can be calculated by comparing the sum of the masses of eight protons and eight neutrons with that of the oxygen nucleus:

$$\text{Mass of } (8 \, ^{1}_{0}n + 8 \, ^{1}_{1}H) = 8(1.67493 \times 10^{-24}\,g) + 8(1.67262 \times 10^{-24}\,g)$$

$$\uparrow \text{Mass of } ^{1}_{0}n \qquad \uparrow \text{Mass of } ^{1}_{1}H$$

$$= 2.67804 \times 10^{-23}\,g$$

$$\text{Mass of } ^{16}_{8}O \text{ nucleus} = 2.65535 \times 10^{-23}\,g$$

The difference in mass for one nucleus is

$$\text{Mass of } ^{16}_{8}O - \text{mass of } (8 \, ^{1}_{0}n + 8 \, ^{1}_{1}H) = -2.269 \times 10^{-25}\,g$$

The difference in mass for formation of 1 mole of $^{16}_{8}O$ nuclei is therefore

$$(-2.269 \times 10^{-25}\,g/\text{nucleus})(6.022 \times 10^{23}\,\text{nuclei/mol}) = -0.1366\,g/\text{mol}$$

Thus 0.1366 g of mass would be lost if 1 mole of oxygen-16 were formed from protons and neutrons. What is the reason for this difference in mass, and how can this information be used to calculate the energy change that accompanies this process?

The answers to these questions can be found in the work of Albert Einstein. As we discussed in Section 7.2, Einstein's theory of relativity showed that energy should be considered a form of matter. His famous equation

Energy is a form of matter.

$$E = mc^2$$

where c is the speed of light, gives the relationship between a quantity of energy and its mass. When a system gains or loses energy, it also gains or loses a quantity of mass, given by E/c^2. Thus the mass of a nucleus is less than that of its component nucleons because the process is so exothermic.

Einstein's equation in the form

$$\text{Energy change} = \Delta E = \Delta mc^2$$

where Δm is the change in mass, or the **mass defect,** can be used to calculate ΔE for the hypothetical formation of a nucleus from its component nucleons.

The energy changes associated with normal chemical reactions are small enough that the corresponding mass changes are not detectable.

Sample Exercise 18.7   ## Nuclear Binding Energy I

Calculate the change in energy if 1 mol $^{16}_{8}O$ nuclei was formed from neutrons and protons.

Solution

We have already calculated that 0.1366 g of mass would be lost in the hypothetical process of assembling 1 mol $^{16}_{8}O$ nuclei from the component nucleons. We can calculate the change in energy for this process from

$$\Delta E = \Delta mc^2$$

where

$$c = 3.00 \times 10^8 \text{ m/s} \quad \text{and} \quad \Delta m = -0.1366 \text{ g/mol} = -1.366 \times 10^{-4} \text{ kg/mol}$$

Thus

$$\Delta E = (-1.366 \times 10^{-4} \text{ kg/mol})(3.00 \times 10^8 \text{ m/s})^2 = -1.23 \times 10^{13} \text{ J/mol}$$

The negative sign for the ΔE value indicates that the process is exothermic. Energy, and thus mass, is lost from the system.

See Exercises 18.35 through 18.37.

The energy changes observed for nuclear processes are extremely large compared with those observed for chemical and physical changes. Thus nuclear processes constitute a potentially valuable energy resource.

The thermodynamic stability of a particular nucleus is normally represented as energy released per nucleon. To illustrate how this quantity is obtained, we will continue to consider $^{16}_{8}O$. First, we calculate ΔE per nucleus by dividing the molar value from Sample Exercise 18.7 by Avogadro's number:

$$\Delta E \text{ per } {}^{16}_{8}O \text{ nucleus} = \frac{-1.23 \times 10^{13} \text{ J/mol}}{6.022 \times 10^{23} \text{ nuclei/mol}} = -2.04 \times 10^{-11} \text{ J/nucleus}$$

In terms of a more convenient energy unit, a million electronvolts (MeV), where

$$1 \text{ MeV} = 1.60 \times 10^{-13} \text{ J}$$

$$\Delta E \text{ per } {}^{16}_{8}O \text{ nucleus} = (-2.04 \times 10^{-11} \text{ J/nucleus})\left(\frac{1 \text{ MeV}}{1.60 \times 10^{-13} \text{ J}}\right)$$

$$= -1.28 \times 10^2 \text{ MeV/nucleus}$$

Next, we can calculate the value of ΔE per nucleon by dividing by A, the sum of neutrons and protons:

$$\Delta E \text{ per nucleon for } {}^{16}_{8}O = \frac{-1.28 \times 10^2 \text{ MeV/nucleus}}{16 \text{ nucleons/nucleus}}$$

$$= -7.98 \text{ MeV/nucleon}$$

FIGURE 18.9
The binding energy per nucleon as a function of mass number. The most stable nuclei are at the top of the curve. The most stable nucleus is $_{26}^{56}$Fe.

This means that 7.98 MeV of energy per nucleon would be *released* if $_{8}^{16}$O were formed from neutrons and protons. The energy required to *decompose* this nucleus into its components has the same numeric value but a positive sign (since energy is required). This is called the **binding energy** per nucleon for $_{8}^{16}$O.

The values of the binding energy per nucleon for the various nuclides are shown in Fig. 18.9. Note that the most stable nuclei (those requiring the largest energy per nucleon to decompose the nucleus) occur at the top of the curve. The most stable nucleus known is $_{26}^{56}$Fe, which has a binding energy per nucleon of 8.79 MeV.

Sample Exercise 18.8 ## Nuclear Binding Energy II

Calculate the binding energy per nucleon for the $_{2}^{4}$He nucleus (atomic masses: $_{2}^{4}$He = 4.0026 amu; $_{1}^{1}$H = 1.0078 amu).

Solution

First, we must calculate the mass defect (Δm) for $_{2}^{4}$He. Since atomic masses (which include the electrons) are given, we must decide how to account for the electron mass:

Since atomic masses include the masses of the electrons, to obtain the mass of a given atomic nucleus from its atomic mass, we must subtract the mass of the electrons.

$$4.0026 = \text{mass of } {}_{2}^{4}\text{He atom} = \text{mass of } {}_{2}^{4}\text{He nucleus} + 2m_{e}$$

Electron mass

$$1.0078 = \text{mass of } {}_{1}^{1}\text{H atom} = \text{mass of } {}_{1}^{1}\text{H nucleus} + m_{e}$$

Thus, since a $_{2}^{4}$He nucleus is "synthesized" from two protons and two neutrons, we see that

$$\Delta m = \underbrace{(4.0026 - 2m_{e})}_{\substack{\text{Mass of } {}_{2}^{4}\text{He} \\ \text{nucleus}}} - [\underbrace{2(1.0078 - m_{e})}_{\substack{\text{Mass of } {}_{1}^{1}\text{H} \\ \text{nucleus (proton)}}} + \underbrace{2(1.0087)}_{\substack{\text{Mass of} \\ \text{neutron}}}]$$

$$= 4.0026 - 2m_{e} - 2(1.0078) + 2m_{e} - 2(1.0087)$$

$$= 4.0026 - 2(1.0078) - 2(1.0087)$$

$$= -0.0304 \text{ amu}$$

Note that in this case the electron mass cancels out in taking the difference. This will always happen in this type of calculation if the atomic masses are used both for the nuclide of interest and for $_{1}^{1}$H. Thus 0.0304 amu of mass is *lost* per $_{2}^{4}$He nucleus formed.

The corresponding energy change can be calculated from

$$\Delta E = \Delta mc^2$$

where

$$\Delta m = -0.0304 \frac{amu}{nucleus} = \left(-0.0304 \frac{amu}{nucleus}\right)\left(1.66 \times 10^{-27} \frac{kg}{amu}\right)$$

$$= -5.04 \times 10^{-29} \frac{kg}{nucleus}$$

and

$$c = 3.00 \times 10^8 \text{ m/s}$$

Thus

$$\Delta E = \left(-5.04 \times 10^{-29} \frac{kg}{nucleus}\right)\left(3.00 \times 10^8 \frac{m}{s}\right)^2$$

$$= -4.54 \times 10^{-12} \text{ J/nucleus}$$

This means that 4.54×10^{-12} J of energy is *released* per nucleus formed and that 4.54×10^{-12} J would be required to decompose the nucleus into the constituent neutrons and protons. Thus the binding energy (BE) per nucleon is

$$\text{BE per nucleon} = \frac{4.54 \times 10^{-12} \text{ J/nucleus}}{4 \text{ nucleons/nucleus}}$$

$$= 1.14 \times 10^{-12} \text{ J/nucleon}$$

$$= \left(1.14 \times 10^{-12} \frac{J}{nucleon}\right)\left(\frac{1 \text{ MeV}}{1.60 \times 10^{-13} \text{ J}}\right)$$

$$= 7.13 \text{ MeV/nucleon}$$

See Exercises 18.38 through 18.40.

18.6 Nuclear Fission and Nuclear Fusion

The graph shown in Fig. 18.9 has very important implications for the use of nuclear processes as sources of energy. Recall that energy is released, that is, ΔE is negative, when a process goes from a less stable to a more stable state. The higher a nuclide is on the curve, the more stable it is. This means that two types of nuclear processes will be exothermic (see Fig. 18.10):

1. Combining two light nuclei to form a heavier, more stable nucleus. This process is called **fusion.**

2. Splitting a heavy nucleus into two nuclei with smaller mass numbers. This process is called **fission.**

Because of the large binding energies involved in holding the nucleus together, both these processes involve energy changes more than a million times larger than those associated with chemical reactions.

Nuclear Fission

Visualization: Nuclear Fission

Nuclear fission was discovered in the late 1930s when $^{235}_{92}U$ nuclides bombarded with neutrons were observed to split into two lighter elements:

$$^{1}_{0}n + ^{235}_{92}U \longrightarrow ^{141}_{56}Ba + ^{92}_{36}Kr + 3\,^{1}_{0}n$$

FIGURE 18.10
Both fission and fusion produce more stable nuclides and are thus exothermic.

This process, shown schematically in Fig. 18.11, releases 3.5×10^{-11} J of energy per event, which translates to 2.1×10^{13} J per mole of $^{235}_{92}U$. Compare this figure with that for the combustion of methane, which releases only 8.0×10^5 J of energy per mole. The fission of $^{235}_{92}U$ produces about 26 million times more energy than the combustion of methane.

The process shown in Fig. 18.11 is only one of the many fission reactions that $^{235}_{92}U$ can undergo. Another is

$$^{1}_{0}n + {}^{235}_{92}U \longrightarrow {}^{137}_{52}Te + {}^{97}_{40}Zr + 2\,{}^{1}_{0}n$$

In fact, over 200 different isotopes of 35 different elements have been observed among the fission products of $^{235}_{92}U$.

In addition to the product nuclides, neutrons are produced in the fission reactions of $^{235}_{92}U$. This makes it possible to have a self-sustaining fission process—a **chain reaction** (see Fig. 18.12). For the fission process to be self-sustaining, at least one neutron from each fission event must go on to split another nucleus. If, on average, *less than one* neutron causes another fission event, the process dies out and the reaction is said to be **subcritical.** If *exactly one* neutron from each fission event causes another fission event, the process sustains itself at the same level and is said to be **critical.** If *more than one* neutron from each fission event causes another fission event, the process rapidly escalates and the heat buildup causes a violent explosion. This situation is described as **supercritical.**

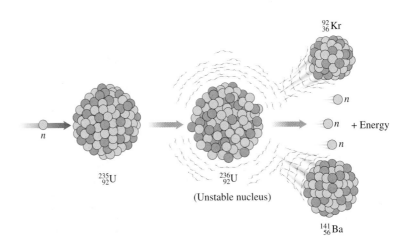

FIGURE 18.11
On capturing a neutron, the $^{235}_{92}U$ nucleus undergoes fission to produce two lighter nuclides, free neutrons (typically three), and a large amount of energy.

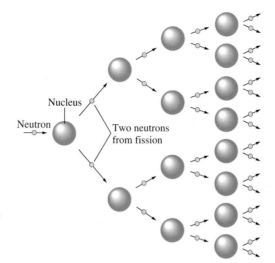

FIGURE 18.12

Representation of a fission process in which each event produces two neutrons, which can go on to split other nuclei, leading to a self-sustaining chain reaction.

To achieve the critical state, a certain mass of fissionable material, called the **critical mass,** is needed. If the sample is too small, too many neutrons escape before they have a chance to cause a fission event, and the process stops. This is illustrated in Fig. 18.13.

During World War II, an intense research effort called the Manhattan Project was carried out by the United States to build a bomb based on the principles of nuclear fission. This program produced the fission bombs that were used with devastating effects on the cities of Hiroshima and Nagasaki in 1945. Basically, a fission bomb operates by suddenly combining subcritical masses of fissionable material to form a supercritical mass, thereby producing an explosion of incredible intensity.

Nuclear Reactors

Because of the tremendous energies involved, it seemed desirable to develop the fission process as an energy source to produce electricity. To accomplish this, reactors were designed in which controlled fission can occur. The resulting energy is used to heat water to produce steam to run turbine generators, in much the same way that a coal-burning power plant generates energy. A schematic diagram of a nuclear power plant is shown in Fig. 18.14.

In the **reactor core,** shown in Fig. 18.15, uranium that has been enriched to approximately 3% $^{235}_{92}U$ (natural uranium contains only 0.7% $^{235}_{92}U$) is housed in cylinders. A **moderator** surrounds the cylinders to slow down the neutrons so that the uranium fuel can capture them more efficiently. **Control rods,** composed of substances that absorb

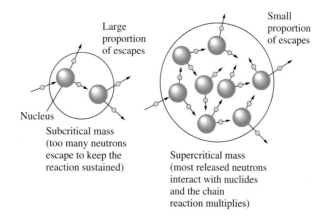

FIGURE 18.13

If the mass of fissionable material is too small, most of the neutrons escape before causing another fission event, and the process dies out.

FIGURE 18.14
A schematic diagram of a nuclear power plant.

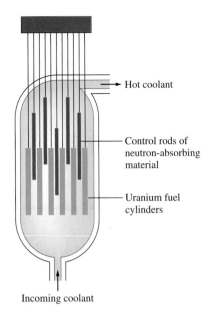

FIGURE 18.15
A schematic of a reactor core. The position of the control rods determines the level of energy production by regulating the amount of fission taking place.

neutrons, are used to regulate the power level of the reactor. The reactor is designed so that should a malfunction occur, the control rods are automatically inserted into the core to stop the reaction. A liquid (usually water) is circulated through the core to extract the heat generated by the energy of fission; the energy can then be passed on via a heat exchanger to water in the turbine system.

Although the concentration of $^{235}_{92}U$ in the fuel elements is not great enough to allow a supercritical mass to develop in the core, a failure of the cooling system can lead to temperatures high enough to melt the core. As a result, the building housing the core must be designed to contain the core even if meltdown occurs. A great deal of controversy now exists about the efficiency of the safety systems in nuclear power plants. Accidents such as the one at the Three Mile Island facility in Pennsylvania in 1979 and in Chernobyl,* Ukraine, in 1986 have led to questions about the wisdom of continuing to build fission-based power plants.

Breeder Reactors

One potential problem facing the nuclear power industry is the supply of $^{235}_{92}U$. Some scientists have suggested that we have nearly depleted those uranium deposits rich enough in $^{235}_{92}U$ to make production of fissionable fuel economically feasible. Because of this possibility, **breeder reactors** have been developed, in which fissionable fuel is actually produced while the reactor runs. In the breeder reactors now being studied, the major component of natural uranium, nonfissionable $^{238}_{92}U$, is changed to fissionable $^{239}_{94}Pu$. The reaction involves absorption of a neutron, followed by production of two β particles:

$$^{1}_{0}n + {}^{238}_{92}U \longrightarrow {}^{239}_{92}U$$
$$^{239}_{92}U \longrightarrow {}^{239}_{93}Np + {}^{0}_{-1}e$$
$$^{239}_{93}Np \longrightarrow {}^{239}_{94}Pu + {}^{0}_{-1}e$$

Uranium oxide (refined uranium).

*See C. A. Atwood, "Chernobyl—What happened?" *J. Chem. Ed.* 65 (1988): 1037.

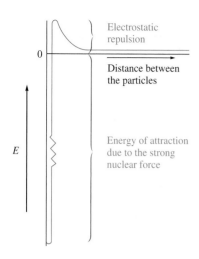

FIGURE 18.16
A plot of energy versus the separation distance for two $_1^2$H nuclei. The nuclei must have sufficient velocities to get over the electrostatic repulsion "hill" and get close enough for the nuclear binding forces to become effective, thus "fusing" the particles into a new nucleus and releasing large quantities of energy. The binding force is at least 100 times the electrostatic repulsion.

Visualization: Nuclear Fusion

As the reactor runs and $_{92}^{235}$U is split, some of the excess neutrons are absorbed by $_{92}^{238}$U to produce $_{94}^{239}$Pu. The $_{94}^{239}$Pu is then separated out and used to fuel another reactor. Such a reactor thus "breeds" nuclear fuel as it operates.

Although breeder reactors are now used in France, the United States is proceeding slowly with their development because of their controversial nature. One problem involves the hazards in handling plutonium, which flames on contact with air and is very toxic.

Fusion

Large quantities of energy are also produced by the fusion of two light nuclei. In fact, stars produce their energy through nuclear fusion. Our sun, which presently consists of 73% hydrogen, 26% helium, and 1% other elements, gives off vast quantities of energy from the fusion of protons to form helium:

$$_1^1H + _1^1H \longrightarrow _1^2H + _1^0e$$
$$_1^1H + _1^2H \longrightarrow _2^3He$$
$$_2^3He + _2^3He \longrightarrow _2^4He + 2\,_1^1H$$
$$_2^3He + _1^1H \longrightarrow _2^4He + _1^0e$$

Intense research is under way to develop a feasible fusion process because of the ready availability of many light nuclides (deuterium, $_1^2$H, in seawater, for example) that can serve as fuel in fusion reactors. The major stumbling block is that high temperatures are required to initiate fusion. The forces that bind nucleons together to form a nucleus are effective only at *very small* distances ($\sim 10^{-13}$ cm). Thus, for two protons to bind together and thereby release energy, they must get very close together. But protons, because they are identically charged, repel each other electrostatically. This means that to get two protons (or two deuterons) close enough to bind together (the nuclear binding force is *not* electrostatic), they must be "shot" at each other at speeds high enough to overcome the electrostatic repulsion.

The electrostatic repulsion forces between two $_1^2$H nuclei are so great that a temperature of 4×10^7 K is required to give them velocities large enough to cause them to collide with sufficient energy that the nuclear forces can bind the particles together and thus release the binding energy. This situation is represented in Fig. 18.16.

Currently, scientists are studying two types of systems to produce the extremely high temperatures required: high-powered lasers and heating by electric currents. At present, many technical problems remain to be solved, and it is not clear which method will prove more useful or when fusion might become a practical energy source. However, there is still hope that fusion will be a major energy source sometime in the future.

18.7 Effects of Radiation

Everyone knows that being hit by a train is very serious. The problem is the energy transfer involved. In fact, any source of energy is potentially harmful to organisms. Energy transferred to cells can break chemical bonds and cause malfunctioning of the cell systems. This fact is behind the concern about the ozone layer in the earth's upper atmosphere, which screens out high-energy ultraviolet radiation from the sun. Radioactive elements, which are sources of high-energy particles, are also potentially hazardous, although the effects are usually quite subtle. The reason for the subtlety of radiation damage is that even though high-energy particles are involved, the quantity of energy actually deposited in tissues *per event* is quite small. However, the resulting damage is no less real, although the effects may not be apparent for years.

The ozone layer is discussed in Section 20.5.

CHEMICAL IMPACT

Nuclear Physics: An Introduction

Nuclear physics is concerned with the fundamental nature of matter. The central focuses of this area of study are the relationship between a quantity of energy and its mass, given by $E = mc^2$, and the fact that matter can be converted from one form (energy) to another (particulate) in particle accelerators. Collisions between high-speed particles have produced a dazzling array of new particles—hundreds of them. These events can best be interpreted as conversions of kinetic energy into particles. For example, a collision of sufficient energy between a proton and a neutron can produce four particles: two protons, one antiproton, and a neutron:

$$\mathstrut_1^1H + \mathstrut_0^1n \longrightarrow 2\,\mathstrut_1^1H + \mathstrut_{-1}^1H + \mathstrut_0^1n$$

where $\mathstrut_{-1}^1H$ is the symbol for an *antiproton,* which has the same mass as a proton but the opposite charge. This process is a little like throwing one baseball at a very high speed into another and having the energy of the collision converted into two additional baseballs.

The results of such accelerator experiments have led scientists to postulate the existence of three types of forces important in the nucleus: the *strong force,* the *weak force,* and the *electromagnetic force.* Along with the *gravitational force,* these forces are thought to account for all types of interactions found in matter. These forces are believed to be generated by the exchange of particles between the interacting pieces of matter. For example, gravitational forces are

thought to be carried by particles called *gravitons.* The electromagnetic force (the classical electrostatic force between charged particles) is assumed to be exerted through the exchange of *photons.* The strong force, not charge-related and effective only at very short distances ($\sim 10^{-13}$ cm), is postulated to involve the exchange of particles called *gluons.* The weak force is 100 times weaker than the strong force and seems to be exerted through the exchange of two types of large particles, the W (has a mass 70 times the proton mass) and the Z (has a mass 90 times the proton mass).

The particles discovered have been classified into several categories. Three of the most important classes are as follows:

1. *Hadrons* are particles that respond to the strong force and have internal structure.

2. *Leptons* are particles that do not respond to the strong force and have no internal structure.

3. *Quarks* are particles with no internal structure that are thought to be the fundamental constituents of hadrons. Neutrons and protons are hadrons that are thought to be composed of three quarks each.

The world of particle physics appears mysterious and complicated. For example, particle physicists have discovered new properties of matter they call "color," "charm,"

Radiation damage to organisms can be classified as somatic or genetic damage. **Somatic damage** is damage to the organism itself, resulting in sickness or death. The effects may appear almost immediately if a massive dose of radiation is received; for smaller doses, damage may appear years later, usually in the form of cancer. **Genetic damage** is damage to the genetic machinery, which produces malfunctions in the offspring of the organism.

The biologic effects of a particular source of radiation depend on several factors:

1. *The energy of the radiation.* The higher the energy content of the radiation, the more damage it can cause. Radiation doses are measured in **rads** (which is short for *rad*iation *a*bsorbed *d*ose), where 1 rad corresponds to 10^{-2} J of energy deposited per kilogram of tissue.

2. *The penetrating ability of the radiation.* The particles and rays produced in radioactive processes vary in their abilities to penetrate human tissue: γ rays are highly penetrating, β particles can penetrate approximately 1 cm, and α particles are stopped by the skin.

3. *The ionizing ability of the radiation.* Extraction of electrons from biomolecules to form ions is particularly detrimental to their functions. The ionizing ability of radiation

and "strangeness" and have postulated conservation laws involving these properties. This area of science is extremely important because it should help us to understand the interactions of matter in a more elegant and unified way. For example, the classification of force into four categories is probably necessary only because we do not understand the true nature of forces. All forces may be special cases of a single, all-pervading force field that governs all of nature. In fact, Einstein spent the last 30 years of his life looking for a way to unify the gravitational and electromagnetic forces—without success. Physicists may now be on the verge of accomplishing what Einstein failed to do.

Although the practical aspects of the work in nuclear physics are not yet totally apparent, a more fundamental understanding of the way nature operates could lead to presently undreamed-of devices for energy production and communication, which could revolutionize our lives.

(left) An aerial view of Fermilab, a high-energy particle accelerator in Batavia, Illinois.
(right) The accelerator tunnel at Fermilab.

varies dramatically. For example, γ rays penetrate very deeply but cause only occasional ionization. On the other hand, α particles, although not very penetrating, are very effective at causing ionization and produce a dense trail of damage. Thus ingestion of an α-particle producer, such as plutonium, is particularly damaging.

4. *The chemical properties of the radiation source.* When a radioactive nuclide is ingested into the body, its effectiveness in causing damage depends on its residence time. For example, $^{85}_{36}\text{Kr}$ and $^{90}_{38}\text{Sr}$ are both β-particle producers. However, since krypton is chemically inert, it passes through the body quickly and does not have much time to do damage. Strontium, being chemically similar to calcium, can collect in bones, where it may cause leukemia and bone cancer.

Because of the differences in the behavior of the particles and rays produced by radioactive decay, both the energy dose of the radiation and its effectiveness in causing biologic damage must be taken into account. The **rem** (which is short for *r*oentgen *equiv*alent for *m*an) is defined as follows:

$$\text{Number of rems} = (\text{number of rads}) \times \text{RBE}$$

where RBE represents the relative effectiveness of the radiation in causing biologic damage.

TABLE 18.6 Effects of Short-Term Exposures to Radiation

Dose (rem)	Clinical Effect
0–25	Nondetectable
25–50	Temporary decrease in white blood cell counts
100–200	Strong decrease in white blood cell counts
500	Death of half the exposed population within 30 days after exposure

TABLE 18.7 Typical Radiation Exposures for a Person Living in the United States (1 millirem = 10^{-3} rem)

	Exposure (millirems/year)
Cosmic radiation	50
From the earth	47
From building materials	3
In human tissues	21
Inhalation of air	5
Total from natural sources	126
X-ray diagnosis	50
Radiotherapy	10
Internal diagnosis/ therapy	1
Nuclear power industry	0.2
TV tubes, industrial wastes, etc.	2
Radioactive fallout	4
Total from human activities	67
Total	193

Table 18.6 shows the physical effects of short-term exposure to various doses of radiation, and Table 18.7 gives the sources and amounts of radiation exposure for a typical person in the United States. Note that natural sources contribute about twice as much as human activities to the total exposure. However, although the nuclear industry contributes only a small percentage of the total exposure, the major controversy associated with nuclear power plants is the *potential* for radiation hazards. These arise mainly from two sources: accidents allowing the release of radioactive materials and improper disposal of the radioactive products in spent fuel elements. The radioactive products of the fission of $^{235}_{92}\text{U}$, although only a small percentage of the total products, have half-lives of several hundred years and remain dangerous for a long time. Various schemes have been advanced for the disposal of these wastes. The one that seems to hold the most promise is the incorporation of the wastes into ceramic blocks and the burial of these blocks in geologically stable formations. At present, however, no disposal method has been accepted, and nuclear wastes continue to accumulate in temporary storage facilities.

Even if a satisfactory method for permanent disposal of nuclear wastes is found, there will continue to be concern about the effects of exposure to low levels of radiation. Exposure is inevitable from natural sources such as cosmic rays and radioactive minerals, and many people are also exposed to low levels of radiation from reactors, radioactive tracers, or diagnostic X rays. Currently, we have little reliable information on the long-term effects of low-level exposure to radiation.

Two models of radiation damage, illustrated in Fig. 18.17, have been proposed: the *linear model* and the *threshold model*. The linear model postulates that damage from radiation is proportional to the dose, even at low levels of exposure. Thus any exposure is dangerous. The threshold model, on the other hand, assumes that no significant damage occurs below a certain exposure, called the *threshold exposure*. Note that if the linear model is correct, radiation exposure should be limited to a bare minimum (ideally at the natural levels). If the threshold model is correct, a certain level of radiation exposure beyond natural levels can be tolerated. Most scientists feel that since there is little evidence available to evaluate these models, it is safest to assume that the linear hypothesis is correct and to minimize radiation exposure.

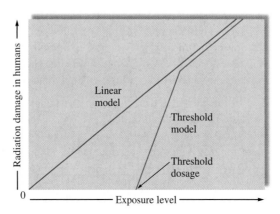

FIGURE 18.17
The two models for radiation damage. In the linear model, even a small dosage causes a proportional risk. In the threshold model, risk begins only after a certain dosage.

Key Terms

neutron
proton
nucleon
atomic number
mass number
isotopes
nuclide

Section 18.1
thermodynamic stability
kinetic stability
radioactive decay
beta (β) particle
zone of stability
alpha (α) particle
α-particle production
spontaneous fission
β-particle production
gamma (γ) ray
positron production
electron capture
decay series

Section 18.2
rate of decay
half-life

Section 18.3
nuclear transformation
particle accelerator
cyclotron
linear accelerator
transuranium elements

Section 18.4
Geiger–Müller counter (Geiger counter)
scintillation counter
radiocarbon dating (carbon-14 dating)
radiotracers

Section 18.5
mass defect
binding energy

Section 18.6
fusion
fission
chain reaction
subcritical reaction
critical reaction
supercritical reaction
critical mass
reactor core
moderator
control rods
breeder reactor

Section 18.7
somatic damage
genetic damage
rad
rem

For Review

Radioactivity

- Certain nuclei decay spontaneously into more stable nuclei
- Types of radioactive decay:
  - α-particle ($_2^4$He) production
  - β-particle ($_{-1}^0$e) production
  - Positron ($_1^0$e) production
  - γ rays are usually produced in a radioactive decay event
- A decay series involves several radioactive decays to finally reach a stable nuclide
- Radioactive decay follows first-order kinetics
  - Half-life of a radioactive sample: the time required for half of the nuclides to decay
- The transuranium elements (those beyond uranium in the periodic table) can be synthesized by particle bombardment of uranium or heavier elements
- Radiocarbon dating employs the $_6^{14}$C/$_6^{12}$C ratio in an object to establish its date of origin

Thermodynamic stability of a nucleus

- Compares the mass of a nucleus to the sum of the masses of its component nucleons
- When a system gains or loses energy, it also gains or loses mass as described by the relationship $E = mc^2$
- The difference between the sum of the masses of the component nucleons and the actual mass of a nucleus (called the mass defect) can be used to calculate the nuclear binding energy

Nuclear energy production

- Fusion: the process of combining two light nuclei to form a heavier, more stable nucleus
- Fission: the process of splitting a heavy nucleus into two lighter, more stable nuclei
  - Current nuclear power reactors employ controlled fission to produce energy

Radiation damage

- Radiation can cause direct (somatic) damage to a living organism or genetic damage to the organism's offspring
- The biologic effects of radiation depend on the energy, the penetrating ability, the ionizing ability of the radiation, and the chemical properties of the nuclide producing the radiation

REVIEW QUESTIONS

1. Define or illustrate the following terms:
   a. thermodynamic stability
   b. kinetic stability
   c. radioactive decay
   d. beta-particle production
   e. alpha-particle production
   f. positron production
   g. electron capture
   h. gamma-ray emissions
   In radioactive decay processes, *A* and *Z* are conserved. What does this mean?
2. Figure 18.1 illustrates the zone of stability. What is the zone of stability? Stable light nuclides have about equal numbers of neutrons and protons. What happens to the neutron-to-proton ratio for stable nuclides as the number of protons

increases? Nuclides that are not already in the zone of stability undergo radioactive processes to get to the zone of stability. If a nuclide has too many neutrons, which process(es) can the nuclide undergo to become more stable? Answer the same question for a nuclide having too many protons.

3. All radioactive decay processes follow first-order kinetics. What does this mean? What happens to the rate of radioactive decay as the number of nuclides is halved? Write the first-order rate law and the integrated first-order rate law. Define the terms in each equation. What is the half-life equation for radioactive decay processes? How does the half-life depend on how many nuclides are present? Are the half-life and rate constant k directly related or inversely related?

4. What is a nuclear transformation? How do you balance nuclear transformation reactions? Particle accelerators are used to perform nuclear transformations. What is a particle accelerator?

5. What is a Geiger counter and how does it work? What is a scintillation counter and how does it work? Radiotracers are used in the medical sciences to learn about metabolic pathways. What are radiotracers? Explain why ^{14}C and ^{32}P radioactive nuclides would be very helpful in learning about metabolic pathways. Why is I-131 useful for diagnosis of diseases of the thyroid? How could you use a radioactive nuclide to demonstrate that chemical equilibrium is a dynamic process?

6. Explain the theory behind carbon-14 dating. What assumptions must be made and what problems arise when using carbon-14 dating?

   The decay of uranium-238 to lead-206 is also used to estimate the age of objects. Specifically, ^{206}Pb-to-^{238}U ratios allow dating of rocks. Why is the ^{238}U decay to ^{206}Pb useful for dating rocks but worthless for dating objects 10,000 years old or younger? Similarly, why is carbon-14 dating useful for dating objects 10,000 years old or younger but worthless for dating rocks?

7. Define *mass defect* and *binding energy*. How do you determine the mass defect for a nuclide? How do you convert the mass defect into the binding energy for a nuclide? Iron-56 has the largest binding energy per nucleon among all known nuclides. Is this good or bad for iron-56? Explain.

8. Define *fission* and *fusion*. How does the energy associated with fission or fusion processes compare to the energy changes associated with chemical reactions? Fusion processes are more likely to occur for lighter elements, whereas fission processes are more likely to occur for heavier elements. Why? (*Hint:* Reference Figure 18.10.) The major stumbling block for turning fusion reactions into a feasible source of power is the high temperature required to initiate a fusion reaction. Why are elevated temperatures necessary to initiate fusion reactions but not fission reactions?

9. The fission of U-235 is used exclusively in nuclear power plants located in the United States. There are many different fission reactions of U-235, but all the fission reactions are self-sustaining chain reactions. Explain. Differentiate between the terms *critical, subcritical,* and *supercritical.* What is the critical mass? How does a nuclear power plant produce electricity? What are the purposes of the moderator and the control rods in a fission reactor? What are some problems associated with nuclear reactors? What are breeder reactors? What are some problems associated with breeder reactors?

10. The biological effects of a particular source of radiation depend on several factors. List some of these factors. Even though ^{85}Kr and ^{90}Sr are both beta-particle emitters, the dangers associated with the decay of ^{90}Sr are much greater than those linked to ^{85}Kr. Why? Although gamma rays are far more penetrating than alpha particles, the latter are more likely to cause damage to an organism. Why? Which type of radiation is more effective at promoting the ionization of biomolecules?

A blue question or exercise number indicates that the answer to that question or exercise appears at the back of this book and a solution appears in the *Solutions Guide*.

Questions

1. When nuclei undergo nuclear transformations, γ rays of characteristic frequencies are observed. How does this fact, along with other information in the chapter on nuclear stability, suggest that a quantum mechanical model may apply to the nucleus?

2. There is a trend in the United States toward using coal-fired power plants to generate electricity rather than building new nuclear fission power plants. Is the use of coal-fired power plants without risk? Make a list of the risks to society from the use of each type of power plant.

3. Which type of radioactive decay has the net effect of changing a neutron into a proton? Which type of decay has the net effect of turning a proton into a neutron?

4. What is annihilation in terms of nuclear processes?

5. What are transuranium elements and how are they synthesized?

6. Scientists have estimated that the earth's crust was formed 4.3 billion years ago. The radioactive nuclide ^{176}Lu, which decays to ^{176}Hf, was used to estimate this age. The half-life of ^{176}Lu is 37 billion years. How are ratios of ^{176}Lu to ^{176}Hf utilized to date very old rocks?

7. Why are the observed energy changes for nuclear processes so much larger than the energy changes for chemical and physical processes?

8. Natural uranium is mostly nonfissionable ^{238}U; it contains only about 0.7% of fissionable ^{235}U. For uranium to be useful as a nuclear fuel, the relative amount of ^{235}U must be increased to about 3%. This is accomplished through a gas diffusion process. In the diffusion process, natural uranium reacts with fluorine to form a mixture of ^{238}UF$_6$(g) and ^{235}UF$_6$(g). The fluoride mixture is then enriched through a multistage diffusion process to produce a 3% ^{235}U nuclear fuel. The diffusion process utilizes Graham's law of effusion (see Chapter 5, Section 5.7). Explain how Graham's law of effusion allows natural uranium to be enriched by the gaseous diffusion process.

9. Strontium-90 and radon-222 both pose serious health risks. ^{90}Sr decays by β-particle production and has a relatively long half-life (28.8 yr). Radon-222 decays by alpha-particle production and has a relatively short half-life (3.82 days). Explain why each decay process poses health risks.

10. A recent study concluded that any amount of radiation exposure can cause biological damage. Explain the differences between the two models of radiation damage, the linear model and the threshold model.

Exercises

In this section similar exercises are paired.

Radioactive Decay and Nuclear Transformations

11. Write balanced equations for each of the processes described below.
    a. Chromium-51, which targets the spleen and is used as a tracer in studies of red blood cells, decays by electron capture.
    b. Iodine-131, used to treat hyperactive thyroid glands, decays by producing a β particle.

12. Write balanced equations for each of the processes described below.
    a. Phosphorus-32, which accumulates in the liver, decays by β-particle production.
    b. Uranium-235, which is used in atomic bombs, decays initially by α-particle production.

13. Write an equation describing the radioactive decay of each of the following nuclides. (The particle produced is shown in parentheses, except for electron capture, where an electron is a reactant.)
    a. ^{68}Ga (electron capture)   c. ^{212}Fr (α)
    b. ^{62}Cu (positron)   d. ^{129}Sb (β)

14. In each of the following nuclear reactions, supply the missing particle.
    a. ^{73}Ga $\rightarrow$ ^{73}Ge + ?   c. ^{205}Bi $\rightarrow$ ^{205}Pb + ?
    b. ^{192}Pt $\rightarrow$ ^{188}Os + ?   d. ^{241}Cm + ? $\rightarrow$ ^{241}Am

15. The radioactive isotope ^{247}Bk decays by a series of α-particle and β-particle productions, taking ^{247}Bk through many transformations to end up as ^{207}Pb. In the complete decay series, how many α particles and β particles are produced?

16. One type of commercial smoke detector contains a minute amount of radioactive americium-241 (^{241}Am), which decays by α-particle production. The α particles ionize molecules in the air, allowing it to conduct an electric current. When smoke particles enter, the conductivity of the air is changed and the alarm buzzes.
    a. Write the equation for the decay of $^{241}_{95}$Am by α-particle production.
    b. The complete decay of ^{241}Am involves successively α, α, β, α, α, β, α, α, α, β, α, and β production. What is the final stable nucleus produced in this decay series?
    c. Identify the 11 intermediate nuclides.

17. There are four stable isotopes of iron with mass numbers 54, 56, 57, and 58. There are also two radioactive isotopes: iron-53 and iron-59. Predict modes of decay for these two isotopes. (See Table 18.2.)

18. The only stable isotope of fluorine is fluorine-19. Predict possible modes of decay for fluorine-21, fluorine-18, and fluorine-17.

19. In 1994 it was proposed (and eventually accepted) that element 106 be named seaborgium, Sg, in honor of Glenn T. Seaborg, discoverer of the transuranium elements.
    a. ^{263}Sg was produced by the bombardment of ^{249}Cf with a beam of ^{18}O nuclei. Complete and balance an equation for this reaction.
    b. ^{263}Sg decays by α emission. What is the other product resulting from the α decay of ^{263}Sg?

20. Many elements have been synthesized by bombarding relatively heavy atoms with high-energy particles in particle accelerators. Complete the following nuclear reactions, which have been used to synthesize elements.
    a. _____ + $^{4}_{2}$He $\rightarrow$ $^{243}_{97}$Bk + $^{1}_{0}$n
    b. $^{238}_{92}$U + $^{12}_{6}$C $\rightarrow$ _____ + 6 $^{1}_{0}$n
    c. $^{249}_{98}$Cf + _____ $\rightarrow$ $^{260}_{105}$Db + 4 $^{1}_{0}$n
    d. $^{249}_{98}$Cf + $^{10}_{5}$B $\rightarrow$ $^{257}_{103}$Lr + _____

Kinetics of Radioactive Decay

21. The rate constant for a certain radioactive nuclide is 1.0×10^{-3} h^{-1}. What is the half-life of this nuclide?

22. Americium-241 is widely used in smoke detectors. The radiation released by this element ionizes particles that are then detected by a charged-particle collector. The half-life of ^{241}Am is 432.2 years, and it decays by emitting alpha particles. How many alpha particles are emitted each second by a 5.00-g sample of ^{241}Am?

23. Krypton consists of several radioactive isotopes, some of which are listed in the following table.

	Half-life
Kr-73	27 s
Kr-74	11.5 min
Kr-76	14.8 h
Kr-81	2.1×10^5 yr

Which of these isotopes is most stable and which isotope is "hottest"? How long does it take for 87.5% of each isotope to decay?

24. Radioactive copper-64 decays with a half-life of 12.8 days.
  a. What is the value of k in s^{-1}?
  b. A sample contains 28.0 mg ^{64}Cu. How many decay events will be produced in the first second? Assume the atomic mass of ^{64}Cu is 64.0.
  c. A chemist obtains a fresh sample of ^{64}Cu and measures its radioactivity. She then determines that to do an experiment, the radioactivity cannot fall below 25% of the initial measured value. How long does she have to do the experiment?

25. Phosphorus-32 is a commonly used radioactive nuclide in biochemical research, particularly in studies of nucleic acids. The half-life of phosphorus-32 is 14.3 days. What mass of phosphorus-32 is left from an original sample of 175 mg of Na$_3{}^{32}$PO$_4$ after 35.0 days? Assume the atomic mass of ^{32}P is 32.0.

26. The curie (Ci) is a commonly used unit for measuring nuclear radioactivity: 1 curie of radiation is equal to 3.7×10^{10} decay events per second (the number of decay events from 1 g of radium in 1 s).
  a. What mass of Na$_2{}^{38}$SO$_4$ has an activity of 10.0 mCi? Sulfur-38 has an atomic mass of 38.0 and a half-life of 2.87 h.
  b. How long does it take for 99.99% of a sample of sulfur-38 to decay?

27. The first atomic explosion was detonated in the desert north of Alamogordo, New Mexico, on July 16, 1945. What fraction of the strontium-90 ($t_{1/2} = 28.8$ years) originally produced by that explosion still remains as of July 16, 2006?

28. Iodine-131 is used in the diagnosis and treatment of thyroid disease and has a half-life of 8.1 days. If a patient with thyroid disease consumes a sample of Na^{131}I containing 10 μg of ^{131}I, how long will it take for the amount of ^{131}I to decrease to 1/100 of the original amount?

29. The Br-82 nucleus has a half-life of 1.0×10^3 min. If you wanted 1.0 g of Br-82 and the delivery time was 3.0 days, what mass of NaBr should you order (assuming all of the Br in the NaBr was Br-82)?

30. Fresh rainwater or surface water contains enough tritium ($^3_1$H) to show 5.5 decay events per minute per 100. g of water. Tritium has a half-life of 12.3 years. You are asked to check a vintage wine that is claimed to have been produced in 1946. How many decay events per minute should you expect to observe in 100. g of that wine?

31. A living plant contains approximately the same fraction of carbon-14 as in atmospheric carbon dioxide. Assuming that the observed rate of decay of carbon-14 from a living plant is 13.6 counts per minute per gram of carbon, how many counts per minute per gram of carbon will be measured from a 15,000-year-old sample? Will radiocarbon dating work well for small samples of 10 mg or less? (For ^{14}C, $t_{1/2} = 5730$ years.)

32. Assume a constant ^{14}C/^{12}C ratio of 13.6 counts per minute per gram of living matter. A sample of a petrified tree was found to give 1.2 counts per minute per gram. How old is the tree? ($t_{1/2} = {}^{14}$C $= 5730$ years.)

33. A rock contains 0.688 mg of ^{206}Pb for every 1.000 mg of ^{238}U present. Assuming that no lead was originally present, that all the ^{206}Pb formed over the years has remained in the rock, and that the number of nuclides in intermediate stages of decay between ^{238}U and ^{206}Pb is negligible, calculate the age of the rock. (For ^{238}U, $t_{1/2} = 4.5 \times 10^9$ years.)

34. The mass ratios of ^{40}Ar to ^{40}K also can be used to date geologic materials. Potassium-40 decays by two processes:

$$^{40}_{19}\text{K} + {}^{0}_{-1}\text{e} \longrightarrow {}^{40}_{18}\text{Ar} \ (10.7\%) \qquad t_{1/2} = 1.27 \times 10^9 \text{ years}$$
$$^{40}_{19}\text{K} \longrightarrow {}^{40}_{20}\text{Ca} + {}^{0}_{-1}\text{e} \ (89.3\%)$$

  a. Why are ^{40}Ar/^{40}K ratios used to date materials rather than ^{40}Ca/^{40}K ratios?
  b. What assumptions must be made using this technique?
  c. A sedimentary rock has an ^{40}Ar/^{40}K ratio of 0.95. Calculate the age of the rock.
  d. How will the measured age of a rock compare to the actual age if some ^{40}Ar escaped from the sample?

Energy Changes in Nuclear Reactions

35. The sun radiates 3.9×10^{23} J of energy into space every second. What is the rate at which mass is lost from the sun?

36. The earth receives 1.8×10^{14} kJ/s of solar energy. What mass of solar material is converted to energy over a 24-h period to provide the daily amount of solar energy to the earth? What mass of coal would have to be burned to provide the same amount of energy? (Coal releases 32 kJ of energy per gram when burned.)

37. Many transuranium elements, such as plutonium-232, have very short half-lives. (For ^{232}Pu, the half-life is 36 minutes.) However, some, like protactinium-231 (half-life $= 3.34 \times 10^4$ years), have relatively long half-lives. Use the masses given in the following table to calculate the change in energy when 1 mol of ^{232}Pu nuclei and 1 mol of ^{231}Pa nuclei are each formed from their respective number of protons and neutrons.

Atom or Particle	Atomic Mass
Neutron	1.67493×10^{-24} g
Proton	1.67262×10^{-24} g
Electron	9.10939×10^{-28} g
Pu-232	3.85285×10^{-22} g
Pa-231	3.83616×10^{-22} g

(Since the masses of ^{232}Pu and ^{231}Pa are atomic masses, they each include the mass of the electrons present. The mass of the nucleus will be the atomic mass minus the mass of the electrons.)

38. The most stable nucleus in terms of binding energy per nucleon is ^{56}Fe. If the atomic mass of ^{56}Fe is 55.9349 amu, calculate the binding energy per nucleon for ^{56}Fe.

39. Calculate the binding energy in J/nucleon for carbon-12 (atomic mass 12.0000) and uranium-235 (atomic mass 235.0439). The atomic mass of $^{1}_{1}$H is 1.00782 amu and the mass of a neutron is 1.00866 amu. The most stable nucleus known is ^{56}Fe (see Exercise 38). Would the binding energy per nucleon for ^{56}Fe be larger or smaller than that of ^{12}C or ^{235}U? Explain.

40. Calculate the binding energy per nucleon for $^{2}_{1}$H and $^{3}_{1}$H. The atomic masses are $^{2}_{1}$H, 2.01410, and $^{3}_{1}$H, 3.01605.

41. The mass defect for a Li-6 nucleus is -0.03434 g/mol. Calculate the atomic mass of Li-6.

42. The binding energy per nucleon for Mg-27 is 1.326×10^{-12} J/nucleon. Calculate the atomic mass of Mg-27.

43. Calculate the amount of energy released per gram of hydrogen nuclei reacted for the following reaction. The atomic masses are $^{1}_{1}$H, 1.00782 amu; $^{2}_{1}$H, 2.01410 amu, and an electron, 5.4858×10^{-4} amu. (*Hint:* Think carefully about how to account for the electron mass.)

$$^{1}_{1}H + ^{1}_{1}H \longrightarrow ^{2}_{1}H + ^{0}_{+1}e$$

44. The easiest fusion reaction to initiate is

$$^{2}_{1}H + ^{3}_{1}H \longrightarrow ^{4}_{2}He + ^{1}_{0}n$$

Calculate the energy released per $^{4}_{2}$He nucleus produced and per mole of $^{4}_{2}$He produced. The atomic masses are $^{2}_{1}$H, 2.01410; $^{3}_{1}$H, 3.01605; and $^{4}_{2}$He, 4.00260. The masses of the electron and neutron are 5.4858×10^{-4} and 1.00866 amu, respectively.

Detection, Uses, and Health Effects of Radiation

45. The typical response of a Geiger–Müller tube is shown below. Explain the shape of this curve.

Disintegrations/s from sample

46. When using a Geiger–Müller counter to measure radioactivity, it is necessary to maintain the same geometrical orientation between the sample and the Geiger–Müller tube to compare different measurements. Why?

47. Photosynthesis in plants can be represented by the following overall reaction:

$$6CO_2(g) + 6H_2O(l) \xrightarrow{\text{Light}} C_6H_{12}O_6(s) + 6O_2(g)$$

Algae grown in water containing some ^{18}O (in $H_2{}^{18}$O) evolve oxygen gas with the same isotopic composition as the oxygen in the water. When algae growing in water containing only ^{16}O were furnished carbon dioxide containing ^{18}O, no ^{18}O was found to be evolved from the oxygen gas produced. What conclusions about photosynthesis can be drawn from these experiments?

48. Consider the following reaction to produce methyl acetate:

$$CH_3OH + CH_3\overset{O}{\overset{\|}{C}}OH \longrightarrow CH_3\overset{O}{\overset{\|}{C}}OCH_3 + H_2O$$
Methyl acetate

When this reaction is carried out with CH_3OH containing oxygen-18, the water produced does not contain oxygen-18. Explain.

49. U-235 undergoes many different fission reactions. For one such reaction, when U-235 is struck with a neutron, Ce-144 and Sr-90 are produced along with some neutrons and electrons. How many neutrons and β-particles are produced in this fission reaction?

50. Breeder reactors are used to convert the nonfissionable nuclide $^{238}_{92}$U to a fissionable product. Neutron capture of the $^{238}_{92}$U is followed by two successive beta decays. What is the final fissionable product?

51. Which do you think would be the greater health hazard: the release of a radioactive nuclide of Sr or a radioactive nuclide of Xe into the environment? Assume the amount of radioactivity is the same in each case. Explain your answer on the basis of the chemical properties of Sr and Xe. Why are the chemical properties of a radioactive substance important in assessing its potential health hazards?

52. Consider the following information:
  i. The layer of dead skin on our bodies is sufficient to protect us from most α-particle radiation.
  ii. Plutonium is an α-particle producer.
  iii. The chemistry of Pu^{4+} is similar to that of Fe^{3+}.
  iv. Pu oxidizes readily to Pu^{4+}.
  Why is plutonium one of the most toxic substances known?

Additional Exercises

53. Predict whether each of the following nuclides is stable or unstable (radioactive). If the nuclide is unstable, predict the type of radioactivity you would expect it to exhibit.
  a. $^{45}_{19}$K **b.** $^{56}_{26}$Fe **c.** $^{20}_{11}$Na **d.** $^{194}_{81}$Tl

54. At a flea market, you've found a very interesting painting done in the style of Rembrandt's "dark period" (1642–1672). You suspect that you really do not have a genuine Rembrandt, but you take it to the local university for testing. Living wood shows a carbon-14 activity of 15.3 counts per minute per gram. Your painting showed a carbon-14 activity of 15.1 counts per minute per gram. Could it be a genuine Rembrandt?

55. Define "third-life" in a similar way to "half-life" and determine the "third-life" for a nuclide that has a half-life of 31.4 years.

56. A proposed system for storing nuclear wastes involves storing the radioactive material in caves or deep mine shafts. One of the most toxic nuclides that must be disposed of is plutonium-239, which is produced in breeder reactors and has a half-life of 24,100 years. A suitable storage place must be geologically stable long enough for the activity of plutonium-239 to decrease to 0.1% of its original value. How long is this for plutonium-239?

57. During World War II, tritium (^{3}H) was a component of fluorescent watch dials and hands. Assume you have such a watch that was made in January 1944. If 17% or more of the original tritium was needed to read the dial in dark places, until what year could you read the time at night? (For ^{3}H, $t_{1/2} = 12.3$ yr.)

58. A positron and an electron can annihilate each other on colliding, producing energy as photons:

$$_{-1}^{0}e + {_{+1}^{0}}e \longrightarrow 2{_0^0}\gamma$$

Assuming that both γ rays have the same energy, calculate the wavelength of the electromagnetic radiation produced.

59. A small atomic bomb releases energy equivalent to the detonation of 20,000 tons of TNT; a ton of TNT releases 4×10^9 J of energy when exploded. Using 2×10^{13} J/mol as the energy released by fission of ^{235}U, approximately what mass of ^{235}U undergoes fission in this atomic bomb?

60. During the research that led to production of the two atomic bombs used against Japan in World War II, different mechanisms for obtaining a supercritical mass of fissionable material were investigated. In one type of bomb, a "gun" shot one piece of fissionable material into a cavity containing another piece of fissionable material. In the second type of bomb, the fissionable material was surrounded with a high explosive that, when detonated, compressed the fissionable material into a smaller volume. Discuss what is meant by critical mass, and explain why the ability to achieve a critical mass is essential to sustaining a nuclear reaction.

61. Using the kinetic molecular theory (Section 5.6), calculate the root mean square velocity and the average kinetic energy of $^2_1$H nuclei at a temperature of 4×10^7 K. (See Exercise 44 for the appropriate mass values.)

Challenge Problems

62. A 0.20-mL sample of a solution containing $^3_1$H that produces 3.7×10^3 cps is injected into the bloodstream of an animal. After allowing circulatory equilibrium to be established, a 0.20-mL sample of blood is found to have an activity of 20. cps. Calculate the blood volume of the animal.

63. A 0.10-cm^3 sample of a solution containing a radioactive nuclide (5.0×10^3 counts per minute per milliliter) is injected into a rat. Several minutes later 1.0 cm^3 of blood is removed. The blood shows 48 counts per minute of radioactivity. Calculate the volume of blood in the rat. What assumptions must be made in performing this calculation?

64. Zirconium is one of the few metals that retains its structural integrity upon exposure to radiation. The fuel rods in most nuclear reactors therefore are often made of zirconium. Answer the following questions about the redox properties of zirconium based on the half-reaction

$$ZrO_2 \cdot H_2O + H_2O + 4e^- \longrightarrow Zr + 4OH^- \qquad \mathscr{E}° = -2.36 \text{ V}$$

a. Is zirconium metal capable of reducing water to form hydrogen gas at standard conditions?

b. Write a balanced equation for the reduction of water by zirconium.

c. Calculate $\mathscr{E}°$, $\Delta G°$, and K for the reduction of water by zirconium metal.

d. The reduction of water by zirconium occurred during the accidents at Three Mile Island in 1979. The hydrogen produced was successfully vented and no chemical explosion occurred. If 1.00×10^3 kg of Zr reacts, what mass of H_2 is produced? What volume of H_2 at 1.0 atm and 1000.°C is produced?

e. At Chernobyl in 1986, hydrogen was produced by the reaction of superheated steam with the graphite reactor core:

$$C(s) + H_2O(g) \longrightarrow CO(g) + H_2(g)$$

It was not possible to prevent a chemical explosion at Chernobyl. In light of this, do you think it was a correct decision to vent the hydrogen and other radioactive gases into the atmosphere at Three Mile Island? Explain.

65. In addition to the process described in the text, a second process called the *carbon–nitrogen cycle* occurs in the sun:

$$^1_1\text{H} + {}^{12}_6\text{C} \longrightarrow {}^{13}_7\text{N} + {}^0_0\gamma$$
$$^{13}_7\text{N} \longrightarrow {}^{13}_6\text{C} + {}^0_{+1}e$$
$$^1_1\text{H} + {}^{13}_6\text{C} \longrightarrow {}^{14}_7\text{N} + {}^0_0\gamma$$
$$^1_1\text{H} + {}^{14}_7\text{N} \longrightarrow {}^{15}_8\text{O} + {}^0_0\gamma$$
$$^{15}_8\text{O} \longrightarrow {}^{15}_7\text{N} + {}^0_{+1}e$$
$$^1_1\text{H} + {}^{15}_7\text{N} \longrightarrow {}^{12}_6\text{C} + {}^4_2\text{He} + {}^0_0\gamma$$

Overall reaction: $\quad 4{}^1_1\text{H} \longrightarrow {}^4_2\text{He} + 2{}^0_{+1}e$

a. What is the catalyst in this process?

b. What nucleons are intermediates?

c. How much energy is released per mole of hydrogen nuclei in the overall reaction? (The atomic masses of $^1_1$H and $^4_2$He are 1.00782 and 4.00260, respectively.)

66. The most significant source of natural radiation is radon-222. ^{222}Rn, a decay product of ^{238}U, is continuously generated in the earth's crust, allowing gaseous Rn to seep into the basements of buildings. Because ^{222}Rn is an α-particle producer with a relatively short half-life of 3.82 days, it can cause biological damage when inhaled.

a. How many α particles and β particles are produced when ^{238}U decays to ^{222}Rn? What nuclei are produced when ^{222}Rn decays?

b. Radon is a noble gas so one would expect it to pass through the body quickly. Why is there a concern over inhaling ^{222}Rn?

c. Another problem associated with ^{222}Rn is that the decay of ^{222}Rn produces a more potent α-particle producer ($t_{1/2} = 3.11$ min) that is a solid. What is the identity of the solid? Give the balanced equation of this species decaying by α-particle production. Why is the solid a more potent α-particle producer?

d. The U.S. Environmental Protection Agency (EPA) recommends that ^{222}Rn levels not exceed 4 pCi per liter of air (1 Ci = 1 curie = 3.7×10^{10} decay events per second; 1 pCi = 1×10^{-12} Ci). Convert 4.0 pCi per liter of air into concentrations units of ^{222}Rn atoms per liter of air and moles of ^{222}Rn per liter of air.

67. To determine the K_{sp} value of Hg_2I_2, a chemist obtained a solid sample of Hg_2I_2 in which some of the iodine is present as radioactive ^{131}I. The count rate of the Hg_2I_2 sample is 5.0×10^{11} counts per minute per mole of I. An excess amount of $Hg_2I_2(s)$ is placed into some water, and the solid is allowed to come to equilibrium with its respective ions. A 150.0-mL sample of the saturated solution is withdrawn and the radioactivity measured at 33 counts per minute. From this information, calculate the K_{sp} value for Hg_2I_2.

$$Hg_2I_2(s) \rightleftharpoons Hg_2^{2+}(aq) + 2I^-(aq) \qquad K_{sp} = [Hg_2^{2+}][I^-]^2$$

68. Estimate the temperature needed to achieve the fusion of deuterium to make an alpha particle. The energy required can be estimated from Coulomb's law [use the form $E = 9.0 \times 10^9 (Q_1Q_2/r)$, using $Q = 1.6 \times 10^{-19}$ C for a proton, and $r = 2 \times 10^{-15}$ m for the helium nucleus; the unit for the proportionality constant in Coloumb's law is $J \cdot m/C^2$.]

Integrative Problems

These problems require the integration of multiple concepts to find the solutions.

69. A recently reported synthesis of the transuranium element bohrium (Bh) involved the bombardment of berkelium-249 with neon-22 to produce bohrium-267. Write a nuclear reaction for this synthesis. The half-life of bohrium-267 is 15.0 seconds. If 199 atoms of bohrium-267 could be synthesized, how much time would elapse before only 11 atoms of bohrium-267 remain? What is the expected electron configuration of elemental bohrium?

70. Radioactive cobalt-60 is used to study defects in vitamin B_{12} absorption because cobalt is the metallic atom at the center of the vitamin B_{12} molecule. The nuclear synthesis of this cobalt isotope involves a three-step process. The overall reaction is iron-58 reacting with two neutrons to produce cobalt-60 along with the emission of another particle. What particle is emitted in this nuclear synthesis? What is the binding energy in J per nucleon for the cobalt-60 nucleus (atomic masses: ^{60}Co = 59.9338 amu; ^1H = 1.00782 amu). What is the de Broglie wavelength of the emitted particle if it has a velocity equal to $0.90c$ where c is the speed of light?

Get help understanding core concepts and visualizing molecular-level interactions, and practice problem solving, by visiting the Online Study Center at **college.hmco.com/ PIC/zumdahl7e.**

19 The Representative Elements: Groups 1A Through 4A

Contents

Scanning electron micrograph of calcium crystals, a representative element in Group 2A.

So far in this book we have covered the major principles and explored the most important models of chemistry. In particular, we have seen that the chemical properties of the elements can be explained very successfully by the quantum mechanical model of the atom. In fact, the most convincing evidence of that model's validity is its ability to relate the observed periodic properties of the elements to the number of valence electrons in their atoms.

We have learned many properties of the elements and their compounds, but we have not discussed in detail the relationship between the chemical properties of a particular element and its position on the periodic table. In this chapter and the next we will explore the chemical similarities and differences among the elements in the several groups of the periodic table and will try to interpret these data using the quantum mechanical model of the atom. In the process we will illustrate a great variety of chemical properties and further demonstrate the practical importance of chemistry.

19.1 A Survey of the Representative Elements

The traditional form of the periodic table is shown in Fig. 19.1. Recall that the **representative elements,** whose chemical properties are determined by the valence-level *s* and *p* electrons, are designated Groups 1A through 8A. The **transition metals,** in the center of the table, result from the filling of *d* orbitals. The elements that correspond to the filling of the 4*f* and 5*f* orbitals are listed separately as the **lanthanides** and **actinides,** respectively.

The heavy black line in Fig. 19.1 divides the metals from the nonmetals. Some elements just on either side of this line, such as silicon and germanium, exhibit both metallic and nonmetallic properties and are often called **metalloids** or **semimetals.** The fundamental chemical difference between a metal and a nonmetal is that metals tend to lose their valence electrons to form *cations,* usually with the valence-electron configuration of the noble gas from the preceding period, and nonmetals tend to gain electrons to

FIGURE 19.1
The periodic table. The elements in the A groups are the representative elements. The elements shown in pink are called *transition metals*. The dark line approximately divides the nonmetals from the metals. The elements that have both metallic and nonmetallic properties (semimetals) are shaded in blue.

form *anions* that exhibit the electron configuration of the noble gas in the same period. Metallic character is observed to increase going down a given group, which is consistent with the trends in ionization energy, electron affinity, and electronegativity discussed earlier (see Sections 7.13 and 8.2).

Atomic Size and Group Anomalies

Although the chemical properties of the members of a group show many similarities, there are also important differences. In fact, the relatively large increase in atomic radius in going from the first to the second member of a group causes the first element to show properties that are often quite different from the others. Consequently, hydrogen, beryllium, boron, carbon, nitrogen, oxygen, and fluorine all have some properties that distinguish them from the other members of their groups. For example, in Group 1A hydrogen is a nonmetal and lithium is a very active metal. This extreme difference results primarily from the very large difference in the atomic radii of hydrogen and lithium, as shown in Fig. 19.2. The small hydrogen atom has a much greater attraction for electrons than do the larger members of Group 1A and forms covalent bonds with nonmetals; the other members of Group 1A lose their valence electrons to nonmetals to form 1+ cations in ionic compounds.

> Metallic character increases going down a group in the periodic table.

This effect of size is also evident in other groups. For example, the oxides of the metals in Group 2A are all quite basic except for the first member of the series; beryllium oxide (BeO) is amphoteric. Recall from Section 14.10 that the basicity of an oxide depends on its ionic character. Ionic oxides contain the O^{2-} ion, which reacts with water to form two OH^- ions. All the oxides of the Group 2A metals are highly ionic except for beryllium oxide, which has considerable covalent character. The small Be^{2+} ion can effectively polarize the electron "cloud" of the O^{2-} ion, producing significant electron sharing. We see the same pattern in Group 3A, where only the small boron atom behaves as a nonmetal, or sometimes as a semimetal, and aluminum and the other members are active metals.

In Group 4A the effect of size is reflected in the dramatic differences between the chemistry of carbon and that of silicon. The chemistry of carbon is dominated by molecules containing chains of C—C bonds, but silicon compounds mainly contain Si—O bonds rather than Si—Si bonds. Carbon forms a wide variety of stable compounds with strong C—C single bonds. Silicon also forms compounds with chains of Si—Si bonds,

FIGURE 19.2
The atomic radii of some atoms in picometers.

but these compounds are much more reactive than the corresponding carbon compounds. The reasons for the difference in reactivity between the carbon and silicon compounds are quite complex but are likely related to the differences in the sizes of the carbon and silicon atoms.

Carbon and silicon differ markedly in their abilities to form π bonds. As we discussed in Section 9.1, carbon dioxide is composed of discrete CO_2 molecules with the Lewis structure

$$\ddot{\text{O}}{=}\text{C}{=}\ddot{\text{O}}$$

where the carbon and oxygen atoms achieve the [Ne] configuration by forming π bonds. In contrast, the structure of silica (empirical formula SiO_2) is based on SiO_4 tetrahedra with Si—O—Si bridges, as shown in Fig. 19.3. The silicon $3p$ valence orbitals do not overlap very effectively with the smaller oxygen $2p$ orbitals to form π bonds; therefore, discrete SiO_2 molecules with the Lewis structure

$$\ddot{\text{O}}{=}\text{Si}{=}\ddot{\text{O}}$$

FIGURE 19.3
The structure of quartz, which has the empirical formula SiO_2. Note that the structure is based on interlocking SiO_4 tetrahedra, where each oxygen atom is shared by two silicon atoms.

are not stable. Instead, the silicon atoms achieve a noble gas configuration by forming several Si—O single bonds.

The importance of π bonding for the relatively small elements of the second period also explains the different elemental forms of the members of Groups 5A and 6A. For example, elemental nitrogen consists of very stable N_2 molecules with the Lewis structure

$$: N \equiv N :$$

Elemental phosphorus forms larger aggregates of atoms, the simplest being the tetrahedral P_4 molecules found in white phosphorus (see Fig. 20.12). Like silicon atoms, the relatively large phosphorus atoms do not form strong π bonds and prefer to achieve a noble gas configuration by forming single bonds to several other phosphorus atoms. In contrast, its very strong π bonds make the N_2 molecule the most stable form of elemental nitrogen. Similarly, in Group 6A the most stable form of elemental oxygen is the O_2 molecule with a double bond, but the larger sulfur atom forms bigger aggregates, such as the cyclic S_8 molecule (see Fig. 20.16), which contains only single bonds.

The relatively large change in size in going from the first to second member of a group also has important consequences for the Group 7A elements. For example, fluorine has a smaller electron affinity than chlorine. This reversal of the expected trend can be attributed to the small fluorine $2p$ orbitals, which result in unusually large electron repulsions. The relative weakness of the bond in the F_2 molecule can be explained in terms of the repulsions among the lone pairs, shown in the Lewis structure:

$$: \ddot{F} — \ddot{F} :$$

The small size of the fluorine atoms allows close approach of the lone pairs, which leads to much greater repulsions than are found in the Cl_2 molecule with its much larger atoms.

Abundance and Preparation

Table 19.1 shows the distribution of elements in the earth's crust, oceans, and atmosphere. The major element is, of course, oxygen, which is found in the atmosphere as O_2, in the oceans in H_2O, and in the earth's crust primarily in silicate and carbonate minerals. The second most abundant element, silicon, is found throughout the earth's crust in the silica and silicate minerals that form the basis of most sand, rocks, and soil. The most abundant metals, aluminum and iron, are found in ores in which they are combined with nonmetals, most commonly oxygen. One notable fact revealed by Table 19.1 is the small incidence of most transition metals. Since many of these relatively rare elements are assuming

Sand dunes in Monument Valley, Arizona.

TABLE 19.1 Distribution (Mass Percent) of the 18 Most Abundant Elements in the Earth's Crust, Oceans, and Atmosphere

Element	Mass Percent	Element	Mass Percent
Oxygen	49.2	Chlorine	0.19
Silicon	25.7	Phosphorus	0.11
Aluminum	7.50	Manganese	0.09
Iron	4.71	Carbon	0.08
Calcium	3.39	Sulfur	0.06
Sodium	2.63	Barium	0.04
Potassium	2.40	Nitrogen	0.03
Magnesium	1.93	Fluorine	0.03
Hydrogen	0.87	All others	0.49
Titanium	0.58		

TABLE 19.2   Abundance of Elements in the Human Body

Major Elements	Mass Percent	Trace Elements (in alphabetical order)
Oxygen	65.0	Arsenic
Carbon	18.0	Chromium
Hydrogen	10.0	Cobalt
Nitrogen	3.0	Copper
Calcium	1.4	Fluorine
Phosphorus	1.0	Iodine
Magnesium	0.50	Manganese
Potassium	0.34	Molybdenum
Sulfur	0.26	Nickel
Sodium	0.14	Selenium
Chlorine	0.14	Silicon
Iron	0.004	Vanadium
Zinc	0.003	

increasing importance in our high-technology society, it is possible that the control of transition metal ores may ultimately have more significance for world politics than the control of petroleum supplies.

The distribution of elements in living materials is very different from that found in the earth's crust. Table 19.2 shows the relative abundance of elements in the human body. Oxygen, carbon, hydrogen, and nitrogen form the basis for all biologically important molecules. The other elements, even though they are found in relatively small amounts, are often crucial for life. For example, zinc is found in over 150 different biomolecules in the human body.

Metallurgy is discussed in more detail in Chapter 21.

Carbon is the cheapest and most readily available industrial reducing agent for metallic ions.

Only about one-fourth of the elements occur naturally in the free state. Most are found in a combined state. The *process of obtaining a metal from its ore* is called **metallurgy.** Since the metals in ores are found in the form of cations, the chemistry of *metallurgy always involves reduction of the ions to the elemental metal (with an oxidation state of zero).* A variety of reducing agents can be used, but carbon is the usual choice because of its wide availability and relatively low cost. As we will see in Chapter 21, carbon is the primary reducing agent in the production of steel. Carbon also can be used to produce tin and lead from their oxides:

$$2SnO(s) + C(s) \xrightarrow{\text{Heat}} 2Sn(s) + CO_2(g)$$
$$2PbO(s) + C(s) \xrightarrow{\text{Heat}} 2Pb(s) + CO_2(g)$$

Hydrogen gas also can be used as a reducing agent for metal oxides, as in the production of tin:

$$SnO(s) + H_2(g) \xrightarrow{\text{Heat}} Sn(s) + H_2O(g)$$

Electrolysis is often used to reduce the most active metals. In Chapter 17 we considered the electrolytic production of aluminum metal. The alkali metals are also produced by electrolysis, usually of their molten halide salts.

The preparation of nonmetals varies widely. Elemental nitrogen and oxygen are usually obtained from the **liquefaction** of air, which is based on the principle that a real gas cools when it expands. After each expansion, part of the cooler gas is compressed, while the rest is used to carry away the heat of the compression. The compressed gas is then allowed to expand again. This cycle is repeated many times. Eventually, the remaining gas becomes cold enough to form the liquid state. Because liquid nitrogen and liquid oxygen have different boiling points, they can be separated by the distillation of liquid air. Both

The preparation of sulfur and the halogens is discussed in Chapter 20.

substances are important industrial chemicals, ranking in the top five in terms of the amounts manufactured in the United States. Hydrogen can be obtained from the electrolysis of water, but more commonly it is obtained from the decomposition of the methane in natural gas. Sulfur is found underground in its elemental form and is recovered using the Frasch process (see Section 20.6). The halogens are obtained by oxidation of the anions from halide salts (see Section 20.7).

19.2 The Group 1A Elements

1A
H
Li
Na
K
Rb
Cs
Fr

Several properties of the alkali metals are given in Table 7.8.

The Group 1A elements with their ns^1 valence-electron configurations are all very active metals (they lose their valence electrons very readily), except for hydrogen, which behaves as a nonmetal. We will discuss the chemistry of hydrogen in the next section. Many of the properties of the **alkali metals** have been described previously (see Section 7.13). The sources and methods of preparation of pure alkali metals are given in Table 19.3. The ionization energies, standard reduction potentials, ionic radii, and melting points for the alkali metals are listed in Table 19.4. Lepidolite, shown in Fig. 19.4, contains several pure alkali metals.

In Section 7.13 we saw that the alkali metals all react vigorously with water to release hydrogen gas:

$$2M(s) + 2H_2O(l) \longrightarrow 2M^+(aq) + 2OH^-(aq) + H_2(g)$$

We will reconsider this process briefly because it illustrates several important concepts. Based on the ionization energies, we might expect lithium to be the weakest of the alkali metals as a reducing agent in water. However, the standard reduction potentials indicate that it is the strongest. This reversal results mainly from the very large energy of hydration

TABLE 19.3 Sources and Methods of Preparation of the Pure Alkali Metals

Element	Source	Method of Preparation
Lithium	Silicate minerals such as spodumene, $LiAl(Si_2O_6)$	Electrolysis of molten LiCl
Sodium	NaCl	Electrolysis of molten NaCl
Potassium	KCl	Electrolysis of molten KCl
Rubidium	Impurity in lepidolite, $Li_2(F,OH)_2Al_2(SiO_3)_3$	Reduction of RbOH with Mg and H_2
Cesium	Pollucite ($Cs_4Al_4Si_9O_{26} \cdot H_2O$) and an impurity in lepidolite (see Fig. 19.4)	Reduction of CsOH with Mg and H_2

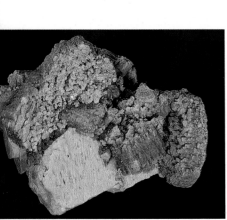

FIGURE 19.4
Lepidolite is composed mainly of lithium, aluminum, silicon, and oxygen, but it also contains significant amounts of rubidium and cesium.

TABLE 19.4 Selected Physical Properties of the Alkali Metals

Element	Ionization Energy (kJ/mol)	Standard Reduction Potential (V) for $M^+ + e^- \rightarrow M$	Radius of M^+ (pm)	Melting Point (°C)
Lithium	520	−3.05	60	180
Sodium	495	−2.71	95	98
Potassium	419	−2.92	133	63
Rubidium	409	−2.99	148	39
Cesium	382	−3.02	169	29

Sodium reacting with water.

Hydrogen peroxide has the Lewis structure

of the small Li^+ ion. Because of its relatively high charge density, the Li^+ ion very effectively attracts water molecules. A large quantity of energy is released in the process, favoring the formation of the Li^+ ion and making lithium a strong reducing agent in aqueous solution.

We also saw in Section 7.13 that lithium, although it is the strongest reducing agent, reacts more slowly with water than does sodium or potassium. From the discussions in Chapters 12 and 16, we know that the *equilibrium position* for a reaction (in this case indicated by the $\mathscr{E}°$ values) is controlled by thermodynamic factors but that the *rate* of a reaction is controlled by kinetic factors. There is *no* direct connection between these factors. Lithium reacts more slowly with water than does sodium or potassium because as a solid it has a higher melting point than either of them. It does not become molten from the heat of reaction with water as sodium and potassium do, and thus it has a smaller area of contact with the water.

The relative ease with which the alkali metals lose electrons to form M^+ cations means that they react with nonmetals to form ionic compounds. Although we might expect the alkali metals to react with oxygen to form regular oxides of the general formula M_2O, lithium is the only one that does so in the presence of excess oxygen gas:

$$4Li(s) + O_2(g) \longrightarrow 2Li_2O(s)$$

Sodium forms solid Na_2O if the oxygen supply is limited, but in excess oxygen it forms *sodium peroxide:*

$$2Na(s) + O_2(g) \longrightarrow Na_2O_2(s)$$

Sodium peroxide contains the basic O_2^{2-} anion and reacts with water to form hydrogen peroxide and hydroxide ions:

$$Na_2O_2(s) + 2H_2O(l) \longrightarrow 2Na^+(aq) + H_2O_2(aq) + 2OH^-(aq)$$

Hydrogen peroxide is a strong oxidizing agent often used as a bleach for hair and as a disinfectant.

Potassium, rubidium, and cesium react with oxygen to produce **superoxides** of the general formula MO_2, which contains the O_2^- anion. For example, potassium reacts with oxygen as follows:

$$K(s) + O_2(g) \longrightarrow KO_2(s)$$

The superoxides release oxygen gas in reactions with water or carbon dioxide:

$$2MO_2(s) + 2H_2O(l) \longrightarrow 2M^+(aq) + 2OH^-(aq) + O_2(g) + H_2O_2(aq)$$
$$4MO_2(s) + 2CO_2(g) \longrightarrow 2M_2CO_3(s) + 3O_2(g)$$

This chemistry makes superoxides very useful in the self-contained breathing apparatuses used by firefighters. These "airpacks" are also used as emergency equipment in labs and production facilities in case toxic fumes are released.

The types of compounds formed by the alkali metals with oxygen are summarized in Table 19.5. Table 19.6 summarizes some important reactions of the alkali metals.

Airpacks are an essential source of oxygen for firefighters.

TABLE 19.5   Types of Compounds Formed by the Alkali Metals with Oxygen

General Formula	Name	Examples
M_2O	Oxide	Li_2O, Na_2O
M_2O_2	Peroxide	Na_2O_2
MO_2	Superoxide	KO_2, RbO_2, CsO_2

Sodium reacts violently with chlorine.

TABLE 19.6 Selected Reactions of the Alkali Metals

Reaction	Comment
$2M + X_2 \rightarrow 2MX$	X_2 = any halogen molecule
$4Li + O_2 \rightarrow 2Li_2O$	Excess oxygen
$2Na + O_2 \rightarrow Na_2O_2$	
$M + O_2 \rightarrow MO_2$	M = K, Rb, or Cs
$2M + S \rightarrow M_2S$	
$6Li + N_2 \rightarrow 2Li_3N$	Li only
$12M + P_4 \rightarrow 4M_3P$	
$2M + H_2 \rightarrow 2MH$	
$2M + 2H_2O \rightarrow 2MOH + H_2$	
$2M + 2H^+ \rightarrow 2M^+ + H_2$	Violent reaction!

The alkali metal ions are very important for the proper functioning of biologic systems, such as nerves and muscles, and Na^+ and K^+ ions are present in all body cells and fluids. In human blood plasma the concentrations are

$$[Na^+] \approx 0.15\ M \quad \text{and} \quad [K^+] \approx 0.005\ M$$

For the fluids *inside* the cells the concentrations are reversed:

$$[Na^+] \approx 0.005\ M \quad \text{and} \quad [K^+] \approx 0.16\ M$$

Since the concentrations are so different inside and outside the cells, an elaborate mechanism is needed to transport Na^+ and K^+ ions through the cell membranes.

Recently, studies have been carried out concerning the role of the Li^+ ion in the human brain, and lithium carbonate has been used extensively in the treatment of manic-depressive patients. The Li^+ ion apparently affects the levels of neurotransmitters, molecules that assist the transmission of messages along the nerve networks. Incorrect concentrations of these molecules can lead to depression or mania.

Sample Exercise 19.1 **Predicting Reaction Products**

Predict the products formed by the following reactants.

a. $Li_3N(s)$ and $H_2O(l)$
b. $KO_2(s)$ and $H_2O(l)$

Solution

a. Solid Li_3N contains the N^{3-} anion, which has a strong attraction for three H^+ ions to form NH_3. Thus the reaction is

$$Li_3N(s) + 3H_2O(l) \longrightarrow NH_3(g) + 3Li^+(aq) + 3OH^-(aq)$$

b. Solid KO_2 is a superoxide that characteristically reacts with water to produce O_2, H_2O_2, and OH^-:

$$2KO_2(s) + 2H_2O(l) \longrightarrow 2K^+(aq) + 2OH^-(aq) + O_2(g) + H_2O_2(aq)$$

See Exercises 19.17 and 19.18.

19.3 Hydrogen

Under ordinary conditions of temperature and pressure, hydrogen is a colorless, odorless gas composed of H_2 molecules. Because of its low molar mass and nonpolarity, hydrogen has a very low boiling point ($-253°C$) and melting point ($-260°C$). Hydrogen gas is highly flammable, and mixtures of air containing from 18% to 60% hydrogen by volume are explosive. In a common lecture demonstration hydrogen and oxygen gases are bubbled into soapy water. The resulting bubbles can be ignited with a candle on a long stick, giving a loud explosion.

The major industrial source of hydrogen gas is the reaction of methane and water at high temperatures ($800-1000°C$) and high pressures ($10-50$ atm) with a metallic catalyst, often nickel:

$$CH_4(g) + H_2O(g) \xrightarrow[\text{Catalyst}]{\text{Heat, pressure}} CO(g) + 3H_2(g)$$

Large quantities of hydrogen are also formed as a by-product of gasoline production, in which hydrocarbons with high molar masses are broken down (*cracked*) to produce smaller molecules more suitable for use as a motor fuel.

Very pure hydrogen can be produced by electrolysis of water (see Section 17.7), but this method is currently not economically feasible for large-scale production because of the relatively high cost of electricity.

The major industrial use of hydrogen is in the production of ammonia by the Haber process. Large quantities of hydrogen are also used for hydrogenating unsaturated vegetable oils (those containing carbon–carbon double bonds) to produce solid shortenings that are saturated (containing carbon–carbon single bonds):

$$\text{\textasciitilde\textasciitilde C}=\text{C\textasciitilde\textasciitilde} \xrightarrow{H_2} \text{\textasciitilde\textasciitilde C}-\text{C\textasciitilde\textasciitilde}$$

The catalysis of this process was discussed in Section 12.8.

Chemically, hydrogen behaves as a typical nonmetal, forming covalent compounds with other nonmetals and forming salts with very active metals. Binary compounds containing hydrogen are called **hydrides,** of which there are three classes. The **ionic**

(left) Hydrogen gas being used to blow soap bubbles. (right) As the bubbles float upward, they are lighted using a candle on a long pole. The orange flame is due to the heat from the reaction of hydrogen with the oxygen in the air that excites sodium ions in the soap solution.

(or **saltlike**) **hydrides** are formed when hydrogen combines with the most active metals, those from Groups 1A and 2A. Examples are LiH and CaH_2, which can best be characterized as containing hydride ions (H^-) and metal cations. Because the presence of two electrons in the small $1s$ orbital produces large electron–electron repulsions and the nucleus has only a 1+ charge, the hydride ion is a strong reducing agent (easily loses electrons). For example, when ionic hydrides are placed in water, a violent reaction takes place. This reaction results in the formation of hydrogen gas, as seen in the equation

$$LiH(s) + H_2O(l) \longrightarrow H_2(g) + Li^+(aq) + OH^-(aq)$$

Boiling points of covalent hydrides are discussed in Section 10.1.

Covalent hydrides are formed when hydrogen combines with other nonmetals. We have encountered many of these compounds already: HCl, CH_4, NH_3, H_2O, and so on. The most important covalent hydride is water. The polarity of the H_2O molecule leads to many of water's unusual properties. Water has a much higher boiling point than is expected from its molar mass. It has a large heat of vaporization and a large heat capacity, both of which make it a very useful coolant. Water has a higher density as a liquid than as a solid. This is due to the open structure of ice, which results from maximizing the hydrogen bonding (see Fig. 19.5). Because water is an excellent solvent for ionic and polar substances, it provides an effective medium for life processes. In fact, water is one of the few covalent hydrides that is nontoxic to organisms.

The third class of hydrides, the **metallic** (or **interstitial**) **hydrides,** are formed when transition metal crystals are treated with hydrogen gas. The hydrogen molecules dissociate at the metal's surface, and the small hydrogen atoms migrate into the crystal structure to occupy holes, or interstices. These metal–hydrogen mixtures are more like solid solutions than true compounds. Palladium can absorb about *900 times* its own volume of hydrogen gas. In fact, hydrogen can be purified by placing it under slight pressure in a vessel containing a thin wall of palladium. The hydrogen diffuses into and through the metal wall, leaving the impurities behind.

Although hydrogen can react with transition metals to form compounds of constant composition, most of the interstitial hydrides have variable compositions (often called *nonstoichiometric compositions*) with formulas such as $LaH_{2.76}$ and $VH_{0.56}$. The compositions of the nonstoichiometric hydrides vary with the length of exposure of the metal to hydrogen gas and other factors.

H_2O

Ice

FIGURE 19.5
The structure of ice, showing the hydrogen bonding.

When interstitial hydrides are heated, much of the absorbed hydrogen is expelled as hydrogen gas. Because of this behavior, these materials offer possibilities for storing hydrogen for use as a portable fuel. The internal combustion engines in current automobiles can burn hydrogen gas with little modification, but storage of enough hydrogen to provide an acceptable mileage range remains a problem. One possible solution might be to use a fuel tank containing a porous solid that includes a transition metal into which the hydrogen gas could be pumped to form the interstitial hydride. The hydrogen gas could then be released as required by the engine.

See Section 6.6 for a discussion of the feasibility of using hydrogen gas as a fuel.

19.4   The Group 2A Elements

The Group 2A elements (with valence-electron configuration ns^2) are very reactive, losing their two valence electrons to nonmetals to form ionic compounds containing M^{2+} cations. These elements are commonly called the **alkaline earth metals** because of the basicity of their oxides:

An amphoteric oxide displays both acidic and basic properties.

$$MO(s) + H_2O(l) \longrightarrow M^{2+}(aq) + 2OH^-(aq)$$

Only beryllium oxide (BeO) also shows some acidic properties, such as dissolving in aqueous solutions containing hydroxide ions:

$$BeO(s) + 2OH^-(aq) + H_2O(l) \longrightarrow Be(OH)_4^{2-}(aq)$$

The more active alkaline earth metals react with water as the alkali metals do, producing hydrogen gas:

$$M(s) + 2H_2O(l) \longrightarrow M^{2+}(aq) + 2OH^-(aq) + H_2(g)$$

Calcium, strontium, and barium react vigorously at 25°C. The less easily oxidized beryllium and magnesium show no observable reaction with water at 25°C, although magnesium reacts with boiling water. Table 19.7 summarizes various properties, sources, and preparations of the alkaline earth metals.

2A
| Be |
| Mg |
| Ca |
| Sr |
| Ba |
| Ra |

TABLE 19.7   Selected Physical Properties, Sources, and Methods of Preparation for the Group 2A Elements

Element	Radius of M^{2+} (pm)	Ionization Energy (kJ/mol) First	Second	$\mathscr{E}°$ (V) for $M^{2+} + 2e^- \rightarrow M$	Source	Method of Preparation
Beryllium	~30	900	1760	−1.70	Beryl ($Be_3Al_2Si_6O_{18}$)	Electrolysis of molten $BeCl_2$
Magnesium	65	738	1450	−2.37	Magnesite ($MgCO_3$), dolomite ($MgCO_3 \cdot CaCO_3$), carnallite ($MgCl_2 \cdot KCl \cdot 6H_2O$)	Electrolysis of molten $MgCl_2$
Calcium	99	590	1146	−2.76	Various minerals containing $CaCO_3$	Electrolysis of molten $CaCl_2$
Strontium	113	549	1064	−2.89	Celestite ($SrSO_4$), strontianite ($SrCO_3$)	Electrolysis of molten $SrCl_2$
Barium	135	503	965	−2.90	Baryte ($BaSO_4$), witherite ($BaCO_3$)	Electrolysis of molten $BaCl_2$
Radium	140	509	979	−2.92	Pitchblende (1 g of Ra/7 tons of ore)	Electrolysis of molten $RaCl_2$

Calcium metal reacting with water to form bubbles of hydrogen gas.

(a)

(b)

(c)

FIGURE 19.6
(a) Solid $BeCl_2$ can be visualized as being formed from many $BeCl_2$ molecules, where lone pairs on the chlorine atoms are used to bond to the beryllium atoms in adjacent $BeCl_2$ molecules. (b) The extended structure of solid $BeCl_2$. (c) The ball-and-stick model of the extended structure.

As we saw in Section 19.1, the small size and relatively high electronegativity of the beryllium atom cause its bonds to be more covalent than is usual for a metal. For example, beryllium chloride with the Lewis structure

$$: \ddot{Cl}—Be—\ddot{Cl} :$$

exists as a linear molecule, as predicted by the VSEPR model. The Be—Cl bonds are covalent, and beryllium is best described as being sp hybridized. As a solid, $BeCl_2$ achieves an octet of electrons around each beryllium atom by forming an extended structure containing Be in a tetrahedral environment, as shown in Fig. 19.6. The lone pairs on the chlorine atoms are used to form Be—Cl bonds.

The alkaline earth metals have great practical importance. Calcium and magnesium ions are essential for human life. Calcium is found primarily in the structural minerals constituting bones and teeth; magnesium (as the Mg^{2+} ion) plays a vital role in metabolism and muscle functions. Also, magnesium was formerly used to produce the bright light for photographic flash bulbs from its reaction with oxygen:

$$2Mg(s) + O_2(g) \longrightarrow 2MgO(s) + \text{light}$$

Because magnesium metal has a relatively low density and moderate strength, it is a useful structural material, especially if alloyed with aluminum.

Table 19.8 summarizes some important reactions of the alkaline earth metals.

Bones contain large amounts of calcium.

TABLE 19.8   Selected Reactions of the Group 2A Elements

Reaction	Comment
$M + X_2 \rightarrow MX_2$	X_2 = any halogen molecule
$2M + O_2 \rightarrow 2MO$	Ba gives BaO_2 as well
$M + S \rightarrow MS$	
$3M + N_2 \rightarrow M_3N_2$	High temperatures
$6M + P_4 \rightarrow 2M_3P_2$	High temperatures
$M + H_2 \rightarrow MH_2$	M = Ca, Sr, or Ba; high temperatures; Mg at high pressure
$M + 2H_2O \rightarrow M(OH)_2 + H_2$	M = Ca, Sr, or Ba
$M + 2H^+ \rightarrow M^{2+} + H_2$	
$Be + 2OH^- + 2H_2O \rightarrow Be(OH)_4^{2-} + H_2$	

(a)

(b)

(c)

FIGURE 19.7
(a) A schematic representation of a typical cation-exchange resin. (b) and (c) When hard water is passed over the cation-exchange resin, the Ca^{2+} and Mg^{2+} bind to the resin.

The Dolomite mountains in Italy. Dolomite is a source of magnesium.

Relatively large concentrations of Ca^{2+} and Mg^{2+} ions are often found in natural water supplies. These ions in this **hard water** interfere with the action of detergents and form precipitates with soap. In Section 14.6 we saw that Ca^{2+} is often removed by precipitation as $CaCO_3$ in large-scale water softening. In individual homes Ca^{2+}, Mg^{2+}, and other cations are removed by **ion exchange.** An **ion-exchange resin** consists of large molecules (polymers) that have many ionic sites. A **cation-exchange resin** is represented schematically in Fig. 19.7(a), showing Na^+ ions bound ionically to the SO_3^- groups that are covalently attached to the resin polymer. When hard water is passed over the resin, Ca^{2+} and Mg^{2+} bind to the resin in place of Na^+, which is released into the solution [Fig. 19.7(b)]. Replacing Mg^{2+} and Ca^{2+} by Na^+ [Fig. 19.7(c)] "softens" the water because the sodium ions interfere much less with the action of soaps and detergents.

| Sample Exercise 19.2 | **Electrolytic Production of Magnesium** |

Calculate the amount of time required to produce 1.00×10^3 kg of magnesium metal by the electrolysis of molten $MgCl_2$ using a current of 1.00×10^2 A.

Solution

The reaction for plating magnesium is

$$Mg^{2+} + 2e^- \longrightarrow Mg$$

which means that 2 moles of electrons are required for each mole of Mg produced. The number of moles of magnesium in 1.00×10^3 kg is

$$1.00 \times 10^3 \text{ kg} \times \frac{1000 \text{ g}}{\text{kg}} \times \frac{1 \text{ mol Mg}}{24.31 \text{ g}} = 4.11 \times 10^4 \text{ mol Mg}$$

Thus $\qquad \dfrac{2 \text{ mol } e^-}{1 \text{ mol Mg}} \times 4.11 \times 10^4 \text{ mol Mg} = 8.22 \times 10^4 \text{ mol } e^-$

Using the faraday (96,485 C/mol e$^-$), we can calculate the coulombs of charge:

$$8.22 \times 10^4 \text{ mol e}^- \times \frac{96,485 \text{ C}}{\text{mol e}^-} = 7.93 \times 10^9 \text{ C}$$

Since an ampere is a coulomb of charge per second, we can now calculate the time required:

$$\frac{7.93 \times 10^9 \text{ C}}{1.00 \times 10^2 \text{ C/s}} = 7.93 \times 10^7 \text{ s} \quad \text{or} \quad 918 \text{ days}$$

See Exercises 19.29 and 19.30.

19.5 The Group 3A Elements

3A

| B |
| Al |
| Ga |
| In |
| Tl |

The Group 3A elements (valence-electron configuration ns^2np^1) generally show the increase in metallic character in going down the group that is characteristic of the representative elements. Some physical properties, sources, and methods of preparation for the Group 3A elements are summarized in Table 19.9.

Boron is a nonmetal, and most of its compounds are covalent. The most interesting compounds of boron are the covalent hydrides called **boranes.** We might expect BH_3 to be the simplest hydride, since boron has three valence electrons to share with three hydrogen atoms. However, this compound is unstable, and the simplest known member of the series is diborane (B_2H_6), with the structure shown in Fig. 19.8(a). In this molecule the terminal B—H bonds are normal covalent bonds, each involving one electron pair. The bridging bonds are three-center bonds using a single pair of electrons to bond all three atoms. Another interesting borane contains the square pyramidal B_5H_9 molecule [Fig. 19.8(b)], which has four three-center bonds around the base of the pyramid. Because the boranes are extremely electron-deficient, they are highly reactive. The boranes react very exothermically with oxygen and were once evaluated as potential fuels for rockets in the U.S. space program.

Aluminum, the most abundant metal on earth, has metallic physical properties, such as high thermal and electrical conductivities and a lustrous appearance, but its bonds to nonmetals are significantly covalent. This covalency is responsible for the amphoteric

TABLE 19.9   Selected Physical Properties, Sources, and Methods of Preparation for the Group 3A Elements

Element	Radius of M^{3+} (pm)	Ionization Energy (kJ/mol)	$\mathscr{E}°$ (V) for $M^{3+} + 3e^- \rightarrow M$	Sources	Method of Preparation
Boron	20	798	—	Kernite, a form of borax ($Na_2B_4O_7 \cdot 4H_2O$)	Reduction by Mg or H_2
Aluminum	51	581	−1.71	Bauxite (Al_2O_3)	Electrolysis of Al_2O_3 in molten Na_3AlF_6
Gallium	62	577	−0.53	Traces in various minerals	Reduction with H_2 or electrolysis
Indium	81	556	−0.34	Traces in various minerals	Reduction with H_2 or electrolysis
Thallium	95	589	0.72	Traces in various minerals	Electrolysis

CHEMICAL IMPACT

Boost Your Boron

Everyone realizes that the body needs protein, carbohydrates, vitamins, and even fat. The importance of several trace elements in our diet, however, is often poorly understood. An example is the element boron. People in the United States have a relatively low intake of boron. For example, the U.S. population consumes a little more than 1 mg of boron per day, which is about 10% less than people living in Great Britain and Egypt and about 35% less than people in Germany and Mexico.

To study the importance of boron intake, Zuo-Fen Zhang and his colleagues in the School of Public Health at the University of California–Los Angeles examined nutrition data collected from thousands of men and women who filled out the National Health and Nutrition Examination Survey (NHANES). Zhang and his coworkers learned that boron seems to protect against prostate cancer. Comparing the diets of men with prostate cancer to those without the disease indicated a strong correlation between boron consumption and the absence of the disease. The prostate cancer risk for men eating at least 1.8 mg boron per day was only one-third that of men who consumed less than 0.9 mg boron per day. The data show that boron offers no apparent protection for other types of cancer, just very specific protection for prostate cancer. Other studies involving animals indicate that boron consumption can furnish protection against autoimmune diseases such as rheumatoid arthritis.

Although boron intake in the neighborhood of 3.0 mg/day seems beneficial, large amounts of boron can be toxic. The best way to obtain extra boron in your diet is by consuming foods such as nuts and noncitrus fruits.

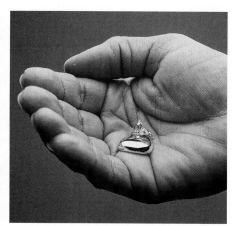

Gallium metal has such a low melting point (30°C) that it melts from the heat of a hand.

nature of Al_2O_3, which dissolves in acidic or basic solution, and for the acidity of $Al(H_2O)_6^{3+}$ (see Section 14.8):

$$Al(H_2O)_6^{3+}(aq) \rightleftharpoons Al(OH)(H_2O)_5^{2+}(aq) + H^+(aq)$$

One especially interesting property of *gallium* is its unusually low melting point at 29.8°C, which is in contrast to the 660°C melting point of aluminum. Gallium's boiling point is approximately 2400°C. This gives gallium the largest liquid range of any metal, which makes it useful for thermometers, especially to measure high temperatures. Gallium, like water, expands when it freezes. The chemistry of gallium is quite similar to that of aluminum. For example, Ga_2O_3 is amphoteric.

Table 19.10 summarizes some important reactions of the Group 3A elements.

The practical importance of the Group 3A elements centers on aluminum. Since the discovery of the electrolytic production process by Hall and Heroult (see Section 17.8), aluminum has become a highly important structural material in a wide variety of applications from aircraft bodies to bicycle components. Aluminum is especially valuable because it has a high strength-to-weight ratio and because it protects itself from corrosion by developing a tough, adherent oxide coating.

(a)   (b)

FIGURE 19.8

(a) The structure of B_2H_6 with its two three-center B—H—B bridging bonds and four "normal" B—H bonds. (b) The structure of B_5H_9. There are five "normal" B—H bonds to terminal hydrogens and four three-center bridging bonds around the base.

Aluminum is used in airplane construction.

TABLE 19.10 Selected Reactions of the Group 3A Elements

Reaction	Comment
$2M + 3X_2 \rightarrow 2MX_3$	X_2 = any halogen molecule; Tl gives TlX as well, but no TlI_3
$4M + 3O_2 \rightarrow 2M_2O_3$	High temperatures; Tl gives Tl_2O as well
$2M + 3S \rightarrow M_2S_3$	High temperatures; Tl gives Tl_2S as well
$2M + N_2 \rightarrow 2MN$	M = Al only
$2M + 6H^+ \rightarrow 2M^{3+} + 3H_2$	M = Al, Ga, or In; Tl gives Tl^+
$2M + 2OH^- + 6H_2O \rightarrow 2M(OH)_4^- + 3H_2$	M = Al or Ga

19.6 The Group 4A Elements

4A

C
Si
Ge
Sn
Pb

Group 4A (with the valence-electron configuration ns^2np^2) contains two of the most important elements on earth: carbon, the fundamental constituent of the molecules necessary for life, and silicon, which forms the basis of the geologic world. The change from nonmetallic to metallic properties seen in Group 3A is also apparent in going down Group 4A from carbon, a typical nonmetal, to silicon and germanium, usually considered semimetals, to the metals tin and lead. Table 19.11 summarizes some physical properties, sources, and methods of preparation for the elements in this group.

All the Group 4A elements can form four covalent bonds to nonmetals—for example, CH_4, SiF_4, $GeBr_4$, $SnCl_4$, and $PbCl_4$. In each of these tetrahedral molecules, the central atom is described as sp^3 hybridized by the localized electron model. All these compounds, except those of carbon, can react with Lewis bases to form two additional covalent bonds. For example, $SnCl_4$, which is a fuming liquid (bp = 114°C), can add two chloride ions:

$$SnCl_4 + 2Cl^- \longrightarrow SnCl_6^{2-}$$

Carbon compounds cannot react in this way because of the small atomic size of carbon and because there are no d orbitals on carbon to accommodate the extra electrons, as there are on the other elements in the group.

TABLE 19.11   Selected Physical Properties, Sources, and Methods of Preparation for the Group 4A Elements

Element	Electronegativity	Melting Point (°C)	Boiling Point (°C)	Sources	Method of Preparation
Carbon	2.5	3727 (sublimes)	—	Graphite, diamond, petroleum, coal	—
Silicon	1.8	1410	2355	Silicate minerals, silica	Reduction of K_2SiF_6 with Al, or reduction of SiO_2 with Mg
Germanium	1.8	937	2830	Germanite (mixture of copper, iron, and germanium sulfides)	Reduction of GeO_2 with H_2 or C
Tin	1.8	232	2270	Cassiterite (SnO_2)	Reduction of SnO_2 with C
Lead	1.9	327	1740	Galena (PbS)	Roasting of PbS with O_2 to form PbO_2 and then reduction with C

Although graphite is thermodynamically more stable than diamond, the transformation of diamond to graphite is not observed under normal conditions.

Fullerenes have been discovered recently by geologists in ancient rocks in Russia.

TABLE 19.12   Strengths of C—C, Si—Si, and Si—O Bonds

Bond	Bond Energy (kJ/mol)
C—C	347
Si—Si	340
Si—O	452

(top) A processed silicon wafer with (bottom) a silicon microchip.

We have seen that carbon also differs markedly from the other members of Group 4A in its ability to form π bonds. This accounts for the completely different structures and properties of CO_2 and SiO_2. Note from Table 19.12 that C—C bonds and Si—O bonds are stronger than Si—Si bonds. This partly explains why the chemistry of carbon is dominated by C—C bonds, whereas that of silicon is dominated by Si—O bonds.

Carbon occurs in the earth's crust mainly in two allotropic forms—graphite and diamond. In addition, new forms of elemental carbon, including buckminsterfullerene (C_{60}) and other related substances, have recently been characterized. The structures of graphite and diamond are given in Section 10.5.

Carbon monoxide (CO), one of three oxides of carbon, is an odorless, colorless, and toxic gas formed as a by-product of the combustion of carbon-containing compounds when there is a limited oxygen supply. Incidents of carbon monoxide poisoning are especially common in the winter in cold areas of the world when blocked furnace vents limit the availability of oxygen. The bonding in carbon monoxide, which has the Lewis structure

$$:C{\equiv}O:$$

is described in terms of *sp* hybridized carbon and oxygen atoms that interact to form one σ and two π bonds.

Carbon dioxide, a linear molecule with the Lewis structure

$$\ddot{O}{=}C{=}\ddot{O}$$

has an *sp* hybridized carbon atom, and is a product of human and animal respiration and of the combustion of fossil fuels. It is also produced by fermentation, a process by which the sugar in fruits and grains is changed to ethanol (C_2H_5OH) and carbon dioxide (see Section 22.4):

$$C_6H_{12}O_6(aq) \xrightarrow{\text{Enzymes}} 2C_2H_5OH(aq) + 2CO_2(g)$$
$$\text{Glucose}$$

Carbon dioxide dissolves in water to produce an acidic solution:

$$CO_2(aq) + H_2O(l) \rightleftharpoons H^+(aq) + HCO_3^-(aq)$$

Carbon suboxide, the third carbon oxide, is a linear molecule with the Lewis structure

$$\ddot{O}{=}C{=}C{=}C{=}\ddot{O}$$

which contains *sp* hybridized carbon atoms.

CHEMICAL IMPACT

Concrete Learning

Concrete has literally paved the way for civilization over the past 5000 years, tracing its roots to the ancient Egyptians. At a cost of about a penny per pound, concrete is ubiquitous in today's world—used in houses, factories, roads, dams, cooling towers, pipes, skyscrapers, and countless other places. In the United States alone there are an estimated $6 trillion worth of concrete-based structures.

Most concretes are based on Portland cement, patented in 1824 by an English bricklayer named J. Aspdin and so named because it forms a product that resembles the natural limestone on the Isle of Portland in England. Portland cement is a powder containing a mixture of calcium silicates [Ca_2SiO_4 (26%) and Ca_3SiO_5 (51%)], calcium aluminate [$Ca_3Al_2O_6$ (11%)], and calcium iron aluminate [$Ca_4Al_2Fe_2O_{10}$ (1%)]. Portland cement is made from a mixture of limestone, sand, shale, clay, and gypsum ($CaSO_4 \cdot 2H_2O$). When the cement is mixed with sand, gravel, and water, it turns into a muddy substance that eventually hardens into the familiar concrete that finds so many uses in our world. The hardening of concrete occurs not through drying but through hydration. The material becomes dry and hard as the water is consumed in building the complex silicate structures present in cured concrete. Although many of the details of this process are poorly understood, the main "glue" that holds the components of concrete together is calcium silicate hydrate, which forms a three-dimensional network mainly responsible for concrete's strength.

Despite its strength when newly produced, concrete contains pockets of air and water dispersed throughout, making it porous and subject to deterioration. Thus, despite all the advantages of concrete, it cracks and deteriorates seriously over time.

Much research is now being carried out to improve the durability of concrete. Most of these efforts are directed toward lowering the porosity of concrete and making it less brittle. One group of additives aimed at solving this problem consists of molecules with carbon atom backbones that have sulfate groups attached. These so-called superplasticizers allow the formation of concrete using much less water, and these chemicals have doubled the strength of ready-mix concrete over the past 20 years.

Researchers also have found that the properties of concrete can be greatly improved by adding fibers of various kinds, including those made of steel, glass, and carbon-based polymers. One type of fiber concrete—called *slurry infiltrated fiber concrete* (SIFCON), which is tough enough to be used to make missile silos and can be formed into complex shapes—may be especially useful for structures in earthquake-prone areas.

Other efforts to improve concrete center on replacing Portland cement with other binders such as carbon-based polymers. Although these polymer-based concretes will burn and do lose their shapes at high temperatures, they are much more resistant to the effects of water, acids, and salts than those made with Portland cement.

Despite the fact that most concrete now used is very similar to that used by the Romans to build the Pantheon, progress is being made, and revolutionary improvements may be just around the corner.

Silicon, the second most abundant element in the earth's crust, is a semimetal found widely distributed in silica and silicates (see Section 10.5). Approximately 85% of the earth's crust is composed of these substances. Although silicon is found in some steel and aluminum alloys, its major use is in semiconductors for electronic devices (see the Chemical Impact in Section 10.5).

Germanium, a relatively rare element, is a semimetal used mainly in the manufacture of semiconductors for transistors and similar electronic devices.

Tin is a soft silvery metal that can be rolled into thin sheets (tin foil) and has been used for centuries in various alloys such as bronze (~20% Sn and ~80% Cu), solder (~33% Sn and ~67% Pb), and pewter (~85% Sn, ~7% Cu, ~6% Bi, and ~2% Sb). Tin exists as three allotropes: *white tin,* stable at normal temperatures; *gray tin,* stable at temperatures below 13.2°C; and *brittle tin,* found at temperatures above 161°C. When tin is exposed to low temperatures, it gradually changes to the powdery gray tin and crumbles away; this process is known as *tin disease.*

The compositions of these alloys vary significantly. For example, the tin content of bronze varies from 5% to 30%, and the tin content of pewter is often as high as 95%.

CHEMICAL IMPACT

Beethoven: Hair Is the Story

Ludwig van Beethoven, arguably the greatest composer who ever lived, led a troubled life fraught with sickness, deafness, and personality aberrations. Now we may know the source of these difficulties: lead poisoning. Scientists have recently reached this conclusion through analysis of Beethoven's hair. When Beethoven died in 1827 at age 56, many mourners took samples of the great man's hair. In fact, it was said at the time that he was practically bald by the time he was buried. The hair that was recently analyzed consisted of 582 strands—3 to 6 inches long—bought for the Center of Beethoven Studies for $7300 in 1994 from Sotheby's auction house in London.

According to William Walsh of the Health Research Institute (HRI) in suburban Chicago, Beethoven's hair showed a lead concentration 100 times the normal levels. The scientists concluded that Beethoven's exposure to lead came as an adult, possibly from the mineral water he drank and swam in when he visited spas.

The lead poisoning may well explain Beethoven's volatile temper—the composer was subject to towering rages and sometimes had the look of a wild animal. In rare cases lead poisoning has been known to cause deafness, but the researchers remain unsure if this problem led to Beethoven's hearing loss.

According to Walsh, the scientists at HRI were originally looking for mercury, a common treatment for syphilis

Portrait of Beethoven by Josef Kari Stieler.

in the early nineteenth century, in Beethoven's hair. The absence of mercury supports the consensus of scholars that Beethoven did not have this disease. Not surprisingly, Beethoven himself wanted to know what made him so ill. In a letter to his brothers in 1802, he asked them to have doctors find the cause of his frequent abdominal pain after his death.

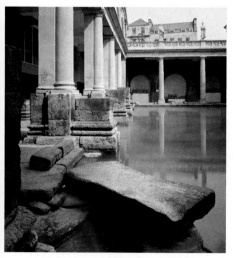

Roman baths such as these in Bath, England, used lead pipes for water.

The major current use for tin is as a protective coating for steel, especially for cans used as food containers. The thin layer of tin, applied electrolytically, forms a protective oxide coating that prevents further corrosion.

Lead is easily obtained from its ore, galena (PbS). Because lead melts at such a low temperature, it may have been the first pure metal obtained from its ore. We know that lead was used as early as 3000 B.C. by the Egyptians and was later used by the Romans to make eating utensils, glazes on pottery, and even intricate plumbing systems. Lead is very toxic, however. In fact, the Romans had so much contact with lead that it may have contributed to the demise of their civilization. Analysis of bones from that era shows significant levels of lead.

Although lead poisoning has been known since at least the second century B.C., the incidences of this problem have been relatively isolated. However, the widespread use of tetraethyl lead, $(C_2H_5)_4Pb$, as an antiknock agent in gasoline increased the lead levels in our environment in the twentieth century. Concern about the effects of this lead pollution has caused the U.S. government to require the gradual replacement of the lead in gasoline with other antiknock agents. The largest commercial use of lead (about 1.3 million tons annually) is for electrodes in the lead storage batteries used in automobiles (see Section 17.5).

Table 19.13 summarizes some important reactions of the Group 4A elements.

Lead(II) oxide, known as *litharge*.

TABLE 19.13   Selected Reactions of the Group 4A Elements

Reaction	Comment
$M + 2X_2 \rightarrow MX_4$	X_2 = any halogen molecule; M = Ge or Sn; Pb gives PbX_2
$M + O_2 \rightarrow MO_2$	M = Ge or Sn; high temperatures; Pb gives PbO or Pb_3O_4
$M + 2H^+ \rightarrow M^{2+} + H_2$	M = Sn or Pb

Key Terms

Section 19.1
representative elements
transition metals
lanthanides
actinides
metalloids (semimetals)
metallurgy
liquefaction

Section 19.2
alkali metals
superoxide

Section 19.3
hydride
ionic (saltlike) hydride
covalent hydride
metallic (interstitial) hydride

Section 19.4
alkaline earth metals
hard water
ion exchange
ion-exchange resin
cation-exchange resin

Section 19.5
boranes

For Review

Representative elements

- Chemical properties are determined by their *s* and *p* valence-electron configurations
- Metallic character increases going down the group
- The properties of the first element in a group usually differ most from the properties of the other elements in the group due to a significant difference in size
  - In Group 1A, hydrogen is a nonmetal and the other members of the group are active metals
  - The first member of a group forms the strongest π bonds, causing nitrogen and oxygen to exist as N_2 and O_2 molecules

Elemental abundances on earth

- Oxygen is the most abundant element, followed by silicon
- The most abundant metals are aluminum and iron, which are found as ores

Group 1A elements (alkali metals)

- Have valence configuration ns^1
- Except for hydrogen, readily lose one electron to form M^+ ions in their compounds with nonmetals
- React vigorously with water to form M^+ and OH^- ions and hydrogen gas
- Form a series of oxides of the types M_2O (oxide), M_2O_2 (peroxide), and MO_2 (superoxide)
  - Not all metals form all types of oxide compounds
- Hydrogen forms covalent compounds with nonmetals
- With very active metals, hydrogen forms hydrides that contain the H^- ion

Group 2A (alkaline earth metals)

- Have valence configuration ns^2
- React less violently with water than alkali metals
- The heavier alkaline earths form nitrides and hydrides
- Hard water contains Ca^{2+} and Mg^{2+} ions
  - Form precipitates with soap
  - Usually removed by ion-exchange resins that replace the Ca^{2+} and Mg^{2+} ions with Na^+

Group 3A

- Have valence configuration ns^2np^1
- Show increasing metallic character going down the group
- Boron is a nonmetal that forms many types of covalent compounds, including boranes, which are highly electron-deficient and thus are very reactive
- The metals aluminum, gallium, and indium show some covalent tendencies

Group 4A
- Have valence configuration ns^2np^2
- Lighter members are nonmetals; heavier members are metals
  - All group members can form covalent bonds to nonmetals
- Carbon forms a huge variety of compounds, most of which are classified as organic compounds

REVIEW QUESTIONS

1. What are the two most abundant elements by mass in the earth's crust, oceans, and atmosphere? Does this make sense? Why? What are the four most abundant elements by mass in the human body? Does this make sense? Why?

2. What evidence supports putting hydrogen in Group 1A of the periodic table? In some periodic tables hydrogen is listed separately from any of the groups. In what ways is hydrogen unlike a typical Group 1A element?

3. What is the valence electron configuration for the alkali metals? List some common properties of alkali metals. How are the pure metals prepared? Predicting formulas for the compound formed when an alkali metal reacts with oxygen can be difficult. Why? What is the difference between an oxide, a peroxide, and a superoxide? Describe how potassium superoxide is used in a self-contained breathing apparatus. Predict the formulas of the compounds formed when an alkali metal reacts with F_2, S, N_2, H_2, and H_2O.

4. List two major industrial uses of hydrogen. Name the three types of hydrides. How do they differ from one another?

5. What is the valence electron configuration for alkaline earth metals? List some common properties of alkaline earth metals. How are alkaline earth metals prepared? What ions are found in hard water? What happens when water is "softened"?

6. Predict the formulas of the compounds formed when an alkaline earth metal reacts with F_2, O_2, S, N_2, H_2, and H_2O.

7. What is the valence electron configuration for the Group 3A elements? How does metallic character change as one goes down this group? How are boron and aluminum different? Al_2O_3 is amphoteric. What does this mean?

8. Predict the formulas of the compounds formed when aluminum reacts with F_2, O_2, S, and N_2.

9. What is the valence electron configuration for Group 4A elements? Group 4A contains two of the most important elements on earth. What are they, and why are they so important? How does metallic character change as one goes down Group 4A? Why is the chemistry of carbon dominated by C—C bonds, whereas that of silicon is dominated by Si—O bonds? What are the two allotropic forms of carbon?

10. List some properties of germanium, tin, and lead. Predict the formulas of the compounds formed when Ge reacts with F_2 and O_2.

A blue question or exercise number indicates that the answer to that question or exercise appears at the back of this book and a solution appears in the *Solutions Guide*.

Questions

1. Although the earth was formed from the same interstellar material as the sun, there is little elemental hydrogen (H_2) in the earth's atmosphere. Explain.

2. Many lithium salts are hygroscopic (absorb water), whereas the corresponding salts of the other alkali metals are not. Explain.

3. How do the acidities of the aqueous solutions of the alkaline earth metal ions (M^{2+}) change in going down the group?

4. What are three-centered bonds?

5. Why is graphite a good lubricant? What advantages does it have over grease- or oil-based lubricants?

6. What are some of the structural differences between quartz and amorphous SiO_2?

7. What type of semiconductor is formed when a Group 3A element is added as an impurity to Si or Ge?

8. Diagonal relationships in the periodic table exist as well as the vertical relationships. For example, Be and Al are similar in some of their properties as are B and Si. Rationalize why these diagonal relationships hold for properties such as size, ionization energy, and electron affinity.

9. Atomic size seems to play an important role in explaining some of the differences between the first element in a group and the subsequent group elements. Explain.

10. What will be the atomic number of the next alkali metal to be discovered? How would you expect the physical properties of the next alkali metal to compare with the properties of the other alkali metals summarized in Table 19.4?

11. In most compounds, the solid phase is denser than the liquid phase. Why isn't this true for water?

12. Beryllium shows some covalent characteristics in some of its compounds, unlike the other alkaline earth halides. Give a possible explanation for this phenomenon.

Exercises

In this section similar exercises are paired.

Group 1A Elements

13. Hydrogen is produced commercially by the reaction of methane with steam:

$$CH_4(g) + H_2O(g) \rightleftharpoons CO(g) + 3H_2(g)$$

a. Calculate $\Delta H°$ and $\Delta S°$ for this reaction (use the data in Appendix 4).
b. What temperatures will favor product formation at standard conditions? Assume $\Delta H°$ and $\Delta S°$ do not depend on temperature.

14. The major industrial use of hydrogen is in the production of ammonia by the Haber process:

$$3H_2(g) + N_2(g) \rightarrow 2NH_3(g)$$

a. Using data from Appendix 4, calculate $\Delta H°$, $\Delta S°$, and $\Delta G°$ for the Haber process reaction.
b. Is the reaction spontaneous at standard conditions?
c. At what temperatures is the reaction spontaneous at standard conditions? Assume $\Delta H°$ and $\Delta S°$ do not depend on temperature.

15. Name each of the following compounds.
a. Li_2O b. KO_2 c. Na_2O_2

16. Write the formula for each of the following compounds.
a. lithium nitride   c. rubidium hydroxide
b. potassium carbonate   d. sodium hydride

17. Complete and balance the following reactions.
a. $Li_2O(s) + H_2O(l) \longrightarrow$
b. $Na_2O_2(s) + H_2O(l) \longrightarrow$
c. $LiH(s) + H_2O(l) \longrightarrow$
d. $KO_2(s) + H_2O(l) \longrightarrow$

18. Write balanced equations describing the reaction of lithium metal with each of the following: O_2, S_8, Cl_2, P_4, H_2, H_2O, and HCl.

19. Lithium reacts with acetylene in liquid ammonia to produce LiC_2H (lithium acetylide, $LiC≡CH$) and hydrogen gas. Write a balanced equation for this reaction. What type of reaction is this?

20. The electrolysis of aqueous sodium chloride (brine) is an important industrial process for the production of chlorine and sodium hydroxide. In fact, this process is the second largest consumer of electricity in the United States, after the production of aluminum. Write a balanced equation for the electrolysis of aqueous sodium chloride (hydrogen gas is also produced).

Group 2A Elements

21. Name each of the following compounds.
a. $MgCO_3$ b. $BaSO_4$ c. $Sr(OH)_2$

22. Write the formula for each of the following compounds.
a. calcium nitride   b. beryllium chloride   c. barium hydride

23. One harmful effect of acid rain is the deterioration of structures and statues made of marble or limestone, both of which are essentially calcium carbonate. The reaction of calcium carbonate with sulfuric acid yields carbon dioxide, water, and calcium sulfate. Because calcium sulfate is marginally soluble in water, part of the object is washed away by the rain. Write a balanced chemical equation for the reaction of sulfuric acid with calcium carbonate.

24. Write balanced equations describing the reaction of Sr with each of the following: O_2, S_8, Cl_2, P_4, H_2, H_2O, and HCl.

25. Predict the structure of BeF_2 in the gas phase. What structure would you predict for $BeF_2(s)$?

26. The beryllium atom in $BeCl_2$ is electron-deficient (only four valence electrons surround it), which makes it very reactive toward electron-pair donors such as ammonia. Draw a Lewis structure for the expected product when $BeCl_2$ reacts with excess ammonia.

27. The U.S. Public Health Service recommends the fluoridation of water as a means for preventing tooth decay. The recommended concentration is 1 mg F^- per liter. The presence of calcium ions in hard water can precipitate the added fluoride. What is the maximum molarity of calcium ions in hard water if the fluoride concentration is at the USPHS recommended level? (K_{sp} for $CaF_2 = 4.0 \times 10^{-11}$)

28. Slaked lime, $Ca(OH)_2$, is used to soften hard water by removing calcium ions from hard water through the reaction

$$Ca(OH)_2(aq) + Ca^{2+}(aq) + 2HCO_3^-(aq) \rightarrow$$
$$2CaCO_3(s) + 2H_2O(l)$$

Although $CaCO_3(s)$ is considered insoluble, some of it does dissolve in aqueous solutions. Calculate the molar solubility of $CaCO_3$ in water ($K_{sp} = 8.7 \times 10^{-9}$).

29. What mass of barium is produced when molten $BaCl_2$ is electrolyzed by a current of 2.50×10^5 A for 6.00 h?

30. Electrolysis of an alkaline earth metal chloride using a current of 5.00 A for 748 s deposits 0.471 g of metal at the cathode. What is the identity of the alkaline earth metal chloride?

Group 3A Elements

31. Write the formula for each of the following compounds.
a. aluminum nitride   b. gallium fluoride   c. gallium sulfide

32. Thallium and indium form +1 and +3 oxidation states when in compounds. Predict the formulas of the possible compounds between thallium and oxygen and between indium and chlorine. Name the compounds.

33. Boron hydrides were once evaluated for possible use as rocket fuels. Complete and balance the following equation for the combustion of diborane.

$$B_2H_6 + O_2 \longrightarrow B(OH)_3$$

34. Elemental boron is produced by reduction of boron oxide with magnesium to give boron and magnesium oxide. Write a balanced equation for this reaction.

35. Ga_2O_3 is an amphoteric oxide, and In_2O_3 is a basic oxide. Write equations for the reactions that illustrate these properties.

36. Aluminum hydroxide is amphoteric and will dissolve in both acidic and basic solutions. Write balanced chemical equations representing each process.

37. Write equations describing the reactions of Ga with each of the following: F_2, O_2, S_8, N_2, and HCl.

38. Write a balanced equation describing the reaction of aluminum metal with concentrated aqueous sodium hydroxide.

Group 4A Elements

39. Draw Lewis structures for CF_4, GeF_4, and GeF_6^{2-}. Predict the molecular structure (including bond angles), and give the expected hybridization of the central atom in these three substances. Explain why CF_6^{2-} does not form.

40. Carbon and sulfur form compounds with the formulas CS_2 and C_3S_2. Draw Lewis structures and predict the shapes of these two compounds.

41. Silicon is produced for the chemical and electronics industries by the following reactions. Give the balanced equation for each reaction.
  a. $SiO_2(s) + C(s) \rightarrow Si(s) + CO(g)$
  b. Silicon tetrachloride is reacted with very pure magnesium, producing silicon and magnesium chloride.
  c. $Na_2SiF_6(s) + Na(s) \rightarrow Si(s) + NaF(s)$

42. Write equations describing the reactions of Sn with each of the following: Cl_2, O_2, and HCl.

43. Why are people advised not to drink hot tap water if their plumbing contains lead solder?

44. Calculate the solubility of $Pb(OH)_2$ ($K_{sp} = 1.2 \times 10^{-15}$) in water. Is $Pb(OH)_2$ more or less soluble in acidic solutions? Explain.

45. The fermentation of glucose produces ethanol and carbon dioxide. Write a balanced equation for this reaction.

46. Tin forms compounds in the +2 and +4 oxidation states. Therefore, when tin reacts with fluorine, two products are possible. Write balanced equations for the production of the two tin halide compounds and name them.

47. The resistivity (a measure of electrical resistance) of graphite is $(0.4 \text{ to } 5.0) \times 10^{-4}$ ohm $\cdot$ cm in the basal plane. (The basal plane is the plane of the six-membered rings of carbon atoms.) The resistivity is 0.2 to 1.0 ohm $\cdot$ cm along the axis perpendicular to the plane. The resistivity of diamond is 10^{14} to 10^{16} ohm $\cdot$ cm and is independent of direction. How can you account for this behavior in terms of the structures of graphite and diamond?

48. Silicon carbide (SiC) is an extremely hard substance. Propose a structure for SiC.

Additional Exercises

49. A 0.250-g chunk of sodium metal is cautiously dropped into a mixture of 50.0 g of water and 50.0 g of ice, both at 0°C. The reaction is

$$2Na(s) + 2H_2O(l) \longrightarrow 2NaOH(aq) + H_2(g) \quad \Delta H = -368 \text{ kJ}$$

Will the ice melt? Assuming the final mixture has a specific heat capacity of 4.18 J/g $\cdot$ °C, calculate the final temperature. The enthalpy of fusion for ice is 6.02 kJ/mol.

50. One of the chemical controversies of the nineteenth century concerned the element beryllium (Be). Berzelius originally claimed that beryllium was a trivalent element (forming Be^{3+} ions) and that it gave an oxide with the formula Be_2O_3. This resulted in a calculated atomic mass of 13.5 for beryllium. In formulating his periodic table, Mendeleev proposed that beryllium was divalent (forming Be^{2+} ions) and that it gave an oxide with the formula BeO. This assumption gives an atomic mass of 9.0. In 1894, A. Combes (*Comptes Rendus* 1894, p. 1221) reacted beryllium with the anion $C_5H_7O_2^-$ and measured the density of the gaseous product. Combes's data for two different experiments are as follows:

	I	II
Mass	0.2022 g	0.2224 g
Volume	22.6 cm³	26.0 cm³
Temperature	13°C	17°C
Pressure	765.2 mm Hg	764.6 mm

If beryllium is a divalent metal, the molecular formula of the product will be $Be(C_5H_7O_2)_2$; if it is trivalent, the formula will be $Be(C_5H_7O_2)_3$. Show how Combes's data help to confirm that beryllium is a divalent metal.

51. It takes 15 kWh (kilowatt-hours) of electrical energy to produce 1.0 kg of aluminum metal from aluminum oxide by the Hall–Heroult process. Compare this to the amount of energy necessary to melt 1.0 kg of aluminum metal. Why is it economically feasible to recycle aluminum cans? (The enthalpy of fusion for aluminum metal is 10.7 kJ/mol [1 watt = 1 J/s].)

52. Borazine ($B_3N_3H_6$) has often been called "inorganic" benzene. Write Lewis structures for borazine. Borazine contains a six-membered ring of alternating boron and nitrogen atoms with one hydrogen bonded to each boron and nitrogen.

53. Carbon monoxide is toxic because it bonds much more strongly to the iron in hemoglobin (Hgb) than does O_2. Consider the following reactions and approximate standard free energy changes:

$$Hgb + O_2 \longrightarrow HgbO_2 \quad \Delta G° = -70 \text{ kJ}$$
$$Hgb + CO \longrightarrow HgbCO \quad \Delta G° = -80 \text{ kJ}$$

Using these data, estimate the equilibrium constant value at 25°C for the following reaction:

$$HgbO_2 + CO \rightleftharpoons HgbCO + O_2$$

54. The three most stable oxides of carbon are carbon monoxide (CO), carbon dioxide (CO_2), and carbon suboxide (C_3O_2). The space-filling models for these three compounds are

For each oxide, draw the Lewis structure, predict the molecular structure, and describe the bonding (in terms of the hybrid orbitals for the carbon atoms).

55. The overall reaction in the lead storage battery is

$$Pb(s) + PbO_2(s) + 2H^+(aq) + 2HSO_4^-(aq) \longrightarrow$$
$$2PbSO_4(s) + 2H_2O(l)$$

Calculate $\mathscr{E}$ at 25°C for this battery when $[H_2SO_4] = 4.5\ M$, that is, $[H^+] = [HSO_4^-] = 4.5\ M$. At 25°C, $\mathscr{E}° = 2.04$ V for the lead storage battery.

56. The bright yellow light emitted by a sodium vapor lamp consists of two emission lines at 589.0 and 589.6 nm. What are the frequency and the energy of a photon of light at each of these wavelengths? What are the energies in kJ/mol?

57. In the 1950s and 1960s, several nations conducted tests of nuclear warheads in the atmosphere. It was customary following each test to monitor the concentration of strontium-90 (a radioactive isotope of strontium) in milk. Why would strontium-90 tend to accumulate in milk?

58. The compound $BeSO_4 \cdot 4H_2O$ cannot be dehydrated easily by heating. It dissolves in water to give an acidic solution. Explain these observations.

59. The inert-pair effect is sometimes used to explain the tendency of heavier members of group 3A to exhibit +1 and +3 oxidation states. What does the inert-pair effect reference? *Hint:* Consider the valence electron configuration for group 3A elements.

60. Assume that element 113 is produced. What is the expected electron configuration for element 113?

61. Calculate the pH of a 0.050 M $Al(NO_3)_3$ solution. The K_a value for $Al(H_2O)_6^{3+}$ is 1.4×10^{-5}.

62. The compound with the formula TlI_3 is a black solid. Given the following standard reduction potentials:

$$Tl^{3+} + 2e^- \longrightarrow Tl^+ \qquad \mathscr{E}° = +1.25\ V$$
$$I_3^- + 2e^- \longrightarrow 3I^- \qquad \mathscr{E}° = +0.55\ V$$

would you formulate this compound as thallium(III) iodide or thallium(I) triiodide?

63. How could you determine experimentally whether the compound Ga_2Cl_4 contains two gallium(II) ions or one gallium(I) and one gallium(III) ion? (*Hint:* Consider the electron configurations of the three possible ions.)

64. Tricalcium aluminate, an important component of Portland cement, is 44.4% calcium and 20.0% aluminum by mass. The remainder is oxygen.
   a. Calculate the empirical formula of tricalcium aluminate.
   b. The structure of tricalcium aluminate was not determined until 1975. The aluminate anion ($Al_6O_{18}^{18-}$) has the following structure:

● = Al
○ = O

What is the molecular formula of tricalcium aluminate?
   c. How would you describe the bonding in the $Al_6O_{18}^{18-}$ anion?

65. In Exercise 107 in Chapter 5, the pressure of CO_2 in a bottle of sparkling wine was calculated assuming that the CO_2 was insoluble in water. This was a bad assumption. Redo this problem by assuming CO_2 obeys Henry's law. Use the data given in that problem to calculate the partial pressure of CO_2 in the gas phase and the solubility of CO_2 in the wine at 25°C. The Henry's law constant for CO_2 is 3.1×10^{-2} mol/L · atm at 25°C with Henry's law in the form $C = kP$, where C is the concentration of the gas in mol/L.

66. The compound Pb_3O_4 (red lead) contains a mixture of lead(II) and lead(IV) oxidation states. What is the mole ratio of lead(II) to lead(IV) in Pb_3O_4?

67. Lead hydrogen arsenate, an inorganic insecticide used against the potato beetle, is produced by the following reaction:

$$Pb(NO_3)_2(aq) + H_3AsO_4(aq) \rightarrow PbHAsO_4(s) + HNO_3(aq)$$

Balance this equation.

Challenge Problems

68. Provide a reasonable estimate for the number of atoms in an average adult human. Explain your answer. Use the information given in Table 19.2.

69. Suppose 10.00 g of an alkaline earth metal reacts with 10.0 L of water to produce 6.10 L of hydrogen gas at 1.00 atm and 25°C. Identify the metal and determine the pH of the solution.

70. Gallium arsenide, GaAs, has gained widespread use in semiconductor devices that convert light and electrical signals in fiber-optic communications systems. Gallium consists of 60.% ^{69}Ga and 40.% ^{71}Ga. Arsenic has only one naturally occurring isotope, ^{75}As. Gallium arsenide is a polymeric material, but its mass spectrum shows fragments with the formulas GaAs and Ga_2As_2. What would the distribution of peaks look like for these two fragments?

71. Consider dissolving 0.50 mol of $CO_2(g)$ to enough water to make a 1.0-L solution. Determine the pH of this solution, and $[CO_3^{2-}]$. Use data from Appendix 5, Table 5.2.

72. a. Many biochemical reactions that occur in cells require relatively high concentrations of potassium ion (K^+). The concentration of K^+ in muscle cells is about 0.15 M. The concentration of K^+ in blood plasma is about 0.0050 M. The high internal concentration in cells is maintained by pumping K^+ from the plasma. How much work must be done to transport 1.0 mol of K^+ from the blood to the inside of a muscle cell at 37°C (normal body temperature)?
   b. When 1.0 mol of K^+ is transferred from blood to the cells, do any other ions have to be transported? Why or why not?
   c. Cells use the hydrolysis of adenosine triphosphate, abbreviated ATP, as a source of energy. Symbolically, this reaction can be represented as

$$ATP(aq) + H_2O(l) \longrightarrow ADP(aq) + H_2PO_4^-(aq)$$

where ADP represents adenosine diphosphate. For this reaction at 37°C, $K = 1.7 \times 10^5$. How many moles of ATP must be hydrolyzed to provide the energy for the transport of 1.0 mol of K^+? Assume standard conditions for the ATP hydrolysis reaction.

73. EDTA is used as a complexing agent in chemical analysis. Solutions of EDTA, usually containing the disodium salt Na_2H_2EDTA, are also used to treat heavy metal poisoning. The equilibrium constant for the following reaction is 1.0×10^{23}:

$$Pb^{2+}(aq) + H_2EDTA^{2-}(aq) \rightleftharpoons PbEDTA^{2-}(aq) + 2H^+(aq)$$

$$EDTA^{4-} =$$

$$\begin{array}{c} ^-O_2C-CH_2 \\ ^-O_2C-CH_2 \end{array} \!\!\! N-CH_2-CH_2-N \!\!\! \begin{array}{c} CH_2-CO_2^- \\ CH_2-CO_2^- \end{array}$$

Ethylenediaminetetraacetate

Calculate $[Pb^{2+}]$ at equilibrium in a solution originally 0.0010 M in Pb^{2+}, 0.050 M in H_2EDTA^{2-}, and buffered at pH = 6.00.

74. The compounds CCl_4 and H_2O do not react with each other. On the other hand, silicon tetrachloride reacts with water according to the equation

$$SiCl_4(l) + 2H_2O(l) \longrightarrow SiO_2(s) + 4HCl(aq)$$

Discuss the importance of thermodynamics and kinetics in the reactivity of water with $SiCl_4$ as compared with its lack of reactivity with CCl_4.

75. One reason suggested to account for the instability of long chains of silicon atoms is that the decomposition involves the transition state shown below:

$$\begin{array}{c} H \; H \\ | \; | \\ H-Si-Si-H \\ | \; | \\ H \; H \end{array} \longrightarrow \left\{ \begin{array}{c} H \\ | \\ H-Si \\ | \\ H \end{array} \!\!\!\!-\!-\!-\!-\!-\!-\!\!\!\! \begin{array}{c} H \\ | \\ Si: \\ | \\ H \end{array} \right\} \longrightarrow SiH_4 + :SiH_2$$

The activation energy for such a process is 210 kJ/mol, which is less than either the Si—Si or Si—H energy. Why would a similar mechanism not be expected to be very important in the decomposition of long carbon chains?

76. From the information on the temperature stability of white and gray tin given in this chapter, which form would you expect to have the more ordered structure?

77. Lead forms compounds in the +2 and +4 oxidation states. All lead(II) halides are known (and are known to be ionic). Only PbF_4 and $PbCl_4$ are known among the possible lead(IV) halides. Presumably lead(IV) oxidizes bromide and iodide ions, producing the lead(II) halide and the free halogen:

$$PbX_4 \longrightarrow PbX_2 + X_2$$

Suppose 25.00 g of a lead(IV) halide reacts to form 16.12 g of a lead(II) halide and the free halogen. Identify the halogen.

Integrative Problems

These problems require the integration of multiple concepts to find the solutions.

78. The heaviest member of the alkaline earth metals is radium (Ra), a naturally radioactive element discovered by Pierre and Marie Curie in 1898. Radium was initially isolated from the uranium ore pitchblende, in which it is present as approximately 1.0 g per 7.0 metric tons of pitchblende. How many atoms of radium can be isolated from 1.75×10^8 g of pitchblende (1 metric ton = 1000 kg)? One of the early uses of radium was as an additive to paint so that watch dials coated with this paint would glow in the dark. The longest-lived isotope of radium has a half-life of 1.60×10^3 years. If an antique watch, manufactured in 1925, contains 15.0 mg of radium, how many atoms of radium will remain in 2025?

79. Indium(III) phosphide is a semiconducting material that has been frequently used in lasers, light-emitting diodes (LED), and fiber-optic devices. This material can be synthesized at 900. K according to the following reaction:

$$In(CH_3)_3(g) + PH_3(g) \longrightarrow InP(s) + 3CH_4(g)$$

a. If 2.56 L of $In(CH_3)_3$ at 2.00 atm is allowed to react with 1.38 L of PH_3 at 3.00 atm, what mass of $InP(s)$ will be produced assuming the reaction is 87% efficient?

b. When an electric current is passed through an optoelectronic device containing InP, the light emitted has an energy of 2.03×10^{-19} J. What is the wavelength of this light and is it visible to the human eye?

c. The semiconducting properties of InP can be altered by doping. If a small number of phosphorus atoms are replaced by atoms with an electron configuration of $[Kr]5s^2 4d^{10} 5p^4$, is this n-type or p-type doping?

80. The chemistry of tin(II) fluoride is particularly complex and demonstrates a wide range of reactivities. For example, in aqueous solutions of tin(II) fluoride containing sodium fluoride, the predominant species is SnF_3^-.

a. What is the molecular geometry of SnF_3^- and the hybridization of the tin atom?

b. When tin(II) fluoride is crystallized from aqueous solutions containing sodium fluoride, one of the products is the polyatomic cluster $Na_4Sn_3F_{10}$. Write a balanced chemical reaction for the formation of $Na_4Sn_3F_{10}$ from tin(II) fluoride and NaF.

c. Assuming complete conversion, what mass of $Na_4Sn_3F_{10}$ can be prepared by mixing 15.5 mL of 1.48 M tin(II) fluoride with 35.0 mL of 1.25 M NaF?

Marathon Problem

This problem is designed to incorporate several concepts and techniques into one situation. Marathon Problems can be used in class by groups of students to help facilitate problem-solving skills.

81. Use the symbols of the elements described in the following clues to fill in the blanks that spell out the name of a famous American scientist. Although this scientist was better known as a physicist than as a chemist, the Philadelphia institute that bears his name does include a biochemistry research facility.

—— —— —— —— —— —— ——
(1)   (2)   (3)   (4)   (5) (6)   (7)

(1) The oxide of this alkaline earth metal is amphoteric.

(2) You might be surprised to learn that a binary compound of sodium with this element has the formula NaX_3, a compound used in airbags.

(3) This alkali metal is radioactive.

(4) This element is the alkali metal with the least negative standard reduction potential. Write its symbol in reverse order.

(5) Potash is an oxide of this alkali metal.

(6) This is the only alkali metal that reacts directly with nitrogen to make a binary compound with formula M_3N.

(7) This element is the first in Group 3A for which the +1 oxidation state is exhibited in stable compounds. Use only the second letter of its symbol.

 Get help understanding core concepts and visualizing molecular-level interactions, and practice problem solving, by visiting the Online Study Center at **college.hmco.com/ PIC/zumdahl7e.**

20 The Representative Elements: Groups 5A Through 8A

Contents

The carnivorous pitcher plant "eats" insects to utilize the nitrogen held in the insect tissue.

*I*n Chapter 19 we saw that vertical groups of elements tend to show similar chemical characteristics because they have identical valence-electron configurations. Generally, metallic character increases going down a group, as the valence electrons are found farther from the nucleus. Also, recall that the most dramatic change in properties occurs after the first group member, mainly because the most dramatic change in size occurs between the first and second group members.

As we proceed from Group 1A to Group 7A, the elements change from active metals (electron donors) to strong nonmetals (electron acceptors). Thus it is not surprising that the middle groups show the most varied chemistry: Some group members behave principally as metals, others behave mainly as nonmetals, and some show both tendencies. The elements in Groups 5A and 6A show great chemical variety and form many compounds of considerable practical value. The halogens (Group 7A) are nonmetals that are also found in many everyday substances such as household bleach, photographic films, and "automatic" sunglasses. The elements in Group 8A (the noble gases) are most useful in their elemental forms, but their ability to form compounds, discovered only within the past 40 years, has provided important tests for the theories of chemical bonding.

In this chapter we give an overview of the elements in Groups 5A through 8A, concentrating on the chemistry of the most important elements in these groups: nitrogen, phosphorus, oxygen, sulfur, and the halogens.

20.1 The Group 5A Elements

The Group 5A elements (with the valence-electron configuration ns^2np^3) are prepared as shown in Table 20.1, and they show remarkably varied chemical properties. As usual, metallic character increases going down the group, as is apparent from the electronegativity values (Table 20.1). *Nitrogen* and *phosphorus* are nonmetals that can gain three electrons to form 3− anions in salts with active metals—for example, magnesium nitride (Mg_3N_2) and beryllium phosphide (Be_3P_2). The chemistry of these two important elements is discussed in the next two sections.

TABLE 20.1 Selected Physical Properties, Sources, and Methods of Preparation for the Group 5A Elements

Element	Electro-negativity	Sources	Method of Preparation
Nitrogen	3.0	Air	Liquefaction of air
Phosphorus	2.1	Phosphate rock $(Ca_3(PO_4)_2)$	$2Ca_3(PO_4)_2 + 6SiO_2 \rightarrow$ $6CaSiO_3 + P_4O_{10}$
		Fluorapatite $(Ca_5(PO_4)_3F)$	$P_4O_{10} + 10C \rightarrow$ $4P + 10CO$
Arsenic	2.0	Arsenopyrite (Fe_3As_2, FeS)	Heating arsenopyrite in the absence of air
Antimony	1.9	Stibnite (Sb_2S_3)	Roasting Sb_2S_3 in air to form Sb_2O_3 and then reduction with carbon
Bismuth	1.9	Bismite (Bi_2O_3), bismuth glance (Bi_2S_3)	Roasting Bi_2S_3 in air to form Bi_2O_3 and then reduction with carbon

Bismuth and *antimony* tend to be metallic, readily losing electrons to form cations. Although these elements have five valence electrons, so much energy is required to remove all five that no ionic compounds containing Bi^{5+} or Sb^{5+} ions are known. Three pentahalides (BiF_5, $SbCl_5$, and SbF_5) are known, but these are molecular rather than ionic compounds.

The Group 5A elements can form molecules or ions that involve three, five, or six covalent bonds to the Group 5A atom. Examples involving three single bonds are NH_3, PH_3, NF_3, and $AsCl_3$. Each of these molecules has a lone pair of electrons (and thus can behave as a Lewis base) and a pyramidal shape as predicted by the VSEPR model (see Fig. 20.1).

All the Group 5A elements except nitrogen can form molecules with five covalent bonds (of general formula MX_5). Nitrogen cannot form such molecules because of its small size and lack of available d orbitals. The MX_5 molecules have a trigonal bipyramidal shape (see Fig. 20.1) as predicted by the VSEPR model, and the central atom is described as dsp^3 hybridized. The MX_5 molecules can accept an additional electron pair to form ionic species containing six covalent bonds. An example is

$$PF_5 + F^- \longrightarrow PF_6^-$$

where the PF_6^- anion has an octahedral shape (see Fig. 20.1) and the phosphorus atom is described as d^2sp^3 hybridized.

Although the MX_5 molecules have a trigonal bipyramidal structure in the gas phase, the solids of many of these compounds contain the ions MX_4^+ and MX_6^- (Fig. 20.2), where the MX_4^+ cation is tetrahedral (the atom represented by M is described as sp^3 hybridized) and the MX_6^- anion is octahedral (the atom represented by M is described as d^2sp^3 hybridized). Examples are PCl_5, which in the solid state contains PCl_4^+ and PCl_6^-, and AsF_3Cl_2, which in the solid state contains $AsCl_4^+$ and AsF_6^-.

As discussed in Section 19.1, the ability of the Group 5A elements to form π bonds decreases dramatically after nitrogen. This explains why elemental nitrogen exists as N_2 molecules, whereas the other elements in the group exist as larger aggregates containing single bonds. For example, in the gas phase, the elements phosphorus, arsenic, and antimony consist of P_4, As_4, and Sb_4 molecules, respectively.

FIGURE 20.1
The molecules of the types MX_3, MX_5, and MX_6 formed by Group 5A elements.

Molecule Type	Molecular structure	Hybridization of M
MX_3	Pyramidal	sp^3
MX_5	Trigonal bipyramidal	dsp^3
MX_6	Octahedral	d^2sp^3

FIGURE 20.2
The structures of the tetrahedral MX_4^+ and octahedral MX_6^- ions.

20.2 The Chemistry of Nitrogen

At the earth's surface, virtually all elemental nitrogen exists as the N_2 molecule with its very strong triple bond (941 kJ/mol). Because of this high bond strength, the N_2 molecule is so unreactive that it can coexist with most other elements under normal conditions without undergoing any appreciable reaction. This property makes nitrogen gas very useful as a medium for experiments involving substances that react with oxygen or water. Such experiments can be done using an inert-atmosphere box of the type shown in Fig. 20.3.

The strength of the triple bond in the N_2 molecule is important both thermodynamically and kinetically. Thermodynamically, the great stability of the $N\equiv N$ bond means that most binary compounds containing nitrogen decompose exothermically to the elements. For example:

$$N_2O(g) \longrightarrow N_2(g) + \tfrac{1}{2}O_2(g) \qquad \Delta H^\circ = -82 \text{ kJ}$$
$$NO(g) \longrightarrow \tfrac{1}{2}N_2(g) + \tfrac{1}{2}O_2(g) \qquad \Delta H^\circ = -90 \text{ kJ}$$
$$NO_2(g) \longrightarrow \tfrac{1}{2}N_2(g) + O_2(g) \qquad \Delta H^\circ = -34 \text{ kJ}$$
$$N_2H_4(g) \longrightarrow N_2(g) + 2H_2(g) \qquad \Delta H^\circ = -95 \text{ kJ}$$
$$NH_3(g) \longrightarrow \tfrac{1}{2}N_2(g) + \tfrac{3}{2}H_2(g) \qquad \Delta H^\circ = +46 \text{ kJ}$$

Of these compounds, only ammonia is thermodynamically more stable than its component elements. That is, only for ammonia is energy required (endothermic process, positive

At the Centers for Disease Control and Prevention in Atlanta, Georgia, a worker checks samples stored in a liquid nitrogen tank.

value of $\Delta H°$) to decompose the molecule to its elements. For the remaining molecules, energy is released when decomposition to the elements occurs as a result of the great stability of N_2.

The importance of the thermodynamic stability of N_2 can be seen clearly in the power of nitrogen-based explosives, such as nitroglycerin ($C_3H_5N_3O_9$), which has the structure

The decomposition of nitroglycerin is a complex process that occurs in many steps. This equation only summarizes the stoichiometry of the reaction.

FIGURE 20.3
An inert-atmosphere box used when working with oxygen- or water-sensitive materials. The box is filled with an inert gas such as nitrogen, and work is done through the ports fitted with large rubber gloves.

When ignited or subjected to sudden impact, nitroglycerin decomposes very rapidly and exothermically:

$$4C_3H_5N_3O_9(l) \longrightarrow 6N_2(g) + 12CO_2(g) + 10H_2O(g) + O_2(g) + \text{energy}$$

An explosion occurs; that is, large volumes of gas are produced in a fast, highly exothermic reaction. Note that 4 moles of liquid nitroglycerin produce 29 (6 + 12 + 10 + 1) moles of gaseous products. This alone produces a large increase in volume. However, also note that the products, including N_2, are very stable molecules with strong bonds. Their formation is therefore accompanied by the release of large quantities of energy as heat, which increases the gaseous volume. The hot, rapidly expanding gases produce a pressure surge and damaging shock wave.

Pure nitroglycerin is quite dangerous because it explodes with little provocation. However, in 1867 the Swedish inventor Alfred Nobel found that if nitroglycerin is absorbed in porous silica, it can be handled quite safely. This tremendously important explosive (see Fig. 20.4), which he called *dynamite,* earned Nobel a great fortune, which he subsequently used to establish the Nobel Prizes.

Most high explosives are organic compounds that, like nitroglycerin, contain nitro ($—NO_2$) groups and produce nitrogen and other gases as products. Another example is *trinitrotoluene,* or TNT, a solid at normal temperatures, which decomposes as follows:

$$2C_7H_5N_3O_6(s) \longrightarrow 12CO(g) + 5H_2(g) + 3N_2(g) + 2C(s) + \text{energy}$$

Note that 2 moles of solid TNT produce 20 moles of gaseous products plus energy.

TNT

Sample Exercise 20.1

Decomposition of NH₄NO₂

When ammonium nitrite is heated, it decomposes to nitrogen gas and water. Calculate the volume of N_2 gas produced from 1.00 g of solid NH_4NO_2 at 250°C and 1.00 atm.

Solution

The decomposition reaction is

$$NH_4NO_2(s) \xrightarrow{\text{Heat}} N_2(g) + 2H_2O(g)$$

Using the molar mass of NH_4NO_2 (64.05 g/mol), we first calculate the moles of NH_4NO_2:

$$1.00 \text{ g } NH_4NO_2 \times \frac{1 \text{ mol } NH_4NO_2}{64.05 \text{ g } NH_4NO_2} = 1.56 \times 10^{-2} \text{ mol } NH_4NO_2$$

Since 1 mol N_2 is produced for each mole of NH_4NO_2, 1.56×10^{-2} mol N_2 will be produced in the given experiment. We can calculate the volume of N_2 from the ideal gas law:

$$PV = nRT$$

In this case we have

$$P = 1.00 \text{ atm}$$
$$n = 1.56 \times 10^{-2} \text{ mol}$$
$$R = 0.08206 \text{ L} \cdot \text{atm/K} \cdot \text{mol}$$
$$T = 250 + 273 = 523 \text{ K}$$

and the volume of N_2 is

$$V = \frac{nRT}{P} = \frac{(1.56 \times 10^{-2} \text{ mol})\left(0.08206 \frac{\text{L} \cdot \text{atm}}{\text{K} \cdot \text{mol}}\right)(523 \text{ K})}{1.00 \text{ atm}}$$

$$= 0.670 \text{ L}$$

FIGURE 20.4
Chemical explosives are used to demolish a building in Miami, Florida.

See Exercises 20.17 and 20.18.

FIGURE 20.5
A schematic diagram of the Haber process for the manufacture of ammonia.

Nodules on the roots of pea plants contain nitrogen-fixing bacteria.

The effect of bond strength on the kinetics of reactions involving the N_2 molecule is illustrated by the synthesis of ammonia from nitrogen and hydrogen, a reaction we have discussed many times before. Because a large quantity of energy is required to disrupt the $N\equiv N$ bond, the ammonia synthesis reaction has a negligible rate at room temperature, even though the equilibrium constant is very large ($K \approx 10^6$) at 25°C. Of course, the most direct way to increase the rate is to raise the temperature, but since the reaction is very exothermic, that is,

$$N_2(g) + 3H_2(g) \longrightarrow 2NH_3(g) \qquad \Delta H° = -92 \text{ kJ}$$

the value of K decreases significantly with a temperature increase (at 500°C, $K \approx 10^{-2}$).

Obviously, the kinetics and the thermodynamics of this reaction are in opposition. A compromise must be reached: high pressure to force the equilibrium to the right and high temperature to produce a reasonable rate. The **Haber process** for manufacturing ammonia illustrates this compromise (see Fig. 20.5). The process is carried out at a pressure of about 250 atm and a temperature of approximately 400°C. Even higher temperatures would be required except that a catalyst, consisting of a solid iron oxide mixed with small amounts of potassium oxide and aluminum oxide, is used to facilitate the reaction.

Nitrogen is essential to living systems. The problem with nitrogen is not one of supply—we are surrounded by it—but of changing it from inert N_2 molecules to a form usable by plants and animals. The process of transforming N_2 to other nitrogen-containing compounds is called **nitrogen fixation.** The Haber process is one example of nitrogen fixation. The ammonia produced can be applied to the soil as a fertilizer, since plants can readily employ the nitrogen in ammonia to make the nitrogen-containing biomolecules essential for their growth.

Nitrogen fixation also results from the high-temperature combustion process in automobile engines. The nitrogen in the air drawn into the engine reacts at a significant rate with oxygen to form nitric oxide (NO), which further reacts with oxygen from the air to form nitrogen dioxide (NO_2). This nitrogen dioxide, which is an important contributor to photochemical smog in many urban areas (see Section 12.8), eventually reacts with moisture in the air and reaches the soil to form nitrate salts, which are plant nutrients.

Nitrogen fixation also occurs naturally. For example, lightning provides the energy to disrupt N_2 and O_2 molecules in the air, producing highly reactive nitrogen and oxygen atoms that attack other N_2 and O_2 molecules to form nitrogen oxides that eventually become nitrates. Although lightning traditionally has been credited with forming about 10% of the total fixed nitrogen, recent studies indicate that lightning may account for as much as half the fixed nitrogen available on earth. Another natural nitrogen fixation process is provided by bacteria that reside in the root nodules of plants such as beans, peas, and alfalfa. These **nitrogen-fixing bacteria** readily allow the conversion of nitrogen to ammonia and other nitrogen-containing compounds useful to plants. The efficiency of these bacteria is intriguing: They produce ammonia at soil temperature and 1 atm of pressure, whereas the Haber process requires severe conditions of 400°C and 250 atm. For obvious reasons, researchers are studying these bacteria intensively.

When plants and animals die, they decompose, and the elements they consist of are returned to the environment. In the case of nitrogen, the return of the element to the atmosphere as nitrogen gas, called **denitrification,** is carried out by bacteria that change nitrates to nitrogen. The complex **nitrogen cycle** is summarized in Fig. 20.6. It has been estimated that as much as 10 million tons per year more nitrogen is currently being fixed by natural and human processes than is being returned to the atmosphere. This fixed nitrogen is accumulating in the soil, lakes, rivers, and oceans, where it can promote the growth of algae and other undesirable organisms.

Nitrogen Hydrides

By far the most important hydride of nitrogen is **ammonia** (NH_3). A toxic, colorless gas with a pungent odor, ammonia is manufactured in huge quantities ($\sim$30 billion pounds per year), mainly for use in fertilizers.

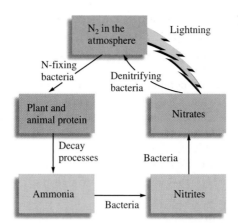

FIGURE 20.6
The nitrogen cycle. To be used by plants and animals, nitrogen must be converted from N_2 to nitrogen-containing compounds, such as nitrates, ammonia, and proteins. The nitrogen is returned to the atmosphere by natural decay processes.

The pyramidal ammonia molecule (see Fig. 20.1) has a lone pair of electrons on the nitrogen atom and polar N—H bonds. This structure leads to a high degree of intermolecular interaction by hydrogen bonding in the liquid state and produces an unusually high boiling point ($-33.4°C$) for a substance of such low molar mass. Note, however, that the hydrogen bonding in liquid ammonia is clearly not as important as that in liquid water, which has about the same molar mass but a much higher boiling point. The water molecule has two polar bonds involving hydrogen and two lone pairs—the right combination for optimal hydrogen bonding—in contrast to the one lone pair and three polar bonds of the ammonia molecule.

As we saw in Chapter 14, ammonia behaves as a base and reacts with acids to produce ammonium salts. For example,

$$NH_3(g) + HCl(g) \longrightarrow NH_4Cl(s)$$

A second nitrogen hydride of major importance is **hydrazine** (N_2H_4). The Lewis structure of hydrazine is

$$\begin{array}{ccc} H & & H \\ \diagdown & \ddots \;\; \ddots & \diagup \\ & N\!-\!N & \\ \diagup & & \diagdown \\ H & & H \end{array}$$

indicating that each nitrogen atom should be sp^3 hybridized with bond angles close to 109.5 degrees (the tetrahedral angle), since the nitrogen atom is surrounded by four electron pairs. The observed structure with bond angles of 112 degrees (see Fig. 20.7) agrees reasonably well with these predictions. Hydrazine, a colorless liquid with an ammonia-like odor, freezes at 2°C and boils at 113.5°C. This boiling point is quite high for a compound with a molar mass of 32 g/mol; this suggests that considerable hydrogen bonding must occur among the polar hydrazine molecules.

Hydrazine is a powerful reducing agent that has been used widely as a rocket propellant. For example, its reaction with oxygen is highly exothermic:

$$N_2H_4(l) + O_2(g) \longrightarrow N_2(g) + 2H_2O(g) \qquad \Delta H° = -622 \text{ kJ}$$

Since hydrazine also reacts vigorously with the halogens, fluorine is often used instead of oxygen as the oxidizer in rocket engines. Substituted hydrazines, where one or more of the hydrogen atoms are replaced by other groups, are also useful rocket fuels. For example, monomethylhydrazine,

$$\begin{array}{ccc} CH_3 & & H \\ \diagdown & & \diagup \\ & N\!-\!N & \\ \diagup & & \diagdown \\ H & & H \end{array}$$

FIGURE 20.7
The molecular structure of hydrazine (N_2H_4). This arrangement minimizes the repulsion between the lone pairs on the nitrogen atoms by placing them on opposite sides.

is used with the oxidizer dinitrogen tetroxide (N_2O_4) to power the U.S. space shuttle orbiter. The reaction is

$$5N_2O_4(l) + 4N_2H_3(CH_3)(l) \longrightarrow 12H_2O(g) + 9N_2(g) + 4CO_2(g)$$

Because of the large number of gaseous molecules produced and the exothermic nature of this reaction, a very high thrust per mass of fuel is achieved. The reaction is also self-starting—it begins immediately when the fuels are mixed—which is a useful property for rocket engines that must be started and stopped frequently.

Heats of Reaction from Bond Energies

Using the bond energies in Table 8.4, calculate the approximate value of ΔH for the reaction between gaseous monomethylhydrazine and dinitrogen tetroxide:

$$5N_2O_4(g) + 4N_2H_3(CH_3)(g) \longrightarrow 12H_2O(g) + 9N_2(g) + 4CO_2(g)$$

The bonding in N_2O_4 is described by resonance structures that predict that the N—O bonds are intermediate in strength between single and double bonds (assume an average N—O bond energy of 440 kJ/mol).

Solution

To calculate ΔH for this reaction, we must compare the energy necessary to break the bonds of the reactants and the energy released by formation of the bonds in the products:

Breaking bonds requires energy (positive sign), and forming bonds releases energy (negative sign). As summarized in the following table,

$$\Delta H = (21.1 \times 10^3 \text{ kJ}) - (26.1 \times 10^3 \text{ kJ}) = -5.0 \times 10^3 \text{ kJ}$$

The reaction is highly exothermic.

Bonds Broken	Energy Required (kJ/mol)	Bonds Formed	Energy Released (kJ/mol)
$5 \times 4 = 20$ N=O	$20 \times 440 = 8.8 \times 10^3$	$12 \times 2 = 24$ O—H	$24 \times 467 = 1.12 \times 10^4$
$5 + 4 = 9$ N—N	$9 \times 160 = 1.4 \times 10^3$	9 N≡N	$9 \times 941 = 8.5 \times 10^3$
$4 \times 3 = 12$ N—H	$12 \times 391 = 4.7 \times 10^3$	$4 \times 2 = 8$ C=O	$8 \times 799 = 6.4 \times 10^3$
$4 \times 3 = 12$ C—H	$12 \times 413 = 5.0 \times 10^3$		
$4 \times 1 = 4$ C—N	$4 \times 305 = 1.2 \times 10^3$		
Total	21.1×10^3	Total	26.1×10^3

See Exercise 20.19.

The use of hydrazine as a rocket propellant is a rather specialized application. The main industrial use of hydrazine is as a "blowing" agent in the manufacture of plastics. Hydrazine decomposes to form nitrogen gas, which causes foaming in the liquid plastic, which results in a porous texture. Another major use of hydrazine is in the production of agricultural pesticides. Of the many hundreds of hydrazine derivatives (substituted hydrazines) that have been tested, 40 are used as fungicides, herbicides, insecticides, and plant growth regulators.

The manufacture of hydrazine involves the oxidation of ammonia by the hypochlorite ion in basic solution:

$$2NH_3(aq) + OCl^-(aq) \longrightarrow N_2H_4(aq) + Cl^-(aq) + H_2O(l)$$

Although this reaction looks straightforward, the actual process involves many steps and requires high pressure, high temperature, and catalysis to optimize the yield of hydrazine in the face of many competing reactions.

Nitrogen Oxides

Nitrogen forms a series of oxides in which it has an oxidation state from +1 to +5, as shown in Table 20.2.

Dinitrogen monoxide (N_2O), more commonly called *nitrous oxide* or "laughing gas," has an inebriating effect and has been used as a mild anesthetic by dentists. Because of its high solubility in fats, nitrous oxide is used widely as a propellant in aerosol cans of whipped cream. It is dissolved in the liquid in the can at high pressure and forms bubbles that produce foaming as the liquid is released from the can. A significant amount of N_2O exists in the atmosphere, mostly produced by soil microorganisms, and its concentration

Blowing agents such as hydrazine, which forms nitrogen gas on decomposition, are used to produce porous plastics like these styrofoam products.

TABLE 20.2 Some Common Nitrogen Compounds

Oxidation State of Nitrogen	Compound	Formula	Lewis Structure*
−3	Ammonia	NH_3	H—N̈—H with H below
−2	Hydrazine	N_2H_4	H—N̈—N̈—H with H below each N
−1	Hydroxylamine	NH_2OH	H—N̈—Ö—H with H below N
0	Nitrogen	N_2	:N≡N:
+1	Dinitrogen monoxide (nitrous oxide)	N_2O	:N̈=N=Ö:
+2	Nitrogen monoxide (nitric oxide)	NO	:N̈=Ö:
+3	Dinitrogen trioxide	N_2O_3	O₂N—N=O structure
+4	Nitrogen dioxide	NO_2	:Ö—N=Ö
+5	Nitric acid	HNO_3	:Ö—N—Ö—H with =Ö below

*In some cases, additional resonance structures are needed to fully describe the electron distribution.

appears to be gradually increasing. Because it can strongly absorb infrared radiation, nitrous oxide plays a small but probably significant role in controlling the earth's temperature in the same way that atmospheric carbon dioxide and water vapor do (see the discussion of the greenhouse effect in Section 6.5). Some scientists fear that the rapid decrease of tropical rain forests resulting from development in countries such as Brazil will significantly affect the rate of production of N_2O by soil organisms and thus will have important effects on the earth's temperature.

In the laboratory, nitrous oxide is prepared by the thermal decomposition of ammonium nitrate:

$$NH_4NO_3(s) \xrightarrow{\text{Heat}} N_2O(g) + 2H_2O(g)$$

Do *not* attempt this experiment unless you have the proper safety equipment.

This experiment must be done carefully because ammonium nitrate can explode. In fact, one of the greatest industrial disasters in U.S. history occurred in 1947 in Texas, when a ship loaded with ammonium nitrate for use as fertilizer exploded and killed nearly 600 people.

Nitrogen monoxide (NO), commonly called *nitric oxide,* is a colorless gas under normal conditions that can be produced in the laboratory by reaction of 6 *M* nitric acid with copper metal:

$$8H^+(aq) + 2NO_3^-(aq) + 3Cu(s) \longrightarrow 3Cu^{2+}(aq) + 4H_2O(l) + 2NO(g)$$

When this reaction is run in the air, the nitric oxide is immediately oxidized to brown nitrogen dioxide (NO_2).

Although nitric oxide is toxic when inhaled, it has been shown to be produced in certain tissues of the human body, where it behaves as a neurotransmitter. Current research indicates that nitric oxide plays a role in regulating blood pressure, blood clotting, and the muscle changes that allow erection of the penis in males.

Since the NO molecule has an odd number of electrons, it is most conveniently described in terms of the molecular orbital model. The molecular orbital energy-level diagram is shown in Fig. 20.8. Note that the NO molecule is paramagnetic and should have a bond order of 2.5, a prediction that is supported by experimental observations. Since the NO molecule has one high-energy electron, it is not surprising that it can be rather easily oxidized to form NO^+, the *nitrosyl ion.* Because an antibonding electron is removed in going from NO to NO^+, the ion should have a stronger bond (the predicted bond order is 3) than the molecule. This is borne out by experiment. The bond lengths and bond

A copper penny reacts with nitric acid to produce NO gas, which is immediately oxidized in air to brown NO_2.

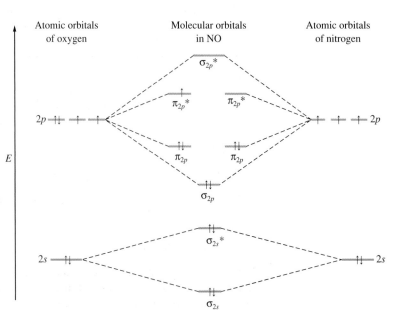

FIGURE 20.8
The molecular orbital energy-level diagram for nitric oxide (NO). The bond order is 2.5, or $(8 - 3)/2$.

TABLE 20.3 Comparison of the Bond Lengths and Bond Energies for Nitric Oxide and the Nitrosyl Ion

	NO	NO$^+$
Bond length (pm)	115	109
Bond energy (kJ/mol)	630	1020
Bond order (predicted by MO model)	2.5	3

energies for nitric oxide and the nitrosyl ion are shown in Table 20.3. The nitrosyl ion is formed when nitric oxide and nitrogen dioxide are dissolved in concentrated sulfuric acid:

$$NO(g) + NO_2(g) + 3H_2SO_4(aq) \longrightarrow 2NO^+(aq) + 3HSO_4^-(aq) + H_3O^+(aq)$$

The ionic compound $NO^+HSO_4^-$ can be isolated from this solution.

Nitric oxide is thermodynamically unstable and decomposes to nitrous oxide and nitrogen dioxide:

$$3NO(g) \longrightarrow N_2O(g) + NO_2(g)$$

Nitrogen dioxide (NO_2) is also an odd-electron molecule and has a V-shaped structure. The brown, paramagnetic NO_2 molecule readily dimerizes to form dinitrogen tetroxide,

$$2NO_2(g) \rightleftharpoons N_2O_4(g)$$

which is diamagnetic and colorless. The value of the equilibrium constant is ~ 1 for this process at 55°C, and since the dimerization is exothermic, K decreases as the temperature increases.

Production of NO_2 by power plants and automobiles leads to smog (see Section 12.8).

| *Sample Exercise 20.3* | **Molecular Orbital Description of NO$^-$** |

Use the molecular orbital model to predict the bond order and magnetism of the NO$^-$ ion.

Solution

Using the energy-level diagram for the NO molecule in Fig. 20.8, we can see that NO$^-$ has one more antibonding electron than NO. Thus there will be unpaired electrons in the two π_{2p}^* orbitals, and NO$^-$ will be paramagnetic with a bond order of $(8 - 4)/2$, or 2. Note that the bond in the NO$^-$ ion is weaker than that in the NO molecule.

See Exercises 20.23 and 20.24.

The least common of the nitrogen oxides are *dinitrogen trioxide* (N_2O_3), a blue liquid that readily dissociates into gaseous nitric oxide and nitrogen dioxide, and *dinitrogen pentoxide* (N_2O_5), which under normal conditions is a solid that is best viewed as a mixture of NO_2^+ and NO_3^- ions. Although N_2O_5 molecules do exist in the gas phase, they readily dissociate to nitrogen dioxide and oxygen:

$$2N_2O_5(g) \rightleftharpoons 4NO_2(g) + O_2(g)$$

This reaction follows first-order kinetics, as was discussed in Section 12.4.

Oxyacids of Nitrogen

Nitric acid is an important industrial chemical (almost 10 million tons is produced annually) used in the manufacture of many products, such as nitrogen-based explosives and ammonium nitrate for use as fertilizer.

CHEMICAL IMPACT

Nitrous Oxide: Laughing Gas That Propels Whipped Cream and Cars

Nitrous oxide (N_2O), more properly called *dinitrogen monoxide,* is a compound with many interesting uses. It was discovered in 1772 by Joseph Priestley (who is also given credit for discovering oxygen gas), and its intoxicating effects were noted almost immediately. In 1798, the 20-year-old Humphry Davy became director of the Pneumatic Institute, which was set up to investigate the medical effects of various gases. Davy tested the effects of N_2O on himself, reporting that after inhaling 16 quarts of the gas in 7 minutes, he became "absolutely intoxicated."

Over the next century "laughing gas," as nitrous oxide became known, was developed as an anesthetic, particularly for dental procedures. Nitrous oxide is still used as an anesthetic, although it has been largely replaced by more modern drugs.

One major use of nitrous oxide today is as the propellant in cans of "instant" whipped cream. The high solubility of N_2O in the whipped cream mixture makes it an excellent candidate for pressurizing the cans of whipped cream.

Another current use of nitrous oxide is to produce "instant horsepower" for hot rods and street racers. Because the reaction of N_2O with O_2 to form NO actually absorbs heat, this reaction has a cooling effect when placed in the fuel mixture in an automobile engine. This cooling effect lowers combustion temperatures, thus allowing the fuel–air mixture to be significantly more dense (the density of a gas is inversely proportional to temperature). This effect can produce a burst of additional power in excess of 200 horsepower. Because engines are not designed to run steadily at such high power levels, the nitrous oxide is injected from a tank when extra power is desired.

FIGURE 20.9
The Ostwald process.

Nitric acid is produced commercially by the oxidation of ammonia in the **Ostwald process** (see Fig. 20.9). In the first step of this process, ammonia is oxidized to nitric oxide:

$$4NH_3(g) + 5O_2(g) \longrightarrow 4NO(g) + 6H_2O(g) \qquad \Delta H° = -905 \text{ kJ}$$

Although this reaction is highly exothermic, it is very slow at 25°C. There is also a side reaction between nitric oxide and ammonia:

$$4NH_3(g) + 6NO(g) \longrightarrow 5N_2(g) + 6H_2O(g)$$

which is particularly undesirable because it traps the nitrogen as very unreactive N_2 molecules. To speed up the desired reaction and minimize the effects of the competing reaction, the ammonia oxidation is carried out using a catalyst of a platinum–rhodium alloy heated to 900°C. Under these conditions, there is a 97% conversion of the ammonia to nitric oxide.

In the second step, nitric oxide reacts with oxygen to produce nitrogen dioxide:

$$2NO(g) + O_2(g) \longrightarrow 2NO_2(g) \qquad \Delta H° = -113 \text{ kJ}$$

This oxidation reaction has a rate that *decreases* with increasing temperature. Because of this very unusual behavior, the reaction is carried out at $\sim$25°C and is kept at this temperature by cooling with water.

The third step in the Ostwald process is the absorption of nitrogen dioxide by water:

$$3NO_2(g) + H_2O(l) \longrightarrow 2HNO_3(aq) + NO(g) \qquad \Delta H° = -139 \text{ kJ}$$

The gaseous NO produced in this reaction is recycled to be oxidized to NO_2. The aqueous nitric acid from this process is about 50% HNO_3 by mass, which can be increased to 68% by distillation to remove some of the water. The maximum concentration attainable this way is 68% because nitric acid and water form an *azeotrope* at this concentration. The solution

FIGURE 20.10
(a) The molecular structure of HNO_3.
(b) The resonance structures of HNO_3.

(a)

(b)

An *azeotrope* is a solution that, like a pure liquid, distills at a constant temperature without a change in composition.

can be further concentrated to 95% HNO_3 by treatment with concentrated sulfuric acid, which strongly absorbs water; H_2SO_4 is often used as a dehydrating (water-removing) agent.

Nitric acid is a colorless, fuming liquid (bp = 83°C) with a pungent odor; it decomposes in sunlight via the following reaction:

$$4HNO_3(l) \xrightarrow{hv} 4NO_2(g) + 2H_2O(l) + O_2(g)$$

As a result, nitric acid turns yellow as it ages because of the dissolved nitrogen dioxide. The common laboratory reagent known as concentrated nitric acid is 15.9 M HNO_3 (70.4% HNO_3 by mass) and is a very strong oxidizing agent. The resonance structures and molecular structure of HNO_3 are shown in Fig. 20.10. Note that the hydrogen is bound to an oxygen atom rather than to nitrogen, as the formula suggests.

Nitric acid reacts with metal oxides, hydroxides, and carbonates and with other ionic compounds containing basic anions to form nitrate salts. For example,

$$Ca(OH)_2(s) + 2HNO_3(aq) \longrightarrow Ca(NO_3)_2(aq) + 2H_2O(l)$$

Nitrate salts are generally very soluble in water.

Nitrous acid (HNO_2) is a weak acid,

$$HNO_2(aq) \rightleftharpoons H^+(aq) + NO_2^-(aq) \qquad K_a = 4.0 \times 10^{-4}$$

that forms pale yellow nitrite (NO_2^-) salts. In contrast to nitrates, which are often used as explosives, nitrites are quite stable even at high temperatures. Nitrites are usually prepared by bubbling equal numbers of moles of nitric oxide and nitrogen dioxide into the appropriate aqueous solution of a metal hydroxide. For example,

$$NO(g) + NO_2(g) + 2NaOH(aq) \longrightarrow 2NaNO_2(aq) + H_2O(l)$$

20.3 The Chemistry of Phosphorus

Visualization: Barking Dogs:
Reaction of Phosphorus

Although phosphorus lies directly below nitrogen in Group 5A of the periodic table, its chemical properties are significantly different from those of nitrogen. The differences arise mainly from four factors: nitrogen's ability to form much stronger π bonds, the greater electronegativity of nitrogen, the larger size of the phosphorus atom, and the availability of empty valence d orbitals on phosphorus.

The chemical differences are apparent in the elemental forms of nitrogen and phosphorus. In contrast to the diatomic form of elemental nitrogen, which is stabilized by strong π bonds, there are several solid forms of phosphorus, all containing aggregates of atoms. *White phosphorus,* which contains discrete tetrahedral P_4 molecules [see Fig. 20.11(a)], is very reactive and bursts into flames on contact with air (it is said to be *pyrophoric*). To prevent this, white phosphorus is commonly stored under water. White phosphorus is quite toxic, and the P_4 molecules are very damaging to tissue, particularly the cartilage and bones of the nose and jaw. The much less reactive forms known as *black phosphorus* and *red phosphorus* are network solids (see Section 10.5). Black phosphorus has a regular crystalline structure [Fig. 20.11(b)], but red phosphorus is amorphous and is thought to consist of chains of P_4 units [Fig. 20.11(c)]. Red phosphorus can be obtained

CHEMICAL IMPACT

Phosphorus: An Illuminating Element

The elemental form of phosphorus was discovered by accident in 1669 by German alchemist Henning Brand when he heated dried urine with sand (alchemists often investigated the chemistry of body fluids in an attempt to better understand the "stuff of life"). When Brand passed the resulting vapors through water, he was able to isolate the form of elemental phosphorus known as *white phosphorus* (contains P_4 molecules). The name *phosphorus* is derived from the Latin *phos*, meaning "light," and *phorus*, meaning "bearing." It seems that when Brand stored the solid white phosphorus in a sealed bottle, it glowed in the dark! This effect—a glow that persists even after the light source has been removed—came to be called *phosphorescence*. Interestingly, the term phosphorescence is derived from the name of an element that really does not phosphoresce. The glow that Brand saw actually was the result of a reaction of oxygen from the air on the surface of white phosphorus. If isolated completely from air, phosphorus does not glow in the dark after being irradiated.

After its discovery, phosphorus became quite a novelty in the seventeenth century. People would deposit a film of phosphorus on their faces and hands so that they would glow in the dark.* This fascination was short-lived—painful, slow-healing burns result from the spontaneous reaction of phosphorus with oxygen from the air.

The greatest consumer use of phosphorus compounds concerns the chemistry of matches. Two kinds of matches are currently available—strike-anywhere matches and safety

---

*An interesting reference to white phosphorus can be found in the Sherlock Holmes mystery, *The Hound of the Baskervilles*, where a large dog was coated with white phosphorus to scare Baskerville family members to death.

---

by heating white phosphorus in the absence of oxygen at 1 atm. Black phosphorus is obtained from either white or red phosphorus by heating at high pressures.

Even though phosphorus has a lower electronegativity than nitrogen, it will form phosphides (ionic substances containing the P^{3-} anion) such as Na_3P and Ca_3P_2. Phosphide salts react vigorously with water to produce *phosphine* (PH_3), a toxic, colorless gas:

$$2Na_3P(s) + 6H_2O(l) \longrightarrow 2PH_3(g) + 6Na^+(aq) + 6OH^-(aq)$$

Phosphine is analogous to ammonia, although it is a much weaker base ($K_b \approx 10^{-26}$) and much less soluble in water. Because phosphine has a relatively small affinity for protons, phosphonium (PH_4^+) salts are very uncommon and not very stable—only PH_4I, PH_4Cl, and PH_4Br are known.

Phosphine has the Lewis structure

$$\left[H - \overset{\cdot\cdot}{\underset{\underset{H}{|}}{P}} - H \right]$$

and a pyramidal molecular structure, as we would predict from the VSEPR model. However, it has bond angles of 94 degrees, rather than 107 degrees, as found in the ammonia

FIGURE 20.11
(a) The P_4 molecule found in white phosphorus. (b) The crystalline network structure of black phosphorus. (c) The chain structure of red phosphorus.

(a)

(b)

(c)

matches. Both types of matches use phosphorus (in different forms) to help initiate a flame at the match head. The chemistry of matches is quite interesting. The tip of a strike-anywhere match is made from a mixture of powdered glass, binder, and tetraphosphorus trisulfide (P_4S_3). When the match is struck, friction ignites the combustion reaction of P_4S_3:

$$P_4S_3(s) + 6O_2(g) \longrightarrow P_4O_6(g) + 3SO_2(g)$$

The heat from this reaction causes an oxidizing agent such as potassium chlorate to decompose:

$$2KClO_3(s) \longrightarrow 2KCl(s) + 3O_2(g)$$

which in turn causes solid sulfur to melt and react with oxygen, producing sulfur dioxide and more heat. This then ignites a paraffin wax that helps to "light" the wooden stem of the match.

The chemistry of a safety match is quite similar, but the location of the reactants is different. The phosphorus needed to initiate all the reactions is found on the striking surface of the box. Thus, in theory, a safety match is able to ignite

The phosphorus in safety matches helps ignite the flame in the match.

only when used with the box. For a safety match, the striking surface contains red phosphorus, which is easily converted to white phosphorus by the friction of the match head on the striking surface. White phosphorus ignites spontaneously in air and generates enough heat to initiate all the other reactions to ignite the match stem.

$$4P \text{ (red)} + \text{energy (friction)} \longrightarrow$$
$$P_4(s)\text{(white)} + 5O_2(g) \longrightarrow P_4O_{10}(s) + \text{heat}$$

molecule. The reasons for this are complex, and we will simply regard phosphine as an exception to the simple version of the VSEPR model that we use.

Phosphorus Oxides and Oxyacids

Phosphorus reacts with oxygen to form oxides in which it has oxidation states of $+5$ and $+3$. The oxide P_4O_6 is formed when elemental phosphorus is burned in a limited supply of oxygen, and P_4O_{10} is produced when the oxygen is in excess. These oxides, as shown in Fig. 20.12, can be pictured as being constructed by adding oxygen atoms to the fundamental P_4 structure. The intermediate states, P_4O_7, P_4O_8, and P_4O_9, which contain one, two, and three terminal oxygen atoms, respectively, are also known.

The terminal oxygens are the nonbridging oxygen atoms.

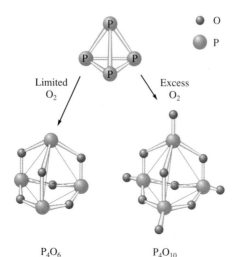

FIGURE 20.12
The structures of P_4O_6 and P_4O_{10}.

P_4O_6 P_4O_{10}

Tetraphosphorus decoxide (P_4O_{10}), which was formerly represented as P_2O_5, has a great affinity for water and thus is a powerful dehydrating agent. For example, it can be used to convert HNO_3 and H_2SO_4 to their parent oxides, N_2O_5 and SO_3, respectively.

When tetraphosphorus decoxide dissolves in water, **phosphoric acid** (H_3PO_4), also called **orthophosphoric acid,** is produced:

$$P_4O_{10}(s) + 6H_2O(l) \longrightarrow 4H_3PO_4(aq)$$

Pure phosphoric acid is a white solid that melts at 42°C. Aqueous phosphoric acid is a much weaker acid ($K_{a_1} \approx 10^{-2}$) than nitric acid or sulfuric acid and is a poor oxidizing agent.

Phosphate minerals are the main source of phosphoric acid. Unlike nitrogen, phosphorus is found in nature exclusively in a combined state, principally as the $PO_4{}^{3-}$ ion in phosphate rock, which is mainly calcium phosphate, $Ca_3(PO_4)_2$, and fluorapatite, $Ca_5(PO_4)_3F$. Fluorapatite can be converted to phosphoric acid by grinding up the phosphate rock and forming a slurry with sulfuric acid:

$Ca_5(PO_4)_3F(s) + 5H_2SO_4(aq) + 10H_2O(l)$
$$\longrightarrow HF(aq) + 5CaSO_4 \cdot 2H_2O(s) + 3H_3PO_4(aq)$$

(A similar reaction can be written for the conversion of calcium phosphate.) The solid product $CaSO_4 \cdot 2H_2O$, called *gypsum,* is used to manufacture wallboard for the construction of buildings.

The process just described, called the *wet process,* produces only impure phosphoric acid. In another procedure, phosphate rock, sand (SiO_2), and coke are heated in an electric furnace to form white phosphorus:

$$12Ca_5(PO_4)_3F + 43SiO_2 + 90C \longrightarrow 9P_4 + 90CO + 20(3CaO \cdot 2SiO_2) + 3SiF_4$$

The white phosphorus obtained is burned in air to form tetraphosphorus decoxide, which is then combined with water to give phosphoric acid.

Phosphoric acid easily undergoes **condensation reactions,** where a molecule of water is eliminated in the joining of two molecules of acid:

The product ($H_4P_2O_7$) is called *pyrophosphoric acid.* Further heating produces polymers, such as *tripolyphosphoric acid* ($H_5P_3O_{10}$), which has the structure

The sodium salt of tripolyphosphoric acid is widely used in detergents because the $P_3O_{10}{}^{5-}$ anion can form complexes with metal ions such as Mg^{2+} and Ca^{2+}, which would otherwise interfere with detergent action.

The mineral hydroxyapatite, $Ca_5(PO_4)_3OH$, the principal component of tooth enamel, can be converted to fluorapatite by reaction with fluoride. Fluoride ions added to drinking water and toothpaste help prevent tooth decay because fluorapatite is less soluble in the acids of the mouth than hydroxyapatite.

Sample Exercise 20.4 | **Structure of Phosphoric Acid**

What are the molecular structure and the hybridization of the central atom of the phosphoric acid molecule?

FIGURE 20.13
(a) The structure of phosphorous acid (H_3PO_3). (b) The structure of hypophosphorous acid (H_3PO_2).

(a)

(b)

Solution

In the phosphoric acid molecule, the hydrogen atoms are attached to oxygens, and the Lewis structure is as shown below. Thus the phosphorus atom is surrounded by four effective pairs, which are arranged tetrahedrally. The atom is described as sp^3 hybridized.

Lewis structure

See Exercises 20.27 and 20.28.

When P_4O_6 is placed in water, **phosphorous acid** (H_3PO_3) is formed [Fig. 20.13(a)]. Although the formula suggests a triprotic acid, phosphorous acid is a *diprotic* acid. The hydrogen atom bonded directly to the phosphorus atom is not acidic in aqueous solution; only those hydrogen atoms bonded to the oxygen atoms in H_3PO_3 can be released as protons.

A third oxyacid of phosphorus is *hypophosphorous acid* (H_3PO_2) [Fig. 20.13(b)], which is a monoprotic acid.

Phosphorus in Fertilizers

Phosphorus is essential for plant growth. Although most soil contains large amounts of phosphorus, it is often present as insoluble minerals, which makes it inaccessible to plants. Soluble phosphate fertilizers are manufactured by treating phosphate rock with sulfuric acid to make **superphosphate of lime,** a mixture of $CaSO_4 \cdot 2H_2O$ and $Ca(H_2PO_4)_2 \cdot H_2O$. If phosphate rock is treated with phosphoric acid, $Ca(H_2PO_4)_2$, or *triple phosphate,* is produced. The reaction of ammonia and phosphoric acid gives *ammonium dihydrogen phosphate* ($NH_4H_2PO_4$), a very efficient fertilizer because it furnishes both phosphorus and nitrogen.

Phosphorus Halides

Phosphorus forms all possible halides of the general formulas PX_3 and PX_5, with the exception of PI_5. The PX_3 molecule has the expected pyramidal structure [Fig. 20.14(a)]. Under normal conditions of temperature and pressure, PF_3 is a colorless gas, PCl_3 is a liquid (bp = 74°C), PBr_3 is a liquid (bp = 175°C), and PI_3 is an unstable red solid (mp = 61°C). All the PX_3 compounds react with water to produce phosphorous acid:

$$PX_3 + 3H_2O(l) \longrightarrow H_3PO_3(aq) + 3HX(aq)$$

In the gaseous and liquid states, the PX_5 compounds have molecules with a trigonal bipyramidal structure [Fig. 20.14(b)]. However, PCl_5 and PBr_5 form ionic solids: Solid

— Unshared electron pair

(a)

(b)

FIGURE 20.14
Structures of the phosphorus halides. (a) The PX_3 compounds have pyramidal molecules. (b) The gaseous and liquid phases of the PX_5 compounds are composed of trigonal bipyramidal molecules.

PCl_5 contains a mixture of octahedral PCl_6^- ions and tetrahedral PCl_4^+ ions, and solid PBr_5 appears to consist of PBr_4^+ and Br^- ions.

The PX_5 compounds react with water to form phosphoric acid:

$$PX_5 + 4H_2O(l) \longrightarrow H_3PO_4(aq) + 5HX(aq)$$

20.4 The Group 6A Elements

6A

O
S
Se
Te
Po

Although in Group 6A (Table 20.4) there is the usual tendency for metallic properties to increase going down the group, none of the Group 6A elements (valence-electron configuration ns^2np^4) behaves as a typical metal. The most common chemical behavior of a Group 6A atom is to achieve a noble gas electron configuration by adding two electrons to become a 2− anion in ionic compounds with metals. In fact, for most metals, the oxides and sulfides constitute the most common minerals.

The Group 6A elements can form covalent bonds with other nonmetals. For example, they combine with hydrogen to form a series of covalent hydrides of the general formula H_2X. Those members of the group that have valence d orbitals available (all except oxygen) commonly form molecules in which they are surrounded by more than eight electrons. Examples are SF_4, SF_6, TeI_4, and $SeBr_4$.

In recent years there has been a growing interest in the chemistry of selenium, an element found throughout the environment in trace amounts. Selenium's toxicity has long been known, but recent medical studies have shown an *inverse* relationship between the incidence of cancer and the selenium levels in soil. It has been suggested that the resulting greater dietary intake of selenium by people living in areas of relatively high levels of selenium somehow furnishes protection from cancer. These studies are only preliminary, but selenium is known to be physiologically important (it is involved in the activity of vitamin E and certain enzymes) and selenium deficiency has been shown to be connected to the occurrence of congestive heart failure. Also of importance is the fact that selenium (along with tellurium) is a semiconductor and therefore finds some application in the electronics industry.

Polonium was discovered in 1898 by Marie and Pierre Curie in their search for the sources of radioactivity in pitchblende. Polonium has 27 isotopes and is highly toxic and very radioactive. It has been suggested that the isotope ^{210}Po, a natural contaminant of tobacco and an α-particle emitter (see Section 18.1), might be at least partly responsible for the incidence of cancer in smokers.

TABLE 20.4 Selected Physical Properties, Sources, and Methods of Preparation for the Group 6A Elements

Element	Electro-negativity	Radius of X^{2-} (pm)	Source	Method of Preparation
Oxygen	3.5	140	Air	Distillation from liquid air
Sulfur	2.5	184	Sulfur deposits	Melted with hot water and pumped to the surface
Selenium	2.4	198	Impurity in sulfide ores	Reduction of H_2SeO_4 with SO_2
Tellurium	2.1	221	Nagyagite (mixed sulfide and telluride)	Reduction of ore with SO_2
Polonium	2.0	230	Pitchblende	

20.5 The Chemistry of Oxygen

It is hard to overstate the importance of oxygen, the most abundant element in and near the earth's crust. Oxygen is present in the atmosphere in oxygen gas and ozone; in soil and rocks in oxide, silicate, and carbonate minerals; in the oceans in water; and in our bodies in water and in a myriad of molecules. In addition, most of the energy we need to live and to run our civilization comes from the exothermic reactions of oxygen and carbon-containing molecules.

The most common elemental form of oxygen (O_2) constitutes 21% of the volume of the earth's atmosphere. Since nitrogen has a lower boiling point than oxygen, nitrogen can be boiled away from liquid air, leaving oxygen and small amounts of argon, another component of air. Liquid oxygen is a pale blue liquid that freezes at $-219°C$ and boils at $-183°C$. The paramagnetism of the O_2 molecule can be demonstrated by pouring liquid oxygen between the poles of a strong magnet, where it "sticks" as it boils away (see Fig. 9.40). The paramagnetism of the O_2 molecule can be accounted for by the molecular orbital model (see Fig. 9.39), which also explains its bond strength.

The other form of elemental oxygen is **ozone** (O_3), a molecule that can be represented by the resonance structures

The bond angle in the O_3 molecule is 117 degrees, in reasonable agreement with the prediction of the VSEPR model (three effective pairs require a trigonal planar arrangement). That the bond angle is slightly less than 120 degrees can be explained by concluding that more space is required for the lone pair than for the bonding pairs.

Ozone can be prepared by passing an electric discharge through pure oxygen gas. The electrical energy disrupts the bonds in some O_2 molecules to give oxygen atoms, which react with other O_2 molecules to form O_3. Ozone is much less stable than oxygen at 25°C and 1 atm. For example, $K \approx 10^{-57}$ for the equilibrium

$$3O_2(g) \rightleftharpoons 2O_3(g)$$

A pale blue, highly toxic gas, ozone is a much more powerful oxidizing agent than oxygen. Because of its oxidizing ability, ozone is being considered as a replacement for chlorine in municipal water purification. Chlorine leaves residues of chloro compounds, such as chloroform ($CHCl_3$), which may cause cancer after long-term exposure. Although ozone effectively kills the bacteria in water, one problem with **ozonolysis** is that the water supply is not protected against recontamination, since virtually no ozone remains after the initial treatment. In contrast, for chlorination, significant residual chlorine remains after treatment.

The oxidizing ability of ozone can be highly detrimental, especially when it is formed in the pollution from automobile exhausts (see Section 5.10).

Ozone exists naturally in the upper atmosphere of the earth. The *ozone layer* is especially important because it absorbs ultraviolet light and thus acts as a screen to prevent this radiation, which can cause skin cancer, from penetrating to the earth's surface. When an ozone molecule absorbs this energy, it splits into an oxygen molecule and an oxygen atom:

$$O_3 \xrightarrow{h\nu} O_2 + O$$

If the oxygen molecule and atom collide, they will not stay together as ozone unless a "third body," such as a nitrogen molecule, is present to help absorb the energy released in the bond formation. The third body absorbs the energy as kinetic energy; its temperature is increased. Therefore, the energy originally absorbed as ultraviolet radiation is eventually changed to thermal energy. Thus the ozone prevents the harmful high-energy ultraviolet light from reaching the earth.

FIGURE 20.15
The Frasch process for recovering sulfur from underground deposits.

20.6 The Chemistry of Sulfur

Sulfur is found in nature both in large deposits of the free element and in widely distributed ores, such as galena (PbS), cinnabar (HgS), pyrite (FeS_2), gypsum ($CaSO_4 \cdot 2H_2O$), epsomite ($MgSO_4 \cdot 7H_2O$), and glauberite ($Na_2SO_4 \cdot CaSO_4$).

About 60% of the sulfur produced in the United States comes from the underground deposits of elemental sulfur found in Texas and Louisiana. This sulfur is recovered using the **Frasch process** developed by Herman Frasch in the 1890s. Superheated water is pumped into the deposit to melt the sulfur (mp = 113°C), which is then forced to the surface by air pressure (see Fig. 20.15). The remaining 40% of sulfur produced in the United States is either a by-product of the purification of fossil fuels before combustion to prevent pollution or comes from the sulfur dioxide (SO_2) scrubbed from the exhaust gases when sulfur-containing fuels are burned.

The scrubbing of sulfur dioxide from exhaust gases was discussed in Section 5.10.

In contrast to oxygen, elemental sulfur exists as S_2 molecules only in the gas phase at high temperatures. Because sulfur atoms form much stronger σ bonds than π bonds, S_2 is less stable at 25°C than larger aggregates such as S_6 and S_8 rings and S_n chains (Fig. 20.16). The most stable form of sulfur at 25°C and 1 atm is called *rhombic sulfur* [see Fig. 20.17(a)], which contains stacked S_8 rings. If rhombic sulfur is melted and heated to 120°C, it forms *monoclinic sulfur* as it cools slowly [Fig. 20.17(b)]. This form also contains S_8 rings, but the rings are stacked differently than they are in rhombic sulfur.

As sulfur is heated beyond its melting point, a relatively nonviscous liquid containing S_8 rings forms initially. With continued heating, the liquid becomes highly viscous as the rings first break and then link up to form long chains. Further heating lowers the viscosity

FIGURE 20.16
(a) The S_8 molecule. (b) Chains of sulfur atoms in viscous liquid sulfur. The chains may contain as many as 10,000 atoms.

(a)

(b)

FIGURE 20.17
(a) Crystals of rhombic sulfur. (b) Crystals of monoclinic sulfur.

Pouring liquid sulfur into water to produce plastic sulfur.

(a)

(b)

FIGURE 20.18
(a) Two of the resonance structures for SO_2. (b) SO_2 is a bent molecule with a 119-degree bond angle, as predicted by the VSEPR model.

FIGURE 20.19
(a) Three of the resonance structures of SO_3. (b) A resonance structure with three double bonds. (c) SO_3 is a planar molecule with 120-degree bond angles.

because the long chains are broken down as the energetic sulfur atoms break loose. If the liquid is suddenly cooled, a substance called *plastic sulfur,* which contains S_n chains and has rubberlike qualities, is formed. Eventually, this form reverts back to the more stable S_8 rings.

Sulfur Oxides

From its position below oxygen in the periodic table, we might expect the simplest stable oxide of sulfur to have the formula SO. However, *sulfur monoxide,* which can be produced in small amounts when gaseous sulfur dioxide (SO_2) is subjected to an electrical discharge, is very unstable. The difference in the stabilities of the O_2 and SO molecules probably reflects the stronger π bonding between oxygen atoms than between sulfur and oxygen atoms.

Sulfur burns in air with a bright blue flame to give *sulfur dioxide* (SO_2), a colorless gas with a pungent odor, which condenses to a liquid at $-10°C$ and 1 atm. Sulfur dioxide is a very effective antibacterial agent and is often used to preserve stored fruit. Its structure is given in Fig. 20.18.

Sulfur dioxide reacts with oxygen to produce *sulfur trioxide* (SO_3):

$$2SO_2(g) + O_2(g) \longrightarrow 2SO_3(g)$$

However, this reaction is very slow in the absence of a catalyst. One of the mysteries during early research on air pollution was how the sulfur dioxide produced from the combustion of sulfur-containing fuels is so rapidly converted to sulfur trioxide. It is now known that dust and other particles can act as heterogeneous catalysts for this process (see Section 12.8). In the preparation of sulfur trioxide for the manufacture of sulfuric acid, a platinum or vanadium(V) oxide (V_2O_5) catalyst is used, and the reaction is carried out at $\sim 500°C$, even though this temperature decreases the value of the equilibrium constant for this exothermic reaction.

The bonding in the SO_3 molecule is usually described in terms of the resonance structures shown in Fig. 20.19. The molecule is trigonal planar, as predicted by the VSEPR

(a)

(b)

(c)

(left) A sulfur deposit. (right) Melted sulfur obtained from underground deposits by the Frasch process.

(a)

(b)

FIGURE 20.20
Different structures for solid SO_3. (a) S_3O_9 rings. (b) $(SO_3)_x$ chains. In both cases the sulfur atoms are surrounded by a tetrahedral arrangement of oxygen atoms.

model. Sulfur trioxide is a corrosive gas with a choking odor that forms white fumes of sulfuric acid when it reacts with moisture in the air. Thus sulfur trioxide and nitrogen dioxide, which reacts with water to form a mixture of nitrous and nitric acids, are the major culprits in the formation of acid rain.

Sulfur trioxide condenses to a colorless liquid at 44.5°C and freezes at 16.8°C to give three solid forms, one containing S_3O_9 rings and the other two containing $(SO_3)_x$ chains (Fig. 20.20).

Oxyacids of Sulfur

Sulfur dioxide dissolves in water to form an acidic solution. The reaction is often represented as

$$SO_2(g) + H_2O(l) \longrightarrow H_2SO_3(aq)$$

where H_2SO_3 is called *sulfurous acid*. However, very little H_2SO_3 actually exists in the solution. The major form of sulfur dioxide in water is SO_2, and the acid dissociation equilibria are best represented as

$$SO_2(aq) + H_2O(l) \rightleftharpoons H^+(aq) + HSO_3^-(aq) \qquad K_{a_1} = 1.5 \times 10^{-2}$$
$$HSO_3^-(aq) \rightleftharpoons H^+(aq) + SO_3^{2-}(aq) \qquad K_{a_2} = 1.0 \times 10^{-7}$$

This situation is analogous to the behavior of carbon dioxide in water (see Section 14.7). Although H_2SO_3 cannot be isolated, salts of SO_3^{2-} (*sulfites*) and HSO_3^- (*hydrogen sulfites*) are well known.

Sulfur trioxide reacts violently with water to produce the diprotic acid **sulfuric acid:**

$$SO_3(g) + H_2O(l) \longrightarrow H_2SO_4(aq)$$

Manufactured in greater amounts than any other chemical, sulfuric acid is usually produced by the *contact process,* which is described at the end of Chapter 3. About 60% of the sulfuric acid manufactured in the United States is used to produce fertilizers from phosphate rock (see Section 20.3). The other 40% is used in lead storage batteries and in petroleum refining, in steel manufacturing, and for various purposes in most of the chemical industries.

Because sulfuric acid has a high affinity for water, it is often used as a dehydrating agent. Gases that do not react with sulfuric acid, such as oxygen, nitrogen, and carbon dioxide, are often dried by bubbling them through concentrated solutions of the acid.

(a) (b) (c)

FIGURE 20.21
(a) A beaker of sucrose (table sugar). (b) Concentrated sulfuric acid reacts with the sucrose to produce a column of carbon (c), accompanied by an intense burnt-sugar odor.

Sulfuric acid is such a powerful dehydrating agent that it will remove hydrogen and oxygen from a substance in a 2:1 ratio even when the substance contains no molecular water. For example, concentrated sulfuric acid reacts vigorously with common table sugar (sucrose), leaving a charred mass of carbon (see Fig. 20.21):

$$C_{12}H_{22}O_{11}(s) + 11H_2SO_4(conc) \longrightarrow 12C(s) + 11H_2SO_4 \cdot H_2O(l)$$
Sucrose

Sulfuric acid is a moderately strong oxidizing agent, especially at high temperatures. Hot concentrated sulfuric acid oxidizes bromide or iodide ions to elemental bromine or iodine. For example,

$$2I^-(aq) + 3H_2SO_4(aq) \longrightarrow I_2(aq) + SO_2(aq) + 2H_2O(l) + 2HSO_4^-(aq)$$

Hot sulfuric acid attacks copper metal:

$$Cu(s) + 2H_2SO_4(aq) \longrightarrow CuSO_4(aq) + 2H_2O(l) + SO_2(aq)$$

The cold acid does not react with copper.

Other Compounds of Sulfur

Sulfur reacts with both metals and nonmetals to form a wide variety of compounds in which it has a +6, +4, +2, 0, or −2 oxidation state (see Table 20.5). The −2 oxidation state occurs in the metal sulfides and in *hydrogen sulfide* (H_2S), a toxic, foul-smelling gas that acts as a diprotic acid when dissolved in water. Hydrogen sulfide is a strong reducing agent in aqueous solution, producing a milky-looking suspension of finely divided sulfur as one of the products. For example, hydrogen sulfide reacts with chlorine in aqueous solution as follows:

The acidic properties of sulfuric acid solutions are discussed in Section 14.7.

$$H_2S(g) + Cl_2(aq) \longrightarrow 2H^+(aq) + 2Cl^-(aq) + S(s)$$

Milky suspension of sulfur

TABLE 20.5   Common Compounds of Sulfur with Various Oxidation States

Oxidation State of Sulfur	Compounds
+6	SO_3, H_2SO_4, SO_4^{2-}, SF_6
+4	SO_2, HSO_3^-, SO_3^{2-}, SF_4
+2	SCl_2
0	S_8 and all other forms of elemental sulfur
−2	H_2S, S^{2-}

The preparation of sulfur trioxide provides an example of the compromise that often must be made between thermodynamics and kinetics.

Sulfur also forms the **thiosulfate ion** ($S_2O_3^{2-}$), which has the Lewis structure

The prefix *thio* means "sulfur."

$$\left[\begin{array}{c} \ddot{:}\ddot{O}\ddot{:} \\ | \\ :\ddot{O}-\overset{}{S}-\ddot{S}: \\ | \\ :\ddot{O}: \end{array} \right]^{2-}$$

Note that this anion can be viewed as a sulfate ion in which one of the oxygen atoms has been replaced by sulfur, which is reflected in the name *thio*sulfate. The thiosulfate ion can be formed by heating sulfur with a sulfite salt in aqueous solution:

$$S(s) + SO_3^{2-}(aq) \longrightarrow S_2O_3^{2-}(aq)$$

One important use of thiosulfate ion is in photography, where $S_2O_3^{2-}$ dissolves solid silver bromide by forming a complex with the Ag^+ ion (see the Chemical Impact in Section 20.7). Thiosulfate ion is also a good reducing agent and is often used to analyze for iodine:

$$2S_2O_3^{2-}(aq) + I_2(aq) \longrightarrow S_4O_6^{2-}(aq) + 2I^-(aq)$$

where $S_2O_6^{2-}$ is called the *tetrathionate ion.*

Sulfur reacts with the halogens to form a variety of compounds, such as S_2Cl_2, SF_4, SF_6, and S_2F_{10}. The structures of these molecules are shown in Fig. 20.22.

20.7 The Group 7A Elements

7A
F
Cl
Br
I
At

In our coverage of the representative elements, we have progressed from groups of metallic elements (Groups 1A and 2A), through groups in which the lighter members are nonmetals and the heavier members are metals (Groups 3A, 4A, and 5A), to a group of all nonmetals (Group 6A—although some might prefer to call polonium a metal). The

FIGURE 20.22
The structures of (a) SF_4, (b) SF_6, (c) S_2F_{10}, and (d) S_2Cl_2.

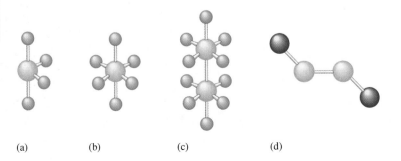

(a)   (b)   (c)   (d)

TABLE 20.6 Trends in Selected Physical Properties of the Group 7A Elements

Element	Electro-negativity	Radius of X⁻ (pm)	$\mathscr{E}°$ (V) for $X_2 + 2e \rightarrow 2X^-$	Bond Energy of X_2 (kJ/mol)
Fluorine	4.0	136	2.87	154
Chlorine	3.0	181	1.36	239
Bromine	2.8	185	1.09	193
Iodine	2.5	216	0.54	149
Astatine	2.2	—	—	—

Group 7A elements, the **halogens** (with the valence-electron configuration ns^2np^5), are also all nonmetals whose properties generally vary smoothly going down the group. The only notable exceptions are the unexpectedly low values for the electron affinity of fluorine and the bond energy of the F_2 molecule (see Section 19.1). Table 20.6 summarizes the trends in some physical properties of the halogens.

Because of their high reactivities, the halogens are not found as the free elements in nature. Instead, they are found as halide ions (X^-) in various minerals and in seawater (see Table 20.7).

Although astatine is a member of Group 7A, its chemistry is of no practical importance because all its known isotopes are radioactive. The longest-lived isotope, ^{210}At, has a half-life of only 8.3 hours.

The halogens, particularly fluorine, have very high electronegativity values (Table 20.6). They tend to form polar covalent bonds with other nonmetals and ionic bonds with metals in their lower oxidation states. When a metal ion is in a higher oxidation state, such as +3 or +4, the metal–halogen bonds are polar covalent ones. For example, $TiCl_4$ and $SnCl_4$ are both covalent compounds that are liquids under normal conditions.

Hydrogen Halides

The hydrogen halides can be prepared by a reaction of the elements:

$$H_2(g) + X_2(g) \longrightarrow 2HX(g)$$

This reaction occurs with explosive vigor when fluorine and hydrogen are mixed. On the other hand, hydrogen and chlorine can coexist with little apparent reaction for relatively

Chlorine, bromine, and iodine.

TABLE 20.7 Some Physical Properties, Sources, and Methods of Preparation for the Group 7A Elements

Element	Color and State	Percentage of Earth's Crust	Melting Point (°C)	Boiling Point (°C)	Sources	Method of Preparation
Fluorine	Pale yellow gas	0.07	−220	−188	Fluorospar (CaF_2), cryolite (Na_3AlF_6), fluorapatite $(Ca_5(PO_4)_3F)$	Electrolysis of molten KHF_2
Chlorine	Yellow-green gas	0.14	−101	−34	Rock salt (NaCl), halite (NaCl), sylvite (KCl)	Electrolysis of aqueous NaCl
Bromine	Red-brown liquid	2.5×10^{-4}	−7.3	59	Seawater, brine wells	Oxidation of Br^- by Cl_2
Iodine	Violet-black solid	3×10^{-5}	113	184	Seaweed, brine wells	Oxidation of I^- by electrolysis or MnO_2

CHEMICAL IMPACT

Photography

In black-and-white photography, light from an object is focused onto a special paper containing an emulsion of solid silver bromide. Silver salts turn dark when exposed to light because the radiant energy stimulates the transfer of an electron to the Ag^+ ion, forming an atom of elemental silver. When photographic paper (film) is exposed to light, the areas exposed to the brightest light form the most silver atoms. The next step is the application of a chemical reducing agent to the film, a process called *developing*. The real advantage of silver-based films is that the silver atoms already present from exposure to light catalyze the reduction of millions of Ag^+ ions in the immediate vicinity in the developing process. Thus the effect of exposure to light is greatly intensified in this chemical reduction process. Once the image has been developed, the unchanged solid silver bromide must be removed so that the film is no longer light-sensitive and the image is fixed. A solution of sodium thiosulfate (called *hypo*) is used in this *fixing process*:

$$AgBr(s) + 2S_2O_3^{2-}(aq) \longrightarrow Ag(S_2O_3)_2^{3-}(aq) + Br^-(aq)$$

After the excess silver bromide is dissolved and washed away, the fixed image (the *negative*) is ready to produce the positive print. By shining light through the negative onto a fresh sheet of film and repeating the developing and fixing processes, a black-and-white photograph can be produced.

Positive and negative images.

A candle burning in an atmosphere of $Cl_2(g)$. The exothermic reaction, which involves breaking C—C and C—H bonds in the wax and forming C—Cl bonds in their places, produces enough heat to make the gases in the region incandescent (a flame results).

long periods in the dark. However, ultraviolet light causes an explosively fast reaction, and this is the basis of a popular lecture demonstration, the "hydrogen–chlorine cannon." Bromine and iodine also react with hydrogen, but more slowly.

The hydrogen halides also can be prepared by treating halide salts with acid. For example, hydrogen fluoride and hydrogen chloride can be prepared as follows:

$$CaF_2(s) + H_2SO_4(aq) \longrightarrow CaSO_4(s) + 2HF(g)$$
$$2NaCl(s) + H_2SO_4(aq) \longrightarrow Na_2SO_4(s) + 2HCl(g)$$

Sulfuric acid is capable of oxidizing Br^- to Br_2 and I^- to I_2 and so cannot be used to prepare hydrogen bromide and hydrogen iodide. However, phosphoric acid, a nonoxidizing acid, can be used to treat bromides and iodides to form the corresponding hydrogen halides.

Some physical properties of the hydrogen halides are listed in Table 20.8. Note the very high boiling point for hydrogen fluoride, which results from extensive hydrogen bonding among the very polar HF molecules (Fig. 20.23). Fluoride ion has such a high affinity for protons that in concentrated aqueous solutions of hydrogen fluoride, the ion $[F—H—F]^-$ exists, in which an H^+ ion is centered between two F^- ions.

When dissolved in water, the hydrogen halides behave as acids, and all except hydrogen fluoride are completely dissociated. Because water is a much stronger base than

FIGURE 20.23
The hydrogen bonding among HF molecules in liquid hydrogen fluoride.

TABLE 20.8   Some Physical Properties of the Hydrogen Halides

HX	Melting Point (°C)	Boiling Point (°C)	H—X Bond Energy (kJ/mol)
HF	−83	20	565
HCl	−114	−85	427
HBr	−87	−67	363
HI	−51	−35	295

Cl^-, Br^-, or I^- ion, the acid strengths of HCl, HBr, and HI cannot be differentiated in water. However, in a less basic solvent, such as glacial (pure) acetic acid, the acids show different strengths of the order

$$H—I > H—Br > H—Cl \gg H—F$$

Strongest Weakest
acid acid

To see why hydrogen fluoride is the only weak acid in water among the HX molecules, let's consider the dissociation equilibrium

$$HX(aq) \rightleftharpoons H^+(aq) + X^-(aq)$$

where

$$K_a = \frac{[H^+][X^-]}{[HX]}$$

from a thermodynamic point of view. Recall that acid strength is reflected by the magnitude of K_a—a small K_a value means a weak acid. Also recall that the value of an equilibrium constant depends on the standard free energy change for the reaction as follows:

$$\Delta G° = -RT \ln(K)$$

As $\Delta G°$ becomes more negative, K becomes larger; a *decrease* in free energy favors a given reaction. As we saw in Chapter 16, free energy depends on enthalpy, entropy, and temperature. For a process at constant temperature,

$$\Delta G° = \Delta H° - T\Delta S°$$

Thus, to explain the various acid strengths of the hydrogen halides, we must focus on the factors that determine $\Delta H°$ and $\Delta S°$ for the acid dissociation reaction.

What energy terms are important in determining $\Delta H°$ for the dissociation of HX in water? (Keep in mind that large positive contributions to the value of $\Delta H°$ will tend to make $\Delta G°$ more highly positive, K_a smaller, and the acid weaker.) One important factor is certainly the H—X bond strength. Note from Table 20.8 that the H—F bond is much stronger than the other H—X bonds. This factor tends to make HF a weaker acid than the others.

Another important contribution to $\Delta H°$ is the enthalpy of hydration (see Section 11.2) of X^- (see Table 20.9). As we would expect, the smallest of the halide ions, F^-, has the most negative value—its hydration is the most exothermic. This term favors the dissociation of HF into its ions more so than it does for the other HX molecules.

So far we have two conflicting factors: The large HF bond energy tends to make HF a weaker acid than the other hydrogen halides, but the enthalpy of hydration favors the dissociation of HF more than that of the others. In comparing data for HF and HCl, the difference in bond energy (138 kJ/mol) is slightly smaller than the difference in the enthalpies of hydration for the anions (144 kJ/mol). If these were the *only* important factors, HF should be a stronger acid than HCl because the large enthalpy of hydration of F^- more than makes up for the large HF bond strength.

When H_2O molecules cluster around an ion, an ordering effect occurs, and $\Delta S°_{hyd}$ is negative.

TABLE 20.9   The Enthalpies and Entropies of Hydration for the Halide Ions

	$X^-(g) \xrightarrow{H_2O} X^-(aq)$	
X^-	$\Delta H°$ (kJ/mol)	$\Delta S°$ (J/K · mol)
F^-	-510	-159
Cl^-	-366	-96
Br^-	-334	-81
I^-	-291	-64

Hydration becomes more exothermic as the charge density of an ion icreases. Thus, for ions of a given charge, the smallest is most strongly hydrated.

Stomach acid is 0.1 *M* HCl.

This Steuben glass design was etched using hydrofluoric acid.

As it turns out, *the deciding factor is entropy*. Note from Table 20.9 that the entropy of hydration for F^- is much more negative than for the other halides because of the high degree of ordering that occurs as the water molecules associate with the small F^- ion. Remember that a negative change in entropy is unfavorable. Thus, although the enthalpy of hydration favors dissociation of HF, the *entropy* of hydration strongly opposes it.

When all these factors are taken into account, $\Delta G°$ for the dissociation of HF in water is positive; that is, K_a is small. In contrast, $\Delta G°$ for dissociation of the other HX molecules in water is negative (K_a is large). This example illustrates the complexity of the processes that occur in aqueous solutions and the importance of entropy effects in that medium.

In practical terms, **hydrochloric acid** is the most important of the **hydrohalic acids,** the aqueous solutions of the hydrogen halides. About 3 million tons of hydrochloric acid is produced annually for use in cleaning steel before galvanizing and in the manufacture of many other chemicals.

Hydrofluoric acid is used to etch glass by reacting with the silica in glass to form the volatile gas SiF_4:

$$SiO_2(s) + 4HF(aq) \longrightarrow SiF_4(g) + 2H_2O(l)$$

Oxyacids and Oxyanions

All the halogens except fluorine combine with various numbers of oxygen atoms to form a series of oxyacids, as shown in Table 20.10. The strengths of these acids vary in direct proportion to the number of oxygen atoms attached to the halogen, as we discussed in Section 14.9.

The only member of the chlorine series that has been obtained in the pure state is *perchloric acid* ($HOClO_3$), a strong acid and powerful oxidizing agent. Because perchloric acid reacts explosively with many organic materials, it must be handled with great caution. The other oxyacids of chlorine are known only in solution, although salts containing their anions are well known (Fig. 20.24).

TABLE 20.10   The Known Oxyacids of the Halogens*

Oxidation State of Halogen	Fluorine	Chlorine	Bromine	Iodine*	General Name of Acids	General Name of Salts
+1	HOF	HOCl	HOBr	HOI	Hypohalous acid	Hypohalites, MOX
+3	**	HOClO	**	**	Halous acid	Halites, MXO_2
+5	**	$HOClO_2$	$HOBrO_2$	$HOIO_2$	Halic acid	Halates, MXO_3
+7	**	$HOClO_3$	$HOBrO_3$	$HOIO_3$	Perhalic acid	Perhalates, MXO_4

*Iodine also forms $H_4I_2O_9$ (mesodiperiodic acid) and H_5IO_6 (paraperiodic acid).

**Compound is unknown.

FIGURE 20.24
The structures of the oxychloro anions.

Hypochlorite ion, OCl^-

Chlorite ion, ClO_2^-

Chlorate ion, ClO_3^-

Perchlorate ion, ClO_4^-

Hypochlorous acid (HOCl) is formed when chlorine gas is dissolved in cold water:

$$Cl_2(aq) + H_2O(l) \rightleftharpoons HOCl(aq) + H^+(aq) + Cl^-(aq)$$

Note that in this reaction chlorine is both oxidized (from 0 in Cl_2 to +1 in HOCl) and reduced (from 0 in Cl_2 to −1 in Cl^-). Such a reaction, *where a given element is both oxidized and reduced,* is called a **disproportionation reaction.** Hypochlorous acid and its salts are strong oxidizing agents, and solutions of them are widely used as household bleaches and disinfectants.

Chlorate salts, such as $KClO_3$, are also strong oxidizing agents and are used as weed killers and as oxidizers in fireworks (see Chapter 7) and explosives.

Fluorine forms only one oxyacid, hypofluorous acid (HOF), but at least two oxides. When fluorine gas is bubbled into a dilute solution of sodium hydroxide, the compound *oxygen difluoride* (OF_2) is formed:

$$4F_2(g) + 3H_2O(l) \longrightarrow 6HF(aq) + OF_2(g) + O_2(g)$$

Oxygen difluoride is a pale yellow gas (bp = −145°C), which is a strong oxidizing agent. The oxide *dioxygen difluoride* (O_2F_2) is an orange solid that can be prepared by passing an electric discharge through an equimolar mixture of fluorine and oxygen gases:

$$F_2(g) + O_2(g) \xrightarrow[\text{discharge}]{\text{Electric}} O_2F_2(s)$$

The name for OF_2 is *oxygen difluoride* rather than difluorine oxide because fluorine has a higher electronegativity than oxygen and thus is named as if it were an anion.

Sample Exercise 20.5   **Bonding Description of OF_2**

Give the Lewis structure, molecular structure, and hybridization of the oxygen atom for OF_2.

Solution

The OF_2 molecule has 20 valence electrons and the Lewis structure is

The four effective pairs around the oxygen are arranged tetrahedrally. Therefore, the oxygen atom is sp^3 hybridized. The molecule is bent (V-shaped), and the bond angle is predicted to be smaller than 109.5 degrees because of the lone-pair repulsions.

See Exercise 20.37.

TABLE 20.11 Some Compounds of the Halogens with Nonmetals

Compounds with Group 3A Nonmetals	Compounds with Group 4A Nonmetals	Compounds with Group 5A Nonmetals	Compounds with Group 6A Nonmetals	Compounds with Group 7A Nonmetals
BX_3 (X = F, Cl, Br, I)	CX_4 (X = F, Cl, Br, I)	NX_3 (X = F, Cl, Br, I)	OF_2	ICl
BF_4^-		N_2F_4	O_2F_2	IBr
	SiF_4		OCl_2	BrF
	SiF_6^{2-}		OBr_2	BrCl
	$SiCl_4$	PX_3 (X = F, Cl, Br, I)		ClF
		PF_5	SF_2	
	GeF_4	PCl_5	SCl_2	ClF_3
	GeF_6^{2-}	PBr_5	S_2F_2	BrF_3
	$GeCl_4$		S_2Cl_2	ICl_3
		AsF_3	SF_4	IF_3
		AsF_5	SCl_4	
		SbF_3	SF_6	ClF_5
		SbF_5		BrF_5
			SeF_4	IF_5
			SeF_6	
			$SeCl_2$	IF_7
			$SeCl_4$	
			$SeBr_4$	
			TeF_4	
			TeF_6	
			$TeCl_4$	
			$TeBr_4$	
			TeI_4	

Other Halogen Compounds

The halogens react readily with most nonmetals to form a variety of compounds, some of which are shown in Table 20.11.

Halogens react with each other to form **interhalogen compounds** with the general formula AB_n, where n is typically 1, 3, 5, or 7 and A is the larger of the two halogens. The structures of these compounds (see Fig. 20.25) are predicted accurately by the VSEPR model. The interhalogens are volatile, highly reactive compounds that act as strong oxidizing agents. They react readily with water, forming the halide ion of the more electronegative halogen and the hypohalous acid of the less electronegative halogen. For example,

$$ICl(s) + H_2O(l) \longrightarrow H^+(aq) + Cl^-(aq) + HOI(aq)$$

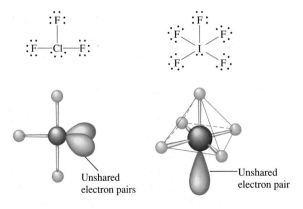

FIGURE 20.25
The idealized structures of the interhalogens ClF_3 and IF_5. In reality, the lone pairs cause the bond angles to be slightly less than 90 degrees.

(a) ClF_3 is "T-shaped" Unshared electron pairs

(b) IF_5 is square pyramidal Unshared electron pair

CHEMICAL IMPACT

Automatic Sunglasses

Sunglasses can be troublesome. It seems they are always getting lost or sat on. One solution to this problem for people who wear glasses is photochromic glass—glass that darkens in response to intense light. Recall that glass is a complex, noncrystalline material that is composed of polymeric silicates (see Chapter 10). Of course, glass transmits visible light—its transparency is its most useful property.

Glass can be made photochromic by adding tiny silver chloride crystals that get trapped in the glass matrix as the glass solidifies. Silver chloride has the unusual property of darkening when struck by light—the property that makes the silver halide salts so useful for photographic films. This darkening occurs because light causes an electron transfer from Cl^- to Ag^+ in the silver chloride crystal, forming a silver atom and a chlorine atom. The silver atoms formed in this way tend to migrate to the surface of the silver chloride crystal, where they aggregate to form a tiny crystal of silver metal, which is opaque to light.

In photography the image defined by the grains of silver is fixed by chemical treatment so that it remains permanent. However, in photochromic glass this process must be reversible—the glass must become fully transparent again when the person goes back indoors. The secret to the reversibility of photochromic glass is the presence of Cu^+ ions. The added Cu^+ ions serve two important functions. First, they reduce the Cl atoms formed in the light-induced reaction. This prevents them from escaping from the crystal:

$$Ag^+ + Cl^- \xrightarrow{h\nu} Ag + Cl$$
$$Cl + Cu^+ \longrightarrow Cu^{2+} + Cl^-$$

Glasses with photosensitive lenses. The right lens has been exposed to light and the left one has not.

Second, when the exposure to intense light ends (the person goes indoors), the Cu^{2+} ions migrate to the surface of the silver chloride crystal, where they accept electrons from silver atoms as the tiny crystal of silver atoms disintegrates:

$$Cu^{2+} + Ag \longrightarrow Cu^+ + Ag^+$$

The Ag^+ ions are re-formed in this way, then return to their places in the silver chloride crystal, making the glass transparent once again.

Typical photochromic glass decreases to about 20% transmittance (transmits 20% of the light that strikes it) in strong sunlight, and then over a period of a few minutes returns to about 80% transmittance indoors (normal glass has 92% transmittance).

20.8 The Group 8A Elements

8A
He
Ne
Ar
Kr
Xe
Rn

The Group 8A elements, the **noble gases,** are characterized by filled *s* and *p* valence orbitals (electron configuration of $2s^2$ for helium and ns^2np^6 for the others). Because of this, these elements are very unreactive. In fact, no noble gas compounds were known 50 years ago. Selected properties of the Group 8A elements are summarized in Table 20.12.

Helium was identified by its characteristic emission spectrum as a component of the sun before it was found on earth. The major sources of helium on earth are natural gas deposits, where helium was formed from α-particle decay of radioactive elements. The α particle is a helium nucleus that can easily pick up electrons from the environment to form a helium atom. Although helium forms no compounds, it is an important substance that is used as a coolant, as a pressurizing gas for rocket fuels, as a diluent in the gases used for deep-sea diving and spaceship atmospheres, and as the gas in lighter-than-air airships (blimps).

Neon, a noble gas, is used in luminescent lighting (neon signs).

TABLE 20.12   Selected Properties of Group 8A Elements

Element	Melting Point (°C)	Boiling Point (°C)	Atmospheric Abundance (% by Volume)	Examples of Compounds
Helium	−270	−269	5×10^{-4}	None
Neon	−249	−246	1×10^{-3}	None
Argon	−189	−186	9×10^{-1}	None
Krypton	−157	−153	1×10^{-4}	KrF_2
Xenon	−112	−107	9×10^{-6}	XeF_4, XeO_3, XeF_6

Like helium, *neon* and *argon* form no compounds but are used extensively. For example, neon is employed in luminescent lighting (neon signs), and argon is used to provide the noncorrosive atmosphere in incandescent light bulbs, which prolongs the life of the tungsten filament.

Of the Group 8A elements, only *krypton* and *xenon* have been observed to form chemical compounds. The first of these was prepared in 1962 by Neil Bartlett, an English chemist who used $Xe(g)$ and $PtF_6(g)$ to make the ionic compound with the empirical formula $XePtF_6$.

Less than a year after Bartlett's report of $XePtF_6$, a group at Argonne National Laboratory near Chicago prepared xenon tetrafluoride by reaction of xenon and fluorine gases in a nickel reaction vessel at 400°C and 6 atm:

$$Xe(g) + 2F_2(g) \longrightarrow XeF_4(s)$$

Xenon tetrafluoride forms stable colorless crystals. Two other xenon fluorides, XeF_2 and XeF_6, were synthesized by the group at Argonne, and a highly explosive xenon oxide (XeO_3) also was found. The xenon fluorides react with water to form hydrogen fluoride and oxycompounds. For example,

$$XeF_6(s) + 3H_2O(l) \longrightarrow XeO_3(aq) + 6HF(aq)$$
$$XeF_6(s) + H_2O(l) \longrightarrow XeOF_4(aq) + 2HF(g)$$

In the past 40 years, other xenon compounds have been prepared—for example, XeO_4 (explosive), XeO_2F_4, XeO_2F_2, and XeO_3F_2. These compounds contain discrete molecules with covalent bonds between the xenon and the other atoms. The structures of some of these xenon compounds are summarized in Fig. 20.26. A few compounds of krypton, such as KrF_2 and KrF_4, also have been observed. There is evidence that radon also reacts with fluorine, but the radioactivity of radon makes its chemistry very difficult to study.

Sample Exercise 20.6

The Structure of XeF₆

Use the VSEPR model to predict whether XeF_6 has an octahedral structure.

Solution

The XeF_6 molecule contains 50 [8 + 6(7)] valence electrons and the Lewis structure is

The xenon atom has seven pairs of electrons around it (one lone pair and six bonding pairs), one more pair than can be accommodated in an octahedral arrangement. Thus XeF_6

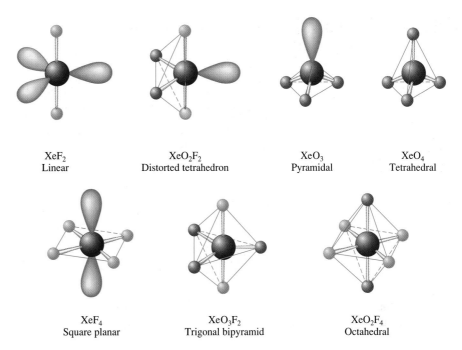

FIGURE 20.26
The structures of several known xenon compounds.

| XeF$_2$
Linear | XeO$_2$F$_2$
Distorted tetrahedron | XeO$_3$
Pyramidal | XeO$_4$
Tetrahedral |

| XeF$_4$
Square planar | XeO$_3$F$_2$
Trigonal bipyramid | XeO$_2$F$_4$
Octahedral |

will not have an octahedral structure, but should be distorted from this geometry by the extra electron pair. There is experimental evidence that the structure of XeF$_6$ is not octahedral.

See Exercises 20.43 and 20.44.

Key Terms

Section 20.2
Haber process
nitrogen fixation
nitrogen-fixing bacteria
denitrification
nitrogen cycle
ammonia
hydrazine
nitric acid
Ostwald process

Section 20.3
phosphoric (orthophosphoric) acid
condensation reactions
phosphorous acid
superphosphate of lime

Section 20.5
ozone
ozonolysis

Section 20.6
Frasch process
sulfuric acid
thiosulfate ion

For Review

Group 5A
- Elements show a wide variety of chemical properties
  - Nitrogen and phosphorus are nonmetals
  - Antimony and bismuth tend to be metallic, although no ionic compounds containing Sb^{5+} and Bi^{5+} are known; the compounds containing Sb(V) and Bi(V) are molecular rather than ionic
  - All group members except N form molecules with five covalent bonds
  - The ability to form π bonds decreases dramatically after N
- Chemistry of nitrogen
  - Most nitrogen-containing compounds decompose exothermically, forming the very stable N$_2$ molecule, which explains the power of nitrogen-based explosives
  - The nitrogen cycle, which consists of a series of steps, shows how nitrogen is cycled in the natural environment
  - Nitrogen fixation changes the N$_2$ in air into compounds useful to plants
    - The Haber process is a synthetic method of nitrogen fixation
    - In the natural world, nitrogen fixation occurs through nitrogen-fixing bacteria in the root nodules of certain plants and through lightning in the atmosphere
  - Ammonia is the most important hydride of nitrogen
    - Contains pyramidal NH$_3$ molecules
    - Widely used as a fertilizer
  - Hydrazine (N$_2$H$_4$) is a powerful reducing agent

- Nitrogen forms a series of oxides including N_2O, NO, NO_2, and N_2O_5
- Nitric acid (HNO_3) is a very important strong acid manufactured by the Ostwald process
- Chemistry of phosphorus
  - Exists in three elemental forms: white (contains P_4 molecules), red, and black
  - Phosphine (PH_3) has bond angles close to 90 degrees
  - Phosphorus forms oxides including P_4O_6 and P_4O_{10} (which dissolves in water to form phosphoric acid, H_3PO_4)

Group 6A
- Metallic character increases going down the group but no element behaves as a typical metal
- The lighter members tend to gain two electrons to form X^{2-} ions in compounds with metals
- Chemistry of oxygen
  - Elemental forms are O_2 and O_3
  - Oxygen forms a wide variety of oxides
  - O_2 and especially O_3 are powerful oxidizing agents
- Chemistry of sulfur
  - The elemental forms are called rhombic and monoclinic sulfur, both of which contain S_8 molecules
  - The most important oxides are SO_2 (which forms H_2SO_3 in water) and SO_3 (which forms H_2SO_4 in water)
  - Sulfur forms a wide variety of compounds in which it shows the oxidation states +6, +4, +2, 0, and −2

Group 7A (halogens)
- All nonmetals
- Form hydrides of the type HX that behave as strong acids in water except for HF, which is a weak acid
- The oxyacids of the halogens become stronger as more oxygen atoms are present
- The interhalogens contain two or more different halogens

Group 8A (noble gases)
- All elements are monatomic gases and are generally very unreactive
- The heavier elements form compounds with electronegative elements such as fluorine and oxygen

REVIEW QUESTIONS

1. What is the valence electron configuration for Group 5A elements? Metallic character increases when going down a group. Give some examples illustrating how Bi and Sb have metallic characteristics not associated with N, P, and As. The Group 5A elements can form molecules or ions that involve three, five, or six covalent bonds; NH_3, $AsCl_5$, and PF_6^- are examples. Draw the Lewis structure for each of these substances and predict the molecular structure and hybridization for each. Why doesn't NF_5 or NCl_6^- form?

2. Table 20.2 lists some common nitrogen compounds having oxidation states ranging from −3 to +5. Rationalize this spread in oxidation states. For each substance listed in Table 20.2, list some of its special properties.

3. Ammonia forms hydrogen-bonding intermolecular forces resulting in an unusually high boiling point for a substance with the small size of NH_3. Can hydrazine, N_2H_4, also form hydrogen-bonding interactions?

   The synthesis of ammonia gas from nitrogen gas and hydrogen gas is a classic case in which a knowledge of kinetics and equilibrium was exploited to make a desired chemical reaction economically feasible. Explain how each of the following conditions helps to maximize the yield of ammonia:

a. running the reaction at an elevated temperature
b. removing the ammonia from the reaction mixture as it forms
c. using a catalyst
d. running the reaction at high pressure

In many natural waters, nitrogen and phosphorus are the least abundant nutrients available for plant life. Some waters that become polluted from agricultural runoff or municipal sewage become infested with algae. The algae consume most of the dissolved oxygen in the water, and fish life dies off as a result. Describe how these events are chemically related.

4. White phosphorus is much more reactive than black or red phosphorus. Explain. How is phosphine's (PH_3) structure different from that of ammonia? Phosphoric acid (H_3PO_4) is a triprotic acid, phosphorous acid (H_3PO_3) is a diprotic acid, and hypophosphorous acid (H_3PO_2) is a monoprotic acid. Explain this phenomenon.

5. What is the valence electron configuration of Group 6A elements? What are some property differences between oxygen and polonium? What are the Lewis structures for the two allotropic forms of oxygen? How can the paramagnetism of O_2 be explained using the molecular orbital model? What is the molecular structure and the bond angle in ozone? Ozone is desirable in the upper atmosphere and undesirable in the lower atmosphere. A dictionary states that ozone has the scent of a fresh spring day. How can these seemingly conflicting statements be reconciled in terms of the chemical properties of ozone?

6. The most stable form of solid sulfur is the rhombic form; however, a solid form called monoclinic sulfur can also form. What is the difference between rhombic and monoclinic sulfur? Explain why O_2 is much more stable than S_2 or SO. When $SO_2(s)$ or $SO_3(g)$ reacts with water, an acidic solution forms. Explain. What are the molecular structures and bond angles in SO_2 and SO_3? Explain the bonding in SO_2 and SO_3. H_2SO_4 is a powerful dehydrating agent: What does this mean?

7. What is the valence electron configuration of the halogens? Why do the boiling points and melting points of the halogens increase steadily from F_2 to I_2? Give two reasons why F_2 is the most reactive of the halogens. Explain why HF is a weak acid, whereas HCl, HBr, and HI are all strong acids.

Explain why the boiling point of HF is much higher than the boiling points of HCl, HBr, and HI. In nature, the halogens are generally found as halide ions in various minerals and seawater. What is a halide ion, and why are halide salts so stable? The oxidation states of the halogens vary from -1 to $+7$. Identify compounds of chlorine that have -1, $+1$, $+3$, $+5$, and $+7$ oxidation states. How does the oxyacid strength of the halogens vary as the number of oxygens in the formula increases?

8. Table 20.11 lists many compounds or ions that halogens form with other nonmetals. For each compound or ion, give the molecular structure, including bond angles, and give the hybridization of the central atom in each species (ignore IF_7). Why does ICl_3 form but not FCl_3?

9. What special property of the noble gases makes them unreactive? The boiling points and melting points of the noble gases increase steadily from He to Xe. Explain. Although He is the second most abundant element in the universe, it is very rare on earth. Why? The noble gases were among the last elements discovered; their existence was not predicted by Mendeleev when he published his first periodic table. Explain. In chemistry textbooks written before 1962, the noble gases were referred to as the inert gases. Why do we no longer use this term?

10. For the structures of the xenon compounds in Figure 20.26, give the bond angles exhibited and the hybridization of the central atom in each compound.

A blue question or exercise number indicates that the answer to that question or exercise appears at the back of this book and a solution appears in the *Solutions Guide*.

Questions

1. Elemental nitrogen exists as N_2, whereas in the gas phase the elements phosphorus, arsenic, and antimony consist of P_4, As_4, and Sb_4 molecules, respectively. Give a possible reason for this difference between N_2 and the other group 5A elements.

2. What is nitrogen fixation? Give some examples of nitrogen fixation.

3. In large doses, selenium is toxic. However, in moderate intake, selenium is a physiologically important element. How is selenium physiologically important?

4. Ozone is a possible replacement for chlorine in municipal water purification. Unlike chlorine, virtually no ozone remains after treatment. This has good and bad consequences. Explain.

5. Sulfur forms a wide variety of compounds in which it has +6, +4, +2, 0, and −2 oxidation states. Give examples of sulfur compounds having each of these oxidation states.

6. When a halogen is a central atom in a compound, the compound typically is sp^3, dsp^3, or d^2sp^3 hybridized. Using bromine as your central atom, give example compounds for each type of hybridization. What is the molecular structure for each of your examples?

7. Explain the following observations regarding reactions of halogens.
   a. In the hydrogen–chlorine cannon lecture demonstration, a lit magnesium strip is held to a mixture of H_2 and Cl_2, resulting in a reaction that sends the stopper to the cannon flying across the lecture room.
   b. When a brown bromine solution is added dropwise to an organic compound called an alkene, the brown color disappears, resulting in a colorless reaction mixture.
   c. When aluminum is reacted with iodine, the reaction container emits sparks and a deep purple colored smoke.

8. There is evidence that radon reacts with fluorine to form compounds similar to those formed by xenon and fluorine. Predict the formulas of these RaF_x compounds. Why is the chemistry of radon difficult to study?

Exercises

In this section similar exercises are paired.

Group 5A Elements

9. The oxyanion of nitrogen in which it has the highest oxidation state is the nitrate ion (NO_3^-). The corresponding oxyanion of phosphorus is PO_4^{3-}. The NO_4^{3-} ion is known but not very stable. The PO_3^- ion is not known. Account for these differences in terms of the bonding in the four anions.

10. In each of the following pairs of substances, one is stable and known, and the other is unstable. For each pair, choose the stable substance, and explain why the other is unstable.
    a. NF_5 or PF_5 b. AsF_5 or AsI_5 c. NF_3 or NBr_3

11. Several important compounds contain only nitrogen and oxygen. Place the following compounds in order of increasing mass percent of nitrogen.
    a. NO, a gas formed by the reaction of N_2 with O_2 in internal combustion engines
    b. NO_2, a brown gas mainly responsible for the brownish color of photochemical smog
    c. N_2O_4, a colorless liquid used as fuel in space shuttles
    d. N_2O, a colorless gas sometimes used as an anesthetic by dentists (known as laughing gas)

12. Nitric acid is produced commercially by the Ostwald process, represented by the following equations:

$$4NH_3(g) + 5O_2(g) \longrightarrow 4NO(g) + 6H_2O(g)$$
$$2NO(g) + O_2(g) \longrightarrow 2NO_2(g)$$
$$3NO_2(g) + H_2O(l) \longrightarrow 2HNO_3(aq) + NO(g)$$

What mass of NH_3 must be used to produce 1.0×10^6 kg HNO_3 by the Ostwald process? Assume 100% yield in each reaction and assume that the NO produced in the third step is not recycled.

13. Complete and balance each of the following reactions.
    a. the decomposition of solid ammonium nitrate
    b. the decomposition of gaseous dinitrogen pentoxide
    c. the reaction between solid potassium phosphide and water
    d. the reaction between liquid phosphorus tribromide and water
    e. the reaction between aqueous ammonia and aqueous sodium hypochlorite

14. Arsenic reacts with oxygen to form oxides that react with water in a manner analogous to that of the phosphorus oxides. Write balanced chemical equations describing the reaction of arsenic with oxygen and the reaction of the resulting oxide with water.

15. Phosphorus occurs naturally in the form of fluorapatite, $CaF_2 \cdot 3Ca_3(PO_4)_2$, where the dot indicates 1 part CaF_2 to 3 parts $Ca_3(PO_4)_2$. This mineral is reacted with an aqueous solution of sulfuric acid in the preparation of a fertilizer. The products are phosphoric acid, hydrogen fluoride, and gypsum, $CaSO_4 \cdot 2H_2O$. Write and balance the chemical equation describing this process.

16. Lewis structures can be used to understand why some molecules react in certain ways. Write the Lewis structure for the reactants and products in the reactions described below.
    a. Nitrogen dioxide dimerizes to produce dinitrogen tetroxide.
    b. Boron trihydride accepts a pair of electrons from ammonia, forming BH_3NH_3.
    Give a possible explanation for why these two reactions occur.

17. Air bags are activated when a severe impact causes a steel ball to compress a spring and electrically ignite a detonator cap. This causes sodium azide (NaN_3) to decompose explosively according to the following reaction:

$$2NaN_3(s) \longrightarrow 2Na(s) + 3N_2(g)$$

How many moles of $NaN_3(s)$ must be reacted to inflate an air bag to 70.0 L at STP?

18. Urea (H_2NCONH_2) is used extensively as a nitrogen source in fertilizers. It is produced commercially from the reaction of ammonia and carbon dioxide:

$$2NH_3(g) + CO_2(g) \longrightarrow H_2NCONH_2(s) + H_2O(g)$$

Ammonia gas at 223°C and 90. atm flows into a reactor at a rate of 500. L/min. Carbon dioxide at 223°C and 45 atm flows into the reactor at a rate of 600. L/min. What mass of urea is produced per minute by this reaction assuming a 100% yield?

19. Hydrazine (N_2H_4) is used as a fuel in liquid-fueled rockets. When hydrazine reacts with oxygen gas, nitrogen gas and water vapor are produced. Write a balanced equation and use bond energies from Table 8.4 to estimate ΔH for this reaction.

20. The space shuttle orbiter utilizes the oxidation of methylhydrazine by dinitrogen tetroxide for propulsion:

$$4N_2H_3CH_3(l) + 5N_2O_4(l) \longrightarrow 12H_2O(g) + 9N_2(g) + 4CO_2(g)$$

Calculate $\Delta H°$ for this reaction using data in Appendix 4. Compare your answer to the ΔH value determined in Sample Exercise 20.2. Explain any discrepancies.

21. Many oxides of nitrogen have positive values for the standard free energy of formation. Using NO as an example, explain why this is the case.

22. Using data from Appendix 4 calculate $\Delta H°$, $\Delta S°$, and $\Delta G°$ for the reaction

$$N_2(g) + O_2(g) \longrightarrow 2NO(g)$$

Why does NO form in an automobile engine but then does not readily decompose back to N_2 and O_2 in the atmosphere?

23. Compare the Lewis structures with the molecular orbital view of the bonding in NO, NO^+, and NO^-. Account for any discrepancies between the two models.

24. The energy to break a particular bond is not always constant. It takes about 200 kJ/mol less energy to break the N—Cl bond in NOCl as compared with NCl_3:

$$NOCl \longrightarrow NO + Cl \qquad \Delta H° = 158 \text{ kJ/mol}$$
$$NCl_3 \longrightarrow NCl_2 + Cl \qquad \Delta H° = 375 \text{ kJ/mol}$$

Why is there such a great discrepancy in the apparent N—Cl bond energies? *Hint:* Consider what happens to the nitrogen–oxygen bond in the first reaction.

25. Predict the relative acid strengths of the following compounds.
   a. H_3PO_4 and H_3PO_3 **b.** H_3PO_4, $H_2PO_4^-$, and HPO_4^{2-}

26. Trisodium phosphate (TSP) is an effective grease remover. Like many cleaners, TSP acts as a base in water. Write a balanced equation to account for this behavior.

27. Isohypophosphonic acid ($H_4P_2O_6$) and diphosphonic acid ($H_4P_2O_5$) are tri- and diprotic acids, respectively. Draw Lewis structures for these acids that are consistent with these facts.

28. One of the most strongly acidic solutions known is a mixture of antimony pentafluoride (SbF_5) and fluorosulfonic acid (HSO_3F). The dominant equilibria are

$$SbF_5 + HSO_3F \rightleftharpoons F_5SbOSO_2FH$$
$$F_5SbOSO_2FH + HSO_3F \rightleftharpoons H_2SO_3F^+ + F_5SbOSO_2F^-$$

a. Draw Lewis structures for all the species shown in the preceding reactions. Predict the hybridization of the central Sb and S atoms in each structure.

b. This *superacid* solution is capable of protonating (adding H^+ to) virtually every known organic compound. What is the active protonating agent in the superacid solution?

Group 6A Elements

29. Use bond energies to estimate the maximum wavelength of light that will cause the reaction

$$O_3 \xrightarrow{hv} O_2 + O$$

30. The xerographic (dry writing) process was invented in 1938 by C. Carlson. In xerography, an image is produced on a photoconductor by exposing it to light. Selenium is commonly used, since its conductivity increases three orders of magnitude upon exposure to light in the range from 400 to 500 nm. What color light should be used to cause selenium to become conductive? (See Figure 7.2.)

31. Complete and balance each of the following reactions.
   a. the reaction between sulfur dioxide gas and oxygen gas
   b. the reaction between sulfur trioxide gas and water
   c. the reaction between aqueous sodium thiosulfate and aqueous iodine
   d. the reaction between copper metal and aqueous hot sulfuric acid

32. Write a balanced equation describing the reduction of H_2SeO_4 by SO_2 to produce selenium.

33. For each of the following, write the Lewis structure(s), predict the molecular structure (including bond angles), and give the expected hybridization of the central atom.
   a. SO_3^{2-} **c.** SCl_2 **e.** TeF_6
   b. O_3 **d.** $SeBr_4$

34. Disulfur dinitride (S_2N_2) exists as a ring of alternating sulfur and nitrogen atoms. S_2N_2 will polymerize to polythiazyl, which acts as a metallic conductor of electricity along the polymer chain. Write a Lewis structure for S_2N_2.

35. Hydrogen peroxide is used as a cleaning agent in the treatment of cuts and abrasions for several reasons. It is an oxidizing agent that can directly kill many microorganisms; it decomposes upon contact with blood, releasing elemental oxygen gas (which inhibits the growth of anaerobic microorganisms); and it foams upon contact with blood, which provides a cleansing action. In the laboratory, small quantities of hydrogen peroxide can be prepared by the action of an acid on an alkaline earth metal peroxide, such as barium peroxide:

$$BaO_2(s) + 2HCl(aq) \longrightarrow H_2O_2(aq) + BaCl_2(aq)$$

What mass of hydrogen peroxide should result when 1.50 g of barium peroxide is treated with 25.0 mL of hydrochloric acid solution containing 0.0272 g of HCl per mL? What mass of which reagent is left unreacted?

36. During the developing process of black-and-white film, silver bromide is removed from photographic film by the fixer. The major component of the fixer is sodium thiosulfate. The net ionic equation for the reaction is

$$AgBr(s) + 2S_2O_3^{2-}(aq) \longrightarrow Ag(S_2O_3)_2^{3-}(aq) + Br^-(aq)$$

What mass of AgBr can be dissolved by 1.00 L of 0.200 M $Na_2S_2O_3$? (Assume the reaction goes to completion.)

Group 7A Elements

37. Write the Lewis structure for O_2F_2. Predict the bond angles and hybridization of the two central oxygen atoms. Assign oxidation states and formal charges to the atoms in O_2F_2. The compound O_2F_2 is a vigorous and potent oxidizing and fluorinating agent. Are oxidation states or formal charges more useful in accounting for these properties of O_2F_2?

38. For each of the following, write the Lewis structure(s), predict the molecular structure (including bond angles), and give the expected hybridization of the central atom.
    a. Freon-12 (CCl_2F_2)   c. iodine trichloride
    b. perchloric acid   d. bromine pentafluoride

39. Complete and balance each of the following reactions.
    a. $BaCl_2(s) + H_2SO_4(aq) \longrightarrow$
    b. $BrF(s) + H_2O(l) \longrightarrow$
    c. $SiO_2(s) + HF(aq) \longrightarrow$

40. Hypofluorous acid is the most recently prepared of the halogen oxyacids. Weighable amounts were first obtained in 1971 by M. H. Studies and E. N. Appelman using the fluorination of ice. Hypofluorous acid is exceedingly unstable, decomposing spontaneously (with a half-life of 30 min) to HF and O_2 in a Teflon container at room temperature. It reacts rapidly with water to produce HF, H_2O_2, and O_2. In dilute acid, H_2O_2 is the major product; in dilute base, O_2 is the major product.
    a. Write balanced equations for the reactions described above.
    b. Assign oxidation states to the elements in hypofluorous acid. Does this suggest why hypofluorous acid is so unstable?

41. Hydrazine is somewhat toxic. Use the following half-reactions to explain why household bleach (highly alkaline solution of sodium hypochlorite) should not be mixed with household ammonia or glass cleansers that contain ammonia.

$$ClO^- + H_2O + 2e^- \longrightarrow 2OH^- + Cl^- \qquad \mathscr{E}° = 0.90 \text{ V}$$
$$N_2H_4 + 2H_2O + 2e^- \longrightarrow 2NH_3 + 2OH^- \qquad \mathscr{E}° = -0.10 \text{ V}$$

42. What is a disproportionation reaction? Use the following reduction potentials

$$ClO_3^- + 3H^+ + 2e^- \longrightarrow HClO_2 + H_2O \qquad \mathscr{E}° = 1.21 \text{ V}$$
$$HClO_2 + 2H^+ + 2e^- \longrightarrow HClO + H_2O \qquad \mathscr{E}° = 1.65 \text{ V}$$

to predict whether $HClO_2$ will disproportionate.

Group 8A Elements

43. The xenon halides and oxides are isoelectronic with many other compounds and ions containing halogens. Give a molecule or ion in which iodine is the central atom that is isoelectronic with each of the following.
    a. xenon tetroxide   d. xenon tetrafluoride
    b. xenon trioxide   e. xenon hexafluoride
    c. xenon difluoride

44. For each of the following, write the Lewis structure(s), predict the molecular structure (including bond angles), and give the expected hybridization of the central atom.
    a. KrF_2 b. KrF_4 c. XeO_2F_2 d. XeO_2F_4

45. Xenon difluoride has proven to be a versatile fluorinating agent. For example, in the reaction

$$C_6H_6(l) + XeF_2(g) \longrightarrow C_6H_5F(l) + Xe(g) + HF(g)$$

the by-products Xe and HF are easily removed, leaving pure C_6H_5F. Xenon difluoride is stored in an inert atmosphere free from oxygen and water. Why is this necessary?

46. Using the data in Table 20.12, calculate the mass of argon at 25°C and 1.0 atm in a room 10.0 m × 10.0 m × 10.0 m. How many Ar atoms are in this room? How many Ar atoms do you inhale in one breath (approximately 2 L) of air at 25°C and 1.0 atm? Argon gas is inert, so it poses no serious health risks. However, if significant amounts of radon were inhaled into the lungs, lung cancer is a possible result. Explain the health-risk differences between argon gas and radon gas.

47. Which do you think would be the greater health hazard, the release of a radioactive nuclide of Sr or a radioactive nuclide of Xe into the environment? Assume the amount of radioactivity is the same in each case. Explain your answer on the basis of the chemical properties of Sr and Xe. Why are the chemical properties of a radioactive substance important in assessing its potential health hazards?

48. The most significant source of natural radiation is radon-222. ^{222}Rn, a decay product of ^{238}U, is continuously generated in the earth's crust, allowing gaseous Rn to seep into the basements of buildings. Because ^{222}Rn is an α-particle producer with a relatively short half-life of 3.82 days, it can cause biological damage when inhaled.
    a. How many α particles and β particles are produced when ^{238}U decays to ^{222}Rn? What nucleus is produced when ^{222}Rn decays?
    b. Radon is a noble gas so one would expect it to pass through the body quickly. Why is there a concern over inhaling ^{222}Rn?

Additional Exercises

49. The compound NF_3 is quite stable, but NCl_3 is very unstable (NCl_3 was first synthesized in 1811 by P. L. Dulong, who lost three fingers and an eye studying its properties). The compounds NBr_3 and NI_3 are rare, although the explosive compound $NI_3 \cdot NH_3$ is known. Account for the instability of these halides of nitrogen.

50. The N_2O molecule is linear and polar.
    a. On the basis of this experimental evidence, which arrangement, NNO or NON, is correct? Explain your answer.
    b. On the basis of your answer in part a, write the Lewis structure of N_2O (including resonance forms). Give the formal charge on each atom and the hybridization of the central atom.
    c. How would the multiple bonding in $:N\equiv N-\ddot{O}:$ be described in terms of orbitals?

51. Oxidation of the cyanide ion produces the stable cyanate ion, OCN^-. The fulminate ion, CNO^-, on the other hand, is very unstable. Fulminate salts explode when struck; $Hg(CNO)_2$ is used in blasting caps. Write the Lewis structures and assign formal charges for the cyanate and fulminate ions. Why is the fulminate ion so unstable?

52. Sodium bismuthate ($NaBiO_3$) is used to test for the presence of Mn^{2+} in solution by the following reaction:

$$Mn^{2+}(aq) + NaBiO_3(s) \longrightarrow MnO_4^-(aq) + BiO_3^{3-}(aq)$$

a. Balance this equation.

b. Given that bismuth does not form double bonds with oxygen in BiO_3^- and that $NaBiO_3$ is relatively insoluble in water, what type of structure must $NaBiO_3$ have to account for this behavior?

53. Bacterial digestion is an economical method of sewage treatment. The reaction

$$5CO_2(g) + 55NH_4^+(aq) + 76O_2(g) \xrightarrow{\text{Bacteria}}$$
$$\underset{\text{Bacterial tissue}}{C_5H_7O_2N(s)} + 54NO_2^-(aq) + 52H_2O(l) + 109H^+(aq)$$

is an intermediate step in the conversion of the nitrogen in organic compounds into nitrate ions. How much bacterial tissue is produced in a treatment plant for every 1.0×10^4 kg of wastewater containing 3.0% NH_4^+ ions by mass? Assume that 95% of the ammonium ions are consumed by the bacteria.

54. An unknown element is a nonmetal and has a valence electron configuration of ns^2np^4.

a. How many valence electrons does this element have?

b. What are some possible identities for this element?

c. What is the formula of the compound this element would form with lithium?

d. Would this element have a larger or smaller radius than barium?

e. Would this element have a greater or smaller ionization energy than fluorine?

55. The structure of TeF_5^- is

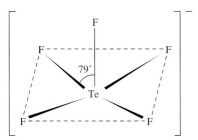

Draw a complete Lewis structure for TeF_5^-, and explain the distortion from the ideal square pyramidal structure.

56. Photogray lenses contain small embedded crystals of solid silver chloride. Silver chloride is light-sensitive because of the reaction

$$AgCl(s) \xrightarrow{h\nu} Ag(s) + Cl$$

Small particles of metallic silver cause the lenses to darken. In the lenses this process is reversible. When the light is removed, the reverse reaction occurs. However, when pure white silver chloride is exposed to sunlight it darkens; the reverse reaction does not occur in the dark.

a. How do you explain this difference?

b. Photogray lenses do become permanently dark in time. How do you account for this?

57. Ammonia is produced by the Haber process, in which nitrogen and hydrogen are reacted directly using an iron mesh impregnated with oxides as a catalyst. For the reaction

$$N_2(g) + 3H_2(g) \rightleftharpoons 2NH_3(g)$$

equilibrium constants (K_p values) as a function of temperature are

300°C, 4.34×10^{-3}
500°C, 1.45×10^{-5}
600°C, 2.25×10^{-6}

Is the reaction exothermic or endothermic?

58. Phosphate buffers are important in regulating the pH of intracellular fluids at pH values generally between 7.1 and 7.2. What is the concentration ratio of $H_2PO_4^-$ to HPO_4^{2-} in intracellular fluid at pH = 7.15?

$$H_2PO_4^-(aq) \rightleftharpoons HPO_4^{2-}(aq) + H^+(aq) \qquad K_a = 6.2 \times 10^{-8}$$

Why is a buffer composed of H_3PO_4 and $H_2PO_4^-$ ineffective in buffering the pH of intracellular fluid?

$$H_3PO_4(aq) \rightleftharpoons H_2PO_4^-(aq) + H^+(aq) \qquad K_a = 7.5 \times 10^{-3}$$

59. Commercial cold packs and hot packs are available for treating athletic injuries. Both types contain a pouch of water and a dry chemical. When the pack is struck, the pouch of water breaks, dissolving the chemical, and the solution becomes either hot or cold. Many hot packs use magnesium sulfate, and many cold packs use ammonium nitrate. Write reactions to show how these strong electrolytes break apart when they dissolve in water.

60. Classify each of the following as a strong acid or a weak acid.

a.   b.   c.   d.

○ H
● O
● Cl
○ S

61. Consider the following Lewis structure where E is an unknown element:

$$\left[:\overset{..}{\underset{..}{O}}-E-\overset{..}{\underset{..}{O}}: \right]^-$$
$$\overset{|}{\underset{..}{\overset{..}{O}:}}$$

What are some possible identities for element E? Predict the molecular structure (including bond angles) for this ion.

62. Consider the following Lewis structure where E is an unknown element:

$$\left[:\overset{..}{\underset{..}{F}}-\overset{\overset{..}{\overset{..}{O}:}}{\underset{\underset{..}{F}:}{E}} \right]^{2-}$$

What are some possible identities for element E? Predict the molecular structure (including bond angles) for this ion.

63. The unit cell for a pure xenon fluoride compound is shown below. What is the formula of the compound?

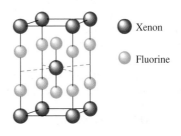

● Xenon
○ Fluorine

Challenge Problems

64. Many structures of phosphorus-containing compounds are drawn with some P=O bonds. These bonds are not the typical π bonds we've considered, which involve the overlap of two p orbitals. Instead, they result from the overlap of a d orbital on the phosphorus atom with a p orbital on oxygen. This type of π bonding is sometimes used as an explanation for why H_3PO_3 has the first structure below rather than the second:

$$
\begin{array}{cc}
\text{O} & \text{OH} \\
\| & | \\
\text{H—P—OH} & \text{HO—P:} \\
| & | \\
\text{OH} & \text{OH}
\end{array}
$$

Draw a picture showing how a d orbital and a p orbital overlap to form a π bond.

65. Use bond energies (Table 8.4) to show that the preferred products for the decomposition of N_2O_3 are NO_2 and NO rather than O_2 and N_2O. (The N—O single bond energy is 201 kJ/mol.) *Hint:* Consider the reaction kinetics.

66. Sodium tripolyphosphate ($Na_5P_3O_{10}$) is used in many synthetic detergents to soften the water by complexing Mg^{2+} and Ca^{2+} ions. It also increases the efficiency of surfactants (wetting agents) that lower a liquid's surface tension. The K value for the formation of $MgP_3O_{10}^{3-}$ is 4.0×10^8. The reaction is

$$Mg^{2+} + P_3O_{10}^{5-} \rightleftharpoons MgP_3O_{10}^{3-}$$

Calculate the concentration of Mg^{2+} in a solution that was originally 50. ppm of Mg^{2+} (50. mg/L of solution) after 40. g $Na_5P_3O_{10}$ is added to 1.0 L of the solution.

67. One pathway for the destruction of ozone in the upper atmosphere is

$$O_3(g) + NO(g) \longrightarrow NO_2(g) + O_2(g) \qquad \text{Slow}$$
$$NO_2(g) + O(g) \longrightarrow NO(g) + O_2(g) \qquad \text{Fast}$$

Overall reaction: $O_3(g) + O(g) \longrightarrow 2O_2(g)$

a. Which species is a catalyst?
b. Which species is an intermediate?
c. The activation energy E_a for the uncatalyzed reaction

$$O_3(g) + O(g) \longrightarrow 2O_2(g)$$

is 14.0 kJ. E_a for the same reaction when catalyzed by the presence of NO is 11.9 kJ. What is the ratio of the rate constant for the catalyzed reaction to that for the uncatalyzed reaction at 25°C? Assume that the frequency factor A is the same for each reaction.
d. One of the concerns about the use of Freons is that they will migrate to the upper atmosphere, where chlorine atoms can be generated by the reaction

$$CCl_2F_2 \xrightarrow{\;hv\;} CF_2Cl + Cl$$
$$\text{Freon-12}$$

Chlorine atoms also can act as a catalyst for the destruction of ozone. The first step of a proposed mechanism for chlorine-catalyzed ozone destruction is

$$Cl(g) + O_3(g) \longrightarrow ClO(g) + O_2(g) \qquad \text{Slow}$$

Assuming a two-step mechanism, propose the second step in the mechanism and give the overall balanced equation.
e. The activation energy for Cl-catalyzed destruction of ozone is 2.1 kJ/mol. Estimate the efficiency with which Cl atoms destroy ozone as compared with NO molecules at 25°C. Assume that the frequency factor A is the same for each catalyzed reaction and assume similar rate laws for each catalyzed reaction.

68. Using data from Appendix 4, calculate $\Delta H°$, $\Delta G°$, and K_p (at 298 K) for the production of ozone from oxygen:

$$3O_2(g) \rightleftharpoons 2O_3(g)$$

At 30 km above the surface of the earth, the temperature is about 230. K, and the partial pressure of oxygen is about 1.0×10^{-3} atm. Estimate the partial pressure of ozone in equilibrium with oxygen at 30 km above the earth's surface. Is it reasonable to assume that the equilibrium between oxygen and ozone is maintained under these conditions? Explain.

69. You travel to a distant, cold planet where the ammonia flows like water. In fact, the inhabitants of this planet use ammonia (an abundant liquid on their planet) much as earthlings use water. Ammonia is also similar to water in that it is amphoteric and undergoes autoionization. The K value for the autoionization of ammonia is 1.8×10^{-12} at the standard temperature of the planet. What is the pH of ammonia at this temperature?

70. Nitrogen gas reacts with hydrogen gas to form ammonia gas. You have an equimolar mixture of nitrogen and hydrogen gases in a 15.0-L container fitted with a piston in a room with a pressure of 1.00 atm. The piston apparatus allows the container volume to change in order to keep the pressure constant at 1.00 atm. Assume ideal behavior, constant temperature, and complete reaction.
a. What is the partial pressure of ammonia in the container when the reaction is complete?
b. What is the mole fraction of ammonia in the container when the reaction is complete?
c. What is the volume of the container when the reaction is complete?

71. A cylinder fitted with a movable piston initially contains 2.00 mol $O_2(g)$ and an unknown amount of $SO_2(g)$. The oxygen is known to be in excess. The density of the mixture is 0.8000 g/L at some T and P. After the reaction has gone to completion, forming $SO_3(g)$, the density of the resulting gaseous mixture is 0.8471 g/L at the same T and P. Calculate the mass of SO_3 formed in the reaction.

72. One way to determine K_{sp} for the salt $Ca(IO_3)_2$ is to titrate it with sodium thiosulfate ($Na_2S_2O_3$). First, make a saturated solution of calcium iodate. Then, add KI and a strong acid (hydrochloric acid and sulfuric acid are generally used). The iodate ion will react according to the equation

$$IO_3^- + 5I^- + 6H^+ \longrightarrow 3I_2 + 3H_2O$$

Note that molecular iodine is a product of this reaction. Adding a starch indicator will turn the solution of I_2 a dark blue-black color. A solution of sodium thiosulfate is added through a buret, which reacts with iodine as follows:

$$I_2 + 2S_2O_3^{2-} \longrightarrow 2I^- + S_4O_6^{2-}$$

The dark blue-black color disappears, when all of the I_2 has reacted. This is the endpoint of the titration.

Consider starting with a 10.0-mL sample of a saturated calcium iodate solution. Upon titrating, you find that 14.9 mL of 0.100 M $Na_2S_2O_3$ is required to reach the end point of the titration. Calculate K_{sp} for $Ca(IO_3)_2$.

Integrative Problems

These problems require the integration of multiple concepts to find the solutions.

73. Although nitrogen trifluoride (NF_3) is a thermally stable compound, nitrogen triiodide (NI_3) is known to be a highly explosive material. NI_3 can be synthesized according to the equation

$$BN(s) + 3IF(g) \longrightarrow BF_3(g) + NI_3(g)$$

a. What is the enthalpy of formation for $NI_3(s)$ given the enthalpy of reaction (-307 kJ) and the enthalpies of formation for $BN(s)$ (-254 kJ/mol), $IF(g)$ (-96 kJ/mol), and $BF_3(g)$ (-1136 kJ/mol)?

b. It is reported that when the synthesis of NI_3 is conducted using 4 mol IF for every 1 mol BN, one of the by-products isolated is $[IF_2]^+[BF_4]^-$. What are the molecular geometries of the species in this by-product? What are the hybridizations of the central atoms in each species in the by-product?

74. While selenic acid has the formula H_2SeO_4 and thus is directly related to sulfuric acid, telluric acid is best visualized as H_6TeO_6 or $Te(OH)_6$.

a. What is the oxidation state of tellurium in $Te(OH)_6$?

b. Despite its structural differences with sulfuric and selenic acid, telluric acid is a diprotic acid with $pK_{a1} = 7.68$ and $pK_{a2} = 11.29$. Telluric acid can be prepared by hydrolysis of tellurium hexafluoride according to the equation

$$TeF_6(g) + 6H_2O(l) \longrightarrow Te(OH)_6(aq) + 6HF(aq)$$

Tellurium hexafluoride can be prepared by the reaction of elemental tellurium with fluorine gas:

$$Te(s) + 3F_2(g) \longrightarrow TeF_6(g)$$

If a cubic block of tellurium (density = 6.240 g/cm³) measuring 0.545 cm on edge is allowed to react with 2.34 L of fluorine gas at 1.06 atm and 25°C, what is the pH of a solution of $Te(OH)_6$ formed by dissolving the isolated $TeF_6(g)$ in 115 mL of water?

Marathon Problem

This problem is designed to incorporate several concepts and techniques into one situation. Marathon Problems can be used in class by groups of students to help facilitate problem-solving skills.

75. Captain Kirk has set a trap for the Klingons who are threatening an innocent planet. He has sent small groups of fighter rockets to sites that are invisible to Klingon radar and put a decoy in the open. He calls this the "fishhook" strategy. Mr. Spock has sent a coded message to the chemists on the fighters to tell the ships what to do next. The outline of the message is

(1)	(2)		(3)		(4)	(5)		(6)
(7)		(8)	(9)		(10)	(11)	(12)	(10)	(11)

Fill in the blanks of the message using the following clues.

(1) Symbol of the halogen whose hydride has the second highest boiling point in the series of HX compounds that are hydrogen halides.

(2) Symbol of the halogen that is the only hydrogen halide, HX, that is a weak acid in aqueous solution.

(3) Symbol of the element whose existence on the sun was known before its existence on earth was discovered.

(4) Symbol of the element whose presence can interfere with the qualitative analysis for Pb^{2+}, Hg_2^{2+}, and Ag^+. When chloride ions are added to an aqueous solution of this metal ion, a white precipitate forms with formula MOCl.

(5) Symbol of the Group 6A element that, like selenium, is a semiconductor.

(6) Symbol for the element known in rhombic and monoclinic forms.

(7) Symbol for the element that exists as diatomic molecules in a yellow-green gas when not combined with another element; its silver, lead, and mercury(I) salts are white and insoluble in water.

(8) Symbol for the most abundant element in and near the earth's crust.

(9) Symbol for the element that seems to give some protection against cancer when a diet rich in this element is consumed.

(10) Symbol for the only noble gas besides xenon that has been shown to form compounds under some circumstances (write the symbol backward and split the letters as shown).

(11) Symbol for the toxic element that, like phosphorus and antimony, forms tetrameric molecules when uncombined with other elements (split the letters of the symbol as shown).

(12) Symbol for the element that occurs as an inert component of air but is a very prominent part of fertilizers and explosives.

 Get help understanding core concepts and visualizing molecular-level interactions, and practice problem solving, by visiting the Online Study Center at **college.hmco.com/PIC/zumdahl7e.**

21 Transition Metals and Coordination Chemistry

Contents

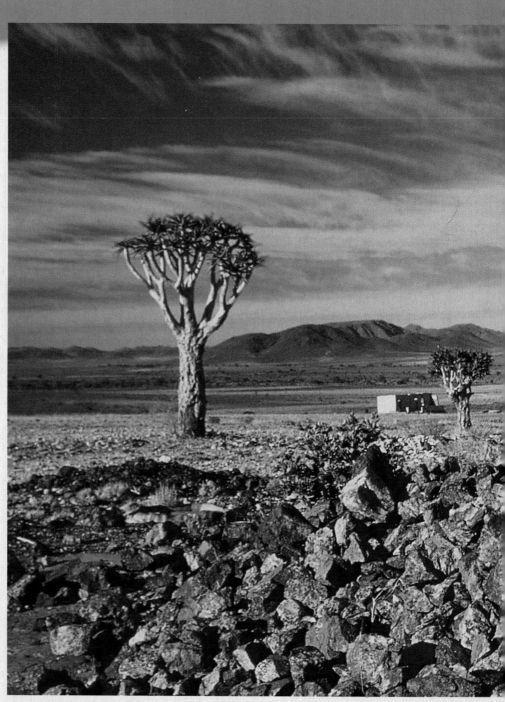

Copper ore deposit in Namibia.

*T*ransition metals have many uses in our society. Iron is used for steel; copper for electrical wiring and water pipes; titanium for paint; silver for photographic paper; manganese, chromium, vanadium, and cobalt as additives to steel; platinum for industrial and automotive catalysts; and so on.

One indication of the importance of transition metals is the great concern shown by the U.S. government for continuing the supply of these elements. In recent years the United States has been a net importer of about 60 "strategic and critical" minerals, including cobalt, manganese, platinum, palladium, and chromium. All these metals play a vital role in the U.S. economy and defense, and approximately 90% of the required amounts must be imported (see Table 21.1).

In addition to being important in industry, transition metal ions play a vital role in living organisms. For example, complexes of iron provide for the transport and storage of oxygen, molybdenum and iron compounds are catalysts in nitrogen fixation, zinc is found in more than 150 biomolecules in humans, copper and iron play a crucial role in the respiratory cycle, and cobalt is found in essential biomolecules such as vitamin B_{12}.

In this chapter we explore the general properties of transition metals, paying particular attention to the bonding, structure, and properties of the complex ions of these metals.

21.1 The Transition Metals: A Survey

General Properties

One striking characteristic of the representative elements is that their chemistry changes markedly across a given period as the number of valence electrons changes. The chemical similarities occur mainly within the vertical groups. In contrast, *the transition metals show great similarities within a given period as well as within a given vertical group.* This difference occurs because the last electrons added for transition metals are inner electrons: *d* electrons for the *d*-block transition metals and *f* electrons for the lanthanides and actinides. These inner *d* and *f* electrons cannot participate as easily in bonding as can the valence *s* and *p* electrons. Thus the chemistry of the transition elements is not affected as greatly by the gradual change in the number of electrons as is the chemistry of the representative elements.

Group designations are traditionally given on the periodic table for the *d*-block transition metals (see Fig. 21.1). However, these designations do not relate as directly to the

TABLE 21.1 Some Transition Metals Important to the U.S. Economy and Defense

Metal	Uses	Percentage Imported
Chromium	Stainless steel (especially for parts exposed to corrosive gases and high temperatures)	~91%
Cobalt	High-temperature alloys in jet engines, magnets, catalysts, drill bits	~93%
Manganese	Steelmaking	~97%
Platinum and palladium	Catalysts	~87%

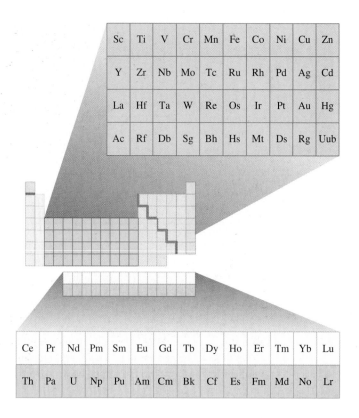

chemical behavior of these elements as they do for the representative elements (the A groups), so we will not use them.

As a class, the transition metals behave as typical metals, possessing metallic luster and relatively high electrical and thermal conductivities. Silver is the best conductor of heat and electric current. However, copper is a close second, which explains copper's wide use in the electrical systems of homes and factories.

FIGURE 21.1

The position of the transition elements on the periodic table. The *d*-block elements correspond to filling the 3*d*, 4*d*, 5*d*, or 6*d* orbitals. The inner transition metals correspond to filling the 4*f* (lanthanides) or 5*f* (actinides) orbitals.

Sterling silver candlesticks and bowl from Japan.

Despite their many similarities, the transition metals do vary considerably in certain properties. For example, tungsten has a melting point of 3400°C and is used for filaments in light bulbs; mercury is a liquid at 25°C. Some transition metals such as iron and titanium are hard and strong and make very useful structural materials; others such as copper, gold, and silver are relatively soft. The chemical reactivity of the transition metals also varies significantly. Some react readily with oxygen to form oxides. Of these metals, some, such as chromium, nickel, and cobalt, form oxides that adhere tightly to the metallic surface, protecting the metal from further oxidation. Others, such as iron, form oxides that scale off, constantly exposing new metal to the corrosion process. On the other hand, the noble metals—primarily gold, silver, platinum, and palladium—do not readily form oxides.

In forming ionic compounds with nonmetals, the transition metals exhibit several typical characteristics:

More than one oxidation state is often found. For example, iron combines with chlorine to form $FeCl_2$ and $FeCl_3$.

The cations are often **complex ions,** species where *the transition metal ion is surrounded by a certain number of ligands* (molecules or ions that behave as Lewis bases). For example, the compound $[Co(NH_3)_6]Cl_3$ contains the $Co(NH_3)_6^{3+}$ cation and Cl^- anions.

The $Co(NH_3)_6^{3+}$ ion

(clockwise from upper left) Calcite stalactites colored by traces of iron. Quartz is often colored by the presence of transition metals such as Mn, Fe, and Ni. Wulfenite contains $PbMoO_4$. Rhodochrosite is a mineral containing $MnCO_3$.

Most compounds are colored, because the transition metal ion in the complex ion can absorb visible light of specific wavelengths.

Many compounds are paramagnetic (they contain unpaired electrons).

In this chapter we will concentrate on the **first-row transition metals** (scandium through zinc) because they are representative of the other transition series and because they have great practical significance. Some important properties of these elements are summarized in Table 21.2 and are discussed in the next section.

Electron Configurations

The electron configurations of the first-row transition metals were discussed in Section 7.11. The $3d$ orbitals begin to fill after the $4s$ orbital is complete, that is, after calcium ($[Ar]4s^2$). The first transition metal, *scandium,* has one electron in the $3d$ orbitals; the second, *titanium,* has two; and the third, *vanadium,* has three. We would expect *chromium,* the fourth transition metal, to have the electron configuration $[Ar]4s^23d^4$. However, the actual configuration is $[Ar]4s^13d^5$, which shows a half-filled $4s$ orbital and a half-filled set of $3d$ orbitals (one electron in each of the five $3d$ orbitals). It is tempting to say that the configuration results because half-filled "shells" are especially stable. Although there are some reasons to think that this explanation might be valid, it is an oversimplification. For instance, tungsten, which is in the same vertical group as chromium, has the configuration $[Xe]6s^24f^{14}5d^4$, where half-filled s and d shells are not found. There are several similar cases.

Basically, the chromium configuration occurs because the energies of the $3d$ and $4s$ orbitals are very similar for the first-row transition elements. We saw in Section 7.11 that when electrons are placed in a set of degenerate orbitals, they first occupy each orbital

(from left to right) Aqueous solutions containing the metal ions Co^{2+}, Mn^{2+}, Cr^{3+}, Fe^{3+}, and Ni^{2+}.

TABLE 21.2 Selected Properties of the First-Row Transition Metals

	Scandium	Titanium	Vanadium	Chromium	Manganese	Iron	Cobalt	Nickel	Copper	Zinc
Atomic number	21	22	23	24	25	26	27	28	29	30
Electron configuration*	$4s^2 3d^1$	$4s^2 3d^2$	$4s^2 3d^3$	$4s^1 3d^5$	$4s^2 3d^5$	$4s^2 3d^6$	$4s^2 3d^7$	$4s^2 3d^8$	$4s^1 3d^{10}$	$4s^2 3d^{10}$
Atomic radius (pm)	162	147	134	130	135	126	125	124	128	138
Ionization energies (eV/atom)										
First	6.54	6.82	6.74	6.77	7.44	7.87	7.86	7.64	7.73	9.39
Second	12.80	13.58	14.65	16.50	15.64	16.18	17.06	18.17	20.29	17.96
Third	24.76	27.49	29.31	30.96	33.67	30.65	33.50	35.17	36.83	39.72
Reduction potential† (V)	−2.08	−1.63	−1.2	−0.91	−1.18	−0.44	−0.28	−0.23	+0.34	−0.76
Common oxidation states	+3	+2,+3, +4	+2,+3, +4,+5	+2,+3, +6	+2,+3, +4,+7	+2,+3	+2,+3	+2	+1,+2	+2
Melting point (°C)	1397	1672	1710	1900	1244	1530	1495	1455	1083	419
Density (g/cm³)	2.99	4.49	5.96	7.20	7.43	7.86	8.9	8.90	8.92	7.14
Electrical conductivity‡	—	2	3	10	2	17	24	24	97	27

*Each atom has an argon inner-core configuration.
†For the reduction process $M^{2+} + 2e^- \rightarrow M$ (except for scandium, where the ion is Sc^{3+}).
‡Compared with an arbitrarily assigned value of 100 for silver.

Chromium has the electron configuration $[Ar]4s^1 3d^5$.

singly to minimize electron repulsions. Since the $4s$ and $3d$ orbitals are virtually degenerate in the chromium atom, we would expect the configuration

$$4s \uparrow \quad 3d \uparrow \uparrow \uparrow \uparrow \uparrow$$

rather than

A set of orbitals with the same energy is said to be *degenerate.*

$$4s \uparrow\downarrow \quad 3d \uparrow \uparrow \uparrow \uparrow \underline{}$$

since the second arrangement has greater electron–electron repulsions and thus a higher energy.

Copper has the electron configuration $[Ar]4s^1 3d^{10}$.

The only other unexpected configuration among the first-row transition metals is that of copper, which is $[Ar]4s^1 3d^{10}$ rather than the expected $[Ar]4s^2 3d^9$.

In transition metal *ions,* the $3d$ orbitals are lower in energy than the $4s$ orbitals.

In contrast to the neutral transition metals, where the $3d$ and $4s$ orbitals have very similar energies, the *energy of the $3d$ orbitals in transition metal ions is significantly less than that of the $4s$ orbital.* This means that the electrons remaining after the ion is formed occupy the $3d$ orbitals, since they are lower in energy. *First-row transition metal ions do not have $4s$ electrons.* For example, manganese has the configuration $[Ar]4s^2 3d^5$, while that of Mn^{2+} is $[Ar]3d^5$. The neutral titanium atom has the configuration $[Ar]4s^2 3d^2$, while that of Ti^{3+} is $[Ar]3d^1$.

Oxidation States and Ionization Energies

The transition metals can form a variety of ions by losing one or more electrons. The common oxidation states of these elements are shown in Table 21.2. Note that for the

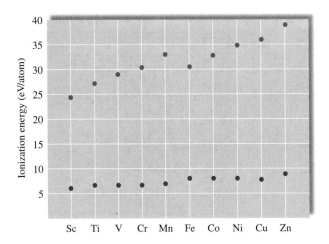

FIGURE 21.2
Plots of the first (red dots) and third (blue dots) ionization energies for the first-row transition metals.

first five metals the maximum possible oxidation state corresponds to the loss of all the $4s$ and $3d$ electrons. For example, the maximum oxidation state of chromium ($[Ar]4s^1 3d^5$) is $+6$. Toward the right end of the period, the maximum oxidation states are not observed; in fact, the $2+$ ions are the most common. The higher oxidation states are not seen for these metals because the $3d$ orbitals become lower in energy as the nuclear charge increases, and the electrons become increasingly difficult to remove. From Table 21.2 we see that ionization energy increases gradually going from left to right across the period. However, the third ionization energy (when an electron is removed from a $3d$ orbital) increases faster than the first ionization energy, clear evidence of the significant decrease in the energy of the $3d$ orbitals going across the period (see Fig. 21.2).

Standard Reduction Potentials

When a metal acts as a *reducing agent,* the half-reaction is

$$M \longrightarrow M^{n+} + ne^-$$

This is the reverse of the conventional listing for half-reactions in tables. Thus, to rank the transition metals in order of reducing ability, it is most convenient to reverse the reactions and the signs given in Table 21.2. The metal with the most positive potential is then the best reducing agent. The transition metals are listed in order of reducing ability in Table 21.3.

Since $\mathscr{E}°$ is zero for the process

$$2H^+ + 2e^- \longrightarrow H_2$$

all the metals except copper can reduce H^+ ions to hydrogen gas in 1 M aqueous solutions of strong acid:

$$M(s) + 2H^+(aq) \longrightarrow H_2(g) + M^{2+}(aq)$$

As Table 21.3 shows, the reducing abilities of the first-row transition metals generally decrease going from left to right across the period. Only chromium and zinc do not follow this trend.

The 4d and 5d Transition Series

In comparing the $3d$, $4d$, and $5d$ transition series, it is instructive to consider the atomic radii of these elements (Fig. 21.3). Note that there is a general, although not regular,

TABLE 21.3 Relative Reducing Abilities of the First-Row Transition Metals in Aqueous Solution

Reaction	Potential (V)
$Sc \rightarrow Sc^{3+} + 3e^-$	2.08
$Ti \rightarrow Ti^{2+} + 2e^-$	1.63
$V \rightarrow V^{2+} + 2e^-$	1.2
$Mn \rightarrow Mn^{2+} + 2e^-$	1.18
$Cr \rightarrow Cr^{2+} + 2e^-$	0.91
$Zn \rightarrow Zn^{2+} + 2e^-$	0.76
$Fe \rightarrow Fe^{2+} + 2e^-$	0.44
$Co \rightarrow Co^{2+} + 2e^-$	0.28
$Ni \rightarrow Ni^{2+} + 2e^-$	0.23
$Cu \rightarrow Cu^{2+} + 2e^-$	−0.34

Reducing ability ↑

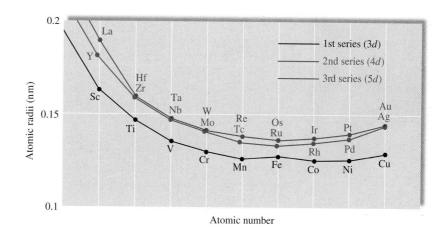

FIGURE 21.3
Atomic radii of the 3d, 4d, and 5d transition series.

decrease in size going from left to right for each of the series. Also note that although there is a significant increase in radius in going from the 3d to the 4d metals, the 4d and 5d metals are remarkably similar in size. This latter phenomenon is the result of the **lanthanide contraction.** In the **lanthanide series,** consisting of the elements between lanthanum and hafnium (see Fig. 21.1), electrons are filling the 4f orbitals. Since the 4f orbitals are buried in the interior of these atoms, the additional electrons do not add to the atomic size. In fact, the increasing nuclear charge (remember that a proton is added to the nucleus for each electron) causes the radii of the lanthanide elements to decrease significantly going from left to right. This lanthanide contraction just offsets the normal increase in size due to going from one principal quantum level to another. Thus the 5d elements, instead of being significantly larger than the 4d elements, are almost identical to them in size. This leads to a great similarity in the chemistry of the 4d and 5d elements in a given vertical group. For example, the chemical properties of hafnium and zirconium are remarkably similar, and they always occur together in nature. Their separation, which is probably more difficult than the separation of any other pair of elements, often requires fractional distillation of their compounds.

In general, the differences between the 4d and 5d elements in a group increase gradually going from left to right. For example, niobium and tantalum are also quite similar, but less so than zirconium and hafnium.

Although generally less well known than the 3d elements, the 4d and 5d transition metals have certain very useful properties. For example, zirconium and zirconium oxide (ZrO_2) have great resistance to high temperatures and are used, along with niobium and molybdenum alloys, for space vehicle parts that are exposed to high temperatures during reentry into the earth's atmosphere. Niobium and molybdenum are also important alloying materials for certain types of steel. Tantalum, which has a high resistance to attack by body fluids, is often used for replacement of bones. The *platinum group metals*—ruthenium, osmium, rhodium, iridium, palladium, and platinum—are all quite similar and are widely used as catalysts for many types of industrial processes.

Niobium was originally called *columbium* and is still occasionally referred to by that name.

21.2 The First-Row Transition Metals

We have seen that the transition metals are similar in many ways but also show important differences. We will now explore some of the specific properties of each of the 3d transition metals.

Scandium is a rare element that exists in compounds mainly in the +3 oxidation state—for example, in $ScCl_3$, Sc_2O_3, and $Sc_2(SO_4)_3$. The chemistry of scandium strongly resembles that of the lanthanides, with most of its compounds being colorless and

An X ray of a patient who has had a hip replacement. The normal hip joint is on the left; the hip joint constructed from tantalum metal is on the right.

$Ti(H_2O)_6^{3+}$ is purple in solution.

The manufacture of sulfuric acid was discussed at the end of Chapter 3.

The most common oxidation state for vanadium is +5.

diamagnetic. This is not surprising; as we will see in Section 21.6, the color and magnetism of transition metal compounds usually arise from the d electrons on the metal ion, and Sc^{3+} has no d electrons. Scandium metal, which can be prepared by electrolysis of molten $ScCl_3$, is not widely used because of its rarity, but it is found in some electronic devices, such as high-intensity lamps.

Titanium is widely distributed in the earth's crust (0.6% by mass). Because of its relatively low density and high strength, titanium is an excellent structural material, especially in jet engines, where light weight and stability at high temperatures are required. Nearly 5000 kg of titanium alloys is used in each engine of a Boeing 747 jetliner. In addition, the resistance of titanium to chemical attack makes it a useful material for pipes, pumps, and reaction vessels in the chemical industry.

The most familiar compound of titanium is no doubt responsible for the white color of this paper. Titanium dioxide, or more correctly, *titanium(IV) oxide* (TiO_2), is a highly opaque substance used as the white pigment in paper, paint, linoleum, plastics, synthetic fibers, whitewall tires, and cosmetics (sunscreens, for example). Approximately 700,000 tons is used annually in these and other products. Titanium(IV) oxide is widely dispersed in nature, but the main ores are rutile (impure TiO_2) and ilmenite ($FeTiO_3$). Rutile is processed by treatment with chlorine to form volatile $TiCl_4$, which is separated from the impurities and burned to form TiO_2:

$$TiCl_4(g) + O_2(g) \longrightarrow TiO_2(s) + 2Cl_2(g)$$

Ilmenite is treated with sulfuric acid to form a soluble sulfate:

$$FeTiO_3(s) + 2H_2SO_4(aq) \longrightarrow Fe^{2+}(aq) + TiO^{2+}(aq) + 2SO_4^{2-}(aq) + 2H_2O(l)$$

When this aqueous mixture is allowed to stand, under vacuum, solid $FeSO_4 \cdot 7H_2O$ forms first and is removed. The mixture is then heated, and the insoluble titanium(IV) oxide hydrate ($TiO_2 \cdot H_2O$) forms. The water of hydration is driven off by heating to form pure TiO_2:

$$TiO_2 \cdot H_2O(s) \xrightarrow{\text{Heat}} TiO_2(s) + H_2O(g)$$

In its compounds, titanium is most often found in the +4 oxidation state. Examples are TiO_2 and $TiCl_4$, the latter a colorless liquid (bp = 137°C) that fumes in moist air to produce TiO_2:

$$TiCl_4(l) + 2H_2O(l) \longrightarrow TiO_2(s) + 4HCl(g)$$

Titanium(III) compounds can be produced by reduction of the +4 state. In aqueous solution, Ti^{3+} exists as the purple $Ti(H_2O)_6^{3+}$ ion, which is slowly oxidized to titanium(IV) by air. Titanium(II) is not stable in aqueous solution but does exist in the solid state in compounds such as TiO and the dihalides of general formula TiX_2.

Vanadium is widely spread throughout the earth's crust (0.02% by mass). It is used mostly in alloys with other metals such as iron (80% of vanadium is used in steel) and titanium. Vanadium(V) oxide (V_2O_5) is used as an industrial catalyst in the production of materials such as sulfuric acid.

Pure vanadium can be obtained from the electrolytic reduction of fused salts, such as VCl_2, to produce a metal similar to titanium that is steel gray, hard, and corrosion resistant. Often the pure element is not required for alloying. For example, *ferrovanadium,* produced by the reduction of a mixture of V_2O_5 and Fe_2O_3 with aluminum, is added to iron to form *vanadium steel,* a hard steel used for engine parts and axles.

The principal oxidation state of vanadium is +5, found in compounds such as the orange V_2O_5 (mp = 650°C) and the colorless VF_5 (mp = 19.5°C). The oxidation states from +5 to +2 all exist in aqueous solution (see Table 21.4). The higher oxidation states,

CHEMICAL IMPACT

Titanium Dioxide—Miracle Coating

Titanium dioxide, more properly called titanium(IV) oxide, is a very important material. Approximately 1.5 million tons of the substance is produced each year in the United States for use as a pigment in paper and paints and as a component of sunscreens.

In recent years, however, scientists have found a new use for TiO_2. When surfaces are coated with titanium dioxide, they become resistant to dirt and bacteria. For example, the Pilkington Glass Company is now making glass coated with TiO_2 that cleans itself. All the glass needs is sun and rain to keep itself clean. The self-cleaning action arises from two effects. First, the coating of TiO_2 acts as a catalyst in the presence of ultraviolet (UV) light to break down carbon-based pollutants to carbon dioxide and water. Second, because TiO_2 reduces surface tension, rainwater "sheets" instead of forming droplets on the glass, thereby washing away the grime on the surface of the glass. Although this self-cleaning glass is bad news for window washers, it could save millions of dollars in maintenance costs for owners of commercial buildings.

Because the TiO_2-treated glass requires UV light for its action, it does not work well for interior surfaces where UV light is present only in small amounts. However, a team of Japanese researchers has found that if the TiO_2 coating is doped with nitrogen atoms, it will catalyze the breakdown of dirt in the presence of visible light as well as UV light. Studies also show that this N-doped TiO_2 surface coating kills many types of bacteria in the presence of visible or ultraviolet light. This discovery could lead to products such as self-sterilizing bathroom tiles, counters, and toilets. In addition, because the TiO_2 on the surface of glass has such a strong attraction for water molecules (greatly lowering the surface tension), water does not bead up to form droplets. Just as this effect produces sheeting action on exterior glass, so it prevents interior windows and mirrors from "fogging up."

Titanium dioxide, a cheap and plentiful material, may prove to be worth its weight in gold as a surface coating.

TABLE 21.4   Oxidation States and Species for Vanadium in Aqueous Solution

Oxidation State of Vanadium	Species in Aqueous Solution
+5	VO_2^+ (yellow)
+4	VO^{2+} (blue)
+3	$V^{3+}(aq)$ (blue-green)
+2	$V^{2+}(aq)$ (violet)

+5 and +4, do not exist as hydrated ions of the type $V^{n+}(aq)$ because the highly charged ion causes the attached water molecules to be very acidic. The H^+ ions are lost to give the oxycations VO_2^+ and VO^{2+}. The hydrated V^{3+} and V^{2+} ions are easily oxidized and thus can function as reducing agents in aqueous solution.

Although *chromium* is relatively rare, it is a very important industrial material. The chief ore of chromium is chromite ($FeCr_2O_4$), which can be reduced by carbon to give *ferrochrome,*

$$FeCr_2O_4(s) + 4C(s) \longrightarrow \underbrace{Fe(s) + 2Cr(s)}_{Ferrochrome} + 4CO(g)$$

which can be added directly to iron in the steelmaking process. Chromium metal, which is often used to plate steel, is hard and brittle and maintains a bright surface by developing a tough invisible oxide coating.

Chromium commonly forms compounds in which it has the oxidation state +2, +3, or +6, as shown in Table 21.5. The Cr^{2+} (chromous) ion is a powerful reducing agent in aqueous solution. In fact, traces of O_2 in other gases can be removed by bubbling through a Cr^{2+} solution:

$$4Cr^{2+}(aq) + O_2(g) + 4H^+(aq) \longrightarrow 4Cr^{3+}(aq) + 2H_2O(l)$$

The chromium(VI) species are excellent oxidizing agents, especially in acidic solution, where chromium(VI) as the dichromate ion ($Cr_2O_7^{2-}$) is reduced to the Cr^{3+} ion:

$$Cr_2O_7^{2-}(aq) + 14H^+(aq) + 6e^- \longrightarrow 2Cr^{3+}(aq) + 7H_2O(l) \qquad \mathscr{E}° = 1.33 \text{ V}$$

TABLE 21.5   Typical Chromium Compounds

Oxidation State of Chromium	Examples of Compounds (X = halogen)
+2	CrX_2
+3	CrX_3
	Cr_2O_3 (green)
	$Cr(OH)_3$ (blue-green)
+6	$K_2Cr_2O_7$ (orange)
	Na_2CrO_4 (yellow)
	CrO_3 (red)

CHEMICAL IMPACT

Titanium Makes Great Bicycles

One of the most interesting characteristics of the world of bicycling is the competition among various frame materials. Bicycle frames are now built from steel, aluminum, carbon fiber composites, and titanium, with each material having advantages and disadvantages. Steel is strong, economical, adaptable, and (unfortunately) "rustable." Aluminum is light and stiff but has relatively low fatigue limits (resistance to repeated stresses). Carbon fiber composites have amazing strength-to-mass ratios and have shock- and vibration-dampening properties superior to any metal; however, they are very expensive. Titanium has a density approximately 43% less than that of steel, a yield strength (when alloyed with metals such as aluminum and tin) that is 30% greater than that of steel, an extraordinary resistance to fatigue, and a high resistance to corrosion, but it is expensive and difficult to work.

Of all these materials, titanium gives the bicycle that fanatics seem to love the most. After their first ride on a bicycle with a titanium frame, most experienced cyclists find themselves shaking their heads and searching hard for the right words to describe the experience. Typically, the word "magic" is used a great deal in the ensuing description.

The magic of titanium results from its combination of toughness, stretchability, and resilience. A bicycle that is built stiff to resist pedaling loads usually responds by giving a harsh, uncomfortable ride. A titanium bike is very stiff against high pedaling torques, but it seems to transmit much less road shock than bikes made of competitive materials. Why titanium excels in dampening vibrations is not entirely clear. Despite titanium's significantly lower density than steel, shock waves travel more slowly in titanium than in steel. Whatever the explanation for its shock-absorbing abilities, titanium provides three things that cyclists find crucial: light weight, stiffness, and a smooth ride—magic.

Titanium is quite abundant in the earth's crust, ranking ninth of all the elements and second among the transition elements. The metallurgy of titanium presents special challenges. Carbon, the reducing agent most commonly used to obtain metals from their oxide ores, cannot be used because it forms intractable interstitial carbides with titanium. These

---

The oxidizing ability of the dichromate ion is strongly pH-dependent, increasing as $[H^+]$ increases, as predicted by Le Châtelier's principle. In basic solution, chromium(VI) exists as the chromate ion, a much less powerful oxidizing agent:

$$CrO_4^{2-}(aq) + 4H_2O(l) + 3e^- \longrightarrow Cr(OH)_3(s) + 5OH^-(aq) \qquad \mathscr{E}° = -0.13 \text{ V}$$

The structures of the $Cr_2O_7^{2-}$ and CrO_4^{2-} ions are shown in Fig. 21.4.

Red chromium(VI) oxide (CrO_3) dissolves in water to give a strongly acidic, red-orange solution:

$$2CrO_3(s) + H_2O(l) \longrightarrow 2H^+(aq) + Cr_2O_7^{2-}(aq)$$

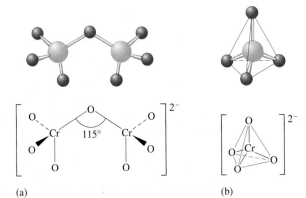

FIGURE 21.4
The structures of the chromium(VI) anions: (a) $Cr_2O_7^{2-}$, which exists in acidic solution, and (b) CrO_4^{2-}, which exists in basic solution.

(a)   (b)

carbides are extraordinarily hard and have melting points close to 3000°C. However, if chlorine gas is used in conjunction with carbon to treat the ore, volatile TiCl$_4$ is formed, which can be distilled off and then reduced with magnesium or sodium at approximately 1000°C to form a titanium "sponge." This sponge is then ground up, cleaned with aqua regia (a 1:3 mixture of concentrated HNO$_3$ and concentrated HCl), melted under a blanket of inert gas (to prevent reaction with oxygen), and cast into ingots. Titanium, a lustrous, silvery metal with a high melting point (1667°C), crystallizes in a hexagonal closest packed structure. Because titanium tends to become quite brittle when trace impurities such as C, N, and O are present, it must be fabricated with great care.

Titanium's unusual ability to stretch makes it hard to machine. It tends to push away even from a very sharp cutting blade, giving a rather unpredictable final dimension. Also, because titanium is embrittled by reaction with oxygen, all welding operations must be carried out under a shielding gas such as argon.

However, the bicycle that results is worth all these difficulties. One woman described a titanium bicycle as "the one God rides on Sunday."

A titanium bicycle.

It is possible to precipitate bright orange dichromate salts, such as K$_2$Cr$_2$O$_7$, from these solutions. When made basic, the solution turns yellow, and chromate salts such as Na$_2$CrO$_4$ can be obtained. A mixture of chromium(VI) oxide and concentrated sulfuric acid, commonly called *cleaning solution,* is a powerful oxidizing medium that can remove organic materials from analytical glassware, yielding a very clean surface.

Manganese is relatively abundant (0.1% of the earth's crust), although no significant sources are found in the United States. The most common use of manganese is in the production of an especially hard steel used for rock crushers, bank vaults, and armor plate. One interesting source of manganese is from *manganese nodules* found on the ocean floor. These roughly spherical "rocks" contain mixtures of manganese and iron oxides as well as smaller amounts of other metals such as cobalt, nickel, and copper. Apparently, the nodules were formed at least partly by the action of marine organisms. Because of the abundance of these nodules, there is much interest in developing economical methods for their recovery and processing.

Manganese can exist in all oxidation states from +2 to +7, although +2 and +7 are the most common. Manganese(II) forms an extensive series of salts with all the common anions. In aqueous solution Mn^{2+} forms Mn(H$_2$O)$_6$$^{2+}$, which has a light pink color. Manganese(VII) is found in the intensely purple permanganate ion (MnO$_4$$^-$). Widely used as an analytical reagent in acidic solution, the MnO$_4$$^-$ ion behaves as a strong oxidizing agent, with the manganese becoming Mn^{2+}:

$$MnO_4^-(aq) + 8H^+(aq) + 5e^- \longrightarrow Mn^{2+}(aq) + 4H_2O(l) \qquad \mathscr{E}° = 1.51 \text{ V}$$

Several typical compounds of manganese are shown in Table 21.6.

TABLE 21.6   Some Compounds of Manganese in Its Most Common Oxidation States

Oxidation State of Manganese	Examples of Compounds
+2	Mn(OH)$_2$ (pink)
	MnS (salmon)
	MnSO$_4$ (reddish)
	MnCl$_2$ (pink)
+4	MnO$_2$ (dark brown)
+7	KMnO$_4$ (purple)

TABLE 21.7 Typical Compounds of Iron

Oxidation State of Iron	Examples of Compounds
+2	FeO (black)
	FeS (brownish black)
	$FeSO_4 \cdot 7H_2O$ (green)
	$K_4Fe(CN)_6$ (yellow)
+3	$FeCl_3$ (brownish black)
	Fe_2O_3 (reddish brown)
	$K_3Fe(CN)_6$ (red)
	$Fe(SCN)_3$ (red)
+2, +3 (mixture)	Fe_3O_4 (black)
	$KFe[Fe(CN)_6]$ (deep blue, "Prussian blue")

Iron is the most abundant heavy metal (4.7% of the earth's crust) and the most important to our civilization. It is a white, lustrous, not particularly hard metal that is very reactive toward oxidizing agents. For example, in moist air it is rapidly oxidized by oxygen to form rust, a mixture of iron oxides.

The chemistry of iron mainly involves its +2 and +3 oxidation states. Typical compounds are shown in Table 21.7. In aqueous solutions iron(II) salts are generally light green because of the presence of $Fe(H_2O)_6^{2+}$. Although the $Fe(H_2O)_6^{3+}$ ion is colorless, aqueous solutions of iron(III) salts are usually yellow to brown in color due to the presence of $Fe(OH)(H_2O)_5^{2+}$, which results from the acidity of $Fe(H_2O)_6^{3+}$ ($K_a = 6 \times 10^{-3}$):

$$Fe(H_2O)_6^{3+}(aq) \rightleftharpoons Fe(OH)(H_2O)_5^{2+}(aq) + H^+(aq)$$

Although *cobalt* is relatively rare, it is found in ores such as smaltite ($CoAs_2$) and cobaltite (CoAsS) in large enough concentrations to make its production economically feasible. Cobalt is a hard, bluish white metal mainly used in alloys such as stainless steel and stellite, an alloy of iron, copper, and tungsten that is used in surgical instruments.

The chemistry of cobalt involves mainly its +2 and +3 oxidation states, although compounds containing cobalt in the 0, +1, or +4 oxidation state are known. Aqueous solutions of cobalt(II) salts contain the $Co(H_2O)_6^{2+}$ ion, which has a characteristic rose color. Cobalt forms a wide variety of coordination compounds, many of which will be discussed in later sections of this chapter. Some typical cobalt compounds are shown in Table 21.8.

Nickel, which ranks twenty-fourth in elemental abundance in the earth's crust, is found in ores, where it is combined mainly with arsenic, antimony, and sulfur. Nickel metal, a silvery white substance with high electrical and thermal conductivities, is quite resistant to corrosion and is often used for plating more active metals. Nickel is also widely used in the production of alloys such as steel.

Nickel in compounds is almost exclusively in the +2 oxidation state. Aqueous solutions of nickel(II) salts contain the $Ni(H_2O)_6^{2+}$ ion, which has a characteristic emerald green color. Coordination compounds of nickel(II) will be discussed later in this chapter. Some typical nickel compounds are shown in Table 21.9.

An aqueous solution containing the Ni^{2+} ion.

TABLE 21.8 Typical Compounds of Cobalt

Oxidation State	Examples of Compounds
+2	$CoSO_4$ (dark blue)
	$[Co(H_2O)_6]Cl_2$ (pink)
	$[Co(H_2O)_6](NO_3)_2$ (red)
	CoS (black)
	CoO (greenish brown)
+3	CoF_3 (brown)
	Co_2O_3 (charcoal)
	$K_3[Co(CN)_6]$ (yellow)
	$[Co(NH_3)_6]Cl_3$ (yellow)

TABLE 21.9 Typical Compounds of Nickel

Oxidation State of Nickel	Examples of Compounds
+2	$NiCl_2$ (yellow)
	$[Ni(H_2O)_6]Cl_2$ (green)
	NiO (greenish black)
	NiS (black)
	$[Ni(H_2O)_6]SO_4$ (green)
	$[Ni(NH_3)_6](NO_3)_2$ (blue)

TABLE 21.10 Alloys Containing Copper	
Alloy	**Composition (% by mass in parentheses)**
Brass	Cu (20–97), Zn (2–80), Sn (0–14), Pb (0–12), Mn (0–25)
Bronze	Cu (50–98), Sn (0–35), Zn (0–29), Pb (0–50), P (0–3)
Sterling silver	Cu (7.5), Ag (92.5)
Gold (18-karat)	Cu (5–15), Au (75), Ag (10–20)
Gold (14-karat)	Cu (12–28), Au (58), Ag (4–30)

Copper roofs and bronze statues, such as the Statue of Liberty, turn green in air because $Cu_3(OH)_4SO_4$ and $Cu_4(OH)_6SO_4$ form.

TABLE 21.11 Typical Compounds of Copper	
Oxidation State of Copper	**Examples of Compounds**
+1	Cu_2O (red)
	Cu_2S (black)
	$CuCl$ (white)
+2	CuO (black)
	$CuSO_4 \cdot 5H_2O$ (blue)
	$CuCl_2 \cdot 2H_2O$ (green)
	$[Cu(H_2O)_6](NO_3)_2$ (blue)

Copper, widely distributed in nature in ores containing sulfides, arsenides, chlorides, and carbonates, is valued for its high electrical conductivity and its resistance to corrosion. It is widely used for plumbing, and 50% of all copper produced annually is used for electrical applications. Copper is a major constituent in several well-known alloys (see Table 21.10).

Although copper is not highly reactive (it will not reduce H^+ to H_2, for example), the reddish metal does slowly corrode in air, producing the characteristic green *patina* consisting of basic copper sulfate

$$3Cu(s) + 2H_2O(l) + SO_2(g) + 2O_2(g) \longrightarrow Cu_3(OH)_4SO_4$$

Basic copper sulfate

and other similar compounds.

The chemistry of copper principally involves the +2 oxidation state, but many compounds containing copper(I) are also known. Aqueous solutions of copper(II) salts are a characteristic bright blue color due to the presence of the $Cu(H_2O)_6^{2+}$ ion. Table 21.11 lists some typical copper compounds.

Although trace amounts of copper are essential for life, copper in large amounts is quite toxic; copper salts are used to kill bacteria, fungi, and algae. For example, paints containing copper are used on ship hulls to prevent fouling by marine organisms.

Widely dispersed in the earth's crust, *zinc* is mainly refined from sphalerite (ZnS), which often occurs with galena (PbS). Zinc is a white, lustrous, very active metal that behaves as an excellent reducing agent and tarnishes rapidly. About 90% of the zinc produced is used for galvanizing steel. Zinc forms colorless salts in the +2 oxidation state.

21.3   Coordination Compounds

Transition metal ions characteristically form coordination compounds, which are usually colored and often paramagnetic. A **coordination compound** typically consists of a *complex ion,* a transition metal ion with its attached ligands (see Section 15.8), and **counterions,** anions or cations as needed to produce a compound with no net charge. The substance $[Co(NH_3)_5Cl]Cl_2$ is a typical coordination compound. The brackets indicate the composition of the complex ion, in this case $Co(NH_3)_5Cl^{2+}$, and the two Cl^- counterions are shown outside the brackets. Note that in this compound one Cl^- acts as a ligand along with the five NH_3 molecules. In the solid state this compound consists of the large $Co(NH_3)_5Cl^{2+}$ cations and twice as many Cl^- anions, all packed together as efficiently as possible. When dissolved in water, the solid behaves like any ionic solid; the cations and anions are assumed to separate and move about independently:

$$[Co(NH_3)_5Cl]Cl_2(s) \xrightarrow{\text{H}_2\text{O}} Co(NH_3)_5Cl^{2+}(aq) + 2Cl^-(aq)$$

TABLE 21.12   Typical Coordination Numbers for Some Common Metal Ions

M$^+$	Coordination Numbers	M^{2+}	Coordination Numbers	M^{3+}	Coordination Numbers
Cu$^+$	2, 4	Mn^{2+}	4, 6	Sc^{3+}	6
Ag$^+$	2	Fe^{2+}	6	Cr^{3+}	6
Au$^+$	2, 4	Co^{2+}	4, 6	Co^{3+}	6
		Ni^{2+}	4, 6		
		Cu^{2+}	4, 6	Au^{3+}	4
		Zn^{2+}	4, 6		

Coordination compounds have been known since about 1700, but their true nature was not understood until the 1890s when a young Swiss chemist named Alfred Werner (1866–1919) proposed that transition metal ions have two types of valence (combining ability). One type of valence, which Werner called the *secondary valence,* refers to the ability of a metal ion to bind to Lewis bases (ligands) to form complex ions. The other type, the *primary valence,* refers to the ability of the metal ion to form ionic bonds with oppositely charged ions. Thus Werner explained that the compound, originally written as $CoCl_3 \cdot 5NH_3$, was really $[Co(NH_3)_5Cl]Cl_2$, where the Co^{3+} ion has a primary valence of 3, satisfied by the three Cl$^-$ ions, and a secondary valence of 6, satisfied by the six ligands (five NH_3 and one Cl$^-$). We now call the primary valence the **oxidation state** and the secondary valence the **coordination number,** which reflects the number of bonds formed between the metal ion and the ligands in the complex ion.

Coordination number	Geometry
2	Linear
4	Tetrahedral Square planar
6	Octahedral

FIGURE 21.5
The ligand arrangements for coordination numbers 2, 4, and 6.

Coordination Number

The number of bonds formed by metal ions to ligands in complex ions varies from two to eight depending on the size, charge, and electron configuration of the transition metal ion. As shown in Table 21.12, 6 is the most common coordination number, followed closely by 4, with a few metal ions showing a coordination number of 2. Many metal ions show more than one coordination number, and there is really no simple way to predict what the coordination number will be in a particular case. The typical geometries for the various common coordination numbers are shown in Fig. 21.5. Note that six ligands produce an octahedral arrangement around the metal ion. Four ligands can form either a tetrahedral or a square planar arrangement, and two ligands give a linear structure.

Ligands

A **ligand** is a *neutral molecule or ion having a lone electron pair that can be used to form a bond to a metal ion.* The formation of a metal–ligand bond therefore can be described as the interaction between a Lewis base (the ligand) and a Lewis acid (the metal ion). The resulting bond is often called a **coordinate covalent bond.**

A *ligand that can form one bond to a metal ion* is called a **monodentate ligand,** or a **unidentate ligand** (from root words meaning "one tooth"). Examples of unidentate ligands are shown in Table 21.13.

Some ligands have more than one atom with a lone electron pair that can be used to bond to a metal ion. Such ligands are said to be **chelating ligands,** or **chelates** (from the

(a)

(b)

FIGURE 21.6
(a) The bidentate ligand ethylenediamine can bond to the metal ion through the lone pair on each nitrogen atom, thus forming two coordinate covalent bonds. (b) Ammonia is a monodentate ligand.

TABLE 21.13   Some Common Ligands

Type	Examples
Unidentate/monodentate	H_2O CN^- SCN^- (thiocyanate) X^- (halides) NH_3 NO_2^- (nitrite) OH^-
Bidentate	Oxalate Ethylenediamine (en)
Polydentate	Diethylenetriamine (dien) $H_2N-(CH_2)_2-NH-(CH_2)_2-NH_2$ Three coordinating atoms Ethylenediaminetetraacetate (EDTA) Six coordinating atoms

FIGURE 21.7
The coordination of EDTA with a 2+ metal ion.

Greek word *chele* for "claw"). A ligand that can form two bonds to a metal ion is called a **bidentate ligand.** A very common bidentate ligand is ethylenediamine (abbreviated en), which is shown coordinating to a metal ion in Fig. 21.6(a). Note the relationship between this ligand and the unidentate ligand ammonia [Fig. 21.6(b)]. Oxalate, another typical bidentate ligand, is shown in Table 21.13.

Ligands that can form more than two bonds to a metal ion are called *polydentate ligands.* Some ligands can form as many as six bonds to a metal ion. The best-known example is ethylenediaminetetraacetate (abbreviated EDTA), which is shown in Table 21.13. This ligand virtually surrounds the metal ion (Fig. 21.7), coordinating through six atoms (a *hexadentate ligand*). As might be expected from the large number of coordination sites, EDTA forms very stable complex ions with most metal ions and is used as a "scavenger" to remove toxic heavy metals such as lead from the human body. It is also used as a reagent to analyze solutions for their metal ion content. EDTA is found in countless consumer products, such as soda, beer, salad dressings, bar soaps, and most cleaners. In these products EDTA ties up trace metal ions that would otherwise catalyze decomposition and produce unwanted precipitates.

Some even more complicated ligands are found in biologic systems, where metal ions play crucial roles in catalyzing reactions, transferring electrons, and transporting and storing oxygen. A discussion of these complex ligands will follow in Section 21.7.

TABLE 21.14 Names of Some Common Unidentate Ligands

Neutral Molecules	
Aqua	H_2O
Ammine	NH_3
Methylamine	CH_3NH_2
Carbonyl	CO
Nitrosyl	NO
Anions	
Fluoro	F^-
Chloro	Cl^-
Bromo	Br^-
Iodo	I^-
Hydroxo	OH^-
Cyano	CN^-

TABLE 21.15 Latin Names Used for Some Metal Ions in Anionic Complex Ions

Metal	Name in an Anionic Complex
Iron	Ferrate
Copper	Cuprate
Lead	Plumbate
Silver	Argentate
Gold	Aurate
Tin	Stannate

Nomenclature

In Werner's lifetime, no system was used to name coordination compounds. Names of the compounds were commonly based on colors and names of discoverers. As the field expanded and more coordination compounds were identified, an orderly system of nomenclature became necessary. A simplified version of this system is summarized by the following rules.

Rules for Naming Coordination Compounds

- As with any ionic compound, *the cation is named before the anion.*

- In naming a complex ion, *the ligands are named before the metal ion.*

- In naming ligands, *an o is added to the root name of an anion.* For example, the halides as ligands are called *fluoro, chloro, bromo,* and *iodo;* hydroxide is *hydroxo;* cyanide is *cyano;* and so on. *For a neutral ligand the name of the molecule is used,* with the exception of H_2O, NH_3, CO, and NO, as illustrated in Table 21.14.

- *The prefixes mono-, di-, tri-, tetra-, penta-, and hexa- are used to denote the number of simple ligands.* The prefixes *bis-, tris-, tetrakis-,* and so on are also used, especially for more complicated ligands or ones that already contain *di-, tri-,* and so on.

- *The oxidation state of the central metal ion is designated by a Roman numeral in parentheses.*

- *When more than one type of ligand is present, they are named alphabetically.* Prefixes do not affect the order.

- *If the complex ion has a negative charge, the suffix -ate is added to the name of the metal.* Sometimes the Latin name is used to identify the metal (see Table 21.15).

The application of these rules is shown in Sample Exercise 21.1.

Sample Exercise 21.1	**Naming Coordination Compounds I**

Give the systematic name for each of the following coordination compounds.

a. $[Co(NH_3)_5Cl]Cl_2$

b. $K_3Fe(CN)_6$

c. $[Fe(en)_2(NO_2)_2]_2SO_4$

Solution

a. To determine the oxidation state of the metal ion, we examine the charges of all ligands and counterions. The ammonia molecules are neutral and each of the chloride ions has a 1− charge, so the cobalt ion must have a 3+ charge to produce a neutral compound. Thus cobalt has the oxidation state +3, and we use cobalt(III) in the name.

The ligands include one Cl^- ion and five NH_3 molecules. The chloride ion is designated as *chloro,* and each ammonia molecule is designated as *ammine.* The prefix *penta-* indicates that there are five NH_3 ligands present. The name of the complex cation is therefore pentaamminechlorocobalt(III). Note that the ligands are named alphabetically,

---

*In an older system the negatively charged ligands were named first, then neutral ligands, with positively charged ligands named last. We will follow the newer convention in this text.

(top) An aqueous solution of [Co(NH₃)₅Cl]Cl₂. (bottom) Solid K₃Fe(CN)₆.

disregarding the prefix. Since the counterions are chloride ions, the compound is named as a chloride salt:

Pentaamminechlorocobalt(III) chloride

Cation   Anion

b. First, we determine the oxidation state of the iron by considering the other charged species. The compound contains three K^+ ions and six CN^- ions. Therefore, the iron must carry a charge of 3+, giving a total of six positive charges to balance the six negative charges. The complex ion present is thus $Fe(CN)_6^{3-}$. The cyanide ligands are each designated *cyano,* and the prefix *hexa-* indicates that six are present. Since the complex ion is an anion, we use the Latin name *ferrate.* The oxidation state is indicated by (III) at the end of the name. The anion name is therefore hexacyanoferrate(III). The cations are K^+ ions, which are simply named potassium. Putting this together gives the name

Potassium hexacyanoferrate(III)

Cation   Anion

(The common name of this compound is potassium ferricyanide.)

c. We first determine the oxidation state of the iron by looking at the other charged species: four NO_2^- ions and one SO_4^{2-} ion. The ethylenediamine is neutral. Thus the two iron ions must carry a total positive charge of 6 to balance the six negative charges. This means that each iron has a +3 oxidation state and is designated as iron(III).

Since the name ethylenediamine already contains *di,* we use *bis-* instead of *di-* to indicate the two en ligands. The name for NO_2^- as a ligand is *nitro,* and the prefix *di-* indicates the presence of two NO_2^- ligands. Since the anion is sulfate, the compound's name is

Bis(ethylenediamine)dinitroiron(III) sulfate

Cation   Anion

Because the complex ion is a cation, the Latin name for iron is not used.

See Exercises 21.29 through 21.32.

Sample Exercise 21.2 | ## Naming Coordination Compounds II

Given the following systematic names, give the formula of each coordination compound.

a. Triamminebromoplatinum(II) chloride
b. Potassium hexafluorocobaltate(III)

Solution

a. *Triammine* signifies three ammonia ligands, and *bromo* indicates one bromide ion as a ligand. The oxidation state of platinum is +2, as indicated by the Roman numeral II. Thus the complex ion is $[Pt(NH_3)_3Br]^+$. One chloride ion is needed to balance the 1+ charge of this cation. The formula of the compound is $[Pt(NH_3)_3Br]Cl$. Note that brackets enclose the complex ion.

b. The complex ion contains six fluoride ligands attached to a Co^{3+} ion to give CoF_6^{3-}. Note that the *-ate* ending indicates that the complex ion is an anion. The cations are K^+ ions, and three are required to balance the 3− charge on the complex ion. Thus the formula is $K_3[CoF_6]$.

See Exercises 21.33 and 21.34.

CHEMICAL IMPACT

Alfred Werner: Coordination Chemist

During the early and middle parts of the nineteenth century, chemists prepared a large number of colored compounds containing transition metals and other substances such as ammonia, chloride ion, cyanide ion, and water. These compounds were very interesting to chemists who were trying to understand the nature of bonding (Dalton's atomic theory of 1808 was very new at this time), and many theories were suggested to explain these substances. The most widely accepted early theory was the *chain theory,* championed by Sophus Mads Jorgensen (1837–1914), professor of chemistry at the University of Copenhagen. The chain theory got its name from the postulate that metal ammine* complexes contain chains of NH_3 molecules. For example, Jorgensen proposed the structure

$$Co\begin{matrix} NH_3-Cl \\ NH_3-NH_3-NH_3-NH_3-Cl \\ NH_3-Cl \end{matrix}$$

for the compound $Co(NH_3)_6Cl_3$. In the late nineteenth century this theory was used in classrooms around the world to explain the nature of metal–ammine compounds.

However, in 1890, a young Swiss chemist named Alfred Werner, who had just obtained a Ph.D. in the field of organic chemistry, became so interested in these compounds that he apparently even dreamed about them. In the middle of one night Werner awoke realizing that he had the correct

explanation for the constitution of these compounds. Writing furiously the rest of that night and into the late afternoon of the following day, he constructed a scientific paper containing his now famous *coordination theory.* This model postulates an octahedral arrangement of ligands around the Co^{3+} ion, producing the $Co(NH_3)_6^{3+}$ complex ion with three Cl^- ions as counterions. Thus Werner's picture of $Co(NH_3)_6Cl_3$ varied greatly from the chain theory.

In his paper on the coordination theory, Werner explained not only the metal–ammine compounds but also most of the other known transition metal compounds, and the importance of his contribution was recognized immediately. He was appointed professor at the University of Zurich, where he spent the rest of his life studying coordination compounds and refining his theory. Alfred Werner was a confident, impulsive man of seemingly boundless energy, who was known for his inspiring lectures, his intolerance of incompetence (he once threw a chair at a student who performed poorly on an oral exam), and his intuitive scientific brilliance. For example, he was the first to show that stereochemistry is a general phenomenon, not one exhibited only by carbon, as was previously thought. He also recognized and named many types of isomerism.

In 1913, for his work on coordination chemistry and stereochemistry, Werner became the fourteenth Nobel Prize winner in chemistry and the first Swiss chemist to be so honored. Werner's work is even more remarkable when one realizes that his ideas preceded by many years any real understanding of the nature of covalent bonds.

*Ammine is the name for NH_3 as a ligand.

21.4 Isomerism

When two or more species have the same formula but different properties, they are said to be **isomers.** Although isomers contain exactly the same types and numbers of atoms, the arrangements of the atoms differ, and this leads to different properties. We will consider two main types of isomerism: **structural isomerism,** where the isomers contain the same atoms but one or more bonds differ, and **stereoisomerism,** where all the bonds in the isomers are the same but the spatial arrangements of the atoms are different. Each of these classes also has subclasses (see Fig. 21.8), which we will now consider.

Structural Isomerism

The first type of structural isomerism we will consider is **coordination isomerism,** in which the composition of the complex ion varies. For example, $[Cr(NH_3)_5SO_4]Br$ and $[Cr(NH_3)_5Br]SO_4$ are coordination isomers. In the first case, SO_4^{2-} is coordinated to Cr^{3+}, and Br^- is the counterion; in the second case, the roles of these ions are reversed.

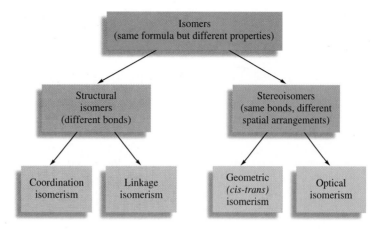

FIGURE 21.8
Some classes of isomers.

(a)

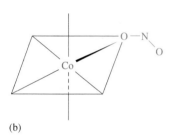

(b)

FIGURE 21.9
As a ligand, NO_2^- can bond to a metal ion (a) through a lone pair on the nitrogen atom or (b) through a lone pair on one of the oxygen atoms.

(a)

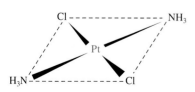

(b)

FIGURE 21.10
(a) The *cis* isomer of $Pt(NH_3)_2Cl_2$ (yellow).
(b) The *trans* isomer of $Pt(NH_3)_2Cl_2$ (pale yellow).

Another example of coordination isomerism is the $[Co(en)_3][Cr(ox)_3]$ and $[Cr(en)_3]$ $[Co(ox)_3]$ pair, where ox represents the oxalate ion, a bidentate ligand shown in Table 21.13.

In a second type of structural isomerism, **linkage isomerism,** the composition of the complex ion is the same, but the point of attachment of at least one of the ligands differs. Two ligands that can attach to metal ions in different ways are thiocyanate (SCN^-), which can bond through lone electron pairs on the nitrogen or the sulfur atom, and the nitrite ion (NO_2^-), which can bond through lone electron pairs on the nitrogen or the oxygen atom. For example, the following two compounds are linkage isomers:

$$[Co(NH_3)_4(NO_2)Cl]Cl$$
Tetraamminechloronitrocobalt(III) chloride
(yellow)

$$[Co(NH_3)_4(ONO)Cl]Cl$$
Tetraamminechloronitritocobalt(III) chloride
(red)

In the first case, the NO_2^- ligand is called *nitro* and is attached to Co^{3+} through the nitrogen atom; in the second case, the NO_2^- ligand is called *nitrito* and is attached to Co^{3+} through an oxygen atom (see Fig. 21.9).

Stereoisomerism

Stereoisomers have the same bonds but different spatial arrangements of the atoms. One type, **geometrical isomerism,** or *cis–trans* **isomerism,** occurs when atoms or groups of atoms can assume different positions around a rigid ring or bond. An important example is the compound $Pt(NH_3)_2Cl_2$, which has a square planar structure. The two possible arrangements of the ligands are shown in Fig. 21.10. In the *trans* **isomer,** the ammonia molecules are across (*trans*) from each other. In the *cis* **isomer,** the ammonia molecules are next (*cis*) to each other.

Geometrical isomerism also occurs in octahedral complex ions. For example, the compound $[Co(NH_3)_4Cl_2]Cl$ has *cis* and *trans* isomers (Fig. 21.11).

A second type of stereoisomerism is called **optical isomerism** because the isomers have opposite effects on plane-polarized light. When light is emitted from a source such as a glowing filament, the oscillating electric fields of the photons in the beam are oriented randomly, as shown in Fig. 21.12. If this light is passed through a polarizer, only the photons with electric fields oscillating in a single plane remain, constituting *plane-polarized light.*

In 1815, a French physicist, Jean Biot (1774–1862), showed that certain crystals could rotate the plane of polarization of light. Later it was found that solutions of certain

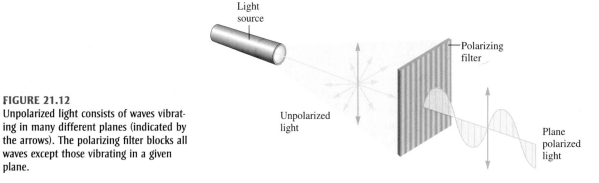

FIGURE 21.11
(a) The *trans* isomer of $[Co(NH_3)_4Cl_2]^+$. The chloride ligands are directly across from each other. (b) The *cis* isomer of $[Co(NH_3)_4Cl_2]^+$. The chloride ligands in this case share an edge of the octahedron. Because of their different structures, the *trans* isomer of $[Co(NH_3)_4Cl_2]Cl$ is green and the *cis* isomer is violet.

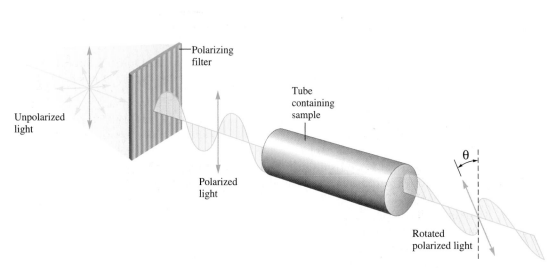

FIGURE 21.12
Unpolarized light consists of waves vibrating in many different planes (indicated by the arrows). The polarizing filter blocks all waves except those vibrating in a given plane.

FIGURE 21.13
The rotation of the plane of polarized light by an optically active substance. The angle of rotation is called theta (θ).

compounds could do the same thing (see Fig. 21.13). Louis Pasteur (1822–1895) was the first to understand this behavior. In 1848 he noted that solid sodium ammonium tartrate ($NaNH_4C_4H_4O_4$) existed as a mixture of two types of crystals, which he painstakingly separated with tweezers. Separate solutions of these two types of crystals rotated plane-polarized light in exactly opposite directions. This led to a connection between optical activity and molecular structure.

CHEMICAL IMPACT

The Importance of Being *cis*

Some of the most important advancements of science are the results of accidental discoveries—for example, penicillin, Teflon, and the sugar substitutes cyclamate and aspartame. Another important chance discovery occurred in 1964, when a group of scientists using platinum electrodes to apply an electric field to a colony of *E. coli* bacteria noticed that the bacteria failed to divide but continued to grow, forming long fibrous cells. Further study revealed that cell division was inhibited by small concentrations of *cis*-$Pt(NH_3)_2Cl_2$ and *cis*-$Pt(NH_3)_2Cl_4$ formed electrolytically in the solution.

Cancerous cells multiply very rapidly because cell division is uncontrolled. Thus these and similar platinum complexes were evaluated as *antitumor agents,* which inhibit the division of cancer cells. The results showed that *cis*-$Pt(NH_3)_2Cl_2$ was active against a wide variety of tumors, including testicular and ovarian tumors, which are very resistant to treatment by more traditional methods. However, although the *cis* complex showed significant antitumor activity, the corresponding *trans* complex had no effect on tumors. This shows the importance of isomerism in biologic systems. When drugs are synthesized, great care must be taken to obtain the correct isomer.

Although *cis*-$Pt(NH_3)_2Cl_2$ has proven to be a valuable drug, unfortunately it has some troublesome side effects, the most serious being kidney damage. As a result, the search continues for even more effective antitumor agents. Promising candidates are shown in Fig. 21.14. Note that they are all *cis* complexes.

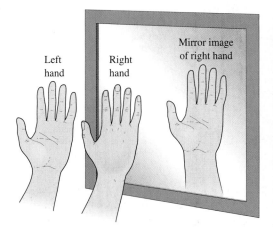

FIGURE 21.14
Some *cis* complexes of platinum and palladium that show significant antitumor activity. It is thought that the *cis* complexes work by losing two adjacent ligands and forming coordinate covalent bonds to adjacent bases on a DNA molecule.

We now realize that optical activity is exhibited by molecules that have *nonsuperimposable mirror images*. Your hands are nonsuperimposable mirror images (Fig. 21.15). The two hands are related like an object and its mirror image; one hand cannot be turned to make it identical to the other. Many molecules show this same feature, such as the

FIGURE 21.15
A human hand exhibits a nonsuperimposable mirror image. Note that the mirror image of the right hand (while identical to the left hand) cannot be turned in any way to make it identical to (superimposable on) the actual right hand.

FIGURE 21.16
Isomers I and II of Co(en)₃³⁺ are mirror images (the image of I is identical to II) that cannot be superimposed. That is, there is no way that I can be turned in space so that it is the same as II.

complex ion $[Co(en)_3]^{3+}$ shown in Fig. 21.16. Objects that have nonsuperimposable mirror images are said to be **chiral** (from the Greek word *cheir,* meaning "hand").

The isomers of $[Co(en)_3]^{3+}$ (Fig. 21.17) are nonsuperimposable mirror images called **enantiomers,** which rotate plane-polarized light in opposite directions and are thus optical isomers. The isomer that rotates the plane of light to the right (when viewed down the beam of oncoming light) is said to be *dextrorotatory,* designated by *d.* The isomer that rotates the plane of light to the left is *levorotatory* (*l*). An equal mixture of the *d* and

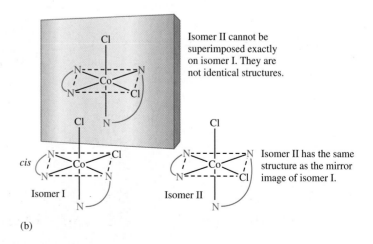

(a)   (b)

FIGURE 21.17
(a) The *trans* isomer of Co(en)₂Cl₂⁺ and its mirror image are identical (superimposable). (b) The *cis* isomer of Co(en)₂Cl₂⁺ and its mirror image are not superimposable and are thus a pair of optical isomers.

l forms in solution, called a *racemic mixture,* does not rotate the plane of the polarized light at all because the two opposite effects cancel each other.

Geometrical isomers are not necessarily optical isomers. For instance, the *trans* isomer of $[Co(en)_2Cl_2]^+$ shown in Fig. 21.17 is identical to its mirror image. Since this isomer is superimposable on its mirror image, it does not exhibit optical isomerism and is not chiral. On the other hand, *cis*-$[Co(en)_2Cl_2]^+$ is *not* superimposable on its mirror image; a pair of enantiomers exists for this complex ion (the *cis* isomer is chiral).

Most important biomolecules are chiral, and their reactions are highly structure dependent. For example, a drug can have a particular effect because its molecules can bind to chiral molecules in the body. To bind correctly, however, the correct optical isomer of the drug must be administered. Just as the right hand of one person requires the right hand of another to perform a handshake, a given isomer in the body requires a specific isomer of the drug to bind together. Because of this, the syntheses of drugs, which are usually very complicated molecules, must be carried out in a way that produces the correct "handedness," a requirement that greatly adds to the synthetic difficulties.

Sample Exercise 21.3	## Geometrical and Optical Isomerism

Does the complex ion $[Co(NH_3)Br(en)_2]^{2+}$ exhibit geometrical isomerism? Does it exhibit optical isomerism?

Solution

The complex ion exhibits geometrical isomerism because the ethylenediamine ligands can be across from or next to each other:

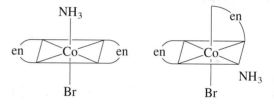

The *cis* isomer of the complex ion also exhibits optical isomerism because its mirror images

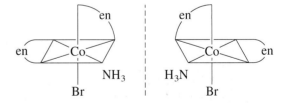

cannot be turned in any way to make them superimposable. Thus these mirror-image isomers of the *cis* complex are shown to be enantiomers that will rotate plane-polarized light in opposite directions.

See Exercises 21.41 and 21.42.

21.5 Bonding in Complex Ions: The Localized Electron Model

In Chapters 8 and 9 we considered the localized electron model, a very useful model for describing the bonding in molecules. Recall that a central feature of this model is the formation of hybrid atomic orbitals that are used to share electron pairs to form σ bonds

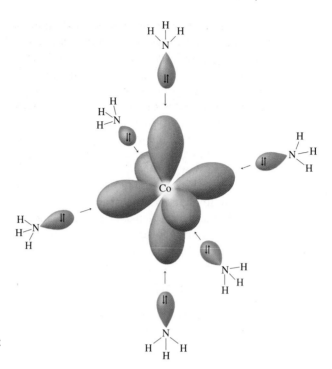

FIGURE 21.18
A set of six d^2sp^3 hybrid orbitals on Co^{3+} can accept an electron pair from each of six NH_3 ligands to form the $Co(NH_3)_6{}^{3+}$ ion.

between atoms. This same model can be used to account for the bonding in complex ions, but there are two important points to keep in mind:

1. The VSEPR model for predicting structure generally *does not work for complex ions*. However, we can safely assume that a complex ion with a coordination number of 6 will have an octahedral arrangement of ligands, and complexes with two ligands will be linear. On the other hand, complex ions with a coordination number of 4 can be either tetrahedral or square planar, and there is no completely reliable way to predict which will occur in a particular case.

2. The interaction between a metal ion and a ligand can be viewed as a Lewis acid–base reaction with the ligand donating a lone pair of electrons to an *empty* orbital of the metal ion to form a coordinate covalent bond:

| Empty metal ion hybrid atomic orbital | Lone pair on the ligand in a hybrid atomic orbital | Coordinate covalent bond |

The hybrid orbitals used by the metal ion depend on the number and arrangement of the ligands. For example, accommodating the lone pairs from the six ammonia molecules in the octahedral $Co(NH_3)_6{}^{3+}$ ion requires a set of six empty hybrid atomic orbitals in an octahedral arrangement. As we discussed in Section 9.1, an octahedral set of orbitals is formed by the hybridization of two d, one s, and three p orbitals to give a set of six d^2sp^3 orbitals (see Fig. 21.18).

The hybrid orbitals required on a metal ion in a four-coordinate complex depend on whether the structure is tetrahedral or square planar. For a tetrahedral arrangement of ligands, an sp^3 hybrid set is required (see Fig. 21.19). For example, in the tetrahedral $CoCl_4{}^{2-}$ ion, the Co^{2+} can be described as sp^3 hybridized. A square planar arrangement of ligands requires a dsp^2 hybrid orbital set on the metal ion (see Fig. 21.19). For example, in the square planar $Ni(CN)_4{}^{2-}$ ion, the Ni^{2+} is described as dsp^2 hybridized.

A linear complex requires two hybrid orbitals 180 degrees from each other. This arrangement is given by an *sp* hybrid set (see Fig. 21.19). Thus, in the linear $Ag(NH_3)_2^+$ ion, the Ag^+ can be described as *sp* hybridized.

Although the localized electron model can account in a general way for metal–ligand bonds, it is rarely used today because it cannot readily account for important properties of complex ions, such as magnetism and color. Thus we will not pursue the model any further.

21.6 The Crystal Field Model

The main reason the localized electron model cannot fully account for the properties of complex ions is that it gives no information about how the energies of the *d* orbitals are affected by complex ion formation. This is critical because, as we will see, the color and magnetism of complex ions result from changes in the energies of the metal ion *d* orbitals caused by the metal–ligand interactions.

The **crystal field model** focuses on the energies of the *d* orbitals. In fact, this model is not so much a bonding model as it is an attempt to account for the colors and magnetic properties of complex ions. In its simplest form, the crystal field model assumes that the ligands can be approximated by *negative point charges* and that metal–ligand bonding is *entirely ionic*.

Octahedral Complexes

We will illustrate the fundamental principles of the crystal field model by applying it to an octahedral complex. Figure 21.20 shows the orientation of the 3*d* orbitals relative to an octahedral arrangement of point-charge ligands. The important thing to note is that two of the orbitals, d_{z^2} and $d_{x^2-y^2}$, point their lobes *directly at* the point-charge ligands and three of the orbitals, d_{xz}, d_{yz}, and d_{xy}, point their lobes *between* the point charges.

To understand the effect of this difference, we need to consider which type of orbital is lower in energy. Because the negative point-charge ligands repel negatively charged electrons, the electrons will first fill the *d* orbitals farthest from the ligands to minimize repulsions. In other words, the d_{xz}, d_{yz}, and d_{xy} orbitals (known as the t_{2g} set) are at a *lower*

Tetrahedral ligand arrangement; sp^3 hybridization

Square planar ligand arrangement; dsp^2 hybridization

Linear ligand arrangement; *sp* hybridization

FIGURE 21.19
The hybrid orbitals required for tetrahedral, square planar, and linear complex ions. The metal ion hybrid orbitals are empty, and the metal ion bonds to the ligands by accepting lone pairs.

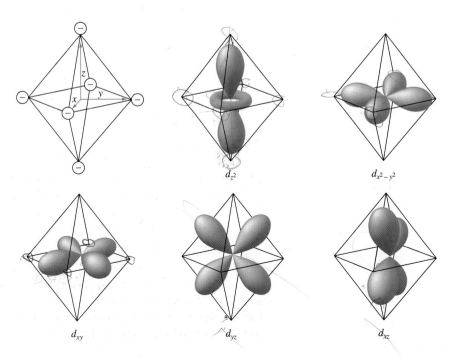

FIGURE 21.20
An octahedral arrangement of point-charge ligands and the orientation of the 3*d* orbitals.

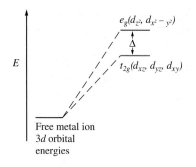

FIGURE 21.21
The energies of the 3d orbitals for a metal ion in an octahedral complex. The 3d orbitals are degenerate (all have the same energy) in the free metal ion. In the octahedral complex the orbitals are split into two sets as shown. The difference in energy between the two sets is designated as Δ (delta).

energy in the octahedral complex than are the d_{z^2} and $d_{x^2-y^2}$ orbitals (the e_g set). This is shown in Fig. 21.21. The negative point-charge ligands increase the energies of all the d orbitals. However, the orbitals that point at the ligands are raised in energy more than those that point between the ligands.

It is this **splitting of the 3d orbital energies** (symbolized by Δ) that explains the color and magnetism of complex ions of the first-row transition metal ions. For example, in an octahedral complex of Co^{3+} (a metal ion with six 3d electrons), there are two possible ways to place the electrons in the split 3d orbitals (Fig. 21.22). If the splitting produced by the ligands is very large, a situation called the **strong-field case,** the electrons will pair in the lower-energy t_{2g} orbitals. This gives a *diamagnetic* complex in which all the electrons are paired. On the other hand, if the splitting is small (the **weak-field case**), the electrons will occupy all five orbitals before pairing occurs. In this case the complex has four unpaired electrons and is *paramagnetic.*

The crystal field model allows us to account for the differences in the magnetic properties of $Co(NH_3)_6^{3+}$ and CoF_6^{3-}. The $Co(NH_3)_6^{3+}$ ion is known to be diamagnetic and thus corresponds to the strong-field case, also called the **low-spin case,** since it yields the *minimum* number of unpaired electrons. In contrast, the CoF_6^{3-} ion, which is known to have four unpaired electrons, corresponds to the weak-field case, also known as the **high-spin case,** since it gives the *maximum* number of unpaired electrons.

| **Sample Exercise 21.4** | **Crystal Field Model I** |

The $Fe(CN)_6^{3-}$ ion is known to have one unpaired electron. Does the CN^- ligand produce a strong or weak field?

Solution

Since the ligand is CN^- and the overall complex ion charge is $3-$, the metal ion must be Fe^{3+}, which has a $3d^5$ electron configuration. The two possible arrangements of the five electrons in the d orbitals split by the octahedrally arranged ligands are

The strong-field case gives one unpaired electron, which agrees with the experimental observation. The CN^- ion is a strong-field ligand toward the Fe^{3+} ion.

See Exercises 21.45 and 21.46.

FIGURE 21.22
Possible electron arrangements in the split 3d orbitals in an octahedral complex of Co^{3+} (electron configuration $3d^6$). (a) In a strong field (large Δ value), the electrons fill the t_{2g} set first, giving a diamagnetic complex. (b) In a weak field (small Δ value), the electrons occupy all five orbitals before any pairing occurs.

From studies of many octahedral complexes, we can arrange ligands in order of their ability to produce d-orbital splitting. A partial listing of ligands in this **spectrochemical series** is

$$CN^- > NO_2^- > en > NH_3 > H_2O > OH^- > F^- > Cl^- > Br^- > I^-$$

Strong-field   Weak-field
ligands   ligands
(large Δ)   (small Δ)

The ligands are arranged in order of decreasing Δ values toward a given metal ion.

It also has been observed that *the magnitude of Δ for a given ligand increases as the charge on the metal ion increases.* For example, NH_3 is a weak-field ligand toward Co^{2+} but acts as a strong-field ligand toward Co^{3+}. This makes sense; as the metal ion charge increases, the ligands will be drawn closer to the metal ion because of the increased charge density. As the ligands move closer, they cause greater splitting of the d orbitals and produce a larger Δ value.

FIGURE 21.23
The visible spectrum.

| Sample Exercise 21.5 | Crystal Field Model II |

Predict the number of unpaired electrons in the complex ion $[Cr(CN)_6]^{4-}$.

Solution

The net charge of 4− means that the metal ion present must be Cr^{2+} ($-6 + 2 = -4$), which has a $3d^4$ electron configuration. Since CN^- is a strong-field ligand (see the spectrochemical series), the correct crystal field diagram for $[Cr(CN)_6]^{4-}$ is

The complex ion will have two unpaired electrons. Note that the CN^- ligand produces such a large splitting that all four electrons will occupy the t_{2g} set even though two of the electrons must be paired in the same orbital.

See Exercises 21.47 and 21.48.

We have seen how the crystal field model can account for the magnetic properties of octahedral complexes. The same model also can explain the colors of these complex ions. For example, $Ti(H_2O)_6^{3+}$, an octahedral complex of Ti^{3+}, which has a $3d^1$ electron configuration, is violet because it absorbs light in the middle of the visible region of the spectrum (see Fig. 21.23). When a substance absorbs certain wavelengths of light in the visible region, the color of the substance is determined by the wavelengths of visible light that remain. We say that the substance exhibits the color *complementary* to those absorbed. The $Ti(H_2O)_6^{3+}$ ion is violet because it absorbs light in the yellow-green region, thus letting red light and blue light pass, which gives the observed violet color. This is shown schematically in Fig. 21.24. Table 21.16 shows the general relationship between the wavelengths of visible light absorbed and the approximate color observed.

Filter absorbs yellow-green light

(a)

$Ti(H_2O)_6^{3+}$

(b)

FIGURE 21.24
(a) When white light shines on a filter that absorbs in the yellow-green region, the emerging light is violet. (b) Because the complex ion $Ti(H_2O)_6^{3+}$ absorbs yellow-green light, a solution of it is violet.

TABLE 21.16   Approximate Relationship of Wavelength of Visible Light Absorbed to Color Observed

Absorbed Wavelength in nm (Color)	Observed Color
400 (violet)	Greenish yellow
450 (blue)	Yellow
490 (blue-green)	Red
570 (yellow-green)	Violet
580 (yellow)	Dark blue
600 (orange)	Blue
650 (red)	Green

CHEMICAL IMPACT

Transition Metal Ions Lend Color to Gems

The beautiful pure color of gems, so valued by cultures everywhere, arises from trace transition metal ion impurities in minerals that would otherwise be colorless. For example, the stunning red of a ruby, the most valuable of all gemstones, is caused by Cr^{3+} ions, which replace about 1% of the Al^{3+} ions in the mineral corundum, which is a form of aluminum oxide (Al_2O_3) that is nearly as hard as diamond. In the corundum structure the Cr^{3+} ions are surrounded by six oxide ions at the vertices of an octahedron. This leads to the characteristic octahedral splitting of chromium's $3d$ orbitals, such that the Cr^{3+} ions absorb strongly in the blue-violet and yellow-green regions of the visible spectrum but transmit red light to give the characteristic ruby color. (On the other hand, if some of the Al^{3+} ions in corundum are replaced by a mixture of Fe^{2+}, Fe^{3+},

and Ti^{4+} ions, the gem is a sapphire with its brilliant blue color; or if some of the Al^{3+} ions are replaced by Fe^{3+} ions, the stone is a yellow topaz.)

Emeralds are derived from the mineral beryl, a beryllium aluminum silicate (empirical formula $3BeO \cdot Al_2O_3 \cdot 6SiO_2$). When some of the Al^{3+} ions in beryl are replaced by Cr^{3+} ions, the characteristic green color of emerald results. In this environment the splitting of the Cr^{3+} $3d$ orbitals causes it to strongly absorb yellow and blue-violet light and to transmit green light.

A gem closely related to ruby and emerald is alexandrite, named after Alexander II of Russia. This gem is based on the mineral chrysoberyl, a beryllium aluminate with the empirical formula $BeO \cdot Al_2O_3$ in which approximately 1% of the Al^{3+} ions are replaced by Cr^{3+} ions. In the chrysoberyl environment Cr^{3+} absorbs strongly in the yellow region of

---

The reason that the $Ti(H_2O)_6^{3+}$ ion absorbs a specific wavelength of visible light can be traced to the transfer of the lone d electron between the split d orbitals, as shown in Fig. 21.25. A given photon of light can be absorbed by a molecule only if the wavelength of the light provides exactly the energy needed by the molecule. In other words, the wavelength absorbed is determined by the relationship

$$\Delta E = \frac{hc}{\lambda}$$

where ΔE represents the energy spacing in the molecule (we have used simply Δ in this chapter) and λ represents the wavelength of light needed. Because the d-orbital splitting in most octahedral complexes corresponds to the energies of photons in the visible region, octahedral complex ions are usually colored.

Since the ligands coordinated to a given metal ion determine the size of the d-orbital splitting, the color changes as the ligands are changed. This occurs because a change in Δ means a change in the wavelength of light needed to transfer electrons between the t_{2g} and e_g orbitals. Several octahedral complexes of Cr^{3+} and their colors are listed in Table 21.17.

Other Coordination Geometries

Using the same principles developed for octahedral complexes, we will now consider complexes with other geometries. For example, Fig. 21.26 shows a tetrahedral arrangement of

TABLE 21.17 Several Octahedral Complexes of Cr^{3+} and Their Colors

Isomer	Color
$[Cr(H_2O)_6]Cl_3$	Violet
$[Cr(H_2O)_5Cl]Cl_2$	Blue-green
$[Cr(H_2O)_4Cl_2]Cl$	Green
$[Cr(NH_3)_6]Cl_3$	Yellow
$[Cr(NH_3)_5Cl]Cl_2$	Purple
$[Cr(NH_3)_4Cl_2]Cl$	Violet

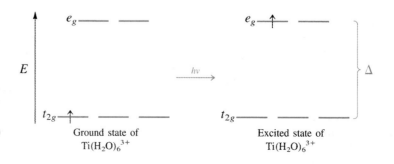

FIGURE 21.25
The complex ion $Ti(H_2O)_6^{3+}$ can absorb visible light in the yellow-green region to transfer the lone d electron from the t_{2g} to the e_g set.

the spectrum. Alexandrite has the interesting property of changing colors depending on the light source. When the first alexandrite stone was discovered deep in a mine in the Russian Ural Mountains in 1831, it appeared to be a deep red color in the firelight of the miners' lamps. However, when the stone was brought to the surface, its color was blue. This seemingly magical color change occurs because the firelight of a miner's helmet is rich in the yellow and red wavelengths of the visible spectrum but does not contain much blue. Absorption of the yellow by the stone produces a reddish color. However, daylight has much more intensity in the blue region than firelight. Thus the extra blue in the light transmitted by the stone gives it bluish color in daylight.

Once the structure of a natural gem is known, it is usually not very difficult to make the gem artificially. For example, rubies and sapphires are made on a large scale by fusing $Al(OH)_3$ with the appropriate transition metal salts at approximately 1200°C to make the "doped" corundum. With these techniques

Alexandrite, a gem closely related to ruby and emerald.

gems of astonishing size can be manufactured: Rubies as large as 10 lb and sapphires up to 100 lb have been synthesized. Smaller synthetic stones produced for jewelry are virtually identical to the corresponding natural stones, and it takes great skill for a gemologist to tell the difference.

point charges in relation to the 3d orbitals of a metal ion. There are two important facts to note:

1. None of the 3d orbitals "point at the ligands" in the tetrahedral arrangement, as the $d_{x^2-y^2}$ and d_{z^2} orbitals do in the octahedral case. Thus the tetrahedrally arranged ligands do not differentiate the d orbitals as much in the tetrahedral case as in the octahedral case. That is, the difference in energy between the split d orbitals will be significantly less in tetrahedral complexes. Although we will not derive it here, the tetrahedral splitting is $\frac{4}{9}$ that of the octahedral splitting for a given ligand and metal ion:

$$\Delta_{tet} = \frac{4}{9}\Delta_{oct}$$

2. Although not exactly pointing at the ligands, the d_{xy}, d_{xz}, and d_{yz} orbitals are closer to the point charges than are the d_{z^2} and $d_{x^2-y^2}$ orbitals. This means that the tetrahedral d-orbital splitting will be opposite to that for the octahedral arrangement. The two arrangements are contrasted in Fig. 21.27. Because the d-orbital splitting is relatively small for the tetrahedral case, the weak-field case (high-spin case) *always* applies. There are no known ligands powerful enough to produce the strong-field case in a tetrahedral complex.

Solutions of $[Cr(NH_3)_6]Cl_3$ (yellow) and $[Cr(NH_3)_5Cl]Cl_2$ (purple).

FIGURE 21.26
(a) Tetrahedral and octahedral arrangements of ligands shown inscribed in cubes. Note that in the two types of arrangements, the point charges occupy opposite parts of the cube; the octahedral point charges are at the centers of the cube faces, and the tetrahedral point charges occupy opposite corners of the cube. (b) The orientations of the 3d orbitals relative to the tetrahedral set of point charges.

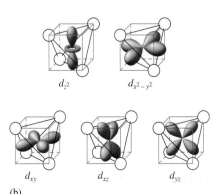

(a)

(b)

FIGURE 21.27
The crystal field diagrams for octahedral and tetrahedral complexes. The relative energies of the sets of d orbitals are reversed. For a given type of ligand, the splitting is much larger for the octahedral complex ($\Delta_{oct} > \Delta_{tet}$) because in this arrangement the d_{z^2} and $d_{x^2-y^2}$ orbitals point their lobes directly at the point charges and are thus relatively high in energy.

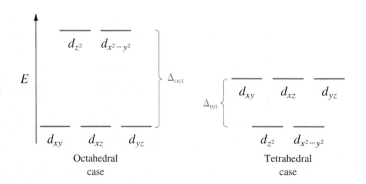

| Sample Exercise 21.6 | **Crystal Field Model III** |

Give the crystal field diagram for the tetrahedral complex ion $CoCl_4^{2-}$.

Solution

The complex ion contains Co^{2+}, which has a $3d^7$ electron configuration. The splitting of the d orbitals will be small, since this is a tetrahedral complex, giving the high-spin case with three unpaired electrons.

See Exercises 21.53 through 21.56.

The crystal field model also applies to square planar and linear complexes. The crystal field diagrams for these cases are shown in Fig. 21.28. The ranking of orbitals in these diagrams can be explained by considering the relative orientations of the point charges and the orbitals. The diagram in Fig. 21.27 for the octahedral arrangement can be used to obtain these orientations. We can obtain the square planar complex by removing the two point charges along the z axis. This will greatly lower the energy of d_{z^2}, leaving only $d_{x^2-y^2}$,

FIGURE 21.28
(a) The crystal field diagram for a square planar complex oriented in the xy plane with ligands along the x and y axes. The position of the d_{z^2} orbital is higher than those of the d_{xz} and d_{yz} orbitals because of the "doughnut" of electron density in the xy plane. The actual position of d_{z^2} is somewhat uncertain and varies in different square planar complexes. (b) The crystal field diagram for a linear complex where the ligands lie along the z axis.

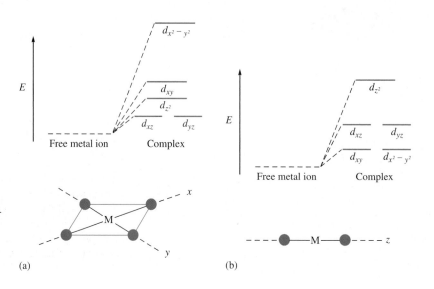

which points at the four remaining ligands as the highest-energy orbital. We can obtain the linear complex from the octahedral arrangement by leaving the two ligands along the z axis and removing the four in the xy plane. This means that only the d_{z^2} points at the ligands and is highest in energy.

21.7 The Biologic Importance of Coordination Complexes

The ability of metal ions to coordinate with and release ligands and to easily undergo oxidation and reduction makes them ideal for use in biologic systems. For example, metal ion complexes are used in humans for the transport and storage of oxygen, as electron-transfer agents, as catalysts, and as drugs. Most of the first-row transition metals are essential for human health, as summarized in Table 21.18. We will concentrate on iron's role in biologic systems, since several of its coordination complexes have been studied extensively.

Iron plays a central role in almost all living cells. In mammals, the principal source of energy comes from the oxidation of carbohydrates, proteins, and fats. Although oxygen is the oxidizing agent for these processes, it does not react directly with these molecules. Instead, the electrons from the breakdown of these nutrients are passed along a complex chain of molecules, called the *respiratory chain,* eventually reaching the O_2 molecule. The principal electron-transfer molecules in the respiratory chain are iron-containing species called **cytochromes,** consisting of two main parts: an iron complex called **heme** and a protein. The structure of the heme complex is shown in Fig. 21.29. Note that it contains an iron ion (it can be either Fe^{2+} or Fe^{3+}) coordinated to a rather complicated planar ligand called a **porphyrin.** As a class, porphyrins all contain the same central ring structure but have different substituent groups at the edges of the rings. The various porphyrin molecules act as tetradentate ligands for many metal ions, including iron, cobalt, and magnesium. In fact, *chlorophyll,* a substance essential to the process of photosynthesis, is a magnesium–porphyrin complex of the type shown in Fig. 21.30.

In addition to participating in the transfer of electrons from nutrients to oxygen, iron plays a principal role in the transport and storage of oxygen in mammalian blood and tissues. Oxygen is stored in a molecule called **myoglobin,** which consists of a heme

A protein is a large molecule assembled from amino acids, which have the general structure in which R represents various groups.

$$H_2N - \underset{\underset{H}{|}}{\overset{\overset{R}{|}}{C}} - COOH$$

TABLE 21.18   The First-Row Transition Metals and Their Biologic Significance

First-Row Transition Metal	Biologic Function(s)
Scandium	None known.
Titanium	None known.
Vanadium	None known in humans.
Chromium	Assists insulin in the control of blood sugar; may also be involved in the control of cholesterol.
Manganese	Necessary for a number of enzymatic reactions.
Iron	Component of hemoglobin and myoglobin; involved in the electron-transport chain.
Cobalt	Component of vitamin B_{12}, which is essential for the metabolism of carbohydrates, fats, and proteins.
Nickel	Component of the enzymes urease and hydrogenase.
Copper	Component of several enzymes; assists in iron storage; involved in the production of color pigments of hair, skin, and eyes.
Zinc	Component of insulin and many enzymes.

FIGURE 21.29
The heme complex, in which an Fe^{2+} ion is coordinated to four nitrogen atoms of a planar porphyrin ligand.

complex and a protein in a structure very similar to that of the cytochromes. In myoglobin, the Fe^{2+} ion is coordinated to four nitrogen atoms of the porphyrin ring and to a nitrogen atom of the protein chain, as shown in Fig. 21.31. Since Fe^{2+} is normally six-coordinate, this leaves one position open for attachment of an O_2 molecule.

One especially interesting feature of myoglobin is that it involves an O_2 molecule attaching directly to Fe^{2+}. However, if gaseous O_2 is bubbled into an aqueous solution containing heme, the Fe^{2+} is immediately oxidized to Fe^{3+}. This oxidation of the Fe^{2+} in heme does not happen in myoglobin. This fact is of crucial importance because Fe^{3+} does

FIGURE 21.30
Chlorophyll is a porphyrin complex of Mg^{2+}. There are two similar forms of chlorophyll, one of which is shown here.

CHEMICAL IMPACT

The Danger of Mercury*

In August 1989, four family members from Lincoln Park, Michigan, died under mysterious circumstances. All four victims had severe tissue damage to the esophagus and lungs, which led doctors to suspect exposure to some type of caustic chemical. Subsequently, local police and fire investigators discovered a crude laboratory in the basement that was used to recover valuable silver from stolen dental amalgams. A dental amalgam is a metal alloy that a dentist uses to fill a tooth. The alloy typically contains silver, tin, copper, and zinc dissolved in liquid mercury. The mixture is placed in a cavity, where it hardens, resulting in a standard "filling."

One of the victims worked at a manufacturing facility for amalgams and was stealing some of the products. At home in his crude lab he heated the amalgam to drive off the mercury (which vaporized at relatively low temperatures) so that he could recover the silver that was left behind. In the process, the colorless, odorless, tasteless mercury vapor entered the ductwork of the home, which was contaminated with mercury at levels 1500 times normal—levels certain to result in death to those exposed. In fact, postmortem analysis revealed extreme levels of mercury in the vital organs of all four victims. Mercury vapor was the silent killer.

The toxicity of mercury varies significantly depending on the route of entry into the body. Inhalation is the most dangerous route because mercury vapor entering the lungs quickly passes across the lung–blood barrier and into the bloodstream, where it can interfere with normal blood chemistry. One of the reactions that takes place in the blood is the decomposition of hydrogen peroxide (a metabolic waste product) by the enzyme peroxidase:

$$2H_2O_2 \xrightarrow{\text{Peroxidase}} 2H_2O + O_2$$

When elemental mercury enters the bloodstream, it reacts with hydrogen peroxide in the presence of peroxidase to produce mercury(II) oxide and water:

$$Hg + H_2O_2 \xrightarrow{\text{Peroxidase}} HgO + H_2O$$

If this conversion to mercury(II) occurs within vital tissues, the mercury(II) cation can denature proteins, inhibit enzyme activity, and disrupt cell membranes. Death often results from respiratory or kidney failure.

If mercury is so toxic, how can it be used in dental fillings? Surprisingly, unlike elemental mercury in the vapor form, mercury bound as a solid in a dental amalgam presents little, if any, risk. Because the mercury is not mobile, even in the harsh environment of the human mouth, the American Dental Association has determined it to be a minimal health risk to dental patients. Even if a filling loosens and is accidentally swallowed, it is passed through the digestive system and excreted before it can pose any risk. The mercury that the four victims in this story were exposed to resulted from heating the amalgam in a smelting furnace, thus vaporizing the mercury and exposing the occupants of the house to the most hazardous route of entry—inhalation.

*Printed with permission, *ChemMatters* magazine. Copyright © 1999, American Chemical Society.

---

not form a coordinate covalent bond with O_2, and myoglobin would not function if the bound Fe^{2+} could be oxidized. Since the Fe^{2+} in the "bare" heme complex can be oxidized, it must be the protein that somehow prevents the oxidation. How? Based on much research, the answer seems to be that the oxidation of Fe^{2+} to Fe^{3+} involves an oxygen bridge between two iron ions (the circles indicate the ligands):

$$Fe^{2+} \quad O{-}O \quad Fe^{2+}$$

The bulky protein around the heme group in myoglobin prevents two molecules from getting close enough to form the oxygen bridge, and so oxidation of the Fe^{2+} is prevented.

The transport of O_2 in the blood is carried out by **hemoglobin,** a molecule consisting of four myoglobin-like units, as shown in Fig. 21.32. Each hemoglobin can therefore

FIGURE 21.31
A representation of the myoglobin molecule. The Fe^{2+} ion is coordinated to four nitrogen atoms in the porphyrin of the heme (represented by the disk in the figure) and on nitrogen from the protein chain. This leaves a sixth coordination position (indicated by the W) available for an oxygen molecule.

bind four O_2 molecules to form a bright red diamagnetic complex. The diamagnetism occurs because oxygen is a strong-field ligand toward Fe^{2+}, which has a $3d^6$ electron configuration. When the oxygen molecule is released, water molecules occupy the sixth coordination position around each Fe^{2+}, giving a bluish paramagnetic complex (H_2O is a weak-field ligand toward Fe^{2+}) that gives venous blood its characteristic bluish tint.

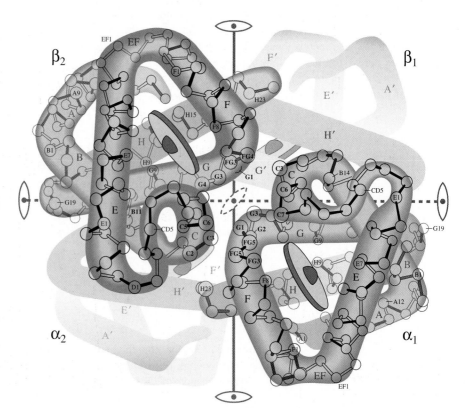

FIGURE 21.32
A representation of the hemoglobin structure. There are two slightly different types of protein chains (α and β). Each hemoglobin has two α chains and two β chains, each with a heme complex near the center. Thus each hemoglobin molecule can complex with four O_2 molecules.

FIGURE 21.33
A normal red blood cell (right) and a sickle cell (left), both magnified 18,000 times.

Hemoglobin dramatically demonstrates how sensitive the function of a biomolecule is to its structure. In certain people, in the synthesis of the proteins needed for hemoglobin, an improper amino acid is inserted into the protein in two places. This may not seem very serious, since there are several hundred amino acids present. However, because the incorrect amino acid has a nonpolar substituent instead of the polar one found on the proper amino acid, the hemoglobin drastically changes its shape. The red blood cells are then sickle-shaped rather than disk-shaped, as shown in Fig. 21.33. The misshapen cells can aggregate, causing clogging of tiny capillaries. This condition, known as *sickle cell anemia,* is the subject of intense research.

Our knowledge of the workings of hemoglobin allows us to understand the effects of high altitudes on humans. The reaction between hemoglobin and oxygen can be represented by the following equilibrium:

$$\text{Hb}(aq) + 4\text{O}_2(g) \rightleftharpoons \text{Hb}(\text{O}_2)_4(aq)$$
$$\text{Hemoglobin} \qquad\qquad\qquad \text{Oxyhemoglobin}$$

At high altitudes, where the oxygen content of the air is lower, the position of this equilibrium will shift to the left, according to Le Châtelier's principle. Because less oxyhemoglobin is formed, fatigue, dizziness, and even a serious illness called *high-altitude sickness* can result. One way to combat this problem is to use supplemental oxygen, as most high-altitude mountain climbers do. However, this is impractical for people who live at high elevations. In fact, the human body adapts to the lower oxygen concentrations by making more hemoglobin, causing the equilibrium to shift back to the right. Someone moving from Chicago to Boulder, Colorado (5300 feet), would notice the effects of the new altitude for a couple of weeks, but as the hemoglobin level increased, the effects would disappear. This change is called *high-altitude acclimatization,* which explains why athletes who want to compete at high elevations should practice there for several weeks prior to the event.

Our understanding of the biologic role of iron also allows us to explain the toxicities of substances such as carbon monoxide and the cyanide ion. Both CO and CN^- are very good ligands toward iron and so can interfere with the normal workings of the iron complexes in the body. For example, carbon monoxide has about 200 times the affinity for the Fe^{2+} in hemoglobin as oxygen does. The resulting stable complex, **carboxyhemoglobin,** prevents the normal uptake of O_2, thus depriving the body of needed oxygen. Asphyxiation can result if enough carbon monoxide is present in the air. The mechanism for the toxicity of the cyanide ion is somewhat different. Cyanide coordinates strongly to cytochrome oxidase, an iron-containing cytochrome enzyme that catalyzes the oxidation–reduction reactions of certain cytochromes. The coordinated cyanide thus prevents the electron-transfer process and rapid death results. Because of its behavior, cyanide is called a *respiratory inhibitor.*

Sherpa and Balti porters are acclimatized to high elevations such as those around the K2 mountain peak in Pakistan.

CHEMICAL IMPACT

Supercharged Blood

During the 1964 Winter Olympics in Innsbruck, Austria, a Finn named Eero Maentyranta won three gold medals in cross-country skiing and immediately became a national hero. His success was due in no small part to the fact that his blood carried 25% to 50% more hemoglobin than the average man's blood. Maentyranta suffered from a rare genetic disorder that results in unusually elevated levels of red blood cells. This extra oxygen-carrying capacity lends itself to increased stamina and endurance, certainly an advantage in the rigorous sport of cross-country skiing. Several years later, geneticists at the University of Helsinki determined that the disorder was due to a mutation of a protein responsible for red blood cell production called the *erythropoietin receptor* (EPO-R). The mutation, which was common in the Maentyranta family, resulted in a protein that was missing 70 amino acids (out of 550). This mutation deleted the portion of the protein that contained the "off switch" for red blood cell production.

Since the discovery of EPO's role in red blood cell production, genetic engineers have been able to synthesize EPO by bioengineering techniques. The protein, marketed in the United States by Amgen of Thousand Oaks, California, is used by kidney dialysis, AIDS, and cancer patients to boost red blood cell production. It has become biotechnology's biggest revenue producer, with over $1 billion in annual sales.

While the potential benefits of this protein are obvious, the potential for abuse may be even greater. The Tour de France, thought by many to be the world's greatest endurance race, was rocked in 1998 by controversy when several riders (including three race favorites) were expelled from the race over allegations of blood doping with the red blood cell–enchancing hormone EPO. EPO has become the drug of choice for many endurance athletes trying to gain an unfair advantage because it is metabolized quickly and, being identical to the body's own EPO, is almost impossible to detect by blood or urine analysis. But the hazards are great. Endurance athletes are especially at risk from abuse of EPO due to extreme water loss during the athletic competition, which, when coupled with elevated levels of EPO, results in an

21.8 Metallurgy and Iron and Steel Production

In the preceding section we saw the importance of iron in biologic systems. Of course, iron is also very important in many other ways in our world. In this section we will discuss the isolation of metals from their natural sources and the formulation of metals into useful materials, with special emphasis on the role of iron.

Metals are very important for structural applications, electrical wires, cooking utensils, tools, decorative items, and many other purposes. However, because the main chemical characteristic of a metal is its ability to give up electrons, almost all metals in nature are found in ores, combined with nonmetals such as oxygen, sulfur, and the halogens. To recover and use these metals, we must separate them from their ores and reduce the metal ions. Then, because most metals are unsuitable for use in the pure state, we must form alloys that have the desired properties. The process of separating a metal from its ore and preparing it for use is known as **metallurgy.** The steps in this process are typically

1. Mining

2. Pretreatment of the ore

3. Reduction to the free metal

4. Purification of the metal (refining)

5. Alloying

A steel mill in Brazil.

An ore can be viewed as a mixture containing **minerals** (relatively pure metal compounds) and **gangue** (sand, clay, and rock). Some typical minerals are listed in Table 21.19. Although silicate minerals are the most common in the earth's crust, they are typically extreme thickening of the blood. This puts an obvious strain on the heart. Since EPO became available in 1986, several world-class athletes (mostly bicyclists and distance runners) have died under mysterious circumstances thought to be associated with abuse of EPO. Because of the widespread abuse of EPO, new methods of detection have been put in place to limit its impact on organized sports and its participants.

The advantage that Eero Maentyranta gained in the 1964 Olympics was the result of a disorder that he had lived with for his entire life. His body had become accustomed to operating with elevated levels of hemoglobin, and it became a natural advantage. Synthetic EPO holds much promise for those suffering conditions that result in hemoglobin deficiency. But as a performance-enhancing drug, EPO's advantages come with enormous risk.

The 1998 Tour de France.

TABLE 21.19 Common Minerals Found in Ores

Anion	Examples
None (free metal)	Au, Ag, Pt, Pd, Rh, Ir, Ru
Oxide	Fe_2O_3 (hematite)
	Fe_3O_4 (magnetite)
	Al_2O_3 (bauxite)
	SnO_2 (cassiterite)
Sulfide	PbS (galena)
	ZnS (sphalerite)
	FeS_2 (pyrite)
	HgS (cinnabar)
	Cu_2S (chalcocite)
Chloride	NaCl (rock salt)
	KCl (sylvite)
	$KCl \cdot MgCl_2$ (carnalite)
Carbonate	$FeCO_3$ (siderite)
	$CaCO_3$ (limestone)
	$MgCO_3$ (magnesite)
	$MgCO_3 \cdot CaCO_3$ (dolomite)
Sulfate	$CaSO_4 \cdot 2H_2O$ (gypsum)
	$BaSO_4$ (barite)
Silicate	$Be_3Al_2Si_6O_{18}$ (beryl)
	$Al_2(Si_2O_8)(OH)_4$ (kaolinite)
	$LiAl(SiO_3)_2$ (spondumene)

FIGURE 21.34
A schematic diagram of a cyclone separator. The ore is pulverized and blown into the separator. The more dense mineral particles are thrown toward the walls by centrifugal force and fall down the funnel. The lighter particles (gangue) tend to stay closer to the center and are drawn out through the top by the stream of air.

very hard and difficult to process, making metal extraction relatively expensive. Therefore, other ores are used when available.

After mining, an ore must be treated to remove the gangue and to concentrate the mineral. The ore is first pulverized and then processed in a variety of devices, including cyclone separators (see Fig. 21.34), inclined vibrating tables, and flotation tanks.

In the **flotation process,** the crushed ore is fed into a tank containing a water–oil–detergent mixture. Because of the difference in the surface characteristics of the mineral particles and the silicate rock particles, the oil wets the mineral particles. A stream of air blown through the mixture causes tiny bubbles to form on the oil-covered pieces, which then float to the surface, where they can be skimmed off.

After the mineral has been concentrated, it is often chemically altered in preparation for the reduction step. For example, nonoxide minerals are often converted to oxides before reduction. Carbonates and hydroxides can be converted by simple heating:

$$CaCO_3(s) \xrightarrow{\text{Heat}} CaO(s) + CO_2(g)$$
$$Mg(OH)_2(s) \xrightarrow{\text{Heat}} MgO(s) + H_2O(g)$$

Sulfide minerals can be converted to oxides by heating in air at temperatures below their melting points, a process called **roasting:**

$$2ZnS(s) + 3O_2(g) \xrightarrow{\text{Heat}} 2ZnO(s) + 2SO_2(g)$$

As we have seen earlier, sulfur dioxide causes severe problems if released into the atmosphere, and modern roasting operations collect this gas and use it in the manufacture of sulfuric acid.

The method chosen to reduce the metal ion to the free metal, a process called **smelting,** depends on the affinity of the metal ion for electrons. Some metals are good enough oxidizing agents that the free metal is produced in the roasting process. For example, the roasting reaction for cinnabar is

$$HgS(s) + O_2(g) \xrightarrow{\text{Heat}} Hg(l) + SO_2(g)$$

where the Hg^{2+} is reduced by electrons donated by the S^{2-} ion, which is then further oxidized by O_2 to form SO_2.

The roasting of a more active metal produces the metal oxide, which must be reduced to obtain the free metal. The most common reducing agents are coke (impure carbon), carbon monoxide, and hydrogen. The following are some common examples of the reduction process:

$$Fe_2O_3(s) + 3CO(g) \xrightarrow{\text{Heat}} 2Fe(l) + 3CO_2(g)$$
$$WO_3(s) + 3H_2(g) \xrightarrow{\text{Heat}} W(l) + 3H_2O(g)$$
$$ZnO(s) + C(s) \xrightarrow{\text{Heat}} Zn(l) + CO(g)$$

The most active metals, such as aluminum and the alkali metals, must be reduced electrolytically, usually from molten salts (see Section 17.8).

The metal obtained in the reduction step is invariably impure and must be refined. The methods of refining include electrolytic refining (see Section 17.8), oxidation of impurities (as for iron, see below), and distillation of low-boiling metals such as mercury and zinc. One process used when highly pure metals are needed is **zone refining.** In this process a bar of the impure metal travels through a heater (see Fig. 21.35), which causes melting and recrystallizing of the metal as the bar cools. Purification of the metal occurs because as the crystal re-forms, the metal ions are likely to fit much better in the crystal lattice than are the atoms of impurities. Thus the impurities tend to be excluded and carried to the end of the bar. Several repetitions of this process give a very pure metal bar.

FIGURE 21.35
A schematic representation of zone refining.

Hydrometallurgy

The metallurgical processes we have considered so far are usually called **pyrometallurgy** (*pyro* means "at high temperatures"). These traditional methods require large quantities of energy and have two other serious problems: atmospheric pollution (mainly by sulfur dioxide) and relatively high costs that make treatment of low-grade ores economically unfeasible.

In the past hundred years, a different process, **hydrometallurgy** (*hydro* means "water"), has been employed to extract metals from ores by use of aqueous chemical solutions, a process called **leaching.** The first two uses of hydrometallurgy were for the extraction of gold from low-grade ores and for the production of aluminum oxide, or alumina, from bauxite, an aluminum-bearing ore.

Gold is sometimes found in ores in the elemental state, but it usually occurs in relatively small concentrations. A process called **cyanidation** treats the crushed ore with an aqueous cyanide solution in the presence of air to dissolve the gold by forming the complex ion $Au(CN)_2^-$:

$$4Au(s) + 8CN^-(aq) + O_2(g) + 2H_2O(l) \longrightarrow 4Au(CN)_2^-(aq) + 4OH^-(aq)$$

Pure gold is then recovered by reaction of the solution of $Au(CN)_2^-$ with zinc powder to reduce Au^+ to Au:

$$2Au(CN)_2^-(aq) + Zn(s) \longrightarrow 2Au(s) + Zn(CN)_4^{2-}(aq)$$

The extraction of alumina from bauxite (the Bayer process) leaches the ore with sodium hydroxide at high temperatures and pressures to dissolve the amphoteric aluminum oxide:

$$Al_2O_3(s) + 2OH^-(aq) \longrightarrow 2AlO_2^-(aq) + H_2O(l)$$

This process leaves behind solid impurities such as SiO_2, Fe_2O_3, and TiO_2, which are not appreciably soluble in basic solution. After the solid impurities are removed, the pH of the solution is lowered, causing the pure aluminum oxide to re-form. It is then electrolyzed to produce aluminum metal (see Section 17.8).

As illustrated by these processes, hydrometallurgy involves two distinct steps: *selective leaching* of a given metal ion from the ore and recovery of the metal ion from the solution by *selective precipitation* as an ionic compound.

Precipitation reactions are discussed in Section 15.7.

The leaching agent can simply be water if the metal-containing compound is a water-soluble chloride or sulfate. However, most commonly, the metal is present in a water-insoluble substance that must somehow be dissolved. The leaching agents used in such cases are usually aqueous solutions containing acids, bases, oxidizing agents, salts, or some combination of these. Often the dissolving process involves the formation of complex ions. For example, when an ore containing water-insoluble lead sulfate is treated with an aqueous sodium chloride solution, the soluble complex ion $PbCl_4^{2-}$ is formed:

$$PbSO_4(s) + 4Na^+(aq) + 4Cl^-(aq) \longrightarrow 4Na^+(aq) + PbCl_4^{2-}(aq) + SO_4^{2-}(aq)$$

TABLE 21.20 Examples of Methods for Recovery of Metal Ions from Leaching Solutions

Method		Examples
Precipitation of a salt		$Cu^{2+}(aq) + S^{2-}(aq) \longrightarrow CuS(s)$
		$Cu^+(aq) + HCN(aq) \longrightarrow CuCN(s) + H^+(aq)$
Reduction	Chemical	$Au^+(aq) + Fe^{2+}(aq) \longrightarrow Au(s) + Fe^{3+}(aq)$
		$Cu^{2+}(aq) + Fe(s) \longrightarrow Cu(s) + Fe^{2+}(aq)$
		$Ni^{2+}(aq) + H_2(g) \longrightarrow Ni(s) + 2H^+(aq)$
	Electrolytic	$Cu^{2+}(aq) + 2e^- \longrightarrow Cu(s)$
		$Al^{3+}(aq) + 3e^- \longrightarrow Al(s)$
Reduction plus precipitation		$2Cu^{2+}(aq) + 2Cl^-(aq) + H_2SO_3(aq) + H_2O(l) \longrightarrow$
		$\quad\quad 2CuCl(s) + 3H^+(aq) + HSO_4^-(aq)$

Formation of a complex ion also occurs in the cyanidation process for the recovery of gold. However, since the gold is present in the ore as particles of metal, it must first be oxidized by oxygen to produce Au^+, which then reacts with CN^- to form the soluble $Au(CN)_2^-$ species. Thus, in this case, the leaching process involves a combination of oxidation and complexation.

Sometimes just oxidation is used. For example, insoluble zinc sulfide can be converted to soluble zinc sulfate by pulverizing the ore and suspending it in water to form a slurry through which oxygen is bubbled:

$$ZnS(s) + 2O_2(g) \longrightarrow Zn^{2+}(aq) + SO_4^{2-}(aq)$$

One advantage of hydrometallurgy over the traditional processes is that sometimes the leaching agent can be pumped directly into the ore deposits in the earth. For example, aqueous sodium carbonate (Na_2CO_3) can be injected into uranium-bearing ores to form water-soluble complex carbonate ions.

Recovering the metal ions from the leaching solution involves forming an insoluble solid containing the metal ion to be recovered. This step may involve addition of an anion to form an insoluble salt, reduction to the solid metal, or a combination of reduction and precipitation of a salt. Examples of these processes are shown in Table 21.20. Because of its suitability for treating low-grade ores economically and without significant pollution, hydrometallurgy is becoming more popular for recovering many important metals such as copper, nickel, zinc, and uranium.

The Metallurgy of Iron

Iron is present in the earth's crust in many types of minerals. *Iron pyrite* (FeS_2) is widely distributed but is not suitable for production of metallic iron and steel because it is almost impossible to remove the last traces of sulfur. The presence of sulfur makes the resulting steel too brittle to be useful. *Siderite* ($FeCO_3$) is a valuable iron mineral that can be converted to iron oxide by heating. The iron oxide minerals are *hematite* (Fe_2O_3), the more abundant, and *magnetite* (Fe_3O_4, really $FeO \cdot Fe_2O_3$). *Taconite* ores contain iron oxides mixed with silicates and are more difficult to process than the others. However, taconite ores are being increasingly used as the more desirable ores are consumed.

To concentrate the iron in iron ores, advantage is taken of the natural magnetism of Fe_3O_4 (hence its name, *magnetite*). The Fe_3O_4 particles can be separated from the gangue by magnets. The ores that are not magnetic are often converted to Fe_3O_4; hematite is partially reduced to magnetite, while siderite is first converted to FeO thermally, then

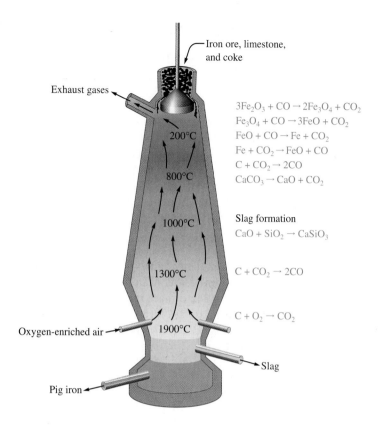

Iron ore, limestone, and coke

Exhaust gases

200°C

800°C

1000°C

1300°C

1900°C

Oxygen-enriched air

Pig iron

Slag

$$3Fe_2O_3 + CO \rightarrow 2Fe_3O_4 + CO_2$$
$$Fe_3O_4 + CO \rightarrow 3FeO + CO_2$$
$$FeO + CO \rightarrow Fe + CO_2$$
$$Fe + CO_2 \rightarrow FeO + CO$$
$$C + CO_2 \rightarrow 2CO$$
$$CaCO_3 \rightarrow CaO + CO_2$$

Slag formation
$$CaO + SiO_2 \rightarrow CaSiO_3$$

$$C + CO_2 \rightarrow 2CO$$

$$C + O_2 \rightarrow CO_2$$

FIGURE 21.36
The blast furnace used in the production of iron.

oxidized to Fe_2O_3, and then reduced to Fe_3O_4:

$$FeCO_3(s) \xrightarrow{\text{Heat}} FeO(s) + CO_2(g)$$
$$4FeO(s) + O_2(g) \longrightarrow 2Fe_2O_3(s)$$
$$3Fe_2O_3(s) + C(s) \longrightarrow 2Fe_3O_4(s) + CO(g)$$

Sometimes the nonmagnetic ores are concentrated by flotation processes.

The most commonly used reduction process for iron takes place in the **blast furnace** (Fig. 21.36). The raw materials required are concentrated iron ore, coke, and limestone (which serves as a *flux* to trap impurities). The furnace, which is approximately 25 feet in diameter, is charged from the top with a mixture of iron ore, coke, and limestone. A very strong blast (~350 mi/h) of hot air is injected at the bottom, where the oxygen reacts with the carbon in the coke to form carbon monoxide, the reducing agent for the iron. The temperature of the charge increases as it travels down the furnace, with reduction of the iron to iron metal occurring in steps:

$$3Fe_2O_3 + CO \longrightarrow 2Fe_3O_4 + CO_2$$
$$Fe_3O_4 + CO \longrightarrow 3FeO + CO_2$$
$$FeO + CO \longrightarrow Fe + CO_2$$

Iron can reduce carbon dioxide,

$$Fe + CO_2 \longrightarrow FeO + CO$$

so complete reduction of the iron occurs only if the carbon dioxide is destroyed by adding excess coke:

$$CO_2 + C \longrightarrow 2CO$$

The limestone ($CaCO_3$) in the charge loses carbon dioxide, or *calcines,* in the hot furnace and combines with silica and other impurities to form **slag,** which is mostly molten calcium silicate, $CaSiO_3$,

$$CaO + SiO_2 \longrightarrow CaSiO_3$$

and alumina (Al_2O_3). The slag floats on the molten iron and is skimmed off. The gas that escapes from the top of the furnace contains carbon monoxide, which is combined with air to form carbon dioxide. The energy released in this exothermic reaction is collected in a heat exchanger and used in heating the furnace.

The iron collected from the blast furnace, called **pig iron,** is quite impure. It contains ~90% iron, ~5% carbon, ~2% manganese, ~1% silicon, ~0.3% phosphorus, and ~0.04% sulfur (from impurities in the coke). The production of 1 ton of pig iron requires approximately 1.7 tons of iron ore, 0.5 ton of coke, 0.25 ton of limestone, and 2 tons of air.

Iron oxide also can be reduced in a **direct reduction furnace,** which operates at much lower temperatures (1300–2000°F) than a blast furnace and produces a solid "sponge iron" rather than molten iron. Because of the milder reaction conditions, the direct reduction furnace requires a higher grade of iron ore (with fewer impurities) than that used in a blast furnace. The iron from the direct reduction furnace is called *DRI (directly reduced iron)* and contains ~95% iron, with the balance mainly silica and alumina.

Production of Steel

Steel is an alloy and can be classified as **carbon steel,** which contains up to about 1.5% carbon, or **alloy steel,** which contains carbon plus other metals such as Cr, Co, Mn, and Mo. The wide range of mechanical properties associated with steel is determined by its chemical composition and by the heat treatment of the final product.

The production of iron from its ore is fundamentally a reduction process, but the conversion of iron to steel is basically an oxidation process in which unwanted impurities are eliminated. Oxidation is carried out in various ways, but the two most common are the open hearth process and the basic oxygen process.

In the oxidation reactions of steelmaking, the manganese, phosphorus, and silicon in the impure iron react with oxygen to form oxides, which in turn react with appropriate fluxes to form slag. Sulfur enters the slag primarily as sulfides, and excess carbon forms carbon monoxide or carbon dioxide. The flux chosen depends on the major impurities present. If manganese is the chief impurity, an acidic flux of silica is used:

$$MnO(s) + SiO_2(s) \xrightarrow{\text{Heat}} MnSiO_3(l)$$

If the main impurity is silicon or phosphorus, a basic flux, usually lime (CaO) or magnesia (MgO), is needed to give reactions such as

$$SiO_2(s) + MgO(s) \xrightarrow{\text{Heat}} MgSiO_3(l)$$
$$P_4O_{10}(s) + 6CaO(s) \xrightarrow{\text{Heat}} 2Ca_3(PO_4)_2(l)$$

Whether an acidic or a basic slag will be needed is a factor that must be considered when a furnace is constructed so that its refractory linings will be compatible with the slag. Silica bricks would deteriorate quickly in the presence of basic slag, and magnesia or lime bricks would dissolve in acid slag.

The **open hearth process** (Fig. 21.37) uses a dishlike container that holds 100 to 200 tons of molten iron. An external heat source is required to keep the iron molten, and a concave roof over the container reflects heat back toward the iron surface. A blast of air or oxygen is passed over the surface of the iron to react with impurities. Silicon

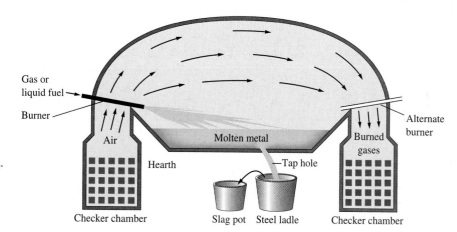

FIGURE 21.37
A schematic diagram of the open hearth process for steelmaking. The checker chambers contain bricks that absorb heat from gases passing over the molten charge. The flow of air and gases is reversed periodically.

and manganese are oxidized first and enter the slag, followed by oxidation of carbon to carbon monoxide, which causes agitation and foaming of the molten bath. The exothermic oxidation of carbon raises the temperature of the bath, causing the limestone flux to calcine:

$$CaCO_3 \xrightarrow{\text{Heat}} CaO + CO_2$$

The resulting lime floats to the top of the molten mixture (an event called the *lime boil*), where it combines with phosphates, sulfates, and silicates. Next comes the refining process, which involves continued oxidation of carbon and other impurities. Because the melting point increases as the carbon content decreases, the bath temperatures must be increased during this phase of the operation. If the carbon content falls below that desired in the final product, coke or pig iron may be added.

The final composition of the steel is "fine-tuned" after the charge is poured. For example, aluminum is sometimes added at this stage to remove trace amounts of oxygen via the reaction

$$4Al + 3O_2 \longrightarrow 2Al_2O_3$$

Alloying metals such as vanadium, chromium, titanium, manganese, and nickel are also added to give the steel the properties needed for a specific application.

The processing of a batch of steel by the open hearth process is quite slow, taking up to 8 hours. The **basic oxygen process** is much faster. Molten pig iron and scrap iron are placed in a barrel-shaped container (Fig. 21.38) that can hold as much as 300 tons of material. A high-pressure blast of oxygen is directed at the surface of the molten iron, oxidizing impurities in a manner very similar to that used in the open hearth process. Fluxes are added after the oxygen blow begins. One advantage of this process is that the exothermic oxidation reactions proceed so rapidly that they produce enough heat to raise the temperature nearly to the boiling point of iron without an external heat source. Also, at these high temperatures only about an hour is needed to complete the oxidation processes.

The **electric arc method,** which was once used only for small batches of specialty steels, is being utilized more and more in the steel industry. In this process an electric arc between carbon electrodes is used to melt the charge. This means that no fuel-borne impurities are added to the steel, since no fuel is needed. Also, higher temperatures are possible than in the open hearth or basic oxygen processes, and this leads to more effective removal of sulfur and phosphorus impurities. Oxygen is added in this process so that the oxide impurities in the steel can be controlled effectively.

FIGURE 21.38
The basic oxygen process for steelmaking.

TABLE 21.21   Percent Composition and Uses of Various Types of Steel

Type of Steel	% Carbon	% Manganese	% Phosphorus	% Sulfur	% Silicon	% Nickel	% Chromium	% Other	Uses
Plain carbon	≤1.35	≤1.65	≤0.04	≤0.05	≤0.60	—	—	—	Sheet steel, tools
High-strength (low-alloy)	≤0.25	≤1.65	≤0.04	≤0.05	0.15– 0.9	0.4–1	0.3–1.3	Cu (0.2–0.6) Sb (0.01–0.08) V (0.01–0.08)	Transportation equipment, structural beams
Alloy	≤1.00	≤3.50	≤0.04	≤0.05	0.15– 2.0	0.25– 10.0	0.25–4.0	Mo (0.08–4.0) V (0–0.2) W (0–18) Co (0–5)	Automobile and aircraft engine parts
Stainless	0.03– 1.2	1.0–10	0.04– 0.06	≤0.03	1–3	1–22	4.0–27	—	Engine parts, steam turbine parts, kitchen utensils
Silicon	—	—	—	—	0.5– 5.0	—	—	—	Electric motors and transformers

Heat Treatment of Steel

One way of producing the desired physical properties in steel is by controlling the chemical composition (see Table 21.21). Another method for tailoring the properties of steel involves heat treatment. Pure iron exists in two different crystalline forms, depending on the temperature. At any temperature below 912°C, iron has a body-centered cubic structure and is called *α-iron*. Between 912°C and 1394°C, iron has a face-centered cubic structure called *austentite,* or *γ-iron*. At 1394°C, iron changes to δ-*iron,* a body-centered cubic structure identical to *α*-iron.

When iron is alloyed with carbon, which fits into holes among the iron atoms to form the interstitial alloy *carbon steel,* the situation becomes even more complex. For example, the temperature at which *α*-iron changes to austentite is lowered by about 200°C. Also, at high temperatures iron and carbon react by an endothermic reversible reaction to form an iron carbide called *cementite*:

$$3Fe + C + energy \rightleftharpoons Fe_3C$$
(Heat)   Cementite

By Le Châtelier's principle, we can predict that cementite will become more stable relative to iron and carbon as the temperature is increased. This is the observed result.

Thus steel is really a mixture of iron metal in one of its crystal forms, carbon, and cementite. The proportions of these components are very important in determining the physical properties of steel.

When steel is heated to temperatures in the region of 1000°C, much of the carbon is converted to cementite. If the steel is then allowed to cool slowly, the equilibrium shown above shifts to the left, and small crystals of carbon precipitate, giving a steel that is relatively ductile. If the cooling is very rapid, the equilibrium does not have time to adjust. The cementite is trapped, and the steel has a high cementite content, making it quite brittle. The proportions of carbon crystals and cementite can be "fine-tuned" to give the desired properties by heating to intermediate temperatures followed by rapid cooling, a process called **tempering.** The rate of heating and cooling determines not only the amounts of cementite present but also the size of its crystals and the form of crystalline iron present.

Refer to Section 10.3 for a review of packing and crystal lattices.

Key Terms

Section 21.1
complex ion
first-row transition metals
lanthanide contraction
lanthanide series

Section 21.3
coordination compound
counterion
oxidation state
coordination number
ligand
coordinate covalent bond
monodentate (unidentate) ligand
chelating ligand (chelate)
bidentate ligand

Section 21.4
isomers
structural isomerism
stereoisomerism
coordination isomerism
linkage isomerism
geometrical (*cis–trans*) isomerism
trans isomer
cis isomer
optical isomerism
chiral
enantiomers

Section 21.6
crystal field model
d-orbital splitting
strong-field (low-spin) case
weak-field (high-spin) case
spectrochemical series

Section 21.7
cytochromes
heme
porphyrin
myoglobin
hemoglobin
carboxyhemoglobin

Section 21.8
metallurgy
minerals
gangue
flotation process
roasting
smelting
zone refining
pyrometallurgy
hydrometallurgy
leaching
cyanidation
blast furnace
slag
pig iron

For Review

First-row transition metals (scandium–zinc)

- All have one or more electrons in the $4s$ orbital and various numbers of $3d$ electrons
- All exhibit metallic properties
  - A particular element often shows more than one oxidation state in its compounds
- Most compounds are colored, and many are paramagnetic
- Most commonly form coordination compounds containing a complex ion involving ligands (Lewis bases) attached to a central transition metal ion
  - The number of attached ligands (called the coordination number) can vary from 2 to 8, with 4 and 6 being most common
- Many transition metal ions have major biologic importance in molecules such as enzymes and those that transport and store oxygen
  - Chelating ligands form more than one bond to the transition metal ion

Isomerism

- Isomers: two or more compounds with the same formula but different properties
  - Coordination isomerism: the composition of the coordination sphere varies
  - Linkage isomerism: the point of attachment of one or more ligands varies
  - Stereoisomerism: isomers have identical bonds but different spatial arrangements
    - Geometric isomerism: ligands assume different relative positions in the coordination sphere; examples are *cis* and *trans* isomers
    - Optical isomerism: molecules with nonsuperimposable mirror images rotate plane-polarized light in opposite directions

Spectral and magnetic properties

- Usually explained in terms of the crystal field model
- Model assumes the ligands are point charges that split the energies of the $3d$ orbitals
- Color and magnetism are explained in terms of how the $3d$ electrons occupy the split $3d$ energy levels
  - Strong-field case: relatively large orbital splitting
  - Weak-field case: relatively small orbital splitting

Metallurgy

- The processes connected with separating a metal from its ore
  - The minerals in ores are often converted to oxides (roasting) before being reduced to the metal (smelting)
- The metallurgy of iron: most common method for reduction uses a blast furnace; process involves iron ore, coke, and limestone
  - Impure product (~90% iron) is called pig iron
- Steel is manufactured by oxidizing the impurities in pig iron

REVIEW QUESTIONS

1. What two first-row transition metals have unexpected electron configurations? A statement in the text says that first-row transition metal ions do not have $4s$ electrons. Why not? Why do transition metal ions often have several oxidation states, whereas representative metals generally have only one?
2. Define each of the following terms:
   a. coordination compound
   b. complex ion
   c. counterions
   d. coordination number

direct reduction furnace
carbon steel
alloy steel
open hearth process
basic oxygen process
electric arc method
tempering

    e. ligand
    f. chelate
    g. bidentate
How would transition metal ions be classified using the Lewis definition of acids and bases? What must a ligand have to bond to a metal? What do we mean when we say that a bond is a "coordinate covalent bond"?

3. When a metal ion has a coordination number of 2, 4, or 6, what are the observed geometries and associated bond angles? For each of the following, give the correct formulas for the complex ions.
    a. linear Ag^+ complex ions having CN^- ligands
    b. tetrahedral Cu^+ complex ions having H_2O ligands
    c. tetrahedral Mn^{2+} complex ions having oxalate ligands
    d. square planar Pt^{2+} complex ions having NH_3 ligands
    e. octahedral Fe^{3+} complex ions having EDTA ligands
    f. octahedral Co^{2+} complex ions having Cl^- ligands
    g. octahedral Cr^{3+} complex ions having ethylenediamine ligands
What is the electron configuration for the metal ion in each of the complex ions in a–g?

4. What is wrong with the following formula–name combinations? Give the correct names for each.
    a. $[Cu(NH_3)_4]Cl_2$ copperammine chloride
    b. $[Ni(en)_2]SO_4$ bis(ethylenediamine)nickel(IV) sulfate
    c. $K[Cr(H_2O)_2Cl_4]$ potassium tetrachlorodiaquachromium(III)
    d. $Na_4[Co(CN)_4C_2O_4]$ tetrasodium tetracyanooxalatocobaltate(II)

5. Define each of the following and give examples of each.
    a. isomer
    b. structural isomer
    c. stereoisomer
    d. coordination isomer
    e. linkage isomer
    f. geometrical isomer
    g. optical isomer
Consider the *cis* and *trans* forms of the octahedral complex $Cr(en)_2Cl_2$. Are both of these isomers optically active? Explain.
    Another way to determine whether a substance is optically active is to look for a plane of symmetry in the molecule. If a substance has a plane of symmetry, then it will not exhibit optical activity (the mirror image will be superimposable). Show the plane of symmetry in the *trans* isomer and prove to yourself that the *cis* isomer does not have a plane of symmetry.

6. What is the major focus of the crystal field model? Why are the *d* orbitals split into two sets for an octahedral complex? What are the two sets of orbitals?
    Define each of the following.
    a. weak-field ligand
    b. strong-field ligand
    c. low-spin complex
    d. high-spin complex
Why is $Co(NH_3)_6^{3+}$ diamagnetic whereas CoF_6^{3-} is paramagnetic? Some octahedral complex ions have the same *d*-orbital splitting diagrams whether they are high-spin or low-spin. For which of the following is this true?
    a. V^{3+}
    b. Ni^{2+}
    c. Ru^{2+}

7. The crystal field model predicts magnetic properties of complex ions and explains the colors of these complex ions. How? Solutions of $[Cr(NH_3)_6]Cl_3$ are yellow, but $Cr(NH_3)_6^{3+}$ does not absorb yellow light. Why? What color light is absorbed by $Cr(NH_3)_6^{3+}$? What is the spectrochemical series, and how can the study of light absorbed by various complex ions be used to develop this series? Would you expect $Co(NH_3)_6^{2+}$ to absorb light of a longer or shorter wavelength than $Co(NH_3)_6^{3+}$? Explain. Compounds of copper(II) are generally colored, but compounds of copper(I) are not colored. Explain. Would you expect $Cd(NH_3)_4Cl_2$ to be colored? Explain. Compounds of Sc^{3+} are not colored, but those of Ti^{3+} and V^{3+} are colored. Explain.

8. Why do tetrahedral complex ions have a different crystal field diagram than octahedral complex ions? What is the tetrahedral crystal field diagram? Why are virtually all tetrahedral complex ions "high spin"?

   Explain the crystal field diagram for square planar complex ions and for linear complex ions.

9. Review Table 21.18, which lists some important biological functions associated with different first-row transition metals. The transport of O_2 in the blood is carried out by hemoglobin. Briefly explain how hemoglobin transports O_2 in the blood. Why are CN^- and CO toxic to humans and animals?

10. Define and give an example of each of the following.
    a. roasting
    b. smelting
    c. flotation
    d. leaching
    e. gangue
    What are the advantages and disadvantages of hydrometallurgy? Describe the process by which a metal is purified by zone refining.

Active Learning Questions

These questions are designed to be used by groups of students in class. The questions allow students to explore their understanding of concepts through discussion and peer teaching. The real value of these questions is the learning that occurs while students talk to each other about chemical concepts.

1. You isolate a compound with the formula $PtCl_4 \cdot 2KCl$. From electrical conductance tests of an aqueous solution of the compound, you find that three ions per formula unit are present, and you also notice that addition of $AgNO_3$ does not cause a precipitate. Give the formula for this compound that shows the complex ion present. Explain your findings. Name this compound.

2. Both $Ni(NH_3)_4^{2+}$ and $Ni(CN)_4^{2-}$ have four ligands. The first is paramagnetic, and the second is diamagnetic. Are the complex ions tetrahedral or square planar? Explain.

3. Which is more likely to be paramagnetic, $Fe(CN)_6^{4-}$ or $Fe(H_2O)_6^{2+}$? Explain.

4. A metal ion in a high-spin octahedral complex has two more unpaired electrons than the same ion does in a low-spin octahedral complex. Name some possible metal ions for which this would be true.

A blue question or exercise number indicates that the answer to that question or exercise appears at the back of this book and a solution appears in the *Solutions Guide*.

Questions

5. Oxalic acid is often used to remove rust stains. What properties of oxalic acid allow it to do this?

6. Four different octahedral chromium coordination compounds exist that all have the same oxidation state for chromium and have H_2O and Cl^- as the ligands and counterions. When 1 mol of each of the four compounds is dissolved in water, how many mol of silver chloride will precipitate upon addition of excess $AgNO_3$?

7. Figure 21.17 shows that the *cis* isomer of $Co(en)_2Cl_2^+$ is optically active while the *trans* isomer is not optically active. Is the same true for $Co(NH_3)_4Cl_2^+$? Explain.

8. A certain first-row transition metal ion forms many different colored solutions. When four coordination compounds of this metal, each having the same coordination number, are dissolved in water, the colors of the solutions are red, yellow, green, and blue. Further experiments reveal that two of the complex ions are paramagnetic with four unpaired electrons and the other two are diamagnetic. What can be deduced from this information about the four coordination compounds?

9. $CoCl_4^{2-}$ forms a tetrahedral complex ion and $Co(CN)_6^{3-}$ forms an octahedral complex ion. What is wrong about the following statements concerning each complex ion and the d orbital splitting diagrams?
   a. $CoCl_4^{2-}$ is an example of a strong-field case having two unpaired electrons.
   b. Because CN^- is a weak field ligand, $Co(CN)_6^{3-}$ will be a low spin case having four unpaired electrons.

10. The following statements discuss some coordination compounds. For each coordination compound, give the complex ion and the counterions, the electron configuration of the transition metal, and the geometry of the complex ion.
    a. $CoCl_2 \cdot 6H_2O$ is a compound used in novelty devices that predict rain.
    b. During the developing process of black-and-white film, silver bromide is removed from photographic film by the fixer. The major component of the fixer is sodium thiosulfate. The equation for the reaction is:

    $$AgBr(s) + 2Na_2S_2O_3(aq) \longrightarrow Na_3[Ag(S_2O_3)_2](aq) + NaBr(aq)$$

    c. The compound cisplatin, $Pt(NH_3)_2Cl_2$, has been studied extensively as an antitumor agent. The reaction for the synthesis of cisplatin is:

    $$K_2PtCl_4(aq) + 2NH_3(aq) \longrightarrow Pt(NH_3)_2Cl_2(s) + 2KCl(aq)$$

    Assume these platinum complex ions have a square planar geometry.

    d. In the production of printed circuit boards for the electronics industry, a thin layer of copper is laminated onto an insulating plastic board. Next, a circuit pattern made of a chemically resistant polymer is printed on the board. The unwanted copper is removed by chemical etching, and the protective polymer is finally removed by solvents. One etching reaction is:

    $$Cu(NH_3)_4Cl_2(aq) + 4NH_3(aq) + Cu(s) \longrightarrow 2Cu(NH_3)_4Cl(aq)$$

    Assume these copper complex ions have tetrahedral geometry.

11. What causes high-altitude sickness and what is high-altitude acclimatization?

12. Almost all metals in nature are found as ionic compounds in ores instead of being in the pure state. Why? What must be done to a sample of ore to obtain a metal substance that has desirable properties?

Exercises

In this section similar exercises are paired.

Transition Metals and Coordination Compounds

13. Write electron configurations for the following metals.
    a. Ni   b. Cd   c. Zr   d. Os

14. Write electron configurations for the following ions.
    a. Ni^{2+} c. Zr^{3+} and Zr^{4+}
    b. Cd^{2+} d. Os^{2+} and Os^{3+}

15. Write electron configurations for each of the following.
    a. Ti, Ti^{2+}, Ti^{4+}
    b. Re, Re^{2+}, Re^{3+}
    c. Ir, Ir^{2+}, Ir^{3+}

16. Write electron configurations for each of the following.
    a. Cr, Cr^{2+}, Cr^{3+} b. Cu, Cu^+, Cu^{2+} c. V, V^{2+}, V^{3+}

17. What is the electron configuration for the transition metal ion in each of the following compounds?
    a. $K_3[Fe(CN)_6]$
    b. $[Ag(NH_3)_2]Cl$
    c. $[Ni(H_2O)_6]Br_2$
    d. $[Cr(H_2O)_4(NO_2)_2]I$

18. What is the electron configuration for the transition metal ion(s) in each of the following compounds?
    a. $(NH_4)_2[Fe(H_2O)_2Cl_4]$
    b. $[Co(NH_3)_2(NH_2CH_2CH_2NH_2)_2]I_2$
    c. $Na_2[TaF_7]$
    d. $[Pt(NH_3)_4I_2][PtI_4]$
    Pt forms +2 and +4 oxidation states in compounds.

19. Molybdenum is obtained as a by-product of copper mining or is mined directly (primary deposits are in the Rocky Mountains in Colorado). In both cases it is obtained as MoS_2, which is then converted to MoO_3. The MoO_3 can be used directly in the production of stainless steel for high-speed tools (which accounts for about 85% of the molybdenum used). Molybdenum can be purified by dissolving MoO_3 in aqueous ammonia and crystallizing ammonium molybdate. Depending on conditions, either $(NH_4)_2Mo_2O_7$ or $(NH_4)_6Mo_7O_{24} \cdot 4H_2O$ is obtained.
    a. Give names for MoS_2 and MoO_3.
    b. What is the oxidation state of Mo in each of the compounds mentioned above?

20. Iron is present in the earth's crust in many types of minerals. The iron oxide minerals are hematite (Fe_2O_3) and magnetite (Fe_3O_4). What is the oxidation state of iron in each mineral? The iron ions in magnetite are a mixture of Fe^{2+} and Fe^{3+} ions. What is the ratio of Fe^{3+} to Fe^{2+} ions in magnetite? The formula for magnetite is usually written as $FeO \cdot Fe_2O_3$. Does this make sense? Explain.

21. What is the lanthanide contraction? How does the lanthanide contraction affect the properties of the $4d$ and $5d$ transition metals?

22. We expect the atomic radius to increase down a group in the periodic table. Can you suggest why the atomic radius of hafnium breaks this rule? (See the following data.)

Element	Atomic Radius (Å)	Element	Atomic Radius (Å)
Sc	1.57	Ti	1.477
Y	1.693	Zr	1.593
La	1.915	Hf	1.476

23. Novelty devices for predicting rain contain cobalt(II) chloride and are based on the following equilibrium:

    $$CoCl_2(s) + 6H_2O(g) \rightleftharpoons CoCl_2 \cdot 6H_2O(s)$$
    Purple   Pink

    What color will such an indicator be if rain is imminent?

24. Chromium(VI) forms two different oxyanions, the orange dichromate ion, $Cr_2O_7^{2-}$, and the yellow chromate ion, CrO_4^{2-}. The equilibrium reaction between the two ions is

    $$Cr_2O_7^{2-}(aq) + H_2O(l) \rightleftharpoons 2CrO_4^{2-}(aq) + 2H^+(aq)$$

The following pictures show what happens when sodium hydroxide is added to a dichromate solution.

Explain what happened.

25. A series of chemicals was added to some $AgNO_3(aq)$. $NaCl(aq)$ was added first to the silver nitrate solution with the end result shown below in test tube 1, $NH_3(aq)$ was then added with the end result shown in test tube 2, and $HNO_3(aq)$ was added last with the end result shown in test tube 3.

Explain the results shown in each test tube. Include a balanced equation for the reaction(s) taking place.

26. When an aqueous solution of KCN is added to a solution containing Ni^{2+} ions, a precipitate forms, which redissolves on addition of more KCN solution. Write reactions describing what happens in this solution. (*Hint:* CN^- is a Brønsted–Lowry base $[K_b \approx 10^{-5}]$ and a Lewis base.)

27. Consider aqueous solutions of the following coordination compounds: $Co(NH_3)_6I_3$, $Pt(NH_3)_4I_4$, Na_2PtI_6, and $Cr(NH_3)_4I_3$. If aqueous $AgNO_3$ is added to separate beakers containing solutions of each coordination compound, how many moles of AgI will precipitate per mole of transition metal present? Assume that each transition metal ion forms an octahedral complex.

28. A coordination compound of cobalt(III) contains four ammonia molecules, one sulfate ion, and one chloride ion. Addition of aqueous $BaCl_2$ solution to an aqueous solution of the compound gives no precipitate. Addition of aqueous $AgNO_3$ to an aqueous solution of the compound produces a white precipitate. Propose a structure for this coordination compound.

29. Name the following complex ions.
    a. $Ru(NH_3)_5Cl^{2+}$ c. $Mn(NH_2CH_2CH_2NH_2)_3^{2+}$
    b. $Fe(CN)_6^{4-}$ d. $Co(NH_3)_5NO_2^{2+}$

30. Name the following complex ions.
    a. $Ni(CN)_4^{2-}$ c. $Fe(C_2O_4)_3^{3-}$
    b. $Cr(NH_3)_4Cl_2^+$ d. $Co(SCN)_2(H_2O)_4^+$

31. Name the following coordination compounds.
    a. $[Co(NH_3)_6]Cl_2$ d. $K_4[PtCl_6]$
    b. $[Co(H_2O)_6]I_3$ e. $[Co(NH_3)_5Cl]Cl_2$
    c. $K_2[PtCl_4]$ f. $[Co(NH_3)_3(NO_2)_3]$

32. Name the following coordination compounds.
    a. $[Cr(H_2O)_5Br]Br_2$ c. $[Fe(NH_2CH_2CH_2NH_2)_2(NO_2)_2]Cl$
    b. $Na_3[Co(CN)_6]$ d. $[Pt(NH_3)_4I_2][PtI_4]$

33. Give formulas for the following.
    a. potassium tetrachlorocobaltate(II)
    b. aquatricarbonylplatinum(II) bromide
    c. sodium dicyanobis(oxalato)ferrate(III)
    d. triamminechloroethylenediaminechromium(III) iodide

34. Give formulas for the following complex ions.
    a. tetrachloroferrate(III) ion
    b. pentaammineaquaruthenium(III) ion
    c. tetracarbonyldihydroxochromium(III) ion
    d. amminetrichloroplatinate(II) ion

35. Draw geometrical isomers of each of the following complex ions.
    a. $[Co(C_2O_4)_2(H_2O)_2]^-$ c. $[Ir(NH_3)_3Cl_3]$
    b. $[Pt(NH_3)_4I_2]^{2+}$ d. $[Cr(en)(NH_3)_2I_2]^+$

36. Draw structures of each of the following.
    a. *cis*-dichloroethylenediamineplatinum(II)
    b. *trans*-dichlorobis(ethylenediamine)cobalt(II)
    c. *cis*-tetraamminechloronitrocobalt(III) ion
    d. *trans*-tetraamminechloronitritocobalt(III) ion
    e. *trans*-diaquabis(ethylenediamine)copper(II) ion

37. Amino acids can act as ligands toward transition metal ions. The simplest amino acid is glycine ($NH_2CH_2CO_2H$). Draw a structure of the glycinate anion ($NH_2CH_2CO_2^-$) acting as a bidentate ligand. Draw the structural isomers of the square planar complex $Cu(NH_2CH_2CO_2)_2$.

38. BAL is a chelating agent used in treating heavy metal poisoning. It acts as a bidentate ligand. What type of linkage isomers are possible when BAL coordinates to a metal ion?

$$CH_2-SH$$
$$|$$
$$CH-SH$$
$$|$$
$$CH_2-OH$$
BAL

39. Which of the following ligands are capable of linkage isomerism? Explain your answer.

$$SCN^-, N_3^-, NO_2^-, NH_2CH_2CH_2NH_2, OCN^-, I^-$$

40. Draw all geometrical and linkage isomers of $Co(NH_3)_4(NO_2)_2$.

41. Acetylacetone, abbreviated acacH, is a bidentate ligand. It loses a proton and coordinates as $acac^-$, as shown below, where M is a transition metal:

Which of the following complexes are optically active: *cis*-Cr(acac)$_2$(H$_2$O)$_2$, *trans*-Cr(acac)$_2$(H$_2$O)$_2$, and Cr(acac)$_3$?

42. Draw all geometrical isomers of Pt(CN)$_2$Br$_2$(H$_2$O)$_2$. Which of these isomers has an optical isomer? Draw the various optical isomers.

Bonding, Color, and Magnetism in Coordination Compounds

43. Draw the *d*-orbital splitting diagrams for the octahedral complex ions of each of the following.
   a. Fe^{2+} (high and low spin)
   b. Fe^{3+} (high spin)
   c. Ni^{2+}

44. Draw the *d*-orbital splitting diagrams for the octahedral complex ions of each of the following.
   a. Zn^{2+}
   b. Co^{2+} (high and low spin)
   c. Ti^{3+}

45. The CrF$_6$$^{4-}$ ion is known to have four unpaired electrons. Does the F$^-$ ligand produce a strong or weak field?

46. The Co(NH$_3$)$_6$$^{3+}$ ion is diamagnetic, but Fe(H$_2$O)$_6$$^{2+}$ is paramagnetic. Explain.

47. How many unpaired electrons are in the following complex ions?
   a. Ru(NH$_3$)$_6$$^{2+}$ (low-spin case)
   b. Ni(H$_2$O)$_6$$^{2+}$
   c. V(en)$_3$$^{3+}$

48. The complex ion Fe(CN)$_6$$^{3-}$ is paramagnetic with one unpaired electron. The complex ion Fe(SCN)$_6$$^{3-}$ has five unpaired electrons. Where does SCN$^-$ lie in the spectrochemical series relative to CN$^-$?

49. Rank the following complex ions in order of increasing wavelength of light absorbed.

$$[Co(H_2O)_6]^{3+}, [Co(CN)_6]^{3-}, [Co(I_6)]^{3-}, [Co(en)_3]^{3+}$$

50. The complex ion [Cu(H$_2$O)$_6$]$^{2+}$ has an absorption maximum at around 800 nm. When four ammonias replace water, [Cu(NH$_3$)$_4$(H$_2$O)$_2$]$^{2+}$, the absorption maximum shifts to around 600 nm. What do these results signify in terms of the relative field splittings of NH$_3$ and H$_2$O? Explain.

51. The following test tubes each contain a different chromium complex ion.

For each compound, predict the predominant color of light absorbed. If the complex ions are Cr(NH$_3$)$_6$$^{3+}$, Cr(H$_2$O)$_6$$^{3+}$, and Cr(H$_2$O)$_4Cl_2$$^+$, what is the identity of the complex ion in each test tube? *Hint:* Reference the spectrochemical series.

52. Consider the complex ions Co(NH$_3$)$_6$$^{3+}$, Co(CN)$_6$$^{3-}$, and CoF$_6$$^{3-}$. The wavelengths of absorbed electromagnetic radiation for these compounds (in no specific order) are 770 nm, 440 nm, and 290 nm. Match the complex ion to the wavelength of absorbed electromagnetic radiation.

53. The wavelength of absorbed electromagnetic radiation for CoBr$_4$$^{2-}$ is 3.4 × 10^{-6} m. Will the complex ion CoBr$_6$$^{4-}$ absorb electromagnetic radiation having a wavelength longer or shorter than 3.4 × 10^{-6} m? Explain.

54. Tetrahedral complexes of Co^{2+} are quite common. Use a *d*-orbital splitting diagram to rationalize the stability of Co^{2+} tetrahedral complex ions.

55. How many unpaired electrons are present in the tetrahedral ion FeCl$_4$$^-$?

56. The complex ion PdCl$_4$$^{2-}$ is diamagnetic. Propose a structure for PdCl$_4$$^{2-}$.

Metallurgy

57. A blast furnace is used to reduce iron oxides to elemental iron. The reducing agent for this reduction process is carbon monoxide.
   a. Given the following data:

$$Fe_2O_3(s) + 3CO(g) \longrightarrow 2Fe(s) + 3CO_2(g) \qquad \Delta H° = -23 \text{ kJ}$$
$$3Fe_2O_3(s) + CO(g) \longrightarrow 2Fe_3O_4(s) + CO_2(g) \qquad \Delta H° = -39 \text{ kJ}$$
$$Fe_3O_4(s) + CO(g) \longrightarrow 3FeO(s) + CO_2(g) \qquad \Delta H° = 18 \text{ kJ}$$

determine $\Delta H°$ for the reaction

$$FeO(s) + CO(g) \longrightarrow Fe(s) + CO_2(g)$$

   b. The CO$_2$ produced in a blast furnace during the reduction process actually can oxidize iron into FeO. To eliminate this reaction, excess coke is added to convert CO$_2$ into CO by the reaction

$$CO_2(g) + C(s) \longrightarrow 2CO(g)$$

Using data from Appendix 4, determine $\Delta H°$ and $\Delta S°$ for this reaction. Assuming $\Delta H°$ and $\Delta S°$ do not depend on temperature, at what temperature is the conversion reaction of CO$_2$ into CO spontaneous at standard conditions?

58. What roles do kinetics and thermodynamics play in the effect that the following reaction has on the properties of steel?

$$3Fe + C \rightleftharpoons Fe_3C$$

59. Silver is sometimes found in nature as large nuggets; more often it is found mixed with other metals and their ores. Cyanide ion is often used to extract the silver by the following reaction that occurs in basic solution:

$$Ag(s) + CN^-(aq) + O_2(g) \xrightarrow{\text{Basic}} Ag(CN)_2^-(aq)$$

Balance this equation by using the half-reaction method.

60. One of the classic methods for the determination of the manganese content in steel involves converting all the manganese to the deeply colored permanganate ion and then measuring the absorption of light. The steel is first dissolved in nitric acid, producing the manganese(II) ion and nitrogen dioxide gas. This solution is then reacted with an acidic solution containing periodate ion; the products are the permanganate and iodate ions. Write balanced chemical equations for both of these steps.

Additional Exercises

61. Ammonia and potassium iodide solutions are added to an aqueous solution of $Cr(NO_3)_3$. A solid is isolated (compound A), and the following data are collected:

  i. When 0.105 g of compound A was strongly heated in excess O_2, 0.0203 g of CrO_3 was formed.

  ii. In a second experiment it took 32.93 mL of 0.100 M HCl to titrate completely the NH_3 present in 0.341 g of compound A.

  iii. Compound A was found to contain 73.53% iodine by mass.

  iv. The freezing point of water was lowered by 0.64°C when 0.601 g of compound A was dissolved in 10.00 g of H_2O (K_f = 1.86°C · kg/mol).

What is the formula of the compound? What is the structure of the complex ion present? (*Hints*: Cr^{3+} is expected to be six-coordinate, with NH_3 and possibly I^- as ligands. The I^- ions will be the counterions if needed.)

62. A transition metal compound contains a cobalt ion, chloride ions, and water molecules. The H_2O molecules are the ligands in the complex ion and the Cl^- ions are the counterions. A 0.256-g sample of the compound was dissolved in water, and excess silver nitrate was added. The silver chloride was filtered, dried, and weighed, and it had a mass of 0.308 g. A second sample of 0.416 g of the compound was dissolved in water, and an excess of sodium hydroxide was added. The hydroxide salt was filtered and heated in a flame, forming cobalt(III) oxide. The mass of cobalt(III) oxide formed was 0.145 g. What is the oxidation state of cobalt in the complex ion and what is the formula of the compound?

63. When aqueous KI is added gradually to mercury(II) nitrate, an orange precipitate forms. Continued addition of KI causes the precipitate to dissolve. Write balanced equations to explain these observations. (*Hint:* Hg^{2+} reacts with I^- to form $HgI_4{}^{2-}$. Would you expect $HgI_4{}^{2-}$ to form colored solutions? Explain.

64. In the production of printed circuit boards for the electronics industry, a 0.60-mm layer of copper is laminated onto an insulating plastic board. Next, a circuit pattern made of a chemically resistant polymer is printed on the board. The unwanted copper is removed by chemical etching, and the protective polymer is finally removed by solvents. One etching reaction is

$$[Cu(NH_3)_4]Cl_2(aq) + 4NH_3(aq) + Cu(s)$$
$$\longrightarrow 2[Cu(NH_3)_4]Cl(aq)$$

  a. Is this reaction an oxidation–reduction process? Explain.

  b. A plant needs to manufacture 10,000 printed circuit boards, each 8.0 × 16.0 cm in area. An average of 80.% of the copper is removed from each board (density of copper = 8.96 g/cm³). What masses of $[Cu(NH_3)_4]Cl_2$ and NH_3 are needed to do this? Assume 100% yield.

65. How many bonds could each of the following chelates form with a metal ion?

a. acetylacetone(acacH)

b. diethylenetriamine

$$NH_2-CH_2-CH_2-NH-CH_2-CH_2-NH_2$$

c. salen

d. porphine

66. Until the discoveries of Werner, it was thought that carbon had to be present in a compound for it to be optically active. Werner prepared the following compound containing OH^- ions as bridging groups and separated the optical isomers.

  a. Draw structures of the two optically active isomers of this compound.

  b. What are the oxidation states of the cobalt ions?

  c. How many unpaired electrons are present if the complex is the low-spin case?

67. The complex ion $Ru(phen)_3{}^{2+}$ has been used as a probe for the structure of DNA. (Phen is a bidentate ligand.)

  a. What type of isomerism is found in $Ru(phen)_3{}^{2+}$?

  b. $Ru(phen)_3{}^{2+}$ is diamagnetic (as are all complex ions of Ru^{2+}). Draw the crystal field diagram for the d orbitals in this complex ion.

Phen = 1,10-phenanthroline =

68. A compound related to acetylacetone is 1,1,1-trifluoroacetyl-acetone (abbreviated Htfa):

$$\underset{CF_3CCH_2CCH_3}{\overset{\overset{O}{\parallel}\ \ \overset{O}{\parallel}}{}}$$

Htfa forms complexes in a manner similar to acetylacetone. (See Exercise 41.) Both Be^{2+} and Cu^{2+} form complexes with tfa$^-$ having the formula $M(tfa)_2$. Two isomers are formed for each metal complex.

a. The Be^{2+} complexes are tetrahedral. Draw the two isomers of $Be(tfa)_2$. What type of isomerism is exhibited by $Be(tfa)_2$?

b. The Cu^{2+} complexes are square planar. Draw the two isomers of $Cu(tfa)_2$. What type of isomerism is exhibited by $Cu(tfa)_2$?

69. Would it be better to use octahedral Ni^{2+} complexes or octahedral Cr^{2+} complexes to determine whether a given ligand is a strong-field or weak-field ligand by measuring the number of unpaired electrons? How else could the relative ligand field strengths be determined?

70. The equilibrium constant, K_a, for the reaction

$$Fe(H_2O)_6^{3+}(aq) + H_2O(l) \rightleftharpoons$$
$$Fe(H_2O)_5(OH)^{2+}(aq) + H_3O^+(aq)$$

is 6.0×10^{-3}.

a. Calculate the pH of a 0.10 M solution of $Fe(H_2O)_6^{3+}$.

b. Will a 1.0 M solution of iron(II) nitrate have a higher or lower pH than a 1.0 M solution of iron(III) nitrate? Explain.

71. Ethylenediaminetetraacetate ($EDTA^{4-}$) is used as a complexing agent in chemical analysis with the structure shown in Figure 21.7. Solutions of $EDTA^{4-}$ are used to treat heavy metal poisoning by removing the heavy metal in the form of a soluble complex ion. The complex ion virtually eliminates the heavy metal ions from reacting with biochemical systems. The reaction of $EDTA^{4-}$ with Pb^{2+} is

$$Pb^{2+}(aq) + EDTA^{4-}(aq) \rightleftharpoons PbEDTA^{2-}(aq) \quad K = 1.1 \times 10^{18}$$

Consider a solution with 0.010 mol $Pb(NO_3)_2$ added to 1.0 L of an aqueous solution buffered at pH = 13.00 and containing 0.050 M Na_4EDTA. Does $Pb(OH)_2$ precipitate from this solution? (K_{sp} for $Pb(OH)_2 = 1.2 \times 10^{-15}$.)

72. Hemoglobin (abbreviated Hb) is a protein that is responsible for the transport of oxygen in the blood of mammals. Each hemoglobin molecule contains four iron atoms that serve as the binding sites for O_2 molecules. The oxygen binding is pH dependent. The relevant equilibrium reaction is

$$HbH_4^{4+}(aq) + 4O_2(g) \rightleftharpoons Hb(O_2)_4(aq) + 4H^+(aq)$$

Use Le Châtelier's principle to answer the following.

a. What form of hemoglobin, HbH_4^{4+} or $Hb(O_2)_4$, is favored in the lungs? What form is favored in the cells?

b. When a person hyperventilates, the concentration of CO_2 in the blood decreases. How does this affect the oxygen-binding equilibrium? How does breathing into a paper bag help to counteract this effect?

c. When a person has suffered a cardiac arrest, an injection of a sodium bicarbonate solution is given. Why is this step necessary?

73. Carbon monoxide is toxic because it binds more strongly to iron in hemoglobin (Hb) than does O_2. Consider the following reactions and approximate standard free energy changes:

$$Hb + O_2 \longrightarrow HbO_2 \qquad \Delta G° = -70 \text{ kJ}$$
$$Hb + CO \longrightarrow HbCO \qquad \Delta G° = -80 \text{ kJ}$$

Using these data, estimate the equilibrium constant value at 25°C for the following reaction:

$$HbO_2 + CO \rightleftharpoons HbCO + O_2$$

74. For the process

$$Co(NH_3)_5Cl^{2+} + Cl^- \longrightarrow Co(NH_3)_4Cl_2^+ + NH_3$$

what would be the expected ratio of *cis* to *trans* isomers in the product?

Challenge Problems

75. The complex *trans*-$[NiA_2B_4]^{2+}$, where A and B represent neutral ligands, is known to be diamagnetic. Do A and B produce very similar or very different crystal fields? Explain.

76. Impure nickel, refined by smelting sulfide ores in a blast furnace, can be converted into metal from 99.90% to 99.99% purity by the Mond process. The primary reaction involved in the Mond process is

$$Ni(s) + 4CO(g) \rightleftharpoons Ni(CO)_4(g)$$

a. Without referring to Appendix 4, predict the sign of $\Delta S°$ for the preceding reaction. Explain.

b. The spontaneity of the preceding reaction is temperature dependent. Predict the sign of ΔS_{surr} for this reaction. Explain.

c. For $Ni(CO)_4(g)$, $\Delta H_f° = -607$ kJ/mol and $S° = 417$ J/K $\cdot$ mol at 298 K. Using these values and data in Appendix 4, calculate $\Delta H°$ and $\Delta S°$ for the preceding reaction.

d. Calculate the temperature at which $\Delta G° = 0$ ($K = 1$) for the preceding reaction, assuming that $\Delta H°$ and $\Delta S°$ do not depend on temperature.

e. The first step of the Mond process involves equilibrating impure nickel with $CO(g)$ and $Ni(CO)_4(g)$ at about 50°C. The purpose of this step is to convert as much nickel as possible into the gas phase. Calculate the equilibrium constant for the preceding reaction at 50.°C.

f. In the second step of the Mond process, the gaseous $Ni(CO)_4$ is isolated and heated at 227°C. The purpose of this step is to deposit as much nickel as possible as pure solid (the reverse of the preceding reaction). Calculate the equilibrium constant for the above reaction at 227°C.

g. Why is temperature increased for the second step of the Mond process?

77. Consider the following data:

$$Co^{3+} + e^- \longrightarrow Co^{2+} \qquad \mathscr{E}° = 1.82 \text{ V}$$
$$Co^{2+} + 3en \longrightarrow Co(en)_3^{2+} \qquad K = 1.5 \times 10^{12}$$
$$Co^{3+} + 3en \longrightarrow Co(en)_3^{3+} \qquad K = 2.0 \times 10^{47}$$

where en = ethylenediamine.

a. Calculate $\mathscr{E}°$ for the half-reaction

$$Co(en)_3^{3+} + e^- \longrightarrow Co(en)_3^{2+}$$

b. Based on your answer to part a, which is the stronger oxidizing agent, Co^{3+} or $Co(en)_3^{3+}$?

c. Use the crystal field model to rationalize the result in part b.

78. Henry Taube, 1983 Nobel Prize winner in chemistry, has studied the mechanisms of the oxidation–reduction reactions of transition metal complexes. In one experiment he and his students studied the following reaction:

$$Cr(H_2O)_6^{2+}(aq) + Co(NH_3)_5Cl^{2+}(aq)$$
$$\longrightarrow Cr(III) \text{ complexes} + Co(II) \text{ complexes}$$

Chromium(III) and cobalt(III) complexes are substitutionally inert (no exchange of ligands) under conditions of the experiment. Chromium(II) and cobalt(II) complexes can exchange ligands very rapidly. One of the products of the reaction is $Cr(H_2O)_5Cl^{2+}$. Is this consistent with the reaction proceeding through formation of $(H_2O)_5Cr—Cl—Co(NH_3)_5$ as an intermediate? Explain.

79. Chelating ligands often form more stable complex ions than the corresponding monodentate ligands with the same donor atoms. For example,

$$Ni^{2+}(aq) + 6NH_3(aq) \rightleftharpoons Ni(NH_3)_6^{2+}(aq) \quad K = 3.2 \times 10^8$$
$$Ni^{2+}(aq) + 3en(aq) \rightleftharpoons Ni(en)_3^{2+}(aq) \quad K = 1.6 \times 10^{18}$$
$$Ni^{2+}(aq) + penten(aq) \rightleftharpoons Ni(penten)^{2+}(aq) \quad K = 2.0 \times 10^{19}$$

where en is ethylenediamine and penten is

$$\begin{array}{c} NH_2CH_2CH_2 \\ NH_2CH_2CH_2 \end{array}\!\!N\!—\!CH_2\!—\!CH_2\!—\!N\!\!\begin{array}{c} CH_2CH_2NH_2 \\ CH_2CH_2NH_2 \end{array}$$

This increased stability is called the *chelate effect*. Based on bond energies, would you expect the enthalpy changes for the above reactions to be very different? What is the order (from least favorable to most favorable) of the entropy changes for the above reactions? How do the values of the formation constants correlate with $\Delta S°$? How can this be used to explain the chelate effect?

80. Qualitatively draw the crystal field splitting of the d orbitals in a trigonal planar complex ion. (Let the z axis be perpendicular to the plane of the complex.)

81. Qualitatively draw the crystal field splitting for a trigonal bipyramidal complex ion. (Let the z axis be perpendicular to the trigonal plane.)

82. Sketch a d-orbital energy diagram for the following.
a. a linear complex with ligands on the x axis
b. a linear complex with ligands on the y axis

83. Sketch and explain the most likely pattern for the crystal field diagram for the complex ion *trans*-diamminetetracyanonickelate(II), where CN^- produces a *much* stronger crystal field than NH_3. Explain completely and label the d orbitals in your diagram. Assume the NH_3 ligands lie on the axis.

84. a. Calculate the molar solubility of AgBr in pure water. K_{sp} for AgBr is 5.0×10^{-13}.
b. Calculate the molar solubility of AgBr in 3.0 M NH_3. The overall formation constant for $Ag(NH_3)_2^+$ is 1.7×10^7, that is,

$$Ag^+(aq) + 2NH_3(aq) \longrightarrow Ag(NH_3)_2^+(aq) \quad K = 1.7 \times 10^7.$$

c. Compare the calculated solubilities from parts a and b. Explain any differences.

d. What mass of AgBr will dissolve in 250.0 mL of 3.0 M NH_3?
e. What effect does adding HNO_3 have on the solubilities calculated in parts a and b?

Integrative Problems

These problems require the integration of multiple concepts to find the solutions.

85. The ferrate ion, FeO_4^{2-}, is such a powerful oxidizing agent that in acidic solution, aqueous ammonia is reduced to elemental nitrogen along with the formation of the iron(III) ion.
a. What is the oxidation state of iron in FeO_4^{2-}, and what is the electron configuration of iron in this polyatomic ion?
b. If 25.0 mL of a 0.243 M FeO_4^{2-} solution is allowed to react with 55.0 mL of 1.45 M aqueous ammonia, what volume of nitrogen gas can form at 25°C and 1.50 atm?

86. a. In the absorption spectrum of the complex ion $[Cr(NCS)_6]^{3-}$, there is a band corresponding to the absorption of a photon of light with an energy of 1.75×10^4 cm^{-1}. Given 1 cm^{-1} = 1.986×10^{-23} J, what is the wavelength of this photon?
b. The Cr—N—C bond angle in $[Cr(NCS)_6]^{3-}$ is predicted to be 180°. What is the hybridization of the N atom in the NCS$^-$ ligand when a Lewis acid–base reaction occurs between Cr^{3+} and NCS$^-$ that would give a 180° Cr—N—C bond angle? $[Cr(NCS)_6]^{3-}$ undergoes substitution by ethylenediammine (en) according to the equation

$$[Cr(NCS)_6]^{3-} + 2en \longrightarrow [Cr(NCS)_2(en)_2]^+ + 4NCS^-$$

Does $[Cr(NCS)_2(en)_2]^+$ exhibit geometric isomerism? Does $[Cr(NCS)_2(en)_2]^+$ exhibit optical isomerism?

Marathon Problem

This problem is designed to incorporate several concepts and techniques into one situation. Marathon Problems can be used in class by groups of students to help facilitate problem-solving skills.

87. There are three salts that contain complex ions of chromium and have the molecular formula $CrCl_3 \cdot 6H_2O$. Treating 0.27 g of the first salt with a strong dehydrating agent resulted in a mass loss of 0.036 g. Treating 270 mg of the second salt with the same dehydrating agent resulted in a mass loss of 18 mg. The third salt did not lose any mass when treated with the same dehydrating agent. Addition of excess aqueous silver nitrate to 100.0-mL portions of 0.100 M solutions of each salt resulted in the formation of different masses of silver chloride; one solution yielded 1430 mg AgCl; another, 2870 mg AgCl; the third, 4300 mg AgCl. Two of the salts are green and one is violet.

Suggest probable structural formulas for these salts, defending your answer on the basis of the preceding observations. State which salt is most likely to be violet. Would a study of the magnetic properties of the salts be helpful in determining the structural formulas? Explain.

 Get help understanding core concepts and visualizing molecular-level interactions, and practice problem solving by visiting the Online Study Center at **college.hmco.com/ PIC/zumdahl7e.**

22 Organic and Biological Molecules

Contents

Polarized light micrograph of crystals of phenylalanine, one of the essential amino acids that the body cannot synthesize.

*T*wo Group 4A elements, carbon and silicon, form the basis of most natural substances. Silicon, with its great affinity for oxygen, forms chains and rings containing Si—O—Si bridges to produce the silica and silicates that form the basis for most rocks, sands, and soils. What silicon is to the geological world, carbon is to the biological world. Carbon has the unusual ability of bonding strongly to itself to form long chains or rings of carbon atoms. In addition, carbon forms strong bonds to other nonmetals such as hydrogen, nitrogen, oxygen, sulfur, and the halogens. Because of these bonding properties, there are a myriad of carbon compounds; several million are now known, and the number continues to grow rapidly. Among these many compounds are the **biomolecules,** those responsible for maintaining and reproducing life.

The study of carbon-containing compounds and their properties is called **organic chemistry.** Although a few compounds involving carbon, such as its oxides and carbonates, are considered to be inorganic substances, the vast majority are organic compounds that typically contain chains or rings of carbon atoms.

Originally, the distinction between inorganic and organic substances was based on whether a compound was produced by living systems. For example, until the early nineteenth century it was believed that organic compounds had some sort of "life force" and could be synthesized only by living organisms. This view was dispelled in 1828 when the German chemist Friedrich Wöhler (1800–1882) prepared urea from the inorganic salt ammonium cyanate by simple heating:

$$NH_4OCN \xrightarrow{\text{Heat}} H_2N—\underset{\displaystyle \underset{O}{\|}}{C}—NH_2$$

Ammonium cyanate   Urea

Urea is a component of urine, so it is clearly an organic material; yet here was clear evidence that it could be produced in the laboratory as well as by living things.

Organic chemistry plays a vital role in our quest to understand living systems. Beyond that, the synthetic fibers, plastics, artificial sweeteners, and drugs that are such an accepted part of modern life are products of industrial organic chemistry. In addition, the energy on which we rely so heavily to power our civilization is based mostly on the organic materials found in coal and petroleum.

Because organic chemistry is such a vast subject, we can provide only a brief introduction to it in this book. We will begin with the simplest class of organic compounds, the hydrocarbons, and then show how most other organic compounds can be considered to be derivatives of hydrocarbons.

22.1 Alkanes: Saturated Hydrocarbons

As the name indicates, **hydrocarbons** are compounds composed of carbon and hydrogen. Those compounds whose carbon–carbon bonds are all single bonds are said to be **saturated,** because each carbon is bound to four atoms, the maximum number. Hydrocarbons containing carbon–carbon multiple bonds are described as being **unsaturated,**

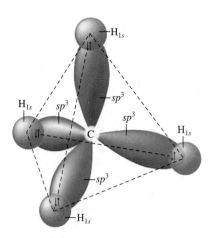

FIGURE 22.1
The C—H bonds in methane.

H—C—C—H structure (a)

(b)

FIGURE 22.2
(a) The Lewis structure of ethane (C_2H_6).
(b) The molecular structure of ethane represented by space-filling and ball-and-stick models.

since the carbon atoms involved in a multiple bond can react with additional atoms, as shown by the *addition* of hydrogen to ethylene:

$$\underset{\text{Unsaturated}}{\begin{array}{c} H \\ \diagdown \\ H \end{array} C = C \begin{array}{c} H \\ \diagup \\ H \end{array}} + H_2 \longrightarrow \underset{\text{Saturated}}{\begin{array}{c} H \quad H \\ | \quad | \\ H - C - C - H \\ | \quad | \\ H \quad H \end{array}}$$

Note that each carbon in ethylene is bonded to three atoms (one carbon and two hydrogens) but that each can bond to one additional atom if one bond of the carbon–carbon double bond is broken.

The simplest member of the saturated hydrocarbons, which are also called the **alkanes,** is *methane* (CH_4). As discussed in Section 9.1, methane has a tetrahedral structure and can be described in terms of a carbon atom using an sp^3 hybrid set of orbitals to bond to the four hydrogen atoms (see Fig. 22.1). The next alkane, the one containing two carbon atoms, is *ethane* (C_2H_6), as shown in Fig. 22.2. Each carbon in ethane is surrounded by four atoms and thus adopts a tetrahedral arrangement and sp^3 hybridization, as predicted by the localized electron model.

The next two members of the series are *propane* (C_3H_8) and *butane* (C_4H_{10}), shown in Fig. 22.3. Again, each carbon is bonded to four atoms and is described as sp^3 hybridized.

Alkanes in which the carbon atoms form long "strings" or chains are called **normal, straight-chain,** or **unbranched hydrocarbons.** As can be seen from Fig. 22.3, the chains in normal alkanes are not really straight but zig-zag, since the tetrahedral C—C—C angle is 109.5°. The normal alkanes can be represented by the structure

$$H - \underset{\underset{H}{|}}{\overset{\overset{H}{|}}{C}} - \left(\underset{\underset{H}{|}}{\overset{\overset{H}{|}}{C}}\right)_n - \underset{\underset{H}{|}}{\overset{\overset{H}{|}}{C}} - H$$

where n is an integer. Note that each member is obtained from the previous one by inserting a *methylene* (CH_2) group. We can condense the structural formulas by omitting some of the C—H bonds. For example, the general formula for normal alkanes shown above can be condensed to

$$CH_3 - (CH_2)_n - CH_3$$

The first ten normal alkanes and some of their properties are listed in Table 22.1. Note that all alkanes can be represented by the general formula C_nH_{2n+2}. For example, nonane, which has nine carbon atoms, is represented by $C_9H_{(2 \times 9)+2}$, or C_9H_{20}. Also note from Table 22.1 that the melting points and boiling points increase as the molar masses increase, as we would expect.

Isomerism in Alkanes

Butane and all succeeding members of the alkanes exhibit **structural isomerism.** Recall from Section 21.4 that structural isomerism occurs when two molecules have the same atoms

FIGURE 22.3
The structures of (a) propane ($CH_3CH_2CH_3$) and (b) butane ($CH_3CH_2CH_2CH_3$). Each angle shown in red is 109.5°.

(a)   (b)

TABLE 22.1 Selected Properties of the First Ten Normal Alkanes

Name	Formula	Molar Mass	Melting Point (°C)	Boiling Point (°C)	Number of Structural Isomers
Methane	CH_4	16	−182	−162	1
Ethane	C_2H_6	30	−183	−89	1
Propane	C_3H_8	44	−187	−42	1
Butane	C_4H_{10}	58	−138	0	2
Pentane	C_5H_{12}	72	−130	36	3
Hexane	C_6H_{14}	86	−95	68	5
Heptane	C_7H_{16}	100	−91	98	9
Octane	C_8H_{18}	114	−57	126	18
Nonane	C_9H_{20}	128	−54	151	35
Decane	$C_{10}H_{22}$	142	−30	174	75

(a)

FIGURE 22.4
(a) Normal butane (abbreviated *n*-butane).
(b) The branched isomer of butane (called isobutane).

(b)

but different bonds. For example, butane can exist as a straight-chain molecule (normal butane, or *n*-butane) or with a branched-chain structure (called isobutane), as shown in Fig. 22.4. Because of their different structures, these molecules exhibit different properties. For example, the boiling point of *n*-butane is −0.5°C, whereas that of isobutane is −12°C.

Sample Exercise 22.1	## Structural Isomerism

Draw the isomers of pentane.

Solution

Pentane (C_5H_{12}) has the following isomeric structures:

1.

$$CH_3-CH_2-CH_2-CH_2-CH_3$$
n-Pentane

2.

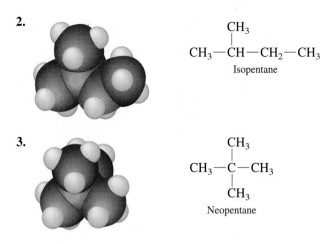

$$CH_3-\overset{\overset{\displaystyle CH_3}{|}}{CH}-CH_2-CH_3$$

Isopentane

3.

$$CH_3-\overset{\overset{\displaystyle CH_3}{|}}{\underset{\underset{\displaystyle CH_3}{|}}{C}}-CH_3$$

Neopentane

Note that the structures

$$CH_3-CH_2-\overset{\overset{\displaystyle CH_3}{|}}{CH}-CH_3 \qquad CH_3-\overset{\overset{\displaystyle CH_3}{|}}{\underset{\underset{\displaystyle CH_3}{|}}{CH}}-CH_2-CH_3$$

$$CH_3-CH_2-\overset{\underset{\underset{\displaystyle CH_3}{|}}{CH}}{}-CH_3$$

which might appear to be other isomers, are actually identical to structure 2.

See Exercise 22.13.

Nomenclature

Because there are literally millions of organic compounds, it would be impossible to remember common names for all of them. We must have a systematic method for naming them. The following rules are used in naming alkanes.

TABLE 22.2   The Most Common Alkyl Substituents and Their Names

Structure*	Name†
—CH_3	Methyl
—CH_2CH_3	Ethyl
—$CH_2CH_2CH_3$	Propyl
$\overset{\overset{\displaystyle |}{}}{CH_3CHCH_3}$	Isopropyl
—$CH_2CH_2CH_2CH_3$	Butyl
$\overset{\overset{\displaystyle |}{}}{CH_3CHCH_2CH_3}$	*sec*-Butyl
—$CH_2-\overset{\overset{\displaystyle H}{|}}{\underset{\underset{\displaystyle CH_3}{|}}{C}}-CH_3$	Isobutyl
—$\overset{\overset{\displaystyle CH_3}{|}}{\underset{\underset{\displaystyle CH_3}{|}}{C}}-CH_3$	*tert*-Butyl

*The bond with one end open shows the point of attachment of the substituent to the carbon chain.
†For the butyl groups, *sec*- indicates attachment to the chain through a secondary carbon, a carbon atom attached to *two* other carbon atoms. The designation *tert*- signifies attachment through a tertiary carbon, a carbon attached to *three* other carbon atoms.

Rules for Naming Alkanes

1. The names of the alkanes beyond butane are obtained by adding the suffix *-ane* to the Greek root for the number of carbon atoms (*pent-* for five, *hex-* for six, and so on). For a branched hydrocarbon, the longest continuous chain of carbon atoms determines the root name for the hydrocarbon. For example, in the alkane

$$CH_3-CH_2-\overset{\overset{\displaystyle CH_3}{\overset{\displaystyle |}{\overset{\displaystyle CH_2}{\overset{\displaystyle |}{\overset{\displaystyle CH_2}{|}}}}}}{CH}-CH_2-CH_3 \quad \text{Six carbons}$$

the longest chain contains six carbon atoms, and this compound is named as a hexane.

2. When alkane groups appear as substituents, they are named by dropping the *-ane* and adding *-yl*. For example, —CH_3 is obtained by removing a hydrogen from methane and is called *methyl*, —C_2H_5 is called *ethyl*, —C_3H_7 is called *propyl*, and so on. The compound above is therefore an ethylhexane. (See Table 22.2.)

3. The positions of substituent groups are specified by numbering the longest chain of carbon atoms sequentially, starting at the end closest to the branching. For example, the compound

$$CH_3CH_2\overset{\overset{\displaystyle CH_3}{|}}{CH}CH_2CH_2CH_3$$

1	2	3	4	5	6	Correct numbering
6	5	4	3	2	1	Incorrect numbering

is called 3-methylhexane. Note that the top set of numbers is correct since the left end of the molecule is closest to the branching, and this gives the smallest number for the position of the substituent. Also, note that a hyphen is written between the number and the substituent name.

4. The location and name of each substituent are followed by the root alkane name. The substituents are listed in alphabetical order, and the prefixes *di-*, *tri-*, and so on, are used to indicate multiple, identical substituents.

Isomerism and Nomenclature

Draw the structural isomers for the alkane C_6H_{14} and give the systematic name for each one.

Solution

We will proceed systematically, starting with the longest chain and then rearranging the carbons to form the shorter, branched chains.

1. $CH_3CH_2CH_2CH_2CH_2CH_3$ Hexane

   Note that although a structure such as

$$\overset{\overset{\displaystyle CH_3}{|}}{CH_2CH_2CH_2CH_2}$$
   $$\overset{|}{CH_3}$$

   Six carbon atoms

   may look different it is still hexane, since the longest carbon chain has six atoms.

2. We now take one carbon out of the chain and make it a methyl substituent.

$$\overset{1}{C}H_3\overset{2}{C}H\overset{3}{C}H_2\overset{4}{C}H_2\overset{5}{C}H_3$$ 2-Methylpentane
   $$\overset{|}{CH_3}$$

   Since the longest chain consists of five carbons, this is a substituted pentane: 2-methylpentane. The 2 indicates the position of the methyl group on the chain. Note that if we numbered the chain from the right end, the methyl group would be on carbon 4. Because we want the smallest possible number, the numbering shown is correct.

3. The methyl substituent can also be on carbon 3 to give

$$\overset{1}{C}H_3\overset{2}{C}H_2\overset{3}{C}H\overset{4}{C}H_2\overset{5}{C}H_3$$ 3-Methylpentane
   $$\overset{|}{CH_3}$$

   Note that we have now exhausted all possibilities for placing a single methyl group on pentane.

4. Next, we can take two carbons out of the original six-member chain:

$$\underset{\underset{\displaystyle CH_3\ \ CH_3}{|\qquad |}}{\overset{1\quad\ 2\quad\ \ 3\quad 4}{CH_3CH-CHCH_3}}\qquad \text{2,3-Dimethylbutane}$$

Since the longest chain now has four carbons, the root name is butane. Since there are two methyl groups, we use the prefix *di*-. The numbers denote that the two methyl groups are positioned on the second and third carbons in the butane chain. Note that when two or more numbers are used, they are separated by a comma.

5. The two methyl groups can also be attached to the same carbon atom as shown here:

$$\underset{\underset{\displaystyle CH_3}{|}}{\overset{\overset{\displaystyle CH_3}{|}}{\underset{1\qquad 2\quad 3\quad\ 4}{CH_3-C-CH_2CH_3}}}\qquad \text{2,2-Dimethylbutane}$$

We might also try ethyl-substituted butanes, such as

$$\underset{\underset{\underset{\displaystyle CH_3}{|}}{\underset{\displaystyle CH_2}{|}}}{CH_3-CHCH_2CH_3}\quad \text{Pentane}$$

However, note that this is instead a pentane (3-methylpentane), since the longest chain has five carbon atoms. Thus it is not a new isomer. Trying to reduce the chain to three atoms provides no further isomers either. For example, the structure

$$\underset{\underset{\underset{\displaystyle CH_3}{|}}{\underset{\displaystyle CH_2}{|}}}{\overset{\overset{\displaystyle CH_3}{|}}{CH_3-C-CH_3}}$$

is actually 2,2-dimethylbutane.

Thus there are only five distinct structural isomers of C_6H_{14}: hexane, 2-methylpentane, 3-methylpentane, 2,3-dimethylbutane, and 2,2-dimethylbutane.

See Exercises 22.15 and 22.16.

Structures from Names

Determine the structure for each of the following compounds.

a. 4-ethyl-3,5-dimethylnonane   **b.** 4-*tert*-butylheptane

Solution

a. The root name *nonane* signifies a nine-carbon chain. Thus we have

$$\underset{\underset{\underset{\displaystyle CH_3}{|}}{\underset{\displaystyle CH_3\ \ CH_2\ \ CH_3}{|\qquad |\qquad |}}}{\overset{1\quad\ \ \ 2\quad\ \ 3\qquad 4\qquad\ 5\ \ 6\quad\ \ 7\quad\ \ 8\quad\ 9}{CH_3CH_2CH-CH-CHCH_2CH_2CH_2CH_3}}$$

b. Heptane signifies a seven-carbon chain, and the *tert*-butyl group is

$$H_3C-\overset{\displaystyle |}{\underset{\displaystyle |}{C}}-CH_3$$
$$CH_3$$

Thus we have

$$\overset{1\quad\ 2\quad\ \ 3\quad\ 4\quad 5\quad\ 6\quad\ 7}{CH_3CH_2CH_2CHCH_2CH_2CH_3}$$
$$H_3C-\overset{\displaystyle |}{\underset{\displaystyle |}{C}}-CH_3$$
$$CH_3$$

See Exercises 22.19 and 22.20.

Reactions of Alkanes

Because they are saturated compounds and because the C—C and C—H bonds are relatively strong, the alkanes are fairly unreactive. For example, at 25°C they do not react with acids, bases, or strong oxidizing agents. This chemical inertness makes them valuable as lubricating materials and as the backbone for structural materials such as plastics.

At a sufficiently high temperature alkanes do react vigorously and exothermically with oxygen, and these **combustion reactions** are the basis for their widespread use as fuels. For example, the reaction of butane with oxygen is

$$2C_4H_{10}(g) + 13O_2(g) \longrightarrow 8CO_2(g) + 10H_2O(g)$$

The alkanes can also undergo **substitution reactions,** primarily where halogen atoms replace hydrogen atoms. For example, methane can be successively chlorinated as follows:

$$CH_4 + Cl_2 \xrightarrow{hv} \underset{\text{Chloromethane}}{CH_3Cl} + HCl$$

$$CH_3Cl + Cl_2 \xrightarrow{hv} \underset{\text{Dichloromethane}}{CH_2Cl_2} + HCl$$

$$CH_2Cl_2 + Cl_2 \xrightarrow{hv} \underset{\substack{\text{Trichloromethane}\\\text{(chloroform)}}}{CHCl_3} + HCl$$

$$CHCl_3 + Cl_2 \xrightarrow{hv} \underset{\substack{\text{Tetrachloromethane}\\\text{(carbon tetrachloride)}}}{CCl_4} + HCl$$

The *hv* above the arrow represents ultraviolet light.

Note that the products of the last two reactions have two names; the systematic name is given first, followed by the common name in parentheses. (This format will be used throughout this chapter for compounds that have common names.) Also, note that ultraviolet light (*hv*) furnishes the energy to break the Cl—Cl bond to produce chlorine atoms:

$$Cl_2 \longrightarrow Cl\cdot + Cl\cdot$$

A butane lighter used for camping.

A chlorine atom has an unpaired electron, as indicated by the dot, which makes it very reactive and able to attack the C—H bond.

Substituted methanes with the general formula CF_xCl_{4-x} containing both chlorine and fluorine as substituents are called chlorofluorocarbons (CFCs) and are also known as *Freons*. These substances are very unreactive and have been extensively used as coolant fluids in refrigerators and air conditioners. Unfortunately, their chemical inertness allows

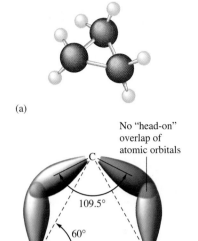

(a)

No "head-on" overlap of atomic orbitals

(b)

FIGURE 22.5
(a) The molecular structure of cyclopropane (C_3H_6). (b) The overlap of the sp^3 orbitals that form the C—C bonds in cyclopropane.

Freons to remain in the atmosphere so long that they eventually reach altitudes where they are a threat to the protective ozone layer (see Section 12.8), and the use of these compounds is being rapidly phased out.

Alkanes can also undergo **dehydrogenation reactions** in which hydrogen atoms are removed and the product is an unsaturated hydrocarbon. For example, in the presence of chromium(III) oxide at high temperatures, ethane can be dehydrogenated, yielding ethylene:

$$CH_3CH_3 \xrightarrow[500°C]{Cr_2O_3} CH_2{=}CH_2 + H_2$$

Ethylene

Cyclic Alkanes

Besides forming chains, carbon atoms also form rings. The simplest of the **cyclic alkanes** (general formula C_nH_{2n}) is cyclopropane (C_3H_6), shown in Fig. 22.5(a). Since the carbon atoms in cyclopropane form an equilateral triangle with 60° bond angles, their sp^3 hybrid orbitals do not overlap head-on as in normal alkanes [Fig. 22.5(b)]. This results in unusually weak, or *strained,* C—C bonds; thus the cyclopropane molecule is much more reactive than straight-chain propane. The carbon atoms in cyclobutane (C_4H_8) form a square with 88° bond angles, and cyclobutane is also quite reactive.

The next two members of the series, cyclopentane (C_5H_{10}) and cyclohexane (C_6H_{12}), are quite stable, because their rings have bond angles very close to the tetrahedral angles, which allows the sp^3 hybrid orbitals on adjacent carbon atoms to overlap head-on and form normal C—C bonds, which are quite strong. To attain the tetrahedral angles, the cyclohexane ring must "pucker"—that is, become nonplanar. Cyclohexane can exist in two forms, the *chair* and the *boat* forms, as shown in Fig. 22.6. The two hydrogen atoms above the ring in the boat form are quite close to each other, and the resulting repulsion between these atoms causes the chair form to be preferred. At 25°C more than 99% of cyclohexane exists in the chair form.

For simplicity, the cyclic alkanes are often represented by the following structures:

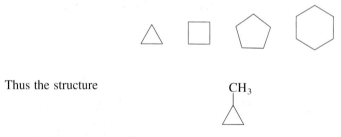

Thus the structure

$$CH_3$$

represents methylcyclopropane.

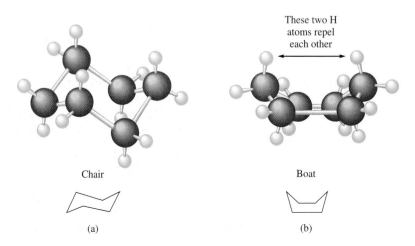

Chair   Boat

These two H atoms repel each other

(a)   (b)

FIGURE 22.6
The (a) chair and (b) boat forms of cyclohexane.

The nomenclature for cycloalkanes follows the same rules as for the other alkanes except that the root name is preceded by the prefix *cyclo-*. The ring is numbered to yield the smallest substituent numbers possible.

Naming Cyclic Alkanes

Name each of the following cyclic alkanes.

a. $CH_3-CH-CH_3$

b. CH_2CH_3
$CH_2CH_2CH_3$

Solution

a. The six-carbon cyclohexane ring is numbered as follows:

$CH_3-CH-CH_3$
CH_3

There is an isopropyl group at carbon 1 and a methyl group at carbon 3. The name is 1-isopropyl-3-methylcyclohexane, since the alkyl groups are named in alphabetical order.

b. This is a cyclobutane ring, which is numbered as follows:

CH_2CH_3
$CH_2CH_2CH_3$

The name is 1-ethyl-2-propylcyclobutane.

See Exercise 22.22.

22.2 Alkenes and Alkynes

Multiple carbon–carbon bonds result when hydrogen atoms are removed from alkanes. Hydrocarbons that contain at least one carbon–carbon double bond are called **alkenes** and have the general formula C_nH_{2n}. The simplest alkene (C_2H_4), commonly known as *ethylene,* has the Lewis structure

H   H
  \   /
   C = C
  /   \
H   H

As discussed in Section 9.1, each carbon in ethylene can be described as sp^2 hybridized. The C—C σ bond is formed by sharing an electron pair between sp^2 orbitals, and the π bond is formed by sharing a pair of electrons between p orbitals (Fig. 22.7).

The systematic nomenclature for alkenes is quite similar to that for alkanes.

1. The root hydrocarbon name ends in *-ene* rather than *-ane.* Thus the systematic name for C_2H_4 is *ethene* and the name for C_3H_6 is *propene.*

2. In alkenes containing more than three carbon atoms, the location of the double bond is indicated by the lowest-numbered carbon atom involved in the bond. Thus $CH_2=CHCH_2CH_3$ is called 1-butene, and $CH_3CH=CHCH_3$ is called 2-butene.

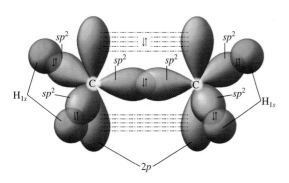

FIGURE 22.7
The bonding in ethylene.

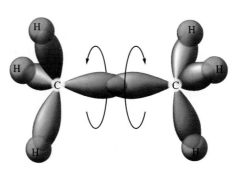

FIGURE 22.8
The bonding in ethane.

Note from Fig. 22.7 that the *p* orbitals on the two carbon atoms in ethylene must be lined up (parallel) to allow formation of the π bond. This prevents rotation of the two CH_2 groups relative to each other at ordinary temperatures, in contrast to alkanes, where free rotation is possible (see Fig. 22.8). The restricted rotation around doubly bonded carbon atoms means that alkenes exhibit *cis–trans* **isomerism.** For example, there are two stereoisomers of 2-butene (Fig. 22.9). Identical substituents on the same side of the double bond are designated *cis* and those on opposite sides are labeled *trans.*

Alkynes are unsaturated hydrocarbons containing at least one triple carbon–carbon bond. The simplest alkyne is C_2H_2 (commonly called *acetylene*), which has the systematic name *ethyne*. As discussed in Section 9.1, the triple bond in acetylene can be described as one σ bond between two *sp* hybrid orbitals on the two carbon atoms and two π bonds involving two 2*p* orbitals on each carbon atom (Fig. 22.10).

The nomenclature for alkynes involves the use of *-yne* as a suffix to replace the *-ane* of the parent alkane. Thus the molecule $CH_3CH_2C{\equiv}CCH_3$ has the name 2-pentyne.

Like alkanes, unsaturated hydrocarbons can exist as ringed structures, for example,

For cyclic alkenes, number through the double bond toward the substituent.

(a)

(b)

FIGURE 22.9
The two stereoisomers of 2-butene: (a) *cis*-2-butene and (b) *trans*-2-butene.

Cyclohexene

4-Methyl-cyclopentene

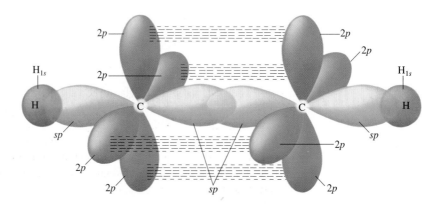

FIGURE 22.10
The bonding in acetylene.

Sample Exercise 22.5 Naming Alkenes and Alkynes

Name each of the following molecules.

a.

$$\begin{array}{c} H \qquad CH_3 \\ \diagdown C{=}C \diagup \\ CH_3CH_2CH \quad\qquad H \\ \vert \\ CH_3 \end{array}$$

b. $CH_3CH_2C{\equiv}CCHCH_2CH_3$
        $\vert$
       CH_2
        $\vert$
       CH_3

A worker using an oxyacetylene torch.

Solution

a. The longest chain, which contains six carbon atoms, is numbered as follows:

$$\begin{array}{c} \qquad\qquad\quad 1 \\ H \quad_3 \quad_2 \quad CH_3 \\ \diagdown C{=}C \diagup \\ {}^{6}\;{}^{5}\;{}^{4} \\ CH_3CH_2CH \qquad H \\ \vert \\ CH_3 \end{array}$$

Thus the hydrocarbon is a 2-hexene. Since the hydrogen atoms are located on opposite sides of the double bond, this molecule corresponds to the *trans* isomer. The name is 4-methyl-*trans*-2-hexene.

b. The longest chain, consisting of seven carbon atoms, is numbered as shown (giving the triple bond the lowest possible number):

$$\begin{array}{c} 1 \quad 2 \quad 3 \quad 4\,5 \quad 6 \quad 7 \\ CH_3CH_2C{\equiv}CCHCH_2CH_3 \\ \vert \\ CH_2 \\ \vert \\ CH_3 \end{array}$$

The hydrocarbon is a 3-heptyne. The full name is 5-ethyl-3-heptyne, where the position of the triple bond is indicated by the lower-numbered carbon atom involved in this bond.

See Exercises 22.25 through 22.28 and 22.44.

Reactions of Alkenes and Alkynes

Because alkenes and alkynes are unsaturated, their most important reactions are **addition reactions.** In these reactions π bonds, which are weaker than the C—C σ bonds, are broken, and new σ bonds are formed to the atoms being added. For example, **hydrogenation reactions** involve the addition of hydrogen atoms:

$$CH_2{=}CHCH_3 + H_2 \xrightarrow{\text{Catalyst}} CH_3CH_2CH_3$$
$$\text{1-Propene} \qquad\qquad\qquad \text{Propane}$$

For this reaction to proceed rapidly at normal temperatures, a catalyst of platinum, palladium, or nickel is used. The catalyst serves to help break the relatively strong H—H bond, as was discussed in Section 12.8. Hydrogenation of alkenes is an important industrial process, particularly in the manufacture of solid shortenings where unsaturated fats (fats containing double bonds), which are generally liquid, are converted to solid saturated fats.

Halogenation of unsaturated hydrocarbons involves addition of halogen atoms. For example,

$$CH_2=CHCH_2CH_2CH_3 + Br_2 \longrightarrow CH_2BrCHBrCH_2CH_2CH_3$$

1-Pentene   1,2-Dibromopentane

Another important reaction involving certain unsaturated hydrocarbons is **polymerization,** a process in which many small molecules are joined together to form a large molecule. Polymerization will be discussed in Section 22.5.

22.3 Aromatic Hydrocarbons

A special class of cyclic unsaturated hydrocarbons is known as the **aromatic hydrocarbons.** The simplest of these is benzene (C_6H_6), which has a planar ring structure, as shown in Fig. 22.11(a). In the localized electron model of the bonding in benzene, resonance structures of the type shown in Fig. 22.11(b) are used to account for the known equivalence of all the carbon–carbon bonds. But as we discussed in Section 9.5, the best description of the benzene molecule assumes that sp^2 hybrid orbitals on each carbon are used to form the C—C and C—H σ bonds, while the remaining $2p$ orbital on each carbon is used to form π molecular orbitals. The delocalization of these π electrons is usually indicated by a circle inside the ring [Fig. 22.11(c)].

The delocalization of the π electrons makes the benzene ring behave quite differently from a typical unsaturated hydrocarbon. As we have seen previously, unsaturated hydrocarbons generally undergo rapid addition reactions. However, benzene does not. Instead, it undergoes substitution reactions in which *hydrogen atoms are replaced by other atoms.* For example,

Chlorobenzene

Nitrobenzene

Toluene

In each case the substance shown over the arrow is needed to catalyze these substitution reactions.

Substitution reactions are characteristic of saturated hydrocarbons, and addition reactions are characteristic of unsaturated ones. The fact that benzene reacts more like a saturated hydrocarbon indicates the great stability of the delocalized π electron system.

FIGURE 22.11
(a) The structure of benzene, a planar ring system in which all bond angles are 120°. (b) Two of the resonance structures of benzene. (c) The usual representation of benzene. The circle represents the electrons in the delocalized π system. All C—C bonds in benzene are equivalent.

The nomenclature of benzene derivatives is similar to the nomenclature for saturated ring systems. If there is more than one substituent present, numbers are used to indicate substituent positions. For example, the compound

is named 1,2-dichlorobenzene. Another nomenclature system uses the prefix *ortho-* (*o-*) for two adjacent substituents, *meta-* (*m-*) for two substituents with one carbon between them, and *para-* (*p-*) for two substituents opposite each other. When benzene is used as a substituent, it is called the **phenyl group.** Examples of some aromatic compounds are shown in Fig. 22.12.

Benzene is the simplest aromatic molecule. More complex aromatic systems can be viewed as consisting of a number of "fused" benzene rings. Some examples are given in Table 22.3.

1,2-Dibromobenzene
(*o*-dibromobenzene)

1,3-Dibromobenzene
(*m*-dibromobenzene)

1,4-Dibromobenzene
(*p*-dibromobenzene)

Methylbenzene
(toluene)

3-Bromonitrobenzene
(*m*-bromonitrobenzene)

3-Chlorotoluene
(*m*-chlorotoluene)

$CH_3CHCH_2CHCH_2CH_3$

Phenyl group

4-Chloro-2-phenylhexane

FIGURE 22.12
Some selected substituted benzenes and their names. Common names are given in parentheses.

TABLE 22.3   More Complex Aromatic Systems

Structural Formula	Name	Use of Effect
	Naphthalene	Formerly used in mothballs
	Anthracene	Dyes
	Phenanthrene	Dyes, explosives, and synthesis of drugs
	3,4-Benzpyrene	Active carcinogen found in smoke and smog

22.4 Hydrocarbon Derivatives

The vast majority of organic molecules contain elements in addition to carbon and hydrogen. However, most of these substances can be viewed as **hydrocarbon derivatives,** molecules that are fundamentally hydrocarbons but that have additional atoms or groups of atoms called **functional groups.** The common functional groups are listed in Table 22.4. Because each functional group exhibits characteristic chemistry, we will consider the groups separately.

Alcohols

$R-CH_2OH$

Primary alcohol
(one R group)

Secondary alcohol
(two R groups)

Tertiary alcohol
(three R groups)

Alcohols are characterized by the presence of the hydroxyl group (—OH). Some common alcohols are shown in Table 22.5. The systematic name for an alcohol is obtained by replacing the final -*e* of the parent hydrocarbon with -*ol*. The position of the —OH group is specified by a number (where necessary) chosen so that it is the smallest of the substituent numbers. Alcohols are classified according to the number of hydrocarbon fragments bonded to the carbon where the —OH group is attached (see margin), where R, R′, and R″ (which may be the same or different) represent hydrocarbon fragments.

Alcohols usually have much higher boiling points than might be expected from their molar masses. For example, both methanol and ethane have a molar mass of 30, but the boiling point for methanol is 65°C while that for ethane is −89°C. This difference can be understood if we consider the types of intermolecular attractions that occur in these liquids. Ethane molecules are nonpolar and exhibit only weak London dispersion interactions. However, the polar —OH group of methanol produces extensive hydrogen bonding similar to that found in water (see Section 10.1), which results in the relatively high boiling point.

Although there are many important alcohols, the simplest ones, methanol and ethanol, have the greatest commercial value. Methanol, also known as *wood alcohol* because it was formerly obtained by heating wood in the absence of air, is prepared industrially

TABLE 22.4   The Common Functional Groups

Class	Functional Group	General Formula*	Example
Halohydrocarbons	—X (F, Cl, Br, I)	R—X	CH_3I Iodomethane (methyl iodide)
Alcohols	—OH	R—OH	CH_3OH Methanol (methyl alcohol)
Ethers	—O—	R—O—R′	CH_3OCH_3 Dimethyl ether
Aldehydes	$\overset{\displaystyle O}{\overset{\displaystyle \|}{-C-H}}$	$\overset{\displaystyle O}{\overset{\displaystyle \|}{R-C-H}}$	CH_2O Methanal (formaldehyde)
Ketones	$\overset{\displaystyle O}{\overset{\displaystyle \|}{-C-}}$	$\overset{\displaystyle O}{\overset{\displaystyle \|}{R-C-R'}}$	CH_3COCH_3 Propanone (dimethyl ketone or acetone)
Carboxylic acids	$\overset{\displaystyle O}{\overset{\displaystyle \|}{-C-OH}}$	$\overset{\displaystyle O}{\overset{\displaystyle \|}{R-C-OH}}$	CH_3COOH Ethanoic acid (acetic acid)
Esters	$\overset{\displaystyle O}{\overset{\displaystyle \|}{-C-O-}}$	$\overset{\displaystyle O}{\overset{\displaystyle \|}{R-C-O-R'}}$	$CH_3COOCH_2CH_3$ Ethyl acetate
Amines	—NH₂	R—NH₂	CH_3NH_2 Aminomethane (methylamine)

*R and R′ represent hydrocarbon fragments.

(approximately 4 million tons annually in the United States) by the hydrogenation of carbon monoxide:

$$CO + 2H_2 \xrightarrow[\text{ZnO/Cr}_2\text{O}_3]{400°C} CH_3OH$$

Methanol is used as a starting material for the synthesis of acetic acid and for many types of adhesives, fibers, and plastics. It is also used (and such use may increase) as a motor fuel. Methanol is highly toxic to humans and can lead to blindness and death if ingested.

Ethanol is the alcohol found in beverages such as beer, wine, and whiskey; it is produced by the fermentation of glucose in corn, barley, grapes, and so on:

$$\underset{\text{Glucose}}{C_6H_{12}O_6} \xrightarrow{\text{Yeast}} \underset{\text{Ethanol}}{2CH_3CH_2OH} + 2CO_2$$

A winemaker drawing off a glass of wine in a modern wine cellar.

TABLE 22.5   Some Common Alcohols

Formula	Systematic Name	Common Name
CH_3OH	Methanol	Methyl alcohol
CH_3CH_2OH	Ethanol	Ethyl alcohol
$CH_3CH_2CH_2OH$	1-Propanol	n-Propyl alcohol
$CH_3\underset{OH}{CHCH_3}$	2-Propanol	Isopropyl alcohol

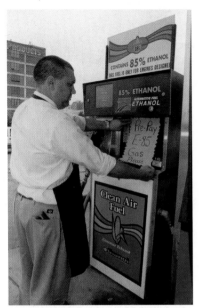

Ethanol is being tested in selected areas as a fuel for automobiles.

The reaction is catalyzed by the enzymes found in yeast. This reaction can proceed only until the alcohol content reaches about 13% (the percentage found in most wines), at which point the yeast can no longer survive. Beverages with higher alcohol content are made by distilling the fermentation mixture.

Ethanol, like methanol, can be burned in the internal combustion engines of automobiles and is now commonly added to gasoline to form gasohol (see Section 6.6). It is also used in industry as a solvent and for the preparation of acetic acid. The commercial production of ethanol (500,000 tons per year in the United States) is carried out by reaction of water with ethylene:

$$CH_2{=}CH_2 + H_2O \xrightarrow[\text{Catalyst}]{\text{Acid}} CH_3CH_2OH$$

Many polyhydroxyl (more than one —OH group) alcohols are known, the most important being *1,2-ethanediol* (ethylene glycol),

$$\begin{array}{c} H_2C{-}OH \\ | \\ H_2C{-}OH \end{array}$$

a toxic substance that is the major constituent of most automobile antifreeze solutions.

The simplest aromatic alcohol is

which is commonly called **phenol.** Most of the 1 million tons of phenol produced annually in the United States is used to make polymers for adhesives and plastics.

Sample Exercise 22.6

Naming and Classifying Alcohols

For each of the following alcohols, give the systematic name and specify whether the alcohol is primary, secondary, or tertiary.

a. CH₃CHCH₂CH₃
　　　|
　　　OH

b. ClCH₂CH₂CH₂OH

c.
　　　CH₃
　　　|
　　CH₃CCH₂CH₂CH₂CH₂Br
　　　|
　　　OH

Solution

a. The chain is numbered as follows:

$$\overset{1}{C}H_3\overset{2}{C}H\overset{3}{C}H_2\overset{4}{C}H_3$$
　　　　|
　　　　OH

The compound is called 2-butanol, since the —OH group is located at the number 2 position of a four-carbon chain. Note that the carbon to which the —OH is attached also has —CH₃ and —CH₂CH₃ groups attached:

$$\begin{array}{c} H \\ | \\ CH_3{-}C{-}CH_2CH_3 \\ | \\ OH \end{array}$$

R　　　　　　R′

Therefore, this is a *secondary* alcohol.

b. The chain is numbered as follows:

$$\overset{3}{Cl}-\overset{2}{CH_2}-\overset{1}{CH_2}-CH_2-OH$$

The name is 3-chloro-1-propanol. This is a *primary* alcohol:

$$
\overset{\displaystyle H}{\underset{\displaystyle H}{\overline{Cl-CH_2CH_2}\big)\!-\!C\!-\!OH}}
$$

One R group attached to the carbon with the —OH group

c. The chain is numbered as follows:

$$
CH_3-\overset{\overset{\displaystyle CH_3}{|}}{\underset{\underset{\displaystyle OH}{|}}{C}}\!\big(\!CH_2-CH_2-CH_2-CH_2Br\!\big)
$$

The name is 6-bromo-2-methyl-2-hexanol. This is a *tertiary* alcohol since the carbon where the —OH is attached also has three other R groups attached.

See Exercises 22.51 and 22.52.

Aldehydes and Ketones

Aldehydes and ketones contain the **carbonyl group,**

$$\diagdown C = O$$

In **ketones** this group is bonded to two carbon atoms, as in acetone,

$$CH_3-\overset{\|}{\underset{\displaystyle O}{C}}-CH_3$$

In **aldehydes** the carbonyl group is bonded to at least one hydrogen atom, as in formaldehyde,

$$H-\overset{\|}{\underset{\displaystyle O}{C}}-H$$

Cinnamaldehyde produces the characteristic odor of cinnamon.

or acetaldehyde,

$$CH_3-\overset{\|}{\underset{\displaystyle O}{C}}-H$$

The systematic name for an aldehyde is obtained from the parent alkane by removing the final -*e* and adding -*al.* For ketones the final -*e* is replaced by -*one,* and a number indicates the position of the carbonyl group where necessary. Examples of common aldehydes and ketones are shown in Fig. 22.13. Note that since the aldehyde functional group always occurs at the end of the carbon chain, the aldehyde carbon is assigned the number 1 when substituent positions are listed in the name.

Ketones often have useful solvent properties (acetone is found in nail polish remover, for example) and are frequently used in industry for this purpose. Aldehydes typically have strong odors. Vanillin is responsible for the pleasant odor in vanilla beans; cinnamaldehyde

Vanillin

Cinnamaldehyde

$CH_3CH_2CH_2C\overset{O}{\underset{H}{}}$

Butyraldehyde

Methanal
(formaldehyde)

Ethanal
(acetaldehyde)

2-Propanone
(acetone)

2-Pentanone

3-Chlorobutanal

Benzaldehyde

2-Butanone
(methyl ethyl ketone,
or MEK)

Methyl phenyl
ketone

FIGURE 22.13
Some common ketones and aldehydes. Note that since the aldehyde functional group always appears at the end of a carbon chain, carbon is assigned the number 1 when the compound is named.

produces the characteristic odor of cinnamon. On the other hand, the unpleasant odor in rancid butter arises from the presence of butyraldehyde.

Aldehydes and ketones are most often produced commercially by the oxidation of alcohols. For example, oxidation of a *primary* alcohol yields the corresponding aldehyde:

$$CH_3CH_2OH \xrightarrow{\text{Oxidation}} CH_3C\overset{O}{\underset{H}{}}$$

Oxidation of a *secondary* alcohol results in a ketone:

$$\underset{\underset{OH}{|}}{CH_3CHCH_3} \xrightarrow{\text{Oxidation}} \underset{\underset{O}{\|}}{CH_3CCH_3}$$

Carboxylic Acids and Esters

Carboxylic acids are characterized by the presence of the **carboxyl group**

$$-C\overset{O}{\underset{O-H}{}}$$

that gives an acid of the general formula RCOOH. Typically, these molecules are weak acids in aqueous solution (see Section 14.5). Organic acids are named from the parent alkane by dropping the final -*e* and adding -*oic*. Thus CH_3COOH, commonly called acetic acid, has the systematic name ethanoic acid, since the parent alkane is ethane. Other examples of carboxylic acids are shown in Fig. 22.14.

Many carboxylic acids are synthesized by oxidizing primary alcohols with a strong oxidizing agent. For example, ethanol can be oxidized to acetic acid by using potassium permanganate:

$$CH_3CH_2OH \xrightarrow{KMnO_4(aq)} CH_3COOH$$

$CH_3CH_2CH_2COOH$

Butanoic acid

COOH

Benzoic acid

$\underset{\underset{Br}{|}}{CH_3CHCH_2CH_2COOH}$

4-Bromopentanoic acid

$Cl-\overset{\overset{Cl}{|}}{\underset{\underset{Cl}{|}}{C}}-COOH$

Trichloroethanoic acid
(trichloroacetic acid)

FIGURE 22.14
Some carboxylic acids.

A carboxylic acid reacts with an alcohol to form an **ester** and a water molecule. For example, the reaction of acetic acid with ethanol produces ethyl acetate and water:

$$CH_3\overset{\overset{\displaystyle O}{\|}}{C}\boxed{-OH \qquad H}-OCH_2CH_3 \longrightarrow CH_3\overset{\overset{\displaystyle O}{\|}}{C}-OCH_2CH_3 + H_2O$$

React to
form water

Esters often have a sweet, fruity odor that is in contrast to the often pungent odors of the parent carboxylic acids. For example, the odor of bananas is caused by *n*-amyl acetate,

$$CH_3C\overset{\displaystyle O}{\underset{\displaystyle OCH_2CH_2CH_2CH_2CH_3}{\diagup}}$$

and that of oranges is caused by *n*-octyl acetate,

$$CH_3\underset{\underset{\displaystyle O}{\|}}{C}-OC_8H_{17}$$

The systematic name for an ester is formed by changing the *-oic* ending of the parent acid to *-oate*. The parent alcohol chain is named first with a *-yl* ending. For example, the systematic name for *n*-octyl acetate is *n*-octylethanoate (from ethanoic acid).

A very important ester is formed from the reaction of salicylic acid and acetic acid:

Salicylic acid   Acetic acid   Acetylsalicylic acid

The product is acetylsalicylic acid, commonly known as *aspirin,* which is used in huge quantities as an analgesic (painkiller).

Amines

Amines are probably best viewed as derivatives of ammonia in which one or more N—H bonds are replaced by N—C bonds. The resulting amines are classified as *primary* if one N—C bond is present, *secondary* if two N—C bonds are present, and *tertiary* if all three N—H bonds in NH_3 have been replaced by N—C bonds (Fig. 22.15). Examples of some common amines are given in Table 22.6.

Common names are often used for simple amines; the systematic nomenclature for more complex molecules uses the name *amino-* for the —NH_2 functional group. For example, the molecule

$$CH_3\underset{\underset{\displaystyle NH_2}{|}}{C}HCH_2CH_3$$

is named 2-aminobutane.

Many amines have unpleasant "fishlike" odors. For example, the odors associated with decaying animal and human tissues are caused by amines such as putrescine ($H_2NCH_2CH_2CH_2NH_2$) and cadaverine ($H_2NCH_2CH_2CH_2CH_2CH_2NH_2$).

Aromatic amines are primarily used to make dyes. Since many of them are carcinogenic, they must be handled with great care.

Aspirin tablets.

Computer-generated space-filling model of acetylsalicylic acid (aspirin).

FIGURE 22.15
The general formulas for primary, secondary, and tertiary amines. R, R′, and R″ represent carbon-containing substituents.

Primary amine

Secondary amine

Tertiary amine

TABLE 22.6   Some Common Amines

Formula	Common Name	Type
CH_3NH_2	Methylamine	Primary
$CH_3CH_2NH_2$	Ethylamine	Primary
$(CH_3)_2NH$	Dimethylamine	Secondary
$(CH_3)_3N$	Trimethylamine	Tertiary
NH_2 (aniline structure)	Aniline	Primary
Diphenylamine structure	Diphenylamine	Secondary

22.5 Polymers

Polymers are large, usually chainlike molecules that are built from small molecules called *monomers*. Polymers form the basis for synthetic fibers, rubbers, and plastics and have played a leading role in the revolution that has been brought about in daily life by chemistry. It has been estimated that about 50% of the industrial chemists in the United States work in some area of polymer chemistry, a fact that illustrates just how important polymers are to our economy and standard of living.

The Development and Properties of Polymers

The development of the polymer industry provides a striking example of the importance of serendipity in the progress of science. Many discoveries in polymer chemistry arose from accidental observations that scientists followed up.

The age of plastics might be traced to a day in 1846 when Christian Schoenbein, a chemistry professor at the University of Basel in Switzerland, spilled a flask containing nitric and sulfuric acids. In his hurry to clean up the spill, he grabbed his wife's cotton apron, which he then rinsed out and hung up in front of a hot stove to dry. Instead of drying, the apron flared and burned.

Very interested in this event, Schoenbein repeated the reaction under more controlled conditions and found that the new material, which he correctly concluded to be nitrated cellulose, had some surprising properties. As he had experienced, the nitrated cellulose is extremely flammable and, under certain circumstances, highly explosive. In addition, he found that it could be molded at moderate temperatures to give objects that were, upon cooling, tough but elastic. Predictably, the explosive nature of the substance was initially of more interest than its other properties, and cellulose nitrate rapidly became the basis for smokeless gun powder. Although Schoenbein's discovery cannot be described as a truly synthetic polymer (because he simply found a way to modify the natural polymer cellulose), it formed the basis for a large number of industries that grew up to produce photographic films, artificial fibers, and molded objects of all types.

The first synthetic polymers were produced as by-products of various organic reactions and were regarded as unwanted contaminants. Thus the first preparations of many of the polymers now regarded as essential to our modern lifestyle were thrown away in

The soybeans on the left are coated with a red acrylic polymer to delay soybean emergence. This allows farmers to plant their crops more efficiently.

A radio from the 1930s made of Bakelite.

Nylon netting magnified 62 times.

disgust. One chemist who refused to be defeated by the "tarry" products obtained when he reacted phenol with formaldehyde was the Belgian-American chemist Leo H. Baekeland (1863–1944). Baekeland's work resulted in the first completely synthetic plastic (called Bakelite), a substance that when molded to a certain shape under high pressure and temperature cannot be softened again or dissolved. Bakelite is a **thermoset polymer.** In contrast, cellulose nitrate is a **thermoplastic polymer;** that is, it can be remelted after it has been molded.

The discovery of Bakelite in 1907 spawned a large plastics industry, producing telephones, billiard balls, and insulators for electrical devices. During the early days of polymer chemistry, there was a great deal of controversy over the nature of these materials. Although the German chemist Hermann Staudinger speculated in 1920 that polymers were very large molecules held together by strong chemical bonds, most chemists of the time assumed that these materials were much like colloids, in which small molecules are aggregated into large units by forces weaker than chemical bonds.

One chemist who contributed greatly to the understanding of polymers as giant molecules was Wallace H. Carothers of the DuPont Chemical Company. Among his accomplishments was the preparation of nylon. The nylon story further illustrates the importance of serendipity in scientific research. When nylon is first prepared, the resulting product is a sticky material with little structural integrity. Because of this, it was initially put aside as having no apparently useful characteristics. However, Julian Hill, a chemist in the Carothers research group, one day put a small ball of this nylon on the end of a stirring rod and drew it away from the remaining sticky mass, forming a string. He noticed the silky appearance and strength of this thread and realized that nylon could be drawn into useful fibers.

The reason for this behavior of nylon is now understood. When nylon is first formed, the individual polymer chains are oriented randomly, like cooked spaghetti, and the substance is highly amorphous. However, when drawn out into a thread, the chains tend to line up (the nylon becomes more crystalline), which leads to increased hydrogen bonding between adjacent chains. This increase in crystallinity, along with the resulting increase in hydrogen-bonding interactions, leads to strong fibers and thus to a highly useful material. Commercially, nylon is produced by forcing the raw material through a *spinneret,* a plate containing small holes, which forces the polymer chains to line up.

Another property that adds strength to polymers is **crosslinking,** the existence of covalent bonds between adjacent chains. The structure of Bakelite is highly crosslinked, which accounts for the strength and toughness of this polymer. Another example of crosslinking occurs in the manufacture of rubber. Raw natural rubber consists of chains of the type

$$\sim\!\!\sim\!\!\sim\!\!CH_2\!-\!CH_2\!-\!CH\!=\!C\!-\!CH_2\!-\!CH_2\!-\!CH\!=\!C\!-\!CH_2\!\sim\!\!\sim\!\!\sim$$
$$\underset{CH_3}{|}\qquad\qquad\underset{CH_3}{|}$$

Charles Goodyear tried for many years to change natural rubber into a useful product. In 1839 he accidentally dropped some rubber containing sulfur on a hot stove. Noting that the rubber did not melt as expected, Goodyear pursued this lead and developed vulcanization.

and is a soft, sticky material unsuitable for tires. However, in 1839 Charles Goodyear (1800–1860), an American chemist, accidentally found that if sulfur is added to rubber and the resulting mixture is heated (a process called **vulcanization**), the resulting rubber is still elastic (reversibly stretchable) but is much stronger. This change in character occurs because sulfur atoms become bonded between carbon atoms on different chains. These sulfur atoms form bridges between the polymer chains, thus linking the chains together.

Types of Polymers

The simplest and one of the best-known polymers is *polyethylene,* which is constructed from ethylene monomers:

$$n CH_2\!=\!CH_2 \xrightarrow{\text{Catalyst}} \left(\!\!\begin{array}{cc} \underset{H}{\overset{H}{|}} & \underset{H}{\overset{H}{|}} \\ C\!-\!C \\ \underset{H}{\overset{|}{}} & \underset{H}{\overset{|}{}} \end{array}\!\!\right)_{\!n}$$

CHEMICAL IMPACT

Heal Thyself

One major problem with structural materials is that they crack and weaken as they age. The human body has mechanisms for healing itself if the skin is cut or a bone is broken. However, inanimate materials have had no such mechanisms—until now. Scientists at the University of Illinois at Urbana–Champaign (UIUC) have invented a plastic that automatically heals microscopic cracks before they can develop into large cracks that would degrade the usefulness of the material. This accomplishment was achieved by an interdisciplinary team of scientists including aeronautical engineering professors Scott White and Philippe Geubelle, applied mechanics professor Nancy Sottos, and chemistry professor Jeffrey Moore.

The self-healing system is based on microcapsules containing liquid dicyclopentadiene

Dicyclopentadiene

that are blended into the plastic. When a microscopic crack develops, it encounters and breaks a microcapsule. The dicyclopentadiene then leaks out, where it encounters a catalyst (blended into the plastic when it was formulated) that mediates a repair polymerization process. This process involves opening the cyclopentadiene rings, which leads to a highly cross-linked repair of the crack.

The trickiest part of the repair mechanism is to get the microcapsules to be the correct size and to have the appropriate wall strength. They must be small enough not to degrade the strength of the plastic. The walls must also be thick enough to survive the molding of the plastic but thin enough to burst as the lengthening crack reaches them.

Self-healing materials should have many applications. The U.S. Air Force, which partially funded the research at UIUC, is interested in using the materials in tanks that hold gases and liquids under pressure. The current materials used for these tanks are subject to microcracks that eventually grow, causing the tanks to leak. Self-healing materials would

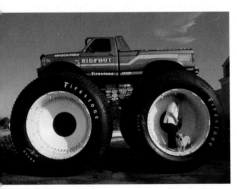

Cross-linking gives the rubber in these tires strength and toughness.

where n represents a large number (usually several thousand). Polyethylene is a tough, flexible plastic used for piping, bottles, electrical insulation, packaging films, garbage bags, and many other purposes. Its properties can be varied by using substituted ethylene monomers. For example, when tetrafluoroethylene is the monomer, the polymer Teflon is obtained:

$$n \begin{pmatrix} F \\ | \\ C \\ | \\ F \end{pmatrix} = \begin{pmatrix} F \\ | \\ C \\ | \\ F \end{pmatrix} \longrightarrow \begin{pmatrix} F & F \\ | & | \\ C - C \\ | & | \\ F & F \end{pmatrix}_n$$

Tetrafluoroethylene   Teflon

The discovery of Teflon, a very important substituted polyethylene, is another illustration of the role of chance in chemical research. In 1938 a DuPont chemist named Roy Plunkett was studying the chemistry of gaseous tetrafluoroethylene. He synthesized about 100 pounds of the chemical and stored it in steel cylinders. When one of the cylinders failed to produce perfluoroethylene gas when the valve was opened, the cylinder was cut open to reveal a white powder. This powder turned out to be a polymer of perfluoroethylene, which was eventually developed into Teflon. Because of the resistance of the strong C—F bonds to chemical attack, Teflon is an inert, tough, and nonflammable material widely used for electrical insulation, nonstick coatings on cooking utensils, and bearings for low-temperature applications.

Other polyethylene-type polymers are made from monomers containing chloro, methyl, cyano, and phenyl substituents, as summarized in Table 22.7 on page 1020. In each case the double carbon–carbon bond in the substituted ethylene monomer becomes a single bond in the polymer. The different substituents lead to a wide variety of properties.

also be valuable in situations where repair is impossible or impractical, such as
electronic circuit boards, components of
deep space probes, and implanted medical devices.

A scanning electron microscope image showing the fractured plane of a self-healing material
with a ruptured microcapsule in a thermosetting matrix.

The polyethylene polymers illustrate one of the major types of polymerization reactions, called **addition polymerization,** in which the monomers simply "add together" to
produce the polymer. No other products are formed. The polymerization process is initiated by a **free radical** (a species with an unpaired electron) such as the hydroxyl radical
(HO·). The free radical attacks and breaks the π bond of an ethylene molecule to form a
new free radical,

which is then available to attack another ethylene molecule:

Repetition of this process thousands of times creates a long-chain polymer. Termination
of the growth of the chain occurs when *two radicals* react to form a bond, a process that
consumes two radicals without producing any others.

TABLE 22.7   Some Common Synthetic Polymers, Their Monomers and Applications

Monomer		Polymer		
Name	*Formula*	*Name*	*Formula*	*Uses*
Ethylene	$H_2C{=}CH_2$	Polyethylene	$-(CH_2-CH_2)_n-$	Plastic piping, bottles, electrical insulation, toys
Propylene	$H_2C{=}C$ with H above and CH_3 below	Polypropylene	$-(CH-CH_2-CH-CH_2)_n-$ with CH_3 groups	Film for packaging, carpets, lab wares, toys
Vinyl chloride	$H_2C{=}C$ with H above and Cl below	Polyvinyl chloride (PVC)	$-(CH_2-CH)_n-$ with Cl	Piping, siding, floor tile, clothing, toys
Acrylonitrile	$H_2C{=}C$ with H above and CN below	Polyacrylonitrile (PAN)	$-(CH_2-CH)_n-$ with CN	Carpets, fabrics
Tetrafluoro ethylene	$F_2C{=}CF_2$	Teflon	$-(CF_2-CF_2)_n-$	Cooking utensils, electrical insulation, bearings
Styrene	$H_2C{=}C$ with H and phenyl group	Polystyrene	$-(CH_2CH)_n-$ with phenyl group	Containers, thermal insulation, toys
Butadiene	$H_2C{=}C-C{=}CH_2$ with H, H	Polybutadiene	$-(CH_2CH{=}CHCH_2)_n-$	Tire tread, coating resin
Butadiene and styrene	(See above.)	Styrene-butadiene rubber	$-(CH-CH_2-CH_2-CH{=}CH-CH_2)_n-$ with phenyl group	Synthetic rubber

Visualization: Synthesis of Nylon

Another common type of polymerization is **condensation polymerization,** in which a small molecule, such as water, is formed for each extension of the polymer chain. The most familiar polymer produced by condensation is *nylon*. Nylon is a **copolymer,** since two different types of monomers combine to form the chain; a **homopolymer** is the result of polymerizing a single type of monomer. One common form of nylon is produced when hexamethylenediamine and adipic acid react by splitting out a water molecule to form a C—N bond:

$$\underset{\text{Hexamethylenediamine}}{\overset{H}{\underset{H}{N}}-(CH_2)_6-\overset{H}{\underset{(H}{N}} \quad \underset{\text{Adipic acid}}{H-O)\overset{O}{C}-(CH_2)_4\overset{O}{C}-O-H} \longrightarrow$$

$$\overset{H}{\underset{H}{N}}-(CH_2)_6-\overset{H}{N}-\overset{O}{C}-(CH_2)_4\overset{O}{C}-O-H \quad + H_2O$$

The molecule formed, called a **dimer** (two monomers joined), can undergo further condensation reactions since it has an amino group at one end and a carboxyl group at the other. Thus both ends are free to react with another monomer. Repetition of this process leads to a long chain of the type

$$\left(\begin{array}{c} H \\ | \\ N-(CH_2)_6 \end{array} \begin{array}{c} H \ \ O \\ |\ \ \ || \\ N-C-(CH_2)_4 \end{array} \begin{array}{c} O \\ || \\ C \end{array}\right)_n$$

which is the basic structure of nylon. The reaction to form nylon occurs quite readily and is often used as a lecture demonstration (see Fig. 22.16). The properties of nylon can be varied by changing the number of carbon atoms in the chain of the acid or amine monomer.

More than 1 million tons of nylon is produced annually in the United States for use in clothing, carpets, rope, and so on. Many other types of condensation polymers are also produced. For example, Dacron is a copolymer formed from the condensation reaction of ethylene glycol (a dialcohol) and *p*-terephthalic acid (a dicarboxylic acid):

FIGURE 22.16
The reaction to form nylon can be carried out at the interface of two immiscible liquid layers in a beaker. The bottom layer contains adipoyl chloride,

$$Cl-\overset{O}{\underset{||}{C}}-(CH_2)_4-\overset{O}{\underset{||}{C}}-Cl$$

dissolved in CCl_4, and the top layer contains hexamethylenediamine,

$$H_2N-(CH_2)_6-NH_2$$

dissolved in water. A molecule of HCl is formed as each C—N bond forms.

$$HOCH_2CH_2O-\boxed{H\quad\quad HO} \qquad O-H$$

Ethylene glycol
H_2O
p-Terephthalic acid

The repeating unit of Dacron is

$$\left(\begin{array}{c} O \qquad\qquad O \\ || \qquad\qquad || \\ OCH_2CH_2-O-C-\bigcirc-C \end{array}\right)_n$$

Note that this polymerization involves a carboxylic acid and an alcohol forming an ester group:

$$R-O-\overset{O}{\underset{||}{C}}-R_1$$

Thus Dacron is called a **polyester.** By itself or blended with cotton, Dacron is widely used in fibers for the manufacture of clothing.

Polymers Based on Ethylene

A large section of the polymer industry involves the production of macromolecules from ethylene or substituted ethylenes. As discussed previously, ethylene molecules polymerize by addition after the double bond has been broken by some initiator:

$$X-\overset{H}{\underset{H}{C}}-\overset{H}{\underset{H}{C}}\cdot \quad \overset{H}{\underset{H}{C}}=\overset{H}{\underset{H}{C}} \longrightarrow X-\overset{H}{\underset{H}{C}}-\overset{H}{\underset{H}{C}}-\overset{H}{\underset{H}{C}}-\overset{H}{\underset{H}{C}}\cdot$$

This process continues by adding new ethylene molecules to eventually give polyethylene, a thermoplastic material.

There are two forms of polyethylene: low-density polyethylene (LDPE) and high-density polyethylene (HDPE). The chains in LDPE contain many branches and thus do not pack as tightly as those in HDPE, which consist of mostly straight-chain molecules.

Traditionally, LDPE has been manufactured under conditions of high pressure ($\approx$20,000 psi) and high temperature (500°C). These severe reaction conditions require specially designed equipment, and for safety reasons the reaction usually has been run behind a reinforced concrete barrier. More recently, lower reaction pressures and

psi is the abbreviation for pounds per square inch: 15 psi $\approx$ 1 atm.

CHEMICAL IMPACT

Wallace Hume Carothers

Wallace H. Carothers. a brilliant organic chemist who was principally responsible for the development of nylon and the first synthetic rubber (Neoprene), was born in 1896 in Burlington, Iowa. As a youth, Carothers was fascinated by tools and mechanical devices and spent many hours experimenting. In 1915 he entered Tarkio College in Missouri. Carothers so excelled in chemistry that even before his graduation, he was made a chemistry instructor.

Carothers eventually moved to the University of Illinois at Urbana–Champaign, where he was appointed to the faculty when he completed his Ph.D. in organic chemistry in 1924. He moved to Harvard University in 1926, and then to DuPont in 1928 to participate in a new program in fundamental research. At DuPont, Carothers headed the organic chemistry division, and during his ten years there played a prominent role in laying the foundations of polymer chemistry.

By the age of 33, Carothers had become a world-famous chemist whose advice was sought by almost everyone working in polymers. He was the first industrial chemist to be elected to the prestigious National Academy of Sciences.

Carothers was an avid reader of poetry and a lover of classical music. Unfortunately, he also suffered from severe bouts of depression that finally led to his suicide in 1937 in a Philadelphia hotel room, where he drank a cyanide

Wallace H. Carothers.

solution. He was 41 years old. Despite the brevity of his career, Carothers was truly one of the finest American chemists of all time. His great intellect, his love of chemistry, and his insistence on perfection produced his special genius.

---

temperatures have become possible through the use of catalysts. One catalytic system using triethylaluminum, $Al(C_2H_5)_3$, and titanium(IV) chloride was developed by Karl Ziegler in Germany and Giulio Natta in Italy. Although this catalyst is very efficient, it catches fire on contact with air and must be handled very carefully. A safer catalytic system was developed at Phillips Petroleum Company. It uses a chromium(III) oxide (Cr_2O_3) and aluminosilicate catalyst and has mainly taken over in the United States. The product of the catalyzed reaction is highly linear (unbranched) and is often called *linear low-density polyethylene.* It is very similar to HDPE.

The major use of LDPE is in the manufacture of the tough transparent film that is used in packaging so many consumer goods. Two-thirds of the approximately 10 billion pounds of LDPE produced annually in the United States are used for this purpose. The major use of HDPE is for blow-molded products, such as bottles for consumer products (see Fig. 22.17).

The useful properties of polyethylene are due primarily to its high molecular weight (molar mass). Although the strengths of the interactions between specific points on the nonpolar chains are quite small, the chains are so long that these small attractions accumulate to a very significant value, so that the chains stick together very tenaciously. There is also a great deal of physical tangling of the lengthy chains. The combination of these interactions gives the polymer strength and toughness. However, a material like polyethylene can be melted and formed into a new shape (thermoplastic behavior), because in the melted state the molecules can readily flow past one another.

Molecular weight (not molar mass) is the common terminology in the polymer industry.

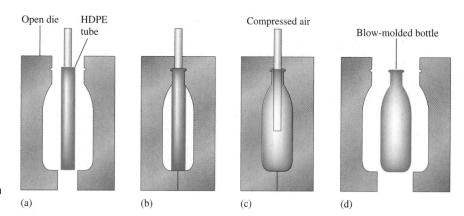

FIGURE 22.17
A major use of HDPE is for blow-molded objects such as bottles for soft drinks, shampoos, bleaches, and so on. (a) A tube composed of HDPE is inserted into the mold (die). (b) The die closes, sealing the bottom of the tube. (c) Compressed air is forced into the warm HDPE tube, which then expands to take the shape of the die. (d) The molded bottle is removed from the die.

Since a high molecular weight gives a polymer useful properties, one might think that the goal would be to produce polymers with chains as long as possible. However, this is not the case—polymers become much more difficult to process as the molecular weights increase. Most industrial operations require that the polymer flow through pipes as it is processed. But as the chain lengths increase, viscosity also increases. In practice, the upper limit of a polymer's molecular weight is set by the flow requirements of the manufacturing process. Thus the final product often reflects a compromise between the optimal properties for the application and those needed for ease of processing.

Although many polymer properties are greatly influenced by molecular weight, some other important properties are not. For example, chain length does not affect a polymer's resistance to chemical attack. Physical properties such as color, refractive index, hardness, density, and electrical conductivity are also not greatly influenced by molecular weight.

We have already seen that one way of altering the strength of a polymeric materials is to vary the chain length. Another method for modifying polymer behavior involves varying the substituents. For example, if we use a monomer of the type

$$\underset{H}{\overset{H}{\underset{|}{}}}C=C\underset{X}{\overset{H}{}}$$

the properties of the resulting polymer depend on the identity of X. The simplest example is polypropylene, whose monomer is

$$\underset{H}{\overset{H}{}}C=C\underset{CH_3}{\overset{H}{}}$$

and that has the form

The CH₃ groups can be arranged on the same side of the chain (called an **isotactic chain**) as shown above, can alternate (called a **syndiotactic chain**) as shown below,

or can be randomly distributed (called an **atactic chain**).

CHEMICAL IMPACT

Plastic That Talks and Listens

Imagine a plastic so "smart" that it can be used to sense a baby's breath, measure the force of a karate punch, sense the presence of a person 100 feet away, or make a balloon that sings. There is a plastic film capable of doing all these things. It's called polyvinylidene difluoride (PVDF), which has the structure

$$
\begin{array}{c}
\text{F} \quad\quad \text{F} \quad\quad \text{F} \quad\quad \text{F} \\
\text{\textasciitilde C — C — C — C\textasciitilde} \\
\text{H} \quad\quad \text{H} \quad\quad \text{H} \quad\quad \text{H}
\end{array}
$$

When this polymer is processed in a particular way, it becomes piezoelectric and pyroelectric. A piezoelectric substance produces an electric current when it is physically deformed or alternatively undergoes a deformation caused by the application of a current. A pyroelectric material is one that develops an electrical potential in response to a change in its temperature.

Because PVDF is piezoelectric, it can be used to construct a paper-thin microphone; it responds to sound by producing a current proportional to the deformation caused by the sound waves. A ribbon of PVDF plastic one-quarter of

an inch wide could be strung along a hallway and used to listen to all the conversations going on as people walk through. On the other hand, electric pulses can be applied to the PVDF film to produce a speaker. A strip of PVDF film glued to the inside of a balloon can play any song stored on a microchip attached to the film—hence a balloon that can sing "Happy Birthday" at a party. The PVDF film can also be used to construct a sleep apnea monitor, which, when placed beside the mouth of a sleeping infant, will set off an alarm if the breathing stops, thus helping to prevent sudden infant death syndrome (SIDS). The same type of film is used by the U.S. Olympic karate team to measure the force of kicks and punches as the team trains. Also, gluing two strips of film together gives a material that curls in response to a current, creating an artificial muscle. In addition, because the PVDF film is pyroelectric, it responds to the infrared (heat) radiation emitted by a human as far away as 100 feet, making it useful for burglar alarm systems.

Making the PVDF polymer piezoelectric and pyroelectric requires some very special processing, which makes it costly ($10 per square foot). This expense seems a small price to pay for its near-magical properties.

The chain arrangement has a significant effect on the polymer's properties. Most polypropylene is made using the Ziegler–Natta catalyst, $Al(C_2H_5)_3 \cdot TiCl_4$, which produces highly isotactic chains that pack together quite closely. As a result, polypropylene is more crystalline, and therefore stronger and harder, than polyethylene. The major uses of polypropylene are for molded parts (40%), fibers (35%), and packaging films (10%). Polypropylene fibers are especially useful for athletic wear because they do not absorb water from perspiration, as cotton does. Rather, the moisture is drawn away from the skin to the surface of the polypropylene garment, where it can evaporate. The annual U.S. production of polypropylene is about 7 billion pounds.

Another related polymer, **polystyrene,** is constructed from the monomer styrene,

$$
\begin{array}{c}
\text{H} \quad\quad\quad \text{H} \\
\text{C=C} \\
\text{H} \quad\quad\quad \bigcirc
\end{array}
$$

Pure polystyrene is too brittle for many uses, so most polystyrene-based polymers are actually *copolymers* of styrene and butadiene,

$$
\begin{array}{c}
\text{H} \quad\quad \text{H} \quad \text{H} \quad\quad \text{H} \\
\text{C=C—C=C} \\
\text{H} \quad\quad\quad\quad\quad\quad \text{H}
\end{array}
$$

thus incorporating bits of butadiene rubber into the polystyrene matrix. The resulting polymer is very tough and is often used as a substitute for wood in furniture.

Another polystyrene-based product is acrylonitrile-butadiene-styrene (ABS), a tough, hard, and chemically resistant plastic used for pipes and for items such as radio housings, telephone cases, and golf club heads, for which shock resistance is an essential property. Originally, ABS was produced by copolymerization of the three monomers:

Acrylonitrile   Styrene   Butadiene

It is now prepared by a special process called *grafting,* in which butadiene is polymerized first, and then the cyanide and phenyl substituents are added chemically.

Another high-volume polymer, **polyvinyl chloride (PVC),** is constructed from the monomer vinyl chloride,

PVC pipe is widely used in industry.

22.6 Natural Polymers

Proteins

We have seen that many useful synthetic materials are polymers. Thus it should not be surprising that a great many natural materials are also polymers: starch, hair, silicate chains in soil and rocks, silk and cotton fibers, and the cellulose in woody plants, to name only a few.

In this section we consider a class of natural polymers, the **proteins,** which make up about 15% of our bodies and have molecular weights (molar masses) that range from about 6000 to over 1,000,000 grams per mole. Proteins perform many functions in the human body. **Fibrous proteins** provide structural integrity and strength for many types of tissue and are the main components of muscle, hair, and cartilage. Other proteins, usually called **globular proteins** because of their roughly spherical shape, are the "worker" molecules of the body. These proteins transport and store oxygen and nutrients, act as catalysts for the thousands of reactions that make life possible, fight invasion by foreign objects, participate in the body's many regulatory systems, and transport electrons in the complex process of metabolizing nutrients.

The building blocks of all proteins are the ***α*-amino acids,** where R may represent H, CH_3, or a more complex substituent. These molecules are called *α*-amino acids because the amino group ($—NH_2$) is always attached to the *α*-carbon, the one next to the carboxyl group ($—CO_2H$). The 20 amino acids most commonly found in proteins are shown in Fig. 22.18.

The protein in muscles enables them to contract.

Nonpolar R groups

Glycine (Gly)

Alanine (Ala)

Proline (Pro)

Phenylalanine (Phe)

Isoleucine (Ile)

Tryptophan (Trp)

Methionine (Met)

Leucine (Leu)

Valine (Val)

Polar R groups

Serine (Ser)

Glutamine (Gln)

Tyrosine (Tyr)

Histidine (His)

Asparagine (Asn)

Threonine (Thr)

Aspartic acid (Asp)

Cysteine (Cys)

Glutamic acid (Glu)

Lysine (Lys)

Arginine (Arg)

FIGURE 22.18
The 20 α-amino acids found in most proteins. The R group is shown in color.

Note from Fig. 22.18 that the amino acids are grouped into polar and nonpolar classes, determined by the R groups, or **side chains.** Nonpolar side chains contain mostly carbon and hydrogen atoms, whereas polar side chains contain large numbers of nitrogen and oxygen atoms. This difference is important, because polar side chains are *hydrophilic* (water-loving), but nonpolar side chains are *hydrophobic* (water-fearing), and this characteristic greatly affects the three-dimensional structure of the resulting protein.

At the pH in biological fluids, the amino acids shown in Fig. 22.18 exist in a different form, with the proton of the —COOH group transferred to the —NH₂ group. For example, glycine would be in the form $H_3^+NCH_2COO^-$.

The protein polymer is built by condensation reactions between amino acids. For example,

Peptide linkage

$$H_2N-CHR-COOH + H_2N-CHR'-COOH \longrightarrow H_2N-CHR-CO-NH-CHR'-COOH + H_2O$$

The product shown above is called a **dipeptide.** This name is used because the structure

$$-\overset{O}{\underset{\parallel}{C}}-\overset{H}{\underset{|}{N}}-$$

The peptide linkage is also found in nylon (see Section 22.5).

is called a **peptide linkage** by biochemists. (The same grouping is called an amide by organic chemists.) Additional condensation reactions lengthen the chain to produce a **polypeptide,** eventually yielding a protein.

You can imagine that with 20 amino acids, which can be assembled in any order, there is essentially an infinite variety possible in the construction of proteins. This flexibility allows an organism to tailor proteins for the many types of functions that must be carried out.

The order, or sequence, of amino acids in the protein chain is called the **primary structure,** conveniently indicated by using three-letter codes for the amino acids (see Fig. 22.18), where it is understood that the terminal carboxyl group is on the right and the terminal amino group is on the left. For example, one possible sequence for a tripeptide containing the amino acids lysine, alanine, and leucine is

$$H_2N-\underset{Lysine}{C}-C-N-\underset{Alanine}{C}-C-N-\underset{Leucine}{C}-COOH$$

A tripeptide containing glycine, cysteine, and alanine.

which is represented in the shorthand notation by

lys-ala-leu

Note from Sample Exercise 22.7 that there are six sequences possible for a polypeptide with three given amino acids. There are three possibilities for the first amino acid (any one of the three given amino acids), there are two possibilities for the second amino acid (one has already been accounted for), but there is only one possibility left for the third amino acid. Thus the number of sequences is $3 \times 2 \times 1 = 6$. The product $3 \times 2 \times 1$ is often written 3! (and is called 3 factorial). Similar reasoning shows that for a polypeptide with four amino acids, there are 4!, or $4 \times 3 \times 2 \times 1 = 24$, possible sequences.

| Sample Exercise 22.7 | **Tripeptide Sequences** |

Write the sequences of all possible tripeptides composed of the amino acids tyrosine, histidine, and cysteine.

Solution

There are six possible sequences:

tyr-his-cys	his-tyr-cys	cys-tyr-his
tyr-cys-his	his-cys-tyr	cys-his-tyr

See Exercise 22.89.

| Sample Exercise 22.8 | **Polypeptide Sequences** |

cys–tyr–|ile|–gln–asn–cys–pro–|leu|–gly
(a)

cys–tyr–|phe|–gln–asn–cys–pro–|arg|–gly
(b)

FIGURE 22.19
The amino acid sequences in (a) oxytocin and (b) vasopressin. The differing amino acids are boxed.

What number of possible sequences exists for a polypeptide composed of 20 different amino acids?

Solution

The answer is 20!, or

$$20 \times 19 \times 18 \times 17 \times 16 \times \cdots \times 5 \times 4 \times 3 \times 2 \times 1 = 2.43 \times 10^{18}$$

See Exercise 22.90.

A striking example of the importance of the primary structure of polypeptides can be seen in the differences between *oxytocin* and *vasopressin*. Both of these molecules are nine-unit polypeptides that differ by only two amino acids (Fig. 22.19), yet they perform completely different functions in the human body. Oxytocin is a hormone that triggers contraction of the uterus and milk secretion. Vasopressin raises blood pressure levels and regulates kidney function.

A second level of structure in proteins, beyond the sequence of amino acids, is the arrangement of the chain of the long molecule. The **secondary structure** is determined to a large extent by hydrogen bonding between lone pairs on an oxygen atom in the carbonyl group of an amino acid and a hydrogen atom attached to a nitrogen of another amino acid:

$$\mathrm{C}{=}\overset{..}{\mathrm{O}} : \text{---}\mathrm{H}\text{---}\mathrm{N}$$
$$\delta^- \qquad \delta^+$$

Such interactions can occur *within* the chain coils to form a spiral structure called an **α-helix,** as shown in Fig. 22.20 and Fig. 22.21. This type of secondary structure gives the protein elasticity (springiness) and is found in the fibrous proteins in wool, hair, and tendons. Hydrogen bonding can also occur *between different* protein chains, joining them together in an arrangement called a **pleated sheet,** as shown in Fig. 22.22. Silk contains this arrangement of proteins, making its fibers flexible yet very strong and resistant to stretching. The pleated sheet is also found in muscle fibers. The hydrogen bonds in the α-helical protein are called *intrachain* (within a given protein chain), and those in the pleated sheet are said to be *interchain* (between protein chains).

As you might imagine, a molecule as large as a protein has a great deal of flexibility and can assume a variety of overall shapes. The specific shape that a protein assumes depends on its function. For long, thin structures, such as hair, wool and silk fibers, and tendons, an elongated shape is required. This may involve an α-helical secondary structure, as found in the protein α-keratin in hair and wool or in the collagen found in tendons [Fig. 22.23(a)], or it may involve a pleated-sheet secondary structure, as found in

● Carbon

● Nitrogen

FIGURE 22.20
Hydrogen bonding within a protein chain causes it to form a stable helical structure called the α-helix. Only the main atoms in the helical backbone are shown here. The hydrogen bonds are not shown.

FIGURE 22.21
Ball-and-stick model of a portion of a protein chain in the α-helical arrangement, showing the hydrogen-bonding interactions.

silk [Fig. 22.23(b)]. Many of the proteins in the body having nonstructural functions are globular, such as myoglobin (see Fig. 21.31). Note that the secondary structure of myoglobin is basically α-helical. However, in the areas where the chain bends to give the protein its compact globular structure, the α-helix breaks down to give a secondary configuration known as the **random-coil arrangement.**

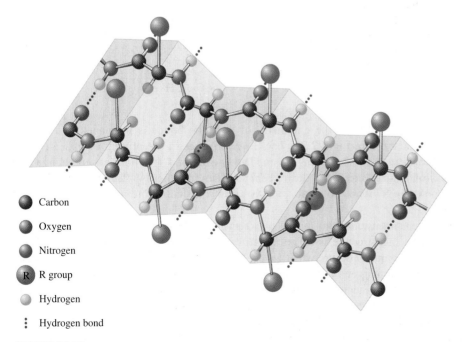

FIGURE 22.22
When hydrogen bonding occurs between protein chains rather than within them, a stable structure (the pleated sheet) results. This structure contains many protein chains and is found in natural fibers, such as silk, and in muscles.

(a)　　　　(b)

FIGURE 22.23
(a) Collagen, a protein found in tendons, consists of three protein chains (each with a helical structure) twisted together to form a superhelix. The result is a long, relatively narrow protein. (b) The pleated-sheet arrangement of many proteins bound together to form the elongated protein found in silk fibers.

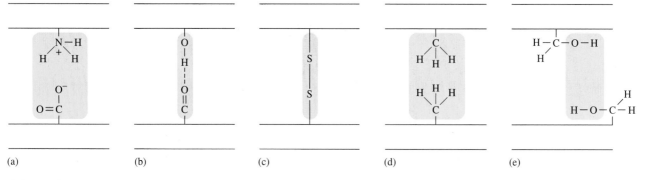

(a)   (b)   (c)   (d)   (e)

FIGURE 22.24
Summary of the various types of interactions that stabilize the tertiary structure of a protein: (a) ionic, (b) hydrogen bonding, (c) covalent, (d) London dispersion, and (e) dipole–dipole.

Natural cysteine
linkages in hair

Reduction

Chains shift

Hair set in curlers
alters tertiary structures

Oxidation

New cysteine linkages
in waved hair

FIGURE 22.25
The permanent waving of hair.

The overall shape of the protein, long and narrow or globular, is called its **tertiary structure** and is maintained by several different types of interactions: hydrogen bonding, dipole–dipole interactions, ionic bonds, covalent bonds, and London dispersion forces between nonpolar groups. These bonds, which represent all the bonding types discussed in this text, are summarized in Fig. 22.24.

The amino acid *cysteine*

plays a special role in stabilizing the tertiary structure of many proteins because the —SH groups on two cysteines can react in the presence of an oxidizing agent to form a S—S bond called a **disulfide linkage:**

A practical application of the chemistry of disulfide bonds is permanent waving of hair, as summarized in Fig. 22.25. The S—S linkages in the protein of hair are broken by treatment with a reducing agent. The hair is then set in curlers to change the tertiary protein structure to the desired shape. Then treatment with an oxidizing agent causes new S—S bonds to form, which allow the hair protein to retain the new structure.

The three-dimensional structure of a protein is crucial to its function. The process of breaking down this structure is called **denaturation** (Fig. 22.26). For example, the denaturation of egg proteins occurs when an egg is cooked. Any source of energy can cause denaturation of proteins and is thus potentially dangerous to living organisms. For example, ultraviolet and X-ray radiation or nuclear radioactivity can disrupt protein structure, which may lead to cancer or genetic damage. Protein damage is also caused by chemicals like benzene, trichloroethane, and 1,2-dibromoethane. The metals lead and mercury, which have a very high affinity for sulfur, cause protein denaturation by disrupting disulfide bonds between protein chains.

The tremendous flexibility in the various levels of protein structure allows the tailoring of proteins for a wide range of specific functions. Proteins are the "workhorse" molecules of living organisms.

FIGURE 22.27
When a tetrahedral carbon atom has four different substituents, there is no way that its mirror image can be superimposed. The lower two forms show other possible orientations of the molecule. Compare these with the mirror image and note that they cannot be superimposed.

FIGURE 22.26
A schematic representation of the thermal denaturation of a protein.

Carbohydrates

Carbohydrates form another class of biologically important molecules. They serve as a food source for most organisms and as a structural material for plants. Because many carbohydrates have the empirical formula CH_2O, it was originally believed that these substances were hydrates of carbon, thus accounting for the name.

Most important carbohydrates, such as starch and cellulose, are polymers composed of monomers called **monosaccharides,** or **simple sugars.** The monosaccharides are polyhydroxy ketones and aldehydes. The most important contain five carbon atoms **(pentoses)** or six carbon atoms **(hexoses).** One important hexose is *fructose,* a sugar found in honey and fruit. Its structure is

$$
\begin{array}{c}
CH_2OH \\
| \\
C=O \\
| \\
HO-\overset{*}{C}-H \\
| \\
H-\overset{*}{C}-OH \\
| \\
H-\overset{*}{C}-OH \\
| \\
CH_2OH
\end{array}
$$

Fructose

where the asterisks indicate chiral carbon atoms. In Section 21.4 we saw that molecules with nonsuperimposable mirror images exhibit optical isomerism. A carbon atom with four *different* groups bonded to it in a tetrahedral arrangement *always* has a nonsuperimposable mirror image (see Fig. 22.27), which gives rise to a pair of optical isomers. For example, the simplest sugar, glyceraldehyde,

$$
\begin{array}{c}
H \quad\quad O \\
\diagdown C \diagup \\
| \\
H-\overset{*}{C}-OH \\
| \\
CH_2OH
\end{array}
$$

which has one chiral carbon, has two optical isomers, as shown in Fig. 22.28.

FIGURE 22.28
The mirror image optical isomers of glyceraldehyde. Note that these mirror images cannot be superimposed.

CHEMICAL IMPACT

Tanning in the Shade

Among today's best-selling cosmetics are self-tanning lotions. Many light-skinned people want to look like they have just spent a vacation in the Caribbean, but they recognize the dangers of too much sun—it causes premature aging and may lead to skin cancer. Chemistry has come to the rescue in the form of lotions that produce an authentic-looking tan. All of these lotions have the same active ingredient: dihydroxyacetone (DHA). DHA, which has the structure

$$\text{H--O--}\overset{\displaystyle H}{\underset{\displaystyle H}{\text{C}}}\text{--}\overset{\displaystyle O}{\text{C}}\text{--}\overset{\displaystyle H}{\underset{\displaystyle H}{\text{C}}}\text{--OH}$$

is a nontoxic, simple sugar that occurs as an intermediate in carbohydrate metabolism in higher-order plants and animals. The DHA used in self-tanners is prepared by bacterial fermentation of glycerine,

$$\text{H--O--}\overset{\displaystyle H}{\underset{\displaystyle H}{\text{C}}}\text{--}\overset{\displaystyle \overset{H}{\underset{}{O}}}{\underset{\displaystyle H}{\text{C}}}\text{--}\overset{\displaystyle H}{\underset{\displaystyle H}{\text{C}}}\text{--O--H}$$

The tanning effects of DHA were discovered by accident in the 1950s at Children's Hospital at the University of Cincinnati, where DHA was being used to treat children with glycogen storage disease. When the DHA was accidentally spilled on the skin, it produced brown spots.

The mechanism of the browning process involves the Maillard reaction, which was discovered by Louis-Camille Maillard in 1912. In this process amino acids react with sugars to create brown or golden brown products. The same reaction is responsible for much of the browning that occurs during the manufacture and storage of foods. It is also the reason that beer is golden brown.

The browning of skin occurs in the stratum corneum—the outermost, dead layer—where the DHA reacts with free amino (—NH$_2$) groups of the proteins found there.

DHA is present in most tanning lotions at concentrations between 2% and 5%, although some products designed to give a deeper tan are more concentrated. Because the lotions themselves turn brown above pH 7, the tanning lotions are buffered at pH 5.

Thanks to these new products, tanning is now both safe and easy.

In fructose each of the three chiral carbon atoms satisfies the requirement of being surrounded by four different groups. This leads to a total of 2^3, or 8, isomers that differ in their ability to rotate polarized light. The particular isomer whose structure is shown in Table 22.8 is called D-fructose. Generally, monosaccharides have one isomer that is more common in nature than the others. The most important pentoses and hexoses are shown in Table 22.8.

| *Sample Exercise 22.9* | **Chiral Carbons in Carbohydrates** |

Determine the number of chiral carbon atoms in the following pentose:

$$\begin{array}{c}
\overset{H}{}\diagdown\overset{O}{} \\
\text{C} \\
| \\
\text{H--C--OH} \\
| \\
\text{H--C--OH} \\
| \\
\text{H--C--OH} \\
| \\
\text{CH}_2\text{OH}
\end{array}$$

Solution

We must look for carbon atoms that have four different substituents. The top carbon has only three substituents and thus cannot be chiral. The three carbon atoms shown in blue

Self-tanning products and a close-up of a label showing the contents.

Ingredients: Water, Aloe Vera Gel, Glycerin, Propylene Glycol, Polysorbate 20, Fragrance, Tocopheryl Acetate (Vitamin E Acetate), Imidazolidinyl Urea, Dihydroxyacetone.

© 1995, 1998 Distributed by Schering-Plough HealthCare Products, Inc., Memphis, TN 38151, USA. All rights Reserved. Made in USA.

www.coppertone.com

21621-C

General Name of Sugar	Number of Carbon Atoms
Triose	3
Tetrose	4
Pentose	5
Hexose	6
Heptose	7
Octose	8
Nonose	9

TABLE 22.8   Some Important Monosaccharides

Pentoses

D-Ribose	D-Arabinose	D-Ribulose
CHO	CHO	CH$_2$OH
H—C—OH	HO—C—H	C=O
H—C—OH	H—C—OH	H—C—OH
H—C—OH	H—C—OH	H—C—OH
CH$_2$OH	CH$_2$OH	CH$_2$OH

Hexoses

D-Glucose	D-Mannose	D-Galactose	D-Fructose
CHO	CHO	CH$_2$OH	CH$_2$OH
H—C—OH	HO—C—H	C=O	C=O
HO—C—H	HO—C—H	HO—C—H	HO—C—H
H—C—OH	H—C—OH	H—C—OH	H—C—OH
H—C—OH	H—C—OH	H—C—OH	H—C—OH
CH$_2$OH	CH$_2$OH	CH$_2$OH	CH$_2$OH

each have four different groups attached to them:

Since the fifth carbon atom has only three types of substituents (it has two hydrogen atoms), it is not chiral.

Thus the three chiral carbon atoms in this pentose are those shown in blue:

Note that D-ribose and D-arabinose, shown in Table 22.8, are two of the eight isomers of this pentose.

See Exercises 22.108 and 22.113 through 22.116.

Although we have so far represented the monosaccharides as straight-chain molecules, they usually cyclize, or form a ring structure, in aqueous solution. Figure 22.29 shows this reaction for fructose. Note that a new bond is formed between the oxygen of the terminal hydroxyl group and the carbon of the ketone group. In the cyclic form fructose is a five-membered ring containing a C—O—C bond. The same type of reaction can occur between a hydroxyl group and an aldehyde group, as shown for D-glucose in Fig. 22.30. In this case a six-membered ring is formed.

More complex carbohydrates are formed by combining monosaccharides. For example, **sucrose,** common table sugar, is a **disaccharide** formed from glucose and fructose by elimination of water to form a C—O—C bond between the rings, which is called a **glycoside linkage** (Fig. 22.31). When sucrose is consumed in food, the above reaction is reversed. An enzyme in saliva catalyzes the breakdown of this disaccharide.

Large polymers consisting of many monosaccharide units, called polysaccharides, can form when each ring forms two glycoside linkages, as shown in Fig. 22.32. Three of the most important of these polymers are starch, cellulose, and glycogen. All these substances are polymers of glucose, differing from each other in the nature of the glycoside linkage, the amount of branching, and molecular weight (molar mass).

Starch, a polymer of α-D-glucose, consists of two parts: *amylose,* a straight-chain polymer of α-glucose [see Fig. 22.32(a)], and *amylopectin,* a highly branched polymer of α-glucose with a molecular weight that is 10 to 20 times that of amylose. Branching occurs when a third glycoside linkage attaches a branch to the main polymer chain.

Starch, the carbohydrate reservoir in plants, is the form in which glucose is stored by the plant for later use as cellular fuel. Glucose is stored in this high-molecular-weight form because it results in less stress on the plant's internal structure by osmotic pressure. Recall

FIGURE 22.29
The cyclization of D-fructose.

FIGURE 22.30
The cyclization of glucose. Two different rings are possible; they differ in the orientation of the hydroxy group and hydrogen on one carbon, as indicated. The two forms are designated α and β and are shown here in two representations.

Bowl of sugar cubes.

from Section 11.6 that it is the concentration of solute molecules (or ions) that determines the osmotic pressure. Combining the individual glucose molecules into one large chain keeps the concentration of solute molecules relatively low, minimizing the osmotic pressure.

Cellulose, the major structural component of woody plants and natural fibers (such as cotton), is a polymer of β-D-glucose and has the structure shown in Fig. 22.32(b). Note that the β-glycoside linkages in cellulose give the glucose rings a different relative orientation than is found in starch. Although this difference may seem minor, it has very important consequences. The human digestive system contains α-glycosidases, enzymes that can catalyze breakage of the α-glycoside bonds in starch. These enzymes are not effective on the β-glycoside bonds of cellulose, presumably because the different structure

FIGURE 22.31
Sucrose is a disaccharide formed from α-D-glucose and fructose.

(a)

(b)

FIGURE 22.32
(a) The polymer amylose is a major component of starch and is made up of α-D-glucose monomers. (b) The polymer cellulose, which consists of β-D-glucose monomers.

results in a poor fit between the enzyme's active site and the carbohydrate. The enzymes necessary to cleave β-glycoside linkages, the β-glycosidases, are found in bacteria that exist in the digestive tracts of termites, cows, deer, and many other animals. Thus, unlike humans, these animals can derive nutrition from cellulose.

Glycogen, the main carbohydrate reservoir in animals, has a structure similar to that of amylopectin but with more branching. It is this branching that is thought to facilitate the rapid breakdown of glycogen into glucose when energy is required.

Nucleic Acids

Life is possible only because each cell, when it divides, can transmit the vital information about how it works to the next generation. It has been known for a long time that this process involves the chromosomes in the nucleus of the cell. Only since 1953, however, have scientists understood the molecular basis of this intriguing cellular "talent."

The substance that stores and transmits the genetic information is a polymer called **deoxyribonucleic acid (DNA),** a huge molecule with a molecular weight as high as several billion grams per mole. Together with other similar nucleic acids called the **ribonucleic acids (RNA),** DNA is also responsible for the synthesis of the various proteins needed by the cell to carry out its life functions. The RNA molecules, which are found in the cytoplasm outside the nucleus, are much smaller than DNA polymers, with molecular weights of only 20,000 to 40,000 grams per mole.

The monomers of the nucleic acids, called **nucleotides,** are composed of three distinct parts:

1. A *five-carbon sugar,* deoxyribose in DNA and ribose in RNA (Fig. 22.33)

2. A *nitrogen-containing organic base* of the type shown in Fig. 22.34

3. A *phosphoric acid molecule* (H_3PO_4)

(a)

(b)

FIGURE 22.33
The structure of the pentoses (a) deoxyribose and (b) ribose. Deoxyribose is the sugar molecule present in DNA; ribose is found in RNA.

A computer image of the base pairs of DNA. The blue lines represent the sugar–phosphate backbone and the colored bars represent the hydrogen bonding between the base pairs.

FIGURE 22.34
The organic bases found in DNA and RNA.

Uracil (U)
RNA

Cytosine (C)
DNA
RNA

Thymine (T)
DNA

Adenine (A)
DNA
RNA

Guanine (G)
DNA
RNA

The base and the sugar combine as shown in Fig. 22.35(a) to form a unit that in turn reacts with phosphoric acid to create the nucleotide, which is an ester [see Fig. 22.35(b)]. The nucleotides become connected through condensation reactions that eliminate water to give a polymer of the type represented in Fig. 22.36; such a polymer can contain a *billion* units.

(a)

Adenine

Ribose

Adenosine

H_2O

(b)

H_2O

Phosphoric acid

Adenosine

Adenosine 5-phosphoric acid

FIGURE 22.35
(a) Adenosine is formed by the reaction of adenine with ribose. (b) The reaction of phosphoric acid with adenosine to form the ester adenosine 5-phosphoric acid, a nucleotide. (At biological pH, the phosphoric acid would not be fully protonated as is shown here.)

The key to DNA's functioning is its *double-helical structure with complementary bases on the two strands.* The bases form hydrogen bonds to each other, as shown in Fig. 22.37. Note that the structures of cytosine and guanine make them perfect partners for hydrogen bonding, and they are *always* found as pairs on the two strands of DNA. Thymine and adenine form similar hydrogen-bonding pairs.

There is much evidence to suggest that the two strands of DNA unwind during cell division and that new complementary strands are constructed on the unraveled strands (Fig. 22.38). Because the bases on the strands always pair in the same way—cytosine with guanine and thymine with adenine—each unraveled strand serves as a template for attaching the complementary bases (along with the rest of the nucleotide). This process results in two double-helix DNA structures that are identical to the original one. Each new double strand contains one strand from the original DNA double helix and one newly synthesized strand. This replication of DNA allows for the transmission of genetic information as the cells divide.

The other major function of DNA is **protein synthesis.** A given segment of the DNA, called a **gene,** contains the code for a specific protein. These codes transmit the primary structure of the protein (the sequence of amino acids) to the construction "machinery" of the cell. There is a specific code for each amino acid in the protein, which ensures that the correct amino acid will be inserted as the protein chain grows. A code consists of a set of three bases called a **codon.**

DNA stores the genetic information, while RNA molecules are responsible for transmitting this information to the ribosomes, where protein synthesis actually occurs. This complex process involves, first, the construction of a special RNA molecule called **messenger RNA (mRNA).** The mRNA is built in the cell nucleus on the appropriate section of DNA (the gene); the double helix is "unzipped," and the complementarity of the bases

FIGURE 22.36

A portion of a typical nucleic acid chain. Note that the backbone consists of sugar–phosphate esters.

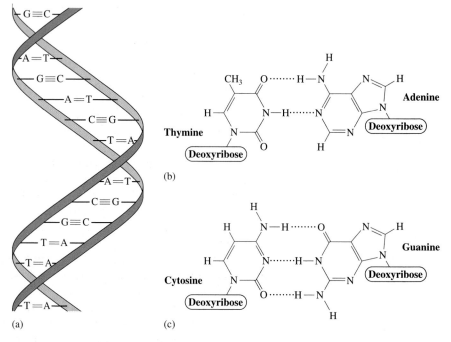

(a)　　(b)　　(c)

FIGURE 22.37

(a) The DNA double helix contains two sugar–phosphate backbones, with the bases from the two strands hydrogen-bonded to each other. The complementarity of the (b) thymine-adenine and (c) cytosine-guanine pairs.

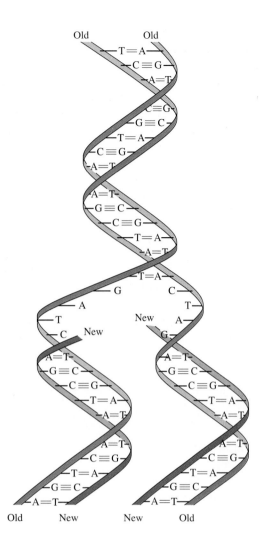

FIGURE 22.38
During cell division the original DNA double helix unwinds and new complementary strands are constructed on each original strand.

is used in a process similar to that used in DNA replication. The mRNA then migrates into the cytoplasm of the cell where, with the assistance of the ribosomes, the protein is synthesized.

Small RNA fragments, called **transfer RNA (tRNA),** are tailored to find specific amino acids and then to attach them to the growing protein chain as dictated by the codons in the mRNA. Transfer RNA has a lower molecular weight than messenger RNA. It consists of a chain of 75 to 80 nucleotides, including the bases adenine, cytosine, guanine, and uracil, among others. The chain folds back onto itself in various places as the complementary bases along the chain form hydrogen bonds. The tRNA decodes the genetic message from the mRNA, using a complementary triplet of bases called an **anticodon.** The nature of the anticodon governs which amino acid will be brought to the protein under construction.

The protein is built in several steps. First, a tRNA molecule brings an amino acid to the mRNA [the anticodon of the tRNA must complement the codon of the mRNA (see Fig. 22.39)]. Once this amino acid is in place, another tRNA moves to the second codon site of the mRNA with its specific amino acid. The two amino acids link via a peptide bond, and the tRNA on the first codon breaks away. The process is repeated down the chain, always matching the tRNA anticodon with the mRNA codon.

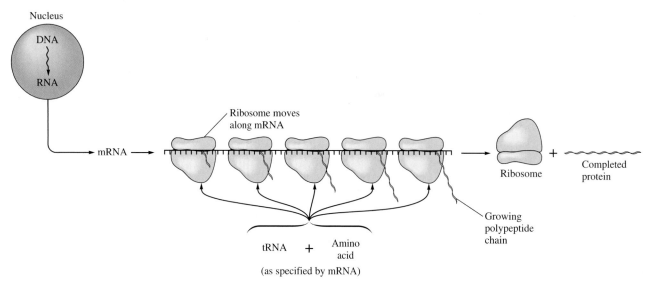

FIGURE 22.39
The mRNA molecule, constructed from a specific gene on the DNA, is used as the pattern to construct a given protein with the assistance of ribosomes. The tRNA molecules attach to specific amino acids and put them in place as called for by the codons on the mRNA.

Key Terms

biomolecule
organic chemistry

Section 22.1

hydrocarbons
saturated
unsaturated
alkanes
normal (straight-chain or unbranched)
    hydrocarbons
structural isomerism
combustion reaction
substitution reaction
dehydrogenation reaction
cyclic alkanes

Section 22.2

alkenes
cis–trans isomerism
alkynes
addition reaction
hydrogenation reaction
halogenation
polymerization

Section 22.3

aromatic hydrocarbons
phenyl group

Section 22.4

hydrocarbon derivatives
functional group
alcohols
phenol
carbonyl group

For Review

Hydrocarbons

- Compounds composed of mostly carbon and hydrogen atoms that typically contain chains or rings of carbon atoms
- Alkanes
  - Contain compounds with only C—C single bonds
  - Can be represented by the formula C_nH_{2n+2}
  - Are said to be saturated because each carbon present is bonded to the maximum number of atoms (4)
  - The carbon atoms are described as being sp^3 hybridized
  - Their structural isomerism involves the formation of branched chains
  - React with O_2 to form CO_2 and H_2O (called a combustion reaction)
  - Undergo substitution reactions
- Alkenes
  - Contain one or more C=C double bonds
  - Simplest alkene is C_2H_4 (ethylene) which is described as containing sp^2 hybridized carbon atoms
  - Restricted rotation about the C=C bonds in alkenes can lead to *cis–trans* isomerism
  - Undergo addition reactions
- Alkynes
  - Contain one or more C≡C triple bonds
  - Simplest example is C_2H_2 (acetylene), described as containing sp-hybridized carbon atoms
  - Undergo addition reactions
- Aromatic hydrocarbons
  - Contain rings of carbon atoms with delocalized π electrons
  - Undergo substitution reactions rather than addition reactions

ketones
aldehydes
carboxylic acids
carboxyl group
ester
amines

Section 22.5
polymers
thermoset polymer
thermoplastic polymer
crosslinking
vulcanization
addition polymerization
free radical
condensation polymerization
copolymer
homopolymer
dimer
polyester
isotactic chain
syndiotactic chain
atactic chain
polystyrene
polyvinyl chloride (PVC)

Section 22.6
proteins
fibrous proteins
globular proteins
α-amino acids
side chains
dipeptide
peptide linkage
polypeptide
primary structure
secondary structure
α-helix
pleated sheet
random-coil arrangement
tertiary structure
disulfide linkage
denaturation
carbohydrates
monosaccharides (simple sugars)
pentoses
hexoses
sucrose
disaccharide
glycoside linkage
starch
cellulose
glycogen
deoxyribonucleic acid (DNA)
ribonucleic acid (RNA)
nucleotides
protein synthesis
gene
codon

Hydrocarbon derivatives
- Contain one or more functional groups
- Alcohols: contain the —OH group
- Aldehydes: contain a $\overset{\diagdown}{\underset{H\diagup}{C}}=O$ group
- Ketones: contain the $\overset{\diagdown}{\underset{\diagup}{C}}=O$ group
- Carboxylic acids: contain the $-\overset{\diagup O}{\underset{\diagdown OH}{C}}$ group

Polymers
- Large molecules formed from many small molecules (called monomers)
  - Addition polymerization: monomers add together by a free radical mechanism
  - Condensation polymerization: monomers connect by splitting out a small molecule, such as water

Proteins
- A class of natural polymers with molar masses ranging from 600 to 1,000,000
- Fibrous proteins form the structural basis of muscle, hair, and cartilage
- Globular proteins perform many biologic functions, including transport and storage of oxygen, catalysis of biologic reactions, and regulation of biologic systems
- Building blocks of proteins (monomers) are α-amino acids, which connect by a condensation reaction to form a peptide linkage
- Protein structure
  - Primary: the order of amino acids in the chain
  - Secondary: the arrangement of the protein chain
    - α-helix
    - pleated sheet
  - Tertiary structure: the overall shape of the protein

Carbohydrates
- Contain carbon, hydrogen, and oxygen
- Serve as food sources for most organisms
- Monosaccharides are most commonly five-carbon and six-carbon polyhydroxy ketones and aldehydes
  - Monosaccharides combine to form more complex carbohydrates, such as sucrose, starch, and cellulose

Genetic processes
- When a cell divides, the genetic information is transmitted via deoxyribonucleic acid (DNA), which has a double helical structure
  - During cell division, the double helix unravels and a new polymer forms along each strand of the original DNA
  - The genetic code is carried by organic bases that hydrogen-bond to each other in specific pairs in the interior of the DNA double helix

REVIEW QUESTIONS

1. What is a hydrocarbon? What is the difference between a saturated hydrocarbon and an unsaturated hydrocarbon? Distinguish between normal and branched hydrocarbons. What is an alkane? What is a cyclic alkane? What are the two general formulas for alkanes? What is the hybridization of carbon atoms in alkanes? What are the bond angles in alkanes? Why are cyclopropane and cyclobutane so reactive?

messenger RNA (mRNA)
transfer RNA (tRNA)
anticodon

The normal (unbranched) hydrocarbons are often referred to as *straight-chain hydrocarbons.* What does this name refer to? Does it mean that the carbon atoms in a straight-chain hydrocarbon really have a linear arrangement? Explain. In the shorthand notation for cyclic alkanes, the hydrogens are usually omitted. How do you determine the number of hydrogens bonded to each carbon in a ring structure?

2. What is an alkene? What is an alkyne? What are the general formulas for alkenes and alkynes, assuming one multiple bond in each? What are the bond angles in alkenes and alkynes? Describe the bonding in alkenes and alkynes using C_2H_4 and C_2H_2 as your examples. Why is there restricted rotation in alkenes and alkynes? Is the general formula for a cyclic alkene C_nH_{2n}? If not, what is the general formula, assuming one multiple bond?

3. What are aromatic hydrocarbons? Benzene exhibits resonance. Explain. What are the bond angles in benzene? Give a detailed description of the bonding in benzene. The π electrons in benzene are delocalized, while the π electrons in alkenes and alkynes are localized. Explain the difference.

4. Summarize the nomenclature rules for alkanes, alkenes, alkynes, and aromatic compounds. Correct the following false statements regarding nomenclature of hydrocarbons.
   a. The root name for a hydrocarbon is based on the shortest continuous chain of carbon atoms.
   b. The suffix used to name all hydrocarbons is *-ane.*
   c. Substituent groups are numbered so as to give the largest numbers possible.
   d. No number is required to indicate the positions of double or triple bonds in alkenes and alkynes.
   e. Substituent groups get the lowest number possible in alkenes and alkynes.
   f. The *ortho-* term in aromatic hydrocarbons indicates the presence of two substituent groups bonded to carbon-1 and carbon-3 in benzene.

5. What functional group distinguishes each of the following hydrocarbon derivatives?
   a. halohydrocarbons
   b. alcohols
   c. ethers
   d. aldehydes
   e. ketones
   f. carboxylic acids
   g. esters
   h. amines

   Give examples of each functional group. What prefix or suffix is used to name each functional group? What are the bond angles in each? Describe the bonding in each functional group. What is the difference between a primary, secondary, and tertiary alcohol? For the functional groups in a–h, when is a number required to indicate the position of the functional group? Carboxylic acids are often written as RCOOH. What does —COOH indicate and what does R indicate? Aldehydes are sometimes written as RCHO. What does —CHO indicate?

6. Distinguish between isomerism and resonance. Distinguish between structural and geometric isomerism. When writing the various structural isomers, the most difficult task is identifying which are different isomers and which are identical to a previously written structure—that is, which are compounds that differ only by the rotation of a carbon single bond. How do you distinguish between structural isomers and those that are identical?

   Alkenes and cycloalkanes are structural isomers of each other. Give an example of each using C_4H_{10}. Another common feature of alkenes and cycloalkanes is that both have restricted rotation about one or more bonds in the compound, so both can exhibit *cis–trans* isomerism. What is required for an alkene or cycloalkane to exhibit *cis–trans* isomerism? Explain the difference between *cis* and *trans* isomers.

Alcohols and ethers are structural isomers of each other, as are aldehydes and ketones. Give an example of each to illustrate. Which functional group in Table 22.4 can be structural isomers of carboxylic acids?

What is optical isomerism? What do you look for to determine whether an organic compound exhibits optical isomerism? 1-Bromo-1-chloroethane is optically active whereas 1-bromo-2-chloroethane is not optically active. Explain.

7. What type of intermolecular forces do hydrocarbons exhibit? Explain why the boiling point of *n*-heptane is greater than that of *n*-butane. A general rule for a group of hydrocarbon isomers is that as the amount of branching increases, the boiling point decreases. Explain why this would be true.

The functional groups listed in Table 22.4 all exhibit London dispersion forces, but they also usually exhibit additional dipole–dipole forces. Explain why this is the case for each functional group. Although alcohols and ethers are structural isomers of each other, alcohols always boil at significantly higher temperatures than similar-size ethers. Explain. What would you expect when comparing the boiling points of similar-size carboxylic acids to esters? $CH_3CH_2CH_3$, CH_3CH_2OH, CH_3CHO, and HCOOH all have about the same molar mass, but they boil at very different temperatures. Why? Place these compounds in order by increasing boiling point.

8. Distinguish between substitution and addition reactions. Give an example of each type of reaction. Alkanes and aromatics are fairly stable compounds. To make them react, a special catalyst must be present. What catalyst must be present when reacting Cl_2 with an alkane or with benzene? Adding Cl_2 to an alkene or alkyne does not require a special catalyst. Why are alkenes and alkynes more reactive than alkanes and aromatic compounds? All organic compounds can be combusted. What is the other reactant in a combustion reaction, and what are the products, assuming the organic compound contains only C, H, and perhaps O?

The following are some other organic reactions covered in Section 22.4. Give an example to illustrate each type of reaction.
a. Adding H_2O to an alkene (in the presence of H^+) yields an alcohol.
b. Primary alcohols are oxidized to aldehydes, which can be further oxidized to carboxylic acids.
c. Secondary alcohols are oxidized to ketones.
d. Reacting an alcohol with a carboxylic acid (in the presence of H^+) produces an ester.

9. Define and give an example of each of the following.
a. addition polymer
b. condensation polymer
c. copolymer
d. homopolymer
e. polyester
f. polyamide

Distinguish between a thermoset polymer and a thermoplastic polymer. How do the physical properties of polymers depend on chain length and extent of chain branching? Explain how crosslinking agents are used to change the physical properties of polymers. Isotactic polypropylene makes stronger fibers than atactic polypropylene. Explain. In which polymer, polyethylene or polyvinyl chloride, would you expect to find the stronger intermolecular forces (assuming the average chain lengths are equal)?

10. Give the general formula for an amino acid. Some amino acids are labeled hydrophilic and some are labeled hydrophobic. What do these terms refer to? Aqueous solutions of amino acids are buffered solutions. Explain. Most of the amino acids in Fig. 22.18 are optically active. Explain. What is a peptide bond? Show how glycine, serine, and alanine react to form a tripeptide. What is a protein, and what are the monomers in proteins? Distinguish between the primary, secondary, and tertiary structures of a protein. Give examples of the types of forces that maintain each type of structure. Describe how denaturation affects the function of a protein.

What are carbohydrates, and what are the monomers in carbohydrates? The monosaccharides in Table 22.8 are all optically active. Explain. What is a *disaccharide?* Which monosaccharide units make up the disaccharide sucrose? What do you call the bond that forms between the monosaccharide units? What forces are responsible for the solubility of starch in water? What is the difference between starch, cellulose, and glycogen?

Describe the structural differences between DNA and RNA. The monomers in nucleic acids are called nucleotides. What are the three parts of a nucleotide? The compounds adenine, guanine, cytosine, and thymine are called the nucleic acid bases. What structural features in these compounds make them bases? DNA exhibits a double-helical structure. Explain. Describe how the complementary base pairing between the two individual strands of DNA forms the overall double-helical structure. How is complementary base pairing involved in the replication of DNA molecule during cell division? Describe how protein synthesis occurs. What is a codon, and what is a gene? The deletion of a single base from a DNA molecule can constitute a fatal mutation, whereas substitution of one base for another is often not as serious a mutation. Explain.

A blue question or exercise number indicates that the answer to that question or exercise appears at the back of this book and a solution appears in the *Solutions Guide.*

Questions

1. A confused student was doing an isomer problem and listed the following six names as different structural isomers of C_7H_{16}.
   a. 1-sec-butylpropane
   b. 4-methylhexane
   c. 2-ethylpentane
   d. 1-ethyl-1-methylbutane
   e. 3-methylhexane
   f. 4-ethylpentane

   How many different structural isomers are actually present in these six names?

2. For the following formulas, what types of isomerism could be exhibited? For each formula, give an example that illustrates the specific type of isomerism. The types of isomerism are structural, geometric, and optical.
   a. C_6H_{12} b. $C_5H_{12}O$ c. $C_6H_4Br_2$

3. What is wrong with the following names? Give the correct name for each compound.
   a. 2-ethylpropane
   b. 5-iodo-5, 6-dimethylhexane
   c. *cis*-4-methyl-3-pentene
   d. 2-bromo-3-butanol

4. The following organic compounds cannot exist. Why?
   a. 2-chloro-2-butyne
   b. 2-methyl-2-propanone
   c. 1,l-dimethylbenzene
   d. 2-pentanal
   e. 3-hexanoic acid
   f. 5,5-dibromo-1-cyclobutanol

5. If you had a group of hydrocarbons, what structural features would you look at to rank the hydrocarbons in order of increasing boiling point?

6. Which of the functional groups in Table 22.4 can exhibit hydrogen bonding intermolecular forces? Can CH_2CF_2 exhibit hydrogen bonding? Explain.

7. A polypeptide is also called a polyamide. What is a polyamide? Consider a polyhydrocarbon, a polyester, and a polyamide. Assuming average chain lengths are equal, which polymer would you expect to make the strongest fibers and which polymer would you expect to make the weakest fibers? Explain.

8. Give an example reaction that would yield the following products. Name the organic reactant and product in each reaction.
   a. alkane
   b. monohalogenated alkane

c. dihalogenated alkane

d. tetrahalogenated alkane

e. monohalogenated benzene

f. alkene

9. Give an example reaction that would yield the following products as major organic products. See Exercises 22.62 and 22.65 for some hints. For oxidation reactions, just write oxidation over the arrow and don't worry about the actual reagent.

a. primary alcohol

b. secondary alcohol

c. tertiary alcohol

d. aldehyde

e. ketone

f. carboxylic acid

g. ester

10. What is polystyrene? The following processes result in a stronger polystyrene polymer. Explain why in each case.

a. addition of catalyst to form syndiotactic polystyrene

b. addition of 1,3-butadiene and sulfur

c. producing long chains of polystyrene

d. addition of a catalyst to make linear polystyrene

11. Answer the following questions regarding the formation of polymers.

a. What structural features must be present in a monomer in order to form a homopolymer polyester?

b. What structural features must be present in the monomers in order to form a copolymer polyamide?

c. What structural features must be present in a monomer that can form both an addition polymer and a condensation polymer?

12. In Section 22.6, three important classes of biologically important natural polymers are discussed. What are the three classes, what are the monomers used to form the polymers, and why are they biologically important?

Exercises

In this section similar exercises are paired.

Hydrocarbons

13. Draw the five structural isomers of hexane (C_6H_{14}).

14. Name the structural isomers in Exercise 13.

15. Draw all the structural isomers for C_8H_{18} that have the following root name (longest carbon chain). Name the structural isomers.

a. heptane   **b.** butane

16. Draw all the structural isomers for C_8H_{18} that have the following root name (longest carbon chain). Name the structural isomers.

a. hexane   **b.** pentane

17. Draw a structural formula for each of the following compounds.

a. 2-methylpropane

b. 2-methylbutane

c. 2-methylpentane

d. 2-methylhexane

18. Draw a structural formula for each of the following compounds.

a. 2,2-dimethylheptane   **c.** 3,3-dimethylheptane

b. 2,3-dimethylheptane   **d.** 2,4-dimethylheptane

19. Draw the structural formula for each of the following.

a. 3-isobutylhexane

b. 2,2,4-trimethylpentane, also called *isooctane.* This substance is the reference (100 level) for octane ratings.

c. 2-*tert*-butylpentane

d. The names given in parts a and c are incorrect. Give the correct names for these hydrocarbons.

20. Draw the structure for 4-ethyl-2,3-diisopropylpentane. This name is incorrect. Give the correct systematic name.

21. Name each of the following:

a.

b.

c.

d.

22. Name each of the following cyclic alkanes, and indicate the formula of the compound.

a.

b.

c.

23. Give two examples of saturated hydrocarbons. How many other atoms are bonded to each carbon in a saturated hydrocarbon?

24. Draw the structures for two examples of *unsaturated* hydrocarbons. What structural feature makes a hydrocarbon unsaturated?

25. Name each of the following alkenes.

a. $CH_2\!=\!CH\!-\!CH_2\!-\!CH_3$

b.

c.

26. Name each of the following alkenes or alkynes.

a.

b.   CH$_3$ CH$_3$
         C≡C—CH—CH$_2$—CH$_3$

c.   CH$_2$=C—CH—CH$_3$
               | |
            CH$_3$ CH$_2$—CH$_3$

---

27. Give the structure for each of the following.
  a. 3-hexene   **b.** 2,4-heptadiene   **c.** 2-methyl-3-octene

28. Give the structure for each of the following.
  a. 4-methyl-1-pentyne
  b. 2,3,3-trimethyl-1-hexene
  c. 3-ethyl-4-decene

---

29. Give the structure of each of the following aromatic hydrocarbons.
  a. *o*-ethyltoluene
  b. *p*-di-*tert*-butylbenzene
  c. *m*-diethylbenzene
  d. 1-phenyl-2-butene

30. Cumene is the starting material for the industrial production of acetone and phenol. The structure of cumene is

                    CH$_3$
                    |
         ⬡—CH
                    |
                    CH$_3$

Give the systematic name for cumene.

---

31. Name each of the following.
  a. Cl—CH$_2$—CH$_2$—CH—CH$_3$
                              |
                              Cl
  b. CH$_3$CH$_2$CH$_2$CCl$_3$
  c. CH$_3$
              \
               CCl—CH—CH—CH$_3$
              / | |
         CH$_3$ Cl   CH$_2$—CH$_3$
  d. CH$_2$FCH$_2$F

32. Name each of the following compounds.
  a. CH$_3$CHCH=CH$_2$
               |
               Cl
  b. CH$_3$
         (cyclopentene ring with CH$_2$CH$_3$)
              CH$_2$CH$_3$
  c. Cl
         (cyclopentene ring)
              —CH$_2$CH$_2$CH$_3$
  d.   CH$_3$
         (cyclohexane ring)
         CH$_3$ CH$_3$
  e. CH$_3$ Br
         (benzene ring)

f. CH$_3$ Br
       (cyclohexane ring)

g. CH$_3$ Br
       (cyclohexene ring)

Isomerism

33. There is only one compound that is named 1,2-dichloroethane, but there are two distinct compounds that can be named 1,2-dichloroethene. Why?

34. Consider the following four structures:

  a. Which of these compounds would have the same physical properties (melting point, boiling point, density, and so on)?
  b. Which of these compounds is (are) *trans* isomers?
  c. Which of these compounds do not exhibit *cis–trans* isomerism?

---

35. Which of the compounds in Exercises 25 and 27 exhibit *cis–trans* isomerism?

36. Which of the compounds in Exercises 26 and 28 exhibit *cis–trans* isomerism?

---

37. Draw all the structural isomers of C$_5$H$_{10}$. Ignore any cyclic isomers.

38. Which of the structural isomers in Exercise 37 exhibit *cis–trans* isomerism?

---

39. Draw all the structural and geometrical (*cis–trans*) isomers of C$_3$H$_5$Cl.

40. Draw all the structural and geometrical (*cis–trans*) isomers of bromochloropropene.

---

41. Draw all structural and geometrical (*cis–trans*) isomers of C$_4$H$_7$F. Ignore any cyclic isomers.

42. *Cis–trans* isomerism is also possible in molecules with rings. Draw the *cis* and *trans* isomers of 1,2-dimethylcyclohexane. In Exercise 41, you drew all of the noncyclic structural and geometric isomers of C$_4$H$_7$F. Now draw the cyclic structural and geometric isomers of C$_4$H$_7$F.

---

43. Draw the following.
  a. *cis*-2-hexene
  b. *trans*-2-butene
  c. *cis*-2,3-dichloro-2-pentene

44. Name the following compounds.

a.

b.

c.

45. If one hydrogen in a hydrocarbon is replaced by a halogen atom, the number of isomers that exist for the substituted compound depends on the number of types of hydrogen in the original hydrocarbon. Thus there is only one form of chloroethane (all hydrogens in ethane are equivalent), but there are two isomers of propane that arise from the substitution of a methyl hydrogen or a methylene hydrogen. How many isomers can be obtained when one hydrogen in each of the compounds named below is replaced by a chlorine atom?

a. *n*-pentane
c. 2,4-dimethylpentane

b. 2-methylbutane
d. methylcyclobutane

46. There are three isomers of dichlorobenzene, one of which has now replaced naphthalene as the main constituent of mothballs.

a. Identify the *ortho,* the *meta,* and the *para* isomers of dichlorobenzene.

b. Predict the number of isomers for trichlorobenzene.

c. It turns out that the presence of one chlorine atom on a benzene ring will cause the next substituent to add *ortho* or *para* to the first chlorine atom on the benzene ring. What does this tell you about the synthesis of *m*-dichlorobenzene?

d. Which of the isomers of trichlorobenzene will be the hardest to prepare?

Functional Groups

47. Identify each of the following compounds as a carboxylic acid, ester, ketone, aldehyde, or amine.

a. Anthraquinone, an important starting material in the manufacture of dyes:

b.

c.

d.

48. Identify the functional groups present in the following compounds.

a.

Testosterone

b.

Vanillin

c.

Aspartame

49. Mimosine is a natural product found in large quantities in the seeds and foliage of some legume plants and has been shown to cause inhibition of hair growth and hair loss in mice.

Mimosine, $C_8H_{10}N_2O_4$

a. What functional groups are present in mimosine?

b. Give the hybridization of the eight carbon atoms in mimosine.

c. How many σ and π bonds are found in mimosine?

50. Minoxidil ($C_9H_{15}N_5O$) is a compound produced by Pharmacia Company that has been approved as a treatment of some types of male pattern baldness.

a. Would minoxidil be more soluble in acidic or basic aqueous solution? Explain.

b. Give the hybridization of the five nitrogen atoms in minoxidil.

c. Give the hybridization of each of the nine carbon atoms in minoxidil.

d. Give approximate values of the bond angles marked *a, b, c, d,* and *e.*

e. Including all the hydrogen atoms, how many σ bonds exist in minoxidil?

f. How many π bonds exist in minoxidil?

---

51. For each of the following alcohols, give the systematic name and specify whether the alcohol is primary, secondary, or tertiary.

a.

CH$_3$CHCH$_2$CH$_2$
with Cl and OH groups

b.
CH$_2$CH$_2$CH$_3$
CH$_3$CCH$_2$CH$_3$
OH

c.

cyclopentane ring with CH$_3$ and OH

52. Draw structural formulas for each of the following alcohols. Indicate whether the alcohol is primary, secondary, or tertiary.

a. 1-butanol   **c.** 2-methyl-1-butanol

b. 2-butanol   **d.** 2-methyl-2-butanol

---

53. Name all the alcohols that have the formula $C_5H_{12}O$. How many ethers have the formula $C_5H_{12}O$?

54. Name all the aldehydes and ketones that have the formula $C_5H_{10}O$.

---

55. Name the following compounds.

a.
Cl   O
CH$_3$CHCHCCH$_2$
Cl   CH$_3$

b.
O   CH$_2$CH$_3$
HCCHCHCH$_3$
CH$_3$

c. CH$_3$
benzene ring with CH$_3$ and CHO (O double bond)

56. Draw the structural formula for each of the following.

a. formaldehyde (methanal)

b. 4-heptanone

c. 3-chlorobutanal

d. 5,5-dimethyl-2-hexanone

---

57. Name the following compounds.

a.

Cl—(benzene ring)—C—OH with O double bond

b.
CH$_3$ O
CH$_3$CH$_2$CHCH—C—OH
CH$_2$CH$_2$CH$_3$

c. HCOOH

58. Draw a structural formula for each of the following.

a. 3-methylpentanoic acid

b. ethyl methanoate

c. methyl benzoate

d. 3-chloro-2,4-dimethylhexanoic acid

---

59. Which of the following statements is (are) false? Explain why the statement(s) is (are) false.

a. CH$_3$CH$_2$CH$_2$COCH$_3$ (with O double bond) is a structural isomer of pentanoic acid.

b. HCCH$_2$CH$_2$CHCH$_3$ (with O double bond and CH$_3$) is a structural isomer of 2-methyl-3-pentanone.

c. CH$_3$CH$_2$OCH$_2$CH$_2$CH$_3$ is a structural isomer of 2-pentanol.

d. CH$_2$=CHCHCH$_3$ (with OH) is a structural isomer of 2-butenal.

e. Trimethylamine is a structural isomer of CH$_3$CH$_2$CH$_2$NH$_2$.

60. Draw the isomer(s) specified. There may be more than one possible isomer for each part.

a. a cyclic compound that is an isomer of *trans*-2-butene

b. an ester that is an isomer of propanoic acid

c. a ketone that is an isomer of butanal

d. a secondary amine that is an isomer of butylamine

e. a tertiary amine that is an isomer of butylamine

f. an ether that is an isomer of 2-methyl-2-propanol

g. a secondary alcohol that is an isomer of 2-methyl-2-propanol

Reactions of Organic Compounds

61. Complete the following reactions.

a. CH$_3$CH=CHCH$_3$ + H$_2$ $\xrightarrow{\text{Pt}}$

b. CH$_2$=CHCHCH=CH + 2Cl$_2$ $\longrightarrow$
CH$_3$ CH$_3$

c.
(benzene ring) + Cl$_2$ $\xrightarrow{\text{FeCl}_3}$

d. CH$_3$C=CH$_2$ + O$_2$ $\xrightarrow{\text{Spark}}$
CH$_3$

62. Reagents such as HCl, HBr, and HOH (H$_2$O) can add across carbon–carbon double and triple bonds, with H forming a bond to one of the carbon atoms in the multiple bond and Cl, Br, or OH forming a bond to the other carbon atom in the multiple bond. In some cases, two products are possible. For the major organic product, the addition occurs so that the hydrogen atom in the reagent attaches to the carbon atom in the multiple bond that already has the greater number of hydrogen atoms bonded to it. With this rule in mind, draw the structure of the major product in each of the following reactions.

a. CH$_3$CH$_2$CH=CH$_2$ + H$_2$O $\longrightarrow$

b. CH$_3$CH$_2$CH=CH$_2$ + HBr $\longrightarrow$

c. CH$_3$CH$_2$C≡CH + 2HBr $\longrightarrow$

d.

cyclopentene ring with CH$_3$ + H$_2$O $\longrightarrow$

e. CH_3CH_2 $C=C$ CH_3 CH_3 H + HCl $\longrightarrow$

63. When toluene ($C_6H_5CH_3$) reacts with chlorine gas in the presence of iron(III) catalyst, the product is a mixture of the *ortho* and *para* isomers of $C_6H_4ClCH_3$. However, when the reaction is light-catalyzed with no Fe^{3+} catalyst present, the product is $C_6H_5CH_2Cl$. Explain.

64. Why is it preferable to produce chloroethane by the reaction of HCl(*g*) with ethene than by the reaction of $Cl_2(g)$ with ethane? (See Exercise 62.)

65. Using appropriate reactants, alcohols can be oxidized into aldehydes, ketones, and/or carboxylic acids. Primary alcohols can be oxidized into aldehydes, which can then be oxidized into carboxylic acids. Secondary alcohols can be oxidized into ketones, while tertiary alcohols do not undergo this type of oxidation. Give the structure of the product(s) resulting from the oxidation of each of the following alcohols.
  a. 3-methyl-1-butanol
  b. 3-methyl-2-butanol
  c. 2-methyl-2-butanol
  d.

OH
CH_2

  e.

OH
CH_3

  f.

HO   OH
CH_3
CH_2
OH

66. Oxidation of an aldehyde yields a carboxylic acid:

$$R-\overset{O}{\overset{\|}{C}H} \xrightarrow{[ox]} R-\overset{O}{\overset{\|}{C}}-OH$$

Draw the structures for the products of the following oxidation reactions.
  a. propanal $\xrightarrow{[ox]}$
  b. 2,3-dimethylpentanal $\xrightarrow{[ox]}$
  c. 3-ethylbenzaldehyde $\xrightarrow{[ox]}$

67. How would you synthesize each of the following?
  a. 1,2-dibromopropane from propene
  b. acetone (2-propanone) from an alcohol
  c. *tert*-butyl alcohol (2-methyl-2-propanol) from an alkene (See Exercise 62.)
  d. propanoic acid from an alcohol

68. What tests could you perform to distinguish between the following pairs of compounds?
  a. $CH_3CH_2CH_2CH_3$, $CH_2=CHCH_2CH_3$
  b.
$CH_3CH_2CH_2COOH$, $CH_3CH_2\overset{O}{\overset{\|}{C}}CH_3$

c.
$CH_3CH_2CH_2OH$, $CH_3\overset{O}{\overset{\|}{C}}CH_3$
  d. $CH_3CH_2NH_2$, CH_3OCH_3

69. How would you synthesize the following esters?
  a. *n*-octylacetate
  b.
$CH_3CH_2CH_2CH_2CH_2CH_2O-\overset{O}{\overset{\|}{C}}CH_2CH_3$

70. Salicylic acid has the following structure:

CO_2H
OH

Since salicylic acid has both an alcohol functional group and a carboxylic acid functional group, it can undergo two different esterification reactions depending on which functional group reacts. For example, when treated with ethanoic acid (acetic acid), salicylic acid behaves as an alcohol and the ester produced is acetylsalicylic acid (aspirin). On the other hand, when reacted with methanol, salicylic acid behaves as an acid and the ester methyl salicylate (oil of wintergreen) is produced. Methyl salicylate is also an analgesic and part of the formulation of many liniments for sore muscles. What are the structures of acetylsalicylic acid and methyl salicylate?

Polymers

71. Kel-F is a polymer with the structure

$$\left(\begin{matrix} F & F & F & F & F & F \\ | & | & | & | & | & | \\ C-C-C-C-C-C \\ | & | & | & | & | & | \\ Cl & F & Cl & F & Cl & F \end{matrix}\right)_n$$

What is the monomer for Kel-F?

72. What monomer(s) must be used to produce the following polymers?
  a.
$\left(CH-CH_2-CH-CH_2-CH-CH_2\right)_n$
  with F, F, F below

  b.
$\left(O-CH_2-CH_2-\overset{O}{\overset{\|}{C}}-O-CH_2-CH_2-\overset{O}{\overset{\|}{C}}\right)_n$

  c.
$\left(\overset{H}{\overset{|}{N}}-CH_2-CH_2-\overset{H}{\overset{|}{N}}-\overset{O}{\overset{\|}{C}}-CH_2-CH_2-\overset{O}{\overset{\|}{C}}\right)_n$

  d.
CH_3, CH_3, CH_3
$\left(C-CH_2-C-CH_2-C-CH_2\right)_n$
with phenyl groups

  e.
$\left(-CH-CH-CH-CH-\right)_n$
with phenyl, CH_3, phenyl, CH_3

f. $-(CClFCF_2CClFCF_2CClFCF_2)_n$

g.

(This polymer is Kodel, used to make fibers of stain-resistant carpeting.)

Classify these polymers as condensation or addition polymers. Which are copolymers?

73. "Super glue" contains methyl cyanoacrylate,

which readily polymerizes upon exposure to traces of water or alcohols on the surfaces to be bonded together. The polymer provides a strong bond between the two surfaces. Draw the structure of the polymer formed by methyl cyanoacrylate.

74. Isoprene is the repeating unit in natural rubber. The structure of isoprene is

$$CH_2=\overset{\overset{\textstyle CH_3}{|}}{C}-CH=CH_2$$

a. Give a systematic name for isoprene.

b. When isoprene is polymerized, two polymers of the form

are possible. In natural rubber, the *cis* configuration is found. The polymer with the *trans* configuration about the double bond is called gutta percha and was once used in the manufacture of golf balls. Draw the structure of natural rubber and gutta percha showing three repeating units and the configuration about the carbon–carbon double bonds.

75. Kevlar, used in bulletproof vests, is made by the condensation copolymerization of the monomers

Draw the structure of a portion of the Kevlar chain.

76. The polyester formed from lactic acid,

$$CH_3-\overset{\overset{\textstyle }{|}}{\underset{\underset{\textstyle OH}{|}}{CH}}-CO_2H$$

is used for tissue implants and surgical sutures that will dissolve in the body. Draw the structure of a portion of this polymer.

77. Polyimides are polymers that are tough and stable at temperatures of up to 400°C. They are used as a protective coating on the quartz fibers used in fiber optics. What monomers were used to make the following polyimide?

78. The Amoco Chemical Company has successfully raced a car with a plastic engine. Many of the engine parts, including piston skirts, connecting rods, and valve-train components, were made of a polymer called *Torlon*:

What monomers are used to make this polymer?

79. Polystyrene can be made more rigid by copolymerizing styrene with divinylbenzene:

How does the divinylbenzene make the copolymer more rigid?

80. Polyesters containing double bonds are often crosslinked by reacting the polymer with styrene.

a. Draw the structure of the copolymer of

$$HO-CH_2CH_2-OH \quad and \quad HO_2C-CH=CH-CO_2H$$

b. Draw the structure of the crosslinked polymer (after the polyester has been reacted with styrene).

81. Which of the following polymers would be stronger or more rigid? Explain your choices.

a. The copolymer of ethylene glycol and terephthalic acid or the copolymer of 1,2-diaminoethane and terephthalic acid ($1,2$-diaminoethane $= NH_2CH_2CH_2NH_2$)

b. The polymer of $HO-(CH_2)_6-CO_2H$ or that of

c. Polyacetylene or polyethylene (The monomer in polyacetylene is ethyne.)

82. Poly(lauryl methacrylate) is used as an additive in motor oils to counter the loss of viscosity at high temperature. The structure is

$$\left(\begin{array}{c} CH_3 \\ | \\ C-CH_2 \\ | \\ C \\ O \diagup \diagdown O-(CH_2)_{11}-CH_3 \end{array}\right)_n$$

The long hydrocarbon chain of poly(lauryl methacrylate) makes the polymer soluble in oil (a mixture of hydrocarbons with mostly 12 or more carbon atoms). At low temperatures the polymer is coiled into balls. At higher temperatures the balls uncoil and the polymer exists as long chains. Explain how this helps control the viscosity of oil.

Natural Polymers

83. Which of the amino acids in Fig. 22.18 contain the following functional groups in their R group?
  a. alcohol   **c.** amine
  b. carboxylic acid   **d.** amide

84. When pure crystalline amino acids are heated, decomposition generally occurs before the solid melts. Account for this observation. (*Hint:* Crystalline amino acids exist as $H_3\overset{+}{N}CRHCOO^-$, called *zwitterions.*)

85. Aspartame, the artificial sweetner marketed under the name Nutra-Sweet, is a methyl ester of a dipeptide:

$$H_2N-CH-\overset{\displaystyle O}{\overset{\|}{C}}-NH-\overset{\displaystyle CO_2CH_3}{\underset{\displaystyle CH_2}{|}}-CH-CH_2- \bigcirc$$
$$\underset{\displaystyle CH_2CO_2H}{|}$$

  a. What two amino acids are used to prepare aspartame?
  b. There is concern that methanol may be produced by the decomposition of aspartame. From what portion of the molecule can methanol be produced? Write an equation for this reaction.

86. Glutathione, a tripeptide found in virtually all cells, functions as a reducing agent. The structure of glutathione is

$$^-OOCCHCH_2CH_2\overset{\displaystyle O}{\overset{\|}{C}}NH\overset{\displaystyle O}{\overset{\|}{CHC}}NHCH_2COO^-$$
$$\underset{\displaystyle \underset{+}{NH_3}}{|} \qquad \underset{\displaystyle CH_2SH}{|}$$

What amino acids make up glutathione?

87. Draw the structures of the two dipeptides that can be formed from serine and alanine.

88. Draw the structures of the tripeptides gly–ala–ser and ser–ala–gly. How many other tripeptides are possible using these three amino acids?

89. Write the sequence of all possible tetrapeptides composed of the following amino acids.
  a. two phenylalanines and two glycines
  b. two phenylalanines, glycine, and alanine

90. How many different pentapeptides can be formed using five different amino acids?

91. Give an example of amino acids that could give rise to the interactions pictured in Fig. 22.24 that maintain the tertiary structures of proteins.

92. What types of interactions can occur between the side chains of the following amino acids that would help maintain the tertiary structure of a protein?
  a. cysteine and cysteine   **c.** glutamic acid and lysine
  b. glutamine and serine   **d.** proline and leucine

93. Oxygen is carried from the lungs to tissues by the protein hemoglobin in red blood cells. Sickle cell anemia is a disease resulting from abnormal hemoglobin molecules in which a valine is substituted for a single glutamic acid in normal hemoglobin. How might this substitution affect the structure of hemoglobin?

94. Over 100 different kinds of mutant hemoglobin molecules have been detected in humans. Unlike sickle cell anemia (see Exercise 93), not all of these mutations are as serious. In one nonlethal mutation, glutamine substitutes for a single glutamic acid in normal hemoglobin. Rationalize why this substitution is nonlethal.

95. Draw cyclic structures for D-ribose and D-mannose.

96. Indicate the chiral carbon atoms found in the monosaccharides D-ribose and D-mannose.

97. In addition to using *numerical* prefixes in the general names of sugars to indicate how many carbon atoms are present, we often use the prefixes *keto-* and *aldo-* to indicate whether the sugar is a ketone or an aldehyde. For example, the monosaccharide fructose is frequently called a *ketohexose* to emphasize that it contains six carbons as well as the ketone functional group. For each of the monosaccharides shown in Table 22.8 classify the sugars as aldohexoses, aldopentoses, ketohexoses, or ketopentoses.

98. Glucose can occur in three forms: two cyclic forms and one open-chain structure. In aqueous solution, only a tiny fraction of the glucose is in the open-chain form. Yet tests for the presence of glucose depend on reaction with the aldehyde group, which is found only in the open-chain form. Explain why these tests work.

99. What are the structural differences between α- and β-glucose? These two cyclic forms of glucose are the building blocks to form two different polymers. Explain.

100. Cows can digest cellulose, but humans can't. Why not?

101. Which of the amino acids in Fig. 22.18 contain more than one chiral carbon atom? Draw the structures of these amino acids and indicate all chiral carbon atoms.

102. Why is glycine not optically active?

103. Which of the noncyclic isomers of bromochloropropene are optically active?

104. How many chiral carbon atoms does the following structure have?

105. Part of a certain DNA sequence is G–G–T–C–T–A–T–A–C. What is the complementary sequence?

106. The codons (words) in DNA (that specify which amino acid should be at a particular point in a protein) are three bases long. How many such three-letter words can be made from the four bases adenine, cytosine, guanine, and thymine?

107. Which base will hydrogen-bond with uracil within an RNA molecule? Draw the structure of this base pair.

108. Tautomers are molecules that differ in the position of a hydrogen atom. A tautomeric form of thymine has the structure

If the tautomer above, rather than the stable form of thymine were present in a strand of DNA during replication, what would be the result?

109. The base sequences in mRNA that code for certain amino acids are

Glu: GAA, GAG
Val: GUU, GUC, GUA, GUG
Met: AUG
Trp: UGG
Phe: UUU, UUC
Asp: GAU, GAC

These sequences are complementary to the sequences in DNA.
a. Give the corresponding sequences in DNA for the amino acids listed above.
b. Give a DNA sequence that would code for the peptide trp–glu–phe–met.
c. How many different DNA sequences can code for the butapeptide in part b?
d. What is the peptide that is produced from the DNA sequence T–A–C–C–T–G–A–A–G?
e. What other DNA sequences would yield the same tripeptide as in part d?

110. The change of a single base in the DNA sequence for normal hemoglobin can encode for the abnormal hemoglobin giving rise to sickle cell anemia. Which base in the codon for glu in DNA is replaced to give the codon(s) for val? (See Exercises 93 and 109.)

Additional Exercises

111. Draw the following incorrectly named compounds and name them correctly.
a. 2-ethyl-3-methyl-5-isopropylhexane
b. 2-ethyl-4-*tert*-butylpentane
c. 3-methyl-4-isopropylpentane
d. 2-ethyl-3-butyne

112. In the presence of light, chlorine can substitute for one (or more) of the hydrogens in an alkane. For the following reactions, draw the possible monochlorination products.
a. 2,2-dimethylpropane + Cl$_2$ $\xrightarrow{hv}$

b. 1,3-dimethylcyclobutane + Cl$_2$ $\xrightarrow{hv}$
c. 2,3-dimethylbutane + Cl$_2$ $\xrightarrow{hv}$

113. Polychlorinated dibenzo-*p*-dioxins (PCDDs) are highly toxic substances that are present in trace amounts as by-products of some chemical manufacturing processes. They have been implicated in a number of environmental incidents—for example, the chemical contamination at Love Canal and the herbicide spraying in Vietnam. The structure of dibenzo-*p*-dioxin, along with the customary numbering convention, is

The most toxic PCCD is 2,3,7,8-tetrachloro-dibenzo-*p*-dioxin. Draw the structure of this compound. Also draw the structures of two other isomers containing four chlorine atoms.

114. Consider the following five compounds.
a. CH$_3$CH$_2$CH$_2$CH$_2$CH$_3$
b.

c. CH$_3$CH$_2$CH$_2$CH$_2$CH$_2$CH$_3$
d.

e.

The boiling points of these five compounds are 9.5°C, 36°C, 69°C, 76°C, and 117°C. Which compound boils at 36°C? Explain.

115. The two isomers having the formula C$_2$H$_6$O boil at −23°C and 78.5°C. Draw the structure of the isomer that boils at −23°C and of the isomer that boils at 78.5°C.

116. Ignoring ring compounds, which isomer of C$_2$H$_4$O$_2$ should boil at the lowest temperature?

117. Explain why methyl alcohol is soluble in water in all proportions, while stearyl alcohol [CH$_3$(CH$_2$)$_{16}$OH] is a waxy solid that is not soluble in water.

118. Is octanoic acid more soluble in 1 *M* HCl, 1 *M* NaOH, or pure water? Explain. Drugs such as morphine (C$_{17}$H$_{19}$NO$_3$) are often treated with strong acids. The most commonly used form of morphine is morphine hydrochloride (C$_{17}$H$_{20}$ClNO$_3$). Why is morphine treated in this way? (*Hint:* Morphine is an amine.)

119. Consider the compounds butanoic acid, pentanal, *n*-hexane, and 1-pentanol. The boiling points of these compounds (in no specific order) are 69°C, 103°C, 137°C, and 164°C. Match the boiling points to the correct compound.

120. Consider the reaction to produce the ester methyl acetate:

When this reaction is carried out with CH_3OH containing radioactive oxygen-18, the water produced does not contain oxygen-18. Explain the results of this radioisotope tracer experiment.

121. A compound containing only carbon and hydrogen is 85.63% C by mass. Reaction of this compound with H_2O produces a secondary alcohol as the major product and a primary alcohol as the minor product (see Exercise 62). If the molar mass of the hydrocarbon is between 50 and 60 g/mol, name the compound.

122. Diborane, B_2H_6, is a highly unstable compound that reacts explosively with oxygen. Ethane, C_2H_6, combines with oxygen only at elevated temperatures. Explain the differences in these two compounds.

123. Three different organic compounds have the formula C_3H_8O. Only two of these isomers react with $KMnO_4$ (a strong oxidizing agent). What are the names of the products when these isomers react with excess $KMnO_4$?

124. Consider the following polymer:

Is this polymer a homopolymer or a copolymer, and is it formed by addition polymerization or condensation polymerization? What is (are) the monomer(s) for this polymer?

125. Nylon is named according to the number of C atoms between the N atoms in the chain. Nylon-46 has 4 C atoms then 6 C atoms, and this pattern repeats. Nylon-6 always has 6 atoms in a row. Speculate as to why nylon-46 is stronger than nylon-6. (*Hint:* Consider the strengths of interchain forces.)

126. The polymer nitrile is a copolymer made from acrylonitrile and butadiene; it is used to make automotive hoses and gaskets. Draw the structure of nitrile. (*Hint:* See Table 22.7.)

127. *Polyaramid* is a term applied to polyamides containing aromatic groups. These polymers were originally made for use as tire cords but have since found many other uses.
   a. Kevlar is used in bulletproof vests and many high-strength

   composites. The structure of Kevlar is
   Which monomers are used to make Kevlar?
   b. Nomex is a polyaramid used in fire-resistant clothing. It is a copolymer of

   Draw the structure of the Nomex polymer. How do Kevlar and Nomex differ in their structures?

128. When acrylic polymers are burned, toxic fumes are produced. For example, in many airplane fires, more passenger deaths have been caused by breathing toxic fumes than by the fire itself. Using polyacrylonitrile as an example, what would you expect to be one of the most toxic, gaseous combustion products created in the reaction?

129. Ethylene oxide,

is an important industrial chemical. Although most ethers are unreactive, ethylene oxide is quite reactive. It resembles C_2H_4 in its reactions in that addition reactions occur across the C—O bond in ethylene oxide.
   a. Why is ethylene oxide so reactive? (*Hint:* Consider the bond angles in ethylene oxide as compared with those predicted by the VSEPR model.)
   b. Ethylene oxide undergoes addition polymerization, forming a polymer used in many applications requiring a nonionic surfactant. Draw the structure of this polymer.

130. Another way of producing highly crosslinked polyesters is to use glycerol. Alkyd resins are a polymer of this type. The polymer forms very tough coatings when baked onto a surface and is used in paints for automobiles and large appliances. Draw the structure of the polymer formed from the condensation of

Explain how crosslinking occurs in this polymer.

131. Monosodium glutamate (MSG) is commonly used as a flavoring in foods. Draw the structure of MSG.

132. a. Use bond energies (Table 8.4) to estimate ΔH for the reaction of two molecules of glycine to form a peptide linkage.
   b. Would you predict ΔS to favor the formation of peptide linkages between two molecules of glycine?
   c. Would you predict the formation of proteins to be a spontaneous process?

133. The reaction to form a phosphate ester linkage between two nucleotides can be approximated as follows:

Would you predict the formation of a dinucleotide from two nucleotides to be a spontaneous process?

134. Considering your answers to Exercises 132 and 133, how can you justify the existence of proteins and nucleic acids in light of the second law of thermodynamics?

135. All amino acids have at least two functional groups with acidic or basic properties. In alanine, the carboxylic acid group has $K_a = 4.5 \times 10^{-3}$ and the amino group has $K_b = 7.4 \times 10^{-5}$. Three ions of alanine are possible when alanine is dissolved in water. Which of these ions would predominate in a solution with $[H^+] = 1.0\ M$? In a solution with $[OH^-] = 1.0\ M$?

136. The average molar mass of one base pair of nucleotides in DNA is approximately 600 g/mol. The spacing between successive base pairs is about 0.34 nm, and a complete turn in the helical structure of DNA occurs about every 3.4 nm. If a DNA molecule has a molar mass of 4.5×10^9 g/mol, approximately how many complete turns exist in the DNA α-helix structure?

137. When heat is added to proteins, the hydrogen bonding in the secondary structure is disrupted. What are the algebraic signs of ΔH and ΔS for the denaturation process?

138. In glycine, the carboxylic acid group has $K_a = 4.3 \times 10^{-3}$ and the amino group has $K_b = 6.0 \times 10^{-5}$. Use these equilibrium constant values to calculate the equilibrium constants for the following.
a. $^+H_3NCH_2CO_2^- + H_2O \rightleftharpoons H_2NCH_2CO_2^- + H_3O^+$
b. $H_2NCH_2CO_2^- + H_2O \rightleftharpoons H_2NCH_2CO_2H + OH^-$
c. $^+H_3NCH_2CO_2H \rightleftharpoons 2H^+ + H_2NCH_2CO_2^-$

Challenge Problems

139. The isoelectric point of an amino acid is the pH at which the molecule has no net charge. For glycine, that point would be the pH at which virtually all glycine molecules are in the form $^+H_3NCH_2CO_2^-$. This form of glycine is amphoteric since it can act as both an acid and a base. If we assume that the principal equilibrium at the isoelectric point has the best acid reacting with the best base present, then the reaction is

$$2\,^+H_3NCH_2CO_2^- \rightleftharpoons H_2NCH_2CO_2^- + \,^+H_3NCH_2CO_2H \quad (i)$$

Assuming this reaction is the principal equilibrium, then the following relationship must hold true:

$$[H_2NCH_2CO_2^-] = [^+H_3NCH_2CO_2H] \quad (ii)$$

Use this result and your answer to part c of Exercise 138 to calculate the pH at which equation (ii) is true. It will be the isoelectric point of glycine.

140. In 1994 chemists at Texas A & M University reported the synthesis of a non-naturally occurring amino acid (*C & E News,* April 18, 1994, pp. 26–27):

a. To which naturally occurring amino acid is this compound most similar?
b. A tetrapeptide, phe–met–arg–phe—NH₂, is synthesized in the brains of rats addicted to morphine and heroin. (The

$$\overset{O}{\underset{\|}{}}$$

—NH₂ indicates that the peptide ends in —C—NH₂ instead of —CO₂H.) The TAMU scientists synthesized a similar tetrapeptide, with the synthetic amino acid above replacing one of the original amino acids. Draw a structure for the tetrapeptide containing the synthetic amino acid.
c. Indicate the chiral carbon atoms in the synthetic amino acid.

141. The structure of tartaric acid is

a. Is the form of tartaric acid pictured below optically active? Explain.

Note: The dashed lines show groups behind the plane of the page. The wedges show groups in front of the plane.
b. Draw the optically active forms of tartaric acid.

142. Using one of the Lewis structures for benzene (C_6H_6), estimate ΔH_f° for $C_6H_6(g)$ using bond energies and given the standard enthalpy of formation of $C(g)$ is 717 kJ/mol. The experimental ΔH_f° value for $C_6H_6(g)$ is 83 kJ/mol. Explain the discrepancy between the experimental value and the calculated ΔH_f° value for $C_6H_6(g)$.

143. Mycomycin, a naturally occurring antibiotic produced by the fungus *Nocardia acidophilus,* has the molecular formula $C_{13}H_{10}O_2$ and the systematic name 3,5,7,8-tridecatetraene-10,12-diynoic acid. Draw the structure of mycomycin.

144. Sorbic acid is used to prevent mold and fungus growth in some food products, especially cheeses. The systematic name for sorbic acid is 2,4-hexadienoic acid. Draw structures for the four geometrical isomers of sorbic acid.

145. Consider the following reactions. For parts b–d, see Exercise 62.
a. When C_5H_{12} is reacted with $Cl_2(g)$ in the presence of ultraviolet light, four different monochlorination products form. What is the structure of C_5H_{12} in this reaction?
b. When C_4H_8 is reacted with H_2O, a tertiary alcohol is produced as the major product. What is the structure of C_4H_8 in this reaction?
c. When C_7H_{12} is reacted with HCl, 1-chloro-1-methylcyclohexane is produced as the major product. What are the two possible structures for C_7H_{12} in this reaction?
d. When a hydrocarbon is reacted with H_2O and the major product of this reaction is then oxidized, acetone (2-propanone) is produced. What is the structure of the hydrocarbon in this reaction?
e. When $C_5H_{12}O$ is oxidized, a carboxylic acid is produced. What are the possible structures for $C_5H_{12}O$ in this reaction?

146. Polycarbonates are a class of thermoplastic polymers that are used in the plastic lenses of eyeglasses and in the shells of bicycle helmets. A polycarbonate is made from the reaction of bisphenol A (BPA) with phosgene ($COCl_2$):

Phenol (C_6H_5OH) is used to terminate the polymer (stop its growth).

a. Draw the structure of the polycarbonate chain formed from the above reaction.

b. Is this reaction a condensation or addition polymerization?

147. A urethane linkage occurs when an alcohol adds across the carbon–nitrogen double bond in an isocyanate:

$$R{-}O{-}H + O{=}C{=}N{-}R' \longrightarrow RO{-}\overset{\overset{\textstyle O}{\|}}{C}{-}\underset{\underset{\textstyle H}{|}}{N}{-}R'$$

Alcohol   Isocyanate   A urethane

Polyurethanes (formed from the copolymerization of a diol with a diisocyanate) are used in foamed insulation and a variety of other construction materials. What is the structure of the polyurethane formed by the following reaction?

$$HOCH_2CH_2OH + O{=}C{=}N{-}\bigcirc{-}N{=}C{=}O \longrightarrow$$

148. ABS plastic is a tough, hard plastic used in applications requiring shock resistance. The polymer consists of three monomer units: acrylonitrile (C_3H_3N), butadiene (C_4H_6), and styrene (C_8H_8).

a. Draw two repeating units of ABS plastic assuming that the three monomer units react in a 1:1:1 mole ratio and react in the same order as the monomers listed above.

b. A sample of ABS plastic contains 8.80% N by mass. It took 0.605 g of Br_2 to react completely with a 1.20-g sample of ABS plastic. What is the percent by mass of acrylonitrile, butadiene, and styrene in this polymer sample?

c. ABS plastic does not react in a 1:1:1 mole ratio among the three monomer units. Using the results from part b, determine the relative numbers of the monomer units in this sample of ABS plastic.

149. Stretch a rubber band while holding it gently to your lips. Then slowly let it relax while still in contact with your lips.

a. What happens to the temperature of the rubber band on stretching?

b. Is the stretching an exothermic or endothermic process?

c. Explain the above result in terms of intermolecular forces.

d. What is the sign of ΔS and ΔG for stretching the rubber band?

e. Give the molecular explanation for the sign of ΔS for stretching.

150. Alcohols are very useful starting materials for the production of many different compounds. The following conversions, starting with 1-butanol, can be carried out in two or more steps. Show the steps (reactants/catalysts) you would follow to carry out the conversions, drawing the formula for the organic product in each step. For each step, a major product must be produced.

See Exercise 62. *Hint:* in the presence of H^+, an alcohol is converted into an alkene and water. This is the exact reverse of the reaction of adding water to an alkene to form an alcohol.

a. 1-butanol $\longrightarrow$ butane

b. 1-butanol $\longrightarrow$ 2-butanone

151. A chemical "breathalyzer" test works because ethyl alcohol in the breath is oxidized by the dichromate ion (orange) to form acetic acid and chromium(III) ion (green). The balanced reaction is

$$3C_2H_5OH(aq) + 2Cr_2O_7^{2-}(aq) + 2H^+(aq) \longrightarrow$$
$$3HC_2H_3O_2(aq) + 4Cr^{3+}(aq) + 11H_2O(l)$$

You analyze a breathalyzer test in which 4.2 mg of $K_2Cr_2O_7$ was reduced. Assuming the volume of the breath was 0.500 L at 30.°C and 750. mm Hg, what was the mole percent alcohol of the breath?

152. Consider a sample of a hydrocarbon at 0.959 atm and 298 K. Upon combusting the entire sample in oxygen, you collect a mixture of gaseous carbon dioxide and water vapor at 1.51 atm and 375 K. This mixture has a density of 1.391 g/L and occupies a volume four times as large as that of the pure hydrocarbon. Determine the molecular formula of the hydrocarbon and name it.

153. Estradiol is a female hormone with the following structure:

How many chiral carbon atoms are in estradiol?

Integrative Problems

These problems require the integration of multiple concepts to find the solutions.

154. Helicenes are extended fused polyaromatic hydrocarbons that have a helical or screw-shaped structure.

a. A 0.1450-g sample of solid helicene is combusted in air to give 0.5063 g of CO_2. What is the empirical formula of this helicene?

b. If a 0.0938-g sample of this helicene is dissolved in 12.5 g of solvent to give a 0.0175 m solution, what is the molecular formula of this helicene?

c. What is the balanced reaction for the combustion of this helicene?

155. An organometallic compound is one containing at least one metal–carbon bond. An example of an organometallic species is (CH_3CH_2)MBr, which contains a metal–ethyl bond.

a. If M^{2+} has the electron configuration [Ar]$3d^{10}$, what is the percent by mass of M in (CH_3CH_2)MBr?

b. One of the reactions in which (CH_3CH_2)MBr becomes involved is the conversion of a ketone to an alcohol as illustrated here:

How does the hybridization of the starred carbon atom change, if at all, in going from reactants to products?

c. What is the systematic name of the product?

Hint: In this shorthand notation, all the C—H bonds have been eliminated and the lines represent C—C bonds, unless shown differently. As is typical of most organic compounds, each carbon atom has four bonds to it and the oxygen atoms have only two bonds.

Marathon Problems

These problems are designed to incorporate several concepts and techniques into one situation. Marathon Problems can be used in class by groups of students to help facilitate problem-solving skills.

156. For each of the following, fill in the blank with the correct response. All of these fill-in-the-blank problems pertain to material covered in the sections on alkanes, alkenes and alkynes, aromatic hydrocarbons, and hydrocarbon derivatives.

a. The first "organic" compound to be synthesized in the laboratory, rather than being isolated from nature, was _____, which was prepared from _____.

b. An organic compound whose carbon–carbon bonds are all single bonds is said to be _____.

c. The general orientation of the four pairs of electrons around the carbon atoms in alkanes is _____.

d. Alkanes in which the carbon atoms form a single unbranched chain are said to be _____ alkanes.

e. Structural isomerism occurs when two molecules have the same number of each type of atom but exhibit different arrangements of the _____ between those atoms.

f. The systematic names of all saturated hydrocarbons have the ending _____ added to a root name that indicates the number of carbon atoms in the molecule.

g. For a branched hydrocarbon, the root name for the hydrocarbon comes from the number of carbon atoms in the _____ continuous chain in the molecule.

h. The positions of substituents along the hydrocarbon framework of a molecule are indicated by the _____ of the carbon atom to which the substituents are attached.

i. The major use of alkanes has been in _____ reactions, as a source of heat and light.

j. With very reactive agents, such as, the halogen elements, alkanes undergo _____ reactions, whereby a new atom replaces one or more hydrogen atoms of the alkane.

k. Alkenes and alkynes are characterized by their ability to undergo rapid, complete _____ reactions, by which other atoms attach themselves to the carbon atoms of the double or triple bond.

l. Unsaturated fats may be converted to saturated fats by the process of _____.

m. Benzene is the parent member of the group of hydrocarbons called _____ hydrocarbons.

n. An atom or group of atoms that imparts new and characteristic properties to an organic molecule is called a _____ group.

o. A _____ alcohol is one in which there is only one hydrocarbon group attached to the carbon atom holding the hydroxyl group.

p. The simplest alcohol, methanol, is prepared industrially by the hydrogenation of _____.

q. Ethanol is commonly prepared by the _____ of certain sugars by yeast.

r. Both aldehydes and ketones contain the _____ group, but they differ in where this group occurs along the hydrocarbon chain.

s. Aldehydes and ketones can be prepared by _____ of the corresponding alcohol.

t. Organic acids, which contain the _____ group, are typically weak acids.

u. The typically sweet-smelling compounds called _____ result from the condensation reaction of an organic acid with an _____.

157. Choose one of the following terms to match the description given in statements (1)–(17). All of the following pertain to proteins or carbohydrates.

a. aldohexose   **g.** disaccharides   **m.** ketohexoses
b. saliva   **h.** disulfide   **n.** oxytocin
c. cellulose   **i.** globular   **o.** pleated sheet
d. CH_2O **j.** glycogen   **p.** polypeptide
e. cysteine   **k.** glycoside linkage   **q.** primary structure
f. denaturation   **l.** hydrophobic

(1) polymer consisting of many amino acids
(2) linkage that forms between two cysteine species
(3) peptide hormone that triggers milk secretion
(4) proteins with roughly spherical shape
(5) sequence of amino acids in a protein
(6) silk protein secondary structure
(7) water-repelling amino acid side chain
(8) amino acid responsible for permanent wave in hair
(9) breakdown of a protein's tertiary and/or secondary structure
(10) animal polymer of glucose
(11) —C—O—C— bond between rings in disaccharide sugars
(12) empirical formula leading to the name carbohydrate
(13) where enzymes catalyzing the breakdown of glycoside linkages are found
(14) six-carbon ketone sugars
(15) structural component of plants, polymer of glucose
(16) sugars consisting of two monomer units
(17) six-carbon aldehyde sugars

158. For each of the following, fill in the blank with the correct response(s). All of the following pertain to nucleic acids.

a. The substance in the nucleus of the cell that stores and transmits genetic information is DNA, which stands for _____.

b. The basic repeating monomer units of DNA and RNA are called _____.

c. The pentose deoxyribose is found in DNA, whereas _____ is found in RNA.

d. The basic linkage in DNA or RNA between the sugar molecule and phosphoric acid is a phosphate _____ linkage.

e. The bases on opposite strands of DNA are said to be _____ to each other, which means the bases fit together specifically by hydrogen bonding to one another.

f. In a strand of normal DNA, the base _____ is always found paired with the base adenine, whereas _____ is always found paired with cytosine.

g. A given segment of the DNA molecule, which contains the molecular coding for a specific protein to be synthesized, is referred to as a _____.

h. During protein synthesis, _____ RNA molecules attach to and transport specific amino acids to the appropriate position on the pattern provided by _____ RNA molecules.

i. The codes specified by _____ are responsible for assembling the correct primary structure of proteins.

Get help understanding core concepts and visualizing molecular-level interactions, and practice problem solving, by visiting the Online Study Center at **college.hmco.com/ PIC/zumdahl7e.**

Appendixes

Mathematical Procedures

A1.1 Exponential Notation

The numbers characteristic of scientific measurements are often very large or very small; thus it is convenient to express them using powers of 10. For example, the number 1,300,000 can be expressed as 1.3×10^6, which means multiply 1.3 by 10 six times, or

$$1.3 \times 10^6 = 1.3 \times \underbrace{10 \times 10 \times 10 \times 10 \times 10 \times 10}_{10^6 = 1\text{ million}}$$

Note that each multiplication by 10 moves the decimal point one place to the right:

$$1.3 \times 10 = 13.$$
$$13 \times 10 = 130.$$
$$130 \times 10 = 1300.$$
$$\vdots$$

Thus the easiest way to interpret the notation 1.3×10^6 is that it means move the decimal point in 1.3 to the right six times:

$$1.3 \times 10^6 = 1\underbrace{300000}_{1\,2\,3\,4\,5\,6} = 1,300,000$$

Using this notation, the number 1985 can be expressed as 1.985×10^3. Note that the usual convention is to write the number that appears before the power of 10 as a number between 1 and 10. To end up with the number 1.985, which is between 1 and 10, we had to move the decimal point three places to the left. To compensate for that, we must multiply by 10^3, which says that to get the intended number we start with 1.985 and move the decimal point three places to the right; that is:

$$1.985 \times 10^3 = 1\underbrace{985.}_{1\,2\,3}$$

Some other examples are given below.

Number	Exponential Notation
5.6	5.6×10^0 or 5.6×1
39	3.9×10^1
943	9.43×10^2
1126	1.126×10^3

So far we have considered numbers greater than 1. How do we represent a number such as 0.0034 in exponential notation? We start with a number between 1 and 10 and *divide* by the appropriate power of 10:

$$0.0034 = \frac{3.4}{10 \times 10 \times 10} = \frac{3.4}{10^3} = 3.4 \times 10^{-3}$$

Division by 10 moves the decimal point one place to the *left*. Thus the number

$$0.\underset{7\;6\;5\;4\;3\;2\;1}{0\;0\;0\;0\;0\;0\;1}\;4$$

can be written as 1.4×10^{-7}.

To summarize, we can write any number in the form

$$N \times 10^{\pm n}$$

where N is between 1 and 10 and the exponent n is an integer. If the sign preceding n is positive, it means the decimal point in N should be moved n places to the right. If a negative sign precedes n, the decimal point in N should be moved n places to the left.

Multiplication and Division

When two numbers expressed in exponential notation are multiplied, the initial numbers are multiplied and the exponents of 10 are added:

$$(M \times 10^m)(N \times 10^n) = (MN) \times 10^{m+n}$$

For example (to two significant figures, as required),

$$(3.2 \times 10^4)(2.8 \times 10^3) = 9.0 \times 10^7$$

When the numbers are multiplied, if a result greater than 10 is obtained for the initial number, the decimal point is moved one place to the left and the exponent of 10 is increased by 1:

$$\begin{aligned}(5.8 \times 10^2)(4.3 \times 10^8) &= 24.9 \times 10^{10}\\ &= 2.49 \times 10^{11}\\ &= 2.5\ \ \times 10^{11} \quad \text{(two significant figures)}\end{aligned}$$

Division of two numbers expressed in exponential notation involves normal division of the initial numbers and *subtraction* of the exponent of the divisor from that of the dividend. For example,

$$\frac{4.8 \times 10^8}{\underset{\text{Divisor}}{\underbrace{2.1 \times 10^3}}} = \frac{4.8}{2.1} \times 10^{(8-3)} = 2.3 \times 10^5$$

If the initial number resulting from the division is less than 1, the decimal point is moved one place to the right and the exponent of 10 is decreased by 1. For example,

$$\begin{aligned}\frac{6.4 \times 10^3}{8.3 \times 10^5} = \frac{6.4}{8.3} \times 10^{(3-5)} &= 0.77 \times 10^{-2}\\ &= 7.7 \times 10^{-3}\end{aligned}$$

Addition and Subtraction

To add or subtract numbers expressed in exponential notation, *the exponents of the numbers must be the same.* For example, to add 1.31×10^5 and 4.2×10^4, we must rewrite one number so that the exponents of both are the same. The number 1.31×10^5 can be written 13.1×10^4, since moving the decimal point one place to the right can be compensated for by decreasing the exponent by 1. Now we can add the numbers:

$$\begin{aligned}13.1 &\times 10^4\\ + 4.2 &\times 10^4\\ \hline 17.3 &\times 10^4\end{aligned}$$

In correct exponential notation the result is expressed as 1.73×10^5.

To perform addition or subtraction with numbers expressed in exponential notation, only the initial numbers are added or subtracted. The exponent of the result is the same as those of the numbers being added or subtracted. To subtract 1.8×10^2 from 8.99×10^3, we write

$$
\begin{array}{r}
8.99 \times 10^3 \\
-0.18 \times 10^3 \\
\hline
8.81 \times 10^3
\end{array}
$$

Powers and Roots

When a number expressed in exponential notation is taken to some power, the initial number is taken to the appropriate power and the exponent of 10 is multiplied by that power:

$$(N \times 10^n)^m = N^m \times 10^{m \cdot n}$$

For example,*

$$
\begin{aligned}
(7.5 \times 10^2)^3 &= 7.5^3 \times 10^{3 \cdot 2} \\
&= 422 \times 10^6 \\
&= 4.22 \times 10^8 \\
&= 4.2 \ \times 10^8 \qquad \text{(two significant figures)}
\end{aligned}
$$

When a root is taken of a number expressed in exponential notation, the root of the initial number is taken and the exponent of 10 is divided by the number representing the root:

$$\sqrt{N \times 10^n} = (n \times 10^n)^{1/2} = \sqrt{N} \times 10^{n/2}$$

For example,

$$
\begin{aligned}
(2.9 \times 10^6)^{1/2} &= \sqrt{2.9} \times 10^{6/2} \\
&= 1.7 \times 10^3
\end{aligned}
$$

Because the exponent of the result must be an integer, we may sometimes have to change the form of the number so that the power divided by the root equals an integer. For example,

$$
\begin{aligned}
\sqrt{1.9 \times 10^3} &= (1.9 \times 10^3)^{1/2} = (0.19 \times 10^4)^{1/2} \\
&= \sqrt{0.19} \times 10^2 \\
&= 0.44 \times 10^2 \\
&= 4.4 \times 10^1
\end{aligned}
$$

In this case, we moved the decimal point one place to the left and increased the exponent from 3 to 4 to make $n/2$ an integer.

The same procedure is followed for roots other than square roots. For example,

$$
\begin{aligned}
\sqrt[3]{6.9 \times 10^5} &= (6.9 \times 10^5)^{1/3} = (0.69 \times 10^6)^{1/3} \\
&= \sqrt[3]{0.69} \times 10^2 \\
&= 0.88 \times 10^2 \\
&= 8.8 \times 10^1
\end{aligned}
$$

and

$$
\begin{aligned}
\sqrt[3]{4.6 \times 10^{10}} &= (4.6 \times 10^{10})^{1/3} = (46 \times 10^9)^{1/3} \\
&= \sqrt[3]{46} \times 10^3 \\
&= 3.6 \times 10^3
\end{aligned}
$$

*Refer to the instruction booklet for your calculator for directions concerning how to take roots and powers of numbers.

A1.2 Logarithms

A logarithm is an exponent. Any number N can be expressed as follows:

$$N = 10^x$$

For example,

$$1000 = 10^3$$
$$100 = 10^2$$
$$10 = 10^1$$
$$1 = 10^0$$

The common, or base 10, logarithm of a number is the power to which 10 must be taken to yield the number. Thus, since $1000 = 10^3$,

$$\log 1000 = 3$$

Similarly,

$$\log 100 = 2$$
$$\log 10 = 1$$
$$\log 1 = 0$$

For a number between 10 and 100, the required exponent of 10 will be between 1 and 2. For example, $65 = 10^{1.8129}$; that is, log $65 = 1.8129$. For a number between 100 and 1000, the exponent of 10 will be between 2 and 3. For example, $650 = 10^{2.8129}$ and log $650 = 2.8129$.

A number N greater than 0 and less than 1 can be expressed as follows:

$$N = 10^{-x} = \frac{1}{10^x}$$

For example,

$$0.001 = \frac{1}{1000} = \frac{1}{10^3} = 10^{-3}$$

$$0.01 = \frac{1}{100} = \frac{1}{10^2} = 10^{-2}$$

$$0.1 = \frac{1}{10} = \frac{1}{10^1} = 10^{-1}$$

Thus

$$\log 0.001 = -3$$
$$\log 0.01 = -2$$
$$\log 0.1 = -1$$

Although common logs are often tabulated, the most convenient method for obtaining such logs is to use an electronic calculator. On most calculators the number is first entered and then the log key is punched. The log of the number then appears in the display.* Some examples are given below. You should reproduce these results on your calculator to be sure that you can find common logs correctly.

Number	Common Log
36	1.56
1849	3.2669
0.156	−0.807
1.68×10^{-5}	−4.775

---

*Refer to the instruction booklet for your calculator for the exact sequence to obtain logarithms.

Note that the number of digits after the decimal point in a common log is equal to the number of significant figures in the original number.

Since logs are simply exponents, they are manipulated according to the rules for exponents. For example, if $A = 10^x$ and $B = 10^y$, then their product is

$$A \cdot B = 10^x \cdot 10^y = 10^{x+y}$$

and

$$\log AB = x + y = \log A + \log B$$

For division, we have

$$\frac{A}{B} = \frac{10^x}{10^y} = 10^{x-y}$$

and

$$\log \frac{A}{B} = x - y = \log A - \log B$$

For a number raised to a power, we have

$$A^n = (10^x)^n = 10^{nx}$$

and

$$\log A^n = nx = n \log A$$

It follows that

$$\log \frac{1}{A^n} = \log A^{-n} = -n \log A$$

or, for $n = 1$,

$$\log \frac{1}{A} = -\log A$$

When a common log is given, to find the number it represents, we must carry out the process of exponentiation. For example, if the log is 2.673, then $N = 10^{2.673}$. The process of exponentiation is also called taking the antilog, or the inverse logarithm. This operation is usually carried out on calculators in one of two ways. The majority of calculators require that the log be entered first and then the keys $\boxed{\text{INV}}$ and $\boxed{\text{LOG}}$ pressed in succession. For example, to find $N = 10^{2.673}$ we enter 2.673 and then press $\boxed{\text{INV}}$ and $\boxed{\text{LOG}}$. The number 471 will be displayed; that is, $N = 471$. Some calculators have a $\boxed{10^x}$ key. In that case, the log is entered first and then the $\boxed{10^x}$ key is pressed. Again, the number 471 will be displayed.

Natural logarithms, another type of logarithm, are based on the number 2.7183, which is referred to as e. In this case, a number is represented as $N = e^x = 2.7183^x$. For example,

$$N = 7.15 = e^x$$

$$\ln 7.15 = x = 1.967$$

To find the natural log of a number using a calculator, the number is entered and then the $\boxed{\text{ln}}$ key is pressed. Use the following examples to check your technique for finding natural logs with your calculator:

Number (e^x)	Natural Log(x)
784	6.664
1.61×10^3	7.384
1.00×10^{-7}	−16.118
1.00	0

If a natural logarithm is given, to find the number it represents, exponentiation to the base e (2.7183) must be carried out. With many calculators this is done using a key marked $\boxed{e^x}$ (the natural log is entered, with the correct sign, and then the $\boxed{e^x}$ key is pressed). The other common method for exponentiation to base e is to enter the natural log and then press the $\boxed{\text{INV}}$ and $\boxed{\text{ln}}$ keys in succession. The following examples will help you check your technique:

ln $N(x)$	$N(e^x)$
3.256	25.9
−5.169	5.69×10^{-3}
13.112	4.95×10^5

Since natural logarithms are simply exponents, they are also manipulated according to the mathematical rules for exponents given earlier for common logs.

A1.3 Graphing Functions

In interpreting the results of a scientific experiment, it is often useful to make a graph. If possible, the function to be graphed should be in a form that gives a straight line. The equation for a straight line (a *linear equation*) can be represented by the general form

$$y = mx + b$$

where y is the *dependent variable*, x is the *independent variable*, m is the *slope*, and b is the *intercept* with the y axis.

To illustrate the characteristics of a linear equation, the function $y = 3x + 4$ is plotted in Fig. A.1. For this equation $m = 3$ and $b = 4$. Note that the y intercept occurs when $x = 0$. In this case the intercept is 4, as can be seen from the equation ($b = 4$).

The slope of a straight line is defined as the ratio of the rate of change in y to that in x:

$$m = \text{slope} = \frac{\Delta y}{\Delta x}$$

For the equation $y = 3x + 4$, y changes three times as fast as x (since x has a coefficient of 3). Thus the slope in this case is 3. This can be verified from the graph. For the triangle shown in Fig. A.1,

$$\Delta y = 34 - 10 = 24 \quad \text{and} \quad \Delta x = 10 - 2 = 8$$

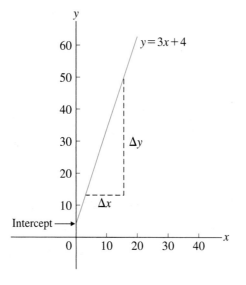

FIGURE A.1
Graph of the linear equation $y = 3x + 4$.

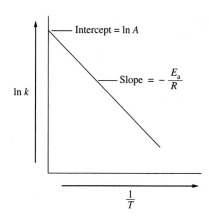

FIGURE A.2
Graph of ln k versus $1/T$.

TABLE A.1   Some Useful Linear Equations in Standard Form

Equation ($y = mx + b$)	What Is Plotted (y vs. x)	Slope (m)	Intercept (b)	Section in Text
$[A] = -kt + [A]_0$	$[A]$ vs. t	$-k$	$[A]_0$	12.4
$\ln[A] = -kt + \ln[A]_0$	$\ln[A]$ vs. t	$-k$	$\ln[A]_0$	12.4
$\dfrac{1}{[A]} = kt + \dfrac{1}{[A]_0}$	$\dfrac{1}{[A]}$ vs. t	k	$\dfrac{1}{[A]_0}$	12.4
$\ln P_{vap} = -\dfrac{\Delta H_{vap}}{R}\left(\dfrac{1}{T}\right) + C$	$\ln P_{vap}$ vs. $\dfrac{1}{T}$	$\dfrac{-\Delta H_{vap}}{R}$	C	10.8

Thus

$$\text{Slope} = \frac{\Delta y}{\Delta x} = \frac{24}{8} = 3$$

The preceding example illustrates a general method for obtaining the slope of a line from the graph of that line. Simply draw a triangle with one side parallel to the y axis and the other parallel to the x axis as shown in Fig. A.1. Then determine the lengths of the sides to give Δy and Δx, respectively, and compute the ratio $\Delta y/\Delta x$.

Sometimes an equation that is not in standard form can be changed to the form $y = mx + b$ by rearrangement or mathematical manipulation. An example is the equation $k = Ae^{-E_a/RT}$ described in Section 12.7, where A, E_a, and R are constants; k is the dependent variable; and $1/T$ is the independent variable. This equation can be changed to standard form by taking the natural logarithm of both sides,

$$\ln k = \ln Ae^{-E_a/RT} = \ln A + \ln e^{-E_a/RT} = \ln A - \frac{E_a}{RT}$$

noting that the log of a product is equal to the sum of the logs of the individual terms and that the natural log of $e^{-E_a/RT}$ is simply the exponent $-E_a/RT$. Thus, in standard form, the equation $k = Ae^{-E_a/RT}$ is written

$$\underset{y}{\underline{\ln k}} = \underset{m}{\underline{-\frac{E_a}{R}}} \underset{x}{\underline{\left(\frac{1}{T}\right)}} + \underset{b}{\underline{\ln A}}$$

A plot of ln k versus $1/T$ (see Fig. A.2) gives a straight line with slope $-E_a/R$ and intercept ln A.

Other linear equations that are useful in the study of chemistry are listed in standard form in Table A.1.

A1.4 Solving Quadratic Equations

A *quadratic equation,* a polynomial in which the highest power of x is 2, can be written as

$$ax^2 + bx + c = 0$$

One method for finding the two values of x that satisfy a quadratic equation is to use the *quadratic formula:*

$$x = \frac{-b \pm \sqrt{b^2 - 4ac}}{2a}$$

where a, b, and c are the coefficients of x^2 and x and the constant, respectively. For example, in determining $[H^+]$ in a solution of 1.0×10^{-4} M acetic acid the following expression arises:

$$1.8 \times 10^{-5} = \frac{x^2}{1.0 \times 10^{-4} - x}$$

which yields

$$x^2 + (1.8 \times 10^{-5})x - 1.8 \times 10^{-9} = 0$$

where $a = 1$, $b = 1.8 \times 10^{-5}$, and $c = -1.8 \times 10^{-9}$. Using the quadratic formula, we have

$$x = \frac{-b \pm \sqrt{b^2 - 4ac}}{2a}$$

$$= \frac{-1.8 \times 10^{-5} \pm \sqrt{3.24 \times 10^{-10} - (4)(1)(-1.8 \times 10^{-9})}}{2(1)}$$

$$= \frac{-1.8 \times 10^{-5} \pm \sqrt{3.24 \times 10^{-10} + 7.2 \times 10^{-9}}}{2}$$

$$= \frac{-1.8 \times 10^{-5} \pm \sqrt{7.5 \times 10^{-9}}}{2}$$

$$= \frac{-1.8 \times 10^{-5} \pm 8.7 \times 10^{-5}}{2}$$

Thus

$$x = \frac{6.9 \times 10^{-5}}{2} = 3.5 \times 10^{-5}$$

and

$$x = \frac{-10.5 \times 10^{-5}}{2} = -5.2 \times 10^{-5}$$

Note that there are two roots, as there always will be, for a polynomial in x^2. In this case x represents a concentration of H^+ (see Section 14.3). Thus the positive root is the one that solves the problem, since a concentration cannot be a negative number.

A second method for solving quadratic equations is by *successive approximations,* a systematic method of trial and error. A value of x is guessed and substituted into the equation everywhere x (or x^2) appears, except for one place. For example, for the equation

$$x^2 + (1.8 \times 10^{-5})x - 1.8 \times 10^{-9} = 0$$

we might guess $x = 2 \times 10^{-5}$. Substituting that value into the equation gives

$$x^2 + (1.8 \times 10^{-5})(2 \times 10^{-5}) - 1.8 \times 10^{-9} = 0$$

or

$$x^2 = 1.8 \times 10^{-9} - 3.6 \times 10^{-10} = 1.4 \times 10^{-9}$$

Thus

$$x = 3.7 \times 10^{-5}$$

Note that the guessed value of $x(2 \times 10^{-5})$ is not the same as the value of x that is calculated (3.7×10^{-5}) after inserting the estimated value. This means that $x = 2 \times 10^{-5}$ is not the correct solution, and we must try another guess. We take the calculated value (3.7×10^{-5}) as our next guess:

$$x^2 + (1.8 \times 10^{-5})(3.7 \times 10^{-5}) - 1.8 \times 10^{-9} = 0$$
$$x^2 = 1.8 \times 10^{-9} - 6.7 \times 10^{-10} = 1.1 \times 10^{-9}$$

Thus

$$x = 3.3 \times 10^{-5}$$

Now we compare the two values of x again:

$$\text{Guessed:} \quad x = 3.7 \times 10^{-5}$$
$$\text{Calculated:} \quad x = 3.3 \times 10^{-5}$$

These values are closer but not close enough. Next we try 3.3×10^{-5} as our guess:

$$x^2 + (1.8 \times 10^{-5})(3.3 \times 10^{-5}) - 1.8 \times 10^{-9} = 0$$
$$x^2 = 1.8 \times 10^{-9} - 5.9 \times 10^{-10} = 1.2 \times 10^{-9}$$

Thus

$$x = 3.5 \times 10^{-5}$$

Again we compare:

$$\text{Guessed:} \quad x = 3.3 \times 10^{-5}$$
$$\text{Calculated:} \quad x = 3.5 \times 10^{-5}$$

Next we guess $x = 3.5 \times 10^{-5}$ to give

$$x^2 + (1.8 \times 10^{-5})(3.5 \times 10^{-5}) - 1.8 \times 10^{-9} = 0$$
$$x^2 = 1.8 \times 10^{-9} - 6.3 \times 10^{-10} = 1.2 \times 10^{-9}$$

Thus

$$x = 3.5 \times 10^{-5}$$

Now the guessed value and the calculated value are the same; we have found the correct solution. Note that this agrees with one of the roots found with the quadratic formula in the first method.

To further illustrate the method of successive approximations, we will solve Sample Exercise 14.17 using this procedure. In solving for $[H^+]$ for 0.010 M H_2SO_4, we obtain the following expression:

$$1.2 \times 10^{-2} = \frac{x(0.010 + x)}{0.010 - x}$$

which can be rearranged to give

$$x = (1.2 \times 10^{-2})\left(\frac{0.010 - x}{0.010 + x}\right)$$

We will guess a value for x, substitute it into the right side of the equation, and then calculate a value for x. In guessing a value for x, we know it must be less than 0.010, since a larger value will make the calculated value for x negative and the guessed and calculated values will never match. We start by guessing $x = 0.005$.

The results of the successive approximations are shown in the following table:

Trial	Guessed Value for x	Calculated Value for x
1	0.0050	0.0040
2	0.0040	0.0051
3	0.00450	0.00455
4	0.00452	0.00453

Note that the first guess was close to the actual value and that there was oscillation between 0.004 and 0.005 for the guessed and calculated values. For trial 3, an average of these values was used as the guess, and this led rapidly to the correct value (0.0045 to the correct number of significant figures). Also, note that it is useful to carry extra digits until the correct value is obtained. That value can then be rounded off to the correct number of significant figures.

The method of successive approximations is especially useful for solving polynomials containing x to a power of 3 or higher. The procedure is the same as for quadratic equations: Substitute a guessed value for x into the equation for every x term but one, and then solve for x. Continue this process until the guessed and calculated values agree.

A1.5 Uncertainties in Measurements

Like all the physical sciences, chemistry is based on the results of measurements. Every measurement has an inherent uncertainty, so if we are to use the results of measurements to reach conclusions, we must be able to estimate the sizes of these uncertainties.

For example, the specification for a commercial 500-mg acetaminophen (the active painkiller in Tylenol) tablet is that each batch of tablets must contain 450 to 550 mg of acetaminophen per tablet. Suppose that chemical analysis gave the following results for a batch of acetaminophen tablets: 428 mg, 479 mg, 442 mg, and 435 mg. How can we use these results to decide if the batch of tablets meets the specification? Although the details of how to draw such conclusions from measured data are beyond the scope of this text, we will consider some aspects of how this is done. We will focus here on the types of experimental uncertainty, the expression of experimental results, and a simplified method for estimating experimental uncertainty when several types of measurement contribute to the final result.

Types of Experimental Error

There are two types of experimental uncertainty (error). A variety of names are applied to these types of errors:

$$\text{Precision} \longleftrightarrow \text{random error} \quad \equiv \text{indeterminate error}$$
$$\text{Accuracy} \longleftrightarrow \text{systematic error} \equiv \text{determinate error}$$

The difference between the two types of error is well illustrated by the attempts to hit a target shown in Fig. 1.7 in Chapter 1.

Random error is associated with every measurement. To obtain the last significant figure for any measurement, we must always make an estimate. For example, we interpolate between the marks on a meter stick, a buret, or a balance. The precision of replicate measurements (repeated measurements of the same type) reflects the size of the random errors. Precision refers to the reproducibility of replicate measurements.

The accuracy of a measurement refers to how close it is to the true value. An inaccurate result occurs as a result of some flaw (systematic error) in the measurement: the presence of an interfering substance, incorrect calibration of an instrument, operator error, and so on. The goal of chemical analysis is to eliminate systematic error, but random errors can only be minimized. In practice, an experiment is almost always done to find an unknown value (the true value is not known—someone is trying to obtain that value by doing the experiment). In this case the precision of several replicate determinations is used to assess the accuracy of the result. The results of the replicate experiments are expressed as an average (which we assume is close to the true value) with an error limit that gives some indication of how close the average value may be to the true value. The error limit represents the uncertainty of the experimental result.

Expression of Experimental Results

If we perform several measurements, such as for the analysis for acetaminophen in painkiller tablets, the results should express two things: the average of the measurements and the size of the uncertainty.

There are two common ways of expressing an average: the mean and the median. The mean $(\bar{x})$ is the arithmetic average of the results, or

$$\text{Mean} = \bar{x} = \sum_{i=1}^{n} \frac{x_i}{n} = \frac{x_1 + x_2 + \cdots + x_n}{n}$$

where Σ means take the sum of the values. The mean is equal to the sum of all the measurements divided by the number of measurements. For the acetaminophen results given previously, the mean is

$$\bar{x} = \frac{428 + 479 + 442 + 435}{4} = 446 \text{ mg}$$

The median is the value that lies in the middle among the results. Half the measurements are above the median and half are below the median. For results of 465 mg, 485 mg, and 492 mg, the median is 485 mg. When there is an even number of results, the median is the average of the two middle results. For the acetaminophen results, the median is

$$\frac{442 + 435}{2} = 438 \text{ mg}$$

There are several advantages to using the median. If a small number of measurements is made, one value can greatly affect the mean. Consider the results for the analysis of acetaminophen: 428 mg, 479 mg, 442 mg, and 435 mg. The mean is 446 mg, which is larger than three of the four weights. The median is 438 mg, which lies near the three values that are relatively close to one another.

In addition to expressing an average value for a series of results, we must express the uncertainty. This usually means expressing either the precision of the measurements or the observed range of the measurements. The range of a series of measurements is defined by the smallest value and the largest value. For the analytical results on the acetaminophen tablets, the range is from 428 mg to 479 mg. Using this range, we can express the results by saying that the true value lies between 428 mg and 479 mg. That is, we can express the amount of acetaminophen in a typical tablet as 446 ± 33 mg, where the error limit is chosen to give the observed range (approximately).

The most common way to specify precision is by the standard deviation, s, which for a small number of measurements is given by the formula

$$s = \left[\frac{\sum_{i=1}^{n} (x_i - \bar{x})^2}{n - 1} \right]^{1/2}$$

where x_i is an individual result, $\bar{x}$ is the average (either mean or median), and n is the total number of measurements. For the acetaminophen example, we have

$$s = \left[\frac{(428 - 446)^2 + (479 - 446)^2 + (442 - 446)^2 + (435 - 446)^2}{4 - 1} \right]^{1/2} = 23$$

Thus we can say the amount of acetaminophen in the typical tablet in the batch of tablets is 446 mg with a sample standard deviation of 23 mg. Statistically this means that any additional measurement has a 68% probability (68 chances out of 100) of being between 423 mg (446 − 23) and 469 mg (446 + 23). Thus the standard deviation is a measure of the precision of a given type of determination.

The standard deviation gives us a means of describing the precision of a given type of determination using a series of replicate results. However, it is also useful to be able to estimate the precision of a procedure that involves several measurements by combining the precisions of the individual steps. That is, we want to answer the following question:

How do the uncertainties propagate when we combine the results of several different types of measurements? There are many ways to deal with the propagation of uncertainty. We will discuss only one simple method here.

A Simplified Method for Estimating Experimental Uncertainty

To illustrate this method, we will consider the determination of the density of an irregularly shaped solid. In this determination we make three measurements. First, we measure the mass of the object on a balance. Next, we must obtain the volume of the solid. The easiest method for doing this is to partially fill a graduated cylinder with a liquid and record the volume. Then we add the solid and record the volume again. The difference in the measured volumes is the volume of the solid. We can then calculate the density of the solid from the equation

$$D = \frac{M}{V_2 - V_1}$$

where M is the mass of the solid, V_1 is the initial volume of liquid in the graduated cylinder, and V_2 is the volume of liquid plus solid. Suppose we get the following results:

$$M = 23.06 \text{ g}$$
$$V_1 = 10.4 \text{ mL}$$
$$V_2 = 13.5 \text{ mL}$$

The calculated density is

$$\frac{23.06 \text{ g}}{13.5 \text{ mL} - 10.4 \text{ mL}} = 7.44 \text{ g/mL}$$

Now suppose that the precision of the balance used is ± 0.02 g and that the volume measurements are precise to ± 0.05 mL. How do we estimate the uncertainty of the density? We can do this by assuming a worst case. That is, we assume the largest uncertainties in all measurements, and see what combinations of measurements will give the largest and smallest possible results (the greatest range). Since the density is the mass divided by the volume, the largest value of the density will be that obtained using the largest possible mass and the smallest possible volume:

Largest possible mass = 23.06 + .02

$$D_{\text{max}} = \frac{23.08}{13.45 - 10.45} = 7.69 \text{ g/mL}$$

Smallest possible V_2 Largest possible V_1

The smallest value of the density is

Smallest possible mass

$$D_{\text{min}} = \frac{23.04}{13.35 - 10.35} = 7.20 \text{ g/mL}$$

Largest possible V_2 Smallest possible V_1

Thus the calculated range is from 7.20 to 7.69 and the average of these values is 7.44. The error limit is the number that gives the high and low range values when added and subtracted from the average. Therefore, we can express the density as 7.44 ± 0.25 g/mL, which is the average value plus or minus the quantity that gives the range calculated by assuming the largest uncertainties.

Analysis of the propagation of uncertainties is useful in drawing qualitative conclusions from the analysis of measurements. For example, suppose that we obtained the preceding results for the density of an unknown alloy and we want to know if it is one of the following alloys:

$$\text{Alloy A:} \quad D = 7.58 \text{ g/mL}$$
$$\text{Alloy B:} \quad D = 7.42 \text{ g/mL}$$
$$\text{Alloy C:} \quad D = 8.56 \text{ g/mL}$$

We can safely conclude that the alloy is not C. But the values of the densities for alloys A and B are both within the inherent uncertainty of our method. To distinguish between A and B, we need to improve the precision of our determination: The obvious choice is to improve the precision of the volume measurement.

The worst-case method is very useful in estimating uncertainties when the results of several measurements are combined to calculate a result. We assume the maximum uncertainty in each measurement and calculate the minimum and maximum possible result. These extreme values describe the range and thus the error limit.

Appendix Two · The Quantitative Kinetic Molecular Model

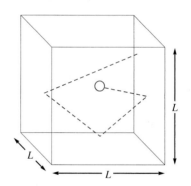

FIGURE A.3
An ideal gas particle in a cube whose sides are of length *L*. The particle collides elastically with the walls in a random, straight-line motion.

We have seen that the kinetic molecular model successfully accounts for the properties of an ideal gas. This appendix will show in some detail how the postulates of the kinetic molecular model lead to an equation corresponding to the experimentally obtained ideal gas equation.

Recall that the particles of an ideal gas are assumed to be volumeless, to have no attraction for each other, and to produce pressure on their container by colliding with the container walls.

Suppose there are *n* moles of an ideal gas in a cubical container with sides each of length *L*. Assume each gas particle has a mass *m* and that it is in rapid, random, straight-line motion colliding with the walls, as shown in Fig. A.3. The collisions will be assumed to be *elastic*—no loss of kinetic energy occurs. We want to compute the force on the walls from the colliding gas particles and then, since pressure is force per unit area, to obtain an expression for the pressure of the gas.

Before we can derive the expression for the pressure of a gas, we must first discuss some characteristics of velocity. Each particle in the gas has a particular velocity *u* that can be divided into components u_x, u_y, and u_z, as shown in Fig. A.4. First, using u_x and u_y and the Pythagorean theorem, we can obtain u_{xy} as shown in Fig. A.4(c):

$$u_{xy}^{2} = u_x^{2} + u_y^{2}$$

Hypotenuse of   Sides of
right triangle   right triangle

Then, constructing another triangle as shown in Fig. A.4(c), we find

$$u^{2} = u_{xy}^{2} + u_z^{2}$$

or

$$u^{2} = u_x^{2} + u_y^{2} + u_z^{2}$$

Now let's consider how an "average" gas particle moves. For example, how often does this particle strike the two walls of the box that are perpendicular to the *x* axis? It is important to realize that only the *x* component of the velocity affects the particle's impacts on these two walls, as shown in Fig. A.5(a). The larger the *x* component of the velocity, the faster the particle travels between these two walls, and the more impacts per unit of time it will make on these walls. Remember, the pressure of the gas is due to these collisions with the walls.

FIGURE A.4

(a) The Cartesian coordinate axes.

(b) The velocity u of any gas particle can be broken down into three mutually perpendicular components, u_x, u_y, and u_z. This can be represented as a rectangular solid with sides u_x, u_y, and u_z and body diagonal u.

(c) In the xy plane,

$$u_x^2 + u_y^2 = u_{xy}^2$$

by the Pythagorean theorem. Since u_{xy} and u_x are also perpendicular,

$$u^2 = u_{xy}^2 + u_z^2 = u_x^2 + u_y^2 + u_z^2$$

The collision frequency (collisions per unit of time) with the two walls that are perpendicular to the x axis is given by

$$(\text{Collision frequency})_x = \frac{\text{velocity in the } x \text{ direction}}{\text{distance between the walls}}$$

$$= \frac{u_x}{L}$$

Next, what is the force of a collision? Force is defined as mass times acceleration (change in velocity per unit of time):

$$F = ma = m\left(\frac{\Delta u}{\Delta t}\right)$$

where F represents force, a represents acceleration, Δu represents a change in velocity, and Δt represents a given length of time.

Since we assume that the particle has constant mass, we can write

$$F = \frac{m\Delta u}{\Delta t} = \frac{\Delta(mu)}{\Delta t}$$

The quantity mu is the momentum of the particle (momentum is the product of mass and velocity), and the expression $F = \Delta(mu)/\Delta t$ implies that force is the change in momentum per unit of time. When a particle hits a wall perpendicular to the x axis, as shown in Fig. A.5(b), an elastic collision results in an *exact reversal* of the x component of velocity. That is, the *sign*, or direction, of u_x reverses when the particle collides with one of the walls perpendicular to the x axis. Thus the final momentum is the *negative*, or opposite, of the initial momentum. Remember that an elastic collision means that there is no change in the *magnitude* of the velocity. The change in momentum in the x direction is then

$$\text{Change in momentum} = \Delta(mu_x) = \text{final momentum} - \text{initial momentum}$$

$$= \underset{\substack{\nearrow \\ \text{Final} \\ \text{momentum} \\ \text{in } x \text{ direction}}}{-mu_x} \underset{\substack{\nwarrow \\ \text{Initial} \\ \text{momentum} \\ \text{in } x \text{ direction}}}{-\ mu_x}$$

$$= -2mu_x$$

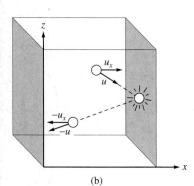

FIGURE A.5

(a) Only the x component of the gas particle's velocity affects the frequency of impacts on the shaded walls, the walls that are perpendicular to the x axis.

(b) For an elastic collision, there is an exact reversal of the x component of the velocity and of the total velocity. The change in momentum (final − initial) is then

$$-mu_x - mu_x = -2mu_x$$

But we are interested in the force the gas particle exerts on the walls of the box. Since we know that every action produces an equal but opposite reaction, the change in momentum with respect to the wall on impact is $-(-2mu_x)$, or $2mu_x$.

Recall that since force is the change in momentum per unit of time,

$$\text{Force}_x = \frac{\Delta(mu_x)}{\Delta t}$$

for the walls perpendicular to the x axis.

This expression can be obtained by multiplying the change in momentum per impact by the number of impacts per unit of time:

$$\text{Force}_x = (2mu_x)\left(\frac{u_x}{L}\right) = \text{change in momentum per unit of time}$$

Change in momentum per impact   Impacts per unit of time

That is,

$$\text{Force}_x = \frac{2mu_x^2}{L}$$

So far we have considered only the two walls of the box perpendicular to the x axis. We can assume that the force on the two walls perpendicular to the y axis is given by

$$\text{Force}_y = \frac{2mu_y^2}{L}$$

and that on the two walls perpendicular to the z axis by

$$\text{Force}_z = \frac{2mu_z^2}{L}$$

Since we have shown that

$$u^2 = u_x^2 + u_y^2 + u_z^2$$

the total force on the box is

$$\begin{aligned}\text{Force}_{\text{TOTAL}} &= \text{force}_x + \text{force}_y + \text{force}_z \\ &= \frac{2mu_x^2}{L} + \frac{2mu_y^2}{L} + \frac{2mu_z^2}{L} \\ &= \frac{2m}{L}(u_x^2 + u_y^2 + u_z^2) = \frac{2m}{L}(u^2)\end{aligned}$$

Now since we want the average force, we use the average of the square of the velocity $(\overline{u^2})$ to obtain

$$\overline{\text{Force}}_{\text{TOTAL}} = \frac{2m}{L}(\overline{u^2})$$

Next, we need to compute the pressure (force per unit of area)

$$\text{Pressure due to "average" particle} = \frac{\overline{\text{force}}_{\text{TOTAL}}}{\text{area}_{\text{TOTAL}}}$$

$$= \frac{\dfrac{2m\overline{u^2}}{L}}{6L^2} = \frac{m\overline{u^2}}{3L^3}$$

The 6 sides of the cube   Area of each side

Since the volume V of the cube is equal to L^3, we can write

$$\text{Pressure} = P = \frac{m\overline{u^2}}{3V}$$

So far we have considered the pressure on the walls due to a single, "average" particle. Of course, we want the pressure due to the entire gas sample. The number of particles in a given gas sample can be expressed as follows:

$$\text{Number of gas particles} = nN_A$$

where n is the number of moles and N_A is Avogadro's number.

The total pressure on the box due to n moles of a gas is therefore

$$P = nN_A \frac{m\overline{u^2}}{3V}$$

Next we want to express the pressure in terms of the kinetic energy of the gas molecules. Kinetic energy (the energy due to motion) is given by $\frac{1}{2}mu^2$, where m is the mass and u is the velocity. Since we are using the average of the velocity squared $(\overline{u^2})$, and since $m\overline{u^2} = 2(\frac{1}{2}m\overline{u^2})$, we have

$$P = \left(\frac{2}{3}\right) \frac{nN_A(\frac{1}{2}m\overline{u^2})}{V}$$

or

$$\frac{PV}{n} = \left(\frac{2}{3}\right) N_A(\frac{1}{2}m\overline{u^2})$$

Thus, based on the postulates of the kinetic molecular model, we have been able to derive an equation that has the same form as the ideal gas equation,

$$\frac{PV}{n} = RT$$

This agreement between experiment and theory supports the validity of the assumptions made in the kinetic molecular model about the behavior of gas particles, at least for the limiting case of an ideal gas.

Appendix Three   Spectral Analysis

Although volumetric and gravimetric analyses are still very commonly used, spectroscopy is the technique most often used for modern chemical analysis. *Spectroscopy* is the study of electromagnetic radiation emitted or absorbed by a given chemical species. Since the quantity of radiation absorbed or emitted can be related to the quantity of the absorbing or emitting species present, this technique can be used for quantitative analysis. There are many spectroscopic techniques, as electromagnetic radiation spans a wide range of energies to include X rays, ultraviolet, infrared, and visible light, and microwaves, to name a few of its familiar forms. We will consider here only one procedure, which is based on the absorption of visible light.

If a liquid is colored, it is because some component of the liquid absorbs visible light. In a solution the greater the concentration of the light-absorbing substance, the more light absorbed, and the more intense the color of the solution.

The quantity of light absorbed by a substance can be measured by a *spectrophotometer,* shown schematically in Fig. A.6. This instrument consists of a source that emits all wavelengths of light in the visible region (wavelengths of ~400 to 700 nm); a monochromator, which selects a given wavelength of light; a sample holder for the solution

FIGURE A.6
A schematic diagram of a simple spectrophotometer. The source emits all wavelengths of visible light, which are dispersed using a prism or grating and then focused, one wavelength at a time, onto the sample. The detector compares the intensity of the incident light (I_0) to the intensity of the light after it has passed through the sample (I).

being measured; and a detector, which compares the intensity of incident light I_0 to the intensity of light after it has passed through the sample I. The ratio I/I_0, called the *transmittance,* is a measure of the fraction of light that passes through the sample. The amount of light absorbed is given by the *absorbance A,* where

$$A = -\log \frac{I}{I_0}$$

The absorbance can be expressed by the *Beer–Lambert law:*

$$A = \epsilon l c$$

where ϵ is the molar absorptivity or the molar extinction coefficient (in L/mol · cm), l is the distance the light travels through the solution (in cm), and c is the concentration of the absorbing species (in mol/L). The Beer–Lambert law is the basis for using spectroscopy in quantitative analysis. If ϵ and l are known, measuring A for a solution allows us to calculate the concentration of the absorbing species in the solution.

Suppose we have a pink solution containing an unknown concentration of $Co^{2+}(aq)$ ions. A sample of this solution is placed in a spectrophotometer, and the absorbance is measured at a wavelength where ϵ for $Co^{2+}(aq)$ is known to be 12 L/mol · cm. The absorbance A is found to be 0.60. The width of the sample tube is 1.0 cm. We want to determine the concentration of $Co^{2+}(aq)$ in the solution. This problem can be solved by a straightforward application of the Beer–Lambert law,

$$A = \epsilon l c$$

where

$$A = 0.60$$

$$\epsilon = \frac{12\ \text{L}}{\text{mol} \cdot \text{cm}}$$

$$l = \text{light path} = 1.0\ \text{cm}$$

Solving for the concentration gives

$$c = \frac{A}{\epsilon l} = \frac{0.60}{\left(12\ \dfrac{\text{L}}{\text{mol} \cdot \text{cm}}\right)(1.0\ \text{cm})} = 5.0 \times 10^{-2}\ \text{mol/L}$$

To obtain the unknown concentration of an absorbing species from the measured absorbance, we must know the product ϵl, since

$$c = \frac{A}{\epsilon l}$$

We can obtain the product ϵl by measuring the absorbance of a solution of *known* concentration, since

$$\epsilon l = \frac{A}{c}$$

Measured using a
spectrophotometer

Known from making up
the solution

However, a more accurate value of the product ϵl can be obtained by plotting A versus c for a series of solutions. Note that the equation $A = \epsilon lc$ gives a straight line with slope ϵl when A is plotted against c.

For example, consider the following typical spectroscopic analysis. A sample of steel from a bicycle frame is to be analyzed to determine its manganese content. The procedure involves weighing out a sample of the steel, dissolving it in strong acid, treating the resulting solution with a very strong oxidizing agent to convert all the manganese to permanganate ion (MnO_4^-), and then using spectroscopy to determine the concentration of the intensely purple MnO_4^- ions in the solution. To do this, however, the value of ϵl for MnO_4^- must be determined at an appropriate wavelength. The absorbance values for four solutions with known MnO_4^- concentrations were measured to give the following data:

Solution	Concentration of MnO_4^- (mol/L)	Absorbance
1	7.00×10^{-5}	0.175
2	1.00×10^{-4}	0.250
3	2.00×10^{-4}	0.500
4	3.50×10^{-4}	0.875

A plot of absorbance versus concentration for the solutions of known concentration is shown in Fig. A.7. The slope of this line (change in A/change in c) is 2.48×10^3 L/mol. This quantity represents the product ϵl.

A sample of the steel weighing 0.1523 g was dissolved and the unknown amount of manganese was converted to MnO_4^- ions. Water was then added to give a solution with a final volume of 100.0 mL. A portion of this solution was placed in a spectrophotometer,

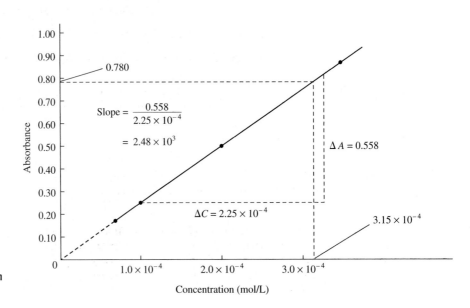

FIGURE A.7
A plot of absorbance versus concentration of MnO_4^- in a series of solutions of known concentration.

and its absorbance was found to be 0.780. Using these data, we want to calculate the percent manganese in the steel. The MnO_4^- ions from the manganese in the dissolved steel sample show an absorbance of 0.780. Using the Beer–Lambert law, we calculate the concentration of MnO_4^- in this solution:

$$c = \frac{A}{\epsilon l} = \frac{0.780}{2.48 \times 10^3 \text{ L/mol}} \times 3.15 \times 10^{-4} \text{ mol/L}$$

There is a more direct way for finding c. Using a graph such as that in Fig. A.7 (often called a *Beer's law plot*), we can read the concentration that corresponds to $A = 0.780$. This interpolation is shown by dashed lines on the graph. By this method, $c = 3.15 \times 10^{-4}$ mol/L, which agrees with the value obtained above.

Recall that the original 0.1523-g steel sample was dissolved, the manganese was converted to permanganate, and the volume was adjusted to 100.0 mL. We now know that $[MnO_4^-]$ in that solution is 3.15×10^{-4} M. Using this concentration, we can calculate the total number of moles of MnO_4^- in that solution:

$$\text{mol of } MnO_4^- = 100.0 \text{ mL} \times \frac{1 \text{ L}}{1000 \text{ mL}} \times 3.15 \times 10^{-4} \frac{\text{mol}}{\text{L}}$$
$$= 3.15 \times 10^{-5} \text{ mol}$$

Since each mole of manganese in the original steel sample yields a mole of MnO_4^-, that is,

$$1 \text{ mol of Mn} \xrightarrow{\text{Oxidation}} 1 \text{ mol of } MnO_4^-$$

the original steel sample must have contained 3.15×10^{-5} mol of manganese. The mass of manganese present in the sample is

$$3.15 \times 10^{-5} \text{ mol of Mn} \times \frac{54.938 \text{ g of Mn}}{1 \text{ mol of Mn}} = 1.73 \times 10^{-3} \text{ g of Mn}$$

Since the steel sample weighed 0.1523 g, the present manganese in the steel is

$$\frac{1.73 \times 10^{-3} \text{ g of Mn}}{1.523 \times 10^{-1} \text{ g of sample}} \times 100 = 1.14\%$$

This example illustrates a typical use of spectroscopy in quantitative analysis. The steps commonly involved are as follows:

1. Preparation of a calibration plot (a Beer's law plot) by measuring the absorbance values of a series of solutions with known concentrations.

2. Measurement of the absorbance of the solution of unknown concentration.

3. Use of the calibration plot to determine the unknown concentration.

Appendix Four   Selected Thermodynamic Data

Note: All values are assumed precise to at least ± 1.

Substance and State	ΔH_f° (kJ/mol)	ΔG_f° (kJ/mol)	S° (J/K · mol)	Substance and State	ΔH_f° (kJ/mol)	ΔG_f° (kJ/mol)	S° (J/K · mol)
Aluminum				Barium			
Al(s)	0	0	28	Ba(s)	0	0	67
$Al_2O_3(s)$	−1676	−1582	51	$BaCO_3(s)$	−1219	−1139	112
$Al(OH)_3(s)$	−1277			BaO(s)	−582	−552	70
$AlCl_3(s)$	−704	−629	111	$Ba(OH)_2(s)$	−946		

(continued)

Appendix Four (continued)

Substance and State	ΔH_f° (kJ/mol)	ΔG_f° (kJ/mol)	S° (J/K · mol)
Barium, *continued*			
$BaSO_4(s)$	−1465	−1353	132
Beryllium			
$Be(s)$	0	0	10
$BeO(s)$	−599	−569	14
$Be(OH)_2(s)$	−904	−815	47
Bromine			
$Br_2(l)$	0	0	152
$Br_2(g)$	31	3	245
$Br_2(aq)$	−3	4	130
$Br^-(aq)$	−121	−104	82
$HBr(g)$	−36	−53	199
Cadmium			
$Cd(s)$	0	0	52
$CdO(s)$	−258	−228	55
$Cd(OH)_2(s)$	−561	−474	96
$CdS(s)$	−162	−156	65
$CdSO_4(s)$	−935	−823	123
Calcium			
$Ca(s)$	0	0	41
$CaC_2(s)$	−63	−68	70
$CaCO_3(s)$	−1207	−1129	93
$CaO(s)$	−635	−604	40
$Ca(OH)_2(s)$	−987	−899	83
$Ca_3(PO_4)_2(s)$	−4126	−3890	241
$CaSO_4(s)$	−1433	−1320	107
$CaSiO_3(s)$	−1630	−1550	84
Carbon			
$C(s)$ (graphite)	0	0	6
$C(s)$ (diamond)	2	3	2
$CO(g)$	−110.5	−137	198
$CO_2(g)$	−393.5	−394	214 ✓
$CH_4(g)$	−75	−51	186
$CH_3OH(g)$	−201	−163	240
$CH_3OH(l)$	−239	−166	127
$H_2CO(g)$	−116	−110	219
$HCOOH(g)$	−363	−351	249
$HCN(g)$	135.1	125	202
$C_2H_2(g)$	227	209	201 ↗
$C_2H_4(g)$	52	68	219
$CH_3CHO(g)$	−166	−129	250
$C_2H_5OH(l)$	−278	−175	161
$C_2H_6(g)$	−84.7	−32.9	229.5
$C_3H_6(g)$	20.9	62.7	266.9
$C_3H_8(g)$	−104	−24	270
$C_2H_4O(g)$ (ethylene oxide)	−53	−13	242
$CH_2{=}CHCN(g)$	185.0	195.4	274
$CH_3COOH(l)$	−484	−389	160
$C_6H_{12}O_6(s)$	−1275	−911	212
CCl_4	−135	−65	216
Chlorine			
$Cl_2(g)$	0	0	223
$Cl_2(aq)$	−23	7	121

Substance and State	ΔH_f° (kJ/mol)	ΔG_f° (kJ/mol)	S° (J/K · mol)
Chlorine, *continued*			
$Cl^-(aq)$	−167	−131	57
$HCl(g)$	−92	−95	187
Chromium			
$Cr(s)$	0	0	24
$Cr_2O_3(s)$	−1128	−1047	81
$CrO_3(s)$	−579	−502	72
Copper			
$Cu(s)$	0	0	33
$CuCO_3(s)$	−595	−518	88
$Cu_2O(s)$	−170	−148	93
$CuO(s)$	−156	−128	43
$Cu(OH)_2(s)$	−450	−372	108
$CuS(s)$	−49	−49	67
Fluorine			
$F_2(g)$	0	0	203
$F^-(aq)$	−333	−279	−14
$HF(g)$	−271	−273	174
Hydrogen			
$H_2(g)$	0	0	131
$H(g)$	217	203	115
$H^+(aq)$	0	0	0
$OH^-(aq)$	−230	−157	−11
$H_2O(l)$	−286	−237	70
$H_2O(g)$	−242	−229	189
Iodine			
$I_2(s)$	0	0	116
$I_2(g)$	62	19	261
$I_2(aq)$	23	16	137
$I^-(aq)$	−55	−52	106
Iron			
$Fe(s)$	0	0	27
$Fe_3C(s)$	21	15	108
$Fe_{0.95}O(s)$ (wustite)	−264	−240	59
FeO	−272	−255	61
$Fe_3O_4(s)$ (magnetite)	−1117	−1013	146
$Fe_2O_3(s)$ (hematite)	−826	−740	90
$FeS(s)$	−95	−97	67
$FeS_2(s)$	−178	−166	53
$FeSO_4(s)$	−929	−825	121
Lead			
$Pb(s)$	0	0	65
$PbO_2(s)$	−277	−217	69
$PbS(s)$	−100	−99	91
$PbSO_4(s)$	−920	−813	149
Magnesium			
$Mg(s)$	0	0	33
$MgCO_3(s)$	−1113	−1029	66
$MgO(s)$	−602	−569	27
$Mg(OH)_2(s)$	−925	−834	64
Manganese			
$Mn(s)$	0	0	32

Appendix Four (continued)

Substance and State	ΔH_f° (kJ/mol)	ΔG_f° (kJ/mol)	S° (J/K · mol)
Manganese, *continued*			
$MnO(s)$	−385	−363	60
$Mn_3O_4(s)$	−1387	−1280	149
$Mn_2O_3(s)$	−971	−893	110
$MnO_2(s)$	−521	−466	53
$MnO_4^-(aq)$	−543	−449	190
Mercury			
$Hg(l)$	0	0	76
$Hg_2Cl_2(s)$	−265	−211	196
$HgCl_2(s)$	−230	−184	144
$HgO(s)$	−90	−59	70
$HgS(s)$	−58	−49	78
Nickel			
$Ni(s)$	0	0	30
$NiCl_2(s)$	−316	−272	107
$NiO(s)$	−241	−213	38
$Ni(OH)_2(s)$	−538	−453	79
$NiS(s)$	−93	−90	53
Nitrogen			
$N_2(g)$	0	0	192
$NH_3(g)$	−46	−17	193
$NH_3(aq)$	−80	−27	111
$NH_4^+(aq)$	−132	−79	113
$NO(g)$	90	87	211
$NO_2(g)$	34	52	240
$N_2O(g)$	82	104	220
$N_2O_4(g)$	10	98	304
$N_2O_4(l)$	−20	97	209
$N_2O_5(s)$	−42	134	178
$N_2H_4(l)$	51	149	121
$N_2H_3CH_3(l)$	54	180	166
$HNO_3(aq)$	−207	−111	146
$HNO_3(l)$	−174	−81	156
$NH_4ClO_4(s)$	−295	−89	186
$NH_4Cl(s)$	−314	−203	96
Oxygen			
$O_2(g)$	0	0	205
$O(g)$	249	232	161
$O_3(g)$	143	163	239
Phosphorus			
$P(s)$ (white)	0	0	41
$P(s)$ (red)	−18	−12	23
$P(s)$ (black)	−39	−33	23
$P_4(g)$	59	24	280
$PF_5(g)$	−1578	−1509	296
$PH_3(g)$	5	13	210
$H_3PO_4(s)$	−1279	−1119	110
$H_3PO_4(l)$	−1267	—	—
$H_3PO_4(aq)$	−1288	−1143	158
$P_4O_{10}(s)$	−2984	−2698	229
Potassium			
$K(s)$	0	0	64
$KCl(s)$	−436	−408	83

Substance and State	ΔH_f° (kJ/mol)	ΔG_f° (kJ/mol)	S° (J/K · mol)
Potassium, *continued*			
$KClO_3(s)$	−391	−290	143
$KClO_4(s)$	−433	−304	151
$K_2O(s)$	−361	−322	98
$K_2O_2(s)$	−496	−430	113
$KO_2(s)$	−283	−238	117
$KOH(s)$	−425	−379	79
$KOH(aq)$	−481	−440	9.20
Silicon			
$SiO_2(s)$ (quartz)	−911	−856	42
$SiCl_4(l)$	−687	−620	240
Silver			
$Ag(s)$	0	0	43
$Ag^+(aq)$	105	77	73
$AgBr(s)$	−100	−97	107
$AgCN(s)$	146	164	84
$AgCl(s)$	−127	−110	96
$Ag_2CrO_4(s)$	−712	−622	217
$AgI(s)$	−62	−66	115
$Ag_2O(s)$	−31	−11	122
$Ag_2S(s)$	−32	−40	146
Sodium			
$Na(s)$	0	0	51
$Na^+(aq)$	−240	−262	59
$NaBr(s)$	−360	−347	84
$Na_2CO_3(s)$	−1131	−1048	136
$NaHCO_3(s)$	−948	−852	102
$NaCl(s)$	−411	−384	72
$NaH(s)$	−56	−33	40
$NaI(s)$	−288	−282	91
$NaNO_2(s)$	−359		
$NaNO_3(s)$	−467	−366	116
$Na_2O(s)$	−416	−377	73
$Na_2O_2(s)$	−515	−451	95
$NaOH(s)$	−427	−381	64
$NaOH(aq)$	−470	−419	50
Sulfur			
$S(s)$ (rhombic)	0	0	32
$S(s)$ (monoclinic)	0.3	0.1	33
$S^{2-}(aq)$	33	86	−15
$S_8(g)$	102	50	431
$SF_6(g)$	−1209	−1105	292
$H_2S(g)$	−21	−34	206
$SO_2(g)$	−297	−300	248
$SO_3(g)$	−396	−371	257
$SO_4^{2-}(aq)$	−909	−745	20
$H_2SO_4(l)$	−814	−690	157
$H_2SO_4(aq)$	−909	−745	20
Tin			
$Sn(s)$ (white)	0	0	52
$Sn(s)$ (gray)	−2	0.1	44
$SnO(s)$	−285	−257	56
$SnO_2(s)$	−581	−520	52

(continued)

Appendix Four (continued)

Substance and State	ΔH_f° (kJ/mol)	ΔG_f° (kJ/mol)	S° (J/K · mol)
Tin, *continued*			
$Sn(OH)_2(s)$	−561	−492	155
Titanium			
$TiCl_4(g)$	−763	−727	355
$TiO_2(s)$	−945	−890	50
Uranium			
$U(s)$	0	0	50
$UF_6(s)$	−2137	−2008	228
$UF_6(g)$	−2113	−2029	380
$UO_2(s)$	−1084	−1029	78
$U_3O_8(s)$	−3575	−3393	282
$UO_3(s)$	−1230	−1150	99

Substance and State	ΔH_f° (kJ/mol)	ΔG_f° (kJ/mol)	S° (J/K · mol)
Xenon			
$Xe(g)$	0	0	170
$XeF_2(g)$	−108	−48	254
$XeF_4(s)$	−251	−121	146
$XeF_6(g)$	−294		
$XeO_3(s)$	402		
Zinc			
$Zn(s)$	0	0	42
$ZnO(s)$	−348	−318	44
$Zn(OH)_2(s)$	−642		
$ZnS(s)$ (wurtzite)	−193		
$ZnS(s)$ (zinc blende)	−206	−201	58
$ZnSO_4(s)$	−983	−874	120

Appendix Five · Equilibrium Constants and Reduction Potentials

A5.1 Values of K_a for Some Common Monoprotic Acids

Name	Formula	Value of K_a
Hydrogen sulfate ion	HSO_4^-	1.2×10^{-2}
Chlorous acid	$HClO_2$	1.2×10^{-2}
Monochloracetic acid	$HC_2H_2ClO_2$	1.35×10^{-3}
Hydrofluoric acid	HF	7.2×10^{-4}
Nitrous acid	HNO_2	4.0×10^{-4}
Formic acid	HCO_2H	1.8×10^{-4}
Lactic acid	$HC_3H_5O_3$	1.38×10^{-4}
Benzoic acid	$HC_7H_5O_2$	6.4×10^{-5}
Acetic acid	$HC_2H_3O_2$	1.8×10^{-5}
Hydrated aluminum(III) ion	$[Al(H_2O)_6]^{3+}$	1.4×10^{-5}
Propanoic acid	$HC_3H_5O_2$	1.3×10^{-5}
Hypochlorous acid	$HOCl$	3.5×10^{-8}
Hypobromous acid	$HOBr$	2×10^{-9}
Hydrocyanic acid	HCN	6.2×10^{-10}
Boric acid	H_3BO_3	5.8×10^{-10}
Ammonium ion	NH_4^+	5.6×10^{-10}
Phenol	HOC_6H_5	1.6×10^{-10}
Hypoiodous acid	HOI	2×10^{-11}

A5.2 Stepwise Dissociation Constants for Several Common Polyprotic Acids

Name	Formula	K_{a_1}	K_{a_2}	K_{a_3}
Phosphoric acid	H_3PO_4	7.5×10^{-3}	6.2×10^{-8}	4.8×10^{-13}
Arsenic acid	H_3AsO_4	5×10^{-3}	8×10^{-8}	6×10^{-10}
Carbonic acid	H_2CO_3	4.3×10^{-7}	5.6×10^{-11}	
Sulfuric acid	H_2SO_4	Large	1.2×10^{-2}	
Sulfurous acid	H_2SO_3	1.5×10^{-2}	1.0×10^{-7}	
Hydrosulfuric acid	H_2S	1.0×10^{-7}	$\sim 10^{-19}$	
Oxalic acid	$H_2C_2O_4$	6.5×10^{-2}	6.1×10^{-5}	
Ascorbic acid (vitamin C)	$H_2C_6H_6O_6$	7.9×10^{-5}	1.6×10^{-12}	
Citric acid	$H_3C_6H_5O_7$	8.4×10^{-4}	1.8×10^{-5}	4.0×10^{-6}

A5.3 Values of K_b for Some Common Weak Bases

Name	Conjugate Formula	Acid	K_b
Ammonia	NH_3	NH_4^+	1.8×10^{-5}
Methylamine	CH_3NH_2	$CH_3NH_3^+$	4.38×10^{-4}
Ethylamine	$C_2H_5NH_2$	$C_2H_5NH_3^+$	5.6×10^{-4}
Diethylamine	$(C_2H_5)_2NH$	$(C_2H_5)_2NH_2^+$	1.3×10^{-3}
Triethylamine	$(C_2H_5)_3N$	$(C_2H_5)_3NH^+$	4.0×10^{-4}
Hydroxylamine	$HONH_2$	$HONH_3^+$	1.1×10^{-8}
Hydrazine	H_2NNH_2	$H_2NNH_3^+$	3.0×10^{-6}
Aniline	$C_6H_5NH_2$	$C_6H_5NH_3^+$	3.8×10^{-10}
Pyridine	C_5H_5N	$C_5H_5NH^+$	1.7×10^{-9}

A5.4 K_{sp} Values at 25°C for Common Ionic Solids

Ionic Solid	K_{sp} (at 25°C)	Ionic Solid	K_{sp} (at 25°C)	Ionic Solid	K_{sp} (at 25°C)
Fluorides		Hg_2CrO_4*	2×10^{-9}	$Co(OH)_2$	2.5×10^{-16}
BaF_2	2.4×10^{-5}	$BaCrO_4$	8.5×10^{-11}	$Ni(OH)_2$	1.6×10^{-16}
MgF_2	6.4×10^{-9}	Ag_2CrO_4	9.0×10^{-12}	$Zn(OH)_2$	4.5×10^{-17}
PbF_2	4×10^{-8}	$PbCrO_4$	2×10^{-16}	$Cu(OH)_2$	1.6×10^{-19}
SrF_2	7.9×10^{-10}			$Hg(OH)_2$	3×10^{-26}
CaF_2	4.0×10^{-11}	Carbonates		$Sn(OH)_2$	3×10^{-27}
		$NiCO_3$	1.4×10^{-7}	$Cr(OH)_3$	6.7×10^{-31}
Chlorides		$CaCO_3$	8.7×10^{-9}	$Al(OH)_3$	2×10^{-32}
$PbCl_2$	1.6×10^{-5}	$BaCO_3$	1.6×10^{-9}	$Fe(OH)_3$	4×10^{-38}
$AgCl$	1.6×10^{-10}	$SrCO_3$	7×10^{-10}	$Co(OH)_3$	2.5×10^{-43}
Hg_2Cl_2*	1.1×10^{-18}	$CuCO_3$	2.5×10^{-10}		
		$ZnCO_3$	2×10^{-10}	Sulfides	
Bromides		$MnCO_3$	8.8×10^{-11}	MnS	2.3×10^{-13}
$PbBr_2$	4.6×10^{-6}	$FeCO_3$	2.1×10^{-11}	FeS	3.7×10^{-19}
$AgBr$	5.0×10^{-13}	Ag_2CO_3	8.1×10^{-12}	NiS	3×10^{-21}
Hg_2Br_2*	1.3×10^{-22}	$CdCO_3$	5.2×10^{-12}	CoS	5×10^{-22}
		$PbCO_3$	1.5×10^{-15}	ZnS	2.5×10^{-22}
Iodides		$MgCO_3$	1×10^{-5}	SnS	1×10^{-26}
PbI_2	1.4×10^{-8}	Hg_2CO_3*	9.0×10^{-15}	CdS	1.0×10^{-28}
AgI	1.5×10^{-16}			PbS	7×10^{-29}
Hg_2I_2*	4.5×10^{-29}	Hydroxides		CuS	8.5×10^{-45}
		$Ba(OH)_2$	5.0×10^{-3}	Ag_2S	1.6×10^{-49}
Sulfates		$Sr(OH)_2$	3.2×10^{-4}	HgS	1.6×10^{-54}
$CaSO_4$	6.1×10^{-5}	$Ca(OH)_2$	1.3×10^{-6}		
Ag_2SO_4	1.2×10^{-5}	$AgOH$	2.0×10^{-8}	Phosphates	
$SrSO_4$	3.2×10^{-7}	$Mg(OH)_2$	8.9×10^{-12}	Ag_3PO_4	1.8×10^{-18}
$PbSO_4$	1.3×10^{-8}	$Mn(OH)_2$	2×10^{-13}	$Sr_3(PO_4)_2$	1×10^{-31}
$BaSO_4$	1.5×10^{-9}	$Cd(OH)_2$	5.9×10^{-15}	$Ca_3(PO_4)_2$	1.3×10^{-32}
		$Pb(OH)_2$	1.2×10^{-15}	$Ba_3(PO_4)_2$	6×10^{-39}
Chromates		$Fe(OH)_2$	1.8×10^{-15}	$Pb_3(PO_4)_2$	1×10^{-54}
$SrCrO_4$	3.6×10^{-5}				

*Contains Hg_2^{2+} ions. $K_{sp} = [Hg_2^{2+}][X^-]^2$ for Hg_2X_2 salts.

A5.5 Standard Reduction Potentials at 25°C (298 K) for Many Common Half-Reactions

Half-Reaction	$\mathscr{E}°$ (V)	Half-Reaction	$\mathscr{E}°$ (V)
$F_2 + 2e^- \rightarrow 2F^-$	2.87	$O_2 + 2H_2O + 4e^- \rightarrow 4OH^-$	0.40
$Ag^{2+} + e^- \rightarrow Ag^+$	1.99	$Cu^{2+} + 2e^- \rightarrow Cu$	0.34
$Co^{3+} + e^- \rightarrow Co^{2+}$	1.82	$Hg_2Cl_2 + 2e^- \rightarrow 2Hg + 2Cl^-$	0.34
$H_2O_2 + 2H^+ + 2e^- \rightarrow 2H_2O$	1.78	$AgCl + e^- \rightarrow Ag + Cl^-$	0.22
$Ce^{4+} + e^- \rightarrow Ce^{3+}$	1.70	$SO_4^{2-} + 4H^+ + 2e^- \rightarrow H_2SO_3 + H_2O$	0.20
$PbO_2 + 4H^+ + SO_4^{2-} + 2e^- \rightarrow PbSO_4 + 2H_2O$	1.69	$Cu^{2+} + e^- \rightarrow Cu^+$	0.16
$MnO_4^- + 4H^+ + 3e^- \rightarrow MnO_2 + 2H_2O$	1.68	$2H^+ + 2e^- \rightarrow H_2$	0.00
$2e^- + 2H^+ + IO_4^- \rightarrow IO_3^- + H_2O$	1.60	$Fe^{3+} + 3e^- \rightarrow Fe$	−0.036
$MnO_4^- + 8H^+ + 5e^- \rightarrow Mn^{2+} + 4H_2O$	1.51	$Pb^{2+} + 2e^- \rightarrow Pb$	−0.13
$Au^{3+} + 3e^- \rightarrow Au$	1.50	$Sn^{2+} + 2e^- \rightarrow Sn$	−0.14
$PbO_2 + 4H^+ + 2e^- \rightarrow Pb^{2+} + 2H_2O$	1.46	$Ni^{2+} + 2e^- \rightarrow Ni$	−0.23
$Cl_2 + 2e^- \rightarrow 2Cl^-$	1.36	$PbSO_4 + 2e^- \rightarrow Pb + SO_4^{2-}$	−0.35
$Cr_2O_7^{2-} + 14H^+ + 6e^- \rightarrow 2Cr^{3+} + 7H_2O$	1.33	$Cd^{2+} + 2e^- \rightarrow Cd$	−0.40
$O_2 + 4H^+ + 4e^- \rightarrow 2H_2O$	1.23	$Fe^{2+} + 2e^- \rightarrow Fe$	−0.44
$MnO_2 + 4H^+ + 2e^- \rightarrow Mn^{2+} + 2H_2O$	1.21	$Cr^{3+} + e^- \rightarrow Cr^{2+}$	−0.50
$IO_3^- + 6H^+ + 5e^- \rightarrow \frac{1}{2}I_2 + 3H_2O$	1.20	$Cr^{3+} + 3e^- \rightarrow Cr$	−0.73
$Br_2 + 2e^- \rightarrow 2Br^-$	1.09	$Zn^{2+} + 2e^- \rightarrow Zn$	−0.76
$VO_2^+ + 2H^+ + e^- \rightarrow VO^{2+} + H_2O$	1.00	$2H_2O + 2e^- \rightarrow H_2 + 2OH^-$	−0.83
$AuCl_4^- + 3e^- \rightarrow Au + 4Cl^-$	0.99	$Mn^{2+} + 2e^- \rightarrow Mn$	−1.18
$NO_3^- + 4H^+ + 3e^- \rightarrow NO + 2H_2O$	0.96	$Al^{3+} + 3e^- \rightarrow Al$	−1.66
$ClO_2 + e^- \rightarrow ClO_2^-$	0.954	$H_2 + 2e^- \rightarrow 2H^-$	−2.23
$2Hg^{2+} + 2e^- \rightarrow Hg_2^{2+}$	0.91	$Mg^{2+} + 2e^- \rightarrow Mg$	−2.37
$Ag^+ + e^- \rightarrow Ag$	0.80	$La^{3+} + 3e^- \rightarrow La$	−2.37
$Hg_2^{2+} + 2e^- \rightarrow 2Hg$	0.80	$Na^+ + e^- \rightarrow Na$	−2.71
$Fe^{3+} + e^- \rightarrow Fe^{2+}$	0.77	$Ca^{2+} + 2e^- \rightarrow Ca$	−2.76
$O_2 + 2H^+ + 2e^- \rightarrow H_2O_2$	0.68	$Ba^{2+} + 2e^- \rightarrow Ba$	−2.90
$MnO_4^- + e^- \rightarrow MnO_4^{2-}$	0.56	$K^+ + e^- \rightarrow K$	−2.92
$I_2 + 2e^- \rightarrow 2I^-$	0.54	$Li^+ + e^- \rightarrow Li$	−3.05
$Cu^+ + e^- \rightarrow Cu$	0.52		

Appendix Six   SI Units and Conversion Factors

Length

SI unit: meter (m)

1 meter	= 1.0936 yards
1 centimeter	= 0.39370 inch
1 inch	= 2.54 centimeters (exactly)
1 kilometer	= 0.62137 mile
1 mile	= 5280 feet
	= 1.6093 kilometers
1 angstrom	= 10^{-10} meter
	= 100 picometers

Mass

SI unit: kilogram (kg)

1 kilogram	= 1000 grams
	= 2.2046 pounds
1 pound	= 453.59 grams
	= 0.45359 kilogram
	= 16 ounces
1 ton	= 2000 pounds
	= 907.185 kilograms
1 metric ton	= 1000 kilograms
	= 2204.6 pounds
1 atomic mass unit	= 1.66056×10^{-27} kilograms

Volume

SI unit: cubic meter (m^3)

1 liter	= 10^{-3} m^3
	= 1 dm^3
	= 1.0567 quarts
1 gallon	= 4 quarts
	= 8 pints
	= 3.7854 liters
1 quart	= 32 fluid ounces
	= 0.94633 liter

Temperature

SI unit: kelvin (K)

$$0 \text{ K} = -273.15°C$$
$$= -459.67°F$$
$$\text{K} = °C + 273.15$$
$$°C = \frac{5}{9}(°F - 32)$$
$$°F = \frac{9}{5}(°C) + 32$$

Energy

SI unit: joule (J)

1 joule	= 1 kg · m^2/s^2
	= 0.23901 calorie
	= 9.4781×10^{-4} btu (British thermal unit)
1 calorie	= 4.184 joules
	= 3.965×10^{-3} btu
1 btu	= 1055.06 joules
	= 252.2 calories

Pressure

SI unit: pascal (Pa)

1 pascal	= 1 N/m^2
	= 1 kg/m · s^2
1 atmosphere	= 101.325 kilopascals
	= 760 torr (mmHg)
	= 14.70 pounds per square inch
1 bar	= 10^5 pascals

Glossary

Accuracy the agreement of a particular value with the true value. (1.4)

Acid a substance that produces hydrogen ions in solution; a proton donor. (2.8; 4.2; 4.8)

Acid–base indicator a substance that marks the end point of an acid–base titration by changing color. (15.5)

Acid dissociation constant (K_a) the equilibrium constant for a reaction in which a proton is removed from an acid by H_2O to form the conjugate base and H_3O^+. (14.1)

Acid rain a result of air pollution by sulfur dioxide. (5.10)

Acidic oxide a covalent oxide that dissolves in water to give an acidic solution. (14.10)

Actinide series a group of 14 elements following actinium in the periodic table, in which the $5f$ orbitals are being filled. (7.11; 19.1)

Activated complex (transition state) the arrangement of atoms found at the top of the potential energy barrier as a reaction proceeds from reactants to products. (12.7)

Activation energy the threshold energy that must be overcome to produce a chemical reaction. (12.7)

Addition polymerization a type of polymerization in which the monomers simply add together to form the polymer, with no other products. (22.5)

Addition reaction a reaction in which atoms add to a carbon–carbon multiple bond. (22.2)

Adsorption the collection of one substance on the surface of another. (12.8)

Air pollution contamination of the atmosphere, mainly by the gaseous products of transportation and production of electricity. (5.10)

Alcohol an organic compound in which the hydroxyl group is a substituent on a hydrocarbon. (22.4)

Aldehyde an organic compound containing the carbonyl group bonded to at least one hydrogen atom. (22.4)

Alkali metal a Group 1A metal. (2.7; 19.2)

Alkaline earth metal a Group 2A metal. (2.7; 19.4)

Alkane a saturated hydrocarbon with the general formula C_nH_{2n+2}. (22.1)

Alkene an unsaturated hydrocarbon containing a carbon–carbon double bond. The general formula is C_nH_{2n}. (22.2)

Alkyne an unsaturated hydrocarbon containing a triple carbon–carbon bond. The general formula is C_nH_{2n-2}. (22.2)

Alloy a substance that contains a mixture of elements and has metallic properties. (10.4)

Alloy steel a form of steel containing carbon plus other metals such as chromium, cobalt, manganese, and molybdenum. (21.8)

Alpha (α) particle a helium nucleus. (18.1)

Alpha-particle production a common mode of decay for radio-active nuclides in which the mass number changes. (18.1)

Amine an organic base derived from ammonia in which one or more of the hydrogen atoms are replaced by organic groups. (14.6; 22.4)

α-Amino acid an organic acid in which an amino group and an R group are attached to the carbon atom next to the carboxyl group. (22.6)

Amorphous solid a solid with considerable disorder in its structure. (10.3)

Ampere the unit of electric current equal to one coulomb of charge per second. (17.7)

Amphoteric substance a substance that can behave either as an acid or as a base. (14.2)

Angular momentum quantum number (ℓ) the quantum number relating to the shape of an atomic orbital, which can assume any integral value from 0 to $n-1$ for each value of n. (7.6)

Anion a negative ion. (2.6)

Anode the electrode in a galvanic cell at which oxidation occurs. (17.1)

Antibonding molecular orbital an orbital higher in energy than the atomic orbitals of which it is composed. (9.2)

Aqueous solution a solution in which water is the dissolving medium or solvent. (4)

Aromatic hydrocarbon one of a special class of cyclic unsaturated hydrocarbons, the simplest of which is benzene. (22.3)

Arrhenius concept a concept postulating that acids produce hydrogen ions in aqueous solution, while bases produce hydroxide ions. (14.1)

Arrhenius equation the equation representing the rate constant as $k = Ae^{-E_a/RT}$, where A represents the product of the collision frequency and the steric factor, and $e^{-E_a/RT}$ is the fraction of collisions with sufficient energy to produce a reaction. (12.7)

Atactic chain a polymer chain in which the substituent groups such as CH_3 are randomly distributed along the chain. (22.5)

Atmosphere the mixture of gases that surrounds the earth's surface. (5.10)

Atomic number the number of protons in the nucleus of an atom. (2.5; 18)

Atomic radius half the distance between the nuclei in a molecule consisting of identical atoms. (7.12)

Atomic solid a solid that contains atoms at the lattice points. (10.3)

Atomic weight the weighted average mass of the atoms in a naturally occurring element. (2.3)

Aufbau principle the principle stating that as protons are added one by one to the nucleus to build up the elements, electrons are similarly added to hydrogen-like orbitals. (7.11)

Autoionization the transfer of a proton from one molecule to another of the same substance. (14.2)

Avogadro's law equal volumes of gases at the same temperature and pressure contain the same number of particles. (5.2)

Avogadro's number the number of atoms in exactly 12 grams of pure ^{12}C, equal to 6.022×10^{23}. (3.3)

Ball-and-stick model a molecular model that distorts the sizes of atoms but shows bond relationships clearly. (2.6)

Band model a molecular model for metals in which the electrons are assumed to travel around the metal crystal in molecular orbitals formed from the valence atomic orbitals of the metal atoms. (10.4)

Barometer a device for measuring atmospheric pressure. (5.1)

Base a substance that produces hydroxide ions in aqueous solution, a proton acceptor. (4.8)

Basic oxide an ionic oxide that dissolves in water to produce a basic solution. (14.10)

Basic oxygen process a process for producing steel by oxidizing and removing the impurities in iron using a high-pressure blast of oxygen. (21.8)

Battery a group of galvanic cells connected in series. (17.5)

Beta (β) particle an electron produced in radioactive decay. (18.1)

Beta-particle production a decay process for radioactive nuclides in which the mass number remains constant and the atomic number changes. The net effect is to change a neutron to a proton. (18.1)

Bidentate ligand a ligand that can form two bonds to a metal ion. (21.3)

Bimolecular step a reaction involving the collision of two molecules. (12.6)

Binary compound a two-element compound. (2.8)

Binding energy (nuclear) the energy required to decompose a nucleus into its component nucleons. (18.5)

Biomolecule a molecule responsible for maintaining and/or reproducing life. (22)

Blast furnace a furnace in which iron oxide is reduced to iron metal by using a very strong blast of hot air to produce carbon monoxide from coke, and then using this gas as a reducing agent for the iron. (21.8)

Bond energy the energy required to break a given chemical bond. (8.1)

Bond length the distance between the nuclei of the two atoms connected by a bond; the distance where the total energy of a diatomic molecule is minimal. (8.1)

Bond order the difference between the number of bonding electrons and the number of antibonding electrons, divided by two. It is an index of bond strength. (9.2)

Bonding molecular orbital an orbital lower in energy than the atomic orbitals of which it is composed. (9.2)

Bonding pair an electron pair found in the space between two atoms. (8.9)

Borane a covalent hydride of boron. (19.5)

Boyle's law the volume of a given sample of gas at constant temperature varies inversely with the pressure. (5.2)

Breeder reactor a nuclear reactor in which fissionable fuel is produced while the reactor runs. (18.6)

Brønsted–Lowry model a model proposing that an acid is a proton donor, and a base is a proton acceptor. (14.1)

Buffered solution a solution that resists a change in its pH when either hydroxide ions or protons are added. (15.2)

Buffering capacity the ability of a buffered solution to absorb protons or hydroxide ions without a significant change in pH; determined by the magnitudes of [HA] and [A$^-$] in the solution. (15.3)

Calorimetry the science of measuring heat flow. (6.2)

Capillary action the spontaneous rising of a liquid in a narrow tube. (10.2)

Carbohydrate a polyhydroxyl ketone or polyhydroxyl aldehyde or a polymer composed of these. (22.6)

Carbon steel an alloy of iron containing up to about 1.5% carbon. (21.8)

Carboxyhemoglobin a stable complex of hemoglobin and carbon monoxide that prevents normal oxygen uptake in the blood. (21.7)

Carboxyl group the —COOH group in an organic acid. (14.2; 22.4)

Carboxylic acid an organic compound containing the carboxyl group; an acid with the general formula RCOOH. (22.4)

Catalyst a substance that speeds up a reaction without being consumed. (12.8)

Cathode the electrode in a galvanic cell at which reduction occurs. (17.1)

Cathode rays the "rays" emanating from the negative electrode (cathode) in a partially evacuated tube; a stream of electrons. (2.4)

Cathodic protection a method in which an active metal, such as magnesium, is connected to steel to protect it from corrosion. (17.6)

Cation a positive ion. (2.6)

Cell potential (electromotive force) the driving force in a galvanic cell that pulls electrons from the reducing agent in one compartment to the oxidizing agent in the other. (17.1)

Ceramic a nonmetallic material made from clay and hardened by firing at high temperature; it contains minute silicate crystals suspended in a glassy cement. (10.5)

Chain reaction (nuclear) a self-sustaining fission process caused by the production of neutrons that proceed to split other nuclei. (18.6)

Charles's law the volume of a given sample of gas at constant pressure is directly proportional to the temperature in kelvins. (5.2)

Chelating ligand (chelate) a ligand having more than one atom with a lone pair that can be used to bond to a metal ion. (21.3)

Chemical bond the force or, more accurately, the energy, that holds two atoms together in a compound. (2.6)

Chemical change the change of substances into other substances through a reorganization of the atoms; a chemical reaction. (1.9)

Chemical equation a representation of a chemical reaction showing the relative numbers of reactant and product molecules. (3.7)

Chemical equilibrium a dynamic reaction system in which the concentrations of all reactants and products remain constant as a function of time. (13)

Chemical formula the representation of a molecule in which the symbols for the elements are used to indicate the types of atoms present and subscripts are used to show the relative numbers of atoms. (2.6)

Chemical kinetics the area of chemistry that concerns reaction rates. (12)

Chemical stoichiometry the calculation of the quantities of material consumed and produced in chemical reactions. (3)

Chirality the quality of having nonsuperimposable mirror images. (21.4)

Chlor–alkali process the process for producing chlorine and sodium hydroxide by electrolyzing brine in a mercury cell. (17.8)

Chromatography the general name for a series of methods for separating mixtures by employing a system with a mobile phase and a stationary phase. (1.9)

Coagulation the destruction of a colloid by causing particles to aggregate and settle out. (11.8)

Codons organic bases in sets of three that form the genetic code. (22.6)

Colligative properties properties of a solution that depend only on the number, and not on the identity, of the solute particles. (11.5)

Collision model a model based on the idea that molecules must collide to react; used to account for the observed characteristics of reaction rates. (12.7)

Colloid (colloidal dispersion) a suspension of particles in a dispersing medium. (11.8)

Combustion reaction the vigorous and exothermic reaction that takes place between certain substances, particularly organic compounds, and oxygen. (22.1)

Common ion effect the shift in an equilibrium position caused by the addition or presence of an ion involved in the equilibrium reaction. (15.1)

Complete ionic equation an equation that shows all substances that are strong electrolytes as ions. (4.6)

Complex ion a charged species consisting of a metal ion surrounded by ligands. (15.8; 21.1)

Compound a substance with constant composition that can be broken down into elements by chemical processes. (1.9)

Concentration cell a galvanic cell in which both compartments contain the same components, but at different concentrations. (17.4)

Condensation the process by which vapor molecules reform a liquid. (10.8)

Condensation polymerization a type of polymerization in which the formation of a small molecule, such as water, accompanies the extension of the polymer chain. (22.5)

Condensation reaction a reaction in which two molecules are joined, accompanied by the elimination of a water molecule. (20.3)

Condensed states of matter liquids and solids. (10.1)

Conjugate acid the species formed when a proton is added to a base. (14.1)

Conjugate acid–base pair two species related to each other by the donating and accepting of a single proton. (14.1)

Conjugate base what remains of an acid molecule after a proton is lost. (14.1)

Continuous spectrum a spectrum that exhibits all the wavelengths of visible light. (7.3)

Control rods rods in a nuclear reactor composed of substances that absorb neutrons. These rods regulate the power level of the reactor. (18.6)

Coordinate covalent bond a metal–ligand bond resulting from the interaction of a Lewis base (the ligand) and a Lewis acid (the metal ion). (21.3)

Coordination compound a compound composed of a complex ion and counter ions sufficient to give no net charge. (21.3)

Coordination isomerism isomerism in a coordination compound in which the composition of the coordination sphere of the metal ion varies. (21.4)

Coordination number the number of bonds formed between the metal ion and the ligands in a complex ion. (21.3)

Copolymer a polymer formed from the polymerization of more than one type of monomer. (22.5)

Core electron an inner electron in an atom; one not in the outermost (valence) principal quantum level. (7.11)

Corrosion the process by which metals are oxidized in the atmosphere. (17.6)

Coulomb's law $E = 2.31 \times 10^{-19} \left(\dfrac{Q_1 Q_2}{r}\right)$, where E is the energy of interaction between a pair of ions, expressed in joules; r is the distance between the ion centers in nm; and Q_1 and Q_2 are the numerical ion charges. (8.1)

Counterions anions or cations that balance the charge on the complex ion in a coordination compound. (21.3)

Covalent bonding a type of bonding in which electrons are shared by atoms. (2.6; 8.1)

Critical mass the mass of fissionable material required to produce a self-sustaining chain reaction. (18.6)

Critical point the point on a phase diagram at which the temperature and pressure have their critical values; the end point of the liquid–vapor line. (10.9)

Critical pressure the minimum pressure required to produce liquefaction of a substance at the critical temperature. (10.9)

Critical reaction (nuclear) a reaction in which exactly one neutron from each fission event causes another fission event, thus sustaining the chain reaction. (18.6)

Critical temperature the temperature above which vapor cannot be liquefied no matter what pressure is applied. (10.9)

Crosslinking the existence of bonds between adjacent chains in a polymer, thus adding strength to the material. (22.5)

Crystal field model a model used to explain the magnetism and colors of coordination complexes through the splitting of the d orbital energies. (21.6)

Crystalline solid a solid with a regular arrangement of its components. (10.3)

Cubic closest packed (ccp) structure a solid modeled by the closest packing of spheres with an *abcabc* arrangement of layers; the unit cell is face-centered cubic. (10.4)

Cyanidation a process in which crushed gold ore is treated with an aqueous cyanide solution in the presence of air to dissolve the gold. Pure gold is recovered by reduction of the ion to the metal. (21.8)

Cyclotron a type of particle accelerator in which an ion introduced at the center is accelerated in an expanding spiral path by the use of alternating electrical fields in the presence of a magnetic field. (18.3)

Cytochromes a series of iron-containing species composed of heme and a protein. Cytochromes are the principal electron-transfer molecules in the respiratory chain. (21.7)

Dalton's law of partial pressures for a mixture of gases in a container, the total pressure exerted is the sum of the pressures that each gas would exert if it were alone. (5.5)

Degenerate orbitals a group of orbitals with the same energy. (7.7)

Dehydrogenation reaction a reaction in which two hydrogen atoms are removed from adjacent carbons of a saturated hydrocarbon, giving an unsaturated hydrocarbon. (22.1)

Denaturation the breaking down of the three-dimensional structure of a protein resulting in the loss of its function. (22.6)

Denitrification the return of nitrogen from decomposed matter to the atmosphere by bacteria that change nitrates to nitrogen gas. (20.2)

Density a property of matter representing the mass per unit volume. (1.8)

Deoxyribonucleic acid (DNA) a huge nucleotide polymer having a double-helical structure with complementary bases on the two strands. Its major functions are protein synthesis and the storage and transport of genetic information. (22.6)

Desalination the removal of dissolved salts from an aqueous solution. (11.6)

Dialysis a phenomenon in which a semipermeable membrane allows transfer of both solvent molecules and small solute molecules and ions. (11.6)

Diamagnetism a type of magnetism, associated with paired electrons, that causes a substance to be repelled from the inducing magnetic field. (9.3)

Differential rate law an expression that gives the rate of a reaction as a function of concentrations; often called the rate law. (12.2)

Diffraction the scattering of light from a regular array of points or lines, producing constructive and destructive interference. (7.2)

Diffusion the mixing of gases. (5.7)

Dilution the process of adding solvent to lower the concentration of solute in a solution. (4.3)

Dimer a molecule formed by the joining of two identical monomers. (22.5)

Dipole–dipole attraction the attractive force resulting when polar molecules line up so that the positive and negative ends are close to each other. (10.1)

Dipole moment a property of a molecule whose charge distribution can be represented by a center of positive charge and a center of negative charge. (8.3)

Direct reduction furnace a furnace in which iron oxide is reduced to iron metal using milder reaction conditions than in a blast furnace. (21.8)

Disaccharide a sugar formed from two monosaccharides joined by a glycoside linkage. (22.6)

Disproportionation reaction a reaction in which a given element is both oxidized and reduced. (20.7)

Distillation a method for separating the components of a liquid mixture that depends on differences in the ease of vaporization of the components. (1.9)

Disulfide linkage an S—S bond that stabilizes the tertiary structure of many proteins. (22.6)

Double bond a bond in which two pairs of electrons are shared by two atoms. (8.8)

Downs cell a cell used for electrolyzing molten sodium chloride. (17.8)

Dry cell battery a common battery used in calculators, watches, radios, and tape players. (17.5)

Dual nature of light the statement that light exhibits both wave and particulate properties. (7.2)

Effusion the passage of a gas through a tiny orifice into an evacuated chamber. (5.7)

Electrical conductivity the ability to conduct an electric current. (4.2)

Electrochemistry the study of the interchange of chemical and electrical energy. (17)

Electrolysis a process that involves forcing a current through a cell to cause a nonspontaneous chemical reaction to occur. (17.7)

Electrolyte a material that dissolves in water to give a solution that conducts an electric current. (4.2)

Electrolytic cell a cell that uses electrical energy to produce a chemical change that would otherwise not occur spontaneously. (17.7)

Electromagnetic radiation radiant energy that exhibits wavelike behavior and travels through space at the speed of light in a vacuum. (7.1)

Electron a negatively charged particle that moves around the nucleus of an atom. (2.4)

Electron affinity the energy change associated with the addition of an electron to a gaseous atom. (7.12)

Electron capture a process in which one of the inner-orbital electrons in an atom is captured by the nucleus. (18.1)

Electron spin quantum number a quantum number representing one of the two possible values for the electron spin; either $+\frac{1}{2}$ or $-\frac{1}{2}$. (7.8)

Electronegativity the tendency of an atom in a molecule to attract shared electrons to itself. (8.2)

Element a substance that cannot be decomposed into simpler substances by chemical or physical means. (1.9)

Elementary step a reaction whose rate law can be written from its molecularity. (12.6)

$E = mc^2$ Einstein's equation proposing that energy has mass; E is energy, m is mass, and c is the speed of light. (7.2)

Empirical formula the simplest whole number ratio of atoms in a compound. (3.6)

Enantiomers isomers that are nonsuperimposable mirror images of each other. (21.4)

Endpoint the point in a titration at which the indicator changes color. (4.8)

Endothermic refers to a reaction where energy (as heat) flows into the system. (6.1)

Energy the capacity to do work or to cause heat flow. (6.1)

Enthalpy a property of a system equal to $E + PV$, where E is the internal energy of the system, P is the pressure of the system, and V is the volume of the system. At constant pressure the change in enthalpy equals the energy flow as heat. (6.2)

Enthalpy (heat) of fusion the enthalpy change that occurs to melt a solid at its melting point. (10.8)

Entropy a thermodynamic function that measures randomness or disorder. (16.1)

Enzyme a large molecule, usually a protein, that catalyzes biological reactions. (12.8)

Equilibrium constant the value obtained when equilibrium concentrations of the chemical species are substituted in the equilibrium expression. (13.2)

Equilibrium expression the expression (from the law of mass action) obtained by multiplying the product concentrations and dividing by the multiplied reactant concentrations, with each concentration raised to a power represented by the coefficient in the balanced equation. (13.2)

Equilibrium point (thermodynamic definition) the position where the free energy of a reaction system has its lowest possible value. (16.8)

Equilibrium position a particular set of equilibrium concentrations. (13.2)

Equivalence point (stoichiometric point) the point in a titration when enough titrant has been added to react exactly with the substance in solution being titrated. (4.9; 15.4)

Ester an organic compound produced by the reaction between a carboxylic acid and an alcohol. (22.4)

Exothermic refers to a reaction where energy (as heat) flows out of the system. (6.1)

Exponential notation expresses a number as $N \times 10^M$, a convenient method for representing a very large or very small number and for easily indicating the number of significant figures. (1.5)

Faraday a constant representing the charge on one mole of electrons; 96,485 coulombs. (17.3)

Filtration a method for separating the components of a mixture containing a solid and a liquid. (1.9)

First law of thermodynamics the energy of the universe is constant; same as the law of conservation of energy. (6.1)

Fission the process of using a neutron to split a heavy nucleus into two nuclei with smaller mass numbers. (18.6)

Flotation process a method of separating the mineral particles in an ore from the gangue that depends on the greater wettability of the mineral pieces. (21.8)

Formal charge the charge assigned to an atom in a molecule or polyatomic ion derived from a specific set of rules. (8.12)

Formation constant (stability constant) the equilibrium constant for each step of the formation of a complex ion by the addition of an individual ligand to a metal ion or complex ion in aqueous solution. (15.8)

Formula equation an equation representing a reaction in solution showing the reactants and products in undissociated form, whether they are strong or weak electrolytes. (4.6)

Fossil fuel coal, petroleum, or natural gas; consists of carbon-based molecules derived from decomposition of once-living organisms. (6.5)

Frasch process the recovery of sulfur from underground deposits by melting it with hot water and forcing it to the surface by air pressure. (20.6)

Free energy a thermodynamic function equal to the enthalpy (H) minus the product of the entropy (S) and the Kelvin temperature (T); $G = H - TS$. Under certain conditions the change in free energy for a process is equal to the maximum useful work. (16.4)

Free radical a species with an unpaired electron. (22.5)

Frequency the number of waves (cycles) per second that pass a given point in space. (7.1)

Fuel cell a galvanic cell for which the reactants are continuously supplied. (17.5)

Functional group an atom or group of atoms in hydrocarbon derivatives that contains elements in addition to carbon and hydrogen. (22.4)

Fusion the process of combining two light nuclei to form a heavier, more stable nucleus. (18.6)

Galvanic cell a device in which chemical energy from a spontaneous redox reaction is changed to electrical energy that can be used to do work. (17.1)

Galvanizing a process in which steel is coated with zinc to prevent corrosion. (17.6)

Gamma (γ) ray a high-energy photon. (18.1)

Gangue the impurities (such as clay or sand) in an ore. (21.8)

Geiger–Müller counter (Geiger counter) an instrument that measures the rate of radioactive decay based on the ions and electrons produced as a radioactive particle passes through a gas-filled chamber. (18.4)

Gene a given segment of the DNA molecule that contains the code for a specific protein. (22.6)

Geometrical (*cis–trans*) isomerism isomerism in which atoms or groups of atoms can assume different positions around a rigid ring or bond. (21.4; 22.2)

Glass an amorphous solid obtained when silica is mixed with other compounds, heated above its melting point, and then cooled rapidly. (10.5)

Glass electrode an electrode for measuring pH from the potential difference that develops when it is dipped into an aqueous solution containing H^+ ions. (17.4)

Glycoside linkage a C—O—C bond formed between the rings of two cyclic monosaccharides by the elimination of water. (22.6)

Graham's law of effusion the rate of effusion of a gas is inversely proportional to the square root of the mass of its particles. (5.7)

Greenhouse effect a warming effect exerted by the earth's atmosphere (particularly CO_2 and H_2O) due to thermal energy retained by absorption of infrared radiation. (6.5)

Ground state the lowest possible energy state of an atom or molecule. (7.4)

Group (of the periodic table) a vertical column of elements having the same valence electron configuration and showing similar properties. (2.7)

Haber process the manufacture of ammonia from nitrogen and hydrogen, carried out at high pressure and high temperature with the aid of a catalyst. (3.10; 20.2)

Half-life (of a radioactive sample) the time required for the number of nuclides in a radioactive sample to reach half of the original value. (18.2)

Half-life (of a reactant) the time required for a reactant to reach half of its original concentration. (12.4)

Half-reactions the two parts of an oxidation–reduction reaction, one representing oxidation, the other reduction. (4.10; 17.1)

Halogen a Group 7A element. (2.7; 20.7)

Halogenation the addition of halogen atoms to unsaturated hydrocarbons. (22.2)

Hard water water from natural sources that contains relatively large concentrations of calcium and magnesium ions. (19.4)

Heat energy transferred between two objects due to a temperature difference between them. (6.1)

Heat capacity the amount of energy required to raise the temperature of an object by one degree Celsius. (6.2)

Heat of fusion the enthalpy change that occurs to melt a solid at its melting point. (10.8)

Heat of hydration the enthalpy change associated with placing gaseous molecules or ions in water; the sum of the energy needed to expand the solvent and the energy released from the solvent–solute interactions. (11.2)

Heat of solution the enthalpy change associated with dissolving a solute in a solvent; the sum of the energies needed to expand both solvent and solute in a solution and the energy released from the solvent–solute interactions. (11.2)

Heat of vaporization the energy required to vaporize one mole of a liquid at a pressure of one atmosphere. (10.8)

Heating curve a plot of temperature versus time for a substance where energy is added at a constant rate. (10.8)

Heisenberg uncertainty principle a principle stating that there is a fundamental limitation to how precisely both the position and momentum of a particle can be known at a given time. (7.5)

Heme an iron complex. (21.7)

Hemoglobin a biomolecule composed of four myoglobin-like units (proteins plus heme) that can bind and transport four oxygen molecules in the blood. (21.7)

Henderson–Hasselbalch equation an equation giving the relationship between the pH of an acid–base system and the concentrations of base and acid: $\text{pH} = \text{p}K_\text{a} + \log\left(\dfrac{[\text{base}]}{[\text{acid}]}\right)$. (15.2)

Henry's law the amount of a gas dissolved in a solution is directly proportional to the pressure of the gas above the solution. (11.3)

Hess's law in going from a particular set of reactants to a particular set of products, the enthalpy change is the same whether the reaction takes place in one step or in a series of steps; in summary, enthalpy is a state function. (6.3)

Heterogeneous equilibrium an equilibrium involving reactants and/or products in more than one phase. (13.4)

Hexagonal closest packed (hcp) structure a structure composed of closest packed spheres with an *ababab* arrangement of layers; the unit cell is hexagonal. (10.4)

Homogeneous equilibrium an equilibrium system where all reactants and products are in the same phase. (13.4)

Homopolymer a polymer formed from the polymerization of only one type of monomer. (22.5)

Hund's rule the lowest energy configuration for an atom is the one having the maximum number of unpaired electrons allowed by the Pauli exclusion principle in a particular set of degenerate orbitals, with all unpaired electrons having parallel spins. (7.11)

Hybrid orbitals a set of atomic orbitals adopted by an atom in a molecule different from those of the atom in the free state. (9.1)

Hybridization a mixing of the native orbitals on a given atom to form special atomic orbitals for bonding. (9.1)

Hydration the interaction between solute particles and water molecules. (4.1)

Hydride a binary compound containing hydrogen. The hydride ion, H^-, exists in ionic hydrides. The three classes of hydrides are covalent, interstitial, and ionic. (19.3)

Hydrocarbon a compound composed of carbon and hydrogen. (22.1)

Hydrocarbon derivative an organic molecule that contains one or more elements in addition to carbon and hydrogen. (22.4)

Hydrogen bonding unusually strong dipole–dipole attractions that occur among molecules in which hydrogen is bonded to a highly electronegative atom. (10.1)

Hydrogenation reaction a reaction in which hydrogen is added, with a catalyst present, to a carbon–carbon multiple bond. (22.2)

Hydrohalic acid an aqueous solution of a hydrogen halide. (20.7)

Hydrometallurgy a process for extracting metals from ores by use of aqueous chemical solutions. Two steps are involved: selective leaching and selective precipitation. (21.8)

Hydronium ion the H_3O^+ ion; a hydrated proton. (14.1)

Hypothesis one or more assumptions put forth to explain the observed behavior of nature. (1.2)

Ideal gas law an equation of state for a gas, where the state of the gas is its condition at a given time; expressed by $PV = nRT$, where P = pressure, V = volume, n = moles of the gas, R = the universal gas constant, and T = absolute temperature. This equation expresses behavior approached by real gases at high T and low P. (5.3)

Ideal solution a solution whose vapor pressure is directly proportional to the mole fraction of solvent present. (11.4)

Indicator a chemical that changes color and is used to mark the end point of a titration. (4.8; 15.5)

Integrated rate law an expression that shows the concentration of a reactant as a function of time. (12.2)

Interhalogen compound a compound formed by the reaction of one halogen with another. (20.7)

Intermediate a species that is neither a reactant nor a product but that is formed and consumed in the reaction sequence. (12.6)

Intermolecular forces relatively weak interactions that occur between molecules. (10.1)

Internal energy a property of a system that can be changed by a flow of work, heat or both; $\Delta E = q + w$, where ΔE is the change in the internal energy of the system, q is heat, and w is work. (6.1)

Ion an atom or a group of atoms that has a net positive or negative charge. (2.6)

Ion exchange (water softening) the process in which an ion-exchange resin removes unwanted ions (for example, Ca^{2+} and Mg^{2+}) and replaces them with Na^+ ions, which do not interfere with soap and detergent action. (19.4)

Ion pairing a phenomenon occurring in solution when oppositely charged ions aggregate and behave as a single particle. (11.7)

Ion-product (dissociation) constant (K_w) the equilibrium constant for the auto-ionization of water; $K_w = [H^+][OH^-]$. At 25°C, K_w equals 1.0×10^{-14}. (14.2)

Ion-selective electrode an electrode sensitive to the concentration of a particular ion in solution. (17.4)

Ionic bonding the electrostatic attraction between oppositely charged ions. (2.6; 8.1)

Ionic compound (binary) a compound that results when a metal reacts with a nonmetal to form a cation and an anion. (8.1)

Ionic solid (salt) a solid containing cations and anions that dissolves in water to give a solution containing the separated ions which are mobile and thus free to conduct electrical current. (2.6; 10.3)

Irreversible process any real process. When a system undergoes the changes State 1 → State 2 → State 1 by any real pathway, the universe is different than before the cyclic process took place in the system. (16.9)

Isoelectronic ions ions containing the same number of electrons. (8.4)

Isomers species with the same formula but different properties. (21.4)

Isotactic chain a polymer chain in which the substituent groups such as CH_3 are all arranged on the same side of the chain. (22.5)

Isotonic solutions solutions having identical osmotic pressures. (11.6)

Isotopes atoms of the same element (the same number of protons) with different numbers of neutrons. They have identical atomic numbers but different mass numbers. (2.5; 18)

Ketone an organic compound containing the carbonyl group bonded

to two carbon atoms. (22.4)

Kinetic energy ($\frac{1}{2}mv^2$) energy due to the motion of an object; dependent on the mass of the object and the square of its velocity. (6.1)

Kinetic molecular theory (KMT) a model that assumes that an ideal gas is composed of tiny particles (molecules) in constant motion. (5.6)

Lanthanide contraction the decrease in the atomic radii of the lanthanide series elements, going from left to right in the periodic table. (21.1)

Lanthanide series a group of 14 elements following lanthanum in the periodic table, in which the 4*f* orbitals are being filled. (7.11; 19.1; 21.1)

Lattice a three-dimensional system of points designating the positions of the centers of the components of a solid (atoms, ions, or molecules). (10.3)

Lattice energy the energy change occurring when separated gaseous ions are packed together to form an ionic solid. (8.5)

Law of conservation of energy energy can be converted from one form to another but can be neither created nor destroyed. (6.1)

Law of conservation of mass mass is neither created nor destroyed. (1.2; 2.2)

Law of definite proportion a given compound always contains exactly the same proportion of elements by mass. (2.2)

Law of mass action a general description of the equilibrium condition; it defines the equilibrium constant expression. (13.2)

Law of multiple proportions a law stating that when two elements form a series of compounds, the ratios of the masses of the second element that combine with one gram of the first element can always be reduced to small whole numbers. (2.2)

Leaching the extraction of metals from ores using aqueous chemical solutions. (21.8)

Lead storage battery a battery (used in cars) in which the anode is lead, the cathode is lead coated with lead dioxide, and the electrolyte is a sulfuric acid solution. (17.5)

Le Châtelier's principle if a change is imposed on a system at equilibrium, the position of the equilibrium will shift in a direction that tends to reduce the effect of that change. (13.7)

Lewis acid an electron-pair acceptor. (14.11)

Lewis base an electron-pair donor. (14.11)

Lewis structure a diagram of a molecule showing how the valence electrons are arranged among the atoms in the molecule. (8.10)

Ligand a neutral molecule or ion having a lone pair of electrons that can be used to form a bond to a metal ion; a Lewis base. (21.3)

Lime–soda process a water-softening method in which lime and soda ash are added to water to remove calcium and magnesium ions by precipitation. (14.6)

Limiting reactant (limiting reagent) the reactant that is completely consumed when a reaction is run to completion. (3.10)

Line spectrum a spectrum showing only certain discrete wavelengths. (7.3)

Linear accelerator a type of particle accelerator in which a changing electrical field is used to accelerate a positive ion along a linear path. (18.3)

Linkage isomerism isomerism involving a complex ion where the ligands are all the same but the point of attachment of at least one of the ligands differs. (21.4)

Liquefaction the transformation of a gas into a liquid. (19.1)

Localized electron (LE) model a model which assumes that a molecule is composed of atoms that are bound together by sharing pairs of electrons using the atomic orbitals of the bound atoms. (8.9)

London dispersion forces the forces, existing among noble gas atoms and nonpolar molecules, that involve an accidental dipole that induces a momentary dipole in a neighbor. (10.1)

Lone pair an electron pair that is localized on a given atom; an electron pair not involved in bonding. (8.9)

Magnetic quantum number m_ℓ, the quantum number relating to the orientation of an orbital in space relative to the other orbitals with the same ℓ quantum number. It can have integral values between ℓ and $-\ell$, including zero. (7.6)

Main-group (representative) elements elements in the groups labeled 1A, 2A, 3A, 4A, 5A, 6A, 7A, and 8A in the periodic table. The group number gives the sum of the valence s and p electrons. (7.11; 18.1)

Major species the components present in relatively large amounts in a solution. (14.3)

Manometer a device for measuring the pressure of a gas in a container. (5.1)

Mass the quantity of matter in an object. (1.3)

Mass defect the change in mass occurring when a nucleus is formed from its component nucleons. (18.5)

Mass number the total number of protons and neutrons in the atomic nucleus of an atom. (2.5; 18)

Mass percent the percent by mass of a component of a mixture (11.1) or of a given element in a compound. (3.5)

Mass spectrometer an instrument used to determine the relative masses of atoms by the deflection of their ions on a magnetic field. (3.2)

Matter the material of the universe. (1.9)

Messenger RNA (mRNA) a special RNA molecule built in the cell nucleus that migrates into the cytoplasm and participates in protein synthesis. (22.6)

Metal an element that gives up electrons relatively easily and is lustrous, malleable, and a good conductor of heat and electricity. (2.7)

Metalloids (semimetals) elements along the division line in the periodic table between metals and nonmetals. These elements exhibit both metallic and nonmetallic properties. (7.13; 19.1)

Metallurgy the process of separating a metal from its ore and preparing it for use. (19.1; 21.8)

Millimeters of mercury (mmHg) a unit of pressure, also called a torr, 760 mm Hg = 760 torr = 101,325 Pa = 1 standard atmosphere. (5.1)

Mineral a relatively pure compound as found in nature. (21.8)

Model (theory) a set of assumptions put forth to explain the observed behavior of matter. The models of chemistry usually involve assumptions about the behavior of individual atoms or molecules. (1.2)

Moderator a substance used in a nuclear reactor to slow down the neutrons. (18.6)

Molal boiling-point elevation constant a constant characteristic of a particular solvent that gives the change in boiling point as a function of solution molality; used in molecular weight determinations. (11.5)

Molal freezing-point depression constant a constant characteristic of a particular solvent that gives the change in freezing point as a function of the solution molality; used in molecular weight determinations (11.5)

Molality the number of moles of solute per kilogram of solvent in a solution. (11.1)

Molar heat capacity the energy required to raise the temperature of one mole of a substance by one degree Celsius. (6.2)

Molar mass the mass in grams of one mole of molecules or formula units of a substance; also called *molecular weight.* (3.4)

Molar volume the volume of one mole of an ideal gas; equal to 22.42 liters at STP. (5.4)

Molarity moles of solute per volume of solution in liters. (4.3; 11.1)

Mole (mol) the number equal to the number of carbon atoms in exactly 12 grams of pure ^{12}C: Avogadro's number. One mole represents 6.022×10^{23} units. (3.3)

Mole fraction the ratio of the number of moles of a given component in a mixture to the total number of moles in the mixture. (5.5; 11.1)

Mole ratio (stoichiometry) the ratio of moles of one substance to moles of another substance in a balanced chemical equation. (3.9)

Molecular formula the exact formula of a molecule, giving the types of atoms and the number of each type. (3.6)

Molecular orbital (MO) model a model that regards a molecule as a collection of nuclei and electrons, where the electrons are assumed to occupy orbitals much as they do in atoms, but having the orbitals extend over the entire molecule. In this model the electrons are assumed to be delocalized rather than always located between a given pair of atoms. (9.2; 10.4)

Molecular orientations (kinetics) orientations of molecules during collisions, some of which can lead to reaction while others cannot. (12.7)

Molecular solid a solid composed of neutral molecules at the lattice points. (10.3)

Molecular structure the three-dimensional arrangement of atoms in a molecule. (8.13)

Molecularity the number of species that must collide to produce the reaction represented by an elementary step in a reaction mechanism. (12.6)

Molecule a bonded collection of two or more atoms of the same or different elements. (2.6)

Monodentate (unidentate) ligand a ligand that can form one bond to a metal ion. (21.3)

Monoprotic acid an acid with one acidic proton. (14.2)

Monosaccharide (simple sugar) a polyhydroxy ketone or aldehyde containing from three to nine carbon atoms. (22.6)

Myoglobin an oxygen-storing biomolecule consisting of a heme complex and a proton. (21.7)

Natural law a statement that expresses generally observed behavior. (1.2)

Nernst equation an equation relating the potential of an electrochemical cell to the concentrations of the cell components:

$$\mathscr{E} = \mathscr{E}° - \frac{0.0591}{n} \log(Q) \text{ at } 25°C \qquad (17.4)$$

Net ionic equation an equation for a reaction in solution, where strong electrolytes are written as ions, showing only those components that are directly involved in the chemical change. (4.6)

Network solid an atomic solid containing strong directional covalent bonds. (10.5)

Neutralization reaction an acid–base reaction. (4.8)

Neutron a particle in the atomic nucleus with mass virtually equal to the proton's but with no charge. (2.5; 18)

Nitrogen cycle the conversion of N_2 to nitrogen-containing compounds, followed by the return of nitrogen gas to the atmosphere by natural decay processes. (20.2)

Nitrogen fixation the process of transforming N_2 to nitrogen-containing compounds useful to plants. (20.2)

Nitrogen-fixing bacteria bacteria in the root nodules of plants that can convert atmospheric nitrogen to ammonia and other nitrogen-containing compounds useful to plants. (20.2)

Noble gas a Group 8A element. (2.7; 20.8)

Node an area of an orbital having zero electron probability. (7.7)

Nonelectrolyte a substance that, when dissolved in water, gives a nonconducting solution. (4.2)

Nonmetal an element not exhibiting metallic characteristics. Chemically, a typical nonmetal accepts electrons from a metal. (2.7)

Normal boiling point the temperature at which the vapor pressure of a liquid is exactly one atmosphere. (10.8)

Normal melting point the temperature at which the solid and liquid states have the same vapor pressure under conditions where the total pressure on the system is one atmosphere. (10.8)

Normality the number of equivalents of a substance dissolved in a liter of solution. (11.1)

Nuclear atom an atom having a dense center of positive charge (the nucleus) with electrons moving around the outside. (2.4)

Nuclear transformation the change of one element into another. (18.3)

Nucleon a particle in an atomic nucleus, either a neutron or a proton. (18)

Nucleotide a monomer of the nucleic acids composed of a five-carbon sugar, a nitrogen-containing base, and phosphoric acid. (22.6)

Nucleus the small, dense center of positive charge in an atom. (2.4)

Nuclide the general term applied to each unique atom; represented by $_Z^A X$, where X is the symbol for a particular element. (18)

Octet rule the observation that atoms of nonmetals tend to form the most stable molecules when they are surrounded by eight electrons (to fill their valence orbitals). (8.10)

Open hearth process a process for producing steel by oxidizing and removing the impurities in molten iron using external heat and a blast of air or oxygen. (21.8)

Optical isomerism isomerism in which the isomers have opposite effects on plane-polarized light. (21.4)

Orbital a specific wave function for an electron in an atom. The square of this function gives the probability distribution for the electron. (7.5)

d-Orbital splitting a splitting of the d orbitals of the metal ion in a complex such that the orbitals pointing at the ligands have higher energies than those pointing between the ligands. (21.6)

Order (of reactant) the positive or negative exponent, determined by experiment, of the reactant concentration in a rate law. (12.2)

Organic acid an acid with a carbon-atom backbone; often contains the carboxyl group. (14.2)

Organic chemistry the study of carbon-containing compounds (typically chains of carbon atoms) and their properties. (22)

Osmosis the flow of solvent into a solution through a semipermeable membrane. (11.6)

Osmotic pressure (π) the pressure that must be applied to a solution to stop osmosis; $\pi = MRT$. (11.6)

Ostwald process a commercial process for producing nitric acid by the oxidation of ammonia. (20.2)

Oxidation an increase in oxidation state (a loss of electrons). (4.9; 17.1)

Oxidation–reduction (redox) reaction a reaction in which one or more electrons are transferred. (4.9; 17.1)

Oxidation states a concept that provides a way to keep track of electrons in oxidation–reduction reactions according to certain rules. (4.9; 21.3)

Oxidizing agent (electron acceptor) a reactant that accepts electrons from another reactant. (4.9; 17.1)

Oxyacid an acid in which the acidic proton is attached to an oxygen atom. (14.2)

Ozone O_3, the form of elemental oxygen in addition to the much more common O_2. (20.5)

Paramagnetism a type of induced magnetism, associated with unpaired electrons, that causes a substance to be attracted into the inducing magnetic field. (9.3)

Partial pressures the independent pressures exerted by different gases in a mixture. (5.5)

Particle accelerator a device used to accelerate nuclear particles to very high speeds. (18.3)

Pascal the SI unit of pressure; equal to newtons per meter squared. (5.1)

Pauli exclusion principle in a given atom no two electrons can have the same set of four quantum numbers. (7.8)

Peptide linkage the bond resulting from the condensation reaction between amino acids; represented by:

$$\begin{matrix} & O & H \\ & \| & | \\ -\!\!\!\!& C & -N- \end{matrix} \qquad (22.6)$$

Percent dissociation the ratio of the amount of a substance that is dissociated at equilibrium to the initial concentration of the substance in a solution, multiplied by 100. (14.5)

Percent yield the actual yield of a product as a percentage of the theoretical yield. (3.10)

Periodic table a chart showing all the elements arranged in columns with similar chemical properties. (2.7)

pH curve (titration curve) a plot showing the pH of a solution being analyzed as a function of the amount of titrant added. (15.4)

pH scale a log scale based on 10 and equal to $-\log[H^+]$; a convenient way to represent solution acidity. (14.3)

Phase diagram a convenient way of representing the phases of a substance in a closed system as a function of temperature and pressure. (10.9)

Phenyl group the benzene molecule minus one hydrogen atom. (22.3)

Photochemical smog air pollution produced by the action of light on oxygen, nitrogen oxides, and unburned fuel from auto exhaust to form ozone and other pollutants. (5.10)

Photon a quantum of electromagnetic radiation. (7.2)

Physical change a change in the form of a substance, but not in its chemical composition; chemical bonds are not broken in a physical change. (1.9)

Pi (π) bond a covalent bond in which parallel p orbitals share an electron pair occupying the space above and below the line joining the atoms. (9.1)

Planck's constant the constant relating the change in energy for a system to the frequency of the electromagnetic radiation absorbed or emitted; equal to 6.626×10^{-34} J s. (7.2)

Polar covalent bond a covalent bond in which the electrons are not shared equally because one atom attracts them more strongly than the other. (8.1)

Polar molecule a molecule that has a permanent dipole moment. (4.1)

Polyatomic ion an ion containing a number of atoms. (2.6)

Polyelectronic atom an atom with more than one electron. (7.9)

Polymer a large, usually chainlike molecule built from many small molecules (monomers). (22.5)

Polymerization a process in which many small molecules (monomers) are joined together to form a large molecule. (22.2)

Polypeptide a polymer formed from amino acids joined together by peptide linkages. (22.6)

Polyprotic acid an acid with more than one acidic proton. It dissociates in a stepwise manner, one proton at a time. (14.7)

Porous disk a disk in a tube connecting two different solutions in a galvanic cell that allows ion flow without extensive mixing of the solutions. (17.1)

Porphyrin a planar ligand with a central ring structure and various substituent groups at the edges of the ring. (21.7)

Positional probability a type of probability that depends on the number of arrangements in space that yield a particular state. (16.1)

Positron production a mode of nuclear decay in which a particle is formed having the same mass as an electron but opposite charge. The net effect is to change a proton to a neutron. (18.1)

Potential energy energy due to position or composition. (6.1)

Precipitation reaction a reaction in which an insoluble substance forms and separates from the solution. (4.5)

Precision the degree of agreement among several measurements of the same quantity; the reproducibility of a measurement. (1.4)

Primary structure (of a protein) the order (sequence) of amino acids in the protein chain. (22.6)

Principal quantum number (n) the quantum number relating to the size and energy of an orbital; it can have any positive integer value. (7.6)

Probability distribution the square of the wave function indicating the probability of finding an electron at a particular point in space. (7.5)

Product a substance resulting from a chemical reaction. It is shown to the right of the arrow in a chemical equation. (3.7)

Protein a natural high-molecular-weight polymer formed by condensation reactions between amino acids. (22.6)

Proton a positively charged particle in an atomic nucleus. (2.5; 18)

Pure substance a substance with constant composition. (1.9)

Pyrometallurgy recovery of a metal from its ore by treatment at high temperatures. (21.8)

Quantization the concept that energy can occur only in discrete units called *quanta*. (7.2)

Rad a unit of radiation dosage corresponding to 10^{-2} J of energy deposited per kilogram of tissue (from *r*adiation *a*bsorbed *d*ose). (18.7)

Radioactive decay (radioactivity) the spontaneous decomposition of a nucleus to form a different nucleus. (2.4; 18.1)

Radiocarbon dating (carbon-14 dating) a method for dating ancient wood or cloth based on the rate of radioactive decay of the nuclide $^{14}_{6}C$. (18.4)

Radiotracer a radioactive nuclide, introduced into an organism for diagnostic purposes, whose pathway can be traced by monitoring its radioactivity. (18.4)

Random error an error that has an equal probability of being high or low. (1.4)

Raoult's law the vapor pressure of a solution is directly proportional to the mole fraction of solvent present. (11.4)

Rate constant the proportionality constant in the relationship between reaction rate and reactant concentrations. (12.2)

Rate of decay the change in the number of radioactive nuclides in a sample per unit time. (18.2)

Rate-determining step the slowest step in a reaction mechanism, the one determining the overall rate. (12.6)

Rate law (differential rate law) an expression that shows how the rate of reaction depends on the concentration of reactants. (12.2)

Reactant a starting substance in a chemical reaction. It appears to the left of the arrow in a chemical equation. (3.7)

Reaction mechanism the series of elementary steps involved in a chemical reaction. (12.6)

Reaction quotient, Q a quotient obtained by applying the law of mass action to initial concentrations rather than to equilibrium concentrations. (13.5)

Reaction rate the change in concentration of a reactant or product per unit time. (12.1)

Reactor core the part of a nuclear reactor where the fission reaction takes place. (18.6)

Reducing agent (electron donor) a reactant that donates electrons to another substance to reduce the oxidation state of one of its atoms. (4.9; 17.1)

Reduction a decrease in oxidation state (a gain of electrons). (4.9; 17.1)

Rem a unit of radiation dosage that accounts for both the energy of the dose and its effectiveness in causing biological damage (from *r*oentgen *e*quivalent for *m*an). (18.7)

Resonance a condition occurring when more than one valid Lewis structure can be written for a particular molecule. The actual electronic structure is not represented by any one of the Lewis structures but by the average of all of them. (8.12)

Reverse osmosis the process occurring when the external pressure on a solution causes a net flow of solvent through a semipermeable membrane from the solution to the solvent. (11.6)

Reversible process a cyclic process carried out by a hypothetical pathway, which leaves the universe exactly the same as it was before the process. No real process is reversible. (16.9)

Ribonucleic acid (RNA) a nucleotide polymer that transmits the genetic information stored in DNA to the ribosomes for protein synthesis. (22.6)

Roasting a process of converting sulfide minerals to oxides by heating in air at temperatures below their melting points. (21.8)

Root mean square velocity the square root of the average of the squares of the individual velocities of gas particles. (5.6)

Salt an ionic compound. (14.8)

Salt bridge a U-tube containing an electrolyte that connects the two compartments of a galvanic cell, allowing ion flow without extensive mixing of the different solutions. (17.1)

Scientific method the process of studying natural phenomena, involving observations, forming laws and theories, and testing of theories by experimentation. (1.2)

Scintillation counter an instrument that measures radioactive decay by sensing the flashes of light produced in a substance by the radiation. (18.4)

Second law of thermodynamics in any spontaneous process, there is always an increase in the entropy of the universe. (16.2)

Secondary structure (of a protein) the three-dimensional structure of the protein chain (for example, α-helix, random coil, or pleated sheet). (22.6)

Selective precipitation a method of separating metal ions from an aqueous mixture by using a reagent whose anion forms a precipitate with only one or a few of the ions in the mixture. (4.7; 15.7)

Semiconductor a substance conducting only a slight electrical current at room temperature, but showing increased conductivity at higher temperatures. (10.5)

Semipermeable membrane a membrane that allows solvent but not solute molecules to pass through. (11.6)

SI system International System of units based on the metric system and units derived from the metric system. (1.3)

Side chain (of amino acid) the hydrocarbon group on an amino acid represented by H, CH_3, or a more complex substituent. (22.6)

Sigma (σ) bond a covalent bond in which the electron pair is shared in an area centered on a line running between the atoms. (9.1)

Significant figures the certain digits and the first uncertain digit of a measurement. (1.4)

Silica the fundamental silicon–oxygen compound, which has the empirical formula SiO_2, and forms the basis of quartz and certain types of sand. (10.5)

Silicates salts that contain metal cations and polyatomic silicon–oxygen anions that are usually polymeric. (10.5)

Single bond a bond in which one pair of electrons is shared by two atoms. (8.8)

Smelting a metallurgical process that involves reducing metal ions to the free metal. (21.8)

Solubility the amount of a substance that dissolves in a given volume of solvent at a given temperature. (4.2)

Solubility product constant the constant for the equilibrium expression representing the dissolving of an ionic solid in water. (15.6)

Solute a substance dissolved in a liquid to form a solution. (4.2; 11.1)

Solution a homogeneous mixture. (1.9)

Solvent the dissolving medium in a solution. (4.2)

Somatic damage radioactive damage to an organism resulting in its sickness or death. (18.7)

Space-filling model a model of a molecule showing the relative sizes of the atoms and their relative orientations. (2.6)

Specific heat capacity the energy required to raise the temperature of one gram of a substance by one degree Celsius. (6.2)

Spectator ions ions present in solution that do not participate directly in a reaction. (4.6)

Spectrochemical series a listing of ligands in order based on their ability to produce *d*-orbital splitting. (21.6)

Spontaneous fission the spontaneous splitting of a heavy nuclide into two lighter nuclides. (18.1)

Spontaneous process a process that occurs without outside intervention. (16.1)

Standard atmosphere a unit of pressure equal to 760 mm Hg. (5.1)

Standard enthalpy of formation the enthalpy change that accompanies the formation of one mole of a compound at 25°C from its elements, with all substances in their standard states at that temperature. (6.4)

Standard free energy change the change in free energy that will occur for one unit of reaction if the reactants in their standard states are converted to products in their standard states. (16.6)

Standard free energy of formation the change in free energy that accompanies the formation of one mole of a substance from its constituent elements with all reactants and products in their standard states. (16.6)

Standard hydrogen electrode a platinum conductor in contact with 1 *M* H^+ ions and bathed by hydrogen gas at one atmosphere. (17.2)

Standard reduction potential the potential of a half-reaction under standard state conditions, as measured against the potential of the standard hydrogen electrode. (17.2)

Standard solution a solution whose concentration is accurately known. (4.3)

Standard state a reference state for a specific substance defined according to a set of conventional definitions. (6.4)

Standard temperature and pressure (STP) the condition 0°C and 1 atmosphere of pressure. (5.4)

Standing wave a stationary wave as on a string of a musical instrument; in the wave mechanical model, the electron in the hydrogen atom is considered to be a standing wave. (7.5)

State function (property) a property that is independent of the pathway. (6.1)

States of matter the three different forms in which matter can exist; solid, liquid, and gas. (1.9)

Stereoisomerism isomerism in which all the bonds in the isomers are the same but the spatial arrangements of the atoms are different. (21.4)

Steric factor the factor (always less than 1) that reflects the fraction of collisions with orientations that can produce a chemical reaction. (12.7)

Stoichiometric quantities quantities of reactants mixed in exactly the correct amounts so that all are used up at the same time. (3.10)

Strong acid an acid that completely dissociates to produce an H^+ ion and the conjugate base. (4.2; 14.2)

Strong base a metal hydroxide salt that completely dissociates into its ions in water. (4.2; 14.6)

Strong electrolyte a material that, when dissolved in water, gives a solution that conducts an electric current very efficiently. (4.2)

Structural formula the representation of a molecule in which the relative positions of the atoms are shown and the bonds are indicated by lines. (2.6)

Structural isomerism isomerism in which the isomers contain the same atoms but one or more bonds differ. (21.4; 22.1)

Subcritical reaction (nuclear) a reaction in which less than one neutron causes another fission event and the process dies out. (18.6)

Sublimation the process by which a substance goes directly from the solid to the gaseous state without passing through the liquid state. (10.8)

Subshell a set of orbitals with a given azimuthal quantum number. (7.6)

Substitution reaction (hydrocarbons) a reaction in which an atom, usually a halogen, replaces a hydrogen atom in a hydrocarbon. (22.1)

Supercooling the process of cooling a liquid below its freezing point without its changing to a solid. (10.8)

Supercritical reaction (nuclear) a reaction in which more than one neutron from each fission event causes another fission event. The process rapidly escalates to a violent explosion. (18.6)

Superheating the process of heating a liquid above its boiling point without its boiling. (10.8)

Superoxide a compound containing the O_2^- anion. (19.2)

Surface tension the resistance of a liquid to an increase in its surface area. (10.2)

Surroundings everything in the universe surrounding a thermodynamic system. (6.1)

Syndiotactic chain a polymer chain in which the substituent groups such as CH_3 are arranged on alternate sides of the chain. (22.5)

Syngas synthetic gas, a mixture of carbon monoxide and hydrogen, obtained by coal gasification. (6.6)

System (thermodynamic) that part of the universe on which attention is to be focused. (6.1)

Systematic error an error that always occurs in the same direction. (1.4)

Tempering a process in steel production that fine-tunes the proportions of carbon crystals and cementite by heating to intermediate temperatures followed by rapid cooling. (21.8)

Termolecular step a reaction involving the simultaneous collision of three molecules. (12.6)

Tertiary structure (of a protein) the overall shape of a protein, long and narrow or globular, maintained by different types of intramolecular interactions. (22.6)

Theoretical yield the maximum amount of a given product that can be formed when the limiting reactant is completely consumed. (3.10)

Theory a set of assumptions put forth to explain some aspect of the observed behavior of matter. (1.2)

Thermal pollution the oxygen-depleting effect on lakes and rivers of using water for industrial cooling and returning it to its natural source at a higher temperature. (11.3)

Thermodynamic stability (nuclear) the potential energy of a particular nucleus as compared to the sum of the potential energies of its component protons and neutrons. (18.1)

Thermodynamics the study of energy and its interconversions. (6.1)

Thermoplastic polymer a substance that when molded to a certain shape under appropriate conditions can later be remelted. (22.5)

Thermoset polymer a substance that when molded to a certain shape under pressure and high temperatures cannot be softened again or dissolved. (22.5)

Third law of thermodynamics the entropy of a perfect crystal at 0 K is zero. (16.5)

Titration a technique in which one solution is used to analyze another. (4.8)

Torr another name for millimeter of mercury (mm Hg). (5.1)

Transfer RNA (tRNA) a small RNA fragment that finds specific amino acids and attaches them to the protein chain as dictated by the codons in mRNA. (22.6)

Transition metals several series of elements in which inner orbitals (d or f orbitals) are being filled. (7.11; 19.1)

Transuranium elements the elements beyond uranium that are made artificially by particle bombardment. (18.3)

Triple bond a bond in which three pairs of electrons are shared by two atoms. (8.8)

Triple point the point on a phase diagram at which all three states of a substance are present. (10.9)

Tyndall effect the scattering of light by particles in a suspension. (11.8)

Uncertainty (in measurement) the characteristic that any measurement involves estimates and cannot be exactly reproduced. (1.4)

Unimolecular step a reaction step involving only one molecule. (12.6)

Unit cell the smallest repeating unit of a lattice. (10.3)

Unit factor method an equivalence statement between units used for converting from one unit to another. (1.6)

Universal gas constant the combined proportionality constant in the ideal gas law; 0.08206 L · atm/K · mol or 8.3145 J/K · mol. (5.3)

Valence electrons the electrons in the outermost principal quantum level of an atom. (7.11)

Valence shell electron-pair repulsion (VSEPR) model a model whose main postulate is that the structure around a given atom in a molecule is determined principally by minimizing electron-pair repulsions. (8.13)

Van der Waals equation a mathematical expression for describing the behavior of real gases. (5.8)

Van't Hoff factor the ratio of moles of particles in solution to moles of solute dissolved. (11.7)

Vapor pressure the pressure of the vapor over a liquid at equilibrium. (10.8)

Vaporization (evaporization) the change in state that occurs when a liquid evaporates to form a gas. (10.8)

Viscosity the resistance of a liquid to flow. (10.2)

Volt the unit of electrical potential defined as one joule of work per coulomb of charge transferred. (17.1)

Voltmeter an instrument that measures cell potential by drawing electric current through a known resistance. (17.1)

Volumetric analysis a process involving titration of one solution with another. (4.8)

Vulcanization a process in which sulfur is added to rubber and the mixture is heated, causing crosslinking of the polymer chains and thus adding strength to the rubber. (22.5)

Wave function a function of the coordinates of an electron's position in three-dimensional space that describes the properties of the electron. (7.5)

Wave mechanical model a model for the hydrogen atom in which the electron is assumed to behave as a standing wave. (7.5)

Wavelength the distance between two consecutive peaks or troughs in a wave. (7.1)

Weak acid an acid that dissociates only slightly in aqueous solution. (4.2; 14.2)

Weak base a base that reacts with water to produce hydroxide ions to only a slight extent in aqueous solution. (4.2; 14.6)

Weak electrolyte a material which, when dissolved in water, gives a solution that conducts only a small electric current. (4.2)

Weight the force exerted on an object by gravity. (1.3)

Work force acting over a distance. (6.1)

X-ray diffraction a technique for establishing the structure of crystalline solids by directing X rays of a single wavelength at a crystal and obtaining a diffraction pattern from which interatomic spaces can be determined. (10.3)

Zone of nuclear stability the area encompassing the stable nuclides on a plot of their positions as a function of the number of protons and the number of neutrons in the nucleus. (18.1)

Zone refining a metallurgical process for obtaining a highly pure metal that depends on continuously melting the impure material and recrystallizing the pure metal. (21.8)

Photo Credits

Answers to Selected Exercises

The answers listed here are from the *Complete Solutions Guide,* in which rounding is carried out at each intermediate step in a calculation in order to show the correct number of significant figures for that step. Therefore, an answer given here may differ in the last digit from the result obtained by carrying extra digits throughout the entire calculation and rounding at the end (the procedure you should follow).

Chapter 1

17. A law summarizes what happens, e.g., law of conservation of mass in a chemical reaction or the ideal gas law, $PV = nRT$. A theory (model) is an attempt to explain why something happens. Dalton's atomic theory explains why mass is conserved in a chemical reaction. The kinetic molecular theory explains why pressure and volume are inversely related at constant temperature and moles of gas. **19.** A qualitative observation expresses what makes something what it is; it does not involve a number; e.g., the air we breathe is a mixture of gases, ice is less dense than water, rotten milk stinks. The SI units are mass in grams, length in meters, and volume in the derived units of m^3. The assumed uncertainty in a number is ± 1 in the last significant figure of the number. The precision of an instrument is related to the number of significant figures associated with an experimental reading on that instrument. Different instruments for measuring mass, length, or volume have varying degrees of precision. Some instruments only give a few significant figures for a measurement while others will give more significant figures. **21.** Significant figures are the digits we associate with a number. They contain all of the certain digits and the first uncertain digit (the first estimated digit). What follows is one thousand indicated to varying numbers of significant figures: 1000 or 1×10^3 (1 S.F.); 1.0×10^3 (2 S.F.); 1.00×10^3 (3 S.F.); 1000. or 1.000×10^3 (4 S.F.). To perform the calculation, the addition/subtraction significant rule is applied to $1.5 - 1.0$. The result of this is the one significant figure answer of 0.5. Next, the multiplication/division rule is applied to 0.5/0.50. A one significant number divided by a two significant number yields an answer with one significant figure (answer = 1). **23.** The slope of the T_F vs. T_C plot is 1.8 (= 9/5) and the y-intercept is 32°F. The slope of T_C vs. T_K plot is one and the y-intercept is -273°C. **25. a.** exact; **b.** inexact; **c.** exact; **d.** inexact **27. a.** 3; **b.** 4; **c.** 4; **d.** 1; **e.** 7; **f.** 1; **g.** 3; **h.** 3 **29. a.** 3.42×10^{-4}; **b.** 1.034×10^4; **c.** 1.7992×10^1; **d.** 3.37×10^5 **31. a.** 641.0; **b.** 1.327; **c.** 77.34; **d.** 3215; **e.** 0.420 **33. a.** 188.1; **b.** 12.; **c.** 4×10^{-7}; **d.** 6.3×10^{-26}; **e.** 4.9; Uncertainty appears in the first decimal place. The average of several numbers can be only as precise as the least precise number. Averages can be exceptions to the significant figure rules. **f.** 0.22 **35. a.** 84.3 mm; **b.** 2.41 m; **c.** 2.945×10^{-5} cm; **d.** 14.45 km; **e.** 2.353×10^5 mm; **f.** 0.9033 μm **37. a.** 8 lb and 9.9 oz; $20\frac{1}{4}$ in; **b.** 4.0×10^4 km, 4.0×10^7 m; **c.** 1.2×10^{-2} m³, 12 L, 730 in³, 0.42 ft³ **39. a.** 4.00×10^2 rods; 10.0 furlongs; 2.01×10^3 m; 2.01 km; **b.** 8390.0 rods; 209.75 furlongs; 42,195 m; 42.195 km **41. a.** 0.373 kg, 0.822 lb; **b.** 31.1 g, 156 carats; **c.** 19.3 cm³ **43.** 2.95×10^9 knots; 3.36×10^9 mi/h **45.** To the proper number of significant figures, the car is traveling at 40. mi/h, which would not violate the speed limit. **47.** 0.68 Canadian/L **49. a.** -273°C, 0 K; **b.** $-40.$°C, 233 K; **c.** 20.°C, 293 K; **d.** 4×10^7 °C, 4×10^7 K **51. a.** 312.4 K; 102.6°F; **b.** 248 K; -13°F; **c.** 0 K; -459°F; **d.** 1074 K; 1470°F **53.** It will float (density = 0.80 g/cm³). **55.** 1×10^6 g/cm³ **57.** 0.28 cm³ **59.** 3.8 g/cm³ **61. a.** Both are the same mass; **b.** 1.0 mL mercury; **c.** Both are the same mass; **d.** 1.0 L benzene **63. a.** 1.0 kg feather; **b.** 100 g water; **c.** same **65.** 2.77 cm **67. a.** Picture iv represents a gaseous compound. Pictures ii and iii also contain a gaseous compound but have a gaseous element present. **b.** Picture vi represents a mixture of two elemental gases. **c.** Picture v represents a solid element. **d.** Pictures ii and iii both represent a mixture of a gaseous element and a gaseous compound. **69. a.** heterogeneous;

b. homogeneous (hopefully); **c.** homogeneous; **d.** homogeneous (hopefully); **e.** heterogeneous; **f.** heterogeneous **71. a.** physical; **b.** chemical; **c.** physical; **d.** chemical **73.** 24 capsules **75.** 1.0×10^5 bags **77.** 56.56°C **79. a.** Volume × density = mass; the orange block is more dense. Since mass (orange) > mass (blue) and volume (orange) < volume (blue), then the density of the orange block must be greater to account for the larger mass of the orange block. **b.** Which block is more dense cannot be determined. Since mass (orange) > mass (blue) and volume (orange) > volume (blue), then the density of the orange block may or may not be larger than the blue block. If the blue block is more dense, then its density cannot be so large that the mass of the smaller blue block becomes larger than the orange block mass. **c.** The blue block is more dense. Since mass (blue) = mass (orange) and volume (blue) < volume (orange), then the density of the blue block must be larger to equate the masses. **d.** The blue block is more dense. Since mass (blue) > mass (orange) and the volumes are equal, then the density of the blue block must be larger to give the blue block the larger mass. **81.** 8.5 ± 0.5 g/cm³ **83. a.** 2%; **b.** 2.2%; **c.** 0.2% **85.** $d_{old} = 8.8$ g/cm³, $d_{new} = 7.17$ g/cm³; $d_{new}/d_{old} = \text{mass}_{new}/\text{mass}_{old} = 0.81$; The difference in mass is accounted for by the difference in the alloy used (if the assumptions are correct). **87.** 7.0% **89. a.** One possibility is that rope B is not attached to anything and rope A and rope C are connected via a pair of pulleys and/or gears; **b.** Try to pull rope B out of the box. Measure the distance moved by C for a given movement of A. Hold either A or C firmly while pulling on the other rope. **91.** $160/person; 3.20×10^3 nickels/person; 85.6 £/person **93.** 200.0°F = 93.33°C; -100.0°F = -73.3°C; 93.33°C = 366.48 K; -73.3°C = 199.9 K; difference of temperatures in °C = 166.6; difference of temperatures in K = 166.6; No, there is not a difference of 300 degrees in °C or K.

Chapter 2

15. A compound will always contain the same numbers (and types) of atoms. A given amount of hydrogen will react only with a specific amount of oxygen. Any excess oxygen will remain unreacted. **17.** Law of conservation of mass: mass is neither created nor destroyed. The mass before a chemical reaction always equals the mass after a chemical reaction. Law of definite proportion: a given compound always contains exactly the same proportion of elements by mass. Water is always 1 g H for every 8 g oxygen. Law of multiple proportions: When two elements form a series of compounds, the ratios of the mass of the second element that combine with one gram of the first element can always be reduced to small whole numbers. For CO_2 and CO discussed in section 2.2, the mass ratios of oxygen that react with 1 g of carbon in each compound are in a 2:1 ratio. **19.** J. J. Thomson's study of cathode-ray tubes led him to postulate the existence of negatively charged particles which we now call electrons. Ernest Rutherford and his alpha bombardment of metal foil experiments led him to postulate the nuclear atom—an atom with a tiny dense center of positive charge (the nucleus) with electrons moving about the nucleus at relatively large distances away; the distance is so large that an atom is mostly empty space. **21.** The number and arrangement of electrons in an atom determines how the atom will react with other atoms. The electrons determine the chemical properties of an atom. The number of neutrons present determine the isotope identity. **23.** Statements a and b are true. Counting over in the periodic table, element 118 will be the next noble gas (a nonmetal). For statement c, hydrogen has mostly nonmetallic properties. For statement d, a family of elements is also known as a group of elements. For statement e, two items are incorrect. When a metal reacts with a nonmetal, an ionic compound is produced and the formula of the compound would be AX_2 (since alkaline earth metals for $+2$ ions and halogens form -1 ions in ionic compounds). The correct statement would be: When alkaline earth metal, A reacts with a halogen, X, the formula of the ionic compound formed should be AX_2. **25. a.** The composition of a substance depends on the number of atoms of each element making up the compound (depends on the formula of the compound) and not on the composition of the mixture from which it was formed. **b.** Avogadro's hypothesis implies that volume ratios are equal to molecule ratios at constant temperature and pressure. $H_2(g) + Cl_2(g) \rightarrow 2\ HCl(g)$; from the balanced equation, the volume of HCl produced will be twice the volume of H_2 (or Cl_2) reacted. **27.** All the masses of hydrogen in these three compounds can be expressed as simple whole-number ratios. The g H/g N in hydrazine, ammonia, and hydrogen azide are in the ratios 6:9:1. **29.** O, 7.94; Na, 22.8; Mg, 11.9; O and Mg are incorrect by a factor of ≈ 2; correct formulas are H_2O, Na_2O, and MgO. **31.** Using $r = 5 \times 10^{-14}$ cm, $d_{nucleus} = 3 \times 10^{15}$ g/cm^3; using $r = 1 \times 10^{-8}$ cm, $d_{atom} = 0.4$ g/cm^3 **33.** 37 **35.** sodium, Na; radium, Ra; iron, Fe; gold, Au; manganese, Mn; lead, Pb **37.** Sn, tin; Pt, platinum; Hg, mercury; Mg, magnesium; K, potassium; Ag, silver **39. a.** Metals: Mg, Ti, Au, Bi, Ge, Eu, Am; nonmetals: Si, B, At, Rn, Br; **b.** metalloids: Si, Ge, B, At. The elements at the boundary between the metals and the nonmetals are B, Si, Ge, As, Sb, Te, Po, and At. These elements are all considered metalloids. Aluminum has mostly properties of metals. **41. a.** 6; **b.** 5; **c.** 4; **d.** 6 **43. a.** 35 p, 44 n, 35 e; **b.** 35 p, 46 n, 35 e; **c.** 94 p, 145 n, 94 e; **d.** 55 p, 78 n, 55 e; **e.** 1 p, 2 n, 1 e; **f.** 26 p, 30 n, 26 e **45. a.** $^{17}_{8}$O; **b.** $^{37}_{17}$Cl; **c.** $^{60}_{27}$Co; **d.** $^{57}_{26}$Fe; **e.** $^{131}_{53}$I; **f.** $^{7}_{3}$Li **47.** $^{151}_{63}$Eu^{3+}; $^{118}_{50}$Sn^{2+} **49.** $^{238}_{92}$U, 92 p, 146 n, 92 e, 0; $^{40}_{20}$Ca^{2+}, 20 p, 20 n, 18 e, 2+; $^{51}_{23}$V^{3+}, 23 p, 28 n, 20 e, 3+; $^{89}_{39}$Y, 39 p, 50 n, 39 e, 0; $^{79}_{35}$Br$^-$, 35 p, 44 n, 36 e, 1−; $^{31}_{15}$P^{3-}, 15 p, 16 n, 18 e, 3− **51. a.** transition metals; **b.** alkaline earth metals; **c.** alkali metals; **d.** noble gases; **e.** halogens **53. a.** lose 2 e$^-$ to form Ra^{2+}; **b.** lose 3 e$^-$ to form In^{3+}; **c.** gain 3 e$^-$ to form P^{3-}; **d.** gain 2 e$^-$ to form Te^{2-}; **e.** gain 1 e$^-$ to form Br$^-$; **f.** lose 1 e$^-$ to form Rb$^+$ **55. a.** sodium bromide; **b.** rubidium oxide; **c.** calcium sulfide; **d.** aluminum iodide; **e.** SrF$_2$; **f.** Al$_2$Se$_3$; **g.** K$_3$N; **h.** Mg$_3$P$_2$ **57. a.** cesium fluoride; **b.** lithium nitride; **c.** silver sulfide (Silver forms only +1 ions so no Roman numerals are needed); **d.** manganese(IV) oxide; **e.** titanium(IV) oxide; **f.** strontium phosphide **59. a.** barium sulfite; **b.** sodium nitrite; **c.** potassium permanganate; **d.** potassium dichromate **61. a.** dinitrogen tetroxide; **b.** iodine trichloride; **c.** sulfur dioxide; **d.** diphosphorus pentasulfide **63. a.** copper(I) iodide; **b.** copper(II) iodide; **c.** cobalt(II) iodide; **d.** sodium carbonate; **e.** sodium hydrogen carbonate or sodium bicarbonate; **f.** tetrasulfur tetranitride; **g.** sulfur hexafluoride; **h.** sodium hypochlorite; **i.** barium chromate; **j.** ammonium nitrate **65. a.** SF$_2$; **b.** SF$_6$; **c.** NaH$_2$PO$_4$; **d.** Li$_3$N; **e.** Cr$_2$(CO$_3$)$_3$; **f.** SnF$_2$; **g.** NH$_4$C$_2$H$_3$O$_2$; **h.** NH$_4$HSO$_4$; **i.** Co(NO$_3$)$_3$; **j.** Hg$_2$Cl$_2$; Mercury(I) exists as Hg$_2^{2+}$ ions. **k.** KClO$_3$; **l.** NaH **67. a.** Na$_2$O; **b.** Na$_2$O$_2$; **c.** KCN; **d.** Cu(NO$_3$)$_2$; **e.** SeBr$_4$; **f.** HIO$_2$; **g.** PbS$_2$; **h.** CuCl; **i.** GaAs (from the positions in the periodic table, Ga^{3+} and As^{3-} are the predicted ions); **j.** CdSe; **k.** ZnS; **l.** HNO$_2$; **m.** P$_2$O$_5$ **69. a.** nitric acid, HNO$_3$; **b.** perchloric acid, HClO$_4$; **c.** acetic acid, HC$_2$H$_3$O$_2$; **d.** sulfuric acid, H$_2$SO$_4$; **e.** phosphoric acid, H$_3$PO$_4$ **71.** Yes, 1.0 g H would react with 37.0 g ^{37}Cl and 1.0 g H would react with 35.0 g ^{35}Cl. No, the mass ratio of H/Cl would always be 1 g H/37 g Cl for ^{37}Cl and 1 g H/35 g Cl for ^{35}Cl. As long as we had pure ^{35}Cl or pure ^{37}Cl, these ratios will always hold. If we have a mixture (such as the natural abundance of chlorine), the ratio will also be constant as long as the composition of the mixture of the two isotopes does not change. **73.** Only statement a is true. For statement b, X has 34 protons. For statement c, X has 45 neutrons. For statement d, X is selenium. **75. a.** lead(II) acetate; **b.** copper(II) sulfate; **c.** calcium oxide; **d.** magnesium sulfate; **e.** magnesium hydroxide; **f.** calcium sulfate; **g.** dinitrogen monoxide or nitrous oxide (common) **77.** X = Ra, 142 neutrons **79. a.** Ca$_3$N$_2$; calcium nitride; **b.** K$_2$O; potassium oxide; **c.** RbF; rubidium fluoride; **d.** MgS; magnesium sulfide; **e.** BaI$_2$; barium iodide; **f.** Al$_2$Se$_3$; aluminum selenide; **g.** Cs$_3$P; cesium phosphide; **h.** InBr$_3$; indium(III) bromide (In forms compounds with +1 and +3 ions. You would predict a +3 ion from the position of In in the periodic table.) **81.** 116 g S; 230. g O **83.** Cu, Ag, and Au **85.** C:H = 8:18 or 4:9 **87.** The ratio of the masses of R that combine with 1.00 g Q is 3:1, as expected by the law of multiple proportions. R$_3$Q is the formula of the first compound. **89. a.** The compounds are isomers of each other. Isomers are compounds with the same formula but the atoms are attached differently, resulting in different properties. **b.** When wood burns,

most of the solid material is converted to gases, which escape. **c.** Atoms are not an indivisible particle. Atoms are composed of electrons, neutrons, and protons. **d.** The two hydride samples contain different isotopes of either hydrogen and/or lithium. Isotopes may have different masses but have similar chemical properties. **91.** tantalum(V) oxide; the formula would have the same subscripts, Ta$_2$S$_5$; 40 protons **93.** Ge^{4+}; ^{99}Tc

Chapter 3

19. From the relative abundances, there would be 9889 atoms of ^{12}C and 111 atoms of ^{13}C in the 10,000-atom sample. The average mass of carbon is independent of the sample size; it will always be 12.01 amu. The total mass would be 1.201×10^5 amu. For one mol of carbon (6.022×10^{23} atoms C), the average mass would still be 12.01 amu. There would be 5.955×10^{23} atoms of ^{12}C and 6.68×10^{21} atoms of ^{13}C. The total mass would be 7.232×10^{24} amu. The total mass in grams is 12.01 g/mol. **21.** Each person would have 100 trillion dollars. **23.** The mass percent of a compound is a constant no matter what amount of substance is present. Compounds always have constant composition. **25.** The information needed is mostly the coefficients in the balanced equation and the molar masses of the reactants and products. For percent yield, we would need the actual yield of the reaction and the amounts of reactants used.

a. mass of CB produced = 1.00×10^4 molecules

$$A_2B_2 \times \frac{1\ \text{mol A}_2\text{B}_2}{6.022 \times 10^{23}\ \text{molecules A}_2\text{B}_2} \times \frac{2\ \text{mol CB}}{1\ \text{mol A}_2\text{B}_2} \times \frac{\text{molar mass of CB}}{\text{mol CB}}$$

b. atoms of A produced = 1.00×10^4 molecules $A_2B_2 \times \dfrac{2\ \text{atoms A}}{1\ \text{molecule A}_2\text{B}_2}$

c. mol of C reacted = 1.00×10^4 molecules

$$A_2B_2 \times \frac{1\ \text{mol A}_2\text{B}_2}{6.022 \times 10^{23}\ \text{molecules A}_2\text{B}_2} \times \frac{2\ \text{mol C}}{1\ \text{mol A}_2\text{B}_2}$$

d. %yield = $\dfrac{\text{actual mass}}{\text{theoretical mass}} \times 100$; The theoretical mass of CB produced

was calculated in part a. If the actual mass of CB produced is given, then the percent yield can be determined for the reaction using the percent-yield equation. **27.** 207.2 amu, Pb **29.** 185 amu **31.** There are three peaks in the mass spectrum, each 2 mass units apart. This is consistent with two isotopes, differing in mass by two mass units. **33.** 4.64×10^{-20} g Fe **35.** 1.00×10^{22} atoms C **37.** Al$_2$O$_3$, 101.96 g/mol; Na$_3$AlF$_6$, 209.95 g/mol **39. a.** 17.03 g/mol; **b.** 32.05 g/mol; **c.** 252.08 g/mol **41. a.** 0.0587 mol NH$_3$; **b.** 0.0312 mol N$_2$H$_4$; **c.** 3.97×10^{-3} mol (NH$_4$)$_2$Cr$_2$O$_7$ **43. a.** 85.2 g NH$_3$; **b.** 160. g N$_2$H$_4$; **c.** 1260 g (NH$_4$)$_2$Cr$_2$O$_7$ **45. a.** 70.1 g N; **b.** 140. g N; **c.** 140. g N **47. a.** 3.54×10^{22} molecules NH$_3$; **b.** 1.88×10^{22} molecules N$_2$H$_4$; **c.** 2.39×10^{21} formula units (NH$_4$)$_2$Cr$_2$O$_7$ **49. a.** 3.54×10^{22} atoms N; **b.** 3.76×10^{22} atoms N; **c.** 4.78×10^{21} atoms N **51.** 176.12 g/mol; 2.839×10^{-3} mol; 1.710×10^{21} molecules **53. a.** 0.9393 mol; **b.** 2.17×10^{-4} mol; **c.** 2.5×10^{-8} mol **55. a.** 4.01×10^{22} atoms N; **b.** 5.97×10^{22} atoms N; **c.** 3.67×10^{22} atoms N; **d.** 6.54×10^{22} atoms N **57. a.** 294.30 g/mol; **b.** 3.40×10^{-2} mol; **c.** 459 g; **d.** 1.0×10^{19} molecules; **e.** 4.9×10^{21} atoms; **f.** 4.9×10^{-13} g; **g.** 4.887×10^{-22} g **59. a.** 50.00% C, 5.595% H, 44.41% O; **b.** 55.80% C, 7.025% H, 37.18% O; **c.** 67.90% C, 5.699% H, 26.40% N **61.** NO$_2$ = N$_2$O$_4$ < NO < N$_2$O **63.** 1360 g/mol **65. a.** 39.99% C, 6.713% H, 53.30% O; **b.** 40.00% C, 6.714% H, 53.29% O; **c.** 40.00% C, 6.714% H, 53.29% O (all the same except for rounding differences) **67. a.** NO$_2$; **b.** CH$_2$; **c.** P$_2$O$_5$; **d.** CH$_2$O **69.** C$_8$H$_{11}$O$_3$N **71.** compound I: HgO; compound II: Hg$_2$O **73.** SN; S$_4$N$_4$ **75.** C$_3$H$_5$O$_2$; C$_6$H$_{10}$O$_4$ **77.** C$_3$H$_8$ **79.** C$_3$H$_4$, C$_9$H$_{12}$ **81. a.** C$_6$H$_{12}$O$_6$(s) + 6O$_2$(g) $\rightarrow$ 6CO$_2$(g) + 6H$_2$O(g); **b.** Fe$_2$S$_3$(s) + 6HCl(g) $\rightarrow$ 2FeCl$_3$(g) + 3H$_2$S(g); **c.** CS$_2$(l) + 2NH$_3$(g) $\rightarrow$ H$_2$S(g) + NH$_4$SCN(s) **83. a.** 3Ca(OH)$_2$(aq) + 2H$_3$PO$_4$(aq) $\rightarrow$ 6H$_2$O(l) + Ca$_3$(PO$_4$)$_2$(s); **b.** Al(OH)$_3$(s) + 3HCl(aq) $\rightarrow$ AlCl$_3$(aq) + 3H$_2$O(l); **c.** 2AgNO$_3$(aq) + H$_2$SO$_4$(aq) $\rightarrow$ Ag$_2$SO$_4$(s) + 2HNO$_3$(aq) **85. a.** 2C$_6$H$_6$(l) + 15O$_2$(g) $\rightarrow$ 12CO$_2$(g) + 6H$_2$O(g); **b.** 2C$_4$H$_{10}$(g) + 13O$_2$(g) $\rightarrow$ 8CO$_2$(g) + 10H$_2$O(g); **c.** C$_{12}$H$_{22}$O$_{11}$(s) +

$12O_2(g) \rightarrow 12CO_2(g) + 11H_2O(g)$; **d.** $4Fe(s) + 3O_2(g) \rightarrow 2Fe_2O_3(s)$; **e.** $4FeO(s) + O_2(g) \rightarrow 2Fe_2O_3(s)$ **87. a.** $SiO_2(s) + 2C(s) \rightarrow Si(s) + 2CO(g)$; **b.** $SiCl_4(l) + 2Mg(s) \rightarrow Si(s) + 2MgCl_2(s)$; **c.** $Na_2SiF_6(s) + 4Na(s) \rightarrow Si(s) + 6NaF(s)$ **89.** 7.26 g Al; 21.5 g Fe_2O_3; 13.7 g Al_2O_3 **91.** 4.355 kg **93.** 32 kg **95. a.** 73.9 g; **b.** 1.30×10^2 g **97.** $2NO(g) + O_2(g) \rightarrow 2NO_2(g)$; NO is limiting. **99.** 0.301 g H_2O_2; 3.6×10^{-2} g HCl in excess **101.** 2.81×10^6 g HCN; 5.63×10^6 g H_2O **103.** 1.96 g (theoretical yield); 76.5% **105.** 1.20×10^3 kg $= 1.20$ metric tons **107.** 6 **109. a.** stoichiometric mixture; **b.** O_2; **c.** H_2; **d.** H_2; **e.** H_2; **f.** stoichiometric mixture; **g.** H_2 **111.** 9.25×10^{22} H atoms **113.** 4.30×10^{-2} mol; 2.50 g **115.** 5 **117.** 42.8% **119.** 81.1 g **121.** 86.2% **123.** $C_{20}H_{30}O$ **125.** $C_7H_5N_3O_6$ **127.** 38.7% **129.** 40.08% **131.** N_4H_6 **133.** 1.8×10^6 g $Cu(NH_3)_4Cl_2$; 5.9×10^5 g NH_3 **135.** 207 amu, Pb **137.** Al_2Se_3 **139.** 0.48 mol **141. a.** 113 Fe atoms; **b.** mass $= 9.071 \times 10^{-20}$ g; **c.** 540 Ru atoms **143.** M = Y, X = Cl, yttrium(III) chloride; 1.84 g

Chapter 4

9. a. Polarity is a term applied to covalent compounds. Polar covalent compounds have an unequal sharing of electrons in bonds that results in an unequal charge distribution in the overall molecule. Polar molecules have a partial negative end and a partial positive end. These are not full charges like in ionic compounds, but are charges much less in magnitude. Water is a polar molecule and dissolves other polar solutes readily. The oxygen end of water (the partial negative end of the polar water molecule) aligns with the partial positive end of the polar solute while the hydrogens of water (the partial positive end of the polar water molecule) align with the partial negative end of the solute. These opposite charged attractions stabilize polar solutes in water. This process is called hydration. Nonpolar solutes do not have permanent partial negative and partial positive ends; nonpolar solutes are not stabilized in water and do not dissolve. **b.** KF is a soluble ionic compound so it is a strong electrolyte. KF(aq) actually exists as separate hydrated K^+ ions and hydrated F^- ions in solution: $C_6H_{12}O_6$ is a polar covalent molecule that is a nonelectrolyte. $C_6H_{12}O_6$ is hydrated as described in part a. **c.** RbCl is a soluble ionic compound so it exists as separate hydrated Rb^+ ions and hydrated Cl^- ions in solution. AgCl is an insoluble ionic compound so the ions stay together in solution and fall to the bottom of the container as a precipitate. **d.** HNO_3 is a strong acid and exists as separate hydrated H^+ ions and hydrated NO_3^- ions in solution. CO is a polar covalent molecule and is hydrated as explained in part a. **11.** Bromides: NaBr, KBr, and HgBr (and others) would be soluble and AgBr, $PbBr_2$, and Hg_2Br_2 would be insoluble. Sulfates: Na_2SO_4, K_2SO_4, and $(NH_4)_2SO_4$ (and others) would be soluble and $BaSO_4$, $CaSO_4$, and $PbSO_4$ (or Hg_2SO_4) would be insoluble. Hydroxides: NaOH, KOH, $Ca(OH)_2$ (and others) would be soluble and $Al(OH)_3$, $Fe(OH)_3$, and $Cu(OH)_2$ (and others) would be insoluble. Phosphates: Na_3PO_4, K_3PO_4, $(NH_4)_3PO_4$ (and others) would be soluble and Ag_3PO_4, $Ca_3(PO_4)_2$, and $FePO_4$ (and others) would be insoluble. Lead: $PbCl_2$, $PbBr_2$, PbI_2, $Pb(OH)_2$, $PbSO_4$, and PbS (and others) would be insoluble. $Pb(NO_3)_2$ would be a soluble Pb^{2+} salt. **13.** The Brønsted-Lowry definitions are best for our purposes. An acid is a proton donor and a base is a proton acceptor. A proton is an H^+ ion. Neutral hydrogen has 1 electron and 1 proton, so an H^+ ion is just a proton. An acid–base reaction is the transfer of an H^+ ion (a proton) from an acid to a base. **15. a.** The species reduced is the element that gains electrons. The reducing agent causes reduction to occur by itself being oxidized. The reducing agent is generally listed as the entire formula of the compound/ion that contains the element oxidized. **b.** The species oxidized is the element that loses electrons. The oxidizing agent causes oxidation to occur by itself being reduced. The oxidizing agent is generally listed as the entire formula of the compound/ion that contains the element reduced. **c.** For simple binary ionic compounds, the actual charge on the ions are the oxidation states. For covalent compounds, nonzero oxidation states are pretend charges the elements would have if they were held together by ionic bonds (assuming the bond is between two different nonmetals). Nonzero oxidation states for elements in covalent compounds are not actual charges. Oxidation states for covalent compounds are a bookkeeping method to keep track of electrons in a reaction.

17.

c. For answers c–i, we will describe what should be in each solution. For c, the drawing should have three times as many NO_3^- anions as Al^{3+} cations. **d.** The drawing should have twice as many NH_4^+ cations as SO_4^{2-} anions. **e.** The drawing should have equal numbers of Na^+ cations and OH^- anions. **f.** The drawing should have equal numbers of Fe^{2+} cations and SO_4^{2-} anions. **g.** The drawing should have equal numbers of K^+ cations and MnO_4^- anions. **h.** The drawing should have equal numbers of H^+ cations and ClO_4^- anions. **i.** The drawing should have equal numbers of NH_4^+ cations and $C_2H_3O_2^-$ anions. **19.** $CaCl_2(s) \rightarrow Ca^{2+}(aq) + 2Cl^-(aq)$ **21. a.** 0.2677 M; **b.** 1.255×10^{-3} M; **c.** 8.065×10^{-3} M **23. a.** $M_{Ca^{2+}} = 1.00$ M, $M_{NO_3^-} = 2.00$ M; **b.** $M_{Na^+} = 4.0$ M, $M_{SO_4^{2-}} = 2.0$ M; **c.** $M_{NH_4^+} = M_{Cl^-} = 0.187$ M; **d.** $M_{K^+} = 0.0564$ M, $M_{PO_4^{3-}} = 0.0188$ M **25.** 100.0 mL of 0.30 M $AlCl_3$ **27.** 4.00 g **29. a.** Place 20.0 g NaOH in a 2-L volumetric flask; add water to dissolve the NaOH and fill to the mark. **b.** Add 500. mL of the 1.00 M NaOH stock solution to a 2-L volumetric flask; fill to the mark with water. **c.** As in a, instead using 38.8 g K_2CrO_4. **d.** As in b, instead using 114 mL of 1.75 M K_2CrO_4 stock solution. **31.** $M_{NH_4^+} = 0.272$ M, $M_{SO_4^{2-}} = 0.136$ M **33.** 5.94×10^{-8} M steroid **35.** Aluminum nitrate, magnesium chloride, and rubidium sulfate are soluble. **37. a.** no precipitate forms; **b.** $Al(OH)_3(s)$; **c.** $CaSO_4(s)$; **d.** $NiS(s)$ **39. a.** No reaction occurs because all possible products are soluble salts. **b.** $2Al(NO_3)_3(aq) + 3Ba(OH)_2(aq) \rightarrow 2Al(OH)_3(s) + 3Ba(NO_3)_2(aq)$; $2Al^{3+}(aq) + 6NO_3^-(aq) + 3Ba^{2+}(aq) + 6OH^-(aq) \rightarrow 2Al(OH)_3(s) + 3Ba^{2+}(aq) + 6NO_3^-(aq)$; $Al^{3+}(aq) + 3OH^-(aq) \rightarrow Al(OH)_3(s)$; **c.** $CaCl_2(aq) + Na_2SO_4(aq) \rightarrow CaSO_4(s) + 2NaCl(aq)$; $Ca^{2+}(aq) + 2Cl^-(aq) + 2Na^+(aq) + SO_4^{2-}(aq) \rightarrow CaSO_4(s) + 2Na^+(aq) + 2Cl^-(aq)$; $Ca^{2+}(aq) + SO_4^{2-}(aq) \rightarrow CaSO_4(s)$; **d.** $K_2S(aq) + Ni(NO_3)_2(aq) \rightarrow 2KNO_3(aq) + NiS(s)$; $2K^+(aq) + S^{2-}(aq) + Ni^{2+}(aq) + 2NO_3^-(aq) \rightarrow 2K^+(aq) + 2NO_3^-(aq) + NiS(s)$; $Ni^{2+}(aq) + S^{2-}(aq) \rightarrow NiS(s)$ **41. a.** $CuSO_4(aq) + Na_2S(aq) \rightarrow CuS(s) + Na_2SO_4(aq)$; $Cu^{2+}(aq) + S^{2-}(aq) \rightarrow CuS(s)$; the grey spheres are the Na^+ spectator ions and the blue-green spheres are the SO_4^{2-} spectator ions; **b.** $CoCl_2(aq) + 2NaOH(aq) \rightarrow Co(OH)_2(s) + 2NaCl(aq)$; $Co^{2+}(aq) + 2OH^-(aq) \rightarrow Co(OH)_2(s)$; the grey spheres are the Na^+ spectator ions and the green spheres are the Cl^- spectator ions; **c.** $AgNO_3(aq) + KI(aq) \rightarrow AgI(s) + KNO_3(aq)$; $Ag^+(aq) + I^-(aq) \rightarrow AgI(s)$; the red spheres are the K^+ spectator ions and the blue spheres are the NO_3^- spectator ions **43. a.** $Ba^{2+}(aq) + SO_4^{2-}(aq) \rightarrow BaSO_4(s)$; **b.** $Pb^{2+}(aq) + 2Cl^-(aq) \rightarrow PbCl_2(s)$; **c.** No reaction; **d.** No reaction; **e.** $Cu^{2+}(aq) + 2OH^-(aq) \rightarrow Cu(OH)_2(s)$ **45.** Ca^{2+}, Sr^{2+}, or Ba^{2+} could all be present. **47.** 0.607 g **49.** 0.520 g $Al(OH)_3$ **51.** 2.9 g AgCl; 0 M Ag^+; 0.10 M NO_3^-; 0.075 M Ca^{2+}; 0.050 M Cl^- **53.** 23 amu; Na **55. a.** $2HClO_4(aq) + Mg(OH)_2(s) \rightarrow Mg(ClO_4)_2(aq) + 2H_2O(l)$; $2H^+(aq) + 2ClO_4^-(aq) + Mg(OH)_2(s) \rightarrow Mg^{2+}(aq) + 2ClO_4^-(aq) + 2H_2O(l)$; $2H^+(aq) + Mg(OH)_2(s) \rightarrow Mg^{2+}(aq) + 2H_2O(l)$; **b.** $HCN(aq) + NaOH(aq) \rightarrow NaCN(aq) + H_2O(l)$; $HCN(aq) + Na^+(aq) + OH^-(aq) \rightarrow Na^+(aq) + CN^-(aq) + H_2O(l)$; $HCN(aq) + OH^-(aq) \rightarrow H_2O(l) + CN^-(aq)$; **c.** $HCl(aq) + NaOH(aq) \rightarrow NaCl(aq) + H_2O(l)$; $H^+(aq) + Cl^-(aq) + Na^+(aq) + OH^-(aq) \rightarrow Na^+(aq) + Cl^-(aq) + H_2O(l)$; $H^+(aq) + OH^-(aq) \rightarrow H_2O(l)$ **57. a.** $KOH(aq) + HNO_3(aq) \rightarrow H_2O(l) + KNO_3(aq)$; $K^+(aq) + OH^-(aq) + H^+(aq) + NO_3^-(aq) \rightarrow H_2O(l) + K^+(aq) + NO_3^-(aq)$; $OH^-(aq) + H^+(aq) \rightarrow H_2O(l)$; **b.** $Ba(OH)_2(aq) + 2HCl(aq) \rightarrow 2H_2O(l) + BaCl_2(aq)$; $Ba^{2+}(aq) + 2OH^-(aq) + 2H^+(aq) + 2Cl^-(aq) \rightarrow Ba^{2+}(aq) + 2Cl^-(aq) + 2H_2O(l)$; $OH^-(aq) + H^+(aq) \rightarrow H_2O(l)$; **c.** $3HClO_4(aq) + Fe(OH)_3(s) \rightarrow 3H_2O(l) + Fe(ClO_4)_3(aq)$; $3H^+(aq) + 3ClO_4^-(aq) + Fe(OH)_3(s) \rightarrow 3H_2O(l) + Fe^{3+}(aq) + 3ClO_4^-(aq)$; $3H^+(aq) + Fe(OH)_3(s) \rightarrow 3H_2O(l) + Fe^{3+}(aq)$ **59. a.** 100. mL; **b.** 66.7 mL; **c.** 50.0 mL **61.** 2.0×10^{-2} M excess OH^- **63.** 0.102 M **65.** 0.4178 g **67. a.** K, +1; O, −2; Mn, +7; **b.** Ni, +4; O, −2; **c.** Na, +1; Fe, +2; O,

−2; H, +1 **d.** H, +1; O, −2; N, −3; P, +5; **e.** P, +3; O, −2; **f.** O, −2; Fe, +$\frac{8}{3}$; **g.** O, −2; F, −1; Xe, −6; **h.** S, +4; F, −1; **i.** C, +2; O, −2; **j.** C, 0; H, +1; O, −2   **69. a.** −3; **b.** −3; **c.** −2; **d.** +2; **e.** +1; **f.** +4; **g.** +3; **h.** +5; **i.** 0

71.

Redox?	Oxidizing Agent	Reducing Agent	Substance Oxidized	Substance Reduced
a. Yes	Ag^+	Cu	Cu	Ag^+
b. No	—	—	—	—
c. No	—	—	—	—
d. Yes	$SiCl_4$	Mg	Mg	$SiCl_4$ (Si)
e. No	—	—	—	—

In b, c, and e, no oxidation numbers change from reactants to products.

73. a. $Zn + 2HCl \rightarrow Zn^{2+} + H_2 + 2Cl^-$; **b.** $2H^+ + 3I^- + ClO^- \rightarrow I_3^- + Cl^- + H_2O$; **c.** $7H_2O + 4H^+ + 3As_2O_3 + 4NO_3^- \rightarrow 4NO + 6H_3AsO_4$; **d.** $16H^+ + 2MnO_4^- + 10Br^- \rightarrow 5Br_2 + 2Mn^{2+} + 8H_2O$; **e.** $8H^+ + 3CH_3OH + Cr_2O_7^{2-} \rightarrow 2Cr^{3+} + 3CH_2O + 7H_2O$ **75. a.** $2H_2O + Al + MnO_4^- \rightarrow Al(OH)_4^- + MnO_2$; **b.** $2OH^- + Cl_2 \rightarrow Cl^- + ClO^- + H_2O$; **c.** $OH^- + H_2O + NO_2^- + 2Al \rightarrow NH_3 + 2AlO_2^-$ **77.** $4NaCl + 2H_2SO_4 + MnO_2 \rightarrow 2Na_2SO_4 + MnCl_2 + Cl_2 + 2H_2O$ **79.** Only statement b is true. **a.** A nonelectrolyte solute can make a concentrated solution. **c.** Weak acids like acetic acid, $HC_2H_3O_2$, are weak electrolytes. **d.** Some ionic compounds do not dissolve in water (are insoluble). These compounds are not strong electrolytes (nor any type of electrolyte). The electrolyte designation refers to solutes that are soluble in water. **81. a.** $AgNO_3$, $Pb(NO_3)_2$, and $Hg_2(NO_3)_2$ would form precipitates with the Cl^- ion; $Ag^+(aq) + Cl^-(aq) \rightarrow AgCl(s)$; $Pb^{2+}(aq) + 2Cl^-(aq) \rightarrow PbCl_2(s)$; $Hg_2^{2+}(aq) + 2Cl^-(aq) \rightarrow Hg_2Cl_2(s)$; **b.** Na_2SO_4, Na_2CO_3, and Na_3PO_4 would form precipitates with the Ca^{2+} ion; $Ca^{2+}(aq) + SO_4^{2-}(aq) \rightarrow CaSO_4(s)$; $Ca^{2+}(aq) + CO_3^{2-}(aq) \rightarrow CaCO_3(s)$; $3Ca^{2+}(aq) + 2PO_4^{3-}(aq) \rightarrow Ca_3(PO_4)_2(s)$; **c.** NaOH, Na_2S, and Na_2CO_3 would form precipitates with the Fe^{3+} ion; $Fe^{3+}(aq) + 3OH^-(aq) \rightarrow Fe(OH)_3(s)$; $2Fe^{3+}(aq) + 3S^{2-}(aq) \rightarrow Fe_2S_3(s)$; $2Fe^{3+}(aq) + 3CO_3^{2-}(aq) \rightarrow Fe_2(CO_3)_3(s)$; **d.** $BaCl_2$, $Pb(NO_3)_2$, and $Ca(NO_3)_2$ would form precipitates with the SO_4^{2-} ion; $Ba^{2+}(aq) + SO_4^{2-}(aq) \rightarrow BaSO_4(s)$; $Pb^{2+}(aq) + SO_4^{2-}(aq) \rightarrow PbSO_4(s)$; $Ca^{2+}(aq) + SO_4^{2-}(aq) \rightarrow CaSO_4(s)$; **e.** Na_2SO_4, NaCl, and NaI would form precipitates with the Hg_2^{2+} ion; $Hg_2^{2+}(aq) + SO_4^{2-}(aq) \rightarrow Hg_2SO_4(s)$; $Hg_2^{2+}(aq) + 2Cl^-(aq) \rightarrow Hg_2Cl_2(s)$; $Hg_2^{2+}(aq) + 2I^-(aq) \rightarrow Hg_2I_2(s)$; **f.** NaBr, Na_2CrO_4, and Na_3PO_4 would form precipitates with the Ag^+ ion; $Ag^+(aq) + Br^-(aq) \rightarrow AgBr(s)$; $2Ag^+(aq) + CrO_4^{2-}(aq) \rightarrow Ag_2CrO_4(s)$; $3Ag^+(aq) + PO_4^{3-}(aq) \rightarrow Ag_3PO_4(s)$ **83.** Ba   **85.** 39.49 mg/tablet; 67.00%   **87.** 2.00 M **89. a.** 0.8393 M; **b.** 5.010%   **91.** $C_6H_8O_6$ **93.** $Ca(OH)_2$, $Sr(OH)_2$, and $Ba(OH)_2$ are possibilities for the base.   **95.** $2H^+(aq) + Mn(s) + 2HNO_3(aq) \rightarrow Mn^{2+}(aq) + 2NO_2(g) + 2H_2O(l)$; $3H_2O(l) + 2Mn^{2+}(aq) + 5IO_4^-(aq) \rightarrow 2MnO_4^-(aq) + 5IO_3^-(aq) + 6H^+(aq)$ **97. a.** 24.8% Co, 29.7% Cl, 5.09% H, 40.4% O; **b.** $CoCl_2 \cdot 6H_2O$; **c.** $CoCl_2 \cdot 6H_2O(aq) + 2AgNO_3(aq) \rightarrow 2AgCl(s) + Co(NO_3)_2(aq) + 6H_2O(l)$, $CoCl_2 \cdot 6H_2O(aq) + 2NaOH(aq) \rightarrow Co(OH)_2(s) + 2NaCl(aq) + 6H_2O(l)$, $4Co(OH)_2(s) + O_2(g) \rightarrow 2Co_2O_3(s) + 4H_2O(l)$ **99. a.** 7.000 M K^+; **b.** 0.750 M CrO_4^{2-} **101.** 0.123 g SO_4^{2-}, 60.0% SO_4^{2-}; 61% K_2SO_4 and 39% Na_2SO_4 **103.** 4.90 M **105.** Y, 2.06 mL/min; Z, 4.20 mL/min   **107.** 57.6 mL   **109. a.** $MgO(s) + 2HCl(aq) \rightarrow MgCl_2(aq) + H_2O(l)$, $Mg(OH)_2(s) + 2HCl(aq) \rightarrow MgCl_2(aq) + 2H_2O(l)$, $Al(OH)_3(s) + 3HCl(aq) \rightarrow AlCl_3(aq) + 3H_2O(l)$; **b.** MgO   **111.** Citric acid has three acidic hydrogens per citric acid molecule.   **113.** 0.07849 ± 0.00016 M or 0.0785 ± 0.0002 M **115.** $3(NH_4)_2CrO_4(aq) + 2Cr(NO_3)_3(aq) \rightarrow 6NH_4NO_2(aq) + Cr_2(CrO_4)_3(s)$; 7.34 g   **117.** X = Se; H_2Se is hydroselenic acid; 0.252 g

Chapter 5

17. higher than; 13.6 times taller; When the pressure of the column of liquid standing on the surface of the liquid is equal to the pressure exerted by air on the rest of the surface of the liquid, then the height of the column of liquid is a measure of atmospheric pressure. Because water is 13.6 times less dense than mercury, the column of water must be 13.6 times longer than that of mercury to match the force exerted by the columns of liquid standing on the surface. **19.** The P versus $1/V$ plot is incorrect. The plot should be linear with positive slope and a y-intercept of zero. $PV = k$ so $P = k(1/V)$, which is in the form of the straight-line equation $y = mx + b$. **21.** $d = $ (molar mass) P/RT; Because d is directly proportional to the molar mass of the gas. Helium, which has the smallest molar mass of all the noble gases, will have the smallest density. **23.** No; At any nonzero Kelvin temperature, there is a distribution of kinetic energies. Similarly, there is a distribution of velocities at any nonzero Kelvin temperature. **25.** $2NH_3(g) \rightarrow N_2(g) + 3H_2(g)$; At constant P and T, volume is directly proportional to the moles of gas present. In the reaction, the moles of gas doubles as reactants are converted to products, so the volume of the container should double. At constant V and T, P is directly proportional to the moles of gas present. As the moles of gas doubles, the pressure will double. The partial pressure of N_2 will be 1/2 the initial pressure of NH_3 and the partial pressure of H_2 will be 3/2 the initial pressure of NH_3. The partial pressure of H_2 will be three times the partial pressure of N_2. **27 a.** 3.6×10^3 mm Hg; **b.** 3.6×10^3 torr; **c.** 4.9×10^5 Pa; **d.** 71 psi **29.** 65 torr, 8.7×10^3 Pa, 8.6×10^{-2} atm **31. a.** 642 torr, 0.845 atm; 8.56×10^4 Pa; **b.** 975 torr; 1.28 atm; 1.30×10^5 Pa; **c.** 517 torr; 850. torr **33.** The balloon will burst. **35.** 0.89 mol **37. a.** 14.0 L; **b.** 4.72×10^{-2} mol; **c.** 678 K; **d.** 133 atm **39.** 4.44×10^3 g He; 2.24×10^3 g H_2 **41. a.** 69.6 K; **b.** 32.3 atm **43.** 1.27 mol **45.** $P_B = 2P_A$ **47.** 5.1×10^4 torr **49.** The volume of the balloon increases from 1.00 L to 2.82 L, so the change in volume is 1.82 L. **51.** 3.21 g Al **53.** 135 g NaN_3 **55.** 1.5×10^7 g Fe, 2.6×10^7 g 98% H_2SO_4 **57.** 2.47 mol H_2O **59. a.** $2CH_4(g) + 2NH_3(g) + 3O_2(g) \rightarrow 2HCN(g) + 6H_2O(g)$; **b.** 13.3 L **61.** Cl_2 **63.** 12.6 g/L **65.** 1.1 atm, $P_{CO_2} = 1.1$ atm, $P_{TOTAL} = 2.1$ atm **67.** $P_{H_2} = 317$ torr, $P_{N_2} = 50.7$ torr, $P_{TOTAL} = 368$ torr **69. a.** $\chi_{CH_4} = 0.412$, $\chi_{O_2} = 0.588$; **b.** 0.161 mol; **c.** 1.06 g CH_4, 3.03 g O_2 **71.** 0.990 atm; 0.625 g **73.** 18.0% **75.** $P_{tot} = 6.0$ atm; $P_{N_2} = 1.5$ atm; $P_{H_2} = 4.5$ atm **77.** Both $CH_4(g)$ and $N_2(g)$ have the same average kinetic energy at the various temperatures. 273 K, 5.65×10^{-21} J/molecule; 546 K, 1.13×10^{-20} J/molecule **79.** CH_4: 652 m/s (273 K); 921 m/s (546 K); N_2: 493 m/s (273 K); 697 m/s (546 K)

81.

Average KE	Average Velocity	Wall-Collision Frequency
a. Increase	Increase	Increase
b. Decrease	Decrease	Decrease
c. Same	Same	Increase
d. Same	Same	Increase

83. a. All the same; **b.** Flask C **85.** CF_2Cl_2 **87.** The relative rates of effusion of $^{12}C^{16}O$, $^{12}C^{17}O$, and $^{12}C^{18}O$ are 1.04, 1.02, and 1.00. Advantage: CO_2 isn't as toxic as CO. Disadvantages: Can get a mixture of oxygen isotopes in CO_2, so some species would effuse at about the same rate. **89. a.** 12.24 atm; **b.** 12.13 atm; **c.** The ideal gas law is high by 0.91%. **91.** 5.2×10^{-6} atm; 1.3×10^{14} atoms He/cm^3 **93.** $2NO_2(g) + H_2O(l) \rightarrow HNO_3(aq) + HNO_2(aq)$; $SO_3(g) + H_2O(l) \rightarrow H_2SO_4(aq)$

95. a.

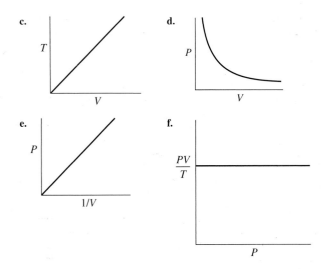

c. T vs V

d. P vs V

e. P vs 1/V

f. PV/T vs P

97. 0.772 atm · L; In Sample Exercise 5.3, 1.0 mol of gas was present at 0°C. The moles of gas and/or the temperature must have been different for Boyle's data. **99.** $MnCl_4$ **101.** 1490 **103.** 24 torr **105.** 4.1×10^6 L air; 7.42×10^5 L H_2 **107.** 490 atm **109.** 13.3% N **111.** $C_{12}H_{21}NO$; $C_{24}H_{42}N_2O_2$ **113.** C_3H_8 should have the largest b constant. Since CO_2 has the largest a constant, CO_2 will have the strongest intermolecular attractions. **115.** 13.4% CaO, 86.6% BaO **117.** C_2H_6 **119. a.** 8.7×10^3 L air/min; **b.** $\chi_{CO} = 0.0017$, $\chi_{CO_2} = 0.032$, $\chi_{O_2} = 0.13$, $\chi_{N_2} = 0.77$, $\chi_{H_2O} = 0.067$ **121. a.** 1.01×10^4 g; **b.** 6.65×10^4 g; **c.** 8.7×10^3 g **123. a.** Due to air's larger average molar mass, a given volume of air at a given set of conditions has a higher density than helium. We need to heat the air to greater than 25°C to lower the air density (by driving air out of the hot-air balloon) until the density is the same as that for helium (at 25°C and 1.00 atm). **b.** 2150 K **125. a.** 0.19 torr; **b.** 6.6×10^{15} molecules CO/cm³ **127.** 0.023 mol **129.** 4.8 g/L; UF_3 will effuse 1.02 times faster.

Chapter 6

9. Path-dependent functions for a trip from Chicago to Denver are those quantities that depend on the route taken. One can fly directly from Chicago to Denver or one could fly from Chicago to Atlanta to Los Angeles and then to Denver. Some path-dependent quantities are miles traveled, fuel consumption of the airplane, time traveling, airplane snacks eaten, etc. State functions are path-independent; they only depend on the initial and final states. Some state functions for an airplane trip from Chicago to Denver would be longitude change, latitude change, elevation change, and overall time zone change.
11. Both q and w are negative.

13.

$H_2O(l) + \frac{1}{2}CO_2(g) \rightarrow \frac{1}{2}CH_4(g) + O_2(g)$	$\Delta H_1 = -\frac{1}{2}(-891 \text{ kJ})$
$\frac{1}{2}CH_4(g) + O_2(g) \rightarrow \frac{1}{2}CO_2(g) + H_2O(g)$	$\Delta H_2 = \frac{1}{2}(-803 \text{ kJ})$
$H_2O(l) \rightarrow H_2O(g)$	$\Delta H = \Delta H_1 + \Delta H_2 = 44 \text{ kJ}$

15. Fossil fuels contain carbon; the incomplete combustion of fossil fuels produces $CO(g)$ instead of $CO_2(g)$. This occurs when the amount of oxygen reacting is not sufficient to convert all of the carbon in fossil fuels to CO_2. Carbon monoxide is a poisonous gas to humans. **17.** 150 J **19.** 1.0 kg object with velocity of 2.0 m/s. **21. a.** 41 kJ; **b.** 35 kJ; **c.** 47 kJ; **d.** part a only **23.** 375 J heat transferred to the system **25.** -13.2 kJ **27.** 11.0 L **29.** $q = 30.9$ kJ, $w = -12.4$ kJ, $\Delta E = 18.5$ kJ **31.** This is an endothermic reaction, so heat must be absorbed to convert reactants into products. The high-temperature environment of internal combustion engines provides the heat. **33. a.** endothermic; **b.** exothermic; **c.** exothermic; **d.** endothermic **35. a.** -1650 kJ; **b.** -826 kJ; **c.** -7.39 kJ; **d.** -34.4 kJ **37.** 4400 g C_3H_8 **39.** When a liquid is converted into a gas, there is an increase in volume.

The 2.5 kJ/mol quantity can be considered as the work done by the vaporization process in pushing back the atmosphere. **41.** $H_2O(l)$; 2.30×10^3 J; $Hg(l)$; 140°C **43.** $Al(s)$ **45.** 311 K **47.** 23.7°C **49.** 0.25 J/g · °C **51.** -66 kJ/mol **53.** 39.2°C **55. a.** 31.5 kJ/°C; **b.** -1.10×10^3 kJ/mol **57.** -220.8 kJ **59.** 1268 kJ; No, because this reaction is very endothermic, it would not be a practical way of making ammonia due to the high energy costs. **61.** -233 kJ **63.** -713 kJ **65.** The enthalpy change for the formation of one mole of a compound from its elements, with all substances in their standard states. $Na(s) + \frac{1}{2}Cl_2(g) \rightarrow NaCl(s)$; $H_2(g) + \frac{1}{2}O_2(g) \rightarrow H_2O(l)$; $6C_{graphite}(s) + 6H_2(g) + 3O_2(g) \rightarrow C_6H_{12}O_6(s)$; $Pb(s) + S(s) + 2O_2(g) \rightarrow PbSO_4(s)$ **67. a.** $-940.$ kJ; **b.** -265 kJ; **c.** -176 kJ **69. a.** -908 kJ, -112 kJ, $-140.$ kJ; **b.** $12NH_3(g) + 21O_2(g) \rightarrow 8HNO_3(aq) + 4NO(g) + 14H_2O(g)$, exothermic **71.** -2677 kJ **73.** -169 kJ/mol **75.** -29.67 kJ/g **77.** For $C_3H_8(g)$, -50.37 kJ/g vs. -47.7 kJ/g for octane. Because of the low boiling point of propane, there are extra safety hazards associated with using the necessary high-pressure compressed gas tanks. **79.** 1.05×10^5 L **81. a.** $2SO_2(g) + O_2(g) \rightarrow 2SO_3(g)$; $w > 0$; **b.** $COCl_2(g) \rightarrow CO(g) + Cl_2(g)$; $w < 0$; **c.** $N_2(g) + O_2(g) \rightarrow 2NO(g)$; $w = 0$; Compare the sum of the coefficients of all the product gases in the balanced equation to the sum of the coefficients of all the reactant gases. When a balanced reaction has more mol of product gases than mol of reactant gases, then the reaction will expand in volume (ΔV is positive) and the system does work on the surroundings ($w < 0$). When a balanced reaction has a decrease in the mol of gas from reactants to products, then the reaction will contract in volume (ΔV is negative) and the surroundings does compression work on the system ($w > 0$). When there is no change in the mol of gas from reactants to products, then $\Delta V = 0$ and $w = 0$. **83.** 25 J **85.** -4.2 kJ heat released **87.** The calculated ΔH value will be less positive (smaller) than it should be. **89.** 25.91°C **91. a.** 632 kJ; **b.** $C_2H_2(g)$ **93. a.** -361 kJ; **b.** -199 kJ; **c.** -227 kJ; **d.** -112 kJ **95. a.** $C_{12}H_{22}O_{11}(s) + 12O_2(g) \rightarrow 12CO_2(g) + 11H_2O(l)$; **b.** -5630 kJ; **c.** -5630 kJ **97.** 37 m² **99.** 1×10^4 steps **101.** 56.9 kJ **103.** 1.74 kJ **105.** 3.3 cm

Chapter 7

15. The equations relating the terms are $\nu\lambda = c$, $E = h\nu$, and $E = hc/\lambda$. From the equations, wavelength and frequency are inversely related, photon energy and frequency are directly related, and photon energy and wavelength are inversely related. The unit of 1 Joule (J) $= 1$ kg m²/s². This is why you must change mass units to kg when using the deBroglie equation. **17.** Sample Exercise 7.3 calculates the deBroglie wavelength of a ball and of an electron. The ball has a wavelength on the order of 10^{-34} m. This is incredibly short and, as far as the wave-particle duality is concerned, the wave properties of large objects are insignificant. The electron, with its tiny mass, also has a short wavelength; on the order of 10^{-10} m. However, this wavelength is significant as it is on the same order as the spacing between atoms in a typical crystal. For very tiny objects like electrons, the wave properties are important. The wave properties must be considered, along with the particle properties, when hypothesizing about the electron motion in an atom. **19.** For the radial probability distribution, the space around the hydrogen nucleus is cut up into a series of thin spherical shells. When the total probability of finding the electron in each spherical shell is plotted versus the distance from the nucleus, we get the radial probability distribution graph. The plot shows a steady increase with distance from the nucleus, maximizes at a certain distance from the nucleus, then shows a steady decrease. Even though it is likely to find an electron near the nucleus, the volume of the spherical shell close to the nucleus is tiny, resulting in a low radial probability. The maximum radial probability distribution occurs at a distance of 5.29×10^{-2} nm from the nucleus; the electron is most likely to be found in the volume of the shell centered at this distance from the nucleus. The 5.29×10^{-2} nm distance is the exact radius of innermost (n = 1) orbit in the Bohr model. **21.** If one more electron is added to a half-filled subshell, electron–electron repulsions will increase because two electrons must now occupy the same atomic orbital. This may slightly decrease the stability of the atom. Hence, half-filled subshells minimize electron–electron repulsions. **23.** The valence electrons are strongly attracted to the nucleus for elements with large ionization energies. One would expect these species to readily accept another electron and have very exothermic electron affinities. The noble gases are an exception; they have a large ionization energy but an endothermic electron affinity. Noble gases have a stable arrangement of electrons. Adding an electron disrupts this stable arrangement, resulting in unfavorable electron affinities. **25.** For hydrogen, all orbitals with the same value of n have the same energy. For polyatomic atoms/ions, the energy of the orbitals also depends on ℓ. Because there are more nondegenerate energy levels for polyatomic atoms/ions as compared with hydrogen, there are many more possible electronic transitions resulting in more complicated line spectra. **27.** Yes, the maximum number of unpaired electrons in any configuration corresponds to a minimum in electron–electron repulsions. **29.** Ionization energy applies to the removal of the electron from the atom in the gas phase. The work function applies to the removal of an electron from the solid. **31.** $4.5 \times 10^{14}\,s^{-1}$ **33.** $3.0 \times 10^{10}\,s^{-1}$, 2.0×10^{-23} J/photon, 12 J/mol **35.** Wave a has the longer wavelength (4.0×10^{-4} m). Wave b has the higher frequency ($1.5 \times 10^{12}\,s^{-1}$) and larger photon energy (9.9×10^{-22} J). Since both of these waves represent electromagnetic radiation, they both should travel at the same speed, c, the speed of light. Both waves represent infrared radiation. **37.** 1.50×10^{23} atoms **39.** 427.7 nm **41. a.** 2.4×10^{-11} m; **b.** 3.4×10^{-34} m **43.** 1.6×10^{-27} kg **45. a.** 656.7 nm (visible); **b.** 486.4 nm (visible); **c.** 121.6 nm (ultraviolet)

47.

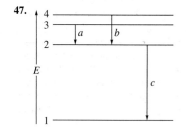

49. $n = 1 \rightarrow n = 5, \lambda = 95.00$ nm; $n = 2 \rightarrow n = 6, \lambda = 410.4$ nm; visible light has sufficient energy for the $n = 2 \rightarrow n = 6$ transition but does not have sufficient energy for the $n = 1 \rightarrow n = 5$ transition. **51.** $n = 1$, 91.20 nm; $n = 2$, 364.8 nm **53.** $n = 2$ **55. a.** 5.79×10^{-4} m; **b.** 3.64×10^{-33} m; **c.** The diameter of an H atom is roughly 1.0×10^{-8} cm. The uncertainty in position is much larger than the size of the atom. **d.** The uncertainty is insignificant compared to the size of a baseball. **57.** $n = 1, 2, 3, \ldots$; $\ell = 0$, $1, 2, \ldots (n - 1); m_\ell = -\ell, \ldots, -2, -1, 0, 1, 2, \ldots, +\ell$. **59. b.** For $\ell = 3$, m_ℓ can range from -3 to $+3$; thus $+4$ is not allowed. **c.** n cannot equal zero. **d.** ℓ cannot be a negative number. **61.** ψ^2 gives the probability of finding the electron at that point. **63.** 3; 1; 5; 25; 16 **65. a.** 32; **b.** 8; **c.** 25; **d.** 10; **e.** 6

67. a.

$\uparrow\downarrow$	$\uparrow\downarrow$	$\uparrow\downarrow$ $\uparrow\downarrow$ $\uparrow\downarrow$	$\uparrow$ or $\downarrow$
$1s$	$2s$	$2p$	$3s$

b.

$\uparrow\downarrow$	$\uparrow\downarrow$	$\uparrow\downarrow$ $\uparrow\downarrow$ $\uparrow\downarrow$	$\uparrow\downarrow$	$\uparrow\downarrow$ $\uparrow\downarrow$ $\uparrow\downarrow$
$1s$	$2s$	$2p$	$3s$	$3p$

$\uparrow\downarrow$	$\uparrow\downarrow$ $\uparrow\downarrow$ $\uparrow$ $\uparrow$ $\uparrow$ or $\uparrow\downarrow$ $\uparrow\downarrow$ $\downarrow$ $\downarrow$ $\downarrow$
$4s$	$3d$

c.

$\uparrow\downarrow$	$\uparrow\downarrow$	$\uparrow\downarrow$ $\uparrow\downarrow$ $\uparrow\downarrow$	$\uparrow\downarrow$	$\uparrow\downarrow$ $\uparrow\downarrow$ $\uparrow\downarrow$
$1s$	$2s$	$2p$	$3s$	$3p$

$\uparrow\downarrow$	$\uparrow\downarrow$ $\uparrow\downarrow$ $\uparrow\downarrow$ $\uparrow\downarrow$ $\uparrow\downarrow$	$\uparrow\downarrow$ $\uparrow\downarrow$ $\uparrow\downarrow$
$4s$	$3d$	$4p$

69. Si: $1s^2 2s^2 2p^6 3s^2 3p^2$ or [Ne]$3s^2 3p^2$; Ga: $1s^2 2s^2 2p^6 3s^2 3p^6 4s^2 3d^{10} 4p^1$ or [Ar]$4s^2 3d^{10} 4p^1$; As: [Ar]$4s^2 3d^{10} 4p^3$; Ge: [Ar]$4s^2 3d^{10} 4p^2$; Al: [Ne]$3s^2 3p^1$; Cd: [Kr]$5s^2 4d^{10}$; S: [Ne]$3s^2 3p^4$; Se: [Ar]$4s^2 3d^{10} 4p^4$ **71.** Sc: $1s^2 2s^2 2p^6 3s^2 3p^6 4s^2 3d^1$; Fe: $1s^2 2s^2 2p^6 3s^2 3p^6 4s^2 3d^6$; P:$1s^2 2s^2 2p^6 3s^2 3p^3$; Cs: $1s^2 2s^2 2p^6 3s^2 3p^6 4s^2 3d^{10} 4p^6 5s^2 4d^{10} 5p^6 6s^1$; Eu: $1s^2 2s^2 2p^6 3s^2 3p^6 4s^2 3d^{10} 4p^6 5s^2 4d^{10} 5p^6 6s^2 4f^6 5d^1$ (Actual: [Xe]$6s^2 4f^7$); Pt: $1s^2 2s^2 2p^6 3s^2 3p^6 4s^2 3d^{10} 4p^6 5s^2 4d^{10} 5p^6 6s^2 4f^{14} 5d^8$ (Actual: [Xe]$6s^1 4f^{14} 5d^9$); Xe: $1s^2 2s^2 2p^6 3s^2 3p^6 4s^2 3d^{10} 4p^6 5s^2 4d^{10} 5p^6$; Br: $1s^2 2s^2 2p^6 3s^2 3p^6 4s^2 3d^{10} 4p^5$; **73. a.** I: [Kr]$5s^2 4d^{10} 5p^5$; **b.** element 120: [Rn]$7s^2 5f^{14} 6d^{10} 7p^6 8s^2$; **c.** Rn: [Xe]$6s^2 4f^{14} 5d^{10} 6p^6$; **d.** Cr: [Ar]$4s^1 3d^5$ **75. a.** 18; **b.** 30; **c.** 10; **d.** 40

77. B: $1s^2 2s^2 2p^1$ N: $1s^2 2s^2 2p^3$

	n	ℓ	m_ℓ	m_s		n	ℓ	m_ℓ	m_s
$1s$	1	0	0	$+\frac{1}{2}$	$1s$	1	0	0	$+\frac{1}{2}$
$1s$	1	0	0	$-\frac{1}{2}$	$1s$	1	0	0	$-\frac{1}{2}$
$2s$	2	0	0	$+\frac{1}{2}$	$2s$	2	0	0	$+\frac{1}{2}$
$2s$	2	0	0	$-\frac{1}{2}$	$2s$	2	0	0	$-\frac{1}{2}$
$2p$	2	1	-1	$+\frac{1}{2}$	$2p$	2	1	-1	$+\frac{1}{2}$
					$2p$	2	1	0	$+\frac{1}{2}$
					$2p$	2	1	$+1$	$+\frac{1}{2}$

For boron, there are six possibilities for the $2p$ electron. For nitrogen, all the $2p$ electrons could have $m_s = -\frac{1}{2}$. **79.** none; an excited state; energy released **81.** C, O, Si, S, Ti, Ni, Ge, Se **83.** Li (1 unpaired electron), N (3 unpaired electrons), Ni (2 unpaired electrons), and Te (2 unpaired electrons) are all expected to be paramagnetic because they have unpaired electrons. **85. a.** S < Se < Te; **b.** Br < Ni; < K; **c.** F < Si < Ba **87. a.** Te < Se < S; **b.** K < Ni < Br; **c.** Ba < Si < F **89. a.** He; **b.** Cl; **c.** element 117; **d.** Si; **e.** Na$^+$ **91. a.** [Rn]$7s^2 5f^{14} 6d^4$; **b.** W; **c.** SgO$_3$ and SgO$_4^{2-}$ probably would form (similar to Cr). **93.** Se is an exception to the general ionization trend. There are extra electron–electron repulsions in Se because two electrons are in the same $4p$ orbital, resulting in a lower ionization energy than expected. **95. a.** C, Br; **b.** N, Ar; **c.** C, Br **97.** Al (-44), Si (-120), P (-74), S (-200.4), Cl (-348.7); Based on the increasing nuclear charge, we would expect the electron affinity (EA) values to become more exothermic as we go from left to right in the period. Phosphorus is out of line. The reaction for the EA of P is

$$P(g) + e^- \rightarrow P^-(g)$$
$$[\text{Ne}]3s^2 3p^3 \qquad [\text{Ne}]3s^2 3p^4$$

The additional electron in P$^-$ will have to go into an orbital that already has one electron. There will be greater repulsions between the paired electrons in P$^-$, causing the EA of P to be less favorable than predicted based solely on attractions to the nucleus. **99. a.** I < Br < F < Cl; **b.** N < O < F **101. a.** Se$^{3+}(g) \rightarrow$ Se$^{4+}(g)$ + e$^-$; **b.** S$^-(g)$ + e$^- \rightarrow$ S$^{2-}(g)$; **c.** Fe$^{3+}(g)$ + e$^- \rightarrow$ Fe$^{2+}(g)$; **d.** Mg$(g) \rightarrow$ Mg$^+(g)$ + e$^-$ **103.** potassium peroxide, K$_2$O$_2$; K^{2+} unstable **105.** $6.582 \times 10^{14}\,s^{-1}$; 4.361×10^{-19} J **107.** Yes; the ionization energy general trend decreases down a group and the atomic radius trend increases down a group. The data in Table 7.8 confirm both of these general trends. **109. a.** $6\text{Li}(s) + \text{N}_2(g) \rightarrow 2\text{Li}_3\text{N}(s)$; **b.** $2\text{Rb}(s) + \text{S}(s) \rightarrow \text{Rb}_2\text{S}(s)$ **111.** 386 nm **113.** 200 s **115.** $\lambda = 4.104 \times 10^{-5}$ cm so violet light is emitted. **117. a.** true for H only; **b.** true for all atoms; **c.** true for all atoms **119.** When the p and d orbital functions are evaluated at various points in space, the results sometimes have positive values and sometimes have negative values. The term *phase* is often associated with the + and − signs. For example, a sine wave has alternating positive and negative phases. This is analogous to the positive and negative values (phases) in the p and d orbitals. **121.** The element with the smallest first ionization energy (I_1) is Al (the green plot), the next highest I_1 belongs to Mg (the blue plot), and Si has the largest I_1 (the red plot). Mg is the element with the huge jump between I_2 and I_3; it has two valence electrons so the third electron removed is an inner-core electron. Inner-core electrons are always much more difficult to remove as compared to valence electrons because they are closer to the nucleus, on average, as compared to the valence electrons. **123.** Valence electrons are easier to remove than inner-core electrons. The large difference in energy between I_2 and I_3 indicates that this element has two valence electrons. The element is most likely an alkaline earth metal because alkaline earth metals have two valence electrons. **125. a.** 146 kJ; **b.** 407 kJ; **c.** 1117 kJ; **d.** 1524 kJ **127. a.** line A, $n = 6$ to $n = 3$; line B, $n = 5$ to $n = 3$; **b.** 121.6 nm **129.** For $r = a_0$ and $\theta = 0°$, $\psi^2 = 2.46 \times 10^{28}$. For $r = a_0$ and $\theta = 90°$, $\psi^2 = 0$. As expected, the xy plane is a node for the $2p_z$, atomic orbital.

131. a.

b. 2, 4, 12, and 20; **c.** There are many possibilities. One example of each formula is $XY = 1 + 11$, $XY_2 = 6 + 11$, $X_2Y = 1 + 10$, $XY_3 = 7 + 11$, and $X_2Y_3 = 7 + 10$; **d.** 6; **e.** 0; **f.** 18 **133.** The ratios for Mg, Si, P, Cl, and Ar are about the same. However, the ratios for Na, Al, and S are higher. For Na, the second IE is extremely high because the electron is taken from $n = 2$ (the first electron is taken from $n = 3$). For Al, the first electron requires a bit less energy than expected by the trend due to the fact it is a $3p$ electron. For S, the first electron requires a bit less energy than expected by the trend due to electrons being paired in one of the p orbitals. **135. a.** As we remove succeeding electrons, the electron being removed is closer to the nucleus and there are fewer electrons left repelling it. The remaining electrons are more strongly attracted to the nucleus and it takes more energy to remove these electrons. **b.** For I_4, we begin removing an electron with $n = 2$. For I_3, we removed an electron with $n = 3$. In going from $n = 3$ to $n = 2$ there is a big jump in ionization energy because the $n = 2$ electrons (inner core) are much closer to the nucleus on the average than the $n = 3$ electrons (valence electrons). Since the $n = 2$ electrons are closer to the nucleus, they are held more tightly and require a much larger amount of energy to remove them. **c.** Al^{4+}; the electron affinity for Al^{4+} is ΔH for the reaction

$$Al^{4+}(g) + e^- \longrightarrow Al^{3+}(g) \qquad \Delta H = -I_4 = -11{,}600 \text{ kJ/mol}$$

d. The greater the number of electrons, the greater the size. So

$$Al^{4+} < Al^{3+} < Al^{2+} < Al^+ < Al$$

137. Solving for the molar mass of the element gives 40.2 g/mol; this is calcium. **139. a.** Fr $= [\text{Rn}]7s^1$, $Fr^+ = [\text{Rn}]$; **b.** 7.7×10^{22} Fr atoms; **c.** 2.27790×10^{-22} g

Chapter 8

13. $(NH_4)_2SO_4$ and $Ca_3(PO_4)_2$ are compounds with both ionic and covalent bonds. **15.** Electronegativity increases left to right across the periodic table and decreases from top to bottom. Hydrogen has an electronegativity value between B and C in the second row, and identical to P in the third row. Going further down the periodic table, H has an electronegativity value between As and Se (row 4) and identical to Te (row 5). It is important to know where hydrogen fits into the electronegativity trend, especially for rows 2 and 3. If you know where H fits into the trend, then you can predict bond dipole directions for nonmetals bonded to hydrogen. **17.** For ions, concentrate on the number of protons and the number of electrons present. The species whose nucleus holds the electrons most tightly will be smallest. For example, compare the size of an anion to the neutral atom. The anion has more electrons held by the same number of protons in the nucleus. These electrons will not be held as tightly, resulting in a bigger size for the anion as compared to the neutral atom. For isoelectronic ions, the same number of electrons are held by different numbers of protons in the various ions. The ion with the most protons holds the electrons tightest and has smallest size. **19.** Fossil fuels contain a lot of carbon and hydrogen atoms. Combustion of fossil fuels (reaction with O_2) produces CO_2 and H_2O. Both these compounds have very strong bonds. Because strong bonds are formed, combustion reactions are very exothermic.

21.

$$\overset{0}{\text{O}}=\overset{0}{\text{C}}=\overset{0}{\text{O}} \longleftrightarrow \overset{-1}{:\ddot{\text{O}}}-\overset{0}{\text{C}}\equiv\overset{+1}{\text{O}}: \longleftrightarrow \overset{+1}{:\text{O}}\equiv\overset{0}{\text{C}}-\overset{-1}{\ddot{\text{O}}:}$$

The formal charges are shown above the atoms in the three Lewis structures. The best Lewis structure for CO_2, from a formal charge standpoint, is the first structure with each oxygen double bonded to carbon. This structure has a formal charge of zero on all atoms (which is preferred). The other two resonance structures have nonzero formal charges on the oxygens, making them less reasonable. For CO_2, we usually ignore the last two resonance structures and think of the first structure as the true Lewis structure for CO_2. **23. a.** $C < N < O$; **b.** $Se < S < Cl$; **c.** $Sn < Ge < Si$; **d.** $Tl < Ge < S$ **25. a.** Ge—F; **b.** P—Cl; **c.** S—F; **d.** Ti—Cl **27.** Order of electronegativity from Fig. 8.3: **a.** C(2.5) $< N$ (3.0) $< O$ (3.5), same; **b.** Se (2.4) $< S$ (2.5) $< Cl$ (3.0), same; **c.** Si $=$ Ge $=$ Sn (1.8), different; **d.** Tl (1.8) $=$ Ge (1.8) $< S$ (2.5), different. Most polar bonds using actual electronegativity values: **a.** Si—F and Ge—F equal polarity (Ge—F predicted); **b.** P—Cl (same as predicted); **c.** S—F (same as predicted); **d.** Ti—Cl (same as predicted) **29.** Incorrect: b, d, e; **b.** $^{\delta-}$Cl—I$^{\delta+}$; **d.** nonpolar bond so no dipole moment; **e.** $^{\delta-}$O—P$^{\delta+}$ **31.** F—H $>$ O—H $>$ N—H $>$ C—H $>$ P—H **33.** Fr^+: $[\text{Xe}]6s^24f^{14}5d^{10}6p^6$; Be^{2+}: $1s^2$; P^{3-} and Cl^-: $[\text{Ne}]3s^23p^6$; Se^{2-}: $[\text{Ar}]4s^23d^{10}4p^6$ **35. a.** Sc^{3+}; **b.** Te^{2-}; **c.** Ce^{4+}, Ti^{4+}; **d.** Ba^{2+} **37.** Sb^{3-}, Te^{2-}, I^-, Cs^+, Ba^{2+}, and La^{3+} are some possibilities. $La^{3+} < Ba^{2+} < Cs^+ < I^- < Te^{2-} < Sb^{3-}$ **39. a.** $Cu > Cu^+ > Cu^{2+}$; **b.** $Pt^{2+} > Pd^{2+} > Ni^{2+}$; **c.** $O^{2-} > O^- > O$; **d.** $La^{3+} > Eu^{3+} > Gd^{3+} > Yb^{3+}$; **e.** $Te^{2-} > I^- > Cs^+ > Ba^{2+} > La^{3+}$ **41. a.** Al_2S_3, aluminum sulfide; **b.** K_3N_1, Potassium nitride; **c.** $MgCl_2$, Magnesium chloride; **d.** CsBr, Cesium bromide **43. a.** NaCl, Na^+ smaller than K^+; **b.** LiF, F^- smaller than Cl^-; **c.** MgO, O^{2-} greater charge than OH^-; **d.** $Fe(OH)_3$, Fe^{3+} greater charge than Fe^{2+}; **e.** Na_2O, O^{2-} greater charge than Cl^-; **f.** MgO, Mg^{2+} smaller than Ba^{2+}, and O^{2-} smaller than S^{2-}. **45.** -437 kJ/mol **47.** The lattice energy for $Mg^{2+}O^{2-}$ will be much more exothermic than for Mg^+O^-. **49.** 181 kJ/mol **51.** Ca^{2+} has greater charge than Na^+, and Se^{2-} is smaller than Te^{2-}. Charge differences affect lattice energy values more than size differences, and we expect the trend from most exothermic to least exothermic to be:

$$\begin{array}{ccccccc} CaSe & > & CaTe & > & Na_2Se & > & Na_2Te \\ (-2862) & & (-2721) & & (-2130) & & (-2095) \end{array}$$

53. a. -183 kJ; **b.** -109 kJ **55.** -42 kJ **57.** -1276 kJ **59.** -295 kJ **61.** 485 kJ/mol **63. a.** Using standard enthalpies of formation, $\Delta H° = -184$ kJ vs. -183 kJ from bond energies; **b.** Using standard enthalpies of formation, $\Delta H = -92$ kJ vs. -109 kJ from bond energies. Bond energies give a reasonably good estimate for ΔH, especially when all reactants and products are gases. **65. a.** Using SF_4 data: $D_{SF} = 342.5$ kJ/mol. Using SF_6 data: $D_{SF} = 327.0$ kJ/mol. **b.** The S—F bond energy in the table is 327 kJ/mol. The value in the table was based on the S—F bond in SF_6. **c.** $S(g)$ and $F(g)$ are not the most stable forms of the elements at 25°C. The most stable forms are $S_8(s)$ and $F_2(g)$; $\Delta H_f° = 0$ for these two species.

67. a. H—C≡N: **b.** H—P̈—H with H below **c.**

d. **e.** :O: **f.** :F̈—Se—F̈:

g. Ö=C=Ö **h.** Ö=Ö **i.** H—Br̈:

69. H—Be—H

71.

PF_5

$$\begin{array}{c} :\!\ddot{F}\!: \\ :\!\ddot{F}\!\diagdown\!\!\overset{\textstyle |}{P}\!\!-\!\ddot{F}\!: \\ :\!\ddot{F}\!\diagup\!\!\underset{\textstyle |}{} \\ :\!\ddot{F}\!: \end{array}$$

SF_4

$$\begin{array}{c} :\!\ddot{F}\!: \\ :\!\ddot{F}\!\diagdown\!\!\overset{\textstyle |}{S}\!: \\ :\!\ddot{F}\!\diagup\!\!\underset{\textstyle |}{} \\ :\!\ddot{F}\!: \end{array}$$

ClF_3

$$\begin{array}{c} :\!\ddot{F}\!: \\ \overset{\textstyle |}{:\!\ddot{Cl}}\!-\!\ddot{F}\!: \\ \underset{\textstyle |}{} \\ :\!\ddot{F}\!: \end{array}$$

Br_3^- $\left[\,:\!\ddot{Br}\!-\!\ddot{Br}\!-\!\ddot{Br}\!:\,\right]^-$

73. a. NO_2^- $\left[\ddot{O}\!=\!\ddot{N}\!-\!\ddot{O}\!:\right]^- \longleftrightarrow \left[:\!\ddot{O}\!-\!\ddot{N}\!=\!\ddot{O}\right]^-$

NO_3^- $\left[\begin{array}{c} :O: \\ \| \\ N \\ \diagup\diagdown \\ :\!\ddot{O}\!\cdot\quad\cdot\!\ddot{O}\!: \end{array}\right]^- \longleftrightarrow$

$$\left[\begin{array}{c} :\!\ddot{O}\!: \\ | \\ N \\ \diagup\diagdown \\ \cdot\ddot{O}\cdot\quad\ddot{O}\cdot \end{array}\right]^- \longleftrightarrow \left[\begin{array}{c} :\!\ddot{O}\!: \\ | \\ N \\ \diagup\diagdown \\ :\!\ddot{O}\cdot\quad\cdot\ddot{O}\cdot \end{array}\right]^-$$

N_2O_4

[Lewis resonance structures for N_2O_4 showing four resonance forms connected by double-headed arrows]

b.

OCN^- $\left[:\!\ddot{O}\!-\!C\!\equiv\!N\!:\right]^- \leftrightarrow \left[:\!\ddot{O}\!=\!C\!=\!\ddot{N}\!:\right]^- \leftrightarrow \left[:O\!\equiv\!C\!-\!\ddot{N}\!:\right]^-$;

SCN^- $\left[:\!\ddot{S}\!-\!C\!\equiv\!N\!:\right]^- \leftrightarrow \left[:\!\ddot{S}\!=\!C\!=\!\ddot{N}\!:\right]^- \leftrightarrow \left[:S\!\equiv\!C\!-\!\ddot{N}\!:\right]^-$;

N_3^- $\left[:\!\ddot{N}\!-\!N\!\equiv\!N\!:\right]^- \leftrightarrow \left[:\!\ddot{N}\!=\!N\!=\!\ddot{N}\!:\right]^- \leftrightarrow \left[:N\!\equiv\!N\!-\!\ddot{N}\!:\right]^-$

75.

[Two resonance structures of benzene (C_6H_6) connected by a double-headed arrow]

77. With resonance all carbon–carbon bonds are equivalent (we indicate this with a circle in the ring), giving three different structures:

[Three structures of dichlorobenzene isomers with circles in the rings]

Localized double bonds give four unique structures.

79. N_2 (triple bond) < N_2F_2 (double bond) < N_2F_4 (single bond)

81. a.–f. and **h.** all have similar Lewis structures:

$$\begin{array}{c} :\!\ddot{Y}\!: \\ | \\ :\!\ddot{Y}\!-\!X\!-\!\ddot{Y}\!: \\ | \\ :\!\ddot{Y}\!: \end{array}$$

g. ClO_3^- $\left[:\!\ddot{O}\!-\!\overset{\textstyle}{\underset{\textstyle :\!\ddot{O}\!:}{\ddot{Cl}}}\!-\!\ddot{O}\!:\right]^-$

Formal charges: **a.** +1; **b.** +2; **c.** +3; **d.** +1; **e.** +2; **f.** +4; **g.** +2; **h.** +1

83. $:\!\ddot{F}\!-\!\ddot{O}\!-\!\ddot{O}\!-\!\ddot{F}\!:$

Formal charge: 0   0   0   0
Oxidation number: −1   +1   +1   −1

Oxidation numbers are more useful. We are forced to assign +1 as the oxidation number for oxygen. Oxygen is very electronegative and +1 is not a stable oxidation state for this element.

85. $:\!\ddot{Cl}\!-\!\ddot{S}\!-\!\ddot{S}\!-\!\ddot{Cl}\!:$

87. [67] **a.** linear, 180°; **b.** trigonal pyramid, <109.5°; **c.** tetrahedral, 109.5°; **d.** tetrahedral, 109.5°; **e.** trigonal planar, 120°; **f.** V-shaped, <109.5°; **g.** linear, 180°; **h.** and **i.** linear, no bond angle in diatomic molecules; [73] **a.** NO_2^-: V-shaped, ~120°; NO_3^-: trigonal planar, 120°; N_2O_4: trigonal planar about both N atoms, 120°; **b.** all are linear, 180°   **89.** Br_3^-: linear; ClF_3: T-shaped; SF_4: see-saw   **91. a.** trigonal planar; 120°; **b.** V-shaped; ~120°   **93. a.** linear; 180°; **b.** T-shaped; ~90°; **c.** see-saw; ~90° and ~120°; **d.** trigonal bipyramid; 90° and 120°   **95.** SeO_2 (bond dipoles do not cancel each other out in SeO_2)   **97.** ICl_3 and TeF_4 (bond dipoles do not cancel each other out in ICl_3 and TeF_4)

99. a. OCl_2 $\left[\begin{array}{c} :\!\ddot{Cl}\!: \\ \diagup\diagdown \\ :\!\ddot{O}\quad\ddot{O}\!: \end{array}\right]$ V-shaped, polar

KrF_2 $\left[:\!\ddot{F}\!-\!\ddot{Kr}\!-\!\ddot{F}\!:\right]$ Linear, nonpolar

BeH$_2$ H—Be—H   Linear, nonpolar

SO$_2$ [Lewis structure: S with two O]   V-shaped, polar

(one other resonance structure possible)

b. SO$_3$ [Lewis structure: S with three O, one double bond]   Trigonal planar, nonpolar

(Two other resonance structures possible)

NF$_3$ [Lewis structure: N with three F and lone pair]   Trigonal pyramid, polar

IF$_3$ [Lewis structure: I with three F]   T-shaped, polar

c. CF$_4$ [Lewis structure: C with four F]   Tetrahedral, nonpolar

SeF$_4$ [Lewis structure: Se with four F and lone pair]   See-saw, polar

KrF$_4$ [Lewis structure: Kr with four F]   Square planar, nonpolar

d. IF$_5$ [Lewis structure: I with five F and lone pair]   Square pyramid, polar

AsF$_5$ [Lewis structure: As with five F]   Trigonal bipyramid, nonpolar

101. Element E is a halogen (F, Cl, Br, or I); trigonal pyramid; <109.5°
103. The polar bonds are symmetrically arranged about the central atoms, and all the individual bond dipoles cancel to give no net dipole moment for each molecule, i.e., the molecules are nonpolar. **105. a.** radius: N$^+$ < N < N$^-$; I.E. N$^-$ < N < N$^+$; **b.** radius: Cl$^+$ < Cl < Se < Se$^-$; I.E. Se$^-$ < Se < Cl < Cl$^+$; **c.** radius: Sr^{2+} < Rb$^+$ < Br$^-$; I.E. Br$^-$ < Rb$^+$ < Sr^{2+}; **107. a.** 1549 kJ; **b.** 1390. kJ **c.** 1312 kJ; **d.** 1599 kJ
109. a. NaBr: In NaBr$_2$, the sodium ion would have a +2 charge assuming each bromine has a −1 charge. Sodium doesn't form stable Na^{2+} compounds. **b.** ClO$_4^-$: ClO$_4$ has 31 valence electrons so it is impossible to satisfy the octet rule for all atoms in ClO$_4$. The extra electron from the −1 charge in ClO$_4^-$ allows for complete octets for all atoms. **c.** XeO$_4$: We can't draw a Lewis

structure that obeys the octet rule for SO$_4$ (30 electrons), unlike XeO$_4$ (32 electrons). **d.** SeF$_4$: Both compounds require the central atom to expand its octet. O is too small and doesn't have low-energy d orbitals to expand its octet (which is true for all row 2 elements). **111. a.** Both have one or more 180° bond angles; both are made up entirely of Xe and Cl; both have the individual bond dipoles arranged so they cancel each other (both are nonpolar); both have lone pairs on the central Xe atom; both have a central Xe atom that has more than 8 electrons around it. **b.** All have lone pairs on the central atom; all have a net dipole moment (all are polar). **113.** Yes, each structure has the same number of effective pairs around the central atom. (We count a multiple bond as a single group of electrons.)

115.

[Lewis structure: TeF$_5^-$, central Te with five F atoms, lone pair]

The lone pair of electrons around Te exerts a stronger repulsion than the bonding pairs. The stronger repulsion pushes the four square planner F atoms away from the lone pair, reducing the bond angles between the axial F atom and the square planar F atoms. **117.** 17 kJ/mol **119.** See Fig. 8.11 to see the data supporting MgO as an ionic compound. Note that the lattice energy is large enough to evercome all of the other processes (removing 2 electrons from Mg, and so on). The bond energy for O$_2$ (247 kJ/mol) and electron affinity (737 kJ/mol) are the same when making CO. However, the energy needed to ionize carbon to form a C^{2+} ion must be too large. Figure 7.30 shows that the first ionization energy for carbon is about 400 kJ/mol greater than the first IE for magnesium. If all other numbers were equal, the overall energy change would be ~200 kJ/mol (see Fig. 8.11). It is not unreasonable to assume that the second ionization energy for carbon is more than 200 kJ/mol greater than the second ionization energy of magnesium. **121.** As the halogen atoms get larger, it becomes more difficult to fit three halogen atoms around the small nitrogen atom, and the NX$_3$ molecule becomes less stable. **123.** reaction i: −2636 kJ; reaction ii: −3471 kJ; reaction iii: −3543 kJ; Reaction iii yields the most energy per kg (−8085 kJ/kg)

125. [Lewis resonance structures with H—C—C—O—O—N and O atoms]   ⟷   [second resonance structure]

⟷   [third structure: H—C—C=O—O=N]   (This form is not important by formal charge arguments.)

127. a. Two possible structures exist; each has a T-shaped molecular structure:

[Lewis structure: Br—I with I atoms]   [Lewis structure: Br—F with I atoms]

90° bond angle between I atoms   180° bond angle between I atoms

b. Three possible structures exist; each has a see-saw molecular structure.

[Lewis structure: Xe with O and F]   [Lewis structure: Xe with F and O]   [Lewis structure: Xe with O and F]

90° bond angle between O atoms   180° bond angle between O atoms   120° bond angle between O atoms

c. Three possible structures exist; each has a square pyramid molecular structure.

One F atom is 180° from lone pair. Both F atoms are 90° from lone pair and 90° from each other. Both F atoms are 90° from lone pair and 180° from each other.

129. $\Delta H = 0$ **131.** X is iodine; square pyramid **133.** $Cr < As < P < Cl$

Chapter 9

7. In hybrid orbital theory, some or all of the valence atomic orbitals of the central atom in a molecule are mixed together to form hybrid orbitals; these hybrid orbitals point to where the bonded atoms and lone pairs are oriented. The σ bonds are formed from the hybrid orbitals overlapping head to head with an appropriate orbital on the bonded atom. The π bonds in hybrid orbital theory are formed from unhybridized p atomic orbitals. The p orbitals overlap side to side to form the π bond where the π electrons occupy the space above and below a line joining the atoms π the internuclear axis). Assuming the z-axis is the internuclear axis, then the p_z atomic orbital will always be hybridized whether the hybridization is sp, sp^2, sp^3, dsp^2 or d^2sp^3. For sp hybridization, the p_x and p_y atomic orbitals are unhybridized; they are used to form two π bonds to the bonded atom(s). For sp^2 hybridization, either the p_x or p_y atomic orbital is hybridized (along with the s and p_z orbitals); the other p orbital is used to form a π bond to a bonded atom. For sp^3 hybridization, the s and all of the p orbitals are hybridized; no unhybridized p atomic orbitals are present, so typical π bonds do not form with sp^3 hybridization. For dsp^3 and d^2sp^3 hybridization, we just mix in one or two d orbitals into the hybridization process. Which specific d orbitals are used is not important to our discussion. **9.** We use d orbitals when we have to; i.e., we use d orbitals when the central atom on a molecule has more than eight electrons around it. The d orbitals are necessary to accommodate the electrons over eight. Row 2 elements never have more than eight electrons around them so they never hybridize d orbitals. We rationalize this by saying there are no d orbitals close in energy to the valence $2s$ and $2p$ orbitals ($2d$ orbitals are forbidden energy levels). However, for row 3 and heavier elements, there are $3d$, $4d$, $5d$, etc. orbitals which will be close in energy to the valence s and p orbitals. It is row 3 and heavier nonmetals that hybridize d orbitals when they have to. For sulfur, the valence electrons are in $3s$ and $3p$ orbitals. Therefore, $3d$ orbitals are closest in energy and are available for hybridization. Arsenic would hybridize $4d$ orbitals to go with the valence $4s$ and $4p$ orbitals while iodine would hybridize $5d$ orbitals since the valence electrons are in $n = 5$. **11.** Bonding and antibonding molecular orbitals are both solutions to the quantum mechanical treatment of the molecule. Bonding orbitals form when in phase orbitals combine to give constructive interference. This results in enhanced electron probability located between the two nuclei. The end result is that a bonding MO is lower in energy than the atomic orbitals of which it is composed. Antibonding orbitals form when out-of-phase orbitals combine. The mismatched phases produce destructive interference leading to a node in the electron probability between the two nuclei. With electron distribution pushed to the outside, the energy of an antibonding orbital is higher than the energy of the atomic orbitals of which it is composed. **13.** The localized electron model does not deal effectively with molecules containing unpaired electrons. We can draw all of the possible resonance structures for NO, but still not have a good feel for whether the bond in NO is weaker or stronger than the bond in NO^-. MO theory can handle odd electron species without any modifications. In addition, hybrid orbital theory does not predict that NO^- is paramagnetic. The MO theory correctly makes this prediction.

15. H_2O:

H_2O has a tetrahedral arrangement of the electron pairs about the O atom that requires sp^3 hybridization. Two of the sp^3 hybrid orbitals are used to form bonds to the two hydrogen atoms, and the other two sp^3 hybrid orbitals hold the two lone pairs on oxygen.

17. H_2CO:

The central carbon atom has a trigonal planar arrangement of the electron pairs that requires sp^2 hybridization. Two of the sp^2 hybrid orbitals are used to form the two bonds to hydrogen. The other sp^2 hybrid orbital forms the σ bond to oxygen. The unchanged (unhybridized) p orbital on carbon is used to form the π bond between carbon and oxygen.

19. Ethane:

The carbon atoms are sp^3 hybridized. The six C—H bonds are formed from the sp^3 hybrid orbitals on C with the $1s$ atomic orbitals from the hydrogen atoms. The carbon–carbon bond is formed from an sp^3 hybrid orbital on each C atom.

Ethanol:

The two C atoms and the O atom are all sp^3 hybridized. All bonds are formed from these sp^3 hybrid orbitals. The C—H and O—H bonds form from sp^3 hybrid orbitals and the $1s$ atomic orbitals from the hydrogen atom. The C—C and C—O bonds are formed from sp^3 hybrid orbitals on each atom. **21.** [67] **a.** sp; **b.** sp^3; **c.** sp^3; **d.** sp^3; **e.** sp^2; **f.** sp^3; **g.** sp; **h.** each O is sp^2 hybridized; **i.** Br is sp^3 hybridized [73] **a.** NO_2^-, sp^2; NO_3^-, sp^2; N_2O_4: both N atoms are sp^2 hybridized; **b.** All are sp hybridized. **23.** All exhibit dsp^3 hybridization. **25.** The molecules in Exercise 91 all exhibit sp^2 hybridization about the central atom; the molecules in Exercise 92 all exhibit sp^3 hybridization about the central atom. **27. a.** tetrahedral, 109.5°, sp^3, nonpolar

b. trigonal pyramid, <109.5°, sp^3, polar

c. V-shaped, <109.5°, sp^3, polar

d. trigonal planar, 120°, sp^2, nonpolar

e. linear, 180°, sp, nonpolar

H—Be—H

f. [structure: :F—Te with F atoms, b and a angles marked] a ≈ 120°, see-saw, dsp^3, polar
b ≈ 90°

g. [structure: As with F atoms, angles a and b marked] a = 90°, trigonal bipyramid, dsp^3, nonpolar
b = 120°

h. :F—Kr—F: linear, 180°, dsp^3, nonpolar

i. [structure: square planar KrF₄] square planar, 90°, d^2sp^3, nonpolar

j. [structure: octahedral SeF₆] octahedral, 90°, d^2sp^3, nonpolar

k. [structure: IF₅]   **l.** [structure: IF₃]

square pyramid, ≈90°; T-shaped, ≈90°;
d^2sp^3, polar dsp^3, polar

29. The π bond forces all six atoms into the same plane. **31.** Biacetyl

[structure: biacetyl with labels sp^2, sp^3]

All CCO angles are 120°. The six atoms are not in the same plane. 11σ and 2π
Acetoin

[structure: acetoin with labels sp^2, sp^3, angles a and b]

angle a = 120°, angle b = 109.5°, 13 σ and 1 π bond **33.** To complete the Lewis structure, add lone pairs to complete octets for each atom. **a.** 6; **b.** 4; **c.** The center N in —N=N=N group; **d.** 33 σ; **e.** 5 π; **f.** 180°; **g.** <109.5°; **h.** sp^3 **35. a.** H_2^+, H_2, H_2^-; **b.** He_2^{2+} and He_2^+ **37. a.** $(\sigma_{2s})^2$; B.O. = 1; diamagnetic (0 unpaired electrons); **b.** $(\sigma_{2s})^2(\sigma_{2s}^*)^2(\pi_{2p})^4$; B.O. = 2; diamagnetic (0 unpaired electrons); **c.** $(\sigma_{3s})^2(\sigma_{3s}^*)^2(\sigma_{3p})^2(\pi_{3p})^4(\pi_{3p}^*)^2$; B.O. = 2; paramagnetic (2 unpaired electrons) **39.** When O_2 loses an electron, it comes from a pi antibonding orbital, which strengthens the bond from a bond order of 2 to a bond order of 2.5. When N_2 loses an electron,

it comes a pi bonding orbital, which changes the bond order from 3 to 2.5 (the bond weakens). **41.** N_2^- and N_2^+ **43. a.** $(\sigma_{2s})^2(\sigma_{2s}^*)^2(\pi_{2p})^4(\sigma_{2p})^2$; B.O. = 3; diamagnetic; **b.** $(\sigma_{2s})^2(\sigma_{2s}^*)^2(\pi_{2p})^4(\sigma_{2p})^1$; B.O. = 2.5; paramagnetic; **c.** $(\sigma_{2s})^2(\sigma_{2s}^*)^2(\pi_{2p})^4$; B.O. = 2; diamagnetic; bond length: CO < CO^+ < CO^{2+}; bond energy: CO^{2+} < CO^+ < CO **45.** H_2; B_2; C_2^{2-}
47.

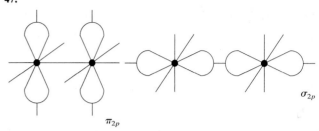

49. a. The electrons would be closer to F on the average. The F atom is more electronegative than the H atom, and the $2p$ orbital of F is lower in energy than the $1s$ orbital of H; **b.** The bonding MO would have more fluorine $2p$ character because it is closer in energy to the fluorine $2p$ orbital; **c.** The antibonding MO would place more electron density closer to H and would have a greater contribution from the higher-energy hydrogen $1s$ atomic orbital. **51.** O_3 and NO_2^- have identical Lewis structures, so we need to discuss only one of them. The Lewis structure for O_3 is

[resonance structures of O_3]

Localized electron model: The central oxygen atom is sp^2 hybridized, which is used to form the two σ bonds and hold the lone pair of electrons. An unchanged (unhybridized) p atomic orbital forms the π bond with the neighboring oxygen atoms. The π bond resonates between the two positions. Molecular orbital model: There are two localized σ bonds and a π bond that is delocalized over the entire surface of the molecule. The delocalized π bond results from overlap of a p atomic orbital on each oxygen atom in O_3.
53. a. Trigonal pyramid; sp^3

[structure: XeO_3]

b. Tetrahedral; sp^3

[structure: XeO_4]

c. Square pyramid; d^2sp^3

[structures: $XeOF_4$ two forms]   or

d. T-shaped; dsp^3

[structures: $XeOF_2$ two forms]   or

e. Trigonal bipyramid; dsp^3

[structures: three forms]   or   or

55.

a. 21 σ bonds; 4 π bonds (The electrons in the 3 π bonds in the ring are delocalized.) **b.** angles a, c, and g: $\approx 109.5°$; angles b, d, e, and f: $\approx 120°$; **c.** 6 sp^2 carbons; **d.** 4 sp^3 atoms; **e.** Yes, the π electrons in the ring are delocalized. The atoms in the ring are all sp^2 hybridized. This leaves a p orbital perpendicular to the plane of the ring from each atom. Overlap of all six of these p orbitals results in a π molecular orbital system where the electrons are delocalized above and below the plane of the ring (similar to benzene in Fig. 9.48 of the text). **57.** 267 kJ/mol; this amount of energy must be supplied to break the π bond.

59. a.

Trigonal planar, nonpolar, 120°, sp^2

b. N_2F_2

V-shaped about both N atoms, $\approx 120°$, sp^2

These are distinctly different molecules.

c.

Trigonal planar about all C atoms, nonpolar, 120°, sp^2

d. ICl_3

T-shaped, polar, $\approx 90°$, dsp^3

61. a. The NNO structure is correct. From the Lewis structures we would predict both NNO and NON to be linear, but NON would be nonpolar. NNO is polar.

b.

$$:N=N=O: \longleftrightarrow :N\equiv N-O: \longleftrightarrow :N-N\equiv O:$$

$$\begin{array}{ccc} -1 \ +1 \ \ 0 & \quad 0 \ +1 \ -1 & \quad -2 \ +1 \ +1 \ \text{Formal} \\ & & \text{charges} \end{array}$$

The central N is sp hybridized. We can probably ignore the third resonance structure on the basis of formal charge. **c.** sp hybrid orbitals on the center N overlap with atomic orbitals (or hybrid orbitals) on the other two atoms to form two σ bonds. The remaining p orbitals on the center N overlap with p orbitals on the other N to form two π bonds. **63.** N_2: $(\sigma_{2s})^2(\sigma_{2s}*)^2(\pi_{2p})^4(\sigma_{2p})^2$ in ground state, B.O. = 3, diamagnetic; 1st excited state: $(\sigma_{2s})^2(\sigma_{2s}*)^2(\pi_{2p})^4(\sigma_{2p})^1(\pi_{2p}*)^1$, B.O. = 2, paramagnetic (two unpaired electrons) **65.** F_2 $(\sigma_{2s})^2(\sigma_{2s}*)^2(\sigma_{2p})^2(\pi_{2p})^4(\pi_{2p}*)^4$; F_2 should have a lower ionization energy than F. The electron removed from F_2 is in a $\pi_{2p}*$ antibonding molecular orbital, which is higher in energy than the $2p$ atomic orbitals from which the electron in atomic fluorine is removed. Since the electron removed from F_2 is higher in energy than the electron removed from F, then it should be easier to remove an electron from F_2 than from F. **67.** π molecular orbital **69.** 6 sp^2; 6 sp^3; 0 sp; 25 σ; 4π **71. a.** No, some atoms are attached differently; **b.** Structure 1: All N = sp^3, all C = sp^2; structure 2: All C and N = sp^2; **c.** The first structure with the carbon–oxygen double bonds is slightly more stable.

73. a. NCN^{2-}:

H_2NCN:

Favored by formal charge

Dicyandiamide:

Favored by formal charge

Melamine:

b. NCN^{2-}: C is sp hybridized. Each resonance structure predicts a different hybridization for the N atoms. For the remaining compounds, we will predict hybrids for the favored resonance structures only.

Melamine: N in NH_2 groups are all sp^3 hybridized. Atoms in ring are all sp^2 hybridized; **c.** NCN^{2-}: 2 σ and 2 π bonds; H_2NCN: 4 σ and 2 π bonds; dicyandiamide: 9 σ and 3 π bonds; melamine: 15 σ and 3 π bonds; **d.** The π system forces the ring to be planar just as the benzene ring is planar.

e. The structure

is the most important because it has three different CN bonds. This structure is also favored on the basis of formal charge. **75. a.** 25-nm light has sufficient energy to ionize N and N_2 and to break the triple bond in N_2. Thus, N_2, N_2^+, N, and N^+ will all be present, assuming excess N_2. **b.** 85.33 nm $< \lambda \le 127$ nm; **c.** The ionization energy of a substance is the energy it takes to completely remove an electron. N_2: $(\sigma_{2s})^2(\sigma_{2s}^*)^2(\pi_{2p})^4(\sigma_{2p})^2$; the electron removed from N_2 is in the σ_{2p} molecular orbital, which is lower in energy than the $2p$ atomic orbital from which the electron in atomic nitrogen is removed. Since the electron removed from N_2 is lower in energy than the electron removed in N, then the ionization energy of N_2 is greater than the ionization energy of N. **77.** Both reactions apparently involve only the breaking of the N—Cl bond. However, in the reaction ONCl → NO + Cl some energy is released in forming the stronger NO bond, lowering the value of ΔH. Therefore, the apparent N—Cl bond energy is artificially low for this reaction. The first reaction involves only the breaking of the N—Cl bond. **79. a.** The CO bond is polar, with the negative end around the more electronegative oxygen atom. We would expect metal cations to be attracted to and to bond to the oxygen end of CO on the basis of electronegativity. **b.** The formal charge on C is −1, and the formal charge on O is +1. From formal charge, we would expect metal cations to bond to the carbon (with the negative formal charge.) **c.** In molecular orbital theory, only orbitals with proper symmetry overlap to form bonding orbitals. The metals that form bonds to CO are usually transition metals, all of which have outer electrons in the d orbitals. The only molecular orbitals of CO that have proper symmetry to overlap with d orbitals are the π_{2p}^* orbitals, whose shape is similar to that of the d orbitals (see Fig. 9.34). Since the antibonding molecular orbitals have more carbon character, one would expect the bond to form through carbon. **81.** The species with the smallest ionization energy has the highest energy electron. O_2, N_2^{2-}, N_2^-, and O_2^+ all have at least one electron in the high-energy π_{2p}^* orbitals. Because N_2^{2-} has the highest ratio of electrons to protons, the π_{2p}^* electrons are least attracted to the nuclei and easiest to remove, translating into the smallest ionization energy. **83. a.** Li_2 bond order = 1; B_2 bond order = 1; **b.** 4 electrons must be removed; **c.** 4.5×10^5 kJ **85.** T-shaped and dsp^3 hybridized

Chapter 10

13. Atoms have an approximately spherical shape. It is impossible to pack spheres together without some empty space between the spheres. **15.** Evaporation takes place when some molecules at the surface of a liquid have enough energy to break the intermolecular forces holding them in the liquid phase. When a liquid evaporates, the molecules that escape have high kinetic energies. The average kinetic energy of the remaining molecules is lower; thus the temperature of the liquid is lower. **17.** An alloy is a substance that contains a mixture of elements and has metallic properties. In a substitutional alloy, some of the host metal atoms are replaced by other metal atoms of similar size (e.g., in brass, pewter, plumber's solder). An interstitial alloy is formed when some of the interstices (holes) in the closest packed metal structure are occupied by smaller atoms (e.g., in carbon steels). **19. a.** As intermolecular forces increase, the rate of evaporation decreases. **b.** increase T: increase rate; **c.** increase surface area: increase rate **21.** Sublimation will occur, allowing water to escape as $H_2O(g)$. **23.** The strength of intermolecular forces determines relative boiling points. The types of intermolecular forces for covalent compounds are London dispersion forces, dipole forces, and hydrogen bonding. Because the three compounds are assumed to have similar molar mass and shape, the strength of the London dispersion forces will be about equal between the three compounds. One of the compounds will be nonpolar so it only has London dispersion forces. The other two compounds will be polar so they have additional dipole forces and will boil at a higher temperature than the

nonpolar compound. One of the polar compounds will have an H covalently bonded to either N, O, or F. This gives rise to the strongest type of covalent intermolecular force, hydrogen bonding. This compound exhibiting hydrogen bonding will have the highest boiling point while the polar compound with no hydrogen bonding will boil at an intermediate temperature. **25. a.** Both CO_2 and H_2O are molecular solids. Both have an ordered array of the individual molecules, with the molecular units occupying the lattice points. A difference within each solid lattice is the strength of the intermolecular forces. CO_2 is nonpolar and only exhibits London dispersion forces. H_2O exhibits the relatively strong hydrogen bonding interactions. The difference in strength is evidenced by the solid phase change that occurs at 1 atm. CO_2 sublimes at a relatively low temperature of −78°C. In sublimation, all of the intermolecular forces are broken. However, H_2O doesn't have a solid phase change until 0°C, and in this phase change from ice to water, only a fraction of the intermolecular forces are broken. The higher temperature and the fact that only a portion of the intermolecular forces are broken are attributed to the strength of the intermolecular forces in H_2O as compared to CO_2. Related to the intermolecular forces is the relative densities of the solid and liquid phases for these two compounds. $CO_2(s)$ is denser than $CO_2(l)$ while $H_2O(s)$ is less dense than $H_2O(l)$. For $CO_2(s)$ and for most solids, the molecules pack together as close as possible, which is why solids are usually more dense than the liquid phase. For H_2O, each molecule has two lone pairs and two bonded hydrogen atoms. Because of the equal number of lone pairs and O—H bonds, each H_2O molecule can form two hydrogen bonding interactions to other H_2O molecules. To keep this symmetric arrangement (which maximizes the hydrogen bonding interactions), the $H_2O(s)$ molecules occupy positions that create empty space in the lattice. This translates into smaller density for $H_2O(s)$ (less mass per unit volume). **b.** Both NaCl and CsCl are ionic compounds with the anions at the lattice points of the unit cell and the cations occupying the empty spaces created by the anions (called holes). In NaCl, the Cl^- anions occupy the lattice points of a face-centered unit cell with the Na^+ cations occupying the octahedral holes. Octahedral holes are the empty spaces created by six Cl^- ions. CsCl has the Cl^- ions at the lattice points of a simple cubic unit cell with the Cs^+ cations occupying the middle of the cube. **27.** In the $\ln P_{vap}$ versus $1/T$ plot, the slope of the straight line is equal to $-\Delta H_{vap}/R$. Because ΔH_{vap} is always positive, the slope of the line will always be negative. **29. a.** LD (London dispersion); **b.** dipole, LD; **c.** hydrogen bonding, LD; **d.** ionic; **e.** LD; **f.** dipole, LD; **g.** ionic **31. a.** OCS; **b.** SeO_2; **c.** $H_2NCH_2CH_2NH_2$; **d.** H_2CO; **e.** CH_3OH **33. a.** Neopentane is more compact than n-pentane. There is less surface area contact among neopentane molecules. This leads to weaker London dispersion forces and a lower boiling point. **b.** HF is capable of hydrogen bonding; HCl is not. **c.** LiCl is ionic, and HCl is a molecular solid with only dipole forces and London dispersion forces. Ionic forces are much stronger than the forces for molecular solids. **d.** n-Hexane is a larger molecule, so it has stronger London dispersion forces. **35. a.** HBr has dipole forces in addition to LD forces; **b.** NaCl, stronger ionic forces; **c.** I_2, larger molecule so stronger LD forces; **d.** N_2, smallest nonpolar compound present, has weakest LD forces; **e.** CH_4, smallest nonpolar compound present, has weakest LD forces; **f.** HF, can form relatively strong hydrogen bonding interactions, unlike the other compounds; **g.** $CH_3CH_2CH_2OH$, unlike others, has relatively strong hydrogen bonding. **37.** H_2O is attracted to glass while Hg is not. **39.** The structure of H_2O_2 produces greater hydrogen bonding than water. Long chains of hydrogen bonded H_2O_2 molecules then get tangled together. **41.** 313 pm **43.** 0.704 Å **45.** 1.54 g/cm³ **47.** 174 pm; 11.6 g/cm³ **49.** edge, 328 pm; radius, 142 pm **51.** face-centered cubic unit cell **53.** For a cubic closest packed structure, 74.06% of the volume of each unit cell is occupied by atoms; in a simple cubic unit cell structure, 52.36% is occupied. The cubic (and hexagonal) closest packed structures provide the most efficient means for packing atoms. **55.** Doping silicon with phosphorus produces an n-type semiconductor. The phosphorus adds electrons at energies near the conduction band of silicon. Electrons do not need as much energy to move from filled to unfilled energy levels so conduction increases. Doping silicon with gallium produces a p-type semiconductor. Because gallium has fewer valence electrons than silicon, holes (unfilled energy levels) at energies in the previously filled molecular orbitals are created, which induces greater electron movement (greater conductivity). **57.** p-type **59.** 5.0×10^2 nm **61.** NaCl: $4Na^+$, $4Cl^-$; CsCl: $1Cs^+$, $1Cl^-$; ZnS: $4Zn^{2+}$, $4S^{2-}$; TiO_2: $2Ti^{4+}$, $4O^{2-}$ **63.** CoF_2 **65.** $ZnAl_2S_4$ **67.** MF_2 **69.** $r_{O^{2-}} = 1.49 \times 10^{-8}$ cm; $r_{Mg^{2+}} = 6.15 \times 10^{-9}$ cm **71. a.** CO_2: molecular; **b.** SiO_2: covalent network; **c.** Si: atomic, covalent network; **d.** CH_4: molecular; **e.** Ru: atomic, metallic; **f.** I_2: molecular; **g.** KBr: ionic; **h.** H_2O: molecular; **i.** NaOH: ionic; **j.** U: atomic, metallic; **k.** $CaCO_3$: ionic; **l.** PH_3: molecular **73. a.** The unit cell consists of Ni at the cube corners and Ti at the body center or Ti at the cube corners and Ni at the body center. **b.** NiTi; **c.** Both have a coordination number of 8. **75.** $CaTiO_3$; six oxygens around each Ti **77. a.** $YBa_2Cu_3O_9$; **b.** The structure of this superconductor material is based on the second perovskite structure. The $YBa_2Cu_3O_9$ structure is three of these cubic perovskite unit cells stacked on top of each other. The oxygens are in the same places, Cu takes the place of Ti, two Ca are replaced by two Ba, and one Ca is replaced by Y. **c.** $YBa_2Cu_3O_7$ **79.** Li, 158 kJ/mol; Mg, 139 kJ/mol. Bonding is stronger in Li. **81.** 89°C **83.** 77°C **85.**

Slope 5 > slope 3 > slope 1

Time 4 = 4 × time 2

87. 1680 kJ **89.** 1490 g **91.** A: solid; B: liquid; C: vapor; D: solid + vapor; E: solid + liquid + vapor (triple point); F: liquid + vapor; G: liquid + vapor (critical point); H: vapor; the first dashed line (at the lower temperature) is the normal melting point, and the second dashed line is the normal boiling point. The solid phase is denser. **93. a.** two; **b.** higher pressure triple point: graphite, diamond, and liquid; lower pressure triple point: graphite, liquid and vapor; **c.** It is converted to diamond (the more dense solid form); **d.** Diamond is more dense, which is why graphite can be converted to diamond by applying pressure. **95.** Because the density of the liquid phase is greater than the density of the solid phase, the slope of the solid–liquid boundary line is negative (as in H_2O). With a negative slope, the melting points increase with a decrease in pressure so the normal melting point of X should be greater than 225°C. **97.** Chalk is composed of the ionic compound calcium carbonate ($CaCO_3$). The electrostatic forces in ionic compounds are much stronger than the intermolecular forces in covalent compounds. Therefore, $CaCO_3$ should have a much higher boiling point than the covalent compounds found in motor oil and in H_2O. Motor oil is composed of nonpolar C—C and C—H bonds. The intermolecular forces in motor oil are therefore London dispersion forces. We generally consider these forces to be weak. However, with compounds that have large molar masses, these London dispersion forces add up significantly and can overtake the relatively strong hydrogen-bonding interactions in water. **99.** A: CH_4; B: SiH_4 C: NH_3 **101.** If TiO_2 conducts electricity as a liquid, then it would be ionic. **103.** B_2H_6, molecular; SiO_2, network; CsI, ionic; W, metallic **105.** 4.65 kg/h **107.** $\Delta E = 27.86$ kJ/mol;

$\Delta H = 30.79$ kJ/mol **109.** 46.7 kJ/mol; 90% **111.** The solids with high melting points (NaCl, $MgCl_2$, NaF, MgF_2, AlF_3) are all ionic solids. $SiCl_4$, SiF_4, Cl_2, F_2, PF_5, and SF_6 are nonpolar covalent molecules with LD forces. PCl_3 and SCl_2 are polar molecules with LD and dipole forces. In these 8 molecular substances the intermolecular forces are weak and the melting points low. $AlCl_3$ is intermediate. The melting point indicates there are stronger forces present than in the nonmetal halides, but not as strong as for an ionic solid. $AlCl_3$ illustrates a gradual transition from ionic to covalent bonding; from an ionic solid to discrete molecules. **113.** $TiO_{1.182}$ or $Ti_{0.8462}O$; 63.7% Ti^{2+}, 36.3% Ti^{3+} **115.** 6.58 g/cm^3

117.

As P is lowered, we go from a to b on the phase diagram. The water boils. The evaporation of the water is endothermic and the water is cooled (b → c), forming some ice. If the pump is left on, the ice will sublime until none is left. This is the basis of freeze drying.

119. The volume of the hole is $\frac{4}{3}\pi\left[\left(\frac{2\sqrt{3}-2}{2}\right)r\right]^3$ **121.** CdS; n-type

123. 2.53 torr; 6.38×10^{22} atoms

Chapter 11

9. 9.74 *M* **11.** 4.5 *M* **13.** As the temperature increases, the gas molecules will have a greater average kinetic energy. A greater fraction of the gas molecules in solution will have kinetic energy greater than the attractive forces between the gas molecules and the solvent molecules. More gas molecules will escape to the vapor phase, and the solubility of the gas will decrease. **15.** The levels of the liquids in each beaker will become constant when the concentration of solute is the same in both beakers. Because the solute is less volatile, the beaker on the right will have a larger volume when the concentrations become equal. Water will initially condense in this beaker in a larger amount than solute is evaporating, while the net change occurring initially in the other beaker is for water to evaporate in a larger amount than solute is condensing. Eventually the rate that solute and H_2O leave and return to each beaker will become equal when the concentrations become equal. **17.** No. For an ideal solution, $\Delta H_{soln} = 0$ **19.** Normality is the number of equivalents per liter of solution. For an acid or a base, an equivalent is the mass of acid or base that can furnish 1 mol of protons (if an acid) or accept 1 mol of protons (if a base). A proton is an H^+ ion. Molarity is defined as the moles of solute per liter of solution. When the number of equivalents equals the number of moles of solute, then normality = molarity. This is true for acids which only have one acidic proton in them and for bases that accept only one proton per formula unit. Examples of acids where equivalents = moles solute are HCl, HNO_3, HF, and $HC_2H_3O_2$. Examples of bases where equivalents = moles solute are NaOH, KOH, and NH_3. When equivalents ≠ moles solute, then normality ≠ molarity. This is true for acids that donate more than one proton (H_2SO_4, H_3PO_4, H_2CO_3, etc.) and for bases that react with more than one proton per formula unit [$Ca(OH)_2$, $Ba(OH)_2$, $Sr(OH)_2$, etc.]. **21.** Only statement b is true. A substance freezes when the vapor pressure of the liquid and solid phases are the same. When a solute is added to water, the vapor pressure of the solution at 0°C is less than the vapor pressure of the solid; the net result is for any ice present to convert to liquid in order to try to equalize the vapor pressures (which never can occur at 0°C). A lower temperature is needed to equalize the vapor pressure of water and ice, hence the freezing point is depressed. For statement a, the vapor pressure of a solution is directly related to the mole fraction of solvent (not solute) by Raoult's law. For statement c, colligative properties depend on the number of solute particles present and not on the identity of the solute. For statement d, the boiling point of water is increased because the sugar solute decreases the vapor pressure of the water; a higher temperature is required for the vapor pressure of the solution to equal the external pressure so boiling can occur. **23.** Isotonic solutions are those which have identical osmotic pressures. Crenation and hemolysis refer to a phenomena that occurs when red blood cells are bathed in solutions having a mismatch in osmotic pressure between the inside and the outside of the cell. When red blood cells are in a solution having a higher osmotic pressure than that of the cells, the cells shrivel as there is a net transfer of water out of the cells. This is called crenation. Hemolysis occurs when the red blood cells are bathed in a solution having lower osmotic pressure than that inside the cell. Here, the cells rupture as there is a net transfer of water to inside the red blood cells. **25.** 1.06 g/mL; 0.0180 mole fraction H_3PO_4, 0.9820 mole fraction H_2O; 0.981 mol/L; 1.02 mol/kg **27.** HCl: 12 M, 17 m, 0.23; HNO_3: 16 M, 37 m, 0.39; H_2SO_4: 18 M, 200 m, 0.76; $HC_2H_3O_2$: 17 M, 2000 m, 0.96; NH_3: 15 M, 23 m, 0.29 **29.** 35%; 0.39; 7.3 m; 3.1 M **31.** 23.9%; 1.6 m, 0.028, 4.11 N **33.** $NaI(s) \rightarrow Na^+(aq) + I^-(aq)$ $\Delta H_{soln} = -8$ kJ/mol **35.** The attraction of water molecules for Al^{3+} and OH^- cannot overcome the larger lattice energy of $Al(OH)_3$. **37. a.** CCl_4; **b.** H_2O; **c.** H_2O; **d.** CCl_4; **e.** H_2O; **f.** H_2O; **g.** CCl_4; **39.** Ability to form hydrogen bonding interactions, ability to break up into ions, and polarity are some factors affecting solute solubility. **a.** CH_3CH_2OH; **b.** $CHCl_3$; **c.** CH_3CH_2OH **41.** As the length of the hydrocarbon chain increases, the solubility decreases because the nonpolar hydrocarbon chain interacts poorly with the polar water molecules. **43.** 1.04×10^{-3} mol/L · atm; 1.14×10^{-3} mol/L **45.** 50.0 torr **47.** 3.0×10^2 g/mol **49. a.** 290 torr; **b.** 0.69 **51.** $X_{methanol} = X_{propanol} = 0.500$ **53.** solution c **55.** $P_{ideal} = 188.6$ torr; $X_{acetone} = 0.512$, $X_{methanol} = 0.488$; the actual vapor pressure of the solution is smaller than the ideal vapor pressure, so this solution exhibits a negative deviation from Raoult's law. This occurs when solute–solvent attractions are stronger than for the pure substances. **57.** 101.5°C **59.** 14.8 g $C_3H_8O_3$ **61.** $T_f = -29.9$°C, $T_b = 108.2$°C **63.** 776 g/mol **65. a.** $\Delta T = 2.0 \times 10^{-5}$°C, $\pi = 0.20$ torr; **b.** Osmotic pressure is better for determining the molar mass of large molecules. A temperature change of 10^{-5}°C is very difficult to measure. A change in height of a column of mercury by 0.2 mm is not as hard to measure precisely. **67.** 0.327 M **69. a.** 0.010 m Na_3PO_4 and 0.020 m KCl; **b.** 0.020 m HF; **c.** 0.020 m $CaBr_2$ **71. a.** $T_f = -0.28$°C; $T_b = 100.077$°C; **b.** $T_f = -0.37$°C; $T_b = 100.10$°C **73.** 2.63 (0.0225 m), 2.60 (0.0910 m), 2.57 (0.278 m); $i_{average} = 2.60$ **75. a.** yes; **b.** no **77. a.** 26.6 kJ/mol; **b.** −657 kJ/mol **79. a.** Water boils when the vapor pressure equals the pressure above the water. In an open pan, $P_{atm} \approx 1.0$ atm. In a pressure cooker, $P_{inside} > 1.0$ atm and water boils at a higher temperature. The higher the cooking temperature, the faster the cooking time. **b.** Salt dissolves in water, forming a solution with a melting point lower than that of pure water ($\Delta T_f = K_f m$). This happens in water on the surface of ice. If it is not too cold, the ice melts. This process won't occur if the ambient temperature is lower than the depressed freezing point of the salt solution. **c.** When water freezes from a solution, if freezes as pure water, leaving behind a more concentrated salt solution. **d.** On the CO_2 phase diagram, the triple point is above 1 atm and $CO_2(g)$ is the stable phase at 1 atm and room temperature. $CO_2(l)$ can't exist at normal atmospheric pressures, which explains why dry ice sublimes rather than boils. In a fire extinguisher, $P > 1$ atm and $CO_2(l)$ can exist. When CO_2 is released from the fire extinguisher, $CO_2(g)$ forms as predicted from the phase diagram. **e.** Adding a solute to a solvent increases the boiling point and decreases the freezing point of the solvent. Thus, the solvent is a liquid over a wider range of temperatures when a solute is dissolved. **81.** 0.600 **83.** $C_2H_4O_3$; 151 g/mol (exp.); 152.10 g/mol (calc.); $C_4H_8O_6$ **85.** 1.97% NaCl **87. a.** 100.77°C; **b.** 23.1 mm Hg; **c.** Assume an ideal solution; assume no ions form (i = 1).

89. 30.% A: $X_A = \dfrac{0.30y}{0.70x - 0.30y}$, $X_B = 1 - X_A$;

50.% A: $X_A = \dfrac{y}{x - y}$, $X_B = 1 - \dfrac{y}{x - y}$;

80.% A: $X_A = \dfrac{0.80y}{0.20x - 0.80y}$, $X_B = 1 - X_A$;

30.% A: $X_A^{\,V} = \dfrac{0.30x}{0.30x + 0.70y}$, $X_B^{\,V} = 1 - \dfrac{0.30x}{0.30x + 0.70y}$;

50.% A: $X_A^{\,V} = \dfrac{x}{x + y}$, $X_B^{\,V} = 1 - X_A^{\,V}$;

80.% A: $X_A^{\,V} = \dfrac{0.80x}{0.80x + 0.20y}$, $X_B^{\,V} = 1 - X_A^{\,V}$

91. 72.7% sucrose and 27.3% NaCl by mass; 0.2 **93.** 0.050 **95.** 44% naphthalene, 56% anthracene **97.** −0.20°C, 100.056°C **99. a.** 46 L; **b.** No; A reverse osmosis system that applies 8.0 atm can purify only water with solute concentrations less than 0.32 mol/L. Salt water has a solute concentration of 2(0.60 M) = 1.2 M ions. The solute concentration of salt water is much too high for this reverse osmosis unit to work. **101.** i = 3.00; $CdCl_2$

Chapter 12

9. In a unimolecular reaction, a single reactant molecule decomposes to products. In a bimolecular reaction, two molecules collide to give products. The probability of the simultaneous collision of three molecules with enough energy and orientation is very small, making termolecular steps very unlikely. **11.** All of these choices would affect the rate of the reaction, but only b and c affect the rate by affecting the value of the rate constant k. The value of the rate constant is dependent on temperature. It also depends on the activation energy. A catalyst will change the value of k because the activation energy changes. Increasing the concentration (partial pressure) of either H_2 or NO does not affect the value of k, but it does increase the rate of the reaction because both concentrations appear in the rate law. **13.** The average rate decreases with time because the reverse reaction occurs more frequently as the concentration of products increase. Initially, with no products present, the rate of the forward reaction is at its fastest; but as time goes on, the rate gets slower and slower since products are converting back into reactants. The instantaneous rate will also decrease with time. The only rate that is constant is the initial rate. This is the instantaneous rate taken at $t \approx 0$. At this time, the amount of products is insignificant and the rate of the reaction only depends on the rate of the forward reaction. **15.** When the rate doubles as the concentration quadruples, the order is 1/2. For a reactant that has an order of −1, the rate will decrease by a factor of 1/2 when the concentrations are doubled. **17.** Two reasons are: **a.** the collision must involve enough energy to produce the reaction; i.e., the collision energy must equal or exceed the activation energy. **b.** the relative orientation of the reactants must allow formation of any new bonds necessary to produce products. **19.** P_4: 6.0×10^{-4} mol/L · s; H_2: 3.6×10^{-3} mol/L · s **21. a.** average rate of decomposition of $H_2O_2 = 2.31 \times 10^{-5}$ mol/L · s, rate of production of $O_2 = 1.16 \times 10^{-5}$ mol/L · s; **b.** average rate of decomposition of $H_2O_2 = 1.16 \times 10^{-5}$ mol/L · s, rate of production of $O_2 = 5.80 \times 10^{-6}$ mol/L · s **23. a.** mol/L · s; **b.** mol/L · s; **c.** s^{-1}; **d.** L/mol · s; **e.** L^2/mol^2 · s **25. a.** rate $= k[NO]^2[Cl_2]$; **b.** 1.8×10^2 L^2/mol^2 · min **27. a.** rate $= k[NOCl]^2$; **b.** 6.6×10^{-29} cm^3/molecules · s; **c.** 4.0×10^{-8} L/mol · s **29. a.** first order in Hb and first order in CO; **b.** rate $= k[Hb][CO]$; **c.** 0.280 L/μmol · s; **d.** 2.26 μmol/L · s **31.** rate $= k[H_2O_2]$; $\ln[H_2O_2] = -kt + \ln[H_2O_2]_0$; $k = 8.3 \times 10^{-4}$ s^{-1}; 0.037 M **33.** rate $= k[NO_2]^2$; $\dfrac{1}{[NO_2]} = kt + \dfrac{1}{[NO_2]_0}$; $k = 2.08 \times 10^{-4}$ L/mol · s; 0.131 M **35. a.** rate $= k$; $[C_2H_5OH] = -kt + [C_2H_5OH]_0$; because slope $= -k$, then $k = 4.00 \times 10^{-5}$ mol/L · s; **b.** 156 s; **c.** 313 s **37.** rate $= k[C_4H_6]^2$; $\dfrac{1}{[C_4H_6]} = kt +$

$\dfrac{1}{[C_4H_6]_0}$; $k = 1.4 \times 10^{-2}$ L/mol · s **39.** second order; 0.1 M **41. a.** [A] = $-kt + [A]_0$; **b.** 1.0×10^{-2} s; **c.** 2.5×10^{-4} M **43. a.** 160. s = $t_{1/2}$ for both the first and second half-life; **b.** 532 s **45.** 12.5 s **47. a.** 1.1×10^{-2} M; **b.** 0.025 M **49. a.** rate = $k[CH_3NC]$; **b.** rate = $k[O_3][NO]$; **c.** rate = $k[O_3]$; **d.** rate = $k[O_3][O]$ **51.** Rate = $k[C_4H_9Br]$; $C_4H_9Br + 2H_2O \rightarrow C_4H_9OH +$ $Br^- + H_3O^+$; the intermediates are $C_4H_9^+$ and $C_4H_9OH_2^+$.

53.

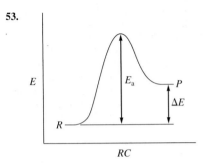

55. 341 kJ/mol **57.** The graph of ln$k$ versus $1/T$ is linear with slope = $-E_a/R = -1.2 \times 10^4$ K; $E_a = 1.0 \times 10^2$ kJ/mol **59.** 9.5×10^{-5} L/mol · s **61.** 51°C **63.** $H_3O^+(aq) + OH^-(aq) \rightarrow 2H_2O(l)$ should have the faster rate. H_3O^+ and OH^- will be electrostatically attracted to each other; Ce^{4+} and Hg_2^{2+} will repel each other (so E_a is much larger). **65. a.** NO; **b.** NO_2; **c.** 2.3 **67.** CH_2D—CH_2D should be the product. If the mechanism is possible, then the reaction must be $C_2H_4 + D_2 \rightarrow CH_2DCH_2D$. If we got this product, then we could conclude that this is a possible mechanism. If we got some other product, e.g., CH_3CHD_2, then we would conclude that the mechanism is wrong. Even though this mechanism correctly predicts the products of the reaction, we cannot say conclusively that this is the correct mechanism; we might be able to conceive of other mechanisms that would give the same product as our proposed one. **69.** 215°C **71.** 5.68×10^{18} molecules/cm^3 · s **73.** 1.0×10^2 kJ/mol **75.** At high [S], the enzyme is completely saturated with substrate. Once the enzyme is completely saturated, the rate of decomposition of ES can no longer increase, and the overall rate remains constant. **77. a.** 115 L^3/mol^3 · s; **b.** 87.0 s; **c.** [A] = 1.27×10^{-5} M, [B] = 1.00 M **79.** rate = $\dfrac{k[I^-][OCl^-]}{[OH^-]}$; $k = 6.0 \times 10^1$ s^{-1} **81. a.** first order with respect to both reactants; **b.** rate = $k[NO][O_3]$; **c.** $k' = 1.8$ s^{-1}; $k'' = 3.6$ s^{-1}; **d.** $k = 1.8 \times 10^{-14}$ cm^3/molecules · s **83. a.** 25 kJ/mol; **b.** 12 s; **c.**

T	Interval	$54 - 2$(Intervals)
21.0°C	16.3 s	21°C
27.8°C	13.0 s	28°C
30.0°C	12 s	30.°C

This rule of thumb gives excellent agreement to two significant figures. **85. a.** [B] $\gg$ [A] so that [B] can be considered constant over the experiments. (This gives us a pseudo-order rate law equation.) **b.** Rate = $k[A]^2[B]$, $k = 0.050$ L^2/mol^2 · s **87.** Rate = $k[A][B]^2$, $k = 1.4 \times 10^{-2}$ L^2/mol^2 · s **89.** 2.20×10^{-5} s^{-1}; 5.99×10^{21} molecules **91.** 1.3×10^{-5} s^{-1}; 112 torr

Chapter 13

9. No, equilibrium is a dynamic process. Both the forward and reverse reactions are occurring at equilibrium, just at equal rates. Thus the forward and reverse reactions will distribute ^{14}C atoms between CO and CO_2. **11.** 4 molecules H_2O, 2 molecules CO, 4 molecules H_2, and 4 molecules CO_2 are present at equilibrium. **13.** K and K_p are equilibrium constants as determined by the law of mass action. For K, the units used for concentrations are mol/L, for K_p, partial pressures in units of atm are used (generally). Q is called the reaction quotient. Q has the exact same form as K or K_p, but instead of equilibrium concentrations, initial concentrations are used to calculate the Q value. Q is of use when it is compared to the K value. When $Q = K$ (or when $Q_p = K_p$), the reaction is at equilibrium. When $Q \neq K$, the reaction is not at equilibrium and one can determine what has to be the net charge for the system to get to equilibrium. **15.** We always try to make good assumptions that simplify the math. In some problems, we can set up the problem so that the net change, x, that must occur to reach equilibrium is a small number. This comes in handy when you have expressions like $0.12 - x$ or $0.727 + 2x$. Since x is small, we assume that it makes little difference when subtracted from or added to some relatively big number. When this is true, $0.12 - x \approx 0.12$ and $0.727 + 2x \approx 0.727$. If the assumption holds by the 5% rule, then the assumption is assumed valid. The 5% rule refers to x (or $2x$ or $3x$, etc.) that was assumed small compared to some number. If x (or $2x$ or $3x$, etc.) is less than 5% of the number the assumption was made against, then the assumption will be assumed valid. If the 5% rule fails to work, one can generally use a math procedure called the method of successive approximations to solve the quadratic or cubic equation.

17. a. $K = \dfrac{[NO]^2}{[N_2][O_2]}$; **b.** $K = \dfrac{[NO_2]^2}{[N_2O_4]}$; **c.** $K = \dfrac{[SiCl_4][H_2]^2}{[SiH_4][Cl_2]^2}$; **d.** $K = \dfrac{[PCl_3]^2[Br_2]^3}{[PBr_3]^2[Cl_2]^3}$ **19. a.** 0.11; **b.** 77; **c.** 8.8; **d.** 4.6×10^{-4} **21.** 4.0×10^6 **23.** 1.7×10^{-5} **25.** 6.3×10^{-13} **27.** 1.1×10^3 **29. a.** $K = \dfrac{[H_2O]}{[NH_3]^2[CO_2]}$, $K_p = \dfrac{P_{H_2O}}{P_{NH_3}^2 \times P_{CO_2}}$; **b.** $K = [N_2][Br_2]^3$, $K_p = P_{N_2} \times P_{Br_2}^3$; **c.** $K = [O_2]^3$, $K_p = P_{O_2}^3$; **d.** $K = \dfrac{[H_2O]}{[H_2]}$, $K_p = \dfrac{P_{H_2O}}{P_{H_2}}$ **31.** 8.0×10^9 **33. a.** $Q > K$, so reaction shifts left to reach equilibrium. **b.** $Q = K$, so reaction is at equilibrium. **c.** $Q < K$, so reaction shifts right to reach equilibrium. **35. a.** decrease; **b.** no change; **c.** no change; **d.** increase **37.** 8.0×10^{-2} M **39.** 3.4 **41.** 0.056 **43.** $[N_2]_0 = 10.0$ M, $[H_2]_0 = 11.0$ M **45.** $[SO_3] = [NO] = 1.06$ M; $[SO_2] = [NO_2] = 0.54$ M **47.** 7.8×10^{-2} atm **49.** $P_{SO_2} = 0.38$ atm; $P_{O_2} = 0.44$ atm; $P_{SO_3} = 0.12$ atm **51. a.** [NO] = 0.032 M, $[Cl_2] = 0.016$ M, [NOCl] = 1.0 M; **b.** [NO] = [NOCl] = 1.0 M, $[Cl_2] = 1.6 \times 10^{-5}$ M; **c.** [NO] = 8.0×10^{-3} M, $[Cl_2] = 1.0$ M, [NOCl] = 2.0 M **53.** $[CO_2] = 0.39$ M, [CO] = 8.6×10^{-3} M, $[O_2] = 4.3 \times 10^{-3}$ M **55.** 0.27 atm **57. a.** no effect; **b.** shifts left; **c.** shifts right **59. a.** right **b.** right; **c.** no effect; **d.** left; **e.** no effect **61. a.** left; **b.** right; **c.** left; **d.** no effect; **e.** no effect; **f.** right **63.** increase **65.** 2.6×10^{81} **67. a.** 0.379 atm; **b.** 0.786 **69. a.** 1.16 atm; **b.** 0.10 atm; **c.** 2.22 atm; **d.** 91.4% **71.** $[H_2] = [F_2] = 0.0251$ M; [HF] = 0.450 M **73.** Added OH^- reacts with H^+ to produce H_2O. As H^+ is removed, the reaction shifts right to produce more H^+ and CrO_4^{2-}. Because more CrO_4^{2-} is produced, the solution turns yellow. **75.** 9.0×10^{-3} M **77.** $P_{PCl_3} = P_{Cl_2} = 0.2230$ atm, $P_{PCl_5} = 0.0259$ atm; $K_p = 1.92$ **79.** [NOCl] = 2.0 M, [NO] = 0.050 M, $[Cl_2] = 0.025$ M **81.** 2.1×10^{-3} atm **83.** $P_{NO_2} = 0.704$ atm, $P_{N_2O_4} = 0.12$ atm **85.** 0.63 **87.** 0.240 atm **89.** 9.17×10^{-3} **91.** 192 g; 0.25 atm **93.** $C_{10}H_8$; 0.0919%

Chapter 14

17. 10.78 (4 significant figures); 6.78 (3 significant figures); 0.78 (2 significant figures); A pH value is a logarithm. The numbers to the left of the decimal place identify the power of 10 to which $[H^+]$ is expressed in scientific notation—for example, 10^{-11}, 10^{-7}, 10^{-1}. The number of decimal places in a pH value identifies the number of significant figures in $[H^+]$. In all three pH values, the $[H^+]$ should be expressed only to two significant figures since these pH values have only two decimal places. **19. a.** These would be 0.10 M solutions of strong acids like HCl, HBr, HI, HNO_3, H_2SO_4 or $HClO_4$. **b.** These are salts of the conjugate acids of the bases in Table 14.3. These conjugate acids are all weak acids. Three examples would be 0.10 M solutions of NH_4Cl, $CH_3NH_3NO_3$, and $C_2H_5NH_3Br$. Note that the anions used to form these salts are conjugate bases of strong acids; this is because they have no acidic or basic properties in water (with the exception of HSO_4^-, which has weak acid properties). **c.** These would be 0.10 M solutions of strong bases like LiOH,

NaOH, KOH, RbOH, CsOH, Ca(OH)$_2$, Sr(OH)$_2$ and Ba(OH)$_2$. **d.** These are salts of the conjugate bases of the neutrally charged weak acids in Table 14.2. The conjugate bases of weak acids are weak bases themselves. Three examples would be 0.10 M solutions of NaClO$_2$, KC$_2$H$_3$O$_2$, and CaF$_2$. The cations used to form these salts are Li$^+$, Na$^+$, K$^+$, Rb$^+$, Cs$^+$, Ca^{2+}, Sr^{2+}, and Ba^{2+} since these cations have no acidic or basic properties in water. Notice that these are the cations in the list of the strong bases listed in part c that you should memorize. **e.** There are two ways to make a neutral salt. The easiest way is to combine a conjugate base of a strong acid (except for HSO$_4^-$) with one of the cations from the strong bases. These ions have no acidic/basic properties in water so salts of these ions are neutral. Three examples would be 0.10 M solutions of NaCl, KNO$_3$, and SrI$_2$. Another type of strong electrolyte that can produce neutral solutions are salts that contain an ion with weak acid properties combined with an ion of opposite charge having weak base properties. If the K_a for the weak acid ion is equal to the K_b for the weak base ion, then the salt will produce a neutral solution. The most common example of this type of salt is ammonium acetate, NH$_4$C$_2$H$_3$O$_2$. For this salt, K_a for NH$_4^+ = K_b$ for C$_2$H$_3$O$_2^- = 5.6 \times 10^{-10}$. This salt, at any concentration, produces a neutral solution.

21. a. H$_2$O(l) + H$_2$O(l) $\rightleftharpoons$ H$_3$O$^+$(aq) + OH$^-$(aq) or

$$\text{H}_2\text{O}(l) \rightleftharpoons \text{H}^+(aq) + \text{OH}^-(aq) \qquad K = K_w = [\text{H}^+][\text{OH}^-]$$

b. HF(aq) + H$_2$O(l) $\rightleftharpoons$ F$^-$(aq) + H$_3$O$^+$(aq) or

$$\text{HF}(aq) \rightleftharpoons \text{H}^+(aq) + \text{F}^-(aq) \qquad K = K_a = \frac{[\text{H}^+][\text{F}^-]}{[\text{HF}]}$$

c. C$_5$H$_5$N(aq) + H$_2$O(l) $\rightleftharpoons$ C$_5$H$_5$NH$^+$(aq) + OH$^-$(aq)

$$K = K_b = \frac{[\text{C}_5\text{H}_5\text{NH}^+][\text{OH}^-]}{[\text{C}_5\text{H}_5\text{N}]}$$

23. a. This expression holds true for solutions of strong acids having a concentration greater than 1.0×10^{-6} M. For example, 0.10 M HCl, 7.8 M HNO$_3$, and 3.6×10^{-4} M HClO$_4$ are solutions where this expression holds true. **b.** This expression holds true for weak acids where the two normal assumptions hold. The two assumptions are that the contribution of H$^+$ from water is negligible and that the acid is less than 5% dissociated in water (from the assumption that x is small compared to some number). This expression will generally hold true for solutions of weak acids having a K_a value less than 1×10^{-4}, as long as there is a significant amount of weak acid present. Three example solutions are 1.5 M HC$_2$H$_3$O$_2$, 0.10 M HOCl, and 0.72 M NH$_4$NO$_3$. **c.** This expression holds true for strong bases that donate 2 OH$^-$ ions per formula unit. As long as the concentration of the base is above 5×10^{-7} M, this expression will hold true. Three examples are 5.0×10^{-3} M Ca(OH)$_2$, 2.1×10^{-4} M Sr(OH)$_2$, and 9.1×10^{-5} M Ba(OH)$_2$. **d.** This expression holds true for solutions of weak bases where the two normal assumptions hold. The assumptions are that the OH$^-$ contribution from water is negligible and that the base is less than 5% ionized in water. For the 5% rule to hold, you generally need bases with $K_b < 1 \times 10^{-4}$ and concentrations of weak base greater than 0.10 M. Three examples are 0.10 M NH$_3$, 0.54 M C$_6$H$_5$NH$_2$, and 1.1 M C$_5$H$_5$N. **25.** One reason HF is a weak acid is that the H—F bond is unusually strong and thus, is difficult to break. This contributes to the reluctance of the HF molecules to dissociate in water. **27. a.** HClO$_4$(aq) + H$_2$O(l) $\rightarrow$ H$_3$O$^+$(aq) + ClO$_4^-$(aq) or HClO$_4$(aq) $\rightarrow$ H$^+$(aq)+ClO$_4^-$(aq); water is commonly omitted from K_a reactions. **b.** CH$_3$CH$_2$CO$_2$H(aq) $\rightleftharpoons$ H$^+$(aq) + CH$_3$CH$_2$CO$_2^-$(aq); **c.** NH$_4^+$(aq) $\rightleftharpoons$H$^+$(aq) + NH$_3$(aq) **29. a.** H$_2$O, base; H$_2$CO$_3$, acid; H$_3$O$^+$, conjugate acid; HCO$_3^-$, conjugate base; **b.** C$_5$H$_5$NH$^+$, acid; H$_2$O, base; C$_5$H$_5$N, conjugate base; H$_3$O$^+$, conjugate acid; **c.** HCO$_3^-$, base; C$_5$H$_5$NH$^+$, acid; H$_2$CO$_3$, conjugate acid; C$_5$H$_5$N, conjugate base **31. a.** HClO$_4$, strong acid; **b.** HOCl, weak acid; **c.** H$_2$SO$_4$, strong acid; **d.** H$_2$SO$_3$, weak acid **33.** HClO$_4$ > HClO$_2$ >NH$_4^+$ > H$_2$O **35. a.** HCl; **b.** HNO$_2$; **c.** HCN since it has a larger K_a value. **37. a.** 1.0×10^{-7} M, neutral; **b.** 12 M, basic; **c.** 8.3×10^{-16} M, acidic; **d.** 1.9×10^{-10} M, acidic **39. a.** endothermic; **b.**[H$^+$] = [OH$^-$] = 2.34×10^{-7} M **41.** [37] **a.** pH = pOH = 7.00; **b.** pH = 15.08, pOH = −1.08; **c.** pH = −1.08, pOH = 15.08; **d.** pH = 4.27, pOH = 9.73 [38] **a.** pH = 14.18, pOH =

−0.18; **b.** pH = −0.44, pOH = 14.44; **c.** pH = pOH = 7.00; **d.** pH = 10.85, pOH = 3.14 **43. a.** pH = 6.88, pOH = 7.12, [H$^+$] = 1.3×10^{-7} M, [OH$^-$] = 7.6×10^{-8} M, acidic; **b.** pH = 0.92, pOH = 13.08, [H$^+$] = 0.12 M, [OH$^-$] = 8.4×10^{-14} M, acidic; **c.** pH = 10.89, pOH = 3.11, [H$^+$] = 1.3×10^{-11} M, [OH$^-$] = 7.8×10^{-4} M, basic; **d.** pH = pOH = 7.00, [H$^+$] = [OH$^-$] = 1.0×10^{-7} M, neutral **45.** pOH = 11.9, [H$^+$] = 8×10^{-3} M, [OH$^-$] = 1×10^{-12} M, acidic **47. a.** H$^+$, ClO$_4^-$, H$_2$O; 0.602; **b.** H$^+$, NO$_3^-$, H$_2$O; 0.602 **49.** [H$^+$] = 0.088 M, [OH$^-$] = 1.1×10^{-13} M, [Cl$^-$] = 0.013 M, [NO$_3^-$] = 0.075 M **51.** Add 4.2 mL of 12 M HCl to water with mixing; add enough water to bring the solution volume to 1600 mL. **53. a.** HNO$_2$ and H$_2$O, 2.00; **b.** HC$_2$H$_3$O$_2$ and H$_2$O, 2.68 **55.** [H$^+$] = [CH$_3$COO$^-$] = 5.8×10^{-4} M, [CH$_3$COOH] = 0.0181 M, pH = 3.24 **57.** [H$^+$] = [F$^-$] = 3.5×10^{-3} M, [OH$^-$] = 2.9×10^{-12} M, [HF] = 0.017 M, 2.46 **59.** 1.96 **61. a.** 1.00; **b.** 1.30 **63. a.** 0.60%; **b.** 1.9%; **c.** 5.8%; **d.** Dilution shifts equilibrium to the side with the greater number of particles (% dissociation increases). **e.** [H$^+$] also depends on initial concentration of weak acid. **65.** 1.4×10^{-4} **67.** 3.5×10^{-4} **69.** 0.024 M

71. a. NH$_3$(aq) + H$_2$O(l) $\rightleftharpoons$ NH$_4^+$(aq) + OH$^-$(aq)

$$K_b = \frac{[\text{NH}_4^+][\text{OH}^-]}{[\text{NH}_3]};$$

b. C$_5$H$_5$N(aq) + H$_2$O(l) $\rightleftharpoons$ C$_5$H$_5$NH$^+$(aq) + OH$^-$(aq)

$$K_b = \frac{[\text{C}_5\text{H}_5\text{NH}^+][\text{OH}^-]}{[\text{C}_5\text{H}_5\text{N}]}$$

73. NH$_3$ > C$_5$H$_5$N > H$_2$O > NO$_3^-$ **75. a.** C$_6$H$_5$NH$_2$; **b.** C$_6$H$_5$NH$_2$; **c.** OH$^-$; **d.** CH$_3$NH$_2$ **77. a.** 13.00; **b.** 7.00; **c.** 14.30 **79. a.** K$^+$, OH$^-$, and H$_2$O, 0.015 M, 12.18; **b.** Ba^{2+}, OH$^-$, and H$_2$O, 0.030 M, 12.48 **81.** 0.16 g **83.** NH$_3$ and H$_2$O, 1.6×10^{-3} M, 11.20 **85. a.** [OH$^-$] = 8.9×10^{-3} M, [H$^+$] = 1.1×10^{-12} M, 11.96; **b.** [OH$^-$] = 4.7×10^{-5} M, [H$^+$] = 2.1×10^{-10} M, 9.68 **87.** 12.00 **89. a.** 1.3%; **b.** 4.2% **91.** 9.2×10^{-7}

93. H$_2$SO$_3$(aq) $\rightleftharpoons$ HSO$_3^-$(aq) + H$^+$(aq) K_{a_1} reaction
HSO$_3^-$(aq) $\rightleftharpoons$ SO$_3^{2-}$(aq) + H$^+$(aq) K_{a_2} reaction

95. a. 1.62; **b.** 3.68 **97.** −0.30 **99.** HCl > NH$_4$Cl > KCl > KCN > KOH **101.** OCl$^-$ **103.** [HN$_3$] = [OH$^-$] = 2.3×10^{-6} M, [Na$^+$] = 0.010 M, [N$_3^-$] = 0.010 M, [H$^+$] = 4.3×10^{-9} M **105. a.** 5.82; **b.** 10.95 **107.** NaF **109.** 3.08 **111. a.** neutral; **b.** basic; NO$_2^-$ + H$_2$O $\rightleftharpoons$ HNO$_2$ + OH$^-$; **c.** acidic; C$_5$H$_5$NH$^+$ $\rightleftharpoons$ C$_5$H$_5$N + H$^+$; **d.** acidic because NH$_4^+$ is a stronger acid than NO$_2^-$ is a base; NH$_4^+$ $\rightleftharpoons$ NH$_3$ + H$^+$; NO$_2^-$ + H$_2$O $\rightleftharpoons$ HNO$_2$ + OH$^-$; **e.** basic; OCl$^-$ + H$_2$O $\rightleftharpoons$ HOCl + OH$^-$; **f.** basic because OCl$^-$ is a stronger base than NH$_4^+$ is an acid; OCl$^-$ + H$_2$O $\rightleftharpoons$ HOCl + OH$^-$, NH$_4^+$ $\rightleftharpoons$ NH$_3$ + H$^+$ **113. a.** HIO$_3$ < HBrO$_3$; as the electronegativity of the central atom increases, acid strength increases. **b.** HNO$_2$ < HNO$_3$; as the number of oxygen atoms attached to the central atom increases, acid strength increases. **c.** HOI < HOCl; same reasoning as in part a. **d.** H$_3$PO$_3$ < H$_3$PO$_4$; same reasoning as in part b. **115. a.** H$_2$O < H$_2$S < H$_2$Se; acid strength increases as bond energy decreases. **b.** CH$_3$CO$_2$H < FCH$_2$CO$_2$H < F$_2$CHCO$_2$H < F$_3$CCO$_2$H; as the electronegativity of the neighboring atoms increases, acid strength increases. **c.** NH$_4^+$ < HONH$_3^+$; same reasoning as in part b. **d.** NH$_4^+$ < PH$_4^+$; same reasoning as in part a. **117. a.** basic; CaO(s) + H$_2$O(l) $\rightarrow$ Ca(OH)$_2$(aq); **b.** acidic; SO$_2$(g) + H$_2$O(l) $\rightarrow$ H$_2$SO$_3$(aq); **c.** acidic; Cl$_2$O(g) + H$_2$O(l) $\rightarrow$ 2HOCl(aq) **119. a.** B(OH)$_3$, acid; H$_2$O, base; **b.** Ag$^+$, acid; NH$_3$, base; **c.** BF$_3$, acid; F$^-$, base **121.** Al(OH)$_3$(s) + 3H$^+$(aq) $\rightarrow$ Al^{3+}(aq) + 3H$_2$O(l); Al(OH)$_3$(s) + OH$^-$(aq) $\rightarrow$ Al(OH)$_4^-$(aq) **123.** Fe^{3+}; because it is smaller with a greater positive charge, Fe^{3+} will be more strongly attracted to a lone pair of electrons from a Lewis base. **125.** 990 mL H$_2$O **127. a.** 2.80; **b.** 1.1×10^{-3} M **129.** NH$_4$Cl **131.** 4.2×10^{-2} M **133.** 3.00 **135. a.** 2.62; **b.** 2.4%; **c.** 8.48 **137. a.** 1.66; **b.** Fe^{2+} ions will produce a less acidic solution (higher pH) due to the lower charge on Fe^{2+} as compared with Fe^{3+}. As the charge on a metal ion increases, acid strength of the hydrated ion increases. **139.** acidic; HSO$_4^-$ $\rightleftharpoons$ SO$_4^{2-}$ + H$^+$; 1.54 **141. a.** Hb(O$_2$)$_4$ in lungs, HbH$_4^{4+}$ in cells; **b.** Decreasing [CO$_2$] will decrease [H$^+$], favoring Hb(O$_2$)$_4$ formation. Breathing into a bag raises [CO$_2$]. **c.** NaHCO$_3$ lowers the acidity from accumulated CO$_2$.

143. a. H_2SO_3; **b.** $HClO_3$; **c.** H_3PO_3; NaOH and KOH are ionic compounds composed of either Na^+ or K^+ cations and OH^- anions. When soluble ionic compounds dissolve in water, they form the ions from which they are formed. The acids in this problem are all covalent compounds. When these acids dissolve in water, the covalent bond between oxygen and hydrogen breaks to form H^+ ions. **145.** 7.20. **147.** 4540 mL **149.** 4.17 **151.** 0.022 M **153.** 2.5×10^{-3} **155.** PO_4^{3-}, $K_b = 0.021$; HPO_4^{2-}, $K_b = 1.6 \times 10^{-7}$; $H_2PO_4^-$, $K_b = 1.3 \times 10^{-12}$; from the K_b values, PO_4^{3-} is the strongest base. **157. a.** basic; **b.** acidic; **c.** basic; **d.** acidic; **e.** acidic **159.** 1.0×10^{-3} **161.** 5.4×10^{-4} **163.** 3.36

Chapter 15

13. When an acid dissociates or when a salt dissolves, ions are produced. A common ion is when one of the product ions in a particular equilibrium is added from an outside source. For a weak acid dissociating to its conjugate base and H^+, the common ion would be the conjugate base; this would be added by dissolving a soluble salt of the conjugate base into the acid solution. The presence of the conjugate base from an outside source shifts the equilibrium to the left so less acid dissociates. For the K_{sp} reaction of a salt dissolving into its respective ions, the common ion would be if one of the ions in the salt was added from an outside source. When a common ion is present, the K_{sp} equilibrium shifts to the left resulting in less of the salt dissolving into its ions. **15.** The more weak acid and conjugate base present, the more H^+ and/or OH^- that can be absorbed by the buffer without significant pH change. When the concentrations of weak acid and conjugate base are equal (so that pH = pK_a), the buffer system is equally efficient at absorbing either H^+ or OH^-. If the buffer is overloaded with weak acid or with conjugate base, then the buffer is not equally efficient at absorbing either H^+ or OH^-. **17.** The three key points to emphasize in your sketch are the initial pH, pH at the halfway point to equivalence, and the pH at the equivalence point. For the two weak bases titrated, pH = pK_a at the halfway point to equivalence (50.0 mL HCl added) because [weak base] = [conjugate acid] at this point. For the initial pH, the strong base has the highest pH (most basic), while the weakest base has the lowest pH (least basic). At the equivalence point, the strong base titration has pH = 7.0. The weak bases titrated have acidic pHs at the equivalence point because the conjugate acids of the weak bases titrated are the major species present. The weakest base has the strongest conjugate acid so its pH will be lowest (most acidic) at the equivalence point.

19. i. This is the result when you have a salt that breaks up into two ions. Examples of these salts (but not all) would be AgCl, $SrSO_4$, $BaCrO_4$, and $ZnCO_3$ **ii.** This is the result when you have a salt that breaks up into three ions, either two cations and one anion or one cation and two anions. Some examples are SrF_2, Hg_2I_2, and Ag_2SO_4. **iii.** This is the result when you have a salt that breaks up into four ions, either three cations and one anion (Ag_3PO_4) or one cation and three anions (ignoring the hydroxides, there are no examples of this type of salt in Table 15.4). **iv.** This is the result when you have a salt that breaks up into five ions, either three cations and two anions $[Sr_3(PO_4)_2]$ or two cations and three anions (no examples of this type of salt are in Table 15.4). **21.** When strong acid or strong base is added to a sodium bicarbonate/sodium carbonate buffer mixture, the strong acid/base is neutralized. The reaction goes to completion resulting in the strong acid/base being replaced with a weak acid/base. This results in a new buffer solution. The reactions are $H^+(aq) + CO_3^{2-}(aq) \rightarrow$

$HCO_3^-(aq)$; $OH^-(aq) + HCO_3^-(aq) \rightarrow CO_3^{2-}(aq) + H_2O(l)$ **23. a.** 2.96; **b.** 8.94; **c.** 7.00; **d.** 4.89 **25.** 1.1% vs. 1.3×10^{-2}% dissociated; the presence of $C_3H_5O_2^-$ in solution 23d greatly inhibits the dissociation of $HC_3H_5O_2$. This is called the *common ion effect*. **27. a.** 1.70; **b.** 5.49; **c.** 1.70; **d.** 4.71 **29. a.** 4.29; **b.** 12.30; **c.** 12.30; **d.** 5.07 **31.** solution d; solution d is a buffer solution that resists pH changes. **33.** 3.40 **35.** 3.48; 3.22 **37.** 4.36 **39. a.** 7.97; **b.** 8.73; both solutions have an initial pH = 8.77. The two solutions differ in their buffer capacity. Solution b with the larger concentrations has the greater capacity to resist pH change. **41.** 15 g **43. a.** 0.19; **b.** 0.59; **c.** 1.0; **d.** 1.9 **45.** HOCl; there are many possibilities. One possibility is a solution with [HOCl] = 1.0 M and [NaOCl] = 0.35 M. **47.** solution d **49. a.** 1.0 mol; **b.** 0.30 mol; **c.** 1.3 mol **51. a.** ~22 mL base added; **b.** buffer region is from ~1 mL to ~21 mL base added. The maximum buffering region would be from ~5 mL to ~17 mL of base added with the halfway point to equivalence (~11 mL) as the best buffer point. **c.** ~11 mL base added; **d.** 0 mL base added; **e.** ~22 mL base added (the stoichiometric point); **f.** any point after the stoichiometric point (volume base added > ~22 mL) **53. a.** 0.699; **b.** 0.854; **c.** 1.301; **d.** 7.00; **e.** 12.15 **55. a.** 2.72; **b.** 4.26; **c.** 4.74; **d.** 5.22; **e.** 8.79; **f.** 12.15

57.

Volume (mL)	pH
0.0	2.43
4.0	3.14
8.0	3.53
12.5	3.86
20.0	4.46
24.0	5.24
24.5	5.6
24.9	6.3
25.0	8.28
25.1	10.3
26.0	11.29
28.0	11.75
30.0	11.96

See *Solutions Guide* for pH plot.

59.

Volume (mL)	pH
0.0	11.11
4.0	9.97
8.0	9.58
12.5	9.25
20.0	8.65
24.0	7.87
24.5	7.6
24.9	6.9
25.0	5.28
25.1	3.7
26.0	2.71
28.0	2.24
30.0	2.04

See *Solutions Guide* for pH plot.
61. a. 4.19, 8.45; **b.** 10.74; 5.96; **c.** 0.89, 7.00 **63.** 2.1×10^{-6} **65. a.** yellow; **b.** 8.0; **c.** blue **67.** phenolphthalein **69.** Phenol red is one possible indicator for the titration in Exercise 53. Phenolphthalein is one possible indicator for the titration in Exercise 55. **71.** Phenolphthalein is one possible indicator for Exercise 57. Bromcresol green is one possible indicator for Exercise 59. **73.** The pH is between 5 and 8. **75. a.** $AgC_2H_3O_2(s) \rightleftharpoons Ag^+(aq) + C_2H_3O_2^-(aq)$; $K_{sp} = [Ag^+][C_2H_3O_2^-]$; **b.** $Al(OH)_3(s) \rightleftharpoons Al^{3+}(aq) + 3OH^-(aq)$; $K_{sp} = [Al^{3+}][OH^-]^3$; **c.** $Ca_3(PO_4)_2(s) \rightleftharpoons 3Ca^{2+}(aq) + 2PO_4^{3-}(aq)$; $K_{sp} = [Ca^{2+}]^3[PO_4^{3-}]^2$ **77. a.** 2.3×10^{-9}; **b.** 8.20×10^{-19} **79.** 3.92×10^{-5} **81. a.** 1.6×10^{-5} mol/L; **b.** 9.3×10^{-5} mol/L; **c.** 6.5×10^{-7} mol/L **83.** 3.30×10^{-43} **85.** 2.5×10^{-22} mol/L **87. a.** CaF_2; **b.** $FePO_4$ **89. a.** 4×10^{-17} mol/L; **b.** 4×10^{-11} mol/L; **c.** 4×10^{-29} mol/L **91.** 2.3×10^{-11} mol/L **93.** 1.5×10^{-19} g **95.** If the anion in the salt can act as a base in water, then the solubility of the salt will increase

as the solution becomes more acidic. Added H^+ will react with the base, forming the conjugate acid. As the basic anion is removed, more of the salt will dissolve to replenish the basic anion. The salts with basic anions are Ag_3PO_4, $CaCO_3$, $CdCO_3$, and $Sr_3(PO_4)_2$. Hg_2Cl_2 and PbI_2 do not have any pH dependence because Cl^- and I^- are terrible bases (the conjugate bases of strong acids).

$$Ag_3PO_4(s) + H^+(aq) \longrightarrow 3Ag^+(aq) + HPO_4^{2-}(aq) \xrightarrow{\text{excess } H^+}$$
$$3Ag^+(aq) + H_3PO_4(aq)$$

$$CaCO_3(s) + H^+(aq) \longrightarrow Ca^{2+}(aq) + HCO_3^-(aq) \xrightarrow{\text{excess } H^+}$$
$$Ca^{2+}(aq) + H_2CO_3(aq)\,[H_2O(l) + CO_2(g)]$$

$$CdCO_3(s) + H^+(aq) \longrightarrow Cd^{2+}(aq) + HCO_3^-(aq) \xrightarrow{\text{excess } H^+}$$
$$Cd^{2+}(aq) + H_2CO_3(aq)\,[H_2O(l) + CO_2(g)]$$

$$Sr_3(PO_4)_2(s) + 2H^+(aq) \longrightarrow 3Sr^{2+}(aq) + 2HPO_4^{2-}(aq) \xrightarrow{\text{excess } H^+}$$
$$3Sr^{2+}(aq) + 2H_3PO_4(aq)$$

97. yes; $Q = 1.9 \times 10^{-4} > K_{sp}$ **99.** $[K^+] = 0.160\ M$, $[C_2O_4^{2-}] = 3.3 \times 10^{-7}$ M, $[Ba^{2+}] = 0.0700\ M$, $[Br^-] = 0.300\ M$ **101.** $[Ag^+] > 5.6 \times 10^{-5}\ M$

103. a.

$Ni^{2+} + CN^- \rightleftharpoons NiCN^+$	K_1
$NiCN^+ + CN^- \rightleftharpoons Ni(CN)_2$	K_2
$Ni(CN)_2 + CN^- \rightleftharpoons Ni(CN)_3^-$	K_3
$Ni(CN)_3^- + CN^- \rightleftharpoons Ni(CN)_4^{2-}$	K_4

$$Ni^{2+} + 4CN^- \rightleftharpoons Ni(CN)_4^{2-}$$

b.

$V^{3+} + C_2O_4^{2-} \rightleftharpoons VC_2O_4^+$	K_1
$VC_2O_4^+ + C_2O_4^{2-} \rightleftharpoons V(C_2O_4)_2^-$	K_2
$V(C_2O_4)_2^- + C_2O_4^{2-} \rightleftharpoons V(C_2O_3)^{3-}$	K_2

$$V^{3+} + 3\,C_2O_4^{2-} \rightleftharpoons V(C_2O_4)_3^{3-}$$

105. 6.2×10^5 **107.** $Hg^{2+}(aq) + 2I^-(aq) \to HgI_2(s)$ (orange precipitate); $HgI_2(s) + 2I^-(aq) \to HgI_4^{2-}(aq)$ (soluble complex ion) **109.** $3.3 \times 10^{-32}\ M$ **111. a.** 1.2×10^{-8} mol/L; **b.** 1.5×10^{-4} mol/L; **c.** The presence of NH_3 increases the solubility of AgI. Added NH_3 removes Ag^+ from solution by forming the complex ion $Ag(NH_3)_2^+$. As Ag^+ is removed, more AgI will dissolve to replenish the Ag^+ concentration. **113.** 4.7×10^{-2} mol/L **115.** Test tube 1: added Cl^- reacts with Ag^+ to form the silver chloride precipitate. The net ionic equation is $Ag^+(aq) + Cl^-(aq) \to AgCl(s)$. Test tube 2: added NH_3 reacts with Ag^+ ions to form the soluble complex ion $Ag(NH_3)_2^+$. As this complex ion forms, Ag^+ is removed from solution, which causes $AgCl(s)$ to dissolve. When enough NH_3 is added, then all of the silver chloride precipitate will dissolve. The equation is $AgCl(s) + 2NH_3(aq) \to Ag(NH_3)_2^+(aq) + Cl^-(aq)$. Test tube 3: added H^+ reacts with the weak base NH_3 to form NH_4^+. As NH_3 is removed, Ag^+ ions are released to solution, which can then react with Cl^- to reform $AgCl(s)$. The equations are $Ag(NH_3)_2^+(aq) + 2H^+(aq) \to Ag^+(aq) + 2NH_4^+(aq)$ and $Ag^+(aq) + Cl^-(aq) \to AgCl(s)$. **117.** pOH $= pK_b + \log\dfrac{[\text{acid}]}{[\text{base}]}$ **119. a.** 10.44; **b.** 10.74 **121. a.** potassium fluoride + HCl; **b.** benzoic acid + NaOH; **c.** acetic acid + sodium acetate; **d.** HOCl + NaOH; **e.** ammonium chloride + NaOH **123. a.** 1.8×10^9; **b.** 5.6×10^4; **c.** 1.0×10^{14} **125.** 4.4 L **127.** 180. g/mol; 3.3×10^{-4}; assume acetylsalicylic acid is a weak monoprotic acid. **129.** 65 mL **131.** 0.210 M **133. a.** 1.6×10^{-6}; **b.** 0.056 mol/L **135.** 2.7×10^{-5} mol/L; the solubility of hydroxyapatite will increase as a solution gets more acidic, since both phosphate and hydroxide can react with H^+. 6×10^{-8} mol/L; the hydroxyapatite in the tooth enamel is converted to the less soluble fluorapatite by fluoride-treated water. The less soluble fluorapatite will then be more difficult to dissolve, making teeth less susceptible to decay. See Chemical Impact on "The Chemistry of Teeth." **137. a.** 6.7×10^{-6} mol/L; **b.** 1.2×10^{-13} mol/L; **c.** $Pb(OH)_2(s)$ will not form since $Q < K_{sp}$ **139.** 49 mL **141.** 3.9 L **143. a.** 200.0 mL; **b.** i. H_2A, H_2O; ii. H_2A, HA^-, H_2O, Na^+; iii. HA^-, H_2O, Na^+; iv. HA^-, A^{2-}, H_2O, Na^+; v. A^{2-}, H_2O, Na^+; vi. A^{2-}, H_2O, Na^+, OH^-;

c. $K_{a_1} = 1 \times 10^{-4}$; $K_{a_2} = 1 \times 10^{-8}$ **145.** pH $\approx$ 5.0; $K_a \approx 1 \times 10^{-10}$ **147.** 3 M **149. a.** 5.8×10^{-4} mol/L; **b.** Greater; F^- is a weak base ($K_b = 1.4 \times 10^{-11}$), so some of the F^- is removed by reaction with water. As F^- is removed, more SrF_2 will dissolve; **c.** 3.5×10^{-3} mol/L **151.** 3.00 **153.** 2.78

Chapter 16

7. Living organisms need an external energy source to produce the necessary "ordering." **9.** ΔS_{univ} **11.** As any process occurs, ΔS_{univ} will increase; ΔS_{univ} cannot decrease. Time also goes in one direction, just as ΔS_{univ} goes in one direction. **13.** Possible arrangements for one molecule:

1 way   1 way

Both are equally probable.
Possible arrangements for two molecules:

1 way   2 ways   1 way
Most probable

Possible arrangement for three molecules:

1 way   3 ways   3 ways   1 way

Equally most probable

15. Note that these substances are not in the solid state, but are in the aqueous state; water molecules are also present. There is an apparent increase in ordering when these ions are placed in water. The hydrating water molecules must be in a highly ordered state when surrounding these anions. **17.** One can determine $\Delta S°$ and $\Delta H°$ for the reaction using the standard entropies and standard enthalpies of formation in Appendix 4, then use the equation $\Delta G° = \Delta H° - T\Delta S°$. One can also use the standard free energies of formation in Appendix 4. And finally, one can use Hess's law to calculate $\Delta G°$. Here, reactions having known $\Delta G°$ values are manipulated to determine $\Delta G°$ for a different reaction. For temperatures other than 25(C, $\Delta G°$ is estimated using the $\Delta G° = \Delta H° - T\Delta S$ equation. The assumptions made are that the $\Delta H°$ and $\Delta S°$ values determined from Appendix 4 data are temperature independent. We use the same $\Delta H°$ and $\Delta S°$ values as determined when $T = 25°C$, then plug in the new temperature in Kelvin into the equation to estimate $\Delta G°$ at the new temperature. **19.** a, b, c **21.** We draw all of the possible arrangements of the two particles in the three levels.

2 kJ	—	—	x	—	x	xx
1 kJ	—	x	—	xx	x	—
0 kJ	xx	x	x	—	—	—
Total $E =$	0 kJ	1 kJ	2 kJ	2 kJ	3 kJ	4 kJ

The most likely total energy is 2 kJ. **23. a.** H_2 at 100°C and 0.5 atm; **b.** N_2 at STP; **c.** $H_2O(l)$ **25. a.** negative; **b.** positive **27.** $\Delta G < 0$ for b, c, d **29.** 89.3 J/K · mol **31. a.** yes ($\Delta G < 0$); **b.** 196 K **33. a.** negative; **b.** positive; **c.** negative; **d.** positive **35. a.** $C_{graphite}(s)$; **b.** $C_2H_5OH(g)$; **c.** $CO_2(g)$ **37. a.** negative, -186 J/K; **b.** positive, 187 J/K; **c.** hard to predict since $\Delta n = 0$.; 138 J/K **39.** 262 J/K · mol **41. a.** ΔH and ΔS are both positive; **b.** $S_{rhombic}$ **43. a.** ΔH and ΔS are both negative; **b.** low temperatures **45. a.** $\Delta H° = -803$ kJ, $\Delta S° = -4$ J/K, $\Delta G° = -802$ kJ; **b.** $\Delta H° = 2802$ kJ, $\Delta S° = -262$ J/K, $\Delta G° = 2880$. kJ; **c.** $\Delta H° = -416$ kJ, $\Delta S° = -209$ J/K, $\Delta G° = -354$ kJ; **d.** $\Delta H° = -176$ kJ, $\Delta S° = -284$ J/K, $\Delta G° = -91$ kJ **47.** -5.40 kJ; 328.6 K; $\Delta G°$ is negative below 328.6 K. **49.** $CH_4(g) + CO_2(g) \rightarrow CH_3CO_2H(l)$, $\Delta H° = -16$ kJ, $\Delta S° = -240$. J/K, $\Delta G° = 56$ KJ; $CH_3OH(g) + CO(g) \rightarrow CH_3CO_2H(l)$, $\Delta H° = -173$ kJ, $\Delta S° = -278$ J/K, $\Delta G° = -90$. kJ; the second reaction is preferred. It should be run at temperatures below 622 K. **51.** -817 kJ **53.** -731 kJ/mol **55.** yes **57.** -188 kJ **59. a.** shifts right; **b.** no shift since the reaction is at equilibrium; **c.** shifts left **61.** 8.72; 0.0789 **63.** 140 kJ **65.** -71 kJ/mol **67.** $\Delta H° = 1.1 \times 10^5$ J/mol; $\Delta S° = 330$ J/K $\cdot$ mol; The major difference in the plot is the slope of the line. An endothermic process has a negative slope for the $\ln(K)$ versus $1/T$ plot, whereas an exothermic process has a positive slope. **69.** -447 J/K $\cdot$ mol **71.** decreases; ΔS will be negative since 2 mol of gaseous reactants form 1 mol of gaseous product. For ΔG to be negative, ΔH must be negative (exothermic). For exothermic reactions, K decreases as T increases, so the ratio of the partial pressure of PCl_5 to the partial pressure of PCl_3 will decrease. **73.** 43.7 K **75.** 60 **77. a.** 1.8×10^4 J/mol; shifts left; **b.** 0; no shift since at equilibrium; **c.** -1.1×10^4 J/mol; shifts right; **d.** 0; no shift since at equilibrium; **e.** 2×10^3 J/mol; shifts left **79. a.** 2.22×10^5; **b.** 94.3; **c.** 0.29 mol ATP **81.** ΔS is more favorable for reaction 2 than for reaction 1, resulting in $K_2 > K_1$. In reaction 1, seven particles in solution form one particle. In reaction 2, four particles form one, which results in a smaller decrease in disorder than for reaction 1. **83.** 725 K **85.** $\Delta H° = 286$ kJ; $\Delta G° = 326$ kJ; $K = 7.22 \times 10^{-58}$; $P_{O_3} = 3.3 \times 10^{-41}$ atm; This partial pressure represents one molecule of ozone per 9.5×10^{17} L of air. Equilibrium is probably not maintained under the conditions because the concentration of ozone is not large enough to maintain equilibrium **87. a.** Because

$$k_f = A \exp\left(\frac{-E_a}{RT}\right) \text{ and } k_r = A \exp\left(\frac{-(E_a - \Delta G°)}{RT}\right),$$

Because $\dfrac{k_f}{k_r} = \exp\left(\dfrac{-E_a}{RT} + \dfrac{(E_a - \Delta G°)}{RT}\right) = \exp\left(\dfrac{-\Delta G°}{RT}\right)$. Because $K = \exp\left(\dfrac{-\Delta G°}{RT}\right)$, then $K = \dfrac{k_f}{k_r}$. **b.** A catalyst increases the value of the rate constant (increases rate) by lowering the activation energy. For the equilibrium constant K to remain constant, both k_f and k_r must increase by the same factor. Therefore, a catalyst must increase the rate of both the forward and the reverse reactions. **89. a.** 0.333; **b.** $P_A = 1.50$ atm; $P_B = 0.50$ atm; **c.** $\Delta G = \Delta G° + RT \ln(P_B/P_A) = 2722$ J $- 2722$ J $= 0$ **91.** at least 7.5 torr **93.** 16 g **95.** 61 kJ **97.** -4.1 kJ/mol

Chapter 17

13. Oxidation: increase in oxidation number, loss of electrons; reduction: decrease in oxidation number, gain of electrons **15.** Reactions a, b, and c are oxidation–reduction reactions.

	Oxidizing Agent	Reducing Agent	Substance Oxidized	Substance Reduced
a.	H_2O	CH_4	$CH_4(C)$	$H_2O(H)$
b.	$AgNO_3$	Cu	Cu	$AgNO_3(Ag)$
c.	HCl	Zn	Zn	$HCl(H)$

17. Magnesium is an alkaline earth metal; Mg will oxidize to Mg^{2+}. The oxidation state of hydrogen in HCl is $+1$. To be reduced, the oxidation state of H must decrease. The obvious choice for the hydrogen product is $H_2(g)$ where hydrogen has a zero oxidation state. The balanced reaction is: $Mg(s) + 2HCl(aq) \rightarrow MgCl_2(aq) + H_2(g)$. Mg goes from the 0 to the $+2$ oxidation state by losing two electrons. Each H atom goes from the 0 to the -1 oxidation state by gaining one electron. Since there are two H atoms in the balanced equation, then a total of two electrons are gained by the H atoms. Hence, two electrons are transferred in the balanced reaction. When the electrons are transferred directly from Mg to H^+, no work is obtained. In order to harness this reaction to do useful work, we must control the flow of

electrons through a wire. This is accomplished by making a galvanic cell which separates the reduction reaction from the oxidation reaction in order to control the flow of electrons through a wire to produce a voltage. **19.** An extensive property is one that depends on the amount of substance. The free energy change for a reaction depends on whether 1 mol of product is produced or 2 mol of product is produced or 1 million mol of product is produced. This is not the case for cell potentials which do not depend on the amount of substance. The equation that relates ΔG to E is $\Delta G = -nFE$. It is the n term that converts the intensive property E into the extensive property ΔG. The n is the number of mol of electrons transferred in the balanced reaction that ΔG is associated with. **21.** A potential hazard when jump-starting a car is that the electrolysis of $H_2O(l)$ can occur. When $H_2O(l)$ is electrolyzed, the products are the explosive gas mixture of $H_2(g)$ and $O_2(g)$. A spark produced during jump starting a car could ignite any $H_2(g)$ and $O_2(g)$ produced. Grounding the jumper cable far from the battery minimizes the risk of a spark nearby the battery where $H_2(g)$ and $O_2(g)$ could be collecting. **23.** You need to know the identity of the metal so you know which molar mass to use. You need to know the oxidation state of metal ion in the salt so the mol of electrons transferred can be determined. And finally, you need to know the amount of current and the time the current was passed through the electrolytic cell. If you know these four quantities, then the mass of metal plated out can be calculated. **25.** See Figure 17.3 of the text for a typical galvanic cell. The anode compartment contains the oxidation half-reaction compounds/ions, and the cathode compartment contains the reduction half-reaction compounds/ions. The electrons flow from the anode to the cathode. For each of the following answers, all solutes are 1.0 M and all gases are at 1.0 atm. **a.** $7H_2O(l) + 2Cr^{3+}(aq) + 3Cl_2(g) \rightarrow Cr_2O_7^{2-}(aq) + 6Cl^-(aq) + 14H^+(aq)$; cathode: Pt electrode; Cl_2 bubbled into solution, Cl^- in solution; anode: Pt electrode; Cr^{3+}, H^+, and $Cr_2O_7^{2-}$ in solution; **b.** $Cu^{2+}(aq) + Mg(s) \rightarrow Cu(s) + Mg^{2+}(aq)$; cathode: Cu electrode; Cu^{2+} in solution; anode: Mg electrode; Mg^{2+} in solution **27. a.** 0.03 V; **b.** 2.71 V **29.** See Exercise 25 for a description of a galvanic cell. For each of the following answers, all solutes are 1.0 M and all gases are at 1.0 atm. In the salt bridge, cations flow to the cathode and anions flow to the anode. **a.** $Cl_2(g) + 2Br^-(aq) \rightarrow Br_2(aq) + 2Cl^-(aq)$, $\mathscr{E}° = 0.27$ V; cathode: Pt electrode; $Cl_2(g)$ bubbled in, Cl^- in solution; anode: Pt electrode; Br_2 and Br^- in solution; **b.** $3H_2O(l) + 5IO_4^-(aq) + 2Mn^{2+}(aq) \rightarrow 5IO_3^-(aq) + 2MnO_4^-(aq) + 6H^+(aq)$, $\mathscr{E}° = 0.09$ V; cathode: Pt electrode; IO_4^-, IO_3^-, and H_2SO_4 (as a source of H^+) in solution; anode: Pt electrode; Mn^{2+}, MnO_4^-, and H_2SO_4 in solution **31.** 25a. $Pt|Cr^{3+}$ (1.0 M), H^+ (1.0 M), $Cr_2O_7^{2-}$ (1.0 M) $\|$ Cl_2 (1.0 atm)$|Cl^-$ (1.0 M) $|$ Pt; 25b. Mg $|$ Mg^{2+} (1.0 M) $\|$ Cu^{2+} (1.0 M) $|$ Cu; 29a. Pt $|$ Br^- (1.0 M), Br_2 (1.0 M) $\|$ Cl_2 (1.0 atm) $|$ Cl^- (1.0 M) $|$ Pt; 29b. Pt $|$ Mn^{2+} (1.0 M), MnO_4^- (1.0 M), H^+ (1.0 M) $\|$ IO_4^- (1.0 M), H^+(1.0 M) IO_3^- (1.0 M), $|$ Pt **33. a.** $Au^{3+}(aq) + 3Cu^+(aq) \rightarrow 3Cu^{2+}(aq) + Au(s)$, $\mathscr{E}° = 1.34$ V; **b.** $2VO_2^+(aq) + 4H^+(aq) + Cd(s) \rightarrow Cd^{2+}(aq) + 2VO^{2+}(aq) + 2H_2O(l)$, $\mathscr{E}° = 1.40$ V **35. a.** $16H^+ + 2MnO_4^- + 10I^- \rightarrow 5I_2 + 2Mn^{2+} + 8H_2O$, $\mathscr{E}°_{cell} = 0.97$ V, spontaneous; **b.** $16H^+ + 2MnO_4^- + 10F^- \rightarrow 5F_2 + 2Mn^{2+} + 8H_2O$, $\mathscr{E}°_{cell} = -1.36$ V, not spontaneous **37.** $\mathscr{E}° = 0.41$ V, $\Delta G° = -79$ kJ **39.** 33a. -388 kJ; 33b. -270. kJ **41.** 1.21 V **43.** $K^+ < H_2O < Cd^{2+} < I_2 < AuCl_4^- < IO_3^-$ **45. a.** no; **b.** yes; **c.** yes; **d.** no **47. a.** $Cr_2O_7^{2-}$, O_2, MnO_2, IO_3^-; **b.** $PbSO_4$, Cd^{2+}, Fe^{2+}, Cr^{3+}, Zn^{2+}, H_2O **49.** $ClO^-(aq) + 2NH_3(aq) \rightarrow Cl^-(aq) + N_2H_4(aq) + H_2O(l)$, $\mathscr{E}°_{cell} = 1.00$ V; Because $\mathscr{E}°_{cell}$ is positive for this reaction, at standard conditions ClO^- can spontaneously oxidize NH_3 to the somewhat toxic N_2H_4. **51. a.** larger; **b.** smaller **53.** Electron flow is always from the anode to the cathode. For the cells with a nonzero cell potential, we will identify the cathode, which means the other compartment is the anode. **a.** 0; **b.** 0.018 V; compartment with $[Ag^+] = 2.0$ M is cathode; **c.** 0.059 V; compartment with $[Ag^+] = 1.0$ M is cathode; **d.** 0.26 V; compartment with $[Ag^+] = 1.0$ M is cathode; **e.** 0 **55.** 2.12 V **57.** 1.09 V **59. a.** 0.23 V; **b.** 1.2×10^{-5} M **61.** 0.16 V, copper is oxidized. **63.** 1.7×10^{-30} **65.** [25] **a.** $\Delta G° = -20$ kJ; 1×10^3; **b.** $\Delta G° = -523$ kJ; 5.12×10^{91}; [29] **a.** $\Delta G° = -52$ kJ; 1.4×10^9; **b.** $\Delta G° = -90$ kJ; 2×10^{15} **67.** 2.5×10^{26} **69. a.** no reaction; **b.** $Cl_2(g) + 2I^-(aq) \rightarrow I_2(s) + 2Cl^-(aq)$, $\mathscr{E}°_{cell} = 0.82$ V; $\Delta G° = -160$ kJ; $K = 5.6 \times 10^{27}$; **c.** no reaction; **d.** $4Fe^{2+}(aq) + 4H^+(aq) + O_2(g) \rightarrow$

$4Fe^{3+}(aq) + 2H_2O(l)$, $\mathscr{E}^\circ_{cell} = 0.46$ V; $\Delta G^\circ = -180$ kJ; $K = 1.3 \times 10^{31}$; **71. a.** $Au^{3+}(aq) + 3Tl(s) \rightarrow Au(s) + 3Tl^+(aq)$; $\mathscr{E}^\circ_{cell} = 1.84$ V; **b.** $\Delta G^\circ = -533$ kJ; $K = 2.52 \times 10^{93}$; **c.** 2.04 V **73.** 5.1×10^{-20} **75.** 6.19×10^{52} **77. a.** 30. hours; **b.** 33 s; **c.** 1.3 hours **79. a.** 16 g; **b.** 25 g; **c.** 71 g; **d.** 4.9 g **81.** Bi **83.** 9.12 L F_2 (anode), 29.2 g K (cathode) **85.** 7.44×10^4 A **87.** 1.14×10^{-2} M **89.** Au followed by Ag followed by Ni followed by Cd **91. a.** cathode: $Ni^{2+} + 2e^- \rightarrow Ni$; anode: $2Br^- \rightarrow Br_2 + 2e^-$; **b.** cathode: $Al^{3+} + 3e^- \rightarrow Al$; anode: $2F^- \rightarrow F_2 + 2e^-$; **c.** cathode: $Mn^{2+} + 2e^- \rightarrow Mn$; anode: $2I^- \rightarrow I_2 + 2e^-$ **93. a.** 0.10 V, SCE is anode; **b.** 0.53 V, SCE is anode; **c.** 0.02 V, SCE is cathode; **d.** 1.90 V, SCE is cathode; **e.** 0.47 V, SCE is cathode **95. a.** decrease; **b.** increase; **c.** decrease; **d.** decrease; **e.** same **97. a.** $\Delta G^\circ = -582$ kJ; $K = 3.45 \times 10^{102}$; $\mathscr{E}^\circ = 1.01$ V; **b.** -0.65 V; **99.** Aluminum has the ability to form a durable oxide coating over its surface. Once the HCl dissolves this oxide coating, Al is exposed to H^+ and is easily oxidized to Al^{3+}. Thus, the Al foil disappears after the oxide coating is dissolved. **101.** The claim is impossible. The strongest oxidizing agent and reducing agent when combined give $\mathscr{E}^\circ$ of only about 6 V. **103.** $w_{max} = -13,200$ kJ; the work done can be no larger than the free energy change. If the process were reversible all of the free energy released would go into work, but this does not occur in any real process. Fuel cells are more efficient in converting chemical energy to electrical energy; they are also less massive. Major disadvantage: They are expensive. **105.** 0.98 V **107.** 0.250 mol **109.** $+3$ **111.** $\mathscr{E}^\circ = \dfrac{T\Delta S^\circ}{nF} - \dfrac{\Delta H^\circ}{nF}$; if we graph $\mathscr{E}^\circ$ versus T, we should get a straight line ($y = mx + b$). The slope of the line is equal to $\Delta S^\circ/nF$ and the y-intercept is equal to $-\Delta H^\circ/nF$. $\mathscr{E}^\circ$ will have little temperature dependence for cell reactions with ΔS° close to zero. **113.** 9.8×10^{-6} **115.** 2.39×10^{-7} **117. a.** ± 0.02 pH units; $\pm 6 \times 10^{-6}$ M H^+; **b.** ± 0.001 V **119. a.** 0.16 V; **b.** 8.6 mol **121.** $[Ag^+] = 4.6 \times 10^{-18}$ M; $[Ni^{2+}] = 1.5$ M **123. a.** 0.12 V; **b.** 0.54 V **125. a.** 5.77×10^{10}; **b.** -12.2 kJ/mol **127.** Osmium(IV) nitrate; $[Ar]4s^13d^{10}$

Chapter 18

1. The characteristic frequencies of energies emitted in a nuclear reaction suggest that discrete energy levels exist in the nucleus. The extra stability of certain numbers of nucleons and the predominance of nuclei with even numbers of nucleons suggest that the nuclear structure might be described by using quantum numbers. **3.** β-particle production has the net effect of turning a neutron into a proton. Radioactive nuclei having too many neutrons typically undergo β-particle decay. Positron production has the net effect of turning a proton into a neutron. Nuclei having too many protons typically undergo positron decay. **5.** The transuranium elements are the elements having more protons than uranium. They are synthesized by bombarding heavier nuclei with neutrons and positive ions in a particle accelerator. **7.** $\Delta E = \Delta mc^2$; The key difference is the mass change when going from reactants to products. In chemical reactions, the mass change is indiscernible. In nuclear processes, the mass change is discernable. It is the conversion of this discernable mass change into energy that results in the huge energies associated with nuclear processes. **9.** Sr-90 is an alkaline earth metal having chemical properties similar to calcium. Sr-90 can collect in bones replacing some of the calcium. Once imbedded inside the human body, β particles can do significant damage. Rn-222 is a noble gas so one would expect Rn to be unreactive and pass through the body quickly; it does. The problem with Rn-222 is the rate at which it produces alpha particles. With a short half-life, the few moments that Rn-222 is in the lungs, a significant number of decay events can occur; each decay event produces an alpha particle which is very effective at causing ionization and can produce a dense trail of damage. **11. a.** $^{51}_{24}Cr + ^{\ 0}_{-1}e \rightarrow ^{51}_{23}V$; **b.** $^{131}_{53}I \rightarrow ^{\ 0}_{-1}e + ^{131}_{54}Xe$ **13. a.** $^{68}_{31}Ga + ^{\ 0}_{-1}e \rightarrow ^{68}_{30}Zn$; **b.** $^{62}_{29}Cu \rightarrow ^{\ 0}_{+1}e + ^{62}_{28}Ni$; **c.** $^{212}_{87}Fr \rightarrow ^{4}_{2}He + ^{208}_{85}At$; **d.** $^{129}_{51}Sb \rightarrow ^{\ 0}_{-1}e + ^{129}_{52}Te$ **15.** 10 α particles; 5 β particles **17.** $^{53}_{26}Fe$ has too many protons. It will undergo positron production, electron capture, and/or alpha-particle production. $^{59}_{26}Fe$ has too many neutrons and will undergo beta-particle production. (See Table 18.2 of the text.)

19. a. $^{249}_{98}Cf + ^{18}_{8}O \rightarrow ^{263}_{106}Sg + 4^{1}_{0}n$; **b.** $^{259}_{104}Rf$ **21.** 690 hours **23.** ^{81}Kr is most stable since it has the longest half-life. ^{73}Kr is "hottest" since it decays very rapidly due to its very short half-life. ^{73}Kr, 81s; ^{74}Kr, 34.5 min; ^{76}Kr, 44.4 h; ^{81}Kr, 6.3×10^5 yr **25.** 6.22 mg ^{32}P remains **27.** 0.230 **29.** 26 g **31.** 2.3 counts per minute per gram of C. No; for a 10.-mg C sample, it would take roughly 40 min to see a single disintegration. This is too long to wait, and the background radiation would probably be much greater than the ^{14}C activity. Thus ^{14}C dating is not practical for very small samples. **33.** 3.8×10^9 yr **35.** 4.3×10^6 kg/s **37.** ^{232}Pu, -1.715×10^{14} J/mol; ^{231}Pa, -1.714×10^{14} J/mol **39.** ^{12}C: 1.23×10^{-12} J/nucleon; ^{235}U: 1.2154×10^{-12} J/nucleon; since ^{56}Fe is the most stable known nucleus, then the binding energy per nucleon for ^{56}Fe would be larger than that of ^{12}C or ^{235}U. (See Fig. 18.9 of the text.) **41.** 6.01513 amu **43.** -2.0×10^{10} J/g of hydrogen nuclei **45.** The Geiger–Müller tube has a certain response time. After the gas in the tube ionizes to produce a "count," some time must elapse for the gas to return to an electrically neutral state. The response of the tube levels off because, at high activities, radioactive particles are entering the tube faster than the tube can respond to them. **47.** All evolved $O_2(g)$ comes from water. **49.** 2 neutrons; 4 β particles **51.** Strontium. Xe is chemically unreactive and not readily incorporated into the body. Sr can be easily oxidized to Sr^{2+}. Strontium is in the same family as calcium and could be absorbed and concentrated in the body in a fashion similar to Ca^{2+}. The chemical properties determine where radioactive material may be concentrated in the body or how easily it may be excreted. **53. a.** unstable; beta production; **b.** stable; **c.** unstable; positron production or electron capture; **d.** unstable, positron production, electron capture, or alpha production. **55.** 49.7 yr **57.** 1975 **59.** 900 g ^{235}U **61.** 7×10^5 m/s; 8×10^{-16} J/nuclei; **63.** Assuming that (1) the radionuclide is long lived enough that no significant decay occurs during the time of the experiment, and (2) the total activity is uniformly distributed only in the rat's blood; $V = 10.$ mL. **65. a.** $^{12}_{6}C$; **b.** ^{13}N, ^{13}C, ^{14}N, ^{15}O, and ^{15}N; **c.** -5.950×10^{11} J/mol ^1H **67.** 4.3×10^{-29} **69.** $^{249}_{97}Bk + ^{22}_{10}Ne \rightarrow ^{267}_{107}Bh + 4^{1}_{0}n$; 62.7s; $[Rn]7s^25f^{14}6d^5$

Chapter 19

1. The gravity of the earth cannot keep H_2 in the atmosphere. **3.** The acidity decreases. Solutions of Be^{2+} are acidic, while solutions of the other M^{2+} ions are neutral. **5.** The planes of carbon atoms slide easily. Graphite is not volatile so the lubricant will not be lost when used in a high vacuum environment. **7.** p-type semiconductor **9.** For groups 1A–3A, the small size of H (as compared to Li), Be (as compared to Mg), and B (as compared to Al) seems to be the reason why these elements have nonmetallic properties, while others in the groups 1A–3A are strictly metallic. The small size of H, Be, and B also causes these species to polarize the electron cloud in nonmetals, thus forcing a sharing of electrons when bonding occurs. For groups 4A–6A, a major difference between the first and second members of a group is the ability to form π bonds. The smaller elements form stable π bonds, while the larger elements do not exhibit good overlap between parallel p orbitals and, in turn, do not form strong π bonds. For group 7A, the small size of F as compared to Cl is used to explain the low electron affinity of F and the weakness of the F—F bond. **11.** In order to maximize hydrogen bonding interactions in the solid phase, ice is forced into an open structure. This open structure is why $H_2O(s)$ is less dense than $H_2O(l)$. **13. a.** $\Delta H^\circ = 207$ kJ, $\Delta S^\circ = 216$ J/K; **b.** $T > 958$ K **15. a.** lithium oxide; **b.** potassium superoxide; **c.** sodium peroxide **17. a.** $Li_2O(s) + H_2O(l) \rightarrow 2LiOH(aq)$; **b.** $Na_2O_2(s) + 2H_2O(l) \rightarrow 2NaOH(aq) + H_2O_2(aq)$; **c.** $LiH(s) + H_2O(l) \rightarrow H_2(g) + LiOH(aq)$; **d.** $2KO_2(s) + 2H_2O(l) \rightarrow 2KOH(aq) + O_2(g) + H_2O_2(aq)$ **19.** $2Li(s) + 2C_2H_2(g) \rightarrow 2LiC_2H(s) + H_2(g)$; oxidation–reduction **21. a.** magnesium carbonate; **b.** barium sulfate; **c.** strontium hydroxide **23.** $CaCO_3(s) + H_2SO_4(aq) \rightarrow CaSO_4(aq) + H_2O(l) + CO_2(g)$ **25.** In the gas phase, linear molecules would exist:

$$:\!\ddot{F}\!\!-\!\!Be\!\!-\!\!\ddot{F}\!:$$

In the solid state, BeF_2 has the following extended structure:

27. 2×10^{-2} M **29.** 3.84×10^6 g Ba **31. a.** AlN; **b.** GaF_3; **c.** Ga_2S_3
33. $B_2H_6(g) + 3O_2(g) \rightarrow 2B(OH)_3(s)$ **35.** $In_2O_3(s) + 6H^+(aq) \rightarrow 2In^{3+}(aq) + 3H_2O(l)$; $In_2O_3(s) + OH^-(aq) \rightarrow$ no reaction; $Ga_2O_3(s) + 6H^+(aq) \rightarrow 2Ga^{3+}(aq) + 3H_2O(l)$; $Ga_2O_3(s) + 2OH^-(aq) + 3H_2O(l) \rightarrow 2Ga(OH)_4^-(aq)$
37. $2Ga(s) + 3F_2(g) \rightarrow 2GaF_3(s)$; $4Ga(s) + 3O_2(g) \rightarrow 2Ga_2O_3(s)$; $16Ga(s) + 3S_8(s) \rightarrow 8Ga_2S_3(s)$; $2Ga(s) + N_2(g) \rightarrow 2GaN(s)$; $2Ga(s) + 6HCl(aq) \rightarrow 2GaCl_3(aq) + 3H_2(g)$

39.

Tetrahedral;	Tetrahedral;	Octahedral;
109.5°; sp^3	109.5°; sp^3	90°; d^2sp^3

To form CF_6^{2-}, carbon would have to expand its octet of electrons. Carbon compounds do not expand their octet because of the small atomic size of carbon and because there are no low energy d orbitals on carbon to accommodate the extra electrons. **41. a.** $SiO_2(s) + 2C(s) \rightarrow Si(s) + 2CO(g)$; **b.** $SiCl_4(l) + 2Mg(s) \rightarrow Si(s) + 2MgCl_2(s)$; **c.** $Na_2SiF_6(s) + 4Na(s) \rightarrow Si(s) + 6NaF(s)$
43. Lead is very toxic. As the temperature of the water increases, the solubility of Pb increases. Drinking hot tap water from pipes containing lead solder could result in higher Pb concentrations in the body. **45.** $C_6H_{12}O_6(aq) \rightarrow 2C_2H_5OH(aq) + 2CO_2(g)$ **47.** The π electrons are free to move in graphite, thus giving it a greater conductivity (lower resistance). The electrons have the greatest mobility within the sheets of carbon atoms. Electrons in diamond are not mobile (high resistance). The structure of diamond is uniform in all directions; thus there is no directional dependence of the resistivity. **49.** Only some of the ice will melt; 0°C **51.** It is feasible to recycle Al by melting the metal because, in theory, it takes less than 1% of the energy required to produce the same amount of Al by the Hall–Heroult process. **53.** 60 **55.** 2.12 V **57.** Strontium and calcium are both alkaline earth metals, so both have similar chemical properties. Since milk is a good source of calcium, strontium could replace some calcium in milk without much difficulty. **59.** The inert-pair effect refers to the difficulty of removing the pair of valence s electrons from some of the elements in the fifth and sixth periods of the periodic table. As a result, multiple oxidation states are exhibited for the heavier elements of Groups 3A (and 4A). In^+, In^{3+}, Tl^+, and Tl^{3+} oxidation states are all important to the chemistry of In and Tl. **61.** 3.08 **63.** If the compound contained Ga(II) it would be paramagnetic and if the compound contained Ga(I) and Ga(III), it would be diamagnetic. Paramagnetic compounds have an apparent greater mass in a magnetic field. **65.** 59 atm in the gas phase; 1.8 mol CO_2/L in the wine **67.** $Pb(NO_3)_2(aq) + H_3AsO_4(aq) \rightarrow PbHAsO_4(s) + 2HNO_3(aq)$ **69.** Ca; 12.698 **71.** $3.34, 5.6 \times 10^{-11}$ M **73.** 2.0×10^{-37} M **75.** Carbon is much smaller than Si and cannot form a fifth bond in the transition state. **77.** I
79. a. 7.1 g; **b.** 979 nm; This electromagnetic radiation is not visible to humans; it is in the infrared region of the electromagnetic radiation spectrum, **c.** n-type

Chapter 20

1. This is due to nitrogen's ability to form strong π bonds whereas heavier group 5A elements do not form strong π bonds. Therefore, P_2, As_2, and Sb_2 do not form since two π bonds are required to form these diatomic substances.
3. There are medical studies that have shown an inverse relationship between the incidence of cancer and the selenium levels in soil. The foods grown in these soils and eventually digested are assumed to somehow furnish protection from cancer. Selenium is also involved in the activity of vitamin E and certain enzymes in the human body. In addition, selenium deficiency has been linked

to the occurrence of congestive heart failure. **5.** +6 oxidation state: SO_4^{2-}, SO_3, SF_6; +4 oxidation state: SO_3^{2-}, SO_2, SF_4; +2 oxidation state: SCl_2; 0 oxidation state: S_8 and all other elemental forms of sulfur; −2 oxidation state: H_2S, Na_2S **7. a.** $H_2(g) + Cl_2(g) \rightarrow 2HCl(g)$; this reaction produces a lot of energy which can be used in a cannon apparatus to send a stopper flying across the room. To initiate this extremely slow reaction, light of specific wavelengths is needed. This is the purpose of lighting the magnesium strip. When magnesium is oxidized to MgO, an intense white light is produced. Some of the wavelengths of this light can break Cl—Cl bonds and get the reaction started. **b.** Br_2 is brown. The disappearance of the brown color indicates that all of the Br_2 has reacted with the alkene (no free Br_2 remains). **c.** $2Al(s) + 3I_2(s) \rightarrow 2AlI_3(s)$; This is a highly exothermic reaction, hence the sparks that accompany this reaction. The purple smoke is excess $I_2(s)$ being vaporized [the purple smoke is $I_2(g)$]. **9.** Nitrogen's small size does not provide room for all four oxygen atoms, making NO_4^{3-} unstable. Phosphorus is larger so PO_4^{3-} is more stable. To form NO_3^-, a pi bond must form. Phosphorus doesn't form strong pi bonds as readily as nitrogen. **11.** $NO_2 = N_2O_4 < NO < N_2O$ **13. a.** $NH_4NO_3(s) \xrightarrow{\text{Heat}} N_2O(g) + 2H_2O(g)$; **b.** $2N_2O_5(g) \rightarrow 4NO_2(g) + O_2(g)$; **c.** $2K_3P(s) + 6H_2O(l) \rightarrow 2PH_3(g) + 6KOH(aq)$; **d.** $PBr_3(l) + 3H_2O(l) \rightarrow H_3PO_3(aq) + 3HBr(aq)$; **e.** $2NH_3(aq) + NaOCl(aq) \rightarrow N_2H_4(aq) + NaCl(aq) + H_2O(l)$
15. $CaF_2 \cdot 3Ca_3(PO_4)_2(s) + 10H_2SO_4(aq) + 20H_2O(l) \rightarrow 6H_3PO_4(aq) + 2HF(aq) + 10CaSO_4 \cdot 2H_2O(s)$ **17.** 2.08 mol **19.** $N_2H_4(l) + O_2(g) \rightarrow N_2(g) + 2H_2O(g)$; $\Delta H = -590.$ kJ **21.** $\frac{1}{2}N_2(g) + \frac{1}{2}O_2(g) \rightarrow NO(g)$ $\Delta G° = \Delta G°_{f(NO)}$; NO (and some other oxides of nitrogen) have weaker bonds as compared with the triple bond of N_2 and the double bond of O_2. Because of this, NO (and some other oxides of nitrogen) has a higher (positive) standard free energy of formation as compared to the relatively stable N_2 and O_2 molecules.
23.

M.O.	Bond order	# unpaired e^-
NO	2.5	1
NO^+	3	0
NO^-	2	2

Lewis

Lewis structures are not adequate for NO and NO^-. The M.O. model gives correct results for all three species. For NO, Lewis structures fail for odd-electron species. For NO^-, Lewis structures fail to predict that NO^- is paramagnetic. **25. a.** $H_3PO_4 > H_3PO_3$; **b.** $H_3PO_4 > H_2PO_4^- > HPO_4^{2-}$
27. The acidic protons are attached to oxygen.

29. 821 nm **31. a.** $2SO_2(g) + O_2(g) \rightarrow 2SO_3(g)$; **b.** $SO_3(g) + H_2O(l) \rightarrow H_2SO_4(aq)$; **c.** $2Na_2S_2O_3(aq) + I_2(aq) \rightarrow Na_2S_4O_6(aq) + 2NaI(aq)$; **d.** $Cu(s) + 2H_2SO_4(aq) \rightarrow CuSO_4(aq) + 2H_2O(l) + SO_2(aq)$
33. a.

Trigonal pyramid; ≈109.5°; sp^3

b.

V-shaped; ≈120°; sp^2

c.

$$:\ddot{C}l\overset{\overset{\displaystyle ..\,S\,..}{|}}{\quad}\ddot{C}l:$$

V-shaped; $\approx 109.5°$; sp^3

d.

See-saw; $a \approx 120°$, $b \approx 90°$; dsp^3

e.

Octahedral; $90°$; d^2sp^3

35. 0.301 g H_2O_2; 3.6×10^{-2} g excess HCl   **37.** From the following Lewis structure, each oxygen atom has a tetrahedral arrangement of electron pairs. Therefore, bond angles $\approx 109.5°$, and each O is sp^3 hybridized.

$$:\ddot{F}-\ddot{O}-\ddot{O}-\ddot{F}:$$

Formal charge: 0   0   0   0
Oxidation state: -1 $+1$ $+1$ -1

Oxidation states are more useful. We are forced to assign $+1$ as the oxidation state for oxygen. Oxygen is very electronegative, and $+1$ is not a stable oxidation state for this element. **39. a.** $BaCl_2(s) + H_2SO_4(aq) \rightarrow BaSO_4(s) + 2HCl(g)$; **b.** $BrF(s) + H_2O(l) \rightarrow HF(aq) + HOBr(aq)$; **c.** $SiO_2(s) + 4HF(aq) \rightarrow SiF_4(g) + 2H_2O(l)$ **41.** ClO^- can oxide NH_3 to the somewhat toxic N_2H_4. **43. a.** IO_4^-; **b.** IO_3^-; **c.** IF_2^-; **d.** IF_4^-; **e.** IF_6^- **45.** XeF_2 can react with oxygen and water to produce explosive xenon oxides and oxy-fluorides. **47.** Release of Sr is probably more harmful. Xe is chemically unreactive. Strontium is in the same family as calcium and could be absorbed and concentrated in the body in a fashion similar to Ca. This puts the radioactive Sr in the bones, and red blood cells are produced in bone marrow. Xe would not be readily incorporated into the body. The chemical properties determine where a radioactive material may concentrate in the body or how easily it may be excreted. The length of time of exposure and the body part exposed to radiation significantly affects the health hazard. **49.** As the halogen atoms get larger, it becomes more difficult to fit three halogens around the small N.
51.

$$\left[:\ddot{O}=C=\ddot{N}:\right]^- \longleftrightarrow \left[:\ddot{\ddot{O}}-C\equiv N:\right]^- \longleftrightarrow \left[:O\equiv C-\ddot{\ddot{N}}:\right]^-$$

Formal charge: 0   0 -1 -1 0   0 $+1$ 0 -2

$$\left[:\ddot{C}=N=\ddot{O}:\right]^- \longleftrightarrow \left[:C\equiv N-\ddot{\ddot{O}}:\right]^- \longleftrightarrow \left[:\ddot{\ddot{C}}-N\equiv O:\right]^-$$

Formal charge: -2 $+1$ 0 -1 $+1$ -1 -3 $+1$ $+1$

All the resonance structures for fulminate involve greater formal charges than in cyanate, making fulminate more reactive (less stable). **53.** 32 kg bacterial tissue
55.

$$\left[\begin{array}{c}:\ddot{F}\quad\ddot{F}\quad\ddot{F}:\\ \diagdown\;|\;\diagup\\ Te\\ \diagup\quad\diagdown\\ :\ddot{F}\quad\quad\ddot{F}:\end{array}\right]^-$$

The lone pair of electrons around Te exerts a stronger repulsion than the bonding pairs, pushing the four square planar F's away from the lone pair.
57. exothermic **59.** $MgSO_4(s) \rightarrow Mg^{2+}(aq) + SO_4^{2-}(aq)$; $NH_4NO_3(s) \rightarrow NH_4^+(aq) + NO_3^-(aq)$ **61.** F, Cl, Br, or I; trigonal pyramid; $\approx 109.5°$
63. XeF_2

65. For the reaction

$$\overset{\displaystyle:\ddot{O}}{\underset{\displaystyle:\ddot{O}}{}}N-N=\ddot{O}: \longrightarrow NO_2 + NO$$

the activation energy must in some way involve the breaking of a nitrogen–nitrogen single bond. For the reaction

$$\overset{\displaystyle:\ddot{O}}{\underset{\displaystyle:\ddot{O}}{}}N-N=\ddot{O}: \longrightarrow O_2 + N_2O$$

at some point nitrogen–oxygen bonds must be broken. N—N single bonds (160 kJ/mol) are weaker than N—O single bonds (201 kJ/mol). In addition, resonance structures indicate that there is more double-bond character in the N—O bonds than in the N—N bond. Thus NO_2 and NO are preferred by kinetics because of the lower activation energy. **67. a.** NO; **b.** NO_2; **c.** $k_{cat}/k_{un} = 2.3$; **d.** $ClO(g) + O(g) \rightarrow O_2(g) + Cl(g)$; $O_3(g) + O(g) \rightarrow 2O_2(g)$; **e.** The Cl-catalyzed reaction is roughly 52 times faster (more efficient) than the NO-catalyzed reaction. **69.** 5.89 **71.** 20. g **73. a.** 287 kJ/mol; **b.** $[IF_2]^+$: V-shaped; sp^3; $[BF_4]^-$: tetrahedral; sp^3

Chapter 21

5. $Fe_2O_3(s) + 6 H_2C_2O_4(aq) \rightarrow 2 Fe(C_2O_4)_3^{3-}(aq) + 3 H_2O(l) + 6 H^+(aq)$; The oxalate anion forms a soluble complex ion with iron in rust (Fe_2O_3), which allows rust stains to be removed. **7.** No; both the *trans* or the *cis* forms of $Co(NH_3)_4Cl_2^+$ have mirror images that are superimposable. For the *cis* form, the mirror image only needs a 90° rotation to produce the original structure. Hence, neither the *trans* nor *cis* forms are optically active.

9. a. $CoCl_4^{2-}$ is an example of a weak-field case having three unpaired electrons.

small Δ

b. CN^- is a strong field ligand so $Co(CN)_6^{3-}$ will be a low-spin case having zero unpaired electrons.

large Δ

11. At high altitudes, the oxygen content of air is lower, so less oxyhemoglobin is formed which diminishes the transport of oxygen in the blood. A serious illness called high-altitude sickness can result from the decrease of O_2 in the blood. High altitude acclimatization is the phenomena that occurs in the human body in response to the lower amounts of oxyhemoglobin in the blood. This response is to produce more hemoglobin, and, hence, increase the oxyhemoglobin in the blood. High-altitude acclimatization takes several weeks to take hold for people moving from lower altitudes to higher altitudes. **13. a.** Ni: $[Ar]4s^23d^8$; **b.** Cd: $[Kr]5s^24d^{10}$; **c.** Zr: $[Kr]5s^24d^2$; **d.** Os: $[Xe]6s^24f^{14}5d^6$ **15. a.** Ti: $[Ar]4s^23d^2$; Ti^{2+}: $[Ar]3d^2$; Ti^{4+}: $[Ne]3s^23p^6$ or $[Ar]$; **b.** Re: $[Xe]6s^24f^{14}5d^5$; Re^{2+}: $[Xe]4f^{14}5d^5$; Re^{3+}: $[Xe]4f^{14}5d^4$; **c.** Ir: $[Xe]6s^24f^{14}5d^7$; Ir^{2+}: $[Xe]4f^{14}5d^7$; Ir^{3+}: $[Xe]4f^{14}5d^6$ **17. a.** Fe^{3+}: $[Ar]3d^5$; **b.** Ag^+: $[Kr]4d^{10}$; **c.** Ni^{2+}: $[Ar]3d^8$; **d.** Cr^{3+}: $[Ar]3d^3$ **19. a.** molybdenum(IV) sulfide, molybdenum(VI) oxide; **b.** MoS_2, $+4$; MoO_3, $+6$; $(NH_4)_2 Mo_2O_7$, $+6$; $(NH_4)_6Mo_7O_{24} \cdot 4H_2O$, $+6$ **21.** The lanthanide elements are located just before the $5d$ transition metals. The lanthanide contraction is the steady decrease in the atomic radii of the lanthanide elements when going from left to right across the periodic table. As a result of the lanthanide contraction, the sizes of the $4d$ and $5d$ elements are very similar. This leads to a greater similarity in the chemistry of the $4d$ and $5d$ elements in a given vertical group. **23.** If rain is imminent, the large amount of water vapor in the air would cause the reaction to shift to the right. The indicator would take on the color of the pink $CoCl_2 \cdot 6H_2O$.   **25.** Test tube 1: added Cl^- reacts with Ag^+ to form the silver chloride precipitate. The net ionic equation is $Ag^+(aq) + Cl^-(aq) \rightarrow AgCl(s)$. Test tube 2: added NH_3 reacts with Ag^+ ions to form the soluble complex ion $Ag(NH_3)_2^+$. As this complex ion forms, Ag^+ is removed from the solution, which causes the $AgCl(s)$ to dissolve. When enough NH_3 is added, then all of the silver chloride precipitate will dissolve. The equation is $AgCl(s) + 2NH_3(aq) \rightarrow Ag(NH_3)_2^+(aq) + Cl^-(aq)$. Test tube 3: added H^+ reacts with the weak base NH_3 to form NH_4^+. As NH_3 is removed, Ag^+ ions are released to solution, which can then react with Cl^- to reform $AgCl(s)$. The equations are $Ag(NH_3)_2^+(aq) + 2H^+(aq) \rightarrow Ag^+(aq) + 2NH_4^+(aq)$ and $Ag^+(aq) + Cl^-(aq) \rightarrow AgCl(s)$.   **27.** $[Co(NH_3)_6]I_3$: 3 mol AgI; $[Pt(NH_3)_4I_2]I_2$: 2 mol AgI; $Na_2[PtI_6]$: 0 mol AgI; $[Cr(NH_3)_4I_2]I$: 1 mol AgI.   **29. a.** pentaamminechlororuthenium(III) ion; **b.** hexacyanoferrate(II) ion; **c.** tris(ethylenediamine)manganese(II) ion; **d.** pentaamminenitrocobalt(III) ion   **31. a.** hexaamminecobalt(II) chloride; **b.** hexaaquacobalt(III) iodide; **c.** potassiumtetrachloro-platinate(II); **d.** potassium hexachloroplatinate(II); **e.** pentaamminechlorocobalt(III) chloride; **f.** triamminetrinitrocobalt(III)   **33. a.** $K_2[CoCl_4]$; **b.** $[Pt(H_2O)(CO)_3]Br_2$; **c.** $Na_3[Fe(CN)_2(C_2O_4)_2]$; **d.** $[Cr(NH_3)_3Cl(H_2NCH_2CH_2NH_2)]I_2$

35. a.

cis   *trans*

b.

cis   *trans*

c.

cis   *trans*

d.

$en = N\frown N = NH_2CH_2CH_2NH_2$

37.

and

39. SCN^-, NO_2^-, and OCN^- can form linkage isomers; all are able to bond to the metal ion in two different ways.   **41.** $Cr(acac)_3$ and *cis*-$Cr(acac)_2(H_2O)_2$ are optically active.

43. a. Fe^{2+}

High spin   Low spin

b. Fe^{3+} **c.** Ni^{2+}

High spin

45. weak field   **47. a.** 0; **b.** 2; **c.** 2   **49.** $[Co(CN)_6]^{3-} < [Co(en)_3]^{3+} < [Co(H_2O)_6]^{3+} < [CoI_6]^{3-}$ **51.** The violet complex ion absorbs yellow-green light ($\lambda \approx 570$ nm), the yellow complex ion absorbs blue light ($\lambda \approx 450$ nm), and the green complex ion absorbs red light ($\lambda \approx 650$ nm). The violet complex ion is $Cr(H_2O)_6^{3+}$, the yellow complex ion is $Cr(NH_3)_6^{3+}$, and the green complex ion is $Cr(H_2O)_4Cl_2^+$.   **53.** $CoBr_4^{2-}$ is a tetrahedral complex ion, while $CoBr_6^{4-}$ is an octahedral complex ion. Since tetrahedral d-orbital splitting is less than one-half the octahedral d-orbital splitting, the octahedral complex ion ($CoBr_6^{4-}$) will absorb higher-energy light, which will have a shorter wavelength than 3.4×10^{-6} m ($E = hc/\lambda$).   **55.** 5   **57. a.** -11 kJ; **b.** $\Delta H^\circ = 172.5$ kJ; $\Delta S^\circ = 176$ J/K; $T > 980$. K   **59.** $8CN^-(aq) + 4Ag(s) + O_2(g) + 2H_2O(l) \rightarrow 4Ag(CN)_2^-(aq) + 4OH^-(aq)$ **61.** $[Cr(NH_3)_5I]I_2$; octahedral   **63.** $Hg^{2+}(aq) + 2I^-(aq) \rightarrow HgI_2(s)$, orange precipitate; $HgI_2(s) + 2I^-(aq) \rightarrow HgI_4^{2-}(aq)$, soluble complex ion   **65. a.** 2; **b.** 3; **c.** 4; **d.** 4   **67. a.** optical isomerism

b.

69. Octahedral Cr^{2+} complexes should be used. Cr^{2+}: [Ar]$3d^4$; High-spin (weak-field) Cr^{2+} complexes have four unpaired electrons and low-spin (strong-field) Cr^{2+} complexes have two unpaired electrons. Ni^{2+}: [Ar]$3d^8$; Octahedral Ni^{2+} complexes will always have two unpaired electrons, whether high or low spin. Therefore, Ni^{2+} complexes cannot be used to distinguish weak- from strong-field ligands by examining magnetic properties. Alternatively, the ligand field strengths can be measured using visible spectra. Either Cr^{2+} or Ni^{2+} complexes can be used for this method.   **71.** $Pb(OH)_2$ will not form since Q is less than K_{sp}.   **73.** 60   **75.** $Ni^{2+} = d^8$; If A and B produced very similar crystal fields, the complex *trans*-$[NiA_2B_4]^{2+}$ would give an octahedral crystal field diagram:

This is paramagnetic. Because the complex ion is diamagnetic, ligands A and B must produce different crystal fields resulting in a unique d-orbital splitting diagram.   **77. a.** -0.26 V; **b.** From standard reduction potentials, Co^{3+} ($\mathscr{E}^\circ = 1.82$ V) is a much stronger oxidizing agent than $Co(en)_3^{3+}$ ($\mathscr{E}^\circ = -0.26$ V); **c.** In aqueous solution, Co^{3+} forms the hydrated transition metal complex, $Co(H_2O)_6^{3+}$. In both complexes, $Co(H_2O)_6^{3+}$ and $Co(en)_3^{3+}$, cobalt exists as Co^{3+}, which has 6 d electrons. If we assume a strong-field case for each complex ion, then the d-orbital splitting diagram for each has the six electrons paired in the lower-energy t_{2g} orbitals. When each complex ion gains an electron, the electron enters the higher-energy e_g orbitals. Since en is a stronger-field ligand than H_2O, then the d-orbital splitting is larger for $Co(en)_3^{3+}$, and it takes more energy to add an electron to $Co(en)_3^{3+}$ than to $Co(H_2O)_6^{3+}$. Therefore, it is more favorable for $Co(H_2O)_6^{3+}$ to gain an electron than for $Co(en)_3^{3+}$ to gain an electron.   **79.** No, since in all three cases six bonds are formed between Ni^{2+} and nitrogen. So ΔH values should be similar. ΔS° for formation of the complex ion is most negative for $6NH_3$ molecules reacting with a metal ion (7 independent species become 1). For penten reacting with a metal ion, 2 independent species become 1, so ΔS° is the least negative. Thus the chelate effect occurs because the more bonds a chelating agent can form to the metal, the more favorable $\Delta S°$ is for the formation of the complex ion, and the larger the formation constant.

81.

$$\begin{array}{ll} \underline{\quad} & d_{z^2} \\ \underline{\quad}\ \underline{\quad} & d_{x^2-y^2},\ d_{xy} \\ \underline{\quad}\ \underline{\quad} & d_{xz},\ d_{yz} \end{array}$$

83. Place the *trans* NH_3 ligands on the z axis with the CN^- ligands oriented as indicated in the following diagram. Since CN^- produces a much stronger crystal field, the diagram will most resemble that of a square planar complex:

$$\begin{array}{ll} d_{x^2-y^2} & \underline{\quad} \\ d_{xy} & \text{\Large ⇈} \\ d_{z^2} & \text{\Large ⇈} \\ d_{xz} & \text{\Large ⇈}\ \text{\Large ⇈}\ d_{yz} \end{array}$$

85. a. +6; $[Ar]3d^2$; **b.** 0.0496 L N_2

Chapter 22

1. a. 1-sec-butylpropane

$$CH_3\overset{\overset{\displaystyle CH_2CH_2CH_3}{|}}{CH}CH_2CH_3$$

3-methylhexane is correct.

c. 2-ethylpentane

$$CH_3\overset{\overset{\displaystyle |}{CH}}{C}H_2CH_2CH_3$$
$$\overset{\displaystyle |}{CH_2CH_3}$$

3-methylhexane is correct.

e. 3-methylhexane

$$CH_3CH_2\overset{\overset{\displaystyle |}{CH}}{CH}CH_2CH_2CH_3$$
$$\overset{\displaystyle |}{CH_3}$$

b. 4-methylhexane

$$CH_3CH_2CH_2\overset{\overset{\displaystyle CH_3}{|}}{CH}CH_2CH_3$$

3-methylhexane is correct.

d. 1-ethyl-1-methylbutane

$$\overset{\displaystyle CH_2CH_3}{\underset{\displaystyle CH_3}{\overset{\displaystyle |}{\underset{\displaystyle |}{CH}}}}CH_2CH_2CH_3$$

3-methylhexane is correct.

f. 4-ethylpentane

$$CH_3CH_2CH_2\overset{\overset{\displaystyle |}{CH}}{CH}CH_3$$
$$\overset{\displaystyle |}{CH_2CH_3}$$

3-methylhexane is correct.

All six of these are the same compound. They only differ from each other by rotations about one or more carbon-carbon single bonds. Only one isomer of C_7H_{16} is present in all of these names, 3-methylhexane.

3. a.

$$CH_3\overset{\overset{\displaystyle |}{CH}}{CH}CH_3$$
$$\overset{\displaystyle |}{CH_2CH_3}$$

The longest chain is 4 carbons long. The correct name is 2-methylbutane.

b.

$$CH_3CH_2CH_2CH_2\overset{\overset{\displaystyle I}{|}}{\underset{\displaystyle |}{C}}\overset{\displaystyle CH_3}{\overset{\displaystyle |}{-}CH_2}$$
$$\overset{\displaystyle |}{CH_3}$$

The longest chain is 7 carbons long and we would start the numbering system at the other end for lowest possible numbers. The correct name is 3-iodo-3-methylheptane.

c.

$$CH_3CH_2CH=\overset{\overset{\displaystyle CH_3}{|}}{C}-CH_3$$

This compound cannot exhibit *cis*–*trans* isomerism since one of the double bonded carbons has the same two groups (CH_3) attached. The numbering system should also start at the other end to give the double bond the lowest possible number. 2-methyl-2-pentene is correct.

d.

$$CH_3\overset{\overset{\displaystyle Br}{|}}{CH}\overset{\overset{\displaystyle OH}{|}}{CH}CH_3$$

The OH functional group gets the lowest number. 3-bromo-2-butanol is correct.

5. Hydrocarbons are nonpolar substances exhibiting only London dispersion forces. Size and shape are the two most important structural features relating to the strength of London dispersion forces. For size, the bigger the molecule (the larger the molar mass), the stronger the London dispersion forces and the higher the boiling point. For shape, the more branching present in a compound, the weaker the London dispersion forces and the lower the boiling point.

7. The correct order of strength is polyhydrocarbon < polyester < polyamide. The difference in strength is related to the types of intermolecular forces present. All of these polymers have London dispersion forces. However, polyhydrocarbons only have London dispersion forces. The polar ester group in polyesters and the polar amide group in polyamides give rise to additional dipole forces. The polyamide has the ability to form relatively strong hydrogen bonding interactions, hence why it would form the strongest fibers.

9. a.

b.

c.

d.

e.

f.

g.

11. a. A polyester forms when an alcohol functional group reacts with a carboxylic acid functional group. The monomer for a homopolymer polyester must have an alcohol functional group and a carboxylic acid functional group present in the structure. **b.** A polyamide forms when an amine functional group reacts with a carboxylic acid functional group. For a copolymer polyamide, one monomer would have at least two amine functional groups present and the other monomer would have at least two carboxylic acid functional groups present. For polymerization to occur, each monomer must have two reactive functional groups present. **c.** To form an addition polymer, a carbon-carbon double bond must be present. To form a polyester, the monomer would need the alcohol and carboxylic acid functional groups present. To form a polyamide, the monomer would need the amine and carboxylic acid functional groups present. The two possibilities are for the monomer to have a carbon-carbon double bond, an alcohol functional group, and a carboxylic acid functional group all present, or to have a carbon-carbon double bond, an amine functional group, and a carboxylic acid functional group present.

13. $CH_3{-}CH_2{-}CH_2{-}CH_2{-}CH_2{-}CH_3$

$$CH_3{-}\underset{\underset{CH_3}{|}}{CH}{-}CH_2{-}CH_2{-}CH_3$$

$$CH_3{-}CH_2{-}\underset{\underset{CH_3}{|}}{CH}{-}CH_2{-}CH_3$$

$$CH_3{-}\underset{\underset{CH_3}{|}}{\overset{\overset{CH_3}{|}}{C}}{-}CH_2{-}CH_3$$

$$CH_3{-}\underset{\underset{CH_3}{|}}{CH}{-}\underset{\underset{CH_3}{|}}{CH}{-}CH_3$$

15. a.
$$CH_3\underset{\underset{CH_3}{|}}{\overset{\overset{CH_3}{|}}{C}H}CH_2CH_2CH_2CH_2CH_3$$
2-methylheptane

$$CH_3CH_2\underset{\underset{CH_3}{|}}{CH}CH_2CH_2CH_2CH_3$$
3-methylheptane

$$CH_3CH_2CH_2\underset{\underset{CH_3}{|}}{CH}CH_2CH_2CH_3$$
4-methylheptane

b.
$$CH_3{-}\underset{\underset{CH_3}{|}}{\overset{\overset{CH_3}{|}}{C}}{-}\underset{\underset{CH_3}{|}}{\overset{\overset{CH_3}{|}}{C}}{-}CH_3$$
2,2,3,3-tetramethylbutane

17. a.
$$CH_3\underset{\underset{CH_3}{|}}{CH}CH_3$$

b.
$$CH_3\underset{\underset{CH_3}{|}}{CH}CH_2CH_3$$

c.
$$CH_3\underset{\underset{CH_3}{|}}{CH}CH_2CH_2CH_3$$

d.
$$CH_3\underset{\underset{CH_3}{|}}{CH}CH_2CH_2CH_2CH_3$$

19. a. $CH_3CH_2{-}CH{-}CH_2CH_2CH_3$
$$\underset{\underset{CH_3}{|}}{\overset{|}{CH_2}}{-}CH{-}CH_3$$

b.
$$CH_3{-}\underset{\underset{CH_3}{|}}{\overset{\overset{CH_3}{|}}{C}}{-}CH_2{-}\underset{\underset{CH_3}{|}}{CH}{-}CH_3$$

c. $CH_3{-}CH{-}CH_2CH_2CH_3$
$$CH_3{-}\underset{\underset{CH_3}{|}}{\overset{|}{C}}{-}CH_3$$

d. 4-ethyl-2-methylheptane; 2,2,3-trimethylhexane

21. a. 2,2,4-trimethylhexane: **b.** 5-methylnonane; **c,** 2,2,4,4-tetramethylpentane; **d.** 3-ethyl-3-methyloctane

23. $CH_3{-}CH_2{-}CH_2{-}CH_3$;

$$\begin{array}{c} H \quad H \\ | \quad\;\; | \\ H{-}C{-}C{-}H \\ | \quad\;\; | \\ H{-}C{-}C{-}H \\ | \quad\;\; | \\ H \quad H \end{array}$$

Each carbon is bonded to four other atoms.

25. a. 1-butene; **b.** 4-methyl-2-hexene; **c.** 2,5-dimethyl-3-heptene

27. a. $CH_3CH_2CH{=}CHCH_2CH_3$; **b.** $CH_3CH{=}CHCH{=}CHCH_2CH_3$;

c. $CH_3\underset{\underset{CH_3}{|}}{CH}CH{=}CHCH_2CH_2CH_2CH_3$

29. a. **b.** **c.** **d.**

31. a. 1,3-dichlorobutane; **b.** 1,1,1-trichlorobutane; **c.** 2,3-dichloro-2,4-dimethylhexane; **d.** 1,2-difluoroethane; **33.** $CH_2Cl{-}CH_2Cl$, 1-2-dichloroethane: There is free rotation about the C—C single bond that doesn't lead to different compounds. $CHCl{=}CHCl$, 1-2-dichloroethene: There is no rotation about the C=C double bond. This creates the *cis* and *trans* isomers, which are different compounds. **35.** [25], compounds b and c; [27], all compounds

37. $CH_2{=}CHCH_2CH_2CH_3$ $CH_3CH{=}CHCH_2CH_3$

$$CH_2{=}\underset{\underset{CH_3}{|}}{C}CH_2CH_3 \qquad CH_3\underset{\underset{CH_3}{|}}{C}{=}CHCH_3$$

$$CH_3\underset{\underset{CH_3}{|}}{CH}CH{=}CH_2$$

39.

41.

43. a.

65. a.

b.

c. No reaction

d.

e.

f.

45. a. 3 monochloro isomers of *n*-pentane; **b.** 4 monochloro isomers of 2-methylbutane; **c.** 3 monochloro isomers of 2,4-dimethylpentane; **d.** 4 monochloro isomers of methylcyclobutane **47. a.** ketone; **b.** aldehyde; **c.** carboxylic acid; **d.** amine

49. a.

b. 5 carbons in ring and the carbon in —CO$_2$H: sp^2; the other two carbons: sp^3; **c.** 24 sigma bonds, 4 pi bonds **51. a.** 3-chloro-1-butanol, primary: **b.** 3-methyl-3-hexanol, tertiary; **c.** 2-methylcyclopentanol, secondary **53.** 1-pentanol; 2-pentanol; 3-pentanol; 2-methyl-1-butanol; 2-methyl-2-butanol; 3-methyl-2-butanol; 3-methyl-1-butanol; 2,2-dimethyl-1-propanol; 6 ethers **55. a.** 4,5-dichloro-3-hexanone; **b.** 2,3-dimethylpentanal; **c.** 3-methylbenzaldehyde or *m*-methylbenzaldehyde **57. a.** 4-chlorobenzoic acid or *p*-chlorobenzoic acid; **b.** 3-ethyl-2-methylhexanoic acid; **c.** methanoic acid (common name = formic acid) **59.** Only statement d is false.

2-butenal: .

The formula of 2-butenal is C$_4$H$_6$O, while the ether has a formula of C$_4$H$_8$O.

61. a. CH$_3$CH$_2$CH$_2$CH$_3$

b.

c.

+ HCl

d. C$_4$H$_8$(g) + 6O$_2$(g) $\longrightarrow$ 4CO$_2$(g) + 4H$_2$O(g)

63. For the iron-catalyzed reaction, one of the *ortho* or *para* hydrogens in benzene is replaced by chlorine. When an iron catalyst is not present, then the benzene hydrogens are unreactive, which is seen for the light-catalyzed reaction where one of the methyl hydrogens is replaced by chlorine.

67. a. CH$_3$CH=CH$_2$ + Br$_2$ $\rightarrow$ CH$_3$CHBrCH$_2$Br;

b.

c.

d.

69. a.

b.

71. CFCl=CF$_2$

73.

75.

77.

H_2N—⬡—NH_2 and HO_2C—⬡(CO_2H, HO_2C, CO_2H)

79. Divinylbenzene inserts itself into two adjacent polymer chains and bonds them together. The chains cannot move past each other because of the crosslinks making the polymer more rigid. **81. a.** The polymer from 1,2-diaminoethane and terephthalic acid is stronger because of the possibility of hydrogen bonding between chains. **b.** The polymer of

HO—⬡—CO_2H

is more rigid because the chains are stiffer due to the rigid benzene rings in the chains. **c.** Polyacetylene is $nHC\equiv CH \rightarrow -(CH=CH)_n$. Polyacetylene is more rigid because the double bonds in the chains make the chains stiffer. **83. a.** serine; tyrosine; threonine; **b.** aspartic acid; glutamic acid; **c.** histidine; lysine; arginine; tryptophan; **d.** glutamine; asparagine **85. a.** aspartic acid and phenylalanine; **b.** Aspartame contains the methyl ester of phenylalanine. This ester can hydrolyze to form methanol, $R-CO_2CH_3 + H_2O \rightleftharpoons RCO_2H + CH_3OH$.

87.

$H_2NCHC-NHCHCO_2H$ (ser–ala) with CH_2, OH and CH_3

$H_2NCHC-NHCHCO_2H$ (ala–ser) with CH_3 and CH_2, OH

89. a. Six tetrapeptides are possible. From NH_2 to CO_2H end: phe–phe–gly–gly, gly–gly–phe–phe, gly–phe–phe–gly, phe–gly–gly–phe, phe–gly–phe–gly, gly–phe–gly–phe **b.** Twelve tetrapeptides are possible. From NH_2 to CO_2H end: phe–phe–gly–ala, phe–phe–ala–gly, phe–gly–phe–ala, phe–gly–ala–phe, phe–ala–phe–gly, phe–ala–gly–phe, gly–phe–phe–ala, gly–phe–ala–phe, gly–ala–phe–phe, ala–phe–phe–gly, ala–phe–gly–phe, ala–gly–phe–phe **91.** Ionic: his, lys, or arg with asp or glu; hydrogen bonding: ser, glu, tyr, his, arg, asn, thr, asp, gln, or lys with any amino acid; covalent: cys with cys; London dispersion: all amino acids with nonpolar R groups (gly, ala, pro, phe, ile, trp, met, leu, val); dipole–dipole: tyr, thr, and ser with each other **93.** Glutamic acid has a polar R group and valine has a nonpolar R group. The change in polarity of the R groups could affect the tertiary structure of hemoglobin and affect the ability of hemoglobin to bond to oxygen.

95.

D-Ribose (ring structure with CH_2OH, H, OH, OH)

D-Mannose (ring structure with CH_2OH, H, OH, HO, OH, H)

97. aldohexose: glucose, mannose, galactose; aldopentose: ribose, arabinose; ketohexose: fructose; ketopentose; ribulose **99.** They differ in the orientation of a hydroxy group on a particular carbon. Starch is composed from α-D-glucose, and cellulose is composed from β-D-glucose.

101. The chiral carbons are marked with asterisks.

Isoleucine: $H_3C-C^*-CH_2CH_3$, $H_2N-C^*-CO_2H$, with H and H

Threonine: H_3C-C^*-OH, $H_2N-C^*-CO_2H$, with H and H

103.

$Br-C^*-CH=CH_2$ with Cl and H

is optically active. The chiral carbon is marked with an asterisk. **105.** C–C–A–G–A–T–A–T–G **107.** Uracil will H-bond to adenine.

Uracil ———— Adenine (hydrogen bonding diagram with Sugar labels)

109. a. glu: CTT, CTC; val: CAA, CAG, CAT, CAC; met: TAC; trp: ACC; phe: AAA, AAG; asp: CTA, CTG; **b.** ACC–CTT–AAA–TAC or ACC–CTC–AAA–TAC or ACC–CTT–AAG–TAC or ACC–CTC–AAG–TAC; **c.** four (see answer in part b); **d.** met–asp–phe **e.** TAC–CTA–AAG; TAC–CTA–AAA; TAC–CTG–AAA **111. a.** 2,3,5,6-tetramethyloctane; **b.** 2,2,3,5-tetramethylheptane; **c.** 2,3,4-trimethylhexane; **d.** 3-methyl-1-pentyne

113.

(dibenzo-p-dioxin structure with four Cl substituents and two O bridges)

There are many possibilities for isomers. Any structure with four chlorines replacing four hydrogens in any of the numbered positions would be an isomer; i.e., 1,2,3,4-tetrachloro-dibenzo-p-dioxin is a possible isomer. **115.** $-23°C$: CH_3-O-CH_3; $78.5°C$: CH_3-CH_2-OH **117.** Alcohols consist of two parts, the polar OH group and the nonpolar hydrocarbon chain attached to the OH group. As the length of the nonpolar hydrocarbon chain increases, the solubility of the alcohol decreases. In methyl alcohol (methanol), the polar OH group can override the effect of the nonpolar CH_3 group, and methyl alcohol is soluble in water. In stearyl alcohol, the molecule consists mostly of the long nonpolar hydrocarbon chain, so it is insoluble in water. **119.** n-hexane, 69°C; pentanal, 103°C; 1-pentanol, 137°C; butanoic acid, 164°C. **121.** 1-butene **123.** ethanoic acid **125.** In nylon, hydrogen-bonding interactions occur due to the presence of N—H bonds in the polymer. For a given polymer chain length, there are more N—H groups in nylon-46 as compared to nylon-6. Hence, nylon-46 forms a stronger polymer compared to nylon-6 due to the increased hydrogen-bonding interactions.

127. a.

H_2N—⬡—NH_2 and HO_2C—⬡—CO_2H

b. Repeating unit:

$(HN$—⬡—NHC(O)—⬡—C(O)$)_n$

The two polymers differ in the substitution pattern on the benzene rings. The Kevlar chain is straighter, and there is more efficient hydrogen bonding between Kevlar chains than between Nomex chains. **129. a.** The bond angles in the ring are about 60°. VSEPR predicts bond angles close to 109°. The bonding electrons are much closer together than they prefer, resulting in strong electron–electron repulsions. Thus ethylene oxide is unstable (reactive). **b.** The ring opens up during polymerization and the monomers link together through the formation of O—C bonds.

$-(O-CH_2CH_2-O-CH_2CH_2-O-CH_2CH_2)_n$

131. $H_2N-CH-CO_2H$ or $H_2N-CH-CO_2^-Na^+$

with $CH_2CH_2CO_2^-Na^+$ and $CH_2CH_2CO_2H$

The first structure is MSG, which is impossible for you to predict.   **133.** In the reaction, P—O and O—H bonds are broken and P—O and O—H bonds are formed. Thus $\Delta H \approx 0$. $\Delta S < 0$, since two molecules are going to form one molecule. Thus $\Delta G > 0$, not spontaneous.
135.

$$1.0\,M\,H^+:\quad H_3\overset{+}{N}-\underset{\underset{CH_3}{|}}{CH}-\overset{\overset{O}{\|}}{C}-OH;$$

$$1.0\,M\,OH^-:\quad H_2N-\underset{\underset{CH_3}{|}}{CH}-\overset{\overset{O}{\|}}{C}-O^-$$

137. Both ΔH and ΔS are positive values.   **139.** 6.07   **141. a.** No; the mirror image is superimposable.

b.

143.

$$HC\equiv C-C\equiv C-HC=C=CH-HC=CH-HC=CH-CH_2-\overset{\overset{O}{\|}}{C}-OH$$

13 12 11 10 9 8 7 6 5 4 3 2 1

145. a.

$$CH_3\underset{\underset{CH_3}{|}}{CH}CH_2CH_3$$

b.

$$CH_2=\underset{\underset{CH_3}{|}}{C}CH_3$$

c.

d. $CH_2=CHCH_3$

e. $\underset{\underset{OH}{|}}{CH_2}CH_2CH_2CH_2CH_3 \quad \underset{\underset{OH}{|}}{CH_2}\underset{\underset{CH_3}{|}}{CH}CH_2CH_3$

$$CH_3\underset{\underset{OH}{|}}{CH}\underset{\underset{CH_3}{|}}{CH}CH_2 \quad CH_2-\underset{\underset{CH_3}{|}}{\overset{\overset{CH_3}{|}}{C}}-CH_3$$

147.

149. a. The temperature of the rubber band increases when it is stretched; **b.** exothermic (heat is released); **c.** As the chains are stretched, they line up more closely resulting in stronger dispersion forces between the chains. Heat is released as the strength of the intermolecular forces increases. **d.** ΔG is positive and ΔS is negative; **e.** The structure of the stretched polymer chains is more ordered than in unstretched rubber. Disorder decreases as the rubber band is stretched.   **151.** 0.11%   **153.** 5   **155. a.** 37.50%; **b.** The hybridization changes from sp^2 to sp^3; **c.** 3,4-dimethyl-3-hexanol

Index

Succeed in College!

WALTER PAUK

Director, Reading Research Center
Cornell University

JOHN P. FIORE

·University of Illinois

Houghton Mifflin Company   **Boston**   **New York**

Contents

To the Student

This book was designed to help you achieve success, not only in this course, but throughout your college career. These five chapters were derived from the bestselling college study skills text, How to Study in College, by Professor Walter Pauk of Cornell University. The chapters present effective methods for mastering areas of interest to every student – managing time, taking good notes, learning from textbooks, and performing well on tests. More than one million students have used Walter Pauk's text. Now you can benefit from the Pauk approach to study skills.

Here's to your success in college – and beyond!

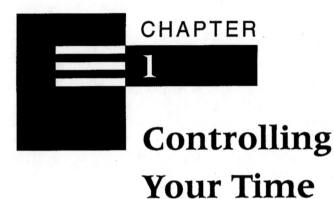

CHAPTER

1

Controlling Your Time

YESTERDAY **is a canceled check.**
TOMORROW **is a promissory note.**
TODAY **is ready cash. Use it!**

Anonymous

Time flies, but that's no reason for you to go through each day simply "winging it." Through conscientious use of time and common-sense planning, you can make the most of your day. This chapter ticks off the important elements of time management, including

- Mastering time
- Scheduling time to gain time
- Principles of scheduling
- Types of schedules
- Scheduling for students with jobs
- Tips for saving time
and finally
- Getting things done

Your success or failure in college depends directly on your use of time. If you use it wisely, you'll prosper. If you use it poorly, you'll fail in the job you came to do. The management of time is the number-one skill to master in college.

Anyone who has paid $30 an hour (50 cents a minute) for a plumber knows that time means money. Actually, time is worth far more than money. Time is life itself, and no price can be put on that. The preciousness of time has never been evoked more convincingly and more succinctly than in the final words of Elizabeth I (1533–1603), queen of England:

All my possessions for a moment of time.

MASTERING TIME

If you want to take control of your life, you must take control of your time. Golda Meir, a schoolteacher in Milwaukee, went on to become prime minister of Israel. Her success was due in part to how she dealt with time. She said, "I must govern the clock, not be governed by it." In order to be the master of time instead of its slave, you must have a *goal*, you must have a *plan*, and you must *take action*.

Formulating a Goal

Nothing will fortify your inner self more than setting personal goals. To succeed in almost anything, you must have a goal. You have to know what you want to be before you can become it, and if you don't know where you're going, you won't get there. Goal setting is not kid stuff. It's student power! It's adult power!

Successful people in all walks of life realize the importance of setting goals. Businesspeople put their goals in writing. They have to show their weekly, monthly, and yearly goals to their immediate supervisors. Even the president of a corporation has to write goals and submit them to the board of directors. Setting goals is almost instinctive behavior. Pioneers heading west painted "California or Bust" on their covered wagons. This slogan was not a magic carpet whisking them across the continent, but it was a constant reminder of their goal.

You *must* express your goal in writing, on a sheet of paper. Your goal should be more specific and less general than simply getting a college education. You need to formulate a clear notion of not only *what* you want in college and life but also *why* you want it. Writing is important. The act of writing will help you clarify your thoughts.

No matter what you want to become—a computer programmer, sales manager, a civil engineer, a teacher, a dentist, a journalist—put your goal in writing and work to achieve it. As a college student you will have to weather some very rough days, and at times things may seem to be falling apart. That's when you'll need a lifeline to hold onto. Focusing on your goal can give you the perspective and strength you need to keep going.

Making a Plan

A plan is the route or approach you want to take in order to reach your goal. A record sheet such as the one shown in Figure 1.1 will help you devise your plan.

On a separate sheet of paper jot down all that comes to mind regarding your goal. Summarize these jottings in a brief statement, and transfer that statement to block 1 in Figure 1.1.

Keeping your goal in mind, on a separate sheet jot down the steps that you must take to reach your goal. Select from your jottings the steps that lead directly to your goal, and list them in block 2 in Figure 1.1.

On another separate sheet list positive factors that will help you accomplish your goal. It helps a lot to know what's working for you. Once you've identified these factors, add them to block 3.

You need to face reality, so think about the problems and obstacles that you have to overcome to reach your goal. List them in block 4.

With your record sheet in hand, take the next step of talking to your academic adviser as well as to a counselor in the career center. Don't underestimate the value of thinking about, writing about, and discussing your goal and plan. Get as much discussion and feedback as you can; then modify your plan if necessary. You will end up with a plan for your future that is realistic and attainable.

Taking Action

Among the saddest words in life are "It might have been." If you take no action, your goals and plans will amount to nothing. Taking action, however, is more easily said than done. In order to take action, you will need a large dose of self-discipline. Adapting to military discipline might even be easier than imposing discipline on yourself, yet self-discipline is what you must have if you are to take the action required to implement your plans. For instance, let's say your particular goal is to excel in your biology course. You think you

1

My Goal

_____

_____

_____

_____

_____

_____

_____

2

Positive Factors

1. _____

2. _____

3. _____

4. _____

5. _____

6. _____

7. _____

3

Steps Leading to My Goal

1. _____

2. _____

3. _____

4. _____

5. _____

6. _____

7. _____

4

Obstacles

1. _____

2. _____

3. _____

4. _____

5. _____

6. _____

7. _____

FIGURE 1.1 Record Sheet for Planning

may have trouble with some of the terms and concepts, so you've decided to seek the assistance of a department tutor. The department identifies the tutor for you, and now it's up to you to contact him or her. If you procrastinate here, all the time and thinking that went into your plan will have been wasted. Taking action simply means taking those steps necessary to complete your plan. When you identify a task, you must go ahead and do it.

SCHEDULING TIME TO GAIN TIME

Lee Iacocca, president of Chrysler Corporation, who became internationally famous as the man who saved the company from almost certain bankruptcy in 1981, made this observation: "I'm constantly amazed by the number of people who can't seem to control their own schedules." The way we use time—or waste it—is largely a matter of habit. It is not easy to change old habits, but if they are bad habits, they put a ceiling on achievement. For example, a professional baseball player with a poor batting stance can become a good hitter, up to a point. Unless he improves his stance, however, progress behind that point is doubtful. To change and begin almost all over again—to break a bad habit and make a good one—takes determination and will, but the decision to change brings the chance for success. If you find that you need more time for all your studies and other activities, consider scheduling your time in order to gain time.

Where Does All the Time Go?

In an effort to find out specifically how he spent his time, a student kept a diary of his daily activities for one week. He found that his "ten-minute" coffee break was nearer forty minutes. Figure 1.2 shows one page of his diary and contains an analysis that demonstrates how the student could avoid dribbling away minutes and save hours for both recreation and study. A time log, or daily diary, is a valuable tool for getting control of time. Without a time log, you really don't know how you are spending your time. Try keeping one for a week or two.

Reasons for Scheduling

How much spare time do you have every day? The student whose activities record appears in Figure 1.2 would probably answer, "None. There are not enough hours in the day for all the things I have to do." That's the way things may seem to you too, but it's not necessarily the way they are.

Time		Time	Activity - Description
Start	End	Used	
7:45	8:15	:30	Dress
8:15	8:40	:25	Breakfast
8:40	9:00	:20	Nothing
9:00	10:00	1:00	Psychology - Lecture
10:00	10:40	:40	Coffee - Talking
10:40	11:00	:20	Nothing
11:00	12:00	1:00	Economics - Lecture
12:00	12:45	:45	Lunch
12:45	2:00	1:15	Reading - Magazine
2:00	4:00	2:00	Biology Lab
4:00	5:30	1:30	Recreation - Volleyball
5:30	6:00	:30	Nothing
6:00	7:00	1:00	Dinner
7:00	8:00	1:00	Nap
8:00	8:50	:50	Study - Statistics
8:50	9:20	:30	Break
9:20	10:00	:40	Study - Statistics
10:00	10:50	:50	Chat with Bob
10:50	11:30	:40	Study - Accounting
11:30	11:45	:15	Ready for bed
11:45	7:45	8:00	Sleep.

Paste 3 X 5 cards on mirror: laws of economics; psychological terms; statistical formulas. Study while brushing teeth, etc.

Look over textbook assignment and previous lecture notes to establish continuity for today's psychology lecture.

Break too long and too soon after breakfast. Work on psychology notes just taken; also look over economics assignment.

Rework the lecture notes on economics while still fresh in mind. Also, look over biology assignment to recall the objective of the coming lab.

Use this time to read a magazine or newspaper.

Not a good idea. Better finish work, then get a good night's sleep.

Break is too long.

Good as a reward if basic work is done.

Insufficient time allotted, but better than no time.

While brushing teeth, study the 3 X 5 cards. Replace cards that have been mastered with new ones.

FIGURE 1.2   Record of One Day's Activities and Suggestions for Making Better Use of Time

TABLE 1.1   Time Spent by Students in a Typical Week

Activity	Hours Spent
Sleep	49.3
Study	19.8
Classes and labs	18.7
Meals	10.7
Total	98.5

Source: From "College Students Report on the Use of Time," by Arthur A. Dole in *The Personnel and Guidance Journal* 37 (May 1959), p. 635. Reprinted by permission of American Association for Counseling & Development.

Table 1.1 shows how students at one university spent time in four main activities during a typical week. The students spent 98.5 hours sleeping, studying, attending classes and labs, and eating their meals. When you subtract that total from 168 (the number of hours in a week), you have 69.5 hours unaccounted for—almost ten hours a day.

You can gain extra time in only two ways: (1) by doing a job in less time than usual, (2) by using small blocks of time that you usually waste. The first way requires you to study more efficiently, and this book provides a great many techniques to help you do just that. The second way requires you to schedule your time, and this chapter offers a number of suggestions.

Although some people believe it's a waste of time to make a schedule, planning actually *saves* time and energy. Sure, it takes time to schedule your time, but the time you spend making a schedule is returned to you several times over when you work—and relax—according to your schedule. Spending a little time to make a schedule saves a lot of time that you would otherwise waste.

Some people feel that maintaining a schedule will make robots or slaves of them. Just the opposite is true. The people you see dashing madly from class to library to gym, or eating a junk-food lunch on the run, are slaves to time because they are not in control of their time. The student who schedules time, who decides how it will be used, is the master of time rather than its slave.

Some people won't schedule their time because they want to be "flexible." But a disorganized person wastes so much time that there really isn't any time left to be flexible with. Scheduling, however, frees up time for a variety of activities, and flexibility can certainly be built into a schedule.

Scheduling actually gives you more time, makes you the master of your time, and provides the flexibility that *you* want. Here are some additional benefits of scheduling.

1. *Gets you started.*   You know how hard it is to get started. Often a well-planned schedule can be the external force that gives you a needed shove.

2. *Prevents avoidance of disliked subjects.*   The mind can play tricks. Without actually deciding to do so, you can keep yourself from doing something you don't like by occupying yourself with favorite subjects.

3. *Monitors the slackening-off process.*   By apportioning time properly, you can keep yourself from slackening off as the semester wears on.

4. *Eliminates the wrong type of cramming.*   If cramming just before exams is to be effective, the original studying and learning must take place day by day.

5. *Makes studying enjoyable.*   When done without the pressure of time, studying and learning can be intensely interesting.

6. *Promotes cumulative review.*   Sandwiching in short review periods is the best way to retain knowledge as well as to prepare for exams. It is less fatiguing and more effective to review a subject in four *distributed* thirty-minute sessions than in a single *massed* two-hour session.

7. *Frees the mind.*   To keep from forgetting details, you may think and rethink them. This often leads to a tense feeling of pressure and confusion. Putting things to do on paper takes them off the mental treadmill.

8. *Controls the study break.*   Rewarding yourself with a ten-minute break when you finish a scheduled block of study helps minimize clock watching. During short breaks, stand up, walk around, or just stare out the window, but keep in mind the subject you're studying. Then you won't need a warm-up period when you resume studying.

9. *Keeps you from overlooking recreation.*   Physical and social activities are needed for a well-balanced personality, good health, and efficient study. On the other hand, allowing extracurricular activities to outweigh studies probably accounts for more failures in college than anything else.

10. *Helps raise your recreational efficiency.*   One of the saddest wastes of time and pleasure is to mix study time and recreation time—that is, when studying, to keep thinking how nice it would be to be playing some game; and when playing, to think about all the studying that needs to be done.

11. *Regulates daily living.*   Without a plan to guide you, assignments are bound to pile up. When they do, you lose control, and your daily living

is thrown into chaos. With a schedule, even weekends and holidays can be free from worry.

PRINCIPLES OF SCHEDULING

Just as there are basic rules for driving a car, no matter how long or short a trip you are taking, so there are basic rules for making a study schedule. The following list includes general principles that apply to all study schedules.

1. *Eliminate dead hours.* Make each block of one hour a productive unit. Some of the most important lessons of our lives are learned in less time.

2. *Use daylight hours.* Research shows that each hour used for study during the day is equal to one and a half hours at night.

3. *Study before recitation-type classes.* For a course in which you recite and discuss, it is an advantage to study just before class. The material will be fresh in your mind.

4. *Study after lecture-type classes.* For a lecture course, retention and understanding are aided by a review of your lecture notes immediately after class.

5. *List according to priorities.* By putting first things first, you are sure to get the most important things done on time.

6. *Avoid too much detail.* Packing a weekly schedule with too many details is a waste of time for two reasons. The time you take to make such a schedule could be better used in studying a subject directly. The chances of your following such a schedule are very slim.

7. *Know your sleep pattern.* We all have daily cycles of sleepiness and alertness. If your work, classes, and circumstances permit, sleep when you're sleepy and study when you're naturally alert.

8. *Discover how long to study.* The rule of thumb that you should study two hours for every hour in class is a rough guide at best. The time required varies from student to student and from subject to subject. Start out allowing two hours of study for every hour in class, but adjust the hours according to your experience, as you find out how long you need to master each assignment.

9. *Plan blocks of time.* Optimum efficiency is reached by planning in blocks of one hour: fifty minutes to study and ten minutes for a break.

10. *Allow time for sleep.* Your need for eight hours of sleep every night is supported by medical evidence. Make no mistake about it: The quality of your education depends on sufficient sleep.

11. *Eat well-balanced meals.*   Take time for good meals. Living on greasy foods or a low-protein diet most of the time is no way to treat your body and brain. Dietary deficiencies result in irritability, fatigue, and lack of pep.

12. *Double your time estimates, and start long jobs ahead of time.*   Most people tend to underestimate the amount of time they need for a project. To avoid discovering the hard way that you cannot bang out a 1500-word paper in three hours the evening before it is due, start ridiculously early, thus allowing yourself more time.

13. *Don't pack your schedule too tightly.*   Be precise, but leave room for last-minute problems that require your time.

14. *Make a plan for living, not merely for studying.*   After all, life, even in college, is many-sided, and its many sides must be recognized.

TYPES OF SCHEDULES

It is important to choose the type of schedule that fits your circumstances best. Some students work best with a detailed schedule; others work best with a brief list of things to do. Circumstances also influence the type of schedule you should make. There are on-campus students, commuting students, married students, employed students, night-class students, and part-time students, and each has different scheduling requirements. You should *adapt* the principles of schedule building to your personal circumstances, rather than *adopt* some ideal model that fits hardly anybody, let alone you.

The schedule for *you* is the schedule that *works*. With time and experience, you can refine your schedule until it is an almost perfect fit for your situation.

Master Schedule _____

Any plan to schedule your time and activities must have at its core a master schedule—that is, a fixed schedule of activities. A master schedule needs to be drawn up only once each semester, unless changes occur in your basic program. Figure 1.3 shows a useful format.

First, fill in all required school activities, such as courses, classes, and laboratory periods. Then add other regular activities, such as a part-time job, commuting time, sports, and regular meetings. Next, add housekeeping chores, sleeping, and eating. When your fixed activities have been accounted for, the blank spaces on the chart are available for weekly or day-by-day planning. Here are some suggestions on how to use some of the time periods represented by the blank spaces in Figure 1.3.

	Mon.	Tues.	Wed.	Thurs.	Fri	Sat.	Sun.
7-8	←————— Dress and Breakfast —————→						
8-9	History		History		History	Dress + Breakfast	
9-10		Phy Ed		Phy Ed.		Phy Ed.	Dress + Breakfast
10-11		Chem		Chem.		Chem	
11-12	French		French		French		
12-1	←——————— Lunch ———————————————→						
1-2	Math	Film making	Math	Film making	Math		
2-3				↑			
3-4				Chem lab.			
4-5	English		English	↓	English		
5-6							
6-7	←——————— Dinner ——————————————→						
7-8							
8-9							
9-10							
10-11							
11-12	←——————— Sleep ———————————————→						

FIGURE 1.3   A Master Schedule

Monday/Wednesday/Friday

9–10 A.M.	Use the free period after history (a lecture course) to study lecture notes.
10–11	Since French (at 11) is a recitation course, prepare by studying during the free period that precedes class.
2–3 P.M.	In math class (1–2) problems are usually discussed and worked out on the blackboard. Take very brief notes on both discussion and blackboard work. Then, because math problems can quickly become "cold," use the free period (2–3) to go over the work covered in class during the preceding hour.
3–4	English (4–5) is often a discussion period. Use the free hour to study and warm up in advance.
7–8	Evening study time begins. Start with English, your last class, so that any notes you have taken can be reviewed before forgetting takes place.
8–9	Study French, giving priority to the notes and assignments of the day.

Such a master schedule, on a 5 × 8 card taped over your desk or carried in your notebook, unclutters your mind. More important, it enables you to visualize the blank boxes as actual blocks of time into which you may fit necessary activities. With the master schedule as your base, you can devise any type of schedule that fits your unique combination of courses, your part-time or full-time job, and your personality.

Detailed Weekly Schedule

Some people work best when they are guided by a weekly schedule that is an expansion of the master schedule. If the demands on your time are both heavy and predictable, you may need a detailed weekly schedule. This kind of schedule needs to be made out only once, early in the semester. A sample weekly schedule is shown in Figure 1.4. The lists that follow indicate how the principles of scheduling were used to set it up.

Monday Through Friday/Saturday

7–8 A.M.	Avoid the frantic dash and the gobbled (or skipped) breakfast by getting up on time.
12–1 P.M.	Take a full, leisurely hour for lunch.
5–6	Relax before dinner—your reward for a day of conscientious work.

Time	Mon.	Tues.	Wed.	Thurs.	Fri.	Sat.	Sun.
7-8	← Dress and Breakfast →						↑
8-9	History	Study Chem.	History	Study Chem.	History	Study Chem.	
9-10	Study History	Phy. Ed.	Study History	Phy. Ed.	Study History	Phy. Ed.	Church, Conversation, Recreation, Recreational Reading
10-11	Study French	Chem.	Study French	Chem.	Study French	Chem.	
11-12	French	Study Chem.	French	Study Chem.	French	Study Chem.	
12-1	← Lunch →					↑	
1-2	Math	Film-Making	Math	Film-Making	Math		
2-3	Study Math	Library: Paper	Study Math	↑	Study Math	Recreation, Conversation, Special Projects, Extra Work on Difficult Subjects	
3-4	Study English	"	Study English	Chem. Lab.	Study English		
4-5	English	"	English	↓	English		
5-6	← Recreation →						
6-7	← Dinner →						↓
7-8	Study English	Study Math	Study English	Study Math	Study English	Recreation, Conversation, Reading, Extra Work, Thorough Review	English Paper
8-9	Study French	Study History	Study French	Study History	Study French		English Paper
9-10	Review English	Review French	Review History	Review Math	Review Chem.		Study History
10-11	← Recreational Reading →						
11-12	← Conversation, Sleep →					↓	

FIGURE 1.4   A Detailed Weekly Schedule Based on a Master Schedule

7–9	Keep up with current notes and assignments by systematic studying.
9–10	To forestall cramming at quiz and examination times, give some time every day to a review of previous assignments and ground covered to date.
10	A cease-study time of 10 P.M. is an incentive to work hard during the day and early evening.
10–12	Devote some time every day to reading books that truly interest you. Recreational reading and conversation help you unwind for a good night's sleep.

Tuesday/Thursday/Saturday

8–9 A.M.	Since chemistry (10–11) is your hard subject, build your morning study program around it. An hour's study before class will make the class period more meaningful.
11–12	Another hour's study immediately after chemistry class will help you remember the work covered in class and move more readily to the next assignment.

Special

Tuesday	2–5 P.M., library: paper
Sunday	7–9 P.M., English paper
	For some assignments you will need to schedule blocks of time to do research or to develop and follow up ideas.
Saturday	From noon on, Saturday is left unscheduled—for recreation, for special projects to which you must devote a concentrated period of time, for extra work on difficult subjects, for thorough review.
Sunday	This is your day until evening. Study history before you go to bed, because it is the first class you'll have on Monday morning.

Assignment-oriented Weekly Schedule _____

Another type of weekly schedule is based primarily on assignments, rather than on available time. It is a supplement to the master schedule and can be used whenever you face unusual or long-term assignments. Because it schedules specific assignments, it covers only one specific week.

Figure 1.5 shows a weekly assignment schedule. The format is simple: Draw a horizontal line to divide a lined sheet of paper approximately in half. In the top half list your subjects, assignments, estimated study times, and due

Subject	Assignment	Estimated Time	Date Due	Time Due
Electronics	Chap. V - 32 pp. - Read	2 hr.	Mon. 13th	8:00
English	Paper to Write	18 hr.	Mon. 20th	9:00
Math	Problems on pp. 110-111	3 hr.	Tues. 14th	10:00
Industrial Safety	Make shop layouts	8 hr.	Fri. 17th	11:00
Graphics	Drawing of TV components	6 hr.	Fri. 17th	1:00
Electronics	Chap. VI - 40 pp. - Read	2½ hr.	Weds. 22nd	8:00

Day	Assignment	Morning	Afternoon	Evening
Sun.	Electronics - Read Chap. V English - Find a Topic			7:30 - 9:30 9:30 - 10:30
Mon	English - Gather Notes Math - Problems		2:00 - 6:00	7:00 - 10:00
Tues	English - Gather Notes Industrial Safety	8:00 - 10:00	3:00 - 6:00	7:00 - 10:00
Wed.	English - First Draft Graphics		2:00 - 6:00	7:00 - 10:00
Thurs	Industrial Safety English - Paper Graphics	8:00 - 10:00	3:00 - 6:00	7:00 - 10:00
Fri	English - Final Copy Electronics		2:00 - 6:00	7:00 - 9:30
Sat				

FIGURE 1.5 A Weekly Schedule Based on Assignments
To provide a time dimension, this schedule is being made out on Saturday, November 11, for the coming week.

dates. Then, using the due dates and estimated times as control factors, check your master schedule for hours available. Choose enough hours to do each job, and write them on the appropriate line on the bottom half of the weekly schedule sheet. *Stick to your schedule.* Give study hours top priority. As long as you do, your remaining free hours will be really free.

FOR MONDAY

8 - 9	Psychology - Review Chapter V and lecture notes
9 - 10	Psychology lecture
10 - 11	Economics lecture
11 - 12	Economics - fix up notes, begin Chapter VII
1 - 2	Campus store - Pick up paper and binder, pen, lead, calculator
2 - 5	Engineering - work on assignment
5 - 6	Exercise - Tennis court with Joan.
7 - 10	Accounting and Math

Review: Just before class is a good time to review the high points of chapters previously studied. Also review the previous lecture for continuity.

Fix up notes: The very best time to fix up lecture notes, and review them simultaneously, is immediately after the lecture.

After lunch: This is a good time to give yourself a semi-break from academic work and do some necessary errands.

2-5 block: This is a valuable block of time during which you should be able to read the assignment and work out the assigned problems without losing continuity.

Exercise: After an entire day with the books, some exercise and a shower will help to put an edge on your appetite, as well as making a definite break between study during the day and study during the evening.

After dinner: Both subjects need unbroken time for efficient production. Use the block of three hours to do a balanced amount of work for each, depending on the assignments.

Breaks: Breaks are not listed. You judge for yourself when a break is best for you. Also, the break should be taken when you arrive at a good stopping point.

FIGURE 1.6   A Daily Schedule

Daily Schedule

You will probably want to have a daily schedule that you can carry around with you. A 3 × 5 card is just the right size. It will fit perfectly into your shirt pocket or shoulder bag and will be at hand when you need it. Every evening before leaving your desk, look at your master schedule to determine your free hours and courses for the next day. Then jot down on the card a plan for the next day: the subjects you plan to study, the errands, appointments, physical exercise, recreation, and any other activities you want to do, and the time you allot for each. The five minutes you spend are important for two reasons. First, you will have a written record to which you can refer, and this will unclutter your mind. Second, you will have mentally thought through your day, thus putting into action a psychological clock that will help keep you on schedule.

Notice in Figure 1.6 that the daily schedule is organized on the basis of blocks of time, rather than fragments of time. By assigning a block of time to each topic or activity, you will ensure that you work at peak efficiency.

Scheduling Long-Term Assignments

Most assignments are not portioned out in bite-size, day-by-day units. Some assignments span a week, some a month, some (research papers and projects) an entire semester. Although it pays to study every day, you must also do some long-term planning.

You are likely to have one or two long-term assignments at all times, and you may get confused if you have too many separate schedules. It is best to keep a record of the full assignments and their due dates in your notebook for each subject. Get started on these assignments early by allotting some time to each of them on your daily schedules. If you still have trouble remembering to do them, you may need to make out a weekly assignment schedule like the one shown in Figure 1.5.

SCHEDULING FOR STUDENTS WITH JOBS

If you have a full-time or part-time job, you probably have less time and less energy for studying than regular full-time students; consequently, you must use your time and energy very carefully. A full-time student can use big blocks of uninterrupted time for studying, but you must find ways to use scattered pieces of time.

If you are a working student, your daily study schedule should simply be a list of things to do, in the order of priority. Figure 1.7 shows a typical daily list for a working student. To be successful, you should have a sense of urgency about referring to your list and studying whenever an opportunity presents itself. Cross off the tasks you complete. Assigning specific times is likely to lead only to frustration. Your study materials should be in a form that permits you to carry them about for use whenever you have some spare time.

Preparing Notes for Study on the Run

To take advantage of moments of spare time, your study materials must be readily available. One way to make them available is to write or type notes on small cards; another way is to record notes on cassettes.

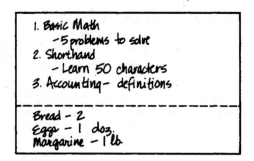

1. Basic Math
   - 5 problems to solve
2. Shorthand
   - Learn 50 characters
3. Accounting - definitions

Bread - 2
Eggs - 1 doz.
Margarine - 1 lb.

FIGURE 1.7   A Things-to-Do Schedule for a Working Student

After reading an assignment or attending a lecture, select from it only the information that you believe is important enough to master. Using your own words, write or type this information on 3 × 5 or 5 × 8 cards. You can then record the same notes, or a portion of them, on cassettes. If you have time for only one of these, use the cards.

How to Study on the Run

Here are some ways to study during time periods that are ordinarily only half-used.

1. Attach small metal or plastic clips near mirrors and on walls, at eye level. Place a note card in each clip. While shaving or combing your hair, or while washing dishes, you can read the notes on the cards. Cards placed in clips can be easily changed; pasting or taping cards to walls is not as practical.

2. To vary the routine and to use your sense of hearing, listen to a cassette or two while going through your morning routine.

3. When you drive to work, listen to several cassettes instead of to music on the car radio. If you have only cards, recite aloud from memory (not verbatim) some of the ideas, formulas, or definitions that are on the cards. After you stop driving, read the cards to check your accuracy.

4. As you walk from the parking lot to your place of work, flip through several of your note cards or listen to a cassette.

5. At lunch, while eating a sandwich in your place of work, do a problem or two in math, or, if you prefer, listen to a cassette.

Knowing how to study on the run will enable you to devote more time to your family, job, and school without scrimping on sleep.

TIPS FOR SAVING TIME

You have twenty-four hours of time every day. You get no more and no less, whether you're rich or poor, stingy or spendthrift, deserving or undeserving. You cannot buy or manufacture more time. There are, however, three ways to accomplish more within the hours you have: (1) by using the mini-size study skills explained in this section; (2) by using the self-discipline strategies explained in this section; and (3) by using the time you once wasted.

Mini-Size Study Skills

Bundle-of-Sticks Technique. A father once tied a bundle of small, thin sticks together with a strand of twine. Handing the bundle to his youngest son, he said, "Son, break these sticks in half." The boy used his hands and knees but could not break the bundle. Sadly, he handed it back to his father. Without a word, the father untied the twine and, using only his fingers, snapped each stick, one by one.

When one of your assignments is long and seems overwhelming, unbundle it and divide it into small, manageable units—units that you can start on immediately. For example, when you're assigned a research paper to write, spring into action immediately by breaking the assignment into small, practical units, and do one or two of them per day:

1. Choose a topic. Remind yourself to choose a topic in which you are interested.

2. Narrow the topic; in fact, make three or four significant narrowings.

3. Look in the *Readers' Guide to Periodical Literature* to see how much current information there is on your topic.

4. Sharpen the focus of the topic to make sure you are answering a question.

5. Buy a stack of 3 × 5 cards or slips of paper for recording your bibliography and notes.

6. Look in the card catalogue, and make bibliographical notes.

7. Look in the reference sections, and make notes.

8. Look in the periodical sections, and make notes.

9. Take separate notes for the bibliography and for detailed information for your paper.

10. Etc. (For more detailed information on researching and writing papers, see Chapter 18 of Pauk: *How to Study in College,* or follow the steps described in any good book on writing papers.)

Right from the beginning, remind yourself that you do not intend to plunge into the main job of writing the paper. After you have divided the assignment, begin your work in the first free study period of the same day, while the full concept is still fresh in your mind. Once underway, the paper will practically write itself.

The secret of the Bundle-of-Sticks Technique is to make the pieces the right size so that each is easy to do. "Divide and conquer" applies to assignments just as it does to military tactics.

Setting a Time Limit for Each Task.   According to Parkinson's Law: Work expands to fill the time available for its completion.[1] To be sure you don't run out of time before you've finished a project, work Parkinson's Law in reverse: For each task, set a deadline that you will find difficult to meet, and then work hard to meet that deadline.

Each time you achieve your goal, reward yourself with a pleasant activity (any behavior that is followed by something pleasant tends to be reinforced and is more likely to happen again). Take a break. Briefly chat with a friend. Get a drink of water. Walk around the room. You may want to keep a special snack, such as a jar of peanuts, in the bottom drawer of your desk, to be opened only as a reward. Lee Iacocca used this principle in college and even as a child:

> As a little kid I had learned how to do my homework right after school so that I could play after supper. By the time I got to college, . . . I used to tell myself: "I'm going to give this my best shot for the next three hours. And when those three hours are up, I'll set this work aside and go to the movies."[2]

Remember these two additional principles:

1. If you fail to meet a deadline, don't punish yourself harshly by, for example, not going to a football game. Your punishment is sufficient if you deprive yourself of the peanuts in your desk. It is *positive* reinforcement that is powerful in effecting a change in behavior.

2. Reward yourself for your small successes, not only for your major ones.

The Pareto Principle.[3]   Named after Vilfredo Pareto (1848–1923), an Italian economist and sociologist, the Pareto Principle states that the truly

---

[1]C. Northcote Parkinson, *Parkinson's Law and Other Studies in Administration* (Boston: Houghton Mifflin, 1957).

[2]Lee Iacocca, with William Novak, *Iacocca: An Autobiography* (New York: Bantam Books, 1984), p. 20.

[3]Reprinted by permission of Charles Scribner's Sons, an imprint of Macmillan Publishing Company and Macdonald & Co. Publishers Ltd. from *Getting Things Done: The ABC's of Time Management* by Edwin C. Bliss. Copyright © 1976 Edwin C. Bliss.

important items in any given group constitute only a small number of the total items in that group. This principle is also known as the 80/20 rule.

For example, in almost any sales force, 80 percent of the business is brought in by 20 percent of the salespeople. In any committee, 80 percent of the ideas come from 20 percent of the members. In a classroom, 80 percent of the teacher's time is taken up by 20 percent of the students.

In any list of things to do, 80 percent of the importance resides in 20 percent of the list. In a list of ten items, 80 percent of the list's value lies in 2 items, which constitute 20 percent of the list. Because of Pareto's Principle, in your lists of things to do always put the most important items first. Then, if you accomplish only the first few items, you will have accomplished the most important tasks on the list.

Keep the Pareto Principle in mind whenever you make up a list or a schedule or must decide which subject to study first. Apply the principle by listing first things first.

Concentrating Your Time and Efforts. Some students jump from subject to subject when they study, scattering their time and efforts. They touch many assignments but finish none. When you focus the sun's rays onto a piece of paper, the rays will burn a hole; unfocused rays, like scattered time and effort, make no impression at all. Pause, make a plan, and then take action. Remember that action without planning won't get you very far.

Planning Ahead. You must not try to play things by ear. No football coach would field a team without a game plan, and no student should try to face a school day without an academic game plan. If you do not have one, other people's actions will determine what you do, and your time will be wasted. By having a plan of your own, you will be able to use your time to achieve *your* goals.

Using a Month-at-a-Glance Calendar. Buy or make—but use—a calendar that shows the entire month on one page. For precise control, you need to see what assignments are due and when at a glance. A page per week won't do. Above all, don't use a page for each day, because assignments hidden from view in next week's pages are out of sight and out of mind.

Taking Study Breaks. Which is better: sticking with a two-hour assignment until you have finished it or breaking the assignment into half-hour periods separated by five-minute breaks? Breaking up a long assignment is better, for several reasons:

1. Study breaks keep you from getting tired and bored.
2. You work harder and concentrate better in short spurts.

3. Five-minute breaks are great motivators.

4. During the rest periods, the material you studied has a chance to sink in.

However, just as some runners need a long time to warm up, some students take a long time to get into a long assignment. If such students broke long assignments into half-hour periods, they would need warming up at the end of every half hour. Such students should study for a full fifty minutes or longer before taking a ten-minute break. It is better for them to be like marathon runners, finishing the long assignment in one continuous stretch.

Before you take a break, review your underlinings and jottings. This will help the facts sink into your long-term memory. Just before a break is also a good time to reread a particularly difficult problem or passage. This gets your mind working on the problem while you rest.

Beating the Sleepy Feeling.   While studying, if you get sleepy before your scheduled sleep time, *don't* take a nap. Instead, pick up your textbook, stand up, and pace the floor, reading aloud as you do. The sleepy feeling will pass. When you go to bed at your scheduled time, you'll be able to fall asleep.

Writing Notes to Yourself.   When you reach the end of a study session, write a note telling yourself where to begin during your next study period. You'll be surprised at how much time this practice will save you each day, and you'll enjoy the boost that such a note provides.

Self-Discipline Strategies

A "yes" answer to any of the following questions is a sure sign of poor planning and poor self-discipline:

1. Did you have to cram for an exam?

2. Did you have to stay up most of the night to finish a term or research paper?

3. Did you have to give up your recreational time?

4. Did you have to miss a basketball or a football game in order to study?

5. Did you have to excuse yourself from going to a good movie with friends?

If you answered "yes" to any of them, take out a sheet of paper and write down why you had this problem; then list specific ways that you could have avoided the problem and ways that you can prevent it from happening again. By taking this action, you show that you are in control of your life.

Here are some other strategies to bolster your self-discipline.

Deciding to Change Your Behavior.   Old habits are difficult to break and new ones difficult to make, but you can do it if you follow these rules:

1. *Develop a strong determination.*   If you want to make or break a habit, your determination must be powerful enough to carry you over rough spots. Every day you succeed, the success of your plan is made more certain.

2. *Never, ever make an exception.*   Making an exception is like dropping a carefully wound ball of string: "A single slip undoes more than a great many turns will wind again."[4] Never willingly lose a battle.

3. *Take every opportunity to put your good habit to work.*   Always practice behavior that you want to come naturally.

Listing Tasks According to Their Importance.   Do you list your priorities according to importance or according to urgency? Should tomorrow's quiz head your list, or should you do some work on that long-range research paper that could make or break your final grade? If your priority lists reflect urgency instead of importance, you have a problem: You began working on such tasks too late, and as time runs out, you must rush frantically to meet your deadline. As a result, you shove aside your heavyweight research paper to make room for a quiz. Avoid this situation. Start early, and work steadily.

Understanding the Relationship Between Time and Goals.   There is a direct relationship between goals and time. When you have a goal firmly in mind, you will think of objectives rather than activities. You will make better decisions, speak and write more forcefully, and treat time as a precious commodity. You will be as serious about time as Ben Franklin, who said, "Time is the stuff of which life is made," and you will avoid falling victim to the four great robbers of time:

1. Laziness: "I don't feel like doing it now."

2. Sidetracks: "I'll wash my hair and then I'll begin working."

3. Procrastination: "Sure, I'll do it later."

4. Daydreaming: "Some day I'll amaze them."

Concentrating on One Task at a Time.   Nothing can help you use time more productively than concentration. Many students never become proficient concentrators because they try to do too many things at once. All your

---

[4]William James, *Psychology* (New York: Holt, 1893), p. 145.

tasks may be important, but you can do only one at a time. To start the time-saving process, you must decide which one task is most important. Push all else aside. Set a realistic deadline, and then work on this task until you have completed it. When you have finished, reward yourself with a five-minute break.

Avoiding Procrastination.   "Nothing [is] so fatiguing as the eternal hanging on of an uncompleted task."[5] These words by William James (1842–1910), distinguished American psychologist, strike at the heart of us all. Every one of us has had many bouts with procrastination.

If a task that you are doing is about three-quarters finished and is finishable, finish it no matter how tired you are. If you delay completion until tomorrow, you'll need extra time to overcome inertia, reread what you have done, pick up your train of thought, and recapture yesterday's momentum.

Make it a habit to save both time and energy by doing a needed task immediately or at the first free opportunity. By doing so, you prove that you are in control of your life.

Obeying the Alarm Clock.   Once you have decided on a time to get up, don't ignore the decision when the alarm goes off. Without stretching, yawning, or groaning, make your feet hit the floor immediately. Five minutes later, you'll be glad you did.

Striving for Excellence.   In *Getting Things Done*, Edwin C. Bliss writes: "There is a difference between striving for excellence and striving for perfection. The first is attainable, gratifying, and healthy. The second is unattainable and frustrating. It's also a terrible waste of time."[6] If you strive for perfection, you will waste time and energy that you could put to good use elsewhere. Trivial errors in your papers, for example, could be corrected neatly in ink; they do not necessitate retyping. In sum, do the best you can; then go on to the next task.

Acknowledging That Everyone Makes Mistakes.   Because we all make many errors in judgment, the words "Everyone makes mistakes" help us preserve our self-image and self-confidence and keep us from giving up on ourselves. Do not use this expression to excuse mistakes that were easily avoidable, however. Try to understand how and why you erred so that you can prevent a reoccurrence. Once you have come to terms with a mistake, put it

---

[5]William James, *The Selected Letters of William James.* Ed. with an introduction by Elizabeth Hardwick (New York: Farrar, Straus & Cudahy, 1960, 1961), p. 125.
[6]Bliss, p. 79.

behind you and concentrate on using the precious minutes of today for today's living.

Having Courage. You need personal courage to follow a good schedule because when you do so, you'll leave some students behind—perhaps some who are your friends. You may feel some loneliness, but you can take pride in the fact that you are controlling your life and achieving your goals.

Using Time Once Wasted

Getting a Head Start. If possible, finalize your class schedule before classes start, so that you can plan the days and weeks that lie ahead. Buy your textbooks early, before the campus store runs out of stock. Being without a textbook for even a little while can throw your study schedule off-balance. Before the first session of each class, visit the building and room where the class is to be held, so that you will know exactly where to go on the hectic, first day.

Carrying Pocket Work. Always carry some work you can do while you are waiting in lines and in places such as bus stations and air terminals, while you are sitting down to rest, while you are eating alone, and so forth. Never be without pocket work such as 3 × 5 cards carrying key words, key concepts, or formulas; a few pages photocopied from an important part of your textbook; or a paperback book. Also carry a few blank cards for jotting down brilliant ideas that occur to you.

Spare-Time Thinking. Use your spare time to think. While you're walking *from* a class, try to recall the main points of the lecture you just heard. If you're walking *to* a class, try to recall the main points of the lecture you heard at the last meeting of the class. At other times—when you're jogging, for example—try to think up interesting topics and titles for your next paper.

Using Your Subconscious. At one time or another, you have awakened during the night with a bright idea or a solution to a problem that you had been thinking about before bedtime. Your subconscious works while your conscious mind is resting in sleep. If you want to capture the ideas or solutions produced by your subconscious, you should write them down as soon as you wake up; otherwise, they'll be lost. Many creative people know this and keep a pad and pencil near their beds. For example, Nobel Prize winner Albert Szent-Györgyi said, "I go to sleep thinking about my problems all the time, and my brain must continue to think about them when I sleep because

I wake up, sometimes in the middle of the night, with answers to questions that have been eluding me all day."[7]

At Stanford University, Dr. William Dement and his colleagues studied the phenomenon of problem solving in dreams. Five hundred students were given the following two problems to solve at two different and separate times. Try to solve these problems before looking at the answers that follow.

> *Problem 1:* The letters O,T,T,F,F . . . form the beginning of an infinite sequence. Find a simple rule for determining any or all successive letters. According to your rule, what would be the next two letters of the sequence?

> *Problem 2:* Consider the letters H,I,J,K,L,M,N,O. The solution to this problem is one word. What is this word?[8]

The students were instructed to read the problem fifteen minutes before going to bed. The correct solutions appeared in the dreams of nine students.

In Problem 1, the letters in the sequence are the first letters of *one, two, three, four,* and *five.* The next two letters in the sequence are therefore S, S.

In Problem 2, the solution is the word *water.* The sequence of letters runs from *H* to *O,* and H_2O is the chemical formula for water.

Working During Prime Time.   There's a certain time of day when you do most of your best work. If you work best from 6 to 8 A.M., set up an early-to-bed and early-to-rise schedule. Remember to schedule your one or two highest-priority assignments for your prime time. Work on other assignments at other times.

GETTING THINGS DONE

A schedule represents a plan. Just as the buzz of an alarm clock is a signal to get up, so sitting down at your desk should be a signal to begin to study. If you make a habit of getting started immediately and then studying vigorously, you will accomplish a great deal, and your feeling of satisfaction will make it easy for you to get started next time.

This vigorous, aggressive approach must become your way of life in the classroom, the laboratory, the library, and elsewhere. Get what you came for! During a lecture, for example, be alert and work hard to capture the lecturer's ideas and get them down on paper.

---

[7]Originally published in SOME MUST WATCH WHILE SOME MUST SLEEP by William C. Dement as a volume in The Portable Stanford series published by the Stanford Alumni Association. Copyright © 1972. Reprinted by permission of the Stanford Alumni Association.
[8]Ibid., pp. 99–100.

In the library, some students wander aimlessly or spend most of their time looking around and watching other students coming and going. If your purpose is to gather data for your research paper, then go to the card catalogue, gather your references, find the books, begin reading and taking notes. Get something done according to plan.

The intelligent use of time is a large part of academic success. Schedule your time wisely, and be sure to follow your plan.

SUMMARY

What's the number-one skill that I need to master in college?

Time management heads the list of skills that you need to learn. It can mean the difference between success and failure in college.

Where does all the time go? I don't feel as though I'm wasting much time, yet I never seem to have enough.

Wasting time becomes such a habit that you don't realize you're wasting it. One excellent way to keep track of where your time goes is with a time log, in which you keep a precise record of how you spend your time, right down to the minute. If you're like most students, you'll be able to reclaim hours of wasted time.

Won't making a schedule consume more time than it saves?

Making a schedule is not busywork. Taking the time to write up a schedule is like making an investment but, unlike the case with most investments, the returns are almost guaranteed. If you spend a few minutes to draw up a schedule, you'll save far more time than you spent scheduling, you'll feel more relaxed, and you'll get more done.

What is the master schedule?

The master schedule is a day-by-day, hour-by-hour breakdown of your typical week. The master schedule should feature the immovables of your semester—the things that aren't going to change from week to week, such as meals, sleep, a job (if you have one), and classes. Once these "obligations" have been filled in, the master schedule should provide you with an excellent illustration of the time you have available.

What is the detailed weekly schedule?

The detailed weekly schedule picks up where the master schedule leaves off. In addition to showing your semester-long obligations, it shows how you intend to use each block of free time. To make a detailed weekly schedule, photocopy your master schedule several times and use it as the foundation for your weekly schedule.

How does the assignment-oriented weekly schedule differ from the detailed weekly schedule?

Instead of being divided up by blocks of time, the assignment-oriented schedule is split into individual assignments. All the information it contains can fit on a single sheet of paper. The top half of the sheet contains a list of your assignments, the time you estimate that each will take, and the date and time due for each. The bottom half of the sheet contains the days of the week, along with the assignments, and splits each day into morning, afternoon, and evening. You write in the day you plan to work on the assignment and the time of day that you want to work on it.

What is the daily schedule?

The daily schedule can usually be squeezed onto a 3 × 5 card. It lists the things you plan to do each day and the time you plan to spend on each. A written record that you carry around with you is an excellent reminder and a great motivator.

How does scheduling differ for students who have jobs?

A working student must use time far more efficiently than a full-time student. Because working students lack the luxury of large blocks of free time, the daily schedule of a working student should simply be a list of things to do, ordered by priority but not limited by time. The tasks can then be crossed off the list whenever free time presents itself.

What is the mini-size study skill called the Bundle-of-Sticks Technique?

Just as a bundle of sticks is easy to break when you break one stick at a time, a large assignment becomes less threatening if you divide it into manageable tasks and work on each task separately.

Why should I set a time limit for my tasks?

The purpose of this mini-size study skill is to prevent you from spending too much time on any one aspect of a project. According to Parkinson's Law, work expands to fill the time available for its completion. You should reverse Parkinson's Law by setting deadlines that you will have difficulty meeting and then reward yourself for meeting them.

What is the Pareto Principle?

Also known as the 80/20 rule, the Pareto Principle tells us a very interesting fact about the tasks we set for ourselves. In any list of things to do, 80 percent of the list's value resides in 20 percent of the items on the list. What that means in concrete terms is that you need to identify the most important tasks to be accomplished. Following the Pareto Principle is a mini-size study skill that will prevent you from spending too much time on relatively unimportant tasks and ignoring the crucial ones.

Are study breaks a good idea?

They can be, and getting the most out of them is an enjoyable mini-size study skill. A short break—five minutes for every half hour of work—gives you a rest, allows you to work in short, efficient spurts, creates motivation that carries you over until the next break, and, most important, gives your brain some time to let new knowledge sink in.

Are there any little tricks of the trade that can help me save time?

Yes. There are five ways to use time that you once wasted. (1) *Get a head start*. Plan your class schedule, buy your books, and locate your classrooms in advance. That way, when the semester begins, you'll be spending time on work instead of on preparations. (2) *Carry pocket work*. If you have some work with you, while the rest of the world is waiting in line and getting more impatient by the minute, you'll be relaxing and accomplishing things as well. (3) *Think in your spare time.* Instead of daydreaming between classes, use that time for real thinking. If you're leaving a class, give some thought to the lecture you just heard. If you're on your way to a class, recall the key points from the last lecture. (4) *Use your subconscious.* Your subconscious is working even when you're asleep. If you wake up with an inspired idea, write it down instead of letting it slip away. (5) *Work during your prime time.* There is a time of day when you do your best work. Use that time to work on high-priority assignments.

HAVE YOU MISSED SOMETHING?

1. *Sentence completion.* Complete the following sentences with one of the three words listed below each sentence.

   a. In order to take control of your life, you must take control of your

   _____

   personality   principles   time

   b. How we spend or waste time is largely a matter of _____ .
   habit   procrastination   priority

2. *Matching.* In each blank space in the left column, write the number preceding the phrase in the right column that matches the left item best.

   _____ a. Procrastination

   _____ b. Parkinson's Law

   _____ c. Pareto Principle

   _____ d. Perfection

   _____ e. Planning

   _____ f. Priorities

   1. A saver of time and energy
   2. Unattainable and frustrating goal
   3. One of the four great robbers of time
   4. Work expands to fill the time available for its completion
   5. Should reflect importance rather than urgency
   6. Also known as the 80/20 rule

3. *True-false.* Write *T* beside the *true* statements and *F* beside the *false* statements.

    _____ a. The master schedule should be updated daily.

    _____ b. It's best to study notes from a lecture course immediately after class.

    _____ c. A leisurely breakfast can start a productive day.

    _____ d. Your goal will be the same whether you put it in writing or keep it in your head.

    _____ e. A month-at-a-glance calendar is recommended for optimum time management.

    _____ f. All assignments should be broken up into half-hour study sessions.

4. *Study breaks.* Write "yes" next to the advantages of study breaks.

    _____ a. Prevent you from getting tired or bored

    _____ b. Give you a chance to take a refreshing nap

    _____ c. Help you work harder and concentrate better

    _____ d. Divide hour-long study sessions into four or five bite-sized pieces

    _____ e. Provide motivation during the work period

    _____ f. Allow work to sink in

5. *Multiple choice.* Choose the phrase that completes the following sentence most accurately, and circle the letter that precedes it.

Of the three steps toward success, action is the

a. easiest to achieve but the most important.
b. hardest to achieve but the least important.
c. hardest to achieve as well as the most important.
d. easiest to achieve as well as the least important.

CHAPTER 2

Note Taking

"The horror of that moment," the King went on, "I shall never, never forget!" "You will, though," the Queen said, "if you don't make a memorandum of it."

Lewis Carroll, pen name of Charles Lutwidge Dodgson (1832–98), author of *Alice's Adventures in Wonderland*

The bright-eyed cub reporter in the old movies really knew what he was doing. He scribbled down facts and ideas in a pocket pad. Although notetaking techniques have changed since then, the reason for taking notes is the same as it's always been: Note taking helps information stick in your memory. Whether you're capturing the words of a world leader or a classroom lecturer, you need to take notes quickly and efficiently. This chapter gives you the scoop on proper note taking. It reports on

- The importance of notes
- Tips and tactics
- The Cornell Note-taking System
- Types of notes
- Combining textbook and lecture notes
and finally
- Abbreviations and symbols

Many students attribute their academic and professional success to what they learned from classroom lectures. This is not surprising because professors and instructors are at their best when they are teaching and inspiring through lecturing. If you expect to learn from lectures, you must take notes. You must, like the cub reporter of old, get the information down in black and white.

THE IMPORTANCE OF NOTES

Forgetting can be *instantaneous* and *complete*. Note taking is a vital skill in college because forgetting occurs so quickly and so thoroughly. Many experiments suggest that unless you mentally rehearse the information you receive, you are unlikely to retain it in your short-term memory for more than about twenty seconds.[1] Hermann Ebbinghaus, the German psychologist who investigated remembering and forgetting, found that almost half of what is learned is forgotten within an hour.[2] Recently, psychologists carrying out experiments similar to Ebbinghaus' confirmed his findings.

The following true story further confirms the rapidity and massiveness of forgetting. Three professors eating lunch in the faculty lounge had this conversation:

CLYDE: Did you hear last night's lecture?
WALTER: No, I was busy.
CLYDE: Well, you missed one of the best lectures in recent years.
LEON: I agree. The four points that he developed were gems.
CLYDE: I never heard anyone make his points so clear.
WALTER: I don't want you to repeat the lecture, but what were those four points?
LEON: (Long silence) Clyde? (Passage of two or three minutes; seems like an hour.)
LEON: Well, I'd better get back to the office.
CLYDE: Me too!
WALTER: Me too!

Neither Leon nor Clyde was able to recall even a fragment of any point made in the previous night's lecture. Each of them forgot the four points because neither of them had transferred the points from short-term memory to long-term memory by silently reciting them. Instead, they both had recited

---

[1]Douglas A. Bernstein, Edward J. Roy, Thomas K. Srull, and Christopher D. Wickens, *Psychology* (Boston: Houghton Mifflin, 1988), p. 293.
[2]Hermann Ebbinghaus, *Memory.* Translated by Henry A. Ruger and Clara E. Bussenius (New York: Dover Publications, 1964 [1913]), p. 76.

that the speaker was clear, forceful, and wise, and that he had made four points—and they remembered only what they had recited.

The only sure way to overcome forgetting is by taking notes, then taking your notes back to your room to study and recite.

TIPS AND TACTICS

If you turn these tips and tactics into habits, your notes will be the envy of your classmates. Use these tips and tactics until they are second nature to you.

Telegraphic Sentences

Sixty years ago, when telephones were not so numerous as they are today, important messages, both personal and business, were sent by telegraph. The sender paid by the word; so the fewer the words, the lower was the cost. A four-word message such as "Will arrive three pm" was a lot less expensive than an eleven-word message: "I will arrive home promptly at 3 o'clock in the afternoon."

When you take notes, use telegraphic sentences. Leave out unnecessary words. Use the key words only. Ignore rules of grammar. Write down a streamlined version of the lecturer's key points. Two examples of the telegraphic style are given in Figure 2.1.

Modified Printing Style

Terrible handwriting need not prevent you from taking legible notes. You can give up your old way of writing and adopt the modified printing style. Your writing will be surprisingly rapid and amazingly clear. Anyone can adopt this style and use it to write neatly and clearly.

Here is how the individual letters look in the modified printing style:

a b c d e f g h i j k l m n o p q r s t u v w x y z

If you have your own way of forming some of the letters, use it. What flows naturally from your pen or pencil will be swifter and easier than a forced change. Figure 2.2 shows the style used in a paragraph.

Lecturer's words in a marketing course

In selling, you can overcome a customer's objections to almost any product if you can come up with a good idea. Here are two examples: first, a lady who objected to a square flyswatter bought it when the sales manager said, "These are square, madam. They get them in the corners." Second, a lady who wanted round clothespins, bought the square ones when the clerk said, "They don't roll out of reach under a sink." So, don't sell the steak - sell the sizzle.

Student's telegraphic sentences

1. People buy ideas, not products.
   a. Ex. square flyswatter = "get in corners."
   b. Ex. square clothespins = "won't roll - sink."
   c. Don't sell steak -- sell sizzle.

Lecturer's words

The US Patent Office has granted numerous patents for perpetual motion machines based upon applications with complete detailed drawings. Some years ago, though, the patent office began requiring working models of such a machine before a patent would be granted. Result: no patents granted for perpetual motion machines since that time.

Student's telegraphic sentence

Perpetual motion machine (drawings) = many patents.
Required working model = no patents since.

FIGURE 2.1 Examples of Telegraphic Sentences

36

> There are four advantages to using this modified printing style. First, it is faster than cursive writing; second, it is neater, permitting easy and direct comprehension; third, it saves time by precluding rewriting or typing; and fourth, it permits easy and clear reforming of letters that are ill-formed due to haste.

FIGURE 2.2 Modified Printing Style

The Two-Page System

When you need to scramble to keep up with a fast-talking lecturer, you may find this two-page system helpful. Here's the way it works: Lay your binder flat on the desk. On the left-hand page, record main ideas only. The left-hand page is your primary page. On the right-hand page, record as many details as you have time for. Place the details opposite the main ideas that they support. After the lecture, remain in your seat for a few minutes and fill in any gaps in your notes while the lecture is still relatively fresh in mind.

The Cassette and Tape Taboo

Do not use a tape or cassette recorder. If you do, you'll be wasting time and not learning very much. When a lecture is on tape, you cannot review it in five or ten minutes; you have to replay the entire lecture. Worst of all, you cannot use the technique of reciting, which is the most effective learning technique known to psychologists. Furthermore, you also lose the advantage of visual learning—that is, seeing the words and seeing the relationship between the written ideas.

Some students create written notes as they listen to the tape in the privacy of their rooms. Don't you see the waste of time? The notes could have been taken directly during the "live" lecture.

No Shorthand

Don't take lecture notes in shorthand. Shorthand notes cannot be studied effectively while they are still in symbol form. Besides, shorthand symbols still have to be transformed into regular words. If you need a fast method to keep up with the lecturer, use the abbreviations and the symbols listed at the end of this chapter.

No Typing

Scribbling is a bad habit. Write legibly the first time. Don't rationalize that you'll type your notes when you return to your room. Typing your notes is a waste of time, opportunity, and energy. You'll need almost a full hour to decipher and type one set of scribbled lecture notes. The hour you spend typing could have been extremely productive if you had spent it reciting notes taken during the lecture. Typing can exhaust you physically, mentally, and emotionally, leaving you unfit for the task of learning.

Contrary to what most people think, almost no learning takes place during the typing of scribbled notes. The act of deciphering and typing requires almost total concentration, leaving scant concentration for comprehending the facts and ideas being typed.

Signal Words and Phrases

Most college lecturers speak about 120 words per minute. In a fifty-minute lecture, you hear up to six thousand words expressing ideas, facts, and details. To impose some recognizable order on those ideas, facts, and details, lecturers use signal words and phrases.

Signal words and phrases themselves do not express ideas, facts, and details. They do, however, convey important information of a directional and relational sort. If you, as a note taker, know the importance and meaning of signal words and phrases, you'll be able to perceive the organization of the lecture, the direction of the lecture, and the relationship among the ideas, facts, and details. A list of signal words and phrases is given in Figure 2.3. Being able to recognize signal words and phrases will improve your reading, writing, speaking, and listening, as well as your note taking.

The Final Barrage

Pay close attention to the end of the lecture. Speakers who do not pace themselves well may have to cram half of the lecture into the last five or ten minutes. Record such packed finales as rapidly as you can. After class, stay in

Categories and Examples	When you hear these words, immediately think . . .
Example Words to illustrate for example for instance	"Here comes an example. The lecturer wants to make clear the point just made. I'd better write this down; otherwise I'll forget it."
Time Words before, after formerly subsequently prior meanwhile	"Hm-m! A time relationship is being established. Let's see, what came first and what came last, and what came in-between?"
Addition Words furthermore in addition moreover also	"After listing everything, they always seem to have one more thing to add. Well, I'd better get it and write it down."
Cause and Effect Words therefore as a result if . . . then accordingly thus, so	"There's that cause and effect word. I'd better quickly write down the word *effect* in my notes at this point. Later, I'll go back and write the word *cause* to label the preceding points."
Contrast Words on the other hand in contrast conversely pros and cons	"Now we're getting the other side of the picture, the other person's story, the research that contradicts what has already been said."
Enumeration Words the four steps . . . first, second, third next finally	"Ten steps is a lot! I'd better number them and list them in order."
Emphasis Words more importantly above all remember this	"Sounds like a hint that this idea is something important and something to remember."
Repeat Words in other words in the vernacular it simply means that is, briefly in essence	"Simplifying a complex idea or simplifying a long-winded explanation. I'd better note this simplified version."

FIGURE 2.3 Signal Words and Phrases

Categories and Examples	When you hear these words, immediately think . . .
Swivel Words however nevertheless yet, but still	"A warning that there's a little bit of doubt or 'give-back' on the point just made. I'd better note this qualifying remark."
Concession Words to be sure of course granted indeed though	"I see. These are similar to the swivel words. The lecturer is admitting that the opposition has a point or two."
Summary Words in a nutshell to sum up in conclusion	"Great! I'll try to get this summary word for word; then I can study it thoroughly when I get to my room."
Test Clues This is important. Remember this. You'll see this again. Here's a pitfall.	"Sounds like a potential test item. I'd better get this one word for word."

FIGURE 2.3   Signal Words and Phrases (continued)

your seat for a few extra minutes to write down as much as you can remember.

Instant Replay

As soon as you leave the lecture room, while walking to your next class, mentally recall the lecture from beginning to end. Visualize the classroom and the lecturer and any blackboard work. After mentally recalling the lecture, ask yourself some questions: What was the lecturer getting at? What really was the central point? What did I learn? How does what I learned fit in with what I already know? If you discover anything you don't quite understand, no matter how small, make a note of it and ask the instructor before the next class to explain it.

Avoiding Ice-Cold Notes

During your first free period after class, or that evening at the latest, read over your notes to fill in gaps and to give yourself an overview of the lecture.

Review your notes while the lecture is still fresh in your mind. Ice-cold notes are frustrating and are time wasters. Days after a lecture, you do not want to be gazing at your own writing and wondering, "What did I mean by that?"

Two Dozen Dos and One Dozen Don'ts

The twenty-four dos and twelve don'ts that follow are the warp and woof of note taking. Weave them into a magic carpet of your own design and glide over all the rough spots of note taking.

Dos

1. Look over previous notes before class. (Maintains continuity.)
2. Attend *all* lectures. (It's a continuing story.)
3. Be academically aggressive. (Sit up straight with "rolled-up sleeves.")
4. Take a front seat to see and hear better. (You won't dare snooze.)
5. Use a large, loose-leaf binder. (Gives ample room.)
6. Carry lined loose-leaf ($8\frac{1}{2} \times 11$) sheets to class. (Insert into binder on return.)
7. Write on only one side of sheet. (Spread out for review.)
8. On top sheet, record course, lecturer, and date. (In case of spill.)
9. Begin taking notes immediately. (Don't wait for inspiration.)
10. Write in short, telegraphic sentences. (Parsimoniously meaningful.)
11. Make notes complete for later understanding. (Don't sit there puzzling.)
12. Use modified printing style. (Clear letters, not scribbles.)
13. Use lecturer's words. (Lecturers like to see their words in exams.)
14. Strive to detect main headings. (As if you peeked at the lecturer's notes.)
15. Capture ideas as well as facts. (Get the drift too.)
16. Keep your note-organization simple. (Easy does it.)
17. Skip lines; leave space between main ideas. (Package the ideas.)
18. Discover the organizational pattern. (Like putting together a puzzle.)
19. If the lecture is too fast, capture fragments. (Jigsaw them together later.)
20. Leave blank spaces for words to fill in later. (Thus avoid voids.)
21. Develop your own abbreviations and symbols. (Not too many, but enough.)
22. Record lecturer's examples. (If you don't, you'll forget.)

23. Identify your own thought-notes. (What's mine? What's the lecturer's?)
24. Keep separate loose-leaf binders for each course. (Don't combine notes yet.)

Don'ts

1. Don't sit near friends. (Can be distracting.)
2. Don't wait for something "important." (Record everything.)
3. Don't convert lecturer's words. (Takes time and invites imprecision.)
4. Don't look for facts only. (See ideas too.)
5. Don't give up if the lecturer is too fast. (Some is better than none.)
6. Don't stop to ponder. (Do so later in your room.)
7. Don't over-indent. (You'll run out of right-side space.)
8. Don't doodle. (Breaks concentration and eye contact.)
9. Don't use spiral-bound notebooks. (Can't insert handouts.)
10. Don't consider any example too obvious. (Copy it!)
11. Avoid using Roman numerals. (You'll get tangled up.)
12. Avoid too many abbreviations. (Trouble deciphering later.)

THE CORNELL NOTE-TAKING SYSTEM

The notes you take in class are really a hand-written textbook. In many instances, your lecture notes are more practical, meaningful, and up-to-date than a textbook. If you keep them neat, complete, and well organized, they'll serve you splendidly.

To help students organize their notes, I developed the Cornell Note-taking System forty years ago at Cornell University. It is used in colleges not only in the United States but also in foreign countries, including China. The keystone of the system is a two-column note sheet.

Use 8½ by 11 paper to create the note sheet (see Figure 2.4). Down the left side, draw a vertical line 2½ inches from the edge of the paper. End this line 2 inches above the bottom of the paper. Draw a horizontal line across the bottom of the paper, 2 inches above the paper's edge. In the narrow (2½") column on the left, you will write cue words or questions. In the wide (6") column on the right, you will write lecture notes. In the space at the bottom of the sheet, you will summarize your notes. Note: You can use this system if you use lined notebook paper, too. You can disregard the red vertical rule and make your own rule 2½" from the left edge of the paper. Or you can make

FIGURE 2.4 Note-Sheet Format for the Cornell Note-taking System
During a lecture class, the student writes notes in the wide (6″) column. To study from the notes, the student writes either cue words or questions in the narrow column and a summary in the space at the bottom of the note sheet.

the rule 2½" from the red rule, leaving yourself 4" for the wide note-taking column. In either case, you will have the 2½" left-hand space for important cue words and questions.

There are two versions of the Cornell System: (1) the Six R version, (2) the One Q/Five R version. Both versions have six steps. The main difference between them is in step 2. The six steps are listed in Table 2.1 and discussed in detail below. Notice that step 2 in the Six R version is *reduce*; in the One Q/Five R version, step 2 is *question*.

When you use the Six R version, you will write cue words in the narrow column of the note sheet (see Figure 2.5). When you use the One Q/Five R version, you will write questions in the narrow column (see Figure 2.6). Which version is better? Give each one a try, and see which one works best for you.

Step 1: Record

In the wide column, record as many facts and ideas as you can. Use telegraphic sentences, but make sure that weeks after the lecture your notes will still make sense. Write legibly. Directly after class or at your first opportunity, fill in any blank spaces that you left and clarify your handwriting if necessary.

Step 2: Reduce (<u>Six R version only</u>)

During your first study opportunity, reread your notes and rethink the entire lecture. Then reduce each fact and idea in your notes to key words and phrases. In the narrow column of the note sheet, jot down the word or phrase that you have extracted from the fact or idea. The key words and phrases will act as memory cues. Later, when you see or hear them, you will recall the full fact or idea.

TABLE 2.1   Steps in the Cornell Note-taking System

Step	Six R Version	One Q/Five R Version
1[a]	Record	Record
2	Reduce	Question
3	Recite	Recite
4	Reflect	Reflect
5	Review	Review
6[a]	Recapitulate	Recapitulate

[a]Notes made in class (step 1) and the summary written during study time (step 6) are placed in the wide column of the note sheet.

Psych. 102 – Prof. Goldsmith – Sept. 14th (Mon.)

	A. Build Self-Confidence –15 steps
Weaknesses & strengths	1. Assess strengths & weaknesses
	a. Set goals accordingly
Life's goal	2. Decide what you'd like your life to be
	a. Rework your thinking to bring inner script up to date
Negatives	3. Bury all <u>negative</u> memories
	a. Forgive others & self
	b. Remember past successes – even minor ones
Guilt & shame	4. Wipe out any guilt & shame
	a. Don't allow these thoughts mental entrance
Personality defects	5. Don't attribute present behavior to personality defects
	a. Real causes might be economic, political, social, etc.
Points of view	6. Events may be seen differently by different people
	a. Rejections or put-downs might not be actual
Negative labels	7. Never label yourself negatively
	a. Such as: stupid, ugly, failure, incorrigible
Criticism	8. Accept criticism of a <u>specific action</u>, but not of <u>you</u> as a person
	a. Accept constructive criticism graciously
Failures blessing	9. Failures can be a blessing -- goals not right for you
	a. Avoids later let-down
Inadequacy	10. Don't tolerate people, jobs, situations that make you feel inadequate
	a. If can't change them or you -- walk out
Relax	11. Take time to relax & meditate -- hobbies
	a. Keep in touch w/ your inner self
Social	12. Be social -- enjoy other people
	a. See their needs and help them
Playing it too cool	13. Don't overprotect your ego -- it's resilient
	a. Better to try & fail, than to clam up -- numbing!

Goals:
  long-range
  short-range
	14. Develop long-ranged goals, also short-ranged ones

	a. Evaluate progress & whisper word of praise in your own ear

Not an object
  – active actor
  – <u>live</u> your life
	15. You're not a passive object -- you can make things happen

	a. You're a product of millions of years of evolution & made in God's image
	b. Don't worry about <u>how</u> to live your life, lose yourself -- be absorbed in <u>living</u> it

Through deep thinking, decide what you want to be. What to do with your life. Write out long-term & short-term goals. Eliminate totally & permanently <u>all</u> <u>negative</u> feelings & occurrences past, present, & future. Do things. Try things. Ego can take set-backs. Don't withdraw to solitary "safety." Enter the stream of life. Be busy swimming in it.

FIGURE 2.5 The Six R Version
The narrow column contains key words and phrases.

Psych. 105 - Prof. Martin - Sept. 14 (Mon.)

MEMORY

A. Memory tricky — Can recall instantly many trivial things of childhood; yet, forget things recently worked hard to learn é retain.

B. Memory Trace
1. Fact that we retain information means that some change was made in the brain.
2. Change called "memory trace."
3. "Trace" probably a molecular arrangement similar to molecular changes in a magnetic recording tape.

C. Three memory systems: sensory, short-term, long-term.
1. Sensory (lasts one second)
Ex. Words or numbers sent to brain by sight (visual image) start to disintegrate within a few tenths of a second é gone in one full second, unless quickly transferred to S-T memory by verbal repetition.
2. Short-term memory [STM] (lasts 30 seconds)
a. Experiments show: a syllable of 3 letters remembered 50% of the time after 3 seconds. Totally forgotten end of 30 seconds.
b. S-T memory — limited capacity = holds average of 7 items.
c. More than 7 items -- jettisons some to make room.
d. To hold items in STM, must rehearse -- must hear sound of words internally or externally.
3. Long-term memory [LTM] (lasts a lifetime or short time).
a. Transfer fact or idea by:
(1) Associating w/information already in LTM
(2) Organizing information into meaningful units
(3) Understanding by comparing é making relationships.
(4) Frameworking - fit pieces in like in a jigsaw puzzle.
(5) Reorganizing - combing new é old into a new unit.
(6) Rehearsing - aloud to keep memory trace strong

How do psychologists account for remembering?

What's a "memory trace"?

What are the three memory systems?

How long does sensory memory retain information?

How is information transferred to STM?

What are the retention times of STM?

What's the capacity of the STM?

How to hold information in STM?

What are the retention times of LTM?

What are the six ways to transfer information from STM to LTM?

Three kinds of memory systems are sensory, which retains information for about one second; short-term, which retains for a maximum of thirty seconds; and long-term, which varies from a lifetime of retention to a relatively short time.

The six ways (activities) to transfer information to the long-term memory are: associating, organizing, understanding, frameworking, reorganizing and rehearsing.

FIGURE 2.6 The One Q/Five R Version
The narrow column contains questions.

Step 2: Question (<u>One Q/Five R version only</u>) _____

During your first opportunity, reread your notes and rethink the entire lecture. Then formulate questions based on your notes. In the narrow column of the note sheet, opposite the fact or idea in your notes, write a brief question that can be answered with the information in your notes. Writing questions helps to clarify meanings, reveal relationships, establish continuity, and strengthen memory. It also sets the stage for studying for exams.

Step 3: Recite _____

Reciting is saying each fact or idea in your notes out loud, in your own words, and from memory. Recitation is an extremely powerful aid to memory. Recitation makes you think, and thinking leaves a trace in your memory. Experiments show that students who recite retain 80 percent of the material; students who reread but do not recite retain only 20 percent when tested two weeks later. Without retention, there is no learning.

Cover up the wide column of your note sheet with a piece of blank paper, exposing only the cue words or questions in the narrow column. Read each cue word or question aloud; then recite *aloud* and in *your own words* the full facts and ideas brought to mind by the cue word or the answer to the question. After reciting, slide the blank sheet down to check your answer. If your answer is incomplete or incorrect, straighten out the information in your mind and then recite your answer aloud again. Recite until you get the answer right. Proceed through the entire lecture in this way.

Why recite aloud? The sound of your voice stimulates your thinking process. It is this thinking that leaves behind in your memory some neural trace to which you may return later, as to a filing cabinet, to retrieve a fact or idea. Reciting aloud is the most powerful single technique known to psychologists for implanting facts and ideas in your memory.

Why recite using your own words? Cognitive theorists have discovered that people do not remember verbatim what they hear or read. Rather, they remember the meaning that they gave to a fact or idea that they heard or read, and the meaning was expressed in words that they used when they were thinking about the fact or idea. In sum, you remember the meaning you gave to a fact or idea as you processed it in your mind through the use of your own words.

Step 4: Reflect _____

Professor Hans Bethe, nuclear physicist and Nobel Prize winner, said that "creativity comes only through reflection." Reflection is thinking about and applying the facts and ideas that you've learned. You reflect by asking yourself questions such as these: What is the significance of these facts? What principles are they based on? How can I apply them? How do they fit in with what I already know? What is beyond these facts and principles?

Reflection leads to advantageous learning—learning that is done voluntarily and with enthusiasm and curiosity, learning that is propelled by a burning desire to know something. What distinguishes advantageous learning from regular learning is your mental attitude. Knowledge gained through advantageous learning will still be with you long after you have taken your final examination.

Step 5: Review

As many students are aware, yesterday's knowledge interferes with today's knowledge and today's knowledge interferes with yesterday's knowledge. The battle between remembering and forgetting goes on continuously. The best way to prepare for examinations is to keep reviewing and keep reciting the sets of notes that you'll be held responsible for.

Every evening, before you settle down to study, quickly review your notes. Pick up a designated set of notes and recite them. Short, fast, frequent reviews will produce far better understanding and far better remembering than long, all-day or all-night sessions can. After reciting, move immediately into your regular study routine.

Step 6: Recapitulate

Writing a recapitulation, or summary, is not easy, but the rewards are great. Recapitulating is a sure-fire way to gain a deep understanding of the facts and ideas in your notes, and reviewing summaries makes studying for exams a breeze. If you take the time to summarize your notes, your understanding deepens because you have the whole picture instead of an assortment of facts.

Write your summary in the space below the horizontal line at the bottom of the note sheet. Summarize according to one of these plans:

1. Summarize the content of each note sheet.
2. Summarize the content of the entire lecture on the last note sheet for that lecture.
3. Do both 1 and 2.

The third option yields the greatest reward. When you review your notes for exams, you'll be able to see the steps you took to arrive at your final, last-page summary.

TYPES OF NOTES

There are various types of notes that you can use: topic-explanation notes, sentence notes, topic-idea notes, paragraph notes. The nature of the subject, the lecturer's style, and your personal preference will determine which you choose. Be sure to use the Cornell System format with all four types.

Topic-Explanation Notes

Take a look at Figure 2.7. When the lecturer said, "There are two kinds of magic used in many primitive societies," the note taker was ready to list and enumerate them. Notice that the note taker fortified the two kinds of magic with good examples. Later, the note taker wrote key words and phrases in the narrow column.

Sentence Notes

In most instances, sentence notes written in a telegraphic style will be the most efficient way to record a lecture. Be flexible, though, because (as Figure 2.8 shows) you might have to switch from one type of notes to another.

	Oct. 10 (Mon.)-Soc.102-Prof. Oxford ①
	A. Two kinds of magic
Sympathetic= clay model	1. Sympathetic-make model or form of a person from clay, etc., then stick pins into object to hurt symbolized person.
Contagious= fingernail clippings	2. Contagious magic a. Need to possess an article belonging to another person. b. Ex. Fingernail clippings. By doing harm to these objects, feel that harm can be thus transmitted.

FIGURE 2.7   Topic-Explanation Notes

	Oct. 10 (Mon.) – Soc. 102 – Prof. Oxford ②
	A. _Animism_
Stick has power	1. Object has supernatural power
Power = mana	2. Power called _mana_ (not limited to objects)
	a. Objects accumulate mana
	Ex. Good canoe – more mana than poor one.
	b. Objects can lose mana
Can gain or	c. People collect objects w/lots of mana
lose mana	d. Good person's objects collect mana
	e. People, animals, plants have mana, too.
Good people have	Ex. Expert canoe builder has mana –
lots of mana	imparts mana to canoe
	f. Chief has lots of mana – dangerous to
	get too close to chief–mana around head.

FIGURE 2.8 Sentence Notes

	Oct. 27 (WED.) – Economics 105 – Prof. Terry ①
	Some Basic Laws & Principles
What is the Law	1. Law of Diminishing Returns
of Diminishing	a. Refers to amount of extra output (pro-
Returns?	duction) we get when we add additional
	inputs; but, after a point, the extra inputs
	yield decreasing amounts of extra output.
What is	b. Malthus's views depended on this law =
Malthus's Law?	Just so much land, but population
	could increase more rapidly than food
	supplies.

FIGURE 2.9 Topic-Idea Notes

FIGURE 2.10 Paragraph Notes

Topic-Idea Notes

The topic-idea format is often useful in history, economics, and philosophy courses. The lecturer mentions a topic and then expands on it. Notice that in Figure 2.9 the "paragraph" about the law of diminishing returns is broken up by two subtopic indicators to show separate ideas.

Paragraph Notes

If the lecturer is expounding on an idea in a straightforward fashion, don't try to impose some sort of topic and subtopic organization where there is none. Instead, write short, telegraphic sentences and end up with an almost solid paragraph, as shown in Figure 2.10.

COMBINING TEXTBOOK AND LECTURE NOTES

The format shown in Figure 2.11 is ideal for lectures that mainly explain and amplify the textbook. First, in the middle column, record your notes on a previously assigned textbook chapter. Then, when you take lecture notes in the right-hand column, you can avoid repeating material you already have,

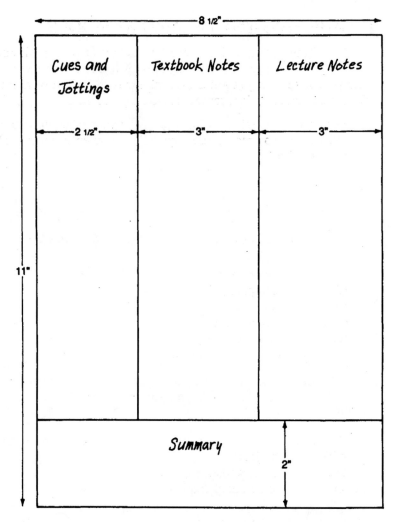

FIGURE 2.11   Cornell System Format for Combining Textbook and Lecture Notes

while you add the lecturer's explanations, examples, and supplementary comments. When you become accustomed to the lecturer's ways, you will be able to judge how much space to leave between items in the middle column in order to keep lecture notes and textbook notes directly opposite each other. The cue words or questions that you write in the left column should pull the two sets of notes together.

ABBREVIATIONS AND SYMBOLS

You should use only the abbreviations that fit your needs and that you will remember easily. A good idea is to introduce only a few abbreviations into your note taking at a time. Overuse may leave you with notes that are difficult to read. Here are some rules to keep in mind.

1. Symbols are especially helpful to students in engineering and mathematics. Lists of commonly used symbols are given in most textbooks and reference books.

   $\neq$ does not equal

   $\underline{f}$ frequency

2. Create a family of symbols.

   $\bigcirc$ organism

   $\odot$ individual

   ⑤   individuals

3. Leave out the periods in standard abbreviations.

   cf   compare

   eg   for example

   dept   department

   NYC   New York City

4. Use only the first syllable of a word.

   pol   politics

   dem   democracy

   lib   liberal

   cap   capitalism

5. Use the entire first syllable and only the first letter of a second syllable.

   subj   subject

   cons   conservative

   tot   totalitarianism

   ind   individual

6. Eliminate final letters. Use just enough of the beginning of a word to form an easily recognizable abbreviation.

   assoc   associate, associated

   ach   achievement

   biol   biological

   info   information

   intro   introduction

   chem   chemistry

   conc   concentration

   max   maximum

   rep   repetition

7. Omit vowels from the middle of words, and retain only enough consonants to provide a recognizable skeleton of the word.

bkgd	background
ppd	prepared
prblm	problem
estmt	estimate
gvt	government

8. Use an apostrophe.

gov't	government
am't	amount
cont'd	continued
educat'l	educational

9. Form the plural of a symbol or abbreviated word by adding "s."

□s	areas
chaps	chapters
co-ops	cooperatives
f̲s	frequencies
/s	ratios

10. Use "g" to represent *ing* endings.

decrg	decreasing
ckg	checking
estg	establishing
exptg	experimenting

11. Use a dot placed over a symbol or word to indicate the word *rate*.

⫶	vibration rate
f̲	frequency rate

12. Generally, spell out short words such as *in, at, to, but, for,* and *key.* Symbols, signs, or abbreviations for short words will make the notes too dense with "shorthand."

13. Leave out unimportant verbs.

14. Leave out the words *a* and *the*.

15. If a term, phrase, or name is initially written out in full during the lecture, substitute initials whenever the term, phrase, or name is used again.
    Initial writing: Modern Massachusetts Party
    Subsequently: MMP

16. Use symbols for commonly recurring connective or transitional words.

&	and
w/	with
w/o	without
vs	against
∴	therefore

SUMMARY

Why should I take notes?	The answer is simple: because forgetting is massive and instantaneous. Forgetting wipes out information like a tornado. Note taking provides disaster relief.
What do the research of Hermann Ebbinghaus and the Leon-Clyde anecdote demonstrate?	Ebbinghaus found that in just twenty minutes we lose nearly half of what we've learned. The Leon-Clyde episode showed how quickly two intelligent men can forget the key points of a lecture that both thought was brilliant. Both point to the necessity of taking notes to combat forgetting.
How do I begin taking notes?	A good way to start is with telegraphic sentences. Students who try to write down a lecture word for word are asking for trouble. The secret is to record only the key words. This streamlined version will save you time, yet provide you with the information you need.
What's the best way to take notes—with printing or with cursive?	Neither. Use the modified printing style. It provides the best of both worlds. It's fast and neat, and it saves you time that you might otherwise spend recopying.
Are there some time wasters in note taking?	Yes. There are at least three that you should avoid: (1) Never tape a lecture. (2) Don't use shorthand. (3) Don't recopy or type your notes.
How can I use the speaker's signals to my advantage?	Expressions such as "in contrast to" or "to sum up" act as signals and help you identify the pattern of organization the speaker is following. If you can follow the speaker's organizational pattern, you'll have little trouble fitting in the facts and ideas along the way.
What do you mean by instant replay?	As soon as you've left the classroom, take a moment to relive the lecture mentally from start to finish. After you've replayed the lecture in your mind, take a few moments to reflect on what the instructor has said and what it all means.

When should I review my notes?

Right away if possible. The longer you wait, the more you'll forget. Review your notes while the lecture is still fresh in your mind.

What is the Cornell Note-taking System?

The Cornell System is a time-honored technique for getting the most out of your notes. The keystone of the system is its format, a 6-inch area for your lecture notes and a 2½-inch left-hand margin for cue words or questions. There are two versions of the Cornell System: the Six R version and the One Q/Five R version. Both have six steps. The main difference between them is in step 2.

What is step 1?

Step 1, recording, simply involves taking notes. The notes go in the 6-inch column. Record as many of the lecturer's key ideas as you can. Use telegraphic sentences to get the information on paper quickly.

What is step 2?

Step 2 in the Six R version is reducing the key facts in your notes to cue words. Step 2 in the One Q/Five R version is formulating some cue questions.

What are cue words?

Cue words are key words or phrases written in the 2½-inch column that act as cues to help you to recall a full fact or idea.

How do I use cue questions?

Simply dream up a question that can be answered with the information from a full fact or idea.

What is involved in step 3, reciting?

When you recite, you say each key fact or idea in your notes out loud, in your own words, and from memory. If you are using the Six R version, your memory will be triggered by the key words in the 2½-inch margin. If you are using the One Q/Five R version, a thoughtful question will focus your response. In either case, the fact that you recite out loud will reveal immediately whether your answer is correct.

What is the reflection step?

Reflection involves thinking about and applying the concepts and ideas that you learn. It triggers advantageous learning—learning that is done voluntarily and with enthusiasm. Advantageous learning has the best chance of lasting.

How often should I follow step 5, reviewing?

As often as possible. Reviewing is really the workhorse of both methods. How much you review will determine whether you will be able to remember important information days and weeks from now. If you make an effort to do a quick review of your notes every evening before you begin studying, you'll do a good job of maintaining your hard-earned knowledge.

What about the sixth and final step, recapitulation?

In short, it means summarizing. If you take the time to summarize your notes, your understanding will deepen because you'll have the whole picture.

Is there more than one way to summarize?

Yes. You have three choices: (1) Summarize the content of each note sheet. (2) Summarize the entire lecture at the bottom of the last note sheet for that lecture. (3) Do both 1 and 2. The third choice is worth the extra effort.

Can lecture and textbook notes be combined?

Yes. Combining lecture and textbook notes is especially important if the lecturer repeats what is in the textbook. Use a three-column format: one column for your lecture notes, another for the notes from your textbook, and the third for your cue words or questions.

Are abbreviations and symbols a help in note taking?

Used sparingly, abbreviations and symbols can be a help. A few key abbreviations can save you time and space. If you use too many abbreviations and symbols, your notes will be difficult to read.

HAVE YOU MISSED SOMETHING?

1. *Sentence completion.* Complete the following sentences with one of the three words listed below each sentence.

   a. Much of the information that a person receives is no longer available after a few _____.

      minutes   hours   weeks

   b. The Leon-Clyde anecdote illustrates the problem of _____.

      note taking   forgetting   recapitulation

2. *Matching.* In each blank space in the left column, write the number preceding the phrase in the right column that matches the left item best.

   _____ a. Two-page system
   _____ b. Forgetting
   _____ c. Cornell System
   _____ d. 2½-inch column
   _____ e. 6-inch column
   _____ f. Recapitulation
   _____ g. Shorthand
   _____ h. Signal words

   1. Can reveal where the lecture is heading
   2. Used cue words or questions
   3. Is both instant and massive
   4. Ideal format for coping with speedy lecturers
   5. Is not recommended as a method of note taking
   6. Used for classroom lecture notes
   7. Time-tested method for taking notes
   8. Note-taking step that involves writing summaries

3. *True-false.* Write *T* beside the *true* statements and *F* beside the *false* statements.

   _____ a. Notes written in the modified printing style must be retyped.

   _____ b. Nearly 47 percent of material learned is forgotten in just twenty minutes.

   _____ c. Taping the lecture is an efficient way to get all the information you need.

   _____ d. Almost no learning takes place during the act of typing.

   _____ e. A well-written stack of notes can function as a second textbook.

   _____ f. The last five or ten minutes of a lecture often contain the greatest concentration of information.

4. *Note-taking dos.* Write "yes" next to the tips that are recommended for optimal note taking.

_____ a. Look over your previous notes before class.

_____ b. Use Roman numerals in outlining your notes.

_____ c. Capture the ideas as well as the facts.

_____ d. Differentiate your thoughts from the lecturer's thoughts.

_____ e. Write on both sides of your note sheets.

_____ f. Skip lines and leave space between main ideas.

_____ g. Begin taking notes immediately.

_____ h. Keep your notes in spiral-bound books.

5. *Multiple choice.* Choose the phrase that completes the following sentence most accurately, and circle the letter that precedes it.

Telegraphic sentences provide you with

a. verbatim notes
b. a secretary-style transcription
c. streamlined information
d. typed documentation

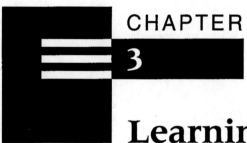

CHAPTER

3

Learning from Your Textbooks

There is a great difference between knowing a thing and understanding it.

Charles Kettering (1876–1958), American electrical engineer and inventor

Are you going hungry? Some students devour their textbook assignments, yet never learn a thing. That's because learning from a textbook involves more than just reading. It means digesting what you read. A textbook assignment needs to be read actively in order to provide food for thought. This chapter discusses

- Getting acquainted with your textbooks
- Mining prefaces and introductions
- Study systems for textbooks
specifically
- The SQ3R Method
- 3Rs for academic survival
and finally
- The Questions-in-the-Margin System

ecause you and your textbooks are going to spend a quarter or a semester together, you'd better become friends. How? By getting acquainted.

GETTING ACQUAINTED WITH YOUR TEXTBOOKS

Buy all your textbooks immediately after you register. This is a wise policy even if your school allows a period in which you can attend many courses before deciding on a final few. Get a head start by reading the tables of contents, prefaces, introductions, and any other up-front material in all your books. Underline important words and sentences, and make notes in the margins. (Of course, if you think you may not ultimately take a course whose books you've bought, don't make these marks! Save your receipts to return all unused books.) Then, while you still have the time, leaf through each of your books. Look at the pictures, tables, and diagrams; read the captions. Read chapter titles and headings and subheadings that interest you. This will give you a good idea of what the book is like and where you will be going during the semester. Later, you'll be glad you did, for you'll be able to see how the various parts of the course fit together.

Reading the Preface

The authors of most textbooks are dealing with serious subjects. Consequently, they write in a serious, scholarly vein. They may be warm and congenial people, but they can appear, in their writing, to be cold and faceless. The only place where most authors can drop their scholarly style and let their hair down is in the preface. There you have a chance to meet and get to know the authors as people. Once you do, you'll find that you can converse and even argue with them as you read the text. Now and then, you'll find yourself saying, "No, I don't agree with that statement" or "What do you mean by that?" You wouldn't make such a statement to a cold, unanswering textbook if you couldn't visualize a live hand behind the writing.

Every textbook would be much more meaningful if the authors could visit your classroom and give a short, informal talk. Thereafter, your textbooks would have far greater meaning. Since personal appearances are usually out of the question, the next best thing is to let the authors talk with you in the preface.

For instance, one student struck pay dirt on page 54 of a ninety-page preface to *A Treatise of Human Nature* by David Hume (1711–76), a Scottish philosopher. Hume wrote in his preface, "If I find the root of human nature, I'll be able to explain all human actions." The student accurately interpreted this sentence to mean that Hume would be using a psychological and not a traditional philosophical approach. Thus, with this proper mental set established, the student was able to read Hume's *Treatise* fairly rapidly and with clear understanding. Students who had not read the author's long preface read the book with a mental set directed at ascertaining Hume's philosophy. Most of those students never understood what David Hume was trying to explain.

In prefaces you can find valuable information such as (1) what the author's objective is, (2) what the author's objective is not, (3) the organizational plan of the book, (4) how and why the book is different from other books about the same subject, and (5) the author's qualifications for writing the book. As a practical exercise, you might find it interesting to read the preface of this book, if you have not already done so. See how much you can gain toward understanding not only the book but also the author.

What the Author's Perspective Is and Is Not

This little book aims to give a certain perspective on the subject of language rather than to assemble facts about it. It has little to say of the ultimate psychological basis of speech and gives only enough of the actual descriptive or historical facts of particular languages to illustrate principles.[1]

It is a tremendous advantage to know the author's objective, for then you'll read and interpret the text from the correct point of view. Otherwise, reading could be quite a struggle, and the facts could seem to be completely unconnected. The author of the quotation just given is saying, "Keep your eye on the *perspective*, not on the facts." Being told what the author is *not* trying to do helps make the objective even clearer. Here, the author says, in effect, "No, this is not a list of facts, as many other books are." Being so warned, you'll refrain from drifting into the wrong pathway of thought while you are reading.

The Organizational Plan of the Book

This book is organized, therefore, neither along chronological lines nor the less obvious logical line of proceeding from simple narration to varying emphases. The arrangement is, if anything, psychological.[2]

Having the organizational plan is like having a road map. You'll know not only what the authors are doing but also where they are going. In the

---

[1]Edward Sapir, *Language* (New York: Harcourt Brace Jovanovich, 1921), p. v.
[2]William M. Sale, Jr., James Hall, and Martin Steinmann, Jr., eds., *Short Stories: Tradition and Direction* (Norfolk, Conn.: New Directions, 1949), p. xii.

example above, you're told what patterns the editors of the anthology are following and not following, which makes the plan of the book especially clear.

How and Why the Book Is Different

Many histories of philosophy exist, and it has not been my purpose merely to add one to their number. My purpose is to exhibit philosophy as an integral part of social and political life; not as the isolated speculations of remarkable individuals.[3]

Knowing how and why the book is different is valuable information. It is easy to think that a new book on a subject is just "more of the same old stuff." When authors point out why their book is different and why their version or approach is necessary, you will read with greater awareness and greater comprehension.

The Author's Qualifications

It is obviously impossible to know as much about every philosopher as can be known about him by a man whose field is less wide; I have no doubt that every single philosopher whom I have mentioned, with the exception of Leibniz, is better known to many men than to me. If, however, this were considered a sufficient reason for respectful silence, it would follow that no man should undertake to treat of more than some narrow strip of history.[4]

Writers usually try, in some subtle way, to let the reader know that their book is written by a scholar, an expert on the subject. In the example above, the writer develops a very fine logical point in an interesting manner. He admits that he is an expert on the German philosopher Leibniz (1646–1716) but not on the broad field of philosophy. He maintains that his lack of knowledge will not prevent him from writing on the broad topic because if writers tackled only their pet subjects, no one would be able to give an overview on any subject.

Reading the Introduction _____

There are four good reasons to read the introduction to a book:

1. The introduction is usually well written, because the writer knows that it is the book's show window—especially for prospective customers looking the book over to decide whether to buy it.

---

[3]Bertrand Russell, *A History of Western Philosophy* (New York: Simon and Schuster, Inc., and London: George Allen Unwin, Ltd., 1945), p. x.
[4]Ibid.

2. Having only limited space, the writer packs the introduction with facts and ideas. As a reader, you will gain a lot from reading a relatively few pages.

3. Reading the introduction puts you on firm footing for the rest of the book, making future assignments easier, requiring less time, and helping you achieve a higher level of mastery than you otherwise would have achieved.

4. With your underlinings and notes in the margin, you can quickly review the introduction time after time, to give yourself a warm-up as well as a door into each assigned chapter.

Figure 3.1 is a densely packed introduction containing information of great and immediate value for the sharper reading of textbooks. It is from a book titled *Six-Way Paragraphs.*[5] The book's sole purpose is to teach students how to spot main ideas. One hundred paragraphs are provided for practice. To prepare students for such practice, the introduction strives to explain the ins and outs of the paragraphs found in textbooks. As you read it, be aware of not only *what* the writer says but also *how* he says it and his *purpose* for saying it.

STUDY SYSTEMS FOR TEXTBOOKS

The old saying "Practice makes perfect" holds true for most activities. Is it true for the reading of textbook chapters? Some say it is not. Others say it is if the reader uses a specially constructed system to read and study the textbook chapters.

In the remainder of this chapter, you will be reading about three specially constructed systems: (1) the SQ3R Method, an old standby; (2) the 3Rs System, which consists of just three essential steps; (3) the Questions-in-the-Margin Technique, which is brand new. If one of these systems fits your personality, style, and academic needs, then adopt it. If you can't find a perfect fit, then select, modify, and adjust the parts of these three systems. Tailor one so that it is right for you.

THE SQ3R METHOD

The SQ3R Method was devised during World War II by Francis P. Robinson, an Ohio State University psychologist. The aim of the system was to help military personnel enrolled in special programs at the university to read

---

[5] Walter Pauk, *Six-Way Paragraphs* (Providence, R.I.: Jamestown Publishers, 1974).

what: wants you to focus on the paragraph - unit

how: brings you and the writer together

purpose: wants you to look at the paragraph through the eyes of the writer

The paragraph! That's the working-unit of both writer and reader. The writer works hard to put meaning into the paragraph; the reader works hard to take meaning out of it. Though they work at opposite tasks, the work of each is closely related. Actually, to understand better the job of the reader, one must first understand better the job of the writer. So, let us look briefly at the writer's job.

what: each paragraph has but one main idea

how: shows you how a writer thinks

purpose: to convince you to look for only one idea per paragraph because writers follow this rule

To make his meaning clear, a writer knows that he must follow certain basic principles. First, he knows that he must develop only one main idea per paragraph. This principle is so important that he knows it backwards, too. He knows that he must not try to develop two main ideas in the same, single paragraph.

what: the topic of the main idea is in the topic sentence, which is usually the first one

how: the writer needs to state a topic sentence to keep his own writing clear and under control

purpose: to instill confidence in you that the topic sentence is an important tool in a writer's kit and convince you it is there, so, look for it!

The next important principle he knows is that the topic of each main idea must be stated in a topic sentence and that such a sentence best serves its function by coming at or near the beginning of its paragraph. He knows, too, that the more clearly he can state the topic of his paragraph in an opening sentence, the more effective he will be in developing a meaningful, well-organized paragraph.

what: developing main ideas through supporting material

how: "more to a writer's job" still keeps you in the writer's shoes

purpose: to announce and advance the new step of supporting materials

Now, there is more to a writer's job than just writing paragraphs consisting of only bare topic sentences and main ideas. The balance of his job deals with *developing* each main idea through the use of supporting material which amplifies and clarifies the main idea and many times makes it more vivid and memorable.

what: (a) main ideas are often supported by examples, (b) other supporting devices listed

how: still through the writer's eyes

To support his main ideas, a writer may use a variety of forms. One of the most common forms to support a main idea is the *example*. Examples help to illustrate the main idea more vividly. Other purpose: to develop the new idea of supporting materials

supporting materials are anecdotes, incidents, jokes, allusions, comparisons, contrasts, analogics, definitions, exceptions, logic, and so forth.

what   paragraph contains (a) topic sentence, (b) main idea, and (c) supporting material

how: transfer the knowledge from the writer to you, the reader

purpose: to summarize all the three steps

To summarize, the reader should have learned from the writer that a textbook-type paragraph usually contains these three elements: a topic sentence, a main idea, and supporting material. Knowing this, the reader should use the topic sentence to lead him to the main idea. Once he grasps the main idea, then everything else is supporting material used to illustrate, amplify, and qualify the main idea. So, in the final analysis, the reader must be able to separate the main idea from the supporting material, yet see the relationship between them.

FIGURE 3.1   The Content of an Introduction
Source: From Six-Way Paragraphs by Walter Pauk. Copyright © 1974 by Jamestown Publishers, Providence, Rhode Island. Reprinted by permission.

faster and to study better. The letters in the name of the system stand for *survey, question, read, recite,* and *review.* Robinson described the SQ3R Method and explained its benefits:

> These five steps of the SQ3R system—survey, question, read, recite, and review—should result in faster reading, and fixing of the important points in the memory. You will find one other worthwhile outcome: Quiz questions will seem familiar because the headings turned into questions are usually the points emphasized in quizzes. By predicting actual quiz questions and looking up the answers beforehand, you know that you are effectively studying what is considered important in the course.[6]

The five steps of the SQ3R Method are described and explained as follows[7]:

---

[6]Francis P. Robinson, *Effective Study,* 4th ed. (New York: Harper & Row, 1970), p. 32.
[7]Explanation and adaptation of five steps of the "SQ3R Method" from *Effective Study* Fourth Edition by Francis P. Robinson. Copyright 1941, 1946 by Harper & Row, Publishers, Inc. Copyright © 1961, 1970 by Francis P. Robinson. Reprinted by permission of Harper & Row, Publishers, Inc.

S Survey

Glance through all the headings in the chapter, and read the final summary paragraph (if the chapter has one). This survey should not take more than a minute, and it will show you the three to six core ideas on which the discussion will be based. This orientation will help you organize the ideas as you read them later.

Q Question

Now begin to work. Turn the first heading into a question. This will arouse your curiosity and thereby increase comprehension. It will bring to mind information you already know, thus helping you understand that section more quickly. The question also will make important points stand out from explanatory details. You can turn a heading into a question as you read the heading, but it demands conscious effort on your part.

R_1 Read

Read so as to answer that question, but read only to the end of the first section. This should not be a passive plodding along each line, but an active search for the answer.

R_2 Recite

Having read the first section, look away from the book and try briefly to recite the answer to your question. Use your own words, and cite an example. If you can do this, you know what is in the book; if you cannot, glance over the section again. An excellent way to do this reciting from memory is to jot down brief cue phrases in outline form on a sheet of paper.

Now repeat the second to fourth steps for each successive section: That is, turn the next heading into a question, read to answer that question, and recite the answer by jotting down cue phrases in your outline. Read in this way until the entire lesson is completed.

R_3 Review

When you have read through in this way, look over your notes to get a bird's-eye view of the points and their relationships to each other. Check your memory by reciting the major subpoints under each heading. This can be done by covering up your notes and trying to recall the main points. Then expose each major point and try to recall the subpoints listed under it.

3Rs FOR ACADEMIC SURVIVAL

The 3Rs System is perfect for students who like to move quickly into a textbook chapter, or for those who face exams with little time for intensive study. The three Rs stand for *read, record,* and *recite*—the three essential steps for mastering textbook assignments. If you like its simplicity, you can also use the 3Rs System to implant facts and ideas in your long-term memory. Just emphasize the third step: Keep reciting the facts and ideas until overlearning occurs.

R₁ Read

Read several paragraphs; then go back to the first paragraph and ask yourself, "What do I need to know in this paragraph?" Read and reread until you find out.

R₂ Record

Once you have identified and can briefly say aloud what you need to know, underline only the key words, phrases, and sentences that identify this information. Later, when you review, your eyes will immediately focus on these, the essential parts of the paragraph. You won't have to reread the whole paragraph again when you review. Then do one more important thing: Jot in the margin an ever-so-brief question that asks for the information underlined. Question forming is very important in this system. Go through the entire chapter paragraph by paragraph.

R₃ Recite

Start at the first page of your assignment and cover up the printed page with a blank sheet of paper, leaving the questions in the margin exposed. Then, in your own words, recite aloud the answers. After reciting, check for accuracy. Recite until you've completed the chapter. Remember: If you don't know the answer now, you won't know it tomorrow in class or be able to write it on an exam. So, while you still have the chance, keep trying until you get the answer right.

THE QUESTIONS-IN-THE-MARGIN SYSTEM

The Questions-in-the-Margin System incorporates seven important steps needed to master any subject. Each step thoroughly done in sequence will

SURVEY	Read the title and speculate about what the chapter will be about. Read the headings to determine what ideas and facts will be presented. Read any summarizing section.
QUESTION	Turn each heading into a question by adding such words as "what," "how," or "who." Then read to answer the question.
READ	Read several paragraphs; then come back to the first paragraph and ask questions such as these: What is the main idea? How do the supporting materials support it? What do I need to know in this paragraph?
QUESTIONS IN MARGINS	Think deeply; then formulate and write a brief, telegraphic question in the margin. Next, underline very sparingly only the key words and phrases that make up the answer. The less underlining, the better.
RECITE	Counteract forgetting by reciting. Cover your textbook page, exposing only your questions in the margin. Then, in your own words, recite aloud the answers. After reciting, check for accuracy. Recite until you've completed the chapter.
REVIEW	Immediately after reciting, take a fresh look at each question; mentally glimpse and hold the answer for a few moments. In this way, work through the entire chapter. This overview of questions and answers will tend to snap the separate parts together like pieces of a jigsaw puzzle, enabling you to see the chapter as a whole. Intersperse reviews throughout the semester.
REFLECT	Manipulate the ideas and facts mentally. Turn them over, speculate on them, compare one with the other, notice where they agree and differ. Organize them under larger categories, or compress them into smaller units. Finally, free them from the chapter by weaving them into your existing knowledge.

FIGURE 3.2   The Questions-in-the-Margin System

help you see the author's facts and ideas more and more clearly. When you finish the seventh step, you will feel as though you had put the last piece of a jigsaw puzzle in place: You will see the full picture, which will image itself indelibly in your memory. Figure 3.2 is an overview of the system.

Step 1: Surveying a Textbook Chapter

Surveying has various uses, but its greatest use is in mastering textbook assignments. It is the grease that makes subsequent reading and studying more efficient. A good scholar would no more begin reading a chapter without first skimming it than an automotive engineer would run a car without first greasing it. The grease does not supply the power, but without it the gasoline would not be of much use.

If you skip this step, you will lose time, not save time. If you burrow directly into one paragraph after another, you'll be unearthing one compartmentalized fact after another, but you won't see how the facts relate to each other. Psychologists call this not-seeing-the-big-picture condition *tunnel vision*.

Here is how a student who had developed the technique of surveying to a fine art described this step:

> I first spend two or three minutes trying to get the full meaning out of the title of the chapter. I even wonder briefly why the author picked such a title. Then I shove off by saying to myself, "Let's see what he has to say about this subject."
>
> Next, I read the first couple of paragraphs in the regular way. If I don't do this, it's like coming into the middle of a conversation: I can't make head or tail of it.
>
> Then I let the printer guide me. My eyes dart to the big-type headings and subheadings. I read them because I know that they are like the small headlines for newspaper items. They are little summaries. I then read a sentence or two underneath these headings. My eyes float over the rest of the material looking for other islands of information. They might be marked by clues such as italicized words, underlined words, and changes in the type.
>
> When I first started to skim, I used to skip all the illustrations, charts, and diagrams. But after getting burned on exams, I found I could learn a lot very easily just by reading the captions and noticing what the lines on the diagrams and graphs meant. At least for me, illustrations stick in my mind better than words do; so during an exam, I take advantage of this. I close my eyes and see the illustration on the blackboard of my mind.
>
> I'm always careful to read the last paragraph or last section marked "summary." That's where the author gathers together all the main ideas of the chapter.
>
> Finally, I pause for a few minutes to bring all these pieces and fragments together before I begin reading and taking notes on the chapter. Sometimes to bring things together, I go back to the beginning of the chapter and leaf through the pages without reading, just looking at what I have already looked at.
>
> There are a few other things that skimming does for me. First, I no longer put off studying. Skimming is easy, so I don't mind getting started. Second, once I get into the chapter, I find that most of the chapters contain some interesting information, so I become interested. Third, because I am interested in the material, I concentrate better. And fourth, the topics that I find by skimming somehow make good topic headings for my notes.

When you skim, don't dawdle. Move along with good comprehension, but go slowly enough to get the facts, ideas, and principles accurately. Once assimilated, a mistake is hard to eradicate.

There are four practical reasons why surveying can make a real and immediate difference in your reading.

1. Surveying Creates a Background.   When you don't have some prior knowledge about the subject matter of an assigned chapter, you read slowly and have difficulty understanding the material. When you come to something that you recognize, your reading speed quickens and your comprehension grows. The difference is your prior knowledge. Surveying prepares you for reading by giving you some background information about a chapter. Surveying counteracts tunnel vision. Once you have viewed the broad canvas, you will see how individual ideas fit into the complete picture.

When you skim a chapter, you spot and pick up topics by reading headings and subheadings. You pick up ideas by reading the first and last sentences of paragraphs. You become familiar with the names of people and places by skimming these names. You grasp the general objective of the chapter by reading the introductory paragraph, and you get an overview by reading the summarizing paragraph at the end of the chapter. You won't know any of these facts and ideas cold, of course. But when you meet them again during your careful reading, you will recognize them, and this familiarity will give you confidence and understanding.

2. Surveying Provides Advance Organizers.   According to David P. Ausubel, a learning-theory psychologist, a preview of the general content of a chapter creates *advance organizers*, which help students learn and remember material they later study closely. The familiar landmarks act as topics or categories under which ideas, facts, and details may be clustered. John Livingston Lowes, a professor of literature at Princeton University, characterized such familiar landmarks as *magnetic centers* around which ideas, facts, and details cluster like iron filings around a magnet.

George Katona, a psychologist, tested the effectiveness of advance organizers with two groups of students. One group was asked to read a selection in which a general principle of economics was stated in the first sentence. The second group was given the same selection, but with the first sentence deleted. When the students in the first group were tested, they not only remembered the specific content of the paragraph better than the second group, but they were able to apply the general principle to all the examples in the selection. Without the first sentence, which was an advance organizer, students in the second group viewed the examples as separate, unrelated entities and were unable to see that the examples could be clustered under the one umbrella of a common principle in economics.

3. Surveying Limbers the Mind.   For an athlete, a pregame warm-up limbers muscles, and it also limbers the psyche and brain. An athlete knows that success comes from the coordination of smoothly gliding muscles, a positive attitude, and a concentrating mind. The prestudy survey of a textbook achieves for the scholar what the pregame warm-up achieves for the athlete.

4. Surveying Overcomes Mental Inertia. How often have you said with impatience and exasperation, "Let's get started!" Getting started is hard. According to Newton's first law of motion, "A body in motion tends to remain in motion; a body at rest tends to remain at rest."

Many students find it difficult to open a textbook and begin to study. If you are one of them, use surveying to ease yourself into studying. Surveying does the job: It gets you started.

You need not always survey an entire chapter as the first step. You may begin by surveying the first part before you read it. Later, as you work your way through the chapter, you may want to skim farther ahead, page by page, as you read and study to understand.

Step 2: Turning Headings into Questions

The people who have *answers to give* when they are finished reading are usually those who had *questions to ask* before and during their reading. Asking questions works for one main reason: The questions force you to concentrate and to observe the words keenly, directly, and selectively as you read. When you don't have a question in mind, your eyes just glide over a paragraph, and you never realize that the printed words are alive with answers. In the words of John Lubbock (1834–1913), naturalist, banker, writer, neighbor of Charles Darwin, and coiner of the words *paleolithic* and *neolithic*, "What we see depends mainly on what we look for."

As you read, you should interrogate the writer, not simply stare at the words. You must approach each paragraph like an inquiring reporter, with definite and searching questions. The better your questions, the better will be your comprehension.

How do you formulate warm-up questions as you read and study a textbook? One technique is to turn each heading into a question. For example, the main heading "Basic Aspects of Memory" could be turned into the question "What are the basic aspects of memory?" The technique is simple, but it works. Here are some additional examples:

Subtopic Heading	*Question Formulated*
The Memory Trace	What is a memory trace?
Rate of Forgetting	How fast do we forget?
Organization of Recall	How is recall organized?
Decay Theory	What is the decay theory?

Once you have turned a heading into a question, you read the material under the heading to answer your question. If the question is answered early in the discussion, ask another, based on what you have read.

There are general questions that you can use in reading about almost any topic. Some readers prefer to ask these general questions to uncover specific facts and ideas. Other readers just enjoy conversing with the writer through the use of a general question-and-answer technique. In either case, an active, searching attitude is created. Here are some of the general questions:

- What does this paragraph tell me?
- What are the important supporting details?
- Does this example make the main point clear?
- What evidence does the writer give?
- What is the underlying principle?
- If this fact or idea is true, then what logically follows?
- If it is true, how does it affect my existing knowledge?
- How does this paragraph fit in with this chapter?
- What questions might I be asked about this paragraph?

Some practical readers ask not only "What is the author saying?" but also "How can I use this information?" If you ask such questions, make it a rule to try to answer them. Say something. Say anything that makes sense to you. Without effort, there's no gain.

A great deal is said these days about learning how to think: Books are written; lectures are given; and teachers exhort. The subject of thinking can be summarized in this one line: Thinking at its highest level is asking the right, relevant question.

Step 3: Reading Paragraph by Paragraph _____

After surveying the chapter, return to the first paragraph and read it thoroughly enough to answer only one question: What did the author say in this paragraph? If you are unable to answer this question at first, you must reread the paragraph until you can; otherwise you will not gain a functional understanding of the paragraph.

This is a crucial step. You must not move ahead to succeeding paragraphs if doing so means leaving the present paragraph unsettled. You may push on beyond a problem paragraph for the purpose of gaining context, but always with the intention of coming back to the problem paragraph. Remember that understanding a succession of paragraphs leads to comprehension of the chapter.

Guard against the habit of moving your eyes over the lines of print without grasping the writer's ideas. Read for the ideas and concepts behind the words. Pause at the end of each paragraph or at the end of a series of paragraphs, and in your own words describe the writer's main idea and the supporting details. Answer the question "What did I learn in this paragraph?" When you have described, you have understood.

The Topic Sentence. Use the topic sentence to help you break into the meaning of each paragraph. The topic sentence often contains the main idea or points to the main idea.

In Figure 3.3, the first sentence, the topic sentence, states the main idea. The rest of the paragraph is a long list of concrete examples supporting the main idea. The last sentence is not a continuation of the list; it rounds out or completes the paragraph. Incidentally (but importantly), notice how the writer sustains the mood of despondency from the opening sentence, through the examples, into the last clause of the last sentence.

Textbook Troubleshooting. As you read and study your textbook, your businesslike side should keep asking, "Am I getting it?" If the answer is, "It's getting pretty vague," you should take immediate action.

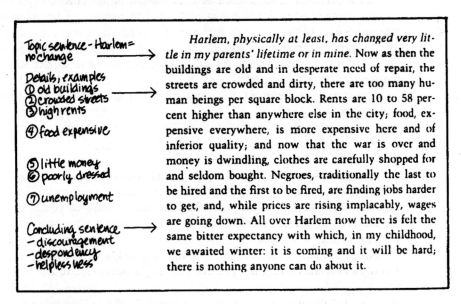

FIGURE 3.3 The Topic Sentence
Source: From Notes of a Native Son *by James Baldwin. Copyright © 1955, renewed 1983 by James Baldwin. Reprinted by permission of Beacon Press.*

1. Go back a couple of paragraphs to pick up the thread of the writer's ideas again.

2. Read ahead a couple of paragraphs to see where you're going.

3. Open your dictionary and look up any words that you are not sure of and that might be holding you back.

4. Reread the troublesome paragraph aloud, using exaggerated expression and emphasis to get at the meaning of what's being said. Such reading aloud, especially with expression, brings concentration back to a 100 percent level.

The Corson Technique.   Dale Corson, former president of Cornell University and dean of the College of Engineering, observed that engineers and other students in science and mathematics must often crack the meaning of an idea or concept one sentence at a time. If comprehension does not occur even at this snail's pace, then you must ask your instructor for help. "But before you do," says Dr. Corson, "ask yourself this question: What is it that I don't understand?"

Under no circumstance should you go to the instructor, open the book, and with a broad sweep of your hand say, "I don't understand this." When you go for help, you should be able to say, "I understand and follow the writer's idea up to this point and even beyond this point, but for some reason this particular section has no meaning for me." That way, the instructor knows not only what you understand and don't understand but also that you did your utmost to achieve understanding. You now have set the stage for a meaningful learning session.

The Corson Technique has a wonderful by-product. After analyzing and verbalizing your problem, after you have viewed it from several angles, you will most likely have solved it yourself. You may not have to discuss it with anyone else.

Additional Reading Strategies.   When you read sentences, make full use of signal words and organizational clues. If a sentence or paragraph begins "on the one hand," watch for the inevitable "on the other hand," which introduces the other side of the argument. Innocent little everyday words such as "since," "because," and "although" are as important in relating parts of a sentence as a plus, minus, or square-root sign is in a math equation. Ignoring or misreading them can get you into serious trouble.

If you get bogged down in a difficult sentence or paragraph, try reading the material without any modifying phrases. Find the simple subject of the sentence, the verb, and the simple object, to avoid getting lost in a maze of language. When the framework shows through clearly, so that you can grasp the main idea, then go back and read the material with all its "trimmings," to get its full sense.

After you finish a paragraph and summarize it, don't plunge immediately into the next paragraph. Pause for a minute or two, to think about the meaning of the paragraph you just read. Such a thinking pause provides time for the main idea to consolidate, to sink into your memory.

Whenever you encounter a difficult, unusual, or new word or term in your textbook, look it up in a glossary or dictionary. Put these words and terms, with their definitions, on 3×5 cards. You can learn these words and terms by carrying the cards and looking them over whenever you have a chance.

When you feel bored, do not reward your boredom by slamming your book shut and leaving empty-minded. Above all, don't reward yourself by going to a movie. If you get bored, give yourself the limited objective of extracting one nugget of knowledge, be it ever so small. Then, with that *accomplished*, you have *earned* the right to a break or a movie.

Step 4: Writing Questions in the Margins

The question-in-the-margin step is different in purpose from the question step of the SQ3R Method. In the SQ3R Method, the purpose of the question is to keep the reader alert, concentrating, and looking for an answer to the limited question that was asked. The question step of SQ3R directs the reader to turn headings and subheadings into questions. Obviously, putting "what" or "how" in front of a heading does not transform it automatically into a deep and searching question. A heading that is limited to begin with will remain limited after the addition of "what" or "how."

To be sure, this does not mean that the question step in SQ3R is not a good one. It serves a definite and valuable purpose when you are reading paragraphs or sections of the textbook for the first time. However, it is hard to imagine that you will be able to formulate a provocative question on textbook material before you have read, understood, and thought about the material. Merely asking a question before reading does not in any way guarantee that an answer will be forthcoming, regardless of how hard you read. Coming up with answers is not easy. Usually you have to dig hard for a comprehensive, accurate answer, and that is why the question-in-the-margin step comes into the system at this time—after you have read a paragraph thoroughly.

Once you have read a paragraph thoroughly and have been able to answer questions such as "What is the main idea here?" or "What are the important points made here?" you are ready to formulate and write a brief, telegraphic question in the margin of your textbook. After writing the question, you should then, for the first time, underline very sparingly only the key words and phrases that make up the answer. The less underlining you do, the better.

Later, when you review for an exam, your eyes and mind will be directed to the words and phrases that deliver the meaning directly and efficiently. When you underline only the key words and phrases, you have to think, and thinking is what makes understanding and remembering possible.

Go through the entire chapter in this way: reading thoroughly to understand the passage; writing a brief, meaningful question; and underlining sparingly. Figure 3.4 shows the questions-in-the-margin technique applied to a textbook page.

Step 5: Reciting Based on the Questions in the Margin

After formulating questions on the entire chapter, go back to the beginning of the chapter and cover the printed text with a blank sheet of paper, exposing only the questions you've written in the margin. Read the first question aloud, and answer the question in your own words. Slide the blank sheet down to check your answer. If your answer is wrong or incomplete, recite it aloud again. Do this until you get the answer right. Go through the entire chapter in this way. Your aim is to establish in your memory an accurate, crystal-clear impression, because that's what you want to return to later

What 2 aspects lead to success?

What 3 elements might make up a paper?

What's the key in choosing a topic?

If not sure of a topic, do what?

WRITING GOOD PAPERS IN COLLEGE

The techniques of writing a good paper are easy to follow. You should remember two important aspects that lead to success. First, start work early on the paper. Second, if you have a choice, choose a subject that you are interested in, or that you can develop an interest in.

Much of your work in college involves absorbing knowledge; when it comes to writing papers, you have the opportunity to put down on paper what you've learned about a subject, and perhaps your opinions and conclusions on the subject.

Writing is an important form of communication. To communicate well you must have something you really want to say. So if you have a choice of topics, choose one that intrigues you. If it isn't one that everyone else is writing on, all the better. If you're not sure about your choice of topic, do a little preliminary research to see what's involved in several topics before you make a final decision. Remember the caution about allowing yourself enough time? Here's where it comes into play. Take enough time to choose a topic carefully (see Chapter 15 for specific pointers).

FIGURE 3.4 Writing Questions in the Margin

during an exam. If the impression in your memory is fuzzy at this time, it will be even fuzzier three or four weeks later.

Why Recite Aloud? Reciting aloud forces you to think, and it is this thinking that leaves behind in your memory a neural trace to come back to. You must believe, without an iota of doubt and without a moment of hesitation, that forgetting is and will continue to be your major academic problem. Forgetting erodes, corrodes, and thwarts learning. Forgetting never lets up. It works continuously to expel from memory what you worked so hard—often far into the night—to put there. Don't let forgetting get the upper hand. You can bring forgetting almost to a standstill by using the power of recitation.

Reciting promotes concentration, forms a sound basis for understanding the next paragraph or the next chapter, provides time for the memory trace to consolidate, ensures that facts and ideas are remembered accurately, and provides immediate feedback on how you're doing (and when you know that you're doing well, you will make progress). Moreover, experiments have shown that the greater the proportion of reciting time to reading time, the greater is the learning. Students who spent 20 percent of their time reading and 80 percent reciting did much better than students who spent less time reciting and more time reading.

When you recite aloud, don't mumble. Express the ideas in complete sentences, using the proper signal words. For example, when you are reciting a list of ideas or facts, enumerate them by saying "first," "second," and so on. Insert words such as "furthermore," "however," and "finally." When you do so in oral practice, you will do so most naturally in writing during an exam.

The New Way: Reciting and Visualizing. Visualizing is a powerful new technique for increasing your learning and your remembering. As you recite, instead of just mouthing the answer, picture yourself as a scholar-orator standing by your seat in the classroom reciting your answer to the instructor. Although you are actually sitting at your desk in your room and reciting in a lively manner, in your mind's eye you are standing in the classroom speaking, explaining, and gesturing.

Many successful athletes use visualization all the time. They burn such a positive image in their minds that it becomes part of the subconscious, and they expect the performance that they visualized to be carried out in actuality. Dwight Stones, a former U.S. Olympic high jumper, is very well known for the way in which he visualizes each jump before he actually makes it. There's nothing subtle about Stones. As he stands staring at the bar, his head bobs and you can almost visualize his jump yourself. His little routine might almost be comical except for one thing: Stones has won countless gold medals in international competition, and so instead of being laughed at for his peculiar routine, he is widely imitated by younger athletes who literally and figuratively are hoping to reach the heights that Stones has achieved.

Picture yourself in a classroom writing the answer to an essay question. Visualize the entire scene: the classroom, the other students, the instructor, the exam being handed out, your reading the questions. Now look at your textbook; read the question in the margin aloud; think for a few moments how you plan to organize and deliver your answer. Then, as if you were in an exam, recite softly to yourself and at the same time write your answer as you would if the exam were real. Try to *see* yourself in the classroom, thinking and writing forcefully and successfully. In this way you'll be creating in your brain cells a deep, well-defined pattern that will be easy to come back to and follow when the real exam is given. To learn more about how to think visually, see Pauk: *How to Study in College*.

Step 6: Reviewing Immediately and Later

Immediately after you have recited the whole chapter, you should finish the session with a general, relaxed overview, using the questions in the margins as cues. The purpose of the general overview is to put together all the separate questions and answers—to snap them together like the parts of a jigsaw puzzle and reveal the chapter as a whole.

This overview is made not by reciting the whole business over again—you've had enough of that for a while. Rather, look thoughtfully at each question in the margin, mentally glimpse the answer, and hold the answer in mind for a few seconds. Proceed through the entire chapter in this way. Don't make this process a chore. Actually, it could be a pleasant process, similar to taking a sweeping glance at a lawn you've finished mowing or a room you've straightened up. Take a last mental look at the questions and answers, and try to see the chapter as a whole.

The immediate review is important—very important—but it is not enough. You should review thoroughly and often. Later reviews should be conducted in the same way as the immediate review: using questions in the margins as cues, one page at a time, aloud, and in your own words. These later reviews will keep you in a state of preparedness for quizzes and exams. There will be no need to cram your head full of ideas and facts on the night before an exam. All you'll need is a refresher, in the same form—one more review.

As you review, look for ways to connect or categorize, to put like things together and to place opposite things opposite each other. Look for common characteristics, differences, or functions by which to categorize facts and ideas. This type of analysis puts you in control and gives you the chance to use your creativity—to bring the textbook to life and bring order to the mass of information you are required to learn. Categorizing also puts to practical use the Magical Number Seven Theory—the finding that the immediate memory seems to be limited to seven categories, which can be as broad as you care to make them.

The best time for a fast review of your textbook is the half hour before going to bed. Things learned then have a way of lingering in the conscious mind during the time before sleep comes and in the subconscious mind after sleep comes.

Step 7: Reflecting on Facts and Ideas

After you learn facts and ideas through recitation and immediate review, let your mind reflect on them. Let it speculate or play with the knowledge you've acquired. To engage in reflection is to bring creativity to your learning. Ask yourself such questions as these: What is the significance of these facts and ideas? What principle or principles are they based on? What else could they be applied to? How do they fit in with what I already know? From these facts and ideas, what else can I learn? When you reflect, you weave new facts and ideas into your existing knowledge. They then become part of your regular stock of thinking tools.

There's a huge difference between proficiency and creativity. You can become proficient by studying your textbooks and lecture notes, but you will never be creative until you try to see beyond the facts, to leap mentally beyond the given. You must reflect on the facts and ideas, because creativity comes only through reflection, not from recitation and review.

To survive academically in college, you have to recite. To grow in creativity and in wisdom, you have to reflect.

The Reciter . . .	*The Reflector . . .*
● Follows strictly the ideas and facts in the textbook	● Pursues ideas and facts through additional reading in the library and goes to original works
● Is bound by the course outline	● Uses the course outline as a point of departure
● Is diligent and disciplined in memorizing but keeps ideas and facts at arm's length	● Is adventuresome and experimental and internalizes facts and ideas
● Is so busy reciting that the framework of the course is vaguely seen or missed	● Is likely to see the framework of the course and to talk to the instructor because of ideas occurring during reflection

- Understands the literal meaning but not the implications of assignments

- Learns and accepts facts and ideas in the sequential order of the textbook

- Applies learning to various situations

- Thinks, hypothesizes, speculates, and then tests ideas independently

Use reflection often. Reflection is a skill you can take with you wherever you go and use in spare moments. You can reflect while walking from one building to another, standing in line, waiting for a friend, or riding a bus. People who have made great discoveries have reported that some of their best insights came in unlikely places and at odd times. A classic example is that of Archimedes (287?–212 B.C.), the greatest mathematician of ancient times, who discovered the natural law of buoyancy while taking a bath. He became so excited that he ran naked through the streets shouting, "Eureka!"

Begin with the facts and ideas you have learned, and become curious about them. Look at them in different ways, combine them, separate them into the basics, try to find out what would happen if the opposite were true, and so on. This may be difficult at first, but it will become easier as your creativity grows. Continue your reflection until your ideas take definite shape. Don't leave them vague. If you need more information, an encyclopedia or a standard source book on the subject will often help you bring fuzzy ideas into focus.

The only type of learning that becomes a permanent part of you and increases your innate wisdom is *advantageous learning*—learning that occurs when you take a voluntary, extra step beyond the mere memorization of facts. That extra step is reflection. In the words of the philosopher Arthur Schopenhauer (1788–1860): "A man may have a great mass of knowledge, but if he has not worked it up by thinking it over for himself, it has much less value than a far smaller amount which he has thoroughly pondered."

SUMMARY

What's the best way to get the semester off to a good start?

Buy all your books just as soon as you've registered, so that you will have time to read the table of contents, preface, introduction, and other up-front material in each textbook.

What good is the preface?

The preface is the one place where most authors drop their scholarly style. As a result, you may get a clear picture of the man or woman who has written your textbook. In addition, the preface provides information not available elsewhere: what the author's objective is and is not, how the book is organized, how and why the book is different from other books on the same subject, and the author's qualifications for writing the book.

With all that information in the preface, what's the point of the introduction?

Whereas the preface deals in matters broad and general, the author's introduction is often narrow and specific. From the introduction you'll learn the underlying principles of the book. Many students refer to the introduction before they tackle each new chapter, just to be sure that they're on the right track.

How does the SQ3R Method of study work?

In five steps—survey, question, read, recite, and review—the SQ3R Method helps you approach reading assignments systematically. First you survey the headings in a chapter and read the summary at the end. Then you turn these headings into questions. Read so as to answer that question, then look away from the book and briefly recite the answer you've found. Review your notes to get a bird's-eye view of all the points you've raised and their relationship to one another. SQ3R should result in faster reading and efficient learning.

How does the 3Rs System work?

The 3Rs System is for students who work well under the pressure of time and exams. The three steps—read, record, and recite—are simple and direct. First read several paragraphs, then return to the first paragraph and ask yourself what you need to know in the paragraph. Then underline key words, phrases, and sentences containing that information. Jot a brief question that asks for this underlined information. Cover

How does the Questions-in-the-Margin System work?

the pages of your assignment and try to answer the questions you've posed in the margins. Recite in this way until you finish the chapter.

This technique combines the simplicity of the 3Rs System with the long-term effectiveness of SQ3R. It has seven clear and helpful steps.

What is the first step in the Questions-in-the-Margin System?

Before you begin to read a textbook assignment in earnest, survey, or skim, it first. The few minutes that you spend surveying a chapter can be invaluable.

Isn't surveying a waste of time?

No. Surveying a chapter can help you in at least four ways: (1) Surveying provides you with background information. (2) Surveying provides advance organizers—familiar landmarks that act as topics or categories around which you can cluster ideas, facts, and details. (3) Surveying readies your mind for the task of reading the textbook chapter. (4) Surveying overcomes mental inertia by easing you into a task (reading your textbook) that you might otherwise have put off.

What is the second step in the Questions-in-the-Margin System?

In the second step, you turn the chapter headings into questions, or you ask some general questions that can be applied to any topic. In either case, you suddenly have a purpose for reading. As a result, you don't simply stare at the words, you interact with them. Remember: Students who have *answers to give* when they finish reading are usually those who had *questions to ask* while they read.

What does the third step, reading paragraph by paragraph, entail?

When you begin to read a textbook chapter, it is crucial for you to understand one paragraph before you move on to the next. You should read and reread until you are able to answer the question "What did the author say in this paragraph?"

Is there a key to understanding the meaning of a paragraph?

Yes. The topic sentence of each paragraph generally contains the main idea or points to the main idea. It is often the first sentence in the paragraph.

What should I do if I can't make sense of a paragraph?

There are five techniques to get yourself out of a jam: (1) Go back a few paragraphs to pick up the thread of the author's ideas. (2) Read ahead a paragraph or two to see what's coming. (3) Grab a dictionary and look up any words that are acting as stumbling blocks. (4) Reread the troublesome paragraph out loud using exaggerated intonation to get at the meaning of the author's words. (5) If the first four techniques don't work, use the Corson Technique: Identify specifically what's causing you trouble. When you take pains to pinpoint a problem, you often wind up solving the problem. If you're still stumped, take your specific question to your instructor.

Are there any other ways to get a lot out of my reading?

Yes. Here are a few: (1) Be on the alert for signal words and organizational clues that tell you where the author is going. (2) To make sense of an especially complex sentence, simplify things by reading the material without any modifiers. (3) Pause after each paragraph so that your mind has a chance to absorb new information. (4) Transfer new and difficult words to 3×5 cards, where they can be studied and mastered so that you won't have to look them up again. (5) If you begin to lose interest in your reading, instead of closing the book and giving up, make an effort to extract at least one more piece of information before you move on to something else.

How does step 4, writing questions in the margins, differ from step 2?

In step 2 you were asked to formulate questions primarily to keep you alert and to keep you reading. When you have read a paragraph carefully and thoroughly, you should be able to ask deep and meaningful questions about it—the kind of questions that you are likely to find on an exam. Once you've written a question in the margin, go back to the text itself and underline the key words and terms that aid in answering your question.

Is there any point in going beyond step 4? Isn't writing questions in the margin the way to gain important information?

If you want to remember information, you must recite it. When you have formulated questions for the entire chapter, go back over the text and read your questions aloud one at a time, answering them correctly before you move on. Reciting out loud forces you to think while you recite and helps keep forgetting in check.

How do I apply step 6, reviewing?

Begin with an immediate review. As soon as you've finished reciting a chapter, take a moment to look over your notes in an effort to pull things together in your mind. Formulating the "big picture" improves the likelihood that the facts from the chapter will remain in your memory.

How do I go about reflecting?

Begin by questioning the things you learn. Wonder about their significance, the principles on which they are based, and other ideas they might be applied to. In short, try to see beyond the facts and ideas in the pages of your textbooks.

HAVE YOU MISSED SOMETHING?

1. *Sentence completion.*   Complete the following sentences with one of the three words listed below each sentence.

    a. Frequent and thorough reviews help to eliminate the need for ____.
        recitation   cramming   reflection

    b. When you use the Questions-in-the-Margin System, you should underline the textbook _____.
        sparingly   frequently   initially

c. Learning is most likely to occur when the proportion of reciting time to reading time is _____.

high   equal   low

2. *Matching.* In each blank space in the left column, write the number preceding the phrase in the right column that matches the left item best.

_____ a. Reflection
_____ b. 3Rs System
_____ c. Recitation
_____ d. Review
_____ e. Preface
_____ f. SQ3R Method
_____ g. Corson Technique
_____ h. Visualization

1. Time-honored way to study textbooks
2. Pinpoints what you don't understand
3. Reveals author's objectives
4. Brings creativity to learning
5. Step not found in the 3Rs System
6. A three-step study method
7. A powerful weapon for combating forgetting
8. Adds a new dimension to the learning process

3. *True-false.* Write *T* beside the *true* statements and *F* beside the *false* statements.

_____ a. The first few pages of a textbook should usually be skipped.

_____ b. The Questions-in-the-Margin System has seven steps.

_____ c. Surveying a chapter provides advance organizers.

_____ d. Visualization will weaken the power of recitation.

_____ e. Answers to questions in the margin may be written as well as recited.

4. *The preface.* Write "yes" next to the common characteristics of a textbook preface.

_____ a. Tells what the author's objective is

_____ b. Deals with matters narrow and specific

_____ c. Explains why the book is different from other books on the same subject

_____ d. Serves as a guide for upcoming chapters

_____ e. Tells what the author's objective is not

_____ f. Presents the organizational plan of the book

5. *Multiple choice.*   Choose the word that completes the following sentence most accurately, and circle the letter that precedes it.

The Questions-in-the-Margin System ultimately aids your mind's ability to

a. recall
b. recognize
c. reflect
d. rephrase

CHAPTER 4

Answering True-False, Multiple-Choice, and Matching Questions

To be able to discern what is true is true and what is false is false; this is the mark and character of intelligence.

Emanuel Swedenborg (1688–1772), Swedish scientist, inventor, and theologian

Do you know right from wrong? Can you recognize a correct answer when you see one? This chapter will help you do both—on tests and exams. It tells you

- What to look for in true-false questions
- How to analyze multiple-choice questions
- How to work through matching questions

True-false questions, multiple-choice questions, and matching questions provide a very efficient way to test a student's knowledge of facts. With these types of questions, a fifty-minute test can cover a great deal of ground. Such questions are easy to grade, and the results depend only on knowledge; the student's writing ability doesn't get in the way of his or her answers.

The three types of questions are similar in one respect: The correct answer is provided; the student must identify it. In spite of this similarity, different techniques are used to analyze and answer true-false, multiple-choice, and matching questions.

WHAT TO LOOK FOR IN TRUE-FALSE QUESTIONS

In its simplest form, a true-false question is a statement that attributes a property or quality to one or more persons or things:

T F   Birds can fly.

T F   Students are creative.

T F   Snakes are poisonous.

In the first statement, the ability to fly is attributed to (or connected with) birds. In the second, the quality of creativeness is connected with students. In the third, the property of being poisonous is attributed to snakes. On an exam you would circle *T* in all three cases, because all three statements are true. There are birds that can fly; there are students who are creative; and there are snakes that are poisonous. You should have no trouble with such simple, straightforward statements. The problem is that very few (if any) true-false statements are written so simply. Most contain qualifiers, negatives, or strings of qualities that make them more difficult to handle.

Watch Out for Qualifiers _____

Here's what happens when we add *qualifiers* to our basic true-false questions:

T F   *All* birds can fly.

T F   *Some* students are creative.

T F   *Most* snakes are poisonous.

In each case, one small word—the qualifier—makes a big difference in the basic statement.

The first statement, "All birds can fly," is false, because birds such as the ostrich and the penguin cannot fly. The qualifier *all* overstates the connection between birds and flying. The second statement is true because *some* students are indeed creative. The qualifier *some* does not overstate or understate the situation. The third statement, "Most snakes are poisonous," is false; of the three thousand different kinds of land snakes, only about 250 are poisonous. Here again the qualifier leads to overstatement.

Qualifiers may be grouped into sets. The six most-used sets are

All—Most—Some—None (No)

Always—Usually—Sometimes—Never

Great—Much—Little—No

More—Equal—Less

Good—Bad

Is—Is Not

Within each set, the qualifiers may overstate a true-false statement, understate it, or make it just right. Memorize the six sets. They will help you answer many true-false questions.

Whenever one qualifier from a set is used in a true-false statement, substitute each of the others for it, in turn. In this way, determine which of the qualifiers in the set fits best (makes the statement just right). If that is the given qualifier, the answer is *true*; otherwise, the answer is *false*.

For example, suppose you are given the question

T   F   All birds can fly.

Substituting the other qualifiers in the "all" set gives you these four statements:

All birds can fly.

Most birds can fly.

Some birds can fly.

No birds can fly.

The statement beginning with the word *most* is just right, but that is not the statement you were given. Therefore, the answer is *false*.

Some qualifiers are "100 percent words." They imply that the statements they appear in are true 100 percent of the time. These words are

No	Every	Only
Never	Always	Entirely
None	All	Invariably
		Best

Such qualifiers are almost always connected with a false statement, because there are very few things in this world that are 100 percent one way or the other. Here are two examples:

All chickens make clucking sounds.

No true chicken can swim.

Always watch out for these qualifying words, but don't automatically consider a statement wrong simply because it contains one of them. To keep you honest and alert, some instructors will occasionally use them in true statements:

All stars are surrounded by space.

All human beings need food to survive.

No human being can live without air.

Qualifying words that fall between the extremes are generally used in true statements. Here are some in-between qualifiers:

Seldom	Most	Usually
Sometimes	Many	Generally
Often	Few	Ordinarily
Frequently	Some	

Here are two items in which these words are used:

T F   *Many* birds fly south for the winter.

T F   A balanced diet *usually* leads to better health.

To test your ability to recognize and work with qualifiers, do the exercise in Figure 4.1.

Check Each Part of the Statement

If any part of a true-false statement is false, then the whole statement is false. Be suspicious of a statement that contains a string of items, but don't conclude that it is false only because it contains the string. Here are two examples of statements with strings:

A long-term sales chart shows the dollar sales and sales trend by weeks, months, and years.

A warm-climate product, cocoa is grown in the Gold Coast of Africa, Nigeria, Brazil, Colombia, Venezuela, and in southern Norway.

The first statement is true because a long-term sales chart does show both dollar sales and the sales trend, which is indicated by the up-and-down

The following quiz, specifically designed both for students who have had a course in psychology and for those who have not, illustrates the importance of key words in objective questions. Take the quiz, picking out the key words and writing them in the space provided. In most cases, there is only one key word, but in a few instances, there are two or three. Also indicate in the right-hand column whether you think the statement is true or false. When you are finished, look below for the correct answers.

1. Geniuses are usually queerer than people of average intelligence. _____ —
2. Only human beings, not animals, have the capacity to think. _____ —
3. Much of human behavior is instinctive. _____ —
4. Slow learners remember what they learn better than fast learners. _____ —
5. Intelligent people form most of their opinions by logical reasoning. _____ —
6. A psychologist is a person who is trained to psychoanalyze people. _____ —
7. You can size up a person very well in an interview. _____ —
8. When one is working for several hours, it is better to take a few long rests than several short ones. _____ —
9. The study of mathematics exercises the mind so that a person can think more logically in other subjects. _____ —
10. Grades in college have little to do with success in business careers. _____ —
11. Alcohol, taken in small amounts, is a stimulant. _____ —
12. There is a clear distinction between the normal person and one who is mentally ill. _____ —
13. Prejudices are mainly due to lack of information. _____ —
14. Competition among people is characteristic of most human societies. _____ —
15. The feature of a job that is most important to employees is the pay they get for their work. _____ —
16. It is possible to classify people very well into introverts and extroverts. _____ —
17. Punishment is usually the best way of eliminating undesirable behavior in children. _____ —
18. By watching closely a person's expression, you can tell quite well the emotion he is experiencing. _____ —
19. The higher one sets his goals in life, the more he is sure to accomplish and the happier he will be. _____ —
20. If a person is honest with you, he usually can tell you what his motives are. _____ —

ANSWERS FOR EXERCISE IN KEY WORDS

The key words for each question were as follows: (1) usually, (2) only, not, (3) much, (4) better, (5) most, (6) psychoanalyze, (7) very well, (8) better, (9) in other subjects, (10) little, (11) stimulant, (12) clear, (13) mainly, (14) most, (15) most important, (16) very well, (17) usually, best, (18) quite well, (19) sure, happier, (20) usually. All the statements are false. The reasons for their being false can be found in the book from which they were taken or, very likely, in any general course in psychology.

FIGURE 4.1   An Exercise in Key Words (Qualifiers)
Source: Clifford T. Morgan, Introduction to Psychology, *copyright 1961. Reprinted by permission of McGraw-Hill Publishing Company.*

movement of the graph. In addition, the time scale on the chart is marked in weeks and months as well as years.

The first nineteen words of the second statement are true. The last two words, "southern Norway," are false because cocoa grows only in warm climates—and Norway, both northern and southern, is freezing cold in winter. This one false item makes the entire statement false.

Some tricky (and usually false) statements are made up of two "substatements," both of which may be true. The two substatements are connected by a conjunction such as *therefore, thus, because, consequently,* or *so,* or a phrase such as *as a result.* What generally makes the statement false is that the second substatement doesn't logically follow from the first. In other words, the two parts are not directly related, although the statement is presented as if they are. For example, consider this statement:

Thomas Edison invented the ticker-tape machine for recording stock prices and, *as a result,* he became famous.

It is true that Edison invented the ticker-tape machine and that he became famous in his lifetime. However, his fame was due not directly to his ticker-tape machine but to other inventions, including the electric light bulb, the phonograph, and the storage battery. For this reason, the statement is false.

Beware of the Negative

True-false statements that contain negative words and prefixes are difficult to sort out and answer. The negatives can upset or complicate your thinking. Negative words include *not* and *cannot,* and the negative prefixes are *dis-, il-, im-, in-, ir-, non-,* and *un-,* as in *inconsequential* or *illogical.*

Notice, in the following three statements, how the addition of negatives increases the difficulty of understanding what the statements mean—let alone deciding whether they are true or false.

Thomas Edison's fame was due to his many practical inventions.

It is illogical to assume that Thomas Edison's fame was due to his many practical inventions.

It is illogical to assume that Thomas Edison's fame was not due to his many practical inventions.

When you are confronted with such a statement, begin by circling the negative words and negative prefixes. Then try to get the meaning of the statement without the negatives. Finally, reread the sentence to find out whether it is true or false in its entirety. Here, the first statement is true, the second is false, and the third is true.

Think "True"—and Guess When You Must _____

Most true-false tests contain more true statements than false statements, simply because they are made up by teachers. Since teachers would rather leave true information in your mind, they tend to stack the test with true statements. Of course, some teachers will fool you, but after the first test you'll know for sure.

On a true-false test, it is a good idea to guess at answers that you don't know, even if credit is subtracted for wrong answers. According to the laws of probability, you should get 50 percent right when you guess, even if you know nothing about the subject matter. If you can make intelligent guesses—knowing that there are more true than false statements—you should be able to do much better than that.

HOW TO ANALYZE MULTIPLE-CHOICE QUESTIONS

Most multiple-choice questions[1] are of the incomplete-statement type. A partial statement (called the *stem*) leads grammatically into four or five sentence endings, or options, listed directly under it. One of the options is the correct answer. The other (incorrect) options are called *distractors* or *decoys*.

Here is an example of a well-constructed multiple-choice question:

 Stem ————→ 1. The almost perfect walls of granite boulders sur-
rounding some lakes in Iowa were formed by
a. American Indians
 Decoys ◁———— b. prehistoric men
Correct ————→ c. huge meteors
Answer ————→ d. thick ice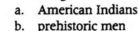

This incomplete-statement question exhibits good construction in the following ways:

1. All options are grammatically consistent.

2. The stem is long, and the options are short.

3. Extraneous material is excluded from the stem.

---

[1]Some of the ideas in this section were inspired by James F. Shepherd, *The Houghton Mifflin Study Skills Handbook* (Boston: Houghton Mifflin, 1982), pp. 230–70.

4. The stem contains one central problem.

5. Double negatives are not used.

6. All options are plausible.

7. The correct option is no longer or shorter than the others.

8. Only one option is the correct or best answer.[2]

When the use of an incomplete statement would lead to an awkward stem or options, the question form is used, and the options are listed below the question.

Answering Multiple-Choice Questions _____

Before you even look at a question on a multiple-choice test, you must *read the directions carefully*. Some say, "Mark the one best answer," whereas others may require that you "Mark all correct answers." You will lose credit if you mark more than one answer in the first case, or if you miss a correct option in the second case. If the directions are not clear, then *ask*.

Begin each question by reading the stem all the way through. Then read the options all the way through. Don't be in a rush to mark the first option that sounds good. In some questions, *all* the options may be correct, and you have to choose the best one; you won't find it unless you read them all.

You should read all the options even when the question seems unfamiliar. One of them might provide you with a hint as to what the question is about. Furthermore, there's information in the options themselves—information that might help you remember what you need to know.

After you read the stem and the options, spend no more than a few seconds puzzling over the question. If it resists answering, cross out any options you have eliminated, mark the question so you will be able to find it easily later, and move on to the next question. But don't leave any question so fast that you do not give it the calm consideration it deserves. If you merely go through the motions, you're wasting time. The idea is to convert the easy questions into quick point-getters and leave enough time to go back to the questions you skipped.

When you have worked your way through the test, go back to the questions that you marked for reconsideration. This time, however, concentrate on eliminating options. The more distractors you can eliminate, the better your chance of finding the correct answer.

---

[2]William D. Hedges, "How to Construct a Good Multiple-Choice Test," *The Clearing House* 39 (September 1964): 9–11.

If you can somehow eliminate all the distractors, then you will have isolated the correct answer. If you can eliminate only one or two of the options, then you should guess at the correct answer. In the long run you will come out ahead by doing so, even if some credit is subtracted for each incorrect answer.

Here are some additional hints that may be of help to you in eliminating distractors and choosing the correct answer.

Try to Apply the True-False Technique

To use the true-false technique, you make a complete statement from the stem and each option, in turn. An option that results in a false statement is eliminated as a distractor. One that results in a true statement is probably the correct answer. As an example, consider this multiple-choice question:

2. Because of its lack of lumber, Syria has many "beehive" homes built of
   a. metal
   b. concrete
   c. marble
   d. mud brick

To judge the correctness of the first option, you would complete the stem as follows: Because of its lack of lumber, Syria has many "beehive" homes built of metal. Because Syria is a hot, dry, and rather poor country, you would probably decide that this statement is false. Metal (and concrete and marble as well) are too expensive and not readily available to the vast majority of people. The last option, *mud brick*, undoubtedly produced locally, would be inexpensive and available and would hold up in a country where rainfall is meager. (The correct answer is *d.*)

When you use this technique, don't be too quick to eliminate options; do so only after sufficient consideration. If you have eliminated three options but don't like the remaining option, you must go back and reconsider them all.

Stick to the Subject Matter of the Course

When a multiple-choice question includes options that you don't recognize or that seem out of place, don't get panicked into choosing one of them. The chances are great that the strange options are distractors. Here's an example:

3. Which of the following does not have satellites (moons)?
   a. Venus
   b. Cassiopeia
   c. Mars
   d. Perseus

You might reason as follows: "We've been studying planets and their rotation around the sun. I've heard of Cassiopeia, but we haven't studied it. I've never heard of Perseus. I bet both are decoys—I'll cross them off. We did study Venus and Mars. They are planets, but I don't remember which one has satellites and which one doesn't. Well, at least I've boiled things down to a fifty-fifty chance. I'll mark this question and come back to it later."

Later, when you return to the question, you might remember that Mars has a ring of satellites or moons around it. That would eliminate Mars, leaving Venus. You still might not remember whether Venus has satellites, but since that's the only option left, you would choose it. (*Venus* is the correct answer.)

Watch Out for Negatives and Extreme Words _____

We discussed negatives and extreme words in relation to true-false questions, and our discussion applies here as well. Whenever you find negative words such as *not* or *except* in the stem or in the options, circle them so they'll stand out. Then make sure you take them into consideration when you choose your answer. Here's an example:

4. Which materials are (not) used in making saddles?
   a. linen, canvas, serge
   b. wood and leather
   c. rubber and cork
   d. iron and steel

(The correct answer is *d*. The materials in *a, b,* and *c* are all used in saddles.)

Always circle 100 percent words such as *never, no, none, best, worst, always, all,* and *every;* and be suspicious of the options in which you find them. In fact, if you have to guess, first eliminate all the options that contain absolute words. Then choose your answer from the remaining options. As an example, see whether you can answer this question:

5. The author suggests that the desert
   a. climate is unpredictable
   b. heat is always unbearable

c.   is totally devoid of rain
d.   earthquakes pose a constant danger

You should have circled *always* in *b*, *totally* in *c*, and *constant* in *d*, to obtain *a* as the correct answer. You didn't even have to know what the question is about.

Foolish Options Are Usually Incorrect

Test writers occasionally include a silly statement as an option. Most likely, they become tired and simply dash off foolish statements to fill space. You should almost always view such statements as distractors worthy of being immediately crossed out. Here's an example:

6. The most important reason why the travel agents tested the Camel Caravan was to
a.   judge the safety aspects of the trip
b.   improve relations with the Arabs
c.   get a free vacation
d.   test the appeal of the Caravan for tourists

The foolish option is *c*. The correct option is *d*. Notice that options *a* and *b* make true statements, but the word *most* in the stem calls for option *d*.

The Option "All the Above" Is Usually Correct

When all the reasonable candidates for options will make the statement true, test writers frequently use "all the above" as an option. Doing so greatly simplifies the writing of such a question. Here's an example:

7. Until the first half of the second millennium B.C., an army laying siege to a city made use of
a.   scaling ladders
b.   siege towers
c.   archery fire
d.   all the above

(The correct option is *d*.)

One way to confirm the choice "all the above" is to find two correct answers in the options. For example, suppose you were sure that ladders and towers were used, but you weren't sure about archery fire. Then, if only one answer were permitted, that answer would have to be *d*, because *d* is the only option that includes *a* and *b*.

Numbers in the Middle Range Are Usually Correct ___

When all the options in a multiple-choice question are numbers, the answer is easy if you have memorized the correct number. Otherwise, you'll probably have to do some guessing. If you have no other information to go on, your chances of guessing correctly are increased if you eliminate the highest and lowest numbers. For some reason, test writers usually include at least one number lower than the correct answer and at least one number higher than the correct answer. This "rule" allows you to eliminate half of the options in the following example:

8. The "Great Pyramid" originally stood how many feet high?
   a.   281
   b.   381
   c.   481
   d.   981

You would eliminate 281 as the lowest number and 981 as the highest, leaving two middle-range numbers, 381 and 481. At this point you have a fifty-fifty chance of choosing correctly. Can you improve the odds?

You could compare the two remaining options to something you know, such as a football field. Then, 381 feet is slightly greater than a football field, perhaps not so high for a pyramid. But 481 feet is over 1½ times as high as a football field is long. That would really make a "Great Pyramid." (If you stuck with 481 feet, you would be correct.)

Check for Look-Alike Options _____

Test makers occasionally include, in one question, two options that are alike except for one word. Such a pair seems to indicate where the test maker's interest was focused, so it is logical to assume that one of the pair is the correct answer. The other options should, of course, be read carefully; they should be eliminated in favor of the look-alikes only in a guessing situation. For example, consider the question:

9. The author considers himself an authority on
   a.   touring the Middle East
   b.   Middle East rug dealers
   c.   Middle East rug bargains
   d.   behavior patterns of tourists

Even if you had no inkling of the correct answer, you would be wise to eliminate *a* and *d* and choose from the similar pair *b* and *c*. (The correct option is *b*.)

The test writer can keep you from using this technique by inserting two pairs of similar options. Then you would have to deal with four options:

10. The author considers himself an authority on
   a. behavior patterns of merchants
   b. Middle East rug dealers
   c. Middle East rug bargains
   d. behavior patterns of tourists

Check for Longer or More Inclusive Options

In multiple-choice questions, the correct option is often longer or more inclusive of qualities or ideas than the distractors. The length or inclusiveness results when the test writer must qualify or amplify a simple statement. So, be alert for a tightly packed or overly long option, as in this question:

11. The author says that rug buying in the Middle East is like courtship in that
   a. both parties fool each other
   b. both parties must trust each other
   c. both parties desire the same thing but begin with expressions of disinterest
   d. in rug buying, as in courtship, one dresses in one's best

(Here option *c* is correct.)

HOW TO WORK THROUGH MATCHING QUESTIONS

Matching questions provide a most efficient way to test knowledge in courses such as history (in which events, dates, names, and places are important) and psychology (for which numerous experiments, experimenters, results, and special terms and definitions have to be remembered). In a matching question, two vertical lists of items are placed next to each other. Each list contains a half dozen or more words or phrases, in random order. The task is to match the items in one list with those in the other list, according to a relation that is given in the directions for answering the question.

Figure 4.2 contains a matching question that will test your knowledge of inventors and their inventions. You may want to try it now, before you read the next section.

Match the inventions in the right-hand column with the inventors in the left-hand column by writing the proper letter in the space provided alongside each inventor's name. Use each item in the right-hand column only once.

Inventor	*Invention*
____ 1. Eli Whitney	a. Automobile assembly line
____ 2. James Watt	b. Telephone
____ 3. Robert Fulton	c. Vulcanizing of rubber
____ 4. Cyrus McCormick	d. Six-shooter revolver
____ 5. Elias Howe	e. Steel plow
____ 6. Henry Ford	f. Steamboat
____ 7. James Hargreaves	g. Motion pictures
____ 8. Richard Arkwright	h. Cotton gin
____ 9. Samuel Colt	i. Dynamite
____ 10. Charles Goodyear	j. Steam engine
____ 11. Alfred Nobel	k. Telegraph
____ 12. Thomas Edison	l. Sewing machine
____ 13. Guglielmo Marconi	m. Spinning frame (textiles)
____ 14. John Deere	n. Radio
____ 15. Samuel Morse	o. Spinning jenny
____ 16. Alexander Bell	p. Grain-reaping machine
	q. Locomotive (train)

Answers: (1) *h*, (2) *j*, (3) *f*, (4) *p*, (5) *l*, (6) *a*, (7) *o*, (8) *m*, (9) *d*, (10) *c*, (11) *i*, (12) *g*, (13) *n*, (14) *e*, (15) *k*, (16) *b*.

FIGURE 4.2 Matching: Inventors and Inventions

How to Answer a Matching Question

The following sequence of steps will help you work through any matching questions systematically and efficiently.

1. Read the directions. Then run your eyes down both columns to get a brief overview of the specific items you will be working with.

2. Read the top item in the left-hand column. Then look carefully and thoughtfully down the right-hand column until you find a match for it. Don't stop at the first likely match; instead, continue through to the end of the right-hand column, to make sure there is not a better match. (If the right-hand column has the longer entries, you can save reading time by looking for the matches in the left-hand column.)

3. When you are certain that you have found a match, fill in the proper letter or number. (If you match the wrong items, you'll not only lose credit on that match, but you will run into more trouble later.) If you're not sure, skip the item and come back to it.

Match the activities in the right-hand column with the names in the left-hand column by writing the proper letter in the space provided alongside each name. Use each item in the right-hand column only once.

Names	Activity
____ 1. Jesse Owens	a. Tennis
____ 2. Pete Rose	b. Swimming
____ 3. Joe Montana	c. Hockey
____ 4. Kareem Abdul-Jabbar	d. Aviation
____ 5. Wayne Gretzky	e. Basketball
____ 6. Althea Gibson	f. Movies
____ 7. Gertrude Ederle	g. Football
____ 8. Amelia Earhart	h. Opera
____ 9. Meryl Streep	i. Baseball
____ 10. Beverly Sills	j. Boxing
____ 11. Joe Louis	k. Track
	l. Soccer

Answers: (1) *k*, (2) *i*, (3) *g*, (4) *e*, (5) *c*, (6) *a*, (7) *b*, (8) *d*, (9) *f*, (10) *h*, (11) *j*.

FIGURE 4.3 Matching: Personalities

4. This is the secret: Continue down the left column, filling in all the matches *that you're sure of*. This will drastically and immediately reduce the number of items that are left when you have to make the more difficult matches. And the fewer the items, the better are your chances of being correct.

5. As you use each item in the right column, circle its letter or number to show that it has been used. (You may also want to add the number or letter of the item with which it has been matched. This keying of your matches will help you check your answers later.)

Don't do any guessing until you are almost absolutely sure you're completely stumped. If you make an incorrect match too soon, you'll remove a "live" item from later consideration; then a second match, which would have made use of that item, will also be wrong. So first do your very best; then, using common sense and hunches, go ahead and guess at the remaining matches.

In case you're not an expert on inventions, Figure 4.3 contains a matching question that features famous personalities of the past and present. If you didn't use the matching-question sequence for Figure 4.2, try it here.

How to Study for Matching Questions

If you know that your instructor includes a long matching question in almost every exam, here's the best way to prepare for it. As you read and mark your textbook, be alert for facts and ideas that are associated with people's names. On a separate sheet, list the names and facts opposite each other, so that you end up with two distinct vertical columns, as in the following example:

Names	Facts or Ideas	(Subject)
Susan B. Anthony	Women's movement	(Sociology)
Jack London	*Call of the Wild*	(Literature)
George Washington Carver	Agricultural chemist	(Science)
Lewis & Clark	American explorers	(History)
George A. Miller	Magic number seven	(Psychology)
William James	Pragmatism	(Philosophy)
Mozart	*Marriage of Figaro*	(Music)

To master your list, cover the fact column with a sheet of paper. Look at each item in the name column, and recite and write the corresponding fact or idea. Then, to make sure that you learn the material both ways, block out the name column and use the facts as your cues. The example given here includes items from various subject areas. The same steps can be taken in any single subject area.

SUMMARY

What makes some true-false questions so hard to answer?

The difficulty often occurs when the test maker uses qualifying words such as *all, most, some,* and *none.* You must know not only the main fact, but also whether the qualifying word overstates or understates the fact, making the statement false. Be especially watchful for words that allow no exceptions—that is, words such as *never, all, always, none,* and *every.* These words can change an otherwise true statement into a false one.

What if half of the statement is true and half is false?

Then the statement is false. Always judge the entire statement. Be especially careful when a statement contains a long list of items.

What else should I watch out for?

Watch out for negative and extreme words within the statement. To make sure you take them into consideration, begin your analysis of the question by drawing a circle around every negative word and prefix.

Should I guess on true-false tests?

Yes. You have a fifty-fifty chance of being right, and knowing something about the subject matter should give you the winning edge.

How should I answer multiple-choice questions?

Begin by reading the directions carefully. Then read each question carefully—both stem and options. Eliminate options (distractors) where you can. Try to use the options as clues, and try the true-false technique.

Should I answer each question before moving on?

No. Don't waste time on a question that you can't answer in a reasonable amount of time. Instead, cross out the options you have eliminated, mark the question so you can come back to it later, and go on to the next question.

What should I do when I return to a multiple-choice question?

Concentrate on eliminating distractors. Make full use of probability techniques by looking for foolish options, "all the above," and look-alike and long options. Guess when you are able to eliminate at least one option in a four-option question or two options in a five-option question.

What's the best way to work a matching question?

First read the instructions and all the listed items. Then mark only the matches you are sure of, one by one. Next, go back to the items that you have skipped, and try to match them. Guess only when you're completely stumped.

Why can I study for matching questions but not for the others?

You *can* study for all types of questions, but you can do some special studying for matching questions by making a list of likely matches and then learning your list.

HAVE YOU MISSED SOMETHING?

1. *Sentence completion.*   Complete the following sentences with one of the three words listed below each sentence.

   a. Negative and absolute words should be _____.
       avoided   circled   defined

   b. In matching questions, the fewer the remaining choices, the better are your chances of being _____.
       incorrect   correct   alert

2. *Matching.*   In each blank space in the left column, write the number preceding the phrase in the right column that matches the left item best.

   _____ a. Stem

   _____ b. Qualifier

   _____ c. Guessing

   _____ d. Distractor

   _____ e. Overstatement

   _____ f. Understatement

   1. Incorrect multiple-choice option
   2. Risk of the word *none*
   3. Correct option makes it a true statement
   4. Risk of the word *all*
   5. A word like *usually* or *some*
   6. A last resort for matching questions

3. *True-false.*   Write *T* beside the *true* statements and *F* beside the *false* statements.

   _____ a. Qualifiers make true-false statements easy to answer.

   _____ b. Complicated true-false statements are usually false.

   _____ c. Guessing is advised when you don't know the answer to a multiple-choice question.

   _____ d. In a well-constructed multiple-choice question, the correct option is always the shortest.

   _____ e. In a matching question, answers you've used should be circled or marked in some fashion.

_____ f. In a matching question, you should immediately guess at matches you are unsure about.

4. *Multiple choice.* Choose the phrase that completes the following sentence most accurately, and circle the letter that precedes it.

In a multiple-choice question, an option is usually correct if it is

a. longer and more inclusive than the other options
b. one of two look-alike options
c. the only nonabsolute option
d. all the above

Studying Science

Kenneth Greisen

The whole of science is nothing more than a refinement of everyday thinking.

Albert Einstein (1879–1955), German-American physicist, formulator of the special theory of relativity

Science has been called the endless frontier, but for some students it seems just plain endless. There are endless lectures, endless textbook assignments, endless problems, endless labs. This chapter presents some techniques to help make science a little less intimidating and a little more exciting. It provides effective methods for

- **Learning from Lectures**
- **Reading a Science Textbook**
- **Working Scientific Problems**
- **Working in the Laboratory**

In every subject that you study, including science, you must learn new terminology, facts, and ideas; then you must develop the ability to apply them to solve various problems. Studying science, however, is different from studying other subjects. First, the terminology, facts, laws, and principles must be learned with extreme precision. Second, the problems are almost always quantitative, and most of the ideas are stated in quantitative (mathematical) terms.

A good example is the definition of *work*, which is learned early in the study of physics: The work W done by a force of magnitude F in moving a body through a distance d in the direction of the force is $W = F \times d$. For a student who is unaccustomed to precise and quantitative terms, such a definition can be intimidating, for the following reasons:

1. The definition is precise, and it must be learned and used precisely. What might seem like a minor rewording could render the definition incorrect and thus useless.
2. The definition contains several parts, and the reasoning underlying each part must be understood if the definition as a whole is to be understood.
3. The definition is quantitative. It makes use of a formula to define *work*, and that formula may be used to calculate work under certain conditions.
4. The student must learn what those conditions are and how to take them into account when using the formula.
5. The scientific meaning of the word *work* is different from the meaning we're used to. Other common words also have special meanings in the sciences; in such cases, the everyday definitions can get in the way of remembering the scientific definitions.

The reason for this degree of precision is that the sciences deal with actual, measurable things. If these things are not described or computed precisely, they will not be described or computed correctly.

You need to learn the precise terminology, facts, and ideas when you study a science. But you should not try to learn a science as if it were a collection of isolated facts. That would be an almost impossible task, and the isolated facts would have little meaning for you. The way to learn science is to fit facts and principles together into groups, or clusters, in your memory. Within each science, facts and principles are related to one another to a much greater extent than in nonscientific subjects, so clustering should be easier.

Actually, much of science is concerned with finding and explaining the relationships among various facts, concepts, and theories. Even our precise definition of *work* is really a relationship; it is given as a formula because the relation is a precise one. Your textbook and teachers will point out many more. Your job is to use these relationships to cluster the factors and ideas in your mind.

As you learn in this way, your knowledge of a few facts in a cluster will easily extend to new facts and ideas that you want to include in the same cluster. You will find yourself becoming more and more comfortable with science and its precision. You may begin to ask yourself questions about how new ideas fit in with old ones, about the patterns that you find in both old and new facts, or about why a principle that you learned in one science course seems so much like a principle you learned in another. Then you really will be learning science.

Learning from Lectures

Your objective is to learn the facts and their interrelationships, and your ears and eyes must be alert to both. Take full, legible notes during lectures, paying particular attention to explanatory diagrams. Don't hesitate to ask questions if you cannot grasp a point after reviewing your lecture notes and reading your text.

Taking Lecture Notes

You should take science lecture notes and study them in the manner described in Chapters 10 and 11.

Taking Notes on Ideas
Do not try to take down the lecture word for word. If you do, the words will get in the way of the ideas. The objective of taking notes is to have a record of the main ideas so that you can study them later for deeper understanding, for review, and for examinations.

Being Systematic
Use the Cornell System for taking notes. The format is shown in Figure 5.1. Write your notes in the right-hand column. Then, as soon as possible after each lecture, put your notes in order by filling in missing steps in the arguments, by correcting errors, and by relating these new notes with the previous lecture's notes. Label each idea on the right with a question, placed in the narrow left-hand column.

Making Master Summary Sheets
Periodically (to prepare for tests or at regular intervals), reorganize your notes on separate sheets of paper by clustering the ideas and details under main topics and categories. By constructing summary sheets, you will be relating facts and ideas to one another and fixing them in your memory.

Figure 5.1

Cornell System Format for Lecture Notes and Notes Based on Textbook Reading

	February 26 (MON.)—Physics 101
What is magnetic polarity? How do magnetic poles interact?	<u>Polarity of Magnets</u> - Magnetism is stronger at ends than at middle. - Like poles repel each other Ex. Two "N" poles, when brought together, fly apart when released. Same for "S" poles. - Unlike poles attract each other

What is Earth's relation to magnets?	- Earth is one big magnet
	  Magnetism stronger at poles
	  Compass needle aligns N to S

What is the iron filings experiment?	- Experiment to show stronger ends
	  1. Place bar magnet under glass
	  2. Pour small iron filings on glass
	  3. Tap glass and filings arrange themselves, showing lines of force

What causes magnetism?	<u>Theory of Magnetism</u> - Not sure what causes it - Believe: way molecules are arranged

Asking Questions

If you have trouble relating concepts, solving assigned problems, or completing lab experiments satisfactorily, there may be gaps in your understanding. In such cases, you should ask questions.

Asking the Teacher at the Start of the Class

The start of the class is usually the best time to ask questions. Well-phrased questions about the previous lecture or the reading assignment can often be cleared up quickly. Moreover, something that presented difficulty for you probably did the same for other members of the class; your teacher may want to discuss the troublesome area during the lecture.

Never worry or feel embarrassed about being the only student who doesn't understand something or about showing that you didn't grasp a particular idea. If you do, you will be underestimating the teacher and yourself, misjudging the purpose of the course, and making it hard for the teacher to keep in touch with the class. Don't, however, ask questions like "How do you do this problem?" Such a question may get you the answer to the problem, but it will do little to increase your understanding. Much better questions are "Did I use the right strategy in attacking this problem? Are there other strategies that I could have used?" Such questions will get you useful information—ideas that you can apply to a broad range of material.

Interrupting a Lecture
Don't be bashful; interrupt a lecture with a question if you need to. Often it is helpful for the whole class to have a lecture slowed down or brought to a halt for a while—especially if some point is obscure. But don't interrupt too often, and make sure your question is important to you.

Asking the Teacher Between Classes
A good teacher's interest in his or her subject and students continues between classes in spite of many other duties. Most teachers enjoy a discussion with an individual student. But remember one thing: Before asking for assistance, do (or at least try) the assignment and think about the problems for yourself. Private sessions with your teacher should only supplement your own work. The major part of learning must be done by you alone.

Asking Other Students
Discussions with other students can be a great help. Friends learning a subject together often share the same difficulties and can thus enlighten one another very effectively.

Reading a Science Textbook

In some ways, studying a science textbook is much the same as studying any other textbook. You should take notes using the Cornell System, review and re-cite them, and from time to time make master summary sheets.

Different sciences, however, call for different attacks and emphases in your reading. Generally, biology and geology place relatively heavy emphasis on key terms and definitions; physics and astronomy, on measurement and mathematics; biology and chemistry, on manipulation; and physics and chemistry, on visualization. Make sure you adapt your study methods accordingly. There are some special techniques that you should use to get the most out of your science textbook. For example, you should keep in mind that science texts are packed with information. You must read them sentence by sentence, making sure you understand each sentence before going on to the next one. Here are four more techniques.

Using Mental Visualization

James Clerk Maxwell (1831–1879), a Scottish mathematical physicist, recognized that different people, as they read and study science, mentally visualize or reconstruct concepts and ideas in their own personal ways. He believed that the concepts and ideas of science can be lifted out of a textbook and placed in one's mind only by the process of mental visualization. Maxwell also believed that although people have different ways of visualizing, everyone does it to varying degrees.

Fortunately, most textbooks and articles in science are heavily illustrated with diagrams to aid the process of visualization. Learn to use the illustrations and text in such a way that they complement one another. When there is no diagram to illustrate a process or an idea, or if a given diagram doesn't work for you, then make your own. This technique is discussed and illustrated in Chapter 8.

Learning New Terms

Your science textbooks contain many terms that are new to you. Because these terms stand for essential concepts, you must know precisely what they mean if you are to understand the subject matter. To help you pick out important new terms, textbooks usually emphasize them by means of italic or boldface type when they first occur. Such terms are specifically defined at that point or in a glossary at the end of the book. Give extra time and attention to the task of memorizing these terms and their definitions. Jot them down on index cards, and master each one as you would any new word.

Learning the Language of Measurement

Learning the language of scientific measurement is important. Most commonly used are the metric system and the Celsius and Fahrenheit temperature scales. Learn to think meaningfully about these quantities and measures.

You should know that the word *metric* comes from *meter*, which is the principal unit of length in this system. The metric system was developed by French scientists in 1799 and it is now used everywhere in the world for scientific work. Table 5.1 compares some metric units with English units of measurement.

You will also want to know about the Celsius and Fahrenheit temperature scales. The thermometers for both look alike, have the same size tubes, and are filled with mercury that rises and falls to the same levels. But Celsius and Fahrenheit thermometers differ in the way their respective scales are graduated. On the Celsius thermometer, the point at which water freezes is marked

Table 5.1

Comparison of Metric and English Units

Metric System			English System		
Length					
Meter	=	1.093 yards	Avoirdupois	=	0.9144 meter
	=	3.281 feet	Foot	=	0.03048 meter
	=	39.370 inches	Inch	=	0.0254 mile
Kilometer	=	0.621 mile	Mile	=	1.609 kilometers
Weight					
Gram	=	15.432 grains	Grain	=	0.0648 gram
	=	0.032 troy ounce	Troy ounce	=	31.1 grams
	=	0.0352 avoirdupois ounce	Avoirdupois		
Kilogram	=	2.2046 pounds avoirdupois	ounce	=	28.35 grams
Metric ton	=	2204.62 pounds avoirdupois	Pound	=	453.6 grams
Carat	=	3.08 grains avoirdupois	Short ton	=	0.907 metric ton

0 (zero); on the Fahrenheit thermometer scale it is marked 32. And on the Celsius scale, the boiling point of water is 100; on the Fahrenheit scale, it is 212.

On the Celsius thermometer, there are 100 equal spaces or degrees between the freezing and boiling points of water. On the Fahrenheit thermometer, there are 180 degrees between the freezing and boiling points. To change Celsius readings to Fahrenheit readings, multiply the Celsius reading by 180/100, or 9/5, and then add 32. To change Fahrenheit readings to Celsius readings, subtract 32 from the Fahrenheit reading and then multiply by 5/9.

Using Study Guides

Study guides accompany the textbooks for many science courses. One type of guide uses what is called a *programmed* approach. In this approach, a section of the guide containing sentence-completion questions corresponds to each section of the textbook. The questions help you evaluate what you've learned and what you still need to review. They also help you rehearse for examinations. In addition, there is a brief summary of each chapter and a list of chapter objectives. The value of the summary is self-evident. And the objectives constitute a ready-made self-test that you can use to make sure you've learned the important concepts in the chapter.

A second type of study guide contains, for each textbook chapter, the following items: an overview, chapter objectives, expanded chapter outline, student study objectives, vocabulary checklist, and self-tests. When using this type of guide, you should read the text chapter *before* attending the lecture on that chapter. Then, after the lecture, read the overview, objectives, and outline in the guide, and summarize the chapter in your own words. Check through the student study objectives, and write out any answers that are called for. Next, make sure you can define all the terms in the vocabulary checklist. Finally, take the self-tests to check that you have mastered the chapter. Use the study guide along with your notes when you review for an examination.

Working Scientific Problems

The Value of Practice

Never skip an assigned practice problem. The most successful way to solve a problem on a test is to remember how you solved a similar problem previously. When you first attempt a new kind of problem, it is natural to be hesitant, to make false starts, to be stumped temporarily—to waste time. But as you work other problems of the same kind, you learn to do them quickly and surely. Because each problem usually has a feature not present in previous ones, you gradually develop the ability to solve a wider and wider range of problems.

Complex problems are usually solved in a series of simple steps. If the steps are so familiar that you do them automatically, you can concentrate on how they fit together to produce a solution to the problem. Then you can proceed from start to finish without confusion. However, if each step is difficult for you, you'll be so involved in details that you won't find the right path to the solution.

In studying a science, therefore, you should do more than just the assigned problems. If your own textbook does not have many extras, look for problems in other books on the same subject, or try to make up appropriate problems for yourself. Making up good problems is hard, but it is an excellent exercise—particularly for two students who are studying together. If you do this, try to anticipate the sorts of problems your teacher will make up for your tests.

Doing Unfamiliar Types of Problems

If you do your assignments faithfully, you will come across new and unfamiliar problems in your homework. Try to approach such problems in this way:

1. Don't start doing problems until you have studied your lecture and textbook notes.
2. Make a list of what is given in the problem and what is to be found.
3. Try to develop a chain of logical steps leading either forward from the known quantities to the unknown you have to find, or backward from the un-

known to the given quantities. If necessary, work from both ends to the middle until you find a logical connection.

4. Express these logical steps in the form of equations.
5. Combine the equations and solve them for the unknown.
6. Check your answer by determining whether it is reasonable in magnitude. If you are unsure, substitute the answer into the original relations and see whether it fits consistently.

Answering Discussion Questions

Discussion questions appear occasionally in quizzes and examinations. Before you answer one, try to understand the purpose and point of view of the person asking the question. Learn to put yourself mentally in his or her place. Ask yourself how the question is related to subjects that were recently discussed in class or in your reading assignments and what principles it is intended to illustrate. If you can visualize the question within your clusters of facts and ideas, you'll be able to determine how you want to answer it. All that remains is to express your answer clearly, using the technical words accurately.

You need practice to become skillful in answering discussion questions. You can develop this skill by taking part in discussions with your friends, by participating in classroom discussions, and by paying careful attention to your *writing* skills. Usually your difficulties will be not in grammar but in vocabulary, in logic, and in ordering the steps in an argument.

Working in the Laboratory

Here are seven hints for laboratory work:

1. *Do not trust your memory.*   Write down everything you think may be pertinent. Some things that you observe in the laboratory may seem so memorable at the time that you see no point in writing them down. But memory fades; if you do not write up an experiment completely when you perform it, you may not be able to recall important items. Figures **5**.2 and **5**.3 show the types of items that you should note immediately.
2. *Make a permanent record of your observations.*   Keep a full record of your calculations, observations, and results in a special notebook. Don't ever write anything down on separate scraps of paper—not even your arithmetical calculations. If you make mistakes, cross them out and go on from there, but keep everything as part of your complete record. Start your record of each experiment or laboratory session on a new page, headed with the

Figure 5.2

Diagram of a Loading-Jig Apparatus, as Part of a Laboratory Report

Experiment #3053 - Strain Measurements
October 27

    The purpose of this experiment is to determine stress sustained by a rectangular bar by means of wire resistance strain gauges. Six of these gauges are taped onto different positions on the bar, then strain readings taken, during both loading and unloading processes, and the results converted to stress by using appropriate equations.

Figure 5.3
A Page from a Record Book,
Showing Raw Data Gathered
Directly from Measurements
Made by Instruments

Experiment 3057 - October 27

Measurement of displacement, velocity and acceleration
EQUIPMENT: (a) Linear Variable Differential Transformer;
(b) an Oscilloscope; (c) an accelerometer; (d) an
Analyzer - Recorder; (e) a Vibrating Table.

- -

Raw Data

FREQ(cps)	DISPLACEMENT	VELOCITY	ACCELERATION
40	Micro (mm) 1.6176 } Δ=101.9 mils 1.358 VIB. MTR. 97 mils	VIB. MTR. 29.2 $\frac{in}{sec}$	V.M. 9300 (in/sec²)
30	Micro (mm) 1.621 } Δ= 96.8 mils 1.375 VIB. MTR. 98 mils	VIB. MTR. 21.9 $\frac{in}{sec}$	V.M. 5700 (in/sec²)
20	Micro (mm) 1.609 } Δ = 94.7 mils 1.369	VIB. MTR. 14.9 $\frac{in}{sec}$	V.M. 2950 (in/sec²)
10	Micro (mm) 1.607 } Δ= 96.3 mils 1.363 VIB MTR. 102 mils	VIB. MTR. 6.9 $\frac{in}{sec}$	V.M. 1020 (in/sec²)

date. This will give you a permanent log of all your data and your thinking for every problem on which you have worked—the raw materials for your final report.

3. *Organize the recorded data.*   Arrange the data so that they will be clear and fully labeled for later reference. The few extra minutes you spend to make neat and orderly records during the lab period will save you time that might otherwise have to be spent deciphering sloppy notes (see Figure **5**.3).

4. *Do not trust yourself or the apparatus too much.*   It is unwise to record a lot of untested numbers, dismantle the apparatus, and leave the laboratory before knowing whether your data are of any use. It is much better to do at least an approximate analysis (including rough graphs) of the data while they are being taken. Such a check will give you a chance to detect anything that is going wrong in time to do something about it—such as readjusting the apparatus, checking or repeating an observation, or asking your instructor for assistance.

5. *Baby the apparatus.*   Poor performance in a laboratory is often due to carelessness, but it may also be the result of an uncooperative attitude. Don't be too ready to say the apparatus doesn't work or to believe it is limited in capability. Treat the apparatus tenderly, and coax out of it all the accuracy it can produce. Make note of its limitations, and watch it like a hawk for signs of strange behavior. No real equipment is quite like the ideal version pictured in a textbook or laboratory manual; each piece of apparatus has an individual "personality."

6. *Keep the purpose of the experiment in mind.*   This can save you much wasted effort and keep you from overlooking the main point of the lab work.

7. *Write up your reports clearly, legibly, and concisely, in the proper form.*   The writing style should be impersonal; in technical reports it is customary to use the passive voice (see Figure **5**.4). A laboratory report usually contains some or all of the following items:

> *Purpose (object):*   A statement explaining what the problem is
> *Theory:*   The background for the problem and the justification for your method of attack
> *Apparatus (equipment, materials):*   A listing and brief description of the essential apparatus, often including a sketch of the apparatus
> *Procedure:*   A step-by-step report of what you did
> *Results:*   A step-by-step record of your observations
> *Conclusion:*   A summary of your findings and an assessment of their accuracy, showing how your results succeed or fail in resolving the problem

Above all, in writing a report, remember that your purpose is to make your findings understandable to a reader. Make full use of your writing skills.

Figure 5.4
Sample Lab Report

Experiment 34

A.   PURPOSE: To observe the increase in birefringence of
nylon by increasing the orientation of fibers through
stretching, despite the thinning of the nylon by necking.

B.   PROCEDURE
(a) A narrow strip of thin transparent nylon sheet,
stretched in some spots and not stretched in others,
was observed between crossed polarizers with low
magnification.
(b) About 1 mm diameter as-extruded nylon monofilament was stretched and the necking observed.
(c) Textile-grade nylon fiber was observed as-
extruded and stretched. The diameters and polarization colors of each region of the fiber were noted.

C.   RESULTS
(a)

unstretched nylon;
polarization colors:
1st order white.

stretched nylon;
polarization colors:
3rd order red and
green.

(b) Nylon monofilament necked abruptly, rather than
breaking, when pulled:

(c) 16 mm objective, 1 eyepiece micrometer division =
16.0 μ

	Diameter	Converted diameter	Retardation
Unstretched	4.3 div.	68.8 μ	200 μ
Stretched	1.9 div.	30.4 μ	1850 μ

	Birefringence
Unstretched	0.003
Stretched	0.059

D.   CONCLUSIONS
Unstretched nylon fiber exhibited a 1st order white
polarization color, i.e., showed very low birefringence. The birefringence was calculated to be
about 0.003.
When pulled in tension, the nylon fiber necked
abruptly. The stretched portion of the sample showed
3rd order and higher polarization colors, despite
decreased thickness. This was due to a marked increase
in birefringence, to about 0.059, resulting from the
parallel orientation of fibers effected by stretching.
Without polarizers, the nylon fiber appeared
slightly greyed or opaqued where stretched. Orienting
the polymer fibers leads to a decrease in clarity. Also,
the stretching results in mechanical discontinuities
which would tend to scatter the light.

SUMMARY

How is learning science different from learning other subjects?
What is meant by learning in clusters?
How can I improve my note taking in science lectures?

There are two differences. First, the terms, facts, and principles must be learned precisely. Second, the facts and problems are quantitative in nature.

Learning in clusters is a matter of finding the relations among various pieces of information and then grouping the information in your mind according to those relations. It makes remembering much easier.

Concentrate on the ideas that are being presented, rather than on the words themselves. Use the Cornell System, which allows you to take, review, recite, and consolidate your notes more easily. Convert your notes into master summary sheets.

What's the best time to ask a question in class?
What's the best way to solve a test problem?

The best time is at the beginning of the lecture. The instructor may make use of your question during the lecture.

The best way is to remember how you solved a similar problem before and to do the same things again. Recall requires experience, and the only way you can get experience is with plenty of practice. Work out all the assigned problems, and then look for more problems to work on.

How should I handle a type of problem that I've never faced before?

Be logical and systematic. First, figure out just what you need to find. Then try to plot a logical course from the given quantities to the unknown quantities, or vice versa. Once you have plotted this course, convert the steps into equations and solve them.

What's the key to answering discussion questions?

Figure out what sort of answer each question requires. Then try to connect the question with your clusters of learned facts and principles. Once you've made the connection, write out your answer in clear, precise language.

What is the objective of the seven hints for doing lab work?

The objective is to make sure you have all the information or data you need, in a logical and legible form, to communicate your lab results clearly and precisely.

HAVE YOU MISSED SOMETHING?

SENTENCE COMPLETION   *Complete the following sentences with one of the three words or phrases listed below each sentence.*

1. The reason for the insistence on precision is that the sciences deal with _____ .

   creative ideas   measurable things   the frontiers of knowledge

2. Science textbooks are packed with information, so read them

   _____ .

   for scientific principles   sentence by sentence   for major ideas

3. In working on experiments in the laboratory, it is important to record _____ .

only the major findings   even the minutest steps
only the steps leading toward proving a principle

MATCHING

In each blank space in the left column, write the letter preceding the phrase in the right column that matches the left item best.

_____ 1. Clustering
_____ 2. Precision
_____ 3. Questioning
_____ 4. Metric system
_____ 5. Writing skills
_____ 6. Maxwell

a. Is used for scientific measurement
b. Realized that people mentally visualize abstract concepts
c. Is characteristic of the sciences.
d. Are needed to do good lab reports
e. Helps to fill gaps in understanding
f. Involves placing facts and ideas into groups and categories

TRUE-FALSE

Write T *beside the* true *statements and* F *beside the* false *statements.*

_____ 1. Complex problems are often made up of simple parts.

_____ 2. No real practice is needed to answer a discussion question.

_____ 3. A science should be studied as if it were made up of isolated facts.

_____ 4. A quantitative principle is one that is stated in mathematical terms.

_____ 5. Your lab equipment is always right and should be trusted.

MULTIPLE CHOICE

Choose the word or phrase that completes each sentence most accurately, and circle the letter that precedes it.

1. The secret of solving science problems is
   a. practice.
   b. genius.
   c. questioning.
   d. creativity.

2. Your science lecture notes should focus less on words and more on
   a. specific data.
   b. facts.
   c. ideas.
   d. formulas.

3. Science is different from many other subjects in that most of the ideas are stated
   a. quantitatively.
   b. repeatedly.
   c. obscurely.
   d. qualitatively.

4. Much of science deals with explaining
   a. isolated facts.
   b. weights and measures.
   c. relationships.
   d. controversial theories.

5. New terms in a science course should be
   a. simplified, if possible.
   b. mastered, as with any new words.
   c. taken only from lectures, not readings.
   d. kept in a separate vocabulary notebook.

SHORT ANSWER   *Supply a brief answer for each of the following items.*

1. Single out a particular science and explain how its orientation and emphases differ from those of other sciences.
2. When and how should you ask questions in a science course?
3. In answering discussion questions, where do the difficulties normally appear?
4. How should you use a laboratory apparatus?

VOCABULARY BUILDING   *Make a light check mark (✓) alongside one of the three words (choices) that most nearly expresses the meaning of the italicized word in the phrases that are in the left-hand column.*

		1	2	3
1.	extreme *precision*	randomness	accuracy	anticipation
2.	can be *intimidating*	suggestive	reassuring	frightening
3.	precise *terminology*	nomenclature	finality	insect study
4.	in *manipulating*	handling	scattering	confirming
5.	write *concisely*	descriptively	succinctly	rationally
6.	appeared *opaque*	translucent	transparent	nontransparent
7.	have been *stymied*	blocked	organized	enlightened
8.	to *wrest* control	seize	give	ruin
9.	number of *allegations*	denials	parables	declarations
10.	*predatory* behavior	predictable	compassionate	rapacious
11.	increase its *scrutiny*	examination	disregard	usefulness
12.	his *diminutive* sidekick	unintelligent	enormous	undersized
13.	a powerful *taboo*	prohibition	endorsement	enchantment
14.	weigh the *credibility*	dubiousness	plausibility	unreasonableness
15.	its *ultimate* goal	private	first	final
16.	*acrimonious* argument	bitter	lively	friendly
17.	*diametrically* opposed	logically	circuitously	exactly oppositely
18.	an *opportunistic* suitor	wealthy	unlucky	taking advantage
19.	*unsolicited* offer	unasked for	sought after	unthoughtful
20.	a *candid* memorandum	diplomatic	truthful	surprising